Washington Information Directory

2000–2001

Washington
Information Directory
2000–2001

A DIVISION OF CONGRESSIONAL QUARTERLY INC.
WASHINGTON, D.C.

Washington Information Directory, 2000–2001
Editor: Jennifer Margiotta
Production Editor: Belinda Josey
Senior Researcher: Scott Kuzner
Cover: Anne Theilgard, Kachergis Book Design
Subject Index: Patricia R. Ruggiero
Electronic Composition: Jessica Forman

The Library of Congress cataloged the first edition of this
   title as follows:
Washington information directory. 1975/76—
Washington. Congressional Quarterly Inc.
   1. Washington, D.C.—Directories. 2. Washington metropol-
   itan area—Directories. 3. United States—Executive
   departments—Directories. I. Congressional Quarterly
   Inc.
F192.3.W33   975.3'0025   75-646321
ISBN 1-56802-498-3
ISSN 0887-8064

Contents

Boxes and Illustrations

Preface

Now in its twenty-fifth year, the *Washington Information Directory* continues to be the primary resource for those interested in the workings of the nation's capital. This newly revised and updated directory identifies the key people, agencies, committees, and nonprofit groups that shape national policy.

Chief among the enhancements for this anniversary edition is a new appendix item, Directory of Government Information on the Internet. Organized by government branch, this section pinpoints the Web sites containing the information you frequently need about cabinet departments, Congress, and the federal courts. Whether you are looking for the regional office of a federal agency or the roll call for a Senate vote, this is your one-stop source for government information.

We have added nearly 100 entries for agencies and organizations, complete with e-mail and Web addresses. New resources on health issues include the National Center for Complementary and Alternative Medicine, the National Center for Policy Research for Women and Families, and a listing of federal agencies that handle minority health issues. The Science and Technology chapter now includes a section that addresses the rights of human and animal subjects in scientific research.

You will find a number of new features in the subject-based chapters. The Government Operations chapter contains a box dealing with the year 2000 decennial census. Pulled together into one spot is useful information about the census, including a list of Web sites for the Census Bureau's regional offices and the racial and ethnic advisory committees. Organizational charts that are new to this edition are the Federal Election Commission, the Federal Emergency Management Agency, and the Customs Service.

Recently updated to include changes made at the start of the second session, the 106th Congress section includes committee assignments and contact information for Capitol Hill and district offices for all members of the Senate and House of Representatives. The appendix provides a listing of governors and other state officials and an up-to-date directory of foreign embassies in Washington, U.S. ambassadors, and country desk officers.

In researching new material and updating existing entries, we have focused on accuracy and relevancy. Every name, address, telephone and fax number, e-mail address, and Web site has been checked and verified. By closely monitoring developments in the government and in the community of nonprofit organizations, we hope to continue the tradition of excellence that has marked the *Washington Information Directory* for a quarter of a century. As always, your comments and suggestions are welcome.

Jennifer Margiotta,
Editor

How to Use This Directory

The *Washington Information Directory* is designed to make your search for information fast and easy.

Each chapter covers a broad topic; within the chapters, information is grouped in more specific subject areas. This subject arrangement allows you to find in one place the departments and agencies of the federal government, congressional committees, and nonprofit organizations that have the information you need.

The directory divides information sources into three categories: (1) agencies, (2) Congress, and (3) nonprofit organizations. Each entry includes the name, address, and telephone number of the organization; the name and title of the director or the best person to contact for information; fax and press numbers, hotlines, and Internet addresses whenever available; and a description of the work performed by the organization.

How Information Is Presented

Here are examples of the three main categories of entries, and of the other resources the directory provides. They are drawn from Parks and Recreation Areas, a subsection in chapter 9, Environment and Natural Resources.

AGENCIES

One main entry—the National Park Service—is a federal agency. It is listed in bold type under its commonly known name, with its government parent, the Interior Dept., shown in parentheses.

National Park Service (NPS), (Interior Dept.), *1849 C St. N.W., #3316 20240; (202) 208-4621. Fax, (202) 208-7889. Robert Stanton, Director. Press, (202) 208-6843. Washington area activities, (202) 619-7275 (recording). Web, www.nps.gov.*

Administers national parks, monuments, historic sites, and recreation areas. Oversees coordination, planning, and financing of public outdoor recreation programs at all levels of government. Conducts recreation research surveys; administers financial assistance program to states for planning and development of outdoor recreation programs. (Some lands designated as national recreation areas are not under NPS jurisdiction.)

CONGRESS

Entries under the Congress heading are usually Senate or House committees. (Also included here are agencies under congressional jurisdiction, such as the General Accounting Office and Library of Congress.) Committee entries include the chair and a key staff member. The descriptions give the committee's jurisdiction or its activities relating to the particular subject. Here is the entry for the Senate committee with jurisdiction over the national park system:

Senate Energy and Natural Resources Committee, *Subcommittee on National Parks, Historic Preservation, and Recreation, SD-354 20510; (202) 224-6969. Fax, (202) 228-0459. Sen. Craig Thomas, R-Wyo., Chair; Jim O'Toole, Professional Staff Member. Web, energy.senate.gov.*

Jurisdiction over legislation on national parks, recreation areas, wilderness areas, trails, wild and scenic rivers, historic sites, and military parks and battlefields.

NONPROFIT

Thousands of nonprofit private and special-interest groups have headquarters or legislative offices in or near Washington. Their staffs are often excellent information sources, and these organizations frequently maintain special libraries or information centers. Here is an example of a group with an interest in parks and recreation areas:

Rails-to-Trails Conservancy, *1100 17th St. N.W., 10th Floor 20036; (202) 331-9696. Fax, (202) 331-9680. David G. Burwell, President. General e-mail, rtrails@transact.org. Web, www.railtrails.org.*
Promotes the conversion of abandoned railroad corridors into hiking and biking trails for public use. Provides public education programs and technical and legal assistance. Publishes trail guides. Monitors legislation and regulations.

BOXES AND CHARTS

The directory includes organization charts to make the hierarchy of federal agencies easier to grasp, as well as boxes that provide essential agency contacts and other quick reference information. On the topic of parks, for example, you can locate the National Park Service within the Interior Dept. (see chart on p. 303) or consult a list of contacts at National Park Service Sites in the Capital Region (see box on p. 161). A general organization chart for the federal government appears on p. 850.

Reference Resources

TABLES OF CONTENTS

The summary table of contents (p. v) lists the directory's chapters and their major subheadings. A list of information boxes and organization charts within the chapters is given on p.viii. At the beginning of each chapter you will find a detailed table of contents that breaks the chapter into general and specific sections; for convenience, here again we list the boxes and charts that appear in the chapter.

CONGRESSIONAL INFORMATION

A special section on the 106th Congress, beginning on p. 725, provides extensive information about members and committees:

State Delegations. Here (p. 727) you can look up senators, representatives, and delegates by state (or territory) and congressional district.

Members' Offices. For both the House (p. 756) and Senate (p. 825), we provide each member's Capitol Hill office address, telephone and fax, Internet address, key professional aide, committee assignments, and district offices.

Committees. These sections provide the jurisdiction and membership for committees and subcommittees of the House (p. 732) and Senate (p. 812), as well as the joint committees of Congress (p. 810). Also included here are partisan committees.

Leadership. Separate sections list the party leadership of the House (p. 754) and Senate (p. 824).

READY REFERENCE LISTS

A special section of reference lists, beginning on p. 845, gives information on the following subjects:

Government Information on the Internet. Organized by branch of government, this section (p. 846) lists Web addresses for locating information on the White House, cabinet departments, Congress, and the judiciary.

State Government. The list of state officials (p. 851) gives the name, address, and telephone number for each governor, lieutenant governor, secretary of state, attorney general, and treasurer.

Diplomats. The foreign embassies section (p. 860) gives the names, official addresses, and telephone numbers of foreign diplomats in Washington; the names of the ranking U.S. diplomatic officials abroad; and the names and phones of State Dept. and Commerce Dept. desk officers.

Federal Laws on Information. Here you will find concise explanations of the Freedom of Information Act (p. 877), which includes the Electronic Freedom of Information Act of 1996, and the Privacy Act (p. 879).

Map of Capitol Hill

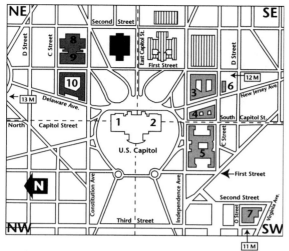

U.S. Capitol, Washington, D.C. 20510 or 20515*
1. Senate Wing
2. House Wing

House Office Buildings, Washington, D.C. 20515
3. Cannon
4. Longworth
5. Rayburn
6. O'Neill
7. Ford

Senate Office Buildings, Washington, D.C. 20510
8. Hart
9. Dirksen
10. Russell

Supreme Court, Washington, D.C. 20543

Library of Congress, Washington, D.C. 20540

Subway System
11. Federal Center SW
12. Capitol South
13. Union Station

* Mail sent to the U.S. Capitol should bear the ZIP code of the chamber to which it is addressed.

Note: Dashed line indicates the city's quadrants, which are noted in the corners of the map.

INDEXES

Use the name index (p. 881) to look up any person mentioned in the directory.

Use the subject index (p. 927) to look up a subject area or a specific organization or agency. If you need information on a particular topic but do not know a specific source, the index has subject entries to help you find where that topic is covered. For example, on the subject of equal employment for women, you can find index entries under both Women and Equal Employment Opportunity.

Reaching Your Information Source

PHONING AND FAXING

Call the information or toll-free number first. Often you can get the answer you need without going further. If not, a quick explanation of your query should put you in touch with the person who can answer your question. Rarely will you need to talk to the top administrator.

Offer to fax your query if it is difficult to explain over the phone, but make sure that the person helping you knows to expect your fax. Faxing promptly and limiting your transmission to a single page should bring the best results.

Remember that publications and documents are often available from a special office (for federal agencies, see p. 125) or, increasingly, by Web sites or special fax-on-demand services. Ask whether there is a faster way than by mail to receive the information you need.

Keep in mind the agency or organization, not the name of the director. Personnel changes are common, but for most inquiries you will want to stay with the organization you call, rather than track down a person who may have moved on to a new job.

With congressional questions, contact your own member of Congress first: your representative has staff people assigned to answer questions from constituents. Contact a committee only if you have a technical question that cannot be answered elsewhere.

WRITING

Address letters to the director of an office or organization—the contact person listed here. Your letter will be directed to the person who can answer your question. Be prepared to follow up by phone.

USING THE INTERNET

Most agencies and nonprofits have sites on the World Wide Web (for federal agencies, see p. 131), as well as e-mail addresses for general inquiries. Information available from these sources is expanding rapidly and is usually free once you are online. If you have Internet access, try the Web site, but bear in mind that this approach is not always faster or better than a phone call: connections can be slow, menus can be complex or confusing, information can be incomplete or out-of-date.

As with faxing, reserve e-mail for inquiries that may be too complex for a phone call, but phone first to establish that someone is ready to help.

Addresses and Area Codes

Listings in the directory include full contact information, including telephone area code and, when available, room or suite number and nine-digit ZIP code. If an office has a mailing address that is different from the physical location, we provide both. Note that a few listings are not a local call from Washington—the Social Security Administration headquarters in Baltimore and a small number of nonprofits in outlying suburbs. Other special cases to take note of:

WASHINGTON, D.C., ADDRESSES

For brevity, entries for agencies, organizations, and congressional offices in the District of Columbia (area code 202) do not include the city and state as part of the address. Here is the beginning of a typical Washington entry:

Federal Communications Commission, *445 12th St. S.W. 20554; (202) 418-1000.*

To complete the mailing address, add "Washington, DC."

BUILDING ADDRESSES

Departments and agencies generally have their own ZIP codes; however, updates to our directory reflect the increasing use of street addresses by the federal government. Federal offices that we list by building name or abbreviation are at the following locations:

The White House. Located at 1600 Pennsylvania Ave. N.W. 20500.

Dwight D. Eisenhower Executive Office Building. Located at 17th St. and Pennsylvania Ave. N.W. 20500.

New Executive Office Building. Located at 725 17th St. N.W. 20505.

Main State Building. Located at 2201 C St. N.W. 20520.

The Pentagon. Located in Arlington, VA, but has a Washington mailing address and special ZIP codes for each branch of the military.

Navy Annex. Located at Columbia Pike and Southgate Rd., Arlington, VA 20370, but most offices use a Washington mailing address.

U.S. Capitol. Abbreviated as CAP; the letters *H* and *S* before the room number indicate the House or Senate side of the building. ZIP codes are 20510 for the Senate, 20515 for the House.

Senate Office Buildings. The ZIP code is 20510. Abbreviations, building names, and street addresses:

SD Dirksen Senate Office Bldg., Constitution Ave. between 1st and 2nd Sts. N.E.

SR Russell Senate Office Bldg., Constitution Ave. between Delaware Ave. and 1st St. N.E.

SH Hart Senate Office Bldg., 2nd St. and Constitution Ave. N.E.

House Office Buildings. The ZIP code is 20515. Abbreviations, building names, and street addresses:

CHOB Cannon House Office Bldg., Independence Ave. between New Jersey Ave. and 1st St. S.E.

FHOB Ford House Office Bldg., 2nd and D Sts. S.W.

LHOB Longworth House Office Bldg., Independence Ave. between S. Capitol St. and New Jersey Ave. S.E.

OHOB O'Neill House Office Bldg., 300 New Jersey Ave. S.E.

RHOB Rayburn House Office Bldg., Independence Ave. between S. Capitol and 1st Sts. S.W.

1 ⚖

Advocacy and Public Service

⚖ CIVIL RIGHTS

See also Constitutional Law and Civil Liberties (chap. 14); Equal Employment Opportunity (chap. 7); Public Interest Law (this chapter); Special Groups in Education (chap. 6)

AGENCIES

Commission on Civil Rights, *624 9th St. N.W., #700 20425; (202) 376-7700. Fax, (202) 376-7672. Mary Frances Berry, Chair; Cruz Reynoso, Vice Chair. Library, (202) 376-8110. Press, (202) 376-8312. TTY, (202) 376-8116. Locator, (202) 376-8177. Complaints, (800) 552-6843; in Washington, (202) 376-8582. Web, www.usccr.gov.*

Assesses federal laws and policies of government agencies and studies legal developments to determine the nature and extent of denial of equal protection under the law on the basis of race, color, religion, sex, national origin, age, or disability in many areas, including employment, voting rights, education, administration of justice, and housing. Reports and makes recommendations to the president and Congress; serves as national clearinghouse for civil rights information. Conducts studies relating to discrimination against certain groups, including women, African Americans, Hispanics, Asians, native Americans, and Pacific Island Americans. Issues public service announcements to discourage discrimination or denials of equal protection of the laws. Library open to the public.

Equal Employment Opportunity Commission, *1801 L St. N.W., #10006 20507; (202) 663-4001. Fax, (202) 663-4110. Ida L. Castro, Chair. Information, (202) 663-4900. Library, (202) 663-4630. TTY, (202) 663-4494. Web, www.eeoc.gov.*

Works to end job discrimination by private and government employers based on race, color, religion, sex, national origin, or age. Works to protect employees against reprisal for protest of employment practices alleged to be unlawful in hiring, promotion, firing, wages, and other terms and conditions of employment. Enforces Title VII of the Civil Rights Act of 1964, as amended, which includes the Pregnancy Discrimination Act; Americans with Disabilities Act; Age Discrimination in Employment Act; Equal Pay Act; and, in the federal sector, rehabilitation laws. Receives charges of discrimination; attempts conciliation or settlement; can bring court action to force compliance; has review and appeals responsibility in the federal sector.

Executive Office of the President, *Public Liaison, Dwight D. Eisenhower Executive Office Bldg., #122 20502; (202) 456-2930. Fax, (202) 456-6218. Mary Beth Cahill, Director.*

Serves as liaison between the administration and the public on issues of domestic and international concern, including women, minorities, and the elderly.

Health and Human Services Dept., *Civil Rights, 200 Independence Ave. S.W., #522A 20201; (202) 619-0403. Fax, (202) 619-3437. Thomas Perez, Director. TTY, (800) 537-7697. Toll-free hotline, (800) 368-1019. Web, www. os.dhhs.gov/progorg/ocr/ocrhmpg.html.*

Administers and enforces laws prohibiting discrimination on the basis of race, color, sex, national origin, religion, age, or disability in programs receiving federal funds from the department; authorized to discontinue funding.

Justice Dept., *Civil Rights, 950 Pennsylvania Ave. N.W., #5643 20530; (202) 514-2151. Fax, (202) 514-0293. Bill Lann Lee, Assistant Attorney General (Acting). Library, (202) 514-3010. Press, (202) 514-2007. TTY, (202) 514-0716. Web, www.usdoj.gov/crt.*

Enforces federal civil rights laws prohibiting discrimination on the basis of race, color, religion, sex, disability, age, or national origin in voting, education, employment, credit, housing, public accommodations and facilities, and federally assisted programs.

CONGRESS

House Government Reform Committee, *Subcommittee on Criminal Justice, Drug Policy, and Human Resources, B373 RHOB 20515; (202) 225-2577. Fax, (202) 225-1154. Rep. John L. Mica, R-Fla., Chair; Sharon Pinkerton, Staff Director. Web, www.house.gov/reform.*

Oversees operations of the Equal Employment Opportunity Commission and the Commission on Civil Rights.

House Judiciary Committee, *Subcommittee on the Constitution, H2-362 FHOB 20515; (202) 226-7680. Fax, (202) 225-3746. Rep. Charles T. Canady, R-Fla., Chair; Cathy Cleaver, Chief Counsel. General e-mail, Judiciary@ mail.house.gov. Web, www.house.gov/judiciary.*

Jurisdiction over constitutional rights and civil liberties legislation. Oversees the U.S. Commission on Civil Rights and the Justice Dept.'s Civil Rights Division.

Senate Health, Education, Labor, and Pensions Committee, *SD-428 20510; (202) 224-5375. Fax, (202) 228-5044. Sen. James M. Jeffords, R-Vt., Chair; Mark Powden, Staff Director. TTY, (202) 224-1975. Web, labor. senate.gov.*

Oversees operations of the Equal Employment Opportunity Commission.

Senate Judiciary Committee, *Subcommittee on the Constitution, Federalism, and Property Rights, SD-524 20510; (202) 224-8081. Fax, (202) 228-0544. Sen. John Ashcroft, R-Mo., Chair; Adam Cingoli, Chief Counsel. Web, judiciary.senate.gov/constitu.htm.*

Jurisdiction over civil and constitutional rights legislation; oversees operations of the Commission on Civil Rights.

NONPROFIT

Citizens' Commission on Civil Rights, *2000 M St. N.W., #400 20036-3307; (202) 659-5565. Fax, (202) 223-5302. Diane M. Piché, Director. General e-mail, citizens@cccr.org. Web, www.cccr.org.*

Bipartisan commission of former federal officials. Monitors compliance of federal agencies and judicial bodies with civil rights laws; conducts social science research and provides technical and legal assistance to other civil rights and public interest groups; interests include low- and moderate-income housing, voting rights, employment, school desegregation, and education of the disadvantaged.

Leadership Conference on Civil Rights, *1629 K St. N.W., #1010 20006; (202) 466-3311. Fax, (202) 466-3435. Wade Henderson, Executive Director.*

Coalition of national organizations representing minorities, women, labor, older Americans, people with disabilities, and religious groups. Works for enactment and enforcement of civil rights and social welfare legislation; acts as clearinghouse for information on civil rights legislation and regulations.

NAACP Legal Defense and Educational Fund, *Washington Office, 1444 Eye St. N.W., 10th Floor 20005; (202) 682-1300. Fax, (202) 682-1312. Janell Byrd, Senior Attorney.*

Civil rights litigation group that provides legal information on civil rights issues, including employment, housing, and educational discrimination; monitors federal enforcement of civil rights laws. Not affiliated with the National Assn. for the Advancement of Colored People (NAACP).

Poverty and Race Research Action Council, *3000 Connecticut Ave. N.W., #200 20008; (202) 387-9887. Fax, (202) 387-0764. Chester W. Hartman, Executive Director. General e-mail, info@prrac.org. Web, www.prrac.org.*

Facilitates cooperative links between researchers and activists who work on race and poverty issues. Provides nonprofit organizations with funding for research on race and poverty.

See also Lawyers' Committee for Civil Rights Under Law (p. 29)

African Americans

See also Caucuses (chap. 20)

NONPROFIT

Blacks in Government, *1820 11th St. N.W. 20001-5015; (202) 667-3280. Fax, (202) 667-3705. Gerald R. Reed, President. Web, www.bignet.org.*

Advocacy organization for public employees. Promotes equal opportunity and career advancement for African American government employees; provides career development information; seeks to eliminate racism in the federal workforce; sponsors programs, business meetings, and social gatherings; represents interests of African American government workers to Congress and the executive branch; promotes voter education and registration.

Congressional Black Caucus Foundation, *1004 Pennsylvania Ave. S.E. 20003; (202) 675-6730. Fax, (202) 547-3806. Ramona H. Edelin, Executive Director. Web, www. cbcfonline.org.*

Conducts research and programs on public policy issues of concern to African Americans. Sponsors fellowship programs in which professionals and academic candidates work on congressional committees and subcommittees. Holds issue forums and leadership seminars. Provides elected officials, organizations, and researchers with statistical, demographic, public policy, and political information. Sponsors internship and scholarship programs.

Joint Center for Political and Economic Studies, *1090 Vermont Ave. N.W., #1100 20005-4961; (202) 789-3500. Fax, (202) 789-6390. Eddie N. Williams, President. Web, www.jointctr.org.*

Researches and analyzes issues of concern to African Americans, focusing on economic and social policy issues and African American political participation. Publishes a biannual profile of African American elected officials in federal, state, and local government; holds forums on public policy issues.

Lincoln Institute for Research and Education, *1001 Connecticut Ave. N.W., #1135 20036; (202) 223-5112. J. A. Parker, President.*

Public policy research group that studies issues of interest to middle-class African Americans, including business, economics, employment, education, national defense, health, and culture. Sponsors seminars.

National Assn. for the Advancement of Colored People, *Washington Office, 1025 Vermont Ave. N.W., #1120 20005; (202) 638-2269. Fax, (202) 638-5936. Hilary O. Shelton, Director. Web, www.naacp.org.*

Membership: persons interested in civil rights for all minorities. Works for the political, educational, social, and economic equality and empowerment of minorities through legal, legislative, and direct action. (Headquarters in Baltimore, Md.)

National Assn. of Colored Women's Clubs, *5808 16th St. N.W. 20011-2898; (202) 726-2044. Fax, (202) 726-0023. Patricia L. Fletcher, President.*

Seeks to promote education of women and youth; protect and enforce civil rights; raise the standard of family living; promote interracial understanding; and enhance leadership development. Awards scholarships; conducts programs in education, social service, and philanthropy.

National Black Caucus of Local Elected Officials, *c/o National League of Cities, 1301 Pennsylvania Ave. N.W., #550 20004; (202) 626-3169. Fax, (202) 626-3043. Roosevelt Coats, President. Press, (202) 626-3000.*

Membership: elected officials at the local level and other interested individuals. Concerned with issues affecting African Americans, including housing, economics, the family, and human rights.

National Black Caucus of State Legislators, *444 N. Capitol St. N.W., #622 20001; (202) 624-5457. Fax, (202) 508-3826. Ivan Lanier, Executive Director.*

Membership: African American state legislators. Promotes effective leadership among African American state legislators; serves as an information network and clearinghouse for members.

National Center for Neighborhood Enterprise, *1424 16th St. N.W., #300 20036; (202) 518-6500. Fax, (202) 588-0314. Robert L. Woodson Sr., Chair. Web, www.ncne.com.*

Seeks new approaches to the problems confronting the African American community. Interests include economic development, the encouragement of entrepreneurship, housing, family development, and education.

National Council of Negro Women, *633 Pennsylvania Ave. N.W. 20004; (202) 737-0120. Fax, (202) 737-0476. Dr. Jane Elaine Smith, President. Web, www.ncnw.com.*

Coalition of domestic and international organizations and individuals interested in issues that affect African American women. Encourages the development of African American women; sponsors programs on family health care, career development, child care, juvenile offenders, housing discrimination against women, teenage pregnancy, and literacy improvement among female heads of households; promotes social and economic well-being of African American women through its Development Projects training program.

National Urban League, *Research and Public Policy, Washington Office, 1111 14th St. N.W., #1001 20005-5603; (202) 898-1604. Fax, (202) 408-1965. William Spriggs, Director. General e-mail, info@nul.org. Web, www.nul.org.*

Social service organization concerned with the social welfare of African Americans and other minorities. Seeks elimination of racial segregation and discrimination; monitors legislation, policies, and regulations to determine impact on minorities; interests include employment, health, welfare, education, housing, and community development.

Project 21, *777 N. Capitol St. N.E., #803 20002; (202) 371-1400. Fax, (202) 408-7773. David Almasi, Director. Web, www.nationalcenter.org.*

Emphasizes spirit of entrepreneurship, sense of family, and traditional values among African Americans. (Initiative of the National Center for Public Policy Research.)

See also Minority Business Enterprise Legal Defense and Education Fund (p. 111)

Hispanics

See also Caucuses (chap. 20)

NONPROFIT

Congressional Hispanic Caucus Institute, *504 C St. N.E. 20002; (202) 543-1771. Fax, (202) 546-2143. Rep. Lucille Roybal-Allard, D-Calif., Chair; Ingrid Duran, Executive Director. Toll-free college scholarship information, (800) 392-3532.*

Addresses issues of concern to Hispanic Americans and fosters awareness of the contributions of Hispanics to American society. Develops programs to familiarize Hispanic students with policy-related careers and to encourage their professional development. Acts as an information clearinghouse on educational opportunities.

League of United Latin American Citizens, *Washington Office, 2000 L St. N.W., #610 20036; (202) 833-6130. Fax, (202) 833-6135. Brent Wilkes, Executive Director. General e-mail, lulac@aol.com. Web, www.lulac.org.*

Seeks full social, political, economic, and educational rights for Hispanics in the United States. Programs include housing projects for the poor, employment and training for youth and women, and political advocacy on issues affecting Hispanics, including immigration. Operates National Educational Service Centers (NESCs) and awards scholarships.

Mexican American Legal Defense and Educational Fund, *Washington Office, 1717 K St. N.W., #311 20036; (202) 628-4074. Fax, (202) 293-2849. Marisa Demeo, Regional Counsel. Web, www.maldef.org.*

Gives legal assistance to Mexican Americans and other Hispanics in such areas as equal employment, voting rights, bilingual education, and immigration; awards scholarship funds to Hispanic law students. Monitors legislation and regulations.

National Conference of Catholic Bishops/U.S. Catholic Conference, *Secretariat for Hispanic Affairs, 3211 4th St. N.E., 4th Floor 20017-1194; (202) 541-3150. Fax, (202) 722-8717. Ronaldo M. Cruz, Director. General e-mail, hispanicaffairs@nccbuscc.org. Web, www.nccbuscc. org.*

Acts as an information clearinghouse on communications and pastoral and liturgical activities; serves as liaison for other church institutions, and government and private agencies concerned with Hispanics; provides information on legislation; acts as advocate for Hispanics within the National Conference of Catholic Bishops.

National Conference of Puerto Rican Women, *5 Thomas Circle N.W. 20005; (202) 387-4716. Fax, (202) 778-0721. Ivonne Cervoni, President. General e-mail, icervoni@prfaa/govpr.org. Web, www.nacoprw.org.*

Promotes equal participation of Puerto Rican and other Hispanic women in the economic, social, and political aspects of life in both the United States and Puerto Rico.

National Council of La Raza, *1111 19th St. N.W., #1000 20036; (202) 785-1670. Fax, (202) 776-1792. Raul Yzaguirre, President. Web, www.nclr.org.*

Offers technical assistance to Hispanic community organizations; operates policy analysis center with interests in education, employment and training, immigration, language issues, civil rights, and housing and community development. Special projects focus on the Hispanic elderly, teenage pregnancy, health, and AIDS. Monitors legislation and regulations.

National Puerto Rican Coalition, *1700 K St. N.W., #500 20006; (202) 223-3915. Fax, (202) 429-2223. Manuel Mirabal, President. General e-mail, nprc@aol.com. Web, www.incacorp.com/nprc.*

Membership: Puerto Rican organizations and individuals. Analyzes and advocates for public policy that benefits Puerto Ricans; offers training and technical assistance to Puerto Rican organizations and individuals; develops national communication network for Puerto Rican community-based organizations and individuals.

See also Aspira Assn. (p. 203); National Alliance of Hispanic Health (p. 402)

Lesbians and Gays

NONPROFIT

And Justice for All, *P.O. Box 53079 20009; (202) 547-0508. Jonathan Zucker, Executive Director. General e-mail, justice@clark.net. Web, www.qrd.org/qrd/www/orgs/aja.*

Seeks to increase the visibility of heterosexuals in the gay, lesbian, bisexual, and transgender rights movement. Coordinates speak-outs and letter writing campaigns; sponsors speeches on college and university campuses; promotes awareness of bisexual, gay, lesbian, and transgender rights at public events and festivals.

Dignity USA, *1500 Massachusetts Ave. N.W., #11 20005; (202) 861-0017. Fax, (202) 429-9808. Mary Louise Cervone, President. Information, (800) 877-8797. General e-mail, dignity@aol.com. Web, www.dignityusa.org.*

Membership: gay, lesbian, bisexual, and transgender Catholics, their families, and friends. Works to promote spiritual development, social interaction, educational outreach, and feminist issues.

Gay and Lesbian Activists Alliance, *P.O. Box 75265 20013-5265; (202) 667-5139. Bob Summersgill, President. General e-mail, equal@glaa.org. Web, www.glaa.org.*

Advances the rights of gays and lesbians within the Washington community. (Affiliated with International Lesbian and Gay Assn., Brussels, Belgium.)

Gay and Lesbian Alliance Against Defamation, *1825 Connecticut Ave. N.W., 5th Floor 20009; (202) 986-1360. Fax, (202) 667-0902. Steve Weisman, Co-Chair; David Steward, Co-Chair. General e-mail, glaad@glaad. org. Web, www.glaad.org.*

Monitors coverage of gay, lesbian, transgender, and bisexual issues in the media. Organizes protests and campaigns against homophobic reporting and stereotyping. Publishes and distributes a media guide.

Gay and Lesbian Victory Fund, *1012 14th St. N.W., #1000 20005; (202) 842-8679. Fax, (202) 289-3863. Brian K. Bond, Executive Director. General e-mail, victory@ victoryfund.org. Web, www.victoryfund.org.*

Supports the candidacy of openly gay and lesbian individuals in federal, state, and local elections.

Human Rights Campaign, *919 18th St. N.W., #800 20006; (202) 628-4160. Fax, (202) 347-5323. Elizabeth Birch, Executive Director. General e-mail, hrc@hrc.org. Web, www.hrc.org.*

Provides campaign support and educates the public to ensure the rights of lesbians and gays at home, work, school, and in the community. Works to prohibit workplace discrimination based on sexual orientation; combat hate crimes; fund AIDS research, care, and prevention; and to repeal the policy on gays and lesbians in the military.

Log Cabin Republicans, *1633 Que St. N.W., #210 20009; (202) 347-5306. Fax, (202) 347-5224. Rich Tafel, Executive Director. General e-mail, info@lcr.org. Web, www.lcr.org.*

Membership: lesbian and gay Republicans. Educates conservative politicians and voters on gay and lesbian issues; disseminates information; conducts seminars for members. Raises campaign funds. Monitors legislation and regulations.

National Gay and Lesbian Task Force and Policy Institute, *1700 Kalorama Rd. 20009; (202) 332-6483. Fax, (202) 332-0207. Kerry Lobel, Executive Director. TTY, (202) 332-6219. General e-mail, ngltf@ngltf.org. Web, www.ngltf.org.*

Educates the media and the public on issues affecting the lesbian and gay community. Interests include grassroots organizations, civil rights, antigay violence, sodomy law reform, and gays on campus. Monitors legislation.

National Lesbian and Gay Journalists Assn., *2120 L St. N.W., #840 20037; (202) 588-9888. Fax, (202) 588-1818. Robert Dodge, President. General e-mail, nlgja@aol. com. Web, www.nlgja.org.*

Fosters fair and accurate coverage of lesbian and gay issues. Provides professional support and networking services; sponsors conferences, seminars, and workshops.

National Organization for Women, *733 15th St. N.W., 2nd Floor 20005; (202) 628-8669. Fax, (202) 785-8576. Patricia Ireland, President. TTY, (202) 331-9002. General e-mail, now@now.org. Web, www.now.org.*

Membership: women and men interested in feminist civil rights. Works to end discrimination against lesbians and gays. Promotes the development and enforcement of legislation prohibiting discrimination on the basis of sexual orientation.

Parents, Families, and Friends of Lesbians and Gays, *1726 M St. N.W., #400 20036; (202) 467-8180. Fax, (202) 638-0243. Kirsten Kingdon, Executive Director. General e-mail, info@pflag.org. Web, www.pflag.org.*

Promotes the health and well-being of gay, lesbian, transgender, and bisexual persons, their families, and their friends through support, education, and advocacy. Works to change public policies and attitudes toward gay, lesbian, and bisexual persons. Monitors legislation and regulations.

Servicemembers Legal Defense Network, *P.O. Box 65301 20035-5301; (202) 328-3244. Fax, (202) 797-1635. Michelle M. Benecke, Co-Director; C. Dixon Osburn, Co-Director. General e-mail, sldn@sldn.org. Web, www.sldn. org.*

Provides legal assistance to individuals affected by the military's policy on gays and lesbians. Monitors legislation and regulations.

Sexual Minority Youth Assistance League, *410 7th St. S.E. 20003-2707; (202) 546-5940. Fax, (202) 544-1306. Craig Bowman, Executive Director. Web, www.smyal.org.*

Provides support to youth who are lesbian, gay, bisexual, transgender, or who may be questioning their sexuality. Facilitates youth center and support groups; promotes HIV/AIDS awareness; assists with foster care opportunities for abused and neglected adolescents who are gay, lesbian, bisexual, and transgender; coordinates public education programs about homophobia.

Native Americans

AGENCIES

Administration for Native Americans *(Health and Human Services Dept.), 200 Independence Ave. S.W., #348F 20201; (202) 690-7776. Fax, (202) 690-7441. Gary N. Kimble, Commissioner.*

Awards grants for locally determined social and economic development strategies; promotes native American economic and social self-sufficiency; funds tribes and native American and native Hawaiian organizations. Commissioner chairs the Intradepartmental Council on Indian Affairs, which coordinates native American-related programs.

Bureau of Indian Affairs *(Interior Dept.), 1849 C St. N.W., #4160, MS 4160 20240; (202) 208-7163. Fax, (202) 208-5320. Kevin Gover, Assistant Secretary. Information, (202) 208-3711. Press, (202) 219-4150. Web, www.doi. gov/bureau-indian-affairs.html.*

Works with federally recognized Indian tribal governments and Alaska native communities in a government-to-government relationship. Encourages and supports tribes' efforts to govern themselves and to provide needed programs and services on the reservations. Manages land held in trust for Indian tribes and individuals. Funds educational benefits, road construction and maintenance, social services, police protection, economic development efforts, and special assistance to develop governmental and administrative skills.

CONGRESS

House Resources Committee, *1324 LHOB 20515-6201; (202) 225-2761. Fax, (202) 225-5929. Rep. Don Young, R-Alaska, Chair; Lloyd Jones, Staff Director. General e-mail, resources.committee@mail.house.gov. Web, www.house.gov/resources.*

Jurisdiction over all matters regarding relations with and welfare of native Americans, including land management and trust responsibilities, education, health, special services, loan programs, and claims against the United States.

Senate Committee on Indian Affairs, *SH-838 20510; (202) 224-2251. Fax, (202) 224-5429. Sen. Ben Nighthorse Campbell, R-Colo., Chair; Paul Moorehead, Staff Director. Web, indian.senate.gov.*

Jurisdiction over legislation on native Americans; oversight of all programs that affect native Americans.

JUDICIARY

U.S. Court of Federal Claims, *717 Madison Pl. N.W. 20005; (202) 219-9668. Fax, (202) 219-9649. Loren A. Smith, Chief Judge; Margaret Ernest, Clerk, (202) 219-9657.*

Deals with native American tribal claims against the government that are founded upon the Constitution, congressional acts, government regulations, and contracts. Examples include claims for land, water, and mineral rights and for the accounting of funds held for native Americans under various treaties.

NONPROFIT

National Congress of American Indians, *1301 Connecticut Ave. N.W., #200 20036; (202) 466-7767. Fax, (202) 466-7797. JoAnn K. Chase, Executive Director. Web, www.ncai.org.*

Membership: native American and Alaska native governments and individuals. Provides information and serves as general advocate for tribes. Monitors legislative and regulatory activities affecting native American affairs.

Native American Rights Fund, *Washington Office, 1712 N St. N.W. 20036; (202) 785-4166. Fax, (202) 822-0068. Lorna Babby, Managing Attorney. Web, www.narf.org.*

Provides native Americans and Alaskan natives with legal assistance in land claims, water rights, hunting, and other areas.

Navajo Nation, *Washington Office, 1101 17th St. N.W., #250 20036; (202) 775-0393. Fax, (202) 775-8075. Estelle Bowman, Executive Director.*

Monitors legislation and regulations affecting the Navajo people; serves as an information clearinghouse on the Navajo Nation.

See also Americans for the Restitution and Righting of Old Wrongs (p. 203); Friends Committee on National Legislation (p. 32)

Senior Citizens

See also Fair Housing/Special Groups (chap. 12); Health Services for Special Groups (chap. 11); Pensions and Benefits (chap. 7); Social Services and Disabilities (chap. 18)

AGENCIES

Administration on Aging *(Health and Human Services Dept.), 200 Independence Ave. S.W., #309F 20201; (202) 401-4634. Fax, (202) 401-7741. Jeanette C. Takamura, Assistant Secretary. Press, (202) 401-4541. General e-mail, AoAInfo@aoa.gov. Web, www.aoa.dhhs.gov.*

Acts as advocate for the elderly; serves as the principal agency for implementing programs under the Older Americans Act. Develops programs to promote the economic welfare and personal independence of older people; provides advice and assistance to promote the development of state-administered, community-based social services for older people; supports curriculum development and training in gerontology.

CONGRESS

House Education and the Workforce Committee, Subcommittee on Early Childhood, Youth, and Families, *2181 RHOB 20515; (202) 225-4527. Fax, (202) 225-9571. Rep. Michael N. Castle, R-Del., Chair; Kevin D. Talley, Staff Director. Web, www.house.gov/ed_workforce.*

Jurisdiction over legislation on all matters dealing with programs and services for the elderly, including health and nutrition programs and the Older Americans Act.

Senate Special Committee on Aging, *SD-G31 20510; (202) 224-5364. Fax, (202) 224-8660. Sen. Charles E. Grassley, R-Iowa, Chair; Ted Totman, Staff Director. Web, aging.senate.gov.*

Oversight of all matters affecting older Americans. Studies and reviews public and private policies and programs that affect the elderly, including retirement income and maintenance, housing, health, welfare, employment, education, recreation, and participation in family and community life; provides other Senate committees with information. Cannot report legislation.

NONPROFIT

AARP, 601 E St. N.W. 20049; (202) 434-2277. Fax, (202) 434-2320. Horace B. Deets, Executive Director. Library, (202) 434-6240. Press, (202) 434-2560. TTY, (202) 434-6561. Web, www.aarp.org.

Membership organization for persons aged fifty and older. Provides members with training, employment information, and volunteer programs; offers financial services, including insurance, investment programs, and consumer discounts; makes grants through AARP Andrus Foundation for research on aging. Monitors legislation and regulations on issues affecting older Americans, including age discrimination, Social Security, Medicaid and Medicare, pensions and retirement, and consumer protection. Formerly the American Association of Retired Persons.

Gray Panthers Project Fund, 733 15th St. N.W., #437 20005; (202) 737-6637. Fax, (202) 737-1160. Tim Fuller, Director. General e-mail, info@graypanthers.org. Web, www.graypanthers.org.

Educational and advocacy organization that promotes national health care and economic and social justice for people of all ages, including the elderly; seeks the preservation of Social Security and jobs for all with a living minimum wage.

National Caucus and Center on Black Aged, 1424 K St. N.W., #500 20005-2407; (202) 637-8400. Fax, (202) 347-0895. Samuel J. Simmons, President.

Concerned with issues that affect elderly African Americans. Sponsors employment and housing programs for the elderly and education and training for professionals in gerontology. Monitors legislation and regulations.

National Council of Senior Citizens, 8403 Colesville Rd., #1200, Silver Spring, MD 20910-3314; (301) 578-8800. Fax, (301) 578-8999. Steve Protulis, Executive Director. Web, www.ncscinc.org.

Federation of senior citizen clubs, associations, councils, and other groups. Seeks to nationalize health care services and to strengthen benefits to the elderly, including improved Social Security payments, increased employment, and education and health programs. Offers prescription drug program, Medicare supplement, and group travel.

National Council on the Aging, 409 3rd St. S.W., 2nd Floor 20024; (202) 479-1200. Fax, (202) 479-0735. James Firman, President. Information, (202) 479-6653. Library,

(202) 479-6669. Press, (202) 479-6975. General e-mail, info@ncoa.org. Web, www.ncoa.org.

Serves as an information clearinghouse on training, technical assistance, advocacy, and research on every aspect of aging. Provides information on social services for older persons. Monitors legislation and regulations. Library open to the public.

National Hispanic Council on Aging, 2713 Ontario Rd. N.W. 20009; (202) 265-1288. Fax, (202) 745-2522. Marta Sotomayor, President. General e-mail, nhcoa@worldnet.att.net. Web, www.nhcoa.org.

Membership: senior citizens, health care workers, professionals in the field of aging, and others in the United States and Puerto Rico who are interested in topics related to Hispanics and aging. Provides research training, consulting, and technical assistance; sponsors seminars, workshops, and management internships.

National Senior Citizens Law Center, 1101 14th St. N.W., #400 20005; (202) 289-6976. Fax, (202) 289-7224. Burton D. Fretz, Executive Director. General e-mail, nsclc@nsclc.org. Web, www.nsclc.org.

Organization funded by the Legal Services Corp. Litigates on behalf of legal services programs and elderly poor clients and client groups. Represents clients before Congress and federal departments and agencies. Interests include Social Security, Medicare, Medicaid, nursing home residents' rights, home health care, pensions, and protective services.

Seniors Coalition, 9001 Braddock Rd., #200, Springfield, VA 22151; (703) 239-1960. Fax, (703) 239-1985. Mary Martin, Executive Director. General e-mail, tsc@senior.org. Web, www.senior.org.

Seeks to protect the quality of life and economic well-being of older Americans. Interests include health care, social security, taxes, pharmaceutical issues, and Medicare. Conducts seminars and monitors legislation and regulations.

60 Plus, 1655 N. Fort Myer Dr., #355, Arlington, VA 22209; (703) 807-2070. Fax, (703) 807-2073. James L. Martin, President. Web, www.60plus.org.

Advocates rights of senior citizens. Interests include free enterprise, less government regulation, and tax reform. Works to eliminate the estate tax. Publishes rating system of members of Congress. Monitors legislation and regulations.

United Seniors Assn., 3900 Jermantown Rd., #450, Fairfax, VA 22030; (703) 359-6500. Fax, (703) 359-6510. Sandra L. Butler, President. Information, (800) 887-2872. Web, www.unitedseniors.org.

Advocates the rights of older Americans. Works to lower taxes, reduce wasteful government spending, and preserve the rights and benefits of senior citizens.

Women

See also Caucuses (chap. 20)

AGENCIES

Office for Women's Initiatives and Outreach *(Executive Office of the President)*, Dwight D. Eisenhower Executive Office Bldg., #15 20502; (202) 456-7300. Fax, (202) 456-7311. Lauren Supina, Director. Web, www. whitehouse.gov/WH/EOP/Women/OWIO/index.html.

Acts as an advocate on issues concerning women; serves as a liaison between the White House offices and women's groups.

NONPROFIT

Assn. for Women in Science, *1200 New York Ave. N.W., #650 20005; (202) 326-8940. Fax, (202) 326-8960. Catherine Didion, Executive Director. General e-mail, awis@awis.org. Web, www.awis.org.*

Promotes equal opportunity for women in scientific professions; provides career and funding information. Interests include international development.

Center for Women Policy Studies, *1211 Connecticut Ave. N.W., #312 20036; (202) 872-1770. Fax, (202) 296-8962. Leslie R. Wolfe, President. General e-mail, cwpsx@ aol.com. Web, www.centerwomenpolicy.org.*

Policy and advocacy organization concerned with women's issues, including educational and employment equity for women, women and AIDS, violence against women, economic opportunity for low-income women, women's health, and reproductive laws.

Church Women United, *100 Maryland Ave. N.E., #100 20002; (202) 544-8747. Fax, (202) 544-9133. Ann Delorey, Legislative Director. Information, (800) CWU-5551. Web, www.churchwomen.org.*

Ecumenical women's organization. Interests include defense policy, employment, family stability, health, human rights, justice, world peace, and hunger and poverty issues, especially as they affect women and children.

Independent Women's Forum, *1319 18th St. N.W. 20036; (202) 833-4553. Fax, (202) 833-4543. Barbara Ledeen, Executive Director. General e-mail, iwf@iwf.org. Web, www.iwf.org.*

Membership: women and men interested in promoting individual responsibility, strong families, freedom, and opportunity. Conducts litigation; publishes periodical and media directory; maintains speakers bureau. Interests include maintaining single-sex schools and eliminating affirmative action programs. Monitors legislation and regulations.

Jewish Women International, *1828 L St. N.W., #250 20036; (202) 857-1300. Fax, (202) 857-1380. Gail Rubinson, Executive Director. General e-mail, jwi@jwi.org. Web, www.jewishwomen.org.*

Organization of Jewish women in the United States and Canada. Interests include emotional health of children and youth; family issues such as choice, family violence, and women's health care; civil and constitutional rights; community services; and anti-Semitism.

Leadership America, *700 N. Fairfax St., #610, Alexandria, VA 22314; (703) 549-1102. Fax, (703) 836-9205. Katha Kissman, President. General e-mail, info@ leadershipamerica.com. Web, www.leadershipamerica.com.*

Educational program designed to increase women's influence in the national decision-making process. Conducts seminars on public policy issues for women in leadership positions and helps launch chapters worldwide.

National Organization for Women, *733 15th St. N.W., 2nd Floor 20005; (202) 628-8669. Fax, (202) 785-8576. Patricia Ireland, President. TTY, (202) 331-9002. General e-mail, now@now.org. Web, www.now.org.*

Membership: women and men interested in feminist civil rights. Uses traditional and nontraditional forms of political activism, including nonviolent civil disobedience, to improve the status of all women regardless of age, income, sexual orientation, or race. Maintains liaisons with counterpart organizations worldwide.

National Partnership for Women and Families, *1875 Connecticut Ave. N.W., #710 20009-5728; (202) 986-2600. Fax, (202) 986-2539. Judith L. Lichtman, President. General e-mail, info@nationalpartnership.org. Web, www. nationalpartnership.org.*

Advocacy organization that advances legal rights of women, primarily in the areas of employment and family leave; conducts research and provides technical expertise and analysis; litigates selected cases.

National Women's Law Center, *11 Dupont Circle N.W., #800 20036; (202) 588-5180. Fax, (202) 588-5185. Marcia D. Greenberger, Co-President; Nancy Duff Campbell, Co-President. Web, www.nwlc.org.*

Works to expand and protect women's legal rights through advocacy and public education. Interests include reproductive rights, health, education, employment, women in prison, income security, and family support.

Older Women's League, *666 11th St. N.W., #700 20001; (202) 783-6686. Fax, (202) 638-2356. Deborah Briceland-Betts, Executive Director.*

Grassroots organization concerned with the social and economic problems of middle-aged and older women. Interests include health care, Social Security, pension rights, housing, employment, women as care givers, effects of budget cuts, and issues relating to death and dying.

Quota International, *1420 21st St. N.W. 20036; (202) 331-9694. Fax, (202) 331-4395. Kathleen Treiber, Executive Director. General e-mail, staff@quota.org. Web, www.quota.org.*

International service organization that links members in thirteen countries in a worldwide network of service and friendship. Interests include deaf, hard-of-hearing, and speech-impaired individuals and disadvantaged women and children.

The Woman Activist, *2310 Barbour Rd., Falls Church, VA 22043; (703) 573-8716. Flora Crater, President.*

Advocacy group that conducts research on individuals and groups in elective and appointive office, especially those who make decisions affecting women and minorities. Publishes legislative record and actions of the Virginia Assembly annually.

Women's Action for New Directions, *Washington Office, 110 Maryland Ave. N.E., #205 20002; (202) 543-8505. Fax, (202) 675-6469. Kimberly Robson, Director. Legislative hotline, (800) 444-9263. General e-mail, wand@wand.org. Web, www.wand.org.*

Monitors legislation affecting women. Interests include the redirection of military spending toward domestic priorities.

Women's Research and Education Institute, *1750 New York Ave. N.W., #350 20006; (202) 628-0444. Fax, (202) 628-0458. Susan Scanlan, President. General e-mail, wrei@wrei.org. Web, www.wrei.org.*

Analyzes policy-relevant information on women's issues. Sponsors fellowships in congressional offices; promotes public education through reports, conferences, and briefings; serves as an information clearinghouse. Interests include women's employment and economic status generally; women in nontraditional occupations; military women; employment opportunities for women veterans; older women; and women's health issues.

*See also the **Fund for the Feminist Majority Foundation** (p. 719)*

Other Minority Groups

See also Religion and Ethics (this chapter); Social Services and Disabilities (chap. 18)

NONPROFIT

American-Arab Anti-Discrimination Committee, *4201 Connecticut Ave. N.W., #300 20008-1158; (202) 244-2990. Fax, (202) 244-3196. Naila Asali, Chair; Hala Maksoud, President. General e-mail, adc@adc.org. Web, www.adc.org.*

Nonsectarian organization that seeks to protect the rights and heritage of Americans of Arab descent. Works to combat discrimination against Arab Americans in employment, education, and political life and to prevent stereotyping of Arabs in the media.

American Muslim Council, *1212 New York Ave. N.W., #400 20005; (202) 789-2262. Fax, (202) 789-2550. Aly Abuzaakouk, Executive Director. Web, www.amconline.org.*

Promotes equal rights and political empowerment for Muslims in the United States. Opposes discrimination against Muslims; fosters cultural understanding and cooperation among organizations.

Anti-Defamation League, *Washington Office, 1100 Connecticut Ave. N.W., #1020 20036; (202) 452-8320. Fax, (202) 296-2371. David Friedman, Regional Director. General e-mail, adlwashdc@aol.com. Web, www.adl.org.*

Jewish organization interested in civil rights and liberties. Seeks to combat anti-Semitism and other forms of bigotry. Interests include discrimination in employment, housing, voting, and education; U.S. foreign policy in the Middle East; and the treatment of Jews worldwide. Monitors legislation and regulations affecting Jewish interests and the civil rights of all Americans.

Japanese American Citizens League, *Washington Office, 1001 Connecticut Ave. N.W., #704 20036; (202) 223-1240. Fax, (202) 296-8082. Kristine Minami, Representative. General e-mail, dc@jacl.org. Web, jacl.org.*

Monitors legislative and regulatory activities affecting the rights of Japanese Americans. Supports civil rights of all Americans, with a focus on Asian and Asian-Pacific Americans.

Organization of Chinese American Women, *4641 Montgomery Ave., #208, Bethesda, MD 20814; (301) 907-3898. Fax, (301) 907-3899. Pauline W. Tsui, Executive Director (Acting). General e-mail, ocawwomen@aol.com.*

Seeks to overcome racial and sexual discrimination and to ensure equal education and employment opportunities in professional and nonprofessional fields; provides members with leadership, skills, and employment training; assists newly arrived immigrants.

Organization of Chinese Americans, *1001 Connecticut Ave. N.W., #601 20036; (202) 223-5500. Fax, (202) 296-0540. Daphne Kwok, Executive Director. General e-mail, oca@ocanatl.org. Web, www.ocanatl.org.*

Advocacy group seeking equal opportunities for Chinese Americans and other Asian Americans. Interests include cultural heritage, education, voter registration, hate crimes, immigration, and civil rights issues; opposes adoption of English as official U.S. language.

⚖ CONSUMER PROTECTION

See also Consumer Education (chap. 6); Food and Nutrition (chap. 2); Public Interest Law (this chapter); Sales and Services (chap. 3)

AGENCIES

Consumer Product Safety Commission, *4330 East-West Hwy., Bethesda, MD 20814; (301) 504-0990. Fax, (301) 504-0281. Ann Brown, Chair; Susan Cox, Executive Director. Information, (301) 504-0580. Library, (301) 504-0044. TTY, (800) 638-8270. Locator, (301) 504-0100. Product safety hotline, (800) 638-2772. General e-mail, info@cpsc.gov. Web, www.cpsc.gov.*

Establishes and enforces product safety standards; collects data; studies the causes and prevention of product-related injuries; identifies hazardous products, including imports, and recalls them from the marketplace. Library open to the public.

General Services Administration, *Consumer Information Center, 1800 F St. N.W., #G142 20405; (202) 501-1794. Fax, (202) 501-4281. Teresa N. Nasif, Director. Web, www.pueblo.gsa.gov.*

Publishes quarterly consumer information catalog that lists free and low-cost federal publications. Copies may be obtained from the Consumer Information Centers, Pueblo, CO 81009. Copies also available at Federal Information Centers.

AGENCY AND DEPARTMENT CONSUMER CONTACTS

Agriculture Dept., *Communication and Governmental Affairs, 3101 Park Center Dr., #808, Alexandria, VA 22302; (703) 305-2282. Fax, (703) 305-2230. Joyce Willis, Director. Web, www.usda.gov/fcs.*

Commission on Civil Rights, *Public Affairs, 624 9th St. N.W. 20425; (202) 376-8312. Fax, (202) 376-8315. Vacant, Chief. TTY, (202) 376-8116. Web, www.usccr.gov.*

Consumer Product Safety Commission, *Information and Public Affairs, 4330 East-West Hwy., Bethesda, MD 20814; (301) 504-0580. Fax, (301) 504-0862. Russell Rader, Director. TTY, (800) 638-8270. Product safety hotline, (800) 638-2772. General e-mail, info@cpsc.gov. Web, www.cpsc.gov.*

Defense Dept., *Morale, Welfare, and Recreation, The Pentagon 20301-4000; (703) 697-7197. Fax, (703) 614-3375. Janis White, Executive Director. Web, www.defenselink.mil.*

Education Dept., *Intergovernmental and Interagency Affairs, 400 Maryland Ave S.W., #5E317 20202-3500; (202) 401-0404. Fax, (202) 401-8607. G. Mario Moreno, Assistant Secretary. Press, (202) 401-1576. TTY, (202) 401-0594. Web, www.ed.gov/offices/OIIA.*

Energy Dept., *Intergovernmental and External Affairs, 1000 Independence Ave. S.W., CI-10, #8G048 20585; (202) 586-5373. Fax, (202) 586-0539. Betty Nolan, Director. Web, www.doe.gov.*

Environmental Protection Agency, *Information Resources Center, 401 M St. S.W., MC 3201 20460; (202) 260-9152. Fax, (202) 260-5153. Susan Westenbargger, Head Librarian. General e-mail, library-hq@epa.gov.*

Federal Communications Commission, *Consumer Information Bureau, 445 12th St. S.W., #7C485 20554; (202) 418-0191. Fax, (202) 418-0232. Martha Contee, Chief. Information, (888) 225-5322. TTY, (888) 835-5322.*

Federal Deposit Insurance Corp., *Compliance and Consumer Affairs, 550 17th St. N.W. 20429; (202) 942-3100. Fax, (202) 942-3427. Stephen M. Cross, Director. Information, (800) 934-3342. TTY, (800) 925-4618. General e-mail, consumer@fdic.gov. Web, www.fdic.gov.*

Federal Maritime Commission, *Informal Inquiries and Complaints, 800 N. Capitol St. N.W., #1052 20573; (202) 523-5807. Fax, (202) 523-0014. Joseph Farrell, Director.*

Federal Reserve System, *Consumer and Community Affairs, 20th and C Sts. N.W. 20551-0001; (202) 452-2631. Fax, (202) 872-4995. Dolores S. Smith, Director. Complaints, (202) 452-3693.*

Food and Drug Administration *(Health and Human Services Dept.), Consumer Affairs, 5600 Fishers Lane,*

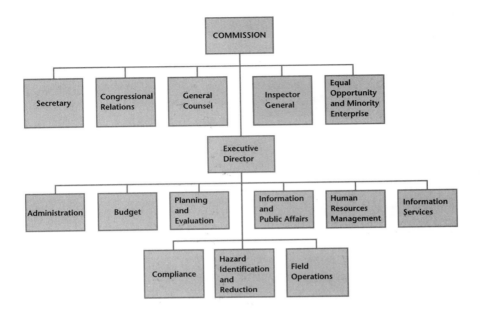

Rockville, MD 20857; (301) 827-5006. Fax, (301) 443-9767. Patricia Kuntze, Associate Director (Acting). Consumer inquiries, (888) 463-6332. Web, www.fda.gov.

General Services Administration, *Consumer Information Center,* 1800 F St. N.W., #G142 20405; (202) 501-1794. Fax, (202) 501-4281. Teresa N. Nasif, Director. Web, www.pueblo.gsa.gov.

Interior Dept., *Communications,* 1849 C St. N.W., #6013 20240; (202) 208-6416. Fax, (202) 208-5133. Michael Gauldin, Director. TTY, (202) 208-4817. Web, www.doi.gov.

Justice Dept., *Civil Division: Consumer Litigation,* 1331 Pennsylvania Ave., #950N 20004; (202) 307-0066. Fax, (202) 514-8742. Eugene M. Thirolf, Director. Web, www.usdoj.gov.

Merit Systems Protection Board, 1615 M St., N.W. 20419; (202) 653-7200. Fax, (202) 653-7130. Robert E. Taylor, Clerk of the Board. TTY, (202) 653-8896. Web, www.mspb.gov.

National Institute of Standards and Technology *(Commerce Dept.),* **Inquiries,** Route I-270 and Quince Orchard Rd., Administrative Bldg., #A-903, Gaithersburg, MD 20899 (mailing address: 100 Bureau Dr., Stop 3460, Gaithersburg, MD 20899-3460); (301) 975-6478. Fax,

(301) 926-1630. Sharon Shaffer, Head. General e-mail, inquiries@nist.gov.

Nuclear Regulatory Commission, *Public Affairs,* 11555 Rockville Pike, Rockville, MD 20852-2738; (301) 415-8200. Fax, (301) 415-3716. Mindy Landau, Coordinator. General e-mail, nrc@nrc.gov. Web, www.nrc.gov/opa.

Postal Rate Commission, *Consumer Advocate,* 1333 H St. N.W. 20268-0001; (202) 789-6830. Fax, (202) 789-6886. Ted Gerarden, Director.

Securities and Exchange Commission, *Filings and Information Services,* 6432 General Greenway, Alexandria, VA 22312; (202) 942-8938. Fax, (703) 914-1005. Kenneth Fogash, Director.

Small Business Administration, *Capital Access,* 409 3rd St. S.W., #8200 20416; (202) 205-6657. Fax, (202) 205-7230. Charles D. Tansey, Associate Deputy Administrator. Web, www.sba.gov.

State Dept., *Coordinator for Business Affairs,* 2201 C St. N.W., #2318 20520-5820; (202) 647-1625. Fax, (202) 647-3953. Sandra Willett Jackson, Senior Coordinator. General e-mail, cbaweb@state.gov. Web, www.state.gov/www/about_state/business/coordin3.html.

Serves as primary contact in the State Dept. for U.S. businesses. Coordinates efforts to facilitate U.S. business interests abroad, ensures that U.S. business interests are given sufficient consideration in foreign policy, and provides assistance to firms with problems overseas (such as claims and trade complaints). Works with agencies in the Trade Promotion Coordinating Committee to support U.S. business interests overseas.

Transportation Dept., *Aviation Consumer Protection,* *400 7th St. S.W., #4107 20590 (mailing address: Transportation Dept., C75 20590); (202) 366-2220. Fax, (202) 366-7907. Norman Strickman, Assistant Director (Acting). General e-mail, airconsumer@ost.dot.gov. Web, www.dot. gov/airconsumer.*

Treasury Dept., *Public Affairs, 1500 Pennsylvania Ave. N.W., #2321 20220; (202) 622-2960. Fax, (202) 622-2808. Michelle Smith, Assistant Secretary. Web, www.ustreas.gov.*

U.S. Postal Service, *Consumer Affairs, 475 L'Enfant Plaza S.W. 20260-2200; (202) 268-2284. Fax, (202) 268-2304. Francia Smith, Vice President. TTY, (202) 268-2310.*

Veterans Affairs Dept., *Consumer Affairs, 810 Vermont Ave. N.W., #915 20420; (202) 273-5772. Fax, (202) 273-5716. Clayton Cochran, Program Analyst; Shirley Mathis, Program Analyst. Web, www.va.gov.*

CONGRESS

House Appropriations Committee, *Subcommittee on Commerce, Justice, State, and Judiciary, H309 CAP 20515; (202) 225-3351. Rep. Harold Rogers, R-Ky., Chair; Jim Kulikowski, Staff Director. Web, www.house.gov/ appropriations.*

Jurisdiction over legislation to appropriate funds for the Federal Trade Commission.

House Appropriations Committee, *Subcommittee on VA, HUD, and Independent Agencies, H143 CAP 20515; (202) 225-3241. Rep. James T. Walsh, R-N.Y., Chair; Frank Cushing, Staff Director. Web, www.house.gov/ appropriations.*

Jurisdiction over legislation to appropriate funds for the Consumer Information Center of the General Services Administration, the Consumer Product Safety Commission, and the U.S. Office of Consumer Affairs of the Health and Human Services Dept.

House Banking and Financial Services Committee, *Subcommittee on Financial Institutions and Consumer Credit, 2129 RHOB 20515; (202) 225-2258. Fax, (202) 225-6984. Rep. Marge Roukema, R-N.J., Chair; Laurie Schaffer, Staff Director. Web, www.house.gov/banking.*

Jurisdiction over legislation on consumer protection, including fair lending and regulatory issues.

House Commerce Committee, *Subcommittee on Health and the Environment, 2125 RHOB 20515; (202) 225-2927. Fax, (202) 225-1919. Rep. Michael Bilirakis, R-Fla., Chair; James E. Derderian, Staff Director. General e-mail, commerce@mail.house.gov. Web, www.house. gov/commerce.*

Jurisdiction over legislation on vaccines; labeling and packaging, including tobacco products and alcohol beverages; and the use of vitamins. Oversight of the Food and Drug Administration.

House Commerce Committee, *Subcommittee on Telecommunications, Trade, and Consumer Protection, 2125 RHOB 20515; (202) 225-2927. Fax, (202) 225-1919. Rep. W. J. "Billy" Tauzin, R-La., Chair; James E. Derderian, Staff Director. General e-mail, commerce@mail.house. gov. Web, www.house.gov/commerce.*

Jurisdiction over product liability and consumer protection legislation, the Consumer Product Safety Commission, the Federal Trade Commission, and interstate and foreign commerce, including general trade matters within the jurisdiction of the full committee.

House Government Reform Committee, *Subcommittee on National Economic Growth, Natural Resources, and Regulatory Affairs, B377 RHOB 20515; (202) 225-4407. Fax, (202) 225-2441. Rep. David M. McIntosh, R-Ind., Chair; Marlo Lewis, Staff Director. Web, www.house.gov/reform.*

Oversight of the Federal Trade Commission and the Consumer Product Safety Commission.

House Science Committee, *Subcommittee on Basic Research, B374 RHOB 20515; (202) 225-7858. Fax, (202) 225-7815. Rep. Nick Smith, R-Mich., Chair; Steve Eule, Staff Director. Web, www.house.gov/science.*

Jurisdiction over legislation related to the U.S. Fire Administration and Building and Fire Research Laboratory of the National Institute of Standards and Technology; oversight of federal fire prevention and the Earthquake Hazards Reduction Act. Jurisdiction over research and development involving government nutritional programs.

Senate Appropriations Committee, *Subcommittee on Commerce, Justice, State, and Judiciary, S-146A CAP 20510; (202) 224-7277. Sen. Judd Gregg, R-N.H., Chair; Jim Morhard, Clerk. Web, appropriations.senate.gov/ commerce.*

Jurisdiction over legislation to appropriate funds for the Federal Trade Commission.

Senate Appropriations Committee, *Subcommittee on VA, HUD, and Independent Agencies, SD-130 20510;*

CONSUMER AND EMERGENCY HOTLINES

DEPARTMENTS

Agriculture

Meat and poultry safety inquiries, (800) 535-4555; (202) 720-3333 in Washington

Commerce

Export enforcement hotline, (800) 424-2980

Trade Information Center, (800) 872-8723

Defense

Army espionage hotline, (800) 225-5779

Education

Student financial aid info., (800) 433-3243

Energy

Energy Efficiency and Renewable Energy and Clearinghouse, (800) 363-3732

Environmental hotline, (800) 541-1625

Health and Human Services

AIDS info., (800) 342-2437; 332-2437 in Washington; TTY, (800) 243-7889. Spanish speaking, (800) 344-7432; (202) 328-0697 in Washington

Civil rights info., (800) 368-1019

General health info., (800) 336-4797

Inspector general hotline, (800) 447-8477

Medicare Fraud hotline, (800) 638-6833

National Adoption Center, (800) 862-3678

National Cancer Institute Cancer info., (800) 422-6237

National Runaway Switchboard, (800) 621-4000

Housing and Urban Development

Housing discrimination hotline, (800) 669-9777

Justice

Americans With Disabilities Act information, (800) 514-0301; TTY, (800) 514-0383

Immigration and Naturalization Service regulations hotline, (800) 375-5283; forms request, (800) 870-3676

Juvenile justice info., (800) 638-8736

National Institute for Corrections Information Center, (800) 877-1461

Office of Justice Programs
Drug and crime data, (800) 666-3332
National Victims Resource Center, (800) 627-6872

Unfair employment hotline, (800) 255-7688

Transportation

Airline safety hotline, (800) 255-1111

Auto safety hotline, (800) 424-9393; (202) 366-0123 in Washington

Federal Aviation Administration consumer hotline, (800) 322-7873

Hazardous material, chemical, and oil spills, (800) 424-8802

USCG Boating hotline, (800) 368-5647

Treasury

Comptroller of the Currency customer assistance hotline, (800) 613-6743

Drug smuggling reports, (800) 232-5378

Explosive materials discovery theft, loss reports, (800) 800-3855; (202) 927-8050 in Washington

Tax form requests, (800) 829-3676

Tax refund info., (800) 829-4477

Taxpayer assistance, (800) 829-1040

Veterans Affairs

Benefits hotline, (800) 827-1000

Debt Management Center, (800) 827-0648

---

(202) 224-7211. Sen. Christopher S. Bond, R-Mo., Chair; Jon Kamarck, Staff Director. Web, appropriations.senate. gov/vahud.

Jurisdiction over legislation to appropriate funds for the Consumer Information Center of the General Services Administration, the Consumer Product Safety Commission, and the U.S. Office of Consumer Affairs.

Senate Banking, Housing, and Urban Affairs Committee, *SD-534 20510; (202) 224-7391. Fax, (202) 224-5137. Sen. Phil Gramm, R-Texas, Chair; Wayne A. Abernathy, Staff Director. Web, banking.senate.gov.*

Jurisdiction over legislation on consumer protection, including the Community Reinvestment Act and the Fair Credit Reporting Act, and regulatory oversight issues.

Senate Commerce, Science, and Transportation Committee, *SD-508 20510; (202) 224-5115. Fax, (202) 224-1259. Sen. John McCain, R-Ariz., Chair; Mark Buse, Staff Director. Web, commerce.senate.gov.*

Jurisdiction over regulation of consumer products and services, including testing related to toxic substances. Jurisdiction over legislation related to the U.S. Fire Administration and the Building and Fire Research Laboratory of the National Institute of Standards and Tech-

CONSUMER AND EMERGENCY HOTLINES (continued)

Fraud, waste, and mismanagement hotline, (800) 488-8244

Life insurance information, (800) 669-8477

Persian Gulf hotline, (800) 749-8387

AGENCIES

Consumer Product Safety Commission

Product safety info., (800) 638-2772

Environmental Protection Agency

Asbestos ombudsman, (800) 368-5888; (202) 260-0490 in Washington

Electric and Magnetic field infoline, (800) 363-2383

Endangered species hotline, (800) 447-3813

National Lead Information Center, (800) 532-3394

National radon hotline, (800) 767-7236

Ozone information hotline, (800) 296-1996

Pesticides and related medical info., (800) 858-7378

Safe drinking water hotline, (800) 426-4791

Superfund hotline, (800) 424-9346; (703) 412-9810 in Washington

Wetlands information hotline, (800) 832-7828

Export-Import Bank

Export finance hotline, (800) 565-3946; (202) 565-3946 in Washington

Federal Deposit Insurance Corporation

Banking complaints and inquiries, (800) 934-3342

Federal Election Commission

Fund-raising laws info., (800) 424-9530; (202) 694-1100 in Washington

Federal Emergency Management Agency

Emergency management and training info., (800) 638-1821; (301) 447-1030 in Maryland

Flood insurance service, (800) 638-6620

General Services Administration

Federal Information Center, (800) 688-9889

National Archives and Records Administration (through NTIS)

Audiovisual material sales and info., (800) 788-6282

Nuclear Regulatory Commission

Nuclear power info., (800) 368-5642

Office of Special Counsel

Prohibited personnel practices info., (800) 872-9855; (202) 653-7188 in Washington

Small Business Administration

Small business assistance, (800) 827-5722

Social Security Administration

Fraud and abuse hotline, (800) 767-0385

Social Security benefits (including Medicare) info., (800) 772-1213

PRIVATE ORGANIZATIONS

GED Hotline on Adult Education, (800) 626-9433

National Center for Missing and Exploited Children, (800) 843-5678

National Insurance Consumer Helpline, (800) 942-4242

National Literacy Hotline, (800) 228-8813

National Organization for Victim Assistance, (800) 879-6682; (202) 232-6682 in Washington

Project Vote Smart, (800) 622-7627

United Network for Organ Sharing, (888) 894-6361

---

nology; oversight of federal fire prevention and the Earthquake Hazards Reduction Act.

Senate Commerce, Science, and Transportation Committee, *Subcommittee on Consumer Affairs, Foreign Commerce, and Tourism, SH-425 20510; (202) 224-5183. Fax, (202) 228-0326. Sen. John Ashcroft, R-Mo., Chair; Rob Taylor, Counsel. Web, commerce.senate.gov.*

Jurisdiction over legislation on the Federal Trade Commission, the Consumer Product Safety Commission, the Food and Drug Administration, the National Highway Traffic Safety Administration, and the U.S. Fire Administration. Jurisdiction over product safety and lia-

bility; flammable products; insurance; and labeling and packaging legislation, including advertising and packaging of tobacco products and alcohol beverages.

Senate Health, Education, Labor, and Pensions Committee, *SD-428 20510; (202) 224-5375. Fax, (202) 228-5044. Sen. James M. Jeffords, R-Vt., Chair; Mark Powden, Staff Director. TTY, (202) 224-1975. Web, labor.senate.gov.*

Jurisdiction over legislation on vaccines, drug labeling and packaging, inspection and certification of fish and processed food, and the use of vitamins.

NONPROFIT

Automotive Consumer Action Program, *8400 West-park Dr., McLean, VA 22102; (703) 821-7144. Fax, (703) 821-7075. Lesley J. Hardesty, National Manager. Press, (703) 827-7407.*

Third-party mediation program that promotes national standards and procedures in resolving auto dealer/manufacturer and consumer disputes.

Center for Auto Safety, *1825 Connecticut Ave., #330 20009; (202) 328-7700. Fax, (202) 387-0140. Clarence M. Ditlow III, Executive Director. Web, www.autosafety.org.*

Public interest organization that receives written consumer complaints against auto manufacturers; monitors federal agencies responsible for regulating and enforcing auto and highway safety rules.

Consumer Alert, *1001 Connecticut Ave. N.W., #1128 20036; (202) 467-5809. Fax, (202) 467-5814. Frances B. Smith, Executive Director. General e-mail, info@consumeralert.org. Web, www.consumeralert.org.*

Membership: individual consumers. Promotes consumer choice and economic competition to advance consumers' interests.

Consumer Federation of America, *1424 16th St. N.W., #604 20036; (202) 387-6121. Fax, (202) 265-7989. Stephen Brobeck, Executive Director.*

Federation of national, regional, state, and local pro-consumer organizations. Promotes consumer interests in banking, credit, and insurance; telecommunications; housing; food, drugs, and medical care; safety; energy and natural resources development; and indoor air quality.

Consumer Federation of America's Insurance Group, *1424 16th St. N.W., #604 20036; (202) 387-6121. Fax, (202) 265-7989. Robert Hunter, Director.*

Public interest organization that conducts research and provides consumers with information on buying insurance. Interests include auto, homeowner, renter, and life insurance. Monitors legislation and regulations.

Consumers Union of the United States, Washington Office, *1666 Connecticut Ave. N.W., #310 20009; (202) 462-6262. Fax, (202) 265-9548. Gene Kimmelman, Co-Director; Mark Silbergeld, Co-Director. Web, www.consumersunion.org.*

Consumer advocacy group that represents consumer interests before Congress and regulatory agencies and litigates consumer affairs cases involving the government. Interests include consumer impact of world trade. Publishes *Consumer Reports* magazine.

Council of Better Business Bureaus, *4200 Wilson Blvd., #800, Arlington, VA 22203-1838; (703) 276-0100. Fax, (703) 525-8277. Kenneth Hunter, President. General e-mail, bbb@bbb.org. Web, www.bbb.org.*

Membership: businesses and Better Business Bureaus in the United States and Canada. Promotes ethical business practices and truth in national advertising; mediates disputes between consumers and businesses.

DANA Foundation, *P.O. Box 1050, Germantown, MD 20875; (301) 540-7295. Joseph Colella, Executive Director.*

Promotes public awareness of child passenger safety issues, including compatibility and proper use of child safety seats.

National Assn. of Consumer Agency Administrators, *1010 Vermont Ave. N.W., #514 20005; (202) 347-7395. Fax, (202) 347-2563. Wendy Weinberg, Executive Director. General e-mail, nacaa@erols.com. Web, www.nacaanet.org.*

Membership: federal, state, and local government consumer affairs professionals. Seeks to enhance consumer services available to the public. Acts as a clearinghouse for consumer information and legislation. Serves as liaison with federal agencies and Congress. Offers training programs, seminars, and conferences.

National Consumers League, *1701 K St. N.W., #1200 20006; (202) 835-3323. Fax, (202) 835-0747. Linda F. Golodner, President. Web, www.nclnet.org.*

Citizens' interest group that engages in research and educational activities related to consumer issues. Interests include health care; child labor; food, drug, and product safety; environment; telecommunications; and financial services.

National SAFE KIDS Campaign, *1301 Pennsylvania Ave. N.W., #1000 20004; (202) 662-0600. Fax, (202) 393-2072. Heather Paul, Executive Director. Web, www.safekids.org.*

Promotes awareness among adults that unintentional injury is the leading cause of death among children ages fourteen and under. Conducts educational programs on childhood injury prevention; sponsors National SAFE KIDS Week.

Public Citizen, *1600 20th St. N.W. 20009; (202) 588-1000. Fax, (202) 588-7798. Joan Claybrook, President. Web, www.citizen.org.*

Public interest consumer advocacy organization comprising the following projects: Buyers Up, Congress Watch, Critical Mass Energy Project, Health Research Group, Litigation Group, and Global Trade Watch.

Trial Lawyers for Public Justice, *1717 Massachusetts Ave. N.W., #800 20036; (202) 797-8600. Fax, (202) 232-7203. Arthur H. Bryant, Executive Director. Web, www.tlpj.org.*

Membership: consumer activists, trial lawyers, and public interest lawyers. Litigates to influence corporate and government decisions about products or activities adversely affecting health or safety. Interests include toxic torts, environmental protection, civil rights and civil liberties, workers' safety, consumer protection, and the preservation of the civil justice system.

U.S. Chamber of Commerce, *Congressional and Public Affairs, 1615 H St. N.W. 20062-2000; (202) 659-6000. Fax, (202) 887-3430. Lonnie P. Taylor, Senior Vice President. Web, www.uschamber.org.*

Monitors legislation and regulations regarding business and consumer issues, including legislation and policies affecting the Federal Trade Commission, the Consumer Product Safety Commission, and other agencies.

U.S. Public Interest Research Group, *218 D St. S.E. 20003; (202) 546-9707. Fax, (202) 546-2461. Gene Karpinski, Executive Director. General e-mail, uspirg@pirg.org. Web, www.pirg.org.*

Conducts research and advocacy on consumer and environmental issues, including telephone rates, banking practices, insurance, campaign finance reform, product safety, toxic and solid waste, safe drinking water, and energy; monitors private and governmental actions affecting consumers; supports efforts to challenge consumer fraud and illegal business practices. Serves as national office for state groups.

See also National Consumer Law Center (p. 29)

Credit Practices

See also Real Estate (chap. 12)

AGENCIES

Comptroller of the Currency *(Treasury Dept.), Community and Consumer Policy, 250 E St. S.W. 20219-0001; (202) 874-5216. Fax, (202) 874-5221. Ralph Sharpe, Deputy Comptroller.*

Develops policy for enforcing consumer laws and regulations that affect national banks, including the Truth-in-Lending, Community Reinvestment, and Equal Credit Opportunity acts.

Comptroller of the Currency *(Treasury Dept.), Law Dept., 250 E St. S.W., 8th Floor 20219; (202) 874-5200. Fax, (202) 874-5374. Julie L. Williams, Chief Counsel. Library, (202) 874-4720.*

Enforces and oversees compliance by nationally chartered banks with laws prohibiting discrimination in credit transactions on the basis of sex or marital status. Enforces regulations concerning bank advertising; may issue cease-and-desist orders.

Comptroller of the Currency *(Treasury Dept.), Public Affairs, 250 E St. S.W. 20219; (202) 874-4970. Fax, (202) 874-5678. Vacant, Senior Deputy Comptroller. Web, www.occ.treas.gov.*

Advises the comptroller on relations with the media, the banking industry, Congress, and consumer and community development groups.

Federal Deposit Insurance Corp., *Compliance and Consumer Affairs, 550 17th St. N.W. 20429; (202) 942-3100. Fax, (202) 942-3427. Stephen M. Cross, Director. Information, (800) 934-3342. TTY, (800) 925-4618. General e-mail, consumer@fdic.gov. Web, www.fdic.gov.*

Coordinates and monitors complaints filed by consumers against federally insured state banks that are not members of the Federal Reserve System; handles complaints concerning truth-in-lending and other fair credit provisions, including charges of discrimination on the basis of sex or marital status; responds to general banking inquiries; answers questions on deposit insurance coverage.

Federal Deposit Insurance Corp., *Supervision, 550 17th St. N.W. 20429; (202) 898-8510. Fax, (202) 898-3638. James L. Sexton, Director.*

Examines and supervises federally insured state banks that are not members of the Federal Reserve System for violations of truth-in-lending and other fair credit provisions.

Federal Reserve System, *Consumer and Community Affairs, 20th and C Sts. N.W. 20551-0001; (202) 452-2631. Fax, (202) 872-4995. Dolores S. Smith, Director. Complaints, (202) 452-3693.*

Receives consumer complaints concerning truth-in-lending, fair credit billing, equal credit opportunity, electronic fund transfer, home mortgage disclosure, consumer leasing, and advertising; receives complaints about unregulated practices; refers complaints to district banks. The Federal Reserve monitors enforcement of fair lending laws with regard to state-chartered banks that are members of the Federal Reserve System.

Federal Trade Commission, *Financial Practices, 601 Pennsylvania Ave. N.W. 20580; (202) 326-3224. Fax, (202) 326-2558. David Medine, Associate Director.*

Enforces truth-in-lending and fair credit billing provisions for creditors not handled by other agencies, such as retail stores and small loan companies; enforces the Fair Credit Reporting Act, which protects consumers from unfair credit ratings and practices; enforces the Fair Debt Collection Practices Act, Electronic Funds Transfer Act, Equal Credit Opportunity Act, Consumer Leasing Act, Holder in Due Course Rule, and Credit Practices Rule.

Justice Dept., *Civil Division: Consumer Litigation,* 1331 Pennsylvania Ave., #950N 20004; (202) 307-0066. Fax, (202) 514-8742. Eugene M. Thirolf, Director. Web, www.usdoj.gov.

Files suits to enforce the Truth-in-Lending Act and other federal statutes protecting consumers, generally upon referral by client agencies.

National Credit Union Administration, *Examination and Insurance,* 1775 Duke St., Alexandria, VA 22314-3428; (703) 518-6360. Fax, (703) 518-6499. David M. Marquis, Director. Toll-free investment hotline, (800) 755-5999.

Oversees and enforces compliance by federally chartered credit unions with the Truth-in-Lending Act, the Equal Credit Opportunity Act, and other federal statutes protecting consumers.

Office of Thrift Supervision *(Treasury Dept.),* *Compliance Policy and Special Exams,* 1700 G St. N.W., 6th Floor 20552; (202) 906-6237. Fax, (202) 906-6326. Richard Riese, Director. Consumer complaints, (800) 842-6929.

Receives and processes complaints filed against savings and loan institutions, including charges of false and deceptive advertising and of discrimination against minorities and women.

Small Business Administration, *Civil Rights Compliance,* 409 3rd St. S.W., #6400 20416; (202) 205-6751. Fax, (202) 205-7580. Carol L. Walker, Deputy Chief. TTY, (202) 205-7150.

Reviews complaints against the Small Business Administration by recipients of its assistance in cases of alleged discrimination in credit transactions; monitors recipients for civil rights compliance.

NONPROFIT

American Bankers Assn., *Communications,* 1120 Connecticut Ave. N.W. 20036; (202) 663-7501. Fax, (202) 663-7578. Virginia Dean, Executive Director. Library, (202) 663-5042. Web, www.aba.com.

Provides information on a wide range of banking issues and financial management. Library open to the public by appointment.

American Financial Services Assn., *919 18th St. N.W., #300 20006; (202) 296-5544. Fax, (202) 223-0321. Randolph Lively, President. General e-mail, afsa@afsamail. com. Web, www.americanfinsvcs.com.*

Membership: consumer installment credit industry including consumer finance, sales finance, and industrial banking companies. Conducts research; provides consumer finance education. Monitors legislation and regulations.

National Retail Federation, *325 7th St. N.W., #1000 20004-2802; (202) 783-7971. Fax, (202) 737-2849. Tracy Mullin, President. Web, www.nrf.com.*

Membership: national and state associations of retailers and major retail corporations. Provides information on credit, truth-in-lending laws, and other fair credit practices.

Fire Prevention and Control

See also Caucuses (chap. 20); Clothing and Textiles (chap. 3)

AGENCIES

Consumer Product Safety Commission, *Hazard Identification and Reduction,* 4330 East-West Hwy., #702, Bethesda, MD 20814; (301) 504-0554. Fax, (301) 504-0407. Ronald L. Medford, Assistant Executive Director.

Proposes, evaluates, and develops standards and test procedures for safety and fire resistance in accordance with the Flammable Fabrics Act and the Federal Hazardous Substances Act. Reports injuries resulting from use of products.

Federal Emergency Management Agency, *National Fire Academy,* 16825 S. Seton Ave., Emmitsburg, MD 21727-8998; (301) 447-1117. Fax, (301) 447-1173. Denis Onieal, Superintendent. Web, www.usfa.fema.gov/nfa.

Trains fire officials and related professionals in fire prevention and management, current fire fighting technologies, and the administration of fire prevention organizations.

Forest Service *(Agriculture Dept.),* *Fire and Aviation Management,* 201 14th St. S.W. 20024 (mailing address: P.O. Box 96090 20090-6090); (202) 205-1483. Fax, (202) 205-1272. Jose Cruz, Director.

Responsible for aviation and fire management programs, including fire control planning and prevention, suppression of fires, and the use of prescribed fires. Provides state foresters with financial and technical assistance for fire protection in forests and on rural lands.

National Institute of Standards and Technology *(Commerce Dept.), Building and Fire Research Laboratory, Route I-270 and Quince Orchard Rd., Gaithersburg, MD 20899; (301) 975-5851. Fax, (301) 975-5433. Jack Snell, Director; James E. Hill, Deputy Director. Web, www.bfrl.nist.gov.*

Conducts basic and applied research on fire and fire resistance of construction materials; develops testing methods, standards, design concepts, and technologies for fire protection and prevention.

National Institute of Standards and Technology *(Commerce Dept.), Fire Safety Engineering, Route I-270 and Quince Orchard Rd., Gaithersburg, MD 20899; (301) 975-6863. Fax, (301) 975-4052. David D. Evans, Chief.*

Conducts research on fire safety. Develops models to measure the behavior and mitigate the impact of large-scale fires. Operates the Fire Research Information Service, Fire Dynamics Group, and a large-scale fire test facility.

National Institute of Standards and Technology *(Commerce Dept.), Fire Science, Route I-270 and Quince Orchard Rd., Bldg. 224, #B250, Gaithersburg, MD 20899; (301) 975-6864. Fax, (301) 975-4052. William Grosshandler, Chief.*

Conducts research on fire and metrology. Studies smoke components of flames, the burning of polymeric materials, and fire detection and suppression systems.

Occupational Safety and Health Administration *(Labor Dept.), Safety Standards, 200 Constitution Ave. N.W., #N3605 20210; (202) 693-2222. Fax, (202) 693-1663. Marthe B. Kent, Director (Acting).*

Administers regulations for fire safety standards; sponsors programs for maritime, fire protection, construction, mechanical, and electrical industries.

U.S. Fire Administration *(Federal Emergency Management Agency), 16825 S. Seton Ave., Emmitsburg, MD 21727; (301) 447-1018. Fax, (301) 447-1270. Carrye B. Brown, Administrator. Web, www.usfa.fema.gov.*

Conducts research and collects, analyzes, and disseminates data on combustion, fire prevention, fire fighter safety, and the management of fire prevention organizations; studies and develops arson prevention programs and fire prevention codes; maintains the National Fire Data System.

NONPROFIT

International Assn. of Fire Chiefs, *4025 Fair Ridge Dr., Fairfax, VA 22033-2868; (703) 273-0911. Fax, (703) 273-9363. Garry L. Briese, Executive Director. General e-mail, iafchq@iafc.org. Web, www.iafc.org.*

Membership: fire fighting chiefs and managers. Conducts research on fire control; testifies before congressional committees. Monitors legislation and regulations affecting fire safety codes.

International Assn. of Fire Fighters, *1750 New York Ave. N.W., 3rd Floor 20006; (202) 737-8484. Fax, (202) 737-8418. Alfred K. Whitehead, General President. Web, www.iaff.org.*

Membership: more than 225,000 professional fire fighters and emergency medical personnel. Assists members with contract negotiation and grievances; conducts training programs and workshops. Monitors legislation and regulations. (Affiliated with the AFL-CIO and the Canadian Labour Congress.)

National Fire Protection Assn., Government Affairs, Washington Office, *1110 N. Glebe Rd., #210, Arlington, VA 22201; (703) 516-4346. Fax, (703) 516-4350. Anthony R. O'Neill, Vice President. General e-mail, wdc@nfpa.org. Web, www.nfpa.org.*

Membership: individuals and organizations interested in fire protection. Develops and updates fire protection codes and standards; sponsors technical assistance programs; collects fire data statistics. Monitors legislation and regulations.

Labeling and Packaging

See also Food and Nutrition (chap. 2); Medical Devices and Technology (chap. 11); Pharmaceuticals (chap. 11); Tobacco (this chapter)

AGENCIES

Consumer Product Safety Commission, Hazard Identification and Reduction, *4330 East-West Hwy., #702, Bethesda, MD 20814; (301) 504-0554. Fax, (301) 504-0407. Ronald L. Medford, Assistant Executive Director.*

Establishes labeling and packaging regulations. Develops standards in accordance with the Poison Prevention Packaging Act, the Federal Hazardous Substances Act, and the Consumer Products Safety Act.

Food and Drug Administration *(Health and Human Services Dept.), Center for Food Safety and Applied Nutrition, 200 C St. S.W. 20204; (202) 205-4850. Fax, (202) 205-5025. Joseph A. Levitt, Director. Press, (202) 205-4241. TTY, (202) 205-4863. Web, vm.cfsan.fda.gov.*

Develops and enforces labeling regulations for foods (except meat and poultry but including fish) and cosmetics; develops and enforces standards on form and fill of packaging for foods and cosmetics; develops and enforces safety regulations for food and cosmetic packaging materials; recommends action to Justice Dept.

Food and Drug Administration *(Health and Human Services Dept.), Drug Marketing, Advertising, and Communications,* 5600 Fishers Lane, HFD-42, #17B-20, Rockville, MD 20857; (301) 827-2828. Fax, (301) 594-6771. Norm Drezin, Director (Acting). Web, www.fda.gov/cder.

Monitors prescription drug advertising and labeling; investigates complaints; conducts market research on health care communications and drug issues.

Food Safety and Inspection Service *(Agriculture Dept.),* 1400 Independence Ave. S.W., #331E 20250; (202) 720-7025. Fax, (202) 205-0158. Thomas J. Billy, Administrator. Press, (202) 720-9113. Consumer inquiries, (800) 535-4555; in Washington, (202) 720-3333. Web, www.usda.gov/fsis.

Inspects meat and poultry products and provides safe handling and labeling guidelines.

National Institute of Standards and Technology *(Commerce Dept.), Weights and Measures,* 820 W. Diamond Ave., #223, Gaithersburg, MD 20878; (301) 975-4004. Fax, (301) 926-0647. Gilbert M. Ugiansky, Chief.

Promotes uniform standards among the states for packaging and labeling products and for measuring devices, including scales and commercial measurement instruments; advises manufacturers on labeling and packaging laws and on measuring device standards.

NONPROFIT

Flexible Packaging Assn., 1090 Vermont Ave. N.W., #500 20005-4960; (202) 842-3880. Fax, (202) 842-3841. John Woolford, President (Interim). General e-mail, fpa@flexpack.org.

Membership: companies that supply or manufacture flexible packaging. Conducts programs to teach students practical applications of science and design; coordinates programs on reducing solid waste for schools.

Glass Packaging Institute, 1627 K St. N.W., #800 20006; (202) 887-4850. Fax, (202) 785-5377. Joseph Cattaneo, Executive Vice President. Web, www.gpi.org.

Membership: manufacturers of glass containers and their suppliers. Promotes industry policies to protect the environment, conserve natural resources, and reduce energy consumption; conducts research; monitors legislation affecting the industry. Interests include glass recycling.

Packaging Machinery Manufacturers Institute, 4350 N. Fairfax Dr., #600, Arlington, VA 22203; (703) 243-8555. Fax, (703) 243-8556. Chuck Yuska, President. Web, www.packexpo.com.

Membership: manufacturers of packaging and packaging-related converting machinery. Provides industry information and statistics; offers educational programs to members.

Privacy

See also Privacy Act (appendix)

AGENCIES

Federal Communications Commission, *Common Carrier Bureau Network Services,* 445 12th St. S.W. 20554; (202) 418-2320. Fax, (202) 418-2345. L. Chuck Keller, Chief.

Establishes federal policy governing interstate caller identification services.

Federal Trade Commission, *Financial Practices,* 601 Pennsylvania Ave. N.W. 20580; (202) 326-3224. Fax, (202) 326-2558. David Medine, Associate Director.

Enforces the Fair Credit Reporting Act, which requires credit bureaus to furnish correct and complete information to businesses evaluating credit, insurance, or job applications.

Office of Management and Budget *(Executive Office of the President), Information Policy and Technology,* 725 17th St. N.W., #10236 20503; (202) 395-3785. Fax, (202) 395-5167. Dan Chenok, Chief (Acting). Web, www.whitehouse.gov/omb.

Oversees implementation of the Privacy Act of 1974. Issues guidelines and regulations.

CONGRESS

House Judiciary Committee, *Subcommittee on the Constitution,* H2-362 FHOB 20515; (202) 226-7680. Fax, (202) 225-3746. Rep. Charles T. Canady, R-Fla., Chair; Cathy Cleaver, Chief Counsel. General e-mail, Judiciary@mail.house.gov. Web, www.house.gov/judiciary.

Jurisdiction over legislation on the release of personal information by government agencies.

Senate Judiciary Committee, *Subcommittee on the Constitution, Federalism, and Property Rights,* SD-524 20510; (202) 224-8081. Fax, (202) 228-0544. Sen. John Ashcroft, R-Mo., Chair; Adam Cingoli, Chief Counsel. Web, judiciary.senate.gov/constitu.htm.

Jurisdiction over legislation on the release of personal information by government agencies.

NONPROFIT

American Civil Liberties Union, *Privacy and Technology,* 122 Maryland Ave. N.E. 20002; (202) 544-1681. Fax,

(202) 546-0738. Laura W. Murphy, Director. Web, www. aclu.org.

Studies the ways in which technology affects privacy. Interests include the Privacy Act of 1974, telecommunications, video and library lists, credit and medical records, criminal justice systems, drug testing, DNA database security, and patient confidentiality.

American Society for Industrial Security, *1625 Prince St., Alexandria, VA 22314; (703) 519-6200. Fax, (703) 519-6299. Michael Stack, Executive Director. Web, www.asisonline.org.*

Membership: security professionals worldwide. Interests include all aspects of security, with emphases on counterterrorism, computer security, privacy issues, government security, and the availability of job-related information for employers determining an employee's suitability for employment.

Assn. of Direct Response Fundraising Counsel, *1612 K St. N.W., #510 20006-2802; (202) 293-9640. Fax, (202) 887-9699. Robert S. Tigner, General Counsel. General e-mail, adrfco@aol.com.*

Membership: businesses in the direct response fundraising industry. Establishes standards of ethical practice in such areas as ownership of direct mail donor lists and mandatory disclosures by fundraising counsel. Educates nonprofit organizations and the public on direct mail fundraising.

Center for Democracy and Technology, *1634 Eye St. N.W., #1100 20006; (202) 637-9800. Fax, (202) 637-0968. Jerry Berman, Executive Director. General e-mail, info@cdt.org. Web, www.cdt.org.*

Promotes civil liberties and democratic values in new computer and communications media, both in the United States and abroad. Interests include free speech, privacy, freedom of information, electronic commerce, and design of the information infrastructure. Monitors legislation and regulations.

Communications Workers of America, *501 3rd St. N.W. 20001; (202) 434-1100. Fax, (202) 434-1279. Morton Bahr, President. Web, www.cwa-union.org.*

Membership: telecommunications, broadcast, and printing and publishing workers. Opposes electronic monitoring of productivity, eavesdropping by employers, and misuse of drug and polygraph tests.

Consumers Union of the United States, *Washington Office, 1666 Connecticut Ave. N.W., #310 20009; (202) 462-6262. Fax, (202) 265-9548. Gene Kimmelman, Co-Director; Mark Silbergeld, Co-Director. Web, www. consumersunion.org.*

Consumer advocacy group active in protecting the privacy of consumers. Interests include credit report accuracy.

Direct Marketing Assn., *Ethics and Consumer Affairs: Government Affairs, Washington Office, 1111 19th St. N.W., #1100 20036; (202) 955-5030. Fax, (202) 955-0085. Jerry Cerasale, Senior Vice President; Patricia Faley, Vice President. Web, www.the-dma.org.*

Membership: telemarketers; users, creators, and producers of direct mail; and suppliers to the industry. Evaluates direct marketing methods that make use of personal consumer information. Offers free service whereby consumers may remove their names from national mailing and telephone marketing lists.

Electronic Privacy Information Center, *666 Pennsylvania Ave. S.E., #301 20003; (202) 544-9240. Fax, (202) 547-5482. Marc Rotenberg, Director. General e-mail, info@epic.org. Web, www.epic.org.*

Public interest research center. Conducts research and conferences on domestic and international civil liberties issues, including privacy, free speech, information access, computer security, and encryption; litigates cases. Monitors legislation and regulations. (Affiliated with the Fund for Constitutional Government.)

National Assn. of State Utility Consumer Advocates, *8300 Colesville Rd., #101, Silver Spring, MD 20910; (301) 589-6313. Fax, (301) 589-6380. Charles Acquard, Executive Director. General e-mail, nasuca@nasuca.org. Web, www.nasuca.org.*

Membership: public advocate offices authorized by states to represent ratepayer interests before state and federal utility regulatory commissions. Supports privacy protection for telephone customers.

National Consumers League, *1701 K St. N.W., #1200 20006; (202) 835-3323. Fax, (202) 835-0747. Linda F. Golodner, President. Web, www.nclnet.org.*

Citizens' interest group concerned with privacy rights of consumers. Interests include credit and financial records, medical records, direct marketing, telecommunications, and workplace privacy.

U.S. Public Interest Research Group, *218 D St. S.E. 20003; (202) 546-9707. Fax, (202) 546-2461. Gene Karpinski, Executive Director. General e-mail, uspirg@ pirg.org. Web, www.pirg.org.*

Coordinates grassroots efforts to advance consumer protection laws. Works for the protection of privacy rights, particularly in the area of fair credit reporting.

See also Information Industry Assn. (p. 134)

Product Safety/Testing

AGENCIES

Consumer Product Safety Commission, *4330 East-West Hwy., Bethesda, MD 20814; (301) 504-0990. Fax, (301) 504-0281. Ann Brown, Chair; Susan Cox, Executive Director. Information, (301) 504-0580. Library, (301) 504-0044. TTY, (800) 638-8270. Locator, (301) 504-0100. Product safety hotline, (800) 638-2772. General e-mail, info@cpsc.gov. Web, www.cpsc.gov.*

Establishes and enforces product safety standards; collects data; studies the causes and prevention of product-related injuries; identifies hazardous products, including imports, and recalls them from the marketplace. Library open to the public.

Consumer Product Safety Commission, *Compliance, 4330 East-West Hwy., Bethesda, MD 20814; (301) 504-0621. Fax, (301) 504-0359. Alan H. Schoem, Director.*

Identifies and acts on any defective consumer product already in distribution; conducts surveillance and enforcement programs to ensure industry compliance with existing safety standards; works to ensure that products imported to the United States comply with existing safety standards; conducts enforcement litigation. Participates in developing standards to ensure that the final result is enforceable; monitors recall of defective products and issues warnings to consumers when appropriate.

Consumer Product Safety Commission, *Engineering Sciences, 4330 East-West Hwy., Bethesda, MD 20814; (301) 504-0504. Fax, (301) 504-0533. Andrew G. Stadnik, Associate Executive Director.*

Develops and evaluates consumer product safety standards, test methods, performance criteria, design specifications, and quality standards; conducts and evaluates engineering tests. Collects scientific and technical data to determine potential hazards of consumer products.

Consumer Product Safety Commission, *Health Sciences, 4330 East-West Hwy., Bethesda, MD 20814; (301) 504-0957. Fax, (301) 504-0079. Mary Ann Danello, Associate Executive Director.*

Collects data on consumer product-related hazards and potential hazards; determines the frequency, severity, and distribution of various types of injuries and investigates their causes; assesses the effects of product safety standards and programs on consumer injuries; conducts epidemiological studies and research in the field of consumer product-related injuries.

National Injury Information Clearinghouse *(Consumer Product Safety Commission), 4330 East-West Hwy., Bethesda, MD 20814; (301) 504-0424. Fax, (301) 504-0124. Ann Montalbano, Director. Fax-on-demand, (301) 504-0051. To report consumer product-related accidents or injuries, (800) 638-2772.*

Analyzes types and frequency of injuries resulting from consumer and recreational products. Collects injury information from consumer complaints, investigations, coroners' reports, death certificates, newspaper clippings, and statistically selected hospital emergency rooms nationwide.

NONPROFIT

American Academy of Pediatrics, *Washington Office, 601 13th St. N.W., #400N 20005; (202) 347-8600. Fax, (202) 393-6137. Jackie Noyes, Director. Information, (800) 336-5475. General e-mail, kids1st@aap.org. Web, www.aap.org.*

Promotes legislation and regulations concerning child health and safety. Committee on Injury and Poison Prevention drafts policy statements and publishes information on toy safety, poisons, and other issues that affect children and adolescents.

Cosmetic Ingredient Review, *1101 17th St. N.W., #310 20036-4702; (202) 331-0651. Fax, (202) 331-0088. F. Alan Andersen, Director. Web, www.cir-safety.org.*

Voluntary self-regulatory program funded by the Cosmetic, Toiletry, and Fragrance Assn. Reviews and evaluates published and unpublished data to assess the safety of cosmetic ingredients.

Product Liability Alliance, *Government Relations, 1725 K St. N.W. 20006; (202) 872-0885. Fax, (202) 785-0586. James A. Anderson Jr., Vice President.*

Membership: manufacturers, product sellers and their insurers, and trade associations. Promotes enactment of federal product liability tort reform legislation.

Tobacco

See also Caucuses (chap. 20); Commodities/Farm Produce (chap. 2)

AGENCIES

Bureau of Alcohol, Tobacco, and Firearms *(Treasury Dept.), Field Operations, 650 Massachusetts Ave. N.W., #8100 20226; (202) 927-7970. Fax, (202) 927-7756. Andrew L. Vita, Assistant Director. Information, (202) 927-7777. Press, (202) 927-9510. Web, www.atf.treas.gov.*

Enforces and administers revenue laws relating to tobacco.

Centers for Disease Control and Prevention *(Health and Human Services Dept.), Smoking and Health/Liaison, 200 Independence Ave. S.W., #317B 20201; (202) 205-8500. Fax, (202) 205-8313. Linda Bailey, Director. Web, www.cdc.gov/tobacco.*

Produces and issues the surgeon general's annual report on smoking and health; conducts public information and education programs on smoking and health. Conducts epidemiological studies, surveys, and analyses on tobacco use. Serves as liaison between governmental and nongovernmental organizations that work on tobacco initiatives.

Federal Trade Commission, *Advertising Practices, 601 Pennsylvania Ave. N.W., #S4002 20580; (202) 326-3090. Fax, (202) 326-3259. C. Lee Peeler, Associate Director.*

Regulates advertising of tobacco products under the Federal Cigarette Labeling and Advertising Act and the Comprehensive Smokeless Tobacco Health Education Act. Regulates labeling and advertising of tobacco products; administers health warnings on packages; monitors and tests claims on tobacco products for validity. Works with the Justice Dept. in enforcing the ban on tobacco advertising in the broadcast media; investigates deceptive claims and violations of laws and may refer violations to the Justice Dept. for criminal prosecution.

Food and Drug Administration *(Health and Human Services Dept.), 5600 Fishers Lane, Rockville, MD 20857; (301) 827-2410. Fax, (301) 443-3100. Dr. Jane E. Henney, Commissioner. Information, (301) 443-3793. Press, (301) 827-6242. Web, www.fda.gov.*

Considers nicotine an addictive drug and issues regulations on the advertising and sale of tobacco products, especially to minors. Regulates smoking cessation products containing nicotine, such as skin patches and chewing gum. Library open to the public.

NONPROFIT

Action on Smoking and Health, *2013 H St. N.W. 20006; (202) 659-4310. Fax, (202) 833-3921. John F. Banzhaf III, Executive Director. Web, ash.org.*

Educational and legal organization that works to protect nonsmokers from cigarette smoking; provides information about smoking hazards and nonsmokers' rights.

Bakery, Confectionery, Tobacco Workers, and Grain Millers International Union, *10401 Connecticut Ave., Kensington, MD 20895; (301) 933-8600. Fax, (301) 946-8452. Frank Hurt, President.*

Membership: approximately 120,000 workers from the bakery and tobacco industries. Helps members negotiate pay, benefits, and better working conditions; conducts training programs and workshops. Monitors legislation and regulations. (Affiliated with the AFL-CIO.)

National Center for Tobacco-Free Kids, *1707 L St. N.W., #800 20036; (202) 296-5469. Fax, (202) 296-5427. Matthew Myers, President. Information, (800) 284-5437. Web, www.tobaccofreekids.org.*

Seeks to reduce tobacco use by children through public policy change and educational programs. Provides technical assistance to state and local programs.

National Smokers Alliance, *901 N. Washington St., #400, Alexandria, VA 22314; (703) 739-1324. Fax, (703) 739-1328. Thomas Humber, President. Information, (800) 224-3322. Web, www.speakup.org.*

Membership: adult smokers. Promotes accommodation of smokers and nonsmokers in public places and at work; opposes discrimination against smokers, government-imposed smoking bans, and excessive taxation and regulation of tobacco products.

PHILANTHROPY, PUBLIC SERVICE, AND VOLUNTARISM

See also Political Advocacy (chap. 20)

AGENCIES

AmeriCorps *(Corporation for National Service), 1201 New York Ave. N.W. 20525; (202) 606-5000. Fax, (202) 565-2784. Harris L. Wofford, Chief Executive Officer. TTY, (202) 565-2799. Volunteer recruiting information, (800) 942-2677. Web, www.americorps.org.*

Provides Americans age seventeen or older with opportunities to serve their communities on a full- or part-time basis. Participants work in the areas of education, public safety, human needs, and the environment and earn education awards for college or vocational training.

AmeriCorps *(Corporation for National Service), National Civilian Community Corps, 1201 New York Ave. N.W. 20525; (202) 606-5000. Fax, (202) 565-2792. Andrew Chambers, Director. TTY, (202) 565-2799. Volunteer recruiting information, (800) 942-2677.*

Provides a residential service and leadership program for young men and women of all social, economic, and educational backgrounds. Works to restore and preserve the environment. Members provide intensive disaster relief, fight forest fires, and restore homes and habitats after natural disasters.

AmeriCorps *(Corporation for National Service), Volunteers in Service to America (VISTA), 1201 New York Ave. N.W., 8th Floor 20525; (202) 606-5000. Fax, (202) 565-2789. Lee Lacy, Deputy Director. TTY, (800) 833-3722. Volunteer recruiting information, (800) 942-2677. Web, www.americorps.org.*

Assigns full-time volunteers to public and private nonprofit organizations to alleviate poverty in local communities. Volunteers receive stipends.

Corporation for National Service, *1201 New York Ave. N.W. 20525; (202) 606-5000. Fax, (202) 565-2784. Harris L. Wofford, Chief Executive Officer. TTY, (202) 565-2799. Volunteer recruiting information, (800) 942-2677. Web, www.cns.gov.*

Independent corporation that administers federally sponsored domestic volunteer programs to provide disadvantaged citizens with services. Engages Americans of all ages and backgrounds in community-based service. Addresses U.S. education, human, public safety, and environmental needs. Works to foster civic responsibility and provide educational opportunity for those who make a substantial commitment to service. Programs include AmeriCorps, AmeriCorps-VISTA (Volunteers in Service to America), AmeriCorps-NCCC (National Civilian Community Corps), Learn and Serve America, and the National Senior Service Corps.

Internal Revenue Service *(Treasury Dept.), Employee Plans and Exempt Organizations, 1111 Constitution Ave. N.W., #1311 20224; (202) 622-6720. Fax, (202) 622-6873. Evelyn Petschek, Commissioner.*

Provides rules for the uniform interpretation and application of federal tax laws affecting tax-exempt organizations and private foundations.

Learn and Serve America *(Corporation for National Service), 1201 New York Ave. N.W. 20525; (202) 606-5000. Fax, (202) 565-2781. Marilyn Smith, Director. TTY, (202) 565-2799. Volunteer recruiting information, (800) 942-2677.*

Coordinates school-based community service programs, including the K–12 Program, for school-age children; the Higher Education Program, for undergraduate and graduate students; and School and Community-based Programs, which support schools and nonprofit organizations that provide school-age children with community service opportunities.

National Senior Service Corps *(Corporation for National Service), Retired and Senior Volunteer Program, Foster Grandparent Program, and Senior Companion Program, 1201 New York Ave. N.W. 20525; (202) 606-5000. Fax, (202) 565-2789. Tom Endres, Director.*

TTY, (202) 565-2799. Volunteer recruiting information, (800) 942-2677. Web, www.cns.gov.

Network of programs that help older Americans find service opportunities in their communities, including the Retired and Senior Volunteer Program, which encourages older citizens to use their talents and experience in community service; the Foster Grandparent Program, which gives older citizens opportunities to work with exceptional children and children with special needs; and the Senior Companion Program, which recruits older citizens to help homebound adults, especially seniors, with special needs.

Peace Corps, *1111 20th St. N.W. 20526; (202) 692-2100. Fax, (202) 692-2101. Mark L. Schneider, Director; Charles R. Baquet III, Deputy Director. Information, (800) 424-8580. Press, (202) 692-2234. Web, www.peacecorps.gov.*

Promotes world peace and mutual understanding between the United States and developing nations. Administers volunteer programs to assist developing countries in education, the environment, health, small business development, agriculture, and urban development.

CONGRESS

General Accounting Office, *Health, Education, and Human Services, 441 G St. N.W. 20548; (202) 512-6806. Fax, (202) 512-5806. Victor S. Rezendes, Assistant Comptroller General.*

Independent, nonpartisan agency in the legislative branch. Audits, analyzes, and evaluates programs of the Corporation for National Service; makes reports available to the public.

House Appropriations Committee, *Subcommittee on VA, HUD, and Independent Agencies, H143 CAP 20515; (202) 225-3241. Rep. James T. Walsh, R-N.Y., Chair; Frank Cushing, Staff Director. Web, www.house.gov/appropriations.*

Appropriates funds for programs of the Corporation for National Service.

House Government Reform Committee, *Subcommittee on Criminal Justice, Drug Policy, and Human Resources, B373 RHOB 20515; (202) 225-2577. Fax, (202) 225-1154. Rep. John L. Mica, R-Fla., Chair; Sharon Pinkerton, Staff Director. Web, www.house.gov/reform.*

Oversight of the Corporation for National Service.

House Ways and Means Committee, *1102 LHOB 20515; (202) 225-3625. Fax, (202) 225-2610. Rep. Bill Archer, R-Texas, Chair; A. L. Singleton, Chief of Staff. Web, www.house.gov/ways_means.*

Jurisdiction over legislation on tax-exempt founda-tions and charitable trusts.

Senate Appropriations Committee, *Subcommittee on Labor, Health and Human Services, and Education, SD-186 20510; (202) 224-7230. Fax, (202) 224-1360. Sen. Arlen Specter, R-Pa., Chair; Bettilou Taylor, Staff Director. Web, appropriations.senate.gov/labor.*

Jurisdiction over legislation to appropriate funds for programs of the Corporation for National Service.

Senate Finance Committee, *SD-219 20510; (202) 224-4515. Fax, (202) 224-5920. Sen. William V. Roth Jr., R-Del., Chair; Frank Polk, Staff Director. Web, finance. senate.gov.*

Jurisdiction over legislation on tax-exempt founda-tions and charitable trusts.

Senate Health, Education, Labor, and Pensions Committee, *SD-428 20510; (202) 224-5375. Fax, (202) 228-5044. Sen. James M. Jeffords, R-Vt., Chair; Mark Powden, Staff Director. TTY, (202) 224-1975. Web, labor. senate.gov.*

Oversight of the Corporation for National Service and domestic activities of the Red Cross.

NONPROFIT

Advocacy Institute, *1707 L St. N.W., #400 20036; (202) 659-8475. Fax, (202) 659-8484. Michael Pertschuk, Co-Director; David Cohen, Co-Director; Kathleen Sheekey, Co-Director. General e-mail, info@advocacy.org. Web, www.advocacy.org.*

Public interest organization that offers counseling and training in advocacy skills and strategies to non-profit groups interested in such issues as civil and human rights, public health, arms control, and environmental and consumer affairs. Aids groups in making better use of resources, such as access to the media and coalition building.

Arca Foundation, *2040 S St. N.W., #200 20009; (202) 822-9193. Donna Edwards, Executive Director. Web, fdncenter.org/grantmaker/arca/index.html.*

Seeks to inform and empower citizens to help shape public policy. Awards grants to nonprofit organizations in the areas of campaign finance reform, U.S. policy with Cuba and Central America, and international labor and education.

Assn. of Junior Leagues International, *Washington Office, 1319 F St. N.W., #604 20004; (202) 393-3364. Fax, (202) 393-4517. Mary Douglass, Director. Web, www.ajli. org.*

Educational and charitable women's organization that promotes voluntarism and works for community improvement through leadership of trained volunteers; includes leagues in Canada, Mexico, and Great Britain. Interests include children, women, domestic violence, aging, education, and child health issues.

Capital Research Center, *1513 16th St. N.W. 20036-1480; (202) 483-6900. Fax, (202) 483-6902. Terrence Scanlon, President. Web, www.capitalresearch.org.*

Researches funding sources of public interest and advocacy groups; analyzes the impact these groups have on public policy; publishes findings in newsletters and reports.

Caring Institute, *228 7th St. S.E. 20003; (202) 547-4273. Fax, (202) 547-3540. Val J. Halamandaris, President. Gen-eral e-mail, caringins@nmaa.org.*

Promotes selflessness and public service. Recognizes the achievements of individuals who have demonstrated a commitment to serving others. Operates the Frederick Douglass Museum and Hall of Fame for Caring Ameri-cans. Sponsors the National Caring Award and offers internships and scholarships to high school and college students.

Center for a New American Dream, *6930 Carroll Ave., #900, Takoma Park, MD 20912; (301) 891-3683. Fax, (301) 891-3684. Betsy Taylor, Executive Director. Informa-tion, (877) 683-7236. General e-mail, newdream@ newdream.org. Web, www.newdream.org.*

Promotes sustainable consumption; distributes edu-cational materials.

Center for Corporate Public Involvement, *1001 Pennsylvania Ave. N.W., #500 20004-2599; (202) 624-2425. Fax, (202) 624-2319. Shawn Hausman, Director.*

Membership: life and health insurance companies and associations. Encourages members to become involved in community projects and voluntarism; pro-vides information on model programs in corporate com-munity involvement. Interests include education, arts and culture, children's health and safety, and crime and violence prevention.

The Congressional Award, *379 FHOB 20515 (mailing address: P.O. Box 77440 20013-8440); (202) 226-0130. Fax, (202) 226-0131. James Manning, National Director. Web, congressionalaward.org.*

Noncompetitive program established by Congress that recognizes the achievements of young people ages fourteen to twenty-three. Participants are awarded gold, silver, and bronze medals for setting and achieving goals in four areas: volunteer public service, personal development, physical fitness, and expeditions and exploration.

Council of Better Business Bureaus, *Philanthropic Advisory Service,* 4200 Wilson Blvd., #800, Arlington, VA 22203-1838; (703) 276-0100. Fax, (703) 525-8277. Bennett M. Weiner, Vice President. Web, www.bbb.org/about/pas.html.

Serves as a donor information service on charities that solicit nationally or have national or international program services; issues reports on the operations of national charitable organizations; provides charities with counseling and educational materials on compliance with the standards for charitable solicitations.

Council on Foundations, 1828 L St. N.W., #300 20036; (202) 466-6512. Fax, (202) 785-3926. Dorothy Ridings, President. Web, www.cof.org.

Membership: independent community, family, and public and company-sponsored foundations; corporate giving programs; and foundations in other countries. Promotes responsible and effective philanthropy through educational programs, publications, government relations, and promulgation of a set of principles and practices for effective grant making.

Earth Share, 3400 International Dr. N.W., #2K 20008; (202) 537-7100. Fax, (202) 537-7101. Kalman Stein, President. Information, (800) 875-3863. General e-mail, info@earthshare.org. Web, www.earthshare.org.

Federation of environmental and conservation organizations. Works with government and private payroll deduction programs to solicit contributions to member organizations for environmental research, education, and community programs. Provides information on establishing environmental giving options in the workplace.

Eugene and Agnes E. Meyer Foundation, 1400 16th St. N.W., #360 20036; (202) 483-8294. Fax, (202) 328-6850. Julie L. Rogers, President.

Seeks to improve the quality of life in Washington, D.C. Awards grants to housing, neighborhood development, and community service groups.

Eugene B. Casey Foundation, 800 S. Frederick Ave., #100, Gaithersburg, MD 20877-4150; (301) 948-4595. Betty Brown Casey, Chair.

Philanthropic organization that supports the arts, education, and social services in the metropolitan Washington area.

Evangelical Council for Financial Accountability, P.O. Box 17456 20041-7456; (703) 713-1414. Fax, (540) 535-0533. Paul D. Nelson, President. Information, (800) 323-9473. General e-mail, webmaster@ecfa.org. Web, www.ecfa.org.

Membership: charitable, religious, international relief, and educational nonprofit organizations committed to evangelical Christianity. Assists members in making appropriate public disclosure of their financial practices and accomplishments. Certifies organizations that conform to standards of financial integrity and Christian ethics.

Foundation Center, *Washington Office,* 1001 Connecticut Ave. N.W., #938 20036; (202) 331-1400. Fax, (202) 331-1739. Vacant, Assistant Director. General e-mail, feedback@fdncenter.org. Web, www.fdncenter.org.

Publishes foundation guides. Serves as a clearinghouse on foundations and corporate giving, nonprofit management, fundraising, and grants for individuals. Provides training and seminars on fundraising and grant writing. Operates libraries in Atlanta, Cleveland, New York, San Francisco, and Washington, D.C.; libraries open to the public.

General Federation of Women's Clubs, 1734 N St. N.W. 20036-2990; (202) 347-3168. Fax, (202) 835-0246. Gabrielle Smith, Executive Director. General e-mail, gfwc@gfwc.org. Web, www.gfwc.org.

Nondenominational, nonpartisan international organization of women volunteers. Interests include conservation, education, international and public affairs, and the arts.

Gifts In Kind International, 333 N. Fairfax St., #100, Alexandria, VA 22314; (703) 836-2121. Fax, (703) 549-1481. Susan Corrigan, President. General e-mail, ProductDonations@giftsinkind.org. Web, www.giftsinkind.org.

Encourages corporations to donate newly manufactured products to domestic and international charities. Works with companies to develop in-kind programs, coordinates the distribution of gifts to nonprofit agencies, collects tax documentation from recipients, and conducts communitywide public relations activities to encourage product giving. Serves schools and health, recreational, housing, arts, and environmental groups.

Grantmakers in Health, *Washington Office,* 1100 Connecticut Ave. N.W., 12th Floor 20036; (202) 452-8331. Fax, (202) 452-8340. Lauren LeRoy, President. Web, www.gih.org.

Seeks to increase the capacity of private sector grantmakers to enhance public health. Fosters information exchange among grant makers. Publications include a bulletin on current news in health and human services and the *Directory of Health Philanthropy.*

Habitat for Humanity International, *Washington Office, 1010 Vermont Ave. N.W., #900 20005; (202) 628-9171. Fax, (202) 628-9169. Thomas L. Jones, Managing Director. Web, www.habitat.org.*

Ecumenical housing ministry that, with the help of volunteers, donors, and its own affiliate offices, builds affordable homes worldwide for low-income persons.

Independent Sector, *1200 18th St. N.W., #200 20036; (202) 467-6100. Fax, (202) 467-6101. Sara E. Melendez, President. Web, www.indepsec.org.*

Membership: corporations, foundations, and national voluntary, charitable, and philanthropic organizations. Encourages volunteering, giving, and not-for-profit initiatives by the private sector for public causes.

Institute for Justice, *1717 Pennsylvania Ave. N.W., #200 20006; (202) 955-1300. Fax, (202) 955-1329. Chip Mellor, President. General e-mail, general@instituteforjustice. org. Web, www.instituteforjustice.org.*

Sponsors seminars to train law students, grassroots activists, and practicing lawyers in applying advocacy strategies in public interest litigation. Seeks to protect from arbitrary government interference in free speech, private property rights, parental school choice, and economic liberty. Litigates cases.

Lutheran Volunteer Corps, *1226 Vermont Ave. N.W., 2nd Floor 20005; (202) 387-3222. Fax, (202) 667-0037. Jennifer Maloney, Executive Director. Web, www.lvchome. org.*

Administers volunteer program in selected U.S. cities; coordinates activities with health and social service agencies, educational institutions, and environmental groups.

Mars Foundation, *6885 Elm St., McLean, VA 22101; (703) 821-4900. Fax, (703) 448-9678. O. O. Otih, Secretary-Treasurer.*

Awards grants to education, arts, and health care concerns.

Morris and Gwendolyn Cafritz Foundation, *1825 K St. N.W., #1400 20006; (202) 223-3100. Fax, (202) 296-7567. Calvin Cafritz, Chair. Web, www.cafritzfoundation. org.*

Awards grants to educational institutions, arts groups, and social services in the metropolitan Washington, D.C., area.

National Assembly of Health and Human Service Organizations, *1319 F St. N.W., #601 20004; (202) 347-2080. Fax, (202) 393-4517. Gordon A. Raley, President. General e-mail, nassembly@nassembly.org. Web, www. nassembly.org.*

Membership: national voluntary health and human service organizations. Provides collective leadership in the areas of health and human service. Provides members' professional staff and volunteers with a forum to share information. Supports public policies, programs, and resources that advance the effectiveness of health and human service organizations and their service delivery.

National Center for Nonprofit Boards, *1828 L St. N.W., #900 20036-5104; (202) 452-6262. Fax, (202) 452-6299. Judith O'Connor, President. General e-mail, ncnb@ncnb.org. Web, www.ncnb.org.*

Works to improve the effectiveness of nonprofit organizations by strengthening their boards of directors. Operates an information clearinghouse; publishes materials on governing nonprofit organizations; assists organizations in conducting training programs, workshops, and conferences for board members and chief executives.

National Committee for Responsive Philanthropy, *2001 S St. N.W., #620 20009; (202) 387-9177. Fax, (202) 332-5084. Rick Cohen, President. General e-mail, info@ncrp.org. Web, www.ncrp.org.*

Directs philanthropic giving to benefit the socially, economically, and politically disenfranchised; advocates for groups that represent the poor, minorities, and women. Conducts research; organizes local coalitions; assists philanthropic groups in other countries. Monitors legislation and regulations.

National Society of Fund Raising Executives, *1101 King St., #700, Alexandria, VA 22314; (703) 684-0410. Fax, (703) 684-0540. Paulette V. Maehara, President. Information, (800) 666-3863. Web, www.nsfre.org.*

Membership: individuals who serve as fundraising executives for nonprofit institutions or as members of counseling firms engaged in fundraising management. Promotes ethical standards; offers workshops; certifies members; monitors legislation and regulations. NSFRE Foundation promotes philanthropy and voluntarism. Library open to the public by appointment.

Points of Light Foundation, *1400 Eye St. N.W., #800 20005; (202) 729-8000. Fax, (202) 829-8100. Robert Goodwin, President. Web, www.pointsoflight.org.*

Promotes mobilization of people for volunteer community service aimed at solving social problems. Offers technical assistance, training, and information services to nonprofit organizations, public agencies, corporations, and others interested in volunteering.

Progressive Policy Institute, *600 Pennsylvania Ave. S.E., #400 20003; (202) 547-0001. Fax, (202) 544-5014. Will Marshall, President. General e-mail, ppiinfo@dlcppi. org. Web, www.dlcppi.org.*

Encourages civic participation in solving U.S. problems through voluntary national service, community-based institutions, and public-private partnerships.

Public Allies, *1015 18th St. N.W., #200 20036; (202) 822-1180. Fax, (202) 822-1199. Chuck J. Supple, President.*

Works in partnership with nonprofit organizations, business, and government to place young adults aged eighteen to thirty in challenging paid positions, provide them with leadership training, and engage them in team projects that serve needs in local neighborhoods.

Support Center of Washington, *2001 O St. N.W. 20036-5955; (202) 833-0300. Fax, (202) 857-0077. Oliver Tessier, Executive Director. General e-mail, info@scw.org. Web, www.scw.org.*

Works to increase the effectiveness and efficiency of nonprofit organizations by providing financial management, accounting, and fundraising assistance. Other services include legal and tax information, marketing and resource development, and training programs.

United Way of America, *701 N. Fairfax St., Alexandria, VA 22314; (703) 836-7100. Fax, (703) 683-7840. Betty Stanley Beene, President. Web, www.unitedway.org.*

Service association for independent local United Way organizations in the United States. Services include staff training; fundraising, planning, and communications assistance; resource management; and national public service advertising.

W. O'Neil Foundation, *5454 Wisconsin Ave., #730, Chevy Chase, MD 20815; (301) 656-5848. Helene O'Neil Cobb, Vice Chair.*

Awards grants to Roman Catholic interests both nationally and internationally.

Youth Service America, *1101 15th St. N.W., #200 20005; (202) 296-2992. Fax, (202) 296-4030. Steven Culbertson, President. General e-mail, info@ysa.org. Web, www.servenet.org.*

Advocates youth service at national, state, and local levels. Promotes opportunities for young people to be engaged in community service. Provides service and conservation corps and school- and university-based programs with technical assistance; acts as a clearinghouse on youth service.

See also Arts and Humanities (chap. 5); Consumer Protection (this chapter); International Trade and Development (chap. 13); Mail Rates and Classification (chap. 10); Small and Disadvantaged Business (chap. 3)

▒ PUBLIC INTEREST LAW

See also Civil Rights (this chapter); Consumer Protection (this chapter); Law and Justice (chap. 14)

AGENCIES

Legal Services Corp., *750 1st St. N.E., 10th Floor 20002-4250; (202) 336-8800. Fax, (202) 336-8959. John McKay, President. Information, (202) 336-8892. Library, (202) 336-8804.*

Independent federal corporation established by Congress. Awards grants to local agencies that provide the poor with legal services. Library open to the public.

CONGRESS

House Government Reform Committee, *Subcommittee on Criminal Justice, Drug Policy, and Human Resources, B373 RHOB 20515; (202) 225-2577. Fax, (202) 225-1154. Rep. John L. Mica, R-Fla., Chair; Sharon Pinkerton, Staff Director. Web, www.house.gov/reform.*

Oversees operations of the Legal Services Corp.

House Judiciary Committee, *Subcommittee on Commercial and Administrative Law, B353 RHOB 20515; (202) 225-2825. Fax, (202) 225-4299. Rep. George W. Gekas, R-Pa., Chair; Ray Smietanka, Counsel. General e-mail, Judiciary@mail.house.gov. Web, www.house.gov/judiciary.*

Jurisdiction over legislation on legal services. Oversees the Legal Services Corp.

Senate Health, Education, Labor, and Pensions Committee, *SD-428 20510; (202) 224-5375. Fax, (202) 228-5044. Sen. James M. Jeffords, R-Vt., Chair; Mark Powden, Staff Director. TTY, (202) 224-1975. Web, labor.senate.gov.*

Legislative and oversight jurisdiction over operations of the Legal Services Corp.

NONPROFIT

Alliance for Justice, *2000 P St. N.W., #712 20036; (202) 822-6070. Fax, (202) 822-6068. Nan Aron, President. General e-mail, alliance@afj.org. Web, www.afj.org.*

Membership: public interest lawyers and advocacy, environmental, civil rights, and consumer organizations. Promotes reform of the legal system to ensure access to the courts; monitors selection of federal judges; works to preserve the rights of nonprofit organizations to advocate on behalf of their constituents.

American Bar Assn., *Commission on Mental and Physical Disability Law, 740 15th St. N.W. 20005; (202)*

662-1570. Fax, (202) 662-1032. John Parry, Director. Web, www.abanet.org/disability/home.html.

Serves as a clearinghouse for information on mental and physical disability law and offers legal research services.

Bazelon Center for Mental Health Law, 1101 15th St. N.W., #1212 20005; (202) 467-5730. Fax, (202) 223-0409. Robert Bernstein, Director. TTY, (202) 467-4232. General e-mail, bazelon@webcom.com. Web, www.bazelon.org.

Public interest law firm. Conducts test case litigation to defend rights of persons with mental disabilities. Provides legal support for legal services offices, protection and advocacy agencies, and private attorneys. Monitors legislation and regulations.

Center for Law and Education, Washington Office, 1875 Connecticut Ave. N.W., #510 20009-5728; (202) 986-3000. Fax, (202) 986-6648. Paul Weckstein, Co-Director. Publications, (202) 462-7688. General e-mail, cle@cleweb.org. Web, www.cleweb.org.

Assists local legal services programs in matters concerning education, civil rights, and provision of legal services to low-income persons; litigates some cases for low-income individuals.

Center for Law and Social Policy, 1616 P St. N.W., #150 20036; (202) 328-5140. Fax, (202) 328-5195. Alan W. Houseman, Director. Web, www.clasp.org.

Public interest organization with expertise in law and policy affecting low-income Americans. Seeks to improve the economic conditions of low-income families with children and to secure access for persons in poverty to the civil justice system.

Center for Study of Responsive Law, 1530 P St. N.W. 20005 (mailing address: P.O. Box 19367 20036); (202) 387-8030. Fax, (202) 234-5176. John Richard, Administrator. Web, www.csrl.org.

Consumer interest clearinghouse that conducts research and holds conferences on public interest law. Interests include white-collar crime, the environment, occupational health and safety, the postal system, banking deregulation, insurance, freedom of information policy, and broadcasting.

Disability Rights Education and Defense Fund, Governmental Affairs, Washington Office, 1629 K St. N.W. 20006; (202) 986-0375. Fax, (202) 775-7465. Pat Wright, Director.

Law and policy center working to protect and advance the civil rights of people with disabilities through legislation, litigation, advocacy, and technical assistance. Educates and trains attorneys, advocates, persons with disabilities, and parents of children with disabilities.

Institute for Justice, 1717 Pennsylvania Ave. N.W., #200 20006; (202) 955-1300. Fax, (202) 955-1329. Chip Mellor, President. General e-mail, general@instituteforjustice.org. Web, www.instituteforjustice.org.

Sponsors seminars to train law students, grassroots activists, and practicing lawyers in applying advocacy strategies in public interest litigation. Seeks to protect from arbitrary government interference in free speech, private property rights, parental school choice, and economic liberty. Litigates cases.

Institute for Public Representation, 600 New Jersey Ave. N.W. 20001; (202) 662-9535. Fax, (202) 662-9634. Douglas L. Parker, Director. TTY, (202) 662-9538.

Public interest law firm funded by Georgetown University Law Center that studies federal administrative law and federal court litigation. Interests include communications law, environmental protection, and disability rights.

Lawyers' Committee for Civil Rights Under Law, 1401 New York Ave. N.W., #400 20005; (202) 662-8600. Fax, (202) 783-0857. Barbara Arnwine, Executive Director. Web, www.lawyerscomm.org.

Provides minority groups and the poor with legal assistance in such areas as voting rights, employment discrimination, education, environment, and equal access to government services and benefits.

Migrant Legal Action Program, P.O. Box 53308 20009; (202) 462-7744. Fax, (202) 462-7914. Roger C. Rosenthal, Executive Director. General e-mail, hn1645@handsnet.org.

Offers support, litigation assistance, and training to local legal services groups and other organizations and private attorneys with migrant farmworker clients. Monitors legislation and regulations.

National Consumer Law Center, Washington Office, 1629 K St. N.W., #600 20006; (202) 986-6060. Fax, (202) 463-9462. Margot Saunders, Managing Attorney.

Provides lawyers funded by the Legal Services Corp. with research and assistance; researches problems of low-income consumers and develops alternative solutions.

National Health Law Program, Washington Office, 1101 14th St. N.W., #405 20005; (202) 289-7661. Fax, (202) 289-7724. Lawrence Lavin, Director. General e-mail, nhelpdc@healthlaw.org. Web, www.healthlaw.org.

Organization of lawyers representing the economically disadvantaged, minorities, and the elderly in issues concerning federal, state, and local health care programs. Offers technical assistance, workshops, seminars, and training for health law specialists.

National Legal Aid and Defender Assn., *1625 K St. N.W., #800 20006; (202) 452-0620. Fax, (202) 872-1031. Clinton Lyons, President. General e-mail, info@nlada.org. Web, www.nlada.org.*

Membership: local organizations and individuals providing indigent clients, including prisoners, with legal aid and defender services. Serves as a clearinghouse for member organizations; publishes directory of legal aid and defender programs.

National Legal Center for the Public Interest, *1000 16th St. N.W., #500 20036; (202) 296-1683. Fax, (202) 293-2118. Ernest B. Hueter, President.*

Public interest law center and information clearinghouse. Studies judicial issues and the impact of the legal system on the private sector; sponsors seminars; does not litigate cases.

Public Citizen Litigation Group, *1600 20th St. N.W. 20009; (202) 588-7721. Fax, (202) 588-7795. David Vladeck, Director. Web, www.citizen.org.*

Conducts litigation for Public Citizen, a citizens' interest group, in the areas of consumer rights, employee rights, health and safety, government and corporate accountability, and separation of powers; represents other individuals and citizens' groups with similar interests.

Trial Lawyers for Public Justice, *1717 Massachusetts Ave. N.W., #800 20036; (202) 797-8600. Fax, (202) 232-7203. Arthur H. Bryant, Executive Director. Web, www.tlpj.org.*

Membership: consumer activists, trial lawyers, and public interest lawyers. Litigates to influence corporate and government decisions about products or activities adversely affecting health or safety. Interests include toxic torts, environmental protection, civil rights and civil liberties, workers' safety, consumer protection, and the preservation of the civil justice system.

⚖ RELIGION AND ETHICS

See also Constitutional Law and Civil Liberties (chap. 14); Private, Parochial, and Home Schooling (chap. 6)

NONPROFIT

Alban Institute, *7315 Wisconsin Ave., #1250 West, Bethesda, MD 20814; (301) 718-4407. Fax, (301) 718-*
1958. Vacant, Executive Vice President. Information, (800) 486-1318. Web, www.alban.org.

Nondenominational research, consulting, and educational membership organization that provides church and synagogue congregations with support and services. Interests include planning and growth, conflict resolution, leadership and staff training, spiritual development, and mission and stewardship. Conducts continuing education programs.

American Assn. of Pastoral Counselors, *9504A Lee Hwy., Fairfax, VA 22301-2303; (703) 385-6967. Fax, (703) 352-7725. C. Roy Woodruff, Executive Director. General e-mail, info@aapc.org. Web, www.aapc.org.*

Membership: mental health professionals with training in both religion and the behavioral sciences. Nonsectarian organization that accredits pastoral counseling centers, certifies pastoral counselors, and approves training programs.

American Baptist Churches U.S.A., *Legislative Advocacy, Washington Office, 110 Maryland Ave. N.E., #504 20002-5694; (202) 544-3400. Fax, (202) 544-0277. Curtis Ramsey Lucas, Director.*

Serves as liaison between American Baptist churches and government organizations. Interests include immigration, foreign and military policy, human services, employment, the environment, and civil rights.

American Ethical Union, *Washington Ethical Action, Washington Office, 7750 16th St. N.W. 20012; (202) 882-6650. Fax, (202) 829-1354. Donald Montagna, Leader. Web, www.aeu.org.*

Federation of ethical culture societies in the United States. Interests include human rights, ethics, world peace, health, welfare, education, and civil and religious liberties. Monitors legislation and regulations.

American Friends Service Committee, *Washington Office, 1822 R St. N.W. 20009-1604; (202) 483-3341. Fax, (202) 232-3197. James Matlack, Director. General e-mail, afscinfo@afsc.org. Web, www.afsc.org.*

Independent organization affiliated with the Religious Society of Friends (Quakers) in America. Sponsors domestic and international service, development, justice, and peace programs. Interests include peace education; arms control and disarmament; social and economic justice; gay and lesbian rights, racism, sexism, and civil rights; refugees and immigration policy; crisis response and relief efforts; and international development efforts, especially in Central America, the Middle East, and southern Africa.

American Jewish Committee, *Government and International Affairs, Washington Office, 1156 15th St. N.W.,*

#1201 20005; (202) 785-4200. Fax, (202) 785-4115. David Bernstein, Director. Web, www.ajc.org.

Human relations agency devoted to protecting civil and religious rights for all people. Interests include church-state issues, research on human behavior, Israel and the Middle East, Jews in the former Soviet Union, immigration, social discrimination, civil and women's rights, employment, education, housing, and international cooperation for peace and human rights.

American Jewish Congress, Washington Office, 2027 Massachusetts Ave. N.W. 20036; (202) 332-4001. Fax, (202) 387-3434. Matt Dorf, Washington Representative. General e-mail, washrep@ajcongress.org. Web, www. ajcongress.org.

Jewish community relations and civil liberties organization. Seeks to combat anti-Semitism and other forms of bigotry in employment, education, housing, and voting. Areas of activity include church-state relations; government involvement in education; public school prayer; gun control policy; constitutional, minority, women's, and human rights; world Jewry; U.S. foreign policy in the Middle East; Arab investment in the United States; and the Arab boycott of Israel. Monitors legislation.

American Muslim Council, 1212 New York Ave. N.W., #400 20005; (202) 789-2262. Fax, (202) 789-2550. Aly Abuzaakouk, Executive Director. Web, www.amconline.org.

Promotes equal rights and political empowerment for Muslims in the United States. Opposes discrimination against Muslims; fosters cultural understanding and cooperation among organizations.

Americans United for Separation of Church and State, 518 C St. N.W. 20002; (202) 466-3234. Fax, (202) 466-2587. Barry W. Lynn, Executive Director. General e-mail, americansunited@au.org. Web, www.au.org.

Citizens' interest group. Opposes federal and state aid to parochial schools; works to ensure religious neutrality in public schools; supports religious free exercise; initiates litigation; maintains speakers bureau. Monitors legislation and regulations.

Baptist Joint Committee on Public Affairs, 200 Maryland Ave. N.E., 3rd Floor 20002; (202) 544-4226. Fax, (202) 544-2094. J. Brent Walker, Executive Director. Web, www.bjcpa.org.

Membership: national Baptist conventions and conferences. Conducts research and operates an information service. Interests include religious liberty, separation of church and state, First Amendment religious issues, and government regulation of religious institutions.

Baptist World Alliance, 6733 Curran St., McLean, VA 22101-6005; (703) 790-8980. Fax, (703) 893-5160. Denton Lotz, General Secretary. General e-mail, bwa@bwanet.org. Web, www.bwanet.org.

International Baptist organization. Conducts religious teaching and works to create a better understanding among nations. Organizes development efforts and disaster relief in less developed nations. Interests include human rights and religious liberty.

B'nai B'rith International, 1640 Rhode Island Ave. N.W. 20036; (202) 857-6500. Fax, (202) 296-0638. Dan Mariaschin, Vice President (Acting). Web, www.bnaibrith. org.

Provides information and coordinates political action on public policy issues important to the international Jewish community. The B'nai B'rith Youth Organization offers educational and leadership training programs for teenagers and counseling and career guidance services. Other interests include community volunteer programs, senior citizen housing, and the security and development of Israel. Partially funds the Foundation for Jewish Campus Life, which offers educational, religious, recreational, and social programs for Jewish college and university students. Operates the B'nai B'rith Klutznick National Jewish Museum.

Catholic Charities USA, 1731 King St., #200, Alexandria, VA 22314; (703) 549-1390. Fax, (703) 549-1656. Fred Kammer (SJ), President. Press, (703) 549-1390. Web, catholiccharitiesusa.org.

Member agencies and institutions provide persons of all backgrounds with social services, including adoption, education, counseling, food, and housing services. National office promotes public policies that address human needs and social injustice. Provides members with advocacy and professional support, including technical assistance, training, and resource development; disseminates publications.

Catholic Information Center, 815 15th St. N.W. 20005-2203; (202) 783-2062. Fax, (202) 783-6667. C. John McCloskey III, Director.

Provides information on Roman Catholicism and the Catholic church. Offers free counseling services.

Christian Science Committee on Publication, 910 16th St. N.W., #700 20006; (202) 857-0427. Fax, (202) 331-0587. Robert D. Miller, Federal Representative. General e-mail, fedrepcs@aol.com.

Public service organization that provides information on the religious convictions and practices of Christian Scientists; maintains a speakers bureau. Monitors legislation and regulations.

Church of the Brethren, *Washington Office,* *337 North Carolina Ave. S.E. 20003; (202) 546-3202. Fax, (202) 544-5852. Loyce Borgmann, Coordinator. General e-mail, washofc@aol.com. Web, www.brethren.org.*

Organizes and coordinates political activities on social policy issues of concern to the church. Interests include military spending; civil rights and liberties; health care; conditions for the poor; refugees and immigrants; world hunger; conditions in the Middle East, Sudan, and Central America; and religious freedom. Sponsors seminars.

Churches' Center for Theology and Public Policy, *4500 Massachusetts Ave. N.W. 20016-5690; (202) 885-8648. Fax, (202) 885-8605. Barbara Green, Director.*

Studies the effect of Christian faith on political life and public policy. Interests include arms control and disarmament, health care, minority rights, and world political economy.

Episcopal Church, *Government Relations, Washington Office,* *110 Maryland Ave. N.E., #309 20002; (202) 547-7300. Fax, (202) 547-4457. Thomas Hart, Director. Web, www.ecusa.anglican.org.*

Informs Congress, the executive branch, and governmental agencies about the actions and resolutions of the Episcopal church. Monitors legislation and regulations.

Episcopal Peace Fellowship, *1317 G St. N.W. 20005 (mailing address: P.O. Box 28156 20038-8156); (202) 783-3380. Fax, (202) 393-3695. Mary H. Miller, Executive Secretary. General e-mail, epf@peacenet.org. Web, www.nonviolence.org/epf.*

Organizes Episcopalians committed to the biblical concept of peace. Supports conscientious objectors who resist military service and who refuse to pay taxes that support the military; opposes nuclear weapons; seeks to end the death penalty. Maintains network of local chapters.

Ethics and Public Policy Center, *Religion and Society Program,* *1015 15th St. N.W., #900 20005; (202) 682-1200. Fax, (202) 408-0632. Elliott Abrams, President. General e-mail, ethics@eppc.org. Web, www.eppc.org.*

Considers implications of Judeo-Christian moral tradition for domestic and foreign policy making.

Ethics and Religious Liberty Commission of the Southern Baptist Convention, *Public Policy, Washington Office,* *505 2nd St. N.E. 20002; (202) 547-8105. Fax, (202) 547-8165. Shannon Royce, Director. Web, www.erlc.com.*

Public policy office of the Southern Baptist Convention. Educates churches and members about moral and

public policy issues in U.S. government. Interests include abortion, pornography, religious liberty, First Amendment, drugs and alcohol, hunger, and race relations.

Evangelical Lutheran Church in America, *Governmental Affairs,* *122 C St. N.W., #125 20001; (202) 783-7507. Fax, (202) 783-7502. Russell Siler, Director. General e-mail, loga@ecunet.org. Web, elca.org.*

Monitors legislation and regulations on public policy issues of interest to the Lutheran church.

Friends Committee on National Legislation (FCNL), *245 2nd St. N.E. 20002-5795; (202) 547-6000. Fax, (202) 547-6019. Joe Volk, Executive Secretary. Recorded information, (202) 547-4343. General e-mail, fcnl@fcnl.org. Web, www.fcnl.org.*

Advocates for economic justice, world disarmament, international cooperation, and religious rights. Advocates on behalf of native Americans in such areas as treaty rights, self-determination, and U.S. trust responsibilities. Conducts research and education activities through the FCNL Education Fund. Opposes the death penalty. Monitors national legislation and policy. Affiliated with the Religious Society of Friends (Quakers).

General Board of Church and Society of the United Methodist Church, *100 Maryland Ave. N.E. 20002; (202) 488-5600. Fax, (202) 488-5619. Thom White Wolf Fassett, General Secretary. Web, www.umc-gbcs.org.*

Conducts research on social, political, and economic issues. Interests include social welfare, the environment, civil liberties, criminal justice, and foreign policy; assists member churches.

General Conference of Seventh-day Adventists, *12501 Old Columbia Pike, Silver Spring, MD 20904-6600; (301) 680-6000. Fax, (301) 680-6090. Jan Paulsen, President. Web, www.adventist.org.*

World headquarters of the Seventh-day Adventist church. Interests include education, health care, humanitarian relief, and development. Supplies educational tools for the blind and the hearing-impaired. Operates schools worldwide. Organizes community service-oriented youth groups.

Institute on Religion and Democracy, *1521 16th St. N.W., #300 20036; (202) 986-1440. Fax, (202) 986-3159. Diane L. Knippers, President. General e-mail, mail@ird-renew.org. Web, www.ird-renew.org.*

Interdenominational bipartisan organization that supports democratic and constitutional forms of government consistent with the values of Christianity. Serves as a resource center to promote Christian perspectives on U.S. foreign policy questions. Interests include international conflicts, religious liberties, and the promotion of democratic forms of government in the United States and worldwide.

Interfaith Alliance, *1012 14th St. N.W., #700 20005; (202) 639-6370. Fax, (202) 639-6375. Jane Holmes-Dixon, President. General e-mail, mail@interfaithalliance.org. Web, www.tialliance.org.*

Membership: Protestant, Catholic, Jewish, and Muslim clergy; laity; and others who favor a positive, nonpartisan role for religious faith in public life. Advocates mainstream religious values; promotes tolerance and social opportunity; opposes the use of religion to promote political extremism at national, state, and local levels. Monitors legislation and regulations.

International Religious Liberty Assn., *12501 Old Columbia Pike, Silver Spring, MD 20904-6600; (301) 680-6680. Fax, (301) 680-6695. John Graz, Secretary General. Web, www.irla.org.*

Seeks to preserve and expand religious liberty and freedom of conscience; advocates separation of church and state; sponsors international and domestic meetings and congresses.

Jesuit Conference, *Social Ministries, 1616 P St. N.W., #400 20036-1405; (202) 462-0400. Fax, (202) 328-9212. British Robinson, Director. General e-mail, brobinson@jesuit.org. Web, www.jesuit.org/advocacy.*

Information and advocacy organization of Jesuits and laypersons concerned with peace and social justice issues in the United States. Interests include peace and disarmament, economic justice, and issues affecting minorities, especially native Americans, Hispanics, and African Americans.

Leadership Conference of Women Religious, *8808 Cameron St., Silver Spring, MD 20910-4169; (301) 588-4955. Fax, (301) 587-4575. Mary Christine Fellerhoff, Executive Director.*

Membership: Roman Catholic women religious who are the principal administrators of their congregations in the United States. Offers programs and support to members; conducts research; serves as an information clearinghouse.

Loyola Foundation, *308 C St. N.E. 20002; (202) 546-9400. Albert G. McCarthy III, Executive Director.*

Assists overseas Catholic mission activities. Awards grants to international missionaries and Catholic dioceses for construction and renovation projects.

Maryknoll Fathers and Brothers (Catholic Foreign Mission Society of America), *Washington Office,*

4834 16th St. N.W. 20011; (202) 726-4252. Fax, (202) 726-0466. Francis Higdon, Regional Director. Web, www.maryknoll.org.

Conducts religious teaching and other mission work for the poor in Africa, Asia, and Latin America.

Mennonite Central Committee, *Washington Office, 110 Maryland Ave. N.E., #502 20002; (202) 544-6564. Fax, (202) 544-2820. J. Daryl Byler, Director. General e-mail, mccwash@mcc.org. Web, www.mennonitecc.ca/mcc.*

Christian organization engaged in service and development projects. Monitors legislation and regulations affecting issues of interest to Mennonite and Brethren in Christ churches. Interests include human rights in developing countries, military spending, the environment, world hunger, poverty, and civil and religious liberties.

National Assn. of Evangelicals, *Washington Office, 1001 Connecticut Ave. N.W., #522 20036; (202) 789-1011. Fax, (202) 842-0392. Rich Cizik, Director. General e-mail, oga@nae.net. Web, www.nae.net.*

Represents fifty Christian evangelical denominations. Interests include religious liberty; economic policy; church-state relations; public health issues, including HIV and AIDS; and immigration and refugee policy. Monitors legislation and regulations.

National Catholic Conference for Interracial Justice, *1200 Varnum St. N.E. 20017; (202) 529-6480. Fax, (202) 526-1262. Joseph Conrad Jr., Executive Director.*

Promotes the Roman Catholic church's teachings on racial justice and multicultural and multiracial understanding.

National Conference of Catholic Bishops/U.S. Catholic Conference, *3211 4th St. N.E. 20017; (202) 541-3000. Fax, (202) 541-3322. Msgr. Dennis M. Schnurr, General Secretary. Press, (202) 541-3200. Web, www.nccbuscc.org.*

Serves as a forum for bishops to exchange ideas, debate concerns of the church, and draft responses to religious and social issues. Provides information on doctrine and policies of the Roman Catholic church; develops religious education and training programs; formulates policy positions on social issues, including the economy, employment, federal budget priorities, voting rights, energy, health, housing, rural affairs, international military and political matters, human rights, the arms race, global economics, and immigration and refugee policy.

National Conference on Soviet Jewry, *1640 Rhode Island Ave. N.W., #501 20036; (202) 898-2500. Fax, (202) 898-0822. Mark B. Levin, Executive Director. General e-mail, ncsj@ncsj.org. Web, www.ncsj.org.*

Promotes religious and personal freedom for Jews wishing to leave the former Soviet Union in accordance with international law and for those choosing to remain. Provides them with legal advice and technical assistance. Organizes conferences, rallies, vigils, commemorations, and letter-writing campaigns; monitors legislation.

National Council of Catholic Women, *1275 K St. N.W., #975 20005; (202) 682-0334. Fax, (202) 682-0338. Annette Kane, Executive Director. General e-mail, nccw@us.net.*

Federation of Roman Catholic women's organizations. Provides a forum for Catholic women to research and discuss issues affecting the church and society; monitors legislation and regulations. Interests include employment, family life, abortion, care for the elderly, day care, world hunger, global water supplies, genetic engineering research, pornography legislation, and substance abuse. Special programs include volunteer respite care, leadership training for women, mentoring of mothers, and drug and alcohol abuse education.

National Council of Churches, *Washington Office, 110 Maryland Ave. N.E., #108 20002; (202) 544-2350. Fax, (202) 543-1297. Vacant, Director. General e-mail, mary@ncccusa.org. Web, www.ncccusa.org.*

Membership: Protestant, Anglican, and Eastern Orthodox churches. Interests include racial and social equality; social welfare, economic justice, and peace issues; church-state relations; prayer in public schools; and federal aid to private schools. (Headquarters in New York.)

National Council of Jewish Women, *Washington Office, 1707 L St. N.W., #950 20036; (202) 296-2588. Fax, (202) 331-7792. Sammie Moshenberg, Director. General e-mail, action@ncjwdc.org. Web, www.ncjw.org.*

Jewish women's education, community service, and advocacy organization. Interests include economic equity for women; reproductive, civil, and constitutional rights; juvenile justice; child care; education and welfare programs; Israel; aging issues; and work and family issues. (Headquarters in New York.)

NETWORK, *801 Pennsylvania Ave. S.E., #460 20003-2167; (202) 547-5556. Fax, (202) 547-5510. Kathy Thornton, National Coordinator. General e-mail, network@ networklobby.org. Web, www.networklobby.org.*

Catholic social justice lobby that coordinates political activity and promotes economic and social justice. Monitors legislation and regulations.

Presbyterian Church (U.S.A.), *Washington Office, 110 Maryland Ave. N.E., #104 20002; (202) 543-1126. Fax, (202) 543-7755. Elenora Giddings Ivory, Director. General*

e-mail, ga_washington_office@pcusa.org. Web, www. pcusa.org.

Provides information on the views of the general assembly of the Presbyterian church on public policy issues; monitors legislation affecting issues of concern. Interests include arms control, budget priorities, foreign policy, civil rights, religious liberty, church-state relations, economic justice, and public policy issues affecting women.

Progressive National Baptist Convention, *601 50th St. N.E. 20019; (202) 396-0558. Fax, (202) 398-4998. Tyrone S. Pitts, General Secretary. Web, www.pnbc.org.*

Baptist denomination that supports missionaries, implements education programs, and advocates for civil and human rights.

Sojourners, *2401 15th St. N.W. 20009; (202) 328-8842. Fax, (202) 328-8757. James E. Wallis, President. Information, (800) 714-7474. General e-mail, sojourners@ sojourners.com. Web, www.sojourners.com.*

Membership: Catholics, Protestants, Evangelicals, and other interested Christians. Grassroots network that focuses on the intersection of faith, politics, and culture. (Affiliated with the Church of the Savior and Call to Renewal.)

Union of American Hebrew Congregations, *Religious Action Center of Reform Judaism, 2027 Massachusetts Ave. N.W. 20036; (202) 387-2800. Fax, (202) 667-9070. Rabbi David Saperstein, Director. General e-mail, rac@uahc.org. Web, rj.org/rac.*

Religious and educational organization concerned with social justice and religious liberty. Mobilizes the American Jewish community and serves as its advocate on issues concerning Jews around the world, including economic justice, civil rights, and international peace.

Unitarian Universalist Assn. of Congregations in North America, *Washington Office, 2026 P St. N.W., #3 20036-6907; (202) 296-4672. Fax, (202) 296-4673. Meg A. Riley, Director. General e-mail, uuawo@aol.com. Web, www.uua.org.*

Monitors public policy and legislation. Interests include civil and religious liberties; the federal budget; international and interfaith affairs; human rights; and public policy affecting women, including reproductive rights policy.

United Church of Christ, *Washington Office, 110 Maryland Ave. N.E., #207 20002; (202) 543-1517. Fax, (202) 543-5994. Jay Lintner, Director. Web, www.ucc.org.*

Studies public policy issues and promotes church policy on these issues; organizes political activity to implement church views. Interests include health care, international peace, economic justice, and civil rights.

United Jewish Communities, *Washington Office,*
1700 K St. N.W., #1150 20006; (202) 785-5900. Fax, (202) 785-4937. Diana Aviv, Director. Web, www. jewishcommunitiesdc.org.

Fundraising organization. Sustains and enhances the quality of Jewish life domestically and internationally. Advocates the needs of the Jewish community abroad. Offers marketing, communications, and public relations support; coordinates a speakers bureau and Israeli emissaries.

Women's Alliance for Theology, Ethics, and Ritual,
8035 13th St., Silver Spring, MD 20910-4803; (301) 589-2509. Fax, (301) 589-3150. Diann Neu, Co-Director; Mary Hunt, Co-Director. General e-mail, water@hers.com. Web, www.hers.com/water.

Feminist theological organization that focuses on issues concerning women and religion. Interests include social issues; work skills for women with disabilities; human rights in Latin America; and liturgies, rituals, counseling, and research.

See also Center of Concern (p. 444); Ethics Resource Center (p. 77)

2

Agriculture and Nutrition

GENERAL POLICY

AGENCIES

Agricultural Marketing Service *(Agriculture Dept.)*, *1400 Independence Ave. S.W., #3071S, MS-0201 20250-0201; (202) 720-5115. Fax, (202) 720-8477. Kathleen Ann Merrigan, Administrator. Information, (202) 720-8998. Web, www.ams.usda.gov.*

Provides domestic and international marketing services to the agricultural industry. Administers marketing, standardization, grading, inspection, and regulatory programs; maintains a market news service to inform producers of price changes; conducts agricultural marketing research and development programs; studies agricultural transportation issues.

Agriculture Dept. (USDA), *1400 Independence Ave. S.W. 20250; (202) 720-3631. Fax, (202) 720-2166. Dan Glickman, Secretary; Richard Rominger, Deputy Secretary, (202) 720-6158. Information, (202) 720-2791. Library, (202) 720-3434. Recorded news, (202) 488-8358. Locator, (202) 720-8732. Web, www.usda.gov.*

Serves as principal adviser to the president on agricultural policy; works to increase and maintain farm income and to develop markets abroad for U.S. agricultural products.

Agriculture Dept., *Board of Contract Appeals,* *1400 Independence Ave. S.W., #2916S 20250-0601; (202) 720-7023. Fax, (202) 720-3059. Edward Houry, Chair. Web, www.usda.gov.*

Considers appeals of decisions made by contracting officers involving agencies within the Agriculture Dept., including decisions on contracts for construction, property, and services.

Agriculture Dept., *Chief Economist,* *1400 Independence Ave. S.W., #112A 20250-3810; (202) 720-5955. Fax, (202) 690-4915. Keith J. Collins, Chief Economist. Web, www.usda.gov/oce.*

Prepares economic and statistical analyses used to plan and evaluate short- and intermediate-range agricultural policy. Evaluates Agriculture Dept. policy, proposals, and legislation for their impact on the agricultural economy. Administers Agriculture Dept. economic agencies, including the Office of Risk Assessment and Cost-Benefit Analysis, the Office of Energy Policy and New Uses, the Global Change Program Office, and the World Agricultural Outlook Board.

Agriculture Dept., *Food, Nutrition, and Consumer Services,* *1400 Independence Ave. S.W., #240E 20250;*
(202) 720-7711. Fax, (202) 690-3100. Shirley R. Watkins, Under Secretary. Web, www.fns.usda.gov/fncs.

Oversees the Food and Consumer Service and the office of the consumer adviser for agricultural products.

Farm Service Agency *(Agriculture Dept.),* *1400 Independence Ave. S.W., MS 0501 20250-0501; (202) 720-3467. Fax, (202) 720-9105. Keith Kelly, Administrator. Information, (202) 720-5237. Web, www.fsa.usda.gov.*

Oversees farm commodity programs that provide crop loans and purchases. Administers price support programs that provide crop payments when market prices fall below specified levels; conducts programs to help obtain adequate farm and commercial storage and drying equipment for farm products; directs conservation and environmental cost sharing projects and programs to assist farmers during natural disasters and other emergencies. Oversees the Federal Crop Insurance Corporation.

See also Domestic Policy Council (p. 319)

CONGRESS

General Accounting Office, *Food and Agriculture Issues,* *441 G St. N.W., #2T23 20548; (202) 512-5138. Fax, (202) 512-9936. Lawrence J. Dyckman, Director.*

Independent, nonpartisan agency in the legislative branch that audits the Agriculture Dept. and analyzes and reports on its handling of food and agriculture issues.

House Agriculture Committee, *1301 LHOB 20515; (202) 225-2171. Fax, (202) 225-0917. Rep. Larry Combest, R-Texas, Chair; Bill O'Conner, Staff Director. General e-mail, agriculture@mail.house.gov. Web, agriculture.house.gov.*

Jurisdiction over legislation on agriculture and forestry in general; agricultural trade matters and international commodity agreements; inspection and certification of livestock, poultry, meat products, and seafood; agricultural research; pests and pesticides; nutrition; and agricultural assistance programs. Oversees Agriculture Dept. operations.

House Agriculture Committee, *Subcommittee on General Farm Commodities, Resource Conservation, and Credit,* *1430 LHOB 20515; (202) 225-0171. Fax, (202) 225-4464. Rep. Bill Barrett, R-Neb., Chair; Mike Neruda, Staff Director. Web, agriculture.house.gov.*

Jurisdiction over legislation on rural development; oversight of Rural Utilities Service. Jurisdiction over legislation on soil conservation; small-scale stream channelization, watershed, and flood control programs; water and air quality; and agricultural credit programs.

AGRICULTURE DEPARTMENT

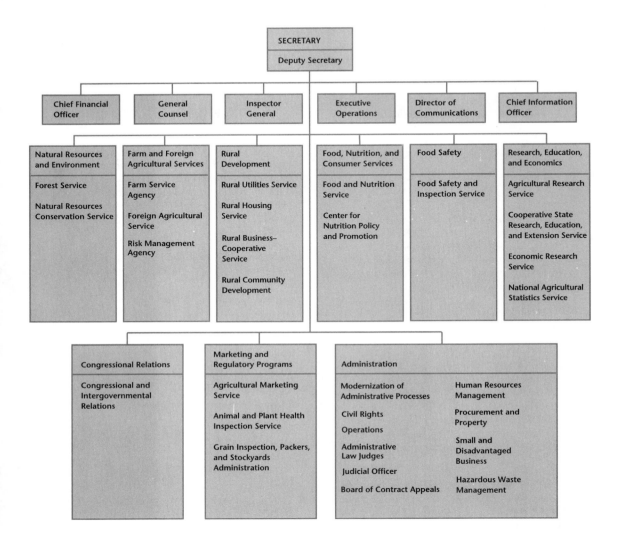

SECRETARY

Deputy Secretary

Chief Financial Officer

General Counsel

Inspector General

Executive Operations

Director of Communications

Chief Information Officer

Natural Resources and Environment

Forest Service

Natural Resources Conservation Service

Farm and Foreign Agricultural Services

Farm Service Agency

Foreign Agricultural Service

Risk Management Agency

Rural Development

Rural Utilities Service

Rural Housing Service

Rural Business– Cooperative Service

Rural Community Development

Food, Nutrition, and Consumer Services

Food and Nutrition Service

Center for Nutrition Policy and Promotion

Food Safety

Food Safety and Inspection Service

Research, Education, and Economics

Agricultural Research Service

Cooperative State Research, Education, and Extension Service

Economic Research Service

National Agricultural Statistics Service

Congressional Relations

Congressional and Intergovernmental Relations

Marketing and Regulatory Programs

Agricultural Marketing Service

Animal and Plant Health Inspection Service

Grain Inspection, Packers, and Stockyards Administration

Administration

Modernization of Administrative Processes

Civil Rights

Operations

Administrative Law Judges

Judicial Officer

Board of Contract Appeals

Human Resources Management

Procurement and Property

Small and Disadvantaged Business

Hazardous Waste Management

House Appropriations Committee, *Subcommittee on Agriculture, Rural Development, FDA, and Related Agencies, 2362 RHOB 20515; (202) 225-2638. Rep. Joe Skeen, R-N.M., Chair; Hank Moore, Staff Director. Web, www.house.gov/appropriations.*

Jurisdiction over legislation to appropriate funds for the Agriculture Dept. (except the Forest Service), the Commodity Futures Trading Commission, and other agriculture-related services and programs.

House Government Reform Committee, *Subcommittee on National Economic Growth, Natural Resources, and Regulatory Affairs, B377 RHOB 20515; (202) 225-4407. Fax, (202) 225-2441. Rep. David M. McIntosh, R-Ind., Chair; Marlo Lewis, Staff Director. Web, www.house.gov/reform.*

Oversees operations of the Agriculture Dept. (except Food and Consumer Service, Food Safety and Inspection Service, and Forest Service).

Senate Agriculture, Nutrition, and Forestry Committee, *SR-328A 20510; (202) 224-2035. Fax, (202) 224-1725. Sen. Richard G. Lugar, R-Ind., Chair; Keith Luse, Staff Director. Web, agriculture.senate.gov.*

Jurisdiction over legislation on agriculture, agricultural economics and research, agricultural extension services and experiment stations, agricultural engineering, animal industry and diseases, forestry, pests and pesticides, rural issues, nutrition, and family farms; oversees Agriculture Dept. operations.

Senate Agriculture, Nutrition, and Forestry Committee, *Subcommittee on Forestry, Conservation, and Rural Revitalization, SR-328A 20510; (202) 224-2752. Fax, (202) 224-1725. Sen. Larry E. Craig, R-Idaho, Chair; Dan Whiting, Staff Contact. Web, agriculture.senate.gov.*

Jurisdiction over legislation on family farming and rural development, including rural electrification and telephone development; oversight of the Rural Utilities Service. Jurisdiction over legislation on irrigation, soil conservation, stream channelization, watershed programs, and flood control programs involving structures of less than 4,000 acre-feet in storage capacity.

Senate Appropriations Committee, *Subcommittee on Agriculture, Rural Development, and Related Agencies, SD-136 20510; (202) 224-5270. Fax, (202) 224-9450. Sen. Thad Cochran, R-Miss., Chair; Rebecca M. Davies, Clerk. Web, appropriations.senate.gov/agriculture.*

Jurisdiction over legislation to appropriate funds for the Agriculture Dept. (except the Forest Service), the Commodity Futures Trading Commission, farm credit, and other agriculture-related services and programs.

Senate Banking, Housing, and Urban Affairs Committee, *Subcommittee on Financial Institutions, SD-534 20510; (202) 224-7391. Fax, (202) 224-5137. Sen. Robert F. Bennett, R-Utah, Chair; Jim Barker, Staff Director. Web, banking.senate.gov.*

Jurisdiction over legislation on economic stabilization and growth, including regulatory relief issues, barriers to development in rural areas, price controls, and asset disposition policies.

NONPROFIT

American Farm Bureau Federation, *Washington Office, 600 Maryland Ave. S.W., #800 20024; (202) 484-3600. Fax, (202) 484-3604. Richard W. Newpher, Executive Director. Web, www.fb.com.*

Federation of state farm bureaus in fifty states and Puerto Rico. Promotes agricultural research. Interests include commodity programs, domestic production, marketing, education, research, financial assistance to the farmer, foreign assistance programs, rural development, the world food shortage, and inspection and certification of food.

National Assn. of State Departments of Agriculture, *1156 15th St. N.W., #1020 20005; (202) 296-9680. Fax, (202) 296-9686. Richard W. Kirchhoff, Executive Vice President. General e-mail, nasda@patriot.net. Web, www.nasda-hq.org/.*

Membership: agriculture commissioners from the fifty states, Puerto Rico, Guam, American Samoa, and the Virgin Islands. Serves as liaison between federal agencies and state governments to coordinate agricultural policies and laws. Seeks to protect consumers and the environment. Monitors legislation and regulations.

National Council of Agricultural Employers, *1112 16th St. N.W., #920 20036; (202) 728-0300. Fax, (202) 728-0303. Sharon M. Hughes, Executive Vice President. General e-mail, ncae@erols.com.*

Membership: employers of agricultural labor. Encourages establishment and maintenance of conditions conducive to an adequate supply of domestic and foreign farm labor.

National Farmers Union (Farmers Educational and Cooperative Union of America), *Washington Office, 400 N. Capitol St. N.W., #790 20001; (202) 554-1600. Fax, (202) 554-1654. Nancy Danielson, Legislative Representative; Tom Buis, Director. Web, www.nfu.org.*

Membership: family farmers belonging to state affiliates. Interests include commodity programs, domestic production, marketing, education, research, energy and natural resources, financial assistance to farmers, Social Security for farmers, foreign programs, rural development, the world food shortage, and inspection and certification of food.

National Grange, *1616 H St. N.W. 20006-4999; (202) 628-3507. Fax, (202) 347-1091. Kermit W. Richardson, Master.*

Membership: farmers and others involved in agricultural production and rural community service activities. Coordinates community service programs with state grange organizations.

Rural Coalition, *1411 K St. N.W., #901 20005; (202) 628-7160. Fax, (202) 628-7165. Lorette Picciano, Executive Director. Web, www.ruralco.org.*

Alliance of organizations that develop public policies benefiting rural communities. Collaborates with community-based groups on agriculture and rural development issues, including health and the environment, minority farmers, farmworkers, native Americans' rights, and rural community development. Provides rural groups with technical assistance.

Union of Concerned Scientists, *Government Relations, Washington Office,* 1616 P St. N.W., #310 20036; (202) 332-0900. Fax, (202) 332-0905. Alden Meyer, Director; Todd Perry, Washington Representative for Arms Control and International Security. General e-mail, ucs@ucsusa.org. Web, www.ucsusa.org.

Advocates policies to encourage low-input sustainable agricultural practices and to reduce the environmental and health effects caused by conventional agricultural practices and high-chemical inputs. Seeks to evaluate future role, risk, and benefits of biotechnology. Monitors legislation and regulations.

United Farm Workers of America, *Washington Office,* c/o AFL-CIO, 815 16th St. N.W. 20006; (202) 637-5212. Fax, (202) 637-5012. Rudy Arredondo, Manager. Web, www.ufw.org.

Membership: approximately 50,000 farm workers. Helps members negotiate pay, benefits, and better working conditions; conducts training programs and workshops. Focus includes immigration and migrant workers. Monitors legislation and regulations. (Affiliated with the AFL-CIO.)

U.S. Chamber of Commerce, *Environment and Regulatory Affairs,* 1615 H St. N.W. 20062-2000; (202) 463-5533. Fax, (202) 887-3445. Bill Kovacs, Manager. Web, www.uschamber.org.

Develops policy on issues affecting production, transportation, and sale of agricultural products. Interests include food safety, pesticides, nutrition labeling, seafood inspection, backhauling, and international trade.

Agricultural Research/Education

See also Botany (chap. 17)

AGENCIES

Agricultural Research Service *(Agriculture Dept.),* 1400 Independence Ave. S.W., #302A 20250-0300; (202) 720-3656. Fax, (202) 720-5427. Edward B. Knipling, Associate Administrator. General e-mail, arsweb@nal.usda.gov. Web, www.ars.usda.gov.

Conducts research on crops, livestock, poultry, soil and water conservation, agricultural engineering, and control of insects and other pests; develops new uses for farm commodities.

Agriculture Dept., *National Agriculture Statistics Service,* 1400 Independence Ave. S.W. 20250-2000; (202) 720-4557. Fax, (202) 720-8738. Steven Wyatt, Director.

Information, (800) 727-9540. General e-mail, nass@nass.usda.gov. Web, www.usda.gov/nass.

Conducts a quinquennial agricultural census that provides data on crops, livestock, operator characteristics, land use, farm production expenditures, machinery and equipment, and irrigation for counties, states, regions, and the nation.

Agriculture Dept., *Research, Education, and Economics,* 1400 Independence Ave. S.W., #217W 20250-0110; (202) 720-5923. Fax, (202) 690-2842. Eileen Kennedy, Deputy Under Secretary, (202) 720-8885. Web, www.usda.gov.

Coordinates agricultural research, extension, and teaching programs in the food and agricultural sciences, including human nutrition, home economics, consumer services, agricultural economics, environmental quality, natural and renewable resources, forestry and range management, animal and plant production and protection, aquaculture, and the processing, distribution, marketing, and utilization of food and agricultural products. Oversees the Agricultural Research Service; the Cooperative State Research, Education, and Extension Service; the Economic Research Service; and the National Agricultural Statistics Service.

Agriculture Dept., *Special Emphasis Outreach Program,* 1400 Independence Ave. S.W., #6420S 20250-9400; (202) 720-7314. Fax, (202) 690-2345. Linda Varner Mount, Chief. Web, www.usda.gov.

Works with state governments to foster participation by minority and disabled individuals and institutions in food and agricultural research, teaching programs, and related areas. Assists the Agriculture Dept. in developing and improving opportunities in agricultural enterprises for minority individuals and institutions.

Cooperative State Research, Education, and Extension Service *(Agriculture Dept.),* 1400 Independence Ave. S.W., #305A 20250-2201; (202) 720-4423. Fax, (202) 720-8987. Charles W. Laughlin, Administrator. Information, (202) 720-6133. TTY, (202) 690-1899. Web, www.reeusda.gov.

Conducts educational programs to assist farmers, processors, and others in efficient production and marketing of agricultural products. Conducts educational programs on sustainable agriculture. Serves as national headquarters for the 4-H youth programs and coordinates activities with state and local clubs.

Cooperative State Research, Education, and Extension Service *(Agriculture Dept.),* *Competitive Research Grants and Awards Management,* 901 D St. S.W., #322 20447; (202) 401-1761. Fax, (202) 401-1782. Sally Rockey, Deputy Administrator.

Administers grants to colleges, universities, small businesses, and other organizations to promote research in food, agriculture, and related areas. Maintains administrative responsibility for programs in aquaculture, small-farm resource development, and higher education.

Cooperative State Research, Education, and Extension Service *(Agriculture Dept.), Science and Education Resources Development, 1400 Independence Ave. S.W., #338A 20250; (202) 720-3377. Fax, (202) 720-3945. K. Jane Coulter, Deputy Administrator.*

Provides national leadership and coordination on issues relating to food and agricultural research, higher education, and extension; assists colleges and universities in developing and maintaining education programs in the food and agricultural sciences. Seeks to ensure that colleges and universities produce the requisite number of graduates to satisfy the nation's need for individuals trained in the field. Maintains research information system covering all publicly supported agriculture, food, human nutrition, and forestry research.

Economic Research Service *(Agriculture Dept.), 1800 M St. N.W. 20036; (202) 694-5200. Fax, (202) 694-5792. Barry Krissoff, Chief, Speciality Crops; Joy Harwood, Chief, Field Crops. Web, www.econ.ag.gov.*

Conducts market research; studies and forecasts domestic supply-and-demand trends for fruits and vegetables.

National Agricultural Library *(Agriculture Dept.), 10301 Baltimore Ave., Beltsville, MD 20705; (301) 504-5248. Fax, (301) 504-7042. Pamela Q. J. André, Director. TTY, (301) 504-6856. Reference desk, (301) 504-5479, 8:30 a.m.–4:30 p.m. Web, www.nal.usda.gov.*

Makes agricultural information available to researchers, educators, policymakers, and the public; coordinates state land-grant and Agriculture Dept. field libraries; promotes international cooperation and exchange of information. Interests include food production, nutrition, animal and plant health, rural development, and agricultural trade.

National Agricultural Library *(Agriculture Dept.), D.C. Reference Center, Washington Office, 14th and Independence Ave. S.W., #1052S 20250; (202) 720-3434. Fax, (202) 720-0342. Alvetta Pindell, Chief. Web, www.nal.usda.gov.*

Maintains an agricultural reference collection and online services for use by department personnel and the public.

National Agricultural Statistics Service *(Agriculture Dept.), 1400 Independence Ave. S.W., #4117S 20250-2001;* *(202) 720-2707. Fax, (202) 720-9013. R. Ronald Bosecker, Administrator. Weekly weather and crop information, bulletin subscriptions, (202) 720-4021. General e-mail, nass@nass.usda.gov. Web, www.usda.gov/nass.*

Prepares estimates and reports on production, supply, prices, and other items relating to the U.S. agricultural economy. Reports include statistics on field crops, fruits and vegetables, cattle, hogs, poultry, and related products.

National Science and Technology Council *(Executive Office of the President), Dwight D. Eisenhower Executive Office Bldg., #435 20502; (202) 456-6100. Fax, (202) 456-6026. Neal Lane, Chair. General e-mail, information@ostp.eop.gov. Web, www.whitehouse.gov/WH/EOP/OSTP/NSTC/html/charge.html.*

Coordinates research and development activities and programs that involve more than one federal agency. Concerns include food, agriculture, and forestry research.

Rural Business-Cooperative Service *(Agriculture Dept.), Cooperative Services, 1400 Independence Ave. S.W., #4016S, MS 3250 20250-3250; (202) 720-7558. Fax, (202) 720-4641. Randall E. Torgerson, Deputy Administrator.*

Conducts economic research and provides technical assistance to help farmers market their products and purchase supplies; helps people living in rural areas to obtain business services through cooperatives.

CONGRESS

House Agriculture Committee, *Subcommittee on Risk Management, Research, and Specialty Crops, 1301 LHOB 20515; (202) 225-4652. Fax, (202) 225-7760. Rep. Thomas W. Ewing, R-Ill., Chair; Stacy C. Carey, Staff Director. Web, agriculture.house.gov.*

Jurisdiction over legislation on agricultural education.

House Science Committee, *Subcommittee on Basic Research, B374 RHOB 20515; (202) 225-7858. Fax, (202) 225-7815. Rep. Nick Smith, R-Mich., Chair; Steve Eule, Staff Director. Web, www.house.gov/science.*

Jurisdiction over legislation concerning agricultural research and development.

Senate Agriculture, Nutrition, and Forestry Committee, *Subcommittee on Research, Nutrition, and General Legislation, SR-328A 20510; (202) 224-2854. Fax, (202) 224-1725. Sen. Peter G. Fitzgerald, R-Ill., Chair; Terry VanDoren, Legislative Assistant. Web, agriculture.senate.gov.*

Jurisdiction over legislation on agricultural education and research.

INTERNATIONAL ORGANIZATIONS

Consultative Group on International Agricultural Research, *1800 G St. N.W. 20006 (mailing address: 1818 H St. N.W. 20433); (202) 473-8951. Fax, (202) 473-8110. Alexander von der Osten, Executive Secretary. General e-mail, cgiar@cgiar.org. Web, www.cgiar.org.*

Promotes sustainable agriculture for food security in developing countries; supports a network of sixteen international agricultural research centers. Interests include agricultural productivity, environmental protection, and biodiversity; promotes effective public policy and strong national research programs.

NONPROFIT

Academy for Educational Development, *Social Development, 1825 Connecticut Ave. N.W., #800 20009-5721; (202) 884-8700. Fax, (202) 884-8701. William Smith, Executive Vice President. Web, www.aed.org.*

Conducts studies of international agricultural development on a contract basis; encourages exchange of agricultural information between researchers and farmers.

Future Farmers of America, *1410 King St., #400, Alexandria, VA 22314 (mailing address: P.O. Box 15160, Alexandria, VA 22309); (703) 838-5889. Fax, (703) 838-5888. Larry D. Case, National Adviser. Toll-free, (800) 772-0939. Web, www.ffa.org.*

Membership: local chapters of high school students enrolled in agricultural education and agribusiness programs. Coordinates leadership training and other activities with local chapters across the United States.

National Council of Farmer Cooperatives, *50 F St. N.W., #900 20001; (202) 626-8700. Fax, (202) 626-8722. David Graves, President. General e-mail, info@ncfc.org. Web, www.ncfc.org.*

Membership: cooperative businesses owned and operated by farmers. Conducts educational programs and encourages research on agricultural cooperatives; provides statistics and analyzes trends; presents awards for research papers.

National 4-H Council, *7100 Connecticut Ave., Chevy Chase, MD 20815-4999; (301) 961-2820. Fax, (301) 961-2894. Richard J. Sauer, President. Press, (301) 961-2915. Web, www.fourhcouncil.edu.*

Educational organization incorporated to strengthen and complement the 4-H program (for young people ages seven to nineteen) of the Agriculture Dept.'s Cooperative Extension Service and state land-grant universities. Programs include citizenship and leadership

training, workforce preparation, and environmental stewardship.

Fertilizer and Pesticides

AGENCIES

Agriculture Dept., *Natural Resources Conservation Service: Pest Management, P.O. Box 2090 20013; (202) 720-7838. Fax, (202) 720-2646. Benjamin Smallwood, Specialist. Web, www.nhq.nrcs.usda.gov/BCS/pest/pest. html.*

Formulates and recommends agency policy in coordination with the Environmental Protection Agency and other USDA agencies for the establishment of standards, procedures, and management of agronomic, forest, and horticultural use of pesticides.

Environmental Protection Agency, *Pesticide Programs, 1921 Jefferson Davis Hwy., Arlington, VA 22202 (mailing address: 401 M St. S.W., MC 7501C 20460); (703) 305-7090. Fax, (703) 308-4776. Marcia Mulkey, Director. National Pesticide Telecommunications Network, (800) 858-7378. Web, www.epa.gov/pesticides.*

Evaluates data to determine the risks and benefits of pesticides; sets standards for safe use of pesticides, including those for use on foods. Develops rules that govern labeling and literature accompanying pesticide products.

Environmental Protection Agency, *Prevention, Pesticides, and Toxic Substances, 401 M St. S.W., MC 7101 20460; (202) 260-2902. Fax, (202) 260-1847. Susan H. Wayland, Assistant Administrator. Pollution prevention and toxic substances control, (202) 260-3810.*

Studies and makes recommendations for regulating chemical substances under the Toxic Substances Control Act; compiles list of chemical substances subject to the act; registers, controls, and regulates use of pesticides and toxic substances.

CONGRESS

House Agriculture Committee, *Subcommittee on Department Operations, Oversight, Nutrition, and Forestry, 1430 LHOB 20515; (202) 225-4913. Fax, (202) 225-4464. Rep. Robert W. Goodlatte, R-Va., Chair; Kevin Kramp, Staff Director. Web, agriculture.house.gov.*

Jurisdiction over legislation on environmental policy, including pesticides.

Senate Environment and Public Works Committee, *Subcommittee on Superfund, Waste Control, and Risk Assessment, SD-410 20510; (202) 224-6176. Fax, (202) 224-5167. Sen. Lincoln Chafee, R-R.I., Chair; Ted*

Michaels, Staff Director. Web, epw.senate.gov.

Jurisdiction over legislation on environmental policy, including pesticides.

NONPROFIT

American Crop Protection Assn., *1156 15th St. N.W., #400 20005; (202) 296-1585. Fax, (202) 463-0474. Jay J. Vroom, President. Web, www.acpa.org.*

Membership: pesticide manufacturers. Provides information on pesticide safety, development, and use. Monitors legislation and regulations.

Entomological Society of America, *9301 Annapolis Rd., Lanham, MD 20706; (301) 731-4535. Fax, (301) 731-4538. James Olmes, Executive Director. General e-mail, esa@entsoc.org. Web, www.entsoc.org.*

Scientific association that promotes the science of entomology and the interests of professionals in the field. Advises on crop protection, food chain, and individual and urban health matters dealing with insect pests.

Fertilizer Institute, *501 2nd St. N.E. 20002; (202) 675-8250. Fax, (202) 544-8123. Gary D. Myers, President. Web, www.tfi.org.*

Membership: manufacturers, dealers, and distributors of fertilizer. Provides statistical data and other information concerning the effects of fertilizer and its relationship to world food production, food supply, and the environment.

Migrant Legal Action Program, *P.O. Box 53308 20009; (202) 462-7744. Fax, (202) 462-7914. Roger C. Rosenthal, Executive Director. General e-mail, hn1645@ handsnet.org.*

Assists local legal services groups and private attorneys representing farm workers. Monitors legislation, regulations, and enforcement activities of the Environmental Protection Agency and the Occupational Safety and Health Administration in the area of pesticide use as it affects the health of migrant farm workers. Litigates cases concerning living and working conditions experienced by migrant farmworkers. Works with local groups on implementation of Medicaid block grants.

National Agricultural Aviation Assn., *1005 E St. S.E. 20003; (202) 546-5722. Fax, (202) 546-5726. James Callan, Executive Director. General e-mail, naaa@aol.com.*

Membership: qualified agricultural pilots; operating companies that seed, fertilize, and spray land by air; and allied industries. Monitors legislation and regulations.

National Coalition Against the Misuse of Pesticides, *701 E St. S.E., #200 20003; (202) 543-5450. Fax,*

(202) 543-4791. Jay Feldman, Executive Director. General e-mail, ncamp@igc.apc.org. Web, www.csn.net/ncamp/.

Coalition of family farmers, farmworkers, consumers, home gardeners, physicians, lawyers, and others concerned about pesticide hazards and safety. Issues information to increase public awareness of environmental, public health, and economic problems caused by pesticide abuse; promotes alternatives to pesticide use, such as the integrated pest management program.

National Food Processors Assn., *1350 Eye St. N.W., #300 20005; (202) 639-5900. Fax, (202) 639-5932. John R. Cady, President. Press, (202) 639-5919.*

Maintains an information clearinghouse on environmental and crop protection; analyzes products for pesticide residue. Monitors legislation and regulations.

National Pest Management Assn., *Government Affairs, 8100 Oak St., Dunn Loring, VA 22027; (703) 573-8330. Fax, (703) 573-4116. Robert M. Rosenberg, Director. Web, www.pestworld.org.*

Membership: pest control operators. Monitors federal regulations that affect pesticide use; provides members with technical information.

Horticulture and Gardening

See also Botany (chap. 17)

AGENCIES

National Arboretum *(Agriculture Dept.), 3501 New York Ave. N.E. 20002; (202) 245-4539. Fax, (202) 245-4575. Thomas S. Elias, Director. Library, (202) 245-4538.*

Maintains public display of plants on 446 acres; provides information and makes referrals concerning cultivated plants (exclusive of field crops and fruits); conducts plant breeding and research; maintains herbarium. Library open to the public by appointment.

Smithsonian Institution, *Horticulture Library, Arts and Industries Bldg., 900 Jefferson Dr. S.W., MRC 420 20560; (202) 357-1544. Fax, (202) 786-2026. Marca L. Woodhams, Chief Librarian. General e-mail, woodhma@ sil.si.edu. Web, www.fil.si.edu.*

Collection includes books, periodicals, trade catalogs, and videotapes on horticulture, garden history, and landscape design. Specializes in American gardens and gardening of the late nineteenth and early twentieth centuries. Open to the public by appointment.

CONGRESS

U.S. Botanic Garden, *245 1st St. S.W. 20024; (202) 225-8333. Fax, (202) 225-1561. Vacant, Executive Director. Web, www.aoc.gov/pages/usbgpage.htm.*

Collects, cultivates, and grows various plants for public display and study; identifies botanic specimens and furnishes information on proper growing methods. Conducts horticultural classes and tours.

NONPROFIT

American Horticultural Society, *7931 E. Boulevard Dr., Alexandria, VA 22308-1300; (703) 768-5700. Fax, (703) 768-8700. Linda Hallman, President. Information, (800) 777-7931. Web, www.ahs.org.*

Promotes the expansion of horticulture in the United States through educational programs for amateur and professional horticulturists. Acts as a horticultural clearinghouse; operates the Gardener's Information Service. Oversees historic house and farm once owned by George Washington, with gardens maintained by plant societies; house and grounds are rented for special occasions.

American Nursery and Landscape Assn., *1250 Eye St. N.W., #500 20005; (202) 789-2900. Fax, (202) 789-1893. Robert J. Dolibois, Executive Vice President. Web, www.anla.org.*

Membership: wholesale growers, garden center retailers, landscape firms, and suppliers to the horticultural community. Monitors legislation and regulations on agricultural, environmental, and small-business issues; conducts educational seminars on business management for members. (Affiliated with the National Assn. of Plant Patent Owners.)

American Society for Horticultural Science, *113 S. West St., #200, Alexandria, VA 22314; (703) 836-4606. Fax, (703) 836-2024. Michael Neff, Executive Director. General e-mail, ashs@ashs.org. Web, www.ashs.org.*

Membership: educators, government workers, firms, associations, and individuals interested in horticultural science. Promotes scientific research and education in horticulture, including international exchange of information.

National Assn. of Plant Patent Owners, *1250 Eye St. N.W., #500 20005-3922; (202) 789-2900. Fax, (202) 789-1893. Craig Regelbrugge, Administrator.*

Membership: owners of patents on newly propagated horticultural plants. Informs members of plant patents issued, provisions of patent laws, and changes in practice. Promotes the development, protection, production, and distribution of new varieties of horticultural plants. Works with international organizations of plant breeders on matters of common interest. (Affiliated with the American Nursery and Landscape Assn.)

Society of American Florists, *1601 Duke St., Alexandria, VA 22314; (703) 836-8700. Fax, (703) 836-8705. Drew Gruenburg, Senior Vice President. Web, www.safnow.org.*

Membership: growers, wholesalers, and retailers in the floriculture and ornamental horticulture industries. Interests include labor, pesticides, the environment, international trade, and toxicity of plants. Mediates industry problems.

Soil and Watershed Conservation

See also Community and Regional Development (chap. 12); Resources Management (chap. 9)

AGENCIES

Farm Service Agency *(Agriculture Dept.), Conservation and Environmental Programs, 1400 Independence Ave. S.W., MS-0513 20250-0513; (202) 720-6221. Fax, (202) 720-4619. Robert Stephenson, Director. Web, www.fsa.usda.gov/pas.*

Directs conservation and environmental projects and programs to help farmers and ranchers prevent soil erosion and contamination of natural resources.

Farm Service Agency *(Agriculture Dept.), Natural Resources Analysis, 1400 Independence Ave. S.W., MS-0519 20250-0519; (202) 720-9685. Fax, (202) 720-8261. Thomas L. Browning, Director. General e-mail, tbrownin@wdc.fsa.usda.gov.*

Studies economic issues relating to conservation and land-use programs.

Interior Dept., *North American Wetlands Conservation Council, 4401 N. Fairfax Dr., #110, Arlington, VA 22203; (703) 358-1784. Fax, (703) 358-2282. David A. Smith, Coordinator. General e-mail, r9arw_nawwo@mail.fws.gov. Web, www.fws.gov.*

Membership: government and private-sector conservation experts. Works to protect, restore, and manage wetlands and other habitats for migratory birds and other animals and to maintain migratory bird and waterfowl populations.

Natural Resources Conservation Service *(Agriculture Dept.), 1400 Independence Ave. S.W. 20013 (mailing address: P.O. Box 2890 20013-2890); (202) 720-4525. Fax, (202) 720-7690. Pearlie S. Reed, Chief. Information, (202) 720-3210. Web, www.ncg.nrcs.usda.gov.*

Responsible for soil and water conservation programs, including watershed protection, flood prevention, river basin surveys, and resource conservation and development. Provides landowners, operators, state and local units of government, and community groups with technical assistance in carrying out local programs. Inventories and monitors soil, water, and related resource data and resource use trends. Provides information about soil surveys, farmlands, and other natural resources.

CONGRESS

House Agriculture Committee, *Subcommittee on General Farm Commodities, Resource Conservation, and Credit,* 1430 LHOB 20515; (202) 225-0171. Fax, (202) 225-4464. Rep. Bill Barrett, R-Neb., Chair; Mike Neruda, Staff Director. Web, agriculture.house.gov.

Jurisdiction over legislation on soil conservation, watershed, and flood control programs.

Senate Agriculture, Nutrition, and Forestry Committee, *Subcommittee on Forestry, Conservation, and Rural Revitalization,* SR-328A 20510; (202) 224-2752. Fax, (202) 224-1725. Sen. Larry E. Craig, R-Idaho, Chair; Dan Whiting, Staff Contact. Web, agriculture.senate.gov.

Jurisdiction over legislation on soil conservation, watershed programs, and flood control programs.

NONPROFIT

American Farmland Trust, 1200 18th St. N.W., #800 20036; (202) 331-7300. Fax, (202) 659-8339. Ralph Grossi, President. General e-mail, info@farmland.org. Web, www.farmland.org.

Works with farmers to promote farming practices that lead to a healthy environment. Interests include preservation of farmlands from urban development, establishment of safeguards against soil erosion, and agricultural resource conservation policy development at all government levels. Initiates local preservation efforts and assists individuals and organizations engaged in safeguarding agricultural properties.

Henry A. Wallace Institute for Alternative Agriculture, 9200 Edmonston Rd., #117, Greenbelt, MD 20770-1551; (301) 441-8777. Fax, (301) 220-0164. Kate Clancy, Executive Director. General e-mail, wallacecenter@ winrock.org. Web, www.hawiaa.org.

Supports the adoption of low-cost, resource-conserving, and environmentally sound farming methods. Provides scientific information and sponsors research and education programs on alternative agricultural methods. Monitors legislation and regulations.

Irrigation Assn., 8260 Willow Oaks Corporate Dr., #120, Fairfax, VA 22031; (703) 573-3551. Fax, (703) 573-1913. Thomas Kimmell, Executive Director. Web, www.irrigation.org.

Membership: companies and individuals involved in irrigation, drainage, and erosion control worldwide. Seeks to improve the products and practices used to manage water resources; interests include economic development and environmental enhancement.

National Assn. of Conservation Districts, 509 Capitol Court N.E. 20002-4937; (202) 547-6223. Fax, (202) 547-6450. Ernest C. Shea, Chief Executive Officer. Web, www.nacdnet.org.

Membership: conservation districts (local subdivisions of state government). Works to promote the conservation of land, forests, and other natural resources. Interests include erosion and sediment control; water quality; forestry, water, flood plain, and range management; rural development; and urban and community conservation.

COMMODITIES/FARM PRODUCE

See also Caucuses (chap. 20)

AGENCIES

Agricultural Marketing Service *(Agriculture Dept.),* **Seed Regulatory and Testing,** Bldg. 306, BARC East, #209, Beltsville, MD 20705; (301) 504-9237. Fax, (301) 504-8098. Richard Payne, Chief. Web, www.ams.usda. gov/lsg/seed/ls-sd.htm.

Administers interstate programs prohibiting false advertising and labeling of seeds. Regulates interstate shipment of seeds. Tests seeds for a fee under the Agricultural Marketing Act.

Agricultural Marketing Service *(Agriculture Dept.),* **Transportation and Marketing,** 1400 Independence Ave. S.W., #4006S 20250 (mailing address: P.O. Box 96456 20090-6456); (202) 690-1300. Fax, (202) 690-0338. Eileen S. Stommes, Deputy Administrator; James A. Caron, Program Manager, SEA, (202) 690-1304. Web, www.ams. usda.gov/tmd/index.htm.

Promotes efficient, cost-effective marketing and transportation for U.S. agricultural products; sets standards for domestic and international marketing of organic products. Shipper and Exporter Assistance (SEA) program provides exporters with market information, educational services, and regulatory representation.

Agricultural Research Service *(Agriculture Dept.),* **National Plant Germplasm System,** 5601 Sunnyside Ave., BLF-4-2200, Beltsville, MD 20705; (301) 504-6252. Fax, (301) 504-5467. Peter Bretting, National Program Leader. Web, www.ars-grin.gov.

Network of organizations and individuals interested in preserving the genetic diversity of crop plants, including cotton, wheat and other grains, fruits and vegetables, rice, sugar, tobacco, and peanuts. Collects, preserves, evaluates, and catalogs germplasm and distributes it for specific purposes.

Agriculture Dept., *Marketing and Regulatory Programs, 1400 Independence Ave. S.W., #228W, MS-0109 20250-0109; (202) 720-4256. Fax, (202) 720-5775. Michael V. Dunn, Under Secretary. Web, www.usda.gov.*

Administers inspection and grading services and regulatory programs for agricultural commodities through the Agricultural Marketing Service; Animal and Plant Health Inspection Service; and Grain Inspection, Packers, and Stockyards Administration.

Animal and Plant Health Inspection Service *(Agriculture Dept.), 1400 Independence Ave. S.W. 20250 (mailing address: Ag. Box 3401 20250); (202) 720-3861. Fax, (202) 720-3054. Craig A. Reed, Administrator. Web, www.aphis.usda.gov.*

Administers quarantine regulations governing imports of agricultural commodities into the United States; certifies that U.S. exports are free of pests and disease.

Commodity Credit Corp. *(Agriculture Dept.), 1400 Independence Ave. S.W. 20250; (202) 720-3467. Fax, (202) 720-8254. August Schumacher Jr., Under Secretary. Web, www.fsa.usda.gov/daco.*

Finances commodity stabilization programs, domestic and export surplus commodity disposal, foreign assistance, storage activities, and related programs.

Commodity Futures Trading Commission, *3 Lafayette Center, 1155 21st St. N.W. 20581; (202) 418-5030. Fax, (202) 418-5525. William J. Rainier, Chair; Don Tendick, Executive Director (Acting). Information, (202) 418-5000. Library, (202) 418-5255. Web, www.cftc.gov.*

Administers the Commodity Exchange Act, which regulates all commodity futures and options to prevent fraudulent trade practices.

Cooperative State Research, Education, and Extension Service *(Agriculture Dept.), 1400 Independence Ave. S.W., #305A 20250-2201; (202) 720-4423. Fax, (202) 720-8987. Charles W. Laughlin, Administrator. Information, (202) 720-6133. TTY, (202) 690-1899. Web, www.reeusda.gov.*

Conducts workshops on management of farmer cooperatives and educational programs on sustainable agriculture. Provides small farmers with management and marketing programs; offers training and assistance to rural communities and local officials.

Farm Service Agency *(Agriculture Dept.), 1400 Independence Ave. S.W., MS 0501 20250-0501; (202) 720-3467. Fax, (202) 720-9105. Keith Kelly, Administrator. Information, (202) 720-5237. Web, www.fsa.usda.gov.*

Administers farm commodity programs providing crop loans and purchases; provides crop payments when market prices fall below specified levels; sets acreage allotments and marketing quotas; assists farmers in areas affected by natural disasters. Oversees the Federal Crop Insurance Corporation.

Foreign Agricultural Service *(Agriculture Dept.), 1400 Independence Ave. S.W., #5071 20250-1001; (202) 720-3935. Fax, (202) 690-2159. Timothy J. Galvin, Administrator; Richard Fritz, General Sales Manager. Information, (202) 720-7115. TTY, (202) 720-1786. Web, www.fas.usda.gov.*

Promotes exports of U.S. commodities and assists with trade negotiations; coordinates activities of U.S. representatives in foreign countries who report on crop and market conditions; sponsors trade fairs in foreign countries to promote export of U.S. agricultural products; analyzes world demand and production of various commodities; monitors sales by private exporters.

Foreign Agricultural Service *(Agriculture Dept.), Commodity and Marketing Programs, 1400 Independence Ave. S.W., #5089 20250; (202) 720-4761. Fax, (202) 690-3606. Gary C. Grove, Administrator (Acting). Web, www.fas.usda.gov/commodity.html.*

Works with nonprofit commodity and trade associations to increase and maintain exports of U.S. agricultural products. Studies and reports on markets for specific commodities and food products, both worldwide and in particular countries; assists with advertising and consumer promotions abroad.

Rural Business-Cooperative Service *(Agriculture Dept.), Cooperative Services, 1400 Independence Ave. S.W., #4016S, MS 3250 20250-3250; (202) 720-7558. Fax, (202) 720-4641. Randall E. Torgerson, Deputy Administrator.*

Provides cooperative enterprises that process and market farm products and other cooperatively owned, rural-based industries with technical and research assistance. Helps to develop new cooperatives.

State Dept., *Agricultural and Textile Trade Affairs: Textiles Trade Policy and Agreements, 2201 C St. N.W., #3526 20520; (202) 647-1813. Fax, (202) 647-2302. James Schollaert, Chief. Web, www.state.gov.*

Negotiates bilateral textile trade agreements with foreign governments concerning cotton, wool, and synthetic textile and apparel products. Develops agricultural trade policy; handles questions pertaining to international negotiations on all agricultural products covered by the World Trade Organization (WTO).

CONGRESS

House Agriculture Committee, *1301 LHOB 20515; (202) 225-2171. Fax, (202) 225-0917. Rep. Larry Combest, R-Texas, Chair; Bill O'Conner, Staff Director. General e-mail, agriculture@mail.house.gov. Web, agriculture. house.gov.*

Jurisdiction over legislation on emergency commodity distribution. Jurisdiction over legislation on international commodity agreements, foreign agricultural trade of commodities, and foreign market development (jurisdiction shared with House International Relations Committee).

House Agriculture Committee, *Subcommittee on General Farm Commodities, Resource Conservation, and Credit, 1430 LHOB 20515; (202) 225-0171. Fax, (202) 225-4464. Rep. Bill Barrett, R-Neb., Chair; Mike Neruda, Staff Director. Web, agriculture.house.gov.*

Jurisdiction over legislation on feed grains, wheat, oilseeds, lentils, peas, soybeans, dry edible beans, cotton, cottonseed, and rice. Jurisdiction over legislation on the Commodity Credit Corp. and agricultural trade matters.

House Agriculture Committee, *Subcommittee on Livestock and Horticulture, 1301 LHOB 20515; (202) 225-1564. Fax, (202) 225-4369. Rep. Richard W. Pombo, R-Calif., Chair; Chris D'Arcy, Staff Director. Web, agriculture.house.gov.*

Jurisdiction over legislation on dairy commodity programs and wool.

House Agriculture Committee, *Subcommittee on Risk Management, Research, and Specialty Crops, 1301 LHOB 20515; (202) 225-4652. Fax, (202) 225-7760. Rep. Thomas W. Ewing, R-Ill., Chair; Stacy C. Carey, Staff Director. Web, agriculture.house.gov.*

Jurisdiction over legislation on tobacco, peanuts, and sugar. Jurisdiction over legislation on the Commodity Futures Trading Commission and the Commodity Exchange Act.

House International Relations Committee, *Subcommittee on International Economic Policy and Trade, 257 FHOB 20515; (202) 225-3345. Fax, (202) 225-0432. Rep. Ileana Ros-Lehtinen, R-Fla., Chair; Mauricio Tamargo, Staff Director. Web, www.house.gov/ international_relations.*

Jurisdiction over legislation on international commodity agreements, foreign agricultural trade of commodities and foreign market development (jurisdiction shared with House Agriculture Committee), and export controls on agricultural commodities.

House Small Business Committee, *Subcommittee on Tax, Finance, and Exports, B363 RHOB 20515; (202) 226-2630. Fax, (202) 225-8950. Rep. Donald Manzullo, R-Ill., Chair; Philip D. Eskeland, Staff Director. General e-mail, smbiz@mail.house.gov. Web, www.house.gov/smbiz.*

Jurisdiction over legislation on export expansion and agricultural development as it relates to the small-business community.

Senate Agriculture, Nutrition, and Forestry Committee, *SR-328A 20510; (202) 224-2035. Fax, (202) 224-1725. Sen. Richard G. Lugar, R-Ind., Chair; Keith Luse, Staff Director. Web, agriculture.senate.gov.*

Jurisdiction over the Commodity Futures Trading Commission and the Commodity Exchange Act.

Senate Agriculture, Nutrition, and Forestry Committee, *Subcommittee on Marketing, Inspection, and Product Promotion, SR-328A 20510; (202) 224-3643. Fax, (202) 224-1725. Sen. Paul Coverdell, R-Ga., Chair; Richard Gupton, Legislative Assistant. Web, agriculture. senate.gov.*

Oversight of international commodity agreements, foreign agricultural trade of commodities, foreign market development, and export controls on agricultural commodities.

Senate Agriculture, Nutrition, and Forestry Committee, *Subcommittee on Production and Price Competitiveness, SR-328A 20510; (202) 224-4774. Sen. Pat Roberts, R-Kan., Chair; Mike Seyfert, Legislative Assistant. Web, agriculture.senate.gov.*

Jurisdiction over legislation on agricultural commodities, including feed grains; wheat; oilseeds, including tung nuts, flaxseed, soybeans, dry edible beans, cotton, cottonseed, and rice; dairy products; wool; tobacco; peanuts; and sugar (jurisdiction over legislation on sugar imports shared with Senate Finance Committee).

Senate Agriculture, Nutrition, and Forestry Committee, *Subcommittee on Research, Nutrition, and General Legislation, SR-328A 20510; (202) 224-2854. Fax, (202) 224-1725. Sen. Peter G. Fitzgerald, R-Ill., Chair; Terry VanDoren, Legislative Assistant. Web, agriculture.senate.gov.*

Jurisdiction over legislation on the inspection and certification of flowers, fruits, and vegetables. Oversight of commodity donations and emergency commodity distribution.

Senate Finance Committee, *SD-219 20510; (202) 224-4515. Fax, (202) 224-5920. Sen. William V. Roth Jr., R-Del., Chair; Frank Polk, Staff Director. Web, finance.senate.gov.*

Jurisdiction over some legislation on sugar, including sugar imports (jurisdiction shared with Senate Agriculture, Nutrition, and Forestry Committee).

Senate Small Business Committee, *SR-428A 20510; (202) 224-5175. Fax, (202) 224-4885. Sen. Christopher S. Bond, R-Mo., Chair; Emilia DiSanto, Staff Director. Web, sbc.senate.gov.*

Jurisdiction over legislation on export expansion and agricultural development as it relates to the small-business community.

NONPROFIT

Agribusiness Council, *1312 18th St. N.W., #300 20036; (202) 296-4563. Fax, (202) 887-9178. Nicholas E. Hollis, President.*

Works to strengthen U.S. competitiveness in overseas agricultural markets. Promotes cooperation between private industry and government to improve international agricultural trade and development. Sponsors trade missions to developing countries. Helps to establish state and local agribusiness councils. (U.S. affiliate of Agri-Energy Roundtable.)

Agri-Energy Roundtable, *1312 18th St. N.W., #300 20036; (202) 887-0528. Fax, (202) 887-9178. Nicholas E. Hollis, Executive Director.*

Membership: companies, international organizations, and affiliated agro-industry associations in emerging countries. International clearinghouse that encourages cooperation in energy and agricultural development between industrialized and developing nations.

American Seed Trade Assn., *601 13th St. N.W., #570S 20005; (202) 638-3128. Fax, (202) 638-3171. Dean Urmston, Executive Vice President. Web, www.amseed.com.*

Membership: producers and merchandisers of seeds. Conducts seminars on research developments in corn, sorghum, soybean, garden seeds, and other farm seeds; promotes overseas seed market development.

International Assn. of Refrigerated Warehouses, *7315 Wisconsin Ave., #1200N, Bethesda, MD 20814; (301) 652-5674. Fax, (301) 652-7269. J. William Hudson, President. Web, www.iarw.org.*

Membership: owners and operators of public refrigerated warehouses. Interests include labor, transportation, taxes, environment, safety, regulatory compliance, and food distribution. Monitors legislation and regulations.

National Cooperative Business Assn., *1401 New York Ave. N.W., #1100 20005-2146; (202) 638-6222. Fax, (202) 638-1374. Paul Hazen, President. General e-mail, ncba@ncba.org. Web, www.cooperative.org.*

Alliance of cooperatives, businesses, and state cooperative associations. Provides information about starting and managing agricultural cooperatives in the United States and in developing nations. Monitors legislation and regulations.

National Council of Farmer Cooperatives, *50 F St. N.W., #900 20001; (202) 626-8700. Fax, (202) 626-8722. David Graves, President. General e-mail, info@ncfc.org. Web, www.ncfc.org.*

Membership: cooperative businesses owned and operated by farmers. Encourages research on agricultural cooperatives; provides statistics and analyzes trends. Monitors legislation and regulations on agricultural trade, transportation, energy, and tax issues.

U.S. Agricultural Export Development Council, *6707 Old Dominion Dr., #315, McLean, VA 22101; (703) 556-9290. Fax, (703) 556-9301. Susan Oderwald, Executive Director (Acting). General e-mail, usaedc@msn.com. Web, www.usaedc.org.*

Membership: producer and agribusiness organizations. Works with the Foreign Agricultural Service on projects to create, expand, and maintain agricultural markets abroad. Sponsors seminars and workshops.

Cotton

AGENCIES

Agricultural Marketing Service *(Agriculture Dept.),* **Cotton,** *1400 Independence Ave. S.W., #2641 20250 (mailing address: P.O. Box 96456 20090-6456); (202) 720-3193. Fax, (202) 690-1718. Norma McDill, Administrator (Acting). Web, www.ams.usda.gov/cotton/index.htm.*

Administers cotton marketing programs; sets cotton grading standards and conducts quality inspections based on those standards. Maintains market news service to inform producers of daily price changes.

Farm Service Agency *(Agriculture Dept.),* **Fibers Analysis,** *1400 Independence Ave. S.W., MS 0515 20250-0515; (202) 720-7954. Fax, (202) 690-1346. Wayne Bjorlie, Director.*

Develops production adjustment and price support programs to balance supply and demand for cotton.

INTERNATIONAL ORGANIZATIONS

International Cotton Advisory Committee, *1629 K St. N.W., #702 20006; (202) 463-6660. Fax, (202) 463-*

6950. *Terry P. Townsend, Executive Director. General e-mail, secretariat@icac.org. Web, www.icac.org.*

Membership: cotton producing and consuming countries. Provides information on cotton production, trade, consumption, stocks, and prices.

NONPROFIT

American Cotton Shippers Assn., *Washington Office, 1725 K St. N.W., #1404 20006; (202) 296-7116. Fax, (202) 659-5322. Neal P. Gillen, Executive Vice President. Web, www.acsa-cotton.org.*

Coalition of four regional cotton shippers' associations. Monitors legislation and regulations concerning international cotton trade.

Cotton Council International, *Washington Office, 1521 New Hampshire Ave. N.W. 20036; (202) 745-7805. Fax, (202) 483-4040. Allen Terhaar, Executive Director. Web, www.cottonusa.org/index.htm.*

Division of National Cotton Council of America. Promotes U.S. raw cotton exports.

Cotton Warehouse Assn. of America, *499 S. Capitol St. S.W., #600 20003; (202) 554-1233. Fax, (202) 554-1230. Donald L. Wallace Jr., Executive Vice President. General e-mail, cwaaoffice@aol.com.*

Membership: cotton compress and warehouse workers. Serves as a liaison between members and government agencies; monitors legislation and regulations.

National Cotton Council of America, *Washington Office, 1521 New Hampshire Ave. N.W. 20036; (202) 745-7805. Fax, (202) 483-4040. John Maguire, Vice President. Web, www.cotton.org/ncc.*

Membership: all segments of the U.S. cotton industry. Provides statistics and information on such topics as cotton history and processing.

Dairy Products and Eggs

AGENCIES

Agricultural Marketing Service *(Agriculture Dept.), Dairy, 1400 Independence Ave. S.W., #2968 20250 (mailing address: P.O. Box 96456 20090-6456); (202) 720-4392. Fax, (202) 690-3410. Richard M. McKee, Deputy Administrator. Web, www.ams.usda.gov/dairy/index.htm.*

Administers dairy product marketing and promotion programs; grades dairy products; maintains market news service on daily price changes; sets minimum price that farmers receive for milk.

Farm Service Agency *(Agriculture Dept.), Dairy and Sweeteners Analysis, 1400 Independence Ave. S.W., MS-0516 20250-0516; (202) 720-6733. Fax, (202) 690-1346. Dan Colacicco, Director.*

Develops production adjustment and price support programs to balance supply and demand for certain commodities, including dairy products, sugar, and honey.

Farm Service Agency *(Agriculture Dept.), Domestic Programs, 1400 Independence Ave. S.W., MS-0551 20250-0551; (202) 720-1696. Fax, (202) 690-0767. William March, Chief. Web, www.fsa.usda.gov.*

Administers dairy and non-perishables stabilization and price support programs, including purchases and dispositions of dairy and non-perishable products acquired under price supports.

NONPROFIT

American Butter Institute, *2101 Wilson Blvd., #400, Arlington, VA 22201; (703) 243-6111. Fax, (703) 841-9328. Jerome J. Kozak, Executive Director.*

Membership: butter manufacturers, packagers, and distributors. Interests include dairy price supports and programs, packaging and labeling, and imports. Monitors legislation and regulations.

Egg Nutrition Center, *1050 17th St. N.W., #560 20036; (202) 833-8850. Fax, (202) 463-0102. Donald McNamara, Director. General e-mail, eggnutr@aol.com. Web, www.enc-online.org.*

Provides information on egg nutrition and related health issues. Disseminates information on cholesterol and heart disease.

International Dairy Foods Assn., *1250 H St. N.W., #900 20005; (202) 737-4332. Fax, (202) 331-7820. E. Linwood Tipton, President. Web, www.idfa.org.*

Membership: processors, manufacturers, marketers, and distributors of dairy foods in the United States and abroad. Provides members with marketing, public relations, training, and management services. Monitors legislation and regulations. (Affiliated with the Milk Industry Foundation, the National Cheese Institute, and the International Ice Cream Assn.)

International Ice Cream Assn., *1250 H St. N.W., #900 20005; (202) 737-4332. Fax, (202) 331-7820. E. Linwood Tipton, President.*

Membership: manufacturers and distributors of ice cream and other frozen desserts. Conducts market research. Monitors legislation and regulations.

Milk Industry Foundation, *1250 H St. N.W., #900 20005; (202) 737-4332. Fax, (202) 331-7820. E. Linwood Tipton, President.*

Membership: processors of fluid milk and fluid-milk products. Conducts market research. Monitors legislation and regulations.

National Cheese Institute, *1250 H St. N.W., #900 20005; (202) 737-4332. Fax, (202) 331-7820. E. Linwood Tipton, President.*

Membership: cheese manufacturers, packagers, processors, and distributors. Interests include dairy price supports and programs, packaging and labeling, and imports. Monitors legislation and regulations.

National Milk Producers Federation, *2101 Wilson Blvd., #400, Arlington, VA 22201; (703) 243-6111. Fax, (703) 841-9328. Jerome J. Kozak, Chief Executive Officer. General e-mail, nmpf@aol.com. Web, www.nmpf.org.*

Membership: dairy farmer cooperatives. Provides information on development and modification of sanitary regulations, product standards, and marketing procedures for dairy products.

United Egg Producers, *Government Relations, Washington Office,* *1 Massachusetts Ave. N.W., #800 20001-1401; (202) 789-2499. Fax, (202) 682-0775. Randy Green, Director. Web, www.unitedegg.org.*

Membership: egg marketing cooperatives and egg producers. Monitors legislation and regulations.

Fruits and Vegetables

AGENCIES

Agricultural Marketing Service *(Agriculture Dept.),* *Fruit and Vegetable,* *1400 Independence Ave. S.W., #2077-50 20250 (mailing address: P.O. Box 96456 20090-6456); (202) 720-4722. Fax, (202) 720-0016. Robert C. Keeney, Deputy Administrator. Web, www.ams.usda.gov/fv/index.htm.*

Administers research, marketing, promotional, and regulatory programs for fruits, vegetables, nuts, ornamental plants, and other specialty crops; focus includes international markets. Sets grading standards for fresh and processed fruits and vegetables; conducts quality inspections; maintains market news service to inform producers of price changes.

Economic Research Service *(Agriculture Dept.),* *1800 M St. N.W. 20036; (202) 694-5200. Fax, (202) 694-5792. Barry Krissoff, Chief, Speciality Crops; Joy Harwood, Chief, Field Crops. Web, www.econ.ag.gov.*

Conducts market research; studies and forecasts domestic supply-and-demand trends for fruits and vegetables.

NONPROFIT

International Banana Assn., *727 N. Washington St., Alexandria, VA 22314; (703) 836-3410. Fax, (703) 836-2049. Fred Heptinstall, Chair.*

Works to improve global distribution and increased consumption of bananas; collects and disseminates information about the banana industry; serves as a liaison between the U.S. government and banana-producing countries on issues of concern to the industry.

United Fresh Fruit and Vegetable Assn., *727 N. Washington St., Alexandria, VA 22314; (703) 836-3410. Fax, (703) 836-7745. Tom Stenzel, President. International Relations fax, (703) 836-2049.*

Membership: growers, shippers, wholesalers, retailers, food service operators, importers, and exporters involved in producing and marketing fresh fruits and vegetables. Represents the industry before the government and the public sector.

U.S. Apple Assn., *6707 Old Dominion Dr., #320, McLean, VA 22101-4556 (mailing address: P.O. Box 1137, McLean, VA 22101-1137); (703) 442-8850. Fax, (703) 790-0845. Kraig Naasz, President. Web, www.usapple.org.*

Membership: U.S. commercial apple growers and processors, distributors, exporters, importers, and retailers of apples. Compiles statistics, including imports and exports; promotes research and marketing; provides information about apples and nutrition to educators. Monitors legislation and regulations.

Wine Institute, *Washington Office,* *601 13th St. N.W., #580 South 20005; (202) 408-0870. Fax, (202) 371-0061. Robert P. Koch, Senior Vice President. Web, www.wineinstitute.org.*

Membership: California wineries and affiliated businesses. Seeks international recognition for California wines; conducts promotional campaigns in other countries. Monitors legislation and regulations.

Grains and Oilseeds

AGENCIES

Agricultural Marketing Service *(Agriculture Dept.),* *Livestock and Seed,* *1400 Independence Ave. S.W., #2092S, Stop 0249 20250-0249; (202) 720-5705. Fax, (202) 720-3499. Barry L. Carpenter, Deputy Administrator. Web, www.ams.usda.gov/lsg/index.htm.*

Administers programs for marketing grain, including rice; maintains market news service to inform producers of grain market situation and daily price changes.

Farm Service Agency *(Agriculture Dept.), Feed Grains and Oilseeds Analysis, 1400 Independence Ave. S.W., MS-0532 20250; (202) 720-4417. Fax, (202) 690-1346. Phil Scronce, Director.*

Develops production adjustment and price support programs to balance supply and demand for certain commodities, including corn, soybeans, and other feed grains and oilseeds.

Farm Service Agency *(Agriculture Dept.), Food Grains, 1400 Independence Ave. S.W., MS-0508 20250; (202) 720-2891. Fax, (202) 690-2186. Thomas Tice, Director. Web, www.fsa.usda.gov.*

Develops production adjustment and price support programs to balance supply and demand for certain commodities, including wheat and rice.

Grain Inspection, Packers, and Stockyards Administration *(Agriculture Dept.), 1400 Independence Ave. S.W., Stop 3601 20250-3601; (202) 720-0219. Fax, (202) 205-9237. James Baker, Administrator. Information, (202) 720-5091. Web, www.usda.gov/gipsa.*

Administers inspection and weighing program for grain, soybeans, rice, sunflower seeds, and other processed commodities; conducts quality inspections based on established standards.

NONPROFIT

American Feed Industry Assn., *1501 Wilson Blvd., #1100, Arlington, VA 22209; (703) 524-0810. Fax, (703) 524-1921. David A. Bossman, President. General e-mail, afia@afia.org. Web, www.afia.org.*

Membership: feed manufacturers and their suppliers. Conducts seminars on feed grain production, marketing, advertising, and quality control; interests include international trade.

American Soybean Assn., *Washington Office, 600 Pennsylvania Ave. S.E., #320 20003; (202) 969-8900. Fax, (202) 969-7036. John Gordley, Washington Representative. Web, www.oilseeds.org/asa.*

Membership: soybean farmers. Promotes expanded world markets and research for the benefit of soybean growers; maintains a network of state and international offices.

Corn Refiners Assn., *1701 Pennsylvania Ave. N.W., #950 20006; (202) 331-1634. Fax, (202) 331-2054. Charles F. Conner, President. General e-mail, details@corn.org. Web, www.corn.org.*

Promotes research on technical aspects of corn refining and product development; acts as a clearinghouse for members who award research grants to colleges and universities. Monitors legislation and regulations.

National Assn. of Wheat Growers, *415 2nd St. N.E., #300 20002; (202) 547-7800. Fax, (202) 546-2638. Jack Eberspacher, Chief Executive Officer. General e-mail, wheatworld@wheatworld.org. Web, www.wheatworld.org.*

Federation of state wheat grower associations. Sponsors annual seminar on legislative issues.

National Corn Growers Assn., *Public Policy, Washington Office, 122 C St. N.W., #510 20001; (202) 628-7001. Fax, (202) 628-1933. Bruce Knight, Vice President. General e-mail, corninfo@ncga.com. Web, www.ncga.com.*

Represents the interests of U.S. corn farmers, including in international trade; promotes the use, marketing, and efficient production of corn; conducts research and educational activities; monitors legislation and regulations.

National Grain and Feed Assn., *1250 Eye St. N.W., #1003 20005; (202) 289-0873. Fax, (202) 289-5388. Kendell Keith, President. Web, www.ngfa.org.*

Membership: firms that process U.S. grains and oilseeds for domestic and export markets. Arbitration panel resolves disputes over trade and commercial regulations.

National Grain Trade Council, *1300 L St. N.W., #925 20005; (202) 842-0400. Fax, (202) 789-7223. Robert R. Petersen, President. Web, www.ngtc.org.*

Federation of grain exchanges and national associations of grain processors, handlers, merchandisers, distributors, exporters, and warehouse workers.

National Institute of Oilseed Products, *1101 15th St. N.W., #202 20005; (202) 785-8450. Fax, (202) 223-9741. Richard Cristol, Washington Representative. General e-mail, niop@assnhq.com. Web, www.oilseed.org.*

Membership: companies and individuals involved in manufacturing and trading oilseed products. Provides statistics on oilseed product imports and exports.

National Oilseed Processors Assn., *1255 23rd St. N.W., #200 20037-1174; (202) 452-8040. Fax, (202) 835-0400. Allen Johnson, President. Web, www.nopa.org.*

Provides information on soybean crops, products, processing, and commodity programs; interests include international trade.

North American Export Grain Assn., *1300 L St. N.W., #900 20005; (202) 682-4030. Fax, (202) 682-4033. Daniel G. Amstutz, President. General e-mail, info@naega.org.*

Membership: grain exporting firms and others interested in the grain export industry. Provides information on grain export allowances, distribution, and current market trends; sponsors foreign seminars. Monitors legislation and regulations.

North American Millers Assn., *600 Maryland Ave. S.W., #305W 20024-2573; (202) 484-2200. Fax, (202) 488-7416. Betsy Faga, President.*

Trade association representing the dry corn, wheat, oats, and rye milling industry. Seeks to inform the public, the industry, and government about issues affecting the domestic milling industry. Monitors legislation and regulations.

Soy Protein Council, *1255 23rd St. N.W., #200 20037-1174; (202) 467-6610. Fax, (202) 833-3636. David Saunders, Director.*

Membership: firms that process and sell vegetable proteins or food products containing vegetable proteins. Provides information on the nutritional properties of vegetable proteins.

Transportation, Elevator, and Grain Merchants Assn., *1300 L St. N.W., #925 20005; (202) 842-0400. Fax, (202) 789-7223. Robert R. Petersen, Secretary.*

Membership: companies owning terminal elevators. Monitors legislation and regulations concerning grain inspection programs, transportation of grain, and general farm policy.

U.S. Grains Council, *1400 K St. N.W., #1200 20005; (202) 789-0789. Fax, (202) 898-0522. Kenneth Hobbie, President. General e-mail, grains@grains.org. Web, www. grains.org.*

Membership: feed grain producers and exporters; railroads; banks; and chemical, machinery, malting, and seed companies interested in feed grain exports. Promotes development of U.S. feed grain markets overseas.

U.S. Wheat Associates, *1620 Eye St. N.W., #801 20006; (202) 463-0999. Fax, (202) 785-1052. Alan Tracy, President. General e-mail, info@uswheat.org. Web, www. uswheat.org.*

Membership: wheat farmers. Develops export markets for the U.S. wheat industry; provides information on wheat production and marketing.

USA Rice Federation, *4301 N. Fairfax Dr., #305, Arlington, VA 22203; (703) 351-8161. Fax, (703) 351-8162. Ellen Terpstra, President. Web, www.usarice.com.*

Membership: rice producers, millers, and related firms. Provides U.S. and foreign rice trade and industry information; assists in establishing quality standards for rice production and milling. Monitors legislation and regulations.

Sugar

AGENCIES

Economic Research Service *(Agriculture Dept.), 1800 M St. N.W. 20036; (202) 694-5200. Fax, (202) 694-5792. Barry Krissoff, Chief, Speciality Crops; Joy Harwood, Chief, Field Crops. Web, www.econ.ag.gov.*

Conducts market research; studies and forecasts domestic supply-and-demand trends for sugar and other sweeteners.

Farm Service Agency *(Agriculture Dept.), Dairy and Sweeteners Analysis, 1400 Independence Ave. S.W., MS 0516 20250-0516; (202) 720-6733. Fax, (202) 690-1346. Dan Colacicco, Director.*

Develops production adjustment and price support programs to balance supply and demand for certain commodities, including dairy products, sugar, and honey.

NONPROFIT

American Sugarbeet Growers Assn., *1156 15th St. N.W., #1101 20005; (202) 833-2398. Fax, (202) 833-2962. Luther Markwart, Executive Vice President. General e-mail, asga@aol.com. Web, members.aol.com/asga/sugar.htm.*

Membership: sugarbeet growers associations. Serves as liaison to U.S. government agencies, including the Agriculture Dept. and the U.S. Trade Representative; interests include international trade. Monitors legislation and regulations.

Chocolate Manufacturers Assn./American Cocoa Research Institute, *7900 Westpark Dr., #A320, McLean, VA 22102; (703) 790-5011. Fax, (703) 790-5752. Lawrence T. Graham, President. Web, www.candyusa.org.*

Membership: U.S. chocolate manufacturers and distributors. Sponsors educational programs; offers grants for cocoa research.

National Confectioners Assn., *7900 Westpark Dr., #A320, McLean, VA 22102; (703) 790-5750. Fax, (703) 790-5752. Lawrence T. Graham, President. Web, www. candyusa.org.*

Membership: confectionery manufacturers and suppliers. Provides information on confectionery consumption and nutrition; sponsors educational programs and research on candy technology. Monitors legislation and regulations.

Sugar Assn., *1101 15th St. N.W., #600 20005; (202) 785-1122. Fax, (202) 785-5019. Richard Keelor, President. General e-mail, sugar@sugar.org. Web, www.sugar.org.*

Membership: sugar processors, growers, refiners, and planters. Provides nutritional information on sugar and information on sugar imports and exports. Library open to the public by appointment.

U.S. Beet Sugar Assn., *1156 15th St. N.W., #1019 20005; (202) 296-4820. Fax, (202) 331-2065. James Johnson, President. General e-mail, beetsugar@aol.com.*

Membership: beet sugar processors. Library open to the public by appointment.

U.S. Cane Sugar Refiners' Assn., *1730 Rhode Island Ave. N.W., #608 20036; (202) 331-1458. Fax, (202) 785-5110. Nicholas Kominus, President. General e-mail, uscsra@worldnet.att.net.*

Membership: independent sugar cane refiners. Monitors legislation and regulations.

Tobacco and Peanuts

AGENCIES

Agricultural Marketing Service *(Agriculture Dept.),* **Tobacco,** *300 12th St. S.W., #502 Annex 20090 (mailing address: P.O. Box 96456 20090-6456); (202) 205-0567. Fax, (202) 205-0009. John P. Duncan III, Deputy Administrator. Web, www.ams.usda.gov/tob/index.htm.*

Administers tobacco marketing programs; sets standards for domestic and imported tobacco; tests imports for prohibited pesticides; conducts voluntary inspections of U.S. tobacco exports; maintains market news service to inform producers of price changes.

Economic Research Service *(Agriculture Dept.), 1800 M St. N.W. 20036; (202) 694-5200. Fax, (202) 694-5792. Barry Krissoff, Chief, Speciality Crops; Joy Harwood, Chief, Field Crops. Web, www.econ.ag.gov.*

Conducts market research; studies and forecasts domestic supply-and-demand trends for tobacco.

Farm Service Agency *(Agriculture Dept.),* **Tobacco and Peanuts,** *1400 Independence Ave. S.W., MS 0514 20250; (202) 720-7413. Fax, (202) 690-2298. Charles Hatcher, Director. Web, www.fsa.usda.gov.*

Develops production adjustment and price support programs to balance supply and demand for tobacco and peanuts.

NONPROFIT

American Peanut Council, *1500 King St., #301, Alexandria, VA 22314-2737; (703) 838-9500. Fax, (703) 838-9089. Jeannette Anderson, President. Web, www. peanutsusa.com.*

Membership: peanut growers, shellers, brokers, and manufacturers, as well as allied companies. Provides information on economic and nutritional value of peanuts; coordinates research; promotes U.S. peanut exports, domestic production, and market development.

Burley and Dark Leaf Tobacco Assn., *1100 17th St. N.W., #900 20036; (202) 296-6820. Fax, (202) 467-6349. Brooke Robinson, Federal Affairs Manager. General e-mail, bdlt@erols.com.*

Membership: growers of burley and dark leaf tobacco. Promotes tobacco sales.

Cigar Assn. of America, *1707 H St. N.W., #800 20006; (202) 223-8204. Fax, (202) 833-0379. Norman F. Sharp, President.*

Membership: growers and suppliers of cigar leaf tobacco and manufacturers, packagers, importers, and distributors of cigars. Monitors legislation and regulations.

Smokeless Tobacco Council, *1627 K St. N.W., #700 20006; (202) 452-1252. Fax, (202) 452-0118. Robert Y. Maples, President.*

Members: smokeless tobacco manufacturers. Monitors legislation and regulations.

Tobacco Associates, *1725 K St. N.W., #512 20006-1401; (202) 828-9144. Fax, (202) 828-9149. Kirk Wayne, President.*

Membership: producers of flue-cured tobacco. Promotes exports; provides information to encourage overseas market development.

FARM LOANS, INSURANCE, AND SUBSIDIES

AGENCIES

Commodity Credit Corp. *(Agriculture Dept.), 1400 Independence Ave. S.W. 20250; (202) 720-3467. Fax, (202) 720-8254. August Schumacher Jr., Under Secretary. Web, www.fsa.usda.gov/daco.*

Administers and finances the commodity stabilization program through loans, purchases, and supplemental payments; sells through domestic and export markets commodities acquired by the government under this program; administers some aspects of foreign food aid through the Food for Peace program; provides storage facilities.

Farm Credit Administration, *1501 Farm Credit Dr., McLean, VA 22102-5090; (703) 883-4000. Fax, (703) 734-*

5784. *Marsha Pyle Martin, Chair. Information, (703) 883-4056. TTY, (703) 883-4444. General e-mail, info-line@fca.gov. Web, www.fca.gov.*

Examines and regulates the cooperative Farm Credit System, which comprises federal land bank associations, production credit associations, federal land credit associations, agriculture credit associations, farm credit banks, and banks for cooperatives. Oversees credit programs and related services for harvesters of aquatic products, farmers, ranchers, producers, and their associations.

Farm Credit Administration, *Examination, 1501 Farm Credit Dr., McLean, VA 22102-5090; (703) 883-4160. Fax, (703) 893-2978. Roland E. Smith, Chief Examiner. Press, (703) 883-4056.*

Enforces and oversees compliance with the Farm Credit Act. Monitors cooperatively owned member banks' and associations' compliance with laws prohibiting discrimination in credit transactions.

Farm Service Agency *(Agriculture Dept.), 1400 Independence Ave. S.W., MS 0501 20250-0501; (202) 720-3467. Fax, (202) 720-9105. Keith Kelly, Administrator. Information, (202) 720-5237. Web, www.fsa.usda.gov.*

Administers farm commodity programs providing crop loans and purchases; provides crop payments when market prices fall below specified levels; sets acreage allotments and marketing quotas; assists farmers in areas affected by natural disasters. Oversees the Federal Crop Insurance Corporation.

Farm Service Agency *(Agriculture Dept.), Farm Loan and Analysis, 1400 Independence Ave. S.W. 20250; (202) 720-4671. Fax, (202) 690-3573. Terry Hickenbotham, Deputy Administrator. Web, www.fsa.usda.gov.*

Provides outreach programs and technical assistance for socially disadvantaged applicants for Agriculture Dept. farm loans.

Federal Agricultural Mortgage Corp., *919 18th St. N.W., #200 20006-5503; (202) 872-7700. Fax, (202) 872-7713. Thomas R. Clark, Vice President. Web, www.farmermac.com.*

Private corporation chartered by Congress to provide a secondary mortgage market for farm and rural housing loans. Guarantees principal and interest repayment on securities backed by farm and rural housing loans.

Risk Management Agency *(Agriculture Dept.), 1400 Independence Ave. S.W., #3053S 20250; (202) 690-2803. Fax, (202) 690-2818. Kenneth D. Ackerman, Administrator. Web, www.act.fcic.usda.gov.*

Provides farmers with insurance against crops lost because of bad weather, insects, disease, and other natural causes.

Rural Development *(Agriculture Dept.), Civil Rights, 1400 Independence Ave. S.W. 20250-3220 (mailing address: Ag. Box 0703 20250-0703); (202) 692-0204. Fax, (202) 692-0276. Cheryl Prejean Greaux, Director.*

Enforces compliance with the Equal Credit Opportunity Act, which prohibits discrimination on the basis of sex, marital status, race, color, religion, disability, or age, in public assistance for rural housing and farm loan programs.

CONGRESS

House Agriculture Committee, *1301 LHOB 20515; (202) 225-2171. Fax, (202) 225-0917. Rep. Larry Combest, R-Texas, Chair; Bill O'Conner, Staff Director. General e-mail, agriculture@mail.house.gov. Web, agriculture.house.gov.*

Jurisdiction over legislation on price supports, natural disaster assistance relating to the farm industry, and production adjustment programs.

House Agriculture Committee, *Subcommittee on Risk Management, Research, and Specialty Crops, 1301 LHOB 20515; (202) 225-4652. Fax, (202) 225-7760. Rep. Thomas W. Ewing, R-Ill., Chair; Stacy C. Carey, Staff Director. Web, agriculture.house.gov.*

Jurisdiction over legislation on commodity futures and crop insurance.

House Small Business Committee, *2361 RHOB 20515; (202) 225-5821. Rep. James M. Talent, R-Mo., Chair; Mark Strand, Chief of Staff. General e-mail, smbiz@mail.house.gov. Web, www.house.gov/smbiz.*

Jurisdiction over rural economy and family farming legislation as it relates to the small-business community.

House Ways and Means Committee, *Subcommittee on Oversight, 1136 LHOB 20515; (202) 225-7601. Fax, (202) 225-9680. Rep. Amo Houghton, R-N.Y., Chair; William McKenney, Staff Director. Web, www.house.gov/ways_means.*

Oversees government-sponsored enterprises, including the Farm Credit Banks and the Federal Agricultural Mortgage Corp., with regard to the financial risk they pose to the federal government.

Senate Agriculture, Nutrition, and Forestry Committee, *Subcommittee on Forestry, Conservation, and Rural Revitalization, SR-328A 20510; (202) 224-2752. Fax, (202) 224-1725. Sen. Larry E. Craig, R-Idaho, Chair; Dan Whiting, Staff Contact. Web, agriculture.senate.gov.*

Jurisdiction over legislation on agricultural credit, loans, natural disaster assistance, and insurance, including crop insurance.

Senate Agriculture, Nutrition, and Forestry Committee, *Subcommittee on Production and Price Competitiveness,* SR-328A 20510; (202) 224-4774. Sen. Pat Roberts, R-Kan., Chair; Mike Seyfert, Legislative Assistant. Web, agriculture.senate.gov.

Jurisdiction over legislation on price supports and production adjustment programs.

Senate Banking, Housing, and Urban Affairs Committee, SD-534 20510; (202) 224-7391. Fax, (202) 224-5137. Sen. Phil Gramm, R-Texas, Chair; Wayne A. Abernathy, Staff Director. Web, banking.senate.gov.

Oversees government-sponsored enterprises, including the Farm Credit Banks and the Federal Agricultural Mortgage Corp., with regard to the financial risk they pose to the federal government.

Senate Small Business Committee, SR-428A 20510; (202) 224-5175. Fax, (202) 224-4885. Sen. Christopher S. Bond, R-Mo., Chair; Emilia DiSanto, Staff Director. Web, sbc.senate.gov.

Jurisdiction over rural economy and family farming legislation as it relates to the small-business community.

NONPROFIT

Environmental Working Group, 1718 Connecticut Ave. N.W., #600 20009; (202) 667-6982. Fax, (202) 232-2592. Kenneth A. Cook, President. General e-mail, info@ewg.org. Web, www.ewg.org.

Research and advocacy group that studies and publishes reports on agricultural subsidies. Monitors legislation and regulations.

Farm Credit Council, 50 F St. N.W., #900 20001; (202) 626-8710. Fax, (202) 626-8718. Ken Auer, President.

Represents the Farm Credit System, a national financial cooperative that makes loans to agricultural producers, rural homebuyers, farmer cooperatives, and rural utilities. Finances the export of U.S. agricultural commodities.

FOOD AND NUTRITION

See also Commodities/Farm Produce (this chapter); Livestock and Poultry (this chapter)

AGENCIES

Agricultural Marketing Service (AMS), *(Agriculture Dept.), Science and Technology,* 1400 Independence Ave. S.W. 20250 (mailing address: P.O. Box 96456 20090-6456); (202) 720-5231. Fax, (202) 720-6496. William J. Franks

Jr., Deputy Administrator. Web, www.ams.usda.gov/science/index.htm.

Provides analytical testing to AMS divisions, federal and state agencies, and the private sector food industry; participates in international food safety organizations. Tests commodities traded with specific countries and regions, including butter, honey, eggs, nuts, poultry, and meat; analyzes nutritional value of U.S. military rations.

Agricultural Research Service *(Agriculture Dept.),* 1400 Independence Ave. S.W., #302A 20250-0300; (202) 720-3656. Fax, (202) 720-5427. Edward B. Knipling, Associate Administrator. General e-mail, arsweb@nal.usda.gov. Web, www.ars.usda.gov.

Conducts studies on agricultural problems of domestic and international concern through nationwide network of research centers. Studies include research on human nutrition; livestock production and protection; crop production, protection, and processing; postharvest technology; and food distribution and market value.

Agriculture Dept., *Food, Nutrition, and Consumer Services,* 1400 Independence Ave. S.W., #240E 20250; (202) 720-7711. Fax, (202) 690-3100. Shirley R. Watkins, Under Secretary. Web, www.fns.usda.gov/fncs.

Oversees the Food and Consumer Service and the office of the consumer adviser for agricultural products.

Animal and Plant Health Inspection Service *(Agriculture Dept.),* 1400 Independence Ave. S.W. 20250 (mailing address: Ag. Box 3401 20250); (202) 720-3861. Fax, (202) 720-3054. Craig A. Reed, Administrator. Web, www.aphis.usda.gov.

Administers animal disease control programs in cooperation with states; inspects imported animals, flowers, and plants; licenses the manufacture and marketing of veterinary biologics to ensure purity and effectiveness.

Cooperative State Research, Education, and Extension Service *(Agriculture Dept.),* 1400 Independence Ave. S.W., #305A 20250-2201; (202) 720-4423. Fax, (202) 720-8987. Charles W. Laughlin, Administrator. Information, (202) 720-6133. TTY, (202) 690-1899. Web, www.reeusda.gov.

Oversees county agents and operation of state offices that provide information on nutrition, diet, food purchase budgeting, food safety, home gardening, and other consumer concerns.

Food and Drug Administration *(Health and Human Services Dept.), Center for Food Safety and Applied Nutrition,* 200 C St. S.W. 20204; (202) 205-4850. Fax, (202) 205-5025. Joseph A. Levitt, Director. Press, (202) 205-4241. TTY, (202) 205-4863. Web, vm.cfsan.fda.gov.

Develops standards of composition and quality of foods (except meat and poultry but including fish); develops safety regulations for food and color additives for foods, cosmetics, and drugs; monitors pesticide residues in foods; conducts food safety and nutrition research; develops analytical methods for measuring food additives, nutrients, pesticides, and chemical and microbiological contaminants; recommends action to Justice Dept.

Food and Drug Administration *(Health and Human Services Dept.), Special Nutritionals, 200 C St. S.W., #2804 20204; (202) 205-4168. Fax, (202) 205-5295. Elizabeth A. Yetley, Director.*

Scientific and technical component of the Center for Food Safety and Applied Nutrition. Conducts research on nutrients; develops regulations and labeling requirements on infant formulas, medical foods, and dietary supplements, including herbs.

Food and Nutrition Service *(Agriculture Dept.), 3101 Park Center Dr., #803, Alexandria, VA 22302; (703) 305-2062. Fax, (703) 305-2908. Samuel Chambers Jr., Administrator. Information, (703) 305-2286. Web, www.usda.gov/fns.*

Administers all Agriculture Dept. domestic food assistance, including the distribution of funds and food for school breakfast and lunch programs (preschool through secondary) to public and nonprofit private schools; the food stamp program; and a supplemental nutrition program for women, infants, and children (WIC).

Food and Nutrition Service *(Agriculture Dept.), Analysis, Nutrition, and Evaluation, 3101 Park Center Dr., #503, Alexandria, VA 22302; (703) 305-2585. Fax, (703) 305-2576. Alberta Frost, Director.*

Administers the Nutrition Education and Training Program, which provides states with grants for disseminating nutrition information to children and for in-service training of food service and teaching personnel; administers the Child Nutrition Labeling Program, which certifies that foods served in school lunch and breakfast programs meet nutritional requirements; provides information and technical assistance in nutrition and food service management.

Food and Nutrition Service *(Agriculture Dept.), Child Nutrition, 3101 Park Center Dr., #1006, Alexandria, VA 22302; (703) 305-2590. Fax, (703) 305-2879. Stanley Garnett, Director. Press, (703) 305-2039.*

Administers the transfer of funds to state agencies for the National School Lunch Program; the School Breakfast Program; the Special Milk Program, which helps

schools and institutions provide children who do not have access to full meals under other child nutrition programs with fluid milk; the Child and Adult Care Food Program, which provides children in nonresidential child-care centers and family day care homes with year-round meal service; and the Summer Food Service Program, which provides children from low-income families with meals during the summer months.

Food and Nutrition Service *(Agriculture Dept.), Food Distribution, 3101 Park Center Dr., #503, Alexandria, VA 22302; (703) 305-2680. Fax, (703) 305-2420. Les Johnson, Director.*

Administers the Emergency Food Assistance Program, under which butter, cheese, milk, rice, and other surplus commodities are distributed to the needy. Administers the National Commodity Processing Program, which facilitates distribution, at reduced prices, of processed foods to state agencies, including charitable institutions, child-care food programs, nutrition programs for the elderly, state correctional institutions, and summer food service programs.

Food and Nutrition Service *(Agriculture Dept.), Food Stamp Program, 3101 Park Center Dr., #710, Alexandria, VA 22302; (703) 305-2026. Fax, (703) 305-2454. Susan Carr Gossman, Deputy Administrator.*

Administers, through state welfare agencies, the Food Stamp Program, which provides needy persons with food coupons to increase food purchasing power. Provides matching funds to cover half the cost of coupon issuance.

Food and Nutrition Service *(Agriculture Dept.), Supplemental Food Program, 3101 Park Center Dr., #540, Alexandria, VA 22302; (703) 305-2746. Fax, (703) 305-2196. Patricia N. Daniels, Director.*

Provides health departments and agencies with federal funding for food supplements and administrative expenses to make food, nutrition education, and health services available to infants, young children, and pregnant, nursing, and postpartum women.

Food Safety and Inspection Service *(Agriculture Dept.), 1400 Independence Ave. S.W., #331E 20250; (202) 720-7025. Fax, (202) 205-0158. Thomas J. Billy, Administrator. Press, (202) 720-9113. Consumer inquiries, (800) 535-4555; in Washington, (202) 720-3333. Web, www.usda.gov/fsis.*

Inspects meat, poultry, and egg products moving in interstate commerce for use as human food to ensure that they are safe, wholesome, and accurately labeled. Provides safe handling and labeling guidelines.

National Agricultural Library *(Agriculture Dept.),* *Food and Nutrition Information Center,* 10301 Baltimore Ave., #304, Beltsville, MD 20705-2351; (301) 504-5719. Fax, (301) 504-6409. Vacant, Coordinator. General e-mail, fnic@nal.usda.gov. Web, www.nal.usda.gov/fnic.

Serves individuals and agencies seeking information or educational materials on food and human nutrition; lends books and audiovisual materials for educational purposes; maintains a database of food and nutrition software and multimedia programs; provides reference services; develops resource lists of health and nutrition publications. Center open to the public.

National Institute of Diabetes and Digestive and Kidney Diseases *(National Institutes of Health), Nutritional Sciences,* 45 Center Dr., Bldg. 45, #6AN-18, Bethesda, MD 20892-6600; (301) 594-8883. Fax, (301) 480-8300. Dr. Van S. Hubbard, Chief.

Supports research on nutritional requirements, dietary fiber, obesity, eating disorders, energy regulation, clinical nutrition, trace minerals, and basic nutrient functions.

National Oceanic and Atmospheric Administration *(Commerce Dept.), Seafood Inspection Program,* 1315 East-West Hwy., Silver Spring, MD 20910; (301) 713-2355. Fax, (301) 713-1081. Samuel L. McKeen, Director. Web, seafood.nmfs.gov.

Administers voluntary inspection program for fish products and fish processing plants; certifies fish for wholesomeness, safety, and condition; grades for quality. Conducts training and workshops to help U.S. importers and foreign suppliers comply with food regulations.

CONGRESS

House Agriculture Committee, *Subcommittee on Department Operations, Oversight, Nutrition, and Forestry,* 1430 LHOB 20515; (202) 225-4913. Fax, (202) 225-4464. Rep. Robert W. Goodlatte, R-Va., Chair; Kevin Kramp, Staff Director. Web, agriculture.house.gov.

Jurisdiction over legislation on nutrition and hunger issues, pesticides, food safety, food stamps, and consumer programs generally.

House Agriculture Committee, *Subcommittee on Livestock and Horticulture,* 1301 LHOB 20515; (202) 225-1564. Fax, (202) 225-4369. Rep. Richard W. Pombo, R-Calif., Chair; Chris D'Arcy, Staff Director. Web, agriculture.house.gov.

Jurisdiction over legislation concerning inspection of aquacultural species (seafood), dairy products, meats, poultry, and livestock.

House Appropriations Committee, *Subcommittee on Agriculture, Rural Development, FDA, and Related Agencies,* 2362 RHOB 20515; (202) 225-2638. Rep. Joe Skeen, R-N.M., Chair; Hank Moore, Staff Director. Web, www.house.gov/appropriations.

Jurisdiction over legislation to appropriate funds for the Food and Drug Administration (FDA), Food Safety and Inspection Service, and Food and Consumer Service.

House Commerce Committee, *Subcommittee on Health and the Environment,* 2125 RHOB 20515; (202) 225-2927. Fax, (202) 225-1919. Rep. Michael Bilirakis, R-Fla., Chair; James E. Derderian, Staff Director. General e-mail, commerce@mail.house.gov. Web, www.house.gov/commerce.

Jurisdiction over legislation on vaccines; labeling and packaging, including tobacco products and alcohol beverages; and the use of vitamins. Oversight of the Food and Drug Administration.

House Education and the Workforce Committee, *Subcommittee on Early Childhood, Youth, and Families,* 2181 RHOB 20515; (202) 225-4527. Fax, (202) 225-9571. Rep. Michael N. Castle, R-Del., Chair; Kevin D. Talley, Staff Director. Web, www.house.gov/ed_workforce.

Jurisdiction over legislation on the National School Lunch Program, the School Breakfast Program, the Summer Food Program for Children, the Special Milk Program for Children, and the Special Supplemental Food Program for Women, Infants, and Children (WIC).

House Government Reform Committee, *Subcommittee on Criminal Justice, Drug Policy, and Human Resources,* B373 RHOB 20515; (202) 225-2577. Fax, (202) 225-1154. Rep. John L. Mica, R-Fla., Chair; Sharon Pinkerton, Staff Director. Web, www.house.gov/reform.

Oversees government food and consumer services, including the Food and Nutrition Service and the Food Safety and Inspection Service.

House Science Committee, *Subcommittee on Basic Research,* B374 RHOB 20515; (202) 225-7858. Fax, (202) 225-7815. Rep. Nick Smith, R-Mich., Chair; Steve Eule, Staff Director. Web, www.house.gov/science.

Jurisdiction over research and development involving government nutritional programs.

Senate Agriculture, Nutrition, and Forestry Committee, *Subcommittee on Research, Nutrition, and General Legislation,* SR-328A 20510; (202) 224-2854. Fax, (202) 224-1725. Sen. Peter G. Fitzgerald, R-Ill., Chair; Terry VanDoren, Legislative Assistant. Web, agriculture.senate.gov.

Jurisdiction over legislation on food, nutrition, and hunger; oversight of the inspection and certification of meat, flowers, fruits, vegetables, and livestock. Jurisdiction over commodity donations, food stamps, school lunch and breakfast programs, nutritional programs for the elderly, and the Special Supplemental Food Program for Women, Infants, and Children (WIC).

Senate Appropriations Committee, *Subcommittee on Agriculture, Rural Development, and Related Agencies,* SD-136 20510; (202) 224-5270. Fax, (202) 224-9450. *Sen. Thad Cochran, R-Miss., Chair; Rebecca M. Davies, Clerk. Web, appropriations.senate.gov/agriculture.*

Jurisdiction over legislation to appropriate funds for the Food and Drug Administration, the Food Safety and Inspection Service, the Food and Consumer Service, and other consumer-related services and programs.

Senate Commerce, Science, and Transportation Committee, *Subcommittee on Consumer Affairs, Foreign Commerce, and Tourism,* SH-425 20510; (202) 224-5183. Fax, (202) 228-0326. Sen. John Ashcroft, R-Mo., Chair; Rob Taylor, Counsel. Web, commerce.senate.gov.

Jurisdiction over legislation on the Food and Drug Administration and over labeling and packaging legislation, including advertising and packaging of tobacco products and alcohol beverages.

Senate Health, Education, Labor, and Pensions Committee, SD-428 20510; (202) 224-5375. Fax, (202) 228-5044. Sen. James M. Jeffords, R-Vt., Chair; Mark Powden, Staff Director. TTY, (202) 224-1975. Web, labor. senate.gov.

Jurisdiction over legislation on vaccines, drug labeling and packaging, inspection and certification of fish and processed food, and the use of vitamins.

INTERNATIONAL ORGANIZATIONS

Codex Alimentarius Commission, *U.S. Codex Office,* 1400 Independence Ave. S.W., South Bldg., #4861 20250; (202) 205-7760. Fax, (202) 720-3157. Patrick Clerkin, Associate Manager; Frank Scarbrough, Codex Manager. General e-mail, uscodex@usda.gov. Web, www.fsis.usda. gov/OA/codex.

The principal U.N. agency concerned with food standards, food safety, and related regulation of international trade. Convenes committees in member countries to address specific commodities and issues including labeling, additives in food and veterinary drugs, pesticide residues and other contaminants, and systems for food inspection. (Located in the USDA Food Safety and Inspection Service; international headquarters in Geneva.)

NONPROFIT

American Dietetic Assn., *Washington Office,* 1225 Eye St. N.W., #1250 20005; (202) 371-0500. Fax, (202) 371-0840. Stephanie Patrick, Vice President. Web, www. eatright.org.

Membership: dietitians and other nutrition professionals. Promotes public health and nutrition; accredits academic programs in clinical nutrition and food service management; sets standards of professional practice. Sponsors the National Center for Nutrition and Dietetics.

American Herbal Products Assn., 8484 Georgia Ave., #370, Silver Spring, MD 20910; (301) 588-1171. Fax, (301) 588-1174. Michael McGuffin, President. General e-mail, ahpa@ahpa.org. Web, www.ahpa.org.

Membership: U.S. companies and individuals that grow, manufacture, and distribute therapeutic herbs and herbal products; and associates in education, law, media, and medicine. Supports research; promotes standardization, consumer protection, competition, and self-regulation in the industry. Monitors legislation and regulations.

American Society for Clinical Nutrition, 9650 Rockville Pike, Bethesda, MD 20814-3998; (301) 530-7110. Fax, (301) 571-1863. Donald Clark, Executive Officer. Web, www.faseb.org/ascn.

Membership: clinical nutritionists. Supports research on the role of human nutrition in health and disease; encourages undergraduate and graduate nutrition education. (Division of American Society for Nutritional Sciences.)

American Society for Nutritional Sciences, 9650 Rockville Pike, Bethesda, MD 20814; (301) 530-7050. Fax, (301) 571-1892. Richard G. Allison, Executive Officer. Web, www.nutrition.org.

Membership: nutrition scientists. Conducts research in nutrition and related fields worldwide and promotes the exchange of information; promotes nutrition education; offers awards for research. Divisions include the Society for International Nutrition Research and the American Society for Clinical Nutrition.

American Society for Parenteral and Enteral Nutrition, 8630 Fenton St., #412, Silver Spring, MD 20910; (301) 587-6315. Fax, (301) 587-2365. Barney Sellers, Executive Director. General e-mail, aspen@nutr.org. Web, www.clinnutr.org.

Membership: health care professionals who provide patients with intravenous nutritional support during hospitalization and rehabilitation at home. Develops nutrition guidelines; provides educational materials; conducts annual meetings.

Center for Science in the Public Interest, *1875 Connecticut Ave. N.W., #300 20009-5728; (202) 332-9110. Fax, (202) 265-4954. Michael Jacobson, Executive Director. General e-mail, cspi@cspinet.org. Web, www.cspinet.org.*

Conducts research on food and nutrition. Interests include eating habits, food safety regulations, food additives, organically produced foods, alcohol beverages, and links between diet and disease. Monitors U.S. and international policy.

Child Nutrition Forum, *1875 Connecticut Ave. N.W., #540 20009-5728; (202) 986-2200. Fax, (202) 986-2525. Ellen Teller, Coordinator.*

Membership: agriculture, labor, education, and health and nutrition specialists; school food service officials; and consumer and religious groups. Supports federal nutrition programs for children; provides information on school nutrition programs. Monitors legislation and regulations concerning hunger issues.

Community Nutrition Institute, *910 17th St. N.W., #413 20006; (202) 776-0595. Fax, (202) 776-0599. Rodney E. Leonard, Executive Director. General e-mail, cni@unidial.com. Web, www.unidial.com/~cni.*

Citizens' interest group that provides information on nutrition, food policy issues, and federally funded food programs. Monitors legislation and regulations affecting food safety and nutrition.

Congressional Hunger Center, *229 1/2 Pennsylvania Ave. S.E. 20003; (202) 547-7022. Fax, (202) 547-7575. John Morrill, Executive Director. General e-mail, nohungr@aol.com. Web, www.hungercenter.org.*

Works to increase public awareness of hunger in the United States and abroad. Develops strategies to combat hunger and facilitates collaborative efforts between organizations.

Council for Responsible Nutrition, *1875 Eye St. N.W., 4th Floor 20006; (202) 872-1488. Fax, (202) 872-9594. John Cordaro, President. Web, www.crnusa.org.*

Membership: manufacturers, distributors, and suppliers of nutritional supplements and products. Provides information to members; monitors Food and Drug Administration, Federal Trade Commission, and Consumer Product Safety Commission regulations.

Food and Drug Law Institute, *1000 Vermont Ave. N.W., #200 20005-4903; (202) 371-1420. Fax, (202) 371-0649. John Villforth, President. General e-mail, comments@fdli.org. Web, www.fdli.org.*

Membership: providers of products and services to the food, drug, medical device, and cosmetics industries, including major food and drug companies; and lawyers working in food and drug law. Arranges conferences on technological and legal developments in the industry; sponsors law courses, fellowships, and legal writing; monitors international regulatory issues. Library open to the public.

Food Research and Action Center, *1875 Connecticut Ave. N.W., #540 20009-5728; (202) 986-2200. Fax, (202) 986-2525. James Weill, President. General e-mail, webmaster@frac.org. Web, www.frac.org.*

Public interest advocacy, research, and legal center that works to end hunger and poverty in the United States; offers legal assistance, organizational aid, training, and information to groups seeking to improve or expand federal food programs, including food stamp, child nutrition, and WIC (women, infants, and children) programs; conducts studies relating to hunger and poverty; coordinates network of antihunger organizations. Monitors legislation and regulations.

International Food Information Council, *1100 Connecticut Ave. N.W., #430 20036; (202) 296-6540. Fax, (202) 296-6547. Sylvia Rowe, President. General e-mail, foodinfo@ific.health.org. Web, ificinfo.health.org.*

Membership: food and beverage companies and manufacturers of food ingredients. Provides the media, health professionals, and consumers with scientific information about food safety, health, and nutrition. Interests include harmonization of international food safety standards.

International Life Sciences Institute, North America, *1126 16th St. N.W., #300 20036; (202) 659-0074. Fax, (202) 659-3859. Sharon Coleman, Administrator. General e-mail, ilsi@ilsi.org. Web, www.ilsi.org.*

Acts as liaison among scientists from international government agencies, concerned industries, research institutes, and universities regarding the safety of foods and chemical ingredients. Conducts research on caffeine, food coloring, oral health, human nutrition, and other food issues. Promotes international cooperation among scientists.

Physicians Committee for Responsible Medicine, *5100 Wisconsin Ave. N.W., #404 20016 (mailing address: P.O. Box 6322 20015); (202) 686-2210. Fax, (202) 686-2216. Dr. Neal D. Barnard, President. General e-mail, pcrm@pcrm.org. Web, www.pcrm.org.*

Membership: health care professionals, medical students, and other individuals. Provides individuals and institutions with nutrition information and low-fat, cholesterol-free recipes; promotes preventive medicine.

Public Citizen, *Health Research Group,* 1600 20th St. N.W. 20009; (202) 588-1000. Fax, (202) 588-7796. Dr. Sidney M. Wolfe, Director. Web, www.citizen.org.

Citizens' interest group that studies and reports on unsafe foods; monitors and petitions the Food and Drug Administration.

United Food and Commercial Workers International Union, *1775 K St. N.W. 20006; (202) 223-3111. Fax, (202) 466-1562. Douglas H. Dority, President. Web, www.ufcw.org.*

Membership: approximately 1.4 million workers in food-related industries, including supermarkets, department stores, insurance and finance, and packing houses and processing plants. Helps members negotiate pay, benefits, and better working conditions; conducts training programs and workshops. Monitors legislation and regulations. (Affiliated with the AFL-CIO and Canadian Labour Congress.)

Vegetarian Resource Group, *P.O. Box 1463, Baltimore, MD 21203; (410) 366-8343. Fax, (410) 366-8804. General e-mail, vrg@vrg.org. Web, www.vrg.org.*

Works to educate the public on vegetarianism and issues of health, nutrition, ecology, ethics, and world hunger.

Vegetarian Union of North America, *P.O. Box 9710 20016; (202) 362-8349. Peter McQueen, President. General e-mail, vuna@ivu.org. Web, www.ivu.org/vuna/english. html.*

Promotes the vegetarian movement throughout North America. Part of a network of vegetarian groups throughout the U.S. and Canada that serve as a liaison with the worldwide vegetarian movement.

Beverages

See also Substance Abuse (chap. 11); Traffic Safety (chap. 19)

Bureau of Alcohol, Tobacco, and Firearms *(Treasury Dept.), Field Operations, 650 Massachusetts Ave. N.W., #8100 20226; (202) 927-7970. Fax, (202) 927-7756. Andrew L. Vita, Assistant Director. Information, (202) 927-7777. Press, (202) 927-9510. Web, www.atf.treas.gov.*

Regulates the advertising and labeling of alcohol beverages, including the size of containers; enforces taxation of alcohol. Authorized to refer violations to Justice Dept. for criminal prosecution.

National Clearinghouse for Alcohol and Drug Information *(Health and Human Services Dept.),*

Center for Substance Abuse Prevention, *11426-28 Rockville Pike, #200, Rockville, MD 20852 (mailing address: P.O. Box 2345, Rockville, MD 20847-2345); (301) 468-2600. Fax, (301) 468-6433. John Noble, Director. Information, (800) 729-6686. TTY, (800) 487-4889. Web, www.health.org.*

Provides information, publications, and grant applications for programs to prevent alcohol and drug abuse.

Beer Institute, *122 C St. N.W., #750 20001; (202) 737-2337. Fax, (202) 737-7004. Jeffrey G. Becker, President. Web, www.beerinst.org.*

Membership: domestic and international brewers and suppliers to the domestic brewing industry. Monitors legislation and regulations.

Center for Science in the Public Interest, *1875 Connecticut Ave. N.W., #300 20009-5728; (202) 332-9110. Fax, (202) 265-4954. Michael Jacobson, Executive Director. General e-mail, cspi@cspinet.org. Web, www.cspinet.org.*

Concerned with U.S. and international policy on food and alcohol, including marketing, labeling, and taxation. Opposes U.S. government promotion of alcohol products overseas.

Distilled Spirits Council of the United States, *1250 Eye St. N.W., #400 20005; (202) 628-3544. Fax, (202) 682-8888. Peter Crebssy, President. Web, www.discus.health.org.*

Membership: manufacturers and marketers of distilled spirits sold in the United States. Provides consumer information on alcohol-related issues and topics. Monitors legislation and regulations.

International Bottled Water Assn., *1700 Diagonal Rd., #650, Alexandria, VA 22314; (703) 683-5213. Fax, (703) 683-4074. Joseph Doss, President. Web, www. bottledwater.org.*

Serves as a clearinghouse for industry-related consumer, regulatory, and technical information; interests include international trade. Monitors state and federal legislation and regulations.

Mothers Against Drunk Driving, *Washington Office, 1001 G St. N.W., #400 East 20001; (202) 638-3735. Fax, (202) 638-3516. Tom Howarth, Washington Contact. General e-mail, peyser@ix.netcom.com.*

Concerned with alcohol policy as it relates to motor vehicle safety. Supports implementation of a nationwide legal intoxication level of 0.08 blood alcohol content.

National Alcohol Beverage Control Assn., *4216 King St. West, Alexandria, VA 22302-1507; (703) 578-4200. Fax, (703) 820-3551. James M. Sgueo, Executive Director.*

Membership: distilleries, trade associations, and state agencies that control the purchase, distribution, and sale of alcohol beverages. Serves as an information clearinghouse. Monitors legislation and regulations.

National Assn. of Beverage Retailers, *5101 River Rd., #108, Bethesda, MD 20816-1508; (301) 656-1494. Fax, (301) 656-7539. John B. Burcham Jr., Executive Director. Web, www.nabronline.org.*

Membership: state associations of on- and off-premise licensees. Monitors legislation and regulations affecting the alcohol beverage industry.

National Assn. of State Alcohol and Drug Abuse Directors, *808 17th St. N.W., #410 20006; (202) 293-0090. Fax, (202) 293-1250. John S. Gustafson, Executive Director.*

Provides information on treatment and prevention of alcohol abuse.

National Beer Wholesalers Assn., *1100 S. Washington St., Alexandria, VA 22314-4494; (703) 683-4300. Fax, (703) 683-8965. David Rehr, President.*

Sponsors programs on preventing alcohol abuse; monitors legislation and regulations for family-owned and family-operated beer distributors.

National Licensed Beverage Assn., *20 S. Quaker Lane, #230, Alexandria, VA 22314-4525; (703) 751-9730. Fax, (703) 751-9748. Debra A. Leach, Executive Director. General e-mail, nlba-mail@nlba.org. Web, www.nlba.org.*

Membership: bars, taverns, restaurants, cocktail lounges, stores, and hotels that sell alcohol beverages. Sponsors program that trains bartenders, waiters, and waitresses to serve alcohol in a responsible manner.

National Soft Drink Assn., *1101 16th St. N.W. 20036-6396; (202) 463-6732. Fax, (202) 463-8172. William L. Ball III, President. Web, www.nsda.org.*

Membership: companies engaged in producing or distributing carbonated soft drinks. Acts as industry liaison with government and the public.

Wine and Spirits Wholesalers of America, *805 15th St. N.W., #430 20005; (202) 371-9792. Fax, (202) 789-2405. Juanita Duggan, Executive Vice President. General e-mail, comments@wswa.org. Web, www.wswa.org.*

Membership: wholesale distributors of domestic and imported wine and distilled spirits. Provides information on drinking awareness.

Wine Institute, *Washington Office, 601 13th St. N.W., #580 South 20005; (202) 408-0870. Fax, (202) 371-0061. Robert P. Koch, Senior Vice President. Web, www.wineinstitute.org.*

Membership: California wineries and affiliated businesses. Seeks international recognition for California wines; conducts promotional campaigns in other countries. Monitors legislation and regulations.

Food Industries

NONPROFIT

American Bakers Assn., *1350 Eye St. N.W., #1290 20005; (202) 789-0300. Fax, (202) 898-1164. Paul C. Abenante, President. General e-mail, info@americanbakers.org. Web, www.americanbakers.org/.*

Membership: wholesale baking companies and their suppliers. Promotes increased consumption of baked goods; provides consumers with nutritional information; conducts conventions. Monitors legislation and regulations.

American Frozen Food Institute, *2000 Corporate Ridge, #1000, McLean, VA 22102; (703) 821-0770. Fax, (703) 821-1350. Leslie G. Sarasin, President. Web, www.affi.com.*

Membership: frozen food packers, distributors, and suppliers. Provides production statistics.

American Meat Institute, *1700 N. Moore St., #1600, Arlington, VA 22209 (mailing address: P.O. Box 3556 20007); (703) 841-2400. Fax, (703) 527-0938. J. Patrick Boyle, President. Web, www.meatami.org.*

Membership: national and international meat and poultry packers, suppliers, and processors. Provides statistics on meat and poultry production and exports. Funds research projects and consumer education programs. Monitors legislation and regulations.

Bakery, Confectionery, Tobacco Workers, and Grain Millers International Union, *10401 Connecticut Ave., Kensington, MD 20895; (301) 933-8600. Fax, (301) 946-8452. Frank Hurt, President.*

Membership: approximately 120,000 workers from the bakery and tobacco industries. Helps members negotiate pay, benefits, and better working conditions; conducts training programs and workshops. Monitors legislation and regulations. (Affiliated with the AFL-CIO.)

Biscuit and Cracker Manufacturers' Assn., *8484 Georgia Ave., #700, Silver Spring, MD 20910; (301) 608-1552. Fax, (301) 608-1557. Frank Rooney, President. Web, www.thebcma.org.*

Membership: companies in the biscuit and cracker industry. Monitors legislation and regulations.

Food Distributors International, *201 Park Washington Court, Falls Church, VA 22046; (703) 532-9400. Fax, (703) 538-4673. John R. Block, President. Web, www.fdi.org.*

Trade association of grocery wholesale distribution companies that supply and service independent grocers throughout the United States and Canada. Provides members with research, technical, educational, and government service programs.

Food Marketing Institute, *655 15th St. N.W., #700 20005; (202) 452-8444. Fax, (202) 429-4519. Timothy Hammonds, President. Library, (202) 220-0687. Web, www.fmi.org.*

Trade association of food retailers and wholesalers. Conducts programs in research, education, industry relations, and public affairs; participates in international conferences. Library open to the public by appointment.

Food Processing Machinery and Supplies Assn., *200 Daingerfield Rd., Alexandria, VA 22314-2800; (703) 684-1080. Fax, (703) 548-6563. George O. Melnykovich, President. General e-mail, fpmsa@clark.net. Web, www.fpmsa.org.*

Membership: manufacturers and suppliers of processing and packaging equipment to the food and beverage industries. Helps members market their products and services.

Grocery Manufacturers of America, *1010 Wisconsin Ave. N.W., #900 20007; (202) 337-9400. Fax, (202) 337-4508. C. Manly Molpus, President. Web, www.gmabrands.com.*

Membership: manufacturers of products sold through the retail grocery trade. Monitors legislation and regulations.

Hotel Employees and Restaurant Employees International, *1219 28th St. N.W. 20007; (202) 393-4373. Fax, (202) 333-0468. John W. Wilhelm, General President. Web, www.hereunion.org.*

Membership: approximately 241,000 hotel and restaurant employees. Helps members negotiate pay, benefits, and better working conditions; conducts training programs and workshops. Monitors legislation and regulations. (Affiliated with the AFL-CIO.)

International Assn. of Food Industry Suppliers, *1451 Dolley Madison Blvd., McLean, VA 22101-3850; (703) 761-2600. Fax, (703) 761-4334. Charles Bray, President. Web, www.iafis.org.*

Membership: equipment manufacturers, suppliers, and servicers for the food and dairy processing industry. Participates in the sanitary standards program for dairy

and food processing; sponsors food engineering scholarships and biennial Food and Dairy Expo.

National Assn. of Convenience Stores, *1605 King St., Alexandria, VA 22314-2792; (703) 684-3600. Fax, (703) 836-4564. Kerley LeBoeuf, President. Web, www.cstorecentral.com.*

Membership: convenience store retailers and industry suppliers. Advocates industry position on labor, tax, environment, alcohol, and food-related issues; conducts research and training programs. Monitors legislation and regulations.

National Food Processors Assn., *1350 Eye St. N.W., #300 20005; (202) 639-5900. Fax, (202) 639-5932. John R. Cady, President. Press, (202) 639-5919.*

Membership: manufacturers and suppliers of processed and packaged food, drinks, and juice. Promotes agricultural interests of food processors; provides research, technical services, education, communications, and crisis management for members. Monitors legislation and regulations.

National Pasta Assn., *2101 Wilson Blvd., #920, Arlington, VA 22201; (703) 841-0818. Fax, (703) 528-6507. Jula J. Kinnaird, President. General e-mail, npa@ibm.net. Web, www.ilovepasta.org.*

Membership: U.S. pasta manufacturers and related suppliers. Represents the industry and provides information on pasta to consumers.

National Restaurant Assn., *1200 17th St. N.W. 20036-3097; (202) 331-5900. Fax, (202) 331-2429. Steven C. Anderson, President. Web, www.restaurant.org.*

Membership: restaurants, cafeterias, clubs, contract feeders, caterers, institutional food services, and other members of the food industry. Supports food service education and research. Monitors legislation and regulations.

Retailer's Bakery Assn., *14239 Park Center Dr., Laurel, MD 20707; (301) 725-2149. Fax, (301) 725-2187. Peter Houstle, Executive Vice President.*

Membership: single- and multiunit retail bakeries and bakery-delis; donut and other specialty shops; supermarket in-store bakeries and bakery-delis; allied companies that offer equipment, ingredients, supplies, or services to these retailers; and students and teachers of secondary or postsecondary school baking programs. Provides business and training aids. Monitors legislation and regulations.

Snack Food Assn., *1711 King St., #1, Alexandria, VA 22314; (703) 836-4500. Fax, (703) 836-8262. James McCarthy, President. Web, www.sfa.org.*

Membership: snack food manufacturers and suppliers. Promotes industry sales; compiles statistics; conducts research and surveys; assists members with training and education; provides consumers with industry information. Monitors legislation and regulations.

Women Grocers of America, *1825 Samuel Morse Dr., Reston, VA 20190; (703) 437-5300. Fax, (703) 437-7768. Thomas K. Zaucha, President.*

Supports the interests of women in the food distribution industry; sponsors seminars. (Affiliated with National Grocers Assn.)

Vegetarianism

NONPROFIT

FARM (Farm Animal Reform Movement), *P.O. Box 30654, Bethesda, MD 20824; (301) 530-1737. Fax, (301) 530-5747. Alex Hershaft, President. General e-mail, farm@farmusa.org. Web, www.farmusa.org.*

Works to end use of animals for food. Interests include animal protection, consumer health, agricultural resources, and environmental quality. Conducts national educational campaigns, including World Farm Animals Day and the Great American Meatout. Monitors legislation and regulations.

Great American Meatout, *P.O. Box 30654, Bethesda, MD 20824. Laurelee Blanchard, Communications Director, (888) 348-6325. Information, (800) 632-8688. Web, www.meatout.org.*

Promotes the dietary elimination of meat. Facilitates information tables, exhibits, cooking demonstrations, and festivals nationwide. (Affiliated with Farm Animal Reform Movement.)

People for the Ethical Treatment of Animals, *501 Front St., Norfolk, VA 23510 (mailing address: P.O. Box 42516 20015); (757) 622-7382. Fax, (757) 622-0457. Ingrid Newkirk, President. Web, www.peta-online.org.*

Educational and activist group supporting animal rights worldwide. Provides information on topics including laboratory research animals, factory farming, cosmetics, and vegetarianism. Monitors legislation; conducts workshops.

Vegetarian Resource Group, *P.O. Box 1463, Baltimore, MD 21203; (410) 366-8343. Fax, (410) 366-8804. General e-mail, vrg@vrg.org. Web, www.vrg.org.*

Works to educate the public on vegetarianism and issues of health, nutrition, ecology, ethics, and world hunger.

Vegetarian Union of North America, *P.O. Box 9710 20016; (202) 362-8349. Peter McQueen, President. General e-mail, vuna@ivu.org. Web, www.ivu.org/vuna/english. html.*

Promotes the vegetarian movement throughout North America. Part of a network of vegetarian groups throughout the U.S. and Canada that serve as a liaison with the worldwide vegetarian movement.

World Food Assistance

See also International Trade and Development (chap. 13)

AGENCIES

Foreign Agricultural Service *(Agriculture Dept.),* **Export Credits,** *1400 Independence Ave. S.W., #4077S 20250; (202) 720-6301. Fax, (202) 690-0727. Mary Chambliss, Deputy Administrator. Web, www.fas.usda.gov.*

Administers Commodity Credit Corporation commercial export programs, including export credit guarantee and export enhancement programs. Administers, with the Agency for International Development, U.S. foreign food aid programs.

Foreign Agricultural Service *(Agriculture Dept.),* **International Cooperation and Development,** *1400 Independence Ave. S.W., #3008S 20250-1081; (202) 690-0776. Fax, (202) 720-6103. Mary Ann Keeffe, Deputy Administrator.*

Coordinates and conducts the department's international cooperation and development programs in agriculture and related fields. Programs include technical assistance and training, scientific and technical cooperation, administration of collaborative research, representation of Agriculture Dept. and U.S. government interests in international organization affairs, and facilitation of private sector involvement in country and regional agricultural development. Programs are conducted cooperatively with other Agriculture Dept. and U.S. government agencies, universities, and the private sector.

State Dept., *Agricultural and Textile Trade Affairs:* **Agricultural Trade Policy and Programs,** *2201 C St. N.W., #3526 20520; (202) 647-3090. Fax, (202) 647-1894. Marc Baas, Director. Web, www.state.gov.*

Makes recommendations on international food policy issues such as the effects of U.S. food aid on foreign policy; studies and drafts proposals on the U.S. role in Food for Peace and World Food programs.

World Agricultural Outlook Board *(Agriculture Dept.), 1400 Independence Ave. S.W., #5143S 20250; (202) 720-6030. Fax, (202) 690-1805. Gerald A. Bange, Chair. Web, www.usda.gov/oce.*

Reports to the USDA Chief Economist. Coordinates the department's commodity forecasting program, which develops the official prognosis of supply, utilization, and prices for commodities worldwide. Works with the National Weather Service to monitor the impact of global weather on agriculture.

CONGRESS

House Agriculture Committee, *1301 LHOB 20515; (202) 225-2171. Fax, (202) 225-0917. Rep. Larry Combest, R-Texas, Chair; Bill O'Conner, Staff Director. General e-mail, agriculture@mail.house.gov. Web, agriculture. house.gov.*

Jurisdiction over international commodity donations and over legislation on U.S. domestic food production for foreign assistance programs under Public Law 480, including the Food for Peace program and the Foreign Agricultural Service. (House International Relations Committee has jurisdiction over legislation on overseas food distribution.)

House International Relations Committee, *2170 RHOB 20515; (202) 225-5021. Fax, (202) 225-2035. Rep. Benjamin A. Gilman, R-N.Y., Chair; Richard J. Garon Jr., Chief of Staff. General e-mail, HIRC@mail.house.gov. Web, www.house.gov/international_relations.*

Jurisdiction over legislation on overseas food distribution for foreign assistance programs under Public Law 480, including the Food for Peace program and the Foreign Agricultural Service. (House Agriculture Committee has jurisdiction over legislation on domestic food production for Public Law 480 programs.)

Senate Agriculture, Nutrition, and Forestry Committee, *Subcommittee on Marketing, Inspection, and Product Promotion, SR-328A 20510; (202) 224-3643. Fax, (202) 224-1725. Sen. Paul Coverdell, R-Ga., Chair; Richard Gupton, Legislative Assistant. Web, agriculture. senate.gov.*

Jurisdiction over legislation on food production and distribution for foreign assistance programs under Public Law 480, including the Food for Peace program and the Foreign Agricultural Service.

Senate Agriculture, Nutrition, and Forestry Committee, *Subcommittee on Research, Nutrition, and General Legislation, SR-328A 20510; (202) 224-2854. Fax, (202) 224-1725. Sen. Peter G. Fitzgerald, R-Ill., Chair; Terry VanDoren, Legislative Assistant. Web, agriculture. senate.gov.*

Jurisdiction over legislation on commodity donations, food, nutrition, and hunger in the United States and in foreign countries.

INTERNATIONAL ORGANIZATIONS

Food and Agriculture Organization of the United Nations, *Liaison Office for North America, 2175 K St. N.W., #300 20437; (202) 653-2400. Fax, (202) 653-5760. Charles H. Riemenschneider, Director. Library, (202) 653-2402. Web, www.fao.org.*

Serves as the main forum of the international community on world food, agriculture, fisheries, and forestry problems. Provides developing nations with technical assistance to improve and increase food and agricultural production; encourages sustainable agriculture and rural development; works to achieve food security, especially in low-income, food-deficient countries; and seeks to control plant and animal disease infestations. Library open to the public by appointment. (International headquarters in Rome.)

International Fund for Agricultural Development, *1775 K St. N.W., #410 20006; (202) 331-9099. Fax, (202) 331-9366. Vera P. Weill-Hallé, Washington Director. General e-mail, v.weillhalle@ifad.org. Web, www.ifad.org.*

Specialized agency of the United Nations which provides the rural poor of developing nations with cost-effective ways of overcoming hunger, poverty, and malnutrition. Advocates a community-based approach to reducing rural poverty. (International headquarters in Rome.)

NONPROFIT

Agricultural Cooperative Development International, *50 F St. N.W., #1100 20001; (202) 638-4661. Fax, (202) 626-8726. Michael Deegan, President.*

Membership: farm supply, processing, and marketing cooperatives; farm credit banks; national farmer organizations; and insurance cooperatives. Provides cooperatives with training and technical, management, and marketing assistance; supports farm credit systems, agribusiness, and government agencies in developing countries. Contracts with the Agency for International Development to start farm cooperatives in other countries. (Affiliated with the National Council of Farmer Cooperatives.)

American Red Cross, *National Headquarters, 430 17th St. N.W., 2nd Floor 20006-2401; (202) 737-8300. Fax, (202) 783-3432. Dr. Bernadine Healy, President. Web, www.redcross.org.*

Humanitarian relief and health education organization chartered by Congress. Provides food and supplies to assist in major disaster and refugee situations worldwide.

Bread for the World, *1100 Wayne Ave., #1000, Silver Spring, MD 20910; (301) 608-2400. Fax, (301) 608-2401. David Beckmann, President. General e-mail, bread@bread. org. Web, www.bread.org.*

Christian citizens' movement that works to eradicate world hunger. Organizes and coordinates political action on issues and public policy affecting the causes of hunger. Interests include domestic food assistance programs, international famine, and hunger relief.

CARE, *Washington Office, 1625 K St. N.W., #200 20006; (202) 223-2277. Fax, (202) 296-8695. Marianne Leach, Executive Director. General e-mail, info@care.org. Web, www.care.org.*

Assists the developing world's poor through emergency assistance and community self-help programs that focus on sustainable development, agriculture, agroforestry, water and sanitation, health, family planning, and income generation. (U.S. headquarters in Atlanta; international headquarters in Brussels.)

International Food Policy Research Institute, *2033 K St. N.W. 20006; (202) 862-5600. Fax, (202) 467-4439. Per Pinstrup-Andersen, Director. Library, (202) 862-5614. General e-mail, ifpri@cgiar.org. Web, www.cgiar.org/ifpri.*

Research organization that analyzes the world food situation and suggests ways of making food more available in developing countries. Provides various governments with information on national and international food policy. Sponsors conferences and seminars; publishes research reports. Library open to the public by appointment.

National Center for Food and Agricultural Policy, *1616 P St. N.W., #100 20036; (202) 328-5048. Fax, (202) 328-5133. Dale E. Hathaway, Director. General e-mail, ncfap@ncfap.org. Web, www.ncfap.org.*

Research and educational organization concerned with international food and agricultural issues. Examines public policy concerning agriculture, food safety and quality, natural resources, and the environment.

Oxfam America, *Washington Office, 733 15th St. N.W., #340 20005; (202) 393-3544. Fax, (202) 783-8739. John Ruthrauff, Director; Bernice Romero, Advocacy Coordinator. Information, (800) 776-9326. Web, www.oxfamamerica.org.*

Funds disaster relief and self-help development projects, primarily at the international level, including food and agriculture programs; supports grass roots and community efforts to combat hunger; conducts an educational campaign and debt relief for foreign countries.

RESULTS, *440 1st St. N.W., #450 20001; (202) 783-7100. Fax, (202) 783-2818. Lynn McMullen, Director. Web, www.resultsusa.org.*

Works to end world hunger; encourages grassroots and legislative support of programs and proposals dealing with hunger and hunger-related issues. Monitors legislation and regulations.

U.S. National Committee for World Food Day, *2175 K St. N.W. 20437; (202) 653-2404. Fax, (202) 653-5760. Patricia Young, National Coordinator.*

Consortium of farm, religious, nutrition, education, consumer, relief, and development organizations. Coordinates widespread community participation in World Food Day. Distributes materials about food and hunger issues and encourages long-term action.

Winrock International Institute for Agricultural Development, *Washington Office, 1611 N. Kent St., #600, Arlington, VA 22209; (703) 525-9430. Fax, (703) 525-1744. Frank Tugwell, President. Web, www.winrock. org.*

Works to increase economic opportunity; sustain natural resources; protect the environment; and increase long-term productivity, equity, and responsible resource management to benefit the world's poor and disadvantaged communities. Matches innovative approaches in agriculture, natural resources management, clean energy, and leadership development with the unique needs of its partners. Links local individuals and communities with new ideas and technology.

Worldwatch Institute, *1776 Massachusetts Ave. N.W., 8th Floor 20036; (202) 452-1999. Fax, (202) 296-7365. Lester R. Brown, President. General e-mail, worldwatch@ worldwatch.org. Web, www.worldwatch.org.*

Research organization that studies the environmental origins of world population growth and health trends; interests include the food supply and malnutrition.

 LIVESTOCK AND POULTRY

See also Animals and Plants (chap. 9); Commodities/Farm Produce (this chapter)

AGENCIES

Agricultural Marketing Service *(Agriculture Dept.),* **Livestock and Seed,** *1400 Independence Ave. S.W., #2092S, Stop 0249 20250-0249; (202) 720-5705. Fax, (202) 720-3499. Barry L. Carpenter, Deputy Administrator. Web, www.ams.usda.gov/lsg/index.htm.*

Administers meat marketing program; maintains market news service to inform producers of meat market situation and daily price changes; develops, establishes, and revises U.S. standards for classes and grades of livestock and meat; grades, examines, and certifies meat and meat products.

Agricultural Marketing Service *(Agriculture Dept.), Poultry,* 1400 Independence Ave. S.W., #3932S 20250 *(mailing address: P.O. Box 96456 20090-6456); (202) 720-4476. Fax, (202) 720-5631. D. Michael Holbrook, Deputy Administrator. General e-mail, dmholbrook@usda.gov. Web, www.ams.usda.gov/poultry/index.htm.*

Sets poultry and egg grading standards and conducts quality inspections based on those standards. Provides promotion and market news services, including for international markets.

Food Safety and Inspection Service *(Agriculture Dept.),* 1400 Independence Ave. S.W., #331E 20250; (202) 720-7025. Fax, (202) 205-0158. Thomas J. Billy, Administrator. Press, (202) 720-9113. Consumer inquiries, (800) 535-4555; in Washington, (202) 720-3333. Web, www. usda.gov/fsis.

Inspects meat and poultry products and provides safe handling and labeling guidelines.

Grain Inspection, Packers, and Stockyards Administration *(Agriculture Dept.),* 1400 Independence Ave. S.W., Stop 3601 20250-3601; (202) 720-0219. Fax, (202) 205-9237. James Baker, Administrator. Information, (202) 720-5091. Web, www.usda.gov/gipsa.

Maintains competition in the marketing of livestock, poultry, grain, and meat by prohibiting deceptive and monopolistic marketing practices; tests market scales and conducts check weighings for accuracy.

CONGRESS

House Agriculture Committee, *Subcommittee on Livestock and Horticulture,* 1301 LHOB 20515; (202) 225-1564. Fax, (202) 225-4369. Rep. Richard W. Pombo, R-Calif., Chair; Chris D'Arcy, Staff Director. Web, agriculture.house.gov.

Jurisdiction over legislation on inspection and certification of meat, livestock, and poultry. Jurisdiction over animal welfare, including animals used for experimentation.

Senate Agriculture, Nutrition, and Forestry Committee, *Subcommittee on Research, Nutrition, and General Legislation,* SR-328A 20510; (202) 224-2854. Fax, (202) 224-1725. Sen. Peter G. Fitzgerald, R-Ill., Chair; Terry VanDoren, Legislative Assistant. Web, agriculture. senate.gov.

Jurisdiction over legislation on inspection and certification of meat, livestock, and poultry, and over animal welfare.

NONPROFIT

American Meat Institute, *1700 N. Moore St., #1600, Arlington, VA 22209 (mailing address: P.O. Box 3556 20007); (703) 841-2400. Fax, (703) 527-0938. J. Patrick Boyle, President. Web, www.meatami.org.*

Membership: national and international meat and poultry packers and processors. Provides statistics on meat and poultry production and consumption, livestock, and feed grains. Funds meat research projects and consumer education programs; sponsors conferences and correspondence courses on meat production and processing. Monitors legislation and regulations.

American Sheep Industry Assn., *Washington Office,* 412 1st St. S.E., #1 Lobby Level 20003; (202) 484-7134. Fax, (202) 484-0770. Fran Boyd, Washington Representative. General e-mail, info@sheepusa.org. Web, www. sheepusa.org.

Membership: sheep, wool, and mohair producers. Interests include sheep breeds, lamb and wool marketing, and wool research. Monitors legislation and regulations.

Animal Health Institute, *1325 G St. N.W., #700 20005-3104; (202) 637-2440. Fax, (202) 393-1667. Alexander S. Mathews, President. Web, www.ahi.org.*

Membership: manufacturers of drugs and other products (including vaccines, pesticides, and vitamins) for pets and food-producing animals. Monitors legislation and regulations.

FARM (Farm Animal Reform Movement), *P.O. Box 30654, Bethesda, MD 20824; (301) 530-1737. Fax, (301) 530-5747. Alex Hershaft, President. General e-mail, farm@ farmusa.org. Web, www.farmusa.org.*

Works to end use of animals for food. Interests include animal protection, consumer health, agricultural resources, and environmental quality. Conducts national educational campaigns, including World Farm Animals Day and the Great American Meatout. Monitors legislation and regulations.

National Cattlemen's Beef Assn., *Public Policy, Washington Office,* 1301 Pennsylvania Ave. N.W., #300 20004; (202) 347-0228. Fax, (202) 638-0607. Chandler Keys, Vice President. Web, www.beef.org.

Membership: individual cattlemen, state cattlemen's groups, and breed associations. Provides information on beef research, agricultural labor, beef grading, foreign trade, taxes, marketing, cattle economics, branding, animal health, and environmental management.

National Chicken Council, *1015 15th St. N.W., #930 20005; (202) 296-2622. Fax, (202) 293-4005. George B. Watts, President. Web, www.eatchicken.com.*

Membership: producers and processors of chickens. Provides information on production, marketing, and consumption of chickens.

National Meat Canners Assn., *1700 N. Moore St., #1600, Arlington, VA 22209; (703) 841-3680. Fax, (703) 841-9656. J. Patrick Boyle, Executive Secretary. Web, www. meatami.org.*

Membership: canners of prepared meats and meat food products. Provides information on the canned meat industry.

National Pork Producers Council, *Public Policy, Washington Office, 122 C St. N.W., #875 20001; (202) 347-3600. Fax, (202) 347-5265. Kirk Ferrell, Vice President. General e-mail, pork@nppc.org. Web, www.nppc.org.*

Membership: pork producers and independent pork producer organizations. Interests include pork production, nutrition, the environment, trade, and federal regulations. Monitors legislation and regulations.

National Renderers Assn., *801 N. Fairfax St., #207, Alexandria, VA 22314; (703) 683-0155. Fax, (703) 683-2626. Thomas M. Cook, Executive Director. General e-mail, renderers@aol.com. Web, www.renderers.org.*

Membership: manufacturers of meat meal and tallow. Compiles industry statistics; sponsors research; conducts seminars and workshops. Monitors legislation and regulations.

National Turkey Federation, *1225 New York Ave. N.W., #400 20005; (202) 898-0100. Fax, (202) 898-0203. Stuart E. Proctor Jr., President. Web, www.turkeyfed.org.*

Membership: turkey growers, hatcheries, breeders, and processors. Promotes turkey consumption. Monitors legislation and regulations.

North American Meat Processors Assn., *1920 Association Dr., #400, Reston, VA 20191; (703) 758-1900. Fax, (703) 758-8001. Deven L. Scott, Executive Vice President. Web, www.namp.com.*

Membership: meat, poultry, fish, and game companies specializing in the food service industry. Conducts seminars; interests include quality standards and procedures for handling meat, poultry, fish, and game.

U.S. Hide, Skin, and Leather Assn., *1700 N. Moore St., #1600, Arlington, VA 22209; (703) 841-5485. Fax, (703) 841-9656. Len Condon, President. Web, www.meatami.org.*

Membership: meatpackers, brokers, dealers, processors, and exporters of hides and skins. Maintains liaison with allied trade associations and participates in programs on export statistics, hide price reporting, and freight rates; conducts seminars and consumer information programs. (Division of American Meat Institute.)

See also Public Lands Council (p. 307)

3

Business and Economics

GENERAL POLICY

See also Caucuses (chap. 20); Community and Regional Development (chap. 12); International Trade and Development (chap. 13)

AGENCIES

Census Bureau *(Commerce Dept.), Economic Programs, Suitland and Silver Hill Rds., #2061-3, Suitland, MD 20233-6000; (301) 457-2112. Fax, (301) 457-8140. Frederick T. Knickerbocker, Associate Director.*

Compiles comprehensive statistics on the level and structure of U.S. economic activity and the characteristics of industrial and business establishments at the national, state, and local levels; collects and publishes foreign trade statistics.

Commerce Dept., *14th St. and Constitution Ave. N.W., #5854 20230; (202) 482-2112. Fax, (202) 482-2741. William M. Daley, Secretary; Robert Mallett, Deputy Secretary. Information, (202) 482-2000. Library, (202) 482-5511. Press, (202) 482-4883. Web, www.doc.gov.*

Acts as principal adviser to the president on federal policy affecting industry and commerce; promotes national economic growth and development, competitiveness, international trade, and technological development; provides business and government with economic statistics, research, and analysis; encourages minority business; promotes tourism. Library reference service staff answers questions about commerce and business.

Commerce Dept., *Business Liaison, 14th St. and Constitution Ave. N.W., #5062 20230; (202) 482-3942. Fax, (202) 482-4054. Lucie Naphin, Director. Information, (202) 482-1360. Web, www.doc.gov.*

Serves as the central office for business assistance. Handles requests for information and services as well as complaints and suggestions from businesses; provides a forum for businesses to comment on federal regulations; initiates meetings on policy issues with industry groups, business organizations, trade and small-business associations, and the corporate community.

Commerce Dept., *STAT-USA, 14th St. and Constitution Ave. N.W., #4886 20230; (202) 482-0434. Fax, (202) 482-3417. Kenneth W. Rogers, Director. Information, (202) 482-1986. Toll-free, (800) STAT-USA. General e-mail, stat-usa@doc.gov. Web, www.stat-usa.gov.*

Maintains and makes available for public use the Economic Bulletin Board (EBB), the National Trade Data Bank (NTDB), and Stat-USA-Internet.

Council of Economic Advisers *(Executive Office of the President), Dwight D. Eisenhower Executive Office Bldg., #314 20502; (202) 395-5042. Fax, (202) 395-6958. Audrey Choi, Chief of Staff; Martin Baily, Chair.*

Advisory body consisting of three members and supporting staff of economists. Monitors and analyzes the economy and advises the president on economic developments, trends, and policies and on the economic implications of other policy initiatives. Prepares the annual *Economic Report of the President* for Congress. Assesses economic implications of international policy.

Economics and Statistics Administration *(Commerce Dept.), 14th St. and Constitution Ave. N.W., #4848 20230; (202) 482-3727. Fax, (202) 482-0432. Robert J. Shapiro, Under Secretary. Information, (202) 482-2235. General e-mail, esa@doc.gov.*

Advises the secretary on economic policy matters, including consumer and capital spending, inventory status, and the short- and long-term outlook in output and unemployment. Seeks to improve economic productivity and growth. Serves as departmental liaison with the Council of Economic Advisers and other government agencies concerned with economic policy. Supervises and sets policy for the Census Bureau and the Bureau of Economic Analysis.

Federal Reserve System, *Board of Governors, 20th and C Sts. N.W. 20551; (202) 452-3201. Fax, (202) 452-3819. Alan Greenspan, Chair; Roger W. Ferguson Jr., Vice Chair. Information, (202) 452-3215. Press, (202) 452-3204. Locator, (202) 452-3000. Web, www.bog.frb.fed.us.*

Sets U.S. monetary policy. Supervises the Federal Reserve System and influences credit conditions through the buying and selling of treasury securities in the open market, by fixing the amount of reserves depository institutions must maintain, and by determining discount rates.

Federal Trade Commission, *6th St. and Pennsylvania Ave. N.W. 20580; (202) 326-2100. Robert Pitofsky, Chair; Rosemarie Straight, Executive Director. Information, (202) 326-2222. Library, (202) 326-2395. Press, (202) 326-2180. Chair's fax, (202) 326-2396. Web, www.ftc.gov.*

Promotes policies designed to maintain strong competitive enterprise within the U.S. economic system. Monitors trade practices and investigates cases involving monopoly, unfair restraints, or deceptive practices. Enforces Truth in Lending and Fair Credit Reporting acts. Library open to the public.

Federal Trade Commission, *Economics, 6th St. and Pennsylvania Ave. N.W. 20580; (202) 326-3429. Jeremy Bulow, Director. Web, www.ftc.gov/be/be.htm.*

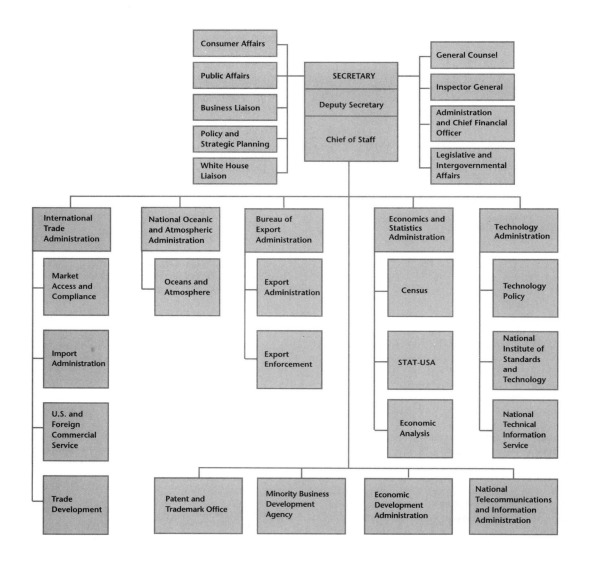

Provides economic analyses for consumer protection and antitrust investigations, cases, and rulemakings; advises the commission on the effect of government regulations on competition and consumers in various industries; develops special reports on competition, consumer protection, and regulatory issues.

National Economic Council *(Executive Office of the President), The White House 20500; (202) 456-6630. Fax, (202) 456-2223. Gene Sperling, National Economic Advisor.*

Comprised of cabinet members and other high-ranking executive branch officials. Coordinates domestic and international economic policy-making process to facilitate the implementation of the president's economic agenda.

National Institute of Standards and Technology *(Commerce Dept.), Standards Information Program, 100 Bureau Dr. MS-2150, Bldg. 820, #164, Gaithersburg, MD 20899; (301) 975-4040. Fax, (301) 926-1559. Joanne*

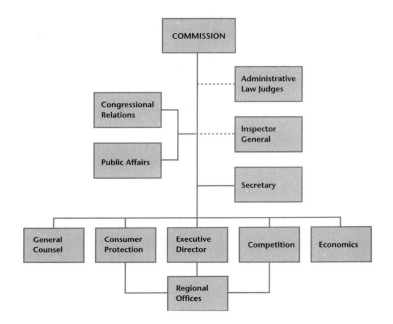

Overman, Chief. Weekly recorded updates: GATT hotline, (301) 975-4041; EU hotline, (301) 921-4164. General e-mail, ncsci@nist.gov. Web, www.nist.gov.

Serves as the national repository for information on voluntary industry standards and regulations for domestic and international products. Provides information on specifications, test methods, domestic and international technical regulations, codes, and recommended practices.

National Women's Business Council, *409 3rd St. S.W., #210 20024; (202) 205-3850. Fax, (202) 205-6825. Kay Koplovitz, Chair; Amy Millman, Executive Director. Web, www.womenconnect.com/nwbc.*

Membership: eight women business owners, six representatives of women business organizations, and one chair appointed by the president. Independent, congressionally mandated council established by the Women's Business Ownership Act of 1988. Reviews the status of women-owned businesses nationwide and makes policy recommendations to the president and Congress. Assesses the role of the federal government in aiding and promoting women-owned businesses.

Small Business Administration, *409 3rd St. S.W., #7000 20416; (202) 205-6605. Fax, (202) 205-6802. Aida*

Alvarez, Administrator; Fred Hochberg, Deputy Administrator. Library, (202) 205-7033. Press, (202) 205-6740. Toll-free information, (800) 827-5722. Locator, (202) 205-6600. Web, www.sba.gov.

Serves as the government's principal advocate of small-business interests through financial, investment, procurement, and management assistance and counseling; evaluates effect of federal programs on and recommends policies for small business.

Treasury Dept., *1500 Pennsylvania Ave. N.W., #3330 20220; (202) 622-1100. Fax, (202) 622-0073. Stuart Eizenstat, Deputy Secretary; Lawrence H. Summers, Secretary. Information, (202) 622-2000. Library, (202) 622-0990. Locator, (202) 622-2111. Web, www.ustreas.gov.*

Serves as chief financial officer of the government and adviser to the president on economic policy. Formulates and recommends domestic and international financial, economic, tax, and broad fiscal policies; manages the public debt. Library open to the public by appointment.

Treasury Dept., *Economic Policy, 1500 Pennsylvania Ave. N.W., #3454 20220; (202) 622-2200. Fax, (202) 622-2633. David W. Wilcox, Assistant Secretary. Web, www. ustreas.gov.*

TREASURY DEPARTMENT

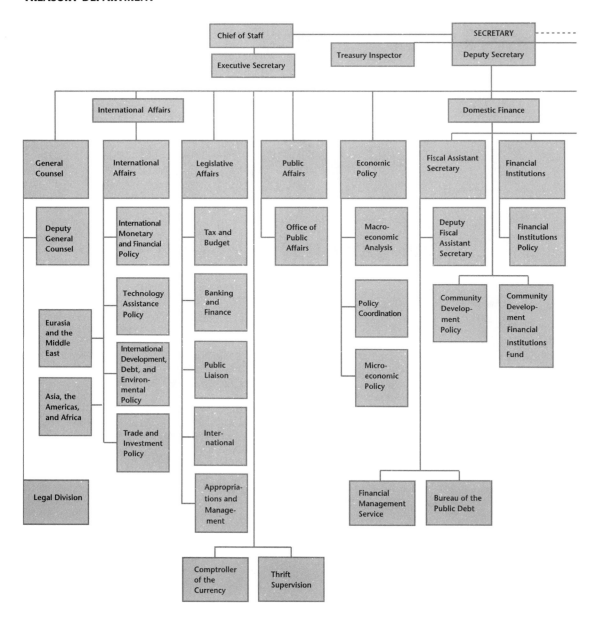

Assists and advises the treasury secretary in the formulation and execution of domestic and international economic policies and programs; helps prepare economic forecasts for the federal budget.

Treasury Dept., *Financial Management Service, 401 14th St. S.W., #548 20227; (202) 874-7000. Fax, (202) 874-6743. Richard Gregg, Commissioner. Press, (202) 874-6604. Web, www.treas.gov/fms.*

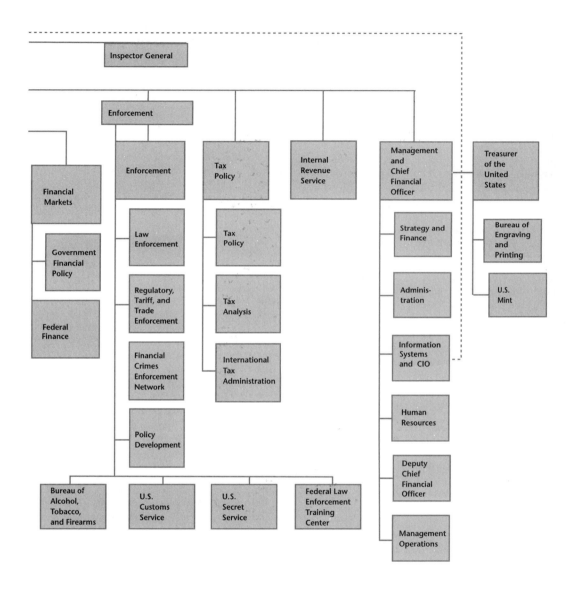

Serves as the government's central financial manager, responsible for cash management and investment of government trust funds, credit administration, and debt collection. Handles central accounting for government fiscal activities; promotes sound financial management practices and increased use of automated payments, collections, accounting, and reporting systems.

Treasury Dept., *Fiscal Policy,* *1500 Pennsylvania Ave. N.W., #2112 20220; (202) 622-0560. Fax, (202) 622-0962. Donald V. Hammond, Fiscal Assistant Secretary. Web, www.ustreas.gov.*

Administers Treasury Dept. financial operations. Supervises the Financial Management Service and the Bureau of the Public Debt.

CONGRESS

General Accounting Office (GAO), *441 G St. N.W. 20548; (202) 512-5500. Fax, (202) 512-5507. David M. Walker, Comptroller General. Information, (202) 512-4800. Library, (202) 512-5180. Documents, (202) 512-6000. Web, www.gao.gov.*

Independent, nonpartisan agency in the legislative branch. Serves as the investigating agency for Congress; carries out legal, accounting, auditing, and claims settlement functions; makes recommendations for more effective government operations; publishes monthly lists of reports available to the public. Library open to the public by appointment.

House Appropriations Committee, *H218 CAP 20515; (202) 225-2771. Rep. C. W. Bill Young, R-Fla., Chair; James W. Dyer, Staff Director. Web, www.house.gov/ appropriations.*

Jurisdiction over legislation to appropriate funds for all government programs; responsible for rescissions of appropriated funds, transfers of surplus allocations, and new spending under the Congressional Budget Act. Maintains data on congressional appropriating process and government spending.

House Appropriations Committee, *Subcommittee on Commerce, Justice, State, and Judiciary, H309 CAP 20515; (202) 225-3351. Rep. Harold Rogers, R-Ky., Chair; Jim Kulikowski, Staff Director. Web, www.house.gov/ appropriations.*

Jurisdiction over legislation to appropriate funds for the Commerce Dept., the Securities and Exchange Commission, the Small Business Administration, the Competitiveness Policy Council, the Federal Trade Commission, the International Trade Commission, and the Office of the U.S. Trade Representative.

House Appropriations Committee, *Subcommittee on Treasury, Postal Service, and General Government, B307 RHOB 20515; (202) 225-5834. Fax, (202) 225-5895. Rep. Jim Kolbe, R-Ariz., Chair; Michelle Mrdeza, Clerk. Web, www.house.gov/appropriations.*

Jurisdiction over legislation to appropriate funds for the Executive Office of the President, including the Council of Economic Advisers and the Office of Management and Budget; the Treasury Dept.; and the U.S. Tax Court.

House Banking and Financial Services Committee, *2129 RHOB 20515; (202) 225-7502. Fax, (202) 226-6052. Rep. Jim Leach, R-Iowa, Chair; Anthony F. Cole, Staff Director. Web, www.house.gov/banking.*

Jurisdiction over legislation dealing with bank regulation and federal monetary policy, including the Federal Reserve System; financial aid to commerce and industry; the measurement of economic activity; federal loan guarantees; economic development; and economic stabilization measures, including wage and price controls.

House Commerce Committee, *2125 RHOB 20515; (202) 225-2927. Fax, (202) 225-1919. Rep. Thomas J. Bliley Jr., R-Va., Chair; James E. Derderian, Staff Director. General e-mail, commerce@mail.house.gov. Web, www. house.gov/commerce.*

Jurisdiction over legislation on interstate and foreign commerce generally (some jurisdiction shared with the House International Relations Committee), including the Federal Trade Commission and many operations of the Commerce Dept.

House Government Reform Committee, *2157 RHOB 20515; (202) 225-5074. Fax, (202) 225-3974. Rep. Dan Burton, R-Ind., Chair; Kevin Binger, Staff Director. Web, www.house.gov/reform.*

Jurisdiction over legislation on government budget and accounting issues other than appropriations; oversight of General Accounting Office operations and of the Office of Management and Budget.

House Government Reform Committee, *Subcommittee on National Economic Growth, Natural Resources, and Regulatory Affairs, B377 RHOB 20515; (202) 225-4407. Fax, (202) 225-2441. Rep. David M. McIntosh, R-Ind., Chair; Marlo Lewis, Staff Director. Web, www.house.gov/reform.*

Oversees operations of the Commerce and Treasury departments, the Federal Reserve System, U.S. Tax Court, and other federal agencies dealing with economic and monetary affairs (jurisdiction shared with House Banking and Financial Services Committee).

House Ways and Means Committee, *1102 LHOB 20515; (202) 225-3625. Fax, (202) 225-2610. Rep. Bill Archer, R-Texas, Chair; A. L. Singleton, Chief of Staff. Web, www.house.gov/ways_means.*

Jurisdiction over legislation dealing with the debt ceiling; investment policy; and taxes, including taxation of savings, interest, and dividends. Oversees the Internal Revenue Service; sets excise tax rates for the Bureau of Alcohol, Tobacco, and Firearms.

Joint Economic Committee, *SD-G01 20510; (202) 224-5171. Fax, (202) 224-0240. Sen. Connie Mack, R-Fla.,*

Chair; Shelley Hymes, Staff Director. General e-mail, jec@jec.house.gov. Web, jec.senate.gov.

Studies and makes recommendations on economic policy, including fiscal policy; maintains data pertaining to aggregate economic activity; analyzes the president's annual economic report to Congress and communicates findings to the House and Senate.

Senate Appropriations Committee, S128 CAP 20510; (202) 224-3471. Sen. Ted Stevens, R-Alaska, Chair; Steve Cortese, Staff Director. Web, appropriations.senate.gov.

Jurisdiction over legislation to appropriate funds for all government programs; responsible for rescissions of appropriated funds, transfers of surplus allocations, and new spending under the Congressional Budget Act. Maintains data on congressional appropriating process and government spending.

Senate Appropriations Committee, *Subcommittee on Commerce, Justice, State, and Judiciary,* S-146A CAP 20510; (202) 224-7277. Sen. Judd Gregg, R-N.H., Chair; Jim Morhard, Clerk. Web, appropriations.senate.gov/commerce.

Jurisdiction over legislation to appropriate funds for the Commerce Dept., the Securities and Exchange Commission, the Small Business Administration, the Competitiveness Policy Council, the Federal Trade Commission, the International Trade Commission, and the Office of the U.S. Trade Representative.

Senate Appropriations Committee, *Subcommittee on Treasury and General Government,* SD-188 20510; (202) 224-7337. Sen. Ben Nighthorse Campbell, R-Colo., Chair; Patricia Raymond, Clerk. Web, appropriations. senate.gov/treasury.

Jurisdiction over legislation to appropriate funds for the Executive Office of the President, including the Council of Economic Advisers and the Office of Management and Budget; the Treasury Dept.; and the U.S. Tax Court.

Senate Banking, Housing, and Urban Affairs Committee, SD-534 20510; (202) 224-7391. Fax, (202) 224-5137. Sen. Phil Gramm, R-Texas, Chair; Wayne A. Abernathy, Staff Director. Web, banking.senate.gov.

Jurisdiction over legislation dealing with bank regulation, federal monetary policy, financial aid to commerce and industry, the measurement of economic activity, federal loan guarantees, economic development, and other economic stabilization measures (including wage and price controls); oversees the Treasury Dept.; oversees the Federal Reserve System.

Senate Commerce, Science, and Transportation Committee, SD-508 20510; (202) 224-5115. Fax, (202)

224-1259. Sen. John McCain, R-Ariz., Chair; Mark Buse, Staff Director. Web, commerce.senate.gov.

Jurisdiction over legislation on interstate and foreign commerce generally, including the Federal Trade Commission, and many operations of the Commerce Dept.

Senate Finance Committee, SD-219 20510; (202) 224-4515. Fax, (202) 224-5920. Sen. William V. Roth Jr., R-Del., Chair; Frank Polk, Staff Director. Web, finance. senate.gov.

Jurisdiction over tax legislation; oversees the Internal Revenue Service and the U.S. Tax Court; sets excise tax rates for the Bureau of Alcohol, Tobacco, and Firearms.

Senate Finance Committee, *Subcommittee on Long-Term Growth, Debt, and Deficit Reduction,* SD-219 20510; (202) 224-4515. Fax, (202) 224-5920. Sen. Frank H. Murkowski, R-Alaska, Chair; Frank Polk, Staff Director. Web, finance.senate.gov.

Holds hearings on debt ceiling legislation.

Senate Finance Committee, *Subcommittee on Taxation and IRS Oversight,* SD-219 20510; (202) 224-4515. Fax, (202) 224-5920. Sen. Orrin G. Hatch, R-Utah, Chair; Mark Prater, Staff Contact. Web, finance.senate.gov.

Holds hearings on legislation relating to investment policy and taxation of savings, interest, and dividends.

Senate Governmental Affairs Committee, SD-340 20510; (202) 224-4751. Fax, (202) 224-9603. Sen. Fred Thompson, R-Tenn., Chair; Hannah Sistare, Staff Director. Web, gov_affairs.senate.gov.

Jurisdiction over legislation on government budget and accounting issues other than appropriations; oversight of General Accounting Office operations and of the Office of Management and Budget.

NONPROFIT

American Business Conference, 1730 K St. N.W., #1200 20006; (202) 822-9300. Fax, (202) 467-4070. Barry K. Rogstad, President. General e-mail, americanbc@aol. com. Web, www.americanbusinessconf.com.

Membership: chief executive officers of midsize, high-growth companies. Seeks a public policy role for growth companies. Studies capital formation, tax policy, regulatory reform, and international trade.

American Chamber of Commerce Executives, 4232 King St., Alexandria, VA 22302; (703) 998-0072. Fax, (703) 931-5624. Paul J. Greeley Jr., President. General e-mail, adminacce@acce.org. Web, www.acce.org.

Membership: managers of local, state, and international chambers of commerce. Conducts for members educational programs and conferences on topics of interest, including economic development, management symposiums, and membership drives. Sponsors special interest groups for members.

American Council for Capital Formation (ACCF), *1750 K St. N.W., #400 20006; (202) 293-5811. Fax, (202) 785-8165. Mark Bloomfield, President. General e-mail, info@accf.org. Web, www.accf.org.*

Advocates tax, trade, and environmental policies conducive to saving, investment, and economic growth. Affiliated with the ACCF Center for Policy Research, which conducts and funds research on capital formation topics.

American Enterprise Institute for Public Policy Research, *Economic Policy Studies, 1150 17th St. N.W. 20036; (202) 862-5814. Fax, (202) 862-7177. Christopher DeMuth, President. Information, (202) 862-5800. Web, www.aei.org.*

Research and educational organization. Interests include monetary, tax, trade, and regulatory policy and labor and social security issues.

American Management Assn. International, *Washington Office, 440 1st St. N.W. 20001; (202) 347-3092. Fax, (202) 347-4549. Judy Doran, Executive Director. Web, www.amanet.org.*

Membership: managers and other corporate professionals. Offers training and education programs to members.

American Society of Assn. Executives, *1575 Eye St. N.W. 20005; (202) 626-2723. Fax, (202) 371-8825. Michael S. Olson, President. Library, (202) 626-2746. Press, (202) 626-2733. TTY, (202) 626-2803. General e-mail, pr@asaenet.org. Web, www.asaenet.org.*

Conducts research and provides educational programs on association management, trends, and developments. Library open to the public.

The Brookings Institution, *Economic Studies Program, 1775 Massachusetts Ave. N.W. 20036-2188; (202) 797-6111. Fax, (202) 797-6181. Robert E. Litan, Director. Information, (202) 797-6302. Web, www.brookings.org/ES/ES_HP.HTM.*

Sponsors economic research and publishes studies on domestic and international economics, worldwide economic growth and stability, public finance, urban economics, industrial organization and regulation, labor economics, social policy, and the economics of human resources.

The Business Council, *888 17th St. N.W., #506 20006; (202) 298-7650. Fax, (202) 785-0296. Philip E. Cassidy, Executive Director.*

Membership: current and former chief executive officers of major corporations. Serves as a forum for business and government to exchange views and explore public policy as it affects U.S. business interests.

Business–Higher Education Forum, *1 Dupont Circle N.W., #800 20036; (202) 939-9345. Fax, (202) 833-4723. Judith Irwin, Managing Director. General e-mail, bhef@ace.nche.edu. Web, www.bhef.com.*

Membership: chief executive officers of major corporations, colleges, and universities. Promotes cooperation between businesses and higher educational institutions. Interests include international economic competitiveness, education and training, research and development, science and technology, and global interdependence.

Business Roundtable, *1615 L St. N.W., #1100 20036-5610; (202) 872-1260. Fax, (202) 466-3509. Samuel L. Maury, President. Web, www.brtable.org.*

Membership: chief executives of the nation's largest corporations. Examines issues of concern to business, including taxation, antitrust law, international trade, employment policy, and the federal budget.

Center for the Study of Public Choice *(George Mason University), Carrow Hall, #1D3, 4400 University Dr., Fairfax, VA 22030; (703) 993-2330. Fax, (703) 993-2323. Roger Congleton, Director. Web, www.gmu.edu/departments/economics.*

Promotes research in public choice, an interdisciplinary approach to the study of the relationship between economic and political institutions. Interests include constitutional economics, public finance, federalism and local government, econometrics, and trade protection and regulation. Sponsors conferences and seminars. Library open to the public.

Citizens for a Sound Economy, *1250 H St. N.W., #700 20005-3908; (202) 783-3870. Fax, (202) 783-4687. Paul Beckner, President. Web, www.cse.org.*

Citizens' advocacy group that promotes reduced taxes, free trade, and deregulation. Advocates deficit reduction through spending restraint, competitiveness in financial markets, and increased private involvement in providing public services. Encourages citizens to petition members of Congress.

Committee for Economic Development, *2000 L St. N.W., #700 20036; (202) 296-5860. Fax, (202) 223-0776. Van Doorn Ooms, Senior Vice President. Web, www.ced.org.*

Research organization that makes recommendations on domestic and international economic policy.

Competitive Enterprise Institute, *1001 Connecticut Ave. N.W., #1250 20036; (202) 331-1010. Fax, (202) 331-0640. Fred L. Smith, President. Web, www.cei.org.*

Advocates free enterprise and limited government. Produces policy analyses on tax, budget, financial services, antitrust, biotechnological, and environmental issues. Monitors legislation and litigates against restrictive regulations through its Free Market Legal Program.

The Conference Board, *Government Affairs, Washington Office, 1255 34th St. N.W. 20007; (202) 625-4733. Fax, (540) 364-4248. Meredith Whiting, Senior Fellow. Web, www.conference-board.org.*

Membership: senior executives from various industries. Researches science and technology policy, environmental affairs, corporate political activity, management-related issues, the integrated market, and European business activities. Headquarters conducts research and provides economic data on business management, trends, and development.

Council for Social and Economic Studies, *1133 13th St. N.W., #C2 20005-4297; (202) 371-2700. Fax, (202) 371-1523. Roger Pearson, Executive Director. General e-mail, socecon@aol.com.*

Conducts research and publishes studies on domestic and international economic, social, and political issues.

Council of State Chambers of Commerce, *c/o Committee on Taxation, 122 C St. N.W., #330 20001; (202) 484-5222. Fax, (202) 484-5229. Doug Lindholm, President.*

Federation of state business organizations. Conducts research on federal spending, state and local taxation, and employee relations and benefits. Represents members and affiliates on corporate state tax issues.

Council on Competitiveness, *1500 K St. N.W., #850 20009; (202) 682-4292. Fax, (202) 682-5150. John N. Yochelson, President. General e-mail, council@compete.org. Web, www.compete.org.*

Membership: executives from business, education, and labor. Seeks increased public awareness of economic competition. Works to set a national action agenda for U.S. competitiveness in global markets.

Economic Policy Institute, *1660 L St. N.W., #1200 20036; (202) 775-8810. Fax, (202) 775-0819. Jeff Faux, President. General e-mail, epi@epinet.org. Web, www.epinet.org.*

Research and educational organization that publishes analyses on economics, economic development, compet-

itiveness, income distribution, industrial competitiveness, and investment. Conducts public conferences and seminars.

Ethics Resource Center, *1747 Pennsylvania Ave. N.W., #400 20006; (202) 737-2258. Fax, (202) 737-2227. Michael G. Daigneault, President. Information, (800) 777-1285. Press, (202) 872-4765. Web, www.ethics.org.*

Nonpartisan educational organization whose vision is an ethical world. Fosters ethical practices among individuals and institutions. Interests include research and knowledge building, education and advocacy, and consulting and technical assistance.

Financial Executives Institute, *Government Relations, 1615 L St. N.W., #1320 20036; (202) 457-6203. Fax, (202) 857-0230. Grace Hinchman, Vice President. Web, www.fei.org.*

Membership: senior financial executives from major companies in the United States and Canada. Provides conferences and professional development programs; publishes the *Financial Executive.* Monitors legislation and regulations affecting business.

Greater Washington Board of Trade, *1129 20th St. N.W., #200 20036; (202) 857-5900. Fax, (202) 223-2648. John Tydings, President. General e-mail, info@bot.org. Web, www.bot.org.*

Promotes and plans economic growth for the capital region. Supports business-government partnerships, technological training, and transportation planning; promotes international trade; works to increase economic viability of the city of Washington. Monitors legislation and regulations at local, state, and federal levels.

National Assn. of Corporate Directors, *1707 L St. N.W., #560 20036; (202) 775-0509. Fax, (202) 775-4857. Roger Rayber, President. Web, www.nacdonline.org.*

Membership: executives of closely held and public companies, outside and inside directors, and stewards of corporate governance. Serves as a clearinghouse on corporate governance and current board practices. Conducts seminars; runs executive search service; sponsors insurance program for directors and officers.

National Assn. of Manufacturers, *1331 Pennsylvania Ave. N.W., #600 20004-1790; (202) 637-3000. Fax, (202) 637-3182. Jerry Jasinowski, President. Press, (202) 637-3094. Web, www.nam.org.*

Represents industry views (mainly of manufacturers) to government on national and international issues. Reviews legislation, administrative rulings, and judicial decisions affecting industry. Sponsors the Human Resources Forum; operates a Web site for members and the public that provides information on legislative and other news; conducts programs on labor relations, occupational safety and health, regulatory and consumer affairs, environmental trade and technology, and other business issues.

National Assn. of State Budget Officers, *444 N. Capitol St. N.W., #642 20001-1501; (202) 624-5382. Fax, (202) 624-7745. Gloria Timmer, Executive Director. Web, www.nasbo.org.*

Membership: state budget and financial officers. Publishes research reports on budget-related issues. (Affiliate of the National Governors' Assn.)

National Chamber Litigation Center, *1615 H St. N.W., #230 20062; (202) 463-5337. Fax, (202) 463-5346. Stephen A. Bokat, Executive Vice President. Web, www. uschamber.com.*

Public policy law firm of the U.S. Chamber of Commerce. Advocates business's positions in court on such issues as employment, environmental, and constitutional law. Provides businesses with legal assistance and representation in legal proceedings before federal courts and agencies.

National Cooperative Business Assn., *1401 New York Ave. N.W., #1100 20005-2146; (202) 638-6222. Fax, (202) 638-1374. Paul Hazen, President. General e-mail, ncba@ncba.org. Web, www.cooperative.org.*

Alliance of cooperatives, businesses, and state cooperative associations. Supports development of cooperative businesses; promotes and develops trade among domestic and international cooperatives. Monitors legislation and regulations.

National Policy Assn., *1424 16th St. N.W., #700 20036; (202) 265-7685. Fax, (202) 797-5516. Anthony C. E. Quainton, President. General e-mail, npa@npa1.org. Web, www.npa1.org.*

Research organization that conducts studies on domestic and international economic policy issues. Interests include agriculture, human resources, employment, international trade, investment and monetary policy, and U.S. economic competitiveness.

National Retail Federation, *325 7th St. N.W., #1000 20004-2802; (202) 783-7971. Fax, (202) 737-2849. Tracy Mullin, President. Web, www.nrf.com.*

Membership: international, national, and state associations of retailers and major retail corporations. Concerned with federal regulatory activities and legislation that affect retailers, including tax, employment, trade, and credit issues. Provides information on retailing through seminars, conferences, and publications.

National Venture Capital Assn., *1655 N. Fort Myer Dr., #850, Arlington, VA 22209; (703) 524-2549. Fax, (703) 524-3940. Mark Heesen, President. Web, www.nvca.org.*

Membership: venture capital organizations and individuals and corporate financiers. Promotes understanding of venture capital investment. Monitors legislation.

The Preamble Center, *1737 21st St. N.W. 20009; (202) 265-3263. Fax, (202) 265-3647. Richard Healey, Executive Director. General e-mail, preamble@rtk.net. Web, www. preamble.org.*

Membership: academics, policy professionals, and community leaders concerned about current social, economic, and political challenges. Promotes discussion of economic problems of working families and possible solutions; researches economic developments and trends; analyzes economic policies; provides information on new policy alternatives and public opinion studies. Interests include economic globalization, job security, living-wage legislation, Social Security, and multilateral trade and investment agreements.

Private Sector Council, *1101 16th St. N.W., #300 20036-4803; (202) 822-3910. Fax, (202) 822-0638. Thomas V. Fritz, President. General e-mail, privsect@ aol.com. Web, www.privatesectorcouncil.org.*

Membership: large corporations, private businesses, and associations, including financial and information technology organizations. Seeks to improve government efficiency, productivity, and management through a cooperative effort of the public and private sectors.

Society of Competitive Intelligence Professionals, *1700 Diagonal Rd., #600, Alexandria, VA 22314; (703) 739-0696. Fax, (703) 739-2524. Guy Kolb, Executive Director. General e-mail, postmaster@scip.org. Web, www.scip.org.*

Promotes businesses' competitiveness through a greater understanding of competitive behaviors and future strategies as well as the market dynamics in which they conduct business. Conducts seminars and conferences. Publishes the *Competitive Intelligence Review.*

U.S. Business and Industrial Council, *910 16th St. N.W., #300 20006; (202) 728-1980. Fax, (202) 728-1981. Kevin L. Kearns, President. General e-mail, usbic@aol.com.*

Advocates energy independence, reindustrialization, and effective use of natural resources and manufacturing capacity. Current issues include business tax reduction, the liability crisis, defense and other federal spending, and the trade deficit. Media network distributes op-ed pieces to newspapers and radio stations.

U.S. Chamber of Commerce, *1615 H St. N.W. 20062-2000; (202) 659-6000. Fax, (202) 463-5328. Thomas J. Donohue, President. Press, (202) 463-5682. Publications, (800) 638-6582. Web, www.uschamber.org.*

Federation of businesses, trade, and professional associations; state and local chambers of commerce; and American chambers of commerce abroad. Develops policy on legislative issues important to American business; sponsors programs on management, business confidence, small business, consumer affairs, economic policy, minority business, and tax policy; maintains a business forecast and survey center and a trade negotiation information service. Monitors legislation and regulations.

U.S. Chamber of Commerce, *Congressional and Public Affairs, 1615 H St. N.W. 20062-2000; (202) 659-6000. Fax, (202) 887-3430. Lonnie P. Taylor, Senior Vice President. Web, www.uschamber.org.*

Advocates business's position on government and regulatory affairs. Monitors legislation and regulations on antitrust and corporate policy, product liability, and business-consumer relations.

U.S. Chamber of Commerce, *Economic Policy, 1615 H St. N.W. 20062-2000; (202) 659-6000. Fax, (202) 463-3188. Martin A. Regalia, Chief Economist. Press, (202) 463-5682. Web, www.uschamber.org.*

Represents business community's views on economic policy, including government spending, the federal budget, and tax issues. Forecasts the economy of the United States and other industrialized nations and projects the impact of major policy changes. Studies economic trends and analyzes their effect on the business community.

Coins and Currency

AGENCIES

Bureau of Engraving and Printing (BEP), *(Treasury Dept.), 14th and C Sts. S.W., #119M 20228; (202) 874-2002. Fax, (202) 874-3879. Thomas Ferguson, Director. Information, (202) 874-3019. Web, www.bep.treas.gov.*

Designs, engraves, and prints Federal Reserve notes, postage stamps, military certificates, White House invitations, presidential portraits, and special security documents for the federal government. Provides information on history, design, and engraving of currency; offers public tours; maintains reading room where materials are brought for special research (for appointment, write to the BEP's Historical Resource Center).

Bureau of Engraving and Printing *(Treasury Dept.), Currency Standards, 14th and C Sts. S.W. 20228 (mailing address: P.O. Box 37048 20013); (202) 874-8897. Fax,*

(202) 874-5362. Carol L. Seegars, Chief. Information, (202) 874-2361. Mutilation redemption, (202) 874-2532. Unfit currency and destruction of currency, (202) 874-2771. Claims, (202) 874-2397.

Redeems U.S. currency that has been mutilated; develops regulations and procedures for the destruction of unfit U.S. currency.

Federal Reserve System, *Board of Governors, 20th and C Sts. N.W. 20551; (202) 452-3201. Fax, (202) 452-3819. Alan Greenspan, Chair; Roger W. Ferguson Jr., Vice Chair. Information, (202) 452-3215. Press, (202) 452-3204. Locator, (202) 452-3000. Web, www.bog.frb.fed.us.*

Influences the availability of money as part of its responsibility for monetary policy; maintains reading room for inspection of records that are available to the public.

National Museum of American History *(Smithsonian Institution), National Numismatic Collection, 14th St. and Constitution Ave. N.W. 20560; (202) 357-1798. Fax, (202) 357-4840. Elvira Clain-Stefanelli, Executive Director. Web, www.si.edu.*

Develops and maintains collections of ancient, medieval, modern, U.S., and world coins; U.S. and world currencies; tokens; medals; orders and decorations; and primitive media of exchange. Conducts research and responds to public inquiries.

Treasury Dept., *1500 Pennsylvania Ave. N.W., #3330 20220; (202) 622-1100. Fax, (202) 622-0073. Lawrence H. Summers, Secretary; Stuart Eizenstat, Deputy Secretary. Information, (202) 622-2000. Library, (202) 622-0990. Locator, (202) 622-2111. Web, www.ustreas.gov.*

Oversees the manufacture of U.S. coins and currency; submits to Congress final reports on the minting of coins or any changes in currency. Library open to the public by appointment.

Treasury Dept., *Financial Management Service, 401 14th St. S.W., #548 20227; (202) 874-7000. Fax, (202) 874-6743. Richard Gregg, Commissioner. Press, (202) 874-6604. Web, www.treas.gov/fms.*

Prepares and publishes for the president, Congress, and the public monthly, quarterly, and annual statements of government financial transactions, including reports on U.S. currency and coins in circulation.

Treasury Dept., *Treasurer of the United States, 1500 Pennsylvania Ave. N.W., #2134 20220; (202) 622-0100. Fax, (202) 622-2258. Mary Ellen Withrow, Treasurer. Web, www.ustreas.gov.*

Spokesperson for the Treasury Dept. in matters dealing with currency, coinage, and savings bonds. Signs currency; promotes selling and holding of savings bonds; oversees operation of the U.S. Mint and the Bureau of Engraving and Printing.

U.S. Mint *(Treasury Dept.),* *801 9th St. N.W. 20220; (202) 354-7200. Fax, (202) 756-6160. Philip N. Diehl, Director. Information, (202) 354-7227. Web, www.usmint. gov.*

Manufactures and distributes all domestic coins; safeguards government's holdings of precious metals; manufactures and sells commemorative coins and medals of historic interest. Maintains a sales area at Union Station in Washington, D.C.

CONGRESS

House Banking and Financial Services Committee, Subcommittee on Domestic and International Monetary Policy, *B304 RHOB 20515; (202) 226-0473. Fax, (202) 226-0537. Rep. Spencer Bachus, R-Ala., Chair; James McCormick, Staff Director. Web, www.house.gov/ banking.*

Jurisdiction over legislation on all matters relating to coins, currency, medals, proof and mint sets, and other special coins. Oversight of the U.S. Mint and the Bureau of Engraving and Printing.

Senate Banking, Housing, and Urban Affairs Committee, *SD-534 20510; (202) 224-7391. Fax, (202) 224-5137. Sen. Phil Gramm, R-Texas, Chair; Wayne A. Abernathy, Staff Director. Web, banking.senate.gov.*

Jurisdiction over legislation on coins and currency, medals, proof and mint sets, and other special coins. Oversight of the U.S. Mint and the Bureau of Engraving and Printing.

Federal Budget

See also Defense Budget (chap. 16)

AGENCIES

Federal Financing Bank *(Treasury Dept.),* *1500 Pennsylvania Ave. N.W., #3054 20220; (202) 622-2470. Fax, (202) 622-0707. Gary H. Burner, Manager; Kerry Lanham, Secretary.*

Coordinates federal agency borrowing by purchasing securities issued or guaranteed by federal agencies; funds its operations by borrowing from the treasury.

Office of Management and Budget *(Executive Office of the President),* *Dwight D. Eisenhower Executive Office Bldg., #252 20503; (202) 395-4840. Fax, (202) 395-3888. Jacob J. Lew, Director. Press, (202) 395-7254. Web, www. whitehouse.gov/omb.*

Prepares president's annual budget; works with the Council of Economic Advisers and the Treasury Dept. to develop the federal government's fiscal program; oversees administration of the budget; reviews government regulations; coordinates administration procurement and management policy.

Treasury Dept., *Bureau of the Public Debt,* *999 E St. N.W. 20239; (202) 691-3500. Fax, (202) 219-4163. Van Zeck, Commissioner. Information, (202) 874-4000. Press, (202) 691-3502. Savings bonds, (202) 447-1775. Web, www.publicdebt.treas.gov.*

Handles public debt securities, treasury notes, and bonds; maintains all records on series EE and HH savings bonds.

Treasury Dept., *Federal Finance Policy Analysis,* *1500 Pennsylvania Ave. N.W., #2034 20220; (202) 622-2680. Fax, (202) 622-0974. Norman Carleton, Director. Web, www.ustreas.gov.*

Analyzes and evaluates economic and financial development, problems and proposals in the areas of treasury financing, public debt management, and related economic matters. Provides analysis and technical assistance on regulatory issues involving government securities and related markets. Monitors and analyzes foreign investment in treasury securities.

Treasury Dept., *Government Financing,* *1500 Pennsylvania Ave. N.W., #3040 20220; (202) 622-2460. Fax, (202) 622-0427. Kerry Lanham, Director. Web, www.ustreas.gov.*

Analyzes federal credit program principles and standards, legislation, and proposals related to government borrowing, lending, and investment. Furnishes actuarial and mathematical analysis required for treasury market financing, the Federal Financing Bank, and other government agencies. Manages the Federal Financing Bank.

Treasury Dept., *Market Finance,* *1500 Pennsylvania Ave. N.W., #2209 20220; (202) 622-2630. Fax, (202) 622-0244. Paul F. Malvey, Director (Acting). Web, www.ustreas. gov.*

Provides financial and economic data on government financing and public debt management. Coordinates, analyzes, and reviews government borrowing, lending, and investment activities. Monitors the volume of funds raised and supplied in the credit market. Determines interest rates for government loan programs.

CONGRESS

Congressional Budget Office, *402 FHOB 20515; (202) 226-2700. Fax, (202) 225-7509. Dan L. Crippen, Director. Information, (202) 226-2600. Web, www.cbo.gov.*

Nonpartisan office that provides the House and Senate with budget-related information and analyses of alternative fiscal policies.

House Budget Committee, *309 CHOB 20515; (202) 226-7270. Fax, (202) 226-7174. Rep. John R. Kasich, R-Ohio, Chair; Wayne Struble, Staff Director. General e-mail, budget@mail.house.gov. Web, www.house.gov/budget.*

Jurisdiction over congressional budget resolutions, which set levels for federal spending, revenues, deficit, and debt. Jurisdiction over reconciliation bills, which alter existing programs to meet budget goals. Oversight of Congressional Budget Office. Studies budget matters; makes available statistics pertaining to budget proposals put forward by the president and Congress.

Senate Budget Committee, *SD-621 20510; (202) 224-0642. Fax, (202) 224-4835. Sen. Pete V. Domenici, R-N.M., Chair; G. William Hoagland, Staff Director. Web, www.senate.gov/~budget.*

Jurisdiction over congressional budget resolutions, which set levels for federal spending, revenues, deficit, and debt. Jurisdiction over reconciliation bills, which alter existing programs to meet budget goals. Oversight of the Congressional Budget Office. Studies budget matters; makes available statistics pertaining to budget proposals put forward by the president and Congress.

NONPROFIT

Committee for a Responsible Federal Budget, *220 1/2 E St. N.E. 20002; (202) 547-4484. Fax, (202) 547-4476. Carol Cox Wait, President. General e-mail, crfb@aol.com.*

Educational organization that works to support and improve the congressional budget process. Seeks to increase public awareness of the dangers of long term financial imbalances. Offers seminars and symposia; commissions studies and policy analyses.

Concord Coalition, *1819 H St. N.W., #800 20006; (202) 467-6222. Fax, (202) 467-6333. Robert L. Bixby, Executive Director. Web, www.concordcoalition.org.*

Nonpartisan, grassroots organization advocating fiscal responsibility and ensuring Social Security, Medicare, and Medicaid are secure for all generations.

Institute for Policy Studies, *National Commission for Economic Conversion and Disarmament, 733 15th St. N.W., #1020 20005; (202) 234-9382. Fax, (202) 387-7915. Miriam Pemberton, Executive Director. Web, www.webcom.com/ncecd.*

Supports cutbacks in the U.S. military budget and reallocation of funds for civilian economic development.

Advocates investment in civilian research and development, transportation, housing, health, education, and the environment.

OMB Watch, *1742 Connecticut Ave. N.W. 20009; (202) 234-8494. Fax, (202) 234-8584. Gary D. Bass, Executive Director. General e-mail, ombwatch@ombwatch.org. Web, www.ombwatch.org/ombwatch.html.*

Research and advocacy organization that monitors and interprets the policies and activities of the Office of Management and Budget (OMB). Sponsors conferences and teaches the governmental decision-making process concerning accountability.

Statistics/Economic Projections

See also Federal Budget (this section)

AGENCIES

Bureau of Economic Analysis *(Commerce Dept.), 1441 L St. N.W., #6006 20230; (202) 606-9600. Fax, (202) 606-5311. J. Steven Landefeld, Director. Information, (202) 606-9900. Web, www.bea.doc.gov.*

Compiles, analyzes, and publishes data on measures of aggregate U.S. economic activity, including gross national product; prices by type of expenditure; personal income and outlays; personal savings; corporate profits; capital stock; U.S. international transactions; and foreign investment. Provides estimates of personal income and employment by industry for regions, states, metropolitan areas, and counties. Refers specific inquiries to economic specialists in the field.

Bureau of Labor Statistics *(Labor Dept.), 2 Massachusetts Ave. N.E., #4040 20212; (202) 691-7800. Fax, (202) 691-7797. Katharine G. Abraham, Commissioner. Press, (202) 606-5902. General e-mail, labstathelpdesk@bls.gov. Web, stats.bls.gov.*

Provides statistical data on labor economics, including labor force, employment and unemployment, hours of work, wages, employee compensation, prices, living conditions, labor-management relations, productivity, technological developments, occupational safety and health, and structure and growth of the economy. Publishes reports on these statistical trends including the Consumer Price Index, Producer Price Index, and Employment and Earnings.

Census Bureau *(Commerce Dept.), Economic Programs, Suitland and Silver Hill Rds., #2061-3, Suitland, MD 20233-6000; (301) 457-2112. Fax, (301) 457-8140. Frederick T. Knickerbocker, Associate Director.*

Provides data and explains proper use of data on county business patterns, classification of industries and commodities, and business statistics. Compiles quarterly reports listing financial data for corporations in certain industrial sectors.

Census Bureau *(Commerce Dept.), Governments Division,* *8905 Presidential Pkwy., Upper Marlboro, MD 20722 (mailing address: Washington Plaza II, #407 20233-6800); (301) 457-1489. Fax, (301) 457-1423. Gordon W. Green Jr., Chief.*

Provides data and explains proper use of data concerning state and local governments, employment, finance, governmental organization, and taxation.

Census Bureau *(Commerce Dept.), Manufacturing and Construction,* *Suitland and Silver Hill Rds., Suitland, MD 20233; (301) 457-4593. Fax, (301) 457-4583. William G. Bostic Jr., Chief.*

Collects and distributes manufacturing, construction, and mineral industry data. Reports are organized by commodity, industry, and geographic area.

Census Bureau *(Commerce Dept.), Service Sector Statistics Division,* *Suitland and Silver Hill Rds., Bldg. 3, #2633, Suitland, MD 20233; (301) 457-2668. Fax, (301) 457-1343. Carole A. Ambler, Chief.*

Provides data of five-year census programs on retail, wholesale, and service industries. Conducts periodic monthly or annual surveys for specific items within these industries.

Council of Economic Advisers *(Executive Office of the President), Statistical Office,* *Dwight D. Eisenhower Executive Office Bldg., #417 20502; (202) 395-5062. Fax, (202) 395-5630. Catherine H. Furlong, Senior Statistician.*

Compiles and reports aggregate economic data, including national income and expenditures, employment, wages, productivity, production and business activity, prices, money stock, credit, finance, government finance, corporate profits and finance, agriculture, and international statistics, including balance of payments and import-export levels by commodity and area. Data published in the *Annual Economic Report* and the monthly *Economic Indicators,* published by the congressional Joint Economic Committee.

Economic Research Service *(Agriculture Dept.), 1800 M St. N.W. 20036; (202) 694-5200. Fax, (202) 694-5792. Barry Krissoff, Chief, Speciality Crops; Joy Harwood, Chief, Field Crops. Web, www.econ.ag.gov.*

Conducts market research; studies and forecasts domestic supply-and-demand trends for fruits and vegetables.

Federal Reserve System, *Monetary Affairs, 20th and C Sts. N.W., #B3022B 20551; (202) 452-3761. Fax, (202) 452-2301. Donald L. Kohn, Director.*

Analyzes monetary policy and issues related to open market operations, reserve requirements, and discount policy. Reports statistics associated with monetary aggregates; issues related to the government securities market; and economic aspects of other regulatory issues closely related to monetary policy, such as banking, loans, and securities.

Federal Reserve System, *Research and Statistics, 20th and C Sts. N.W., #B3048 20551; (202) 452-3301. Fax, (202) 452-5296. Michael J. Prell, Director. Publications, (202) 452-3245.*

Publishes statistical data on business finance, real estate credit, consumer credit, industrial production, construction, and flow of funds.

Internal Revenue Service *(Treasury Dept.), Statistics of Income, 500 N. Capitol St. N.W. 20001 (mailing address: P.O. Box 2608 20013-2608); (202) 874-0700. Fax, (202) 874-0983. Daniel Skelly, Director. Publications, (202) 874-0410.*

Provides the public and the Treasury Dept. with statistical information on tax laws. Prepares statistical information for the Commerce Dept. to use in formulating the gross national product (GNP). Publishes *Statistics of Income,* a series available at cost to the public.

International Trade Administration *(Commerce Dept.), Trade and Economic Analysis, 14th St. and Constitution Ave. N.W., #2815 20230; (202) 482-5145. Fax, (202) 482-4614. Jonathan C. Menes, Director. Web, www. ita.doc.gov/tradestats.*

Monitors developments in major U.S. industrial sectors. Produces studies, including *U.S. Industrial Outlook,* which reports business planning and marketing data on more than 350 industries and projects economic trends for selected industries.

National Agricultural Statistics Service *(Agriculture Dept.), 1400 Independence Ave. S.W., #4117S 20250-2001; (202) 720-2707. Fax, (202) 720-9013. R. Ronald Bosecker, Administrator. Weekly weather and crop information, bulletin subscriptions, (202) 720-4021. General e-mail, nass@ nass.usda.gov. Web, www.usda.gov/nass.*

Prepares estimates and reports on production, supply, prices, and other items relating to the U.S. agricultural economy. Reports include statistics on field crops, fruits and vegetables, cattle, hogs, poultry, and related products.

Office of Management and Budget *(Executive Office of the President), Statistical Policy,* New Executive Office Bldg., #10201 20503; (202) 395-3093. Fax, (202) 395-7245. Katherine K. Wallman, Chief. Web, www. whitehouse.gov/omb.

Carries out the statistical policy and coordination functions under the Paperwork Reduction Act of 1995; develops long-range plans for improving federal statistical programs; develops policy standards and guidelines for statistical data collection, classification, and publication; evaluates statistical programs and agency performance.

Securities and Exchange Commission, *Economic Analysis,* 450 5th St. N.W. 20549; (202) 942-8020. Fax, (202) 942-9657. Vacant, Chief Economist.

Publishes data on trading volume of the stock exchanges; compiles statistics on financial reports of brokerage firms.

U.S. International Trade Commission, *Industries,* 500 E St. S.W. 20436; (202) 205-3296. Fax, (202) 205-3161. Vern Simpson, Director. Press, (202) 205-1819. Web, www.usitc.gov.

Identifies, analyzes, and develops data on economic and technical matters related to the competitive position of the United States in domestic and world markets in agriculture, chemicals and energy, electronics and transportation, services and investments, mining, and manufacturing.

CONGRESS

Joint Economic Committee, SD-G01 20510; (202) 224-5171. Fax, (202) 224-0240. Sen. Connie Mack, R-Fla., Chair; Shelley Hymes, Staff Director. General e-mail, jec@jec.house.gov. Web, jec.senate.gov.

Maintains statistics on nearly all facets of economic activity; provides information to the public or refers individuals to office where information is available; provides statistics on economy pertaining to energy and environment; publishes monthly *Economic Indicators* from data supplied by the Council of Economic Advisers.

NONPROFIT

American Statistical Assn., 1429 Duke St., Alexandria, VA 22314; (703) 684-1221. Fax, (703) 684-2037. Ray Waller, Executive Director. General e-mail, asainfo@ amstat.org. Web, www.amstat.org.

Membership: individuals interested in statistics and related quantitative fields. Advises government agencies on statistics and methodology in agency research; promotes development of statistical techniques for use in business, industry, finance, government, agriculture, and science.

Taxes and Tax Reform

See also Business and Tax Law (chap. 14)

AGENCIES

Bureau of Alcohol, Tobacco, and Firearms *(Treasury Dept.), Field Operations,* 650 Massachusetts Ave. N.W., #8100 20226; (202) 927-7970. Fax, (202) 927-7756. Andrew L. Vita, Assistant Director. Information, (202) 927-7777. Press, (202) 927-9510. Web, www.atf.treas.gov.

Enforces and administers revenue laws relating to firearms, explosives, alcohol, and tobacco.

Internal Revenue Service (IRS), *(Treasury Dept.),* 1111 Constitution Ave. N.W. 20224; (202) 622-4115. Fax, (202) 622-5756. Charles Rossotti, Commissioner. Information, (800) 829-1040. Press, (202) 622-4000. TTY, (800) 829-4059. Problem resolution, (877) 777-4778. Web, www. irs.ustreas.gov.

Administers and enforces internal revenue laws (except those relating to firearms, explosives, alcohol, and tobacco).

Internal Revenue Service *(Treasury Dept.), Employee Plans and Exempt Organizations,* 1111 Constitution Ave. N.W., #1311 20224; (202) 622-6720. Fax, (202) 622-6873. Evelyn Petschek, Commissioner.

Provides rules for the uniform interpretation and application of federal tax laws affecting tax-exempt organizations and private foundations.

Internal Revenue Service *(Treasury Dept.), Operations,* 1111 Constitution Ave. N.W. 20224; (202) 622-6860. Fax, (202) 622-8393. John M. Dalrymple, Chief Operations Officer. TTY, (800) 829-4059. Forms and publications, (800) 829-3676. Recorded tax and refund information, (800) 829-4477. Tax information and notice inquiries, (800) 829-1040.

Oversees field offices that provide information and guidance on tax matters, including group assistance in the preparation of returns and assistance to taxpayers who telephone, write, or visit IRS district offices. Arranges tax courses for groups of taxpayers through an IRS taxpayer education coordinator. Provides businesses with a tax kit, which includes tax regulations and forms. Assists foreign-based Americans and foreign nationals who pay U.S. taxes.

Justice Dept., *Tax Division,* 950 Pennsylvania Ave. N.W., #4143 20530; (202) 514-2901. Fax, (202) 514-5479. Paula Jounghanf, Assistant Attorney General (Acting). Web, www.usdoj.gov/tax/tax.html.

Acts as counsel for the Internal Revenue Service in court litigation between the government and taxpayers (other than those handled by the IRS in the U.S. Tax Court).

Multistate Tax Commission, *444 N. Capitol St. N.W., #425 20001-1538; (202) 624-8699. Fax, (202) 624-8819. Dan R. Bucks, Executive Director. General e-mail, mtc@mtc.gov. Web, www.mtc.gov.*

Membership: state governments that have enacted the Multistate Tax Compact. Promotes fair, effective, and efficient state tax systems for interstate and international commerce; works to preserve state tax sovereignty. Encourages uniform state tax laws and regulations for multistate and multinational enterprises. Maintains three regional audit offices that monitor compliance with state tax laws and encourage uniformity in taxpayer treatment. Administers program to identify businesses that do not file tax returns with states.

Treasury Dept., *Tax Policy, 1500 Pennsylvania Ave. N.W., #1334 20220; (202) 622-0050. Fax, (202) 622-0605. Jonathan Talisman, Assistant Secretary (Acting). Web, www.ustreas.gov/taxpolicy.*

Formulates and implements domestic and international tax policies and programs; conducts analyses of proposed tax legislation and programs; participates in international tax treaty negotiations; responsible for receipts estimates for the annual budget of the United States.

CONGRESS

Joint Committee on Taxation, *1015 LHOB 20515; (202) 225-3621. Fax, (202) 225-0832. Sen. William V. Roth Jr., R-Del, Chair; Lindy Paull, Chief of Staff. Web, www.house.gov/jct.*

Performs staff work for House Ways and Means and Senate Finance committees on domestic and international tax matters in the Internal Revenue Code, the public debt limit, and savings bonds under the Second Liberty Bond Act. Provides those committees with general economic and budgetary analysis. Provides revenue estimates for all tax legislation.

JUDICIARY

U.S. Tax Court, *400 2nd St. N.W. 20217; (202) 606-8700. Mary Ann Cohen, Chief Judge; Charles S. Casazza, Clerk of the Court, (202) 606-8754.*

Tries and adjudicates disputes involving income, estate, and gift taxes and personal holding company surtaxes in cases in which deficiencies have been determined by the Internal Revenue Service.

NONPROFIT

American Enterprise Institute for Public Policy Research, *Fiscal Policy Studies, 1150 17th St. N.W.*

20036; (202) 862-5800. Fax, (202) 862-7177. John Makin, Director. Information, (202) 862-7158. Press, (202) 862-5829. Web, www.aei.org.

Research and educational organization that conducts studies on fiscal policy, taxes, and budget issues.

Americans for Tax Reform, *1920 L St. N.W., #200 20036; (202) 785-0266. Fax, (202) 785-0261. Grover G. Norquist, President. Information, (888) 785-0266. Web, www.atr.org.*

Advocates reduction of federal and state taxes; encourages candidates for public office to pledge their opposition to income tax increases through a national pledge campaign.

Citizens for a Sound Economy, *1250 H St. N.W., #700 20005-3908; (202) 783-3870. Fax, (202) 783-4687. Paul Beckner, President. Web, www.cse.org.*

Citizens' advocacy group that promotes reduced taxes, free trade, and deregulation.

Citizens for Tax Justice, *1311 L St. N.W., #400 20005; (202) 626-3780. Fax, (202) 638-3486. Robert S. McIntyre, Director. Web, www.ctj.org.*

Coalition that works for progressive taxes at the federal, state, and local levels.

Council of State Chambers of Commerce, *c/o Committee on Taxation, 122 C St. N.W., #330 20001; (202) 484-5222. Fax, (202) 484-5229. Doug Lindholm, President.*

Federation of state business organizations. Conducts research on federal spending, state and local taxation, and employee relations and benefits. Represents members and affiliates on corporate state tax issues.

Federation of Tax Administrators, *444 N. Capitol St. N.W., #348 20001; (202) 624-5890. Fax, (202) 624-7888. Harley T. Duncan, Executive Director. Web, www.taxadmin.org.*

Membership: state tax agencies. Provides information upon written request on tax-related issues, including court decisions and legislation. Conducts research and sponsors workshops.

Institute for Research on the Economics of Taxation, *1730 K St. N.W., #910 20006; (202) 463-1400. Fax, (202) 463-6199. Stephen Entin, Executive Director. General e-mail, irettex@ibm.net. Web, www.iret.org.*

Research organization that analyzes all aspects of taxation. Conducts research on the economic effects of federal tax policies; publishes studies on domestic and international economic policy issues.

National Assn. of Manufacturers, *Taxation and Economic Policy, 1331 Pennsylvania Ave. N.W., #600 20004;*

(202) 637-3073. Fax, (202) 637-3182. Monica McGuire, Senior Policy Director.

Represents industry views (mainly of manufacturers) on federal tax and budget policies; conducts conferences. Monitors legislation and regulations.

National Center for Fair Competition, *8421 Frost Way, Annandale, VA 22003; (703) 280-4622. Fax, (703) 280-0942. Kenton Pattie, President. General e-mail, kentonp1@aol.com.*

Membership: trade and professional associations and individual businesses. Concerned with the economic effect of commercial activity by tax-exempt and governmental entities. Supports privatization and contracting out by governmental agencies. Advocates passage of fair competition laws for state legislatures.

National Taxpayers Union, *Communications,* 108 N. *Alfred St., 3rd Floor, Alexandria, VA 22314; (703) 683-5700. Fax, (703) 683-5722. Peter Sepp, Vice President. Web, www.ntu.org.*

Citizens' interest group that promotes tax and spending reduction at all levels of government. Supports constitutional amendments to balance the federal budget and limit taxes.

Tax Council, *1301 K St. N.W., #800W 20005; (202) 822-8062. Fax, (202) 414-1301. Roger J. LeMaster, Executive Director.*

Organization of corporations concerned with tax policy and legislation. Interests include tax rate, capital formation, capital gains, foreign source income, and capital cost recovery.

Tax Executives Institute, *1200 G St. N.W., #300 20005-3814; (202) 638-5601. Fax, (202) 638-5607. Michael J. Murphy, Executive Director. Web, www.tei.org.*

Membership: accountants, lawyers, and other corporate and business employees dealing with tax issues. Sponsors seminars and conferences on federal, state, local, and international tax issues. Develops and monitors tax legislation, regulations, and administrative procedures.

Tax Foundation, *1250 H St. N.W., #750 20005-3908; (202) 783-2760. Fax, (202) 783-6868. J. D. Foster, Executive Director. Web, www.taxfoundation.org.*

Membership: individuals and businesses interested in federal, state, and local fiscal matters. Conducts research and prepares reports on taxes and government expenditures.

U.S. Conference of Mayors, *1620 Eye St. N.W., #400 20006; (202) 293-7330. Fax, (202) 293-2352. J. Thomas*

Cochran, Executive Director. General e-mail, uscm@cais. com. Web, www.usmayors.org/uscm.

Membership: mayors of cities with populations of 30,000 or more. Monitors tax policy and legislation.

FINANCE AND INVESTMENTS
Banking

AGENCIES

Antitrust Division *(Justice Dept.), Computers and Finance, 600 E St. N.W., #9500 20530; (202) 307-6122. Fax, (202) 616-8544. Nancy M. Goodman, Chief.*

Investigates and litigates certain antitrust cases involving financial institutions, including banking, securities, commodity futures, and insurance; participates in agency proceedings and rulemaking in these areas; monitors and analyzes legislation.

Comptroller of the Currency *(Treasury Dept.), 250 E St. S.W. 20219; (202) 874-4900. Fax, (202) 874-4950. John D. Hawke Jr., Comptroller. Information, (202) 874-5000. Library, (202) 874-4720. Press, (202) 874-5770. Web, www.occ.treas.gov.*

Regulates and examines operations of national banks; establishes guidelines for bank examinations; handles mergers of national banks with regard to antitrust law. Library open to the public.

Comptroller of the Currency *(Treasury Dept.), Washington Directed Licensing, 250 E St. S.W. 20219; (202) 874-5060. Fax, (202) 874-5293. Julie L. Williams, Chief Counsel. Library, (202) 874-4720. Web, www.occ.treas.gov.*

Advises the comptroller on policy matters and programs related to bank corporate activities, and is the primary decision maker on national bank corporate applications, including charters, mergers, and acquisitions, conversions, and operating subsidiaries.

Federal Deposit Insurance Corp. (FDIC), *550 17th St. N.W. 20429; (202) 898-6974. Fax, (202) 898-3778. Donna Tanoue, Chair; Andrew C. Hove Jr., Vice Chair. Information, (800) 374-3405. Library, (202) 898-3631. Press, (202) 898-6993. Web, www.fdic.gov.*

Insures deposits in national banks, state banks, and savings and loans. Conducts examinations of insured state banks that are not members of the Federal Reserve System.

Federal Deposit Insurance Corp., *Resolutions and Receiverships, 1776 F St. N.W. 20429 (mailing address: 550 17th St. N.W. 20429); (202) 898-6779. Fax, (202) 898-7024. Gail Patelunas, Deputy Director.*

FEDERAL DEPOSIT INSURANCE CORPORATION

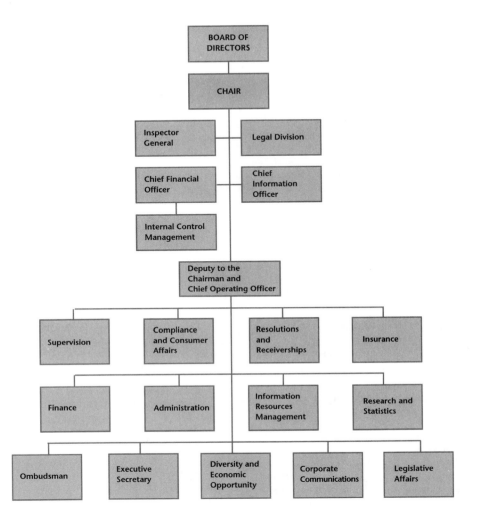

Plans, executes, and monitors the orderly and least cost resolution of failing FDIC insured institutions. Manages remaining liability of the federal savings and loan resolution fund.

Federal Deposit Insurance Corp., *Supervision, 550 17th St. N.W. 20429; (202) 898-8510. Fax, (202) 898-3638. James L. Sexton, Director.*

Serves as the federal regulator and supervisor of insured state banks that are not members of the Federal Reserve System. Conducts regular examinations and investigations of banks under the jurisdiction of FDIC;

advises bank managers on improving policies and practices. Administers the Bank Insurance Fund, which insures deposits in commercial and savings banks, and the Savings Association Insurance Fund, which insures deposits in savings and loan institutions.

Federal Reserve System, *Banking Supervision and Regulation, 20th and C Sts. N.W., #M3142 20551; (202) 452-2773. Fax, (202) 452-2770. Richard Spillenkothen, Director. Web, www.bog.frb.fed.us.*

Supervises and regulates state banks that are members of the Federal Reserve System; supervises and

FEDERAL RESERVE SYSTEM

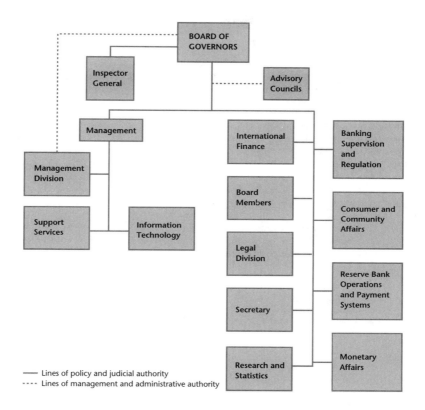

— Lines of policy and judicial authority
---- Lines of management and administrative authority

inspects all bank holding companies; monitors banking practices; approves bank mergers, consolidations, and other changes in bank structure.

Federal Reserve System, *Board of Governors,* *20th and C Sts. N.W. 20551; (202) 452-3201. Fax, (202) 452-3819. Alan Greenspan, Chair; Roger W. Ferguson Jr., Vice Chair. Information, (202) 452-3215. Press, (202) 452-3204. Locator, (202) 452-3000. Web, www.bog.frb.fed.us.*

Serves as the central bank and fiscal agent for the government. Examines Federal Reserve banks and state member banks; supervises bank holding companies. Controls wire system transfer operations and supplies currency for depository institutions.

National Credit Union Administration, *1775 Duke St., Alexandria, VA 22314-3428; (703) 518-6300. Fax, (703) 518-6319. Norman E. D'Amours, Chair. Information, (703) 518-6330. Electronic bulletin board, (703) 518-6480. Web, www.ncua.gov.*

Regulates all federally chartered credit unions; charters new credit unions; supervises and examines federal credit unions and insures their member accounts up to $100,000. Insures state-chartered credit unions that apply and are eligible. Manages the Central Liquidity Facility, which supplies emergency short-term loans to members. Conducts research on economic trends and their effect on credit unions and advises the administration's board on economic and financial policy and regulations.

Office of Management and Budget *(Executive Office of the President), Financial Institutions, New Executive Office Bldg., #9235 20503; (202) 395-7241. Fax, (202) 395-1292. James Boden, Chief. Web, www.whitehouse.gov/omb.*

Monitors the financial condition of deposit insurance funds including the Bank Insurance Fund, the Savings Association Insurance Fund, and the Federal Savings and Loan Insurance Corp. (FSLIC) Resolution Fund. Moni-

SECURITIES AND EXCHANGE COMMISSION

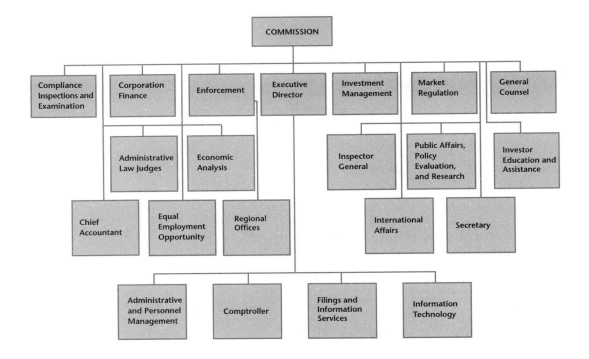

tors the Securities and Exchange Commission. Has limited oversight over the Federal Housing Finance Board and the Federal Home Loan Bank System.

Office of Thrift Supervision *(Treasury Dept.), 1700 G St. N.W. 20552; (202) 906-6280. Fax, (202) 898-0230. Ellen Seidman, Director. Information, (202) 906-6000. Library, (202) 906-6470. Press, (202) 906-6913. Mortgage rates recording, (202) 906-6988. Web, www.ots.treas.gov.*

Charters, regulates, and examines the operations of savings and loan institutions. Library open to the public.

Securities and Exchange Commission (SEC), *Corporation Finance, 450 5th St. N.W. 20549; (202) 942-2800. Fax, (202) 942-9525. David Martin, Director. Information, (202) 942-8088.*

Receives and examines disclosure statements and other information from publicly held companies, including bank holding companies.

Securities and Exchange Commission, *Economic Analysis, 450 5th St. N.W. 20549; (202) 942-8020. Fax, (202) 942-9657. Vacant, Chief Economist.*

Provides the commission with economic analyses of proposed rule and policy changes and other information to guide the SEC in influencing capital markets. Evaluates the effect of policy and other factors on competition within the securities industry and among competing securities markets; compiles financial statistics on capital formation and the securities industry.

Treasury Dept., *Financial Institutions, 1500 Pennsylvania Ave. N.W., #2326 20220; (202) 622-2600. Fax, (202) 622-2027. Gregory Baer, Assistant Secretary. Web, www. ustreas.gov.*

Advises the under secretary for domestic finance and the treasury secretary on financial institutions, banks, and thrifts.

CONGRESS

House Appropriations Committee, *Subcommittee on VA, HUD, and Independent Agencies, H143 CAP 20515; (202) 225-3241. Rep. James T. Walsh, R-N.Y., Chair; Frank Cushing, Staff Director. Web, www.house.gov/ appropriations.*

Jurisdiction over legislation to appropriate funds for the National Credit Union Administration.

House Banking and Financial Services Committee, Subcommittee on Financial Institutions and Consumer Credit, 2129 RHOB 20515; (202) 225-2258. Fax, (202) 225-6984. Rep. Marge Roukema, R-N.J., Chair; Laurie Schaffer, Staff Director. Web, www.house.gov/banking.

Jurisdiction over legislation regulating banking and financial institutions.

House Government Reform Committee, Subcommittee on National Economic Growth, Natural Resources, and Regulatory Affairs, B377 RHOB 20515; (202) 225-4407. Fax, (202) 225-2441. Rep. David M. McIntosh, R-Ind., Chair; Marlo Lewis, Staff Director. Web, www.house.gov/reform.

Oversees federal bank regulatory agencies, including the Federal Deposit Insurance Corp., National Credit Union Administration, and Export-Import Bank.

House Ways and Means Committee, Subcommittee on Oversight, 1136 LHOB 20515; (202) 225-7601. Fax, (202) 225-9680. Rep. Amo Houghton, R-N.Y., Chair; William McKenney, Staff Director. Web, www.house.gov/ ways_means.

Oversees government-sponsored enterprises, including the Federal Home Loan Bank System, with regard to the financial risk posed to the federal government.

Senate Appropriations Committee, Subcommittee on VA, HUD, and Independent Agencies, SD-130 20510; (202) 224-7211. Sen. Christopher S. Bond, R-Mo., Chair; Jon Kamarck, Staff Director. Web, appropriations.senate. gov/vahud.

Jurisdiction over legislation to appropriate funds for the National Credit Union Administration.

Senate Banking, Housing, and Urban Affairs Committee, SD-534 20510; (202) 224-7391. Fax, (202) 224-5137. Sen. Phil Gramm, R-Texas, Chair; Wayne A. Abernathy, Staff Director. Web, banking.senate.gov.

Jurisdiction over legislation regulating banking and financial institutions. Oversees federal bank regulatory agencies, including the Federal Deposit Insurance Corp., National Credit Union Administration, and Office of Thrift Supervision; also oversees government-sponsored enterprises, including the Federal Home Loan Bank System, with regard to the financial risk posed to the federal government.

NONPROFIT

American Bankers Assn., 1120 Connecticut Ave. N.W. 20036; (202) 663-5000. Fax, (202) 663-7533. Donald G.

Ogilvie, Executive Vice President. Information, (202) 663-5221. Library, (202) 663-5040. Web, www.aba.com.

Membership: commercial banks. Operates schools to train banking personnel; conducts conferences; formulates government relations policies for the banking community. Library open to the public by appointment.

American Council of State Savings Supervisors, P.O. Box 34175 20043-4175; (703) 922-5153. Fax, (703) 922-6237. Diane Homiak, Executive Director.

Membership: supervisors and regulators of state-chartered savings associations; associate members include state-chartered savings associations and state savings banks. Monitors legislation and regulations affecting the state-chartered thrift industry.

American Institute of Certified Public Accountants, Washington Office, 1455 Pennsylvania Ave. N.W., 4th Floor 20004-1081; (202) 737-6600. Fax, (202) 638-4512. John E. Hunnicutt, Senior Vice President. Press, (202) 434-9214. Web, www.aicpa.org.

Establishes voluntary professional and ethical regulations for the profession; sponsors conferences and training workshops. Answers technical auditing and accounting questions.

American League of Financial Institutions, 900 19th St. N.W., #400 20006-2105; (202) 857-5094. Fax, (202) 296-8716. Dina Curtis, President. Web, www.alfi.org.

Membership: minority-controlled community savings banks and savings associations. Helps promote small business; offers on-site technical assistance. Monitors legislative and regulatory issues.

American Savings Education Council, 2121 K St. N.W., #600 20037; (202) 659-0670. Fax, (202) 775-6360. Don M. Blandin, President. Web, www.asec.org.

Seeks to raise public awareness about long-term personal financial independence and encourage retirement savings. Sponsors workshops.

America's Community Bankers, 900 19th St. N.W., #400 20006; (202) 857-3100. Fax, (202) 296-8716. Diane M. Casey, President. Press, (202) 857-3103. General e-mail, info@acbankers.org. Web, www.acbankers.org.

Membership: insured depository institutions involved in community finance. Provides information and statistics on issues that affect the industry; sponsors conferences with international banks and savings and loan institutions. Monitors economic issues affecting savings institutions. Monitors legislation and regulations.

Assn. of Financial Services Holding Companies, 888 17th St. N.W., #312 20006; (202) 223-6575. Fax, (202)

331-3836. Patrick A. Forte, President. General e-mail, afshc@ibm.net.

Defends the authority of companies to affiliate with federally insured depository institutions while remaining outside the scope of the Bank Holding Company Act.

Associated Credit Bureaus, *1090 Vermont Ave. N.W., #200 20005-4905; (202) 371-0910. Fax, (202) 371-0134. Barry Connelly, President. Press, (202) 408-7406. General e-mail, acb@acb-credit.com. Web, www.acb-credit.com.*

Membership: credit reporting, mortgage reporting, and collection service companies. Provides information about credit rights to consumers. Monitors legislation and regulations.

Bank Marketing Assn., *1120 Connecticut Ave. N.W., 3rd Floor 20036; (202) 663-5268. Fax, (202) 828-4540. Douglas Adamson, Managing Director. Information, (800) 433-9013. Web, www.bmanet.org.*

Membership: financial institutions and firms that provide products and services to the financial industry. (Affiliate of the American Bankers Assn.)

Bankers' Assn. for Foreign Trade, *2121 K St. N.W., #701 20037; (202) 452-0952. Fax, (202) 452-0959. Mary Condeelis, Executive Director. Web, www.baft.org.*

Membership: U.S. commercial banks with major international operations; foreign banks with U.S. operations are affiliated as nonvoting members. Monitors activities that affect the operation of U.S. commercial banks.

Bankers' Roundtable, *805 15th St. N.W., #600 20005; (202) 289-4322. Fax, (202) 289-1903. Richard Whiting, Executive Director. Web, www.bankersround.org.*

Membership: bank holding companies registered with the Federal Reserve Board under the Bank Holding Company Act. Conducts research and provides information on banking and financial issues.

Conference of State Bank Supervisors, *1015 18th St. N.W., #1100 20036-5725; (202) 296-2840. Fax, (202) 296-1928. Neil Milner, President. Web, www.csbs.org.*

Membership: state officials responsible for supervision of state-chartered banking institutions. Conducts educational programs. Monitors legislation.

Consumer Bankers Assn., *1000 Wilson Blvd., #2500, Arlington, VA 22209; (703) 276-1750. Fax, (703) 528-1290. Joe Belew, President. Press, (703) 276-3880. Web, www.cbanet.org.*

Membership: federally insured financial institutions. Provides information on retail banking, including industry trends. Operates the Graduate School of Retail Bank

Management to train banking personnel; sponsors conferences.

Credit Union National Assn., *Washington Office, 805 15th St. N.W., #300 20005-2207; (202) 682-4200. Fax, (202) 682-9054. Daniel A. Mica, President. Web, www.cuna.org.*

Confederation of credit unions from every state, the District of Columbia, and Puerto Rico. Represents federal and state chartered credit unions. Monitors legislation and regulations.

Electronic Funds Transfer Assn., *950 Herndon Pkwy., #390, Herndon, VA 20170; (703) 435-9800. Fax, (703) 435-7157. H. Kurt Helwig, Executive Director. Web, www.efta.org.*

Membership: financial institutions, electronic funds transfer hardware and software providers, automatic teller machine networks, and others engaged in electronic commerce. Promotes electronic payments and commerce technologies; sponsors industry analysis. Monitors legislation and regulations.

Independent Bankers Assn. of America, *1 Thomas Circle N.W., #400 20005; (202) 659-8111. Fax, (202) 659-9216. Kenneth A. Guenther, Executive Vice President. Information, (800) 422-8439. General e-mail, info@ibaa.org.*

Membership: medium-sized and smaller community banks. Interests include farm credit, deregulation, interstate banking, deposit insurance, and financial industry standards.

Mortgage Bankers Assn. of America, *1919 Pennsylvania Ave. N.W. 20006; (202) 557-2700. Fax, (202) 721-0204. Paul Reid, Executive Vice President.*

Membership: institutions involved in real estate finance. Maintains School of Mortgage Banking and sponsors educational seminars; collects statistics on the industry. Library open to the public by appointment.

National Assn. of Federal Credit Unions, *3138 N. 10th St., Arlington, VA 22201; (703) 522-4770. Fax, (703) 524-1082. Fred Becker, President. Web, www.nafcunet.org.*

Membership: federally chartered credit unions. Represents interests of federal credit unions before Congress and regulatory agencies and provides legislative alerts for its members. Sponsors educational meetings focusing on current financial trends, changes in legislation and regulations, and management techniques.

National Assn. of State Credit Union Supervisors, *1655 N. Fort Meyer Dr., #300, Arlington, VA 22209; (703)*

528-8351. Fax, (703) 528-3248. Douglas Duerr, President. General e-mail, offices@nascus.org. Web, www.nascus.org.

Membership: state credit union supervisors, state-chartered credit unions, and credit union leagues. Interests include state regulatory systems; conducts educational programs for examiners.

National Automated Clearing House Assn., 13665 Dulles Technology Dr., #300, Herndon, VA 20171; (703) 561-1100. Fax, (703) 787-0996. Elliott C. McEntee, President. Web, www.nacha.org.

Membership: financial institutions involved in the automated clearing house (ACH) payment system. Establishes rules and standards for the ACH system; works for the development of technological and service innovation in electronic funds transfers; provides information for members. Sponsors workshops and seminars.

National Bankers Assn., 1513 P St. N.W. 20005; (202) 588-5432. Fax, (202) 588-5443. Norma Alexander Hart, President. Web, www.nationalbankers.org.

Membership: minority-owned banks and minority banking personnel. Monitors legislation and regulations affecting minority banking.

National Society of Accountants, 1010 N. Fairfax St., Alexandria, VA 22314-1574; (703) 549-6400. Fax, (703) 549-2984. William R. Mathisen, Executive Vice President. Web, www.nsacct.org.

Seeks to improve the accounting profession and to enhance the status of individual practitioners. Sponsors seminars and correspondence courses on accounting, auditing, business law, and estate planning; monitors legislation and regulations affecting accountants and their small-business clients.

Treasury Management Assn., 7315 Wisconsin Ave., #600W, Bethesda, MD 20814; (301) 907-2862. Fax, (301) 907-2864. James A. Kaitz, President. Web, www.tma-net.org.

Professional association that provides forum for ideas and perspectives on the treasury management profession and its role in the business environment. Supports treasury professionals through continuing education, professional certification (Certified Cash Manager and Certified Treasury Executive), publishing and information services, industry standards, and government relations.

Stocks, Bonds, and Securities

See also Federal Budget (this chapter)

AGENCIES

Bureau of the Public Debt *(Treasury Dept.), Savings Bonds Marketing,* 999 E St. N.W., #314 20226; (202) 691-3535. Fax, (202) 208-1574. Dino DeConcini, Executive Director. Information, (202) 219-3302. Web, www.savingsbonds.gov.

Promotes the sale and retention of U.S. savings bonds through educational and volunteer programs; administers the payroll savings plan for savings bonds.

Federal Reserve System, *Board of Governors,* 20th and C Sts. N.W. 20551; (202) 452-3201. Fax, (202) 452-3819. Alan Greenspan, Chair; Roger W. Ferguson Jr., Vice Chair. Information, (202) 452-3215. Press, (202) 452-3204. Locator, (202) 452-3000. Web, www.bog.frb.fed.us.

Regulates amount of credit that may be extended and maintained on certain securities in order to prevent excessive use of credit for purchase or carrying of securities.

Securities and Exchange Commission, 450 5th St. N.W. 20549; (202) 942-0100. Fax, (202) 942-9646. Arthur Levitt, Chair; James M. McConnell, Executive Director, (202) 942-4300. Press, (202) 942-0020. Investor Education and Assistance, (202) 942-7040. Locator, (202) 942-4150. Public Reference, (202) 942-8090. Web, www.sec.gov.

Requires public disclosure of financial and other information about companies whose securities are offered for public sale, traded on exchanges, or traded over the counter; issues and enforces regulations to prevent fraud in securities markets and investigates securities frauds and violations; supervises operations of stock exchanges and activities of securities dealers, investment advisers, and investment companies; regulates purchase and sale of securities, properties, and other assets of public utility holding companies and their subsidiaries; participates in bankruptcy proceedings involving publicly held companies; has some jurisdiction over municipal securities trading. Public Reference Section, (202) 942-8090, makes available corporation reports and statements filed with SEC. The information also is available via the Web (www.sec.gov/edgarhp.htm).

Securities and Exchange Commission, *Economic Analysis,* 450 5th St. N.W. 20549; (202) 942-8020. Fax, (202) 942-9657. Vacant, Chief Economist.

Provides the commission with economic analyses of proposed rule and policy changes and other information to guide the SEC in influencing capital markets. Evaluates the effect of policy and other factors on competition within the securities industry and among competing securities markets; compiles financial statistics on capital formation and the securities industry.

Securities and Exchange Commission, *Market Regulation,* 450 5th St. N.W. 20549; (202) 942-0090. Fax, (202) 942-9643. Anette Nazareth, Director. Library, (202) 942-7090.

Oversees and regulates the operations of securities markets, brokers, dealers, and transfer agents. Promotes the establishment of a national system for clearing and settling securities transactions. Works for standards among and oversees self-regulatory organizations, such as national securities exchanges, registered clearing agencies, and the National Assn. of Securities Dealers. Facilitates the development of a national market system.

Treasury Dept., *Financial Institutions Policy, 1500 Pennsylvania Ave. N.W., #3025 20220; (202) 622-2740. Fax, (202) 622-0256. Joan Affleck-Smith, Director. Web, www.ustreas.gov.*
Coordinates department efforts on all legislation affecting financial institutions and the government agencies that regulate them. Develops department policy on all matters relating to agencies responsible for supervising financial institutions and financial markets.

CONGRESS

House Commerce Committee, *Subcommittee on Telecommunications, Trade, and Consumer Protection, 2125 RHOB 20515; (202) 225-2927. Fax, (202) 225-1919. Rep. W. J. "Billy" Tauzin, R-La., Chair; James E. Derderian, Staff Director. General e-mail, commerce@mail.house. gov. Web, www.house.gov/commerce.*
Jurisdiction over stocks, bonds, stock exchanges, over-the-counter markets, mergers and acquisitions, and securities legislation; the Securities Investor Protection Corp.; the Federal Trade Commission; and the Securities and Exchange Commission.

House Government Reform Committee, *Subcommittee on National Economic Growth, Natural Resources, and Regulatory Affairs, B377 RHOB 20515; (202) 225-4407. Fax, (202) 225-2441. Rep. David M. McIntosh, R-Ind., Chair; Marlo Lewis, Staff Director. Web, www.house.gov/reform.*
Investigates investment fraud schemes and commodities and securities fraud. Oversees operations of the Securities and Exchange Commission.

Senate Banking, Housing, and Urban Affairs Committee, *Subcommittee on Securities, SD-534 20510; (202) 224-7391. Fax, (202) 224-5137. Sen. Rod Grams, R-Minn., Chair; Mark Olson, Staff Director. Web, banking. senate.gov.*
Jurisdiction over stocks, bonds, stock exchanges, over-the-counter markets, mergers and acquisitions, and securities legislation; the Securities Investor Protection Corp.; and the Securities and Exchange Commission.

Senate Governmental Affairs Committee, *Permanent Subcommittee on Investigations, SR-100 20510;* *(202) 224-3721. Fax, (202) 224-7042. Sen. Susan Collins, R-Maine, Chair; K. Lee Blalack, Staff Director. General e-mail, PSI@govt-aff.senate.gov. Web, gov_affairs.senate. gov/psi.htm.*
Investigates investment fraud schemes and commodities and securities fraud.

NONPROFIT

Assn. of Publicly Traded Companies, *1200 G St. N.W. 20005; (202) 434-8983. Fax, (202) 828-6042. Brian T. Borders, President.*
Membership: companies that issue stock into public capital markets. Promotes fair and efficient capital markets and the ability to manage corporate affairs free from unnecessary government interference. Interests include taxation and accounting rules under the purview of the Financial Accounting Standards Board. Monitors legislation and regulations.

Bond Market Assn., *Washington Office, 1445 New York Ave. N.W., 8th Floor 20005; (202) 434-8400. Fax, (202) 737-4744. John Vogt, Executive Vice President. Web, www. bondmarket.com.*
Membership: banks, dealers, and brokers who underwrite, trade, and sell municipal securities, mortgage-backed securities, and government and federal agency securities. Acts as an information and education center for the public securities industry.

Council of Institutional Investors, *1730 Rhode Island Ave. N.W., #512 20036; (202) 822-0800. Fax, (202) 822-0801. Sarah Teslik, Executive Director. Web, www. ciicentral.com.*
Membership: public, union, and corporate pension funds. Studies investment issues that affect pension plan assets. Monitors legislation and regulations.

Futures Industry Assn., *2001 Pennsylvania Ave. N.W., #600 20006; (202) 466-5460. Fax, (202) 296-3184. John M. Damgard, President. Web, www.fiafii.org.*
Membership: commodity futures brokerage firms and others interested in commodity futures. Serves as a forum for discussion of futures industry; provides market information and statistical data; offers educational programs; works to establish professional and ethical standards for members.

Investment Company Institute, *1401 H St. N.W., 12th Floor 20005-2148; (202) 326-5800. Fax, (202) 326-5806. Matthew P. Fink, President. Web, www.ici.org.*
Membership: mutual funds and closed-end funds registered under the Investment Company Act of 1940 (including investment advisers to and underwriters of such companies) and the unit investment trust industry.

Conducts research and disseminates information on issues affecting mutual funds.

Investment Program Assn., *1101 17th St. N.W., #703 20036; (202) 775-9750. Fax, (202) 331-8446. Christopher L. Davis, President. Web, www.ipa-dc.org.*

Membership: broker/dealer organizations and sponsors, law and accounting firms, financial planners, and partnership consultants. Works to preserve limited partnerships and real estate investment trusts as a form of investment and a source of new capital for the economy. Conducts economic research. Monitors legislation and regulations, especially those concerning tax policy.

Investor Responsibility Research Center, *1350 Connecticut Ave. N.W., #700 20036-1702; (202) 833-0700. Fax, (202) 833-3555. Scott Fenn, Executive Director. General e-mail, irrc@aol.com. Web, www.irrc.org.*

Research organization that reports on and analyzes business and public policy issues affecting corporations and investors.

Municipal Securities Rulemaking Board, *1150 18th St. N.W., #400 20036; (202) 223-9347. Fax, (202) 872-0347. Christopher A. Taylor, Executive Director. Web, www.msrb.org.*

Writes rules, subject to approval by the Securities and Exchange Commission, applicable to municipal securities brokers and dealers, in such areas as conduct, industry practices, and professional qualifications. Serves as a self-regulatory agency for the municipal securities industry.

National Assn. of Bond Lawyers, *Governmental Affairs, Washington Office, 601 13th St., #800-S 20005-3875; (202) 682-1498. Fax, (202) 637-0217. William L. Larsen, Director. Web, www.nabl.org.*

Membership: municipal finance lawyers. Provides members with information on laws relating to the borrowing of money by states and municipalities and to the issuance of state and local government bonds. Monitors legislation and regulations.

National Assn. of Real Estate Investment Trusts, *1875 Eye St. N.W., #600 20006; (202) 739-9400. Fax, (202) 739-9401. Steve Wechsler, President. Web, www. nareit.com.*

Membership: real estate investment trusts and corporations, partnerships, and individuals interested in real estate securities and the industry. Monitors federal and state legislation, federal taxation, securities regulation, standards and ethics, and housing and education; compiles industry statistics.

National Assn. of Securities Dealers (NASD), *1735 K St. N.W. 20006-1506; (202) 728-8000. Fax, (202) 728-8075. Frank G. Zarb, President. Member services, (301) 590-6500. Public disclosure, (800) 289-9999. Web, www.nasd.com.*

Membership: investment brokers and dealers authorized to conduct transactions of the investment banking and securities business under federal and state laws. Serves as the self-regulatory mechanism in the over-the-counter securities market. Operates speakers bureau. (Affiliated with NASD Regulation Inc. and Nasdaq Stock Market.)

National Investor Relations Institute, *8045 Leesburg Pike, #600, Vienna, VA 22182; (703) 506-3570. Fax, (703) 506-3571. Louis M. Thompson Jr., President. Web, www.niri.org.*

Membership: executives engaged in investor relations and financial communications. Provides publications, educational training sessions, and research on investor relations for members; offers conferences and workshops; maintains job placement and referral services for its members.

New York Stock Exchange, *Washington Office, 801 Pennsylvania Ave. N.W., #603 20004; (202) 347-4300. Fax, (202) 347-4370. Sheila Bair, Senior Vice President. Web, www.nyse.com.*

Provides limited information on operations of the New York Stock Exchange; Washington office monitors legislation and regulations.

North American Securities Administrators Assn., *10 G St. N.E., #710 20002; (202) 737-0900. Fax, (202) 783-3571. Marc Beauchamp, Executive Director. Web, www. nasaa.org.*

Membership: state, provincial, and territorial securities administrators of the United States, Canada, and Mexico. Serves as the national representative of the state agencies responsible for investor protection. Works to prevent fraud in securities markets and provides a national forum to increase the efficiency and uniformity of state regulation of capital markets. Operates the Central Registration Depository, a nationwide computer link for agent registration and transfers, in conjunction with the National Assn. of Securities Dealers. Monitors legislation and regulations.

Securities Industry Assn., *Washington Office, 1401 Eye St. N.W., #1000 20005-2225; (202) 296-9410. Fax, (202) 296-9775. Marc E. Lackritz, President. General e-mail, info@sia.com. Web, www.sia.com.*

Membership: investment bankers, securities underwriters, and dealers in stocks and bonds. Represents all segments of the securities industry. Monitors legislation, regulations, and international agreements.

Securities Investor Protection Corp., *805 15th St. N.W., #800 20005-2207; (202) 371-8300. Fax, (202) 371-6728. Clifford Hudson, Chair; Debbie D. Branson, Vice Chair. Web, www.sipc.org.*

Private corporation established by Congress to administer the Securities Investor Protection Act. Provides financial protection for customers of member broker-dealers that fail financially.

Tangible Assets

See also Coins and Currency (this chapter)

AGENCIES

Census Bureau *(Commerce Dept.), Manufacturing and Construction: Construction and Minerals, #2229, Bldg. 4 20233; (301) 457-4680. Fax, (301) 457-2059. Patricia L. Horning, Chief.*

Collects, tabulates, and publishes statistics for the mining and construction sectors of the Economic Census; collects and tabulates data for manufacturing energy consumption survey for the Energy Dept. concerning the domestic construction minerals industry.

Commodity Futures Trading Commission, *3 Lafayette Center, 1155 21st St. N.W. 20581; (202) 418-5030. Fax, (202) 418-5525. William J. Rainier, Chair; Don Tendick, Executive Director (Acting). Information, (202) 418-5000. Library, (202) 418-5255. Web, www.cftc.gov.*

Enforces federal statutes relating to commodity futures and options, including gold and silver futures and options. Monitors and regulates gold and silver leverage contracts, which provide for deferred delivery of the commodity and the payment of an agreed portion of the purchase price on margin.

Defense Logistics Agency *(Defense Dept.), Defense National Stockpile Center, 8725 John Jay Kingman Rd., #4528, Fort Belvoir, VA 22060-6223; (703) 767-5500. Fax, (703) 767-5538. Richard J. Connelly, Administrator. Web, www.dnsc.dla.mil.*

Manages the national defense stockpile of strategic and critical materials. Purchases strategic materials including beryllium and newly developed high-tech alloys. Disposes of excess materials including tin, silver, industrial diamond stones, tungsten, and vegetable tannin.

Federal Reserve System, *Accounting and Budgets, 20th and C Sts. N.W., MS-194 20551; (202) 452-2265. Fax, (202) 872-7574. Dorothy Lachatelle, Manager.*

Monitors gold certificate accounts and budgets of Federal Reserve Banks. (Gold certificate accounts are credits issued by the Treasury Dept. against gold held by the Treasury.)

U.S. Geological Survey *(Interior Dept.), Metals, 12201 Sunrise Valley Dr., MS 989, Reston, VA 20192; (703) 648-4968. Fax, (703) 648-7757. Mike McKinley, Chief; Earle B. Amey, Gold; Henry E. Hilliard, Silver and Platinum Group Metals; Daniel Edelstein, Copper. Web, minerals. usgs.gov/minerals.*

Studies supply and demand of copper, precious metals (including gold, silver, and platinum group metals), and ferrous metals (iron, iron ore, steel, chromium, and nickel); collects and provides statistical data on production and consumption of precious metals; provides information on gold and silver research, production, and processing methods. (CD-ROMs may be purchased from the Government Printing Office, [202] 512-1800.)

U.S. Mint *(Treasury Dept.), 801 9th St. N.W. 20220; (202) 354-7200. Fax, (202) 756-6160. Philip N. Diehl, Director. Information, (202) 354-7227. Web, www.usmint. gov.*

Produces gold, silver, and platinum coins for sale to investors.

See also Census Bureau, Foreign Trade (p. 252)

CONGRESS

House Banking and Financial Services Committee, *Subcommittee on Domestic and International Monetary Policy, B304 RHOB 20515; (202) 226-0473. Fax, (202) 226-0537. Rep. Spencer Bachus, R-Ala., Chair; James McCormick, Staff Director. Web, www.house.gov/ banking.*

Jurisdiction over legislation to regulate transactions in gold and precious metals.

Senate Banking, Housing, and Urban Affairs Committee, *Subcommittee on International Trade and Finance, SD-534 20510; (202) 224-7391. Fax, (202) 224-5137. Sen. Michael B. Enzi, R-Wyo., Chair; Katherine McGuire, Staff Director. Web, banking.senate.gov.*

Jurisdiction over legislation to regulate international transactions in gold and precious metals.

NONPROFIT

Gold Institute, *1112 16th St. N.W., #240 20036; (202) 835-0185. Fax, (202) 835-0155. John Lutley, President. Web, www.goldinstitute.org.*

Membership: companies that mine, refine, fabricate, or manufacture gold or gold-containing products; wholesalers of physical gold investment products; banks; and gold bullion dealers. Conducts research on new technological and industrial uses for gold. Compiles statistics by country on mine production of gold; coinage use; and the production, distribution, and use of refined gold.

Silver Institute, *1112 16th St. N.W., #240 20036; (202) 835-0185. Fax, (202) 835-0155. Paul Bateman, Executive Director. Web, www.silverinstitute.org.*

Membership: companies that mine, refine, fabricate, or manufacture silver or silver-containing products. Conducts research on new technological and industrial uses for silver. Compiles statistics by country on mine production of silver; coinage use; the production, distribution, and use of refined silver; and the conversion of refined silver into other forms, such as silverware and jewelry.

Silver Users Assn., *1730 M St. N.W., #911 20036-4505; (202) 785-3050. Walter L. Frankland Jr., Executive Vice President.*

Membership: users of silver, including the photographic industry, silversmiths, and other manufacturers. Conducts research on silver market; monitors government activities in silver; analyzes government statistics on silver consumption and production.

See also American Society of Appraisers and Appraisal Institute (p. 434)

☑ INDUSTRIAL PRODUCTION/ MANUFACTURING

See also Construction (chap. 12); Motor Vehicles (chap. 19)

AGENCIES

Bureau of Export Administration (*Commerce Dept.*), *Strategic Industries and Economic Security,* 14th St. and Constitution Ave. N.W., #3876 20230; (202) 482-4506. Fax, (202) 482-5650. William Denk, Director (Acting). Web, www.bxa.doc.gov.

Assists in providing for an adequate supply of strategic and critical materials for defense activities and civilian needs, including military requirements, and other domestic energy supplies; develops plans for industry to meet national emergencies. Studies the effect of imports on national security and recommends actions.

Census Bureau (*Commerce Dept.*), *Manufacturing and Construction,* Suitland and Silver Hill Rds., Suitland, MD 20233; (301) 457-4593. Fax, (301) 457-4583. William G. Bostic Jr., Chief.

Collects and distributes manufacturing, construction, and mineral industry data. Reports are organized by commodity, industry, and geographic area.

Economic Development Administration (*Commerce Dept.*), *Trade Adjustment Assistance,* 14th St. and Constitution Ave. N.W., #7315 20230; (202) 482-2127. Fax, (202) 482-0466. Tony Meyer, Coordinator.

Assists U.S. firms in increasing their competitiveness against foreign imports. Certifies eligibility and provides domestic firms and industries adversely affected by foreign trade with technical assistance under provisions of the Trade Act of 1974. Administers twelve regional Trade Adjustment Administrative Centers which offer consulting services to eligible U.S. firms.

Economics and Statistics Administration (*Commerce Dept.*), 14th St. and Constitution Ave. N.W., #4848 20230; (202) 482-3727. Fax, (202) 482-0432. Robert J. Shapiro, Under Secretary. Information, (202) 482-2235. General e-mail, esa@doc.gov.

Advises the secretary on economic policy matters, including consumer and capital spending, inventory status, and the short- and long-term outlook in output and unemployment. Seeks to improve economic productivity and growth. Serves as departmental liaison with the Council of Economic Advisers and other government agencies concerned with economic policy. Supervises and sets policy for the Census Bureau and the Bureau of Economic Analysis.

International Trade Administration (*Commerce Dept.*), *Basic Industries,* 14th St. and Constitution Ave. N.W., #4043 20230; (202) 482-0614. Fax, (202) 482-5666. Alan S. Bowser, Deputy Assistant Secretary.

Analyzes and maintains data on domestic and international industries, including metals, materials, chemicals, construction, forest products, energy, automotives, and industrial machinery; responds to government and business inquiries about materials shortages in specific industries. Analyzes supply and demand, capacity and production capability, and capital formation requirements.

Technology Administration (*Commerce Dept.*), *Technology Competitiveness,* 1401 Constitution Ave. N.W., #4418 20230; (202) 482-2100. Fax, (202) 219-8667. Jon Paugh, Director, (202) 482-6101. Library, (202) 482-1288. Press, (202) 482-8321. Law library, (202) 482-5517. Publications request, (202) 482-1397. Web, www.ta.doc.gov.

Encourages industrial research to promote U.S. competitiveness and economic security. Increases private access to federally developed technology by encouraging industry involvement in research conducted at federal laboratories.

CONGRESS

Senate Commerce, Science, and Transportation Committee, *Subcommittee on Manufacturing and Competitiveness, SD-508 20510 (mailing address: SD-508 20510); (202) 224-1745. Fax, (202) 224-8834. Sen. Spencer Abraham, R-Mich., Chair; Gregg Willhauck, Legislative Counsel. Web, commerce.senate.gov.*

Jurisdiction over industrial policy and general manufacturing issues, including investment, innovation, job creation, deregulation, corporate subsidies, and competitiveness.

NONPROFIT

American National Standards Institute (ANSI), *Conformity Assessment, Washington Office, 1819 L St. N.W., #600 20006; (301) 469-3360. John Donaldson, Vice President. Customer service, (888) 267-4783. General e-mail, info@ansi.org. Web, www.ansi.org.*

Administers and coordinates the voluntary standardization system for the U.S. private sector; maintains staff contacts for specific industries. Serves as U.S. member of the International Organization for Standardization (ISO) and hosts the U.S. National Committee of the International Electrotechnical Commission (IEC). (ANSI headquarters in New York.)

APICS, The Educational Society for Resource Management, *5301 Shawnee Rd., Alexandria, VA 22312; (703) 354-8851. Fax, (703) 354-8785. Jeffry Raynes, Executive Director. Web, www.apics.org.*

Membership: integrated resource management professionals in the manufacturing and service industries. Offers certification exams in production and inventory management and integrated resource management; provides job placement assistance; conducts workshops and symposia. Formerly the American Production and Inventory Control Society.

Assn. for Manufacturing Technology, *7901 Westpark Dr., McLean, VA 22102; (703) 893-2900. Fax, (703) 893-1151. Don Carlson, President. Web, www.mfgtech.org.*

Supports the U.S. manufacturing industry; sponsors workshops and seminars; fosters safety and technical standards. Monitors legislation and regulations.

Envelope Manufacturers Assn., *300 N. Washington St., #500, Alexandria, VA 22314-2530; (703) 739-2200. Fax, (703) 739-2209. Maynard H. Benjamin, President. Web, www.envelope.org.*

Membership: envelope manufacturers and suppliers. Monitors legislation and regulations.

Flexible Packaging Assn., *1090 Vermont Ave. N.W., #500 20005-4960; (202) 842-3880. Fax, (202) 842-3841.*

John Woolford, President (Interim). General e-mail, fpa@flexpack.org.

Researches packaging trends and technical developments; compiles industry statistics. Monitors legislation and regulations.

Independent Lubricant Manufacturers Assn., *651 S. Washington St., Alexandria, VA 22314; (703) 684-5574. Fax, (703) 836-8503. Richard H. Ekfelt, Executive Director. Web, www.ilma.org.*

Membership: U.S. and international companies that manufacture automotive, industrial, and metalworking lubricants; associates include suppliers and related businesses. Conducts workshops and conferences; compiles statistics. Monitors legislation and regulations.

Independent Office Products and Furniture Dealers Assn., *301 N. Fairfax St., Alexandria, VA 22314; (703) 549-9040. Fax, (703) 683-7552. Jim McGarry, President. Information, (800) 542-6672. Web, www.bpia.org.*

Membership: independent dealers of office products and office furniture. Serves independent dealers and works with their trading partners to develop programs and opportunities that help strengthen the dealer position in the marketplace.

Industrial Designers Society of America, *1142 Walker Rd., Great Falls, VA 22066-1836; (703) 759-0100. Fax, (703) 759-7679. Robert Schwartz, Executive Director. General e-mail, idsa@erols.com. Web, www.idsa.org.*

Membership: designers of products, equipment, instruments, furniture, transportation, packages, exhibits, information services, and related services. Provides the Bureau of Labor Statistics with industry information. Monitors legislation and regulations.

Industrial Research Institute, *1550 M St. N.W., #1100 20005-1712; (202) 296-8811. Fax, (202) 776-0756. Charles F. Larson, President. Web, www.iriinc.org.*

Membership: companies that maintain laboratories for industrial research. Seeks to improve the process of industrial research by promoting cooperative efforts among companies, between the academic and research communities, and between industry and the government. Monitors legislation and regulations concerning technology, industry, and national competitiveness.

Institute of Packaging Professionals, *481 Carlisle Dr., Herndon, VA 20170-4823; (703) 318-8970. Fax, (703) 814-4961. William C. Pflaum, Executive Director. General e-mail, info@pkgmatters.com. Web, www.packinfo-world.org.*

Represents the interests of packaging professionals. Conducts an annual packaging design competition. Publishes journals and newsletters.

International Sleep Products Assn., *501 Wythe St., Alexandria, VA 22314; (703) 683-8371. Fax, (703) 683-4503. Russell L. Abolt, Executive Vice President. Web, www.sleepproducts.org.*

Membership: manufacturers of bedding and mattresses. Compiles statistics on the industry. (Affiliated with Sleep Products Safety Council and the Better Sleep Council.)

International Union of Electronic, Electrical, Salaried, Machine, and Furniture Workers, *1126 16th St. N.W. 20036; (202) 785-7200. Fax, (202) 785-7441. Edward L. Fire, President, (202) 785-7201. Web, www.iue.org.*

Membership: approximately 125,000 workers in the field of industrial electronics and furniture and general manufacturing. Helps members negotiate pay, benefits, and better working conditions; conducts training programs and workshops. (Affiliated with the AFL-CIO.)

Manufacturers' Alliance for Productivity and Innovation, *1525 Wilson Blvd., #900, Arlington, VA 22209; (703) 841-9000. Fax, (703) 841-9514. Tom Duesterberg, President. Web, www.mapi.net.*

Membership: companies involved in high technology industries, including electronics, telecommunications, precision instruments, computers, and the automotive and aerospace industries. Seeks to increase industrial productivity. Conducts research; organizes discussion councils. Monitors legislation and regulations.

National Assn. of Manufacturers, *1331 Pennsylvania Ave. N.W., #600 20004-1790; (202) 637-3000. Fax, (202) 637-3182. Jerry Jasinowski, President. Press, (202) 637-3094. Web, www.nam.org.*

Represents industry views (mainly of manufacturers) to government on national and international issues. Reviews legislation, administrative rulings, and judicial decisions affecting industry. Sponsors the Human Resources Forum; operates a Web site for members and the public that provides information on legislative and other news; conducts programs on labor relations, occupational safety and health, regulatory and consumer affairs, environmental trade and technology, and other business issues.

National Coalition for Advanced Manufacturing, *1201 New York Ave., #725 20005; (202) 216-2740. Fax, (202) 289-7618. Leo Reddy, President. Information, (800) 622-3260. General e-mail, NACFAM@aol.com. Web, www. nacfam.org.*

Seeks a public policy environment more supportive of advanced manufacturing and industrial modernization as keys to global economic competitiveness. Advo-cates greater national focus on industrial base modernization, increased investment in plant and equipment, accelerated development and deployment of advanced manufacturing technology, and reform of technical education and training. (Affiliated with the Foundation for Industrial Modernization.)

National Industrial Council, *1331 Pennsylvania Ave. N.W., #600 20004-1790; (202) 637-3053. Fax, (202) 637-3182. Barry Buzby, Executive Director, State Associations, (202) 637-3054; Mark Stuart, Executive Director, Employer Associations, (202) 637-3052. Web, www.nam.org.*

Membership: employer associations at the regional, state, and local levels. Works to strengthen U.S. competitive enterprise system. Represents views of industry on business and economic issues; sponsors conferences and seminars. (Affiliated with the National Assn. of Manufacturers.)

Paper Allied-Industrial, Chemical, and Energy Workers International Union, *Washington Office, 1155 15th St. N.W., #405 20005; (703) 876-9300. Fax, (703) 876-8952. Paula R. Littles, Legislative Director.*

Membership: approximately 310,000 workers in the energy, chemical, pharmaceutical, and allied industries. Assists members with contract negotiation and grievances; conducts training programs and workshops. Monitors legislation and regulations.

Rubber Manufacturers Assn., *1400 K St. N.W., #900 20005; (202) 682-4800. Fax, (202) 682-4854. Donald Shea, President. Information, (800) 220-7622. Web, www.rma.org.*

Membership: manufacturers of tires, tubes, roofing, sporting goods, and mechanical and industrial products. Interests include recycling.

U.S. Business and Industrial Council, *910 16th St. N.W., #300 20006; (202) 728-1980. Fax, (202) 728-1981. Kevin L. Kearns, President. General e-mail, usbic@aol.com.*

Advocates energy independence, reindustrialization, and effective use of natural resources and manufacturing capacity. Current issues include business tax reduction, the liability crisis, defense and other federal spending, and the trade deficit. Media network distributes op-ed pieces to newspapers and radio stations.

Clothing and Textiles

See also Cotton (chap. 2)

AGENCIES

Federal Trade Commission, *Consumer Protection: Enforcement, 601 Pennsylvania Ave. N.W., 4th Floor*

20580; (202) 326-3238. Fax, (202) 326-2558. Joan Z. Bernstein, Director. Identity Fraud report line, (877) IDTHEFT. Web, www.ftc.gov.

Enforces regulations dealing with unfair or deceptive business practices in advertising, credit, marketing, and service industries; educates consumers and business about these regulations; conducts investigations and litigation.

International Trade Administration *(Commerce Dept.), Textiles, Apparel, and Consumer Goods Industries, 14th St. and Constitution Ave. N.W., #3001A 20230; (202) 482-3737. Fax, (202) 482-2331. Troy H. Cribb, Deputy Assistant Secretary.*

Participates in negotiating bilateral textile and apparel import restraint agreements; responsible for textile, apparel, and consumer goods export expansion programs and reduction of nontariff barriers; provides data on economic conditions in the domestic textile, apparel, and consumer goods markets, including impact of imports.

NONPROFIT

American Apparel Manufacturers Assn., *2500 Wilson Blvd., #301, Arlington, VA 22201; (703) 524-1864. Fax, (703) 522-6741. Larry K. Martin, President. Information, (800) 520-2262. Web, www.americanapparel.org.*

Membership: manufacturers of apparel and allied needle-trade products. Interests include product flammability.

American Fiber Manufacturers Assn., *1150 17th St. N.W., #310 20036; (202) 296-6508. Fax, (202) 296-3052. Paul T. O'Day, President. General e-mail, afma@afma.org. Web, www.fibersource.com.*

Membership: U.S. producers of manufactured (man-made) fibers, filaments, and yarns. Interests include international trade, education, and environmental and technical services. Monitors legislation and regulations.

American Textile Machinery Assn., *111 Park Pl., Falls Church, VA 22046; (703) 538-1789. Fax, (703) 241-5603. Harry W. Buzzerd Jr., Executive Vice President. Web, www. atmanet.org.*

Membership: U.S.-based manufacturers of textile machinery and related parts and accessories. Interests include competitiveness and expansion of foreign markets. Monitors legislation and regulations.

American Textile Manufacturers Institute, *1130 Connecticut Ave. N.W., #1200 20036-3954; (202) 862-0500. Fax, (202) 862-0570. Carlos F. J. Moore, Executive Vice President. Web, www.atmi.org.*

Membership: U.S. companies that spin, weave, knit, or finish textiles from natural fibers, and associate members from affiliated industries. Interests include domestic and world markets. Monitors legislation and regulations.

Footwear Distributors and Retailers of America, *1319 F St. N.W., #700 20004; (202) 737-5660. Fax, (202) 638-2615. Peter T. Mangione, President. Web, www.fdra. org.*

Membership: companies that operate shoe retail outlets. Provides business support and government relations to members. Interests include intellectual property rights, ocean shipping rates, trade with China, and labeling regulations.

Footwear Industries of America, *1420 K St. N.W., #600 20005; (202) 789-1420. Fax, (202) 789-4058. Fawn Evenson, President. General e-mail, Info@fia.org. Web, www.fia.org.*

Membership: manufacturers of footwear and their suppliers, importers, and distributors. Provides members with information on the industry, including import and export data. Monitors legislation and regulations.

International Fabricare Institute, *12251 Tech Rd., Silver Spring, MD 20904; (301) 622-1900. Fax, (301) 236-9320. William E. Fisher, Executive Vice President. Web, www.ifi.org.*

Membership: dry cleaners and launderers. Conducts research and provides information on products and services. Monitors legislation and regulations.

National Cotton Council of America, *Washington Office, 1521 New Hampshire Ave. N.W. 20036; (202) 745-7805. Fax, (202) 483-4040. John Maguire, Vice President. Web, www.cotton.org/ncc.*

Membership: all segments of the U.S. cotton industry. Formulates positions on trade policy and negotiations; seeks to improve competitiveness of U.S. exports; sponsors programs to educate the public about flammable fabrics.

Uniform and Textile Service Assn., *1300 N. 17th St., #750, Arlington, VA 22209; (703) 247-2600. Fax, (703) 841-4750. David F. Hobson, President. General e-mail, info@utsa.com. Web, www.utsa.com.*

Membership: companies that provide uniforms and textile products to commercial and government enterprises. Sponsors seminars and conferences; provides information on environmental policy and procedures to members. Monitors legislation and regulations.

Union of Needletrades Industrial and Textile Employees, *Washington Office, 888 16th St. N.W., #303*

20006; (202) 347-7417. Fax, (202) 347-0708. Ann Hoff-man, Legislative Director. General e-mail, stopsweatshops@uniteunion.org. Web, www.uniteunion.org.

Membership: approximately 285,000 workers in basic apparel and textiles, millinery, shoe, laundry, retail, and related industries; and in auto parts and auto supply. Assists members with contract negotiation and griev-ances; conducts training programs and workshops. Mon-itors legislation and regulations.

Electronics and Appliances

NONPROFIT

Consumer Electronics Assn., 2500 Wilson Blvd., Arlington, VA 22201-3834; (703) 907-7600. Fax, (703) 907-7601. Gary Shapiro, President. Web, www.ce.org.

Membership: U.S. consumer electronics manufactur-ers. Promotes the industry; sponsors seminars and con-ferences; conducts research; consults with member companies. Monitors legislation and regulations. (Affili-ated with Electronic Industries Alliance.)

Electronic Industries Alliance, 2500 Wilson Blvd., #400, Arlington, VA 22201-3834; (703) 907-7500. Fax, (703) 907-7501. Dave McCurdy, President. Web, www.eia.org.

Membership: manufacturers, dealers, installers, and distributors of consumer electronics products. Provides consumer information and data on industry trends; advocates an open market. Monitors legislation and reg-ulations.

Gas Appliance Manufacturers Assn., 1901 N. Moore St., #1100, Arlington, VA 22209; (703) 525-9565. Fax, (703) 525-0718. C. Reuben Autery, President. General e-mail, information@gamanet.org. Web, www.gamanet.org.

Membership: manufacturers of gas appliances and equipment for residential and commercial use and related industries. Advocates product improvement; pro-vides market statistics. Monitors legislation and regula-tions.

National Electrical Contractors Assn., 3 Bethesda Metro Center, #1100, Bethesda, MD 20814; (301) 657-3110. Fax, (301) 215-4500. John Grau, Executive Vice President. Web, www.necanet.org.

Membership: electrical contractors who build and service electrical wiring, equipment, and appliances. Represents members in collective bargaining with union workers; sponsors research and educational programs.

Optoelectronics Industry Development Assn., 2010 Massachusetts Ave. N.W., #200 20036-1023; (202) 785-4426. Fax, (202) 785-4428. Fred Welsh, Executive Director. Web, www.oida.org.

Membership: users and suppliers of optoelectronics in North America. Promotes the global competitiveness of members; provides a forum for exchange of informa-tion; conducts workshops and conferences; sponsors research. Monitors legislation and regulations.

Steel, Metalworking, Machinery

NONPROFIT

American Boiler Manufacturers Assn., 950 N. Glebe Rd., #160, Arlington, VA 22203; (703) 522-7350. Fax, (703) 522-2665. Russell N. Mosher, President. Web, www.abma.com.

Membership: manufacturers of boiler systems and boiler-related products, including fuel-burning systems. Interests include energy and environmental issues.

American Gear Manufacturers Assn., 1500 King St., #201, Alexandria, VA 22314; (703) 684-0211. Fax, (703) 684-0242. Joe T. Franklin, President. Web, www.agma.org.

Membership: gear manufacturers, suppliers, and industry consultants. Conducts workshops, seminars, and conferences; develops industry standards; sponsors research. Monitors legislation and regulations.

American Institute for International Steel, 1325 G St. N.W., #980 20005; (202) 628-3878. Fax, (202) 737-3134. David Phelps, Executive Director. General e-mail, aiis@msn.com. Web, www.aiis.org.

Membership: importers and exporters of steel. Con-ducts research on manufacturing processes. Holds annual conferences.

American Machine Tool Distributors Assn., 1445 Research Blvd., #450, Rockville, MD 20850; (301) 738-1200. Fax, (301) 738-9499. Ralph Nappi, President. Infor-mation, (800) 878-2683. Web, www.amtda.org.

Membership: distributors of machine tools. Supports advances in manufacturing and expansion of interna-tional trade. Monitors legislation and regulations.

American Wire Producers Assn., 6232 Roudsby Lane, Alexandria, VA 22315-5285; (703) 971-6454. Fax, (703) 971-6997. Kimberly Korbel, Executive Director. General e-mail, info@awpa.org. Web, www.awpa.org.

Membership: companies that produce carbon, alloy, and stainless steel wire and wire products in the United States. Interests include imports of rod, wire, and wire products and enforcement of antidumping and counter-vailing duty laws. Publishes survey of the domestic wire industry. Monitors legislation and regulations.

Cold Finished Steel Bar Institute, *111 Park Pl., Falls Church, VA 22046; (703) 538-1788. Fax, (703) 241-5603. Lane Pate, President. Web, www.cfsbi.com.*

Promotes the industry of cold finished steel bar production. Conducts research; sponsors annual award. Monitors legislation and regulations.

International Assn. of Bridge, Structural, Ornamental, and Reinforcing Iron Workers, *1750 New York Ave. N.W., #400 20006; (202) 383-4800. Fax, (202) 638-4856. Jake West, President.*

Membership: approximately 82,000 iron workers. Helps members negotiate pay, benefits, and better working conditions; conducts training programs and workshops. Monitors legislation and regulations. (Affiliated with the AFL-CIO.)

International Assn. of Machinists and Aerospace Workers, *9000 Machinists Pl., Upper Marlboro, MD 20772-2687; (301) 967-4500. Fax, (301) 967-4588. Thomas Buffenbarger, President. Web, www.iamaw.org.*

Membership: machinists in more than 200 industries. Helps members negotiate pay, benefits, and better working conditions; conducts training programs and workshops. Monitors legislation and regulations. (Affiliated with the AFL-CIO, the Canadian Labour Congress, the Railway Labor Executives Assn., the International Metalworkers Federation, and the International Transport Workers' Federation.)

International Magnesium Assn., *1303 Vincent Pl., #1, McLean, VA 22101; (703) 442-8888. Fax, (703) 821-1824. Byron B. Clow, Executive Director. General e-mail, ima@bellatlantic.net. Web, www.intlmag.org.*

Membership: national and international magnesium producers, processors, and suppliers. Promotes the magnesium industry. (Operates an office in Cologne, Germany.)

Machinery Dealers National Assn., *315 S. Patrick St., Alexandria, VA 22314; (703) 836-9300. Fax, (703) 836-9303. Darryl D. McEwen, Executive Vice President. Web, www.mdna.org.*

Membership: companies that buy and sell used capital equipment. Establishes a code of ethics for members; publishes a buyer's guide that lists members by types of machinery they sell.

National Tooling and Machining Assn., *9300 Livingston Rd., Ft. Washington, MD 20744-4998; (301) 248-6200. Fax, (301) 248-7104. Matthew B. Coffey, President. Web, www.ntma.org.*

Membership: members of the contract precision metalworking industry, including tool, die, mold,

diecasting die, and special machining companies. Assists members in developing and expanding their domestic and foreign markets. Offers training programs, insurance, and legal advice; compiles statistical information. Monitors legislation and regulations.

Outdoor Power Equipment Institute, *341 S. Patrick St., Alexandria, VA 22314; (703) 549-7600. Fax, (703) 549-7604. William G. Harley, President. General e-mail, opei.mow@aol.com. Web, opei.mow.org.*

Membership: manufacturers of powered lawn and garden maintenance products, components and attachments, and their suppliers. Promotes safe use of outdoor power equipment; keeps statistics on the industry; fosters exchange of information. Monitors legislation and regulations.

Sheet Metal Workers' International Assn., *1750 New York Ave. N.W. 20006; (202) 783-5880. Fax, (202) 662-0880. Michael J. Sullivan, General President. Web, smwia.org.*

Membership: more than 130,000 U.S. and Canadian workers in the building and construction trades, manufacturing, and the railroad and shipyard industries. Assists members with contract negotiation and grievances; conducts training programs and workshops. Monitors legislation and regulations. (Affiliated with the Sheet Metal and Air Conditioning Contractors' Assn., the AFL-CIO, and the Canadian Labour Congress.)

Specialty Steel Industry of North America, *3050 K St. N.W., #400 20007; (202) 342-8630. Fax, (202) 342-8451. David Hartquist, Counsel. Information, (800) 982-0355. General e-mail, ssina@ssina.com. Web, www. ssina.com.*

Membership: manufacturers of products in stainless and other specialty steels. Establishes quality standards and manufacturing techniques; sponsors workshops; operates a hotline for technical questions.

Steel Manufacturers Assn., *1730 Rhode Island Ave. N.W., #907 20036-3101; (202) 296-1515. Fax, (202) 296-2506. Thomas A. Danjczek, President. Web, www.steelnet. org.*

Membership: steel producers in North America and abroad. Helps members exchange information on technical matters; provides information on the steel industry to the public and government. Monitors legislation and regulations.

United Steelworkers of America, *Washington Office, 1150 17th St. N.W., #300 20036; (202) 778-4384. Fax, (202) 293-5308. William Klinefelter, Legislative and Political Director. Web, www.uswa.org.*

Membership: more than 700,000 steelworkers in the United States and Canada. Helps members negotiate pay, benefits, and better working conditions; conducts training programs and workshops. Monitors legislation and regulations.

 INSURANCE

See also Health (chap. 11); Military Personnel and Veterans (chap. 15); Pensions and Benefits (chap. 7); Real Estate (chap. 12)

AGENCIES

Federal Insurance Administration *(Federal Emergency Management Agency)*, 500 C St. S.W., #430 20472; (202) 646-2781. Fax, (202) 646-7970. Jo Ann Howard, Administrator. Web, www.fema.gov/nfip.

Administers federal crime and flood insurance programs, including the National Flood Insurance Program. Makes available to eligible homeowners low-cost flood and crime insurance.

Small Business Administration, *Disaster Assistance,* 409 3rd St. S.W., #6050 20416; (202) 205-6734. Fax, (202) 205-7728. Bernard Kulik, Associate Administrator. Web, www.sba.gov.

Provides victims of physical disasters with disaster and economic injury loans for homes, businesses, and personal property. Lends funds to individual homeowners, business concerns of all sizes, and nonprofit institutions to repair or replace damaged structures and furnishings, business machinery, equipment, and inventory.

CONGRESS

House Banking and Financial Services Committee, *Subcommittee on Housing and Community Opportunity,* B303 RHOB 20515; (202) 225-6634. Rep. Rick A. Lazio, R-N.Y., Chair; Joseph M. Ventrone, Staff Director. Web, www.house.gov/banking.

Jurisdiction over federal flood, fire, and earthquake insurance programs; oversees activities of the insurance industry pertaining to these programs.

House Commerce Committee, *Subcommittee on Finance and Hazardous Materials,* 2125 RHOB 20515; (202) 225-2927. Fax, (202) 225-1919. Rep. Michael G. Oxley, R-Ohio, Chair; James E. Derderian, Staff Director. General e-mail, commerce@mail.house.gov. Web, www.house.gov/commerce.

Jurisdiction over legislation on insurance, except health insurance.

Senate Banking, Housing, and Urban Affairs Committee, *Subcommittee on Housing and Transportation,* SD-534 20510; (202) 224-7391. Fax, (202) 224-5137. Sen. Wayne Allard, R-Colo., Chair; John Carson, Staff Director. Web, banking.senate.gov.

Jurisdiction over federal flood, crime, fire, and earthquake insurance programs; oversees activities of the insurance industry pertaining to these programs.

NONPROFIT

Alliance of American Insurers, *Federal Affairs, Washington Office,* 1211 Connecticut Ave. N.W., #400 20036; (202) 822-8811. Fax, (202) 872-1885. David M. Farmer, Senior Vice President. Web, www.allianceai.org.

Membership: property and casualty insurance companies. Provides educational and advisory services for members on insurance issues.

American Academy of Actuaries, 1100 17th St. N.W., 7th Floor 20036; (202) 223-8196. Fax, (202) 872-1948. Rick Lawson, Executive Director. Web, www.actuary.org.

Membership: professional actuaries practicing in the areas of life, health, liability, property, and casualty insurance; pensions; government insurance plans; and general consulting. Provides information on actuarial matters, including insurance and pensions; develops professional standards; advises public policymakers.

American Council of Life Insurance, 1001 Pennsylvania Ave. N.W., #500S 20004-2599; (202) 624-2000. Fax, (202) 624-2319. Carroll A. Campbell Jr., President. Press, (202) 624-2416. National Insurance Consumer Helpline, (800) 942-4242. Web, www.acli.com.

Membership: life insurance companies authorized to do business in the United States. Conducts research and compiles statistics at state and federal levels. Monitors legislation and regulations.

American Insurance Assn., 1130 Connecticut Ave. N.W., #1000 20036; (202) 828-7100. Fax, (202) 293-1219. Robert E. Vagley, President. Library, (202) 828-7183. Press, (202) 828-7116. Web, www.aiadc.org.

Membership: companies providing property and casualty insurance. Conducts public relations and educational activities; provides information on issues related to property and casualty insurance. Library open to the public by appointment.

American Society of Pension Actuaries, 4245 N. Fairfax Dr., #750, Arlington, VA 22203-1619; (703) 516-9300. Fax, (703) 516-9308. Brian Graff, Executive Director. Web, www.aspa.org.

Membership: professional pension plan actuaries, administrators, consultants, and other benefits professionals. Sponsors educational programs to prepare actuaries and consultants for professional exams. Monitors legislation.

Assn. for Advanced Life Underwriting, *1922 F St. N.W. 20006-4387; (202) 331-6081. Fax, (202) 331-2164. David J. Stertzer, Executive Vice President. Web, www.aalu. org.*

Membership: specialized underwriters in the fields of estate analysis, charitable planning, business insurance, pension planning, and employee benefit plans. Monitors legislation and regulations on small-business taxes and capital formation.

Assn. of Trial Lawyers of America, *1050 31st St. N.W. 20007-4499; (202) 965-3500. Fax, (202) 342-5484. Thomas H. Henderson Jr., Executive Director. Web, www. atlanet.org.*

Membership: attorneys, judges, law professors, and students. Interests include aspects of legal and legislative activity relating to the adversary system and trial by jury, including property and casualty insurance.

Consumer Federation of America's Insurance Group, *1424 16th St. N.W., #604 20036; (202) 387-6121. Fax, (202) 265-7989. Robert Hunter, Director.*

Public interest organization that conducts research and provides consumers with information on buying insurance. Interests include auto, homeowner, renter, and life insurance. Monitors legislation and regulations.

Council of Insurance Agents and Brokers, *701 Pennsylvania Ave. N.W., #750 20004; (202) 783-4400. Fax, (202) 783-4410. Ken A. Crerar, President. General e-mail, ciab@ciab.com. Web, www.ciab.com.*

Represents commercial property and casualty insurance agencies and brokerage firms. Members offer insurance products and risk management services to business, government, and the public.

ERISA Industry Committee, *1400 L St. N.W., #350 20005; (202) 789-1400. Fax, (202) 789-1120. Mark J. Ugoretz, President. General e-mail, eric@eric.org. Web, www.eric.org.*

Membership: major U.S. employers. Advocates members' positions on employee retirement, health care coverage, and welfare benefit plans; promotes flexibility and cost-effectiveness in employee benefits. Monitors legislation and regulations.

GAMA International, *1922 F St. N.W. 20006; (202) 331-6088. Fax, (202) 785-5712. Mary K. Hindle, Director. Information, (800) 345-2687. Web, www.gamaweb.com.*

Membership: general agents and managers who provide life insurance and related financial products and services. Provides information, education, and training for members.

Independent Insurance Agents of America, *Government Relations: Industry and State Relations, 127 S. Peyton St., Alexandria, VA 22314; (703) 683-4422. Fax, (703) 683-7556. Jeff Yates, Executive Officer. Web, www. iiaa.org.*

Provides educational and advisory services; researches issues pertaining to auto, home, business, life, and health insurance; offers cooperative advertising program to members. Political action committee monitors legislation and regulations.

Insurance Information Institute, *Washington Office, 1730 Rhode Island Ave. N.W., #710 20036; (202) 833-1580. Fax, (202) 223-5779. Carolyn Gorman, Vice President. Web, www.iii.org.*

Membership: property and casualty insurance companies. Monitors state and federal issues concerning insurance. Serves as a primary source for information, analysis, and referral concerning property and casualty insurance.

Mortgage Insurance Companies of America, *727 15th St. N.W. 20005; (202) 393-5566. Fax, (202) 393-5557. Suzanne C. Hutchinson, Executive Vice President.*

Membership: companies that provide guarantee insurance on residential mortgage loans.

National Assn. of Independent Insurers, *Washington Office, 444 N. Capitol St. N.W., #801 20001; (202) 639-0490. Fax, (202) 639-0494. Robert Dibblee, Senior Vice President. Web, www.naii.org.*

Membership: companies providing property and casualty insurance. Monitors legislation and compiles statistics; interests include auto and no-fault insurance and personal lines.

National Assn. of Independent Life Brokerage Agencies, *8201 Greensboro Dr., #300, McLean, VA 22102; (703) 610-9020. Fax, (703) 610-9005. Joe Normandy, Executive Director. Web, www.nailba.com.*

Membership: owners of independent life insurance agencies. Fosters the responsible and effective distribution of life and health insurance and related financial services; provides a forum for exchange of information among members. Monitors legislation and regulations.

National Assn. of Insurance and Financial Advisors, *1922 F St. N.W. 20006-4387; (202) 331-6000. Fax, (202) 835-9601. Arthur Kraus, Executive Vice President. Web, www.naifa.org.*

Federation of affiliated state and local life underwriters. Provides information on life and health insurance and other financial services; sponsors education and training programs. Formerly the National Assn. of Life Underwriters.

National Assn. of Insurance Commissioners, *Washington Office*, 444 N. Capitol St. N.W., #701 20001-1512; (202) 624-7790. Fax, (202) 624-8579. David Wetmore, Washington Director. Web, www.naic.org.

Membership: state insurance commissioners, directors, and supervisors. Provides members with information on computer information services, legal and market conduct, and financial services; publishes research and statistics on the insurance industry. Monitors legislation and regulations.

National Assn. of Professional Insurance Agents, 400 N. Washington St., Alexandria, VA 22314-2353; (703) 836-9340. Fax, (703) 836-1279. Gary Eberhart, Executive Vice President. Information, (800) 742-6900. Press, (703) 518-1351. Web, www.pianet.com.

Membership: independent insurance agents and brokers. Operates schools to provide agents with basic training; offers seminars and provides educational materials. Monitors legislation and regulations.

Nonprofit Risk Management Center, 1001 Connecticut Ave. N.W., #410 20036; (202) 785-3891. Fax, (202) 296-0349. Melanie Herman, Executive Director. General e-mail, info@nonprofitrisk.org. Web, www.nonprofitrisk.org.

Assists all groups engaged in charitable service, including nonprofit organizations, government entities, and corporate volunteer programs, to improve the quality of and reduce the cost of their insurance. Provides information on insurance and risk management issues through conferences and publications.

Product Liability Alliance, *Government Relations*, 1725 K St. N.W. 20006; (202) 872-0885. Fax, (202) 785-0586. James A. Anderson Jr., Vice President.

Membership: manufacturers, product sellers and their insurers, and trade associations. Promotes enactment of federal product liability tort reform legislation.

Reinsurance Assn. of America, 1301 Pennsylvania Ave. N.W., #900 20004; (202) 638-3690. Fax, (202) 638-0936. Franklin W. Nutter, President. Web, www.raanet.org.

Membership: companies writing property and casualty reinsurance. Serves as an information clearinghouse.

PATENTS, COPYRIGHTS, AND TRADEMARKS

AGENCIES

Justice Dept., *Civil Division: Intellectual Property*, 1100 L St. N.W., #11116 20005; (202) 514-7223. Fax, (202) 307-0345. Vito J. DiPietro, Director. Web, www.usdoj.gov.

Represents the United States in patent, copyright, and trademark cases. Includes the defense of patent infringement suits; legal proceedings to establish government priority of invention; defense of administrative acts of the Register of Copyrights; and actions on behalf of the government involving the use of trademarks.

Patent and Trademark Office *(Commerce Dept.)*, 2121 Crystal Dr., Crystal Park II, #906, Arlington, VA 22202; (703) 305-8600. Fax, (703) 305-8664. Q. Todd Dickinson, Commissioner. Information, (703) 308-4357. Press, (703) 305-8341. TTY, (703) 305-7785. Toll-free, (800) 786-9199. Trademark search library, (703) 308-9800. Patent search library, (703) 305-4463. Copyright search library, (202) 707-3000. Web, www.uspto.gov.

Grants patents, registers trademarks, and provides patent and trademark information. Scientific library and search file of U.S. and foreign patents available for public use.

State Dept., *Intellectual Property and Competition*, 2201 C St. N.W., #3829 20520; (202) 647-3251. Fax, (202) 647-1537. James Roberts, Division Chief. Web, www.state.gov.

Handles multilateral and bilateral policy formulation involving patents, copyrights, and trademarks, and international industrial property of U.S. nationals.

U.S. Customs Service *(Treasury Dept.)*, *Intellectual Property Rights*, 1300 Pennsylvania Ave. N.W., 3rd Floor 20229; (202) 927-2330. Fax, (202) 927-1873. Joanne Roman Stump, Chief.

Responsible for Customs recordation of registered trademarks and copyrights. Enforces rules and regulations pertaining to intellectual property rights. Coordinates enforcement of International Trade Commission exclusion orders against unfairly competing goods. Determines admissibility of restricted merchandise and cultural properties. Provides support to and coordinates with international organizations and the Office of the U.S. Trade Representative.

CONGRESS

House Judiciary Committee, *Subcommittee on Courts and Intellectual Property,* B351A RHOB 20515; (202) 225-5741. Fax, (202) 225-3673. Rep. Howard Coble, R-N.C., Chair; Blaine Merritt, Chief Counsel. General e-mail, Judiciary@mail.house.gov. Web, www.house.gov/ judiciary.

Jurisdiction over patent, trademark, and copyright legislation, including legislation on home audio and video taping, intellectual property rights, and financial syndication. Oversees the Patent and Trademark Office, Copyright Office, and Copyright Royalty Tribunal. (Some jurisdictions shared with House Science Committee.)

House Science Committee, *Subcommittee on Technology,* 2319 RHOB 20515; (202) 225-8844. Fax, (202) 225-4438. Rep. Constance A. Morella, R-Md., Chair; Jeffrey Grove, Staff Director. Web, www.house.gov/science.

Jurisdiction over patent and intellectual property policies (shared with House Judiciary Committee).

Library of Congress, *Copyright Office: Licensing,* 101 Independence Ave. S.E., #403 20559; (202) 707-8350. Fax, (202) 707-8366. Walter D. Sampson, Chief; Marybeth Peters, Register of Copyrights. Information, (202) 707-3000. Web, www.loc.gov/copyright.

Provides information on copyright registration procedures and requirements, copyright law, and international copyrights; registers copyright claims and maintains public records of copyright registrations. Copyright record searches conducted on an hourly fee basis. Files open to public for research during weekday business hours. Does not give legal advice on copyright matters.

Senate Judiciary Committee, SD-224 20510; (202) 224-5225. Fax, (202) 224-9102. Sen. Orrin G. Hatch, R-Utah, Chair; Manus Cooney, Chief Counsel. Web, judiciary.senate.gov.

Jurisdiction over patent, trademark, and copyright legislation, including legislation on home audio and video taping, intellectual property rights, and financial syndication.

JUDICIARY

U.S. Court of Appeals for the Federal Circuit, 717 Madison Pl. N.W. 20439; (202) 633-6556. Fax, (202) 633-6353. Haldane Robert Mayer, Chief Judge; Jan Horbaly, Clerk, (202) 633-9614. Electronic bulletin board, (202) 633-9608 or (202) 786-6584.

Reviews decisions of U.S. Patent and Trademark Office on applications and interferences regarding patents and trademarks; hears appeals on patent infringement cases from district courts.

NONPROFIT

American Bar Assn., *Intellectual Property Law,* 740 15th St. N.W., 9th Floor 20005; (202) 662-1000. Fax, (202) 662-1732. Hayden Gregory, Staff Legislative Consultant. Web, www.abanet.org.

Membership: attorneys practicing intellectual property law, including patent, trademark, copyright, and related unfair competition law. Promotes development and improvement of intellectual property treaties, laws, and regulations, and monitors their enforcement; conducts continuing legal education programs.

American Intellectual Property Law Assn., 2001 Jefferson Davis Hwy., #203, Arlington, VA 22202; (703) 415-0780. Fax, (703) 415-0786. Michael K. Kirk, Executive Director. General e-mail, aipla@aipla.org. Web, www. aipla.org.

Membership: lawyers practicing in the field of patents, trademarks, and copyrights (intellectual property law). Holds continuing legal education conferences.

Assn. of American Publishers, *Copyright and New Technology,* 50 F St. N.W., 4th Floor 20001; (202) 347-3375. Fax, (202) 347-3690. Carol A. Risher, Vice President. Web, www.publishers.org.

Monitors copyright activity in government, Congress, and international forums and institutions; sponsors seminars open to the public for a fee.

Digital Futures Coalition, P.O. Box 7679 20004-7679; (202) 538-2004. Fax, (202) 628-9227. Skip Lockwood, Coordinator. General e-mail, dfc@dfc.org. Web, www.dfc.org.

Membership: educational, scholarly, library, and consumer groups as well as trade associations. Advocates a fair and balanced approach to implementing the World Intellectual Property Organization treaties. Monitors legislation and regulations.

Intellectual Property Owners, 1255 23rd St. N.W., #200 20037; (202) 466-2396. Fax, (202) 466-2893. Herbert C. Wamsley, Executive Director. Web, www.ipo.org.

Monitors legislation and conducts educational programs to protect intellectual property through patents, trademarks, copyrights, and trade secret laws.

National Assn. of Manufacturers, *Intellectual Property Subcommittee,* 1331 Pennsylvania Ave. N.W., #600 20004-1790; (202) 637-3147. Fax, (202) 637-3182. Roger May, Chair. Web, www.nam.org.

Develops policy and legislation on patents, copyrights, trademarks, and trade secrets.

National School Boards Assn., 1680 Duke St., Alexandria, VA 22314; (703) 838-6722. Fax, (703) 683-7590.

Anne Bryant, Executive Director; Julie Underwood, General Counsel. Web, www.nsba.org.

Promotes a broad interpretation of copyright law to permit legitimate scholarly use of published and musical works, videotaped programs, and materials for computer-assisted instruction.

U.S. Chamber of Commerce, *Congressional and Public Affairs, 1615 H St. N.W. 20062-2000; (202) 659-6000. Fax, (202) 887-3430. Lonnie P. Taylor, Senior Vice President. Web, www.uschamber.org.*

Monitors legislation and regulations on patents, copyrights, and trademarks.

See also Council of Scientific Society Presidents (p. 595); Information Industry Assn. (p. 134); National Assn. of Plant Patent Owners (p. 44); Recording Industry Assn. of America (p. 158)

SALES AND SERVICES

See also Antitrust (chap. 14); Consumer Protection (chap. 1); Food and Nutrition (chap. 2)

AGENCIES

Bureau of Labor Statistics *(Labor Dept.), Prices and Living Conditions, 2 Massachusetts Ave. N.E., #3120 20212; (202) 691-6960. Fax, (202) 691-7080. Kenneth V. Dalton, Associate Commissioner.*

Collects, processes, analyzes, and disseminates data relating to prices and consumer expenditures; maintains the Consumer Price Index.

Census Bureau *(Commerce Dept.), Service Sector Statistics Division, Suitland and Silver Hill Rds., Bldg. 3, #2633, Suitland, MD 20233; (301) 457-2668. Fax, (301) 457-1343. Carole A. Ambler, Chief.*

Provides data of five-year census programs on retail, wholesale, and service industries. Conducts periodic monthly or annual surveys for specific items within these industries.

NONPROFIT

American Wholesale Marketers Assn., *1128 16th St. N.W. 20036; (202) 463-2124. Fax, (202) 467-0559. David Strachan, President. Web, www.awmanet.org.*

Membership: wholesalers, manufacturers, retailers, and brokers who sell or distribute convenience products. Conducts education programs. Monitors legislation and regulations.

Assn. of Sales and Marketing Companies, *2100 Reston Pkwy., #400, Reston, VA 20191-1218; (703) 758-7790. Fax, (703) 758-7787. Mark Baum, President. General e-mail, info@asmc.org. Web, www.asmc.org.*

Membership: sales and marketing agents and retail merchandisers of food and consumer products worldwide. Sponsors research, training, and educational programs for members and their trading partners. Monitors legislation and regulations.

Cosmetic, Toiletry, and Fragrance Assn., *1101 17th St. N.W., #300 20036; (202) 331-1770. Fax, (202) 331-1969. E. Edward Kavanaugh, President. Web, www.ctfa.org.*

Membership: manufacturers and distributors of finished personal care products. Represents the industry at the local, state, and national levels. Interests include scientific research, legal issues, international trade, legislation, and regulatory policy.

Council of Better Business Bureaus, *4200 Wilson Blvd., #800, Arlington, VA 22203-1838; (703) 276-0100. Fax, (703) 525-8277. Kenneth Hunter, President. General e-mail, bbb@bbb.org. Web, www.bbb.org.*

Membership: businesses and Better Business Bureaus in the United States and Canada. Promotes ethical business practices and truth in national advertising; mediates disputes between consumers and businesses.

Equipment Leasing Assn. of America, *4301 N. Fairfax Dr., #550, Arlington, VA 22203; (703) 527-8655. Fax, (703) 527-2649. Michael Fleming, Chief Executive Officer. Web, elaonline.com.*

Promotes the interests of the equipment leasing and finance industry; assists in the resolution of industry problems; encourages standards. Monitors legislation and regulations.

International Cemetery and Funeral Assn., *1895 Preston White Dr., #220, Reston, VA 20191; (703) 391-8400. Fax, (703) 391-8416. Linda Christenson, Executive Vice President. Information, (800) 645-7700. Web, www.icfa.org.*

Membership: owners and operators of cemeteries, funeral homes, mausoleums, and columbariums. Promotes the building and proper maintenance of modern interment places; promotes high ethical standards in the industry; encourages pre-arrangement of funerals.

International Council of Shopping Centers, *Government Relations, Washington Office, 1033 N. Fairfax St., #404, Alexandria, VA 22314; (703) 549-7404. Fax, (703) 549-8712. Becky Sullivan, Vice President. Web, www.icsc.org.*

Membership: shopping center owners, developers, managers, retailers, contractors, and others in the industry worldwide. Provides information, including research data. Monitors legislation and regulations.

International Franchise Assn., *1350 New York Ave. N.W., #900 20005; (202) 628-8000. Fax, (202) 628-0812. Don J. DeBolt, President. Web, www.franchise.org.*

Membership: national and international franchisers. Sponsors seminars, workshops, trade shows, and conferences. Monitors legislation and regulations.

International Mass Retail Assn., *1700 N. Moore St., #2250, Arlington, VA 22209-1998; (703) 841-2300. Fax, (703) 841-1184. Robert J. Verdisco, President. Web, www. imra.org.*

Membership: discount, specialty, home center, wholesale club, and mass retailers in the United States and abroad. Interests include industry research, trade, and government relations. Monitors legislation and regulations.

National Assn. of Convenience Stores, *1605 King St., Alexandria, VA 22314-2792; (703) 684-3600. Fax, (703) 836-4564. Kerley LeBoeuf, President. Web, www. cstorecentral.com.*

Membership: convenience store retailers and industry suppliers. Advocates industry position on labor, tax, environment, alcohol, and food-related issues; conducts research and training programs. Monitors legislation and regulations.

National Assn. of Wholesaler-Distributors, *1725 K St. N.W., #300 20006; (202) 872-0885. Fax, (202) 785-0586. Dirk Van Dongen, President.*

Membership: wholesale distributors and trade associations. Provides members and government policymakers with research, education, and government relations information. Monitors legislation and regulations.

National Burglar and Fire Alarm Assn., *8300 Colesville Rd., #750, Silver Spring, MD 20910; (301) 585-1855. Fax, (301) 585-1866. Brad Shipp, Executive Director. General e-mail, staff@alarm.org. Web, www.alarm.org.*

Promotes the electronic security industry. Conducts professional training and certification; compiles industry statistics; disseminates information to consumers regarding home security systems; sponsors seminars. Monitors legislation and regulations.

National Retail Federation, *325 7th St. N.W., #1000 20004-2802; (202) 783-7971. Fax, (202) 737-2849. Tracy Mullin, President. Web, www.nrf.com.*

Membership: international, national, and state associations of retailers and major retail corporations. Con-

cerned with federal regulatory activities and legislation that affect retailers, including tax, employment, trade, and credit issues. Provides information on retailing through seminars, conferences, and publications.

Security Industry Assn., *635 Slaters Lane, #110, Alexandria, VA 22314; (703) 683-2075. Fax, (703) 683-2469. Ronald F. Spiller, Executive Director. Web, www. siaonline.org.*

Promotes expansion and professionalism in the security industry. Sponsors trade shows, develops industry standards, supports educational programs and job training, and publishes statistical research. Serves as an information source for the media and the industry.

Service Station Dealers of America, *9420 Annapolis Rd., #307, Lanham, MD 20706; (301) 577-4956. Fax, (301) 731-0039. Don Sadler, President. Web, www.ssda-at. org.*

Membership: state associations of gasoline retailers. Interests include environmental issues, retail marketing, oil allocation, imports and exports, prices, and taxation.

Society of Consumer Affairs Professionals in Business, *801 N. Fairfax St., #404, Alexandria, VA 22314-1757; (703) 519-3700. Fax, (703) 549-4886. Louis Garcia, Executive Director. Web, www.socap.org.*

Membership: managers and supervisors who are responsible for consumer affairs, customer service, market research, and sales and marketing operations. Provides information on customer service techniques, market trends, and industry statistics; sponsors seminars and conferences. Monitors legislation and regulations.

Trade Show Exhibitors Assn., *5501 Backlick Rd., #105, Springfield, VA 22151; (703) 941-3725. Fax, (703) 941-8275. Michael J. Bandy, President. Web, www.tsea.org.*

Membership: organizations that use exhibits as a marketing medium. Members share information on matters affecting exhibit programs.

Advertising

See also Credit Practices (chap. 1)

AGENCIES

Federal Highway Administration *(Transportation Dept.), Real Estate Services, 400 7th St. S.W. 20590; (202) 366-0142. Fax, (202) 366-3713. Susan Lauffer, Director.*

Administers laws concerning outdoor advertising along interstate and federally aided primary highways.

Federal Trade Commission, *Advertising Practices,* 601 *Pennsylvania Ave. N.W., #S4002 20580; (202) 326-3090. Fax, (202) 326-3259. C. Lee Peeler, Associate Director.*

Monitors advertising claims of products for validity; investigates allegations of deceptive advertising practices; handles complaints from consumers, public interest groups, businesses, and Congress regarding the truthfulness and fairness of advertising practices. Enforces statutes and rules preventing misrepresentations in print and broadcast advertising.

Food and Drug Administration *(Health and Human Services Dept.), Drug Marketing, Advertising, and Communications, 5600 Fishers Lane, HFD-42, #17B-20, Rockville, MD 20857; (301) 827-2828. Fax, (301) 594-6771. Norm Drezin, Director (Acting). Web, www.fda.gov/cder.*

Monitors prescription drug advertising and labeling; investigates complaints; conducts market research on health care communications and drug issues.

NONPROFIT

American Advertising Federation, *1101 Vermont Ave. N.W., #500 20005; (202) 898-0089. Fax, (202) 898-0159. Wallace Snyder, President. Web, www.aaf.org.*

Membership: advertising companies (ad agencies, advertisers, media, and services), clubs, associations, and college chapters. A founder of the National Advertising Review Board, a self-regulatory body. Sponsors annual awards for outstanding advertising.

American Assn. of Advertising Agencies, *Washington Office, 1899 L St. N.W., #700 20036-3891; (202) 331-7345. Fax, (202) 857-3675. Hal Shoup, Executive Vice President. General e-mail, wash@aaaadc.org. Web, www. AAAA.org.*

Co-sponsors the National Advertising Review Board (a self-regulatory body), the Advertising Council, and the Media/Advertising Partnership for a Drug Free America. Monitors legislation and regulations.

Assn. of National Advertisers, *Washington Office, 700 11th St. N.W., #650 20001; (202) 626-7800. Fax, (202) 626-6161. Daniel L. Jaffe, Executive Vice President. Web, www.ana.net.*

Co-sponsors the National Advertising Review Board, a self-regulatory body. Monitors legislation and regulations.

Color Marketing Group, *5904 Richmond Hwy., #408, Alexandria, VA 22303; (703) 329-8500. Fax, (703) 329-0155. Hall Dillon, President. General e-mail, cmg@ colormarketing.org. Web, www.colormarketing.org.*

Provides a forum for the exchange of noncompetitive information on color marketing. Holds meetings; sponsors special events in the United States as well as abroad.

Direct Marketing Assn., *Ethics and Consumer Affairs: Government Affairs, Washington Office, 1111 19th St. N.W., #1100 20036; (202) 955-5030. Fax, (202) 955-0085. Jerry Cerasale, Senior Vice President; Patricia Faley, Vice President. Web, www.the-dma.org.*

Membership: telemarketers; users, creators, and producers of direct mail; and suppliers to the industry. Conducts research and promotes knowledge and use of direct response marketing; interests include international business. Handles consumer complaints about telephone and mail-order purchases. Operates a mail preference service, which removes consumer names from unwanted mailing lists, and a telephone preference service, which helps consumers handle unsolicited telephone sales calls.

International Sign Assn., *707 N. Saint Asaph St., Alexandria, VA 22314; (703) 836-4012. Fax, (703) 836-8353. Mark Lappen, President. Web, www.signs.org.*

Membership: manufacturers and distributors of signs. Promotes the sign industry; conducts workshops and seminars; sponsors annual competition.

Outdoor Advertising Assn. of America, *1850 M St. N.W., #1040 20036; (202) 833-5566. Fax, (202) 833-1522. Nancy Fletcher, President. Web, www.oaaa.org.*

Membership: outdoor advertising companies, operators, suppliers, and affiliates. Serves as a clearinghouse for public service advertising campaigns. Monitors legislation and regulations.

🔲 SMALL AND DISADVANTAGED BUSINESS

AGENCIES

Agency for International Development, *Small and Disadvantaged Business Utilization/Minority Resource Center, 1300 Pennsylvania Ave. N.W., #7.8-E 20523; (202) 712-1500. Fax, (202) 216-3056. Ivan R. Ashley, Director. Web, www.info.usaid.gov/procurement_bus_opp/osdbu/.*

Provides information and counseling to U.S. business firms seeking export sales and technical service contracts. Devotes special attention to assisting small businesses and minority-owned firms.

Commerce Dept., *Business Liaison, 14th St. and Constitution Ave. N.W., #5062 20230; (202) 482-3942. Fax,*

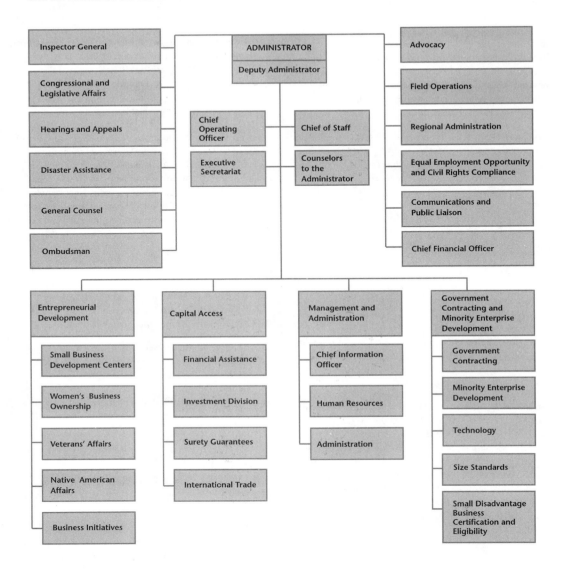

(202) 482-4054. *Lucie Naphin, Director. Information,* (202) 482-1360. *Web, www.doc.gov.*

Serves as the central office for business assistance. Handles requests for information and services as well as complaints and suggestions from businesses; provides a forum for businesses to comment on federal regulations; initiates meetings on policy issues with industry groups, business organizations, trade and small-business associations, and the corporate community.

Federal Insurance Administration *(Federal Emergency Management Agency), 500 C St. S.W., #430 20472; (202) 646-2781. Fax, (202) 646-7970. Jo Ann Howard, Administrator. Web, www.fema.gov/nfip.*

Administers federal crime and flood insurance programs. Makes available to eligible small businesses low-cost flood and crime insurance.

General Services Administration (GSA), *Enterprise Development, 1800 F St. N.W., #6029 20405; (202) 501-*

1021. Fax, (202) 208-5938. *Marinda Jackson, Associate Administrator (Acting).*

Works to increase small-business procurement of government contracts. Provides policy guidance and direction for GSA Business Service Centers, which offer advice and assistance to businesses interested in government procurement.

Minority Business Development Agency *(Commerce Dept.), 14th St. and Constitution Ave. N.W., #5055 20230; (202) 482-5061. Fax, (202) 501-4698. Courtland Cox, Director.*

Assists minority business owners in obtaining federal loans and contract awards; produces an annual report on federal agencies' performance in procuring from minority-owned businesses.

National Science Foundation (NSF), *Small Business Innovation Research Program, 4201 Wilson Blvd., #550, Arlington, VA 22230; (703) 306-1391. Fax, (703) 306-0298. Kesh Narayanan, Senior Adviser.*

Serves as liaison between the small-business community and NSF offices awarding grants and contracts. Administers the Small Business Innovation Research Program, which funds research proposals from small science/high technology firms and offers incentives for commercial development of NSF-funded research.

National Women's Business Council, *409 3rd St. S.W., #210 20024; (202) 205-3850. Fax, (202) 205-6825. Kay Koplovitz, Chair; Amy Millman, Executive Director. Web, www.womenconnect.com/nwbc.*

Membership: eight women business owners, six representatives of women business organizations, and one chair appointed by the president. Independent, congressionally mandated council established by the Women's Business Ownership Act of 1988. Reviews the status of women-owned businesses nationwide and makes policy recommendations to the president and Congress. Assesses the role of the federal government in aiding and promoting women-owned businesses.

Securities and Exchange Commission, *Economic Analysis, 450 5th St. N.W. 20549; (202) 942-8020. Fax, (202) 942-9657. Vacant, Chief Economist.*

Provides the commission with economic analyses of proposed rule and policy changes and other information to guide the SEC in influencing capital markets. Evaluates the effect of policy and other factors on competition within the securities industry and among competing securities markets; compiles financial statistics on capital formation and the securities industry.

Small Business Administration (SBA), *409 3rd St. S.W., #7000 20416; (202) 205-6605. Fax, (202) 205-6802.*

SMALL AND DISADVANTAGED BUSINESS CONTACTS AT FEDERAL AGENCIES

DEPARTMENTS

Agriculture, Sharron Harris, (202) 720-7117

Commerce, Brenda Black, (202) 482-1472

Defense, Robert L. Neal Jr., (703) 588-8631

    Air Force, Anthony J. DeLuca, (703) 697-1950

    Army, Tracey L. Pinson, (703) 695-9800

    Navy, Nancy Tarrant, (202) 685-6485

Education, Viola J. Jaramillo, (202) 708-9820

Energy, Sarah Summerville (acting), (202) 586-7377

Health and Human Services, Verl Zanders, (202) 690-7300

Housing and Urban Development, Casmir Bonkowski, (202) 708-1428

Interior, Ralph Rausch (acting), (202) 208-3493

Justice, Ken Bryan, (202) 616-0521

State, Durie N. White, (703) 875-6824

Transportation, Luz A. Hopewell, (202) 366-1930

Treasury, Kevin Boshears (acting), (202) 622-0376

    Office of Thrift Supervision, John Connors, (202) 906-6666

Veterans Affairs, Scott F. Denniston, (202) 565-8124

AGENCIES

Agency for International Development, Ivan R. Ashley, (202) 712-1500

Consumer Product Safety Commission, Ann Brown, (301) 504-0570

Environmental Protection Agency, Jeanette L. Brown, (202) 564-4100

General Services Administration, Marinda Jackson (acting), (202) 501-1021

National Aeronautics and Space Administration, Ralph C. Thomas III, (202) 358-2088

Nuclear Regulatory Commission, Von Deloatch, (301) 415-7380

Social Security Administration, Wanda Eley, (410) 965-9457

Aida Alvarez, Administrator; Fred Hochberg, Deputy Administrator. Library, (202) 205-7033. Press, (202) 205-6740. Toll-free information, (800) 827-5722. Locator, (202) 205-6600. Web, www.sba.gov.

Provides small businesses with financial and management assistance; offers loans to victims of floods, natural disasters, and other catastrophes; licenses, regulates, and guarantees some financing of small-business investment companies; conducts economic and statistical research on small businesses. SBA Answer Desk is an information and referral service. District or regional offices can be contacted for specific loan information.

Small Business Administration, *Advocacy,* *409 3rd St. S.W., #7800 20416; (202) 205-6533. Fax, (202) 205-6928. Jere W. Glover, Chief Counsel. General e-mail, agh@adv. sba.gov. Web, www.sba.gov/ADVO.*

Acts as an advocate for small-business viewpoints in regulatory and legislative proceedings. Economic Research Office analyzes the effects of government policies on small business and documents the contributions of small business to the economy.

Small Business Administration, *Business Initiatives,* *409 3rd St. S.W., #6100 20416; (202) 205-6665. Fax, (202) 205-7416. Monika Edwards Harrison, Associate Administrator. Web, www.sba.gov/BI.*

Provides small businesses with instruction and counseling in marketing, accounting, product analysis, production methods, research and development, and management problems.

Small Business Administration, *Capital Access,* *409 3rd St. S.W., #8200 20416; (202) 205-6657. Fax, (202) 205-7230. Charles D. Tansey, Associate Deputy Administrator. Web, www.sba.gov.*

Provides financial assistance to small business; focus includes surety guarantees, investment, and international trade. Makes microloans to start-up businesses and loans to established businesses for purchase of new equipment or facilities.

Small Business Administration, *Entrepreneurial Development,* *409 3rd St. S.W., #6200 20416; (202) 205-6706. Fax, (202) 205-6903. Daryl Dennis, Associate Administrator. Web, www.sba.gov.*

Responsible for business development programs of the Small Business Development Centers and the offices of Business Initiatives, Veterans Affairs, native American Affairs, Women's Business Ownership, and Welfare to Work.

Small Business Administration, *Financial Assistance,* *409 3rd St. S.W., #8300 20416; (202) 205-6490. Fax, (202) 205-7722. Jane Butler, Associate Administrator. Web, www.sba.gov.*

Makes available guaranteed loans to aid in developing small businesses.

Small Business Administration, *Minority Enterprise Development,* *409 3rd St. S.W., #8000 20416; (202) 205-*

6410. Fax, (202) 205-7267. Della Ford, Associate Administrator (Acting). Web, www.sba.gov/MED.

Coordinates the services provided by private industry, banks, the SBA, and other government agencies—such as business development and management and technical assistance—to increase the number of small businesses owned by socially and economically disadvantaged Americans.

Small Business Administration, *Women's Business Ownership,* *409 3rd St. S.W., 4th Floor 20416; (202) 205-6673. Fax, (202) 205-7287. Sherrye Henry, Assistant Administrator. Web, www.sba.gov/womeninbusiness.*

Advocates for current and potential women business owners throughout the federal government and in the private sector. Provides training and counseling; offers information on national and local resources.

CONGRESS

House Government Reform Committee, *Subcommittee on National Economic Growth, Natural Resources, and Regulatory Affairs,* *B377 RHOB 20515; (202) 225-4407. Fax, (202) 225-2441. Rep. David M. McIntosh, R-Ind., Chair; Marlo Lewis, Staff Director. Web, www.house.gov/reform.*

Reviews regulatory process and effect of specific regulations and paperwork on the small-business community. Oversees operations of the Small Business Administration. (Shared with House Small Business Committee.)

House Small Business Committee, *2361 RHOB 20515; (202) 225-5821. Rep. James M. Talent, R-Mo., Chair; Mark Strand, Chief of Staff. General e-mail, smbiz@mail.house.gov. Web, www.house.gov/smbiz.*

Jurisdiction over legislation dealing with the Small Business Administration (shared with House Government Reform Committee). Studies and makes recommendations on problems of American small business.

House Small Business Committee, *Subcommittee on Empowerment,* *B363 RHOB 20515; (202) 226-2630. Fax, (202) 225-8950. Rep. Joseph R. Pitts, R-Pa., Chair; Stephanie O'Donnell, Professional Staff Member. General e-mail, smbiz@mail.house.gov. Web, www.house.gov/smbiz.*

Jurisdiction over development of economically depressed areas, including regulations and licensing policies, that affect small businesses in high-risk communities.

House Small Business Committee, *Subcommittee on Government Programs and Oversight,* *B363 RHOB*

20515; (202) 226-2630. Fax, (202) 225-8950. Rep. Roscoe G. Bartlett, R-Md., Chair; Nelson Crowther, Staff Director. General e-mail, smbiz@mail.house.gov. Web, www.house.gov/smbiz.

Jurisdiction over legislation on opportunities for women and minority-owned businesses, and federal government programs designed to assist small businesses.

House Small Business Committee, Subcommittee on Tax, Finance, and Exports, B363 RHOB 20515; (202) 226-2630. Fax, (202) 225-8950. Rep. Donald Manzullo, R-Ill., Chair; Philip D. Eskeland, Staff Director. General e-mail, smbiz@mail.house.gov. Web, www.house.gov/smbiz.

Jurisdiction over legislation on programs affecting small business; studies impact of tax policy on small business.

Senate Small Business Committee, SR-428A 20510; (202) 224-5175. Fax, (202) 224-4885. Sen. Christopher S. Bond, R-Mo., Chair; Emilia DiSanto, Staff Director. Web, sbc.senate.gov.

Jurisdiction over and oversight of the Small Business Administration. Studies and makes recommendations on problems of American small business and on programs involving minority enterprise. Reviews regulatory process and effect of specific regulations and paperwork on the small-business community.

NONPROFIT

Latin American Management Assn., 419 New Jersey Ave. S.E. 20003-4007; (202) 546-3803. Fax, (202) 546-3807. Stephen Denlinger, President.

Membership: Hispanic manufacturing and technical firms. Promotes Hispanic enterprise, industry, and technology throughout the United States. Supports public policy beneficial to minority businesses. Monitors legislation and regulations.

Minority Business Enterprise Legal Defense and Education Fund, 900 2nd St. N.E., #8 20002; (202) 289-1700. Fax, (202) 289-1701. Anthony W. Robinson, President.

Acts as an advocate for the minority business community. Represents minority businesses in class action suits; conducts legal research; serves as an information clearinghouse on business and legal trends. Monitors legislation and regulations.

National Assn. of Investment Companies, 733 15th St. N.W., #700 20005; (202) 289-4336. Fax, (202) 289-4329. Betty Lynn Smith, President. General e-mail, NAICHQTRS@aol.com. Web, www.naichq.org.

Membership: investment companies that provide minority-owned small businesses with venture capital and management guidance. Provides technical assistance; monitors legislation affecting small business.

National Assn. of Negro Business and Professional Women's Clubs, 1806 New Hampshire Ave. N.W. 20009; (202) 483-4206. Fax, (202) 462-7253. Clair Patra Vaughn, President. Web, www.afrika.com/nanbpwc.

Promotes opportunities for African American women in business; sponsors workshops; maintains a job bank. Monitors legislation and regulations.

National Assn. of Small Business Investment Companies, 666 11th St. N.W., #750 20001; (202) 628-5055. Fax, (202) 628-5080. Lee W. Mercer, President. Web, www.nasbic.org.

Membership: companies licensed by the Small Business Administration to provide small businesses with advisory services, equity financing, and long-term loans.

National Federation of Independent Business, 600 Maryland Ave. S.W., #700 20024; (202) 554-9000. Fax, (202) 554-0496. Jackson Faris, President. Web, www.nfibonline.com.

Membership: independent business and professional people. Monitors public policy issues and legislation affecting small and independent businesses, including taxation, government regulation, labor-management relations, and liability insurance.

National Small Business United, 1156 15th St. N.W., #1100 20005; (202) 293-8830. Fax, (202) 872-8543. Todd McCracken, President. General e-mail, nsbu@nsbu.org. Web, www.nsbu.org.

Membership: manufacturing, wholesale, retail, service, and other small-business firms and regional small-business organizations. Represents the interests of small business before Congress, the administration, and federal agencies. Services to members include a toll-free legislative hotline and group insurance.

Research Institute for Small and Emerging Business, 722 12th St. N.W. 20005; (202) 628-8382. Fax, (202) 628-8392. Mark Shultz, President. General e-mail, rise@bellatlantic.net. Web, www.riseb.org.

Seeks to enhance the formation and growth of the small and emerging business sector by developing and sponsoring research on small and emerging businesses, and then ensuring its effective dissemination.

Service Corps of Retired Executives Assn., 409 3rd St. S.W., 6th Floor 20024; (202) 205-6762. Fax, (202) 205-

7636. *W. Kenneth Yancey Jr., Executive Director. Information, (800) 634-0245. Web, www.score.org.*

Independent voluntary organization funded by the Small Business Administration through which retired, semiretired, and active business executives use their knowledge and experience to counsel small businesses.

Small Business Legislative Council, *1010 Massachusetts Ave. N.W., #400 20001; (202) 639-8500. Fax, (202) 296-5333. John Satagaj, President. General e-mail, email@sblc.org. Web, www.sblc.org.*

Membership: trade associations that represent small businesses in the manufacturing, wholesale, retail, service, and other sectors. Monitors and proposes legislation and regulations to benefit small businesses.

Small Business Survival Committee, *1920 L St. N.W., #200 20036; (202) 785-0238. Fax, (202) 822-8118. Christopher Wysocki, President. Web, www.sbsc.org.*

Membership: small businesses throughout the United States. Promotes small business economic growth through limited government. Acts as an educational resource for members. Monitors legislation and regulations.

U.S. Chamber of Commerce, *Small Business Center, 1615 H St. N.W. 20062-2000; (202) 463-5503. Fax, (202) 887-3445. David Voight, Director. Web, www.uschamber. com/smallbiz/index.html.*

Seeks to enhance visibility of small business within the national chamber and the U.S. business community. Provides members with information on national small-business programs.

4

Communications and the Media

GENERAL POLICY

AGENCIES

Federal Communications Commission (FCC),
445 12th St. S.W. 20554; (202) 418-1000. Fax, (202) 418-2801. William Kennard, Chair. Library, (202) 418-0450. Press, (202) 418-0500. Locator, (202) 418-0126. Web, www.fcc.gov.

Regulates interstate and foreign communications by radio, television, wire, cable, microwave, and satellite; consults with other government agencies and departments on national and international matters involving wire and radio telecommunications and with state regulatory commissions on telegraph and telephone matters; reviews applications for construction permits and licenses for such services. Library open to the public.

Federal Communications Commission, *Complaints and Political Programming*, 445 12th St. S.W., 3rd Floor 20554; (202) 418-1440. Fax, (202) 418-2053. Robert Baker, Chief. Information, (202) 418-0200.

Handles complaints and inquiries concerning the equal time rule, which requires equal broadcast opportunities for all legally qualified candidates for the same office. Enforces related Communications Act provisions, including the requirement for sponsorship identification of all paid broadcast announcements.

National Telecommunications and Information Administration *(Commerce Dept.)*, *14th St. and Constitution Ave. N.W., #4898 20230; (202) 482-1840. Fax, (202) 482-1635. Gregory Rohde, NTIA Administrator. Information, (202) 482-7002. Web, www.ntia.doc.gov.*

Develops domestic and international telecommunications policy for the executive branch; manages federal use of radio spectrum; conducts research on radiowave transmissions and other aspects of telecommunications; serves as information source for federal and state agencies on the efficient use of telecommunications resources; provides noncommercial telecommunications services with grants for construction of facilities.

CONGRESS

House Appropriations Committee, *Subcommittee on Commerce, Justice, State, and Judiciary*, H309 CAP 20515; (202) 225-3351. Rep. Harold Rogers, R-Ky., Chair; Jim Kulikowski, Staff Director. Web, www.house.gov/appropriations.

Jurisdiction over legislation to appropriate funds for the Federal Communications Commission, the Board for International Broadcasting, and the National Telecommunications and Information Administration.

House Appropriations Committee, *Subcommittee on Labor, Health and Human Services, and Education*, 2358 RHOB 20515; (202) 225-3508. Fax, (202) 225-3509. Rep. John Edward Porter, R-Ill., Chair; Tony McCann, Staff Director. Web, www.house.gov/appropriations.

Jurisdiction over legislation to appropriate funds for the Corporation for Public Broadcasting.

House Commerce Committee, *Subcommittee on Telecommunications, Trade, and Consumer Protection*, 2125 RHOB 20515; (202) 225-2927. Fax, (202) 225-1919. Rep. W. J. "Billy" Tauzin, R-La., Chair; James E. Derderian, Staff Director. General e-mail, commerce@mail.house. gov. Web, www.house.gov/commerce.

Jurisdiction over legislation related to interstate and foreign telecommunications, including television, cable television, local and long-distance telephone service, radio, wire, microwave, and satellite communications. Jurisdiction over the Federal Communications Commission and the Corporation for Public Broadcasting.

House Government Reform Committee, *Subcommittee on Government Management, Information, and Technology*, B373 RHOB 20515; (202) 225-5147. Fax, (202) 225-2373. Rep. Steve Horn, R-Calif., Chair; J. Russell George, Staff Director. Web, www.house.gov/reform.

Oversees operations of the National Telecommunications and Information Administration, the Federal Communications Commission, and the Board for International Broadcasting.

House Judiciary Committee, 2138 RHOB 20515; (202) 225-3951. Fax, (202) 225-7682. Rep. Henry J. Hyde, R-Ill., Chair; Thomas Mooney, Chief of Staff. General e-mail, Judiciary@mail.house.gov. Web, www.house.gov/judiciary.

Jurisdiction over legislation related to anticompetitive practices and to monopolies in communications, including cable telecommunications and network practices.

Library of Congress, *Copyright Office: Licensing*, 101 Independence Ave. S.E., #403 20559; (202) 707-8350. Fax, (202) 707-8366. Walter D. Sampson, Chief; Marybeth Peters, Register of Copyrights. Information, (202) 707-3000. Web, www.loc.gov/copyright.

Licenses cable television companies and satellite carriers; collects and distributes royalty payments under the copyright law. Distributes licenses for making and distributing phonorecords and for use of certain noncommercial broadcasting. Administers Section 115 licensing for making and distributing phonorecords.

Senate Appropriations Committee, *Subcommittee on Commerce, Justice, State, and Judiciary*, S-146A CAP

FEDERAL COMMUNICATIONS COMMISSION

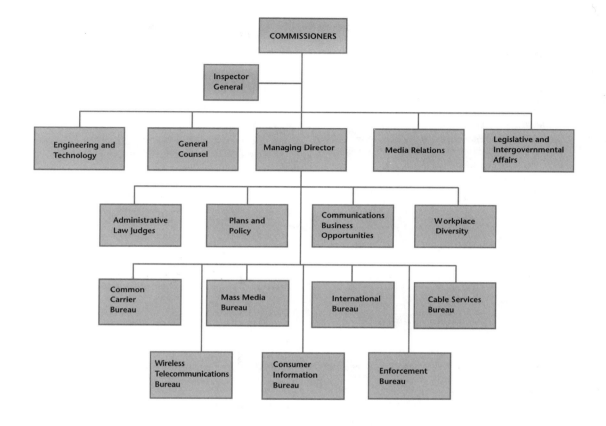

20510; (202) 224-7277. Sen. Judd Gregg, R-N.H., Chair; Jim Morhard, Clerk. Web, appropriations.senate.gov/ commerce.

Jurisdiction over legislation to appropriate funds for the Federal Communications Commission, the Board for International Broadcasting, and the National Telecommunications and Information Administration.

Senate Appropriations Committee, *Subcommittee on Labor, Health and Human Services, and Education,* SD-186 20510; (202) 224-7230. Fax, (202) 224-1360. Sen. Arlen Specter, R-Pa., Chair; Bettilou Taylor, Staff Director. Web, appropriations.senate.gov/labor.

Jurisdiction over legislation to appropriate funds for the Corporation for Public Broadcasting.

Senate Commerce, Science, and Transportation Committee, *Subcommittee on Communications,* SH-227 20510; (202) 224-5184. Fax, (202) 224-9334. Sen.

Conrad Burns, R-Mont., Chair; Lauren Belvin, Senior Counsel. Web, commerce.senate.gov.

Jurisdiction over legislation related to interstate and foreign communications, including television, cable television, local and long-distance telephone service, radio, wire, microwave, and satellite communications. Oversight of the Federal Communications Commission, the National Telecommunications and Information Administration, and the Corporation for Public Broadcasting.

Senate Foreign Relations Committee, *Subcommittee on International Operations,* SD-450 20510; (202) 224-4651. Fax, (202) 224-0836. Sen. Rod Grams, R-Minn., Chair; Steve Biegun, Staff Director. Web, foreign.senate.gov.

Oversight of the Board for International Broadcasting.

Senate Judiciary Committee, *Subcommittee on Antitrust, Business Rights, and Competition,* SD-161

20510; (202) 224-9494. Fax, (202) 228-0463. Sen. Mike DeWine, R-Ohio, Chair; Pete Levitas, Chief Counsel. Web, judiciary.senate.gov/antibusn.htm.

Jurisdiction over legislation related to anticompetitive practices and to monopolies in communications, including cable telecommunication and network practices.

INTERNATIONAL ORGANIZATIONS

Inter-American Telecommunications Commission (Organization of American States), *1889 F St. N.W., #250-A 20006; (202) 458-3004. Fax, (202) 458-6854. William Moran, Executive Secretary (Acting). General e-mail, citel@oas.org. Web, www.oas.org.*

Works with the public and private sectors to facilitate the development of telecommunications in the Americas.

NONPROFIT

Accuracy in Media, *4455 Connecticut Ave. N.W., #330 20008; (202) 364-4401. Fax, (202) 364-4098. Reed J. Irvine, Board Chair. General e-mail, ar@aim.org. Web, www.aim.org.*

Analyzes print and electronic news media for bias, omissions, and errors in news; approaches media with complaints. Maintains speakers bureau.

Alliance for Public Technology, *919 18th St. N.W., #900 20006; (202) 263-2970. Fax, (202) 263-2960. Jennings Bryant, Chair. Main phone is voice and TTY accessible. General e-mail, apt@apt.org. Web, www.apt.org.*

Membership: public groups and individuals concerned with developing affordable access to information services and telecommunications technology, particularly for the elderly, residential consumers, low-income groups, and people with disabilities.

Alliance for Telecommunications Industry Solutions, *1200 G St. N.W., #500 20005; (202) 628-6380. Fax, (202) 393-5453. Susan Miller, President. General e-mail, atispr@atis.org. Web, www.atis.org.*

Promotes the timely resolution of national and international issues involving telecommunications standards and operational guidelines. Sponsors industry forums; serves as an information clearinghouse. Monitors legislation and regulations.

Center for Media and Public Affairs, *2100 L St. N.W., #300 20037-1525; (202) 223-2942. Fax, (202) 872-4014. Christine Messina-Boyer, Managing Director. Web, www.cmpa.com.*

Nonpartisan research and educational organization that studies media coverage of social and political issues

and campaigns. Conducts surveys; publishes materials and reports.

Center for Media Education, *2120 L St. N.W., #200 20037; (202) 331-7833. Fax, (202) 331-7841. Kathryn C. Montgomery, President. Web, www.cme.org.*

Promotes public interest in media policies and access to new educational technologies for all children. Provides nonprofit groups with educational and informational services. Maintains a speakers bureau.

Computer and Communications Industry Assn., *666 11th St. N.W., #600 20001; (202) 783-0070. Fax, (202) 783-0534. Edward J. Black, President. General e-mail, ccia@aol.com. Web, www.ccianet.org.*

Membership: manufacturers and suppliers of computer data processing and communications-related products and services. Interests include telecommunications policy, capital formation and tax policy, federal procurement policy, communications and computer industry standards, intellectual property policies, encryption, international trade, and antitrust reform.

Institute for Public Representation, *600 New Jersey Ave. N.W. 20001; (202) 662-9535. Fax, (202) 662-9634. Douglas L. Parker, Director. TTY, (202) 662-9538.*

Public interest law firm funded by Georgetown University Law Center that specializes in communications regulatory policy. Assists citizens' groups that seek input into local and federal regulation of the electronic media; interests include freedom of information.

International Communications Industries Assn., *11242 Waples Mill Rd., #200, Fairfax, VA 22030; (703) 273-7200. Fax, (703) 278-8082. Walter Blackwell, Executive Director. Information, (800) 659-7469. General e-mail, icia@icia.org. Web, www.icia.org.*

Membership: video, audiovisual, and microcomputer dealers; manufacturers and producers; and individuals. Interests include international trade, small business issues, postal rates, copyright, education, and taxation. Monitors legislation and regulations.

Media Access Project, *950 18th St. N.W., #200 20006; (202) 232-4300. Fax, (202) 466-7656. Andrew Jay Schwartzman, President.*

Public interest telecommunications law firm that represents the right of the public to speak and to receive information from the mass media. Interests include media ownership, access to new technologies, and the fairness doctrine.

Media Institute, *1000 Potomac St. N.W., #301 20007; (202) 298-7512. Fax, (202) 337-7092. Patrick D. Maines,*

President. General e-mail, tmi@clark.net. Web, www. mediainst.org.

Conducts conferences, files court briefs and regulatory comments, and sponsors programs on communications topics. Advocates free-speech rights for individuals, media, and corporate speakers.

Media Research Center, *325 S. Patrick St., Alexandria, VA 22314; (703) 683-9733. Fax, (703) 683-9736. L. Brent Bozell III, Chair. Web, www.mediaresearch.org.*

Media-watch organization working for balanced news coverage of political issues. Records and analyzes network news programs; analyzes print media; maintains profiles of media executives and library of recordings.

National Assn. of Broadcasters, *1771 N St. N.W. 20036-2891; (202) 429-5300. Fax, (202) 429-5343. Edward O. Fritts, President. Library, (202) 429-5490. Press, (202) 429-5350. General e-mail, register@nab.org. Web, www.nab.org.*

Membership: radio and television broadcast stations and broadcast networks holding an FCC license or construction permit; associate members include producers of equipment and programs. Assists members in areas of management, engineering, and research. Interests include privatization abroad and related business opportunities. Monitors legislation and regulations.

National Assn. of Regulatory Utility Commissioners, *1101 Vermont Ave. N.W., #200 20005; (202) 898-2200. Fax, (202) 898-2213. Charles Gray, Executive Director. Press, (202) 898-2205. Web, www.naruc.org.*

Membership: members of federal, state, municipal, and Canadian regulatory commissions that have jurisdiction over utilities and carriers. Interests include telecommunications regulation.

National Captioning Institute, *1900 Gallows Rd., Vienna, VA 22182; (703) 917-7600. Fax, (703) 917-9878. Bill Merriam, Chief Executive Officer. Main phone is voice and TTY accessible. General e-mail, mail@ncicap.org. Web, www.ncicap.org.*

Captions television programs for the deaf and hard-of-hearing on behalf of public and commercial broadcast television networks, cable network companies, syndicators, program producers, advertisers, and home video distributors. Produces and disseminates information about the national closed-captioning service.

Telecommunications for the Deaf, *8630 Fenton St., #604, Silver Spring, MD 20910; (301) 589-3786. Fax, (301) 589-3797. Claude Stout, Executive Director. TTY, (301) 589-3006. Voice via relay, (800) 735-2258. General e-mail, info@tdi-online.org. Web, www.tdi-online.org.*

Membership: individuals, organizations, and businesses using text telephone (TTY) equipment. Provides information on TTY equipment. Interests include closed captioning for television, emergency access (911), TTY relay services, visual alerting systems, and TTY/computer conversion. Publishes a national TTY telephone directory.

Telecommunications Industry Assn., *2500 Wilson Blvd., #300, Arlington, VA 22201-3834; (703) 907-7700. Fax, (703) 907-7727. Matthew J. Flanigan, President. Press, (703) 907-7723. General e-mail, tia@tia.eia.org. Web, www.tiaonline.org.*

Membership: telecommunications equipment manufacturers, suppliers, and distributors. Represents members in telecommunications manufacturing issues; helps to develop standards for products; sponsors a job-matching service; cohosts trade shows worldwide. (Affiliated with the Electronic Industries Assn.)

See also National Assn. of State Utility Consumer Advocates (p. 21)

Cable Services

AGENCIES

Federal Communications Commission, *Cable Services Bureau, 445 12th St. S.W., 3rd Floor 20554; (202) 418-7200. Fax, (202) 418-2376. Deborah Lathen, Chief. Library, (202) 418-0450. Web, www.fcc.gov/csb.*

Makes and enforces rules governing cable television and other video distribution services; promotes industry growth, competition, and availability to the public; ensures reasonable rates for consumers in areas that do not have competition in cable service.

Federal Communications Commission, *Cable Services Bureau, Engineering and Technical Services, 445 12th St. S.W. 20554; (202) 418-7000. Fax, (202) 418-1189. John Wong, Chief.*

Processes applications and notifications for licensing of cable television relay service stations (CARS); registers cable television systems; develops, administers, and enforces regulation of cable television and CARS.

NONPROFIT

Alliance for Community Media, *666 11th St. N.W., #740 20001; (202) 393-2650. Fax, (202) 393-2653. Bunnie Riedel, Executive Director. General e-mail, acm@alliancem.org. Web, www.alliancecm.org.*

Membership: cable television companies, programming managers and producers, independent producers, cable administrators and regulators, media access centers, and others involved in community communications. Promotes local programming and participation in cable television. Interests include freedom of expression, diversity of information, and developing technologies. Monitors legislation and regulations.

CTAM, *201 N. Union St., Alexandria, VA 22314; (703) 549-4200. Fax, (703) 684-1167. Char Beales, President. Web, www.ctam.com.*

Promotes innovation in the cable and related industries in areas of marketing, research, management, and new product development. Sponsors annual marketing conference; interests include international markets.

National Cable Television Assn., *1724 Massachusetts Ave. N.W. 20036-1969; (202) 775-3550. Fax, (202) 775-1055. Robert Sachs, President.*

Membership: companies that operate cable television systems, cable television programmers, and manufacturers and suppliers of hardware and software for the industry. Represents the industry before federal regulatory agencies and Congress and in the courts; provides management and promotional aids and information on legal, legislative, and regulatory matters.

Enforcement, Judicial, and Legal Actions

AGENCIES

Antitrust Division, *Telecommunications, 1401 H St. N.W., #8000 20530; (202) 514-5621. Fax, (202) 514-6381. Donald J. Russell, Chief. Information, (888) 736-5287. Web, www.usdoj.gov/atr/index.html.*

Investigates and litigates antitrust cases dealing with communications; participates in agency proceedings and rulemaking concerning communications; monitors and analyzes legislation.

Federal Bureau of Investigation *(Justice Dept.),* **CALEA Implementation Section,** *14800 Conference Center Dr., #300, Chantilly, VA 20151; (703) 814-4800. Fax, (703) 814-4720. H. Michael Warren, Chief.*

Administers enforcement of the Communications Assistance for Law Enforcement Act (CALEA). Promotes cooperation between the telecommunications industry and law enforcement officials to ensure the appropriate use of code-authorized electronic surveillance.

Federal Communications Commission, *Administrative Law Judges, 445 12th St. S.W. 20554; (202) 418-2259. Fax, (202) 418-0195. Joseph Chachkin, Chief Judge.*

Presides over hearings and issues initial decisions in disputes over FCC regulations and applications for licensing.

Federal Communications Commission, *Enforcement Information Bureau, 445 12th St. S.W. 20554-0001; (202) 418-1105. David H. Solomon, Chief. Information, (888) 225-5322. TTY, (888) 835-5322. Web, www.fcc.gov/cib.*

See also General Counsels box (chap. 14)

NONPROFIT

Federal Communications Bar Assn., *1020 19th St. N.W., #325 20036-6101; (202) 293-4000. Fax, (202) 293-4317. Stan Zenor, Executive Director (Acting). General e-mail, fcba@fcba.org. Web, www.fcba.org.*

Membership: attorneys, nonattorneys, and law students in communications law who practice before the Federal Communications Commission, the courts, and state and local regulatory agencies. Cooperates with the FCC and other members of the bar on legal aspects of communications issues.

International and Satellite Communications

AGENCIES

Federal Communications Commission, *Common Carrier Bureau, 445 12th St. S.W. 20554; (202) 418-1500. Fax, (202) 418-2825. Lawrence Strickling, Chief. Web, www.fcc.gov/ccb.*

Develops, recommends, and administers FCC policies involving common carriers (wireline facilities that furnish interstate communications services for hire). Policy areas include long-distance and local exchange telephone companies and proposals to introduce or expand competition in telecommunications markets.

Federal Communications Commission, *International Bureau, 445 12th St. S.W., 6th Floor 20554; (202) 418-0437. Fax, (202) 418-2818. Donald Abelson, Chief. Web, www.fcc.gov/ib.*

Coordinates the FCC's collection and dissemination of information on communications and telecommunications policy, regulation, and market developments in other countries and the policies and regulations of international organizations. Coordinates the FCC's international policy activities; represents the FCC in international forums.

State Dept., *International Communications and Information Policy, 2201 C St. N.W., #4826 20520-5818; (202) 647-5212. Fax, (202) 647-5957. Richard Beaird, U.S. Coordinator (Acting). Web, www.state.gov.*

Develops and manages international communication and information policy for the State Dept. Acts as a liaison for other federal departments and agencies and the private sector in international communications issues. Trade-related telecommunications issues are handled by the Bureau of Economic and Business Affairs.

INTERNATIONAL ORGANIZATIONS

International Telecommunications Satellite Organization, *3400 International Dr. N.W. 20008-3098; (202) 944-6800. Fax, (202) 944-7898. Conny Kullman, Director General. Web, www.intelsat.int.*

Membership: more than 140 nations. Owns and operates a global international satellite communications system.

NONPROFIT

International Assn. of Satellite Users and Suppliers, *45681 Oakbrook Court, #107, Sterling, VA 20166; (703) 759-2094. A. Fred Dassler, Executive Director. Library, (703) 406-2744. General e-mail, iasus@erols.com.*

Membership: satellite users and suppliers. Provides information on the business application of satellites, new technological developments, and federal regulatory and policy actions. Assists corporations, developing countries, and consortia in efficient satellite usage. Brokers new and reconditioned telecommunications equipment; acts as a liaison between satellite users and suppliers.

Satellite Broadcasting and Communications Assn., *225 Reinekers Lane, #600, Alexandria, VA 22314; (703) 549-6990. Fax, (703) 549-7640. Charles Hewitt, President. Fax-on-demand, (888) 629-7222. Web, www.sbca.com.*

Membership: owners, operators, manufacturers, dealers, and distributors of satellite receiving stations; software and program suppliers; and others in the home satellite industry. Promotes use of satellite earth stations for television programming and as part of the national and global information infrastructure. Monitors legislation and regulations.

Society of Satellite Professionals International, *225 Reinekers Lane, #600, Alexandria, VA 22314; (703) 549-8696. Fax, (703) 549-9728. Constance Beck, Executive Director. Web, www.sspi.org.*

Membership: professionals in satellite communications. Promotes worldwide growth of the industry; encourages professional development, information exchange, and research.

Radio and Television

See also Broadcasting (this chapter)

AGENCIES

Corporation for Public Broadcasting, *901 E St. N.W. 20004-2037; (202) 879-9600. Fax, (202) 789-9700. Robert*

T. Coonrod, President. General e-mail, comments@cpb.org. Web, www.cpb.org.

Private corporation chartered by Congress under the Public Broadcasting Act of 1967 and funded by the federal government. Supports public broadcasting through grants for public radio and television stations; provides general support for national program production and operation; helps fund projects on U.S. and international news, culture, history, and natural history; studies emerging technologies, such as cable and satellite transmission, for possible use by public telecommunications; supports training activities.

Federal Communications Commission, *Enforcement Information Bureau, 445 12th St. S.W. 20554-0001; (202) 418-1105. David H. Solomon, Chief. Information, (888) 225-5322. TTY, (888) 835-5322. Web, www.fcc.gov/cib.*

Monitors the radio spectrum and inspects broadcast stations; ensures that U.S. radio laws and FCC rules are observed. Develops activities to inform, assist, and educate licensees; provides presentations and information. Manages the Emergency Alert System. Operates the National Call Center in Gettysburg, Pa.; toll-free (888) numbers handle inquiries and complaints.

Federal Communications Commission, *Engineering and Technology, 445 12th St. S.W. 20554; (202) 418-2470. Fax, (202) 418-1944. Dale N. Hatfield, Chief. Web, www. fcc.gov/oet.*

Advises the FCC on technical and spectrum matters and assists in developing U.S. telecommunications policy. Identifies and reviews developments in telecommunications and related technologies. Studies characteristics of radio frequency spectrum. Certifies radios and other electronic equipment to meet FCC standards.

Federal Communications Commission, *Mass Media Bureau, 455 12th St. S.W., #2C337 20554; (202) 418-2600. Fax, (202) 418-2828. Roy J. Stewart, Chief. Web, www.fcc.gov/mmb.*

Licenses, regulates, and develops audio and video services in traditional broadcasting and emerging television delivery systems, including high-definition television; processes applications for licensing commercial and noncommercial radio and television broadcast equipment and facilities; handles renewals and changes of ownership; investigates public complaints.

National Endowment for the Arts *(National Foundation on the Arts and the Humanities), Dance, Design, Media Arts, Museums, and Visual Arts, 1100 Pennsylvania Ave. N.W. 20506-0001; (202) 682-5452. Fax, (202) 682-5721. Saralyn Reece Hardy, Director. Web, arts.endow. gov.*

Awards grants to nonprofit organizations for film, video, and radio productions; supports arts programming broadcast nationally on public television and radio.

NONPROFIT

Assn. for Interactive Media, *1301 Connecticut Ave. N.W., 5th Floor 20036; (202) 408-0008. Fax, (202) 408-0111. Benjamin Isaacson, Executive Director (Acting). Web, www.interactivehq.org.*

Membership: companies and organizations involved in production and broadband delivery of interactive television and personal computer-based media. Informs members about changes in technology, marketing opportunities, information and product distribution channels, and international policy concerning the Internet. Sponsors the Open Internet Congress.

Assn. for Maximum Service Television, *1776 Massachusetts Ave. N.W., #310 20036; (202) 861-0344. Fax, (202) 861-0342. Margita E. White, President. Web, www. mstv.org.*

Membership: commercial and educational television stations. Participates in FCC rulemaking proceedings; specializes in television engineering and other matters concerning the transmission structure of the nation's television system.

Assn. of America's Public Television Stations, *1350 Connecticut Ave. N.W., #200 20036; (202) 887-1700. Fax, (202) 293-2422. David J. Brugger, President. General e-mail, info@apts.org. Web, www.apts.org.*

Membership: public television licensees. Provides information on licensees' operating characteristics, financing, and facilities; conducts research; assists licensees in local and regional planning efforts. Monitors legislation and regulations.

Assn. of Local Television Stations, *1320 19th St. N.W., #300 20036; (202) 887-1970. Fax, (202) 887-0950. James B. Hedlund, President. Web, www.altv.com.*

Membership: local and independent television stations. Monitors legislation and regulations affecting the industry. Interests include the must-carry rules, copyright laws, and television advertising and syndication issues.

Commercial Alert, *1611 Connecticut Ave. N.W., #3A 20009; (202) 296-2787. Fax, (202) 833-2406. Gary Ruskin, Director. General e-mail, alert@essential.org. Web, www. essential.org/alert.*

Advocates for the reduction of excessive commercialism, advertising, and marketing. Promotes a decrease in the amount of television watched by Americans. Inter-ests include the effects of television, video games, and films on children.

Electronic Industries Alliance, *2500 Wilson Blvd., #400, Arlington, VA 22201-3834; (703) 907-7500. Fax, (703) 907-7501. Dave McCurdy, President. Web, www. eia.org.*

Membership: U.S. electronics manufacturers. Interests include common distribution, government procurement, high-definition television, and home recording rights; promotes trade, competitiveness, and export expansion through the International Business Council. Monitors legislation and regulations.

National Assn. of Broadcasters, *1771 N St. N.W. 20036-2891; (202) 429-5300. Fax, (202) 429-5343. Edward O. Fritts, President. Library, (202) 429-5490. Press, (202) 429-5350. General e-mail, register@nab.org. Web, www.nab.org.*

Membership: radio and television broadcast stations and broadcast networks holding an FCC license or construction permit; associate members include producers of equipment and programs. Assists members in areas of management, engineering, and research. Interests include privatization abroad and related business opportunities. Monitors legislation and regulations.

National Coalition on Television Violence, *5132 Newport Ave., Bethesda, MD 20816; (301) 986-0362. Fax, (301) 656-7031. Mary Ann Banta, Vice President. General e-mail, nctvmd@aol.com. Web, www.nctvv.org.*

Analyzes reports prepared by the broadcast and cable industries; monitors levels of violence in media.

National Public Radio, *635 Massachusetts Ave. N.W. 20001-3753; (202) 414-2000. Fax, (202) 414-3329. Kevin Klose, President. Press, (202) 414-2300. Audience services (tapes, transcripts, and listener inquiries), (202) 414-3232. General e-mail, nprlist@npr.org. Web, www.npr.org.*

Membership: public radio stations nationwide. Produces and distributes news and public affairs programming, congressional hearings, speeches, cultural and dramatic presentations, and programs for specialized audiences. Provides program distribution service via satellite. Represents member stations before Congress, the FCC, and other regulatory agencies.

Public Broadcasting Service, *1320 Braddock Pl., Alexandria, VA 22314; (703) 739-5000. Fax, (703) 739-0775. John Swope, President (Acting). General e-mail, pbs@pbs.org. Web, www.pbs.org.*

Membership: public television stations nationwide. Selects, schedules, promotes, and distributes national programs; provides public television stations with educational, instructional, and cultural programming; also provides news and public affairs, science and nature, fundraising, and children's programming. Assists members with technology development and fundraising.

T.V.-Free America, *1611 Connecticut Ave. N.W., #3A 20009; (202) 887-0436. Fax, (202) 518-5560. Frank Vespe, Executive Director. General e-mail, tvfa@essential.org. Web, www.tvfa.org.*

Promotes a voluntary and dramatic reduction in the amount of television watched by Americans. Sponsors National TV Turn-off Week.

Telephone and Telegraph

For cellular telephones, see Wireless Telecommunications (this chapter)

AGENCIES

Federal Communications Commission, *Common Carrier Bureau, 445 12th St. S.W. 20554; (202) 418-1500. Fax, (202) 418-2825. Lawrence Strickling, Chief. Web, www.fcc.gov/ccb.*

Develops, recommends, and administers FCC policies involving common carriers (wireline facilities that furnish interstate communications services for hire). Policy areas include long-distance and local exchange telephone companies and proposals to introduce or expand competition in telecommunications markets.

General Services Administration, *Federal Telecommunications Service, 10304 Eaton Pl., Fairfax, VA 22030; (703) 306-6020. Fax, (703) 306-6029. Dennis J. Fischer, Commissioner. Web, www.gsa.gov.*

Purchases and leases telecommunications equipment and services for the federal government. Monitors the transition from federal telecommunications direct service to private provider partnerships for government telephone service.

NONPROFIT

Assn. for Local Telecommunications Services, *888 17th St. N.W., #900 20006; (202) 969-2587. Fax, (202) 969-2581. Tricia Breckenridge, Chair. Web, www.alts.org.*

Seeks to open local telecommunications market to full and fair facilities-based competition. Monitors legislation and regulations.

CompTel, *1900 M St. N.W., #800 20036; (202) 296-6650. Fax, (202) 296-7585. Russell Frisby, President. Web, www.comptel.org.*

Membership: providers of long-distance telecommunications services and suppliers to the industry. Analyzes domestic and international issues affecting competitive long-distance carriers, including mergers. Monitors legislation and regulations.

MultiMedia Telecommunications Assn., *2500 Wilson Blvd., #300, Arlington, VA 22201; (703) 907-7470. Fax, (703) 907-7478. Mary I. Bradshaw, President. General e-mail, info@mmta.org. Web, www.mmta.org.*

Membership: manufacturers, suppliers, distributors, and users of computer and communications systems. Serves as an information source and provides members with a benefits program and legal counsel; conducts training program. Monitors legislation and regulations.

National Telephone Cooperative Assn., *4121 Wilson Blvd., 10th Floor, Arlington, VA 22203; (703) 351-2000. Fax, (703) 351-2001. Michael E. Brunner, Executive Vice President. General e-mail, contact@ntca.org. Web, www. ntca.org.*

Membership: locally owned and controlled telecommunications cooperatives and companies serving rural and small-town areas. Offers educational seminars, workshops, technical assistance, and a benefits program to members. Monitors legislation and regulations.

Organization for the Protection and Advancement of Small Telephone Companies, *21 Dupont Circle N.W., #700 20036; (202) 659-5990. Fax, (202) 659-4619. John N. Rose, President. General e-mail, opastco@opastco. org. Web, www.opastco.org.*

Membership: local exchange carriers with 50,000 or fewer access lines. Provides members with educational materials and information on regulatory, legislative, and judicial issues in the telecommunications industry. Operates Foundation for Rural Education and Development.

U.S. Telecom Assn., *1401 H St. N.W., #600 20005; (202) 326-7300. Fax, (202) 326-7333. Roy Neel, President. Web, www.usta.org.*

Membership: local telephone companies and manufacturers and suppliers for these companies. Provides members with information on the industry; conducts seminars; participates in FCC regulatory proceedings.

Wireless Telecommunications

AGENCIES

Federal Communications Commission, *Wireless Telecommunications Bureau, 445 12th St. S.W., #3-C207 20554; (202) 418-0600. Fax, (202) 418-0787. Tom Sugrue, Chief. Library, (202) 418-0450. Web, www.fcc.gov/wtb.*

Regulates wireless communications, including cellular telephone, paging, personal communications services, public safety, air and maritime navigation, and other commercial and private radio services. Assesses new uses of wireless technologies, including electronic commerce. Gettysburg office handles all licensing applications and concerns: FCC Wireless Telecommunications Bureau, Licensing Division, 1270 Fairfield Rd., Gettysburg, PA 17325; (717) 338-2510.

U.S. Secret Service *(Treasury Dept.), Financial Crimes, 950 H St. N.W., #5300 20001; (202) 406-5850. Fax, (202) 406-5031. Gregory Regan, Special Agent in Charge. Web, www.ustreas.gov/usss/financial_crimes.htm.*
Investigates reports of cellular phone and credit fraud.

NONPROFIT

American Mobile Telecommunications Assn., *1150 18th St. N.W., #250 20036; (202) 331-7773. Fax, (202) 331-9062. Alan R. Shark, President. Web, www.amtausa. org.*
Membership: mobile telecommunications companies, including dispatch services. Serves as an information source on radio frequencies, licensing, new products and technology, and market conditions; offers research service of FCC records. Promotes the industry abroad through the International Mobile Telecommunications Assn. Monitors legislation and regulations.

Cellular Telecommunications Industry Assn., *1250 Connecticut Ave. N.W., #800 20036; (202) 785-0081. Fax, (202) 776-0540. Thomas E. Wheeler, President. Web, www. wow-com.com.*
Membership: system operators, equipment manufacturers, engineering firms, and others engaged in the cellular telephone and mobile communications industry in domestic and world markets. Provides information for consumers and persons with disabilities. Monitors legislation and regulations.

Council of Independent Communication Suppliers, *1110 N. Glebe Rd., #500, Arlington, VA 22201-5720; (703) 528-5115. Fax, (703) 524-1074. Samuel J. Klein, Chair. General e-mail, sharpe@ita-relay.com. Web, www.ita-relay. com.*
Represents independent radio sales and service organizations, communications service providers, and telecommunications consultants and engineers serving the Private Land Mobile Radio Services industry. Informs members of FCC and industry activities; solicits members' views on FCC regulatory proceedings. (Affiliated with Industrial Telecommunications Assn.)

Industrial Telecommunications Assn., *1110 N. Glebe Rd., #500, Arlington, VA 22201-5720; (703) 528-5115.*

Fax, (703) 524-1074. Mark E. Crosby, President. General e-mail, info@ita-relay.com. Web, www.ita-relay.com.
FCC-certified frequency advisory committee for the Special Industrial Radio Service and Industrial/Land Transportation pools. Provides frequency coordination, licensing, research, and telecommunications engineering services to Private Land Mobile Radio Services licensees and applicants. Represents telecommunications interests of Special Industrial, Video Production, and Telephone Maintenance Radio Service licensees and informs members of FCC rule changes and industry activities.

Personal Communications Industry Assn., *500 Montgomery St., #700, Alexandria, VA 22314; (703) 739-0300. Fax, (703) 836-1608. E. B. "Jay" Kitchen Jr., President. Information, (800) 759-0300. Fax-on-demand, (800) 680-7242. Web, www.pcia.com.*
Membership: individuals; institutions; independent two-way radio dealers; and FCC-licensed carriers who provide the public with personal communications services, including pagers, cellular telephones, and conventional radio telephones. Provides members with information, technical assistance, and educational programs. Serves as the FCC-recognized coordinator for frequencies in the Business Radio Service. Interests include technological standards and development of international markets. Library offers fee-based services by appointment. Monitors legislation and regulations.

United Telecom Council, *1140 Connecticut Ave. N.W., #1140 20036; (202) 872-0030. Fax, (202) 872-1331. Denise Bartlow, Member Services Manager. Web, www.utc.org.*
Membership: electric, gas, and water utility companies and natural gas pipelines. Participates in FCC rulemaking proceedings. Interests include radio spectrum for fixed and mobile communication and technological, legislative, and regulatory developments affecting telecommunications operations of energy utilities.

Wireless Communications Assn. International, *1140 Connecticut Ave. N.W., #810 20036; (202) 452-7823. Fax, (202) 452-0041. Andrew Kreig, President. Web, www.wcai. com.*
Membership: system operators, program suppliers, equipment and service providers, engineers, and others involved in delivery of subscription television programming over a terrestrial microwave platform. Develops standards; promotes technological advancement and worldwide growth of the industry. Monitors legislation and regulations.

GOVERNMENT INFORMATION

See also Access to Congressional Information (chap. 20); Internet and Related Technologies (this chapter: for list of agency Web sites); Libraries and Educational Media (chap. 6)

AGENCIES

General Services Administration, *Federal Information Center, P.O. Box, #600, Cumberland, MD 21501-0600. Fax, (301) 722-0066. Warren Snaider, Staff Contact. Information, (800) 688-9889. TTY, (800) 326-2996. Web, fic.info.gov.*

Operates a toll-free hotline which provides information on all federal government agencies, programs, and services.

General Services Administration, *Federal Relay Service, 13221 Woodland Park Rd., 3rd Floor, Herndon, VA 20171-3022; (703) 306-6360. Carolyn Thomas, Director. TTY, (800) 877-8339. Customer service, (800) 877-0996. Web, www.gsa.gov/frs.*

Assures that the federal telecommunications system is fully accessible to deaf, hearing-impaired, and speech-impaired individuals, including federal workers. Operates twenty-four hours a day, seven days a week. Produces a directory of TDD/TTY services within the federal government.

National Archives and Records Administration, *8601 Adelphi Rd., #4200, College Park, MD 20740-6001; (301) 713-6410. Fax, (301) 713-7141. John Carlin, Archivist of the United States; Lewis J. Bellardo, Deputy Archivist. Press, (301) 713-7360.*

Identifies, preserves, and makes available federal government documents of historic value; administers a network of regional storage centers and archives and operates the presidential library system. Collections include photographs, graphic materials, and films; holdings include records generated by foreign governments (especially in wartime) and by international conferences, commissions, and exhibitions.

National Archives and Records Administration, *Center for Legislative Archives, 700 Pennsylvania Ave. N.W., #8E 20408; (202) 501-5350. Fax, (202) 219-2176. Michael Gillette, Director.*

Collects and maintains records of congressional committees and legislative files from 1789 to the present. Publishes inventories and guides to these records.

National Archives and Records Administration, *Electronic and Special Media Records, 8601 Adelphi Rd.,*

#5320, College Park, MD 20740-6001; (301) 713-6630. Fax, (301) 713-6911. Michael Carlson, Director. Reference service, (301) 713-6645. General e-mail, cer@nara.gov. Web, www.nara.gov/nara/electronic.

Preserves, maintains, and makes available electronic records of the U.S. government in all subject areas. Provides researchers with magnetic tape copies of records on a cost-recovery basis. Distributes lists of holdings.

National Archives and Records Administration, *Federal Register, 800 N. Capitol St., #700 20408; (202) 523-5230. Fax, (202) 523-6866. Frances D. McDonald, Editor-in-Chief. TTY, (202) 523-5229. Public Laws Update Service (PLUS), (202) 523-6641. Web, www.nara.gov/fedreg/.*

Assigns public law numbers to enacted legislation, executive orders, and proclamations; responds to inquiries on public law numbers; assists inquirers in finding presidential signing or veto messages in the *Weekly Compilation of Presidential Documents* and the *Public Papers of the Presidents* series; compiles slip laws and annual *United States Statutes at Large;* compiles indexes for finding statutory provisions. Operates Public Laws Update Service (PLUS), which provides information by telephone on new legislation. Publications available from the U.S. Government Printing Office.

National Archives and Records Administration, *Modern Records Program, 8601 Adelphi Rd., College Park, MD 20740; (301) 713-7100. Fax, (301) 713-6850. Michael L. Miller, Director. General e-mail, Records. Management@arch2.nara.gov.*

Administers programs that establish standards, guidelines, and procedures for agency records administration. Manages training programs; inspects records management practices; monitors certain records not contained in National Archives depositories.

National Archives and Records Administration, *Presidential Libraries, 8601 Adelphi Rd., #2200, College Park, MD 20740; (301) 713-6050. Fax, (301) 713-6045. David F. Peterson, Assistant Archivist. Web, www.nara.gov.*

Directs all programs relating to acquisition, preservation, publication, and research use of materials in presidential libraries; conducts oral history projects; publishes finding aids for research sources; provides reference service, including information from and about documentary holdings.

National Archives and Records Administration, *Regional Records Services, 8601 Adelphi Rd., College Park, MD 20740-6001; (301) 713-7200. Fax, (301) 713-7205. Richard L. Claypoole, Assistant Archivist.*

CHIEF INFORMATION OFFICERS FOR FEDERAL AGENCIES

DEPARTMENTS

Agriculture, Anne Reed, (202) 720-8833

Commerce, Roger W. Baker, (202) 482-4797

Defense, Arthur L. Money, (703) 695-0348

   Air Force, Lt. Gen. Gregory S. Martin, (703) 697-6363

   Army, Lt. Gen. William H. Campbell, (703) 697-7494

   Navy, Daniel E. Porter, (703) 602-1800, (703) 602-2104

Education, Craig Luygart, (202) 401-0085

Energy, John M. Gilligan, (202) 586-0166

Health and Human Services, John J. Callahan, (202) 690-6396

Housing and Urban Development, Gloria Parker, (202) 708-1008

Interior, Daryl W. White, (202) 208-6194

Justice, Stephen R. Colgate, (202) 514-3101

Labor, Patricia Lattimore, (202) 693-4040

State, Fernando Burbano, (202) 647-2226

Transportation, Eugene Taylor, (202) 366-9201

Treasury, Jim Flyzik, (202) 622-1200

Veterans Affairs, Harold Gracey, (202) 273-8842

AGENCIES

Environmental Protection Agency, Alvin Pesachowitz, (202) 260-6665

Federal Emergency Management Agency, George Haddow, (202) 646-4600

Federal Trade Commission, Richard G. Turner, (202) 326-2898

General Accounting Office, John Harmon, (202) 512-6623

General Services Administration, William C. Piatt, (202) 501-1000

Intelligence Community, John Young, (703) 482-1100

National Aeronautics and Space Administration, Lee Holcomb, (202) 358-1824

National Science Foundation, Linda Massaro, (703) 306-1100

Nuclear Regulatory Commission, Stuart Reiter, (301) 415-8700

Office of Personnel Management, Janet L. Barnes, (202) 606-2150

Securities and Exchange Commission, Michael E. Bartell, (202) 942-8800

Small Business Administration, Lawrence E. Barrett, (202) 205-6708

Social Security Administration, John R. Dyer, (410) 965-9000

Stores federal records and assists agencies in microfilming records, protecting vital operating records, improving filing and classification systems, and developing disposition schedules. (See appendix for list of regional records facilities.)

National Archives and Records Administration, *Textual Reference, 8601 Adelphi Rd., College Park, MD 20740-6001; (301) 713-7250. Fax, (301) 713-6907. James Hastings, Director.*

Provides reference service for unpublished civil and military federal government records. Maintains central catalog of all library materials. Compiles comprehensive bibliographies of materials related to archival administration and records management. Permits research in American history, archival science, and records management. Maintains collections of the papers of the Continental Congress (1774–1789), U.S. State Dept. diplomatic correspondence (1789–1963), and general records of the U.S. government.

National Technical Information Service *(Commerce Dept.), 5285 Port Royal Rd., #200F, Springfield, VA 22161; (703) 605-6400. Fax, (703) 605-6715. Ron R. Lawson, Director. TTY, (703) 605-6043. Sales center, (703) 605-6000; rush orders, (800) 553-6847. Web, www.ntis.gov.*

Distribution center that catalogs and sells U.S. and foreign government-sponsored research, development, and scientific engineering reports and other technical analyses prepared by federal and local government agencies. Offers microfiche and computerized bibliographic search services. Online database available through commercial vendors and in machine-readable form through lease agreement.

National Technical Information Service *(Commerce Dept.), National Audiovisual Center, 5285 Port Royal Rd., Springfield, VA 22161; (703) 605-6000. Fax, (703) 605-6900. Ron R. Lawson, Director. Web, www.ntis.gov.*

Serves as a clearinghouse for video cassettes, slide sets, audiotapes, interactive video disks, and multimedia kits produced by federal agencies on a wide range of

PUBLICATIONS OFFICES AT FEDERAL AGENCIES

DEPARTMENTS

Agriculture, Orders, (202) 720-2791

Commerce, Orders (via NTIS), (703) 605-6000

Defense, Orders, (703) 697-5737

  Army, Orders, (703) 325-6297

Energy, Orders, (202) 586-5575

Health and Human Services, Orders, (301) 458-4636

Housing and Urban Development, Orders, (800) 767-7468; Fax orders, (202) 708-2313

Justice, Orders, (202) 514-2007

Labor, Statistic orders, (202) 606-7828

State, Orders, (202) 647-6575; Fax-on-demand, (202) 736-7720

Transportation, Orders, (301) 322-4961; Fax orders, (301) 386-5394

Treasury, Orders, (202) 622-2970; Fax-on-demand, (202) 622-2040

Veterans Affairs, Orders, (202) 273-5700

AGENCIES

Census Bureau, Orders, (301) 457-4100

Commission on Civil Rights, Orders, (202) 376-8128

Consumer Product Safety Commission, Orders, (301) 504-0785

Corporation for National Service (AmeriCorps), Orders, (800) 942-2677

Energy Information Administration, Orders, (202) 586-8800

Environmental Protection Agency, Orders, (202) 260-5922

Equal Employment Opportunity Commission, Orders, (800) 669-3362

Federal Communications Commission, Orders, (202) 857-3800; Fax orders, (202) 857-3805; Fax-on-demand, (202) 418-2830

Federal Election Commission, Orders, (800) 424-9530

Federal Emergency Management Agency, Orders, (202) 646-3484

Federal Reserve System, Orders, (202) 452-3244

Federal Trade Commission, Orders, (202) 326-2222

General Accounting Office, Orders, (202) 512-6000

General Services Administration, Orders, (202) 501-1235

Government Printing Office, Orders, (202) 512-1800

International Bank for Reconstruction and Development (World Bank), Orders, (202) 473-1155

International Trade Administration Orders from NTIS and GPO, (202) 482-5487

National Aeronautics and Space Administration, Orders, (301) 621-0390

National Archives and Records Administration, Orders, (202) 501-5235; Toll-free, (800) 234-8861

National Endowment for the Humanities, Orders, (202) 606-8400

National Institute of Standards and Technology, Information (orders from NTIS and GPO), (301) 975-6478

National Labor Relations Board, Pamphlets, (202) 273-1991; Orders from GPO, (202) 512-1800

National Oceanic and Atmospheric Administration, Information and orders, (800) 638-8975; Fax orders, (301) 436-6829

National Park Service, Information (orders by mail only), (202) 208-4747

National Science Foundation, Orders, (301) 947-2722

National Technical Information Service, Orders, (703) 605-6000

National Transportation Safety Board, Orders, (202) 314-6551

Nuclear Regulatory Commission, Orders from GPO, (202) 512-1800

Occupational Safety and Health Administration, Orders, (202) 693-1888

Office of Personnel Management, Information (orders from GPO), (202) 606-1822; Retirement and insurance information, (202) 606-0623

Peace Corps, Orders from NTIS, (703) 605-6000 or ERIC, (800) 538-3742; Information, (202) 692-2636

Securities and Exchange Commission, Information, (202) 942-4040; Orders, (202) 942-4046

Smithsonian Institution, Orders: Smithsonian books, recordings, videos, (800) 669-1559; Orders: Smithsonian University Press, (800) 782-4612; Customer service, (202) 287-3738

Social Security Administration, Orders, (410) 965-4155

U.S. Fish and Wildlife Service, Orders, (304) 876-7203

U.S. Geological Survey, Orders, (888) ASK-USGS

U.S. Institute of Peace, Book orders, (800) 868-8064; Other orders, (202) 457-1700

Women's Bureau (Labor Dept.), Orders, (202) 219-6652

FREEDOM OF INFORMATION CONTACTS

DEPARTMENTS

Agriculture, Andrea Fowler, (202) 720-8164

Commerce, Brenda Dolan, (202) 482-4115

Defense, H. J. McIntyre, (703) 697-4026

Air Force, Rhonda Jenkins, (703) 696-7263

Army, Rosemary Christianson, (703) 806-5698

Navy, Doris M. Lama, (202) 685-6545

Education, Maria-Teresa Cueva, (202) 708-9263

Energy, Abel Lopez, (202) 586-6025

Health and Human Services, Rosario Cirrincione, (202) 690-7453

Housing and Urban Development, Sharri Weaver, (202) 708-3866

Interior, Alexandra Mallus, (202) 208-5342

Justice, Patricia D. Harris, (301) 436-1018

Labor, Miriam Miller, (202) 219-8188

State, Margaret Grafeld, (202) 647-7740

Transportation, Vacant, (202) 366-4542

Treasury, Lana Johnson, (202) 622-0930

Veterans Affairs, Donald L. Nielson, (202) 273-8135

AGENCIES

Agency for International Development, Willette Smith, (202) 712-5027

Central Intelligence Agency, Kathryn Dyer, (703) 613-1287

Commission on Civil Rights, Emma Monroig, (202) 376-8351

Commodity Futures Trading Commission, Edward Colbert, (202) 418-5105

Consumer Product Safety Commission, Todd A. Stevenson, (301) 504-0785

Environmental Protection Agency, Jeralene B. Green, (202) 260-4048

Equal Employment Opportunity Commission, J. C. Thurmond, (202) 663-4669

Export-Import Bank, Howard Schweitzer, (202) 565-3229

Farm Credit Administration, Deborah Buccolo, (703) 883-4020

Federal Communications Commission, Patricia Quartey, (202) 418-0440

Federal Deposit Insurance Corp., Lisa Snider, (202) 898-3822

Federal Election Commission, Ron Harris, (202) 694-1220

Federal Emergency Management Agency, Sandra Jackson, (202) 646-3840

Federal Labor Relations Authority, David M. Smith, (202) 482-6620

Federal Maritime Commission, Bryant Van Brakle, (202) 523-5725

Federal Reserve, Martha Connor, (202) 452-3684

Federal Trade Commission, William Golden, (202) 326-2494

General Services Administration, Mary Cunningham, (202) 501-3415

Legal Services Corp., Shannon Adaway, (202) 336-8813

Merit Systems Protection Board, Michael Hoxie, (202) 653-7200

National Aeronautics and Space Administration, Patricia M. Riep-Dice, (202) 358-1764

National Archives and Records Administration, Mary Ronan, (301) 713-6025

National Credit Union Administration, Patricia Slye, (703) 518-6565

National Endowment for the Humanities, Laura Nelson, (202) 606-8322

National Labor Relations Board, John W. Hornbeck, (202) 273-3847

National Mediation Board, Judy Femi, (202) 692-5040

National Science Foundation, Leslie Crawford, (703) 306-1060

National Transportation Safety Board, Melba Moye, (202) 314-6551

Nuclear Regulatory Commission, Russell Powell, (301) 415-7169

Office of Personnel Management, Mary Beth Smith-Toomey, (202) 606-8358

Peace Corps, Joy Hazel, (202) 692-1125

Pension Benefit Guaranty Corp., Bill Fitzgerald, (202) 326-4040

Securities and Exchange Commission, Betty Lopez (acting), (202) 942-4320

Selective Service, Paula Sweeney, (703) 605-4046

Small Business Administration, Beverly Linden, (202) 401-8203

Social Security Administration, Darrell Blevins, (410) 966-6645

U.S. International Trade Commission, Donna R. Koehnke, (202) 205-2000

U.S. Postal Service, Betty Sheriff, (202) 268-2608

subjects, including languages, health and safety, and training programs. Publishes catalogs of audiovisual materials produced by all agencies of the U.S. government.

CONGRESS

General Accounting Office, *Document Distribution Center,* 441 G St. N.W. 20548 (mailing address: P.O. Box 37050 20013); (202) 512-6000. Fax, (202) 512-6061. *Angela Childs, Supervisor. Press, (202) 512-4800. Locator, (202) 512-3000. General e-mail, info@www.gao.gov. Web, www.gao.gov.*

Provides information to the public on many federal programs. GAO publications and information about GAO publications are available upon request.

Government Printing Office (GPO), *732 N. Capitol St. N.W. 20402; (202) 512-2034. Fax, (202) 512-1347. Michael F. DiMario, Public Printer. Press, (202) 512-1991. Congressional documents, (202) 512-1808. General government publications, (202) 512-1800. General e-mail, publicprinter@gpo.gov. Web, www.gpo.gov.*

Prints, distributes, and sells selected publications of the U.S. Congress, government agencies, and executive departments. Makes available, for a fee, the *Monthly Catalog of U.S. Government Publications,* a comprehensive listing of all publications issued by the various departments and agencies each month. Publications are distributed to GPO Regional Depository Libraries; some titles also may be purchased at GPO bookstores in larger cities.

House Administration Committee, *1309 LHOB 20515; (202) 225-8281. Fax, (202) 225-9957. Rep. Bill Thomas, R-Calif., Chair; Cathy Abernathy, Staff Director. Web, www.house.gov/cha.*

Jurisdiction over the printing, cost of printing, binding, and distribution of congressional publications; jurisdiction (in conjunction with the Senate Rules and Administration Committee and the Joint Committee on Printing) over the Government Printing Office, executive papers and depository libraries; jurisdiction over federal election law.

Joint Committee on Printing, *1309 LHOB 20515; (202) 225-8281. Rep. Bill Thomas, R-Calif., Chair; Eric C. Peterson, Staff Director. Web, www.house.gov/jcp.*

Oversees public printing, binding, and distribution of government publications; executive papers and depository libraries; and activities of the Government Printing Office (in conjunction with the House Administration and Senate Rules and Administration committees).

Legislative Resource Center, *Resource and Reference, B-106 CHOB 20515; (202) 226-5200. Fax, (202) 226-5208. Lea Uhre, Manager.*

Conducts historical research. Advises members on the disposition of their records and papers; maintains information on manuscript collections of former members; maintains biographical files on former members. Print publications include *Biographical Directory of the United States Congress, 1774–1989; Guide to Research Collections of Former Members of the United States House of Representatives, 1789–1987; Black Americans in Congress, 1870–1989;* and *Women in Congress, 1917–1989.*

Library of Congress, *Federal Library and Information Center Committee,* 101 Independence Ave. S.E., #217 20540-4935; (202) 707-4800. Fax, (202) 707-4818. *Susan Tarr, Executive Director. General e-mail, flicc@loc.gov. Web, locweb.loc.gov/flicc.*

Membership: one representative from each major federal agency, one representative each from the Library of Congress and the national libraries of medicine and agriculture, and one representative from each of the major Federal Information Centers. Coordinates planning, development, operations, and activities among federal libraries.

Library of Congress, *Serial and Government Publications,* 101 Independence Ave. S.E. 20540; (202) 707-5647. *Fax, (202) 707-6128. Karen Renninger, Chief. Information, (202) 707-5690.*

Operates Newspaper and Periodical Reading Room; maintains library's collection of current domestic and foreign newspapers, current periodicals, and serially issued publications of federal, state, and foreign governments; has maintained full government publication depository since 1979. Responds to written or telephone requests for information on government publications.

Senate Historical Office, *SH-201 20510; (202) 224-6900. Fax, (202) 224-5329. Richard Baker, Historian. Web, www.senate.gov.*

Serves as an information clearinghouse on Senate history, traditions, and members. Collects, organizes, and distributes to the public previously unpublished Senate documents; collects and preserves photographs and pictures related to Senate history; conducts an oral history program; advises senators and Senate committees on the disposition of their noncurrent papers and records. Produces publications on the history of the Senate.

Senate Rules and Administration Committee, *SR-305 20510; (202) 224-6352. Fax, (202) 224-3036. Sen. Mitch McConnell, R-Ky., Chair; Tamara Somerville, Staff Director. Web, rules.senate.gov.*

Jurisdiction over the printing, cost of printing, binding, and distribution of congressional publications; jurisdiction (in conjunction with the House Administration

PUBLIC AFFAIRS CONTACTS FOR FEDERAL AGENCIES

DEPARTMENTS

Agriculture, Andy Solomon, (202) 720-4623

Commerce, Morrie Goodman, (202) 482-4883

Defense, Kenneth H. Bacon, (703) 697-9312

  Air Force, Col. Ronald T. Rand, (703) 697-6061

  Army, Maj. Gen. John G. Meyer Jr., (703) 695-5135

  Marine Corps, Brig. Gen. William A. Whitlow, (703) 614-2958

  Navy, Rear Adm. Thomas Jurkowsky, (703) 697-7391

Education, Alex Wohl, (202) 401-3026

Energy, Brooke D. Anderson, (202) 586-4940

Health and Human Services, Melissa T. Skolfield, (202) 690-7850

Housing and Urban Development, David Egner (acting), (202) 708-0980

Interior, Michael G. Gauldin, (202) 208-6416

Justice, Myron Marlin, (202) 616-2777

Labor, Howard Waddell (acting), (202) 693-4676

State, Vacant, (202) 647-7191

Transportation, Mary Trupo (acting), (202) 366-4570

Treasury, Michelle Smith, (202) 622-2910

Veterans Affairs, John T. Hanson, (202) 273-5750

AGENCIES

Agency for International Development, Joseph Crapa, (202) 712-4300

Commission on Civil Rights, Marcia Tyler, (202) 376-8312

Commodity Futures Trading Commission, John C. Phillips, (202) 418-5080

Consumer Product Safety Commission, Russ Rader (acting), (301) 504-0580

Corporation for National Service, Tara Murphy, (202) 606-5000, ext. 158

Environmental Protection Agency, Margaret Morgan-Hubbard, (202) 260-4454

Equal Employment Opportunity Commission, Reginald Welch, (202) 663-4900

Export–Import Bank, Sandy Jackson (acting), (202) 565-3200

Farm Credit Administration, Eileen M. McMahon, (703) 883-4235

Federal Communication Commission, Joy Howell, (202) 418-0500

Federal Deposit Insurance Corporation, Philip Battey, (202) 898-7192

Federal Election Commission, Ronald M. Harris, (202) 694-1220

Federal Emergency Management Agency, George Haddow, (202) 646-4600

Federal Labor Relations Authority, Patty Reilly, (202) 482-6690, ext. 403

Federal Mediation and Conciliation Services, David L. Helfert, (202) 606-8080

Committee and the Joint Committee on Printing) over the Government Printing Office, executive papers, and depository libraries.

Freedom of Information

AGENCIES

Each agency has rules governing public access to its documents. Grants for access are determined initially by the agency; contact the freedom of information officer of the agency involved. (See appendix for explanation of Freedom of Information Act.)

Justice Dept., *Information and Privacy, 950 Pennsylvania Ave. N.W., #570 20530; (202) 514-3642. Fax, (202) 514-1009. Daniel J. Metcalfe, Co-Director; Richard L.*

Huff, Co-Director. Information, (202) 514-2000. TTY, (202) 514-1888. Web, www.usdoj.gov.

Provides federal agencies with advice and policy guidance on matters related to implementing and interpreting the Freedom of Information Act (FOIA). Litigates selected FOIA and Privacy Act cases; adjudicates administrative appeals from Justice Dept. denials of public requests for access to documents; conducts FOIA training for government agencies.

National Archives and Records Administration,
Information Security Oversight, 700 Pennsylvania Ave. N.W., #18N 20408-0001; (202) 219-5250. Fax, (202) 219-5385. Steven Garfinkel, Director. General e-mail, isoo@arch1.nara.gov.

Oversees government policy on security classification of documents for federal agencies and industry; reviews

PUBLIC AFFAIRS CONTACTS FOR FEDERAL AGENCIES (continued)

Federal Reserve System, Lynn Fox, (202) 452-3204

Federal Trade Commission, Victoria A. Streitfeld, (202) 326-2180

General Accounting Office, Cleve E. Corlett, (202) 512-4800

General Services Administration, Beth W. Newburger, (202) 501-0705

Government Printing Office, Andrew M. Sherman, (202) 512-1991

Institute of Museum and Library Services, Mary Ann Bittner, (202) 606-8536

National Aeronautics and Space Administration, Peggy Wilhide, (202) 358-1898

National Archives and Records Administration, Susan Cooper, (301) 713-6000

National Capital Planning Commission, Denise H. Liebowitz, (202) 482-7200

National Credit Union Administration, Robert E. Loftus, (703) 518-6330

National Endowment for the Arts, Cherie Simon, (202) 682-5570

National Endowment for the Humanities, Roberta Heine, (202) 606-8624

National Labor Relations Board, David B. Parker, (202) 273-1991

National Science Foundation, Julia A. Moore, (703) 306-1070

National Transportation Safety Board, Jamie Finch, (202) 314-6100

Nuclear Regulatory Commission, William M. Beecher, (301) 415-8200

Occupational Safety and Health Review Commission, Linda A. Smith-Whitsett, (202) 606-5398

Office of Personnel Management, Jon-Christopher Bua, (202) 606-1800

Office of Special Counsel, Jane McFarland, (202) 653-7984

Pension Benefit Guaranty Corporation, Judith Welles, (202) 326-4040

Securities and Exchange Commission, Christophe Ullman, (202) 942-0020

Selective Service System, Lewis C. Brodsky, (703) 605-4100

Small Business Administration, Debra Silimeo, (202) 205-6606

Social Security Administration, Charles H. Mullen, (410) 965-2739

U.S. International Trade Commission, Margaret M. O'Laughlin, (202) 205-1819

U.S. Postal Service, Judy deTorok, (202) 268-3615

---

procedures; monitors declassification programs of federal agencies.

National Archives and Records Administration, *Initial Processing/Declassification,* 8601 Adelphi Rd., College Park, MD 20740; (301) 713-7160. Fax, (301) 713-6908. Jeanne Schauble, Director.

Directs the review and declassification of records and security-classified materials in the National Archives in accordance with Executive Order 12958 and the Freedom of Information Act; assists other federal archival agencies in declassifying security-classified documents in their holdings.

CONGRESS

House Government Reform Committee, *Subcommittee on Government Management, Information, and Technology,* B373 RHOB 20515; (202) 225-5147. Fax, (202) 225-2373. Rep. Steve Horn, R-Calif., Chair; J. Russell George, Staff Director. Web, www.house.gov/reform.

Jurisdiction over Freedom of Information Act.

Senate Judiciary Committee, *Subcommittee on Technology, Terrorism, and Government Information,* SH-325 20510; (202) 224-6791. Fax, (202) 228-0542. Sen. Jon Kyl, R-Ariz., Chair; Stephen Higgins, Chief Counsel. Web, judiciary.senate.gov/techterr.htm.

Jurisdiction over Freedom of Information Act.

NONPROFIT

American Civil Liberties Union, *Washington Office,* 122 Maryland Ave. N.E. 20002; (202) 544-1681. Fax, (202) 546-0738. Laura W. Murphy, Director. Web, www. aclu.org.

Initiates test court cases and advocates legislation to guarantee constitutional rights and civil liberties. Monitors agency compliance with the Freedom of Information Act, the Privacy Act, and other access statutes. Produces publications.

American Society of Access Professionals, *1444 Eye St. N.W., #700 20005; (202) 712-9054. Fax, (202) 216-9646. Claire Shamley, Executive Director. Web, www.podi. com/asap.*

Membership: federal employees, attorneys, journalists, and others working with or interested in access-to-information laws. Seeks to improve the administration of the Freedom of Information Act, the Privacy Act, and other access statutes.

Center for National Security Studies, *Gelman Library, 2130 H St. N.W., #701 20037; (202) 994-7060. Fax, (202) 994-1446. Kate Martin, Director. Web, gwis.circ. gwu.edu/~cnss.*

A project of the Fund for Peace. Specializes in the Freedom of Information Act as it relates to national security matters and access to government information issues in the United States and abroad. Affiliated with the National Security Archive. Collection open to the public by appointment.

Radio-Television News Directors Assn., *1000 Connecticut Ave. N.W., #615 20036; (202) 659-6510. Fax, (202) 223-4007. Barbara Cochran, President. General e-mail, rtnda@rtnda.org. Web, www.rtnda.org.*

Membership: local and network news executives in broadcasting, cable, and other electronic media. Operates the Freedom of Information Committee, which assists members with news access.

▦ INTERNET AND RELATED TECHNOLOGIES

AGENCIES

Criminal Division *(Justice Dept.),* **Computer Crime and Intellectual Property,** *1301 New York Ave. N.W., #600 20005; (202) 514-1026. Fax, (202) 514-6113. Martha Stansell-Gamm, Chief. Web, www.usdoj.gov/criminal/ cybercrime.*

Investigates and litigates criminal and civil cases involving computers and the Internet; provides specialized technical and legal assistance to other Justice Dept. divisions; coordinates international efforts; formulates policies and proposes legislation on computer crime issues.

Defense Advanced Research Projects Agency *(Defense Dept.),* *3701 N. Fairfax Dr., Arlington, VA 22203-1714; (703) 696-2400. Fax, (703) 696-2209. F. L. Fernandez, Director; Jane A. Alexander, Deputy Director, (703) 696-2402. Press, (703) 696-2404. Web, www. darpa.mil.*

Helps maintain U.S. technological superiority in support of national security. Conducts ongoing research to develop the World Wide Web; funds Web-related research at other organizations.

Federal Bureau of Investigation *(Justice Dept.),* **Financial Institution Fraud,** *935 Pennsylvania Ave. N.W., #4997 20535; (202) 324-5594. Fax, (202) 324-6248. Laura Laughlin, Chief. Press, (202) 324-3691. Web, www. fbi.gov.*

Investigates crimes of fraud, theft, or embezzlement within or against financial institutions. Priorities include frauds involving computers and nationally significant intrusions into computer networks.

Federal Communications Commission, *Plans and Policy: New Technology and Policy, 445 12th St. S.W., #7-C347 20554; (202) 418-2030. Fax, (202) 418-2807. Vacant, Counsel. Web, www.fcc.gov/opp.*

Monitors developments in expansion of the global Internet.

General Services Administration, *Governmentwide Information Technology Management, 1800 F St. N.W. 20405; (202) 501-0202. Fax, (202) 219-1533. Joan Steyaert, Deputy Associate Administrator.*

Reviews agencies' information resources management and procurement of information technology.

Government E-Mail Steering Subcommittee, *200 Independence Ave. S.W., #531H 20201; (202) 690-6162. Fax, (202) 690-8715. Brian Burns, Deputy Assistant Secretary.*

Oversees implementation of governmentwide e-mail services; coordinates proposals and assists agencies in expanding electronic mail and electronic commerce capabilities.

National Science Foundation (NSF), *Computer and Information Sciences and Engineering, 4201 Wilson Blvd., Arlington, VA 22230; (703) 306-1900. Fax, (703) 306-0577. Ruzena Bajesy, Assistant Director. Web, www.cise.nsf.gov.*

Directorate that promotes basic research and education in computer and information sciences and engineering; helps maintain U.S. preeminence in these fields. Coordinates NSF involvement in the High-Performance Computing and Communications (HPCC) program;

WORLD WIDE WEB SITES OF FEDERAL AGENCIES

CONGRESS

General Accounting Office, www.gao.gov

House of Representatives, www.house.gov

Library of Congress, www.loc.gov

Senate, www.senate.gov

WHITE HOUSE

General Information, www.whitehouse.gov

DEPARTMENTS

Agriculture, www.usda.gov

Commerce, www.doc.gov

Defense, www.defenselink.mil

  Air Force, www.af.mil

  Army, www.army.mil

  Marine Corps, www.usmc.mil

  Navy, www.navy.mil

Education, www.ed.gov

Energy, www.doe.gov

Health and Human Services, www.dhhs.gov

Housing and Urban Development, www.hud.gov

Interior, www.doi.gov

Justice, www.usdoj.gov

Labor, www.dol.gov

State, www.state.gov

Transportation, www.dot.gov

Treasury, www.ustreas.gov

Veterans Affairs, www.va.gov

AGENCIES

Consumer Product Safety Commission,
www.cpsc.gov

Corporation for Public Broadcasting, www.cpb.org

Drug Enforcement Administration,
www.usdoj.gov/dea

Environmental Protection Agency, www.epa.gov

Export-Import Bank, www.exim.gov

Federal Aviation Administration, www.faa.gov

Federal Bureau of Investigation, www.fbi.gov

Federal Communications Commission, www.fcc.gov

Federal Deposit Insurance Corporation, www.fdic.gov

Federal Election Commission, www.fec.gov

Federal Emergency Management Agency,
www.fema.gov

Federal Energy Regulatory Commission,
www.ferc.fed.us

Federal Reserve System, www.bog.frb.fed.us

Federal Trade Commission, www.ftc.gov

Food and Drug Administration, www.fda.gov

General Services Administration, www.gsa.gov

Government Printing Office, www.gpo.gov

Internal Revenue Service, www.irs.ustreas.gov

National Aeronautics and Space Administration,
www.nasa.gov

National Archives and Records Administration,
www.nara.gov

National Institute of Standards and Technology,
www.nist.gov

National Institutes of Health, www.nih.gov

National Oceanic and Atmospheric Administration,
www.noaa.gov

National Park Service, www.nps.gov

National Performance Review, www.npr.gov

National Railroad Passenger Corporation (Amtrak),
www.amtrak.com

National Science Foundation, www.nsf.gov

National Technical Information Services,
www.ntis.gov

National Transportation Safety Board, www.ntsb.gov

Nuclear Regulatory Commission, www.nrc.gov

Occupational Safety and Health Administration,
www.osha.gov

Patent and Trademark Office, www.uspto.gov

Peace Corps, www.peacecorps.gov

Pension Benefit Guaranty Corporation,
www.pbgc.gov

Securities and Exchange Commisssion, www.sec.gov

Small Business Administration, www.sba.gov

Smithsonian Institution, www.si.edu

Social Security Administration, www.ssa.gov

U.S. Fish and Wildlife Service, www.fws.gov

U.S. Geological Survey, www.usgs.gov

U.S. International Trade Commission, www.usitc.gov

U.S. Postal Service, www.usps.gov

develops computer resources for scholarly communication, including links with foreign research and education networks; helps set Internet policy.

National Telecommunications and Information Administration *(Commerce Dept.), 14th St. and Constitution Ave. N.W., #4898 20230; (202) 482-1840. Fax, (202) 482-1635. Gregory Rohde, NTIA Administrator. Information, (202) 482-7002. Web, www.ntia.doc.gov.*

Promotes private-sector development of the National Information Infrastructure (NII) and market access for U.S. firms in developing the Global Information Infrastructure (GII). Makes grants to public and nonprofit entities for innovative use of the Internet and related technologies.

Office of Management and Budget *(Executive Office of the President), Information Policy and Technology, 725 17th St. N.W., #10236 20503; (202) 395-3785. Fax, (202) 395-5167. L. Chuck Keller, Chief. Web, www.whitehouse.gov/omb.*

Oversees implementation and policy development under the Information Technology Reform Act of 1996 and the Paperwork Reduction Act of 1995; focuses on information technology management and substantive information policy, including records management, privacy, and computer security.

CONGRESS

General Accounting Office, *Federal Management and Workforce Issues, 441 G St. N.W. 20548; (202) 512-8676. Fax, (202) 512-4516. L. Nye Stevens, Director.*

Assesses the quality of the nation's major statistical databases and helps adapt the government's dissemination of information to a new technological environment.

General Accounting Office, *Information Resources Management Policies and Issues, 441 G St. N.W. 20548; (202) 512-6406. Fax, (202) 512-6450. Jack Brock, Director.*

Seeks to make the federal government more effective in its information management. Assesses practices in the public and private sectors; makes recommendations to government agencies. Interests include information security.

House Commerce Committee, *Subcommittee on Telecommunications, Trade, and Consumer Protection, 2125 RHOB 20515; (202) 225-2927. Fax, (202) 225-1919. Rep. W. J. "Billy" Tauzin, R-La., Chair; James E. Derderian, Staff Director. General e-mail, commerce@mail.house.gov. Web, www.house.gov/commerce.*

Jurisdiction over legislation on communications, including computer communications and the Internet.

Senate Commerce, Science, and Transportation Committee, *Subcommittee on Communications, SH-227 20510; (202) 224-5184. Fax, (202) 224-9334. Sen. Conrad Burns, R-Mont., Chair; Lauren Belvin, Senior Counsel. Web, commerce.senate.gov.*

Jurisdiction over legislation on communications, including computer communications and the Internet.

NONPROFIT

American Electronics Assn., *Washington Office, 601 Pennsylvania Ave. N.W., North Bldg., #600 20004; (202) 682-9110. Fax, (202) 682-9111. William T. Archey, President. Web, www.aeanet.org.*

Membership: companies in the software, electronics, telecommunications, and information technology industries. Interests include international trade and investment, export controls, and U.S. competitiveness internationally. Holds conferences. Monitors legislation and regulations.

American Library Assn., *Information Technology Policy, 1301 Pennsylvania Ave. N.W., #403 20004; (202) 628-8421. Fax, (202) 628-8424. Frederick Weingarten, Director. Information, (800) 941-8478. General e-mail, oitp@alawash.org. Web, www.ala.org/oitp.*

Provides policy analysis and development in technology and telecommunications; interests include free expression on the Internet, equitable access to new media, and treaty negotiations of the World Intellectual Property Organization.

American Society for Information Science, *8720 Georgia Ave., #501, Silver Spring, MD 20910; (301) 495-0900. Fax, (301) 495-0810. Richard Hill, Executive Director. General e-mail, asis@asis.org. Web, www.asis.org.*

Membership: librarians, computer scientists, management specialists, behavioral scientists, engineers, and individuals concerned with access to information. Conducts research and educational programs.

Assn. of Research Libraries, *21 Dupont Circle N.W., #800 20036; (202) 296-2296. Fax, (202) 872-0884. Duane Webster, Executive Director. Web, www.arl.org.*

Membership: major research libraries, mainly at universities, in the United States and Canada. Interests include computer information systems and other bibliographic tools; publishing and scholarly communication; and worldwide policy on information, copyrights, and intellectual property.

Business Software Alliance, *1150 18th St. N.W., #700 20036; (202) 872-5500. Fax, (202) 872-5501. Robert Holleyman, President. Anti-piracy hotline, (800) 667-4722. General e-mail, software@bsa.org. Web, www.bsa.org.*

Membership: personal computer software publishing companies. Promotes growth of the software industry worldwide; helps develop electronic commerce. Operates a toll-free hotline to report software piracy; investigates claims of software theft within corporations, financial institutions, academia, state and local governments, and nonprofit organizations. Provides legal counsel and initiates litigation on behalf of members.

Capcon Library Network, *1990 M St. N.W., #200 20036; (202) 331-5771. Fax, (202) 331-5788. Robert Drescher, President. General e-mail, info@capcon.net. Web, www.capcon.net.*

Serves as a resource to libraries and other organizations on the information technology industry. Provides Internet access and training, education programs, and bibliographic services. Sponsors workshops and product demonstrations.

Center for Democracy and Technology, *1634 Eye St. N.W., #1100 20006; (202) 637-9800. Fax, (202) 637-0968. Jerry Berman, Executive Director. General e-mail, info@cdt.org. Web, www.cdt.org.*

Promotes civil liberties and democratic values in new computer and communications media, both in the United States and abroad. Interests include free speech, privacy, freedom of information, electronic commerce, and design of the information infrastructure. Monitors legislation and regulations.

Communications and Policy Technology Network, *919 18th St. N.W., 10th Floor 20006; (202) 263-2951. Fax, (202) 263-2960. Phil Attey, Director. General e-mail, captn@captn.org. Web, www.captn.org.*

Membership: Internet strategy and production specialists from public affairs, public relations, and issue advocacy groups; unions; political parties; candidate campaigns; think tanks; and governmental agencies. Supports and provides career development for professionals using the Internet and other new and emerging technologies for policy and political work and public affairs. Conducts online support center and workshops.

Computer and Communications Industry Assn., *666 11th St. N.W., #600 20001; (202) 783-0070. Fax, (202) 783-0534. Edward J. Black, President. General e-mail, ccia@aol.com. Web, www.ccianet.org.*

Membership: manufacturers and suppliers of computer data processing and communications-related products and services. Interests include telecommunications policy, capital formation and tax policy, federal procurement policy, communications and computer industry standards, intellectual property policies, encryption, international trade, and antitrust reform.

Computer Law Assn., *3028 Javier Rd., #402, Fairfax, VA 22031-4622; (703) 560-7747. Fax, (703) 207-7028. Barbara Fieser, Executive Director. General e-mail, clanet@aol.com. Web, www.cla.org.*

Membership: lawyers, law students, and nonattorneys concerned with the legal aspects of computers and computer communications. Sponsors programs and provides information on such issues as software protection, contracting, telecommunications, international distribution, financing, taxes, copyrights, patents, and electronic data interchange. Focus includes the Internet and e-commerce.

Cyberspace Policy Institute, *George Washington University School of Engineering and Applied Science, 2033 K St. N.W. 20006; (202) 994-5512. Fax, (202) 994-5505. Michael A. Stankosky, Director. General e-mail, cpi@seas.gwu.edu. Web, www.cpi.seas.gwu.edu.*

Conducts research on telecommunications delivery systems, management information systems, computer networks, compensation for electronic intellectual property, ethics and values among users of new media, and related cultural and geopolitical issues. Works with government and private organizations.

Data Interchange Standards Assn., *333 John Carlyle St., #600, Alexandria, VA 22314-2852; (703) 548-7005. Fax, (703) 548-5738. Jerry Connors, President (Acting). Web, www.disa.org.*

Supports the development and the use of electronic data interchange standards in electronic commerce. Sponsors workshops, seminars, and conferences. Helps develop international standards.

Electronic Privacy Information Center, *666 Pennsylvania Ave. S.E., #301 20003; (202) 544-9240. Fax, (202) 547-5482. Marc Rotenberg, Director. General e-mail, info@epic.org. Web, www.epic.org.*

Public interest research center. Conducts research and conferences on domestic and international civil liberties issues, including privacy, free speech, information access, computer security, and encryption; litigates cases. Monitors legislation and regulations. (Affiliated with the Fund for Constitutional Government.)

EMA–E-Business Forum, *1655 N. Fort Myer Dr., #500, Arlington, VA 22209; (703) 524-5550. Fax, (703) 524-5558. Kerry Stackpole, Chief Executive Officer. General e-mail, info@ema.org. Web, www.ema.org.*

Membership: corporations, government, academia, and organizations involved in software development, mainframe, mini-computer, LAN messaging, and network communication. Seeks to advance messaging technologies, information exchange, and electronic commerce worldwide. Sponsors annual conference.

Graphic Communications Assn., *100 Daingerfield Rd., Alexandria, VA 22314-2888; (703) 519-8160. Fax, (703) 548-2867. Norm Scharpf, President. Web, www.gca.org.*

Membership: firms and customers in printing, publishing, and related industries. Helps set industry standards for electronic commerce and conducts studies on new information technologies. (Affiliated with Printing Industries of America.)

Highway 1, *601 Pennsylvania Ave. N.W. North Bldg., #250 20004-2601; (202) 628-3900. Fax, (202) 628-3922. Mike Hernon, President. Web, www.highway1.org.*

Works with Congress, the White House, and federal agencies to provide information on emerging technologies and solutions. Provides seminars and workshops on technology-related issues and develops demonstration projects with federal agencies.

Information Industry Assn., *1730 M. St. N.W., #700 20036-4510; (202) 452-1600. Fax, (202) 223-8756. Ken Walsh, President. Web, www.infoindustry.org.*

Membership: companies involved in creating, distributing, and using information products, services, and technologies. Helps formulate global business strategies; interests include telecommunications, government procurement, taxation, intellectual property rights, and privacy. Monitors legislation and regulations.

Information Sciences Institute, *Washington Office, 4350 N. Fairfax Dr., #770, Arlington, VA 22203; (703) 243-9422. Fax, (703) 812-3731. Terry Shaulis, Senior Business Manager. Web, www.isi.edu or www.east.isi.edu.*

Conducts research in advanced computer, communications, and information processing technologies; serves as the Internet Assigned Numbers Authority (IANA). Specific projects support development of the Internet, related software, and electronic commerce.

Information Technology Assn. of America, *1616 N. Fort Myer Dr., #1300, Arlington, VA 22209; (703) 284-5300. Fax, (703) 525-2279. Harris N. Miller, President. Web, www.itaa.org.*

Membership: organizations in the computer, communications, and data industries. Conducts research; holds seminars and workshops; interests include small business, government procurement, competitive practices, communications, software, trade, and international copyright issues. Monitors legislation and regulations.

Information Technology Industry Council, *1250 Eye St. N.W., #200 20005; (202) 737-8888. Fax, (202) 638-4922. Rhett Dawson, President. Press, (202) 626-5725. General e-mail, webmaster@itic.org. Web, www.itic.org.*

Membership: providers of information technology products and services. Promotes the global competitiveness of its members and advocates free trade. Seeks to protect intellectual property and encourages the use of voluntary standards.

Interactive Digital Software Assn., *1775 Eye St. N.W., #420 20006; (202) 833-4372. Fax, (202) 833-4431. Douglas Lowenstein, President. General e-mail, info@idsa.com. Web, www.idsa.com.*

Membership: publishers of interactive entertainment software. Distributes marketing statistics and information. Administers an independent rating system for the industry and a worldwide anti-piracy program. Monitors legislation and regulations.

International Communications Industries Assn., *11242 Waples Mill Rd., #200, Fairfax, VA 22030; (703) 273-7200. Fax, (703) 278-8082. Walter Blackwell, Executive Director. Information, (800) 659-7469. General e-mail, icia@icia.org. Web, www.icia.org.*

Membership: video, audiovisual, and microcomputer dealers; manufacturers and producers; and individuals. Interests include international trade, small business issues, postal rates, copyright, education, and taxation. Monitors legislation and regulations.

International Council for Computer Communication, *P.O. Box 9745 20016; (703) 836-7787. John D. McKendree, Treasurer. Web, www.icccgovernors.org.*

Membership: industry, government, and academic leaders interested in computer communications issues. Promotes scientific research in and development of computer communication; encourages evaluation of applications of computer communication for educational, scientific, medical, economic, legal, cultural, and other peaceful purposes; sponsors international conferences, seminars, and workshops. (Affiliated with the International Federation for Information Processing in Vienna, Austria.)

International Telework Assn., *204 E St. N.E. 20002; (202) 547-6157. Fax, (202) 546-3289. John Edwards, President. Web, www.telecommute.org.*

Membership: individuals, corporations, government agencies, educators, consultants, and vendors involved in telecommuting. Promotes the economic, social, and environmental benefits of telecommuting. Seeks to facilitate the development of telecommuting programs internationally.

International Webcasting Assn., *8403 Colesville Rd., #865, Silver Spring, MD 20910; (301) 650-2467. Fax, (301) 495-4959. Robert L. Smith Jr., Executive Director;*

Peggy Miles, Founding Chair. General e-mail, info@webcasters.org. Web, www.webcasters.org.

Membership: companies providing webcasting products, services, and content in the United States and abroad. Promotes the webcasting industry. Sponsors seminars and electronic mailing lists; conducts research. Monitors legislation and regulations.

Internet Alliance, 1825 Eye St. N.W., #400 20006 (mailing address: P.O. Box 65782 20035-5782); (202) 955-8091. Fax, (202) 955-8081. Jeff B. Richards, Executive Director. General e-mail, ia@internetalliance.org. Web, www.internetalliance.org.

Membership: Internet and online companies, advertising agencies, cable companies, consulting and research organizations, computer and terminal manufacturers, entrepreneurs, financial institutions, interactive service providers, publishers, software vendors, telecommunications companies, service bureaus, and packagers. Promotes customer-focused development of the Internet.

Internet Engineering Task Force, Secretariat, 1895 Preston White Dr., #100, Reston, VA 20191-5434; (703) 620-8990. Fax, (703) 620-0913. Steve Coya, Executive Director. General e-mail, ietf-info@ietf.org. Web, www.ietf.org.

Membership: network designers, operators, vendors, and researchers from around the world who are concerned with the evolution, smooth operation, and continuing development of the Internet. Establishes working groups to address technical concerns.

Internet Society, 11150 Sunset Hills Rd., #100, Reston, VA 20190-5321; (703) 326-9880. Fax, (703) 326-9881. Donald M. Heath, President. Information, (800) 468-9507. General e-mail, isoc@isoc.org. Web, www.isoc.org.

Membership: individuals, corporations, nonprofit organizations, and government agencies. Promotes development and availability of the Internet and its associated technologies and applications; promulgates international standards. Conducts research and educational programs; assists technologically developing countries in achieving Internet usage; provides information about the Internet.

Progress and Freedom Foundation, 1301 K St. N.W., #550E 20005; (202) 289-8928. Fax, (202) 289-6079. Jeffrey A. Eisenach, President. General e-mail, mail@pff.org. Web, www.pff.org.

Studies the impact of the digital revolution and its implications for public policy; sponsors seminars, conferences, and broadcasts.

Public Service Telecommunications Corporation, 4900 Seminary Rd., #1120, Alexandria, VA 22311; (703)

998-1703. Fax, (703) 998-8480. Louis Bransford, President. General e-mail, info@pstc.net.

Membership: educational and public service organizations. Represents the interests of members in the use of new and advanced technologies. Conducts telecommunications policy research.

Recreational Software Advisory Council on the Internet, 3460 Olney-Laytonsville Rd., #202, Olney, MD 20832; (301) 260-8669. Fax, (301) 260-8677. Stephen Balkam, Founding President. General e-mail, info@rsac.org. Web, www.rsac.org.

Provides the public with information about the level of sex, nudity, and violence in software games and on the Internet. Assists parents through programs that rate the content of software.

Software and Information Industry Assn., 1730 M St. N.W., #700 20036; (202) 452-1600. Fax, (202) 223-8756. Ken Walsh, President. Web, www.siia.net.

Membership: publishers of microcomputer software. Promotes the industry worldwide; conducts investigations and litigation to protect members' copyrights; collects data, including monthly sales information; offers contracts reference and credit information exchange services; sponsors conferences and seminars. Monitors legislation and regulations.

Unison Institute, 1742 Connecticut Ave. N.W. 20009; (202) 797-7200. Fax, (202) 234-8584. John Chelen, Executive Director. General e-mail, unison@unison.org. Web, www.rtk.net.

Information technology public interest group. Provides policy analysis, strategic and program planning, technical assistance, training, and targeted software services. Holds conferences.

U.S. Internet Industry Assn., 1901 N. Fort Myer Dr., Arlington, VA 22209; (703) 312-1111. Fax, (703) 312-1113. David P. McClure, Executive Director. General e-mail, info@usiia.org. Web, www.usiia.org.

Membership: U.S. Internet access, business, and electronic commerce companies. Fosters the growth and development of online commerce and communications. Monitors legislation and regulations.

▦ MEDIA PROFESSIONS AND RESOURCES

AGENCIES

Federal Communications Commission, Communications Business Opportunity, 445 12th St. S.W. 20554;

(202) 418-0990. Fax, (202) 418-0235. Francisco R. Montero, Director. Web, www.fcc.gov/ocbo.

Provides technical and legal guidance and assistance to the small, minority, and female business community in the telecommunications industry. Advises the FCC chairman on small, minority, and female business issues. Serves as liaison between federal agencies, state and local governments, and trade associations representing small, minority, and female enterprises concerning FCC policies, procedures, and rulemaking activities.

Federal Communications Commission, *Equal Employment Opportunity, 445 12th St. S.W., #3B443 20554; (202) 418-1450. Fax, (202) 418-1797. Vacant, Chief.*

Responsible for the annual certification of cable television equal employment opportunity compliance. Oversees broadcast employment practices. Publishes annual report on employment trends in cable television and broadcast industries.

NONPROFIT

American News Women's Club, *1607 22nd St. N.W. 20008; (202) 332-6770. Fax, (202) 265-6477. Donna Kaulkin, President. General e-mail, anwc@sprynet.com. Web, www.anwc.org.*

Membership: writers, reporters, photographers, cartoonists, and professionals in print and broadcast media, government and private industry, publicity, and public relations. Promotes the advancement of women in all media. Sponsors professional receptions and seminars.

Communications Workers of America, *501 3rd St. N.W. 20001; (202) 434-1100. Fax, (202) 434-1279. Morton Bahr, President. Web, www.cwa-union.org.*

Membership: approximately 600,000 workers in telecommunications, printing and news media, public service, cable television, electronics, and other fields. Assists members with contract negotiation and grievances; conducts training programs and workshops. Monitors legislation and regulations. (Affiliated with the AFL-CIO.)

Education and Research Institute, *800 Maryland Ave. N.E. 20002; (202) 546-1710. Fax, (202) 546-1638. M. Stanton Evans, Chair. Web, www.eri-njc.org.*

Educational organization that conducts seminars and operates the National Journalism Center to train interns in basic skills of media work.

Freedom Forum, *1101 Wilson Blvd., Arlington, VA 22209; (703) 528-0800. Fax, (703) 284-3770. Charles L. Overby, Chair. Publications fax, (703) 284-3570. General e-mail, news@freedomforum.org. Web, www.freedomforum.org.*

Sponsors conferences, educational activities, training, and research that promote free press, free speech, and freedom of information and that enhance the teaching and practice of journalism, both in the United States and abroad.

Fund for Investigative Journalism, *P.O. Box 40339 20016; (202) 362-0260. Peg Lotito, Executive Director. General e-mail, fundfij@aol.com. Web, www.fij.org.*

Provides investigative reporters with grants for articles, broadcasts, photojournalism, and books.

National Assn. of Black Journalists, *University of Maryland, 8701-A Adelphi Rd., Adelphi, MD 20783; (301) 445-7100. Fax, (301) 445-7101. Antoinette Samuel, Executive Director. General e-mail, nabj@nabj.org. Web, www.nabj.org.*

Membership: African American journalists working for radio and television stations, newspapers, and magazines, and others in the field of journalism. Works to increase recognition of the achievements of minority journalists, to expand opportunities for minority students entering the field, and to promote balanced coverage of the African American community by the media. Sponsors scholarships and internship program.

National Assn. of Government Communicators, *10301 Democracy Lane, #203, Fairfax, VA 22030; (703) 691-0377. Fax, (703) 691-0896. Joni Iman, President. General e-mail, info@nagc.com. Web, www.nagc.com.*

Membership: federal, state, and local government communications employees. Promotes job standards for the government communications profession.

National Assn. of Hispanic Journalists, *1193 National Press Bldg., 529 14th St. N.W. 20045; (202) 662-7145. Fax, (202) 662-7144. Anna Lopez, Executive Director. Web, www.nahj.org.*

Membership: professional journalists, educators, students, and others interested in encouraging Hispanics to study and enter the field of journalism. Promotes fair representation of Hispanics by the news media. Provides computerized job referral service; compiles and updates national directory of Hispanics in the media; sponsors national high school essay contest, journalism awards, and scholarships.

National Black Media Coalition, *1738 Elton Rd., Silver Spring, MD 20903; (301) 445-2600. Fax, (301) 445-1693. Pluria W. Marshall, Chair. Web, www.nbmc.org.*

Advocates African American involvement in communications at local and national levels. Maintains an employment resource center. Conducts training classes; negotiates affirmative action plans with large media corporations.

MEDIA CONTACTS IN WASHINGTON

MAGAZINES

CQ Weekly, 1414 22nd St. N.W. 20037; (202) 887-8500

National Journal, 1501 M St. N.W., #300 20005; (202) 739-8400

Newsweek, 1750 Pennsylvania Ave. N.W., #1220 20006; (202) 626-2000

Time, 1050 Connecticut Ave. N.W., #850 20036; (202) 861-4000

U.S. News & World Report, 1050 Thomas Jefferson St. N.W. 20007; (202) 955-2000

NEWSPAPERS

Baltimore Sun, 1627 K St. N.W., #1100 20006; (202) 452-8250

Christian Science Monitor, 910 16th St. N.W. 20006; (202) 785-4400

Los Angeles Times, 1875 Eye St. N.W., #1100 20006; (202) 293-4650

New York Times, 1627 Eye St. N.W. 20006; (202) 862-0300

USA Today, 1000 Wilson Blvd., Arlington, VA 22229; (703) 276-3400

Wall Street Journal, 1025 Connecticut Ave. N.W., #800 20036; (202) 862-9200

Washington Post, 1150 15th St. N.W. 20071; (202) 334-6000

Washington Times, 3600 New York Ave. N.E. 20002; (202) 636-3000

NEWS SERVICES

Agence France-Presse, 1015 15th St. N.W., #500 20005; (202) 289-0700

Associated Press, 2021 K St. N.W., 6th Floor 20006; (202) 776-9400

Gannett News Service, 1000 Wilson Blvd., Arlington, VA 22229; (703) 276-5800

Knight-Ridder Newspapers, 700 National Press Bldg., 529 14th St. N.W. 20045; (202) 383-6000

Newhouse News Service, 1101 Connecticut Ave. N.W., #300 20036; (202) 383-7800

Reuters, 1333 H St. N.W., #500 20005; (202) 898-8300

Scripps-Howard Newspapers, 1090 Vermont Ave. N.W., #1000 20005; (202) 408-1484

States News Service, 1333 F St. N.W., 4th Floor 20004; (202) 628-3100

United Press International, 1510 H St. N.W. 20005; (202) 898-8000

TELEVISION/RADIO NETWORKS

ABC News, 1717 DeSales St. N.W. 20036; (202) 222-7777

Cable News Network (CNN), 820 1st St. N.E. 20002; (202) 898-7900

CBS News, 2020 M St. N.W. 20036; (202) 457-4321

C-SPAN, 400 N. Capitol St. N.W., #650 20001; (202) 737-3220

Fox News, 400 N. Capitol St. N.W., #550 20001; (202) 824-6300

Mutual/NBC Radio Network, 1755 S. Jefferson Davis Highway, Arlington, VA 22202; (703) 413-8300

National Public Radio, 635 Massachusetts Ave. N.W. 20001; (202) 414-2000

NBC News, 4001 Nebraska Ave. N.W. 20016; (202) 885-4200

Public Broadcasting Service, 1320 Braddock Place, Alexandria, VA 22314; (703) 739-5000

National Conference of Editorial Writers, *6223 Executive Blvd., Rockville, MD 20852; (301) 984-3015. Fax, (301) 231-0026. Cora Everett, Executive Secretary. Web, www.ncew.org.*

Membership: editorial writers, editors, syndicated columnists, broadcasters, students, journalism professors at accredited universities, and commentators on general circulation newspapers and television and radio stations in the United States and Canada. Sponsors critique exchange workshops. Provides critique service upon request.

National Lesbian and Gay Journalists Assn., *2120 L St. N.W., #840 20037; (202) 588-9888. Fax, (202) 588-1818. Robert Dodge, President. General e-mail, nlgja@ aol.com. Web, www.nlgja.org.*

Fosters fair and accurate coverage of lesbian and gay issues. Provides professional support and networking services; sponsors conferences, seminars, and workshops.

National Press Foundation, *1211 Connecticut Ave. N.W. 20036; (202) 721-9100. Fax, (202) 530-2855. Bob Meyers, President. General e-mail, npf@natpress.org. Web, www.natpress.org.*

Works to enhance the professional competence of journalists through in-career education projects. Sponsors conferences, seminars, fellowships, and awards; conducts public forums and international exchanges. Supports the National Press Club library; includes the Washington Journalism Center.

Pew Center for Civic Journalism, *1101 Connecticut Ave. N.W., #420 20036-4303; (202) 331-3200. Fax, (202) 347-6440. Jan Schaffer, Executive Director. General e-mail, news@pccj.org. Web, www.pewcenter.org.*

Seeks to advance the field of civic journalism through workshops, publications, videos, and other outreach programs.

Regional Reporters Assn., *2037 National Press Bldg. 20045; (202) 408-2728. Jennifer Maddox, President. General e-mail, maddox@shns.com. Web, www.rra.org.*

Membership: Washington-based reporters for regional newspapers and radio and television stations. Works to improve regional correspondents' access to all branches of the federal government; encourages professional development.

Society for Technical Communication, *901 N. Stuart St., #904, Arlington, VA 22203-1854; (703) 522-4114. Fax, (703) 522-2075. William C. Stolgitis, Executive Director. General e-mail, stc@stc-va.org. Web, www.stc-va.org.*

Membership: writers, publishers, educators, editors, illustrators, and others involved in technical communication in the print and broadcast media. Encourages research and develops training programs for technical communicators; aids educational institutions in devising curricula; awards scholarships.

Statistical Assessment Service, *2100 L St. N.W., #300 20037; (202) 223-3193. Fax, (202) 872-4014. S. Robert Lichter, President. Web, www.stats.org.*

Promotes accurate use of statistical and quantitative data in public policy debate. Provides journalists with analysis of current statistical disputes.

Washington Press Club Foundation, *529 14th St. N.W., #1067 20045; (202) 393-0613. Fax, (202) 783-0841. Julia D. Whiston, Executive Director.*

Seeks to advance professionalism in journalism. Awards minority grants and scholarships. Administers an oral history of women in journalism. Sponsors annual Salute to Congress Dinner in late January to welcome Congress back into session. Maintains speakers bureau.

White House Correspondents Assn., *1067 National Press Bldg. 20045; (202) 737-2934. Fax, (202) 783-0841. Arlene Dillon, President.*

Membership: reporters who cover the White House. Acts as a link between reporters and White House staff.

Women in Communications Foundation, *1244 Richie Hwy., #6, Arnold, MD 21012; (410) 544-7442. Fax, (410) 544-4640. Pat Troy, Executive Director.*

Membership: professionals and students in communications. Maintains job hotline for members and supports women in communications. Works for freedom of expression for all communicators.

Women's Institute for Freedom of the Press, *3306 Ross Pl. N.W. 20008; (202) 966-7783. Martha Allen, Director. General e-mail, wifponline@igc.org. Web, www.igc.org/ wifp.*

Conducts research and publishes in areas of communications and the media that are of particular interest to women.

See also Council on Hemispheric Affairs (p. 485); Washington Center for Politics and Journalism (p. 180)

Accreditation in Washington

Most federal agencies and courts do not require special press credentials.

AGENCIES

Defense Dept., *Public Affairs, The Pentagon, #2E800 20301-1400; (703) 697-9312. Fax, (703) 695-4299. Kenneth H. Bacon, Assistant Secretary. Press, (703) 697-5131. National Media Pool, (703) 693-1075. Web, www. defenselink.mil.*

Grants accreditation to Washington-based media organizations to form the National Media Pool. Selected staff of accredited groups are assigned to the media pool on a rotating basis and put on alert for short-notice deployment to the site of military operations.

Foreign Press Center *(State Dept.), 529 14th St. N.W., #898 20045; (202) 724-1640. Fax, (202) 724-0007. Marjorie Ransom, Director. Alternate fax, (202) 724-0122. Fax-on-demand, (202) 724-0050. Web, www.fpc.gov.*

Provides foreign journalists with access to news sources, including wire services and daily briefings from the White House, State Dept., and Pentagon. Holds live news conferences. Foreign journalists wishing to use the center must present a letter from their organization and a letter from the embassy of the country in which their paper is published.

Metropolitan Police Dept., *Police Public Information, 300 Indiana Ave. N.W., #4048 20001; (202) 727-4383. Fax, (202) 727-0437. Sgt. Joseph Gentile, Director.*

Provides application forms and issues press passes required for crossing police lines within the city of Washington. Passes are issued on a yearly basis; applicants should allow four to six weeks for processing of passes.

National Park Service *(Interior Dept.), National Capital Region,* 1100 Ohio Dr. S.W., #336 20242; (202) 619-7000. Fax, (202) 619-7220. Terry Carlstrom, Director. Information, (202) 619-7222. Recorded information, (202) 619-7275. Permits, (202) 619-7225. Web, www.nps.gov/ncro.

Regional office that administers national parks, monuments, historic sites, and recreation areas in the Washington metropolitan area. Issues special permits required for commercial filming on public park lands. Media representatives covering public events that take place on park lands should notify the Office of Public Affairs and Tourism in advance. A White House or metropolitan police press pass is required in some circumstances.

State Dept., *Public Affairs Press Office,* 2201 C St. N.W., #2109 20520; (202) 647-2492. Fax, (202) 647-0244. Vacant, Assistant Secretary. Fax-on-demand, (202) 736-7720. General e-mail, publicaffairs@panet.us-state.gov. Web, www.state.gov/www/dept/publicaffairs/index.html.

U.S. journalists seeking building passes must apply in person with a letter from their editor or publisher and a passport-size photograph. In addition, foreign correspondents need a letter from the embassy of the country in which their organization is based. All journalists must reside in the Washington, D.C., area and must cover the State Dept.'s daily briefing on a regular basis. Applicants should allow three months for security clearance.

White House, *Press Office,* 1600 Pennsylvania Ave. N.W. 20500; (202) 456-2580. Fax, (202) 456-6210. Joe Lockhart, Press Secretary. Fax-on-demand, (202) 395-9088. Comments and information, (202) 456-1111. Web, www. whitehouse.gov.

Journalists seeking permanent accreditation must be accredited by the House or Senate press galleries, must be residents of the Washington, D.C., area, and must be full-time employees of a news-gathering organization, expecting to cover the White House on a nearly daily basis. A journalist's editor, publisher, or employer must write to the press office requesting accreditation. Journalists wishing temporary accreditation should have their assignment desk call a day ahead to be cleared for a one-day pass. Press Office also maintains an index of journalists with permanent specialized White House accreditation. Applicants must undergo a Secret Service investigation.

CONGRESS

House Periodical Press Gallery, *H304 CAP 20515;* (202) 225-2941. Richard E. Maze, Chair (Army Times). General e-mail, periodical.press@mail.house.gov.

Open by application to periodical correspondents whose chief occupation is gathering and reporting news for periodicals not affiliated with lobbying organizations. Accreditation with the House Gallery covers accreditation with the Senate Gallery.

Press Photographers Gallery, *Standing Committee of Press Photographers,* S317 CAP 20510; (202) 224-6548. Fax, (202) 224-0280. Tim Dillon, Chair (USA Today).

Open by application to bona fide news photographers and to heads of photographic bureaus. Accreditation by the standing committee covers both the House and Senate.

Senate Press Gallery, *Standing Committee of Correspondents,* S316 CAP 20510; (202) 224-0241. John D. Diamond, Chair (Chicago Tribune).

Open by application to Washington-based reporters who earn more than half their income from news services or from newspapers published at least five times a week. Accreditation with the Senate Gallery covers accreditation with the House Gallery.

Senate Radio and Television Gallery, *Executive Committee of the Radio and Television Correspondents' Galleries,* S325 CAP 20510; (202) 224-6421. Fax, (202) 224-4882. Lew Ketcham, Chair (C-Span). Web, www. senate.gov/galleries/radiotv/index.htm.

Open by application to Washington-based radio and television correspondents and technicians who earn more than half their income from or spend at least half their time in the news gathering profession. Accreditation with the Senate Gallery covers accreditation with the House Gallery.

JUDICIARY

Supreme Court of the United States, *1 1st St. N.E.* 20543; (202) 479-3000. William H. Rehnquist, Chief Justice; Kathleen Arberg, Public Information Officer, (202) 479-3050. Library, (202) 479-3037. Opinions and information, (202) 479-3211.

Journalists seeking to cover the Court must be accredited by either the White House or the House or Senate press galleries. Contact the public information office to make arrangements.

CONGRESSIONAL NEWS MEDIA GALLERIES

The congressional news media galleries serve as liaisons between members of Congress and their staffs and accredited newspaper, magazine, and broadcasting correspondents. The galleries provide accredited correspondents with facilities to cover activities of Congress, and gallery staff members ensure that congressional press releases reach appropriate correspondents. Independent committees of correspondents working through the press galleries are responsible for accreditation of correspondents; see Accreditation in Washington, Legislative Branch (p. 138–140).

House Periodical Press Gallery, H304 CAP 20515; (202) 225-2941. David W. Holmes, Director.

House Press Gallery, H315 CAP 20515; (202) 225-3945. Jerry Gallegos, Superintendent.

House Radio and Television Gallery, H321 CAP 20515; (202) 225-5214. Tina Tate, Director.

Press Photographers Gallery, S317 CAP 20510; (202) 224-6548. Jeffrey Kent, Director.

Senate Periodical Press Gallery, S320 CAP 20510; (202) 224-0265. Jim Talbert, Superintendent.

Senate Press Gallery, S316 CAP 20510; (202) 224-0241. Robert E. Petersen Jr., Superintendent.

Senate Radio and Television Gallery, S325 CAP 20510; (202) 224-6421. Larry Janezich, Director.

Broadcasting

See also Radio and Television (this chapter)

NONPROFIT

American Federation of Television and Radio Artists, *4340 East-West Hwy., #204, Bethesda, MD 20814; (301) 657-2560. Fax, (301) 657-4517. Patricia O'Donnell, Executive Director. Web, www.aftra.org.*

Membership: television and radio reporters, anchors, editors, staff announcers, disc jockeys, and freelancers. Labor organization that advocates a professional performing arts union. Monitors legislation and regulations.

American Women in Radio and Television, *1595 Spring Hill Rd., #330, Tyson's Corner, Vienna, VA 22182; (703) 506-3290. Fax, (703) 506-3266. Jacci Duncan, Executive Director. Web, www.awrt.org.*

Membership: professionals in the electronic media and full-time students in accredited colleges and universities. Promotes industry cooperation and advancement

of women. Maintains foundation for educational and charitable purposes.

Broadcast Education Assn., *1771 N St. N.W. 20036-2891; (202) 429-5354. Fax, (202) 775-2981. Louisa A. Nielsen, Executive Director. Web, www.beaweb.org.*

Membership: universities, colleges, and faculty members offering specialized training in radio and television broadcasting. Promotes improvement of curriculum and teaching methods. Fosters working relationships among academics, students, and professionals in the industry.

National Academy of Television Arts and Sciences, Washington Office, *9405 Russell Rd., Silver Spring, MD 20910; (301) 587-3993. Fax, (301) 587-3993. Dianne Bruno, Administrator.*

Membership: professionals in television and related fields and students in communications. Works to upgrade television programming; awards scholarship to a junior, senior, or graduate student in communications. Sponsors annual Emmy Awards.

National Assn. of Black-Owned Broadcasters, *1155 Connecticut Ave. N.W., 6th Floor 20036; (202) 463-8970. Fax, (202) 429-0657. James L. Winston, Executive Director.*

Membership: minority owners and employees of radio and television stations and telecommunications properties. Provides members and the public with information on the broadcast industry and the FCC. Provides members with legal and advertising research facilities. Monitors legislation and regulations.

National Assn. of Broadcast Employees and Technicians, *501 3rd St. N.W., 8th Floor 20001; (202) 434-1254. Fax, (202) 434-1426. John S. Clark, President.*

Membership: approximately 10,000 commercial television and radio personnel. Helps members negotiate pay, benefits, and better working conditions; conducts training programs and workshops. Monitors legislation and regulations.

National Assn. of Broadcasters, *1771 N St. N.W. 20036-2891; (202) 429-5300. Fax, (202) 429-5343. Edward O. Fritts, President. Library, (202) 429-5490. Press, (202) 429-5350. General e-mail, register@nab.org. Web, www.nab.org.*

Membership: radio and television broadcast stations and broadcast networks holding an FCC license or construction permit; associate members include producers of equipment and programs. Assists members in areas of management, engineering, and research. Interests include privatization abroad and related business opportunities. Monitors legislation and regulations.

Radio and Television Correspondents Assn., *S-325 CAP 20510; (202) 224-6421. Fax, (202) 224-4882. Larry Janezich, Director.*

Membership: broadcast correspondents who cover the White House. Sponsors annual dinner.

Radio-Television News Directors Assn., *1000 Connecticut Ave. N.W., #615 20036; (202) 659-6510. Fax, (202) 223-4007. Barbara Cochran, President. General e-mail, rtnda@rtnda.org. Web, www.rtnda.org.*

Membership: local and network news executives in broadcasting, cable, and other electronic media in more than thirty countries. Serves as information source for members; provides advice on legislative, political, and judicial problems of electronic journalism; conducts international exchanges.

Press Freedom

CONGRESS

House Judiciary Committee, *Subcommittee on the Constitution,* *H2-362 FHOB 20515; (202) 226-7680. Fax, (202) 225-3746. Rep. Charles T. Canady, R-Fla., Chair; Cathy Cleaver, Chief Counsel. General e-mail, Judiciary@ mail.house.gov. Web, www.house.gov/judiciary.*

Jurisdiction over press shield legislation.

Senate Judiciary Committee, *Subcommittee on the Constitution, Federalism, and Property Rights,* *SD-524 20510; (202) 224-8081. Fax, (202) 228-0544. Sen. John Ashcroft, R-Mo., Chair; Adam Cingoli, Chief Counsel. Web, judiciary.senate.gov/constitu.htm.*

Jurisdiction over press shield legislation.

NONPROFIT

Joint Washington Media Committee, *c/o Cohn and Marks, 1920 N St. N.W., #300 20036; (202) 452-4837. Fax, (202) 293-4827. Richard M. Schmidt Jr., Chair.*

Membership: representatives of media organizations. Consulting group that acts as a clearinghouse and forum for exchange of information on legislative and judicial developments affecting freedom of the press.

Reporters Committee for Freedom of the Press, *1815 N. Fort Myer Dr., #900, Arlington, VA 22209; (703) 807-2100. Fax, (703) 807-2109. Gregg Leslie, Executive Director (Acting). Freedom of information hotline, (800) 336-4243. General e-mail, rcfp@rcfp.org. Web, www.rcfp. org/.*

Membership: reporters, news editors, publishers, and lawyers from the print and broadcast media. Maintains a legal defense and research fund for members of the news media involved in freedom of the press court cases; interests include freedom of speech abroad.

Student Press Law Center, *1815 N. Fort Myer Dr., #900, Arlington, VA 22209; (703) 807-1904. Fax, (703) 807-2109. Mark Goodman, Executive Director. General e-mail, splc@splc.org. Web, www.splc.org.*

Collects, analyzes, and distributes information on free expression and freedom of information rights of student journalists (print and broadcast) and on violations of those rights in high schools and colleges. Provides free legal assistance to students and faculty advisers experiencing censorship.

World Press Freedom Committee, *11690-C Sunrise Valley Dr., Reston, VA 22191; (703) 715-9811. Fax, (703) 620-6790. Marilyn J. Greene, Executive Director. General e-mail, freepress@wpfc.org. Web, www.wpfc.org.*

Worldwide organization of print and broadcast groups. Promotes freedom of the press and opposes government censorship. Conducts training programs and assists journalists in central and eastern Europe and the developing world. Participates in international conferences.

See also Freedom Forum (p. 136)

Print Media

NONPROFIT

American Press Institute, *11690 Sunrise Valley Dr., Reston, VA 22191; (703) 620-3611. Fax, (703) 620-5814. William L. Winter, President. General e-mail, api@ apireston.org. Web, www.newspaper.org/api.*

Promotes the continuing education and career development of newspaper men and women. Conducts seminars, workshops, and conferences. Programs include an intensive computerized newspaper management simulation.

American Society of Newspaper Editors, *11690-B Sunrise Valley Dr., Reston, VA 22191; (703) 453-1122. Fax, (703) 453-1133. Scott Bosley, Executive Director. General e-mail, asne@asne.org. Web, www.asne.org.*

Membership: directing editors of daily newspapers. Campaigns against government secrecy; works to improve the racial mix of newsroom staff; sponsors work/training program for journalists from developing countries; serves as information clearinghouse for newsrooms of daily newspapers.

Assn. for Suppliers of Printing and Publishing Technologies, *Communications, 1899 Preston White Dr., Reston, VA 20191-4367; (703) 264-7200. Fax, (703) 620-0994. Carol J. Hurlburt, Director. Documents-on-demand, (800) 874-0858. General e-mail, npes@npes.org. Web, www.npes.org.*

Trade association representing companies that manufacture and distribute equipment, supplies, systems, software, and services for printing and publishing.

Assn. of American Publishers, *Copyright and New Technology, 50 F St. N.W., 4th Floor 20001; (202) 347-3375. Fax, (202) 347-3690. Carol A. Risher, Vice President. Web, www.publishers.org.*

Membership: U.S. publishers of books, journals, tests, and software. Provides members with information on domestic and international trade and market conditions; interests include library and educational funding, educational reform, postal rates, new technology, taxes, copyright, censorship, and libel matters. Monitors legislation and regulations.

Document Management Industries Assn., *433 E. Monroe Ave., Alexandria, VA 22301-1693; (703) 836-6225. Fax, (703) 836-2241. Chuck Calman, President. Web, www.dmia.org.*

Membership: manufacturers, suppliers, and distributors of business forms, labels, commercial printing, advertising specialties, electronic forms, or document products. Conducts workshops, seminars, and conferences; sponsors industry research. Monitors legislation and regulations.

Essential Information, *P.O. Box 19405 20036; (202) 387-8030. Fax, (202) 234-5176. John Richard, Director. General e-mail, EI@essential.org. Web, www.essential. org/EI.html.*

Provides writers and the public with information on public policy matters; awards grants to investigative reporters; sponsors conference on investigative journalism. Interests include activities of multinational corporations in developing countries.

Graphic Communications Assn., *100 Daingerfield Rd., Alexandria, VA 22314-2888; (703) 519-8160. Fax, (703) 548-2867. Norm Scharpf, President. Web, www.gca.org.*

Membership: firms and customers in printing, publishing, and related industries. Assists members in production of color graphics and conducts studies on print media management methods. (Affiliated with Printing Industries of America.)

Graphic Communications International Union, *1900 L St. N.W. 20036; (202) 462-1400. Fax, (202) 721-0600. James J. Norton, President. Web, www.gciu.org.*

Membership: approximately 150,000 members of the print industry, including lithographers, photoengravers, and bookbinders. Assists members with contract negotiation and grievances; conducts training programs and workshops. Monitors legislation and regulations. (Affiliated with the AFL-CIO.)

Greeting Card Assn., *1030 15th St. N.W., #870 20005; (202) 393-1778. Fax, (202) 393-0336. Marianne McDermott, Executive Vice President. Web, www.greetingcard.org.*

Membership: publishers, printers, and others interested in the greeting card industry. Monitors legislation and regulations.

International Newspaper Financial Executives, *21525 Ridgetop Circle, #200, Dulles, VA 20166; (703) 421-4060. Fax, (703) 421-4068. Robert J. Kasabian, Vice President. General e-mail, membership@infe.org. Web, www. infe.org.*

Membership: controllers and chief financial officers of newspapers. Disseminates information on financial aspects of publishing newspapers. Provides members with information on business office technology, including accounting software and spreadsheet applications. Produces publications, conducts seminars, and sponsors an annual convention.

Magazine Publishers of America, *Government Affairs, Washington Office, 1211 Connecticut Ave. N.W., #610 20036; (202) 296-7277. Fax, (202) 296-0343. Jim Creegan, Executive Vice President. Web, www.magazine. org.*

Washington office represents members in all aspects of government relations in Washington and state capitals.

National Newspaper Assn., *1010 N. Glebe Rd., #450, Arlington, VA 22201; (703) 525-7900. Fax, (703) 907-7901. Kenneth B. Allen, Executive Vice President.*

Membership: community, weekly, and daily newspapers. Provides members with advisory services; informs members of legislation and regulations that affect their business. Educational arm, the National Newspaper Foundation, conducts management seminars and conferences.

National Newspaper Publishers Assn., *3200 13th St. N.W. 20010; (202) 588-8764. Fax, (202) 588-5029. Benjamin Jealous, Executive Director. General e-mail, nnpadc@nnpa.org. Web, www.nnpa.org.*

Membership: newspapers owned by African Americans serving an African American audience. Assists in improving management and quality of the African American press through workshops and merit awards.

Newsletter Publishers Assn., *1501 Wilson Blvd., #509, Arlington, VA 22209; (703) 527-2333. Fax, (703) 841-0629. Patricia M. Wysocki, Executive Director. Web, www.newsletters.org.*

Membership: newsletter publishers and specialized information services. Serves as information clearinghouse; interests include international marketing. Monitors legislation and regulations. Library open to the public.

Newspaper Assn. of America, *1921 Gallows Rd., #600, Vienna, VA 22182; (703) 902-1600. Fax, (703) 917-0636. John Sturm, President. Library, (703) 902-1692. Web, www.naa.org.*

Membership: daily and weekly newspapers and other papers published in the United States, Canada, other parts of the Western Hemisphere, and Europe. Conducts research and disseminates information on newspaper publishing, including labor relations, legal matters, government relations, technical problems and innovations, telecommunications, economic and statistical data, training programs, and public relations. Library open to the public.

Printing Industries of America, *100 Daingerfield Rd., Alexandria, VA 22314; (703) 519-8100. Fax, (703) 548-3227. Ray Roper, President. Web, www.printing.org.*

Membership: printing firms and businesses that service printing industries. Represents members before Congress and regulatory agencies. Assists members with labor relations, human resources management, and other business management issues. Sponsors graphic arts competition. Monitors legislation and regulations.

Screen Printing Technical Foundation, *10015 Main St., Fairfax, VA 22031-3489; (703) 385-1335. Fax, (703) 273-0456. John M. Crawford, Managing Director. Web, www.sgia.org.*

Provides screen printers, suppliers, manufacturers, and schools with technical support and training; conducts research on production practices and standards. Offers scholarships for college students, grants to schools and teachers, and workshops. (Affiliated with Screenprinting and Graphic Imaging Assn. International.)

Screenprinting and Graphic Imaging Assn. International, *10015 Main St., Fairfax, VA 22031-3489; (703) 385-1335. Fax, (703) 273-0456. John M. Crawford, President. Web, www.sgia.org.*

Provides screen printers, graphic imagers, digital imagers, suppliers, manufacturers, and educators with technical guidebooks, training videos, managerial support, and guidelines for safety programs. Monitors legislation and regulations.

Society of National Assn. Publications, *1650 Tysons Blvd., #200, McLean, VA 22102; (703) 506-3285. Fax, (703) 506-3266. Laura Skoff, Director. Web, www.snaponline.org.*

Membership: publications owned or controlled by voluntary organizations. Works to develop high publishing standards, including high quality editorial and advertising content in members' publications. Compiles statistics; bestows editorial and graphics awards; monitors postal regulations.

See also The Writer's Center (p. 152)

5

Culture and Recreation

ARTS AND HUMANITIES

AGENCIES

Commission of Fine Arts, *441 F St. N.W., #312 20001; (202) 504-2200. Fax, (202) 504-2195. J. Carter Brown, Chair; Charles H. Atherton, Secretary.*

Advises the president, congressional committees, and government agencies on designs of public buildings, parks, and statuary.

General Services Administration, *Environmental Division, 1800 F St. N.W., #4207 20405; (202) 501-1811. Fax, (202) 501-3203. Debra Yap, Director.*

Administers the Art and Historic Preservation Program, which sets aside for art projects a percentage of the estimated construction costs for new buildings or renovation costs for existing ones; manages a collection of fine arts.

General Services Administration, *Living Buildings Program, 18th and F St. 20405; (202) 501-0514. Fax, (202) 208-5912. Peter Ford, Staff Contact.*

Provides information on the opening of federal buildings for public use for cultural, educational, and recreational activities, including conferences, performing arts functions, and art exhibits.

John F. Kennedy Center for the Performing Arts, *20566-0001; (202) 416-8000. Fax, (202) 416-8205. James A. Johnson, Chair; Lawrence J. Wilker, President, (202) 416-8010. Press, (202) 416-8448. TTY, (202) 416-8524. Performance and ticket information, (202) 467-4600; toll-free, (800) 444-1324. Web, kennedy-center.org.*

Independent bureau of the Smithsonian Institution administered by a separate board of trustees. Sponsors educational programs; presents American and international performances in theater, music, dance, and film; sponsors the John F. Kennedy Center Education Program, which produces the annual American College Theater Festival; presents and subsidizes events for young people. Library open to the public.

National Endowment for the Arts *(National Foundation on the Arts and the Humanities), 1100 Pennsylvania Ave. N.W. 20506-0001; (202) 682-5414. Fax, (202) 682-5639. Bill Ivey, Chair. Information, (202) 682-5400. Library, (202) 682-5485. Press, (202) 682-5570. TTY, (202) 682-5496. Web, arts.endow.gov.*

Independent federal grant-making agency. Awards grants to nonprofit arts organizations in four areas: creation and presentation; education and access; heritage and preservation; and partnership, planning, and stabi-

lization. Organizations must choose one of the four theme areas for submission of project proposals. Library open to the public by appointment.

National Endowment for the Arts *(National Foundation on the Arts and the Humanities), Arts Education, Music, Opera, Presenting, and Multidisciplinary, 1100 Pennsylvania Ave. N.W. 20506-0001; (202) 682-5438. Fax, (202) 682-5002. Jan Stunkard, Division Coordinator. Web, arts.endow.gov.*

Grant-making theme program for projects which expand awareness and appreciation of art and art education for people of all ages.

National Endowment for the Arts *(National Foundation on the Arts and the Humanities), Dance, Design, Media Arts, Museums, and Visual Arts, 1100 Pennsylvania Ave. N.W. 20506-0001; (202) 682-5452. Fax, (202) 682-5721. Saralyn Reece Hardy, Director. Web, arts.endow. gov.*

Grant-making theme program for the creation of new work and the presentation of new and existing works of any culture, period, or discipline.

National Endowment for the Arts *(National Foundation on the Arts and the Humanities), Folk and Traditional Arts, Literature, Theater, Musical Theater, and Planning and Stabilization, 1100 Pennsylvania Ave. N.W. 20506-0001; (202) 682-5428. Fax, (202) 682-5669. Barry Bergey, Division Coordinator. Web, arts.endow.gov.*

Grant-making theme program for projects in the arts which preserve nationally significant artistic accomplishments and works of art.

National Endowment for the Arts *(National Foundation on the Arts and the Humanities), Partnership, 1100 Pennsylvania Ave. N.W. 20506-0001; (202) 682-5429. Fax, (202) 682-5602. Jeff Watson, Division Coordinator. Web, arts.endow.gov.*

Grant-making program for projects which focus on organizational planning, sustaining the arts, building partnerships, and developing resources. Works to increase worldwide recognition of U.S. arts; provides U.S. artists and arts organizations with information on exchanges and other international arts activities; supports international endeavors that increase public understanding of the arts, including cultural influences from abroad.

National Endowment for the Humanities *(National Foundation on the Arts and the Humanities), 1100 Pennsylvania Ave. N.W., #503 20506; (202) 606-8310. Fax, (202) 606-8588. William R. Ferris, Chair; Juan E. Mestas, Deputy Chair, (202) 606-8273. Information, (202) 606-*

8400. *Library, (202) 606-8244. Press, (202) 606-8446.*
TTY, (202) 606-8282. General e-mail, info@neh.gov. Web,
www.neh.gov.

Independent federal grant-making agency. Awards
grants to individuals and institutions for research, scholarship, educational programs, and public programs
(including broadcasts, museum exhibitions, lectures, and
symposia) in the humanities (defined as study of archeology; history; jurisprudence; language; linguistics; literature; philosophy; comparative religion; ethics; the history,
criticism, and theory of the arts; and humanistic aspects
of the social sciences). Funds preservation of books,
newspapers, historical documents, and photographs.

President's Committee on the Arts and the
Humanities, *1100 Pennsylvania Ave. N.W., #526 20506;*
(202) 682-5409. Fax, (202) 682-5668. Harriet Mayor Ful-
bright, Executive Director.

Recommends to the president, the National Endowment for the Arts, and the National Endowment for the
Humanities ways to promote private sector support for
the arts, humanities, and international cultural
exchanges; analyzes the effectiveness of federal support.

CONGRESS

House Administration Committee, *1309 LHOB*
20515; (202) 225-8281. Fax, (202) 225-9957. Rep. Bill
Thomas, R-Calif., Chair; Cathy Abernathy, Staff Director.
Web, www.house.gov/cha.

Jurisdiction over legislation related to and operations
of the Smithsonian Institution (jurisdiction shared with
House Government Reform Committee).

House Appropriations Committee, *Subcommittee on*
Interior, B308 RHOB 20515; (202) 225-3081. Fax, (202)
225-9069. Rep. Ralph Regula, R-Ohio, Chair; Deborah A.
Weatherly, Clerk. Web, www.house.gov/appropriations.

Jurisdiction over legislation to appropriate funds for
the Interior Dept. and government programs for the arts
and the humanities, including the Smithsonian Institution, the National Foundation on the Arts and the
Humanities, the Commission of Fine Arts, the Advisory
Council on Historic Preservation, and the Institute of
Museum and Library Services.

House Education and the Workforce Committee,
Subcommittee on Postsecondary Education, Training,
and Life-Long Learning, 2181 RHOB 20515; (202) 225-
4527. Fax, (202) 225-9571. Rep. Howard P. "Buck"
McKeon, R-Calif., Chair; Kevin D. Talley, Staff Director.
Web, www.house.gov/ed_workforce.

Jurisdiction over programs related to the arts and
humanities, museum services, and arts and artifacts

indemnity. Jurisdiction over the National Foundation on
the Arts and Humanities Act.

House Government Reform Committee, *Subcom-*
mittee on Civil Service, B371C RHOB 20515; (202) 225-
6427. Fax, (202) 225-2392. Rep. Joe Scarborough, R-Fla.,
Chair; George Nesterczuk, Staff Director. Web, www.house.
gov/reform.

Jurisdiction over legislation on holidays and celebrations.

House Government Reform Committee, *Subcom-*
mittee on Government Management, Information, and
Technology, B373 RHOB 20515; (202) 225-5147. Fax,
(202) 225-2373. Rep. Steve Horn, R-Calif., Chair; J. Rus-
sell George, Staff Director. Web, www.house.gov/reform.

Oversees operations of the Smithsonian Institution
(jurisdiction shared with House Administration Committee) and the National Foundation on the Arts and the
Humanities.

Senate Appropriations Committee, *Subcommittee*
on Interior, SD-131 20510; (202) 224-7233. Sen. Slade
Gorton, R-Wash., Chair; Bruce Evans, Clerk. Web,
appropriations.senate.gov/interior.

Jurisdiction over legislation to appropriate funds for
government programs for the arts and the humanities,
including the Commission of Fine Arts; the National
Foundation on the Arts and the Humanities; and the
operations and programs of the Smithsonian Institution,
the Institute of Museum and Library Services, and the
Advisory Council on Historic Preservation.

Senate Health, Education, Labor, and Pensions
Committee, *SD-428 20510; (202) 224-5375. Fax, (202)*
228-5044. Sen. James M. Jeffords, R-Vt., Chair; Mark
Powden, Staff Director. TTY, (202) 224-1975. Web, labor.
senate.gov.

Jurisdiction over legislation on government programs
for the arts and the humanities, including the National
Endowment for the Arts, the National Endowment for
the Humanities, and the Institute of Museum and
Library Services. Jurisdiction over the Library Services
and Construction Act.

Senate Judiciary Committee, *SD-224 20510; (202)*
224-5225. Fax, (202) 224-9102. Sen. Orrin G. Hatch, R-
Utah, Chair; Manus Cooney, Chief Counsel. Web,
judiciary.senate.gov.

Jurisdiction over legislation on holidays and celebrations.

Senate Rules and Administration Committee, *SR-*
305 20510; (202) 224-6352. Fax, (202) 224-3036. Sen.

Mitch McConnell, R-Ky., Chair; Tamara Somerville, Staff Director. Web, rules.senate.gov.

Jurisdiction over legislation concerning the Smithsonian Institution and the U.S. Botanic Garden.

NONPROFIT

America the Beautiful Fund, *1730 K St. N.W., #1002 20006; (202) 638-1649. Fax, (202) 638-1687. Nanine Bilski, President. Web, www.america-the-beautiful.org.*

National service organization that promotes community self-help. Offers advisory services; grants; free seeds for civic and charitable volunteer programs; and national recognition awards to local community groups for activities that promote America's heritage, culture, environment, public parks, and human services.

American Arts Alliance, *805 15th St. N.W., #500 20005; (202) 289-1776. Fax, (202) 371-6601. Alvin Lam, Executive Director. General e-mail, aaa@artswire.org. Web, www.artswire.org/~aaa.*

Membership: symphony orchestras; art museums; arts presenters; and theater, dance, and opera companies. Advocates national policies that recognize the important role played by the arts in American life.

Americans for the Arts, *1000 Vermont Ave. N.W., 12th Floor 20005; (202) 371-2830. Fax, (202) 371-0424. Robert L. Lynch, President. Web, www.artsusa.org.*

Membership: groups and individuals dedicated to advancing the arts and culture in U.S. communities. Provides information on programs, activities, and administration of local arts agencies; on funding sources and guidelines; and on government policies and programs. Monitors legislation and regulations.

Aspen Institute, *Policy Programs, 1 Dupont Circle N.W., #700 20036; (202) 736-5818. Fax, (202) 467-0790. Charles M. Firestone, Executive Vice President. Information, (202) 736-5800. Web, www.aspeninst.org.*

Conducts seminars on Western civilization and other traditions and cultures; conducts studies and workshops on critical contemporary issues. Fields of interest include communications, energy, justice and the law, science and technology, education, international relations, social policies, rural economy, and the environment.

Assn. of Performing Arts Presenters, *1112 16th St. N.W., #400 20036; (202) 833-2787. Fax, (202) 833-1543. Tom Tomlinson, President. General e-mail, artpres@artspresenters.org. Web, www.artspresenters.org.*

Connects performing artists to audiences and communities around the world. Facilitates the work of presenters, artist managers, and consultants through

continuing education, regranting programs, and legislative advocacy.

Federation of State Humanities Councils, *1600 Wilson Blvd., #902, Arlington, VA 22209; (703) 908-9700. Fax, (703) 908-9706. Gail Leftwich, President. Web, www.acls.org/fshc.htm.*

Membership: humanities councils from U.S. states and territories. Provides members with information; forms partnerships with other organizations and with the private sector to promote the humanities. Monitors legislation and regulations.

International Network of Performing and Visual Arts Schools, *5505 Connecticut Ave. N.W., #280 20015; (202) 966-2216. Fax, (202) 966-2283. Ronald Daniel, Executive Director.*

Membership: schools of the arts, universities, and allied arts organizations from around the world. Supports and serves the leaders of specialized arts schools, fosters communications, and promotes development of new schools of the arts.

National Assembly of State Arts Agencies, *1029 Vermont Ave. N.W., 2nd Floor 20005; (202) 347-6352. Fax, (202) 737-0526. Jonathan Katz, Chief Executive Officer. General e-mail, nasaa@nasaa-arts.org. Web, nasaa-arts.org.*

Membership: state and jurisdictional arts agencies. Provides members with information, resources, and representation. Interests include arts programs for rural and underserved populations, and the arts as a catalyst for economic development. Monitors legislation and regulations.

National Campaign for Freedom of Expression, *1429 G St. N.W., PMB 416 20005; (202) 393-2787. Fax, (703) 685-7675. Michelle Coffey, Executive Director. Information, (800) 477-6233. General e-mail, ncfe@ncfe.net. Web, www.ncfe.net.*

Membership: artists, artists' organizations, and concerned individuals. Opposes censorship; promotes political empowerment of artists; seeks to increase funding for the arts. Monitors legislation and regulations.

National Humanities Alliance, *21 Dupont Circle N.W., #800 20036; (202) 296-4994. Fax, (202) 872-0884. John H. Hammer, Executive Director. Web, www.nhalliance.org.*

Represents scholarly and professional humanities associations; associations of museums, libraries, and historical societies; higher education institutions; state humanities councils; and independent and university-based research centers. Promotes the interests of individuals engaged in research, writing, and teaching.

National League of American Pen Women, *1300 17th St. N.W. 20036-1973; (202) 785-1997. Judith LaFourest, National President. Web, members.aol.com/penwomen/pen.htm.*

Promotes the development of the creative talents of professional women in the fields of art, letters, and music composition. Conducts and promotes literary, educational, and charitable activities. Offers scholarships, workshops, discussion groups, and professional lectures.

Wolf Trap Foundation for the Performing Arts, *1624 Trap Rd., Vienna, VA 22182; (703) 255-1920. Fax, (703) 255-1918. Terrence D. Jones, President. Information, (703) 255-1900. Web, www.wolf-trap.org.*

Established by Congress to administer Wolf Trap Farm Park for the Performing Arts. Sponsors performances in theater, music, and dance. Conducts educational programs for children, internships for college students, career-entry programs for young singers, and professional training for teachers and performers.

Education

See also Museums (this chapter)

AGENCIES

Education Dept., *Arts in Education, 400 Maryland Ave. S.W. 20202-6510 (mailing address: 600 Independence Ave. S.W. 20202-6140); (202) 260-2487. Fax, (202) 205-5630. Shelton Allen, Program Specialist. Web, www.ed.gov.*

Provides information on arts education programs. Awards grants to the Kennedy Center's arts and education program and to Very Special Arts, a program for the disabled.

John F. Kennedy Center for the Performing Arts, *Alliance for Arts Education Network, 20566-0001; (202) 416-8845. Fax, (202) 416-8802. Kathi Levin, Director. TTY, (202) 416-8822. Web, kennedy-center.org/education/kcaaen.*

Supports state alliances with operating and program grants and information. Alliances are statewide arts education organizations that provide communities with services including teacher professional development, conferences, and arts education programming.

John F. Kennedy Center for the Performing Arts, *Education, 20566-0004; (202) 416-8800. Fax, (202) 416-8802. Derek Gordon, Vice President. Press, (202) 416-8448. TTY, (202) 416-8822. Web, kennedy-center.org/education.*

Establishes and supports state committees to encourage arts education in schools (Kennedy Center Alliance for Arts Education Network); promotes community partnerships between performing arts centers and school systems (Performing Arts Centers and Schools); provides teachers with professional development opportunities; offers performances for young people and families; arranges artist and company residencies in schools; sponsors the National Symphony Orchestra education program; presents lectures, demonstrations, and classes in the performing arts for the general public; offers internships in arts management and fellowships for visiting artists; and produces annually the Kennedy Center American College Theater Festival.

National Endowment for the Arts *(National Foundation on the Arts and the Humanities), Arts Education, Music, Opera, Presenting, and Multidisciplinary, 1100 Pennsylvania Ave. N.W. 20506-0001; (202) 682-5438. Fax, (202) 682-5002. Jan Stunkard, Division Coordinator. Web, arts.endow.gov.*

Awards grants to state arts agencies and arts organizations to support arts education of students in grades pre-K through 12. Awards grants to nonprofit groups for development of community-based educational arts programs that reflect the culture of minority, inner city, rural, and tribal communities. Supports projects that create, present, or teach art. Awards grants to presenting organizations.

National Endowment for the Humanities *(National Foundation on the Arts and the Humanities), Research and Education, 1100 Pennsylvania Ave. N.W., #302 20506; (202) 606-8373. Fax, (202) 606-8394. James Herbert, Director. General e-mail, education@neh.gov. Web, www.neh.gov.*

Advocates the improvement of education in the humanities. Projects supported include curricula and materials development and faculty training and development. Offers fellowships, stipends, seminars, and institutes for higher education faculty, school teachers, and independent scholars. Conducts research.

National Gallery of Art, *Education Resources, 6th St. and Constitution Ave. N.W. 20565; (202) 842-6273. Fax, (202) 842-6935. Ruth Perlin, Head. Information, (202) 842-6273. TTY, (202) 842-6176. Order desk, (202) 842-6263. Web, www.nga.gov.*

Serves as an educational arm of the gallery; lends audiovisual educational materials free of charge to schools, colleges, community groups, libraries, and individuals on a free loan basis. Answers written and telephone inquiries about European and American art.

Smithsonian Institution, *Smithsonian Associates, 1100 Jefferson Dr. S.W., MRC 701 20560; (202) 357-3030.*

Fax, (202) 786-2034. Mara Mayor, Director. TTY, (202) 633-9467. General e-mail, tsa.rap@ic.si.edu. Web, www.si.edu/tsa/rap.

National cultural and educational membership organization that offers courses and lectures for adults and young people. Presents films and offers study tours on arts-, humanities-, and science-related subjects; sponsors performances, studio arts workshops, and research.

Smithsonian Office of Education, 900 Jefferson Dr. S.W. MRC 402 20560; (202) 357-3049. Fax, (202) 357-2116. Ann Bay, Director. Information, (202) 357-2425. TTY, (202) 357-1696. General e-mail, education@soe.si.edu.

Serves as the Smithsonian's central education office. Provides elementary and secondary teachers with programs, publications, audiovisual materials, regional workshops, and summer courses on using museums and primary source materials as teaching tools. Publishes books and other educational materials for teachers.

NONPROFIT

National Art Education Assn., 1916 Association Dr., Reston, VA 20191-1590; (703) 860-8000. Fax, (703) 860-2960. Thomas A. Hatfield, Executive Director. General e-mail, naea@dgs.dgsys.com. Web, www.naea-reston.org.

Membership: art teachers (elementary through university), museum staff, and manufacturers and suppliers of art materials. Issues publications on art education theory and practice, research, and current trends; provides technical assistance to art educators. Sponsors awards.

National Assn. of Schools of Art and Design, 11250 Roger Bacon Dr., #21, Reston, VA 20190; (703) 437-0700. Fax, (703) 437-6312. Samuel Hope, Executive Director. Web, www.arts-accredit.org.

Accrediting agency for educational programs in art and design. Provides information on art and design programs at the postsecondary level; offers professional development for executives of art and design programs.

Young Audiences, 1200 29th St. N.W., Lower Level 20007; (202) 944-2790. Fax, (202) 944-2793. Marie C. Barksdale, Executive Director.

Sponsors professional musicians, actors, and dancers who present arts education programs in U.S. schools; promotes career opportunities in the performing arts. Seeks to enhance the education of students through exposure to the performing arts. Researches techniques and disseminates information on developing arts education programs.

Film, Photography, and Broadcasting

See also Media Professions and Resources (chap. 4)

AGENCIES

American Film Institute Theater *(John F. Kennedy Center for the Performing Arts),* 20566-0001; (202) 416-7815. Fax, (202) 659-1970. Jean Firstenberg, Director. Recorded information, (202) 785-4600. General e-mail, NFT@afionline.org. Web, www.afionline.org/nft.

Preserves and catalogs films; supports research. Shows films of historical and artistic importance. Theater open to the public. (Administrative offices and Center for Advanced Film and Television Studies located in Los Angeles.)

National Archives and Records Administration, Motion Picture, Sound, and Video, 8601 Adelphi Rd., #3340, College Park, MD 20740-6001; (301) 713-7060. Fax, (301) 713-6904. Les Waffen, Manager. General e-mail, mopix@nara.gov. Web, www.nara.gov/nara/nail.html.

Selects and preserves audiovisual records produced or acquired by federal agencies; maintains collections from private sector, including newsreels. Research room open to the public.

National Archives and Records Administration, Still Pictures, 8601 Adelphi Rd., #5360, College Park, MD 20740-6001; (301) 713-6660. Fax, (301) 713-7436. Robert Richardson, Director. Fax-on-demand, (301) 713-6905. General e-mail, stillpix@nara.gov.

Provides the public with copies of still pictures from around the world; supplies guides to these materials. Collection includes still pictures from more than 150 federal agencies.

National Endowment for the Arts *(National Foundation on the Arts and the Humanities),* ***Dance, Design, Media Arts, Museums, and Visual Arts,*** 1100 Pennsylvania Ave. N.W. 20506-0001; (202) 682-5452. Fax, (202) 682-5721. Saralyn Reece Hardy, Director. Web, arts.endow.gov.

Awards grants to nonprofit organizations for film, video, and radio productions; supports film and video exhibitions and workshops.

National Endowment for the Humanities (NEH), *(National Foundation on the Arts and the Humanities),* ***Public Programs,*** 1100 Pennsylvania Ave. N.W., #426 20506; (202) 606-8267. Fax, (202) 606-8557. Nancy Rodger, Director. General e-mail, publicpgms@neh.gov.

Promotes public appreciation of the humanities through support of quality public programs of broad significance, reach, and impact. Awards grants for projects that meet NEH goals and standards, including excellence in content and format, broad public appeal, and wide access to diverse audiences.

National Technical Information Service *(Commerce Dept.), National Audiovisual Center, 5285 Port Royal Rd., Springfield, VA 22161; (703) 605-6000. Fax, (703) 605-6900. Ron R. Lawson, Director. Web, www.ntis.gov.*

Serves as a clearinghouse for video cassettes, slide sets, audiotapes, interactive video disks, and multimedia kits produced by federal agencies on a wide range of subjects, including languages, health and safety, and training programs. Publishes catalogs of audiovisual materials produced by all agencies of the U.S. government.

CONGRESS

Library of Congress, *Motion Picture, Broadcasting, and Recorded Sound, 101 Independence Ave. S.E. 20540-4690; (202) 707-5840. Fax, (202) 707-2371. David Francis, Chief. Recorded sound reference center, (202) 707-7833. Web, www.loc.gov/rr/mopic.*

Collections include archives of representative motion pictures (1942–present); historic films (1894–1915); early American films (1898–1926); German, Italian, and Japanese features, newsreels, and documentary films (1930–1945); and a selected collection of stills, newspaper reviews, and U.S. government productions. Collection also includes television programs of all types (1948–present), radio broadcasts (1924–present), and sound recordings (1890–present). Tapes the library's concert series and other musical events for radio broadcast; produces recordings of music and poetry for sale to the public. American Film Institute film archives are interfiled with the division's collections. Use of collections restricted to scholars and researchers; reading room open to the public.

Library of Congress, *National Film Preservation Board, 101 Independence Ave. S.E. 20540-4710 (mailing address: National Film Registry, Library of Congress 20540); (202) 707-6240. Fax, (202) 707-6269. Winston Tabb, Administrator. TTY, (202) 707-6362. Web, www. loc.gov/film.*

Administers the National Film Preservation Plan. Establishes guidelines and receives nominations for the annual selection of twenty-five films of cultural, historical, or aesthetic significance; selections are entered in the National Film Registry to ensure archival preservation in their original form.

Library of Congress, *Prints and Photographs, 101 Independence Ave. S.E. 20540-4730; (202) 707-5836. Fax,*

(202) 707-6647. Ellen Hahn, Chief. TTY, (202) 707-9051. Reading Room, (202) 707-6394. Web, lcweb.loc.gov/rr/ print.

Maintains Library of Congress's collection of pictorial material, not in book format, totaling more than 13.5 million items. U.S. and international collections include artists' prints; historical prints, posters, and drawings; photographs (chiefly documentary); political and social cartoons; and architectural plans, drawings, prints, and photographs. Reference service provided in the Prints and Photographs Reading Room. Reproductions of nonrestricted material available through the Library of Congress's Photoduplication Service; prints and photographs may be borrowed through the Exhibits Office for exhibits by qualified institutions. A portion of the collections and an overview of reference services are available on the World Wide Web.

NONPROFIT

Council on International Nontheatrical Events, *1001 Connecticut Ave. N.W., #625 20036; (202) 785-1136. Fax, (202) 785-4114. Donna Tschiffely, Executive Director. Web, www.cine.org.*

Selects and enters nontheatrical films in international film festivals; holds semiannual screening competitions and annual showcase and awards ceremonies.

Library of American Broadcasting, *University of Maryland, Hornbake Library, College Park, MD 20742; (301) 405-9160. Fax, (301) 314-2634. Chuck Howell, Curator.*

Maintains library and archives on the history of radio and television. Open to the public.

Motion Picture Assn., *1600 Eye St. N.W. 20006; (202) 293-1966. Fax, (202) 452-9823. Jack Valenti, President. Anti-piracy hotline, (800) 662-6797. Web, www.mpaa.org.*

Membership: motion picture producers and distributors. Advises state and federal governments on copyrights, censorship, cable broadcasting, and other topics; administers volunteer rating system for motion pictures; works to prevent video piracy.

Screen Actors Guild, *Washington Office, 4340 East-West Hwy., #204, Bethesda, MD 20814; (301) 657-2560. Fax, (301) 656-3615. Patricia O'Donnell, Chapter Executive Director. Web, www.sag.com.*

Membership: approximately 76,000 actors in television, theater, and commercials. Helps members negotiate pay, benefits, and better working conditions; conducts training programs and workshops. Monitors legislation and regulations. (Headquarters in Los Angeles.)

Language and Literature

See also Special Topics in Education (chap. 6)

AGENCIES

National Endowment for the Arts *(National Foundation on the Arts and the Humanities), Folk and Traditional Arts, Literature, Theater, Musical Theater, and Planning and Stabilization, 1100 Pennsylvania Ave. N.W. 20506-0001; (202) 682-5428. Fax, (202) 682-5669. Barry Bergey, Division Coordinator. Web, arts.endow.gov.*

Awards grants to published writers, poets, and translators of prose and poetry; awards grants to small presses and literary magazines that publish poetry and fiction.

CONGRESS

Library of Congress, *Center for the Book, 101 Independence Ave. S.E., #650 20540-4920; (202) 707-5221. Fax, (202) 707-0269. John Y. Cole, Director. Web, www.loc.gov/loc/cfbook.*

Seeks to broaden public appreciation of books, reading, and libraries; sponsors lectures and conferences on the educational and cultural role of the book worldwide, including the history of books and printing, television and the printed word, and the publishing and production of books; cooperates with state centers and with other organizations. Projects and programs are privately funded except for basic administrative support from the Library of Congress.

Library of Congress, *Children's Literature Center, 10 1st St. S.E. 20540-4620; (202) 707-5535. Fax, (202) 707-4632. Sybille Jagusch, Chief.*

Provides reference and information services by telephone, by correspondence, and in person; maintains reference materials on all aspects of the study of children's literature, including critical reviews of current books; sponsors lectures, symposia, and exhibits. Reading room open to the public.

Library of Congress, *Poetry and Literature, 10 1st St. S.E. 20540-8910; (202) 707-5394. Fax, (202) 707-9946. Robert Pinsky, Poet Laureate.*

Advises the library on public literary programs and on the acquisition of literary materials. Arranges for poets to record readings of their work for the library's tape archive. The poet laureate is appointed by the Librarian of Congress on the basis of literary distinction.

NONPROFIT

Alliance Française de Washington DC, *2142 Wyoming Ave. N.W. 20008; (202) 234-7911. Fax, (202)*
234-0125. *Laurent Mellier, Executive Director. General e-mail, alliance@francedc.org. Web, www.francedc.org.*

Offers courses in French language and literature; presents lectures and cultural events; maintains library of French-language publications for members; offers corporate language training programs.

American Councils for International Education, *American Council of Teachers of Russian, 1776 Massachusetts Ave. N.W., #700 20036; (202) 833-7522. Fax, (202) 833-7523. Dan Davidson, President. General e-mail, general@actr.org. Web, www.actr.org.*

Conducts educational exchanges for high school, university, and graduate school students as well as scholars with the countries of the former Soviet Union and Eastern Europe. Assists the countries of the former Soviet Union in implementing education reforms, advises them on academic testing, and provides them with language instruction materials.

American Poetry and Literacy Project, *P.O. Box 53445 20009; (202) 338-1109. Andrew Carroll, Executive Director.*

Donates new books of poetry to schools, libraries, hospitals, homeless shelters, nursing homes, hotels, and other public places around the country to promote literacy.

Brazilian-American Cultural Institute, *4103 Connecticut Ave. N.W. 20008; (202) 362-8334. Fax, (202) 362-8337. José M. Neistein, Executive Director.*

Conducts courses in Portuguese language and Brazilian literature; sponsors art exhibitions, films, concerts, and other public presentations on Brazilian culture. Library open to the public.

Center for Applied Linguistics, *4646 40th St. N.W., #200 20016-1859; (202) 362-0700. Fax, (202) 362-3740. Donna Christian, President. General e-mail, webmaster@cal.org. Web, www.cal.org.*

Research and technical assistance organization that serves as clearinghouse on application of linguistics to practical language problems. Interests include English as a second language (ESL), teacher training and material development, language education, language proficiency test development, bilingual education, and sociolinguistics.

English First, *8001 Forbes Pl., #102, Springfield, VA 22151; (703) 321-8818. Fax, (703) 321-8408. Jim Boulet Jr., Executive Director. Web, www.englishfirst.org.*

Seeks to make English the official language of the United States. Advocates policies which make English education available to all children. Monitors legislation and regulations. Opposes bilingual education and ballots.

Folger Shakespeare Library, *201 E. Capitol St. S.E. 20003-1094; (202) 544-4600. Fax, (202) 544-4623. Werner Gundersheimer, Director. Web, www.folger.edu.*

Administered by the trustees of Amherst College. Maintains major Shakespearean and Renaissance materials; awards fellowships for postdoctoral research; presents concerts, poetry and fiction readings, exhibits, and other public events. Offers educational programs for elementary and secondary school students and teachers.

Japan-America Society of Washington, *1020 19th St. N.W., Lower Lobby #40 20036; (202) 833-2210. Fax, (202) 833-2456. JoAnna Phillips, Executive Director. General e-mail, jaswdc@intr.net. Web, www.us-japan.org/dc.*

Assists Japanese performing artists; offers lectures and films on Japan; operates a Japanese-language school and an annual language competition for high school students; awards scholarships to college students studying in the Washington area. Maintains library for members.

Joint National Committee for Language, *4646 40th St. N.W., #310 20016; (202) 966-8477. Fax, (202) 966-8310. J. David Edwards, Executive Director. General e-mail, info@languagepolicy.org. Web, www.languagepolicy. org.*

Membership: translators, interpreters, and associations of language teachers (primary through postsecondary level). Supports a national policy on language study and international education. Provides forum and clearinghouse for professional language and international education associations. National Council for Languages and International Studies is the political arm.

Linguistic Society of America, *1325 18th St. N.W., #211 20036; (202) 835-1714. Fax, (202) 835-1717. Margaret W. Reynolds, Executive Director. General e-mail, lsa@lsadc.org. Web, www.lsadc.org.*

Membership: individuals and institutions interested in the scientific analysis of language. Holds linguistic institutes every other year.

National Foreign Language Center *(Johns Hopkins University), 1619 Massachusetts Ave. N.W., 4th Floor 20036; (202) 667-8100. Fax, (202) 667-6907. Richard Brecht, Director. Web, www.nflc.org.*

Research and policy organization that develops new strategies to strengthen foreign language competence in the United States. Conducts research on national language needs and assists policymakers in identifying priorities, allocating resources, and designing programs. Interests include the role of foreign language in higher education, national competence in critical languages, ethnic language maintenance, and K–12 and postsecondary language programs.

PEN/Faulkner Foundation, *c/o Folger Shakespeare Library, 201 E. Capitol St. S.E. 20003-1094; (202) 675-0345. Fax, (202) 608-1719. Robert Stone, Chair; Janice Delaney, Executive Director.*

Sponsors an annual juried award for American fiction. Brings authors to Washington-area public schools to teach classes. Holds readings by authors of new American fiction.

U.S. English, *1747 Pennsylvania Ave. N.W., #1100 20006; (202) 833-0100. Fax, (202) 833-0108. Mauro E. Mujica, Chair. Web, www.us-english.org.*

Advocates English as the official language of federal and state government. Affiliates U.S. English Foundation promotes English language education for immigrants.

The Writer's Center, *4508 Walsh St., Bethesda, MD 20815; (301) 654-8664. Fax, (301) 654-8667. Jane Fox, Executive Director. General e-mail, postmaster@writer.org. Web, www.writer.org.*

Membership: writers, editors, graphic artists, and interested individuals. Sponsors workshops in writing and graphic arts, and a reading series of poetry, fiction, and plays. Provides access to word processing, desktop publishing, and design equipment; maintains a book gallery.

See also Teachers of English to Speakers of Other Languages (p. 183)

Museums

See also History and Preservation (this chapter)

AGENCIES

Anacostia Museum and Center for African American History and Culture *(Smithsonian Institution), Arts and Industry Bldg., #1130, 900 Jefferson Dr. S.W., MRC 431 20560; (202) 287-3306. Fax, (202) 287-3183. Steven Newsome, Director. TTY, (202) 357-1729. Recorded information, (202) 357-4500. Web, www.si.edu/organiza/ museums/anacost/start.htm.*

Researches, interprets, and documents the history of African Americans, placing special emphasis on the experiences of residents of Georgia, Maryland, North Carolina, South Carolina, Virginia, and the District of Columbia.

MUSEUM EDUCATION PROGRAMS

Alexandria Archaeology, (703) 838-4399

American Assn. of Museums, Museum Assessment Program, (202) 289-9118

Arlington Arts Center, (703) 524-1494

Assn. of Science-Technology Centers, (202) 783-7200

B'nai B'rith Klutznick Museum, (202) 857-6583

C & O Canal, (301) 739-4200

Capital Children's Museum, (202) 675-4120

Corcoran Gallery of Art, (202) 639-1700

Daughters of the American Revolution (DAR) Museum, (202) 879-3241

Decatur House, (202) 842-0915

Dumbarton Oaks, (202) 339-6409

Federal Reserve Board, (202) 452-3686

Folger Shakespeare Library, (202) 675-0306

Gadsby's Tavern Museum, (703) 838-4242

Historical Society of Washington, DC, (202) 785-2068

J.F.K. Center for the Performing Arts—Alliance for Arts Education, (202) 416-8800

Lyceum, (703) 838-4994

Mount Vernon, (703) 780-2000

National Arboretum, (202) 245-2726

National Archives, (301) 713-6275

National Building Museum, (202) 272-2448

National Gallery of Art, (202) 842-6246

National Museum of Women in the Arts, (202) 783-7370

Navy Museum, (202) 433-4882

Octagon Museum, (202) 638-3221

Phillips Collection, (202) 387-2151

Smithsonian Institution

  Central education office, (202) 357-3049

  Anacostia Museum, (202) 287-3369

  Arthur M. Sackler Gallery, (202) 357-4880

  Freer Gallery of Art, (202) 357-4880

  Friends of the National Zoo, (202) 673-4954

  Hirshhorn Museum and Sculpture Garden, (202) 357-3235

  National Air and Space Museum, (202) 786-2106

  National Museum of African Art, (202) 357-4600

  National Museum of American Art, (202) 357-3095

  National Museum of American History, (202) 357-3229

  National Museum of Natural History, (202) 357-2747

  National Portrait Gallery, (202) 357-2920

  Renwick Gallery, (202) 357-2531

Textile Museum, (202) 483-0981

Woodrow Wilson House, (202) 387-4062

Arthur M. Sackler Gallery *(Smithsonian Institution), 1050 Independence Ave. S.W. 20560-0707; (202) 357-2700. Fax, (202) 357-4911. Milo C. Beach, Director. Press, (202) 357-4880. TTY, (202) 786-2374. Public programs, (202) 357-3200 (recording). Web, www.si.edu/asia.*

Exhibits Asian and Near Eastern art drawn from collections in the United States and abroad; features international exhibitions and public programs. Presents films, lectures, and concerts. Library open to the public.

Federal Council on the Arts and the Humanities *(National Foundation on the Arts and the Humanities), 1100 Pennsylvania Ave. N.W. 20506; (202) 682-5574. Fax, (202) 682-5603. Alice M. Whelihan, Indemnity Administrator.*

Membership: leaders of federal agencies sponsoring arts-related activities. Administers the Arts and Artifacts Indemnity Act, which helps museums reduce the costs of commercial insurance for international exhibits.

Frederick Douglass National Historic Site, *1411 W St. S.E. 20020; (202) 426-5961. Fax, (202) 426-0880. Lawerence Burgess, Site Manager. Web, www.nps.gov/frdo.*

Administered by the National Park Service. Museum of the life and work of abolitionist Frederick Douglass and his family. Offers tours of the home and special programs, such as documentary films, videos, and slide presentations; maintains visitor's center and bookstore.

Freer Gallery of Art *(Smithsonian Institution), 12th St. and Jefferson Dr. S.W. 20560-0707; (202) 357-2700. Fax, (202) 357-4911. Milo C. Beach, Director. Press, (202) 357-4880. TTY, (202) 786-2374. Public programs, (202) 357-3200 (recording). Web, www.si.edu/asia.*

Exhibits Asian art from the Mediterranean to Japan and late nineteenth and early twentieth century American art from its permanent collection, including works by James McNeill Whistler. Presents films, lectures, and concerts. Library open to the public.

Hirshhorn Museum and Sculpture Garden *(Smithsonian Institution), 7th St. and Independence Ave. S.W. 20560; (202) 357-3091. Fax, (202) 786-2682. James T. Demetrion, Director. Information, (202) 357-2700. Press, (202) 357-1618. TTY, (202) 633-8043. Web, www.si.edu/ hirshhorn.*

Preserves and exhibits contemporary American and European paintings and sculpture. Offers films, lectures, concerts, and tours of the collection.

Institute of Museum and Library Services, *1100 Pennsylvania Ave. N.W. 20506; (202) 606-8536. Fax, (202) 606-8591. Diane Frankel, Director. Information, (202) 606-8539. TTY, (202) 606-8636. General e-mail, imlsinfo@imls.fed.us. Web, www.imls.gov.*

Independent agency established by Congress to assist museums and libraries in increasing and improving their services. Awards grants for general operating support, conservation projects, and museum assessment to museums of all disciplines and budget sizes; helps fund museum associations.

National Endowment for the Arts *(National Foundation on the Arts and the Humanities), Dance, Design, Media Arts, Museums, and Visual Arts, 1100 Pennsylvania Ave. N.W. 20506-0001; (202) 682-5452. Fax, (202) 682-5721. Saralyn Reece Hardy, Director. Web, arts. endow.gov.*

Awards grants to museums for installing and cataloging permanent and special collections; traveling exhibits; training museum professionals; conserving and preserving museum collections; and developing arts-related educational programs.

National Gallery of Art, *6th St. and Constitution Ave. N.W. 20565; (202) 737-4215. Fax, (202) 842-2356. Earl A. Powell III, Director. Information, (202) 842-6191. Press, (202) 842-6353. TTY, (202) 842-6176. Web, www.nga.gov.*

Autonomous bureau of the Smithsonian Institution administered by a separate board of trustees. Preserves and exhibits European and American paintings, sculpture, and decorative and graphic arts. Offers concerts, demonstrations, lectures, symposia, films, tours, and teachers' workshops to enhance exhibitions, the permanent collection, and related topics. Lends art to museums in all fifty states and abroad through the National Lending Service. Publishes monthly calendar of events.

National Museum of African Art *(Smithsonian Institution), 950 Independence Ave. S.W. 20560-0708; (202) 357-4600. Fax, (202) 357-4879. Roslyn A. Walker, Director, (202) 357-4858. TTY, (202) 357-4814. Web, www.si. edu/nmafa.*

Collects, studies, and exhibits traditional and contemporary arts of Africa. Exhibits feature objects from the permanent collection and from private and public collections worldwide. Library and photo archive open to the public by appointment.

National Museum of American Art *(Smithsonian Institution), 8th and G Sts. N.W. 20560; (202) 357-1959. Fax, (202) 357-2528. Elizabeth Broun, Director. Information, (202) 357-2700. Press, (202) 357-2247. TTY, (202) 786-2393. Web, www.nmaa.si.edu.*

Exhibits and interprets American painting, sculpture, photographs, folk art, and graphic art from eighteenth century to present in permanent collection and temporary exhibition galleries.

National Museum of American History *(Smithsonian Institution), 14th St. and Constitution Ave. N.W. 20560; (202) 357-2510. Fax, (202) 786-2624. Spencer R. Crew, Director. Information, (202) 357-3129. Library, (202) 357-2414. TTY, (202) 357-1563. General e-mail, viarcmx@sivm.si.edu. Web, www.americanhistory.si.edu.*

Collects and exhibits objects representative of American cultural history, applied arts, industry, national and military history, and science and technology. Library open to the public by appointment.

National Museum of Health and Medicine *(Defense Dept.), Walter Reed Medical Center, Bldg. 54 South 20307 (mailing address: 6825 16th St. N.W. 20036-6000); (202) 782-2200. Fax, (202) 782-3573. Dr. Adrianne Noe, Director.*

Collects and exhibits medical models, tools, and teaching aids. Maintains permanent exhibits on the human body, AIDS, Civil War medicine, and military contributions to medicine; collects specimens illustrating a broad range of pathological conditions. Open to the public. Study collection available for scholars by appointment.

National Museum of the American Indian *(Smithsonian Institution), 470 L'Enfant Plaza, #7102 20560; (202) 287-2523. Fax, (202) 287-2538. W. Richard West, Director. Web, www.si.edu/nmai.*

Established by Congress in 1989 to plan and coordinate development of the National Museum of the American Indian. The museum, scheduled to open in the year 2002, will collect, preserve, study, and exhibit American Indian languages, literature, history, art, and culture.

National Portrait Gallery *(Smithsonian Institution), 8th and F Sts. N.W. 20560-0213; (202) 3571915. Fax, (202) 357-2307. Carolyn K. Carr, Director (Acting). Library, (202) 357-1886. TTY, (202) 357-1729. Web, www.npg.si.edu.*

Exhibits paintings, photographs, sculpture, drawings, and prints of individuals who have made significant contributions to the history, development, and culture of the United States. Library open to the public.

Renwick Gallery *(Smithsonian Institution), 17th St. and Pennsylvania Ave. N.W. 20560; (202) 357-2531. Fax, (202) 786-2810. Kenneth Trapp, Curator-in-Charge. Information, (202) 357-2247. TTY, (202) 357-4522.*

Curatorial department of the National Museum of American Art. Exhibits late twentieth century American crafts.

Smithsonian Institution, *1000 Jefferson Dr. S.W., #205 20560; (202) 357-1846. Fax, (202) 786-2515. I. Michael Heyman, Secretary; Constance B. Newman, Under Secretary, (202) 357-3258. Information, (202) 357-2700. Library, (202) 357-2240. Press, (202) 357-2627. TTY, (202) 357-1729. Recorded daily museum highlights, (202) 357-2020. Locator, (202) 357-1300. Web, www.si.edu.*

Conducts research; publishes results of studies, explorations, and investigations; maintains study and reference collections on science, culture, and history; maintains exhibitions in the arts, American history, technology, aeronautics and space exploration, and natural history. Smithsonian Institution sites in Washington, D.C., include the Anacostia Museum, Archives of American Art, Arthur M. Sackler Gallery, Arts & Industries Building, Freer Gallery of Art, Hirshhorn Museum and Sculpture Garden, National Air & Space Museum, National Museum of African Art, National Museum of American Art, National Museum of American History, National Museum of Natural History, National Portrait Gallery, National Postal Museum, National Zoological Park, S. Dillon Ripley Center, Smithsonian Institution Building, and Renwick Gallery. Supports affiliates in New York, Arizona, Florida, Maryland, Massachusetts, and Panama. Autonomous bureaus affiliated with the Smithsonian Institution include John F. Kennedy Center for the Performing Arts, National Gallery of Art, and Woodrow Wilson International Center for Scholars. Libraries open to the public by appointment.

Smithsonian Institution, *Center for Museum Studies, 900 Jefferson Dr. S.W., #2235 20560; (202) 357-3101. Fax, (202) 357-3346. Bruce Craig, Director. Library, (202) 786-2271. Web, www.si.edu/cms.*

Provides training, services, information, and assistance for the professional enhancement of museum personnel and institutions in the United States; sponsors museum training workshops; maintains museum reference center; offers career counseling.

Smithsonian Institution, *International Relations, 1100 Jefferson Dr. S.W., #3123, MRC 705 20560; (202) 357-4282. Fax, (202) 786-2557. Francine C. Berkowitz, Director.*

Fosters the development and coordinates the international aspects of Smithsonian cultural activities; facilitates basic research in history and art and encourages international collaboration among individuals and institutions.

Smithsonian Institution, *Internship Programs and Services, 900 Jefferson Dr. S.W., #2235 20560-0427; (202) 357-3102. Fax, (202) 357-3346. Elena Mayberry, Coordinator. General e-mail, siintern@sms.si.edu.*

Provides internship placements to high school students over sixteen years of age, undergraduate and graduate students, and museum professionals. Emphasizes methods and current practices employed by museum professionals.

CONGRESS

Library of Congress, *Interpretive Programs, 101 Independence Ave. S.E. 20540-4950; (202) 707-5223. Fax, (202) 707-9063. Irene Chambers, Interpretive Programs Officer. Web, www.loc.gov.*

Handles exhibits within the Library of Congress; establishes and coordinates traveling exhibits; handles loans of library material.

NONPROFIT

American Assn. of Museums, *1575 Eye St. N.W., #400 20005-1105; (202) 289-1818. Fax, (202) 289-6578. Edward H. Able Jr., President. TTY, (202) 289-8439. General e-mail, aaminfo@aam-us.org. Web, www.aam-us.org.*

Membership: individuals, institutions, museums, and museum professionals. Accredits museums; conducts educational programs; promotes international professional exchanges.

Art, Science, and Technology Institute, *1400 S. Joyce St., #226, Arlington, VA 22202; (703) 892-2226. Laurent Bussaut, President.*

Research and educational organization. Displays a permanent collection on the art, science, and technology of holography. Conducts research on holographic applications, laser, and photonics imaging, and new forms of expression that combine art, science, and technology.

Art Services International, *700 N. Fairfax St., #220, Alexandria, VA 22314; (703) 548-4554. Fax, (703) 548-3305. Lynn K. Rogerson, Director. Web, www.artservicesintl.org.*

Organizes and circulates fine arts exhibitions to museums worldwide.

Capital Children's Museum, *800 3rd St. N.E. 20002; (202) 675-4120. Fax, (202) 675-4140. Catherine Martens, Executive Director. Press, (202) 675-4183. Museum desk, (202) 675-4170. Web, www.ccm.org.*

Offers exhibits that involve participation by children. Integrates art, science, the humanities, and technology through "hands-on" learning experiences. (A program of the National Learning Center.)

Corcoran Gallery of Art, *500 17th St. N.W. 20006; (202) 639-1700. Fax, (202) 639-1768. David C. Levy, Director. Web, www.corcoran.org.*

Exhibits paintings, sculpture, and drawings, primarily American. Collections include European art and works of local Washington artists. The affiliated Corcoran School of Art offers a BFA degree and a continuing education program. Library open to the public by appointment.

Dumbarton Oaks, *1703 32nd St. N.W. 20007; (202) 339-6410. Edward L. Keenan, Director. Information, (202) 339-6400. Recorded information, (202) 339-6401. Web, www.doaks.org.*

Administered by the trustees for Harvard University. Exhibits Byzantine and pre-Columbian art and artifacts; conducts advanced research and maintains publication programs and library in Byzantine and pre-Columbian studies and in landscape architecture. Gardens open to the public daily (fee charged April through October); library open to qualified scholars by advance application.

Freedom Forum Newseum, *1101 Wilson Blvd., 10th Floor, Arlington, VA 22209; (703) 284-3700. Fax, (703) 284-3777. Joe Urschel, Executive Director. Web, www.newseum.org.*

World's only interactive museum of news. Collects items related to the history of news coverage; offers multimedia presentations and exhibits on the past, present, and future of news coverage; emphasizes the importance of the First Amendment to news coverage. (Affiliated with Freedom Forum.)

Hillwood Museum and Gardens, *4155 Linnean Ave. N.W. 20008; (202) 686-8500. Fax, (202) 966-7846. Frederick Fisher, Director. TTY, (202) 363-3056.*

Former residence of Marjorie Merriweather Post. Maintains and exhibits collection of French and Russian decorative arts, including portraits, liturgical objects, and furniture. Gardens and museum open to the public by appointment.

Museum Services International, *1716 17th St. N.W. 20009; (202) 462-6176. Fax, (202) 462-2380. Roger Wulff, Director. General e-mail, museplan@erols.com. Web, www.washingtonpost.com/yp/museumshopint.*

Provides consulting services to museums around the world. Interests include museum security and value engineering (federally mandated cost analysis of architecture and construction of federal buildings, including museums).

National Building Museum, *401 F St. N.W. 20001; (202) 272-2448. Fax, (202) 272-2564. Susan Henshaw Jones, President. Press, (202) 272-3606. Web, www.nbm.org.*

Celebrates American achievements in building, architecture, urban planning, engineering, and historic preservation through educational programs, exhibitions, tours, lectures, workshops, and publications.

National Museum of Women in the Arts, *1250 New York Ave. N.W. 20005; (202) 783-5000. Fax, (202) 393-3235. Nancy Risque Rohrbach, Director. Information, (800) 222-7270. Library, (202) 783-7365. Web, www.nmwa.org.*

Acquires, researches, and presents the works of women artists from the Renaissance to the present. Promotes greater representation and awareness of women in the arts. Library open to the public by appointment.

Octagon Museum, *1799 New York Ave. N.W. 20006-5291; (202) 638-3221. Fax, (202) 879-7764. Eryl J. Platzer, Director. TTY, (202) 638-1538. Web, www.aafpages.org.*

Federal period house open for tours; served as the executive mansion following the War of 1812. Presents temporary exhibits on architecture, decorative arts, and Washington history. Sponsors lectures, scholarly research, publications, and educational programs. (Owned by the American Architectural Foundation.)

Phillips Collection, *1600 21st St. N.W. 20009; (202) 387-2151. Fax, (202) 387-2436. Jay Gates, Director. Membership, (202) 387-3036. Shop, (202) 387-2151, ext. 239. Web, www.phillipscollection.org.*

Maintains permanent collection of European and American paintings, primarily of the nineteenth and twentieth centuries, and holds special exhibits from the same period. Sponsors lectures, gallery talks, and special events, including Sunday concerts (September–May). Library open to researchers and members by appointment.

Textile Museum, *2320 S St. N.W. 20008; (202) 667-0441. Fax, (202) 483-0994. Ursula E. McCracken, Director.*

Exhibits historic and handmade textiles and carpets. Sponsors symposia, conferences, workshops, lectures, and an annual rug convention. Library open to the public.

Trust for Museum Exhibitions, *1424 16th St. N.W., #600 20036; (202) 745-2566. Fax, (202) 745-0103. Ann Van Devanter Townsend, President. General e-mail, thetrust@tme.org. Web, www.tme.org.*

Provides lending and exhibiting institutions with traveling exhibition services, which include negotiating loans, engaging guest curators, scheduling tours, fundraising, and managing registrarial details and catalog production.

U.S. Holocaust Memorial Museum, *100 Raoul Wallenberg Pl. S.W. 20024-2126; (202) 488-0400. Fax, (202) 488-2690. Sara Bloomfield, Director. Library, (202) 488-9717. TTY, (202) 488-0406. Web, www.ushmm.org.*

Works to preserve documentation about the Holocaust; encourages research; provides educational resources, including conferences, publications, and public programming. Responsible for the annual Days of Remembrance of the Victims of the Holocaust.

Woodrow Wilson House *(National Trust for Historic Preservation), 2340 S St. N.W. 20008; (202) 387-4062. Fax, (202) 483-1466. Frank Aucella, Director (Acting). General e-mail, wilsondc@worldweb.net.*

Georgian Revival home that exhibits furnishings and memorabilia from President Woodrow Wilson's political and retirement years.

See also Assn. of Science-Technology Centers (p. 153); National Geographic Society (p. 210)

Music

AGENCIES

National Archives and Records Administration, *Public Program, 700 Pennsylvania Ave. N.W., #G6 20408; (202) 501-5210. Fax, (202) 501-5239. Edith James, Director. Web, www.nara.gov.*

Plans and directs activities to acquaint the public with materials of the National Archives; conducts tours, workshops, and classes; stages exhibits; produces books and pamphlets; issues teaching packets using historic documents.

National Endowment for the Arts *(National Foundation on the Arts and the Humanities), Arts Education, Music, Opera, Presenting, and Multidisciplinary, 1100 Pennsylvania Ave. N.W. 20506-0001; (202) 682-*

5438. Fax, (202) 682-5002. Jan Stunkard, Division Coordinator. Web, arts.endow.gov.

Awards grants to music professional training and career development institutions and to music performing, presenting, recording, and service organizations; awards fellowship grants to professional jazz musicians. Awards grants to professional opera and musical theater companies for regional touring and to organizations that provide services for opera and musical theater professionals.

National Museum of American History *(Smithsonian Institution), Cultural History, 12th St. and Constitution Ave. N.W. 20560; (202) 357-1707. Fax, (202) 786-2883. Rex Ellis, Chair. General e-mail, info@info. si.edu. Web, www.americanhistory.si.edu.*

Handles exhibits, including construction, and audiovisual services. Presents concerts that feature jazz by regional artists and ensembles, American popular songs, and American theater music on topics related to the museum's collections and current exhibitions. The chamber music program uses a collection of historic European and American musical instruments in performances.

National Symphony Orchestra Education Program *(John F. Kennedy Center for the Performing Arts), 20566-0004; (202) 416-8820. Fax, (202) 416-8802. Carole J. Wysocki, Director. TTY, (202) 416-8822. Web, kennedy-center.org/nso/nsoed.html.*

Presents concerts for students, grades K–12; sponsors fellowship program for talented high school musicians and a young associates program for high school students interested in arts management and professional music careers; holds an annual soloist competition open to college and high school pianists, orchestral instrumentalists, and college vocalists; sponsors Youth Orchestra Day for area youth orchestra members selected by their conductors.

CONGRESS

Library of Congress, *Motion Picture, Broadcasting, and Recorded Sound, 101 Independence Ave. S.E. 20540-4690; (202) 707-5840. Fax, (202) 707-2371. David Francis, Chief. Recorded sound reference center, (202) 707-7833. Web, www.loc.gov/rr/mopic.*

Maintains library's collection of musical and vocal recordings; tapes the library's concert series and other musical events for radio broadcast; produces recordings of music and poetry for sale to the public. Collection also includes sound recordings (1890–present). Reading room open to the public; listening and viewing by appointment.

Library of Congress, *Music Division, 101 Independence Ave. S.E. 20540-4710; (202) 707-5503. Fax, (202) 707-0621. John Newsom, Chief. Concert information, (202) 707-5502. Reading room, (202) 707-5507.*

Maintains and services, through the Performing Arts Reading Room, the library's collection of music manuscripts, sheet music, books, and instruments. Coordinates the library's chamber music concert series; produces radio broadcasts and, for sale to the public, recordings of concerts sponsored by the division; issues publications relating to the field of music and to division collections.

NONPROFIT

American Music Therapy Assn., *8455 Colesville Rd., #1000, Silver Spring, MD 20910; (301) 589-3300. Fax, (301) 589-5175. Andrea Farbman, Executive Director. General e-mail, info@musictherapy.org. Web, www. musictherapy.org.*

Promotes the therapeutic use of music by approving degree programs and clinical training sites for therapists, setting standards for certification of music therapists, and conducting research in the music therapy field.

American Symphony Orchestra League, *1156 15th St. N.W., #805 20005-1704; (202) 776-0212. Fax, (202) 776-0224. Charles Olton, President. General e-mail, league@symphony.org. Web, www.symphony.org.*

Service and educational organization dedicated to strengthening symphony and chamber orchestras. Provides artistic, organizational, and financial leadership and service to the music directors, musicians, direct service and governance volunteers, managers, and staff of member orchestras.

Music Educators National Conference, *1806 Robert Fulton Dr., Reston, VA 20191-4348; (703) 860-4000. Fax, (703) 860-1531. John J. Mahlmann, Executive Director. Web, www.menc.org.*

Membership: music educators (preschool through university). Holds biennial conference. Publishes books and teaching aids for music educators.

National Assn. of Schools of Music, *11250 Roger Bacon Dr., #21, Reston, VA 20190; (703) 437-0700. Fax, (703) 437-6312. Samuel Hope, Executive Director.*

Accrediting agency for educational programs in music. Provides information on music education programs; offers professional development for executives of music programs.

OPERA America, *1156 15th St. N.W., #810 20005-1704; (202) 293-4466. Fax, (202) 393-0735. Marc A. Scorca,*

President. General e-mail, frontdesk@operaam.org. Web, www.operaam.org.

Membership: professional opera companies in the United States and abroad, producing and presenting organizations, artists, and others affiliated with professional opera. Advises and assists opera companies in daily operations; encourages development of opera and musical theater; produces educational programs; implements programs to increase awareness and appreciation of opera and opera companies.

Recording Industry Assn. of America, *1330 Connecticut Ave. N.W., #300 20036; (202) 775-0101. Fax, (202) 775-7253. Hilary B. Rosen, President. Web, www.riaa.com.*

Membership: creators, manufacturers, and marketers of sound recordings. Educates members about new technology in the music industry. Advocates copyright protection and opposes censorship. Works to prevent recording piracy, counterfeiting, bootlegging, and unauthorized record rental and imports. Certifies gold, platinum, and multiplatinum recordings. Publishes statistics on the recording industry.

Rhythm and Blues Foundation, *1555 Connecticut Ave. N.W., #401 20036-1111; (202) 588-5566. Fax, (202) 588-5549. Bob Wade, Executive Director (Interim). General e-mail, randbfdn@aol.com. Web, www.rhythm-n-blues.org.*

Fosters wider recognition, financial support, and historic and cultural preservation of rhythm and blues music through various grants and programs in support of artists from the 1940s, '50s, and '60s.

Washington Area Music Assn., *1101 17th St. N.W., #1100 20036; (202) 338-1134. Fax, (703) 237-7923. Mike Schreibman, Executive Director. Information, (703) 237-9500. General e-mail, dcmusic@wamadc.com. Web, www. wamadc.com.*

Membership: musicians, concert promoters, lawyers, recording engineers, managers, contractors, and other music industry professionals. Sponsors workshops on industry-related topics. Represents professionals from all musical genres. Serves as a liaison between the Washington-area music community and music communities nationwide.

Theater and Dance

AGENCIES

Ford's Theatre National Historic Site, *511 10th St. N.W. 20004; (202) 426-6924. Fax, (202) 426-1845. Suzanne Kelley, Site Manager. TTY, (202) 426-1749. Recorded ticket information, (202) 347-4833. General e-mail, NACC_FOTH_Interpretation@nps.gov. Web, www. nps.gov/foth.*

Administered by the National Park Service. Manages Ford's Theatre, Ford's Theatre Museum, and the Peterson House (house where Lincoln died). Presents interpretive talks, exhibits, and tours; research library open by appointment. Functions as working stage for theatrical productions.

Fund for New American Plays *(John F. Kennedy Center for the Performing Arts), 20566; (202) 416-8024. Fax, (202) 416-8205. Rebecca Foster, Co-Manager; Max Woodward, Co-Manager. Web, www.kennedy-center.org/newwork/fnap.*

Encourages playwrights to write and nonprofit professional theaters to produce new American plays; gives playwrights financial support and provides grants to cover some expenses that exceed standard production costs. Submissions must come from the producing theater.

National Endowment for the Arts *(National Foundation on the Arts and the Humanities), Dance, Design, Media Arts, Museums, and Visual Arts, 1100 Pennsylvania Ave. N.W. 20506-0001; (202) 682-5452. Fax, (202) 682-5721. Saralyn Reece Hardy, Director. Web, arts.endow. gov.*

Awards grants to dance services organizations and companies.

National Endowment for the Arts *(National Foundation on the Arts and the Humanities), Folk and Traditional Arts, Literature, Theater, Musical Theater, and Planning and Stabilization, 1100 Pennsylvania Ave. N.W. 20506-0001; (202) 682-5428. Fax, (202) 682-5669. Barry Bergey, Division Coordinator. Web, arts.endow.gov.*

Awards grants to professional theater companies and theater service organizations.

Smithsonian Institution, *Discovery Theater, 900 Jefferson Dr. S.W. 20560; (202) 357-1502. Fax, (202) 357-2588. Roberta Gasbarre, Director. Reservations, (202) 357-1500.*

Presents live theatrical performances, including storytelling, dance, music, puppetry, and plays, for young people and their families.

See also John F. Kennedy Center for the Performing Arts and National Endowment for the Humanities (p. 145)

NONPROFIT

National Assn. of Schools of Dance, *11250 Roger Bacon Dr., #21, Reston, VA 20190; (703) 437-0700. Fax, (703) 437-6312. Samuel Hope, Executive Director.*

Accrediting agency for educational programs in dance. Provides information on dance education programs; offers professional development for executives of dance programs.

National Assn. of Schools of Theatre, *11250 Roger Bacon Dr., #21, Reston, VA 20190; (703) 437-0700. Fax, (703) 437-6312. Samuel Hope, Executive Director.*

Accrediting agency for educational programs in theater. Provides information on theater education programs; offers professional development for executives of theater programs.

National Conservatory of Dramatic Arts, *1556 Wisconsin Ave. N.W. 20007; (202) 333-2202. Fax, (202) 333-1753. Dennis A. Dulmage, President.*

Offers an accredited two-year program in postsecondary professional actor training and a one-year program in advanced professional training. Emphasizes both physical and mental preparedness for acting in the professional entertainment industry.

Shakespeare Theatre, *450 7th St. N.W. 20004 (mailing address: 516 8th St. S.E. 20003); (202) 547-3230. Fax, (202) 547-0226. Sam Sweet, Managing Director. TTY, (202) 638-3863. Box office, (202) 547-1122. Web, www.shakespearedc.org.*

Professional resident theater that presents Shakespearean and other classical plays. Offers actor training program for youths, adults, and professional actors. Produces free outdoor summer Shakespeare plays and free Shakespeare plays for schools.

Visual Arts

See also Architecture and Design (chap. 12); Film, Photography, and Broadcasting (this chapter); Museums (this chapter)

AGENCIES

National Endowment for the Arts *(National Foundation on the Arts and the Humanities), Dance, Design, Media Arts, Museums, and Visual Arts, 1100 Pennsylvania Ave. N.W. 20506-0001; (202) 682-5452. Fax, (202) 682-5721. Saralyn Reece Hardy, Director. Web, arts.endow.gov.*

Awards grants to nonprofit organizations for creative works and programs in the visual arts, including painting, sculpture, crafts, video, photography, printmaking, drawing, artists' books, and performance art.

National Endowment for the Arts *(National Foundation on the Arts and the Humanities), Folk and Traditional Arts, Literature, Theater, Musical Theater, and Planning and Stabilization, 1100 Pennsylvania Ave. N.W. 20506-0001; (202) 682-5428. Fax, (202) 682-5669. Barry Bergey, Division Coordinator. Web, arts.endow.gov.*

Awards grants for design arts projects in architecture; landscape architecture; urban design and planning; historic preservation; and interior, graphic, industrial, product, and costume and fashion design.

State Dept., *Art in Embassies,* *2201 C St. N.W., #3491 20520; (202) 647-5321. Fax, (202) 647-4080. Gwen Berlin, Director. Information, (202) 647-5723. Web, www.state. gov.*

Exhibits American art in U.S. ambassadorial residences. Acquires art works from artists, collectors, galleries, and museums either as loans or as gifts.

CONGRESS

Library of Congress, *Prints and Photographs,* *101 Independence Ave. S.E. 20540-4730; (202) 707-5836. Fax, (202) 707-6647. Ellen Hahn, Chief. TTY, (202) 707-9051. Reading Room, (202) 707-6394. Web, lcweb.loc.gov/rr/ print.*

Maintains Library of Congress's collection of pictorial material, not in book format, totaling more than 13.5 million items. U.S. and international collections include artists' prints; historical prints, posters, and drawings; photographs (chiefly documentary); political and social cartoons; and architectural plans, drawings, prints, and photographs. Reference service provided in the Prints and Photographs Reading Room. Reproductions of non-restricted material available through the Library of Congress's Photoduplication Service; prints and photographs may be borrowed through the Exhibits Office for exhibits by qualified institutions. A portion of the collections and an overview of reference services are available on the World Wide Web.

NONPROFIT

American Institute of Architects, *1735 New York Ave. N.W. 20006; (202) 626-7310. Fax, (202) 626-7426. Norman L. Koonce, Chief Executive Officer. Information, (202) 626-7300. Library, (202) 626-7492. Web, www.aiaonline. com.*

Membership: registered American architects. Works to advance the standards of architectural education, training, and practice. Promotes the aesthetic, scientific, and practical efficiency of architecture, urban design, and planning; monitors international developments. Offers continuing and professional education programs; sponsors scholarships, internships, and awards. Houses archival collection, including documents and drawings of American architects and architecture. Library open to the public. Monitors legislation and regulations.

Friends of Art and Preservation in Embassies, *2715 M St. N.W., #100 20007; (202) 337-1573. Fax, (202) 337-*

0856. Lee Kimche McGrath, Director. General e-mail, fapenindc@aol.com.

Foundation established to assist the State Dept.'s Office of Foreign Buildings and Art in Embassies programs. Acquires and exhibits American art and preserves high-value furnishings in U.S. embassies and other diplomatic facilities.

National Assn. of Artists' Organizations, *1718 M St. N.W., PMB 239 20036; (202) 319-1107. Fax, (202) 319-1107. Roberto Bedoya, Executive Director. General e-mail, naao@artswire.org. Web, www.naao.org.*

Provides technical assistance and sponsors conferences to ensure the continuation and growth of artists' organizations and publications. Monitors legislation and regulations affecting art, artists' organizations, and individual artists.

National Assn. of Schools of Art and Design, *11250 Roger Bacon Dr., #21, Reston, VA 20190; (703) 437-0700. Fax, (703) 437-6312. Samuel Hope, Executive Director. Web, www.arts-accredit.org.*

Accrediting agency for educational programs in art and design. Provides information on art and design programs at the postsecondary level; offers professional development for executives of art and design programs.

⬛ HISTORY AND PRESERVATION

See also Military History and Honors (chap. 15); Museums (this chapter)

AGENCIES

Most federal agencies have historic preservation officers who ensure that agencies protect historic buildings and other cultural resources that are on or eligible for nomination to the National Register of Historic Places, including nonfederal property that may be affected by agency activities.

Advisory Council on Historic Preservation, *1100 Pennsylvania Ave. N.W., #809 20004; (202) 606-8503. Fax, (202) 606-8672. Cathryn Buford Slater, Chair; John M. Fowler, Executive Director. General e-mail, achp@achp.gov. Web, www.achp.gov.*

Advises the president and Congress on historic preservation; reviews and comments on federal projects and programs affecting historic, architectural, archeological, and cultural resources.

Bureau of Land Management *(Interior Dept.),* **Cultural Heritage, Wilderness, Special Areas, and Paleon-**

tology, 1620 L St. N.W., #204 20240 (mailing address: 1849 C St. N.W., #204-LS 20240); (202) 452-0330. Fax, (202) 452-7701. Marilyn Nickels, Group Manager. TTY, (202) 452-0326.

Develops bureau policy on historic preservation, archeological resource protection, consultation with native Americans, curation of artifacts and records, heritage education, and paleontological resource management.

Millennium Council *(Executive Office of the President)*, 708 Jackson Pl. N.W. 20503; (202) 456-2000. Fax, (202) 456-2008. Ellen McCullock-Lovel, Director. General e-mail, millennium@whitehouse.gov. Web, www. whitehouse.gov/Initiatives/Millennium/index.shtml.

Multiyear initiative to celebrate the accomplishments of America and individual Americans in the twentieth century. Sponsors a lecture series and special events.

National Archives and Records Administration, *Advisory Committee on Preservation,* 8601 Adelphi Rd., #2800, College Park, MD 20740-6001; (301) 713-6705. Fax, (301) 713-6653. Alan Calmes, Preservation Officer.

Advises the archivist of the United States on preservation technology and research and on matters related to the continued preservation of records of the National Archives of the United States.

National Archives and Records Administration, *Cartographic and Architectural Branch,* 8601 Adelphi Rd., #3320, College Park, MD 20740-6001; (301) 713-7030. Fax, (301) 713-7488. Robert Richardson, Director. TTY, (301) 713-7030. General e-mail, carto@arch2. nara.gov.

Preserves and makes available historical records of federal agencies, including maps, charts, aerial photographs, architectural drawings, patents, and ships' plans. Research room open to the public. Records may be reproduced for a fee.

National Archives and Records Administration, *Preservation Programs,* 8601 Adelphi Rd., #2800, College Park, MD 20740-6001; (301) 713-6705. Fax, (301) 713-6653. Maida Loescher, Director. Information, (301) 713-6719.

Responsible for conserving textual and nontextual records in the archives. Nontextual records include videotapes, sound recordings, motion pictures, still photos, and preservation microfilming. Conducts research and testing for materials purchased by and used in the archives.

National Capital Planning Commission, 801 Pennsylvania Ave. N.W., #301 20576; (202) 482-7200. Fax, (202)

NATIONAL PARK SERVICE SITES IN THE CAPITAL REGION

The National Park Service administers most parks, circles, and monuments in the District of Columbia, as well as sites in nearby Maryland, Virginia, and West Virginia. For information on facilities not listed here, call (202) 619-7005. Web, www.nps.gov/ncro/index.htm.

Antietam National Battlefield, (301) 432-5124

Arlington House, Robert E. Lee Memorial, (703) 557-0613

C&O Canal National Historic Park, (301) 739-4200
  Great Falls Area, Maryland, (301) 299-3613

Catoctin Mountain Park, (301) 663-9330

Clara Barton National Historic Site, (301) 492-6245

Ford's Theatre National Historic Site, (202) 426-6924

Fort Washington Park, (301) 763-4600 (includes Piscataway Park)

Frederick Douglass National Historic Site, (202) 426-5960

George Washington Parkway, (703) 289-2500 (includes memorials to Theodore Roosevelt, Lyndon Johnson, and U.S. Marine Corps)
  Glen Echo Park, (301) 492-6229
  Great Falls Park, Virginia, (703) 285-2966

Greenbelt Park, (301) 344-3948

Harpers Ferry National Historic Park, (304) 535-6223

Manassas National Battlefield Park, (703) 754-1861

Mary McLeod Bethune National Historic Site, (202) 673-2402

Monocacy National Battlefield, (301) 662-3515

National Mall, (202) 426-6841 (includes presidential and war memorials and Pennsylvania Avenue National Historic Site)

Potomac Heritage American Hiking Association, (301) 565-6704

Prince William Forest Park, (703) 221-7181

Rock Creek Park, (202) 282-1063

Thomas Stone National Historic Site, (301) 934-6027

White House, (202) 456-7041

Wolf Trap Farm Park, (703) 255-1800

482-7272. Reginald W. Griffith, Executive Director. Web, www.ncpc.gov.

Central planning agency for the federal government in the national capital region, which includes the District of Columbia and suburban Maryland and Virginia. Reviews and approves plans for the preservation of certain historic and environmental features in the national capital region, including the annual federal capital improvement plan.

National Endowment for the Arts *(National Foundation on the Arts and the Humanities), Folk and Traditional Arts, Literature, Theater, Musical Theater, and Planning and Stabilization, 1100 Pennsylvania Ave. N.W. 20506-0001; (202) 682-5428. Fax, (202) 682-5669. Barry Bergey, Division Coordinator. Web, arts.endow.gov.*

Grant-making theme program for projects in the arts which preserve nationally significant artistic accomplishments and works of art.

National Endowment for the Humanities *(National Foundation on the Arts and the Humanities), Preservation and Access, 1100 Pennsylvania Ave. N.W., #411 20506; (202) 606-8570. Fax, (202) 606-8639. George Farr, Director. General e-mail, preservation@neh.gov. Web, www.neh.gov.*

Sponsors preservation and access projects, the stabilization and documentation of material culture collections, and the U.S. newspaper program.

National Museum of American History *(Smithsonian Institution), Cultural History, 12th St. and Constitution Ave. N.W. 20560; (202) 357-1707. Fax, (202) 786-2883. Rex Ellis, Chair. General e-mail, info@info. si.edu. Web, www.americanhistory.si.edu.*

Collects and preserves artifacts related to U.S. cultural heritage; supports research, exhibits, performances, and educational programs. Areas of focus include ethnic and religious communities; sports, recreation, and leisure; popular entertainment and mass media; business and commercial culture; musical instruments; hand tools; and educational, civic, and voluntary organizations.

National Park Service *(Interior Dept.), Cultural Resource Stewardship and Partnerships, 1849 C St. N.W., #3128 20240; (202) 208-7625. Fax, (202) 273-3237. Katherine H. Stevenson, Associate Director.*

Oversees preservation of federal historic sites and administration of buildings programs. Programs include the National Register of Historic Places, National Historic and National Landmark Programs, Historic American Building Survey, Historic American Engineering Record, Archeology and Antiquities Act Program, and Technical Preservation Services. Gives grant and aid assistance and tax benefit information to properties listed in the National Register of Historic Places.

CONGRESS

House Resources Committee, *Subcommittee on National Parks and Public Lands, 140 CHOB 20515; (202) 226-7736. Fax, (202) 226-2301. Rep. James V. Hansen, R-Utah, Chair; Allen Freemyer, Staff Director. General e-mail, parks.subcommittee@mail.house.gov. Web, www.house.gov/resources/parks.*

Jurisdiction over historic preservation legislation.

Senate Energy and Natural Resources Committee, *Subcommittee on National Parks, Historic Preservation, and Recreation, SD-354 20510; (202) 224-6969. Fax, (202) 228-0459. Sen. Craig Thomas, R-Wyo., Chair; Jim O'Toole, Professional Staff Member. General e-mail, parks@energy.senate.gov. Web, energy.senate.gov.*

Jurisdiction over historic preservation legislation.

Senate Office of Conservation and Preservation, *S410 CAP 20510; (202) 224-4550. Carl Fritter, Bookbinder.*

Develops and coordinates programs related to the conservation and preservation of Senate records and materials for the Secretary of the Senate.

NONPROFIT

American Historical Assn., *400 A St. S.E. 20003; (202) 544-2422. Fax, (202) 544-8307. Arnita Jones, Executive Director. General e-mail, aha@theaha.org. Web, chnm. gmu.edu/aha.*

Supports public access to government information; publishes original historical research, journal, bibliographies, historical directories, and job placement bulletin. Committee on Women Historians seeks to improve the status of women in the profession as well as promotes the teaching of women's history.

American Institute for Conservation of Historic and Artistic Works, *1717 K St. N.W., #200 20006; (202) 452-9545. Fax, (202) 452-9328. Elizabeth Jones, Executive Director. General e-mail, info@aic-faic.org. Web, aic. stanford.edu.*

Membership: professional conservators, scientists, students, administrators, cultural institutions, and others. Promotes the knowledge and practice of the conservation of cultural property; supports research; and disseminates information on conservation.

American Studies Assn., *1120 19th St. N.W., #301 20036; (202) 467-4783. Fax, (202) 467-4786. John F. Stephens, Executive Director. General e-mail, asastaff@erols.com. Web, www.georgetown.edu/crossroads.*

Fosters exchange of ideas about American life; supports and assists programs for teaching American studies abroad and encourages teacher and student exchanges; awards annual prizes for contributions to American studies; provides curriculum resources.

Children of the American Revolution, *1776 D St. N.W., #224 20006-5392; (202) 638-3153. Fax, (202) 737-3162. JoAnn Schiefer, Office Manager.*

Membership: descendants, age twenty-two years and under, of American soldiers or patriots of the American Revolution. Conducts historical, educational, and patriotic activities; preserves places of historical interest.

Civil War Preservation Trust, *1515 Wilson Blvd., #350, Arlington, VA 22209; (703) 682-2350. Fax, (703) 682-2350. Elliot Gruber, Executive Vice President. Web, www. civilwar.org.*

Promotes the appreciation and stewardship of America's cultural and environmental heritage through the preservation of historic Civil War battlefields.

Council on America's Military Past-U.S.A., *P.O. Box 1151, Fort Myer, VA 22211-1151; (703) 912-6124. Fax, (703) 912-5666. Herbert M. Hart, Executive Director. Information, (800) 398-4693.*

Membership: historians, archeologists, curators, writers, and others interested in military history and preservation of historic military establishments and ships.

Heritage Preservation, *1730 K St. N.W., #566 20006; (202) 634-1422. Fax, (202) 634-1435. Larry Reger, President. General e-mail, info@heritagepreservation.org. Web, www.heritagepreservation.org.*

Membership: museums, libraries, archives, historic preservation organizations, historical societies, and conservation groups. Advocates the conservation and preservation of works of art, anthropological artifacts, documents, historic objects, architecture, and natural science specimens. Programs include Save Outdoor Sculpture, which works to inventory all U.S. outdoor sculpture, and the Conservation Assessment Program, which administers grants to museums for conservation surveys of their collections.

National Conference of State Historic Preservation Officers, *444 N. Capitol St. N.W., #342 20001-1512; (202) 624-5465. Fax, (202) 624-5419. Nancy Miller, Executive Director.*

Membership: state and territorial historic preservation officers and deputy officers. Conducts research and compiles statistics on programs; monitors legislation and regulations.

National Preservation Institute, *P.O. Box 1702, Alexandria, VA 22313; (703) 765-0100. Constance Werner-*

Ramirez, President. General e-mail, info@npi.org. Web, www.npi.org.

Provides specialized education research, technical assistance, and professional training for the management, development, and preservation of historic, cultural, and environmental resources.

National Society, Colonial Dames XVII Century, *1300 New Hampshire Ave. N.W. 20036; (202) 293-1700. Fax, (202) 466-6099. Sandra Quimby, Office Manager.*

Membership: American women who are lineal descendants of persons who rendered civil or military service and lived in America or one of the British colonies before 1701. Preserves records and shrines; encourages historical research; awards scholarships to undergraduate and graduate students and scholarships in medicine to persons of native American descent.

National Society, Daughters of the American Revolution, *1776 D St. N.W. 20006-5392; (202) 628-1776. Fax, (202) 879-3252. Dale K. Love, President. Web, www.dar.org.*

Membership: women descended from American Revolutionary War patriots. Conducts historical, educational, and patriotic activities; maintains a genealogical library, American museum, and documentary collection antedating 1830. Library open to the public (nonmembers charged fee for use).

National Society of the Colonial Dames of America, *2715 Que St. N.W. 20007; (202) 337-2288. Fax, (202) 337-0348. Bill Birdseye, Director.*

Membership: descendants of colonists in America before 1750. Conducts historical and educational activities; maintains Dumbarton House, a museum open to the public.

National Trust for Historic Preservation, *1785 Massachusetts Ave. N.W. 20036-2117; (202) 588-6000. Fax, (202) 588-6038. Richard Moe, President. Web, www.nthp.org.*

Conducts seminars, workshops, and conferences on topics related to preservation, including neighborhood conservation, main street revitalization, rural conservation, and preservation law; offers financial assistance through loan and grant programs; provides advisory services; operates historic house museums, which are open to the public.

Preservation Action, *1350 Connecticut Ave. N.W., #401 20036; (202) 659-0915. Fax, (202) 659-0189. Susan West Montgomery, President. Web, www.preservationaction.org.*

Monitors legislation affecting historic preservation and neighborhood conservation; promotes effective management of historic preservation programs.

Society for American Archaeology, *900 2nd St. N.E., #12 20002; (202) 789-8200. Fax, (202) 789-0284. Tobi Brimsek, Executive Director. General e-mail, info@saa.org. Web, www.saa.org.*

Promotes greater awareness, understanding, and research of archaeology on the American continents; works to preserve and publish results of scientific data and research; serves as information clearinghouse for members.

Archives and Manuscripts

See also Film, Photography, and Broadcasting (this chapter); Music (this chapter)

AGENCIES

National Archives and Records Administration, *8601 Adelphi Rd., #4200, College Park, MD 20740-6001; (301) 713-6410. Fax, (301) 713-7141. John Carlin, Archivist of the United States; Lewis J. Bellardo, Deputy Archivist. Press, (301) 713-7360.*

Identifies, preserves, and makes available federal government documents of historic value; administers a network of regional storage centers and archives and operates the presidential library system. Collections include photographs, graphic materials, and films; holdings include records generated by foreign governments (especially in wartime) and by international conferences, commissions, and exhibitions. (Headquarters in College Park, Md.)

National Archives and Records Administration, *Center for Legislative Archives, 700 Pennsylvania Ave. N.W., #8E 20408; (202) 501-5350. Fax, (202) 219-2176. Michael Gillette, Director.*

Collects and maintains records of congressional committees and legislative files from 1789 to the present. Publishes inventories and guides to these records.

National Archives and Records Administration, *Presidential Libraries, 8601 Adelphi Rd., #2200, College Park, MD 20740; (301) 713-6050. Fax, (301) 713-6045. David F. Peterson, Assistant Archivist. Web, www.nara.gov.*

Directs all programs relating to acquisition, preservation, publication, and research use of materials in presidential libraries; conducts oral history projects; publishes finding aids for research sources; provides reference service, including information from and about documentary holdings.

National Historical Publications and Records Commission *(National Archives and Records Administration), 700 Pennsylvania Ave. N.W., #111 20408; (202)*

501-5610. Fax, (202) 501-5601. Ann C. Newhall, Executive Director. General e-mail, nhprc@arch1.nara.gov.

Makes plans and recommendations and provides cost estimates for preserving and publishing documentation of U.S. history. Awards grants to government and private cultural institutions that preserve, arrange, edit, and publish documents of historical importance, including the papers of outstanding Americans.

National Museum of American History *(Smithsonian Institution), Archives Center, 12th St. and Constitution Ave. N.W., #C340, MRC 601 20560-0601; (202) 357-3270. Fax, (202) 786-2453. John A. Fleckner, Chief Archivist. TTY, (202) 357-1729. General e-mail, archivescenter@nmah.si.edu.*

Acquires, organizes, preserves, and makes available for research the museum's archival and documentary materials relating to American history and culture. (Three-dimensional objects and closely related documents are in the care of curatorial divisions.)

Smithsonian Institution, *Archives of American Art, 901 D St. S.W., #704 20560-0937; (202) 314-3900. Fax, (202) 314-3988. Richard J. Wattenmaker, Director. TTY, (202) 633-9320. General e-mail, aaaemref@sivm.si.edu. Web, www.si.edu/artarchives.*

Collects and preserves manuscript items, such as notebooks, sketchbooks, letters, and journals; photos of artists and works of art; tape-recorded interviews with artists, dealers, and collectors; exhibition catalogs; directories; and biographies on the history of visual arts in the United States. Library open to scholars and researchers. Reference centers that maintain microfilm copies of a selection of the Archives' collection include New York; San Francisco; and San Marino, Calif.

CONGRESS

Legislative Resource Center, *Resource and Reference, B-106 CHOB 20515; (202) 226-5200. Fax, (202) 226-5208. Lea Uhre, Manager.*

Conducts historical research. Advises members on the disposition of their records and papers; maintains information on manuscript collections of former members; maintains biographical files on former members. Print publications include *Biographical Directory of the United States Congress, 1774–1989; Guide to Research Collections of Former Members of the United States House of Representatives, 1789–1987; Black Americans in Congress, 1870–1989;* and *Women in Congress, 1917–1989.*

Library of Congress, *Manuscript Division, 101 Independence Ave. S.E., #LM102 20540-4780; (202) 707-5383. Fax, (202) 707-6336. James H. Hutson, Chief. Reading Room, (202) 707-5387.*

Maintains, describes, and provides reference service on the library's manuscript collections, including the papers of U.S. presidents and other eminent Americans. Manuscript Reading Room primarily serves serious scholars and researchers; historians and reference librarians are available for consultation.

Library of Congress, *Rare Book and Special Collections Division,* 10 1st St. S.E., #239 20540-4742; (202) 707-5434. Fax, (202) 707-4142. Mark Dimunation, Chief. Reading room, (202) 707-3348. Web, lcweb.loc.gov/rr/rarebook.

Maintains collections of incunabula (books printed before 1501) and other early printed books; early imprints of American history and literature; illustrated books; early Spanish American, Russian, and Bulgarian imprints; Confederate states imprints; libraries of famous personalities (including Thomas Jefferson, Woodrow Wilson, and Oliver Wendell Holmes); special format collections (miniature books, broadsides, almanacs, and pre-1870 copyright records); special interest collections; and special provenance collections. Reference assistance is provided in the Rare Book and Special Collections Reading Room.

Senate Historical Office, SH-201 20510; (202) 224-6900. Fax, (202) 224-5329. Richard Baker, Historian. Web, www.senate.gov.

Serves as an information clearinghouse on Senate history, traditions, and members. Collects, organizes, and distributes to the public previously unpublished Senate documents; collects and preserves photographs and pictures related to Senate history; conducts an oral history program; advises senators and Senate committees on the disposition of their noncurrent papers and records. Produces publications on the history of the Senate.

NONPROFIT

Council on Library and Information Resources, 1755 Massachusetts Ave. N.W., #500 20036-2124; (202) 939-4750. Fax, (202) 939-4765. Deanna B. Marcum, President. General e-mail, info@clir.org. Web, www.clir.org.

Acts on behalf of the nation's libraries, archives, and universities to develop and encourage collaborative strategies for preserving the nation's intellectual heritage and strengthening its information system.

Moorland-Spingarn Research Center *(Howard University),* 500 Howard Pl. N.W. 20059; (202) 806-7239. Fax, (202) 806-6405. Thomas C. Battle, Director. Web, www.founders.howard.edu/moorland-spingarn.

Collects, preserves, and makes available for study numerous artifacts, books, manuscripts, newspapers, photographs, prints, recordings, and other materials documenting black history and culture in the United States, Africa, Europe, Latin America, and the Caribbean. Maintains extensive collections of black newspapers and magazines; contains the works of African American and African scholars, poets, and novelists; maintains collections on the history of Howard University.

Genealogy

AGENCIES

National Archives and Records Administration, *Archives 1, Research Room Services Branch,* 700 Pennsylvania Ave. N.W., #406 20408; (202) 501-5402. Fax, (202) 501-7154. Jo Ann Williamson, Branch Chief. TTY, (202) 501-5404. Web, www.nara.gov.

Assists individuals interested in researching record holdings of the National Archives, including genealogical records; issues research cards to prospective genealogical, biographical, and other researchers who present photo identification. Users must be fourteen. Still and motion picture research rooms located in College Park, Md.

National Archives and Records Administration, *Public Program,* 700 Pennsylvania Ave. N.W., #G6 20408; (202) 501-5210. Fax, (202) 501-5239. Edith James, Director. Web, www.nara.gov.

Co-sponsors the National Institute of Genealogical Research, a genealogical research class taught annually by National Archives staff and outside professionals; conducts workshops.

CONGRESS

Library of Congress, *Local History and Genealogy Reading Room,* 10 1st St. S.E. 20540; (202) 707-5537. Fax, (202) 707-1957. Judith Reid, Head. TTY, (202) 707-9958. Web, www.loc.gov.

Provides reference and referral service on topics related to local history, genealogy, and heraldry throughout the United States.

NONPROFIT

Family History Center, *Church of Jesus Christ of Latter-day Saints,* 10000 Stoneybrook Dr., Kensington, MD 20895 (mailing address: P.O. Box 49, Kensington, MD 20895); (301) 587-0042. Susan Frazier, Director.

Maintains genealogical library for research. Collection includes international genealogical index, family group record archives, microfiche registers, and the Family Search Computer Program. Library open to the public.

National Genealogical Society, *4527 17th St. North, Arlington, VA 22207-2399; (703) 525-0050. Fax, (703) 525-0052. Francis J. Shane, Executive Director. Information, (800) 473-0060. General e-mail, membership@ ngsgenealogy.org. Web, www.ngsgenealogy.org.*

Encourages study of genealogy and publication of all records that are of genealogical interest. Maintains a genealogical library for research; provides an accredited home study online program; holds an annual conference. Library open to the public (closed Tuesday and Thursday; nonmembers charged fee for use).

National Society, Daughters of the American Colonists, *2205 Massachusetts Ave. N.W. 20008; (202) 667-3076. Mary Ann Hepler, President.*

Membership: women descended from men and women who gave civil or military service to the colonies prior to the Revolutionary War. Maintains library of colonial and genealogical records.

National Society, Daughters of the American Revolution, *1776 D St. N.W. 20006-5392; (202) 628-1776. Fax, (202) 879-3252. Dale K. Love, President. Web, www. dar.org.*

Membership: women descended from American Revolutionary War patriots. Maintains a genealogical library, which is open to the public (nonmembers charged fee for use).

Specific Cultures

See also Language and Literature (this chapter)

AGENCIES

Interior Dept., *Indian Arts and Crafts Board,* *1849 C St. N.W. 20240-0001; (202) 208-3773. Fax, (202) 208-5196. Meredith Stanton, Director (Acting). Web, www.doi. gov.*

Advises native American artisans and craft guilds; produces a source directory on arts and crafts of native Americans (including Alaskan natives); maintains museums of native crafts in Montana, South Dakota, and Oklahoma; provides information on native American crafts.

National Endowment for the Arts *(National Foundation on the Arts and the Humanities), Folk and Traditional Arts, Literature, Theater, Musical Theater, and Planning and Stabilization,* *1100 Pennsylvania Ave. N.W. 20506-0001; (202) 682-5428. Fax, (202) 682-5669. Barry Bergey, Division Coordinator. Web, arts.endow.gov.*

Seeks to preserve and enhance multicultural artistic heritage through grants for folk arts projects.

National Museum of American History *(Smithsonian Institution), History Department,* *12th St. and Constitution Ave. N.W., #4601, MRC 638 20560; (202) 357-1963. Fax, (202) 633-8192. Jim Gardner, Assistant Director. Information, (202) 357-3129. Web, www.si. edu/nmah.*

Conducts research, develops collections, and creates exhibits on political, community, and domestic life, based on collections of folk and popular arts, ethnic and craft objects, textiles, coins, costumes and jewelry, ceramics and glass, graphic arts, musical instruments, photographs, appliances, and machines.

Smithsonian Institution, *Center for Folklife and Cultural Heritage,* *955 L'Enfant Plaza S.W., #2600, MRC 914 20560; (202) 287-3424. Fax, (202) 287-3699. Richard Kurin, Director. General e-mail, cspcs.csp@ic.si.edu. Web, www.si.edu/organiza/offices/folklife.*

Conducts research into traditional U.S. cultures and foreign folklife traditions; produces folkways recordings, films, monographs, and educational programs; presents annual Smithsonian Folklife Festival in Washington, D.C.

CONGRESS

Library of Congress, *American Folklife Center,* *101 Independence Ave. S.E. 20540-4610; (202) 707-5510. Fax, (202) 707-2076. Margaret Bulger, Director. Archive of Folk Culture, (202) 707-5510. General e-mail, folklife@loc.gov. Web, www.loc.gov/folklife.*

Coordinates national, regional, state and local government, and private folklife activities; contracts with individuals and groups for research and field studies in American folklife and for exhibits and workshops; maintains the National Archive of Folk Culture (an ethnographic collection of American and international folklore, grassroots oral histories, and ethnomusicology); conducts internships at the archive; sponsors summer concerts of traditional and ethnic music.

NONPROFIT

American Indian Heritage Foundation, *6051 Arlington Blvd., Falls Church, VA 22044; (703) 237-7500. Fax, (703) 532-1921. Princess Pale Moon, President. Recorded information, (202) 463-4267. Web, www.indians.org.*

Promotes national and international cultural programs for native Americans. Sponsors the National American Indian Heritage Month and the Miss Indian USA Scholarship Program; notes outstanding achievement among young native Americans; assists tribes in meeting emergency needs.

National Council for the Traditional Arts, *1320 Fenwick Lane, #200, Silver Spring, MD 20910; (301) 565-*

0654. Fax, (301) 565-0472. Joseph T. Wilson, Executive Director. General e-mail, info@ncta.net. Web, www.ncta. net.

Presents and provides consultation for regional and national folk festivals; offers training programs for park officials on folk culture; conducts ethnocultural surveys; coordinates exhibitions and tours of traditional folk artists with the support of the National Endowment for the Arts. Produces films and videos on traditional arts; sponsors annual national folk festival.

National Italian American Foundation, *1860 19th St. N.W. 20009; (202) 387-0600. Fax, (202) 387-0800. Alfred M. Rotondaro, Executive Director. Web, www.niaf.org.*

Membership: U.S. citizens of Italian ancestry. Promotes recognition of Italian American contributions to American society. Funds cultural events, educational symposia, antidefamation programs, and scholarships. Represents the interests of Italian Americans before Congress. Serves as an umbrella organization for local Italian American clubs throughout the United States.

Washington Area

See also Museums (this chapter)

AGENCIES

National Park Service *(Interior Dept.), National Capital Region, 1100 Ohio Dr. S.W., #336 20242; (202) 619-7000. Fax, (202) 619-7220. Terry Carlstrom, Director. Information, (202) 619-7222. Recorded information, (202) 619-7275. Permits, (202) 619-7225. Web, www.nps.gov/ncro.*

Provides visitors with information on Washington-area parks, monuments, and Civil War battlefields; offers press services for the media and processes special event applications and permits.

White House Visitors Center, *1450 Pennsylvania Ave. N.W. 20230; (202) 208-1631. Fax, (202) 208-1643. Tom Payton, Manager. Information, (202) 456-7041. TTY, (202) 208-1636.*

Administered by the National Park Service. Educates visitors about the White House through videos, exhibits, and historical artifacts. Distributes White House tour tickets daily starting at 7:30 a.m. Tuesday through Saturday, from March through Labor Day (tickets not required for the rest of the year). Tours conducted 10:00 a.m. to noon.

CONGRESS

Architect of the Capitol, *Office of the Curator, HT3 CAP 20515; (202) 228-1222. Fax, (202) 228-4602.*

Barbara A. Wolanin, Curator. Press, (202) 228-1205. Web, www.aoc.gov.

Preserves artwork; maintains collection of drawings, photographs, and manuscripts on and about the Capitol and the House and Senate office buildings. Maintains records of the architect of the Capitol. Library open to the public.

Senate Commission on Art, *S411 CAP 20510-7102; (202) 224-2955. Fax, (202) 224-8799. Sen. Trent Lott, R-Miss., Chair; Diane K. Skvarla, Curator of the Senate. Web, www.senate.gov/learning/learn_art_about.html.*

Accepts artwork and historical objects for display in Senate office buildings and the Senate wing of the Capitol. Maintains and exhibits Senate collections (paintings, sculpture, furniture, and manuscripts); oversees and maintains old Senate and Supreme Court chambers.

NONPROFIT

Assn. for Preservation of Historic Congressional Cemetery, *1801 E St. S.E. 20003; (202) 543-0539. Fax, (202) 543-5966. Jim Oliver, Chair. General e-mail, congressionalcemetery@mail.org. Web, www.geocities.com/heartland/Meadows/4633.*

Administers and maintains the Washington Parish Burial Ground (commonly known as the Congressional Cemetery).

D.C. Preservation League, *1815 Pennsylvania Ave. N.W., #200 20006; (202) 955-5616. Fax, (202) 955-5456. Julianne Mueller, President.*

Participates in planning and preserving buildings and sites in Washington, D.C. Programs include protection and enhancement of the city's landmarks; educational lectures, tours, and seminars; and technical assistance to neighborhood groups. Monitors legislation and regulations.

Historical Society of Washington, D.C., *1307 New Hampshire Ave. N.W. 20036; (202) 785-2068. Fax, (202) 887-5785. Barbara Franco, Executive Director. General e-mail, heurich@ibm.net. Web, www.hswdc.org.*

Maintains research collections on the District of Columbia, including photographs, manuscripts, archives, books, and prints and graphics of Washington (1790–present); publishes *Metro D.C. History News* and *Washington History* magazine; operates a historic house museum in the Heurich mansion. Museum and library open to the public.

Martin Luther King Memorial Library, *Washingtoniana Division, 901 G St. N.W., #307 20001; (202) 727-1213. Fax, (202) 727-1129. Susan Malbin, Chief.*

Maintains reference collections of District of Columbia current laws and regulations, history, and culture. Collections include biographies; travel books; memoirs and diaries; family, church, government, and institutional histories; maps (1612–present); plat books; city, telephone, and real estate directories (1822–present); census schedules; newspapers and periodicals (including the *Washington Star* collection of clippings and photographs, 1940–1981); photographs; and oral history materials on local neighborhoods, ethnic groups, and businesses.

National Assn. to Restore Pride in America's Capital, *2 Wisconsin Circle, #700, Chevy Chase, MD 20815; (301) 229-6076. Fax, (301) 229-6077. Leonard Sullivan, President. Web, www.narpac.org.*

Operates as an information clearinghouse on the city's history and its major current issues.

Supreme Court Historical Society, *224 E. Capitol St. N.E. 20003; (202) 543-0400. Fax, (202) 547-7730. David T. Pride, Executive Director. Web, www.supremecourthistory. org.*

Acquires, preserves, and displays historic items associated with the Court; conducts and publishes scholarly research. Conducts lecture programs; promotes and supports educational activities in the Court.

U.S. Capitol Historical Society, *200 Maryland Ave. N.E. 20002; (202) 543-8919. Fax, (202) 544-8244. Ron Sarasin, President. Information, (800) 887-9318. Library, (202) 543-8919, ext. 27. General e-mail, uschs@uschs.org. Web, www.uschs.org.*

Membership: members of Congress, individuals, and organizations interested in the preservation of the history and traditions of the U.S. Capitol. Conducts historical research; offers tours, lectures, and films; maintains information centers in the Capitol; publishes an annual historical calendar.

White House Historical Assn., *740 Jackson Pl. N.W. 20503; (202) 737-8292. Fax, (202) 789-0440. Neil W. Horstman, Executive Vice President. Web, www. whitehousehistory.org.*

Seeks to enhance the understanding and appreciation of the White House. Publishes books on the White House, including a historical guide, a description of ceremonial events, two volumes of biographical sketches and illustrations of the presidents and first ladies, a book on White House glassware, and a book on White House paintings and sculptures. Net proceeds from book sales go toward the purchase of historic items, such as paintings and furniture, for the White House permanent collection.

RECREATION AND SPORTS

See also Parks and Recreation Areas (chap. 9)

AGENCIES

Health and Human Services Dept., *President's Council on Physical Fitness and Sports, Humphrey Bldg. #738H, 200 Independence Ave. S.W. 20201; (202) 690-9000. Fax, (202) 690-5211. Sandra Perlmutter, Executive Director, (202) 690-5187. Web, www.dhhs.gov.*

Provides schools, state and local governments, recreation agencies, and employers with information on designing and implementing physical fitness programs; conducts award programs for children and adults and for schools, clubs, and other institutions.

U.S. Armed Forces Sports Council, *4700 King St., 4th Floor, Alexandria, VA 22302-4418; (703) 681-7232. Fax, (703) 681-1616. Suba Saty, Secretariat.*

Membership: one representative from each of the four armed services. Administers and coordinates interservice, national, and international sports activities and competitions for military personnel from the intramural level to the world class athlete program.

NONPROFIT

American Alliance for Health, Physical Education, Recreation, and Dance, *1900 Association Dr., Reston, VA 20191; (703) 476-3400. Fax, (703) 476-9527. Michael Davis, Executive Vice President. General e-mail, info@ aahperd.org. Web, www.aahperd.org.*

Membership: teachers and others who work with school health, physical education, athletics, recreation, dance, and safety education programs (kindergarten through postsecondary levels). Member associations are American Assn. for Leisure and Recreation, National Assn. for Girls and Women in Sport, American Assn. for Health Education, National Dance Assn., National Assn. for Sport and Physical Education, and American Assn. for Active Lifestyles and Fitness.

American Canoe Assn., *7432 Alban Station Blvd., #B-232, Springfield, VA 22150; (703) 451-0141. Fax, (703) 451-2245. Jeffrey Yeager, Executive Director. General e-mail, acadirect@aol.com. Web, www.aca-paddler.org.*

Membership: individuals and organizations interested in the promotion of canoeing, kayaking, and other paddle sports. Works to preserve the nation's recreational waterways. Sponsors programs in safety education, competition, recreation, public awareness, conservation, and public policy. Monitors legislation and regulations.

American Gaming Assn., *555 13th St. N.W., #1010E 20004-1109; (202) 637-6501. Fax, (202) 637-6507. Frank J. Fahrenkopf Jr., President. Information, (202) 637-6500. Web, www.americangaming.org.*

Membership: casinos, casino and gaming equipment manufacturers, and financial services companies. Compiles statistics and serves as an information clearinghouse on the gaming industry. Administers a task force to study gambling addiction, raise public awareness, and develop assistance programs. Monitors legislation and regulations.

American Hiking Society, *1422 Fenwick Lane, Silver Spring, MD 20910; (301) 565-6704. Fax, (301) 565-6714. David Lillard, President. General e-mail, info@ americanhiking.org. Web, www.americanhiking.org.*

Membership: individuals and clubs interested in preserving America's trail system and protecting the interests of hikers and other trail users. Sponsors research on trail construction and a trail maintenance summer program. Provides information on outdoor volunteer opportunities on public lands.

American Medical Athletic Assn., *4405 East-West Hwy., #405, Bethesda, MD 20814; (301) 913-9517. Fax, (301) 913-9520. Susan Kalish, Executive Director. Information, (800) 776-2732. General e-mail, amasportsmed@ aol.com. Web, www.americanrunning.org.*

Membership: sports medicine and allied health professionals. Assists members in promoting physical fitness to their patients and in developing their own physical fitness programs. Promotes and reports on sports medicine research and discussion. (Affiliated with the American Running and Fitness Assn.)

American Recreation Coalition, *1225 New York Ave. N.W., #450 20005; (202) 682-9530. Fax, (202) 682-9529. Derrick A. Crandall, President. General e-mail, arc@ funoutdoors.com. Web, www.funoutdoors.com.*

Membership: organized recreationists, national and regional corporations offering recreational products and services, and recreation industry trade associations. Works to increase public and private sector activity in public recreation, land and water management, and energy policy. Provides information on innovative recreational planning.

American Resort Development Assn., *1220 L St. N.W., #500 20005; (202) 371-6700. Fax, (202) 289-8544. Vacant, President. Web, www.arda.org.*

Membership: U.S. and international developers, builders, financiers, marketing companies, and others involved in resort, recreational, and community development. Serves as an information clearinghouse; monitors

federal and state legislation affecting land, time share, and community development industries.

American Running and Fitness Assn., *4405 East-West Hwy., #405, Bethesda, MD 20814; (301) 913-9517. Fax, (301) 913-9520. Susan Kalish, Executive Director. Information, (800) 776-2732. General e-mail, run@ americanrunning.org. Web, www.arfa.org.*

Membership: athletes, health clubs, businesses, and individuals. Promotes proper nutrition and regular exercise. Provides members with medical advice and referrals, fitness information, and assistance in developing fitness programs.

American Sportfishing Assn., *1033 N. Fairfax St., #200, Alexandria, VA 22314; (703) 519-9691. Fax, (703) 519-1872. Mike Hayden, President. General e-mail, info@ asafishing.org. Web, www.asafishing.org.*

Works to ensure healthy and sustainable fish resources, to increase participation in sport fishing, and to make its members more profitable.

Bicycle Federation of America, *1506 21st St. N.W., #200 20036; (202) 463-6622. Fax, (202) 463-6625. William C. Wilkinson III, Executive Director. General e-mail, bikefed@aol.com. Web, www.bikefed.org.*

Promotes bicycle use; conducts research, planning, and training projects; develops safety education and public information materials. Works to increase public awareness of the benefits and opportunities of bicycling and walking. Manages the Campaign to Make America Walkable.

Boat Owners Assn. of the United States, *Government Affairs, 880 S. Pickett St., Alexandria, VA 22304; (703) 461-2864. Fax, (703) 461-2845. Michael Sciulla, Director.*

Membership: owners of recreational boats. Represents boat-owner interests before the federal government; offers consumer protection and other services to members.

Disabled Sports USA, *451 Hungerford Dr., #100, Rockville, MD 20850; (301) 217-0960. Fax, (301) 217-0968. Kirk M. Bauer, Executive Director. TTY, (301) 217-0963. General e-mail, dsusa@dsusa.org. Web, www.dsusa.org.*

Conducts sports and recreation activities and physical fitness programs for people with disabilities and their families and friends; conducts workshops and competitions; participates in world championships.

Future Fisherman Foundation, *1033 N. Fairfax St., #200, Alexandria, VA 22314; (703) 519-9691. Fax, (703)*

519-1872. Kathleen McKee, Director. General e-mail, info@asafishing.org. Web, www.asafishing.org.

Promotes sportfishing to youth through programs such as the Aquatic Resources Education Program and the Hooked on Fishing, Not Drugs Campaign. (Affiliated with the American Sportfishing Assn.)

National Aeronautic Assn., *1815 N. Fort Myer Dr., #700, Arlington, VA 22209; (703) 527-0226. Fax, (703) 527-0229. Donald J. Koranda, President. General e-mail, naa@naa-usa.org. Web, www.naa-usa.org.*

Membership: persons interested in development of general and sporting aviation. Supervises sporting aviation competitions; oversees and approves official U.S. aircraft, aeronautics, and astronautics records. Interests include aeromodeling, aerobatics, helicopters, ultralights, home-built aircraft, parachuting, soaring, hang gliding, and ballooning. Serves as U.S. representative to the International Aeronautical Federation in Lausanne, Switzerland.

National Assn. for Girls and Women in Sport, *1900 Association Dr., Reston, VA 20191-1599; (703) 476-3452. Fax, (703) 476-4566. MaryAnn Borysowicz, Director. General e-mail, nagws@aahperd.org. Web, www.aahperd.org.*

Membership: students, coaches, physical education teachers, athletes, athletic directors, and trainers for girls' and women's sports programs. Seeks to increase sports opportunity for women and girls; provides information on laws relating to equality of sports funds and facilities for women; hosts training sites and rates officials; publishes sports guides; maintains speakers bureau.

National Collegiate Athletic Assn., *Federal Relations, Washington Office, 1 Dupont Circle N.W., #310 20036; (202) 293-3050. Fax, (202) 293-3075. Doris Dixon, Director. Web, www.ncaa.org.*

Membership: senior colleges and universities, conferences, and organizations interested in the administration of intercollegiate athletics. Certifies institutions' athletic programs; compiles records and statistics; produces publications and television programs; administers youth development programs; awards student athletes with postgraduate scholarships and degree-completion grants. (Headquarters in Overland Park, Kan.)

National Football League Players Assn., *2021 L St. N.W., #600 20036; (202) 463-2200. Fax, (202) 857-0380. Gene Upshaw, Executive Director. Web, www.nflplayers. com.*

Membership: professional football players. Represents members in matters concerning wages, hours, and working conditions. Provides assistance to charitable and community organizations. Sponsors programs and events to promote the image of professional football and its players.

National Recreation and Park Assn., *22377 Belmont Ridge Rd., Ashburn, VA 20148; (703) 858-0784. Fax, (703) 858-0794. Dean Tice, Executive Director. General e-mail, info@nrpa.org. Web, www.nrpa.org.*

Membership: park and recreation professionals and interested citizens. Provides technical assistance for park and recreational programs.

National Spa and Pool Institute, *2111 Eisenhower Ave., Alexandria, VA 22314-4698; (703) 838-0083. Fax, (703) 549-0493. Roger Galvin, Chief Executive Officer. Web, www.nspi.org.*

Membership: manufacturers, dealers, and distributors of pools, spas, and hot tubs. Promotes the industry; compiles statistics; establishes construction standards for pools and spas. Monitors legislation and regulations.

Road Runners Club of America, *1150 S. Washington St., #250, Alexandria, VA 22314; (703) 836-0558. Fax, (703) 836-4430. Henley Gabeau, Executive Director. Information, (703) 683-7722. General e-mail, execdir@rrca.org. Web, www.rrca.org.*

Develops and promotes road races and fitness programs, including the Children's Running Development Program. Issues guidelines on road races. Interests include safety, wheelchair participation, and baby joggers/strollers in races; facilitates communication between clubs. Supports running for people with disabilities.

Snowsports Industries America, *8377-B Greensboro Dr., McLean, VA 22102; (703) 556-9020. Fax, (703) 821-8276. David Ingemie, President. Web, www.snowlink.com.*

Membership: manufacturers and distributors of ski and other outdoor sports equipment, apparel, accessories, and footwear. Interests include international markets.

Society of State Directors of Health, Physical Education, and Recreation, *1900 Association Dr., Reston, VA 20191; (703) 476-3402. Fax, (703) 476-9527. Bill Dateman, Executive Director.*

Membership: state directors, supervisors, and coordinators for physical and health education and recreation activities in state education departments, and other interested individuals. Seeks to improve school programs on comprehensive health, physical education, athletics, outdoor education, recreation, and safety.

Special Olympics International, *1325 G St. N.W., #500 20005; (202) 628-3630. Fax, (202) 824-0200. Robert Sargent Shriver Jr., Chair. General e-mail, soimail@aol.com. Web, www.specialolympics.org.*

Offers individuals with mental retardation opportunities for year-round sports training; sponsors athletic competition worldwide in twenty-two individual and team sports.

U.S. Combined Training Assn., *525 Old Waterford Rd. N.W., Leesburg, VA 20176; (703) 779-0440. Fax, (703) 779-0550. Jo Whitehouse, Executive Director. General e-mail, uscta4u@uscta.com. Web, www.eventingusa.com.*

Membership: individuals interested in combined training, an Olympic-recognized equestrian sport. Registers all national events to ensure that they meet the standards set by the American Horse Show Assn. Sponsors three-day events for members from novice to Olympic levels. Provides educational materials on competition, riding, and care of horses.

U.S. Olympic Committee, *Washington Office, 1150 18th St. N.W., #300 20036; (202) 466-3399. Fax, (202) 466-5068. Stephen Bull, Director, Government Relations. Web, www.olympic-usa.org.*

Responsible for training, entering, and underwriting the full expenses for U.S. teams in the Olympic and Pan American Games. Supports the bid of U.S. cities to host the Olympic and Pan American Games; recognizes the national governing body of each sport in these games. Promotes international athletic competition. (Headquarters in Colorado Springs, Colo.)

U.S. Parachute Assn., *1440 Duke St., Alexandria, VA 22314; (703) 836-3495. Fax, (703) 836-2843. Christopher Needels, Executive Director. Information, (800) 371-8772. General e-mail, uspa@uspa.org. Web, www.uspa.org.*

Membership: individuals and organizations interested in skydiving. Develops safety procedures; maintains training programs; issues skydiving licenses and ratings; certifies skydiving instructors; sanctions national competitions; and documents record attempts. Offers liability insurance to members. Monitors legislation and regulations.

⬛ TRAVEL AND TOURISM

See also Americans Abroad (chap. 13); Caucuses (chap. 20); Information and Exchange Programs (chap. 13)

AGENCIES

Immigration and Naturalization Service *(Justice Dept.), 425 Eye St. N.W., #7100 20536; (202) 514-1900. Fax, (202) 514-3296. Doris Meissner, Commissioner. Press,* (202) 514-2648. Form requests, (800) 870-3676. Web, www.ins.usdoj.gov.

Clears aliens and U.S. citizens for entry into the United States. Compiles statistics on tourists.

International Trade Administration *(Commerce Dept.), Tourism Industries, 14th St. and Constitution Ave. N.W., #2073 20230; (202) 482-0140. Fax, (202) 482-2887. Leslie R. Doggett, Deputy Assistant Secretary. Web, tinet.ita.doc.gov.*

Fosters tourism trade development, including public-private partnerships; represents the United States in tourism-related meetings with foreign government officials. Assembles, analyzes, and disseminates data and statistics on travel and tourism.

State Dept., *Passport Services, 2201 C St. N.W., #6811 20520; (202) 647-5366. Fax, (202) 647-0341. George Lannon, Deputy Assistant Secretary. Passport information, (800) 225-5674. Web, travel.state.gov.*

Administers passport laws and issues passports. (Most branches of the U.S. Postal Service and most U.S. district and state courts are authorized to accept applications and payment for passports and to administer the required oath to U.S. citizens. Completed applications are sent from the post office or court to the nearest State Dept. regional passport office for processing.) Maintains a variety of records received from the Overseas Citizens Services, including consular certificates of witness to marriage and reports of birth and death.

CONGRESS

House Commerce Committee, *Subcommittee on Finance and Hazardous Materials, 2125 RHOB 20515; (202) 225-2927. Fax, (202) 225-1919. Rep. Michael G. Oxley, R-Ohio, Chair; James E. Derderian, Staff Director. General e-mail, commerce@mail.house.gov. Web, www. house.gov/commerce.*

Jurisdiction over legislation affecting tourism.

Senate Commerce, Science, and Transportation Committee, *Subcommittee on Consumer Affairs, Foreign Commerce, and Tourism, SH-425 20510; (202) 224-5183. Fax, (202) 228-0326. Sen. John Ashcroft, R-Mo., Chair; Rob Taylor, Counsel. Web, commerce.senate.gov.*

Jurisdiction over legislation affecting tourism.

INTERNATIONAL ORGANIZATIONS

Organization of American States, *Inter-Sectoral Unit for Tourism, 1889 F St. N.W., #300A 20006; (202) 458-3196. Fax, (202) 458-3190. Claude Larreur, Director (Acting). General e-mail, Tourism@oas.org. Web, www.oas. org/tourism.*

Responsible for matters related to tourism and its development in the hemisphere. Provides support to the Inter-American Travel Congress; works for sustainable tourism development; promotes cooperation among international, regional, and subregional tourism offices.

NONPROFIT

American Hotel and Motel Assn., *1201 New York Ave. N.W., #600 20005-3931; (202) 289-3100. Fax, (202) 289-3199. William P. Fisher, President. Library, (202) 289-3193. Web, www.ahma.com.*

Provides operations, technical, educational, marketing, and communications services to members; focus includes international travel. Library open to the public by appointment. Monitors legislation and regulations.

American Society of Travel Agents, *1101 King St., #200, Alexandria, VA 22314-2944; (703) 739-2782. Fax, (703) 684-8319. Joe Galloway, President. Consumer affairs, (703) 739-8739. Web, www.astanet.com.*

Membership: representatives of the travel industry. Works to safeguard the traveling public against fraud, misrepresentation, and other unethical practices. Offers training programs for travel agents. Consumer affairs department offers help for anyone with a travel complaint against a member of the association.

Hostelling International—American Youth Hostels, *733 15th St. N.W., #840 20005; (202) 783-6161. Fax, (202) 783-6171. Richard Martyr, Executive Director. General e-mail, hiayhserv@hiayh.org. Web, www.hiayh.org.*

Provides opportunities for outdoor recreation and inexpensive educational travel through hostelling. Member of the International Youth Hostel Federation.

Hotel Employees and Restaurant Employees International, *1219 28th St. N.W. 20007; (202) 393-4373. Fax, (202) 333-0468. John W. Wilhelm, General President. Web, www.hereunion.org.*

Membership: approximately 241,000 hotel and restaurant employees. Helps members negotiate pay, benefits, and better working conditions; conducts training programs and workshops. Monitors legislation and regulations. (Affiliated with the AFL-CIO.)

International Assn. of Amusement Parks and Attractions, *1448 Duke St., Alexandria, VA 22314; (703)* 836-4800. Fax, (703) 836-4801. John Graff, Director. Web, www.iaapa.org.

Membership: companies from around the world in the amusement parks and attractions industry. Conducts an international exchange program for members. Monitors legislation and regulations.

International Assn. of Convention and Visitor Bureaus, *2000 L St. N.W., #702 20036-4990; (202) 296-7888. Fax, (202) 296-7889. Edward Nielsen, President. Web, www.iacvb.org.*

Membership: travel- and tourism-related businesses, convention and meeting professionals, and tour operators. Encourages business travelers and tourists to visit local historic, cultural, and recreational areas; assists in meeting preparations. Monitors legislation and regulations.

National Business Travel Assn., *1650 King St., #401, Alexandria, VA 22314; (703) 684-0836. Fax, (703) 684-0263. Norman R. Sherlock, Executive Director. General e-mail, info@nbta.org. Web, www.nbta.org.*

Membership: corporate travel managers. Promotes educational advancement of members and provides a forum for exchange of information on U.S. and international travel. Monitors legislation and regulations.

Passenger Vessel Assn., *1600 Wilson Blvd., #1000A, Arlington, VA 22209; (703) 807-0100. Fax, (703) 807-0103. John R. Groundwater, Executive Director. Web, www.passengervessel.com.*

Membership: owners, operators, and suppliers for U.S. and Canadian passenger vessels; and international vessel companies. Interests include dinner and excursion boats, car and passenger ferries, overnight cruise ships, and riverboat casinos. Monitors legislation and regulations.

Travel Industry Assn. of America, *1100 New York Ave. N.W., #450 20005; (202) 408-8422. Fax, (202) 408-1255. William Norman, President. Web, www.tia.org.*

Membership: business, professional, and trade associations of the travel industry and state and local associations (including official state government tourism offices) promoting tourism to a specific region or site. Encourages travel to and within the United States.

6

Education

![icon] GENERAL POLICY

AGENCIES

Education Dept., *400 Maryland Ave. S.W. 20202; (202) 401-3000. Fax, (202) 401-0596. Richard W. Riley, Secretary; Frank Holleman, Deputy Secretary. Information, (202) 401-2000. TTY, (800) 437-0833. Web, www.ed.gov.*

Establishes education policy and acts as principal adviser to the president on education matters; administers and coordinates most federal assistance programs on education.

Education Dept., *Goals 2000: Educate America, 400 Maryland Ave. S.W., #3E241 20202-6400; (202) 401-0039. Fax, (202) 205-5870. Patricia W. Gore, Director. Information, (800) 872-5327. Press, (202) 401-1576. TTY, (800) 437-0833.*

Provides a coordinated strategy to focus federal resources on supporting improvements in schools; promotes development and implementation of comprehensive improvement plans that direct resources toward improved achievement for all students.

Education Dept., *National Assessment of Educational Progress, 555 New Jersey Ave. N.W. 20208; (202) 219-1690. Web, nces.ed.gov/nationsreportcard/site/home.asp.*

Assesses the abilities of U.S. students in various subject areas on national and state levels. Makes findings available to policymakers at the national, state, and local levels.

Educational Resources Information Center *(Education Dept.), 2277 Research Blvd., #6L, Rockville, MD 20850-3172; (301) 519-5157. Fax, (301) 519-6760. Lynn Smarte, Project Director. Information, (800) 538-3742. General e-mail, accesseric@accesseric.org. Web, www.accesseric.org.*

Coordinates a national information system comprising sixteen clearinghouses on specific subjects. Documents available in microfiche form at most university libraries. Answers queries and offers referrals to individuals on all facets of education.

For a list of clearinghouses on the Web, see box (p. 176).

CONGRESS

General Accounting Office, *Health, Education, and Human Services, 441 G St. N.W. 20548; (202) 512-6806. Fax, (202) 512-5806. Victor S. Rezendes, Assistant Comptroller General.*

Independent, nonpartisan agency in the legislative branch. Audits, analyzes, and evaluates Education Dept. programs; makes reports available to the public.

House Appropriations Committee, *Subcommittee on Labor, Health and Human Services, and Education, 2358 RHOB 20515; (202) 225-3508. Fax, (202) 225-3509. Rep. John Edward Porter, R-Ill., Chair; Tony McCann, Staff Director. Web, www.house.gov/appropriations.*

Jurisdiction over legislation to appropriate funds for federal education programs (except native American education programs), including adult education, compensatory education, and education for the disadvantaged and disabled.

House Education and the Workforce Committee, *Subcommittee on Early Childhood, Youth, and Families, 2181 RHOB 20515; (202) 225-4527. Fax, (202) 225-9571. Rep. Michael N. Castle, R-Del., Chair; Kevin D. Talley, Staff Director. Web, www.house.gov/ed_workforce.*

Jurisdiction over legislation on preschool, elementary, and secondary education; adult basic education (family literacy); and overseas dependent schools.

House Education and the Workforce Committee, *Subcommittee on Postsecondary Education, Training, and Life-Long Learning, 2181 RHOB 20515; (202) 225-4527. Fax, (202) 225-9571. Rep. Howard P. "Buck" McKeon, R-Calif., Chair; Kevin D. Talley, Staff Director. Web, www.house.gov/ed_workforce.*

Jurisdiction over legislation on education beyond the high school level, including training and apprenticeship programs, vocational education, rehabilitation, postsecondary student assistance, domestic volunteer programs, and library services and construction. Oversees the Robert A. Taft Institute and the U.S. Institute of Peace.

House Government Reform Committee, *Subcommittee on Criminal Justice, Drug Policy, and Human Resources, B373 RHOB 20515; (202) 225-2577. Fax, (202) 225-1154. Rep. John L. Mica, R-Fla., Chair; Sharon Pinkerton, Staff Director. Web, www.house.gov/reform.*

Oversees operations of the Education Dept.

Senate Appropriations Committee, *Subcommittee on Labor, Health and Human Services, and Education, SD-186 20510; (202) 224-7230. Fax, (202) 224-1360. Sen. Arlen Specter, R-Pa., Chair; Bettilou Taylor, Staff Director. Web, appropriations.senate.gov/labor.*

Jurisdiction over legislation to appropriate funds for federal education programs, including adult education, compensatory education, and education for the disadvantaged and disabled.

Senate Health, Education, Labor, and Pensions Committee, *SD-428 20510; (202) 224-5375. Fax, (202) 228-5044. Sen. James M. Jeffords, R-Vt., Chair; Mark Powden, Staff Director. TTY, (202) 224-1975. Web, labor.senate.gov.*

EDUCATION DEPARTMENT

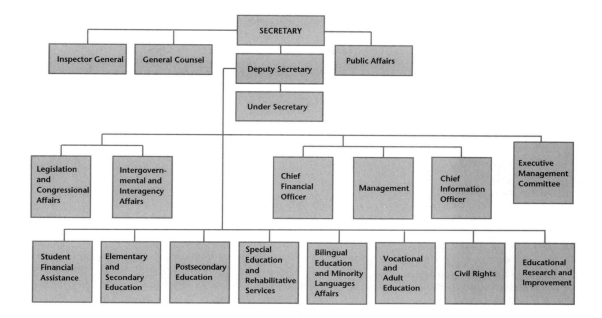

Inspector General | **General Counsel** | **SECRETARY** | **Public Affairs**

Deputy Secretary

Under Secretary

Legislation and Congressional Affairs | **Intergovernmental and Interagency Affairs** | **Chief Financial Officer** | **Management** | **Chief Information Officer** | **Executive Management Committee**

Student Financial Assistance | **Elementary and Secondary Education** | **Postsecondary Education** | **Special Education and Rehabilitative Services** | **Bilingual Education and Minority Languages Affairs** | **Vocational and Adult Education** | **Civil Rights** | **Educational Research and Improvement**

Jurisdiction over legislation on preschool, elementary, secondary, and vocational education, including community schools, aid to private schools, the Office of Educational Research and Improvement, education technology, and drug and alcohol abuse education. Jurisdiction over legislation on postsecondary education, libraries, and education of people with disabilities; jurisdiction over legislation barring discrimination in education. Oversees operations of the Education Dept.

NONPROFIT

Annenberg Public Policy Center, *529 14th St. N.W. 20045; (202) 879-6700. Fax, (202) 879-6707. Lorie Slass, Director. General e-mail, appcdc@appcpenn.org. Web, appcpenn.org.*

Supports research on public policy issues at the local, state, and federal levels. Sponsors lectures and conferences.

Capital Children's Museum, *800 3rd St. N.E. 20002; (202) 675-4120. Fax, (202) 675-4140. Catherine Martens, Executive Director. Press, (202) 675-4183. Museum desk, (202) 675-4170. Web, www.ccm.org.*

Designs, implements, and conducts studies in education. Interests include the creation and development of new educational methods, materials, and structures. Maintains the Options School.

Center for Education Reform, *1001 Connecticut Ave. N.W., #204 20036; (202) 822-9000. Fax, (202) 822-5077. Jeanne Allen, President. General e-mail, cer@edreform. com. Web, www.edreform.com.*

Provides support and guidance to individuals, community and civic groups, policymakers, and others who are working to bring fundamental reforms to their schools.

Center for Law and Education, *Washington Office, 1875 Connecticut Ave. N.W., #510 20009-5728; (202) 986-3000. Fax, (202) 986-6648. Paul Weckstein, Co-Director. Publications, (202) 462-7688. General e-mail, cle@cleweb. org. Web, www.cleweb.org.*

Works to advance the right of all students, and low income students in particular, to a high-quality education. Interests include testing and tracking; bilingual education; discriminatory discipline; special education; special needs for native Americans, migrants, and Hispanics; parent, community, and student participation in education; and vocational and compensatory education. (Headquarters in Boston.)

Charles F. Kettering Foundation, *Washington Office, 444 N. Capitol St. N.W., #434 20001-1512; (202) 393-4478. Fax, (202) 393-7644. James C. Wilder, Director. Information, (800) 221-3657. Web, www.kettering.org.*

EDUCATIONAL RESOURCES INFORMATION CENTER (ERIC) CLEARINGHOUSES

ERIC, supported by the Education Dept.'s Office of Educational Research and Improvement and the National Library of Education, provides users with access to a national information system of education related literature. Its clearinghouses collect, abstract, index, and disseminate information in sixteen subject-specific categories.

Adult, Career, and Vocational Education
Web, ericacve.org

AskERIC
Web, ericir.syr.edu

Assessment and Evaluation
Web, ericae.net

Community College
Web, www.gseis.ucla.edu/ERIC/eric.html

Counseling and Student Services
Web, www.uncg.edu/edu/ericcass

Disabilities and Gifted Education
Web, www.cec.sped.org/ericec.htm

Educational Management
Web, eric.uoregon.edu

Elementary and Early Childhood Education
Web, ericeece.org

Higher Education
Web, www.eriche.org

Information and Technology
Web, ericir.syr.edu/ithome

Languages and Linguistics
Web, www.cal.org/ericcll

National Parent Information Network
Web, npin.org

Reading, English, and Communication
Web, www.indiana.edu/~eric_rec

Rural Education and Small Schools
Web, www.ael.org/eric

Science, Mathematics, and Environmental Education
Web, www.ericse.org

Social Studies/Social Education
Web, www.indiana.edu/~ssdc/eric_chess.htm

Teaching and Teacher Education
Web, www.ericsp.org

Urban Education
Web, eric-web.tc.columbia.edu

Works to improve the domestic policy-making process. Supports international program focusing on unofficial, citizen-to-citizen diplomacy. Encourages greater citizen involvement in formation of public policy. Interests include public education and at-risk youths. (Headquarters in Dayton, Ohio.)

Council for Advancement and Support of Education, *1307 New York Ave. N.W. 20005; (202) 328-5900. Fax, (202) 387-4973. Eustace Theodore, President. General e-mail, membership@case.org. Web, www.case.org.*

Membership: two- and four-year colleges, universities, and independent schools. Offers professional education and training programs to members; advises members on institutional advancement issues, including fundraising, alumni affairs, public relations programs, government relations, and management. Library open to the public by appointment.

Distributive Education Clubs of America, *1908 Association Dr., Reston, VA 20191-1594; (703) 860-5000. Fax, (703) 860-4013. Edward L. Davis, Executive Director. Web, www.deca.org.*

Educational organization that helps high school and college students develop skills in marketing, management, and entrepreneurship. Promotes business and education partnerships.

Education Policy Institute, *4401-A Connecticut Ave. N.W. 20008; (202) 244-7535. Fax, (202) 244-7584. Charlene K. Haar, President; Myron Lieberman, Chair. General e-mail, info@educationpolicy.org. Web, www. educationpolicy.org.*

Seeks to improve education through research, policy analysis, and the development of alternatives to current policies and practices. Promotes greater parental choice in education, a more competitive education industry, and an increase in the creative role of for-profit schools.

Ethics Resource Center, *1747 Pennsylvania Ave. N.W., #400 20006; (202) 737-2258. Fax, (202) 737-2227. Michael G. Daigneault, President. Information, (800) 777-1285. Press, (202) 872-4765. Web, www.ethics.org.*

Nonpartisan educational organization whose vision is an ethical world. Fosters ethical practices among individuals and institutions. Interests include research and knowledge building, education and advocacy, and consulting and technical assistance.

Institute for Educational Leadership, *1001 Connecticut Ave. N.W., #310 20036; (202) 822-8405. Fax, (202) 872-4050. Michael Usdan, President. General e-mail, iel@iel.org. Web, www.iel.org.*

Works with educators, human services personnel, government officials, and association executives to improve educational opportunities for youths; conducts research on education issues.

National Assn. of State Boards of Education, *277 S. Washington St., #100, Alexandria, VA 22314; (703) 684-4000. Fax, (703) 836-2313. Brenda L. Welburn, Executive Director. Web, www.nasbe.org.*

Membership: members of state boards of education, state board attorneys, and executives to state boards. Interests include strengthening state leadership in educational policy making; promoting excellence in the education of all students; advocating equality of access to educational opportunity; and assuring continued citizen support for public education.

National Center for Education Information, *4401 Connecticut Ave. N.W. 20008; (202) 362-3444. Fax, (202) 362-3493. Emily Feistritzer, President. General e-mail, nceicef@aol.com. Web, www.ncei.com.*

Specializes in survey research and data analysis of alternative teacher preparation and certification. Conducts national and state surveys of teachers, school administrators, school board presidents, state departments of education, local school districts, and individuals interested in becoming teachers.

National Center on Education and the Economy, *America's Choice District and School Design, 700 11th St. N.W., #750 20001; (202) 783-3668. Fax, (202) 783-3672. Mary Ann Mays, Director. General e-mail, info@ncee.org. Web, www.ncee.org.*

Partnership of states, school districts, corporations, foundations, and nonprofit organizations that provides tools and technical assistance to help school systems improve student performance. Areas of focus include standards, assessments, curriculum, and instruction.

National Clearinghouse for Corporate Matching Gifts Information, *1307 New York Ave. N.W. 20005-4701; (202) 478-5634. Fax, (202) 387-4973. Greg Humpert, Director. General e-mail, matchgifts@ns.case.org. Web, www.case.org.*

Provides companies and educational institutions with information on matching gift programs, in which companies match employee contributions to educational and other nonprofit institutions. Sponsored by the Council for Advancement and Support of Education.

National Community Education Assn., *3929 Old Lee Hwy., #91-A, Fairfax, VA 22030-2401; (703) 359-8973. Fax, (703) 359-0972. Starla Jewell-Kelly, Executive Director. General e-mail, ncea@ncea.com. Web, www.ncea.com.*

Works for greater recognition of community education programs, services, and personnel. Interests include business-education partnerships to improve schools; lifelong learning; school-site child care and latchkey programs; and parental involvement in public education.

National Humanities Institute, *214 Massachusetts Ave. N.E., #303 20002; (202) 544-3158. Fax, (202) 544-3158. Joseph Baldacchino, President. General e-mail, mail@nhumanities.org. Web, www.nhumanities.org.*

Promotes research, publishing, and teaching in the humanities. Interests include the effect of the humanities on society.

National School Public Relations Assn., *15948 Derwood Rd., Rockville, MD 20855; (301) 519-0496. Fax, (301) 519-0494. Richard D. Bagin, Executive Director.*

Membership: educators and individuals interested in improving communications in education. Works to improve communication between educators and the public on the needs of schools; provides educators with information on public relations and policy developments.

New American Schools, *1616 Wilson Blvd., #901, Arlington, VA 22209; (703) 908-9500. Fax, (703) 908-0622. Donald Feuerstein, President. Web, www.naschools.org.*

Promotes comprehensive education reform through programs that reorganize an entire school. Conducts research and provides technical assistance.

Internships, Fellowships, Grants

See also Arts and Humanities (chap. 5); Post-secondary Education (this chapter); Special Topics in Education (this chapter)

AGENCIES

Harry S. Truman Scholarship Foundation, *712 Jackson Pl. N.W., 3rd Floor 20006-4901; (202) 395-4831. Fax, (202) 395-6995. Louis H. Blair, Executive Secretary. General e-mail, staff@truman.gov. Web, www.truman.gov.*

Memorial to Harry S. Truman established by Congress. Provides students preparing for careers in public service with scholarships. (Candidates are nominated by their respective colleges or universities while in their third year of undergraduate study.)

National Endowment for the Arts *(National Foundation on the Arts and the Humanities), 1100 Pennsylvania Ave. N.W. 20506-0001; (202) 682-5414. Fax, (202) 682-5639. Bill Ivey, Chair. Information, (202) 682-5400. Library, (202) 682-5485. Press, (202) 682-5570. TTY, (202) 682-5496. Web, arts.endow.gov.*

Independent federal grant-making agency. Awards grants to nonprofit arts organizations in four areas: creation and presentation; education and access; heritage and preservation; and partnership, planning, and stabilization. Organizations must choose one of the four theme areas for submission of project proposals. Library open to the public by appointment.

National Endowment for the Humanities *(National Foundation on the Arts and the Humanities), 1100 Pennsylvania Ave. N.W., #503 20506; (202) 606-8310. Fax, (202) 606-8588. William R. Ferris, Chair. Information, (202) 606-8400. Library, (202) 606-8244. Press, (202) 606-8446. TTY, (202) 606-8282. General e-mail, info@neh.gov. Web, www.neh.gov.*

Independent federal grant-making agency. Awards grants to individuals and institutions for research, scholarship, educational programs, and public programs (including broadcasts, museum exhibitions, lectures, and symposia) in the humanities (defined as study of archeology; history; jurisprudence; language; linguistics; literature; philosophy; comparative religion; ethics; the history, criticism, and theory of the arts; and humanistic aspects of the social sciences). Funds preservation of books, newspapers, historical documents, and photographs.

National Endowment for the Humanities *(National Foundation on the Arts and the Humanities), Research and Education, 1100 Pennsylvania Ave. N.W., #302 20506; (202) 606-8373. Fax, (202) 606-8394. James Herbert, Director. General e-mail, education@neh.gov. Web, www.neh.gov.*

Offers fellowships, stipends, seminars, and institutes for higher education faculty, school teachers, and independent scholars. Conducts research.

National Science Foundation, *Graduate Education, 4201 Wilson Blvd., Arlington, VA 22230; (703) 306-1630. Fax, (703) 306-0468. Susan W. Duby, Director. TTY, (703) 306-0090. Web, www.nsf.gov/EHR/DGE/dge.htm.*

Supports activities to strengthen the education of research scientists and engineers; promotes career development; offers pre- and postdoctoral fellowships for study and research; manages the Graduate fellowships and the Travel Awards for NATO–Advanced Study Institute.

President's Commission on White House Fellowships, *712 Jackson Pl. N.W. 20503; (202) 395-4522. Fax, (202) 395-6179. Jacqueline Blumenthal, Director. Web, www.whitehouse.gov/WH_Fellows.*

Nonpartisan commission that provides professionals from all sectors of national life with the opportunity to observe firsthand the processes of the federal government. Fellows work for one year as special assistants to cabinet members or to principal members of the White House staff. Qualified applicants have demonstrated superior accomplishments early in their careers and have a commitment to community service.

Smithsonian Institution, *Fellowships and Grants, 955 L'Enfant Plaza S.W., #7000 20560-0902; (202) 287-3271. Fax, (202) 287-3691. Roberta Rubinoff, Director. General e-mail, siofg@ofg.si.edu. Web, www.si.edu/research+study.*

Administers fellowships in residence that provide pre- and postdoctoral appointments for study and research at the Smithsonian Institution in history of science and technology, American and cultural history, history of art, anthropology, evolutionary and systematic biology, environmental sciences, astrophysics and astronomy, earth sciences, and tropical biology.

Woodrow Wilson International Center for Scholars, *Fellowships, 1300 Pennsylvania Ave. N.W., Pennsylvania Ave. N.W. 20004-3027; (202) 691-4000. Fax, (202) 691-4001. Rosemary Lyon, Director. General e-mail, fellowships@wwic.si.edu. Web, wwics.si.edu.*

Awards fellowships to established scholars and professionals from the United States and abroad for humanities and social science research at the center. Publishes guides to scholarly research material in the Washington area.

NONPROFIT

American Assn. of University Women Educational Foundation, *1111 16th St. N.W. 20036; (202) 728-7602. Fax, (202) 463-7169. Karen Lebovich, Director. General e-mail, foundation@aauw.org. Web, www.aauw.org/7000/aboutef.html.*

Awards fellowships and grants to women for various areas of study and educational pursuit. Offers fellowships to foreign women coming to the United States for one year of graduate study. Awards grants to women returning to school for postbaccalaureate education or professional development. Administers the Eleanor Roosevelt Fund, which supports a teacher sabbatical program for women who teach girls math and science in grades K–12. (Affiliate of the American Assn. of University Women.)

American Institute of Architects, *American Architectural Foundation, 1735 New York Ave. N.W. 20006; (202) 626-7500. Fax, (202) 626-7420. William Chapin, President. Library, (202) 626-7492. Web, www.aafpages.org.*

Seeks to advance the quality of American architecture. Works to increase public awareness and under-

INTERNSHIPS IN WASHINGTON

The following are some key organizations offering internships in the Washington area. For Congressional internships, contact the individual member's office (see appendix).

Alexis de Tocqueville Institution, (703) 351-4969

American Civil Liberties Union, (202) 544-1681

American Enterprise Institute for Public Policy Research, (202) 862-5800

Amnesty International USA, (202) 544-0200

Brookings Institution, (202) 797-6096

C-SPAN, (202) 737-3220

Cato Institute, (202) 842-0200

Center for Defense Information, (202) 332-0600

Center for Policy Alternatives, (202) 387-6030

Center for Science in the Public Interest, (202) 332-9110

Center for Strategic and International Studies, (202) 775-3165

Center for Study of Responsive Law, (202) 387-8030

Central Intelligence Agency, (703) 482-0677

Children's Defense Fund, (202) 628-8787

Concord Coalition, (202) 467-6222

Conservative Caucus, (703) 938-9626

Democratic National Committee, (202) 863-8000

Empower America, (202) 452-8200

Environmental Protection Agency, (202) 260-7690

Fund for the Feminist Majority, (703) 522-2214

General Accounting Office, (202) 512-3429

The Heritage Foundation, (202) 546-4400

Institute for Policy Studies, (202) 234-9382

John F. Kennedy Center for the Performing Arts, (202) 416-8807

Joint Center for Political and Economic Studies, (202) 789-3500

Library of Congress, (202) 707-2087

National Audubon Society, (202) 861-2242

National Institutes of Health, (301) 402-2176

National Public Radio, (202) 414-2909

National Wildlife Federation, (202) 797-6800

Office of Personnel Management, (202) 606-2525

Progress & Freedom Foundation, (202) 289-8928

Public Defender Service, (800) 341-2582

Republican National Committee, (202) 863-8563

Smithsonian Institution, (202) 357-3102

State Dept., (703) 875-7490

Supreme Court of the United States, (202) 479-3374

The Urban Institute, (202) 833-7200

The White House, (202) 456-2742

---

standing, and apply new technology to create more humane environments. Acts as liaison between the profession and the public; awards grants for architecture-oriented projects. Serves as the educational arm of the American Institute of Architects. Also operates the historic Octagon Museum.

American Political Science Assn., *Congressional Fellowship Program, 1527 New Hampshire Ave. N.W. 20036-1290; (202) 483-2512. Fax, (202) 483-2657. Jeff Biggs, Administrative Director. Web, www.apsanet.org.*

Places political scientists, journalists, faculty of medical schools (Robert Wood Johnson Fellowships), and federal agency executives in congressional offices and committees for nine-month fellowships. Individual government agencies nominate federal executive participants.

Business and Professional Women's Foundation, *2012 Massachusetts Ave. N.W. 20036; (202) 293-1200. Fax, (202) 861-0298. Robin Robinson, President. Web, www.bpwusa.org.*

Works to improve women's economic status by promoting their employment at all levels in all occupations. Provides mature women seeking training and education with scholarships and loans to increase their job skills. Awards grants for doctoral research on women's economic issues. Library open to the public. (Affiliate of Business and Professional Women U.S.A.)

Congressional Black Caucus Foundation, *1004 Pennsylvania Ave. S.E. 20003; (202) 675-6730. Fax, (202) 547-3806. Ramona H. Edelin, Executive Director. Web, www.cbcfonline.org.*

Conducts public policy research on issues of concern to African Americans. Sponsors fellowship programs in which professionals and academic candidates work on congressional committees and subcommittees. Sponsors internship and scholarship programs.

Council for International Exchange of Scholars, *3007 Tilden St. N.W., #5L 20008-3009; (202) 686-4000. Fax, (202) 362-3442. Patti McGill Peterson, Executive*

Director. General e-mail, info@ciesnet.cies.org. Web, www. cies.org.

Cooperates with the U.S. government in administering Fulbright grants for university teaching and advanced research abroad. (Affiliated with the American Council of Learned Societies.)

Council on Foundations, *1828 L St. N.W., #300 20036; (202) 466-6512. Fax, (202) 785-3926. Dorothy Ridings, President. Web, www.cof.org.*

Membership: independent community, family, and public and company-sponsored foundations; corporate giving programs; and foundations in other countries. Acts as clearinghouse for information on private philanthropy; sponsors conferences and workshops on effective grant making.

Foundation Center, *Washington Office, 1001 Connecticut Ave. N.W., #938 20036; (202) 331-1400. Fax, (202) 331-1739. Vacant, Assistant Director. General e-mail, feedback@fdncenter.org. Web, www.fdncenter.org.*

Publishes foundation guides. Serves as a clearinghouse on foundations and corporate giving, nonprofit management, fundraising, and grants for individuals. Provides training and seminars on fundraising and grant writing. Operates libraries in Atlanta, Cleveland, New York, San Francisco, and Washington, D.C.; libraries open to the public. (Headquarters in New York.)

Fund for American Studies, *1706 New Hampshire Ave. N.W. 20009; (202) 986-0384. Fax, (202) 986-0390. Roger Ream, President. Toll-free, (800) 741-6964 (outside D.C. area). General e-mail, feedback@tfas.org. Web, www.tfas. org.*

Educational foundation that sponsors summer institutes on comparative political and economic systems, business and government affairs, and political journalism; grants scholarships to qualified students for study-internship programs.

Institute of International Education, *National Security Education Program, 1400 K St. N.W., 6th Floor 20005-2403; (202) 326-7697. Fax, (202) 326-7698. Leslie Anderson, Director. Information, (800) 618-6737. Web, www.iie.org/nsep.*

Provides scholarships, fellowships, and institutional grants to academics with in an interest in foreign affairs and national security.

National Journalism Center, *800 Maryland Ave. N.E. 20002; (202) 546-1710. Fax, (202) 546-1638. M. Stanton Evans, Director.*

Sponsors extensive internship program in journalism; provides a stipend for living expenses; offers job

placement service. Funded by the Education and Research Institute.

Washington Center, *2000 M St. N.W., #750 20036-3307; (202) 336-7600. Fax, (202) 336-7609. William M. Burke, President. Information, (800) 496-8921. General e-mail, info@twc.edu. Web, www.twc.edu.*

Arranges congressional, agency, and public service internships for college students for credit. Fee for internship and housing assistance. Sponsors classes and lectures as part of the internship program. Scholarships and stipends available.

Washington Center for Politics and Journalism, *1901 L St. N.W., #300 20036 (mailing address: P.O. Box 15201 20003); (800) 858-8365. Fax, (202) 466-7598. Terry Michael, Executive Director. General e-mail, pol-jrn@wcpj. org. Web, www.wcpj.org.*

Offers internships in political journalism to undergraduate and graduate students; provides a stipend for living expenses. Sixteen-week fall and winter/spring sessions include full-time work in Washington news bureaus and seminars in campaign, governance, and interest group politics for future political reporters.

Women's Research and Education Institute, *1750 New York Ave. N.W., #350 20006; (202) 628-0444. Fax, (202) 628-0458. Susan Scanlan, President. General e-mail, wrei@wrei.org. Web, www.wrei.org.*

Analyzes policy-relevant information on issues that concern or affect women; serves as a resource for federal and state policymakers, the media, and the public. Sponsors Congressional Fellowships on Women and Public Policy for graduate students, who are placed in congressional offices for one academic year to work on policy issues affecting women.

Youth Policy Institute, *1333 Green Court N.W. 20005-4113; (202) 638-2144. Fax, (202) 638-2325. David L. Hackett, Executive Director. General e-mail, corpsnet@ mnsinc.com.*

Seeks to involve everyone, especially youth, in public policy decision making.

Professional Interests and Benefits

See also Postsecondary Education (this chapter)

NONPROFIT

AARP, *National Retired Teachers Assn., 601 E St. N.W. 20049; (202) 434-2380. Fax, (202) 434-6451. Annette Norsman, Director. General e-mail, aarpwrit@aol.com. Web, www.aarp.org.*

Membership: active and retired teachers and other school personnel (elementary through postsecondary) over age fifty. Provides members with information on relevant national issues. Provides state associations of retired school personnel with technical assistance.

American Assn. of Colleges for Teacher Education, *1307 New York Ave. N.W., #300 20005-4701; (202) 293-2450. Fax, (202) 457-8095. David G. Imig, Executive Director. Web, www.aacte.org.*

Membership: colleges and universities with teacher education programs. Informs members of state and federal policies affecting teacher education and of professional issues such as accreditation, certification, and assessment. Collects and analyzes information on education.

American Assn. of School Administrators, *1801 N. Moore St., Arlington, VA 22209-9988; (703) 528-0700. Fax, (703) 841-1543. Paul D. Houston, Executive Director. Web, www.aasa.org.*

Membership: chief school executives, administrators at district or higher level, and teachers of school administration. Promotes opportunities for minorities, women, and the disabled in educational administration and organization.

American Federation of School Administrators, *1729 21st St. N.W. 20009; (202) 986-4209. Fax, (202) 986-4211. Joe L. Greene, President. Web, www.admin.org.*

Membership: approximately 12,000 school administrators, including principals, vice principals, directors, and superintendents. Helps members negotiate pay, benefits, and better working conditions; conducts training programs and workshops. Monitors legislation and regulations. (Affiliated with the AFL-CIO.)

American Federation of Teachers, *555 New Jersey Ave. N.W., 10th Floor 20001; (202) 879-4400. Fax, (202) 879-4545. Sandra Feldman, President. Web, www.aft.org/index.htm.*

Membership: public and private school teachers, higher education faculty, and school-related personnel. Assists members with contract negotiation and grievances; conducts training programs and workshops. Monitors legislation and regulations. (Affiliated with the AFL-CIO.)

American Political Science Assn., *1527 New Hampshire Ave. N.W. 20036; (202) 483-2512. Fax, (202) 483-2657. Catherine E. Rudder, Executive Director. General e-mail, apsa@apsanet.org. Web, www.apsanet.org.*

Membership: political scientists, primarily college and university professors. Promotes scholarly inquiry into all aspects of political science, including international affairs and comparative government. Works to increase public understanding of politics; provides services to facilitate and enhance research, teaching, and professional development of its members. Acts as liaison with federal agencies, Congress, and the public. Seeks to improve the status of women and minorities in the profession. Offers congressional fellowships, workshops, and awards. Provides information on political science issues.

Assn. of School Business Officials International, *11401 N. Shore Dr., Reston, VA 20190-4232; (703) 478-0405. Fax, (703) 478-0205. Don I. Tharpe, Executive Director. Web, www.asbointl.org.*

Membership: administrators, directors, and others involved in school business management. Works to educate members on tools, techniques, and procedures of school business management. Researches, analyzes, and disseminates information; conducts workshops.

Assn. of Teacher Educators, *1900 Association Dr., Reston, VA 20191-1502; (703) 620-3110. Fax, (703) 620-9530. Lynn Montgomery, Executive Director (Acting). Web, www.siu.edu/departments/coe/ate.*

Membership: individuals and public and private agencies involved with teacher education. Seeks to improve teacher education at all levels; conducts workshops and conferences; produces and disseminates publications.

Council of Chief State School Officers, *1 Massachusetts Ave. N.W., #700 20001-1431; (202) 408-5505. Fax, (202) 408-8072. Gordon M. Ambach, Executive Director. Press, (202) 326-8680. General e-mail, info@ccsso.org. Web, www.ccsso.org.*

Membership: state superintendents and commissioners of education. Works to achieve equal education for all children and to improve ways to measure school performance; provides state education agency personnel and others with leadership, technical assistance, and training. Offers seminars, educational travel, and study programs for members.

Federal Education Assn., *1101 15th St. N.W., #1002 20005; (202) 822-7850. Fax, (202) 822-7816. Jan Mohr, President. Web, www.feaonline.org.*

Membership: teachers and personnel of Defense Dept. schools for military dependents in the United States and abroad. Helps members negotiate pay, benefits, and better working conditions. Monitors legislation and regulations. (Affiliated with the National Education Assn.)

International Test and Evaluation Assn., *4400 Fair Lakes Court, #104, Fairfax, VA 22033-3899; (703) 631-6220. Fax, (703) 631-6221. R. Alan Plishker, Executive Director. Web, www.itea.org.*

Membership: engineers, scientists, managers, and other industry, government, and academic professionals interested in testing and evaluating products and complex systems. Provides a forum for information exchange; monitors international research.

National Assn. for Women in Education, *1325 18th St. N.W., #210 20036; (202) 659-9330. Fax, (202) 457-0946. Lynn Gangone, Executive Director. General e-mail, nawe@nawe.org. Web, www.nawe.org.*

Membership: women in educational administration, teaching, and research, mainly in higher education. Interests include career mobility for women administrators, equitable pensions, and equal educational opportunity and training.

National Assn. of Biology Teachers, *12030 Sunrise Valley Dr., #110, Reston, VA 20190; (703) 264-9696. Fax, (703) 264-7778. Wayne Carley, Executive Director. Information, (800) 406-0775. General e-mail, NABTer@aol.com. Web, www.nabt.org.*

Membership: biology teachers and others interested in biology and life sciences education at the elementary, secondary, and collegiate levels. Provides professional development opportunities through its publication program, summer workshops, conventions, and national award programs. Interests include teaching standards, science curriculum, and issues affecting biology and life sciences education.

National Assn. of School Psychologists, *4340 East-West Hwy., #402, Bethesda, MD 20814; (301) 657-0270. Fax, (301) 657-0275. Susan Gorin, Executive Director. TTY, (301) 657-4155. Web, www.naspweb.org.*

Advocates for the mental health and educational needs of children; encourages professional growth of members. Monitors legislation and regulations.

National Business Education Assn., *1914 Association Dr., Reston, VA 20191-1596; (703) 860-8300. Fax, (703) 620-4483. Janet M. Treichel, Executive Director. General e-mail, nbea@nbea.org. Web, www.nbea.org.*

Membership: business education teachers and others interested in the field. Provides information on business education; offers teaching materials; sponsors conferences. Monitors legislation and regulations affecting business education.

National Certification Commission, *P.O. Box 15282, Chevy Chase, MD 20825-0282; (301) 588-1212. Richard*

C. Jaffeson, Executive Director. Fax-on-demand, (301) 588-1211. General e-mail, certusa@usa.net.

Provides information on the development and improvement of professional certification programs.

National Council for Accreditation of Teacher Education, *2010 Massachusetts Ave. N.W., #500 20036-1023; (202) 466-7496. Fax, (202) 296-6620. Arthur E. Wise, President. General e-mail, art@ncate.org. Web, www.ncate.org.*

Evaluates and accredits schools, colleges, and academic departments at higher education institutions; publishes list of accredited institutions and standards for accreditation.

National Council for the Social Studies, *3501 Newark St. N.W. 20016-3167; (202) 966-7840. Fax, (202) 966-2061. Susan Griffith, Executive Director (Acting). Web, www.ncss.org.*

Membership: curriculum developers, educational administrators, state supervisors, and social studies educators, including teachers of history, political science, geography, economics, civics, psychology, sociology, and anthropology. Promotes the teaching of social studies; encourages research; sponsors publications; works with other organizations to advance social studies education.

National Council of State Education Assns., *1201 16th St. N.W., #816 20036; (202) 822-7745. Fax, (202) 822-7624. Larry Diebold, Executive Director.*

Membership: presidents, vice presidents, secretary-treasurers, and executive directors of state education associations. Holds meetings and training programs for officers and staff of state education associations.

National Council of Teachers of Mathematics, *1906 Association Dr., Reston, VA 20191-9988; (703) 620-9840. Fax, (703) 476-2970. John A. Thorpe, Executive Director. General e-mail, infocentral@nctm.org. Web, www.nctm.org.*

Membership: teachers of mathematics in elementary and secondary schools and two-year colleges; university teacher education faculty; students; and other interested persons. Works for the improvement of classroom instruction at all levels. Serves as forum and information clearinghouse on issues related to mathematics education. Offers educational materials and conferences. Monitors legislation and regulations.

National Education Assn., *1201 16th St. N.W. 20036; (202) 833-4000. Fax, (202) 822-7767. Don Cameron, Executive Director. Web, www.nea.org.*

Membership: more than 2.4 million educators from preschool to university graduate programs. Promotes the interest of the profession of teaching and the cause of education in the United States. Monitors legislation and regulations at state and national levels.

National Foundation for the Improvement of Education, *1201 16th St. N.W., #416 20036-3207; (202) 822-7840. Fax, (202) 822-7779. Judith Rényi, Executive Director. Web, www.nfie.org.*

Educational and charitable organization created by the National Education Assn. Awards grants to teachers to improve teaching techniques and professional development; provides teachers with assistance to integrate computer and telecommunications technology into classroom instruction, curriculum management, and administration.

National Science Resources Center, *Smithsonian Institution Arts and Industries Bldg. 20560-0403; (202) 357-4892. Fax, (202) 786-2028. Douglas M. Lapp, Executive Director. Web, www.si.edu/nsrc.*

Sponsored by the Smithsonian Institution and the National Academy of Sciences. Works to improve science teaching in the nation's schools. Disseminates information; develops curriculum materials; seeks to increase public support for reform of science education.

National Science Teachers Assn., *1840 Wilson Blvd., Arlington, VA 22201-3000; (703) 243-7100. Fax, (703) 243-7177. Gerry Wheeler, Executive Director. General e-mail, publicinfo@nsta.org. Web, www.nsta.org.*

Membership: science teachers from elementary through college levels. Seeks to improve science education; provides forum for exchange of information. Monitors legislation and regulations.

Teachers of English to Speakers of Other Languages, *700 S. Washington St., #200, Alexandria, VA 22314-4287; (703) 836-0774. Fax, (703) 836-7864. Charles Amorosino, Executive Director. General e-mail, tesol@tesol.edu. Web, www.tesol.edu.*

Promotes scholarship and provides information on instruction and research in the teaching of English to speakers of other languages. Offers placement service.

Research

AGENCIES

Education Dept., *Educational Research and Improvement, 555 New Jersey Ave. N.W., #600 20208; (202) 219-1385. Fax, (202) 219-1402. C. Kent McGuire, Assistant Secretary. Library, (202) 401-2199. Toll-free education statistics and trends, (800) 424-1616. Web, www.ed.gov/NLE.*

Gathers, analyzes, and disseminates information, statistics, and research findings on the conditions and practices of American education. Supports nationally significant model projects, including the National Assessment of Educational Progress (the Nation's Report Card), a survey of the knowledge, skills, understanding, and attitudes of nine, thirteen, and seventeen year olds.

Education Dept., *National Center for Education Statistics, 555 New Jersey Ave. N.W., #400 20208-5574; (202) 219-1828. Fax, (202) 219-1736. Lauress L. Wise II, Commissioner (Nominee). Information, (800) 424-1616. Web, www.ed.gov/NCES.*

Gathers, analyzes, synthesizes, and disseminates qualitative and quantitative data on the characteristics and effectiveness of American education. Helps state and local education agencies improve statistical gathering and processing methods.

Education Dept., *National Institute on Student Achievement, Curriculum, and Assessment, 555 New Jersey Ave. N.W., #510 20208-5573; (202) 219-2079. Fax, (202) 219-2135. Joseph Conaty, Director. Web, www.ed.gov.*

Supports fundamental research at every institutional level of education on topics such as the processes of teaching and learning; school organization and improvement; curriculum; and factors that contribute to excellence in education.

Education Dept., *National Library of Education, 400 Maryland Ave. S.W. 20202; (202) 205-5015. Fax, (202) 401-0547. Blane Dessy, Director. Information, (800) 424-1616. ED Pubs, (877) 4ED-PUBS. General e-mail, library@inet.ed.gov. Web, www.ed.gov/NLE.*

Dedicated to presenting information on education to teachers, students, parents, and other interested parties. Houses all publications produced or funded by the Education Dept., including Educational Resources Information Center (ERIC) materials. Provides information and answers questions on education statistics and research. Operates the ED Pubs program, which provides to the public more than 1,200 department publications, including books, brochures, and posters.

Education Dept., *Reform Assistance and Dissemination, 555 New Jersey Ave. N.W., #500 20208-5572; (202) 219-2164. Fax, (202) 219-2106. Peirce A. Hammond, Director. Web, www.ed.gov.*

Supports comprehensive education reform by linking teachers, parents, administrators, and policymakers with information from education research, statistics, and practice. Provides technical and financial assistance for development and demonstration programs; supports applied research that assists states and local school districts.

NONPROFIT

Academy for Educational Development, *1825 Connecticut Ave. N.W., #900 20009; (202) 884-8000. Fax, (202) 884-8400. Stephen F. Moseley, President. General e-mail, admin@aed.org. Web, www.aed.org.*

Conducts studies on domestic and international education, on a contract basis. Interests include finance; management of educational institutions; application of communications technology to health education, agricultural extension, and other development problems; exchange of information; and use of telecommunications for social services. Operates international exchange programs.

American Educational Research Assn., *1230 17th St. N.W. 20036; (202) 223-9485. Fax, (202) 775-1824. William J. Russell, Executive Officer. Web, www.aera.net.*

Membership: educational researchers affiliated with universities and colleges, school systems, and federal and state agencies. Publishes original research in education; sponsors publication of reference works in educational research; conducts continuing education programs; studies status of women and minorities in the education field.

Council on Governmental Relations, *1200 New York Ave. N.W., #320 20005; (202) 289-6655. Fax, (202) 289-6698. Milton Goldberg, President. Web, www.cogr.edu.*

Membership: research universities maintaining federally supported programs. Advises members and makes recommendations to government agencies regarding policies and regulations affecting university research.

Ethics and Public Policy Center, *Education and Society Program, 1015 15th St. N.W., #900 20005; (202) 682-1200. Fax, (202) 408-0632. Elliott Abrams, President. General e-mail, ethics@eppc.org. Web, www.eppc.org.*

Conducts research and holds conferences on the role of formal education and morality in teaching facts, ideas, attitudes, and values.

National Assn. of Independent Colleges and Universities, *Research and Policy, 1025 Connecticut Ave. N.W., #700 20036; (202) 785-8866. Fax, (202) 835-0003. Frank J. Balz, Vice President.*

Conducts research on national attitudes and policies concerning independent higher education; surveys student aid programs and federal tax policies affecting institutional financing; acts as a clearinghouse for state associations.

National Education Knowledge Industry Assn., *1718 Connecticut Ave. N.W., #700 20009-1162; (202) 518-0847. Fax, (202) 785-3849. C. Todd Jones, President. Web, www.nekia.org.*

Membership: regional educational laboratories and university-based educational research and development organizations. Serves as a clearinghouse for information on research conducted by members on various education issues. Formerly the Council for Educational Development and Research.

National Research Council, *Board on International Comparative Studies in Education, 2101 Constitution Ave. N.W., HA 450 20418; (202) 334-3010. Fax, (202) 334-2210. Colette Chabbot, Director. Web, www2.nas.edu/delhp/216a.html.*

Helps plan and implement U.S. participation in comparative international research in education. Interests include the scope of specific projects, funding, and the supply and quality of U.S. statistics for use in research.

Rand Corporation, *Education and Human Resources Program, 1333 H St. N.W., #800 20005; (202) 296-5000. Fax, (202) 296-7960. Bruce Hoffman, Director. Web, www.rand.org.*

Research organization partially funded by federal agencies. Conducts research on education policy.

See also American Institutes for Research (p. 618); Institute for Educational Leadership (p. 176)

🔲 LIBRARIES AND EDUCATIONAL MEDIA

See also Internet and Related Technologies (chap. 4)

AGENCIES

Institute of Museum and Library Services, *Library Services, 1100 Pennsylvania Ave. N.W., #802 20506; (202) 606-8536. Fax, (202) 606-8591. Elizabeth Sywetz, Deputy Director.*

Awards federal grants to support public, academic, research, school, and special libraries. Promotes access to information through electronic networks, links between libraries, and services to individuals having difficulty using a library. Provides funding for improved library services to native American tribal communities, Alaska native villages, and native Hawaiian library users.

National Commission on Libraries and Information Science, *1110 Vermont Ave. N.W., #820 20005-3552; (202) 606-9200. Fax, (202) 606-9203. Jeanne Hurley Simon, Chair; Martha Gould, Vice Chair. Web, www.nclis.gov.*

Advises Congress and the president on national and international information and library policy issues;

works with other agencies, the private sector, libraries, and information networks to improve access to library and information resources for all Americans, including the elderly, disadvantaged, illiterate, and geographically isolated; promotes effective local use of information generated by the federal government.

National Endowment for the Humanities *(National Foundation on the Arts and the Humanities), Public Programs and Enterprise, 1100 Pennsylvania Ave. N.W., #426 20506; (202) 606-8305. Fax, (202) 606-8557. Thomas C. Phelps, Program Officer. General e-mail, info@ neh.fed.us.*

Awards grants to libraries for projects that enhance public appreciation and understanding of the humanities through books and other resources in American library collections. Projects include conferences, exhibitions, essays, and lecture series.

Smithsonian Institution, *Central Reference and Loan Services, 10th St. and Constitution Ave. N.W., MRC 154 20560; (202) 357-2139. Fax, (202) 786-2443. Martin A. Smith, Chief Librarian. TTY, (202) 357-2328.*

Maintains collection of general reference, biographical, and interdisciplinary materials; serves as an information resource on institution libraries.

CONGRESS

House Administration Committee, *1309 LHOB 20515; (202) 225-8281. Fax, (202) 225-9957. Rep. Bill Thomas, R-Calif., Chair; Cathy Abernathy, Staff Director. Web, www.house.gov/cha.*

Oversight of and jurisdiction over legislation on the Library of Congress.

House Appropriations Committee, *Subcommittee on Legislative Branch, H147 CAP 20515; (202) 225-5338. Rep. Charles H. Taylor, R-N.C., Chair; Edward E. Lombard, Staff Assistant. Web, www.house.gov/appropriations.*

Jurisdiction over legislation to appropriate funds for the Library of Congress, including the Congressional Research Service.

House Education and the Workforce Committee, *Subcommittee on Postsecondary Education, Training, and Life-Long Learning, 2181 RHOB 20515; (202) 225-4527. Fax, (202) 225-9571. Rep. Howard P. "Buck" McKeon, R-Calif., Chair; Kevin D. Talley, Staff Director. Web, www.house.gov/ed_workforce.*

Jurisdiction over legislation on libraries, including the Library Services and Construction Act.

Joint Committee on the Library of Congress, *SR-305 20510; (202) 224-6352. Sen. Ted Stevens, R-Alaska, Chair; Ed Edens, Staff Contact.*

Studies and makes recommendations on legislation dealing with the Library of Congress.

Library of Congress, *101 Independence Ave. S.E. 20540-1000; (202) 707-5205. Fax, (202) 707-1714. James H. Billington, Librarian of Congress. Information, (202) 707-2905. Web, www.loc.gov.*

Main book repository of the United States.

Library of Congress, *Center for the Book, 101 Independence Ave. S.E., #650 20540-4920; (202) 707-5221. Fax, (202) 707-0269. John Y. Cole, Director. Web, www.loc.gov/ loc/cfbook.*

Seeks to broaden public appreciation of books, reading, and libraries; sponsors lectures and conferences on the educational and cultural role of the book worldwide, including the history of books and printing, television and the printed word, and the publishing and production of books; cooperates with state centers and with other organizations. Projects and programs are privately funded except for basic administrative support from the Library of Congress.

Library of Congress, *Federal Library and Information Center Committee, 101 Independence Ave. S.E., #217 20540-4935; (202) 707-4800. Fax, (202) 707-4818. Susan Tarr, Executive Director. General e-mail, flicc@loc.gov. Web, locweb.loc.gov/flicc.*

Membership: one representative from each major federal agency, one representative each from the Library of Congress and the national libraries of medicine and agriculture, and one representative from each of the major Federal Information Centers. Coordinates planning, development, operations, and activities among federal libraries.

Library of Congress, *Preservation, 101 Independence Ave. S.E., #G21 20540; (202) 707-5213. Fax, (202) 707-3434. Diane N. Kresh, Director. General e-mail, preserve@loc.gov.*

Responsible for preserving book and paper materials in the library's collections.

Senate Appropriations Committee, *Subcommittee on Legislative Branch, S125 CAP 20510; (202) 224-8921. Sen. Robert F. Bennett, R-Utah, Chair; Christine Ciccone, Staff Director. Web, appropriations.senate.gov/leg.*

Jurisdiction over legislation to appropriate funds for the Library of Congress, including the Congressional Research Service.

LIBRARY OF CONGRESS DIVISIONS AND PROGRAMS

African and Middle Eastern Division, (202) 707-7937

American Folklife Center, (202) 707-5510

American Memory Project, (202) 707-6233

Asian Division, (202) 707-5420

Cataloging Distribution Service, (202) 707-9797

The Center for the Book, (202) 707-5221

Children's Literature Center, (202) 707-5535

Computer Catalog Center, (202) 707-3370

Concert Office, (202) 707-5502

Copyright Office, (202) 707-3000

European Division, (202) 707-5414

Federal Library and Information Center Committee, (202) 707-4800

Geography and Map Division, (202) 707-8530

Hispanic Division, (202) 707-5400

Humanities and Social Science Division, (202) 707-5530

Interlibrary Loans, (202) 707-5444

Interpretative Programs, (202) 707-5223

Law Library, (202) 707-5065

Law Library Reading Room, (202) 707-5079

Local History and Genealogy Reading Room, (202) 707-5537

Manuscript Division, (202) 707-5383

Mary Pickford Theater, (202) 707-5677

Microform Reading Room, (202) 707-5471

Motion Picture, Broadcasting, and Recorded Sound Division, (202) 707-5840

Music Division, (202) 707-5503

National Library Service for the Blind and Physically Handicapped, (202) 707-5104

Photoduplication Service, (202) 707-5640

Poetry and Literature Center, (202) 707-5394

Preservation Office, (202) 707-5213

Prints and Photographs Division, (202) 707-5836

Rare Book and Special Collections Division, (202) 707-5434

Science, Technology, and Business Division, (202) 707-5664

Serial and Government Publications Division, (202) 707-5647

Senate Health, Education, Labor, and Pensions Committee, *SD-428 20510; (202) 224-5375. Fax, (202) 228-5044. Sen. James M. Jeffords, R-Vt., Chair; Mark Powden, Staff Director. TTY, (202) 224-1975. Web, labor.senate.gov.*

Jurisdiction over legislation on libraries, including the Library Services and Construction Act.

Senate Rules and Administration Committee, *SR-305 20510; (202) 224-6352. Fax, (202) 224-3036. Sen. Mitch McConnell, R-Ky., Chair; Tamara Somerville, Staff Director. Web, rules.senate.gov.*

Oversight of and jurisdiction over legislation on the Library of Congress.

NONPROFIT

American Chemical Society, *Project Bookshare, 1155 16th St. N.W. 20036; (202) 872-6285. Fax, (202) 872-6317. J. C. Torio, Coordinator. Web, www.acs.org.*

Collects used books; distributes the books to tribal libraries or small, low-income high schools in the United States and other educational institutions in developing countries.

American Library Assn., *Washington Office, 1301 Pennsylvania Ave. N.W., #403 20004; (202) 628-8410. Fax, (202) 628-8419. Emily Sheketoff, Executive Director. General e-mail, alawash@alawash.org. Web, www.ala.org.*

Educational organization of librarians, trustees, and educators. Washington office monitors legislation and regulations on libraries and information science. (Headquarters in Chicago.)

American Society for Information Science, *8720 Georgia Ave., #501, Silver Spring, MD 20910; (301) 495-0900. Fax, (301) 495-0810. Richard Hill, Executive Director. General e-mail, asis@asis.org. Web, www.asis.org.*

Membership: librarians, computer scientists, management specialists, behavioral scientists, engineers, and individuals concerned with access to information. Conducts research and educational programs.

Assn. for Information and Image Management, *1100 Wayne Ave., #1100, Silver Spring, MD 20910; (301) 587-8202. Fax, (301) 587-2711. John Mancini, President. General e-mail, aiim@aiim.org. Web, www.aiim.org.*

Membership: manufacturers and users of image-based information systems. Works to advance the

LIBRARIES AT FEDERAL AGENCIES

DEPARTMENTS

Agriculture, (301) 504-6778

Commerce, (202) 482-5511

Defense, (703) 697-4301

Education, (202) 205-5019

Energy, (202) 586-9534

Health and Human Services, (202) 619-0190

Housing and Urban Development, (202) 708-3728

Interior, (202) 208-5815

Justice, (202) 514-3775

Labor, (202) 219-6992

State, (202) 647-1099

Transportation, (202) 366-0746

Treasury, (202) 622-0990

Veterans Affairs, (202) 273-8523

  Law (202) 273-6558

AGENCIES

Agency for International Development, (202) 712-0579

Commission on Civil Rights, (202) 376-8110

Commodity Futures Trading Commission, (202) 418-5255

Consumer Product Safety Commission, (301) 504-0044

Drug Enforcement Administration, (202) 307-8932

Environmental Protection Agency, (202) 260-5922

Equal Employment Opportunity Commission, (202) 663-4630

Export-Import Bank, (202) 565-3980

Farm Credit Administration, (703) 883-4296

Federal Communications Commission, (202) 418-0450

Federal Deposit Insurance Corporation, (202) 898-3631

Federal Election Commission, (202) 694-1600

Federal Emergency Management Agency, (202) 646-3771

Federal Labor Relation Authority, (202) 482-6552

Federal Maritime Commission, (202) 523-5762

Federal Reserve System, (202) 452-3332

Federal Trade Commission, (202) 326-2395

General Accounting Office

  Law (202) 512-2585

  Technical (202) 512-5180

General Services Administration, (202) 501-0788

International Bank for Reconstruction and Development (World Bank) and International Monetary Fund, (202) 623-7054

Merit Systems Protection Board, (202) 653-7132

National Aeronautics and Space Administration, (202) 358-0168

National Credit Union Administration, (703) 518-6540

National Endowment for the Arts, (202) 682-5485

National Endowment for the Humanities, (202) 606-8244

National Labor Relations Board, (202) 273-3720

National Library of Medicine, (301) 496-5501

National Science Foundation, (703) 306-0658

Nuclear Regulatory Commission, (301) 415-5610

Occupational Safety and Health Review Commission, (202) 606-5100, ext. 261

Office of Personnel Management, (202) 606-1381

Office of Thrift Supervision (202) 906-6470

Overseas Private Investment Corporation, (202) 336-8565

Peace Corps, (202) 692-2635

Postal Rate Commission, (202) 789-6877

Public Health Library, (301) 443-2673

Securities and Exchange Commission, (202) 942-7090

Small Business Administration

  Main Library (202) 205-7033

  Law (202) 205-6849

Smithsonian Institution, (202) 357-2139

Social Security Administration

  Main Library (410) 965-6113

  Law (410) 965-6108

U.S. International Trade Commission

  Main Library (202) 205-2630

  Law (202) 205-3287

U.S. Postal Service, (202) 268-2904

profession of information management; develops standards on such technologies as microfilm and electronic imaging. Library open to the public.

Assn. of Research Libraries, *21 Dupont Circle N.W., #800 20036; (202) 296-2296. Fax, (202) 872-0884. Duane Webster, Executive Director. Web, www.arl.org.*

Membership: major research libraries, mainly at universities, in the United States and Canada. Interests include development of library resources in all formats, subjects, and languages; computer information systems and other bibliographic tools; management of research libraries; preservation of library materials; worldwide information policy; and publishing and scholarly communication.

Council on Library and Information Resources, *1755 Massachusetts Ave. N.W., #500 20036-2124; (202) 939-4750. Fax, (202) 939-4765. Deanna B. Marcum, President. General e-mail, info@clir.org. Web, www.clir.org.*

Acts on behalf of the nation's libraries, archives, and universities to develop and encourage collaborative strategies for preserving the nation's intellectual heritage and strengthening its information system.

Gallaudet University, *Library, 800 Florida Ave. N.E. 20002; (202) 651-5231. Fax, (202) 651-5213. John Day, Librarian. Information, (202) 651-5217. Archives, (202) 651-5209. Some numbers require state relay service for voice transmission.*

Maintains extensive special collection on deafness, including archival materials relating to deaf cultural history and Gallaudet University.

Information Industry Assn., *1730 M St. N.W., #700 20036-4510; (202) 452-1600. Fax, (202) 223-8756. Ken Walsh, President. Web, www.infoindustry.org.*

Membership: companies involved in creating, distributing, and using information products, services, and technologies. Helps formulate global business strategies; interests include telecommunications, government procurement, taxation, intellectual property rights, and privacy. Monitors legislation and regulations.

International Communications Industries Assn., *11242 Waples Mill Rd., #200, Fairfax, VA 22030; (703) 273-7200. Fax, (703) 278-8082. Walter Blackwell, Executive Director. Information, (800) 659-7469. General e-mail, icia@icia.org. Web, www.icia.org.*

Membership: manufacturers, dealers, and specialists in educational communications products. Provides educators with information on federal funding for audio-visual, video, and computer equipment and materials; monitors trends in educational technology; conducts

educational software conference on microcomputers and miniaturization.

Kidsnet, *6856 Eastern Ave. N.W., #208 20012; (202) 291-1400. Fax, (202) 882-7315. Karen W. Jaffe, Executive Director. General e-mail, kidsnet@aol.com. Web, www.kidsnet.org.*

Computerized clearinghouse that provides information about audio, video, radio, multimedia, and television programming for preschool through high school. Publishes study and media guides for classroom use. Information available by subscription and electronically.

Society for Imaging Science and Technology, *7003 Kilworth Lane, Springfield, VA 22151; (703) 642-9090. Fax, (703) 642-9094. Calva A. Leonard, Executive Director. General e-mail, info@imaging.org. Web, www.imaging.org.*

Membership: individuals and companies worldwide in fields of imaging science and technology, including photofinishing, nonimpact printing, electronic imaging, silver halide, image preservation, and hybrid imaging systems. Gathers and disseminates technical information; fosters professional development.

Special Libraries Assn., *1700 18th St. N.W. 20009-2514; (202) 234-4700. Fax, (202) 265-9317. David R. Bender, Executive Director. General e-mail, sla@sla.org. Web, www.sla.org.*

Membership: librarians and information managers serving institutions that use or produce information in specialized areas, including business, engineering, law, the arts and sciences, government, museums, and universities. Conducts professional development programs and research projects; provides a consultation service; sponsors International Special Libraries Day. Monitors legislation and regulations.

POSTSECONDARY EDUCATION

See also Professional Interests and Benefits (this chapter); Health Professions (chap. 11); Military Education and Training (chap. 15)

AGENCIES

Education Dept., *Fund for the Improvement of Postsecondary Education, 1900 K St. N.W., 8th Floor 20006; (202) 502-7509. Fax, (202) 502-7877. Sandra Newkirk, Director (Acting). Web, www.ed.gov/offices/OPE/FIPSE.*

Works to improve postsecondary education by administering grant competitions, including the Com-

COLLEGES AND UNIVERSITIES IN WASHINGTON

Agriculture Dept. Graduate School, 600 Maryland Ave. S.W. 20024

Switchboard: (202) 314-3320

Director: Philip Hudson, (202) 720-2077

American University, 4400 Massachusetts Ave. N.W. 20016

Switchboard: (202) 885-1000

President: Benjamin Ladner, (202) 885-2121

Catholic University, 620 Michigan Ave. N.E. 20064

Switchboard: (202) 319-5000

President: Rev. David M. O'Connell C.M., (202) 319-5100

Columbia Union College, 7600 Flower Ave., Takoma Park, MD 20912

Switchboard: (301) 891-4000

President: Charles Scriven, (301) 891-4128

Gallaudet University, 800 Florida Ave. N.E. 20002

Switchboard: (202) 651-5000 (voice and TDD)

President: I. King Jordan, (202) 651-5005 (voice and TDD)

George Mason University, 4400 University Dr., Fairfax, VA 22030

Switchboard: (703) 993-1000

President: Alan G. Merton, (703) 993-8700

George Washington University, 2121 Eye St. N.W. 20052

Switchboard: (202) 994-1000

President: Stephen Joel Trachtenberg, (202) 994-6500

Georgetown University, 37th and O Sts. N.W. 20057

Switchboard: (202) 687-0100

President: Leo O'Donovan, (202) 687-4134

Howard University, 2400 6th St. N.W. 20059

Switchboard: (202) 806-6100

President: H. Patrick Swygert, (202) 806-2500

Marymount University, 2807 N. Glebe Rd., Arlington, VA 22207

Switchboard: (703) 522-5600

President: Sister Eymard Gallagher, (703) 284-1598

Mount Vernon College, 2100 Foxhall Rd. N.W. 20007

Switchboard: (202) 625-0400

Executive Dean: Grae Baxter, (202) 625-4600

Paul H. Nitze School of Advanced International Studies (Johns Hopkins University), 1740 Massachusetts Ave. N.W. 20036

Switchboard: (202) 663-5600

Dean: Paul D. Wolfowitz, (202) 663-5624

Protestant Episcopal Theological Seminary, 3737 Seminary Rd., Alexandria, VA 22304

Switchboard: (703) 370-6600

Dean: Martha J. Horne, (703) 461-1701

Trinity College, 125 Michigan Ave. N.E. 20017

Switchboard: (202) 884-9000

President: Patricia McGuire, (202) 884-9050

University of Maryland, Rt. 1, College Park Campus, College Park, MD 20742

Switchboard: (301) 405-1000

President: C. D. Mote Jr., (301) 405-5803

University of the District of Columbia, 4200 Connecticut Ave. N.W. 20008

Switchboard: (202) 274-5000

President: Julius F. Nimmons Jr., (202) 274-5100

University of Virginia/Virginia Tech Northern Virginia Center, 7054 Haycock Rd., Falls Church, VA 22043

UVA Switchboard: (703) 536-1100

UVA Director: Steve Gladis, (703) 536-1100

VT Switchboard: (703) 538-8324

VT Director: Elizabeth Holford (interim), (703) 538-8310

---

prehensive Program for improvements in postsecondary education; the European Community/United States (ECUS) Joint Consortia for Cooperation in Higher Education and Vocational Education; the Program for North American Mobility in Higher Education; and the Disseminating Proven Reforms Program.

Education Dept., *Postsecondary Education, 1900 K St. N.W., #7113 20006; (202) 502-7714. Fax, (202) 502-7677. A. Lee Fritschler, Assistant Secretary. Information, (202) 502-7750. TTY, (800) 848-0978. Web, www.ed.gov.*

Administers federal assistance programs for public and private postsecondary institutions; provides financial support for faculty development, construction of facilities, and improvement of graduate, continuing, cooperative, and international education; awards grants and loans for financial assistance to eligible students.

CONGRESS

House Education and the Workforce Committee, *Subcommittee on Postsecondary Education, Training, and Life-Long Learning, 2181 RHOB 20515; (202) 225-*

4527. Fax, (202) 225-9571. Rep. Howard P. "Buck" McKeon, R-Calif., Chair; Kevin D. Talley, Staff Director. Web, www.house.gov/ed_workforce.

Jurisdiction over legislation on postsecondary education, including community and junior colleges, the Construction Loan Program, construction of school facilities, and financial aid, and over legislation barring discrimination in postsecondary education.

Senate Banking, Housing, and Urban Affairs Committee, SD-534 20510; (202) 224-7391. Fax, (202) 224-5137. Sen. Phil Gramm, R-Texas, Chair; Wayne A. Abernathy, Staff Director. Web, banking.senate.gov.

Oversees government-sponsored enterprises, including the Student Loan Marketing Assn. and the College Construction Loan Insurance Assn., with regard to the financial risk posed to the federal government.

Senate Health, Education, Labor, and Pensions Committee, SD-428 20510; (202) 224-5375. Fax, (202) 228-5044. Sen. James M. Jeffords, R-Vt., Chair; Mark Powden, Staff Director. TTY, (202) 224-1975. Web, labor. senate.gov.

Jurisdiction over legislation on postsecondary education, including community and junior colleges, the Construction Loan Program, construction of school facilities, and financial aid, and over legislation barring discrimination in postsecondary education, including the Women's Educational Equity Act of 1974 as it applies to postsecondary education.

NONPROFIT

ACT (American College Testing), *Washington Office, 1 Dupont Circle N.W., #340 20036-1170; (202) 223-2318. Fax, (202) 293-2223. Daniel Minchew, Director. Web, www.act.org.*

Administers American College Test (ACT) entrance examination for colleges and universities. Provides colleges and universities with testing, counseling, research, and student aid processing services. (Headquarters in Iowa City, Iowa.)

American Assn. for Higher Education, *1 Dupont Circle N.W., #360 20036; (202) 293-6440. Fax, (202) 293-0073. Margaret Miller, President. Web, www.aahe.org.*

Membership: college and university educators, students, public officials, and others interested in postsecondary education. Evaluates issues in higher education; interests include statewide and institutional assessment, school-college collaboration, improvement of teaching and learning, and student community service. Conducts studies, conferences, and an annual convention.

American Assn. of Colleges of Pharmacy, *1426 Prince St., Alexandria, VA 22314-2841; (703) 739-2330. Fax, (703) 836-8982. Richard Penna, Executive Vice President. General e-mail, pthompson@aacp.org. Web, www.aacp.org.*

Represents and advocates for pharmacists in the academic community. Conducts programs and activities in cooperation with other national health and higher education associations.

American Assn. of Collegiate Registrars and Admissions Officers, *1 Dupont Circle N.W., #520 20036-1135; (202) 293-9161. Fax, (202) 872-8857. Jerry Sullivan, Executive Director. General e-mail, info@aacrao. com. Web, www.aacrao.com.*

Membership: degree-granting postsecondary institutions, government agencies, higher education coordinating boards, private education organizations, and education-oriented businesses. Promotes higher education and contributes to the professional development of members working in admissions, enrollment management, financial aid, institutional research, records, and registration.

American Assn. of Community Colleges, *1 Dupont Circle N.W., #410 20036-1176; (202) 728-0200. Fax, (202) 223-9390. David Pierce, President. Web, www.aacc.nche.edu.*

Membership: accredited, two-year community technical and junior colleges, corporate foundations, international associates, and institutional affiliates. Studies include policies for lifelong education, workforce training programs and partnerships, international curricula, enrollment trends, and cooperative programs with public schools and communities.

American Assn. of State Colleges and Universities, *1307 New York Ave. N.W., 5th Floor 20005; (202) 293-7070. Fax, (202) 296-5819. Constantine W. Curris, President. Web, www.aascu.org.*

Membership: presidents and chancellors of state colleges and universities. Promotes equity in education; fosters information exchange among members; interests include minority participation in higher education, student financial aid, international education programs, academic affairs, and teacher education. Monitors legislation and regulations.

American Assn. of University Professors, *1012 14th St. N.W., #500 20005; (202) 737-5900. Fax, (202) 737-5526. Mary Burgan, General Secretary. Information, (800) 424-2973. General e-mail, aaup@aaup.org. Web, www. aaup.org.*

Membership: college and university faculty members. Defends faculties' academic freedom and tenure; advocates collegial governance; assists in the development of policies ensuring due process. Conducts workshops and education programs. Monitors legislation and regulations.

American Conference of Academic Deans, *1818 R St. N.W. 20009; (202) 387-3760. Fax, (202) 265-9532. Carol Geary Schneider, President.*

Membership: academic deans of two- and four-year accredited colleges, universities, and community colleges (private and public). Fosters information exchange among members on college curricular and administrative issues.

American Council of Trustees and Alumni, *1776 M St. N.W., #800 20036; (202) 467-6787. Fax, (202) 467-6784. Lynne V. Cheney, Chair; Jerry L. Martin, President. General e-mail, naf@naf.org. Web, www.naf.org.*

Membership: college and university alumni and trustees interested in promoting academic freedom and excellence. Seeks to help alumni and trustees direct their financial contributions to programs that will raise educational standards at their alma maters. Promotes the role of alumni and trustees in shaping higher education policies.

American Council on Education, *1 Dupont Circle N.W., #800 20036-1193; (202) 939-9300. Fax, (202) 833-4760. Stanley O. Ikenberry, President. Library, (202) 939-9405. Press, (202) 939-9365. Web, www.acenet.edu.*

Membership: colleges, universities, education associations, students with disabilities, and businesses. Conducts and publishes research; maintains offices dealing with government relations, women and minorities in higher education, management of higher education institutions, adult learning and educational credentials (academic credit for nontraditional learning, especially in the armed forces), leadership development, and international education. Library open to the public by appointment.

Assn. for Supervision and Curriculum Development, *1703 N. Beauregard St., Alexandria, VA 22311-1714; (703) 578-9600. Fax, (703) 575-5400. Gene R. Carter, Executive Director. Information, (800) 933-2723. General e-mail, member@ascd.org. Web, www.ascd.org.*

Membership: teachers, supervisors, directors of instruction, school principals (kindergarten through secondary), university and college faculty, and individuals interested in curriculum development. Sponsors institutes and conferences. Monitors legislation and regulations.

Assn. of American Colleges and Universities, *1818 R St. N.W. 20009; (202) 387-3760. Fax, (202) 265-9532. Carol Geary Schneider, President. Web, www.aacu-edu.org.*

Membership: public and private colleges, universities, and postsecondary consortia. Works to develop effective academic programs and improve undergraduate curricula and services. Seeks to encourage, enhance, and support the development of broadly based intellectual skills through the study of liberal arts and sciences.

Assn. of American Law Schools, *1201 Connecticut Ave. N.W., #800 20036; (202) 296-8851. Fax, (202) 296-8869. Carl C. Monk, Executive Director. Web, www.aals.org.*

Membership: schools of law, subject to approval by association. Represents member organizations before federal government and private agencies; evaluates member institutions; conducts workshops on the teaching of law; assists law schools with faculty recruitment; publishes faculty placement bulletin and annual directory of law teachers.

Assn. of American Universities, *1200 New York Ave. N.W., #550 20005; (202) 408-7500. Fax, (202) 408-8184. Nils Hasselmo, President. Web, www.tulane.edu/~aau.*

Membership: public and private universities with emphasis on graduate and professional education and research. Fosters information exchange among presidents of member institutions.

Assn. of Catholic Colleges and Universities, *1 Dupont Circle N.W., #650 20036; (202) 457-0650. Fax, (202) 728-0977. Monika K. Hellwig, Executive Director. General e-mail, accu@accunet.org. Web, www.accunet.org.*

Membership: regionally accredited Catholic colleges and universities and individuals interested in Catholic higher education. Acts as a clearinghouse for information on Catholic institutions of higher education. (Affiliated with the National Catholic Educational Assn.)

Assn. of Community College Trustees, *1740 N St. N.W. 20036; (202) 775-4667. Fax, (202) 223-1297. Ray Taylor, President. Web, www.acct.org.*

Provides members of community college governing boards with training in educational programs. Monitors federal education programs.

Assn. of Governing Boards of Universities and Colleges, *1 Dupont Circle N.W., #400 20036-1190; (202) 296-8400. Fax, (202) 223-7053. Richard T. Ingram, President. Web, www.agb.org.*

Membership: presidents, boards of trustees, regents, commissions, and other groups governing colleges, universities, and institutionally related foundations. Interests include the relationship between the president and board of trustees and other subjects relating to governance. Zwingle Information Center open to the public.

Assn. of Higher Education Facilities Officers, *1643 Prince St., Alexandria, VA 22314-2818; (703) 684-1446. Fax, (703) 549-2772. E. Lander Medlin, Executive Vice President. General e-mail, info@appa.org. Web, www.appa. org.*

Membership: professionals involved in the administration, maintenance, planning, and development of buildings and facilities used by colleges and universities. Interests include maintenance and upkeep of housing facilities. Provides information on campus energy management programs and campus accessibility for people with disabilities.

Assn. of Jesuit Colleges and Universities, *1 Dupont Circle N.W., #405 20036-1136; (202) 862-9893. Fax, (202) 862-8523. Charles L. Currie (SJ), President. General e-mail, blkrobe@aol.com. Web, www.AJCUnet.edu.*

Membership: American Jesuit colleges and universities. Monitors government regulatory and policy-making activities affecting higher education. Publishes directory of Jesuit colleges, universities, and high schools and monthly report on the state of higher education. Promotes international cooperation among Jesuit higher education institutions.

Business–Higher Education Forum, *1 Dupont Circle N.W., #800 20036; (202) 939-9345. Fax, (202) 833-4723. Judith Irwin, Managing Director. General e-mail, bhef@ ace.nche.edu. Web, www.bhef.com.*

Membership: chief executive officers of major corporations, colleges, and universities. Promotes cooperation between businesses and higher educational institutions. Interests include international economic competitiveness, education and training, research and development, science and technology, and global interdependence.

Career College Assn., *10 G St. N.E., #750 20002-4213; (202) 336-6700. Fax, (202) 336-6828. Nick Glakas, President. General e-mail, cca@career.org. Web, www.career.org.*

Membership: private postsecondary colleges and career schools in the United States. Works to expand the accessibility of postsecondary career education and to improve the quality of education offered by member schools.

Coalition for Christian Colleges and Universities, *321 8th St. N.E. 20002; (202) 546-8713. Fax, (202) 546-8913. Robert Andringa, President. General e-mail, council@cccu.org. Web, www.cccu.org.*

Membership: accredited four-year Christian liberal arts colleges. Offers faculty development conferences on faith and the academic disciplines. Coordinates annual gathering of college administrators. Sponsors intership/

seminar programs for students at member colleges. Interests include religious and educational freedom.

College and University Personnel Assn., *1233 20th St. N.W., #301 20036-1250; (202) 429-0311. Fax, (202) 429-0149. Susan Jurow, Executive Director. Web, www. cupa.org.*

Membership: college and university human resource administrators. Conducts seminars and workshops; responds to inquiries on human resource administration. Monitors legislation and regulations.

College Board, *Communications and Government Relations, Washington Office, 1233 20th St. N.W., #600 20036-2304; (202) 822-5900. Fax, (202) 822-5920. Lezli Baskerville, Vice President. Web, www.collegeboard.org.*

Membership: colleges and universities, secondary schools, school systems, and education associations. Provides direct student support programs and professional development for educators; conducts policy analysis and research; and advocates public policy positions that support educational excellence and promote student access to higher education. Library open to the public. (Headquarters in New York.)

Council for Resource Development, *1 Dupont Circle N.W., #410 20036-1176; (202) 822-0750. Fax, (202) 822-5014. Joy Rafey, Executive Director; Mike Gaudette, President. Web, www.slcc.edu/crd.*

Membership: college presidents, administrators, fundraisers, grantwriters, and development officers at two-year colleges. Educates members on how to secure resources for their institution; conducts workshops and training programs. Monitors legislation and regulations. (Affiliated with the American Assn. of Community Colleges.)

Council of Graduate Schools, *1 Dupont Circle N.W., #430 20036-1173; (202) 223-3791. Fax, (202) 331-7157. Debra Stewart, President. Web, www.cgsnet.org.*

Membership: private and public colleges and universities with significant involvement in graduate education. Produces publications and information about graduate education; provides a forum for member schools to exchange information and ideas.

Council of Independent Colleges, *1 Dupont Circle N.W., #320 20036; (202) 466-7230. Fax, (202) 466-7238. Allen P. Splete, President. General e-mail, cic@cic.nche.edu. Web, www.cic.edu.*

Membership: private four-year liberal arts colleges. Sponsors management development institutes for college presidents and deans; conducts faculty development programs; sponsors national projects on leadership, curriculum development, and related topics. Holds workshops and produces publications.

Educational Testing Service, *State and Federal Relations, Washington Office,* *1800 K St. N.W., #900 20006; (202) 659-0616. Fax, (202) 659-8075. Patricia McAllister, Director. Web, www.ets.org.*

Administers examinations for admission to educational programs and for graduate and licensing purposes; conducts instructional programs in testing, evaluation, and research in education fields. Washington office handles government and professional relations. Fee for services. (Headquarters in Princeton, N.J.)

National Assn. for College Admission Counseling, *1631 Prince St., Alexandria, VA 22314; (703) 836-2222. Fax, (703) 836-8015. Joyce Smith, Executive Director. Web, www.nacac.com.*

Membership: high school guidance counselors, independent counselors, college and university admissions officers, and financial aid officers. Assists counselors who serve students in the college admission process. Promotes and funds research on admission counseling and on the transition from high school to college. Advocates for the rights of students in the college admission process. Sponsors national college fairs and continuing education for members.

National Assn. of College and University Attorneys, *1 Dupont Circle N.W., #620 20036; (202) 833-8390. Fax, (202) 296-8379. Sheila Trice Bell, Executive Director. General e-mail, nacua@nacua.org. Web, www.nacua.org.*

Provides information on legal developments affecting postsecondary education. Operates a clearinghouse through which attorneys on campuses are able to network with their counterparts on current legal problems.

National Assn. of College and University Business Officers, *2501 M St. N.W., #400 20037; (202) 861-2500. Fax, (202) 861-2583. James E. Morley Jr., President. Web, www.nacubo.org.*

Membership: chief business officers at higher education institutions. Provides members with information on financial management, federal regulations, and other subjects related to the business administration of universities and colleges; conducts workshops on issues such as student aid, institutional budgeting, and accounting.

National Assn. of Independent Colleges and Universities, *1025 Connecticut Ave. N.W., #700 20036-5405; (202) 785-8866. Fax, (202) 835-0003. David L. Warren, President.*

Membership: independent colleges and universities and related state associations. Counsels members on federal education programs and tax policy.

National Assn. of State Universities and Land Grant Colleges, *1307 New York Ave. N.W., #400 20005; (202) 478-6040. Fax, (202) 478-6046. C. Peter Magrath, President. Web, www.nasulgc.org.*

Membership: land grant colleges and state universities. Serves as clearinghouse on issues of public higher education.

National Assn. of Student Personnel Administrators, *1875 Connecticut Ave. N.W., #418 20009-5728; (202) 265-7500. Fax, (202) 797-1157. Gwen Dungy, Executive Director. General e-mail, office@naspa.org. Web, www.naspa.org.*

Membership: deans, student affairs administrators, faculty, and graduate students. Seeks to develop leadership and improve practices in student affairs administration. Initiates and supports programs and legislation to improve student affairs administration.

National Council of University Research Administrators, *1 Dupont Circle N.W., #220 20036; (202) 466-3894. Fax, (202) 223-5573. Kathleen Larmett, Executive Director. General e-mail, info@ncura.edu. Web, www.ncura.edu.*

Membership: individuals engaged in administering research, training, and educational programs, primarily at colleges and universities. Encourages development of effective policies and procedures in the administration of these programs.

U.S. Student Assn., *1413 K St. N.W., 9th Floor 20005; (202) 347-8772. Fax, (202) 393-5886. Kendra Fox-Davis, President. General e-mail, prs@usstudent.org. Web, www.essential.org/ussa.*

Represents postsecondary students, student government associations, and state student lobby associations. Interests include civil rights on campus and the financing of higher education. Maintains student coalitions of women, racial, ethnic, and sexual minorities. Serves as clearinghouse for information on student problems, activities, and government; holds conferences emphasizing student lobbying techniques.

Washington Higher Education Secretariat, *1 Dupont Circle N.W., #800 20036; (202) 939-9345. Fax, (202) 833-4723. Judith Irwin, Executive Secretary. Web, www.whes.org.*

Membership: national higher education associations representing the different sectors and functions in postsecondary institutions. Provides forum for discussion on national and local education issues.

Women's College Coalition, *125 Michigan Ave. N.E. 20017; (202) 234-0443. Fax, (202) 234-0445. Jadwiga S. Sebrechts, President. Web, www.womenscolleges.org.*

Membership: public and private, independent and church-related, two- and four-year women's colleges. Interests include the role of women's colleges as model institutions for educating women, gender equity issues, and retention of women in math, science, and engineering. Maintains an information clearinghouse on U.S. undergraduate women's colleges. Conducts research on gender equity issues in education and positive learning environments.

College Accreditation

Many college- or university-based and independent postsecondary education programs are accredited by member associations. See specific subject headings and associations within the chapter.

AGENCIES

Education Dept., *Accreditation and Eligibility Determination, 1990 K St. N.W. 20006; (202) 219-7011. Fax, (202) 219-7005. Karen W. Kershenstein, Division Director. Web, www.ed.gov.*

Reviews accrediting agencies and state approval agencies that seek initial or renewed recognition by the secretary; provides the National Advisory Committee on Institutional Quality and Integrity with staff support.

NONPROFIT

American Academy for Liberal Education (AALE), *1700 K St. N.W., #901 20006; (202) 452-8611. Fax, (202) 452-8620. Jeffrey Wallin, President.*

Accredits colleges and universities whose general education program in the liberal arts meets the academy's accreditation requirements. Provides support for institutions that maintain substantial liberal arts programs and which desire to raise requirements to meet AALE standards.

Council for Higher Education Accreditation, *1 Dupont Circle N.W., #510 20036-1135; (202) 955-6126. Fax, (202) 955-6129. Judith Eaton, President. General e-mail, chea@chea.org. Web, www.chea.org.*

Advocates voluntary self-regulation of colleges and universities through accreditation; coordinates research, debate, and processes that improve accreditation; mediates disputes and fosters communications among accrediting bodies and the higher education community.

Financial Aid to Students

See also Internships, Fellowships, Grants (this chapter)

AGENCIES

Education Dept., *Student Financial Assistance, 400 Maryland Ave. S.W. 20202; (202) 260-6536. Fax, (202) 708-7970. Greg Woods, Chief Operating Officer. Student Aid Information Center, (800) 433-3243. Web, www.ed.gov.*

Administers federal loan, grant, and work-study programs for postsecondary education to eligible individuals. Administers the Pell Grant Program, the Perkins Loan Program, the Stafford Student Loan Program (Guaranteed Student Loan)/PLUS Program, the College Work-Study Program, the Supplemental Loans for Students (SLS), and the Supplemental Educational Opportunity Grant Program.

NONPROFIT

Alliance to Save Student Aid, *Public Affairs, c/o American Council on Education, 1 Dupont Circle N.W., #800 20036-1193; (202) 939-9365. Fax, (202) 833-4762. Laura Wilcox, Assistant Director. General e-mail, web@ace.nche.edu. Web, www.acenet.edu.*

Membership: more than sixty organizations representing students, administrators, and faculty members from all sectors of higher education. Seeks to ensure adequate funding of federal aid programs. Monitors legislation and regulations.

College Board, *Communications and Government Relations, Washington Office, 1233 20th St. N.W., #600 20036-2304; (202) 822-5900. Fax, (202) 822-5920. Lezli Baskerville, Vice President. Web, www.collegeboard.org.*

Membership: colleges and universities, secondary schools, school systems, and education associations. Provides direct student support programs and professional development for educators; conducts policy analysis and research; and advocates public policy positions that support educational excellence and promote student access to higher education. Library open to the public. (Headquarters in New York.)

College Parents of America, *700 13th St. N.W., #950 20005; (202) 661-2170. Fax, (202) 661-2189. Richard M. Flaherty, President. Information, (888) 256-4627. Web, www.collegeparents.org.*

Provides information on savings strategies and financial aid to families with children in college. Monitors legislation and regulation on national and state levels.

Education Finance Council, *1155 15th St. N.W., #801 20005; (202) 466-8621. Fax, (202) 466-8643. William D. Hansen, Executive Director. Web, www.efc.org.*

Membership: nonprofit educational loan secondary market organizations. Works to maintain and expand student access to higher education through tax-exempt funding for loans.

National Assn. of Student Financial Aid Administrators, *1129 20th St. N.W., #400 20036; (202) 785-0453. Fax, (202) 785-1487. Dallas Martin, President. Web, www.nasfaa.org.*

Membership: more than 3,500 educational institutions, organizations, and individuals at postsecondary institutions who administer student financial aid. Works to ensure adequate funding for individuals seeking postsecondary education and to ensure proper management and administration of public and private financial aid funds.

National Council of Higher Education Loan Programs, *1100 Connecticut Ave. N.W., 12th Floor 20036; (202) 822-2106. Fax, (202) 822-2142. Brett Lief, President.*

Membership: agencies and organizations involved in making, servicing, and collecting Guaranteed Student Loans. Works with the Education Dept. to develop forms and procedures for administering the Federal Family Education Loan Program. Fosters information exchange among members.

Student Loan Marketing Assn. (Sallie Mae), *901 E St. N.W., #410 20004; (202) 969-8000. Fax, (202) 969-8030. Al Lord, President. Web, www.salliemae.com.*

Government-sponsored private corporation. Provides funds to financial and educational institutions (such as commercial banks, colleges, and universities) that make Stafford Student Loans and other educational loans administered by the Education Dept. available to students.

✏️ PRESCHOOL, ELEMENTARY, SECONDARY EDUCATION

See also Children and Families (chap. 18); Food and Nutrition (chap. 2); Museums (chap. 5); Professional Interests and Benefits (this chapter)

AGENCIES

Education Dept., *Bilingual Education and Minority Languages Affairs, 330 C St. S.W., #5086 20202-6510; (202) 205-5463. Fax, (202) 205-8737. Bouy Te, Deputy Director. Web, www.ed.gov/offices/OBEMLA.*

Administers bilingual education programs in elementary and secondary schools to help students of limited English proficiency learn the English language. The program is designed to give students of limited English proficiency better opportunities to achieve academic success and meet grade promotion and graduation requirements.

Education Dept., *Elementary and Secondary Education, 400 Maryland Ave. S.W., #3W300 20202-6100; (202) 401-0113. Fax, (202) 205-0303. Michael Cohen, Assistant Secretary. Web, www.ed.gov.*

Administers federal assistance programs for elementary and secondary education (both public and private). Program divisions are Compensatory Education (including Chapter 1 aid for disadvantaged children); School Improvement; Migrant Education; Indian Education; Impact Aid; Goals 2000; and Safe Drug-Free Schools.

Education Dept., *Even Start, 400 Maryland Ave. S.W., #3W 20202-6132; (202) 260-0826. Fax, (202) 260-7764. Patricia McKee, Coordinator, (202) 260-0991. Web, www.ed.gov.*

Develops family-centered education projects to encourage parents of economic and educationally disadvantaged families to become involved in the education of their children; helps children reach their full potential as learners and offers literacy training to parents.

Education Dept., *Impact Aid, 400 Maryland Ave. S.W., #3E105 20202-6244; (202) 260-3858. Fax, (202) 205-0088. Catherine Schagh, Director. Web, www.ed.gov.*

Provides funds for elementary and secondary educational activities to school districts in federally impacted areas (where federal activities such as military bases enlarge staff and reduce taxable property).

Education Dept., *Safe and Drug-Free Schools, 400 Maryland Ave. S.W. 20202-6123; (202) 260-3954. Fax, (202) 260-7767. William Modzeleski, Director. Web, www.ed.gov/offices/oese/sdfs.*

Develops policy for the department's drug and violence prevention initiatives for students in elementary and secondary schools and institutions of higher education. Coordinates education efforts in drug and violence prevention with those of other federal departments and agencies.

Environmental Protection Agency, *Pollution Prevention and Toxics, 401 M St. S.W., #527 East Tower 20460; (202) 260-3810. Fax, (202) 260-0575. William H. Sanders III, Director. Information, (202) 554-1404.*

Administers the Asbestos Loan and Grant Program by awarding loans and grants to needy public and private elementary and secondary schools to eliminate friable asbestos materials that pose a health threat to building occupants.

Health and Human Services Dept., *Head Start, 330 C St. S.W., #2212 20447; (202) 205-8572. Fax, (202) 260-9336. Helen Taylor, Associate Commissioner. Web, www. acf.dhhs.gov/programs/hsb/index.htm.*

Awards grants to nonprofit organizations and local governments for operating community Head Start programs (comprehensive development programs for children, ages three to five, of low-income families); manages a limited number of parent and child centers for families with children up to age three. Conducts research and manages demonstration programs, including those under the Comprehensive Child Care Development Act of 1988; administers the Child Development Associate scholarship program, which trains individuals for careers in child development, often as Head Start teachers.

National Agricultural Library *(Agriculture Dept.),* **Food and Nutrition Information Center,** *10301 Baltimore Ave., #304, Beltsville, MD 20705-2351; (301) 504-5719. Fax, (301) 504-6409. Vacant, Coordinator. General e-mail, fnic@nal.usda.gov. Web, www.nal.usda.gov/fnic.*

Serves as a resource center for school and child nutrition program personnel who need information on food service management and nutrition education. Center open to the public.

White House Commission on Presidential Scholars *(Education Dept.), 400 Maryland Ave. S.W. 20202-3500; (202) 205-0512. Fax, (202) 205-0676. Kimberly Watkins-Foote, Executive Director. Information, (202) 401-0961.*

Honorary recognition program that selects high school seniors of outstanding achievement in academics, community service, artistic ability, and leadership to receive the Presidential Scholars Award. Scholars travel to Washington for national recognition week.

CONGRESS

House Education and the Workforce Committee, *Subcommittee on Early Childhood, Youth, and Families, 2181 RHOB 20515; (202) 225-4527. Fax, (202) 225-9571. Rep. Michael N. Castle, R-Del., Chair; Kevin D. Talley, Staff Director. Web, www.house.gov/ed_workforce.*

Jurisdiction over preschool, elementary, and secondary education legislation, including impact aid legislation and food programs for children in schools.

Senate Agriculture, Nutrition, and Forestry Committee, *Subcommittee on Research, Nutrition, and General Legislation, SR-328A 20510; (202) 224-2854. Fax, (202) 224-1725. Sen. Peter G. Fitzgerald, R-Ill., Chair;*

Terry VanDoren, Legislative Assistant. Web, agriculture. senate.gov.

Jurisdiction over legislation on food programs for children in schools.

Senate Health, Education, Labor, and Pensions Committee, *SD-428 20510; (202) 224-5375. Fax, (202) 228-5044. Sen. James M. Jeffords, R-Vt., Chair; Mark Powden, Staff Director. TTY, (202) 224-1975. Web, labor. senate.gov.*

Jurisdiction over preschool, elementary, and secondary education legislation, including impact aid legislation; and legislation barring discrimination in schools. Oversight of the Follow Through Act, which aids children in making the transition from preschool to elementary grades.

NONPROFIT

American School Food Service Assn., *700 S. Washington St., #300, Alexandria, VA 22314-4787; (703) 739-3900. Fax, (703) 739-3915. Barbara Borschow, Executive Director. Information, (800) 877-8822. Web, www.asfsa.org.*

Membership: state and local food service workers and supervisors, school cafeteria managers, nutrition educators, and others interested in school food programs and child nutrition. Sponsors National School Lunch Week.

Assn. for Childhood Education International, *17904 Georgia Ave., #215, Olney, MD 20832; (301) 570-2111. Fax, (301) 570-2212. Gerald C. Odland, Executive Director. Information, (800) 423-3563. General e-mail, aceihq@aol.com. Web, www.udel.edu/bateman/acei.*

Membership: educators, parents, and professionals who work with children (infancy to adolescence). Works to promote the rights, education, and well-being of children worldwide. Holds annual conference.

Assn. for Supervision and Curriculum Development, *1703 N. Beauregard St., Alexandria, VA 22311-1714; (703) 578-9600. Fax, (703) 575-5400. Gene R. Carter, Executive Director. Information, (800) 933-2723. General e-mail, member@ascd.org. Web, www.ascd.org.*

Membership: teachers, supervisors, directors of instruction, school principals (kindergarten through secondary), university and college faculty, and individuals interested in curriculum development. Sponsors institutes and conferences. Monitors legislation and regulations.

Council for Basic Education, *1319 F St. N.W., #900 20004-1152; (202) 347-4171. Fax, (202) 347-5047. Christopher T. Cross, President. General e-mail, info@ c-b-e.org. Web, www.c-b-e.org.*

Promotes liberal arts education in elementary and secondary schools; seeks to improve liberal arts instruction of teachers and administrators; conducts workshops, seminars, and independent summer study programs for elementary and secondary school teachers; works to establish and maintain high academic standards; serves as information clearinghouse on education issues.

Council of the Great City Schools, *1301 Pennsylvania Ave. N.W., #702 20004; (202) 393-2427. Fax, (202) 393-2400. Mike Casserly, Executive Director. Web, www.cgcs.org.*

Membership: superintendents and school board members of large urban school districts. Provides research, legislative, and support services for members; interests include elementary and secondary education and school finance.

Home and School Institute, *MegaSkills Education Center, 1500 Massachusetts Ave. N.W. 20005; (202) 466-3633. Fax, (202) 833-1400. Dorothy Rich, President. Web, www.megaskillshsi.org.*

Works to improve the quality of education for children and parents by integrating the resources of the home, the school, and the community. Develops family training curricula and materials for home use, and training programs and conferences for professionals. Interests include special, bilingual, and career education; character development; and working, single, and teenage parents.

National Alliance of Business, *Education Reform, 1201 New York Ave. N.W., #700 20005-3917; (202) 289-2888. Fax, (202) 289-1303. Milton Goldberg, Executive Vice President. Web, www.nab.com.*

Encourages business leaders, government officials, and educators to work together to upgrade the educational system. Provides information on state and local education improvement initiatives; helps build relationships between academic standards and workplace requirements.

National Assessment Governing Board, *800 N. Capitol St. N.W., #825 20002-4233; (202) 357-6938. Fax, (202) 357-6945. Roy Truby, Executive Director. Web, www.nagb.org.*

Independent board of local, state, and federal officials, educators, and others appointed by the secretary of education and funded under the National Assessment of Educational Progress (NAEP) program. Sets policy for NAEP, a series of tests measuring achievements in U.S. schools since 1969.

National Assn. for College Admission Counseling, *1631 Prince St., Alexandria, VA 22314; (703) 836-2222.*

Fax, (703) 836-8015. Joyce Smith, Executive Director. Web, www.nacac.com.

Membership: high school guidance counselors, independent counselors, college and university admissions officers, and financial aid officers. Assists counselors who serve students in the college admission process. Promotes and funds research on admission counseling and on the transition from high school to college. Advocates for the rights of students in the college admission process. Sponsors national college fairs and continuing education for members.

National Assn. for the Education of Young Children, *1509 16th St. N.W. 20036-1426; (202) 232-8777. Fax, (202) 328-1846. Mark R. Ginsberg, Executive Director. Web, www.naeyc.org.*

Membership: teachers, parents, and directors of early childhood programs. Works to improve the education of and the quality of services to children from birth through age eight. Sponsors professional development opportunities for early childhood educators. Offers an accreditation program and conducts an annual conference; issues publications.

National Assn. of Elementary School Principals, *1615 Duke St., Alexandria, VA 22314-3483; (703) 684-3345. Fax, (703) 548-6021. Vincent Ferrandino, Executive Director. General e-mail, naesp@naesp.org. Web, www.naesp.org.*

Membership: elementary and middle school principals. Conducts workshops for members on federal and state policies and programs and on professional development. Offers assistance in contract negotiations.

National Assn. of Partners in Education, *901 N. Pitt St., #320, Alexandria, VA 22314; (703) 836-4880. Fax, (703) 836-6941. Daniel W. Merenda, President. General e-mail, NAPEhq@NAPEhq.org. Web, www.partnersineducation.org.*

Membership: teachers, administrators, volunteers, businesses, community groups, and others seeking to help students achieve academic excellence. Creates and strengthens volunteer and partnership programs. Advocates community involvement in schools.

National Assn. of Secondary School Principals, *1904 Association Dr., Reston, VA 20191-1537; (703) 860-0200. Fax, (703) 476-5432. Gerald Triozzi, Executive Director. Web, www.nassp.org.*

Membership: principals and assistant principals of middle and senior high schools, both public and private, and college-level teachers of secondary education. Conducts training programs for members; serves as clearinghouse for information on secondary school administration. Student activities office provides student councils, student activity advisers, and national and junior honor societies with information on national associations.

National Congress of Parents and Teachers, Legislation, Washington Office, 1090 Vermont Ave. N.W., #1200 20005; (202) 289-6790. Fax, (202) 289-6791. Maribeth Oakes, Director. Web, www.pta.org.

Membership: parent-teacher associations at the preschool, elementary, and secondary levels. Washington office represents members' interests on education, funding for education, parent involvement, child protection and safety, comprehensive health care for children, AIDS, the environment, children's television and educational technology, child care, and nutrition. (Headquarters in Chicago.)

National Head Start Assn., 1651 Prince St., Alexandria, VA 22314; (703) 739-0875. Fax, (703) 739-0878. Sarah M. Greene, Chief Executive Officer. Web, www.nhsa.org.

Membership organization that represents Head Start children, families, and staff. Recommends strategies on issues affecting Head Start programs; provides training and professional development opportunities. Monitors legislation and regulations.

National School Boards Assn., 1680 Duke St., Alexandria, VA 22314; (703) 838-6722. Fax, (703) 683-7590. Anne Bryant, Executive Director; Julie Underwood, General Counsel. Web, www.nsba.org.

Federation of state school board associations. Interests include funding of public education, local governance, and quality of education programs. Sponsors seminars, an annual conference, and an information center. Monitors legislation and regulations. Library open to the public by appointment.

National Urban Coalition, 2120 L St. N.W., #510 20037; (202) 986-1460. Fax, (202) 986-1468. Rhett Louis, President (Acting).

Membership: urban community action groups. Operates Say Yes to a Youngster's Future, a community-based education program for low-income students in math, science, and technology. M. Carl Holman Leadership Development Institute gives students opportunities to learn from local and national leaders, including scholars, entrepreneurs, and other experts.

Reading Is Fundamental, 600 Maryland Ave. S.W., #600 20024; (202) 287-3371. Fax, (202) 287-3196. William Trueheart, President. Information, (202) 287-3220. Web, www.rif.org.

Conducts programs and workshops to motivate young people to read. Provides young people with books and parents with services to encourage reading at home.

Teach for America, Washington Office, 1328 Florida Ave. N.W., #110 20009; (202) 463-6122. Fax, (202) 293-7273. Kaya Henderson, Executive Director. Information, (800) 832-1230. General e-mail, tfadcw@aol.com. Web, www.teachforamerica.org.

A national teacher corps of recent college graduates from all academic majors and cultural backgrounds. Participants teach for a minimum of two years in under-funded urban and rural public schools. Promotes outstanding teaching and educational equity. Monitors legislation and regulations. (Headquarters in New York.)

Private, Parochial, and Home Schooling

AGENCIES

Education Dept., Non-Public Education, 400 Maryland Ave. S.W., #5E318 20202-3600; (202) 401-1365. Fax, (202) 401-1368. Michelle L. Doyle, Director. Web, www.ed.gov.

Acts as ombudsman for interests of teachers and students in non-public schools (elementary and secondary levels); reports to the secretary on matters relating to non-public education.

NONPROFIT

Americans United for Separation of Church and State, 518 C St. N.W. 20002; (202) 466-3234. Fax, (202) 466-2587. Barry W. Lynn, Executive Director. General e-mail, americansunited@au.org. Web, www.au.org.

Citizens' interest group. Opposes federal and state aid to parochial schools; works to ensure religious neutrality in public schools; supports religious free exercise; initiates litigation; maintains speakers bureau. Monitors legislation and regulations.

Council for American Private Education, 13017 Wysteria Dr., #457, Germantown, MD 20874; (301) 916-8460. Fax, (301) 916-8485. Joe McTighe, Executive Director. General e-mail, cape@impresso.com. Web, www.capenet.org.

Coalition of national private school associations serving private elementary and secondary schools. Acts as a liaison between private education and government, other educational organizations, the media, and the public. Seeks greater access to private schools for all families. Monitors legislation and regulations.

Home School Legal Defense Assn., 17333 Pickwick Dr., Purcellville, VA 20134 (mailing address: P.O. Box 3000, Purcellville, VA 20134); (540) 338-5600. Fax, (540)

338-2733. Michael P. Farris, President. In Washington, (703) 478-8585. General e-mail, mailroom@hslda.org. Web, www.hslda.org.

Membership: families who practice home schooling. Provides members with legal consultation and defense. Initiates civil rights litigation on behalf of members. Monitors legislation and regulations.

Lutheran Educational Conference of North America, 1001 Connecticut Ave. N.W., #504 20036; (202) 463-6486. Fax, (202) 463-6609. Donald A. Stoike, Executive Director. Web, www.lutherancolleges.org.

Membership: private Lutheran-related colleges and boards of higher education. Supports federal aid to private higher education.

National Assn. of Independent Schools, *Government Relations,* 1620 L St. N.W., #1100 20036-5605; (202) 973-9700. Fax, (202) 973-9790. Jefferson G. Burnett, Director. Press, (202) 973-9716. Web, www.nais.org.

Membership: independent elementary and secondary schools in the United States and abroad. Provides statistical and educational information to members. Monitors legislation and regulations.

National Catholic Educational Assn., 1077 30th St. N.W., #100 20007-3852; (202) 337-6232. Fax, (202) 333-6706. Leonard DeFiore, President. Web, www.ncea.org.

Membership: Catholic schools (preschool through college and seminary) and school administrators. Provides consultation services to members for administration, curriculum, continuing education, religious education, campus ministry, boards of education, and union and personnel negotiations; conducts workshops; supports federal aid for private education. (Affiliated with the Assn. of Catholic Colleges and Universities.)

National Congress of Parents and Teachers, *Legislation, Washington Office,* 1090 Vermont Ave. N.W., #1200 20005; (202) 289-6790. Fax, (202) 289-6791. Maribeth Oakes, Director. Web, www.pta.org.

Membership: parent-teacher associations at the preschool, elementary, and secondary levels. Coordinates the National Coalition for Public Education, which opposes tuition tax credits and vouchers for private education. (Headquarters in Chicago.)

National Council of Churches, *Washington Office,* 110 Maryland Ave. N.E., #108 20002; (202) 544-2350. Fax, (202) 543-1297. Vacant, Director. General e-mail, mary@ncccusa.org. Web, www.ncccusa.org.

Membership: Protestant, Anglican, and Eastern Orthodox churches. Opposes federal aid to private schools. (Headquarters in New York.)

National Home Education Research Institute, *Washington Office,* 12221 Van Brady Rd., Upper Marlboro, MD 20772-7924; (301) 372-2889. Fax, (301) 372-0086. Bill Lloyd, Manager. Web, www.nheri.org.

Serves as an information clearinghouse for researchers, home educators, attorneys, legislators, policymakers, and the public. Conducts research on home education. Monitors legislation and regulations. (Headquarters in Salem, Ore.)

U.S. Catholic Conference, 3211 4th St. N.E. 20017; (202) 541-3130. Fax, (202) 541-3390. Lords Sheehan (RSM), Contact. Press, (202) 541-3200. TTY, (202) 740-0424. Web, www.nccbuscc.org.

Represents the Catholic church in the United States in educational matters; advises Catholic schools on federal programs; assists church organizations with religious education.

SPECIAL GROUPS IN EDUCATION

Gifted and Talented

AGENCIES

Education Dept., *Gifted and Talented Education,* 555 New Jersey Ave. N.W. 20208-5572; (202) 219-2210. Fax, (202) 219-2053. Elizabeth Barnes, Program Analyst. Web, www.ed.gov/prog_info/javits.

Awards grants for developing programs for gifted and talented students, including the limited-English-speaking, economically disadvantaged, and disabled. Oversees the National Research Center, which administers grants for research and analysis of gifted and talented programs. Conducts seminars and produces publications on issues related to gifted and talented programs.

NONPROFIT

Council for Exceptional Children, 1920 Association Dr., Reston, VA 20191-1589; (703) 620-3660. Fax, (703) 264-9494. Nancy Safer, Executive Director. TTY, (703) 264-9446. Web, www.cec.sped.org.

Provides information on gifted and talented education nationwide; maintains clearinghouse of information on the gifted; provides lawmakers with technical assistance. Monitors legislation and regulations affecting gifted and talented education. Library open to the public.

Foundation for Exceptional Children, 1920 Association Dr., Reston, VA 20191; (703) 264-3507. Fax, (703) 264-9494. Kenneth L. Collins, Executive Director. Web, www.cec.sped.org/fd-menu.htm.

Membership: individuals interested in meeting the needs of gifted children and children with disabilities. Provides information and assists educators and parents; works to protect the rights of exceptional children; develops education programs and faculty standards. Awards scholarships and grants.

National Assn. for Gifted Children, *1707 L St. N.W., #550 20036; (202) 785-4268. Fax, (202) 785-4248. Peter D. Rosenstein, Executive Director. Web, www.nagc.org.*

Membership: teachers, administrators, state coordinators, and parents. Works for programs for intellectually and creatively gifted children in public and private schools.

See also National Assn. of Private Schools for Exceptional Children (p. 201)

Learning and Physically Disabled

See also Social Services and Disabilities (chap. 18)

AGENCIES

Education Dept., *Special Education and Rehabilitative Services, 330 C St. S.W. 20202-2500; (202) 205-5465. Fax, (202) 205-9252. Judith Heumann, Assistant Secretary. TTY, (202) 205-5465. Main phone is voice and TTY accessible. Web, www.ed.gov.*

Administers federal assistance programs for the education and rehabilitation of people with disabilities, which are administered by the National Institute of Disability and Rehabilitation Research, the Office of Special Education Programs, and the Rehabilitation Services Administration; maintains a national information clearinghouse on people with disabilities.

Education Dept., *Special Education Programs, 330 C St. S.W. 20202-5175; (202) 205-5507. Fax, (202) 260-0416. Kenneth Warlick, Director. Web, www.ed.gov.*

Responsible for special education programs and services designed to meet the needs and develop the full potential of children with disabilities. Programs include support for training of teachers and other professional personnel; grants for research; financial aid to help states initiate and improve their resources; and media services and captioned films for hearing impaired persons.

Smithsonian Institution, *Accessibility Program, 900 Jefferson Dr. S.W., #1239 20560-0426; (202) 786-2942. Fax, (202) 786-2210. Janice Majewski, Coordinator. TTY, (202) 786-2414.*

Coordinates Smithsonian efforts to improve accessibility of its programs and facilities to visitors and staff with disabilities. Serves as a resource for museums and individuals nationwide.

CONGRESS

House Education and the Workforce Committee, *Subcommittee on Early Childhood, Youth, and Families, 2181 RHOB 20515; (202) 225-4527. Fax, (202) 225-9571. Rep. Michael N. Castle, R-Del., Chair; Kevin D. Talley, Staff Director. Web, www.house.gov/ed_workforce.*

Jurisdiction over legislation on special education programs including, but not limited to, alcohol and drug abuse and education of the disabled.

Library of Congress, *National Library Service for the Blind and Physically Handicapped, 1291 Taylor St. N.W. 20542; (202) 707-5104. Fax, (202) 707-0712. Frank Kurt Cylke, Director. TTY, (202) 707-0744. Reference, (202) 707-5100; outside D.C. area, (800) 424-8567. General e-mail, nls@loc.gov. Web, www.loc.gov/nls.*

Administers a national program of free library services for persons with physical disabilities in cooperation with regional and subregional libraries. Produces and distributes full-length books and magazines in recorded form (disc and cassette) and in Braille. Reference section answers questions relating to blindness and physical disabilities and on library services available to persons with disabilities.

Senate Health, Education, Labor, and Pensions Committee, *SD-428 20510; (202) 224-5375. Fax, (202) 228-5044. Sen. James M. Jeffords, R-Vt., Chair; Mark Powden, Staff Director. TTY, (202) 224-1975. Web, labor.senate.gov.*

Jurisdiction over legislation on education of people with disabilities, including Gallaudet University and the National Technical Institute for the Deaf; jurisdiction over the Americans with Disabilities Act.

NONPROFIT

American Assn. of University Affiliated Programs for Persons with Developmental Disabilities, *8630 Fenton St., #410, Silver Spring, MD 20910; (301) 588-8252. Fax, (301) 588-2842. George Jesien, Executive Director. Web, www.aauap.org.*

Network of facilities that diagnose and treat the developmentally disabled. Trains graduate students and professionals in the field; helps state and local agencies develop services. Interests include interdisciplinary training and services, early screening to prevent developmental disabilities, and development of equipment and programs to serve persons with disabilities.

Assn. for Education and Rehabilitation of the Blind and Visually Impaired, *P.O. Box 22397, Alexandria, VA 22304; (703) 823-9690. Fax, (703) 823-9695. Denise Rozell, Executive Director. General e-mail, aer@ aerbvi.org. Web, www.aerbvi.org.*

Membership: professionals and paraprofessionals who work with the blind and visually impaired. Provides information on services for people who are blind and visually impaired and on employment opportunities for those who work with them. Works to improve quality of education and rehabilitation services. Monitors legislation and regulations.

Council for Exceptional Children, *1920 Association Dr., Reston, VA 20191-1589; (703) 620-3660. Fax, (703) 264-9494. Nancy Safer, Executive Director. TTY, (703) 264-9446. Web, www.cec.sped.org.*

Provides information on the education of exceptional children; maintains clearinghouse of information on disabilities, learning disorders, and special education topics; provides lawmakers with technical assistance. Monitors legislation and regulations affecting special education. Library open to the public.

Foundation for Exceptional Children, *1920 Association Dr., Reston, VA 20191; (703) 264-3507. Fax, (703) 264-9494. Kenneth L. Collins, Executive Director. Web, www.cec.sped.org/fd-menu.htm.*

Membership: individuals interested in meeting the needs of gifted children and children with disabilities. Provides information and assists educators and parents; works to protect the rights of exceptional children; develops education programs and faculty standards. Awards scholarships and grants.

Gallaudet University, *800 Florida Ave. N.E. 20002-3695; (202) 651-5000. Fax, (202) 651-5508. I. King Jordan, President, (202) 651-5005. Phone numbers are voice and TTY accessible. Web, www.gallaudet.edu.*

Offers undergraduate and graduate degree programs for the deaf and hard of hearing and graduate training for teachers and other professionals who work with the deaf; conducts research; maintains outreach and regional centers and demonstration doctoral, continuing education, secondary, elementary, and preschool programs (Model Secondary School for the Deaf, Kendall Demonstration Elementary School). Sponsors the Center for Global Education, the National Information Center on Deafness, and the National Center for the Law and the Deaf.

National Assn. of Private Schools for Exceptional Children, *1522 K St. N.W., #1032 20005-1202; (202) 408-3338. Fax, (202) 408-3340. Sherry L. Kolbe, Executive*

Director. General e-mail, napsec@aol.com. Web, www. napsec.com.

Promotes greater education opportunities for children with disabilities; provides legislators and agencies with information and testimony; formulates and disseminates positions and statements on special education issues.

National Assn. of State Directors of Special Education, *1800 Diagonal Rd., #320, Alexandria, VA 22314; (703) 519-3800. Fax, (703) 519-3808. Bill East, Executive Director. TTY, (703) 519-7008. Web, www.nasdse.org.*

Membership: state education agency special education administrators, consultants, and supervisors. Coordinates and provides state education agency personnel with in-service training programs; manages federally sponsored clearinghouse on professions in special education. Monitors legislation and research developments in special education.

Very Special Arts, *1300 Connecticut Ave. N.W., #700 20036; (202) 628-2800. Fax, (202) 737-0725. John Kemp, Chief Executive Officer. Information, (800) 933-8721. TTY, (202) 737-0645. Web, www.vsarts.org.*

Initiates and supports research and program development providing arts training and demonstration for persons with disabilities. Provides technical assistance and training to Very Special Arts state organizations; acts as an information clearinghouse for arts and persons with disabilities. (Affiliated with the Kennedy Center education office.)

See also Home and School Institute (p. 197)

Minorities and Women

See also Civil Rights (chap. 1); Special Topics in Education (this chapter)

AGENCIES

Bureau of Indian Affairs *(Interior Dept.),* **Indian Education Programs,** *1849 C St. N.W., #3512 20240; (202) 208-6123. Fax, (202) 208-3312. Joann Morris, Director.*

Operates schools for native Americans, including people with disabilities. Provides special assistance to native American pupils in public schools; aids native American college students; sponsors adult education programs.

Commission on Civil Rights, *Civil Rights Evaluation, 624 9th St. N.W. 20425; (202) 376-8582. Fax, (202) 376-8315. Vacant, Assistant Staff Director. Library, (202) 376-8110.*

Researches federal policy on education, including desegregation. Library open to the public.

Education Dept., *Civil Rights,* 330 C St. S.W., #5000 20202-1100 (mailing address: 400 Maryland Ave. S.W. 20202); (202) 205-5413. Fax, (202) 205-9862. Norma Cantù, Assistant Secretary. Web, www.ed.gov.

Enforces laws prohibiting use of federal funds for education programs or activities that discriminate on the basis of race, color, sex, national origin, age, or disability; authorized to discontinue funding.

Education Dept., *Compensatory Education Programs,* 400 Maryland Ave. S.W., #3W230 20202-6132; (202) 260-0826. Fax, (202) 260-7764. Mary Jean LeTendre, Director. Press, (202) 401-1008. Web, www.ed.gov.

Administers the Chapter 1 federal assistance program for education of educationally deprived children (preschool through secondary), including native American children, homeless children, delinquents, and residents in state institutions. Administers the Even Start program.

Education Dept., *Federal TRIO Programs,* 1900 K St. N.W., #7000 20006; (202) 502-7600. Fax, (202) 502-7857. Linda Byrd-Johnson, Team Leader. TTY, (202) 502-7600. Web, www.ed.gov.

Administers programs for disadvantaged students, including Upward Bound, Talent Search, Student Support Services, the Ronald E. McNair Post-Baccalaureate Achievement Program, and educational opportunity centers; provides special programs personnel with training.

Education Dept., *Indian Education Programs,* 400 Maryland Ave. S.W., #FB6 20202-6335; (202) 260-3774. Fax, (202) 260-7779. David Beaulieu, Director. Web, www.ed.gov.

Aids local school districts with programs for native American students; funds schools operated by the Bureau of Indian Affairs and native American-controlled schools and programs.

Education Dept., *Intergovernmental and Constituent Services,* 400 Maryland Ave. S.W., #5E301 20202; (202) 401-3049. Fax, (202) 401-8607. Leo Coco, Deputy Assistant Secretary. Web, www.ed.gov.

Acts as ombudsman for Asian-Pacific, African American, Hispanic, and women's organizations concerned with education issues. Disseminates information on government programs to organizations and educators; reports to the secretary on interests of special populations.

Education Dept., *Migrant Education,* 400 Maryland Ave. S.W., #3E329 20202-6135; (202) 260-1164. Fax, (202) 205-0089. Francisco Garcia, Director. Web, www.ed.gov.

Administers programs that fund education (preschool through postsecondary) for children of migrant workers.

Education Dept., *White House Initiative on Historically Black Colleges and Universities,* 1990 K St. N.W., #8099 20006; (202) 502-7900. Fax, (202) 502-7869. Catherine LeBlanc, Executive Director. Web, www.ed.gov.

Supervises and seeks to increase involvement of the private sector in historically black colleges and universities. Works to eliminate barriers to the participation of these colleges and universities in federal and private programs.

Education Dept., *Women's Educational Equity Act Program,* 400 Maryland Ave. S.W., #3E228 20202-6140; (202) 260-2502. Fax, (202) 205-5630. Madeline Vaggett, Program Specialist. Web, www.ed.gov.

Administers the Women's Educational Equity Act; awards grants and contracts to individuals, higher education institutions, and public and nonprofit private organizations promoting issues related to educational equity for women; maintains liaison with national women's organizations. (Program does not offer financial aid directly to students.)

Justice Dept., *Educational Opportunity,* 601 D St. N.W., #4300 20530; (202) 514-4092. Fax, (202) 514-8337. Jeremiah Glassman, Chief. Web, www.usdoj.gov.

Initiates litigation to ensure equal opportunities in public education; enforces laws dealing with civil rights in public education.

Office of Personnel Management, *Diversity,* 1900 E St. N.W., #2445 20415-0001; (202) 606-2817. Fax, (202) 606-0927. Maria Mercedes Olivieri, Director.

Develops and provides guidance to federal agencies on the employment of minorities and women. Administers the Federal Equal Opportunity Recruitment Program and the Disabled Veterans Affirmative Action Program.

CONGRESS

House Appropriations Committee, *Subcommittee on Interior,* B308 RHOB 20515; (202) 225-3081. Fax, (202) 225-9069. Rep. Ralph Regula, R-Ohio, Chair; Deborah A. Weatherly, Clerk. Web, www.house.gov/appropriations.

Jurisdiction over legislation to appropriate funds for all native American education activities of the Education Dept. and for the Bureau of Indian Affairs.

House Education and the Workforce Committee, *2181 RHOB 20515; (202) 225-4527. Fax, (202) 225-9571. Rep. Bill Goodling, R-Pa., Chair; Kevin D. Talley, Staff Director. Web, www.house.gov/ed_workforce.*

Jurisdiction over legislation pertaining to native American education; oversight of native American education programs (jurisdiction shared with the House Resources Committee).

House Education and the Workforce Committee, *Subcommittee on Early Childhood, Youth, and Families, 2181 RHOB 20515; (202) 225-4527. Fax, (202) 225-9571. Rep. Michael N. Castle, R-Del., Chair; Kevin D. Talley, Staff Director. Web, www.house.gov/ed_workforce.*

Jurisdiction over legislation barring discrimination in education, including the Women's Educational Equity Act of 1974.

House Education and the Workforce Committee, *Subcommittee on Postsecondary Education, Training, and Life-Long Learning, 2181 RHOB 20515; (202) 225-4527. Fax, (202) 225-9571. Rep. Howard P. "Buck" McKeon, R-Calif., Chair; Kevin D. Talley, Staff Director. Web, www.house.gov/ed_workforce.*

Jurisdiction over legislation barring discrimination in postsecondary education.

House Resources Committee, *1324 LHOB 20515-6201; (202) 225-2761. Fax, (202) 225-5929. Rep. Don Young, R-Alaska, Chair; Lloyd Jones, Staff Director. General e-mail, resources.committee@mail.house.gov. Web, www.house.gov/resources.*

Jurisdiction over legislation pertaining to native American education; oversight of native American education programs (jurisdiction shared with House Education and the Workforce Committee).

Senate Appropriations Committee, *Subcommittee on Interior, SD-131 20510; (202) 224-7233. Sen. Slade Gorton, R-Wash., Chair; Bruce Evans, Clerk. Web, appropriations.senate.gov/interior.*

Jurisdiction over legislation to appropriate funds for all native American education activities and for the Bureau of Indian Affairs.

Senate Committee on Indian Affairs, *SH-838 20510; (202) 224-2251. Fax, (202) 224-5429. Sen. Ben Nighthorse Campbell, R-Colo., Chair; Paul Moorehead, Staff Director. Web, indian.senate.gov.*

Jurisdiction over legislation pertaining to native American education; oversight of native American education programs.

Senate Health, Education, Labor, and Pensions Committee, *SD-428 20510; (202) 224-5375. Fax, (202) 228-5044. Sen. James M. Jeffords, R-Vt., Chair; Mark Powden, Staff Director. TTY, (202) 224-1975. Web, labor.senate.gov.*

Jurisdiction over legislation barring discrimination in education, including the Women's Educational Equity Act of 1974.

NONPROFIT

American Assn. of University Women, *1111 16th St. N.W. 20036-4873; (202) 785-7700. Fax, (202) 872-1425. Vacant, Executive Director. Library, (202) 785-7763. TTY, (202) 785-7777. General e-mail, info@aauw.org. Web, www.aauw.org.*

Membership: graduates of accredited colleges, universities, and recognized foreign institutions. Interests include equity for women and girls in education, the workplace, health care, and the family. Library open to the public by appointment.

Americans for the Restitution and Righting of Old Wrongs, *1000 Connecticut Ave. N.W., #1204 20036; (202) 296-0685. Fax, (202) 659-4377. Hazel Elbert, Executive Director. General e-mail, arrow1949@aol.com.*

Administers scholarship program for native Americans engaged in post-graduate study.

Aspira Assn., *1444 Eye St. N.W., #800 20005; (202) 835-3600. Fax, (202) 835-3613. Ronald Blackburn-Moreno, President. General e-mail, info@aspira.org. Web, www.aspira.org.*

Provides Latino youth with resources necessary for them to remain in school and contribute to their community. Interests include math, science, and leadership development, parental involvement, and research. Monitors legislation and regulations.

Assn. of American Colleges and Universities, *1818 R St. N.W. 20009; (202) 387-3760. Fax, (202) 265-9532. Carol Geary Schneider, President. Web, www.aacu-edu.org.*

Serves as clearinghouse for information on women professionals in higher education. Interests include women's studies, women's centers, and women's leadership and professional development.

Council for Opportunity in Education, *1025 Vermont Ave. N.W., #900 20005; (202) 347-7430. Fax, (202) 347-0786. Arnold L. Mitchem, President. Web, www.hqcoe.org.*

Represents institutions of higher learning, administrators, counselors, teachers, and others committed to advancing equal educational opportunity in colleges and universities. Works to sustain and improve educational opportunity programs such as the federally funded TRIO program, designed to help low-income, first-generation immigrant, and physically disabled students enroll in and graduate from college.

East Coast Migrant Head Start Project, *4245 Fairfax Dr., #800, Arlington, VA 22203; (703) 243-7522. Fax, (703) 243-1259. Raphael Guerra, Executive Director. Web, www.ecmhsp.org.*

Establishes Head Start programs for migrant children and offers training and technical assistance to established centers that enroll migrant children.

League of United Latin American Citizens, *Washington Office, 2000 L St. N.W., #610 20036; (202) 833-6130. Fax, (202) 833-6135. Brent Wilkes, Executive Director. General e-mail, lulac@aol.com. Web, www.lulac.org.*

Seeks to increase the number of minorities, especially Hispanics, attending postsecondary schools; supports legislation to increase educational opportunities for Hispanics and other minorities; provides scholarship funds and educational and career counseling. Educational arm of the League of United Latin American Citizens. (Headquarters in El Paso, Texas.)

The Links Inc., *1200 Massachusetts Ave. N.W. 20005-4501; (202) 842-8686. Fax, (202) 842-4020. Vacant, Executive Director. Web, www.linksinc.org.*

Predominantly African American women's service organization that works with the educationally disadvantaged and culturally deprived; focuses on arts, services for youth, and national and international trends and services.

NAACP Legal Defense and Educational Fund, *Washington Office, 1444 Eye St. N.W., 10th Floor 20005; (202) 682-1300. Fax, (202) 682-1312. Janell Byrd, Senior Attorney.*

Civil rights litigation group that provides legal information about civil rights and advice on educational discrimination against women and minorities; monitors federal enforcement of civil rights laws. Not affiliated with the National Association for the Advancement of Colored People (NAACP). (Headquarters in New York.)

National Alliance of Black School Educators, *2816 Georgia Ave. N.W. 20001; (202) 483-1549. Fax, (202) 483-8323. Quentin Lawson, Executive Director.*

Promotes the education of African American youth and adults; seeks to raise the academic achievement level of all African American students. Sponsors workshops and conferences on major issues in education affecting African American students and educators.

National Assn. for Equal Opportunity in Higher Education, *8701 Georgia Ave., #200, Silver Spring, MD 20910; (301) 650-2440. Fax, (301) 495-3306. Henry Ponder, President. Web, www.nafeo.org.*

Membership: historically and predominantly black colleges and universities (HBCU). Works for increased federal and private support for member institutions and for increased minority representation in private and governmental education agencies; serves as a clearinghouse for information on federal contracts and grants for member institutions; collects, analyzes, and publishes data on member institutions; operates internship program.

National Assn. for the Advancement of Colored People, *Washington Office, 1025 Vermont Ave. N.W., #1120 20005; (202) 638-2269. Fax, (202) 638-5936. Hilary O. Shelton, Director. Web, www.naacp.org.*

Membership: persons interested in civil rights for all minorities. Works for equal opportunity for minorities in all areas, including education; seeks to ensure a quality desegregated education for all through litigation and legislation. (Headquarters in Baltimore.)

National Assn. of Colored Women's Clubs, *5808 16th St. N.W. 20011-2898; (202) 726-2044. Fax, (202) 726-0023. Patricia L. Fletcher, President.*

Seeks to promote education of women and youth; protect and enforce civil rights; raise the standard of family living; promote interracial understanding; and enhance leadership development. Awards scholarships; conducts programs in education, social service, and philanthropy.

National Assn. of State Universities and Land Grant Colleges, *Advancement of Public Black Colleges, 1307 New York Ave. N.W., #400 20005; (202) 478-6041. Fax, (202) 478-6046. Joyce Payne, Director. Web, www.nasulgc.org.*

Seeks to heighten awareness and visibility of public African American colleges; promotes institutional advancement. Conducts research and provides information on issues of concern; acts as a liaison with African American public colleges and universities, the federal government, and private associations. Monitors legislation and regulations.

National Clearinghouse for Bilingual Education, *2011 Eye St. N.W., #200 20006; (202) 467-0867. Fax, (202) 467-4283. Minerva Gorena, Director. General e-mail, askncbe@ncbe.gwu.edu. Web, www.ncbe.gwu.edu.*

Collects, analyzes, and disseminates information relating to the effective education of linguistically and culturally diverse learners in the U.S. Interests include foreign language programs, ESL programs, Head Start, Title I, migrant education, and adult education programs.

National Council of La Raza, *1111 19th St. N.W., #1000 20036; (202) 785-1670. Fax, (202) 776-1792. Raul Yzaguirre, President. Web, www.nclr.org.*

Provides research, policy analysis, and advocacy on educational status and needs of Hispanics; promotes education reform benefiting Hispanics; develops and tests community-based models for helping Hispanic students succeed in school. Interests include counseling, testing, and bilingual, vocational, preschool through postsecondary, and migrant education.

National Women's Law Center, *11 Dupont Circle N.W., #800 20036; (202) 588-5180. Fax, (202) 588-5185. Marcia D. Greenberger, Co-President; Nancy Duff Campbell, Co-President. Web, www.nwlc.org.*

Works to expand and protect women's legal rights in education through advocacy and public education.

United Negro College Fund, *8260 Willow Oaks Corporate Dr., Fairfax, VA 22031-4511 (mailing address: P.O. Box 10444, Fairfax, VA 22031); (703) 205-3400. Fax, (703) 205-3575. William H. Gray III, President. Press, (703) 205-3553. Web, www.uncf.org.*

Membership: private colleges and universities with historically black enrollment. Raises money for member institutions; monitors legislation and regulations.

See also Center for Law and Education (p. 29); U.S. Student Assn. (p. 193); Women's College Coalition (p. 194)

SPECIAL TOPICS IN EDUCATION

See also Recreation and Sports (chap. 5); Information and Exchange Programs (chap. 13)

Bilingual and Multicultural

See also Special Groups in Education (this chapter); Language and Literature (chap. 5)

AGENCIES

Education Dept., *Bilingual Education and Minority Languages Affairs, 330 C St. S.W., #5086 20202-6510; (202) 205-5463. Fax, (202) 205-8737. Bouy Te, Deputy Director. Web, www.ed.gov/offices/OBEMLA.*

Provides school districts and state education agencies with grants to establish, operate, and improve programs for people with limited English proficiency; promotes development of resources for such programs, including training for parents and education personnel. Administers assistance programs for refugee and immigrant children.

NONPROFIT

National Assn. for Bilingual Education, *1220 L St. N.W., #605 20005-4018; (202) 898-1829. Fax, (202) 789-2866. Delia Pompa, Executive Director. General e-mail, NABE@nabe.org. Web, www.nabe.org.*

Membership: educators, policymakers, paraprofessionals, publications personnel, students, researchers, and interested individuals. Works to improve educational programs for non-English-speaking students and to promote bilingualism among American students. Conducts annual conference and workshops.

National MultiCultural Institute, *3000 Connecticut Ave. N.W., #438 20008-2556; (202) 483-0700. Fax, (202) 483-5233. Elizabeth Salett, President. General e-mail, nmci@nmci.org. Web, www.nmci.org.*

Encourages understanding and communication among people of various backgrounds; seeks to increase awareness of different perspectives and experiences; provides multicultural training, education, and counseling programs for organizations and institutions working with diverse cultural groups.

Teachers of English to Speakers of Other Languages, *700 S. Washington St., #200, Alexandria, VA 22314-4287; (703) 836-0774. Fax, (703) 836-7864. Charles Amorosino, Executive Director. General e-mail, tesol@tesol.edu. Web, www.tesol.edu.*

Promotes scholarship and provides information on instruction and research in the teaching of English to speakers of other languages. Offers placement service.

See also Center for Law and Education (p. 29); Home and School Institute (p. 197); Organization of Chinese Americans (p. 11)

Citizenship Education

NONPROFIT

Close Up Foundation, *44 Canal Center Plaza, #500, Alexandria, VA 22314; (703) 706-3300. Fax, (703) 706-0000. Stephen A. Janger, President. Web, www.closeup.org.*

Sponsors week-long programs on American government for high school students, teachers, older Americans, new Americans, native Americans, Alaskan natives, and Pacific Islanders; offers fellowships for participation in the programs; produces television series for secondary schools; conducts the national Citizen Bee, an academic social studies competition for high school students, and the Civic Achievement Award Program for elementary and junior high school students. Develops specialized programs such as the U.S.-Japan Educational Initiative; summer institutes on energy, environment, and policy choices; and Active Citizenship Today, a program that promotes community service.

Horatio Alger Assn., *99 Canal Center Plaza, #320, Alexandria, VA 22314; (703) 684-9444. Fax, (703) 548-3822. Terrence J. Giroux, Executive Director. General e-mail, horatioaa@aol.com. Web, www.horatioalger.com.*

Educates young people about the economic and personal opportunities available in the American free enterprise system. Conducts seminars on careers in public and community service; operates speakers bureau and internship program. Presents the Horatio Alger Youth Award to outstanding high school students and the Horatio Alger Award to professionals who have achieved success in their respective fields. Awards college scholarships.

League of Women Voters Education Fund, *1730 M St. N.W., #1000 20036; (202) 429-1965. Fax, (202) 429-0854. Jane Gruenebaum, Director. Web, www.lwv.org.*

Public foundation established by League of Women Voters of the United States. Promotes citizen knowledge of and involvement in representative government; conducts citizen education on current public policy issues; seeks to increase voter registration and turnout; sponsors candidate forums and debates.

National 4-H Council, *7100 Connecticut Ave., Chevy Chase, MD 20815-4999; (301) 961-2820. Fax, (301) 961-2894. Richard J. Sauer, President. Press, (301) 961-2915. Web, www.fourhcouncil.edu.*

Citizenship education organization that conducts programs for youth and adult groups in Washington. Programs on American government include Wonders of Washington, Citizenship-Washington Focus, and Know America.

Presidential Classroom for Young Americans, *119 Oronoco St., Alexandria, VA 22314-2015; (703) 683-5400. Fax, (703) 548-5728. Jay D. Wickliff, Executive Director. Information, (800) 441-6533. General e-mail, prezclass@aol.com. Web, www.presidentialclassroom.org.*

Offers civic education programs for high school students and volunteer opportunities for college students and adults. Provides week-long series of seminars featuring representatives of each branch of government, the diplomatic community, the military, the media, private interest groups, and both major political parties.

Washington Workshops Foundation, *3222 N St. N.W., #340 20007; (202) 965-3434. Fax, (202) 965-1018. Sharon E. Sievers, President. Information, (800) 368-5688. Web, www.workshops.org.*

Educational foundation that provides introductory seminars on American government and politics to junior and senior high school students; congressional seminars to secondary and postsecondary students; and seminars on diplomacy and global affairs to secondary students.

Consumer Education

For a list of federal consumer contacts, see chap. 1

AGENCIES

Agriculture Dept., *Research, Education, and Economics, 1400 Independence Ave. S.W., #217W 20250-0110; (202) 720-5923. Fax, (202) 690-2842. Eileen Kennedy, Deputy Under Secretary, (202) 720-8885. Web, www.usda.gov.*

Coordinates agricultural research, extension, and teaching programs in the food and agricultural sciences, including human nutrition, home economics, consumer services, agricultural economics, environmental quality, natural and renewable resources, forestry and range management, animal and plant production and protection, aquaculture, and the production, distribution, and utilization of food and agricultural products. Oversees the Cooperative State Research, Education, and Extension Service.

Consumer Product Safety Commission (CPSC), *Information and Public Affairs, 4330 East-West Hwy., Bethesda, MD 20814; (301) 504-0580. Fax, (301) 504-0862. Russell Rader, Director. TTY, (800) 638-8270. Product safety hotline, (800) 638-2772. General e-mail, info@cpsc.gov. Web, www.cpsc.gov.*

Provides information concerning consumer product safety; works with local and state governments, school systems, and private groups to develop product safety information and education programs. Toll-free hotline accepts consumer complaints on hazardous products and injuries associated with a product and offers recorded information on product recalls and CPSC safety recommendations.

Cooperative State Research, Education, and Extension Service *(Agriculture Dept.), 1400 Independence Ave. S.W., #305A 20250-2201; (202) 720-4423. Fax, (202) 720-8987. Charles W. Laughlin, Administrator. Information, (202) 720-6133. TTY, (202) 690-1899. Web, www.reeusda.gov.*

Oversees county agents and operation of state offices that provide information on home economics, including diet and nutrition, food budgeting, food safety, home gardening, clothing care, and other consumer concerns.

Federal Trade Commission (FTC), *Consumer and Business Education,* 600 Pennsylvania Ave. N.W., #H403 20580-0001; (202) 326-3650. Fax, (202) 326-3574. Carolyn Shanoff, Director. TTY, (202) 326-2502. Consumer Response Center, (202) FTC-HELP or (887) FTC-HELP. Web, www.ftc.gov.

Develops educational material about FTC activities for consumers and businesses.

Food and Drug Administration *(Health and Human Services Dept.),* **Consumer Affairs,** 5600 Fishers Lane, Rockville, MD 20857; (301) 827-5006. Fax, (301) 443-9767. Patricia Kuntze, Associate Director (Acting). Consumer inquiries, (888) 463-6332. Web, www.fda.gov.

Responds to inquiries on issues related to the FDA. Conducts consumer health education programs for specific groups, including women, the elderly, and the educationally and economically disadvantaged. Serves as liaison with national health and consumer organizations.

Food Safety and Inspection Service *(Agriculture Dept.),* 1400 Independence Ave. S.W., #331E 20250; (202) 720-7025. Fax, (202) 205-0158. Thomas J. Billy, Administrator. Press, (202) 720-9113. Consumer inquiries, (800) 535-4555; in Washington, (202) 720-3333. Web, www. usda.gov/fsis.

Sponsors food safety educational programs to inform the public about measures to prevent foodborne illnesses; sponsors lectures, publications, public service advertising campaigns, exhibits, and audiovisual presentations. Toll-free hotline answers food safety questions.

NONPROFIT

American Assn. of Family and Consumer Sciences, 1555 King St., Alexandria, VA 22314; (703) 706-4600. Fax, (703) 706-4663. Ann Chadwick, Executive Director. General e-mail, staff@aafcs.org. Web, www.aafcs.org.

Membership: professional home economists. Supports family and consumer sciences education; develops accrediting standards for undergraduate family and consumer science programs; trains and certifies family and consumer science professionals. Monitors legislation and regulations concerning family and consumer issues.

Family, Career, and Community Leaders of America, 1910 Association Dr., Reston, VA 20191-1584; (703) 476-4900. Fax, (703) 860-2713. Alan T. Rains Jr., Executive Director. General e-mail, nationalheadquarters@ fcclainc.org. Web, www.fcclainc.org.

National student organization that helps young men and women address personal, family, work, and social issues through family and consumer sciences education.

Literacy/Basic Skills

AGENCIES

AmeriCorps *(Corporation for National Service),* **Volunteers in Service to America (VISTA),** 1201 New York Ave. N.W., 8th Floor 20525; (202) 606-5000. Fax, (202) 565-2789. Lee Lacy, Deputy Director. TTY, (800) 833-3722. Volunteer recruiting information, (800) 942-2677. Web, www.americorps.org.

Assigns volunteers to local and state education departments, to public agencies, and to private, non-profit organizations that have literacy programs. Other activities include tutor recruitment and training and the organization and expansion of local literacy councils, workplace literacy programs, and intergenerational literacy programs.

Education Dept., *Adult Education and Literacy,* 330 C St. S.W., #4428 20202-6510 (mailing address: 400 Maryland Ave. S.W. 20202); (202) 205-8270. Fax, (202) 205-8973. Ronald S. Pugsley, Director. Literacy clearinghouse, (202) 205-9996. Web, www.ed.gov.

Provides state and local education agencies and the general public with information on establishing, expanding, improving, and operating adult education and literacy programs. Emphasizes basic and life skills attainment and high school completion. Awards grants to state education agencies for adult education and literacy programs, including grants for workplace literacy partnerships. Coordinates homeless and adult literacy programs.

Education Dept., *National Institute for Literacy,* 1775 Eye St. N.W., #730 20006; (202) 233-2025. Fax, (202) 233-2050. Andy Hartman, Director. Web, www.nifl.gov.

Operates a literacy clearinghouse and an electronic national literacy and communications system; provides private literacy groups, educational institutions, and federal, state, and local agencies working on illiteracy with assistance; awards grants and fellowships to literacy programs and individuals pursuing careers in the literacy field.

Employment and Training Administration *(Labor Dept.),* **Workplace Literacy,** 200 Constitution Ave. N.W., #N5637 20210; (202) 219-5472. Fax, (202) 219-5455. Vacant, Chief.

Coordinates workplace literacy projects, including technical and basic skills effectiveness training, technology training, adult education studies, and literacy surveys; sponsors, with the Education and Health and Human Services departments, the National Institute for Literacy.

CONGRESS

Library of Congress, *Center for the Book,* 101 Independence Ave. S.E., #650 20540-4920; (202) 707-5221. Fax, (202) 707-0269. John Y. Cole, Director. Web, www.loc.gov/loc/cfbook.

Promotes family and adult literacy; encourages the study of books and stimulates public interest in books, reading, and libraries; sponsors publication of a directory describing national organizations that administer literacy programs. Affiliated state centers sponsor projects and hold events that call attention to the importance of literacy.

NONPROFIT

AFL-CIO Working for America Institute, 1101 14th St. N.W., #320 20005; (202) 638-3912. Fax, (202) 783-6536. Bruce Herman, Executive Director. General e-mail, info@workingforamerica.org.

Provides labor unions, employers, education agencies, and community groups with technical assistance for workplace education programs focusing on adult literacy, basic skills, and job training. Interests include new technologies and workplace innovations.

American Bar Assn., *Standing Committee on Law and Literacy,* 740 15th St. N.W. 20005; (202) 662-1020. Fax, (202) 662-1751. Susan Kidd, Director. Web, www.abanet.org.

Seeks to involve lawyers in literacy programs at the local, state, and national levels; sponsors conferences on literacy and publishes a literacy program manual for state and local bars.

American Poetry and Literacy Project, P.O. Box 53445 20009; (202) 338-1109. Andrew Carroll, Executive Director.

Donates new books of poetry to schools, libraries, hospitals, homeless shelters, nursing homes, hotels, and other public places around the country to promote literacy.

American Society for Training and Development, 1640 King St., Alexandria, VA 22313-2043; (703) 683-8100. Fax, (703) 683-1523. Tina Sung, President. Web, www.astd.org.

Membership: trainers and human resource developers. Publishes information on workplace literacy.

Barbara Bush Foundation for Family Literacy, 4646 40th St. N.W. 20016; (202) 362-0700. Fax, (202) 362-3740. Donna Christiansan, Director. Web, www.barbarabushfoundation.com.

Seeks to establish literacy as a value in every family and to develop and expand family literacy programs nationwide.

Center for Applied Linguistics, *National Clearinghouse for ESL Literacy Education,* 4646 40th St. N.W. 20016; (202) 362-0700. Fax, (202) 362-3740. Vacant, Assistant Director. General e-mail, ncle@cal.org. Web, www.cal.org.

Provides information and referral service on literacy instruction for adults and out-of-school youth learning English as a second language. Operates English language training programs internationally.

General Federation of Women's Clubs, 1734 N St. N.W. 20036-2990; (202) 347-3168. Fax, (202) 835-0246. Gabrielle Smith, Executive Director. General e-mail, gfwc@gfwc.org. Web, www.gfwc.org.

Nondenominational, nonpartisan international organization of women volunteers. Develops literacy projects in response to community needs; sponsors tutoring.

National Alliance of Business, *Workforce Adjustment,* 1201 New York Ave. N.W., #700 20005; (202) 289-2905. Fax, (202) 289-1303. Roberts T. Jones, President. Press, (202) 289-2860. General e-mail, info@nab.com. Web, www.nab.com.

Builds business partnerships with government, labor, and education to improve the quality of the American workforce. Provides technical assistance and information on workplace literacy.

Newspaper Assn. of America Foundation, *Educational Programs,* 1921 Gallows Rd., #600, Vienna, VA 22182; (703) 902-1600. Fax, (703) 917-0636. Jim Abbott, Manager. Web, www.naa.org.

Publishes a handbook for starting newspaper literacy projects; promotes intergenerational literacy through its Family Focus program; acts as a clearinghouse for literacy information.

Reading Is Fundamental, 600 Maryland Ave. S.W., #600 20024; (202) 287-3371. Fax, (202) 287-3196. William Trueheart, President. Information, (202) 287-3220. Web, www.rif.org.

Conducts programs and workshops to motivate young people to read. Provides young people with books and parents with services to encourage reading at home.

United Way of America, *Education and Literacy Initiative, 701 N. Fairfax St., Alexandria, VA 22314-2045; (703) 836-7112. Fax, (703) 549-9152. Robbin Sorensen, Director. Web, www.unitedway.org.*

Produces and distributes literacy information to local United Way chapters; conducts regional forums on literacy for state and local United Way chapters and their communities; provides communities with technical assistance, financial support, and training and scholarships for local literacy professionals.

See also Correctional Education Assn. (p. 519); Institute for Alternative Futures (p. 389)

Science and Mathematics Education

AGENCIES

Education Dept., *Higher Education: Minority Science and Engineering Improvement, 1990 K St. N.W., 6th Floor 20006; (202) 502-7777. Fax, (202) 502-7861. Argelia Velez-Rodriguez, Senior Officer. Web, www.ed.gov.*

Funds programs to improve science and engineering education in predominantly minority colleges and universities; promotes increased participation by minority students and faculty in science and engineering fields; encourages minority schools and universities to apply for grants that will generate precollege student interest in science.

Education Dept., *School Improvement Program: Eisenhower Professional Development Program, 400 Maryland Ave. S.W., #3C106 20202-6140; (202) 260-2434. Fax, (202) 205-5630. Arthur Cole, Director. Web, www.ed.gov.*

Administers formula grant program for states; implements the state entitlement section of the Dwight D. Eisenhower Professional Development Program, which funds programs for improving teacher education in mathematics and science, and programs for improving instruction for the underrepresented and underserved, including women, minorities, people with disabilities, individuals with limited English proficiency, and migrants.

National Museum of Natural History *(Smithsonian Institution), Naturalist Center, 741 Miller Dr. S.E., #G2, Leesburg, VA 20175; (703) 779-9712. Fax, (703) 779-9715. Richard H. Efthim, Manager. Information, (800) 729-7725. General e-mail, natcenter@aol.com. Web, nmnhgoph.si.edu/museum/learn.html.*

Maintains natural history research and reference library with books and more than 30,000 objects, including minerals, rocks, plants, animals, shells and corals,

insects, invertebrates, micro- and macrofossil materials, and microbiological and anthropological materials. Facilities include study equipment such as microscopes, dissecting instruments, and plant presses. Operates a teachers' reference center. Library open to the public. Reservations required for groups of six or more.

National Oceanic and Atmospheric Administration *(Commerce Dept.), National Sea Grant College Program, 1315 East-West Hwy., Silver Spring, MD 20910; (301) 713-2448. Fax, (301) 713-0799. Ronald C. Baird, Director.*

Provides grants, primarily to colleges and universities, for marine resource development; sponsors undergraduate and graduate education and the training of technicians at the college level.

National Science Foundation, *Education and Human Resources, 4201 Wilson Blvd., #805, Arlington, VA 22230; (703) 306-1600. Fax, (703) 306-0399. Judith Sunley, Assistant Director (Interim). Web, www.ehr.nsf.gov.*

Directorate that develops and supports programs to strengthen science and mathematics education. Provides fellowships and grants for graduate research and teacher education, instructional materials, and studies on the quality of existing science and mathematics programs. Participates in international studies.

National Science Foundation, *Science Resources Studies, 4201 Wilson Blvd., #965, Arlington, VA 22230; (703) 306-1780. Fax, (703) 306-0510. Linda T. Carlson, Director. Web, www.nsf.gov/sbe/srs.*

Develops and analyzes U.S. and international statistics and models on training, use, and characteristics of scientists, engineers, and technicians.

Office of Science and Technology Policy *(Executive Office of the President), Science, Dwight D. Eisenhower Executive Office Bldg., #436 20502; (202) 456-6130. Fax, (202) 456-6027. Arthur Bienenstock, Associate Director. Web, www.whitehouse.gov/WH/EOP/OSTP/html/OSTP_Home.html.*

Analyzes policies and advises the president on science education issues; coordinates executive office and federal agency actions related to these issues. Evaluates the effectiveness of science education programs.

NONPROFIT

American Assn. for the Advancement of Science, *Education and Human Resources Programs, 1200 New York Ave. N.W. 20005; (202) 326-6670. Fax, (202) 371-9849. Shirley M. Malcom, Head. Main phone is voice and TTY accessible. Web, www.aaas.org.*

Membership: scientists, scientific organizations, and others interested in science and technology education. Works to increase and provide information on the status of women, minorities, and people with disabilities in the sciences and engineering; focuses on expanding science education opportunities for women, minorities, and people with disabilities.

American Assn. of Physics Teachers, *1 Physics Ellipse, College Park, MD 20740-3845; (301) 209-3300. Fax, (301) 209-0845. Bernard V. Khoury, Executive Officer. General e-mail, aapt@acp.org. Web, www.aapt.org.*

Membership: physics teachers and others interested in physics education. Seeks to advance the institutional and cultural role of physics education. Sponsors seminars and conferences; provides educational information and materials. (Affiliated with the American Institute of Physics.)

American Society for Engineering Education, *1818 N St. N.W., #600 20036; (202) 331-3500. Fax, (202) 265-8504. Frank L. Huband, Executive Director. Press, (202) 331-3537. Web, www.asee.org.*

Membership: engineering faculty and administrators, professional engineers, government agencies, and engineering colleges, corporations, and professional societies. Conducts research, conferences, and workshops on engineering education. Monitors legislation and regulations.

Assn. of Science-Technology Centers, *Government Relations, 1025 Vermont Ave. N.W., #500 20005-3516; (202) 783-7200. Fax, (202) 783-7207. Ellen Griffee, Director. General e-mail, info@astc.org. Web, www.astc.org.*

Membership: science centers and science museums in forty-four countries around the world. Strives to enhance the ability of its members to engage visitors in intriguing science activities and explorations of scientific phenomena. Sponsors conferences and informational exchanges on interactive exhibits, hands-on science experiences, and educational programs for children, families, and teachers.

Challenger Center for Space Science Education, *1250 N. Pitt St., Alexandria, VA 22314; (703) 683-9740. Fax, (703) 683-7546. Vance Ablott, President. Web, www.challenger.org.*

Educational organization designed to stimulate interest in science, math, and technology among middle school and elementary school students. Students participate in interactive mission simulations that require training and classroom preparation. Sponsors Challenger Learning Centers across the United States and Canada.

Commission on Professionals in Science and Technology, *1200 New York Ave. N.W., #390 20005; (202) 326-7080. Fax, (202) 842-1603. Eleanor Babco, Executive Director. Web, www.cpst.org.*

Membership: scientific societies, corporations, academicians, and individuals. Analyzes and publishes data on scientific and engineering human resources in the United States. Interests include employment of minorities and women, salary ranges, and supply and demand of scientists and engineers.

Mathematical Assn. of America, *1529 18th St. N.W. 20036-1358; (202) 387-5200. Fax, (202) 265-2384. Tina H. Straley, Executive Director. General e-mail, maahq@maa.org. Web, www.maa.org.*

Membership: mathematics professors and individuals worldwide with a professional interest in mathematics. Seeks to improve the teaching of collegiate mathematics. Conducts professional development programs.

National Assn. of Biology Teachers, *12030 Sunrise Valley Dr., #110, Reston, VA 20190; (703) 264-9696. Fax, (703) 264-7778. Wayne Carley, Executive Director. Information, (800) 406-0775. General e-mail, NABTer@aol.com. Web, www.nabt.org.*

Membership: biology teachers and others interested in biology and life sciences education at the elementary, secondary, and collegiate levels. Provides professional development opportunities through its publication program, summer workshops, conventions, and national award programs. Interests include teaching standards, science curriculum, and issues affecting biology and life sciences education.

National Council of Teachers of Mathematics, *1906 Association Dr., Reston, VA 20191-9988; (703) 620-9840. Fax, (703) 476-2970. John A. Thorpe, Executive Director. General e-mail, infocentral@nctm.org. Web, www.nctm.org.*

Membership: teachers of mathematics in elementary and secondary schools and two-year colleges; university teacher education faculty; students; and other interested persons. Works for the improvement of classroom instruction at all levels. Serves as forum and information clearinghouse on issues related to mathematics education. Offers educational materials and conferences. Monitors legislation and regulations.

National Geographic Society, *1145 17th St. N.W. 20036-4688; (202) 857-7000. Fax, (202) 775-6141. John Fahey, President. Information, (800) 647-5463. Library, (202) 857-7783. Press, (202) 857-7027. TTY, (202) 857-7198. Web, www.nationalgeographic.com.*

Educational and scientific organization. Publishes *National Geographic, Research and Exploration, National*

Geographic Traveler, and *World* magazines; produces maps, books, and films; maintains an exhibit hall; offers film-lecture series; produces television specials. Library open to the public.

National Science Resources Center, *Smithsonian Institution Arts and Industries Bldg. 20560-0403; (202) 357-4892. Fax, (202) 786-2028. Douglas M. Lapp, Executive Director. Web, www.si.edu/nsrc.*

Sponsored by the Smithsonian Institution and the National Academy of Sciences. Works to improve science teaching in the nation's schools. Disseminates information; develops curriculum materials; seeks to increase public support for reform of science education.

National Science Teachers Assn., *1840 Wilson Blvd., Arlington, VA 22201-3000; (703) 243-7100. Fax, (703) 243-7177. Gerry Wheeler, Executive Director. General e-mail, publicinfo@nsta.org. Web, www.nsta.org.*

Membership: science teachers from elementary through college levels. Seeks to improve science education; provides forum for exchange of information. Monitors legislation and regulations.

Science Service, *1719 N St. N.W. 20036; (202) 785-2255. Fax, (202) 785-3751. Donald R. Harless, President. Web, www.sciserv.org.*

Seeks to increase public understanding of science and to distribute scientific information. Publishes *Science News;* administers the Intel Science Talent Search and the Intel International Science and Engineering Fair.

World Future Society, *7910 Woodmont Ave., #450, Bethesda, MD 20814; (301) 656-8274. Fax, (301) 951-0394. Edward Cornish, President. Web, www.wfs.org/wfs.*

Scientific and educational organization interested in future social and technological developments on a global scale. Publishes magazines and journals.

Vocational and Adult

See also Employment and Training Programs (chap. 7)

AGENCIES

Agriculture Dept., *Graduate School,* 600 Maryland Ave. S.W., #129 20024-2520; (202) 314-3680. Fax, (202) 479-4894. Philip Hudson, Director. Information, (202) 314-3300. General e-mail, pubaffairs@grad.usda.gov. Web, www.grad.usda.gov.

Self-supporting educational institution that is open to the public. Offers continuing education courses for career advancement and personal fulfillment; offers training at agency locations.

Education Dept., *National Programs,* 400 Maryland Ave. S.W., #4512 20202-7242; (202) 205-9650. Fax, (202) 205-8793. Dennis Berry, Director. Web, www.ed.gov.

Awards contracts and grants on a competitive basis to individuals, state and local education agencies, institutions of higher education, and other organizations for research, demonstration, and training projects in adult and vocational education.

Education Dept., *Vocational and Adult Education,* 330 C St. S.W., #4090 20202-5175 (mailing address: 400 Maryland Ave. S.W. 20202-7100); (202) 205-5451. Fax, (202) 205-8748. Patricia W. McNeil, Assistant Secretary. Web, www.ed.gov.

Coordinates and recommends national policy for improving vocational and adult education. Administers grants, contracts, and technical assistance for programs in adult education, dropout prevention, literacy, and occupational training.

Education Dept., *Vocational Technical Education,* 330 C St. S.W., #4317 20202-5175 (mailing address: 400 Maryland Ave. S.W. 20202-7241); (202) 205-9441. Fax, (202) 205-5522. Ronald Castaldi, Director. Web, www.ed.gov.

Provides state and local education agencies with information on establishment, expansion, improvement, and operation of vocational technical education programs. Awards grants to state education agencies for vocational technical education programs.

NONPROFIT

Accrediting Commission of Career Schools and Colleges of Technology, *2101 Wilson Blvd., #302, Arlington, VA 22201; (703) 247-4212. Fax, (703) 247-4533. Elise Scanlon, Executive Director. General e-mail, info@accsct.org. Web, www.accsct.org.*

Serves as the national accrediting agency for private, postsecondary institutions offering occupational and vocational programs. Sponsors workshops and meetings on academic excellence and ethical practices in career education.

American Assn. for Adult and Continuing Education, *4380 Forbes Blvd., Lanham, MD 20706; (301) 918-1913. Fax, (301) 918-1846. John Doulmetis, President. Web, www.albany.edu/aaace.*

Membership: adult and continuing education professionals. Acts as an information clearinghouse; evaluates adult and continuing education programs; sponsors conferences, seminars, and workshops.

Assn. for Career and Technical Education, *1410 King St., Alexandria, VA 22314; (703) 683-3111. Fax, (703)*

683-7424. Bret D. Lovejoy, Executive Director. Information, (800) 826-9972. Web, www.acteonline.org.

Membership: teachers, students, supervisors, administrators, and others working or interested in vocational education (middle school through postgraduate). Interests include the impact of high school graduation requirements on vocational education; private sector initiatives; and improving the quality and image of vocational education. Offers conferences, workshops, and an annual convention. Monitors legislation and regulations.

Career College Assn., *10 G St. N.E., #750 20002-4213; (202) 336-6700. Fax, (202) 336-6828. Nick Glakas, President. General e-mail, cca@career.org. Web, www.career.org.*

Acts as an information clearinghouse on trade and technical schools.

Distance Education and Training Council, *1601 18th St. N.W. 20009-2529; (202) 234-5100. Fax, (202) 332-1386. Michael P. Lambert, Executive Director. General e-mail, detc@detc.org. Web, www.detc.org.*

Membership: accredited correspondence schools. Accredits home study schools, many of which offer vocational training.

International Assn. for Continuing Education and Training, *1620 Eye St. N.W., #615 20006; (202) 463-2905. Fax, (202) 463-8498. James Clawson, Executive Director. General e-mail, iacet@moinc.com. Web, www.iacet.org.*

Membership: education and training organizations and individuals who use the Continuing Education Unit. (The C.E.U. is defined as ten contact hours of participation in an organized continuing education program that is noncredit.) Certifies organizations which issue the C.E.U.; develops criteria and guidelines for use of the C.E.U.

International Technology Education Assn., *1914 Association Dr., #201, Reston, VA 20191-1539; (703) 860-2100. Fax, (703) 860-0353. Kendall N. Starkweather, Executive Director. General e-mail, itea@iris.org. Web, www.iteawww.org.*

Membership: technology education teachers, supervisors, teacher educators, and individuals studying to be technology education teachers. Technology education includes the curriculum areas of manufacturing, construction, communications, transportation, and energy.

National Assn. of Manufacturers, *Employment Policy, 1331 Pennsylvania Ave. N.W., 6th Floor 20004-1790; (202) 637-3133. Fax, (202) 637-3182. Jenny Krese, Director.*

Works to enhance the quality of vocational education and to increase support from the business community.

Interests include opportunities for dislocated workers, legislation affecting vocational education, and the impact of high technology on the workforce.

National Assn. of State Directors of Vocational/ Technical Education Consortium, *444 N. Capitol St. N.W., #830 20001; (202) 737-0303. Fax, (202) 737-1106. Kimberly Green, Executive Director. General e-mail, nasdvtec@iris.org. Web, www.iris.org/~nasdvtec.*

Membership: state vocational education agency heads, senior staff, and business, labor, and other education officials. Advocates state and national policy to strengthen vocational-technical education to create a foundation of skills for American workers and provide them with opportunities to acquire new and advanced skills.

National Institute for Work and Learning, *1825 Connecticut Ave. N.W., 7th Floor 20009-1202; (202) 884-8186. Fax, (202) 884-8422. Ivan Charner, Vice President.*

Public policy research organization that seeks to improve collaboration between educational and business institutions. Conducts demonstration projects with communities throughout the country on employer-funded tuition aid, youth transition from school to work, and employee education and career development. Conducts research on education and work issues. Library open to the public. (Affiliated with the Academy for Educational Development.)

University Continuing Education Assn., *1 Dupont Circle N.W., #615 20036; (202) 659-3130. Fax, (202) 785-0374. Kay Kohl, Executive Director. Web, www.nucea.edu.*

Membership: higher education institutions and nonprofit organizations involved in postsecondary continuing education. Prepares statistical analyses and produces data reports for members; recognizes accomplishments in the field. Monitors legislation and regulations.

Vocational Industrial Clubs of America, *14001 James Monroe Hwy., Leesburg, VA 20177-0300 (mailing address: P.O. Box 3000, Leesburg, VA 20177-0300); (703) 777-8810. Fax, (703) 777-8999. Stephen Denby, Executive Director. Web, www.vica.org.*

Membership: students, teachers, and administrators of trade, industrial, technical, and health occupations programs at public high schools, vocational schools, and two-year colleges. Promotes strong work skills, workplace ethics, understanding of free enterprise, and lifelong education.

See also American Assn. of Community Colleges (p. 190); Correctional Education Assn. (p. 519); National Community Education Assn. (p. 177)

7 Employment and Labor

GENERAL POLICY

AGENCIES

Labor Dept., *200 Constitution Ave. N.W., #S2018 20210; (202) 693-6000. Fax, (202) 693-6111. Alexis Herman, Secretary; Edward Montgomery, Deputy Secretary (Acting), (202) 693-6002. Information, (202) 693-4650. Library, (202) 219-6992. Locator, (202) 219-8191. Web, www.dol. gov.*

Promotes and develops the welfare of U.S. wage earners; administers federal labor laws; acts as principal adviser to the president on policies relating to wage earners, working conditions, and employment opportunities. Library open to the public.

Labor Dept., *Administrative Law Judges, 800 K St. N.W., #400 20001-8002; (202) 565-5330. Fax, (202) 565-5325. John Vittone, Chief Administrative Law Judge; Beverly Queen, Docket Clerk. Web, www.oalj.dol.gov.*

Presides over formal hearings to determine violations of minimum wage requirements, overtime payments, compensation benefits, employee discrimination, grant performance, alien certification, employee protection, and health and safety regulations set forth under numerous statutes, executive orders, and regulations. With few exceptions, hearings are required to be conducted in accordance with the Administrative Procedure Act.

Labor Dept., *Administrative Review Board, 200 Constitution Ave. N.W., #S4309 20210; (202) 219-4728. Fax, (202) 219-9315. Paul Greenberg, Chair. Web, www.dol.gov.*

Issues final decisions on appeals under the Service Contract Act, the Comprehensive Employment and Training Act, the Job Training Partnership Act, the Davis-Bacon Act, the Trade Act, the Surface Transportation Assistance Act, the Energy Reorganization Act, and several environmental laws, unemployment insurance conformity proceedings, and cases brought by the Office of Federal Contract Compliance Programs.

CONGRESS

General Accounting Office, *Health, Education, and Human Services, 441 G St. N.W. 20548; (202) 512-6806. Fax, (202) 512-5806. Victor S. Rezendes, Assistant Comptroller General.*

Independent, nonpartisan agency in the legislative branch. Audits, analyzes, and evaluates Labor Dept. programs; makes reports available to the public.

House Appropriations Committee, *Subcommittee on Labor, Health and Human Services, and Education, 2358 RHOB 20515; (202) 225-3508. Fax, (202) 225-3509.*

Rep. John Edward Porter, R-Ill., Chair; Tony McCann, Staff Director. Web, www.house.gov/appropriations.

Jurisdiction over legislation to appropriate funds for the Labor Dept., the National Labor Relations Board, National Mediation Board, Federal Mediation and Conciliation Service, and other labor-related agencies.

House Education and the Workforce Committee, *2181 RHOB 20515; (202) 225-4527. Fax, (202) 225-9571. Rep. Bill Goodling, R-Pa., Chair; Kevin D. Talley, Staff Director. Web, www.house.gov/ed_workforce.*

Jurisdiction over labor and employment legislation.

House Education and the Workforce Committee, *Subcommittee on Postsecondary Education, Training, and Life-Long Learning, 2181 RHOB 20515; (202) 225-4527. Fax, (202) 225-9571. Rep. Howard P. "Buck" McKeon, R-Calif., Chair; Kevin D. Talley, Staff Director. Web, www. house.gov/ed_workforce.*

Jurisdiction over public- and full-employment legislation.

Senate Appropriations Committee, *Subcommittee on Labor, Health and Human Services, and Education, SD-186 20510; (202) 224-7230. Fax, (202) 224-1360. Sen. Arlen Specter, R-Pa., Chair; Bettilou Taylor, Staff Director. Web, appropriations.senate.gov/labor.*

Jurisdiction over legislation to appropriate funds for the Labor Dept., National Labor Relations Board, National Mediation Board, Federal Mediation and Conciliation Service, and other labor-related agencies.

Senate Health, Education, Labor, and Pensions Committee, *Subcommittee on Employment, Safety, and Training, SH-607 20510; (202) 224-7229. Sen. Michael B. Enzi, R-Wyo., Chair; Raissa Geary, Staff Director. Web, labor.senate.gov.*

Jurisdiction over labor and employment legislation, including public- and full-employment legislation.

NONPROFIT

AFL-CIO (American Federation of Labor—Congress of Industrial Organizations), *815 16th St. N.W. 20006; (202) 637-5000. John J. Sweeney, President. General e-mail, feedback@aflcio.org. Web, www.aflcio.org.*

Voluntary federation of national and international labor unions in the United States. Represents members before Congress and other branches of government. Each member union conducts its own contract negotiations. Library open to the public.

American Civil Liberties Union, *National Capital Area, 1400 20th St. N.W. 20036; (202) 457-0800. Fax,*

LABOR DEPARTMENT

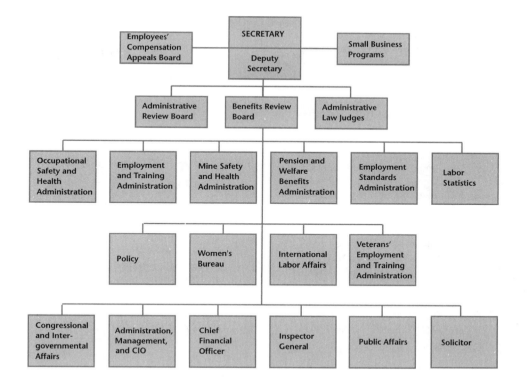

SECRETARY

Deputy Secretary

Employees' Compensation Appeals Board

Small Business Programs

Administrative Review Board

Benefits Review Board

Administrative Law Judges

Occupational Safety and Health Administration

Employment and Training Administration

Mine Safety and Health Administration

Pension and Welfare Benefits Administration

Employment Standards Administration

Labor Statistics

Policy

Women's Bureau

International Labor Affairs

Veterans' Employment and Training Administration

Congressional and Inter-governmental Affairs

Administration, Management, and CIO

Chief Financial Officer

Inspector General

Public Affairs

Solicitor

---

(202) 452-1868. Mary Jane DeFrank, Executive Director; Arthur B. Spitzer, Legal Director. Web, www.aclu.org.

Protects the civil rights and liberties of the citizens, including federal employees, of the Washington metropolitan area. Interests include First Amendment rights, privacy, and due process.

American Enterprise Institute for Public Policy Research, *Economic Policy Studies, 1150 17th St. N.W. 20036; (202) 862-5814. Fax, (202) 862-7177. Christopher DeMuth, President. Information, (202) 862-5800. Web, www.aei.org.*

Research and educational organization that studies trends in employment, earnings, the environment, health care, and income in the United States.

American Staffing Assn., *277 S. Washington St., #200, Alexandria, VA 22314; (703) 253-2020. Fax, (703) 253-2053. Richard Wahlquist, Executive Vice President. Web, www.asa.net.*

Membership: companies supplying other companies with workers on a temporary basis. Monitors legislation and regulations.

Campaign for America's Future, *1025 Connecticut Ave. N.W., #205 20036; (202) 955-5665. Fax, (202) 955-5606. Robert L. Borosage, Co-Director; Roger Hickey, Co-Director. General e-mail, info@ourfuture.org. Web, www. ourfuture.org.*

Operates the Campaign for America's Future and the Institute for America's Future. Advocates policies to help working people. Supports improved employee benefits, including health care, child care, and paid family leave; promotes lifelong education and training of workers. Seeks full employment, higher wages, and increased productivity. Monitors legislation and regulations.

Employment Policy Foundation, *1015 15th St. N.W., #1200 20005; (202) 789-8685. Fax, (202) 789-8684. Edward E. Potter, President. General e-mail, info@epfnet. org. Web, www.epfnet.org.*

Research and education foundation. Seeks employment policy that facilitates U.S. economic growth; increases productivity, job creation, and job security; and raises the standard of living of the American workforce. Interests include global competitiveness.

International Telework Assn., *204 E St. N.E. 20002; (202) 547-6157. Fax, (202) 546-3289. John Edwards, President. Web, www.telecommute.org.*

Membership: individuals, corporations, government agencies, educators, consultants, and vendors involved in telecommuting. Promotes the economic, social, and environmental benefits of telecommuting. Seeks to facilitate the development of telecommuting programs internationally.

Labor Policy Assn., *1015 15th St. N.W., #1200 20005; (202) 789-8670. Fax, (202) 789-0064. Jeffrey C. McGuiness, President. Web, www.lpa.org.*

Membership: corporate vice presidents in charge of employee relations. Promotes research in employee relations, particularly in federal employment policy and implementation. Interests include international labor issues, including immigration and child labor.

National Assn. of Personnel Services, *3133 Mount Vernon Ave., Alexandria, VA 22305; (703) 684-0180. Fax, (703) 684-0071. Dianne Callis, President. Web, www.napsweb.org.*

Membership: owners and managers of private personnel services companies, including permanent and temporary service firms. Monitors legislation and regulations concerning the personnel services industry.

National Assn. of Professional Employer Organizations, *901 N. Pitt St., #150, Alexandria, VA 22314; (703) 836-0466. Fax, (703) 836-0976. Milan P. Yager, Executive Vice President. Web, www.napeo.org.*

Membership: professional employer organizations. Conducts research; sponsors seminars and conferences for members. Monitors legislation and regulations.

Society for Human Resource Management, *1800 Duke St., Alexandria, VA 22314; (703) 548-3440. Fax, (703) 836-0367. Michael R. Losey, President. Information, (800) 283-7476. TTY, (703) 548-6999. General e-mail, shrm@shrm.org. Web, www.shrm.org.*

Membership: human resource management professionals. Monitors legislation and regulations concerning recruitment, training, and employment practices; occupational safety and health; compensation and benefits; employee and labor relations; and equal employment opportunity. Sponsors seminars and conferences.

U.S. Chamber of Commerce, *Economic Policy, 1615 H St. N.W. 20062-2000; (202) 659-6000. Fax, (202) 463-3188. Martin A. Regalia, Chief Economist. Press, (202) 463-5682. Web, www.uschamber.org.*

Monitors legislation and regulations affecting the business community, including employee benefits, health care, legal and regulatory affairs, transportation and telecommunications infrastructure, defense conversion, and equal employment opportunity.

International Issues

AGENCIES

Bureau of Labor Statistics *(Labor Dept.),* **Foreign Labor Statistics,** *2 Massachusetts Ave. N.E., #2120 20212; (202) 691-5654. Fax, (202) 691-5679. Mark Sherwood, Chief. Web, stats.bls.gov/flshome.htm.*

Issues statistical reports on labor force, productivity, employment, prices, and labor costs in foreign countries adjusted to U.S. concepts.

Commerce Dept., *Policy Analysis, 14th St. and Constitution Ave. N.W., #4862 20230; (202) 482-5703. Fax, (202) 482-0325. David A. Peterson, Senior Policy Adviser. Web, www.doc.gov.*

Responsible with the Labor Dept. and the State Dept. for U.S. government relations with the Geneva-based International Labor Organization (ILO), an agency of the United Nations that deals with worldwide labor issues.

Employment and Training Administration *(Labor Dept.),* **Trade Adjustment Assistance,** *200 Constitution Ave. N.W., #C4318 20210; (202) 219-5555. Fax, (202) 219-5753. Edward A. Tomchick, Director. Web, www.doleta.gov.*

Assists American workers who are totally or partially unemployed because of increased imports; offers training, job search and relocation assistance, weekly benefits at state unemployment insurance levels, and other reemployment services.

Labor Dept., *Foreign Relations, 200 Constitution Ave. N.W., #S5006 20210; (202) 219-7632. Fax, (202) 219-5613. Jim Perlmutter, Director. Web, www.dol.gov.*

Provides foreign governments with technical assistance in labor-related activities on a reimbursable basis. (Funding is provided by the U.S. Agency for International Development, international organizations, and foreign governments.) Participates with the State Dept. in managing the U.S. labor attaché program; conducts the U.S. International Visitors Program. Provides information on foreign labor developments, including foreign labor trends.

Labor Dept., *International Economic Affairs, 200 Constitution Ave. N.W., #S5325 20210; (202) 219-7597. Fax, (202) 219-5071. Jorge Perez-Lopez, Director. Web, www.dol.gov.*

Assists in developing U.S. foreign economic policy; examines the effect of foreign trade investment and immigration on income and job opportunities of American workers, domestic production, consumption, and the competitiveness of U.S. products.

Labor Dept., *International Labor Affairs,* *200 Constitution Ave. N.W., #S2235 20210; (202) 693-4770. Fax, (202) 693-4780. Andrew James Samet, Deputy Under Secretary. Web, www.dol.gov.*

Assists in developing international economic policy relating to labor; helps represent the United States in multilateral and bilateral trade negotiations. Evaluates the effects of immigration policy on the wages and employment of U.S. workers.

Labor Dept., *Office of International Organizations,* *200 Constitution Ave. N.W., #S5311 20210; (202) 219-6241. Fax, (202) 219-9074. H. Charles Spring, Director. Web, www.dol.gov.*

Provides administrative support for U.S. participation in the International Labor Organization (ILO) and at the Paris-based Organization for Economic Cooperation and Development (OECD), which studies and reports on world economic issues.

Labor Dept., *U.S. International Visitors Program,* *200 Constitution Ave. N.W., #S5006 20210; (202) 219-7632. Fax, (202) 219-5613. Linda Bates-Brooks, Director. Web, www.dol.gov.*

Works with the State Dept., the Agency for International Development, and other agencies in arranging visits and training programs for foreign officials interested in U.S. labor and trade unions.

President's Committee on the International Labor Organization *(Labor Dept.),* *200 Constitution Ave. N.W., #S5311 20210; (202) 219-6241. Fax, (202) 219-9074. Alexis Herman, Chair; Andrew James Samet, U.S. ILO Representative, (202) 693-4770.*

Advisory committee of government, employer, and worker representatives, including secretaries of state, commerce, and labor, the president's national security adviser, the president of the U.S. Council for International Business, and the president of the AFL-CIO. Formulates and coordinates policy on the International Labor Organization (ILO); advises the president and the secretary of labor.

State Dept., *International Labor Affairs,* *2201 C St. N.W., #4829A 20520; (202) 647-3663. Fax, (202) 647-0431. Edmond McWilliams, Director. Web, www.state.gov.*

Uses bilateral and multilateral diplomacy and works with trade unions and the U.S. business community to promote worker rights around the world. Concerned with issues of core labor standards such as child labor, forced labor, and freedom of association.

State Dept., *International Organization Affairs,* *2201 C St. N.W., #6323 20520-6319; (202) 647-9600. Fax, (202) 736-4116. C. David Welch, Assistant Secretary. Press, (202) 647-8490. Web, www.state.gov.*

Responsible, with the Labor Dept. and the Commerce Dept., for U.S. government relations with the International Labor Organization (ILO).

CONGRESS

House Ways and Means Committee, *Subcommittee on Trade,* *1104 LHOB 20515; (202) 225-6649. Fax, (202) 226-0158. Rep. Philip M. Crane, R-Ill., Chair; Angela Paolini Ellard, Staff Director. Web, www.house.gov/ ways_means.*

Jurisdiction over legislation on foreign trade, including its impact on U.S. workers.

Senate Finance Committee, *Subcommittee on International Trade,* *SD-219 20510; (202) 224-4515. Fax, (202) 224-5920. Sen. Charles E. Grassley, R-Iowa, Chair; Frank Polk, Staff Director. Web, finance.senate.gov.*

Holds hearings on legislation concerning foreign trade, including its impact on U.S. workers.

INTERNATIONAL ORGANIZATIONS

International Labor Organization, *Washington Office,* *1828 L St. N.W., #600 20036; (202) 653-7652. Fax, (202) 653-7687. Anthony G. Freeman, Director. Web, www.us.ilo.org.*

Specialized agency of the United Nations. Works to improve working conditions, create employment, and promote human rights worldwide. Establishes international labor standards; conducts training and technical assistance. Washington office serves as liaison between the ILO and U.S. government, employer, and worker groups. Library open to the public. (Headquarters in Geneva.)

NONPROFIT

American Center for International Labor Solidarity, *1925 K St. N.W., #300 20006; (202) 778-4500. Fax, (202) 778-4525. Harry Kamberis, Executive Director. General e-mail, acils@acils.org.*

Provides assistance to free and democratic trade unions worldwide. Provides trade union leadership courses in collective bargaining, union organization, trade integration, labor-management cooperation, union administration, and political theories. Sponsors social and community development projects; focus includes, child labor, human and worker rights, and the role of women in labor unions.

International Labor Rights Fund, *733 15th St. N.W., #920 20005; (202) 347-4100. Fax, (202) 347-4885. Pharis J. Harvey, Executive Director. General e-mail, laborrights@ igc.org. Web, www.laborrights.org.*

Promotes the enforcement of international labor rights. Pursues legal and administrative actions on behalf of working people; advocates for better protection of workers. Concerns include child labor, sweatshops, and exploited workers. Monitors legislation and regulations on national and international levels.

Society for Human Resource Management, *Institute for International Human Resources, 1800 Duke St., Alexandria, VA 22314-3499; (703) 548-3440. Fax, (703) 836-0367. Brian Glade, Vice President. General e-mail, intldiv@shrm.org. Web, www.shrmglobal.org.*

Provides human resources professionals with specialized, timely information on the worldwide business environment and its implications on the human resources profession.

Labor Standards and Practices

See also Equal Employment Opportunity (this chapter)

AGENCIES

Bureau of Labor Statistics *(Labor Dept.), Compensation and Working Conditions, 2 Massachusetts Ave. N.E. 20212; (202) 691-6300. Fax, (202) 691-6310. Kathleen MacDonald, Associate Commissioner. Web, www.bls.gov/ comhome.*

Conducts annual area wage surveys to determine occupational pay information in individual labor markets. Conducts industry wage surveys, which provide wage and employee benefit information; presents data for selected white- and blue-collar jobs.

Employment Standards Administration *(Labor Dept.), 200 Constitution Ave. N.W. 20210; (202) 693-0200. Fax, (202) 693-0218. Bernard Anderson, Assistant Secretary.*

Administers and enforces employment laws and regulations. Responsibilities include ensuring compliance among federal contractors, administering benefits claims for federal employees and other workers, and protecting workers' wages and working conditions.

Employment Standards Administration *(Labor Dept.), Fair Labor Standards Act Enforcement, 200 Constitution Ave. N.W., #S3516 20210; (202) 693-0067. Fax,*

(202) 693-1432. Daniel F. Sweeney, Chief. Web, www.dol. gov/dol/esa.

Issues interpretations and rulings of the Fair Labor Standards Act of 1938, as amended (Federal Minimum Wage and Overtime Pay Law).

Employment Standards Administration *(Labor Dept.), Federal Contract Compliance Programs, 200 Constitution Ave. N.W., #C3325 20210; (202) 693-0101. Fax, (202) 693-1304. Shirley J. Wilcher, Deputy Assistant Secretary.*

Monitors and enforces government contractors' compliance with federal laws and regulations on equal employment opportunities and affirmative action, including employment rights of minorities, women, persons with disabilities, and disabled and Vietnam-era veterans.

Employment Standards Administration *(Labor Dept.), Government Contracts, 200 Constitution Ave. N.W., #S3018 20210; (202) 693-0064. Fax, (202) 693-1432. Timothy Helm, Team Leader.*

Enforces the Davis-Bacon Act, the Walsh-Healey Public Contracts Act, the Contract Work Hours and Safety Standards Act, the Service Contract Act, and other related government contract labor standards statutes.

Employment Standards Administration *(Labor Dept.), Special Employment, 200 Constitution Ave. N.W., #S3510 20210; (202) 693-0072. Fax, (202) 693-1432. Arthur M. Kerschner Jr., Team Leader.*

Authorizes subminimum wages under the Fair Labor Standards Act for certain categories of workers, including full-time students, student learners, and workers with disabilities. Administers the Fair Labor Standards Act restrictions on working at home in certain industries. Administers special minimum wage provisions applicable in Puerto Rico and American Samoa.

Employment Standards Administration *(Labor Dept.), Wage and Hour Division, 200 Constitution Ave. N.W., #S3502 20210; (202) 693-0051. Fax, (202) 693-1406. T. Michael Kerr, Administrator. Web, www.dol.gov/ dol/esa.*

Enforces the minimum-wage and overtime provisions of the Fair Labor Standards Act.

Employment Standards Administration *(Labor Dept.), Wage Determinations, 200 Constitution Ave. N.W. 20210; (202) 693-0062. Fax, (202) 693-1425. Nila Stovall, Chief, Service Contract Wage Determinations, (202) 693-0073; Carl Poleskey, Chief, Construction Wage Determinations, (202) 693-0086; William Gross, Director.*

Issues prevailing wage determinations under the Service Contract Act of 1965, the Davis-Bacon Act, and related acts.

House Education and the Workforce Committee, *Subcommittee on Workforce Protections,* 2181 RHOB 20515; (202) 225-4527. Fax, (202) 225-9571. Rep. Cass Ballenger, R-N.C., Chair; Kevin D. Talley, Staff Director. Web, www.house.gov/ed_workforce.

Jurisdiction over legislation on minimum wage and wage and hour standards, including the Davis-Bacon Act, the Walsh-Healey Public Contracts Act, and the Fair Labor Standards Act; jurisdiction over mandated benefits, including those for government contractors. Jurisdiction over legislation on job discrimination by government contractors, electronic monitoring, and polygraph testing.

Senate Health, Education, Labor, and Pensions Committee, *Subcommittee on Employment, Safety, and Training,* SH-607 20510; (202) 224-7229. Sen. Michael B. Enzi, R-Wyo., Chair; Raissa Geary, Staff Director. Web, labor.senate.gov.

Jurisdiction over legislation on job discrimination by government contractors, minimum wage, wage and hour standards, and mandated benefits, including those for government contractors.

Statistics and Information

AGENCIES

Bureau of Labor Statistics *(Labor Dept.),* 2 Massachusetts Ave. N.E., #4040 20212; (202) 691-7800. Fax, (202) 691-7797. Katharine G. Abraham, Commissioner. Press, (202) 606-5902. General e-mail, labstathelpdesk@bls.gov. Web, stats.bls.gov.

Collects, analyzes, and publishes data on labor economics, including employment, unemployment, hours of work, wages, employee compensation, prices, consumer expenditures, labor-management relations, productivity, technological developments, occupational safety and health, and structure and growth of the economy. Publishes reports on these statistical trends, including the Consumer Price Index, the Producer Price Index, and Employment and Earnings.

Bureau of Labor Statistics *(Labor Dept.), Employment and Unemployment Statistics,* 2 Massachusetts Ave. N.E., #4945 20212; (202) 691-6400. Fax, (202) 691-6425. John M. Galvin, Associate Commissioner. General e-mail, labstathelpdesk@bls.gov. Web, www.bls.gov.

Monitors employment and unemployment trends on national and local levels; compiles data on worker and industry employment and earnings.

Bureau of Labor Statistics *(Labor Dept.), Employment Projections,* 2 Massachusetts Ave. N.E., #2135 20212; (202) 691-5700. Fax, (202) 691-5745. Neal H. Rosenthal, Associate Commissioner. Web, stats.bls.gov.

Develops economic, industrial, and demographic employment projections according to industry and occupation. Provides career guidance material.

Bureau of Labor Statistics *(Labor Dept.), Foreign Labor Statistics,* 2 Massachusetts Ave. N.E., #2120 20212; (202) 691-5654. Fax, (202) 691-5679. Mark Sherwood, Chief. Web, stats.bls.gov/flshome.htm.

Issues statistical reports on labor force, productivity, employment, prices, and labor costs in foreign countries adjusted to U.S. concepts.

Bureau of Labor Statistics *(Labor Dept.), Local Area Unemployment Statistics,* 2 Massachusetts Ave. N.E., #4675 20212; (202) 691-6390. Fax, (202) 691-6459. Sharon P. Brown, Chief. Information, (202) 691-6392. General e-mail, labstathelpdesk@bls.gov.

Issues labor force and unemployment statistics for states, metropolitan statistical areas, cities with populations of 25,000 or more, counties, and other areas covered under federal assistance programs.

Bureau of Labor Statistics *(Labor Dept.), Monthly Industry Employment Statistics,* 2 Massachusetts Ave. N.E., #4860 20212; (202) 691-6528. Fax, (202) 691-6644. Patricia Getz, Chief. Information, (202) 691-6555.

Analyzes and publishes national-level employment, hour, and earnings statistics based on data submitted by the states; develops statistical information on employment, hours, and earnings by industry for the nation, states, and metropolitan statistical areas.

Bureau of Labor Statistics *(Labor Dept.), Productivity and Technology,* 2 Massachusetts Ave. N.E., #2150 20212; (202) 691-5600. Fax, (202) 691-5664. Marlyn Manser, Associate Commissioner. TTY, (202) 691-6034.

Develops and analyzes productivity measures for U.S. industries and total economy; adjusts productivity measures of foreign countries for comparison with U.S. standards; studies implications of technological changes on employment and occupational distribution.

Census Bureau *(Commerce Dept.), Demographic Surveys,* 4700 Silver Hill Rd., Suitland, MD 20233-8400; (301) 457-3773. Fax, (301) 457-2306. Chester E. Bowie, Chief.

Conducts surveys and compiles official monthly employment and unemployment statistics for the Labor Dept.'s Bureau of Labor Statistics.

Employment and Training Administration *(Labor Dept.), Office of Workforce Security: Actuarial Services,* 200 Constitution Ave. N.W., #S4231 20210; (202) 219-

6209. Fax, (202) 219-8506. Cynthia L. Ambler, Statistician; Grace Kilbane, Director.

Compiles statistics on state unemployment insurance programs. Studies unemployment issues related to benefits.

Occupational Safety and Health Administration (OSHA), *(Labor Dept.),* **Statistics,** *200 Constitution Ave. N.W., #N3507 20210; (202) 693-1702. Fax, (202) 693-1631. Scott Richardson, Director.*

Compiles and provides all statistical data for OSHA, such as occupational injury and illness records, which are used in setting standards and making policy.

CONGRESS

House Education and the Workforce Committee, *Subcommittee on Employer-Employee Relations, 2181 RHOB 20515; (202) 225-4527. Fax, (202) 225-9571. Rep. John A. Boehner, R-Ohio, Chair; Kevin D. Talley, Staff Director. Web, www.house.gov/ed_workforce.*

Jurisdiction over legislation on the Bureau of Labor Statistics.

Senate Health, Education, Labor, and Pensions Committee, *Subcommittee on Employment, Safety, and Training, SH-607 20510; (202) 224-7229. Sen. Michael B. Enzi, R-Wyo., Chair; Raissa Geary, Staff Director. Web, labor.senate.gov.*

Jurisdiction over legislation on the Bureau of Labor Statistics.

Unemployment Benefits

See also Statistics and Information (this section)

AGENCIES

Employment and Training Administration *(Labor Dept.),* **Office of Workforce Security: Actuarial Services,** *200 Constitution Ave. N.W., #S4231 20210; (202) 219-6209. Fax, (202) 219-8506. Grace Kilbane, Director; Cynthia L. Ambler, Statistician.*

Directs and reviews the state-administered system that provides income support for unemployed workers nationwide; advises state and federal employment security agencies on wage-loss, worker dislocation, and adjustment assistance compensation programs.

Employment and Training Administration *(Labor Dept.),* **Trade Adjustment Assistance,** *200 Constitution Ave. N.W., #C4318 20210; (202) 219-5555. Fax, (202) 219-5753. Edward A. Tomchick, Director. Web, www.doleta.gov.*

Assists American workers who are totally or partially unemployed because of increased imports; offers train-

ing, job search and relocation assistance, weekly benefits at state unemployment insurance levels, and other reemployment services.

CONGRESS

House Ways and Means Committee, *Subcommittee on Human Resources, B317 RHOB 20515; (202) 225-1025. Fax, (202) 225-9480. Rep. Nancy L. Johnson, R-Conn., Chair; Ronald Haskins, Staff Director. Web, www.house.gov/ways_means.*

Jurisdiction over unemployment benefits legislation.

Senate Finance Committee, *Subcommittee on Social Security and Family Policy, SD-219 20510; (202) 224-4515. Fax, (202) 224-5920. Sen. Don Nickles, R-Okla., Chair; Alec Bachon, Staff Contact. Web, finance.senate.gov.*

Holds hearings on unemployment benefits legislation.

NONPROFIT

Interstate Conference of Employment Security Agencies, *444 N. Capitol St. N.W., #142 20001; (202) 434-8020. Fax, (202) 434-8033. Emily DeRocco, Executive Director. Web, www.icesa.org.*

Membership: state employment security administrators. Informs members of unemployment insurance programs and legislation. Provides unemployment insurance and reemployment professionals with opportunities for networking and information exchange.

◼ EMPLOYMENT AND TRAINING PROGRAMS

See also Civil Service (chap. 10); Equal Employment Opportunity (this chapter); Military Personnel and Veterans (chap. 15); Social Services and Disabilities (chap. 18)

AGENCIES

Employment and Training Administration *(Labor Dept.), 200 Constitution Ave. N.W., #S2307 20210; (202) 693-2700. Fax, (202) 693-2725. Ray Bramucci, Assistant Secretary. Public Affairs, (202) 219-6871. Web, www.doleta.gov.*

Responsible for employment, training, and trade adjustment programs for economically disadvantaged, unemployed, and dislocated workers. Administers and directs policy for the U.S. Employment Service, the Unemployment Insurance Service, and the Office of Work-Based Learning. Administers and directs programs for native Americans, migrants, youth, older workers, and workers with disabilities.

Employment and Training Administration *(Labor Dept.), U.S. Employment Service, 200 Constitution Ave. N.W., #N4464 20210; (202) 219-5257. Fax, (202) 208-5854. Timothy Sullivan, Director.*

Assists states in maintaining a system of local employment-service centers for job seekers and employers.

Employment and Training Administration *(Labor Dept.), Work-Based Learning, 200 Constitution Ave. N.W., #N5426 20210; (202) 219-5339. Fax, (202) 219-5938. Shirley Smith, Administrator.*

Responsible for Worker Retraining and Adjustment programs (including the Trade Adjustment Assistance Program and the Economic Dislocation and Worker Adjustment Assistance Act); examines training initiatives and technology.

National Occupational Information Coordinating Committee, *2100 M St. N.W., #156 20037; (202) 653-5665. Fax, (202) 653-2123. Juliette N. Lester, Executive Director. General e-mail, lester-juliette@dol.gov. Web, www.noicc.gov.*

Interagency group that works with the departments of Agriculture, Commerce, Defense, Education, and Labor; provides information on civilian and military occupations, educational institutions, and training programs; develops systems to provide labor market and occupational information to vocational education and employment-related program planners and administrators at the state level; supports state efforts to provide citizens with career information and guidance.

CONGRESS

House Education and the Workforce Committee, *2181 RHOB 20515; (202) 225-4527. Fax, (202) 225-9571. Rep. Bill Goodling, R-Pa., Chair; Kevin D. Talley, Staff Director. Web, www.house.gov/ed_workforce.*

Jurisdiction over work incentive, education, and job training programs for youth and public assistance recipients, including the Job Opportunities and Basic Skills Training Program and the Job Training Partnership Act.

House Education and the Workforce Committee, *Subcommittee on Early Childhood, Youth, and Families, 2181 RHOB 20515; (202) 225-4527. Fax, (202) 225-9571. Rep. Michael N. Castle, R-Del., Chair; Kevin D. Talley, Staff Director. Web, www.house.gov/ed_workforce.*

Jurisdiction over legislation on employment training programs for elderly workers.

House Education and the Workforce Committee, *Subcommittee on Postsecondary Education, Training,*

and Life-Long Learning, 2181 RHOB 20515; (202) 225-4527. Fax, (202) 225-9571. Rep. Howard P. "Buck" McKeon, R-Calif., Chair; Kevin D. Talley, Staff Director. Web, www. house.gov/ed_workforce.

Jurisdiction over employment training legislation, including legislation on apprenticeship programs, on-the-job training, dislocated workers and plant shutdowns, displaced homemakers, rural workers, and vocational rehabilitation and education for workers with disabilities. Jurisdiction over youth and young adult conservation corps programs.

House Education and the Workforce Committee, *Subcommittee on Workforce Protections, 2181 RHOB 20515; (202) 225-4527. Fax, (202) 225-9571. Rep. Cass Ballenger, R-N.C., Chair; Kevin D. Talley, Staff Director. Web, www.house.gov/ed_workforce.*

Jurisdiction over legislation on minimum wage and wage and hour standards, including the Davis-Bacon Act, the Walsh-Healey Act, and the Fair Labor Standards Act; jurisdiction over mandated benefits, including those for government contractors.

House Judiciary Committee, *Subcommittee on Immigration and Claims, B370B RHOB 20515; (202) 225-5727. Fax, (202) 225-3672. Rep. Lamar Smith, R-Texas, Chair; George Fishman, Counsel. General e-mail, Judiciary@mail.house.gov. Web, www.house.gov/judiciary.*

Jurisdiction over legislation on foreign laborers once they are in the United States and on employer sanctions for not complying with the Immigration and Refugee Control Act of 1986.

Senate Finance Committee, *Subcommittee on Social Security and Family Policy, SD-219 20510; (202) 224-4515. Fax, (202) 224-5920. Sen. Don Nickles, R-Okla., Chair; Alec Bachon, Staff Contact. Web, finance.senate.gov.*

Holds hearings on legislation affecting the Job Opportunities and Basic Skills Training Program.

Senate Health, Education, Labor, and Pensions Committee, *Subcommittee on Aging, SH-608 20510; (202) 224-2962. Fax, (202) 228-0412. Sen. Mike DeWine, R-Ohio, Chair; Karla Carpenter, Staff Director. Web, labor. senate.gov.*

Jurisdiction over legislation on employment training programs for elderly workers.

Senate Health, Education, Labor, and Pensions Committee, *Subcommittee on Employment, Safety, and Training, SH-607 20510; (202) 224-7229. Sen. Michael B. Enzi, R-Wyo., Chair; Vacant, Staff Director. Web, labor.senate.gov.*

Jurisdiction over education and job training programs for youth and public assistance recipients, including the Job Training Partnership Act and legislation on apprenticeship programs, on-the-job training, and displaced homemakers.

Senate Judiciary Committee, *Subcommittee on Immigration, SD-323 20510; (202) 224-6098. Fax, (202) 228-4506. Sen. Spencer Abraham, R-Mich., Chair; Lee Lieberman Otis, Chief Counsel. Web, judiciary.senate. gov/immigrat.htm.*

Jurisdiction over legislation on nonimmigrant foreign laborers once they are in the United States.

Senate Special Committee on Aging, *SD-G31 20510; (202) 224-5364. Fax, (202) 224-8660. Sen. Charles E. Grassley, R-Iowa, Chair; Ted Totman, Staff Director. Web, aging.senate.gov.*

Studies and makes recommendations on legislation and federal programs affecting older Americans, including the areas of age discrimination, compensation, and unemployment; oversees Older Americans Act programs.

NONPROFIT

AFL-CIO Working for America Institute, *1101 14th St. N.W., #320 20005; (202) 638-3912. Fax, (202) 783-6536. Bruce Herman, Executive Director. General e-mail, info@workingforamerica.org.*

Provides technical assistance to labor unions, employers, education agencies, and community groups for workplace programs focusing on dislocated workers, economically disadvantaged workers, and skill upgrading. Interests include new technologies and workplace innovations.

American Labor Education Center, *2000 P St. N.W., #300 20036; (202) 828-5170. Fax, (202) 785-3862. Karen Ohmans, Director. General e-mail, amlabor@mindspring. com.*

Produces materials for workers and unions. Interests include occupational health and safety, communication skills, and other labor issues.

American Society for Training and Development, *1640 King St., Alexandria, VA 22313-2043; (703) 683-8100. Fax, (703) 683-1523. Tina Sung, President. Web, www.astd.org.*

Membership: trainers and human resource developers. Promotes workplace training programs and human resource development. Interests include productivity, job training and retraining, participative management, and unemployment. Holds conferences and provides information on technical and skills training.

Employee Relocation Council, *1720 N St. N.W. 20036; (202) 857-0857. Fax, (202) 466-2384. H. Cris Collie, Executive Vice President. Web, www.erc.org.*

Membership: corporations that relocate employees and moving, real estate, and relocation management companies. Researches and recommends policies that provide a smooth transition for relocated employees and their families. Holds conferences and issues publications on employee relocation issues.

International Federation of Training and Development Organizations, *1800 Duke St., Alexandria, VA 22314; (703) 535-6011. Fax, (703) 836-0367. David A. Waugh, Secretary General. General e-mail, iftdo@shrm. org. Web, www.iftdo.org.*

Operates a worldwide network that seeks to identify, develop, and transfer knowledge skills and technology to enhance organizational growth and workplace productivity.

Interstate Conference of Employment Security Agencies, *444 N. Capitol St. N.W., #142 20001; (202) 434-8020. Fax, (202) 434-8033. Emily DeRocco, Executive Director. Web, www.icesa.org.*

Membership: state employment security administrators. Informs members of federal legislation on job placement, veterans' affairs, and employment and training programs. Distributes labor market information; trains new state administrators and executive staff. Provides employment and training professionals with opportunities for networking and information exchange.

National Alliance of Business, *Workforce Adjustment, 1201 New York Ave. N.W., #700 20005; (202) 289-2905. Fax, (202) 289-1303. Roberts T. Jones, President. Press, (202) 289-2860. General e-mail, info@nab.com. Web, www.nab.com.*

Represents the interests of business in developing a quality workforce. Promotes partnerships between government and business at the federal, state, and local levels. Interests include improving public education, addressing the employment and training needs of individuals in a globally competitive economy, and easing the transition from school to the workplace.

National Assn. of Counties, *Employment and Training Program, 440 1st St. N.W., 8th Floor 20001; (202) 393-6226. Fax, (202) 737-0480. Gary Gortenberg, Director. Web, www.naco.org.*

Oversees, directs, and offers technical assistance to members participating in federal job training programs; informs members of related legislation. Assists county officials, private industry councils, workforce development boards, and service delivery areas in implementing workforce development systems.

National Assn. of Manufacturers, *Employment Policy, 1331 Pennsylvania Ave. N.W., 6th Floor 20004-1790;*

(202) 637-3133. Fax, (202) 637-3182. Jenny Krese, Director.

Interests include opportunities for dislocated workers, striker replacement, vocational education, matters relating to the National Labor Relations Act, and the effect of high technology on the workforce.

National Assn. of Private Industry Councils, *1201 New York Ave. N.W., #350 20005; (202) 289-2950. Fax, (202) 289-2846. Robert F. Knight, President. Web, www. work-web.com/napic.*

Membership: private industry councils and state job training coordinating councils established under the Job Training Partnership Act of 1982. Interests include job training opportunities for youth and unemployed, economically disadvantaged, and dislocated workers; and private sector involvement in federal employment and training policy. Provides members with technical assistance; holds conferences and seminars.

National Assn. of Workforce Development Professionals, *1620 Eye St. N.W., Lower Level 30 20006-4005; (202) 887-6120. Fax, (202) 887-8216. Paul Mendez, Executive Director. General e-mail, nawdp@aol.com. Web, www.nawdp.org.*

Membership: professionals and policymakers in the employment and training field. Promotes professionalism, information exchange, networking, and professional growth in the workforce development field.

National Center on Education and the Economy, *America's Choice District and School Design, 700 11th St. N.W., #750 20001; (202) 783-3668. Fax, (202) 783-3672. Mary Ann Mays, Director. General e-mail, info@ ncee.org. Web, www.ncee.org.*

Partnership of states, school districts, corporations, foundations, and nonprofit organizations that provides tools and technical assistance for school districts to improve education and training for the workplace.

National Governors' Assn., *Center for Policy Research: Training and Employment Program, 444 N. Capitol St. N.W., #267 20001-1512; (202) 624-5345. Fax, (202) 624-5313. Martin Simon, Director. Press, (202) 624-5331.*

Provides information and technical assistance to members participating in federal job training programs, including programs authorized under the federal workforce development programs; informs members of related legislation. Provides technical assistance to members in areas of work and welfare programs, youth programs, employment services, dislocated workers, and dropout prevention.

National Institute for Work and Learning, *1825 Connecticut Ave. N.W., 7th Floor 20009-1202; (202) 884-8186. Fax, (202) 884-8422. Ivan Charner, Vice President.*

Public policy research organization that seeks to improve collaboration between educational and business institutions. Conducts demonstration projects with communities throughout the country on employer-funded tuition aid, youth transition from school to work, and employee education and career development. Conducts research on education and work issues. Library open to the public. (Affiliated with the Academy for Educational Development.)

U.S. Chamber of Commerce, *Center for Workforce Preparation, 1615 H St. N.W. 20062-2000; (202) 463-5525. Fax, (202) 822-2468. Beth Buehlmann, Executive Director. Web, www.uschamber.com/cwp.*

Works with state and local chambers on educational reform, human resource, and job training issues.

U.S. Conference of Mayors, *Employment and Training Council, 1620 Eye St. N.W., #400 20006; (202) 861-6724. Fax, (202) 293-2352. Joan Crigger, Assistant Executive Director.*

Offers technical assistance to members participating in federal job training programs; monitors related legislation; acts as an information clearinghouse on employment and training programs.

See also Corporation for Enterprise Development (p. 414)

Aliens

AGENCIES

Administration for Children and Families *(Health and Human Services Dept.), Refugee Resettlement, 901 D St. S.W., 6th Floor 20447; (202) 401-9246. Fax, (202) 401-5487. Lavinia Limon, Director.*

Directs a domestic resettlement program for refugees; reimburses states for costs incurred in giving refugees monetary and medical assistance; awards funds to private resettlement agencies for providing refugees with monetary assistance and case management; provides states and nonprofit agencies with grants for social services such as English and employment training.

Employment and Training Administration *(Labor Dept.), Foreign Labor Certification, 200 Constitution Ave. N.W., #N4456 20210; (202) 219-5263. Fax, (202) 208-5844. James Norris, Chief.*

Sets policies and guidelines for regional offices that certify applications for alien employment in the United

States; determines whether U.S. citizens are available for those jobs and whether employment of aliens will adversely affect similarly employed U.S. citizens.

Apprenticeship Programs

AGENCIES

Employment and Training Administration *(Labor Dept.), Apprenticeship and Training,* 200 Constitution Ave. N.W., #N4649 20210; (202) 219-5921. Fax, (202) 219-5011. Anthony Swoope, Administrator, (202) 219-5921. Library, (202) 219-6992. Web, www.doleta.gov/bat.

Promotes establishment of apprenticeship programs in private industry and the public sector. Library open to the public.

Employment and Training Administration *(Labor Dept.), Federal Committee on Apprenticeship,* 200 Constitution Ave. N.W., #N4649 20210; (202) 219-5943. Fax, (202) 219-5011. Anthony Swoope, Administrator, (202) 219-5921.

Advises the secretary of labor on the role of apprenticeship programs in employment training and on safety standards for those programs; encourages sponsors to include these standards in planning apprenticeship programs.

Dislocated Workers

AGENCIES

Employment and Training Administration *(Labor Dept.), Work-Based Learning,* 200 Constitution Ave. N.W., #N5426 20210; (202) 219-5339. Fax, (202) 219-5938. Shirley Smith, Administrator.

Responsible for dislocated worker retraining programs.

NONPROFIT

National Assn. of Manufacturers, *Employment Policy,* 1331 Pennsylvania Ave. N.W., 6th Floor 20004-1790; (202) 637-3133. Fax, (202) 637-3182. Jenny Krese, Director.

Interests include opportunities for dislocated workers and vocational education.

National Assn. of Private Industry Councils, 1201 New York Ave. N.W., #350 20005; (202) 289-2950. Fax, (202) 289-2846. Robert F. Knight, President. Web, www.work-web.com/napic.

Membership: private industry councils and state job training coordinating councils established under the Job Training Partnership Act of 1982. Interests include job training opportunities for dislocated workers.

National Governors' Assn., *Center for Policy Research: Training and Employment Program,* 444 N. Capitol St. N.W., #267 20001-1512; (202) 624-5345. Fax, (202) 624-5313. Martin Simon, Director. Press, (202) 624-5331.

Provides technical assistance to members participating in employment and training activities for dislocated workers.

Migrant and Seasonal Farm Workers

AGENCIES

Employment and Training Administration *(Labor Dept.), Migrant Seasonal Farm Worker Programs,* 200 Constitution Ave. N.W., #N4645 20210; (202) 219-5500. Fax, (202) 219-6338. Licia Fernandez-Mott, Chief.

Provides funds for programs that help seasonal farm workers and their families find better jobs in agriculture and other areas. Services include occupational training, education, and job development and placement.

Employment Standards Administration *(Labor Dept.), Farm Labor Programs,* 200 Constitution Ave. N.W., #S3510 20210; (202) 693-0070. Fax, (202) 693-1432. Mike Hancock, Chief.

Administers and enforces the Migrant and Seasonal Agricultural Worker Protection Act, which protects migrant and seasonal agricultural workers from substandard labor practices by farm labor contractors, agricultural employers, and agricultural associations.

NONPROFIT

Assn. of Farmworker Opportunity Programs, 1611 N. Kent St., #910, Arlington, VA 22209-2111; (703) 528-4141. Fax, (703) 528-4145. Lynda D. Mull, Executive Director. General e-mail, afop@afop.org. Web, www.afop.org.

Represents state-level organizations that provide services and support to migrant and guest workers. Monitors legislation and conducts research.

Migrant Legal Action Program, P.O. Box 53308 20009; (202) 462-7744. Fax, (202) 462-7914. Roger C. Rosenthal, Executive Director. General e-mail, hn1645@handsnet.org.

Supports and assists local legal services, migrant education, migrant health issues, and other organizations and private attorneys with respect to issues involving the living and working conditions of migrant farm workers. Monitors legislation and regulations.

United Farm Workers of America, *Washington Office,* c/o AFL-CIO, 815 16th St. N.W. 20006; (202) 637-

5212. Fax, (202) 637-5012. Rudy Arredondo, Manager. Web, www.ufw.org.

Membership: approximately 50,000 farm workers. Helps members negotiate pay, benefits, and better working conditions; conducts training programs and workshops. Focus includes immigration and migrant workers. Monitors legislation and regulations. (Headquarters in Keene, Calif.; affiliated with the AFL-CIO.)

See also National Council of Agricultural Employers (p. 39)

Older Workers

AGENCIES

Employment and Training Administration *(Labor Dept.), Older Worker Programs,* 200 Constitution Ave. N.W., #N4641 20210; (202) 219-5904. Fax, (202) 219-6338. Erich W. Larisch, Chief.

Administers the Senior Community Service Employment Program, which provides funds for part-time, community service work-training programs; the programs pay minimum wage and are operated by national sponsoring organizations and state and territorial governments. The program is aimed at economically disadvantaged persons age fifty-five and over.

NONPROFIT

AARP, *Senior Community Service Employment Program,* 601 E St. N.W. 20049; (202) 434-2020. Fax, (202) 434-6446. Jim Seith, Director. Web, www.aarp.org.

Conducts a federally funded work-experience program for economically disadvantaged older persons; places trainees in community service jobs and helps them reenter the labor force.

National Council on the Aging, *Senior Community Service Employment Program,* 409 3rd St. S.W., 2nd Floor 20024; (202) 479-6631. Fax, (202) 479-0735. Donald Davis, Vice President. Web, www.maturityworks.org.

Works with the Labor Dept. under the authority of the Older Americans Act to provide workers age fifty-five and over with employment, community service, and training opportunities in their resident communities. Library open to the public.

National Senior Citizens Educational and Research Center, *Employment and Community Programs,* 8403 Colesville Rd., #1200, Silver Spring, MD 20910-3314; (301) 578-8800. Fax, (301) 578-8999. Dorinda Fox, Director.

Operates the Labor Dept.'s Senior Community Service Employment Program, which provides funds for part-time, community service work-training programs and is aimed at low-income individuals age fifty-five and over.

Workers with Disabilities

AGENCIES

Committee for Purchase from People Who Are Blind or Severely Disabled, 1215 Jefferson Davis Hwy., #310, Arlington, VA 22202-4302; (703) 603-7740. Fax, (703) 603-0655. Leon Wilson, Executive Director.

Presidentially appointed committee. Determines which products and services are suitable for federal procurement from qualified nonprofit agencies that employ people who are blind or have other severe disabilities; seeks to increase employment opportunities for these individuals.

Employment Standards Administration *(Labor Dept.), Special Employment,* 200 Constitution Ave. N.W., #S3510 20210; (202) 693-0072. Fax, (202) 693-1432. Arthur M. Kerschner Jr., Team Leader.

Administers certification of special lower minimum wage rates for workers with disabilities and impaired earning capacity; wage applies in industry, sheltered workshops, hospitals, institutions, and group homes.

Equal Employment Opportunity Commission (EEOC), *Interagency Committee on Employees with Disabilities,* 1801 L St. N.W. 20507; (202) 663-4560. Fax, (202) 663-7004. Philip Calkins, Executive Director. TTY, (202) 663-4593.

Established by the Rehabilitation Act of 1973, as amended, and cochaired by the Office of Personnel Management and the EEOC. Works for increased employment of persons with disabilities, affirmative action by the federal government, and an equitable work environment for employees with mental and physical disabilities.

Office of Personnel Management, *Diversity,* 1900 E St. N.W., #2445 20415-0001; (202) 606-2817. Fax, (202) 606-0927. Maria Mercedes Olivieri, Director.

Develops policies, programs, and procedures to promote opportunities for qualified workers with disabilities, including veterans, to obtain and advance in federal employment. Administers the Disabled Veterans Affirmative Action Program.

President's Committee on Employment of People with Disabilities, 1331 F St. N.W., #300 20004-1107; (202) 376-6200. Fax, (202) 376-6219. John Lancaster, Executive Director. TTY, (202) 376-6205. General e-mail, info@pcepd.gov. Web, www.pcepd.gov.

Promotes training, rehabilitation, and employment opportunities for people with disabilities.

Rehabilitation Services Administration *(Education Dept.), 330 C St. S.W. 20202-2531; (202) 205-5482. Fax, (202) 205-9874. Fredric K. Schroeder, Commissioner. TTY, (202) 205-9295.*

Coordinates and directs federal services for eligible persons with physical or mental disabilities, with emphasis on programs that promote employment opportunities. Provides vocational training and job placement; supports projects with private industry; administers grants for the establishment of supported-employment programs.

NONPROFIT

Inter-National Assn. of Business, Industry, and Rehabilitation, *P.O. Box 15242 20003; (202) 543-6353. Fax, (202) 546-2854. Charles Harles, Executive Director. General e-mail, inabir@harles.com. Web, www.harles.com/inabir.*

Membership: corporations, organized labor, state government agencies, rehabilitation service organizations, and other groups that work to provide competitive employment for persons with disabilities.

Mainstream, *6930 Carroll Ave., #240, Takoma Park, MD 20912; (301) 891-8777. Fax, (301) 891-8778. David Pichette, Executive Director. TTY, (301) 891-8777. General e-mail, mainstrm@aol.com. Web, www.mainstreaminc.org.*

Seeks to bring persons with disabilities into the workforce; directs a demonstration placement program in competitive employment for persons with disabilities; provides publications, videos, and employment services; holds conferences on disability issues. Library open to the public.

NISH, *2235 Cedar Lane, Vienna, VA 22182-5200; (703) 560-6800. Fax, (703) 849-8916. Daniel W. McKinnon Jr., President. TTY, (703) 560-6512.*

Assists work centers that employ people with severe disabilities in obtaining federal contracts under the Javits-Wagner-O'Day Act; supports community rehabilitation programs employing persons with severe disabilities.

Youth

AGENCIES

Employment and Training Administration *(Labor Dept.), Job Corps, 200 Constitution Ave. N.W., #N4510 20210; (202) 219-8550. Fax, (202) 219-5183. Mary Silva, Director. Information, (800) 733-5627. Web, www.jobcorps.org.*

Administers with the Interior Dept. a national program of comprehensive job training for disadvantaged youth at residential centers.

Employment Standards Administration *(Labor Dept.), Child Labor and Special Employment Team, 200 Constitution Ave. N.W., #S3510 20210; (202) 693-0072. Fax, (202) 693-1432. Arthur M. Kerschner Jr., Team Leader. Press, (202) 693-0023.*

Administers and enforces child labor, special minimum wage and other provisions of Section 14 of the Fair Labor Standards Act. Administers the Work Experience and Career Exploration Program aimed at reducing the number of high school dropouts.

Forest Service *(Agriculture Dept.), Youth Conservation Corps, 1621 N. Kent St., Arlington, VA 22209 (mailing address: P.O. Box 96090 20090-6090); (703) 605-4854. Fax, (703) 605-5115. Ransom Hughes, Program Manager.*

Administers with the National Park Service and the Fish and Wildlife Service the Youth Conservation Corps, a summer employment and training, public works program for youths ages fifteen to eighteen. The program is conducted in national parks, in national forests, and on national wildlife refuges.

NONPROFIT

Joint Action in Community Service, *5225 Wisconsin Ave. N.W., #404 20015-2021; (202) 537-0996. Fax, (202) 363-0239. Harvey Wise, Executive Director. Information, (800) 522-7773. Web, www.jacsinc.org.*

Volunteer organization that works with the Labor Dept.'s Job Corps program for disadvantaged youths ages sixteen to twenty-four. Provides follow-up assistance to help these youths make the transition from training to jobs.

National Alliance of Business, *Workforce Adjustment, 1201 New York Ave. N.W., #700 20005; (202) 289-2905. Fax, (202) 289-1303. Roberts T. Jones, President. Press, (202) 289-2860. General e-mail, info@nab.com. Web, www.nab.com.*

Represents the interests of business in developing a quality workforce. Promotes partnerships between government and business at the federal, state, and local levels. Interests include improving public education, addressing the employment and training needs of individuals in a globally competitive economy, and easing the transition from school to the workplace.

National Assn. of Service and Conservation Corps, *666 11th St. N.W., #1000 20001-4542; (202) 737-6272. Fax, (202) 737-6277. Kathleen Selz, President. General e-mail, nascc@nascc.org. Web, www.nascc.org.*

Membership: youth corps programs. Produces publications on starting and operating youth corps. Offers technical assistance to those interested in launching programs and sponsors professional development workshops. Holds annual conference. Monitors legislation and regulations.

Work, Achievement, Values, and Education, *525 School St. S.W., #500 20024; (202) 484-0103. Fax, (202) 488-7595. Lawrence C. Brown, President. General e-mail, mail@waveinc.org. Web, www.waveinc.org.*

Public service corporation that provides high school dropouts and students at risk, ages twelve to twenty-one, with a program of education and employment services. Provides educational institutions with training and technical assistance.

EQUAL EMPLOYMENT OPPORTUNITY

See also Civil Rights (chap. 1); Military Personnel and Veterans (chap. 15)

AGENCIES

Commission on Civil Rights, *Civil Rights Evaluation, 624 9th St. N.W. 20425; (202) 376-8582. Fax, (202) 376-8315. Vacant, Assistant Staff Director. Library, (202) 376-8110.*

Researches federal policy in areas of equal employment and job discrimination; monitors the economic status of minorities and women, including their employment and earnings. Library open to the public.

Employment Standards Administration *(Labor Dept.), Federal Contract Compliance Programs, 200 Constitution Ave. N.W., #C3325 20210; (202) 693-0101. Fax, (202) 693-1304. Shirley J. Wilcher, Deputy Assistant Secretary.*

Monitors and enforces government contractors' compliance with federal laws and regulations on equal employment opportunities and affirmative action, including employment rights of minorities, women, persons with disabilities, and disabled and Vietnam-era veterans.

Equal Employment Opportunity Commission, *1801 L St. N.W., #10006 20507; (202) 663-4001. Fax, (202) 663-4110. Ida L. Castro, Chair. Information, (202) 663-4900. Library, (202) 663-4630. TTY, (202) 663-4494. Web, www.eeoc.gov.*

Works to end job discrimination by private and government employers based on race, color, religion, sex,

national origin, or age. Works to protect employees against reprisal for protest of employment practices alleged to be unlawful in hiring, promotion, firing, wages, and other terms and conditions of employment. Enforces Title VII of the Civil Rights Act of 1964, as amended, which includes the Pregnancy Discrimination Act; Americans with Disabilities Act; Age Discrimination in Employment Act; Equal Pay Act; and, in the federal sector, rehabilitation laws. Receives charges of discrimination; attempts conciliation or settlement; can bring court action to force compliance; has review and appeals responsibility in the federal sector.

Equal Employment Opportunity Commission, *Field Programs, 1801 L St. N.W., #8002 20507; (202) 663-4801. Fax, (202) 663-7190. Elizabeth M. Thornton, Director.*

Provides guidance and technical assistance to employees who suspect discrimination and to employers who are working to comply with equal employment laws.

Justice Dept., *Civil Rights: Employment Litigation, 601 D St. N.W., #4040 20004; (202) 514-3831. Fax, (202) 514-1105. Katherine Baldwin, Chief. Library, (202) 616-5564. Web, www.usdoj.gov/crt.*

Investigates, negotiates, and litigates allegations of employment discrimination by public schools, universities, state and local governments, and federally funded employers; has enforcement power. Library open to the public by appointment.

Office of Personnel Management, *Diversity, 1900 E St. N.W., #2445 20415-0001; (202) 606-2817. Fax, (202) 606-0927. Maria Mercedes Olivieri, Director.*

Develops policies and guidelines for government recruiting programs, including diversity employment efforts related to women, minorities, persons with disabilities, and veterans. Collects and maintains statistics on the federal employment of these groups. Administers the Federal Equal Opportunity Recruitment Program and the Disabled Veterans Affirmative Action Program.

CONGRESS

House Education and the Workforce Committee, *Subcommittee on Employer-Employee Relations, 2181 RHOB 20515; (202) 225-4527. Fax, (202) 225-9571. Rep. John A. Boehner, R-Ohio, Chair; Kevin D. Talley, Staff Director. Web, www.house.gov/ed_workforce.*

Jurisdiction over legislation on discrimination based on race, color, religion, sex, age, or national origin in employment where public funds are involved. Oversight of federal equal opportunity, age discrimination, and equal pay laws.

EQUAL EMPLOYMENT CONTACTS AT FEDERAL AGENCIES

DEPARTMENTS

Agriculture, Rosalind D. Gray, (202) 720-5212

Commerce, Kimberly Walton, (202) 482-0625

Defense, William E. Leftwich III, (703) 695-0105

  Air Force, Vacant, (703) 697-6586

  Army, Luther L. Santiful, (703) 607-1976

  Marines, Howard Mathews, (703) 784-9379

  Navy, Betty Welch, (703) 695-2248

Education, James R. White, (202) 401-3560

Energy, William L. Garrett (acting), (202) 586-2218

Health and Human Services, Tom Perez, (202) 619-0403

Housing and Urban Development, Sandra Hobson, (202) 708-5921

Interior, E. Melodee Stith, (202) 208-5693

Justice, Ted McBurrows, (202) 616-4800

Labor, Annabelle Lockhart, (202) 219-6362

State, Deidre Davis, (202) 647-9294

Transportation, Ronald A. Stroman, (202) 366-4648

Treasury, Mariam Harvey, (202) 622-1160

Veterans Affairs, Ellis Jones Hodges, (202) 273-5888

AGENCIES

Commission on Civil Rights, Edward A. Hailes Jr., (202) 376-8351

Commodity Futures Trading Commission, Frank Alston, (202) 418-5011

Consumer Product Safety Commission, Felipa Coleman, (301) 504-0570

Corporation for National Service, Nancy Voss, (202) 606-5000, ext. 309

Environmental Protection Agency, Ann Goode, (202) 260-4575

Equal Employment Opportunity Commission, Robbie Dix III, (202) 663-7081

Export-Import Bank, Cynthia B. Wilson, (202) 565-3590

Farm Credit Administration, Eric Howard, (703) 883-4481

Federal Communications Commission, Jack W. Gravely, (202) 418-1799

Federal Deposit Insurance Corporation, D. Michael Collins, (202) 416-6925

Federal Election Commission, Patricia Brown, (202) 694-1228

Federal Emergency Management Agency, Pauline Campbell, (202) 646-4122

Federal Labor Relations Authority, Michele Pilipovich, (202) 482-6640

Federal Maritime Commission, Alice Blackman, (202) 523-5806

Federal Mediation and Conciliation Service, Bill Carlisle, (202) 606-5460

Federal Reserve Board, Sheila Clark, (202) 452-2883

Federal Trade Commission, Barbara B. Wiggs, (202) 326-2196

General Services Administration, Larry Roush, (202) 501-0767

Merit Systems Protection Board, Janice E. Pirkle, (202) 653-6180

National Aeronautics and Space Administration, George E. Reese, (202) 358-2167

National Credit Union Administration, Robert French (acting), (703) 518-6325

National Endowment for the Humanities, Willie McGhee, (202) 606-8233

National Labor Relations Board, Lori Suto-Goldsby, (202) 273-3891

National Science Foundation, Ann Ortiz, (703) 306-1020

National Transportation Safety Board, Bob Barlett (acting), (202) 314-6190

Nuclear Regulatory Commission, Irene P. Little, (301) 415-7380

Occupational Safety and Health Review Commission, Ledia E. Bernall, (202) 606-5390

Office of Personnel Management, Barbara J. Mathews-Beck, (202) 606-2460

Peace Corps, Brenda Gooch, (202) 692-2130

Securities and Exchange Commission, Deborah Balducchi, (202) 942-0040

Small Business Administration, Erline M. Patrick, (202) 205-6750

Smithsonian Institution, Era Marshall, (202) 287-3508

Social Security Administration, Miguel Torrado, (410) 965-1977

U.S. International Trade Commission, Jackie Waters, (202) 205-2240

U.S. Postal Service, Peter L. Garwood, (202) 268-3994

House Government Reform Committee, *Subcommittee on Criminal Justice, Drug Policy, and Human Resources,* B373 RHOB 20515; (202) 225-2577. Fax, (202) 225-1154. Rep. John L. Mica, R-Fla., Chair; Sharon Pinkerton, Staff Director. Web, www.house.gov/reform.

Oversees operations of the Equal Employment Opportunity Commission and other federal agencies concerned with racial and sexual discrimination in employment.

Office of Compliance, *Education and Training,* 110 2nd St. S.E., #LA-200 20540-1999; (202) 724-9250. Fax, (202) 426-1913. Teresa James, Director. Information, (202) 724-9260. TTY, (202) 426-1912. Web, www.compliance.gov.

Provides general information to covered employees, applicants, and former employees of the legislative branch about their equal employment rights and protections under the Congressional Accountability Act of 1995.

Senate Governmental Affairs Committee, SD-340 20510; (202) 224-4751. Fax, (202) 224-9603. Sen. Fred Thompson, R-Tenn., Chair; Hannah Sistare, Staff Director. Web, gov_affairs.senate.gov.

Jurisdiction over legislation on discrimination based on race, color, religion, sex, age, or national origin in employment where federal employees are involved.

Senate Health, Education, Labor, and Pensions Committee, *Subcommittee on Employment, Safety, and Training,* SH-607 20510; (202) 224-7229. Sen. Michael B. Enzi, R-Wyo., Chair; Raissa Geary, Staff Director. Web, labor.senate.gov.

Jurisdiction over legislation on discrimination based on race, color, religion, sex, age, or national origin in employment except where federal employees are involved. Oversight of federal equal pay laws and of federal agencies concerned with racial and sexual discrimination in employment. Oversees operation of the Equal Employment Opportunity Commission.

NONPROFIT

Center for Equal Opportunity, 815 15th St. N.W., #928 20005; (202) 639-0803. Fax, (202) 639-0827. Linda Chavez, President. General e-mail, comment@ceousa.org. Web, www.ceousa.org.

Research organization concerned with issues of race, ethnicity, and assimilation; opposes racial preferences in employment and education. Monitors legislation and regulations.

Equal Employment Advisory Council, 1015 15th St. N.W., #1200 20005; (202) 789-8650. Fax, (202) 789-2291.

Jeffrey A. Norris, President. TTY, (202) 789-8645. Web, www.eeac.org.

Membership: principal equal employment officers and lawyers. Files amicus curiae (friend of the court) briefs; conducts research and provides information on equal employment law and policy. Monitors legislation and regulations.

NAACP Legal Defense and Educational Fund, *Washington Office,* 1444 Eye St. N.W., 10th Floor 20005; (202) 682-1300. Fax, (202) 682-1312. Director; Janell Byrd, Senior Attorney.

Civil rights litigation group that provides legal information about civil rights legislation and advice on employment discrimination against women and minorities; monitors federal enforcement of equal opportunity rights laws. Not affiliated with the National Association for the Advancement of Colored People (NAACP). (Headquarters in New York.)

National Assn. of Manufacturers, *Employment Policy,* 1331 Pennsylvania Ave. N.W., 6th Floor 20004-1790; (202) 637-3133. Fax, (202) 637-3182. Jenny Krese, Director.

Monitors Equal Employment Opportunity Commission and Office of Federal Contract Compliance programs. Studies equal employment regulations, human resources, equal rights issues, comparable worth, pregnancy disability, privacy issues, and employment and training.

National Committee on Pay Equity, 1126 16th St. N.W., #411 20036; (202) 331-7343. Fax, (202) 331-7406. Susan Bianchi-Sand, Executive Director. General e-mail, fairpay@aol.com. Web, feminist.com/fairpay.htm.

Coalition of labor, women's, and civil rights groups. Works to eliminate wage discrimination based on race and sex and to achieve equitable pay for all workers. Acts as an information clearinghouse on pay equity activities throughout the world and provides technical assistance on pay equity matters.

See also American Institutes for Research (p. 618); Lawyers' Committee for Civil Rights Under Law (p. 29); Society for Human Resource Management (p. 216)

Minorities

AGENCIES

Bureau of Indian Affairs *(Interior Dept.),* *Economic Development,* 1849 C St. N.W., #4640 20240; (202) 208-5324. Fax, (202) 208-7419. Dominic Nessi, Director (Acting).

Develops policies and programs to promote the achievement of economic goals for members of federally recognized tribes who live on or near reservations. Provides job training; assists those who have completed job training programs in finding employment; provides loan guarantees; enhances contracting opportunities for individuals and tribes.

Employment and Training Administration *(Labor Dept.), Indian and Native American Programs,* 200 Constitution Ave. N.W., #N4645 20210; (202) 219-8502. Fax, (202) 219-6338. James DeLuca, Chief.

Administers grants for training and employment-related programs to promote employment opportunity; provides unemployed, underemployed, or economically disadvantaged native Americans and Alaskan and Hawaiian natives with funds for training, job placement, and support services.

NONPROFIT

Coalition of Black Trade Unionists, *1625 L St. N.W. 20036 (mailing address: P.O. Box 66268 20035); (202) 429-1203. Fax, (202) 429-1102. Wil Duncan, Executive Director.*

Monitors legislation affecting African American and other minority trade unionists. Focuses on equal employment opportunity, unemployment, and voter education and registration.

Labor Council for Latin American Advancement, *815 16th St. N.W., #310 20006; (202) 347-4223. Fax, (202) 347-5095. Oscar Sanchez, Executive Director. Web, www. lclaa.org.*

Membership: Hispanic trade unionists. Encourages equal employment opportunity, voter registration and education, and participation in the political process. (Affiliated with the AFL-CIO.)

Mexican American Legal Defense and Educational Fund, *Washington Office,* 1717 K St. N.W., #311 20036; (202) 628-4074. Fax, (202) 293-2849. Marisa Demeo, Regional Counsel. Web, www.maldef.org.

Provides Mexican Americans and other Hispanics involved in class-action employment discrimination suits or complaints with legal assistance. Monitors legislation and regulations. (Headquarters in Los Angeles.)

National Assn. for the Advancement of Colored People, *Washington Office,* 1025 Vermont Ave. N.W., #1120 20005; (202) 638-2269. Fax, (202) 638-5936. Hilary O. Shelton, Director. Web, www.naacp.org.

Membership: persons interested in civil rights for all minorities. Advises individuals with employment discrimination complaints. Seeks to eliminate job discrimination and to bring about full employment for all Americans through legislation and litigation. (Headquarters in Baltimore.)

National Assn. of Negro Business and Professional Women's Clubs, *1806 New Hampshire Ave. N.W. 20009; (202) 483-4206. Fax, (202) 462-7253. Clair Patra Vaughn, President. Web, www.afrika.com/nanbpwc.*

Promotes opportunities for African American women in business; sponsors workshops; maintains a job bank. Monitors legislation and regulations.

National Council of La Raza, *1111 19th St. N.W., #1000 20036; (202) 785-1670. Fax, (202) 776-1792. Raul Yzaguirre, President. Web, www.nclr.org.*

Provides research, policy analysis, and advocacy on Hispanic employment status and programs; provides Hispanic community-based groups with technical assistance to help develop effective employment programs with strong educational components. Works to promote understanding of Hispanic employment needs in the private sector. Interests include women in the workplace, affirmative action, equal opportunity employment, and youth employment. Monitors federal employment legislation and regulations.

National Urban League, *Research and Public Policy, Washington Office,* 1111 14th St. N.W., #1001 20005-5603; (202) 898-1604. Fax, (202) 408-1965. William Spriggs, Director. General e-mail, info@nul.org. Web, www.nul.org.

Social service organization concerned with the social welfare of African Americans and other minorities. Testifies before congressional committees and federal agencies on equal employment; studies and evaluates federal enforcement of equal employment laws and regulations. (Headquarters in New York.)

Women

AGENCIES

Agriculture Dept., *Women's Executive Leadership Program,* 600 Maryland Ave. S.W., #330 20024; (202) 314-3580. Fax, (202) 479-6813. Debra Eddington, Director. Web, www.usda.gov.

Trains federally employed men and women with managerial potential for executive positions in the government. The program is geared toward GS-11 and GS-12 employees.

Labor Dept., *Women's Bureau,* 200 Constitution Ave. N.W., #S3002 20210; (202) 219-6611. Fax, (202) 219-0173. Irasema Garza, Director. Information, (800) 827-5335. Web, www.dol.gov/dol/wb/welcome.html.

Monitors women's employment issues. Promotes employment opportunities for women; sponsors workshops, job fairs, symposia, demonstrations, and pilot projects. Offers technical assistance; conducts research and provides publications on issues that affect working women; represents working women in international forums.

Office of Personnel Management, *Federal Women's Program, 1900 E St. N.W. 20415; (202) 606-2605. Fax, (202) 606-0927. Maria Mercedes Olivieri, Director.*

Promotes opportunities for women to obtain and advance in federal employment; assists federal agencies in the recruitment and employment of women. Collects and maintains statistics on women's employment.

NONPROFIT

Business and Professional Women U.S.A., *2012 Massachusetts Ave. N.W. 20036; (202) 293-1100. Fax, (202) 861-0298. Gail Shaffer, Executive Director; Robin Robinson, President.*

Seeks to improve the status of working women through education, legislative action, and local projects. Sponsors Business and Professional Women's Foundation, which awards grants and loans, based on need, to mature women reentering the workforce or entering nontraditional fields. Library open to the public.

Federally Employed Women, *1400 Eye St. N.W., #425 20005; (202) 898-0994. Fax, (202) 898-0998. Jeanette Miller, President. Web, www.few.org.*

Membership: women and men who work for the federal government. Works to eliminate sex discrimination in government employment and to increase job opportunities for women; offers training program. Monitors legislation and regulations.

Federation of Organizations for Professional Women, *P.O. Box 6234, Falls Church, VA 22040; (202) 328-1415. Fax, (202) 429-9574. Viola Young-Horvath, Executive Director.*

Membership: women's organizations, women's caucuses and committees in professional associations, and people interested in equal educational and employment opportunities for women. Monitors federal programs affecting women; organizes workshops to exchange information; publishes directory of women's organizations nationwide; maintains professional women's legal fund.

Institute for Women's Policy Research, *1707 L St. N.W., #750 20036; (202) 785-5100. Fax, (202) 833-4362. Heidi I. Hartmann, Director. Web, www.iwpr.org.*

Public policy research organization that focuses on women's issues, including welfare reform, family and work policies, employment and wages, and discrimination based on gender, race, or ethnicity.

National Women's Law Center, *11 Dupont Circle N.W., #800 20036; (202) 588-5180. Fax, (202) 588-5185. Marcia D. Greenberger, Co-President; Nancy Duff Campbell, Co-President. Web, www.nwlc.org.*

Works to expand and protect women's legal rights in education through advocacy and public education.

Wider Opportunities for Women, *815 15th St. N.W., #916 20005; (202) 638-3143. Fax, (202) 638-4885. Lina Frescas Dobbs, Executive Director.*

Promotes equal employment opportunities for women through equal access to jobs and training, equal incomes, and an equitable workplace. Conducts nontraditional skills training programs; monitors public policy relating to jobs, affirmative action, vocational education, training opportunities, and welfare reform.

Women in Community Service, *1900 N. Beauregard St., #103, Alexandria, VA 22311; (703) 671-0500. Fax, (703) 671-4489. Ruth C. Herman, President. Information, (800) 442-9427. General e-mail, wicsnatl@wics.org. Web, www.wics.org.*

Seeks to reduce the number of women living in poverty by promoting self-reliance and economic independence. Interests include job training and welfare reform. Holds contract with Labor Dept. for outreach, support service, and job placement for the Job Corps. Sponsors the Lifeskills Program to assist at-risk women in such areas as job training and money management.

Women Work!, *1625 K St. N.W., #300 20006; (202) 467-6346. Fax, (202) 467-5366. Jill Miller, Executive Director. Information, (800) 235-2732. General e-mail, womenwork@womenwork.org. Web, www.womenwork.org.*

Fosters the development of programs and services for former homemakers reentering the job market and provides information about public policy issues that affect displaced homemakers and single parents. Refers individuals to local services. Monitors legislation.

See also Assn. for Women in Science (p. 9); Business and Professional Women's Foundation (p. 179)

 LABOR-MANAGEMENT RELATIONS

See also Civil Service (chap. 10); Postal Service (chap. 10); and specific industries within each chapter

AGENCIES

Bureau of Labor Statistics *(Labor Dept.), Compensation and Working Conditions,* 2 Massachusetts Ave. N.E. 20212; (202) 691-6300. Fax, (202) 691-6310. Kathleen MacDonald, Associate Commissioner. Web, www.bls.gov/comhome.

Provides data on collective bargaining agreements, wage structures, industrial relations, and work stoppages. Compiles data for *Employment Cost Index,* published quarterly.

Criminal Division *(Justice Dept.), Organized Crime and Racketeering: Labor-Management Racketeering,* 1301 New York Ave., #510 20530; (202) 514-3666. Fax, (202) 514-9837. Gerald A. Toner, Assistant Chief.

Reviews and advises on prosecutions of criminal violations involving labor-management relations and internal affairs of labor unions.

Employment Standards Administration *(Labor Dept.), Labor-Management Standards,* 200 Constitution Ave. N.W., #N5605 20210; (202) 693-0122. Fax, (202) 693-1340. John Kotch, Director. Web, gatekeeper.dol.gov/dol/esa/public/olms_org.htm.

Administers and enforces the Labor-Management Reporting and Disclosure Act of 1959 (Landrum-Griffin Act), which guarantees union members certain rights; sets rules for electing union officers, handling union funds, and using trusteeships; requires unions to file annual financial reports with the Labor Dept. Regulatory authority over Foreign Service Act of 1980.

Federal Mediation and Conciliation Service, 2100 K St. N.W. 20427; (202) 606-8100. Fax, (202) 606-3679. C. Richard Barnes, Director; Vella M. Traynham, Deputy Director. Information, (202) 606-8080. Web, www.fmcs.gov.

Assists labor and management representatives in resolving disputes in collective bargaining contract negotiation through voluntary mediation and arbitration services; awards competitive grants to joint labor-management committees; trains other federal agencies in mediating administrative disputes under the Administrative Dispute Resolution Act of 1996 and the Negotiated Rulemaking Act of 1996; provides training to unions and management in cooperative processes.

National Labor Relations Board, 1099 14th St. N.W. 20570-0001; (202) 273-1790. Fax, (202) 273-4276. John C. Truesdale, Chair; John Toner, Executive Secretary, (202) 273-1940. Information, (202) 273-1991. Library, (202) 273-3720. Locator, (202) 273-1000. Web, www.nlrb.gov.

Works to prevent and remedy unfair labor practices by employers and labor unions; conducts elections among employees to determine whether they wish to be represented by a labor union for collective bargaining purposes. Library open to the public.

National Mediation Board, 1301 K St. N.W., #250E 20572; (202) 692-5000. Fax, (202) 692-5080. Stephen E. Crable, Chief of Staff, (202) 692-5030; Ernest DuBester, Chair. Information, (202) 692-5050. TTY, (202) 692-5001.

Mediates labor disputes in the railroad and airline industries; determines and certifies labor representatives for those industries.

CONGRESS

House Education and the Workforce Committee, *Subcommittee on Employer-Employee Relations,* 2181 RHOB 20515; (202) 225-4527. Fax, (202) 225-9571. Rep. John A. Boehner, R-Ohio, Chair; Kevin D. Talley, Staff Director. Web, www.house.gov/ed_workforce.

Jurisdiction over legislation on labor-management issues and unfair labor practices and the National Labor Relations Act.

House Government Reform Committee, *Subcommittee on Civil Service,* B371C RHOB 20515; (202) 225-6427. Fax, (202) 225-2392. Rep. Joe Scarborough, R-Fla., Chair; George Nesterczuk, Staff Director. Web, www.house.gov/reform.

Jurisdiction over legislation on federal civil service labor-management issues; oversees the Federal Labor Relations Authority.

House Government Reform Committee, *Subcommittee on Criminal Justice, Drug Policy, and Human Resources,* B373 RHOB 20515; (202) 225-2577. Fax, (202) 225-1154. Rep. John L. Mica, R-Fla., Chair; Sharon Pinkerton, Staff Director. Web, www.house.gov/reform.

Oversight of the Federal Mediation and Conciliation Service, the Labor Dept., and the National Labor Relations Board.

House Government Reform Committee, *Subcommittee on National Economic Growth, Natural Resources, and Regulatory Affairs,* B377 RHOB 20515; (202) 225-4407. Fax, (202) 225-2441. Rep. David M. McIntosh, R-Ind., Chair; Marlo Lewis, Staff Director. Web, www.house.gov/reform.

Oversees operations of the National Mediation Board.

Senate Governmental Affairs Committee, *Subcommittee on International Security, Proliferation, and Federal Services,* SH-442 20510; (202) 224-2254. Fax, (202)

228-3796. Sen. Thad Cochran, R-Miss., Chair; Mitch Kugler, Staff Director. Web, gov_affairs.senate.gov/ispfs.htm.

Jurisdiction over legislation on federal civil service labor-management issues, including classification, compensation, and benefits.

Senate Health, Education, Labor, and Pensions Committee, *Subcommittee on Employment, Safety, and Training, SH-607 20510; (202) 224-7229. Sen. Michael B. Enzi, R-Wyo., Chair; Raissa Geary, Staff Director. Web, labor.senate.gov.*

Jurisdiction over the National Labor Relations Act and over legislation on labor-management issues and unfair labor practices. Oversight of the Labor Dept., the National Mediation Board, the Federal Mediation and Conciliation Service, and the National Labor Relations Board.

NONPROFIT

AFL-CIO (American Federation of Labor—Congress of Industrial Organizations), *815 16th St. N.W. 20006; (202) 637-5000. John J. Sweeney, President. General e-mail, feedback@aflcio.org. Web, www.aflcio.org.*

Voluntary federation of national and international labor unions in the United States. Represents members before Congress and other branches of government. Each member union conducts its own contract negotiations. Library open to the public.

American Arbitration Assn., *Washington Office, 8201 Greensboro Dr., #610, McLean, VA 22102-3810; (703) 760-4820. Fax, (703) 760-4847. Arnold B. Crews, Regional Vice President. General e-mail, webmaster@adr.org. Web, www.adr.org.*

Provides dispute resolution services worldwide, including arbitration, mediation, minitrials, and elections. (Headquarters in New York.)

American Federation of Musicians, *Washington Office, 501 3rd St. N.W. 20001; (202) 628-5460. Fax, (202) 628-5461. Steve Young, President. Web, www.afm.org.*

Seeks to improve the working conditions and salary of musicians. Monitors legislation and regulations affecting musicians and the arts.

American Foreign Service Assn., *2101 E St. N.W. 20037; (202) 338-4045. Fax, (202) 338-6820. Susan Reardon, Executive Director. General e-mail, afsa@afsa.org. Web, www.afsa.org.*

Membership: active and retired foreign service employees of federal agencies. Represents active duty foreign service personnel in labor-management negotia-

---

AFL-CIO

DEPARTMENTS

Civil Rights, Richard Womack, Director; (202) 637-5270

Education, Bill Fletcher, Director; (202) 637-5143

Field Mobilization, Marilyn Sneiderman, Director; (202) 637-5356

International Affairs, Barbara Shailor, Director; (202) 637-5050

Legal Dept., Jonathan Hiatt, General Counsel; (202) 637-5053

Legislation, Peggy Taylor, Director; (202) 637-5090

Occupational Safety and Health, Peg Seminario, Director; (202) 637-5366

Organizing, Kirk Adams, Director; (202) 639-6200

Political Dept., Steve Rosenthal, Director; (202) 637-5102

Public Affairs, Denise Mitchell, Special Assistant to the President; (202) 637-5340

Public Policy, David Smith, Director; (202) 637-5172

Working Women, Karen Nussbaum, Director; (202) 637-5064

TRADE AND INDUSTRIAL DEPARTMENTS

Building and Construction Trades, Robert A. Georgine, President; (202) 347-1461

Food and Allied Service Trades, Jeffrey Fiedler, President; (202) 737-7200

Maritime Trades, Michael Sacco, President; (202) 628-6300

Metal Trades, John Meese, President; (202) 347-7255

Professional Employees, Jack Golodner, President; (202) 638-0320

Transportation Trades, Sonny Hall, President; (202) 628-9262

Union Label and Service Trades, Charles E. Mercer, President; (202) 628-2131

---

tions; seeks to ensure adequate resources for foreign service operations and personnel. Monitors legislation and regulations.

Coalition of Black Trade Unionists, *1625 L St. N.W. 20036 (mailing address: P.O. Box 66268 20035); (202) 429-1203. Fax, (202) 429-1102. Wil Duncan, Executive Director.*

Monitors legislation affecting African American and other minority trade unionists. Focuses on equal employment opportunity, unemployment, and voter education and registration.

Coalition of Labor Union Women, *1126 16th St. N.W., #104 20036; (202) 466-4610. Fax, (202) 776-0537. Gloria T. Johnson, President.*

Seeks to make unions more responsive to the needs of women in the workplace; advocates affirmative action and the active participation of women in unions. Monitors legislation and regulations.

George Meany Center for Labor Studies and the George Meany Memorial Archives, *10000 New Hampshire Ave., Silver Spring, MD 20903; (301) 431-6400. Fax, (301) 434-0371. Susan Sherman, Executive Director. Web, www.georgemeany.org.*

Educational institute that offers classes, workshops, and an undergraduate degree program to AFL-CIO–affiliated officers, representatives, and staff. Maintains the AFL-CIO archives and the Institute for the Study of Labor Organizations.

International Brotherhood of Teamsters, *25 Louisiana Ave. N.W. 20001; (202) 624-6800. Fax, (202) 624-8102. James P. Hoffa, President. Web, www.teamster.org.*

Membership: more than 1.4 million workers in the transportation and construction industries, factories, offices, hospitals, warehouses, and other workplaces. Helps members negotiate pay, benefits, and better working conditions; conducts training programs and workshops. Monitors legislation and regulations. (Affiliated with the AFL-CIO.)

Labor Council for Latin American Advancement, *815 16th St. N.W., #310 20006; (202) 347-4223. Fax, (202) 347-5095. Oscar Sanchez, Executive Director. Web, www. lclaa.org.*

Membership: Hispanic trade unionists. Encourages equal employment opportunity, voter registration and education, and participation in the political process. (Affiliated with the AFL-CIO.)

Laborers' International Union of North America, *905 16th St. N.W. 20006; (202) 737-8320. Fax, (202) 737-2754. Terence O'Sullivan, President. Web, www.liuna.org.*

Membership: approximately 750,000 construction workers; federal, state, and local government employees; health care professionals; mail handlers; custodial service personnel; shipbuilders; and hazardous waste handlers. Helps members negotiate pay, benefits, and better working conditions; conducts training programs and workshops. Monitors legislation and regulations. (Affiliated with the AFL-CIO.)

National Assn. of Manufacturers, *Human Resources Policy, 1331 Pennsylvania Ave. N.W., #600N 20004-1790; (202) 637-3100. Fax, (202) 637-3182. Jenny Krese, Director.*

Provides information on corporate industrial relations, including collective bargaining, labor standards, international labor relations, productivity, employee benefits, health care, and other current labor issues; monitors legislation and regulations.

National Public Employer Labor Relations Assn., *1620 Eye St. N.W. 20006. Fax, (202) 293-2352. Roger E. Dahl, Executive Director. Information, (800) 296-2230. Web, www.npelra.org.*

Represents professional public employees in federal, state, and local governments and school and special districts in a wide range of areas including, individual relationships with employees, state labor relations boards, bargaining with employee unions and associations, conducting impasse proceedings with mediators and arbitrators, and working with arbitrators under grievance and arbitration procedures.

National Right to Work Committee, *8001 Braddock Rd., Springfield, VA 22160; (703) 321-9820. Fax, (703) 321-7342. Reed E. Larson, President. Information, (800) 325-7892. General e-mail, info@nrtw.org. Web, www.nrtw.org.*

Citizens' organization opposed to compulsory union membership. Supports right-to-work legislation.

National Right to Work Legal Defense Foundation, *8001 Braddock Rd., #600, Springfield, VA 22160; (703) 321-8510. Fax, (703) 321-9613. Rex H. Reed, Executive Vice President. General e-mail, info@nrtw.org. Web, www. nrtw.org.*

Provides free legal aid for employees in cases of compulsory union membership abuses.

Office and Professional Employees International Union, *Washington Office, 1660 L St. N.W., #801 20036; (202) 393-4464. Fax, (202) 347-0649. Michael Goodwin, President. Web, www.opeiu.org.*

Membership: 130,000 workers, including computer analysts, programmers, and data entry operators; copywriters; nurses and other health care personnel; attorneys; law enforcement officers and security guards; accountants; secretaries; bank employees; and insurance workers and agents. Helps members negotiate pay, benefits, and better working conditions; conducts training program and workshops. Monitors legislation and regulations. (Headquarters in New York; affiliated with the AFL-CIO and the Canadian Labour Congress.)

Public Service Research Council, *320D Maple Ave. East, Vienna, VA 22180; (703) 242-3575. Fax, (703) 242-3579. David Y. Denholm, President. Web, www.psrf.org.*

Independent, nonpartisan research and educational organization. Opposes collective bargaining, strikes, and binding arbitration in the public sector. Sponsors conferences and seminars. Library open to the public by appointment.

Service Employees International Union, *1313 L St. N.W. 20005; (202) 898-3200. Fax, (202) 898-3402. Andrew L. Stern, President. Web, www.seiu.org.*

Membership: more than one million service providers, including teachers; nurses, doctors, and other health care professionals; school bus drivers; janitors; and others. Helps members negotiate pay, benefits, and better working conditions; conducts training programs and workshops. Monitors legislation and regulations. (Affiliated with the AFL-CIO.)

United Auto Workers, *Washington Office, 1757 N St. N.W. 20036; (202) 828-8500. Fax, (202) 293-3457. Stephen P. Yokich, President. Toll-free, (800) 243-8829; in Canada, (800) 387-0538. Web, www.uaw.org.*

Membership: approximately 775,000 active and 500,000 retired North American workers in aerospace, automotive, defense, manufacturing, steel, technical, and other industries. Assists members with contract negotiation and grievances; conducts training programs and workshops. Monitors legislation and regulations. (Headquarters in Detroit; affiliated with the AFL-CIO.)

United Electrical, Radio and Machine Workers of America, *1800 Diagonal Rd., #600, Alexandria, VA 22314; (703) 684.3123. Fax, (703) 519-8982. John H. Hovis, President. General e-mail, ue@ranknfile-ue.org. Web, www.ranknfile-ue.org.*

Represents over 35,000 workers in electrical, metal working, and plastic manufacturing public sector and private nonprofit sector jobs. Membership: plastic injection molders, tool and die makers, sheet metal workers, truck drivers, warehouse workers, custodians, clerical workers, graduate instructors, graduate researchers, scientists, librarians, and day care workers.

United Steelworkers of America, *Washington Office, 1150 17th St. N.W., #300 20036; (202) 778-4384. Fax, (202) 293-5308. William Klinefelter, Legislative and Political Director. Web, www.uswa.org.*

Membership: more than 700,000 steelworkers in the United States and Canada. Helps members negotiate pay, benefits, and better working conditions; conducts training programs and workshops. Monitors legislation and regulations. (Headquarters in Pittsburgh; affiliated with the AFL-CIO.)

U.S. Chamber of Commerce, *Labor and Employee Benefits, 1615 H St. N.W. 20062-2000; (202) 463-5522.*

Fax, (202) 463-3194. Randel K. Johnson, Vice President. Press, (202) 463-5682. Web, www.uschamber.org.

Monitors legislation and regulations affecting labor-management relations and employee benefits.

PENSIONS AND BENEFITS

See also Civil Service (chap. 10); Insurance (chap. 3); Social Security (chap. 18)

AGENCIES

Advisory Council on Employee Welfare and Pension Benefit Plans (ERISA Advisory Council) *(Labor Dept.), 200 Constitution Ave. N.W., #N5677 20210; (202) 219-8753. Fax, (202) 219-6531. Sharon Morrissey, Executive Secretary. Information, (202) 219-8776.*

Advises and makes recommendations to the secretary of labor under the Employee Retirement Income Security Act of 1974 (ERISA).

Bureau of Labor Statistics *(Labor Dept.), Compensation and Working Conditions, 2 Massachusetts Ave. N.E. 20212; (202) 691-6300. Fax, (202) 691-6310. Kathleen MacDonald, Associate Commissioner. Web, www.bls.gov/comhome.*

Provides data on pensions and related work benefits.

Criminal Division *(Justice Dept.), Organized Crime and Racketeering: Labor-Management Racketeering, 1301 New York Ave., #510 20530; (202) 514-3666. Fax, (202) 514-9837. Gerald A. Toner, Assistant Chief.*

Reviews and advises on prosecutions of criminal violations concerning the operation of employee benefit plans in the private sector.

Federal Retirement Thrift Investment Board, *1250 H St. N.W., #200 20005; (202) 942-1600. Fax, (202) 942-1676. Roger W. Mehle, Executive Director.*

Administers the Thrift Savings Plan, a tax-deferred, defined contribution plan that permits federal employees to save for additional retirement security under a program similar to private 401(k) plans.

Internal Revenue Service *(Treasury Dept.), Employee Plans and Exempt Organizations, 1111 Constitution Ave. N.W., #1311 20224; (202) 622-6720. Fax, (202) 622-6873. Evelyn Petschek, Commissioner.*

Administers tax aspects of private and self-employed pension plans; determines tax-exempt status; enforces related regulations and minimum standards for funding participation and beneficiary rights under the Employee Retirement Income Security Act of 1974 (ERISA).

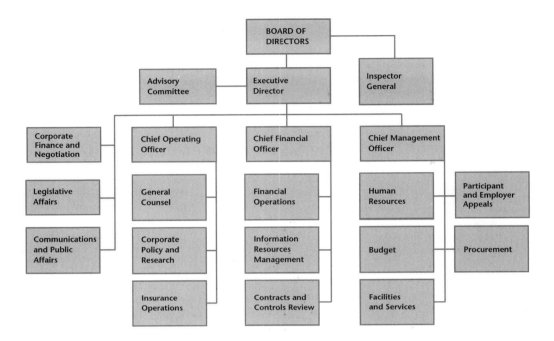

Joint Board for the Enrollment of Actuaries,
1111 Constitution Ave. N.W., C:AP:DOP, Internal Revenue Service 20224; (202) 694-1891. Fax, (202) 694-1876. Patrick W. McDonough, Executive Director.

Joint board, with members from the departments of Labor and Treasury and the Pension Benefit Guaranty Corp., established under the Employee Retirement Income Security Act of 1974 (ERISA). Promulgates regulations for the enrollment of pension actuaries; examines applicants and grants certificates of enrollment; disciplines enrolled actuaries who have engaged in misconduct in the discharge of duties under ERISA.

Office of Personnel Management, *Retirement Information, 1900 E St. N.W. 20415-0001; (202) 606-0500. Fax, (202) 606-0145. Valerie Wagner-Hippen, Chief. TTY, (202) 606-0551.*

Provides civil servants with information and assistance on federal retirement payments.

Pension and Welfare Benefits Administration
(Labor Dept.), 200 Constitution Ave. N.W., #S2524 20210; (202) 219-8233. Fax, (202) 219-5526. Leslie B. Kramerich, Secretary (Acting). Information, (202) 219-8921. Web, www.dol.gov.

Administers, regulates, and enforces private employee benefit plan standards established by the Employee Retirement Income Security Act of 1974 (ERISA), with particular emphasis on fiduciary obligations; receives and maintains required reports from employee benefit plan administrators pursuant to ERISA.

Pension Benefit Guaranty Corp., *1200 K St. N.W., #210 20005-4026; (202) 326-4010. Fax, (202) 326-4016. David Strauss, Executive Director; Joseph Grant, Deputy Executive Director. Information, (202) 326-4000. Locator, (202) 326-4110.*

Self-financed U.S. government corporation. Insures private-sector, defined-benefit pension plans; guarantees payment of retirement benefits subject to certain limitations established in the Employee Retirement Income Security Act of 1974 (ERISA). Provides insolvent multiemployer pension plans with financial assistance to enable them to pay guaranteed retirement benefits.

See also Railroad Retirement Board (p. 684)

CONGRESS

General Accounting Office, *Health, Education, and Human Services, 441 G St. N.W. 20548; (202) 512-6806.*

Fax, (202) 512-5806. Victor S. Rezendes, Assistant Comptroller General.

Independent, nonpartisan agency in the legislative branch. Audits, analyzes, and evaluates federal agency and private sector pension programs; makes reports available to the public.

House Education and the Workforce Committee, *Subcommittee on Employer-Employee Relations,* *2181 RHOB 20515; (202) 225-4527. Fax, (202) 225-9571. Rep. John A. Boehner, R-Ohio, Chair; Kevin D. Talley, Staff Director. Web, www.house.gov/ed_workforce.*

Jurisdiction over pension plan, fringe benefit, and retirement income security legislation, including the Employee Retirement Income Security Act of 1974 (ERISA) and the Labor-Management Reporting and Disclosure Act.

House Ways and Means Committee, *1102 LHOB 20515; (202) 225-3625. Fax, (202) 225-2610. Rep. Bill Archer, R-Texas, Chair; A. L. Singleton, Chief of Staff. Web, www.house.gov/ways_means.*

Jurisdiction over legislation related to taxation of pension contributions.

House Ways and Means Committee, *Subcommittee on Oversight,* *1136 LHOB 20515; (202) 225-7601. Fax, (202) 225-9680. Rep. Amo Houghton, R-N.Y., Chair; William McKenney, Staff Director. Web, www.house.gov/ways_means.*

Oversees the Pension Benefit Guaranty Corp.

Senate Finance Committee, *SD-219 20510; (202) 224-4515. Fax, (202) 224-5920. Sen. William V. Roth Jr., R-Del., Chair; Frank Polk, Staff Director. Web, finance.senate.gov.*

Jurisdiction over legislation related to taxation of pension contributions.

Senate Finance Committee, *Subcommittee on Taxation and IRS Oversight,* *SD-219 20510; (202) 224-4515. Fax, (202) 224-5920. Sen. Orrin G. Hatch, R-Utah, Chair; Mark Prater, Staff Contact. Web, finance.senate.gov.*

Holds hearings on pension reform legislation; investigates private and self-employed pension plan problems. Oversees the Pension Benefit Guaranty Corp.

Senate Governmental Affairs Committee, *Permanent Subcommittee on Investigations,* *SR-100 20510; (202) 224-3721. Fax, (202) 224-7042. Sen. Susan Collins, R-Maine, Chair; K. Lee Blalack, Staff Director. General e-mail, PSI@govt-aff.senate.gov. Web, gov_affairs.senate.gov/psi.htm.*

Investigates labor racketeering, including pension and health and welfare fund frauds.

Senate Health, Education, Labor, and Pensions Committee, *Subcommittee on Employment, Safety, and Training,* *SH-607 20510; (202) 224-7229. Sen. Michael B. Enzi, R-Wyo., Chair; Raissa Geary, Staff Director. Web, labor.senate.gov.*

Jurisdiction over pension plan and retirement income security legislation and over the Labor-Management Reporting and Disclosure Act.

Senate Special Committee on Aging, *SD-G31 20510; (202) 224-5364. Fax, (202) 224-8660. Sen. Charles E. Grassley, R-Iowa, Chair; Ted Totman, Staff Director. Web, aging.senate.gov.*

Studies and makes recommendations on private and self-employed pension plan legislation and mandatory retirement.

NONPROFIT

AARP, *601 E St. N.W. 20049; (202) 434-2277. Fax, (202) 434-2320. Horace B. Deets, Executive Director. Library, (202) 434-6240. Press, (202) 434-2560. TTY, (202) 434-6561. Web, www.aarp.org.*

Researches and testifies on private, federal, and other government employee pension legislation and regulations; conducts seminars; provides information on pre-retirement preparation. Library open to the public.

American Academy of Actuaries, *1100 17th St. N.W., 7th Floor 20036; (202) 223-8196. Fax, (202) 872-1948. Rick Lawson, Executive Director. Web, www.actuary.org.*

Membership: professional actuaries practicing in the areas of life, health, liability, property, and casualty insurance; pensions; government insurance plans; and general consulting. Provides information on actuarial matters, including insurance and pensions; develops professional standards; advises public policymakers.

American Society of Pension Actuaries, *4245 N. Fairfax Dr., #750, Arlington, VA 22203-1619; (703) 516-9300. Fax, (703) 516-9308. Brian Graff, Executive Director. Web, www.aspa.org.*

Membership: professional pension plan actuaries, administrators, consultants, and other benefits professionals. Sponsors educational programs to prepare actuaries and consultants for professional exams. Monitors legislation.

Assn. of Private Pension and Welfare Plans, *1212 New York Ave. N.W., #1250 20005; (202) 289-6700. Fax, (202) 289-4582. James A. Klein, Executive Director. General e-mail, appwp@aol.com. Web, www.appwp.org.*

Membership: employers, consultants, banks, and service organizations. Informs members of private pension benefits and compensation.

Center for Economic Organizing, *1522 K St. N.W., #406 20005; (202) 775-9072. Fax, (202) 775-9074. Randy Barber, Director.*

Research, consulting, and training organization. Interests include the investment and control of pension funds and the role of unions and the private sector in administering these funds.

Employee Benefit Research Institute, *2121 K St. N.W., #600 20037-1896; (202) 659-0670. Fax, (202) 775-6312. Dallas L. Salisbury, President; Jack Vanderhei, Research Associate. Web, www.ebri.org.*

Researches proposed policy changes on employee benefits. Sponsors studies on retirement income and on health, work, family, and other benefits.

Employers Council on Flexible Compensation, *927 15th St. N.W., #1000 20005; (202) 659-4300. Kenneth E. Feltman, Executive Director. Web, www.ecfc.org.*

Represents employers who have or are considering flexible compensation plans. Supports the preservation and expansion of employee choice in savings and pension plans. Monitors legislation and regulations. Interests include cafeteria plans and 401(K).

ERISA Industry Committee, *1400 L St. N.W., #350 20005; (202) 789-1400. Fax, (202) 789-1120. Mark J. Ugoretz, President. General e-mail, eric@eric.org. Web, www.eric.org.*

Membership: major U.S. employers. Advocates members' positions on employee retirement, health care coverage, and welfare benefit plans; promotes flexibility and cost-effectiveness in employee benefits. Monitors legislation and regulations.

National Assn. of Manufacturers, *Human Resource Policy, 1331 Pennsylvania Ave. N.W., #600 20004-1790; (202) 637-3137. Fax, (202) 637-3182. Karen Wargo, Executive Assistant.*

Studies the Social Security system to ensure that its long-term status remains compatible with private sector retirement plans. Other interests include health care, pensions, cost containment, mandated benefits, and Medicare and other federal programs that affect employers. Opposed to government involvement in health care and proposed expansion of health care liability.

National Employee Benefits Institute, *1350 Connecticut Ave. N.W., #600 20036; (202) 822-6432. Fax, (202) 466-5109. Joseph Semo, Executive Director. Information, (888) 822-1344.*

Membership: large self-insured companies interested in employee benefits. Provides a forum for members and serves as a clearinghouse for information on employee benefits. Monitors legislation and regulations.

Pension Rights Center, *1140 19th St. N.W., #602 20036-6608; (202) 296-3776. Fax, (202) 833-2472. Karen W. Ferguson, Director. General e-mail, pnsnrights@ aol.com.*

Works to preserve and expand pension rights; provides information and technical assistance on pensions.

Retirement Policy Institute, *2158 Florida Ave. N.W. 20008; (202) 483-3140. A. Haeworth Robertson, President.*

Researches and educates the public about retirement policy issues. Interests include trends, pension reform, Social Security, and policy alternatives.

Society of Professional Benefit Administrators, *2 Wisconsin Circle, #670, Chevy Chase, MD 20815-7003; (301) 718-7722. Fax, (301) 718-9440. Frederick D. Hunt Jr., President.*

Membership: independent third-party administration firms that manage outside claims and benefit plans for client employers. Monitors government compliance requirements. Interests include pensions and retirement policy and funding, health coverage, and the Employee Retirement Income Security Act of 1974 (ERISA).

United Mine Workers of America Health and Retirement Funds, *4455 Connecticut Ave. N.W. 20008; (202) 895-3700. Fax, (202) 895-3703. Elliot Segal, Executive Director (Acting).*

Labor/management trust fund that provides health and retirement benefits to coal miners. Health benefits are provided to pensioners, their dependents, and, in some cases, their survivors.

Women's Institute for Secure Retirement, *1201 Pennsylvania Ave. N.W., #619 20004; (202) 393-5452. Fax, (202) 393-5890. Cindy Hounsell, Executive Director. General e-mail, wiserwomen@aol.com. Web, www.wiser.heinz. org.*

Provides information on women's retirement issues; conducts workshops and seminars. Monitors legislation and regulations.

See also National Council of Senior Citizens (p. 8); National Council on the Aging (p. 8)

◪ WORKPLACE SAFETY AND HEALTH

See also Coal (chap. 8)

AGENCIES

Bureau of Labor Statistics *(Labor Dept.),* **Compensation and Working Conditions,** *2 Massachusetts Ave. N.E.*

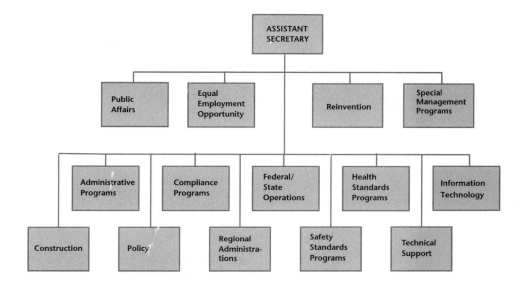

20212; (202) 691-6300. Fax, (202) 691-6310. Kathleen MacDonald, Associate Commissioner. Web, www.bls.gov/comhome.

Compiles data on occupational safety and health.

Environment, Safety, and Health *(Energy Dept.),* **Worker Health and Safety,** *20300 Century Blvd., Germantown, MD 20854 (mailing address: 19901 Germantown Rd., EH5 270CC, Germantown, MD 20874); (301) 903-5532. Fax, (301) 903-3189. Joseph E. Fitzgerald Jr., Deputy Assistant Secretary.*

Develops policy and establishes standards to ensure safety and health protection in all department activities.

Federal Mine Safety and Health Review Commission, *1730 K St. N.W., #600 20006; (202) 653-5660. Fax, (202) 653-5030. Mary Lu Jordan, Chair; Richard L. Baker, Executive Director, (202) 653-5625. Information, (202) 653-5633. Library, (202) 653-5002.*

Independent agency established by the Federal Mine Safety and Health Act of 1977. Holds fact-finding hearings and issues orders affirming, modifying, or vacating the labor secretary's enforcement actions regarding mine safety and health. Library open to the public.

Mine Safety and Health Administration *(Labor Dept.), 4015 Wilson Blvd., #622, Arlington, VA 22203; (703) 235-1385. Fax, (703) 235-4369. J. Davitt McAteer, Assistant Secretary. Information, (703) 235-1452. Web, www.msha.gov.*

Administers and enforces the health and safety provisions of the Federal Mine Safety and Health Act of 1977.

National Institute for Occupational Safety and Health (NIOSH), *(Centers for Disease Control and Prevention), 200 Independence Ave. S.W. 20201; (202) 401-6997. Fax, (202) 260-4464. Dr. Linda Rosenstock, Director. Information, (800) 356-4674. Press, (202) 401-3749. General e-mail, pubstaft@cdc.gov. Web, www.cdc.gov/niosh.*

Entity within the Centers for Disease Control and Prevention in Atlanta. Supports and conducts research on occupational safety and health issues; provides technical assistance and training; develops recommendations for the Labor Dept. Operates an occupational safety and health bibliographic database (mailing address: NIOSH Clearinghouse for Occupational Safety and Health Information, 4676 Columbia Pkwy., Cincinnati, OH 45226).

Occupational Safety and Health Administration *(Labor Dept.), 200 Constitution Ave. N.W., #S2315 20210; (202) 693-1900. Fax, (202) 693-2106. Charles Jeffress, Assistant Secretary. Information, (202) 693-2000. Web, www.osha.gov.*

Sets and enforces rules and regulations for workplace safety and health. Implements the Occupational Safety and Health Act of 1970. Provides federal agencies and private industries with compliance guidance and assistance.

Occupational Safety and Health Administration *(Labor Dept.),* **Compliance Programs,** *200 Constitution*

Ave. N.W., #N3603 20210; (202) 693-2100. Fax, (202) 693-1681. Richard Fairfax, Director. Web, www.osha.gov.

Interprets compliance safety standards for agency field personnel and private employees and employers.

Occupational Safety and Health Administration

(Labor Dept.), Construction, 200 Constitution Ave. N.W., #N3468 20210; (202) 693-2020. Fax, (202) 693-1689. Russell B. Swanson, Director.

Provides technical expertise to OSHA's enforcement personnel; initiates studies to determine causes of construction accidents; works with private sector to promote construction safety.

Occupational Safety and Health Administration

(Labor Dept.), Federal/State Operations, 200 Constitution Ave. N.W., #N3700 20210; (202) 693-2200. Fax, (202) 693-1671. Paula White, Director.

Makes grants to nonprofit organizations under the New Directions Grant Program to assist in providing education, training, and technical assistance to meet the workplace safety and health needs of employers and employees; administers state enforcement and consultation programs; trains federal and private employees, OSHA and state inspectors, and state consultants.

Occupational Safety and Health Administration

(Labor Dept.), Health Standards Programs, 200 Constitution Ave. N.W., #N3718 20210; (202) 693-1950. Fax, (202) 693-1678. Marthe B. Kent, Director (Acting).

Develops new or revised occupational health standards for toxic, hazardous, and carcinogenic substances, biological hazards, or other harmful physical agents, such as vibration, noise, and radiation.

Occupational Safety and Health Administration

(Labor Dept.), Public Affairs, 200 Constitution Ave. N.W., #N3647 20210; (202) 693-1999. Fax, (202) 693-1634. Bonnie Friedman, Director. Emergency hotline, (800) 321-OSHA. Web, www.osha.gov.

Conducts public hearings on proposed workplace safety and health standards; provides information, staff assistance and support for the National Advisory Committee for Occupational Safety and Health and the Construction Advisory Committee. Advises the assistant secretary of labor for occupational safety and health on consumer affairs matters.

Occupational Safety and Health Administration

(Labor Dept.), Safety Standards, 200 Constitution Ave. N.W., #N3605 20210; (202) 693-2222. Fax, (202) 693-1663. Marthe B. Kent, Director (Acting).

Develops new or revised occupational safety standards.

Occupational Safety and Health Review Commission,

1120 20th St. N.W., 9th Floor 20036-3419; (202) 606-5374. Fax, (202) 606-5050. Stuart E. Weisberg, Chair; William J. Gainer, Executive Director, (202) 606-5380. Information, (202) 606-5398. Locator, (202) 606-5100.

Independent executive branch agency that adjudicates disputes between private employers and the Occupational Safety and Health Administration arising under the Occupational Safety and Health Act of 1970.

CONGRESS

House Appropriations Committee, *Subcommittee on Labor, Health and Human Services, and Education, 2358 RHOB 20515; (202) 225-3508. Fax, (202) 225-3509. Rep. John Edward Porter, R-Ill., Chair; Tony McCann, Staff Director. Web, www.house.gov/appropriations.*

Jurisdiction over legislation to appropriate funds for the Federal Mine Safety and Health Review Commission and the Occupational Safety and Health Review Commission.

House Education and the Workforce Committee, *Subcommittee on Workforce Protections, 2181 RHOB 20515; (202) 225-4527. Fax, (202) 225-9571. Rep. Cass Ballenger, R-N.C., Chair; Kevin D. Talley, Staff Director. Web, www.house.gov/ed_workforce.*

Jurisdiction over legislation on workers' compensation and related wage loss; occupational safety and health; mine safety and health; youth camp safety; and migrant and agricultural labor health and safety.

House Small Business Committee, *Subcommittee on Regulatory Reform and Paperwork Reduction, B363 RHOB 20515; (202) 226-2630. Fax, (202) 225-8950. Rep. Sue W. Kelly, R-N.Y., Chair; Meredith Matty, Staff Director. General e-mail, smbiz@mail.house.gov. Web, www.house.gov/smbiz.*

Investigates oversight over the Occupational Safety and Health Administration as it affects small business.

Senate Appropriations Committee, *Subcommittee on Labor, Health and Human Services, and Education, SD-186 20510; (202) 224-7230. Fax, (202) 224-1360. Sen. Arlen Specter, R-Pa., Chair; Bettilou Taylor, Staff Director. Web, appropriations.senate.gov/labor.*

Jurisdiction over legislation to appropriate funds for the Federal Mine Safety and Health Review Commission and the Occupational Safety and Health Review Commission.

Senate Health, Education, Labor, and Pensions Committee, *Subcommittee on Public Health, SD-424 20510; (202) 224-7139. Fax, (202) 228-0928. Sen. Bill*

Frist, R-Tenn., Chair; Anne Phelps, Staff Director. Web, labor.senate.gov.

Jurisdiction over legislation on occupational safety and health, including workers' compensation and related wage loss, and on migrant and agricultural labor safety and health.

Senate Small Business Committee, *SR-428A 20510; (202) 224-5175. Fax, (202) 224-4885. Sen. Christopher S. Bond, R-Mo., Chair; Emilia DiSanto, Staff Director. Web, sbc.senate.gov.*

Jurisdiction over the Occupational Safety and Health Administration as it affects small business.

NONPROFIT

American Industrial Health Council, *2001 Pennsylvania Ave. N.W., #760 20006; (202) 833-2131. Fax, (202) 833-2201. Gaylen M. Camera, Executive Director. General e-mail, membershipservices@aihc.org.*

Membership: chemical companies and manufacturers of pharmaceutical, petroleum, aerospace, consumer, and metal products. Monitors regulations affecting methods for assessing health risks in these industries.

American Industrial Hygiene Assn., *2700 Prosperity Ave., #250, Fairfax, VA 22031; (703) 849-8888. Fax, (703) 207-3561. O. Gordon Banks, Executive Director. Web, www.aiha.org.*

Membership: scientists and engineers who practice industrial hygiene in government, labor, academic institutions, and independent organizations. Promotes health and safety standards in the workplace and the community; conducts research to identify potential dangers; educates workers about job-related risks; monitors safety regulations. Interests include international standards and information exchange.

Institute for a Drug-Free Workplace, *1225 Eye St. N.W., #1000 20005; (202) 842-7400. Fax, (202) 842-0011. Mark A. de Bernardo, Executive Director. Web, www. drugfreeworkplace.org.*

Coalition of businesses, business organizations, and individuals. Seeks to increase productivity, improve safety, and control insurance costs through detection and treatment of drug and alcohol abuse. Promotes fair and consistent implementation of drug abuse prevention programs; supports the right of employers to test for drugs. Monitors legislation and regulations.

ISEA—The Safety Equipment Assn., *1901 N. Moore St., #808, Arlington, VA 22209; (703) 525-1695. Fax, (703) 528-2148. Daniel K. Shipp, President. Web, www.safetycentral. org/isea.*

Trade organization that drafts industry standards for employee personal safety and protective equipment; encourages development and use of proper equipment to deal with industrial hazards; works to influence international standards, especially in North America. Monitors legislation and regulations.

National Assn. of Manufacturers, *Human Resources Policy, 1331 Pennsylvania Ave. N.W., #600N 20004-1790; (202) 637-3100. Fax, (202) 637-3182. Jenny Krese, Director.*

Conducts research, develops policy, and informs members of toxic injury compensation systems, and occupational safety and health legislation, regulations, and standards. Offers mediation service to business members.

National Safety Council, *Public Affairs, Washington Office, 1025 Connecticut Ave. N.W., #1200 20036; (202) 293-2270. Fax, (202) 293-0032. Charles A. Hurley, Executive Director. Web, www.nsc.org.*

Chartered by Congress. Conducts research and provides educational and informational services on highway safety, child passenger safety, and occupational safety and health; promotes policies to reduce accidental deaths and injuries and preventable illnesses. Monitors legislation and regulations. (Headquarters in Itasca, Ill.)

Public Citizen, *Health Research Group, 1600 20th St. N.W. 20009; (202) 588-1000. Fax, (202) 588-7796. Dr. Sidney M. Wolfe, Director. Web, www.citizen.org.*

Citizens' interest group that studies and reports on occupational diseases; monitors the Occupational Safety and Health Administration and participates in OSHA enforcement proceedings.

See also National AIDS Fund (p. 391)

Workers' Compensation

AGENCIES

Bureau of Labor Statistics *(Labor Dept.),* **Safety, Health, and Working Conditions,** *2 Massachusetts Ave. N.E., #4130 20212-0001; (202) 606-6304. Fax, (202) 606-6310. William L. Weber, Assistant Commissioner.*

Compiles and publishes statistics on occupational injuries, illnesses, and fatalities.

Employment Standards Administration *(Labor Dept.),* **Coal Mine Workers' Compensation,** *200 Constitution Ave. N.W., #C3520 20210; (202) 693-0046. Fax, (202) 693-1395. James L. DeMarce, Director.*

Provides direction for administration of the black lung benefits program. Adjudicates claims filed on or after July 1, 1973; certifies these benefit payments and maintains black lung beneficiary rolls.

Employment Standards Administration *(Labor Dept.), Workers' Compensation Programs, 200 Constitution Ave. N.W., #S3524 20210; (202) 693-0031. Fax, (202) 693-1378. Vacant, Deputy Assistant Secretary.*

Administers three federal workers' compensation laws: the Federal Employees' Compensation Act; the Longshore and Harbor Workers' Compensation Act and extensions; and Title IV (Black Lung Benefits Act) of the Federal Coal Mine Health and Safety Act.

Labor Dept., *Benefits Review Board, 200 Constitution Ave. N.W., #N5101 20210 (mailing address: P.O. Box 37601 20013-7601); (202) 565-7501. Fax, (202) 565-4137. Betty Jean Hall, Chief Administrative Appeals Judge. Web, www.dol.gov.*

Reviews appeals of workers seeking benefits under the Longshore and Harbor Workers' Compensation Act and its extensions, including the District of Columbia Workers' Compensation Act, and Title IV (Black Lung Benefits Act) of the Federal Coal Mine Health and Safety Act.

Labor Dept., *Employees' Compensation Appeals Board, 200 Constitution Ave. N.W., #N-2609 20210; (202) 208-1900. Fax, (202) 208-1876. Michael J. Walsh, Chair. Web, www.dol.gov.*

Reviews and determines appeals of final determinations of benefits claims made by the Office of Workers' Compensation Programs under the Federal Employees' Compensation Act.

NONPROFIT

American Insurance Assn., *1130 Connecticut Ave. N.W., #1000 20036; (202) 828-7100. Fax, (202) 293-1219. Robert E. Vagley, President. Library, (202) 828-7183. Press, (202) 828-7116. Web, www.aiadc.org.*

Membership: companies providing property and casualty insurance. Offers information on workers' compensation legislation and regulations; conducts educational activities. Library open to the public by appointment.

National Assn. of Manufacturers, *Human Resources Policy, 1331 Pennsylvania Ave. N.W., #600N 20004-1790; (202) 637-3100. Fax, (202) 637-3182. Jenny Krese, Director.*

Conducts research, develops policy, and informs members of workers' compensation law; provides feedback to government agencies

8 Energy

⚜ GENERAL POLICY

AGENCIES

Bureau of Land Management *(Interior Dept.)*, *Minerals, Realty, and Resource Protection*, 1849 C St. N.W., #5627 20240; (202) 208-4201. Fax, (202) 208-4800. Carson W. Culp, Assistant Director.

Evaluates and classifies onshore oil, natural gas, geothermal resources, and all solid energy and mineral resources, including coal and uranium on federal lands. Develops and administers regulations for fluid and solid mineral leasing on national lands and on the subsurface of land where fluid and solid mineral rights have been reserved for the federal government.

Economic Research Service *(Agriculture Dept.)*, 1800 M St. N.W. 20036; (202) 694-5200. Fax, (202) 694-5792. Barry Krissoff, Chief, Specialty Crops; Joy Harwood, Chief, Field Crops. Web, www.econ.ag.gov.

Conducts market research; studies and forecasts domestic supply-and-demand trends for fruits and vegetables.

Energy Dept., 1000 Independence Ave. S.W. 20585; (202) 586-6210. Fax, (202) 586-4403. Bill Richardson, Secretary. Information, (202) 586-5575. Press, (202) 586-4940. Locator, (202) 586-5000. Web, www.doe.gov.

Decides major energy policy issues and acts as principal adviser to the president on energy matters, including trade issues, strategic reserves, and nuclear power; acts as principal spokesperson for the department.

Energy Dept., 1000 Independence Ave. S.W. 20585; (202) 586-6210. Fax, (202) 586-4403. T. J. Glauthier, Deputy Secretary. Information, (202) 586-5575. Press, (202) 586-4940. Locator, (202) 586-5000. Web, www.doe.gov.

Manages departmental programs in energy efficiency and renewable energy, fossil energy, the Energy Information Administration, nuclear energy, civilian radioactive waste management, and the power marketing administrations.

Energy Dept., 1000 Independence Ave. S.W. 20585; (202) 586-6210. Fax, (202) 586-4403. Ernest J. Moniz, Under Secretary. Information, (202) 586-5575. Press, (202) 586-4940. Locator, (202) 586-5000. Web, www.doe.gov.

Manages departmental programs in defense, environmental safety and health, and waste management (including radioactive and nuclear waste); responsible for all administration and management matters and for regulatory and information programs.

Energy Dept., *Economic Impact and Diversity*, 1000 Independence Ave. S.W., #5B110 20585; (202) 586-8383. Fax, (202) 586-3075. James B. Lewis, Director. Web, www.doe.gov.

Researches the effects of government energy policies on minority businesses; offers technical and financial assistance to minority businesses, educational institutions, and developmental organizations to encourage their participation in energy research, development, and conservation; acts as an information clearinghouse.

Energy Dept., *Emergency Operations*, 1000 Independence Ave. S.W., #GH060 20585; (202) 586-9892. Fax, (202) 586-3904. Gen. John M. McBroom, Director.

Works to ensure coordinated Energy Dept. responses to energy-related emergencies. Recommends policies to mitigate the effects of energy supply crises on the United States; recommends government responses to energy emergencies.

Energy Dept., *Energy Advisory Board*, 1000 Independence Ave. S.W., #8E044 20585; (202) 586-7092. Fax, (202) 586-6279. Andrew Athy, Chair. Web, www.hr.doe.gov/seab.

Provides the secretary with advice and long-range guidance on the department's research and development, energy, environmental, and national defense-related activities.

Energy Dept., *Inventions and Innovation*, 1000 Independence Ave. S.W. 20585; (202) 586-2097. Marsha Quinn, Director. Web, www.oit.doe.gov/inventions.

Provides financial assistance for establishing technical performance and conducting early development of innovative ideas and inventions that have a significant energy saving impact and future commercial market potential. Offers technical guidance and commercialization support to successful applicants.

Energy Dept., *Nonproliferation and National Security*, 1000 Independence Ave. S.W., #7A049 20585; (202) 586-0645. Fax, (202) 586-0862. Rose Gottemoeller, Assistant Secretary. Web, www.nn.doe.gov.

Provides intelligence community with technical and analytical expertise on foreign nuclear and energy issues. Oversees programs to prevent the spread of weapons of mass destruction, to protect the U.S. nuclear deterrent, and to respond to nuclear and energy emergencies.

Energy Dept., *Office of Policy*, 1000 Independence Ave. S.W., #7C034 20585; (202) 586-5316. Fax, (202) 586-3047. Mark J. Mazur, Director. Web, www.osti.gov/policy/home.html.

ENERGY DEPARTMENT

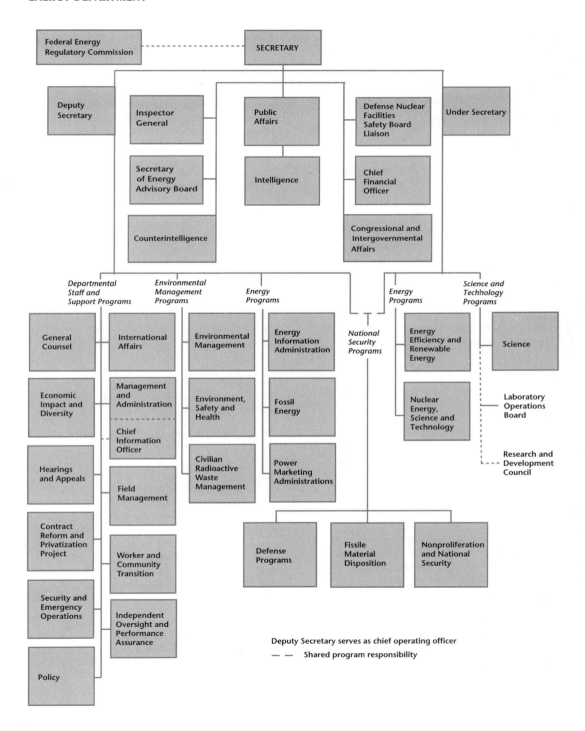

Deputy Secretary serves as chief operating officer

— — Shared program responsibility

Serves as principal adviser to the secretary, deputy secretary, and undersecretary in formulating and evaluating departmental policy. Reviews programs, budgets, regulations, and legislative proposals to ensure consistency with departmental policy.

Energy Information Administration (EIA), *(Energy Dept.), 1000 Independence Ave. S.W. 20585; (202) 586-4361. Fax, (202) 586-0329. Jay Hakes, Administrator. Web, www.eia.doe.gov.*

Collects and publishes data on national and international energy reserves, financial status of energy-producing companies, production, demand, consumption, and other areas; provides long- and short-term analyses of energy trends and data.

Energy Information Administration *(Energy Dept.), Energy Markets and End Use, 1000 Independence Ave. S.W., #2G-090 20585; (202) 586-1617. Fax, (202) 586-9753. W. Calvin Kilgore, Director. General e-mail, infoctr@eia.doe.gov. Web, www.eia.doe.gov.*

Designs, develops, and maintains statistical and short-term forecasting information systems concerning consumption and other subjects that cut across energy sources. Formulates and administers financial data reporting requirements for major energy companies. Maintains survey on energy supply and use.

Energy Information Administration *(Energy Dept.), Integrated Analysis and Forecasting, 1000 Independence Ave. S.W., EI-80, #2F081 20585; (202) 586-2222. Fax, (202) 586-3045. Mary J. Hutzler, Director (Acting). Library, (202) 586-9534. Web, www.eia.doe.gov.*

Analyzes and forecasts alternative energy futures. Develops, applies, and maintains modeling systems for analyzing the interactions of demand, conversion, and supply for all energy sources and their economic and environmental impacts. Concerned with emerging energy markets and U.S. dependence on petroleum imports.

Environment, Safety, and Health *(Energy Dept.), 1000 Independence Ave. S.W., #7A097 20585; (202) 586-6151. Fax, (202) 586-0956. David Michaels, Assistant Secretary. Web, www.eh.doe.gov.*

Ensures that Energy Dept. programs comply with federal policies and standards designed to protect the environment and government property. Approves all environmental impact statements prepared by the department. Oversees health and nonnuclear safety conditions at Energy Dept. facilities.

Federal Energy Regulatory Commission *(Energy Dept.), 888 1st St. N.E., #11A 20426; (202) 208-0000. Fax,*

(202) 208-0151. James J. Hoecker, Chair. Information, (202) 208-0200. Press, (202) 208-1088. Dockets, (202) 208-0715. Web, www.ferc.fed.us.

Establishes and enforces: interstate oil pipeline rates, charges, and valuations; and rates and charges for wholesale electric power transmission, sale, and interconnection. Regulates the construction and operation of interstate natural gas facilities and the interstate rates for resale and transportation of natural gas. Issues licenses for nonfederal hydroelectric projects and establishes accounting rules and procedures for utilities.

Interior Dept., *Land and Minerals Management, 1849 C St. N.W., MS-6628 20240; (202) 208-5676. Fax, (202) 208-3144. Sylvia Baca, Assistant Secretary. Web, www.doi.gov.*

Directs and supervises the Bureau of Land Management, the Minerals Management Service, and the Office of Surface Mining and Reclamation Enforcement. Supervises programs associated with land use planning, onshore and offshore minerals, surface mining reclamation and enforcement, and outer continental shelf minerals management.

Office of Management and Budget *(Executive Office of the President), Energy and Science, New Executive Office Bldg., #8002 20503; (202) 395-3404. Fax, (202) 395-3049. Kathleen Peroff, Deputy Associate Director. Web, www.whitehouse.gov/omb.*

Advises and assists the president in preparing the budget for energy programs; coordinates OMB energy policy and programs.

Office of Science *(Energy Dept.), 1000 Independence Ave. S.W., #7B058 20585; (202) 586-5430. Fax, (202) 586-4120. James Decker, Director (Acting).*

Advises the secretary on the department's physical science research and energy research and development programs; the use of multipurpose laboratories (except weapons laboratories); and education and training for basic and applied research activities, including fellowships for university researchers. Manages the department's high energy and nuclear physics programs and the fusion energy program. Conducts environmental and health-related research and development programs, including studies of energy-related pollutants and hazardous materials.

Office of Science and Technology Policy *(Executive Office of the President), Dwight D. Eisenhower Executive Office Bldg., #424 20502; (202) 456-7116. Fax, (202) 456-6021. Neal Lane, Director. General e-mail, information@ostp.pop.gov. Web, www.whitehouse.gov/WH/EOP/OSTP/html/OSTP_Home.html.*

Provides the president with policy analysis on scientific and technological matters, including energy policy and technology issues; coordinates executive office and federal agency responses to these issues; evaluates the effectiveness of scientific and technological programs.

Treasury Dept., *Tax Analysis: Business Taxation,* 1500 Pennsylvania Ave. N.W., #4217 20220; (202) 622-1782. Fax, (202) 622-2969. Geraldine Gerardi, Director. Web, www.ustreas.gov.

Develops and provides economic analysis of business taxation policy relating to energy matters, including tax incentives for alternative energy usage and development, gasoline and automobile efficiency taxes, and tax incentives designed to encourage industrial conversion from oil to coal in industrial facilities.

See also Domestic Policy Council (p. 319)

CONGRESS

General Accounting Office, *Energy, Resources, and Science,* 441 G St. N.W., #2T23 20548; (202) 512-3841. Fax, (202) 512-6880. Jim Wells, Director.

Independent, nonpartisan agency in the legislative branch that audits, analyzes, and reports on efficiency and effectiveness of federal energy and natural resource programs. Addresses governmentwide science issues and the production, regulation, and consumption of all forms of energy.

House Appropriations Committee, *Subcommittee on Energy and Water Development,* 2362 RHOB 20515; (202) 225-3421. Rep. Ron Packard, R-Calif., Chair; Robert Schmidt, Staff Director. Web, www.house.gov/appropriations.

Jurisdiction over legislation to appropriate funds for the Energy Dept. (except for the Economic Regulatory Administration; Energy Information Administration; strategic petroleum reserve; naval petroleum and oil shale reserves; fossil energy research and development; energy conservation; alternative fuels production; and related matters), the Nuclear Regulatory Commission, the Tennessee Valley Authority, the Federal Energy Regulatory Commission, and the federal power marketing administrations.

House Appropriations Committee, *Subcommittee on Interior,* B308 RHOB 20515; (202) 225-3081. Fax, (202) 225-9069. Rep. Ralph Regula, R-Ohio, Chair; Deborah A. Weatherly, Clerk. Web, www.house.gov/appropriations.

Jurisdiction over legislation to appropriate funds for the Interior Dept.; strategic petroleum reserve and naval petroleum and oil shale reserves; clean coal technology;

fossil energy research and development; energy conservation; alternate fuels production; and related matters.

House Commerce Committee, *Subcommittee on Energy and Power,* 2125 RHOB 20515; (202) 225-2927. Fax, (202) 225-1919. Rep. Joe L. Barton, R-Texas, Chair; James E. Derderian, Staff Director. General e-mail, commerce@mail.house.gov. Web, www.house.gov/commerce.

Jurisdiction over legislation on energy policy, regulation, conservation, exploration, production, distribution, storage, and pricing; commercialization and utilization of new technologies, including liquefied natural gas projects; and measures relating to the Energy Dept., and the Federal Energy Regulatory Commission.

House Government Reform Committee, *Subcommittee on National Economic Growth, Natural Resources, and Regulatory Affairs,* B377 RHOB 20515; (202) 225-4407. Fax, (202) 225-2441. Rep. David M. McIntosh, R-Ind., Chair; Marlo Lewis, Staff Director. Web, www.house.gov/reform.

Oversight of Energy Dept., Nuclear Regulatory Commission, and Tennessee Valley Authority.

House Resources Committee, *Subcommittee on Energy and Mineral Resources,* 1626 LHOB 20515; (202) 225-9297. Fax, (202) 225-5255. Rep. Barbara Cubin, R-Wyo., Chair; William Condit, Staff Director. General e-mail, resources.committee@mail.house.gov. Web, www.house.gov/resources/energy.

Jurisdiction over conservation of the U.S. uranium supply, the U.S. Geological Survey (except water-related programs), mineral land laws, mining, and mineral resources on public lands.

House Resources Committee, *Subcommittee on Water and Power,* 1522 LHOB 20515; (202) 225-8331. Fax, (202) 226-6953. Rep. John T. Doolittle, R-Calif., Chair; Robert Faber, Staff Director. General e-mail, water.power@mail.house.gov. Web, www.house.gov/resources/water.

Jurisdiction over water-related programs of the U.S. Geological Survey, saline water research and development, water resources research programs, and matters related to the Water Resources Planning Act.

House Science Committee, 2320 RHOB 20515; (202) 225-6371. Fax, (202) 226-0891. Rep. F. James Sensenbrenner Jr., R-Wis., Chair; Todd Schultz, Chief of Staff. Web, www.house.gov/science.

Jurisdiction over legislation on all nonmilitary energy research and development.

House Small Business Committee, *2361 RHOB 20515; (202) 225-5821. Rep. James M. Talent, R-Mo., Chair; Mark Strand, Chief of Staff. General e-mail, smbiz@mail.house.gov. Web, www.house.gov/smbiz.*

Studies and makes recommendations on energy allocation and marketing, and energy research and development contracts as they relate to small business.

House Ways and Means Committee, *1102 LHOB 20515; (202) 225-3625. Fax, (202) 225-2610. Rep. Bill Archer, R-Texas, Chair; A. L. Singleton, Chief of Staff. Web, www.house.gov/ways_means.*

Jurisdiction over legislation on taxes, tariffs, and trade measures relating to energy.

Joint Committee on Taxation, *1015 LHOB 20515; (202) 225-3621. Fax, (202) 225-0832. Sen. William V. Roth Jr., R-Del., Chair; Lindy Paull, Chief of Staff. Web, www.house.gov/jct.*

Performs staff work for House Ways and Means and Senate Finance committees on legislation involving internal revenue, including taxation of energy producers, transporters, and consumers. Provides revenue estimates for all tax legislation.

Senate Appropriations Committee, *Subcommittee on Energy and Water Development, SD-127 20510; (202) 224-7260. Sen. Pete V. Domenici, R-N.M., Chair; Clay Sell, Clerk. Web, appropriations.senate.gov/energy.*

Jurisdiction over legislation to appropriate funds for the Energy Dept. (except for the Energy Regulatory Administration; Energy Information Administration; strategic petroleum reserve; fossil energy research, development, and construction; and energy conservation); the Federal Energy Regulatory Commission; the federal power marketing administrations; the Nuclear Regulatory Commission; and the Tennessee Valley Authority.

Senate Appropriations Committee, *Subcommittee on Interior, SD-131 20510; (202) 224-7233. Sen. Slade Gorton, R-Wash., Chair; Bruce Evans, Clerk. Web, appropriations.senate.gov/interior.*

Jurisdiction over legislation to appropriate funds for the Energy Information Administration; economic regulation; strategic petroleum reserve; energy production, demonstration, and distribution; fossil energy research, development, and construction; energy conservation; civilian (nonnuclear) programs in the Energy Dept.; and related matters.

Senate Energy and Natural Resources Committee, *SD-364 20510; (202) 224-4971. Fax, (202) 224-6163. Sen. Frank H. Murkowski, R-Alaska, Chair; Andrew Lundquist, Staff Director. General e-mail, committee@energy.senate.gov. Web, energy.senate.gov.*

Jurisdiction over legislation on energy policy, regulation, and conservation; research and development; nonmilitary development of nuclear energy; oil and gas production and distribution (including price); energy-related aspects of deepwater ports; hydroelectric power; coal production and distribution; mining, mineral land laws, and mineral conservation; leasing and the extraction of minerals from the ocean and outer continental shelf lands; and naval petroleum reserves in Alaska. Jurisdiction over legislation on the Federal Energy Regulatory Commission. Oversees the Energy Dept., Tennessee Valley Authority, and the U.S. Geological Survey.

Senate Energy and Natural Resources Committee, *Subcommittee on Energy Research, Development, Production, and Regulation, SD-308 20510; (202) 224-6567. Fax, (202) 228-0302. Sen. Don Nickles, R-Okla., Chair; Howard Useem, Professional Staff Member. General e-mail, erdpr@energy.senate.gov. Web, energy.senate.gov.*

Jurisdiction over legislation on regulatory functions of nuclear energy; nonmilitary energy research and development; commercialization and utilization of new technologies; global climate changes; energy conservation; and liquefied natural gas projects.

Senate Finance Committee, *SD-219 20510; (202) 224-4515. Fax, (202) 224-5920. Sen. William V. Roth Jr., R-Del., Chair; Frank Polk, Staff Director. Web, finance.senate.gov.*

Holds hearings on legislation concerning taxes, tariffs, and trade measures relating to energy, such as oil import fees.

Senate Special Committee on Aging, *SD-G31 20510; (202) 224-5364. Fax, (202) 224-8660. Sen. Charles E. Grassley, R-Iowa, Chair; Ted Totman, Staff Director. Web, aging.senate.gov.*

Studies and makes recommendations on the availability of energy to older people and on the adequacy of federal energy programs for the elderly.

NONPROFIT

American Assn. of Blacks in Energy, *927 15th St. N.W., #200 20005; (202) 371-9530. Fax, (202) 371-9218. Dorita M. Dixon, National Project Director. General e-mail, aabe@erols.com. Web, www.aabe.org.*

Encourages participation of African Americans and other minorities in formulating energy policy.

American Boiler Manufacturers Assn., *950 N. Glebe Rd., #160, Arlington, VA 22203; (703) 522-7350. Fax, (703) 522-2665. Russell N. Mosher, President. Web, www.abma.com.*

Membership: manufacturers of boiler systems and boiler-related products, including fuel-burning systems. Interests include energy and environmental issues.

Consumer Energy Council of America Research Foundation, *2000 L St. N.W., #802 20036-4907; (202) 659-0404. Fax, (202) 659-0407. Ellen Berman, President. Web, www.cecarf.org.*

Analyzes economic and social effects of energy policies; develops long-range conservation and load-management strategies for utilities; designs pilot programs for and conducts research on conservation initiatives. Builds consensus among public- and private-sector organizations, state and local groups, businesses, utilities, consumers, environmentalists, government agencies, and others on energy policy issues. Interests include transportation policies, transmission siting and certification, air pollution emissions trading, oil overcharge funds, and appliance rebate programs. Conducts consumer education campaigns.

Energy Bar Assn., *1350 Connecticut Ave. N.W., #300 20036; (202) 223-5625. Fax, (202) 833-5596. Lorna Wilson, Administrator. Web, www.eba-net.org.*

Membership: lawyers interested in all areas of energy law. Interests include administration of laws covering production, development, conservation, transmission, and economic regulation of energy.

National Assn. of Energy Service Companies, *1615 M St. N.W., #800 20036; (202) 822-0950. Fax, (202) 822-0955. Terry E. Singer, Executive Director. Web, www.naesco. org.*

Membership: energy service companies, equipment manufacturers, affiliates of utilities, financial institutions, and governmental and other organizations involved in energy conservation and alternative energy projects. Acts as an energy information clearinghouse; sponsors conferences and seminars. Monitors legislation and regulations affecting the industry.

National Assn. of Regulatory Utility Commissioners, *1101 Vermont Ave. N.W., #200 20005; (202) 898-2200. Fax, (202) 898-2213. Charles Gray, Executive Director. Press, (202) 898-2205. Web, www.naruc.org.*

Membership: members of federal, state, municipal, and Canadian regulatory commissions that have jurisdiction over utilities and carriers. Interests include electricity, natural gas, and nuclear power.

National Governors' Assn., *Natural Resources, 444 N. Capitol St. N.W., #267 20001-1512; (202) 624-5339. Fax, (202) 624-5313. Diane S. Shea, Staff Director. Web, www.nga.org.*

Develops governors' recommendations on energy and environmental issues and presents these policies to Congress and federal agencies.

Paper Allied-Industrial, Chemical, and Energy Workers International Union, *Washington Office, 1155 15th St. N.W., #405 20005; (703) 876-9300. Fax, (703) 876-8952. Paula R. Littles, Legislative Director.*

Membership: approximately 310,000 workers in the energy, chemical, pharmaceutical, and allied industries. Assists members with contract negotiation and grievances; conducts training programs and workshops. Monitors legislation and regulations. (Headquarters in Lakewood, Colo.; affiliated with the AFL-CIO.)

Southern States Energy Board, *Washington Office, P.O. Box 34606 20043; (202) 667-7303. Fax, (202) 667-7313. Carolyn C. Drake, Director. General e-mail, sseb@sseb.org. Web, www.sseb.org.*

Interstate compact organization that serves as regional representative of sixteen southern states, Puerto Rico, and the Virgin Islands for energy and environmental issues. (Headquarters in Norcross, Ga.)

SRI International, *Washington Office, 1611 N. Kent St., #700, Arlington, VA 22209; (703) 524-2053. Fax, (703) 247-8569. William Mohr, Director. Web, www.sri.com.*

Research organization that conducts policy-related energy studies and scientific research. Projects include surveys of energy supply and demand; analyses of fossil fuel, solar, and nuclear energy; the environmental effects of advanced energy technology; and energy management. (Headquarters in Menlo Park, Calif.)

U.S. Chamber of Commerce, *Environment and Regulatory Affairs, 1615 H St. N.W. 20062-2000; (202) 463-5533. Fax, (202) 887-3445. Bill Kovacs, Manager. Web, www.uschamber.org.*

Develops policy on all issues affecting the production, use, and conservation of energy, including transportation, energy taxes, and on- and offshore mining of energy resources.

U.S. Conference of Mayors, *Municipal Waste Management Assn., 1620 Eye St. N.W., 6th Floor 20006; (202) 293-7330. Fax, (202) 293-2352. J. Thomas Cochran, Executive Director; David Gatton, Deputy Executive Director. Web, www.usmayors.org/uscm/about/affiliate_ organizations/non-elected_affiliates/municip.html.*

Membership: mayors of cities with populations of 30,000 or more. Works with Congress and the executive branch to promote urban policy on energy and environment issues; analyzes federal legislation, programs, and policies from an urban perspective.

Utility Workers Union of America, *815 16th St. N.W. 20006; (202) 347-8105. Fax, (202) 347-4872. Donald E. Wightman, President. Web, www.uwua.org.*

Membership: approximately 50,000 workers in utilities and related industries. Helps members negotiate pay, benefits, and better working conditions; conducts training programs and workshops. Monitors legislation and regulations. (Affiliated with the AFL-CIO.)

See also Federation of American Scientists (p. 568); National Academy of Sciences (p. 595); Rand Corporation (p. 499)

Energy Conservation

See also Environment and Natural Resources (chap. 9)

AGENCIES

Energy Efficiency and Renewable Energy *(Energy Dept.), 1000 Independence Ave. S.W., #6C016 20585; (202) 586-9220. Fax, (202) 586-9260. Dan W. Reicher, Assistant Secretary. Information, (800) 363-3732. Web, www.eren.doe.gov.*

Develops and manages programs to improve foreign and domestic markets for renewable energy sources including solar, biomass, wind, geothermal, and hydropower and to increase efficiency of energy use among residential, commercial, transportation, utility, and industrial users. Administers financial and technical assistance for state energy programs, weatherization for low-income households, and implementation of energy conservation measures by schools, hospitals, local governments, and public care institutions.

Energy Efficiency and Renewable Energy *(Energy Dept.), Building Technologies, 1000 Independence Ave. S.W., #EE40 20585; (202) 586-1510. Fax, (202) 586-5954. Mark Ginsberg, Deputy Assistant Secretary.*

Supports private and government efforts to improve the energy efficiency of buildings and increase use of renewable energy sources. Conducts research to make information and energy technologies available.

Energy Efficiency and Renewable Energy *(Energy Dept.), Industrial Technologies, 1000 Independence Ave. S.W., #5F065, EE20 20585; (202) 586-9232. Fax, (202) 586-9234. Denise F. Swink, Deputy Assistant Secretary.*

Conducts research and disseminates information to increase energy end-use efficiency, promote renewable energy use and industrial applications, and reduce the volume of industrial and municipal waste.

Energy Efficiency and Renewable Energy *(Energy Dept.), Transportation Technologies, 1000 Independence Ave. S.W., #5G086, EE30 20585; (202) 586-8027. Fax, (202) 586-1637. Thomas J. Gross, Deputy Assistant Secretary.*

Conducts research and development programs to improve transportation energy efficiency. Programs include electric and hybrid vehicles, advanced propulsion systems, advanced materials research, and alternative fuels, including biofuels.

Energy Information Administration *(Energy Dept.), Energy Consumption, 1000 Independence Ave. S.W., #2F065, MS 2G-090, EI-63 20585; (202) 586-1112. Fax, (202) 586-0018. Dwight K. French, Director.*

Maintains data on energy consumption in the residential, commercial, industrial, and transportation sectors. Prepares analyses on energy consumption by sector and fuel type, including the impact of conservation measures.

Housing and Urban Development Dept., *Community Viability, 451 7th St. S.W., #7240 20410; (202) 708-2894. Fax, (202) 708-3363. Richard H. Broun, Director. Web, www.hud.gov.*

Develops policies promoting energy efficiency, conservation, and renewable sources of supply in housing and community development programs, including district heating and cooling systems and waste-to-energy cogeneration projects.

National Institute of Standards and Technology *(Commerce Dept.), Building and Fire Research Laboratory, Route I-270 and Quince Orchard Rd., Gaithersburg, MD 20899; (301) 975-5851. Fax, (301) 975-5433. Jack Snell, Director; James E. Hill, Deputy Director. Web, www.bfrl.nist.gov.*

Develops measurement techniques, test methods, and mathematical models to encourage energy conservation in large buildings. Interests include refrigeration, lighting, infiltration and ventilation, heating and air conditioning, indoor air quality, and heat transfer in the building envelope.

CONGRESS

House Commerce Committee, *Subcommittee on Energy and Power, 2125 RHOB 20515; (202) 225-2927. Fax, (202) 225-1919. Rep. Joe L. Barton, R-Texas, Chair; James E. Derderian, Staff Director. General e-mail, commerce@ mail.house.gov. Web, www.house.gov/commerce.*

Jurisdiction over legislation on proposals to label appliances to indicate energy consumption and on emergency fuel allocation. Jurisdiction over legislation on energy conservation measures in housing (jurisdiction shared with House Banking and Financial Service Committee).

House Science Committee, *Subcommittee on Energy and Environment, 389 FHOB 20515; (202) 225-9662. Fax, (202) 226-6983. Rep. Ken Calvert, R-Calif., Chair; Harlan Watson, Staff Director. Web, www.house.gov/science.*

Jurisdiction over legislation on research and development of energy sources and over Energy Dept. basic research programs, including those in energy conservation and utilization; jurisdiction over legislation related to the Energy Dept.'s transportation energy conservation programs.

Joint Economic Committee, *SD-G01 20510; (202) 224-5171. Fax, (202) 224-0240. Sen. Connie Mack, R-Fla., Chair; Shelley Hymes, Staff Director. General e-mail, jec@jec.house.gov. Web, jec.senate.gov.*

Studies and makes recommendations on the conservation and expansion of energy supplies.

Senate Energy and Natural Resources Committee, *SD-364 20510; (202) 224-4971. Fax, (202) 224-6163. Sen. Frank H. Murkowski, R-Alaska, Chair; Andrew Lundquist, Staff Director. General e-mail, committee@energy.senate.gov. Web, energy.senate.gov.*

Jurisdiction over mineral conservation and over energy conservation measures, such as emergency fuel allocation, proposals to label appliances to indicate energy consumption, gasoline rationing, and coal conversion. Jurisdiction over legislation on energy research and development, including petroleum on public lands and the U.S. uranium supply.

NONPROFIT

Alliance to Save Energy, *1200 18th St. N.W., #900 20036; (202) 857-0666. Fax, (202) 331-9588. David Nemtzow, President. General e-mail, info@ase.org. Web, www.ase.org.*

Coalition of government, business, consumer, and labor leaders concerned with increasing the efficiency of energy use. Advocates efficient use of energy; conducts research, demonstration projects, and public education programs.

American Council for an Energy-Efficient Economy, *1001 Connecticut Ave. N.W., #801 20036; (202) 429-8873. Fax, (202) 429-2248. Howard Geller, Executive Director. General e-mail, info@aceee.org. Web, aceee.org.*

Independent research organization concerned with energy policy, technologies, and conservation. Interests include energy efficiency in buildings and appliances, improved transportation efficiency, industrial efficiency, utility issues, and conservation in developing countries.

Environmental Defense Fund, *Washington Office, 1875 Connecticut Ave. N.W., #1016 20009-5728; (202) 387-3500. Fax, (202) 234-6049. Senta Boardley, Office Manager. Web, www.edf.org.*

Citizens' interest group staffed by lawyers, economists, and scientists. Provides information on energy issues and advocates energy conservation measures. Interests include Antarctica and the Amazon rain forest. Provides utilities and environmental organizations with energy conservation computer models. (Headquarters in New York.)

Friends of the Earth, *1025 Vermont Ave. N.W., #300 20005-6303; (202) 783-7400. Fax, (202) 783-0444. Brent Blackwelder, President. General e-mail, foe@foe.org. Web, www.foe.org.*

Environmental advocacy group. Interests include conservation and renewable energy resources and air and water pollution, including international water projects. Specializes in federal budget and tax issues related to the environment; ozone layer and ground water protection; and World Bank and International Monetary Fund reform. Library open to the public by appointment.

International Institute for Energy Conservation, *1015 15th St. N.W., #600 20005; (202) 842-3388. Fax, (202) 789-2943. Griffin Thompson, President. Web, www.cerf.org/iiec.*

Works with developing nations to establish sustainable growth through efficient uses of energy. Seeks to counteract air and water pollution and the threat of global warming.

National Conference of States on Building Codes and Standards, *505 Huntmar Park Dr., #210, Herndon, VA 20170; (703) 437-0100. Fax, (703) 481-3596. Robert Wible, Executive Director. Web, www.ncsbcs.org.*

Membership: delegates appointed by the governors of the states and territories, and individuals and organizations concerned with building standards. Prepares code reports under contract. Works with national and state organizations and governmental agencies to promote the updating and adoption of model energy conservation codes for new and existing buildings. Maintains library of national, state, and local government energy conservation codes. Library open to members.

National Insulation Assn., *99 Canal Center Plaza, #222, Alexandria, VA 22314; (703) 683-6422. Fax, (703) 549-4838. Bill Pitkin, Executive Vice President. General e-mail, niainfo@insulation.org. Web, www.insulation.org.*

Membership: companies in the commercial and industrial insulation and asbestos abatement industries. Monitors legislation and regulations.

North American Insulation Manufacturers Assn., *44 Canal Center Plaza, #310, Alexandria, VA 22314; (703) 684-0084. Fax, (703) 684-0427. Kenneth D. Mentzer, President. General e-mail, insulation@naima.org. Web, www. naima.org.*

Membership: manufacturers of insulation products for use in homes, commercial buildings, and industrial facilities. Provides information on the use of insulation for thermal efficiency, sound control, and fire safety; monitors research in the industry. Monitors legislation and regulations.

Resources for the Future, *1616 P St. N.W. 20036; (202) 328-5000. Fax, (202) 939-3460. Paul Portney, President. Library, (202) 328-5089. General e-mail, info@rff.org. Web, www.rff.org.*

Research organization that conducts studies on economic and policy aspects of energy, conservation, and development of natural resources, including effects on the environment. Interests include hazardous waste, the Superfund, and biodiversity.

Sierra Club, *Washington Office, 408 C St. N.E. 20002; (202) 547-1141. Fax, (202) 547-6009. Debbie Sease, Legislative Director. Legislative hotline, (202) 675-2394. General e-mail, information@sierraclub.org. Web, www. sierraclub.org.*

Citizens' interest group that promotes protection and responsible use of the Earth's ecosystems and its natural resources. Focuses on combating global warming/greenhouse effect through energy conservation, efficient use of renewable energy resources, auto efficiency, and constraints on deforestation. Monitors federal, state, and local legislation relating to the environment and natural resources. (Headquarters in San Francisco.)

Union of Concerned Scientists, *Government Relations, Washington Office, 1616 P St. N.W., #310 20036; (202) 332-0900. Fax, (202) 332-0905. Alden Meyer, Director; Todd Perry, Washington Representative for Arms Control and International Security. General e-mail, ucs@ ucsusa.org. Web, www.ucsusa.org.*

Independent group of scientists and others that advocates safe and sustainable international, national, and state energy policies. Conducts research, advocacy, and educational outreach focusing on market-based strategies for the development of renewable energy and alternative fuels, transportation policy, carbon reduction, global warming, and energy efficiency. (Headquarters in Cambridge, Mass.)

Worldwatch Institute, *1776 Massachusetts Ave. N.W., 8th Floor 20036; (202) 452-1999. Fax, (202) 296-7365. Lester R. Brown, President. General e-mail, worldwatch@ worldwatch.org. Web, www.worldwatch.org.*

Research organization that focuses on interdisciplinary approach to solving global environmental problems. Interests include energy conservation, renewable resources, solar power, and energy use in developing countries.

International Trade and Cooperation

See also Energy Conservation (this chapter); International Affairs (chap. 13)

AGENCIES

Agency for International Development, *Center for Environment, 1300 Pennsylvania Ave. N.W., #3.08-B, USAID/G/ENV 20523-3800; (202) 712-1750. Fax, (202) 216-3174. David Hales, Deputy Assistant Administrator. Web, www.info.usaid.gov.*

Assists with the economic growth of developing countries by providing policy, technical, and financial assistance for cost-effective, reliable, and environmentally sound energy programs. Focuses on the Global Warming Initiative, private initiatives, renewable energy, energy efficiency and conservation, technology innovation, and training officials in developing countries.

Census Bureau *(Commerce Dept.), Foreign Trade, Suitland and Silver Hill Rds., Suitland, MD 20772 (mailing address: 4700 Silver Hill Rd. 20233-6700); (301) 457-2203. Fax, (301) 457-2867. C. Harvey Monk Jr., Chief. Trade data inquiries, (301) 457-2227. Web, www.census.gov/ foreign-trade/www.*

Provides information on imports and exports of energy commodities, including coal, oil, and natural gas.

Commerce Dept., *Balance of Payments, 1441 L St. N.W., BE-58 20230; (202) 606-9545. Fax, (202) 606-5314. Christopher L. Bach, Chief. Web, www.stat-usa.gov.*

Provides statistics on U.S. balance of trade, including figures on energy commodities.

Energy Dept., *Emergency Operations, 1000 Independence Ave. S.W., #GH060 20585; (202) 586-9892. Fax, (202) 586-3904. Gen. John M. McBroom, Director.*

Monitors international energy situations as they affect domestic market conditions; recommends policies on and government responses to energy emergencies; represents the United States in the International Energy Agency's emergency programs and NATO civil emergency preparedness activities.

Energy Dept., *International Affairs: International Energy Policy, 1000 Independence Ave. S.W., #7C034, PO-7 20585; (202) 586-5493. Fax, (202) 586-3047. Theresa Fariello, Deputy Assistant Secretary. Web, www.doe.gov/international.*

Monitors and evaluates energy policies of foreign nations to determine the effect on international trade; works with industry associations and the Commerce Dept. on promoting U.S. energy exports.

Energy Dept., *Office of Policy,* *1000 Independence Ave. S.W., #7C034 20585; (202) 586-5316. Fax, (202) 586-3047. Mark J. Mazur, Director. Web, www.osti.gov/policy/home.html.*

Advises the secretary on developing and implementing international energy policies consistent with U.S. foreign policy. Evaluates Energy Dept. programs. Represents the department in international discussions on energy matters, including the Organization for Economic Cooperation and Development's International Energy Agency. Assesses world energy price and supply trends and technological developments; studies effects of international actions on U.S. energy supply.

Energy Information Administration *(Energy Dept.),* ***International Economic and Greenhouse Gases,*** *1000 Independence Ave. S.W., #2F081, EI81 20585; (202) 586-1441. Fax, (202) 586-3045. Mary J. Hutzler, Director (Acting).*

Compiles, interprets, and reports international energy statistics and U.S. energy data for international energy organizations. Analyzes international energy markets; makes projections concerning world prices and trade for energy sources, including oil, natural gas, coal, and electricity; monitors world petroleum market to determine U.S. vulnerability.

Fossil Energy *(Energy Dept.),* ***Coal and Power Import and Export,*** *FE-27, 19901 Germantown Rd., Germantown, MD 20874-1290; (301) 903-4497. Fax, (301) 903-1591. Barbara McKee, Director. Web, www.fe.doe.gov/international.*

Responsible for coal and technology import and export promotion activities for the Office of Fossil Energy; assesses fossil energy markets; evaluates international research development activities.

International Trade Administration *(Commerce Dept.),* ***Energy,*** *14th St. and Constitution Ave. N.W., #4056 20230; (202) 482-1466. Fax, (202) 482-0170. Helen Burroughs, Director. Web, www.ita.doc.gov/energy.*

Conducts research on the effect of federal energy policy on the business community; monitors overseas trade and investment opportunities; promotes improved market competitiveness and participation in international trade by the basic energy fuels industries. Provides export counseling; develops strategies to remove foreign trade barriers; conducts conferences and workshops.

Nonproliferation *(Energy Dept.),* ***International Nuclear Safety,*** *1000 Independence Ave. S.W., #4F094 20585; (202) 586-7313. Fax, (202) 586-8272. Dan Geissing, Associate Director.*

Seeks to improve the safety of nuclear activities internationally and coordinates other departmental offices and government agencies in the implementation of U.S. nonproliferation policy. Promotes nuclear safety in the former Soviet Union and Eastern Europe and assists in the shutdown of plutonium production reactors. Works with other agencies to open new markets for U.S. nuclear technology.

Nuclear Regulatory Commission, *Nonproliferation, Exports, and Multilateral Relations, 11555 Rockville Pike, Rockville, MD 20852; (301) 415-2344. Fax, (301) 415-2395. Janice Dunn Lee, Director.*

Coordinates application review process for exports and imports of nuclear materials, facilities, and components. Makes recommendations on licensing upon completion of review process. Conducts related policy reviews.

Office of Science *(Energy Dept.), 1000 Independence Ave. S.W., #7B058 20585; (202) 586-5430. Fax, (202) 586-4120. James Decker, Director.*

Coordinates energy research, science, and technology programs among producing and consuming nations; analyzes existing international research and development activities; pursues international collaboration in research and in the design, development, construction, and operation of new facilities and major scientific experiments; participates in negotiations for international cooperation activities.

State Dept., *International Energy and Commodities Policy, 2201 C St. N.W., #3529 20520; (202) 647-3036. Fax, (202) 647-4037. Stephen J. Gallogly, Director; Stephen Muller, Chief. Web, www.state.gov.*

Coordinates U.S. international energy policy related to commodities, including energy supply, and U.S. participation in the International Energy Agency; monitors cooperative multilateral and bilateral agreements related to energy; coordinates energy-related aspects of U.S. relations with other countries.

State Dept., *Nuclear Energy Affairs, 2201 C St. N.W., #7828 20520; (202) 647-3310. Fax, (202) 647-0775. Richard J. K. Stratford, Director. Web, www.state.gov.*

Coordinates and supervises international nuclear energy policy for the State Dept. Advises the secretary on policy matters relating to nonproliferation and export controls, nuclear technology and safeguards, and nuclear safety. Promotes adherence to the Nuclear Nonproliferation Treaty and other international agreements. Chairs the Subgroup on Nuclear Export Coordination, the interagency group that reviews nuclear export license applications. Enforces the Atomic Energy Act.

Treasury Dept., *International Affairs: Middle East and South Asian Nations, 1500 Pennsylvania Ave. N.W., #5041 20220; (202) 622-2140. Fax, (202) 622-0037. Maureen Grewe, Director. Web, www.ustreas.gov.*

Represents the department in the International Energy Agency, World Bank, International Monetary Fund, and other international institutions that address energy matters. Analyzes oil market and provides economic analyses of Arabian peninsular and South Asian countries.

U.S. International Trade Commission, *Energy, Petroleum, Benzenoid, Chemicals, Rubber, and Plastics, 500 E St. S.W. 20436; (202) 205-3368. Fax, (202) 205-2150. Edmund Cappuccilli, Chief.*

Advisory fact-finding agency on tariffs, commercial policy, and foreign trade matters. Analyzes data on oil, petrochemical, coal, coke, and natural gas products traded internationally; investigates effects of tariffs on certain chemical and energy imports.

U.S. Trade Representative *(Executive Office of the President), 600 17th St. N.W., #209 20508; (202) 395-6890. Fax, (202) 395-3911. Charlene Barshefsky, U.S. Trade Representative. Information, (202) 395-8787. Press, (202) 395-3230. Web, www.ustr.gov.*

Serves as principal adviser to the president and primary trade negotiator on international trade policy. Develops and coordinates energy trade matters among government agencies.

CONGRESS

House International Relations Committee, *2170 RHOB 20515; (202) 225-5021. Fax, (202) 225-2035. Rep. Benjamin A. Gilman, R-N.Y., Chair; Richard J. Garon Jr., Chief of Staff. General e-mail, HIRC@mail.house.gov. Web, www.house.gov/international_relations.*

Jurisdiction over most legislation on U.S. participation in international energy programs and legislation related to the economic aspects of trading nuclear technology and materials with foreign countries.

House Ways and Means Committee, *1102 LHOB 20515; (202) 225-3625. Fax, (202) 225-2610. Rep. Bill Archer, R-Texas, Chair; A. L. Singleton, Chief of Staff. Web, www.house.gov/ways_means.*

Jurisdiction over legislation on taxes, tariffs, and trade measures relating to energy, such as oil import fees.

Senate Energy and Natural Resources Committee, *SD-364 20510; (202) 224-4971. Fax, (202) 224-6163. Sen. Frank H. Murkowski, R-Alaska, Chair; Andrew Lundquist, Staff Director. General e-mail, committee@ energy.senate.gov. Web, energy.senate.gov.*

Jurisdiction over legislation relating to U.S. participation in international energy programs (jurisdiction shared with Senate Foreign Relations Committee).

Senate Finance Committee, *SD-219 20510; (202) 224-4515. Fax, (202) 224-5920. Sen. William V. Roth Jr., R-Del., Chair; Frank Polk, Staff Director. Web, finance. senate.gov.*

Holds hearings on legislation concerning taxes, tariffs, and trade measures relating to energy, such as oil import fees.

Senate Foreign Relations Committee, *SD-450 20510; (202) 224-4651. Fax, (202) 224-0836. Sen. Jesse Helms, R-N.C., Chair; Steve Biegun, Staff Director. Web, foreign. senate.gov.*

Jurisdiction over legislation related to the economic aspects of trading nuclear technology and materials. Jurisdiction over legislation relating to U.S. participation in international energy programs (jurisdiction shared with Senate Energy and Natural Resources Committee).

INTERNATIONAL ORGANIZATIONS

European Commission, *Press and Public Affairs, Washington Office, 2300 M St. N.W. 20037; (202) 862-9500. Fax, (202) 429-1766. Willy Helin, Director; Günter Burghardt, Ambassador. Press, (202) 862-9540. Web, www. europa.eu.int.*

Information and public affairs office in the United States for the European Union, which includes the European Economic Community, the European Coal and Steel Community, and the European Atomic Energy Community. Provides energy information, statistics, and documents on member countries. Library open to the public by appointment. (Headquarters in Brussels.)

International Energy Agency *(Organization for Economic Cooperation and Development), Washington Office, 2001 L St. N.W., #650 20036-4922; (202) 785-6323. Fax, (202) 785-0350. Matthew Brosius, Co-Director. General e-mail, washington.contact@oecd.org. Web, www. oecdwash.org.*

Promotes cooperation in energy research among developed nations; assists developing countries in negotiations with energy-producing nations; prepares plans for international emergency energy allocation. Publishes statistics and analyses on most aspects of energy. Washington Center maintains reference library open to the public; offers for sale publications of the International Energy Agency. (Headquarters in Paris.)

United Nations Information Centre, *1775 K St. N.W., #400 20006; (202) 331-8670. Fax, (202) 331-9191. Cathryn O'Neill, Director. Web, www.un.org.*

Center for reference publications of the United Nations; publications include *World Energy Statistics, Energy Balances and Electricity Profiles,* and other statistical material on energy. Library open to the public.

NONPROFIT

Atlantic Council of the United States, *Energy and Environment Program, 910 17th St. N.W., 10th Floor 20006; (202) 778-4942. Fax, (202) 463-7241. Eliane Lomax, Associate Director. Information, (202) 463-7226. General e-mail, info@acus.org. Web, www.acus.org.*

Studies and makes policy recommendations on international energy relationships for all energy sources, including oil, natural gas, coal, synthetic and renewable fuels, and nuclear power.

U.S. Energy Assn., *1300 Pennsylvania Ave. N.W., #550, Mailbox 142 20004-3022; (202) 312-1230. Fax, (202) 682-1682. Barry K. Worthington, Executive Director.*

Membership: energy-related organizations, including professional, trade, and government groups. Participates in the World Energy Council (headquartered in London). Sponsors seminars and conferences on energy resources, policy management, technology, utilization, and conservation.

World Energy Efficiency Assn., *910 17th St. N.W., #1010 20006; (202) 778-4961. Fax, (202) 463-0017. Donald L. Guertin, Executive Director. General e-mail, info@weea.org. Web, www.weea.org.*

Assists developing countries in accessing information on energy efficiency programs, technologies, and measures; fosters international cooperation in energy efficiency efforts.

Statistics

See also specific energy resources (this chapter)

AGENCIES

Bureau of Labor Statistics *(Labor Dept.),* **Industrial Prices and Price Indexes,** *2 Massachusetts Ave. N.E., #3840 20212-0001; (202) 691-7705. Fax, (202) 691-7704. Joseph Kelley, Energy Analyst.*

Compiles statistics on energy for the Producer Price Index; analyzes movement of prices for natural gas, petroleum, coal, and electric power in the primary commercial and industrial markets.

Energy Information Administration *(Energy Dept.),* **National Energy Information Center,** *1000 Independence Ave. S.W., #1E238, EI-30 20585; (202) 586-8800. Fax, (202) 586-0727. Sandra Wilkins, Chief. Web, www.eia.doe.gov.*

Catalogs and distributes energy data; acts as a clearinghouse for statistical information on energy; makes referrals for technical information. Reading room of EIA publications open to the public.

NONPROFIT

American Gas Assn., *Statistics, 400 N. Capitol St. N.W., 4th Floor 20001; (202) 824-7000. Fax, (202) 824-7115. Paul Pierson, Manager. Web, www.aga.org.*

Issues statistics on the gas utility industry, including supply and reserves.

American Petroleum Institute, *Policy Analysis and Statistics, 1220 L St. N.W. 20005; (202) 682-8532. Fax, (202) 962-4730. John Fellmy, Director. Information, (202) 682-8520. Library, (202) 682-8042. Web, www.api.org.*

Provides basic statistical information on petroleum industry operations, market conditions, and environmental, health, and safety performance. Includes data on supply and demand of crude oil and petroleum products, exports and imports, refinery operations, drilling activities and costs, environmental expenditures, injuries, illnesses and fatalities, oil spills, and emissions.

Edison Electric Institute, *Statistics, 701 Pennsylvania Ave. N.W. 20004; (202) 508-5574. Fax, (202) 508-5380. Linda Spencer, Manager.*

Provides statistics on electric utility operations, including the *Statistical Yearbook of the Electric Utility Industry,* which contains data on the capacity, generation, sales, customers, revenue, and finances of the electric utility industry.

National Mining Assn., *Policy Analysis, 1130 17th St. N.W. 20036-4677; (202) 463-2654. Fax, (202) 833-9636. Constance D. Holmes, Senior Vice President. Web, www.nma.org.*

Collects, analyzes, and distributes statistics on the mining industry, including statistics on the production, transportation, and consumption of coal.

ELECTRICITY

AGENCIES

Energy Dept., *Bonneville Power Administration, Washington Office, 1000 Independence Ave. S.W., #8G061 20585; (202) 586-5640. Fax, (202) 586-6762. Jeffrey K. Stier, Vice President. Web, www.bpa.gov.*

Coordinates marketing of electric power and energy for the Bonneville Power Administration; serves as liaison between the Bonneville Power Administration and Congress. (Headquarters in Portland, Ore.)

Energy Dept., *Power Marketing Liaison Office,* 1000 Independence Ave. S.W., #8G027 20585; (202) 586-5581. Fax, (202) 586-6261. Timothy Meeks, Assistant Administrator. Web, www.doe.gov.

Serves as a liaison among the Southeastern, Southwestern, and Western area power administrations; other federal agencies; and Congress. Coordinates marketing of electric power from federally owned hydropower projects.

Energy Information Administration *(Energy Dept.),* *Coal, Nuclear, Electric, and Alternate Fuels,* 950 L'Enfant Plaza S.W. 20024 (mailing address: 1000 Independence Ave. S.W. 20585); (202) 426-1200. Fax, (202) 426-1280. John Geidl, Director.

Prepares analyses and forecasts on electric power supplies, including the effects of government policies and regulatory actions on capacity, consumption, finances, and rates. Publishes statistics on electric power industry.

Tennessee Valley Authority, *Government Affairs, Washington Office,* 1 Massachusetts Ave. N.W., #300 20444; (202) 898-2999. Fax, (202) 898-2998. David Withrow, Vice President. Web, www.tva.gov.

Coordinates resource conservation, development, and land-use programs in the Tennessee River Valley. Produces and supplies wholesale power to municipal and cooperative electric systems, federal installations, and some industries.

CONGRESS

House Commerce Committee, *Subcommittee on Energy and Power,* 2125 RHOB 20515; (202) 225-2927. Fax, (202) 225-1919. Rep. Joe L. Barton, R-Texas, Chair; James E. Derderian, Staff Director. General e-mail, commerce@mail.house.gov. Web, www.house.gov/commerce.

Jurisdiction over legislation on electric utilities regulation, energy plant siting (including nuclear facilities), and proposals to label appliances to indicate energy consumption.

House Resources Committee, *Subcommittee on Water and Power,* 1522 LHOB 20515; (202) 225-8331. Fax, (202) 226-6953. Rep. John T. Doolittle, R-Calif., Chair; Robert Faber, Staff Director. General e-mail, water.power@mail.house.gov. Web, www.house.gov/resources/water.

Jurisdiction over legislation on the federal power administrations.

House Science Committee, *Subcommittee on Energy and Environment,* 389 FHOB 20515; (202) 225-9662. Fax, (202) 226-6983. Rep. Ken Calvert, R-Calif., Chair; Harlan Watson, Staff Director. Web, www.house.gov/science.

Jurisdiction over legislation on electric energy research and development.

House Transportation and Infrastructure Committee, *Subcommittee on Water Resources and Environment,* B376 RHOB 20515; (202) 225-4360. Fax, (202) 226-5435. Rep. Sherwood Boehlert, R-N.Y., Chair; Ben Grumbles, Counsel. General e-mail, transcomm@mail.house.gov. Web, www.house.gov/transportation.

Jurisdiction over the Tennessee Valley Authority.

Senate Energy and Natural Resources Committee, *Subcommittee on Energy Research, Development, Production, and Regulation,* SD-308 20510; (202) 224-6567. Fax, (202) 228-0302. Sen. Don Nickles, R-Okla., Chair; Howard Useem, Professional Staff Member. General e-mail, erdpr@energy.senate.gov. Web, energy.senate.gov.

Jurisdiction over legislation on electric energy research and development.

Senate Energy and Natural Resources Committee, *Subcommittee on Water and Power,* SD-308 20510; (202) 224-4971. Sen. Gordon H. Smith, R-Ore., Chair; Colleen Deegan, Majority Counsel. General e-mail, water&power@energy.senate.gov. Web, energy.senate.gov.

Jurisdiction over the federal power marketing administrations, hydroelectric power, and the impact of energy development on water resources.

Senate Environment and Public Works Committee, *Subcommittee on Clean Air, Wetlands, Private Property, and Nuclear Safety,* SD-410 20510; (202) 224-6176. Fax, (202) 224-5167. Sen. James M. Inhofe, R-Okla., Chair; Andy Wheeler, Staff Contact. Web, epw.senate.gov.

Jurisdiction over Tennessee Valley Authority legislation.

NONPROFIT

Center for Energy and Economic Development, 1800 Diagonal Rd., #370, Alexandria, VA 22314; (703) 684-6292. Fax, (703) 684-6297. Stephen L. Miller, President. Web, www.ceednet.org.

Membership: coal, railroad, and electric utility companies. Educates the public and policymakers about economic, technological, and scientific research on energy resources employed in generating electricity.

Citizens for State Power, *122 S. Patrick St., Alexandria, VA 22314; (703) 739-5920. Fax, (703) 739-5924. Craig Shirley, Consulting Director. General e-mail, csp@craigshirley.com.*

Coalition of conservative policy organizations that seeks to increase competition in the electric utility industry through federal and state deregulation.

Electric Power Supply Assn., *1401 H St. N.W., #760 20005; (202) 789-7200. Fax, (202) 789-7201. Lynne H. Church, Executive Director. Web, www.epsa.org.*

Membership: power generators active in U.S. and global markets, power marketers, and suppliers of goods and services to the industry. Promotes competition in the delivery of electricity to consumers.

Electricity Consumers Resource Council, *1333 H St. N.W., West Tower, 8th Floor 20005; (202) 682-1390. Fax, (202) 289-6370. John A. Anderson, Executive Director. General e-mail, elcon@elcon.org. Web, www.elcon.org.*

Membership: large industrial users of electricity. Promotes development of coordinated federal, state, and local policies concerning electrical supply for industrial users; studies rate structures and their impact on consumers.

Electrification Council, *701 Pennsylvania Ave. N.W. 20004-2696; (202) 508-5900. Fax, (202) 508-5335. Susan Mitchell, Executive Director. General e-mail, tec@eei.org. Web, www.eei.org/tec.*

Membership: electric utilities and independent manufacturers. Facilitates partnerships among members; provides products and services that increase their marketing and sales capabilities.

National Electrical Contractors Assn., *3 Bethesda Metro Center, #1100, Bethesda, MD 20814; (301) 657-3110. Fax, (301) 215-4500. John Grau, Executive Vice President. Web, www.necanet.org.*

Membership: electrical contractors who build and service electrical wiring, equipment, and appliances. Represents members in collective bargaining with union workers; sponsors research and educational programs.

National Electrical Manufacturers Assn., *1300 N. 17th St., #1847, Rosslyn, VA 22209; (703) 841-3200. Fax, (703) 841-3300. Malcolm O'Hagan, President. Web, www.nema.org.*

Membership: manufacturers of electrical products. Develops and promotes use of electrical standards; compiles and analyzes industry statistics. Interests include efficient energy management, product safety and liability, occupational safety, and the environment. Monitors international trade activities, legislation, and regulations.

National Hydropower Assn., *1 Massachusetts Ave. N.W., #850 20001; (202) 682-1700. Fax, (202) 682-9478. Linda Church Ciocci, Executive Director. Fax-on-demand, (800) 964-1093. General e-mail, info@hydro.org. Web, www.hydro.org.*

Membership: investor-owned utilities and municipal and independent companies that generate hydroelectric power; consulting, engineering, and law firms; and equipment suppliers and manufacturers. Focus includes regulatory relief, international marketing, and coalition building. Monitors legislation and regulations.

See also Institute of Electrical and Electronics Engineers (p. 607)

Public Utilities

AGENCIES

Federal Energy Regulatory Commission *(Energy Dept.), Hydropower Licensing, 888 1st St. N.E., #6A03 20426; (202) 219-2700. Fax, (202) 219-0205. Carol L. Sampson, Director.*

Issues licenses, permits, and exemptions for hydroelectric power projects. Ensures safety of licensed dams and safeguards the environment.

Federal Energy Regulatory Commission *(Energy Dept.), Markets, Tariffs, and Rates, 888 1st St. N.E. 20426; (202) 208-0700. Fax, (202) 208-0193. Dan Larcamp, Director.*

Establishes rates and power charges for electric energy transmission, sale, and interconnections. Regulates wholesale electric rates in interstate commerce.

Rural Utilities Service *(Agriculture Dept.), 1400 Independence Ave. S.W. 20250-1500; (202) 720-9540. Fax, (202) 720-1725. Christopher A. McLean, Administrator (Acting). Information, (202) 720-1255. Web, www.usda.gov/rus.*

Makes loans and loan guarantees to rural electric utilities providing service in rural areas.

NONPROFIT

American Public Power Assn., *2301 M St. N.W. 20037; (202) 467-2900. Fax, (202) 467-2910. Alan H. Richardson, Executive Director. Library, (202) 467-2957. Web, www.appanet.org.*

Membership: local, publicly owned electric utilities nationwide. Represents industry interests before Congress, federal agencies, and the courts; provides educational programs; collects and disseminates information; funds energy research and development projects. Library open to the public by appointment.

Edison Electric Institute, *701 Pennsylvania Ave. N.W. 20004; (202) 508-5000. Fax, (202) 508-5759. Thomas R. Kuhn, President. Web, www.eei.org.*

Membership: investor-owned electric power companies and electric utility holding companies. Interests include electric utility operation and concerns, including conservation and energy management, energy analysis, resources and environment, cogeneration and renewable energy resources, nuclear power, and research. Provides information and statistics relating to electric energy; aids member companies in generating and selling electric energy; and conducts information forums. Library open to the public by appointment.

National Assn. of Regulatory Utility Commissioners, *1101 Vermont Ave. N.W., #200 20005; (202) 898-2200. Fax, (202) 898-2213. Charles Gray, Executive Director. Press, (202) 898-2205. Web, www.naruc.org.*

Membership: members of federal, state, municipal, and Canadian regulatory commissions that have jurisdiction over utilities. Interests include electric utilities.

National Assn. of State Utility Consumer Advocates, *8300 Colesville Rd., #101, Silver Spring, MD 20910; (301) 589-6313. Fax, (301) 589-6380. Charles Acquard, Executive Director. General e-mail, nasuca@nasuca.org. Web, www.nasuca.org.*

Membership: public advocate offices authorized by states to represent ratepayer interests before state and federal utility regulatory commissions. Monitors legislation and regulatory agencies with jurisdiction over electric utilities, telecommunications, natural gas, and water; conducts conferences and workshops.

National Rural Electric Cooperative Assn., *4301 Wilson Blvd., Arlington, VA 22203-1860; (703) 907-5500. Fax, (703) 907-5516. Glenn English, Chief Executive Officer. Web, www.nreca.org.*

Membership: rural electric cooperative systems and public power and utility districts. Provides members with legislative, legal, and regulatory services. Supports energy and environmental research and offers technical advice and assistance to developing countries.

Research and Development

AGENCIES

Energy Dept., *Office of Science: Fusion Energy Sciences, 19901 Germantown Rd., Germantown, MD 20874-1290; (301) 903-4941. Fax, (301) 903-8584. N. Anne Davies, Associate Director. Web, wwwofe.er.doe.gov.*

Conducts research and development on fusion energy for electric power generation.

National Institute of Standards and Technology (Commerce Dept.), *Electricity Division, 100 Bureau Dr., MS-8110, Gaithersburg, MD 20899-8110; (301) 975-2400. Fax, (301) 926-3972. Bruce Field, Chief (Acting). Web, www.eeel.nist.gov.*

Conducts research to characterize and define performance parameters of electrical/electronic systems, components, and materials; applies research to advance measurement instrumentation and the efficiency of electric power transmission and distribution; develops and maintains national electrical reference standards, primarily for power, energy, and related measurements, to assist in the development of new products and promote international competitiveness.

National Institute of Standards and Technology (Commerce Dept.), *Electronics and Electrical Engineering Laboratory, 100 Bureau Dr., Bldg. 220, #B358, MS 8100, Gaithersburg, MD 20899; (301) 975-2220. Fax, (301) 975-4091. William E. Anderson, Director (Acting). General e-mail, eeel@nist.gov. Web, www.eeel.nist.gov.*

Provides focus for research, development, and applications in the fields of electrical, electronic, quantum electric, and electromagnetic materials engineering. Interests include fundamental physical constants, practical data, measurement methods, theory, standards, technology, technical services, and international trade.

NONPROFIT

Electric Power Research Institute, *Washington Office, 2000 L St. N.W., #805 20036; (202) 872-9222. Fax, (202) 293-2697. Barbara Bauman, Director, Government Relations. Web, www.epri.com.*

Membership: investor- and municipal-owned electric utilities and rural cooperatives. Conducts research and development in power generation and delivery technologies, including fossil fuel, nuclear, and renewable energy sources used by electric utilities. Studies energy management and utilization, including conservation and environmental issues. (Headquarters in Palo Alto, Calif.)

 FOSSIL FUELS

See also International Trade and Cooperation (this chapter)

AGENCIES

Fossil Energy (Energy Dept.), *1000 Independence Ave. S.W., #4G084 20585; (202) 586-6660. Fax, (202) 586-7847. Robert W. Gee, Assistant Secretary. Web, www.fe.doe. gov.*

Responsible for policy and management of high-risk, long-term research and development in recovering, converting, and using fossil energy, including coal, petroleum, oil shale, and unconventional sources of natural gas. Handles the petroleum reserve and the naval petroleum and oil shale reserve programs; oversees the Clean Coal Program to design and construct environmentally clean coal-burning facilities.

U.S. Geological Survey *(Interior Dept.), Energy Resources, 12201 Sunrise Valley Dr., Reston, VA 20192 (mailing address: 915A National Center, Reston, VA 20192); (703) 648-6470. Fax, (703) 648-5464. Suzanne D. Weedman, Program Coordinator. Web, energy.usgs.gov.*

Conducts research on fossil energy resources of the United States and the world, including assessments of the quality, quantity, and geographic locations of natural gas, oil, and coal resources. Estimates energy resource availability and recoverability; anticipates and mitigates deleterious environmental impacts of energy resource extraction and use.

CONGRESS

House Commerce Committee, *Subcommittee on Energy and Power, 2125 RHOB 20515; (202) 225-2927. Fax, (202) 225-1919. Rep. Joe L. Barton, R-Texas, Chair; James E. Derderian, Staff Director. General e-mail, commerce@mail.house.gov. Web, www.house.gov/commerce.*

Jurisdiction over legislation dealing with coal, oil, and natural gas, including proposed emergency presidential energy authority (such as rationing), proposals to create civilian petroleum reserves, petroleum and natural gas pricing and pipelines, natural gas imports, regulation of public utilities, energy plant siting, and low head hydro projects.

House Resources Committee, *Subcommittee on Energy and Mineral Resources, 1626 LHOB 20515; (202) 225-9297. Fax, (202) 225-5255. Rep. Barbara Cubin, R-Wyo., Chair; William Condit, Staff Director. General e-mail, resources.committee@mail.house.gov. Web, www.house.gov/resources/energy.*

Jurisdiction over legislation on mineral land laws; mining policy; coal, oil and gas, and mineral leasing on publicly owned land; and conservation and development of energy and natural resources in the ocean and outer continental shelf. Jurisdiction over oil and coal slurry pipelines (shared with House Transportation and Infrastructure Committee).

House Science Committee, *Subcommittee on Energy and Environment, 389 FHOB 20515; (202) 225-9662. Fax, (202) 226-6983. Rep. Ken Calvert, R-Calif., Chair;*

Harlan Watson, Staff Director. Web, www.house.gov/science.

Jurisdiction over legislation on research and development of fossil fuel energy (including coal, petroleum, natural gas, oil shale, tar sand, and synthetic fuels such as liquefied and gasified coal) and over Energy Dept. basic research programs.

House Transportation and Infrastructure Committee, *Subcommittee on Economic Development, Public Buildings, Hazardous Materials, Pipeline Transportation, 586 FHOB 20515; (202) 225-3014. Fax, (202) 226-1898. Rep. Bob Franks, R-N.J., Chair; Richard C. Barnett, Staff Director. General e-mail, transcomm@mail.house.gov. Web, www.house.gov/transportation.*

Jurisdiction over legislation on oil and coal slurry pipelines (jurisdiction shared with House Resources Committee).

Senate Commerce, Science, and Transportation Committee, *Subcommittee on Oceans and Fisheries, SH-428 20510; (202) 224-8172. Fax, (202) 228-0326. Sen. Olympia J. Snowe, R-Maine, Chair; Sloan Rapoport, Counsel. Web, commerce.senate.gov.*

Jurisdiction over legislation on production and development of deep seabed mining and deepwater ports (jurisdiction shared with Senate Energy and Natural Resources Committee).

Senate Energy and Natural Resources Committee, *SD-364 20510; (202) 224-4971. Fax, (202) 224-6163. Sen. Frank H. Murkowski, R-Alaska, Chair; Andrew Lundquist, Staff Director. General e-mail, committee@energy.senate.gov. Web, energy.senate.gov.*

Jurisdiction over legislation on fossil fuel research and development, including Energy Dept. programs; mining policy, including mineral leasing; and interstate aspects of production and distribution of coal, natural gas, and petroleum. Jurisdiction over deep seabed mining and deepwater ports (jurisdiction shared with Senate Commerce, Science, and Transportation Committee).

Coal

AGENCIES

Bureau of Land Management *(Interior Dept.), Solid Minerals Group, 1620 L St. N.W., #501 20240 (mailing address: 1849 C St. N.W., #LS501 20240); (202) 452-0350. Fax, (202) 452-0399. Brenda Aird, Group Manager.*

Evaluates and classifies coal resources on federal lands; develops and administers leasing programs. Supervises coal mining operations on federal lands; oversees pre- and postlease operations, including production phases of coal development. Oversees implementation of the Mining Law of 1872 and the Mineral Materials Act of 1955.

Energy Information Administration *(Energy Dept.), Coal, Nuclear, Electric, and Alternate Fuels,* 950 L'Enfant Plaza S.W. 20024 (mailing address: 1000 Independence Ave. S.W. 20585); (202) 426-1200. Fax, (202) 426-1280. John Geidl, Director.

Collects data, compiles statistics, and prepares analyses and forecasts on domestic coal supply, including availability, production, costs, processing, transportation, and distribution. Publishes data on the export and import of coal; makes forecasts and provides analyses on coal imports and exports.

Federal Mine Safety and Health Review Commission, 1730 K St. N.W., #600 20006; (202) 653-5660. Fax, (202) 653-5030. Mary Lu Jordan, Chair; Richard L. Baker, Executive Director, (202) 653-5625. Information, (202) 653-5633. Library, (202) 653-5002.

Independent agency established by the Federal Mine Safety and Health Act of 1977. Holds fact-finding hearings and issues orders affirming, modifying, or vacating the labor secretary's enforcement actions regarding mine safety and health. Library open to the public.

Fossil Energy *(Energy Dept.), Coal Fuels and Industrial Systems,* 19901 Germantown Rd., Germantown, MD 20874; (301) 903-9451. Fax, (301) 903-2238. C. Lowell Miller, Director.

Fosters the development and implementation of clean coal technologies in the private sector. Monitors economic and commercial efficiency program and disseminates results. Cofunded by private industry.

Interior Dept., *Surface Mining Reclamation and Enforcement,* 1951 Constitution Ave. N.W. 20240; (202) 208-4006. Fax, (202) 219-3106. Kathy Karpen, Director. Information, (202) 208-2719. Web, www.osmre.gov/osm. htm.

Administers the Surface Mining Control and Reclamation Act of 1977. Establishes and enforces national standards for the regulation and reclamation of surface coal mining and the surface effects of underground coal mining; oversees state implementation of these standards.

Mine Safety and Health Administration *(Labor Dept.),* 4015 Wilson Blvd., #622, Arlington, VA 22203; (703) 235-1385. Fax, (703) 235-4369. J. Davitt McAteer, Assistant Secretary. Information, (703) 235-1452. Web, www.msha.gov.

Administers and enforces the health and safety provisions of the Federal Mine Safety and Health Act of 1977.

Monitors underground mining and processing operations of minerals, including minerals used in construction materials; produces educational materials in engineering; and assists with rescue operations following mining accidents.

CONGRESS

House Education and the Workforce Committee, *Subcommittee on Workforce Protections,* 2181 RHOB 20515; (202) 225-4527. Fax, (202) 225-9571. Rep. Cass Ballenger, R-N.C., Chair; Kevin D. Talley, Staff Director. Web, www.house.gov/ed_workforce.

Jurisdiction over legislation on coal mining health and safety.

Senate Health, Education, Labor, and Pensions Committee, *Subcommittee on Public Health,* SD-424 20510; (202) 224-7139. Fax, (202) 228-0928. Sen. Bill Frist, R-Tenn., Chair; Anne Phelps, Staff Director. Web, labor.senate.gov.

Jurisdiction over legislation on coal mining health and safety.

NONPROFIT

American Coal Ash Assn., 6940 S. King Hwy., #207, Alexandria, VA 22310-3344; (703) 317-2400. Fax, (703) 317-2409. Samuel Tyson, Executive Director. Web, www. acaa-usa.org.

Membership: electric utilities that use coal to produce electricity, marketers or brokers of coal ash, coal companies, and suppliers of ash-related equipment. Compiles statistics and provides information on coal ash production and utilization. Library publications available online.

American Coke and Coal Chemicals Institute, 1255 23rd St. N.W. 20037; (202) 452-1140. Fax, (202) 833-3636. David Saunders, President. Web, www.accci.org.

Membership: producers of oven coke, metallurgical coal, and chemicals; coke sales agents; tar distillers; and builders of coke ovens and coke oven byproduct plants. Maintains committees on chemicals, coke, manufacturing and environment, safety and health, and traffic.

Assn. of Bituminous Contractors, 1747 Pennsylvania Ave. N.W., #1050 20006; (202) 785-4440. Fax, (202) 331-8049. William H. Howe, General Counsel.

Membership: independent and general contractors that build coal mines. Represents members before the Federal Mine Safety and Health Review Commission and in collective bargaining with the United Mine Workers of America.

Bituminous Coal Operators Assn., *1500 K St. N.W., #875 20005; (202) 783-3195. Fax, (202) 783-4862. David M. Young, President.*

Membership: firms that mine bituminous coal. Represents members in collective bargaining with the United Mine Workers of America.

Coal Exporters Assn. of the United States Inc., *1130 17th St. N.W. 20036; (202) 463-2639. Fax, (202) 833-9636. Moya Phelleps, Executive Director. Web, www.nma. org/Coal%20Exporters%20Association.html.*

Membership: exporters of coal. Provides information on coal exports. Monitors legislation and regulations. (Affiliate of the National Mining Assn.)

National Coal Council, *2000 N. 15th St., #500, Arlington, VA 22201; (703) 527-1191. Fax, (703) 527-1195. Robert A. Beck, Executive Director. Web, www. nationalcoalcouncil.org.*

Membership: individuals appointed by the secretary of energy. Represents coal producers, transporters, women and minorities in mining, and manufacturers of coal-producing equipment. Makes recommendations to the secretary on issues involving coal. Library open to the public.

National Mining Assn., *1130 17th St. N.W. 20036-4677; (202) 463-2625. Fax, (202) 463-6152. Richard L. Lawson, President. Press, (202) 463-2651. General e-mail, nma@ prime.planetcom.com. Web, www.nma.org.*

Membership: coal producers, coal sales and transportation companies, equipment manufacturers, consulting firms, coal resource developers and exporters, coal-burning electric utility companies, and other energy companies. Collects, analyzes, and distributes industry statistics; conducts special studies of competitive fuels, coal markets, production and consumption forecasts, and industry planning. Interests include exports, coal leasing programs, coal transportation, environmental issues, health and safety, national energy policy, slurry pipelines, and research and development, including synthetic fuels.

United Mine Workers of America, *8315 Lee Hwy., Fairfax, VA 22031; (703) 208-7200. Fax, (703) 842-7227. Cecil E. Roberts, President. Web, www.umwa.org.*

Membership: coal miners and other mining workers. Represents members in collective bargaining with industry. Conducts educational, housing, and health and safety training programs; monitors federal coal mining safety programs.

Oil and Natural Gas

AGENCIES

Energy Information Administration *(Energy Dept.), Collection and Dissemination, 1000 Independence Ave.*

S.W., #2E068 20585; (202) 586-6401. Fax, (202) 586-4419. Kendrick E. Brown Jr., Director.

Collects natural gas and petroleum publications; disseminates publications in print and via the Web; collects and disseminates EIA forms.

Energy Information Administration *(Energy Dept.), Natural Gas, 1000 Independence Ave. S.W., #BE054 20585; (202) 586-6401. Fax, (202) 586-4420. Joan Heinkel, Director. Web, www.eia.doe.gov.*

Collects and publishes monthly and annual estimates of domestic crude oil, natural gas, and natural gas liquids. Performs analyses of the natural gas industry.

Energy Information Administration *(Energy Dept.), Oil and Gas, 1000 Independence Ave. S.W., #2G024 20585; (202) 586-6401. Fax, (202) 586-9739. Ken Vagts, Director.*

Collects, interprets, and publishes data on domestic production, use, and distribution of oil and natural gas; analyzes and projects oil and gas reserves, resources, production, capacity, and supply; surveys and monitors alternative fuel needs during emergencies; publishes statistics.

Energy Information Administration *(Energy Dept.), Petroleum, 1000 Independence Ave. S.W., #2G051 20585; (202) 586-5986. Fax, (202) 586-3873. John Cook, Director. Web, www.eia.doe.gov.*

Collects, compiles, interprets, and publishes data on domestic production, distribution, and prices of crude oil and refined petroleum products; analyzes and projects availability of petroleum supplies. Publishes statistics, including import and export data.

Fossil Energy *(Energy Dept.), Natural Gas and Petroleum Technology, 1000 Independence Ave. S.W., #3E028 20585; (202) 586-5600. Fax, (202) 586-6221. Guido DeHoratiis, Director (Acting).*

Responsible for research and development programs in oil and gas exploration, production, processing, and storage; studies ways to improve efficiency of oil recovery in depleted reservoirs; coordinates and evaluates research and development among government, universities, and industrial research organizations.

Fossil Energy *(Energy Dept.), Naval Petroleum and Oil Shale Reserves, 1000 Independence Ave. S.W., #3H076 20585; (202) 586-4685. Fax, (202) 586-4446. Anton R. Dammer, Director.*

Develops, conserves, operates, and maintains oil shale reserves for producing oil, natural gas, and other petroleum products.

Internal Revenue Service *(Treasury Dept.), Passthrough and Special Industries, Branch 8, 1111*

Constitution Ave. N.W., #5314 20224; (202) 622-3130. Fax, (202) 622-4524. Richard A. Kocak, Chief.

Administers excise tax programs, including taxes on diesel, gasoline, and special fuels. Advises district offices, internal IRS offices, and general inquirers on tax policy, rules, and regulations.

Minerals Management Service *(Interior Dept.), Engineering and Operations,* 381 Elden St., Herndon, VA 20170-4817; (703) 787-1598. Fax, (703) 787-1093. E. P. Danenberger, Chief.

Administers the Outer Continental Shelf Land Act. Supervises oil and gas operations on outer continental shelf lands; oversees lease operations including exploration, drilling, and production phases of offshore oil and gas development; administers lease provisions for offshore oil and gas.

National Oceanic and Atmospheric Administration (NOAA), *(Commerce Dept.), Policy and Strategic Planning,* 14th St. and Constitution Ave. N.W., #6117 20230; (202) 482-5181. Fax, (202) 501-3024. Susan Fruchter, Director.

Makes recommendations to NOAA concerning environmental and ecological problems. Assesses the accuracy and coordinates the implementation of environmental impact statements for all federal projects, including offshore oil and natural gas facilities.

NONPROFIT

American Gas Assn., 400 N. Capitol St. N.W. 20001; (202) 824-7000. Fax, (202) 824-7115. David Parker, President. Web, www.aga.org.

Membership: natural gas utilities and pipeline companies. Interests include all technical and operational aspects of the gas industry. Publishes comprehensive statistical record of gas industry; conducts national standard testing for gas appliances. Monitors legislation and regulations.

American Petroleum Institute, 1220 L St. N.W. 20005; (202) 682-8100. Fax, (202) 682-8110. Red Cavaney, President. Library, (202) 682-8042. Press, (202) 682-8120. Web, www.api.org.

Membership: producers, refiners, marketers, and transporters of oil, natural gas, and related products such as gasoline. Provides information on the industry, including data on exports and imports, taxation, transportation, weekly refinery operations (stock levels, output, and input), and drilling activity and costs; conducts research on petroleum and publishes statistical and drilling reports.

American Petroleum Institute, *Taxation,* 1220 L St. N.W., 12th Floor 20005; (202) 682-8465. Fax, (202) 682-8049. Andy Yood, Director.

Provides information on petroleum taxation.

American Public Gas Assn., 11094-D Lee Hwy., #102, Fairfax, VA 22030-5014; (703) 352-3890. Fax, (703) 352-1271. Robert S. Cave, Executive Director. General e-mail, apga@apga.org. Web, www.apga.org.

Membership: municipally owned gas distribution systems. Provides information on federal developments affecting natural gas. Promotes efficiency and works to protect the interests of public gas systems. Sponsors workshops and conferences.

Compressed Gas Assn., 1725 Jefferson Davis Hwy., #1004, Arlington, VA 22202-4102; (703) 412-0900. Fax, (703) 412-0128. Carl T. Johnson, President. Web, www.cganet.com.

Membership: all segments of the compressed gas industry, including producers and distributors of compressed and liquefied gases. Promotes and coordinates technical development and standardization of the industry. Monitors legislation and regulations.

Gas Appliance Manufacturers Assn., 1901 N. Moore St., #1100, Arlington, VA 22209; (703) 525-9565. Fax, (703) 525-0718. C. Reuben Autery, President. General e-mail, information@gamanet.org. Web, www.gamanet.org.

Membership: manufacturers of gas appliances and equipment for residential and commercial use and related industries. Advocates product improvement; provides market statistics. Monitors legislation and regulations.

Gas Research Institute, *Policy and Regulatory Affairs, Washington Office,* 1600 Wilson Blvd., #900, Arlington, VA 22209; (703) 526-7800. Fax, (703) 526-7805. David O. Webb, Senior Vice President.

Membership: all segments of the natural gas industry, including producers, pipelines, and distributors. Conducts research and develops new technology for gas customers and the industry. (Headquarters in Chicago.)

Independent Liquid Terminals Assn., 1133 15th St. N.W., #650 20005; (202) 659-2301. Fax, (202) 466-4166. John Prokop, President. Web, www.ilta.org.

Membership: commercial operators of for-hire bulk liquid terminals and tank storage facilities, including those for crude oil and petroleum. Promotes the safe and efficient handling of various types of bulk liquid commodities. Sponsors workshops and seminars; maintains speakers bureau; publishes directories. Monitors legislation and regulations.

Independent Petroleum Assn. of America, *1101 16th St. N.W., 2nd Floor 20036; (202) 857-4722. Fax, (202) 857-4799. Gil Thurm, President. Web, www.ipaa. org.*

Membership: independent oil and gas producers; land and royalty owners; and others with interests in domestic exploration, development, and production of oil and natural gas. Interests include leasing, prices and taxation, foreign trade, environmental restrictions, and improved recovery methods.

Independent Terminal Operators Assn., *1150 Connecticut Ave. N.W., 9th Floor 20036; (202) 862-4100. Fax, (202) 828-4130. William H. Bode, General Counsel.*

Membership: independent operators of petroleum storage facilities. Interests include oil imports. Monitors legislation and regulations.

International Assn. of Drilling Contractors, *Government Affairs, Washington Office, 1901 L St. N.W., #702 20036; (202) 293-0670. Fax, (202) 872-0047. Brian T. Petty, Senior Vice President. General e-mail, info@iadc. org. Web, www.iadc.org.*

Membership: drilling contractors, oil and gas producers, and others in the industry worldwide. Promotes safe exploration and production of hydrocarbons, advances in drilling technology, and preservation of the environment. Monitors legislation and regulations. (Headquarters in Houston.)

National Ocean Industries Assn., *1120 G St. N.W., #900 20005; (202) 347-6900. Fax, (202) 347-8650. Robert B. Stewart, President. General e-mail, noia@noia.org. Web, www.noia.org.*

Membership: manufacturers, producers, suppliers, and support and service companies involved in marine, offshore, and ocean work. Interests include offshore oil and gas supply and production.

National Petrochemical and Refiners Assn., *1899 L St. N.W., #1000 20036; (202) 457-0480. Fax, (202) 457-0486. Urvan Sternfels, President. Web, www.npradc.org.*

Membership: petroleum, petrochemical, and refining companies. Interests include allocation, imports, refining technology, petrochemicals, and environmental regulations.

National Petroleum Council, *1625 K St. N.W., #600 20006; (202) 393-6100. Fax, (202) 331-8539. Marshall W. Nichols, Executive Director. Web, www.npc.org.*

Advisory committee to the secretary of energy on matters relating to the petroleum industry, including oil and natural gas. Publishes reports concerning technical aspects of the oil and gas industries.

National Propane Gas Assn., *Government Relations, Washington Office, 1101 17th St. N.W., #1004 20036; (202) 466-7200. Fax, (202) 466-7205. Richard R. Roldan, Vice President. Web, www.npga.org.*

Membership: retail marketers, producers, wholesale distributors, appliance and equipment manufacturers, equipment fabricators, and distributors and transporters of liquefied petroleum gas. Conducts research, safety, and educational programs; provides statistics on the industry. (Headquarters in Lisle, Ill.)

Natural Gas Supply Assn., *805 15th St. N.W., #510 20005; (202) 326-9300. Fax, (202) 326-9330. Ralph Horvath, President. Web, www.ngsa.org.*

Membership: major and independent producers of domestic natural gas. Interests include the production, consumption, marketing, and regulation of natural gas. Monitors legislation and regulations.

Natural Gas Vehicle Coalition, *1100 Wilson Blvd., #850, Arlington, VA 22209; (703) 527-3022. Fax, (703) 527-3025. Richard R. Kolodziej, President. Web, www.ngvc. org.*

Membership: natural gas distributors; pipeline, automobile, and engine manufacturers; environmental groups; research and development organizations; and state and local government agencies. Advocates installation of compressed natural gas fuel stations and development of industry standards. Helps market new natural gas products and equipment.

Petroleum Marketers Assn. of America, *1901 N. Fort Myer Dr., #1200, Arlington, VA 22209-1604; (703) 351-8000. Fax, (703) 351-9160. Dan Gilligan, President. Web, www.pmaa.org.*

Membership: state and regional associations representing independent branded and nonbranded marketers of petroleum products. Provides information on all aspects of petroleum marketing. Monitors legislation and regulations.

Public Citizen, *Buyers Up, 1600 20th St. N.W. 20009; (202) 588-7780. Fax, (202) 588-7798. Garland Auton, Program Manager. General e-mail, publiccitizen@citizen. org. Web, www.citizen.org/buyersup.htm.*

Administers cooperative purchasing program for consumers of heating oil and heating and cooling services. Promotes energy conservation; helps consumers save on energy bills.

Service Station Dealers of America, *9420 Annapolis Rd., #307, Lanham, MD 20706; (301) 577-4956. Fax, (301) 731-0039. Don Sadler, President. Web, www. ssda-at.org.*

Membership: state associations of gasoline retailers. Interests include environmental issues, retail marketing, oil allocation, imports and exports, prices, and taxation.

Society of Independent Gasoline Marketers of America, *11911 Freedom Dr., #590, Reston, VA 20190; (703) 709-7000. Fax, (703) 709-7007. Kenneth A. Doyle, Executive Vice President. Web, www.sigma.org.*

Membership: marketers and wholesalers of brand and nonbrand gasoline. Seeks to ensure adequate supplies of gasoline at competitive prices. Monitors legislation and regulations affecting gasoline supply and price.

U.S. Oil and Gas Assn., *801 Pennsylvania Ave. N.W., #840 20004-2615; (202) 638-4400. Fax, (202) 638-5967. Wayne Gibbens, President.*

Membership: major and independent petroleum companies. Monitors legislation and regulations affecting the petroleum industry.

Pipelines

AGENCIES

Federal Energy Regulatory Commission *(Energy Dept.), Markets, Tariffs, and Rates, 888 1st St. N.E. 20426; (202) 208-0700. Fax, (202) 208-0193. Kevin P. Madden, Deputy Director.*

Establishes and enforces maximum rates and charges for oil and natural gas pipelines; establishes oil pipeline operating rules; issues certificates for and regulates construction, sale, and acquisition of natural gas pipeline facilities. Ensures compliance with the Natural Gas Policy Act, the Natural Gas Act, and other statutes.

National Transportation Safety Board, *Pipeline and Hazardous Material Safety, 490 L'Enfant Plaza S.W. 20594; (202) 314-6460. Fax, (202) 314-6482. Bob Chipkevich, Director.*

Investigates natural gas and petroleum pipeline accidents.

Research and Special Programs Administration *(Transportation Dept.), Hazardous Materials Safety, 400 7th St. S.W., #8321 20590; (202) 366-0656. Fax, (202) 366-5713. Robert McGuire, Associate Administrator (Acting). Web, hazmat.dot.gov.*

Designates fuels, chemicals, and other substances as hazardous materials and regulates their transportation in interstate commerce; coordinates international standards regulations.

Research and Special Programs Administration *(Transportation Dept.), Pipeline Safety, 400 7th St. S.W., #7128 20590; (202) 366-4595. Fax, (202) 366-4566.*

Richard B. Felder, Associate Administrator. Web, ops.dot. gov.

Issues and enforces federal regulations for oil, natural gas, and petroleum products pipeline safety.

NONPROFIT

Assn. of Oil Pipe Lines, *1101 Vermont Ave. N.W., #604 20005; (202) 408-7970. Fax, (202) 408-7983. Ben Cooper, Executive Director. General e-mail, aopl@aopl.org. Web, www.aopl.org.*

Membership: oil pipeline companies. Analyzes industry statistics. Monitors legislation and regulations.

Coal Technology Assn., *104 Edith Dr., Rockville, MD 20850; (301) 294-6080. Fax, (301) 294-7480. Stuart D. Serkin, Executive Director. Web, www.coaltechnologies. com.*

Membership: government and business professionals interested in transportation, energy, economic, and environmental policies and regulations. Seeks to improve coal utilization technologies and to develop coal cleaning technologies. Facilitates the exchange of technical information on coal technologies.

Interstate Natural Gas Assn. of America, *10 G St. N.E., #700 20002; (202) 216-5900. Fax, (202) 216-0877. Jerry V. Halvorsen, President. Web, www.ingaa.org.*

Membership: U.S. interstate and Canadian interprovincial natural gas pipeline companies. Commissions studies and provides information on the natural gas pipeline industry.

⚛ NUCLEAR ENERGY

See also International Trade and Cooperation (this chapter); Nuclear Weapons and Power (chap. 16)

AGENCIES

Energy Information Administration *(Energy Dept.), Coal, Nuclear, Electric, and Alternate Fuels, 950 L'Enfant Plaza S.W. 20024 (mailing address: 1000 Independence Ave. S.W. 20585); (202) 426-1200. Fax, (202) 426-1280. John Geidl, Director.*

Prepares analyses and forecasts on the availability, production, prices, processing, transportation, and distribution of nuclear energy, both domestically and internationally. Collects and publishes data concerning the uranium supply and market.

Nuclear Energy, Science, and Technology *(Energy Dept.), 1000 Independence Ave. S.W. 20585; (202) 586-*

6450. Fax, (202) 586-8353. William D. Magwood IV, Director.

Administers nuclear fission power generation and fuel technology programs; develops and provides nuclear power sources to meet national civilian requirements. Develops, interprets, and coordinates nuclear safety policy for all Energy Dept. reactors and nuclear facilities. Encourages public involvement in programs and provides information to increase public knowledge.

Nuclear Energy, Science, and Technology (*Energy Dept.*), *Isotope Programs,* 19901 Germantown Rd., #B-432, NE-70, Germantown, MD 20874-1290; (301) 903-5161. Fax, (301) 903-5434. Owen W. Lowe, Associate Director.

Directs all isotope production and distribution activities within the Energy Dept.; ensures a reliable supply of medical, research, and industrial isotopes consistent with customer needs.

Nuclear Energy, Science, and Technology (*Energy Dept.*), *Nuclear Facilities Management,* 19901 Germantown Rd., #E-468, Germantown, MD 20874-1290; (301) 903-2915. Fax, (301) 903-5005. Robert G. Lange, Associate Director.

Manages the design, construction, and operation of nuclear energy test facilities and Office of Energy Research reactor and supporting facilities, assuring their safe, reliable, and environmentally sound operation and cost-effective use. Interests include international nuclear safety.

Nuclear Regulatory Commission, 11555 Rockville Pike, Rockville, MD 20852; (301) 415-1759. Fax, (301) 415-1672. Richard A. Meserve, Chair; William D. Travers, Executive Director, (301) 415-1700. Information, (301) 415-8200. General e-mail, opa@nrc.gov. Web, www.nrc. gov.

Regulates commercial uses of nuclear energy; responsibilities include licensing, inspection, and enforcement; monitors and regulates the imports and exports of nuclear material and equipment.

Tennessee Valley Authority, *Government Affairs, Washington Office,* 1 Massachusetts Ave. N.W., #300 20444; (202) 898-2999. Fax, (202) 898-2998. David Withrow, Vice President. Web, www.tva.gov.

Coordinates resource conservation, development, and land-use programs in the Tennessee River Valley. Produces and supplies wholesale power to municipal and cooperative electric systems, federal installations, and some industries; interests include nuclear power generation.

CONGRESS

House Commerce Committee, *Subcommittee on Energy and Power,* 2125 RHOB 20515; (202) 225-2927. Fax, (202) 225-1919. Rep. Joe L. Barton, R-Texas, Chair; James E. Derderian, Staff Director. General e-mail, commerce@mail.house.gov. Web, www.house.gov/commerce.

Jurisdiction over regulation of commercial nuclear facilities and special oversight functions with respect to all laws, programs, and government activities affecting nonmilitary aspects of nuclear energy.

House Science Committee, *Subcommittee on Energy and Environment,* 389 FHOB 20515; (202) 225-9662. Fax, (202) 226-6983. Rep. Ken Calvert, R-Calif., Chair; Harlan Watson, Staff Director. Web, www.house.gov/ science.

Jurisdiction over legislation and international cooperation on nuclear energy research and development. Oversight responsibilities over the uranium supply and the operation of nonmilitary Energy Dept. laboratories, including toxic waste cleanup.

Senate Energy and Natural Resources Committee, SD-364 20510; (202) 224-4971. Fax, (202) 224-6163. Sen. Frank H. Murkowski, R-Alaska, Chair; Andrew Lundquist, Staff Director. General e-mail, committee@energy.senate. gov. Web, energy.senate.gov.

Jurisdiction over nonmilitary and nonregulatory aspects of nuclear energy.

Senate Energy and Natural Resources Committee, *Subcommittee on Energy Research, Development, Production, and Regulation,* SD-308 20510; (202) 224-6567. Fax, (202) 228-0302. Sen. Don Nickles, R-Okla., Chair; Howard Useem, Professional Staff Member. General e-mail, erdpr@energy.senate.gov. Web, energy.senate.gov.

Jurisdiction over nuclear energy research and development, including uranium enrichment and nuclear fuel cycle policy.

Senate Environment and Public Works Committee, *Subcommittee on Clean Air, Wetlands, Private Property, and Nuclear Safety,* SD-410 20510; (202) 224-6176. Fax, (202) 224-5167. Sen. James M. Inhofe, R-Okla., Chair; Andy Wheeler, Staff Contact. Web, epw.senate.gov.

Legislative jurisdiction over nonmilitary environmental regulation and control of nuclear energy, including plant licensing and siting, radiological health and safety, security and safeguards, nuclear waste disposal, and licensing of certain nuclear exports.

Senate Governmental Affairs Committee, SD-340 20510; (202) 224-4751. Fax, (202) 224-9603. Sen. Fred Thompson, R-Tenn., Chair; Hannah Sistare, Staff Director. Web, gov_affairs.senate.gov.

Jurisdiction over organization and management of nuclear export policy; jurisdiction over legislation on the reform of nuclear licensing procedures and nuclear waste and spent fuel policy, physical security at nuclear installations, and nuclear proliferation.

NONPROFIT

American Physical Society, *Public Information, Washington Office, 529 14th St. N.W., #1050 20045; (202) 662-8700. Fax, (202) 662-8711. Robert L. Park, Director. General e-mail, opa@aps.org. Web, www.aps.org.*

Scientific and educational society of educators, students, citizens, and scientists, including industrial scientists. Sponsors studies on issues of public concern related to physics, such as reactor safety and energy use. Informs members of national and international developments. (Headquarters in College Park, Md.)

Nuclear Energy Institute, *1776 Eye St. N.W., #400 20006-3708; (202) 739-8000. Fax, (202) 785-4019. Joe Colvin, President. Web, www.nei.org.*

Membership: utilities; industries; labor, service, and research organizations; law firms; universities; and government agencies interested in peaceful uses of nuclear energy, including the generation of electricity. Acts as a spokesperson for the nuclear power industry; provides information on licensing and plant siting, research and development, safety and security, waste disposal, and legislative and policy issues.

Nuclear Information and Resource Service, *1424 16th St. N.W., #404 20036; (202) 328-0002. Fax, (202) 462-2183. Michael Mariotte, Executive Director. General e-mail, nirsnet@igc.org. Web, www.nirs.org.*

Membership: organizations and individuals concerned about nuclear energy and nuclear waste. Information clearinghouse on nuclear power plants, nuclear waste, and radiation effects. Library open to the public by appointment.

Public Citizen, *Critical Mass Energy Project, 215 Pennsylvania Ave. S.E. 20003-1155; (202) 546-4996. Fax, (202) 547-7392. Wenonah Hauter, Director. General e-mail, cmep@citizen.org. Web, www.citizen.org/cmep.*

Public interest group that promotes energy efficiency and renewable energy technologies; opposes nuclear energy. Interests include nuclear plant safety and energy policy issues. Library open to the public by appointment.

Safe Energy Communication Council, *1717 Massachusetts Ave. N.W., #106 20036; (202) 483-8491. Fax, (202) 234-9194. Scott Denman, Executive Director. General e-mail, safeenergy@erols.com. Web, www.safeenergy.org.*

Coalition of national energy, environmental, and public interest media groups that works to increase public awareness of both the ability of energy efficiency and renewable energy sources to meet an increasing share of U.S. energy needs and of the economic and environmental liabilities of nuclear power. Provides local, state, and national organizations with technical assistance through media skills training and outreach strategies.

Union of Concerned Scientists, *Government Relations, Washington Office, 1616 P St. N.W., #310 20036; (202) 332-0900. Fax, (202) 332-0905. Alden Meyer, Director; Todd Perry, Washington Representative for Arms Control and International Security. General e-mail, ucs@ucsusa.org. Web, www.ucsusa.org.*

Independent group of scientists and others concerned with U.S. energy policy, including nuclear policy and nuclear plant safety. (Headquarters in Cambridge, Mass.)

See also Electric Power Research Institute (p. 258); National Rural Electric Cooperative Assn. (p. 258)

Licensing and Plant Siting

AGENCIES

Federal Emergency Management Agency, *Preparedness, Training, and Exercises, 500 C St. S.W. 20472; (202) 646-3487. Fax, (202) 646-4557. Kay Goss, Associate Director.*

Reviews off-site preparedness for commercial nuclear power facilities; evaluates emergency plans before plant licensing and submits findings to the Nuclear Regulatory Commission.

Nuclear Regulatory Commission, *Nuclear Material Safety and Safeguards, 11555 Rockville Pike, Rockville, MD 20852; (301) 415-7800. Fax, (301) 415-5370. William S. Kane, Director.*

Licenses all nuclear facilities and materials except power reactors; directs principal licensing and regulation activities for the management of nuclear waste.

Nuclear Regulatory Commission, *Nuclear Reactor Regulation, 11555 Rockville Pike, Rockville, MD 20852; (301) 415-1270. Fax, (301) 415-8333. Samuel J. Collins, Director.*

Licenses nuclear power plants and operators.

Research and Development

AGENCIES

Energy Dept., *Office of Science: Fusion Energy Sciences, 19901 Germantown Rd., Germantown, MD 20874-*

NUCLEAR REGULATORY COMMISSION

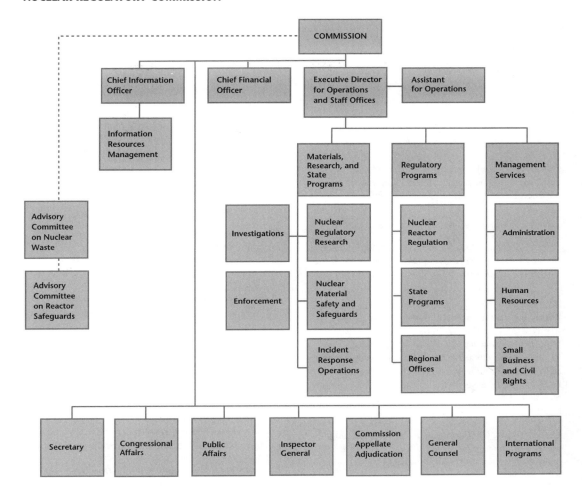

1290; (301) 903-4941. Fax, (301) 903-8584. N. Anne Davies, Associate Director. Web, wwwofe.er.doe.gov.

Conducts research and development on fusion energy for electric power generation.

National Institute of Standards and Technology (Commerce Dept.), Physics Laboratory, 100 Bureau Dr., Bldg. 221, #B160, Gaithersburg, MD 20899-8400; (301) 975-4200. Fax, (301) 975-3038. Katharine B. Gebbie, Director. Web, physics.nist.gov.

Provides national standards for radiation measurement methods and technology. Conducts research in measurement science in the fields of electron physics; ionizing radiation dosimetry; neutron physics; and

optical, ultraviolet, x-ray, gamma-ray, and infrared radiometry.

Nuclear Energy, Science, and Technology (Energy Dept.), **Management and Planning,** 1000 Independence Ave. S.W., NE-2.2 20585; (202) 586-6450. Fax, (202) 586-8353. Robert Knipp, Deputy Director.

Responsible for uranium activities and management of fuel cycle issues. Supplies reactor fuel to university reactors; manages conversion of university reactors from highly enriched uranium fuel to low enriched fuel; supports university reactor instrumentation and equipment upgrades; provides general support to nuclear engineering programs at U.S. universities.

Nuclear Energy, Science, and Technology *(Energy Dept.), Space and Defense Power Systems, 19901 Germantown Rd., Germantown, MD 20874; (301) 903-3456. Fax, (301) 903-1510. Earl Wahlquist, Associate Director.*

Develops and produces radio isotopes power systems for space applications in support of NASA.

Nuclear Regulatory Commission, *Nuclear Regulatory Research, 11545 Rockville Pike, Rockville, MD 20852-2738; (301) 415-6641. Fax, (301) 415-5153. Ashok Thadani, Director.*

Plans, recommends, and implements nuclear regulatory research, standards development, and resolution of safety issues for nuclear power plants and other facilities regulated by the Nuclear Regulatory Commission; develops and promulgates all technical regulations.

Safety, Security, and Waste Disposal

See also Hazardous Materials (chap. 9); International Trade and Cooperation (this chapter); Radiation Protection (chap. 9)

AGENCIES

Defense Nuclear Facilities Safety Board, *625 Indiana Ave. N.W., #700 20004; (202) 694-7080. Fax, (202) 208-6518. John T. Conway, Chair. Web, www.dnfsb.gov.*

Independent board created by Congress and appointed by the president to provide external oversight of Energy Dept. defense nuclear facilities and make recommendations to the secretary of energy regarding public health and safety.

Energy Dept., *Civilian Radioactive Waste Management, 1000 Independence Ave. S.W., #5A085 20585; (202) 586-6842. Fax, (202) 586-6638. Ivan Itkin, Director. Web, www.doe.gov.*

Responsible for developing the waste disposal system for commercial spent nuclear fuels and some military high-level radioactive waste. Sites, licenses, constructs, and operates a permanent repository. Monitors and reports on the adequacy of congressional appropriations for the Nuclear Waste Fund to finance nuclear waste disposal through fees collected from private utility companies that generate electricity.

Energy Information Administration *(Energy Dept.), Coal, Nuclear, Electric, and Alternate Fuels, 950 L'Enfant Plaza S.W. 20024 (mailing address: 1000 Independence Ave. S.W. 20585); (202) 426-1200. Fax, (202) 426-1280. John Geidl, Director.*

Directs collection of spent fuel data and validation of spent nuclear fuel discharge data for the Civilian Radioactive Waste Management Office.

Environment, Safety, and Health *(Energy Dept.), Environment, 1000 Independence Ave. S.W., #7A075 20585; (202) 586-5680. Fax, (202) 586-2268. Ray Berube, Deputy Assistant Secretary.*

Establishes policies and guidance for environmental protection and compliance; provides technical assistance to departmental program and field offices in complying with environmental requirements.

Environment, Safety, and Health *(Energy Dept.), Health Studies, 19901 Germantown Rd., EH-6/27OCC, Germantown, MD 20874-1290; (301) 903-5926. Fax, (301) 903-3445. Paul J. Seligman, Deputy Assistant Secretary.*

Evaluates and establishes standards related to radiation, industrial hygiene, and occupational medicine. Oversees epidemiologic studies.

Environment, Safety, and Health *(Energy Dept.), Nuclear and Facility Safety, 1000 Independence Ave. S.W., #7A121 20585; (202) 586-2407. Fax, (202) 586-6010. Orin Pearson, Deputy Assistant Secretary. Web, tis-nt.eh.doe.gov/eh-3/sect-3.htm.*

Provides technical assistance to Energy Dept. facilities; reviews accidents, risk assessments, emergency preparedness plans, and radiological protection programs.

Environment, Safety, and Health *(Energy Dept.), Worker Health and Safety, 20300 Century Blvd., Germantown, MD 20874 (mailing address: 19901 Germantown Rd., EH5 270CC, Germantown, MD 20874); (301) 903-5532. Fax, (301) 903-3189. Joseph E. Fitzgerald Jr., Deputy Assistant Secretary.*

Develops policy and establishes standards to ensure safety and health protection in all department activities.

Environmental Management *(Energy Dept.), Environmental Restoration, 1000 Independence Ave. S.W., #5B050 20585; (202) 586-6331. Fax, (202) 586-6523. James Fiore, Assistant Secretary.*

Manages Energy Dept. programs that treat and stabilize radioactive waste including the decontamination and decommissioning of nongovernment facilities and sites; works to develop a reliable national system for low-level waste management and techniques for treatment and immobilization of waste from former nuclear weapons complex sites.

Environmental Management *(Energy Dept.), Project Completion Environmental Management, 1000 Independence Ave. S.W., #5B-040 20585; (202) 586-0370. Fax, (202) 586-0449. Mark Frei, Deputy Assistant Secretary.*

Provides policy guidance for and oversees waste management operations.

Environmental Management *(Energy Dept.), Science and Technology,* 1000 Independence Ave. S.W., #5B014 20585; (202) 586-6382. Fax, (202) 586-6773. Gerald Boyd, Deputy Assistant Secretary.

Performs research, development, testing, demonstration, and evaluation for innovative, safe, and cost-effective solutions to the problems of hazardous waste and contamination of soils and groundwater.

Environmental Protection Agency, *Radiation and Indoor Air,* 501 3rd St. N.W. 20001 (mailing address: 401 M St. S.W., #6601J 20460); (202) 564-9320. Fax, (202) 565-2043. Stephen D. Page, Director.

Establishes standards to regulate the amount of radiation discharged into the environment from uranium mining and milling projects, and other activities that result in radioactive emissions; and to ensure the safe disposal of radioactive waste. Fields a Radiological Emergency Response Team to respond to radiological incidents.

Federal Emergency Management Agency, 500 C St. S.W. 20472; (202) 646-3923. Fax, (202) 646-3930. James Lee Witt, Director. Press, (202) 646-4600. Locator, (202) 646-2500. Disaster assistance, (800) 462-9029. Radio network, (800) 323-5248. Fax-on-demand, (202) 646-3362. Web, www.fema.gov.

Assists state and local governments in preparing for and responding to natural and man-made emergencies, including accidents at nuclear power facilities and accidents involving transportation of radioactive materials; provides planning guidance in the event of such accidents; operates the National Emergency Training Center. Coordinates emergency preparedness and planning for all federal agencies and departments.

National Transportation Safety Board, *Pipeline and Hazardous Material Safety,* 490 L'Enfant Plaza S.W. 20594; (202) 314-6460. Fax, (202) 314-6482. Bob Chipkevich, Director.

Investigates accidents involving the transportation of hazardous materials.

Nuclear Regulatory Commission, *Advisory Committee on Nuclear Waste,* 11545 Rockville Pike, Rockville, MD 20852; (301) 415-7360. Fax, (301) 415-5422. John T. Larkins, Executive Director.

Oversees handling and disposal of high- and low-level nuclear waste, especially the disposal of high-level waste in the Yucca Mountain Repository.

Nuclear Regulatory Commission, *Advisory Committee on Reactor Safeguards,* 11545 Rockville Pike, Rockville, MD 20852; (301) 415-7360. Fax, (301) 415-5422. John T. Larkins, Executive Director.

Established by Congress to review and report on safety aspects of proposed and existing nuclear reactor facilities and the adequacy of proposed reactor safety standards; directs the Safety Research Program.

Nuclear Regulatory Commission, *Nuclear Material Safety and Safeguards,* 11555 Rockville Pike, Rockville, MD 20852; (301) 415-7800. Fax, (301) 415-5370. William S. Kane, Director.

Develops and implements safeguards programs; directs licensing and regulation activities for the management and disposal of nuclear waste.

Nuclear Regulatory Commission, *Nuclear Reactor Regulation,* 11555 Rockville Pike, Rockville, MD 20852; (301) 415-1270. Fax, (301) 415-8333. Samuel J. Collins, Director.

Conducts safety inspections of nuclear reactors. Regulates nuclear materials used or produced at nuclear power plants.

Nuclear Regulatory Commission, *Nuclear Regulatory Research,* 11545 Rockville Pike, Rockville, MD 20852-2738; (301) 415-6641. Fax, (301) 415-5153. Ashok Thadani, Director.

Plans, recommends, and implements resolution of safety issues for nuclear power plants and other facilities regulated by the Nuclear Regulatory Commission.

Nuclear Waste Technical Review Board, 2300 Clarendon Blvd., #1300, Arlington, VA 22201-3367; (703) 235-4473. Fax, (703) 235-4495. William D. Barnard, Executive Director. General e-mail, info@nwtrb.gov. Web, www.nwtrb.gov.

Independent board of scientists and engineers appointed by the president to review, evaluate, and report on Energy Dept. development of waste disposal systems and repositories for spent fuel and high-level radioactive waste. Oversees siting, packaging, and transportation of waste, in accordance with the Nuclear Waste Policy Act of 1987.

Research and Special Programs Administration *(Transportation Dept.), Hazardous Materials Safety,* 400 7th St. S.W., #8321 20590; (202) 366-0656. Fax, (202) 366-5713. Robert McGuire, Associate Administrator (Acting). Web, hazmat.dot.gov.

Issues safety regulations and exemptions for the transportation of hazardous materials; works with the International Atomic Energy Agency on standards for international shipments of radioactive materials.

⬛ RENEWABLE ENERGIES/ ALTERNATIVE FUELS

AGENCIES

Energy Efficiency and Renewable Energy *(Energy Dept.), Clearinghouse, P.O. Box 3048, Merrifield, VA 22116-3048. Fax, (703) 893-0400. Larry Goldberg, Project Manager. Information, (800) 363-3732. TTY, (800) 273-2957. General e-mail, doe.erec@nciinc.com. Web, www. eren.doe.gov/consumerinfo.*

Provides information on renewable energy and energy efficiency; makes referrals to other organizations for technical information on renewable energy resources. Serves as repository of information for the President's Council on Sustainability and the Federal Energy Management Program.

Energy Efficiency and Renewable Energy *(Energy Dept.), Power Technologies, 1000 Independence Ave. S.W., #5H021 20585; (202) 586-9275. Fax, (202) 586-1640. Robert K. Dixon, Assistant Secretary (Acting).*

Conducts research, development, and deployment activities to facilitate use of renewable energy resources, including solar, wind, photovoltaic, biomass, geothermal, and hydropower.

Energy Efficiency and Renewable Energy *(Energy Dept.), Technology Utilization, 1000 Independence Ave. S.W., #5G086, EE34 20585; (202) 586-9118. Fax, (202) 586-1610. David Rodgers, Director.*

Conducts research on and develops technology for alternative fuels (including methanol, ethanol, natural gas, propane, and bio-diesel) for use in heavy and light duty transportation vehicles.

Energy Information Administration *(Energy Dept.), Coal, Nuclear, Electric, and Alternate Fuels, 950 L'Enfant Plaza S.W. 20024 (mailing address: 1000 Independence Ave. S.W. 20585); (202) 426-1200. Fax, (202) 426-1280. John Geidl, Director.*

Prepares analyses on the availability, production, costs, processing, transportation, and distribution of uranium and alternative energy supplies, including biomass, solar, wind, waste, wood, and alcohol.

Environmental Management *(Energy Dept.), Project Completion Environmental Management, 1000 Independence Ave. S.W., #5B-040 20585; (202) 586-0370. Fax, (202) 586-0449. Mark Frei, Deputy Assistant Secretary.*

Conducts research on municipal waste conversion for use as an energy source.

CONGRESS

House Commerce Committee, *Subcommittee on Energy and Power, 2125 RHOB 20515; (202) 225-2927. Fax, (202) 225-1919. Rep. Joe L. Barton, R-Texas, Chair; James E. Derderian, Staff Director. General e-mail, commerce@mail.house.gov. Web, www.house.gov/ commerce.*

Jurisdiction over legislation on regulation, commercialization, and utilization of hydroelectric power, synthetic and alcohol fuels, and renewable energy resources, including wind, solar, and ocean thermal energy.

House Resources Committee, *Subcommittee on Energy and Mineral Resources, 1626 LHOB 20515; (202) 225-9297. Fax, (202) 225-5255. Rep. Barbara Cubin, R-Wyo., Chair; William Condit, Staff Director. General e-mail, resources.committee@mail.house.gov. Web, www. house.gov/resources/energy.*

Jurisdiction over legislation concerning the development and conservation of energy and natural resources found in the ocean and the outer continental shelf. Jurisdiction over legislation affecting the use of geothermal resources.

House Resources Committee, *Subcommittee on Water and Power, 1522 LHOB 20515; (202) 225-8331. Fax, (202) 226-6953. Rep. John T. Doolittle, R-Calif., Chair; Robert Faber, Staff Director. General e-mail, water.power@mail.house.gov. Web, www.house.gov/ resources/water.*

Jurisdiction over legislation on irrigation and reclamation projects and electrical power marketing administrations.

House Science Committee, *Subcommittee on Energy and Environment, 389 FHOB 20515; (202) 225-9662. Fax, (202) 226-6983. Rep. Ken Calvert, R-Calif., Chair; Harlan Watson, Staff Director. Web, www.house.gov/ science.*

Jurisdiction over Energy Dept. basic research programs, including legislation on research and development of solar, wind, geothermal, and fossil fuel energy (including synthetic fuels such as liquefied and gasified coal) and other nonfossil and nonnuclear energy sources.

Senate Commerce, Science, and Transportation Committee, *Subcommittee on Oceans and Fisheries, SH-428 20510; (202) 224-8172. Fax, (202) 228-0326. Sen. Olympia J. Snowe, R-Maine, Chair; Sloan Rapoport, Counsel. Web, commerce.senate.gov.*

Studies ocean resources development and conservation. (Subcommittee does not report legislation.)

Senate Energy and Natural Resources Committee, *SD-364 20510; (202) 224-4971. Fax, (202) 224-6163. Sen. Frank H. Murkowski, R-Alaska, Chair; Andrew Lundquist, Staff Director. General e-mail, committee@energy.senate. gov. Web, energy.senate.gov.*

Jurisdiction over legislation on energy and nonfuel mineral resources, including hydroelectric power, irrigation and reclamation projects, power marketing administrations, and the impact of energy developments on water resources. Jurisdiction over legislation on synfuels research and development and over Energy Dept. basic research programs.

NONPROFIT

Electric Power Supply Assn., *1401 H St. N.W., #760 20005; (202) 789-7200. Fax, (202) 789-7201. Lynne H. Church, Executive Director. Web, www.epsa.org.*

Membership: companies that generate electricity, steam, and other forms of energy using a broad spectrum of fossil fuel-fired and renewable technologies.

Energy Frontiers International, *1110 N. Glebe Rd., #610, Arlington, VA 22201; (703) 276-6655. Fax, (703) 276-7662. Michael Koleda, President.*

Membership: companies interested in technologies for converting solid, liquid, and gaseous fossil fuels and biomass into other forms. Interests include coal gasification, combined cycle power generation, and liquid transportation fuels from coal, natural gas, and biomass.

Hearth Products Assn., *1601 N. Kent St., #1001, Arlington, VA 22209; (703) 522-0086. Fax, (703) 522-0548. Carter E. Keithley, President. Web, www.hearthassociation. org.*

Membership: all sectors of the hearth products industry. Provides industry training programs to its members on the safe and efficient use of alternative fuels and appliances. Works with the Hearth Education Foundation, which certifies gas hearth, fireplace, pellet stove, and wood stove appliances and venting design specialists.

National BioEnergy Industries Assn., *1616 H St. N.W., 8th Floor 20006; (202) 628-7745. Fax, (202) 628-7779. Scott Sklar, Executive Director. Web, www.bioenergy. org/index.html.*

Membership: landowners, foresters, harvesters, fuel transporters, processors, equipment manufacturers, and others involved in the U.S. biomass energy industry. Encourages public and private participation in the development of renewable bioenergy resources worldwide. (Affiliated with Solar Energy Industries Assn.)

National Hydrogen Assn., *1800 M St. N.W., #300 20036; (202) 223-5547. Fax, (202) 223-5537. Bob Mauro,*

Vice President. General e-mail, nha@ttcorp.com. Web, www.ttcorp.com/nha.

Membership: industry, small businesses, universities, and research institutions. Promotes use of hydrogen as an energy carrier; fosters the development and application of hydrogen technologies.

See also Edison Electric Institute (p. 255); Electric Power Research Institute (p. 258); Public Citizen, Critical Mass Energy Project (p. 266); World Resources Institute (p. 284)

Alcohol Fuels

AGENCIES

Bureau of Alcohol, Tobacco, and Firearms *(Treasury Dept.), Regulations, 650 Massachusetts Ave. N.W., #5000 20226; (202) 927-8210. Fax, (202) 927-8602. Richard A. Mascolo, Chief.*

Develops guidelines for regional offices responsible for issuing permits for producing gasohol and other ethyl alcohol fuels, whose uses include heating and operating machinery. Writes and interprets regulations for distilleries that produce ethyl alcohol fuels.

Rural Business-Cooperative Service *(Agriculture Dept.), Business, 1400 Independence Ave. S.W., #5050 20250-3220; (202) 720-7287. Fax, (202) 690-0097. William F. Hagy III, Deputy Administrator. Web, www.rurder.usda.gov/rbs.*

Makes loan guarantees to rural businesses, including those seeking to develop alcohol fuels production facilities.

NONPROFIT

American Methanol Institute, *800 Connecticut Ave. N.W., #620 20006; (202) 467-5050. Fax, (202) 331-9055. John E. Lynn, President. General e-mail, ami@methanol. org. Web, www.methanol.org.*

Membership: methanol producers and related industries. Encourages use of methanol fuels and development of chemical-derivative markets. Monitors legislation and regulations.

Renewable Fuels Assn., *1 Massachusetts Ave. N.W., #820 20001-1431; (202) 289-3835. Fax, (202) 289-7519. Eric Vaughn, President. General e-mail, etohrfa@erols.com. Web, www.ethanolrfa.org.*

Membership: companies and state governments involved in developing the domestic ethanol industry. Distributes publications on ethanol performance.

Geothermal Energy

AGENCIES

Energy Efficiency and Renewable Energy *(Energy Dept.)*, *Geothermal,* 1000 Independence Ave. S.W., #5H072, EE-12 20585-0121; (202) 586-5340. Fax, (202) 586-8185. Peter Goldman, Director.

Responsible for long-range research and technology development of geothermal energy resources.

U.S. Geological Survey *(Interior Dept.)*, *Volcano Hazards,* 12201 Sunrise Valley Dr., Reston, VA 20192 (mailing address: 905 National Center, Reston, VA 20192); (703) 648-6708. Fax, (703) 648-5483. Marianne C. Guffanti, Program Coordinator. Web, volcanoes.usgs.gov.

Provides staff support to the U.S. Geological Survey through programs in geothermal research and volcano hazards.

Solar, Ocean, and Wind Energy

AGENCIES

Energy Efficiency and Renewable Energy *(Energy Dept.)*, *Geothermal and Wind Technologies,* 1000 Independence Ave. S.W., #5H072 20585; (202) 586-5348. Peter Goldman, Director.

Conducts research on geothermal and wind technologies. Works with U.S. industries to develop geothermal and wind technologies.

Energy Efficiency and Renewable Energy *(Energy Dept.)*, *Solar Energy Technologies,* 1000 Independence Ave. S.W., #5H095 20585; (202) 586-1720. Fax, (202) 586-8148. James Rannels, Director.

Supports research and development, through national laboratories and partnerships with industry, of small and utility scale wind energy systems; new photovoltaic devices, and improved manufacturing processes.

National Oceanic and Atmospheric Administration *(Commerce Dept.)*, *Ocean and Coastal Resource Management,* 1305 East-West Hwy., SSMC4, Silver Spring, MD 20910; (301) 713-3155. Fax, (301) 713-4012. Jeff Benoit, Director. Web, www.nos.noaa.gov/programs/ocrm.html.

Administers the Coastal Zone Management Act, the National Estuarine Research Reserve System, the National Marine Sanctuary Program, the Deep Seabed Hard Mineral Resources Act, and the Ocean Thermal Energy Conversion Act to carry out NOAA's goals for preservation, conservation, and restoration management of the ocean and coastal environment.

NONPROFIT

American Wind Energy Assn., 122 C St. N.W., #380 20001; (202) 383-2500. Fax, (202) 383-2505. Randall S. Swisher, Executive Director. General e-mail, windmail@awea.org. Web, www.awea.org.

Membership: manufacturers, developers, operators, and distributors of wind machines; utility companies; and others interested in wind energy. Advocates wind energy as an alternative energy source; makes industry data available to the public and to federal and state legislators. Promotes export of wind energy technology.

National Ocean Industries Assn., 1120 G St. N.W., #900 20005; (202) 347-6900. Fax, (202) 347-8650. Robert B. Stewart, President. General e-mail, noia@noia.org. Web, www.noia.org.

Membership: manufacturers, producers, suppliers, and support and service companies involved in marine, offshore, and ocean work. Interests include ocean thermal energy and new energy sources.

Solar Electric Light Fund, 1775 K St. N.W., #595 20006; (202) 234-7265. Fax, (202) 328-9512. Robert A. Freling, Executive Director. General e-mail, solarlectric@self.org. Web, www.self.org.

Promotes and develops solar rural electrification and energy self-sufficiency in developing countries. Assists developing world communities and governments in acquiring, financing, and installing decentralized household solar electric systems.

Solar Energy Industries Assn., 1616 H St. N.W., 8th Floor 20006; (202) 628-7745. Fax, (202) 628-7779. Scott Sklar, Director. General e-mail, plowenth@seia.org. Web, www.seia.org.

Membership: industries with interests in the production and use of solar energy. Promotes growth of U.S. and international markets; interests include photovoltaic, solar thermal power, solar hot water, and solar space heating and cooling technologies. Monitors legislation and regulations. (Affiliated with National BioEnergy Industries Assn.)

Solartherm, 1315 Apple Ave., Silver Spring, MD 20910; (301) 587-8686. Fax, (301) 587-8688. Carl Schleicher, President. General e-mail, mankindrf@aol.com. Web, members.aol.com/mankindrf.

Membership: scientists and scientific organizations. Conducts research and market development activities for low-cost solar energy systems and for alternative energy systems, including high-temperature solar, solid waste, ocean, and wind energy systems.

Sustainable Building Industries Council, *1331 H St. N.W., #1000 20005; (202) 628-7400. Fax, (202) 393-5043. Helen English, Executive Director. General e-mail, sbic@sbicouncil.org. Web, www.sbicouncil.org.*

Membership: building industry associations, corporations, small businesses, and independent professionals.

Provides information on sustainable design and construction. Interests include passive solar industry and related legislation, regulations, and programs.

9 ◨

Environment and Natural Resources

GENERAL POLICY

AGENCIES

Agriculture Dept., *Natural Resources and Environment,* 1400 Independence Ave. S.W., #217E 20250-0108; (202) 720-7173. Fax, (202) 720-4732. James R. Lyons, Under Secretary. Web, www.usda.gov.

Formulates and promulgates policy relating to environmental activities and management of natural resources; administers forest, conservation, and natural resource aspects of the National Environmental Policy Act. Oversees the Forest Service and the Natural Resources Conservation Service.

Council on Environmental Quality *(Executive Office of the President),* 722 Jackson Pl. N.W. 20503; (202) 456-6224. Fax, (202) 456-2710. George T. Frampton, Chair (Acting). Web, www.whitehouse.gov/CEQ.

Advises the president on environmental issues and prepares annual report on environmental quality for Congress; develops regulations for implementation of environmental impact statement law; provides information on environmental affairs.

Environment, Safety, and Health *(Energy Dept.),* 1000 Independence Ave. S.W., #7A097 20585; (202) 586-6151. Fax, (202) 586-0956. David Michaels, Assistant Secretary. Web, www.eh.doe.gov.

Ensures that Energy Dept. programs comply with federal policies and standards designed to protect the environment and government property. Approves all environmental impact statements prepared by the department. Oversees health and nonnuclear safety conditions at Energy Dept. facilities.

Environmental Protection Agency (EPA), *401 M St. S.W. 20460; (202) 260-4700. Fax, (202) 260-4309. Carol Browner, Administrator; Michael McCabe, Deputy Administrator (Acting), (202) 564-4711 . Information, (202) 260-2090. Press, (202) 260-4355. Web, www.epa.gov.*

Administers federal environmental policies, research, and regulations; provides information on environmental subjects, including water pollution, pollution prevention, hazardous and solid waste disposal, air and noise pollution, pesticides and toxic substances, and radiation.

Environmental Protection Agency, *Children's Health Protection,* 401 M St. S.W., MC 1107, #913, West Tower 20460; (202) 260-7778. Fax, (202) 260-4103. E. Ramona Trovato, Director. Web, www.epa.gov.

Supports and facilitates EPA's efforts to protect children's health from environmental threats.

Environmental Protection Agency, *National Center for Environmental Assessment,* 808 17th St. N.W., #400 20006; (202) 564-3322. Fax, (202) 567-0090. William H. Farland, Director.

Evaluates animal and human health data to define environmental health hazards and estimate risk to humans.

Environmental Protection Agency, *Policy,* 401 M St. S.W., 1013 West Tower 20460; (202) 260-4332. Fax, (202) 260-1849. Richard Farrell, Assistant Administrator.

Coordinates agency policy development and standard-setting activities.

Environmental Protection Agency, *Research and Development,* 1200 Pennsylvania Ave. N.W. 20460; (202) 564-6620. Fax, (202) 565-2431. Norine E. Noonan, Assistant Administrator.

Develops scientific data and methods to support EPA standards and regulations; conducts exposure and risk assessments; researches applied and long-term technologies to reduce risks from pollution.

Environmental Protection Agency, *Science Advisory Board,* 1200 Pennsylvania Ave. N.W., MC 1400A 20460; (202) 564-4533. Fax, (202) 501-0323. Donald G. Barnes, Staff Director.

Coordinates nongovernment scientists and engineers who advise the administrator on scientific and technical aspects of environmental problems and issues. Evaluates EPA research projects, the technical basis of regulations and standards, and policy statements.

Housing and Urban Development Dept. (HUD), *Community Viability,* 451 7th St. S.W., #7240 20410; (202) 708-2894. Fax, (202) 708-3363. Richard H. Broun, Director. Web, www.hud.gov.

Issues policies and sets standards for environmental and land-use planning and environmental management practices. Oversees HUD implementation of requirements on environment, historic preservation, archeology, flood plain management, coastal zone management, sole source aquifers, farmland protection, endangered species, airport clear zones, explosive hazards, radon, and noise.

Interior Dept., *1849 C St. N.W., #6156 20240; (202) 208-7351. Fax, (202) 208-6956. Bruce Babbitt, Secretary; David Hayes, Deputy Secretary. Information, (202) 208-3100. Library, (202) 208-5815. Locator, (202) 208-3100. Web, www.doi.gov.*

Principal U.S. conservation agency. Manages most federal land; responsible for conservation and development of mineral and water resources; responsible for con-

ENVIRONMENTAL PROTECTION AGENCY

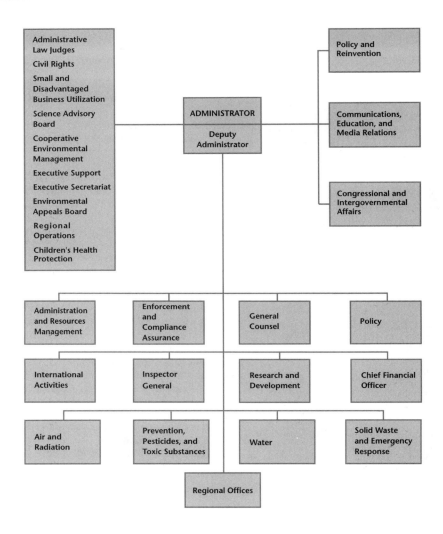

servation, development, and use of fish and wildlife resources; operates recreation programs for federal parks, refuges, and public lands; preserves and administers the nation's scenic and historic areas; reclaims arid lands in the West through irrigation; administers native American lands and relationships with tribal governments.

Interior Dept., *Policy Analysis, 1849 C St. N.W., #4411, MS 4426 20240; (202) 208-5978. Fax, (202) 208-4867. James Pipkin, Director. Web, www.doi.gov.*

Analyzes how policies affect the department; makes recommendations and develops policy options for resolving natural resource problems.

Justice Dept., *Environment and Natural Resources, 950 Pennsylvania Ave. N.W., #2718 20530-0001; (202) 514-2701. Fax, (202) 514-0557. Lois J. Schiffer, Assistant Attorney General. Web, www.usdoj.gov/enrd.*

Handles civil suits involving the federal government in all areas of the environment and natural resources; handles some criminal suits involving pollution control.

National Institute of Environmental Health Sciences *(National Institutes of Health), Bldg. 31, #B1C02, 31 Center Dr., MSC 2256, Bethesda, MD 20892-2256; (301) 496-3511. Fax, (301) 496-0563. Kenneth Olden,*

Director; Chris Schonwalder, Director, International Programs. Web, www.niehs.nih.gov.

Conducts and supports fundamental research on the effects of chemical, biological, and physical factors in the environment on human health. Participates in international research. (Most operations located in Research Triangle Park, N.C.)

National Oceanic and Atmospheric Administration (NOAA), *(Commerce Dept.),* *14th St. and Constitution Ave. N.W. 20230; (202) 482-3436. Fax, (202) 408-9674. D. James Baker, Under Secretary. Information, (202) 482-2000. Press, (202) 482-6090. Web, www.noaa.gov.*

Conducts research in marine and atmospheric sciences; issues weather forecasts and warnings vital to public safety and the national economy; surveys resources of the sea; analyzes economic aspects of fisheries operations; develops and implements policies on international fisheries; provides states with grants to conserve coastal zone areas; protects marine mammals; maintains a national environmental center with data from satellite observations and other sources including meteorological, oceanic, geodetic, and seismological data centers; provides colleges and universities with grants for research, education, and marine advisory services; prepares and provides nautical and aeronautical charts and maps.

National Oceanic and Atmospheric Administration *(Commerce Dept.),* *National Environmental Satellite, Data, and Information Service, 1335 East-West Hwy., Silver Spring, MD 20910; (301) 713-3578. Fax, (301) 713-1249. Gregory W. Withee, Assistant Administrator. Web, www.nesdis.noaa.gov.*

Provides satellite observations of the environment by operating polar orbiting and geostationary satellites; develops satellite techniques; increases the utilization of satellite data in environmental services.

National Science and Technology Council *(Executive Office of the President),* *Dwight D. Eisenhower Executive Office Bldg., #435 20502; (202) 456-6100. Fax, (202) 456-6026. Neal Lane, Chair. General e-mail, information@ostp.eop.gov. Web, www.whitehouse.gov/WH/EOP/OSTP/NSTC/html/charge.html.*

Coordinates research and development activities and programs that involve more than one federal agency. Activities concern earth sciences, materials, forestry research, and radiation policy.

Office of Science and Technology Policy *(Executive Office of the President),* *Environment, Dwight D. Eisenhower Executive Office Bldg., #443 20502; (202) 456-6202. Fax, (202) 456-6025. Rosina Bierbaum, Associate Director.*

Web, www.whitehouse.gov/WH/EOP/OSTP/html/OSTP_Home.html.

Provides the president with policy analysis and assistance on issues related to the environment and natural resources.

Transportation Dept., *Environmental Policies Team, 400 7th St. S.W., #10309 20590-0001; (202) 366-4861. Fax, (202) 366-7610. Camille Mittelholtz, Team Leader. Web, www.dot.gov.*

Develops environmental policy and makes recommendations to the secretary; monitors Transportation Dept. implementation of environmental legislation; serves as liaison with other federal agencies and state and local governments on environmental matters related to transportation.

U.S. Geological Survey *(Interior Dept.),* *12201 Sunrise Valley Dr., Reston, VA 20192; (703) 648-7411. Fax, (703) 648-4454. Charles G. Groat, Director. Library, (703) 648-4302. Press, (703) 648-4460. Outreach, (703) 648-4460. Web, www.usgs.gov.*

Provides reports, maps, and databases that describe and analyze water, energy, biological, and mineral resources; the land surface; and the underlying geological structure and dynamic processes of the earth.

CONGRESS

General Accounting Office, *Energy, Resources, and Science, 441 G St. N.W., #2T23 20548; (202) 512-3841. Fax, (202) 512-6880. Jim Wells, Director.*

Independent, nonpartisan agency in the legislative branch that audits, analyzes, and reports on efficiency and effectiveness of Interior Dept. programs concerned with managing natural resources.

General Accounting Office, *Environmental Protection Issues, 441 G St. N.W., #2085 20548; (202) 512-6111. Fax, (202) 512-9925. Peter F. Guerrero, Director.*

Independent, nonpartisan agency in the legislative branch. Audits, analyzes, and evaluates programs of the Environmental Protection Agency; makes reports available to the public.

House Appropriations Committee, *Subcommittee on Commerce, Justice, State, and Judiciary, H309 CAP 20515; (202) 225-3351. Rep. Harold Rogers, R-Ky., Chair; Jim Kulikowski, Staff Director. Web, www.house.gov/appropriations.*

Jurisdiction over legislation to appropriate funds for the Marine Mammal Commission and the Commerce Dept., including the National Oceanic and Atmospheric Administration.

House Appropriations Committee, *Subcommittee on Energy and Water Development, 2362 RHOB 20515; (202) 225-3421. Rep. Ron Packard, R-Calif., Chair; Robert Schmidt, Staff Director. Web, www.house.gov/ appropriations.*

Jurisdiction over legislation to appropriate funds for the Bureau of Reclamation in the Interior Dept., the federal power marketing administrations in the Energy Dept., the civil programs of the Army Corps of Engineers, the Tennessee Valley Authority, and related agencies.

House Appropriations Committee, *Subcommittee on Interior, B308 RHOB 20515; (202) 225-3081. Fax, (202) 225-9069. Rep. Ralph Regula, R-Ohio, Chair; Deborah A. Weatherly, Clerk. Web, www.house.gov/appropriations.*

Jurisdiction over legislation to appropriate funds for the Interior Dept. (except the Bureau of Reclamation), the Forest Service in the Agriculture Dept., clean coal technology, fossil energy, naval petroleum and oil shale reserves, and other natural resources-related services and programs.

House Appropriations Committee, *Subcommittee on VA, HUD, and Independent Agencies, H143 CAP 20515; (202) 225-3241. Rep. James T. Walsh, R-N.Y., Chair; Frank Cushing, Staff Director. Web, www.house.gov/ appropriations.*

Jurisdiction over legislation to appropriate funds for the Environmental Protection Agency, Office of Environmental Policy, Council on Environmental Quality, National Science Foundation, and other environment-related services and programs.

House Commerce Committee, *Subcommittee on Finance and Hazardous Materials, 2125 RHOB 20515; (202) 225-2927. Fax, (202) 225-1919. Rep. Michael G. Oxley, R-Ohio, Chair; James E. Derderian, Staff Director. General e-mail, commerce@mail.house.gov. Web, www. house.gov/commerce.*

Jurisdiction over legislation on solid waste disposal, pollution, toxic substances, noise pollution control, and hazardous materials (except EPA research and development programs). Jurisdiction over the Comprehensive Environmental Response, Compensation, and Liability Act (the Superfund), the Resource Conservation and Recovery Act, and the Toxic Substances Control Act (jurisdiction shared with House Science Committee).

House Commerce Committee, *Subcommittee on Health and the Environment, 2125 RHOB 20515; (202) 225-2927. Fax, (202) 225-1919. Rep. Michael Bilirakis, R-Fla., Chair; James E. Derderian, Staff Director. General e-mail, commerce@mail.house.gov. Web, www.house.gov/ commerce.*

Jurisdiction over legislation concerning environmental affairs, including global warming.

House Government Reform Committee, *Subcommittee on National Economic Growth, Natural Resources, and Regulatory Affairs, B377 RHOB 20515; (202) 225-4407. Fax, (202) 225-2441. Rep. David M. McIntosh, R-Ind., Chair; Marlo Lewis, Staff Director. Web, www.house.gov/reform.*

Oversight of the Interior Dept., the Environmental Protection Agency, the Office of Environmental Policy, the Nuclear Regulatory Commission, the U.S. Fish and Wildlife Service, and the Council on Environmental Quality.

House Resources Committee, *1324 LHOB 20515-6201; (202) 225-2761. Fax, (202) 225-5929. Rep. Don Young, R-Alaska, Chair; Lloyd Jones, Staff Director. General e-mail, resources.committee@mail.house.gov. Web, www.house.gov/resources.*

Jurisdiction over legislation on natural resource issues, including water control.

House Resources Committee, *Subcommittee on Fisheries, Conservation, Wildlife, and Oceans, H2-187 FHOB 20515; (202) 226-0200. Fax, (202) 225-1542. Rep. H. James Saxton, R-N.J., Chair; Harry Burroughs, Staff Director. General e-mail, fishery.subcommittee@mail. house.gov. Web, www.house.gov/resources/fisheries.*

Jurisdiction over legislation on many natural resource issues, including conservation, marine sanctuaries, and wildlife resources.

House Science Committee, *Subcommittee on Energy and Environment, 389 FHOB 20515; (202) 225-9662. Fax, (202) 226-6983. Rep. Ken Calvert, R-Calif., Chair; Harlan Watson, Staff Director. Web, www.house.gov/ science.*

Jurisdiction over legislation on research and development related to natural resources, including Energy Dept. environmental science activities and Environmental Protection Agency programs concerning air, water, noise, and solid waste pollution. Jurisdiction over research and development programs of the National Environmental Policy Act, the Comprehensive Environmental Response, Compensation, and Liability Act (the Superfund), the Resource Conservation and Recovery Act, and the Toxic Substances Control Act (jurisdiction shared with House Commerce Committee).

House Small Business Committee, *2361 RHOB 20515; (202) 225-5821. Rep. James M. Talent, R-Mo., Chair; Mark Strand, Chief of Staff. General e-mail, smbiz@mail.house.gov. Web, www.house.gov/smbiz.*

Studies and makes recommendations on environmental and pollution issues as they relate to small business.

Senate Agriculture, Nutrition, and Forestry Committee, *Subcommittee on Forestry, Conservation, and Rural Revitalization, SR-328A 20510; (202) 224-2752. Fax, (202) 224-1725. Sen. Larry E. Craig, R-Idaho, Chair; Dan Whiting, Staff Contact. Web, agriculture.senate.gov.*

Jurisdiction over legislation on many natural resources issues, including conservation, forestry, and water control; oversight of the Interior Dept. and the Agriculture Dept.'s Forest Service.

Senate Appropriations Committee, *Subcommittee on Commerce, Justice, State, and Judiciary, S-146A CAP 20510; (202) 224-7277. Sen. Judd Gregg, R-N.H., Chair; Jim Morhard, Clerk. Web, appropriations.senate.gov/ commerce.*

Jurisdiction over legislation to appropriate funds for the Marine Mammal Commission and the Commerce Dept., including the National Oceanic and Atmospheric Administration.

Senate Appropriations Committee, *Subcommittee on Energy and Water Development, SD-127 20510; (202) 224-7260. Sen. Pete V. Domenici, R-N.M., Chair; Clay Sell, Clerk. Web, appropriations.senate.gov/energy.*

Jurisdiction over legislation to appropriate funds for the Bureau of Reclamation in the Interior Dept., the federal power marketing administrations in the Energy Dept., the civil programs of the Army Corps of Engineers, the Tennessee Valley Authority, and related agencies.

Senate Appropriations Committee, *Subcommittee on Interior, SD-131 20510; (202) 224-7233. Sen. Slade Gorton, R-Wash., Chair; Bruce Evans, Clerk. Web, appropriations.senate.gov/interior.*

Jurisdiction over legislation to appropriate funds for the Interior Dept.; the Forest Service in the Agriculture Dept.; the National Park Service; clean coal technology; fossil energy; naval petroleum and oil shale reserves; and other natural resources-related services and programs.

Senate Appropriations Committee, *Subcommittee on VA, HUD, and Independent Agencies, SD-130 20510; (202) 224-7211. Sen. Christopher S. Bond, R-Mo., Chair; Jon Kamarck, Staff Director. Web, appropriations.senate. gov/vahud.*

Jurisdiction over legislation to appropriate funds for the Environmental Protection Agency, Office of Environmental Policy, Council on Environmental Quality, National Science Foundation, and other environment-related services and programs.

Senate Energy and Natural Resources Committee, *SD-364 20510; (202) 224-4971. Fax, (202) 224-6163. Sen. Frank H. Murkowski, R-Alaska, Chair; Andrew Lundquist, Staff Director. General e-mail, committee@energy.senate. gov. Web, energy.senate.gov.*

Jurisdiction over legislation on many aspects of natural resources, including research and development.

Senate Environment and Public Works Committee, *SD-410 20510; (202) 224-6176. Fax, (202) 224-5167. Sen. Robert C. Smith, R-N.H., Chair; Dave Conover, Staff Director. Web, epw.senate.gov.*

Jurisdiction over most legislation relating to environmental affairs, including global warming and Environmental Protection Agency research and development programs concerning air, water, noise, solid waste, hazardous materials, and toxic substances; jurisdiction over legislation relating to the National Environmental Policy Act, the Comprehensive Environmental Response, Compensation, and Liability Act (the Superfund), the Resource Conservation and Recovery Act, and the Toxic Substances Control Act. Oversight of the Environmental Protection Agency, the Office of Environmental Policy, the Nuclear Regulatory Commission, the U.S. Fish and Wildlife Service, and the Council on Environmental Quality.

Senate Small Business Committee, *SR-428A 20510; (202) 224-5175. Fax, (202) 224-4885. Sen. Christopher S. Bond, R-Mo., Chair; Emilia DiSanto, Staff Director. Web, sbc.senate.gov.*

Studies and makes recommendations on environmental and pollution issues as they relate to small businesses.

NONPROFIT

American Bar Assn. (ABA), *Standing Committee on Environmental Law, 740 15th St. N.W. 20005; (202) 662-1693. Fax, (202) 638-3844. Elissa Lichtenstein, Director. Web, www.abanet.org/publicserv/environmental.html.*

Conducts domestic and international projects in environmental law and policy; coordinates environmental law activities throughout the ABA.

Americans for the Environment, *1400 16th St. N.W., Box 24 20036-2266; (202) 797-6665. Fax, (202) 797-6563. Roy Morgan, President. General e-mail, afore@afore.org. Web, www.afore.org.*

Seeks to protect natural resources by influencing public policy. Encourages citizen involvement in ballot measures and the electoral process; offers training, education, and information in environmental fields and in political campaign management.

Citizens for a Sound Economy, *1250 H St. N.W., #700 20005-3908; (202) 783-3870. Fax, (202) 783-4687. Paul Beckner, President. Web, www.cse.org.*

Education and research organization that seeks market-oriented solutions to environmental problems. Develops initiatives to balance environmental and economic considerations; supports private efforts to manage wildlife habitats.

Concern, *1794 Columbia Rd. N.W. 20009; (202) 328-8160. Fax, (202) 387-3378. Susan Boyd, Executive Director. General e-mail, concern@igc.org. Web, www. sustainable.org.*

Environmental education organization interested in issues such as sustainable communities, global warming, energy, agriculture, pesticides, water resources, and waste reduction.

Conservation Fund, *1800 N. Kent St., #1120, Arlington, VA 22209-2156; (703) 525-6300. Fax, (703) 525-4610. John F. Turner, President. Web, www.conservationfund.org.*

Creates partnerships with the private sector, non-profit organizations, and public agencies to promote land and water conservation.

Co-op America, *1612 K St. N.W., #600 20006; (202) 872-5307. Fax, (202) 331-8166. Alisa Gravitz, Executive Director. Information, (800) 584-7336. General e-mail, info@coopamerica.org. Web, www.coopamerica.org.*

Educates consumers and businesses about social and environmental responsibility. Publishes a directory of environmentally responsible businesses, a financial planning guide for investment, and boycott information.

Earth Share, *3400 International Dr. N.W., #2K 20008; (202) 537-7100. Fax, (202) 537-7101. Kalman Stein, President. Information, (800) 875-3863. General e-mail, info@earthshare.org. Web, www.earthshare.org.*

Federation of environmental and conservation organizations. Works with government and private payroll deduction programs to solicit contributions to member organizations for environmental research, education, and community programs. Provides information on establishing environmental giving options in the workplace.

Edison Electric Institute, *701 Pennsylvania Ave. N.W. 20004; (202) 508-5000. Fax, (202) 508-5759. Thomas R. Kuhn, President. Web, www.eei.org.*

Membership: investor-owned electric power companies and electric utility holding companies. Interests include electric utility operation and concerns, including conservation and energy management, energy analysis, resources and environment, cogeneration and renewable energy resources, nuclear power, and research. Library open to the public by appointment.

Environmental and Energy Study Institute, *122 C St. N.W., #700 20001-2109; (202) 628-1400. Fax, (202) 628-1825. Carol Werner, Director. General e-mail, eesi@eesi.org. Web, www.eesi.org.*

Nonpartisan policy education and analysis group established by members of Congress to foster informed debate on environmental and energy issues. Interests include policies for sustainable development, energy, climate change, transportation, and fiscal policy reform.

Environmental Council of the States, *444 N. Capitol St. N.W., #445 20001; (202) 624-3660. Fax, (202) 624-3666. Robert E. Roberts, Executive Director. General e-mail, ecos@sso.org. Web, www.sso.org/ecos.*

Works to improve the environment by providing for the exchange of ideas and experiences among states and territories; fosters cooperation and coordination among environmental management professionals.

Environmental Defense Fund, Washington Office, *1875 Connecticut Ave. N.W., #1016 20009-5728; (202) 387-3500. Fax, (202) 234-6049. Senta Boardley, Office Manager. Web, www.edf.org.*

Citizens' interest group staffed by lawyers, economists, and scientists. Takes legal action on environmental issues; provides information on pollution prevention, environmental health, wetlands, toxic substances, acid rain, tropical rain forests, and litigation of water pollution standards. (Headquarters in New York.)

Environmental Law Institute, *1616 P St. N.W., #200 20036; (202) 939-3800. Fax, (202) 939-3868. J. William Futrell, President. General e-mail, law@eli.org. Web, www.eli.org.*

Research and education organization with an interdisciplinary staff of lawyers, economists, scientists, and journalists. Publishes materials on environmental issues, sponsors education and training courses, issues policy recommendations, and cosponsors conferences on environmental law.

Environmental Media Services, *1320 18th St., 5th Floor 20036; (202) 463-6670. Fax, (202) 463-6671. Arlie Schardt, President; Chris DeCardy, Executive Director. Web, www.ems.org.*

Advocates expanded and improved coverage of environmental issues in the nation's media. Conducts educational workshops.

Environmental Working Group, *1718 Connecticut Ave. N.W., #600 20009; (202) 667-6982. Fax, (202) 232-2592. Kenneth A. Cook, President. General e-mail, info@ewg.org. Web, www.ewg.org.*

Research and advocacy organization that studies and reports on the presence of herbicides and pesticides in food and drinking water. Monitors legislation and regulations.

Friends of the Earth, *1025 Vermont Ave. N.W., #300 20005-6303; (202) 783-7400. Fax, (202) 783-0444. Brent Blackwelder, President. General e-mail, foe@foe.org. Web, www.foe.org.*

Environmental advocacy group concerned with environmental, public health, and energy-related issues, including clean air, water, and groundwater; energy conservation; international water projects; transportation of hazardous wastes; global warming; and toxic substances and pesticides. Specializes in federal budget and tax issues related to the environment; ozone layer and ground water protection; and World Bank and International Monetary Fund reform. Library open to the public by appointment.

Izaak Walton League of America, *707 Conservation Lane, Gaithersburg, MD 20878-2983; (301) 548-0150. Fax, (301) 548-0146. Paul W. Hansen, Executive Director. General e-mail, general@iwla.org. Web, www.iwla.org.*

Grassroots organization that promotes conservation of natural resources and the environment. Interests include air and water pollution and wildlife habitat protection. Provides information on acid rain and stream cleanup efforts at the local level.

League of Conservation Voters, *1920 L St. N.W., #800 20036; (202) 785-8683. Fax, (202) 835-0491. Debra J. Callahan, President. Web, www.lcv.org.*

Works to support the environmental movement by helping elect environmentally concerned candidates to public office.

League of Women Voters Education Fund, *Natural Resources, 1730 M St. N.W., #1000 20036; (202) 429-1965. Fax, (202) 429-0854. Jane Gruenebaum, Director. Web, www.lwv.org.*

Education foundation affiliated with the League of Women Voters. Promotes citizen understanding of nuclear and solid waste issues; holds regional workshops to educate community leaders on these issues.

National Assn. of Conservation Districts, *509 Capitol Court N.E. 20002-4937; (202) 547-6223. Fax, (202) 547-6450. Ernest C. Shea, Chief Executive Officer. Web, www.nacdnet.org.*

Membership: conservation districts (local subdivisions of state government). Works to promote the conservation of land, forests, and other natural resources. Interests include erosion and sediment control; water quality; forestry, water, flood plain, and range management; rural development; and urban and community conservation.

National Audubon Society, *Public Policy, Washington Office, 1901 Pennsylvania Ave. N.W., #1100 20006; (202) 861-2242. Fax, (202) 861-4290. Dan Beard, Senior Vice President. Web, www.audubon.org.*

Citizens' interest group that promotes environmental preservation. Provides information on water resources, public lands, rangelands, forests, parks, wildlife and marine conservation, and the national wildlife refuge system. (Headquarters in New York.)

National Environmental Development Assn., *818 Connecticut Ave. N.W., 2nd Floor 20006; (202) 289-0966. Fax, (202) 289-1327. Steve Hellem, Director. General e-mail, strat@comm.net.*

Membership: corporations and individuals. Provides information on balancing environmental and economic needs. Manages projects concerning clean air regulation, new federal and state environmental relationships, and international environmental advocacy.

National Environmental Trust, *1200 18th St. N.W., #500 20036; (202) 887-8800. Fax, (202) 887-8877. Phil Clapp, President. General e-mail, netinfo@environet.org. Web, environet.policy.net.*

Organization that identifies and publicizes environmental issues at the national and local levels. Interests include climate change, endangered species, hazardous chemicals, and campaign finance reform; opposes efforts to weaken environmental laws. Monitors legislation and regulations.

National Wilderness Institute, *P.O. Box 25766 20007; (703) 836-7404. Fax, (703) 836-7405. Robert Gordon, Executive Director. General e-mail, nwi@nwi.org. Web, www.nwi.org.*

Works to inform the public, the media, educators, and public officials about environmental issues including endangered species, land use rights, and environmental regulations.

National Wildlife Federation, *8925 Leesburg Pike, Vienna, VA 22184; (703) 790-4000. Fax, (703) 790-4040. Mark Van Putten, President. General e-mail, info@nwf. org. Web, www.nwf.org.*

Promotes conservation of natural resources; provides information on the environment and resource management; takes legal action on environmental issues. Laurel Ridge Conservation Education Center in Vienna, Va., provides educational materials and outdoor programs.

Natural Resources Defense Council, *Washington Office, 1200 New York Ave. N.W., #400 20005-4709; (202) 289-6868. Fax, (202) 289-1060. Leslie Rosenberg, Office Manager. General e-mail, nycnrdcinfo@nrdc.org. Web, www.nrdc.org.*

Environmental organization staffed by lawyers and scientists who undertake litigation and research. Interests include air, water, land use, forests, toxic materials, natural resources management and conservation, preservation of endangered plant species, and ozone pollution. (Headquarters in New York.)

Nature Conservancy, *4245 N. Fairfax Dr., #100, Arlington, VA 22203; (703) 841-5300. Fax, (703) 841-1283. John C. Sawhill, President. Web, www.tnc.org.*

Acquires land to protect endangered species and habitats; maintains international system of natural sanctuaries; operates the Heritage Program, a cooperative effort with state governments to identify and inventory threatened and endangered plants and animals.

Population-Environment Balance, *2000 P St. N.W., #600 20036; (202) 955-5700. Fax, (202) 955-6161. Maria Sepulveda, Executive Director. General e-mail, uspop@balance.org. Web, www.balance.org.*

Grassroots organization that advocates U.S. population stabilization to safeguard the environment.

Renew America, *1200 18th St. N.W., #1100 20036; (202) 721-1545. Fax, (202) 467-5780. Anna Slafer, Executive Director. General e-mail, renewamerica@counterpart.org. Web, www.crest.org/renew_america.*

Advances solutions to environmental problems by encouraging the replication of successful community-based initiatives.

Resources for the Future, *1616 P St. N.W. 20036; (202) 328-5000. Fax, (202) 939-3460. Paul Portney, President. Library, (202) 328-5089. General e-mail, info@rff.org. Web, www.rff.org.*

Engages in research and education on environmental and natural resource issues, including forestry, multiple use of public lands, costs and benefits of pollution control, endangered species, environmental risk management, energy and national security, and climate resources. Interests include hazardous waste, the Superfund, and biodiversity. Library open to the public.

Sierra Club, *Washington Office, 408 C St. N.E. 20002; (202) 547-1141. Fax, (202) 547-6009. Debbie Sease, Legislative Director. Legislative hotline, (202) 675-2394. General e-mail, information@sierraclub.org. Web, www.sierraclub.org.*

Citizens' interest group that promotes protection of natural resources. Interests include the Clean Air Act; the Arctic National Wildlife Refuge; protection of national forests, parks, and wilderness; toxins; global warming; promotion of responsible international trade; and international development lending reform. Monitors legislation and regulations. (Headquarters in San Francisco.)

Union of Concerned Scientists, *Government Relations, Washington Office, 1616 P St. N.W., #310 20036; (202) 332-0900. Fax, (202) 332-0905. Alden Meyer, Director; Todd Perry, Washington Representative for Arms Control and International Security. General e-mail, ucs@ucsusa.org. Web, www.ucsusa.org.*

Membership: scientists and others who advocate a comprehensive approach to resolving global environmental and resource concerns. Educates and mobilizes citizens on the linkages between resource depletion, environmental degradation, climate changes, consumption patterns, and population growth. Fosters cooperative efforts between the scientific, environmental, and religious communities through the National Religious Partnership for the Environment. (Headquarters in Cambridge, Mass.)

U.S. Chamber of Commerce, *Environmental and Regulatory Affairs, 1615 H St. N.W. 20062-2000; (202) 659-6000. Fax, (202) 463-5327. Thomas J. Donohue, President. Web, www.uschamber.org.*

Monitors operations of federal departments and agencies responsible for environmental programs, policies, regulatory issues, and food safety. Analyzes and evaluates legislation and regulations that affect the environment.

U.S. Public Interest Research Group, *218 D St. S.E. 20003; (202) 546-9707. Fax, (202) 546-2461. Gene Karpinski, Executive Director. General e-mail, uspirg@pirg.org. Web, www.pirg.org.*

Coordinates grassroots efforts to advance environmental and consumer protection laws; conducts research on environmental issues, including toxic and solid waste, air and water pollution, pesticides, endangered species, forest and wildlife preservation, alternative energy sources, and energy conservation; compiles reports and disseminates information on such issues; drafts and monitors environmental laws; testifies on behalf of proposed environmental legislation.

Wilderness Society, *900 17th St. N.W. 20006-2506; (202) 833-2300. Fax, (202) 429-3958. William H. Meadows III, President. Information, (202) 833-2300. General e-mail, tws@tws.org. Web, www.wilderness.org.*

Promotes preservation of wilderness and the responsible management of all federal lands, including national parks and forests, wilderness areas, wildlife refuges, and land administered by the Interior Dept.'s Bureau of Land Management.

International Issues

AGENCIES

Environmental Protection Agency, *International Activities,* 1300 Pennsylvania Ave. N.W., #31207 20004 (mailing address: 401 M St. S.W., MC 2610R 20460); (202) 564-6600. Fax, (202) 565-2407. William Nitze, Assistant Administrator. Web, www.epa.gov.

Coordinates the agency's work on international environmental issues and programs, including management of bilateral agreements and participation in multilateral organizations and negotiations.

International Trade Administration *(Commerce Dept.),* **Environmental Technologies Exports,** 14th St. and Constitution Ave. N.W., #1003 20230; (202) 482-5225. Fax, (202) 482-5665. Carlos Montoulieu, Deputy Assistant Secretary (Acting). Web, www.infoserv2.ita.doc.gov/ete.

Works to facilitate and increase exports of U.S. environmental technologies, including both goods and services. Conducts market analysis, business counseling, and trade promotion.

State Dept., *Ecology and Terrestrial Conservation,* 2201 C St. N.W., #4333 20520; (202) 647-2418. Fax, (202) 736-7351. Barbara Tobias, Director; Stephanie J. Caswell, Deputy Director. Web, www.state.gov.

Represents the United States in international affairs relating to natural resources. Interests include wildlife, tropical forests, and biological diversity and decertification.

State Dept., *Environmental Policy,* 2201 C St. N.W., #4325 20520; (202) 647-9266. Fax, (202) 647-5947. Daniel Fantozzi, Director. Web, www.state.gov.

Advances U.S. interests internationally regarding multilateral environmental organizations, chemical wastes and other pollutants, and bilateral and regional environmental policies.

State Dept., *Oceans and International Environmental and Scientific Affairs,* 2201 C St. N.W., #7831 20520-7818; (202) 647-1554. Fax, (202) 647-0217. David Sandalow, Assistant Secretary. Press, (202) 647-3486. Web, www.state.gov.

Concerned with foreign policy as it affects natural resources and the environment, human health, the global climate, energy production, and oceans and fisheries.

U.S.-Asia Environmental Partnership, 1720 Eye St. N.W., #700 20006; (202) 835-0333. Fax, (202) 835-0366. Peter Kim, Director. General e-mail, usasia@usaep.org. Web, www.usaep.org.

Interagency program, led by the Agency for International Development (AID), which uses U.S. technology and services to help address environmental degradation and sustainable development issues in Asia and the Pacific. Focuses on pulp and paper, food processing, electroplating, petrochemical, and textile industries. (Secretariat located within the Asia and Near East Bureau at AID.)

CONGRESS

House International Relations Committee, *Subcommittee on International Economic Policy and Trade,* 257 FHOB 20515; (202) 225-3345. Fax, (202) 225-0432. Rep. Ileana Ros-Lehtinen, R-Fla., Chair; Mauricio Tamargo, Staff Director. Web, www.house.gov/international_relations.

Jurisdiction over legislation on international environmental agreements and policy (jurisdiction shared with Subcommittee on International Operations and Human Rights).

Senate Foreign Relations Committee, *Subcommittee on International Economic Policy, Export, and Trade Promotion,* SD-450 20510; (202) 224-4651. Fax, (202) 224-0836. Sen. Chuck Hagel, R-Neb., Chair; Steve Biegun, Staff Director. Web, foreign.senate.gov.

Jurisdiction over legislation on international environmental agreements and policy, including international marine affairs in the Antarctic and Arctic areas.

INTERNATIONAL ORGANIZATIONS

International Joint Commission, United States and Canada, *U.S. Section,* 1250 23rd St. N.W., #100 20440; (202) 736-9000. Fax, (202) 736-9015. Gerald Galloway, Secretary (Acting).

Deals with disputes between the United States and Canada on transboundary water and air resources. Investigates issues upon request of the governments of the United States and Canada. Reviews applications for water resource projects. (Canadian section in Ottawa.)

Organization of American States (OAS), *Sustainable Development and Environment,* 1889 F St. N.W., #340-I 20006; (202) 458-3567. Fax, (202) 458-3560. Richard Meganck, Director. Web, www.oas.org.

Provides support to OAS technical cooperation projects. Promotes integrated and sustainable development of natural resources; interests include international river basins, border areas, coastal zones, and emerging trade corridors.

World Conservation Union, *U.S. Office, Washington Office,* 1630 Connecticut Ave. N.W., 3rd Floor 20009;

(202) 387-4826. Fax, (202) 387-4823. Scott Hajost, Executive Director. General e-mail, postmaster@iucnus.org. Web, www.iucn.org.

Membership: world governments, their environmental agencies, and nongovernmental organizations. Studies conservation issues from local to global levels; interests include protected areas, forests, oceans, polar regions, biodiversity, species survival, environmental law, sustainable use of resources, and the impact of trade on the environment. (Headquarters in Gland, Switzerland.)

NONPROFIT

Antarctica Project, *1630 Connecticut Ave. N.W., 3rd Floor 20009 (mailing address: P.O. Box 76920 20013); (202) 234-2480. Fax, (202) 234-2482. Beth Clark, Director. General e-mail, antarctica@igc.org. Web, www.asoc. org.*

Promotes effective implementation of the Antarctic Treaty System; works to protect the environment of the Antarctic continent. Interests include depletion of ozone in polar regions.

Conservation International, *2501 M St. N.W., #200 20037; (202) 429-5660. Fax, (202) 887-5188. Russell Mittermeier, President. Web, www.conservation.org.*

Works to conserve tropical rain forests through economic development; promotes exchange of debt relief for conservation programs that involve local people and organizations. Provides private groups and governments with information and technical advice on conservation efforts; supports conservation data gathering in Latin America, Africa, Asia, and the Caribbean.

Global Climate Coalition, *1275 K St. N.W., #890 20005; (202) 682-9161. Fax, (202) 638-1043. Glenn Kelly, President. General e-mail, gcc@globalclimate.org. Web, www.globalclimate.org.*

Membership: business trade associations and private companies. Promotes scientific research on global climate change; analyzes economic and social impacts of policy options; produces educational materials and conducts programs.

Greenpeace USA, *Washington Office, 1436 U St. N.W. 20009; (202) 462-1177. Fax, (202) 462-4507. Kristen Engberg, Executive Director. General e-mail, greenpeace.usa@ wdc.greenpeace.org. Web, www.greenpeaceusa.org.*

Seeks to protect the environment through research, education, and grassroots organizing. Interests include chemical and nuclear waste dumping, solid and hazardous waste disposal, and protection of marine mammals and endangered species. Supports the establishment of Antarctica as a world park, free of industry, military presence, and nuclear power and weaponry. Monitors

legislation and regulations. (Headquarters in Amsterdam, Netherlands.)

Pinchot Institute for Conservation, *1616 P St. N.W., #100 20036; (202) 797-6580. Fax, (202) 797-6583. V. Alaric Sample, President. General e-mail, pinchot@pinchot.org. Web, www.pinchot.org.*

Seeks to advance the conservation of natural resources throughout the world. Promotes cooperation among resource managers, scientists, policymakers, and the American public. Conducts conservation research.

World Resources Institute, *10 G St. N.E., #800 20002; (202) 729-7600. Fax, (202) 729-7610. Jonathan Lash, President. Press, (202) 729-7745. Web, www.wri.org.*

International organization that conducts research on environmental problems and studies the inter-relationships of natural resources, economic growth, and human needs. Interests include forestry and land use, renewable energy, fisheries, and sustainable agriculture. Assesses environmental policies of aid agencies.

World Wildlife Fund, *1250 24th St. N.W., #400 20037; (202) 293-4800. Fax, (202) 293-9211. Kathryn S. Fuller, President. Web, www.wwf.org.*

Conducts scientific research and analyzes policy on environmental and conservation issues, including pollution reduction, land use, forestry and wetlands management, parks, soil conservation, and sustainable development. Supports projects to promote biological diversity and to save endangered species and their habitats, including tropical forests in Latin America, Asia, and Africa. Awards grants and provides technical assistance to local conservation groups.

Worldwatch Institute, *1776 Massachusetts Ave. N.W., 8th Floor 20036; (202) 452-1999. Fax, (202) 296-7365. Lester R. Brown, President. General e-mail, worldwatch@ worldwatch.org. Web, www.worldwatch.org.*

Research organization that focuses on interdisciplinary approach to solving global environmental problems. Interests include natural resources and human needs, environmental threats to food production, and quality of life.

 ## ANIMALS AND PLANTS

See also Livestock and Poultry (chap. 2); Zoology (chap. 17)

AGENCIES

Animal and Plant Health Inspection Service *(Agriculture Dept.), Animal Care, 4700 River Rd., Unit 84,*

Riverdale, MD 20737-1234; (301) 734-7833. Fax, (301) 734-4978. Dr. William Ron DeHaven, Deputy Administrator. Web, www.aphis.usda.gov/ac.

Administers laws that regulate the handling, breeding, and care of animals raised for sale, used in research, transported commercially, or exhibited to the public. Conducts inspections; works to prevent neglect and inhumane treatment.

Animal and Plant Health Inspection Service *(Agriculture Dept.), Investigative and Enforcement Services,* 4700 River Rd., Unit 85, Riverdale, MD 20737-1234; (301) 734-8684. Fax, (301) 734-4328. Alan Christian, Director (Acting). Web, www.aphis.usda.gov/ies.

Provides investigative and enforcement services and leadership, direction, and support for compliance activities within the service.

Food and Drug Administration *(Health and Human Services Dept.), Center for Veterinary Medicine,* 7500 Standish Pl., Rockville, MD 20855-2764; (301) 594-1740. Fax, (301) 594-1830. Dr. Stephen F. Sundlof, Director. Web, www.fda.gov/cvm.

Regulates the manufacture and marketing of drugs, food additives, feed ingredients, and devices for animals, including both livestock and pets. Conducts research; works to ensure animal health and the safety of food derived from animals.

National Institutes of Health *(Health and Human Services Dept.), Protection from Research Risks,* 6100 Executive Blvd., #3B01, Rockville, MD 20892-7507; (301) 496-7005. Fax, (301) 402-2071. Gary B. Ellis, Director. Human subjects, (301) 496-7041. Animal welfare, (301) 496-7163. Web, www.grants.nih.gov/grants/oprr/oprr.htm.

Monitors the use of animals in research to ensure that programs and procedures comply with Public Health Service and Health and Human Services Dept. (HHS) regulations; conducts and develops educational programs and materials; evaluates the effectiveness of HHS policies and programs for the humane care and use of laboratory animals; helps other organizations address ethical issues in medicine and research.

National Zoological Park *(Smithsonian Institution),* 3001 Connecticut Ave. N.W. 20008; (202) 673-4721. Fax, (202) 673-4607. Michael H. Robinson, Director. Information, (202) 673-4821. Library, (202) 673-4771. TTY, (202) 673-4823. Recorded information, (202) 673-4800. Web, www.si.edu/natzoo.

Maintains a public zoo for exhibiting animals. Conducts research on animal behavior, ecology, nutrition, reproductive physiology, pathology, and veterinary medicine; operates an annex near Front Royal, Va., for the

long-term propagation and study of endangered species. Houses a unit of the Smithsonian Institution library with volumes in zoology, biology, ecology, animal behavior, and veterinary medicine; makes interlibrary loans. Library open to qualified researchers by appointment.

CONGRESS

House Agriculture Committee, *Subcommittee on Livestock and Horticulture,* 1301 LHOB 20515; (202) 225-1564. Fax, (202) 225-4369. Rep. Richard W. Pombo, R-Calif., Chair; Chris D'Arcy, Staff Director. Web, agriculture.house.gov.

Jurisdiction over legislation on inspection and certification of meat, livestock, and poultry. Jurisdiction over animal welfare, including animals used for experimentation.

Senate Agriculture, Nutrition, and Forestry Committee, *Subcommittee on Research, Nutrition, and General Legislation,* SR-328A 20510; (202) 224-2854. Fax, (202) 224-1725. Sen. Peter G. Fitzgerald, R-Ill., Chair; Terry VanDoren, Legislative Assistant. Web, agriculture. senate.gov.

Jurisdiction over legislation on inspection and certification of meat, livestock, and poultry and over animal welfare.

NONPROFIT

American Herbal Products Assn., 8484 Georgia Ave., #370, Silver Spring, MD 20910; (301) 588-1171. Fax, (301) 588-1174. Michael McGuffin, President. General e-mail, ahpa@ahpa.org. Web, www.ahpa.org.

Membership: U.S. companies and individuals that grow, manufacture, and distribute therapeutic herbs and herbal products; and associates in education, law, media, and medicine. Supports research; promotes standardization, consumer protection, competition, and self-regulation in the industry. Monitors legislation and regulations.

American Horse Protection Assn., 1000 29th St. N.W., #T100 20007; (202) 965-0500. Fax, (202) 965-9621. Robin C. Lohnes, Executive Director.

Membership: individuals, corporations, and foundations interested in protecting wild and domestic horses.

American Humane Assn., *Washington Office,* 236 Massachusetts Ave. N.E., #203 20002; (202) 543-7780. Fax, (202) 546-3266. Adele Douglass, Director. General e-mail, ahaeast@aol.com. Web, www.americanhumane.org.

Membership: humane societies, government agencies, and individuals. Monitors legislation and regulations to ensure the proper treatment of all animals;

assists local societies in establishing shelters and investigating cruelty cases; maintains training programs for humane society personnel; assists in public school education programs. (Headquarters in Denver.)

American Society for the Prevention of Cruelty to Animals, *Washington Legislative Office, Washington Office,* 1755 Massachusetts Ave. N.W., #418 20036; (202) 232-5020. Fax, (202) 797-8947. Nancy Blaney, Director. Web, www.aspca.org.

Works for the humane treatment and protection of both domestic and wild animals. Interests include animal adoption and spaying and neutering of pets. Monitors legislation and regulations. (Headquarters in New York.)

American Veterinary Medical Assn., *Governmental Relations, Washington Office,* 1101 Vermont Ave. N.W., #710 20005-3521; (202) 789-0007. Fax, (202) 842-4360. Niall Finnegan, Director. General e-mail, avmagrg@avma.org. Web, www.avma.org.

Monitors legislation and regulations affecting veterinary medicine. (Headquarters in Schaumburg, Ill.)

Americans for Medical Progress Educational Foundation, 421 King St., #401, Alexandria, VA 22314-3121; (703) 836-9595. Fax, (703) 836-9594. Jacqueline Calnan, President. General e-mail, ampef@aol.com. Web, www.amprogress.org.

Seeks to promote and protect animal-based medical research. Serves as a media resource by fact-checking claims of animal rights groups. Conducts public education campaign on the link between animal research and medical advances.

Animal Health Institute, 1325 G St. N.W., #700 20005-3104; (202) 637-2440. Fax, (202) 393-1667. Alexander S. Mathews, President. Web, www.ahi.org.

Membership: manufacturers of drugs and other products (including vaccines, pesticides, and vitamins) for pets and food-producing animals. Monitors legislation and regulations.

Animal Welfare Institute, P.O. Box 3650 20007; (202) 337-2332. Fax, (202) 338-9478. Christine Stevens, President. General e-mail, awi@animalwelfare.com. Web, www.animalwelfare.com.

Educational group that opposes cruel treatment of animals used in research. Seeks to curtail animal experimentation and favors research methods that rely on non-animal subjects whenever possible.

Assn. of American Veterinary Medical Colleges, 1101 Vermont Ave. N.W., #710 20005-3521; (202) 371-9195. Fax, (202) 842-0773. Curt Mann, Executive Director. Web, www.aavmc.org.

Membership: U.S. and Canadian schools and colleges of veterinary medicine, departments of comparative medicine, and departments of veterinary science in agricultural colleges. Produces veterinary reports; sponsors continuing education programs.

The Fund for Animals, *Washington Office,* 8121 Georgia Ave., #301, Silver Spring, MD 20910; (301) 585-2591. Fax, (301) 585-2595. Heidi Prescott, National Director. Web, www.fund.org.

Works for the humane treatment and protection of both domestic and wild animals. (Headquarters in New York.)

Humane Society of the United States, 2100 L St. N.W. 20037; (202) 452-1100. Fax, (202) 778-6132. Paul Irwin, Chief Executive. Web, www.hsus.org.

Citizens' interest group that seeks to reduce suffering of animals used in medical research and testing. Promotes the use of nonanimal alternatives, elimination of unnecessary testing, and refinement of procedures to minimize pain. Interests include legislation regulating the use of live animals in research and testing.

National Assn. for Biomedical Research, 818 Connecticut Ave. N.W., #303 20006; (202) 857-0540. Fax, (202) 659-1902. Frankie L. Trull, President. Web, www.nabr.org.

Membership: scientific and medical professional societies, academic institutions, and research-oriented corporations. Supports the humane use of animals in medical research, education, and product safety testing.

National Assn. of Professional Pet Sitters, 1030 15th St. N.W., #870 20005; (202) 393-3317. Fax, (202) 393-0336. Marianne McDermott, Executive Director. Referrals, (800) 296-PETS. Web, www.petsitters.org.

Promotes in-home pet care and supports professionals engaged in the industry of pet sitting. Conducts education programs for certification, seminars, and conferences; provides referral service.

National Research Council, *Institute for Laboratory Animal Research,* 2101 Constitution Ave. N.W. 20418; (202) 334-2590. Fax, (202) 334-1687. Dr. Ralph B. Dell, Director. General e-mail, ILAR@nas.edu. Web, www4.nas.edu/cls/ilarhome.nsf.

Maintains an information center and answers inquiries concerning animal models for use in biomedical research, location of unique animal colonies, and availability of animals and genetic stocks from colonies and breeders. Develops guidelines on topics related to animal care and use in research, testing, and education; conducts conferences.

Physicians Committee for Responsible Medicine, 5100 Wisconsin Ave. N.W., #404 20016 (mailing address: P.O. Box 6322 20015); (202) 686-2210. Fax, (202) 686-2216. Dr. Neal D. Barnard, President. General e-mail, pcrm@pcrm.org. Web, www.pcrm.org.

Membership: health professionals, medical students, and other individuals. Investigates alternatives to animal use in medical research experimentation, product testing, and education.

Society for Animal Protective Legislation, P.O. Box 3719 20007; (202) 337-2334. Fax, (202) 338-9478. Christine Stevens, Secretary. General e-mail, sapl@animalwelfare.com. Web, www.animalwelfare.com.

Citizens' interest group that supports legislation to ensure the proper treatment of animals.

Fish

See also Fishing/Law of the Sea (chap. 13)

AGENCIES

Atlantic States Marine Fisheries Commission, 1444 Eye St. N.W., 6th Floor 20005; (202) 289-6400. Fax, (202) 289-6051. John H. Dunnigan, Executive Director. Web, www.asmfc.org.

Interstate compact commission of marine fisheries representatives from fifteen states along the Atlantic seaboard. Assists states in developing joint fisheries programs; works with other fisheries organizations and the federal government on environmental, natural resource, and conservation issues.

Interior Dept., *Fish, Wildlife, and Parks,* 1849 C St. N.W., #3156 20240; (202) 208-4416. Fax, (202) 208-4684. Donald Barry, Assistant Secretary. Web, www.doi.gov.

Responsible for programs associated with the development, conservation, and use of fish, wildlife, recreational, historical, and national park system resources. Coordinates marine environmental quality and biological resources programs with other federal agencies.

Justice Dept., *Wildlife and Marine Resources,* 601 Pennsylvania Ave. N.W., #5000 20004 (mailing address: P.O. Box 7369, Ben Franklin Station 20044-7369); (202) 305-0210. Fax, (202) 305-0275. Jean E. Williams, Chief. Web, www.usdoj.gov.

Supervises both civil and criminal cases under federal maritime laws and other laws protecting marine fish and mammals. Focuses on smugglers and black market dealers of protected wildlife.

National Oceanic and Atmospheric Administration *(Commerce Dept.), National Marine Fisheries Service,* 1315 East-West Hwy., Silver Spring, MD 20910; (301) 713-2239. Fax, (301) 713-2258. Penelope Dalton, Assistant Administrator. Press, (301) 713-2370. Web, www.nmfs.gov.

Administers marine fishing regulations, including offshore fishing rights and international agreements; conducts marine resources research; studies use and management of these resources; administers the Magnuson Fishery Conservation and Management Act; manages and protects marine resources, especially endangered species and marine mammals, within the exclusive economic zone.

U.S. Fish and Wildlife Service *(Interior Dept.),* 1849 C St. N.W., #3256 20240; (202) 208-4717. Fax, (202) 208-6965. Jamie R. Clark, Director. Information, (202) 208-4131. Web, www.fws.gov.

Works with federal and state agencies and nonprofits to conserve, protect, and enhance fish and wildlife and their habitats for continuing benefit of the American people.

U.S. Fish and Wildlife Service *(Interior Dept.), Ecological Services,* 1849 C St. N.W., #3242 20240; (202) 208-4646. Fax, (202) 208-6916. Gary D. Frazer, Assistant Director. Web, www.fws.gov.

Monitors federal policy on fish and wildlife. Reviews all federal and federally licensed projects to determine environmental effect on fish and wildlife; responsible for maintaining the endangered species list and for protecting and restoring species to healthy numbers.

U.S. Fish and Wildlife Service *(Interior Dept.), Fisheries,* 1849 C St. N.W., #3245 20240; (202) 208-6394. Fax, (202) 208-4674. Cathleen Short, Assistant Director. Web, www.fws.gov.

Develops, manages, and protects interstate and international fisheries, including fisheries of the Great Lakes, fisheries on federal lands, aquatic ecosystems, endangered species of fish, and anadromous species. Administers the National Fish Hatchery System and the National Fish and Wildlife Resource Management Offices.

U.S. Geological Survey *(Interior Dept.), Biological Resources,* 12201 Sunrise Valley Dr., Reston, VA 20192; (703) 648-4050. Fax, (703) 648-7031. Dennis B. Fenn, Chief Biologist. Web, www.nbs.gov.

Performs research in support of biological resource management. Monitors and reports on the status of the nation's biotic resources, including fish resources. Conducts research on fish diseases, nutrition, and culture techniques; studies ecology of the Great Lakes and the effects of pesticides and herbicides on fish.

CONGRESS

House Resources Committee, *Subcommittee on Fisheries, Conservation, Wildlife, and Oceans, H2-187 FHOB 20515; (202) 226-0200. Fax, (202) 225-1542. Rep. H. James Saxton, R-N.J., Chair; Harry Burroughs, Staff Director. General e-mail, fishery.subcommittee@mail. house.gov. Web, www.house.gov/resources/fisheries.*

Jurisdiction over legislation on fish and fish hatcheries, fisheries promotion, the Magnuson-Stevens Fishery Conservation and Management Act, fisheries research, aquaculture, and seafood safety.

Senate Commerce, Science, and Transportation Committee, *Subcommittee on Oceans and Fisheries, SH-428 20510; (202) 224-8172. Fax, (202) 228-0326. Sen. Olympia J. Snowe, R-Maine, Chair; Sloan Rapoport, Counsel. Web, commerce.senate.gov.*

Studies all aspects of fish and fish hatcheries, including the Magnuson Fishery Conservation and Management Act, fisheries research, aquaculture, and seafood safety. (Subcommittee does not report legislation.)

NONPROFIT

American Fisheries Society, *5410 Grosvenor Lane, #110, Bethesda, MD 20814-2199; (301) 897-8616. Fax, (301) 897-8096. Gus Rassam, Executive Director. General e-mail, main@fisheries.org. Web, www.fisheries.org.*

Membership: biologists and other scientists interested in fisheries. Promotes the fisheries profession, the advancement of fisheries science, and conservation of renewable aquatic resources. Monitors legislation and regulations.

Center for Marine Conservation, *1725 DeSales St. N.W., #600 20036; (202) 429-5609. Fax, (202) 872-0619. Roger T. Rufe, President. General e-mail, cmc@dccmc.org. Web, www.cmc-ocean.org.*

Works to prevent the overexploitation of living marine resources, including fisheries, and to restore depleted marine wildlife populations.

International Assn. of Fish and Wildlife Agencies, *444 N. Capitol St. N.W., #544 20001; (202) 624-7890. Fax, (202) 624-7891. R. Max Peterson, Executive Vice President. General e-mail, iafwa@sso.org. Web, www.sso.org/ iafwa.*

Membership: federal, state, and provincial fish and wildlife management agencies in the United States, Canada, and Mexico. Encourages balanced fish and wildlife resource management.

National Fisheries Institute, *1901 N. Fort Myer Dr., #700, Arlington, VA 22209; (703) 524-8880. Fax, (703)*

524-4619. *Dick Gutting, Executive Vice President. General e-mail, office@nfi.org. Web, www.nfi.org.*

Membership: vessel owners and distributors, processors, wholesalers, importers, traders, and brokers of fish and shellfish. Monitors legislation and regulations on fisheries.

National Food Processors Assn., *1350 Eye St. N.W., #300 20005; (202) 639-5900. Fax, (202) 639-5932. John R. Cady, President. Press, (202) 639-5919.*

Membership: manufacturers and suppliers of processed and packaged food, drinks, and juice. Serves as industry liaison between seafood processors and the federal government.

Trout Unlimited, *1500 Wilson Blvd., #310, Arlington, VA 22209-2404; (703) 522-0200. Fax, (703) 284-9400. Charles Gauvin, President. Web, www.tu.org.*

Membership: individuals interested in the protection and enhancement of cold-water fish and their habitat. Sponsors research projects with federal and state fisheries agencies; maintains programs for water quality surveillance and cleanup of streams and lakes.

U.S. Tuna Foundation, *1101 17th St. N.W., #609 20036; (202) 857-0610. Fax, (202) 331-9686. David G. Burney, Executive Director.*

Membership: tuna processors, vessel owners, and fishermen's unions. Interests include fishing legislation and government relations.

Wildlife and Marine Mammals

AGENCIES

Animal and Plant Health Inspection Service *(Agriculture Dept.),* **Wildlife Services,** *1400 Independence Ave. S.W., #1624S 20250-3402; (202) 720-2054. Fax, (202) 690-0053. William Clay, Deputy Administrator (Acting). Web, www.aphis.usda.gov/ws.*

Works to minimize damage caused by wildlife to crops and livestock, natural resources, and human health and safety. Removes or eliminates predators and nuisance birds; interests include aviation safety and coexistence of people and wildlife in suburban areas. Oversees the National Wildlife Research Center, located in Ft. Collins, Colo.

Forest Service *(Agriculture Dept.),* **Wildlife, Fisheries, and Rare Plants,** *1400 Independence Ave. S.W. 20024 (mailing address: P.O. Box 96090 20090-6090); (202) 205-1205. Fax, (202) 205-1599. Joel D. Holtrop, Director. Web, www.fs.fed.us.*

Provides national policy direction and management for fish, endangered species, wildlife, and rare plants programs on lands managed by the Forest Service.

Interior Dept., *Fish, Wildlife, and Parks,* 1849 C St. N.W., #3156 20240; (202) 208-4416. Fax, (202) 208-4684. *Donald Barry, Assistant Secretary. Web, www.doi.gov.*

Responsible for programs associated with the development, conservation, and use of fish, wildlife, recreational, historical, and national park system resources. Coordinates marine environmental quality and biological resources programs with other federal agencies.

Interior Dept., *North American Wetlands Conservation Council,* 4401 N. Fairfax Dr., #110, Arlington, VA 22203; (703) 358-1784. Fax, (703) 358-2282. *David A. Smith, Coordinator. General e-mail, r9arw_nawwo@mail. fws.gov. Web, www.fws.gov.*

Membership: government and private-sector conservation experts. Works to protect, restore, and manage wetlands and other habitats for migratory birds and other animals and to maintain migratory bird and waterfowl populations.

Justice Dept., *Wildlife and Marine Resources,* 601 Pennsylvania Ave. N.W., #5000 20004 (mailing address: P.O. Box 7369, Ben Franklin Station 20044-7369); (202) 305-0210. Fax, (202) 305-0275. *Jean E. Williams, Chief. Web, www.usdoj.gov.*

Responsible for criminal enforcement and civil litigation under federal fish and wildlife conservation statutes, including protection of wildlife, fish, and plant resources within U.S. jurisdiction; monitors interstate and foreign commerce of these resources.

Marine Mammal Commission, 4340 East-West Hwy., #905, Bethesda, MD 20814; (301) 504-0087. Fax, (301) 504-0099. *John R. Twiss Jr., Executive Director; Robert J. Hofman, Scientific Program Director.*

Established by Congress to ensure protection and conservation of marine mammals; conducts research and makes recommendations on federal programs that affect marine mammals.

National Oceanic and Atmospheric Administration *(Commerce Dept.),* **Protected Resources,** 1315 East-West Hwy., #13701, Silver Spring, MD 20910; (301) 713-2332. Fax, (301) 713-0376. *Art Jeffers, Deputy Director; Donald R. Knowles, Director. Web, www.nmfs.gov/prot_res.*

Provides guidance on the conservation and protection of marine mammals and endangered species and on the conservation and restoration of their habitats. Develops national guidelines and policies for relevant research programs; prepares and reviews management and recovery plans and environmental impact analyses.

U.S. Fish and Wildlife Service *(Interior Dept.),* 1849 C St. N.W., #3256 20240; (202) 208-4717. Fax, (202) 208-6965. *Jamie R. Clark, Director. Information, (202) 208-4131. Web, www.fws.gov.*

Works with federal and state agencies and nonprofits to conserve, protect, and enhance fish and wildlife and their habitats for continuing benefit of the American people.

U.S. Fish and Wildlife Service *(Interior Dept.),* **Ecological Services,** 1849 C St. N.W., #3242 20240; (202) 208-4646. Fax, (202) 208-6916. *Gary D. Frazer, Assistant Director. Web, www.fws.gov.*

Monitors federal policy on fish and wildlife. Reviews all federal and federally licensed projects to determine environmental effect on fish and wildlife; responsible for maintaining the endangered species list and for protecting and restoring species to healthy numbers.

U.S. Fish and Wildlife Service *(Interior Dept.),* **Migratory Bird Conservation Commission,** 4401 N. Fairfax Dr., #622, Arlington, VA 22203; (703) 358-1716. Fax, (703) 358-2223. *Jeffery M. Donahoe, Secretary. Web, www.fws.gov.*

Established by the Migratory Bird Conservation Act of 1929. Decides which areas to purchase for use as migratory bird refuges.

U.S. Fish and Wildlife Service *(Interior Dept.),* **North American Waterfowl and Wetlands,** 4401 N. Fairfax Dr., #110, Arlington, VA 22203; (703) 358-1784. Fax, (703) 358-2282. *David A. Smith, Executive Director. General e-mail, r9arw_nawwo@fws.gov. Web, www.northamerican. fws.gov.*

Coordinates U.S. activities with Canada and Mexico to protect waterfowl habitats, restore waterfowl populations, and set research priorities under the North American Waterfowl Management Plan.

U.S. Fish and Wildlife Service *(Interior Dept.),* **Refuges and Wildlife,** 1849 C St. N.W., #3251 20240; (202) 208-5333. Fax, (202) 208-3082. *Daniel M. Ashe, Assistant Director. Web, www.fws.gov.*

Determines policy for the management of wildlife, including migratory birds; administers hunting regulations and establishes hunting seasons for migratory birds; marks and bands waterfowl; manages the National Wildlife Refuge System; manages land acquisition for wildlife refuges; and oversees the federal duck stamp program, which generates revenue for wetlands acquisition.

U.S. Geological Survey *(Interior Dept.),* **Biological Resources,** 12201 Sunrise Valley Dr., Reston, VA 20192; (703) 648-4050. Fax, (703) 648-7031. *Dennis B. Fenn, Chief Biologist. Web, www.nbs.gov.*

Performs research in support of biological resource management. Monitors and reports on the status of the nation's biotic resources. Conducts research on fish and wildlife, including the effects of disease and environmental contaminants on wildlife populations. Studies endangered and other species.

CONGRESS

House Government Reform Committee, *Subcommittee on National Economic Growth, Natural Resources, and Regulatory Affairs, B377 RHOB 20515; (202) 225-4407. Fax, (202) 225-2441. Rep. David M. McIntosh, R-Ind., Chair; Marlo Lewis, Staff Director. Web, www.house.gov/reform.*

Oversight of the U.S. Fish and Wildlife Service.

House Resources Committee, *Subcommittee on Fisheries, Conservation, Wildlife, and Oceans, H2-187 FHOB 20515; (202) 226-0200. Fax, (202) 225-1542. Rep. H. James Saxton, R-N.J., Chair; Harry Burroughs, Staff Director. General e-mail, fishery.subcommittee@mail. house.gov. Web, www.house.gov/resources/fisheries.*

Jurisdiction over legislation on fisheries and wildlife, habitat preservation and research programs, endangered species and marine mammal protection, wildlife refuges, estuarine protection, wetlands conservation, and biological diversity. General oversight of the U.S. Fish and Wildlife Service, the National Marine Fisheries Service, the Office of Environmental Policy, and the Marine Mammal Commission, and certain programs of the National Oceanic and Atmospheric Administration.

Senate Environment and Public Works Committee, *Subcommittee on Fisheries, Wildlife, and Drinking Water, SD-410 20510; (202) 224-6176. Fax, (202) 224-5167. Sen. Michael D. Crapo, R-Idaho, Chair; Sharla Moffett, Staff Contact. Web, epw.senate.gov.*

Jurisdiction over legislation on fisheries and wildlife, habitat preservation and research programs, endangered species and marine mammal protection, wildlife refuges, estuarine protection, wetlands conservation, and biological diversity; oversight of the U.S. Fish and Wildlife Service, the Office of Environmental Policy, and the Marine Mammal Commission.

NONPROFIT

Animal Welfare Institute, *P.O. Box 3650 20007; (202) 337-2332. Fax, (202) 338-9478. Christine Stevens, President. General e-mail, awi@animalwelfare.com. Web, www.animalwelfare.com.*

Educational group that opposes steel jaw leghold animal traps and supports the protection of marine mammals. Interests include preservation of endangered

species, reform of cruel methods of raising food animals, and humane treatment of laboratory animals.

Center for Marine Conservation, *1725 DeSales St. N.W., #600 20036; (202) 429-5609. Fax, (202) 872-0619. Roger T. Rufe, President. General e-mail, cmc@dccmc.org. Web, www.cmc-ocean.org.*

Works to conserve the diversity and abundance of life in the oceans and coastal areas, to prevent the overexploitation of living marine resources and the degradation of marine ecosystems, and to restore depleted marine wildlife populations and their ecosystems.

Defenders of Wildlife, *1101 14th St. N.W., #1400 20005; (202) 682-9400. Fax, (202) 682-1331. Rodger Schlickeisen, President. Web, www.defenders.org.*

Advocacy group that works to protect wild animals and plants in their natural communities. Interests include endangered species and biodiversity. Monitors legislation and regulations.

Ducks Unlimited, *Governmental Affairs, Washington Office, 1301 Pennsylvania Ave. N.W., #402 20004; (202) 347-1530. Fax, (202) 347-1533. Scott Sutherland, Director. Web, www.ducks.org.*

Promotes waterfowl and other wildlife conservation through activities aimed at developing and restoring natural nesting and migration habitats. (Headquarters in Memphis.)

Greenpeace USA, *Washington Office, 1436 U St. N.W. 20009; (202) 462-1177. Fax, (202) 462-4507. Kristen Engberg, Executive Director. General e-mail, greenpeace. usa@wdc.greenpeace.org. Web, www.greenpeaceusa.org.*

Seeks to protect the environment through research, education, and grassroots organizing. Works to stop commercial slaughter of whales, seals, and dolphins; to preserve marine habitats; and to establish Antarctica as a world park, free of industry, military presence, and nuclear power and weaponry. Monitors legislation and regulations. (Headquarters in Amsterdam, Netherlands.)

Humane Society of the United States, *2100 L St. N.W. 20037; (202) 452-1100. Fax, (202) 778-6132. Paul Irwin, Chief Executive. Web, www.hsus.org.*

Works for the humane treatment and protection of animals. Interests include protecting endangered wildlife and marine mammals and their habitats and ending inhumane or cruel conditions in zoos.

International Assn. of Fish and Wildlife Agencies, *444 N. Capitol St. N.W., #544 20001; (202) 624-7890. Fax, (202) 624-7891. R. Max Peterson, Executive Vice President. General e-mail, iafwa@sso.org. Web, www.sso.org/ iafwa.*

Membership: federal, state, and provincial fish and wildlife management agencies in the United States, Canada, and Mexico. Encourages balanced fish and wildlife resource management.

Jane Goodall Institute, *P.O. Box 14890, Silver Spring, MD 20911-4890; (301) 565-0086. Fax, (301) 565-3188. Stewart Hudson, Executive Director. General e-mail, JGIinformation@janegoodall.org. Web, www.janegoodall. org.*

Seeks to increase primate habitat conservation, expand noninvasive primate research, and promote activities that ensure the well-being of primates. (Affiliated with Jane Goodall Institutes in Canada, Europe, Asia, and Africa.)

National Fish and Wildlife Foundation, *1120 Connecticut Ave. N.W., #900 20036; (202) 857-0166. Fax, (202) 857-0162. Alex Echols, Executive Director (Acting). Web, www.nfwf.org.*

Forges partnerships between the public and private sectors in support of national and international conservation activities that identify the root causes of environmental problems.

National Wildlife Federation, *8925 Leesburg Pike, Vienna, VA 22184; (703) 790-4000. Fax, (703) 790-4040. Mark Van Putten, President. General e-mail, info@nwf. org. Web, www.nwf.org.*

Educational organization that promotes preservation of natural resources; provides information on wildlife.

National Wildlife Refuge Assn., *1010 Wisconsin Ave. N.W., #200 20007; (202) 965-6972. Fax, (202) 333-9077. David Tobin, President. General e-mail, nwra@refugenet. org. Web, www.refugenet.org.*

Works to improve management and protection of the Refuge System by providing information to administrators, Congress, and the public. Advocates adequate funding and improved policy guidance for the Refuge System; assists individual refuges with particular needs.

Nature Conservancy, *4245 N. Fairfax Dr., #100, Arlington, VA 22203; (703) 841-5300. Fax, (703) 841-1283. John C. Sawhill, President. Web, www.tnc.org.*

Acquires land to protect endangered species and habitats; maintains international system of natural sanctuaries; operates the Heritage Program, a cooperative effort with state governments to identify and inventory threatened and endangered plants and animals.

Wildlife Habitat Council, *1010 Wayne Ave., #920, Silver Spring, MD 20910; (301) 588-8994. Fax, (301) 588-4629. William Howard, President. General e-mail, whc@ wildlifehc.org. Web, www.wildlifehc.org.*

Membership: corporations, conservation groups, and individuals. Supports use of underdeveloped private lands for the benefit of wildlife, fish, and plant life. Provides technical assistance and educational programs; fosters information sharing among members.

Wildlife Management Institute, *1101 14th St. N.W., #801 20005; (202) 371-1808. Fax, (202) 408-5059. Rollin D. Sparrowe, President. Web, www.wildlifemgt.org/wmi.*

Research and consulting organization that provides technical services and information on natural resources, particularly on wildlife management. Interests include threatened and endangered species, nongame and hunted wildlife, waterfowl, large land mammals, and predators.

Wildlife Society, *5410 Grosvenor Lane, #200, Bethesda, MD 20814-2197; (301) 897-9770. Fax, (301) 530-2471. Harry E. Hodgdon, Executive Director. General e-mail, tws@wildlife.org. Web, www.wildlife.org.*

Membership: wildlife biologists and resource management specialists. Provides information on management techniques; sponsors conferences; maintains list of job opportunities for members.

World Wildlife Fund, *1250 24th St. N.W., #400 20037; (202) 293-4800. Fax, (202) 293-9211. Kathryn S. Fuller, President. Web, www.wwf.org.*

International conservation organization that supports and conducts scientific research and conservation projects to promote biological diversity and to save endangered species and their habitats. Awards grants for habitat protection.

See also National Audubon Society (p. 179)

POLLUTION AND TOXINS

See also Energy (chap. 8); Environmental and Earth Sciences (chap. 17)

AGENCIES

Environmental Protection Agency, *Enforcement and Compliance Assurance, 1200 Pennsylvania Ave. N.W., #3204 20004; (202) 564-2440. Fax, (202) 501-3842. Steven A. Herman, Assistant Administrator. Web, www.epa.gov.*

Principal adviser to the administrator on enforcement of standards for air, water, toxic substances and pesticides, hazardous and solid waste management, radiation, and emergency preparedness programs. Investigates criminal and civil violations of environmental standards; oversees federal facilities' environmental compliance and site cleanup; serves as EPA's liaison office for federal agency compliance with the National Environmental Policy Act; manages environmental review of other agencies' projects and activities and coordinates EPA native American environmental programs.

Justice Dept., *Environmental Crimes, 601 Pennsylvania Ave. N.W., #6101 20004 (mailing address: P.O. Box 23985 20026-3985); (202) 305-0321. Fax, (202) 305-0397. Steven P. Solow, Chief. Web, www.usdoj.gov.*

Conducts criminal enforcement actions on behalf of the United States for all environmental protection statutes, including air, water, pesticides, hazardous wastes, wetland matters investigated by the Environmental Protection Agency, and other criminal environmental enforcement.

Justice Dept., *Environmental Defense, 601 D St. N.W., #8000 20004 (mailing address: P.O. Box 23986 20026-3986); (202) 514-2219. Fax, (202) 514-8865. Letitia J. Grishaw, Chief. Web, www.usdoj.gov.*

Conducts litigation on air, water, noise, pesticides, solid waste, toxic substances, Superfund, and wetlands in cooperation with the Environmental Protection Agency; represents the EPA in suits involving judicial review of EPA actions; represents the U.S. Army Corps of Engineers in cases involving dredge-and-fill activity in navigable waters and adjacent wetlands; represents the Coast Guard in oil and hazardous spill cases; defends all federal agencies in environmental litigation.

Justice Dept., *Environmental Enforcement, 1425 New York Ave. N.W., 13th Floor 20005 (mailing address: P.O. Box 7611, Ben Franklin Station 20044-7611); (202) 514-1604. Fax, (202) 353-0296. Joel M. Gross, Chief. Web, www.usdoj.gov.*

Conducts civil enforcement actions on behalf of the United States for all environmental protection statutes, including air, water, pesticides, hazardous waste, wetland matters investigated by the Environmental Protection Agency, and other civil environmental enforcement.

See also Domestic Policy Council (p. 319)

NONPROFIT

American Academy of Environmental Engineers,
130 Holiday Court, #100, Annapolis, MD 21401; (410) 266-3311. Fax, (410) 266-7653. William C. Anderson, Executive Director. General e-mail, academy@aaee.net. Web, www.aaee.net.

Membership: state-licensed environmental engineers who have passed examinations in environmental engineering specialties, including general environment, air

pollution control, solid waste management, hazardous waste management, industrial hygiene, radiation protection, water supply, and wastewater.

Environmental Industry Assns., *4301 Connecticut Ave. N.W., #300 20008; (202) 244-4700. Fax, (202) 966-4818. Bruce Parker, President. Web, www.envasns.org.*

Membership: trade associations from the waste services and environmental technology industries. Represents the National Solid Waste Management Assn. and the Waste Equipment Technology Assn.

See also America the Beautiful Fund (p. 147); Earth Share (p. 26); National Governors' Assn., Natural Resources (p. 249); Zero Population Growth (p. 396)

Air Pollution

AGENCIES

Environmental Protection Agency, *Air and Radiation, 401 M St. S.W., West Tower, MC 6101 20460; (202) 260-7400. Fax, (202) 260-5155. Robert Brenner, Deputy Administrator (Acting). Docket and Information Center, (202) 260-7548; fax, (202) 260-4400.*

Administers air quality standards and planning programs of the Clean Air Act Amendment of 1990; operates the Air and Radiation Docket and Information Center. Supervises the Office of Air Quality Planning and Standards in Durham, N.C., which develops air quality standards and provides information on air pollution control issues, including industrial air pollution. Administers the Air Pollution Technical Information Center in Research Triangle Park, N.C., which collects and provides technical literature on air pollution.

Environmental Protection Agency, *Atmospheric Programs, 501 3rd St. N.W. 20001 (mailing address: 1200 Pennsylvania Ave. N.W. 20460); (202) 564-9140. Fax, (202) 565-2147. Paul Stolpman, Director.*

Responsible for acid rain and stratospheric ozone programs; examines strategies for preventing atmospheric pollution and mitigating climate change.

Environmental Protection Agency, *Manufacturing, Energy, and Transportation, 1200 Pennsylvania Ave. N.W., 7th Floor 20004 (mailing address: 1200 Pennsylvania Ave. N.W. 20460); (202) 564-2300. Fax, (202) 564-0050. John B. Rasnic, Director. Web, www.epa.gov.*

Administers Clean Air Act provisions for extraction of fuels and minerals; electric and gas utilities; petroleum refining; transport operations; and manufacturing of textiles, wood and paper products, steel and construction materials, transportation equipment, and electronics.

Maintains data on the compliance status of various sources.

Environmental Protection Agency, *Radiation and Indoor Air,* 501 3rd St. N.W. 20001 (mailing address: 401 M St. S.W., #6601J 20460); (202) 564-9320. Fax, (202) 565-2043. Stephen D. Page, Director.

Administers indoor air quality control programs, including those regulating radon and environmental tobacco smoke; trains building managers in sound operation practices to promote indoor air quality.

Federal Aviation Administration *(Transportation Dept.), Environment and Energy,* 800 Independence Ave. S.W., #900W 20591; (202) 267-3576. Fax, (202) 267-5594. James Erickson, Director. Web, www.faa.aee.gov.

Enforces government standards for aircraft noise and emissions; conducts research on ozone depletion and high-altitude aircraft.

U.S. Geological Survey *(Interior Dept.), Energy Resources,* 12201 Sunrise Valley Dr., Reston, VA 20192 (mailing address: 915A National Center, Reston, VA 20192); (703) 648-6470. Fax, (703) 648-5464. Suzanne D. Weedman, Program Coordinator. Web, energy.usgs.gov.

Conducts research on fossil energy resources of the United States and the world; estimates energy resource availability and recoverability; anticipates and mitigates deleterious environmental impacts of energy resource extraction and use.

CONGRESS

House Commerce Committee, *Subcommittee on Health and the Environment,* 2125 RHOB 20515; (202) 225-2927. Fax, (202) 225-1919. Rep. Michael Bilirakis, R-Fla., Chair; James E. Derderian, Staff Director. General e-mail, commerce@mail.house.gov. Web, www.house.gov/ commerce.

Jurisdiction over legislation on indoor and outdoor air pollution, including the Clean Air Act.

Senate Environment and Public Works Committee, *Subcommittee on Clean Air, Wetlands, Private Property, and Nuclear Safety,* SD-410 20510; (202) 224-6176. Fax, (202) 224-5167. Sen. James M. Inhofe, R-Okla., Chair; Andy Wheeler, Staff Contact. Web, epw.senate.gov.

Jurisdiction over legislation on indoor and outdoor air pollution, including the Clean Air Act.

NONPROFIT

Alliance for Responsible Atmospheric Policy, 2111 Wilson Blvd., #850, Arlington, VA 22201; (703) 243-0344. Fax, (703) 243-2874. David Stirpe, Executive Director. Web, www.alcalde-fay.com.

Coalition of users and producers of chlorofluorocarbons (CFCs). Seeks further study of the ozone depletion theory.

Asbestos Information Assn./North America, 1745 Jefferson Davis Hwy., #406, Arlington, VA 22202; (703) 412-1150. Fax, (703) 412-1152. B. J. Pigg, President.

Membership: firms that manufacture, sell, and use products containing asbestos fiber and those that mine, mill, and sell asbestos. Provides information on asbestos and health and on industry efforts to eliminate problems associated with asbestos dust; serves as liaison between the industry and federal and state governments.

Assn. of Local Air Pollution Control Officials, 444 N. Capitol St. N.W., #307 20001; (202) 624-7864. Fax, (202) 624-7863. S. William Becker, Executive Director. General e-mail, 4cleanair@sso.org. Web, www.4cleanair. org.

Membership: local representatives of air pollution control programs nationwide that are responsible for implementing provisions of the Clean Air Act. Disseminates policy and technical information; analyzes air pollution issues; conducts seminars, workshops, and conferences. Monitors legislation and regulations.

Center for Auto Safety, 1825 Connecticut Ave., #330 20009; (202) 328-7700. Fax, (202) 387-0140. Clarence M. Ditlow III, Executive Director. Web, www.autosafety.org.

Public interest organization that conducts research on air pollution caused by auto emissions; monitors fuel economy regulations.

Center for Clean Air Policy, 750 1st St. N.E., #1140 20002; (202) 408-9260. Fax, (202) 408-8896. Edward Helme, Executive Director. General e-mail, general@ccap. org. Web, www.ccap.org.

Membership: governors, corporations, environmentalists, and academicians. Analyzes economic and environmental effects of air pollution and related environmental problems. Serves as a liaison among government, corporate, community, and environmental groups.

Climate Institute, 333 1/2 Pennsylvania Ave. S.E. 20003-1148; (202) 547-0104. Fax, (202) 547-0111. John C. Topping Jr., President. General e-mail, info@climate.org. Web, www.climate.org.

Educates the public and policymakers on climate change (greenhouse effect or global warming) and on the depletion of the ozone layer. Develops strategies on mitigating climate change in developing countries.

Environmental Defense Fund, *Washington Office,* 1875 Connecticut Ave. N.W., #1016 20009-5728; (202)

387-3500. Fax, (202) 234-6049. Senta Boardley, Office Manager. Web, www.edf.org.

Citizens' interest group staffed by lawyers, economists, and scientists. Conducts research and provides information on pollution prevention, environmental health, and protection of the Amazon rain forest and the ozone layer. (Headquarters in New York.)

Manufacturers of Emission Controls Assn., *1660 L St. N.W., #1100 20036; (202) 296-4797. Fax, (202) 331-1388. Bruce I. Bertelsen, Executive Director. Web, www. meca.org.*

Membership: manufacturers of motor vehicle and stationary source emission control equipment. Provides information on emission technology and industry capabilities.

State and Territorial Air Pollution Program Administrators, *444 N. Capitol St. N.W., #307 20001; (202) 624-7864. Fax, (202) 624-7863. S. William Becker, Executive Director. Web, www.4cleanair.org.*

Membership: state territorial and local officials responsible for implementing programs established under state and local legislation and the Clean Air Act. Disseminates policy and technical information and analyzes air quality issues; conducts seminars, workshops, and conferences. Monitors legislation and regulations.

See also American Council for an Energy-Efficient Economy (p. 251)

Hazardous Materials

See also Fertilizer and Pesticides (chap. 2); Water Pollution (this section)

AGENCIES

Agency for Toxic Substances and Disease Registry *(Health and Human Services Dept.), Washington Office, 200 Independence Ave. S.W., #719B 20201; (202) 690-7536. Fax, (202) 690-6985. Andrea A. Wargo, Associate Administrator. Web, atsdr.cdc.gov.*

Works with federal, state, and local agencies to minimize or eliminate adverse effects of exposure to toxic substances at spill and waste disposal sites; maintains a registry of persons exposed to hazardous substances and of diseases and illnesses resulting from exposure to hazardous or toxic substances; maintains inventory of hazardous substances; maintains registry of sites closed or restricted because of contamination by hazardous material. (Headquarters in Atlanta.)

Defense Dept., *Environmental Security, 3400 Defense Pentagon, #3E792 20301-3400; (703) 695-6639. Fax, (703)*

693-7011. Sherri W. Goodman, Deputy Under Secretary. Web, www.acq.osd.mil/ens.

Integrates environmental, safety, and occupational health considerations into U.S. defense and economic policies. Works to ensure responsible performance in defense operations, to maintain quality installations, to reduce the costs of complying with environmental laws, and to clean up past contamination.

Environmental Protection Agency, *Chemical Control, 401 M St. S.W., MC 7405 20460; (202) 260-3749. Fax, (202) 260-8168. Charlie M. Auer, Director.*

Selects and implements control measures for new and existing chemicals that present a risk to human health and the environment. Oversees and manages regulatory evaluation and decision-making processes. Evaluates alternative remedial control measures under the Toxic Substances Control Act and makes recommendations concerning the existence of unreasonable risk from exposure to chemicals. Develops generic and chemical-specific rules for new chemicals.

Environmental Protection Agency, *Chemical Emergency Preparedness and Prevention, 401 M St. S.W., Southeast 311, MC 5104 20460; (202) 260-8600. Fax, (202) 260-7906. Jim Makris, Director. Toll-free hotline, (800) 535-0202. Web, www.epa.gov.*

Develops and administers chemical emergency preparedness and prevention programs; reviews effectiveness of programs; prepares community right-to-know regulations. Provides guidance materials, technical assistance, and training. Implements the preparedness and community right-to-know provisions of the Superfund Amendments and Reauthorization Act of 1986.

Environmental Protection Agency, *Enforcement and Compliance Assurance, 1200 Pennsylvania Ave. N.W., #3204 20004; (202) 564-2440. Fax, (202) 501-3842. Steven A. Herman, Assistant Administrator. Web, www.epa.gov.*

Enforces laws that protect public health and the environment from hazardous materials, pesticides, and toxic substances.

Environmental Protection Agency, *Pollution Prevention and Toxics, 401 M St. S.W., #527 East Tower 20460; (202) 260-3810. Fax, (202) 260-0575. William H. Sanders III, Director. Information, (202) 554-1404.*

Assesses the health and environmental hazards of existing chemical substances and mixtures; collects information on chemical use, exposure, and effects; maintains inventory of existing chemical substances; reviews new chemicals and regulates the manufacture, distribution, use, and disposal of harmful chemicals.

Environmental Protection Agency, *Prevention, Pesticides, and Toxic Substances,* 401 M St. S.W., MC 7101 20460; (202) 260-2902. Fax, (202) 260-1847. James V. Aidala, Assistant Administrator (Nominee). Pollution prevention and toxic substances control, (202) 260-3810.

Studies and makes recommendations for regulating chemical substances under the Toxic Substances Control Act; compiles list of chemical substances subject to the act; registers, controls, and regulates use of pesticides and toxic substances.

Environmental Protection Agency, *Solid Waste and Emergency Response,* 401 M St. S.W., #5101, MC 360 20460; (202) 260-4610. Fax, (202) 260-3527. Timothy Fields Jr., Assistant Administrator. Superfund/Resource conservation and recovery hotline, (800) 424-9346; in Washington, (703) 412-9810. TTY, (800) 553-7672; in Washington, (703) 412-3323. Web, www.epa.gov/swerrims.

Administers and enforces the Superfund Act; manages the handling, cleanup, and disposal of hazardous wastes.

Housing and Urban Development Dept., *Lead Hazard Control,* 451 7th St. S.W., #P3202 20410; (202) 755-1785. Fax, (202) 755-1000. David E. Jacobs, Director. Community Outreach, (202) 755-1785, ext. 114. Web, www.hud.gov/lea/leahome.html.

Advises HUD offices, other agencies, health authorities, and the housing industry on lead poisoning prevention. Develops regulations for lead-based paint; conducts research; makes grants to state and local governments for hazard reduction and inspection of housing.

Justice Dept., *Environmental Enforcement,* 1425 New York Ave. N.W., 13th Floor 20005 (mailing address: P.O. Box 7611, Ben Franklin Station 20044-7611); (202) 514-1604. Fax, (202) 353-0296. Joel M. Gross, Chief. Web, www.usdoj.gov.

Represents the United States in civil cases under environmental laws that involve the handling, storage, treatment, transportation, and disposal of hazardous waste. Recovers federal money spent to clean up hazardous waste sites or sues defendants to clean up sites under Superfund.

National Response Center *(Transportation Dept.),* 2100 2nd St. S.W., #2611 20593; (202) 267-2675. Fax, (202) 267-2165. Syed Qadir, Director. Toll-free hotline, (800) 424-8802. Web, www.nrc.uscg.mil.

Maintains 24-hour hotline for reporting oil spills or hazardous materials accidents. Notifies appropriate federal officials to reduce the effects of accidents.

National Transportation Safety Board, *Pipeline and Hazardous Material Safety,* 490 L'Enfant Plaza S.W. 20594; (202) 314-6460. Fax, (202) 314-6482. Bob Chipkevich, Director.

Investigates natural gas and liquid pipeline accidents and other accidents involving the transportation of hazardous materials.

Research and Special Programs Administration *(Transportation Dept.),* 400 7th St. S.W., #8410 20590; (202) 366-4433. Fax, (202) 366-3666. Kelley Coyner, Administrator. Web, www.rspa.dot.gov.

Coordinates research and development programs to improve safety of transportation systems; focus includes hazardous materials shipments, pipeline safety, and preparedness for transportation emergencies. Oversees Volpe National Transportation Systems Center in Cambridge, Mass., and Transportation Safety Institute in Oklahoma City.

Research and Special Programs Administration *(Transportation Dept.),* *Hazardous Materials Safety,* 400 7th St. S.W., #8321 20590; (202) 366-0656. Fax, (202) 366-5713. Robert McGuire, Associate Administrator (Acting). Web, hazmat.dot.gov.

Designates substances as hazardous materials and regulates their transportation in interstate commerce; coordinates international standards regulations.

Research and Special Programs Administration *(Transportation Dept.),* *Pipeline Safety,* 400 7th St. S.W., #7128 20590; (202) 366-4595. Fax, (202) 366-4566. Richard B. Felder, Associate Administrator. Web, ops.dot.gov.

Issues and enforces federal regulations for hazardous liquids pipeline safety.

State Dept., *Environmental Policy,* 2201 C St. N.W., #4325 20520; (202) 647-9266. Fax, (202) 647-5947. Daniel Fantozzi, Director. Web, www.state.gov.

Advances U.S. interests internationally regarding multilateral environmental organizations, chemical wastes and other pollutants, and bilateral and regional environmental policies.

CONGRESS

House Commerce Committee, *Subcommittee on Finance and Hazardous Materials,* 2125 RHOB 20515; (202) 225-2927. Fax, (202) 225-1919. Rep. Michael G. Oxley, R-Ohio, Chair; James E. Derderian, Staff Director. General e-mail, commerce@mail.house.gov. Web, www. house.gov/commerce.

Jurisdiction over legislation on pollution; toxic substances, including the Toxic Substances Control Act; hazardous substances, including the Comprehensive Environmental Response, Compensation, and Liability Act (the Superfund); and other hazardous materials programs (jurisdiction shared with House Science and House Transportation and Infrastructure committees).

House Science Committee, *Subcommittee on Energy and Environment, 389 FHOB 20515; (202) 225-9662. Fax, (202) 226-6983. Rep. Ken Calvert, R-Calif., Chair; Harlan Watson, Staff Director. Web, www.house.gov/ science.*

Jurisdiction over legislation and environmental research and development on pollution; toxic substances, including the Toxic Substances Control Act; and the Comprehensive Environmental Response, Compensation, and Liability Act (the Superfund) (jurisdiction shared with House Commerce and House Transportation and Infrastructure committees).

House Transportation and Infrastructure Committee, *Subcommittee on Water Resources and Environment, B376 RHOB 20515; (202) 225-4360. Fax, (202) 226-5435. Rep. Sherwood Boehlert, R-N.Y., Chair; Ben Grumbles, Counsel. General e-mail, transcomm@mail. house.gov. Web, www.house.gov/transportation.*

Shares jurisdiction over the Comprehensive Environmental Response, Compensation, and Liability Act (the Superfund) with the House Commerce and House Science committees.

Senate Environment and Public Works Committee, *Subcommittee on Superfund, Waste Control, and Risk Assessment, SD-410 20510; (202) 224-6176. Fax, (202) 224-5167. Sen. Lincoln Chafee, R-R.I., Chair; Ted Michaels, Staff Director. Web, epw.senate.gov.*

Jurisdiction over legislation on pollution; environmental research and development; pesticides; and toxic substances, including the Toxic Substances Control Act. Oversight of the Comprehensive Environmental Response, Compensation, and Liability Act (the Superfund) and of hazardous materials programs.

NONPROFIT

Center for Health, Environment, and Justice, *150 S. Washington St., #300, Falls Church, VA 22046 (mailing address: P.O. Box 6806, Falls Church, VA 22040); (703) 237-2249. Fax, (703) 237-8389. Lois Marie Gibbs, Executive Director. General e-mail, cchw@essential.org. Web, www.essential.org/cchw.*

Provides citizens' groups, individuals, and municipalities with support and information on solid and haz-

ardous waste. Sponsors workshops, speakers bureau, leadership development conference, and convention. Operates a toxicity data bank on environmental and health effects of common chemical compounds; maintains a registry of technical experts to assist in solid and hazardous waste problems; gathers information on polluting corporations.

Chemical Specialties Manufacturers Assn., *1913 Eye St. N.W. 20006; (202) 872-8110. Fax, (202) 872-8114. Christopher Cathart, President. General e-mail, info@ csma.org. Web, www.csma.org.*

Membership: manufacturers, marketers, packagers, and suppliers in the chemical specialties industry. Specialties include cleaning compounds and detergents, insecticides, disinfectants, automotive and industrial products, polishes and floor finishes, antimicrobials, and aerosol products. Monitors scientific developments; conducts surveys and research; provides chemical safety information and consumer education programs; sponsors National Inhalants and Poisons Awareness and Aerosol Education Bureau. Monitors legislation and regulations.

Chlorine Institute Inc., *2001 L St. N.W., #506 20036-4919; (202) 775-2790. Fax, (202) 223-7225. Robert G. Smerko, President. Web, www.cl2.com.*

Safety, health, and environmental protection center of the chlor-alkali (chlorine, caustic soda, caustic potash, and hydrogen chloride) industry. Interests include employee health and safety, resource conservation and pollution abatement, control of chlorine emergencies, product specifications, and public and community relations. Publishes technical pamphlets and drawings.

Environmental Technology Council, *734 15th St. N.W., #720 20005; (202) 783-0870. Fax, (202) 737-2038. David Case, Executive Director. Web, www.etc.org.*

Membership: environmental service firms. Interests include the recycling, detoxification, and disposal of hazardous and industrial waste and cleanup of contaminated industrial sites; works to encourage permanent and technology-based solutions to environmental problems. Provides the public with information.

Greenpeace USA, *Washington Office, 1436 U St. N.W. 20009; (202) 462-1177. Fax, (202) 462-4507. Kristen Engberg, Executive Director. General e-mail, greenpeace.usa@ wdc.greenpeace.org. Web, www.greenpeaceusa.org.*

Seeks to protect the environment through research, education, and grassroots organizing. Works to prevent careless disposal and incineration of hazardous waste; encourages the development of methods to reduce production of hazardous waste. Monitors legislation and regulations. (Headquarters in Amsterdam, Netherlands.)

Hazardous Materials Advisory Council, *1101 Vermont Ave. N.W., #301 20005; (202) 289-4550. Fax, (202) 289-4074. Jonathan Collom, President. General e-mail, hmacinfo@hmac.org. Web, www.hmac.org.*

Membership: shippers, carriers, container manufacturers, and emergency response and spill cleanup companies. Promotes safety in the domestic and international transportation of hazardous materials. Provides information and educational services; sponsors conferences, workshops, and seminars. Advocates uniform hazardous materials regulations.

International Assn. of Heat and Frost Insulators and Asbestos, *1776 Massachusetts Ave. N.W., #301 20036-1989; (202) 785-2388. Fax, (202) 429-0568. William G. Bernard, President. Web, www.insulators.org.*

Membership: approximately 18,000 workers in insulation industries. Helps members negotiate pay, benefits, and better working conditions; conducts training programs and workshops. Monitors legislation and regulations. (Affiliated with the AFL-CIO.)

National Insulation Assn., *99 Canal Center Plaza, #222, Alexandria, VA 22314; (703) 683-6422. Fax, (703) 549-4838. Bill Pitkin, Executive Vice President. General e-mail, niainfo@insulation.org. Web, www.insulation.org.*

Membership: companies in the commercial and industrial insulation and asbestos abatement industries. Monitors legislation and regulations.

Rachel Carson Council, *8940 Jones Mill Rd., Chevy Chase, MD 20815; (301) 652-1877. Diana Post, Executive Director. General e-mail, rccouncil@aol.com. Web, members.aol.com/rccouncil/ourpage.*

Acts as a clearinghouse for information on pesticides and alternatives to their use; maintains extensive data on toxicity and the effects of pesticides on humans and domestic animals. Library open to the public by appointment.

See also Chemical Manufacturers Assn. (p. 614); League of Women Voters Education Fund, Natural Resources (p. 281)

Radiation Protection

See also Nuclear Energy (chap. 8)

AGENCIES

Armed Forces Radiobiology Research Institute *(Defense Dept.), 8901 Wisconsin Ave., Bethesda, MD*

20889-5603; (301) 295-1210. Fax, (301) 295-4967. Col. Robert Eng (MSUSA), Director. Web, www.afrri.usuhs.mil.

Serves as the principal ionizing radiation radiobiology research laboratory under the jurisdiction of the Uniformed Services University of the Health Sciences. Participates in international conferences and projects. Library open to the public.

Environment, Safety, and Health *(Energy Dept.), Nuclear and Facility Safety, 1000 Independence Ave. S.W., #7A121 20585; (202) 586-2407. Fax, (202) 586-6010. Orin Pearson, Deputy Assistant Secretary. Web, tis-nt.eh.doe.gov/eh-3/sect-3.htm.*

Reviews radiological protection standards and programs at Energy Dept. facilities; provides department with technical assistance in the area of nuclear and facility safety.

Environmental Protection Agency, *Radiation and Indoor Air, 501 3rd St. N.W. 20001 (mailing address: 401 M St. S.W., #6601J 20460); (202) 564-9320. Fax, (202) 565-2043. Stephen D. Page, Director.*

Establishes standards to regulate the amount of radiation discharged into the environment from uranium mining and milling projects and other activities that result in radioactive emissions; and to ensure safe disposal of radioactive waste. Fields a Radiological Emergency Response Team. Administers the nationwide Environmental Radiation Ambient Monitoring System (ERAMS), which analyzes environmental radioactive contamination.

Food and Drug Administration *(Health and Human Services Dept.), Center for Devices and Radiological Health, 9200 Corporate Blvd., #100, Rockville, MD 20850; (301) 443-4690. Fax, (301) 594-1320. David W. Feigal Jr., Director. International Reference System, (301) 827-3993. Web, www.fda.gov/cdrh.*

Administers national programs to control exposure to radiation; establishes standards for emissions from consumer and medical products; conducts factory inspections. Accredits and certifies mammography facilities and personnel; provides physicians and consumers with guidelines on radiation-emitting products. Conducts research, training, and educational programs. Library open to the public.

NONPROFIT

Institute for Science and International Security, *236 Massachusetts Ave. N.E., #500 20002; (202) 547-3633. Fax, (202) 547-3634. David Albright, Director. General e-mail, isis@isis-online.org. Web, www.isis-online.org.*

Analyzes scientific and policy issues affecting national and international security, including the problems of war, regional and global arms races, the spread of nuclear weapons, and the environmental, health, and safety hazards of nuclear weapons production.

NAHB Research Center, *Radon Research and Indoor Air Quality: Laboratory Services,* *400 Prince George's Blvd., Upper Marlboro, MD 20774; (301) 249-4000. Fax, (301) 249-0305. Tom Kenney, Director. Web, www.nahbrc. org.*

Conducts building research to lower the cost and improve the quality of housing and other types of buildings; labels and certifies building products.

National Council on Radiation Protection and Measurements, *7910 Woodmont Ave., #800, Bethesda, MD 20814; (301) 657-2652. Fax, (301) 907-8768. William M. Beckner, Executive Director. Information, (800) 229-2652. Web, www.ncrp.com.*

Corporation chartered by Congress that collects and analyzes information and provides recommendations on radiation protection and measurement. Studies radiation emissions from household items and from office and medical equipment. Holds annual conference; publishes reports on radiation protection and measurement.

See also American College of Radiology (p. 374); Public Citizen, Health Research Group (p. 60)

Recycling and Solid Waste

AGENCIES

Environmental Protection Agency, *Solid Waste and Emergency Response,* *401 M St. S.W., #5101, MC 360 20460; (202) 260-4610. Fax, (202) 260-3527. Timothy Fields Jr., Assistant Administrator. Superfund/Resource conservation and recovery hotline, (800) 424-9346; in Washington, (703) 412-9810. TTY, (800) 553-7672; in Washington, (703) 412-3323. Web, www.epa.gov/swerrims.*

Administers and enforces the Resource Conservation and Recovery Act.

CONGRESS

House Commerce Committee, *Subcommittee on Finance and Hazardous Materials,* *2125 RHOB 20515; (202) 225-2927. Fax, (202) 225-1919. Rep. Michael G. Oxley, R-Ohio, Chair; James E. Derderian, Staff Director. General e-mail, commerce@mail.house.gov. Web, www. house.gov/commerce.*

Jurisdiction over legislation on solid waste disposal, including the Resource Conservation and Recovery Act. (Jurisdiction shared with House Science and House Transportation and Infrastructure committees.)

House Science Committee, *Subcommittee on Energy and Environment,* *389 FHOB 20515; (202) 225-9662. Fax, (202) 226-6983. Rep. Ken Calvert, R-Calif., Chair; Harlan Watson, Staff Director. Web, www.house.gov/ science.*

Jurisdiction over legislation and research and development on solid waste disposal, including the Resource Conservation and Recovery Act. (Jurisdiction shared with House Commerce and House Transportation and Infrastructure committees.)

House Transportation and Infrastructure Committee, *Subcommittee on Water Resources and Environment,* *B376 RHOB 20515; (202) 225-4360. Fax, (202) 226-5435. Rep. Sherwood Boehlert, R-N.Y., Chair; Ben Grumbles, Counsel. General e-mail, transcomm@mail. house.gov. Web, www.house.gov/transportation.*

Shares jurisdiction over the Comprehensive Environmental Response, Compensation, and Liability Act (the Superfund) with the House Commerce and House Science committees.

Senate Environment and Public Works Committee, *Subcommittee on Superfund, Waste Control, and Risk Assessment,* *SD-410 20510; (202) 224-6176. Fax, (202) 224-5167. Sen. Lincoln Chafee, R-R.I., Chair; Ted Michaels, Staff Director. Web, epw.senate.gov.*

Jurisdiction over research and development and legislation on solid waste disposal, including the Resource Conservation and Recovery Act.

NONPROFIT

Alliance of Foam Packaging Recyclers, *2128 Espey Court, #4, Crofton, MD 21114; (410) 451-8340. Fax, (410) 451-8343. Betsy DeCampos, Executive Director. Information, (800) 944-8448. Web, www.epspackaging.org.*

Membership: companies that recycle foam packaging material. Coordinates national network of collection centers for postconsumer foam packaging products; helps to establish new collection centers.

American Plastics Council, *1300 Wilson Blvd., #800, Arlington, VA 22209; (703) 253-0700. Fax, (703) 253-0701. Ronald H. Yocum, President. Web, www.plastics.org.*

Seeks to increase plastics recycling; conducts research on disposal of plastic products; sponsors research on waste-handling methods, incineration, and degradation; supports programs that test alternative waste management technologies. Monitors legislation and regulations. (Affiliated with the Society of the Plastics Industry.)

Assn. of State and Territorial Solid Waste Management Officials, *444 N. Capitol St. N.W., #315 20001; (202) 624-5828. Fax, (202) 624-7875. Thomas Kennedy,*

Executive Director. General e-mail, swmtrina@sso.org. Web, www.astswmo.org.

Membership: state and territorial solid waste management officials. Works with the Environmental Protection Agency to develop policy on solid and hazardous waste.

Container Recycling Institute, *1911 Fort Myer Dr., #900, Arlington, VA 22209-1603; (703) 276-9800. Fax, (703) 276-9587. Pat Franklin, Executive Director. General e-mail, cri@igc.org. Web, www.container_recycling.org.*

Studies alternatives for reducing container and packaging waste; researches container and packaging reuse and recycling options; serves as an information clearinghouse.

Environmental Industry Assns., *4301 Connecticut Ave. N.W., #300 20008; (202) 244-4700. Fax, (202) 966-4818. Bruce Parker, President. Web, www.envasns.org.*

Membership: organizations engaged in refuse collection, processing, and disposal. Provides information on solid and hazardous waste management and waste equipment; sponsors workshops.

Flexible Packaging Assn., *1090 Vermont Ave. N.W., #500 20005-4960; (202) 842-3880. Fax, (202) 842-3841. John Woolford, President (Interim). General e-mail, fpa@flexpack.org.*

Coordinates environmental programs on reducing solid waste for schools and the public.

Foodservice and Packaging Institute, *1550 Wilson Blvd., #701, Arlington, VA 22209; (703) 527-7505. Fax, (703) 527-7512. John Burke, President. General e-mail, fpi@fpi.org. Web, www.fpi.org.*

Membership: manufacturers, suppliers, and distributors of disposable products used in food service, packaging, and consumer products. Promotes the use of disposables for commercial and home use; sponsors research on recycling and composting technology. Monitors environmental legislation.

Glass Packaging Institute, *1627 K St. N.W., #800 20006; (202) 887-4850. Fax, (202) 785-5377. Joseph Cattaneo, Executive Vice President. Web, www.gpi.org.*

Membership: manufacturers of glass containers and their suppliers. Promotes industry policies to protect the environment, conserve natural resources, and reduce energy consumption; conducts research; monitors legislation affecting the industry. Interests include glass recycling.

Institute for Local Self-Reliance, *2425 18th St. N.W. 20009-2096; (202) 232-4108. Fax, (202) 332-0463. Neil Seldman, President. General e-mail, ilsr@igc.org. Web, www.ilsr.org.*

Conducts research and provides technical assistance on environmentally sound economic development for government, small businesses, and community organizations. Advocates the development of a materials policy at local, state, and regional levels to reduce per capita consumption of raw materials and to shift from dependence on fossil fuels to reliance on renewable resources.

Institute of Scrap Recycling Industries, *1325 G St. N.W., #1000 20005; (202) 737-1770. Fax, (202) 626-0900. Robin Wiener, Executive Director. General e-mail, isri@isri.org. Web, www.isri.org.*

Represents processors, brokers, and consumers of scrap paper, glass, plastic, textiles, rubber, and ferrous and nonferrous metals.

Integrated Waste Services Assn., *1401 H St. N.W., #220 20005; (202) 467-6240. Fax, (202) 467-6225. Maria Zannes, President. General e-mail, iwsa@ix.netcom.com. Web, www.wte.org.*

Membership: companies that design, build, and operate resource recovery facilities. Promotes integrated solutions to municipal solid waste management issues. Encourages the use of waste-to-energy technology.

National Assn. of Chemical Recyclers, *1900 M St. N.W., #750 20036; (202) 296-1725. Fax, (202) 296-2530. Joann Wright, Administrator (Acting). Web, www.nacr-r2.org.*

Membership: commercial chemical recyclers and others interested in the industry. Promotes the recovery and reuse of spent solvent as an alternative to waste disposal. Seeks to educate members on the safest and most efficient methods of recycling. Sponsors seminars and conferences. Monitors legislation and regulations.

National Recycling Coalition, *1727 King St., #105, Alexandria, VA 22314; (703) 683-9025. Fax, (703) 683-9026. William M. Ferretti, Executive Director. Web, www.nrc-recycle.org.*

Membership: public officials; community recycling groups; local, state, and national agencies; environmentalists; waste haulers; solid waste disposal consultants; and private recycling companies. Encourages recycling to reduce waste, preserve resources, and promote economic development.

Polystyrene Packaging Council, *1300 Wilson Blvd., #800, Arlington, VA 22209; (703) 253-0649. Fax, (703) 253-0651. Michael Levy, Executive Director. Web, www.polystyrene.org.*

Membership: manufacturers and suppliers of polystyrene foam products. Promotes effective use and recycling of polystyrene; studies and reports on solid waste disposal issues, including waste-to-energy incineration and use of landfills. Serves as an information clearinghouse. Monitors legislation and regulations.

Shippers of Recycled Textiles, *7910 Woodmont Ave., #1130, Bethesda, MD 20814; (301) 656-1077. Fax, (301) 656-1079. Bernard D. Brill, Executive Vice President. General e-mail, smartasn@erols.com. Web, www.smartasn.org.*

Membership: organizations and individuals involved in shipping and distributing recycled textiles and other textile products. Publishes statistics on the amount of waste material recycled. (Affiliated with the Secondary Materials and Recycled Textiles Assn.)

Solid Waste Assn. of North America, *1100 Wayne Ave., #700, Silver Spring, MD 20910 (mailing address: P.O. Box 7219, Silver Spring, MD 20907); (301) 585-2898. Fax, (301) 589-7068. John Skinner, Executive Director. Web, www.swana.org.*

Membership: government officials who manage municipal solid waste programs. Interests include waste reduction, collection, recycling, combustion, and disposal. Conducts training and certification programs. Operates solid waste information clearinghouse. Monitors legislation and regulations.

U.S. Conference of Mayors, *Municipal Waste Management Assn., 1620 Eye St. N.W., 6th Floor 20006; (202) 293-7330. Fax, (202) 293-2352. J. Thomas Cochran, Executive Director; David Gatton, Deputy Executive Director. Web, www.usmayors.org/uscm/about/affiliate_organizations/non-elected_affiliates/municip.html.*

Organization of local governments and private companies involved in planning and developing solid waste management programs, including pollution prevention, waste-to-energy, and recycling. Assists communities with financing, environmental assessments, and associated policy implementation.

See also Automotive Recyclers Assn. (p. 679)

Water Pollution

See also Water Resources (this chapter)

AGENCIES

Environmental Protection Agency, *Ground and Drinking Water, 401 M St. S.W., 1209 East Tower, MC 4601 20460; (202) 260-5543. Fax, (202) 260-4383. Cynthia Dougherty, Director. Toll-free hotline, (800) 426-4791. Web, www.epa.gov/ogwdw.*

Develops standards for the quality of drinking water supply systems; regulates underground injection of waste and protection of groundwater wellhead areas under the Safe Drinking Water Act; provides information on public water supply systems.

Environmental Protection Agency, *Municipal Support, 1200 Pennsylvania Ave. N.W. 20460; (202) 260-5859. Fax, (202) 260-1827. Richard T. Kuhlman, Director (Acting).*

Directs programs to assist in the design and construction of municipal sewage systems; develops programs to ensure efficient operation and maintenance of municipal wastewater treatment facilities; implements programs for prevention of water pollution.

Environmental Protection Agency, *Science and Technology, 401 M St. S.W., MC4301, 635 West Tower 20460; (202) 260-5400. Fax, (202) 260-5394. Geoffrey H. Grubbs, Director.*

Develops and coordinates water pollution control programs for the Environmental Protection Agency; monitors water quality nationwide and maintains a data collection system; assists state and regional agencies in establishing water quality standards and planning local water resources management; develops guidelines for industrial wastewater discharge.

Environmental Protection Agency, *Wastewater Management, 1200 Pennsylvania Ave. N.W. 20460; (202) 260-5850. Fax, (202) 260-1040. Michael B. Cook, Director.*

Oversees the issuance of water permits. Responsible for the Pretreatment Program regulating industrial discharges to local sewage treatment. Oversees the State Revolving Funds Program, which provides assistance for the construction of wastewater treatment plants.

National Drinking Water Advisory Council, *401 M St. S.W., MC 4601, 1209 East Tower 20460; (202) 260-2285. Fax, (202) 260-4383. Charlene Shaw, Officer. Web, www.epa.gov/OGWDW.*

Advises the EPA administrator on activities, functions, and policies relating to implementation of the Safe Drinking Water Act.

National Oceanic and Atmospheric Administration *(Commerce Dept.), Office of Response and Restoration, 1305 East-West Hwy., Silver Spring, MD 20910; (301) 713-2989. Fax, (301) 713-4389. David Kennedy, Director. Web, www.nos.noaa.gov/programs/orr.html.*

Provides information on damage to marine ecosystems caused by pollution. Offers information on spill trajectory projections and chemical hazard analyses. Researches trends of toxic contamination on U.S. coastal regions.

U.S. Coast Guard *(Transportation Dept.), National Pollution Funds Center, 4200 Wilson Blvd., #1000, Arlington, VA 22203; (202) 493-6700. Fax, (202) 493-6900. Daniel F. Sheehan, Director. Web, www.uscg.mil/hq/npfc/npfc.htm.*

Certifies the financial responsibility of vessels and companies involved in oil exploration and transportation in U.S. waters and on the outer continental shelf; manages the Oil Spill Liability Trust Fund under the Oil Pollution Act of 1990.

U.S. Coast Guard *(Transportation Dept.), Response, 2100 2nd St. S.W., #2100 20593; (202) 267-0518. Fax, (202) 267-4085. Capt. Larry L. Hereth, Chief. Web, www.uscg.mil/hq/g-m/mor/default.html.*

Oversees cleanup operations after spills of oil and other hazardous substances in U.S. waters, on the outer continental shelf, and in international waters. Reviews coastal zone management and enforces international standards for pollution prevention and response.

CONGRESS

House Commerce Committee, *Subcommittee on Health and the Environment, 2125 RHOB 20515; (202) 225-2927. Fax, (202) 225-1919. Rep. Michael Bilirakis, R-Fla., Chair; James E. Derderian, Staff Director. General e-mail, commerce@mail.house.gov. Web, www.house.gov/commerce.*

Jurisdiction over legislation on drinking water purity, including the Safe Drinking Water Act.

House Resources Committee, *Subcommittee on Fisheries, Conservation, Wildlife, and Oceans, H2-187 FHOB 20515; (202) 226-0200. Fax, (202) 225-1542. Rep. H. James Saxton, R-N.J., Chair; Harry Burroughs, Staff Director. General e-mail, fishery.subcommittee@mail.house.gov. Web, www.house.gov/resources/fisheries.*

Jurisdiction over legislation concerning coastal marine pollution, including the Magnuson-Stevens Fishery Conservation and Management Act, and elements of the Clean Water Act and the National Environmental Policy Act.

House Transportation and Infrastructure Committee, *Subcommittee on Coast Guard and Maritime Transportation, 507 FHOB 20515; (202) 226-3552. Fax, (202) 226-2524. Rep. Wayne T. Gilchrest, R-Md., Chair; Rebecca Dye, Counsel. General e-mail, transcomm@mail.house.gov. Web, www.house.gov/transportation.*

Jurisdiction over legislation on ocean dumping, oil spills and financial responsibility requirements, and marine pollution control and abatement. (Jurisdiction shared with the Subcommittee on Water Resources and Environment.)

House Transportation and Infrastructure Committee, *Subcommittee on Water Resources and Environment, B376 RHOB 20515; (202) 225-4360. Fax, (202) 226-5435. Rep. Sherwood Boehlert, R-N.Y., Chair; Ben Grumbles, Counsel. General e-mail, transcomm@mail.house.gov. Web, www.house.gov/transportation.*

Jurisdiction over most legislation on water pollution, including the Clean Water Act. Shares jurisdiction on oil spills and financial responsibility requirements with the Subcommittee on Coast Guard and Maritime Transportation.

Senate Environment and Public Works Committee, *SD-410 20510; (202) 224-6176. Fax, (202) 224-5167. Sen. Robert C. Smith, R-N.H., Chair; Dave Conover, Staff Director. Web, epw.senate.gov.*

Jurisdiction over legislation on ocean dumping and ocean pollution research; drinking water purity; water pollution; oil spill laws and financial responsibility requirements; and marine pollution control and abatement; jurisdiction over the Clean Water Act, National Environmental Policy Act, Safe Drinking Water Act, and Ocean Dumping Act.

NONPROFIT

Alliance for Environmental Technology, *1250 24th St. N.W., #300 20037; (202) 835-1688. Fax, (202) 835-1601. Douglas C. Pryke, Executive Director. General e-mail, info@aet.org. Web, www.aet.org.*

Membership: U.S. and Canadian chemical manufacturers and forest products companies. Seeks to improve environmental performance of the pulp and paper industry, particularly in waste water; supports use of chlorine dioxide to prevent pollution. Monitors legislation and regulations.

Assn. of State and Interstate Water Pollution Control Administrators, *750 First St. N.E., #1010 20002; (202) 898-0905. Fax, (202) 898-0929. Roberta Haley Savage, Executive Director. General e-mail, admin1@asiwpca.org. Web, www.asiwpca.org.*

Membership: administrators of state water pollution agencies and related associations. Represents the states' concerns on implementation, funding, and reauthorization of the Clean Water Act. Monitors legislation and regulations.

Center for Marine Conservation, *1725 DeSales St. N.W., #600 20036; (202) 429-5609. Fax, (202) 872-0619. Roger T. Rufe, President. General e-mail, cmc@dccmc.org. Web, www.cmc-ocean.org.*

Protects the health of oceans and seas. Advocates policies that restrict discharge of pollutants harmful to marine ecosystems.

Clean Water Action, 4455 Connecticut Ave. N.W., #A300 20008; (202) 895-0420. Fax, (202) 895-0438. David R. Zwick, President. General e-mail, cwa@essential.org. Web, www.essential.org/cwa.

Citizens' organization interested in clean, safe, and affordable water. Works to influence public policy through education, technical assistance, and grassroots organizing. Interests include toxins and pollution, drinking water, water conservation, sewage treatment, pesticides, mass burn incineration, bay and estuary protection, and consumer water issues. Monitors legislation and regulations.

League of Women Voters Education Fund, *Natural Resources,* 1730 M St. N.W., #1000 20036; (202) 429-1965. Fax, (202) 429-0854. Jane Gruenebaum, Director. Web, www.lwv.org.

Education foundation affiliated with the League of Women Voters. Conducts a national project concerning community drinking water systems and groundwater. Sponsors research and develops educational materials on water issues; helps local leagues manage demonstration programs.

Water Environment Federation, 601 Wythe St., Alexandria, VA 22314-1994; (703) 684-2400. Fax, (703) 684-2492. Quincalee Brown, Executive Director. Web, www.wef.org.

Membership: civil and environmental engineers, wastewater treatment plant operators, scientists, government officials, and others concerned with water quality. Works to preserve and improve water quality worldwide. Provides the public with technical information and educational materials. Monitors legislation and regulations.

▣ RESOURCES MANAGEMENT

See also Energy (chap. 8)

AGENCIES

Bureau of Land Management *(Interior Dept.),* *Renewable Resources and Planning,* 1849 C St. N.W., #5650 20240; (202) 208-4896. Fax, (202) 208-5010. Henri Bisson, Assistant Director. Web, www.blm.gov.

Develops and implements natural resource programs for renewable resources use and protection, including management of forested land, rangeland, wild horses and burros, wildlife habitats, endangered species, soil and water quality, rights of way, recreation, and cultural programs.

Interior Dept., 1849 C St. N.W., #6156 20240; (202) 208-7351. Fax, (202) 208-6956. Bruce Babbitt, Secretary; David Hayes, Deputy Secretary. Information, (202) 208-3100. Library, (202) 208-5815. Locator, (202) 208-3100. Web, www.doi.gov.

Manages most federal land through its component agencies; responsible for conservation and development of mineral, water, and fish and wildlife resources; operates recreation programs for federal parks, refuges, and public lands; preserves and administers the scenic and historic areas; administers native American lands and relationships with tribal governments.

Tennessee Valley Authority, *Government Affairs,* *Washington Office,* 1 Massachusetts Ave. N.W., #300 20444; (202) 898-2999. Fax, (202) 898-2998. David Withrow, Vice President. Web, www.tva.gov.

Coordinates resource conservation, development, and land-use programs in the Tennessee River Valley. Activities include forestry and wildlife development.

NONPROFIT

National Assn. of Conservation Districts, 509 Capitol Court N.E. 20002-4937; (202) 547-6223. Fax, (202) 547-6450. Ernest C. Shea, Chief Executive Officer. Web, www.nacdnet.org.

Membership: conservation districts (local subdivisions of state government). Works to promote the conservation of land, forests, and other natural resources. Interests include erosion and sediment control; water quality; forestry, water, flood plain, and range management; rural development; and urban and community conservation.

Renewable Natural Resources Foundation, 5430 Grosvenor Lane, Bethesda, MD 20814-2193; (301) 493-9101. Fax, (301) 493-6148. Robert D. Day, Executive Director. General e-mail, rnrf@aol.com. Web, rnrf.org.

Consortium of professional, scientific, and education organizations working to advance scientific and public education in renewable natural resources. Encourages the application of sound scientific practices to resource management and conservation. Fosters interdisciplinary cooperation among its member organizations.

U.S. Chamber of Commerce, *Environment and Regulatory Affairs,* 1615 H St. N.W. 20062-2000; (202) 463-5533. Fax, (202) 887-3445. Bill Kovacs, Manager. Web, www.uschamber.org.

Develops policy on all issues affecting the production, use, and conservation of natural resources, including fuel and nonfuel minerals, timber, water, public lands, on- and offshore energy, wetlands, and endangered species.

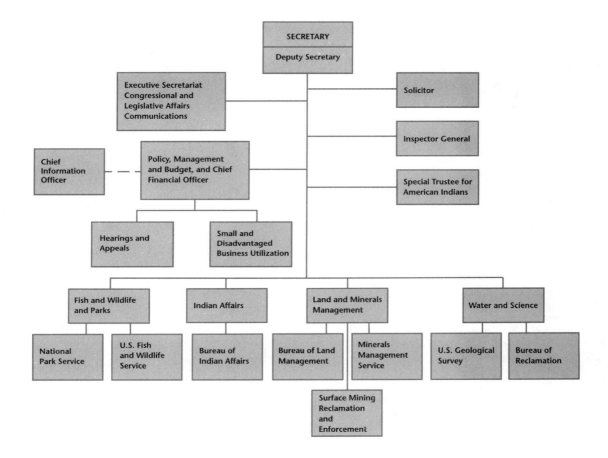

Wildlife Management Institute, *1101 14th St. N.W., #801 20005; (202) 371-1808. Fax, (202) 408-5059. Rollin D. Sparrowe, President. Web, www.wildlifemgt.org/wmi.*

Research and consulting organization that provides technical services and information about natural resources. Interests include forests, rangelands, and land, water, and wildlife resources.

See also Rand Corporation (p. 499)

Forests and Rangelands

AGENCIES

Forest Service *(Agriculture Dept.), 201 14th St. S.W., #4NW 20024 (mailing address: P.O. Box 96090 20090-6090); (202) 205-1661. Fax, (202) 205-1765. Mike Dombeck, Chief. Web, www.fs.fed.us.*

Manages national forests and grasslands for outdoor recreation and sustained yield of renewable natural resources, including timber, water, forage, fish, and wildlife. Cooperates with state and private foresters; conducts forestry research.

Forest Service *(Agriculture Dept.), International Programs, 201 14th St. S.W. 20024 (mailing address: P.O. Box 96090 20090-6090); (202) 205-1650. Fax, (202) 205-1603. Valdis Mezainis, Director. Web, www.fs.fed.us/global.*

Responsible for the Forest Service's involvement in international forest conservation efforts. Analyzes international resource issues; promotes information exchange; provides planning and technical assistance. Interests include tropical forests and sustainable forest management.

Forest Service *(Agriculture Dept.), National Forest System,* *201 14th St. S.W., #3NW 20024 (mailing address: P.O. Box 96090 20090-6090); (202) 205-1523. Fax, (202) 205-1758. James Furnish, Deputy Chief. Web, www.fs.fed.us.*

Manages 191 million acres of forests and rangelands. Products and services from these lands include timber, water, forage, wildlife, minerals, and recreation.

Forest Service *(Agriculture Dept.), Research and Development,* *201 14th St. S.W., #1NW Yates Bldg. 20024 (mailing address: P.O. Box 96090 20090-6090); (202) 205-1665. Fax, (202) 205-1530. Robert Lewis Jr., Deputy Chief. Web, www.fs.fed.us.*

Conducts biological, physical, and economic research related to forestry, including studies on harvesting methods, acid deposition, international forestry, the effects of global climate changes on forests, and forest products. Provides information on the establishment, improvement, and growth of trees, grasses, and other forest vegetation. Works to protect forest resources from fire, insects, diseases, and animal pests. Examines the effect of forest use activities on water quality, soil erosion, and sediment production. Conducts continuous forest survey and analyzes outlook for future supply and demand.

Forest Service *(Agriculture Dept.), State and Private Forestry,* *1400 Independence Ave. S.W., #2NW 20024 (mailing address: P.O. Box 96090 20090-6090); (202) 205-1657. Fax, (202) 205-1174. Janice McDougle, Deputy Chief. Web, www.fs.fed.us.*

Assists state and private forest owners with the protection and management of 574 million acres of forest and associated watershed lands. Assistance includes fire control, protecting forests from insects and diseases, land-use planning, developing multiple-use management, and improving practices in harvesting, processing, and marketing of forest products.

Forest Service *(Agriculture Dept.), Youth Conservation Corps,* *1621 N. Kent St., Arlington, VA 22209 (mailing address: P.O. Box 96090 20090-6090); (703) 605-4854. Fax, (703) 605-5115. Ransom Hughes, Program Manager.*

Administers with the National Park Service and the Fish and Wildlife Service the Youth Conservation Corps, a summer employment and training, public works program for youths ages fifteen to eighteen. The program is conducted in national parks, in national forests, and on national wildlife refuges.

CONGRESS

House Agriculture Committee, *Subcommittee on Department Operations, Oversight, Nutrition, and Forestry,* *1430 LHOB 20515; (202) 225-4913. Fax, (202)*

225-4464. Rep. Robert W. Goodlatte, R-Va., Chair; Kevin Kramp, Staff Director. Web, agriculture.house.gov.

Jurisdiction over legislation on forestry in general and forest reserves acquired from state, local, or private sources. Oversight of Forest Service.

House Resources Committee, *1324 LHOB 20515-6201; (202) 225-2761. Fax, (202) 225-5929. Rep. Don Young, R-Alaska, Chair; Lloyd Jones, Staff Director. General e-mail, resources.committee@mail.house.gov. Web, www.house.gov/resources.*

Jurisdiction over legislation on forest reserves and public lands in Alaska.

House Resources Committee, *Subcommittee on Forests and Forest Health,* *1337 LHOB 20515; (202) 225-0691. Fax, (202) 225-0521. Rep. Helen Chenoweth-Hage, R-Idaho, Chair; Doug Crandall, Staff Director. General e-mail, resources.committee@mail.house.gov. Web, www. house.gov/resources/forests.*

Jurisdiction over legislation on public forest lands (except in Alaska), including issues of forestry, wilderness preservation, forest reserve, water rights, national trails and rivers, and recreation.

House Resources Committee, *Subcommittee on National Parks and Public Lands,* *140 CHOB 20515; (202) 226-7736. Fax, (202) 226-2301. Rep. James V. Hansen, R-Utah, Chair; Allen Freemyer, Staff Director. General e-mail, parks.subcommittee@mail.house.gov. Web, www.house.gov/resources/parks.*

Jurisdiction over legislation on public lands (except lands in Alaska and forests), the national park system, the establishment of wildlife refuges on public lands, and the Bureau of Land Management.

Senate Agriculture, Nutrition, and Forestry Committee, *Subcommittee on Forestry, Conservation, and Rural Revitalization,* *SR-328A 20510; (202) 224-2752. Fax, (202) 224-1725. Sen. Larry E. Craig, R-Idaho, Chair; Dan Whiting, Staff Contact. Web, agriculture.senate.gov.*

Jurisdiction over legislation on forestry in general and forest reserves acquired from state, local, or private sources.

Senate Energy and Natural Resources Committee, *Subcommittee on Forest and Public Land Management,* *SD-306 20510; (202) 224-6170. Fax, (202) 228-0539. Sen. Larry E. Craig, R-Idaho, Chair; Mark Rey, Professional Staff Member. General e-mail, forests@energy.senate.gov. Web, energy.senate.gov.*

Jurisdiction over legislation on forest reserves, public lands, the national forest system, the establishment of wildlife refuges on public lands, and the Bureau of Land Management.

NONPROFIT

American Forest and Paper Assn., *Regulatory Affairs, 1111 19th St. N.W., #800 20036; (202) 463-2700. Fax, (202) 463-2785. Sharon Kneiss, Vice President. Web, www.afandpa.org.*

Membership: manufacturers of wood and specialty products and related associations. Interests include tax, housing, environmental, international trade, natural resources, and land-use issues that affect the wood products industry.

American Forests, *910 17th St. N.W., #600 20006 (mailing address: P.O. Box 2000 20013-2000); (202) 955-4500. Fax, (202) 955-4588. Deborah Gangloff, Executive Vice President. Web, www.amfor.org.*

Citizens' interest group that promotes protection and responsible management of forests and natural resources. Provides information on conservation, public land policy, urban forestry, and timber management. Runs an international tree planting campaign to help mitigate global warming.

American Hardwood Export Council, *1111 19th St. N.W., #800 20036; (202) 463-2720. Fax, (202) 463-2787. Michael Snow, Executive Director. Web, www.ahec.org.*

Trade association of companies and associations that export hardwood products. Aids members in developing and expanding export capabilities in new and existing markets.

American Wood Preservers Institute, *2750 Prosperity Ave. #550, Fairfax, VA 22031-4312; (703) 204-0500. Fax, (703) 204-4610. Scott Ramminger, President. General e-mail, info@awpi.org. Web, www.awpi.org.*

Membership: wood preservers, including manufacturers, formulators of wood preservatives, wood treating companies, and environmental technology companies. Monitors legislation and regulations.

Forest Resources Assn., *600 Jefferson Plaza, #350, Rockville, MD 20852; (301) 838-9385. Fax, (301) 838-9481. Richard Lewis, President. Web, www.forestresources.org.*

Membership: logging contractors, pulpwood dealers, suppliers, and consumers. Administers programs to improve the productivity, safety, and efficiency of pulpwood harvesting and transport; provides information on new equipment, tools, and methods; works to ensure continued access to the timberland base. Monitors legislation and regulations.

International Wood Products Assn., *4214 King St., Alexandria, VA 22302; (703) 820-6696. Fax, (703) 820-8550. Wendy Baer, Executive Vice President. General e-mail, info@iwpawood.org. Web, www.iwpawood.org.*

Membership: companies that handle imported wood products. Encourages environmentally responsible forest management and international trade in wood products. Sponsors research and environmental education on tropical forestry. (Affiliated with the Tropical Forest Foundation.)

National Assn. of State Foresters, *444 N. Capitol St. N.W., #540 20001; (202) 624-5415. Fax, (202) 624-5407. Bill Imbergamo, Executive Director. General e-mail, nasf@sso.org. Web, www.stateforesters.org.*

Membership: directors of state forestry agencies from all states, the District of Columbia, and U.S. territories. Members manage and protect over two thirds of the nation's forests, as well as assist private landowners in managing their forests. Monitors legislation and regulations.

National Forest Foundation, *1050 17th St. N.W., #600 20036; (202) 216-9750. Fax, (202) 219-6585. William Possiel, President. Web, www.nffweb.org.*

Established by Congress to support the U.S. Forest Service in its management of public lands. Promotes research and multiple-use, cooperative forestry. Interests include conservation, preservation, recreation, wildlife, and environmental education.

National Lumber and Building Material Dealers Assn., *40 Ivy St. S.E. 20003; (202) 547-2230. Fax, (202) 547-7640. Gary W. Donnelly, President. General e-mail, nlbmda@dealer.org. Web, www.dealer.org.*

Membership: federated associations of retailers in the lumber and building material industries. Monitors legislation and regulations.

Save America's Forests, *4 Library Court S.E. 20003; (202) 544-9219. Fax, (202) 544-7462. Carl Ross, Executive Director. Web, www.saveamericasforests.org.*

Coalition of environmental and public interest groups, businesses, and individuals. Advocates recycling and comprehensive nationwide laws to prevent deforestation and to protect forest ecosystems.

Society of American Foresters, *5400 Grosvenor Lane, Bethesda, MD 20814-2198; (301) 897-8720. Fax, (301) 897-3690. William H. Banzhaf, Executive Vice President. Web, www.safnet.org.*

Association of forestry professionals. Provides technical information on forestry; accredits forestry programs in universities and colleges.

See also Alliance for Environmental Technology (p. 301); International Center (p. 445)

Land Resources and Rights

See also Rural Areas (chap. 12); Soil and Watershed Conservation (chap. 2)

AGENCIES

Bureau of Land Management *(Interior Dept.),* 1849 C St. N.W., #5660 20240; (202) 208-3801. Fax, (202) 208-5242. Tom Fry, Director (Acting). Web, www.blm.gov.

Manages public lands and federally owned mineral resources, including oil, gas, and coal. Resources managed and leased include wildlife habitats, timber, minerals, open space, wilderness areas, forage, and recreational resources. Surveys federal lands and maintains public land records.

Bureau of Land Management *(Interior Dept.),* **Lands and Realty,** 1620 L St. N.W. 20240 (mailing address: 1849 C St. N.W., MC 1000LS 20240); (202) 452-7780. Fax, (202) 452-7708. Ray Brady, Manager. Web, www.blm.gov.

Oversees use, acquisition, and disposal of public lands. Conducts the Public Lands Survey; authorizes rights-of-way on public lands, including roads and power lines.

Bureau of Reclamation *(Interior Dept.),* 1849 C St. N.W., #7659 20240; (202) 208-4157. Fax, (202) 208-3484. Eluid Martinez, Commissioner. Information, (202) 208-4215. Web, www.usbr.gov.

Responsible for acquisition, administration, management, and disposal of lands in seventeen western states associated with bureau water resource development projects.

Interior Dept., *Board of Land Appeals,* 4015 Wilson Blvd., #1007A, Arlington, VA 22203; (703) 235-3750. Fax, (703) 235-8349. James L. Byrnes, Chief Administrative Judge. Web, www.doi.gov.

Adjunct office of the interior secretary that decides appeals from decisions rendered by the Bureau of Land Management, the Minerals Management Service, the Office of Surface Mining, and the Bureau of Indian Affairs concerning the use and disposition of public lands and minerals; issues final decisions concerning the Surface Mining Control and Reclamation Act of 1977.

Interior Dept., *Land and Minerals Management,* 1849 C St. N.W., MS-6628 20240; (202) 208-5676. Fax, (202) 208-3144. Sylvia Baca, Assistant Secretary. Web, www. doi.gov.

Directs and supervises the Bureau of Land Management, the Minerals Management Service, and the Office of Surface Mining and Reclamation Enforcement. Supervises programs associated with land-use planning, onshore and offshore minerals, surface mining reclamation and enforcement, and outer continental shelf minerals management.

Interior Dept., *North American Wetlands Conservation Council,* 4401 N. Fairfax Dr., #110, Arlington, VA 22203; (703) 358-1784. Fax, (703) 358-2282. David A. Smith, Coordinator. General e-mail, r9arw_nawwo@mail. fws.gov. Web, www.fws.gov.

Membership: government and private-sector conservation experts. Works to protect, restore, and manage wetlands and other habitats for migratory birds and other animals and to maintain migratory bird and waterfowl populations.

Interior Dept., *Surface Mining Reclamation and Enforcement,* 1951 Constitution Ave. N.W. 20240; (202) 208-4006. Fax, (202) 219-3106. Kathy Karpen, Director. Information, (202) 208-2719. Web, www.osmre.gov/osm.htm.

Regulates surface mining of coal and surface effects of underground coal mining. Responsible for reclamation of abandoned coal mine lands.

Natural Resources Conservation Service *(Agriculture Dept.),* 1400 Independence Ave. S.W. 20013 (mailing address: P.O. Box 2890 20013-2890); (202) 720-4525. Fax, (202) 720-7690. Pearlie S. Reed, Chief. Information, (202) 720-3210. Web, www.ncg.nrcs.usda.gov.

Responsible for soil and water conservation programs, including watershed protection, flood prevention, river basin surveys, and resource conservation and development. Provides landowners, operators, state and local units of government, and community groups with technical assistance in carrying out local programs.

Tennessee Valley Authority, *Government Affairs, Washington Office,* 1 Massachusetts Ave. N.W., #300 20444; (202) 898-2999. Fax, (202) 898-2998. David Withrow, Vice President. Web, www.tva.gov.

Coordinates resource conservation, development, and land-use programs in the Tennessee River Valley. Provides information on land usage in the region.

U.S. Geological Survey *(Interior Dept.),* **Critical Ecosystems,** National Center M.S. 913, Reston, VA 20192; (703) 648-6895. Fax, (703) 648-6647. Sarah Gerould, Assistant Program Coordinator, Minerals.

Provides hydrologic, geologic, geochemical, cartographic, and ecological information to assist land and resource managers in restoring critical ecosystems in south Florida, the San Francisco Bay, the Mohave Desert, Platte River, Yellowstone, and the Chesapeake Bay areas.

CONGRESS

House Resources Committee, *Subcommittee on Energy and Mineral Resources,* 1626 LHOB 20515; (202) 225-9297. Fax, (202) 225-5255. Rep. Barbara Cubin, R-Wyo., Chair; William Condit, Staff Director. General e-mail, resources.committee@mail.house.gov. Web, www. house.gov/resources/energy.

Jurisdiction over legislation on land use planning, including surface mining and development of public lands.

House Resources Committee, *Subcommittee on National Parks and Public Lands,* 140 CHOB 20515; (202) 226-7736. Fax, (202) 226-2301. Rep. James V. Hansen, R-Utah, Chair; Allen Freemyer, Staff Director. General e-mail, parks.subcommittee@mail.house.gov. Web, www.house.gov/resources/parks.

Jurisdiction over legislation on public lands (except in Alaska), the land and water conservation fund, and the Bureau of Land Management.

Senate Energy and Natural Resources Committee, SD-364 20510; (202) 224-4971. Fax, (202) 224-6163. Sen. Frank H. Murkowski, R-Alaska, Chair; Andrew Lundquist, Staff Director. General e-mail, committee@energy.senate. gov. Web, energy.senate.gov.

Jurisdiction over legislation on public lands, the land and water conservation fund, the Bureau of Land Management, and the Alaska National Interest Lands Conservation Act.

Senate Energy and Natural Resources Committee, *Subcommittee on Energy Research, Development, Production, and Regulation,* SD-308 20510; (202) 224-6567. Fax, (202) 228-0302. Sen. Don Nickles, R-Okla., Chair; Howard Useem, Professional Staff Member. General e-mail, erdpr@energy.senate.gov. Web, energy.senate.gov.

Jurisdiction over legislation on land use planning, including surface mining; coal production, distribution, and utilization; and coal severance tax.

Senate Environment and Public Works Committee, *Subcommittee on Clean Air, Wetlands, Private Property, and Nuclear Safety,* SD-410 20510; (202) 224-6176. Fax, (202) 224-5167. Sen. James M. Inhofe, R-Okla., Chair; Andy Wheeler, Staff Contact. Web, epw.senate.gov.

Jurisdiction over legislation on wetlands.

NONPROFIT

American Geological Institute, 4220 King St., Alexandria, VA 22302; (703) 379-2480. Fax, (703) 379-7563. Marcus E. Milling, Executive Director. Web, www.agiweb. org.

Membership: earth science societies and associations. Maintains computerized database of the world's geoscience literature (available to the public for a fee).

American Resort Development Assn., 1220 L St. N.W., #500 20005; (202) 371-6700. Fax, (202) 289-8544. Vacant, President. Web, www.arda.org.

Membership: U.S. and international developers, builders, financiers, marketing companies, and others involved in resort, recreational, and community development. Serves as an information clearinghouse; monitors federal and state legislation affecting land, time share, and community development industries.

Defenders of Property Rights, 1350 Connecticut Ave. N.W., #410 20036; (202) 822-6770. Fax, (202) 822-6774. Nancie Marzulla, President; Roger Marzulla, Chair. Web, www.defendersproprights.org.

Advocates private property rights. Works to ensure that federal and state governments compensate property owners for property seizures and for effects on property value due to government regulations. Conducts litigation on behalf of property owners.

Land Trust Alliance, 1319 F St. N.W., #501 20004-1106; (202) 638-4725. Fax, (202) 638-4730. Jean Hocker, President. Web, www.lta.org.

Membership: organizations and individuals who work to conserve land resources. Serves as a forum for the exchange of information; conducts research and public education programs. Monitors legislation and regulations.

National Assn. of Conservation Districts, 509 Capitol Court N.E. 20002-4937; (202) 547-6223. Fax, (202) 547-6450. Ernest C. Shea, Chief Executive Officer. Web, www.nacdnet.org.

Membership: conservation districts (local subdivisions of state government). Works to promote the conservation of land, forests, and other natural resources. Interests include erosion and sediment control; water quality; forestry, water, flood plain, and range management; rural development; and urban and community conservation.

Public Lands Council, 1301 Pennsylvania Ave. N.W., #300 20004-1701; (202) 347-5355. Fax, (202) 737-4086. K. Jason Campbell, Executive Director. Web, www. cowtown.org.

Membership: cattle and sheep ranchers who hold permits and leases to graze livestock on public lands.

Scenic America, 801 Pennsylvania Ave. S.E., #300 20003-2152; (202) 543-6200. Fax, (202) 543-9130. Meg Maguire, President. Web, www.scenic.org.

Membership: national, state, and local groups concerned with land-use control, growth management, and landscape protection. Works to enhance the scenic quality of America's communities and countryside. Provides information and technical assistance on scenic byways, tree preservation, economics of aesthetic regulation, billboard and sign control, scenic areas preservation, and growth management.

Wallace Genetic Foundation, *4900 Massachusetts Ave. N.W., #220 20016; (202) 966-2932. Fax, (202) 966-3370. Carolyn Sand, Co-Executive Director; Kate Lee, Co-Executive Director. Web, www.wallacegenetic.org.*

Supports national and international nonprofits in the areas of agricultural research, land conservation and preservation, and environmental concerns.

See also National Cattlemen's Beef Assn. (p. 66)

Metals and Minerals

AGENCIES

Bureau of Land Management *(Interior Dept.), Minerals, Realty, and Resource Protection, 1849 C St. N.W., #5627 20240; (202) 208-4201. Fax, (202) 208-4800. Carson W. Culp, Assistant Director.*

Evaluates and classifies onshore oil, natural gas, geothermal resources, and all solid energy and mineral resources, including coal and uranium on federal lands. Develops and administers regulations for fluid and solid mineral leasing on national lands and on the subsurface of land where fluid and solid mineral rights have been reserved for the federal government.

Federal Emergency Management Agency, *Partnerships and Outreach, 500 C St. S.W., #633 20472; (202) 646-3544. Fax, (202) 646-3397. Thomas R. McQuillan, Director.*

Supports the enhancement and availability of a mineral resources base to respond to national emergencies; administers the Defense Production Act; promotes inter- and intra-agency development of mineral resource mobilization plans and policies.

Interior Dept., *Board of Land Appeals, 4015 Wilson Blvd., #1007A, Arlington, VA 22203; (703) 235-3750. Fax, (703) 235-8349. James L. Byrnes, Chief Administrative Judge. Web, www.doi.gov.*

Adjunct office of the interior secretary that decides appeals from decisions rendered by the Bureau of Land Management, the Minerals Management Service, the Office of Surface Mining, and the Bureau of Indian Affairs concerning the use and disposition of public lands and minerals; issues final decisions concerning the Surface Mining Control and Reclamation Act of 1977.

Interior Dept., *Land and Minerals Management, 1849 C St. N.W., MS-6628 20240; (202) 208-5676. Fax, (202) 208-3144. Sylvia Baca, Assistant Secretary. Web, www. doi.gov.*

Directs and supervises the Bureau of Land Management, the Minerals Management Service, and the Office of Surface Mining and Reclamation Enforcement. Supervises programs associated with land-use planning, onshore and offshore minerals, surface mining reclamation and enforcement, and outer continental shelf minerals management.

Interior Dept., *Water and Science, 1849 C St. N.W., #6657, MS 6640 20240; (202) 208-3186. Fax, (202) 208-3324. Mark Schaefer, Assistant Secretary (Acting). Web, www.doi.gov.*

Administers departmental water, scientific, and research activities. Directs and supervises the Bureau of Reclamation and the U.S. Geological Survey.

Minerals Management Service *(Interior Dept.), 1849 C St. N.W., MS 4230 20240; (202) 208-3500. Fax, (202) 208-7242. Walt Rosenbusch, Director. Web, www.mms.gov.*

Collects and accounts for revenues from onshore and offshore minerals production; disburses royalties to the federal government and native American groups; oversees development of offshore resources, especially oil and natural gas.

Minerals Management Service *(Interior Dept.), Engineering and Operations, 381 Elden St., Herndon, VA 20170-4817; (703) 787-1598. Fax, (703) 787-1093. E. P. Danenberger, Chief.*

Oversees postlease operations, including exploration, drilling, and production phases of oil and gas development. Ensures compliance with environmental statutes and regulations.

Minerals Management Service *(Interior Dept.), Royalty Management Program: Washington Royalty Office, Washington Office, 1849 C St. N.W., #4245, MS 4230 20240; (202) 208-3512. Fax, (202) 208-3982. R. Dale Fazio, Chief. Web, www.mms.gov.*

Collects and manages royalties on minerals produced on federal and native American lands. (Headquarters and accounting center in Denver.)

State Dept., *International Energy and Commodities Policy, 2201 C St. N.W., #3529 20520; (202) 647-3036. Fax, (202) 647-4037. Stephen J. Gallogly, Director; Stephen Muller, Chief. Web, www.state.gov.*

Coordinates U.S. international energy policy related to commodities, including energy supply, and U.S. participation in the International Energy Agency; monitors cooperative multilateral and bilateral agreements related to energy; coordinates energy-related aspects of U.S. relations with other countries.

U.S. Geological Survey *(Interior Dept.), Mineral Resource Program,* 12201 Sunrise Valley Dr., MS 913, Reston, VA 20192; (703) 648-6110. Fax, (703) 648-6057. Kathleen Johnson, Program Coordinator. Web, www. minerals.usgs.gov.

Coordinates mineral resource activities for the Geological Survey, including geochemical and geophysical instrumentation and application research.

CONGRESS

House Resources Committee, *Subcommittee on Energy and Mineral Resources,* 1626 LHOB 20515; (202) 225-9297. Fax, (202) 225-5255. Rep. Barbara Cubin, R-Wyo., Chair; William Condit, Staff Director. General e-mail, resources.committee@mail.house.gov. Web, www. house.gov/resources/energy.

Jurisdiction over legislation on metallic and non-metallic minerals; oversight and legislative jurisdiction over the Minerals Management Service, mineral aspects of the Office of Surface Mining, mineral leasing of the Bureau of Land Management, and offshore hardrock mineral development programs.

Senate Energy and Natural Resources Committee, *Subcommittee on Forest and Public Land Management,* SD-306 20510; (202) 224-6170. Fax, (202) 228-0539. Sen. Larry E. Craig, R-Idaho, Chair; Mark Rey, Professional Staff Member. General e-mail, forests@energy.senate.gov. Web, energy.senate.gov.

Jurisdiction over legislation on metallic and non-metallic minerals, including mineral supply and leasing; oversight and legislative jurisdiction over the Minerals Management Service and offshore hardrock mineral development programs. Jurisdiction over the Bureau of Land Management.

NONPROFIT

Aluminum Assn., 900 19th St. N.W., #300 20006; (202) 862-5100. Fax, (202) 862-5164. J. Stephen Larkin, President. Web, www.aluminum.org.

Represents the aluminum industry. Develops voluntary standards and technical data; compiles statistics concerning the industry.

American Iron and Steel Institute, 1101 17th St. N.W., 13th Floor 20036-4700; (202) 452-7100. Fax, (202)

463-6573. Andrew G. Sharkey III, President. Web, www. steel.org.

Represents the iron and steel industry. Publishes statistics on iron and steel production; promotes the use of steel; conducts research. Monitors legislation and regulations.

American Zinc Assn., 1112 16th St. N.W., #240 20036; (202) 835-0164. Fax, (202) 835-0155. George F. Vary, Executive Director. Web, www.zinc.org.

Provides information on zinc. Monitors legislation and regulations.

Mineralogical Society of America, 1015 18th St. N.W., #601 20036; (202) 775-4344. Fax, (202) 775-0018. Bill Carlson, President. Web, www.minsocam.org.

Membership: mineralogists, petrologists, crystallographers, geochemists, educators, students, and others interested in mineralogy. Conducts research; sponsors educational programs; promotes industrial application of mineral studies.

National Mining Assn., 1130 17th St. N.W. 20036-4677; (202) 463-2625. Fax, (202) 463-6152. Richard L. Lawson, President. Press, (202) 463-2651. General e-mail, nma@ prime.planetcom.com. Web, www.nma.org.

Membership: domestic producers of coal and industrial-agricultural minerals and metals; manufacturers of mining equipment; engineering and consulting firms; and financial institutions. Interests include mine leasing programs, mine health and safety, research and development, public lands, and minerals availability. Monitors legislation and regulations.

Salt Institute, 700 N. Fairfax St., #600, Alexandria, VA 22314; (703) 549-4648. Fax, (703) 548-2194. Richard L. Hanneman, President. General e-mail, info@ saltinstitute.org. Web, www.saltinsitute.org.

Membership: North American salt companies and overseas companies that produce dry salt for use in food, animal feed, highway deicing, water softening, and chemicals. Sponsors education and training projects with the Bureau of Mines and the Food and Drug Administration. Monitors legislation and regulations.

Native American Trust Resources

See also Civil Rights (chap. 1)

AGENCIES

Bureau of Indian Affairs *(Interior Dept.), Trust Responsibilities,* 1849 C St. N.W., MS 4513 20240; (202) 208-5831. Fax, (202) 219-1255. Terrance Virden, Director.

Assists in developing and managing bureau programs involving native American trust resources (agriculture, minerals, forestry, wildlife, water, transportation, irrigation, energy, geographic data services, environmental services, and real property management).

Interior Dept., *Office of the Solicitor: Indian Affairs,* 1849 C St. N.W., MS 6456 20240; (202) 208-3401. Fax, (202) 219-1791. Derril Jordan, Associate Solicitor. Web, www.doi.gov.

Advises the Bureau of Indian Affairs and the secretary of interior on all legal matters, including its trust responsibilities toward native Americans and their natural resources.

Justice Dept., *Indian Resources,* 601 Pennsylvania Ave. N.W., #6702 20530 (mailing address: P.O. Box 44378, L'Enfant Plaza 20004); (202) 305-0259. Fax, (202) 305-0271. James J. Clear, Chief. Web, www.usdoj.gov.

Represents the United States in suits, including trust violations, brought on behalf of individual native Americans and native American tribes against the government. Also represents the Unites States as trustee for native Americans in court actions involving protection of native American land and resources.

Minerals Management Service *(Interior Dept.), Royalty Management Program: Washington Royalty Office,* 1849 C St. N.W., #4245, MS 4230 20240; (202) 208-3512. Fax, (202) 208-3982. R. Dale Fazio, Chief. Web, www.mms.gov.

Collects and manages royalties on minerals produced on federal and native American lands. (Headquarters and accounting center in Denver.)

CONGRESS

House Resources Committee, *1324 LHOB 20515-6201;* (202) 225-2761. Fax, (202) 225-5929. Rep. Don Young, R-Alaska, Chair; Lloyd Jones, Staff Director. General e-mail, resources.committee@mail.house.gov. Web, www.house.gov/resources.

Jurisdiction over native American legislation, including land management and trust responsibilities and claims against the United States.

Senate Committee on Indian Affairs, *SH-838 20510;* (202) 224-2251. Fax, (202) 224-5429. Sen. Ben Nighthorse Campbell, R-Colo., Chair; Paul Moorehead, Staff Director. Web, indian.senate.gov.

Jurisdiction over native American legislation, including land management and trust responsibilities and claims against the United States.

NONPROFIT

Native American Rights Fund, *Washington Office,* 1712 N St. N.W. 20036; (202) 785-4166. Fax, (202) 822-0068. Lorna Babby, Managing Attorney. Web, www.narf.org.

Provides native Americans and Alaskan natives with legal assistance in land claims, water rights, hunting, and other areas. (Headquarters in Boulder.)

See also Rural Coalition (p. 39)

Ocean Resources

See also Fishing/Law of the Sea (chap. 13); Oceanography (chap. 16)

AGENCIES

National Oceanic and Atmospheric Administration *(Commerce Dept.), Commissioned Corps,* 1315 East-West Hwy., 12th Floor, Bldg. #3, Silver Spring, MD 20910-3282; (301) 713-1045. Fax, (301) 713-1541. Rear Adm. Evelyn J. Fields, Director. Recruiting, (301) 713-3470. Web, www.noaa.gov/nchome.

Uniformed service of the Commerce Dept. that operates and manages NOAA's fleet of hydrographic, oceanographic, and fisheries research ships and aircraft. Supports NOAA's scientific programs.

National Oceanic and Atmospheric Administration *(Commerce Dept.), National Environmental Satellite, Data, and Information Service,* 1335 East-West Hwy., Silver Spring, MD 20910; (301) 713-3578. Fax, (301) 713-1249. Gregory W. Withee, Assistant Administrator. Web, www.nesdis.noaa.gov.

Disseminates worldwide environmental data through a system of meteorological, oceanographic, geophysical, and solar-terrestrial data centers.

National Oceanic and Atmospheric Administration *(Commerce Dept.), National Sea Grant College Program,* 1315 East-West Hwy., Silver Spring, MD 20910; (301) 713-2448. Fax, (301) 713-0799. Ronald C. Baird, Director.

Provides institutions with grants for marine research, education, and advisory services; provides marine environmental information.

National Oceanic and Atmospheric Administration *(Commerce Dept.), Ocean and Coastal Resource Management,* 1305 East-West Hwy., SSMC4, Silver Spring, MD 20910; (301) 713-3155. Fax, (301) 713-4012. Jeff Benoit, Director. Web, www.nos.noaa.gov/programs/ocrm.html.

Administers the Coastal Zone Management Act, the National Estuarine Research Reserve System, the National Marine Sanctuary Program, the Deep Seabed Hard Mineral Resources Act, and the Ocean Thermal Energy Conversion Act to carry out NOAA's goals for preservation, conservation, and restoration management of the ocean and coastal environment.

National Oceanic and Atmospheric Administration *(Commerce Dept.), Office of Special Projects,* 1305 East-West Hwy., Silver Spring, MD 20910; (301) 713-3000. Fax, (301) 713-4384. Dan Basta, Director. Web, www.nos.noaa. gov.

Conducts national studies and develops policies on ocean management and use along the U.S. coastline and the exclusive economic zone.

National Oceanic and Atmospheric Administration *(Commerce Dept.), Sanctuaries and Reserves,* 1305 East-West Hwy., 11th Floor, Silver Spring, MD 20910; (301) 713-3125. Fax, (301) 713-0404. Dan Basta, Director.

Administers the National Marine Sanctuary program, which seeks to protect the ecology and the recreational and cultural resources of marine and Great Lakes waters. Administers (in cooperation with state governments) the National Estuarine Research Reserve System, which helps to acquire, develop, and operate estuarine areas as natural field laboratories for research and education.

CONGRESS

House Resources Committee, *Subcommittee on Fisheries, Conservation, Wildlife, and Oceans,* H2-187 FHOB 20515; (202) 226-0200. Fax, (202) 225-1542. Rep. H. James Saxton, R-N.J., Chair; Harry Burroughs, Staff Director. General e-mail, fishery.subcommittee@mail. house.gov. Web, www.house.gov/resources/fisheries.

Jurisdiction over legislation concerning research on ocean life and the National Environmental Policy Act as it applies to ocean resources. Jurisdiction over ocean environment and charting, ocean engineering, coastal barriers, coastal zone management, Law of the Sea, Sea Grant programs and extension services, and all matters relating to the protection of coastal and marine environments.

Senate Commerce, Science, and Transportation Committee, SD-508 20510; (202) 224-5115. Fax, (202) 224-1259. Sen. John McCain, R-Ariz., Chair; Mark Buse, Staff Director. Web, commerce.senate.gov.

Jurisdiction over legislation concerning research on ocean life, the National Environmental Policy Act as it applies to ocean resources, deep seabed mining, ocean environment and charting, coastal zone management, Law of the Sea, Sea Grant programs and extension ser-

vices, and commerce and transportation aspects of outer continental shelf lands.

Senate Commerce, Science, and Transportation Committee, *Subcommittee on Oceans and Fisheries,* SH-428 20510; (202) 224-8172. Fax, (202) 228-0326. Sen. Olympia J. Snowe, R-Maine, Chair; Sloan Rapoport, Counsel. Web, commerce.senate.gov.

Studies all aspects of ocean policy, including marine science funding and the outer continental shelf. Studies issues involving marine research, coastal zone management, ocean environment, and the Law of the Sea. Studies deep seabed mining, ocean charting, and the National Environmental Policy Act as it applies to ocean resources. (Subcommittee does not report legislation.)

NONPROFIT

Coastal States Organization, 444 N. Capitol St. N.W., #322 20001; (202) 508-3860. Fax, (202) 508-3843. Anthony MacDonald, Executive Director. General e-mail, cso@sso.org. Web, www.sso.org/cso.

Nonpartisan organization that represents governors of U.S. coastal states, territories, and commonwealths on management of coastal, Great Lakes, and marine resources. Interests include ocean dumping, coastal pollution, wetlands preservation and restoration, national oceans policy, and the outer continental shelf. Gathers and analyzes data to assess state coastal needs; sponsors and participates in conferences and workshops.

Marine Technology Society, 1828 L St. N.W., #906 20036-5104; (202) 775-5966. Fax, (202) 429-9417. Judith Krauthames, Executive Director. General e-mail, mtsadmin@erols.com. Web, www.mtsociety.org.

Membership: scientists, engineers, technologists, and others interested in marine science and technology. Provides information on marine science, technology, and education.

National Ocean Industries Assn., 1120 G St. N.W., #900 20005; (202) 347-6900. Fax, (202) 347-8650. Robert B. Stewart, President. General e-mail, noia@noia.org. Web, www.noia.org.

Membership: manufacturers, producers, suppliers, and support and service companies involved in marine, offshore, and ocean work. Interests include offshore oil and gas supply and production, deep-sea mining, ocean thermal energy, and new energy sources.

Outer Continental Shelf

AGENCIES

Minerals Management Service *(Interior Dept.), Offshore Minerals Management,* 1849 C St. N.W., MS 4230

20240; (202) 208-3530. Fax, (202) 208-6048. Carolita Kallaur, Associate Director. Web, www.mms.gov.

Administers the Outer Continental Shelf Lands Act. Evaluates, classifies, and supervises oil, gas, and other mineral reserves and operations on outer continental shelf lands; manages the submerged lands of the outer continental shelf.

Minerals Management Service *(Interior Dept.),* *Resources and Environmental Management,* *381 Elden St., Herndon, VA 20170; (703) 787-1211. Fax, (703) 787-1209. Thomas A. Readinger, Deputy Associate Director. Web, www.mms.gov.*

Oversees prelease operations; administers offshore oil and gas leasing.

U.S. Geological Survey *(Interior Dept.), Marine and* *Coastal Geologic Surveys,* *12201 Sunrise Valley Dr., Reston, VA 20192 (mailing address: 915B National Center, Reston, VA 20192); (703) 648-6511. Fax, (703) 648-5464. S. Jeffress Williams, Program Coordinator.*

Handles resource assessment, exploration research, and marine geologic and environmental studies on the U.S. outer continental shelf.

CONGRESS

House Resources Committee, *Subcommittee on* *Energy and Mineral Resources,* *1626 LHOB 20515; (202) 225-9297. Fax, (202) 225-5255. Rep. Barbara Cubin, R-Wyo., Chair; William Condit, Staff Director. General e-mail, resources.committee@mail.house.gov. Web, www. house.gov/resources/energy.*

Jurisdiction over legislation on leasing and development of the outer continental shelf under the Outer Continental Shelf Lands Act.

Senate Commerce, Science, and Transportation Committee, *Subcommittee on Oceans and Fisheries,* *SH-428 20510; (202) 224-8172. Fax, (202) 228-0326. Sen. Olympia J. Snowe, R-Maine, Chair; Sloan Rapoport, Counsel. Web, commerce.senate.gov.*

Studies outer continental shelf matters related to coastal zone management, marine research, and ocean environment. (Jurisdiction shared with the Senate Energy and Natural Resources and the Senate Environmental and Public Works committees.)

Senate Energy and Natural Resources Committee, *SD-364 20510; (202) 224-4971. Fax, (202) 224-6163. Sen. Frank H. Murkowski, R-Alaska, Chair; Andrew Lundquist, Staff Director. General e-mail, committee@energy.senate. gov. Web, energy.senate.gov.*

Jurisdiction over legislation on ocean environment and coastal zone matters, including leasing and develop-

ment of the outer continental shelf under the Outer Continental Shelf Lands Act; and on the environmental impact of offshore drilling on the outer continental shelf (jurisdiction shared with Senate Commerce, Science, and Transportation and Senate Environment and Public Works committees).

Senate Environment and Public Works Committee, *Subcommittee on Clean Air, Wetlands, Private Property, and Nuclear Safety,* *SD-410 20510; (202) 224-6176. Fax, (202) 224-5167. Sen. James M. Inhofe, R-Okla., Chair; Andy Wheeler, Staff Contact. Web, epw.senate.gov.*

Jurisdiction over legislation on the environmental impact of offshore drilling on the outer continental shelf. (Jurisdiction shared with Senate Commerce, Science, and Transportation and Senate Energy and Natural Resources committees.)

Parks and Recreation Areas

See also History and Preservation (chap. 5); Recreation and Sports (chap. 5)

AGENCIES

Bureau of Land Management *(Interior Dept.), Cultural Heritage, Wilderness, Special Areas, and Paleontology,* *1620 L St. N.W., #204 20240 (mailing address: 1849 C St. N.W., #204-LS 20240); (202) 452-0330. Fax, (202) 452-7701. Marilyn Nickels, Group Manager. TTY, (202) 452-0326.*

Identifies and manages cultural heritage and recreation programs on public lands.

Bureau of Reclamation *(Interior Dept.), 1849 C St. N.W., #7659 20240; (202) 208-4157. Fax, (202) 208-3484. Eluid Martinez, Commissioner. Information, (202) 208-4215. Web, www.usbr.gov.*

Responsible for acquisition, administration, management, and disposal of lands in seventeen western states associated with bureau water resource development projects. Provides overall policy guidance for land use, including agreements with public agencies for outdoor recreation, fish and wildlife enhancement, and land-use authorizations such as leases, licenses, permits, and rights of way.

Forest Service *(Agriculture Dept.), Recreation Management,* *201 14th St. S.W., 4th Floor Central 20250 (mailing address: P.O. Box 96090 20090-6090); (202) 205-1706. Fax, (202) 205-1145. Dennis E. Bschor, Director. Web, www.fs.fed.us.*

Develops policy and sets guidelines on administering national forests and grasslands for recreational purposes.

(The Forest Service administers some of the lands designated as national recreation areas.)

Interior Dept., *Fish, Wildlife, and Parks,* *1849 C St. N.W., #3156 20240; (202) 208-4416. Fax, (202) 208-4684. Donald Barry, Assistant Secretary. Web, www.doi.gov.*

Responsible for programs associated with the development, conservation, and use of fish, wildlife, recreational, historical, and national park system resources. Coordinates marine environmental quality and biological resources programs with other federal agencies.

National Park Service (NPS), *(Interior Dept.), 1849 C St. N.W., #3316 20240; (202) 208-4621. Fax, (202) 208-7889. Robert Stanton, Director. Press, (202) 208-6843. Washington area activities, (202) 619-7275 (recording). Web, www.nps.gov.*

Administers national parks, monuments, historic sites, and recreation areas. Oversees coordination, planning, and financing of public outdoor recreation programs at all levels of government. Conducts recreation research surveys; administers financial assistance program to states for planning and development of outdoor recreation programs. (Some lands designated as national recreation areas are not under NPS jurisdiction.)

National Park Service *(Interior Dept.), Policy, 1849 C St. N.W., #2414 20240; (202) 208-7456. Fax, (202) 219-8835. Loran G. Fraser, Chief.*

Researches and develops management policy on matters relating to the National Park Service; makes recommendations on the historical significance of national trails and landmarks.

Tennessee Valley Authority, *Government Affairs, Washington Office, 1 Massachusetts Ave. N.W., #300 20444; (202) 898-2999. Fax, (202) 898-2998. David Withrow, Vice President. Web, www.tva.gov.*

Operates Land Between the Lakes, a national recreation and environmental education area located in western Kentucky and Tennessee.

U.S. Fish and Wildlife Service *(Interior Dept.), Refuges and Wildlife, 1849 C St. N.W., #3251 20240; (202) 208-5333. Fax, (202) 208-3082. Daniel M. Ashe, Assistant Director. Web, www.fws.gov.*

Manages the National Wildlife Refuge System. Most refuges are open to public use; activities include bird and wildlife watching, fishing, hunting, and environmental education.

CONGRESS

House Resources Committee, *Subcommittee on Forests and Forest Health, 1337 LHOB 20515; (202) 225-*0691. Fax, (202) 225-0521. Rep. Helen Chenoweth-Hage, R-Idaho, Chair; Doug Crandall, Staff Director. General e-mail, resources.committee@mail.house.gov. Web, www.house.gov/resources/forests.*

Jurisdiction over legislation on public forest lands (except in Alaska), including issues of forestry, wilderness preservation, forest reserve, water rights, national trails and rivers, and recreation.

House Resources Committee, *Subcommittee on National Parks and Public Lands, 140 CHOB 20515; (202) 226-7736. Fax, (202) 226-2301. Rep. James V. Hansen, R-Utah, Chair; Allen Freemyer, Staff Director. General e-mail, parks.subcommittee@mail.house.gov. Web, www.house.gov/resources/parks.*

Jurisdiction over legislation on the national park system, the Bureau of Land Management, and related parks and recreation.

Senate Energy and Natural Resources Committee, *Subcommittee on National Parks, Historic Preservation, and Recreation, SD-354 20510; (202) 224-6969. Fax, (202) 228-0459. Sen. Craig Thomas, R-Wyo., Chair; Jim O'Toole, Professional Staff Member. General e-mail, parks@energy.senate.gov. Web, energy.senate.gov.*

Jurisdiction over legislation on national parks, recreation areas, wilderness areas, trails, wild and scenic rivers, historic sites, and military parks and battlefields.

NONPROFIT

American Hiking Society, *1422 Fenwick Lane, Silver Spring, MD 20910; (301) 565-6704. Fax, (301) 565-6714. David Lillard, President. General e-mail, info@americanhiking.org. Web, www.americanhiking.org.*

Membership: individuals and clubs interested in preserving America's trail system and protecting the interests of trail users. Provides information on outdoor volunteer opportunities on public lands.

American Recreation Coalition, *1225 New York Ave. N.W., #450 20005; (202) 682-9530. Fax, (202) 682-9529. Derrick A. Crandall, President. General e-mail, arc@funoutdoors.com. Web, www.funoutdoors.com.*

Membership: organized recreationists, national and regional corporations offering recreational products and services, and recreation industry trade associations. Works to increase public and private sector activity in public recreation, land and water management, and energy policy. Provides information on innovative recreational planning.

National Park Foundation, *1101 17th St. N.W., #1102 20036-4704; (202) 785-4500. Fax, (202) 785-3539. James D. Maddy, President. Web, www.nationalparks.org.*

Chartered by Congress and chaired by the interior secretary. Encourages private-sector support of the national park system; provides grants and sponsors educational and cultural activities.

National Parks and Conservation Assn., *1300 19th St. N.W., #300 20036-6404; (202) 223-6722. Fax, (202) 659-0650. Tom Kiernan, President. Information, (800) 628-7275. General e-mail, npca@npca.org. Web, www. npca.org.*

Citizens' interest group that seeks to protect national parks and other park system areas.

National Recreation and Park Assn., *22377 Belmont Ridge Rd., Ashburn, VA 20148; (703) 858-0784. Fax, (703) 858-0794. Dean Tice, Executive Director. General e-mail, info@nrpa.org. Web, www.nrpa.org.*

Membership: park and recreation professionals and interested citizens. Provides technical assistance for park and recreational programs.

Rails-to-Trails Conservancy, *1100 17th St. N.W., 10th Floor 20036; (202) 331-9696. Fax, (202) 331-9680. David G. Burwell, President. General e-mail, rtrails@transact.org. Web, www.railtrails.org.*

Promotes the conversion of abandoned railroad corridors into hiking and biking trails for public use. Provides public education programs and technical and legal assistance. Publishes trail guides. Monitors legislation and regulations.

Scenic America, *801 Pennsylvania Ave. S.E., #300 20003-2152; (202) 543-6200. Fax, (202) 543-9130. Meg Maguire, President. Web, www.scenic.org.*

Membership: national, state, and local groups concerned with land-use control, growth management, and landscape protection. Works to enhance the scenic quality of America's communities and countryside. Provides information and technical assistance on scenic byways, tree preservation, economics of aesthetic regulation, billboard and sign control, scenic areas preservation, and growth management.

Student Conservation Assn., *Washington Office, 1800 N. Kent St., #1260, Arlington, VA 22209; (703) 524-2441. Fax, (703) 524-2451. Reginald Hagood, National Director. Web, www.sca-inc.org.*

Educational organization that provides youth and adults with opportunities for training and work experience in natural resource management and conservation. Volunteers serve in national parks, forests, wildlife refuges, and other public lands. (Headquarters in Charlestown, N.H.)

World Wildlife Fund, *1250 24th St. N.W., #400 20037; (202) 293-4800. Fax, (202) 293-9211. Kathryn S. Fuller, President. Web, www.wwf.org.*

International conservation organization that provides funds and technical assistance for establishing and maintaining parks.

Water Resources

See also Rural Areas (chap. 2); Soil and Watershed Conservation (chap. 2); Water Pollution (this chapter)

AGENCIES

Army Corps of Engineers *(Defense Dept.), 20 Massachusetts Ave. N.W., #8228 20314-1000; (202) 761-0001. Fax, (202) 761-4463. Lt. Gen. Joe N. Ballard (USACE), Chief of Engineers. Web, www.usace.army.mil.*

Provides local governments with disaster relief, flood control, navigation, and hydroelectric power services.

Bureau of Reclamation *(Interior Dept.), 1849 C St. N.W., #7659 20240; (202) 208-4157. Fax, (202) 208-3484. Eluid Martinez, Commissioner. Information, (202) 208-4215. Web, www.usbr.gov.*

Administers federal programs for water and power resource development and management in seventeen western states; oversees municipal and industrial water supply, hydroelectric power generation, irrigation, flood control, water quality improvement, river regulation, fish and wildlife enhancement, and outdoor recreation.

Environmental Protection Agency, *Wetlands Protection, 499 S. Capitol St. S.W., #708 20003 (mailing address: 1200 Pennsylvania Ave. N.W. 20460); (202) 260-7791. Fax, (202) 260-2356. John W. Meagher, Director.*

Manages dredge-and-fill program under section 404 of the Clean Water Act. Coordinates federal policies affecting wetlands. Promotes public awareness of wetland preservation and management. Encourages the development of stronger wetland programs at the state level.

Interstate Commission on the Potomac River Basin, *6110 Executive Blvd., #300, Rockville, MD 20852; (301) 984-1908. Fax, (301) 984-5841. Joseph K. Hoffman, Executive Director. Web, www.potomacriver.org.*

Nonregulatory interstate compact commission established by Congress to control and reduce water pollution and to restore and protect living resources in the Potomac River and its tributaries. Monitors water quality; assists metropolitan water utilities; seeks innovative methods to solve water supply and land resource problems. Provides information and educational materials on the Potomac River basin.

Office of Management and Budget (*Executive Office of the President*), *Water and Power,* New Executive Office Bldg., #8002 20503; (202) 395-4590. Fax, (202) 395-4817. Rick Mertens, Chief. Web, www.whitehouse.gov/omb.

Reviews all plans and budgets related to federal or federally assisted water power and related land resource projects.

Rural Utilities Service (*Agriculture Dept.*), 1400 Independence Ave. S.W. 20250-1500; (202) 720-9540. Fax, (202) 720-1725. Christopher A. McLean, Administrator (Acting). Information, (202) 720-1255. Web, www.usda.gov/rus.

Makes loans and provides technical assistance for development, repair, and replacement of water and waste disposal systems in rural areas.

Smithsonian Environmental Research Center (*Smithsonian Institution*), 647 Contees Wharf Rd., Edgewater, MD 21037 (mailing address: P.O. Box 28, Edgewater, MD 21037); (410) 798-4424. Fax, (301) 261-7954. Ross B. Simons, Director. Web, www.serc.si.edu.

Studies the interaction of the Rhode River with its watershed, the effect of humans on the system, and the long-term effects of water quality on the plant and animal population.

Tennessee Valley Authority, *Government Affairs, Washington Office,* 1 Massachusetts Ave. N.W., #300 20444; (202) 898-2999. Fax, (202) 898-2998. David Withrow, Vice President. Web, www.tva.gov.

Coordinates resource conservation, development, and land-use programs in the Tennessee River Valley. Operates the river control system; projects include flood control, navigation development, and multiple-use reservoirs.

U.S. Geological Survey (*Interior Dept.*), *Water Resources,* 12201 Sunrise Valley Dr., Reston, VA 20192; (703) 648-5215. Fax, (703) 648-7031. Robert M. Hirsch, Chief Hydrologist. Web, www.usgs.gov.

Administers the Water Resources Research Act of 1990. Assesses the quantity and quality of surface and groundwater resources; collects, analyzes, and disseminates data on water use and the effect of human activity and natural phenomena on hydrologic systems. Provides federal agencies, state and local governments, international organizations, and foreign governments with scientific and technical assistance.

CONGRESS

House Agriculture Committee, *Subcommittee on General Farm Commodities, Resource Conservation,*

and Credit, 1430 LHOB 20515; (202) 225-0171. Fax, (202) 225-4464. Rep. Bill Barrett, R-Neb., Chair; Mike Neruda, Staff Director. Web, agriculture.house.gov.

Jurisdiction over legislation on small watershed programs, including stream channelization.

House Commerce Committee, *Subcommittee on Energy and Power,* 2125 RHOB 20515; (202) 225-2927. Fax, (202) 225-1919. Rep. Joe L. Barton, R-Texas, Chair; James E. Derderian, Staff Director. General e-mail, commerce@mail.house.gov. Web, www.house.gov/commerce.

Jurisdiction over legislation on hydroelectric power and ocean thermal energy resource commercialization, utilization, and conversion.

House Resources Committee, *Subcommittee on Water and Power,* 1522 LHOB 20515; (202) 225-8331. Fax, (202) 226-6953. Rep. John T. Doolittle, R-Calif., Chair; Robert Faber, Staff Director. General e-mail, water.power@mail.house.gov. Web, www.house.gov/resources/water.

Jurisdiction over legislation on water rights, including federally reserved water rights on public lands; irrigation and reclamation projects; compacts relating to use and apportionment of interstate water resources; and power marketing administrations.

House Science Committee, *Subcommittee on Energy and Environment,* 389 FHOB 20515; (202) 225-9662. Fax, (202) 226-6983. Rep. Ken Calvert, R-Calif., Chair; Harlan Watson, Staff Director. Web, www.house.gov/science.

Jurisdiction over drinking water resources research legislation.

House Transportation and Infrastructure Committee, *Subcommittee on Water Resources and Environment,* B376 RHOB 20515; (202) 225-4360. Fax, (202) 226-5435. Rep. Sherwood Boehlert, R-N.Y., Chair; Ben Grumbles, Counsel. General e-mail, transcomm@mail.house.gov. Web, www.house.gov/transportation.

Jurisdiction over legislation on water resources; watershed and flood control programs; U.S. Army Corps of Engineers water resources projects; wetlands protection; navigation and river basin programs; small watershed programs within the Agriculture Dept.; groundwater programs; construction, operation, and maintenance of harbors and inland waterways; and hydroelectric power.

Senate Agriculture, Nutrition, and Forestry Committee, *Subcommittee on Forestry, Conservation, and Rural Revitalization,* SR-328A 20510; (202) 224-2752.

Fax, (202) 224-1725. Sen. Larry E. Craig, R-Idaho, Chair; Dan Whiting, Staff Contact. Web, agriculture.senate.gov.

Jurisdiction over legislation on small watershed programs, including stream channelization, and on flood control programs that involve structures of less than 4,000 acre-feet in storage capacity.

Senate Energy and Natural Resources Committee, Subcommittee on Water and Power, SD-308 20510; (202) 224-4971. Sen. Gordon H. Smith, R-Ore., Chair; Colleen Deegan, Majority Counsel. General e-mail, water&power@energy.senate.gov. Web, energy.senate.gov.

Jurisdiction over legislation on hydroelectric power; irrigation and reclamation projects; water rights, including federally reserved water rights on public lands; compacts relating to use and apportionment of interstate water resources; and power marketing administrations.

Senate Environment and Public Works Committee, SD-410 20510; (202) 224-6176. Fax, (202) 224-5167. Sen. Robert C. Smith, R-N.H., Chair; Dave Conover, Staff Director. Web, epw.senate.gov.

Jurisdiction over water resources and water resources research legislation; watershed and flood control programs; U.S. Army Corps of Engineers water resources projects; navigation and river basin programs; small watershed programs of the Natural Resources Conservation Service; wetlands protection and groundwater programs; and construction, operation, and maintenance of harbors.

NONPROFIT

American Rivers, 1025 Vermont Ave. N.W., #720 20005; (202) 347-7550. Fax, (202) 347-9240. Rebecca Wodder, President. Web, www.amrivers.org.

Works to preserve and protect the nation's river systems.

American Water Works Assn., Washington Office, 1401 New York Ave. N.W., #640 20005; (202) 628-8303. Fax, (202) 628-2846. Tom Curtis, Deputy Executive Director. Web, www.awwa.org.

Membership: municipal water utilities, manufacturers of equipment for water industries, water treatment companies, and individuals. Provides information on drinking water treatment; publishes voluntary standards for the water industry. (Headquarters in Denver.)

Assn. of State Drinking Water Administrators, 1025 Connecticut Ave. N.W., #903 20036; (202) 293-7655. Fax, (202) 293-7656. Vanessa Leiby, Executive Director. General e-mail, asdwa@erols.com. Web, www.asdwa.org.

Membership: state officials responsible for the drinking water supply and enforcement of safety standards. Monitors legislation and regulations.

Environmental Defense Fund, Washington Office, 1875 Connecticut Ave. N.W., #1016 20009-5728; (202) 387-3500. Fax, (202) 234-6049. Senta Boardley, Office Manager. Web, www.edf.org.

Citizens' interest group staffed by lawyers, economists, and scientists. Takes legal action on environmental issues; provides information on pollution prevention, environmental health, water resources, and water marketing. (Headquarters in New York.)

Irrigation Assn., 8260 Willow Oaks Corporate Dr., #120, Fairfax, VA 22031; (703) 573-3551. Fax, (703) 573-1913. Thomas Kimmell, Executive Director. Web, www. irrigation.org.

Membership: companies and individuals involved in irrigation, drainage, and erosion control worldwide. Seeks to improve the products and practices used to manage water resources; interests include economic development and environmental enhancement.

Izaak Walton League of America, 707 Conservation Lane, Gaithersburg, MD 20878-2983; (301) 548-0150. Fax, (301) 548-0146. Paul W. Hansen, Executive Director. General e-mail, general@iwla.org. Web, www.iwla.org.

Grassroots organization that promotes conservation of natural resources and the environment. Coordinates a citizen action program to monitor and improve the condition of local streams.

National Assn. of Conservation Districts, 509 Capitol Court N.E. 20002-4937; (202) 547-6223. Fax, (202) 547-6450. Ernest C. Shea, Chief Executive Officer. Web, www.nacdnet.org.

Membership: conservation districts (local subdivisions of state government). Develops national policies and works to promote the conservation of water resources. Interests include erosion and sediment control and control of nonpoint source pollution.

National Assn. of Flood and Stormwater Management Agencies, 1299 Pennsylvania Ave. N.W., 8th Floor, West 20004; (202) 218-4122. Fax, (202) 785-5277. Susan Gilson, Executive Director. Web, www.nafma.org.

Membership: state, county, and local governments concerned with management of water resources. Monitors legislation and regulations.

National Assn. of Regulatory Utility Commissioners, 1101 Vermont Ave. N.W., #200 20005; (202) 898-2200. Fax, (202) 898-2213. Charles Gray, Executive Director. Press, (202) 898-2205. Web, www.naruc.org.

Membership: members of federal, state, municipal, and Canadian regulatory commissions that have jurisdiction over utilities. Interests include water.

National Assn. of Water Companies, *1725 K St. N.W., #1212 20006; (202) 833-8383. Fax, (202) 331-7442. Peter L. Cook, Executive Director. Web, www.nawc.org.*

Membership: privately owned, regulated water companies. Provides members with information on legislative and regulatory issues and other subjects.

National Rural Community Assistance Program, *722 East Market St., #105, Leesburg, VA 20176; (703) 771-8636. Fax, (703) 771-8753. Randolph A. Adams, Executive Director. General e-mail, rcap@rcap.org. Web, www.rcap.org.*

Federally funded organization that conducts program to improve water delivery and disposal of waste water for rural residents, particularly low-income families.

National Utility Contractors Assn., *4301 N. Fairfax Dr., #360, Arlington, VA 22203-1627; (703) 358-9300. Fax, (703) 358-9307. Peggie Woodward, Executive Director. Web, www.nuca.com.*

Membership: contractors who perform water, sewer, and other underground utility construction. Sponsors conferences; conducts surveys. Monitors public works legislation and regulations.

National Water Resources Assn., *3800 N. Fairfax Dr., #4, Arlington, VA 22203; (703) 524-1544. Fax, (703) 524-1548. Thomas F. Donnelly, Executive Vice President. General e-mail, nwra@nwra.org. Web, www.nwra.org.*

Membership: conservation and irrigation districts, municipalities, and others interested in water resources. Works for the development and maintenance of water resource projects in the western reclamation states. Represents interests of members before Congress and regulatory agencies.

River Network, *Washington Office, 4000 Albemarle St. N.W., #303 20016; (202) 364-2550. Fax, (202) 364-2520. Pat Munoz, Program Manager. General e-mail, dc@rivernetwork.org. Web, www.rivernetwork.org.*

Acquires and conserves watersheds of rivers used for drinking water supply, floodplain management, fish and wildlife habitats, and recreation. Works to build and support citizen watershed councils. (Headquarters in Portland, Ore.)

See also Irrigation Assn. (p. 45)

10 Government Operations

🏛 GENERAL POLICY

See also Civil Service (this chapter); Government Information (chap. 4)

AGENCIES

Domestic Policy Council *(Executive Office of the President),* The White House 20502; (202) 456-2216. Fax, (202) 456-7028. Bruce Reed, Assistant to the President for Domestic Policy.

Comprises cabinet officials and staff members. Coordinates the domestic policy-making process to facilitate the implementation of the president's domestic agenda in such areas as agriculture, education, energy, environment, health, housing, labor, and veterans affairs.

Federal Bureau of Investigation *(Justice Dept.),* **Administrative Services,** 935 Pennsylvania Ave. N.W., #6012 20535; (202) 324-3514. Fax, (202) 324-1091. William F. Welby, Assistant Director.

Performs background investigations of presidential appointees.

General Services Administration (GSA), 1800 F St. N.W., #6137 20405; (202) 501-0800. David J. Barram, Administrator; Thurman M. Davis Sr., Deputy Administrator, (202) 501-1226. Information, (202) 708-5082. Library, (202) 501-0788. Press, (202) 501-1231. Web, www.gsa.gov.

Establishes policies for managing federal government property, including construction and operation of buildings and procurement and distribution of supplies and equipment; manages transportation and telecommunications. Manages disposal of surplus federal property.

General Services Administration, *Acquisition Policy,* 1800 F St. N.W., #4040 20405; (202) 501-1043. Fax, (202) 501-1986. J. Les Davison, Deputy Associate Administrator (Acting). Web, policyworks.gov/org/main/mv/oap.htm.

Develops and implements federal government acquisition policies and procedures; conducts preaward and postaward contract reviews; administers federal acquisition regulations for civilian agencies; suspends and debars contractors for unsatisfactory performance; coordinates and promotes governmentwide career management and training programs for contracting personnel.

General Services Administration, *Federal Information Center,* P.O. Box, #600, Cumberland, MD 21501-0600. Fax, (301) 722-0066. Warren Snaider, Staff Contact. Information, (800) 688-9889. TTY, (800) 326-2996. Web, fic.info.gov.

Responds to inquiries about federal programs and services. Gives information or locates particular agencies or persons best suited to help with specific concerns.

General Services Administration, *Governmentwide Policy,* 1800 F St. N.W., #5240 20405; (202) 501-8880. Fax, (202) 501-8898. G. Martin Wagner, Associate Administrator. Web, policyworks.gov.

Coordinates GSA policy-making activities; promotes collaboration between government and the private sector in developing policy and management techniques; works to integrate acquisition, management, and disposal of government property.

National Archives and Records Administration, *Federal Register,* 800 N. Capitol St., #700 20408; (202) 523-5230. Fax, (202) 523-6866. Frances D. McDonald, Editor-in-Chief. TTY, (202) 523-5229. Public Laws Update Service (PLUS), (202) 523-6641. Web, www.nara.gov/fedreg/.

Assigns public law numbers to enacted legislation, executive orders, and proclamations; responds to inquiries on public law numbers; assists inquirers in finding presidential signing or veto messages in the *Weekly Compilation of Presidential Documents* and the *Public Papers of the Presidents* series; compiles slip laws and annual *United States Statutes at Large;* compiles indexes for finding statutory provisions. Operates Public Laws Update Service (PLUS), which provides information by telephone on new legislation. Publications available from the U.S. Government Printing Office.

Office of Administration *(Executive Office of the President),* 725 17th St. N.W., #5001 20503; (202) 395-7235. Fax, (202) 456-7921. Michael J. Lyle, Director (Acting). Web, www.whitehouse.gov/WH/EOP/html/other/OA.html.

Provides administrative support services to the Executive Office of the President, including personnel and financial management, data processing, library services, and general office operations.

Office of Management and Budget *(Executive Office of the President),* **Federal Procurement Policy,** Dwight D. Eisenhower Executive Office Bldg., #352 20503; (202) 395-5802. Fax, (202) 395-3242. Vacant, Administrator. Web, www.whitehouse.gov/omb.

Coordinates government procurement policies, regulations, and procedures. Responsible for cost accounting rules governing federal contractors and subcontractors.

Office of Management and Budget *(Executive Office of the President),* **Information and Regulatory Affairs,** Dwight D. Eisenhower Executive Office Bldg., #350 20503; (202) 395-4852. Fax, (202) 395-3047. John Spotila, Administrator. Web, www.whitehouse.gov/omb.

Oversees development of federal regulatory programs. Supervises agency information management activities in accordance with the Paperwork Reduction

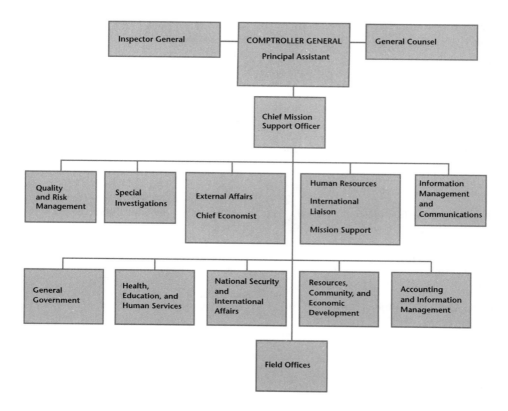

Act of 1995, as amended; reviews agency analyses of the effect of government regulatory activities on the U.S. economy.

Office of Management and Budget *(Executive Office of the President)*, Personnel, Postal, EXOP, *725 17th St. N.W., #7236 20503; (202) 395-5017. Fax, (202) 395-5738. Lisa Fairhall, Chief. Web, www.whitehouse.gov/omb.*

Examines, evaluates, and suggests improvements for agencies and programs within the Office of Personnel Management, the U.S. Postal Service, and the Executive Office of the President.

Office of Management and Budget *(Executive Office of the President)*, Treasury, *New Executive Office Bldg., #9236 20503; (202) 395-6156. Fax, (202) 395-6825. Mark Schwartz, Chief. Web, www.whitehouse.gov/omb.*

Examines, evaluates, and suggests improvements for agencies and programs within the Treasury Dept. (including the Internal Revenue Service and the Customs Dept.), and the District of Columbia government.

Regulatory Information Service Center *(General Services Administration)*, *1800 F St. N.W., #3033 20405; (202) 482-7350. Fax, (202) 482-7360. Ronald Kelly, Executive Director. Information, (202) 482-7340. General e-mail, risc@gsa.gov. Web, reginfo.gov.*

Provides the president, Congress, and the public with information on federal regulatory policies; recommends ways to make regulatory information more accessible to government officials and the public.

CONGRESS

General Accounting Office, *441 G St. N.W. 20548; (202) 512-5500. Fax, (202) 512-5507. David M. Walker, Comptroller General. Information, (202) 512-4800. Library, (202) 512-5180. Documents, (202) 512-6000. Web, www.gao.gov.*

Independent, nonpartisan agency in the legislative branch. Serves as the investigating agency for Congress; carries out legal, accounting, auditing, and claims settlement functions; makes recommendations for more effec-

WHITE HOUSE OFFICES

OFFICE OF THE PRESIDENT

President, Bill Clinton

    1600 Pennsylvania Ave. N.W. 20500; (202) 456-1414

    president@whitehouse.gov or www.whitehouse.gov

Chief of Staff, John D. Podesta, Chief of Staff, (202) 456-6797

    Maria Echaveste, Deputy Chief of Staff, (202) 456-1960

Communications, Loretta Ucelli, Director, (202) 456-2640

Speechwriting, J. Terry Edmonds, Director, (202) 456-2777

Cabinet Affairs, Thurgood Marshall Jr., Cabinet Secretary, (202) 456-2572

General Counsel, Beth Nolan, Counsel, (202) 456-2632

Intergovernmental Affairs, Mickey Ibarra, Director, (202) 456-7060

Legislative Affairs, Charles Brain, Deputy Director, (202) 456-2230

    House Liaison, Broderick Johnson, Director, (202) 456-6620

    Senate Liaison, Tracey E. Thornton, Director, (202) 456-6493

Management and Administration, Mark F. Lindsay, Director, (202) 456-2861

    White House Intern Program, Patrick Crawford, Director, (202) 456-2742

    White House Military Office, Joseph J. Simmons IV, Director, (202) 456-2150

Oval Office Operations, Nancy V. Hernreich, Director, (202) 456-6610

Political Affairs, Minyon Moore, Director, (202) 456-1125

Presidential Personnel, J. Robert Nash, Director, (202) 456-6676

Press Secretary, Joe Lockhart, Press Secretary, (202) 456-2673

    Media Affairs, James Kennedy, Deputy Press Secretary, (202) 456-2580

Public Liaison, Mary Beth Cahill, Director, (202) 456-2930

Scheduling and Advance, Stephanie Streett, Director, (202) 456-7560

Staff Secretary, Sean Maloney, Staff Secretary, (202) 456-2702

    Correspondence, Daniel W. Burkhardt, Director, (202) 456-7610

OFFICE OF THE FIRST LADY

First Lady, Hillary Rodham Clinton

    1600 Pennsylvania Ave. N.W. 20500; (202) 456-6266

    first.lady@whitehouse.gov

Chief of Staff, Melanne S. Verveer, Chief of Staff, (202) 456-6266

Communications, Lissa Muscatine, Director, (202) 456-2960

OFFICE OF THE VICE PRESIDENT

Vice President, Albert Gore Jr.

    Old Executive Office Bldg. 20501; (202) 456-2326

    vice-president@whitehouse.gov

Chief of Staff, Charles Burson, Chief of Staff, (202) 456-6605

Communications, Vacant, Director, (202) 456-7035

Mrs. Gore, Tipper Gore, Wife of the Vice President, (202) 456-6640

---

tive government operations; publishes monthly lists of reports available to the public. Library open to the public by appointment.

House Appropriations Committee, *Subcommittee on Treasury, Postal Service, and General Government,* B307 RHOB 20515; (202) 225-5834. Fax, (202) 225-5895. Rep. Jim Kolbe, R-Ariz., Chair; Michelle Mrdeza, Clerk. Web, www.house.gov/appropriations.

Jurisdiction over legislation to appropriate funds for the Office of Management and Budget, the General Services Administration (except the Consumer Information Center), the National Archives and Records Administration, and the Executive Office of the President.

House Government Reform Committee, *2157 RHOB 20515; (202) 225-5074. Fax, (202) 225-3974. Rep. Dan Burton, R-Ind., Chair; Kevin Binger, Staff Director. Web, www.house.gov/reform.*

Jurisdiction over legislation on all procurement practices. Also examines the efficiency of government operations, including federal regulations and program management.

FINANCIAL OFFICERS FOR FEDERAL AGENCIES

DEPARTMENTS

Agriculture, Sally Thompson, (202) 720-5539

Commerce, Linda J. Bilmes, (202) 482-4951

Defense, William J. Lynn, (703) 695-3237

  Air Force, Robert F. Hale, (703) 693-6457

  Army, Helen T. McCoy, (703) 697-8121

  Navy, Vacant, (703) 697-2325

Education, Tom Skelly, (202) 401-0085

Energy, Michael L. Telson, (202) 586-4171

Health and Human Services, John Callahan, (202) 690-6396

Housing and Urban Development, David Gibbons (acting), (202) 708-3296

Interior, John Berry, (202) 208-4203

Justice, Steven Colgate, (202) 514-3101

Labor, Kenneth M. Bresnahan, (202) 219-6891

State, Bert Edwards, (202) 647-7490

Transportation, David Kleinberg, (202) 366-9192

Treasury

  Comptroller of the Currency, Edward Hanley, (202) 874-5080

Veterans Affairs, Edward A. Powell Jr., (202) 273-5589

AGENCIES

Advisory Council on Historic Preservation, Carol McLain, (202) 606-8503

Agency for International Development, Tony Cully (acting), (202) 712-1890

Central Intelligence Agency, Michael Kennedy, (703) 482-4456

Commission on Civil Rights, George Harbison, (202) 376-8356

Commodity Futures Trading Commission, Madge Bolinger, (202) 418-5190

Consumer Product Safety Commission, Edward E. Quist, (301) 504-0029

Corporation for National Service, Tony Musick, (202) 606-5000, ext. 530

Corporation for Public Broadcasting, Rita Jankovich, (202) 879-9831

Environmental Protection Agency, Michael W. S. Ryan, (202) 564-9673

Equal Employment Opportunity Commission, Allen M. Fisher, (202) 663-4200

Export-Import Bank, James K. Hess, (202) 565-3240

Farm Credit Administration, Donald P. Clark, (703) 883-4200

Federal Bureau of Investigation, William J. Stollhans, (202) 324-1345

Federal Communications Commission, Mark Reger, (202) 418-1925

Federal Deposit Insurance Corporation, Chris Sale (acting), (202) 416-6965

Federal Election Commission, Richard Pullen, (202) 694-1230

Federal Emergency Management Agency, Gary D. Johnson, (202) 646-3545

Federal Energy Regulatory Commission, Thomas R. Herlihy, (202) 208-0300

Federal Home Loan Mortgage Corporation, John Gibbons, (703) 903-4200

Federal Labor Relations Authority, Kevin K. Copper, (202) 482-6640

Federal Maritime Commission, Sandra Kusumoto, (202) 523-5866

Federal Mediation and Conciliation Service, Fran Leonard, (202) 606-3661

House Government Reform Committee, *Subcommittee on Government Management, Information, and Technology, B373 RHOB 20515; (202) 225-5147. Fax, (202) 225-2373. Rep. Steve Horn, R-Calif., Chair; J. Russell George, Staff Director. Web, www.house.gov/reform.*

Jurisdiction over legislation concerning the efficiency and management of government operations and activities; oversight responsibilities for operations of the White House, the Executive Office of the President, and the Office of Management and Budget. Jurisdiction over leg-islation for the General Services Administration and General Accounting Office.

Senate Appropriations Committee, *Subcommittee on Treasury and General Government, SD-188 20510; (202) 224-7337. Sen. Ben Nighthorse Campbell, R-Colo., Chair; Patricia Raymond, Clerk. Web, appropriations.senate.gov/treasury.*

Jurisdiction over legislation to appropriate funds for the General Services Administration (except the Consumer Information Center), National Archives and

FINANCIAL OFFICERS FOR FEDERAL AGENCIES (continued)

Federal National Mortgage Association, Timothy Howard, (202) 752-7140

Federal Reserve System, Stephen J. Clark, (202) 452-2304

Federal Trade Commission, Henry Hoffman, (202) 326-2664

General Accounting Office, Gene Dodaro, (202) 512-5600

General Services Administration, William B. Early Jr., (202) 501-1721

International Bank for Reconstruction and Development (World Bank), Jules W. Muis, (202) 458-1674

John F. Kennedy Center for the Performing Arts, Leslie M. Frank, (202) 416-8603

Merit Systems Protection Board, Robert Lawshe, (202) 653-6772, ext. 1105

National Academy of Sciences, Archie Turner, (202) 334-3110

National Aeronautics and Space Administration, Arnold G. Holz, (202) 358-2262

National Archives and Records Administration, David M. Millane, (301) 713-6810

National Credit Union Administration, Dennis Winans, (703) 518-6571

National Endowment for the Arts, Marvin Marks, (202) 682-5407

National Endowment for the Humanities, Jeffrey Thomas, (202) 606-8428

National Labor Relations Board, Karl Rohrbaugh, (202) 273-4230

National Mediation Board, June D. W. King, (202) 692-5010

National Railroad Passenger Corporation (Amtrak), Arlene Friner, (202) 906-3300

National Science Foundation, Joseph L. Kull, (703) 306-1201

National Transportation Safety Board, Craig Keller, (202) 314-6210

Nuclear Regulatory Commission, Jesse L. Funchez, (301) 415-7501

Occupational Safety and Health Review Commission, Ledia E. Bernall, (202) 606-5390

Office of Management and Budget, Sally Katzen, (202) 395-6190

Office of Personnel Management, J. Gilbert Seaux, (202) 606-1390

Overseas Private Investment Corporation, Mildred O. Callear, (202) 336-8450

Peace Corps, Lana Hurdle, (202) 692-1600

Pension Benefit Guaranty Corporation, N. Anthony Calhoun, (202) 326-4170

Postal Rate Commission, Margaret P. Crenshaw, (202) 789-6840

Securities and Exchange Commission, Margaret Carpenter, (202) 942-0360

Small Business Administration, Joseph Loddo, (202) 205-6449

Smithsonian Institution, Rick Johnson, (202) 357-4610

Social Security Administration, Yvette Jackson, (410) 965-2910

United States International Trade Commission, Queen E. Cox, (202) 205-2678

United States Postal Service, M. Richard Porras, (202) 268-2454

Records Administration, and Executive Office of the President.

Senate Environment and Public Works Committee, *Subcommittee on Transportation and Infrastructure,* SD-410 20510; (202) 224-6176. Fax, (202) 224-5167. Sen. George V. Voinovich, R-Ohio, Chair; Ellen Stein, Staff Contact. Web, epw.senate.gov.

Oversight of the public buildings service of the General Services Administration.

Senate Governmental Affairs Committee, *Subcommittee on Oversight of Government Management, Restructuring, and the District of Columbia,* SH-601 20510; (202) 224-3682. Fax, (202) 224-3328. Sen. George V. Voinovich, R-Ohio, Chair; Kristine Simmons, Staff Director. General e-mail, ogm@govt-aff.senate.gov. Web, gov_affairs.senate.gov/ogm.htm.

Jurisdiction over legislation for the General Services Administration and the National Archives and Records Administration; government procurement and legislation to reduce the volume of federal paperwork; and the improvement of federal information management. Oversight responsibilities for operations of the White House and the Office of Management and Budget. Jurisdiction over the Ethics and Government Act of 1978. Examines the efficiency of government operations, including federal regulations and program management.

NONPROFIT

The Brookings Institution, *Center for Public Service, 1775 Massachusetts Ave. N.W. 20036; (202) 797-6425. Fax, (202) 797-6144. Paul Light, Director. Information, (202) 797-6000. Web, www.brookings.org/gs/cps/research. htm.*

Conducts research on public service and critical problems of federal, state, and local governance; offers training programs in leadership and public service for government executives.

Council for Excellence in Government, *1301 K St. N.W., #450 West 20005; (202) 728-0418. Fax, (202) 728-0422. Patricia G. McGinnis, President. Web, www.excelgov. org.*

Membership: business and professional leaders with previous executive-level government experience. Works to improve public-sector performance by strengthening federal leadership and management; seeks to build a public understanding of and confidence in government.

Federal Managers Assn., *1641 Prince St., Alexandria, VA 22314; (703) 683-8700. Fax, (703) 683-8707. J. Drew Hiatt, Chief Operating Officer. General e-mail, info@ fedmanagers.org.*

Seeks to improve the effectiveness of federal supervisors and managers and the operations of the federal government.

Private Sector Council, *1101 16th St. N.W., #300 20036-4803; (202) 822-3910. Fax, (202) 822-0638. Thomas V. Fritz, President. General e-mail, privsect@aol. com. Web, www.privatesectorcouncil.org.*

Membership: large corporations, private businesses, and associations, including financial and information technology organizations. Seeks to improve government efficiency, productivity, and management through a cooperative effort of the public and private sectors.

Buildings and Services

AGENCIES

General Services Administration, *Business Performance, 1800 F St. N.W., #4340 20405; (202) 501-0971. Fax, (202) 501-3296. Kevin Kampschroer, Assistant Commissioner.*

Oversees safety programs for federal buildings, employees, and visitors to federal buildings.

General Services Administration, *Federal Acquisition Institute, 1800 F St. N.W. 20405; (202) 501-0964. Fax, (202) 501-3341. Deborah O'Neill, Director. Web, www.gsa.gov/staff/v/training.htm.*

Fosters development of a professional acquisition workforce governmentwide; collects and analyzes acquisition workforce data; helps agencies identify and recruit candidates for the acquisitions field; develops instructional materials; evaluates training and career development programs.

General Services Administration, *Federal Protective Service, 1800 F St. N.W., #2341 20405; (202) 501-0907. Fax, (202) 208-5866. Clarence Edwards, Assistant Commissioner.*

Oversees security and law enforcement programs for federal buildings, employees, and visitors to federal buildings.

General Services Administration, *Federal Supply Service, 1941 Jefferson Davis Hwy., Arlington, VA 22202; (703) 305-6667. Fax, (703) 305-5500. Frank P. Pugliese Jr., Commissioner. Web, www.fss.gsa.gov.*

Responsible for providing federal agencies with common-use goods and nonpersonal services and for procurement and supply, transportation and travel management, and disposal of surplus personal property.

General Services Administration, *National Capital Region, 7th and D Sts. S.W., #7022 20407; (202) 708-9100. Fax, (202) 708-9966. Nelson B. Alcalde, Regional Administrator.*

Provides federal agencies with space, supplies, telecommunications, transportation, data processing, and construction services; has equal status with regional offices.

General Services Administration, *Public Buildings Service, 1800 F St. N.W., #6344 20405; (202) 501-1100. Fax, (202) 219-2310. Robert A. Peck, Commissioner.*

Administers the construction, maintenance, and operation of buildings owned or leased by the federal government. Manages and disposes of federal real estate.

General Services Administration, *Transportation and Property Management, 1941 Jefferson Davis Hwy., #815, Arlington, VA 22202; (703) 305-7660. Fax, (703) 305-6905. Allan Zaic, Assistant Commissioner.*

Manages governmentwide programs and activities relating to the use of excess personal property (except Automated Data Processing [ADP] equipment); provides transportation, travel, aircraft, mail, relocation, and vehi-

CHIEF MANAGEMENT OFFICERS AT FEDERAL AGENCIES

Agriculture, Sally Thompson, (202) 720-5539

Commerce, Linda J. Bilmes, (202) 482-4951

Defense, David O. Cooke, (703) 695-4436

Education, Willie H. Gilmore, (202) 401-0690

Energy, David Klaus, (202) 586-8010

Health and Human Services, John Callahan, (202) 690-6396

Housing and Urban Development, Joseph F. Smith, (202) 708-0940

Interior, Paul A. Denett, (202) 208-3668

Justice, Stephen R. Colgate, (202) 514-3101

Labor, Patricia Lattimore, (202) 693-4040

State, Bonnie R. Cohen, (202) 647-1500

Transportation, Melissa J. Allen, (202) 366-2332

Treasury, Nancy Killefer, (202) 622-0410

Veterans Affairs, Robert W. Schultz, (202) 273-5356

AGENCIES

Commission on Civil Rights, George Harbison, (202) 376-8356

Congressional Budget Office, David M. Delquadro, (202) 226-2600

Consumer Product Safety Commission, Mauna V. Kammer, (301) 504-0075

Environmental Protection Agency, Romulo L. Diaz, (202) 564-4600

Equal Employment Opportunity Commission, Allen M. Fisher, (202) 663-4200

Export-Import Bank, Dolores Bartning, (202) 565-3561

Federal Communications Commission, Jeffrey R. Ryan, (202) 418-1950

Federal Election Commission, James A. Pehrkon, (202) 694-1007

Federal Housing Finance Board, William W. Ginsberg, (202) 408-2890

Federal Labor Relations Authority, Judy Mullen, (202) 482-6650

Federal Maritime Commission, Edward Patrick Walsh, (202) 523-5800

Federal Reserve System, Stephen Malthrus, (202) 452-3764

Federal Trade Commission, Sherron G. Greulich, (202) 326-2271

Government Ethics Office, Robert E. Lammon, (202) 208-8000

National Credit Union Administration, James L. Baylen, (703) 518-6410

National Endowment for the Arts, Laurence M. Baden, (202) 682-5408

National Endowment for the Humanities, Barry Maynes, (202) 606-8233

National Transportation Safety Board, Peter Goelz, (202) 314-6060

Nuclear Regulatory Commission, Michael L. Springer, (301) 415-6222

Occupational Safety and Health Review Commission, Ledia E. Bernall, (202) 606-5390

Overseas Private Investment Corporation, Michael C. Cushing, (202) 336-8520

Peace Corps, William Piatt, (202) 692-1100

Pension Benefit Guaranty Corporation, John C. Seal, (202) 326-4180

Securities and Exchange Commission, Jayne L. Seidman, (202) 942-4000

Small Business Administration, Elizabeth Montoya, (202) 205-6610

Social Security Administration, Carolyn W. Colvin, (410) 965-3143

---

cle fleet services. Produces *Federal Travel Regulations* and *Federal Travel Directory*.

Ethics in Government

See also Inspectors General list (this section)

AGENCIES

Office of Government Ethics, *1201 New York Ave. N.W., #500 20005-3917; (202) 208-8000. Fax, (202) 208-* 8037. *Stephen D. Potts, Director; Gary Davis, Deputy Director. Web, www.usoge.gov.*

Administers executive branch policies relating to financial disclosure, employee conduct, and conflict-of-interest laws.

Office of Special Counsel, *Congressional and Public Affairs, 1730 M St. N.W., #216 20036-4505; (202) 653-7122. Fax, (202) 653-5161. Jane McFarland, Director; Elaine D. Kaplan, Special Counsel. Information, (202)*

653-7188. *Issues relating to the Hatch Act, (800) 854-2824. Web, www.osc.gov.*

Investigates allegations of prohibited personnel practices and prosecutes individuals who violate civil service regulations. Receives and refers federal employee disclosures of waste, fraud, inefficiency, mismanagement, and other violations in the federal government. Enforces the Hatch Act, which limits political activity by most federal and District of Columbia employees.

CONGRESS

House Appropriations Committee, *Subcommittee on Treasury, Postal Service, and General Government, B307 RHOB 20515; (202) 225-5834. Fax, (202) 225-5895. Rep. Jim Kolbe, R-Ariz., Chair; Michelle Mrdeza, Clerk. Web, www.house.gov/appropriations.*

Jurisdiction over legislation to appropriate funds for the Office of Government Ethics.

House Government Reform Committee, *Subcommittee on the Census, H1-114 OHOB 20515; (202) 226-1973. Rep. Dan Miller, R-Fla., Chair; Jane Cobb, Staff Director. Web, www.house.gov/reform.*

Jurisdiction over legislation on civil service issues, including code of ethics.

House Government Reform Committee, *Subcommittee on Government Management, Information, and Technology, B373 RHOB 20515; (202) 225-5147. Fax, (202) 225-2373. Rep. Steve Horn, R-Calif., Chair; J. Russell George, Staff Director. Web, www.house.gov/reform.*

Oversight of the Office of Government Ethics.

Senate Appropriations Committee, *Subcommittee on Treasury and General Government, SD-188 20510; (202) 224-7337. Sen. Ben Nighthorse Campbell, R-Colo., Chair; Patricia Raymond, Clerk. Web, appropriations. senate.gov/treasury.*

Jurisdiction over legislation to appropriate funds for the Office of Government Ethics.

Senate Governmental Affairs Committee, *SD-340 20510; (202) 224-4751. Fax, (202) 224-9603. Sen. Fred Thompson, R-Tenn., Chair; Hannah Sistare, Staff Director. Web, gov_affairs.senate.gov.*

Jurisdiction over legislation on civil service issues, including code of ethics and right to privacy. Oversight of the Office of Government Ethics.

NONPROFIT

Center for Public Integrity, *910 17th St. N.W., 7th Floor 20006; (202) 466-1300. Fax, (202) 466-1101. Charles Lewis, Executive Director. General e-mail, contact@ publicintegrity.org. Web, www.publicintegrity.org.*

Educational foundation supported by corporations, labor unions, foundations, and individuals. Publishes comprehensive reports concerning ethics-related issues.

Council for Citizens Against Government Waste, *1301 Connecticut Ave. N.W., #400 20036; (202) 467-5300. Fax, (202) 467-4253. Thomas A. Schatz, President. Information, (800) 232-6479. Web, www.cagw.org.*

Nonpartisan organization that seeks to eliminate waste, mismanagement, and inefficiency in the federal government. Monitors legislation and regulations.

Fund for Constitutional Government, *122 Maryland Ave. N.E., 3rd Floor 20002; (202) 546-3799. Fax, (202) 543-3156. Anne B. Zill, President. General e-mail, funcongov@aol.com. Web, www.epic.org/fcg/.*

Seeks to expose and correct corruption in the federal government and private sector through research and public education. Sponsors the Electronic Privacy Information Center, the Government Accountability Project, and the Project on Government Oversight.

Government Accountability Project, *1612 K St. N.W., #400 20006; (202) 408-0034. Fax, (202) 408-9855. Louis Clark, Executive Director. General e-mail, gap1@ erols.com. Web, www.whistleblower.org.*

Membership: federal employees, union members, professionals, and interested citizens. Provides legal and strategic counsel to public and private employees who seek to expose corporate and government actions that are illegal, wasteful, or repressive; aids such employees in personnel action taken against them; assists grassroots organizations investigating corporate wrongdoing, government inaction, or corruption.

Project on Government Oversight, *1900 L St. N.W., #314 20036-5027; (202) 466-5539. Fax, (202) 466-5596. Danielle Brian, Executive Director. General e-mail, pogo@pogo.org. Web, www.pogo.org.*

Public interest organization that works to expose waste, fraud, abuse, and conflicts of interest in all aspects of federal spending.

Executive Reorganization

AGENCIES

National Partnership for Reinventing Government, *750 17th St. N.W., #200 20006; (202) 694-0001. Fax, (202) 632-0390. John Kamensky, Deputy Director. General e-mail, rego.news@npr.gsa.gov. Web, www.npr.gov.*

Initiated by Vice President Al Gore; formerly the National Performance Review. Assesses the operation and functions of government in an attempt to make it more efficient. Assists federal agencies in evaluating their

INSPECTORS GENERAL FOR FEDERAL AGENCIES

Departmental and agency inspectors general are responsible for identifying and reporting program fraud and abuse, criminal activity, and unethical conduct in the federal government. In the legislative branch the General Accounting Office also has fraud and abuse hotlines: (800) 424-5454; (202) 512-7470 in Washington.

DEPARTMENTS

Agriculture, Roger C. Viadero, (202) 720-8001

Hotline, (800) 424-9121; (202) 690-1622 in Washington

Commerce, Johnnie Frazier, (202) 482-4661

Hotline, (800) 424-5197; (202) 482-2495 in Washington

Defense, Donald Mancuso (acting), (703) 604-8300

Hotline, (800) 424-9098; (703) 604-8555 in Washington

Education, Loraine Lewis, (202) 205-5439

Hotline, (800) 647-8733

Energy, Gregory H. Friedman, (202) 586-4393

Hotline, (800) 541-1625; (202) 586-4073 in Washington

Health and Human Services, June Gibbs Brown, (202) 619-3148

Hotline, (800) 447-8477

Housing and Urban Development, Susan Gaffney, (202) 708-0430

Hotline, (800) 347-3735; (202) 708-4200 in Washington

Interior, Earl D. Devancy, (202) 208-5745

Hotline, or (800) 424-5081; (202) 208-5300 in Washington

Justice, Robert Ashbaugh (acting), (202) 514-3435

Hotline, (800) 869-4499

Labor, Gordon S. Heddell (nominee), (202) 693-5100

Hotline, (800) 347-3756; (202) 219-5227 in Washington

State, Jacquelyn Williams-Bridgers, (202) 647-9450

Hotline, (202) 647-3320

Transportation, Kenneth Mead, (202) 366-1959

Hotline, (800) 424-9071; (202) 366-1461 in Washington

Treasury, Jeffrey Rush, (202) 622-1090

Hotline, (800) 359-3898

Veterans Affairs, Richard Griffin, (202) 565-8620

Hotline, (800) 488-8244

AGENCIES

Agency for International Development, Everett L. Mosley (acting), (202) 712-1150

Hotline, (800) 230-6539

Central Intelligence Agency, L. Britt Snider, (703) 874-2553

Environmental Protection Agency, Nikki Tinsley, (202) 260-3137

Hotline, (202) 260-4977

Federal Deposit Insurance Corporation, Gaston L. Gianni, (202) 416-2026

Hotline, (800) 964-3342

Federal Emergency Management Agency, George Opfer, (202) 646-3910

Hotline, (800) 323-8603

General Services Administration, William Barton, (202) 501-0450

Hotline, (800) 424-5210; (202) 501-1780 in Washington

National Aeronautics and Space Administration, Roberta L. Gross, (202) 358-1220

Hotline, (800) 424-9183

National Science Foundation, Philip Sunshine (acting), (703) 306-2100

Nuclear Regulatory Commission, Hubert Bell, (301) 415-5930

Hotline, (800) 233-3497

Office of Personnel Management, Patrick E. McFarland, (202) 606-1200

Hotline, (202) 606-2423

Small Business Administration, Phyllis K. Song, (202) 205-6580

Hotline, (800) 767-6580

Social Security Administration, James G. Huse Jr., (410) 966-8385

U.S. Postal Service, Carla Corcoran, (202) 268-4267

Hotline, (800) 654-8896; (888) 877-7644; (202) 268-5746 in Washington

missions, simplifying the bureaucratic process, and reforming the regulatory system. Staffed by workers from federal agencies.

Office of Management and Budget *(Executive Office of the President),* **President's Management Council,** *Dwight D. Eisenhower Executive Office Bldg., #260 20503; (202) 395-6190. Fax, (202) 395-5730. Sally Katzen, Chair. Web, www.whitehouse.gov/omb.*

Membership: chief operating officers of federal government departments and agencies. Responsible for implementing the management improvement initiatives of the administration. Develops and oversees improved governmentwide management and administrative systems; formulates long-range plans to promote these systems; works to resolve interagency management problems and to implement reforms.

Office of Personnel Management, *National Partnership Council: Office of Labor and Employee Relations, 1900 E St. N.W., #7H28 20415-0001; (202) 606-2930. Fax, (202) 606-2613. Jeffrey Sumberg, Director.*

Membership: officials of executive departments, government agencies, federal labor unions, the Federal Managers' Assn., and the Senior Executives' Assn. Advises the president on labor-management relations in the executive branch. (Affiliated with the National Partnership Clearinghouse.)

CONGRESS

General Accounting Office, *Federal Management and Workforce Issues, 441 G St. N.W. 20548; (202) 512-8676. Fax, (202) 512-4516. L. Nye Stevens, Director.*

Assesses the effectiveness of the National Performance Review efforts, implementation of the Government Performance and Results Act, and opportunities to introduce market-based incentives and reorganization into federal personnel management.

General Accounting Office, *Information Resources Management Policies and Issues, 441 G St. N.W. 20548; (202) 512-6406. Fax, (202) 512-6450. Jack Brock, Director.*

Seeks to make the federal government more effective in its information management. Assesses practices in the public and private sectors; makes recommendations to government agencies. Interests include information security.

House Government Reform Committee, *Subcommittee on Civil Service, B371C RHOB 20515; (202) 225-6427. Fax, (202) 225-2392. Rep. Joe Scarborough, R-Fla., Chair; George Nesterczuk, Staff Director. Web, www.house.gov/reform.*

Studies the effect of reorganization of agencies on federal employees.

House Government Reform Committee, *Subcommittee on Government Management, Information, and Technology, B373 RHOB 20515; (202) 225-5147. Fax, (202) 225-2373. Rep. Steve Horn, R-Calif., Chair; J. Russell George, Staff Director. Web, www.house.gov/reform.*

Jurisdiction over executive and legislative reorganization legislation.

Senate Governmental Affairs Committee, *SD-340 20510; (202) 224-4751. Fax, (202) 224-9603. Sen. Fred Thompson, R-Tenn., Chair; Hannah Sistare, Staff Director. Web, gov_affairs.senate.gov.*

Jurisdiction over executive and legislative reorganization legislation; studies the effect of reorganization of agencies on federal employees.

NONPROFIT

Alliance for Redesigning Government, *1120 G St. N.W., #850 20005-3801; (202) 347-3190. Fax, (202) 347-3252. Mary Ann Troanovitch, Senior Project Manager. General e-mail, innovate@napawash.org. Web, www.alliance.napawash.org.*

Advocates a smaller, more efficient, and more effective government. Serves as an information clearinghouse; sponsors projects that seek innovation in government. (Affiliated with the National Academy of Public Administration.)

🏛 CENSUS/POPULATION DATA

The Census Bureau publishes a pamphlet, "Telephone Contacts for Data Users," that lists key Census Bureau personnel and their fields of specialty. Copies may be obtained from the Census Bureau, Public Information Office, Washington, DC 20233; (301) 457-2822. For a specific inquiry about computer data, call (301) 457-4100.

AGENCIES

Census Bureau *(Commerce Dept.),* *Suitland and Silver Hill Rds., Suitland, MD 20746; (301) 457-2135. Fax, (301) 457-3761. Kenneth Prewitt, Director. Information, (301) 457-4608. Library, (301) 457-2511. Press, (301) 457-3030. Web, www.census.gov.*

Conducts surveys and censuses (including the decennial census of population and housing); collects and analyzes demographic, social, economic, housing, agricultural, and foreign trade data and data on governments;

CENSUS 2000

As provided for in Article 1, section 2 of the Constitution, the United States conducts a census every ten years for the purpose of apportioning the U.S. House of Representatives. Federal and state policymakers will use the results of the 2000 Decennial Census to allocate funding for entitlement programs, schools, roads, hospitals, and police forces. A census is a complete enumeration of a population or the business and commercial establishments, farms, or governments in an area. The 2000 census begins April 1, 2000.

U.S. CENSUS BUREAU

Home Page
Web, www.census.gov

Census Field Divisions
Web, www.census.gov/field/www/index.txt.html

Plans and directs the collection of national sample survey, census, and other data at the local level. Data are collected through regional offices in twelve major cities across the country. The offices employ part-time interviewers who gather data from households who have not returned their census forms. During major censuses, the division administers temporary regional census centers, district offices, and other offices.

Census Information Centers
Web, www.census.gov/clo/www/cic.html

Represents the interests of racial and ethnic communities to make census information and data available to participating organizations for analysis and policy planning.

Census Regional Offices
Web, www.census.gov/field/www/

Twelve permanent offices that collect economic and demographic data for an area that covers several million housing units.

State Data Centers
Web, www.census.gov/sdc/www

A state agency or university facility identified by the governor of each state and state equivalent to disseminate census data to the public.

Federal State Cooperative Program for Population Estimates
Web, www.census.gov/population/www/coop/fscpe.html

Race and Ethnic Census Advisory Committees
Web, www.census.gov/dmd/www/minority-2.html

African Americans
Web, www.census.gov/dmd/www/dateaap.html

American Indians and Alaska Natives
Web, www.census.gov/dmd/www/dateaian.html

Asians and Pacific Islanders
Web, www.census.gov/dmd/www/dateapi.html

Hispanic
Web, www.census.gov/dmd/www/datehis.html

Accessing Census Bureau Data
Web, www.census.gov/mso/www/npr/access.html

Frequently Asked Questions
Web, www.census.gov/dmd/www/faqquest.htm

Glossary of Census Terms
Web, www.census.gov/dmd/www/glossary.html

General E-mail Address
2000usa@census.gov

CONGRESSIONAL WEB SITES

House Government Reform Committee, Subcommittee on the Census
Web, www.house.gov/danmiller/census/

Census Monitoring Board
Web, 206.183.6.96/index.asp

Established by Congress in 1997, the Census Monitoring Board is an eight member bipartisan oversight board charged with observing and monitoring all aspects of the preparation and implementation of the 2000 decennial census.

---

publishes statistics for use by Congress, business, state and local governments, planners, and the public. Library open to the public.

Census Bureau *(Commerce Dept.), Decennial Census, Suitland and Silver Hill Rds., Suitland, MD 20746; (301) 457-3946. Fax, (301) 457-3024. John Thompson, Associate Director.*

Provides data from the 1990 decennial census (including general plans and procedures); economic, demographic, and population statistics; and information on trends.

Census Bureau *(Commerce Dept.), Demographic Surveys, 4700 Silver Hill Rd., Suitland, MD 20233-8400; (301) 457-3773. Fax, (301) 457-2306. Chester E. Bowie, Chief.*

Provides and explains proper use of data on consumer spending, crime, employment and unemployment, income, and housing. Conducts surveys on various subjects, including population, prisoners, health, and travel.

Census Bureau *(Commerce Dept.), Housing and Household Economic Statistics, 4700 Silver Hill Rd., Suitland, MD 20746; (301) 457-3234. Fax, (301) 457-3248. Daniel H. Weinberg, Chief.*

Develops statistical programs for the decennial census and for other surveys on housing, income, poverty, and the labor force. Collects and explains the proper use of economic, social, and demographic data. Responsible for the technical planning, analysis, and publication of data from current surveys, including the decennial census, the American Housing Survey, Current Population Survey, and Survey of Income and Program Participation.

Census Bureau *(Commerce Dept.), Population, Suitland and Silver Hill Rds., Suitland, MD 20746; (301) 457-2071. Fax, (301) 457-2644. John F. Long, Chief.*

Prepares population estimates and projections for national, state, and local areas and congressional districts. Provides data on demographic and social statistics in the following areas: families and households, marital status and living arrangements, farm population, migration and mobility, population distribution, ancestry, fertility, child care, race and ethnicity, language patterns, school enrollment, educational attainment, and voting.

CONGRESS

House Appropriations Committee, *Subcommittee on Commerce, Justice, State, and Judiciary, H309 CAP 20515; (202) 225-3351. Rep. Harold Rogers, R-Ky., Chair; Jim Kulikowski, Staff Director. Web, www.house.gov/appropriations.*

Jurisdiction over legislation to appropriate funds for the Commerce Dept., including the Census Bureau.

House Government Reform Committee, *Subcommittee on the Census, H1-114 OHOB 20515; (202) 226-1973. Rep. Dan Miller, R-Fla., Chair; Jane Cobb, Staff Director. Web, www.house.gov/reform.*

Jurisdiction over census legislation and statistics collection, demography, and population issues; oversight of the Census Bureau.

Senate Appropriations Committee, *Subcommittee on Commerce, Justice, State, and Judiciary, S-146A CAP 20510; (202) 224-7277. Sen. Judd Gregg, R-N.H., Chair; Jim Morhard, Clerk. Web, appropriations.senate.gov/commerce.*

Jurisdiction over legislation to appropriate funds for the Commerce Dept., including the Census Bureau.

Senate Governmental Affairs Committee, *SD-340 20510; (202) 224-4751. Fax, (202) 224-9603. Sen. Fred Thompson, R-Tenn., Chair; Hannah Sistare, Staff Director. Web, gov_affairs.senate.gov.*

Jurisdiction over census legislation and statistics collection, demography, and population issues; oversight of the Census Bureau.

NONPROFIT

Population Assn. of America, *721 Ellsworth Dr., #303, Silver Spring, MD 20910; (301) 565-6710. Fax, (301) 565-7850. Stephanie Dudley, Executive Director. General e-mail, info@popassoc.org. Web, www.popassoc.org.*

Membership: university, government, and industry researchers in demography. Holds annual technical sessions to present papers on domestic and international population issues and statistics.

Population Reference Bureau, *1875 Connecticut Ave. N.W., #520 20009; (202) 483-1100. Fax, (202) 328-3937. Peter J. Donaldson, President. General e-mail, popref@prb.org. Web, www.prb.org.*

Educational organization engaged in information dissemination, training, and policy analysis on domestic and international population trends and issues. Interests include international development and family planning programs, the environment, and U.S. social and economic policy. Library open to the public.

🏛 CIVIL SERVICE

AGENCIES

National Archives and Records Administration, *Information Security Oversight, 700 Pennsylvania Ave. N.W., #18N 20408-0001; (202) 219-5250. Fax, (202) 219-5385. Steven Garfinkel, Director. General e-mail, isoo@arch1.nara.gov.*

Oversees the security classification system throughout the executive branch; reports to the president on implementation of the security classification system. Develops and disseminates security education materials. Oversees the Classified Information Nondisclosure Agreement, which bars federal employees from disclosing classified and sensitive government information.

Office of Personnel Management (OPM), *1900 E St. N.W., #7353 20415-0001; (202) 606-1000. Fax, (202) 606-0082. Janice R. Lachance, Director; John Sepulveda, Deputy Director.*

Administers civil service rules and regulations; sets policy for personnel management, labor-management relations, workforce effectiveness, and employment within the executive branch; manages federal personnel activities, including recruitment, pay comparability, and benefit programs. Library open to the public (10 a.m.–2 p.m., Monday–Friday).

Office of Personnel Management, *Compensation Administration,* *1900 E St. N.W., #7H31 20415; (202) 606-2880. Fax, (202) 606-0824. Donald J. Winstead, Assistant Director. General e-mail, payleave@opm.gov. Web, www.opm.gov/oca/index.htm.*

Responsible for policy development and administration of compensation systems for almost two million federal civilian white-collar and blue-collar employees.

Office of Personnel Management, *Merit Systems Oversight and Effectiveness,* *1900 E St. N.W., #7470 20415-0001; (202) 606-1575. Fax, (202) 606-1798. Carol J. Okin, Associate Director.*

Monitors federal agencies' personnel practices and ensures that they abide by the Merit Systems Principles.

Office of Personnel Management, *Statistical Analysis and Services,* *1900 E St. N.W., #7439 20415-0001; (202) 606-2850. Fax, (202) 606-1719. George Kelly Croft, Director.*

Produces information for the Office of Personnel Management, Congress, and the public on statistical aspects of the federal civilian workforce, including trends in composition, grade levels, minority employment, sizes of agencies, and salaries.

Office of Personnel Management, *Workforce Compensation and Performance Service,* *1900 E St. N.W., #7508 20415-0001; (202) 606-2800. Fax, (202) 606-1443. Henry Romero, Associate Director.*

Works to improve personnel management within agencies by developing and implementing policy on white- and blue-collar pay systems, incentive awards, labor-management relations, employee benefits, and information systems.

Office of Special Counsel, *Congressional and Public Affairs,* *1730 M St. N.W., #216 20036-4505; (202) 653-7122. Fax, (202) 653-5161. Jane McFarland, Director; Elaine D. Kaplan, Special Counsel. Information, (202) 653-7188. Issues relating to the Hatch Act, (800) 854-2824. Web, www.osc.gov.*

Interprets federal laws, including the Hatch Act, concerning political activities allowed by certain federal employees; investigates allegations of Hatch Act violations and conducts prosecutions. Investigates and prosecutes complaints under the Whistleblower Protection Act.

CONGRESS

House Appropriations Committee, *Subcommittee on Treasury, Postal Service, and General Government,* *B307 RHOB 20515; (202) 225-5834. Fax, (202) 225-5895. Rep. Jim Kolbe, R-Ariz., Chair; Michelle Mrdeza, Clerk. Web, www.house.gov/appropriations.*

Jurisdiction over legislation to appropriate funds for the Office of Personnel Management and the Merit Systems Protection Board.

House Education and the Workforce Committee, *Subcommittee on Workforce Protections,* *2181 RHOB 20515; (202) 225-4527. Fax, (202) 225-9571. Rep. Cass Ballenger, R-N.C., Chair; Kevin D. Talley, Staff Director. Web, www.house.gov/ed_workforce.*

Jurisdiction over legislation on federal employees' compensation.

House Government Reform Committee, *Subcommittee on Civil Service,* *B371C RHOB 20515; (202) 225-6427. Fax, (202) 225-2392. Rep. Joe Scarborough, R-Fla., Chair; George Nesterczuk, Staff Director. Web, www.house.gov/reform.*

Jurisdiction over legislation on civil service labor-management issues, job classifications, hiring and recruiting, pay and compensation, benefits, retirement, rights of privacy, and code of ethics; and legislation related to the Hatch Act, which deals with the political activity of civil service employees. Oversight of the Senior Executive Service and intergovernmental personnel programs. Studies the effects of reorganization of agencies on federal employees.

House Government Reform Committee, *Subcommittee on Criminal Justice, Drug Policy, and Human Resources,* *B373 RHOB 20515; (202) 225-2577. Fax, (202) 225-1154. Rep. John L. Mica, R-Fla., Chair; Sharon Pinkerton, Staff Director. Web, www.house.gov/reform.*

Oversight of the Office of Personnel Management and the Merit Systems Protection Board.

Senate Appropriations Committee, *Subcommittee on Treasury and General Government,* *SD-188 20510; (202) 224-7337. Sen. Ben Nighthorse Campbell, R-Colo., Chair; Patricia Raymond, Clerk. Web, appropriations. senate.gov/treasury.*

Jurisdiction over legislation to appropriate funds for the Office of Personnel Management and the Merit Systems Protection Board.

OFFICE OF PERSONNEL MANAGEMENT

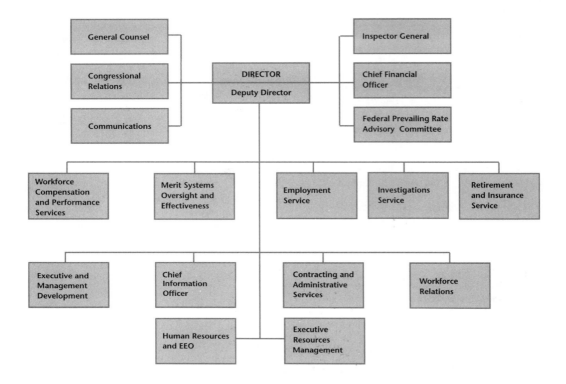

Senate Governmental Affairs Committee, *SD-340 20510; (202) 224-4751. Fax, (202) 224-9603. Sen. Fred Thompson, R-Tenn., Chair; Hannah Sistare, Staff Director. Web, gov_affairs.senate.gov.*

Jurisdiction over legislation on civil service labor-management issues; hiring, recruiting, and job classifications; compensation, including pay allowances and benefits; code of ethics; rights of privacy; intergovernmental personnel programs; effects of reorganization; leave and retirement; and legislation related to the Hatch Act, which deals with the political activity of civil service employees. Oversight of the Senior Executive Service, the Office of Personnel Management, and the Merit Systems Protection Board.

NONPROFIT

American Council of the Blind Government
Employees, *1155 15th St. N.W., #1004 20005; (202) 467-5081. Fax, (202) 467-5085. Mitch Pomerantz, President. Information, (800) 424-8666. Web, www.acb.org.*

Membership: federal, state, and local government employees and retirees who are blind or visually impaired and other interested persons. Seeks to improve government employment opportunities for visually disabled persons. Offers technical assistance. (Affiliated with American Council of the Blind.)

American Federation of Government Employees,
80 F St. N.W. 20001; (202) 737-8700. Fax, (202) 639-6490. Bobby L. Harnage, President. Membership, (202) 639-6411. Web, www.afge.org.

Membership: approximately 700,000 federal government employees. Provides legal services to members; assists members with contract negotiations and grievances. Monitors legislation and regulations. (Affiliated with the AFL-CIO.)

Blacks in Government, *1820 11th St. N.W. 20001-5015; (202) 667-3280. Fax, (202) 667-3705. Gerald R. Reed, President. Web, www.bignet.org.*

Advocacy organization for public employees. Promotes equal opportunity and career advancement for African American government employees; provides career development information; seeks to eliminate racism in the federal workforce; sponsors programs, business meetings, and social gatherings; represents interests of African American government workers to Congress and the executive branch; promotes voter education and registration.

Council for Excellence in Government, *1301 K St. N.W., #450 West 20005; (202) 728-0418. Fax, (202) 728-0422. Patricia G. McGinnis, President. Web, www.excelgov. org.*

Membership: business and professional leaders with previous executive-level government experience. Works to improve public-sector performance by strengthening federal leadership and management; seeks to build a public understanding of and confidence in government.

Federal Managers Assn., *1641 Prince St., Alexandria, VA 22314; (703) 683-8700. Fax, (703) 683-8707. J. Drew Hiatt, Chief Operating Officer. General e-mail, info@ fedmanagers.org.*

Seeks to improve the effectiveness of federal supervisors and managers and the operations of the federal government.

Federally Employed Women, *1400 Eye St. N.W., #425 20005; (202) 898-0994. Fax, (202) 898-0998. Jeanette Miller, President. Web, www.few.org.*

Membership: women and men who work for the federal government. Works to eliminate sex discrimination in government employment and to increase job opportunities for women; offers training program. Monitors legislation and regulations.

Public Employees Roundtable, *500 N. Capitol St., #1204 20001 (mailing address: P.O. Box 75248 20013-5248); (202) 927-4926. Fax, (202) 927-4920. Arvid Knutsen, Executive Director. General e-mail, info@ theroundtable.org. Web, www.theroundtable.org.*

Membership: professional and managerial associations and unions representing a wide range of public employees at all levels. Sponsors conferences, celebrations, and publicity events to educate the public about the contributions of public employees. Sponsors annual scholarship program for college students pursuing a public service career.

Senior Executives Assn., *P.O. Box 44808 20026; (202) 927-7000. Fax, (202) 927-5192. Carol A. Bonosaro, President. Web, www.seniorexecs.com.*

Professional association representing Senior Executive Service members and other federal career executives. Sponsors professional education. Interests include management improvement. Monitors legislation and regulations.

See also American Foreign Service Assn. (p. 233)

Dismissals and Disputes

AGENCIES

Merit Systems Protection Board, *1615 M St., N.W. 20419; (202) 653-7200. Fax, (202) 653-7130. Beth Slavet, Chair (nominee), (202) 653-7105. TTY, (202) 653-8896. Web, www.mspb.gov.*

Independent quasi-judicial agency that handles hearings and appeals involving federal employees; protects the integrity of federal merit systems and ensures adequate protection for employees against abuses by agency management. Library open to the public.

Merit Systems Protection Board, *Appeals Counsel, 1615 M St., N.W. 20419; (202) 653-6772. Fax, (202) 653-2260. Stephen E. Alpern, Director. General e-mail, settlement@mspb.gov. Web, www.mspb.gov/offices/appeals. html.*

Analyzes and processes petitions for review of appeals decisions from the regional offices; prepares opinions and orders for board consideration; analyzes and processes cases that are reopened and prepares proposed dispositions.

Merit Systems Protection Board, *Policy and Evaluations, 1615 M St., N.W. 20419; (202) 653-7208. Fax, (202) 653-7211. John M. Palguta, Director. General e-mail, studies@mspb.gov. Web, www.mspb.gov/studies/studies. html.*

Conducts studies on the civil service and other executive branch merit systems; reports to the president and Congress on whether federal employees are adequately protected against political abuses and prohibited personnel practices. Conducts annual oversight review of the Office of Personnel Management.

Merit Systems Protection Board, *Washington Regional Office, 5203 Leesburg Pike, #1109, Falls Church, VA 22041; (703) 756-6250. Fax, (703) 756-7112. P. J. Winzer, Director. General e-mail, washingtonregion@ mspb.gov.*

Hears and decides appeals of adverse personnel actions (such as removals, suspensions for more than fourteen days, and reductions in grade or pay), retirement, and performance-related actions for federal civilian employees who work in the Washington area or in overseas areas not covered by other board regional offices. Federal civilian employees who work outside Washington should contact the Merit Systems Protection Board regional office in their area.

Office of Personnel Management, *1900 E St. N.W., #7353 20415-0001; (202) 606-1000. Fax, (202) 606-0082. Suzanne Seiden, General Counsel.*

PERSONNEL OFFICES AT FEDERAL AGENCIES

DEPARTMENTS

Agriculture, (202) 720-3327

Commerce, recording, (202) 482-5138

Defense (civilian), (703) 696-2720

  Air Force (civilian), (703) 697-3127

  Navy (civilian), (703) 695-2633

  Defense Logistics Agency, (703) 767-7150

Education, (202) 401-0553
vacancies, (202) 401-0559

Energy, (202) 586-2731;
Fax-on-demand, (202) 586-1705

Health and Human Services, (301) 504-3301

  Food and Drug Administration, (301) 827-4070

  Health Resources and Services Administration,
  recording, (301) 443-1230

  National Institutes of Health, recording,
  (301) 496-2403

  Public Health and Science, (202) 619-0146

  **Substance Abuse and Mental Health
  Services Administration,** (301) 443-5407
  recording, (301) 443-2282

Housing and Urban Development, (202) 708-0408
recording, (202) 708-3203

Interior, recording, (800) 336-4562

Justice, (202) 514-6877

Labor, recording, (202) 219-6646

State, (202) 647-7252
civil service recording, (202) 647-7284
foreign service recording, (703) 875-7490

Transportation, (202) 366-9392
recording, (202) 366-9391
toll-free, (800) 525-2878

Treasury, recording, (202) 622-1029

Veterans Affairs, (202) 273-4920

AGENCIES

Administrative Office of the U.S. Courts,
recording, (202) 502-1271

Commodity Futures Trading Commission,
(202) 418-5010

Consumer Product Safety Commission,
(301) 504-0100

Corporation for National Service, (202) 606-5000,
ext. 330

Environmental Protection Agency, (202) 260-3267

Equal Employment Opportunity Commission,
(202) 663-4337

Export-Import Bank, (202) 565-3300

Farm Credit Administration, recording,
(703) 883-4139

Federal Communications Commission, (202) 418-0130
recording, (202) 418-0101

Federal Deposit Insurance Corporation,
(202) 942-3311

Federal Election Commission, (202) 694-1080

Federal Emergency Management Agency,
(202) 646-4040

Federal Labor Relations Authority, (202) 482-6660

Federal Mediation and Conciliation Service, (202)
606-5460

Federal Reserve Board, (202) 452-3880; recording,
(202) 452-3038; (800) 448-4894

Federal Trade Commission, recording, (202) 326-2020

General Accounting Office, (202) 512-4500
recording, (202) 512-6092

General Services Administration, (202) 501-0370

Government Printing Office, (202) 512-1200

National Aeronautics and Space Administration,
(202) 358-0520

National Archives and Records Administration,
(301) 713-6760

National Credit Union Administration,
(703) 518-6510

National Endowment for the Arts, (202) 682-5405

National Endowment for the Humanities,
(202) 606-8415

National Labor Relations Board, (202) 273-3980

National Mediation Board, (202) 692-5008

National Science Foundation, (703) 306-1182

National Transportation Safety Board, (202) 314-6268

Nuclear Regulatory Commission, (301) 415-7400

Office of Personnel Management, recording,
(202) 606-2424

Securities and Exchange Commission,
recording, (202) 942-4150

Small Business Administration, (202) 205-6780

Smithsonian Institution, (202) 287-3100
recording, (202) 287-3102

Social Security Administration, (410) 965-3318

U.S. International Trade Commission, (202) 205-2651

U.S. Postal Service, (202) 268-3646

Represents the federal government before the Merit Systems Protection Board, other administrative tribunals, and the courts.

Office of Special Counsel, *Congressional and Public Affairs,* *1730 M St. N.W., #216 20036-4505; (202) 653-7122. Fax, (202) 653-5161. Jane McFarland, Director; Elaine D. Kaplan, Special Counsel. Information, (202) 653-7188. Issues relating to the Hatch Act, (800) 854-2824. Web, www.osc.gov.*

Investigates allegations of prohibited personnel practices, including reprisals against whistleblowers (federal employees who disclose waste, fraud, inefficiency, and wrongdoing by supervisors of federal departments and agencies). Initiates necessary corrective or disciplinary action. Enforces the Hatch Act, which limits political activity by most federal and District of Columbia employees.

JUDICIARY

U.S. Court of Appeals for the Federal Circuit, *717 Madison Pl. N.W. 20439; (202) 633-6556. Fax, (202) 633-6353. Haldane Robert Mayer, Chief Judge; Jan Horbaly, Clerk, (202) 633-9614. Electronic bulletin board, (202) 633-9608 or (202) 786-6584.*

Reviews decisions of the Merit Systems Protection Board.

Hiring, Recruitment, and Training

AGENCIES

The Career America Connection in Washington, (202) 606-2700, the U.S. government's official employment service, provides the public with information on applications for civil service jobs. This automated service is available twenty-four hours a day. See also list of personnel offices under Civil Service, above.

Office of Personnel Management, *Classification,* *1900 E St. N.W., #6H31 20415; (202) 606-2950. Fax, (202) 606-4891. Judy Davis, Chief. Web, www.opm.gov.*

Develops job classification standards for agencies within the federal government.

Office of Personnel Management, *Diversity, 1900 E St. N.W., #2445 20415-0001; (202) 606-2817. Fax, (202) 606-0927. Maria Mercedes Olivieri, Director.*

Develops policies and guidelines for government recruiting programs, including diversity employment efforts related to women, minorities, persons with disabilities, and veterans. Collects and maintains statistics on the federal employment of these groups. Administers

the Federal Equal Opportunity Recruitment Program and the Disabled Veterans Affirmative Action Program.

Office of Personnel Management, *Employment Service, 1900 E St. N.W., #6500 20415; (202) 606-0800. Fax, (202) 606-1637. Mary Lou Lindholm, Associate Director.*

Develops civil service tests for most federal jobs through GS-15; develops qualification standards and governmentwide staffing policies; administers special programs to find jobs for displaced federal employees, minorities, veterans, women, youth, and persons with disabilities; administers the Administrative Law Judges program, federal recruitment efforts, and special personnel programs.

Office of Personnel Management, *Executive Resources Management, 1900 E St. N.W., #6484 20415; (202) 606-1610. Fax, (202) 606-0557. K. Joyce Edwards, Director. Web, www.opm.gov.*

Responsible for training and curriculum development programs for government executives and supervisors. Administers executive personnel systems, including those for the Senior Executive Service (SES) and personnel in executive positions not in SES.

Office of Personnel Management, *Intergovernmental Personnel Act Mobility Program, 1900 E St. N.W., #7463 20415; (202) 606-1181. Fax, (202) 606-3577. Tony Ryan, Program Head. Web, www.opm.gov.*

Implements temporary personnel exchanges between federal agencies and nonfederal entities including state and local governments, institutions of higher education, and other organizations.

Office of Personnel Management, *Investigations Service, 1900 E St. N.W., #5416 20415; (202) 606-1042. Fax, (202) 606-2390. Richard Ferris, Associate Director. Web, www.opm.gov.*

Initiates and conducts investigations of new federal employees; determines whether applicants and appointees are suitable for positions other than those involving national security.

Labor-Management Relations

See also Labor-Management Relations (chap. 7)

AGENCIES

Federal Labor Relations Authority, *607 14th St. N.W., #410 20424-0001; (202) 482-6500. Fax, (202) 482-6635. Solly J. Thomas Jr., Executive Director, (202) 482-6560; Donald Wasserman, Chair. Web, www.flra.gov.*

Oversees the federal labor-management relations program; administers the law that protects the right of federal employees to organize, bargain collectively, and participate through labor organizations of their own choosing.

Federal Service Impasses Panel *(Federal Labor Relations Authority)*, *607 14th St. N.W., #220 20424-1000; (202) 482-6670. Fax, (202) 482-6674. H. Joseph Schimansky, Executive Director; Bonnie P. Castrey, Chair.*

Assists in resolving contract negotiation impasses between federal agencies and labor organizations representing federal employees.

Office of Personnel Management, *1900 E St. N.W., #7353 20415-0001; (202) 606-1000. Fax, (202) 606-0082. Suzanne Seiden, General Counsel.*

Advises the government on law and legal policy relating to federal labor-management relations; represents the government before the Merit Systems Protection Board.

Office of Personnel Management, *Labor and Employee Relations, 1900 E St. N.W., #7H28 20415; (202) 606-2930. Fax, (202) 606-2613. Jeffrey Sumberg, Director.*

Provides government agencies and unions with information and advice on employee- and labor-management relations.

Office of Personnel Management, *National Partnership Council: Office of Labor and Employee Relations, 1900 E St. N.W., #7H28 20415-0001; (202) 606-2930. Fax, (202) 606-2613. Jeffrey Sumberg, Director.*

Membership: officials of executive departments, government agencies, federal labor unions, the Federal Managers' Assn., and the Senior Executives' Assn. Advises the president on labor-management relations in the executive branch. (Affiliated with the National Partnership Clearinghouse.)

NONPROFIT

National Alliance of Postal and Federal Employees, *1628 11th St. N.W. 20001; (202) 939-6325. Fax, (202) 939-6389. James M. McGee, President. General e-mail, napfe@patriot.net. Web, www.napfe.com.*

Membership: approximately 70,000 postal and federal employees. Helps members negotiate pay, benefits, and better working conditions; conducts training programs and workshops. Monitors legislation and regulations.

National Assn. of Government Employees, *Washington Office, 317 S. Patrick St., Alexandria, VA 22314; (703) 519-0300. Fax, (703) 519-0311. Susanne Pooler, Regional Director. General e-mail, nage@erols.com. Web, www.nage.org.*

Membership: approximately 200,000 federal government employees. Helps members negotiate pay, benefits, and better working conditions; conducts training programs and workshops. Monitors legislation and regulations. (Headquarters in Quincy, Mass.; affiliated with the AFL-CIO.)

National Federation of Federal Employees, *1016 16th St. N.W., #300 20036; (202) 862-4400. Fax, (202) 862-4432. Richard Brown, National President. Web, www.nffe.org.*

Membership: approximately 52,000 federal government employees. Helps members negotiate pay, benefits, and better working conditions; conducts training programs and workshops. Monitors legislation and regulations.

National Treasury Employees Union, *901 E St. N.W., #600 20004; (202) 783-4444. Fax, (202) 783-4085. Colleen Kelly, President. General e-mail, nteuinfo@nteuhq1.nteu.org. Web, www.nteu.org.*

Membership: approximately 150,000 employees from the Treasury Dept. and eighteen other federal agencies. Helps members negotiate pay, benefits, and better working conditions; conducts training programs and workshops. Monitors legislation and regulations.

Public Service Research Council, *320D Maple Ave. East, Vienna, VA 22180; (703) 242-3575. Fax, (703) 242-3579. David Y. Denholm, President. Web, www.psrf.org.*

Independent, nonpartisan research and educational organization. Opposes collective bargaining, strikes, and binding arbitration in the public sector. Sponsors conferences and seminars. Library open to the public by appointment.

Pay and Employee Benefits

AGENCIES

Bureau of Labor Statistics *(Labor Dept.), Survey, Data Analysis, and Publications, 2 Massachusetts Ave. N.E., #4175 20212; (202) 691-6199. Fax, (202) 691-6647. Frances Harris, Chief. General e-mail, ocltinfo@bls.gov.*

Develops occupational pay surveys on area and national industries; analyzes, distributes, and disseminates information.

Labor Dept., *Federal Employees' Compensation, 200 Constitution Ave. N.W., #S3229 20210; (202) 693-0040. Fax, (202) 693-1497. Dennis L. Mankin, Director (Acting). Web, www.dol.gov/dol/esa/public/owcp_org.htm.*

Administers the Federal Employees Compensation Act, which provides workers' compensation for federal employees.

Office of Personnel Management, *Compensation Administration,* 1900 E St. N.W., #7H31 20415; (202) 606-2880. Fax, (202) 606-0824. Donald J. Winstead, Assistant Director. General e-mail, payleave@opm.gov. Web, www.opm.gov/oca/index.htm.

Administers governmentwide pay systems for federal civilian employees, family pay and leave policies, and assists federal agencies and employees in administering governmentwide compensation systems.

Office of Personnel Management, *Employee Relations and Health Services Center,* 1900 E St. N.W. 20415; (202) 606-1740. Fax, (202) 606-0967. Ken Bates, Director.

Sets policy and guides federal agencies in establishing and maintaining programs on alcohol and drug abuse, drug-free workplaces, AIDS issues, workplace violence, and fitness programs.

Office of Personnel Management (OPM), *Federal Prevailing Rate Advisory Committee,* 1900 E St. N.W., #5559 20415; (202) 606-1500. Fax, (202) 606-5104. John F. Leyden, Chair (Acting).

Advises OPM on pay systems for federal blue-collar workers.

Office of Personnel Management, *Insurance Programs,* 1900 E St. N.W., #3400 20415; (202) 606-0770. Fax, (202) 606-4640. Frank D. Titus, Assistant Director.

Administers group life insurance for federal employees and retirees; negotiates rates and benefits with health insurance carriers; settles disputed claims.

Office of Personnel Management, *Performance Management and Incentive Awards,* 1900 E St. N.W., #7412 20415; (202) 606-2720. Fax, (202) 606-2395. Margaret M. Higgins, Chief.

Performance Management division sets policy and implements the performance appraisal and pay-for-performance system for all federal employees. Consults with agencies to help them develop their own systems; reviews and approves agencies' plans before implementation. Sets policy for performance appraisal and awards for federal employees. Incentive Awards division provides agencies with technical assistance and guidance on the Federal Incentive Awards Program and other awards programs that recognize achievements of federal workers.

Office of Personnel Management, *Retirement and Insurance Service,* 1900 E St. N.W., #4A10 20415; (202) 606-0600. Fax, (202) 606-2711. William E. Flynn III, Associate Director.

Develops and interprets federal policy and regulations on retirement benefits.

Office of Personnel Management, *Retirement Information,* 1900 E St. N.W. 20415-0001; (202) 606-0500. Fax, (202) 606-0145. Valerie Wagner-Hippen, Chief. TTY, (202) 606-0551.

Responds to telephone inquiries on retirement law and health and life insurance; handles reports of annuitants' deaths; conducts interviews on individual cases; makes appropriate referrals.

Office of Personnel Management, *Retirement Programs,* 1900 E St. N.W., #3305 20415; (202) 606-0300. Fax, (202) 606-1998. Sidney M. Conley, Assistant Director.

Administers the civil service and federal employees' retirement systems; responsible for monthly annuity payments and other benefits; organizes and maintains retirement records; distributes information on retirement and on insurance programs for annuitants.

Office of Personnel Management, *Salary and Wage Systems,* 1900 E St. N.W., #7H31 20415; (202) 606-2838. Fax, (202) 606-4264. Jerome D. Mikowicz, Chief. Web, www.opm.gov/oca/payrates/index.htm.

Responsible for the annual pay adjustment review process and for local adjustment allowances (locality pay) for federal white-collar workers. Works jointly with the Office of Management and Budget and the Labor Dept. to aid the director of OPM in the role of "pay agent" for the president. Report available to the public after presidential consideration. Administers the federal wage system that establishes pay scales for federal blue-collar employees and the non-foreign area cost of living allowance program for federal employees in offshore areas. Responds to inquiries on federal blue-collar pay rates and pay administration matters.

NONPROFIT

National Assn. of Retired Federal Employees, 606 N. Washington St., Alexandria, VA 22314; (703) 838-7760. Fax, (703) 838-7785. Frank Atwater, President. Member relations, (800) 456-8410. General e-mail, natlhq@narfe.org. Web, www.narfe.org.

Works to preserve the integrity of the civil service retirement system. Provides members with information about benefits for retired federal employees and for survivors of deceased federal employees. Monitors legislation and regulations.

🏛 FEDERAL CONTRACTS AND PROCUREMENT

See also General Policy (this chapter); Labor Standards and Practices (chap. 7); Procurement, Acquisition, and Logistics (chap. 16)

AGENCIES

Agencies and departments have their own contracting offices to deal with firms, organizations, and individuals seeking to sell goods and services to the government. Government solicitations for bids on goods and services are published in Commerce Business Daily issued by the Commerce Dept., Publishing Division, (202) 482-0632. See also list of procurement officers (this section).

Committee for Purchase from People Who Are Blind or Severely Disabled, *1215 Jefferson Davis Hwy., #310, Arlington, VA 22202-4302; (703) 603-7740. Fax, (703) 603-0655. Leon Wilson, Executive Director.*

Presidentially appointed committee. Determines which products and services are suitable for federal procurement from qualified nonprofit agencies that employ people who are blind or have other severe disabilities; seeks to increase employment opportunities for these individuals.

Comptroller of the Currency *(Treasury Dept.),* **Acquisition Services,** *250 E St. S.W. 20219; (202) 874-5040. Fax, (202) 874-5625. Karen Waters, Small Business Specialist.*

Ensures that businesses owned and controlled by minorities, women, and individuals with disabilities are given the opportunity to participate in contracts with the Comptroller of the Currency.

General Services Administration, *Acquisition Policy, 1800 F St. N.W., #4040 20405; (202) 501-1043. Fax, (202) 501-1986. J. Les Davison, Deputy Associate Administrator (Acting). Web, policyworks.gov/org/main/mv/oap.htm.*

Develops and implements federal government acquisition policies and procedures; conducts preaward and postaward contract reviews; administers federal acquisition regulations for civilian agencies; suspends and debars contractors for unsatisfactory performance; coordinates and promotes governmentwide career management and training programs for contracting personnel.

General Services Administration, *Board of Contract Appeals, 1800 F St. N.W., #7022 20405; (202) 501-0585. Fax, (202) 501-0664. Stephen M. Daniels, Chair. For filings, (202) 501-0116.*

Resolves disputes arising out of contracts with the General Services Administration, the Treasury Dept., the Education Dept., the Commerce Dept., and other independent agencies.

General Services Administration, *Enterprise Development, 1800 F St. N.W., #6029 20405; (202) 501-1021. Fax, (202) 208-5938. Marinda Jackson, Associate Administrator (Acting).*

Works to increase small-business procurement of government contracts. Provides policy guidance and direction for GSA Business Service Centers, which offer advice and assistance to businesses interested in government procurement.

General Services Administration, *Governmentwide Information Systems, 7th and D Sts. S.W., #5652 20407; (202) 401-1529. Fax, (202) 401-1546. Jim Adams, Director.*

Makes available quarterly information about government procurement contracts over $25,000; collects and disseminates data on the amount of business that companies do with each federal department and agency.

General Services Administration, *Governmentwide Policy, 1800 F St. N.W., #5240 20405; (202) 501-8880. Fax, (202) 501-8898. G. Martin Wagner, Associate Administrator. Web, policyworks.gov.*

Coordinates GSA policy-making activities; promotes collaboration between government and the private sector in developing policy and management techniques; works to integrate acquisition, management, and disposal of government property.

Minority Business Development Agency *(Commerce Dept.), 14th St. and Constitution Ave. N.W., #5055 20230; (202) 482-5061. Fax, (202) 501-4698. Courtland Cox, Director.*

Assists minority business owners in obtaining federal loans and contract awards; produces an annual report on federal agencies' performance in procuring from minority-owned businesses.

Office of Management and Budget *(Executive Office of the President), Federal Procurement Policy, Dwight D. Eisenhower Executive Office Bldg., #352 20503; (202) 395-5802. Fax, (202) 395-3242. Vacant, Administrator. Web, www.whitehouse.gov/omb.*

Coordinates government procurement policies, regulations, and procedures. Responsible for cost accounting rules governing federal contractors and subcontractors.

CONGRESS

General Accounting Office, *Procurement Law Division, 441 G St. N.W. 20548; (202) 512-6071. Fax, (202)*

PROCUREMENT OFFICERS FOR FEDERAL AGENCIES

DEPARTMENTS

Agriculture, Russ Ashworth, (202) 720-9448

Commerce, Howard Price, (202) 482-4185

Defense, Deidre A. Lee, (703) 695-7145

Education, Glenn Perry, (202) 708-8488

Energy, Richard H. Hopf, (202) 586-8613

Health and Human Services, Debra Peters, (202) 690-8457

Housing and Urban Development, V. Stephen Carberry, (202) 708-1290

Interior, Paul Denett, (202) 208-3668

Justice, James W. Johnston, (202) 307-2000

Labor, Daniel P. Murphy, (202) 219-4631

State, Michael Rafferty, (703) 875-6037

Transportation, Dom Telet, (202) 366-4953

Treasury, Annelie Kuhn (acting), (202) 622-0540

Veterans Affairs, David Derr, (202) 273-6047

AGENCIES

Consumer Product Safety Commission, Robert Frost, (301) 504-0444

Corporation for National Service, Simon Woodward, (202) 606-5000, ext. 114

Export-Import Bank, Mark Pitra, (202) 565-3338

Farm Credit Administration, Jim Judge, (703) 883-4135

Federal Communications Commission, Sonna B. Stampone, (202) 418-0992

Federal Deposit Insurance Corporation, Rodney Cartwright, (202) 942-3680

Federal Maritime Commission, Michael Kilby, (202) 523-5900

Federal Mediation and Conciliation Service, Sam Baumgardner, (202) 606-8111

Federal Reserve System, Michael E. Kelly, (202) 452-3296

Federal Trade Commission, Jean Sefchick, (202) 326-2258

General Services Administration, J. Les Davison (acting), (202) 501-1043

National Aeronautics and Space Administration, Thomas Lvedtke, (202) 358-2090

National Labor Relations Board, Paula M. Roy, (202) 273-4210

National Mediation Board, Jan Smith, (202) 692-5010

National Science Foundation, Veronica Bankins, (703) 306-1122

Nuclear Regulatory Commission, Timothy F. Hagan, (301) 415-6732

Office of Personnel Management, Alfred Chatterton, (202) 606-2240

Securities and Exchange Commission, Linda Sudhoff, (202) 942-4990

Social Security Administration, James Fornataro, (410) 965-9459

Small Business Administration, Sharon Gurley, (202) 205-6622

U.S. International Trade Commission, Michael Boling, (202) 205-2734

U.S. Postal Service, A. Keith Strange, (202) 268-4040

512-9749. *Anthony Gamboa, Senior Associate General Counsel.*

Considers and rules on the proposed or actual award of a government contract upon receipt of a written protest.

House Government Reform Committee, *Subcommittee on Government Management, Information, and Technology, B373 RHOB 20515; (202) 225-5147. Fax, (202) 225-2373. Rep. Steve Horn, R-Calif., Chair; J. Russell George, Staff Director. Web, www.house.gov/reform.*

Jurisdiction over legislation on the federal procurement system; oversees rules and regulations concerning government procurement.

House Small Business Committee, *Subcommittee on Tax, Finance, and Exports, B363 RHOB 20515; (202) 226-2630. Fax, (202) 225-8950. Rep. Donald Manzullo, R-Ill., Chair; Philip D. Eskeland, Staff Director. General e-mail, smbiz@mail.house.gov. Web, www.house.gov/smbiz.*

Jurisdiction over legislation on programs affecting small business and the federal procurement system; oversees rules and regulations concerning government procurement.

Senate Governmental Affairs Committee, *Subcommittee on Oversight of Government Management, Restructuring, and the District of Columbia, SH-601 20510; (202) 224-3682. Fax, (202) 224-3328. Sen. George V. Voinovich, R-Ohio, Chair; Kristine Simmons, Staff*

Director. General e-mail, ogm@govt-aff.senate.gov. Web, gov_affairs.senate.gov/ogm.htm.

Jurisdiction over legislation on the federal procurement system; oversees rules and regulations concerning government procurement.

Senate Small Business Committee, *SR-428A 20510; (202) 224-5175. Fax, (202) 224-4885. Sen. Christopher S. Bond, R-Mo., Chair; Emilia DiSanto, Staff Director. Web, sbc.senate.gov.*

Studies and makes recommendations on legislation concerning government procurement as it affects small business.

NONPROFIT

Some nongovernmental groups provide members with information about government contracts. Contact representative group for information.

Coalition for Government Procurement, *1990 M St. N.W., #400 20036; (202) 331-0975. Fax, (202) 822-9788. Larry Allen, Executive Director. General e-mail, coalgovpro@aol.com. Web, www.washmg.com/cgp.*

Alliance of business firms that sell to the federal government. Seeks equal opportunities for businesses to sell to the government; monitors practices of the General Services Administration and government procurement legislation and regulations.

Contract Services Assn., *1200 G St. N.W., #510 20005; (202) 347-0600. Fax, (202) 347-0608. Gary Engebretson, President. Web, www.csa-dc.org.*

Membership: companies that, under contract, provide federal, state, and local governments and other agencies with various technical and support services (particularly in defense, space, transportation, environment, energy, and health care). Analyzes the process by which the government awards contracts to private firms. Monitors legislation and regulations.

National Contract Management Assn., *1912 Woodford Rd., Vienna, VA 22182; (703) 448-9231. Fax, (703) 448-0939. Jim Goggins, Executive Vice President. Information, (800) 344-8096. Web, www.ncmahq.org.*

Membership: individuals concerned with administering, procuring, negotiating, and managing government contracts and subcontracts. Sponsors Certified Professional Contracts Manager Program and various educational and professional programs.

National Institute of Governmental Purchasing, *151 Spring St., #300, Herndon, VA 20170; (703) 736-8900. Fax, (703) 736-9644. Rick Grimm, Executive Vice President. Information, (800) 367-6447. Web, www.nigp.org.*

Membership: governmental purchasing departments, agencies, and organizations at the federal, state, and local levels in the United States and Canada. Provides public procurement officers with technical assistance and information, training seminars, and professional certification.

Professional Services Council, *2101 Wilson Blvd., #750, Arlington, VA 22201; (703) 875-8059. Fax, (703) 875-8922. Bert M. Concklin, President. Web, www. pscouncil.org.*

Membership: associations and firms that provide local, state, federal, and international governments with professional and technical services. Promotes reform of the procurement system; seeks to improve the compilation of data and statistics about the professional and technical services industry.

See also National Industries for the Blind (p. 647)

🏛 POSTAL SERVICE

AGENCIES

U.S. Postal Service, *475 L'Enfant Plaza S.W. 20260-0001; (202) 268-2000. Fax, (202) 268-4860. William J. Henderson, Postmaster General, (202) 268-2500. Library, (202) 268-2904. Press, (202) 268-2156. Locator, (202) 268-2020. Web, www.usps.gov.*

Offers postal service throughout the country as an independent establishment of the executive branch. Library open to the public.

U.S. Postal Service, *Inspection Service, 475 L'Enfant Plaza S.W., #3100 20260; (202) 268-4267. Fax, (202) 268-4563. Kenneth C. Weaver, Chief Postal Inspector. Fraud and abuse hotline, (888) 877-7644.*

Investigates criminal violations of postal laws, such as theft of mail or posted valuables, assaults on postal employees, organized crime in postal-related matters, and prohibited mailings. Conducts internal audits; investigates postal activities to determine effectiveness of procedures; monitors compliance of individual post offices with postal regulations; functions as the inspector general for the postal service.

CONGRESS

House Appropriations Committee, *Subcommittee on Treasury, Postal Service, and General Government, B307 RHOB 20515; (202) 225-5834. Fax, (202) 225-5895. Rep. Jim Kolbe, R-Ariz., Chair; Michelle Mrdeza, Clerk. Web, www.house.gov/appropriations.*

Jurisdiction over legislation to appropriate funds for the U.S. Postal Service and the Postal Rate Commission.

House Government Reform Committee, *Subcommittee on the Postal Service,* B349C RHOB 20515; (202) 225-3741. Fax, (202) 225-2544. Rep. John M. McHugh, R-N.Y., Chair; Robert Taub, Staff Director. Web, www.house.gov/reform.

Jurisdiction over postal service legislation; oversight of the U.S. Postal Service and the Postal Rate Commission. Analyzes the impact on federal jobs of the use of mail consultants and contractors by government agencies.

Senate Appropriations Committee, *Subcommittee on Treasury and General Government,* SD-188 20510; (202) 224-7337. Sen. Ben Nighthorse Campbell, R-Colo., Chair; Patricia Raymond, Clerk. Web, appropriations.senate.gov/treasury.

Jurisdiction over legislation to appropriate funds for the U.S. Postal Service and the Postal Rate Commission.

Senate Governmental Affairs Committee, *Permanent Subcommittee on Investigations,* SR-100 20510; (202) 224-3721. Fax, (202) 224-7042. Sen. Susan Collins, R-Maine, Chair; K. Lee Blalack, Staff Director. General e-mail, PSI@govt-aff.senate.gov. Web, gov_affairs.senate.gov/psi.htm.

Investigates postal fraud.

Senate Governmental Affairs Committee, *Subcommittee on International Security, Proliferation, and Federal Services,* SH-442 20510; (202) 224-2254. Fax, (202) 228-3796. Sen. Thad Cochran, R-Miss., Chair; Mitch Kugler, Staff Director. Web, gov_affairs.senate.gov/ispfs.htm.

Jurisdiction over postal service legislation, including legislation on postal service consumer protection, labor relations, automation of postal facilities, postal fraud, mail rates, and classifications for the postal service and philately; postal finances and expenditures; and mail transportation and military mail. Oversight of the U.S. Postal Service and the Postal Rate Commission. Analyzes the impact on federal jobs of the use of mail consultants and contractors by government agencies.

Consumer Services

AGENCIES

U.S. Postal Service, *Consumer Affairs,* 475 L'Enfant Plaza S.W. 20260-2200; (202) 268-2284. Fax, (202) 268-2304. Francia Smith, Vice President. TTY, (202) 268-2310.

Handles consumer complaints; oversees investigations into consumer problems; intercedes in local areas when problems are not adequately resolved; provides information on specific products and services; represents consumers' viewpoint before postal management bodies; initiates projects to improve postal service.

U.S. Postal Service, *Consumer Protection,* 475 L'Enfant Plaza S.W., #6347 20260-1127; (202) 268-2965. Fax, (202) 268-5287. Elizabeth Martin, Chief Counsel.

Initiates civil administrative proceedings to stop mail delivery that solicits money by lottery or misrepresentation; enforces statutes designed to prevent receipt of unwanted sexual material.

U.S. Postal Service, *Enforcement Law,* 475 L'Enfant Plaza S.W. 20260-1127; (202) 268-3075. Fax, (202) 268-5287. George C. Davis, Chief Counsel.

Reviews and processes cases falling under the Program Fraud Civil Remedies Act of 1986.

U.S. Postal Service, *Stamp Distribution,* 475 L'Enfant Plaza S.W., #4474E 20260-2436; (202) 268-2325. Fax, (202) 268-5978. Lawrence L. Lum, Manager.

Distributes postage stamps and postal stationery; develops inventory controls.

U.S. Postal Service, *Strategic Marketing,* 475 L'Enfant Plaza S.W., #5014 20260-1400; (202) 268-2203. Fax, (202) 268-3428. John R. Wargo, Vice President.

Develops policies, plans, and programs for commercial mailers to improve customer satisfaction. Directs the Business Partners program. Activities include the local postal customer councils, the National Postal Forum, and the Mailers' Technical Advisory Committee.

Employee and Labor Relations

AGENCIES

U.S. Postal Service, *Diversity Development,* 475 L'Enfant Plaza S.W., #3821 20260-5600; (202) 268-6567. Fax, (202) 268-6573. Benjamin Paul O'Casio, Vice President (Acting).

Responsible for policy and planning with regard to affirmative action hiring and supplier/vendor selection.

U.S. Postal Service, *Human Resources,* 475 L'Enfant Plaza S.W., #9840 20260-4200; (202) 268-3783. Fax, (202) 268-3803. Yvonne D. Maguire, Vice President.

Drafts and implements employment policies and practices, safety and health guidelines, training and development programs, and compensation guidelines.

U.S. Postal Service, *Labor Relations,* 475 L'Enfant Plaza S.W., #9021 20260-4100; (202) 268-3622. Fax, (202) 268-3074. Anthony Vegliante, Vice President.

Handles collective bargaining and contract administration for the U.S. Postal Service and processes complaints regarding equal employment opportunity.

U.S. Postal Service, *Personnel Operations Support,* *475 L'Enfant Plaza S.W., #1831 20260-4261; (202) 268-4255. Fax, (202) 268-6195. Janet Qualters, Manager.*

Matches needs of U.S. Postal Service with career goals and job preferences of its executive employees.

NONPROFIT

American Postal Workers Union, *1300 L St. N.W. 20005; (202) 842-4200. Fax, (202) 842-8530. Moe Biller, President. Web, www.apwu.org.*

Membership: approximately 366,000 postal employees, including clerks, motor vehicle operators, special delivery messengers, and other employees. Assists members with contract negotiation and grievances; conducts training programs and workshops. Monitors legislation and regulations. (Affiliated with the Postal, Telegraph, and Telephone International and the AFL-CIO.)

National Alliance of Postal and Federal Employees, *1628 11th St. N.W. 20001; (202) 939-6325. Fax, (202) 939-6389. James M. McGee, President. General e-mail, napfe@patriot.net. Web, www.napfe.com.*

Membership: approximately 70,000 postal and federal employees. Helps members negotiate pay, benefits, and better working conditions; conducts training programs and workshops. Monitors legislation and regulations.

National Assn. of Letter Carriers, *100 Indiana Ave. N.W. 20001; (202) 393-4695. Fax, (202) 737-1540. Vincent R. Sombrotto, President. General e-mail, nalcinf@nalc.org. Web, www.nalc.org.*

Membership: approximately 315,000 city letter carriers working for, or retired from, the U.S. Postal Service. Assists members with contract negotiation and grievances; conducts training programs and workshops. Monitors legislation and regulations. (Affiliated with the AFL-CIO and the Union Network International.)

National Assn. of Postal Supervisors, *1727 King St., #400, Alexandria, VA 22314-2753; (703) 836-9660. Fax, (703) 836-9665. Vincent Palladino, President. Web, www.naps.org.*

Membership: present and former postal supervisors. Cooperates with other postal management associations, unions, and the U.S. Postal Service to improve the efficiency of the postal service; promotes favorable working conditions and broader career opportunities for all postal employees; provides members with information on current functions and legislative issues of the postal service.

National Assn. of Postmasters of the United States, *8 Herbert St., Alexandria, VA 22305-2600; (703)*

683-9027. Fax, (703) 683-6820. Ed Baer, Executive Director. Hotline, (703) 683-9038. General e-mail, napus6@napus.org. Web, www.napus.org.

Membership: present and former postmasters of the United States. Promotes quality mail service and favorable relations between the postal service and the public; works with other postal groups and levels of management in the interest of postal matters and the welfare of its members.

National League of Postmasters, *1023 N. Royal St., Alexandria, VA 22314; (703) 548-5922. Fax, (703) 836-8937. Joseph W. Cinadr, President. Information, (800) 524-4771.*

Membership: state and area postmaster associations. Promotes effective postal management; sponsors insurance plans for members; operates a 24-hour help line, which makes confidential referrals for those experiencing stress. Monitors legislation and regulations.

National Rural Letter Carriers' Assn., *1630 Duke St., 4th Floor, Alexandria, VA 22314-5545; (703) 684-5545. Fax, (703) 548-8735. Steven R. Smith, President. Web, www.nrlca.org.*

Membership: approximately 100,000 rural letter carriers working for, or retired from, the U.S. Postal Service. Seeks to improve rural mail delivery. Helps members negotiate pay, benefits, and better working conditions; conducts training programs and workshops. Monitors legislation and regulations.

National Star Route Mail Contractors Assn., *324 E. Capitol St. 20003-3897; (202) 543-1661. Fax, (202) 543-8863. John V. Maraney, Executive Director.*

Membership: contractors for highway mail transport and selected rural route deliverers. Acts as liaison between contractors and the U.S. Postal Service, the Transportation Dept., and the Labor Dept. concerning contracts, wages, and other issues. Monitors legislation and regulations.

Mail Rates and Classification

AGENCIES

Postal Rate Commission, *1333 H St. N.W., #300 20268-0001; (202) 789-6800. Fax, (202) 789-6886. Edward J. Gleiman, Chair; George Omas, Vice Chair, (202) 789-6871.*

Submits recommendations to the governors of the U.S. Postal Service concerning proposed changes in postage rates, fees, and mail classifications; issues advisory opinions on proposed changes in postal services; studies and submits recommendations on public complaints concerning postal rates and nationwide service. Reviews appeals of post office closings.

U.S. Postal Service, *Business Mail Acceptance,* 475 *L'Enfant Plaza S.W., #6801 20260-6808; (202) 268-2161. Fax, (202) 268-4404. John Sadler, Manager.*

Implements policies on and answers customer inquiries about domestic mail classification matters.

U.S. Postal Service, *Mail Preparation and Standards,* 475 *L'Enfant Plaza S.W., #6800 20260-2405; (202) 268-6249. Fax, (202) 268-4336. Sherry Suggs, Manager.*

Issues policy statements on domestic mail classification matters. Ensures the accuracy of policies developed by the Postal Rate Commission with respect to domestic mail classification schedules.

U.S. Postal Service, *Pricing and Product Design,* 475 *L'Enfant Plaza S.W., #5016 20260-2401; (202) 268-7841. Fax, (202) 268-3428. Anita Bizzotto, Vice President.*

Sets prices for postal service product lines using competitive pricing methods.

NONPROFIT

Alliance of Nonprofit Mailers, *1211 Connecticut Ave. N.W., #620 20036-2701; (202) 462-5132. Fax, (202) 462-0423. Neal Denton, Executive Director. General e-mail, npmailers@aol.com. Web, www.nonprofitmailers.org.*

Works to maintain reasonable mail rates for nonprofit organizations. Represents member organizations before Congress, the U.S. Postal Service, the Postal Rate Commission, and the courts on nonprofit postal rate and mail classification issues.

Assn. for Postal Commerce, *1901 N. Fort Myer Dr., #401, Arlington, VA 22209-1609; (703) 524-0096. Fax, (703) 524-1871. Gene A. Del Polito, President. Web, www. postcom.org.*

Membership: companies and organizations interested in advertising (Standard Mail A) mail. Provides members with information about postal policy, postal rates, and legislation regarding postal regulations.

Direct Marketing Assn., *Ethics and Consumer Affairs: Government Affairs, Washington Office,* 1111 19th St. N.W., #1100 20036; (202) 955-5030. Fax, (202) 955-0085. Jerry Cerasale, Senior Vice President; Patricia Faley, Vice President. Web, www.the-dma.org.*

Membership: telemarketers; users, creators, and producers of direct mail; and suppliers to the industry. Serves as liaison between members and the U.S. Postal Service. Monitors federal legislation and regulations concerning postal rates. (Headquarters in New York.)

Mail Advertising Service Assn., *1421 Prince St., Alexandria, VA 22314-2806; (703) 836-9200. Fax, (703) 548-8204. David A. Weaver, President. Web, www.masa. org.*

Membership: U.S. and foreign letter and printing shops that engage in direct mail advertising. Serves as a clearinghouse for members on improving methods of using the mail for advertising.

National Federation of Nonprofits, *815 15th St. N.W., #822 20005-2201; (202) 628-4380. Fax, (202) 628-4383. Lee M. Cassidy, Executive Director. General e-mail, nfndc@ aol.com. Web, www.federationofnonprofits.org.*

Membership: educational, cultural, fraternal, religious, and scientific organizations that mail nonprofit second-, third-, or fourth-class mail. Serves as liaison between members and the U.S. Postal Service; represents nonprofit members' interests on the Mailers' Technical Advisory Committee. Monitors legislation and regulations.

Parcel Shippers Assn., *1211 Connecticut Ave. N.W., #610 20036; (202) 296-3690. Fax, (202) 296-0343. J. Pierce Myers, Executive Vice President. Web, www.parcelshippers. org.*

Voluntary organization of business firms concerned with the shipment of small parcels. Works to improve parcel post rates and service; represents members before the Postal Rate Commission in matters regarding parcel post rates. Monitors legislation and regulations.

Stamps/Postal History

AGENCIES

National Postal Museum *(Smithsonian Institution), Smithsonian Institution,* 2 Massachusetts Ave. N.E., MRC 570 20560; (202) 633-9360. Fax, (202) 633-9393. James H. Bruns, Director.*

Exhibits postal history and philatelic collections; provides information on world postal and philatelic history.

U.S. Postal Service, *Citizens' Stamp Advisory Committee,* 475 L'Enfant Plaza S.W., #4474 East Bldg. 20260-2437; (202) 268-2312. Fax, (202) 268-2714. Virginia Noelke Jr., Chair.*

Reviews stamp subject nominations. Develops the annual Stamp Program and makes subject and design recommendations to the Postmaster General.

U.S. Postal Service, *Stamp Acquisition,* 475 L'Enfant Plaza S.W., #4474 E 20260-2436; (202) 268-2321. Fax, (202) 268-6710. Catherine Caggiano, Manager.*

Manufactures postage stamps and postal stationery.

U.S. Postal Service, *Stamp Development,* 475 L'Enfant Plaza S.W. 20260-2437; (202) 268-2312. Fax, (202) 268-2714. *Terry McCaffrey, Manager.*

Manages the stamp selection function; develops the basic stamp pre-production design; manages relationship with philatelic community.

🏛 PUBLIC ADMINISTRATION

AGENCIES

Office of Management and Budget *(Executive Office of the President), President's Management Council,* Dwight D. Eisenhower Executive Office Bldg., #260 20503; (202) 395-6190. Fax, (202) 395-5730. *Sally Katzen, Chair.* Web, www.whitehouse.gov/omb.

Membership: chief operating officers of federal government departments and agencies. Responsible for implementing the management improvement initiatives of the administration. Develops and oversees improved governmentwide management and administrative systems; formulates long-range plans to promote these systems; works to resolve interagency management problems and to implement reforms.

President's Commission on White House Fellowships, 712 Jackson Pl. N.W. 20503; (202) 395-4522. Fax, (202) 395-6179. *Jacqueline Blumenthal, Director.* Web, www.whitehouse.gov/WH_Fellows.

Nonpartisan commission that provides professionals from all sectors of national life with the opportunity to observe firsthand the processes of the federal government. Fellows work for one year as special assistants to cabinet members or to principal members of the White House staff. Qualified applicants have demonstrated superior accomplishments early in their careers and have a commitment to community service.

CONGRESS

House Government Reform Committee, *Subcommittee on Government Management, Information, and Technology,* B373 RHOB 20515; (202) 225-5147. Fax, (202) 225-2373. *Rep. Steve Horn, R-Calif., Chair; J. Russell George, Staff Director.* Web, www.house.gov/reform.

Jurisdiction over legislation on all procurement practices. Also examines the efficiency of government operations, including federal regulations and program management.

House Government Reform Committee, *Subcommittee on National Economic Growth, Natural Resources, and Regulatory Affairs,* B377 RHOB 20515;

(202) 225-4407. Fax, (202) 225-2441. *Rep. David M. McIntosh, R-Ind., Chair; Marlo Lewis, Staff Director.* Web, www.house.gov/reform.

Jurisdiction over legislation involving the efficiency and management of government operations, including federal paperwork reduction.

House Standards of Official Conduct Committee, HT-2 CAP 20515; (202) 225-7103. Fax, (202) 225-7392. *Rep. Lamar Smith, R-Texas, Chair; Robert Walker, Chief Counsel.* Web, www.house.gov/ethics/.

Jurisdiction over the Ethics in Government Act of 1978.

Senate Governmental Affairs Committee, *Subcommittee on Oversight of Government Management, Restructuring, and the District of Columbia,* SH-601 20510; (202) 224-3682. Fax, (202) 224-3328. *Sen. George V. Voinovich, R-Ohio, Chair; Kristine Simmons, Staff Director.* General e-mail, ogm@govt-aff.senate.gov. Web, gov_affairs.senate.gov/ogm.htm.

Jurisdiction over the Ethics in Government Act of 1978 and over legislation on all procurement practices. Examines the efficiency of government operations, including federal regulations and program management.

NONPROFIT

American Society for Public Administration, 1120 G St. N.W., #700 20005; (202) 393-7878. Fax, (202) 638-4952. *Mary Hamilton, Executive Director.* Web, www.aspanet.org.

Membership: government administrators, public officials, educators, researchers, and others interested in public administration. Presents awards to distinguished professionals in the field; sponsors workshops and conferences; disseminates information about public administration. Promotes high ethical standards for public service.

Assn. of Government Accountants, 2208 Mount Vernon Ave., Alexandria, VA 22301; (703) 684-6931. Fax, (703) 548-9367. *Charles Culkin, Executive Director.* Web, www.agacgfm.org.

Membership: individuals engaged in government accounting, auditing, budgeting, and information systems.

Federally Employed Women, 1400 Eye St. N.W., #425 20005; (202) 898-0994. Fax, (202) 898-0998. *Jeanette Miller, President.* Web, www.few.org.

Membership: women and men who work for the federal government. Works to eliminate sex discrimination in government employment and to increase job opportunities for women; offers training program. Monitors legislation and regulations.

International City/County Management Assn., *777 N. Capitol St. N.E., #500 20002; (202) 289-4262. Fax, (202) 962-3500. William H. Hansell Jr., Executive Director. Web, www.icma.org.*

Membership: city and county managers, council of government directors, and municipal administrators. Sponsors a professional development institute that offers courses and workshops in municipal administration; maintains an information service on local government management practices.

International Personnel Management Assn., *1617 Duke St., Alexandria, VA 22314; (703) 549-7100. Fax, (703) 684-0948. Neil Reichenberg, Executive Director. General e-mail, ipma@ipma.hr.org. Web, www.ipma.hr.org.*

Membership: personnel professionals from federal, state, and local governments. Provides information on training procedures, management techniques, and legislative developments on the federal, state, and local levels.

National Academy of Public Administration, *1120 G St. N.W., #850 20005-3801; (202) 347-3190. Fax, (202) 393-0993. Robert O'Neill, President. Web, www.napawash. org.*

Membership: scholars and administrators in public management. Offers assistance to federal, state, and local government agencies, public officials, foreign governments, foundations, and corporations on problems related to public administration.

National Assn. of Schools of Public Affairs and Administration, *1120 G St. N.W., #730 20005; (202) 628-8965. Fax, (202) 626-4978. Michael Brintnall, Executive Director. General e-mail, office@naspa.org. Web, www. naspa.org.*

Membership: universities and government agencies interested in the advancement of education, research, and training in public management. Serves as a clearinghouse for information on public administration and public affairs programs in colleges and universities. Accredits masters degree programs.

National Women's Political Caucus, *1630 Connecticut Ave. N.W., #201 20009; (202) 785-1100. Fax, (202) 785-3605. Nick Demeter, Political Director; Roselyn O'Connell, President. General e-mail, mailnwpc@aol.com. Web, www. nwpc.org.*

Seeks to increase the number of women in policy-making positions in federal, state, and local government. Identifies, recruits, trains, and supports pro-choice women candidates for public office. Monitors agencies

and provides names of qualified women for high- and midlevel appointments.

Women in Government Relations, *1029 Vermont Ave. N.W., #510 20005-3527; (202) 347-5432. Fax, (202) 347-5434. Phyllis Hughes, Director. General e-mail, info@wgr. org. Web, www.wgr.org.*

Membership: professionals in business, trade associations, and government whose jobs involve governmental relations at the federal, state, or local level. Serves as a forum for exchange of information among its members.

🏛 **STATE AND LOCAL GOVERNMENT**

See also Community and Regional Development (chap. 12); State Officials list (appendix)

AGENCIES

Census Bureau *(Commerce Dept.),* **Governments Division,** *8905 Presidential Pkwy., Upper Marlboro, MD 20722 (mailing address: Washington Plaza II, #407 20233-6800); (301) 457-1489. Fax, (301) 457-1423. Gordon W. Green Jr., Chief.*

Compiles annual *Federal Expenditures by State* (available to the public), which provides information on overall federal grants-in-aid expenditures to state and local governments; collects data on finances, employment, and structure of the public sector; and serves as national clearinghouse on state and local audit reports. Computer data obtainable from Data User Services, (301) 457-4100.

Executive Office of the President, *Intergovernmental Affairs, White House 20502; (202) 456-7060. Fax, (202) 456-6220. Mickey Ibarra, Director.*

Serves as liaison with state, local, and tribal governments; provides information on administration programs and policies.

General Services Administration, *Federal Domestic Assistance Catalog Staff, 300 7th St. S.W., #101 20407; (202) 708-5126. Jim Adams, Director.*

Prepares *Catalog of Federal Domestic Assistance* (published annually in June and updated in December), which lists all types of federal aid and explains types of assistance, eligibility requirements, application process, and suggestions for writing proposals. Copies may be ordered from the Superintendent of Documents, U.S. Government Printing Office, Washington, D.C. 20402; (202) 512-1800. Also available on CD-ROM and floppy diskettes.

Housing and Urban Development Dept., *Policy Development and Research,* 451 7th St. S.W., #8100 20410-6000; (202) 708-1600. Fax, (202) 619-8000. Susan Wachter, Assistant Secretary. Web, www.huduser.org.

Assesses urban economic development and the fiscal capacity of state and local governments.

Multistate Tax Commission, 444 N. Capitol St. N.W., #425 20001-1538; (202) 624-8699. Fax, (202) 624-8819. Dan R. Bucks, Executive Director. General e-mail, mtc@ mtc.gov. Web, www.mtc.gov.

Membership: state governments that have enacted the Multistate Tax Compact. Promotes fair, effective, and efficient state tax systems for interstate and international commerce; works to preserve state tax sovereignty. Encourages uniform state tax laws and regulations for multistate and multinational enterprises. Maintains three regional audit offices that monitor compliance with state tax laws and encourage uniformity in taxpayer treatment. Administers program to identify businesses that do not file tax returns with states.

Office of Management and Budget *(Executive Office of the President), Federal Financial Management,* New Executive Office Bldg., #6025 20503; (202) 395-3993. Fax, (202) 395-3952. Joshua Gotbaum, Controller. Web, www. whitehouse.gov/omb.

Facilitates exchange of information on financial management standards, techniques, and processes among officers of state and local governments.

CONGRESS

General Accounting Office, *Health, Education, and Human Services,* 441 G St. N.W. 20548; (202) 512-6806. Fax, (202) 512-5806. Victor S. Rezendes, Assistant Comptroller General.

Independent, nonpartisan agency in the legislative branch. Responsible for intergovernmental relations activities. Reviews the effects of federal grants and regulations on state and local governments; works to reduce intergovernmental conflicts and costs; seeks to improve the allocation and targeting of federal funds to state and local governments through changes in federal funding formulas.

House Government Reform Committee, *Subcommittee on Criminal Justice, Drug Policy, and Human Resources,* B373 RHOB 20515; (202) 225-2577. Fax, (202) 225-1154. Rep. John L. Mica, R-Fla., Chair; Sharon Pinkerton, Staff Director. Web, www.house.gov/reform.

Jurisdiction over legislation dealing with the interrelationship among federal, state, and local governments.

Senate Finance Committee, SD-219 20510; (202) 224-4515. Fax, (202) 224-5920. Sen. William V. Roth Jr., R-Del., Chair; Frank Polk, Staff Director. Web, finance. senate.gov.

Jurisdiction over legislation dealing with the interrelationship among federal, state, and local governments, including revenue sharing legislation (jurisdiction shared with Senate Governmental Affairs Committee).

Senate Governmental Affairs Committee, SD-340 20510; (202) 224-4751. Fax, (202) 224-9603. Sen. Fred Thompson, R-Tenn., Chair; Hannah Sistare, Staff Director. Web, gov_affairs.senate.gov.

Jurisdiction over legislation dealing with the interrelationship between federal, state, and local governments, including revenue sharing legislation (jurisdiction shared with Senate Finance Committee).

NONPROFIT

Academy for State and Local Government, 444 N. Capitol St. N.W., #345 20001; (202) 434-4850. Fax, (202) 434-4851. Dawn Hatzer, Coordinator.

Offers technical assistance, training, and research to the Council of State Governments, International City/County Management Assn., National Assn. of Counties, National Conference of State Legislatures, National Governors' Assn., National League of Cities, and U.S. Conference of Mayors. Promotes cooperation among federal, state, and local governments; the private sector; and researchers. Interests include tax policy, finance, and state and local relations. Works to improve state and local litigation in the Supreme Court. Promotes the exchange of information from overseas with state and local officials.

American Legislative Exchange Council, 910 17th St. N.W., 5th Floor 20006; (202) 466-3800. Fax, (202) 466-3801. Duane Parde, Executive Director. General e-mail, info@alec.org. Web, www.alec.org.

Bipartisan educational and research organization for state legislators. Conducts research and provides information and model state legislation on public policy issues. Supports the development of state policies to limit government, expand free markets, promote economic growth, and preserve individual liberty.

Assn. of Metropolitan Sewerage Agencies, 1816 Jefferson Pl. N.W. 20036; (202) 833-2672. Fax, (202) 833-3743. Ken Kirk, Executive Director. Web, www. amsa-cleanwater.org.

Represents the interests of the country's publicly owned wastewater treatment works. Sponsors conferences. Monitors legislation and regulations.

Center for Policy Alternatives, *1875 Connecticut Ave. N.W., #710 20009-5728; (202) 387-6030. Fax, (202) 986-2539. Linda Tarr-Whelan, President. Web, www.stateaction. org.*

Clearinghouse and research center that assists state and local officials in developing policy initiatives. Interests include state and local economic development and tax reform, governmental reform, health policy, leadership issues, voter registration, and women's rights issues; provides technical assistance.

Coalition of Northeastern Governors, *Policy Research Center, Inc., 400 N. Capitol St. N.W., #382 20001; (202) 624-8450. Fax, (202) 624-8463. Anne D. Stubbs, Executive Director. General e-mail, coneg@sso.org. Web, www.coneg.org.*

Membership: governors of seven northeastern states (Connecticut, Maine, Massachusetts, New Hampshire, New York, Rhode Island, and Vermont). Addresses common issues of concern such as energy, economic development, transportation, and the environment; serves as an information clearinghouse and liaison among member states and with the federal government.

Council of State Governments, *Washington Office, 444 N. Capitol St. N.W., #401 20001; (202) 624-5460. Fax, (202) 624-5452. James Brown, Director. General e-mail, csg-dc@csg.org. Web, www.csg.org.*

Membership: governing bodies of states, commonwealths, and territories. Promotes interstate, federal-state, and state-local cooperation; interests include education, transportation, human services, housing, natural resources, and economic development. Provides services to affiliates and associated organizations, including the National Assn. of State Treasurers, National Assn. of Government Labor Officials, and other state administrative organizations in specific fields. Monitors legislation and executive policy. (Headquarters in Lexington, Ky.)

Government Finance Officers Assn., *Federal Liaison Center, Washington Office, 1750 K St. N.W., #350 20006; (202) 429-2750. Fax, (202) 429-2755. Betsy Dotson, Director. General e-mail, federalliaison@gfoa.org. Web, www. gfoa.org.*

Membership: state and local government finance managers. Offers training and publications in public financial management. Conducts research in public fiscal management, design and financing of government programs, and formulation and analysis of government fiscal policy. (Headquarters in Chicago.)

International Municipal Lawyers Assn., *1110 Vermont Ave. N.W., #200 20005; (202) 466-5424. Fax, (202)*

785-0152. Henry W. Underhill Jr., General Counsel. General e-mail, info@imla.org. Web, www.imla.org.

Membership: chief legal officers of cities and municipalities. Acts as a research service for members in all areas of municipal law; participates in litigation of municipal and constitutional law issues.

Municipal Treasurers' Assn. of the United States and Canada, *1029 Vermont Ave. N.W., #710 20005; (202) 737-0660. Fax, (202) 737-0662. Stacey Crane, Executive Director. General e-mail, info@mtausc.org. Web, www.mtausc.org.*

Provides continuing education and certification programs. Monitors legislation and regulations.

National Assn. of Bond Lawyers, *Governmental Affairs, Washington Office, 601 13th St., #800-S 20005-3875; (202) 682-1498. Fax, (202) 637-0217. William L. Larsen, Director. Web, www.nabl.org.*

Membership: municipal finance lawyers. Provides members with information on laws relating to the borrowing of money by states and municipalities and to the issuance of state and local government bonds. Monitors legislation and regulations. (Headquarters in Wheaton, Ill.)

National Assn. of Counties, *440 1st St. N.W., 8th Floor 20001-2080; (202) 393-6226. Fax, (202) 393-2630. Larry Naake, Executive Director. Press, (202) 942-4212. Web, www.naco.org.*

Membership: county officials. Conducts research, provides information, and offers technical assistance on issues affecting counties. Monitors legislation and regulations.

National Assn. of Regional Councils, *1700 K St. N.W., #1300 20006; (202) 457-0710. Fax, (202) 296-9352. William Dodge, Executive Director. General e-mail, narc@ clark.net. Web, www.narc.org.*

Membership: regional councils of local governments. Works to improve local governments' ability to deal with common public needs, address regional issues, and reduce public expense. Interests include housing, urban and rural planning, transportation, the environment, workforce development, economic development, and aging.

National Assn. of State Budget Officers, *444 N. Capitol St. N.W., #642 20001-1501; (202) 624-5382. Fax, (202) 624-7745. Gloria Timmer, Executive Director. Web, www.nasbo.org.*

Membership: state budget and financial officers. Publishes research reports on budget-related issues. (Affiliate of the National Governors' Assn.)

National Assn. of Towns and Townships, *444 N. Capitol St. N.W., #208 20001; (202) 624-3550. Fax, (202) 624-3554. Thomas Halicki, Executive Director. General e-mail, natat@sso.org. Web, www.natat.org.*

Membership: towns, townships, small communities, and others interested in supporting small town government. Provides local government officials from small jurisdictions with technical assistance, educational services, and public policy support; conducts research and coordinates training for local government officials nationwide. Holds an annual conference.

National Black Caucus of State Legislators, *444 N. Capitol St. N.W., #622 20001; (202) 624-5457. Fax, (202) 508-3826. Ivan Lanier, Executive Director.*

Membership: African American state legislators. Promotes effective leadership among African American state legislators; serves as an information network and clearinghouse for members.

National Conference of State Legislatures, *Washington Office, 444 N. Capitol St. N.W., #515 20001; (202) 624-5400. Fax, (202) 737-1069. Carl Tubbesing, Deputy Executive Director. Web, www.ncsl.org.*

Coordinates and represents state legislatures at the federal level; conducts research, produces videos, and publishes reports in areas of interest to state legislatures; conducts an information exchange program on intergovernmental relations; sponsors seminars for state legislators and their staffs. Monitors legislation and regulations. (Headquarters in Denver.)

National Governors' Assn., *444 N. Capitol St. N.W., #267 20001; (202) 624-5300. Fax, (202) 624-5313. Raymond C. Scheppach, Executive Director. Press, (202) 624-5364. Web, www.nga.org.*

Membership: governors of states, commonwealths, and territories. Provides members with policy and technical assistance. Makes policy recommendations to Congress and the president in community and economic development; education; international trade and foreign relations; energy and the environment; health care and welfare reform; agriculture; transportation, commerce, and technology; communications; criminal justice; public safety; and workforce development.

National League of Cities, *1301 Pennsylvania Ave. N.W., #550 20004-1763; (202) 626-3000. Fax, (202) 626-3043. Donald J. Borut, Executive Director. Information, (202) 626-3120. Press, (202) 626-3158. Web, www.nlc.org.*

Membership: cities and state municipal leagues. Provides city leaders with training, technical assistance, and publications; investigates needs of local governments in implementing federal programs that affect cities. Holds

an annual conference; conducts research; sponsors awards. (Affiliates include National Black Caucus of Local Elected Officials.)

Public Risk Management Assn., *1815 N. Fort Myer Dr., #1020, Arlington, VA 22209; (703) 528-7701. Fax, (703) 528-7966. James F. Coyle, Executive Director. General e-mail, info@primacentral.org. Web, www.primacentral.org.*

Membership: state and local government risk management practitioners, including benefits and insurance managers. Develops and teaches cost-effective management techniques for handling public liability issues; promotes professional development of its members. Gathers and disseminates information about risk management to public and private sectors.

Public Technology, *1301 Pennsylvania Ave. N.W., #800 20004; (202) 626-2400. Fax, (202) 626-2498. Costis Toregas, President. Information, (800) 852-4934. Library, (202) 626-2456. Press, (202) 626-2412. General e-mail, press@pti.nw.dc.us. Web, pti.nw.dc.us.*

Cooperative research, development, and technology-transfer organization of cities and counties in North America. Assists local governments in increasing efficiency, reducing costs, improving services, and developing public enterprise programs to help local officials create revenues and serve citizens. Participates in international conferences.

Southern Governors' Assn., *444 N. Capitol St. N.W., #200 20001; (202) 624-5897. Fax, (202) 624-7797. Elizabeth G. Schneider, Executive Director. General e-mail, sga@sso.org. Web, www.southerngovernors.org.*

Membership: governors of seventeen southern states, including the territories of Puerto Rico and the U.S. Virgin Islands. Provides a regional, bipartisan forum for governors to help formulate and implement national policy; works to enhance the region's competitiveness nationally and internationally.

U.S. Conference of Mayors, *1620 Eye St. N.W., #400 20006; (202) 293-7330. Fax, (202) 293-2352. J. Thomas Cochran, Executive Director. General e-mail, uscm@cais.com. Web, www.usmayors.org/uscm.*

Membership: mayors of cities with populations of 30,000 or more. Promotes city-federal cooperation; publishes reports and conducts meetings on federal programs, policies, and initiatives that affect urban and suburban interests. Serves as a clearinghouse for information on urban and suburban problems.

Western Governors' Assn., *Washington Office, 400 N. Capitol St. N.W., #388 20001; (202) 624-5402. Fax, (202)*

624-7707. *Richard Bechtel, Director. Web, www.westgov. org.*

Independent, nonpartisan organization of governors from eighteen western states, two Pacific territories, and one commonwealth. Identifies and addresses key policy and governance issues in natural resources, the environment, human services, economic development, international relations, and public management. (Headquarters in Denver.)

Women In Government, *2600 Virginia Ave. N.W., #709 20037; (202) 333-0825. Fax, (202) 333-0875. Joy N. Newton, Executive Director. Web, www.womeningovernment. org.*

Membership: women serving in state legislatures. Acts as a forum for discussion of women in politics; sponsors seminars; conducts educational research.

See also Coastal States Organization (p. 311); Multistate Tax Commission (p. 84); National Assn. of State Development Agencies (p. 411)

Washington Area

AGENCIES

See Local Government box (this section). See also Airports (chap. 19); Transit Systems (chap. 19)

CONGRESS

House Appropriations Committee, *Subcommittee on the District of Columbia, H147 CAP 20515; (202) 225-5338. Fax, (202) 225-8044. Rep. Ernest Istook, R-Okla., Chair; Americo S. Miconi, Staff Assistant. Web, www. house.gov/appropriations.*

Jurisdiction over legislation to appropriate funds for the District of Columbia.

House Government Reform Committee, *Subcommittee on the District of Columbia, B-349A RHOB 20515; (202) 225-6751. Rep. Thomas M. Davis III, R-Va., Chair; Peter Sirh, Staff Director. Web, www.house.gov/ reform.*

Jurisdiction over all measures relating to the municipal affairs of the District of Columbia, other than appropriations.

Senate Appropriations Committee, *Subcommittee on the District of Columbia, S128 CAP 20510; (202) 224-1526. Sen. Kay Bailey Hutchison, R-Texas, Chair; Mary Beth Nethercutt, Clerk. Web, appropriations.senate.gov/dc.*

Jurisdiction over legislation to appropriate funds for the District of Columbia and St. Elizabeth's Hospital.

LOCAL GOVERNMENT IN THE WASHINGTON AREA

DISTRICT OF COLUMBIA

Executive Office of the Mayor
Anthony A. Williams, Mayor
441 4th St. N.W., #1100 20001; (202) 727-2980; fax, (202) 727-9561
Web, ci.washington.dc.us

Financial Responsibility and Management Assistance Authority (D.C. Control Board)
Alice Rivlin, Chair
1 Thomas Circle N.W., #900 20005; (202) 504-3400; fax, (202) 504-3431
Web, www.dcfra.gov

MARYLAND

Montgomery County
Douglas M. Duncan, County Executive
101 Monroe St., 2nd Floor, Rockville, MD 20850; (240) 777-2500; fax, (240) 777-2517
Web, www.co.mo.md.us

Prince George's County
Wayne K. Curry, County Executive
14741 Gov. Oden Bowie Dr., #5032, Upper Marlboro, MD 20772, (301) 952-4131; fax, (301) 952-3784
Web, www.co.pg.md.us

VIRGINIA

City of Alexandria
Kerry J. Donley, Mayor
301 King St., City Hall, Alexandria, VA 22314; (703) 838-4500; fax, (703) 838-6433
Web, ci.alexandria.va.us

Arlington County
Paul Ferguson, Board Chair
2100 Clarendon Blvd., #300, Arlington, VA 22201; (703) 228-3130; fax, (703) 228-7430
Web, www.co.arlington.va.us

Fairfax County
Anthony H. Griffin, County Executive
12000 Government Center Pkwy., #552, Fairfax, VA 22035; (703) 324-2531; fax, (703) 324-3956
Web, www.co.fairfax.va.us

City of Falls Church
David Snyder, Mayor
300 Park Ave., Falls Church, VA 22046; (703) 241-5014; fax, (703) 241-5146
Web, ci.falls-church.va.us

Senate Governmental Affairs Committee, *Subcommittee on Oversight of Government Management, Restructuring, and the District of Columbia, SH-601 20510; (202) 224-3682. Fax, (202) 224-3328. Sen. George V. Voinovich, R-Ohio, Chair; Kristine Simmons, Staff Director. General e-mail, ogm@govt-aff.senate.gov. Web, gov_affairs.senate.gov/ogm.htm.*

Jurisdiction over all measures relating to the municipal affairs of the District of Columbia, other than appropriations.

NONPROFIT

Metropolitan Washington Council of Governments, *777 N. Capitol St. N.E., #300 20002-4239; (202) 962-3200. Fax, (202) 962-3201. Michael Rogers, Executive Director. TTY, (202) 962-3213. General e-mail, infocntr@ mwcog.org. Web, www.mwcog.org.*

Membership: local governments in the Washington area, plus members of the Maryland and Virginia legislatures and the U.S. Congress. Analyzes and develops regional responses to issues such as the environment, affordable housing, economic development, population growth, human and social services, public safety, and transportation.

Washington Convention Center Authority, *900 9th St. N.W. 20001; (202) 789-1600. Lewis H. Dawley III, Chief Executive Officer. Information, (800) 368-9000. Web, www.dcconvention.com.*

Promotes national and international conventions and trade shows; hosts local events; fosters redevelopment of downtown Washington.

11 Health

⊕ GENERAL POLICY

See also Food and Nutrition (chap. 2); Recreation and Sports (chap. 5); Caucuses (chap. 20)

AGENCIES

Agency for Health Care Policy and Research *(Health and Human Services Dept.), 2101 E. Jefferson St., #600, Rockville, MD 20852; (301) 594-6662. Fax, (301) 594-2168. John M. Eisenberg, Administrator. TTY, (888) 586-6340. General e-mail, info@ahcpr.gov. Web, www.ahcpr.gov.*

Works to enhance the quality, appropriateness, and effectiveness of health care services and to improve access to services. Promotes improvements in clinical practices and in organizing, financing, and delivering health care services. Conducts and supports research, demonstration projects, evaluations, and training; disseminates information on a wide range of activities.

Centers for Disease Control and Prevention *(Health and Human Services Dept.), Washington Office, 200 Independence Ave. S.W., #746-G 20201-0004; (202) 690-8598. Fax, (202) 690-7519. Donald E. Shriber, Associate Director. Web, www.cdc.gov.*

Surveys national and international disease trends, epidemics, and environmental health problems; administers block grants to states for preventive health services; promotes national health education program; administers foreign quarantine program and occupational safety and health programs; assists state and local health departments and programs with control of sexually transmitted diseases, treatment of tuberculosis, childhood immunization, and health promotion regarding chronic diseases and injury. (Headquarters in Atlanta: 1600 Clifton Rd. N.E. 30333. Public inquiries, [404] 639-3534.)

Food and Drug Administration (FDA), *(Health and Human Services Dept.), 5600 Fishers Lane, Rockville, MD 20857; (301) 827-2410. Fax, (301) 443-3100. Dr. Jane E. Henney, Commissioner. Information, (301) 443-3793. Press, (301) 827-6242. Web, www.fda.gov.*

Conducts research and develops standards on the composition, quality, and safety of drugs, cosmetics, medical devices, radiation-emitting products, foods, food additives, and infant formulas, including imports. Develops labeling and packaging standards; conducts inspections of manufacturers; issues orders to companies to recall and/or cease selling or producing hazardous products; enforces rulings and recommends action to Justice Dept. when necessary. Library open to the public.

Food and Drug Administration *(Health and Human Services Dept.), International Relations Staff, 5600 Fishers Lane, Rockville, MD 20857; (301) 827-4480. Fax, (301) 443-0235. Walter Batts, Director. Web, www.fda.gov/opacom/morechoices/oia.html.*

Serves as the principal FDA liaison with foreign counterpart agencies, international organizations, and U.S. government agencies on international issues. Coordinates agency involvement in international trade, harmonization, and technical assistance; administers programs for foreign scientists and other international visitors.

Food and Drug Administration *(Health and Human Services Dept.), Regulatory Affairs, 5600 Fishers Lane, #1490, Rockville, MD 20857; (301) 827-3101. Fax, (301) 443-6591. Dennis Baker, Associate Commissioner. Web, www.fda.gov.*

Directs and coordinates the FDA's compliance activities; manages field offices; advises FDA commissioner on domestic and international regulatory policies.

Health and Human Services Dept. (HHS), *National Committee on Vital and Health Statistics, 6525 Belcrest Rd., #1100, Hyattsville, MD 20782; (301) 458-4200. Fax, (301) 458-4022. Marjorie S. Greenberg, Executive Secretary. Web, www.ncvhs.hhs.gov.*

Advises the secretary on health problem statistics; works with agencies and committees of other nations on health problems of mutual concern.

Health and Human Services Dept., *Planning and Evaluation, 200 Independence Ave. S.W., #415F 20201; (202) 690-7858. Fax, (202) 690-7383. Dr. Margaret A. Hamburg, Assistant Secretary. Web, aspe.os.dhhs.gov.*

Provides policy advice and makes recommendations to the secretary on the full range of department planning, including Medicare, Medicaid, health care services, human resources, health care facilities development and financing, biomedical research, and health care planning.

Health Resources and Services Administration *(Health and Human Services Dept.), 5600 Fishers Lane, #1405, Rockville, MD 20857; (301) 443-2216. Fax, (301) 443-1246. Dr. Claude Earl Fox, Administrator. Information, (301) 443-3376. Press, (301) 443-2086.*

Administers federal health service programs related to access, quality, equity, and cost of health care. Supports state and community efforts to deliver care to underserved areas and groups with special health needs.

Health Resources and Services Administration *(Health and Human Services Dept.), Rural Health Policy, 5600 Fishers Lane, #9A55, Rockville, MD 20857; (301)*

HEALTH AND HUMAN SERVICES DEPARTMENT

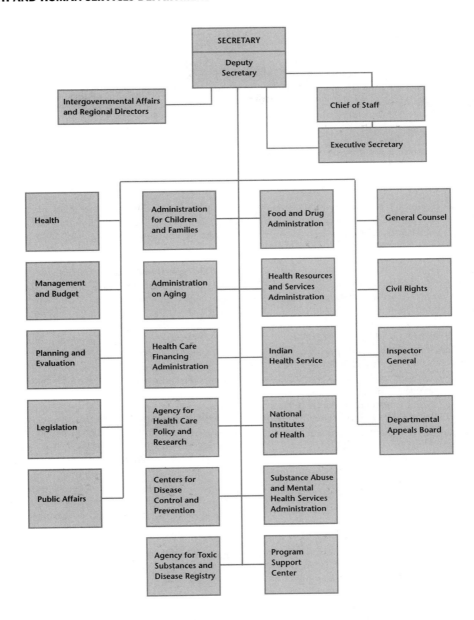

443-0835. Fax, (301) 443-2803. Dr. Wayne Myers, Director. Web, www.nal.usda.gov/ric/richs/orhp.htm.

Works with federal agencies, states, and the private sector to develop solutions to health care problems in rural communities. Administers grants to rural communities and supports rural health services research. Studies the effects of Medicare and Medicaid programs on rural access to health care. Provides the National Advisory Committee on Rural Health with staff support.

National Center for Health Statistics (*Centers for Disease Control and Prevention*), *6525 Belcrest Rd., #1140, Hyattsville, MD 20782; (301) 458-4500. Fax, (301) 458-4020. Edward J. Sondik, Director. Information, (301) 458-4636. Press, (301) 458-4800. Web, www.cdc.gov/ nchswww/nchshome.htm.*

Compiles, analyzes, and disseminates national statistics on population health characteristics, health facilities and human resources, health costs and expenditures, and health hazards. Interests include international health statistics.

National Clearinghouse for Primary Care Information (*Health and Human Services Dept.*), *2070 Chain Bridge Rd., #450, Vienna, VA 22182; (800) 400-2742. Fax, (703) 821-2098. Judy A. Cramer, Project Director.*

Supports the planning, development, and delivery of ambulatory health care to urban and rural areas in need of medical personnel and services; gives information to health care providers, administrators, and other interested persons.

National Institute for Occupational Safety and Health (*Centers for Disease Control and Prevention*), *200 Independence Ave. S.W. 20201; (202) 401-6997. Fax, (202) 260-4464. Dr. Linda Rosenstock, Director. Information, (800) 356-4674. Press, (202) 401-3749. General e-mail, pubstaft@cdc.gov. Web, www.cdc.gov/niosh.*

Supports and conducts research on occupational safety and health issues; provides technical assistance and training; organizes international conferences and symposia; develops recommendations for the Labor Dept. Operates occupational safety and health bibliographic databases; publishes documents on occupational safety and health.

National Institutes of Health (*Health and Human Services Dept.*), *1 Center Dr., Bldg. 1, #126, Bethesda, MD 20892-0148; (301) 496-2433. Fax, (301) 402-2700. Ruth L. Kirschstein, Director (Acting). Press, (301) 496-4461. Web, www.nih.gov.*

Supports and conducts biomedical research into the causes and prevention of diseases and furnishes information to health professionals and the public. Comprises research institutes (*see Health Topics: Research and Advocacy, this chapter*), and other components (the National Library of Medicine, the Warren Grant Magnuson Clinical Center, the National Center for Research Resources, the John E. Fogarty International Center, the Division of Research Grants, and the Division of Computer Research and Technology). All institutes are located in Bethesda except the National Institute of Environmental Health Sciences, P.O. Box 12233, Research Triangle Park, NC 27709.

Public Health and Science (*Health and Human Services Dept.*), *200 Independence Ave. S.W., #716G 20201; (202) 690-7694. Fax, (202) 690-6960. Dr. David Satcher, Surgeon General. Web, www.surgeongeneral.gov.*

Directs activities of the Public Health Service. Serves as the secretary's principal adviser on health concerns; exercises specialized responsibilities in various health areas, including population affairs and international health.

Public Health and Science (*Health and Human Services Dept.*), *Disease Prevention and Health Promotion, 200 Independence Ave. S.W., #738G 20201; (202) 401-6295. Fax, (202) 205-9478. Randolph F. Wykoff, Director. Publications, (301) 468-5960. Web, odphp.osophs.dhhs.gov.*

Develops national policies for disease prevention, clinical preventive services, and health promotion; assists the private sector and agencies with disease prevention, clinical preventive services, and health promotion activities.

Public Health and Science (*Health and Human Services Dept.*), *National Health Information Center, 5640 Nicholson Lane, Rockville, MD 20852 (mailing address: P.O. Box 1133 20013-1133); (301) 565-4167. Fax, (301) 984-4256. Bill Keating, Project Director. Information, (800) 336-4797. General e-mail, nhicinfo@health.org. Web, nhic-nt.health.org.*

A project of the office of Disease Prevention and Health Promotion; provides referrals on health topics and resources.

Public Health and Science (*Health and Human Services Dept.*), *Surgeon General, 5600 Fishers Lane, #18-66, Rockville, MD 20857; (301) 443-4000. Fax, (301) 443-3574. Dr. David Satcher, Surgeon General.*

Advises the public on health issues such as smoking, AIDS, immunization, diet, nutrition, disease prevention, and general health issues. Oversees activities of all members of the Public Health Service Commissioned Corps.

CONGRESS

General Accounting Office, *Health, Education, and Human Services, 441 G St. N.W. 20548; (202) 512-6806. Fax, (202) 512-5806. Victor S. Rezendes, Assistant Comptroller General.*

Independent, nonpartisan agency in the legislative branch. Audits all federal government health programs, including those administered by the departments of Defense, Health and Human Services, and Veterans Affairs.

House Appropriations Committee, *Subcommittee on Agriculture, Rural Development, FDA, and Related*

Agencies, 2362 RHOB 20515; (202) 225-2638. Rep. Joe Skeen, R-N.M., Chair; Hank Moore, Staff Director. Web, www.house.gov/appropriations.

Jurisdiction over legislation to appropriate funds for the Food and Drug Administration, Food Safety and Inspection Service, and Food and Consumer Service.

House Appropriations Committee, *Subcommittee on Labor, Health and Human Services, and Education,* 2358 RHOB 20515; (202) 225-3508. Fax, (202) 225-3509. Rep. John Edward Porter, R-Ill., Chair; Tony McCann, Staff Director. Web, www.house.gov/appropriations.

Jurisdiction over legislation to appropriate funds for health agencies in the Health and Human Services Dept. (excluding the Food and Drug Administration and native American health and health facilities construction activities); the National Commission on Acquired Immune Deficiency Syndrome; and the National Council on Disability.

House Commerce Committee, *Subcommittee on Health and the Environment,* 2125 RHOB 20515; (202) 225-2927. Fax, (202) 225-1919. Rep. Michael Bilirakis, R-Fla., Chair; James E. Derderian, Staff Director. General e-mail, commerce@mail.house.gov. Web, www.house.gov/commerce.

Jurisdiction over most health legislation, including Medicaid, national health insurance proposals (jurisdiction shared with the House Ways and Means Committee), public health and quarantine, alcohol abuse, drug abuse including medical and psychological rehabilitation programs for drug abusers, dental health, medical devices, long-term and nursing home care, orphan drugs, preventive health and emergency medical care, family planning, population research, mental health, and prenatal, maternal, and child health care. Oversight of the Food and Drug Administration.

House Government Reform Committee, *Subcommittee on Criminal Justice, Drug Policy, and Human Resources,* B373 RHOB 20515; (202) 225-2577. Fax, (202) 225-1154. Rep. John L. Mica, R-Fla., Chair; Sharon Pinkerton, Staff Director. Web, www.house.gov/reform.

Oversees operations of the Health and Human Services Dept.

House Ways and Means Committee, *Subcommittee on Health,* 1136 LHOB 20515; (202) 225-3943. Fax, (202) 226-1765. Rep. Bill Thomas, R-Calif., Chair; Vacant, Staff Director. Web, www.house.gov/ways_means.

Jurisdiction over legislation dealing with health care research and delivery programs supported by tax revenues, including Medicare, and proposals to establish a national health insurance system (jurisdiction shared with the House Commerce Committee).

Senate Appropriations Committee, *Subcommittee on Agriculture, Rural Development, and Related Agencies,* SD-136 20510; (202) 224-5270. Fax, (202) 224-9450. Sen. Thad Cochran, R-Miss., Chair; Rebecca M. Davies, Clerk. Web, appropriations.senate.gov/agriculture.

Jurisdiction over legislation to appropriate funds for the Food and Drug Administration, the Food Safety and Inspection Service, the Food and Consumer Service, and other consumer-related services and programs.

Senate Appropriations Committee, *Subcommittee on Labor, Health and Human Services, and Education,* SD-186 20510; (202) 224-7230. Fax, (202) 224-1360. Sen. Arlen Specter, R-Pa., Chair; Bettilou Taylor, Staff Director. Web, appropriations.senate.gov/labor.

Jurisdiction over legislation to appropriate funds for health agencies in the Health and Human Services Dept. (excluding the Food and Drug Administration and native American health programs).

Senate Finance Committee, SD-219 20510; (202) 224-4515. Fax, (202) 224-5920. Sen. William V. Roth Jr., R-Del., Chair; Frank Polk, Staff Director. Web, finance.senate.gov.

Jurisdiction over health programs supported by tax revenues, including Medicaid and Medicare.

Senate Health, Education, Labor, and Pensions Committee, SD-428 20510; (202) 224-5375. Fax, (202) 228-5044. Sen. James M. Jeffords, R-Vt., Chair; Mark Powden, Staff Director. TTY, (202) 224-1975. Web, labor.senate.gov.

Jurisdiction over most health legislation, including insurance, dental health, emergency medical care, mental health, medical devices, public health and quarantine, family planning, population research, prenatal, and some maternal and child health care legislation, including the dangers of lead-based paint and sudden infant death syndrome. Jurisdiction over legislation on radiation hazards of consumer products and machines used in industry. Jurisdiction over alcohol and drug abuse legislation. Oversees operations of the Health and Human Services Dept.

Senate Judiciary Committee, SD-224 20510; (202) 224-5225. Fax, (202) 224-9102. Sen. Orrin G. Hatch, R-Utah, Chair; Manus Cooney, Chief Counsel. Web, judiciary.senate.gov.

Jurisdiction over legislation on drug abuse, which includes regulatory aspects of federal drug abuse programs and criminal justice system rehabilitation programs for juvenile drug abusers.

INTERNATIONAL ORGANIZATIONS

International Bank for Reconstruction and Development, *Human Development, 1818 H St. N.W., #G8005 20433 (mailing address: 1818 H St. N.W., #S9035 20433); (202) 473-3437. Fax, (202) 522-3235. Eduardo Doryan, Vice President. Web, www.worldbank.org.*

Provides developing member countries with loans to help improve citizens' primary health care and nutrition and to help slow population growth through family planning.

Pan American Health Organization, *525 23rd St. N.W. 20037; (202) 974-3000. Fax, (202) 974-3663. Dr. George A. O. Alleyne, Director. Information, (202) 974-3458. Library, (202) 974-3305. Web, www.paho.org.*

Regional office for the Americas of the World Health Organization, headquartered in Geneva, Switzerland. Works to extend health services to underserved populations of its member countries and to control or eradicate communicable diseases; promotes cooperation among governments to solve public health problems. Library open to the public by appointment.

World Federation of Public Health Assns., *800 Eye St. N.W. 20001-3710; (202) 777-2487. Fax, (202) 777-2534. Dr. Alan Jones, Executive Secretary.*

International health organization composed of national public health associations whose membership includes health professionals and laypersons interested in improving community health. Sponsors triennial international congress.

NONPROFIT

American Assn. for World Health, *1825 K St. N.W., #1208 20006-1202; (202) 466-5883. Fax, (202) 466-5896. Richard L. Wittenberg, President. Web, www. aawhworldhealth.org.*

Serves as the U.S. Committee for the World Health Organization and the Pan American Health Organization. Informs the public about major health challenges that affect people both in the United States and abroad; promotes cooperative solutions that emphasize grassroots involvement.

American Clinical Laboratory Assn., *1250 H St. N.W., #880 20005; (202) 637-9466. Fax, (202) 637-2050. Dr. David N. Sundwall, President. Web, www.clinicallabs.com.*

Membership: laboratories and laboratory service companies. Advocates laws and regulations that recognize the role of laboratory services in cost-effective health care. Works to ensure the confidentiality of patient test results. Provides education, information, and research materials to members.

American Industrial Health Council, *2001 Pennsylvania Ave. N.W., #760 20006; (202) 833-2131. Fax, (202) 833-2201. Gaylen M. Camera, Executive Director. General e-mail, membershipservices@aihc.org.*

Coalition of industrial firms and trade associations concerned about potential health effects associated with industrial and commercial activities. Advocates using scientific information to evaluate and assess health risks; promotes the development and use of scientifically valid risk assessment data by regulatory agencies. Provides information on health hazards of toxic substances, genetic testing, and causes of cancer and birth defects.

American Public Health Assn., *800 Eye St. N.W. 20001; (202) 777-2742. Fax, (202) 777-2534. Dr. Mohammad Akhter, Executive Director. Web, www.apha.org.*

Membership: health care professionals, educators, environmentalists, social workers, industrial hygienists, and individuals. Interests include all aspects of health care and education. Establishes standards for scientific procedures in public health; conducts research on the causes and origin of communicable diseases. Produces data on the number of women and minority workers in public health and on their health status.

Assn. of State and Territorial Health Officials, *1275 K St. N.W., #800 20005-4006; (202) 371-9090. Fax, (202) 371-9797. George Hardy Jr., Executive Director. Web, www. astho.org.*

Membership: executive officers of state and territorial health departments. Serves as legislative review agency and information source for members.

The Brookings Institution, *Economic Studies Program, 1775 Massachusetts Ave. N.W. 20036-2188; (202) 797-6111. Fax, (202) 797-6181. Robert E. Litan, Director. Information, (202) 797-6302. Web, www.brookings.org/ ES/ES_HP.HTM.*

Studies federal health care issues and health programs, including Medicare, Medicaid, and long-term care.

Center for Patient Advocacy, *1350 Beverly Rd., #108, McLean, VA 22101; (703) 748-0400. Fax, (703) 748-0402. Terre McFillen Hall, Executive Director. Information, (800) 846-7444. General e-mail, patientadv@erols.com. Web, www.patientadvocacy.org.*

Represents the interests of patients nationwide. Dedicated to ensuring that patients have timely access to state-of-the-art health care.

Global Health Council, *1701 K St. N.W., #600 20006; (202) 833-5900. Fax, (202) 833-0075. Dr. Nils Daulaire, President. General e-mail, ghc@globalhealth.org. Web, www.globalhealth.org.*

FOOD AND DRUG ADMINISTRATION

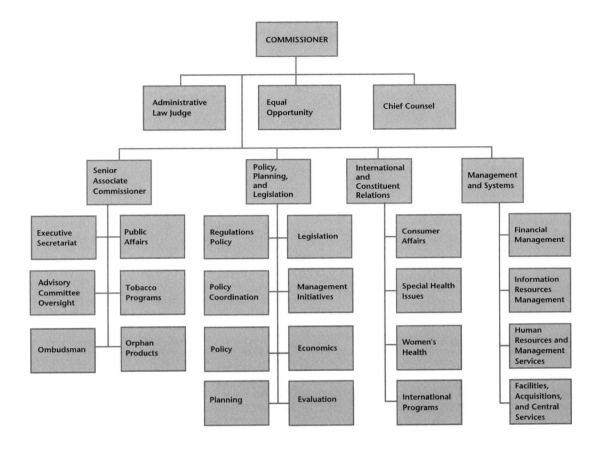

Seeks to strengthen U.S. participation in international health activities, especially in developing countries. Serves as an information clearinghouse for the international health community. Promotes cooperation among private and public organizations involved in international health activities. Provides policy analysis and public education. Holds the annual International Health Conference. Sponsors career services program and international health seminars.

Grantmakers in Health, *Washington Office,* 1100 Connecticut Ave. N.W., 12th Floor 20036; (202) 452-8331. Fax, (202) 452-8340. Lauren LeRoy, President. Web, www. gih.org.

Seeks to increase the capacity of private sector grantmakers to enhance public health. Fosters information exchange among grantmakers. Publications include a bulletin on current news in health and human services and the *Directory of Health Philanthropy.* (Headquarters in New York.)

Health Education Foundation, *2600 Virginia Ave. N.W., #502 20037; (202) 338-3501. Fax, (202) 965-6520. Dr. Morris Chafetz, President. General e-mail, hefmona@ erols.com.*

Develops health information programs. Promotes responsible drinking behavior.

Healthcare Leadership Council, *900 17th St. N.W., #600 20006; (202) 452-8700. Fax, (202) 296-9561. Mary Grealy, President. Web, www.hlc.org.*

Membership: health care leaders who examine major health issues, including access and affordability. Works to implement new public policies.

Institute for Health Care Research and Policy, *2233 Wisconsin Ave. N.W., #525 20007; (202) 687-0880. Fax, (202) 687-3110. James Reuter, Director.*

Research branch of Georgetown University School of Medicine. Interests include quality of care, cost effectiveness, outcomes research, structure and impact of managed care, and access to care.

Intergovernmental Health Policy Project, *444 N. Capitol St. N.W., #515 20001; (202) 624-8698. Fax, (202) 737-1069. Richard Merritt, Director. Web, www.ncsl.org.*

Researches state health laws and programs. Provides health policymakers, administrators, and others with information on state health programs and policies. (Affiliated with the National Conference of State Legislatures.)

National Assn. of Counties, *Health, 440 1st St. N.W., 8th Floor 20001-2028; (202) 393-6226. Fax, (202) 942-4281. Sally McElroy, Associate Legislative Director. Web, www.naco.org.*

Promotes federal understanding of county government's role in providing, funding, and overseeing health care services at the local level. Interests include indigent health care, Medicaid and Medicare, prevention of and services for HIV infection and AIDS, long-term care, mental health, maternal and child health, and traditional public health programs conducted by local health departments.

National Assn. of County and City Health Officials, *1100 17th St. N.W., 2nd Floor 20036; (202) 783-5550. Fax, (202) 783-1583. Thomas L. Milne, Executive Director. Web, www.naccho.org.*

Represents local health departments. Promotes partnership among local, state, and federal health agencies. Works to improve the capacity of local health departments to assess health needs, develop public health policies, and ensure delivery of community services. Submits health policy proposals to the federal government.

National Governors' Assn., *Health Policy Studies, 444 N. Capitol St. N.W., #267 20001; (202) 624-5319. Fax, (202) 624-5313. Randy Desonia, Director. Information, (202) 624-5300. Web, www.nga.org.*

Provides technical assistance regarding the Title 21 Program, state oversight of managed care, public/private efforts to improve health care quality, and long-term care services.

National Health Council, *1730 M St. N.W., #500 20036-4505; (202) 785-3910. Fax, (202) 785-5923. Myrl Weinberg, President. Web, www.nhcouncil.org.*

Membership: voluntary health agencies, associations, and business, insurance, and government groups interested in health. Conducts research on health and health-related issues; serves as an information clearinghouse on health careers. Monitors legislation and regulations.

National Health Policy Forum, *2021 K St. N.W., #800 20006; (202) 872-1390. Fax, (202) 862-9837. Judith Miller Jones, Director.*

Nonpartisan policy analysis and research organization that provides executive branch and congressional staff with information on financing and delivery of health care services. Affiliated with George Washington University.

Partnership for Prevention, *1233 20th St. N.W., #200 20036; (202) 833-0009. Fax, (202) 833-0113. Ashley Coffield, President. Web, www.prevent.org.*

Seeks to make prevention a priority in national health policy and practice. Coordinates the prevention-oriented efforts of federal health agencies, corporations, states, and nonprofit organizations in order to achieve the Healthy People 2010 national prevention goals.

Public Citizen, *Health Research Group, 1600 20th St. N.W. 20009; (202) 588-1000. Fax, (202) 588-7796. Dr. Sidney M. Wolfe, Director. Web, www.citizen.org.*

Citizens' interest group that conducts policy-oriented research on health care issues. Interests include hospital quality and costs, doctors' fees, physician discipline and malpractice, state administration of Medicare programs, workplace safety and health, unnecessary surgery, comprehensive health planning, dangerous drugs, carcinogens, and medical devices. Favors a single-payer (Canadian-style), comprehensive health program.

Rand Corporation, *Health Program, Washington Office, 1333 H St. N.W., #800 20005-4707; (202) 296-5000. Fax, (202) 296-7960. Bruce Hoffman, Director. Web, www.rand.org.*

Research organization that assesses health issues, including alternative reimbursement schemes for health care. Monitors national and international trends. (Headquarters in Santa Monica, Calif.)

Regulatory Affairs Professionals Society, *12300 Twinbrook Pkwy., #350, Rockville, MD 20852; (301) 770-2920. Fax, (301) 770-2924. Sherry Keramidas, Executive Director. General e-mail, raps@raps.org. Web, www.raps.org.*

Membership: regulatory professionals in the pharmaceutical, medical device, biologic, biotechnology, and related industries. Fosters cooperation among health care regulatory professionals; sponsors seminars. Monitors legislation and regulations.

Robert Wood Johnson Foundation, *Center for Study-ing Health System Change,* 600 Maryland Ave. S.W., #550 20024-2512; (202) 484-5261. Fax, (202) 484-9258. Paul B. Ginsburg, Director. Web, www.hschange.com.

Studies change in the health care system; conducts and monitors research; disseminates information to researchers, health care professionals, and national, state, and local policymakers. Sponsors workshops and conferences. (Foundation headquarters in Princeton, N.J.)

Health Insurance/Managed Care

See also Insurance (chap. 3); Medicaid and Medicare (this chapter)

AGENCIES

Health Care Financing Administration *(Health and Human Services Dept.), Health Plans and Providers,* 7500 Security Blvd., C5-24-27, Baltimore, MD 21244; (410) 786-5674. Fax, (410) 786-4490. Robert Berenson, Director.

Sets national policies for federally qualified health maintenance organizations (HMOs) and competitive medical plans; monitors HMO compliance with federal regulations. Administers and promotes prepaid health plan participation in Medicare and Medicaid programs.

CONGRESS

Congressional Budget Office, *Health and Human Resources,* 418A FHOB 20515; (202) 226-2668. Fax, (202) 225-3149. Joseph Antos, Assistant Director.

Analyzes program and budget issues in the areas of health, education, employment and training, and social services. Examines the potential effects on the private sector of proposed federal mandates in those areas.

House Commerce Committee, *Subcommittee on Health and the Environment,* 2125 RHOB 20515; (202) 225-2927. Fax, (202) 225-1919. Rep. Michael Bilirakis, R-Fla., Chair; James E. Derderian, Staff Director. General e-mail, commerce@mail.house.gov. Web, www.house.gov/commerce.

Jurisdiction over national health insurance proposals (jurisdiction shared with the House Ways and Means Committee) and legislation on malpractice insurance, Medicaid, and health maintenance organizations.

House Ways and Means Committee, *Subcommittee on Health,* 1136 LHOB 20515; (202) 225-3943. Fax, (202) 226-1765. Rep. Bill Thomas, R-Calif., Chair; Vacant, Staff Director. Web, www.house.gov/ways_means.

Jurisdiction over national health insurance proposals (jurisdiction shared with the House Commerce Com-

mittee) and legislation on health insurance supported by tax revenues, including Medicare.

Senate Finance Committee, *Subcommittee on Health Care,* SD-219 20510; (202) 224-4515. Fax, (202) 224-5920. Sen. Paul Coverdell, R-Ga., Chair; Kathy Means, Staff Contact. Web, finance.senate.gov.

Holds hearings on national health insurance proposals (jurisdiction shared with the Senate Health, Education, Labor, and Pensions Committee) and on legislation on health insurance and Medicaid for low-income individuals.

Senate Health, Education, Labor, and Pensions Committee, SD-428 20510; (202) 224-5375. Fax, (202) 228-5044. Sen. James M. Jeffords, R-Vt., Chair; Mark Powden, Staff Director. TTY, (202) 224-1975. Web, labor.senate.gov.

Jurisdiction over national health insurance proposals (jurisdiction shared with the Senate Finance Committee) and legislation on malpractice insurance and health maintenance organizations.

NONPROFIT

Alliance for Health Reform, 1900 L St. N.W., #512 20036; (202) 466-5626. Fax, (202) 466-6525. Edward Howard, Executive Vice President. Web, www.allhealth.org.

Nonpartisan organization that advocates health care reform, including cost containment and universal coverage. Sponsors conferences and seminars for journalists, business leaders, policymakers, and the public.

American Assn. of Health Plans, 1129 20th St. N.W., #600 20036-3421; (202) 778-3200. Fax, (202) 331-7487. Karen Ignagni, President. Press, (202) 778-3274. Web, www.aahp.org.

Membership: managed health care plans and organizations. Provides legal counsel and conducts educational programs. Conducts research and analysis of managed care issues; produces publications. Monitors legislation and regulations.

American Medical Assn., *Public and Private Sector Advocacy, Washington Office,* 1101 Vermont Ave. N.W., 12th Floor 20005; (202) 789-7400. Fax, (202) 789-7485. Lee Stillwell, Senior Vice President. Web, www.ama-assn.org.

Membership: physicians, residents, and medical students. Provides information on health care. Monitors legislation and regulations. (Headquarters in Chicago.)

Blue Cross and Blue Shield Assn., *Washington Office,* 1310 G St. N.W. 20005; (202) 626-4780. Fax, (202) 626-4833. Scott Serota, President (Acting). Web, www.bluecares.com.

Membership: Blue Cross and Blue Shield insurance plans, which operate autonomously at the local level. Certifies member plans; acts as consultant to plans in evaluating new medical technologies and contracting with doctors and hospitals. Operates a national telecommunications network to collect, analyze, and disseminate data. (Headquarters in Chicago.)

Council for Affordable Health Insurance, *112 S. West St., #400, Alexandria, VA 22314; (703) 836-6200. Fax, (703) 836-6550. Nona Wagner, President. General e-mail, mail@cahi.org. Web, www.cahi.org.*

Membership: insurance carriers in the small group, individual, and senior markets; business groups; doctors; actuaries; and insurance brokers. Research and advocacy organization devoted to free market solutions to America's health care problems. Promotes reform measures, including establishment of medical savings accounts, tax equity, universal access, medical price disclosure prior to treatment, and caps on malpractice awards. Serves as a liaison with businesses, provider organizations, and public interest groups. Monitors legislation and regulations at state and federal levels.

Employee Benefit Research Institute, *2121 K St. N.W., #600 20037-1896; (202) 659-0670. Fax, (202) 775-6312. Dallas L. Salisbury, President; Jack Vanderhei, Research Associate. Web, www.ebri.org.*

Conducts research on health insurance coverage, health care utilization, and health care cost containment; studies health care delivery and financing alternatives, including long-term care, flexible benefits, and retiree health financing options.

Employers Council on Flexible Compensation, *927 15th St. N.W., #1000 20005; (202) 659-4300. Kenneth E. Feltman, Executive Director. Web, www.ecfc.org.*

Represents employers who have or are considering flexible compensation plans. Supports the preservation and expansion of employee choice in health insurance coverage. Monitors legislation and regulations.

Employers Managed Health Care Assn., *1299 Pennsylvania Ave. N.W., 8th Floor, West 20004; (202) 218-4121. Fax, (202) 842-0621. Pamela Kalen, Executive Director. Web, www.emhca.org.*

Organization of public- and private-sector employers that promotes the expansion and improvement of managed health care. Provides health care management professionals with education and training. Supports innovation in the design and operation of managed care programs. Provides a forum for information exchange among employers, managed care organizations, and health care providers. Serves as a technical resource on managed health care systems.

Health Insurance Assn. of America, *555 13th St. N.W., #600E 20004-1109; (202) 824-1600. Fax, (202) 824-1722. Charles N. Kahn III, President. Web, www.hiaa.org.*

Membership: health insurance companies that write and sell health insurance policies. Promotes effective management of health care expenditures; provides statistical information on health insurance issues. Monitors legislation and regulations.

National Academy of Social Insurance, *1776 Massachusetts Ave. N.W., #615 20036-1904; (202) 452-8097. Fax, (202) 452-8111. Pamela J. Larson, Executive Vice President. General e-mail, nasi@nasi.org. Web, www.nasi.org.*

Promotes research and education on Social Security, health care financing, and related public and private programs; assesses social insurance programs and their relationship to other programs; supports research and leadership development. Acts as a clearinghouse for social insurance information.

National Assn. of Health Underwriters, *2000 N. 14th St., #450, Arlington, VA 22201; (703) 276-0220. Fax, (703) 841-7797. Kevin Corcoran, Executive Vice President. General e-mail, nahu@nahu.org. Web, www.nahu.org.*

Promotes the health insurance industry; certifies health underwriters; conducts advanced health insurance underwriting and research seminars at universities; maintains a speakers bureau.

National Assn. of Manufacturers, *Human Resource Policy, 1331 Pennsylvania Ave. N.W., #600 20004; (202) 637-3131. Fax, (202) 637-3182. Pat Cleary, Vice President.*

Interests include health care, Social Security, pensions, employee benefits, cost containment, mandated benefits, Medicare, and other federal programs that affect employers. Opposed to government involvement in health care.

National Health Care Anti-Fraud Assn., *1255 23rd St. N.W., #200 20037-1174; (202) 659-5955. Fax, (202) 785-6764. William J. Mahon, Executive Director. Web, www.nhcaa.org.*

Membership: health insurance companies and regulatory and law enforcement agencies. Members work to identify, investigate, and prosecute individuals defrauding health care reimbursement systems.

Society of Professional Benefit Administrators, *2 Wisconsin Circle, #670, Chevy Chase, MD 20815-7003; (301) 718-7722. Fax, (301) 718-9440. Frederick D. Hunt Jr., President.*

Membership: independent third-party administration firms that manage employee benefit plans for client employers. Interests include health care and insurance legislation and regulations, revision of Medicare programs, and health care cost containment. Monitors industry trends, government compliance requirements, and developments in health care financing.

Washington Business Group on Health, *777 N. Capitol St. N.E., #800 20002-4239; (202) 408-9320. Fax, (202) 408-9332. Mary Jane England, President. TTY, (202) 408-9333. Web, www.wbgh.com.*

Membership: large corporations with an interest in health. Monitors health care legislation and regulations of interest to large corporations. Interests include reimbursement policies, Medicare, retiree medical cost, hospital cost containment, health planning, and corporate health education.

Hospitals

AGENCIES

Health Care Financing Administration *(Health and Human Services Dept.), Disabled and Elderly Health Programs, 7500 Security Blvd., S2-14-27, Baltimore, MD 21244; (410) 786-9493. Fax, (410) 786-9004. Thomas Hamilton, Director.*

Enforces health care and safety standards for hospitals, nursing homes, and other long-term care facilities; clinical and other laboratories; clinics; and other health care facilities.

Health Resources and Services Administration *(Health and Human Services Dept.), Health Resources Development, 5600 Fishers Lane, Parklawn Bldg., #705, Rockville, MD 20857; (301) 443-1993. Fax, (301) 443-9645. William H. Aspden Jr., Deputy Associate Administrator.*

Reviews applications for hospital mortgage insurance; monitors repayment of insured mortgages and direct and guaranteed loans; publishes guidelines for constructing and equipping health facilities; directs efforts to improve their operational effectiveness and efficiency. Plans, directs, coordinates, and monitors activities relating to emergency medical services and trauma system planning and implementation.

See also National Clearinghouse for Primary Care Information (p. 354)

CONGRESS

House Banking and Financial Services Committee, *Subcommittee on Capital Markets, Securities, and Government-Sponsored Enterprises, 2129 RHOB 20515; (202) 226-0469. Fax, (202) 225-6518. Rep. Richard H. Baker, R-La., Chair; Greg Wierzynski, Staff Director. Web, www.house.gov/banking.*

Oversees government-sponsored enterprises, including the College Construction Loan Insurance Assn. (Connie Lee), with regard to the financial risk posed to the federal government. Connie Lee insures loans for teaching hospitals.

House Commerce Committee, *Subcommittee on Health and the Environment, 2125 RHOB 20515; (202) 225-2927. Fax, (202) 225-1919. Rep. Michael Bilirakis, R-Fla., Chair; James E. Derderian, Staff Director. General e-mail, commerce@mail.house.gov. Web, www.house.gov/commerce.*

Jurisdiction over legislation on health planning, health facilities construction, and government-run health care facilities, including Public Health Service hospitals.

Senate Banking, Housing, and Urban Affairs Committee, *SD-534 20510; (202) 224-7391. Fax, (202) 224-5137. Sen. Phil Gramm, R-Texas, Chair; Wayne A. Abernathy, Staff Director. Web, banking.senate.gov.*

Oversees government-sponsored enterprises, including the College Construction Loan Insurance Assn. (Connie Lee), with regard to the financial risk posed to the federal government. Connie Lee insures loans for teaching hospitals.

Senate Health, Education, Labor, and Pensions Committee, *SD-428 20510; (202) 224-5375. Fax, (202) 228-5044. Sen. James M. Jeffords, R-Vt., Chair; Mark Powden, Staff Director. TTY, (202) 224-1975. Web, labor.senate.gov.*

Jurisdiction over legislation on health planning, health facilities construction, and government-run health care facilities, including Public Health Service hospitals.

NONPROFIT

American Hospital Assn., *325 7th St. N.W., #700 20004; (202) 638-1100. Fax, (202) 626-2345. Richard J. Davidson, President. Web, www.aha.org.*

Membership: hospitals, other inpatient care facilities, outpatient centers, Blue Cross plans, areawide planning agencies, regional medical programs, hospital schools of nursing, and individuals. Conducts research and education projects in such areas as provision of comprehensive care, hospital economics, hospital facilities and design, and community relations; participates with other health care associations in establishing hospital care standards. Monitors legislation and regulations.

Assn. of Academic Health Centers, *1400 16th St. N.W., #720 20036; (202) 265-9600. Fax, (202) 265-7514. Dr. Roger J. Bulger, President. Web, www.ahcnet.org.*

Membership: academic health centers (composed of a medical school, a teaching hospital, and at least one other health professional school or program). Participates in studies and public debates on health professionals' training and education, patient care, and biomedical research.

Federation of American Health Systems, *801 Pennsylvania Ave. N.W., #245 20004-2604; (202) 624-1500. Fax, (202) 737-6462. Thomas A. Scully, President. Web, www.fahs.com.*

Membership: investor-owned, for-profit hospitals and health care systems. Interests include health care reform, cost containment, and Medicare and Medicaid reforms. Maintains speakers bureau; compiles statistics on investor-owned hospitals. Monitors legislation and regulations.

National Assn. of Children's Hospitals and Related Institutions, *401 Wythe St., Alexandria, VA 22314; (703) 684-1355. Fax, (703) 684-1589. Lawrence A. McAndrews, President.*

Advocates and promotes education and research on child health care related to children's hospitals; compiles statistics and provides information on pediatric hospitalizations.

National Assn. of Public Hospitals, *1301 Pennsylvania Ave. N.W., #950 20004; (202) 585-0100. Fax, (202) 585-0101. Larry S. Gage, President. General e-mail, naph@naph.org. Web, www.naph.org.*

Membership: city and county public hospitals, state universities, and hospital districts and authorities. Works to improve and expand health care in hospitals; interests include Medicaid patients and vulnerable populations, including AIDS patients, the homeless, the mentally ill, and non-English-speaking patients. Holds annual regional meetings. Monitors legislation and regulations.

See also American Osteopathic Healthcare Assn. (p. 369); Assn. for Healthcare Philanthropy (p. 369)

Medicaid and Medicare

See also Health Insurance/Managed Care (this chapter); Health Services for Special Groups, Elderly (this chapter); Social Security (chap. 18)

AGENCIES

Health Care Financing Administration *(Health and Human Services Dept.), 200 Independence Ave. S.W., #314G 20201; (202) 690-6726. Fax, (202) 690-6262. Nancy-Ann Min DeParle, Administrator. Information, (202) 690-6105. Web, www.hcfa.gov.*

Administers Medicare (a health insurance program for persons with disabilities or age sixty-five or older, who are eligible to participate) and Medicaid (a health insurance program for persons judged unable to pay for health services).

Health Care Financing Administration *(Health and Human Services Dept.), Clinical Standards and Quality, 7500 Security Blvd., S3-02-01, Baltimore, MD 21244; (410) 786-6842. Fax, (410) 786-6857. Jeff Kang, Director.*

Develops, establishes, and enforces standards that regulate the quality of care of hospitals and other health care facilities under Medicare and Medicaid programs. Administers operations of survey and peer review organizations that enforce health care standards, primarily for institutional care. Oversees clinical laboratory improvement programs and end stage renal disease networks. Monitors providers' and suppliers' compliance with standards.

Health Care Financing Administration *(Health and Human Services Dept.), Disabled and Elderly Health Programs, 7500 Security Blvd., S2-14-27, Baltimore, MD 21244; (410) 786-9493. Fax, (410) 786-9004. Thomas Hamilton, Director.*

Certifies facilities that participate in federal Medicare and Medicaid programs. Determines whether facilities meet federal health and safety standards required for participation in such programs.

Health Care Financing Administration *(Health and Human Services Dept.), Health Plans and Providers, 7500 Security Blvd., C5-24-27, Baltimore, MD 21244; (410) 786-5674. Fax, (410) 786-4490. Robert Berenson, Director.*

Issues regulations and guidelines for administration of the Medicare program.

Health Care Financing Administration *(Health and Human Services Dept.), Information Services, 7500 Security Blvd., N3-15-25, Baltimore, MD 21244-1850; (410) 786-1800. Fax, (410) 786-1810. Gary Christoph, Director.*

Serves as primary federal statistical office for disseminating economic data on Medicare.

Health Care Financing Administration *(Health and Human Services Dept.), Medicaid, 7500 Security Blvd., #C52223, Baltimore, MD 21244; (410) 786-3230. Fax, (410) 786-0025. Rachel Block, Deputy Director.*

Administers and monitors Medicaid programs to ensure program quality and financial integrity; promotes beneficiary awareness and access to services.

Health Care Financing Administration *(Health and Human Services Dept.), Medicare Contractor Management,* 7500 Security Blvd., S1-01-26, Baltimore, MD 21244; (410) 786-0338. Fax, (410) 786-1978. Geraldine Nicholson, Director.

Manages the contractual framework for the Medicare program; establishes and enforces performance standards for contractors who process and pay Medicare claims.

Health Resources and Services Administration *(Health and Human Services Dept.), Rural Health Policy,* 5600 Fishers Lane, #9A55, Rockville, MD 20857; (301) 443-0835. Fax, (301) 443-2803. Dr. Wayne Myers, Director. Web, www.nal.usda.gov/ric/richs/orhp.htm.

Studies the effects of Medicare and Medicaid programs on rural access to health care.

NONPROFIT

Blue Cross and Blue Shield Assn., Washington Office, 1310 G St. N.W. 20005; (202) 626-4780. Fax, (202) 626-4833. Scott Serota, President (Acting). Web, www. bluecares.com.

Acts as the primary contractor for the federal government in administration of Medicare Part A, which covers hospitalization and institutional care for persons with disabilities and persons age sixty-five or older. (Headquarters in Chicago.)

Federation of American Health Systems, 801 Pennsylvania Ave. N.W., #245 20004-2604; (202) 624-1500. Fax, (202) 737-6462. Thomas A. Scully, President. Web, www.fahs.com.

Membership: investor-owned, for-profit hospitals and health care systems. Studies Medicaid and Medicare reforms. Maintains speakers bureau; compiles statistics on investor-owned hospitals. Monitors legislation and regulations.

National Committee to Preserve Social Security and Medicare, 10 G St. N.E., #600 20002; (202) 216-0420. Fax, (202) 216-0451. Martha McSteen, President. Web, www.ncpssm.org.

Educational and advocacy organization that focuses on Social Security and Medicare programs and on related income security and health issues. Interests include retirement income protection, health care reform, and the quality of life of seniors. Monitors legislation and regulations.

See also AARP, Health and Long-Term Care (p. 381)

Medical Devices and Technology

See also Health Services for Special Groups (this chapter); Labeling and Packaging (chap. 1)

AGENCIES

Food and Drug Administration *(Health and Human Services Dept.), Center for Devices and Radiological Health,* 9200 Corporate Blvd., #100, Rockville, MD 20850; (301) 443-4690. Fax, (301) 594-1320. David W. Feigal Jr., Director. International Reference System, (301) 827-3993. Web, www.fda.gov/cdrh.

Evaluates safety, efficacy, and labeling of medical devices; classifies devices; establishes performance standards; assists in legal actions concerning medical devices; coordinates research and testing; conducts training and educational programs. Maintains an international reference system, to facilitate trade in devices. Library open to the public.

Food and Drug Administration *(Health and Human Services Dept.), Small Manufacturers Assistance,* 1350 Piccard Dr., HFZ-220, Rockville, MD 20850; (301) 443-6597. Fax, (301) 443-8818. John F. Stigi, Director. Information, (800) 638-2041. Fax-on-demand, (800) 899-0381. General e-mail, dsma@cdrh.fda.gov. Web, www.fda.gov/cdrh.

Serves as liaison between small-business manufacturers of medical devices and the FDA. Assists manufacturers in complying with FDA regulatory requirements; sponsors seminars.

NONPROFIT

American Assn. for Homecare, 625 Slaters Lane, #200, Alexandria, VA 22314-1171; (703) 836-6263. Fax, (703) 836-6730. Galen Powers, President (Acting). Web, www. aahomecare.org.

Membership: home medical equipment suppliers, manufacturers, and state associations. Promotes legislative and regulatory policy that improves access to quality home medical equipment.

American Institute of Ultrasound in Medicine, 14750 Sweitzer Lane, #100, Laurel, MD 20707-5906; (301) 498-4100. Fax, (301) 498-4450. Carmine Valente, Executive Director. General e-mail, admin@aium.org. Web, www.aium.org.

Membership: medical professionals who use ultrasound technology in their practices. Promotes multidisciplinary research and education in the field of diagnostic ultrasound through conventions and educational programs. Monitors international research.

American Medical Informatics Assn., *4915 St. Elmo Ave., #401, Bethesda, MD 20814; (301) 657-1291. Fax, (301) 657-1296. Dennis Reynolds, Executive Director. Document-on-Request, (800) 819-2334. General e-mail, mail@mail.amia.org. Web, www.amia.org.*

Membership: doctors and other medical professionals in the applied informatics field. Provides members information on medical systems and the use of computers in the health care field. Promotes use of computers and information systems in patient care; conducts and promotes research on medical technology; encourages development of universal standards, terminology, and coding systems.

American Orthotic and Prosthetic Assn., *1650 King St., #500, Alexandria, VA 22314; (703) 836-7116. Fax, (703) 836-0838. Lance O. Hoxie, Executive Director. Web, www.opoffice.org.*

Membership: companies that manufacture or supply artificial limbs and braces. Provides information on the profession.

American Roentgen Ray Society, *44211 Slatestone Court, Leesburg, VA 20176-5109; (703) 729-3353. Fax, (703) 729-4839. Susan Cappitelli, Executive Director. Toll-free, (800) 438-2777. Web, www.arrs.org.*

Membership: physicians and researchers in radiology and allied sciences. Publishes research; conducts conferences; presents scholarships and awards; monitors international research.

Health Industry Distributors Assn., *66 Canal Center, #520, Alexandria, VA 22314-1591; (703) 549-4432. Fax, (703) 549-6495. Matthew Rowan, President. Web, www.hida.org.*

Membership: medical products distributors and home health care providers. Administers educational programs and conducts training seminars. Monitors legislation and regulations.

Health Industry Manufacturers Assn., *1200 G St. N.W., #400 20005-3814; (202) 783-8700. Fax, (202) 783-8750. Pamela Bailey, President. Web, www.himanet.com.*

Membership: manufacturers of medical devices, diagnostic products, and health care information systems. Interests include safe and effective medical devices; conducts educational seminars. Monitors legislation, regulations, and international issues.

Optical Society of America, *2010 Massachusetts Ave. N.W. 20036; (202) 223-8130. Fax, (202) 223-1096. John Thorner, Executive Director. Web, www.osa.org.*

Membership: researchers, educators, manufacturers, students, and others interested in optics and photonics

worldwide. Promotes research and information exchange; conducts conferences. Interests include use of optics in medical imaging and surgery.

Program for Appropriate Technology in Health, Washington Office, *1990 M St. N.W., #700 20036; (202) 822-0033. Fax, (202) 457-1466. Vacant, Director. General e-mail, info@path-dc.org. Web, www.path.org.*

Seeks to improve the safety and availability of health products and technologies worldwide, particularly in developing countries. Interests include reproductive health, immunization, maternal-child health, AIDS, and nutrition. (Headquarters in Seattle.)

> *See also Center for Patient Advocacy (p. 356); Johns Hopkins University Applied Physics Laboratory (p. 389); Public Citizen, Health Research Group (p. 358)*

Nursing Homes and Hospices

> *See also Health Services for Special Groups, Elderly (this chapter)*

AGENCIES

Health Care Financing Administration *(Health and Human Services Dept.), Disabled and Elderly Health Programs, 7500 Security Blvd., S2-14-27, Baltimore, MD 21244; (410) 786-9493. Fax, (410) 786-9004. Thomas Hamilton, Director.*

Enforces health care and safety standards for hospitals, nursing homes, and other long-term care facilities; clinical and other laboratories; clinics; and other health care facilities.

Health Care Financing Administration *(Health and Human Services Dept.), Outcomes and Improvements, 7500 Security Blvd., S2-11-07, Baltimore, MD 21244-1850; (410) 786-7304. Fax, (410) 786-6730. Helene Fredeking, Director.*

Monitors compliance of nursing homes, psychiatric hospitals, and long-term and intermediate care facilities with government standards. Focus includes quality of care, environmental conditions, and participation in Medicaid and Medicare programs. Coordinates health care programs for the mentally retarded.

NONPROFIT

American College of Health Care Administrators, *1800 Diagonal Rd., Alexandria, VA 22314; (703) 549-5822. Fax, (703) 739-7901. Karen Tucker, President. General e-mail, info@achca.org. Web, www.achca.org.*

Membership: administrators of long-term health care organizations and facilities, including home health care programs, hospices, day care centers for the elderly, nursing and hospital facilities, retirement communities, and mental health care centers. Conducts research on statistical characteristics of nursing home and other medical administrators; conducts seminars; offers education courses; provides certification for administrators. Library open to the public by appointment.

American Health Care Assn., *1201 L St. N.W. 20005; (202) 842-4444. Fax, (202) 842-3860. Charles H. Roadman II, President. Publication orders, (800) 321-0343. Web, www.ahca.org.*

Federation of associations representing assisted living nursing facilities and subacute care providers. Sponsors and provides educational programs and materials. Library open to the public by appointment.

Assisted Living Federation of America, *10300 Eaton Pl., #400, Fairfax, VA 22030; (703) 691-8100. Fax, (703) 691-8106. Karen Wayne, Executive Director.*

Promotes the development of standards and increased awareness for the assisted living industry. Provides members with information on policy, funding access, and quality of care. Interests include funding alternatives to make assisted living available to all who need it. Monitors legislation and regulations.

Hospice Foundation of America, *Washington Office, 2001 S St. N.W., #300 20009; (202) 638-5419. Fax, (202) 638-5312. Lisa Veglahn, Vice President for Programs. Toll-free, (800) 854-3402. General e-mail, hfa@ hospicefoundation.org. Web, www.hospicefoundation.org.*

Promotes hospice care for terminally ill people. Disseminates information; conducts education and training; awards small grants. (Headquarters in Miami Beach, Fla.)

National Assn. for Homecare, *228 7th St. S.E. 20003; (202) 547-7424. Fax, (202) 547-3540. Val J. Halamandaris, President. Web, www.nahc.org.*

Promotes high-quality hospice, home care, and other community services for those with chronic health problems or life-threatening illness. Conducts research and provides information on related issues. Works to educate the public concerning health and social policy matters. Oversees the National HomeCaring Council, which provides training, education, accreditation, and certification in the field. Monitors legislation and regulations.

National Citizens' Coalition for Nursing Home Reform, *1424 16th St. N.W., #202 20036-2211; (202) 332-2275. Fax, (202) 332-2949. Sarah Greene Burger, Executive Director.*

Seeks to improve the long-term care system and quality of life for residents in nursing homes and other facilities for the elderly; coordinates the Campaign for Quality Care. Promotes citizen participation in all aspects of nursing homes; acts as clearinghouse for nursing home advocacy.

National Hospice Organization, *1700 Diagonal Rd., #300, Alexandria, VA 22314; (703) 243-5900. Fax, (703) 525-5762. Karen Davie, President. Toll-free information and referral helpline, (800) 658-8898. Web, www.nho.org.*

Membership: institutions and individuals providing hospice care and other interested organizations and individuals. Promotes supportive care for the terminally ill and their families; sets hospice program standards; provides information on hospices. Monitors legislation and regulations.

See also American Assn. of Homes and Services for the Aging (p. 381)

Pharmaceuticals

See also Labeling and Packaging (chap. 1); Health Topics: Research and Advocacy, Substance Abuse (this chapter)

AGENCIES

Food and Drug Administration *(Health and Human Services Dept.), Center for Drug Evaluation and Research, 1451 Rockville Pike, Rockville, MD 20852; (301) 594-5400. Fax, (301) 594-6197. Dr. Janet Woodcock, Director. Information, (301) 827-4573. Press, (301) 827-6242.*

Reviews and approves applications to investigate and market new drugs; monitors prescription drug advertising; works to harmonize drug approval internationally.

Food and Drug Administration *(Health and Human Services Dept.), Generic Drugs, 7500 Standish Pl., Rockville, MD 20855; (301) 827-5845. Fax, (301) 594-0183. Gary Buehler, Director (Acting).*

Oversees generic drug review process to ensure the safety and effectiveness of approved drugs.

Public Health Service *(Health and Human Services Dept.), Orphan Products Development, 5600 Fishers Lane, #8-73, Rockville, MD 20857; (301) 827-3666. Fax, (301) 443-4915. Dr. Marlene E. Haffner, Director. Web, www.fda.gov/orphan.*

Promotes the development of drugs, devices, and alternative medical food therapies for rare diseases or conditions. Coordinates activities on the development of orphan drugs among federal agencies, manufacturers, and organizations representing patients.

American Assn. of Colleges of Pharmacy, *1426 Prince St., Alexandria, VA 22314-2841; (703) 739-2330. Fax, (703) 836-8982. Richard Penna, Executive Vice President. General e-mail, pthompson@aacp.org. Web, www. aacp.org.*

Represents and advocates for pharmacists in the academic community. Conducts programs and activities in cooperation with other national health and higher education associations.

American Assn. of Pharmaceutical Scientists, *2107 Wilson Blvd., Arlington, VA 22201-3045; (703) 548-3000. Fax, (703) 684-7349. Amy Miller, Public Relations. General e-mail, aaps@aaps.org. Web, www.aaps.org.*

Membership: pharmaceutical scientists from biomedical, biotechnological, and health care fields. Promotes pharmaceutical sciences as an industry; represents scientific interests within academia and public and private institutions. Monitors legislation and regulations.

American Pharmaceutical Assn., *2215 Constitution Ave. N.W. 20037-2985; (202) 628-4410. Fax, (202) 783-2351. Dr. John A. Gans, Executive Vice President. Information, (800) 237-2742. Library, (202) 429-7524. Web, www. aphanet.org.*

Membership: practicing pharmacists, pharmaceutical scientists, and pharmacy students. Promotes professional education and training; publishes scientific journals and handbook on nonprescription drugs; monitors international research. Library open to the public by appointment.

American Society for Pharmacology and Experimental Therapeutics, *9650 Rockville Pike, Bethesda, MD 20814-3995; (301) 530-7060. Fax, (301) 530-7061. Dr. Christine Carrico, Executive Officer. General e-mail, aspetinfo@faseb.org. Web, www.faseb.org/aspet.*

Membership: researchers and teachers involved in basic and clinical pharmacology primarily in the United States and Canada.

American Society of Health-System Pharmacists, *7272 Wisconsin Ave., Bethesda, MD 20814; (301) 657-3000. Fax, (301) 657-1251. Henri Manasse, Chief Executive Officer. Web, www.ashp.com.*

Membership: pharmacists who practice in organized health care settings such as hospitals, health maintenance organizations, and long-term care facilities. Provides publishing and educational programs designed to help members improve pharmaceutical services; accredits pharmacy residency and pharmacy technician training programs. Monitors legislation and regulations.

Consumer Health Care Products Assn., *1150 Connecticut Ave. N.W., #1200 20036-4193; (202) 429-9260. Fax, (202) 223-6835. Dr. Michael Maves, President.*

Membership: manufacturers and distributors of nonprescription medicines; associate members include suppliers, advertising agencies, and research and testing laboratories. Promotes the role of self-medication in health care. Monitors legislation and regulations.

Drug Policy Foundation, *4455 Connecticut Ave. N.W., #B500 20008-2328; (202) 537-5005. Fax, (202) 537-3007. Ruth Lampi, Administrative Director. General e-mail, dpf@dpf.org. Web, www.dpf.org.*

Seeks to broaden debate on drug policy to include consideration of alternatives to incarceration, expanding maintenance therapies, and restoring constitutional protections. Studies drug policy in other countries. Monitors legislation and regulations.

Food and Drug Law Institute, *1000 Vermont Ave. N.W., #200 20005-4903; (202) 371-1420. Fax, (202) 371-0649. John Villforth, President. General e-mail, comments@ fdli.org. Web, www.fdli.org.*

Membership: providers of products and services to the food, drug, medical device, and cosmetics industries, including major food and drug companies; and lawyers working in food and drug law. Arranges conferences on technological and legal developments in the industry; sponsors law courses, fellowships, and legal writing; monitors international regulatory issues. Library open to the public.

Generic Pharmaceutical Industry Assn., *1620 Eye St. N.W., #800 20006-4005; (202) 833-9070. Fax, (202) 833-9612. Alice E. Till, President. General e-mail, info@gpia. org. Web, www.gpia.org.*

Represents the generic pharmaceutical industry in legislative, regulatory, scientific, and health care policy matters. Attempts to increase availability and public awareness of generic medicines.

National Assn. of Chain Drug Stores, *413 N. Lee St., Alexandria, VA 22314 (mailing address: P.O. Box 1417-D49, Alexandria, VA 22313); (703) 549-3001. Fax, (703) 836-4869. Craig L. Fuller, President. Web, www.nacds.org.*

Membership: chain drug retailers; associate members include manufacturers, suppliers, publishers, and advertising agencies. Provides information on the pharmacy profession, community pharmacy practice, and retail prescription drug economics.

National Community Pharmacists Assn., *205 Daingerfield Rd., Alexandria, VA 22314; (703) 683-8200. Fax, (703) 683-3619. Calvin Anthony, Executive Vice President. Web, www.ncpanet.org.*

Membership: independent drug store owners and pharmacists working in retail drugstores. Interests include drug regulation and national health insurance. Provides consumer information on such issues as prescription drugs, poison control, and mail order drug fraud.

National Council on Patient Information and Education, *4915 St. Elmo Ave., #505, Bethesda, MD 20814-6053; (301) 656-8565. Fax, (301) 655-4464. W. Ray Bullman, Executive Vice President. General e-mail, ncpie@ erols.com. Web, www.talkaboutrx.org.*

Membership: organizations of health care professionals, pharmaceutical manufacturers, federal agencies, voluntary health organizations, and consumer groups. Works to improve communication between health care professionals and patients about the appropriate use of medicines; produces educational resources; conducts public affairs programs; sponsors awards program.

National Pharmaceutical Council, *1894 Preston White Dr., Reston, VA 20191-5433; (703) 620-6390. Fax, (703) 476-0904. Karen Williams, President. General e-mail, main@npcnow.com. Web, www.npcnow.org.*

Membership: pharmaceutical manufacturers that research and produce trade-name prescription medication and other pharmaceutical products. Provides information on the quality and cost-effectiveness of pharmaceutical products and the economics of drug programs.

National Wholesale Druggists' Assn., *1821 Michael Faraday Dr., #400, Reston, VA 20190 (mailing address: P.O. Box 2219, Reston, VA 20195-0219); (703) 787-0000. Fax, (703) 787-6930. Ronald J. Streck, President. Web, www.nwda.org.*

Membership: full-service drug wholesalers. Works to improve relations among supplier and customer industries; serves as a forum on major industry issues; researches and disseminates information on management practices for drug wholesalers. Monitors legislation and regulations.

Parenteral Drug Assn., *7500 Old Georgetown Rd., #620, Bethesda, MD 20814; (301) 986-0293. Fax, (301) 986-0296. Edmund M. Fry, President. Web, www.pda.org.*

Educates pharmaceutical professionals on parenteral and sterile-product technologies. Promotes pharmaceutical research. Serves as a liaison with pharmaceutical manufacturers, suppliers, users, academics, and government regulatory officials.

Pharmaceutical Care Management Assn., *2300 9th St. South, #210, Arlington, VA 22204-2320; (703) 920-*

8480. Fax, (703) 920-8491. Delbert D. Konnor, President. Web, PCMAnet.org.

Membership: companies providing managed care pharmacy and pharmacy benefits management. Promotes legislation, research, education, and practice standards that foster quality, affordable pharmaceutical care.

Pharmaceutical Research and Manufacturers of America, *1100 15th St. N.W., #900 20005; (202) 835-3400. Fax, (202) 785-4834. Alan F. Holmer, President. Web, www.phrma.org.*

Membership: companies that discover, develop, and manufacture prescription drugs. Provides consumer information on drug abuse, the safe and effective use of prescription medicines, and developments in important areas, including AIDS. Provides pharmaceutical industry statistics.

U.S. Pharmacopeial Convention, *12601 Twinbrook Pkwy., Rockville, MD 20852; (301) 881-0666. Fax, (301) 816-8299. Roger Williams, Executive Director. Web, www.usp.org.*

Establishes and revises standards for drug strength, quality, purity, packaging, labeling, and storage. Publishes drug use information, official drug quality standards, patient education materials, and consumer drug references. Interests include international standards.

See also Animal Health Institute (p. 66); Center for Patient Advocacy (p. 356); Institute for Alternative Futures (p. 389)

✚ HEALTH PROFESSIONS

AGENCIES

Health Care Financing Administration *(Health and Human Services Dept.), Clinical Standards and Quality, 7500 Security Blvd., S3-02-01, Baltimore, MD 21244; (410) 786-6842. Fax, (410) 786-6857. Jeff Kang, Director.*

Oversees professional review and other medical review programs; establishes guidelines; prepares issue papers relating to legal aspects of professional review and quality assurance.

Health Resources and Services Administration *(Health and Human Services Dept.), Health Education Assistance Loan Branch, 5600 Fishers Lane, #8-37, Parklawn Bldg., Rockville, MD 20857; (301) 443-1540. Fax, (301) 594-6911. Stephen J. Boehlert, Associate Director.*

Administers federal program of insured loans to graduate students in medicine, osteopathy, dentistry, veterinary medicine, optometry, podiatry, public health, pharmacy, clinical psychology, chiropractics, and health administration under the Health Professions Education Assistance Act of 1976.

Health Resources and Services Administration *(Health and Human Services Dept.), Health Professions,* 5600 Fishers Lane, #805, Rockville, MD 20857; (301) 443-5794. Fax, (301) 443-2111. Dr. Vincent C. Rogers, Associate Administrator. Web, www.hrsa.dhhs. gov/bhpr.

Promotes primary care and public health education and practice. Advocates recruitment of health care professionals, including nursing and allied health professionals, for underserved populations. Administers categorical training programs, scholarship and loan programs, and minority and disadvantaged assistance programs. Oversees national practitioner data bank and vaccine injury compensation program.

Health Resources and Services Administration *(Health and Human Services Dept.), Health Services Corps Scholarship Program,* 4350 East-West Hwy., 10th Floor, Bethesda, MD 20814; (301) 594-4410. Fax, (301) 594-4985. Dr. Marilyn H. Gaston, Director. Toll-free information hotlines, (800) 638-0824 and (800) 783-1547.

Administers service-obligated scholarship and loan repayment programs that support students in medical and health professional schools.

Health Resources and Services Administration *(Health and Human Services Dept.), National Health Service Corps,* 4350 East-West Hwy., 8th Floor, Bethesda, MD 20814; (301) 594-4130. Fax, (301) 594-4076. Dr. Donald L. Weaver, Director.

Supplies communities experiencing a shortage of health care personnel with doctors and other medical professionals.

Health Resources and Services Administration *(Health and Human Services Dept.), National Practitioners Data Bank,* 5600 Fishers Lane, Parklawn Bldg., #8A-55, Rockville, MD 20857; (301) 443-2300. Fax, (301) 443-6725. Thomas C. Croft, Director, Quality Assurance. Information, (800) 767-6732.

Provides information on reports of malpractice payments, adverse state licensure, clinical privileges, and society membership actions (only to eligible state licensing boards, hospitals, and other health care entities) about physicians, dentists, and other licensed health care practitioners.

National Institutes of Health *(Health and Human Services Dept.), Minority Opportunities in Research,*
45 Center Dr., Bldg. 45, #2AS.37, Bethesda, MD 20892; (301) 594-3900. Fax, (301) 480-2753. Dr. Clifton A. Poodry, Director.

Awards grants to eligible minority universities and colleges to support biomedical research by minority students and faculty; funds development of research facilities.

Program Support Center, Human Resources Service *(Health and Human Services Dept.), Commissioned Personnel,* 5600 Fishers Lane, #4A15, Rockville, MD 20857; (301) 594-3000. Fax, (301) 443-8207. Rear Adm. R. Michael Davidson (CC), Director.

Develops policies and procedures related to the payroll and personnel system of the Public Health Service Commissioned Corps.

See also National Clearinghouse for Primary Care Information (p. 354)

CONGRESS

House Commerce Committee, *Subcommittee on Health and the Environment,* 2125 RHOB 20515; (202) 225-2927. Fax, (202) 225-1919. Rep. Michael Bilirakis, R-Fla., Chair; James E. Derderian, Staff Director. General e-mail, commerce@mail.house.gov. Web, www.house.gov/commerce.

Jurisdiction over legislation on the education, training, and distribution of health professionals.

House Ways and Means Committee, *Subcommittee on Health,* 1136 LHOB 20515; (202) 225-3943. Fax, (202) 226-1765. Rep. Bill Thomas, R-Calif., Chair; Vacant, Staff Director. Web, www.house.gov/ways_means.

Jurisdiction over Professional Standards Review Organizations legislation.

Senate Health, Education, Labor, and Pensions Committee, *Subcommittee on Public Health,* SD-424 20510; (202) 224-7139. Fax, (202) 228-0928. Sen. Bill Frist, R-Tenn., Chair; Anne Phelps, Staff Director. Web, labor.senate.gov.

Jurisdiction over legislation on the education, training, and distribution of health professionals.

NONPROFIT

American Assn. for Health Education, 1900 Association Dr., Reston, VA 20191-1599; (703) 476-3437. Fax, (703) 476-6638. Becky J. Smith, Executive Director. General e-mail, aahe@aahperd.org. Web, www.aahperd.org/aahe.html.

Membership: health educators and allied health professionals in community and volunteer health agencies, educational institutions, and businesses. Develops health education programs; monitors legislation.

American Assn. of Colleges of Pharmacy, *1426 Prince St., Alexandria, VA 22314-2841; (703) 739-2330. Fax, (703) 836-8982. Richard Penna, Executive Vice President. General e-mail, pthompson@aacp.org. Web, www. aacp.org.*

Membership: teachers and administrators representing colleges of pharmacy accredited by the American Council on Pharmaceutical Education. Sponsors educational programs; conducts research; provides career information; helps administer the Pharmacy College Admissions Test.

American Assn. of Healthcare Consultants, *11208 Waples Mill Rd., #109, Fairfax, VA 22030-6077; (703) 691-2242. Fax, (703) 691-2247. Vaughan A. Smith, President. Toll-free, (800) 362-4674. General e-mail, info@aahc.net. Web, www.aahc.net.*

Membership organization that develops credentials and standards for consulting services in all aspects of health planning and management; supports continuing education and training of health care consultants. Enforces code of professional ethics.

American College of Health Care Administrators, *1800 Diagonal Rd., Alexandria, VA 22314; (703) 549-5822. Fax, (703) 739-7901. Karen Tucker, President. General e-mail, info@achca.org. Web, www.achca.org.*

Membership: administrators of long-term health care organizations and facilities, including home health care programs, hospices, day care centers for the elderly, nursing and hospital facilities, retirement communities, and mental health care centers. Conducts research on statistical characteristics of nursing home and other medical administrators; conducts seminars; offers education courses; provides certification for administrators. Library open to the public by appointment.

American Health Lawyers Assn., *1025 Connecticut Ave. N.W., #600 20036; (202) 833-1100. Fax, (202) 833-1105. Peter Leibold, President. General e-mail, memberservice@healthlawyers.org. Web, www. healthlawyers.org.*

Membership: corporate, institutional, and government lawyers interested in the health field; law students; and health professionals. Serves as an information clearinghouse on health law; sponsors health law educational programs and seminars.

American Medical Group Assn., *1422 Duke St., Alexandria, VA 22314-3430; (703) 838-0033. Fax, (703) 548-1890. Donald W. Fisher, Chief Executive Officer. Web, www.amga.org.*

Membership: medical and dental group practices. Compiles statistics on group practice; sponsors a foundation for research and education programs.

American Osteopathic Healthcare Assn., *5550 Friendship Blvd., #300, Chevy Chase, MD 20815-7201; (301) 968-2642. Fax, (301) 968-4995. David Kushner, President. Web, www.aoha.org.*

Conducts educational programs on management techniques for executives of member hospitals. Monitors legislation and regulations.

American Society of Consultant Pharmacists, *1321 Duke St., 4th Floor, Alexandria, VA 22314-3563; (703) 739-1300. Fax, (703) 739-1321. R. Tim Webster, Executive Director. Web, www.ascp.com.*

Membership: dispensing and clinical pharmacists who provide services to long-term care facilities. Makes grants and conducts research in the science and practice of consultant pharmacy. Monitors legislation and regulations.

American Speech-Language-Hearing Assn., *10801 Rockville Pike, Rockville, MD 20852; (301) 897-5700. Fax, (301) 571-0457. Frederick T. Spahr, Executive Director. Press, (301) 897-0156. TTY, (301) 897-0157. Toll-free hotline (except Alaska, Hawaii, and Maryland), (800) 638-8255 (voice and TTY accessible). General e-mail, actioncenter@asha.org. Web, www.asha.org.*

Membership: specialists in speech-language pathology and audiology. Sponsors professional education programs; acts as accrediting agent for graduate college programs and for public clinical education programs in speech-language pathology and audiology. Advocates the rights of the communicatively disabled; provides information on speech, hearing, and language problems. Provides referrals to speech-language pathologists and audiologists. Interests include national and international standards for bioacoustics and noise.

Assn. for Healthcare Philanthropy, *313 Park Ave., #400, Falls Church, VA 22046; (703) 532-6243. Fax, (703) 532-7170. William C. McGinly, President. General e-mail, ahp@go.ahp.org. Web, www.go-ahp.org.*

Membership: hospital and health care executives who manage fundraising activities.

Assn. of Reproductive Health Professionals, *2401 Pennsylvania Ave. N.W., #350 20037-1718; (202) 466-3825. Fax, (202) 466-3826. Wayne Shields, President. Web, www.arhp.org.*

Membership: obstetricians, gynecologists, other physicians, researchers, clinicians, educators, and others. Educates health professionals and the public on reproductive health issues, including family planning, contraception, HIV/AIDS, other sexually transmitted diseases, abortion, menopause, infertility, and cancer prevention and detection.

Assn. of Schools of Allied Health Professions, *1730 M St. N.W., #500 20036; (202) 293-4848. Fax, (202) 293-4852. Thomas Elwood, Executive Director. General e-mail, asahp1@asahp.org. Web, www.asahp.org.*

Membership: two- and four-year colleges and academic health science centers with allied health professional training programs; administrators, educators, and practitioners; and professional societies. Serves as information resource; works with the Health and Human Services Dept. to conduct surveys of allied health education programs. Interests include health promotion and disease prevention, ethics in health care, and the participation of women and persons with disabilities in allied health. Monitors legislation and regulations.

Assn. of Schools of Public Health, *1660 L St. N.W., #204 20036; (202) 296-1099. Fax, (202) 296-1252. Michael K. Gemmell, Executive Director. General e-mail, info@asph.org. Web, www.asph.org.*

Membership: accredited graduate schools of public health. Promotes improved education and training of professional public health personnel; interests include international health.

Assn. of State and Territorial Health Officials, *1275 K St. N.W., #800 20005-4006; (202) 371-9090. Fax, (202) 371-9797. George Hardy Jr., Executive Director. Web, www.astho.org.*

Membership: executive officers of state and territorial health departments. Serves as legislative review agency and information source for members.

Assn. of Teachers of Preventive Medicine, *1660 L St. N.W., #208 20036; (202) 463-0550. Fax, (202) 463-0555. Barbara J. Calkins, Executive Director. General e-mail, info@atpm.org. Web, www.atpm.org.*

Membership: medical educators, practitioners, administrators, students, and health care agencies. Works to advance education in preventive medicine; interests include public health, international health, clinical prevention, and aerospace and occupational medicine. Promotes collaborative research and programs; fosters information exchange.

Assn. of University Programs in Health Administration, *730 11th St. N.W. 20001; (202) 638-1448. Fax, (202) 638-3429. Jeptha W. Dalston, President. General e-mail, aupha@aupha.org. Web, www.aupha.org.*

Membership: colleges and universities with programs in health administration. Offers consultation services to health administration programs; maintains task forces on undergraduate education, educational outcomes, ethics, epidemiology, health law, health facilities, long-term care, international development, institutional research, information management, quality improvement, and technology assessment.

Council on Education for Public Health, *800 Eye St. N.W., #202 20001; (202) 789-1050. Fax, (202) 789-1895. Patricia P. Evans, Executive Director. Web, www.ceph.org.*

Accredits schools of public health and graduate programs in community health education and community health preventive medicine. Works to strengthen public health programs through consultation, research, and other services.

Federation of Nurses and Health Professionals, *555 New Jersey Ave. N.W. 20001; (202) 879-4491. Fax, (202) 879-4597. Sandra Feldman, President. General e-mail, fnhpaft@aft.org. Web, www.aft.org/fnhp/index.htm.*

Membership: nurses and other technical health care workers. Assists members with contract negotiation and grievances; conducts training programs and workshops. Monitors legislation and regulations. (Division of the American Federation of Teachers.)

Healthcare Financial Management Assn., *Washington Office, 1301 Connecticut Ave. N.W., #300 20036-5503; (202) 296-2920. Fax, (202) 223-9771. Elizabeth Propp, Vice President. Information, (800) 252-4362. Web, www.hfma.org.*

Membership: health care financial management specialists. Offers educational programs; provides information on financial management of health care. (Headquarters in Westchester, Ill.)

Hispanic Serving Health Professions Schools Inc., *1700 17th St. N.W., #405 20009; (202) 667-9788. Fax, (202) 234-5468. Elena Rios, Executive Director. Web, www.hshps.com.*

Seeks to increase representation of Hispanics in all health care professions. Monitors legislation and regulations.

National Assn. of County and City Health Officials, *1100 17th St. N.W., 2nd Floor 20036; (202) 783-5550. Fax, (202) 783-1583. Thomas L. Milne, Executive Director. Web, www.naccho.org.*

Membership: city, county, and district health officers. Provides members with information on national, state, and local health developments. Works to develop the technical competence, managerial capacity, and leadership potential of local public health officials.

National Assn. of Healthcare Access Management, *2025 M St. N.W. 20036-3309; (202) 857-1125. Fax, (202) 857-1115. Steven Kemp, Executive Director. General e-mail, info@naham.org. Web, www.naham.org.*

Promotes professional growth and recognition of health care patient access managers; provides instructional videotapes; sponsors educational programs.

National Center for Homeopathy, *801 N. Fairfax St., #306, Alexandria, VA 22314; (703) 548-7790. Fax, (703) 548-7792. Sharon Stevenson, Executive Director. General e-mail, info@homeopathic.org. Web, www.homeopathic.org.*

Educational organization for professionals, groups, associations, and individuals interested in homeopathy and homeotherapeutics. Promotes health through homeopathy; conducts education programs; holds annual conference.

National Organization for Competency Assurance, *2025 M St. N.W. 20036-3309; (202) 857-1165. Fax, (202) 223-4579. Bonnie Aubin, Executive Director. General e-mail, info@noca.org. Web, www.noca.org.*

Membership: certifying agencies and other groups that issue credentials to health professionals. Promotes public understanding of competency assurance certification programs for health professions and occupations. Oversees commission that establishes certification program standards. Monitors regulations.

See also Assn. of Academic Health Centers (p. 361); Health Volunteers Overseas (p. 450)

Chiropractors

NONPROFIT

American Chiropractic Assn., *1701 Clarendon Blvd., Arlington, VA 22209; (703) 276-8800. Fax, (703) 243-2593. Garret F. Cuneo, Executive Vice President. General e-mail, memberinfo@amerchiro.org. Web, www.amerchiro.org.*

Promotes professional growth and recognition for chiropractors. Interests include health care coverage, sports injuries, physical fitness, internal disorders, and orthopedics. Supports foundation for chiropractic education and research. Monitors legislation and regulations.

International Chiropractors Assn., *1110 N. Glebe Rd., #1000, Arlington, VA 22201; (703) 528-5000. Fax, (703) 528-5023. Ronald Hendrickson, Executive Director. General e-mail, chiro@chiropractic.org. Web, www.chiropractic.org.*

Membership: chiropractors, students, educators, and laypersons. Seeks to increase public awareness of chiropractic care. Supports research on health issues; administers scholarship program; monitors legislation and regulations.

Dental Care

AGENCIES

National Institute of Dental and Craniofacial Research *(National Institutes of Health), 31 Center Dr., MSC-2290, Bldg. 31, #2C39, Bethesda, MD 20892-2290; (301) 496-3571. Fax, (301) 402-2185. Dr. Harold C. Slavkin, Director. Information, (301) 496-4261. Web, www.nidcr.nih.gov.*

Conducts and funds research on the causes, prevention, and treatment of oral diseases and conditions. Monitors international research.

NONPROFIT

American Assn. of Dental Education, *1625 Massachusetts Ave. N.W., #600 20036-2212; (202) 667-9433. Fax, (202) 667-0642. Dr. Richard Valachovic, Executive Director. General e-mail, aads@aads.jhu.edu. Web, www.aads.jhu.edu.*

Membership: individuals interested in dental education; undergraduate and graduate schools of dentistry; hospital dental education programs; and allied dental education programs in the United States, Canada, and Puerto Rico. Provides information on dental teaching and research and on admission requirements of U.S. and Canadian dental schools; publishes a directory of dental educators.

American College of Dentists, *839 Quince Orchard Blvd., Suite J, Gaithersburg, MD 20878; (301) 977-3223. Fax, (301) 977-3330. Stephen Ralls, Executive Director. General e-mail, info@facd.org. Web, www.acdentists.org.*

Honorary society of dentists. Fellows are elected based on their contributions to education, research, dentistry, and community and civic organizations. Interests include ethics, professionalism, and dentistry in health care.

American Dental Assn., *Government Relations, Washington Office, 1111 14th St. N.W., #1100 20005; (202) 898-2400. Fax, (202) 898-2437. Dorothy Moss, Director. Web, www.ada.org.*

Conducts research; provides dental education materials; compiles statistics on dentistry and dental care. Monitors legislation and regulations. (Headquarters in Chicago.)

American Dental Trade Assn., *4222 King St. West, Alexandria, VA 22302-1597; (703) 379-7755. Fax, (703) 931-9429. Robert S. Bolan, President (Acting). Web, www.adta.com.*

Membership: dental laboratories and distributors and manufacturers of dental equipment and supplies. Collects and disseminates statistical and management information; conducts studies, programs, and projects of interest to the industry; acts as liaison with government agencies.

International Assn. for Dental Research, *1619 Duke St., Alexandria, VA 22314-3406; (703) 548-0066. Fax, (703) 548-1883. Dr. Eli Schwarz, Executive Director. Toll-free, (800) 950-1150. General e-mail, research@iadr.com. Web, www.iadr.com.*

Membership: professionals engaged in dental research worldwide. Conducts annual convention, conferences, and symposia.

National Assn. of Dental Laboratories, *8201 Greensboro Rd., #300, McLean, VA 22102; (703) 610-9035. Fax, (703) 610-9005. Terry Peters, Executive Director. General e-mail, nadl@nadl.org. Web, www.nadl.org.*

Provides programs, services, and networking opportunities responsive to the evolving technical, professional, and business needs of its members. Promotes high standards and acts as a unified voice for the dental laboratory industry.

National Dental Assn., *3517 16th St. N.W. 20010; (202) 588-1697. Fax, (202) 588-1224. Robert S. Johns, Executive Director. Web, www.natdent.org.*

Promotes the interests of African American and other minority dentists through educational programs and federal legislation and programs.

Medical Researchers

NONPROFIT

American Assn. for Clinical Chemistry, *2101 L St. N.W., #202 20037-1526; (202) 857-0717. Fax, (202) 887-5093. Richard G. Flaherty, Executive Vice President. Web, www.aacc.org.*

International society of chemists, physicians, and other scientists specializing in clinical chemistry. Provides educational and professional development services; presents awards for outstanding achievement. Monitors legislation and regulations.

American Assn. of Immunologists, *9650 Rockville Pike, Bethesda, MD 20814-3994; (301) 530-7178. Fax,*

(301) 571-1816. M. M. Hogan, Executive Director. General e-mail, info@aai.org. Web, www.aai.org.

Membership: scientists working in virology, bacteriology, biochemistry, genetics, immunology, and related disciplines. Conducts training courses and workshops; compiles statistics; participates in international conferences.

American Society for Clinical Laboratory Science, *7910 Woodmont Ave., #530, Bethesda, MD 20814-3015; (301) 657-2768. Fax, (301) 657-2909. Elissa Passiment, Executive Director. General e-mail, ascls@ascls.org. Web, www.ascls.org.*

Membership: laboratory technologists. Conducts continuing education programs for medical technologists and laboratory workers. Monitors legislation and regulations.

American Society of Clinical Pathologists, *Washington Office, 1225 New York Ave. N.W., #250 20005; (202) 347-4450. Fax, (202) 347-4453. Robin E. Stombler, Director. Information, (800) 621-4142. General e-mail, info@ascp.org. Web, www.ascp.wash.org.*

Membership: pathologists, residents, and other physicians; clinical scientists; registered certified medical technologists; and technicians. Promotes continuing education, educational standards, and research in pathology. Monitors legislation, regulations, and international research. (Headquarters in Chicago.)

Assn. of Public Health Laboratories, *1211 Connecticut Ave. N.W., #608 20036; (202) 822-5227. Fax, (202) 887-5098. James Pearson, President. Web, www.aphl.org.*

Membership: state and territorial public health laboratories. Administers the National Laboratory Training Network, which assesses, develops, and delivers continuing education for laboratory practitioners. Implements international training and assistance programs for developing nations. Acts as a liaison to the Centers for Disease Control.

Society of Toxicology, *1767 Business Center Dr., #302, Reston, VA 20190; (703) 438-3115. Fax, (703) 438-3113. Shawn Lamb, Executive Director. General e-mail, sothq@toxicology.org. Web, www.toxicology.org.*

Membership: scientists from academic institutions, government, and industry worldwide who work in toxicology. Promotes professional development, exchange of information, public health, and protection of the environment.

See also American Roentgen Ray Society (p. 364)

Nurses and Physician Assistants

AGENCIES

National Institute of Nursing Research *(National Institutes of Health)*, 31 Center Dr., Bldg. 31, #5B10, MSC 2178, Bethesda, MD 20892-2178; (301) 496-8230. Fax, (301) 480-8845. Dr. Patricia A. Grady, Director. Information, (301) 496-0207.

Provides grants and awards for nursing research and research training. Programs include research to prevent the onset of disease or disability and to find effective approaches to achieving and sustaining good health.

NONPROFIT

American Academy of Physician Assistants, 950 N. Washington St., Alexandria, VA 22314; (703) 836-2272. Fax, (703) 684-1924. Stephen C. Crane, Executive Vice President. General e-mail, aapa@aapa.org. Web, www. aapa.org.

Membership: physician assistants and people interested in physician assistant issues. Sponsors continuing medical education programs for recertification of physician assistants; offers malpractice insurance; Interests include federal support for physician assistants' education programs; health issues related to underserved populations, Medicare coverage of physician assistants' services, and state laws regulating practice. Maintains speakers bureau. Monitors legislation and regulations.

American Assn. of Colleges of Nursing, 1 Dupont Circle N.W., #530 20036; (202) 463-6930. Fax, (202) 785-8320. Geraldine Bednash, Executive Director. Web, www. aacn.nche.edu.

Promotes quality baccalaureate and graduate nursing education; works to secure federal support of nursing education, nursing research, and student financial assistance; operates databank providing information on enrollments, graduations, salaries, and other conditions in nursing higher education. Interests include international practices.

American College of Nurse-Midwives, 818 Connecticut Ave. N.W., #900 20006; (202) 728-9860. Fax, (202) 728-9897. Deanne Williams, Executive Director. Press, (202) 728-9875. General e-mail, info@acnm.org. Web, www.midwife.org.

Membership: certified nurse-midwives who preside at deliveries. Interests include preventive health care for women.

American Nurses Assn., 600 Maryland Ave. S.W., #100W 20024-2571; (202) 651-7000. Fax, (202) 651-7001. David Hennage, Executive Director. General e-mail, info@ana.org. Web, www.nursingworld.org.

Membership: registered nurses. Sponsors the American Nurses Foundation. Monitors legislation and regulations.

Federation of Nurses and Health Professionals, 555 New Jersey Ave. N.W. 20001; (202) 879-4491. Fax, (202) 879-4597. Sandra Feldman, President. General e-mail, fnhpaft@aft.org. Web, www.aft.org/fnhp/index.htm.

Membership: nurses and other technical health care workers. Assists members with contract negotiation and grievances; conducts training programs and workshops. Monitors legislation and regulations. (Division of the American Federation of Teachers.)

Physical and Occupational Therapy

See also Health Services for Special Groups (this chapter)

NONPROFIT

American Occupational Therapy Assn., 4720 Montgomery Lane, Bethesda, MD 20814 (mailing address: P.O. Box 31220, Bethesda, MD 20824-1220); (301) 652-2682. Fax, (301) 652-7711. Chris Bluhm, Executive Director (Acting). TTY, (800) 377-8555. Web, www.aota.org.

Membership: registered occupational therapists, certified occupational therapy assistants, and students. Associate members include businesses and organizations supportive of occupational therapy. Accredits colleges and universities and certifies therapists.

American Physical Therapy Assn., 1111 N. Fairfax St., Alexandria, VA 22314-1488; (703) 684-2782. Fax, (703) 684-7343. Francis Mallon, Executive Vice President. Information, (800) 999-2782. TTY, (703) 683-6748. General e-mail, svcctr@apta.org. Web, www.apta.org.

Membership: physical therapists, assistants, and students. Establishes professional standards and accredits physical therapy programs; seeks to improve physical therapy education, practice, and research.

Physicians

For veterinary medicine, see Animals and Plants (chap. 9)

NONPROFIT

American Academy of Family Physicians, *Washington Office*, 2021 Massachusetts Ave. N.W. 20036; (202) 232-9033. Fax, (202) 232-9044. Rosemarie Sweeney, Vice President. General e-mail, fp@aafp.org. Web, www.aafp. org.

Membership: family physicians, family practice residents, and medical students. Sponsors continuing medical education programs; promotes family practice residency programs. Monitors legislation and regulations. (Headquarters in Kansas City, Mo.)

American Academy of Otolaryngology–Head and Neck Surgery, *1 Prince St., Alexandria, VA 22314; (703) 836-4444. Fax, (703) 683-5100. Dr. G. Richard Holt, Executive Vice President. Press, (703) 519-1563. TTY, (703) 519-1585. Web, www.entnet.org.*

Coordinates research in ear, nose, and throat disorders and head and neck surgery; provides continuing education. Related interests include allergies, plastic and reconstructive surgery, and medical problems resulting from the use of tobacco. Monitors legislation, regulations, and international research.

American Assn. of Colleges of Osteopathic Medicine, *5550 Friendship Blvd., #310, Chevy Chase, MD 20815-4101; (301) 968-4100. Fax, (301) 968-4101. Dr. Douglas L. Wood, President. Web, www.aacom.org.*

Administers a centralized application service for osteopathic medical colleges; supports increase in the number of minority and economically disadvantaged students in osteopathic colleges; maintains an information database; sponsors recruitment and retention programs. Monitors legislation and regulations.

American Assn. of Colleges of Podiatric Medicine, *1350 Piccard Dr., #322, Rockville, MD 20850-4307; (301) 990-7400. Fax, (301) 990-2807. Anthony J. McNevin, President. Information, (800) 922-9266. Web, www.aacpm.org.*

Membership: schools of podiatric medicine and affiliate teaching hospitals in the United States. Serves as an information clearinghouse on podiatric medical education; conducts research and policy analysis; administers centralized admissions program to colleges of podiatric medicine and to graduate residency programs; advises on establishing new colleges of podiatric medicine.

American College of Cardiology, *9111 Old Georgetown Rd., Bethesda, MD 20814-1699; (301) 897-5400. Fax, (301) 897-9745. Christine McEntee, Executive Vice President. Web, www.acc.org.*

Membership: physicians, surgeons, and scientists specializing in cardiovascular health care. Sponsors programs in continuing medical education; collaborates with national and international cardiovascular organizations. Library open to the public by appointment.

American College of Emergency Physicians, Government Affairs, Washington Office, *1111 19th St. N.W., #650 20036; (202) 728-0610. Fax, (202) 728-0617. Gordon B. Wheeler, Director. Web, www.acep.org.*

Monitors legislation affecting emergency medicine and practitioners. Interests include Medicare and Medicaid legislation and regulations, graduate medical education, indigent care, prehospital care, drunk driving, public health, tax policy, domestic violence, and the ban on assault weapons. (Headquarters in Dallas.)

American College of Obstetricians and Gynecologists, *409 12th St. S.W. 20024 (mailing address: P.O. Box 96920 20090-6920); (202) 638-5577. Fax, (202) 484-5107. Dr. Ralph Hale, Executive Director. Press, (202) 484-2527. Web, www.acog.org.*

Membership: medical specialists in obstetrics and gynecology. Monitors legislation, regulations, and international research on maternal and child health care.

American College of Osteopathic Surgeons, *123 N. Henry St., Alexandria, VA 22314-2903; (703) 684-0416. Fax, (703) 684-3280. Guy D. Beaumont, Executive Director.*

Membership: osteopathic surgeons in disciplines of orthopedics, neurosurgery, thoracic surgery, cardiovascular surgery, urology, plastic surgery, and general surgery. Offers members continuing education programs.

American College of Preventive Medicine, *1660 L St. N.W., #206 20036; (202) 466-2044. Fax, (202) 466-2662. Jordan Richland, Executive Director. General e-mail, info@acpm.org. Web, www.acpm.org.*

Membership: physicians in general preventive medicine, public health, international health, occupational medicine, and aerospace medicine. Provides educational opportunities; advocates public policies consistent with scientific principles of the discipline; supports the investigation and analysis of issues relevant to the field.

American College of Radiology, *1891 Preston White Dr., Reston, VA 20191; (703) 648-8900. Fax, (703) 262-9312. John J. Curry, Executive Director. General e-mail, info@acr.org. Web, www.acr.org.*

Membership: certified radiologists in the United States and Canada. Develops programs in radiation protection, technologist training, practice standards, and health care insurance; maintains a placement service for radiologists; participates in international conferences.

American College of Surgeons, Washington Office, *1640 Wisconsin Ave. N.W. 20007; (202) 337-2701. Fax, (202) 337-4271. Cynthia A. Brown, Manager. Web, www.facs.org.*

Monitors legislation and regulations concerning surgery; conducts continuing education programs and sponsors scholarships for graduate medical education. Interests include hospital cancer programs, trauma care, hospital accreditation, and international research. (Headquarters in Chicago.)

American Health Quality Assn., *1140 Connecticut Ave. N.W., #1050 20036; (202) 331-5790. Fax, (202) 331-9334. David Schulke, Director. General e-mail, ahqa@ahqa.org. Web, www.ahqa.org.*

Seeks to improve physicians' ability to assess the quality of medical care services; assists in developing methods to monitor the appropriateness of medical care. Monitors legislation.

American Medical Assn., *Public and Private Sector Advocacy, Washington Office,* *1101 Vermont Ave. N.W., 12th Floor 20005; (202) 789-7400. Fax, (202) 789-7485. Lee Stillwell, Senior Vice President. Web, www.ama-assn. org.*

Membership: physicians, residents, and medical students. Provides information on the medical profession and health care; cooperates in setting standards for medical schools and hospital intern and residency training programs; offers physician placement service and counseling on management practices; provides continuing medical education. Interests include international research and peer review. Monitors legislation and regulations. (Headquarters in Chicago.)

American Medical Women's Assn., *801 N. Fairfax St., #400, Alexandria, VA 22314-1767; (703) 838-0500. Fax, (703) 549-3864. Eileen McGrath, Executive Director. General e-mail, info@amwa-doc.org. Web, www.amwa-doc. org.*

Membership: female physicians, interns, residents, and medical students. Promotes continuing education; evaluates manufacturers' research on products for women's health; provides student educational loans. Monitors legislation and regulations.

American Osteopathic Assn., *Washington Office,* *1090 Vermont Ave. N.W., #510 20005; (202) 414-0140. Fax, (202) 544-3525. Sydney Olson, Director. Information, (800) 962-9008. Web, www.am-osteo-assn.org.*

Membership: osteopathic physicians. Promotes general health and education; accredits osteopathic educational institutions. Monitors legislation and regulations. (Headquarters in Chicago.)

American Podiatric Medical Assn., *9312 Old Georgetown Rd., Bethesda, MD 20814-1698; (301) 581-9200. Fax, (301) 530-2752. Dr. Glenn Gastwirth, Executive Director. Web, www.apma.org.*

Membership: podiatrists. Accredits colleges of podiatric medicine and podiatric residency programs. Interests include the status of podiatrists in the military, fed-

erally supported financial assistance for podiatric students, and national health care initiatives.

American Psychiatric Assn., *1400 K St. N.W. 20005; (202) 682-6000. Fax, (202) 682-6850. Dr. Steven Mirin, Medical Director. Library, (202) 682-6080. Press, (202) 682-6142. General e-mail, apa@psych.org. Web, www. psych.org.*

Membership: psychiatrists. Promotes availability of high-quality psychiatric care; provides the public with information; assists state and local agencies; conducts educational programs for professionals and students in the field; participates in international meetings and research. Library open to the public by appointment.

American Society of Addiction Medicine, *4601 N. Park Ave., Upper Arcade, #101, Chevy Chase, MD 20815-4520; (301) 656-3920. Fax, (301) 656-3815. James F. Callahan, Executive Vice President. General e-mail, email@asam.org. Web, www.asam.org.*

Membership: physicians and medical students. Supports the study and provision of effective treatment and care for people with alcohol and drug dependencies; educates physicians; administers certification program in addiction medicine. Monitors legislation and regulations.

American Society of Nuclear Cardiology, *9111 Old Georgetown Rd., Bethesda, MD 20814-1699; (301) 493-2360. Fax, (301) 493-2376. William D. Nelligan, Executive Director. Web, www.asnc.org.*

Membership: physicians and scientists engaged in nuclear cardiology practice or research. Provides professional education programs; establishes standards and guidelines for training and practice; promotes research worldwide. Monitors user-licensing requirements of the Nuclear Regulatory Commission.

Assn. for Hospital Medical Education, *2025 M St. N.W. 20036-3309; (202) 857-1196. Fax, (202) 223-4579. Dennis Smeage, Executive Director. Web, ahme.med.edu.*

Membership: physicians and others engaged in graduate and continuing medical education at community teaching hospitals. Conducts graduate and continuing education programs.

Assn. of American Medical Colleges, *2450 N St. N.W. 20037; (202) 828-0400. Fax, (202) 828-1125. Dr. Jordan J. Cohen, President. Web, www.aamc.org.*

Membership: U.S. schools of medicine, councils of deans, teaching hospitals, academic societies, medical students, and residents. Administers Medical College Admissions Test.

Assn. of Professors of Medicine, *2501 M St. N.W., #550 20037-1308; (202) 861-7700. Fax, (202) 861-9731. Tod Ibrahim, Executive Director. General e-mail, apm@im. org. Web, www.im.org.*

Membership: chairs of internal medicine departments at all U.S medical schools and several affiliated teaching hospitals.

Clerkship Directors in Internal Medicine, *2501 M St. N.W., #550 20037-1308; (202) 861-8600. Fax, (202) 861-9731. Tod Ibrahim, Executive Director. General e-mail, cdim@im.org. Web, www.im.org/cdim.*

Membership: directors of third-year internal medicine clerkships at U.S. medical schools.

College of American Pathologists, *Washington Office, 1350 Eye St. N.W., #590 20005-3305; (202) 354-7100. Fax, (202) 354-7155. John Scott, Vice President. Information, (800) 392-9994. Web, www.cap.org.*

Membership: physicians who are board certified in clinical or anatomic pathology. Accredits laboratories and provides them with proficiency testing programs; promotes the practice of pathology and laboratory medicine worldwide. (Headquarters in Northfield, Ill.)

International Council of Societies of Pathology, *7001 Georgia St., Chevy Chase, MD 20815; (202) 782-2759. Fax, (202) 782-3056. Dr. F. K. Mostofi, Secretary-Treasurer.*

Seeks to develop and maintain international cooperative research and education programs in pathology. Assists the World Health Organization and other international organizations in the delivery of medical care.

National Medical Assn., *1012 10th St. N.W. 20001; (202) 347-1895. Fax, (202) 842-3293. Lorraine Cole, Executive Director.*

Membership: minority physicians. Supports increased participation of minorities in the health professions, especially medicine.

Vision Care

See also Blind and Visually Impaired (chap. 18)

AGENCIES

National Eye Institute *(National Institutes of Health), 31 Center Dr., MSC-2510, #6A03, Bethesda, MD 20892-2510; (301) 496-2234. Fax, (301) 496-9970. Dr. Carl Kupfer, Director. Information, (301) 496-5248. Web, www. nei.nih.gov.*

Conducts and funds research on the eye and visual disorders. Participates in international research.

NONPROFIT

American Academy of Ophthalmology, *Governmental Affairs, Washington Office, 1101 Vermont Ave. N.W., #700 20005-3570; (202) 737-6662. Fax, (202) 737-7061. Cathy G. Cohen, Vice President. Web, www.eyenet.org.*

Membership: eye physicians and surgeons. Provides information on eye diseases. Monitors legislation, regulations, and international research. (Headquarters in San Francisco.)

American Academy of Optometry, *6110 Executive Blvd., #506, Rockville, MD 20852; (301) 984-1441. Fax, (301) 984-4737. Lois Schoenbrun, Executive Director. Web, www.aaopt.org.*

Membership: optometrists and students of optometry. Conducts research and continuing education; participates in international meetings; interests include primary care optometry, contact lenses, low vision, and diseases of the eye.

American Board of Opticianry and National Contact Lens Examiners Board, *6506 Loisdale Rd., Springfield, VA 22150; (703) 691-8356. Fax, (703) 691-4152. Michael Robey, Executive Manager. Information, (703) 715-6435. Web, www.abo.org.*

Establishes standards for opticians who dispense eyeglasses and contact lenses. Administers professional exams and awards certification; maintains registry of certified eyeglass and contact lens dispensers. Adopts and enforces continuing education requirements; assists state licensing boards; approves educational offerings for recertification requirements.

American Optometric Assn., *Washington Office, 1505 Prince St., Alexandria, VA 22314; (703) 739-9200. Fax, (703) 739-9497. Jeffrey G. Mays, Director. Web, www. aoanet.org.*

Membership: optometrists and optometry students. Monitors legislation and regulations and acts as liaison with international optometric groups and government optometrists; conducts continuing education programs for optometrists and provides information on eye care. (Headquarters in St. Louis.)

Assn. for Research in Vision and Ophthalmology, *9650 Rockville Pike, Bethesda, MD 20814-3998; (301) 571-1844. Fax, (301) 571-8311. Joanne Angle, Executive Director. General e-mail, mem@arvo.arvo.org. Web, www. arvo.org/arvo.*

Promotes eye and vision research; issues awards for significant research and administers research grant program.

Assn. of Schools and Colleges of Optometry, *6110 Executive Blvd., #510, Rockville, MD 20852; (301) 231-5944. Fax, (301) 770-1828. Martin A. Wall, Executive Director. General e-mail, admini@opted.org. Web, www.opted.org.*

Membership: U.S. and Puerto Rican optometry schools and colleges, and foreign affiliates. Provides information about the Optometry College Admissions Test to students. Monitors legislation and regulations.

Contact Lens Society of America, *441 Carlisle Dr., Reston, VA 20170; (703) 437-5100. Fax, (703) 437-0727. Tina M. Schott, Executive Director. General e-mail, clsa@huskynet.com. Web, www.theclsa.com.*

Membership: contact lens professionals. Conducts courses and continuing education seminars for contact lens fitters and technicians.

Eye Bank Assn. of America, *1015 18th St. N.W., #1010 20036-5504; (202) 775-4999. Fax, (202) 429-6036. Patricia Aiken-O'Neill, President. General e-mail, sightebaa@aol.com. Web, www.restoresight.org.*

Membership: eye banks in Canada, England, Saudi Arabia, and the United States. Sets and enforces medical standards for eye banking; seeks to increase donations to eye, tissue, and organ banks; conducts training and certification programs for eye bank technicians; compiles statistics.

International Eye Foundation, *7801 Norfolk Ave., Bethesda, MD 20814; (301) 986-1830. Fax, (301) 986-1876. Victoria M. Sheffield, Executive Director. General e-mail, ief@iefusa.org. Web, www.iefusa.org.*

Operates eye health care and blindness prevention programs in developing countries. Sends volunteer surgeons and public health specialists to provide care; trains paramedical and public health personnel in developing countries in various aspects of public eye health care. Implements programs to control vitamin A deficiency and onchocerciasis (river blindness). Provides technology transfer and ophthalmic equipment and medicines.

Optical Laboratories Assn., *11096B Lee Hwy., #102, Fairfax, VA 22030 (mailing address: P.O. Box 2000, Merrifield, VA 22116-2000); (703) 359-2830. Fax, (703) 359-2834. Robert Dziuban, Executive Vice President. Web, www.ola-labs.org.*

Membership: optical laboratories. Promotes the eyewear industry; sponsors conferences. Monitors legislation and regulations.

Opticians Assn. of America, *10341 Democracy Lane, Fairfax, VA 22030-2521; (703) 691-8355. Fax, (703) 691-3929. Joyce M. Otto, Executive Director. General e-mail, oaa@opticians.org. Web, www.oaa.org.*

Membership: independent retail optical firms, optical corporations, state societies of opticians, and individual optical dispensers. Conducts education programs for members. Monitors legislation and regulations.

Vision Council of America, *1655 N. Fort Myer Dr., #200, Arlington, VA 22209; (703) 243-1508. Fax, (703) 243-1537. Bill Thomas, CEO. General e-mail, vca@visionsite.org. Web, www.visionsite.org.*

Sponsors trade shows and public relations programs for the ophthalmic industry. Educates the public on developments in the optical industry. Represents manufacturers and distributors of lenses and frames.

See also AARP Andrus Foundation (p. 381)

✚ HEALTH SERVICES FOR SPECIAL GROUPS

AGENCIES

Administration for Children and Families *(Health and Human Services Dept.),* 901 D St. S.W. 20447 *(mailing address: 370 L'Enfant Promenade S.W. 20447); (202) 401-9200. Fax, (202) 401-5770. Olivia A. Golden, Assistant Secretary. Information, (202) 401-9215. Web, www.acf.dhhs.gov.*

Administers and funds programs for native Americans, children, youth, families, and those with developmental disabilities. Responsible for Social Services Block Grants to the states. Provides agencies with technical assistance; administers Head Start program; funds the National Runaway Switchboard, (800) 621-4000, the Domestic Violence Hotline, (800) 799-7233, and programs for abused children.

Health Care Financing Administration *(Health and Human Services Dept.), Outcomes and Improvements,* *7500 Security Blvd., S2-11-07, Baltimore, MD 21244-1850; (410) 786-7304. Fax, (410) 786-6730. Helene Fredeking, Director.*

Monitors compliance of nursing homes, psychiatric hospitals, and long-term and intermediate care facilities with government standards. Focus includes quality of care, environmental conditions, and participation in Medicaid and Medicare programs. Coordinates health care programs for the mentally retarded.

Health Resources and Services Administration *(Health and Human Services Dept.), Community and Migrant Health,* *4350 East-West Hwy., 7th Floor, Bethesda, MD 20814; (301) 594-4300. Fax, (301) 594-4997. Richard C. Bohrer, Director.*

Awards grants to public and nonprofit migrant, community, and health care centers to provide direct health care services in areas that are medically underserved. Administers National Migrant Health Advisory Council.

Health Resources and Services Administration
(Health and Human Services Dept.), Health Resources Development, 5600 Fishers Lane, Parklawn Bldg., #705, Rockville, MD 20857; (301) 443-1993. Fax, (301) 443-9645. William H. Aspden Jr., Deputy Associate Administrator.

Administers programs that provide communities with grants for the delivery of health care services to persons infected with the HIV virus; supports health facilities for uncompensated care, construction grants, and loans; provides grants to organ procurement transplantation programs; plans, directs, coordinates, and monitors activities relating to emergency medical services and trauma system planning and implementation.

Health Resources and Services Administration
(Health and Human Services Dept.), Immigration Health Services, 801 Eye St. N.W., 8th Floor 20536; (202) 514-3339. Fax, (202) 514-0095. Gene Migliaccio, Director.

Division of the Bureau of Primary Health Care. Works to improve the health of new immigrants and detained aliens in the United States; promotes increased access to comprehensive primary and preventive health care.

Health Resources and Services Administration
(Health and Human Services Dept.), Primary Health Care, 4350 East-West Hwy., #11-10, Bethesda, MD 20814; (301) 594-4110. Fax, (301) 594-4072. Dr. Marilyn H. Gaston, Director.

Advocates accessible primary health care for underserved communities and individuals. Promotes partnerships in public and private health care delivery communities. Researches and analyzes effectiveness of community-based systems of care.

Health Resources and Services Administration
(Health and Human Services Dept.), Special Populations, 4350 East-West Hwy., West Towers Bldg., 9th Floor, Bethesda, MD 20814; (301) 594-4420. Fax, (301) 594-4989. Regan Crump, Director.

Awards grants to community-based organizations to provide primary health care services to special populations, including HIV-infected persons, women considered to be at risk, homeless individuals, substance abusers, elderly people, and native Hawaiian and Pacific Basin residents. Focus includes Alzheimer's disease.

Indian Health Service *(Health and Human Services Dept.),* 5600 Fishers Lane, #6-05 Parklawn Bldg.,

Rockville, MD 20857; (301) 443-1083. Fax, (301) 443-4794. Dr. Michael H. Trujillo, Director. Information, (301) 443-3593. Web, www.tucson.ihs.gov.

Operates hospitals and health centers that provide native Americans and Alaska natives with preventive and remedial health care. Provides or improves sanitation and water supply systems in native American communities.

National Institute of Child Health and Human Development *(National Institutes of Health), National Center for Medical Rehabilitation Research,* 6100 Executive Blvd., Bldg. 6100E, #2A-03, Bethesda, MD 20852; (301) 402-2242. Fax, (301) 402-0832. Dr. Michael Weinrich, Director. Web, silk.nih.gov/silk/NCMRR.

Conducts and supports research to develop improved technologies, techniques, and prosthetic and orthotic devices for people with disabilities; promotes medical rehabilitation training.

National Institute on Deafness and Other Communication Disorders *(National Institutes of Health),* 31 Center Dr., MSC-2320, #3C02, Bethesda, MD 20892-2320; (301) 402-0900. Fax, (301) 402-1590. Dr. James F. Battey Jr., Director. Information, (301) 496-7243. TTY, (301) 496-6596. Web, www.nih.gov/nidcd.

Conducts and supports research and research training and disseminates information on hearing disorders and other communication processes, including diseases that affect hearing, balance, smell, taste, voice, speech, and language. Monitors international research.

Public Health and Science *(Health and Human Services Dept.), Minority Health,* 5515 Security Lane, #1000, Rockwall II Bldg., Rockville, MD 20852; (301) 443-5084. Fax, (301) 594-0767. Nathan Stinson, Deputy Assistant Secretary (Acting). Information, (800) 444-6472. General e-mail, info@omhrc.gov. Web, www.omhrc.gov.

Oversees the implementation of the secretary's Task Force on Black and Minority Health and legislative mandates; develops programs to meet the health care needs of minorities; awards grants to coalitions of minority community organizations and to minority AIDS education and prevention projects.

Rehabilitation Services Administration *(Education Dept.),* 330 C St. S.W. 20202-2531; (202) 205-5482. Fax, (202) 205-9874. Fredric K. Schroeder, Commissioner. TTY, (202) 205-9295.

Allocates funds to state agencies and nonprofit organizations for programs serving eligible physically and mentally disabled persons; services provided by these funds include medical and psychological treatment as well as establishment of supported-employment and independent-living programs.

CONGRESS

House Commerce Committee, *Subcommittee on Health and the Environment,* 2125 RHOB 20515; (202) 225-2927. Fax, (202) 225-1919. Rep. Michael Bilirakis, R-Fla., Chair; James E. Derderian, Staff Director. General e-mail, commerce@mail.house.gov. Web, www.house.gov/ commerce.

Jurisdiction over legislation on the mentally retarded, migrant health care, the disabled, long-term and nursing home programs, health care for the poor (including Medicaid and national health insurance proposals), and medical research on aging. (Jurisdiction over native American health care shared with House Resources Committee.)

House Education and the Workforce Committee, *Subcommittee on Postsecondary Education, Training, and Life-Long Learning,* 2181 RHOB 20515; (202) 225-4527. Fax, (202) 225-9571. Rep. Howard P. "Buck" McKeon, R-Calif., Chair; Kevin D. Talley, Staff Director. Web, www.house.gov/ed_workforce.

Jurisdiction over legislation on all matters dealing with programs and services for the elderly, including health and nutrition programs and the Older Americans Act.

House Education and the Workforce Committee, *Subcommittee on Workforce Protections,* 2181 RHOB 20515; (202) 225-4527. Fax, (202) 225-9571. Rep. Cass Ballenger, R-N.C., Chair; Kevin D. Talley, Staff Director. Web, www.house.gov/ed_workforce.

Jurisdiction over workers' health and safety legislation, including migrant and agricultural labor matters.

House Resources Committee, 1324 LHOB 20515-6201; (202) 225-2761. Fax, (202) 225-5929. Rep. Don Young, R-Alaska, Chair; Lloyd Jones, Staff Director. General e-mail, resources.committee@mail.house.gov. Web, www.house.gov/resources.

Jurisdiction over legislation pertaining to native American health care and special services; oversight of native American health care programs. (Jurisdiction shared with House Commerce Committee.)

Senate Committee on Indian Affairs, SH-838 20510; (202) 224-2251. Fax, (202) 224-5429. Sen. Ben Nighthorse Campbell, R-Colo., Chair; Paul Moorehead, Staff Director. Web, indian.senate.gov.

Jurisdiction over legislation pertaining to native American health care; oversight of native American health care programs.

Senate Finance Committee, *Subcommittee on Health Care,* SD-219 20510; (202) 224-4515. Fax, (202) 224-

5920. Sen. Paul Coverdell, R-Ga., Chair; Kathy Means, Staff Contact. Web, finance.senate.gov.

Holds hearings on health legislation for low-income individuals, including Medicaid and national health insurance proposals (jurisdiction shared with the Senate Health, Education, Labor, and Pensions Committee).

Senate Health, Education, Labor, and Pensions Committee, SD-428 20510; (202) 224-5375. Fax, (202) 228-5044. Sen. James M. Jeffords, R-Vt., Chair; Mark Powden, Staff Director. TTY, (202) 224-1975. Web, labor. senate.gov.

Jurisdiction over legislation on migrant health care, health care for the poor and elderly (excluding Medicaid and Medicare), health care for individuals with physical and developmental disabilities, government-run health care facilities, and medical research on aging.

Senate Special Committee on Aging, SD-G31 20510; (202) 224-5364. Fax, (202) 224-8660. Sen. Charles E. Grassley, R-Iowa, Chair; Ted Totman, Staff Director. Web, aging.senate.gov.

Studies and makes recommendations on the overall health problems of the elderly, including quality and cost of long-term care, and on access to and quality of health care for minority elderly; oversight of federally funded programs for the elderly, including Medicare, Medicaid, and programs concerning day-to-day care.

NONPROFIT

Americans for the Restitution and Righting of Old Wrongs, 1000 Connecticut Ave. N.W., #1204 20036; (202) 296-0685. Fax, (202) 659-4377. Hazel Elbert, Executive Director. General e-mail, arrow1949@aol.com.

Recruits physicians and nurses to volunteer their services on reservation health care facilities; maintains personnel bank of volunteers. Works to prevent drug, alcohol, and child abuse.

Brain Injury Assn., 105 N. Alfred St., Alexandria, VA 22314; (703) 236-6000. Fax, (703) 236-6001. Allan I. Bergman, President. Family helpline, (800) 444-6443.

Works to improve the quality of life for persons with traumatic brain injuries and for their families. Promotes the prevention of head injuries through public awareness and education programs. Offers state-level support services for individuals and their families. Monitors legislation and regulations.

Catholic Health Assn. of the United States, 1875 Eye St. N.W., #1000 20006; (202) 296-3993. Fax, (202) 296-3997. Michael Place, President. Web, www.chausa.org.

Concerned with the health care needs of the poor and disadvantaged. Promotes health care reform, including universal insurance coverage, and more cost-effective, affordable health care.

Center on Disability and Health, *1522 K St. N.W., #800 20005; (202) 842-4408. Fax, (202) 842-2402. Bob Griss, Director. General e-mail, bgrisscdh@aol.com.*

Promotes changes in the financing and delivery of health care to meet the needs of persons with disabilities and other chronic health conditions. Conducts research; provides technical assistance to disability groups and agencies. Monitors legislation and regulations.

Farm Worker Health Services, *1234 Massachusetts Ave. N.W., #C-1017 20005-4526; (202) 347-7377. Fax, (202) 347-6385. Oscar Gomez, Executive Director. General e-mail, farmwlths@aol.com. Web, www.farmworkerhealth.org.*

Funded by the Health and Human Services Dept. Assigns health professionals and allied health care personnel to health facilities along the East Coast. Assists migrants in addressing health and social needs and familiarizes providers with migrants' special health care needs.

National Alliance of Hispanic Health, *1501 16th St. N.W. 20036; (202) 387-5000. Fax, (202) 265-8027. Jane L. Delgado, President. Web, www.cossmho.org.*

Assists agencies and groups serving the Hispanic community in general health care and in targeting health and psychosocial problems; provides information, technical assistance, health care provider training, and policy analysis; coordinates and supports research. Interests include mental health, chronic diseases, substance abuse, maternal and child health, youth issues, juvenile delinquency, and access to care.

National Assn. of Community Health Centers, *1330 New Hampshire Ave. N.W., #122 20036; (202) 659-8008. Fax, (202) 659-8519. Thomas Van Coverden, President. Web, www.nachc.com.*

Membership: community health centers, migrant and homeless health programs, and other community health care programs. Provides the medically underserved with health services; seeks to ensure the continued development of community health care programs through policy analysis, research, technical assistance, publications, education, and training.

National Easter Seal Society, *Washington Office, 700 13th St. N.W., #200 20005; (202) 347-3066. Fax, (202) 737-7914. Joseph D. Romer, Executive Vice President. TTY, (202) 347-7385. Web, www.easter-seals.org.*

Federation of state and local groups with programs that help people with disabilities achieve independence.

Washington office monitors legislation and regulations. Affiliates assist individuals with a broad range of disabilities, including muscular dystrophy, cerebral palsy, stroke, speech and hearing loss, blindness, amputation, and learning disabilities. Services include physical, occupational, vocational, and speech therapy; speech, hearing, physical, and vocational evaluation; psychological testing and counseling; personal and family counseling; and special education programs. (Headquarters in Chicago.)

National Health Law Program, *Washington Office, 1101 14th St. N.W., #405 20005; (202) 289-7661. Fax, (202) 289-7724. Lawrence Lavin, Director. General e-mail, nhelpdc@healthlaw.org. Web, www.healthlaw.org.*

Organization of lawyers representing the economically disadvantaged, minorities, and the elderly in issues concerning federal, state, and local health care programs. Offers technical assistance, workshops, seminars, and training for health law specialists. (Headquarters in Los Angeles.)

Spina Bifida Assn. of America, *4590 MacArthur Blvd. N.W., #250 20007-4226; (202) 944-3285. Fax, (202) 944-3295. Lawrence Pencak, Executive Director. Information, (800) 621-3141. General e-mail, sbaa@sbaa.org. Web, www.sbaa.org.*

Membership: individuals with spina bifida, their supporters, and concerned professionals. Offers educational programs, scholarships, and support services; acts as a clearinghouse; provides referrals. Serves as U.S. member of the International Federation for Hydrocephalus and Spina Bifida, which is headquartered in Geneva. Monitors legislation and regulations.

White House Initiative on Asian Americans and Pacific Islanders, *5600 Fisher's Lane, #1042, Rockville, MD 20857-0259; (301) 443-2492. Fax, (301) 443-7853. Shamina Singh, Executive Director. General e-mail, api@hrsa.gov. Web, www.hrsa.gov/_whaapi.*

Advises the HHS secretary on the implementation and coordination of federal programs and how they relate to Asian Americans and Pacific Islanders; oversees federal interagency working group and presidential advisory commission (advisory commission will serve until June 7, 2001). Interests include health, education, housing, and economic and community development.

Elderly

See also Medicaid and Medicare (this chapter); Nursing Homes and Hospices (this chapter); Senior Citizens (chap. 1); Social Services and Disabilities (chap. 18)

AGENCIES

National Institute on Aging *(National Institutes of Health),* *31 Center Dr., MSC-2292, Bldg. 31, #5C35, Bethesda, MD 20892-2292; (301) 496-9265. Fax, (301) 496-2525. Dr. Richard J. Hodes, Director; Marta Welsh, Director, International Activities, (301) 496-0767. Information, (301) 496-1752. Web, www.nih.gov/nia.*

Conducts and funds research and disseminates information on the biological, medical, behavioral, and social aspects of aging and the common problems of the elderly. Participates in international research.

NONPROFIT

AARP, *Health and Long-Term Care, 601 E St. N.W., #A5 20049; (202) 434-2230. Fax, (202) 434-7683. Michael McKean, Manager (Acting). Web, www.aarp.org.*

Promotes good health habits among older persons and encourages effective use of the health care system through educational and voluntary programs. Assists older adults in making health care decisions.

AARP Andrus Foundation, *601 E St. N.W. 20049; (202) 434-6200. Fax, (202) 434-6483. Dr. John Feather, Director. General e-mail, andrus@aarp.org. Web, www.andrus.org.*

Awards grants for applied research projects in gerontology. Disseminates research findings to professionals, policymakers, the media, and the public. Interests include aging and living environments and living with chronic health conditions. (Affiliated with American Assn. of Retired Persons.)

Alliance for Aging Research, *2021 K St. N.W., #305 20006; (202) 293-2856. Fax, (202) 785-8574. Daniel Perry, Executive Director. General e-mail, info@agingresearch. org. Web, www.agingresearch.org.*

Membership: senior corporate and foundation executives, science leaders, and congressional representatives. Citizen advocacy organization that seeks to improve the health and independence of older Americans through public and private research.

Alzheimer's Assn., *Public Policy, Washington Office, 1319 F St. N.W., #710 20004-1106; (202) 393-7737. Fax, (202) 393-2109. Stephen R. McConnell, Vice President. Information, (800) 272-3900. Web, www.alz.org.*

Offers family support services and educates the public about Alzheimer's disease, a neurological disorder mainly affecting the brain tissue in older adults. Promotes research and long-term care protection; maintains liaison with Alzheimer's associations abroad. Monitors legislation and regulations. (Headquarters in Chicago.)

American Assn. of Homes and Services for the Aging, *Policy and Governmental Affairs, 901 E St.*

N.W., #500 20004-2011; (202) 783-2242. Fax, (202) 783-2255. Michael F. Rodgers, Senior Vice President. Web, www.aahsa.org.

Membership: nonprofit homes, housing, and health-related facilities for the elderly sponsored by religious, fraternal, labor, private, and governmental organizations. Conducts research on long-term care for the elderly; sponsors institutes and workshops on accreditation, financing, and institutional life. Monitors legislation and regulations.

Gerontological Society of America, *1030 15th St. N.W., #250 20005-1503; (202) 842-1275. Fax, (202) 842-1150. Carol Schutz, Executive Director. General e-mail, geron@geron.org. Web, www.geron.org.*

Scientific organization of researchers, educators, and professionals in the field of aging. Promotes the study of aging and the application of research to public policy; interests include international aging and migration.

National Assn. for Homecare, *228 7th St. S.E. 20003; (202) 547-7424. Fax, (202) 547-3540. Val J. Halaman-daris, President. Web, www.nahc.org.*

Membership: home care professionals and paraprofessionals. Advocates the rights of the elderly, infirm, and terminally ill to remain independent in their own homes as long as possible. Monitors legislation and regulations.

National Citizens' Coalition for Nursing Home Reform, *1424 16th St. N.W., #202 20036-2211; (202) 332-2275. Fax, (202) 332-2949. Sarah Greene Burger, Executive Director.*

Seeks to improve the long-term care system and quality of life for residents in nursing homes and other facilities for the elderly; coordinates the Campaign for Quality Care. Promotes citizen participation in all aspects of nursing homes; acts as clearinghouse for nursing home advocacy.

National Council of Senior Citizens, *8403 Colesville Rd., #1200, Silver Spring, MD 20910-3314; (301) 578-8800. Fax, (301) 578-8999. Steve Protulis, Executive Director. Web, www.ncscinc.org.*

Supports expansion of Medicare, improved health programs, national health care, and reduced cost of drugs. Nursing Home Information Service provides information on nursing home standards and regulations.

National Council on the Aging, *409 3rd St. S.W., 2nd Floor 20024; (202) 479-1200. Fax, (202) 479-0735. James Firman, President. Information, (202) 479-6653. Library, (202) 479-6669. Press, (202) 479-6975. General e-mail, info@ncoa.org. Web, www.ncoa.org.*

Promotes the physical, mental, and emotional health of older persons and studies adult day care and community-based long-term care. Monitors legislation and regulations. Library open to the public.

National Hispanic Council on Aging, *2713 Ontario Rd. N.W. 20009; (202) 265-1288. Fax, (202) 745-2522. Marta Sotomayor, President. General e-mail, nhcoa@worldnet.att.net. Web, www.nhcoa.org.*

Membership: senior citizens, health care workers, professionals in the field of aging, and others in the United States and Puerto Rico who are interested in topics related to Hispanics and aging.

National Long-Term Care Ombudsman Resource Center, *1424 16th St. N.W., #202 20036-2211; (202) 332-2275. Fax, (202) 332-2949. Alice Hedt, Director. Web, www.nccnhr.org.*

Provides technical assistance, management guidance, policy analysis, and program development information in behalf of state and substate ombudsman programs. (Affiliate of the National Citizens' Coalition for Nursing Home Reform.)

National Osteoporosis Foundation, *1232 22nd St. N.W. 20037-1292; (202) 223-2226. Fax, (202) 223-2237. Sandra C. Raymond, Executive Director. Web, www.nof. org.*

Seeks to reduce osteoporosis through educational programs, research, and patient advocacy. Monitors international research.

United Seniors Health Cooperative, *409 3rd St. S.W., 2nd Floor 20024-3212; (202) 479-6973. Fax, (202) 479-6660. Anne Werner, President. Web, www.ushc-online.org.*

Provides members with health care information and health insurance counseling. Publishes on health issues affecting older Americans.

Prenatal, Maternal, and Child Health Care

See also Children and Families (chap. 18)

AGENCIES

Centers for Disease Control and Prevention *(Health and Human Services Dept.), Washington Office, 200 Independence Ave. S.W., #746-G 20201-0004; (202) 690-8598. Fax, (202) 690-7519. Donald E. Shriber, Associate Director. Web, www.cdc.gov.*

Assists state and local health agencies that receive grants for the control of childhood diseases preventable by immunization. Studies childhood diseases worldwide. (Headquarters in Atlanta: 1600 Clifton Rd. N.E. 30333. Public inquiries, [404] 639-3534.)

Environmental Protection Agency (EPA), *Children's Health Protection, 401 M St. S.W., MC 1107, #913, West Tower 20460; (202) 260-7778. Fax, (202) 260-4103. E. Ramona Trovato, Director. Web, www.epa.gov.*

Supports and facilitates EPA's efforts to protect children's health from environmental threats.

Health Care Financing Administration *(Health and Human Services Dept.), Medicaid, 7500 Security Blvd., #C52223, Baltimore, MD 21244; (410) 786-3230. Fax, (410) 786-0025. Rachel Block, Deputy Director.*

Develops health care policies and programs for needy children under Medicaid; works with the Public Health Service and other related agencies to coordinate the department's child health resources.

Health Resources and Services Administration *(Health and Human Services Dept.), Maternal and Child Health, 5600 Fishers Lane, #18-05, Rockville, MD 20857; (301) 443-2170. Fax, (301) 443-1797. Dr. Peter C. van Dyck, Associate Administrator. Web, www.mchb.hrsa.gov.*

Administers block grants to states for mothers and children and for children with special health needs; awards funding for research training, genetic disease testing, counseling and information dissemination, hemophilia diagnostic and treatment centers, and demonstration projects to improve the health of mothers and children. Interests also include pediatric AIDS health care and emergency medical services for children.

Health Resources and Services Administration *(Health and Human Services Dept.), National Maternal and Child Health Clearinghouse, 2070 Chain Bridge Rd., #450, Vienna, VA 22182; (703) 356-1964. Fax, (703) 821-2098. Larry Silver, Project Director. Toll-free, (888) 434-4624. Web, www.nmchc.org.*

Disseminates information on various aspects of maternal and child health and genetics.

Health Resources and Services Administration *(Health and Human Services Dept.), National Sudden Infant Death Syndrome Resource Center, 2070 Chain Bridge Rd., #450, Vienna, VA 22182; (703) 821-8955. Fax, (703) 821-2098. Olivia Cowdrill, Director. General e-mail, sids@circsol.com. Web, www.circsol.com/sids.*

A component of the National Maternal and Child Health Clearinghouse. Provides information about sudden infant death syndrome (SIDS), apnea, and related issues; makes referrals to local SIDS programs and parent support groups; publishes educational information about SIDS; distributes literature for the National Institute of Child Health and Human Development's "Back to Sleep" campaign.

Health Resources and Services Administration *(Health and Human Services Dept.), National Vaccine Injury Compensation Program,* 5600 Fishers Lane, Park-lawn Bldg., #8A-46, Rockville, MD 20857; (301) 443-6593. Fax, (301) 443-8196. Thomas E. Balbier Jr., Director. Toll-free hotline, (800) 338-2382. Web, www.hrsa.gov/bhpr/vicp.

Provides no-fault compensation to individuals injured by certain childhood vaccines (rotavirus vaccine; diphtheria and tetanus toxoids and pertussis vaccine; measles, mumps, and rubella vaccine; varicella, hepatitis B, HiB vaccine; and oral polio and inactivated polio vaccine).

National Institute of Child Health and Human Development *(National Institutes of Health),* Center Dr., Bldg. 31, #2A03 MSC-2425, Bethesda, MD 20892-2425; (301) 496-3454. Fax, (301) 402-1104. Dr. Duane F. Alexander, Director. Information, (301) 496-5133. Web, www.nih.gov/nichd.

Conducts research and research training on biological and behavioral human development. Studies reproduction and population statistics, perinatal biology and infant mortality, congenital defects, nutrition, human learning and behavior, medical rehabilitation, and mental retardation. Interests include UNICEF and other international organizations.

National Institute of Child Health and Human Development *(National Institutes of Health), Center for Research for Mothers and Children,* 6100 Executive Blvd., #4B05, Bethesda, MD 20892-7510; (301) 496-5097. Fax, (301) 480-7773. Dr. Sumner J. Yaffe, Director.

Supports biomedical and behavioral science research and training for maternal and child health care. Areas of study include fetal development, maternal-infant health problems, HIV-related diseases in childbearing women, roles of nutrients and hormones in child growth, developmental disabilities, and behavioral development.

Public Health and Science *(Health and Human Services Dept.), Adolescent Pregnancy Programs,* 4350 East-West Hwy., #200, Bethesda, MD 20814; (301) 594-4004. Fax, (301) 594-5981. Patrick J. Sheeran, Director (Acting). Web, www.dhhs.gov/progorg/opa/oapp.html.

Awards, administers, and evaluates research and demonstration grants through the Adolescent Family Life Program, which funds community health care and pregnancy prevention programs. Administers a program that provides pregnant adolescents and children of teenage parents with comprehensive health education and social services, and a program that focuses on sexual abstinence. Interests include adolescent sexual behavior, adoption, and early childbearing.

NONPROFIT

Advocates for Youth, 1025 Vermont Ave. N.W., #200 20005; (202) 347-5700. Fax, (202) 347-2263. James Wag-oner, Executive Director. General e-mail, info@ advocatesforyouth.org. Web, www.advocatesforyouth.org.

Seeks to reduce the incidence of unintended teenage pregnancy and AIDS through public education, training and technical assistance, research, and media programs.

Alan Guttmacher Institute, *Public Policy, Washington Office,* 1120 Connecticut Ave. N.W., #460 20036-3902; (202) 296-4012. Fax, (202) 223-5756. Cory L. Richards, Vice President. General e-mail, info@agi-usa.org. Web, www.agi-usa.org.

Conducts research, policy analysis, and public education in reproductive health issues, including maternal and child health. (Headquarters in New York.)

Alliance to End Childhood Lead Poisoning, 227 Massachusetts Ave. N.E., #200 20002; (202) 543-1147. Fax, (202) 543-4466. Don Ryan, Executive Director. General e-mail, aeclp@aeclp.org. Web, www.aeclp.org.

Works to increase awareness of childhood lead poisoning and to develop and implement prevention programs.

American Academy of Child and Adolescent Psychiatry, 3615 Wisconsin Ave. N.W., 2nd Floor 20016-2037; (202) 966-7300. Fax, (202) 966-2891. Virginia Q. Anthony, Executive Director. Web, www.aacap.org.

Membership: psychiatrists working with children and adolescents. Sponsors annual meeting and review for medical board examinations; provides information on child abuse, youth suicide, and drug abuse; monitors international research and U.S. legislation concerning mentally ill children.

American Academy of Pediatrics, *Washington Office,* 601 13th St. N.W., #400N 20005; (202) 347-8600. Fax, (202) 393-6137. Jackie Noyes, Director. Information, (800) 336-5475. General e-mail, kids1st@aap.org. Web, www.aap.org.

Advocates for maternal and child health legislation and regulations. Interests include increased access and coverage for persons under age twenty-one, immunizations, injury prevention, environmental hazards, child abuse, emergency medical services, biomedical research, Medicaid, disabilities, pediatric AIDS, substance abuse, and nutrition. (Headquarters in Elk Grove Village, Ill.)

American Assn. of Children's Residential Centers, 122 C St. N.W., #820 20001; (202) 628-1816. Fax, (202) 638-0973. Allison Vickery, Executive Director. General e-mail, aacrc@dc.net.

Membership: mental health out-of-home agencies and individuals interested in clinical practice in residential care for children with emotional disturbance. Represents interests of children with emotional disturbance and their families before the federal government; conducts educational conferences; provides information on residential treatment.

American College of Nurse-Midwives, *818 Connecticut Ave. N.W., #900 20006; (202) 728-9860. Fax, (202) 728-9897. Deanne Williams, Executive Director. Press, (202) 728-9875. General e-mail, info@acnm.org. Web, www.midwife.org.*

Membership: certified nurse-midwives who preside at deliveries. Interests include preventive health care for women.

American College of Obstetricians and Gynecologists, *409 12th St. S.W. 20024 (mailing address: P.O. Box 96920 20090-6920); (202) 638-5577. Fax, (202) 484-5107. Dr. Ralph Hale, Executive Director. Press, (202) 484-2527. Web, www.acog.org.*

Membership: medical specialists in obstetrics and gynecology. Monitors legislation, regulations, and international research on maternal and child health care.

Children's Defense Fund, *25 E St. N.W. 20001; (202) 628-8787. Fax, (202) 662-3510. Marian Wright Edelman, President. Web, www.childrensdefense.org.*

Advocacy group concerned with programs for children and youth. Assesses adequacy of the Early and Periodic Screening, Diagnosis, and Treatment Program for Medicaid-eligible children. Promotes adequate prenatal care for adolescent and lower-income women; works to prevent adolescent pregnancy.

Lamaze International, *2025 M St. N.W. 20036-3309; (202) 857-1128. Fax, (202) 828-6051. Linda Harmon, Executive Director. Information, (800) 368-4404. General e-mail, lamaze@dc.sba.com. Web, www.lamaze-childbirth.com.*

Membership: supporters of the Lamaze method of childbirth, including parents, physicians, childbirth educators, and other health professionals. Trains and certifies Lamaze educators. Provides referral service for parents seeking Lamaze classes.

March of Dimes, *Government Affairs, Washington Office, 1901 L St. N.W., #260 20036; (202) 659-1800. Fax, (202) 296-2964. Marina Weiss, Senior Vice President. Web, www.modimes.org.*

Works to prevent birth defects, low birth weight, and infant mortality. Awards grants for research and provides funds for treatment of birth defects. Medical services

grantees provide prenatal counseling. Monitors legislation and regulations. (Headquarters in White Plains, NY.)

National Assn. of Children's Hospitals and Related Institutions, *401 Wythe St., Alexandria, VA 22314; (703) 684-1355. Fax, (703) 684-1589. Lawrence A. McAndrews, President.*

Advocates and promotes education and research on child health care related to children's hospitals; compiles statistics and provides information on pediatric hospitalizations.

National Center for Education in Maternal and Child Health, *2000 15th St. North, #701, Arlington, VA 22201-2617; (703) 524-7802. Fax, (703) 524-9335. Dr. Rochelle Mayer, Director. General e-mail, info@ncemch.org. Web, www.ncemch.org.*

Collects and disseminates information about maternal and child health to health professionals and the general public. Carries out special projects for the U.S. Maternal and Child Health Bureau. Library open to the public by appointment. (Affiliated with Georgetown University.)

National Consortium for Child Mental Health Services, *3615 Wisconsin Ave. N.W., 2nd Floor 20016-2037; (202) 966-7300. Fax, (202) 966-2891. Virginia Q. Anthony, Executive Director.*

Membership: organizations interested in developing mental health services for children. Fosters information exchange; advises local, state, and federal agencies that develop children's mental health services. (Affiliated with American Academy of Child and Adolescent Psychiatry.)

National Organization on Adolescent Pregnancy, Parenting, and Prevention, *2401 Pennsylvania Ave. N.W., #350 20037; (202) 293-8370. Fax, (202) 293-8805. Mary Jean Schumann, Executive Director. General e-mail, noappp@noappp.org. Web, www.noappp.org.*

Membership: health and social work professionals, community and state leaders, and individuals. Promotes services to prevent and resolve problems associated with adolescent sexuality, pregnancy, and parenting. Helps to develop stable and supportive family relationships through program support and evaluation. Monitors legislation and regulations.

National Organization on Fetal Alcohol Syndrome, *216 G St. N.E. 20002; (202) 785-4585. Fax, (202) 466-6456. Tom Donaldson, Executive Director. Information, (800) 666-6327. General e-mail, nofas@erols.com. Web, www.nofas.org.*

Works to eradicate fetal alcohol syndrome and alcohol-related birth defects through public education, conferences, medical school curricula, and partnerships with federal programs interested in fetal alcohol syndrome.

Zero to Three/National Center for Infants, Toddlers, and Families, *734 15th St. N.W., 10th Floor 20005; (202) 638-1144. Fax, (202) 638-0851. Matthew Melmed, Executive Director. Publications, (800) 899-4301. Web, www.zerotothree.org.*

Works to improve infant health, mental health, and development. Sponsors training programs for professionals; offers fellowships. Provides private and government organizations with information on infant development issues.

See also Assn. of Reproductive Health Professionals (p. 369); Cystic Fibrosis Foundation (p. 397); Program for Appropriate Technology in Health (p. 364)

✚ HEALTH TOPICS: RESEARCH AND ADVOCACY

See also Animals and Plants (chap. 9); General Policy: Medical Devices and Technology (this chapter); Mental Health (this chapter). For research on aging, see Health Services for Special Groups, Elderly (this chapter)

AGENCIES

Armed Forces Institute of Pathology *(Defense Dept.), 14th St. and Alaska Ave. N.W. 20306-6000; (202) 782-2100. Fax, (202) 782-9376. Capt. Glenn Wagner (USN), Director. Web, www.afip.org.*

Maintains a central laboratory of pathology for consultation and diagnosis of pathologic tissue for the Defense Dept., other federal agencies, and civilian pathologists. Conducts research and provides instruction in advanced pathology and related subjects; monitors international research.

Armed Forces Radiobiology Research Institute *(Defense Dept.), 8901 Wisconsin Ave., Bethesda, MD 20889-5603; (301) 295-1210. Fax, (301) 295-4967. Col. Robert Eng (MSUSA), Director. Web, www.afrri.usuhs.mil.*

Serves as the principal ionizing radiation radiobiology research laboratory under the jurisdiction of the Uniformed Services University of the Health Sciences. Participates in international conferences and projects. Library open to the public.

Environment, Safety, and Health *(Energy Dept.), Health Studies, 19901 Germantown Rd., EH-6/27OCC, Germantown, MD 20874-1290; (301) 903-5926. Fax,*

(301) 903-3445. Paul J. Seligman, Deputy Assistant Secretary.

Manages the federal program that addresses the potential health effects of electric and magnetic fields. Oversees the epidemiologic studies programs, the international health studies programs, and the occupational medicine and medical surveillance programs of the Energy Dept.

Fogarty International Center *(National Institutes of Health), 9000 Rockville Pike, Bldg. 31, #B2C02, Bethesda, MD 20892-2220; (301) 496-1415. Fax, (301) 402-2173. Dr. Gerald T. Keusch, Director. Web, www.nih.gov/fic.*

Coordinates international epidemiologic research on chronic and infectious diseases. Disseminates information on biomedical research in the United States and abroad; studies international health issues. Directs John E. Fogarty International Center/World Health Organization programs in biomedical research and training.

Health Resources and Services Administration *(Health and Human Services Dept.), Special Programs: Transplantation, 5600 Fishers Lane, #7C22, Rockville, MD 20857; (301) 443-7577. Fax, (301) 594-6095. John L. Nelson, Deputy Administrator.*

Implements provisions of the National Organ Transplant Act. Provides information on federal, state, and private programs involved in transplantation; supports a national computerized network for organ procurement and matching; maintains information on transplant recipients; awards grants to organ procurement organizations. Administers the National Marrow Donor Program, which maintains a registry of potential unrelated bone marrow donors.

National Heart, Lung, and Blood Institute *(National Institutes of Health), 9000 Rockville Pike, Bldg. 31, #5A52, Bethesda, MD 20892-2486; (301) 496-5166. Fax, (301) 402-0818. Dr. Claude Lenfant, Director; Dr. Ruth Hegyeli, Director, International Programs, (301) 496-5375. Web, www.nhlbi.nih.gov.*

Collects and disseminates information on diseases of the heart, lungs, and blood, on sleep disorders, and on transfusion medicine, with an emphasis on disease prevention. Conducts educational programs for scientists and clinicians; participates in international research.

National Institute of Diabetes and Digestive and Kidney Diseases *(National Institutes of Health), Chronic Renal Disease, 31 Center Dr., MSC 2560, Bldg. 31, #9A52, Bethesda, MD 20892-2560; (301) 496-5877. Fax, (301) 402-2125. Dr. Allen M. Spiegel, Director.*

Conducts and supports research on kidney, urologic, hematologic, digestive, metabolic, and endocrine dis-

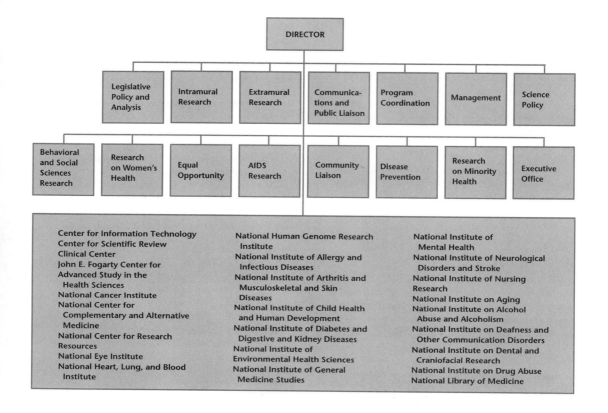

eases, as well as on diabetes and nutrition. Provides health information to the public; participates in international research.

National Institute of General Medical Sciences *(National Institutes of Health), 45 Center Dr., MSC-6200, #2AN12B, Bethesda, MD 20892-6200; (301) 594-2172. Fax, (301) 402-0156. Marvin Cassman, Director. Web, www.nih.gov/nigms.*

Supports basic biomedical research and training that are not targeted to specific diseases; focus includes cell biology, genetics, pharmacology, and systemic response to trauma and anesthesia.

National Institutes of Health (NIH), *(Health and Human Services Dept.), 1 Center Dr., Bldg. 1, #126, Bethesda, MD 20892-0148; (301) 496-2433. Fax, (301) 402-2700. Ruth L. Kirschstein, Director (Acting). Press, (301) 496-4461. Web, www.nih.gov.*

Supports and conducts biomedical research on the causes and prevention of diseases; furnishes health professionals and the public with information.

National Institutes of Health *(Health and Human Services Dept.), Center for Information Technology, 9000 Rockville Pike, Bldg. 12A, #3033, Bethesda, MD 20892-5654; (301) 496-5703. Fax, (301) 402-1754. Alan Graeff, Director. Information, (301) 496-6203. Web, www.cit.nih.gov/home.asp.*

Responsible for incorporating computers into biomedical research and administrative procedures of NIH. Serves as the primary scientific and technological resource for NIH in the areas of high performance computing, database applications, mathematics, statistics, laboratory automation, engineering, computer science and technology, telecommunications, and information resources management.

National Institutes of Health *(Health and Human Services Dept.), Center for Scientific Review, 6701 Rockledge Dr. MSC-7776, Rockledge II Bldg., #3109, Bethesda, MD 20892-7776; (301) 435-1114. Fax, (301) 480-3965. Dr. Ellie Ehrenfeld, Director.*

Conducts scientific merit review of research grant and fellowship applications submitted to NIH. Assists in formulating grant and award policies.

National Institutes of Health *(Health and Human Services Dept.), Minority Opportunities in Research, 45 Center Dr., Bldg. 45, #2AS.37, Bethesda, MD 20892; (301) 594-3900. Fax, (301) 480-2753. Dr. Clifton A. Poodry, Director.*

Awards grants to eligible minority universities and colleges to support biomedical research by minority students and faculty; funds development of research facilities.

National Institutes of Health *(Health and Human Services Dept.), National Center for Complementary and Alternative Medicine, 31 Center Dr., Bldg. 31, #5B38, Bethesda, MD 20892-2182; (301) 435-5042. Fax, (301) 402-4741. Dr. Stephen E. Straus, Director. Information, (888) 644-6226. TTY, (888) 644-6226. General e-mail, nccam-info@nccam.nih.gov. Web, nccam.nih.gov.*

Conducts and supports complementary and alternative medicine research and training; disseminates information to practitioners and the public; works with the Food and Drug Administration (FDA) to evaluate the current rules and regulations governing research on and the use of devices, acupuncture needles, herbs, and homeopathic remedies.

National Institutes of Health *(Health and Human Services Dept.), National Center for Research Resources, 31 South Dr. MSC-2128, Bldg. 31, #3B11, Bethesda, MD 20892-2128; (301) 496-5793. Fax, (301) 402-0006. Dr. Judith L. Vaitukaitis, Director. Web, www.ncrr.nih.gov.*

Discovers, develops, and provides biomedical researchers with access to critical research technologies and resources, including sophisticated instrumentation, models of human disease, and clinical research environments.

National Institutes of Health *(Health and Human Services Dept.), Protection from Research Risks, 6100 Executive Blvd., #3B01, Rockville, MD 20892-7507; (301) 496-7005. Fax, (301) 402-2071. Gary B. Ellis, Director. Human subjects, (301) 496-7041. Animal welfare, (301) 496-7163. Web, www.grants.nih.gov/grants/oprr/oprr.htm.*

Monitors the use of humans and animals in research to ensure that programs and procedures comply with Public Health Service and Health and Human Services Dept. regulations; conducts and develops educational programs for the protection of human subjects and the humane care and use of laboratory animals; helps other organizations address ethical issues in medicine and research.

National Institutes of Health *(Health and Human Services Dept.), Research on Minority Health, 1 Center Dr., Bldg. 1, #258, Bethesda, MD 20892-0164; (301) 402-1366. Fax, (301) 402-7040. Dr. John Ruffin, Associate Director.*

Coordinates the development of NIH policies and objectives related to minority health research and research training programs. Encourages minorities to work in the biomedical research field.

National Library of Medicine *(National Institutes of Health), 8600 Rockville Pike, Bldg. 38, #2E17, Bethesda, MD 20894-0002; (301) 496-6221. Fax, (301) 496-4450. Dr. Donald A. B. Lindberg, Director. Web, www.nlm.nih.gov.*

Offers medical library services and computer-based reference service to the public, health professionals, libraries in medical schools and hospitals, and research institutions; operates a toxicology information service for the scientific community, industry, and federal agencies; assists medical libraries through the National Network of Libraries of Medicines with research in medical library science. Assists in the improvement of basic library resources.

National Library of Medicine *(National Institutes of Health), Health Information Programs Development, 8600 Rockville Pike, Bldg. 38, #2S20, Bethesda, MD 20894; (301) 496-2311. Fax, (301) 496-4450. Elliot R. Siegel, Associate Director.*

Facilitates worldwide use of the library's medical databases, through agreements with individual nations, international organizations, and commercial vendors. Helps the library acquire and share international biomedical literature; promotes international collaboration in creating new databases. Conducts programs for international visitors.

Naval Medical Research Center *(Defense Dept.), 503 Robert Grant Ave., Silver Spring, MD 20910-7500; (301) 319-7400. Fax, (301) 319-7410. Capt. Richard Hibbs, Commanding Officer. Web, www.nmri.nnmc.navy.mil.*

Performs basic and applied biomedical research in areas of military importance, including infectious diseases, hyperbaric medicine, wound repair enhancement, environmental stress, and immunobiology. Provides support to field laboratories and naval hospitals; monitors research internationally.

Walter Reed Army Institute of Research *(Defense Dept.)*, 6825 16th St. N.W., #1103 20307-5100; (202) 782-3551. Fax, (202) 782-3114. Col. Martin H. Crumrine, Director. Web, wrair-www.army.mil.

Provides research, education, and training in support of the Defense Dept.'s health care system. Interests include biochemistry, biometrics, pathology, surgery, veterinary medicine, naturally occurring infectious diseases of military importance, battle casualties, operational hazards, and defense against biological and chemical agents.

Warren Grant Magnuson Clinical Center *(National Institutes of Health)*, 9000 Rockville Pike, Bldg. 10, #2C146, Bethesda, MD 20892-1504; (301) 496-4114. Fax, (301) 402-0244. Dr. John I. Gallin, Director. Web, www.cc.nih.gov.

Serves as a clinical research center for the NIH; patients are referred by physicians and self-referred throughout the United States and overseas.

CONGRESS

House Commerce Committee, *Subcommittee on Health and the Environment,* 2125 RHOB 20515; (202) 225-2927. Fax, (202) 225-1919. Rep. Michael Bilirakis, R-Fla., Chair; James E. Derderian, Staff Director. General e-mail, commerce@mail.house.gov. Web, www.house.gov/commerce.

Jurisdiction over legislation on health research, the treatment of cancer, AIDS, medical research on human subjects, and developmental disabilities (including epilepsy, cerebral palsy, autism, and mental retardation).

House Science Committee, *Subcommittee on Basic Research,* B374 RHOB 20515; (202) 225-7858. Fax, (202) 225-7815. Rep. Nick Smith, R-Mich., Chair; Steve Eule, Staff Director. Web, www.house.gov/science.

Jurisdiction over legislation on research and development involving health, nutrition, and medical programs.

Senate Health, Education, Labor, and Pensions Committee, *Subcommittee on Public Health,* SD-424 20510; (202) 224-7139. Fax, (202) 228-0928. Sen. Bill Frist, R-Tenn., Chair; Anne Phelps, Staff Director. Web, labor.senate.gov.

Jurisdiction over legislation on health research and health professions education. Oversight of public health programs, including the National Institutes of Health, Agency for Health Care Policy and Research, and Substance Abuse and Mental Health Services Administration.

NONPROFIT

American Physiological Society, 9650 Rockville Pike, Bethesda, MD 20814-3991; (301) 530-7118. Fax, (301)

571-8305. Dr. Martin Frank, Executive Director. General e-mail, info@aps.faseb.org. Web, www.faseb.org/aps.

Researches how the body and its organ systems function. Promotes scientific research, education, and dissemination of information through publication of peer-reviewed journals; monitors international research. Offers travel fellowships for scientific meetings; encourages minority participation in physiological research. Works to establish standards for the humane care and use of laboratory animals.

American Trauma Society, 8903 Presidential Pkwy., #512, Upper Marlboro, MD 20772-2656; (301) 420-4189. Fax, (301) 420-0617. Harry Teter, Executive Director. General e-mail, atstrauma@aol.com. Web, www.amtrauma.org.

Seeks to prevent trauma and improve its treatment. Coordinates programs aimed at reducing the incidence and severity of trauma; sponsors research; provides training to nurses and others involved in the trauma field. Monitors legislation and regulations.

Assn. for Health Services Research, 1130 Connecticut Ave. N.W., #700 20036; (202) 223-2477. Fax, (202) 835-8972. W. David Helms, Chief Executive Officer. Web, www.ahsr.org.

Membership: individuals and organizations with an interest in health services research, including universities, private research organizations, professional associations, consulting firms, advocacy organizations, insurers, managed care companies, health care systems, and pharmaceutical companies. Serves as an information clearinghouse on health services research; works to increase public and private funding for research. Monitors legislation and regulations.

Center for Patient Advocacy, 1350 Beverly Rd., #108, McLean, VA 22101; (703) 748-0400. Fax, (703) 748-0402. Terre McFillen Hall, Executive Director. Information, (800) 846-7444. General e-mail, patientadv@erols.com. Web, www.patientadvocacy.org.

Represents the interests of patients nationwide. Dedicated to ensuring that patients have timely access to state-of-the-art health care.

Howard Hughes Medical Institute, 4000 Jones Bridge Rd., Chevy Chase, MD 20815-6789; (301) 215-8500. Fax, (301) 215-8663. Dr. Thomas Cech, President. Web, www.hhmi.org.

Conducts biomedical research programs in major academic medical centers and universities. Areas of research include cell biology, genetics, immunology, neuroscience, and structural biology. Maintains a grants program in science education, including postgraduate, graduate, undergraduate, and precollege levels. Supports selected biomedical researchers in foreign countries.

Impotence World Assn., *6911 Laurel-Bowie Rd., #301, Bowie, MD 20715 (mailing address: P.O. Box 410, Bowie, MD 20718-0410); (301) 262-2400. Fax, (301) 262-6825. Victoria Tate, Executive Director. Information, (800) 669-1603. Web, www.impotenceworld.org.*

Represents impotent men and their partners, physicians who treat impotence, and the industry that develops products for treatment. Provides members with medical referrals and educational materials. Sponsors national support group, Impotence Anonymous; maintains toll-free help line.

Institute for Alternative Futures, *100 N. Pitt St., #235, Alexandria, VA 22314-3134; (703) 684-5880. Fax, (703) 684-0640. Clement Bezold, President. General e-mail, futurist@altfutures.com. Web, www.altfutures.com.*

Research and educational organization that explores the implications of scientific developments. Works with state and local governments, Congress, and associations; conducts seminars. Interests include pharmaceutical research, health care, telecommunications, artificial intelligence, and the environment.

Institute of Medicine, *2101 Constitution Ave. N.W. 20418; (202) 334-3300. Fax, (202) 334-3851. Kenneth I. Shine, President. Information, (202) 334-2169. Library, (202) 334-2125. Press, (202) 334-2138. Web, www.national-academies.org.*

Independent research organization chartered by the National Academy of Sciences. Studies policy issues related to health and medicine and issues position statements; interests include international health. National Academy of Sciences library open to the public by appointment.

Johns Hopkins University Applied Physics Laboratory, *11100 Johns Hopkins Rd., Laurel, MD 20723-6099; (240) 228-5000. Fax, (240) 228-1093. Richard Roca, Director. Information, (240) 228-5021. Web, www.jhuapl.edu.*

Organization that, with affiliated medical centers, conducts research and develops engineering-related biomedical programs and high technology systems to improve medical care.

National Sleep Foundation, *729 15th St. N.W., 5th Floor 20005-1253; (202) 347-3471. Fax, (202) 347-3472. Richard Gelula, Executive Director. General e-mail, natsleep@erols.com. Web, www.sleepfoundation.org.*

Promotes research to understand sleep disorders, including insomnia, sleep apnea, and narcolepsy. Works

to prevent sleep-related accidents, especially those that involve driving.

Research!America, *908 King St., #400 East, Alexandria, VA 22314-3067; (703) 739-2577. Fax, (703) 739-2372. Mary Woolley, President. Information, (800) 366-2873. Web, www.researchamerica.org.*

Membership: academic institutions, professional societies, voluntary health organizations, corporations, and individuals interested in promoting medical research. Provides information on the benefits of medical research and seeks to increase funding for research.

SRI International, *Washington Office, 1611 N. Kent St., #700, Arlington, VA 22209; (703) 524-2053. Fax, (703) 247-8569. William Mohr, Director. Web, www.sri.com.*

Research and consulting organization. Conducts studies on biotechnology, genetic engineering, drug metabolism, cancer, toxicology, disease control systems, and other areas of basic and applied research; monitors international research. (Headquarters in Menlo Park, Calif.)

Undersea and Hyperbaric Medical Society, *10531 Metropolitan Ave., Kensington, MD 20895-2627; (301) 942-2980. Fax, (301) 942-7804. Leon J. Greenbaum Jr., Executive Director. General e-mail, uhms@uhms.org. Web, www.uhms.org.*

Works internationally to advance undersea and hyperbaric medicine and its supporting sciences. Studies the effect of greater than normal atmospheric pressure on the human body. Serves as a forum for information exchange on scientific issues.

Whitaker Foundation, *1700 N. Moore St., #2200, Rosslyn, VA 22209; (703) 528-2430. Fax, (703) 528-2431. Dr. Peter Katona, President. General e-mail, info@whitaker.org. Web, www.whitaker.org.*

Dedicated to improving human health through the support of biomedical engineering. Awards grants and fellowships to universities in the fields of biomedical engineering research, development, and education.

See also American Institutes for Research (p. 618); American Roentgen Ray Society (p. 364)

AIDS and HIV

See also Blood and Bone Marrow (this chapter)

AGENCIES

Centers for Disease Control and Prevention *(Health and Human Services Dept.), Washington Office, 200 Independence Ave. S.W., #746-G 20201-0004; (202) 690-*

8598. Fax, (202) 690-7519. Donald E. Shriber, Associate Director. Web, www.cdc.gov.

Conducts research to prevent and control acquired immune deficiency syndrome (AIDS); promotes public awareness through guidelines for health care workers, educational packets for schools, and monthly reports on incidences of AIDS. (Headquarters in Atlanta: 1600 Clifton Rd. N.E. 30333. Public inquiries, [404] 639-3534.)

Food and Drug Administration (FDA), *(Health and Human Services Dept.), Center for Biologics Evaluation and Research, 1401 Rockville Pike, #200 North, Rockville, MD 20852-1448; (301) 827-0372. Fax, (301) 827-0440. Kathryn C. Zoon, Director; Dr. Elaine C. Esber, Associate Director, Medical and International Affairs, (301) 827-0641. Press, (301) 827-2000. Web, www.fda.gov/cber.*

Develops testing standards for vaccines, blood supply, and blood products and derivatives to prevent transmission of the human immunodeficiency virus (HIV); regulates biological therapeutics; helps formulate international standards. Serves as the focus for AIDS activities within the FDA.

Food and Drug Administration *(Health and Human Services Dept.), Center for Drug Evaluation and Research, 1451 Rockville Pike, Rockville, MD 20852; (301) 594-5400. Fax, (301) 594-6197. Dr. Janet Woodcock, Director. Information, (301) 827-4573. Press, (301) 827-6242.*

Approves new drugs for AIDS and AIDS-related diseases. Reviews and approves applications to investigate and market new drugs; works to harmonize drug approval internationally.

Health Resources and Services Administration *(Health and Human Services Dept.), HIV/AIDS Bureau, 5600 Fishers Lane, #705, Rockville, MD 20857; (301) 443-1993. Fax, (301) 443-9645. Joseph F. O'Neill, Associate Administrator.*

Administers grants to support health care programs for AIDS patients, including those that reimburse low-income patients for drug expenses. Provides patients with AIDS and HIV-related disorders with ambulatory and community-based care. Conducts AIDS/HIV education and training activities for health professionals.

National Institute of Allergy and Infectious Diseases *(National Institutes of Health), AIDS, 6700-B Rockledge Dr., #4142, Bethesda, MD 20892-7620; (301) 496-0545. Fax, (301) 402-1505. Dr. John Killen, Director. Toll-free hotline, (800) 342-2437. Web, www.niaid.nih.gov/research/daids.htm.*

Primary institute at NIH for AIDS research. Conducts a network of AIDS clinical trials and preclinical drug development research. Supports epidemiological studies and research into AIDS vaccines. Studies the pathogenesis of HIV infection.

Office of National AIDS Policy *(Executive Office of the President), 736 Jackson Pl. N.W. 20503; (202) 456-2437. Fax, (202) 456-2438. Sandra L. Thurman, Director.*

Advises the president and formulates policy on matters related to AIDS and AIDS treatment.

Public Health and Science *(Health and Human Services Dept.), HIV/AIDS Policy, 200 Independence Ave. S.W., #736E 20201; (202) 690-5560. Fax, (202) 690-7560. Dr. Eric Goosby, Director.*

Coordinates national AIDS policy, sets priorities, recommends funding, and helps implement all Public Health Service HIV programs. Monitors progress of prevention and control programs; serves as a liaison with governmental and private organizations.

Public Health and Science *(Health and Human Services Dept.), Minority Health, 5515 Security Lane, #1000, Rockwall II Bldg., Rockville, MD 20852; (301) 443-5084. Fax, (301) 594-0767. Nathan Stinson, Deputy Assistant Secretary (Acting). Information, (800) 444-6472. General e-mail, info@omhrc.gov. Web, www.omhrc.gov.*

Awards grants to minority AIDS education and prevention projects to administer health promotion, education, and disease prevention programs.

Walter Reed Army Institute of Research *(Defense Dept.), Combined Military Diagnostic Retrovirology Service, 1600 E. Gude Dr., Rockville, MD 20850-5318; (301) 251-5000. Fax, (301) 309-8346. Dr. Deborah Birx, Director.*

Conducts and funds AIDS research for the military's retrovirus program; oversees AIDS testing for Defense Dept. personnel.

Warren Grant Magnuson Clinical Center *(National Institutes of Health), Transfusion Medicine, 10 Center Dr. MSC-1184, Bldg. 10, #1C711, Bethesda, MD 20892-1184; (301) 496-9702. Fax, (301) 594-1981. Dr. Harvey Klein, Chief. Information, (301) 496-4506.*

Supplies blood and blood components for patient care and research. Conducts research on diseases transmissible by blood, primarily AIDS and hepatitis.

***See also National Museum of Health and Medicine** (p. 154)*

NONPROFIT

AIDS Action, *1906 Sunderland Pl. N.W. 20036; (202) 530-8030. Fax, (202) 530-8031. Claudia French, Executive*

Director (Acting). General e-mail, aidsaction@aidsaction. org. Web, www.aidsaction.org.

Promotes and monitors legislation on AIDS research and education and on related public policy issues.

AIDS Alliance for Children, Youth, and Families, *1600 St. N.W., #300 20006; (202) 785-3564. Fax, (202) 785-3579. David C. Harvey, Executive Director. General e-mail, info@aids-alliance.org. Web, www.aids-alliance.org.*

Conducts research and disseminates information on health care and HIV issues. Develops and promotes policy aimed at improving the health and welfare of children, youth, and families affected by HIV. Provides training and technical assistance to health care providers and consumers.

AIDS National Interfaith Network, *110 Maryland Ave., #504 20002; (202) 546-0807. Scott Harrison, Executive Director (Acting). General e-mail, aninscott@aol.com. Web, www.anin.org.*

Coordinates national network of faith-based, AIDS-specific ministries. Maintains a database on the HIV/AIDS activities of religious organizations. Educates AIDS service organizations, the religious community, and the general public about AIDS and AIDS ministries. (Affiliated with the Council of Religious AIDS Networks.)

American Foundation for AIDS Research, *Public Policy, Washington Office, 1828 L St. N.W., #802 20036; (202) 331-8600. Fax, (202) 331-8606. Jane Silver, Director. Information, (800) 392-6327. Web, www.amfar.org.*

Supports funding for basic biomedical and clinical AIDS research; promotes AIDS prevention education worldwide; advocates effective AIDS-related public policy. Monitors legislation, regulations, and international research. (Headquarters in New York.)

American Red Cross, *National Headquarters, 430 17th St. N.W., 2nd Floor 20006-2401; (202) 737-8300. Fax, (202) 783-3432. Dr. Bernadine Healy, President. Web, www.redcross.org.*

Humanitarian relief and health education organization chartered by Congress. Conducts public education campaigns on AIDS.

Human Rights Campaign, *919 18th St. N.W., #800 20006; (202) 628-4160. Fax, (202) 347-5323. Elizabeth Birch, Executive Director. General e-mail, hrc@hrc.org. Web, www.hrc.org.*

Promotes legislation to fund AIDS research.

National AIDS Fund, *1400 Eye St. N.W., #1220 20005-2208; (202) 408-4848. Fax, (202) 408-1818. Mary Wilson-*

Byrom, President (Acting). Toll-free, (888) 234-AIDS. General e-mail, info@aidsfund.org. Web, www.aidsfund.org.

Provides grants to support state HIV/AIDS programs. Assists public health agencies in developing new models of community-based care and prevention. Supports community leadership with financial, program, and technical assistance. Administers the Workplace Resource Center, which works with businesses to create AIDS policies, guidelines, and education programs.

National Assn. of People with AIDS, *1413 K St. N.W., 7th Floor 20005; (202) 898-0414. Fax, (202) 898-0435. Terje Anderson, Executive Director (Acting). Fax-on-demand, (202) 789-2222. Web, www.napwa.org.*

Membership: people with AIDS or HIV disease. Provides persons infected by AIDS or HIV disease with information and social service referrals; contributes to educational campaigns about AIDS; maintains speakers bureau.

National Minority AIDS Council, *1931 13th St. N.W. 20009; (202) 483-6622. Fax, (202) 483-1135. Paul A. Kawata, Executive Director. Web, www.nmac.org.*

Works to encourage leadership within minority communities responding to the HIV/AIDS epidemic; provides community-based AIDS programs with technical assistance. Disseminates information on AIDS, especially information on the impact of the disease on minority communities. Monitors legislation and regulations.

Arthritis

AGENCIES

National Institute of Arthritis and Musculoskeletal and Skin Diseases *(National Institutes of Health), 31 Center Dr., MSC-2350, #4C32, Bethesda, MD 20892-2350; (301) 496-4353. Fax, (301) 480-6069. Dr. Stephen I. Katz, Director. Information, (301) 496-8190. Web, www.nih.gov/niams.*

Conducts and funds research on arthritis, rheumatic, skin, muscle, and bone diseases and musculoskeletal disorders. Funds national arthritis centers.

National Institute of Arthritis and Musculoskeletal and Skin Diseases Information Clearinghouse *(National Institutes of Health), 1 AMS Circle, Bethesda, MD 20892-3675; (301) 495-4484. Fax, (301) 718-6366. Kelly Collins, Project Manager. TTY, (301) 565-2966. Toll-free, (877) 226-4267. Web, www.nih.gov/niams.*

Provides physicians and the public with educational materials related to rheumatic, musculoskeletal, and skin diseases.

Blood and Bone Marrow

In this chapter, see also AIDS and HIV; Genetic Disorders; Heart Disease, Strokes

AGENCIES

Health Resources and Services Administration *(Health and Human Services Dept.), Special Programs: Transplantation,* 5600 Fishers Lane, #7C22, Rockville, MD 20857; (301) 443-7577. Fax, (301) 594-6095. John L. Nelson, Deputy Administrator.

Administers the National Marrow Donor Program, which maintains a registry of potential unrelated bone marrow donors.

National Heart, Lung, and Blood Institute *(National Institutes of Health), Blood Diseases and Resources,* 6701 Rockledge Dr., MSC-7950, Bethesda, MD 20892-7950; (301) 435-0080. Fax, (301) 480-0867. Dr. Barbara Alving, Director.

Administers and conducts research and training programs to improve the diagnosis, prevention, and treatment of blood diseases and related disorders. Works to ensure the efficient and safe use and adequate supply of high-quality blood and blood products.

National Heart, Lung, and Blood Institute *(National Institutes of Health), Blood Resources Program,* 6701 Rockledge Dr., MSC-7950, Bethesda, MD 20892-7950; (301) 435-0075. Fax, (301) 480-0868. Dr. Henry Chang, Director.

Promotes and supports research on bone marrow and stem cell transplantation technology and on transplantation procedure-related complications.

National Heart, Lung, and Blood Institute *(National Institutes of Health), Information Center,* P.O. Box 30105, Bethesda, MD 20824-0105; (301) 592-8573. Fax, (301) 592-8563. Brian Marquis, Manager. Press, (301) 496-4236. Web, www.nhlbi.nih.gov.

Acquires, maintains, and disseminates information on cholesterol and high blood pressure. Provides reference and referral services.

National Institute of Diabetes and Digestive and Kidney Diseases *(National Institutes of Health), Hematology,* 45 Center Dr., Natcher Bldg., #6AS-13C, Bethesda, MD 20892-6600; (301) 594-7717. Fax, (301) 480-3510. David G. Badman, Director.

Supports basic research on and clinical studies of the states of blood cell formation, mobilization, and release. Interests include anemia associated with chronic diseases, iron and white blood cell metabolism, and genetic control of hemoglobin.

Warren Grant Magnuson Clinical Center *(National Institutes of Health), Transfusion Medicine,* 10 Center Dr. MSC-1184, Bldg. 10, #1C711, Bethesda, MD 20892-1184; (301) 496-9702. Fax, (301) 594-1981. Dr. Harvey Klein, Chief. Information, (301) 496-4506.

Supplies blood and blood components for research and patient care. Provides training programs and conducts research in the preparation and transfusion of blood and blood products. Research topics include hepatitis, automated cell separation, immunohematology, and AIDS transmittal through transfusions.

NONPROFIT

American Assn. of Blood Banks, 8101 Glenbrook Rd., Bethesda, MD 20814-2749; (301) 907-6977. Fax, (301) 907-6895. Karen Shoos-Lipton, Executive Officer. General e-mail, aabb@aabb.org. Web, www.aabb.org.

Membership: hospital and community blood centers, transfusion and transplantation services, and individuals involved in transfusion and transplantation medicine. Supports high medical standards, scientific investigation, clinical application, and education. Encourages the voluntary donation of blood and other tissues and organs through education and public information.

American Red Cross, *National Headquarters,* 430 17th St. N.W., 2nd Floor 20006-2401; (202) 737-8300. Fax, (202) 783-3432. Dr. Bernadine Healy, President. Web, www.redcross.org.

Humanitarian relief and health education organization chartered by Congress; provides services in the United States and internationally. Collects blood and maintains blood centers; conducts research; operates the national bone marrow registry and a rare-donor registry; operates transfusion alternative program. Conducts training programs in nursing and first aid; trains volunteers. Serves as U.S. member of the International Federation of Red Cross and Red Crescent Societies.

Cancer

See also Nursing Homes and Hospices (this chapter)

AGENCIES

National Cancer Institute *(National Institutes of Health),* 31 Center Dr., MSC-2590, #11A48, Bethesda, MD 20892; (301) 496-5615. Fax, (301) 402-0338. Dr. Richard D. Klausner, Director; Dr. Joe Harford, Associate Director, Special Projects, (301) 496-5534. Information, (301) 435-7782. Press, (301) 496-6641. Web, www.nci.nih.gov.

Conducts and funds research on the causes, diagnosis, treatment, prevention, control, and biology of cancer and the rehabilitation of cancer patients; administers the National Cancer Program; coordinates international research activities. Sponsors regional and national cancer information services.

National Cancer Institute *(National Institutes of Health), Cancer Prevention, 31 Center Dr., MSC-2580, #10A52, Bethesda, MD 20892-2580; (301) 496-6616. Fax, (301) 496-9931. Dr. Peter Greenwald, Director.*

Funds projects for innovative and effective approaches to preventing and controlling cancer. Coordinates support for establishing multidisciplinary cancer care and clinical research activities in community hospitals. Supports cancer research training, clinical and continuing education, and career development.

National Cancer Institute *(National Institutes of Health), International Cancer Information Center, 9030 Old Georgetown Rd., Bldg. 82, Bethesda, MD 20892; (301) 496-9096. Fax, (301) 480-8105. Dr. Anne Thurn, Director (Acting). Web, www.nci.nih.gov.*

Collects and disseminates scientific information on cancer biology, etiology, screening, prevention, treatment, and supportive care. Evaluates and develops new media formats for cancer information.

National Cancer Institute *(National Institutes of Health), Organ Systems Branch, 6116 Executive Blvd., #7008, MSC 8347, Rockville, MD 20852; (301) 496-8528. Fax, (301) 402-5319. Dr. Jorge Gomez, Chief.*

Encourages the study of cancers in solid tumors. Encourages multidisciplinary research linking laboratory and clinical medicine.

President's Cancer Panel, *c/o National Cancer Institute, 31 Center Dr., #4A48, MSC-2473, Bethesda, MD 20892-2473; (301) 496-1148. Fax, (301) 402-1508. Dr. Maureen O. Wilson, Executive Secretary. General e-mail, prescan@nih.gov. Web, www.deainfo.nci.nih.gov/advisory/pop/pcp.htm.*

Presidentially appointed committee that monitors and evaluates the National Cancer Program; reports to the president and Congress.

NONPROFIT

American Cancer Society, *National Government Relations, Washington Office, 701 Pennsylvania Ave. N.W., #650 20004; (202) 661-5700. Fax, (202) 661-5750. Lisa Halpern, Director. Information, (800) 227-2345. Web, www.cancer.org.*

Nationwide community-based voluntary health organization dedicated to eliminating cancer as a major health problem by preventing cancer, saving lives, and diminishing suffering from cancer through research, education, advocacy, and service. Monitors legislation. (Headquarters in Atlanta.)

American Institute for Cancer Research, *1759 R St. N.W. 20009-2583; (202) 328-7744. Fax, (202) 328-7226. Marilyn Gentry, Executive Director. Information, (800) 843-8114. Web, www.aicr.org.*

Funds cancer research in areas of diet and nutrition; sponsors education programs. Library open to the public by appointment.

American Society for Therapeutic Radiology and Oncology, *12500 Fair Lakes Circle, #375, Fairfax, VA 22033-3882; (703) 502-1550. Fax, (703) 502-7852. Frank Malouff, Executive Director. Toll-free, (800) 962-7876. Web, www.astro.org.*

Seeks to advance the practice of radiation oncology; disseminates data on scientific research; sponsors workshops and conferences. Monitors legislation and regulations.

American Society of Clinical Oncology, *225 Reinekers Lane, #650, Alexandria, VA 22314; (703) 299-0150. Fax, (703) 299-1044. Dr. Charles Balch, Executive Vice President. Web, www.asco.org.*

Membership: physicians and scientists specializing in cancer prevention, treatment, education, and research. Promotes exchange of information in clinical research and patient care relating to all stages of cancer; monitors international research.

Assn. of Community Cancer Centers, *11600 Nebel St., #201, Rockville, MD 20852-2538; (301) 984-9496. Fax, (301) 770-1949. Lee E. Mortenson, Executive Director. Web, www.accc-cancer.org.*

Membership: individuals from community hospitals involved in multidisciplinary cancer programs, including physicians, administrators, nurses, medical directors, pharmacists, and other members of the cancer care team.

Candlelighters Childhood Cancer Foundation, *3910 Warner St., Kensington, MD 20895; (301) 962-3520. Fax, (301) 962-3521. Ruth Hoffman, Executive Director. Information, (800) 366-2223. General e-mail, info@ candlelighters.org. Web, www.candlelighters.org.*

Membership: families of children with cancer, survivors of childhood cancer, and health and education professionals. Serves as an information and educational network; sponsors self-help groups for parents of children and adolescents with cancer. Monitors legislation and regulations.

Leukemia and Lymphoma Society of America, *Washington Office, 5845 Richmond Hwy., #630, Alexandria, VA 22303; (703) 960-1100. Fax, (703) 960-0920. David M. Timko, Executive Director. Information, (800) 955-4572. Web, www.leukemia.org.*

Seeks to expand knowledge of leukemia, lymphoma, and allied diseases. Conducts research; provides research scholarships and fellowships; maintains speakers bureau. Local chapters provide leukemia and lymphoma patients with financial assistance, counseling, and referrals. (Headquarters in New York.)

National Breast Cancer Coalition, *1707 L St. N.W., #1060 20036; (202) 296-7477. Fax, (202) 265-6854. Fran Visco, President. Web, www.stopbreastcancer.org.*

Membership: organizations, local coalitions, and individuals. Advocates increased funding for research to prevent and treat breast cancer; promotes better access to screening and care; conducts training for breast cancer activists.

National Coalition for Cancer Survivorship, *1010 Wayne Ave., #700, Silver Spring, MD 20910-5600; (301) 650-9127. Fax, (301) 565-9670. Ellen L. Stovall, Executive Director. Information, (888) 937-6227. General e-mail, info@cansearch.org. Web, www.cansearch.org.*

Membership: survivors of cancer (newly diagnosed to long-term), their families and friends, health care providers, and support organizations. Disseminates information about living with cancer; works to reduce cancer-based discrimination in employment and insurance; operates Cansearch, a guide to cancer resources on the Internet.

See also AARP Andrus Foundation (p. 381); Drug Policy Foundation (p. 366)

Diabetes, Digestive Diseases

AGENCIES

National Diabetes Information Clearinghouse *(National Institutes of Health), 1 Information Way, Bethesda, MD 20892-3560; (301) 654-3327. Fax, (301) 907-8906. Faith Osgard, Senior Information Specialist. Web, www.niddk.nih.gov.*

Provides health professionals and the public with information on the symptoms, causes, treatments, and general nature of diabetes.

National Digestive Diseases Information Clearinghouse *(National Institutes of Health), 2 Information Way, Bethesda, MD 20892-3570; (301) 654-3810. Fax, (301) 907-8906. Ruth Ann Speir, Senior Information Specialist. Web, www.niddk.nih.gov.*

Provides health professionals and the public with information on the symptoms, causes, treatments, and general nature of digestive ailments.

National Institute of Diabetes and Digestive and Kidney Diseases *(National Institutes of Health), Diabetes, Endocrinology, and Metabolic Diseases, 31 Center Dr., MSC-2560, #9A16, Bethesda, MD 20892-2560; (301) 496-7348. Fax, (301) 480-6792. Dr. Richard Eastman, Director.*

Awards grants and contracts to support basic and clinical research of diabetes mellitus and its complications.

National Institute of Diabetes and Digestive and Kidney Diseases *(National Institutes of Health), Digestive Diseases and Nutrition, 31 Center Dr., MSC-2560, #9A23, Bethesda, MD 20892-2560; (301) 496-1333. Fax, (301) 496-2830. Dr. Jay H. Hoofnagle, Director.*

Awards grants and contracts to support basic and clinical research on digestive diseases.

NONPROFIT

American Diabetes Assn., *1701 N. Beauregard St., Alexandria, VA 22311; (703) 549-1500. Fax, (703) 836-7439. John H. Graham IV, Chief Executive Officer. Information, (800) 232-3472. Web, www.diabetes.org.*

Conducts and funds research on diabetes; monitors international research. Provides local affiliates with education, information, and referral services.

American Gastroenterological Assn., *7910 Woodmont Ave., 7th Floor, Bethesda, MD 20814; (301) 654-2055. Fax, (301) 654-5920. Robert Greenberg, Executive Vice President. Web, www.gastro.org.*

Membership: gastroenterology clinicians, scientists, health care professionals, and educators. Sponsors scientific research on digestive diseases; disseminates information on new methods of prevention and treatment. Monitors legislation and regulations. (Affiliated with the American Digestive Health Foundation.)

Endocrine Society, *4350 East-West Hwy., #500, Bethesda, MD 20814-4426; (301) 941-0200. Fax, (301) 941-0259. Scott Hunt, Executive Director. Web, www.endo-society.org.*

Membership: scientists, doctors, health care educators, clinicians, nurses, and others interested in endocrine glands and their disorders. Promotes endocrinology research and clinical practice; sponsors seminars and conferences; gives awards and travel grants.

Juvenile Diabetes Foundation, *Governmental Relations, Washington Office, 1400 Eye St. N.W., #530 20005;*

(202) 371-9746. Fax, (202) 371-2760. William T. Schmidt, Director. Information, (800) 533-1868. Web, www.jdfcure. org.

Conducts research, education, and public awareness programs aimed at improving the lives of people with diabetes and finding a cure for diabetes. Monitors legislation and regulations. (Headquarters in New York.)

Family Planning and Population

See also Abortion and Reproductive Issues (chap. 14); Census/Population Data (chap. 10); Prenatal, Maternal, and Child Health Care (this chapter)

AGENCIES

Agency for International Development, *Population, 1300 Pennsylvania Ave. N.W., 3rd Floor 20723-3600; (202) 712-0540. Fax, (202) 216-3046. Margaret Neuse, Director. Web, www.info.usaid.gov/pop_health.*

Division of the AID Center for Population, Health, and Nutrition. Supports family planning and reproductive health programs; conducts research.

Census Bureau *(Commerce Dept.), Fertility and Family Statistics, 4700 Silver Hill Rd., Bldg. 3, #2351, Suitland, MD 20746-8500; (301) 457-2416. Fax, (301) 457-2396. Martin O'Connell, Chief.*

Provides data and statistics on fertility and family composition. Conducts census and survey research on the number of children, households and living arrangements, and current child spacing patterns of women in the United States, especially working mothers. Conducts studies on child care.

National Institute of Child Health and Human Development *(National Institutes of Health), Center for Population Research, 6100 Executive Blvd., #8B-07, Bethesda, MD 20892-7510; (301) 496-1101. Fax, (301) 496-0962. Dr. Florence P. Haseltine, Director.*

Supports biomedical and behavioral research on reproductive processes influencing human fertility and infertility; develops methods for regulating fertility; evaluates the safety and effectiveness of contraceptive methods; conducts research on the reproductive motivation of individuals and the causes and consequences of population change.

Public Health and Science *(Health and Human Services Dept.), Population Affairs, 4350 East-West Hwy., #200, Bethesda, MD 20814; (301) 594-4001. Fax, (301) 594-5980. Denese Shervington, Deputy Assistant Secretary. Web, www.osophs.dhhs.gov.*

Responsible for planning, monitoring, and evaluating population research, voluntary family planning, and adolescent family life programs.

Public Health and Science *(Health and Human Services Dept.), Population Affairs Clearinghouse, P.O. Box 30686, Bethesda, MD 20824-0686; (301) 654-6190. Fax, (301) 215-7731. Cathy House, Project Manager. Web, www.dhhs.gov/progorg/opa.*

Federally contracted program that collects and disseminates information on family planning general reproductive health care and related topics, including adoption, adolescent pregnancy prevention, contraception, HIV/AIDS, sexually transmitted diseases, and abstinence.

INTERNATIONAL ORGANIZATIONS

International Bank for Reconstruction and Development, *Human Development, 1818 H St. N.W., #G8005 20433 (mailing address: 1818 H St. N.W., #S9035 20433); (202) 473-3437. Fax, (202) 522-3235. Eduardo Doryan, Vice President. Web, www.worldbank.org.*

Provides member countries with loans and technical advice for family planning projects designed to slow population growth. (Works in conjunction with regional World Bank offices.)

NONPROFIT

Advocates for Youth, *1025 Vermont Ave. N.W., #200 20005; (202) 347-5700. Fax, (202) 347-2263. James Wagoner, Executive Director. General e-mail, info@ advocatesforyouth.org. Web, www.advocatesforyouth.org.*

Seeks to reduce the incidence of unintended teenage pregnancy and AIDS through public education, training and technical assistance, research, and media programs.

Alan Guttmacher Institute, *Public Policy, Washington Office, 1120 Connecticut Ave. N.W., #460 20036-3902; (202) 296-4012. Fax, (202) 223-5756. Cory L. Richards, Vice President. General e-mail, info@agi-usa.org. Web, www.agi-usa.org.*

Conducts research, policy analysis, and public education in reproductive health, fertility regulation, population, and related areas of U.S. and international health. (Headquarters in New York.)

National Abortion Federation, *1755 Massachusetts Ave. N.W., #600 20036; (202) 667-5881. Fax, (202) 667-5890. Vicki Saporta, Executive Director. Information, (800) 772-9100. Web, www.prochoice.org.*

Federation of facilities providing abortion services. Offers information on medical, legal, and social aspects of abortion; sets quality standards for abortion care.

Conducts training workshops and seminars. Monitors legislation and regulations.

National Family Planning and Reproductive Health Assn., *1627 K St. N.W., 12th Floor 20006-1702; (202) 293-3114. Fax, (202) 293-1990. Judith DeSarno, President. General e-mail, info@nfprha.org. Web, www.nfprha.org.*

Membership: health professionals and others interested in family planning and reproductive health. Operates a network for information, referral, research, policy analysis, and training designed to improve and expand the delivery of family planning services and reproductive health care.

Planned Parenthood Federation of America, *Public Policy, Washington Office, 1120 Connecticut Ave. N.W., #461 20036; (202) 785-3351. Fax, (202) 293-4349. Jacquelyn Lendsey, Vice President. Web, www.plannedparenthood. org.*

Educational, research, and medical services organization. Washington office conducts research and monitors legislation on fertility-related health topics, including abortion, reproductive health, contraception, family planning, and international population control. (Headquarters in New York accredits affiliated local centers, which offer medical services, birth control, and family planning information.)

Population Action International, *1300 19th St. N.W., #200 20036; (202) 557-3400. Fax, (202) 728-4177. Amy Coen, President. General e-mail, pai@popact.org. Web, www.populationaction.org.*

Promotes population stabilization through public education and universal access to voluntary family planning. Library open to the public by appointment.

Population-Environment Balance, *2000 P St. N.W., #600 20036; (202) 955-5700. Fax, (202) 955-6161. Maria Sepulveda, Executive Director. General e-mail, uspop@ balance.org. Web, www.balance.org.*

Grassroots organization that advocates U.S. population stabilization to safeguard the environment.

Population Institute, *107 2nd St. N.E. 20002; (202) 544-3300. Fax, (202) 544-0068. Werner Fornos, President. General e-mail, web@populationinstitute.org. Web, www. populationinstitute.org.*

Encourages leaders of developing nations to balance population growth through resource management; works with leaders of industrial nations to help achieve a balance between population and natural resources.

Population Reference Bureau, *1875 Connecticut Ave. N.W., #520 20009; (202) 483-1100. Fax, (202) 328-3937.*

Peter J. Donaldson, President. General e-mail, popref@prb. org. Web, www.prb.org.

Educational organization engaged in information dissemination, training, and policy analysis on domestic and international population trends and issues. Interests include international development and family planning programs, the environment, and U.S. social and economic policy. Library open to the public.

Zero Population Growth, *1400 16th St. N.W., #320 20036; (202) 332-2200. Fax, (202) 332-2302. Peter Kostmayer, Executive Director. General e-mail, info@zpg.org. Web, www.zpg.org.*

Membership: persons interested in sustainable world populations. Promotes the expansion of domestic and international family planning programs; supports a voluntary population stabilization policy and women's access to abortion and family planning services; works to protect the earth's resources and environment.

See also Assn. of Reproductive Health Professionals (p. 369); Program for Appropriate Technology in Health (p. 364)

Genetic Disorders

See also Biotechnology (chap. 17)

AGENCIES

Health Resources and Services Administration *(Health and Human Services Dept.), Genetic Services, 5600 Fishers Lane, #18A19, Rockville, MD 20857; (301) 443-1080. Fax, (301) 443-8604. Dr. Michele Puryear, Chief.*

Awards funds, including demonstration grants, to develop or enhance regional, local, and state genetic screening, diagnostic, counseling, and follow-up programs; assists states in their newborn screening programs; provides funding for regional hemophilia treatment centers. Supports comprehensive care for individuals and families with Cooley's anemia, and those with sickle cell anemia identified through newborn screening. Supports educational programs.

National Heart, Lung, and Blood Institute *(National Institutes of Health), Blood Disease Program, 6701 Rockledge Dr., 10th Floor, Bethesda, MD 20892-7950; (301) 435-0050. Fax, (301) 480-0868. Charles M. Peterson, Director.*

Supports research into the diagnosis and treatment of sickle cell anemia and other genetic blood disorders and continuing education programs for professionals and the public.

National Human Genome Research Institute
(National Institutes of Health), 31 Center Dr., MSC-2152, #4B09, Bethesda, MD 20892-2152; (301) 496-0844. Fax, (301) 402-0837. Dr. Francis S. Collins, Director. Information, (301) 402-0911. Web, www.nhgri.nih.gov.

Responsible, with the Energy Dept., for U.S. involvement in the international Human Genome Project, which seeks to map all genes in human DNA, as well as those of model organisms. Works to improve techniques for cloning, storing, and handling DNA and to enhance data processing and analysis; promotes exchange of information.

National Institute of Allergy and Infectious Diseases *(National Institutes of Health), Allergy, Immunology, and Transplantation, 6700 B Rockledge Dr., #5142, Bethesda, MD 20892-7640; (301) 496-1886. Fax, (301) 402-0175. Dr. Daniel Rotrosen, Director. Information, (301) 496-5717. Web, www.niaid.nih.gov/research/dait.htm.*

Focuses on the immune system as it functions to maintain health and as it malfunctions to produce disease; interests include allergies, asthma, immune deficiencies (other than AIDS), transplantation of organs and tissue, and genetics. Monitors international research.

National Institute of Diabetes and Digestive and Kidney Diseases *(National Institutes of Health), Hematology, 45 Center Dr., Natcher Bldg., #6AS-13C, Bethesda, MD 20892-6600; (301) 594-7717. Fax, (301) 480-3510. David G. Badman, Director.*

Supports basic research on and clinical studies of the states of blood cell formation, mobilization, and release. Interests include anemia associated with chronic diseases, iron and white blood cell metabolism, and genetic control of hemoglobin.

National Institute of General Medical Sciences *(National Institutes of Health), Genetics and Developmental Biology, 45 Center Dr., MSC-6200, #2AS25N, Bethesda, MD 20892-6200; (301) 594-0943. Fax, (301) 480-2228. Judith H. Greenberg, Director. Web, www.nih.gov/nigms/about_nigms/gdb.html.*

Supports research and research training in genetics.

National Institutes of Health *(Health and Human Services Dept.), Biotechnology Activities, 6000 Executive Blvd., #302, MSC 7010, Bethesda, MD 20892-7010; (301) 496-9838. Fax, (301) 496-9839. Amy Patterson, Director. Web, www.nih.gov/od/oba.*

Reviews requests submitted to NIH involving genetic testing, recombinant DNA technology, and xenotransplantation, and implements research guidelines.

NONPROFIT

Center for Sickle Cell Disease *(Howard University), 2121 Georgia Ave. N.W. 20059; (202) 806-7930. Fax, (202) 806-4517. Dr. Oswaldo Castro, Director.*

Screens and tests for sickle cell disease; conducts research; promotes public education and community involvement; provides counseling and patient care.

Cystic Fibrosis Foundation, *6931 Arlington Rd., Bethesda, MD 20814; (301) 951-4422. Fax, (301) 951-6378. Robert J. Beall, President. Information, (800) 344-4823. General e-mail, info@cff.org. Web, www.cff.org.*

Conducts research on cystic fibrosis, an inherited genetic disease affecting the respiratory and digestive systems. Provides funding for care centers; publishes and disseminates information on the disease.

Genetics Society of America, *9650 Rockville Pike, Bethesda, MD 20814; (301) 571-1825. Fax, (301) 530-7079. Elaine Strass, Executive Director. General e-mail, society@genetics.faseb.org. Web, www.faseb.org/genetics/gsa/gsamenu.htm.*

Encourages professional cooperation among persons working in genetics and related sciences; participates in international conferences.

Kennedy Institute of Ethics *(Georgetown University), Healy Hall, 4th Floor, 37th and O Sts. N.W. 20057; (202) 687-8099. Fax, (202) 687-8089. Dr. Leroy Walters, Director. Library, (800) 633-3849; in Washington, (202) 687-3885. Web, www.georgetown.edu/research/kie.*

Sponsors research on medical ethics, including legal and ethical definitions of death, allocation of scarce health resources, and recombinant DNA and human gene therapy. Supplies National Library of Medicine with online database on bioethics; publishes annual bibliography; conducts international programs and free bibliographic searches. Library open to the public.

March of Dimes, *Government Affairs, Washington Office, 1901 L St. N.W., #260 20036; (202) 659-1800. Fax, (202) 296-2964. Marina Weiss, Senior Vice President. Web, www.modimes.org.*

Works to prevent and treat birth defects. Awards grants for research and provides funds for treatment of birth defects. Monitors legislation and regulations. (Headquarters in White Plains, NY.)

See also American Assn. of Immunologists (p. 372); Howard Hughes Medical Institute (p. 388); National Research Council, Institute for Laboratory Animal Research (p. 286); SRI International (p. 249)

Heart Disease, Strokes

AGENCIES

National Heart, Lung, and Blood Institute *(National Institutes of Health), Heart and Vascular Diseases,* 6701 Rockledge Dr., #9160, Bethesda, MD 20892-7940; (301) 435-0466. Fax, (301) 480-1336. Dr. Stephen C. Mockrin, Director (Acting).

Conducts and funds research on the prevention, causes, and treatment of heart and vascular diseases.

National Heart, Lung, and Blood Institute *(National Institutes of Health), Information Center,* P.O. Box 30105, Bethesda, MD 20824-0105; (301) 592-8573. Fax, (301) 592-8563. Brian Marquis, Manager. Press, (301) 496-4236. Web, www.nhlbi.nih.gov.

Acquires, maintains, and disseminates information on cholesterol, high blood pressure, heart attack awareness, and asthma to the public and health professionals. Provides reference and referral services. Library open to the public.

National Institute of Neurological Disorders and Stroke *(National Institutes of Health),* 31 Center Dr., MSC-2540, #8A52, Bethesda, MD 20892-2540; (301) 496-9746. Fax, (301) 496-0296. Dr. Gerald Fischbach, Director. Information, (301) 496-5751. Web, www.ninds.nih.gov.

Conducts and funds stroke research. Monitors international research.

NONPROFIT

American Heart Assn., *Washington Office,* 1150 Connecticut Ave. N.W., #810 20036; (202) 785-7900. Fax, (202) 785-7950. Diane Canova, Vice President. Information, (800) 242-1793. Web, www.americanheart.org.

Membership: physicians, scientists, and other interested individuals. Supports cardiovascular research, treatment, and community service programs that provide information about heart disease and stroke; participates in international conferences and research. Monitors legislation and regulations. (Headquarters in Dallas.)

Citizens for Public Action on Blood Pressure and Cholesterol, P.O. Box 30374, Bethesda, MD 20824; (202) 362-7563. Fax, (202) 362-7565. Gerald J. Wilson, Executive Director. General e-mail, libbase@aol.com.

Works to ensure public health resources for cholesterol and blood pressure education, screening, and treatment; prepares patient and professional educational materials and programs. Monitors legislation and regulations on heart disease research, programs, and services available through the public health system.

Infectious Diseases, Allergies

AGENCIES

National Institute of Allergy and Infectious Diseases *(National Institutes of Health),* 31 Center Dr., MSC-2520, #7A03, Bethesda, MD 20892-2520; (301) 496-2263. Fax, (301) 496-4409. Dr. Anthony S. Fauci, Director. Information, (301) 496-5717. General e-mail, niaidoc@flash.niaid.nih.gov. Web, www.niaid.nih.gov.

Conducts and funds research on infectious diseases, allergies, and other immunological disorders. Participates in international research, especially on AIDS and HIV.

NONPROFIT

Allergy and Asthma Network/Mothers of Asthmatics Inc., 2751 Prosperity Ave., #150, Fairfax, VA 22031; (703) 641-9595. Fax, (703) 573-7794. Nancy Sander, President. Information, (800) 878-4403. General e-mail, aanma@aol.com. Web, www.aanma.org.

Membership: families dealing with asthma and allergies. Promotes research; provides information on treatments and therapies, new products, support groups, and coping techniques.

Asthma and Allergy Foundation of America, 1233 20th St. N.W., #402 20036; (202) 466-7643. Fax, (202) 466-8940. Mary Worstell, Executive Director. Information, (800) 727-8462. General e-mail, info@aafa.org. Web, www.aafa.org.

Provides information on asthma and allergies; offers a self-management program for asthmatic children and their parents; awards research grants to health care professionals; offers in service training in school and occupational nurses, teachers, and others with in-service training. Interests include international air standards.

National Foundation for Infectious Diseases, 4733 Bethesda Ave., #750, Bethesda, MD 20814-5228; (301) 656-0003. Fax, (301) 907-0878. Len Novick, Executive Director. General e-mail, info@nfid.org. Web, www.nfid.org.

Raises, receives, maintains, and disburses funds to support research on infectious diseases; educates the public and health professionals about infectious diseases; conducts prevention programs, including an annual adult immunization awareness campaign; coordinates activities for the National Coalition for Adult Immunization. Monitors international research.

Kidney Disease

AGENCIES

Health Care Financing Administration *(Health and Human Services Dept.), Chronic Care Management,*

7500 Security Blvd., C5-05-27, Baltimore, MD 21244-1850; (410) 786-4533. Fax, (410) 786-0594. Lana K. Price, Director. Information, (410) 786-4567.

Administers coverage policy for Medicare persons with renal disease, chronic kidney failure, and the program for all inclusive care for the elderly. Coordinates coverage under new treatment methods.

National Institute of Allergy and Infectious Diseases *(National Institutes of Health), Allergy, Immunology, and Transplantation,* 6700 B Rockledge Dr., #5142, Bethesda, MD 20892-7640; (301) 496-1886. Fax, (301) 402-0175. Dr. Daniel Rotrosen, Director. Information, (301) 496-5717. Web, www.niaid.nih.gov/research/dait.htm.

Focuses on the immune system as it functions to maintain health and as it malfunctions to produce disease; interests include allergies, asthma, immune deficiencies (other than AIDS), transplantation of organs and tissue, and genetics. Monitors international research.

National Institute of Diabetes and Digestive and Kidney Diseases *(National Institutes of Health), Kidney, Urologic, and Hematological Diseases,* 45 Center Dr. MSC-6600, Natcher Bldg., #6AS-19, Bethesda, MD 20892-6600; (301) 594-7717. Fax, (301) 480-3510. Dr. Gladys H. Hirschman, Director. Information, (301) 496-3583.

Funds research on the prevention, diagnosis, and treatment of renal disorders. Conducts research and reviews grant proposals concerning maintenance therapy for persons with chronic renal disease.

National Institute of Diabetes and Digestive and Kidney Diseases *(National Institutes of Health), National Kidney and Urologic Diseases Information Clearinghouse,* 3 Information Way, Bethesda, MD 20892-3580; (301) 654-4415. Fax, (301) 907-8906. Sarah Johnson, Senior Information Specialist. Web, www.niddk.nih.gov.

Supplies health care providers and the public with information on the symptoms, causes, treatments, and general nature of kidney and urologic diseases.

NONPROFIT

American Kidney Fund, 6110 Executive Blvd., #1010, Rockville, MD 20852; (301) 881-3052. Fax, (301) 881-0898. Karen Sendelback, Executive Director. Information, (800) 638-8299.

Voluntary health organization that gives financial assistance to kidney disease victims. Disseminates public service announcements and public education materials;

sponsors research grants and conferences for professionals; promotes organ donation for transplantation.

National Kidney Foundation, *Government Relations, Washington Office,* 1911 N. Fort Myer Dr., #801, Arlington, VA 22209-1603; (703) 522-8544. Fax, (703) 522-8586. Troy Zimmerman, Director. Information, (800) 889-9559. Web, www.kidney.org.

Supports funding for kidney dialysis and other forms of treatment for kidney disease; provides information on detection and screening of kidney diseases. Monitors legislation, regulations, and international research. (Headquarters in New York.)

Lung Diseases

AGENCIES

National Heart, Lung, and Blood Institute *(National Institutes of Health), Information Center,* P.O. Box 30105, Bethesda, MD 20824-0105; (301) 592-8573. Fax, (301) 592-8563. Brian Marquis, Manager. Press, (301) 496-4236. Web, www.nhlbi.nih.gov.

Acquires, maintains, and disseminates information on asthma and other lung ailments. Provides reference and referral services.

National Heart, Lung, and Blood Institute *(National Institutes of Health), Lung Diseases,* 6701 Rockledge Dr., #10018, Bethesda, MD 20892; (301) 435-0233. Fax, (301) 480-3547. James P. Kiley, Director. Information, (301) 592-8573. Press, (301) 496-4236. Web, www.nhlbi.nih.gov.

Plans and directs research and training programs in lung diseases including research on causes, treatments, prevention, and health education.

NONPROFIT

American Assn. for Respiratory Care, *Government Affairs, Washington Office,* 1225 King St., 2nd Floor, Alexandria, VA 22314; (703) 548-8538. Fax, (703) 548-8499. Cheryl West, Director, (703) 548-8506. General e-mail, west@aarc.org. Web, www.aarc.org.

Membership: respiratory therapists; educators; and managers of respiratory and cardiopulmonary services. Monitors legislation and regulations. (Headquarters in Dallas.)

American Lung Assn., *Washington Office,* 1726 M St. N.W., #902 20036-4502; (202) 785-3355. Fax, (202) 452-1805. Fran Du Melle, Director. Web, www.lungusa.org.

Fights lung disease through research, educational programs, and public awareness campaigns. Interests include antismoking campaigns, lung-related biomedical research, air pollution, school health education, and all lung diseases, including tuberculosis and occupational lung diseases. Participates in international research. (Headquarters in New York.)

Cystic Fibrosis Foundation, *6931 Arlington Rd., Bethesda, MD 20814; (301) 951-4422. Fax, (301) 951-6378. Robert J. Beall, President. Information, (800) 344-4823. General e-mail, info@cff.org. Web, www.cff.org.*

Conducts research on cystic fibrosis, an inherited genetic disease affecting the respiratory and digestive systems. Provides funding for care centers; publishes and disseminates information on the disease.

Neurological and Muscular Disorders

AGENCIES

National Institute of Neurological Disorders and Stroke *(National Institutes of Health), 31 Center Dr., MSC-2540, #8A52, Bethesda, MD 20892-2540; (301) 496-9746. Fax, (301) 496-0296. Dr. Gerald Fischbach, Director. Information, (301) 496-5751. Web, www.ninds.nih.gov.*

Conducts and funds research on neurological diseases. Monitors international research.

NONPROFIT

Alzheimer's Assn., *Public Policy, Washington Office, 1319 F St. N.W., #710 20004-1106; (202) 393-7737. Fax, (202) 393-2109. Stephen R. McConnell, Vice President. Information, (800) 272-3900. Web, www.alz.org.*

Offers family support services and educates the public about Alzheimer's disease, a neurological disorder mainly affecting the brain tissue in older adults. Promotes research and long-term care protection; maintains liaison with Alzheimer's associations abroad. Monitors legislation and regulations. (Headquarters in Chicago.)

Epilepsy Foundation, *4351 Garden City Dr., Landover, MD 20785; (301) 459-3700. Fax, (301) 577-2684. Eric Hargis, Chief Executive Officer. Information, (800) 332-1000. Library, (800) 332-4050. General e-mail, postmaster@ efa.org. Web, www.epilepsyfoundation.org.*

Promotes research and treatment of epilepsy; makes research grants; disseminates information and educational materials. Affiliates provide direct services for people with epilepsy and make referrals when necessary. Library open to the public by appointment.

Foundation for the Advancement of Chiropractic Tenets and Science, *1110 N. Glebe Rd., #1000, Arlington, VA 22201-5722; (703) 528-5000. Fax, (703) 528-5023. Ronald Hendrickson, Executive Director. Web, www. chiropractic.org.*

Offers financial aid for education and research programs in colleges and independent institutions; studies chiropractic services in the United States. (Affiliate of the International Chiropractors Assn.)

International Rett Syndrome Assn., *9121 Piscataway Rd., #2B, Clinton, MD 20735; (301) 856-3334. Fax, (301) 856-3336. Kathy Hunter, President. Information, (800) 818-7388. General e-mail, irsa@rettsyndrome.org. Web, www.rettsyndrome.org.*

Provides information and support to families of children with Rett syndrome, a severe neurological disorder causing mental and physical disabilities. Awards grants nationally and internationally. Promotes research on causes and treatment.

National Coalition for Research in Neurological Disorders, *1250 24th St. N.W., #300 20037; (202) 293-5453. Fax, (202) 466-0585. Lawrence S. Hoffheimer, Executive Director. Web, www.brainnet.org/ncr.htm.*

Coalition of voluntary agencies, physicians, and scientists. Works to increase federal funding for neurological disorder research; conducts educational programs.

National Foundation for Brain Research, *1250 24th St. N.W., #300 20037; (202) 293-5453. Fax, (202) 466-0585. Lawrence S. Hoffheimer, Executive Director. Web, www.brainnet.org/nfbr.htm.*

Membership: professional societies, voluntary organizations, and businesses that support research into neurological and addictive brain disorders, including Alzheimer's disease, obsessive-compulsive behavior, dyslexia, drug addiction and alcoholism, stroke, Tay-Sachs disease, and depression. Sponsors programs that heighten public and professional awareness of brain disorders. Serves as a liaison with government agencies, medical and scientific societies, volunteer health organizations, and industry.

National Multiple Sclerosis Society, *Washington Office, 2021 K St. N.W., #715 20006-1003; (202) 296-9891. Fax, (202) 296-3425. Jeanne Oates Angulo, President. Web, www.msandyou.org.*

Seeks to advance medical knowledge of multiple sclerosis, a disease of the central nervous system; disseminates information worldwide. Patient services include individual and family counseling, exercise programs, equipment loans, medical and social service referrals, transportation assistance, back-to-work training programs, and in-service training seminars for nurses, homemakers, and physical and occupational therapists. (Headquarters in New York.)

Neurofibromatosis Inc., *8855 Annapolis Rd., #110, Lanham, MD 20706-2924; (301) 577-8984. Fax, (301) 577-0016. John Vickerman, Executive Director. Information, (800) 942-6825. General e-mail, nfinc1@aol.com. Web, www.nfinc.org.*

Provides information and assistance to health care professionals, individuals, and families affected by neurofibromatosis and related disorders. Promotes research; maintains a database of resources; makes referrals to physicians, service providers, and peer counselors.

Society for Neuroscience, *11 Dupont Circle N.W., #500 20036; (202) 462-6688. Fax, (202) 234-9770. Lorne Mendell, President. Web, www.sfn.org.*

Membership: scientists and physicians worldwide who research the brain, spinal cord, and nervous system. Interests include the molecular and cellular levels of the nervous system; systems within the brain, such as vision and hearing; and behavior produced by the brain. Promotes education in the neurosciences and the application of research to treat nervous system disorders.

United Cerebral Palsy Assns., *1660 L St. N.W., #700 20036-5602; (202) 776-0406. Fax, (202) 776-0414. Kirsten Nyrop, Executive Director. Information, (800) 872-5827. Main phone is voice and TTY accessible. Web, www.ucpa. org.*

National network of state and local affiliates that assists individuals with cerebral palsy and other developmental disabilities and their families. Provides parent education, early intervention, employment services, family support and respite programs, therapy, assistive technology, and vocational training. Promotes research on cerebral palsy; supports the use of assistive technology and community-based living arrangements for persons with cerebral palsy and other developmental disabilities.

See also National Easter Seal Society (p. 380)

People of Color

AGENCIES

Health and Human Services Dept., *Civil Rights, 200 Independence Ave. S.W., #522A 20201; (202) 619-0403. Fax, (202) 619-3437. Thomas Perez, Director. TTY, (800) 537-7697. Toll-free hotline, (800) 368-1019. Web, www.os. dhhs.gov/progorg/ocr/ocrhmpg.html.*

Administers and enforces laws prohibiting discrimination on the basis of race, color, sex, national origin, religion, age, or disability in programs receiving federal funds from the department; authorized to discontinue funding.

Health and Human Services Dept., *Minority Health, Rockwall II Bldg., #1000, 5515 Security Lane, Rockville, MD 20852; (301) 443-5084. Fax, (301) 443-8280. Dr. Nathan Stinson, Deputy Assistant Secretary. Information, (800) 444-6472. General e-mail, info@omhrc.gov. Web, www.omhrc.gov/AboutOMH.HTM.*

Promotes improved health among racial and ethnic minority populations. Advises the secretary and the Office of Public Health and Science on public health program activities affecting American Indian and Alaska Native, African American, Asian American and Pacific Islander, and Hispanic populations.

Health and Human Services Dept., *Minority Health Resource Center, 5515 Security Lane, #101, Rockville, MD 20852 (mailing address: P.O. Box 37337 20013-7337); (301) 230-7874. Fax, (301) 230-7198. Jose Tarcisio M. Carneiro, Director. Information, (800) 444-6472. TTY, (301) 230-7199. General e-mail, info@omhrc.gov. Web, www.omhrc.gov/frames.htm.*

Serves as a national resource and referral service on minority health issues. Distributes information on health topics such as substance abuse, cancer, heart disease, violence, diabetes, HIV/AIDS, and infant mortality. Provides free services, including customized database searches, publications, mailing lists, and referrals regarding American Indian and Alaska Native, African American, Asian American and Pacific Islander, and Hispanic populations.

Health Resources and Services Administration, *Minority Health, 5600 Fishers Lane, #1049, Rockville, MD 20857; (301) 443-2964. Fax, (301) 443-7853. M. June Horner, Director. General e-mail, comments@hrsa.gov. Web, www.hrsa.gov/hrsa/omh/main1_overview.HTM.*

Sponsors programs and activities that address the special health needs of racial and ethnic minorities. Advises the administrator on minority health issues affecting the Health Resources and Services Administration (HRSA) and policy development; collects data on minority health activities within HRSA; represents HRSA programs affecting the health of racial and ethnic minorities to the health community, and organizations in the public, private, and international sectors.

Indian Health Service *(Health and Human Services Dept.), 5600 Fishers Lane, #6-05 Parklawn Bldg., Rockville, MD 20857; (301) 443-1083. Fax, (301) 443-4794. Dr. Michael H. Trujillo, Director. Information, (301) 443-3593. Web, www.tucson.ihs.gov.*

Operates hospitals and health centers that provide native Americans and Alaska natives with preventive and remedial health care. Provides or improves sanitation and water supply systems in native American communities.

National Institutes of Health *(Health and Human Services Dept.), Research on Minority Health, 1 Center Dr., Bldg. 1, #258, Bethesda, MD 20892-0164; (301) 402-1366. Fax, (301) 402-7040. Dr. John Ruffin, Associate Director.*

Coordinates the development of NIH policies and objectives related to minority health research and research training programs. Encourages minorities to work in the biomedical research field.

Public Health and Science *(Health and Human Services Dept.), Minority Health, 5515 Security Lane, #1000, Rockwall II Bldg., Rockville, MD 20852; (301) 443-5084. Fax, (301) 594-0767. Nathan Stinson, Deputy Assistant Secretary (Acting). Information, (800) 444-6472. General e-mail, info@omhrc.gov. Web, www.omhrc.gov.*

Awards grants to minority AIDS education and prevention projects to administer health promotion, education, and disease prevention programs.

NONPROFIT

National Alliance of Hispanic Health, *1501 16th St. N.W. 20036; (202) 387-5000. Fax, (202) 265-8027. Jane L. Delgado, President. Web, www.cossmho.org.*

Assists agencies and groups serving the Hispanic community in general health care and in targeting health and psychosocial problems; provides information, technical assistance, health care provider training, and policy analysis; coordinates and supports research. Interests include mental health, chronic diseases, substance abuse, maternal and child health, youth issues, juvenile delinquency, and access to care.

Skin Disorders

AGENCIES

National Institute of Arthritis and Musculoskeletal and Skin Diseases *(National Institutes of Health), 31 Center Dr., MSC-2350, #4C32, Bethesda, MD 20892-2350; (301) 496-4353. Fax, (301) 480-6069. Dr. Stephen I. Katz, Director. Information, (301) 496-8190. Web, www.nih.gov/niams.*

Supports research on the causes and treatment of skin diseases, including psoriasis, eczema, and acne.

NONPROFIT

American Academy of Facial Plastic and Reconstructive Surgery, *310 S. Henry St., Alexandria, VA 22314; (703) 299-9291. Fax, (703) 299-8895. Stephen C. Duffy, Executive Vice President. Toll-free information and*

physician referral, (800) 332-3223. General e-mail, aafprs@aol.com. Web, www.facial-plastic-surgery.org.

Promotes research and study in the field. Helps train residents in facial plastic and reconstructive surgery; offers continuing medical education. Sponsors scientific and medical meetings, international symposia, fellowship training program, seminars, and workshops. Provides videotapes on facial plastic and reconstructive surgery.

Substance Abuse

See also Tobacco (chap. 1); Drug Control (chap. 14)

AGENCIES

Education Dept., *Safe and Drug-Free Schools, 400 Maryland Ave. S.W. 20202-6123; (202) 260-3954. Fax, (202) 260-7767. William Modzeleski, Director. Web, www.ed.gov/offices/oese/sdfs.*

Develops policy for the department's drug and violence prevention initiatives for students in elementary and secondary schools and institutions of higher education. Coordinates education efforts in drug and violence prevention with those of other federal departments and agencies.

Health Resources and Services Administration *(Health and Human Services Dept.), Special Populations, 4350 East-West Hwy., West Towers Bldg., 9th Floor, Bethesda, MD 20814; (301) 594-4420. Fax, (301) 594-4989. Regan Crump, Director.*

Funds a program that links primary care and substance abuse treatment.

National Institute on Alcohol Abuse and Alcoholism *(National Institutes of Health), 6000 Executive Blvd., Willco Bldg., #400, MSC 7003, Bethesda, MD 20892-7003; (301) 443-3885. Fax, (301) 443-7043. Dr. Enoch Gordis, Director. Information, (301) 443-3860. Web, www.niaaa.nih.gov.*

Supports basic and applied research on preventing and treating alcoholism and alcohol-related problems; conducts research and disseminates findings on alcohol abuse and alcoholism. Participates in international research.

National Institute on Drug Abuse *(National Institutes of Health), 6001 Executive Blvd., #5274, MSC 9581, Rockville, MD 20859; (301) 443-6480. Fax, (301) 443-9127. Alan I. Leshner, Director. Information, (301) 443-1124. Press, (301) 443-6245. TTY, (888) 889-6432. Toll-free fax-on-demand, (888) 644-6432. Web, www.nida.nih.gov.*

Conducts and sponsors research on the prevention, effects, and treatment of drug abuse. Monitors international policy and research.

Office of National Drug Control Policy *(Executive Office of the President)*, *750 17th St. N.W. 20503; (202) 395-6700. Fax, (202) 395-6708. Barry McCaffrey, Director. Web, www.whitehousedrugpolicy.gov.*

Establishes policies and oversees the implementation of a national drug control strategy; recommends changes to reduce demand for and supply of illegal drugs; advises the National Security Council on drug control policy.

Office of Personnel Management, *Employee Relations and Health Services Center, 1900 E St. N.W. 20415; (202) 606-1740. Fax, (202) 606-0967. Ken Bates, Director.*

Sets policy and guides federal agencies in establishing and maintaining alcohol and drug abuse programs and drug-free workplaces.

Substance Abuse and Mental Health Services Administration *(Health and Human Services Dept.), 5600 Fishers Lane, #12-105, Rockville, MD 20857; (301) 443-4795. Fax, (301) 443-0284. Nelba Chavez, Administrator. Information, (301) 443-8956. Web, www.samhsa. gov.*

Coordinates activities of the Center for Substance Abuse Treatment, Center for Mental Health Services, and Center for Substance Abuse Prevention, which sponsors the National Clearinghouse for Alcohol and Drug Information.

Substance Abuse and Mental Health Services Administration *(Health and Human Services Dept.), Center for Substance Abuse Prevention, 5515 Security Lane, Rockwall 2, #900, Rockville, MD 20857; (301) 443-0365. Fax, (301) 443-5447. Karol Kumpher, Director; John Noble, Clearinghouse Director, (301) 468-2600. Information, (800) 729-6686. TTY, (800) 487-4889. Web, www. samhsa.gov.*

Promotes strategies to prevent alcohol and drug abuse. Operates the National Clearinghouse for Alcohol and Drug Information, which provides information, publications, and grant applications for programs to prevent substance abuse. (Clearinghouse address: P.O. Box 2345, Rockville, MD 29847.)

Substance Abuse and Mental Health Services Administration *(Health and Human Services Dept.), Center for Substance Abuse Treatment, 5515 Security Lane, Rockwall 2, #615, Rockville, MD 20852 (mailing address: 5600 Fishers Lane, Rockwall 2, Rockville, MD 20857); (301) 443-5700. Fax, (301) 443-8751. Dr. H. Westley Clark, Director. Information, (301) 443-5052.*

Treatment referral, literature, and reports: (800) 662-4357; (800) 487-4889 (hearing-impaired).

Develops and supports policies and programs that improve and expand treatment services for alcoholism and substance abuse addiction. Administers grants that support private and public addiction prevention and treatment services. Conducts research on and evaluates alcohol treatment programs and other drug treatment programs and delivery systems.

INTERNATIONAL ORGANIZATIONS

International Commission for the Prevention of Alcoholism and Drug Dependency, *12501 Old Columbia Pike, Silver Spring, MD 20904; (301) 680-6719. Fax, (301) 680-6707. Thomas R. Neslund, Executive Director. General e-mail, 74617.2242@compuserve.com. Web, www.adventist.org/ICPA.*

Membership: health officials, physicians, educators, clergy, and judges worldwide. Promotes scientific research on prevention of alcohol and drug dependencies; provides information about medical effects of alcohol and drugs; conducts world congresses.

NONPROFIT

American Society of Addiction Medicine, *4601 N. Park Ave., Upper Arcade, #101, Chevy Chase, MD 20815-4520; (301) 656-3920. Fax, (301) 656-3815. James F. Callahan, Executive Vice President. General e-mail, email@asam.org. Web, www.asam.org.*

Membership: physicians and medical students. Supports the study and provision of effective treatment and care for people with alcohol and drug dependencies; educates physicians; administers certification program in addiction medicine. Monitors legislation and regulations.

Employee Assistance Professionals Assn., *2101 Wilson Blvd., #500, Arlington, VA 22201; (703) 387-1000. Fax, (703) 522-4585. Sylvia Straub, Chief Operating Officer. General e-mail, eapamain@aol.com. Web, www. eap-association.org.*

Represents professionals in the workplace who assist employees and their family members with personal and behavioral problems, including health, marital, family, financial, alcohol, drug, legal, emotional, stress, or other personal problems that adversely affect employee job performance and productivity.

National Assn. of Alcoholism and Drug Abuse Counselors, *1911 N. Fort Myer Dr., #900, Arlington, VA 22209; (703) 741-7686. Fax, (703) 741-7698. William McColl, Executive Director (Acting). Information, (800) 548-0497. General e-mail, naadac@naadac.org. Web, www.naadac.org.*

Provides information on drug dependency treatment, research, and resources. Works with private groups and federal agencies concerned with treating and preventing alcoholism and drug abuse; certifies addiction counselors; holds workshops and conferences for treatment professionals.

National Assn. of State Alcohol and Drug Abuse Directors, *808 17th St. N.W., #410 20006; (202) 293-0090. Fax, (202) 293-1250. John S. Gustafson, Executive Director.*

Membership: state alcohol and drug abuse agencies. Provides information on alcohol and other drug abuse treatment and prevention services and resources; contracts with federal and state agencies to design and conduct research on alcohol and drug abuse programs.

National Council on Alcoholism and Drug Dependence, *Public Policy, Washington Office, 1010 Vermont Ave. N.W., #710 20005; (202) 737-8122. Fax, (202) 628-4731. Sarah Kayson, Director. General e-mail, publicpolicy@ncadd.org. Web, www.ncadd.org.*

Membership: local affiliates and individuals interested in alcoholism, other drug dependencies, and their related problems. Monitors legislation and regulations. Affiliates offer information and referral services. (Headquarters in New York.)

Therapeutic Communities of America, *1611 Connecticut Ave. N.W., #4B 20009; (202) 296-3503. Fax, (202) 518-5475. Linda R. Wolf Jones, Executive Director. Web, www.tcanet.org.*

Membership: substance abuse treatment and rehabilitation agencies. Provides policy analysis and educates the public on substance abuse and treatment issues. Promotes the interests of therapeutic communities, their clients, and staffs. Monitors legislation and regulations.

See also National Organization on Fetal Alcohol Syndrome (p. 384)

Women's Health

AGENCIES

National Institutes of Health *(Health and Human Services Dept.), Research on Women's Health, 1 Center Dr., #201, Bethesda, MD 20892-0161; (301) 402-1770. Fax, (301) 402-1798. Dr. Vivian W. Pinn, Director. Web, www4.od.nih.gov/orwh.*

Collaborates with NIH institutes and centers to establish NIH goals and policies for research related to women's health; supports expansion of research on diseases, conditions, and disorders that affect women; monitors inclusion of women and minorities in clinical research; develops opportunities and support for recruitment and advancement of women in biomedical careers.

Public Health and Science *(Health and Human Services Dept.), Women's Health, 200 Independence Ave. S.W., #730B 20201; (202) 690-7650. Fax, (202) 401-4005. Dr. Wanda K. Jones, Deputy Assistant Secretary.*

Coordinates HHS activities in women's health research and medical care, including professional education and advancement of women; works with other agencies and organizations; participates in international conferences. Oversees the National Women's Health Information Center; interests include breast cancer.

NONPROFIT

American Medical Women's Assn., *801 N. Fairfax St., #400, Alexandria, VA 22314-1767; (703) 838-0500. Fax, (703) 549-3864. Eileen McGrath, Executive Director. General e-mail, info@amwa-doc.org. Web, www.amwa-doc.org.*

Membership: female physicians, interns, residents, and medical students. Promotes continuing education; evaluates manufacturers' research on products for women's health; provides student educational loans. Monitors legislation and regulations.

Institute for Women's Policy Research, *1707 L St. N.W., #750 20036; (202) 785-5100. Fax, (202) 833-4362. Heidi I. Hartmann, Director. Web, www.iwpr.org.*

Public policy research organization that focuses on women's issues, including health care and comprehensive family and medical leave programs.

National Center For Policy Research For Women and Families, *1444 Eye St. N.W., #900 20005; (202) 216-9507. Fax, (202) 216-9845. Diana Zuckerman, Executive Director. General e-mail, cpr4wf@gateway.net. Web, www.cpr4womenandfamilies.org.*

Utilizes scientific and medical research to improve the quality of women's lives and the lives of family members. Seeks to educate policymakers about medical and scientific research through hearings, meetings, and publications.

National Women's Health Network, *514 10th St. N.W., #400 20004-1410; (202) 347-1140. Fax, (202) 347-1168. Cynthia Pearson, Executive Director. Web, www.womenshealthnetwork.org.*

Acts as an information clearinghouse on women's health issues; monitors federal health policies and legislation. Interests include older women's health issues, contraception, breast cancer, abortion, unsafe drugs, and AIDS.

Society for Women's Health Research, *1828 L St. N.W., #625 20036; (202) 223-8224. Fax, (202) 833-3472. Phyllis Greenberger, Executive Director. Web, www. womens-health.org.*

Promotes public and private funding for women's health research and changes in public policies affecting women's health. Seeks to advance women as leaders in the health professions and to inform policymakers, educators, and the public of research outcomes. Sponsors meetings; produces reports and educational videotapes.

See also Assn. of Reproductive Health Professionals (p. 369); National Breast Cancer Coalition (p. 394)

 MENTAL HEALTH

AGENCIES

National Institute of Mental Health *(National Institutes of Health),* *6001 Executive Blvd., #8235, Rockville, MD 20852; (301) 443-3673. Fax, (301) 443-2578. Dr. Steven E. Hyman, Director. Information, (301) 443-4513. Press, (301) 443-4536. TTY, (301) 443-4229. Web, www. nimh.nih.gov.*

Conducts research on the cause, diagnosis, treatment, and prevention of mental disorders; provides information on mental health problems and programs. Participates in international research.

National Institute of Mental Health *(National Institutes of Health), Developmental Psychpathology and Prevention Research, 6001 Executive Blvd., #6200, Bethesda, MD 20892; (301) 443-5944. Fax, (301) 480-4415. Doreen Koretz, Chief.*

Promotes research programs concerning the prevention of mental disorders and the promotion of mental health.

National Institute of Mental Health *(National Institutes of Health), Neuroscience and Basic Behavioral Science, 6001 Executive Blvd., #7S-7204, Rockville, MD 20852; (301) 443-3563. Fax, (301) 443-1731. Stephen L. Foote, Director.*

Directs, plans, and supports programs of basic and clinical neuroscience research, genetics and therapeutics research, research training, resource development, and research dissemination to further understand the treatment and prevention of brain disorders. Interests include: behavioral and integrative neuroscience; molecular and cellular neuroscience; genetics; and preclinical

and clinical therapeutics. Analyzes national needs and research opportunities.

National Institute of Mental Health *(National Institutes of Health), Special Populations, 6001 Executive Blvd., #8125, Rockville, MD 20852; (301) 443-3533. Fax, (301) 443-8022. Juan Ramos, Director.*

Sets research policy on women and underrepresented racial and ethnic minorities. Administers the minority institutions programs, which support research on and research training for minorities in the mental health field.

Substance Abuse and Mental Health Services Administration *(Health and Human Services Dept.), 5600 Fishers Lane, #12-105, Rockville, MD 20857; (301) 443-4795. Fax, (301) 443-0284. Nelba Chavez, Administrator. Information, (301) 443-8956. Web, www.samhsa. gov.*

Coordinates activities of the Center for Substance Abuse Treatment, Center for Mental Health Services, and Center for Substance Abuse Prevention, which sponsors the National Clearinghouse for Alcohol and Drug Information.

Substance Abuse and Mental Health Services Administration *(Health and Human Services Dept.), Center for Mental Health Services, 5600 Fishers Lane, #17-99, Rockville, MD 20857; (301) 443-0001. Fax, (301) 443-1563. Dr. Bernard S. Arons, Director. Information, (301) 443-2792. TTY, (301) 443-9006.*

Works with federal agencies and state and local governments to demonstrate, evaluate, and disseminate service delivery models to treat mental illness, promote mental health, and prevent the developing or worsening of mental illness.

NONPROFIT

American Academy of Child and Adolescent Psychiatry, *3615 Wisconsin Ave. N.W., 2nd Floor 20016-2037; (202) 966-7300. Fax, (202) 966-2891. Virginia Q. Anthony, Executive Director. Web, www.aacap.org.*

Membership: psychiatrists working with children and adolescents. Sponsors annual meeting and review for medical board examinations; provides information on child abuse, youth suicide, and drug abuse; monitors international research and U.S. legislation concerning mentally ill children.

American Assn. of Pastoral Counselors, *9504A Lee Hwy., Fairfax, VA 22301-2303; (703) 385-6967. Fax, (703) 352-7725. C. Roy Woodruff, Executive Director. General e-mail, info@aapc.org. Web, www.aapc.org.*

Membership: mental health professionals with training in both religion and the behavioral sciences. Nonsectarian organization that accredits pastoral counseling centers, certifies pastoral counselors, and approves training programs.

American Assn. of Suicidology, *4201 Connecticut Ave. N.W., #408 20008; (202) 237-2280. Fax, (202) 237-2282. Dr. Alan Berman, Executive Director. General e-mail, debbiehu@ix.netcom.com. Web, www.suicidology.org.*

Membership: educators, researchers, suicide prevention centers, school districts, volunteers, and survivors affected by suicide. Works to understand and prevent suicide; serves as an information clearinghouse.

American Bar Assn., *Commission on Mental and Physical Disability Law, 740 15th St. N.W. 20005; (202) 662-1570. Fax, (202) 662-1032. John Parry, Director. Web, www.abanet.org/disability/home.html.*

Serves as a clearinghouse for information on mental and physical disability law and offers legal research services.

American Counseling Assn., *5999 Stevenson Ave., Alexandria, VA 22304-3300; (703) 823-9800. Fax, (703) 823-0252. Richard Yep, Executive Director. Information, (800) 347-6647. Web, www.counseling.org.*

Membership: professional counselors and counselor educators. Provides members with leadership training, continuing education programs, and advocacy services; develops professional and ethical standards for the counseling profession; accredits counselor education programs. Monitors legislation and regulations. Library open to the public.

American Mental Health Counselors Assn., *801 N. Fairfax St., #304, Alexandria, VA 22314; (703) 548-6002. Fax, (703) 548-4775. Dr. W. Mark Hamilton, Executive Director. Toll-free, (800) 326-2642. Web, www.amhca.org.*

Membership: professional counselors and graduate students in the mental health field. Sponsors leadership training and continuing education programs for members. Monitors legislation and regulations. (Affiliated with the American Counseling Assn.)

American Psychiatric Assn., *1400 K St. N.W. 20005; (202) 682-6000. Fax, (202) 682-6850. Dr. Steven Mirin, Medical Director. Library, (202) 682-6080. Press, (202) 682-6142. General e-mail, apa@psych.org. Web, www. psych.org.*

Membership: psychiatrists. Promotes availability of high-quality psychiatric care; provides the public with information; assists state and local agencies; conducts educational programs for professionals and students in the field; participates in international meetings and research. Library open to the public by appointment.

American Psychological Assn., *750 1st St. N.E. 20002-4242; (202) 336-5500. Fax, (202) 336-6069. Raymond D. Fowler, Executive Vice President. Library, (202) 336-5640. TTY, (202) 336-6123. Web, www.apa.org.*

Membership: professional psychologists, educators, and behavioral research scientists. Supports research, training, and professional services; works toward improving the qualifications, competence, and training programs of psychologists. Monitors international research and U.S. legislation on mental health.

Anxiety Disorders Assn. of America, *11900 Parklawn Dr., #100, Rockville, MD 20852-2624; (301) 231-9350. Fax, (301) 231-7392. Lawson Hockman, Chief Operating Officer. Web, www.adaa.org.*

Membership: people with phobias and anxiety disorders, their support persons, and mental health professionals. Provides self-help groups with technical and networking support; encourages research and treatment for anxiety disorders.

Assn. of Black Psychologists, *821 Kennedy St. N.W. 20011 (mailing address: P.O. Box 55999 20040-5999); (202) 722-0808. Fax, (202) 722-5941. Dr. Anthony Young, President. Web, www.abpsi.org.*

Membership: psychologists and psychology students. Develops policies to foster mental health in the African American community.

Bazelon Center for Mental Health Law, *1101 15th St. N.W., #1212 20005; (202) 467-5730. Fax, (202) 223-0409. Robert Bernstein, Director. TTY, (202) 467-4232. General e-mail, bazelon@webcom.com. Web, www.bazelon.org.*

Public interest law firm. Conducts test case litigation to defend rights of persons with mental disabilities. Provides legal support for legal services offices, protection and advocacy agencies, and private attorneys. Monitors legislation and regulations.

International Assn. of Psychosocial Rehabilitation Services, *10025 Gov. Warfield Pkwy., #301, Columbia, MD 21044-3357; (410) 730-7190. Fax, (410) 730-5965. Ruth A. Hughes, Chief Executive Officer. TTY, (410) 730-1723. General e-mail, general@iapsrs.org. Web, www. iapsrs.org.*

Membership: agencies, mental health practitioners, policymakers, family groups, and consumer organizations. Supports the community adjustment of persons with psychiatric disabilities; promotes the role of rehabilitation in mental health systems; opposes discrimination based on mental disability.

National Alliance for the Mentally Ill, *2107 Wilson Blvd., Colonial Pl. III, #300, Arlington, VA 22201-3042; (703) 524-7600. Fax, (703) 524-9094. Laurie M. Flynn, Executive Director. Helpline, (800) 950-6264. General e-mail, membership@nami.org. Web, www.nami.org.*

Membership: mentally ill individuals and their families and friends. Works to eradicate mental illness and improve the lives of those affected by brain diseases; sponsors public education and research. Monitors legislation and regulations.

National Assn. of Psychiatric Health Systems, *325 7th St. N.W., #625 20004-2802; (202) 393-6700. Fax, (202) 783-6041. Mark Covall, Executive Director. Web, www.naphs.org.*

Membership: behavioral health care systems that are committed to the delivery of responsive, accountable, and clinically effective treatment and prevention programs for children, adolescents, and adults with mental and substance use disorders.

National Assn. of State Mental Health Program Directors, *66 Canal Center Plaza, #302, Alexandria, VA 22314-1591; (703) 739-9333. Fax, (703) 548-9517. Robert W. Glover, Executive Director. Web, www.nasmhpd.org.*

Membership: officials in charge of state mental health agencies. Compiles data on state mental health programs. Fosters collaboration among members; provides technical assistance and consultation. Maintains research institute.

National Consortium for Child Mental Health Services, *3615 Wisconsin Ave. N.W., 2nd Floor 20016-2037; (202) 966-7300. Fax, (202) 966-2891. Virginia Q. Anthony, Executive Director.*

Membership: organizations interested in developing mental health services for children. Fosters information exchange; advises local, state, and federal agencies that develop children's mental health services. (Affiliated with American Academy of Child and Adolescent Psychiatry.)

National Council for Community Behavior Healthcare, *12300 Twinbrook Pkwy., #320, Rockville, MD 20852; (301) 984-6200. Fax, (301) 881-7159. Charles G. Ray, Chief Executive Officer. Web, www.nccbh.org.*

Membership: community mental health agencies and state community mental health associations. Conducts research on community mental health activities; provides information, technical assistance, and referrals. Operates a job bank; publishes newsletters and a membership directory. Monitors legislation and regulations affecting community mental health facilities.

National Mental Health Assn., *1021 Prince St., Alexandria, VA 22314-2971; (703) 684-7722. Fax, (703) 684-5968. Michael Faenza, President. Information, (800) 969-6642. General e-mail, infoctr@nmha.org. Web, www. nmha.org.*

Works to increase accessible and appropriate care for adults and children with mental disorders. Informs and educates public about mental illnesses and available treatment. Supports research on illnesses and services.

12 🏠

Housing and Development

GENERAL POLICY

AGENCIES

Economic Development Administration *(Commerce Dept.)*, *14th St. and Constitution Ave. N.W., #7800 20230; (202) 482-5081. Fax, (202) 273-4781. Chester Straub, Assistant Secretary (Acting). Information, (202) 482-2309. Web, www.doc.gov/eda.*

Advises the commerce secretary on domestic economic development. Administers development assistance programs that provide financial and technical aid to economically distressed areas to stimulate economic growth and create jobs. Awards public works and technical assistance grants to public institutions, nonprofit organizations, and native American tribes; assists state and local governments with economic adjustment problems caused by long-term or sudden economic dislocation.

General Services Administration, *Federal Domestic Assistance Catalog Staff, 300 7th St. S.W., #101 20407; (202) 708-5126. Jim Adams, Director.*

Prepares *Catalog of Federal Domestic Assistance* (published annually in June and updated in December), which lists all types of federal aid and explains types of assistance, eligibility requirements, application process, and suggestions for writing proposals. Copies may be ordered from the Superintendent of Documents, U.S. Government Printing Office, Washington, DC 20402; (202) 512-1800. Also available on CD-ROM and floppy diskettes.

Housing and Urban Development Dept. (HUD), *451 7th St. S.W., #10000 20410; (202) 708-0417. Fax, (202) 619-8365. Andrew Cuomo, Secretary; Saul Ramirez, Deputy Secretary. Information, (202) 708-0980. Library, (202) 708-3180. Press, (202) 708-0685. TTY, (202) 708-1455. Web, www.hud.gov.*

Responsible for federal programs concerned with housing needs, fair housing opportunity, and improving and developing the nation's urban and rural communities. Administers mortgage insurance, rent subsidy, preservation, rehabilitation, and antidiscrimination in housing programs. Advises the president on federal policy and makes legislative recommendations on housing and community development issues.

Housing and Urban Development Dept., *HUD USER, P.O. Box 6091, Rockville, MD 20849; (301) 519-5154. Fax, (301) 519-5767. Tony Cain, Director. Information, (800) 245-2691. General e-mail, huduser@aspensys.com. Web, www.huduser.org.*

Research information service and clearinghouse for HUD research reports. Provides information on past and current HUD research; maintains HUD USER, an in-house database. Performs custom search requests for a nominal fee; blueprints available upon request. Some documents available online.

Housing and Urban Development Dept., *Policy Development and Research, 451 7th St. S.W., #8100 20410-6000; (202) 708-1600. Fax, (202) 619-8000. Susan Wachter, Assistant Secretary. Web, www.huduser.org.*

Studies ways to improve the effectiveness and equity of HUD programs; analyzes housing and urban issues, including national housing goals, the operation of housing financial markets, the management of housing assistance programs, and statistics on federal and housing insurance programs; conducts the American Housing Survey; develops policy recommendations to improve federal housing programs. Works to increase the affordability of rehabilitated and newly constructed housing through technological and regulatory improvements.

Housing and Urban Development Dept., *Program Evaluation, 451 7th St. S.W., #8140 20410; (202) 708-0574. Fax, (202) 708-5873. Kevin J. Neary, Director. Web, www.hud.gov.*

Conducts research, program evaluations, and demonstrations for all HUD housing, community development, and fair housing and equal opportunity programs.

Office of Management and Budget (OMB), *(Executive Office of the President), Housing, New Executive Office Bldg., #9226 20503; (202) 395-4610. Fax, (202) 395-1307. F. Stevens Redburn, Chief. Web, www.whitehouse.gov/omb.*

Assists and advises the OMB director in budget preparation, reorganizations, and evaluations of Housing and Urban Development Dept. programs.

CONGRESS

House Appropriations Committee, *Subcommittee on VA, HUD, and Independent Agencies, H143 CAP 20515; (202) 225-3241. Rep. James T. Walsh, R-N.Y., Chair; Frank Cushing, Staff Director. Web, www.house.gov/appropriations.*

Jurisdiction over legislation to appropriate funds for all programs of the Housing and Urban Development Dept., the Federal Emergency Management Agency, the National Credit Union Administration, and the Neighborhood Reinvestment Corporation.

House Banking and Financial Services Committee, *Subcommittee on Housing and Community Opportunity, B303 RHOB 20515; (202) 225-6634. Rep. Rick A. Lazio, R-N.Y., Chair; Joseph M. Ventrone, Staff Director. Web, www.house.gov/banking.*

Jurisdiction over all housing legislation, including construction standards and materials, condominiums and cooperatives, home ownership aid, manufactured homes, single and multifamily housing, and rural housing; oversees the Rural Housing Service in the Agriculture Dept. and other housing-related services and programs.

House Government Reform Committee, *Subcommittee on Criminal Justice, Drug Policy, and Human Resources,* B373 RHOB 20515; (202) 225-2577. Fax, (202) 225-1154. Rep. John L. Mica, R-Fla., Chair; Sharon Pinkerton, Staff Director. Web, www.house.gov/reform.

Oversight of the Housing and Urban Development Dept.

House Small Business Committee, *Subcommittee on Empowerment,* B363 RHOB 20515; (202) 226-2630. Fax, (202) 225-8950. Rep. Joseph R. Pitts, R-Pa., Chair; Stephanie O'Donnell, Professional Staff Member. General e-mail, smbiz@mail.house.gov. Web, www.house.gov/smbiz.

Jurisdiction over development of economically depressed areas, including regulations and licensing policies, that affect small businesses in high-risk communities.

Senate Appropriations Committee, *Subcommittee on VA, HUD, and Independent Agencies,* SD-130 20510; (202) 224-7211. Sen. Christopher S. Bond, R-Mo., Chair; Jon Kamarck, Staff Director. Web, appropriations.senate.gov/vahud.

Jurisdiction over legislation to appropriate funds for all programs of the Housing and Urban Development Dept., the Federal Emergency Management Agency, the National Credit Union Administration, and the Neighborhood Reinvestment Corporation.

Senate Banking, Housing, and Urban Affairs Committee, *Subcommittee on Financial Institutions,* SD-534 20510; (202) 224-7391. Fax, (202) 224-5137. Sen. Robert F. Bennett, R-Utah, Chair; Jim Barker, Staff Director. Web, banking.senate.gov.

Jurisdiction over legislation on economic stabilization and growth, including regulatory relief issues and barriers to development in rural areas.

Senate Banking, Housing, and Urban Affairs Committee, *Subcommittee on Housing and Transportation,* SD-534 20510; (202) 224-7391. Fax, (202) 224-5137. Sen. Wayne Allard, R-Colo., Chair; John Carson, Staff Director. Web, banking.senate.gov.

Jurisdiction over legislation concerning housing issues, including rural housing, construction standards and materials, condominiums and cooperatives, home

ownership aid, manufactured homes, and single and multifamily housing. Oversees the Housing and Urban Development Dept. and housing programs in the Agriculture Dept.

Senate Small Business Committee, SR-428A 20510; (202) 224-5175. Fax, (202) 224-4885. Sen. Christopher S. Bond, R-Mo., Chair; Emilia DiSanto, Staff Director. Web, sbc.senate.gov.

Jurisdiction over small and disadvantaged business and related economic development.

NONPROFIT

Center for Housing Policy, 815 15th St. N.W., #538 20005; (202) 393-5772. Fax, (202) 393-5656. Robert J. Reid, Executive Director. General e-mail, chp@nhc.org. Web, www.nhc.org.

Researches and develops fundamentals of housing policy. Seeks to create new policies that integrate housing into overall social and economic goals. Sponsors educational forums. (Affiliated with the National Housing Conference.)

Housing and Development Law Institute, 630 Eye St. N.W. 20001; (202) 289-3400. Fax, (202) 289-3401. William F. Maher, Executive Director.

Assists public agencies that administer assisted housing and community development programs in addressing common legal concerns and problems; publishes legal periodicals concerning affordable housing issues; conducts seminars on legal issues and practices in the housing and community development field. (Affiliated with the National Assn. of Housing and Redevelopment Officials.)

Institute for Local Self-Reliance, 2425 18th St. N.W. 20009-2096; (202) 232-4108. Fax, (202) 332-0463. Neil Seldman, President. General e-mail, ilsr@igc.org. Web, www.ilsr.org.

Conducts research and provides technical assistance on environmentally sound economic development for government, small businesses, and community organizations.

National Assn. of Housing and Redevelopment Officials, 630 Eye St. N.W. 20001; (202) 289-3500. Fax, (202) 289-8181. Richard Y. Nelson Jr., Executive Director. Web, www.nahro.org.

Membership: housing, community, and urban development practitioners and organizations, and state and local government agencies and personnel. Works with federal government agencies to improve community development and housing programs; conducts training programs.

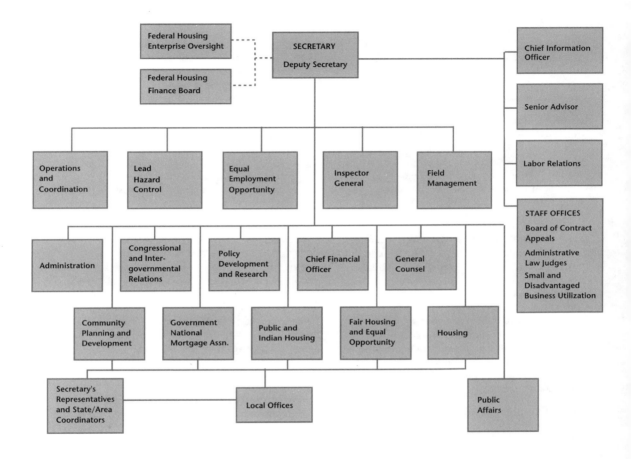

National Assn. of State Development Agencies, 750 1st St. N.E., #710 20002-4241; (202) 898-1302. Fax, (202) 898-1312. Miles Friedman, President. Web, www.nasda. com.

Membership: directors of state economic development agencies. Provides economic development consulting service; sponsors conferences and seminars. Interests include financing techniques, job training programs, aid to small business, and state-local coordination strategies.

Statistics

AGENCIES

Census Bureau *(Commerce Dept.), Governments Division,* 8905 Presidential Pkwy., Upper Marlboro, MD 20722 (mailing address: Washington Plaza II, #407 20233-6800);

(301) 457-1489. Fax, (301) 457-1423. Gordon W. Green Jr., Chief.

Compiles the annual *Federal Expenditures by State,* which provides information on federal domestic spending, federal grants programs, and federal aid to states.

Census Bureau *(Commerce Dept.), Housing and Household Economic Statistics,* 4700 Silver Hill Rd., Suitland, MD 20746 (mailing address: 1071-3 20233-8500); (301) 457-3234. Fax, (301) 457-3248. Daniel H. Weinberg, Chief.

Publishes decennial census of housing and the American Housing Survey, which describe housing inventory characteristics. Also publishes a quarterly survey of market absorption. Survey on housing vacancy is available on the Internet.

Census Bureau *(Commerce Dept.), Manufacturing and Construction,* Suitland and Silver Hill Rds., Suitland, MD 20233; (301) 457-4593. Fax, (301) 457-4583. William G. Bostic Jr., Chief.

Publishes statistics on the value of construction put in place; housing starts, sales, and completions; building permits; price index of single-family homes sold; characteristics of new housing; and expenditures for residential improvements. Conducts a census of construction industries every five years.

Housing and Urban Development Dept., *Economic Affairs,* 451 7th St. S.W., #8204 20410-6000; (202) 708-3080. Fax, (202) 708-1159. Frederick J. Eggers, Deputy Assistant Secretary. Web, www.hud.gov.

Directs research in public finance and urban economic development; assembles data on housing markets; conducts annual housing surveys; analyzes financial instruments used in housing.

International Trade Administration *(Commerce Dept.), Basic Industries,* 14th St. and Constitution Ave. N.W., #4043 20230; (202) 482-0614. Fax, (202) 482-5666. Alan S. Bowser, Deputy Assistant Secretary.

Analyzes and maintains data on international construction and engineering. Monitors production costs, prices, financial and labor conditions, technological changes, distribution, markets, trade patterns, and other aspects of these industries. Promotes international trade, develops competitive assessments, and assists engineering and construction companies in obtaining overseas construction projects.

Office of Thrift Supervision *(Treasury Dept.), Financial Reporting,* 1700 G St. N.W. 20552; (202) 906-6720. Fax, (202) 906-5735. Patrick Berbakos, Director.

Provides housing and mortgage statistics, including terms and rates of conventional home mortgages, and asset and liability information for thrift institutions insured by the Savings Association Insurance Fund.

▨ COMMUNITY AND REGIONAL DEVELOPMENT

AGENCIES

Administration for Children and Families *(Health and Human Services Dept.), Community Services,* 901 D St. S.W. 20447 (mailing address: 370 L'Enfant Promenade S.W. 20447); (202) 401-9333. Fax, (202) 401-4694. Donald Sykes, Director.

Administers the Community Services Block Grant and Discretionary Grant programs.

Administration for Native Americans *(Health and Human Services Dept.),* 200 Independence Ave. S.W., #348F 20201; (202) 690-7776. Fax, (202) 690-7441. Gary N. Kimble, Commissioner.

Awards grants for locally determined social and economic development strategies; promotes native American economic and social self-sufficiency; funds tribes and native American and native Hawaiian organizations. Commissioner chairs the Intradepartmental Council on Indian Affairs, which coordinates native American-related programs.

Army Corps of Engineers *(Defense Dept.),* 20 Massachusetts Ave. N.W., #8228 20314-1000; (202) 761-0001. Fax, (202) 761-4463. Lt. Gen. Joe N. Ballard (USACE), Chief of Engineers. Web, www.usace.army.mil.

Provides local governments with disaster relief, flood control, navigation, and hydroelectric power services.

Defense Dept., *Base Closure and Community Reinvestment,* 400 Army-Navy Dr., #200, Arlington, VA 22202-2884; (703) 604-6020. Fax, (703) 604-5843. Paul J. Dempsey, Director. Web, www.defenselink.mil.

Civilian office that helps community officials develop strategies and coordinate plans to alleviate the economic effect of major defense program changes, including base closings, reductions in forces, and contract cutbacks. Assists communities where defense activities are being expanded. Serves as the staff for the Economic Adjustment Committee, an interagency group that coordinates federal defense economic adjustment activities.

Housing and Urban Development Dept., *Block Grant Assistance,* 451 7th St. S.W., #7286 20410; (202) 708-3587. Fax, (202) 401-2044. Richard Kennedy, Director. Press, (202) 708-0685. Web, www.hud.gov.

Develops regulations and procedures for the Community Development Block Grant Program and the Section 108 Loan Guarantee Program. Manages close-out functions of the Urban Renewal Program.

Housing and Urban Development Dept., *Community Planning and Development,* 451 7th St. S.W., #7100 20410; (202) 708-2690. Fax, (202) 708-3336. Cardell Cooper, Assistant Secretary. Information, (202) 708-0980. Web, www.hud.gov.

Provides cities and states with community and economic development and housing assistance, including community development block grants. Encourages public-private partnerships in urban development and private sector initiatives. Oversees enterprise zone development program.

Housing and Urban Development Dept., *Community Viability,* 451 7th St. S.W., #7240 20410; (202) 708-

2894. Fax, (202) 708-3363. Richard H. Broun, Director. Web, www.hud.gov.

Issues policies and sets standards for environmental and land-use planning and for environmental management practices. Develops policies promoting energy efficiency, conservation, and renewable sources of supply in housing and community development programs, including district heating and cooling systems and wastes-to-energy cogeneration projects.

Housing and Urban Development Dept., *Field Management,* *451 7th St. S.W., #7150 20410; (202) 708-2565. Fax, (202) 401-9681. Nadeb O. Bynum, Director. Web, www.hud.gov.*

Acts as liaison and coordinates all activities between the Office of Community Planning and Development and regional and field offices; evaluates the performance of regional and field offices. Conducts policy analyses and evaluations of community planning and development programs, including the Community Development Block Grant Program, the Empowerment Zones/Enterprise Communities Program, and the McKinney Act programs.

Housing and Urban Development Dept., *State and Small Cities,* *451 7th St. S.W., #7184 20410; (202) 708-1322. Fax, (202) 708-3363. Steve Johnson, Director. Web, www.hud.gov.*

Provides states with grants for distribution to small cities and counties with fewer than 50,000 persons that are not entitled to community development block grants; insular areas also are eligible. Funds community development programs in low- and moderate-income communities and communities with urgent needs.

Housing and Urban Development Dept., *Technical Assistance,* *451 7th St. S.W., #7216 20410; (202) 708-3176. Fax, (202) 708-3363. Lyn T. Whitcomb, Director. Web, www.hud.gov.*

Develops program policies and designs and implements technical assistance plans for state and local governments for use in community planning and development programs.

Interagency Empowerment Zone/Enterprise Community Task Force, *300 7th St. S.W., #701 20024; (202) 619-7980. Fax, (202) 401-7420. Rick Wetherill, Director. Information, (800) 645-4712. TTY, (202) 720-7807. Web, www.ezec.gov.*

Provides information about federal empowerment zones and enterprise communities in economically distressed urban and rural areas.

CONGRESS

House Banking and Financial Services Committee, *Subcommittee on Housing and Community Opportunity,* *B303 RHOB 20515; (202) 225-6634. Rep. Rick A. Lazio, R-N.Y., Chair; Joseph M. Ventrone, Staff Director. Web, www.house.gov/banking.*

Jurisdiction over all community development legislation; urban planning, design, and research; urban redevelopment and relocation; and community development training and fellowships. Jurisdiction over Urban Development Action Grants and enterprise zones. Oversees the Housing and Urban Development Dept. and housing programs in the Agriculture Dept.

House Transportation and Infrastructure Committee, *Subcommittee on Economic Development, Public Buildings, Hazardous Materials, and Pipeline Transportation,* *586 FHOB 20515; (202) 225-3014. Fax, (202) 226-1898. Rep. Bob Franks, R-N.J., Chair; Richard C. Barnett, Staff Director. General e-mail, transcomm@ mail.house.gov. Web, www.house.gov/transportation.*

Jurisdiction over legislation on development of economically depressed areas, including Appalachia, and legislation designed to create jobs, often with public works and water resource development projects; jurisdiction over the Economic Development Administration.

Senate Banking, Housing, and Urban Affairs Committee, *Subcommittee on Housing and Transportation,* *SD-534 20510; (202) 224-7391. Fax, (202) 224-5137. Sen. Wayne Allard, R-Colo., Chair; John Carson, Staff Director. Web, banking.senate.gov.*

Jurisdiction over community development legislation (including Urban Development Action Grants and enterprise zones); federal insurance (including flood insurance); urban planning, design, and research; and urban redevelopment and relocation. Oversees the Housing and Urban Development Dept. and housing programs in the Agriculture Dept.

Senate Environment and Public Works Committee, *SD-410 20510; (202) 224-6176. Fax, (202) 224-5167. Sen. Robert C. Smith, R-N.H., Chair; Dave Conover, Staff Director. Web, epw.senate.gov.*

Jurisdiction over legislation on development of economically depressed areas, including Appalachia, and over legislation designed to create jobs, often with public works and water resource development projects; jurisdiction over the Economic Development Administration.

Senate Finance Committee, *SD-219 20510; (202) 224-4515. Fax, (202) 224-5920. Sen. William V. Roth Jr., R-Del., Chair; Frank Polk, Staff Director. Web, finance.senate.gov.*

Jurisdiction over revenue sharing legislation (jurisdiction shared with Senate Governmental Affairs Committee).

Senate Governmental Affairs Committee, *SD-340 20510; (202) 224-4751. Fax, (202) 224-9603. Sen. Fred Thompson, R-Tenn., Chair; Hannah Sistare, Staff Director. Web, gov_affairs.senate.gov.*

Jurisdiction over revenue sharing legislation (jurisdiction shared with Senate Finance Committee).

NONPROFIT

American Planning Assn., *1776 Massachusetts Ave. N.W., #400 20036-1904; (202) 872-0611. Fax, (202) 872-0643. Frank So, Executive Director. Web, www.planning. org.*

Membership: professional planners and others interested in urban and rural planning. Serves as a clearinghouse for planners. Sponsors professional development workshops conducted by the American Institute of Certified Planners. Prepares studies and technical reports; conducts seminars and conferences.

American Resort Development Assn., *1220 L St. N.W., #500 20005; (202) 371-6700. Fax, (202) 289-8544. Vacant, President. Web, www.arda.org.*

Membership: U.S. and international developers, builders, financiers, marketing companies, and others involved in resort, recreational, and community development. Serves as an information clearinghouse; monitors federal and state legislation affecting land, time share, and community development industries.

Center for Community Change, *1000 Wisconsin Ave. N.W. 20007; (202) 342-0519. Fax, (202) 342-1132. Andy Mott, Executive Director.*

Provides community-based organizations serving minorities and the economically disadvantaged with technical assistance. Areas of assistance include community development block grants, housing, economic and resource development, rural development projects, and program planning.

Corporation for Enterprise Development, *777 N. Capitol St. N.E., #410 20002; (202) 408-9788. Fax, (202) 408-9793. Brian Dabson, President. General e-mail, cfed@ cfed.org. Web, www.cfed.org.*

Research and consulting organization that promotes economic self-sufficiency among low-income people through enterprise development, including microbusinesses to generate self-employment for the unemployed. Provides technical assistance and policy analysis to state and local governments and community organizations.

Council of State Community Development Agencies, *444 N. Capitol St. N.W., #224 20001-1512; (202) 624-3630. Fax, (202) 624-3639. John M. Sidor, Executive Director. Web, www.coscda.org.*

Membership: directors and staff of state community development agencies. Promotes common interests among the states, including community and economic development, housing, homelessness, infrastructure, and state and local planning.

International Institute of Site Planning, *715 G St. S.E. 20003; (202) 546-2322. Fax, (202) 546-2722. Beatriz de W. Coffin, Director. General e-mail, iisitep@aol.com.*

Directs research and provides information on site planning development and design of sites and buildings; conducts study/travel programs.

Land Trust Alliance, *1319 F St. N.W., #501 20004-1106; (202) 638-4725. Fax, (202) 638-4730. Jean Hocker, President. Web, www.lta.org.*

Membership: organizations and individuals who work to conserve land resources. Serves as a forum for the exchange of information; conducts research and public education programs. Monitors legislation and regulations.

Local Initiatives Support Corp., *Washington Office, 1825 K St. N.W., #1100 20006; (202) 785-2908. Fax, (202) 835-8931. Michael Tierney, Senior Vice President. Web, www.liscnet.org.*

Provides community development corporations with financial and technical assistance to build affordable housing and revitalize distressed neighborhoods. (Headquarters in New York.)

National Assn. of Conservation Districts, *509 Capitol Court N.E. 20002-4937; (202) 547-6223. Fax, (202) 547-6450. Ernest C. Shea, Chief Executive Officer. Web, www.nacdnet.org.*

Membership: conservation districts (local subdivisions of state government). Works to promote the conservation of land, forests, and other natural resources. Interests include erosion and sediment control; water quality; forestry, water, flood plain, and range management; rural development; and urban and community conservation.

National Assn. of Counties, *Community and Economic Development, 440 1st St. N.W., 8th Floor 20001-2028; (202) 393-6226. Fax, (202) 393-2630. Dianne Taylor, Associate Legislative Director. Information, (202) 393-6226. Web, www.naco.org.*

Membership: county governments. Conducts research and provides information on community development block grants, assisted low-income housing, and other housing and economic development programs. Monitors legislation and regulations.

National Assn. of Development Organizations, *400 N. Capitol St. N.W., #390 20001; (202) 624-7806. Fax, (202) 624-8813. Aliceann Wohlbruck, Executive Director. General e-mail, nado@sso.org. Web, www.nado.org.*

Membership: organizations interested in regional, local, and rural economic development. Provides information on federal, state, and local development programs and revolving loan funds; sponsors conferences and seminars.

National Assn. of Regional Councils, *1700 K St. N.W., #1300 20006; (202) 457-0710. Fax, (202) 296-9352. William Dodge, Executive Director. General e-mail, narc@clark.net. Web, www.narc.org.*

Membership: regional councils of local governments. Works with member local governments to encourage areawide economic growth and cooperation between public and private sectors, with emphasis on community development.

National Community Development Assn., *522 21st St. N.W., #120 20006; (202) 293-7587. Fax, (202) 887-5546. John A. Sasso, Executive Secretary. General e-mail, ncda@ncdaonline.org. Web, www.ncdaonline.org.*

Membership: local governments that administer federally supported community and economic development, housing, and human service programs.

National Congress for Community Economic Development, *1030 15th St. N.W., #325 20005; (202) 289-9020. Fax, (202) 289-7051. Roy Priest, President. Information, (877) 446-2233. Web, www.ncced.org.*

Membership: organizations engaged in revitalizing economically distressed communities. Services include advocacy, fundraising and technical assistance, information and referrals, conferences, and training. Conducts research and compiles statistics on industry issues and trends. Library open to the public.

National Trust for Historic Preservation, *1785 Massachusetts Ave. N.W. 20036-2117; (202) 588-6000. Fax, (202) 588-6038. Richard Moe, President. Web, www.nthp.org.*

Conducts seminars, workshops, and conferences on topics related to preservation, including neighborhood conservation, main street revitalization, rural conservation, and preservation law; offers financial assistance through loan and grant programs; provides advisory services; operates historic house museums, which are open to the public.

Partners for Livable Communities, *1429 21st St. N.W., 2nd Floor 20036; (202) 887-5990. Fax, (202) 466-4845. Robert H. McNulty, President. General e-mail, partners@livable.com. Web, www.livable.com.*

Promotes working partnerships among public, private, and governmental sectors to improve the quality of life and economic development at local and regional levels. Conducts conferences and workshops; maintains referral clearinghouse.

Scenic America, *801 Pennsylvania Ave. S.E., #300 20003-2152; (202) 543-6200. Fax, (202) 543-9130. Meg Maguire, President. Web, www.scenic.org.*

Membership: national, state, and local groups concerned with land-use control, growth management, and landscape protection. Works to enhance the scenic quality of America's communities and countryside. Provides information and technical assistance on scenic byways, tree preservation, economics of aesthetic regulation, billboard and sign control, scenic areas preservation, and growth management.

Rural Areas

AGENCIES

Agriculture Dept., Rural Development, *1400 Independence Ave. S.W., #206W 20250; (202) 720-4581. Fax, (202) 720-2080. Jill Long Thompson, Under Secretary. Information, (202) 720-4323. Web, www.rurdev.usda.gov.*

Acts as chief adviser to the secretary on agricultural credit and related matters; coordinates rural development policies and programs throughout the federal government; supervises the Rural Utilities Service, Rural Housing Service, and Rural Business-Cooperative Service.

Farm Service Agency (Agriculture Dept.), Farm Loan and Analysis, *1400 Independence Ave. S.W. 20250; (202) 720-4671. Fax, (202) 690-3573. Terry Hickenbotham, Deputy Administrator. Web, www.fsa.usda.gov.*

Supports rural development through farm program loans, including real estate, farm production, and emergency loans.

Rural Business-Cooperative Service (Agriculture Dept.), *1400 Independence Ave. S.W., #5045 20250-3201; (202) 690-4730. Fax, (202) 690-4737. Dayton J. Watkins, Administrator. Web, www.rurdev.usda.gov/rbs/index.html.*

Promotes rural economic development by financing community facilities and assisting community businesses.

Rural Housing Service (Agriculture Dept.), *1400 Independence Ave. S.W., #5014, MS 0701 20250-0701; (202)*

690-1533. Fax, (202) 690-0500. James C. Kearney, Administrator. Web, www.rurdev.usda.gov/rhs/index.html.

Offers financial assistance to apartment dwellers and homeowners in rural areas; provides funds to construct or improve community facilities.

Rural Utilities Service (*Agriculture Dept.*), *1400 Independence Ave. S.W. 20250-1500; (202) 720-9540. Fax, (202) 720-1725. Christopher A. McLean, Administrator (Acting). Information, (202) 720-1255. Web, www.usda. gov/rus.*

Makes loans and loan guarantees to rural electric and telephone utilities providing service in rural areas. Administers the Rural Telephone Bank, which provides supplemental financing from federal sources. Makes loans for economic development and creation of jobs in rural areas, for water and waste disposal, and for distance learning and telemedicine.

CONGRESS

House Agriculture Committee, *Subcommittee on General Farm Commodities, Resource Conservation, and Credit, 1430 LHOB 20515; (202) 225-0171. Fax, (202) 225-4464. Rep. Bill Barrett, R-Neb., Chair; Mike Neruda, Staff Director. Web, agriculture.house.gov.*

Jurisdiction over legislation on rural development; oversight of Rural Utilities Service. Jurisdiction over legislation on soil conservation, small-scale stream channelization, watershed, and flood control programs, water and air quality, and agricultural credit programs.

Senate Agriculture, Nutrition, and Forestry Committee, *Subcommittee on Forestry, Conservation, and Rural Revitalization, SR-328A 20510; (202) 224-2752. Fax, (202) 224-1725. Sen. Larry E. Craig, R-Idaho, Chair; Dan Whiting, Staff Contact. Web, agriculture.senate.gov.*

Jurisdiction over legislation on rural development; oversight of Rural Utilities Service. Jurisdiction over legislation on soil conservation, small-scale stream channelization, watershed, and flood control programs, water and air quality, and agricultural credit programs.

NONPROFIT

Farm Credit Council, *50 F St. N.W., #900 20001; (202) 626-8710. Fax, (202) 626-8718. Ken Auer, President.*

Represents the Farm Credit System, a national financial cooperative that makes loans to agricultural producers, rural homebuyers, farmer cooperatives, and rural utilities. Finances the export of U.S. agricultural commodities.

Housing Assistance Council, *1025 Vermont Ave. N.W., #606 20005-3516; (202) 842-8600. Fax, (202) 347-3441.*

Moises Loza, Executive Director. Information, (800) 989-4422. General e-mail, hac@ruralhome.org.

Operates in rural areas and in cities of fewer than 25,000 citizens. Advises low-income and minority groups seeking federal assistance for improving rural housing and community facilities; studies and makes recommendations for state and local housing policies; makes low-interest loans for housing programs for low-income and minority groups living in rural areas, including native Americans and farm workers.

Irrigation Assn., *8260 Willow Oaks Corporate Dr., #120, Fairfax, VA 22031; (703) 573-3551. Fax, (703) 573-1913. Thomas Kimmell, Executive Director. Web, www.irrigation. org.*

Membership: companies and individuals involved in irrigation, drainage, and erosion control worldwide. Seeks to improve the products and practices used to manage water resources; interests include economic development and environmental enhancement.

National Cooperative Business Assn., *1401 New York Ave. N.W., #1100 20005-2146; (202) 638-6222. Fax, (202) 638-1374. Paul Hazen, President. General e-mail, ncba@ ncba.org. Web, www.cooperative.org.*

Alliance of cooperatives, businesses, and state cooperative associations. Provides information about starting and managing agricultural cooperatives in the United States and in developing nations. Monitors legislation and regulations.

National Council of Farmer Cooperatives, *50 F St. N.W., #900 20001; (202) 626-8700. Fax, (202) 626-8722. David Graves, President. General e-mail, info@ncfc.org. Web, www.ncfc.org.*

Membership: cooperative businesses owned and operated by farmers. Encourages research on agricultural cooperatives; provides statistics and analyzes trends. Monitors legislation and regulations on agricultural trade, transportation, energy, and tax issues.

National Rural Community Assistance Program, *722 East Market St., #105, Leesburg, VA 20176; (703) 771-8636. Fax, (703) 771-8753. Randolph A. Adams, Executive Director. General e-mail, rcap@rcap.org. Web, www.rcap. org.*

Federally funded organization that conducts program to improve water delivery and disposal of waste water for rural residents, particularly low-income families.

National Rural Electric Cooperative Assn., *4301 Wilson Blvd., Arlington, VA 22203-1860; (703) 907-5500. Fax, (703) 907-5516. Glenn English, Chief Executive Officer. Web, www.nreca.org.*

Membership: rural electric cooperative systems and public power and utility districts. Provides members with legislative, legal, and regulatory services.

National Telephone Cooperative Assn., *4121 Wilson Blvd., 10th Floor, Arlington, VA 22203; (703) 351-2000. Fax, (703) 351-2001. Michael E. Brunner, Executive Vice President. General e-mail, contact@ntca.org. Web, www. ntca.org.*

Membership: locally owned and controlled telecommunications cooperatives and companies serving rural and small-town areas. Offers educational seminars, workshops, technical assistance, and a benefits program to members. Monitors legislation and regulations.

Rural Coalition, *1411 K St. N.W., #901 20005; (202) 628-7160. Fax, (202) 628-7165. Lorette Picciano, Executive Director. Web, www.ruralco.org.*

Alliance of organizations that develop public policies benefiting rural communities. Collaborates with community-based groups on agriculture and rural development issues, including health and the environment, minority farmers, farmworkers, native Americans' rights, and rural community development. Provides rural groups with technical assistance.

Specific Regions

AGENCIES

Appalachian Regional Commission, *1666 Connecticut Ave. N.W., #600 20235; (202) 884-7660. Fax, (202) 884-7693. Jesse White, Federal Co-Chair; Thomas Hunter, Executive Director, (202) 884-7700. Information, (202) 884-7773. Press, (202) 884-7770. Web, www.arc.gov.*

Federal-state-local partnership for economic development of the region including West Virginia and parts of Alabama, Georgia, Kentucky, Maryland, Mississippi, New York, North Carolina, Ohio, Pennsylvania, South Carolina, Tennessee, and Virginia. Plans and provides technical and financial assistance and coordinates federal and state efforts for economic development of Appalachia.

Bureau of Reclamation *(Interior Dept.), 1849 C St. N.W., #7659 20240; (202) 208-4157. Fax, (202) 208-3484. Eluid Martinez, Commissioner. Information, (202) 208-4215. Web, www.usbr.gov.*

Administers federal programs for water and power resource development and management in seventeen western states; oversees municipal and industrial water supply, hydroelectric power generation, irrigation, flood control, water quality improvement, river regulation, fish and wildlife enhancement, and outdoor recreation.

Interstate Commission on the Potomac River Basin, *6110 Executive Blvd., #300, Rockville, MD 20852; (301) 984-1908. Fax, (301) 984-5841. Joseph K. Hoffman, Executive Director. Web, www.potomacriver.org.*

Nonregulatory interstate compact commission established by Congress to control and reduce water pollution and to restore and protect living resources in the Potomac River and its tributaries. Monitors water quality; assists metropolitan water utilities; seeks innovative methods to solve water supply and land resource problems. Provides information and educational materials on the Potomac River basin.

National Capital Planning Commission, *801 Pennsylvania Ave. N.W., #301 20576; (202) 482-7200. Fax, (202) 482-7272. Reginald W. Griffith, Executive Director. Web, www.ncpc.gov.*

Central planning agency for the federal government in the national capital region, which includes the District of Columbia and suburban Maryland and Virginia. Reviews and approves plans for the physical growth and development of the national capital area, using environmental, historic, and land-use criteria.

Tennessee Valley Authority, *Government Affairs, Washington Office, 1 Massachusetts Ave. N.W., #300 20444; (202) 898-2999. Fax, (202) 898-2998. David Withrow, Vice President. Web, www.tva.gov.*

Coordinates resource conservation, development, and land-use programs in the Tennessee River Valley. Produces and supplies wholesale power to municipal and cooperative electric systems, federal installations, and some industries.

NONPROFIT

Greater Washington Board of Trade, *1129 20th St. N.W., #200 20036; (202) 857-5900. Fax, (202) 223-2648. John Tydings, President. General e-mail, info@bot.org. Web, www.bot.org.*

Promotes and plans economic growth for the capital region. Supports business-government partnerships, technological training, and transportation planning; promotes international trade; works to increase economic viability of the city of Washington. Monitors legislation and regulations at local, state, and federal levels.

New England Council, *Government Relations, Washington Office, 331 Constitution Ave. N.E. 20002; (202) 547-0048. Fax, (202) 547-9149. Deidre W. Savage, Vice President. General e-mail, newenglandcouncildc@msn. com. Web, www.newenglandcouncil.org.*

Provides information on business and economic issues concerning New England; serves as liaison between the New England congressional delegations and business community. (Headquarters in Boston.)

Northeast-Midwest Institute, *218 D St. S.E., 1st Floor 20003; (202) 544-5200. Fax, (202) 544-0043. Dick Munson, Executive Director. Web, www.nemw.org.*

Public policy research organization that promotes the economic vitality of the northeast and midwest regions. Interests include distribution of federal funding to regions, economic development, human resources, energy, and natural resources.

Urban Areas

AGENCIES

Housing and Urban Development Dept., *Affordable Housing Programs, 451 7th St. S.W., #7164 20410; (202) 708-2685. Fax, (202) 708-1744. Mary Kolesar, Director. Web, www.hud.gov.*

Coordinates with cities to convey publicly owned, abandoned property to low-income families in exchange for their commitment to repair, occupy, and maintain property.

Housing and Urban Development Dept., *Economic Development, 451 7th St. S.W., #7136 20410; (202) 708-2290. Fax, (202) 708-7543. Nelson R. Bregon, Director. Web, www.ezec.gov.*

Manages economic development programs, including Urban Development Action Grants, Empowerment Zones/Enterprise Communities, and YOUTHBUILD. Encourages private-public partnerships for development through neighborhood development corporations. Formulates policies and legislative proposals on economic development.

Neighborhood Reinvestment Corp., *1325 G St. N.W., #800 20005; (202) 220-2300. Fax, (202) 376-2600. George Knight, Executive Director. Web, www.nw.org.*

Chartered by Congress to assist localities in developing and operating local neighborhood-based programs designed to reverse decline in urban residential neighborhoods and rural communities. Oversees the National NeighborWorks Network, an association of local non-profit organizations concerned with urban and rural development.

NONPROFIT

Council for Urban Economic Development, *1730 K St. N.W., #700 20006; (202) 223-4735. Fax, (202) 223-4745. Jeffrey Finkle, President. General e-mail, mail@urbandevelopment.com. Web, www.cued.org.*

Membership: public economic development directors, chamber of commerce staff, utility executives, aca-demicians, and others who design and implement development programs. Provides information to members on job creation, attraction, and retention.

International Downtown Assn., *910 17th St. N.W., #210 20006; (202) 293-4505. Fax, (202) 293-4509. Elizabeth Jackson, President. General e-mail, question@ida-downtown.org. Web, www.ida-downtown.org.*

Membership: organizations, corporations, public agencies, and individuals interested in the development and management of city downtown areas. Supports cooperative efforts between the public and private sectors to revitalize downtowns and adjacent neighborhoods; provides members with information, technical assistance, and advice; administers the Downtown Development Foundation.

Milton S. Eisenhower Foundation, *1660 L St. N.W., #200 20036; (202) 429-0440. Fax, (202) 452-0169. Lynn A. Curtis, President. General e-mail, mseinsenhower@msn. com. Web, www.eisenhowerfoundation.org.*

Strives to help inner city communities combat violence by supporting programs with proven records of success. Provides funding, technical assistance, evaluation, and supervision to communities wishing to replicate successful programs.

National Assn. for the Advancement of Colored People, *Washington Office, 1025 Vermont Ave. N.W., #1120 20005; (202) 638-2269. Fax, (202) 638-5936. Hilary O. Shelton, Director. Web, www.naacp.org.*

Membership: persons interested in civil rights for all minorities. Works to eliminate discrimination in housing and urban affairs. Interests include programs for urban redevelopment, urban homesteading, and low-income housing. Supports programs that make affordable rental housing available to minorities and that maintain African American ownership of urban and rural land. (Headquarters in Baltimore.)

National Assn. of Neighborhoods, *1651 Fuller St. N.W. 20009; (202) 332-7766. Fax, (202) 332-2314. Ricardo C. Byrd, Executive Director. Web, www. consumermortgage.org.*

Federation of neighborhood groups that provides technical assistance to local governments, neighborhood groups, and businesses. Seeks to increase influence of grassroots groups on decisions affecting neighborhoods; sponsors training workshops promoting neighborhood awareness.

National Center for Neighborhood Enterprise, *1424 16th St. N.W., #300 20036; (202) 518-6500. Fax, (202) 588-0314. Robert L. Woodson Sr., Chair. Web, www.ncne. com.*

Public policy research and demonstration organization. Interests include economic development, education, family preservation, and crime prevention. Attempts to identify model neighborhood-based economic and social development projects. Gives technical assistance to enterprises undertaking neighborhood development.

National Center for Urban Ethnic Affairs, *P.O. Box 20, Cardinal Station 20064; (202) 319-5128. Fax, (202) 319-6289. John A. Kromkowski, President. Information, (202) 232-3600.*

Educational and research organization that preserves and revitalizes urban neighborhoods through community organization and development; provides technical support and encourages interethnic and interracial cooperation, particularly between recent and older immigrants. Publishes monographs.

National League of Cities, *1301 Pennsylvania Ave. N.W., #550 20004-1763; (202) 626-3000. Fax, (202) 626-3043. Donald J. Borut, Executive Director. Information, (202) 626-3120. Press, (202) 626-3158. Web, www.nlc.org.*

Membership: cities and state municipal leagues. Aids city leaders in developing programs; investigates needs of local governments in implementing federal community development programs.

National Neighborhood Coalition, *1875 Connecticut Ave. N.W., #410 20009; (202) 986-2096. Fax, (202) 986-1941. Betty Weiss, Executive Director. General e-mail, nncnnc@erols.com. Web, www.neighborhoodcoalition.org.*

Membership: national and regional organizations that have neighborhood-based affiliates. Provides technical assistance to neighborhood groups, or conduct research on issues affecting neighborhoods. Monitors national programs and policies that affect inner-city neighborhoods; conducts monthly information forums.

National Urban League, *Research and Public Policy, Washington Office, 1111 14th St. N.W., #1001 20005-5603; (202) 898-1604. Fax, (202) 408-1965. William Spriggs, Director. General e-mail, info@nul.org. Web, www.nul.org.*

Social service organization concerned with the social welfare of African Americans and other minorities. Conducts legislative and policy analysis on housing and urban affairs. Operates a job bank. (Headquarters in New York.)

Urban Institute, *Metropolitan Housing and Communities Policy Center, 2100 M St. N.W., #500 20037; (202) 833-7200. Fax, (202) 728-0232. Margery Austin Turner, Director. Web, www.urban.org.*

Research organization that deals with urban problems. Researches federal, state, and local policies; focus includes community development block grants, neighborhood rehabilitation programs, and housing issues. Conducts economic research on the infrastructure of urban areas.

Urban Land Institute, *1025 Thomas Jefferson St. N.W., #500W 20007-5201; (202) 624-7000. Fax, (202) 624-7140. Richard Rosan, President. Information, (800) 321-5011. Library, (202) 624-7117. Web, www.uli.org.*

Membership: land developers, planners, state and federal agencies, financial institutions, home builders, consultants, and realtors. Provides responsible leadership in the use of land in order to enhance the total environment; monitors trends in new community development. Library open to the public by appointment for a fee.

U.S. Conference of Mayors, *1620 Eye St. N.W., #400 20006; (202) 293-7330. Fax, (202) 293-2352. J. Thomas Cochran, Executive Director. General e-mail, uscm@ cais.com. Web, www.usmayors.org/uscm.*

Membership: mayors of cities with populations of 30,000 or more. Promotes city-federal cooperation; publishes reports and conducts meetings on federal programs, policies, and initiatives that affect urban and suburban interests. Serves as a clearinghouse for information on urban and suburban problems.

CONSTRUCTION

See also Military Installations (chap. 16); Transportation (chap. 19)

AGENCIES

Census Bureau *(Commerce Dept.), Manufacturing and Construction, Suitland and Silver Hill Rds., Suitland, MD 20233; (301) 457-4593. Fax, (301) 457-4583. William G. Bostic Jr., Chief.*

Publishes statistics on the value of construction put in place; housing starts, sales, and completions; building permits; price index of single-family homes sold; characteristics of new housing; and expenditures for residential improvements. Conducts a census of construction industries every five years.

General Services Administration, *Public Buildings Service, 1800 F St. N.W., #6344 20405; (202) 501-1100. Fax, (202) 219-2310. Robert A. Peck, Commissioner.*

Administers the construction, maintenance, and operation of buildings owned or leased by the federal government. Manages and disposes of federal real estate.

International Trade Administration *(Commerce Dept.), Basic Industries, 14th St. and Constitution Ave. N.W., #4043 20230; (202) 482-0614. Fax, (202) 482-5666. Alan S. Bowser, Deputy Assistant Secretary.*

Analyzes and maintains data on international construction and engineering. Monitors production costs, prices, financial and labor conditions, technological changes, distribution, markets, trade patterns, and other aspects of these industries. Promotes international trade, develops competitive assessments, and assists engineering and construction companies in obtaining overseas construction projects.

NONPROFIT

American Public Works Assn., *Washington Office, 1401 K St. N.W., 11th Floor 20005; (202) 408-9541. Fax, (202) 408-9542. Peter B. King, Executive Director. General e-mail, apwa.dc@apwa.net. Web, www.apwa.net.*

Membership: engineers, architects, and others who maintain and manage public works facilities and services. Conducts research and promotes exchange of information on transportation and infrastructure-related issues. (Headquarters in Kansas City.)

American Subcontractors Assn., *1004 Duke St., Alexandria, VA 22314-3588; (703) 684-3450. Fax, (703) 836-3482. Colette Nelson, Executive Vice President. General e-mail, asaoffice@aol.com. Web, www.asaonline.com.*

Membership: construction subcontractors, specialty contractors, and their suppliers. Addresses business, contract, and payment issues affecting all subcontractors. Interests include procurement laws, payment practices, and lien laws. Monitors legislation and regulations.

Associated Builders and Contractors, *1300 N. 17th St., 8th Floor, Rosslyn, VA 22209; (703) 812-2000. Fax, (703) 812-8202. Bob Hepner, Executive Vice President. Web, www.abc.org.*

Membership: construction contractors engaged primarily in nonresidential construction, subcontractors, and suppliers. Sponsors apprenticeship, safety, and training programs. Provides labor relations information; compiles statistics. Monitors legislation and regulations.

Associated General Contractors of America, *333 John Carlyle St., #200, Alexandria, VA 22314; (703) 548-3118. Fax, (703) 548-3119. Stephen E. Sandherr, Executive Vice President. General e-mail, sanders@agc.org. Web, www.agc.org.*

Membership: general contractors engaged primarily in nonresidential construction; subcontractors; suppliers; accounting, insurance and bonding, and law firms. Conducts training programs, conferences, seminars, and market development activities for members. Produces position papers on construction issues. Monitors legislation and regulations.

Associated Landscape Contractors of America, *150 Elden St., #270, Herndon, VA 20170; (703) 736-9666. Fax, (703) 736-9668. Debra H. Holder, Executive Director. Web, www.alca.org.*

Represents the interior and exterior landscape contracting industry. Monitors legislation and regulations.

Construction Management Assn. of America, *7918 Jones Branch Dr., #540, McLean, VA 22102; (703) 356-2622. Fax, (703) 356-6388. Bruce D'Agostino, Executive Vice President. Web, www.cmaanet.org.*

Promotes the development of construction management as a profession through publications, education, a certification program, and an information network. Serves as an advocate for construction management in the legislative, executive, and judicial branches of government.

Construction Specifications Institute, *99 Canal Center Plaza, #300, Alexandria, VA 22314-1588; (703) 684-0300. Fax, (703) 684-0465. Gregory Balestrero, Executive Director. Information, (800) 689-2900. Web, www.csinet.org.*

Membership: architects, engineers, contractors, and others in the construction industry. Promotes construction technology; maintains speakers bureau; publishes reference materials to help individuals prepare construction documents; sponsors certification programs for construction specifiers and manufacturing representatives.

Mechanical Contractors Assn. of America, *1385 Piccard Dr., Rockville, MD 20850; (301) 869-5800. Fax, (301) 990-9690. John R. Gentille, Executive Vice President. Web, www.mcaa.org.*

Membership: mechanical contractors and members of related professions. Seeks to improve building standards and codes. Provides information, publications, and training programs; conducts seminars and annual convention. Monitors legislation and regulations.

National Assn. of Home Builders, *1201 15th St. N.W. 20005-2800; (202) 822-0200. Fax, (202) 822-0559. Thomas M. Downs, Executive Vice President. Press, (202) 822-0253. Web, www.nahb.com.*

Membership: contractors, builders, architects, engineers, mortgage lenders, and others interested in home building and commercial real estate construction. Participates in updating and developing building codes and standards; offers technical information. Library open to the public.

National Assn. of Minority Contractors, *666 11th St. N.W., #520 20001; (202) 347-8259. Fax, (202) 628-1876. Vacant, Executive Director.*

Membership: minority businesses and related firms, associations, and individuals serving those businesses in the construction industry. Advises members on commercial and government business; develops resources for technical assistance and training; provides bid information on government contracts.

National Assn. of Plumbing-Heating-Cooling Contractors, *180 S. Washington St., Falls Church, VA 22046 (mailing address: P.O. Box 6808, Falls Church, VA 22040); (703) 237-8100. Fax, (703) 237-7442. Allen Inlow, Chief Executive Officer. Information, (800) 533-7694. Web, www.naphcc.org.*

Provides education and training for plumbing, heating, and cooling contractors and their employees. Offers career information, internships, and scholarship programs for business and engineering students to encourage careers in the plumbing and mechanical contracting field.

National Assn. of the Remodeling Industry, *4900 Seminary Rd., #320, Alexandria, VA 22311-1811; (703) 575-1100. Fax, (703) 575-1121. Randall Scott, Executive Vice President. Web, www.remodeltoday.com.*

Membership: remodeling contractors, manufacturers, wholesalers, distributors, lenders, and utilities. Sponsors educational programs on construction products and techniques; provides information on industry statistics and small-business practices; publishes consumer information. Monitors legislation and regulations.

National Constructors Assn., *1730 M St. N.W., #503 20036; (202) 466-8880. Fax, (202) 466-7512. Nicholas A. Fiore, President.*

Membership: designers and builders of oil refineries, chemical plants, steel mills, power plants, and other industrial facilities. Interests include governmental energy policies, regulations, worker safety and health, and labor relations.

National Electrical Contractors Assn., *3 Bethesda Metro Center, #1100, Bethesda, MD 20814; (301) 657-3110. Fax, (301) 215-4500. John Grau, Executive Vice President. Web, www.necanet.org.*

Membership: electrical contractors who build and service electrical wiring, equipment, and appliances.

Represents members in collective bargaining with union workers; sponsors research and educational programs.

National Utility Contractors Assn., *4301 N. Fairfax Dr., #360, Arlington, VA 22203-1627; (703) 358-9300. Fax, (703) 358-9307. Peggie Woodward, Executive Director. Web, www.nuca.com.*

Membership: contractors who perform water, sewer, and other underground utility construction. Sponsors conferences; conducts surveys. Monitors public works legislation and regulations.

Rebuild America Coalition, *c/o American Public Works Assn., 1401 K St. N.W., 11th Floor 20005; (202) 408-1325. Fax, (202) 408-9542. Ann McCulloch, Coalition Manager. Web, www.rebuildamerica.org.*

Coalition of public and private organizations concerned with maintaining the infrastructure of the United States. Advocates government encouragement of innovative technology, financing, and public-private partnerships to build and rebuild public facilities.

Sheet Metal and Air Conditioning Contractors National Assn., *4201 Lafayette Center Dr., Chantilly, VA 20151-1209; (703) 803-2980. Fax, (703) 803-3732. John W. Sroka, Executive Vice President. Web, www.smacna.org.*

Membership: unionized sheet metal and air conditioning contractors. Provides information on standards and installation and fabrication methods. Operates the National Environmental Balancing Bureau with the Mechanical Contractors Assn. of America.

Society for Marketing Professional Services, *99 Canal Center Plaza, #250, Alexandria, VA 22314-1588; (703) 549-6117. Fax, (703) 549-2498. Ronald Worth, Vice President. Information, (800) 292-7677. Web, www.smps.org.*

Membership: individuals who provide professional services to the building industry. Assists individuals who market design services in the areas of architecture, engineering, planning, interior design, landscape architecture, and construction management. Provides seminars, workshops, and publications for members. Maintains job banks.

Women Construction Owners and Executives USA, *4423 Lehigh Rd., #325, College Park, MD 20740; (435) 404-5354. Fax, (435) 404-5354. Carole L. Bionda, National Administrator. Information, (800) 788-3548. General e-mail, wcoeusa@aol.com. Web, www.wcoeusa.org.*

Promotes the interests of women who own their own construction companies or who are in policy-making positions within construction firms. Sponsors national conferences. Monitors legislation and regulation.

Architecture and Design

AGENCIES

General Services Administration, *Environmental Division, 1800 F St. N.W., #4207 20405; (202) 501-1811. Fax, (202) 501-3203. Debra Yap, Director.*

Administers the Art and Historic Preservation Program, which sets aside for art projects a percentage of the estimated construction costs for new buildings or renovation costs for existing ones; manages a collection of fine arts.

National Endowment for the Arts *(National Foundation on the Arts and the Humanities), Folk and Traditional Arts, Literature, Theater, Musical Theater, and Planning and Stabilization, 1100 Pennsylvania Ave. N.W. 20506-0001; (202) 682-5428. Fax, (202) 682-5669. Barry Bergey, Division Coordinator. Web, arts.endow.gov.*

Awards grants for design arts projects in architecture; landscape architecture; urban design and planning; historic preservation; and interior, graphic, industrial, product, and costume and fashion design.

NONPROFIT

American Institute of Architects, *1735 New York Ave. N.W. 20006; (202) 626-7310. Fax, (202) 626-7426. Norman L. Koonce, Chief Executive Officer. Information, (202) 626-7300. Library, (202) 626-7492. Web, www.aiaonline.com.*

Membership: registered American architects. Works to advance the standards of architectural education, training, and practice. Promotes the aesthetic, scientific, and practical efficiency of architecture, urban design, and planning; monitors international developments. Offers continuing and professional education programs; sponsors scholarships, internships, and awards. Houses archival collection, including documents and drawings of American architects and architecture. Library open to the public. Monitors legislation and regulations.

American Nursery and Landscape Assn., *1250 Eye St. N.W., #500 20005; (202) 789-2900. Fax, (202) 789-1893. Robert J. Dolibois, Executive Vice President; Warren Quinn, Director. Web, www.anla.org.*

Serves as an information clearinghouse on the technical aspects of nursery and landscape business and design.

American Society of Interior Designers, *608 Massachusetts Ave. N.E. 20002-6006; (202) 546-3480. Fax, (202) 546-3240. Michael Alin, Executive Director. General e-mail, network@asid.noli.com. Web, www.asid.org.*

Offers certified professional development courses addressing the technical, professional, and business needs of designers; bestows annual scholarships, fellowships, and awards; supports licensing efforts at the state level.

American Society of Landscape Architects, *636 Eye St. N.W. 20001; (202) 898-2444. Fax, (202) 898-1185. James Tolliver, Executive Vice President (Acting). Web, www.asla.org.*

Membership: professional landscape architects. Advises government agencies on land-use policy and environmental matters. Accredits university-level programs in landscape architecture; conducts professional education seminars for members.

Assn. of Collegiate Schools of Architecture, *1735 New York Ave. N.W. 20006; (202) 785-2324. Fax, (202) 628-0448. Stephanie U. Vierra, Executive Director. Web, www.acsa-arch.org.*

Conducts workshops and seminars for architecture school faculty; presents awards for student and faculty excellence in architecture; publishes directory of architecture professors and a guide to architecture schools in North America.

Industrial Designers Society of America, *1142 Walker Rd., Great Falls, VA 22066-1836; (703) 759-0100. Fax, (703) 759-7679. Robert Schwartz, Executive Director. General e-mail, idsa@erols.com. Web, www.idsa.org.*

Membership: designers of products, equipment, instruments, furniture, transportation, packages, exhibits, information services, and related services. Provides the Bureau of Labor Statistics with industry information. Monitors legislation and regulations.

Landscape Architecture Foundation, *636 Eye St. N.W. 20001; (202) 898-2444. Fax, (202) 898-1185. Susan Everett, Contact. Web, www.asla.org.*

Conducts research and provides educational and scientific information on landscape architecture and related fields. Awards scholarships and fellowships in landscape architecture. (Affiliated with the American Society of Landscape Architects.)

National Architectural Accrediting Board, *1735 New York Ave. N.W. 20006; (202) 783-2007. Fax, (202) 783-2822. Elliott Pavlos, Executive Director. General e-mail, info@naab.org. Web, www.naab.org.*

Accredits Bachelor and Master of Architecture degree programs.

National Assn. of Schools of Art and Design, *11250 Roger Bacon Dr., #21, Reston, VA 20190; (703) 437-0700.*

Fax, (703) 437-6312. Samuel Hope, Executive Director. Web, www.arts-accredit.org.

Accrediting agency for educational programs in art and design. Provides information on art and design programs at the postsecondary level; offers professional development for executives of art and design programs.

National Council of Architectural Registration Boards, *1735 New York Ave. N.W., #700 20006; (202) 783-6500. Fax, (202) 783-0290. Lenore M. Lucey, Executive Vice President. Web, www.ncarb.org.*

Membership: state architectural licensing boards. Develops examination used in U.S. states and territories for licensing architects; certifies architects.

Codes, Standards, and Research

AGENCIES

Architectural and Transportation Barriers Compliance Board (Access Board), *1331 F St. N.W., #1000 20004-1111; (202) 272-5434. Fax, (202) 272-5447. Lawrence W. Roffee, Executive Director. TTY, (202) 272-5449. Toll-free technical assistance, (800) 872-2253. Web, www.access-board.gov.*

Enforces standards requiring that buildings and telecommunications and transportation systems be accessible to persons with disabilities; provides technical assistance and information on designing these facilities; sets accessibility guidelines for the Americans with Disabilities Act and the Telecommunications Act of 1996.

Environmental Protection Agency, *Radiation and Indoor Air, 501 3rd St. N.W. 20001 (mailing address: 401 M St. S.W., #6601J 20460); (202) 564-9320. Fax, (202) 565-2043. Stephen D. Page, Director.*

Establishes standards for measuring radon; develops model building codes for state and local governments; provides states and building contractors with technical assistance and training on radon detection and mitigation.

Federal Housing Administration *(Housing and Urban Development Dept.), Manufactured Housing and Standards, 451 7th St. S.W. #9152 20410; (202) 708-6409. Fax, (202) 708-4213. Elizabeth A. Cocke, Director. Consumer complaints, (800) 927-2891. Web, www.hud.gov/fha/mhs/mhshome.html.*

Establishes and maintains standards for selection of new materials and methods of construction; evaluates technical suitability of products and materials; develops uniform, preemptive, and mandatory national standards for manufactured housing; enforces standards through design review and quality control inspection of factories; administers a national consumer protection program.

Housing and Urban Development Dept., *Affordable Housing Research and Technology, 451 7th St. S.W., #8132 20410; (202) 708-4370. Fax, (202) 708-5873. David Engel, Director. Web, www.hud.gov.*

Studies regulatory barriers to housing, such as land development and building zones. Conducts building technology research on radon, other environmental hazards, and energy efficiency. Reviews and assesses changes in building codes and standards. Conducts demonstrations on innovative building construction techniques.

Housing and Urban Development Dept., *Lead Hazard Control, 451 7th St. S.W., #P3202 20410; (202) 755-1785. Fax, (202) 755-1000. David E. Jacobs, Director. Community Outreach, (202) 755-1785, ext. 114. Web, www.hud.gov/lea/leahome.html.*

Advises HUD offices, other agencies, health authorities, and the housing industry on lead poisoning prevention. Develops regulations for lead-based paint; conducts research; makes grants to state and local governments for hazard reduction and inspection of housing.

National Institute of Building Sciences, *1090 Vermont Ave. N.W., #700 20005-4905; (202) 289-7800. Fax, (202) 289-1092. David A. Harris, President. General e-mail, nibs@nibs.org. Web, www.nibs.org.*

Public-private partnership authorized by Congress to improve the regulation of building construction, facilitate the safe introduction of innovative building technology, and disseminate performance criteria and other technical information.

National Institute of Standards and Technology *(Commerce Dept.), Building and Fire Research Laboratory, Route I-270 and Quince Orchard Rd., Gaithersburg, MD 20899; (301) 975-5851. Fax, (301) 975-5433. Jack Snell, Director; James E. Hill, Deputy Director. Web, www.bfrl.nist.gov.*

Performs analytical, laboratory, and field research in the area of building technology and its applications for building usefulness, safety, and economy; produces performance criteria and evaluation, test, and measurement methods for building owners, occupants, designers, manufacturers, builders, and federal, state, and local regulatory authorities.

Occupational Safety and Health Administration *(Labor Dept.), Safety Standards, 200 Constitution Ave. N.W., #N3605 20210; (202) 693-2222. Fax, (202) 693-1663. Marthe B. Kent, Director (Acting).*

Administers regulations for fire safety standards; sponsors programs for maritime, fire protection, construction, mechanical, and electrical industries.

U.S. Fire Administration *(Federal Emergency Management Agency)*, 16825 S. Seton Ave., Emmitsburg, MD 21727; (301) 447-1018. Fax, (301) 447-1270. Carrye B. Brown, Administrator. Web, www.usfa.fema.gov.

Conducts research and collects, analyzes, and disseminates data on combustion, fire prevention, fire fighter safety, and the management of fire prevention organizations; studies and develops arson prevention programs and fire prevention codes; maintains the National Fire Data System.

NONPROFIT

Air Conditioning and Refrigeration Institute, *Legislative and Regulatory Affairs,* 4301 N. Fairfax Dr., #425, Arlington, VA 22203; (703) 524-8800. Fax, (703) 528-3816. Lake Coulson, Director. General e-mail, ari@dgsys.com. Web, www.ari.org.

Represents manufacturers of central air conditioning and commercial refrigeration equipment. Develops product performance rating standards and administers programs to verify manufacturers' certified ratings.

American Society of Civil Engineers, 1801 Alexander Bell Dr., Reston, VA 20191-4400; (703) 295-6300. Fax, (703) 295-6333. James E. Davis, Executive Director. Information, (800) 548-2723. Web, www.asce.org.

Membership: professionals and students in civil engineering. Develops and produces consensus standards for construction documents and building codes. Maintains the Civil Engineering Research Foundation, which focuses national attention and resources on the research needs of the civil engineering profession. Participates in international conferences.

American Society of Heating, Refrigerating, and Air Conditioning Engineers, *Government Affairs,* 1828 L St. N.W., #906 20036-3146; (202) 833-1830. Fax, (202) 833-0118. J. E. Cox, Director. Web, www.ashrae.org.

Membership: engineers for the heating and cooling industry in the United States and abroad, including students. Sponsors research, meetings, and educational activities. Develops industry standards; publishes technical data. Monitors legislation and regulations.

Center for Auto Safety, 1825 Connecticut Ave., #330 20009; (202) 328-7700. Fax, (202) 387-0140. Clarence M. Ditlow III, Executive Director. Web, www.autosafety.org.

Monitors Federal Trade Commission warranty regulations and HUD implementation of federal safety and construction standards for manufactured mobile homes.

International Code Council, 5203 Leesburg Pike, Falls Church, VA 22041; (703) 931-4533. Fax, (703) 379-1546.

Richard P. Kuchnicki, Executive Vice President. Web, www.intlcode.org.

Seeks to ensure consistency among model codes; encourages uniformity in administration of building regulations; maintains a one- and two-family dwelling code, a model energy code, and manufactured home construction and safety standards; provides review board for the American National Standards Institute disabled accessibility standards.

NAHB Research Center, 400 Prince George's Blvd., Upper Marlboro, MD 20774; (301) 249-4000. Fax, (301) 430-6180. Liza K. Bowles, President. Web, www.nahbrc.org.

Conducts contract research and product labeling and certification for U.S. industry, government, and trade associations related to home building and light commercial industrial building. Interests include energy conservation, new technologies, international research, public health issues, affordable housing, special needs housing for the elderly and persons with disabilities, building codes and standards, land development, and environmental issues. (Affiliated with the National Assn. of Home Builders [NAHB].)

National Conference of States on Building Codes and Standards, 505 Huntmar Park Dr., #210, Herndon, VA 20170; (703) 437-0100. Fax, (703) 481-3596. Robert Wible, Executive Director. Web, www.ncsbcs.org.

Membership: individuals and organizations concerned with building standards. Works with HUD to ensure that manufactured housing conforms to HUD standards and codes; assists states in improving their building codes, standards, and regulations; promotes local, state, and interstate cooperation.

National Fire Protection Assn., *Government Affairs, Washington Office,* 1110 N. Glebe Rd., #210, Arlington, VA 22201; (703) 516-4346. Fax, (703) 516-4350. Anthony R. O'Neill, Vice President. General e-mail, wdc@nfpa.org. Web, www.nspa.org.

Membership: individuals and organizations interested in fire protection. Develops and updates fire protection codes and standards; sponsors technical assistance programs; collects fire data statistics. Monitors legislation and regulations. (Headquarters in Quincy, Mass.)

National Spa and Pool Institute, 2111 Eisenhower Ave., Alexandria, VA 22314-4698; (703) 838-0083. Fax, (703) 549-0493. Roger Galvin, Chief Executive Officer. Web, www.nspi.org.

Membership: manufacturers, dealers, and distributors of pools, spas, and hot tubs. Promotes the industry;

compiles statistics; establishes construction standards for pools and spas. Monitors legislation and regulations.

Materials and Labor

See also Codes, Standards, and Research (this section); Employment and Labor (chap. 7)

NONPROFIT

American Forest and Paper Assn., *Regulatory Affairs, 1111 19th St. N.W., #800 20036; (202) 463-2700. Fax, (202) 463-2785. Sharon Kneiss, Vice President. Web, www.afandpa.org.*

Membership: manufacturers of wood and specialty products and related associations. Interests include tax, housing, environmental, international trade, natural resources, and land-use issues that affect the wood and paper products industry.

American Portland Cement Alliance, *1225 Eye St. N.W., #300 20005-5955; (202) 408-9494. Fax, (202) 408-0877. Richard C. Creighton, President.*

Membership: producers of portland cement. Monitors legislation and regulations.

Architectural Woodwork Institute, *1952 Isaac Newton Square West, Reston, VA 20190; (703) 733-0600. Fax, (703) 733-0584. Judith B. Durham, Executive Vice President. Web, www.awinet.org.*

Promotes the use of architectural woodworking; establishes industry standards; conducts seminars and workshops; certifies professionals in the industry. Monitors legislation and regulations.

Asbestos Information Assn./North America, *1745 Jefferson Davis Hwy., #406, Arlington, VA 22202; (703) 412-1150. Fax, (703) 412-1152. B. J. Pigg, President.*

Membership: firms that manufacture, sell, and use products containing asbestos fiber and those that mine, mill, and sell asbestos. Provides information on asbestos and health and on industry efforts to eliminate problems associated with asbestos dust; serves as liaison between the industry and federal and state governments.

Asphalt Roofing Manufacturers Assn., *4041 Powder Mill Rd., #404, Calverton, MD 20705; (301) 348-2002. Fax, (301) 348-2020. Russell K. Snyder, Executive Vice President. Web, www.asphaltroofing.org.*

Membership: manufacturers of bitumen-based roofing products. Assists in developing local building codes and standards for asphalt roofing products. Provides technical information; supports research. Monitors legislation and regulations.

Assn. of the Wall and Ceiling Industries, *803 W. Broad St., #600, Falls Church, VA 22046-3108; (703) 534-8300. Fax, (703) 534-8307. Steven A. Etkin, Executive Vice President. Web, www.awci.org.*

Membership: contractors and suppliers working in the wall and ceiling industries. Sponsors conferences and seminars. Monitors legislation and regulations.

Brick Industry Assn., *11490 Commerce Park Dr., #300, Reston, VA 20191-1525; (703) 620-0010. Fax, (703) 620-3928. Nelson J. Cooney, President. Web, www.bia.org.*

Membership: manufacturers of clay brick. Provides technical expertise and assistance; promotes bricklaying vocational education programs; maintains collection of technical publications on brick masonry construction. Monitors legislation and regulations.

Building Systems Councils of the National Assn. of Home Builders, *1201 15th St. N.W., 4th Floor 20005-2800; (202) 822-0576. Fax, (202) 861-2141. Barbara K. Martin, Executive Director.*

Membership: manufacturers and suppliers of home building products and services. Represents all segments of the industry. Assists in developing National Assn. of Home Builders policies regarding building codes, legislation, and government regulations affecting manufacturers of model code complying, factory-built housing; sponsors educational programs; conducts plant tours of member operations.

Composite Panel Assn., *18928 Premiere Court, Gaithersburg, MD 20879; (301) 670-0604. Fax, (301) 840-1252. Jack O'Leary, President. General e-mail, pbmdf@ pbmdf.com. Web, www.pbmdf.com.*

Membership: manufacturers of particleboard and medium-density fiberboard. Promotes use of these materials; conducts industry education through the Composite Wood Council. Monitors legislation and regulations.

Door and Hardware Institute, *14150 Newbrook Dr., #200, Chantilly, VA 20151-2223; (703) 222-2010. Fax, (703) 222-2410. Jerry Heppes, Executive Director. Web, www.dhi.org.*

Membership: companies and individuals that manufacture or distribute doors and related fittings. Promotes the industry. Interests include building security, life safety and exit devices, and compliance with the Americans with Disabilities Act. Monitors legislation and regulations.

Gypsum Assn., *810 1st St. N.E., #510 20002; (202) 289-5440. Fax, (202) 289-3707. Jerry A. Walker, Executive Director. Web, www.gypsum.org.*

Membership: manufacturers of gypsum wallboard and plaster. Assists members, code officials, builders, designers, and others with technical problems and building code questions; publishes Fire Resistance Design Manual referenced by major building codes; conducts safety programs for member companies. Monitors legislation and regulations.

Hardwood, Plywood, and Veneer Assn., *1825 Michael Faraday Dr., Reston, VA 20190-5350 (mailing address: P.O. Box 2789, Reston, VA 20195-0789); (703) 435-2900. Fax, (703) 435-2537. E. T. Altman, President. Web, www.hpva.org.*

Membership: distributors, wholesalers, suppliers, and sales agents of plywood, veneer, and laminated wood floor. Disseminates business information; sponsors workshops and seminars; conducts research.

International Assn. of Bridge, Structural, Ornamental, and Reinforcing Iron Workers, *1750 New York Ave. N.W., #400 20006; (202) 383-4800. Fax, (202) 638-4856. Jake West, President.*

Membership: approximately 82,000 iron workers. Helps members negotiate pay, benefits, and better working conditions; conducts training programs and workshops. Monitors legislation and regulations. (Affiliated with the AFL-CIO.)

International Assn. of Heat and Frost Insulators and Asbestos, *1776 Massachusetts Ave. N.W., #301 20036-1989; (202) 785-2388. Fax, (202) 429-0568. William G. Bernard, President. Web, www.insulators.org.*

Membership: approximately 18,000 workers in insulation industries. Helps members negotiate pay, benefits, and better working conditions; conducts training programs and workshops. Monitors legislation and regulations. (Affiliated with the AFL-CIO.)

International Brotherhood of Boilermakers, Iron Ship Builders, Blacksmiths, Forgers, and Helpers, *Legislative Affairs, Washington Office, 2722 Merrilee Dr., #360, Fairfax, VA 22031; (703) 560-1493. Fax, (703) 560-2584. Andy Abbott, Director. Web, www.boilermakers. org.*

Membership: approximately 80,000 workers in construction, repair, maintenance, manufacturing, and related industries in the United States and Canada. Helps members negotiate pay, benefits, and better working conditions; conducts training programs and workshops. Monitors legislation and regulations. (Headquarters in Kansas City, Kan.; affiliated with the AFL-CIO.)

International Brotherhood of Electrical Workers, *1125 15th St. N.W. 20005; (202) 833-7000. Fax, (202) 467-6316. John J. Barry, President. General e-mail, postmaster@ibew.org. Web, www.ibew.org.*

Helps members negotiate pay, benefits, and better working conditions; conducts training programs and workshops. Monitors legislation and regulations. (Affiliated with the AFL-CIO.)

International Brotherhood of Teamsters, *25 Louisiana Ave. N.W. 20001; (202) 624-6800. Fax, (202) 624-8102. James P. Hoffa, President. Web, www.teamster. org.*

Membership: more than 1.4 million workers in the transportation and construction industries, factories, offices, hospitals, warehouses, and other workplaces. Helps members negotiate pay, benefits, and better working conditions; conducts training programs and workshops. Monitors legislation and regulations. (Affiliated with the AFL-CIO.)

International Union of Bricklayers and Allied Craftworkers, *815 15th St. N.W. 20005; (202) 783-3788. Fax, (202) 393-0219. John J. Flynn, President. Web, www. bacweb.org.*

Membership: bricklayers, stonemasons, and other skilled craftworkers in the building industry. Helps members negotiate pay, benefits, and better working conditions; conducts training programs and workshops. Monitors legislation and regulations. (Affiliated with the AFL-CIO and the International Masonry Institute.)

International Union of Operating Engineers, *1125 17th St. N.W. 20036; (202) 429-9100. Fax, (202) 778-2616. Frank Hanley, President. Web, www.iuoe.org.*

Membership: approximately 400,000 operating engineers, including heavy equipment operators, mechanics, and surveyors in the construction industry, and stationary engineers, including operations and building maintenance staff. Helps members negotiate pay, benefits, and better working conditions; conducts training programs and workshops. Monitors legislation and regulations. (Affiliated with the AFL-CIO.)

International Union of Painters and Allied Trades, *1750 New York Ave. N.W., 8th Floor 20006; (202) 637-0700. Fax, (202) 637-0771. Michael E. Monroe, President. Web, www.ibpat.org.*

Membership: more than 130,000 painters, paint makers, drywall finishers, decorators, carpet and soft tile layers, scenic artists, and workers in allied trades. Helps members negotiate pay, benefits, and better working conditions; conducts training programs and workshops. Monitors legislation and regulations. (Affiliated with the AFL-CIO.)

Kitchen Cabinet Manufacturers Assn., *1899 Preston White Dr., Reston, VA 20191-5435; (703) 264-1690. Fax,*

(703) 620-6530. *C. Richard Titus, Executive Vice President. Web, www.kcma.org.*

Represents cabinet manufacturers and suppliers to the industry. Provides government relations, management statistics, marketing information, and plant tours. Administers cabinet testing and certification programs.

National Concrete Masonry Assn., *2302 Horse Pen Rd., Herndon, VA 20171-3499; (703) 713-1900. Fax, (703) 713-1910. Mark B. Hogan, President. Web, www.ncma.org.*

Membership: producers of concrete masonry and suppliers of related goods and services. Conducts research; provides members with technical, marketing, government relations, and communications assistance.

National Glass Assn., *8200 Greensboro Dr., #302, McLean, VA 22102-3881; (703) 442-4890. Fax, (703) 442-0630. Phillip J. James, President. General e-mail, nga@glass.org. Web, www.glass.org.*

Membership: companies in flat (architectural and automotive) glass industry, including manufacturers, fabricators, distributors, retailers, and installers of glass used in a structure. Conducts conferences; provides information on industry codes. Monitors legislation and regulations.

National Insulation Assn., *99 Canal Center Plaza, #222, Alexandria, VA 22314; (703) 683-6422. Fax, (703) 549-4838. Bill Pitkin, Executive Vice President. General e-mail, niainfo@insulation.org. Web, www.insulation.org.*

Membership: companies in the commercial and industrial insulation and asbestos abatement industries. Monitors legislation and regulations.

National Lumber and Building Material Dealers Assn., *40 Ivy St. S.E. 20003; (202) 547-2230. Fax, (202) 547-7640. Gary W. Donnelly, President. General e-mail, nlbmda@dealer.org. Web, www.dealer.org.*

Membership: federated associations of retailers in the lumber and building material industries. Monitors legislation and regulations.

National Paint and Coatings Assn., *1500 Rhode Island Ave. N.W. 20005; (202) 462-6272. Fax, (202) 462-8549. J. Andrew Doyle, President. General e-mail, npca@paint.org. Web, www.paint.org.*

Membership: paint and coatings manufacturers, raw materials suppliers, and distributors. Provides educational and public outreach programs for the industry; interests include health, safety, and the environment. Monitor legislation and regulations.

North American Insulation Manufacturers Assn., *44 Canal Center Plaza, #310, Alexandria, VA 22314; (703)*

684-0084. *Fax, (703) 684-0427. Kenneth D. Mentzer, President. General e-mail, insulation@naima.org. Web, www.naima.org.*

Membership: manufacturers of insulation products for use in homes, commercial buildings, and industrial facilities. Provides information on the use of insulation for thermal efficiency, sound control, and fire safety; monitors research in the industry. Monitors legislation and regulations.

Operative Plasterers' and Cement Masons' International Assn. of the United States and Canada, *14405 Laurel Pl., #300, Laurel, MD 20707; (301) 470-4200. Fax, (301) 470-2502. John Dougherty, President. Web, www.opcmia.org.*

Membership: approximately 58,000 concrete masons and terrazzo workers. Helps members negotiate pay, benefits, and better working conditions; conducts training programs and workshops. Monitors legislation and regulations. (Affiliated with the AFL-CIO.)

Painting and Decorating Contractors of America, *3913 Old Lee Hwy., #33B, Fairfax, VA 22030; (703) 359-0826. Fax, (703) 359-2576. Brandt Domas, President. Web, www.pdca.org.*

Promotes the painting and decorating industry; sponsors workshops and seminars. Monitors legislation and regulations.

Roof Coatings Manufacturers Assn., *4041 Powder Mill Rd., #404, Calverton, MD 20705; (301) 348-2003. Fax, (301) 348-2020. Russell K. Snyder, Executive Vice President. General e-mail, info@roofcoatings.org. Web, www.roofcoatings.org.*

Represents the manufacturers of cold-applied protective roof coatings, cements, and systems, and the suppliers of products, equipment, and services to and for the roof coating manufacturing industry.

Sheet Metal Workers' International Assn., *1750 New York Ave. N.W. 20006; (202) 783-5880. Fax, (202) 662-0880. Michael J. Sullivan, General President. Web, smwia.org.*

Membership: more than 130,000 U.S. and Canadian workers in the building and construction trades, manufacturing, and the railroad and shipyard industries. Assists members with contract negotiation and grievances; conducts training programs and workshops. Monitors legislation and regulations. (Affiliated with the Sheet Metal and Air Conditioning Contractors' Assn., the AFL-CIO, and the Canadian Labour Congress.)

United Assn. of Journeymen and Apprentices of the Plumbing and Pipe Fitting Industry of the

United States and Canada, *901 Massachusetts Ave. N.W. 20001-4397; (202) 628-5823. Fax, (202) 628-5024. Martin J. Maddaloni, General President. Web, www.ua.org.*

Membership: approximately 300,000 workers who fabricate, install, and service piping systems. Assists members with contract negotiation and grievances; sponsors training programs, apprenticeships, and workshops. Monitors legislation and regulations. (Affiliated with the AFL-CIO and the Canadian Federation of Labour.)

United Brotherhood of Carpenters and Joiners of America, *101 Constitution Ave. N.W. 20001; (202) 546-6206. Fax, (202) 543-5724. William G. Luddy, Treasurer.*

Membership: approximately 500,000 carpenters and joiners. Helps members negotiate pay, benefits, and better working conditions; conducts training programs and workshops. Monitors legislation and regulations. (Affiliated with the AFL-CIO.)

United Union of Roofers, Waterproofers, and Allied Workers, *1660 L St. N.W., #800 20036; (202) 463-7663. Fax, (202) 463-6906. Earl Kruse, President. Web, www.unionroofers.com.*

Membership: approximately 25,000 roofers, waterproofers, and allied workers. Helps members negotiate pay, benefits, and better working conditions; conducts training programs and workshops. Monitor legislation and regulations. (Affiliated with the AFL-CIO.)

Utility Workers Union of America, *815 16th St. N.W. 20006; (202) 347-8105. Fax, (202) 347-4872. Donald E. Wightman, President. Web, www.uwua.org.*

Membership: approximately 50,000 workers in utilities and related industries. Helps members negotiate pay, benefits, and better working conditions; conducts training programs and workshops. Monitors legislation and regulations. (Affiliated with the AFL-CIO.)

▣ HOUSING

See also Homelessness (chap. 18); Statistics (this chapter)

AGENCIES

Federal Housing Administration *(Housing and Urban Development Dept.), Insured Single Family Housing, 451 7th St. S.W., #9162 20410; (202) 708-3046. Fax, (202) 708-2582. Morris Carter, Director (Acting).*

Offers a mortgage insurance program for new and existing single-family dwellings (one to four units), including certain cooperatives and condominiums.

Federal Housing Administration *(Housing and Urban Development Dept.), Multifamily Business Products, 451 7th St. S.W., #6134 20410-8000; (202) 708-3000. Fax, (202) 708-3104. Willie Spearmon, Director. Web, www.hud.gov/fha/mfh/fhamfbus.html.*

Establishes procedures for the development of housing under the multifamily mortgage insurance programs. Administers the mortgage insurance programs for rental, cooperative, and condominium housing.

Federal Housing Administration *(Housing and Urban Development Dept.), Multifamily Housing Programs, 451 7th St. S.W., #6106 20410; (202) 708-2495. Fax, (202) 708-2583. Robert Reavis, Deputy Assistant Secretary (Acting). Web, www.hud.gov.*

Determines risk and administers programs associated with government-insured mortgage programs, architectural procedures, and land development programs for multifamily housing. Administers the Rural Rental Housing Program and the development of congregate housing facilities that provide affordable housing, adequate space for meals, and supportive services.

Federal Housing Administration *(Housing and Urban Development Dept.), Single Family Housing, 451 7th St. S.W., #9282 20410; (202) 708-3175. Fax, (202) 708-2582. Frederick C. Douglas Jr., Deputy Assistant Secretary.*

Determines risk and administers programs associated with government-insured mortgage programs, architectural procedures, land development programs, and interstate land sales for single family housing. Administers requirements to obtain and maintain federal government approval of mortgages.

Housing and Urban Development Dept., *Entitlement Communities, 451 7th St. S.W., #7282 20410; (202) 708-1577. Fax, (202) 401-2044. Barbara Neal, Director. Web, www.hud.gov.*

Provides entitled cities and counties with block grants to provide housing and economic opportunity for low- and moderate-income people.

Housing and Urban Development Dept., *Housing— Federal Housing Commissioner, 451 7th St. S.W., #9100 20410; (202) 708-3600. Fax, (202) 708-2580. William C. Apgar, Assistant Secretary. Web, www.hud.gov/fha/fhahome.html.*

Administers housing programs including the production, financing, and management of housing; directs preservation and rehabilitation of the housing stock; manages regulatory programs.

Rural Housing Service *(Agriculture Dept.), 1400 Independence Ave. S.W., #5014, MS 0701 20250-0701; (202)*

690-1533. Fax, (202) 690-0500. James C. Kearney, Administrator. Web, www.rurdev.usda.gov/rhs/index.html.

Offers financial assistance to apartment dwellers and homeowners in rural areas.

Rural Housing Service *(Agriculture Dept.), Housing Programs,* 1400 Independence Ave. S.W., #5013 20250-0780; (202) 720-5177. Fax, (202) 690-3025. David J. Villano, Deputy Administrator. Press, (202) 720-6903.

Makes loans and grants in rural communities (population under 20,000) to low-income borrowers, including the elderly and persons with disabilities, for buying, building, or improving single-family houses. Makes grants to communities for rehabilitating single-family homes or rental units.

CONGRESS

House Banking and Financial Services Committee, *Subcommittee on Housing and Community Opportunity,* B303 RHOB 20515; (202) 225-6634. Rep. Rick A. Lazio, R-N.Y., Chair; Joseph M. Ventrone, Staff Director. Web, www.house.gov/banking.

Jurisdiction over all housing legislation, including housing allowances, housing for the elderly and persons with disabilities, public housing, and subsidized housing.

House Judiciary Committee, *Subcommittee on the Constitution,* H2-362 FHOB 20515; (202) 226-7680. Fax, (202) 225-3746. Rep. Charles T. Canady, R-Fla., Chair; Cathy Cleaver, Chief Counsel. General e-mail, Judiciary@mail.house.gov. Web, www.house.gov/judiciary.

Jurisdiction over fair housing legislation pertaining to discrimination against minorities.

Senate Banking, Housing, and Urban Affairs Committee, *Subcommittee on Housing and Transportation,* SD-534 20510; (202) 224-7391. Fax, (202) 224-5137. Sen. Wayne Allard, R-Colo., Chair; John Carson, Staff Director. Web, banking.senate.gov.

Jurisdiction over all housing legislation, including housing allowances, housing for the elderly and persons with disabilities, public housing, and subsidized housing.

Senate Judiciary Committee, *Subcommittee on the Constitution, Federalism, and Property Rights,* SD-524 20510; (202) 224-8081. Fax, (202) 228-0544. Sen. John Ashcroft, R-Mo., Chair; Adam Cingoli, Chief Counsel. Web, judiciary.senate.gov/constitu.htm.

Jurisdiction over fair housing legislation, including legislation pertaining to discrimination against minorities.

Senate Special Committee on Aging, SD-G31 20510; (202) 224-5364. Fax, (202) 224-8660. Sen. Charles E.

Grassley, R-Iowa, Chair; Ted Totman, Staff Director. Web, aging.senate.gov.

Studies and makes recommendations on housing access for the elderly.

NONPROFIT

Center for Housing Policy, 815 15th St. N.W., #538 20005; (202) 393-5772. Fax, (202) 393-5656. Robert J. Reid, Executive Director. General e-mail, chp@nhc.org. Web, www.nhc.org.

Researches and develops fundamentals of housing policy. Seeks to create new policies that integrate housing into overall social and economic goals. Sponsors educational forums. (Affiliated with the National Housing Conference.)

Enterprise Foundation, 10227 Wincopin Circle, #500, Columbia, MD 21044; (410) 964-1230. Fax, (410) 964-1918. Rey Ramsey, President. Web, www.enterprisefoundation.org.

Works with local groups to help provide decent, affordable housing for low-income individuals and families.

Habitat for Humanity International, *Washington Office,* 1010 Vermont Ave. N.W., #900 20005; (202) 628-9171. Fax, (202) 628-9169. Thomas L. Jones, Managing Director. Web, www.habitat.org.

Ecumenical housing ministry that, with the help of volunteers, donors, and its own affiliate offices, builds affordable homes worldwide for low-income persons. (Headquarters in Americus, Ga.)

Housing Assistance Council, 1025 Vermont Ave. N.W., #606 20005-3516; (202) 842-8600. Fax, (202) 347-3441. Moises Loza, Executive Director. Information, (800) 989-4422. General e-mail, hac@ruralhome.org.

Operates in rural areas and in cities of fewer than 25,000 citizens. Advises low-income and minority groups seeking federal assistance for improving rural housing and community facilities; studies and makes recommendations for state and local housing policies; makes low-interest loans for housing programs for low-income and minority groups living in rural areas, including native Americans and farm workers.

National Housing and Rehabilitation Assn., 1625 Massachusetts Ave. N.W., #601 20036-2244; (202) 939-1750. Fax, (202) 265-4435. Peter H. Bell, Executive Director. Web, www.housingonline.com.

Membership: development firms and organizations and city, state, and local agencies concerned with affordable multifamily housing. Monitors government policies affecting multifamily development and rehabilitation.

National Housing Conference, *815 15th St. N.W., #538 20005; (202) 393-5772. Fax, (202) 393-5656. Robert J. Reid, Executive Director. General e-mail, nhc@nhc.org.*

Membership: state and local housing officials, community development specialists, builders, bankers, lawyers, civic leaders, tenants, architects and planners, labor and religious groups, and national housing and housing-related organizations. Mobilizes public support for community development and affordable housing programs; conducts educational sessions.

National Leased Housing Assn., *1818 N St. N.W., #405 20036; (202) 785-8888. Fax, (202) 785-2008. Denise Muha, Executive Director. General e-mail, hudnlha@worldweb.net. Web, www.worldweb.net/~hudnlha/index.html.*

Membership: public and private organizations and individuals concerned with multifamily, government-assisted housing programs. Conducts training seminars. Monitors legislation and regulations.

National Low Income Housing Coalition, *1012 14th St. N.W., #610 20005; (202) 662-1530. Fax, (202) 393-1973. Sheila Crowley, President. Web, www.nlihc.org.*

Membership: individuals and organizations interested in low-income housing. Works for decent, affordable housing and freedom of housing choice for low-income citizens. Provides information and technical assistance through the Low Income Housing Information Service. Monitors legislation.

National Rural Housing Coalition, *1250 Eye St. N.W., #902 20005; (202) 393-5229. Fax, (202) 393-3034. Robert A. Rapoza, Legislative Director.*

Advocates improved housing for low-income rural families; works to increase public awareness of rural housing problems; monitors legislation.

Fair Housing/Special Groups

AGENCIES

Bureau of Indian Affairs *(Interior Dept.),* **Housing Assistance,** *1849 C St. N.W., #4660 20240; (202) 208-3667. Fax, (202) 208-5113. June Henkel, Chief.*

Provides assistance to native American families who have limited resources, live on or near a reservation community, and do not qualify or receive assistance from other housing programs.

Federal Housing Administration *(Housing and Urban Development Dept.),* **Portfolio Management,** *451 7th St. S.W., #6160 20410; (202) 708-3730. Fax, (202) 401-5978. Frank Malone, Director. Web, www.hud.gov.*

Administers rental assistance, moderate rehabilitation, and housing programs for the elderly and people

with disabilities. Manages grants for housing for the elderly and the disabled under Sections 202 and 811 of the Housing Act of 1959.

Housing and Urban Development Dept., *Fair Housing and Equal Opportunity, 451 7th St. S.W., #5100 20410; (202) 708-4252. Fax, (202) 708-4483. Eva M. Plaza, Assistant Secretary. Housing discrimination hotline, (800) 669-9777. Web, www.hud.gov.*

Monitors compliance with legislation requiring equal opportunities in housing for minorities, persons with disabilities, and families with children. Monitors compliance with construction codes to accommodate people with disabilities in multifamily dwellings. Hotline answers inquiries about housing discrimination.

Housing and Urban Development Dept., *FHIP/FHAP Support, 451 7th St. S.W., #5222 20410; (202) 708-2288. Fax, (202) 708-4445. Ivy Davis, Director. Web, www.hud.gov.*

Awards grants to public and private organizations and to state and local agencies. Funds projects work to educate the public about fair housing rights; programs are designed to prevent or eliminate discriminatory housing practices. Administers the Fair Housing Initiative and the Fair Housing Assistance Programs (FHIP/FHAP).

Housing and Urban Development Dept., *Native American Programs, 451 7th St. S.W. 20410-6000 (mailing address: 451 7th St. S.W., #4126 20410); (202) 401-7914. Fax, (202) 401-7909. Jacqueline Johnson, Deputy Assistant Secretary. Web, www.hud.gov.*

Administers federal assistance for American Indian tribes. Assistance programs focus on housing and community and economic development through competitive and formula grants. Funds for approved activities are provided directly to tribes or Alaska native villages or to a tribally designated housing authority.

Justice Dept., *Civil Rights, 950 Pennsylvania Ave. N.W., #5643 20530; (202) 514-2151. Fax, (202) 514-0293. Bill Lann Lee, Assistant Attorney General (Acting). Library, (202) 514-3010. Press, (202) 514-2007. TTY, (202) 514-0716. Web, www.usdoj.gov/crt.*

Enforces federal civil rights laws prohibiting discrimination on the basis of race, color, religion, sex, disability, age, or national origin in housing, public accommodations and facilities, and credit and federally assisted programs.

Office of Thrift Supervision *(Treasury Dept.),* **Compliance Policy and Special Exams,** *1700 G St. N.W., 6th Floor 20552; (202) 906-6237. Fax, (202) 906-6326.*

Richard Riese, Director. Consumer complaints, (800) 842-6929.

Handles complaints of discrimination against minorities and women by savings and loan associations; assists minority-owned or minority-controlled savings and loan institutions.

Rural Development *(Agriculture Dept.), Civil Rights,* 1400 Independence Ave. S.W. 20250-3220 (mailing address: Ag. Box 0703 20250-0703); (202) 692-0204. Fax, (202) 692-0276. Cheryl Prejean Greaux, Director.

Enforces compliance with laws prohibiting discrimination in credit transactions on the basis of sex, marital status, race, color, religion, age, or disability. Ensures equal opportunity in granting Rural Economic and Community Development housing, farm ownership, and operating loans, and a variety of community and business program loans.

NONPROFIT

AARP, *Consumer Issues,* 601 E St. N.W. 20049; (202) 434-6030. Fax, (202) 434-6466. Jane King, Manager. Web, www.aarp.org.

Offers consultation and information services to organizations and consumers interested in home modification and universal design for older persons. Supports affordable and appropriate housing for older Americans, including shared housing, continuing care, retirement and assisted living communities, and home equity conversion.

American Assn. of Homes and Services for the Aging, *Policy and Governmental Affairs,* 901 E St. N.W., #500 20004-2011; (202) 783-2242. Fax, (202) 783-2255. Michael F. Rodgers, Senior Vice President. Web, www.aahsa.org.

Membership: nonprofit nursing homes, housing, and health-related facilities for the elderly. Provides research and technical assistance on housing and long-term care for the elderly; conducts certification program for retirement housing professionals. Operates a capital formation program to procure financing for new housing facilities for the elderly. Monitors legislation and regulations.

Assn. of Community Organizations for Reform Now, *Washington Office,* 739 8th St. S.E. 20003; (202) 547-2500. Fax, (202) 547-2483. Melanie Marcus, Head. General e-mail, natacorndc@acorn.org. Web, www.acorn.org.

Works to advance the interests of minority and low-income families through community organizing and action. Interests include jobs, living wages, housing, welfare reform, and community reinvestment. (Headquarters in New Orleans.)

B'nai B'rith International, *Senior Housing Committee,* 1640 Rhode Island Ave. N.W. 20036-3278; (202) 857-6581. Fax, (202) 857-0980. Mark D. Olshan, Director. General e-mail, seniors@bnaibrith.org. Web, bnaibrith.org.

Works with local groups to sponsor federally assisted housing for independent low-income senior citizens and persons with disabilities, regardless of race or religion.

Center for Community Change, 1000 Wisconsin Ave. N.W. 20007; (202) 342-0519. Fax, (202) 342-1132. Andy Mott, Executive Director.

Provides community-based organizations serving minorities and the economically disadvantaged with technical assistance. Areas of assistance include community development block grants, housing, economic and resource development, rural development projects, and program planning.

National American Indian Housing Council, 900 2nd St. N.E., #305 20002; (202) 789-1754. Fax, (202) 789-1758. Christopher Boesen, Executive Director. Web, www.naihc.indian.com.

Membership: native American housing authorities. Clearinghouse for information on native American housing issues; works for safe and sanitary dwellings for native American and Alaska native communities; monitors HUD policies and housing legislation; provides members with training and technical assistance in managing housing assistance programs.

National Assn. for the Advancement of Colored People, *Washington Office,* 1025 Vermont Ave. N.W., #1120 20005; (202) 638-2269. Fax, (202) 638-5936. Hilary O. Shelton, Director. Web, www.naacp.org.

Membership: persons interested in civil rights for all minorities. Works to eliminate discrimination in housing and urban affairs. Supports programs that make affordable rental housing available to minorities and that maintain African American ownership of land. (Headquarters in Baltimore.)

National Assn. of Real Estate Brokers, 1629 K St. N.W., #602 20006-1635; (202) 785-4477. Fax, (202) 785-1244. Ernest Clark, President. Web, www.nareb.com.

Membership: minority real estate brokers, appraisers, contractors, property managers, and salespersons. Works to prevent discrimination in housing policies and practices; conducts regional seminars on federal policy, legislation, and regulations; advises members on procedures for procuring federal contracts.

National Council of La Raza, 1111 19th St. N.W., #1000 20036; (202) 785-1670. Fax, (202) 776-1792. Raul Yzaguirre, President. Web, www.nclr.org.

Helps Hispanic community-based groups obtain funds, develop and build low-income housing and community facilities, and develop and finance community economic development projects; conducts research and provides policy analysis on the housing status and needs of Hispanics; monitors legislation on fair housing and government funding for low-income housing.

National Council on the Aging, *409 3rd St. S.W., 2nd Floor 20024; (202) 479-1200. Fax, (202) 479-0735. James Firman, President. Information, (202) 479-6653. Library, (202) 479-6669. Press, (202) 479-6975. General e-mail, info@ncoa.org. Web, www.ncoa.org.*

Serves as an information clearinghouse on aging. Works to ensure quality housing for older persons. Monitors legislation and regulations. Library open to the public.

Public and Subsidized Housing

AGENCIES

Housing and Urban Development Dept., *Public and Assisted Housing Delivery, 451 7th St. S.W., #4130 20410-5000; (202) 708-1380. Fax, (202) 708-0690. Gloria Cousar, Deputy Assistant Secretary. Web, www.hud.gov.*

Establishes policies and procedures for low-income public housing and rental assistance programs, including special needs for the elderly and disabled, standards for rental and occupancy, utilities and maintenance engineering, and financial management.

Housing and Urban Development Dept., *Public Housing Investment, 451 7th St. S.W., #4130 20410-5000; (202) 401-8812. Fax, (202) 401-2370. Elinor R. Bacon, Deputy Assistant Secretary. Web, www.hud.gov.*

Establishes development policies and procedures for low-income housing programs, including criteria for site approval and construction standards; oversees administration of the Comprehensive Improvement Assistance Program for modernizing existing public housing. Administers the HOPE 6 Program.

Public and Indian Housing *(Housing and Urban Development Dept.), Rental Assistance, 451 7th St. S.W., #4210 20410; (202) 708-0477. Fax, (202) 401-7974. Gerald Benoit, Director.*

Administers certificate, housing voucher programs, and moderate rehabilitation authorized by Section 8 of the Housing Act of 1937, as amended. Provides rental subsidies to lower income families.

NONPROFIT

Public Housing Authorities Directors Assn., *511 Capitol Court N.E., #200 20002-4937; (202) 546-5445. Fax, (202) 546-2280. Timothy G. Kaiser, Executive Direc-*

tor. *General e-mail, advnews@phada.org. Web, www. phada.org.*

Membership: executive directors of public housing authorities. Serves as liaison between members and the Housing and Urban Development Dept. and Congress; conducts educational seminars and conferences. Monitors legislation and regulations.

Urban Institute, *Metropolitan Housing and Communities Policy Center, 2100 M St. N.W., #500 20037; (202) 833-7200. Fax, (202) 728-0232. Margery Austin Turner, Director. Web, www.urban.org.*

Research organization that deals with urban problems. Researches housing policy problems, including housing management, public housing programs, finance, and rent control.

REAL ESTATE

See also Military Installations (chap. 16); Statistics (this chapter)

AGENCIES

Federal Highway Administration *(Transportation Dept.), Real Estate Services, 400 7th St. S.W. 20590; (202) 366-0142. Fax, (202) 366-3713. Susan Lauffer, Director.*

Funds and oversees acquisition of land by states for federally assisted highways; provides financial assistance to relocate people and businesses forced to move by highway construction; cooperates in administering program for the use of air rights in connection with federally aided highways; administers Highway Beautification Act to control billboards and junkyards along interstate and federally aided primary highways.

Federal Insurance Administration *(Federal Emergency Management Agency), 500 C St. S.W., #430 20472; (202) 646-2781. Fax, (202) 646-7970. Jo Ann Howard, Administrator. Web, www.fema.gov/nfip.*

Administers federal crime and flood insurance programs, including the National Flood Insurance Program. Makes available to eligible homeowners low-cost flood and crime insurance.

General Services Administration, *Public Buildings Service, 1800 F St. N.W., #6344 20405; (202) 501-1100. Fax, (202) 219-2310. Robert A. Peck, Commissioner.*

Administers the construction, maintenance, and operation of buildings owned or leased by the federal government. Manages and disposes of federal real estate.

Housing and Urban Development Dept., *Affordable Housing Programs,* 451 7th St. S.W., #7164 20410; (202) 708-2685. Fax, (202) 708-1744. Mary Kolesar, Director. Web, www.hud.gov.

Administers the Uniform Relocation Assistance and Real Property Acquisition Policies Act of 1970, as amended, and other laws requiring that relocation assistance be given to persons displaced by federally assisted housing and community development programs.

Housing and Urban Development Dept., *Interstate Land Sales/RESPA (Real Estate Settlement Procedure Act),* 451 7th St. S.W., #9146 20410; (202) 708-0502. Fax, (202) 708-4559. Rebecca J. Holtz, Director. Web, www.hud.gov.

Administers the Interstate Land Sales Full Disclosure Act, which requires land developers who sell undeveloped land through interstate commerce or the mails to disclose required information about the land to the purchaser prior to signing a sales contract and to file information with the federal government.

Small Business Administration, *Disaster Assistance,* 409 3rd St. S.W., #6050 20416; (202) 205-6734. Fax, (202) 205-7728. Bernard Kulik, Associate Administrator. Web, www.sba.gov.

Provides victims of physical disasters with disaster and economic injury loans for homes, businesses, and personal property. Lends funds to individual homeowners, business concerns of all sizes, and nonprofit institutions to repair or replace damaged structures and furnishings, business machinery, equipment, and inventory.

CONGRESS

House Banking and Financial Services Committee, *Subcommittee on Financial Institutions and Consumer Credit,* 2129 RHOB 20515; (202) 225-2258. Fax, (202) 225-6984. Rep. Marge Roukema, R-N.J., Chair; Laurie Schaffer, Staff Director. Web, www.house.gov/banking.

Jurisdiction over legislation on federal financial regulatory agencies and authorized activities of federally chartered and supervised financial institutions.

House Banking and Financial Services Committee, *Subcommittee on Housing and Community Opportunity,* B303 RHOB 20515; (202) 225-6634. Rep. Rick A. Lazio, R-N.Y., Chair; Joseph M. Ventrone, Staff Director. Web, www.house.gov/banking.

Jurisdiction over mortgage banking legislation, including mortgage insurance, secondary mortgage markets, and mortgage credit (except programs administered by the Veterans Affairs Dept.). Jurisdiction over federal insurance, including flood insurance.

House Ways and Means Committee, *Subcommittee on Oversight,* 1136 LHOB 20515; (202) 225-7601. Fax, (202) 225-9680. Rep. Amo Houghton, R-N.Y., Chair; William McKenney, Staff Director. Web, www.house.gov/ways_means.

Oversees government-sponsored enterprises, including the Federal Home Loan Mortgage Corp. and the Federal National Mortgage Assn., with regard to the financial risk posed to the federal government.

Senate Banking, Housing, and Urban Affairs Committee, SD-534 20510; (202) 224-7391. Fax, (202) 224-5137. Sen. Phil Gramm, R-Texas, Chair; Wayne A. Abernathy, Staff Director. Web, banking.senate.gov.

Jurisdiction over legislation on federal financial regulatory agencies and authorized activities of federally chartered and supervised financial institutions. Oversees government-sponsored enterprises, including the Federal Home Loan Mortgage Corp. and the Federal National Mortgage Assn.

Senate Banking, Housing, and Urban Affairs Committee, *Subcommittee on Economic Policy,* SD-534 20510; (202) 224-7391. Fax, (202) 224-5137. Sen. Connie Mack, R-Fla., Chair; Bob Stein, Staff Director. Web, banking.senate.gov.

Jurisdiction over legislation on mortgage insurance and secondary mortgage markets.

NONPROFIT

American Homeowners Foundation, 6776 Little Falls Rd., Arlington, VA 22213-1213; (703) 536-7776. Bruce Hahn, President. Web, www.americanhomeowners.org.

Conducts research and compiles statistics on home ownership; sponsors seminars and workshops; publishes model contracts.

American Land Title Assn., 1828 L St. N.W., #705 20036; (202) 296-3671. Fax, (202) 223-5843. James R. Maher, Executive Vice President. Web, www.alta.org.

Membership: land title insurance underwriting companies, abstracters, and title insurance agents. Searches, reviews, and insures land titles to protect real estate investors, including home buyers and mortgage lenders; provides industry information. Monitors legislation and regulations.

American Resort Development Assn., 1220 L St. N.W., #500 20005; (202) 371-6700. Fax, (202) 289-8544. Vacant, President. Web, www.arda.org.

Membership: U.S. and international developers, builders, financiers, marketing companies, and others involved in resort, recreational, and community development. Serves as an information clearinghouse; monitors federal and state legislation.

American Society of Appraisers, *555 Herndon Pkwy., #125, Herndon, VA 20170 (mailing address: P.O. Box 17265 20041); (703) 478-2228. Fax, (703) 742-8471. Edwin W. Baker, Executive Director. Information, (800) 272-8258. General e-mail, asainfo@apo.com. Web, www.appraisers.org.*

Membership: accredited appraisers of real property, including land, houses, and commercial buildings; businesses; machinery and equipment; yachts; aircraft; public utilities; personal property, including antiques, fine art, residential contents, gems, and jewelry. Affiliate members include students and professionals interested in appraising. Provides technical information; accredits appraisers; provides consumer information program.

Appraisal Foundation, *1029 Vermont Ave. N.W., #900 20005; (202) 347-7722. Fax, (202) 347-7727. David S. Bunton, Executive Vice President. Web, www.appraisalfoundation.org.*

Seeks to ensure that appraisers are qualified to offer their services by promoting uniform appraisal standards and establishing education, experience, and examination requirements.

Appraisal Institute, *Public Affairs, Washington Office, 2600 Virginia Ave. N.W., #123 20037; (202) 298-6449. Fax, (202) 298-5547. Donald E. Kelly, Vice President. Web, www.appraisalinstitute.org.*

Provides Congress, regulatory agencies, and the executive branch with information on appraisal matters. (Headquarters in Chicago.)

Assn. of Foreign Investors in Real Estate, *1300 Pennsylvania Ave. N.W., #880 20004-3020; (202) 312-1400. Fax, (202) 312-1401. James A. Fetgatter, Chief Executive. General e-mail, afireinfo@afire.org. Web, www.afire.org.*

Represents foreign institutions that are interested in the laws, regulations, and economic trends affecting the U.S. real estate market. Informs the public and the government of the contributions foreign investment makes to the U.S. economy. Examines current issues and organizes seminars for members.

International Real Estate Federation, *American Chapter, 2000 N. 15th St., #101, Arlington, VA 22201; (703) 524-4279. Fax, (703) 528-2392. Owen Gwyn Jr., President. General e-mail, info@fiabci-usa.com. Web, www.fiabci-usa.com.*

Membership: real estate professionals in the fields of appraisal, brokerage, counseling, development, financ-

ing, and property management. Sponsors seminars, workshops, and conferences. (International headquarters in Paris.)

Investment Program Assn., *1101 17th St. N.W., #703 20036; (202) 775-9750. Fax, (202) 331-8446. Christopher L. Davis, President. Web, www.ipa-dc.org.*

Represents the partnership industry, public and private investments that employ partnerships, Real Estate Investment Trusts (REIT), limited liability companies, and other direct investment programs. Conducts conferences and seminars.

Manufactured Housing Institute, *2101 Wilson Blvd., #610, Arlington, VA 22201-3062; (703) 558-0400. Fax, (703) 558-0401. Christopher Stinebert, President. Web, www.mfghome.org.*

Represents park owners, financial lenders, and builders, suppliers, and retailers of manufactured homes. Provides information on manufactured home construction standards, finance, site development, property management, and marketing.

National Assn. of Home Builders, *1201 15th St. N.W. 20005-2800; (202) 822-0200. Fax, (202) 822-0559. Thomas M. Downs, Executive Vice President. Press, (202) 822-0253. Web, www.nahb.com.*

Membership: contractors, builders, architects, engineers, mortgage lenders, and others interested in home building and commercial real estate construction. Offers educational programs and information on housing policy and mortgage finance in the United States. Library open to the public.

National Assn. of Real Estate Brokers, *1629 K St. N.W., #602 20006-1635; (202) 785-4477. Fax, (202) 785-1244. Ernest Clark, President. Web, www.nareb.com.*

Membership: minority real estate brokers, appraisers, contractors, property managers, and salespersons. Works to prevent discrimination in housing policies and practices; conducts regional seminars on federal policy, legislation, and regulations; advises members on procedures for procuring federal contracts.

National Assn. of Real Estate Investment Trusts, *1875 Eye St. N.W., #600 20006; (202) 739-9400. Fax, (202) 739-9401. Steve Wechsler, President. Web, www.nareit.com.*

Membership: real estate investment trusts and corporations, partnerships, and individuals interested in real estate securities and the industry. Monitors federal and state legislation, federal taxation, securities regulation, standards and ethics, and housing and education; compiles industry statistics.

National Assn. of Realtors, *Government Affairs, Washington Office, 700 11th St. N.W. 20001-4507; (202) 383-1238. Fax, (202) 383-7850. Lee L. Verstandig, Senior Vice President. Web, www.realtor.com.*

Sets standards of ethics for the real estate business; promotes education, research, and exchange of information. Monitors legislation and regulations. (Headquarters in Chicago.)

National Home Buyers and Home Owners Assn., *1050 17th St. N.W., #1100 20036; (202) 659-6500. Fax, (202) 293-2608. Benny L. Kass, General Counsel.*

Promotes consumer interests in housing, including condominiums; publishes a homebuyer's checklist in English and Spanish.

The Real Estate Roundtable, *1420 New York Ave. N.W., #1100 20005-2159; (202) 639-8400. Fax, (202) 639-8442. Jeffrey D. DeBoer, President. General e-mail, info@rer.org.*

Membership: real estate owners, advisers, builders, investors, lenders, and managers. Serves as forum for public policy issues including taxes, the environment, capital, credit, and investments.

Society of Industrial and Office Realtors, *700 11th St. N.W., #510 20001-4507; (202) 737-1150. Fax, (202) 737-8796. Pam Hinton, Executive Vice President. Web, www.sior.com.*

Membership: commercial and industrial real estate brokers worldwide. Certifies brokers; sponsors seminars and conferences; mediates and arbitrates business disputes for members; sponsors a speakers bureau. (Affiliated with the National Assn. of Realtors.)

Mortgages and Finance

AGENCIES

Federal Agricultural Mortgage Corp., *919 18th St. N.W., #200 20006-5503; (202) 872-7700. Fax, (202) 872-7713. Thomas R. Clark, Vice President. Web, www.farmermac.com.*

Private corporation chartered by Congress to provide a secondary mortgage market for farm and rural housing loans. Guarantees principal and interest repayment on securities backed by farm and rural housing loans.

Federal Home Loan Mortgage Corp., *8200 Jones Branch Dr., McLean, VA 22102-3107; (703) 903-2701. Fax, (703) 903-3495. David W. Glenn, President; Leland C. Brendsel, Chair, (703) 903-3001. Information, (703) 903-3000. Press, (703) 903-2411. Web, www.fhlmc.com.*

Chartered by Congress to increase the flow of funds for residential mortgages by buying conforming mortgages and selling mortgage securities to major investors.

Federal Housing Administration *(Housing and Urban Development Dept.), Insured Single Family Housing, 451 7th St. S.W., #9162 20410; (202) 708-3046. Fax, (202) 708-2582. Morris Carter, Director (Acting).*

Establishes acceptable financial risks for the operation of government-insured mortgage programs for single-family properties (one to four units); monitors and oversees HUD-approved local counseling agencies for Federal Housing Administration programs.

Federal Housing Administration *(Housing and Urban Development Dept.), Multifamily Business Products, 451 7th St. S.W., #6134 20410-8000; (202) 708-3000. Fax, (202) 708-3104. Willie Spearmon, Director. Web, www.hud.gov/fha/mfh/fhamfbus.html.*

Establishes procedures for the development of housing under the multifamily mortgage insurance programs. Administers the mortgage insurance programs for rental, cooperative, and condominium housing.

Federal Housing Administration *(Housing and Urban Development Dept.), Title I Insurance, 451 7th St. S.W., #9272 20410; (202) 708-6396. Fax, (202) 401-8951. Mary Worthy, Loan Specialist.*

Sets policy for Title I loans on manufactured home and property improvement loans. Provides information to lenders on policy issues.

Federal Housing Enterprise Oversight *(Housing and Urban Development Dept.), 1700 G St. N.W., 4th Floor 20552-0100; (202) 414-3800. Fax, (202) 414-3823. Armando Falcon Jr., Director. Web, www.ofheo.gov.*

Works to ensure the financial soundness of the Federal National Mortgage Assn. (Fannie Mae) and the Federal Home Loan Mortgage Corp. (Freddie Mac).

Federal Housing Finance Board, *1777 F St. N.W. 20006; (202) 408-2587. Fax, (202) 408-1435. Bruce A. Morrison, Chair; William W. Ginsberg, Managing Director, (202) 408-2890. Information, (202) 408-2500. Press, (202) 408-2986. TTY, (202) 408-2579. Public reading room, (202) 408-2969. Web, www.fhfb.gov.*

Regulates and supervises the credit and financing operations of the twelve Federal Home Loan Banks, which provide a flexible credit reserve for member institutions engaged in home mortgage lending. Member institutions of the Federal Home Loan Banks include savings and loans, savings banks, commercial banks, credit unions, insurance companies, and other financial intermediaries.

Federal National Mortgage Assn., *3900 Wisconsin Ave. N.W. 20016; (202) 752-7000. Fax, (202) 752-3616. Franklin D. Raines, Chair; Vacant, President. Information, (800) 732-6643. Library, (202) 752-7750. Press, (202) 752-7928. TTY, (202) 752-1324. Web, www.fanniemae.com.*

Congressionally chartered, shareholder-owned corporation. Makes mortgage funds available by buying conventional and government-insured mortgages in the secondary mortgage market; raises capital through sale of short- and long-term obligations, mortgages, and stock; issues and guarantees mortgage-backed securities. Library open to the public by appointment.

Government National Mortgage Assn. *(Housing and Urban Development Dept.), 451 7th St. S.W., #6100 20410; (202) 708-0926. Fax, (202) 708-0490. George S. Anderson, Executive Vice President; Vacant, President.*

Supports government housing objectives by establishing secondary markets for residential mortgages. Serves as a vehicle for channeling funds from the securities markets into the mortgage market through mortgage-backed securities programs and helps to increase the supply of credit available for housing. Guarantees privately issued securities backed by Federal Housing Administration, Veterans Affairs Dept., and Farmers Home Administration mortgages.

Housing and Urban Development Dept., *Housing— Federal Housing Commissioner, 451 7th St. S.W., #9100 20410; (202) 708-3600. Fax, (202) 708-2580. William C. Apgar, Assistant Secretary. Web, www.hud.gov/fha/fhahome.html.*

Administers all Federal Housing Administration (FHA) mortgage insurance programs; approves and monitors all lending institutions that conduct business with HUD.

Office of Thrift Supervision *(Treasury Dept.), 1700 G St. N.W. 20552; (202) 906-6280. Fax, (202) 898-0230. Ellen Seidman, Director. Information, (202) 906-6000. Library, (202) 906-6470. Press, (202) 906-6913. Mortgage rates recording, (202) 906-6988. Web, www.ots.treas.gov.*

Charters, regulates, and examines the operations of savings and loan institutions; focus includes mortgage rates. Library open to the public.

NONPROFIT

American League of Financial Institutions, *900 19th St. N.W., #400 20006-2105; (202) 857-5094. Fax, (202) 296-8716. Dina Curtis, President. Web, www.alfi.org.*

Membership: minority-controlled community savings associations and savings banks. Offers on-site technical assistance to resolve problems in operations.

Encourages financing of low- and moderate-income housing and promotes community reinvestment activities. Monitors legislative and regulatory issues.

America's Community Bankers, *900 19th St. N.W., #400 20006; (202) 857-3100. Fax, (202) 296-8716. Diane M. Casey, President. Press, (202) 857-3103. General e-mail, info@acbankers.org. Web, www.acbankers.org.*

Membership: insured depository institutions involved in community finance. Provides information on issues that affect the industry. Monitors economic issues affecting savings institutions; publishes homebuyers survey. Monitors legislation and regulations.

Assn. of Local Housing Finance Agencies, *1200 19th St. N.W., #300 20036-2422; (202) 857-1197. Fax, (202) 223-4579. John C. Murphy, Executive Director. Web, www.alhfa.org.*

Membership: professionals of city and county government that finance affordable housing. Provides professional development programs in new housing finance and other areas. Monitors legislation and regulations.

Mortgage Bankers Assn. of America, *1919 Pennsylvania Ave. N.W. 20006; (202) 557-2700. Fax, (202) 721-0204. Paul Reid, Executive Vice President.*

Membership: institutions involved in real estate finance. Maintains School of Mortgage Banking; collects statistics on the industry. Conducts seminars and workshops in specialized areas of mortgage finance. Monitors legislation and regulations. Library open to the public by appointment.

Mortgage Insurance Companies of America, *727 15th St. N.W. 20005; (202) 393-5566. Fax, (202) 393-5557. Suzanne C. Hutchinson, Executive Vice President.*

Membership: companies that provide guarantee insurance on residential, high-ratio mortgage loans. Insures members against loss from default on low down payment home mortgages and provides coverage that acts as a credit enhancement on mortgage securities.

National Assn. of Affordable Housing Lenders, *2121 K St. N.W., #700 20037; (202) 293-9850. Fax, (202) 293-9852. Judith A. Kennedy, President. General e-mail, naahl@naahl.org.*

Membership: lenders who specialize in providing financing for affordable housing and community development, including regulated financial institutions, insurance companies, mortgage banking companies, and loan funds. Serves as an information clearinghouse; provides education, training, and direct technical assistance. Monitors legislation and regulations.

National Assn. of Mortgage Brokers, *8201 Greensboro Dr., #300, McLean, VA 22102; (703) 610-9009. Fax, (703) 610-9005. Brian J. Kinsella, Executive Vice President. Web, www.namb.org.*

Membership: mortgage brokers. Seeks to improve the mortgage broker industry. Offers educational programs to members. Provides referrals. Monitors legislation and regulations.

National Council of State Housing Agencies, *444 N. Capitol St. N.W., #438 20001; (202) 624-7710. Fax, (202) 624-5899. John McEvoy, Executive Director. Web, www.ncsha.org.*

Membership: state housing finance agencies. Promotes greater opportunities for lower-income people to rent or buy affordable housing.

Property Management

AGENCIES

Bureau of Land Management *(Interior Dept.),* **Lands and Realty,** *1620 L St. N.W. 20240 (mailing address: 1849 C St. N.W., MC 1000LS 20240); (202) 452-7780. Fax, (202) 452-7708. Ray Brady, Manager. Web, www.blm.gov.*

Oversees use, acquisition, and disposal of public lands. Conducts the Public Lands Survey; authorizes rights-of-way on public lands, including roads and power lines.

Federal Housing Administration *(Housing and Urban Development Dept.),* **Portfolio Management,** *451 7th St. S.W., #6160 20410; (202) 708-3730. Fax, (202) 401-5978. Frank Malone, Director. Web, www.hud.gov.*

Services mortgages developed under HUD's multifamily mortgage insurance programs, including the Community Disposal Program; reviews management of multifamily housing projects and administers project-based subsidy programs; advises state housing agencies that administer multifamily projects.

Federal Housing Administration *(Housing and Urban Development Dept.),* **Procurement,** *451 7th St. S.W., #2220 20410; (202) 708-4466. Fax, (202) 708-3698. Thomas R. Vincent, Director.*

Develops policies and procedures for procurement contracting related to the rehabilitation, repair, rental, maintenance, management, demolition, and sale of acquired multifamily and single-family properties and properties under the federal surplus land program.

NONPROFIT

Building Owners and Managers Assn. International, *1201 New York Ave. N.W., #300 20005; (202) 408-*2662. Fax, (202) 371-0181. Robert Angle, Executive Vice President. Web, www.boma.org.*

Membership: office building owners and managers. Reviews changes in model codes and building standards; conducts seminars and workshops on building operation and maintenance issues; sponsors educational and training programs. Monitors legislation and regulations.

Building Service Contractors Assn. International, *10201 Lee Hwy., #225, Fairfax, VA 22030; (703) 359-7090. Fax, (703) 352-0493. Carol A. Dean, Executive Vice President. Web, www.bscai.org.*

Membership: building service contractors. Promotes industry practices that are professional and environmentally responsive.

Community Associations Institute, *225 Reinekers St., Alexandria, VA 22314; (703) 548-8600. Fax, (703) 684-1581. Barbara Keenan, President. Fax-on-demand, (703) 836-6904. Web, www.caionline.org.*

Membership: homeowner associations, builders, lenders, owners, managers, realtors, insurance companies, and public officials. Provides members with information on creating, financing, and maintaining common facilities and services in condominiums and other planned developments.

Cooperative Housing Foundation, *8300 Colesville Rd., #420, Silver Spring, MD 20910; (301) 587-4700. Fax, (301) 587-2626. Michael Doyle, President. General e-mail, mailbox@chfhq.com. Web, www.chfhq.org.*

Works under contract with the Agency for International Development, United Nations, and World Bank to strengthen government housing departments abroad. Develops and strengthens nonprofit technical service organizations; conducts training workshops; assists tenant groups in converting units into cooperatives; conducts research.

NAIOP, National Assn. of Industrial and Office Properties, *2201 Cooperative Way, 3rd Floor, Herndon, VA 20171-3024; (703) 904-7100. Fax, (703) 904-7942. Thomas J. Bisacquino, President. Web, www.naiop.org.*

Membership: developers, planners, designers, builders, financiers, and managers of industrial and office properties. Provides research and continuing education programs. Monitors legislation and regulations on capital gains, real estate taxes, impact fees, growth management, environmental issues, and hazardous waste liability.

National Apartment Assn., *201 N. Union St., #200, Alexandria, VA 22314; (703) 518-6141. Fax, (703) 518-6191. James Hepfner, President. Web, www.naahq.org.*

Membership: state and local associations of owners, managers, investors, developers, and builders of apartment houses or other rental properties; conducts educational and professional certification programs. Monitors legislation and regulations.

National Assn. of Home Builders, *1201 15th St. N.W. 20005-2800; (202) 822-0200. Fax, (202) 822-0559. Thomas M. Downs, Executive Vice President. Press, (202) 822-0253. Web, www.nahb.com.*

Membership: contractors, builders, architects, engineers, mortgage lenders, and others interested in home building and commercial real estate construction. Offers a Registered Apartment Managers certification program; provides educational programs and information on apartment construction and management, condominiums and cooperatives, multifamily rehabilitation, and low-income and federally assisted housing. Library open to the public.

National Assn. of Housing and Redevelopment Officials, *630 Eye St. N.W. 20001; (202) 289-3500. Fax, (202) 289-8181. Richard Y. Nelson Jr., Executive Director. Web, www.nahro.org.*

Membership: housing, community, and urban development practitioners and organizations, and state and local government agencies and personnel. Conducts studies and provides training and certification in the operation and management of rental housing; develops performance standards for low-income rental housing operations.

National Assn. of Housing Cooperatives, *1401 New York Ave. N.W., #100 20005-0797; (703) 737-0797. Fax, (703) 783-7869. Douglas M. Kleine, Executive Director. General e-mail, info@coophousing.org. Web, www. coophousing.org.*

Membership: housing cooperative professionals, developers, and individuals. Promotes housing cooperatives; sets standards; provides technical assistance in all phases of cooperative housing; sponsors educational programs and on-site training; monitors legislation;

maintains an information clearinghouse on housing cooperatives.

National Center for Housing Management, *National Training Center, 1010 N., Glebe Rd., #160, Arlington, VA 22201; (703) 516-4070. Fax, (703) 516-4069. W. Glenn Stevens, President. Web, www.nchm.org.*

Private corporation created by executive order to meet housing management and training needs. Conducts research, demonstrations, and educational and training programs in all types of multifamily housing management. Develops and implements certification systems for housing management programs.

National Cooperative Business Assn., *1401 New York Ave. N.W., #1100 20005-2146; (202) 638-6222. Fax, (202) 638-1374. Paul Hazen, President. General e-mail, ncba@ ncba.org. Web, www.cooperative.org.*

Alliance of cooperatives, businesses, and state cooperative associations. Provides information about starting and managing housing cooperatives. Monitors legislation and regulations.

National Multi Housing Council, *1850 M St. N.W., #540 20036; (202) 974-2300. Fax, (202) 775-0112. Jonathan L. Kempner, President. Web, www.nmhc.org.*

Membership: owners, financiers, managers, and developers of multifamily housing. Advocates policies and programs at the federal, state, and local levels to increase the supply and quality of multifamily units in the United States; serves as a clearinghouse on rent control, condominium conversion, taxes, fair housing, housing for seniors, and environmental issues.

Property Management Assn., *7900 Wisconsin Ave., #204, Bethesda, MD 20814; (301) 657-9200. Fax, (301) 907-9326. Thomas B. Cohn, Executive Vice President. General e-mail, pma@erols.com. Web, www.pma-dc.org.*

Membership: property managers and firms that offer products and services needed in the property management field. Promotes information exchange on property management practices.

13 International Affairs

🌏 GENERAL POLICY

See also Military Aid and Peacekeeping (chap. 16)

AGENCIES

Defense Dept., International Security Affairs, The Pentagon, #4E838 20301-2400; (703) 695-4351. Fax, (703) 697-7230. Franklin D. Kramer, Assistant Secretary. Web, www.defenselink.mil.

Advises the secretary of defense and recommends policies on regional security issues (except those involving countries of the former Soviet Union).

National Security Council (*Executive Office of the President*), *Defense Policy/Arms Control: International Economic Affairs,* The White House 20502; (202) 456-9281. Fax, (202) 456-9280. Malcolm Lee, Director. Web, www.whitehouse.gov/WH/EOP/NSC/html/nschome.html.

Advises the president and the National Security Adviser on all aspects of U.S. foreign policy dealing with U.S. international economic policies.

Office of Science and Technology Policy (*Executive Office of the President*), *National Security and International Affairs,* Dwight D. Eisenhower Executive Office Bldg., #494 20502; (202) 456-2894. Fax, (202) 456-6028. Neal Lane, Director. Web, www.whitehouse.gov/WH/EOP/OSTP/html/OSTP_Home.html.

Advises the president on international science and technology matters as they affect national security; coordinates international science and technology initiatives at the interagency level.

President's Foreign Intelligence Advisory Board (*Executive Office of the President*), Dwight D. Eisenhower Executive Office Bldg., #340 20502; (202) 456-2352. Fax, (202) 395-3403. Warren Rudman, Chair; Randy Deitering, Executive Director.

Members appointed by the president. Assesses the quality, quantity, and adequacy of foreign intelligence collection and of counterintelligence activities by all government agencies; advises the president on matters concerning intelligence and national security.

State Dept., 2201 C St. N.W. 20520; (202) 647-5291. Fax, (202) 647-6434. Madeleine K. Albright, Secretary; Strobe Talbott, Deputy Secretary, (202) 647-9640. Information, (202) 647-4000. Press, (202) 647-2492. Web, www.state.gov.

Directs and coordinates U.S. foreign relations and interdepartmental activities of the U.S. government overseas.

State Dept., Consular Affairs, 2201 C St. N.W., #6811 20520-4818; (202) 647-9576. Fax, (202) 647-0341. Mary A. Ryan, Assistant Secretary. Passport services, (202) 647-0518. Assistance to U.S. citizens overseas, (202) 647-5225. Web, travel.state.gov.

Issues passports to U.S. citizens and visas to immigrants and nonimmigrants seeking to enter the United States. Provides protection, assistance, and documentation for American citizens abroad.

State Dept., Global Affairs, 2201 C St. N.W., #7250 20520; (202) 647-6240. Fax, (202) 647-0753. Frank E. Loy, Under Secretary. Web, www.state.gov.

Advises the secretary on international issues. Divisions include Democracy, Human Rights, and Labor; International Narcotics and Law Enforcement Affairs; Oceans and International Environmental and Scientific Affairs; and Population, Refugees, and Migration.

State Dept., Intelligence and Research, 2201 C St. N.W., #6531 20520-6531; (202) 647-9177. Fax, (202) 736-4688. J. Stapleton Roy, Assistant Secretary. Web, www.state.gov.

Coordinates foreign policy-related research, analysis, and intelligence programs for the State Dept. and other federal agencies.

State Dept., International Conferences, 2201 C St. N.W., #1517 20520-6319; (202) 647-6875. Fax, (202) 647-5996. Frank R. Provyn, Managing Director. Web, www.state.gov.

Coordinates U.S. participation in international conferences.

State Dept., International Organization Affairs, 2201 C St. N.W., #6323 20520-6319; (202) 647-9600. Fax, (202) 736-4116. C. David Welch, Assistant Secretary. Press, (202) 647-8490. Web, www.state.gov.

Coordinates and develops policy guidelines for U.S. participation in the United Nations and in other international organizations and conferences.

State Dept., Management, 2201 C St. N.W., #7207 20520; (202) 647-1500. Fax, (202) 647-0168. Bonnie R. Cohen, Under Secretary. Web, www.state.gov.

Serves as principal adviser to the secretary on management matters, including budgetary, administrative, and personnel policies of the department and the Foreign Service.

State Dept., Policy Planning Staff, 2201 C St. N.W., #7311 20520; (202) 647-2372. Fax, (202) 647-4147. Morton H. Halperin, Director. Web, www.state.gov.

Advises the secretary and other State Dept. officials on foreign policy matters.

State Dept., *Political Affairs*, *2201 C St. N.W., #7240 20520; (202) 647-2471. Fax, (202) 647-4780. Thomas R. Pickering, Under Secretary. Web, www.state.gov.*

Assists in the formulation and conduct of foreign policy and in the overall direction of the department; coordinates interdepartmental activities of the U.S. government abroad.

State Dept., *Public Diplomacy and Public Affairs, 2201 C St. N.W., #7325 20520; (202) 647-9199. Fax, (202) 647-9140. Evelyn Lieberman, Under Secretary. Web, www.state.gov/www/outreach/index.html.*

Seeks to broaden public affairs discussion on foreign policy with American citizens, media, and institutions. Provides cultural and educational exchange opportunities and international information programs to people in the United States and abroad.

State Dept., *Public Diplomacy and Public Affairs: Bureau of Educational and Cultural Affairs, 301 4th St. S.W., #336 20547; (202) 619-4949. Fax, (202) 205-2457. David Whitten, Executive Director. Web, e.usia.gov/education.*

Seeks to promote mutual understanding between the people of the U.S. and other countries through international educational and training programs. Promotes personal, professional, and institutional ties between private citizens and organizations in the U.S. and abroad; presents U.S. history, society, art, and culture to overseas audiences.

U.S. Institute of Peace, *1200 17th St. N.W., #200 20036; (202) 457-1700. Fax, (202) 429-6063. Chester Crocker, Chair; Richard H. Solomon, President. TTY, (202) 457-1719. Web, www.usip.org.*

Independent organization created and funded by Congress to promote the peaceful resolution of international conflict through negotiation and mediation. Provides federal agencies and individuals with training, research programs, and information; awards grants to institutions and individuals; and provides fellowships to scholars from the United States and abroad. Library open to the public by appointment.

CONGRESS

General Accounting Office, *National Security and International Affairs, 441 G St. N.W., #4035 20548; (202) 512-2800. Fax, (202) 512-7686. Henry L. Hinton, Assistant Comptroller General.*

Independent, nonpartisan agency in the legislative branch. Audits, analyzes, and evaluates international programs; makes unclassified reports available to the public.

House Appropriations Committee, *Subcommittee on Commerce, Justice, State, and Judiciary, H309 CAP 20515; (202) 225-3351. Rep. Harold Rogers, R-Ky., Chair; Jim Kulikowski, Staff Director. Web, www.house.gov/appropriations.*

Jurisdiction over legislation to appropriate funds for the State Dept. (except migration and refugee assistance), the Foreign Claims Settlement Commission, the Commission on Security and Cooperation in Europe, and the Japan–United States Friendship Commission.

House Appropriations Committee, *Subcommittee on Foreign Operations, Export Financing, and Related Programs, H150 CAP 20515; (202) 225-2041. Rep. Sonny Callahan, R-Ala., Chair; Charles O. Flickner, Staff Director. Web, www.house.gov/appropriations.*

Jurisdiction over legislation to appropriate funds for foreign operations, including migration, refugee, economic, and military assistance programs of the State Dept.; the Export-Import Bank; the International Bank for Reconstruction and Development (World Bank); the Inter-American Development Bank; the International Monetary Fund; the Agency for International Development; the Peace Corps; and related international organizations.

House Government Reform Committee, *Subcommittee on National Security, Veterans Affairs, and International Affairs, B372 RHOB 20515; (202) 225-2548. Fax, (202) 225-2382. Rep. Christopher Shays, R-Conn., Chair; Lawrence Halloran, Staff Director. Web, www.house.gov/reform.*

Oversees operations of the State Dept., the Peace Corps, the Agency for International Development, and other agencies concerned with foreign affairs.

House International Relations Committee, *2170 RHOB 20515; (202) 225-5021. Fax, (202) 225-2035. Rep. Benjamin A. Gilman, R-N.Y., Chair; Richard J. Garon Jr., Chief of Staff. General e-mail, HIRC@mail.house.gov. Web, www.house.gov/international_relations.*

Jurisdiction over legislation on and operations of the State Dept. and U.S. foreign embassies. Jurisdiction over authorization of budget for the Agency for International Development and U.S. contributions to the United Nations and other international organizations. Oversight of State and Defense departments' operations regarding arms transfers, export licenses, sales, administration of security assistance, and foreign military training and advisory programs.

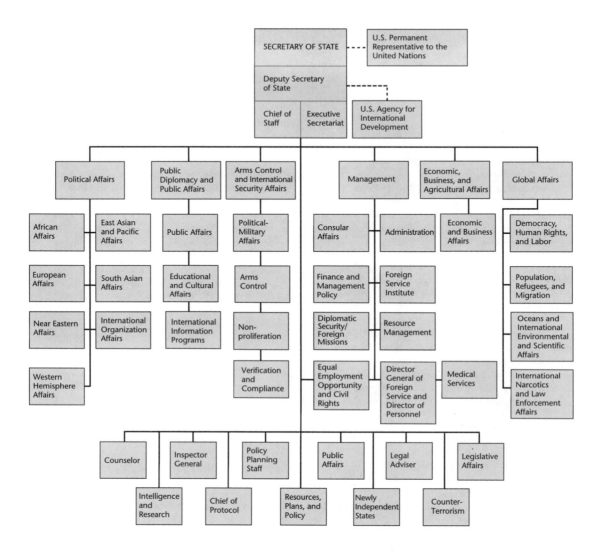

Library of Congress, *Serial and Government Publications,* *101 Independence Ave. S.E. 20540; (202) 707-5647. Fax, (202) 707-6128. Karen Renninger, Chief. Information, (202) 707-5690.*

Collects and maintains information on governmental and nongovernmental organizations that are internationally based, financed, and sponsored. Responds to written or telephone requests to provide information on the history, structure, operation, and activities of these organizations. Some book material available for interlibrary loan through the Library of Congress Loan Division.

Senate Appropriations Committee, *Subcommittee on Commerce, Justice, State, and Judiciary, S-146A CAP 20510; (202) 224-7277. Sen. Judd Gregg, R-N.H., Chair; Jim Morhard, Clerk. Web, appropriations.senate.gov/ commerce.*

Jurisdiction over legislation to appropriate funds for the State Dept. (except counterterrorism, migration and refugee assistance, and international narcotics control), the Foreign Claims Settlement Commission, and other programs related to foreign policy and foreign aid.

Senate Appropriations Committee, *Subcommittee on Foreign Operations, SD-142 20510; (202) 224-2104. Fax, (202) 228-1323. Sen. Mitch McConnell, R-Ky., Chair; Robin Cleveland, Staff Director. Web, appropriations. senate.gov/foreignops.*

Jurisdiction over legislation to appropriate funds for foreign operations, including migration, refugee, development, economic, and military assistance programs of the State Dept.

Senate Foreign Relations Committee, *SD-450 20510; (202) 224-4651. Fax, (202) 224-0836. Sen. Jesse Helms, R-N.C., Chair; Steve Biegun, Staff Director. Web, foreign. senate.gov.*

Jurisdiction over legislation on foreign affairs, including economic and military assistance programs. Oversight responsibilities for operations of the State Dept., the Foreign Service, U.S. participation in the United Nations, and other agencies concerned with foreign affairs.

Senate Foreign Relations Committee, *Subcommittee on Western Hemisphere, Peace Corps, Narcotics, and Terrorism, SD-450 20510; (202) 224-4651. Fax, (202) 224-0836. Sen. Lincoln Chafee, R-R.I., Chair; Roger Noriega, Senior Professional Staff Member. Web, www.senate. gov/~foreign.*

Jurisdiction over foreign affairs legislation dealing with the Americas; oversight of all matters of the Peace Corps and the U.S. delegation to the Organization of American States.

INTERNATIONAL ORGANIZATIONS

European Commission, *Press and Public Affairs, Washington Office, 2300 M St. N.W. 20037; (202) 862-9500. Fax, (202) 429-1766. Willy Helin, Director; Günter Burghardt, Ambassador. Press, (202) 862-9540. Web, www.europa.eu.int.*

Information and public affairs office in the United States for the European Union, which includes the European Economic Community, the European Coal and Steel Community, and the European Atomic Energy Community. Member countries are Austria, Belgium, Denmark, Finland, France, Germany, Great Britain, Greece, Ireland, Italy, Luxembourg, the Netherlands, Portugal, Spain, and Sweden. Provides social policy data on the European Union and provides statistics and documents on member countries, including those related to energy, economics, development and cooperation, commerce, agriculture, industry, and technology. Library open to the public by appointment. (Headquarters in Brussels.)

International Bank for Reconstruction and Development, *1818 H St. N.W., MC12-750 20433; (202) 477-1234. Fax, (202) 522-3031. James D. Wolfensohn, President. Press, (202) 473-1804. Publications, (202) 473-1956. Web, www.worldbank.org.*

International development institution funded by membership subscriptions and borrowings on private capital markets. Encourages the flow of public and private foreign investment into developing countries through loans and technical assistance. Finances foreign economic development projects in agriculture, environmental protection, education, public utilities, telecommunications, water supply, sewerage, public health, and other areas.

International Monetary Fund, *700 19th St. N.W. 20431; (202) 623-7759. Fax, (202) 623-4940. Karin Lissakers, U.S. Executive Director. Information, (202) 623-7000. Press, (202) 623-7300. Web, www.imf.org.*

Intergovernmental organization that maintains funds, contributed and available for use by members, to promote world trade and aid members with temporary balance-of-payments problems.

Organization for Economic Cooperation and Development, *Washington Office, 2001 L St. N.W., #650 20036-4922; (202) 785-6323. Fax, (202) 785-0350. Matthew Brosius, Co-Director. Web, www.oecdwash.org.*

Membership: twenty-nine nations including Australia, Canada, Japan, Mexico, New Zealand, the United States, and western European nations. Serves as a forum for members to exchange information and attempt to coordinate their economic policies. Washington Center maintains reference library open to the public. (Headquarters in Paris.)

Organization of American States, *17th St. and Constitution Ave. N.W. 20006 (mailing address: 1889 F St. N.W. 20006); (202) 458-3000. Fax, (202) 458-3967. Cesar Gaviria, Secretary General. Information, (202) 458-3756. Library, (202) 458-6037. Web, www.oas.org.*

Membership: the United States, Canada, and all independent Latin American and Caribbean countries. Funded by quotas paid by member states and by contributions to special multilateral funds. Works to promote democracy, eliminate poverty, and resolve disputes among member nations. Provides member states with technical and advisory services in cultural, educational, scientific, social, and economic areas. Library open to the public.

United Nations Information Centre, *1775 K St. N.W., #400 20006; (202) 331-8670. Fax, (202) 331-9191. Cathryn O'Neill, Director. Web, www.un.org.*

Lead United Nations (U.N.) office in Washington. Center for reference publications of the U.N. Library, open to the public, includes all official U.N. records and publications.

NONPROFIT

American Enterprise Institute for Public Policy Research, *Foreign and Defense Policy Studies, 1150 17th St. N.W., #1100 20036; (202) 862-5814. Fax, (202) 862-7177. Jeane Kirkpatrick, Director. Information, (202) 862-5800. Press, (202) 862-5829. Web, www.aei.org.*

Research and educational organization that conducts conferences, seminars, and debates and sponsors research on international affairs.

Assn. on Third World Affairs, *1629 K St. N.W., #802 20006; (202) 331-8455. Fax, (202) 775-7465. Lorna Hahn, Executive Director.*

Membership: individuals and groups interested in developing nations. Promotes research projects; arranges lectures and conferences; sponsors student interns.

Assn. to Unite the Democracies, *502 H St. S.W. 20024-2726; (202) 544-5150. Fax, (202) 544-3742. Tom Hudgens, President. Information, (800) 288-6483. General e-mail, atunite@aol.com. Web, www.iaud.org.*

Educational organization that promotes and conducts research on unity among the industrial democracies, including the United States, Japan, western European countries, and new and emerging democracies in the former Soviet bloc. Advocates a federation of these states.

Atlantic Council of the United States, *910 17th St. N.W., 10th Floor 20006; (202) 463-7226. Fax, (202) 463-7241. Christopher J. Makins, President. General e-mail, info@acus.org. Web, www.acus.org.*

Conducts studies and makes policy recommendations on American foreign security and international economic policies in the Atlantic and Pacific communities; sponsors conferences and educational exchanges.

The Brookings Institution, *Foreign Policy Studies, 1775 Massachusetts Ave. N.W. 20036-2188; (202) 797-6400. Fax, (202) 797-6003. Richard N. Haass, Director. Information, (202) 797-6000. Press, (202) 797-6105. Publications, (202) 797-6258. Web, www.brook.edu.*

Conducts studies on foreign policy, national security, regional and global affairs, and economic policies.

Carnegie Endowment for International Peace, *1779 Massachusetts Ave. N.W. 20036; (202) 483-7600. Fax, (202) 483-1840. Jessica T. Mathews, President. General e-mail, carnegie@ceip.org. Web, www.ceip.org.*

Conducts research on international affairs and American foreign policy. Program activities cover a broad range of military, political, and economic issues; sponsors panel discussions. (Affiliate office in Moscow.)

Center for Democracy, *1101 15th St. N.W., #505 20005-5002; (202) 429-9141. Fax, (202) 293-1768. Allen Weinstein, President. General e-mail, center@ centerfordemocracy.org. Web, www.centerfordemocracy.org.*

Nonpartisan organization that works to promote the democratic process and strengthen democratic institutions in the United States and worldwide. Monitors elections and provides democratizing governments with technical and informational assistance.

Center for Strategic and International Studies, *1800 K St. N.W. 20006; (202) 887-0200. Fax, (202) 775-3199. John J. Hamre, President. Publications, (202) 775-3119. Web, www.csis.org.*

Independent nonpartisan research institute that studies international and domestic policy issues. Interests include science and technology, international business and economics, political-military affairs, arms control, international communications, and fiscal policy.

Center of Concern, *1225 Otis St. N.E. 20017; (202) 635-2757. Fax, (202) 832-9494. James Hug, President. General e-mail, coc@coc.org. Web, www.coc.org/coc.*

Independent, interdisciplinary organization that conducts social analysis, theological reflection, policy advocacy, and public education on issues of international justice and peace.

Charles F. Kettering Foundation, *Washington Office, 444 N. Capitol St. N.W., #434 20001-1512; (202) 393-4478. Fax, (202) 393-7644. James C. Wilder, Director. Information, (800) 221-3657. Web, www.kettering.org.*

Works to improve the domestic policy-making process. Supports international program focusing on unofficial, citizen-to-citizen diplomacy. Encourages greater citizen involvement in formation of public policy. Interests include public education and at-risk youths. (Headquarters in Dayton, Ohio.)

Citizens Network for Foreign Affairs, *1111 19th St. N.W., #900 20036; (202) 296-3920. Fax, (202) 296-3948. John H. Costello, President. General e-mail, cohend@ cnfa.com. Web, www.cnfa.com.*

Public policy and education organization that works to involve Americans in the foreign policy process. Advocates a more collaborative partnership between the public and private sectors to promote global economic growth.

Council on Foreign Relations, *Washington Office,* 1779 Massachusetts Ave. N.W. 20036; (202) 518-3400. Fax, (202) 986-2984. Paula J. Dobriansky, Director. Web, www.foreignrelations.org.

Promotes understanding of U.S. foreign policy and international affairs. Awards research grants through its International Affairs Fellowship Program. (Headquarters in New York.)

Democracy International, 2803 Whirlaway Circle, Oak Hill, VA 20171; (703) 620-9258. Fax, (202) 620-0647. Ira Straus, Executive Director.

Seeks to encourage democracy and protect human rights throughout the world.

Eisenhower World Affairs Institute, 1620 Eye St. N.W., #703 20006; (202) 223-6710. Fax, (202) 452-1837. Carl W. Reddel, President.

Sponsors public policy and educational programs for future leaders designed to improve understanding of the presidency and world affairs.

Friends Committee on National Legislation, 245 2nd St. N.E. 20002-5795; (202) 547-6000. Fax, (202) 547-6019. Joe Volk, Executive Secretary. Recorded information, (202) 547-4343. General e-mail, fcnl@fcnl.org. Web, www.fcnl.org.

Seeks to broaden public interest and affect legislation and policy concerning regional and global institutions, peace processes, international development, and the work of the United Nations. Affiliated with the Religious Society of Friends (Quakers).

Institute for Foreign Policy Analysis, 1725 DeSales St. N.W., #402 20036; (202) 463-7942. Fax, (202) 785-2785. Robert Pfaltzgraff Jr., President. Web, www.ifpa.org.

Trains policy analysts in the fields of foreign policy and national security. Sponsors research and workshops.

Institute for Policy Studies, 733 15th St. N.W., #1020 20005; (202) 234-9382. Fax, (202) 387-7915. John Cavanagh, Director. Web, www.ips-dc.org.

Research and educational organization. Interests include foreign policy, the U.S. military-industrial complex, international development, human rights, and national security.

Institute of International Education, *National Security Education Program,* 1400 K St. N.W., 6th Floor 20005-2403; (202) 326-7697. Fax, (202) 326-7698. Leslie Anderson, Director. Information, (800) 618-6737. Web, www.iie.org/nsep.

Provides scholarships, fellowships, and institutional grants to academics with an interest in foreign affairs and national security.

Institute of World Politics, 1521 16th St. N.W. 20036; (202) 462-2101. Fax, (202) 462-7031. John Lenczowski, Director. General e-mail, info@iwp.edu. Web, www.iwp.edu.

Offers graduate programs in international affairs, foreign policy, methods of statecraft, and political philosophy.

International Center, 731 8th St. S.E. 20003; (202) 547-3800. Fax, (202) 546-4784. Lindsay Mattison, Executive Director. General e-mail, icnfp@erols.com. Web, www.internationalcenter.com.

Research organization concerned with U.S. foreign policy. Sponsored U.S. delegation to more than twenty countries. Current projects include: Commission on U.S.-Russian Relations, New Forests Project, U.S.-Vietnam Trade Council, U.S.-Vietnam Forum, and the U.S.-Bulgaria Council.

International Foundation for Election Systems, 1101 15th St. N.W., 3rd Floor 20005; (202) 828-8507. Fax, (202) 452-0804. Richard W. Soudriette, President. Web, www.ifes.org.

Supports electoral and other democratic institutions in emerging democracies. Holds conferences; observes election activities in more than ninety countries. Provides technical assistance. Conducts education and training programs and conferences.

International Republican Institute, 1212 New York Ave. N.W., #900 20005-3987; (202) 408-9450. Fax, (202) 408-9462. Lorne Craner, President. Web, www.iri.org.

Created under the National Endowment for Democracy Act. Fosters democratic self-rule through closer ties and cooperative programs with political parties and other nongovernmental institutions overseas.

National Defense Council Foundation, 1220 King St., #230, Alexandria, VA 22314; (703) 836-3443. Fax, (703) 836-5402. Milton R. Copulos, President. General e-mail, ndcf@erols.com. Web, www.ndcf.org.

Studies defense and foreign affairs issues that face the U.S. Informs Congress and the media on socioeconomic, political, and military issues that affect the U.S. Interests include low-intensity conflict, drug control, and energy concerns.

National Democratic Institute for International Affairs, 1717 Massachusetts Ave. N.W., #503 20036; (202) 328-3136. Fax, (202) 939-3166. Kenneth Wollack, President. General e-mail, demos@ndi.org. Web, www.ndi.org.

Conducts nonpartisan international programs to help maintain and strengthen democratic institutions worldwide. Focuses on party building, governance, and electoral systems.

National Endowment for Democracy, *1101 15th St. N.W., #700 20005-1650; (202) 293-9072. Fax, (202) 223-6042. Carl Gershman, President; Barbara Haig, Program Director. Web, www.ned.org.*

Grant-making organization that receives funding from Congress. Awards grants to private organizations involved in democratic development abroad, including the areas of democratic political processes; pluralism; and education, culture, and communications.

National Peace Foundation, *1819 H St. N.W., #1200 20006-3603; (202) 223-1770. Fax, (202) 223-1718. Stephen P. Strickland, President. Web, www.nationalpeace. org.*

Supports conflict resolution education and the U.S. Institute of Peace. Holds conferences and provides information on peace education and managing and resolving conflict.

National Security Archive, *Gelman Library, 2130 H St. N.W., #701 20037; (202) 994-7000. Fax, (202) 994-7005. Thomas Blanton, Executive Director. General e-mail, nsarchiv@gwu.edu. Web, www.gwu.edu/~nsarchiv.*

Research institute and library that provides information on U.S. foreign policy and national security affairs. Maintains collection of declassified and unclassified national security documents. Archive open to the public by appointment.

Paul H. Nitze School of Advanced International Studies, *1740 Massachusetts Ave. N.W. 20036; (202) 663-5624. Fax, (202) 663-5621. Paul D. Wolfowitz, Dean. Information, (202) 663-5600. Press, (202) 663-5626.*

Offers graduate programs in international relations and public policy. Sponsors the Johns Hopkins Foreign Policy Institute and centers for international business and public policy; central Asia and the Caucasus; and Canadian, Brazilian, East Asian, and Sino-American studies.

United Nations Assn. of the USA, *Washington Office, 1779 Massachusetts Ave. N.W., #610 20036; (202) 462-3446. Fax, (202) 462-3448. Steven A. Dimoff, Vice President. General e-mail, unadc@unausa.org. Web, www. unausa.org.*

Research and educational organization focusing on international institutions, multilateral diplomacy, U.S. foreign policy, and international economics. Coordinates Model United Nations program for high school and university students. Monitors legislation and regulations. (Headquarters in New York.)

U.S. Catholic Conference, *International Justice and Peace, 3211 4th St. N.E. 20017-1194; (202) 541-3199. Fax,*

(202) 541-3339. Gerard Powers, Director. Web, www. nccbuscc.org/sdwp.

Works with the U.S. State Dept., foreign government offices, and international organizations on issues of peace, justice, and human rights.

Washington Institute of Foreign Affairs, *2121 Massachusetts Ave. N.W. 20008; (202) 966-1061. Fax, (202) 966-0945. Marina G. Fischer, Executive Secretary.*

Membership: former government officials, retired military professionals, educators, and others concerned with foreign affairs. Promotes greater understanding of foreign affairs by the American public.

Women in International Security, *University of Maryland, CISSM, SPA, 4133F Van Munching Hall, College Park, MD 20742; (301) 405-7612. Fax, (301) 403-8107. Peggy Knudson, Executive Director. Web, www.puaf. umd.edu/WIIS.*

Seeks to advance women in the field of international relations. Maintains a database of women foreign and defense policy specialists worldwide; organizes conferences in Europe, the former Soviet Union, and Asia; disseminates information on jobs, internships, and fellowships for women in international affairs.

Women's Foreign Policy Group, *1825 Connecticut Ave. N.W., #660 20009-5728; (202) 986-8862. Fax, (202) 986-8869. Patricia Ellis, Executive Director. General e-mail, wfpg@wfpg.org. Web, www.wfpg.org.*

Promotes the leadership of women in international affairs professions. Conducts policy programs, mentoring, and research.

World Federalist Assn., *418 7th St. S.E. 20003-2796; (202) 546-3950. Fax, (202) 546-3749. John B. Anderson, President. Information, (800) 923-0123. Web, www.wfa. org.*

Sponsors projects and conducts research related to international affairs; seeks to broaden public support for world order organizations and a restructured United Nations.

Diplomats and Foreign Agents

See also Americans Abroad (this chapter); Foreign Embassies, U.S. Ambassadors, and Country Desk Officers (appendix)

AGENCIES

For information on the annual foreign service exam, contact FSO (Foreign Service Officer) Exam, State Dept., P.O. Box 12226, Arlington, VA 22219; (703) 875-

7490. Exam information is also available via the Internet at www.state.gov/www/careers/rexamcontents.html.

Foreign Service Institute (*State Dept.*), *Professional and Area Studies*, 4000 Arlington Blvd., Arlington, VA 22204-1500; (703) 302-6703. Fax, (703) 302-7461. Ruth A. Davis, Director; Steven A. Browning, Dean, (703) 302-6940. Student messages and course information, (703) 302-7143.

Provides training for U.S. government personnel involved in foreign affairs agencies, including employees of the State Dept., the Agency for International Development, the Defense Dept., and other agencies.

Justice Dept., *Foreign Agents Registration Unit*, 1400 New York Ave. N.W., #9500 20530; (202) 514-1216. Fax, (202) 514-2836. Marshall Williams, Chief. Web, www.usdoj.gov/criminal/fara.

Receives and maintains the registration of agents representing foreign countries, companies, organizations, and individuals. Compiles semi-annual report on foreign agent registrations. Foreign agent registration files are open for public inspection.

State Dept., *Career Development and Assignments*, 2201 C St. N.W., #2328 20520-6258 (mailing address: PER/CDA 20520-2810); (202) 647-1692. Fax, (202) 647-0277. Vincent M. Battle, Director. Web, www.state.gov.

Coordinates programs related to the professional development of American members of the Foreign Service, including career development and assignment counseling programs; training; and presidential appointments and resignations.

State Dept., *Diplomatic Security Bureau*, 2201 C St. N.W., #6316 20520; (202) 647-6290. Fax, (202) 647-0953. David G. Carpenter, Assistant Secretary. Web, www.state.gov.

Provides a secure environment for conducting American diplomacy and promoting American interests abroad and in the United States.

State Dept., *Family Liaison*, 2201 C St. N.W., #1212A 20520-7512; (202) 647-1076. Fax, (202) 647-1670. Faye Barnes, Director. Web, www.state.gov/www/flo.

Provides support for U.S. foreign affairs personnel and their families in Washington, D.C. and abroad. Maintains liaison offices that give support services to the U.S. foreign affairs community overseas. Services include dependent employment assistance and continuing education programs; educational assistance for families with children; and information on adoption and separation, regulations, allowance, and finances. Assists families in emergencies.

State Dept., *Foreign Missions*, 2201 C St. N.W., #2238 20520; (202) 647-4554. Fax, (202) 647-1919. Theodore A. Strickler, Deputy Director. Web, www.state.gov.

Regulates the benefits, privileges, and immunities granted to foreign missions and their personnel in the United States on the basis of the treatment accorded U.S. missions abroad and considerations of national security and public safety.

State Dept., *Foreign Service*, 2201 C St. N.W., #6218 20520; (202) 647-9898. Fax, (202) 647-5080. Marc Grossman, Director General (Nominee). Web, www.state.gov.

Administers the Foreign Service.

State Dept., *Medical Services*, 2401 E St. N.W., #L209 20522-0102; (202) 663-1611. Fax, (202) 663-1613. Dr. Cedric E. Dumont, Medical Director. Web, www.state.gov.

Operates a worldwide primary health care system for American citizen employees, and eligible family members, of the U.S. government residing abroad. Conducts physical examinations of Foreign Service officers and candidates; provides clinical services; assists with medical evacuation of patients overseas.

State Dept., *Protocol*, 2201 C St. N.W., #1238 20520; (202) 647-4543. Fax, (202) 647-3980. Mary Mel French, Chief. Press, (202) 647-1685. Web, www.state.gov.

Serves as principal adviser to the president, vice president, the secretary, and other high-ranking government officials on matters of diplomatic procedure governed by law or international customs and practice.

CONGRESS

House International Relations Committee, *Subcommittee on International Operations and Human Rights,* B-358 RHOB 20515; (202) 225-5748. Fax, (202) 225-7485. Rep. Christopher H. Smith, R-N.J., Chair; Grover Joseph Rees, Staff Director. Web, www.house.gov/international_relations.

Jurisdiction over legislation on the foreign service, the United Nations, other international organizations, and educational and cultural exchange programs.

Senate Foreign Relations Committee, *Subcommittee on International Operations,* SD-450 20510; (202) 224-4651. Fax, (202) 224-0836. Sen. Rod Grams, R-Minn., Chair; Steve Biegun, Staff Director. Web, foreign.senate.gov.

Jurisdiction over legislation on the foreign service, the United Nations, other international organizations and conferences, and educational and cultural exchange programs.

NONPROFIT

American Foreign Service Assn., *2101 E St. N.W. 20037; (202) 338-4045. Fax, (202) 338-6820. Susan Reardon, Executive Director. General e-mail, afsa@afsa.org. Web, www.afsa.org.*

Membership: active and retired foreign service employees of the State Dept., Agency for International Development, Foreign Commercial Service, and the Foreign Agricultural Service. Offers scholarship program; maintains club for members; represents active duty foreign service personnel in labor-management negotiations. Seeks to ensure adequate resources for foreign service operations and personnel. Interests include business-government collaboration and international trade. Monitors legislation and regulations.

Council of American Ambassadors, *888 17th St. N.W., #901 20006-3939; (202) 296-3757. Fax, (202) 296-0926. Carolyn M. Gretzinger, Executive Director; Keith L. Brown, President. General e-mail, council@his.com. Web, www.his.com/~council.*

Membership: U.S. ambassadors. Seeks to advance the understanding of the American ambassador's role in serving U.S. interests abroad; assists in the ambassadorial selection process.

Executive Council on Diplomacy, *818 Connecticut Ave. N.W., #1200 20006-2702; (202) 466-5199. Fax, (202) 872-8696. Alan Robbins, Deputy Director.*

Brings foreign diplomats from international organizations such as the United Nations and World Bank into contact with their American counterparts. Provides a forum for discussion on issues such as agriculture, international trade, education, and the arts.

Institute for the Study of Diplomacy *(Georgetown University), 801 Intercultural Center, 37th and O Sts. N.W. 20057; (202) 687-6279. Fax, (202) 687-8312. Casimir A. Yost, Director. Web, www.georgetown.edu/sfs/programs/isd.*

Part of the Edmund A. Walsh School of Foreign Service. Focuses on the practical implementation of foreign policy objectives; draws on academic research and the concrete experience of diplomats and other members of the foreign service.

Humanitarian Aid

See also Development Assistance (this chapter); Emergency Preparedness (chap. 16); World Food Assistance (chap. 2)

AGENCIES

Administration for Children and Families *(Health and Human Services Dept.), Refugee Resettlement, 901 D St. S.W., 6th Floor 20447; (202) 401-9246. Fax, (202) 401-5487. Lavinia Limon, Director.*

Directs a domestic resettlement program for refugees; reimburses states for costs incurred in giving refugees monetary and medical assistance; awards funds to private resettlement agencies for providing refugees with monetary assistance and case management; provides states and nonprofit agencies with grants for social services such as English and employment training.

Agency for International Development, *Center for Population, Health, and Nutrition, 1300 Pennsylvania Ave. N.W., G/PHN 20523-3600; (202) 712-4120. Fax, (202) 216-3485. Duff Gillespie, Deputy Assistant Director. Web, www.info.usaid.gov/pop_health.*

Participates in global efforts to stabilize world population growth and support women's reproductive rights. Focus includes family planning; reproductive health care; infant, child, and maternal health; and prevention of sexually transmitted diseases, especially AIDS. Conducts demographic and health surveys; educates girls and women.

Agency for International Development, *Humanitarian Response Bureau, 1300 Pennsylvania Ave. N.W., #8.06 20523; (202) 712-0100. Fax, (202) 216-3397. Hugh Q. Parmer, Assistant Administrator. Web, www.info.usaid.gov.*

Manages U.S. foreign disaster assistance, U.S. government food aid programs, grants to private voluntary and cooperative development organizations, and American sponsored schools and hospitals around the world.

Agency for International Development, *U.S. Foreign Disaster Assistance, 1300 Pennsylvania Ave. N.W., #8.06A 20523-0008; (202) 712-0400. Fax, (202) 216-3707. Tami Halmrast-Sanchez, Deputy Director. Web, www.info.usaid.gov.*

Division of the Humanitarian Response Bureau. Administers disaster relief and preparedness assistance to foreign countries to save lives and alleviate human suffering. Aids displaced persons in disaster situations and helps other countries manage natural and complex disasters.

Defense Dept., *Peacekeeping and Humanitarian Assistance, The Pentagon, #4B680, ODASD (PK-HA) 20301-2500; (703) 614-0446. Fax, (703) 614-0442. James A. Schear, Deputy Assistant Secretary. Web, www.defenselink.mil.*

Develops policy and plans for department provision of humanitarian assistance, refugee affairs, U.S. international information programs, and international peacekeeping and peace enforcement activities. Develops policy related to creating, identifying, training, exercising, and committing military forces for peacekeeping and peace enforcement activities.

Public Health and Science *(Health and Human Services Dept.), International and Refugee Health, 5600 Fishers Lane, #18105, Rockville, MD 20857-1750; (301) 443-1774. Fax, (301) 443-6288. Thomas Novotny, Director. Web, www.surgeongeneral.gov/ophs/oirh.htm.*

Represents the Health and Human Services Dept. before other governments, U.S. government agencies, international organizations, and the private sector on international and refugee health issues. Promotes international cooperation; provides health-related humanitarian and developmental assistance.

State Dept., *Population, Refugees, and Migration, 2201 C St. N.W., #5824 20520-5824; (202) 647-7360. Fax, (202) 647-8162. Julia V. Taft, Assistant Secretary. Information, (202) 663-1014. Web, www.state.gov.*

Develops and implements policies and programs on international refugee matters, including repatriation and resettlement programs; funds and monitors overseas relief, assistance, and repatriation programs; manages refugee admission to the United States.

CONGRESS

House International Relations Committee, *2170 RHOB 20515; (202) 225-5021. Fax, (202) 225-2035. Rep. Benjamin A. Gilman, R-N.Y., Chair; Richard J. Garon Jr., Chief of Staff. General e-mail, HIRC@mail.house.gov. Web, www.house.gov/international_relations.*

Jurisdiction over international disaster assistance legislation, including the Foreign Assistance Act.

House Judiciary Committee, *Subcommittee on Immigration and Claims, B370B RHOB 20515; (202) 225-5727. Fax, (202) 225-3672. Rep. Lamar Smith, R-Texas, Chair; George Fishman, Counsel. General e-mail, Judiciary@mail.house.gov. Web, www.house.gov/judiciary.*

Jurisdiction over legislation on immigration, refugees, and repatriated Americans; oversight of private immigration relief bills.

Senate Foreign Relations Committee, *SD-450 20510; (202) 224-4651. Fax, (202) 224-0836. Sen. Jesse Helms, R-N.C., Chair; Steve Biegun, Staff Director. Web, foreign. senate.gov.*

Jurisdiction over international disaster assistance legislation, including the International Emergency Economic Powers Act.

Senate Judiciary Committee, *Subcommittee on Immigration, SD-323 20510; (202) 224-6098. Fax, (202) 228-4506. Sen. Spencer Abraham, R-Mich., Chair; Lee Lieberman Otis, Chief Counsel. Web, judiciary.senate. gov/immigrat.htm.*

Jurisdiction over legislation on refugees, repatriated Americans, immigration, and naturalization. Oversight of private immigration relief bills.

INTERNATIONAL ORGANIZATIONS

International Organization for Migration, *Washington Office, 1752 N St. N.W., #700 20036; (202) 862-1826. Fax, (202) 862-1879. Luca Dall'Oglio, Regional Representative. General e-mail, srowashington@iom.int. Web, www.iom.int.*

Nonpartisan organization that plans and operates refugee resettlement, national migration, and humanitarian assistance programs at the request of its member governments. Recruits skilled professionals for developing countries. (Headquarters in Geneva.)

Pan American Health Organization, *525 23rd St. N.W. 20037; (202) 974-3000. Fax, (202) 974-3663. Dr. George A. O. Alleyne, Director. Information, (202) 974-3458. Library, (202) 974-3305. Web, www.paho.org.*

Regional office for the Americas of the World Health Organization, headquartered in Geneva, Switzerland. Works to extend health services to underserved populations of its member countries and to control or eradicate communicable diseases; promotes cooperation among governments to solve public health problems. Library open to the public by appointment.

United Nations High Commissioner for Refugees, *Washington Office, 1775 K St. N.W., #300 20006-1502; (202) 296-5191. Fax, (202) 296-5660. Karen AbuZayd, Washington Representative. Web, www.unhcr.ch.*

Works with governments and voluntary organizations to protect and assist refugees worldwide. Promotes long-term alternatives to refugee camps, including voluntary repatriation, local integration, and resettlement overseas. (Headquarters in Geneva.)

U.S. Fund for the United Nations Children's Fund, *Public Policy and Advocacy, Washington Office, 1775 K St. N.W., #360 20006; (202) 296-4242. Fax, (202) 296-4060. Martin S. Rendon, Vice President. Information, (800) 367-5437. Web, www.unicefusa.org.*

Serves as information reference service on UNICEF; advocates policies to advance the well-being of the world's children. Interests include international humanitarian assistance, U.S. voluntarism, child survival, and international health. (Headquarters in New York.)

See also Pan American Development Foundation (p. 485)

NONPROFIT

American Red Cross, National Headquarters, *430 17th St. N.W., 2nd Floor 20006-2401; (202) 737-8300. Fax, (202) 783-3432. Dr. Bernadine Healy, President. Web, www.redcross.org.*

Service organization chartered by Congress to provide domestic and international disaster relief and to act as a medium of communication between the U.S. armed forces and their families in time of war. Coordinates the distribution of supplies, funds, and technical assistance for relief in major foreign disasters through the International Federation of Red Cross and Red Crescent Societies and the International Committee of the Red Cross, both headquartered in Geneva.

Central American Resource Center, *1459 Columbia Rd. N.W. 20009; (202) 328-9799. Fax, (202) 328-0023. Saul Solorzano, Executive Director. General e-mail, carecendc2@aol.com.*

Human rights organization that seeks recognition of refugees' rights, including the right not to be deported. Provides legal representation for refugees seeking asylum; encourages church congregations to assist refugees in applying for political asylum. Interests include community education, documentation of human rights abuses, and social services.

Christian Children's Fund, *Washington Office, 1400 16th St. N.W., #715 20036; (202) 462-2161. Fax, (202) 462-0601. Betty Meyer, Director. General e-mail, ccfwash@ aol.com. Web, www.christianchildrensfund.org.*

Nonsectarian humanitarian organization that promotes improved child welfare standards and services worldwide by supporting long-term sustainable development. Provides children in emergency situations brought on by war, natural disaster, and other circumstances with education, medical care, food, clothing, and shelter. Provides aid to children of all backgrounds. (Headquarters in Richmond, Va.)

Church World Service, *Development Policy, Washington Office, 110 Maryland Ave. N.E. 20002; (202) 543-6336. Fax, (202) 546-6232. Lisa Wright, Director.*

International relief, refugee, and development agency of the National Council of Churches. Provides food and medical assistance in drought- and famine-stricken areas; disaster relief services in the United States; and development assistance in developing countries. Monitors legislation and regulations. (Headquarters in New York.)

Health Volunteers Overseas, *1001 Connecticut Ave. N.W., #622 20036 (mailing address: Washington Station, P.O. Box 65157 20035-5157); (202) 296-0928. Fax, (202) 296-8018. Nancy Kelly, Executive Director. General e-mail, info@hvousa.org. Web, www.hvousa.org.*

Operates training programs in developing countries for health professionals who wish to teach low-cost health care delivery practices.

Holy Childhood Assn., *1720 Massachusetts Ave. N.W. 20036; (202) 775-8637. Fax, (202) 429-2987. Rev. Francis W. Wright, National Director.*

Religious education and relief organization that provides educational materials to teach American children about underprivileged children in foreign countries. Provides financial aid for programs and facilities that benefit underprivileged children abroad under age fourteen.

International Rescue Committee, *Government Relations, Washington Office, 1612 K St. N.W., #700 20006; (202) 822-0043. Fax, (202) 822-0089. Sheppie Abramowitz, Vice President. Web, www.intrescom.org.*

Provides worldwide emergency aid, resettlement services, and educational support for refugees; recruits volunteers. (Headquarters in New York.)

Jesuit Refugee Service/USA, *1616 P St. N.W., #400 20036-1405; (202) 462-5200. Fax, (202) 328-9212. Richard Ryscavage (SJ), National Coordinator. General e-mail, united.states@jesref.org. Web, www.jesref.org.*

U.S. Jesuit organization that aids refugees in Africa, Southeast Asia, Central America, and Mexico. Provides information on refugee problems; places individual Jesuits, sisters, and lay people in refugee work abroad. Monitors refugee- and immigration-related legislation. (International headquarters in Rome.)

Program for Appropriate Technology in Health, *Washington Office, 1990 M St. N.W., #700 20036; (202) 822-0033. Fax, (202) 457-1466. Anne Wilson, Director. General e-mail, info@path-dc.org. Web, www.path.org.*

Seeks to improve the safety and availability of health products and technologies worldwide, particularly in developing countries. Interests include reproductive health, immunization, maternal-child health, AIDS, and nutrition. (Headquarters in Seattle.)

Refugee Policy Group, *P.O. Box 37, Kensington, MD 20895; (301) 588-6555. Fax, (301) 588-6709. Dennis Gal-*

lagher, Executive Director. General e-mail, refugeePG@ worldnet.att.net.

Conducts policy analyses and research on domestic and international refugee issues; sponsors symposia. Library open to the public by appointment.

Refugee Voices, *1717 Massachusetts Ave. N.W., #200 20036; (202) 347-3507. Fax, (202) 347-3418. Melissa Wyers, Director. Information, (800) 688-7338. Web, www. refugees.org.*

Advocates on behalf of refugees; produces radio programs to educate Americans about the plight of refugees; coordinates information network. Monitors legislation and regulations. (Affiliated with U.S. Committee for Refugees.)

Southeast Asia Resource Action Center, *1628 16th St. N.W., 3rd Floor 20009; (202) 667-4690. Fax, (202) 667-6449. KaYing Yang, Executive Director. General e-mail, searacdc@aol.com. Web, www.searac.org.*

Assists Southeast Asians in the United States with resettlement. Advocates for refugee rights. Interests include education, citizenship development, Indochinese self-help organizations, and economic development.

U.S. Catholic Conference (USCC), *Migration and Refugee Services, 3211 4th St. N.E. 20017; (202) 541-3352. Fax, (202) 541-3399. Mark Franken, Executive Director. Web, www.nccbuscc.org/mrs.*

Provides refugees and immigrants with resettlement services and legal counseling; operates training programs for volunteers and professionals; develops and implements USCC policy on migration, immigration, and refugee issues.

U.S. Committee for Refugees, *1717 Massachusetts Ave. N.W., #200 20036; (202) 347-3507. Fax, (202) 347-3418. Roger P. Winter, Executive Director. Web, www. refugees.org.*

Public information and educational organization that monitors the world refugee situation and informs the public about refugee issues. Interests include human rights abuses. Publishes position papers and an annual survey. (Affiliated with Refugee Voices.)

World Mercy Fund, *P.O. Box 227, Waterford, VA 20197; (540) 882-4425. Fax, (540) 882-3226. Patrick Leonard, President.*

Provides the developing world with medical, educational, agricultural, and other forms of aid.

World Vision, *Washington Office, 220 Eye St. N.E., #270 20002; (202) 547-3743. Fax, (202) 547-4834. Bruce Wilkinson, Vice President. Web, www.worldvision.org.*

Provides children and families around the world with aid, including emergency disaster relief; helps impoverished communities become self-sustaining through agriculture, health care, community organization, food programming, nutritional training, income generation and credit, and other development projects. (Headquarters in Seattle.)

Information and Exchange Programs

See also International Programs (chap. 17); Language and Literature (chap. 5); Regional Affairs (this chapter)

AGENCIES

Broadcasting Board of Governors, *330 Independence Ave. S.W., #3360 20237; (202) 401-3736. Fax, (202) 401-6605. Marc Nathanson, Chair; John Lindburg, Executive Director (Acting).*

Established by Congress to direct and supervise all U.S. government nonmilitary international broadcasting, including Voice of America, Radio and TV Marti, Worldnet Television, Radio Free Europe/Radio Liberty, and Radio Free Asia. Assesses the quality and effectiveness of broadcasts with regard to U.S. foreign policy objectives; reports annually to the president and to Congress.

USDA Graduate School *(Agriculture Dept.),* **International Institute,** *600 Maryland Ave. S.W., #320 20024-2520; (202) 314-3500. Fax, (202) 479-6803. Jack Maykowski, Director (Acting). Web, www.grad.usda.gov.*

Offers professional training and educational services to employees of foreign governments, international organizations, nongovernmental agencies, and employees of U.S. agencies engaged in international activities. Areas of concentration include governance and democratization, international conflict resolution, privatization, environmental management, and management skills and systems development. Conducts courses in Washington, D.C., San Francisco, and other locations worldwide.

Voice of America *(International Broadcasting Bureau),* *330 Independence Ave. S.W., #3300 20237; (202) 619-3375. Fax, (202) 260-2228. Sanford Ungar, Director. Information, (202) 619-2538. Locator, (202) 619-4700.*

Official radio broadcast service of the International Broadcasting Bureau. Offers overseas broadcasts of news, editorials, and features dealing with developments in American foreign and domestic affairs. Operates African, East Asian and Pacific, European, Eurasian, Latin American, North African, and Near East and South Asian affairs offices, as well as the World English program.

Alliance for International Educational and Cultural Exchange, *1776 Massachusetts Ave. N.W., #620 20036; (202) 293-6141. Fax, (202) 293-6144. Michael McCarry, Executive Director. General e-mail, info@ alliance-exchange.org. Web, www.alliance-exchange.org.*

Promotes public policies that support the growth of international exchange between the United States and other countries. Provides professional representation, resource materials, publications, and public policy research for those involved in international exchanges.

American Bar Assn., *International Legal Exchange Program,* *740 15th St. N.W. 20005-1022; (202) 662-1670. Fax, (202) 662-1669. Jesus Izquierdo, Executive Director. Web, www.abanet.org/intlaw.*

Organizes the exchange of lawyers between the United States and other countries and arranges short-term placements for foreign lawyers with law firms nationwide. Coordinates briefing trips for U.S. lawyers overseas.

American Council of Young Political Leaders, *1612 K St. N.W., #300 20006; (202) 857-0999. Fax, (202) 857-0027. Mark Poole, Executive Director. General e-mail, acypl@erols.com. Web, www.acypl.org.*

Bipartisan political education organization that promotes understanding of foreign policy between state and local leaders and their counterparts abroad. Sponsors conferences and political study tours for U.S. and foreign political leaders between the ages of twenty-five and forty-one.

Business–Higher Education Forum, *1 Dupont Circle N.W., #800 20036; (202) 939-9345. Fax, (202) 833-4723. Judith Irwin, Managing Director. General e-mail, bhef@ ace.nche.edu. Web, www.bhef.com.*

Membership: chief executive officers of major corporations, colleges, and universities. Promotes the development of industry-university alliances around the world. Provides countries in central and eastern Europe with technical assistance in enterprise development, management training, market economics, education, and infrastructure development.

Center for Intercultural Education and Development, *3307 M St. N.W., #302 20007 (mailing address: P.O. Box 579400, Georgetown University 20057-9400); (202) 687-1400. Fax, (202) 687-2555. Julio Giulietti (SJ), Director. Web, www.georgetown.edu/CIED.*

Designs and administers programs aimed at improving the quality of life of economically disadvantaged people; provides technical education, job training, leadership skill development, and business management training; runs programs in Central America, the Caribbean, Central Europe, and Southeast Asia.

Council for International Exchange of Scholars, *3007 Tilden St. N.W., #5L 20008-3009; (202) 686-4000. Fax, (202) 362-3442. Patti McGill Peterson, Executive Director. General e-mail, info@ciesnet.cies.org. Web, www.cies.org.*

Cooperates with the U.S. government in administering Fulbright grants for university teaching and advanced research abroad. (Affiliated with the American Council of Learned Societies.)

Delphi International, *1015 18th St. N.W., #1000 20036-8104; (202) 898-0950. Fax, (202) 842-0885. Nalini Shetty, President. General e-mail, postmaster@delphi-int.org. Web, www.delphi-int.org.*

Assists public and private organizations engaged in international cooperation and business. Works with governments and private counterparts to support foreign professional exchanges. Develops technical training programs and educational curricula for foreign visitors. Provides technical expertise, management support, travel, and business development services.

English-Speaking Union, *Washington Office,* *15 Dupont Circle, 4th Floor 20036; (202) 234-4602. Fax, (202) 234-4639. Diana Nicholson, Executive Director. General e-mail, esuwdc@erols.com. Web, www.esu-dc.org.*

International educational and cultural organization that promotes cultural exchange programs with countries in which English is a major language; offers free English conversational tutoring to persons for whom English is a second language; sponsors scholarships for studies in English-speaking countries; sponsors annual Shakespeare competition among D.C. schools. (Headquarters in New York.)

Foreign Services Research Institute, *2718 Unicorn Lane N.W. 20015-2234 (mailing address: P.O. Box 6317 20015-0317); (202) 362-1588. John E. Whiteford Boyle, President.*

Provides information on American culture to embassies, foreign business firms, and foreign educational establishments. Advises on placement of foreign students; maintains library on U.S. educational and cultural data. Represents the International Academy of Independent Scholars, which aids retired scholars in research, library access, and travel, and the Essentialist Philosophical Society.

Institute of International Education, *Washington Office,* *1400 K St. N.W., 6th Floor 20005-2403; (202) 898-*

KEEP YOUR COLLECTION CURRENT —
SIGN UP FOR CQ'S STANDING ORDER PLAN

Now that you have CQ's *Washington Information Directory*, be sure you are signed up for our standing order plan on this title. As new editions of *Washington Information Directory* are published **every year**, you will automatically receive your copy—without having to order again.

All you have to do to join is check the box below and drop this postage-paid card in the mail.

☐ Add me to your standing order file for CQ's *Washington Information Directory* (Institutions only, please). As new editions of this title are published, I will be among the first to receive my copy, and I will be billed. I understand that I can return any CQ book within 30 days for a full refund.

Name	
Title	
Organization	
Address	
City	State ZIP
	Phone ( )

CQ Press

Call (800) 638-1710 or Fax (800) 380-3810

If you already have this title on standing order, you do not need to return this card. You will automatically receive new editions in the series.

L0WDB4-CQ

BUSINESS REPLY MAIL

First Class   Permit No.10182   Washington, D.C.

Postage Will Be Paid By Addressee

CQ Press
Attn: Customer Service Dept. L0WDB4-CQ
1414 22nd Street, N.W.
Washington, D.C. 20077-6778

CQ PRESS

0600. Fax, (202) 326-7696. *Jeanne Thum, Administrative Officer; Allan Goodman, President,* (202) 326-7840. *Web, www.iie.org.*

Educational exchange, technical assistance, and training organization that arranges professional programs for international visitors; conducts training courses in energy, environment, journalism, human resource development, educational policy and administration, and business-related fields; provides developing countries with short- and long-term technical assistance in human resource development; arranges professional training and support for staff of human rights organizations; sponsors fellowships and applied internships for midcareer professionals from developing countries; implements contracts and cooperative agreements for organizations, including the U.S. Agency for International Development, philanthropic foundations, multilateral banks, and other organizations. (Headquarters in New York.)

International Research and Exchanges Board, *1616 H St. N.W. 20006; (202) 628-8188. Fax, (202) 628-8189. Daniel C. Matuszewski, President. General e-mail, irex@ irex.org. Web, www.irex.org.*

Administers academic exchanges between the United States and Russia, the new independent states, central and eastern Europe, Mongolia, and China. Exchange efforts include professional training, institution building, technical assistance, and policy development.

Meridian International Center, *1630 Crescent Pl. N.W. 20009; (202) 667-6800. Fax, (202) 667-1475. Walter L. Cutler, President. Information, (202) 667-6670. General e-mail, meridian@meridian.org. Web, www. meridian.org.*

Conducts international educational and cultural programs; provides foreign visitors and diplomats in the United States with services, including cultural orientation, seminars, and language assistance. Offers world affairs programs and international exhibitions for Americans.

NAFSA: Assn. of International Educators, *1307 New York Ave. N.W., #800 20005-4701; (202) 737-3699. Fax, (202) 737-3657. Marlene Johnson, Executive Director. Publications, (800) 836-4994. General e-mail, inbox@ nafsa.org. Web, www.nafsa.org.*

Membership: individuals, educational institutions, and others interested in international educational exchange. Seeks to increase awareness of and support for international education in colleges and universities, government, and the community. Provides information on evaluating exchange programs; assists members in complying with federal regulations affecting foreign students and scholars; administers grant programs with an international education focus.

National Council for International Visitors, *1420 K St. N.W., #800 20005-2501; (202) 842-1414. Fax, (202) 289-4625. Sherry L. Mueller, Executive Director. Information, (800) 523-8101. Web, www.nciv.org.*

National network of nonprofit and community organizations that provides hospitality to international visitors. Seeks to improve international relations through professional and personal communications and exchanges. Provides training, networking, and information services.

Radio Free Europe/Radio Liberty, *Washington Office, 1201 Connecticut Ave. N.W., #1100 20036-2605; (202) 457-6900. Fax, (202) 457-6992. Jane Lester, Corporate Secretary. Information, (202) 457-6914. Press, (202) 457-6947. General e-mail, goblep@rferl.org. Web, www.rferl. org.*

Independent radio broadcast service funded by federal grants to promote and support democracy. Radio Free Europe broadcasts programs to Bulgaria, the Czech Republic, Estonia, Latvia, Lithuania, Poland, Romania, and Slovakia; programming includes entertainment, news, and specials on political developments in eastern Europe. Radio Liberty broadcasts similar programming to the former Soviet Union. Research materials available to the public by appointment. (Headquarters in Prague.)

Town Affiliation Assn. of the U.S., *Sister Cities International, 1424 K St. N.W., #600 20005; (202) 347-8630. Fax, (202) 393-6524. Ned Benner, Executive Director. General e-mail, info@sister-cities.org. Web, www.sister-cities.org.*

Assists U.S. and foreign cities in establishing formal city-to-city affiliations, including exchanges of people, ideas, and materials; serves as program coordinator and information clearinghouse; sponsors youth programs and scholarships.

Youth for Understanding, *3501 Newark St. N.W. 20016; (202) 966-6800. Fax, (202) 895-1104. Sally Grooms Cowal, President. TTY, (800) 787-8000. Teen Information, (800) TEENAGE. Web, www.youthforunderstanding.org.*

Educational organization that administers cross-cultural exchange programs for secondary school students. Administers scholarship programs that sponsor student exchanges, including the Congress-Bundestag Scholarship Program.

🏛 IMMIGRATION AND NATURALIZATION

AGENCIES

Administration for Children and Families *(Health and Human Services Dept.)*, *Refugee Resettlement*, 901 D St. S.W., 6th Floor 20447; (202) 401-9246. Fax, (202) 401-5487. Lavinia Limon, Director.

Directs a domestic resettlement program for refugees; reimburses states for costs incurred in giving refugees monetary and medical assistance; awards funds to private resettlement agencies for providing refugees with monetary assistance and case management; provides states and nonprofit agencies with grants for social services such as English and employment training.

Immigration and Naturalization Service *(Justice Dept.)*, 425 Eye St. N.W., #7100 20536; (202) 514-1900. Fax, (202) 514-3296. Doris Meissner, Commissioner. Press, (202) 514-2648. Form requests, (800) 870-3676. Web, www.ins.usdoj.gov.

Administers and enforces immigration and naturalization laws relating to the admission, exclusion, deportation, and naturalization of aliens; responsible for preventing illegal entry into the United States; investigates, apprehends, and deports illegal aliens; oversees Border Patrol enforcement activities. Field offices provide aliens with information on application for asylum and U.S. citizenship.

Justice Dept., 950 Pennsylvania Ave. N.W., #5111 20530-0001; (202) 514-2001. Fax, (202) 307-6777. Janet Reno, Attorney General; Eric H. Holder Jr., Deputy Attorney General, (202) 514-2101. Information, (202) 514-2000. Web, www.usdoj.gov.

Administers immigration and naturalization laws through the Immigration and Naturalization Service and the Executive Office for Immigration Review.

Justice Dept., *Civil Division: Immigration Litigation*, 1331 Pennsylvania Ave. N.W., #7022 20530; (202) 616-4952. Fax, (202) 616-4948. Thomas W. Hussey, Director. Information, (202) 514-2007. Web, www.usdoj.gov/civil.

Handles most civil litigation arising under immigration and nationality laws.

Justice Dept., *Executive Office for Immigration Review*, 5107 Leesburg Pike, #2400, Falls Church, VA 22041; (703) 305-0169. Fax, (703) 305-0985. Kevin D. Rooney, Director. Web, www.usdoj.gov.

Quasi-judicial body which includes the Board of Immigration Appeals and is separate from the Immigra-tion and Naturalization Service. Interprets immigration laws; conducts hearings and hears appeals on immigration issues.

Justice Dept., *Special Investigations*, 1301 New York Ave. N.W., #200 20530; (202) 616-2492. Fax, (202) 616-2491. Eli M. Rosenbaum, Director. Web, www.usdoj.gov.

Identifies Nazi war criminals who illegally entered the United States after World War II. Handles legal action to ensure denaturalization and/or deportation.

Labor Dept., *International Economic Affairs*, 200 Constitution Ave. N.W., #S5325 20210; (202) 219-7597. Fax, (202) 219-5071. Jorge Perez-Lopez, Director. Web, www.dol.gov.

Assists in developing U.S. immigration policy.

State Dept., *Visa Services*, 2401 E St. N.W., SA-1 #L-703 20522-0106; (202) 663-1225. Fax, (202) 663-1247. Nancy Sambaiew, Deputy Assistant Secretary, (202) 647-9584. Web, travel.state.gov/visa_services.html.

Supervises visa issuance system, which is administered by U.S. consular offices abroad.

CONGRESS

House Judiciary Committee, *Subcommittee on Immigration and Claims*, B370B RHOB 20515; (202) 225-5727. Fax, (202) 225-3672. Rep. Lamar Smith, R-Texas, Chair; George Fishman, Counsel. General e-mail, Judiciary@mail.house.gov. Web, www.house.gov/judiciary.

Jurisdiction over immigration and naturalization legislation.

Senate Judiciary Committee, *Subcommittee on Immigration*, SD-323 20510; (202) 224-6098. Fax, (202) 228-4506. Sen. Spencer Abraham, R-Mich., Chair; Lee Lieberman Otis, Chief Counsel. Web, judiciary.senate.gov/immigrat.htm.

Jurisdiction over legislation on refugees, immigration, and naturalization. Oversight of the Immigration and Naturalization Service, the U.S. Board of Immigration Appeals, international migration and refugee laws and policies, and private immigration relief bills.

INTERNATIONAL ORGANIZATIONS

International Organization for Migration, *Washington Office*, 1752 N St. N.W., #700 20036; (202) 862-1826. Fax, (202) 862-1879. Luca Dall'Oglio, Regional Representative. General e-mail, srowashington@iom.int. Web, www.iom.int.

Nonpartisan organization that plans and operates refugee resettlement, national migration, and humanitarian assistance programs at the request of its member governments. Recruits skilled professionals for developing countries. (Headquarters in Geneva.)

NONPROFIT

Alexis de Tocqueville Institution, *1611 N. Kent St., #901, Arlington, VA 22209; (703) 351-4969. Fax, (703) 351-0090. Christian Braunlich, President. Web, www. adti.net.*

Works to increase public understanding of the cultural and economic benefits associated with legal immigration. Supports pro-immigration policy reform.

American Immigration Lawyers Assn., *1400 Eye St. N.W., #1200 20005; (202) 371-9377. Fax, (202) 371-9449. Jeanne Butterfield, Executive Director. Web, www.aila.org.*

Bar association for attorneys interested in immigration law. Provides information and continuing education programs on immigration law and policy; offers workshops and conferences. Monitors legislation and regulations.

Center for Immigration Studies, *1522 K St. N.W., #820 20005-1202; (202) 466-8185. Fax, (202) 466-8076. Mark Krikorian, Executive Director. General e-mail, center@cis.org. Web, www.cis.org.*

Nonpartisan organization that conducts research and policy analysis of the economic, social, demographic, and environmental impact of immigration on the United States. Sponsors symposiums.

Federation for American Immigration Reform, *1666 Connecticut Ave. N.W., #400 20009; (202) 328-7004. Fax, (202) 387-3447. Daniel A. Stein, Executive Director. General e-mail, fair@fairus.org. Web, www.fairus.org.*

Organization of individuals interested in immigration reform. Monitors immigration laws and policies.

Immigration and Refugees Services of America, *1717 Massachusetts Ave. N.W., #200 20036; (202) 347-3507. Fax, (202) 347-3418. Roger P. Winter, Executive Director. Web, www.refugees.org.*

Helps immigrants and refugees adjust to American society; assists in resettling recently arrived immigrants and refugees; offers information, counseling services, and temporary living accommodations through its member agencies nationwide; issues publications on immigration law, refugees, and refugee resettlement. Operates U.S. Committee for Refugees, which collects and disseminates information on refugee issues in the United States and abroad. Monitors legislation and regulations.

Lutheran Immigration and Refugee Service, *Washington Office, 122 C St. N.W., #125 20001-2172; (202) 783-7509. Fax, (202) 783-7502. Philip Anderson, Washington Representative. General e-mail, lirswdc@aol.com. Web, www.lirs.org.*

Provides refugees in the United States with resettlement assistance, follow-up services, and immigration counseling. Funds local projects that provide social and legal services to all refugees, including undocumented persons. (Headquarters in New York.)

National Council of La Raza, *1111 19th St. N.W., #1000 20036; (202) 785-1670. Fax, (202) 776-1792. Raul Yzaguirre, President. Web, www.nclr.org.*

Provides research, policy analysis, and advocacy relating to immigration policy and programs. Monitors federal legislation on immigration, legalization, employer sanctions, employment discrimination, and eligibility of immigrants for federal benefit programs. Assists community-based groups involved in immigration and education services and educates employers about immigration laws.

U.S. Catholic Conference, *Migration and Refugee Services, 3211 4th St. N.E. 20017; (202) 541-3352. Fax, (202) 541-3399. Mark Franken, Executive Director. Web, www. nccbuscc.org/mrs.*

Provides refugees and immigrants with resettlement services and legal counseling; operates training programs for volunteers and professionals; develops and implements USCC policy on migration, immigration, and refugee issues.

See also Institute for Public Representation (p. 29); National Center for Urban Ethnic Affairs (p. 418)

🌐 INTERNATIONAL LAW AND AGREEMENTS

See also Intelligence and Counterterrorism (chap. 16)

AGENCIES

Commission on Security and Cooperation in Europe *(Helsinki Commission), 234 FHOB 20515; (202) 225-1901. Fax, (202) 226-4199. Rep. Christopher H. Smith, R-N.J., Chair; Sen. Ben Nighthorse Campbell, R-Colo., Co-Chair; Ronald McNamara, Deputy Chief of Staff. Web, www.house.gov/csce.*

Independent agency created by Congress. Membership includes individuals from the executive and legislative branches. Monitors and encourages compliance with the Helsinki Accords, a series of agreements with provisions on security, economic, environmental, human rights, and humanitarian issues; conducts hearings; serves as an information clearinghouse for issues in eastern and western Europe, Canada, and the United States relating to the Helsinki Accords.

Federal Bureau of Investigation *(Justice Dept.),* ***International Operations,*** *935 Pennsylvania Ave. N.W., #7443 20535; (202) 324-5904. Fax, (202) 324-5292. James K. Weber, Deputy Assistant Director.*

Supports FBI involvement in international investigations; oversees liaison offices in U.S. embassies abroad. Maintains contacts with other federal agencies; Interpol; foreign police and security officers based in Washington, D.C.; and national law enforcement associations.

Securities and Exchange Commission, *International Affairs, 450 5th St. N.W. 20549-1104; (202) 942-2770. Fax, (202) 942-9524. Marisa Lago, Director. Web, www.sec.gov.*

Acts as liaison with enforcement and diplomatic officials abroad; coordinates international enforcement activities for the securities market; obtains evidence from abroad relating to investigations and litigation. Develops agreements with foreign countries to assist commission enforcement and regulatory efforts.

State Dept., *International Claims and Investment Disputes, 2430 E St. N.W., #203 20037-2800; (202) 776-8360. Fax, (202) 776-8389. Ronald J. Bettauer, Assistant Legal Adviser. Web, www.state.gov.*

Handles claims by foreign governments and their nationals against the U.S. government, as well as claims against the State Dept. for negligence under the Federal Tort Claims Act. Administers the Iranian claims program and negotiates agreements with other foreign governments on claims settlements.

State Dept., *Law Enforcement and Intelligence Affairs, 2201 C St. N.W., #5419 20520; (202) 647-7324. Fax, (202) 647-4802. Samuel Witten, Assistant Legal Adviser. Web, www.state.gov.*

Negotiates extradition treaties, legal assistance treaties in criminal matters, and other agreements relating to international criminal matters.

State Dept., *Legal Adviser, 2201 C St. N.W., #6423 20520-6310; (202) 647-9598. Fax, (202) 647-7096. David R. Andrews, Legal Adviser. Web, www.state.gov.*

Provides the department with legal advice on international problems; participates in international negotiations; represents the U.S. government in international litigation and in international conferences related to legal issues.

State Dept., *Political-Military Affairs, 2201 C St. N.W., #7325 20520; (202) 647-9022. Fax, (202) 736-4779. Eric D. Newsom, Assistant Secretary. Web, www.state.gov.*

Negotiates U.S. military base and operating rights overseas; acts as liaison between the Defense Dept. and State Dept.; controls military travel to sensitive or restricted areas abroad; arranges diplomatic clearance for overflights and ship visits.

State Dept., *Treaty Affairs, 2201 C St. N.W., #5420 20520; (202) 647-1345. Fax, (202) 736-7541. Robert E. Dalton, Assistant Legal Adviser. Web, www.state.gov.*

Provides legal advice on treaties and other international agreements, including constitutional questions, drafting, negotiation, and interpretation of treaties; maintains records of treaties and executive agreements.

Technology Administration *(Commerce Dept.),* ***International Technology Policy,*** *14th St. and Constitution Ave. N.W., #4412 20230; (202) 482-6351. Fax, (202) 501-6849. Cathy Campbell, Director.*

Provides information on foreign research and development; coordinates, on behalf of the Commerce Dept., negotiation of international science and technology agreements.

Transportation Dept., *International Aviation, 400 7th St. S.W., #6402 20590; (202) 366-2423. Fax, (202) 366-3694. Paul L. Gretch, Director. Web, www.dot.gov.*

Responsible for international aviation regulation and negotiations, including fares, tariffs, and foreign licenses; represents the United States at international aviation meetings.

CONGRESS

House International Relations Committee, *2170 RHOB 20515; (202) 225-5021. Fax, (202) 225-2035. Rep. Benjamin A. Gilman, R-N.Y., Chair; Richard J. Garon Jr., Chief of Staff. General e-mail, HIRC@mail.house.gov. Web, www.house.gov/international_relations.*

Jurisdiction over legislation on international law enforcement, including narcotics control; boundaries; international terrorism (jurisdiction shared with House Judiciary Committee); international human rights, including implementation of the Universal Declaration of Human Rights; executive agreements; regional security agreements; protection of Americans abroad, including the Foreign Airports Security Act; embassy security; and United Nations organizations.

House Judiciary Committee, *Subcommittee on Immigration and Claims, B370B RHOB 20515; (202) 225-5727. Fax, (202) 225-3672. Rep. Lamar Smith, R-Texas,*

Chair; George Fishman, Counsel. General e-mail, Judiciary@mail.house.gov. Web, www.house.gov/judiciary.

Jurisdiction over legislation on treaties, conventions, and international agreements; diplomatic immunity; foreign sovereign immunity; and admission and resettlement of refugees.

Senate Foreign Relations Committee, *SD-450 20510; (202) 224-4651. Fax, (202) 224-0836. Sen. Jesse Helms, R-N.C., Chair; Steve Biegun, Staff Director. Web, foreign.senate.gov.*

Jurisdiction over legislation on human rights; international boundaries; regional security; executive agreements; international narcotics control; embassy security; international terrorism (jurisdiction shared with Senate Judiciary Committee); and exchange of prisoners with Canada and Mexico.

Senate Governmental Affairs Committee, *Permanent Subcommittee on Investigations, SR-100 20510; (202) 224-3721. Fax, (202) 224-7042. Sen. Susan Collins, R-Maine, Chair; K. Lee Blalack, Staff Director. General e-mail, PSI@govt-aff.senate.gov. Web, gov_affairs.senate.gov/psi.htm.*

Investigates international narcotics trafficking.

INTERNATIONAL ORGANIZATIONS

INTERPOL, *Washington Office, 600 E St. N.W. 20530-1022 (mailing address: INTERPOL-USNCB U.S. Justice Dept. 20530); (202) 616-9000. Fax, (202) 616-8400. Edgar A. Adamson, Chief. Web, www.usdoj.gov/usncb.*

U.S. national central bureau for INTERPOL; participates in international investigations on behalf of U.S. police; coordinates the exchange of investigative information on crimes, including drug trafficking, counterfeiting, missing persons, and terrorism. Coordinates law enforcement requests for investigative assistance in the United States and abroad. Assists with extradition processes. Serves as liaison between foreign and U.S. law enforcement agencies at federal, state, and local levels. (Headquarters in Lyons, France.)

NONPROFIT

American Arbitration Assn., *Washington Office, 8201 Greensboro Dr., #610, McLean, VA 22102-3810; (703) 760-4820. Fax, (703) 760-4847. Arnold B. Crews, Regional Vice President. General e-mail, webmaster@adr.org. Web, www.adr.org.*

Provides dispute resolution services and information. Administers international arbitration and mediation systems. (Headquarters in New York.)

American Bar Assn., *International Law and Practice, 740 15th St. N.W. 20005; (202) 662-1660. Fax, (202) 662-*

1669. Cynthia Price, Director. Web, www.abanet.org/intlaw.

Monitors domestic and international policy developments that affect the practice of public and private international law. Conducts seminars and provides information for members.

American Society of International Law, *2223 Massachusetts Ave. N.W. 20008-2864; (202) 939-6000. Fax, (202) 797-7133. Charlotte Ku, Executive Director. Web, www.asil.org.*

Membership: lawyers, political scientists, economists, government officials, and students. Conducts research and study programs on international law; sponsors the International Law Students Assn. Library open to the public.

Antarctica Project, *1630 Connecticut Ave. N.W., 3rd Floor 20009 (mailing address: P.O. Box 76920 20013); (202) 234-2480. Fax, (202) 234-2482. Beth Clark, Director. General e-mail, antarctica@igc.org. Web, www.asoc.org.*

Promotes effective implementation of the Antarctic Treaty System; works to protect the environment of the Antarctic continent. Interests include depletion of ozone in polar regions.

Inter-American Bar Assn., *1211 Connecticut Ave. N.W., #202 20036; (202) 393-1217. Fax, (202) 393-1241. Louis Ferrand, Secretary General. General e-mail, iaba@iaba.org. Web, www.iaba.org.*

Membership: lawyers and bar associations in the Western Hemisphere with associate members in Europe and Asia. Works to promote uniformity of national and international laws; holds conferences; makes recommendations to national governments and organizations. Library open to the public.

World Jurist Assn., *1000 Connecticut Ave. N.W., #202 20036-5302; (202) 466-5428. Fax, (202) 452-8540. Margaret M. Henneberry, Executive Vice President. General e-mail, wja@worldjurist.org. Web, www.worldjurist.org.*

Membership: lawyers, law professors, judges, law students, and nonlegal professionals worldwide. Conducts research; promotes world peace through adherence to international law; holds biennial world conferences. (Affiliates, at same address, include World Assn. of Judges, World Assn. of Law Professors, and World Assn. of Lawyers.)

Americans Abroad

See also Diplomats and Foreign Agents (this chapter); Travel and Tourism (chap. 5)

Administration for Children and Families *(Health and Human Services Dept.), Repatriate Program,* 901 D St. S.W., 6th Floor 20447; (202) 401-9246. Fax, (202) 401-5487. *Lavinia Limon, Director.*

Administers and operates a repatriation program available to State Dept.-certified U.S. citizens returning from foreign countries because of destitution, illness, or emergencies. Reimburses state and local governments and community-based organizations for transportation from port of entry and for the temporary costs of food, shelter, and clothing; and medical care, including hospitalization.

Foreign Claims Settlement Commission of the United States *(Justice Dept.),* 600 E St. N.W., #6002 20579; (202) 616-6975. Fax, (202) 616-6993. *Vacant, Chair; Judith H. Lock, Administrative Officer,* (202) 616-6986.

Processes claims by U.S. nationals against foreign governments for property losses sustained.

State Dept., *American Citizens Services and Crisis Management,* 2201 C St. N.W., #4811 20520-4818; (202) 647-9019. Fax, (202) 647-3732. *Patrick Hegarty, Director. Recorded consular information,* (202) 647-5225. *Web,* travel.state.gov.

Handles matters involving protective services for Americans abroad, including arrests, assistance in death cases, financial assistance, medical emergencies, welfare and whereabouts inquiries, travel warnings and consular information, nationality and citizenship determination, document issuance, judicial and notarial services, estates, property claims, third-country representation, and disaster assistance.

State Dept., *Children's Issues,* 2201 C St. N.W., #4811 20520-4800; (202) 647-1046. Fax, (202) 647-2835. *Mary B. Marshall, Director. Recorded consular information,* (202) 736-7000. *Fax-on-demand,* (202) 647-3000. *Web,* travel.state.gov/officeofchildissues.html.

Assists with consular aspects of children's services and fulfills U.S. treaty obligations relating to the abduction of children. Advises foreign service posts on international parental child abduction and transnational adoption.

State Dept., *International Claims and Investment Disputes,* 2430 E St. N.W., #203 20037-2800; (202) 776-8360. Fax, (202) 776-8389. *Ronald J. Bettauer, Assistant Legal Adviser. Web,* www.state.gov.

Handles claims by U.S. government and citizens against foreign governments; handles claims by owners of U.S. flag vessels for reimbursements of fines, fees, licenses, and other direct payments for illegal seizures by foreign governments in international waters under the Fishermen's Protective Act.

State Dept., *Passport Services,* 2201 C St. N.W., #6811 20520; (202) 647-5366. Fax, (202) 647-0341. *George Lannon, Deputy Assistant Secretary. Passport information,* (800) 225-5674. *Web,* travel.state.gov.

Administers passport laws and issues passports. (Most branches of the U.S. Postal Service and most U.S. district and state courts are authorized to accept applications and payment for passports and to administer the required oath to U.S. citizens. Completed applications are sent from the post office or court to the nearest State Dept. regional passport office for processing.) Maintains a variety of records received from the Overseas Citizens Services, including consular certificates of witness to marriage and reports of birth and death.

State Dept., *Policy Review and Interagency Liaison,* 2201 C St. N.W., #4817 20520-4818; (202) 647-3666. Fax, (202) 647-6201. *Ed Betancourt, Director. Recorded consular information,* (202) 647-5225. *Web,* www.state.gov.

Offers guidance concerning the administration and enforcement of laws on citizenship and on the appropriate documentation of Americans traveling and residing abroad; gives advice on legislative matters, including implementation of new laws, and on treaties and agreements; reconsiders the acquisition and loss of U.S. citizenship in complex cases; and administers the overseas federal benefits program.

Boundaries

Saint Lawrence Seaway Development Corp. *(Transportation Dept.),* 400 7th St. S.W., #5424 20590; (202) 366-0118. Fax, (202) 366-7147. *Albert S. Jacquez, Administrator. Information,* (202) 366-0091. *Web,* www.dot.gov/slsdc.

Operates and maintains the Saint Lawrence Seaway within U.S. territorial limits; conducts development programs and coordinates activities with its Canadian counterpart.

State Dept., *Mexican Affairs: U.S.-Mexico Border,* 2201 C St. N.W., #4258 20520-6258; (202) 647-8529. Fax, (202) 647-5752. *David E. Randolph, Coordinator. Web,* www.state.gov/www/regions/wha/mexico.html.

Acts as liaison between the State Dept. and the U.S. section of the International Boundary and Water Commission, United States and Mexico (based in El Paso,

Texas), in international boundary and water matters as defined by binational treaties and agreements.

INTERNATIONAL ORGANIZATIONS

International Boundary Commission, United States and Canada, *U.S. Section, 1250 23rd St. N.W., #100 20440; (202) 736-9100. Fax, (202) 736-9015. Thomas Baldini, Commissioner.*

Defines and maintains the international boundary line between the United States and Canada. Rules on applications for approval of projects affecting boundary or transboundary waters. Assists the United States and Canada in protecting the transboundary environment, including implementation of the Great Lakes Water Quality Agreement and the improvement of transboundary air quality. Alerts the governments to emerging issues that may give rise to bilateral disputes. Commissioners represent only the commission, not the government that appointed them. (Canadian section in Ottawa.)

International Joint Commission, United States and Canada, *U.S. Section, 1250 23rd St. N.W., #100 20440; (202) 736-9000. Fax, (202) 736-9015. Gerald Galloway, Secretary (Acting).*

Handles disputes concerning the use of boundary waters; negotiates questions dealing with the rights, obligations, and interests of the United States and Canada along the border; establishes procedures for the adjustment and settlement of questions. (Canadian section in Ottawa.)

Extradition

AGENCIES

Justice Dept., *International Affairs, 1301 New York Ave. N.W., #800 20005 (mailing address: P.O. Box 27330 20038-7330); (202) 514-0000. Fax, (202) 514-0080. John Harris, Director. Web, www.usdoj.gov.*

Performs investigations necessary for extradition of fugitives from the United States and other nations. Handles U.S. and foreign government requests for legal assistance, including documentary evidence.

State Dept., *Law Enforcement and Intelligence Affairs, 2201 C St. N.W., #5419 20520; (202) 647-7324. Fax, (202) 647-4802. Samuel Witten, Assistant Legal Adviser. Web, www.state.gov.*

Negotiates and approves extradition of fugitives between the United States and other nations.

NONPROFIT

Center for National Security Studies, *Gelman Library, 2130 H St. N.W., #701 20037; (202) 994-7060.*

Fax, (202) 994-1446. Kate Martin, Director. Web, gwis.circ. gwu.edu/~cnss.

A project of the Fund for Peace. Monitors and conducts research on extradition, intelligence, national security, and civil liberties.

Fishing/Law of the Sea

AGENCIES

National Oceanic and Atmospheric Administration *(Commerce Dept.), National Marine Fisheries Service, 1315 East-West Hwy., Silver Spring, MD 20910; (301) 713-2239. Fax, (301) 713-2258. Penelope Dalton, Assistant Administrator. Press, (301) 713-2370. Web, www.nmfs.gov.*

Administers marine fishing regulations, including offshore fishing rights and international agreements.

State Dept., *Oceans, Science, and Technology, 2201 C St. N.W., #7831 20520-7831; (202) 647-2396. Fax, (202) 647-0217. R. Tucker Scully, Deputy Assistant Secretary. Web, www.state.gov.*

Coordinates U.S. negotiations concerning international fishing and oceans issues. Handles both foreign fleets fishing in U.S. waters and U.S. fleets fishing in foreign waters or the open seas.

CONGRESS

House International Relations Committee, *2170 RHOB 20515; (202) 225-5021. Fax, (202) 225-2035. Rep. Benjamin A. Gilman, R-N.Y., Chair; Richard J. Garon Jr., Chief of Staff. General e-mail, HIRC@mail.house.gov. Web, www.house.gov/international_relations.*

Jurisdiction over legislation concerning international fisheries agreements and Law of the Sea. (Jurisdiction shared with House Resources and House Transportation and Infrastructure committees.)

House Resources Committee, *Subcommittee on Fisheries, Conservation, Wildlife, and Oceans, H2-187 FHOB 20515; (202) 226-0200. Fax, (202) 225-1542. Rep. H. James Saxton, R-N.J., Chair; Harry Burroughs, Staff Director. General e-mail, fishery.subcommittee@mail. house.gov. Web, www.house.gov/resources/fisheries.*

Jurisdiction over legislation concerning international fisheries agreements and the U.N. Convention on the Law of the Sea. (Jurisdiction shared with House International Relations and House Transportation and Infrastructure committees.)

House Transportation and Infrastructure Committee, *Subcommittee on Coast Guard and Maritime Transportation, 507 FHOB 20515; (202) 226-3552. Fax, (202) 226-2524. Rep. Wayne T. Gilchrest, R-Md., Chair;*

*Rebecca Dye, Counsel. General e-mail, transcomm@mail.
house.gov. Web, www.house.gov/transportation.*

Jurisdiction over legislation concerning Law of the
Sea, international arrangements to prevent collisions at
sea, and enforcement of laws and treaties on marine pollution control and abatement. (Jurisdiction shared with
House International Relations and House Resources
committees.)

**Senate Commerce, Science, and Transportation
Committee,** *Subcommittee on Oceans and Fisheries,
SH-428 20510; (202) 224-8172. Fax, (202) 228-0326. Sen.
Olympia J. Snowe, R-Maine, Chair; Sloan Rapoport,
Counsel. Web, commerce.senate.gov.*

Studies issues concerning international fishing laws
and Law of the Sea. (Jurisdiction shared with Senate Foreign Relations Committee. Subcommittee does not
report legislation.)

Senate Foreign Relations Committee, *SD-450 20510;
(202) 224-4651. Fax, (202) 224-0836. Sen. Jesse Helms,
R-N.C., Chair; Steve Biegun, Staff Director. Web, foreign.
senate.gov.*

Oversight of Law of the Sea matters (jurisdiction
shared with Senate Commerce, Science, and Transportation Committee).

NONPROFIT

U.S. Tuna Foundation, *1101 17th St. N.W., #609 20036;
(202) 857-0610. Fax, (202) 331-9686. David G. Burney,
Executive Director.*

Membership: tuna processors, vessel owners, and
fishermen's unions. Provides members with information
and research on the tuna industry; offers advice on fisheries to the U.S. delegation to the United Nations Law of
the Sea Conference and to other U.S. delegations.

Human Rights

*See also Humanitarian Aid (this chapter); Regional
Affairs (this chapter)*

AGENCIES

**Commission on Security and Cooperation in
Europe** *(Helsinki Commission), 234 FHOB 20515; (202)
225-1901. Fax, (202) 226-4199. Rep. Christopher H. Smith,
R-N.J., Chair; Sen. Ben Nighthorse Campbell, R-Colo., Co-
Chair; Ronald McNamara, Deputy Chief of Staff. Web,
www.house.gov/csce.*

Independent agency created by Congress. Membership includes individuals from the executive and legislative branches. Monitors and encourages compliance with
the human rights provisions of the Helsinki Accords;

conducts hearings; serves as an information clearing-
house for human rights issues in eastern and western
Europe, Canada, and the United States relating to the
Helsinki Accords.

State Dept., *Democracy, Human Rights, and Labor,
2201 C St. N.W., #7802 20520-7812; (202) 647-2126. Fax,
(202) 647-5283. Harold Hongju Koh, Assistant Secretary.
Web, www.state.gov.*

Implements U.S. policies relating to human rights;
prepares annual review of human rights worldwide; provides the Immigration and Naturalization Service with
advisory opinions regarding asylum petitions.

State Dept., *Global Affairs: President's Interagency
Council on Women, 2201 C St. N.W., #6936 20520; (202)
647-5440. Fax, (202) 647-5337. Theresa Loar, Senior
Coordinator. Web, secretary.state.gov/www/picw/index.
html.*

Works to promote the human rights of women
within U.S. foreign policy. Participates in international
organizations and conferences; advises other U.S. agencies; disseminates information. Reports to under secretary for global affairs.

NONPROFIT

Amnesty International USA, *Washington Office, 600
Pennsylvania Ave. S.E., 5th Floor 20003; (202) 544-0200.
Fax, (202) 546-7142. Stephen Rickard, Director. Web,
www.amnesty-usa.org.*

International organization that works for the release
of men and women imprisoned anywhere in the world
for their beliefs, political affiliation, color, ethnic origin,
sex, language, or religion, provided they have neither
used nor advocated violence. Opposes torture and the
death penalty; urges fair and prompt trials for all political prisoners. Library open to the public. (U.S. headquarters in New York.)

Center for Human Rights and Humanitarian Law,
*4801 Massachusetts Ave. N.W., #310 20016-8084; (202)
274-4180. Fax, (202) 274-4130. Robert Guitteau Jr., Executive Director. Web, www.wcl.american.edu/pub/
humright.*

Seeks to promote human rights and humanitarian
law. Establishes training programs for judges, lawyers,
and law schools; assists emerging democracies and other
nations in developing laws and institutions that protect
human rights; organizes conferences with public and private institutions.

Human Rights Watch, *Washington Office, 1630 Connecticut Ave. N.W., #500 20009; (202) 612-4321. Fax,*

(202) 612-4333. Allyson Collins, Associate Director. General e-mail, hrwdc@hrw.org. Web, www.hrw.org.

International, nonpartisan human rights organization that monitors human rights violations worldwide. Subdivided into five regional concentrations—Africa, Americas, Asia, Europe and Central Asia, and Middle East. Coordinates thematic projects on women's rights, arms sales, and prisons. Sponsors fact-finding missions to various countries; publicizes violations and encourages international protests; maintains file on human rights violations. (Headquarters in New York.)

International Assn. of Official Human Rights Agencies, 444 N. Capitol St. N.W., #536 20001; (202) 624-5410. Fax, (202) 624-8185. Jannie Campbell, Office Manager. General e-mail, iaohra@sso.org. Web, www.fairhousing.com/iaohra.

Works with government and human rights agencies worldwide to identify needs common to civil rights enforcement. Offers management training for human rights executives and civil rights workshops for criminal justice agencies; develops training programs in investigative techniques, settlement and conciliation, and legal theory. Serves as an information clearinghouse on human rights laws and enforcement.

International Human Rights Law Group, 1200 18th St. N.W., #602 20036; (202) 822-4600. Fax, (202) 822-4606. Gay McDougall, Executive Director. General e-mail, humanrights@hrlawgroup.org. Web, www.hrlawgroup.org.

Public interest law center concerned with promoting and protecting international human rights. Conducts educational programs and conferences; provides information and legal assistance regarding human rights violations; monitors the electoral and judicial process in several countries.

Lawyers Committee for Human Rights, *Washington Office,* 100 Maryland Ave. N.E., #500 20002-5614; (202) 547-5692. Fax, (202) 543-5999. Elisa Massimino, Director. General e-mail, wdc@lchr.org. Web, www.lchr.org.

Promotes human rights as guaranteed by the International Bill of Human Rights. Mobilizes the legal community to protect the rule of law. (Headquarters in New York.)

Robert F. Kennedy Memorial, *Center for Human Rights,* 1367 Connecticut Ave. N.W., #200 20036; (202) 463-7575. Fax, (202) 463-6606. Lynn Delaney, Director. General e-mail, hrcenter@rfkmemorial.org. Web, www.rfkmemorial.org.

Presents annual human rights award and carries out programs that support the work of the award laureates in their countries. Investigates and reports on human

rights; campaigns to heighten awareness of these issues, stop abuses, and encourage governments, international organizations, and corporations to adopt policies that ensure respect for human rights.

Narcotics Trafficking

See also Drug Control (chap. 14)

AGENCIES

Defense Dept., *Counter-Narcotics,* The Pentagon, #2B913 20318-3000; (703) 695-1476. Fax, (703) 695-1727. Capt. Bruce T. Van Belle (USN), Captain. Web, www.defenselink.mil.

Responsible for countering the importation of narcotics into the United States.

Defense Dept., *Drug Enforcement Policy and Support,* The Pentagon, #2E538 20301-1510; (703) 695-7996. Fax, (703) 693-7588. Ana Maria Salazar, Deputy Assistant Secretary. Web, www.defenselink.mil.

Coordinates and monitors Defense Dept. support of civilian drug law enforcement agencies and interagency efforts to detect and monitor the maritime and aerial transit of illegal drugs into the United States. Represents the secretary on drug control matters outside the department.

Drug Enforcement Administration *(Justice Dept.),* 700 Army-Navy Dr., Arlington, VA 22202; (202) 307-8000. Fax, (202) 307-7965. Donnie R. Marshall, Administrator (Acting). Press, (202) 307-7977. Locator, (202) 307-4132. Web, www.usdoj.gov/dea.

Assists foreign narcotics agents; cooperates with the State Dept., embassies, the Agency for International Development, and international organizations to strengthen narcotics law enforcement and to reduce supply and demand in developing countries; trains and advises narcotics enforcement officers in developing nations.

State Dept., *International Narcotics and Law Enforcement Affairs,* 2201 C St. N.W., #7333 20520-7512; (202) 647-8464. Fax, (202) 736-4885. Rand Beers, Assistant Secretary. Web, www.state.gov.

Coordinates international drug control activities, including policy development, diplomatic initiatives, bilateral and multilateral assistance for crop control, interdiction and related enforcement activities in producer and transit nations, development assistance, technical assistance for demand reduction, and training for foreign personnel in narcotics enforcement and related procedures.

U.S. Coast Guard *(Transportation Dept.), Law Enforcement,* 2100 2nd St. S.W., #3110 20593-0001; (202) 267-1890. Fax, (202) 267-4082. Capt. Anthony S. Tangeman, Chief. Web, www.uscg.mil/hq/g-o/g-opl/mle/welcome.htm.

Enforces or assists in the enforcement of federal laws and treaties and other international agreements to which the United States is party, on, over, and under the high seas and waters subject to the jurisdiction of the United States; conducts investigations into suspected violations of laws and international agreements concerning narcotics and migration interdiction, and the enforcement of fisheries.

✈ INTERNATIONAL TRADE AND DEVELOPMENT

See also Business and Economics (chap. 3); Regional Affairs (this chapter)

AGENCIES

Advisory Committee for Trade Policy and Negotiations *(Executive Office of the President),* 1724 F St. N.W. 20508; (202) 395-6120. Fax, (202) 395-3692. Pate Felts, Public Liaison. Web, www.ustr.gov.

Serves as chief private sector advisory committee for the president, U.S. trade representative, and Congress on all matters concerning U.S. trade policy. Interests include the North American Free Trade Agreement (NAFTA) and the World Trade Organization (WTO).

Agency for International Development, *Global Technology Network: G/EGAD/BD-GTN Program,* 1300 Pennsylvania Ave. N.W. 20523; (202) 712-0469. Fax, (202) 216-3526. Ken Rogers, Program Director. General e-mail, gtn1@usgtn.org. Web, www.usgtn.org.

Facilitates the transfer of U.S. technology and services to developing countries by matching a local company's needs with U.S. firms equipped to provide the appropriate technical solutions. Focuses primarily on agriculture, communications, information technology, environment and energy, and health technology industries.

Antitrust Division *(Justice Dept.), Foreign Commerce,* 601 D St. N.W., #10024 20530; (202) 514-2464. Fax, (202) 514-4508. Charles S. Stark, Chief.

Acts as the division's liaison with foreign governments and international organizations including the European Union. Works with the State Dept. to exchange information with foreign governments concerning investigations involving foreign corporations and nationals.

Bureau of Export Administration *(Commerce Dept.),* 14th St. and Constitution Ave. N.W., #3898 20230; (202) 482-1427. Fax, (202) 482-2387. William Alan Reinsch, Under Secretary. Press, (202) 482-2721. Export licensing information, (202) 482-4811. Web, www.bxa.doc.gov.

Administers Export Administration Act; coordinates export administration programs of federal departments and agencies; maintains control lists and performs export licensing for the purposes of national security, foreign policy, and short supply. Monitors impact of foreign boycotts on the United States; ensures availability of goods and services essential to industrial performance on contracts for national defense. Assesses availability of foreign products and technology to maintain control lists and licensing.

Census Bureau *(Commerce Dept.), Foreign Trade,* Suitland and Silver Hill Rds., Suitland, MD 20772 (mailing address: 4700 Silver Hill Rd. 20233-6700); (301) 457-2203. Fax, (301) 457-2867. C. Harvey Monk Jr., Chief. Trade data inquiries, (301) 457-2227. Web, www.census.gov/foreign-trade/www.

Provides data on all aspects of foreign trade in commodities.

Commerce Dept., *International Investment,* 1441 L St. N.W., #7005 20230; (202) 606-9807. Fax, (202) 606-5318. R. David Belli, Chief. Information, (202) 606-9800. Web, www.stat-usa.gov.

Compiles statistics under the International Investment and Trade in Services Act for an ongoing study of foreign direct investment in the United States and direct investment abroad by the United States.

Economic Development Administration *(Commerce Dept.), Trade Adjustment Assistance,* 14th St. and Constitution Ave. N.W., #7315 20230; (202) 482-2127. Fax, (202) 482-0466. Tony Meyer, Coordinator.

Assists U.S. firms in increasing their competitiveness against foreign imports. Certifies eligibility and provides domestic firms and industries adversely affected by foreign trade with technical assistance under provisions of the Trade Act of 1974. Administers twelve regional Trade Adjustment Administrative Centers which offer consulting services to eligible U.S. firms.

Export-Import Bank of the United States, 811 Vermont Ave. N.W. 20571; (202) 565-3500. Fax, (202) 565-3505. James A. Harmon, Chair; Jackie M. Clegg, Vice Chair. Press, (202) 565-3200. TTY, (202) 565-3377. Toll-free hotline, (800) 565-3946; in Washington, D.C., (202) 565-3900. Web, www.exim.gov.

Independent agency of the U.S. government. Aids in financing exports of U.S. goods and services; offers direct

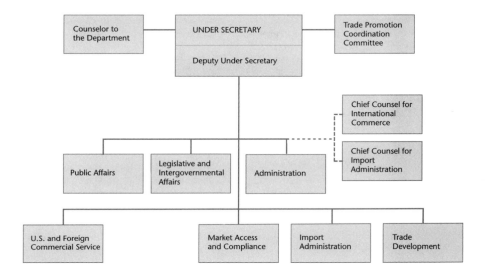

credit to borrowers outside the United States; guarantees export loans made by commercial lenders, working capital guarantees, and export credit insurance; conducts an intermediary loan program. Hotline advises businesses in using U.S. government export programs.

Federal Trade Commission, *Competition: International Antitrust,* *600 Pennsylvania Ave. N.W., #H382 20580; (202) 326-3051. Fax, (202) 326-2884. Randolph W. Tritell, Assistant Director. Web, www.ftc.gov.*

Enforces antitrust laws and investigates possible violations involving international cases; seeks voluntary compliance and pursues civil judicial remedies; reviews premerger filings; coordinates activities with Antitrust Division of the Justice Dept.

Foreign Trade Zones Board *(Commerce Dept.), 14th St. and Constitution Ave. N.W., #4008 20230; (202) 482-2862. Fax, (202) 482-0002. Dennis Puccinelli, Executive Secretary (Acting). Web, www.ita.doc.gov/ia.*

Authorizes public and private corporations to establish foreign trade zones to which foreign and domestic goods can be brought without being subject to customs duties.

International Trade Administration *(Commerce Dept.), 14th St. and Constitution Ave. N.W., #3850 20230; (202) 482-2867. Fax, (202) 482-4821. David L. Aaron, Under Secretary. Information, (202) 482-3808. Press, (202)*

482-3809. Publications, (202) 482-5487. Trade information, (800) 872-8723. Web, www.ita.doc.gov.

Serves as the focal point of operational responsibilities in nonagricultural world trade. Participates in formulating international trade policy and implements programs to promote world trade and strengthen the international trade and investment position of the United States. Library open to the public.

International Trade Administration *(Commerce Dept.), Export Promotion Services, 14th St. and Constitution Ave. N.W., #2810 20230; (202) 482-6220. Fax, (202) 482-2526. Valerie G. Blatnik-Sigel, Deputy Assistant Secretary. Web, www.ita.doc.gov.*

Promotes and directs programs to expand exports abroad; manages overseas trade missions; conducts trade fair certification programs. Participates in trade fairs and technology seminars to introduce American products abroad. Provides the business community with sales and trade information through an automated system, which allows a direct connection between U.S. and overseas offices.

International Trade Administration *(Commerce Dept.), Import Administration, 14th St. and Constitution Ave. N.W., #3099B 20230; (202) 482-1780. Fax, (202) 482-0947. Robert LaRussa, Assistant Secretary.*

Enforces antidumping and countervailing duty statutes if foreign goods are subsidized or sold at less than fair market value. Evaluates and processes applications by U.S. international air- and seaport communities seeking to establish limited duty-free zones. Administers the Statutory Import Program, which governs specific tariff schedules and imports and determines whether property left abroad by U.S. agencies may be imported back into the United States.

International Trade Administration *(Commerce Dept.), Market Access and Compliance, 14th St. and Constitution Ave. N.W., #3868A 20230; (202) 482-3022. Fax, (202) 482-5444. Patrick A. Mulloy, Assistant Secretary. Web, www.ita.doc.gov.*

Develops and implements trade and investment policies affecting countries, regions, or international organizations to improve U.S. market access abroad. Provides information and analyses of foreign business and economic conditions to the U.S. private sector; monitors consultation and renegotiation of the MTN (Multilateral Trade Negotiations) affecting specific areas; represents the United States in many other trade negotiations.

International Trade Administration *(Commerce Dept.), NAFTA and Inter-American Affairs, 14th St. and Constitution Ave. N.W., #3022 20230; (202) 482-0393. Fax, (202) 482-5865. Juliet Bender, Director. Web, www.mac.doc.gov/nafta/nafta2.htm.*

Coordinates Commerce Dept. activities regarding NAFTA (North American Free Trade Agreement). Maintains, with Latin America office of International Trade Administration, a fax-on-demand system for information on NAFTA and on doing business in Latin America and the Caribbean, including Haiti.

International Trade Administration *(Commerce Dept.), Trade and Economic Analysis, 14th St. and Constitution Ave. N.W., #2815 20230; (202) 482-5145. Fax, (202) 482-4614. Jonathan C. Menes, Director. Web, www.ita.doc.gov/tradestats.*

Monitors and analyzes U.S. international trade and competitive performance, foreign direct investment in the United States, and international economic factors affecting U.S. trade; identifies future trends and problems. Annual reports include *U.S. Industrial Outlook* and *Foreign Direct Investment in the United States: Transactions.* Foreign Trade Reference Room open to the public.

International Trade Administration *(Commerce Dept.), Trade Development, 14th St. and Constitution Ave. N.W., #3832 20230; (202) 482-1461. Fax, (202) 482-5697. Michael J. Copps, Assistant Secretary. Web, www.ita.doc.gov.*

Seeks to strengthen the international competitiveness of U.S. businesses; coordinates export promotion programs and trade missions; compiles and analyzes trade data. Divisions focus on basic industries; service industries and finance; technology and aerospace; textiles, apparel, and consumer goods; tourism; and environmental technologies exports.

International Trade Administration *(Commerce Dept.), Trade Information Center, 14th St. and Constitution Ave. N.W., #M800RRB 20230; (202) 482-0543. Fax, (202) 482-4473. Wendy Smith, Director. Information, (800) 872-8723. TTY, (800) 833-8723. General e-mail, tic@ita.doc.gov. Web, tradeinfo.doc.gov.*

Counsels U.S. business firms on export matters and on programs and services provided by the agencies that are members of the Trade Promotion Coordinating Committee to facilitate exports. Agencies include the Agriculture and Commerce departments, Export-Import Bank, Overseas Private Investment Corp., Agency for International Development, and others.

International Trade Administration *(Commerce Dept.), U.S. and Foreign Commercial Service, 14th St. and Constitution Ave. N.W., #3802 20230; (202) 482-5777. Fax, (202) 482-5013. Marjory E. Searing, Director General (Acting). Web, www.ita.doc.gov.*

Promotes the export of U.S. goods and services; protects and advocates U.S. business interests abroad; provides counseling and information on overseas markets, international contacts, and trade promotion.

National Institute of Standards and Technology *(Commerce Dept.), Technical Standards Activities, Bldg. 820, #161, Gaithersburg, MD 20899-2150; (301) 975-4029. Fax, (301) 926-1559. Samuel Chappell, Chief. GATT hotline, (301) 975-4041. National Center for Standards and Certification Information, (301) 975-4040. Web, ts.nist.gov.*

Compiles information on proposed foreign technical regulations. Provides recorded information on selected international trade regulation matters from the World Trade Organization secretariat in Switzerland. Maintains National Center for Standards and Certification Information to provide U.S. exporters with information on product standards in foreign countries.

Overseas Private Investment Corp., *1100 New York Ave. N.W. 20527; (202) 336-8400. Fax, (202) 408-9859. George Muñoz, President. Information, (202) 336-8799. Press, (202) 336-8680. Web, www.opic.gov.*

Provides assistance through political risk insurance, direct loans, and loan guarantees to qualified U.S. private investors to support their investments in less developed countries. Offers preinvestment information and counseling. Provides insurance against the risks of inconvertibility of local currency; expropriation; and war, revolution, insurrection, or civil strife.

President's Export Council *(Commerce Dept.)*, *14th St. and Constitution Ave. N.W., #2015B 20230; (202) 482-1124. Fax, (202) 482-4452. J. Marc Chittum, Director. Web, www.ita.doc.gov/pec.*

Advises the president on all aspects of export trade including export controls, promotion, and expansion.

Small Business Administration, *International Trade, 409 3rd St. S.W., 8th Floor 20416; (202) 205-6720. Fax, (202) 205-7272. James Wilfong, Assistant Administrator. Web, www.sba.gov/oit.*

Offers instruction, assistance, and information on exporting through counseling and conferences. Helps businesses gain access to export financing through loan guarantee programs.

State Dept., *Coordinator for Business Affairs, 2201 C St. N.W., #2318 20520-5820; (202) 647-1625. Fax, (202) 647-3953. Sandra Willett Jackson, Senior Coordinator. General e-mail, cbaweb@state.gov. Web, www.state.gov/ www/about_state/business/coordin3.html.*

Serves as primary contact in the State Dept. for U.S. businesses. Coordinates efforts to facilitate U.S. business interests abroad, ensures that U.S. business interests are given sufficient consideration in foreign policy, and provides assistance to firms with problems overseas (such as claims and trade complaints). Works with agencies in the Trade Promotion Coordinating Committee to support U.S. business interests overseas.

State Dept., *Economic and Business Affairs Bureau, 2201 C St. N.W., #6828 20520; (202) 647-7971. Fax, (202) 647-5713. Vacant, Assistant Secretary. Web, www.state. gov/www/issues/economic/index.html.*

Formulates and implements policies related to U.S. economic relations with foreign countries, including international business practices, communications and information, trade, finance, investment, development, natural resources, energy, and transportation.

State Dept., *Economic, Business, and Agricultural Affairs, 2201 C St. N.W., #7256 20520; (202) 647-7575. Fax, (202) 647-9763. Alan Larson, Under Secretary. Web, www.state.gov.*

Advises the secretary on formulation and conduct of foreign economic policies and programs, including international monetary and financial affairs, trade, telecommunications, energy, agriculture, commodities, investments, and international transportation issues. Coordinates economic summit meetings.

State Dept., *Economic Sanctions Policy, 2201 C St. N.W., #3329 20520; (202) 647-5673. Fax, (202) 647-4064. Brian J. Mohler, Director. Web, www.state.gov.*

Develops and implements U.S. foreign policy sanctions of embargo and terrorist listed countries. Coordinates U.S. participation in multilateral strategic trade control and revisions related to the export of strategically critical high-technology goods. Cooperates with the Commerce, Defense, and Treasury departments regarding export controls.

State Dept., *Investment Affairs, 2201 C St. N.W., #3336 20520; (202) 736-4247. Fax, (202) 647-0320. Wesley Scholz, Director. Web, www.state.gov.*

Develops U.S. investment policy. Makes policy recommendations regarding multinational enterprises and the expropriation of and compensation for U.S. property overseas. Negotiates bilateral and multilateral investment agreements.

State Dept., *Trade Policy and Programs, 2201 C St. N.W., #3831A, EB/TPP 20520; (202) 647-2532. Fax, (202) 647-1537. Bryan Samuel, Deputy Assistant Secretary. Web, www.state.gov.*

Develops and administers policies and programs on international trade, including trade negotiations and agreements, import relief, unfair trade practices, trade relations with developing countries, export development, and export controls (including controls imposed for national security or foreign policy purposes).

Trade Promotion Coordinating Committee, *14th St. and Constitution Ave. N.W., #3051 20230; (202) 482-5455. Fax, (202) 482-2741. William M. Daley, Chair; Jeri Jensen-Moran, Director.*

Coordinates all export promotion and export financing activities of the U.S. government. Composed of representatives from the Depts. of Commerce, State, Treasury, Defense, Interior, Agriculture, Labor, Transportation, and Energy, OMB, U.S. Trade Representative, Council of Economic Advisers, EPA, Small Business Administration, AID, Export-Import Bank, Overseas Private Investment Corporation, and the U.S. Trade and Development Agency.

Treasury Dept., *Foreign Assets Control, 1500 Pennsylvania Ave. N.W., Annex Bldg., 2nd Floor 20220; (202) 622-2510. Fax, (202) 622-1657. R. Richard Newcomb, Director. Fax-on-demand, (202) 622-0077. Web, www.treas.gov/ofac.*

Has authority under the revised Trading with the Enemy Act, the International Emergency Economic Powers Act, and the United Nations Participation Act to control financial and commercial dealings with certain countries and their foreign nationals in times of war or

CUSTOMS SERVICE

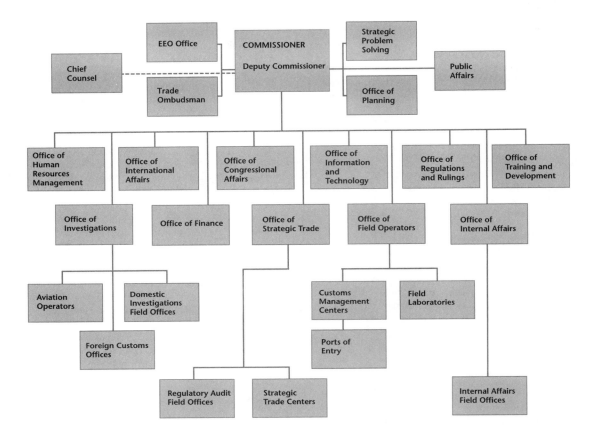

emergencies. Regulations involving foreign assets control and commercial transactions currently apply in varying degrees to Cuba, Iran, Iraq, Libya, North Korea, and Angola.

Treasury Dept., *International Investment,* *1440 New York Ave. N.W., #4209 20220; (202) 622-1860. Fax, (202) 622-0391. Gay Sills Hoar, Director. Web, www.ustreas.gov.*

Advises senior department officials on direct foreign investment.

Treasury Dept., *International Trade,* *1440 New York Ave. N.W., #4109 20220; (202) 622-0141. Fax, (202) 622-1731. Mary E. Chaves, Director. Web, www.ustreas.gov.*

Formulates Treasury Dept. foreign trade policies and coordinates them with other agencies through the U.S. Trade Representative.

U.S. Customs Service *(Treasury Dept.),* *1300 Pennsylvania Ave. N.W., #4.4A 20229; (202) 927-2001. Fax, (202) 927-1380. Raymond W. Kelly, Commissioner. Library, (202) 927-1350. Press, (202) 927-1770. Web, www.customs.ustreas.gov.*

Assesses and collects duties and taxes on imported merchandise; processes persons and baggage entering the United States; collects import and export data for international trade statistics; controls export carriers and goods to prevent fraud and smuggling. Library open to the public.

U.S. Customs Service *(Treasury Dept.),* *Trade Compliance,* *1300 Pennsylvania Ave. N.W., #5.2A 20229; (202) 927-0300. Fax, (202) 927-1096. Elizabeth Durant, Director. Web, www.customs.ustreas.gov.*

Enforces compliance with all commercial import requirements; collects import statistics; assesses and collects countervailing and antidumping duties after determinations have been made by the Commerce Dept. in conjunction with the U.S. International Trade Commission.

U.S. International Trade Commission, *500 E St. S.W. 20436; (202) 205-2000. Fax, (202) 205-2338. Lynn M. Bragg, Chair, (202) 205-2250; Marcia E. Miller, Vice Chair, (202) 205-2021. Press, (202) 205-1819. Web, www. usitc.gov.*

Provides Congress, the president, and government agencies with technical information and advice on trade and tariff matters. Determines the impact of imports on U.S. industries in antidumping and countervailing duty investigations. Directs actions against certain unfair trade practices, such as intellectual property infringement. Investigates and reports on U.S. industries and the global trends that affect them. Publishes the *Harmonized Tariff Schedule of the United States.* Library open to the public.

U.S. Trade and Development Agency, *1621 N. Kent St., #200, Rosslyn, VA 22209-2131; (703) 875-4357. Fax, (703) 875-4009. J. Joseph Grandmaison, Director; Barbara Bradford, Deputy Director. General e-mail, info@tda.gov. Web, www.tda.gov.*

Assists U.S. companies exporting to developing and middle-income countries. Provides grants for feasibility studies. Offers technical assistance and identifies commercial opportunities in these countries.

U.S. Trade Representative *(Executive Office of the President), 600 17th St. N.W., #209 20508; (202) 395-6890. Fax, (202) 395-3911. Charlene Barshefsky, U.S. Trade Representative. Information, (202) 395-8787. Press, (202) 395-3230. Web, www.ustr.gov.*

Serves as principal adviser to the president and primary trade negotiator on international trade policy. Develops and coordinates U.S. trade policy including commodity and direct investment matters; import remedies; East-West trade policy; U.S. export expansion policy; and the implementation of MTN (Multilateral Trade Negotiations) agreements. Conducts international trade negotiations and represents the United States in World Trade Organization (WTO) matters.

CONGRESS

House Appropriations Committee, *Subcommittee on Commerce, Justice, State, and Judiciary, H309 CAP 20515; (202) 225-3351. Rep. Harold Rogers, R-Ky., Chair; Jim Kulikowski, Staff Director. Web, www.house.gov/ appropriations.*

Jurisdiction over legislation to appropriate funds for the Commerce Dept., the Office of the U.S. Trade Representative, and the International Trade Commission.

House Commerce Committee, *Subcommittee on Telecommunications, Trade, and Consumer Protection, 2125 RHOB 20515; (202) 225-2927. Fax, (202) 225-1919. Rep. W. J. "Billy" Tauzin, R-La., Chair; James E. Derderian, Staff Director. General e-mail, commerce@mail.house. gov. Web, www.house.gov/commerce.*

Jurisdiction over legislation on foreign investment in the United States (jurisdiction shared with House International Relations Committee).

House Government Reform Committee, *Subcommittee on National Economic Growth, Natural Resources, and Regulatory Affairs, B377 RHOB 20515; (202) 225-4407. Fax, (202) 225-2441. Rep. David M. McIntosh, R-Ind., Chair; Marlo Lewis, Staff Director. Web, www.house.gov/reform.*

Jurisdiction over operations of the Export-Import Bank, Overseas Private Investment Corp., U.S. International Trade Commission, and the Office of the U.S. Trade Representative. (Some jurisdictions shared with House International Relations Committee.)

House International Relations Committee, *Subcommittee on International Economic Policy and Trade, 257 FHOB 20515; (202) 225-3345. Fax, (202) 225-0432. Rep. Ileana Ros-Lehtinen, R-Fla., Chair; Mauricio Tamargo, Staff Director. Web, www.house.gov/international_relations.*

Jurisdiction over legislation on foreign investment in the United States (shares jurisdiction with House Commerce Committee) and foreign trade, including activities of U.S. firms abroad, the Export Administration Act, the International Emergency Economic Powers Act, the Overseas Private Investment Corp., and the revised Trading with the Enemy Act, which authorizes trade restrictions. Oversees the Export-Import Bank of the United States, international financial and monetary institutions, and customs. (Some jurisdictions shared with House Government Reform Committee.)

House Small Business Committee, *Subcommittee on Tax, Finance, and Exports, B363 RHOB 20515; (202) 226-2630. Fax, (202) 225-8950. Rep. Donald Manzullo, R-Ill., Chair; Philip D. Eskeland, Staff Director. General e-mail, smbiz@mail.house.gov. Web, www.house.gov/ smbiz.*

Jurisdiction over legislation on export expansion as it relates to small business.

House Ways and Means Committee, *Subcommittee on Oversight, 1136 LHOB 20515; (202) 225-7601. Fax,*

(202) 225-9680. *Rep. Amo Houghton, R-N.Y., Chair; William McKenney, Staff Director. Web, www.house.gov/ ways_means.*

Oversees the U.S. Customs Service.

House Ways and Means Committee, *Subcommittee on Trade, 1104 LHOB 20515; (202) 225-6649. Fax, (202) 226-0158. Rep. Philip M. Crane, R-Ill., Chair; Angela Paolini Ellard, Staff Director. Web, www.house.gov/ ways_means.*

Jurisdiction over legislation on tariffs, trade, and customs. Authorizes budgets for the U.S. Customs Service, U.S. International Trade Commission, and the Office of the U.S. Trade Representative.

Joint Economic Committee, *SD-G01 20510; (202) 224-5171. Fax, (202) 224-0240. Sen. Connie Mack, R-Fla., Chair; Shelley Hymes, Staff Director. General e-mail, jec@ jec.house.gov. Web, jec.senate.gov.*

Studies and makes recommendations on international economic policy and programs, trade, and foreign investment policy; monitors economic policy in foreign countries.

Senate Appropriations Committee, *Subcommittee on Commerce, Justice, State, and Judiciary, S-146A CAP 20510; (202) 224-7277. Sen. Judd Gregg, R-N.H., Chair; Jim Morhard, Clerk. Web, appropriations.senate.gov/ commerce.*

Jurisdiction over legislation to appropriate funds for the Commerce Dept., the Office of the U.S. Trade Representative, International Trade Commission, and other international economics-related agencies, services, and programs.

Senate Banking, Housing, and Urban Affairs Committee, *Subcommittee on International Trade and Finance, SD-534 20510; (202) 224-7391. Fax, (202) 224-5137. Sen. Michael B. Enzi, R-Wyo., Chair; Katherine McGuire, Staff Director. Web, banking.senate.gov.*

Jurisdiction over legislation on international monetary and exchange rate policies, international capital flows, foreign investments in the United States, export control, foreign trade promotion, the Export-Import Bank, the Export Administration Act, and the revised Trading with the Enemy Act, which authorizes trade restrictions (some jurisdictions shared with Senate Finance and Foreign Relations committees).

Senate Finance Committee, *Subcommittee on International Trade, SD-219 20510; (202) 224-4515. Fax, (202) 224-5920. Sen. Charles E. Grassley, R-Iowa, Chair; Frank Polk, Staff Director. Web, finance.senate.gov.*

Holds hearings on tariff and trade legislation; oversees the U.S. Customs Service.

Senate Foreign Relations Committee, *Subcommittee on International Economic Policy, Export, and Trade Promotion, SD-450 20510; (202) 224-4651. Fax, (202) 224-0836. Sen. Chuck Hagel, R-Neb., Chair; Steve Biegun, Staff Director. Web, foreign.senate.gov.*

Jurisdiction over legislation to encourage foreign trade and to protect American business interests abroad. Jurisdiction over legislation affecting multinational corporations; balance of payments; the African Development Bank; the World Bank; the Asian Development Bank; the Inter-American Development Bank; the Overseas Private Investment Corp.; the Trade Development Agency; the International Monetary Fund, the Export-Import Bank, and other international monetary organizations; international economic and monetary policy as it relates to U.S. foreign policy (jurisdiction shared with the Senate Finance and Senate Banking, Housing, and Urban Affairs committees).

Senate Small Business Committee, *SR-428A 20510; (202) 224-5175. Fax, (202) 224-4885. Sen. Christopher S. Bond, R-Mo., Chair; Emilia DiSanto, Staff Director. Web, sbc.senate.gov.*

Jurisdiction over legislation on export expansion as it relates to small business.

INTERNATIONAL ORGANIZATIONS

European Commission, *Press and Public Affairs, Washington Office, 2300 M St. N.W. 20037; (202) 862-9500. Fax, (202) 429-1766. Willy Helin, Director; Günter Burghardt, Ambassador. Press, (202) 862-9540. Web, www. europa.eu.int.*

Information and public affairs office in the United States for the European Union, which includes the European Economic Community, the European Coal and Steel Community, and the European Atomic Energy Community. Provides commercial policy data on the European Union and provides information and documents on member countries, including economic, development and cooperation, industry, and technology data. Library open to the public by appointment. (Headquarters in Brussels.)

Food and Agriculture Organization of the United Nations, *Liaison Office for North America, 2175 K St. N.W., #300 20437; (202) 653-2400. Fax, (202) 653-5760. Charles H. Riemenschneider, Director. Library, (202) 653-2402. Web, www.fao.org.*

Serves as the main forum of the international community on world food, agriculture, fisheries, and forestry problems; provides developing nations with technical assistance to improve and increase agricultural productivity. Library open to the public by appointment. (International headquarters in Rome.)

Inter-American Development Bank, *1300 New York Ave. N.W. 20577; (202) 623-1100. Fax, (202) 623-3096. Enrique V. Iglesias, President; Lawrence Harrington, U.S. Executive Director, (202) 623-1031. Information, (202) 623-1000. Library, (202) 623-3211. Press, (202) 623-1371. Web, www.iadb.org.*

Promotes, through loans and technical assistance, the investment of public and private capital in member countries for social and economic development purposes. Facilitates economic integration of the Latin American region. Library open to the public by appointment.

International Bank for Reconstruction and Development, *1818 H St. N.W., MC12-750 20433; (202) 477-1234. Fax, (202) 522-3031. James D. Wolfensohn, President. Press, (202) 473-1804. Publications, (202) 473-1956. Web, www.worldbank.org.*

International development institution funded by membership subscriptions and borrowings on private capital markets. Encourages the flow of public and private foreign investment into developing countries through loans and technical assistance; collects data on selected economic indicators, world trade, and external public debt. Finances economic development projects in agriculture, environmental protection, education, public utilities, telecommunications, water supply, sewerage, public health, and other areas.

International Centre for Settlement of Investment Disputes, *1818 H St. N.W. 20433; (202) 458-1601. Fax, (202) 477-5828. Ibrahim F. I. Shihata, Secretary General. Information, (202) 477-1234. Web, www.worldbank.org.*

World Bank affiliate that handles the conciliation and arbitration of investment disputes between contracting states and foreign investors.

International Development Assn., *1818 H St. N.W. 20433; (202) 477-1234. Fax, (202) 477-6391. James D. Wolfensohn, President. Press, (202) 473-1804. Web, www.worldbank.org.*

Affiliate of the World Bank funded by membership contributions and transfers of funds from the World Bank. Extends interest-free credit to poorest member countries for high-priority development projects.

International Monetary Fund, *Statistics, 1825 Eye St. N.W. 20006 (mailing address: 700 19th St. N.W. 20431); (202) 623-7900. Fax, (202) 623-6460. Carol S. Carson, Director. Publications, (202) 623-7430.*

Publishes monthly *International Financial Statistics (IFS),* which includes comprehensive financial data for most countries, and *Direction of Trade Statistics,* a quarterly publication, which includes the distribution of exports and imports for 152 countries. Annual statistical publications include the *Balance of Payments Statistics Yearbook, Direction of Trade Statistics Yearbook,* the *Government Finance Statistics Yearbook,* and the *International Financial Statistics Yearbook.* Subscriptions available to the public. IFS also is available on CD-ROM.

Organization for Economic Cooperation and Development, *Washington Office, 2001 L St. N.W., #650 20036-4922; (202) 785-6323. Fax, (202) 785-0350. Matthew Brosius, Co-Director. Web, www.oecdwash.org.*

Membership: twenty-nine nations including Australia, Canada, Japan, Mexico, New Zealand, the United States, and western European nations. Funded by membership contributions. Serves as a forum for members to exchange information and coordinate their economic policies; compiles statistics. Washington Center sells OECD publications and software; maintains reference library that is open to the public. (Headquarters in Paris.)

United Nations Information Centre, *1775 K St. N.W., #400 20006; (202) 331-8670. Fax, (202) 331-9191. Cathryn O'Neill, Director. Web, www.un.org.*

Lead United Nations office in Washington. Center for reference publications of the U.N.; publications include statistical compilations on international trade and development, national accounts, growth of world industry, and demographic statistics. Library open to the public.

JUDICIARY

U.S. Court of Appeals for the Federal Circuit, *717 Madison Pl. N.W. 20439; (202) 633-6556. Fax, (202) 633-6353. Haldane Robert Mayer, Chief Judge; Jan Horbaly, Clerk, (202) 633-9614. Electronic bulletin board, (202) 633-9608 or (202) 786-6584.*

Reviews decisions of U.S. Court of International Trade (located in New York) on classifications of and duties on imported merchandise; settles legal questions about unfair practices in import trade (such as anti-dumping cases) found by the U.S. International Trade Commission and on import duties found by the Commerce Dept.

NONPROFIT

Assn. of Foreign Investors in Real Estate, *1300 Pennsylvania Ave. N.W., #880 20004-3020; (202) 312-1400. Fax, (202) 312-1401. James A. Fetgatter, Chief Executive. General e-mail, afireinfo@afire.org. Web, www.afire.org.*

Represents foreign institutions that are interested in the laws, regulations, and economic trends affecting the U.S. real estate market. Informs the public and the government of the contributions foreign investment makes to the U.S. economy. Examines current issues and organizes seminars for members.

Assn. of Women in International Trade, *P.O. Box 65962 20035; (202) 785-9842. Melissa Coyle, President, (202) 624-2895. Web, www.embassy.org/wiit.*

Membership: women and men from all sectors concerned with international trade, including import-export firms, government, corporations, and nonprofit organizations. Provides members with opportunities for professional development. Maintains job bank and conducts an annual public opinion poll on international trade.

Business Alliance for International Economic Development, *601 13th St. N.W., #900-S 20005; (202) 783-5588. Fax, (202) 783-5595. Terrence L. Bracy, Executive Director. Web, www.milcom.com/alliance.*

Studies the relation between foreign economic assistance and the expansion of U.S. exports and jobs. Supports proper implementation of foreign aid by the U.S. government and multilateral development banks.

Center for International Private Enterprise, *1155 15th St. N.W., #700 20005-2706; (202) 721-9200. Fax, (202) 721-9250. Willard A. Workman, Vice President; John Sullivan, Executive Director. General e-mail, cipe@ cipe.org. Web, www.cipe.org.*

Works to strengthen private voluntary business organizations worldwide and to promote participation in the formation of public policy. Cooperates with local, national, regional, and multilateral institutions promoting private enterprise. (Affiliate of the U.S. Chamber of Commerce.)

Coalition for Employment Through Exports, *1100 Connecticut Ave. N.W., #810 20036-4101; (202) 296-6107. Fax, (202) 296-9709. Edmund B. Rice, President.*

Alliance of governors and representatives of business and organized labor. Works to ensure adequate lending authority for the Export-Import Bank and other trade finance facilities as well as aggressive export financing policies for the United States.

Consumers for World Trade, *2000 L St. N.W., #200 20036; (202) 785-4835. Fax, (202) 416-1734. Doreen L. Brown, President.*

Consumer organization that advocates open and competitive trade policies. Represents consumer views in the formulation of foreign trade policy.

Economic Strategy Institute, *1401 H St. N.W., #750 20005; (202) 289-1288. Fax, (202) 289-1319. Clyde V. Prestowitz Jr., President. General e-mail, esidc@aol.com. Web, www.econstrat.org.*

Works to increase U.S. economic competitiveness through research on domestic and international economic policies, industrial and technological developments, and global security issues. Testifies before Congress and government agencies.

Emergency Committee for American Trade, *1211 Connecticut Ave. N.W., #801 20036-2703; (202) 659-5147. Fax, (202) 659-1347. Calman J. Cohen, President.*

Membership: U.S. corporations and banks interested in international trade and investment. Supports open trade and opposes restrictions on U.S. exports and imports.

Federation of International Trade Assns., *11800 Sunrise Valley Dr., Reston, VA 20191; (703) 620-1588. Fax, (703) 620-4922. Nelson T. Joyner, Chair. Toll-free fax, (800) 926-FITA. General e-mail, info@fita.org. Web, www. fita.org.*

Membership: local, regional, and national trade associations throughout North America that have an international mission. Works to increase North American exports.

G7 Council, *1133 Connecticut Ave. N.W., #901 20036; (202) 223-0774. Fax, (202) 861-0790. David Smick, Co-Chair; Manuel Johnson, Co-Chair.*

Membership: international economic policy experts and business leaders, including former G7 officials. Advocates promoting the international economy over national economies. Promotes cooperation and coordination among the G7 countries and other industrial nations.

Institute for International Economics, *11 Dupont Circle N.W., 6th Floor 20036; (202) 328-9000. Fax, (202) 328-5432. C. Fred Bergsten, Director. Web, www.iie.com.*

Conducts studies and makes policy recommendations on international monetary affairs, trade, investment, energy, exchange rates, commodities, and North-South and East-West economic relations.

International Management and Development Institute, *1615 L St. N.W., #900 20036; (202) 337-1022. Fax, (202) 337-6678. Don Bonker, President. General e-mail, imdimail@aol.com. Web, members.aol.com/ imdiweb.*

Educational organization that works to improve government-business understanding and international economic and trade cooperation worldwide through policy seminars and research on international economic and trade issues.

National Assn. of Manufacturers, *Economic Policy,* *1331 Pennsylvania Ave. N.W., #600 20004-1790; (202) 637-3144. Fax, (202) 637-3182. Howard Lewis III, Vice President. Web, www.nam.org.*

Represents manufacturing business interests on international economic issues, including trade and technology, international investment and financial affairs, and multinational corporations.

National Assn. of State Development Agencies, *750 1st St. N.E., #710 20002-4241; (202) 898-1302. Fax, (202) 898-1312. Miles Friedman, President. Web, www.nasda.com.*

Membership: directors of state economic development agencies. Assists member agencies in encouraging direct capital investment by foreign firms intending to manufacture goods in the United States. Aids in development of export promotion strategies.

National Customs Brokers and Forwarders Assn. of America, *1200 18th St. N.W., #901 20036; (202) 466-0222. Fax, (202) 466-0226. Barbara Reilly, Executive Vice President. General e-mail, staff@ncbfaa.org. Web, www.ncbfaa.org.*

Membership: customs brokers and freight forwarders in the United States. Fosters information exchange within the industry. Monitors legislation and regulations.

National Foreign Trade Council, *1625 K St. N.W., #1090 20006-1604; (202) 887-0278. Fax, (202) 452-8160. Frank D. Kittredge, President.*

Membership: U.S. companies engaged in international trade and investment. Advocates open international trading, export expansion, and policies to assist U.S. companies competing in international markets. Provides members with information on international trade topics. Sponsors seminars and conferences.

National Policy Assn., *1424 16th St. N.W., #700 20036; (202) 265-7685. Fax, (202) 797-5516. Anthony C. E. Quainton, President. General e-mail, npa@npa1.org. Web, www.npa1.org.*

Research organization that conducts studies and makes policy recommendations on international economic issues, including international trade, investment, monetary policy, and U.S. economic competitiveness.

Overseas Development Council, *1875 Connecticut Ave. N.W., #1012 20009-5728; (202) 234-8701. Fax, (202) 745-0067. John W. Sewell, President. Web, www.odc.org.*

Research and educational organization that encourages review of U.S. policy toward developing nations by

the business community, educators, policymakers, specialists, the public, and the media. Library open to the public by appointment.

United States Council for International Business, *Washington Office, 1015 15th St. N.W., #975 20005-2605; (202) 371-1316. Fax, (202) 371-8249. Timothy Deal, Senior Vice President. General e-mail, info@uscib.org. Web, www.uscib.org.*

Membership: multinational corporations, service companies, law firms, and business associations. Represents U.S. business positions before intergovernmental bodies, foreign governments, and business communities. Promotes an open system of world trade, finance, and investment. (Headquarters in New York.)

U.S. Chamber of Commerce, *International Division, 1615 H St. N.W., #635 20062-2000; (202) 463-5455. Fax, (202) 463-3114. Willard A. Workman, Vice President. Information, (202) 463-5460. General e-mail, custsvc@uschamber.com. Web, www.uschamber.com.*

Provides liaison with network of American chambers of commerce abroad; administers multilateral business councils; responsible for international economic policy development; informs members of developments in international affairs, business economics, and trade; sponsors seminars and conferences.

Washington International Trade Assn., *1300 Pennsylvania Ave. N.W., #350 20004; (202) 312-1600. Fax, (202) 312-1601. Libby Bingham, Executive Director. Web, www.wita.org.*

Membership: trade professionals. Conducts programs and provides neutral forums to discuss international trade issues. Monitors legislation and regulations.

See also Atlantic Council of the United States (p. 444)

Development Assistance

See also Humanitarian Aid (this chapter); World Food Assistance (chap. 2)

AGENCIES

Agency for International Development, *Center for Human Capacity Development, 1300 Pennsylvania Ave. N.W., #3.09-036 20523-3901; (202) 712-4273. Fax, (202) 216-3229. Emily Vargas-Baron, Director. Web, www.info.usaid.gov.*

Administers the AID Participant Training Program, which provides students and midcareer professionals from developing countries with academic and technical training; the Entrepreneur International Initiative, a short-term training/trade program that matches developing country entrepreneurs with American counterparts to familiarize them with American goods, services, and technology.

Agency for International Development, *Global Programs, Field Support, and Research Bureau,* 1300 Pennsylvania Ave. N.W., #3.09 20523-3901; (202) 712-1479. Fax, (202) 216-3235. Barbara Turner, Assistant Administrator (Acting). Web, www.info.usaid.gov.

Administers grants to research and educational institutions for development of foreign assistance programs. Divisions focus on economic growth (including business, agriculture, microenterprise development, and institutional reform); the environment (including energy use); population, health, and nutrition; democracy and governance; human capacity development (including education and training); and women in development.

Foreign Agricultural Service *(Agriculture Dept.),* 1400 Independence Ave. S.W., #5071 20250-1001; (202) 720-3935. Fax, (202) 690-2159. Timothy J. Galvin, Administrator; Richard Fritz, General Sales Manager. Information, (202) 720-7115. TTY, (202) 720-1786. Web, www.fas.usda.gov.

Administers the U.S. foreign food aid program with the Agency for International Development. Responsible for Title I of the Food for Peace program, the Food for Progress program, and the Section 416(b) program, which provides developing countries with surplus commodities.

Peace Corps, 1111 20th St. N.W. 20526; (202) 692-2100. Fax, (202) 692-2101. Mark L. Schneider, Director; Charles R. Baquet III, Deputy Director. Information, (800) 424-8580. Press, (202) 692-2234. Web, www.peacecorps.gov.

Promotes world peace and mutual understanding between the United States and developing nations. Administers volunteer programs to assist developing countries in education, the environment, health, small business development, agriculture, and urban development.

State Dept., *Development Finance,* 2201 C St. N.W., #3425 20520-5820; (202) 647-9426. Fax, (202) 647-5585. J. Paul Reid, Director. Web, www.state.gov.

Provides liaison between the International Bank for Reconstruction and Development (World Bank), regional development banks, and the U.S. Export-Import Bank to facilitate U.S. assistance to developing nations. Helps to formulate State Dept. and U.S. government positions on multilateral lending.

Treasury Dept., *Multilateral Development Banks,* 1440 New York Ave. N.W., #3426 20220; (202) 622-1231. Fax,

(202) 622-1228. Joe Eichenberger, Director. Information, (202) 622-1810. Web, www.ustreas.gov.

Provides support for U.S. participation in multilateral development banks: the World Bank Group, the Inter-American Development Bank, the African Development Bank/Fund, the Asian Development Bank, and the European Bank for Reconstruction and Development.

INTERNATIONAL ORGANIZATIONS

United Nations Development Programme, *Washington Office,* 1775 K St. N.W., #420 20006; (202) 331-9130. Fax, (202) 331-9363. Michael Marek, Director. Web, www.undp.org.

Funded by voluntary contributions from member nations and by nonmember recipient nations. Administers and coordinates technical assistance programs provided through the United Nations system. Seeks to increase economic and social development in developing nations. (Headquarters in New York.)

NONPROFIT

Academy for Educational Development, 1825 Connecticut Ave. N.W., #900 20009; (202) 884-8000. Fax, (202) 884-8400. Stephen F. Moseley, President. General e-mail, admin@aed.org. Web, www.aed.org.

Distributes information on basic education programs in developing countries and on education-related issues.

Adventist Development and Relief Agency International, 12501 Old Columbia Pike, Silver Spring, MD 20904; (301) 680-6380. Fax, (301) 680-6370. Ralph S. Watts Jr., President. Information, (800) 424-2372. Press, (301) 680-6340.

Worldwide humanitarian agency of the Seventh-day Adventist church. Works to alleviate poverty in developing countries and responds to disasters. Sponsors activities that improve health, foster economic and social well-being, and build self-reliance.

Alliance for Communities in Action, P.O. Box 30154, Bethesda, MD 20824-0154; (301) 229-7707. Fax, (301) 229-0457. Richard Schopfer, Executive Director.

Collaborates with local and international development organizations to promote self-help projects for small Latin American communities and small-business projects for skilled workers. Arranges funding, technical assistance, and supplies for health, housing, food production, and water projects. Promotes microenterprise development projects.

Ashoka: Innovators for the Public, 1700 N. Moore St., #2000, Arlington, VA 22209; (703) 527-8300. Fax, (703) 527-8383. William Drayton, President. General e-mail, info@ashoka.org. Web, www.ashoka.org.

Supports fellowships for individuals with ideas for social change in thirty-six developing nations. Provides fellows with research support, organizational networking, legal counseling, and business consulting. Seeks to educate the public about the developing world and the work of its fellows.

Assn. for the Advancement of Policy, Research, and Development in the Third World, *1730 K St. N.W., #304 20006; (202) 296-0947. Fax, (202) 331-3759. Mekki Mtewa, Executive Director.*

Serves as a forum for the exchange of scientific and technological information to aid developing countries; conducts research; sponsors workshops, seminars, and an annual conference on international development.

CARE, *Washington Office, 1625 K St. N.W., #200 20006; (202) 223-2277. Fax, (202) 296-8695. Marianne Leach, Executive Director. General e-mail, info@care.org. Web, www.care.org.*

Assists the developing world's poor through emergency assistance and community self-help programs that focus on sustainable development, agriculture, agroforestry, water and sanitation, health, family planning, and income generation. (U.S. headquarters in Atlanta; international headquarters in Brussels.)

Center for Intercultural Education and Development, *3307 M St. N.W., #302 20007 (mailing address: P.O. Box 579400, Georgetown University 20057-9400); (202) 687-1400. Fax, (202) 687-2555. Julio Giulietti (SJ), Director. Web, www.georgetown.edu/CIED.*

Designs and administers programs aimed at improving the quality of life of economically disadvantaged people; provides technical education, job training, leadership skill development, and business management training; runs programs in Central America, the Caribbean, Central Europe, and Southeast Asia.

Citizens Democracy Corps, *1400 Eye St. N.W., #1125 20005; (202) 872-0933. Fax, (202) 872-0923. Michael Levett, President. Information, (800) 394-1945. General e-mail, info@cdc.org. Web, www.cdc.org.*

Mobilizes volunteers in the U.S. private sector to assist in the development of market economies and democratic societies worldwide. Through the Business Entrepreneur Program, American volunteers assist private and privatizing businesses and public and nonprofit institutions that support business development.

Cooperative Housing Foundation, *8300 Colesville Rd., #420, Silver Spring, MD 20910; (301) 587-4700. Fax, (301) 587-2626. Michael Doyle, President. General e-mail, mailbox@chfhq.com. Web, www.chfhq.org.*

Works under contract with the Agency for International Development, United Nations, and World Bank to strengthen local government housing departments abroad.

Development Group for Alternative Policies, *927 15th St. N.W., 4th Floor 20005; (202) 898-1566. Fax, (202) 898-1612. Douglas Hellinger, Executive Director. General e-mail, dgap@igc.org. Web, www.developmentgap.org.*

Works with grassroots organizations in developing countries to promote changes in international economic policies to benefit the poor.

InterAction, *1717 Massachusetts Ave. N.W., #701 20036; (202) 667-8227. Fax, (202) 667-8236. Jim Moody, President. General e-mail, ia@interaction.org. Web, www.interaction.org.*

Provides a forum for exchange of information among private U.S. voluntary agencies on development assistance issues, including food aid and other relief services, migration, and refugee affairs. Monitors legislation and regulations.

International Center for Research on Women, *1717 Massachusetts Ave. N.W., #302 20036; (202) 797-0007. Fax, (202) 797-0020. Geeta Rao Gupta, President. General e-mail, icrw@igc.apc.org. Web, www.icrw.org.*

Seeks to advance women's rights and opportunities. Promotes social and economic development with participation of women; provides technical assistance on women's productive and reproductive roles; advocates with governments and agencies.

International Voluntary Services, *1601 Connecticut Ave. N.W., #402D 20009; (202) 387-5533. Fax, (202) 387-4291. Anne D. Shirk, Chief Operating Officer. General e-mail, ivs.inc@erols.com.*

Provides developing countries with volunteers and technical assistance in the areas of health, agriculture, small business, and community and rural development.

National Peace Corps Assn., *1900 L St. N.W., #205 20036-5002; (202) 293-7728. Fax, (202) 293-7554. Dane Smith, President. Web, www.rpcv.org.*

Membership: returned Peace Corps volunteers, staff, and interested individuals. Promotes a global perspective in the United States; seeks to educate the public about the developing world; supports Peace Corps programs; maintains network of returned volunteers.

New TransCentury Foundation, *17002 Waterfall Rd., Haymarket, VA 20169-1702; (703) 753-3785. Fax, (703) 753-3785. Lisa Wiggins, President. General e-mail, transcentury@compuserve.com.*

International development research and consulting organization. Provides developing countries with technical assistance. Interests include agriculture, health, labor and migration, refugee resettlement, credit entrepreneurship (loans to entrepreneurs to start businesses), and assistance to private voluntary and nongovernmental organizations.

Partners for Livable Communities, *1429 21st St. N.W., 2nd Floor 20036; (202) 887-5990. Fax, (202) 466-4845. Robert H. McNulty, President. General e-mail, partners@livable.com. Web, www.livable.com.*

Provides technical assistance, support services, and information to assist communities in creating better living environments. Works in the Caribbean area, South America, and Europe on public/private partnerships and resource development to improve living environments. Conducts conferences and workshops; maintains referral clearinghouse.

Pax World Service, *1730 Rhode Island Ave. N.W., #715 20036; (202) 463-0486. Fax, (202) 463-7322. Malcolm Butler, President. General e-mail, info@paxworld.org. Web, www.paxworld.org.*

Initiates and supports community-based sustainable development projects. Supports educational activities and facilitates citizen diplomacy through people-to-people tours, a program that allows individuals to develop a better understanding of the culture and diverse viewpoints of people living in regions of conflict.

Planning Assistance, *1832 Jefferson Pl. N.W. 20036; (202) 466-3290. Fax, (202) 466-3293. Robert Learmonth, Executive Director. General e-mail, planasst@igc.org.*

Provides managerial assistance to governmental and nongovernmental organizations seeking to create, expand, or improve their social and economic development programs. Interests include health, family planning, environmental programming, and municipal development. Focuses on development in Africa, Asia, and Latin America.

Salvation Army World Service Office, *615 Slaters Lane, Alexandria, VA 22313 (mailing address: P.O. Box 269, Alexandria, VA 22313); (703) 684-5528. Fax, (703) 684-5536. Harden White, Executive Director.*

Works in Russia and the new independent states, Latin America, the Caribbean, Africa, Asia, and the South Pacific to provide technical assistance in support of local Salvation Army programs of health services (including HIV/AIDS), community development, education, institutional development, microenterprise, and relief and reconstruction assistance. (International headquarters in London.)

United Way International, *701 N. Fairfax St., Alexandria, VA 22314-2045; (703) 519-0092. Fax, (703) 519-0097. Robert Beggan, President. General e-mail, uwi@unitedway.org. Web, www.wwint.org.*

Membership: independent United Way organizations in other countries. Provides United Way fundraising campaigns with technical assistance; trains volunteers and professionals; operates an information exchange for affiliated organizations.

Volunteers in Overseas Cooperative Assistance, *50 F St. N.W., #1075 20001; (202) 383-4961. Fax, (202) 783-7204. Michael Deegan, President. Web, www.acdivoca.org.*

Recruits professionals for voluntary, short-term technical assistance to cooperatives, environmental groups, and agricultural enterprises, upon request, in developing countries and emerging democracies.

Finance/Monetary Affairs

AGENCIES

Commerce Dept., *Balance of Payments, 1441 L St. N.W., BE-58 20230; (202) 606-9545. Fax, (202) 606-5314. Christopher L. Bach, Chief. Web, www.stat-usa.gov.*

Compiles, analyzes, and publishes quarterly U.S. balance-of-payments figures.

Federal Reserve System, *International Finance, 20th and C Sts. N.W., #B1242C 20551-2345; (202) 452-2345. Fax, (202) 452-6424. Karen H. Johnson, Director.*

Provides the Federal Reserve's board of governors with economic analyses of international developments. Compiles data on balance of payments, international trade, and exchange rates.

State Dept., *International Finance and Development, 2201 C St. N.W., #3336 20520; (202) 647-9496. Fax, (202) 647-0320. Melinda L. Kimble, Deputy Assistant Secretary. Web, www.state.gov.*

Formulates and implements policies related to multinational investment and insurance; activities of the World Bank and regional banks in the financial development of various countries; bilateral aid; international monetary reform; international antitrust cases; and international debt, banking, and taxation.

State Dept., *Monetary Affairs, 2201 C St. N.W., #3425 20520; (202) 647-5935. Fax, (202) 647-7453. David Nelson, Director. Web, www.state.gov.*

Formulates balance-of-payments and debt rescheduling policies. Monitors balance-of-payments developments in other countries.

Treasury Dept., *Foreign Exchange Operations,* 1500 Pennsylvania Ave. N.W., #2409 20220; (202) 622-2650. Fax, (202) 622-2021. Timothy Dulaney, Director. Web, www.ustreas.gov.

Monitors foreign exchange market developments; manages the Exchange Stabilization Fund to counter disruptive market conditions and to provide developing countries with bridge loans.

Treasury Dept., *International Affairs,* 1500 Pennsylvania Ave. N.W., #3430 20220; (202) 622-1270. Fax, (202) 622-0417. Timothy Geithner, Under Secretary; Edwin M. Truman, Assistant Secretary. Web, www.ustreas.gov.

Coordinates and implements U.S. international economic policy in cooperation with other government agencies. Works to improve the structure and stabilizing operations of the international monetary and investment system; monitors developments in international gold and foreign exchange operations; coordinates policies and programs of development lending institutions; coordinates Treasury Dept. participation in direct and portfolio investment by foreigners in the United States; studies international monetary, economic, and financial issues; analyzes data on international transactions.

Treasury Dept., *Trade Finance,* 1500 Pennsylvania Ave. N.W. 20220; (202) 622-2120. Fax, (202) 622-0967. Steven F. Tvardek, Director. Web, www.ustreas.gov.

Reviews lending policies of the Export-Import Bank, the Commodity Credit Corp., and the Defense Dept.'s foreign military sales program. Serves as U.S. representative to the Export Credits Group, a committee of the Organization for Economic Cooperation and Development, and negotiates international arrangements for export credits.

CONGRESS

House Banking and Financial Services Committee, *Subcommittee on Domestic and International Monetary Policy,* B304 RHOB 20515; (202) 226-0473. Fax, (202) 226-0537. Rep. Spencer Bachus, R-Ala., Chair; James McCormick, Staff Director. Web, www.house.gov/banking.

Jurisdiction over legislation on international monetary policy, international capital flows, and foreign investment in the United States as they affect domestic monetary policy and the economy; exchange rates; the African, Asian, European, and Inter-American Development Banks; the World Bank; legislation on international trade, investment, and monetary policy and export expansion matters related to the International Monetary Fund and the Export-Import Bank.

Senate Banking, Housing, and Urban Affairs Committee, *Subcommittee on International Trade and Finance,* SD-534 20510; (202) 224-7391. Fax, (202) 224-5137. Sen. Michael B. Enzi, R-Wyo., Chair; Katherine McGuire, Staff Director. Web, banking.senate.gov.

Jurisdiction over legislation on international monetary and exchange rate policies, international capital flows, foreign investments in the United States, export control, foreign trade promotion, the Export-Import Bank, the Export Administration Act, and the revised Trading with the Enemy Act, which authorizes trade restrictions (some jurisdictions shared with Senate Finance and Foreign Relations committees).

Senate Finance Committee, SD-219 20510; (202) 224-4515. Fax, (202) 224-5920. Sen. William V. Roth Jr., R-Del., Chair; Frank Polk, Staff Director. Web, finance.senate.gov.

Jurisdiction over legislation on international monetary matters (shares jurisdiction with the Senate Foreign Relations and Banking, Housing, and Urban Affairs committees).

Senate Foreign Relations Committee, *Subcommittee on International Economic Policy, Export, and Trade Promotion,* SD-450 20510; (202) 224-4651. Fax, (202) 224-0836. Sen. Chuck Hagel, R-Neb., Chair; Steve Biegun, Staff Director. Web, foreign.senate.gov.

Jurisdiction over legislation to encourage foreign trade and to protect American business interests abroad. Jurisdiction over legislation affecting multinational corporations; balance of payments; international monetary organizations; and international economic and monetary policy as it relates to U.S. foreign policy (jurisdiction shared with the Senate Finance and Senate Banking, Housing, and Urban Affairs committees).

INTERNATIONAL ORGANIZATIONS

International Finance Corp., 2121 Pennsylvania Ave. N.W. 20433 (mailing address: 1818 H St. N.W. 20433); (202) 477-1234. Fax, (202) 477-6391. James D. Wolfensohn, President; Peter Woicke, Executive Vice President. Web, www.ifc.org.

Promotes private enterprise in developing countries through direct investments in projects that establish new businesses or expand, modify, or diversify existing businesses; provides its own financing or recruits financing from other sources. Gives developing countries technical assistance in capital market development, privatization, corporate restructuring, and foreign investment. Affiliated with the World Bank.

International Monetary Fund, 700 19th St. N.W. 20431; (202) 623-7759. Fax, (202) 623-4940. Karin Lissakers, U.S. Executive Director. Information, (202) 623-7000. Press, (202) 623-7300. Web, www.imf.org.

Intergovernmental organization that maintains funds, contributed and available for use by members, to promote world trade and aid members with temporary balance-of-payments problems.

Multilateral Investment Guarantee Agency, *1818 H St. N.W., #U12001 20433; (202) 473-6138. Fax, (202) 522-2620. Motomichi Ikawa, Executive Vice President. Web, www.miga.org.*

World Bank affiliate that seeks to encourage foreign investment in developing countries. Provides guarantees against losses due to currency transfer, expropriation, war, revolution, civil disturbance, and breach of contract. Advises member developing countries on means of improving their attractiveness to foreign investors. Membership open to World Bank member countries and Switzerland.

NONPROFIT

Bankers' Assn. for Foreign Trade, *2121 K St. N.W., #701 20037; (202) 452-0952. Fax, (202) 452-0959. Mary Condeelis, Executive Director. Web, www.baft.org.*

Membership: U.S. commercial banks with major international operations; foreign banks with U.S. operations are affiliated as nonvoting members. Monitors activities that affect the operation of U.S. commercial banks.

Bretton Woods Committee, *1990 M St. N.W., #450 20036; (202) 331-1616. Fax, (202) 785-9423. James C. Orr, Executive Director. Web, www.brettonwoods.org.*

Works to increase public understanding of the World Bank, the regional development institutions, the International Monetary Fund, and the World Trade Organization.

Institute of International Finance, *2000 Pennsylvania Ave. N.W., #8500 20006-1812; (202) 857-3600. Fax, (202) 775-1430. Charles Dallara, Managing Director. Press, (202) 331-8183. Web, www.iif.com.*

Membership: international commercial banks, multinational corporations, and official lending agencies. Promotes better understanding of international lending transactions by improving the availability and quality of financial information on major country borrowers. Collects and analyzes information to help members evaluate credit risks of public and private borrowers in developing and middle-income countries. Studies and develops alternative solutions to the developing-country debt problem. Examines factors affecting the future of international lending.

🌍 REGIONAL AFFAIRS

See also Foreign Embassies, U.S. Ambassadors, and Country Desk Officers (appendix); Language and Literature (chap. 5)

Africa

For North Africa, see Near East and South Asia

AGENCIES

African Development Foundation, *1400 Eye St. N.W., 10th Floor 20005-2208; (202) 673-3916. Fax, (202) 673-3810. William R. Ford, President. General e-mail, info@ adf.gov. Web, www.adf.gov.*

Established by Congress to work with and fund organizations and individuals involved in development projects at the local level in Africa. Gives preference to projects involving extensive participation by local Africans.

Agency for International Development, Africa Bureau, *1300 Pennsylvania Ave. N.W., #4.08C 20523-4801; (202) 712-0500. Fax, (202) 216-3008. Vivian Lowery Derryck, Assistant Administrator. Web, www.info. usaid.gov.*

Advises AID administrator on U.S. policy toward developing countries in Africa.

State Dept., Bureau of African Affairs, *2201 C St. N.W., #6234A 20520; (202) 647-4440. Fax, (202) 647-6301. Susan E. Rice, Assistant Secretary. Press, (202) 647-7371. Web, www.state.gov.*

Advises the secretary on U.S. policy toward sub-Saharan Africa. Directors, assigned to different regions in Africa, aid the assistant secretary.

State Dept., Central African Affairs, *2201 C St. N.W., #4246 20520-2902; (202) 647-2080. Fax, (202) 647-1726. Roger Meece, Director. Web, www.state.gov.*

Includes Burundi, Cameroon, Central African Republic, Chad, Congo, Equatorial Guinea, Gabon, Rwanda, São Tomé and Principe, and Zaire.

State Dept., East African Affairs, *2201 C St. N.W., #5240 20520; (202) 647-9742. Fax, (202) 647-0810. Jeffrey Millington, Director. Web, www.state.gov.*

Includes Comoros, Djibouti, Eritrea, Ethiopia, Kenya, Madagascar, Mauritius, Seychelles, Somalia, Sudan, Tanzania, Uganda, and Indian Ocean Territory.

State Dept., Southern African Affairs, *2201 C St. N.W., #4238 20520; (202) 647-9836. Fax, (202) 647-5007. John W. Blaney, Director. Web, www.state.gov.*

Includes Angola, Botswana, Lesotho, Malawi,

Mozambique, Namibia, South Africa, Swaziland, Zambia, and Zimbabwe.

State Dept., *West African Affairs,* 2201 C St. N.W., #4250 20520-3430; (202) 647-2637. Fax, (202) 647-4855. Sharon Wilkinson, Director. Web, www.state.gov.

Includes Benin, Burkina Faso, Cape Verde, Côte d'Ivoire, Gambia, Ghana, Guinea, Guinea-Bissau, Liberia, Mali, Mauritania, Niger, Nigeria, Senegal, Sierra Leone, and Togo.

CONGRESS

House International Relations Committee, *Subcommittee on Africa,* 255 FHOB 20515; (202) 226-7812. Fax, (202) 225-7491. Rep. Ed Royce, R-Calif., Chair; Thomas Sheehy, Staff Director. Web, www.house.gov/international_relations.

Jurisdiction over foreign affairs legislation dealing with Africa, except Egypt. Concurrent jurisdiction over matters assigned to the functional House International Relations subcommittees insofar as they affect the region.

Library of Congress, *African and Middle Eastern Division,* 110 2nd St. S.E., #220 20540; (202) 707-7937. Fax, (202) 252-3180. Beverly Gray, Chief.

Maintains collections of African, Near Eastern, and Hebraic material. Prepares bibliographies and special studies relating to Africa and the Middle East. Reference service and reading rooms available to the public.

Senate Foreign Relations Committee, *Subcommittee on African Affairs,* SD-450 20510; (202) 224-4651. Fax, (202) 224-0836. Sen. Bill Frist, R-Tenn., Chair; Michael Westphal, Majority Professional Staff Member. Web, foreign.senate.gov.

Jurisdiction over foreign affairs legislation dealing with Africa, with the exception of countries bordering on the Mediterranean Sea from Egypt to Morocco.

INTERNATIONAL ORGANIZATIONS

International Bank for Reconstruction and Development, *Africa,* 1818 H St. N.W., #J5093 20433; (202) 458-2858. Fax, (202) 477-0380. Callisto E. Madavo, Vice President, (202) 458-2856; Jean-Louis Sarbib, Vice President, (202) 473-4946. Information, (202) 473-4619.

Encourages public and private foreign investment in the countries of sub-Saharan Africa through loans, loan guarantees, and technical assistance. Finances economic development projects in agriculture, environmental protection, education, public utilities, telecommunications, water supply, sewage treatment, public health, and other areas.

NONPROFIT

Africa-America Institute, *Washington Office,* 1625 Massachusetts Ave. N.W., #400 20036-2246; (202) 667-5636. Fax, (202) 265-6332. Jerry L. Drew, Director. Web, www.aaionline.org.

Designs exchange and visitor programs which bring together African and American professionals and policymakers to discuss areas of mutual concern. Sponsors policy studies program to educate Congress on African issues. Promotes trade and investment in Africa. (Headquarters in New York.)

Africare, 440 R St. N.W. 20001; (202) 462-3614. Fax, (202) 387-1034. C. Payne Lucas, President. General e-mail, africare@africare.org. Web, www.africare.org.

Seeks to improve the quality of life in rural Africa through development of water resources, increased food production, and delivery of health services. Resource center open to the public by appointment.

American African Affairs Assn., 1001 Connecticut Ave. N.W., #1135 20036; (202) 223-5110. J. A. Parker, Co-Chair.

Educational organization that provides information on African states. Interests include world communism and the role of the United States in development.

TransAfrica, 1744 R St. N.W. 20009-2410; (202) 797-2301. Fax, (202) 797-2382. Randall Robinson, President. General e-mail, transforum@igc.org. Web, www.igc.org/transafrica.

Focuses on U.S. foreign policy toward African nations, the Caribbean, and peoples of African descent. Provides members with information on foreign policy issues; conducts educational training programs for minority students considering careers in international affairs; affiliated with the TransAfrica Forum, which includes the Arthur R. Ashe Foreign Policy Library.

Washington Office on Africa, 212 E. Capitol St. 20003; (202) 547-7503. Fax, (202) 547-7505. Leon Spencer, Executive Director. General e-mail, woa@igc.org. Web, www.woaafrica.org.

Promotes a just American policy toward Africa. Monitors legislation and executive actions concerning Africa; issues action alerts.

East Asia and the Pacific

See also Russia and New Independent States

AGENCIES

Agency for International Development, *Asia and Near East Bureau,* 1300 Pennsylvania Ave. N.W., #4.09-

034 20523-4900; (202) 712-0200. Fax, (202) 216-3386. Robert C. Randolph, Assistant Administrator. General e-mail, rrandolph@usaid.gov. Web, www.info.usaid.gov.

Advises AID administrator on U.S. economic development policy in Asia and the Near East.

Defense Dept., *Asian and Pacific Affairs*, The Pentagon, #4C839 20301-2400; (703) 695-4175. Fax, (703) 695-8222. Kurt M. Campbell, Deputy Assistant Secretary. Web, www.defenselink.mil.

Advises the assistant secretary for international security affairs on matters dealing with Asia and the Pacific.

Japan-United States Friendship Commission, 1120 Vermont Ave. N.W., #925 20005; (202) 418-9800. Fax, (202) 418-9802. Eric J. Gangloff, Executive Director. General e-mail, jusfc@jusfc.gov. Web, www.jusfc.gov.

Independent agency established by Congress that makes grants and administers funds and programs promoting educational and cultural exchanges between Japan and the United States. Consults with public and private organizations in both countries.

State Dept., *Bureau of East Asian and Pacific Affairs*, 2201 C St. N.W., #6205 20520-6205; (202) 647-9596. Fax, (202) 647-7350. Stanley Roth, Assistant Secretary. Press, (202) 647-2538. Web, www.state.gov.

Advises the secretary on U.S. policy toward East Asian and Pacific countries. Director assigned to specific countries within the bureau aid the assistant secretary.

State Dept., *Australia, New Zealand, and Pacific Island Affairs*, 2201 C St. N.W., #4206 20520; (202) 736-4741. Fax, (202) 647-0118. Emil Skodon, Director. Web, www.state.gov.

State Dept., *Burma, Cambodia, Laos, Thailand, and Vietnam Affairs*, 2201 C St. N.W., #5206 20520-6310; (202) 647-3132. Fax, (202) 647-3069. Neil Silver, Director. Web, www.state.gov.

Handles issues related to Americans missing in action in Indochina; serves as liaison with Congress, international organizations, and foreign governments on developments in these countries.

State Dept., *Chinese and Mongolian Affairs*, 2201 C St. N.W., #4318 20520; (202) 647-6803. Fax, (202) 647-6820. Steve Schlaikjer, Director. Web, www.state.gov.

State Dept., *Japanese Affairs*, 2201 C St. N.W., #4206 20520; (202) 647-2913. Fax, (202) 647-4402. Robin White, Director. Web, www.state.gov.

State Dept., *Korean Affairs*, 2201 C St. N.W., #5313 20520; (202) 647-7719. Fax, (202) 647-7388. Evans Revere, Director. Web, www.state.gov.

State Dept., *Philippines, Indonesia, Malaysia, Brunei, and Singapore Affairs*, 2201 C St. N.W., #5210 20520; (202) 647-3276. Fax, (202) 736-4559. Douglas Hartwick, Director. Web, www.state.gov.

State Dept., *Taiwan Coordination Staff*, 2201 C St. N.W., #4312 20520; (202) 647-7711. Fax, (202) 647-0076. John Norris, Director. Web, www.state.gov.

CONGRESS

House International Relations Committee, *Subcommittee on Asia and the Pacific*, B-359 RHOB 20515; (202) 226-7825. Fax, (202) 226-7829. Rep. Doug Bereuter, R-Neb., Chair; Michael Ennis, Staff Director. Web, www.house.gov/international_relations.

Jurisdiction over foreign affairs legislation dealing with East Asia and the Pacific, the Near East, and South Asia, from Afghanistan to the Far East. Concurrent jurisdiction over matters assigned to the functional House International Relations subcommittees insofar as they affect the region.

Library of Congress, *Asian Division*, 110 2nd St. S.E., #LJ150 20540-4810; (202) 707-5420. Fax, (202) 707-1724. Mya Thanda Poe, Chief.

Maintains collections of Chinese, Korean, Japanese, Southeast Asian, and South Asian material covering all subjects except law, technical agriculture, and clinical medicine. Reference service is provided in the Asian Reading Room.

Senate Foreign Relations Committee, *Subcommittee on East Asian and Pacific Affairs*, SD-450 20510; (202) 224-4651. Fax, (202) 224-0836. Sen. Craig Thomas, R-Wyo., Chair; Jim Doran, Senior Professional Staff Member. Web, foreign.senate.gov.

Jurisdiction over foreign affairs legislation dealing with East Asia and the Pacific, including the mainland of Asia from China and Korea to Burma, Japan, the Philippines, Malaysia, Indonesia, Australia and New Zealand, Oceania, and the South Pacific islands.

INTERNATIONAL ORGANIZATIONS

International Bank for Reconstruction and Development, *East Asia and Pacific*, 1818 H St. N.W., MC9-123 20433; (202) 473-7723. Fax, (202) 477-0169. Jemal-ud-Din Kassum, Vice President.

Encourages public and private investment in the countries of East Asia and the Pacific through loans, loan guarantees, and technical assistance. Finances economic development projects in agriculture, environmental protection, education, public utilities, telecommunications, water supply, sewerage, public health, and other areas.

NONPROFIT

American Institute in Taiwan, *1700 N. Moore St., #1700, Arlington, VA 22209; (703) 525-8474. Fax, (703) 841-1385. Barbara Schrage, Deputy Director. Web, www. ait.org.tw.*

Chartered by Congress to coordinate commercial, cultural, and other activities between the people of the United States and Taiwan. Represents U.S. interests and maintains offices in Taiwan.

Asia Foundation, *Washington Office, 1779 Massachusetts Ave. N.W., #815 20036; (202) 588-9420. Fax, (202) 588-9409. Nancy Yuan, Director. Web, www.asiafoundation. org.*

Provides grants and technical assistance in Asia and the Pacific islands (excluding the Middle East). Seeks to strengthen legislatures, legal and judicial systems, market economies, the media, and nongovernmental organizations. (Headquarters in San Francisco.)

Asia Pacific Center for Justice and Peace, *110 Maryland Ave. N.E., Box #70 20002; (202) 543-1094. Fax, (202) 546-5103. Miriam A. Young, Director. General e-mail, apcjp@igc.apc.org. Web, www.apcjp.org.*

Nonprofit organization that supports justice and peace throughout Asia and the Pacific. Focuses on the policies of the U.S. government, corporations, international institutions, and religious bodies as they impact Asia and the Pacific. Monitors countries and issues; sponsors public education forums; supports people-to-people relationships.

Asia Society, *Washington Office, 1800 K St. N.W., #1102 20006; (202) 833-2742. Fax, (202) 833-0189. Judith Sloan, Director. Web, www.asiasociety.org.*

Membership: individuals interested in Asia and the Pacific (excluding the Middle East). Sponsors seminars and lectures on political, economic, and cultural issues. (Headquarters in New York.)

Heritage Foundation, *Asian Studies Center, 214 Massachusetts Ave. N.E. 20002; (202) 608-6081. Fax, (202) 675-1779. Larry Wortzel, Director.*

Conducts research and provides information on U.S. policies in Asia and the Pacific. Interests include economic and security issues in the Asia Pacific region. Hosts speakers and visiting foreign policy delegations; sponsors conferences.

Japan-America Society of Washington, *1020 19th St. N.W., Lower Lobby #40 20036; (202) 833-2210. Fax, (202) 833-2456. JoAnna Phillips, Executive Director. General e-mail, jaswdc@intr.net. Web, www.us-japan.org/dc.*

Conducts programs on U.S.-Japan trade, politics, and economic issues. Cultural programs include lectures, films, a Japanese-language school, scholarships to college students studying in the Washington, D.C., area, and assistance to Japanese performing artists. Maintains library for members. Sponsors national Cherry Blossom Festival.

Japan Economic Institute of America, *1000 Connecticut Ave. N.W., #211 20036; (202) 296-5633. Fax, (202) 296-8333. Arthur J. Alexander, President. General e-mail, jei_info@jei.org. Web, www.jei.org.*

Research organization supported by Japan's Ministry of Foreign Affairs. Publishes current information on the Japanese economy and U.S.-Japan economic relations. Library open to the public.

Japan Information Access Project, *2000 P St. N.W., #620 20036; (202) 822-6040. Fax, (202) 822-6044. Mindy Kotler, Director. General e-mail, access@nmjc.org. Web, www.nmjc.org/jiap.*

Studies Japanese and Northeast Asian Security and public policy. Researches and analyzes issues affecting Japan's relationship with the West.

Japan Productivity Center for Socio-Economic Development, *Washington Office, 1001 Connecticut Ave. N.W., #425 20036; (202) 955-5663. Fax, (202) 955-6125. Daisaku Harada, Director. General e-mail, jpc@cais. com.*

Promotes education and exchange of information between Japanese and American businesspeople by coordinating overseas meetings and visits for participating countries. (Headquarters in Tokyo.)

Pacific Economic Cooperation Council, *1112 16th St. N.W., #520 20036; (202) 293-3995. Fax, (202) 293-1402. Mark Borthwick, Executive Director. General e-mail, uspecc@pecc.org. Web, www.pecc.org.*

Membership: business, government, and research representatives from twenty-two Asia-Pacific economies. Works on practical government and business policy issues to increase trade, investment, and economic development in the region. Serves as one of three observer organizations to the government forum on Asia Pacific Economic Cooperation (APEC).

Taipei Economic and Cultural Representative Office, *4201 Wisconsin Ave. N.W. 20016; (202) 895-1800. Fax, (202) 966-0825. Stephen Chen, Representative. Press, (202) 895-1850.*

Represents political, economic, and cultural interests of the government of the Republic of China (Taiwan) in the United States; handles former embassy functions.

U.S.-Asia Institute, *232 E. Capitol St. N.E. 20003; (202) 544-3181. Fax, (202) 543-1748. Joji Konoshima, President.*

Organization of individuals interested in Asia. Encourages communication among political and business leaders in the United States and Asia. Interests include foreign policy, international trade, Asian and American cultures, education, and employment. Conducts research and sponsors conferences and workshops in cooperation with the State Dept. to promote greater understanding between the United States and Asian nations. Conducts programs that take congressional staff members to Japan and China.

U.S.-China Business Council, *1818 N St. N.W., #200 20036-2406; (202) 429-0340. Fax, (202) 775-2476. Robert A. Kapp, President. Web, www.uschina.org.*

Member-supported organization that represents U.S. companies engaged in business relations with the People's Republic of China. Participates in U.S. policy issues relating to China and other international trade. Publishes research reports. (Maintains offices in Beijing, Shanghai, and Hong Kong.)

Europe

(Includes the Baltic states)

AGENCIES

Agency for International Development, *Europe and Eurasia Bureau, 1300 Pennsylvania Ave. N.W., #5.06 20523-5600; (202) 712-5123. Fax, (202) 216-3057. Donald Pressley, Assistant Administrator. Web, www.info. usaid.gov.*

Advises AID administrator on U.S. economic development policy in Europe and the new independent states.

Defense Dept., *European and NATO Affairs, The Pentagon, #4D800 20301-2400; (703) 697-7207. Fax, (703) 697-5992. Lisa Bronson, Deputy Assistant Secretary. Web, www.defenselink.mil.*

Advises the assistant secretary for international security affairs on matters dealing with Europe and NATO.

International Trade Administration *(Commerce Dept.), Central and Eastern Europe Business Information Center, 1401 Constitution Ave. N.W. 20230; (202) 482-2645. Fax, (202) 482-3898. Jay Burgess, Director. Toll-free, (800) USATRADE. General e-mail, ceebic@ita. doc.gov. Web, www.mac.doc.gov/eebic/ceebic.html.*

Provides information on trade and investment in central and eastern Europe, includes the reconstruction of Kosovo and southeastern Europe. Disseminates information on potential trade partners, regulations and incentives, and trade promotion; encourages private enterprise in the region.

State Dept., *Bureau of European Affairs, 2201 C St. N.W., #6226 20520; (202) 647-9626. Fax, (202) 647-0967. Marc Grossman, Assistant Secretary. Information, (202) 647-6925. Web, www.state.gov.*

Advises the secretary on U.S. policy toward European countries and Canada. Directors assigned to specific countries within the bureau aid the assistant secretary.

State Dept., *European Security and Political Affairs, 2201 C St. N.W., #6227 20520; (202) 647-1626. Fax, (202) 647-1369. Richard A. Morford, Director. Web, www. state.gov.*

Coordinates and advises, with the Defense Dept. and other agencies, the U.S. mission to the North Atlantic Treaty Organization and the U.S. delegation to the Organization on Security and Cooperation in Europe regarding political, military, and arms control matters.

State Dept., *European Union and Regional Affairs, 2201 C St. N.W., #6519 20520-6511; (202) 647-3932. Fax, (202) 647-9959. Joseph M. DeThomas, Director. Web, www.state.gov.*

Handles all matters concerning the European Union, the Council of Europe, and the Organization for Economic Cooperation and Development, with emphasis on trade issues. Monitors export controls and economic activities for the North Atlantic Treaty Organization and the Conference on Security and Cooperation in Europe.

State Dept., *German, Austrian, and Swiss Affairs, 2201 C St. N.W., #4228 20520; (202) 647-1484. Fax, (202) 647-5117. James Warlick, Director. Web, www.state.gov.*

Includes Austria, Germany, Liechtenstein, and Switzerland.

State Dept., *Nordic and Baltic Affairs, 2201 C St. N.W., #5229 20520; (202) 647-5669. Fax, (202) 736-4170. Debi Graze, Director. Web, www.state.gov.*

Includes Denmark, Estonia, Finland, Iceland, Latvia, Lithuania, Norway, and Sweden.

State Dept., *North Central European Affairs, 2201 C St. N.W., #5220 20520; (202) 647-4136. Fax, (202) 736-4853. Joyce B. Rabens, Director. Web, www.state.gov.*

Includes Czech Republic, Hungary, Poland, Romania, Slovakia, and Slovenia.

State Dept., *South Central European Affairs, 2201 C St. N.W., #5221 20520; (202) 647-0608. Fax, (202) 647-0555. Thomas M. Countryman, Director. Web, www.state. gov.*

Includes Albania, Bosnia-Herzegovina, Bulgaria, Croatia, Macedonia, and the former Republic of Yugoslavia (Serbia-Montenegro).

State Dept., *Southern European Affairs,* 2201 C St. N.W., #5511 20520; (202) 647-6112. Fax, (202) 647-5087. *Morton R. Dworken, Director. Web, www.state.gov.*

Includes Cyprus, Greece, and Turkey.

State Dept., *United Kingdom, Benelux, and Ireland Affairs,* 2201 C St. N.W., #4513 20520; (202) 647-5687. Fax, (202) 647-3463. *Anna Borg, Director. Web, www. state.gov.*

Includes Belgium, Bermuda, Ireland, Luxembourg, the Netherlands, and the United Kingdom.

State Dept., *Western European Affairs,* 2201 C St. N.W., #5226 20520-6511; (202) 647-3072. Fax, (202) 647-3459. *Carolee Heileman, Director. Web, www.state.gov.*

Includes Andorra, France, Italy, Malta, Monaco, Portugal, Réunion, San Marino, Spain, and the Vatican.

CONGRESS

House International Relations Committee, 2170 RHOB 20515; (202) 225-5021. Fax, (202) 225-2035. *Rep. Benjamin A. Gilman, R-N.Y., Chair; Richard J. Garon Jr., Chief of Staff. General e-mail, HIRC@mail.house.gov. Web, www.house.gov/international_relations.*

Jurisdiction over foreign affairs legislation dealing with Europe. Concurrent jurisdiction over matters assigned to the functional House International Relations subcommittees insofar as they affect the region.

House International Relations Committee, *Subcommittee on the Western Hemisphere,* 2401A RHOB 20515; (202) 226-7820. Fax, (202) 226-2722. *Rep. Elton Gallegly, R-Calif., Chair; Vince Morelli, Staff Director. Web, www. house.gov/international_relations.*

Jurisdiction over foreign affairs legislation dealing with Canada.

Library of Congress, *European Division,* 101 Independence Ave. S.E. 20540-4830; (202) 707-5414. Fax, (202) 707-8482. *John Van Oudenaren, Chief. Reference desk, (202) 707-4515. Web, lcweb.loc.gov/rr/european.*

Provides reference service on the library's European collections (except collections on Spain, Portugal, and the British Isles). Prepares bibliographies and special studies relating to European countries, including Russia and the new independent states. Maintains current unbound Slavic language periodicals and newspapers, which are available at the European Reference Desk.

Senate Foreign Relations Committee, *Subcommittee on European Affairs,* SD-450 20510; (202) 224-4651. Fax, (202) 224-0836. *Sen. Gordon H. Smith, R-Ore., Chair; Beth Stewart, Senior Professional Staff Member. Web, foreign.senate.gov.*

Jurisdiction over foreign affairs legislation dealing with Europe (including Greece and Turkey), the United Kingdom, Greenland, Iceland, the former Soviet Union, and the North Polar region.

Senate Foreign Relations Committee, *Subcommittee on Western Hemisphere, Peace Corps, Narcotics, and Terrorism,* SD-450 20510; (202) 224-4651. Fax, (202) 224-0836. *Sen. Lincoln Chafee, R-R.I., Chair; Roger Noriega, Senior Professional Staff Member. Web, www.senate. gov/~foreign.*

Jurisdiction over foreign affairs legislation dealing with Canada.

INTERNATIONAL ORGANIZATIONS

European Commission, *Press and Public Affairs, Washington Office,* 2300 M St. N.W. 20037; (202) 862-9500. Fax, (202) 429-1766. *Willy Helin, Director; Günter Burghardt, Ambassador. Press, (202) 862-9540. Web, www. europa.eu.int.*

Information and public affairs office in the United States for the European Union, which includes the European Economic Community, the European Coal and Steel Community, and the European Atomic Energy Community. Provides social policy data on the European Union and provides statistics and documents on member countries, including those related to energy, economics, development and cooperation, commerce, agriculture, industry, and technology. Library open to the public by appointment. (Headquarters in Brussels.)

International Bank for Reconstruction and Development, *Europe and Central Asia,* 600 19th St. N.W. 20431 (mailing address: 1818 H St. N.W., #H12211 20433); (202) 458-0602. Fax, (202) 522-2758. *Johannes F. Linn, Vice President.*

Encourages public and private foreign investment in the countries of eastern Europe through loans, loan guarantees, and technical assistance. Finances economic development projects in agriculture, environmental protection, education, energy, public utilities, telecommunications, water supply, sewerage, public health, and other areas.

NONPROFIT

American Bar Assn., *Central and East European Law Initiative,* 740 15th St. N.W., 8th Floor 20005-1022; (202) 662-1950. Fax, (202) 662-1597. *Mark Ellis, Executive*

Director. General e-mail, ceeli@abanet.org. Web, www.abanet.org/ceeli.

Promotes the rule of law and specific legal reforms in the emerging democracies of central and eastern Europe, Russia, and the new independent states; recruits volunteer legal professionals from the United States and western Europe. Interests include civil, criminal, commercial, and environmental law; judicial restructuring; bar development; and legal education and research.

American Czech and Slovak Assn., *8201 16th St., #418, Silver Spring, MD 20910; (301) 650-0612. Fax, (301) 565-3882. Robert J. Miller, President. General e-mail, czechusa@erols.com.*

Seeks to develop U.S.–Czech and Slovak cooperation in the areas of art, business, human rights, rule of law, and international trade. Operates a speakers bureau and awards program; holds biennial convention.

American Hellenic Institute, *1220 16th St. N.W. 20036; (202) 785-8430. Fax, (202) 785-5178. Eugene Rossides, General Counsel. General e-mail, info@ahiworld.org. Web, www.ahiworld.org.*

Works to strengthen trade and commerce between Greece and Cyprus and the United States and within the American Hellenic community.

British-American Business Assn., *P.O. Box 17482 20041; (202) 293-0010. Fax, (202) 296-3332. Courtenay Ellis, President. Web, www.baba-dc.org.*

Membership: organizations dedicated to the development of business relations between the United Kingdom and the United States.

British American Security Information Council, *1900 L St. N.W., #401 20036; (202) 785-1266. Fax, (202) 387-6298. Daniel T. Plesch, Director. Web, www.basicint.org.*

Research organization that analyzes international security policy in Europe and North America. Promotes public awareness of defense and disarmament issues. Monitors and reports on the activities of Congress and the Depts. of State and Defense.

European-American Business Council, *1333 H St. N.W., #630 20005; (202) 347-9292. Fax, (202) 628-5498. Willard M. Berry, President. General e-mail, eabc@eabc.org. Web, www.eabc.org.*

Membership: American companies with operations in Europe and European companies with operations in the United States. Works for free and fair trade and investment between the United States and the European Union.

European Institute, *5225 Wisconsin Ave. N.W., #200 20015-2014; (202) 895-1670. Fax, (202) 362-1088. Jacqueline Grapin, President. Web, www.europeaninstitute.org.*

Membership: governments and multinational corporations. Provides an independent forum for business leaders, government officials, journalists, academics, and policy experts. Organizes seminars and conferences. Interests include international finance, economics, energy, telecommunications, defense and procurement policies, the integration of Central Europe into the European Union and NATO, and relations with Asia and Latin America.

French-American Chamber of Commerce, *1600 K St. N.W., #406 20006; (202) 775-0256. Fax, (202) 785-4604. Chantal Attias, Executive Director. General e-mail, faccwdc@msn.com. Web, www.fachamber.org.*

Membership: small and large enterprises based in France and the United States. Promotes trade and investment between the United States and France. Provides seminars and various cultural events.

German American Business Council, *1524 18th St. N.W., #200 20036; (202) 371-0555. Fax, (202) 408-9369. Leo G. B. Welt, Executive Director.*

Promotes trade, investment, and business relationships between the United States and Germany. Provides seminars and opportunities for members to meet with industry leaders and government officials.

German Marshall Fund of the United States, *11 Dupont Circle N.W. 20036; (202) 745-3950. Fax, (202) 265-1662. Craig Kennedy, President. General e-mail, info@gmfus.org. Web, www.gmfus.org.*

U.S. foundation funded by the Federal Republic of Germany as a memorial to the Marshall Plan. Seeks to strengthen U.S.-European relations; explores changing U.S.-European economic roles; supports reform in central and eastern Europe; builds environmental partnerships; promotes contacts between individuals with similar responsibilities in different countries; awards grants; offers fellowships.

Irish American Unity Conference, *529 14th St. N.W., #837 20045; (202) 662-8830. Fax, (202) 662-8831. James Gallagher, President. Information, (800) 947-4282. General e-mail, iauc@iauc.org. Web, www.iauc.org.*

Nationwide organization that encourages nonviolent means of resolving conflict in Northern Ireland. Conducts symposia and provides information on Northern Ireland. Monitors legislation and regulations.

Irish National Caucus, *413 E. Capitol St. S.E. 20003-3810; (202) 544-0568. Fax, (202) 543-2491. Sean*

McManus, President. General e-mail, inc@knight-hub. com. Web, www.knight-hub.com/inc.

Educational organization concerned with protecting human rights in Northern Ireland. Seeks to end anti-Catholic discrimination in Northern Ireland through implementation of the McBride principles, initiated in 1984. Advocates nonviolence. Monitors legislation and regulations.

Joint Baltic American National Committee, *400 Hurley Ave., Rockville, MD 20850; (301) 340-1954. Fax, (301) 309-1406. Janis Bolsteins, Chair; Karl Altau, Managing Director. General e-mail, jbanc@jbanc.org. Web, www.jbanc.org.*

Washington representative of the Estonian, Latvian, and Lithuanian American communities in the United States; acts as a representative on issues affecting the Baltic states.

National Federation of Croatian Americans, *1329 Connecticut Ave. N.W., #3 20036; (202) 331-2830. Fax, (202) 331-0050. Steve Rukavina, President. General e-mail, NFCAhdq@aol.com.*

Membership: Croatian American organizations. Promotes independence, democracy, human rights, and a free-market economy in Croatia and Bosnia-Herzegovina. Supports equal rights in these countries regardless of ethnicity or religious beliefs.

Latin America, Canada, and the Caribbean

AGENCIES

Agency for International Development, *Latin America and the Caribbean Bureau, 1300 Pennsylvania Ave. N.W., #5.8-A 20523-5900; (202) 712-4800. Fax, (202) 216-3012. Carl H. Leonard, Assistant Administrator (Acting). Web, www.info.usaid.gov.*

Advises AID administrator on U.S. policy toward developing Latin American and Caribbean countries. Designs and implements assistance programs for developing nations.

Defense Dept., *Inter-American Affairs, The Pentagon, #4C800 20301-2500; (703) 697-5884. Fax, (703) 695-8404. Pedro Pablo Permuy, Deputy Assistant Secretary. Web, www.defenselink.mil.*

Advises the assistant secretary for international security affairs on inter-American matters; aids in the development of U.S. policy toward Latin America.

Inter-American Foundation, *901 N. Stuart St., 10th Floor, Arlington, VA 22203; (703) 306-4301. Fax, (703) 306-4365. George A. Evans, President. Web, www.iaf.gov.*

Supports small-scale Latin American and Caribbean social and economic development efforts through grass-roots development programs, grants, and fellowships.

International Trade Administration (*Commerce Dept.*), *NAFTA and Inter-American Affairs, 14th St. and Constitution Ave. N.W., #3022 20230; (202) 482-0393. Fax, (202) 482-5865. Juliet Bender, Director. Web, www. mac.doc.gov/nafta/nafta2.htm.*

Coordinates Commerce Dept. activities regarding NAFTA (North American Free Trade Agreement). Maintains, with Latin America office of International Trade Administration, a fax-on-demand system for information on NAFTA and on doing business in Latin America and the Caribbean, including Haiti.

Panama Canal Commission, *1850 Eye St. N.W., #1030 20006; (202) 634-6441. Fax, (202) 634-6439. William J. Connolly, Deputy Director. Web, www.pananet.com/ pancanal.*

Independent federal agency that manages, operates, and maintains the Panama Canal and its complementary works, installations, and equipment; provides for the orderly transit of vessels through the canal.

State Dept., *Bureau of Western Hemisphere Affairs, 2201 C St. N.W., #6263 20520-6258; (202) 647-5780. Fax, (202) 647-0791. Peter F. Romero, Assistant Secretary (Acting). Web, www.state.gov.*

Advises the secretary on U.S. policy toward Canada, Latin America, and the Caribbean. Directors assigned to specific countries within the bureau aid the assistant secretary.

State Dept., *Andean Affairs, 2201 C St. N.W., #5906 20520-6258; (202) 647-1715. Fax, (202) 647-2628. Phillip Chicola, Director. Web, www.state.gov.*

Includes Bolivia, Colombia, Ecuador, Peru, and Venezuela.

State Dept., *Brazilian, Southern Cone Affairs, 2201 C St. N.W., #5911 20520-6258; (202) 647-2407. Fax, (202) 736-4475. James Curtis Struble, Director. Web, www.state.gov.*

Includes Argentina, Brazil, Chile, Paraguay, and Uruguay.

State Dept., *Canadian Affairs, 2201 C St. N.W., #3917 20520; (202) 647-3135. Fax, (202) 647-4088. Paul J. Saxton, Director. Web, www.state.gov.*

State Dept., *Caribbean Affairs, 2201 C St. N.W., #4908 20520-6258; (202) 647-2620. Fax, (202) 647-4477. Marsha E. Barnes, Director. Web, www.state.gov.*

Includes Anguilla, Antigua and Barbuda, Aruba, Bahamas, Barbados, British Virgin Islands, Cayman

Islands, Dominica, Dominican Republic, Grenada, Guyana, Haiti, Jamaica, Martinique, Montserrat, Netherlands Antilles, St. Kitts and Nevis, St. Lucia, St. Vincent and the Grenadines, Suriname, Trinidad and Tobago, and Turks and Caicos Islands.

State Dept., *Central American Affairs, 2201 C St. N.W., #4915 20520-6258; (202) 647-4010. Fax, (202) 647-2597. John Keane, Director. Web, www.state.gov.*

Includes Belize, Costa Rica, El Salvador, Guatemala, Honduras, Nicaragua, and Panama.

State Dept., *Cuban Affairs, 2201 C St. N.W., #3234 20520-3234; (202) 647-9272. Fax, (202) 736-4476. Charles Shapiro, Director. Web, www.state.gov.*

State Dept., *Mexican Affairs: U.S.-Mexico Border, 2201 C St. N.W., #4258 20520-6258; (202) 647-8529. Fax, (202) 647-5752. David E. Randolph, Coordinator. Web, www.state.gov/www/regions/wha/mexico.html.*

Acts as liaison between the State Dept. and the U.S. section of the International Boundary and Water Commission, United States and Mexico, in international boundary and water matters as defined by binational treaties and agreements.

State Dept., *U.S. Mission to the Organization of American States, 2201 C St. N.W., #6494 20520-6258; (202) 647-9376. Fax, (202) 647-0911. Luis Lauredo, U.S. Permanent Representative. Press, (202) 647-9378. Web, www.state.gov.*

Formulates U.S. policy and represents U.S. interests at the Organization of American States (OAS).

CONGRESS

House International Relations Committee, *Subcommittee on the Western Hemisphere, 2401A RHOB 20515; (202) 226-7820. Fax, (202) 226-2722. Rep. Elton Gallegly, R-Calif., Chair; Vince Morelli, Staff Director. Web, www.house.gov/international_relations.*

Jurisdiction over foreign affairs legislation dealing with Latin America, the Caribbean, Mexico, and Canada. Concurrent jurisdiction over matters assigned to the functional House International Relations subcommittees insofar as they affect the region.

Library of Congress, *Hispanic Division, 101 Independence Ave. S.E., #LJ-240 20540-4850; (202) 707-5400. Fax, (202) 707-2005. Georgette Dorn, Chief. Reference staff and reading room, (202) 707-5397. Web, lcweb.loc.gov/rr/hispanic.*

Reading room staff (in the Hispanic Division Room) orients researchers and scholars in the area of Iberian, Latin American, Caribbean, and U.S. Latino studies. Primary and secondary source materials are available in the library's general collections for the study of all periods, from pre-Columbian to the present. All major subject areas are represented with emphasis on history, literature, and the social sciences; the "Archive of Hispanic Literature on Tape" is available in the reading room.

Senate Foreign Relations Committee, *Subcommittee on Western Hemisphere, Peace Corps, Narcotics, and Terrorism, SD-450 20510; (202) 224-4651. Fax, (202) 224-0836. Sen. Lincoln Chafee, R-R.I., Chair; Roger Noriega, Senior Professional Staff Member. Web, www.senate.gov/~foreign.*

Jurisdiction over foreign affairs legislation dealing with Latin America, the Caribbean, Mexico, and Canada; oversight of all matters of the Peace Corps and the U.S. delegation to the Organization of American States.

INTERNATIONAL ORGANIZATIONS

Inter-American Development Bank, *1300 New York Ave. N.W. 20577; (202) 623-1100. Fax, (202) 623-3096. Enrique V. Iglesias, President; Lawrence Harrington, U.S. Executive Director, (202) 623-1031. Information, (202) 623-1000. Library, (202) 623-3211. Press, (202) 623-1371. Web, www.iadb.org.*

Promotes, through loans and technical assistance, the investment of public and private capital in member countries for social and economic development purposes. Facilitates economic integration of the Latin American region. Library open to the public by appointment.

International Bank for Reconstruction and Development, *Latin America and the Caribbean, 1850 Eye St. N.W. 20433 (mailing address: 1818 H St. N.W. 20433); (202) 473-8729. Fax, (202) 676-9271. David de Ferranti, Vice President.*

Encourages public and private foreign investment in the countries of Latin America and the Caribbean through loans, loan guarantees, and technical assistance. Finances economic development projects in agriculture, environmental protection, education, public utilities, telecommunications, water supply, sewerage, public health, and other areas.

Organization of American States, *17th St. and Constitution Ave. N.W. 20006 (mailing address: 1889 F St. N.W. 20006); (202) 458-3000. Fax, (202) 458-3967. Cesar Gaviria, Secretary General. Information, (202) 458-3756. Library, (202) 458-6037. Web, www.oas.org.*

Membership: the United States, Canada, and all independent Latin American and Caribbean countries. Funded by quotas paid by member states and by contributions to special multilateral funds. Works to promote democracy, eliminate poverty, and resolve disputes among member nations. Provides member states with technical and advisory services in cultural, educational, scientific, social, and economic areas. Library open to the public.

United Nations Economic Commission for Latin America and the Caribbean, *Washington Office, 1825 K St. N.W., #1120 20006; (202) 955-5613. Fax, (202) 296-0826. Inés Bustillo, Director. General e-mail, info@eclac. org. Web, www.eclac.org.*

Membership: Latin American and some industrially developed Western nations. Seeks to strengthen economic relations between countries both within and outside Latin America through research and analysis of socioeconomic problems, training programs, and advisory services to member governments. (Headquarters in Santiago, Chile.)

NONPROFIT

Caribbean/Latin American Action, *1818 N St. N.W., #500 20036; (202) 466-7464. Fax, (202) 822-0075. Donald J. Planty, Executive Director. General e-mail, info@claa. org. Web, www.claa.org.*

Promotes trade and investment in Caribbean Basin countries; encourages democratic public policy in member countries and works to strengthen private initiatives.

Center for International Policy, *1755 Massachusetts Ave. N.W., #312 20036; (202) 232-3317. Fax, (202) 232-3440. William Goodfellow, Executive Director. General e-mail, cip@ciponline.org. Web, www.ciponline.org.*

Research and educational organization concerned with peace and security worldwide. Special interests include military spending, U.S. intelligence policy, and U.S. policy toward Cuba and Haiti. Publishes the *International Policy Report.*

Council of the Americas, Americas Society, *Washington Office, 1310 G St. N.W., #690 20005; (202) 639-0724. Fax, (202) 639-0794. William Price, Managing Director. Web, www.counciloftheamericas.org.*

Membership: businesses with interests and investments in Latin America. Seeks to expand the role of private enterprise in development of the region. (Headquarters in New York.)

Council on Hemispheric Affairs, *1444 Eye St. N.W., #211 20005; (202) 216-9261. Fax, (202) 216-9193. Laurence R. Birns, Director. General e-mail, coha@coha.org. Web, www.coha.org.*

Seeks to expand interest in Inter-American relations and increase press coverage of Latin America and

Canada. Monitors U.S., Latin American, and Canadian relations, with emphasis on human rights, trade, growth of democratic institutions, freedom of the press, and hemispheric economic and political developments; provides educational materials and analyzes issues. Issues annual survey on human rights and freedom of the press.

Cuban American National Foundation, *Washington Office, 1000 Thomas Jefferson St. N.W., #505 20007; (202) 265-2822. Fax, (202) 338-0308. Jose Cardenas, Director. General e-mail, canfnet@icanect.net. Web, www.canfnet.org.*

Conducts research and provides information on Cuba; supports the establishment of a democratic government in Cuba. Library open to the public by appointment. (Headquarters in Miami.)

Guatemala Human Rights Commission/USA, *3321 12th St. N.E. 20017-4008; (202) 529-6599. Fax, (202) 526-4611. Alice Zachmann, Coordinator. General e-mail, ghrc-usa@ghrc-usa.org.*

Provides information and collects and makes available reports on human rights violations in Guatemala; publishes a biweekly report of documented cases of specific abuses and a quarterly bulletin of human rights news and analysis. Takes on special projects to further sensitize the public and the international community to human rights abuses in Guatemala.

Inter-American Dialogue, *1211 Connecticut Ave. N.W., #510 20036-2701; (202) 822-9002. Fax, (202) 822-9553. Peter Hakim, President. General e-mail, iad@thedialogue. org. Web, www.thedialogue.org.*

Serves as a forum for communication and exchange among leaders of the Americas. Provides analyses and policy recommendations on issues of hemispheric concern. Interests include economic integration and the strengthening of democracy in Latin America. Sponsors conferences and seminars.

Network in Solidarity with the People of Guatemala, *1830 Connecticut Ave. N.W. 20009; (202) 518-7638. Fax, (202) 223-8221. Christine Keith, Executive Director. General e-mail, nisgua@igc.org. Web, www. nisgua.org.*

Membership: organizations interested in promoting social justice and human rights in Central America. Opposes U.S. intervention in Central America; seeks to inform the public about human rights and U.S. policy in Guatemala.

Pan American Development Foundation, *2600 16th St. N.W., 4th Floor 20009-4202; (202) 458-3969. Fax, (202) 458-6316. John Sambrailo, Executive Director.*

Works with the public and private sectors to improve the quality of life throughout the Caribbean and Latin America. Associated with the Organization of American States (OAS).

Partners of the Americas, *1424 K St. N.W., #700 20005; (202) 628-3300. Fax, (202) 628-3306. Norman Brown, President, (202) 637-6202. Web, www.partners.net.*

Membership: individuals in the United States, Latin America, and the Caribbean. Sponsors technical assistance projects and exchanges between the United States, Latin America, and the Caribbean; supports self-help projects in agriculture, public health, education, and democratic participation.

Religious Task Force on Central America and Mexico, *3053 4th St. N.E. 20017; (202) 529-0441. Margaret Swedish, Director. General e-mail, rtfca@igc.org. Web, www.igc.org/rtfcam.*

Network of religious-based organizations and individuals concerned about Central America and Mexico. Provides information and promotes human rights and social justice in the region.

U.S.-Mexico Chamber of Commerce, *1300 Pennsylvania Ave. N.W., #270 20004-3021; (202) 371-8680. Fax, (202) 371-8686. Albert C. Zapanta, President. Web, www. usmcoc.org.*

Promotes trade and investment between the United States and Mexico. Provides members with information and expertise on conducting business between the two countries. Serves as a clearinghouse for information.

Washington Office on Latin America, *1630 Connecticut Ave. N.W., #200 20009; (202) 797-2171. Fax, (202) 797-2172. George Vickers, Director. General e-mail, wola@ wola.org. Web, www.wola.org.*

Acts as a liaison between government policymakers and groups and individuals concerned with human rights and U.S. policy in Latin America. Serves as an information resource center; monitors legislation.

Near East and South Asia

(Includes North Africa)

AGENCIES

Agency for International Development, *Asia and Near East Bureau, 1300 Pennsylvania Ave. N.W., #4.09-034 20523-4900; (202) 712-0200. Fax, (202) 216-3386. Robert C. Randolph, Assistant Administrator. General e-mail, rrandolph@usaid.gov. Web, www.info.usaid.gov.*

Advises AID administrator on U.S. economic development policy in Asia and the Near East.

Defense Dept., *Near East and South Asia Affairs, The Pentagon, #4D765 20301; (703) 697-5146. Fax, (703) 693-6795. Alina Romanowski, Deputy Assistant Secretary. Web, www.defenselink.mil.*

Advises the assistant secretary for international security affairs on matters dealing with the Near East and South Asia.

State Dept., *Bureau of Near Eastern Affairs, 2201 C St. N.W., #6241 20520-6243; (202) 647-7209. Fax, (202) 736-4462. Edward S. Walker Jr., Assistant Secretary. Information, (202) 647-5150. Web, www.state.gov.*

Advises the secretary on U.S. policy toward countries of the Near East and North Africa. Directors, assigned to specific countries within the bureau, aid the assistant secretary.

State Dept., *Bureau of South Asian Affairs, 2201 C St. N.W., #6254 20520-6258; (202) 736-4325. Fax, (202) 736-4333. Karl F. Inderfurth, Assistant Secretary. Information, (202) 736-4255. Web, www.state.gov.*

Advises the secretary on U.S. policy toward South Asian countries. Directors, assigned to specific countries within the bureau, aid the assistant secretary.

State Dept., *Arabian Peninsula Affairs, 2201 C St. N.W., #4224 20520-6243; (202) 647-6184. Fax, (202) 736-4459. Allen Keiswetter, Director. Web, www.state.gov.*

Includes Bahrain, Kuwait, Oman, Qatar, Saudi Arabia, United Arab Emirates, and Yemen.

State Dept., *Egyptian and North African Affairs, 2201 C St. N.W., #5250A 20520-6243; (202) 647-2300. Fax, (202) 647-4458. Ronald L. Schlicher, Director. Web, www.state.gov.*

Includes Algeria, Egypt, Libya, Morocco, and Tunisia.

State Dept., *India, Nepal, Sri Lanka Affairs, 2201 C St. N.W., #5251 20520-6243; (202) 647-2141. Fax, (202) 736-4463. Gary S. Usrey, Director. Web, www.state.gov.*

Includes Bhutan, India, Maldives, Nepal, and Sri Lanka.

State Dept., *Israel and Arab-Israeli Affairs, 2201 C St. N.W., #6251 20520; (202) 647-3672. Fax, (202) 736-4461. Jacob Walles, Director. Web, www.state.gov.*

State Dept., *Lebanon, Jordan, Palestine, and Syria Affairs, 2201 C St. N.W., #6250 20520-6243; (202) 647-2670. Fax, (202) 647-0989. Sharon Wiener, Director. Web, www.state.gov.*

State Dept., *Northern Gulf Affairs, 2201 C St. N.W., #4515 20520; (202) 647-5692. Fax, (202) 736-4464. Philo Dibble, Director. Web, www.state.gov.*

Includes Iran and Iraq.

State Dept., *Pakistan, Afghanistan, and Bangladesh Affairs,* 2201 C St. N.W., #5247 20520-6258; (202) 647-7593. Fax, (202) 647-3001. Jeffrey Lunstead, Director. Web, www.state.gov.

CONGRESS

House International Relations Committee, *Subcommittee on Asia and the Pacific,* B-359 RHOB 20515; (202) 226-7825. Fax, (202) 226-7829. Rep. Doug Bereuter, R-Neb., Chair; Michael Ennis, Staff Director. Web, www.house.gov/international_relations.

Jurisdiction over foreign affairs legislation dealing with East Asia and the Pacific, the Near East, and South Asia, from Afghanistan to the Far East. Concurrent jurisdiction over matters assigned to the functional House International Relations subcommittees insofar as they affect the region.

Library of Congress, *African and Middle Eastern Division,* 110 2nd St. S.E., #220 20540; (202) 707-7937. Fax, (202) 252-3180. Beverly Gray, Chief.

Maintains collections of African, Near Eastern, and Hebraic material. Prepares bibliographies and special studies relating to Africa and the Middle East. Reference service and reading rooms available to the public.

Library of Congress, *Asian Division,* 110 2nd St. S.E., #LJ150 20540-4810; (202) 707-5420. Fax, (202) 707-1724. Mya Thanda Poe, Chief.

Maintains collections of Chinese, Korean, Japanese, Southeast Asian, and South Asian material covering all subjects except law, technical agriculture, and clinical medicine. Reference service is provided in the Asian Reading Room.

Senate Foreign Relations Committee, *Subcommittee on Near Eastern and South Asian Affairs,* SD-450 20510; (202) 224-4651. Fax, (202) 224-0836. Sen. Sam Brownback, R-Kan., Chair; Danielle Pletka, Senior Professional Staff Member. Web, foreign.senate.gov.

Jurisdiction over foreign affairs legislation dealing with the Near East and South Asia, including the Arab states and Israel, Bhutan, Bangladesh, India, Pakistan, Afghanistan, Nepal, Sri Lanka, and across North Africa from Egypt to Morocco.

INTERNATIONAL ORGANIZATIONS

International Bank for Reconstruction and Development, *Middle East and North Africa,* 600 19th St. N.W. 20433 (mailing address: 1818 H St. N.W., #H10-211 20433); (202) 473-2776. Fax, (202) 477-0810. Kemal Dervis, Vice President.

Encourages public and private foreign investment in the countries of the Middle East and North Africa

through loans, loan guarantees, and technical assistance. Finances economic development projects in agriculture, education, public utilities, telecommunications, water supply, sewerage, and other areas.

International Bank for Reconstruction and Development, *South Asia,* 1818 H St. N.W., MC10-829 20433; (202) 458-0600. Fax, (202) 522-3707. Mieko Nishimizu, Vice President.

Encourages public and private foreign investment in the countries of South Asia through loans, loan guarantees, and technical assistance. Finances economic development projects in agriculture, environmental protection, education, public utilities, telecommunications, water supply, sewerage, public health, and other areas.

League of Arab States, *Washington Office,* 1100 17th St. N.W., #602 20036; (202) 265-3210. Fax, (202) 331-1525. Khalid M. Abdalla, Director.

Membership: Arab countries in the Near East, North Africa, and the Indian Ocean. Coordinates members' policies in political, cultural, economic, and social affairs; mediates disputes among members and between members and third parties. Washington office maintains the Arab Information Center. (Headquarters in Cairo.)

NONPROFIT

American Israel Public Affairs Committee, 440 1st St. N.W., #600 20001; (202) 639-5200. Fax, (202) 347-4889. Howard Kohr, Executive Director. General e-mail, help@aipac.org. Web, www.aipac.org.

Works to maintain and improve relations between the United States and Israel.

American Jewish Congress, *Washington Office,* 2027 Massachusetts Ave. N.W. 20036; (202) 332-4001. Fax, (202) 387-3434. Matt Dorf, Washington Representative. General e-mail, washrep@ajcongress.org. Web, www.ajcongress.org.

National Jewish organization that advocates the maintenance and improvement of U.S.-Israeli relations through legislation, public education, and joint economic ventures. Interests include the Arab boycott of Israel and foreign investment in the United States. (Headquarters in New York.)

American Kurdish Information Network, 2600 Connecticut Ave. N.W., #1 20008-1558; (202) 483-6444. Fax, (202) 483-6476. Kani Xulam, Director. General e-mail, akin@kurdish.org. Web, www.kurdistan.org.

Membership: Americans of Kurdish origin, recent Kurdish immigrants and refugees, and others. Collects and disseminates information about the Kurds, an ethnic group living in parts of Turkey, Iran, Iraq, and Syria. Monitors human rights abuses against Kurds; promotes self-determination in Kurdish homelands; fosters Kurdish American friendship and understanding.

American Near East Refugee Aid, *1522 K St. N.W., #202 20005-1270; (202) 347-2558. Fax, (202) 682-1637. Peter Gubser, President. General e-mail, anera@mail. anera.org. Web, www.anera.org.*

Assists Palestinian and Lebanese grassroots organizations in providing their communities with health and welfare services, employment, and educational opportunities. Provides relief in response to civilian emergencies. (Field offices in Jerusalem and Gaza.)

AMIDEAST, *1730 M St. N.W., #1100 20036; (202) 776-9600. Fax, (202) 776-7000. William Rugh, President. Web, www.amideast.org.*

Promotes understanding and cooperation between Americans and the people of the Middle East and North Africa through education, information, and development programs. Produces educational material to help improve teaching about the Arab world in American schools and colleges.

Asia Foundation, *Washington Office, 1779 Massachusetts Ave. N.W., #815 20036; (202) 588-9420. Fax, (202) 588-9409. Nancy Yuan, Director. Web, www.asiafoundation. org.*

Provides grants and technical assistance in Asia and the Pacific islands (excluding the Middle East). Seeks to strengthen legislatures, legal and judicial systems, market economies, the media, and nongovernmental organizations. (Headquarters in San Francisco.)

Asia Society, *Washington Office, 1800 K St. N.W., #1102 20006; (202) 833-2742. Fax, (202) 833-0189. Judith Sloan, Director. Web, www.asiasociety.org.*

Membership: individuals interested in Asia and the Pacific (excluding the Middle East). Sponsors seminars and lectures on political, economic, and cultural issues. (Headquarters in New York.)

Center for Contemporary Arab Studies *(Georgetown University), 241 Intercultural Center 20057-1020; (202) 687-5793. Fax, (202) 687-7001. Michael C. Hudson, Director. General e-mail, ccasinfo@gunet.georgetown.edu. Web, www.georgetown.edu/sfs/programs/ccas.*

Sponsors lecture series, seminars, and conferences. Conducts a community outreach program which assists secondary school teachers in the development of instructional materials on the Middle East; promotes the study of the Arabic language in area schools.

Center for Middle East Peace and Economic Cooperation, *633 Pennsylvania Ave. N.W. 20004; (202) 624-0850. Fax, (202) 624-0855. S. Daniel Abraham, Chair. General e-mail, sahana@centerpeace.org. Web, www. centerpeace.org.*

Membership: Middle Eastern policymakers, American government officials, and international business leaders. Serves as a mediator to encourage a peaceful resolution to the Arab-Israeli conflict; sponsors travel to the region, diplomatic exchanges, and conferences for Middle Eastern and American leaders interested in the peace process.

Council on American-Islamic Relations, *453 New Jersey Ave. S.E. 20003; (202) 659-2247. Fax, (202) 659-2254. Nihad Awad, Executive Director. General e-mail, cair1@ ix.netcom.com. Web, www.cair-net.org.*

Promotes an Islamic perspective on issues of importance to the American public. Seeks to empower the Muslim community in America through political and social activism.

Foundation for Middle East Peace, *1761 N St. N.W. 20036; (202) 835-3650. Fax, (202) 835-3651. Lucius D. Battle, President; Jean Newsom, Executive Director. General e-mail, info@fmep.org. Web, www.fmep.org.*

Educational organization that seeks to promote understanding and resolution of the Israeli-Palestinian conflict. Publishes a bimonthly report, *Israeli Settlement in the Occupied Territories*; provides media with information.

Institute for Palestine Studies, *Washington Office, 3501 M St. N.W. 20007-2624; (202) 342-3990. Fax, (202) 342-3927. Philip Mattar, Executive Director. General e-mail, jps@ipsjps.org. Web, www.ipsjps.org.*

Scholarly research institute that specializes in the history and development of the Palestine problem, the Arab-Israeli conflict, and their peaceful resolution. (Headquarters in Beirut, Lebanon.)

Institute of Turkish Studies *(Georgetown University), Intercultural Center, Box 571033 20057-1033; (202) 687-0295. Fax, (202) 687-3780. Sabri Sayari, Executive Director. Web, www.turkishstudies.org.*

Supports and encourages the development of Turkish studies in American colleges and universities. Awards grants to individual scholars and educational institutions in the United States.

Kashmiri-American Council, *733 15th St. N.W., #1100 20005; (202) 628-6789. Fax, (202) 393-0062. Ghulam Nabi Fai, Executive Director. Web, www.erols.com/gfai.*

Promotes self-determination for Jammu and Kashmir, a region claimed by both India and Pakistan; monitors human rights violations in the region; fosters unity and social interaction among people of Kashmiri ancestry, regardless of religious or political affiliations.

Middle East Institute, *1761 N St. N.W. 20036-2882; (202) 785-1141. Fax, (202) 331-8861. Roscoe Suddarth, President. Library, (202) 785-0183. Language Dept., (202) 785-2710. General e-mail, mei@mideasti.org. Web, www. mideasti.org/mei.*

Membership: individuals interested in the Middle East. Seeks to broaden knowledge of the Middle East through research, conferences and seminars, language classes, lectures, and exhibits. Library open to the public.

Middle East Policy Council, *1730 M St. N.W., #512 20036-4505; (202) 296-6767. Fax, (202) 296-5791. Charles W. Freeman Jr., President. General e-mail, info@ mepc.org. Web, www.mepc.org.*

Encourages public discussion and understanding of issues affecting U.S. policy in the Middle East. Sponsors conferences for the policy community; conducts workshops for high school teachers nationwide.

Middle East Research and Information Project, *1500 Massachusetts Ave. N.W., #119 20005; (202) 223-3677. Fax, (202) 223-3604. Terry Walz, Executive Director. General e-mail, merip@merip.org. Web, www.merip.org.*

Works to educate the public about the contemporary Middle East. Focuses on U.S. policy in the region and issues of human rights and social justice.

National Council on U.S.-Arab Relations, *1140 Connecticut Ave. N.W., #1210 20036; (202) 293-0801. Fax, (202) 293-0903. John Duke Anthony, President. General e-mail, info@ncusar.org. Web, www.ncusar.org.*

Educational organization that works to improve mutual understanding between the United States and the Arab world. Serves as a clearinghouse on Arab issues and maintains speakers bureau. Coordinates trips for U.S. professionals and congressional delegations to the Arab world.

National U.S.-Arab Chamber of Commerce, *1100 New York Ave. N.W., #550, E. Tower 20005; (202) 289-5920. Fax, (202) 289-5938. Richard Holmes, President. Web, www.nusacc.org.*

Promotes trade between the United States and the Arab world. Offers members informational publications, research and certification services, and opportunities to meet with international delegations.

New Israel Fund, *1625 K St. N.W., #500 20006-1604; (202) 223-3333. Fax, (202) 659-2789. Norman Rosenberg, Executive Director. General e-mail, info@nif.org. Web, www.nif.org.*

International philanthropic partnership of North Americans, Israelis, and Europeans. Supports activities that defend civil and human rights, promote Jewish-Arab equality and coexistence, advance the status of women, nurture tolerance, bridge social and economic gaps, encourage government accountability, and assist citizen efforts to protect the environment. Makes grants and provides capacity-building assistance to Israeli public interest groups; trains civil rights and environmental lawyers.

United Palestinian Appeal, *2100 M St. N.W., #409 20037; (202) 659-5007. Fax, (202) 296-0224. Makboula Yasin, Deputy Director. General e-mail, upa@cais.com. Web, www.helpupa.com.*

Charitable organization dedicated to improving the quality of life for Palestinians in the Middle East, particularly those in the West Bank, the Gaza Strip, and refugee camps. Provides funding for community development projects, health care, education, children's services, and emergency relief. Funded by private donations from individuals and foundations in the United States and Arab world.

Washington Institute for Near East Policy, *1828 L St. N.W., #1050 20036; (202) 452-0650. Fax, (202) 223-5364. Robert Satloff, Executive Director. General e-mail, info@washingtoninstitute.org. Web, www. washingtoninstitute.org.*

Research and educational organization that seeks to improve the effectiveness of American policy in the Near East by promoting debate among policymakers, journalists, and scholars.

Russia and New Independent States

For the Baltic states, see Europe

AGENCIES

Agency for International Development, *Europe and Eurasia Bureau, 1300 Pennsylvania Ave. N.W., #5.06 20523-5600; (202) 712-5123. Fax, (202) 216-3057. Donald Pressley, Assistant Administrator. Web, www.info. usaid.gov.*

Advises AID administrator on U.S. economic development policy in Europe and the new independent states.

Kennan Institute for Advanced Russian Studies, *1300 Pennsylvania Ave. N.W. 20004-3027; (202) 691-4100. Fax, (202) 691-4247. Blair A. Ruble, Director. General e-mail, kiars@wwics.si.edu. Web, wwics.si.edu/ PROGRAMS/REGION/KENNAN/KENMAIN.HTM.*

Offers residential research scholarships to academic scholars and to specialists from government, media, and the private sector for studies to improve American knowledge about Russia and the former Soviet Union. Sponsors lectures; publishes reports; promotes dialogue between academic specialists and policymakers. (Affiliated with the Woodrow Wilson International Center for Scholars.)

State Dept., *Ambassador-at-Large (NIS)*, 2201 C St. N.W., #7531 20520-7512; (202) 647-3112. Fax, (202) 647-2699. Stephen R. Sestanovich, Ambassador-at-Large. Web, www.state.gov.

Handles relations with Russia and other countries of the former Soviet Union, except the Baltic states; assists other agencies in dealings with the new independent states. Directors, assigned to specific countries, aid the ambassador-at-large.

State Dept., *Caucasus and Central Eurasian Affairs*, 2201 C St. N.W., #4217 20520-7512; (202) 647-9370. Fax, (202) 736-4710. Clifford Bond, Director. Web, www.state.gov.

Includes Armenia, Azerbaijan, Georgia, and other newly independent states.

State Dept., *Russian Affairs*, 2201 C St. N.W., #4223 20520-7512; (202) 647-9806. Fax, (202) 647-3506. David A. Russell, Director. Web, www.state.gov.

State Dept., *Western Slavic and Moldovan Affairs*, 2201 C St. N.W., #4225 20520-7512; (202) 647-8671. Fax, (202) 647-3506. Mary Warlick, Director. Web, www.state.gov.

Includes Belarus, Moldova, and Ukraine.

CONGRESS

House International Relations Committee, 2170 RHOB 20515; (202) 225-5021. Fax, (202) 225-2035. Rep. Benjamin A. Gilman, R-N.Y., Chair; Richard J. Garon Jr., Chief of Staff. General e-mail, HIRC@mail.house.gov. Web, www.house.gov/international_relations.

Jurisdiction over legislation dealing with Russia and the new independent states. Concurrent jurisdiction over matters assigned to the functional House International Relations subcommittees insofar as they affect the region.

Library of Congress, *European Division*, 101 Independence Ave. S.E. 20540-4830; (202) 707-5414. Fax, (202) 707-8482. John Van Oudenaren, Chief. Reference desk, (202) 707-4515. Web, lcweb.loc.gov/rr/european.

Provides reference service on the library's European collections (except collections on Spain, Portugal, and the British Isles). Prepares bibliographies and special studies relating to European countries, including Russia and the new independent states. Maintains current unbound Slavic language periodicals and newspapers, which are available at the European Reference Desk.

Senate Foreign Relations Committee, SD-450 20510; (202) 224-4651. Fax, (202) 224-0836. Sen. Jesse Helms, R-N.C., Chair; Steve Biegun, Staff Director. Web, foreign.senate.gov.

Jurisdiction over legislation dealing with Russia and the new independent states. Concurrent jurisdiction over matters assigned to the functional Senate Foreign Relations subcommittees insofar as they affect the region.

INTERNATIONAL ORGANIZATIONS

International Bank for Reconstruction and Development, *Europe and Central Asia*, 600 19th St. N.W. 20431 (mailing address: 1818 H St. N.W., #H12211 20433); (202) 458-0602. Fax, (202) 522-2758. Johannes F. Linn, Vice President.

Encourages public and private foreign investment in eastern Europe and central Asia, including the former Soviet Union, through loans, loan guarantees, and technical assistance. Finances economic development projects in agriculture, environmental protection, education, energy, public utilities, telecommunications, water supply, sewerage, public health, and other areas.

NONPROFIT

American Bar Assn., *Central and East European Law Initiative*, 740 15th St. N.W., 8th Floor 20005-1022; (202) 662-1950. Fax, (202) 662-1597. Mark Ellis, Executive Director. General e-mail, ceeli@abanet.org. Web, www.abanet.org/ceeli.

Promotes the rule of law and specific legal reforms in the emerging democracies of central and eastern Europe, Russia, and the new independent states; recruits volunteer legal professionals from the United States and western Europe. Interests include civil, criminal, commercial, and environmental law; judicial restructuring; bar development; and legal education and research.

American Councils for International Education, *American Council of Teachers of Russian*, 1776 Massachusetts Ave. N.W., #700 20036; (202) 833-7522. Fax, (202) 833-7523. Dan Davidson, President. General e-mail, general@actr.org. Web, www.actr.org.

Conducts educational exchanges for high school, university, and graduate school students as well as scholars with the countries of the former Soviet Union and Eastern Europe. Assists the countries of the former Soviet Union in implementing education reforms, advises them on academic testing, and provides them with language instruction materials.

Armenian Assembly of America, *122 C St. N.W., #350 20001; (202) 393-3434. Fax, (202) 638-4904. Ross Vartian, Executive Director. Web, www.aaainc.org.*

Promotes public understanding and awareness of Armenian issues; advances research and data collection and disseminates information on the Armenian people; advocates greater Armenian American participation in the American democratic process; works to alleviate human suffering of Armenians.

Eurasia Foundation, *1350 Connecticut Ave. N.W., #1000 20036; (202) 234-7370. Fax, (202) 234-7377. Charles Williams Maynes, President. General e-mail, eurasia@ eurasia.org. Web, www.eurasia.org.*

Grant-making organization that funds programs that build democratic and free market institutions in the new independent states. Interests include economic and governmental reform, development of the nonprofit sector, and projects in media and communications.

Free Congress Research and Education Foundation, *717 2nd St. N.E. 20002-4368; (202) 546-3000. Fax, (202) 543-5605. Paul M. Weyrich, President. General e-mail, info@freecongress.org. Web, www.freecongress.org.*

Public policy research and education foundation. Through the Krieble Institute, provides citizens of the former Soviet bloc with training in democratic processes and free enterprise.

Institute for European, Russian, and Eurasian Studies *(George Washington University), 2013 G St. N.W., #401 20052; (202) 994-6340. Fax, (202) 994-5436. James Goldgeier, Director (Acting).*

Studies and researches European, Russian, and Eurasian affairs. Sino-Soviet Information Center open to the public.

ISAR: Initiative for Social Action and Renewal in Eurasia, *1601 Connecticut Ave. N.W., #301 20009; (202) 387-3034. Fax, (202) 667-3291. Eliza K. Klose, Executive Director. Web, www.isar.org.*

Encourages cooperation between America and the former Soviet Union. Operates an information clearinghouse on issues such as agriculture and the environment. Library open to the public.

Jamestown Foundation, *1528 18th St. N.W. 20036; (202) 483-8888. Fax, (202) 483-8337. William Geimer, President. Web, www.jamestown.org.*

Monitors the development of the republics of the former Soviet Union. Provides information on trends in

Russia that affect U.S. interests; sponsors conferences; promotes development of democracy and free enterprise.

National Conference on Soviet Jewry, *1640 Rhode Island Ave. N.W., #501 20036; (202) 898-2500. Fax, (202) 898-0822. Mark B. Levin, Executive Director. General e-mail, ncsj@ncsj.org. Web, www.ncsj.org.*

Membership: national Jewish organizations and local federations. Coordinates efforts by members to aid Jews in the former Soviet Union, including Jewish families attempting to emigrate.

Ukrainian National Information Service, *Washington Office, 311 Massachusetts Ave. N.E. 20002; (202) 547-0018. Fax, (202) 543-5502. Michael Sawkiw, Director. General e-mail, unis@worldnet.att.net. Web, www.ucca. org.*

Information bureau of the Ukrainian Congress Committee of America in New York. Provides information and monitors U.S. policy on Ukraine and the Ukrainian community in the United States and abroad. (Headquarters in New York.)

U.S.-Russia Business Council, *1701 Pennsylvania Ave. N.W., #520 20006; (202) 739-9180. Fax, (202) 659-5920. Eugene K. Lawson, President. Press, (202) 739-9184.*

Membership: U.S. companies involved in trade and investment in Russia. Promotes commercial ties between the United States and Russia.

U.S. Territories and Associated States

AGENCIES

Interior Dept., *Insular Affairs, 1849 C St. N.W., #4311, Mail Drop 4328 20240; (202) 208-4736. Fax, (202) 501-7759. Danny Aranza, Director. Web, www.doi.gov.*

Promotes economic, social, and political development of U.S. territories (Guam, American Samoa, the Virgin Islands, and the Commonwealth of the Northern Mariana Islands). Supervises federal programs for the freely associated states (Federated States of Micronesia, Republic of the Marshall Islands, and Republic of Palau).

CONGRESS

American Samoa's Delegate to Congress, *2422 RHOB 20515; (202) 225-8577. Fax, (202) 225-8757. Del. Eni F. H. Faleomavaega, D-Am. Samoa, Delegate.*

Represents American Samoa in Congress.

Guam's Delegate to Congress, *2418 RHOB 20515; (202) 225-1188. Fax, (202) 226-0341. Del. Robert A. Underwood, D-Guam, Delegate.*

Represents Guam in Congress.

House Appropriations Committee, *Subcommittee on Interior, B308 RHOB 20515; (202) 225-3081. Fax, (202) 225-9069. Rep. Ralph Regula, R-Ohio, Chair; Deborah A. Weatherly, Clerk. Web, www.house.gov/appropriations.*

Jurisdiction over legislation to appropriate funds for territorial affairs.

House Resources Committee, *1324 LHOB 20515-6201; (202) 225-2761. Fax, (202) 225-5929. Rep. Don Young, R-Alaska, Chair; Lloyd Jones, Staff Director. General e-mail, resources.committee@mail.house.gov. Web, www.house.gov/resources.*

Jurisdiction, oversight, and investigative authority over activities, policies, and programs for U.S. territories (Guam, American Samoa, Puerto Rico, the Northern Mariana Islands, and the Virgin Islands) and for the freely associated states (Federated States of Micronesia, Republic of the Marshall Islands, Republic of Palau).

Puerto Rican Resident Commissioner, *2443 RHOB 20515; (202) 225-2615. Fax, (202) 225-2154. Del. Carlos A. Romero-Barceló, D-P.R., Resident Commissioner.*

Represents the Commonwealth of Puerto Rico in Congress.

Senate Appropriations Committee, *Subcommittee on Interior, SD-131 20510; (202) 224-7233. Sen. Slade Gorton, R-Wash., Chair; Bruce Evans, Clerk. Web, appropriations.senate.gov/interior.*

Jurisdiction over legislation to appropriate funds for territorial and Pacific island affairs.

Senate Energy and Natural Resources Committee, *SD-364 20510; (202) 224-4971. Fax, (202) 224-6163. Sen.*

Frank H. Murkowski, R-Alaska, Chair; Andrew Lundquist, Staff Director. General e-mail, committee@energy.senate.gov. Web, energy.senate.gov.

Jurisdiction, oversight, and investigative authority over activities, policies, and programs for U.S. territories (Guam, American Samoa, Puerto Rico, the Northern Mariana Islands, and the Virgin Islands) and for the freely associated states (Federated States of Micronesia, Republic of the Marshall Islands, and Republic of Palau).

Virgin Islands Delegate to Congress, *1711 LHOB 20515; (202) 225-1790. Fax, (202) 225-5517. Del. Donna M. C. Christensen, D-Virgin Is., Delegate.*

Represents the Virgin Islands in Congress.

NONPROFIT

Puerto Rico Federal Affairs Administration, *1100 17th St. N.W., #800 20036; (202) 778-0710. Fax, (202) 778-0721. Alcides Ortiz, Director. Web, www.prfaa.com.*

Represents the governor and the government of the Commonwealth of Puerto Rico before Congress and the executive branch; conducts research; serves as official press information center for the Commonwealth of Puerto Rico. Monitors legislation and regulations.

U.S. Virgin Islands Department of Tourism, *Washington Office, 444 N. Capitol St. N.W., #298 20001; (202) 624-3590. Fax, (202) 624-3594. Nicholas Berry, Regional Manager. Web, www.usvi.net.*

Provides information about the U.S. Virgin Islands; promotes tourism. (Headquarters in St. Thomas.)

14 ⚖

Law and Justice

⚖ GENERAL POLICY

See also Public Interest Law (chap. 1)

AGENCIES

Executive Office for U.S. Attorneys *(Justice Dept.),* *950 Pennsylvania Ave. N.W., #2244 20530; (202) 514-2121. Fax, (202) 616-2278. Mary H. Murguia, Director. Information, (202) 514-1020. Web, www.usdoj.gov/usao/eousa.*

Provides the offices of U.S. attorneys with technical assistance and supervision in areas of legal counsel, personnel, and training. Publishes the *U.S. Attorneys' Manual.* Administers the Attorney General's Advocacy Institute, which conducts workshops and seminars to develop the litigation skills of the department's attorneys in criminal and civil trials. Develops and implements Justice Dept. procedures and policy for collecting criminal fines.

Justice Dept., *950 Pennsylvania Ave. N.W., #5111 20530-0001; (202) 514-2001. Fax, (202) 307-6777. Janet Reno, Attorney General; Eric H. Holder Jr., Deputy Attorney General, (202) 514-2101. Information, (202) 514-2000. Web, www.usdoj.gov.*

Investigates and prosecutes violations of federal laws; represents the government in federal cases and interprets laws under which other departments act. Supervises federal corrections system; administers immigration and naturalization laws. Justice Dept. organization includes divisions on antitrust, civil law, civil rights, criminal law, environment and natural resources, and tax, as well as the Federal Bureau of Investigation, Federal Bureau of Prisons, Office of Legal Counsel, Office of Policy Development, Office of Professional Responsibility, U.S. Parole Commission, Immigration and Naturalization Service, Board of Immigration Appeals, Executive Office for Immigration Review, Drug Enforcement Administration, Foreign Claims Settlement Commission of the United States, Office of Justice Programs, U.S. Marshals Service, and U.S. Trustees.

Justice Dept., *Policy Development, 950 Pennsylvania Ave. N.W., #4234 20530; (202) 514-4601. Fax, (202) 514-2424. Eleanor Dean Acheson, Assistant Attorney General. Web, www.usdoj.gov.*

Studies, develops, and coordinates Justice Dept. policy. Drafts and reviews legislative proposals. Oversees implementation of the Freedom of Information and Privacy acts.

Justice Dept., *Professional Responsibility, 950 Pennsylvania Ave. N.W., #4304 20530; (202) 514-3365. Fax, (202)*

514-4371. H. Marshall Jarrett, Counsel. Web, www.usdoj.gov.

Receives and reviews allegations of misconduct by Justice Dept. employees; refers cases that warrant further review to appropriate investigative agency or unit; makes recommendations to the attorney general for action on certain misconduct cases.

Justice Dept., *Solicitor General, 950 Pennsylvania Ave. N.W., #5712 20530; (202) 514-2201. Fax, (202) 514-9769. Seth P. Waxman, Solicitor General. Information on pending cases, (202) 514-2218. Web, www.usdoj.gov/osg.*

Represents the federal government before the Supreme Court of the United States.

Office of Justice Programs *(Justice Dept.), 810 7th St. N.W. 20531; (202) 307-5933. Fax, (202) 514-7805. Mary Lou Leary, Assistant Attorney General (Acting). Web, www.ojp.usdoj.gov.*

Sets program policy, provides staff support, and coordinates administration for the National Institute of Justice, which conducts research on criminal justice; the Bureau of Justice Statistics, which gathers and evaluates national crime data; the Office for Victims of Crime, which funds state victim compensation and assistance programs; the Office of Juvenile Justice and Delinquency Prevention, which administers federal juvenile delinquency programs; and the Bureau of Justice Assistance, which provides funds for anticrime programs.

State Justice Institute, *1650 King St., #600, Alexandria, VA 22314; (703) 684-6100. Fax, (703) 684-7618. David I. Tevelin, Executive Director. Web, www.statejustice.org.*

Quasi-governmental corporation established by Congress. Awards grants to state courts and to state agencies working to improve judicial administration in the state courts. Interests include judicial education, court technology, victim assistance, prevention of violence against women, and federal-state relations.

CONGRESS

General Accounting Office, *General Government, 441 G St. N.W., #2A38 20548; (202) 512-8777. Fax, (202) 512-8692. Laurie E. Ekstrand, Director. Documents, (202) 512-6000.*

Independent, nonpartisan agency in the legislative branch. Audits, analyzes, and evaluates federal administration of justice programs and activities; makes some reports available to the public.

House Appropriations Committee, *Subcommittee on Commerce, Justice, State, and Judiciary, H309 CAP 20515; (202) 225-3351. Rep. Harold Rogers, R-Ky., Chair;*

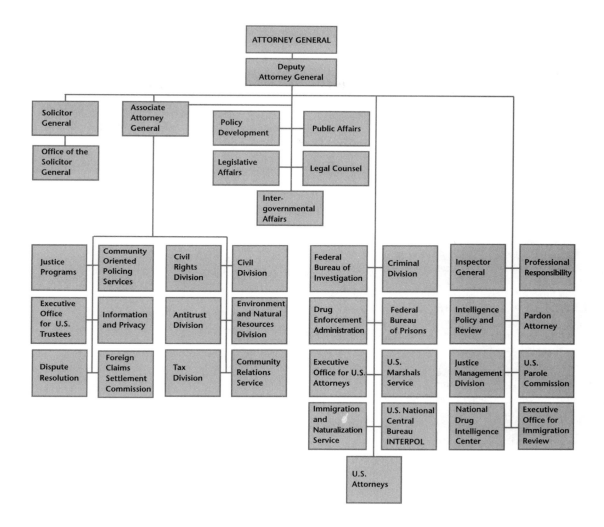

Jurisdiction over legislation to appropriate funds for the Justice Dept., the federal judiciary, the Legal Services Corp., the State Justice Institute, juvenile justice and delinquency prevention, district courts, and other judicial-related services and programs.

House Government Reform Committee, *Subcommittee on Criminal Justice, Drug Policy, and Human Resources,* B373 RHOB 20515; (202) 225-2577. Fax, (202) 225-1154. Rep. John L. Mica, R-Fla., Chair; Sharon Pinkerton, Staff Director. Web, www.house.gov/reform.

Oversees operations of the Justice Dept., the federal judiciary (except the U.S. Tax Court), the Legal Services Corp., and the State Justice Institute.

House Judiciary Committee, *2138 RHOB 20515; (202) 225-3951. Fax, (202) 225-7682. Rep. Henry J. Hyde, R-Ill., Chair; Thomas Mooney, Chief of Staff. General e-mail, Judiciary@mail.house.gov. Web, www.house.gov/judiciary.*

Jurisdiction over legislation on judicial proceedings, constitutional amendments, civil liberties, ethics in government, federal judiciary, federal corrections system, interstate compacts, patents, copyrights and trademarks, bankruptcy, mutiny, espionage and counterfeiting, immigration and naturalization, revision and codification of the statutes of the United States, internal security, local courts in the territories and possessions, protection of trade and commerce against unlawful restraints and monopolies, legislation relating to claims against the United States, and state and territorial boundary lines.

House Judiciary Committee, *Subcommittee on Courts and Intellectual Property,* B351A RHOB 20515; (202) 225-5741. Fax, (202) 225-3673. Rep. Howard Coble, R-N.C., Chair; Blaine Merritt, Chief Counsel. General e-mail, Judiciary@mail.house.gov. Web, www.house.gov/ judiciary.

Jurisdiction over legislation on court administration and management and over rules of civil judicial procedure. Oversees the Administrative Office of the U.S. Courts.

Senate Appropriations Committee, *Subcommittee on Commerce, Justice, State, and Judiciary,* S-146A CAP 20510; (202) 224-7277. Sen. Judd Gregg, R-N.H., Chair; Jim Morhard, Clerk. Web, appropriations.senate.gov/ commerce.

Jurisdiction over legislation to appropriate funds for the Justice Dept., the federal judiciary, the Legal Services Corp., the State Justice Institute, juvenile justice and delinquency prevention, district courts, and other judicial-related services and programs.

Senate Judiciary Committee, SD-224 20510; (202) 224-5225. Fax, (202) 224-9102. Sen. Orrin G. Hatch, R-Utah, Chair; Manus Cooney, Chief Counsel. Web, judiciary.senate.gov.

Jurisdiction over legislation on judicial proceedings, constitutional amendments, civil liberties, ethics in government, federal judiciary, federal corrections system, interstate compacts, government information, patents, copyrights and trademarks, bankruptcy, mutiny, espionage and counterfeiting, immigration and naturalization, revision and codification of the statutes of the United States, internal security, local courts in the territories and possessions, protection of trade and commerce against unlawful restraints and monopolies, legislation relating to claims against the United States, and state and territorial boundary lines. Oversees operations of the Justice Dept., the federal judiciary (except the U.S. Tax Court), the Legal Services Corp., and the State Justice Institute.

Senate Judiciary Committee, *Subcommittee on Administrative Oversight and the Courts,* SH-308 20510; (202) 224-6736. Fax, (202) 228-0536. Sen. Charles E. Grassley, R-Iowa, Chair; Kolan L. Davis, Chief Counsel. Web, judiciary.senate.gov/admnover.htm.

Jurisdiction over legislation on court administration and management and over rules of civil judicial procedure.

JUDICIARY

Administrative Office of the U.S. Courts, 1 Columbus Circle N.E., #7-100 20544; (202) 273-3000. Leonidas Ralph Mecham, Director. Information, (202) 502-2600. Web, www.uscourts.gov.

Provides administrative support to the federal courts including the procurement of supplies and equipment, the administration of personnel, budget, and financial control services, and the compilation and publication of statistical data and reports on court business. Implements the policies of the Judicial Conference of the United States and supports its committees. Recommends plans and strategies to manage court business. Supports judicial officers, including active and senior appellate and district court judges, bankruptcy judges, and magistrate judges.

Federal Judicial Center, 1 Columbus Circle N.E. 20002-8003; (202) 502-4000. Fax, (202) 502-4099. Fern M. Smith, Director. Press, (202) 502-4153. Web, www.fjc.gov.

Conducts research on the operations of the federal court system; develops and conducts continuing education and training programs for judges and judicial personnel; and makes recommendations to improve the administration of the courts.

Judicial Conference of the United States, 1 Columbus Circle N.E., #7-425 20544; (202) 502-2400. Fax, (202) 502-1144. William H. Rehnquist, Chief Justice of the United States, Chair; Leonidas Ralph Mecham, Secretary. Web, www.uscourts.gov.

Serves as the policy-making and governing body for the administration of the federal judicial system; advises Congress on the creation of new federal judgeships. Interests include international judicial relations.

Supreme Court of the United States, 1 1st St. N.E. 20543; (202) 479-3000. William H. Rehnquist, Chief Justice. Library, (202) 479-3037. Opinions and information, (202) 479-3211.

Highest appellate court in the federal judicial system. Interprets the U.S. Constitution, federal legislation, and treaties. Provides information on new cases filed, the status of pending cases, and admissions to the Supreme Court Bar. Library open to Supreme Court bar members only.

NONPROFIT

Alliance for Justice, 2000 P St. N.W., #712 20036; (202) 822-6070. Fax, (202) 822-6068. Nan Aron, President. General e-mail, alliance@afj.org. Web, www.afj.org.

Membership: public interest lawyers and advocacy, environmental, civil rights, and consumer organizations. Promotes reform of the legal system to ensure access to the courts; monitors selection of federal judges; works to preserve the rights of nonprofit organizations to advocate on behalf of their constituents.

American Bar Assn., *Washington Office, 740 15th St. N.W. 20005-1022; (202) 662-1000. Fax, (202) 662-1032. Robert D. Evans, Director. Information, (202) 662-1010. Library, (202) 662-1011. TTY, (202) 662-1012. Web, www. abanet.org.*

Comprised of the Public Service Division, the Government and Public Sector Division, International Law and Practice Section, Criminal Justice Section, Taxation Section, Individual Rights and Responsibilities Section, Dispute Resolution Section, Administrative Law and Regulatory Practice Section, and others. Acts as a clearinghouse for the association's legislative activities and communicates the status of important bills and regulations to state and local bar associations and to all sections concerned with major governmental activities that affect the legal profession. (Headquarters in Chicago.)

American Tort Reform Assn., *1850 M St. N.W., #1095 20036-5803; (202) 682-1163. Fax, (202) 682-1022. Sherman Joyce, President. Web, www.atra.org.*

Membership: businesses, associations, trade groups, professional societies, and individuals interested in reforming the civil justice system in the United States. Develops model state legislation and position papers on tort reform. Works with state coalitions in support of tort reform legislation.

Assn. of Trial Lawyers of America, *1050 31st St. N.W. 20007-4499; (202) 965-3500. Fax, (202) 342-5484. Thomas H. Henderson Jr., Executive Director. Web, www. atlanet.org.*

Membership: attorneys, judges, law professors, and students. Works to strengthen the civil justice system and the right to trial by jury. Interests include victims' rights, property and casualty insurance, revisions of federal rules of evidence, criminal code, jurisdictions of courts, juries, and consumer law.

Center for Study of Responsive Law, *1530 P St. N.W. 20005 (mailing address: P.O. Box 19367 20036); (202) 387-8030. Fax, (202) 234-5176. John Richard, Administrator. Web, www.csrl.org.*

Consumer interest clearinghouse that conducts research and holds conferences on public interest law. Interests include white-collar crime, the environment, occupational health and safety, the postal system, banking deregulation, insurance, freedom of information policy, and broadcasting.

Death Penalty Information Center, *1320 18th St. N.W., 5th Floor 20036; (202) 293-6970. Fax, (202) 822-4787. Richard C. Dieter, Executive Director. General e-mail, dpic@essential.org. Web, www.essential.org/dpic.*

Provides the media and public with analysis and information on issues concerning capital punishment. Conducts briefings for journalists; prepares reports; issues press releases.

Federal Bar Assn., *2215 M St. N.W. 20037; (202) 785-1614. Fax, (202) 785-1568. Jack D. Lockridge, Executive Director. General e-mail, fba@fedbar.org. Web, www. fedbar.org.*

Membership: attorneys employed by the federal government or practicing before federal courts or agencies. Conducts research and programs in fields including tax, native American, antitrust, immigration, and international law; concerns include professional ethics, legal education (primarily continuing education), and legal services.

The Federalist Society, *1015 18th St. N.W., #425 20036; (202) 822-8138. Fax, (202) 296-8061. Gary Lawson, Director. General e-mail, fedsoc@radix.net. Web, www. fed-soc.org.*

Promotes awareness of federalist principles among lawyers, judges, law professors, and the general public. Sponsors lectures and seminars.

Help Abolish Legal Tyranny—An Organization of Americans for Legal Reform, *1612 K St. N.W., #510 20006; (202) 887-8255. Fax, (202) 887-9699. James C. Turner, Executive Director. Web, www.halt.org.*

Public interest organization concerned with legal reform. Conducts research on alternative dispute resolution programs for delivery of legal services, including arbitration, legal clinics, and mediation services; provides educational and self-help manuals on the use of the legal system. Operates The Law Store, a legal document preparation service created to research, test, and promote innovative techniques for improving access to legal services for the average citizen.

Lawyers for Civil Justice, *1140 Connecticut Ave. N.W., #503 20006; (202) 429-0045. Fax, (202) 429-6982. Barry Bauman, Executive Director.*

Membership: defense trial lawyers and corporate and insurance attorneys. Interests include tort reform, litigation cost containment, and tort and product liability. Monitors legislation and regulations affecting the civil justice system.

GENERAL COUNSELS FOR FEDERAL AGENCIES

DEPARTMENTS

Agriculture, Charles R. Rawls, (202) 720-3351

Commerce, Andrew J. Pincus, (202) 482-4772

Defense, Douglas Dworkin (acting), (703) 695-3341

  Air Force, J. Charles Johnson, (703) 697-0941

  Army, Charles Blanchard, (703) 697-9235

  Navy, Stephen Preston, (703) 614-1994

Education, Judith Winston, (202) 401-6000

Energy, Mary Anne Sullivan, (202) 586-5281

Health and Human Services, Harriet S. Rabb, (202) 690-7741

Housing and Urban Development, Gail Laster, (202) 708-2244

Interior, John Leshy, (202) 208-4423

Justice, Randy Moss, (202) 514-2051

Labor, Henry L. Solano, (202) 693-5260

State, David R. Andrews, (202) 647-9598

Transportation, Nancy E. McFadden, (202) 366-4702

Treasury, Neal Wolin, (202) 622-0287

Veterans Affairs, Leigh A. Bradley, (202) 273-6660

AGENCIES

Advisory Council on Historic Preservation, John M. Fowler, (202) 606-8503

Agency for International Development, Singleton McAllister, (202) 712-4476

Central Intelligence Agency, Robert M. McNamara Jr., (703) 482-1951

Commission on Civil Rights, Stephanie Moore, (202) 376-8351

Commodity Futures Trading Commission, C. Robert Paul, (202) 418-5120

Consumer Product Safety Commission, Jeffrey S. Bromme, (301) 504-0980

Corporation for National Service, Thomasenia P. Duncan, (202) 606-5000

Environmental Protection Agency, Gary Guzy (acting), (202) 564-8040

Equal Employment Opportunity Commission, Clifford Gregory Stewart, (202) 663-4702

Export-Import Bank, John Neihuss, (202) 565-3430

Farm Credit Administration, Jean Noonan, (703) 883-4020

Federal Communications Commission, Christopher J. Wright, (202) 418-1700

Federal Deposit Insurance Corporation, William F. Kroener III, (202) 898-3680

Federal Election Commission, Lawrence M. Noble, (202) 694-1650

Federal Emergency Management Agency, Ernest Abbott, (202) 646-4105

Federal Energy Regulatory Commission, Douglas W. Smith, (202) 208-1000

Federal Labor Relations Authority, Joseph Swerdzewski, (202) 482-6600

Federal Maritime Commission, Thomas Panebianco, (202) 523-5740

National Assn. for the Advancement of Colored People, *Washington Office*, 1025 Vermont Ave. N.W., #1120 20005; (202) 638-2269. Fax, (202) 638-5936. Hilary O. Shelton, Director. Web, www.naacp.org.

Membership: persons interested in civil rights for all minorities. Seeks, through litigation, to end discrimination in all areas, including discriminatory practices in the administration of justice. Studies and recommends policy on court administration and jury selection. Maintains branch offices in many state and federal prisons. (Headquarters in Baltimore.)

National Bar Assn., *1225 11th St. N.W. 20001-4217; (202) 842-3900. Fax, (202) 289-6170. John Crump, Executive Director. Web, www.nationalbar.org.*

Membership: primarily minority attorneys, legal professionals, judges, and law students. Interests include legal education and improvement of the judicial process.

Sponsors legal education seminars in all states that require continuing legal education for lawyers.

National Center for State Courts, *Government Relations, 2425 Wilson Blvd., #350, Arlington, VA 22201; (703) 841-0200. Fax, (703) 841-0206. Thomas A. Henderson, Executive Director. Web, www.ncsc.dni.us.*

Works to improve state court systems through research, technical assistance, and training programs. Monitors legislation affecting court systems; interests include state-federal jurisdiction and automated information systems. Serves as secretariat for several state court organizations, including the Conference of Chief Justices, Conference of State Court Administrators, American Judges Assn., and National Assn. for Court Management.

National Legal Center for the Public Interest, *1000 16th St. N.W., #500 20036; (202) 296-1683. Fax, (202) 293-2118. Ernest B. Hueter, President.*

GENERAL COUNSELS FOR FEDERAL AGENCIES (continued)

Federal Mediation and Conciliation Service, Jane Lorber, (202) 606-5443

Federal Reserve System, J. Virgil Mattingly Jr., (202) 452-3430

Federal Trade Commission, Debra A. Valentine, (202) 326-2480

General Services Administration, Stephanie Foster, (202) 501-2200

International Bank for Reconstruction and Development (World Bank), Kuyung Tung, (202) 458-1601

Merit Systems Protection Board, Mary L. Jennings, (202) 653-7171

National Aeronautics and Space Administration, Edward A. Frankle, (202) 358-2450

National Credit Union Administration, Robert M. Fenner, (703) 518-6540

National Endowment for Humanities, Virginia Canter, (202) 606-8322

National Endowment for the Arts, Hope O'Keeffe (acting), (202) 682-5654

National Labor Relations Board, Fred Feinstein, (202) 273-3700

National Mediation Board, Leonard R. Page, (703) 993-8025

National Railroad Passenger Corporation (Amtrak), James Lloyd, (202) 906-3402

National Science Foundation, Lawrence Rudolph, (703) 306-1060

National Transportation Safety Board, Ronald S. Battochi, (202) 314-6080

Nuclear Regulatory Commission, Karen D. Cyr, (301) 415-1743

Occupational Safety and Health Review Commission, Earl R. Ohman Jr., (202) 606-5410

Office of Personnel Management, Suzanne B. Ceiden, (202) 606-1700

Overseas Private Investment Corporation, Jane Chalmers, (202) 336-8421

Peace Corps, Nancy Hendry, (202) 692-2150

Pension Benefit Guaranty Corporation, James Keightley, (202) 326-4020

Postal Rate Commission, Stephen Sharfman, (202) 789-6820

Securities and Exchange Commission, Harvey J. Goldschmid, (202) 942-0900

Small Business Administration, Michael D. Schattman, (202) 205-6642

Smithsonian Institution, John E. Huerta, (202) 357-2583

Social Security Administration, Arthur Fried, (410) 965-0600

U.S. International Trade Commission, Lyn M. Schlitt, (202) 205-3061

U.S. Postal Service, Mary S. Elcano, (202) 268-2950

Public interest law center and information clearinghouse. Studies judicial issues and the impact of the legal system on the private sector; sponsors seminars; does not litigate cases.

Rand Corporation, *Washington Office, 1333 H St. N.W., #800 20005; (202) 296-5000. Fax, (202) 296-7960. Bruce Hoffman, Director. Web, www.rand.org.*

Analyzes current problems of the American civil and criminal justice systems and evaluates recent and pending changes and reforms. (Headquarters in Santa Monica, Calif.)

U.S. Chamber of Commerce, *Congressional and Public Affairs, 1615 H St. N.W. 20062-2000; (202) 659-6000. Fax, (202) 887-3430. Lonnie P. Taylor, Senior Vice President. Web, www.uschamber.org.*

Federation of individuals, firms, corporations, trade and professional associations, and local, state, and

regional chambers of commerce. Monitors legislation and regulations in administrative law, antitrust policy, civil justice reform, and product liability reform.

Washington Legal Foundation, *2009 Massachusetts Ave. N.W. 20036; (202) 588-0302. Fax, (202) 588-0386. Daniel J. Popeo, General Counsel. Web, www.wlf.org.*

Public interest law and policy center. Interests include constitutional law, government regulation, media law, and criminal justice; litigates on behalf of small businesses, members of Congress, and victims of violent crimes who bring civil suits against their attackers.

Women's Bar Assn., *815 15th St. N.W., #815 20005; (202) 639-8880. Fax, (202) 639-8889. Julie C. Almacy, Executive Director. Web, www.wbadc.org.*

Membership: women and men who are judges, attorneys in the public and private sectors, law students, and lawyers at home who remain professionally active. Pro-

See also Product Liability Alliance (p. 22)

SUPREME COURT JUSTICES

CHIEF JUSTICE

William H. Rehnquist

Appointed Associate Justice by President Nixon, sworn in Jan. 7, 1972; appointed Chief Justice by President Reagan, sworn in Sept. 26, 1986.

ASSOCIATE JUSTICES

in order of appointment

John Paul Stevens

Appointed by President Ford, sworn in Dec. 17, 1975.

Sandra Day O'Connor

Appointed by President Reagan, sworn in Sept. 25, 1981.

Antonin Scalia

Appointed by President Reagan, sworn in Aug. 17, 1986.

Anthony M. Kennedy

Appointed by President Reagan, sworn in Feb. 18, 1988.

David H. Souter

Appointed by President Bush, sworn in Oct. 9, 1990.

Clarence Thomas

Appointed by President Bush, sworn in Oct. 23, 1991.

Ruth Bader Ginsburg

Appointed by President Clinton, sworn in Aug. 19, 1993.

Stephen G. Breyer

Appointed by President Clinton, sworn in Aug. 3, 1994.

motes appointment of members to positions in government and legislative policies that assist women in the workplace.

World Jurist Assn., *1000 Connecticut Ave. N.W., #202 20036-5302; (202) 466-5428. Fax, (202) 452-8540. Margaret M. Henneberry, Executive Vice President. General e-mail, wja@worldjurist.org. Web, www.worldjurist.org.*

Membership: lawyers, law professors, judges, law students, and nonlegal professionals worldwide. Conducts research; promotes world peace through adherence to international law; holds biennial world conferences. (Affiliates, at same address, include World Assn. of Judges, World Assn. of Law Professors, and World Assn. of Lawyers.)

Dispute Resolution

AGENCIES

Justice Dept., *Dispute Resolution, 950 Pennsylvania Ave. N.W., #5240 20530; (202) 616-9471. Fax, (202) 616-9570. Peter R. Steenland Jr., Senior Counsel. Web, www.usdoj.gov.*

Division of the office of the associate attorney general. Coordinates Justice Dept. activities related to dispute resolution.

NONPROFIT

American Arbitration Assn., *Washington Office, 8201 Greensboro Dr., #610, McLean, VA 22102-3810; (703) 760-4820. Fax, (703) 760-4847. Arnold B. Crews, Regional Vice President. General e-mail, webmaster@adr.org. Web, www.adr.org.*

Provides dispute resolution services worldwide, including arbitration, mediation, minitrials, and elections. (Headquarters in New York.)

American Bar Assn., *Dispute Resolution, 740 15th St. N.W. 20005; (202) 662-1680. Fax, (202) 662-1683. Jack Hanna, Director. Web, www.abanet.org.*

Acts as a clearinghouse on dispute resolution; supports methods for resolving disputes other than litigation; provides technical assistance.

Center for Dispute Settlement, *1666 Connecticut Ave. N.W., #500 20009; (202) 265-9572. Fax, (202) 328-9162. Linda R. Singer, Executive Director.*

Designs, implements, and evaluates alternative and nonjudicial methods of dispute resolution; mediates disputes; provides training in dispute resolution.

Conflict Resolution Education Network, *1527 New Hampshire Ave. N.W., 3rd Floor 20036; (202) 667-9700. Fax, (202) 667-8629. Heather Prichard, Director. General e-mail, crenet@crenet.org. Web, www.crenet.org.*

Promotes knowledge and public awareness of the value of alternative dispute resolution methods including mediation, negotiation, and arbitration. Fosters the use of such processes and programs in new arenas locally, nationally, and internationally; stimulates innovative approaches to the resolution of future conflict. Provides educators and conflict resolution professionals with information and technical assistance regarding the use of dispute resolution processes. Develops approaches to youth conflict and alternatives to violence.

Council of Better Business Bureaus, *Alternative Dispute Resolution, 4200 Wilson Blvd., #800, Arlington, VA*

22203; (703) 247-9361. Fax, (703) 276-0634. Charles I. Underhill, Senior Vice President. General e-mail, bbb@bbb.org. Web, www.bbb.org/complaints.

Administers mediation and arbitration programs through Better Business Bureaus nationwide to assist in resolving disputes between businesses and consumers. Assists with unresolved disputes between car owners and automobile manufacturers. Maintains pools of certified arbitrators nationwide. Provides mediation training.

Help Abolish Legal Tyranny—An Organization of Americans for Legal Reform, 1612 K St. N.W., #510 20006; (202) 887-8255. Fax, (202) 887-9699. James C. Turner, Executive Director. Web, www.halt.org.

Public interest organization concerned with legal reform. Conducts research on alternative dispute resolution programs for delivery of legal services, including arbitration, legal clinics, and mediation services; provides educational and self-help manuals on the use of the legal system. Operates The Law Store, a legal document preparation service created to research, test, and promote innovative techniques for improving access to legal services for the average citizen.

National Assn. for Community Mediation, 1527 New Hampshire Ave. N.W. 20036-1206; (202) 667-9700. Fax, (202) 667-8629. Anne Pokras, Executive Director (Interim). General e-mail, nafcm@nafcm.org. Web, www.nafcm.org.

Supports the maintenance and growth of community-based mediation programs and processes. Provides information on the development and practice of community mediation; encourages regional and national collaborative projects among community mediation programs.

Judicial Appointments

AGENCIES

Justice Dept., *Policy Development,* 950 Pennsylvania Ave. N.W., #4234 20530; (202) 514-4601. Fax, (202) 514-2424. Eleanor Dean Acheson, Assistant Attorney General. Web, www.usdoj.gov.

Investigates and processes prospective candidates for presidential appointment (subject to Senate confirmation) to the federal judiciary.

CONGRESS

House Judiciary Committee, *Subcommittee on Courts and Intellectual Property,* B351A RHOB 20515; (202) 225-5741. Fax, (202) 225-3673. Rep. Howard Coble, R-N.C., Chair; Blaine Merritt, Chief Counsel. General e-mail, Judiciary@mail.house.gov. Web, www.house.gov/judiciary.

Jurisdiction over legislation on federal judicial appointments, which includes legislation to create new federal judgeships.

Senate Judiciary Committee, SD-224 20510; (202) 224-5225. Fax, (202) 224-9102. Sen. Orrin G. Hatch, R-Utah, Chair; Manus Cooney, Chief Counsel. Web, judiciary.senate.gov.

Jurisdiction over legislation on federal judicial appointments, which includes legislation to create new federal judgeships; conducts hearings on presidential appointees to federal judgeships, including Supreme Court nominees.

JUDICIARY

Administrative Office of the U.S. Courts, 1 Columbus Circle N.E., #7-100 20544; (202) 273-3000. Leonidas Ralph Mecham, Director. Information, (202) 502-2600. Web, www.uscourts.gov.

Supervises all administrative matters of the federal court system, except the Supreme Court. Transmits to Congress the recommendations of the Judicial Conference of the United States concerning creation of federal judgeships and other legislative proposals.

Judicial Conference of the United States, 1 Columbus Circle N.E., #7-425 20544; (202) 502-2400. Fax, (202) 502-1144. William H. Rehnquist, Chief Justice of the United States, Chair; Leonidas Ralph Mecham, Secretary. Web, www.uscourts.gov.

Serves as the policy-making and governing body for the administration of the federal judicial system; advises Congress on the creation of new federal judgeships. Interests include international judicial relations.

NONPROFIT

Alliance for Justice, *Judicial Selection Project,* 2000 P St. N.W., #712 20036-6919; (202) 822-6070. Fax, (202) 822-6068. Nancy Marcus, Director (Acting). General e-mail, alliance@afj.org. Web, www.afj.org.

Monitors candidates for vacancies in the federal judiciary; independently reviews nominees' records; maintains statistics on the judiciary.

BUSINESS AND TAX LAW

See also Business and Economics (chap. 3)

Antitrust

AGENCIES

Antitrust Division *(Justice Dept.),* 950 Pennsylvania Ave. N.W., #3109 20530; (202) 514-2401. Fax, (202) 616-2645. Joel I. Klein, Assistant Attorney General. Web, www.usdoj.gov/atr.

Enforces antitrust laws to prevent monopolies and unlawful restraint of trade; has civil and criminal jurisdiction; coordinates activities with Bureau of Competition of the Federal Trade Commission.

Antitrust Division *(Justice Dept.), Civil Task Force,* 325 7th St. N.W., #300 20530; (202) 616-5935. Fax, (202) 514-7308. Mary Jean Moltenbrey, Chief.

Investigates and litigates certain antitrust cases involving sports groups, music publishing, and other segments of the publishing industry. Handles certain violations of antitrust laws that involve patents, copyrights, and trademarks.

Antitrust Division *(Justice Dept.), Computers and Finance,* 600 E St. N.W., #9500 20530; (202) 307-6122. Fax, (202) 616-8544. Nancy M. Goodman, Chief.

Investigates and litigates certain antitrust cases involving either communications industries or financial institutions, including banking, securities, commodity futures, and insurance firms; participates in agency proceedings and rulemaking in these areas.

Antitrust Division *(Justice Dept.), Documents,* 325 7th St. N.W., #215 20530; (202) 514-2481. Fax, (202) 514-3763. Janie Ingalls, Chief.

Maintains files and handles requests for information on federal civil and criminal antitrust cases; provides the president and Congress with copies of statutory reports prepared by the division on a variety of competition-related issues; issues opinion letters on whether certain business activity violates antitrust laws.

Antitrust Division *(Justice Dept.), Health Care Task Force,* 325 7th St. N.W., 4th Floor 20530; (202) 307-5799. Fax, (202) 514-1517. Gail Kursh, Chief.

Litigates certain antitrust cases involving health care and pharmaceutical industries.

Antitrust Division *(Justice Dept.), Transportation, Energy, and Agriculture,* 325 7th St. N.W., #500 20530; (202) 307-6351. Fax, (202) 307-2784. Roger W. Fones, Chief.

Enforces antitrust laws in the airline, railroad, motor carrier, barge line, ocean carrier, and energy industries; litigates antitrust cases pertaining to agriculture and related commodities.

Comptroller of the Currency *(Treasury Dept.),* 250 E St. S.W. 20219; (202) 874-4900. Fax, (202) 874-4950. John D. Hawke Jr., Comptroller. Information, (202) 874-5000. Library, (202) 874-4720. Press, (202) 874-5770. Web, www.occ.treas.gov.

Regulates and examines operations of national banks; establishes guidelines for bank examinations; handles mergers of national banks with regard to antitrust law. Library open to the public.

Federal Communications Commission, *Common Carrier Bureau,* 445 12th St. S.W. 20554; (202) 418-1500. Fax, (202) 418-2825. Lawrence Strickling, Chief. Web, www.fcc.gov/ccb.

Regulates mergers involving common carriers (wireline facilities that furnish interstate communications services).

Federal Deposit Insurance Corp., *Supervision,* 550 17th St. N.W. 20429; (202) 898-8510. Fax, (202) 898-3638. James L. Sexton, Director.

Studies and analyzes applications for mergers, consolidations, acquisitions, and assumption transactions between insured banks.

Federal Energy Regulatory Commission *(Energy Dept.),* 888 1st St. N.E., #11A 20426; (202) 208-0000. Fax, (202) 208-0151. James J. Hoecker, Chair. Information, (202) 208-0200. Press, (202) 208-1088. Dockets, (202) 208-0715. Web, www.ferc.fed.us.

Regulates mergers, consolidations, and acquisitions of electric utilities; regulates the acquisition of interstate natural gas pipeline facilities.

Federal Maritime Commission, 800 N. Capitol St. N.W., #1046 20573-0001; (202) 523-5725. Fax, (202) 523-0014. Bruce A. Dombrowski, Managing Director; Harold J. Creel Jr., Chair. Library, (202) 523-5762. TTY, (800) 877-8339. Locator, (202) 523-5773. Web, www.fmc.gov.

Regulates foreign ocean shipping of the United States; reviews agreements (on rates, schedules, and other matters) filed by common carriers for compliance with antitrust laws and grants antitrust immunity. Library open to the public.

Federal Reserve System, *Banking Supervision and Regulation,* 20th and C Sts. N.W., #M3142 20551; (202) 452-2773. Fax, (202) 452-2770. Richard Spillenkothen, Director. Web, www.bog.frb.fed.us.

Approves bank mergers, consolidations, and other alterations in bank structure.

Federal Trade Commission, *Competition,* 600 Pennsylvania Ave. N.W., #H374 20580; (202) 326-2932. Fax, (202) 326-2884. Richard G. Parker, Director. Information, (202) 326-2180.

Enforces antitrust laws and investigates possible violations, including international cases; seeks voluntary compliance and pursues civil judicial remedies; reviews premerger filings; coordinates activities with Antitrust Division of the Justice Dept.

Surface Transportation Board *(Transportation Dept.)*, 1925 K St. N.W. 20423-0001; (202) 565-1500. Fax, (202) 565-9004. Wayne Burkes, Vice Chair; Linda J. Morgan, Chair. Web, www.stb.dot.gov.

Regulates rail rate disputes, railroad consolidations, rail line construction proposals, line abandonments, rail car service, and motor carrier undercharge cases.

CONGRESS

House Banking and Financial Services Committee, *Subcommittee on Financial Institutions and Consumer Credit,* 2129 RHOB 20515; (202) 225-2258. Fax, (202) 225-6984. Rep. Marge Roukema, R-N.J., Chair; Laurie Schaffer, Staff Director. Web, www.house.gov/banking.

Jurisdiction over legislation on mergers, acquisitions, consolidations, and conversions of financial institutions.

House Judiciary Committee, 2138 RHOB 20515; (202) 225-3951. Fax, (202) 225-7682. Rep. Henry J. Hyde, R-Ill., Chair; Thomas Mooney, Chief of Staff. General e-mail, Judiciary@mail.house.gov. Web, www.house.gov/judiciary.

Jurisdiction over legislation affecting anticompetitive and monopolistic practices and over Justice Dept. antitrust enforcement policies. Oversight of the Sherman Act and the Clayton Act.

House Small Business Committee, *Subcommittee on Regulatory Reform and Paperwork Reduction,* B363 RHOB 20515; (202) 226-2630. Fax, (202) 225-8950. Rep. Sue W. Kelly, R-N.Y., Chair; Meredith Matty, Staff Director. General e-mail, smbiz@mail.house.gov. Web, www.house.gov/smbiz.

Investigates anticompetitive and monopolistic practices.

Senate Judiciary Committee, *Subcommittee on Antitrust, Business Rights, and Competition,* SD-161 20510; (202) 224-9494. Fax, (202) 228-0463. Sen. Mike DeWine, R-Ohio, Chair; Pete Levitas, Chief Counsel. Web, judiciary.senate.gov/antibusn.htm.

Jurisdiction over legislation affecting anticompetitive and monopolistic practices and over Justice Dept. antitrust enforcement polices. Oversight of the Sherman Act and the Clayton Act.

Senate Small Business Committee, SR-428A 20510; (202) 224-5175. Fax, (202) 224-4885. Sen. Christopher S. Bond, R-Mo., Chair; Emilia DiSanto, Staff Director. Web, sbc.senate.gov.

Investigates antitrust matters relating to small business; investigates anticompetitive and monopolistic practices.

NONPROFIT

American Corporate Counsel Assn., 1025 Connecticut Ave. N.W., #200 20036-5425; (202) 293-4103. Fax, (202) 293-4701. Frederick J. Krebs, President. Web, www.acca.com.

Membership: practicing attorneys in corporate law departments. Provides information on corporate law issues, including securities, health and safety, the environment, intellectual property, litigation, international legal affairs, pro bono work, and labor benefits. Monitors legislation and regulations, with primary focus on issues affecting in-house attorneys' ability to practice law.

Business Roundtable, 1615 L St. N.W., #1100 20036-5610; (202) 872-1260. Fax, (202) 466-3509. Samuel L. Maury, President. Web, www.brtable.org.

Membership: chief executives of the nation's largest corporations. Examines issues of concern to business, including antitrust law.

Bankruptcy

AGENCIES

Executive Office for U.S. Trustees *(Justice Dept.)*, 901 E St. N.W., #700 20004; (202) 307-1391. Fax, (202) 307-0672. Kevyn Orr, Director (Acting). Web, www.usdoj.gov/ust.

Handles the administration and oversight of bankruptcy and liquidation cases filed under the Bankruptcy Reform Act. Provides individual U.S. trustee offices with administrative and management support.

Justice Dept., *Policy Development,* 950 Pennsylvania Ave. N.W., #4234 20530; (202) 514-4601. Fax, (202) 514-2424. Eleanor Dean Acheson, Assistant Attorney General. Web, www.usdoj.gov.

Studies and develops policy for improvement of the criminal and civil justice systems, including bankruptcy reform policy.

CONGRESS

House Judiciary Committee, *Subcommittee on Commercial and Administrative Law,* B353 RHOB 20515; (202) 225-2825. Fax, (202) 225-4299. Rep. George W. Gekas, R-Pa., Chair; Ray Smietanka, Counsel. General e-mail, Judiciary@mail.house.gov. Web, www.house.gov/judiciary.

Jurisdiction over bankruptcy legislation. Oversees the bankruptcy court.

Senate Judiciary Committee, *Subcommittee on Administrative Oversight and the Courts,* SH-308 20510; (202) 224-6736. Fax, (202) 228-0536. Sen. Charles

E. Grassley, R-Iowa, Chair; Kolan L. Davis, Chief Counsel. Web, judiciary.senate.gov/admnover.htm.

Jurisdiction over bankruptcy legislation.

JUDICIARY

Administrative Office of the U.S. Courts, *Bankruptcy Judges Division,* *1 Columbus Circle N.E., #4-250 20544; (202) 502-1900. Fax, (202) 502-1988. Francis F. Szczebak, Chief.*

Provides administrative assistance and support in the operation of the U.S. Bankruptcy Courts.

NONPROFIT

American Bankruptcy Institute, *44 Canal Center Plaza, #404, Alexandria, VA 22314-1592; (703) 739-0800. Fax, (703) 739-1060. Samuel Gerdano, Executive Director. Web, www.abiworld.org.*

Membership: lawyers; federal and state legislators; and representatives of accounting and financial services firms, lending institutions, credit organizations, and consumer groups. Provides information and educational services on insolvency, reorganization, and bankruptcy issues; sponsors conferences, seminars, and workshops.

Tax Violations

See also Taxes and Tax Reform (chap. 5)

AGENCIES

Internal Revenue Service *(Treasury Dept.), Field Service, 1111 Constitution Ave. N.W., #4050 20224; (202) 622-7800. Fax, (202) 622-7722. Deborah Butler, Assistant Chief Counsel.*

Oversees field office litigation of civil cases that involve underpayment of taxes when the taxpayer chooses to challenge the determinations of the Internal Revenue Service (IRS) in the U.S. Tax Court, or when the taxpayer chooses to pay the amount in question and sue the IRS for a refund. Reviews briefs and defense letters prepared by field offices for tax cases; prepares tax litigation advice memoranda; formulates litigation strategy. Makes recommendations concerning appeal and certiorari. Litigates insurance and declaratory judgment cases in the U.S. Tax Court.

Justice Dept., *Tax Division, 950 Pennsylvania Ave. N.W., #4143 20530; (202) 514-2901. Fax, (202) 514-5479. Paula Jounghanf, Assistant Attorney General (Acting). Web, www.usdoj.gov/tax/tax.html.*

Authorizes prosecution of all criminal cases involving tax violations investigated and developed by the Internal Revenue Service (IRS); represents IRS in civil litigation

except in U.S. Tax Court proceedings; represents other agencies, including the departments of Defense and Interior, in cases with state or local tax authorities.

CONGRESS

House Ways and Means Committee, *1102 LHOB 20515; (202) 225-3625. Fax, (202) 225-2610. Rep. Bill Archer, R-Texas, Chair; A. L. Singleton, Chief of Staff. Web, www.house.gov/ways_means.*

Jurisdiction over legislation concerning changes in enforcement of tax laws.

Senate Finance Committee, *Subcommittee on Taxation and IRS Oversight, SD-219 20510; (202) 224-4515. Fax, (202) 224-5920. Sen. Orrin G. Hatch, R-Utah, Chair; Mark Prater, Staff Contact. Web, finance.senate.gov.*

Holds hearings on legislation concerning changes in enforcement of tax laws.

JUDICIARY

U.S. Tax Court, *400 2nd St. N.W. 20217; (202) 606-8700. Mary Ann Cohen, Chief Judge; Charles S. Casazza, Clerk of the Court, (202) 606-8754.*

Tries and adjudicates disputes involving income, estate, and gift taxes and personal holding company surtaxes in cases in which deficiencies have been determined by the Internal Revenue Service.

NONPROFIT

American Bar Assn., *Taxation Section, 740 15th St. N.W., 10th Floor 20005-1022; (202) 662-8670. Fax, (202) 662-8682. Christine A. Brunswick, Director. Web, www. abanet.org.*

Studies and recommends policies on taxation; provides information on tax issues; sponsors continuing legal education programs; monitors tax laws and legislation.

⚖ CONSTITUTIONAL LAW AND CIVIL LIBERTIES

See also Public Interest Law (chap. 1)

AGENCIES

Commission on Civil Rights, *624 9th St. N.W., #700 20425; (202) 376-7700. Fax, (202) 376-7672. Mary Frances Berry, Chair; Cruz Reynoso, Vice Chair. Library, (202) 376-8110. Press, (202) 376-8312. TTY, (202) 376-8116. Locator, (202) 376-8177. Complaints, (800) 552-6843; in Washington, (202) 376-8582. Web, www.usccr.gov.*

Assesses federal laws and policies of government agencies and reviews legal developments to determine the nature and extent of denial of equal protection on the basis of race, color, religion, sex, national origin, age, or disability; investigates complaints of denials of voting rights. Library open to the public.

Education Dept., *Civil Rights,* 330 C St. S.W., #5000 20202-1100 (mailing address: 400 Maryland Ave. S.W. 20202); (202) 205-5413. Fax, (202) 205-9862. Norma Cantù, Assistant Secretary. Web, www.ed.gov.

Enforces laws prohibiting use of federal funds for education programs or activities that discriminate on the basis of race, color, sex, national origin, age, or disability; authorized to discontinue funding.

Health and Human Services Dept., *Civil Rights,* 200 Independence Ave. S.W., #522A 20201; (202) 619-0403. Fax, (202) 619-3437. Thomas Perez, Director. TTY, (800) 537-7697. Toll-free hotline, (800) 368-1019. Web, www.os. dhhs.gov/progorg/ocr/ocrhmpg.html.

Administers and enforces laws prohibiting discrimination on the basis of race, color, sex, national origin, religion, age, or disability in programs receiving federal funds from the department; authorized to discontinue funding.

Justice Dept., *Civil Rights,* 950 Pennsylvania Ave. N.W., #5643 20530; (202) 514-2151. Fax, (202) 514-0293. Bill Lann Lee, Assistant Attorney General (Acting). Library, (202) 514-3010. Press, (202) 514-2007. TTY, (202) 514-0716. Web, www.usdoj.gov/crt.

Enforces federal civil rights laws prohibiting discrimination on the basis of race, color, religion, sex, disability, age, or national origin in voting, education, employment, credit, housing, public accommodations and facilities, and federally assisted programs.

Justice Dept., *Legal Counsel,* 950 Pennsylvania Ave. N.W., #3266 20530; (202) 514-2041. Fax, (202) 514-0539. Randolph Moss, Assistant Attorney General (Acting). Web, www.usdoj.gov.

Advises the attorney general, the president, and executive agencies on questions regarding constitutional law.

Labor Dept., *Civil Rights Center,* 200 Constitution Ave. N.W., #N4123 20210; (202) 219-8927. Fax, (202) 219-5658. Annabelle Lockhart, Director. TTY, (202) 219-7773. Web, www.dol.gov.

Resolves complaints of discrimination on the basis of race, color, religion, sex, national origin, age, or disability in programs funded by the department.

CONGRESS

House Government Reform Committee, *Subcommittee on National Security, Veterans Affairs, and International Affairs,* B372 RHOB 20515; (202) 225-2548. Fax, (202) 225-2382. Rep. Christopher Shays, R-Conn., Chair; Lawrence Halloran, Staff Director. Web, www.house.gov/reform.

Oversees operations of the Commission on Civil Rights.

House Judiciary Committee, 2138 RHOB 20515; (202) 225-3951. Fax, (202) 225-7682. Rep. Henry J. Hyde, R-Ill., Chair; Thomas Mooney, Chief of Staff. General e-mail, Judiciary@mail.house.gov. Web, www.house.gov/judiciary.

Jurisdiction over legislation on proposed amendments to the Constitution; subcommittee jurisdiction determined by subject of proposed amendment.

House Judiciary Committee, *Subcommittee on the Constitution,* H2-362 FHOB 20515; (202) 226-7680. Fax, (202) 225-3746. Rep. Charles T. Canady, R-Fla., Chair; Cathy Cleaver, Chief Counsel. General e-mail, Judiciary@ mail.house.gov. Web, www.house.gov/judiciary.

Jurisdiction over legislation dealing with civil rights enforcement, civil liberties, and constitutional issues. Oversees the Justice Dept.'s Civil Rights Division and the Commission on Civil Rights.

Senate Judiciary Committee, *Subcommittee on the Constitution, Federalism, and Property Rights,* SD-524 20510; (202) 224-8081. Fax, (202) 228-0544. Sen. John Ashcroft, R-Mo., Chair; Adam Cingoli, Chief Counsel. Web, judiciary.senate.gov/constitu.htm.

Jurisdiction over legislation on proposed amendments to the Constitution, civil rights enforcement, the Voting Rights Act and affirmative action, civil liberties (including the First Amendment, excluding computers), constitutional issues involving criminal law, habeas corpus, the death penalty, and the exclusionary rule; oversees operations of the Commission on Civil Rights.

JUDICIARY

Supreme Court of the United States, 1 1st St. N.E. 20543; (202) 479-3000. William H. Rehnquist, Chief Justice. Library, (202) 479-3037. Opinions and information, (202) 479-3211.

Highest appellate court in the federal judicial system. Interprets the U.S. Constitution, federal legislation, and treaties. Provides information on new cases filed, the status of pending cases, and admissions to the Supreme Court Bar. Library open to Supreme Court bar members only.

NONPROFIT

American Civil Liberties Union, *Washington Office,* *122 Maryland Ave. N.E. 20002; (202) 544-1681. Fax, (202) 546-0738. Laura W. Murphy, Director. Web, www. aclu.org.*

Initiates test court cases and advocates legislation to guarantee constitutional rights and civil liberties. Focuses on First Amendment rights, minority and women's rights, gay and lesbian rights, and privacy; supports legalized abortion, opposes government-sponsored school prayer and legislative restrictions on television content. Washington office monitors legislative and regulatory activities and public policy. Library open to the public by appointment. (Headquarters in New York maintains docket of cases.)

Center for Individual Rights, *1233 20th St. N.W., #300 20036; (202) 833-8400. Fax, (202) 833-8410. Michael S. Greve, Chief Executive Officer. General e-mail, cir@mail. wdn.com. Web, www.cir-usa.org.*

Public interest law firm that supports reform of the civil justice system on the basis of private rights and individual responsibility. Interests include economic regulation, freedom of speech, and libel law.

Ethics and Public Policy Center, *Law and Society Program, 1015 15th St. N.W., #900 20005; (202) 682-1200. Fax, (202) 408-0632. Elliott Abrams, President; Alex Acosta, Director. General e-mail, ethics@eppc.org. Web, www.eppc.org.*

Examines current issues of jurisprudence, especially those relating to constitutional interpretation.

Institute for Justice, *1717 Pennsylvania Ave. N.W., #200 20006; (202) 955-1300. Fax, (202) 955-1329. Chip Mellor, President. General e-mail, general@instituteforjustice. org. Web, www.instituteforjustice.org.*

Sponsors seminars to train law students, grassroots activists, and practicing lawyers in applying advocacy strategies in public interest litigation. Seeks to protect from arbitrary government interference in free speech, private property rights, parental school choice, and economic liberty. Litigates cases.

Legal Affairs Council Freedom Center, *10560 Main St., #217, Fairfax, VA 22030; (703) 591-7767. Fax, (703) 273-4514. Richard A. Delgaudio, President. Web, www. stardot.com/lac/lac.html.*

Provides financial and legal assistance to people challenging in court alleged violations of human and civil rights, especially First Amendment rights.

NAACP Legal Defense and Educational Fund, *Washington Office, 1444 Eye St. N.W., 10th Floor 20005;* *(202) 682-1300. Fax, (202) 682-1312. Janell Byrd, Senior Attorney.*

Civil rights litigation group that provides legal information on civil rights issues, including employment, housing, and educational discrimination; monitors federal enforcement of civil rights laws. Not affiliated with the National Assn. for the Advancement of Colored People (NAACP). (Headquarters in New York.)

National Assn. for the Advancement of Colored People, *Washington Office, 1025 Vermont Ave. N.W., #1120 20005; (202) 638-2269. Fax, (202) 638-5936. Hilary O. Shelton, Director. Web, www.naacp.org.*

Membership: persons interested in civil rights for all minorities. Works for the political, educational, social, and economic equality and empowerment of minorities through legal, legislative, and direct action. (Headquarters in Baltimore.)

National Organization for Women, *733 15th St. N.W., 2nd Floor 20005; (202) 628-8669. Fax, (202) 785-8576. Patricia Ireland, President. TTY, (202) 331-9002. General e-mail, now@now.org. Web, www.now.org.*

Membership: women and men interested in civil rights for women. Works to end discrimination based on gender, to preserve abortion rights, and to pass an equal rights amendment to the Constitution.

See also Lawyers' Committee for Civil Rights Under Law (p. 29)

Abortion and Reproductive Issues

See also Family Planning and Population (chap. 11)

CONGRESS

House Judiciary Committee, *Subcommittee on the Constitution, H2-362 FHOB 20515; (202) 226-7680. Fax, (202) 225-3746. Rep. Charles T. Canady, R-Fla., Chair; Cathy Cleaver, Chief Counsel. General e-mail, Judiciary@ mail.house.gov. Web, www.house.gov/judiciary.*

Jurisdiction over proposed abortion amendments to the Constitution.

Senate Judiciary Committee, *Subcommittee on the Constitution, Federalism, and Property Rights, SD-524 20510; (202) 224-8081. Fax, (202) 228-0544. Sen. John Ashcroft, R-Mo., Chair; Adam Cingoli, Chief Counsel. Web, judiciary.senate.gov/constitu.htm.*

Jurisdiction over proposed abortion amendments to the Constitution.

NONPROFIT

Assn. of Reproductive Health Professionals, *2401 Pennsylvania Ave. N.W., #350 20037-1718; (202) 466-3825. Fax, (202) 466-3826. Wayne Shields, President. Web, www.arhp.org.*

Membership: obstetricians, gynecologists, other physicians, researchers, clinicians, educators, and others. Educates health professionals and the public on reproductive health issues, including family planning, contraception, HIV/AIDS, other sexually transmitted diseases, abortion, menopause, infertility, and cancer prevention and detection.

Catholics for a Free Choice, *1436 U St. N.W., #301 20009-3997; (202) 986-6093. Fax, (202) 332-7995. Frances Kissling, President. General e-mail, cffc@igc.apc. org. Web, www.cath4choice.org.*

Works to change church positions and public policies that limit individual freedom, particularly those related to sexuality and reproduction. Provides the public, policymakers, and groups working for change with information and analysis.

Feminists for Life of America, *733 15th St. N.W., #1100 20005; (202) 737-3352. Fax, (202) 737-0414. Serrin M. Foster, President. Web, www.feministsforlife.org.*

Membership: women and men who advocate classical feminism, including its pro-life position. Opposes abortion, euthanasia, and capital punishment; seeks to redress economic and social conditions that cause women to choose abortion.

March for Life Fund, *P.O. Box 90300 20090; (202) 543-3377. Fax, (202) 543-8202. Nellie J. Gray, President. Web, www.marchforlife.org.*

Membership: individuals and organizations that support government action prohibiting abortion. Sponsors annual march in Washington each January 22. Monitors legislation and regulations.

National Abortion and Reproductive Rights Action League, *1156 15th St. N.W., 7th Floor 20005; (202) 973-3000. Fax, (202) 973-3099. Kate Michelman, President. Press, (202) 973-3032. Web, www.naral.org.*

Membership: persons favoring legalized abortion. Promotes grassroots support of political candidates in favor of legalized abortion.

National Abortion Federation, *1755 Massachusetts Ave. N.W., #600 20036; (202) 667-5881. Fax, (202) 667-5890. Vicki Saporta, Executive Director. Information, (800) 772-9100. Web, www.prochoice.org.*

Membership: abortion providers. Seeks to preserve and enhance the quality and accessibility of abortion care.

National Committee for a Human Life Amendment, *733 15th St. N.W., #926 20005; (202) 393-0703. Fax, (202) 347-1383. Michael A. Taylor, Executive Director.*

Supports legislation and a constitutional amendment prohibiting abortion.

National Conference of Catholic Bishops/U.S. Catholic Conference, *Secretariat for Pro-Life Activities, 3211 4th St. N.E. 20017-1194; (202) 541-3070. Fax, (202) 541-3054. Gail Quinn, Executive Director. Web, www.nccbuscc.org/prolife.*

Provides information on the position of the Roman Catholic Church on abortion; monitors legislation on abortion and related issues; provides alternatives to abortion through Catholic charities.

National Right to Life Committee, *419 7th St. N.W. 20004; (202) 626-8800. Fax, (202) 737-9189. David N. O'Steen, Executive Director. General e-mail, nrlc@nrlc.org. Web, www.nrlc.org.*

Association of fifty state right-to-life organizations. Opposes abortion, infanticide, and euthanasia; supports legislation prohibiting abortion except when the life of the mother is endangered. Operates an information clearinghouse and speakers bureau. Monitors legislation and regulations.

National Women's Health Network, *514 10th St. N.W., #400 20004-1410; (202) 347-1140. Fax, (202) 347-1168. Cynthia Pearson, Executive Director. Web, www.womenshealthnetwork.org.*

Advocacy organization interested in women's health. Seeks to preserve legalized abortion; monitors legislation and regulations; testifies before Congress.

National Women's Political Caucus, *1630 Connecticut Ave. N.W., #201 20009; (202) 785-1100. Fax, (202) 785-3605. Nick Demeter, Political Director; Roselyn O'Connell, President. General e-mail, mailnwpc@aol.com. Web, www.nwpc.org.*

Advocacy group that seeks greater involvement of women in politics. Supports legalized abortion.

Operation Rescue, *Press Relations, Washington Office, 2020 Pennsylvania Ave. N.W. 20006; (202) 546-0054. Troy Newman, Director. General e-mail, operationrescue@ netzero.net. Web, www.operationrescue.org.*

Advocates active stand against abortion. Seeks repeal of the Freedom of Access to Clinic Entrances law. Monitors legislation and regulations. (Headquarters in Dallas.)

Religious Coalition for Reproductive Choice, *1025 Vermont Ave. N.W., #1130 20005; (202) 628-7700. Fax, (202) 628-7716. Carlton Wadsworth Veazey, President. General e-mail, info@rcrc.org. Web, www.rcrc.org.*

Coalition of religious groups favoring legalized abortion. Opposes constitutional amendments and federal and state legislation restricting access to abortion services.

Voters for Choice, *1010 Wisconsin Ave. N.W., #410 20007-3679; (202) 944-5080. Fax, (202) 944-5081. Julie Burton, Executive Director. General e-mail, vfc@ibm.net.*

Independent, nonpartisan political committee that supports candidates favoring legalized abortion. Provides candidates at all levels of government with campaign strategy information; opposes constitutional amendments and legislation restricting abortion.

See also American Civil Liberties Union (p. 129); National Council of Catholic Women (p. 34); National Organization for Women (p. 6)

Claims Against the Government

AGENCIES

Justice Dept., *Civil Division: Federal Claims, 1331 Pennsylvania Ave. N.W., #3744 20530; (202) 514-3301. Fax, (202) 514-8071. David M. Cohen, Director. Information, (202) 514-2007.*

Represents the United States in the U.S. Court of Federal Claims, except in cases involving taxes, lands, or native American claims.

Justice Dept., *Environment and Natural Resources, 950 Pennsylvania Ave. N.W., #2718 20530-0001; (202) 514-2701. Fax, (202) 514-0557. Lois J. Schiffer, Assistant Attorney General. Web, www.usdoj.gov/enrd.*

Represents the United States in the U.S. Court of Federal Claims in cases arising from acquisition of property or related matters.

Justice Dept., *Tax Division, 950 Pennsylvania Ave. N.W., #4143 20530; (202) 514-2901. Fax, (202) 514-5479. Paula Jounghanf, Assistant Attorney General (Acting). Web, www.usdoj.gov/tax/tax.html.*

Represents the United States and its officers in all civil and criminal litigation arising under the internal revenue laws, other than proceedings in the United States Tax Court.

State Dept., *International Claims and Investment Disputes, 2430 E St. N.W., #203 20037-2800; (202) 776-8360. Fax, (202) 776-8389. Ronald J. Bettauer, Assistant Legal Adviser. Web, www.state.gov.*

Handles claims by U.S. government and citizens against foreign governments, as well as claims by foreign governments and their nationals against the U.S. government; negotiates international claims agreements. Han-

dles claims against the State Dept. for negligence (under the Federal Tort Claims Act) and claims by owners of U.S. flag vessels due to illegal seizures by foreign governments in international waters (under the Fishermen's Protective Act).

CONGRESS

House Judiciary Committee, *Subcommittee on Immigration and Claims, B370B RHOB 20515; (202) 225-5727. Fax, (202) 225-3672. Rep. Lamar Smith, R-Texas, Chair; George Fishman, Counsel. General e-mail, Judiciary@mail.house.gov. Web, www.house.gov/judiciary.*

Jurisdiction over legislation related to claims against the United States.

Senate Judiciary Committee, *SD-224 20510; (202) 224-5225. Fax, (202) 224-9102. Sen. Orrin G. Hatch, R-Utah, Chair; Manus Cooney, Chief Counsel. Web, judiciary.senate.gov.*

Jurisdiction over legislation related to claims against the United States.

JUDICIARY

U.S. Court of Federal Claims, *717 Madison Pl. N.W. 20005; (202) 219-9668. Fax, (202) 219-9649. Loren A. Smith, Chief Judge; Margaret Ernest, Clerk, (202) 219-9657.*

Renders judgment on any nontort claims for monetary damages against the United States founded upon the Constitution, statutes, government regulations, and government contracts. Examples include compensation for taking of property, claims arising under construction and supply contracts, certain patent cases, and cases involving the refund of federal taxes. Hears cases involving native American claims.

Interstate Compacts

CONGRESS

House Judiciary Committee, *Subcommittee on Commercial and Administrative Law, B353 RHOB 20515; (202) 225-2825. Fax, (202) 225-4299. Rep. George W. Gekas, R-Pa., Chair; Ray Smietanka, Counsel. General e-mail, Judiciary@mail.house.gov. Web, www.house.gov/judiciary.*

Jurisdiction over all interstate compacts, including hazardous waste transportation, water rights, and boundaries. (Congressional approval of interstate compacts is required by the Constitution.)

Senate Judiciary Committee, *Subcommittee on the Constitution, Federalism, and Property Rights, SD-524 20510; (202) 224-8081. Fax, (202) 228-0544. Sen. John*

Ashcroft, R-Mo., Chair; Adam Cingoli, Chief Counsel. Web, judiciary.senate.gov/constitu.htm.

Jurisdiction over interstate compacts dealing with such matters as hazardous waste transportation, water rights, and boundaries. (Congressional approval of interstate compacts is required by the Constitution.)

Religious Freedom

See also Private, Parochial, and Home Schooling (chap. 6); Religion and Ethics (chap. 1)

CONGRESS

House Judiciary Committee, *Subcommittee on the Constitution,* H2-362 FHOB 20515; (202) 226-7680. Fax, (202) 225-3746. Rep. Charles T. Canady, R-Fla., Chair; Cathy Cleaver, Chief Counsel. General e-mail, Judiciary@ mail.house.gov. Web, www.house.gov/judiciary.

Jurisdiction over proposed constitutional amendments; oversight of the First Amendment right to religious freedom.

Senate Judiciary Committee, *Subcommittee on the Constitution, Federalism, and Property Rights,* SD-524 20510; (202) 224-8081. Fax, (202) 228-0544. Sen. John Ashcroft, R-Mo., Chair; Adam Cingoli, Chief Counsel. Web, judiciary.senate.gov/constitu.htm.

Jurisdiction over proposed constitutional amendments; oversight of the First Amendment right to religious freedom.

NONPROFIT

American Jewish Congress, *Washington Office,* 2027 Massachusetts Ave. N.W. 20036; (202) 332-4001. Fax, (202) 387-3434. Matt Dorf, Washington Representative. General e-mail, washrep@ajcongress.org. Web, www. ajcongress.org.

Advocacy organization that seeks to uphold civil and constitutional rights. Litigates cases involving prayer in public schools, tuition tax credits, equal access, and religious symbols on public property. (Headquarters in New York.)

Americans for Religious Liberty, P.O. Box 6656, Silver Spring, MD 20916; (301) 598-2447. Fax, (301) 438-8424. Edd Doerr, Executive Director. General e-mail, arlinc@ erols.com.

Educational organization concerned with issues involving the separation of church and state. Opposes government-sponsored school prayer and tax support for religious institutions; supports religious neutrality in public education; defends abortion rights. Provides legal services in litigation cases. Maintains speakers bureau.

Americans United for Separation of Church and State, 518 C St. N.W. 20002; (202) 466-3234. Fax, (202) 466-2587. Barry W. Lynn, Executive Director. General e-mail, americansunited@au.org. Web, www.au.org.

Citizens' interest group that opposes government-sponsored prayer in public schools and tax aid for parochial schools.

Christian Legal Society, 4208 Evergreen Lane, #222, Annandale, VA 22003; (703) 642-1070. Fax, (703) 642-1075. Samuel B. Casey, Executive Director. General e-mail, clshq@clsnet.org. Web, www.christianlegalsociety.org.

Membership: attorneys, judges, law professors, and law students. Seeks to create and mobilize a national network of Christians to advocate justice and religious freedom.

Council on Religious Freedom, 110 N. Washington St., #404, Rockville, MD 20850; (301) 294-8766. Fax, (301) 294-8909. Nicholas P. Miller, Executive Director. General e-mail, freedom@c-r-f.org. Web, www.c-r-f.org.

Seeks to preserve principles of religious liberty through litigation and educational programs. Opposes prayer in public schools.

International Religious Liberty Assn., 12501 Old Columbia Pike, Silver Spring, MD 20904-6600; (301) 680-6680. Fax, (301) 680-6695. John Graz, Secretary General. Web, www.irla.org.

Seeks to preserve and expand religious liberty and freedom of conscience; advocates separation of church and state; sponsors international and domestic meetings and congresses.

National Assn. of Evangelicals, *Washington Office,* 1001 Connecticut Ave. N.W., #522 20036; (202) 789-1011. Fax, (202) 842-0392. Rich Cizik, Director. General e-mail, oga@nae.net. Web, www.nae.net.

Membership: evangelical churches, organizations (including schools), and individuals. Supports religious freedom. Monitors legislation and regulations. (Headquarters in Wheaton, Ill.)

National Council of Churches, *Washington Office,* 110 Maryland Ave. N.E., #108 20002; (202) 544-2350. Fax, (202) 543-1297. Vacant, Director. General e-mail, mary@ncccusa.org. Web, www.ncccusa.org.

Membership: Protestant, Anglican, and Orthodox churches. Opposes government-sponsored prayer in public schools. Provides information on the school prayer issue. (Headquarters in New York.)

See also American Civil Liberties Union (p. 129)

Separation of Powers

CONGRESS

House Government Reform Committee, *Subcommittee on Criminal Justice, Drug Policy, and Human Resources, B373 RHOB 20515; (202) 225-2577. Fax, (202) 225-1154. Rep. John L. Mica, R-Fla., Chair; Sharon Pinkerton, Staff Director. Web, www.house.gov/reform.*

Jurisdiction over legislation on some aspects of executive privilege and separation of powers (jurisdiction over separation of powers shared with House Judiciary Committee).

House Judiciary Committee, *2138 RHOB 20515; (202) 225-3951. Fax, (202) 225-7682. Rep. Henry J. Hyde, R-Ill., Chair; Thomas Mooney, Chief of Staff. General e-mail, Judiciary@mail.house.gov. Web, www.house.gov/judiciary.*

Jurisdiction over legislation dealing with separation of powers and presidential succession (jurisdiction over separation of powers shared with House Government Reform Committee).

Senate Judiciary Committee, *Subcommittee on the Constitution, Federalism, and Property Rights, SD-524 20510; (202) 224-8081. Fax, (202) 228-0544. Sen. John Ashcroft, R-Mo., Chair; Adam Cingoli, Chief Counsel. Web, judiciary.senate.gov/constitu.htm.*

Jurisdiction over legislation on separation of powers, presidential succession, and some aspects of executive privilege.

NONPROFIT

Public Citizen Litigation Group, *1600 20th St. N.W. 20009; (202) 588-7721. Fax, (202) 588-7795. David Vladeck, Director. Web, www.citizen.org.*

Conducts litigation for Public Citizen, a citizens' interest group, in cases involving separation of powers; represents individuals and groups with similar interests.

 CRIMINAL LAW

AGENCIES

Criminal Division *(Justice Dept.), 950 Pennsylvania Ave. N.W., #2107 20530; (202) 514-2601. Fax, (202) 514-9412. James K. Robinson, Assistant Attorney General. Web, www.usdoj.gov/criminal.*

Enforces all federal criminal laws except those specifically assigned to the antitrust, civil rights, environment and natural resources, and tax divisions of the Justice Dept. Supervises and directs U.S. attorneys in the field on criminal matters and litigation; supervises interna-

tional extradition proceedings. Coordinates federal enforcement efforts against white-collar crime, fraud, and child pornography; handles civil actions under customs, liquor, narcotics, gambling, and firearms laws; coordinates enforcement activities against organized crime. Directs the National Asset Forfeiture Program for seizing the proceeds of criminal activity. Investigates and prosecutes criminal offenses involving public integrity and subversive activities, including treason, espionage, and sedition; Nazi war crimes; and related criminal offenses. Handles all civil cases relating to internal security and counsels federal departments and agencies regarding internal security matters. Drafts responses on proposed and pending criminal law legislation.

Criminal Division *(Justice Dept.), Enforcement Operations: International Prisoner Transfers, P.O. Box 7600, Ben Franklin Station 20044-7600; (202) 514-3173. Fax, (202) 514-9003. Sylvia Royce, Chief.*

Implements prisoner transfer treaties with foreign countries.

Federal Bureau of Investigation *(Justice Dept.), 935 Pennsylvania Ave. N.W. 20535; (202) 324-3444. Fax, (202) 324-4705. Louis J. Freeh, Director. Information, (202) 324-3000. Web, www.fbi.gov.*

Investigates all violations of federal criminal laws except those assigned specifically to other federal agencies. Exceptions include alcohol, counterfeiting, tobacco, and customs violations (departments of Treasury and Commerce); postal violations (U.S. Postal Service); and illegal entry of aliens (Justice Dept.'s Immigration and Naturalization Service). Services provided to other law enforcement agencies include fingerprint identification, laboratory services, police training, and the National Crime Information Center (communications network among FBI, state, and local police agencies).

Office of Justice Programs *(Justice Dept.), National Institute of Justice, 810 7th St. N.W. 20531; (202) 307-2942. Fax, (202) 307-6394. Jeremy Travis, Director. Web, www.ojp.usdoj.gov/nij.*

Conducts research on all aspects of criminal justice, including crime prevention, enforcement, adjudication, and corrections; evaluates programs; develops model programs using new techniques. Serves as an affiliated institute of the United Nations Crime Prevention and Criminal Justice Programme (UNCPCJ); studies transnational issues, especially within the Western Hemisphere. Maintains the National Criminal Justice Reference Service, which provides information on criminal justice research: (800) 851-3420; in Maryland, (301) 251-5500; Web, www.ncjrs.org.

Office of Justice Programs *(Justice Dept.), Victims of Crime,* 810 7th St. N.W., 8th Floor 20531; (202) 307-5983. Fax, (202) 514-6383. Kathryn M. Turman, Director. TTY, (202) 514-7863. Resource Center, (800) 627-6872. Web, www.ojp.usdoj.gov/ovc.

Provides funds to state victim compensation and assistance programs, including counseling for victims of rape, child abuse, and spouse abuse; supports victim assistance programs for native Americans. Operations are financed by the crime victims fund, which is financed by federal criminal fines, penalties, and bond forfeitures. Provides information on victim and witness services.

CONGRESS

House Commerce Committee, *Subcommittee on Health and the Environment,* 2125 RHOB 20515; (202) 225-2927. Fax, (202) 225-1919. Rep. Michael Bilirakis, R-Fla., Chair; James E. Derderian, Staff Director. General e-mail, commerce@mail.house.gov. Web, www.house.gov/commerce.

Jurisdiction over legislation on drug abuse and rehabilitation of drug abusers, including narcotics addicts who have had contact (arrest or conviction) with the federal criminal justice system.

House Education and the Workforce Committee, *Subcommittee on Early Childhood, Youth, and Families,* 2181 RHOB 20515; (202) 225-4527. Fax, (202) 225-9571. Rep. Michael N. Castle, R-Del., Chair; Kevin D. Talley, Staff Director. Web, www.house.gov/ed_workforce.

Jurisdiction over legislation on juvenile justice and related issues, including the role of children in the courts (jurisdiction shared with House Judiciary Committee). Oversight of the Juvenile Justice and Delinquency Prevention Act, the Runaway Youth Act, and juvenile justice programs administered by the Office of Justice Programs.

House Government Reform Committee, *Subcommittee on the Postal Service,* B349C RHOB 20515; (202) 225-3741. Fax, (202) 225-2544. Rep. John M. McHugh, R-N.Y., Chair; Robert Taub, Staff Director. Web, www.house.gov/reform.

Jurisdiction over legislation on postal fraud.

House Judiciary Committee, 2138 RHOB 20515; (202) 225-3951. Fax, (202) 225-7682. Rep. Henry J. Hyde, R-Ill., Chair; Thomas Mooney, Chief of Staff. General e-mail, Judiciary@mail.house.gov. Web, www.house.gov/judiciary.

Jurisdiction over internal security legislation.

House Judiciary Committee, *Subcommittee on Crime,* 207 CHOB 20515; (202) 225-3926. Fax, (202) 225-3737. Rep. Bill McCollum, R-Fla., Chair; Daniel Bryant, Chief

Counsel. General e-mail, Judiciary@mail.house.gov. Web, www.house.gov/judiciary.

Responsible for all aspects of criminal law and procedure, and revision of the U.S. criminal code (jurisdiction over juvenile justice and the role of children in the courts shared with House Education and the Workforce Committee). Oversees federal law enforcement agencies, including the Federal Bureau of Investigation (shares intelligence operations jurisdiction with the House Select Committee on Intelligence); the Drug Enforcement Administration; the Bureau of Alcohol, Tobacco, and Firearms; the Federal Bureau of Prisons; the U.S. Parole Commission; the U.S. Marshals Service; and the Secret Service. Jurisdiction over legislation concerning the Criminal Division of the Justice Dept.

House Permanent Select Committee on Intelligence, H405 CAP 20515; (202) 225-4121. Fax, (202) 225-1991. Rep. Porter J. Goss, R-Fla., Chair; John I. Millis, Staff Director.

Jurisdiction over legislation on control of domestic terrorism; oversight of the intelligence operations of the Federal Bureau of Investigation (jurisdiction shared with House Judiciary Committee).

Senate Foreign Relations Committee, *Subcommittee on Western Hemisphere, Peace Corps, Narcotics, and Terrorism,* SD-450 20510; (202) 224-4651. Fax, (202) 224-0836. Sen. Lincoln Chafee, R-R.I., Chair; Roger Noriega, Senior Professional Staff Member. Web, www.senate.gov/~foreign.

Jurisdiction over legislation dealing with the international flow of illegal drugs.

Senate Governmental Affairs Committee, SD-340 20510; (202) 224-4751. Fax, (202) 224-9603. Sen. Fred Thompson, R-Tenn., Chair; Hannah Sistare, Staff Director. Web, gov_affairs.senate.gov.

Oversight of Bureau of Alcohol, Tobacco, and Firearms.

Senate Governmental Affairs Committee, *Permanent Subcommittee on Investigations,* SR-100 20510; (202) 224-3721. Fax, (202) 224-7042. Sen. Susan Collins, R-Maine, Chair; K. Lee Blalack, Staff Director. General e-mail, PSI@govt-aff.senate.gov. Web, gov_affairs.senate.gov/psi.htm.

Investigates organized criminal activity, national and international narcotics trafficking, postal fraud, prison crime, child pornography, government contracts fraud, insurance fraud, entitlement fraud, fraud involving the use of computers, and securities theft and fraud. Investigates federal arson prevention and control activities.

Senate Health, Education, Labor, and Pensions Committee, *SD-428 20510; (202) 224-5375. Fax, (202) 228-5044. Sen. James M. Jeffords, R-Vt., Chair; Mark Powden, Staff Director. TTY, (202) 224-1975. Web, labor. senate.gov.*

Jurisdiction over legislation on drug abuse and reha-bilitation of drug abusers, including narcotics addicts who have had contact (arrest or conviction) with the federal criminal justice system.

Senate Judiciary Committee, *SD-224 20510; (202) 224-5225. Fax, (202) 224-9102. Sen. Orrin G. Hatch, R-Utah, Chair; Manus Cooney, Chief Counsel. Web, judiciary.senate.gov.*

Responsible for all aspects of criminal law and proce-dure and revision of the U.S. criminal code. Jurisdiction over legislation on internal security, speedy trials and pretrial procedures, grand juries, federal trial juries, fed-eral corrections institutions (including prisoner health care), sentences, parole, pardons, the U.S. Parole Com-mission, and capital punishment. Jurisdiction over legis-lation dealing with organized crime, including the Rack-eteer Influenced and Corrupt Organizations Act (RICO); judicial ethics; gun control; control of domestic terror-ism; some aspects of narcotics abuse, including control, enforcement, and criminal penalties; and regulation of trade.

Senate Judiciary Committee, *Subcommittee on Youth Violence, SD-G13 20510; (202) 224-7572. Fax, (202) 228-0545. Sen. Jeff Sessions, R-Ala., Chair; Kristi Lee, Chief Counsel. Web, judiciary.senate.gov/youth.htm.*

Jurisdiction over legislation on juvenile justice and related issues, including the role of children in the courts. Oversight of the Juvenile Justice and Delinquency Prevention Act, the Runaway and Homeless Youth Act, and juvenile justice programs administered by the Office of Justice Programs.

Senate Select Committee on Intelligence, *SH-211 20510; (202) 224-1700. Fax, (202) 224-1772. Sen. Richard C. Shelby, R-Ala., Chair; Nick Rostow, Staff Director. Web, intelligence.senate.gov.*

Studies, makes recommendations, and proposes leg-islation on intelligence agencies' activities, policies, and funds; oversees the Central Intelligence Agency, National Security Agency, Defense Intelligence Agency, the intelli-gence activities of the Federal Bureau of Investigation, and other intelligence operations of the U.S. government to ensure conformity with the U.S. Constitution and laws; authorizes appropriations for the intelligence com-munity. Oversight of directives and procedures govern-ing intelligence activities affecting the rights of Ameri-cans abroad.

INTERNATIONAL ORGANIZATIONS

INTERPOL, *Washington Office, 600 E St. N.W. 20530-1022 (mailing address: INTERPOL-USNCB U.S. Justice Dept. 20530); (202) 616-9000. Fax, (202) 616-8400. Edgar A. Adamson, Chief. Web, www.usdoj.gov/usncb.*

U.S. national central bureau for INTERPOL; partici-pates in international investigations on behalf of U.S. police; coordinates the exchange of investigative infor-mation on crimes, including drug trafficking, counter-feiting, missing persons, and terrorism. Coordinates law enforcement requests for investigative assistance in the United States and abroad. Assists with extradition processes. Serves as liaison between foreign and U.S. law enforcement agencies at federal, state, and local levels. (Headquarters in Lyons, France.)

NONPROFIT

American Bar Assn., *Criminal Justice, Washington Office, 740 15th St. N.W. 20005-1022; (202) 662-1500. Fax, (202) 662-1501. Thomas C. Smith, Director. Web, www.abanet.org.*

Responsible for all matters pertaining to criminal law and procedure for the association. Studies and makes recommendations on all facets of the criminal and juve-nile justice system, including sentencing, juries, pretrial procedures, grand juries, white-collar crime, and the Racketeer Influenced and Corrupt Organizations Act (RICO). (Headquarters in Chicago.)

American Prosecutors Research Institute, *99 Canal Center Plaza, #510, Alexandria, VA 22314; (703) 549-4253. Fax, (703) 836-3195. Kevin O'Brien, Deputy Direc-tor. Web, www.ndaa-apri.org.*

Conducts research, provides information, and ana-lyzes policies related to improvements in criminal prose-cution. (Affiliated with the National District Attorneys' Assn.)

Justice Policy Institute, *2208 Martin Luther King Jr. Ave. S.E. 20020; (202) 678-9282. Fax, (202) 678-9321. Vincent Schiraldi, Director. Web, www.cjcj.org/jpi.*

Research, advocacy, and policy development organi-zation. Analyzes current and emerging criminal justice problems; works to develop new initiatives; educates the public about criminal justice issues. Interests include new prison construction, alternatives to incarceration, and curfew laws.

National Assn. of Attorneys General, *750 1st St. N.E., #1100 20002; (202) 326-6053. Fax, (202) 408-7014. Chris-tine Milliken, Executive Director. Press, (202) 326-6047.*

Membership: attorneys general of the states, territo-ries, and commonwealths. Fosters interstate cooperation on legal and law enforcement issues, conducts policy research and analysis, and facilitates communication between members and all levels of government.

(For list of attorneys general, see Governors and Other State Officials in appendix.)

National Assn. of Crime Victim Compensation Boards, *P.O. Box 16003, Alexandria, VA 22302-8003; (703) 370-2996. Fax, (703) 370-2996. Dan Eddy, Executive Director.*

Provides state compensation agencies with training and technical assistance. Provides public information on victim compensation.

National Assn. of Criminal Defense Lawyers, *1025 Connecticut Ave. N.W., #901 20036; (202) 872-8600. Fax, (202) 872-8690. Stuart M. Statler, Executive Director. Web, www.criminaljustice.org.*

Membership: criminal defense attorneys. Provides members with continuing legal education programs, a brief bank, an ethics hotline, and specialized assistance in areas such as DNA and Section 8300 cash reporting requirements. Offers free legal assistance to members who are harassed, charged with contempt, or receive a bar grievance for providing ethical but aggressive representation. Interests include eliminating mandatory minimum sentencing, reforming the FBI laboratories, opposing the death penalty, and minimizing the effect on civil liberties of the war on drugs. Monitors legislation and regulations.

National Center For Victims of Crime, *2111 Wilson Blvd., #300, Arlington, VA 22201; (703) 276-2880. Fax, (703) 276-2889. Susan Herman, Executive Director. Web, www.ncvc.org.*

Works with victims' groups and criminal justice agencies to protect the rights of crime victims through state and federal statutes and policies. Promotes greater responsiveness to crime victims through training and education; provides research and technical assistance in the development of victim-related legislation.

National Crime Prevention Council, *1700 K St. N.W., 2nd Floor 20006-3817; (202) 466-6272. Fax, (202) 296-1356. John A. Calhoun, Executive Director. Fulfillment office, (800) 627-2911. Web, www.weprevent.org.*

Educates public on crime prevention through media campaigns, supporting materials, and training workshops; sponsors McGruff public service campaign; runs demonstration programs in schools.

National District Attorneys' Assn., *99 Canal Center Plaza, #510, Alexandria, VA 22314; (703) 549-9222. Fax,*

(703) 836-3195. Newman Flanagan, Executive Director. Web, www.ndaa-apri.org.

Sponsors conferences and workshops on criminal justice; provides information on district attorneys, criminal justice, the courts, child abuse, environmental crime, and national traffic laws.

National Organization for Victim Assistance, *1757 Park Rd. N.W. 20010; (202) 232-6682. Fax, (202) 462-2255. Marlene A. Young, Executive Director. Toll-free information hotline, (800) 879-6682; (202) 232-6682 in Washington area. General e-mail, nova@try-nova.org. Web, www.try-nova.org.*

Membership: persons involved with victim and witness assistance programs, criminal justice professionals, researchers, crime victims, and others interested in victims' rights. Monitors legislation; provides victims and victim support programs with technical assistance, referrals, and program support; provides information on victims' rights.

Child Abuse, Domestic Violence, and Sexual Assault

See also Children and Families (chap. 18)

AGENCIES

Administration for Children, Youth, and Families *(Health and Human Services Dept.), Family and Youth Services, 330 C St. S.W. 20447 (mailing address: P.O. Box 1182 20013); (202) 205-8102. Fax, (202) 260-9333. Gilda Lambert, Associate Commissioner.*

Administers federal discretionary grant programs for projects serving runaway and homeless youth and for projects that deter youth involvement in gangs. Provides youth service agencies with training and technical assistance. Monitors federal policies, programs, and legislation. Supports research on youth development issues, including gangs, runaways, and homeless youth. Operates national clearinghouse on families and youth.

Criminal Division *(Justice Dept.), Child Exploitation and Obscenity Section, 1331 F St. N.W., #637 20530; (202) 514-5780. Terry Lord, Chief. Web, www.usdoj.gov/ criminal/CEOS.*

Enforces federal obscenity and child pornography laws; prosecutes cases involving violations of these laws. Maintains collection of briefs, pleadings, and other material for use by federal, state, and local prosecutors.

Office of Justice Programs *(Justice Dept.), National Institute of Justice, 810 7th St. N.W. 20531; (202) 307-2942. Fax, (202) 307-6394. Jeremy Travis, Director. Web, www.ojp.usdoj.gov/nij.*

Conducts research on all aspects of criminal justice, including AIDS issues for law enforcement officials. Studies on rape and domestic violence available from the National Criminal Justice Reference Service: (800) 851-3420; in Maryland, (301) 251-5500; Web, www.ncjrs.org.

Office of Justice Programs *(Justice Dept.), Violence Against Women,* 800 K St. N.W., #920 20001; (202) 616-8894. Fax, (202) 307-3911. Bonnie Campbell, Director. Web, www.usdoj.gov/vawo.

Seeks more effective policies and services to combat domestic violence, sexual assault, stalking, and other crimes against women. Helps administer grants to states to fund shelters, crisis centers, and hotlines, and to hire law enforcement officers, prosecutors, and counselors specializing in cases of sexual violence and other violent crimes against women.

NONPROFIT

American Bar Assn., *Center on Children and the Law,* 740 15th St. N.W., 9th Floor 20005-1009; (202) 662-1720. Fax, (202) 662-1755. Howard Davidson, Director. General e-mail, ctrchildlaw@abanet.org. Web, www.abanet.org/child.

Provides state and private child welfare organizations with training and technical assistance. Interests include child abuse and neglect, adoption, foster care, and medical neglect.

National Center for Prosecution of Child Abuse, 99 Canal Center Plaza, #510, Alexandria, VA 22314; (703) 739-0321. Fax, (703) 549-6259. Victor Veith, Director. Web, www.ndaa-apri.org.

Provides prosecutors involved in child abuse cases with training, technical assistance, and information. Monitors legislation concerning child abuse.

Rape, Abuse, and Incest National Network (RAINN), 635-B Pennsylvania Ave. S.E. 20003-4303; (202) 544-1034. Fax, (202) 544-3556. Debbie Andrews, Executive Director. Toll-free, (800) 656-HOPE. General e-mail, rainnmail@aol.com. Web, www.rainn.org.

Publicizes the issue of sexual assault and the availability of local counseling services for rape and incest survivors. RAINN's 24-hour sexual assault hotline provides free counseling services through a national network of rape crisis centers.

See also Center for Women Policy Studies (p. 9)

Drug Control

See also Narcotics Trafficking (chap. 13); Substance Abuse (chap. 11)

AGENCIES

Criminal Division *(Justice Dept.), Narcotic and Dangerous Drugs,* 1400 New York Ave. N.W., #1100 20530; (202) 514-0917. Fax, (202) 514-6112. John Roth, Chief.

Investigates and prosecutes participants in criminal syndicates involved in the large-scale importation, manufacture, shipment, or distribution of illegal narcotics and other dangerous drugs. Trains agents and prosecutors in the techniques of major drug litigation.

Defense Dept., *Drug Enforcement Policy and Support,* The Pentagon, #2E538 20301-1510; (703) 695-7996. Fax, (703) 693-7588. Ana Maria Salazar, Deputy Assistant Secretary. Web, www.defenselink.mil.

Advises the secretary on Defense Dept. policies and programs in support of federal counternarcotics operations and the implementation of the president's National Drug Control Policy.

Drug Enforcement Administration *(Justice Dept.),* 700 Army-Navy Dr., Arlington, VA 22202; (202) 307-8000. Fax, (202) 307-7965. Donnie R. Marshall, Administrator (Acting). Press, (202) 307-7977. Locator, (202) 307-4132. Web, www.usdoj.gov/dea.

Enforces federal laws and statutes relating to narcotics and other dangerous drugs, including addictive drugs, depressants, stimulants, and hallucinogens; manages the National Narcotics Intelligence System in cooperation with federal, state, and local officials; investigates violations and regulates legal trade in narcotics and dangerous drugs. Provides school and community officials with drug abuse policy guidelines. Provides information on drugs and drug abuse.

Federal Bureau of Investigation *(Justice Dept.),* 935 Pennsylvania Ave. N.W. 20535; (202) 324-3444. Fax, (202) 324-4705. Louis J. Freeh, Director. Information, (202) 324-3000. Web, www.fbi.gov.

Shares responsibility with the Drug Enforcement Administration for investigating violations of federal criminal drug laws; investigates organized crime involvement with illegal narcotics trafficking.

Food and Drug Administration *(Health and Human Services Dept.), Center for Drug Evaluation and Research,* 1451 Rockville Pike, Rockville, MD 20852; (301) 594-5400. Fax, (301) 594-6197. Dr. Janet Woodcock, Director. Information, (301) 827-4573. Press, (301) 827-6242.

Makes recommendations to the Justice Dept.'s Drug Enforcement Administration on narcotics and dangerous drugs to be controlled.

Interior Dept., *Managing Risk and Public Safety*, 1849 C St. N.W., #7358 20240-4108; (202) 208-7702. Fax, (202) 208-5078. L. Michael Kaas, Director. Web, www.doi.gov/mrps.

Administers drug and law enforcement programs for the Interior Dept., including programs in national parks, ranges, and fish and wildlife refuges. Cooperates with local law enforcement agencies, state park rangers, and other drug enforcement agencies.

Office of Justice Programs *(Justice Dept.)*, *Justice Assistance*, 810 7th St. N.W., 4th Floor 20531; (202) 514-6278. Fax, (202) 305-1367. Nancy E. Gist, Director. Web, www.ojp.usdoj.gov/BJA.

Awards grants and provides eligible state and local governments with training and technical assistance to enforce laws relating to narcotics and other dangerous drugs.

Office of National Drug Control Policy *(Executive Office of the President)*, 750 17th St. N.W. 20503; (202) 395-6700. Fax, (202) 395-6708. Barry McCaffrey, Director. Web, www.whitehousedrugpolicy.gov.

Establishes policies and oversees the implementation of a national drug control strategy; recommends changes to reduce demand for and supply of illegal drugs; advises the National Security Council on drug control policy.

U.S. Coast Guard *(Transportation Dept.)*, *Law Enforcement*, 2100 2nd St. S.W., #3110 20593-0001; (202) 267-1890. Fax, (202) 267-4082. Capt. Anthony S. Tangeman, Chief. Web, www.uscg.mil/hq/g-o/g-opl/mle/welcome.htm.

Combats smuggling of narcotics and other dangerous drugs into the United States via the Atlantic and Pacific oceans and the Gulf of Mexico; works with U.S. Customs Service on drug law enforcement; interdicts illegal migrants; enforces fisheries.

U.S. Customs Service *(Treasury Dept.)*, *Investigations*, 1300 Pennsylvania Ave. N.W., #6.5EA 20229; (202) 927-1600. Fax, (202) 927-1948. Bonni G. Tischler, Assistant Commissioner. Information, (202) 927-1770. Web, www.customs.ustreas.gov.

Interdicts and seizes contraband, including narcotics and other dangerous drugs smuggled into the United States. To report information on drug smuggling, call (800) 232-5378.

NONPROFIT

Common Sense for Drug Policy, 3619 Tallwood Terrace, Falls Church, VA 22041; (703) 354-5694. Fax, (703) 354-5695. Kevin B. Zeese, President. Web, www.csdp.org.

Provides comprehensive information on drug policy related questions to media and other interested parties. Offers technical assistance, fundraising, and public relations advice to groups that promote health-based strategies of drug control. Seeks to encourage development of an effective drug policy and to reduce drug-related harms, including spread of AIDS and other diseases, crime and violence, and social dysfunction; focus includes international drug policy.

Drug Policy Foundation, 4455 Connecticut Ave. N.W., #B500 20008-2328; (202) 537-5005. Fax, (202) 537-3007. Ruth Lampi, Administrative Director. General e-mail, dpf@dpf.org. Web, www.dpf.org.

Supports reform of current drug control policy. Advocates medical treatment to control drug abuse; opposes random drug testing. Sponsors the International Conference on Drug Policy Reform annually.

Marijuana Policy Project, *Government Relations*, P.O. Box 77492 20013; (202) 462-5747. Fax, (202) 232-0442. Robert D. Kampia, Director. General e-mail, mpp@mpp.org. Web, www.mpp.org.

Promotes reform of marijuana policies and regulations. Opposes the prohibition of responsible growing and use of marijuana by adults. Interests include allowing doctors to prescribe marijuana to seriously ill patients and reforming federal sentencing policies.

National Assn. of Chiefs of Police, *Washington Office*, 1090 Vermont Ave. N.W., #800 20005; (202) 293-9088. Donna Shepherd, Director. Web, www.aphf.org.

Conducts research and provides organizations interested in reducing drug demand with information, programs, and training. (Affiliated with the National Police Hall of Fame in Miami, [305] 573-0070.)

National Assn. of State Alcohol and Drug Abuse Directors, 808 17th St. N.W., #410 20006; (202) 293-0090. Fax, (202) 293-1250. John S. Gustafson, Executive Director.

Provides information on drug abuse treatment and prevention; contracts with federal and state agencies for design of programs to fight drug abuse.

National Organization for the Reform of Marijuana Laws, 1001 Connecticut Ave. N.W., #710 20036; (202) 483-5500. Fax, (202) 483-0057. Keith Stroup, Executive Director. General e-mail, natlnorml@norml.org. Web, www.norml.org.

Works to reform federal, state, and local marijuana laws and policies. Educates the public and conducts litigation on behalf of marijuana consumers. Monitors legislation and regulations.

Rand Corporation, *Drug Policy Research Center,* ***Washington Office,*** *1333 H St. N.W., #800 20005-4707; (202) 296-5000. Fax, (202) 296-7960. Barbara Williams, Senior Adviser. Web, www.rand.org/centers/dprc.*

Studies and analyzes the nation's drug problems and policies; interests include international policy, trafficking, and interdiction. Provides policymakers with information. (Headquarters in Santa Monica, Calif.)

Gun Control

AGENCIES

Bureau of Alcohol, Tobacco, and Firearms *(Treasury Dept.),* **Field Operations,** *650 Massachusetts Ave. N.W., #8100 20226; (202) 927-7970. Fax, (202) 927-7756. Andrew L. Vita, Assistant Director. Information, (202) 927-7777. Press, (202) 927-9510. Web, www.atf.treas.gov.*

Enforces and administers laws to eliminate illegal possession and use of firearms. Investigates criminal violations and regulates legal trade, including imports and exports. To report thefts, losses, or discoveries of explosive materials, call (800) 800-3855.

NONPROFIT

Center to Prevent Handgun Violence, *1225 Eye St. N.W., #1100 20005; (202) 289-7319. Fax, (202) 408-1851. Vacant, President. Web, www.cphv.org.*

Educational, research, and legal action organization that seeks to allay handgun violence, especially among children, through gun control legislation. (Affiliated with Handgun Control, Inc.)

Citizens Committee for the Right to Keep and Bear Arms, *Publications and Public Affairs, Washington Office, 1090 Vermont Ave. N.W., #800 20005; (202) 326-5259. Fax, (202) 898-1939. John M. Snyder, Director.*

Concerned with rights of gun owners. Maintains National Advisory Council, comprising members of Congress and other distinguished Americans, which provides advice on issues concerning the right to keep and bear arms. (Headquarters in Bellevue, Wash.)

Coalition to Stop Gun Violence, *1000 16th St. N.W., #603 20036; (202) 530-0340. Fax, (202) 530-0331. Michael K. Beard, President. General e-mail, noguns@aol. com. Web, www.csgv.org.*

Membership: organizations and individuals seeking to ban handguns. Provides national, state, and local groups operating handgun education programs with materials; engages in research and field work to support legislation to ban or control handguns.

Educational Fund to End Handgun Violence, *1000 16th St. N.W., #603 20036; (202) 530-5888. Fax, (202)*

530-0331. Joshua Horwitz, Executive Director. General e-mail, edfund@aol.com. Web, www.endhandgunviolence. org.

Works to reduce handgun violence through education; assists schools and organizations in establishing antiviolence programs; maintains a firearms litigation clearinghouse.

Gun Owners of America, *8001 Forbes Pl., #102, Springfield, VA 22151; (703) 321-8585. Fax, (703) 321-8408. Lawrence D. Pratt, Executive Director. Web, www. gunowners.org.*

Seeks to preserve the right to bear arms and to protect the rights of law-abiding gun owners. Administers foundation that provides gun owners with legal assistance in suits against the federal government. Monitors legislation, regulations, and international agreements.

Handgun Control Inc., *1225 Eye St. N.W., #1100 20005; (202) 898-0792. Fax, (202) 371-9615. Sarah Brady, Chair. Web, www.handguncontrol.org.*

Public interest organization that works for handgun control legislation and serves as an information clearinghouse.

National Rifle Assn. of America, *11250 Waples Mill Rd., Fairfax, VA 22030; (703) 267-1000. Fax, (703) 267-3976. Wayne LaPierre Jr., Executive Vice President. Press, (703) 267-3820. Web, www.nra.org.*

Membership: target shooters, hunters, gun collectors, gunsmiths, police officers, and others interested in firearms. Promotes shooting sports and recreational shooting and safety; studies and makes recommendations on firearms laws. Opposes gun control legislation.

Juvenile Justice

See also Children and Families (chap. 18)

AGENCIES

Education Dept., *Compensatory Education Programs, 400 Maryland Ave. S.W., #3W230 20202-6132; (202) 260-0826. Fax, (202) 260-7764. Mary Jean LeTendre, Director. Press, (202) 401-1008. Web, www.ed.gov.*

Funds state and local institutions responsible for providing neglected or delinquent children with free public education.

Office of Justice Programs *(Justice Dept.),* **Juvenile Justice and Delinquency Prevention,** *810 7th St. N.W., 8th Floor 20531; (202) 307-5911. Fax, (202) 307-2093. Shay Bilchik, Administrator. Technical information, (202) 307-0751. Clearinghouse, (800) 638-8736. Web, www. ncjrs.org/ojjhome.htm.*

Administers federal programs related to prevention and treatment of juvenile delinquency, missing and exploited children, child victimization, and research and evaluation of juvenile justice system; coordinates with youth programs of the departments of Agriculture, Education, Housing and Urban Development, Interior, and Labor, and of the Substance Abuse and Mental Health Services Administration, including the Center for Studies of Crime and Delinquency. Operates the Juvenile Justice Clearinghouse.

NONPROFIT

Coalition for Juvenile Justice, *1211 Connecticut Ave. N.W., #414 20036; (202) 467-0864. Fax, (202) 887-0738. David Doi, Executive Director. General e-mail, juvjustice@ aol.com.*

Represents state juvenile justice advisory groups. Promotes the improvement of the juvenile justice system and the prevention of juvenile delinquency.

Robert F. Kennedy Memorial, *National Youth Project, 1367 Connecticut Ave. N.W., #200 20036-1819; (202) 463-7575. Fax, (202) 463-6606. Michael White, Director. General e-mail, info@rfkmemorial.org. Web, www. rfkmemorial.org.*

Develops new approaches to the problems of drug and alcohol addiction, crime and violence, school failures, and family disorder. Develops youth leadership skills through service and training programs, including the RFK Fellowship Program.

Organized Crime

AGENCIES

Criminal Division *(Justice Dept.), Narcotic and Dangerous Drugs, 1400 New York Ave. N.W., #1100 20530; (202) 514-0917. Fax, (202) 514-6112. John Roth, Chief.*

Investigates and prosecutes participants in criminal syndicates involved in the large-scale importation, manufacture, shipment, or distribution of illegal narcotics and other dangerous drugs. Trains agents and prosecutors in the techniques of major drug litigation.

Criminal Division *(Justice Dept.), Organized Crime and Racketeering, 1301 New York Ave. N.W., #700 20530; (202) 514-3594. Fax, (202) 305-1448. Bruce Ohr, Chief.*

Enforces federal criminal laws when subjects under investigation are alleged racketeers or part of syndicated criminal operations; coordinates efforts of federal, state, and local law enforcement agencies against organized crime, including emerging international groups. Cases include infiltration of legitimate businesses and labor unions, public corruption, labor-management racke-

teering, and violence that disrupts the criminal justice process.

Other Violations

See also Campaigns and Elections (chap. 20)

AGENCIES

Bureau of Alcohol, Tobacco, and Firearms *(Treasury Dept.), Field Operations, 650 Massachusetts Ave. N.W., #8100 20226; (202) 927-7970. Fax, (202) 927-7756. Andrew L. Vita, Assistant Director. Information, (202) 927-7777. Press, (202) 927-9510. Web, www.atf.treas.gov.*

Enforces and administers laws relating to alcohol (beer, wine, and distilled spirits), tobacco, firearms, arson, explosives, and destructive devices; investigates criminal violations and regulates legal trade. To report thefts, losses, or discoveries of explosive materials, call (800) 800-3855.

Criminal Division *(Justice Dept.), Asset Forfeiture and Money Laundering, 1400 New York Ave. N.W., #10100 20005; (202) 514-1263. Fax, (202) 514-5522. Gerald E. McDowell, Chief.*

Investigates and prosecutes money-laundering and criminal and civil forfeiture offenses involving illegal transfer of funds within the United States and from the United States to other countries. Oversees and coordinates legislative policy proposals. Advises U.S. attorney's offices in multi-district money laundering and criminal and civil forfeiture prosecutions. Represents Justice Dept. in international anti-money laundering and criminal and civil forfeiture initiatives.

Criminal Division *(Justice Dept.), Fraud, 1400 New York Ave. N.W., #2100 20005; (202) 514-0640. Fax, (202) 514-6118. Joshua R. Hochberg, Chief. Web, www.usdoj.gov/ criminal/fraud.*

Administers federal enforcement activities related to fraud and white-collar crime. Focuses on frauds against government programs, transnational and multidistrict fraud, and cases involving the security and commodity exchanges, banking practices, and consumer victimization.

Criminal Division *(Justice Dept.), Terrorism and Violent Crime, 601 D St. N.W., #6500 20530; (202) 514-0849. Fax, (202) 514-8714. James S. Reynolds, Chief.*

Investigates and prosecutes incidents of international terrorism involving U.S. interests, domestic violent crime, firearms, and explosives violations. Provides legal advice on federal statutes relating to murder, assault, kidnapping, threats, robbery, weapons and explosives control, malicious destruction of property, and aircraft and sea piracy.

Federal Bureau of Investigation *(Justice Dept.)*, *Economic Crimes,* 935 Pennsylvania Ave. N.W., #7373 20535; (202) 324-6352. Fax, (202) 324-8072. Helen L. Schumacher, Chief. Press, (202) 324-3691. Web, www.fbi.gov.

Investigates crimes of fraud, theft, or embezzlement within or against the national or international financial community, excluding frauds against financial institutions. Priorities include insurance, securities and commodities, bankruptcy, Internet fraud, and telemarketing.

U.S. Customs Service *(Treasury Dept.)*, *Investigations,* 1300 Pennsylvania Ave. N.W., #6.5EA 20229; (202) 927-1600. Fax, (202) 927-1948. Bonni G. Tischler, Assistant Commissioner. Information, (202) 927-1770. Web, www.customs.ustreas.gov.

Combats smuggling and the unreported transportation of funds in excess of $10,000; enforces statutes relating to the processing and regulation of people, carriers, cargo, and mail into and out of the United States. Investigates counterfeiting, child pornography, and commercial fraud cases.

U.S. Postal Service, *Inspection Service,* 475 L'Enfant Plaza S.W., #3100 20260; (202) 268-4267. Fax, (202) 268-4563. Kenneth C. Weaver, Chief Postal Inspector. Fraud and abuse hotline, (888) 877-7644.

Protects mail, postal funds, and property from violations of postal laws, such as mail fraud or distribution of obscene materials.

U.S. Secret Service *(Treasury Dept.)*, 950 H St. N.W., #8000 20001; (202) 406-5700. Fax, (202) 406-5246. Brian Stafford, Director. Information, (202) 406-5708. Web, www.treas.gov/usss.

Enforces and administers counterfeiting and forgery laws. Investigates electronic fund transfer, credit card, and other types of access fraud, and threats against the president, vice president, and foreign heads of state visiting the United States.

Sentencing and Corrections

AGENCIES

Federal Bureau of Prisons *(Justice Dept.)*, 320 1st St. N.W. 20534; (202) 307-6300. Fax, (202) 514-6878. Kathleen Hawk Sawyer, Director. Press, (202) 307-3198. Inmate locator service, (202) 307-3126. Web, www.bop.gov.

Supervises operations of federal correctional institutions and community treatment facilities, and commitment and management of federal inmates; oversees contracts with local institutions for confinement and support of federal prisoners. Regional offices are responsible for administration; central office in Washington coordinates operations and issues standards and policy guidelines. Central office includes Federal Prison Industries, a government corporation providing prison-manufactured goods and services for sale to federal agencies, and the National Institute of Corrections, an information and technical assistance center on state and local corrections programs.

Federal Bureau of Prisons *(Justice Dept.)*, *Health Services,* 320 1st St. N.W., #1054 20534; (202) 307-3055. Fax, (202) 307-0826. Dr. Newton E. Kendig, Medical Director; Phillip S. Wise, Assistant Director.

Administers health care and treatment programs for prisoners in federal institutions.

Federal Bureau of Prisons *(Justice Dept.)*, *Industries, Education, and Vocational Training—UNICOR,* 400 1st St. N.W. 20534 (mailing address: 320 1st St. N.W. 20534); (202) 305-3500. Fax, (202) 305-7340. Steve Schwalb, Chief Operating Officer. Web, www.unicor.gov.

Administers program whereby inmates in federal prisons produce goods and services that are sold to the federal government.

Federal Bureau of Prisons *(Justice Dept.)*, *National Institute of Corrections,* 320 1st St. N.W. 20534; (202) 307-3106. Fax, (202) 307-3361. Morris L. Thigpen, Director.

Offers technical assistance and training for upgrading state and local corrections systems through staff development, research, and evaluation of correctional operations and programs. Acts as a clearinghouse on correctional information.

Justice Dept., *Pardon Attorney,* 500 1st St. N.W., #400 20530; (202) 616-6070. Fax, (202) 616-6069. Roger C. Adams, Pardon Attorney. Web, www.usdoj.gov/offices/opa.html.

Receives and reviews petitions to the president for all forms of executive clemency, including pardons and sentence reductions; initiates investigations and prepares the deputy attorney general's recommendations to the president on petitions.

Office of Justice Programs *(Justice Dept.)*, *Justice Assistance,* 810 7th St. N.W., 4th Floor 20531; (202) 514-6278. Fax, (202) 305-1367. Nancy E. Gist, Director. Web, www.ojp.usdoj.gov/BJA.

Provides states and communities with funds and technical assistance for corrections demonstration projects.

Office of Justice Programs *(Justice Dept.)*, *National Institute of Justice,* 810 7th St. N.W. 20531; (202) 307-

2942. Fax, (202) 307-6394. Jeremy Travis, Director. Web, www.ojp.usdoj.gov/nij.

Conducts research on all aspects of criminal justice, including crime prevention, enforcement, adjudication, and corrections. Maintains the National Criminal Justice Reference Service, which provides information on corrections research: (800) 851-3420; in Maryland, (301) 251-5500; Web, www.ncjrs.org.

U.S. Parole Commission *(Justice Dept.)*, 5550 Friendship Blvd., #420, Chevy Chase, MD 20815-7286; (301) 492-5990. Fax, (301) 492-5307. Michael Gaines, Chair. Web, www.usdoj.gov/uspc.

Makes release decisions for all federal prisoners serving sentences of more than one year; jurisdiction over paroled federal prisoners and over other prisoners on mandatory release under the "good time" statutes. U.S. probation officers supervise parolees and mandatory releases.

U.S. Sentencing Commission, 1 Columbus Circle N.E., #2-500 South Lobby 20002-8002; (202) 502-4500. Fax, (202) 502-4699. Diana E. Murphy, Chair. Web, www.ussc.gov.

Establishes sentencing guidelines and policy for all federal courts, including guidelines prescribing the appropriate form and severity of punishment for those convicted of federal crimes. Provides training and research on sentencing-related issues. Serves as an information resource.

JUDICIARY

Administrative Office of the U.S. Courts, 1 Columbus Circle N.E., #7-100 20544; (202) 273-3000. Leonidas Ralph Mecham, Director. Information, (202) 502-2600. Web, www.uscourts.gov.

Supervises all administrative matters of the federal court system, except the Supreme Court; collects statistical data on business of the courts.

Administrative Office of the U.S. Courts, *Federal Corrections and Supervision,* 1 Columbus Circle N.E., #4-300 20544; (202) 502-1600. Fax, (202) 502-1677. John M. Hughes, Chief.

Supervises federal probation and pretrial services officers, subject to primary control by the respective district courts in which they serve. Responsible for general oversight of field offices; tests new probation programs such as probation teams and deferred prosecution.

NONPROFIT

American Bar Assn., *Criminal Justice, Washington Office,* 740 15th St. N.W. 20005-1022; (202) 662-1500.

Fax, (202) 662-1501. Thomas C. Smith, Director. Web, www.abanet.org.

Studies and makes recommendations on all aspects of the correctional system, including overcrowding in prisons and the privatization of prisons and correctional institutions. (Headquarters in Chicago.)

American Civil Liberties Union Foundation, *National Prison Project,* 1875 Connecticut Ave. N.W., #410 20009-5728; (202) 234-4830. Fax, (202) 234-4890. Elizabeth Alexander, Executive Director.

Litigates on behalf of prisoners through class action suits. Seeks to improve prison conditions and the penal system; serves as resource center for prisoners' rights; operates an AIDS education project.

American Correctional Assn., 4380 Forbes Blvd., Lanham, MD 20706-4322; (301) 918-1800. Fax, (301) 918-1900. James A. Gondles Jr., Executive Director. Information, (800) 222-5646. Web, www.corrections.com/aca.

Membership: corrections administrators and staff in juvenile and adult institutions, community corrections facilities, and jails; affiliates include state and regional corrections associations in the United States and Canada. Conducts and publishes research; provides state and local governments with technical assistance. Interests include criminal justice issues, correctional standards, and accreditation programs. Library open to the public.

Amnesty International USA, *Washington Office,* 600 Pennsylvania Ave. S.E., 5th Floor 20003; (202) 544-0200. Fax, (202) 546-7142. Stephen Rickard, Director. Web, www.amnesty-usa.org.

International organization that opposes retention or reinstitution of the death penalty; advocates humane treatment of all prisoners. (U.S. headquarters in New York.)

Correctional Education Assn., 4380 Forbes Blvd., Lanham, MD 20706-4322; (301) 918-1915. Fax, (301) 918-1846. Stephen J. Steurer, Executive Director. Web, www.ceainternational.org.

Membership: educators and administrators who work with students in correctional settings. Provides members with information and technical assistance to improve quality of educational programs and services offered in correctional settings. Interests include post-secondary and vocational education, special education, jail education, and libraries and literacy.

Families Against Mandatory Minimums, 1612 K St. N.W., #1400 20006; (202) 822-6700. Fax, (202) 822-6704. Julie Stewart, President. General e-mail, famm@famm.org. Web, www.famm.org.

Seeks to repeal statutory mandatory minimum prison sentences. Works to increase public awareness of inequity of mandatory minimum sentences through grassroots efforts and media outreach programs.

NAACP Legal Defense and Educational Fund, *Washington Office, 1444 Eye St. N.W., 10th Floor 20005; (202) 682-1300. Fax, (202) 682-1312. Janell Byrd, Senior Attorney.*

Civil rights litigation group that supports abolition of capital punishment; assists attorneys representing prisoners on death row; focuses public attention on race discrimination in the application of the death penalty. Not affiliated with the National Assn. for the Advancement of Colored People (NAACP). (Headquarters in New York.)

National Center on Institutions and Alternatives, *3125 Mt. Vernon Ave., Alexandria, VA 22305; (703) 684-0373. Fax, (703) 684-6037. Jerome G. Miller, President. General e-mail, info@ncianet.org. Web, www.sentencing. org.*

Seeks to reduce incarceration as primary form of punishment imposed by criminal justice system; advocates use of extended community service, work-release, and halfway house programs; operates residential programs; provides defense attorneys and courts with specific recommendations for sentencing and parole.

National Coalition to Abolish the Death Penalty, *1436 U St. N.W., #104 20009; (202) 387-3890. Fax, (202) 387-5590. Steven Hawkins, Executive Director. General e-mail, info@ncadp.org. Web, www.ncadp.org.*

Membership: organizations and individuals opposed to the death penalty. Maintains collection of death penalty research. Provides training, resources, and conferences. Works with families of murder victims; tracks execution dates. Monitors legislation and regulations.

Prison Fellowship Ministries, *1856 Old Reston Ave., Reston, VA 20190-3321 (mailing address: P.O. Box 17500 20041-0500); (703) 478-0100. Fax, (703) 478-0452. Thomas C. Pratt, President. Web, www.pfm.org.*

Religious organization that ministers to prisoners and ex-prisoners, victims, and the families involved. Offers counseling, seminars, and postrelease support for readjustment; works to increase the fairness and effectiveness of the criminal justice system.

Sentencing Project, *1516 P St. N.W. 20005; (202) 628-0871. Fax, (202) 628-1091. Malcolm Young, Executive Director. Web, www.sentencingproject.org.*

Develops and promotes sentencing programs that reduce reliance on incarceration; provides technical assistance to sentencing programs; compares domestic and international rates of incarceration; publishes research and information on criminal justice policy.

LAW ENFORCEMENT

See also Criminal Law (this chapter); Legal Professions and Resources (this chapter)

AGENCIES

Criminal Division *(Justice Dept.), Computer Crime and Intellectual Property, 1301 New York Ave. N.W., #600 20005; (202) 514-1026. Fax, (202) 514-6113. Martha Stansell-Gamm, Chief. Web, www.usdoj.gov/criminal/ cybercrime.*

Investigates and litigates criminal and civil cases involving computers and the Internet; provides specialized technical and legal assistance to other Justice Dept. divisions; coordinates international efforts; formulates policies and proposes legislation on computer crime issues.

Federal Law Enforcement Training Center *(Treasury Dept.), Washington Office, 650 Massachusetts Ave. N.W., #3100 20226; (202) 927-8940. Fax, (202) 927-8782. John C. Dooher, Associate Director. General e-mail, jdooher@fletc.treas.gov. Web, www.ustreas.gov/treasury/ bureaus/fletc.*

Trains federal law enforcement personnel from seventy agencies, excluding the Federal Bureau of Investigation and the Drug Enforcement Administration. (Headquarters in Glynco, Ga.)

National Institute of Standards and Technology *(Commerce Dept.), Law Enforcement Standards, Route I-270 and Quince Orchard Rd., Bldg. 225, #A323, Gaithersburg, MD 20899 (mailing address: 100 Bureau Dr., MS 8102, Gaithersburg, MD 20899-8102); (301) 975-2757. Fax, (301) 948-0978. Kathleen Higgins, Director. General e-mail, oles@nist.gov.*

Answers inquiries and makes referrals concerning the application of science and technology to the criminal justice community; maintains information on standards and current research; prepares reports and formulates standards for the National Institute of Justice, the Federal Bureau of Investigation, and the National Highway Traffic Safety Administration.

Office of Justice Programs *(Justice Dept.), Justice Assistance, 810 7th St. N.W., 4th Floor 20531; (202) 514-6278. Fax, (202) 305-1367. Nancy E. Gist, Director. Web, www.ojp.usdoj.gov/BJA.*

Provides funds to eligible state and local governments and to nonprofit organizations for criminal justice programs, primarily those that combat drug trafficking and other drug-related crime.

Treasury Dept., *Financial Crimes Enforcement Network,* *2070 Chain Bridge Rd., #200, Vienna, VA 22182; (703) 905-3591. Fax, (703) 905-3690. James F. Sloan, Director. Web, www.treas.gov/fincen.*

Administers information network to aid federal, state, local, and foreign law enforcement agencies in the detection, investigation, and prosecution of money-laundering operations and other financial crimes.

U.S. Marshals Service *(Justice Dept.), 600 Army-Navy Dr., #1200, Arlington, VA 22202-4210; (202) 307-9001. Fax, (703) 557-9788. John W. Marshall, Director. TTY, (202) 307-9525. Public Affairs, (202) 307-9065.*

Provides the federal judiciary system and the attorney general with support services, including court and witness security, prisoner custody and transportation, prisoner support, maintenance and disposal of seized and forfeited property, and special operations. Administers the Federal Witness Protection program. Apprehends fugitives, including those wanted by foreign nations and believed to be in the United States; oversees the return of fugitives apprehended abroad and wanted by U.S. law enforcement.

CONGRESS

House Judiciary Committee, *Subcommittee on the Constitution, H2-362 FHOB 20515; (202) 226-7680. Fax, (202) 225-3746. Rep. Charles T. Canady, R-Fla., Chair; Cathy Cleaver, Chief Counsel. General e-mail, Judiciary@ mail.house.gov. Web, www.house.gov/judiciary.*

Jurisdiction over legislation dealing with the use, collection, evaluation, and release of U.S. and international criminal justice data. Oversight of legislation on information policy, electronic privacy, computer security, and trade and licensing.

House Judiciary Committee, *Subcommittee on Crime, 207 CHOB 20515; (202) 225-3926. Fax, (202) 225-3737. Rep. Bill McCollum, R-Fla., Chair; Daniel Bryant, Chief Counsel. General e-mail, Judiciary@mail.house.gov. Web, www.house.gov/judiciary.*

Jurisdiction over legislation related to Office of Justice Programs and the Criminal Division at the Justice Dept. Oversees federal assistance to state and local law enforcement; the Federal Bureau of Investigation; the Drug Enforcement Administration; the Bureau of Alcohol, Tobacco, and Firearms; the U.S. Marshals Service; and the Secret Service.

Senate Judiciary Committee, *SD-224 20510; (202) 224-5225. Fax, (202) 224-9102. Sen. Orrin G. Hatch, R-Utah, Chair; Manus Cooney, Chief Counsel. Web, judiciary.senate.gov.*

Jurisdiction over legislation related to Office of Justice Programs, which includes the Bureau of Justice Assistance, Bureau of Justice Statistics, National Institute of Justice, Office of Juvenile Justice and Delinquency Prevention, and the Office for Victims of Crime.

Senate Judiciary Committee, *Subcommittee on Technology, Terrorism, and Government Information, SH-325 20510; (202) 224-6791. Fax, (202) 228-0542. Sen. Jon Kyl, R-Ariz., Chair; Stephen Higgins, Chief Counsel. Web, judiciary.senate.gov/techterr.htm.*

Jurisdiction over legislation dealing with the use, collection, evaluation, and release of U.S. and international criminal justice data. Oversight of legislation on information policy, electronic privacy, computer security, and trade and licensing.

NONPROFIT

American Federation of Police, *Washington Office, 1090 Vermont Ave. N.W., #800 20005; (202) 293-9088. Donna Shepherd, Director. Web, aphf.org.*

Membership: governmental and private law enforcement officers. Provides members with insurance benefits and training programs. (Affiliated with the National Police Hall of Fame in Miami, [305] 573-0070.)

International Assn. of Chiefs of Police, *515 N. Washington St., Alexandria, VA 22314-2357; (703) 836-6767. Fax, (703) 836-4543. Daniel N. Rosenblatt, Executive Director. Web, www.theiacp.org.*

Membership: foreign and U.S. police executives and administrators. Consults and conducts research on all aspects of police activity; conducts training programs and develops educational aids; conducts public education programs.

International Union of Police Assns., *1421 Prince St., #330, Alexandria, VA 22314; (703) 549-7473. Fax, (703) 683-9048. Sam Cabral, President. Web, www.sddi.com/ iupa.*

Membership: about 80,000 law enforcement officers and personnel. Helps members negotiate pay, benefits, and better working conditions; conducts training programs and workshops; offers legal services to members. Monitors legislation and regulations. (Affiliated with the AFL-CIO.)

Law Enforcement Alliance of America, *7700 Leesburg Pike, #421, Falls Church, VA 22043; (703) 847-2677.*

Fax, (703) 556-6485. Jim Fotis, Executive Director. General e-mail, info@leaa.org. Web, www.leaa.org.

Membership: law enforcement professionals, citizens, and victims of crime. Advocacy group on law and order issues.

National Assn. of Chiefs of Police, Washington Office, 1090 Vermont Ave. N.W., #800 20005; (202) 293-9088. Donna Shepherd, Director. Web, www.aphf.org.

Membership: U.S. chiefs of police and supervisory command rank officers. Conducts educational and in-service training programs; conducts research. (Affiliated with the National Police Hall of Fame in Miami, [305] 573-0070.)

National Black Police Assn., 3251 Mt. Pleasant St. N.W., 2nd Floor 20010-2103; (202) 986-2070. Fax, (202) 986-0410. Ronald Hampton, Executive Director. General e-mail, nbpanatofc@worldnet.att.net.

Membership: local, state, and regional African American police associations. Works to improve the relationship between police departments and minorities; to evaluate the effect of criminal justice policies and programs on the minority community; to recruit minority police officers; to eliminate police corruption, brutality, and racial discrimination; and to educate and train police officers.

National Criminal Justice Assn., 444 N. Capitol St. N.W., #618 20001; (202) 624-1440. Fax, (202) 508-3859. Cabell Cropper, Executive Director. Web, www.sso.org/ncja.

Membership: criminal justice organizations and professionals. Provides members and interested individuals with technical assistance and information.

National Law Enforcement Council, 888 16th St. N.W., #700 20006; (202) 835-8020. Fax, (202) 331-4291. Donald Baldwin, Executive Director.

Membership: national law enforcement organizations. Fosters information exchange and explores the effects of public policy on law enforcement. Monitors legislation and regulations.

National Organization of Black Law Enforcement Executives, 4609 Pine Crest Office Park Dr., Suite F, Alexandria, VA 22312-1442; (703) 658-1529. Fax, (703) 658-9479. Robert Stewart, Executive Director. Web, www. noblenatl.org.

Membership: minority police chiefs and senior law enforcement executives. Works to increase community involvement in the criminal justice system and to enhance the role of minorities in law enforcement. Provides urban police departments with assistance in police operations, community relations, and devising strategies to combat urban and hate crimes.

National Sheriffs' Assn., 1450 Duke St., Alexandria, VA 22314; (703) 836-7827. Fax, (703) 683-6541. Aldine N. Moser Jr., Executive Director. Information, (800) 424-7827. Web, www.sheriffs.org.

Membership: sheriffs and other municipal, state, and federal law enforcement officers. Conducts research and training programs for members in law enforcement, court procedures, and corrections. Publishes Sheriff magazine.

Police Executive Research Forum, 1120 Connecticut Ave. N.W., #930 20036; (202) 466-7820. Fax, (202) 466-7826. Chuck Wexler, Executive Director. Web, www. PoliceForum.org.

Membership: law enforcement executives from moderate to large police departments. Conducts research on law enforcement issues and methods of disseminating criminal justice and law enforcement information.

Police Foundation, 1201 Connecticut Ave. N.W., #200 20036; (202) 833-1460. Fax, (202) 659-9149. Hubert Williams, President. Web, www.policefoundation.org.

Research and education foundation that conducts studies to improve police procedures; provides technical assistance for innovative law enforcement strategies, including community-oriented policing. Houses the National Center for the Study of Police and Civil Disorder.

⚖ LEGAL PROFESSIONS AND RESOURCES

See also Criminal Law (this chapter); Public Interest Law (chap. 1)

NONPROFIT

American Bar Assn., International Law and Practice, 740 15th St. N.W. 20005; (202) 662-1660. Fax, (202) 662-1669. Cynthia Price, Director. Web, www.abanet.org/intlaw.

Monitors domestic and international policy developments that affect the practice of public and private international law. Conducts seminars and provides information for members.

American Blind Lawyers Assn., 1155 15th St. N.W., #1004 20005; (202) 467-5081. Fax, (202) 467-5085. Gary Austin, President.

Membership: blind lawyers and law students. Provides members with legal information; acts as an information clearinghouse on legal materials available in Braille, in large print, on computer disc, and on tape. (Affiliated with American Council of the Blind.)

American Health Lawyers Assn., *1025 Connecticut Ave. N.W., #600 20036; (202) 833-1100. Fax, (202) 833-1105. Peter Leibold, President. General e-mail, memberservice@ healthlawyers.org. Web, www.healthlawyers.org.*

Membership: corporate, institutional, and government lawyers interested in the health field; law students; and health professionals. Serves as an information clearinghouse on health law; sponsors health law educational programs and seminars.

American Inns of Court Foundation, *127 S. Peyton St., #201, Alexandria, VA 22314; (703) 684-3590. Fax, (703) 684-3607. Don Stumbaugh, Executive Director. Web, www.innsofcourt.org.*

Promotes professionalism, ethics, civility, and legal skills of judges, lawyers, academicians, and law students in order to improve the quality and efficiency of the justice system.

Assn. of American Law Schools, *1201 Connecticut Ave. N.W., #800 20036; (202) 296-8851. Fax, (202) 296-8869. Carl C. Monk, Executive Director. Web, www.aals.org.*

Membership: schools of law, subject to approval by association. Represents member organizations before federal government and private agencies; evaluates member institutions; conducts workshops on the teaching of law; assists law schools with faculty recruitment; publishes faculty placement bulletin and annual directory of law teachers.

Friends of the Jessup, *2223 Massachusetts Ave. N.W. 20008-2864; (202) 939-6030. Fax, (202) 265-0386. Steven Schneebaum, Chair; M. Elizabeth Atkins, Executive Director. General e-mail, ilsa@iamdigex.net. Web, www. foj.org.*

Membership: supporters and former participants of the Philip C. Jessup International Law Moot Court Competition. Raises funds for the competition, helps to organize and support teams from disadvantaged countries, and conducts educational programs for competition participants. (Affiliated with the International Law Students Assn.)

Hispanic National Bar Fund, *1700 K St. N.W., #1005 20006; (202) 293-1507. Fax, (202) 293-1508. Alexander M. Sanchez, Executive Director. General e-mail, hnba@ aol.com. Web, www.hnba.com.*

Membership: Hispanic American attorneys, judges, professors, and law students. Seeks to increase professional opportunities in law for Hispanic Americans and to increase Hispanic American representation in law school. (Affiliated with National Hispanic Leadership Agenda and the American Bar Assn.)

International Law Institute, *1615 New Hampshire Ave. N.W. 20009-2520; (202) 483-3036. Fax, (202) 483-3029. Stuart Kerr, Executive Director. Web, www.ili.org.*

Performs scholarly research, offers training programs, and provides technical assistance in the area of international law. Sponsors international conferences.

International Law Students Assn., *2223 Massachusetts Ave. N.W. 20008-2864; (202) 939-6030. Fax, (202) 265-0386. M. Elizabeth Atkins, Executive Director. General e-mail, ilsa@iamdigex.net. Web, www.ilsa.org.*

Promotes the study and understanding of international law and related issues. Encourages communication and cooperation among law students and lawyers internationally; works to expand opportunities for learning about legal systems worldwide.

National Consumer Law Center, *Washington Office, 1629 K St. N.W., #600 20006; (202) 986-6060. Fax, (202) 463-9462. Margot Saunders, Managing Attorney.*

Provides lawyers funded by the Legal Services Corp. with research and assistance; provides lawyers with training in consumer and energy law. (Headquarters in Boston.)

National Court Reporters Assn., *8224 Old Courthouse Rd., Vienna, VA 22182-3808; (703) 556-6272. Fax, (703) 556-6291. Mark J. Golden, Executive Director. TTY, (703) 556-6289. Membership Service and Information, (800) 272-6272. Web, www.verbatimreporters.com.*

Membership organization that certifies and offers continuing education for court reporters. Acts as a clearinghouse on technology and information for and about court reporters; certifies legal video specialists.

Street Law, *1600 K St. N.W., #602 20006-2801; (202) 293-0088. Fax, (202) 293-0089. Edward L. O'Brien, Executive Director.*

Educational organization that promotes public understanding of the law and the legal system, particularly through citizen participation. Provides information, curriculum materials, training, and technical assistance to public and private school systems at elementary and secondary levels, law schools, departments of corrections, local juvenile justice systems, bar associations, community groups, and state and local governments interested in establishing law-related education programs, including mediation.

Data and Research

AGENCIES

Office of Justice Programs *(Justice Dept.),* **Bureau of Justice Statistics,** *810 7th St. N.W., #2400 20531; (202)*

307-0765. Fax, (202) 307-5846. Jan M. Chaiken, Director. Web, www.ojp.usdoj.gov/bjs.

Collects, evaluates, publishes, and provides statistics on criminal justice. Data available from the National Criminal Justice Reference Service, P.O. Box 6000, Rockville, Md. 20857; toll-free, (800) 732-3277; in Maryland, (301) 519-5500.

Office of Justice Programs *(Justice Dept.), National Institute of Justice, 810 7th St. N.W. 20531; (202) 307-2942. Fax, (202) 307-6394. Jeremy Travis, Director. Web, www.ojp.usdoj.gov/nij.*

Conducts research on all aspects of criminal justice, including crime prevention, enforcement, adjudication, and corrections; evaluates programs; develops model programs using new techniques. Serves as an affiliated institute of the United Nations Crime Prevention and Criminal Justice Programme (UNCPCJ); studies transnational issues. Maintains the National Criminal Justice Reference Service, which provides information on criminal justice, including activities of the Office of National Drug Control Policy and law enforcement in Latin America: (800) 851-3420 or (301) 251-5500; Web, www.ncjrs.org.

CONGRESS

Library of Congress, *Law Library, 101 Independence Ave. S.E., #LM240 20540; (202) 707-5065. Fax, (202) 707-1820. Rubens Medina, Law Librarian. Reading room, (202) 707-5080.*

Maintains collections of foreign, international, and comparative law organized jurisdictionally by country; covers all legal systems—common, civil, Roman, canon, religious, and ancient and medieval law. Services include a public reading room; a microtext facility, with readers and printers for microfilm and microfiche; and foreign law/rare book reading areas. Staff of legal specialists is competent in approximately forty languages; does not provide advice on legal matters.

JUDICIARY

Administrative Office of the U.S. Courts, *1 Columbus Circle N.E., #7-100 20544; (202) 273-3000. Leonidas Ralph Mecham, Director. Information, (202) 502-2600. Web, www.uscourts.gov.*

Supervises all administrative matters of the federal court system, except the Supreme Court; prepares statistical data and reports on the business of the courts, including reports on juror utilization, caseloads of federal, public, and community defenders, and types of cases adjudicated.

Administrative Office of the U.S. Courts, *Statistics, 1 Columbus Circle N.E., #2-250 20544; (202) 502-1440. Fax, (202) 502-1411. Steven R. Schlesinger, Chief. Press, (202) 502-2600.*

Compiles information and statistics from civil, criminal, appeals, and bankruptcy cases. Publishes statistical reports on court management; juror utilization; federal offenders; equal access to justice; the Financial Privacy Act; caseloads of federal, public, and community defenders; and types of cases adjudicated.

Supreme Court of the United States, *Library, 1 1st St. N.E. 20543; (202) 479-3037. Fax, (202) 479-3477. Shelley L. Dowling, Librarian.*

Maintains collection of Supreme Court documents dating from the mid-1800s. Records, briefs, and depository documents available for public use.

See also Federal Judicial Center (p. 496)

NONPROFIT

Justice Research and Statistics Assn., *777 N. Capitol St. N.E., #801 20002; (202) 842-9330. Fax, (202) 842-9329. Joan C. Weiss, Executive Director. General e-mail, cjinfo@jrsa.org. Web, www.jrsa.org.*

Provides information on the collection, analysis, dissemination, and use of data concerning crime and criminal justice at the state level; serves as liaison between the Justice Dept. Bureau of Justice Statistics and the states; develops standards for states on the collection, analysis, and use of statistics. Offers courses in criminal justice software and in research and evaluation methodologies in conjunction with its annual conference.

15

Military Personnel and Veterans

AGENCIES

Air Force Dept. *(Defense Dept.), Force Management and Personnel,* The Pentagon, #5E977 20330-1660; (703) 614-4752. Fax, (703) 693-4244. Mary Lou Keener, Deputy Assistant Secretary. Web, www.af.mil.

Civilian office that coordinates military and civilian personnel policies of the Air Force Dept. Focus includes pay; health care; education and training; commissaries, PXs, and service clubs; recruitment; retirement; and veterans affairs.

Air Force Dept. *(Defense Dept.), Personnel,* 1040 Air Force Pentagon, #4E194 20330-1040; (703) 697-6088. Fax, (703) 697-6091. Lt. Gen. Donald L. Peterson, Deputy Chief of Staff. Toll-free casualty assistance, (800) 433-0048. Web, www.af.mil.

Military office that coordinates military and civilian personnel policies of the Air Force Dept.

Army Dept. *(Defense Dept.), Manpower and Reserve Affairs,* The Pentagon 20310-0111; (703) 697-9253. Fax, (703) 692-9000. Patrick T. Henry, Assistant Secretary. Web, www.army.mil.

Civilian office that reviews policies and programs for Army personnel and reserves; makes recommendations to the secretary of the Army.

Army Dept. *(Defense Dept.), Military Personnel Management and Equal Opportunity Policy,* 111 Army Pentagon 20310-0111; (703) 697-2631. Fax, (703) 614-5975. John P. McLaurin III, Deputy Assistant Secretary. Web, www.army.mil.

Civilian office that coordinates military personnel policies of the Army. Focus includes pay; health care; equal opportunity; drug and alcohol abuse; recruitment; retirement; and commissaries, PXs, and service clubs.

Army Dept. *(Defense Dept.), Personnel,* The Pentagon, #2E736 20310-0300; (703) 695-6003. Fax, (703) 693-6607. Lt. Gen. David H. Ohly, Deputy Chief of Staff. Web, www.army.mil.

Military office that coordinates military personnel policies of the Army Dept.

Army Dept. *(Defense Dept.), U.S. Army Service Center for the Armed Forces,* The Pentagon, #1B866 20310-6604; (703) 695-5643. Fax, (703) 697-9756. Lacy E. Saunders, Director. Web, www.army.mil.

Assists Defense Dept. personnel (military, civilian, retirees, and dependents) with travel requests, movement of household goods, and processing of passports; provides support for the Armed Forces Hostess Assn. and for the chaplain's office. Operates the Pentagon library and motorpool and the Pentagon Athletic Center.

Defense Dept., *Equal Opportunity Policy,* The Pentagon, #3A272 20301-4000; (703) 695-0105. Fax, (703) 697-7534. William E. Leftwich III, Deputy Assistant Secretary. Web, www.defenselink.mil.

Develops military equal opportunity policy and civilian equal employment opportunity policy for the Defense Dept.

Defense Dept., *Military Personnel Policy,* The Pentagon, #3E767 20301-4000; (703) 697-4166. Fax, (703) 614-7046. Vice Adm. Patricia A. Tracey (USN), Deputy Assistant Secretary. Web, www.defenselink.mil.

Military office that coordinates military personnel policies of the Defense Dept. and reviews military personnel policies of the individual services.

Defense Dept., *Personnel and Readiness,* The Pentagon, #3E764 20301-4000; (703) 695-5254. Fax, (703) 693-0171. Bernard D. Rostker, Under Secretary (Nominee). Web, www.defenselink.mil.

Coordinates civilian and military personnel policies of the Defense Dept. and reviews personnel policies of the individual services. Handles equal opportunity policies; serves as focal point for all readiness issues.

Defense Dept., *Public Communication,* The Pentagon, #1E757 20301-1400; (703) 697-5737. Fax, (703) 695-1149. Harold Heilsnis, Director. Web, www.defenselink.mil.

Responds to public inquiries on Defense Dept. personnel, including those listed as missing in action.

Navy Dept. *(Defense Dept.), Manpower,* The Pentagon, #4E792 20350-1000; (703) 695-4350. Fax, (703) 614-4103. Karen S. Heath, Principal Deputy Assistant Secretary. Web, www.navy.mil.

Civilian office that coordinates military personnel policies of the Navy and the Marine Corps. Focus includes pay, health care, education and training, family services, recruitment, retirement, and veterans affairs.

Navy Dept. *(Defense Dept.), Military Personnel Plans and Policy Division N13,* 2 Navy Annex, #1825 20370; (703) 614-5571. Fax, (703) 614-5595. Rear Adm. William L. Putnam, Deputy Director. Web, www.navy.mil.

Military office that coordinates naval personnel policies, including promotions, professional development, and compensation, for officers and enlisted personnel.

Navy Dept. *(Defense Dept.), Naval Personnel,* 2 Navy Annex 20370; (703) 614-1101. Fax, (703) 693-1746. Rear Adm. Norbert R. Ryan Jr., Chief. Web, www.navy.mil.

Military office that coordinates Navy Dept.'s military personnel policies of the Navy Dept.

Selective Service System, *1515 Wilson Blvd., Arlington, VA 22209-2425; (703) 605-4010. Fax, (703) 605-4006. Gil Coronado, Director; Willie L. Blanding Jr., Executive Director. Locator, (703) 605-4000. Web, www.sss.gov.*

Supplies the armed forces with manpower when authorized; registers male citizens of the United States ages eighteen to twenty-five. In an emergency, would institute a draft and would provide alternative service assignments to men classified as conscientious objectors.

U.S. Coast Guard *(Transportation Dept.),* **Human Resources,** *2100 2nd St. S.W. 20593-0001; (202) 267-0905. Fax, (202) 267-4205. Rear Adm. Fred L. Ames, Chief. Web, www.uscg.mil/hq/g-w/hrhome.htm.*

Responsible for hiring, recruiting, and training all military and nonmilitary Coast Guard personnel.

CONGRESS

House Armed Services Committee, *Subcommittee on Military Personnel, 2340 RHOB 20515; (202) 225-7560. Fax, (202) 226-0789. Rep. Steve Buyer, R-Ind., Chair; John Chapla, Professional Staff Member. Web, www.house. gov/hasc.*

Jurisdiction over legislation on military personnel, including drug and alcohol abuse, equal opportunity, banking and insurance, family services, medical care and benefits, pay and compensation, recruitment, military reserve strength, and retirement benefits. Jurisdiction over legislation on civilian personnel of the armed forces.

Senate Armed Services Committee, *Subcommittee on Personnel, SR-228 20510; (202) 224-3871. Sen. Tim Hutchinson, R-Ark., Chair; Charles S. Abell, Professional Staff Member. Web, armed_services.senate.gov.*

Jurisdiction over legislation on military personnel, including drug and alcohol abuse, equal opportunity, banking and insurance, family services, medical care and benefits, Americans missing in action (MIAs), education of overseas dependents, pay and compensation, recruitment, military reserve strength, and retirement benefits. Jurisdiction over legislation on civilian personnel of the armed forces.

NONPROFIT

Air Force Assn., *1501 Lee Hwy., Arlington, VA 22209-1198; (703) 247-5800. Fax, (703) 247-5853. John A. Shaud, Executive Director. Library, (703) 247-5829. Press, (703) 247-5850. General e-mail, custserv@afa.org. Web, www.afa.org.*

Membership: civilians and active, reserve, retired, and cadet personnel of the Air Force. Informs members and the public of developments in the aerospace field. Monitors legislation and Defense Dept. policies. Library on aviation history open to the public by appointment.

Air Force Sergeants Assn., *5211 Auth Rd., Suitland, MD 20746; (301) 899-3500. Fax, (301) 899-8136. James D. Staton, Executive Director. Web, www.afsahq.org.*

Membership: active duty, reserve, National Guard, and retired enlisted Air Force personnel. Monitors defense policies and legislation on issues such as the proposed phasing out of federal subsidies for medical and retirement benefits and commissaries.

Assn. of the United States Army, *2425 Wilson Blvd., Arlington, VA 22201; (703) 841-4300. Fax, (703) 525-9039. Gordon R. Sullivan, President. Web, www.ausa.org.*

Membership: civilians and active and retired members of the armed forces. Conducts symposia on defense issues and researches topics that affect the military.

Fleet Reserve Assn., *125 N. West St., Alexandria, VA 22314-2754; (703) 683-1400. Fax, (703) 549-6610. Charles L. Calkins, National Executive Secretary. Information, (800) 372-1924. General e-mail, news-fra@fra.org. Web, www.fra.org.*

Membership: active duty, reserve, and retired Navy, Marine Corps, and Coast Guard personnel. Works to safeguard the compensation, benefits, and entitlements of Sea Services personnel. Recognized by the Veterans Affairs Dept. to assist veterans and widows of veterans with benefit claims.

Marine Corps League, *8626 Lee Hwy., #201, Fairfax, VA 22031 (mailing address: P.O. Box 3070, Merrifield, VA 22116); (703) 207-9588. Fax, (703) 207-0047. William "Brooks" Corley Jr., Executive Director. General e-mail, mcl@mcleague.org. Web, www.mcleague.org.*

Membership: active duty, retired, and reserve Marine Corps groups. Promotes the interests of the Marine Corps and works to preserve its traditions; assists veterans and their survivors. Monitors legislation and regulations.

Military Order of the World Wars, *435 N. Lee St., Alexandria, VA 22314; (703) 683-4911. Fax, (703) 683-4501. George G. Kundahl, Chief of Staff. General e-mail, mowwhq@aol.com. Web, www.militaryorder.org.*

Membership: retired and active duty commissioned officers, warrant officers, and flight officers. Supports a strong national defense; supports patriotic education in schools; presents awards to outstanding Reserve Officers Training Corps (ROTC) cadets.

National Assn. for Uniformed Services, *5535 Hempstead Way, Springfield, VA 22151-4094; (703) 750-1342. Fax, (703) 354-4380. Richard D. Murray, President. Information, (800) 842-3451. Web, www.naus.org.*

Membership: active, reserve, and retired officers and enlisted personnel of all uniformed services and their families and survivors. Supports legislation that benefits military personnel and veterans. (Affiliated with the Society of Military Widows.)

National Interreligious Service Board for Conscientious Objectors, *Center for Conscience and War, 1830 Connecticut Ave. N.W. 20009; (202) 483-2220. Fax, (202) 483-1246. J. E. McNeil, Executive Director. General e-mail, nisbco@igc.apc.org. Web, www.nisbco.org.*

Seeks to defend and extend the rights of conscientious objectors. Provides information and advocacy about the military draft and national selective service. Offers counseling and information to military personnel seeking discharge or transfer to noncombatant positions within the military.

Navy League of the United States, *2300 Wilson Blvd., Arlington, VA 22201; (703) 528-1775. Fax, (703) 528-2333. Charles L. Robinson, Executive Director. General e-mail, mail@navyleague.org. Web, www.navyleague.org.*

Membership: retired and reserve military personnel and civilians interested in the U.S. Navy, Marine Corps, Coast Guard, and Merchant Marine. Distributes literature, provides speakers, and conducts seminars to promote interests of the sea services. Monitors legislation.

Non-Commissioned Officers Assn., *Washington Office, 225 N. Washington St., Alexandria, VA 22314; (703) 549-0311. Fax, (703) 549-0245. David W. Sommers, President. Web, www.ncoausa.org.*

Congressionally chartered fraternal organization of active and retired enlisted military personnel. Sponsors job fairs to assist members in finding employment. (Headquarters in San Antonio.)

United Service Organizations, *Washington Navy Yard, 1008 Eberle Pl. S.E., #301 20374-5096; (202) 610-5700. Fax, (202) 610-5699. Carl E. Mundy Jr., President. Web, www.uso.org.*

Voluntary civilian organization chartered by Congress. Provides military personnel and their families in the United States and overseas with social, educational, and recreational programs.

U.S. Army Warrant Officers Assn., *462 Herndon Pkwy., #207, Herndon, VA 20170-5235; (703) 742-7727. Fax, (703) 742-7728. Raymond A. Bell, Executive Director. General e-mail, usawoa@erols.com. Web, www.penfed.org/usawoa.*

Membership: active duty, reserve, and retired Army warrant officers. Monitors and makes recommendations to Defense Dept., Army Dept., and Congress on policies and programs affecting Army warrant officers.

DEFENSE PERSONNEL

See also Military Installations (chap. 16)

Chaplains

AGENCIES

Air Force Dept. *(Defense Dept.),* **Chief of the Chaplain Service,** *Boiling Air Force Base, 112 Luke Ave. 20332-9050; (202) 767-4577. Fax, (202) 404-7841. Maj. Gen. William J. Dendinger, Chief. Web, www.af.mil.*

Oversees chaplains and religious services with the Air Force; maintains liaison with religious denominations.

Armed Forces Chaplain Board *(Defense Dept.),* *4000 Defense Pentagon, #1B652 20301-4000; (703) 697-9015. Fax, (703) 697-8256. Capt. R. O. Gunter (USN), Executive Director; Rear Adm. A. Bryon Holderby (USN), Chair.*

Membership: chiefs and deputy chiefs of chaplains of the armed services; works to coordinate religious policies and services among the military branches.

Army Dept. *(Defense Dept.),* **Chief of Chaplains,** *2700 Army Pentagon, #1E712 20310-2700; (703) 695-1133. Fax, (703) 695-9834. Gaylord T. Gunhus, Chief. Web, www.army.mil.*

Oversees chaplains and religious services within the Army; maintains liaison with religious denominations.

Marine Corps *(Defense Dept.),* **Chaplain,** *2 Navy Annex, #3024, FB2 20380-1775; (703) 614-5630. Fax, (703) 614-4491. Capt. J. R. Lamonde (USN), Chaplain. Web, www.hqmc.usmc.mil.*

Oversees chaplains and religious services within the Marine Corps; maintains liaison with religious denominations.

National Guard Bureau *(Defense Dept.),* **Air National Guard: Chaplain Service,** *1411 Jefferson Davis Hwy., Arlington, VA 22202-3231; (703) 607-5279. Fax, (703) 607-5295. Col. John B. Ellington Jr., Chief Chaplain.*

Oversees chaplains and religious services within the Air National Guard; maintains liaison with religious denominations.

National Guard Bureau *(Defense Dept.),* **Army National Guard: Chaplain Service,** *1411 Jefferson Davis*

Hwy., #9500, Arlington, VA 22202-3231; (703) 607-7072. Fax, (703) 607-8621. Col. Donald W. Hill, Chief Chaplain.

Oversees chaplains and religious services with the Army National Guard; maintains liaison with religious denominations; serves as policy leader for chaplains.

Navy Dept. *(Defense Dept.), Chief of Chaplains, N097,* 2 Navy Annex, #1056 20370-0400; (703) 614-4043. Fax, (703) 614-4725. Rear Adm. A. Byron Holderby (USN), Chief. Web, www.navy.mil.

Oversees chaplains and religious services within the Navy; maintains liaison with religious denominations.

NONPROFIT

Military Chaplains Assn. of the United States of America, P.O. Box 42660 20015-0660; (202) 574-2423. David E. White, Executive Director. General e-mail, chaplains@erols.com. Web, www.mca-usa.org.

Membership: chaplains of all faiths in all branches of the armed services and chaplains of veterans affairs and civil air patrol. Sponsors workshops and conventions; coordinates a speakers' bureau.

National Conference on Ministry to the Armed Forces, 4141 N. Henderson Rd., Arlington, VA 22203; (703) 276-7905. Fax, (703) 276-7906. Jack Williamson, Coordinator.

Offers support to the Armed Forces Chaplains Board and the chief of chaplains of each service; disseminates information on matters affecting service personnel welfare.

Civilian Employees

AGENCIES

Air Force Dept. *(Defense Dept.), Civilian Policy, The* Pentagon 20330-1040; (703) 695-7381. Fax, (703) 692-9939. Gary T. Beavers, Chief. Web, www.af.mil.

Civilian office that monitors and reviews Air Force equal employment opportunity programs and policies, benefits and entitlements, civilian pay, career programs, and external and internal placement of staff.

Air Force Dept. *(Defense Dept.), Personnel Force Management, The Pentagon,* #4E228 20330-1040; (703) 695-6770. Fax, (703) 614-8523. Maj. Gen. Susan L. Pamerleau, Director. Web, www.af.mil.

Implements and evaluates Air Force civilian personnel policies; serves as the principal adviser to the Air Force personnel director on civilian personnel matters and programs.

Army Dept. *(Defense Dept.), Civilian Personnel, The* Pentagon 20310-0111; (703) 695-4237. Fax, (703) 693-

3513. David L. Snyder, Deputy Assistant Secretary. Web, www.army.mil.

Develops and reviews Army civilian personnel policies and advises the secretary of the Army on civilian personnel matters.

Army Dept. *(Defense Dept.), Equal Employment Opportunity Agency,* Crystal Mall 4, #207, 1941 Jefferson Davis Hwy., Arlington, VA 22202-4508; (703) 607-1976. Fax, (703) 607-2042. Luther L. Santiful, Director. Main phone is voice and TTY accessible. Web, www.army.mil.

Civilian office that administers equal employment opportunity programs and policies for civilian employees of the Army.

Defense Dept., *Civilian Assistance and Re-Employment (CARE),* 1400 Key Blvd., B-200, Arlington, VA 22209-5144; (703) 696-1799. Fax, (703) 696-5416. G. Jorge Araiza, Chief (Acting). Web, www.defenselink.mil.

Manages transition programs for Defense Dept. civilians, including placement, early retirement, and transition assistance programs.

Marine Corps *(Defense Dept.), Civilian Human Resources,* 1213, Code HRH, Arlington, VA 20380-1775; (703) 614-2046. Fax, (703) 697-7682. William T. Catsonis, Head; Deborah Summers, Deputy Equal Employment Opportunities Officer.

Develops and implements personnel and equal employment opportunity programs for civilian employees of the Marine Corps.

Navy Dept. *(Defense Dept.), Civilian Human Resources/Equal Employment Opportunity, The Penta-gon,* #4E789 20350-1000; (703) 695-2248. Fax, (703) 614-4103. Betty Welch, Deputy Assistant Secretary. Web, www.donhr.navy.mil.

Civilian office that develops and reviews Navy and Marine Corps civilian personnel and equal opportunity programs and policies.

U.S. Coast Guard *(Transportation Dept.), Civil Rights: Military Equal Opportunity,* 2100 2nd St. S.W., #2400 20593-0001; (202) 267-0042. Fax, (202) 267-4282. Cruz Sedillo, Director.

Administers the Affirmative Employment Program relating to civilian Coast Guard positions; processes complaints.

Equal Opportunity

AGENCIES

Air Force Dept. *(Defense Dept.), Military Equal Opportunity,* 1040 Air Force Pentagon, #5C238 20330-

1040; (703) 614-8488. Fax, (703) 695-4083. Lt. Col. Terry R. Hankerson, Chief. Web, www.af.mil.

Military office that develops and administers Air Force equal opportunity programs and policies.

Army Dept. *(Defense Dept.), Equal Opportunity Programs: Leadership Division,* The Pentagon, #2C655 20310-0300; (703) 697-2874. Fax, (703) 697-2407. Col. John S. Westwood, Director. Web, www.army.mil.

Military office that develops and administers equal opportunity programs and policies for the Army.

Defense Dept., *Force Management Policy—Defense Advisory Committee on Women in the Services,* The Pentagon, #3D769 20301-4000; (703) 697-2122. Fax, (703) 614-6233. Capt. Barbara L. Brehm (USN), Military Director. Web, www.dtic.mil/dacowits.

Advises the secretary of defense and provides the public with information on matters relating to women and men in the military, including recruitment and retention.

Defense Dept., *Military Equal Opportunity,* The Pentagon, #3A272 20301-4000; (703) 697-6381. Fax, (703) 695-4619. Jimmy Love, Director (Acting). Web, www.dticaw.dtic.mil/trhome/das_eo.html.

Receives civil rights complaints from military personnel and assists in seeking corrective action.

Marine Corps *(Defense Dept.), Equal Opportunity,* HQMC, MNRA (MPE), 3280 Russell Rd., Quantico, VA 22134-5108; (703) 784-9371. Fax, (703) 784-9814. Aaron X. Butler, Head. Web, www.usmc.mil.

Military office that develops, monitors, and administers Marine Corps equal opportunity programs.

Navy Dept. *(Defense Dept.), Minority Affairs,* Navy Annex, Arlington, VA 20370; (703) 695-2623. Fax, (703) 695-9922. Cmdr. Ron R. Evan, Director. Web, www.navy.mil.

Military office that develops and administers Navy equal opportunity programs and policies.

U.S. Coast Guard *(Transportation Dept.), Civil Rights: Military Equal Opportunity,* 2100 2nd St. S.W., #2400 20593-0001; (202) 267-0042. Fax, (202) 267-4282. Cruz Sedillo, Director.

Administers equal opportunity regulations for Coast Guard military personnel.

NONPROFIT

Human Rights Campaign, 919 18th St. N.W., #800 20006; (202) 628-4160. Fax, (202) 347-5323. Elizabeth Birch, Executive Director. General e-mail, hrc@hrc.org. Web, www.hrc.org.

Promotes legislation affirming the rights of lesbians and gays. Focus includes discrimination in the military.

Minerva Center, 20 Granada Rd., Pasadena, MD 21122-2708; (410) 437-5379. Linda Grant De Pauw, Director. Web, www.minervacenter.com.

Encourages the study of women in the military. Focus includes current U.S. servicewomen; women veterans; women, war, and military abroad; and the preservation of artifacts, oral history, and first-hand accounts of women's experience in military service.

Servicemembers Legal Defense Network, P.O. Box 65301 20035-5301; (202) 328-3244. Fax, (202) 797-1635. Michelle M. Benecke, Co-Director; C. Dixon Osburn, Co-Director. General e-mail, sldn@sldn.org. Web, www.sldn.org.

Provides legal assistance to individuals affected by the military's policy on gays and lesbians. Monitors legislation and regulations.

Family Services

AGENCIES

Air Force Dept. *(Defense Dept.), Family Matters,* The Pentagon, #5C236, Headquarters AF/DPDFF 20330-1040; (703) 697-4720. Fax, (703) 695-4083. Lt. Col. David L. Rothwell, Chief. Web, www.af.mil.

Military office that monitors and reviews services provided to Air Force families and civilian employees with family concerns; oversees family support centers.

Air Force Dept. *(Defense Dept.), Personnel,* 1040 Air Force Pentagon, #4E194 20330-1040; (703) 697-6088. Fax, (703) 697-6091. Lt. Gen. Donald L. Peterson, Deputy Chief of Staff. Toll-free casualty assistance, (800) 433-0048. Web, www.af.mil.

Military office that responds to inquiries concerning deceased Air Force personnel and their beneficiaries; refers inquiries to the Military Personnel Center at Randolph Air Force Base in San Antonio, Texas.

Army Dept. *(Defense Dept.), Casualty Operations,* 2461 Eisenhower Ave., #920, Alexandria, VA 22331-0481; (703) 325-7990. Fax, (703) 325-0134. Lt. Col. Rita Salley, Chief. Web, www.army.mil.

Verifies beneficiaries of deceased Army personnel for benefits distribution.

Army Dept. *(Defense Dept.), Community and Family Support Center,* 4700 King St., Alexandria, VA 22302-

4401; (703) 681-7469. Fax, (703) 681-7446. Brig. Gen. Craig B. Whelden, Commanding General. Web, www.army. mil.

Military office that directs operations of Army recreation, community service, child development, and youth activity centers. Handles dependent education in conjunction with the Defense Dept.

Defense Dept., *Dependents Education Activity*, 4040 N. Fairfax Dr., Arlington, VA 22203-1635; (703) 696-4247. Fax, (703) 696-8918. Ray Tolleson, Director (Acting). Web, www.odedodea.edu.

Civilian office that maintains school system for dependents of all military personnel and eligible civilians in the U.S. and abroad; advises the secretary of defense on overseas education matters; supervises selection of teachers in schools for military dependents.

Defense Dept., *Quality of Life*, The Pentagon, #3B916 20301-4000; (703) 697-7191. Fax, (703) 695-1977. Jane C. Burke, Director. Web, www.defenselink.mil.

Coordinates policies of the individual services relating to the families of military personnel.

Marine Corps *(Defense Dept.), Casualty Section*, HQUSMC, 3280 Russell Rd., Quantico, VA 22134; (703) 784-9501. Fax, (703) 784-7823. Maj. M. L. Ward, Head.

Confirms beneficiaries of deceased Marine Corps personnel for benefits distribution.

Marine Corps *(Defense Dept.), Family Programs*, HQUSMC, M and RA, 3280 Russell Rd., Quantico, VA 22134-5103; (703) 784-9501. Fax, (703) 784-9816. Col. Joel Eissinger, Deputy Director. Web, www.usmc-mccs.org.

Sponsors family service centers located on major Marine Corps installations. Oversees the administration of policies affecting the quality of life of Marine Corps military families. Administers relocation assistance programs.

Navy Dept. *(Defense Dept.), Force Support and Families*, The Pentagon 20350-1000; (703) 693-0484. Fax, (703) 693-4957. Buster Tate, Staff Director. Web, www.navy.mil.

Civilian office that oversees the administration of all policies affecting the quality of life of families of Navy military personnel.

Navy Dept. *(Defense Dept.), Personal Readiness and Community Support: Personnel 6 Washington Liaison*, Navy Annex, #1612, Arlington, VA 20370; (703) 614-4259. Fax, (703) 614-4199. Capt. Bernard Jackson, Liaison. Web, www.navy.mil.

Oversees Navy family service centers; provides naval personnel and families being sent overseas with information and support; addresses problems of abuse and sexual assault within families; helps Navy spouses find employment; facilitates communication between Navy families and Navy officials. Assists in relocating Navy families during transition from military to civilian life.

U.S. Coast Guard *(Transportation Dept.), Individual and Family Support*, 2100 2nd St. S.W., #6320 20593-0001; (202) 267-6263. Fax, (202) 267-4798. Cmdr. Ruth I. Torres, Chief.

Offers broad array of human services to individuals in the Coast Guard and their families, including child care, elderly care, educational services, domestic violence counseling, health care, and special needs.

CONGRESS

House Armed Services Committee, *Subcommittee on Military Personnel*, 2340 RHOB 20515; (202) 225-7560. Fax, (202) 226-0789. Rep. Steve Buyer, R-Ind., Chair; John Chapla, Professional Staff Member. Web, www.house. gov/hasc.

Jurisdiction over legislation on education of overseas military dependents (jurisdiction shared with House Education and the Workforce Committee).

House Education and the Workforce Committee, *Subcommittee on Early Childhood, Youth, and Families*, 2181 RHOB 20515; (202) 225-4527. Fax, (202) 225-9571. Rep. Michael N. Castle, R-Del., Chair; Kevin D. Talley, Staff Director. Web, www.house.gov/ed_workforce.

Jurisdiction over legislation concerning overseas and domestic military dependents' education programs (jurisdiction shared with House Armed Services Committee).

Senate Armed Services Committee, *Subcommittee on Personnel*, SR-228 20510; (202) 224-3871. Sen. Tim Hutchinson, R-Ark., Chair; Charles S. Abell, Professional Staff Member. Web, armed_services.senate.gov.

Jurisdiction over legislation concerning military dependents' education programs.

NONPROFIT

Air Force Aid Society Inc., 1745 Jefferson Davis Hwy., #202, Arlington, VA 22202-3410; (703) 607-3072. Fax, (703) 607-3022. Robert T. Marsh, Director. Web, www. afas.org.

Membership: Air Force active duty, reserve, and retired military personnel and their dependents. Provides active duty and retired Air Force military personnel with personal emergency loans for basic needs, travel, or dependents' health expenses; assists families of active, deceased, or retired Air Force personnel with post-secondary education, loans, and grants.

American Red Cross, *Armed Forces Emergency Services,* *8111 Gatehouse Rd., Falls Church, VA 22042; (703) 206-7481. Fax, (703) 206-8533. Sue A. Richter, Vice President. Web, www.crossnet.org.*

Provides emergency services for active duty armed forces personnel and their families, including reporting and communications, financial assistance, information and referral, and counseling.

American Red Cross, *Emergency Communications,* *8111 Gatehouse Rd., Falls Church, VA 22042; (800) 926-6001. Fax, (703) 206-6181. Rick Davis, Director.*

Contacts military personnel in family emergencies; provides military personnel with verification of family situations for emergency leave applications.

Armed Forces Hostess Assn., *The Pentagon, #1A736 20310-6604; (703) 697-3180. Fax, (703) 693-9510. Gayl Taylor, President.*

Volunteer office staffed by wives of military personnel of all services. Serves as an information clearinghouse for military and civilian Defense Dept. families; maintains information on military bases in the United States and abroad; issues information handbook for families in the Washington area.

Army Distaff Foundation, *6200 Oregon Ave. N.W. 20015-1543; (202) 541-0105. Fax, (202) 364-2856. Calvert P. Benedict, Executive Director. Information, (800) 541-4255.*

Nonprofit continuing care retirement community for career military officers and their families. Provides retirement housing and health care services.

EXPOSE, Ex-partners of Servicemembers for Equality, *P.O. Box 11191, Alexandria, VA 22312; (703) 941-5844. Fax, (703) 212-6951. Kathleen Rogers, Director. General e-mail, ex-pose@juno.com.*

Membership: former spouses of military personnel, both officers and enlisted, and other interested parties. Seeks federal laws to restore to ex-spouses benefits lost through divorce, including retirement pay; survivors' benefits; and medical, commissary, and exchange benefits. Provides information concerning related federal laws and regulations. Serves as an information clearinghouse.

Federal Education Assn., *1101 15th St. N.W., #1002 20005; (202) 822-7850. Fax, (202) 822-7816. Jan Mohr, President. Web, www.feaonline.org.*

Membership: teachers and personnel of Defense Dept. schools for military dependents in the United States and abroad. Helps members negotiate pay, benefits, and better working conditions. Monitors legislation and regulations. (Affiliated with the National Education Assn.)

National Military Family Assn., *6000 Stevenson Ave., #304, Alexandria, VA 22304-3526; (703) 823-6632. Fax, (703) 751-4857. Nancy J. Alsheimer, President. General e-mail, families@nmfa.org. Web, www.nmfa.org.*

Membership: active duty and retired military, National Guard, and reserve personnel of all U.S. uniformed services, their families, and interested individuals. Works to improve the quality of life for military families.

Navy-Marine Corps Relief Society, *801 N. Randolph St., #1228, Arlington, VA 22203-1978; (703) 696-4904. Fax, (703) 696-0144. Jerome L. Johnson, President. Web, www.nmcrs.org.*

Assists active and retired Navy and Marine Corps personnel and their families in times of need. Disburses interest-free loans and grants. Provides educational scholarships and loans, visiting nurse services, thrift shops, food lockers, budget counseling, and volunteer training.

Navy Services FamilyLine, *Washington Navy Yard, 1254 9th St. S.E., #104 20374-5067; (202) 433-2333. Fax, (202) 433-4622. David F. Tuma, Chair. General e-mail, nsfamline@aol.com.*

Offers support services to spouses of Navy, Marine Corps, and Coast Guard personnel; disseminates information on all aspects of military life; fosters sense of community among naval personnel and their families.

Financial Services

AGENCIES

Air Force Dept. *(Defense Dept.), Financial Management, The Pentagon 20330-1130; (703) 697-1974. Fax, (703) 693-1996. Robert F. Hale, Assistant Secretary. Web, www.af.mil.*

Advises the secretary of the Air Force on policies relating to financial services for military and civilian personnel.

Defense Dept., *Accounting Policy, The Pentagon, #3A882 20301-1100; (703) 697-3200. Fax, (703) 697-4608. De Ritchie, Director. Web, www.defenselink.mil.*

Develops accounting policy for the Defense Dept. including banks and credit unions on military installations for all service branches.

CONGRESS

House Banking and Financial Services Committee, *Subcommittee on Financial Institutions and Consumer Credit,* 2129 RHOB 20515; (202) 225-2258. Fax, (202) 225-6984. Rep. Marge Roukema, R-N.J., Chair; Laurie Schaffer, Staff Director. Web, www.house.gov/banking.

Jurisdiction over legislation regulating banking and credit unions on military bases (jurisdiction shared with Subcommittee on General Oversight and Investigations).

House Banking and Financial Services Committee, *Subcommittee on General Oversight and Investigations,* 212 OHOB 20515; (202) 226-3280. Rep. Peter T. King, R.-N.Y., Chair; Jim Clinger, Staff Director. Web, www.house.gov/banking.

Oversight of banking and credit unions on military bases (jurisdiction shared with Subcommittee on Financial Institutions and Consumer Credit).

Senate Banking, Housing, and Urban Affairs Committee, SD-534 20510; (202) 224-7391. Fax, (202) 224-5137. Sen. Phil Gramm, R-Texas, Chair; Wayne A. Abernathy, Staff Director. Web, banking.senate.gov.

Oversees and has jurisdiction over legislation regulating banking and credit unions on military bases.

NONPROFIT

Armed Forces Benefit Assn., 909 N. Washington St., Alexandria, VA 22314; (703) 549-4455. Fax, (703) 548-6497. C. C. Blanton, President. Web, www.afba.com.

Membership: active and retired personnel of the uniformed services, federal civilian employees, and dependents. Offers low-cost health and life insurance and financial, banking, and investment services worldwide.

Army and Air Force Mutual Aid Assn., 102 Sheridan Ave., Fort Myer, VA 22211-1110; (703) 522-3060. Fax, (703) 522-1336. Bradley J. Snyder, President. Information, (800) 336-4538. General e-mail, info@aafmaa.com. Web, www.aafmaa.com.

Private service organization that offers member and family insurance services to active duty and reserve Army and Air Force officers, warrant officers, noncommissioned officers, and retired officers under age sixty-six.

Defense Credit Union Council, 805 15th St. N.W., #300 20005-2007; (202) 682-5993. Fax, (202) 682-9054. Roland Arteaga, President. General e-mail, dcuc1@cuna.com. Web, www.dcuc.org.

Trade association of credit unions serving the Defense Dept.'s military and civilian personnel. Works with the National Credit Union Administration to solve problems concerning the operation of credit unions for

the military community; maintains liaison with the Defense Dept.

Health Care

AGENCIES

Air Force Dept. *(Defense Dept.), Managed Care,* 110 Luke Ave., #400, Bolling Air Force Base 20332-7050; (202) 767-4699. Fax, (202) 404-7366. Donald E. Taylor, Chief. Web, www.af.mil.

Military office that develops and administers health benefits and policies for Air Force military personnel. Oversees modernization of Air Force medical facilities.

Air Force Dept. *(Defense Dept.), Surgeon General,* 110 Luke Ave. Bldg. 5681, #400, Bolling Air Force Base 20332-7050; (202) 767-4444. Fax, (202) 404-7084. Lt. Gen Paul K. Carlton Jr., Surgeon General. Web, www.satx.disa.mil.

Directs the provision of medical and dental services for Air Force personnel and their dependents.

Army Dept. *(Defense Dept.), Health Services,* 5109 Leesburg Pike, Falls Church, VA 22041-3258; (703) 681-3113. Fax, (703) 681-3163. Col. Tony Carter, Senior Medical Officer. Web, www.army.mil.

Military office that administers medical benefits programs for Army military personnel; answers inquiries regarding eligibility and formulates clinical policy.

Army Dept. *(Defense Dept.), Personnel Readiness,* The Pentagon, DAPE-HR-PR 20310-0300; (703) 614-7701. Fax, (703) 223-0212. Lt. Col. Claude A. Wood, Chief. Web, www.army.mil.

Military office that develops Army policies on HIV-positive Army personnel, suicide prevention, and general health promotion. Develops policies for combating alcohol and drug abuse; monitors and evaluates programs of the major Army commands.

Army Dept. *(Defense Dept.), Surgeon General,* 5109 Leesburg Pike, #672, Falls Church, VA 22041-3258; (703) 681-3000. Fax, (703) 681-3167. Lt. Gen. Ronald R. Blanck, Surgeon General. Information, (703) 681-8020. Web, www.armymedicine.army.mil.

Directs the provision of medical and dental services for Army personnel and their dependents.

Defense Dept., *Health Affairs: Clinical Program Policy,* The Pentagon 20301-1200; (703) 697-2111. Fax, (703) 697-4197. Sue Bailey, Assistant Secretary. Web, www.defenselink.mil.

Administers the medical benefits programs for active duty and retired military personnel and dependents in the Defense Dept.; develops policies relating to medical programs.

Defense Dept., *Health Affairs: Clinical Program Policy,* The Pentagon 20301-1200; (703) 697-2111. Fax, (703) 697-4197. Dr. John F. Mazzuchi, Deputy Assistant Secretary. Web, www.defenselink.mil.

Reviews and directs drug and alcohol abuse identification, education, prevention, treatment, and rehabilitation programs within the Defense Dept.

Marine Corps *(Defense Dept.),* **Personal and Family Readiness Division,** HQMC, MNRA (MRT), 3280 Russell Rd., Quantico, VA 22134-5103; (703) 784-9546. Fax, (703) 784-9826. P. G. Short, Head.

Military office that directs Marine Corps health care and drug and alcohol abuse policies and programs.

Naval Medical Research Center *(Defense Dept.),* 503 Robert Grant Ave., Silver Spring, MD 20910-7500; (301) 319-7400. Fax, (301) 319-7410. Capt. Richard Hibbs, Commanding Officer. Web, www.nmri.nnmc.navy.mil.

Performs basic and applied biomedical research in areas of military importance, including infectious diseases, hyperbaric medicine, wound repair enhancement, environmental stress, and immunobiology. Provides support to field laboratories and naval hospitals; monitors research internationally.

Navy Dept. *(Defense Dept.),* **Health Affairs,** The Pentagon, #5D825 20350-1000; (703) 693-0238. Fax, (703) 693-4959. Cmdr. Kelly J. McConville, Director. Web, www.navy.mil.

Reviews medical programs for Navy and Marine Corps military personnel and develops and reviews policies relating to these programs.

Navy Dept. *(Defense Dept.),* **Patient Administration,** 23rd and E Sts. N.W. 20372-5300; (202) 762-3152. Fax, (202) 762-3743. Cmdr. Ron Luca, Head. Web, www.navy.mil.

Military office that assists in the development of eligibility policy for medical benefits programs for Navy and Marine Corps military personnel. Interprets and oversees the implementation of Navy health care policy.

Navy Dept. *(Defense Dept.),* **Surgeon General,** 23rd and E Sts. N.W., #1112 20372-5120; (202) 762-3701. Fax, (202) 762-3714. Vice Adm. Richard A. Nelson, Surgeon General. Web, www.navy.mil.

Directs the provision of medical and dental services for Navy and Marine Corps personnel and their dependents; oversees the Navy's Bureau of Medicine and Surgery.

U.S. Coast Guard *(Transportation Dept.),* **Health and Safety,** 2100 2nd St. S.W., G-WK 20593-0001; (202) 267-1098. Fax, (202) 267-4512. Rear Adm. Joyce M. Johnson, Director.

Oversees all health and safety aspects of the Coast Guard, including the operation of medical and dental clinics, sick bays on ships, and mess halls and galleys. Investigates Coast Guard accidents, such as the grounding of ships and downing of aircraft.

Walter Reed Army Institute of Research *(Defense Dept.),* 6825 16th St. N.W., #1103 20307-5100; (202) 782-3551. Fax, (202) 782-3114. Col. Martin H. Crumrine, Director. Web, wrair-www.army.mil.

Provides research, education, and training in support of the Defense Dept.'s health care system. Interests include biochemistry, biometrics, pathology, surgery, veterinary medicine, naturally occurring infectious diseases of military importance, battle casualties, operational hazards, and defense against biological and chemical agents.

NONPROFIT

Assn. of Military Surgeons of the United States, 9320 Old Georgetown Rd., Bethesda, MD 20814-1653; (301) 897-8800. Fax, (301) 530-5446. Frederic G. Sanford, Executive Director. Web, www.amsus.org.

Membership: health professionals, including nurses, dentists, pharmacists, and physicians, who work or have worked for the U.S. Public Health Service, the VA, or the Army, Navy, or Air Force, and students. Works to improve all phases of federal health services.

Commissioned Officers Assn. of the U.S. Public Health Service, 8201 Corporate Dr., #560, Landover, MD 20785; (301) 731-9080. Fax, (301) 731-9084. Michael W. Lord, Executive Director. General e-mail, membercoa@aol.com. Web, www.coausphs.org.

Membership: commissioned officers of the U.S. Public Health Service. Supports expansion of federal health care facilities, including military facilities.

Missing in Action/Prisoners of War

AGENCIES

Air Force Dept. *(Defense Dept.),* **Personnel,** 1040 Air Force Pentagon, #4E194 20330-1040; (703) 697-6088. Fax, (703) 697-6091. Lt. Gen. Donald L. Peterson, Deputy Chief of Staff. Toll-free casualty assistance, (800) 433-0048. Web, www.af.mil.

Military office that responds to inquiries about missing in action (MIA) personnel for the Air Force; refers inquiries to the Military Personnel Center at Randolph Air Force Base in San Antonio, Texas.

Army Dept. *(Defense Dept.), Repatriation and Family Affairs: POWs and MIAs,* 2461 Eisenhower Ave., Alexandria, VA 22331-0482; (703) 325-5305. Fax, (703) 325-1808. Lt. Col. Rosemary Salak, Chief. Web, www.army.mil.

Military office that responds to inquiries about prisoner of war (POW) and missing in action (MIA) personnel for the Army and distributes information about Army POWs and MIAs to the next of kin.

Defense Dept., *Prisoners of War and Missing Personnel,* 1745 Jefferson Davis Hwy., CSQ4, #800, Arlington, VA 22202; (703) 602-2102. Fax, (703) 602-4375. Robert L. Jones, Deputy Assistant Secretary. Web, www.dtic.mil/dpmo.

Civilian office responsible for policy matters relating to prisoners of war and missing personnel issues. Represents the Defense Dept. before Congress, the media, veterans organizations, and prisoner of war and missing personnel families.

Defense Dept., *Public Communication,* The Pentagon, #1E757 20301-1400; (703) 697-5737. Fax, (703) 695-1149. Harold Heilsnis, Director. Web, www.defenselink.mil.

Responds to public inquiries on Defense Dept. personnel, including those listed as missing in action.

Marine Corps *(Defense Dept.), Casualty Section,* HQUSMC, 3280 Russell Rd., Quantico, VA 22134; (703) 784-9501. Fax, (703) 784-7823. Maj. M. L. Ward, Head.

Military office that responds to inquiries about missing in action (MIA) personnel for the Marine Corps and distributes information about Marine Corps MIAs to the next of kin.

Navy Dept. *(Defense Dept.), Naval Personnel,* 2 Navy Annex 20370; (703) 614-1101. Fax, (703) 693-1746. Rear Adm. Norbert R. Ryan Jr., Chief. Web, www.navy.mil.

Military office that responds to inquiries about missing in action (MIA) personnel for the Navy and distributes information about Navy MIAs.

State Dept., *Burma, Cambodia, Laos, Thailand, and Vietnam Affairs,* 2201 C St. N.W., #5206 20520-6310; (202) 647-3132. Fax, (202) 647-3069. Neil Silver, Director. Web, www.state.gov.

Handles issues related to Americans missing in action in Indochina; serves as liaison with Congress, international organizations, and foreign governments on developments in these countries.

CONGRESS

House Armed Services Committee, *Subcommittee on Military Personnel,* 2340 RHOB 20515; (202) 225-7560.

Fax, (202) 226-0789. Rep. Steve Buyer, R-Ind., Chair; John Chapla, Professional Staff Member. Web, www.house.gov/hasc.

Jurisdiction over legislation on Americans missing in action (MIAs).

Senate Armed Services Committee, *Subcommittee on Personnel,* SR-228 20510; (202) 224-3871. Sen. Tim Hutchinson, R-Ark., Chair; Charles S. Abell, Professional Staff Member. Web, armed_services.senate.gov.

Jurisdiction over legislation on Americans missing in action (MIAs).

NONPROFIT

American Defense Institute, *Pride in America,* 1055 N. Fairfax St., #200, Alexandria, VA 22314; (703) 519-7000. Fax, (703) 519-8627. Eugene B. McDaniel, President. General e-mail, rdt2@americandefinst.org. Web, www.ajc.org/adi/.

Nonpartisan organization that seeks to educate young Americans on matters of national security and foreign policy, including POW/MIA issues.

National League of Families of American Prisoners and Missing in Southeast Asia, 1001 Connecticut Ave. N.W., #919 20036-5504; (202) 223-6846. Fax, (202) 785-9410. Ann Mills Griffiths, Executive Director. Recording, (202) 659-0133. General e-mail, powmiafam@aol.com. Web, www.pow-miafamilies.org.

Membership: family members of MIAs and POWs and returned POWs of the Vietnam War. Works for the release of all prisoners of war, an accounting of the missing, and repatriation of the remains of those who have died serving their country in Southeast Asia. Works to raise public awareness of these issues; maintains regional and state coordinators; sponsors an annual recognition day.

Pay and Compensation

AGENCIES

Air Force Dept. *(Defense Dept.), Legislation and Compensation Division,* The Pentagon, #4C236 20330-1040; (703) 695-1111. Fax, (703) 614-0099. Jim Wilkinson, Chief. Web, www.af.mil.

Military office that develops and administers Air Force military personnel pay and compensation policies.

Army Dept. *(Defense Dept.), Military Compensation and Entitlements,* The Pentagon, #2D677 20310-0300; (703) 695-2491. Fax, (703) 693-1832. Lt. Col. Curtis W. Crutchfield, Chief. Web, www.army.mil.

Military office that develops and administers Army military personnel pay and compensation policies.

Defense Dept., *Compensation,* *The Pentagon, #2B279 20301-4000; (703) 695-3176. Fax, (703) 697-8725. Capt. Elliot L. Bloxom (USN), Director. Web, www.defenselink. mil.*

Coordinates military pay and compensation policies with the individual service branches and advises the secretary of defense on compensation policy.

Marine Corps *(Defense Dept.), Manpower Policy,* *3280 Russell Rd., Quantico, VA 22134-5103; (703) 784-9386. Fax, (703) 784-9815. Karl Hackbarth, Compensation/ Incentive Officer.*

Military office that develops and administers Marine Corps personnel pay and compensation policies.

Navy Dept. *(Defense Dept.), Military Compensation and Policy Coordination,* *Navy Annex, Arlington, VA 20370; (703) 614-7797. Fax, (703) 695-3311. Capt. Ronald Alsbrooks, Director. Web, www.navy.mil.*

Military office that develops and administers Navy military pay, compensation, and personnel policies.

Recruitment

AGENCIES

Air Force Dept. *(Defense Dept.), Accession Policy,* *The Pentagon, #4E161 20330-1040; (703) 697-2388. Fax, (703) 614-1436. Lt. Col. Roxanne Lehr, Chief. Web, www.af.mil.*

Military office that coordinates Air Force recruiting activities with the recruitment service at Randolph Air Force Base in San Antonio, Texas.

Army Dept. *(Defense Dept.), Army Career and Alumni Program,* *200 Stovall St., #3N17, Alexandria, VA 22332-0476; (703) 325-3591. Fax, (703) 325-8092. James T. Hoffman, Chief. Information, (800) 445-2049. Web, www.army.mil.*

Military office that provides Army military personnel with information concerning transition benefits and job assistance for those separating service members and their families.

Army Dept. *(Defense Dept.), Enlisted Accessions,* *300 Army Pentagon 20310-0300; (703) 697-6744. Fax, (703) 695-0183. Jeffrey L. Spara, Chief. Web, www.army.mil.*

Military office that develops policies and administers Army recruitment programs.

Defense Dept., *Accession Policy,* *The Pentagon, #2B271 20301-4000; (703) 695-5525. Fax, (703) 614-9272. Wayne S. Sellman, Director. Web, www.defenselink.mil.*

Civilian office that develops Defense Dept. recruiting programs and policies, including advertising, market research, and enlistment standards. Coordinates with

the individual services on recruitment of military personnel.

Marine Corps *(Defense Dept.), Recruiting Command,* *3280 Russell Rd., Quantico, VA 22134-5103; (703) 784-9400. Fax, (703) 784-9863. Maj. Gen. Garry L. Parks, Commanding General. Web, www.mcrc.usmc.mil.*

Military office that administers and develops policies for Marine Corps officer and enlisted recruitment programs.

Retirement

See also Veterans (this chapter)

AGENCIES

Army Dept. *(Defense Dept.), Retirement Services,* *200 Stovall St., #3N33, Alexandria, VA 22332; (703) 325-9158. Fax, (703) 325-8947. Gary F. Smith, Chief. Information, (800) 336-4909. Web, www.army.mil.*

Military office that administers retirement programs for Army military personnel.

Defense Dept., *Compensation,* *The Pentagon, #2B279 20301-4000; (703) 695-3176. Fax, (703) 697-8725. Capt. Elliot L. Bloxom (USN), Director. Web, www.defenselink. mil.*

Develops retirement policies and reviews administration of retirement programs for all Defense Dept. military personnel.

Marine Corps *(Defense Dept.), Retired Activities,* *3280 Russell Rd., Quantico, VA 22134-5103; (703) 784-9310. Fax, (703) 784-9834. Anthony C. Orlando, Head. Web, tripoli.manpower.usmc.mil.*

Military office that administers retirement programs and benefits for Marine Corps retirees.

Marine Corps *(Defense Dept.), Separation and Retirement,* *3280 Russell Rd., Quantico, VA 22134-5103; (703) 784-9304. Fax, (703) 784-9834. James P. Rathbun, Head. Web, tripoli.manpower.usmc.mil.*

Military office that processes Marine Corps military personnel retirements but does not administer benefits.

U.S. Soldiers' and Airmen's Home, *3700 N. Capitol St. N.W. 20317; (202) 730-3229. Fax, (202) 730-3127. Donald C. Hilbert, Director. Information, (202) 730-3556. Web, www.afrh.com.*

Gives domiciliary and medical care to retirees and members of the armed services or career service personnel unable to earn a livelihood. (U.S. Naval Home in Gulfport, Miss., also serves all branches of the armed services.)

NONPROFIT

Army Distaff Foundation, *6200 Oregon Ave. N.W. 20015-1543; (202) 541-0105. Fax, (202) 364-2856. Calvert P. Benedict, Executive Director. Information, (800) 541-4255.*

Nonprofit continuing care retirement community for career military officers and their families. Provides retirement housing and health care services.

🎖 MILITARY EDUCATION AND TRAINING

AGENCIES

Air Force Dept. *(Defense Dept.), Air Force Academy Admissions Liaison, HQ USAFA/OL-C, The Pentagon, #4C174 20330-1040; (703) 695-4005. Fax, (703) 695-7999. Karen E. Parker, Director. Web, www.af.mil.*

Military office that receives congressional nominations for the Air Force Academy; counsels congressional offices on candidate selection.

Air Force Dept. *(Defense Dept.), Force Management and Personnel, The Pentagon, #5E977 20330-1660; (703) 614-4752. Fax, (703) 693-4244. Mary Lou Keener, Deputy Assistant Secretary. Web, www.af.mil.*

Civilian office that monitors and reviews education policies of the U.S. Air Force Academy at Colorado Springs and officer candidates' training and Reserve Officers Training Corps (ROTC) programs for the Air Force. Advises the secretary of the Air Force on education matters, including graduate education, voluntary education programs, and flight, specialized, and recruit training.

Air Force Dept. *(Defense Dept.), Personnel Force Management, The Pentagon, #4E228 20330-1040; (703) 695-6770. Fax, (703) 614-8523. Maj. Gen. Susan L. Pamerleau, Director. Web, www.af.mil.*

Supervises operations and policies of all professional military education, including continuing education programs. Oversees operations and policies of Air Force service schools, including technical training for newly enlisted Air Force personnel.

Army Dept. *(Defense Dept.), Collective Training Division, The Pentagon 20310-0450; (703) 697-4109. Fax, (703) 697-0936. Lt. Col. Robert L. Harrison, Chief. Web, www.army.mil.*

Military office that runs civilian and military training readiness programs; monitors and reviews operations and policies of Army service schools and advises the chief of staff of the Army on education matters; adminis-

ters certain service schools and serves as an information source for others.

Army Dept. *(Defense Dept.), Education, 2461 Eisenhower Ave., Attn.: TAPC-PDE #922, Alexandria, VA 22331-0472; (703) 325-9800. Fax, (703) 325-7476. Dian L. Stoskopf, Chief.*

Military office that manages the operations and policies of voluntary education programs for active Army personnel. Administers the tuition assistance program and basic army special skills program.

Army Dept. *(Defense Dept.), Military Personnel Management, The Pentagon 20310-0300; (703) 695-2497. Fax, (703) 693-5980. Brig. Gen. Dee A. McWilliams, Director. Web, www.army.mil.*

Military office that supervises operations and policies of the U.S. Military Academy and officer candidates' training and Reserve Officers Training Corps (ROTC) programs. Advises the chief of staff of the Army on academy and education matters.

Army Dept. *(Defense Dept.), West Point Liaison, 200 Stovall St., Attn.: TAPC-OPD-CM, Alexandria, VA 22332-0413; (703) 325-7414. Fax, (703) 325-6073. Jorja L. Graves, Chief. Web, www.army.mil.*

Military office that receives congressional nominations for West Point; counsels congressional offices on candidate selection.

Civil Air Patrol, *National Capital Wing, Washington Office, Bolling Air Force Base, 222 Luke Ave., #2 20332-5114; (202) 767-4405. Fax, (202) 767-5695. Col. Roland Butler, Wing Commander.*

Official auxiliary of the U.S. Air Force. Sponsors a cadet training and education program for junior and senior high school age students. Cadets who have earned the Civil Air Patrol's Mitchell Award are eligible to enter the Air Force at an advanced pay grade. Conducts an aerospace education program for adults. (Headquarters at Maxwell Air Force Base, Ala.)

Defense Dept., *Accession Policy, The Pentagon, #2B271 20301-4000; (703) 695-5525. Fax, (703) 614-9272. Wayne S. Sellman, Director. Web, www.defenselink.mil.*

Reviews and develops education policies of the service academies, service schools, graduate and voluntary education programs, education programs for active duty personnel, tuition assistance programs, and officer candidates' training and Reserve Officers Training Corps (ROTC) programs for the Defense Dept. Advises the secretary of defense on education matters.

Defense Dept., *Readiness and Training, The Pentagon, #1C757 20301-4000; (703) 695-2618. Fax, (703) 693-*

7382. Michael A. Parmentier, Director. Web, www. defenselink.mil.

Develops, reviews, and analyzes legislation, policies, plans, programs, resource levels, and budgets for the training of military personnel and military units.

Defense Systems Management College *(Defense Dept.),* 9820 Belvoir Rd., #G38, Fort Belvoir, VA 22060-5565; (703) 805-3360. Fax, (703) 805-2639. Brig. Gen. Frank J. Anderson (USAF), Commandant. Registrar, (703) 805-2227. Web, www.dsmc.dsm.mil.

Academic institution that offers courses to military and civilian personnel who specialize in acquisition and procurement. Conducts research to support and improve management of defense systems acquisition programs.

Industrial College of the Armed Forces *(Defense Dept.),* Fort Lesley J. McNair, 408 4th Ave., Bldg. #59 20319-5062; (202) 685-4333. Fax, (202) 685-4175. Maj. Gen. Richard L. Engel (USA), Commandant, (202) 685-4337. Web, www.ndu.edu.

Division of National Defense University. Offers professional level courses for senior military officers and senior civilian government officials. Academic program focuses on management of national resources, mobilization, and industrial preparedness.

Marine Corps *(Defense Dept.), Training and Education,* 3300 Russell Rd., Code MCCDC (C46), Quantico, VA 22134-5001; (703) 784-3730. Fax, (703) 784-3724. Brig. Gen. T. S. Jones, Director.

Military office that develops and implements training and education programs for regular and reserve personnel and units.

National Defense University *(Defense Dept.),* Fort Lesley J. McNair, 4th and P Sts. S.W. 20319-5066; (202) 685-3922. Fax, (202) 685-3931. Lt. Gen. Richard A. Chilcoat (USAF), President. Press, (202) 685-4220. Web, www.ndu.edu.

Specialized university sponsored by the Joint Chiefs of Staff to prepare individuals for senior executive duties in the national security establishment. Offers master of science degrees in national resource strategy and national security strategy, as well as nondegree programs and courses.

National War College *(Defense Dept.),* Fort Lesley J. McNair, Bldg. #61 20319-5078; (202) 685-4341. Fax, (202) 685-3993. Rear Adm. Daniel R. Bowler (USN), Commandant. Information, (202) 685-3715. Web, www.ndu.edu/ndu/nducat22.html.

Division of National Defense University. Offers professional level courses for senior military officers, senior civil-

ian government officials, and foreign officers. Academic program focuses on the formulation and implementation of national security policy and military strategy.

Navy Dept. *(Defense Dept.), Manpower,* The Pentagon, #4E792 20350-1000; (703) 695-4350. Fax, (703) 614-4103. Karen S. Heath, Principal Deputy Assistant Secretary. Web, www.navy.mil.

Civilian office that reviews policies of the U.S. Naval Academy, Navy and Marine Corps service schools, and officer candidates' training and Reserve Officer Training Corps (ROTC) programs. Advises the secretary of the Navy on education matters, including voluntary education programs.

Navy Dept. *(Defense Dept.), Naval Training,* The Pentagon 20350-2000; (703) 697-4071. Fax, (703) 693-6480. Vice Adm. John W. Craine Jr., Director. Web, www.navy.mil.

Develops and implements naval training policies. Oversees Navy service college and graduate school programs. Administers training programs for Naval Reserve Officer Training Corps, Naval Junior ROTC, and officer and enlisted personnel.

Uniformed Services University of the Health Sciences *(Defense Dept.),* 4301 Jones Bridge Rd., Bethesda, MD 20814-4799; (301) 295-3013. Fax, (301) 295-1960. Dr. James A. Zimble, President. Information, (301) 295-3166. Registrar, (301) 295-3101. Web, www.usuhs.mil.

Fully accredited four-year medical school under the auspices of the Defense Dept. Awards doctorates and master's degrees in health- and science-related fields. The Graduate School of Nursing awards a masters of science (nursing).

U.S. Coast Guard *(Transportation Dept.), Human Resources,* 2100 2nd St. S.W. 20593-0001; (202) 267-0905. Fax, (202) 267-4205. Rear Adm. Fred L. Ames, Chief. Web, www.uscg.mil/hq/g-w/hrhome.htm.

Responsible for hiring, recruiting, and training all military and nonmilitary Coast Guard personnel.

U.S. Naval Academy *(Defense Dept.),* 106 Maryland Ave., Annapolis, MD 21402-5023; (410) 293-1000. Fax, (410) 293-2303. Adm. John R. Ryan, Superintendent, (410) 293-1500; David A. Vetter, Dean of Admissions, (410) 293-1801. Press, (410) 293-2293. Visitors information, (410) 263-6933. Candidate guidance, (800) 638-9156. General e-mail, navy@nadn.navy.mil. Web, www.usna.navy.mil.

Provides undergraduate education for young men and women who have been nominated by members of their state's congressional delegation, or, in some cases, the president or vice president of the United States. Graduates receive bachelor of science degrees and are commissioned as either an ensign in the U.S. Navy or a second lieutenant in the U.S. Marine Corps.

CONGRESS

House Armed Services Committee, *Subcommittee on Military Personnel,* 2340 RHOB 20515; (202) 225-7560. Fax, (202) 226-0789. Rep. Steve Buyer, R-Ind., Chair; John Chapla, Professional Staff Member. Web, www.house. gov/hasc.

Jurisdiction over legislation on precommissioning programs and on military service academies and schools.

Senate Armed Services Committee, *Subcommittee on Personnel,* SR-228 20510; (202) 224-3871. Sen. Tim Hutchinson, R-Ark., Chair; Charles S. Abell, Professional Staff Member. Web, armed_services.senate.gov.

Jurisdiction over legislation on precommissioning programs and on military service academies and schools.

NONPROFIT

Assn. of Military Colleges and Schools of the U.S., 9429 Garden Court, Potomac, MD 20854-3964; (301) 765-0695. Lewis Sorley (USA, ret.), Executive Director. Web, www.amcsus.org.

Membership: nonfederal military colleges, junior colleges, and secondary schools that emphasize character development, leadership, and knowledge. Interests include: Reserve Officers Training Corps (ROTC); publishes a newsletter; sponsors an annual meeting and outreach activities.

George and Carol Olmsted Foundation, 103 W. Broad St., #330, Falls Church, VA 22046; (703) 536-3500. Larry R. Marsh, Executive Vice President.

Administers grants for military academies and scholarship programs for selected officers of the armed forces.

Military Order of the World Wars, 435 N. Lee St., Alexandria, VA 22314; (703) 683-4911. Fax, (703) 683-4501. George G. Kundahl, Chief of Staff. General e-mail, mowwhq@aol.com. Web, www.militaryorder.org.

Membership: retired and active duty commissioned officers, warrant officers, and flight officers. Presents awards to outstanding Reserve Officers Training Corps (ROTC) cadets; gives awards to Boy Scouts and Girl Scouts; conducts youth leadership conferences.

Navy League of the United States, 2300 Wilson Blvd., Arlington, VA 22201; (703) 528-1775. Fax, (703) 528-2333. Charles L. Robinson, Executive Director. General e-mail, mail@navyleague.org. Web, www.navyleague.org.

Sponsors Naval Sea Cadet Corps and Navy League Sea Cadet Corps for young people ages eleven through eighteen years. Graduates are eligible to enter the Navy at advanced pay grades.

Servicemembers Opportunity Colleges, 1307 New York Ave. N.W., 5th Floor 20005; (202) 667-0079. Fax, (202) 667-0622. Steve F. Kime, Director. Information, (800) 368-5622. General e-mail, socmail@aascu.org. Web, www.soc.aascu.org.

Partnership of higher education associations, educational institutions, the Defense Dept., and the military services. Offers credit courses and degree programs to military personnel and their families stationed in the United States and around the world.

⬛ MILITARY GRIEVANCES AND DISCIPLINE

AGENCIES

Air Force Dept. *(Defense Dept.), Air Force Personnel Council,* 1535 Command Dr., EE Wing, Andrews AFB, MD 20762-7002; (240) 857-5739. Fax, (240) 857-9282. Raymond C. Chapman, Director. Web, www.af.mil.

Military office that administers boards that review appeal cases. Administers the Air Force Board of Review, Disability Review Board, Clemency and Parole Board, Discharge Review Board, Decorations Board, Personnel Board, and the Physical Disability Appeal Board.

Air Force Dept. *(Defense Dept.), Air Force Review Boards,* 1535 Command Dr., #E302, Andrews AFB, MD 20762-7002; (240) 857-3137. Fax, (240) 857-3136. Joe G. Lineberger, Director. Web, www.af.mil.

Civilian office that responds to complaints from Air Force military personnel and assists in seeking corrective action.

Air Force Dept. *(Defense Dept.), Inquiries Directorate,* The Pentagon 20330-1140; (703) 588-1531. Fax, (703) 696-2555. Edward N. McKinney, Chief. Web, www.af.mil.

Military office that handles complaints and requests for assistance from civilians and Air Force and other military personnel.

Army Dept. *(Defense Dept.), Army Review Boards Agency,* 1941 Jefferson Davis Hwy., 2nd Floor, Arlington, VA 22202-4508; (703) 607-1607. Fax, (703) 607-2036. Col. Thomas J. Allen, Director. Information, (703) 607-1600. Web, www.army.mil.

Military office that administers boards that review appeal cases. Administers the Ad Hoc Review Board,

Army Grade Determination Board, Disability Rating Review Board, Discharge Review Board, Elimination Review Board, Security Review Board, and Physical Disability Appeal Board.

Army Dept. *(Defense Dept.), Military Personnel Management and Equal Opportunity Policy,* 111 Army Pentagon 20310-0111; (703) 697-2631. Fax, (703) 614-5975. John P. McLaurin III, Deputy Assistant Secretary. Web, www.army.mil.

Civilian office that receives complaints from Army military personnel and assists in seeking corrective action.

Defense Dept., *Legal Policy,* The Pentagon, #4C759 20301-4000; (703) 697-3387. Fax, (703) 693-6708. Col. Paul Black (USAF), Director. Web, www.defenselink.mil.

Coordinates policy for the discharge review boards of the armed services.

Defense Dept., *Military Equal Opportunity,* The Pentagon, #3A272 20301-4000; (703) 697-6381. Fax, (703) 695-4619. Jimmy Love, Director (Acting). Web, www.dticaw.dtic.mil/trhome/das_eo.html.

Receives civil rights complaints from military personnel and assists in seeking corrective action.

Marine Corps *(Defense Dept.), Inspection,* Navy Annex, Arlington, VA 20370 (mailing address: Headquarters, U.S. Marine Corps, Code IG 20380-1775); (703) 614-1698. Fax, (703) 697-6690. Timothy Ghormley, Inspector General. Web, www.hqmc.usmc.mil/ig/ig.nsf.

Military office that investigates complaints from Marine Corps personnel and assists in seeking corrective action.

Navy Dept. *(Defense Dept.), Manpower and Reserve Affairs,* The Pentagon 20350-1000; (703) 697-2180. Fax, (703) 614-4103. Carolyn H. Becraft, Assistant Secretary. Web, www.navy.mil.

Civilian office that receives complaints from Navy and Marine Corps military personnel and assists in seeking corrective action.

Navy Dept. *(Defense Dept.), Naval Council of Personnel Boards,* Washington Navy Yard, 720 Kennon St. S.E., #309 20374-5023; (202) 685-6408. Fax, (202) 685-6610. Capt. William F. Eckert, Director. Web, www.navy.mil.

Military office that administers boards that review appeal cases for the Navy and the Marine Corps. Composed of the Physical Evaluation Boards, the Naval Discharge Review Board, and the Naval Clemency and Parole Board.

CONGRESS

House Armed Services Committee, *Subcommittee on Military Personnel,* 2340 RHOB 20515; (202) 225-7560. Fax, (202) 226-0789. Rep. Steve Buyer, R-Ind., Chair; John Chapla, Professional Staff Member. Web, www.house.gov/hasc.

Jurisdiction over legislation on military personnel matters, including courts martial and appeals and military grievance procedures.

Senate Armed Services Committee, *Subcommittee on Personnel,* SR-228 20510; (202) 224-3871. Sen. Tim Hutchinson, R-Ark., Chair; Charles S. Abell, Professional Staff Member. Web, armed_services.senate.gov.

Jurisdiction over legislation on military personnel matters, including courts martial and appeals and military grievance procedures.

NONPROFIT

National Institute of Military Justice, c/o Feldesman, Tucker, 2001 L St. N.W., #200 20036; (202) 466-8960. Fax, (202) 293-8103. Eugene R. Fidell, President. General e-mail, efidell@feldesmantucker.com.

Advances the administration of military justice within the U.S. armed services; fosters improved public understanding of the military justice system.

National Interreligious Service Board for Conscientious Objectors, *Center for Conscience and War,* 1830 Connecticut Ave. N.W. 20009; (202) 483-2220. Fax, (202) 483-1246. J. E. McNeil, Executive Director. General e-mail, nisbco@igc.apc.org. Web, www.nisbco.org.

Seeks to defend and extend the rights of conscientious objectors. Provides information and advocacy about the military draft and national selective service. Offers counseling and information to military personnel seeking discharge or transfer to noncombatant positions within the military.

Servicemembers Legal Defense Network, P.O. Box 65301 20035-5301; (202) 328-3244. Fax, (202) 797-1635. Michelle M. Benecke, Co-Director; C. Dixon Osburn, Co-Director. General e-mail, sldn@sldn.org. Web, www.sldn.org.

Provides legal assistance to individuals affected by the military's policy on gays and lesbians. Monitors legislation and regulations.

Correction of Military Records

AGENCIES

Air Force Dept. *(Defense Dept.), Board for the Correction of Military Records,* 1535 Command Dr., EE Wing,

3rd Floor, Andrews AFB, MD 20762-7002; (240) 857-3502. Fax, (240) 857-9207. Mack Burton, Executive Director. Web, www.af.mil.

Civilian board that reviews appeals for corrections to Air Force personnel records and makes recommendations to the secretary of the Air Force.

Army Dept. *(Defense Dept.), Board for the Correction of Military Records,* 1941 Jefferson Davis Hwy., 2nd Floor, Arlington, VA 22202-4508; (703) 607-1611. Fax, (703) 602-0935. Loren G. Harrell, Director. Web, www.army.mil.

Civilian board that reviews appeals for corrections to Army personnel records and makes recommendations to the secretary of the Army.

Defense Dept., *Legal Policy,* The Pentagon, #4C759 20301-4000; (703) 697-3387. Fax, (703) 693-6708. Col. Paul Black (USAF), Director. Web, www.defenselink.mil.

Coordinates policy for armed services boards charged with correcting military records.

Navy Dept. *(Defense Dept.), Board for Correction of Naval Records,* 2 Navy Annex, #2432 20370-5100; (703) 614-1402. Fax, (703) 614-9857. W. Dean Pfeiffer, Executive Director. Web, www.navy.mil.

Civilian board that reviews appeals for corrections to Navy and Marine Corps personnel records and makes recommendations to the secretary of the Navy.

U.S. Coast Guard *(Transportation Dept.), Board for Correction of Military Records,* 400 7th St. S.W., #4100 20590-0001; (202) 366-9335. Fax, (202) 366-7152. Robert H. Joost, Chair. Web, www.dot.gov/ost/ogc.

Civilian board that reviews appeals for corrections to Coast Guard personnel records and makes recommendations to the general counsel of the Transportation Dept.

Legal Proceedings

AGENCIES

Air Force Dept. *(Defense Dept.), Air Force Personnel Council,* 1535 Command Dr., EE Wing, Andrews AFB, MD 20762-7002; (240) 857-5739. Fax, (240) 857-9282. Raymond C. Chapman, Director. Web, www.af.mil.

Military office that administers review boards, including the Clemency and Parole Board, which in turn reviews cases of military prisoners and makes recommendations to the secretary of the Air Force.

Air Force Dept. *(Defense Dept.), Judge Advocate General,* The Pentagon 20330-1420; (703) 614-5732. Fax, (703) 614-8894. Maj. Gen. William A. Moorman, Judge Advocate General. Web, www.af.mil.

Military office that prosecutes and defends Air Force personnel during military legal proceedings. Gives legal advice and assistance to Air Force staff.

Army Dept. *(Defense Dept.), Army Clemency and Parole Board,* Crystal Mall 4, 1941 Jefferson Davis Hwy., #109A, Arlington, VA 22202-4508; (703) 607-1504. Fax, (703) 607-2047. James E. Vick, Chair. Web, www.army.mil.

Civilian and military board that reviews cases of military prisoners and makes recommendations to the secretary of the Army; reviews suspension of less-than-honorable discharges and restoration of prisoners to active duty or parole.

Army Dept. *(Defense Dept.), Judge Advocate General,* The Pentagon 20310-2200; (703) 697-5151. Fax, (703) 693-0600. Maj. Gen. Walter B. Huffman, Judge Advocate General. Web, www.army.mil.

Military office that prosecutes and defends Army personnel during military legal proceedings. Serves as an administrative office for military appeals court, which hears legal proceedings involving Army personnel.

Defense Dept., *U.S. Court of Appeals for the Armed Forces,* 450 E St. N.W. 20442-0001; (202) 761-1448. Fax, (202) 761-4672. Thomas F. Granahan, Clerk of the Court. Library, (202) 761-1466. Web, www.defenselink.mil.

Serves as the appellate court for cases involving dishonorable or bad conduct discharges, confinement of a year or more, and the death penalty, and for cases certified to the court by the judge advocate general of an armed service. Less serious cases are reviewed by the individual armed services. Library open to the public.

Navy Dept. *(Defense Dept.), Judge Advocate General,* Washington Navy Yard, 1322 Patterson Ave. S.E., #3000 20374-5066; (703) 614-7420. Fax, (703) 697-4610. Rear Adm. John D. Hutson, Judge Advocate General. Web, www.navy.mil.

Military office that administers legal proceedings involving Navy and Marine personnel.

Navy Dept. *(Defense Dept.), Naval Clemency and Parole Board,* 720 Kennon St. S.E., Bldg. 36, #322 20374-5023; (202) 685-6455. Fax, (202) 685-6629. Capt. Jeffrey Keho (USN), President. Web, www.navy.mil.

Military board that reviews cases of Navy and Marine Corps prisoners and makes recommendations to the secretary of the Navy.

Military Police and Corrections

AGENCIES

Army Dept. *(Defense Dept.), Security Force Protection and Law Enforcement,* 400 Army Pentagon, DAMO-

ODL, #BF758 20310-0400; (703) 693-6580. Col. Manolito Garabato, Chief. Web, www.army.mil.

Develops policies and supports military police and corrections programs in all branches of the U.S. military. Operates the Military Police Management Information System (MPMIS), which automates incident reporting and tracks information on facilities, staff, and inmates, including enemy prisoners of war.

Army Dept. *(Defense Dept.), Security Force Protection and Law Enforcement: Federal Liaison, HQDA, ODC-SOPS DAMO-ODL, 400 Army Pentagon 22301-0400; (703) 681-4868. Fax, (703) 693-6580. Jeffrey Porter, Federal Liaison Officer. Web, www.army.mil.*

Military office that develops Army policies and responds to inquiries relating to deserters.

Defense Dept., *Legal Policy, The Pentagon, #4C759 20301-4000; (703) 697-3387. Fax, (703) 693-6708. Col. Paul Black (USAF), Director. Web, www.defenselink.mil.*

Coordinates and reviews Defense Dept. policies and programs relating to deserters.

Marine Corps *(Defense Dept.), Corrections, CMC HQMC POS-40, 2 Navy Annex 20380-1775; (703) 614-1375. Fax, (703) 614-3499. Tim Purcell, Head.*

Military office that develops Marine Corps policies and responds to inquiries relating to deserters. Oversees Marine Corps brigs (correctional facilities).

▨ MILITARY HISTORY AND HONORS

AGENCIES

Air Force Dept. *(Defense Dept.), Air Force History, Bolling Air Force Base, 200 McChord St., #94 20332-1111; (202) 404-2167. Fax, (202) 404-2270. Richard P. Hallion, Historian. Library, (202) 404-2264. Web, www.af.mil.*

Publishes histories, studies, monographs, and reference works; directs worldwide Air Force History Program and provides guidance to the Air Force Historical Research Agency at Maxwell Air Force Base in Alabama; supports Air Force Air Staff agencies and responds to inquiries from the public and the U.S. government. Library open to the public.

Army Dept. *(Defense Dept.), Institute of Heraldry, 9325 Gunston Rd., Bldg. 1466, #S-112, Fort Belvoir, VA 22060-5579; (703) 806-4968. Fax, (703) 806-4964. Fred N. Eichorn, Director. Information, (703) 806-4971. Web, www.army.mil.*

Furnishes heraldic services to the Armed Forces and other U.S. government agencies, including the Executive Office of the President. Responsible for research, design, development, and standardization of official symbolic items, including seals, decorations, medals, insignias, badges, flags, and other items awarded to or authorized for official wear or display by government personnel and agencies. Limited research and information services on these items are provided to the general public.

Army Dept. *(Defense Dept.), U.S. Center of Military History, 103 3rd Ave., Bldg. 35, Fort Lesley J. McNair 20319-5058; (202) 685-2706. Fax, (202) 685-4570. Brig. Gen. John S. Brown, Chief. Information, (202) 761-5421. Library, (202) 685-3573. Web, www.army.mil/cmh-pg.*

Publishes the official history of the Army. Provides information on Army history; coordinates Army museum system and art program. Works with Army school system to ensure that history is included in curriculum. Sponsors professional appointments, fellowships, and awards.

Defense Dept., *Historical Office, 1777 N. Kent St., #500, Arlington, VA 22209; (703) 588-7890. Fax, (703) 588-7572. Alfred Goldberg, Historian. Web, www.defenselink.mil.*

Collects, compiles, and publishes documents and data on the history of Defense Dept. and the office of the secretary; coordinates historical activities of the Defense Dept. and prepares special studies at the request of the secretary.

Defense Dept., *Joint History Office, The Pentagon, #1B707 20318-9999; (703) 695-2114. Fax, (703) 614-6243. Brig. Gen. David A. Armstrong (USA, ret.), Director. Web, www.defenselink.mil.*

Provides historical support services to the Joint Chiefs of Staff, including research; writes the official history of the Joint Chiefs.

Marine Corps *(Defense Dept.), Historical Center, Washington Navy Yard, 1254 Charles Morris St. S.E. 20374-5040; (202) 433-0731. Fax, (202) 433-7265. Col. Michael F. Monigan (USMC), Director. Information, (202) 433-3840. Library, (202) 433-3447. Reference, (202) 433-3483. Web, www.usmc.mil.*

Maintains official Marine Corps archives; writes official histories of the corps for government agencies and the public; answers inquiries about Marine Corps history; maintains museum; conducts prearranged tours of the historical center and museum. Library open to the public.

National Archives and Records Administration, *Textual Reference, 8601 Adelphi Rd., College Park, MD 20740-6001; (301) 713-7250. Fax, (301) 713-6907. James Hastings, Director.*

Contains Army records from the Revolutionary War to the Vietnam War, Navy records from the Revolutionary War to the Korean War, and Air Force records from 1947–1954. Handles records captured from enemy powers at the end of World War II and a small collection of records captured from the Vietnamese. Conducts research in response to specific inquiries; makes records available for reproduction or examination in research room.

National Museum of American History *(Smithsonian Institution), Armed Forces History Collections, 14th St. and Constitution Ave. N.W., NMAH-4012, MRC 620 20560-0620; (202) 357-1883. Fax, (202) 357-1853. Jennifer Locke, Assistant Chair. Web, www.si.edu/organiza/ museums/nmah/csr/cadht.htm.*

Maintains collections relating to the history of the U.S. armed forces and the American flag; includes manuscripts, documents, correspondence, uniforms, ordnance material of European and American origin, and other personal memorabilia of armed forces personnel of all ranks.

National Museum of Health and Medicine *(Defense Dept.), Walter Reed Medical Center, Bldg. 54 South 20307 (mailing address: 6825 16th St. N.W. 20036-6000); (202) 782-2200. Fax, (202) 782-3573. Dr. Adrianne Noe, Director.*

Maintains exhibits related to pathology and the history of medicine, particularly military medicine during the Civil War. Open to the public. Study collection available for scholars by appointment.

National Park Service *(Interior Dept.), 1849 C St. N.W., #3316 20240; (202) 208-4621. Fax, (202) 208-7889. Robert Stanton, Director. Press, (202) 208-6843. Washington area activities, (202) 619-7275 (recording). Web, www.nps.gov.*

Administers national parks, monuments, historic sites, and recreation areas. Responsible for national battlefields, selected historic forts, and other sites associated with U.S. military history.

Navy Dept. *(Defense Dept.), Naval Historical Center, 805 Kidder Breese St. S.E. 20374-5060; (202) 433-2210. Fax, (202) 433-3593. William S. Dudley, Director. Library, (202) 433-4132. Museum, (202) 433-6897; Art Gallery, (202) 433-3815; Archives, (202) 433-3224. Web, www. history.navy.mil.*

Produces publications on naval history. Maintains historical files on Navy ships, operations, shore installations, and aviation. Collects Navy art, artifacts, and photographs. Library and archives open to the public.

U.S. Coast Guard *(Transportation Dept.), Historian, 2100 2nd St. S.W. 20593-0001; (202) 267-2596. Fax, (202)* 267-4309. Robert M. Browning, Chief Historian. Web, www.uscg.mil/hq/g-cp/history/collect.html.

Collects and maintains Coast Guard historical materials, including service artifacts, documents, photographs, and books. Publishes historical inserts in the Coast Guard magazine. Archives are available to the public by appointment only.

NONPROFIT

Aerospace Education Foundation, *1501 Lee Hwy., Arlington, VA 22209; (703) 247-5839. Fax, (703) 247-5853. Dan Marrs, Managing Director (Acting). Information, (800) 727-3337. General e-mail, aefstaff@aef.org. Web, www.aef.org.*

Promotes knowledge of U.S. military and civilian aerospace development and history. Sponsors educational symposia and scholarships for enlisted personnel and officers on active duty or in the National Guard and Reserves. (Affiliated with the Air Force Assn.)

Air Force Historical Foundation, *1535 Command Dr., #A-122, Andrews AFB, MD 20762; (301) 981-4728. Fax, (301) 981-3574. Col. Maynard Y. Binge, Executive Director.*

Membership: individuals interested in the history of the U.S. Air Force and U.S. air power. Bestows awards on Air Force Academy and Air War College students and to other active duty personnel. Funds research and publishes books on aviation and Air Force history.

Council on America's Military Past-U.S.A., *P.O. Box 1151, Fort Myer, VA 22211-1151; (703) 912-6124. Fax, (703) 912-5666. Herbert M. Hart, Executive Director. Information, (800) 398-4693.*

Membership: historians, archeologists, curators, writers, and others interested in military history and preservation of historic military establishments and ships.

National Museum of American Jewish Military History, *1811 R St. N.W. 20009; (202) 265-6280. Fax, (202) 234-5662. Herb Rosenbleeth, Executive Director. Web, www.pemfed.org/jwv/home.htm.*

Collects, preserves, and displays memorabilia of Jewish men and women in the military; conducts research; sponsors seminars; provides information on the history of Jewish participation in the U.S. armed forces.

Naval Historical Foundation, *Washington Navy Yard, 1306 Dahlgren Ave. S.E. 20374-5055; (202) 678-4333. Fax, (202) 889-3565. Robert F. Dunn, President. Web, www.mil. org/navyhist/.*

Collects private documents and artifacts relating to naval history; maintains collection on deposit with the

Library of Congress for public reference; raises funds to support the Navy Museum and historical programs.

Cemeteries and Memorials

AGENCIES

American Battle Monuments Commission, *2300 Clarendon Blvd., #500, Arlington, VA 22201-3367; (703) 696-6900. Fax, (703) 696-6666. John D. Herrling, Secretary. Web, www.usabmc.com/.*

Maintains military cemeteries and memorials on foreign soil and certain memorials in the United States; provides next of kin with grave site and related information.

Army Dept. *(Defense Dept.), Arlington National Cemetery: Interment Services,, Arlington, VA 22211; (703) 695-3250. Fax, (703) 614-6339. Vicki Tanner, Chief. Web, www.army.mil.*

Arranges interment services and provides eligibility information for burials at Arlington National Cemetery.

Veterans Affairs Dept. (VA), *National Cemetery Administration, 810 Vermont Ave. N.W., #400 20420; (202) 273-5145. Fax, (202) 273-6696. Robert M. Walker, Under Secretary for Memorial Affairs (Acting). Web, www.va.gov.*

Administers VA national cemeteries; furnishes markers and headstones for deceased veterans; administers state grants to establish, expand, and improve veterans' cemeteries. Provides presidential memorial certificates to next of kin.

CONGRESS

House Appropriations Committee, *Subcommittee on VA, HUD, and Independent Agencies, H143 CAP 20515; (202) 225-3241. Rep. James T. Walsh, R-N.Y., Chair; Frank Cushing, Staff Director. Web, www.house.gov/appropriations.*

Jurisdiction over legislation to appropriate funds for the American Battle Monuments Commission and for cemeterial expenses for the Army Dept., including Arlington National Cemetery.

Senate Appropriations Committee, *Subcommittee on VA, HUD, and Independent Agencies, SD-130 20510; (202) 224-7211. Sen. Christopher S. Bond, R-Mo., Chair; Jon Kamarck, Staff Director. Web, appropriations.senate.gov/vahud.*

Jurisdiction over legislation to appropriate funds for the American Battle Monuments Commission and for cemeterial expenses for the Army Dept., including Arlington National Cemetery.

Senate Veterans' Affairs Committee, *SR-412 20510; (202) 224-9126. Fax, (202) 224-8908. Sen. Arlen Specter, R-Pa., Chair; William Tuerk, Staff Director. Web, veterans.senate.gov.*

Jurisdiction over legislation on national cemeteries, including Arlington National Cemetery.

NONPROFIT

Air Force Memorial Foundation, *1501 Lee Hwy., #120, Arlington, VA 22209-1198; (703) 247-5808. Fax, (703) 247-5819. Charles D. Link, President. Web, www.airforcememorial.org.*

Plans to design and construct an Air Force Memorial to honor the achievements of men and women who have served in the U.S. Air Force, or its predecessors, such as the Army Air Forces.

The Black Revolutionary War Patriots Foundation, *1612 K St. N.W., #1104 20006-2802; (202) 452-1776. Fax, (202) 728-0770. Wayne F. Smith, President. Web, www.blackpatriots.org.*

Private corporation authorized by Congress to fund and build a national memorial to honor black patriots who served in the militia or provided civilian assistance during the American Revolution.

No Greater Love, *1750 New York Ave. N.W. 20006; (202) 783-4665. Fax, (202) 783-1168. Carmella LaSpada, Chief Executive Officer. Web, www.ngl.org.*

Provides programs of remembrance, friendship, and care for families of Americans killed in war or by acts of terrorism.

U.S. Navy Memorial Foundation, *701 Pennsylvania Ave. N.W., #123 20004-2608; (202) 737-2300. Fax, (202) 737-2308. Henry C. McKinney, President. General e-mail, ahoy@lonesailor.org. Web, www.lonesailor.org.*

Educational foundation authorized by Congress. Focuses on American naval history; built and supports the Navy memorial to honor those who serve or have served in the naval services.

Women in Military Service for America Memorial Foundation, *5510 Columbia Pike, #302, Arlington, VA 22204 (mailing address: Dept. 560 20042-0560); (703) 533-1155. Fax, (703) 931-4208. Wilma L. Vaught, President. Information, (800) 222-2294. General e-mail, wimsa@aol.com. Web, www.womensmemorial.org.*

Authorized by Congress to create, support, and build the national memorial to honor women who serve or have served in the U.S. armed forces from the revolutionary war to the present.

Ceremonies/Military Bands

AGENCIES

Air Force Dept. *(Defense Dept.), Air Force Band,* Bolling Air Force Base, 201 McChord St. 20332-0202; (202) 767-5255. Fax, (202) 767-0686. Col. Lowell E. Graham, Commander. Web, www.bolling.af.mil/band/band. htm.

Supports the Air Force by providing musical services for official military ceremonies and community events.

Air Force Dept. *(Defense Dept.), Bands and Music,* 901 N. Stuart St., #803, Arlington, VA 22203; (703) 695-0019. Fax, (703) 696-0125. Maj. Mark R. Peterson, Chief. Web, www.af.mil/band/home.htm.

Disseminates information to the public regarding various Air Force bands; coordinates their schedules and performances.

Army Dept. *(Defense Dept.), Army Field Band,* 4214 Field Band Dr., Fort Meade, MD 20755-5330; (301) 677-6231. Fax, (301) 677-6533. Col. Finley R. Hamilton, Commander. Web, www.mdw.army.mil/fband/usafb.htm.

Supports the Army by providing musical services for official military ceremonies and community events. Sponsors vocal and instrumental clinics for high school and college students.

Army Dept. *(Defense Dept.), Ceremonies and Special Events,* Fort Lesley J. McNair, 4th and P Sts. S.W. 20319-5050; (202) 685-2983. Fax, (202) 685-3379. Thomas L. Groppel, Special Events Coordinator. Web, www.army.mil.

Coordinates and schedules public ceremonies and special events, including appearances of all armed forces bands and honor guards.

Army Dept. *(Defense Dept.), Ceremonies and Special Events,* Fort Lesley J. McNair, 4th and P Sts. S.W. 20319-5050; (202) 685-2983. Fax, (202) 685-3379. Thomas L. Groppel, Special Events Coordinator. Web, www.army.mil.

Responsible for ceremonies at the Tomb of the Unknown Soldier in Arlington National Cemetery; arranges for military ceremonies at civilian cemeteries in the military district of Washington and surrounding area.

Army Dept. *(Defense Dept.), The U.S. Army Band,* Attn: ANAB, Bldg. 400, 204 Lee Ave., Fort Myer, VA 22211-1199; (703) 696-3647. Fax, (703) 696-3904. Col. Gary F. Lamp, Commander. Web, www.army.mil/armyband.

Supports the Army by providing musical services for official military ceremonies and community events.

Defense Dept., *Community Relations,* 1400 Defense Pentagon, 1E776 20301-1400; (703) 697-7385. Fax, (703) 697-2577. Michael W. Byers, Civilian Public Affairs Officer, (703) 695-6108; William Harris, Military Public Affairs Officer; Celia Hoke, Director. Web, www.defenselink.mil.

Provides armed forces bands with policy guidance for related public events.

Marine Corps *(Defense Dept.), Marine Band,* 8th and Eye Sts. S.E. 20390; (202) 433-4044. Fax, (202) 433-4752. Col. T. W. Foley, Director. Web, www.marineband.hqmc. usmc.mil.

Supports the Marines by providing musical services for official military ceremonies and community events.

Navy Dept. *(Defense Dept.), Navy Band,* Washington Navy Yard, 617 Warrington Ave. S.E. 20374-5054; (202) 433-3366. Fax, (202) 433-4108. Cmdr. Ralph M. Gambone, Officer in Charge. Web, www.navyband.navy.mil.

Supports the Navy by providing musical services for official military ceremonies and community events.

U.S. Naval Academy *(Defense Dept.), Band,* c/o U.S. Naval Academy, 101 Buchanan Rd., Annapolis, MD 21402-5080; (410) 293-1253. Fax, (410) 293-2116. Cmdr. J. M. Alverson, Director. Concert information, (410) 293-0263. Web, www.nadn.navy.mil/USNABand.

The Navy's oldest continuing musical organization. Supports the Navy by providing musical services for official military ceremonies and community events.

U.S. Naval Academy *(Defense Dept.), Drum and Bugle Corps,* c/o U.S. Naval Academy, Stop 3A, Annapolis, MD 21402; (410) 293-4508. Jeff Weir, Civilian Director. General e-mail, drumbug@nadn.navy.mil. Web, www.usna. navy.mil/USNADB.

The oldest drum and bugle corps in existence in the United States. Plays for Brigade of Midshipmen at sporting events, pep rallies, parades, and daily formations. Supports the Navy by providing musical services for official military ceremonies and community events.

RESERVES AND NATIONAL GUARD

AGENCIES

Air Force Dept. *(Defense Dept.), Air Force Reserve,* The Pentagon 20330-1150; (703) 695-9225. Fax, (703) 695-8959. Maj. Gen. James E. Sherrard, Chief. Information, (703) 697-1761. Web, www.af.mil.

Military office that coordinates and directs Air Force Reserve matters (excluding the Air National Guard).

Air Force Dept. *(Defense Dept.), Reserve Affairs, The Pentagon 20330-1660; (703) 697-6375. Fax, (703) 695-2701. Bryan E. Sharratt, Deputy Assistant Secretary. Web, www.af.mil.*

Civilian office that reviews and monitors Air Force Reserve, Air National Guard, and Civil Air Patrol policies.

Army Dept. *(Defense Dept.), Army Reserve, 2400 Army Pentagon 20310-2400; (703) 697-1784. Fax, (703) 697-1891. Maj. Gen. Thomas J. Plewes, Chief. Web, www.army.mil.*

Military office that coordinates and directs Army Reserve matters (excluding the Army National Guard).

Army Dept. *(Defense Dept.), Reserve Affairs, Mobilization, Readiness, and Training, 111 Army Pentagon 20310-0111; (703) 697-0919. Fax, (703) 614-5975. Col. Wendell Long, Assistant Deputy. Web, www.army.mil.*

Oversees training, military preparedness, and mobilization for all active and reserve members of the Army.

Defense Dept., Reserve Affairs, *The Pentagon 20301-1500; (703) 697-6631. Fax, (703) 697-1682. Charles L. Cragin, Principal Deputy Assistant Secretary. Web, www.defenselink.mil.*

Civilian office that addresses national guard and reserve component issues.

Marine Corps *(Defense Dept.), Reserve Affairs, 3280 Russell Rd., Quantico, VA 22134-5103; (703) 784-9102. Fax, (703) 784-9805. Maj. Gen. Dennis M. McCarthy, Assistant Deputy Chief of Staff. Web, www.usmc.mil.*

Military office that coordinates and directs Marine Corps Reserve matters.

National Guard Bureau *(Defense Dept.), 1411 Jefferson Davis Hwy., Arlington, VA 22202-3231; (703) 607-2200. Fax, (703) 607-3671. Lt. Gen. Russell C. Davis (USA), Chief. Web, www.ngb.dtic.mil.*

Military office that oversees and coordinates activities of the Air National Guard and Army National Guard.

National Guard Bureau *(Defense Dept.), Air National Guard, NGB/CF 1411 Jefferson Davis Hwy., Arlington, VA 22202-3231; (703) 607-2370. Fax, (703) 607-3678. Gen. Paul A. Weaver Jr., Director. Web, www.ngb.mil.*

Military office that coordinates and directs Air National Guard matters.

National Guard Bureau *(Defense Dept.), Air National Guard: Chaplain Service, 1411 Jefferson Davis Hwy., Arlington, VA 22202-3231; (703) 607-5279. Fax, (703) 607-5295. Col. John B. Ellington Jr., Chief Chaplain.*

Oversees chaplains and religious services within the Air National Guard; maintains liaison with religious denominations.

National Guard Bureau *(Defense Dept.), Army National Guard, 1411 Jefferson Davis Hwy., Arlington, VA 22202-3231; (703) 607-2365. Fax, (703) 607-7088. Maj. Gen. Roger C. Schultz, Director. Web, www.ngb.mil.*

Military office that coordinates and directs Army National Guard matters.

National Guard Bureau *(Defense Dept.), Army National Guard: Chaplain Service, 1411 Jefferson Davis Hwy., #9500, Arlington, VA 22202-3231; (703) 607-7072. Fax, (703) 607-8621. Col. Donald W. Hill, Chief Chaplain.*

Oversees chaplains and religious services with the Army National Guard; maintains liaison with religious denominations; serves as policy leader for chaplains.

Navy Dept. *(Defense Dept.), Naval Reserve, The Pentagon, CNO-N095 20350-2000; (703) 695-5353. Fax, (703) 695-3357. Rear Adm. John B. Totushek, Director. Web, www.navy.mil.*

Military office that coordinates and directs Naval Reserve matters.

Navy Dept. *(Defense Dept.), Reserve Affairs, The Pentagon 20350-1000; (703) 614-5410. Fax, (703) 614-4103. Mark H. Davidson, Deputy Assistant Secretary. Web, www.navy.mil.*

Civilian office that reviews Navy and Marine Corps Reserve policies.

U.S. Coast Guard *(Transportation Dept.), Reserve and Training, 2100 2nd St. S.W. 20593-0001; (202) 267-2350. Fax, (202) 267-4243. Rear Adm. R. Dennis Sirois, Director. Web, www.uscg.mil/reserve.*

Oversees and ensures Coast Guard readiness to perform its peacetime mission and its wartime role. Responsible for training all reserve and active duty forces.

NONPROFIT

Adjutants General Assn. of the United States, *1 Massachusetts Ave. N.W. 20001-1431; (202) 789-0031. Fax, (202) 682-9358. Richard C. Alexander, President; Capt. John Goheen, Director of Communications. Web, www.ngaus.org.*

Organization of the adjutants general of the National Guard. Works to promote a strong national defense and National Guard with the Congress, governors, and Defense Dept.

Assn. of Civilian Technicians, *12510-B Lake Ridge Dr., Lake Ridge, VA 22192-2354; (703) 690-1330. Fax, (703) 494-0961. John T. Hunter, President. Web, www.actnat.com.*

Membership: federal civil service employees of the National Guard. Represents members before federal agencies and Congress.

Enlisted Assn. of the National Guard of the United States, *1219 Prince St., Alexandria, VA 22314-2754; (703) 519-3846. Fax, (703) 519-3849. Michael P. Cline, Executive Director. Information, (800) 234-3264. General e-mail, eangus@eangus.org. Web, www.eangus.org.*

Membership: active and retired enlisted members and veterans of the National Guard. Promotes a strong national defense and National Guard. Sponsors scholarships, conducts seminars, and provides information concerning members and their families.

Marine Corps Reserve Officers Assn., *110 N. Royal St., #406, Alexandria, VA 22314-3234; (703) 548-7607. Fax, (703) 519-8779. Vernon J. Leubecker, Executive Director (Acting). Information, (800) 927-6270. Web, www. mcroa.com.*

Membership: active and retired Marine Corps Reserve officers. Promotes the interests of the Marine Corps and the Marine Corps Reserve.

National Guard Assn. of the United States, *1 Massachusetts Ave. N.W. 20001-1431; (202) 789-0031. Fax, (202) 682-9358. Richard C. Alexander, Executive Director. General e-mail, ngaus@ngaus.org. Web, www.ngaus.org.*

Membership: active duty and retired officers of the National Guard. Works to promote a strong national defense and to maintain a strong, ready National Guard.

Naval Reserve Assn., *1619 King St., Alexandria, VA 22314-2793; (703) 548-5800. Fax, (703) 683-3647. Thomas F. Hall, Executive Director. Web, www. navy-reserve.org.*

Membership: active duty, inactive, and retired Navy and Naval Reserve officers. Supports and promotes U.S. military and naval policies, particularly the interests of the Navy and Naval Reserve. Offers education programs for naval reservists and potential naval commissioned officers. Provides the public with information on national security issues. Assists members with Naval Reserve careers, military retirement, and veterans' benefits.

Reserve Officers Assn. of the United States, *1 Constitution Ave. N.E. 20002-5655; (202) 479-2200. Fax, (202) 479-0416. Jayson Spiegel, Executive Director. Information, (800) 809-9448. Web, www.roa.org.*

Membership: active and inactive commissioned officers of all uniformed services. Supports continuation of a reserve force to enhance national security.

VETERANS

AGENCIES

Center for Women Veterans *(Veterans Affairs Dept.), 810 Vermont Ave. N.W., #700 20420; (202) 273-6193. Fax, (202) 273-7092. Joan A. Furey, Director. Web, www.va.gov/ womenvet/center.htm.*

Advises the secretary and promotes research on matters related to women veterans; seeks to assure that women veterans receive benefits and services on par with men.

U.S. Soldiers' and Airmen's Home, *3700 N. Capitol St. N.W. 20317; (202) 730-3229. Fax, (202) 730-3127. Donald C. Hilbert, Director. Information, (202) 730-3556. Web, www.afrh.com.*

Gives domiciliary and medical care to retirees and members of the armed services or career service personnel unable to earn a livelihood. (U.S. Naval Home in Gulfport, Miss., also serves all branches of the armed services.)

Veterans Affairs Dept. (VA), *810 Vermont Ave. N.W. 20420; (202) 273-4800. Fax, (202) 273-4877. Togo D. West Jr., Secretary; Hershel W. Gober, Deputy Secretary, (202) 273-4817. Information, (202) 273-5700. Locator, (202) 273-5400. Web, www.va.gov.*

Administers programs benefiting veterans, including disability compensation, pensions, education, home loans, insurance, vocational rehabilitation, medical care at veterans' hospitals and outpatient facilities, and burial benefits.

Veterans Affairs Dept., *Compensation and Pension Service, 810 Vermont Ave. N.W., MC 21 20420; (202) 273-7203. Fax, (202) 275-1728. Robert J. Epley, Director. Web, www.va.gov.*

Administers disability payments; handles claims for burial and plot allowances by veterans' survivors. Provides information on and assistance with benefits legislated by Congress for veterans of active military, naval, or air service.

Veterans Affairs Dept., *National Cemetery Administration, 810 Vermont Ave. N.W., #400 20420; (202) 273-5145. Fax, (202) 273-6696. Robert M. Walker, Under Secretary for Memorial Affairs (Acting). Web, www.va.gov.*

Administers VA national cemeteries; furnishes markers and headstones for deceased veterans; administers state grants to establish, expand, and improve veterans' cemeteries. Provides presidential memorial certificates to next of kin.

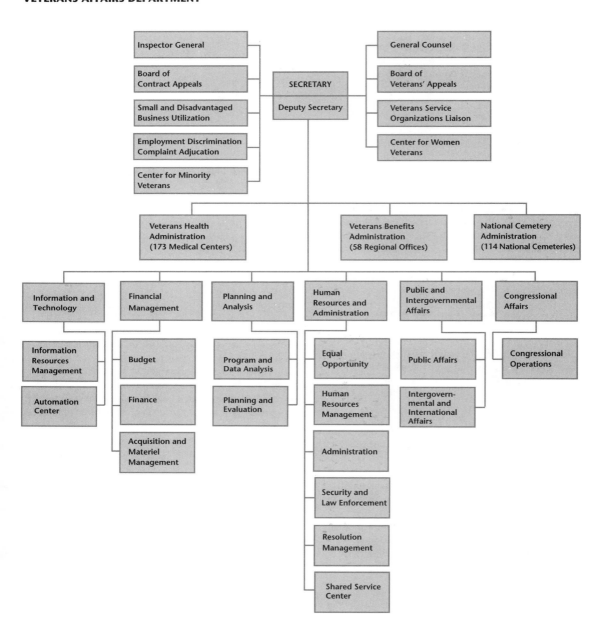

Veterans Affairs Dept., *Planning and Analysis,* 810 Vermont Ave. N.W., #300 MC 008 20420; (202) 273-5033. Fax, (202) 273-5993. Dennis M. Duffy, Assistant Secretary. Web, www.va.gov.

Develops policy and provides policymakers with analytical reports on improving services to veterans and their families.

Veterans Affairs Dept., *Program and Data Analysis,* *810 Vermont Ave. N.W. 20420; (202) 273-5182. Fax, (202) 273-5993. Patricia O'Neil, Deputy Assistant Secretary. Web, www.va.gov.*

Serves as the single, departmentwide repository, clearinghouse, and publication source for veterans' demographic and statistical information.

Veterans Benefits Administration *(Veterans Affairs Dept.), 810 Vermont Ave. N.W., #520, MC 20 20420; (202) 273-6761. Fax, (202) 275-3591. Joseph Thompson, Under Secretary. Information, (202) 418-4343. Toll-free insurance hotline, (800) 669-8477. Web, www.va.gov.*

Administers nonmedical benefits programs for veterans and their dependents and survivors. Benefits include veterans' compensation and pensions, survivors' benefits, education and rehabilitation assistance, home loan benefits, insurance coverage, and burials. (Directs benefits delivery nationwide through regional offices and veterans' insurance offices in Philadelphia and St. Paul.)

CONGRESS

General Accounting Office, *Health, Education, and Human Services, 441 G St. N.W. 20548; (202) 512-6806. Fax, (202) 512-5806. Victor S. Rezendes, Assistant Comptroller General.*

Independent, nonpartisan agency in the legislative branch that audits, analyzes, and evaluates Veterans Affairs Dept. programs; makes reports available to the public.

House Appropriations Committee, *Subcommittee on VA, HUD, and Independent Agencies, H143 CAP 20515; (202) 225-3241. Rep. James T. Walsh, R-N.Y., Chair; Frank Cushing, Staff Director. Web, www.house.gov/ appropriations.*

Jurisdiction over legislation to appropriate funds for the Veterans Affairs Dept., the Board of Veterans Appeals, the U.S. Court of Veterans Appeals, and other veterans' programs.

House Government Reform Committee, *Subcommittee on Criminal Justice, Drug Policy, and Human Resources, B373 RHOB 20515; (202) 225-2577. Fax, (202) 225-1154. Rep. John L. Mica, R-Fla., Chair; Sharon Pinkerton, Staff Director. Web, www.house.gov/reform.*

Oversight jurisdiction of the Veterans Affairs Dept. (shares oversight jurisdiction with the House Veterans' Affairs Committee).

House Veterans' Affairs Committee, *335 CHOB 20515; (202) 225-3527. Rep. Bob Stump, R-Ariz., Chair; Carl Commenator, Staff Director. Web, veterans.house.gov.*

Jurisdiction over the Veterans Affairs Dept. (jurisdiction shared with House Government Reform Committee).

House Veterans' Affairs Committee, *Subcommittee on Benefits, 337 CHOB 20515; (202) 225-9164. Fax, (202) 225-6392. Rep. Jack Quinn, R-N.Y., Chair; Darryl Kehrer, Staff Director. Web, veterans.house.gov.*

Jurisdiction over legislation on veterans' pensions and life insurance; service-connected disability payments to veterans, survivors, and dependents; and burial benefits for veterans. Jurisdiction over legislation on education, training, vocational rehabilitation, employment, housing loans, special housing for paraplegics, readjustment to civilian life for veterans and disabled veterans and educational assistance for survivors of deceased veterans.

Senate Appropriations Committee, *Subcommittee on VA, HUD, and Independent Agencies, SD-130 20510; (202) 224-7211. Sen. Christopher S. Bond, R-Mo., Chair; Jon Kamarck, Staff Director. Web, appropriations.senate. gov/vahud.*

Jurisdiction over legislation to appropriate funds for the Veterans Affairs Dept., the Board of Veterans Appeals, the U.S. Court of Veterans Appeals, and other veterans' programs.

Senate Veterans' Affairs Committee, *SR-412 20510; (202) 224-9126. Fax, (202) 224-8908. Sen. Arlen Specter, R-Pa., Chair; William Tuerk, Staff Director. Web, veterans. senate.gov.*

Jurisdiction over veterans' legislation, including pensions; service-connected disability payments to veterans, survivors, and dependents; education and training; vocational rehabilitation for disabled veterans; veterans' life insurance, hospitals, medical programs, and outpatient programs; construction of medical facilities; readjustment to civilian life; housing loans and special housing loans for paraplegics; employment; cemetery and burial benefits; state veterans' homes; and educational assistance for survivors of deceased veterans. Oversight of and legislative jurisdiction over the Veterans Affairs Dept.

NONPROFIT

American Legion National Organization, *1608 K St. N.W. 20006; (202) 861-2700. Fax, (202) 861-2728. John F. Sommer Jr., Executive Director. Web, www.legion.org.*

Membership: honorably discharged wartime veterans of World War I, World War II, the Korean War, the Vietnam War, or conflicts in Lebanon, Grenada, Panama, and the Persian Gulf. Chartered by Congress to assist veterans with claims for benefits.

American Red Cross, Armed Forces Emergency Services, 8111 Gatehouse Rd., Falls Church, VA 22042; (703) 206-7481. Fax, (703) 206-8533. Sue A. Richter, Vice President. Web, www.crossnet.org.

Assists veterans and their dependents with claims for benefits on a limited basis; provides emergency services for active duty armed forces personnel and their families.

American Veterans Committee, 6309 Bannockburn Dr., Bethesda, MD 20817; (301) 320-6490. June A. Willenz, Executive Director.

Membership: veterans of the World Wars and the Korean, Vietnam, and Persian Gulf wars. Promotes the philosophy, "citizens first, veterans second"; works for international cooperation and peace. (Affiliated with World Veterans Federation, headquartered in Paris.)

American Veterans of World War II, Korea, and Vietnam, 4647 Forbes Blvd., Lanham, MD 20706-4380; (301) 459-9600. Fax, (301) 459-7924. Dave Woodbury, Executive Director. Web, www.amvets.org.

Membership: those who served honorably in the military after September 15, 1940. Helps members obtain benefits; participates in community programs; operates a volunteer service that donates time to hospitalized veterans. Monitors legislation and regulations.

Blinded Veterans Assn., 477 H St. N.W. 20001-2699; (202) 371-8880. Fax, (202) 371-8258. John Williams, Director. Information, (800) 669-7079. General e-mail, bva@bva.org. Web, www.bva.org.

Chartered by Congress to assist veterans with claims for benefits. Seeks out blinded veterans to make them aware of benefits and services available to them.

Catholic War Veterans U.S.A., 441 N. Lee St., Alexandria, VA 22314-2344; (703) 549-3622. Fax, (703) 684-5196. Gilman Udell, Executive Director.

Recognized by the Veterans Affairs Dept. to assist veterans with claims for benefits. Conducts community service programs; offers scholarships for children; supports benefits for Vietnam veterans commensurate with those received by World War II veterans.

Coast Guard Combat Veterans Assn., 17728 Striley Dr., Ashton, MD 20861-9763; (301) 570-5664. Joseph L. Kleinpeter, President.

Membership: Coast Guard combat veterans. Maintains records of Coast Guard combat veterans; sponsors biennial conference; conducts fundraising campaigns.

Disabled American Veterans, 807 Maine Ave. S.W. 20024-2410; (202) 554-3501. Fax, (202) 554-3581. Arthur H. Wilson, National Adjutant. Web, www.dav.org.

Chartered by Congress to assist veterans with claims for benefits; represents veterans seeking to correct alleged errors in military records. Assists families of veterans with disabilities.

Jewish War Veterans of U.S.A., 1811 R St. N.W. 20009; (202) 265-6280. Fax, (202) 234-5662. Herb Rosenbleeth, National Executive Director. Web, www.penfed.org/jwv/home.htm.

Recognized by the Veterans Affairs Dept. to assist veterans with claims for benefits. Offers programs in community relations and services, foreign affairs, national defense, and veterans' affairs. Monitors legislation and regulations that affect veterans.

Marine Corps League, 8626 Lee Hwy., #201, Fairfax, VA 22031 (mailing address: P.O. Box 3070, Merrifield, VA 22116); (703) 207-9588. Fax, (703) 207-0047. William "Brooks" Corley Jr., Executive Director. General e-mail, mcl@mcleague.org. Web, www.mcleague.org.

Membership: active duty, retired, and reserve Marine Corps groups. Chartered by Congress to assist veterans with claims for benefits. Operates a volunteer service program in VA hospitals.

Military Order of the Purple Heart of the U.S.A., 5413-B Backlick Rd., Springfield, VA 22151-3960; (703) 642-5360. Fax, (703) 642-2054. John B. Kirby, Adjutant General. Web, www.purpleheart.org.

Membership: veterans awarded the Purple Heart for combat wounds. Chartered by Congress to assist veterans with claims for benefits. Conducts service and welfare work on behalf of disabled and needy veterans and their families.

National Coalition for Homeless Veterans, 333 1/2 Pennsylvania Ave. S.E. 20003-1148; (202) 546-1969. Fax, (202) 546-2063. Linda Boone, Executive Director. General e-mail, nchv@nchv.org. Web, www.nchv.org.

Provides technical assistance to service providers; advocates on behalf of homeless veterans.

National Veterans Legal Services Program, 2001 S St. N.W., #610 20009-1125; (202) 265-8305. Fax, (202) 328-0063. David F. Addlestone, Joint Executive Director; Barton F. Stichman, Joint Executive Director. General e-mail, nvlsp@nvlsp.org. Web, www.nvlsp.org.

Represents the interests of veterans through educational programs, advocacy, public policy programming, and litigation.

Non-Commissioned Officers Assn., Washington Office, 225 N. Washington St., Alexandria, VA 22314; (703) 549-0311. Fax, (703) 549-0245. David W. Sommers, President. Web, www.ncoausa.org.

Congressionally chartered and accredited by the Veterans Affairs Dept. to assist veterans and widows of veterans with claims for benefits. (Headquarters in San Antonio.)

Paralyzed Veterans of America, *801 18th St. N.W. 20006-3517; (202) 872-1300. Fax, (202) 785-4452. Gordon H. Mansfield, Executive Director. Information, (800) 424-8200. TTY, (202) 416-7622. Web, www.pva.org.*

Congressionally chartered organization that assists veterans with claims for benefits. Distributes information on special education for paralyzed veterans; supports and raises funds for medical research.

Retired Enlisted Assn., *Washington Office,* 909 N. Washington St., #301, Alexandria, VA 22314-1555; (703) 684-1981. Fax, (703) 548-4876. Mark H. Olanoff, National Legislative Director. General e-mail, treadc@ trea.org. Web, www.trea.org.

Membership: enlisted personnel who have retired for length of service or medical reasons from the active, reserve, or guard components of the armed forces. Runs scholarship, legislative, and veterans service programs. (Headquarters in Aurora, Colo.)

Retired Officers Assn., *201 N. Washington St., Alexandria, VA 22314-2539; (703) 549-2311. Fax, (703) 838-8173. Michael A. Nelson, President. General e-mail, troa@troa.org. Web, www.troa.org.*

Membership: officers and former officers of the uniformed services. Assists members, their dependents, and survivors with service status and retirement problems; provides employment assistance. Monitors legislation affecting veterans affairs, health, and military compensation issues.

Veterans of Foreign Wars of the United States, *National Veterans Service,* 200 Maryland Ave. N.E. 20002; (202) 543-2239. Fax, (202) 547-3196. Frederico Juarbe Jr., Director. General e-mail, vfw@vfw.org. Web, www.vfw.org.

Chartered by Congress to assist veterans with claims for benefits.

Veterans of the Battle of the Bulge, *P.O. Box 11129, Arlington, VA 22210-2129; (703) 528-4058. Nancy Monson, Administrative Director.*

Membership: veterans who were awarded the Ardennes Campaign battle star and their families. Maintains historical data on the Battle of the Bulge; sponsors reunions, memorial services, and educational programs; fosters international peace.

Veterans of World War I of the U.S.A., *P.O. Box 8027, Alexandria, VA 22306; (703) 780-5660. Fax, (703) 780-8465. Muriel Sue Parkhurst, Executive Director.*

Fraternal organization of veterans of wartime service in World War I. Chartered by Congress to assist veterans with claims for benefits. Maintains representatives in VA hospitals.

Vietnam Veterans of America, *1224 M St. N.W. 20005-5183; (202) 628-2700. Fax, (202) 628-5880. George C. Duggins, President. Information, (800) 882-1316. General e-mail, vva@vva.org. Web, www.vva.org.*

Membership organization that provides information on legislation that affects Vietnam era veterans and their families. Engages in legislative and judicial advocacy in areas relevant to Vietnam era veterans.

Appeals of VA Decisions

AGENCIES

Defense Dept., *Legal Policy,* The Pentagon, #4C759 20301-4000; (703) 697-3387. Fax, (703) 693-6708. Col. Paul Black (USAF), Director. Web, www.defenselink.mil.

Coordinates policy for armed services boards charged with correcting military records and reviewing discharges.

Veterans Affairs Dept., *Board of Veterans Appeals,* 810 Vermont Ave. N.W., #845 20420; (202) 565-5001. Fax, (202) 565-5587. Eligah Dane Clark, Chair. Web, www. va.gov.

Final appellate body within the department; reviews claims for veterans' benefits on appeal from agencies of original jurisdiction. Decisions of the board are subject to review by the U.S. Court of Veterans Appeals.

JUDICIARY

U.S. Court of Appeals for the Federal Circuit, *717 Madison Pl. N.W. 20439; (202) 633-6556. Fax, (202) 633-6353. Haldane Robert Mayer, Chief Judge; Jan Horbaly, Clerk, (202) 633-9614. Electronic bulletin board, (202) 633-9608 or (202) 786-6584.*

Reviews decisions concerning the Veteran's Judicial Review Provisions.

U.S. Court of Appeals for Veteran's Claims, *625 Indiana Ave. N.W., #900 20004-2950; (202) 501-5970. Fax, (202) 501-5849. Frank Q. Nebeker, Chief Judge. Toll-free, (800) 869-8654.*

Independent court that reviews decisions of the VA's Board of Veterans Appeals concerning benefits. Focuses primarily on disability benefits claims.

American Legion National Organization, *Claims Service,* 1608 K St. N.W. 20006; (202) 861-2700. Fax, (202) 861-2728. *Philip R. Wilkerson, Deputy Director. Web, www.legion.org.*

Membership: honorably discharged wartime veterans of World War I, World War II, the Korean War, the Vietnam War, or conflicts in Lebanon, Grenada, Panama, and the Persian Gulf. Assists veterans with appeals before the Veterans Affairs Dept. for benefits claims.

American Legion National Organization, *Review and Correction Boards Unit,* 1608 K St. N.W. 20006; (202) 861-2700. Fax, (202) 861-2728. *Thomas Holland, Supervisor. Web, www.legion.org.*

Membership: honorably discharged wartime veterans of World War I, World War II, the Korean War, the Vietnam War, or conflicts in Lebanon, Grenada, Panama, and the Persian Gulf. Represents before the Defense Dept. former military personnel seeking to upgrade less-than-honorable discharges and to correct alleged errors in military records.

National Veterans Legal Services Program, 2001 S St. N.W., #610 20009-1125; (202) 265-8305. Fax, (202) 328-0063. *David F. Addlestone, Joint Executive Director; Barton F. Stichman, Joint Executive Director. General e-mail, nvlsp@nvlsp.org. Web, www.nvlsp.org.*

Represents the interests of veterans through educational programs, advocacy, public policy programming, and litigation.

Veterans of Foreign Wars of the United States, *Appeals,* 200 Maryland Ave. N.E. 20002; (202) 543-2239. Fax, (202) 547-3196. *George Estry, Chief of Appeals. Web, www.vfw.org.*

Assists veterans and their dependents and survivors with appeals before the Veterans Affairs Dept. for benefits claims. Assists with cases in the U.S. Court of Veterans Appeals.

Veterans of Foreign Wars of the United States, *Military Claims Consultant,* 1120 Vermont Ave. N.W., #1121 20421; (202) 691-3196. Fax, (202) 833-9475. *William G. Crawford, Service Officer.*

Represents before the Defense Dept. veterans seeking to upgrade less-than-honorable discharges.

Education/Economic Opportunity

AGENCIES

Office of Personnel Management, *Diversity,* 1900 E St. N.W., #2445 20415-0001; (202) 606-2817. Fax, (202) 606-0927. *Maria Mercedes Olivieri, Director.*

Responsible for government recruiting policies and guidelines. Advises and assists federal agency offices in the recruitment and employment of minorities, women, veterans, and people with disabilities. Collects and maintains statistics on the federal employment of these groups. Administers the Disabled Veterans Affirmative Action Program.

Small Business Administration, *Veterans Affairs,* 409 3rd St. S.W., #6500 20416; (202) 205-6773. Fax, (202) 205-7292. *Cliff Toulson, Assistant Administrator. TTY, (202) 205-6189.*

Coordinates programs to give special consideration to veterans in loan, counseling, procurement, and training programs and in transition training sessions.

Veterans Affairs Dept., *Education Service,* 1800 G St. N.W. 20006 (mailing address: 810 Vermont Ave. N.W. 20420); (202) 273-7132. Fax, (202) 275-1653. *Celia P. Dollarhide, Director. Information, (800) 827-1000. GI Bill information, (888) 442-4551. General e-mail, wasco22@vba.va.gov. Web, www.va.gov/education.*

Administers VA's education program, including financial support for veterans' education and for spouses and dependent children of disabled and deceased disabled veterans; provides eligible veterans and dependents with educational assistance under the G.I. Bill and Veterans Educational Assistance Program. Provides postsecondary institutions with funds, based on their eligible veterans' enrollment.

Veterans Affairs Dept., *Loan Guaranty Service,* 810 Vermont Ave. N.W., #525 20420; (202) 273-7332. Fax, (202) 275-3523. *R. Keith Pedigo, Director. Web, www.va.gov.*

Guarantees private institutional financing of home loans (including manufactured home loans) for veterans; provides disabled veterans with direct loans and grants for specially adapted housing; administers a direct loan program for native American veterans living on trust land.

Veterans Affairs Dept., *Vocational Rehabilitation and Employment Service,* 1800 G St. N.W., #501 20006 (mailing address: 810 Vermont Ave. N.W. 20420); (202) 273-7419. Fax, (202) 275-5122. *Julius M. Williams Jr., Director. TTY, (202) 275-5119. Web, www.va.gov.*

Administers VA's vocational rehabilitation and employment program, which provides service-disabled veterans with services and assistance; helps veterans to become employable and to obtain and maintain suitable employment.

Veterans' Employment and Training Service (*Labor Dept.*), 200 Constitution Ave. N.W., #S1313 20210; (202)

693-4700. Fax, (202) 693-4754. Al Borrego, Assistant Secretary. Web, www2.dol.gov/dol/vets.

Works with and monitors state employment offices to see that preference is given to veterans seeking jobs; advises the secretary on veterans' issues.

Veterans' Employment and Training Service *(Labor Dept.), Operations and Programs, 200 Constitution Ave. N.W., #S1316 20210; (202) 693-4701. Fax, (202) 693-4755. Stan Seidel, Director. Web, www2.dol.gov/dol/vets.*

Investigates veterans' complaints of job or benefits loss because of active or reserve duty military service.

NONPROFIT

Blinded Veterans Assn., *477 H St. N.W. 20001-2699; (202) 371-8880. Fax, (202) 371-8258. John Williams, Director. Information, (800) 669-7079. General e-mail, bva@bva.org. Web, www.bva.org.*

Provides blind and disabled veterans with vocational rehabilitation and employment services.

Disabled American Veterans, *Employment, 807 Maine Ave. S.W. 20024; (202) 554-3501. Fax, (202) 554-3581. Anthony L. Baskerville, Deputy Director.*

Recommends veterans' employment policy to federal agencies. Monitors legislation and regulations on veterans' employment.

Interstate Conference of Employment Security Agencies, *444 N. Capitol St. N.W., #142 20001; (202) 434-8020. Fax, (202) 434-8033. Emily DeRocco, Executive Director. Web, www.icesa.org.*

Membership: state employment security administrators. Provides veterans' employment and training professionals with opportunities for networking and information exchange. Monitors legislation and regulations that affect veterans' employment and training programs involving state employment security agencies.

Paralyzed Veterans of America, *801 18th St. N.W. 20006-3517; (202) 872-1300. Fax, (202) 785-4452. Gordon H. Mansfield, Executive Director. Information, (800) 424-8200. TTY, (202) 416-7622. Web, www.pva.org.*

Congressionally chartered organization that assists veterans with claims for benefits. Promotes access to educational and public facilities and to public transportation for people with disabilities; seeks modification of workplaces.

Health Care/VA Hospitals

AGENCIES

Defense Dept., *Special Assistant for Gulf War Illnesses, 5113 Leesburg Pike, #901, Falls Church, VA 22041-3226;*

(703) 578-8500. Fax, (703) 578-8501. Bernard D. Rostker, Special Assistant. Incident reporting line, (800) 497-6261. Web, www.gulflink.osd.mil.

Coordinates Defense Dept. investigation of illnesses suffered by Gulf War veterans. Researches links between these illnesses and possible exposure to Iraqi nerve agents. Responds to inquiries from veterans and their families.

Public Health and Science *(Health and Human Services Dept.), Veterans Affairs and Military Liaison, 200 Independence Ave. S.W., #719H 20201; (202) 260-0576. Fax, (202) 260-1570. Capt. Peter P. Mazzella, Director.*

Advises the assistant secretary on health issues that affect veterans and military personnel. Works to identify the health-related needs of veterans and their families and to facilitate the delivery of services.

Veterans Affairs Dept., *Advisory Committee on the Readjustment of Veterans, c/o American Legion, 1608 K St. N.W. 20006; (202) 861-2711. Fax, (202) 861-2786. John F. Sommer Jr., Chair. Web, www.va.gov.*

Studies veteran readjustment issues such as medical service, compensation, and pension for posttraumatic stress disorder; examines Vet Center operations and veteran employment issues.

Veterans Health Administration *(Veterans Affairs Dept.), 810 Vermont Ave. N.W., #800 20420; (202) 273-5781. Fax, (202) 273-5787. Thomas Garthwaite, Deputy Under Secretary for Health.*

Recommends policy and administers medical and hospital services for eligible veterans. Publishes guidelines on treatment of veterans exposed to Agent Orange.

Veterans Health Administration *(Veterans Affairs Dept.), Academic Affiliations, 810 Vermont Ave. N.W. 20420; (202) 273-8946. Fax, (202) 273-9031. Timothy C. Flynn, Chief Academic Affiliations Officer (Acting).*

Administers education and training programs for health professionals, students, and residents through partnerships with affiliated academic institutions.

Veterans Health Administration *(Veterans Affairs Dept.), Dentistry, 810 Vermont Ave. N.W., MC 112-D 20420; (202) 273-8503. Fax, (202) 273-9105. Dr. Robert T. Frame, Assistant Under Secretary.*

Administers VA oral health care programs; coordinates oral research, education, and training of VA oral health personnel and outpatient dental care in private practice.

Veterans Health Administration *(Veterans Affairs Dept.), Facilities Management, 810 Vermont Ave. N.W.,*

MC 18 20420; (202) 565-5009. Fax, (202) 565-4155. C. V. Yarbrough, Chief.

Reviews construction policies for VA hospitals.

Veterans Health Administration *(Veterans Affairs Dept.), Geriatrics and Extended Care, 810 Vermont Ave. N.W., MC 114 20420; (202) 273-8540. Fax, (202) 273-9131. Dr. Judith Salerno, Chief Consultant. Web, www.va.gov.*

Administers research, educational, and clinical health care programs in geriatrics, including VA and community nursing homes, personal care homes, VA domiciliaries, state veterans' homes, and hospital-based home care.

Veterans Health Administration *(Veterans Affairs Dept.), Mental Health Strategic Health Care Group, 810 Vermont Ave. N.W., MC 116 20420; (202) 273-8440. Fax, (202) 273-9069. Dr. Laurent S. Lehmann, Chief Consultant.*

Develops ambulatory and inpatient psychiatry and psychology programs for the mentally ill and for drug and alcohol abusers; programs are offered in VA facilities and networks. Incorporates special programs for veterans suffering from post-traumatic stress disorders, serious mental illness, addictive disorders, and homelessness.

Veterans Health Administration *(Veterans Affairs Dept.), Patient Care Services, 810 Vermont Ave. N.W., MC 11 20420; (202) 273-8474. Fax, (202) 273-9274. Dr. Thomas Holohan, Chief Officer.*

Manages clinical programs of the VA medical care system.

Veterans Health Administration *(Veterans Affairs Dept.), Policy, Planning, and Performance, 810 Vermont Ave. N.W., MC 105 20420; (202) 273-8932. Fax, (202) 273-9030. Greg A. Pane, Director.*

Coordinates and develops departmental planning to distribute funds to VA field facilities.

Veterans Health Administration *(Veterans Affairs Dept.), Readjustment Counseling, 810 Vermont Ave. N.W., MC 15 20420; (202) 273-8967. Fax, (202) 273-9071. Alfonso R. Batres, Chief.*

Responsible for community-based centers for veterans nationwide. Provides outreach and counseling services for war-related psychological problems.

Veterans Health Administration *(Veterans Affairs Dept.), Research and Development, 810 Vermont Ave. N.W., MC 12 20420; (202) 273-8284. Fax, (202) 273-6536. Dr. John Feussner, Chief Medical Director.*

Formulates and implements policy for the research and development program of the Veterans Health Administration; advises the undersecretary for health on research-related matters and on management of the VA's health care system; represents the VA in interactions with external organizations in matters related to biomedical and health services research.

Veterans Health Administration *(Veterans Affairs Dept.), Voluntary Service, 810 Vermont Ave. N.W., MC 10C2 20420; (202) 273-8952. Fax, (202) 273-9040. Jim W. Delgado, Director.*

Supervises volunteer programs in VA medical centers.

CONGRESS

House Veterans' Affairs Committee, *Subcommittee on Health, 338 CHOB 20515; (202) 225-9154. Fax, (202) 226-4536. Rep. Cliff Stearns, R-Fla., Chair; Ralph Ibson, Staff Director. Web, veterans.house.gov.*

Jurisdiction over legislation on hospitals, medical programs, outpatient programs, state veterans' homes, and construction of medical facilities.

Senate Veterans' Affairs Committee, *Special Investigations Unit on Gulf War Illnesses, SD B40-2 20510; (202) 224-4316. Michael J. Rotko, Special Counsel. Web, www.senate.gov/~veterans.*

Coordinates committee efforts to determine the causes and incidence of Gulf War illnesses; provides liaison to the Veterans Affairs Dept. and the General Accounting Office.

NONPROFIT

National Assn. of VA Physicians and Dentists, *1414 Prince St., #202, Alexandria, VA 22314; (703) 548-0280. Fax, (703) 548-8024. Robert M. Conroy, President. General e-mail, navapd@dgsys.com. Web, www.navapd.org.*

Seeks to improve the quality of care and conditions at VA hospitals. Monitors legislation and regulations on veterans' health care.

National Conference on Ministry in the Armed Forces, *Endorsers Conference for Veterans Affairs Chaplaincy, 4141 N. Henderson Rd., #13, Arlington, VA 22203; (703) 276-7905. Fax, (703) 276-7906. Jack Williamson, Coordinator.*

Encourages religious ministry to veterans in VA hospitals and centers.

National Gulf War Resource Center, *1224 M St. N.W. 20005; (202) 628-2700. Fax, (202) 628-6997. Chris Kornkven, President; Paul Sullivan, Director. General e-mail, ngwrc@gulfweb.org. Web, www.gulfweb.org/ngwrc.*

Supports grassroots efforts of national and international Gulf War veterans associations. Provides information and referrals on health and benefits. Monitors legislation and regulations.

Paralyzed Veterans of America, *801 18th St. N.W. 20006-3517; (202) 872-1300. Fax, (202) 785-4452. Gordon H. Mansfield, Executive Director. Information, (800) 424-8200. TTY, (202) 416-7622. Web, www.pva.org.*

Congressionally chartered veterans' service organization. Consults with the Veterans Affairs Dept. on the establishment and operation of spinal cord injury treatment centers.

Spouses, Dependents, and Survivors

AGENCIES

Air Force Dept. *(Defense Dept.), Personnel,* 1040 Air Force Pentagon, #4E194 20330-1040; (703) 697-6088. Fax, (703) 697-6091. Lt. Gen. Donald L. Peterson, Deputy Chief of Staff. Toll-free casualty assistance, (800) 433-0048. Web, www.af.mil.

Military office that responds to inquiries concerning deceased Air Force personnel and their beneficiaries; refers inquiries to the Military Personnel Center at Randolph Air Force Base in San Antonio, Texas.

Army Dept. *(Defense Dept.), Casualty Operations,* 2461 Eisenhower Ave., #920, Alexandria, VA 22331-0481; (703) 325-7990. Fax, (703) 325-0134. Lt. Col. Rita Salley, Chief. Web, www.army.mil.

Verifies beneficiaries of deceased Army personnel for benefits distribution.

Marine Corps *(Defense Dept.), Casualty Section,* HQUSMC, 3280 Russell Rd., Quantico, VA 22134; (703) 784-9501. Fax, (703) 784-7823. Maj. M. L. Ward, Head.

Confirms beneficiaries of deceased Marine Corps personnel for benefits distribution.

NONPROFIT

American Gold Star Mothers, *2128 LeRoy Pl. N.W. 20008-1893; (202) 265-0991. Jeanne K. Penfold, National Service Officer. General e-mail, agsms@aol.com. Web, www.goldstarmoms.com.*

Membership: mothers who have lost sons or daughters in military service (World War I to the present). Members serve as volunteers in VA hospitals.

American War Mothers, *2615 Woodley Pl. N.W. 20008; (202) 462-2791. Lorena K. DeRoin, President.*

Membership: mothers and stepmothers of military personnel from all branches of service. Members serve as volunteers in VA hospitals.

Army and Air Force Mutual Aid Assn., *102 Sheridan Ave., Fort Myer, VA 22211-1110; (703) 522-3060. Fax, (703) 522-1336. Bradley J. Snyder, President. Information, (800) 336-4538. General e-mail, info@aafmaa.com. Web, www.aafmaa.com.*

Private service organization that offers member and family insurance services to Army and Air Force officers. Recognized by the Veterans Affairs Dept. to assist veterans and their survivors with claims for benefits.

Army Distaff Foundation, *6200 Oregon Ave. N.W. 20015-1543; (202) 541-0105. Fax, (202) 364-2856. Calvert P. Benedict, Executive Director. Information, (800) 541-4255.*

Nonprofit continuing care retirement community for career military officers and their families. Provides retirement housing and health care services.

EXPOSE, Ex-partners of Servicemembers for Equality, *P.O. Box 11191, Alexandria, VA 22312; (703) 941-5844. Fax, (703) 212-6951. Kathleen Rogers, Director. General e-mail, ex-pose@juno.com.*

Membership: former spouses of military personnel, both officers and enlisted, and other interested parties. Seeks federal laws to restore to ex-spouses benefits lost through divorce, including retirement pay; survivors' benefits; and medical, commissary, and exchange benefits. Provides information concerning related federal laws and regulations. Serves as an information clearinghouse.

National Assn. of Military Widows, *4023 N. 25th Rd., Arlington, VA 22207; (703) 527-4565. Jean Arthurs, President.*

Provides military widows with referral information on survivor benefit programs; helps locate widows eligible for benefits. Interests include health and education. Monitors legislation.

No Greater Love, *1750 New York Ave. N.W. 20006; (202) 783-4665. Fax, (202) 783-1168. Carmella LaSpada, Chief Executive Officer. Web, www.ngl.org.*

Provides programs of remembrance, friendship, and care for families of Americans killed in war or by acts of terrorism.

Society of Military Widows, *5535 Hempstead Way, Springfield, VA 22151; (703) 750-1342. Fax, (703) 354-4380. Jeanne Thompson, President. General e-mail, naus@ix.netcom.com.*

Serves the interests of widows of servicemen who died while in active military service; provides support programs and information. Monitors legislation concerning military widows' benefits. (Affiliated with the National Assn. for Uniformed Services.)

16

National Security

GENERAL POLICY

See also Caucuses (chap. 20); International Law and Agreements (chap. 13)

AGENCIES

Air Force Dept. *(Defense Dept.),* The Pentagon, #4E871 20330-1670; (703) 697-7376. Fax, (703) 695-8809. F. Whitten Peters, Secretary (Acting). Web, www.af.mil.

Civilian office that develops and reviews Air Force national security policies in conjunction with the chief of staff of the Air Force and the secretary of defense.

Air Force Dept. *(Defense Dept.), Chief of Staff,* The Pentagon, #4E924 20330-1670; (703) 697-9225. Fax, (703) 693-9297. Gen. Michael E. Ryan, Chief of Staff. Web, www. hq.af.mil.

Military office that develops and directs Air Force national security policies in conjunction with the secretary of the Air Force and the secretary of defense.

Army Dept. *(Defense Dept.),* The Pentagon, #3E700 20310-0101; (703) 695-1717. Fax, (703) 697-8036. Louis Caldera, Secretary; Gregory R. Dahlberg, Under Secretary (Nominee). Press, (703) 697-2564. Web, www.army.mil.

Civilian office that develops and reviews Army national security policies in conjunction with the chief of staff of the Army and the secretary of defense.

Army Dept. *(Defense Dept.), Chief of Staff,* The Pentagon, #3E668 20310-0200; (703) 695-2077. Fax, (703) 614-5268. Eric K. Shinseki, Chief of Staff. Press, (703) 697-7589. Web, www.army.mil.

Military office that develops and administers Army national security policies in conjunction with the secretary of the Army and the secretary of defense.

Defense Dept., The Pentagon 20301-1000; (703) 692-7100. Fax, (703) 697-9080. William S. Cohen, Secretary; Rudy de Leon, Deputy Secretary. Information, (703) 697-5737. Press, (703) 695-0192 (defense information); (703) 695-3324 (tours). Web, www.defenselink.mil.

Civilian office that develops national security policies and has overall responsibility for administering national defense; responds to public and congressional inquiries about national defense matters.

Defense Dept., *Environmental Security,* 3400 Defense Pentagon, #3E792 20301-3400; (703) 695-6639. Fax, (703) 693-7011. Sherri W. Goodman, Deputy Under Secretary. Web, www.acq.osd.mil/ens.

Integrates environmental, safety, and occupational health considerations into U.S. defense and economic policies. Works to ensure responsible performance in defense operations, to maintain quality installations, to reduce the costs of complying with environmental laws, and to clean up past contamination.

Defense Dept., *Joint Chiefs of Staff,* The Pentagon, #2E872 20318-9999; (703) 697-9121. Fax, (703) 697-8758. Gen. Henry H. Shelton (USA), Chair; Lt. Gen. Carlton W. Fulford, Joint Staff Director. Information, (703) 697-4272. Web, www.dtic.mil/jcs.

Joint military staff office that assists the president, the National Security Council, and the secretary of defense in developing national security policy and in coordinating operations of the individual armed services.

Defense Dept., *Policy,* The Pentagon, #4E808 20301-2000; (703) 697-7200. Fax, (703) 697-6602. Walter B. Slocombe, Under Secretary. Web, www.defenselink.mil.

Civilian office responsible for policy matters relating to international security issues and political-military affairs. Oversees such areas as arms control, foreign military sales, intelligence collection and analysis, and NATO and regional security affairs.

Defense Dept., *Special Operations and Low Intensity Conflict,* The Pentagon, #2E258 20301-2500; (703) 693-2895. Fax, (703) 693-6335. Brian E. Sheridan, Assistant Secretary. Web, www.defenselink.mil.

Serves as special staff assistant and civilian adviser to the defense secretary on matters related to special operations and low intensity conflict. Responsible for the Army's Green Berets, the Navy Seals, and other special operations forces. Oversees counterdrug efforts and humanitarian and refugee affairs for the Defense Dept.

Defense Dept., *Strategy and Threat Reduction,* The Pentagon, #4E817 20301-2900; (703) 697-7728. Fax, (703) 693-9146. Edward L. Warner III, Assistant Secretary. Web, www.defenselink.mil.

Develops and coordinates national security strategy and defense strategy and advises on the resources, forces, and contingency plans necessary to implement those strategies. Ensures the integration of defense strategy into the department's resource allocation, force structure development, weapons system acquisition, and budgetary processes. Evaluates the capability of forces to accomplish defense strategy.

Marine Corps *(Defense Dept.), Commandant,* Navy Annex, Arlington, VA 20370 (mailing address: Marine Corps Headquarters 20380-1775); (703) 614-2500. Fax, (703) 697-7246. Gen. James L. Jones, Commandant. Information, (703) 614-8010. Press, (703) 614-1492. Web, www.hqmc.usmc.mil.

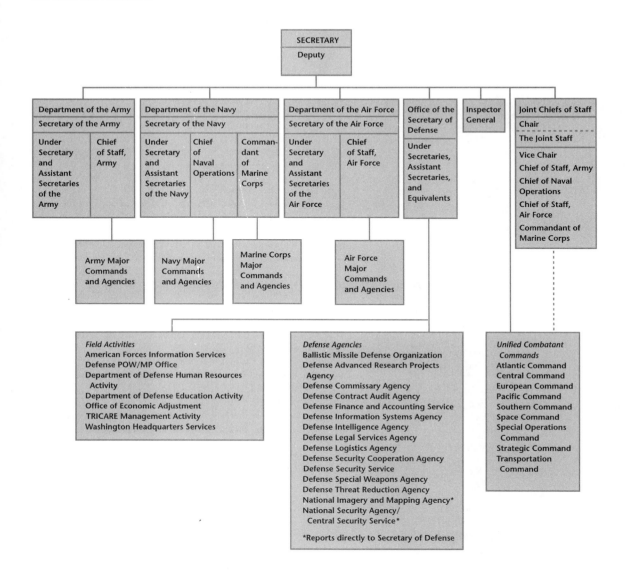

Military office that develops and directs Marine Corps national security policies in conjunction with the secretary of defense and the secretary of the Navy.

National Security Council *(Executive Office of the President), Defense Policy/Arms Control: International Economic Affairs, The White House 20502; (202) 456-9281. Fax, (202) 456-9280. Malcolm Lee, Director. Web, www.whitehouse.gov/WH/EOP/NSC/html/nschome.html.*

Advises the president and the National Security Adviser on all aspects of U.S. foreign policy dealing with U.S. international economic policies.

Navy Dept. *(Defense Dept.), The Pentagon, #4E686 20350-1000; (703) 695-3131. Fax, (703) 614-3477. Richard Danzig, Secretary; Jerry Hultin, Under Secretary, (703) 695-3141. Information, (703) 695-0965. Press, (703) 697-5342. Web, www.navy.mil.*

Civilian office that develops and reviews Navy and Marine Corps national security policies in conjunction with the chief of naval operations, the commandant of the Marine Corps, and the secretary of defense.

Navy Dept. *(Defense Dept.), Naval Operations,* The Pentagon, #4E660 20350-2000; (703) 695-6007. Fax, (703) 697-6290. Adm. Vernon Clark (Nominee), Chief. Information, (703) 695-0965. Press, (703) 697-5342. Web, www. navy.mil.

Military office that develops Navy national security policies in conjunction with the secretary of defense and the secretary of the Navy and in cooperation with the commandant of the Marine Corps.

State Dept., *Political-Military Affairs,* 2201 C St. N.W., #7325 20520; (202) 647-9022. Fax, (202) 736-4779. Eric D. Newsom, Assistant Secretary. Web, www.state.gov.

Responsible for security affairs policy; acts as a liaison between the Defense Dept. and the State Dept.

U.S. Coast Guard *(Transportation Dept.),* 2100 2nd St. S.W. 20593-0001; (202) 267-2390. Fax, (202) 267-4158. Adm. James M. Loy, Commandant. Information, (202) 267-1587. Web, www.uscg.mil.

Carries out search-and-rescue missions in and around navigable waters and on the high seas; enforces federal laws on the high seas and navigable waters of the United States and its possessions; conducts marine environmental protection programs; administers boating safety programs; inspects and regulates construction, safety, and equipment of merchant marine vessels; establishes and maintains a system of navigation aids; carries out domestic icebreaking activities; maintains a state of military readiness to assist the Navy in time of war or when directed by the president.

CONGRESS

House Appropriations Committee, *Subcommittee on Defense,* H149 CAP 20515; (202) 225-2847. Fax, (202) 225-2822. Rep. Jerry Lewis, R-Calif., Chair; Kevin M. Roper, Staff Director. Web, www.house.gov/appropriations.

Jurisdiction over legislation to appropriate funds for the Defense Dept. (excluding military construction, civil defense, military assistance to foreign countries, and nuclear warhead program), the Central Intelligence Agency, and the intelligence community.

House Appropriations Committee, *Subcommittee on Treasury, Postal Service, and General Government,* B307 RHOB 20515; (202) 225-5834. Fax, (202) 225-5895. Rep. Jim Kolbe, R-Ariz., Chair; Michelle Mrdeza, Clerk. Web, www.house.gov/appropriations.

Jurisdiction over legislation to appropriate funds for the Executive Office of the President, including the National Security Council.

House Armed Services Committee, *2120 RHOB 20515; (202) 225-4151. Fax, (202) 225-9077. Rep. Floyd D. Spence, R-S.C., Chair; Robert S. Rangel, Staff Director. Web, www.house.gov/hasc.*

Jurisdiction over defense legislation. Oversight of the Defense Dept., including the Army, Navy, and Air Force departments.

Senate Appropriations Committee, *Subcommittee on Defense,* SD-119 20510; (202) 224-7255. Sen. Ted Stevens, R-Alaska, Chair; Steve Cortese, Staff Director. Web, appropriations.senate.gov/defense.

Jurisdiction over legislation to appropriate funds for the Defense Dept. (excluding military construction, family housing, civil defense, nuclear materials, and military assistance to foreign countries), the Central Intelligence Agency, and the intelligence community.

Senate Armed Services Committee, *SR-228 20510; (202) 224-3871. Sen. John W. Warner, R-Va., Chair; Les Brownlee, Staff Director. Web, armed_services.senate.gov.*

Jurisdiction over defense legislation. Oversight of the Defense Dept., including the Army, Navy, and Air Force departments.

Senate Armed Services Committee, *Subcommittee on Airland Forces,* SR-228 20510; (202) 224-3871. Sen. Rick Santorum, R-Pa., Chair; John Barnes, Professional Staff Member. Web, armed_services.senate.gov.

Jurisdiction over legislation concerning NATO and East Asia defenses, cooperation with allies, defense modeling and simulation, equipment requirements and programs for reserve forces, and to the extent not covered by the full committee, issues of peacekeeping and peace enforcement.

Senate Armed Services Committee, *Subcommittee on Seapower,* SR-228 20510; (202) 224-3871. Sen. Olympia J. Snowe, R-Maine, Chair; Eric Thoemmes, Professional Staff Member. Web, armed_services.senate.gov.

Jurisdiction over legislation concerning Southwest Asia defenses and defense-related programs of the U.S. Coast Guard. Oversees policy aspects of security assistance programs and the Defense Security Assistance Agency; oversees the Military Sealift Command, Military Transportation Command, and budget accounts for research, development, and procurement of airlift and sealift capability.

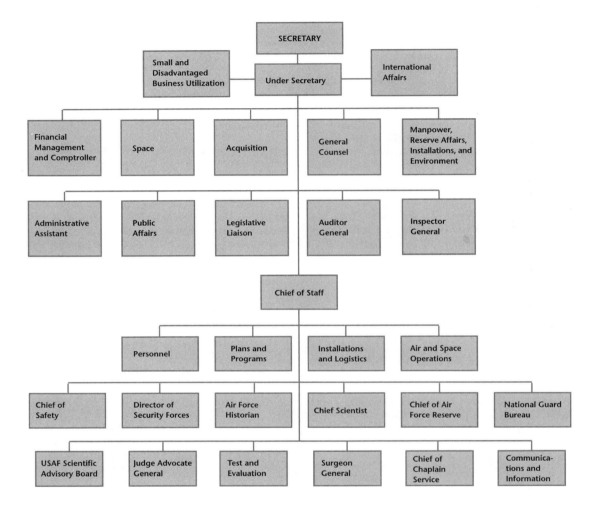

Senate Governmental Affairs Committee, *SD-340 20510; (202) 224-4751. Fax, (202) 224-9603. Sen. Fred Thompson, R-Tenn., Chair; Hannah Sistare, Staff Director. Web, gov_affairs.senate.gov.*

Oversees operations of the National Security Council.

NONPROFIT

Air Force Assn., *1501 Lee Hwy., Arlington, VA 22209-1198; (703) 247-5800. Fax, (703) 247-5853. John A. Shaud, Executive Director. Library, (703) 247-5829. Press, (703) 247-5850. General e-mail, custserv@afa.org. Web, www.afa.org.*

Membership: civilians and active, reserve, retired, and cadet personnel of the Air Force. Informs members and the public of developments in the aerospace field. Monitors legislation and Defense Dept. policies. Library on aviation history open to the public by appointment.

American Conservative Union, *1007 Cameron St., Alexandria, VA 22314; (703) 836-8602. Fax, (703) 836-8606. Christian Josi, Executive Director. Information, (800) 228-7345. General e-mail, acu@conservative.org. Web, www.conservative.org.*

Legislative interest organization concerned with national defense policy, legislation related to nuclear weapons, U.S. strategic position vis-à-vis the former Soviet Union, missile defense programs, U.S. troops under U.N. command, and U.S. strategic alliance commitments.

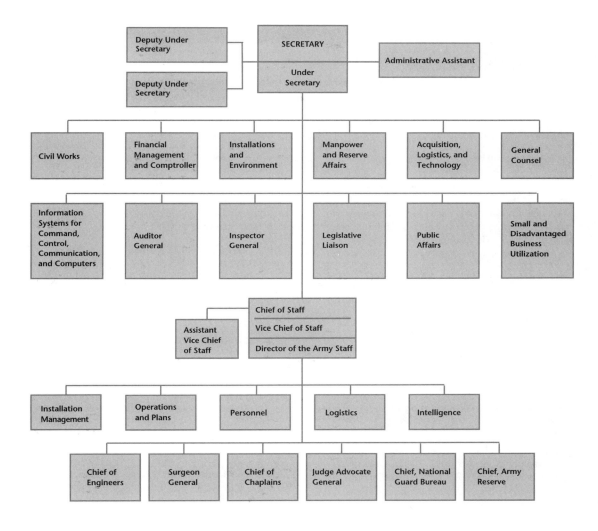

American Defense Institute, *Pride in America,* 1055 N. Fairfax St., #200, Alexandria, VA 22314; (703) 519-7000. Fax, (703) 519-8627. Eugene B. McDaniel, President. General e-mail, rdt2@americandefinst.org. Web, www.ajc.org/adi/.

Nonpartisan organization that advocates a strong national defense. Acts as an information clearinghouse on issues related to national security. Seeks to educate young Americans on matters of defense and foreign policy.

American Enterprise Institute for Public Policy Research, *Foreign and Defense Policy Studies,* 1150 *17th St. N.W., #1100 20036; (202) 862-5814. Fax, (202) 862-7177. Jeane Kirkpatrick, Director. Information, (202) 862-5800. Press, (202) 862-5829. Web, www.aei.org.*

Research and educational organization that conducts conferences, seminars, and debates and sponsors research on national security, defense policy, and arms control.

American Security Council, *5545 Security Circle, Boston, VA 22713 (mailing address: P.O. Box 8, Boston, VA 22713); (540) 547-1776. Fax, (540) 547-9737. John M. Fisher, Chair.*

Bipartisan, prodefense organization that advocates continuation of the strategic modernization program and stable funding for the space program, new technologies, and conventional forces. Monitors legislation and conducts educational activities.

Assn. of the United States Army, *2425 Wilson Blvd., Arlington, VA 22201; (703) 841-4300. Fax, (703) 525-9039. Gordon R. Sullivan, President. Web, www.ausa.org.*

Membership: civilians and active and retired members of the armed forces. Conducts symposia on defense issues and researches topics that affect the military.

Atlantic Council of the United States, *910 17th St. N.W., 10th Floor 20006; (202) 463-7226. Fax, (202) 463-7241. Christopher J. Makins, President. General e-mail, info@acus.org. Web, www.acus.org.*

Conducts studies and makes policy recommendations on American foreign security and international economic policies in the Atlantic and Pacific communities; sponsors conferences and educational exchanges.

The Brookings Institution, *Foreign Policy Studies, 1775 Massachusetts Ave. N.W. 20036-2188; (202) 797-6400. Fax, (202) 797-6003. Richard N. Haass, Director. Information, (202) 797-6000. Press, (202) 797-6105. Publications, (202) 797-6258. Web, www.brook.edu.*

Research and educational organization that focuses on major national security topics, including U.S. armed forces, weapons decisions, employment policies, and the security aspects of U.S. foreign relations.

Center for Defense Information, *1779 Massachusetts Ave. N.W., #615 20036; (202) 332-0600. Fax, (202) 462-4559. Bruce Blair, Director. Information, (800) 234-3334. General e-mail, info@cdi.org. Web, www.cdi.org.*

Educational organization that advocates a strong defense while opposing excessive expenditures for weapons and policies that increase the risk of war. Interests include the defense budget, weapons systems, and troop levels. Provides Congress, the Pentagon, State Dept., media, and public with appraisals of military matters. Library open to the public.

Center for Naval Analyses, *4401 Ford Ave., Alexandria, VA 22302-0268; (703) 824-2000. Fax, (703) 824-2942. Robert J. Murray, President. Web, www.cna.org.*

Conducts research on weapons acquisitions, tactical problems, and naval operations.

Center for Security Policy, *1920 L St. N.W., #210 20036; (202) 835-9077. Fax, (202) 835-9066. Frank J. Gaffney Jr., Director. Web, www.security-policy.org.*

Educational institution concerned with U.S. defense and foreign policy. Interests include relations between the United States and the former Soviet Union, arms control compliance and verification policy, and technology transfer policy.

Conservative Caucus, *450 Maple Ave. East, #309, Vienna, VA 22180; (703) 938-9626. Fax, (703) 281-4108. Howard Phillips, Chair. Web, www.conservativeusa.org.*

Legislative interest organization that promotes grassroots activity on national defense and foreign policy.

Defense Orientation Conference Assn., *9271 Old Keene Mill Rd., #200, Burke, VA 22015-4202; (703) 451-1200. Fax, (703) 451-1201. John W. Ohlsen, Executive Vice President. General e-mail, doca@erols.com. Web, www.doca.org.*

Membership: citizens interested in national defense. Promotes continuing education of members on national security issues through tours of defense installations in the United States and abroad.

Ethics and Public Policy Center, *Foreign Policy Program, 1015 15th St. N.W., #900 20005; (202) 682-1200. Fax, (202) 408-0632. Elliott Abrams, President. General e-mail, ethics@eppc.org. Web, www.eppc.org.*

Considers implications of Judeo-Christian moral tradition for domestic and foreign policy making. Conducts research and holds conferences on foreign policy, including the role of the U.S. military abroad.

Henry L. Stimson Center, *11 Dupont Circle N.W., 9th Floor 20036; (202) 223-5956. Fax, (202) 238-9604. Michael Krepon, President. General e-mail, info@stimson.org. Web, www.stimson.org.*

Research and educational organization that studies arms control and international security, focusing on policy, technology, and politics.

Hudson Institute, *National Security Studies, Washington Office, 1015 18th St. N.W., #300 20036; (202) 223-7770. Fax, (202) 223-8537. William E. Odom, Director. Web, www.hudson.org.*

Public policy research organization that conducts studies on U.S. overseas bases, U.S.-NATO relations, and missile defense programs. Focuses on long-range implications for U.S. national security. (Headquarters in Indianapolis.)

Institute for Foreign Policy Analysis, *1725 DeSales St. N.W., #402 20036; (202) 463-7942. Fax, (202) 785-2785. Robert Pfaltzgraff Jr., President. Web, www.ifpa.org.*

Trains policy analysts in the fields of foreign policy and national security. Sponsors research and workshops.

Institute of International Education, *National Security Education Program, 1400 K St. N.W., 6th Floor*

20005-2403; (202) 326-7697. Fax, (202) 326-7698. Leslie Anderson, Director. Information, (800) 618-6737. Web, www.iie.org/nsep.

Provides scholarships, fellowships, and institutional grants to academics with in an interest in foreign affairs and national security.

Jewish Institute for National Security Affairs, 1717 K St. N.W., #800 20036; (202) 833-0020. Fax, (202) 296-6452. Tom Neumann, Executive Director. General e-mail, info@jinsa.org. Web, www.jinsa.org.

Seeks to educate the public about the importance of effective U.S. defense capability and inform the U.S. defense and foreign affairs community about Israel's role in Mediterranean and the Middle Eastern affairs. Sponsors lectures and conferences; facilitates dialogue between security policymakers, military officials, diplomats, and the general public.

Marine Corps League, 8626 Lee Hwy., #201, Fairfax, VA 22031 (mailing address: P.O. Box 3070, Merrifield, VA 22116); (703) 207-9588. Fax, (703) 207-0047. William "Brooks" Corley Jr., Executive Director. General e-mail, mcl@mcleague.org. Web, www.mcleague.org.

Membership: active duty, retired, and reserve Marine Corps groups. Promotes the interests of the Marine Corps and works to preserve its traditions; assists veterans and their survivors. Monitors legislation and regulations.

National Institute for Public Policy, 3031 Javier Rd., #300, Fairfax, VA 22031; (703) 698-0563. Fax, (703) 698-0566. Keith B. Payne, President. Web, www.nipp.org.

Studies public policy and its relation to national security. Interests include arms control, strategic weapons systems and planning, and foreign policy.

Navy League of the United States, 2300 Wilson Blvd., Arlington, VA 22201; (703) 528-1775. Fax, (703) 528-2333. Charles L. Robinson, Executive Director. General e-mail, mail@navyleague.org. Web, www.navyleague.org.

Membership: retired and reserve military personnel and civilians interested in the U.S. Navy, Marine Corps, Coast Guard, and Merchant Marine. Distributes literature, provides speakers, and conducts seminars to promote interests of the sea services. Monitors legislation.

Rand Corporation, Washington Office, 1333 H St. N.W., #800 20005; (202) 296-5000. Fax, (202) 296-7960. Bruce Hoffman, Director. Web, www.rand.org.

Conducts research on national security issues, including political/military affairs of the former Soviet Union and U.S. strategic policy. (Headquarters in Santa Monica, Calif.)

U.S. Naval Fire Support Assn. Inc., 10416 Rockville Pike, #301, Bethesda, MD 20852-3322; (301) 493-5192. William L. Stearman, Executive Director. Web, www.usnfsa.com.

Advocates credible and effective naval surface fire support for soldiers and Marines in littoral conflicts. Conducts research; provides analyses, educational materials, and briefings. Monitors legislation and regulations.

Defense Budget

See also Federal Budget (chap. 3)

AGENCIES

Defense Contract Audit Agency (*Defense Dept.*), 8725 John Jay Kingman Rd., #2135, Fort Belvoir, VA 22060-6219; (703) 767-3200. Fax, (703) 767-3267. William H. Reed, Director; Michael J. Thibault, Deputy Director, (703) 767-3272. Web, www.dcaai.mil.

Performs all contract audits for the Defense Dept. Provides Defense Dept. personnel responsible for procurement and contract administration with accounting and financial advisory services regarding the negotiation, administration, and settlement of contracts and subcontracts.

Defense Dept., *Comptroller,* The Pentagon, #3E822 20301-1100; (703) 695-3237. Fax, (703) 693-0582. William J. Lynn, Comptroller. Web, www.defenselink.mil.

Supervises and reviews the preparation and implementation of the defense budget. Advises the secretary of defense on fiscal matters. Collects and distributes information on the department's management of resources.

Office of Management and Budget (*Executive Office of the President*), *National Security,* New Executive Office Bldg., #10001 20503; (202) 395-3884. Fax, (202) 395-3307. David H. Morrison, Deputy Associate Director. Web, www.whitehouse.gov/omb.

Supervises preparation of the Defense Dept.'s portion of the federal budget.

CONGRESS

General Accounting Office, *National Security and International Affairs,* 441 G St. N.W., #4035 20548; (202) 512-2800. Fax, (202) 512-7686. Henry L. Hinton, Assistant Comptroller General.

Independent, nonpartisan agency in the legislative branch. Audits, analyzes, and evaluates defense spending programs; makes unclassified reports available to the public.

Center for Strategic and Budgetary Assessments,
1730 Rhode Island Ave., #912 20036; (202) 331-7990. Fax, (202) 331-8019. Andrew F. Krepinevich, Director. Web, www.csbahome.com.

Conducts detailed analyses of defense spending; makes results available to members of Congress, the executive branch, the media, academics, other organizations, and the general public.

Institute for Policy Studies, *National Commission for Economic Conversion and Disarmament*, *733 15th St. N.W., #1020 20005; (202) 234-9382. Fax, (202) 387-7915. Miriam Pemberton, Executive Director. Web, www.webcom.com/ncecd.*

Supports cutbacks in the U.S. military budget and reallocation of funds for civilian economic development. Advocates investment in civilian research and development, transportation, housing, health, education, and the environment.

National Campaign for a Peace Tax Fund, *2121 Decatur Pl. N.W. 20008; (202) 483-3751. Fax, (202) 986-0667. Marian Franz, Executive Director. General e-mail, peacetaxfund@igc.org. Web, www.nonviolence.org/peacetax.*

Membership: individuals opposed to military spending. Supports legislation permitting taxpayers who are conscientiously opposed to military expenditures to have the military portion of their income tax money placed in a separate, nonmilitary fund.

Women's Action for New Directions, *Washington Office*, *110 Maryland Ave. N.E., #205 20002; (202) 543-8505. Fax, (202) 675-6469. Kimberly Robson, Director. Legislative hotline, (800) 444-9263. General e-mail, wand@wand.org. Web, www.wand.org.*

Seeks to redirect federal spending priorities from military spending toward domestic needs; works to develop citizen expertise through education and political involvement; provides educational programs and material about nuclear and conventional weapons; monitors defense legislation, budget policy legislation, and legislation affecting women. (Headquarters in Arlington, Mass.)

Military Aid and Peacekeeping

See also Regional Affairs (chap. 13)

AGENCIES

Commission on Security and Cooperation in Europe *(Helsinki Commission)*, *234 FHOB 20515; (202) 225-1901. Fax, (202) 226-4199. Rep. Christopher H. Smith, R-N.J., Chair; Sen. Ben Nighthorse Campbell,*

R-Colo., Co-Chair; Ronald McNamara, Deputy Chief of Staff. Web, www.house.gov/csce.

Independent agency created by Congress. Membership includes individuals from the executive and legislative branches. Studies and evaluates international peacekeeping and peace enforcement operations, particularly as they relate to the Helsinki Accords.

Defense Dept., *Defense Security Cooperation Agency*, *Crystal Gateway North, #303, 1111 Jefferson Davis Hwy., Arlington, VA 22202-4306; (703) 604-6604. Fax, (703) 602-5403. Lt. Gen. Michael S. Davison (USA), Director. Information, (703) 604-6633. Web, www.defenselink.mil.*

Develops budgetary proposals and Defense Dept. policies on arms transfers. Selects and manages U.S. personnel in security assistance assignments overseas; manages weapons systems sales; maintains special defense acquisition funds and priority defense items information systems. Administers foreign military sales programs.

Defense Dept., *European and NATO Affairs*, *The Pentagon, #4D800 20301-2400; (703) 697-7207. Fax, (703) 697-5992. Lisa Bronson, Deputy Assistant Secretary. Web, www.defenselink.mil.*

Advises the assistant secretary for international security affairs on matters dealing with Europe and NATO.

Defense Dept., *International Security Affairs*, *The Pentagon, #4E838 20301-2400; (703) 695-4351. Fax, (703) 697-7230. Franklin D. Kramer, Assistant Secretary. Web, www.defenselink.mil.*

Advises the secretary of defense and recommends policies on regional security issues (except those involving countries of the former Soviet Union).

State Dept., *Arms Control and International Security*, *2201 C St. N.W., #7208 20520-7512; (202) 647-1049. Fax, (202) 736-4397. Vacant, Under Secretary; John D. Holum, Senior Adviser. Web, www.state.gov.*

Works with the secretary of state to develop policy on foreign security assistance programs and technology transfer.

State Dept., *European Security and Political Affairs*, *2201 C St. N.W., #6227 20520; (202) 647-1626. Fax, (202) 647-1369. Richard A. Morford, Director. Web, www.state.gov.*

Coordinates and advises, with the Defense Dept. and other agencies, the U.S. mission to the North Atlantic Treaty Organization and the U.S. delegation to the Organization on Security and Cooperation in Europe regarding political, military, and arms control matters.

State Dept., *International Organization Affairs*, *2201 C St. N.W., #6323 20520-6319; (202) 647-9600. Fax, (202)*

NAVY DEPARTMENT

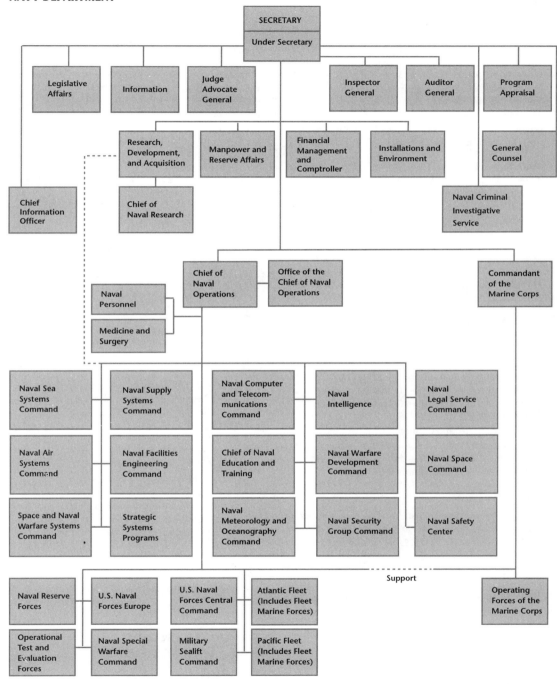

736-4116. C. David Welch, Assistant Secretary. Press, (202) 647-8490. Web, www.state.gov.

Coordinates and develops policy guidelines for U.S. participation in the United Nations and in other international organizations and conferences.

State Dept., Policy Planning Staff, 2201 C St. N.W., #7311 20520; (202) 647-2372. Fax, (202) 647-4147. Morton H. Halperin, Director. Web, www.state.gov.

Advises the secretary and other State Dept. officials on foreign policy matters, including international peace-keeping and peace enforcement operations.

State Dept., Political-Military Affairs, 2201 C St. N.W., #7325 20520; (202) 647-9022. Fax, (202) 736-4779. Eric D. Newsom, Assistant Secretary. Web, www.state.gov.

Responsible for security affairs policy and operations for the non-European area.

State Dept., United Nations Political Affairs, 2201 C St. N.W., #6334 20520-6319; (202) 647-2392. Fax, (202) 647-0039. William Stanton, Director. Web, www.state.gov.

Deals with United Nations political and institutional matters and international security affairs.

U.S. Institute of Peace, 1200 17th St. N.W., #200 20036; (202) 457-1700. Fax, (202) 429-6063. Chester Crocker, Chair; Richard H. Solomon, President. TTY, (202) 457-1719. Web, www.usip.org.

Independent organization created and funded by Congress to promote the peaceful resolution of international conflict through negotiation and mediation. Provides federal agencies and individuals with training, research programs, and information. Awards grants to institutions and individuals and provides fellowships to scholars from the United States and abroad. Library open to the public by appointment.

CONGRESS

General Accounting Office, National Security and International Affairs, 441 G St. N.W., #4035 20548; (202) 512-2800. Fax, (202) 512-7686. Henry L. Hinton, Assistant Comptroller General.

Independent, nonpartisan agency in the legislative branch. Audits, analyzes, and evaluates international programs, including U.S. participation in international peacekeeping and peace enforcement operations; makes unclassified reports available to the public.

INTERNATIONAL ORGANIZATIONS

Inter-American Defense Board, 2600 16th St. N.W. 20441; (202) 939-6600. Fax, (202) 939-6620. Maj. Gen. John C. Thompson (USA), Chair. Web, www.jid.org.

Membership: military officers from twenty countries of the Western Hemisphere. Plans for the collective self-defense of the American continents. Develops procedures for standardizing military organization and operations; operates the Inter-American Defense College.

Joint Mexican–United States Defense Commission, U.S. Section, The Pentagon, #2D959, 5134 Joint Staff 20318-5134; (703) 695-8162. Fax, (703) 614-8945. Maj. Gen. Timothy A. Kinnan (USAF), Chair.

Composed of military delegates of the two countries. Studies problems concerning the common defense of the United States and Mexico.

Permanent Joint Board on Defense/United States and Canada, 1111 Jefferson Davis Hwy., #511, Arlington, VA 22202-4306; (703) 604-0487. Fax, (703) 604-0486. Dwight N. Mason, Chair; Col. Michael J. Muolo (USAF), Military Secretary.

Comprises representatives from the State Dept. and Defense Dept.; chair appointed by the president. Conducts studies relating to sea, land, and air defense problems. (Canadian counterpart located in Ottawa.)

NONPROFIT

National Peace Foundation, 1819 H St. N.W., #1200 20006-3603; (202) 223-1770. Fax, (202) 223-1718. Stephen P. Strickland, President. Web, www.nationalpeace. org.

Supports conflict resolution education and the U.S. Institute of Peace. Holds conferences and provides information on peace education and managing and resolving conflict.

Peace Links, 666 11th St. N.W., #202 20001; (202) 783-7030. Fax, (202) 783-7040. Deedie Runkel, Director. General e-mail, peacelinks1@erols.com. Web, www. peacelinksusa.org.

Seeks to educate Americans about alternatives to war as a means of resolving conflicts; promotes improved relations between people from the former Soviet Union and Americans through an exchange program and a letter-writing program; provides educational information, primarily to women's groups, concerning the arms race and national security issues.

⬛ ARMS CONTROL AND DISARMAMENT

AGENCIES

Defense Dept., Chemical and Biological Defense Programs, The Pentagon, #3C257 20301-3050; (703) 693-

9410. Fax, (703) 695-0476. Col. Stanley H. Lillie, Director. Web, www.defenselink.mil.

Coordinates, integrates, and provides oversight for the Joint Services Chemical and Biological Defense Program. Provides oversight for the Chemical Weapons Demilitarization Program and the Counterproliferation Support Program.

Defense Dept., *Requirements, Plans, and Counterproliferation Policy,* The Pentagon, #4B856 20301-2900; (703) 697-6963. Fax, (703) 693-5193. James N. Miller Jr., Deputy Assistant Secretary. Web, www.defenselink.mil.

Formulates national policies to prevent and counter the proliferation of nuclear, chemical, and biological weapons; missiles; and conventional technologies. Devises arms control agreements, export controls, technology transfer policies, and military planning policies.

Defense Dept., *Strategy and Threat Reduction,* The Pentagon, #4E817 20301-2900; (703) 697-7728. Fax, (703) 693-9146. Edward L. Warner III, Assistant Secretary. Web, www.defenselink.mil.

Advises the secretary on reducing and countering nuclear, biological, chemical, and missile threats to the United States and its forces and allies; arms control negotiations, implementation, and verification policy; nuclear weapons policy, denuclearization, threat reduction, and nuclear safety, and security; and technology transfer.

Defense Threat Reduction Agency *(Defense Dept.),* 45045 Aviation Dr., Dulles, VA 20166-7517; (703) 810-4883. Fax, (703) 810-4343. Jay Davis, Director; Gen. Frank Moore, Deputy Director, (703) 810-4551. Web, www.dtra.mil.

Seeks to reduce the threat of the U.S. and its allies from nuclear, biological, chemical, conventional, and special weapons; conducts technology security activities, cooperative threat reduction programs, arms control treaty monitoring, and on-site inspection; provides technical support on weapons of mass destruction matters to the Defense Dept. components.

National Security Council *(Executive Office of the President),* **Defense Policy/Arms Control,** The White House 20502; (202) 456-9191. Fax, (202) 456-9190. Hans Binnendijk, Senior Director. Web, www.whitehouse.gov/WH/EOP/NSC/html/nschome.html.

Advises the assistant to the president for national security affairs on matters concerning nuclear weapons policy.

State Dept., *Policy, Plans, and Analysis,* 2201 C St. N.W., #7418 20520; (202) 647-7775. Fax, (202) 647-8998. Robert Maggi, Director (Acting). Web, www.state.gov.

Develops policies related to nuclear and conventional arms control, strategic defenses, nuclear testing, and assistance to the former Soviet Union aimed toward eliminating weapons of mass destruction.

CONGRESS

House Armed Services Committee, 2120 RHOB 20515; (202) 225-4151. Fax, (202) 225-9077. Rep. Floyd D. Spence, R-S.C., Chair; Robert S. Rangel, Staff Director. Web, www.house.gov/hasc.

Oversight of international arms control and disarmament matters (jurisdiction shared with House International Relations Committee).

House International Relations Committee, *Subcommittee on International Operations and Human Rights,* B-358 RHOB 20515; (202) 225-5748. Fax, (202) 225-7485. Rep. Christopher H. Smith, R-N.J., Chair; Grover Joseph Rees, Staff Director. Web, www.house.gov/international_relations.

Jurisdiction over arms control, disarmament, and nuclear nonproliferation legislation. Oversight of State and Defense department activities involving arms transfers and arms sales.

Senate Armed Services Committee, SR-228 20510; (202) 224-3871. Sen. John W. Warner, R-Va., Chair; Les Brownlee, Staff Director. Web, armed_services.senate.gov.

Oversight of arms control and disarmament matters (jurisdiction shared with Senate Foreign Relations Committee).

Senate Foreign Relations Committee, SD-450 20510; (202) 224-4651. Fax, (202) 224-0836. Sen. Jesse Helms, R-N.C., Chair; Steve Biegun, Staff Director. Web, foreign.senate.gov.

Jurisdiction over arms control, disarmament, and nuclear nonproliferation legislation (jurisdiction shared with Senate Armed Services Committee).

NONPROFIT

Arms Control Assn., 1726 M St. N.W., #201 20036; (202) 463-8270. Fax, (202) 463-8273. Spurgeon M. Keeny Jr., Executive Director. General e-mail, aca@armscontrol.org. Web, www.armscontrol.org.

Nonpartisan organization interested in arms control. Seeks to broaden public interest in arms control, disarmament, and national security policy.

Center for Defense Information, 1779 Massachusetts Ave. N.W., #615 20036; (202) 332-0600. Fax, (202) 462-4559. Bruce Blair, Director. Information, (800) 234-3334. General e-mail, info@cdi.org. Web, www.cdi.org.

Educational organization that advocates a strong defense while opposing excessive expenditures for weapons and policies that increase the risk of war. Interests include the defense budget, weapons systems, and troop levels. Provides Congress, the Pentagon, State Dept., media, and public with appraisals of military matters. Library open to the public.

Chemical and Biological Arms Control Institute, *2111 Eisenhower Ave., #302, Alexandria, VA 22314; (703) 739-1538. Fax, (703) 739-1525. Michael L. Moodie, President. General e-mail, info@edi.org. Web, www.cbaci.org.*

Promotes arms control, nonproliferation, and the elimination of chemical, biological, and other weapons of mass destruction through research, analysis, technical support, and education.

Council for a Livable World, *110 Maryland Ave. N.E., #409 20002; (202) 543-4100. Fax, (202) 543-6297. John Isaacs, President. General e-mail, clw@clw.org. Web, www.clw.org.*

Citizens' interest group that supports arms control treaties, reduced military spending, peacekeeping, and tight restrictions on international arms sales.

Federation of American Scientists, *307 Massachusetts Ave. N.E. 20002; (202) 546-3300. Fax, (202) 675-1010. Jeremy J. Stone, President. General e-mail, fas@fas.org. Web, www.fas.org.*

Opposes the global arms race and supports nuclear disarmament. Conducts studies and monitors legislation on U.S. nuclear arms policy; provides the public with information on arms control and related issues.

Friends Committee on National Legislation, *245 2nd St. N.E. 20002-5795; (202) 547-6000. Fax, (202) 547-6019. Joe Volk, Executive Secretary. Recorded information, (202) 547-4343. General e-mail, fcnl@fcnl.org. Web, www.fcnl.org.*

Supports world disarmament; international cooperation; domestic, economic, peace, and social justice issues; and improvement in relations between the United States and the former Soviet Union. Opposes conscription. Affiliated with the Religious Society of Friends (Quakers).

High Frontier, *2800 Shirlington Rd., #405, Arlington, VA 22206-3601; (703) 671-4111. Fax, (703) 931-6432. Henry Cooper, Chair. General e-mail, hifront@erols.com. Web, www.highfrontier.org.*

Educational organization that provides information on missile defense programs and proliferation. Advocates development of a single-stage-to-orbit space vehicle and research of space solar power. Operates speakers bureau. Monitors defense legislation.

Lawyers Alliance for World Security, *1901 Pennsylvania Ave. N.W., #201 20006; (202) 745-2450. Fax, (202) 667-0444. Thomas Graham Jr., President. General e-mail, laws@lawscns.org. Web, www.lawscns.org.*

Public education organization that seeks to broaden interest in and understanding of arms control and disarmament with regard to nuclear, conventional, chemical, and biological weapons. Sponsors educational programs for government officials, including legislators from the Commonwealth of Independent States.

Peace Action, *1819 H St. N.W., #420 20006-3603; (202) 862-9740. Fax, (202) 862-9762. Gordon Clark, Executive Director. General e-mail, pamembers@igc.apc.org. Web, www.peace-action.org.*

Grassroots organization that supports a negotiated comprehensive test ban treaty. Seeks a reduction in the military budget and a transfer of those funds to nonmilitary programs. Works for an end to international arms trade. Formerly Sane/Freeze.

Physicians for Social Responsibility, *1101 14th St. N.W., #700 20005; (202) 898-0150. Fax, (202) 898-0172. Robert K. Musil, Executive Director. General e-mail, psrnatl@psr.org. Web, www.psr.org.*

Membership: doctors, dentists, and other individuals. Works toward the elimination of nuclear and other weapons of mass destruction, the achievement of a sustainable environment, and the reduction of violence and its causes. Conducts public education programs, monitors policy decisions on arms control, and serves as a liaison with other concerned groups.

Union of Concerned Scientists, *Government Relations, Washington Office, 1616 P St. N.W., #310 20036; (202) 332-0900. Fax, (202) 332-0905. Alden Meyer, Director; Todd Perry, Washington Representative for Arms Control and International Security. General e-mail, ucs@ucsusa.org. Web, www.ucsusa.org.*

Works to advance the international security policies and agreements that restrict the spread of weapons of mass destruction and reduce the risk of war. Promotes international nonproliferation through reductions in fissile materials, arms control measures including a comprehensive nuclear testing ban, restrictions on ballistic missile defenses and dismantlement of nuclear warheads. Encourages the use of collective security forces such as the United Nations to alleviate conflicts. (Headquarters in Cambridge, Mass.)

Nuclear Weapons and Power

See also Nuclear Energy (chap. 8)

AGENCIES

Defense Threat Reduction Agency *(Defense Dept.)*, 45045 Aviation Dr., Dulles, VA 20166-7517; (703) 810-4883. Fax, (703) 810-4343. Jay Davis, Director; Gen. Frank Moore, Deputy Director, (703) 810-4551. Web, www.dtra.mil.

Seeks to reduce the threat of the U.S. and its allies from nuclear, biological, chemical, conventional, and special weapons; conducts technology security activities, cooperative threat reduction programs, arms control treaty monitoring, and on-site inspection; provides technical support on weapons of mass destruction matters to the Defense Dept. components.

Energy Dept., *Arms Control and Nonproliferation: Nuclear Transfer and Supplier Policy,* 1000 Independence Ave. S.W. 20585-0001; (202) 586-2331. Fax, (202) 586-1348. Anatoli Welihozkiy, Director (Acting). Web, www.doe.gov.

Develops and implements policies concerning nuclear materials and equipment; participates in international negotiations involving nuclear policy; supports activities of the International Atomic Energy Agency; develops policies concerning nuclear reprocessing requests.

Energy Dept., *Defense Programs,* 1000 Independence Ave. S.W., #4A019 20585; (202) 586-2177. Fax, (202) 586-1567. Brig. Gen. Thomas F. Giconda, Assistant Secretary (Acting). Web, www.doe.gov.

Responsible for nuclear weapons research, development, and engineering; performs laser fusion research and development.

Energy Dept., *Naval Reactors,* National Center 2, 2521 Jefferson Davis Hwy., Arlington, VA 22242-5160; (703) 603-7321. Fax, (703) 603-1906. Adm. F. L. Bowman, Director. Web, www.doe.gov.

Designs, develops, and maintains naval nuclear propulsion plants.

Navy Dept. *(Defense Dept.), Naval Sea Systems Command: Naval Nuclear Propulsion,* National Center 2, 2521 Jefferson Davis Hwy., Arlington, VA 22242-5160; (703) 602-3887. Fax, (703) 603-1906. Adm. F. L. Bowman, Director. Web, www.navy.mil.

Responsible for naval nuclear propulsion.

State Dept., *Nuclear Energy Affairs,* 2201 C St. N.W., #7828 20520; (202) 647-3310. Fax, (202) 647-0775. Richard J. K. Stratford, Director. Web, www.state.gov.

Coordinates U.S. government activities that support safeguards against proliferation of nuclear weapons.

CONGRESS

House Appropriations Committee, *Subcommittee on Energy and Water Development,* 2362 RHOB 20515; (202) 225-3421. Rep. Ron Packard, R-Calif., Chair; Robert Schmidt, Staff Director. Web, www.house.gov/appropriations.

Jurisdiction over legislation to appropriate funds for atomic energy defense activities within the Energy Dept., Defense Nuclear Facilities Safety Board, Nuclear Regulatory Commission, Nuclear Waste Technical Review Board, and Nuclear Safety Oversight Commission.

House Armed Services Committee, *Subcommittee on Military Procurement,* 2340 RHOB 20515; (202) 225-4440. Fax, (202) 226-0105. Rep. Duncan Hunter, R-Calif., Chair; Steve Thompson, Professional Staff Member. Web, www.house.gov/hasc.

Jurisdiction over military applications of nuclear energy.

Senate Appropriations Committee, *Subcommittee on Energy and Water Development,* SD-127 20510; (202) 224-7260. Sen. Pete V. Domenici, R-N.M., Chair; Clay Sell, Clerk. Web, appropriations.senate.gov/energy.

Jurisdiction over legislation to appropriate funds for the Nuclear Regulatory Commission, Nuclear Waste Technical Review Board, Defense Nuclear Facilities Safety Board, and atomic energy defense activities within the Energy Dept.

Senate Armed Services Committee, SR-228 20510; (202) 224-3871. Sen. John W. Warner, R-Va., Chair; Les Brownlee, Staff Director. Web, armed_services.senate.gov.

Jurisdiction over national security aspects of nuclear energy.

NONPROFIT

Institute for Science and International Security, 236 Massachusetts Ave. N.E., #500 20002; (202) 547-3633. Fax, (202) 547-3634. David Albright, Director. General e-mail, isis@isis-online.org. Web, www.isis-online.org.

Conducts research and analysis on nuclear weapons production and nonproliferation issues.

Nuclear Control Institute, 1000 Connecticut Ave. N.W., #804 20036; (202) 822-8444. Fax, (202) 452-0892. Paul Leventhal, President. General e-mail, nci@nci.org. Web, www.nci.org.

Promotes nuclear nonproliferation; works to prevent the use of nuclear explosive materials (plutonium and highly enriched uranium) as reactor fuels; advocates terminating the export of nuclear technologies and facilities that could be used in the manufacture of nuclear weaponry; works to reduce the nuclear arsenals of nuclear weapons states; studies and recommends measures to prevent nuclear terrorism.

Women Strike for Peace, *110 Maryland Ave. N.E., #102 20002; (202) 543-2660. Fax, (202) 544-9613. Edith Villastrigo, Legislative Director.*

Promotes opposition to nuclear weapons, nuclear power plants, and U.S. intervention in developing countries. Supports nuclear disarmament with international controls. Provides the public with information on foreign policy and prevention of nuclear war.

⬛ DEFENSE TRADE AND TECHNOLOGY

See also Procurement, Acquisition, and Logistics (this chapter)

AGENCIES

Bureau of Export Administration *(Commerce Dept.), 14th St. and Constitution Ave. N.W., #3898 20230; (202) 482-1427. Fax, (202) 482-2387. William Alan Reinsch, Under Secretary. Press, (202) 482-2721. Export licensing information, (202) 482-4811. Web, www.bxa.doc.gov.*

Administers Export Administration Act; maintains control lists and performs export licensing for the purposes of national security, foreign policy, and prevention of short supply.

Bureau of Export Administration *(Commerce Dept.), Export Enforcement, 14th St. and Constitution Ave. N.W., #3721 20230; (202) 482-3618. Fax, (202) 482-4173. F. Amanda DeBusk, Assistant Secretary. Web, www.bxa. doc.gov.*

Enforces dual-use export controls on exports of U.S. goods and technology for purposes of national security, nonproliferation, counterterrorism, foreign policy, and short supply. Enforces the antiboycott provisions of the Export Administration Regulations.

Defense Threat Reduction Agency *(Defense Dept.), Technology Security, 400 Army-Navy Dr., #300, Arlington, VA 22202-2884; (703) 604-5215. Fax, (703) 602-5838. Dave Tarbell, Director. Web, www.dtra.mil/security/ security.html.*

Analyzes export control factors affecting national security; develops and implements Defense Dept. policies for trade security and for the transfer and control of advanced military technology.

Energy Dept., *Arms Control and Nonproliferation: Nuclear Transfer and Supplier Policy, 1000 Independence Ave. S.W. 20585-0001; (202) 586-2331. Fax, (202) 586-1348. Anatoli Welihozkiy, Director (Acting). Web, www.doe.gov.*

Develops policies concerning nuclear material and equipment exports, nuclear material transfers and retransfers, and regional nonproliferation.

Export Administration Review Board *(Commerce Dept.), 14th St. and Constitution Ave. N.W., #2639 20230; (202) 482-5863. Fax, (202) 501-2815. Carol A. Kalinoski, Executive Secretary. Web, www.bxa.doc.gov.*

Committee of cabinet-level secretaries and heads of other government offices. Considers export licensing policies and actions, especially those concerning national security and other major policy matters; advises the secretary of commerce on export licensing; reviews export licensing applications.

National Security Council *(Executive Office of the President), Defense Policy/Arms Control: International Economic Affairs, The White House 20502; (202) 456-9281. Fax, (202) 456-9280. Malcolm Lee, Director. Web, www.whitehouse.gov/WH/EOP/NSC/html/nschome.html.*

Advises the president and the National Security Adviser on all aspects of U.S. foreign policy dealing with U.S. international economic policies.

Nuclear Regulatory Commission, *Nonproliferation, Exports, and Multilateral Relations, 11555 Rockville Pike, Rockville, MD 20852; (301) 415-2344. Fax, (301) 415-2395. Janice Dunn Lee, Director.*

Coordinates application review process for exports and imports of nuclear materials, facilities, and components. Makes recommendations on licensing upon completion of review process. Conducts related policy reviews.

President's Export Council *(Commerce Dept.), Subcommittee on Export Administration, 14th St. and Constitution Ave. N.W., #3876 20230; (202) 482-2583. Fax, (202) 501-8024. Lee Ann Carpenter, Committee Control Officer.*

Advises the president and secretary of commerce on matters related to the Export Administration Act of 1979, which deals with controlling trade for reasons of national security, foreign policy, and short supply. Seeks ways to minimize the negative effect of export controls while protecting U.S. national security and foreign policy interests.

State Dept., *Bureau of Nonproliferation, 320 21st St. N.W., #4936 20451; (202) 647-2208. Fax, (202) 647-3259.*

Norman Wolf, Representative to the President for Nuclear Proliferation. Web, www.state.gov.

Serves as U.S. representative to preparatory committee meetings and reviews conferences for the Treaty on the Nonproliferation of Nuclear Weapons. Interests include the International Atomic Energy Agency and nuclear weapon free zones.

State Dept., *Defense Trade Controls, 2201 C St. N.W. 20520-6258 (mailing address: State Dept., Rm. 200, PM/DTC, SA-6 20520-0602); (703) 875-6644. Fax, (703) 875-6647. William J. Lowell, Director. Web, www.pmdtc.org.*

Controls the commercial export of defense articles, services, and related technical data; authorizes the permanent export and temporary import of such items.

State Dept., *Economic Sanctions Policy, 2201 C St. N.W., #3329 20520; (202) 647-5673. Fax, (202) 647-4064. Brian J. Mohler, Director. Web, www.state.gov.*

Develops and implements U.S. foreign policy sanctions of embargo and terrorist listed countries. Coordinates U.S. participation in multilateral strategic trade control and revisions related to the export of strategically critical high-technology goods. Cooperates with the Commerce, Defense, and Treasury departments regarding export controls.

Treasury Dept., *Foreign Assets Control, 1500 Pennsylvania Ave. N.W., Annex Bldg., 2nd Floor 20220; (202) 622-2510. Fax, (202) 622-1657. R. Richard Newcomb, Director. Fax-on-demand, (202) 622-0077. Web, www.treas.gov/ofac.*

Authorized under the revised Trading with the Enemy Act, the International Emergency Economic Powers Act, and the United Nations Participation Act to control financial and commercial dealings with certain countries and their foreign nationals in times of war or emergencies. Regulations involving foreign assets control and commercial transactions currently apply in varying degrees to Cuba, Iran, Iraq, Libya, North Korea, and Angola.

CONGRESS

House Armed Services Committee, *Subcommittee on Military Procurement, 2340 RHOB 20515; (202) 225-4440. Fax, (202) 226-0105. Rep. Duncan Hunter, R-Calif., Chair; Steve Thompson, Professional Staff Member. Web, www.house.gov/hasc.*

Jurisdiction over legislation on foreign military sales and the proliferation of weapons technology.

House International Relations Committee, *Subcommittee on International Economic Policy and Trade, 257 FHOB 20515; (202) 225-3345. Fax, (202) 225-0432. Rep.*

Ileana Ros-Lehtinen, R-Fla., Chair; Mauricio Tamargo, Staff Director. Web, www.house.gov/international_relations.

Has authority under the revised Trading with the Enemy Act, the International Emergency Economic Powers Act, and the United Nations Participation Act to control financial and commercial dealings with certain countries and their foreign nationals in times of war or emergencies. Regulations involving foreign assets control and commercial transactions currently apply in varying degrees to Cuba, Iran, Iraq, Libya, North Korea, and Angola.

House Science Committee, *Subcommittee on Technology, 2319 RHOB 20515; (202) 225-8844. Fax, (202) 225-4438. Rep. Constance A. Morella, R-Md., Chair; Jeffrey Grove, Staff Director. Web, www.house.gov/science.*

Jurisdiction over legislation on transfers of technology between the United States and foreign countries (jurisdiction shared with House International Relations Committee).

Senate Armed Services Committee, *Subcommittee on Emerging Threats and Capabilities, SR-228 20510; (202) 224-3871. Sen. Pat Roberts, R-Kan., Chair; Pamela Farrel, Professional Staff Member. Web, armed_services. senate.gov.*

Jurisdiction over legislation on foreign military sales and the proliferation of weapons technology.

Senate Banking, Housing, and Urban Affairs Committee, *Subcommittee on International Trade and Finance, SD-534 20510; (202) 224-7391. Fax, (202) 224-5137. Sen. Michael B. Enzi, R-Wyo., Chair; Katherine McGuire, Staff Director. Web, banking.senate.gov.*

Jurisdiction over foreign trade legislation and legislation related to export control, including the Export Administration Act and the revised Trading with the Enemy Act, which authorize trade restrictions.

Senate Foreign Relations Committee, *SD-450 20510; (202) 224-4651. Fax, (202) 224-0836. Sen. Jesse Helms, R-N.C., Chair; Steve Biegun, Staff Director. Web, foreign. senate.gov.*

Oversight of State and Defense department operations regarding arms transfers, export licenses, and sales.

Senate Governmental Affairs Committee, *Permanent Subcommittee on Investigations, SR-100 20510; (202) 224-3721. Fax, (202) 224-7042. Sen. Susan Collins, R-Maine, Chair; K. Lee Blalack, Staff Director. General e-mail, PSI@govt-aff.senate.gov. Web, gov_affairs.senate. gov/psi.htm.*

Investigates transfers of technology between the United States and foreign countries.

Business Executives for National Security, *1717 Pennsylvania Ave. N.W., #350 20006; (202) 296-2125. Fax, (202) 296-2490. Stanley Weiss, Chair. Web, www.bens.org.*

Monitors legislation on national security issues from a business perspective; holds conferences, congressional forums, and other meetings on national security issues; works with other organizations on defense policy issues.

Research and Development

AGENCIES

Air Force Dept. *(Defense Dept.), Acquisition, 1060 Air Force Pentagon 20330-1060; (703) 697-6361. Fax, (703) 693-6400. Lawrence J. Delaney, Assistant Secretary. Web, www.af.mil.*

Civilian office that directs and reviews Air Force research, development, and acquisition of weapons systems.

Air Force Dept. *(Defense Dept.), Scientific Research, 801 N. Randolph St., #732, Arlington, VA 22203-1977; (703) 696-7554. Fax, (703) 696-9556. Joseph F. Janni, Director. Web, www.afosr.af.mil.*

Sponsors and sustains basic research; assists in the transfer of research results to the fleet; supports Air Force goals of control and maximum utilization of air and space.

Army Corps of Engineers *(Defense Dept.), Research and Development, 20 Massachusetts Ave. N.W., #6207 20314; (202) 761-1839. Fax, (202) 761-0907. Lewis E. Link, Director. Web, www.usace.army.mil.*

Coordinates the Corps of Engineers' research efforts; acts as advocate for its research laboratories in the Pentagon and with Congress; develops management procedures for laboratories.

Army Dept. *(Defense Dept.), Acquisition Logistics and Technology, The Pentagon 20310-0103; (703) 695-6153. Fax, (703) 697-4003. Paul J. Hoeper, Assistant Secretary. Web, www.army.mil.*

Civilian office that directs and reviews Army research and development of weapons systems and missiles.

Army Dept. *(Defense Dept.), Research and Technology, 2511 Jefferson Davis Hwy., Arlington, VA 22202; (703) 601-1500. Fax, (703) 607-5988. A. Michael Andrews, Deputy Assistant Secretary. Web, www.army.mil.*

Sponsors and supports basic research at Army laboratories, universities, and other public and private organizations; assists in the transfer of research and technology to the field.

Defense Advanced Research Projects Agency *(Defense Dept.), 3701 N. Fairfax Dr., Arlington, VA 22203-1714; (703) 696-2400. Fax, (703) 696-2209. F. L. Fernandez, Director; Jane A. Alexander, Deputy Director, (703) 696-2402. Press, (703) 696-2404. Web, www.darpa.mil.*

Helps maintain U.S. technological superiority and guard against unforeseen technological advances by potential adversaries; determines which proposals for future projects related to national security deserve further research.

Defense Dept., *Ballistic Missile Defense Organization, The Pentagon 20301-7100; (703) 695-8743. Fax, (703) 614-7059. Maj. Gen. Peter C. Franklin (USA), Deputy Director; Lt. Gen. Ronald T. Kadish (USAF), Director. Web, www.acq.osd.mil/bmdo.*

Manages and directs the ballistic missile defense acquisition and research and development programs. Seeks to deploy improved theater missile defense systems and to develop options for effective national missile defenses while increasing the contribution of defensive systems to U.S. and allied security.

Defense Dept., *Defense Research and Engineering, The Pentagon, #3E808 20301-3030; (703) 695-0598. Fax, (703) 693-7167. Hans Mark, Director. Web, www.dtic.mil/ddre/index.html.*

Civilian office responsible for policy, guidance, and oversight of the Defense Dept.'s Science and Technology Program. Serves as focal point for in-house laboratories, university research, and other science and technology matters.

Defense Technical Information Center *(Defense Dept.), 8725 John Jay Kingman Rd., #0944, Fort Belvoir, VA 22060-6221; (703) 767-9100. Fax, (703) 767-9183. Kurt N. Molholm, Administrator. Registration, (703) 767-8273. Web, www.dtic.mil.*

Acts as a central repository for the Defense Dept.'s collection of current and completed research and development efforts in all fields of science and technology. Disseminates research and development information to contractors, grantees, and registered organizations working on government research and development projects, particularly for the Defense Dept. Users must register with the center.

Marine Corps *(Defense Dept.), Systems Command, 2033 Barnett Ave., #315, Quantico, VA 22134-5010; (703) 784-2411. Fax, (703) 784-3792. Brig. Gen. James M. Feigley, Commander.*

Military office that directs Marine Corps research, development, and acquisition.

Naval Research Laboratory *(Defense Dept.),* **Research,** *4555 Overlook Ave. S.W. 20375-5320; (202) 767-3301. Fax, (202) 404-2676. Timothy Coffey, Director. Web, www.nrl.navy.mil.*

Conducts scientific research and develops advanced technology for the Navy. Areas of research include radar systems, radiation technology, tactical electronic warfare, and weapons guidance systems.

Navy Dept. *(Defense Dept.),* **Naval Research,** *800 N. Quincy St., #907, Arlington, VA 22217-5660; (703) 696-4767. Fax, (703) 696-4065. Rear Adm. Paul G. Gaffney II, Chief. Web, www.onr.navy.mil.*

Oversees the offices of Naval Research, Naval Technology, and Advanced Technology; works to ensure transition of research and technology to the fleet; sponsors and supports basic research at Navy laboratories, universities, and other public and private organizations.

Navy Dept. *(Defense Dept.),* **Research, Development, and Acquisition,** *The Pentagon 20350-1000; (703) 695-6315. Fax, (703) 693-4618. H. Lee Buchanan III, Assistant Secretary. Web, www.navy.mil.*

Civilian office that directs and reviews Navy and Marine Corps research and development of weapons systems.

Navy Dept. *(Defense Dept.),* **Test Evaluation and Technology Requirements,** *The Pentagon 20350-2000; (703) 601-1870. Fax, (703) 601-2011. Rear Adm. Paul G. Gaffney II, Director. Web, www.onr.navy.mil.*

Military office that directs Navy testing, evaluation, and science and technology.

Office of Science and Technology Policy *(Executive Office of the President),* **National Security and International Affairs,** *Dwight D. Eisenhower Executive Office Bldg., #494 20502; (202) 456-2894. Fax, (202) 456-6028. Neal Lane, Director. Web, www.whitehouse.gov/WH/EOP/OSTP/html/OSTP_Home.html.*

Advises the president on international science and technology matters as they affect national security; coordinates international science and technology initiatives at the interagency level.

President's National Security Telecommunications Advisory Committee, *c/o National Communications System, 701 S. Courthouse Rd., Arlington, VA 22204-2198; (703) 607-6221. Fax, (703) 607-4826. Janet S. Jefferson, Program Manager. Web, www.ncs.gov.*

Advises the president on specific measures to improve national security telecommunications.

State Dept., *Intelligence and Research, 2201 C St. N.W., #6531 20520-6531; (202) 647-9177. Fax, (202) 736-*
4688. J. Stapleton Roy, Assistant Secretary. Web, www.state.gov.

Coordinates foreign policy-related research, analysis, and intelligence programs for the State Dept. and other federal agencies.

U.S. Coast Guard *(Transportation Dept.),* **Systems,** *2100 2nd St. S.W., #6120 20593-0001; (202) 267-1844. Fax, (202) 267-4245. Rear Adm. John T. Tozzi, Assistant Commandant.*

Develops and maintains engineering standards for the building of ships and other Coast Guard craft.

CONGRESS

House Armed Services Committee, *Subcommittee on Military Research and Development, 2120 RHOB 20515; (202) 225-1967. Fax, (202) 226-0105. Rep. Curt Weldon, R-Pa., Chair; Steve Ansley, Professional Staff Member. Web, www.house.gov/hasc.*

Jurisdiction over legislation on military research and development, reinvestment, and conversion.

Senate Armed Services Committee, *SR-228 20510; (202) 224-3871. Sen. John W. Warner, R-Va., Chair; Les Brownlee, Staff Director. Web, armed_services.senate.gov.*

Jurisdiction over military research and development legislation.

NONPROFIT

American Society of Naval Engineers, *1452 Duke St., Alexandria, VA 22314-3458; (703) 836-6727. Fax, (703) 836-7491. Dennis K. Kruse, Executive Director. General e-mail, asnehq@navalengineers.org. Web, www.navalengineers.org.*

Membership: civilian, active duty, and retired naval engineers. Provides forum for an exchange of information between industry and government involving all phases of naval engineering.

ANSER (Analytic Services), *1215 Jefferson Davis Hwy., #800, Arlington, VA 22202-3251; (703) 416-2000. Fax, (703) 416-4451. Ruth David, President. Web, www.anser.org.*

Systems analysis organization funded by government contracts. Conducts weapon systems analysis.

Armed Forces Communications and Electronics Assn., *4400 Fair Lakes Court, Fairfax, VA 22033-3899; (703) 631-6100. Fax, (703) 631-4693. C. Norman Wood, President. Web, www.afcea.com.*

Membership: industrial organizations, scientists, and military and government personnel in the fields of communications, electronics, computers, and electrical engineering. Consults with the Defense Dept. and other federal agencies on design and maintenance of command, control, communications, computer, and intelligence systems; holds shows displaying latest communications products.

Institute for Defense Analyses, *1801 N. Beauregard St., Alexandria, VA 22311-1772; (703) 845-2300. Fax, (703) 845-2569. Larry D. Welch, President. Web, www. ida.org.*

Federally funded research and development center that focuses on national security and defense. Conducts research, systems evaluation, and policy analysis for Defense Dept. and other agencies.

Johns Hopkins University Applied Physics Laboratory, *11100 Johns Hopkins Rd., Laurel, MD 20723-6099; (240) 228-5000. Fax, (240) 228-1093. Richard Roca, Director. Information, (240) 228-5021. Web, www.jhuapl. edu.*

Research and development organization that conducts research for the Defense Dept. (primarily the Navy) and other state and federal agencies. Interests include weapons systems and satellites.

Logistics Management Institute, *2000 Corporate Ridge, McLean, VA 22102-7805; (703) 917-9800. Fax, (703) 917-7591. William G. T. Tuttle Jr., President. Library, (703) 917-7249. Web, www.lmi.org.*

Conducts research on military and nonmilitary logistics, including transportation, supply and maintenance, force management, weapons support, acquisition, health systems, international programs, energy and environment, mathematical modeling, installations, operations, and information systems. Library open to the public by appointment.

Military Operations Research Society, *101 S. Whiting St., #202, Alexandria, VA 22304-3416; (703) 751-7290. Fax, (703) 751-8171. Richard I. Wiles, Executive Vice President. Web, www.mors.org.*

Membership: professional analysts of military operations. Fosters information exchange; promotes professional development and high ethical standards; educates members on emerging issues, analytical techniques, and applications of research.

Society of American Military Engineers, *607 Prince St., Alexandria, VA 22314-3117; (703) 549-3800. Fax, (703) 684-0231. Maj. Gen. Pat M. Stevens III (USA, ret.), Executive Director. Web, www.same.org.*

Membership: military and civilian engineers and architects. Conducts research on subjects related to military engineering.

SRI International, *Washington Office, 1611 N. Kent St., #700, Arlington, VA 22209; (703) 524-2053. Fax, (703) 247-8569. William Mohr, Director. Web, www.sri.com.*

Research organization supported by government and private contracts. Conducts research on military technology, including lasers and computers. Other interests include strategic planning and armed forces interdisciplinary research. (Headquarters in Menlo Park, Calif.)

EMERGENCY PREPAREDNESS

AGENCIES

Army Corps of Engineers *(Defense Dept.), Civil Emergency Management, 20 Massachusetts Ave. N.W., #6215 20314; (202) 761-0409. Fax, (202) 761-4150. Edward J. Hecker, Chief.*

Assists in repairing and restoring damaged flood control structures and federally authorized hurricane and shore protection projects damaged by wind or water; provides emergency assistance during floods or coastal storms. Supplies emergency power, removes debris, provides temporary housing, rebuilds public infrastructure, and performs other services at request of the Federal Emergency Management Agency.

Civil Air Patrol, *National Capital Wing, Washington Office, Bolling Air Force Base, 222 Luke Ave., #2 20332-5114; (202) 767-4405. Fax, (202) 767-5695. Col. Roland Butler, Wing Commander.*

Official auxiliary of the U.S. Air Force. Conducts search-and-rescue missions for the Air Force; participates in emergency airlift and disaster relief missions. (Headquarters at Maxwell Air Force Base, Ala.)

Energy Dept., *Emergency Operations, 1000 Independence Ave. S.W., #GH060 20585; (202) 586-9892. Fax, (202) 586-3904. Gen. John M. McBroom, Director.*

Works to ensure coordinated Energy Dept. responses to energy-related emergencies. Recommends policies to mitigate the effects of energy supply crises on the United States; recommends government responses to energy emergencies.

Federal Emergency Management Agency, *500 C St. S.W. 20472; (202) 646-3923. Fax, (202) 646-3930. James Lee Witt, Director. Press, (202) 646-4600. Locator, (202) 646-2500. Disaster assistance, (800) 462-9029. Radio network, (800) 323-5248. Fax-on-demand, (202) 646-3362. Web, www.fema.gov.*

Assists state and local governments in preparing for and responding to natural, man-made, and national security-related emergencies. Develops plans and policies for hazard mitigation, preparedness planning, emergency response, and recovery. Coordinates emergency preparedness and planning for all federal agencies and departments.

Federal Emergency Management Agency, *Emergency Management Institute, 16825 S. Seton Ave., Emmitsburg, MD 21727; (301) 447-1286. Fax, (301) 447-1497. Stephen Sharrow, Superintendent (Acting). Web, www.fema.gov/home/emi/index.htm.*

Provides federal, state, and local government personnel and private organizations engaged in emergency management with technical, professional, and vocational training. Educational programs include hazard mitigation, emergency preparedness, and disaster response.

Federal Emergency Management Agency, *FEMA Operations, 500 C St. S.W. 20472 (mailing address: P.O. Box 129, Berryville, VA 22611); (202) 898-6100. Fax, (202) 898-6175. Ralph Hersko, Chief, Operations Center. Press, (202) 646-4600. Operations, (202) 646-2400. Web, www.fema.gov.*

Serves as a central point of contact for federal agencies and members of Congress for coordinating national response to disasters and emergencies.

Federal Emergency Management Agency, *Response and Recovery, 500 C St. S.W. 20472; (202) 646-3692. Fax, (202) 646-4060. Lacy E. Suiter, Executive Director. Press, (202) 646-4600. Web, www.fema.gov.*

Administers the president's disaster relief program, including disaster research, preparedness, temporary housing, funding for repair of damaged public facilities, debris removal, and hazard mitigation; provides financial and technical assistance in the event of natural or technological disasters including earthquakes; assists in developing civil emergency planning. Coordinates other federal agency disaster assistance activities.

Federal Insurance Administration *(Federal Emergency Management Agency), 500 C St. S.W., #430 20472; (202) 646-2781. Fax, (202) 646-7970. Jo Ann Howard, Administrator. Web, www.fema.gov/nfip.*

Administers federal crime and flood insurance programs, including the National Flood Insurance Program. Makes available to eligible homeowners low-cost flood and crime insurance.

Public Health and Science *(Health and Human Services Dept.), Emergency Preparedness, 12300 Twinbrook Pkwy., #360, Rockville, MD 20852; (301) 443-1167. Fax, (301) 443-5146. Robert F. Knouss, Director. Web, www.oep_ndms.dhhs.gov.*

Works with the Federal Emergency Management Agency and other federal agencies and departments to develop plans and maintain operational readiness for responding to requests for assistance during presidentially declared disasters; develops and coordinates medical equipment and training plans for catastrophic disasters; maintains logistical plans and communication networks with federal, state, and local emergency preparedness organizations.

Research and Special Programs Administration *(Transportation Dept.), Emergency Transportation, 400 7th St. S.W., #8404 20590-0001; (202) 366-5270. Fax, (202) 366-3769. William M. Medigovich, Director. Web, www.rspa.dot.gov/oet.*

Develops, coordinates, and reviews transportation emergency preparedness programs for use in emergencies affecting national defense and in emergencies caused by natural disasters and crisis situations.

Small Business Administration, *Disaster Assistance, 409 3rd St. S.W., #6050 20416; (202) 205-6734. Fax, (202) 205-7728. Bernard Kulik, Associate Administrator. Web, www.sba.gov.*

Provides victims of physical disasters with disaster and economic injury loans for homes, businesses, and personal property. Lends funds to individual homeowners, business concerns of all sizes, and nonprofit institutions to repair or replace damaged structures and furnishings, business machinery, equipment, and inventory.

U.S. Coast Guard *(Transportation Dept.), Defense Operations, 2100 2nd St. S.W. 20593; (202) 267-1502. Fax, (202) 267-4278. Capt. Keith Coddington, Chief.*

Ensures that the Coast Guard can mobilize effectively during national emergencies, including those resulting from enemy military attack. (The Coast Guard is part of the Transportation Dept. during peacetime; in certain emergency circumstances, including war, some of its functions become components of the Navy and come under the jurisdiction of the Defense Dept.)

CONGRESS

House Appropriations Committee, *Subcommittee on VA, HUD, and Independent Agencies, H143 CAP 20515; (202) 225-3241. Rep. James T. Walsh, R-N.Y., Chair; Frank Cushing, Staff Director. Web, www.house.gov/appropriations.*

Jurisdiction over legislation to appropriate funds for the Federal Emergency Management Agency.

House Armed Services Committee, *2120 RHOB 20515; (202) 225-4151. Fax, (202) 225-9077. Rep. Floyd*

FEDERAL EMERGENCY MANAGEMENT AGENCY

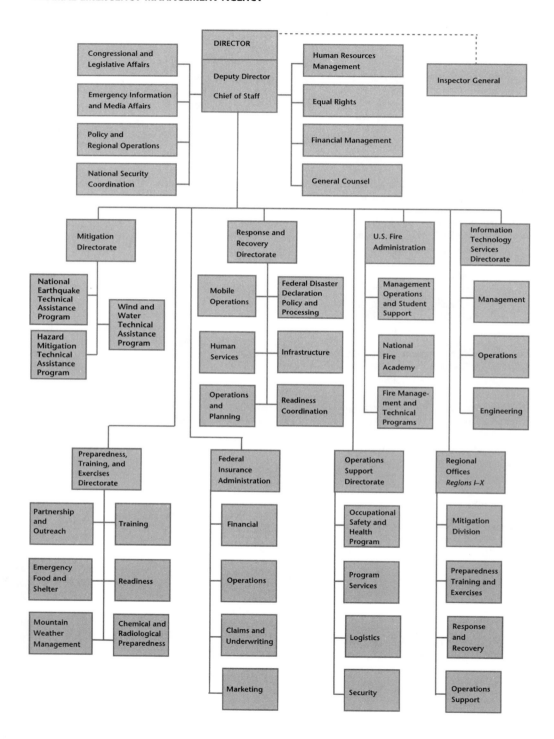

D. Spence, R-S.C., Chair; Robert S. Rangel, Staff Director. Web, www.house.gov/hasc.

Jurisdiction over legislation for emergency communications and industrial planning and mobilization.

House Armed Services Committee, *Subcommittee on Military Readiness,* 2117 RHOB 20515; (202) 225-6288. Fax, (202) 225-7102. Rep. Herbert H. Bateman, R-Va., Chair; Peter Steffes, Professional Staff Member. Web, www. house.gov/hasc.

Jurisdiction over legislation concerning civil defense, emergency mobilization of merchant fleets, and national defense stockpiles, including military, civilian, and industrial requirements.

House Banking and Financial Services Committee, *Subcommittee on Housing and Community Opportunity,* B303 RHOB 20515; (202) 225-6634. Rep. Rick A. Lazio, R-N.Y., Chair; Joseph M. Ventrone, Staff Director. Web, www.house.gov/banking.

Jurisdiction over federal flood, fire, and earthquake insurance programs; oversees activities of the insurance industry pertaining to these programs.

House Transportation and Infrastructure Committee, *Subcommittee on Oversight, Investigations, and Emergency Management,* 586 FHOB 20515; (202) 225-5504. Fax, (202) 226-4623. Rep. Tillie Fowler, R-Fla., Chair; Charles Zeigler, Chief Counsel. General e-mail, transcomm@mail.house.gov. Web, www.house.gov/transportation.

Jurisdiction over disaster relief and emergency response programs of the Federal Emergency Management Agency.

Senate Appropriations Committee, *Subcommittee on VA, HUD, and Independent Agencies,* SD-130 20510; (202) 224-7211. Sen. Christopher S. Bond, R-Mo., Chair; Jon Kamarck, Staff Director. Web, appropriations.senate. gov/vahud.

Jurisdiction over legislation to appropriate funds for the Federal Emergency Management Agency.

Senate Armed Services Committee, *Subcommittee on Readiness and Management Support,* SR-228 20510; (202) 224-3871. Sen. James M. Inhofe, R-Okla., Chair; Cord Sterling, Professional Staff Member. Web, armed_ services.senate.gov.

Jurisdiction over legislation concerning national defense stockpiles, including military, civilian, and industrial requirements. Jurisdiction over emergency preparedness legislation, including civil defense, emergency mobilization of merchant fleets, emergency communications, and industrial planning and mobilization.

Senate Banking, Housing, and Urban Affairs Committee, *Subcommittee on Housing and Transportation,* SD-534 20510; (202) 224-7391. Fax, (202) 224-5137. Sen. Wayne Allard, R-Colo., Chair; John Carson, Staff Director. Web, banking.senate.gov.

Jurisdiction over federal flood, crime, fire, and earthquake insurance programs; oversees activities of the insurance industry pertaining to these programs.

Senate Environment and Public Works Committee, *Subcommittee on Clean Air, Wetlands, Private Property, and Nuclear Safety,* SD-410 20510; (202) 224-6176. Fax, (202) 224-5167. Sen. James M. Inhofe, R-Okla., Chair; Andy Wheeler, Staff Contact. Web, epw.senate.gov.

Jurisdiction over the Federal Emergency Management Agency.

NONPROFIT

American Red Cross, *Disaster Services,* 8111 Gatehouse Rd., Falls Church, VA 22042; (703) 206-8672. Fax, (703) 206-8835. John A. Clizbe, Vice President. Web, www.redcross.org/disaster.

Chartered by Congress to administer disaster relief. Provides disaster victims with food, clothing, shelter, first aid, and medical care; promotes disaster preparedness and prevention.

International Assn. of Chiefs of Police, *Advisory Committee for Patrol and Tactical Operations,* 515 N. Washington St., Alexandria, VA 22314-2357; (703) 836-6767. Fax, (703) 836-4543. Matt Snyder, Staff Liaison. Web, www.theiacp.org.

Membership: foreign and U.S. police executives and administrators. Maintains liaison with civil defense and emergency service agencies; prepares guidelines for police cooperation with emergency and disaster relief agencies during emergencies.

Salvation Army Disaster Service, 2626 Pennsylvania Ave. N.W. 20037; (202) 756-2600. Fax, (202) 756-2663. Bruce Smith, Emergency Disaster Services Coordinator. Web, www.salvationarmyusa.org.

Provides disaster victims and rescuers with emergency support, including food, clothing, and counseling services.

Emergency Communications

AGENCIES

Air Force Dept. *(Defense Dept.), Communications and Information,* The Pentagon, #4B1060 20330-1250; (703) 695-6324. Fax, (703) 614-0156. Lt. Gen. William J. Donahue, Director. Web, www.af.mil.

Responsible for policy, planning, programming, and evaluating performance of the Air Force's C-4 system.

Army Dept. *(Defense Dept.), Information Systems for Command, Control, Communications, and Computers,* The Pentagon, #1A271 20310-0107; (703) 695-4366. Fax, (703) 695-3091. Lt. Gen. William H. Campbell, Director. Web, www.army.mil.

Oversees policy and budget for the Army's information systems and programs.

Defense Dept., *Command, Control, Communications, and Computer Systems,* The Pentagon, #2D866 20318-6000; (703) 695-6478. Fax, (703) 614-2945. Lt. Gen. John L. Woodward, Director. Web, www.defenselink.mil.

Military office that sets policy throughout the Defense Dept. for C-4 matters.

Defense Dept., *Command, Control, Communications, and Intelligence,* The Pentagon, #3E172 20301-6000; (703) 695-0348. Fax, (703) 693-8060. Arthur L. Money, Assistant Secretary. Web, www.c3i.osd.mil.

Civilian office with policy oversight for all C3I matters.

Defense Dept., *White House Communications Agency,* U.S. Naval Station—Anacostia, 2743 Defense Blvd. S.W. 20373-5815; (202) 757-5530. Fax, (202) 757-5529. Col. Dennis C. Moran (USA), Commander. Web, www. defenselink.mil.

Responsible for presidential communications.

Federal Communications Commission, *Emergency Alert System,* 445 12th St. S.W. 20554; (202) 418-1220. Fax, (202) 418-2817. John R. Winston, Assistant Chief. Web, www.fcc.gov/eb/eas.

Develops rules and regulations for the Emergency Alert System, which issues radio reports during local, state, and national emergencies, including war, natural disasters, or major accidents involving hazardous materials. Assists officials of state and local emergency communications committees.

National Communications System *(Defense Dept.),* 701 S. Courthouse Rd., Arlington, VA 22204-2199; (703) 607-6100. Fax, (703) 607-4802. Lt. Gen. David J. Kelley (USA), Manager. Information, (703) 607-6900. Web, www.disa.mil.

Ensures that the federal government has the necessary communications capabilities to permit its continued operation during a national emergency, including war; provides the Federal Emergency Management Agency with communications support as it directs the nation's recovery from a major disaster.

Navy Dept. *(Defense Dept.), Naval Computer and Telecommunications Command,* 4234 Seminary Dr. N.W., #19122 20394-5460; (202) 764-0550. Fax, (202) 764-0357. Charles G. Cooper III, Commander. Web, www.navy.mil.

Provides, operates, and maintains all Navy onshore communications resources; nontactical information resources for command, control, and administration of the Navy; and the Defense Communication System.

President's National Security Telecommunications Advisory Committee, *c/o National Communications System,* 701 S. Courthouse Rd., Arlington, VA 22204-2198; (703) 607-6221. Fax, (703) 607-4826. Janet S. Jefferson, Program Manager. Web, www.ncs.gov.

Advises the president on specific measures to improve national security telecommunications.

Industrial Planning and Mobilization

AGENCIES

Bureau of Export Administration *(Commerce Dept.), Strategic Industries and Economic Security,* 14th St. and Constitution Ave. N.W., #3876 20230; (202) 482-4506. Fax, (202) 482-5650. William Denk, Director (Acting). Web, www.bxa.doc.gov.

Administers the Defense Production Act and provides industry with information on the allocation of resources falling under the jurisdiction of the act; conducts studies on industrial mobilization for the federal government.

Defense Dept., *International Cooperation,* The Pentagon, #3A280 20301-3070; (703) 697-4172. Fax, (703) 693-2026. Alfred Volkman, Director. Web, www.acq.osd.mil/ic.

Advises the under secretary of defense on cooperative research and development, production, procurement, and follow-on support programs with foreign nations; monitors the transfer of secure technologies to foreign nations.

Defense Logistics Agency *(Defense Dept.), Defense Logistics Support Command,* 8725 John Jay Kingman Rd., Fort Belvoir, VA 22060-6221; (703) 767-1600. Fax, (703) 767-1588. Rear Adm. Daniel H. Stone (USN), Commander. Information, (703) 767-6200. Web, www.supply. dla.mil.

Oversees operations of Emergency Supply Operations Centers that acquire, maintain, and distribute items used in first-line weapons systems worldwide.

Maritime Administration *(Transportation Dept.), National Security Plans,* 400 7th St. S.W., #PI-1303

20590; (202) 366-5900. Fax, (202) 366-5904. Thomas M. P. Christensen, Director. Web, marad.dot.gov/offices/national_security.html.

Plans for the transition of merchant shipping from peacetime to wartime operations under the direction of the National Shipping Authority. (The National Shipping Authority is a stand-by organization that is activated upon the declaration of a war or other national emergency.)

Maritime Administration *(Transportation Dept.),* **Ship Operations,** *400 7th St. S.W., #2122 20590; (202) 366-1875. Fax, (202) 366-3954. William F. Trost, Director. Web, marad.dot.gov/offices/ship_operations.html.*

Maintains the National Defense Reserve Fleet, a fleet of older vessels traded in by U.S. flag operators that are called into operation during emergencies; manages and administers the Ready Reserve Force, a fleet of ships available for operation within four to twenty days, to meet the nation's sealift readiness requirements.

NONPROFIT

National Defense Industrial Assn., *2111 Wilson Blvd., #400, Arlington, VA 22201-3061; (703) 522-1820. Fax, (703) 522-1885. Lawrence F. Skibbie, President. Web, www.ndia.org.*

Membership: U.S. citizens and businesses interested in national security. Also open to individuals and businesses in nations that have defense agreements with the United States. Provides information and expertise on defense preparedness issues; works to increase public awareness of national defense preparedness through education programs; serves as a forum for dialogue between the defense industry and the government.

National Defense Transportation Assn., *50 S. Pickett St., #220, Alexandria, VA 22304-7296; (703) 751-5011. Fax, (703) 823-8761. Edward Honor, President.*

Membership: transportation service and manufacturing companies. Maintains liaison with the Defense Dept., Transportation Dept., and Federal Emergency Management Agency to prepare emergency transportation plans.

Shipbuilders Council of America, *1600 Wilson Blvd., #1000, Arlington, VA 22209; (703) 351-6734. Fax, (703) 351-6736. Allen Walker, President. Web, www.shipbuilders.org.*

Membership: commercially focused shipyards that repair and build ships, and allied industries and associations. National trade association representing the competitive shipyard industry that makes up the core shipyard industrial base in the United States. Monitors legislation and regulations.

Selective Service

AGENCIES

Selective Service System, *1515 Wilson Blvd., Arlington, VA 22209-2425; (703) 605-4010. Fax, (703) 605-4006. Willie L. Blanding Jr., Executive Director; Gil Coronado, Director. Locator, (703) 605-4000. Web, www.sss.gov.*

Supplies the armed forces with manpower when authorized; registers male citizens of the United States ages eighteen to twenty-five. In an emergency, would institute a draft and would provide alternative service assignments to men classified as conscientious objectors.

CONGRESS

House Appropriations Committee, *Subcommittee on VA, HUD, and Independent Agencies, H143 CAP 20515; (202) 225-3241. Rep. James T. Walsh, R-N.Y., Chair; Frank Cushing, Staff Director. Web, www.house.gov/appropriations.*

Jurisdiction over legislation to appropriate funds for the Selective Service System.

House Armed Services Committee, *Subcommittee on Military Personnel, 2340 RHOB 20515; (202) 225-7560. Fax, (202) 226-0789. Rep. Steve Buyer, R-Ind., Chair; John Chapla, Professional Staff Member. Web, www.house.gov/hasc.*

Jurisdiction over selective service legislation.

House Government Reform Committee, *Subcommittee on National Security, Veterans Affairs, and International Affairs, B372 RHOB 20515; (202) 225-2548. Fax, (202) 225-2382. Rep. Christopher Shays, R-Conn., Chair; Lawrence Halloran, Staff Director. Web, www.house.gov/reform.*

Oversees operations of the Selective Service System.

Senate Appropriations Committee, *Subcommittee on VA, HUD, and Independent Agencies, SD-130 20510; (202) 224-7211. Sen. Christopher S. Bond, R-Mo., Chair; Jon Kamarck, Staff Director. Web, appropriations.senate.gov/vahud.*

Jurisdiction over legislation to appropriate funds for the Selective Service System.

Senate Armed Services Committee, *Subcommittee on Personnel, SR-228 20510; (202) 224-3871. Sen. Tim Hutchinson, R-Ark., Chair. Web, armed_services.senate.gov.*

Oversees operations of the Selective Service System.

NONPROFIT

National Interreligious Service Board for Conscientious Objectors, *Center for Conscience and War, 1830*

Connecticut Ave. N.W. 20009; (202) 483-2220. Fax, (202) 483-1246. J. E. McNeil, Executive Director. General e-mail, nisbco@igc.apc.org. Web, www.nisbco.org.

Seeks to defend and extend the rights of conscientious objectors. Provides information and advocacy about the military draft and national selective service. Offers counseling and information to military personnel seeking discharge or transfer to noncombatant positions within the military.

Strategic Stockpiles

AGENCIES

Defense Dept., *Industrial Affairs*, The Pentagon, #3E1060 20301-3330; (703) 695-7178. Fax, (703) 695-4277. Jeffrey P. Bialos, Deputy Under Secretary. Web, www.acq.osd.mil.

Develops and oversees strategic and critical materials policies including oversight of the National Defense Stockpile.

Defense Logistics Agency *(Defense Dept.)*, *Defense National Stockpile Center*, 8725 John Jay Kingman Rd., #4528, Fort Belvoir, VA 22060-6223; (703) 767-5500. Fax, (703) 767-5538. Richard J. Connelly, Administrator. Web, www.dnsc.dla.mil.

Manages the national defense stockpile of strategic and critical materials. Purchases strategic materials including beryllium and newly developed high-tech alloys. Disposes of excess materials including tin, silver, industrial diamond stones, tungsten, and vegetable tannin.

Fossil Energy *(Energy Dept.)*, *Naval Petroleum and Oil Shale Reserves*, 1000 Independence Ave. S.W., #3H076 20585; (202) 586-4685. Fax, (202) 586-4446. Anton R. Dammer, Director.

Develops, conserves, operates, and maintains oil shale reserves for producing oil, natural gas, and other petroleum products.

National Institute of Standards and Technology *(Commerce Dept.)*, *Materials Science and Engineering Laboratory*, 100 Bureau Dr., MS 8500, Gaithersburg, MD 20899-8500 (mailing address: Bldg. 223, #B309, Gaithersburg, MD 20899); (301) 975-5658. Fax, (301) 975-5012. Leslie E. Smith, Director.

Advises the secretary and Congress on strategic resources issues. Conducts studies; coordinates development of departmental positions on federal policies and programs; and develops and maintains consultation program with business interests.

INTELLIGENCE AND COUNTERTERRORISM

AGENCIES

Air Force Dept. *(Defense Dept.)*, *Intelligence*, The Pentagon, #4A932 20330-1480; (703) 695-5613. Fax, (703) 697-4903. Brig. Gen. Glen Shaffer, Director. Web, www.af.mil.

Military office that directs Air Force intelligence activities and coordinates activities with other intelligence agencies.

Army Dept. *(Defense Dept.)*, *Intelligence*, The Pentagon, #1E713 20310-1000; (703) 695-3033. Fax, (703) 697-7605. Lt. Gen. Claudia J. Kennedy, Deputy Chief of Staff. Web, www.army.mil.

Military office that directs Army intelligence activities and coordinates activities with other intelligence agencies.

Central Intelligence Agency, CIA Headquarters, Langley, VA 23665; (703) 482-1100. Fax, (703) 482-6790. George J. Tenet, Director. Information, (703) 482-7677. Web, www.cia.gov.

Coordinates the intelligence functions of government agencies as they relate to national security and advises the National Security Council on those functions; gathers and evaluates intelligence relating to national security and distributes the information to government agencies in the national security field.

Criminal Division *(Justice Dept.)*, *Terrorism and Violent Crime*, 601 D St. N.W., #6500 20530; (202) 514-0849. Fax, (202) 514-8714. James S. Reynolds, Chief.

Investigates and prosecutes incidents of international terrorism involving U.S. interests, domestic violent crime, firearms, and explosives violations. Provides legal advice on federal statutes relating to murder, assault, kidnapping, threats, robbery, weapons and explosives control, malicious destruction of property, and aircraft and sea piracy.

Defense Dept., *Command, Control, Communications, and Intelligence*, The Pentagon, #3E172 20301-6000; (703) 695-0348. Fax, (703) 693-8060. Arthur L. Money, Assistant Secretary. Web, www.c3i.osd.mil.

Civilian office that advises and makes recommendations to the secretary of defense on the management of all Defense Dept. intelligence and communications programs, resources, and activities.

Defense Dept., *Intelligence Oversight*, 4035 Ridgetop Rd., #210, Fairfax, VA 22030; (703) 275-6552. Fax, (703)

275-6590. *George B. Lotz II, Assistant to the Secretary.* Web, *www.dtic.mil/atsdio.*

Responsible for the independent oversight of all Defense Dept. intelligence, counterintelligence, and related activities and for the formulation of intelligence oversight policy; reviews intelligence operations and investigates and reports on possible violations of federal law or regulations.

Defense Dept., *Special Operations and Low Intensity Conflict,* The Pentagon, #2E258 20301-2500; (703) 693-2895. Fax, (703) 693-6335. *Brian E. Sheridan, Assistant Secretary.* Web, *www.defenselink.mil.*

Serves as special staff assistant and civilian adviser to the defense secretary on matters related to special operations and international terrorism.

Defense Information Systems Agency (DISA), *(Defense Dept.), 701 S. Courthouse Rd., Arlington, VA 22204-2199; (703) 607-6100. Fax, (703) 607-4802. Lt. Gen. David J. Kelley (USA), Director. Information, (703) 607-6900.* Web, *www.disa.mil.*

Division of Command, Control, Communications, and Intelligence; the Defense Dept. agency responsible for information technology and the central manager for major portions of the defense information infrastructure. Units include the White House Communications Agency; the DISA director is also manager of the National Communications System.

Defense Intelligence Agency *(Defense Dept.),* The Pentagon, #3E258 20301-7400; (703) 695-7353. Fax, (703) 695-7336. *Vice Adm. Thomas R. Wilson, Director.* Web, *www.dia.osis.com.*

Collects and evaluates foreign military-related intelligence information to satisfy the requirements of the secretary of defense, Joint Chiefs of Staff, selected components of the Defense Dept., and other authorized agencies.

Energy Dept., *Office of Intelligence: Intelligence Support Division,* 1000 Independence Ave. S.W., #GA-301 20585; (202) 586-2610. Fax, (202) 586-0751. *Lawrence Sanchez, Director.* Web, *www.doe.gov.*

Gathers and maintains information as it relates to national security, including military applications of nuclear energy.

Federal Bureau of Investigation *(Justice Dept.),* ***International Terrorism Operations,*** 935 Pennsylvania Ave. N.W., #5222 20535; (202) 324-4664. Fax, (202) 324-4624. *Michael E. Rolince, Chief. Press, (202) 324-3691.*

Federal law enforcement agency with primary jurisdiction over the U.S. government's counterterrorism activities. Responsible for preventing, interdicting, and investigating the criminal activities of international terrorist groups and individuals.

Justice Dept., *Intelligence Policy and Review,* 950 Pennsylvania Ave. N.W., #3305 20530; (202) 514-5600. Fax, (202) 514-7858. *Frances Fragos Townsend, Counsel.* Web, *www.usdoj.gov.*

Provides the attorney general with legal advice and recommendations on national security matters. Reviews executive orders, directives, and procedures relating to the intelligence community; approves certain intelligence-gathering activities. Provides interpretations and applications of the Constitution, statutes, regulations, and directives relating to U.S. national security activities. Represents the United States before the Foreign Intelligence Surveillance Court.

Marine Corps *(Defense Dept.),* ***Intelligence,*** 2 Navy Annex 20380-1775; (703) 614-2522. Fax, (703) 614-5888. *Brig. Gen. Robert M. Shea, Director.*

Military office that directs Marine Corps intelligence activities and coordinates activities with other intelligence agencies.

National Imagery and Mapping Agency *(Defense Dept.),* 4600 Sangamore Rd., Bethesda, MD 20816; (301) 227-7300. Fax, (301) 227-3696. *Lt. Gen. James C. King, Director.* Web, *www.nima.mil.*

Combat support agency that provides imagery and geospatial information to national policymakers and military forces in support of national defense objectives; incorporates the missions and functions of the former Defense Mapping Agency, Central Imaging Office, and Defense Dissemination Program Office.

National Reconnaissance Office *(Defense Dept.),* 14675 Lee Rd., Chantilly, VA 20151-1715; (703) 808-1198. Fax, (703) 808-1171. *Keith R. Hall, Director. Press, (703) 808-1015.* Web, *www.nro.odci.gov.*

Researches, develops, and operates intelligence satellites. Gathers intelligence for various purposes, including indications and warning, monitoring of arms control agreements, military operations and exercises, and monitoring of natural disasters and other environmental issues.

National Security Agency *(Defense Dept.),* 9800 Savage Rd., Fort Meade, MD 20755-6000; (301) 688-6311. Fax, (301) 688-6198. *Lt. Gen. Kenneth A. Minihan (USAF), Director; Barbara A. McNamara, Deputy Director. Information, (301) 688-6524.* Web, *www.nsa.gov.*

Provides technical advice and services to protect classified and unclassified national security systems against exploitation through interception, unauthorized access, or related technical intelligence threats. Collects data on foreign signals and transmissions in the United States.

National Security Council (*Executive Office of the President*), **Defense Policy/Arms Control: International Economic Affairs,** *The White House 20502; (202) 456-9281. Fax, (202) 456-9280. Malcolm Lee, Director. Web, www.whitehouse.gov/WH/EOP/NSC/html/nschome.html.*

Advises the president and the National Security Adviser on all aspects of U.S. foreign policy dealing with U.S. international economic policies.

Navy Dept. (*Defense Dept.*), **Naval Intelligence,** *The Pentagon, #5C600 20350-2000; (703) 695-0124. Fax, (703) 614-0230. P. M. Ratliff, Director. Web, www.navy.mil.*

Military office that directs Navy intelligence activities and coordinates activities with other intelligence agencies.

President's Foreign Intelligence Advisory Board (*Executive Office of the President*), *Dwight D. Eisenhower Executive Office Bldg., #340 20502; (202) 456-2352. Fax, (202) 395-3403. Warren Rudman, Chair; Randy Deitering, Executive Director.*

Members appointed by the president. Assesses the quality, quantity, and adequacy of foreign intelligence collection and of counterintelligence activities by all government agencies; advises the president on matters concerning intelligence and national security.

State Dept., *Counterterrorism,* *2201 C St. N.W., #2507 20520; (202) 647-9892. Fax, (202) 647-0221. Michael A. Sheehan, Coordinator. Press, (202) 647-8682. Web, www.state.gov.*

Implements U.S. counterterrorism policy and coordinates activities with foreign governments; responds to terrorist acts; works to promote a stronger counterterrorism stance worldwide.

State Dept., *Diplomatic Security Bureau,* *2201 C St. N.W., #6316 20520; (202) 647-6290. Fax, (202) 647-0953. David G. Carpenter, Assistant Secretary. Web, www.state.gov.*

Conducts Anti-Terrorism Assistance Program, which provides training to foreign governments fighting terrorism.

State Dept., *Intelligence and Research,* *2201 C St. N.W., #6531 20520-6531; (202) 647-9177. Fax, (202) 736-4688. J. Stapleton Roy, Assistant Secretary. Web, www.state.gov.*

Coordinates foreign policy-related research, analysis, and intelligence programs for the State Dept. and other federal agencies.

Transportation Dept., *Intelligence and Security,* *400 7th St. S.W., #10401 20590; (202) 366-6535. Fax, (202) 366-7261. Rear Adm. J. A. Kinghorn (USCG), Director. Web, www.dot.gov.*

Advises the secretary on transportation intelligence and security policy. Acts as liaison with the intelligence community, federal agencies, corporations, and interest groups; administers counterterrorism strategic planning processes.

U.S. Coast Guard (*Transportation Dept.*), *Intelligence,* *2100 2nd St. S.W. 20593-0001; (202) 267-2126. Fax, (202) 267-6954. Dennis L. Hager, Chief. Web, www.uscg.mil.*

Manages all Coast Guard intelligence activities and programs.

CONGRESS

House Armed Services Committee, *Subcommittee on Military Procurement,* *2340 RHOB 20515; (202) 225-4440. Fax, (202) 226-0105. Rep. Duncan Hunter, R-Calif., Chair; Steve Thompson, Professional Staff Member. Web, www.house.gov/hasc.*

Jurisdiction over military intelligence activities affecting national security (jurisdiction shared with the House Permanent Select Committee on Intelligence).

House Government Reform Committee, *Subcommittee on National Security, Veterans Affairs, and International Affairs,* *B372 RHOB 20515; (202) 225-2548. Fax, (202) 225-2382. Rep. Christopher Shays, R-Conn., Chair; Lawrence Halloran, Staff Director. Web, www.house.gov/reform.*

Oversight responsibilities for the operations of agencies related to intelligence and security, including the Defense Dept., Central Intelligence Agency, National Security Agency, and Defense Intelligence Agency.

House International Relations Committee, *2170 RHOB 20515; (202) 225-5021. Fax, (202) 225-2035. Rep. Benjamin A. Gilman, R-N.Y., Chair; Richard J. Garon Jr., Chief of Staff. General e-mail, HIRC@mail.house.gov. Web, www.house.gov/international_relations.*

Jurisdiction over legislation on international terrorism, including counterterrorism policy, embassy security, and the Anti-Terrorism Assistance Program (jurisdiction shared with House Judiciary Committee).

House Judiciary Committee, *2138 RHOB 20515; (202) 225-3951. Fax, (202) 225-7682. Rep. Henry J. Hyde, R-Ill., Chair; Thomas Mooney, Chief of Staff. General e-mail, Judiciary@mail.house.gov. Web, www.house.gov/judiciary.*

Jurisdiction over legislation on control of international terrorism (shared with House International Relations Committee).

House Permanent Select Committee on Intelligence, H405 CAP 20515; (202) 225-4121. Fax, (202) 225-1991. Rep. Porter J. Goss, R-Fla., Chair; John I. Millis, Staff Director.

Studies, makes recommendations, and proposes legislation on intelligence agencies' activities and policies, including the attorney general's implementation of guidelines for Federal Bureau of Investigation intelligence activities and the conduct of electronic surveillance for foreign intelligence purposes; oversees the Central Intelligence Agency, National Security Agency, Defense Intelligence Agency, and other intelligence activities of the U.S. government to ensure conformity with the U.S. Constitution and laws; authorizes budgets for the intelligence community.

Senate Armed Services Committee, *Strategic Forces Subcommittee,* SR-228 20510; (202) 224-3871. Sen. Wayne Allard, R-Colo., Chair; Eric Thoemmes, Professional Staff Member. Web, armed_services.senate.gov.

Jurisdiction over military intelligence activities affecting national security.

Senate Foreign Relations Committee, SD-450 20510; (202) 224-4651. Fax, (202) 224-0836. Sen. Jesse Helms, R-N.C., Chair; Steve Biegun, Staff Director. Web, foreign.senate.gov.

Oversight of foreign intelligence activities. Jurisdiction over international counterterrorism policy, including the Anti-Terrorism Assistance Program (jurisdiction shared with the Senate Judiciary Committee).

Senate Judiciary Committee, SD-224 20510; (202) 224-5225. Fax, (202) 224-9102. Sen. Orrin G. Hatch, R-Utah, Chair; Manus Cooney, Chief Counsel. Web, judiciary.senate.gov.

Jurisdiction over legislation relating to the control of international terrorism (jurisdiction shared with the Senate Foreign Relations Committee).

Senate Select Committee on Intelligence, SH-211 20510; (202) 224-1700. Fax, (202) 224-1772. Sen. Richard C. Shelby, R-Ala., Chair; Nick Rostow, Staff Director. Web, intelligence.senate.gov.

Studies, makes recommendations, and proposes legislation on intelligence agencies' activities, policies, and funds; oversees the Central Intelligence Agency, National Security Agency, Defense Intelligence Agency, the intelligence activities of the Federal Bureau of Investigation, and other intelligence operations of the U.S. government to ensure conformity with the U.S. Constitution and laws; authorizes appropriations for the intelligence community. Oversight of directives and procedures governing intelligence activities affecting the rights of Americans abroad.

INTERNATIONAL ORGANIZATIONS

INTERPOL, *Washington Office,* 600 E St. N.W. 20530-1022 (mailing address: INTERPOL-USNCB U.S. Justice Dept. 20530); (202) 616-9000. Fax, (202) 616-8400. Edgar A. Adamson, Chief. Web, www.usdoj.gov/usncb.

U.S. national central bureau for INTERPOL; interacts in international investigations of terrorism on behalf of U.S. police. Serves as liaison between foreign and U.S. law enforcement agencies. Headquarters office sponsors forums enabling foreign governments to discuss counterterrorism policy. (Headquarters in Lyons, France.)

NONPROFIT

American Society for Industrial Security, 1625 Prince St., Alexandria, VA 22314; (703) 519-6200. Fax, (703) 519-6299. Michael Stack, Executive Director. Web, www.asisonline.org.

Membership: security administrators from around the world who protect the assets and personnel of private and public organizations. Sponsors seminars and workshops on counterterrorism.

Assn. of Former Intelligence Officers, 6723 Whittier Ave., #303A, McLean, VA 22101; (703) 790-0320. Fax, (703) 790-0264. Roy K. Jonkers, Executive Director. Information, (800) 234-6717. General e-mail, afio@his.com. Web, www.afio.com.

Membership: former military and civilian intelligence officers. Encourages public support for intelligence agencies; supports increased intelligence education in colleges and universities.

Center for National Security Studies, Gelman Library, 2130 H St. N.W., #701 20037; (202) 994-7060. Fax, (202) 994-1446. Kate Martin, Director. Web, gwis.circ.gwu.edu/~cnss.

A project of the Fund for Peace. Monitors and conducts research on civil liberties and intelligence and national security, including activities of the Central Intelligence Agency and the Federal Bureau of Investigation.

National Security Archive, Gelman Library, 2130 H St. N.W., #701 20037; (202) 994-7000. Fax, (202) 994-7005. Thomas Blanton, Executive Director. General e-mail, nsarchiv@gwu.edu. Web, www.gwu.edu/~nsarchiv.

Research institute and library that provides information on U.S. foreign policy and national security affairs. Maintains collection of declassified and unclassified national security documents. Archive open to the public by appointment.

Internal Security

See also Defense Trade and Technology (this chapter); Emergency Preparedness (this chapter)

AGENCIES

Air Force Dept. *(Defense Dept.), Special Investigations,* The Pentagon, #4E1081 20330-1140; (703) 697-1955. Fax, (703) 695-4346. Col. Charles P. Azukas, Director. Web, www.af.mil.

Develops and implements policy with regard to investigations of foreign intelligence, terrorism, and other crimes as they relate to Air Force security.

Army Dept. *(Defense Dept.), Counterintelligence and Human Intelligence,* 2511 Jefferson Davis Hwy., 9th Floor, Arlington, VA 22202; (703) 601-1962. Fax, (703) 601-0730. Col. Glenn M. DeSoto (USA), Director (Acting). Web, www.dami.army.pentagon.mil/offices/dami_ch.html.

Responsible for policy formation, planning, programming, oversight, and representation for counterintelligence, human intelligence, and security countermeasures of the Army.

Defense Dept., *Counterintelligence and Investigations,* The Pentagon, #3C260 20301-6000; (703) 614-2195. Fax, (703) 695-8217. David A. Burtt II, Director. Web, www.defenselink.mil.

Conducts counterintelligence activities to protect against espionage and other foreign intelligence activities, sabotage, international terrorist activities, and assassination efforts of foreign powers, organizations, or persons directed against the Defense Dept.

Defense Security Service *(Defense Dept.),* 1340 Braddock Pl., Alexandria, VA 22314-1651; (703) 325-5308. Fax, (703) 325-3916. Charles J. Cunningham Jr., Director. Web, www.dss.mil.

Administers programs to protect classified government information and resources, including the Personnel Security Investigations and Defense Industrial Security programs. Serves the Defense Dept. and other executive departments and agencies.

Federal Bureau of Investigation *(Justice Dept.), National Security,* 935 Pennsylvania Ave. N.W., #7110 20535; (202) 324-4880. Neil J. Gallagher, Assistant Director. Information, (202) 324-3000. Press, (202) 324-2727.

Investigates violations of federal law relating to sabotage, espionage, treason, sedition, and other matters affecting national security. Conducts counterespionage activities against hostile intelligence services and their agents in the United States.

Justice Dept., *Internal Security,* 1400 New York Ave. N.W., 9th Floor 20530; (202) 514-1187. Fax, (202) 514-2836. John J. Dion, Chief (Acting). Web, www.usdoj.gov.

Enforces criminal statutes relating to national security, including treason, espionage, sedition, sabotage, and the export of military and strategic commodities and technology; supervises registration requirements of the Foreign Agents Registration Act.

National Archives and Records Administration, *Information Security Oversight,* 700 Pennsylvania Ave. N.W., #18N 20408-0001; (202) 219-5250. Fax, (202) 219-5385. Steven Garfinkel, Director. General e-mail, isoo@arch1.nara.gov.

Administers governmentwide national security classification program under which information is classified, declassified, and safeguarded for national security purposes.

National Security Agency *(Defense Dept.),* 9800 Savage Rd., Fort Meade, MD 20755-6000; (301) 688-6311. Fax, (301) 688-6198. Lt. Gen. Kenneth A. Minihan (USAF), Director; Barbara A. McNamara, Deputy Director. Information, (301) 688-6524. Web, www.nsa.gov.

Maintains and operates the Defense Dept.'s Computer Security Center; ensures communications and computer security within the government.

Navy Dept. *(Defense Dept.), Naval Criminal Investigative Service,* Washington Navy Yard, Bldg. 111, 716 Sicard St. S.E. 20388-5380; (202) 433-8800. Fax, (202) 433-9619. David L. Brant, Director. Information, (202) 433-9624. Web, www.ncis.navy.mil.

Handles investigative responsibilities for naval counterintelligence and security; processes security clearances for the Navy.

State Dept., *Countermeasures and Information Security,* 2121 Virginia Ave. N.W. 20037; (202) 663-0538. Fax, (202) 663-0653. Wayne S. Rychak, Deputy Assistant Secretary. Web, www.state.gov.

Safeguards all electronic information and systems in the State Dept., both domestically and abroad. Also responsible for Physical Security Program for State Dept. officials and for the Diplomatic Courier Service.

State Dept., *Diplomatic Security Service: Intelligence and Threat Analysis,* 2121 Virginia Ave. N.W. 20037; (202) 663-0787. Fax, (202) 663-0852. Joe D. Morton, Director. Web, www.state.gov.

Oversees the safety and security of all U.S. government employees at U.S. embassies and consulates abroad. Responsible for the safety of the secretary of state and all foreign dignitaries. Conducts background investigations of potential government employees, investigates passport and visa fraud, and warns government employees of any counterintelligence dangers they might encounter.

State Dept., *Foreign Missions*, 2201 C St. N.W., #2238 20520; (202) 647-4554. Fax, (202) 647-1919. Theodore A. Strickler, Deputy Director. Web, www.state.gov.

Authorized to control the numbers, locations, and travel privileges of foreign diplomats and diplomatic staff in the United States.

🪖 MILITARY INSTALLATIONS

AGENCIES

Defense Dept., *Environmental Security*, 3400 Defense Pentagon, #3E792 20301-3400; (703) 695-6639. Fax, (703) 693-7011. Sherri W. Goodman, Deputy Under Secretary. Web, www.acq.osd.mil/ens.

Integrates environmental, safety, and occupational health considerations into U.S. defense and economic policies. Works to ensure responsible performance in defense operations, to maintain quality installations, to reduce the costs of complying with environmental laws, and to clean up past contamination.

Defense Dept., *International Security Affairs*, The Pentagon, #4E838 20301-2400; (703) 695-4351. Fax, (703) 697-7230. Franklin D. Kramer, Assistant Secretary. Web, www.defenselink.mil.

Negotiates and monitors defense cooperation agreements, including base rights, access and prepositioning, exchange programs, and status of forces agreements with foreign governments in assigned geographic areas of responsibility.

CONGRESS

House Armed Services Committee, *Subcommittee on Military Installations and Facilities*, 2340 RHOB 20515; (202) 225-7120. Fax, (202) 226-0789. Rep. Joel Hefley, R-Colo., Chair; Philip Grone, Professional Staff Member. Web, www.house.gov/hasc.

Jurisdiction over legislation on military base operations and closings, military construction, military housing, and military real estate leasing and buying.

Senate Armed Services Committee, *Subcommittee on Readiness and Management Support*, SR-228 20510; (202) 224-3871. Sen. James M. Inhofe, R-Okla., Chair; Cord Sterling, Professional Staff Member. Web, armed_services.senate.gov.

Jurisdiction over legislation on military base operations and closings, military construction, military housing, and military real estate leasing and buying.

Base Closings/Economic Impact

AGENCIES

Air Force Dept. *(Defense Dept.)*, *Base Realignment and Transition*, The Pentagon, #5D973 20330-1660; (703) 695-6766. Fax, (703) 693-9707. Lt. Col. Will Selden, Chief. Web, www.af.mil.

Military office that plans for the closing of Air Force bases.

Air Force Dept. *(Defense Dept.)*, *Bases and Units*, The Pentagon, #4B267 20330-1260; (703) 697-7356. Fax, (703) 697-5143. Lt. Col. Chris M. Hazen, Chief. Web, www.af.mil.

Manages Air Force bases and units worldwide.

Air Force Dept. *(Defense Dept.)*, *SAF/MII*, 1660 Air Force Pentagon, #4C940 20330-1660; (703) 695-3592. Fax, (703) 693-7568. Jimmy G. Dishner, Deputy Assistant Secretary. Web, www.af.mil.

Civilian office that plans and reviews the closing of Air Force bases.

Army Dept. *(Defense Dept.)*, *Installations and Housing*, The Pentagon, #3E581 20310-0110; (703) 697-8161. Fax, (703) 614-7394. Paul W. Johnson, Deputy Assistant Secretary. Web, www.army.mil.

Civilian office that manages all Army installations and reviews the closing of Army facilities.

Army Dept. *(Defense Dept.)*, *Policy and Program Development*, 200 Stovall St., #4S43, Alexandria, VA 22322-0300; (703) 325-9650. Fax, (703) 325-2601. Elizabeth B. Throckmorton, Chief (Acting). Web, www.army.mil.

Military office responsible for employment policies to assist civilian personnel in cases of Defense Dept. program changes, including base closings.

Defense Dept., *Base Closure and Community Reinvestment*, 400 Army-Navy Dr., #200, Arlington, VA 22202-2884; (703) 604-6020. Fax, (703) 604-5843. Paul J. Dempsey, Director. Web, www.defenselink.mil.

Civilian office that helps community officials develop strategies and coordinate plans to alleviate the economic effect of major defense program changes, including base closings, reductions in forces, and contract cutbacks. Assists communities where defense activities are being expanded. Serves as the staff for the Economic Adjustment Committee, an interagency group that coordinates federal defense economic adjustment activities.

Defense Dept., *Civilian Assistance and Re-Employment (CARE)*, 1400 Key Blvd., B-200, Arlington, VA 22209-5144; (703) 696-1799. Fax, (703) 696-5416. G. Jorge Araiza, Chief (Acting). Web, www.defenselink.mil.

Manages transition programs for Defense Dept. civilians, including placement, early retirement, and transition assistance programs.

Marine Corps *(Defense Dept.), Land Use and Military Construction,* 2 Navy Annex 20380-1775; (703) 695-8202. Fax, (703) 695-8550. Richard P. Hobbs, Head.

Military office that reviews studies on base closings.

Navy Dept. *(Defense Dept.), Installations and Facilities,* The Pentagon, #4E765 20350-1000; (703) 588-6686. Fax, (703) 588-8431. Duncan Holaday, Deputy Assistant Secretary. Web, www.navy.mil.

Civilian office that assists in planning Navy energy, real estate, and housing programs.

Navy Dept. *(Defense Dept.), Naval Facilities Engineering Command,* Washington Navy Yard, 1322 Patterson Ave. S.E., #1000 20374-5065; (202) 685-9499. Fax, (202) 685-1463. Rear Adm. Louis M. Smith (USN), Commander. Web, www.navy.mil.

Military command that plans, designs, and constructs facilities for Navy and other Defense Dept. activities around the world and manages Navy public works, utilities, environmental, real estate, and housing programs.

Commissaries, PXs, and Service Clubs

AGENCIES

Air Force Dept. *(Defense Dept.), Defense Commissary Liaison Office,* The Pentagon, #1B657G 20330-1000; (703) 695-3265. Fax, (703) 695-3650. Dan W. Sclater, Legislative Liaison; Harry Witt, Operations Liaison. Web, www.af.mil.

Serves as a liaison for defense commissary services. Monitors legislation and regulations.

Army Dept. *(Defense Dept.), Troop Support,* The Pentagon, #1E583 20310-0500; (703) 695-2711. Fax, (703) 614-4031. Larry W. Matthews, Chief. Web, www.army.mil.

Military office that monitors Army operations and policies regarding clothing, equipment, food, field, and commissary services.

Defense Dept., *Army and Air Force Exchange, Washington Office,* 2511 Jefferson Davis Hwy., #11600, Arlington, VA 22202-3922; (703) 604-7523. Fax, (703) 604-7510. Robert Ellis, Director. Web, www.aafes.com.

Coordinates Army and Air Force PX matters with other Defense Dept. offices. (Headquarters in Miami.)

Defense Dept., *Morale, Welfare, and Recreation,* The Pentagon 20301-4000; (703) 697-7197. Fax, (703) 614-3375. Janis White, Executive Director. Web, www.defenselink.mil.

Directs the operations and policies of armed forces commissaries, PXs, and service clubs.

Navy Dept. *(Defense Dept.), Manpower and Reserve Affairs,* The Pentagon 20350-1000; (703) 697-2180. Fax, (703) 614-4103. Carolyn H. Becraft, Assistant Secretary. Web, www.navy.mil.

Civilian office that develops policies for Navy and Marine Corps commissaries, exchanges, and service clubs and reviews their operations.

Navy Dept. *(Defense Dept.), Navy Exchange Service Command, Washington Office,* 1213 Jefferson Davis Hwy, #1400, Arlington, VA 22202; (703) 607-0072. Fax, (703) 607-1167. Alexander Douvres, Director. Web, www.navy-nex.com.

Civilian office that serves as a liaison between the Navy Exchange Service Command, Navy Supply Systems Command, Congress, and the Defense Dept. (Headquarters located in Virginia Beach, Va.)

CONGRESS

House Armed Services Committee, *Panel on Morale, Welfare, and Recreation,* 2120 RHOB 20515; (202) 226-2843. Fax, (202) 226-0789. Rep. John M. McHugh, R-N.Y., Chair; Tom Hawley, Staff Director. Web, www.house.gov/hasc.

Oversight responsibility on military commissaries, PXs, and service clubs.

Senate Armed Services Committee, *Subcommittee on Personnel,* SR-228 20510; (202) 224-3871. Sen. Tim Hutchinson, R-Ark., Chair; Charles S. Abell, Professional Staff Member. Web, armed_services.senate.gov.

Jurisdiction over legislation on military commissaries, PXs, and service clubs.

NONPROFIT

American Logistics Assn., 1133 15th St. N.W., #640 20005; (202) 466-2520. Fax, (202) 296-4419. Alan Burton, President. Web, www.ala-natl.org.

Membership: suppliers of military commissaries, PXs, and service clubs. Acts as liaison between the Defense Dept. and service contractors; monitors legislation and testifies on issues of interest to members.

International Military Community Executives Assn., 1125 Duke St., Alexandria, VA 22314; (703) 548-0093. Fax, (703) 548-0095. Donald Pavlik, Executive Director. Web, www.imcea.com.

Provides members with education and training seminars on government affairs, public relations, hospitality and recreation management, and communication. Operates certification program.

United Service Organizations, *Washington Navy Yard, 1008 Eberle Pl. S.E., #301 20374-5096; (202) 610-5700. Fax, (202) 610-5699. Carl E. Mundy Jr., President. Web, www.uso.org.*

Voluntary civilian organization chartered by Congress. Provides military personnel and their families in the United States and overseas with social, educational, and recreational programs.

Construction, Housing, and Real Estate

AGENCIES

Air Force Dept. *(Defense Dept.), Civil Engineering, Headquarters USAF/ILE, The Pentagon 20330-1260; (703) 607-0200. Fax, (703) 604-0610. Maj. Gen. Ernest O. Robbins II, Director. Web, www.af.mil.*

Military office that plans and directs construction of Air Force facilities (except housing) in the United States and overseas.

Air Force Dept. *(Defense Dept.), Housing, The Pentagon 20330-1260; (703) 601-0478. Fax, (703) 604-2484. Col. Emmitt G. Smith, Director. Web, www.af.mil.*

Military office that plans and manages construction of Air Force housing on military installations in the United States and overseas.

Air Force Dept. *(Defense Dept.), Real Estate Agency, 112 Luke Ave. #104, AFREA/DR, Bolling Air Force Base 20332-8020; (202) 767-4275. Fax, (202) 767-4384. William E. Edwards, Director. Web, www.af.mil.*

Acquires, manages, and disposes of land for the Air Force worldwide. Maintains a complete land and facilities inventory; establishes instructions and operating procedures.

Air Force Dept. *(Defense Dept.), SAF/MII, 1660 Air Force Pentagon, #4C940 20330-1660; (703) 695-3592. Fax, (703) 693-7568. Jimmy G. Dishner, Deputy Assistant Secretary. Web, www.af.mil.*

Civilian office that plans and reviews construction policies and programs of Air Force military facilities (including the Military Construction Program), housing programs, and real estate buying, selling, and leasing in the United States.

Army Corps of Engineers *(Defense Dept.), 20 Massachusetts Ave. N.W., #8228 20314-1000; (202) 761-0001. Fax, (202) 761-4463. Lt. Gen. Joe N. Ballard (USACE), Chief of Engineers. Web, www.usace.army.mil.*

Military office that establishes policy and designs, directs, and manages civil works and military construction projects of the Army Corps of Engineers; directs the Army's real estate leasing and buying for military installations and civil works projects.

Army Dept. *(Defense Dept.), Army Housing, DAIM-FDH, 7701 Telegraph Rd., Alexandria, VA 22315-3802; (703) 428-6401. Fax, (703) 428-8359. George F. McKimmie, Chief. Web, www.hqda.army.mil.*

Military office that plans, directs, and administers the construction and maintenance of Army family housing. Also responsible for unaccompanied personnel.

Army Dept. *(Defense Dept.), Installations and Housing, The Pentagon, #3E581 20310-0110; (703) 697-8161. Fax, (703) 614-7394. Paul W. Johnson, Deputy Assistant Secretary. Web, www.army.mil.*

Civilian office that reviews construction of Army military facilities, housing programs, and the buying and leasing of real estate in the United States and overseas.

Defense Dept., *Installation Management, 400 Army-Navy Dr., #206, Arlington, VA 22202-2884; (703) 604-5774. Fax, (703) 604-5934. Steve Kleiman, Director. Web, www.defenselink.mil.*

Develops Defense Dept. policy for acquisition, management, and disposal of military real property. Ensures responsiveness of military physical plant to the changing needs of the military; seeks to improve business and management processes on military installations; monitors Defense Dept. experiment with decentralized management of military commands.

Marine Corps *(Defense Dept.), Facilities, 3250 Catlin Ave., #235, Quantico, VA 22134-5001; (703) 784-2331. Fax, (703) 784-2332. Lt. Col. K. H. Leeman, Director. Web, www.usmc.mil.*

Control point for the Marine Corps divisions of facilities maintenance, public works, support, family housing, bachelor housing, and natural resources and environmental affairs.

Marine Corps *(Defense Dept.), Land Use and Military Construction, 2 Navy Annex 20380-1775; (703) 695-8202. Fax, (703) 695-8550. Richard P. Hobbs, Head.*

Military office responsible for military construction and the acquisition, management, and disposal of Marine Corps real property.

Navy Dept. *(Defense Dept.), Installations and Facilities, The Pentagon, #4E765 20350-1000; (703) 588-6686. Fax, (703) 588-8431. Duncan Holaday, Deputy Assistant Secretary. Web, www.navy.mil.*

Civilian office that monitors and reviews construction of Navy military facilities and housing and the buying and leasing of real estate in the United States and overseas.

Navy Dept. *(Defense Dept.), Naval Facilities Engineering Command,* Washington Navy Yard, 1322 Patterson Ave. S.E., #1000 20374-5065; (202) 685-9499. Fax, (202) 685-1463. Rear Adm. Louis M. Smith (USN), Commander. Web, www.navy.mil.

Military command that plans, designs, and constructs facilities for Navy and other Defense Dept. activities around the world and manages Navy public works, utilities, environmental, real estate, and housing programs.

Navy Dept. *(Defense Dept.), Real Estate,* Washington Navy Yard, 1322 Patterson Ave. S.E., #1000 20374-5065; (202) 685-9202. Fax, (202) 685-1585. Howard D. Kelsey, Director. Web, www.navy.mil.

Military office that directs the Navy's real estate leasing and buying for military installations.

U.S. Coast Guard *(Transportation Dept.), Housing Programs,* 2100 2nd St. S.W., #5313, G-WPM-4 20593-0001; (202) 267-2223. Fax, (202) 267-4862. Herbert Levin, Chief.

Provides temporary housing for active personnel and their families.

CONGRESS

House Appropriations Committee, *Subcommittee on Military Construction,* B300 RHOB 20515; (202) 225-3047. Fax, (202) 225-3099. Rep. David L. Hobson, R-Ohio, Chair; Elizabeth G. Dawson, Staff Director. Web, www.house.gov/appropriations.

Jurisdiction over legislation to appropriate funds for military construction, including family housing and NATO infrastructure.

Senate Appropriations Committee, *Subcommittee on Military Construction,* SD-140 20510; (202) 224-7204. Sen. Conrad Burns, R-Mont., Chair; Sid Ashworth, Staff Director. Web, appropriations.senate.gov/milcon.

Jurisdiction over legislation to appropriate funds for military construction, including family housing and NATO infrastructure.

🖼 PROCUREMENT, ACQUISITION, AND LOGISTICS

See also Defense Trade and Technology (this chapter); Federal Contracts and Procurement (chap. 10)

AGENCIES

Air Force Dept. *(Defense Dept.), Acquisition,* 1060 Air Force Pentagon 20330-1060; (703) 697-6361. Fax, (703) 693-6400. Lawrence J. Delaney, Assistant Secretary. Web, www.af.mil.

Civilian office that directs and reviews Air Force procurement policies and programs.

Air Force Dept. *(Defense Dept.), Contracting,* The Pentagon 20330-1060; (703) 588-7004. Fax, (703) 588-1067. Timothy A. Beyland, Deputy Assistant Secretary (Acting). Web, www.af.mil.

Develops, implements, and enforces contracting policies on Air Force acquisitions worldwide, including research and development services, weapons systems, logistics services, and operational contracts.

Air Force Dept. *(Defense Dept.), Global Power Programs,* The Pentagon 20330-1060; (703) 588-7170. Fax, (703) 588-6196. Maj. Gen. Raymond P. Huot, Director. Web, www.af.mil.

Military office that directs Air Force acquisition and development programs within the tactical arena.

Army Dept. *(Defense Dept.), Operations Research,* 102 Army Pentagon, #2E660 20310-0102; (703) 695-0083. Fax, (703) 693-3897. Walter W. Hollis, Deputy Under Secretary. Web, www.odusa-or.army.mil.

Establishes policy for operations research and systems analysis activities for the Army. Supports acquisition review committees within the Army and the Defense Dept.

Army Dept. *(Defense Dept.), Procurement,* The Pentagon 20310-0103; (703) 695-2488. Fax, (703) 614-9505. Kenneth J. Oscar, Deputy Assistant Secretary. Web, www.army.mil.

Directs and reviews Army procurement policies and programs.

Criminal Division *(Justice Dept.), Federal Procurement Fraud,* 1400 New York Ave. N.W., #3100 20530 (mailing address: P.O. Box 28188 20038); (202) 616-0440. Fax, (202) 514-0152. Barbara Corprew, Deputy Chief.

Interdepartmental unit that investigates fraud in federal procurement contracting.

Defense Contract Audit Agency *(Defense Dept.),* 8725 John Jay Kingman Rd., #2135, Fort Belvoir, VA 22060-6219; (703) 767-3200. Fax, (703) 767-3267. William H. Reed, Director; Michael J. Thibault, Deputy Director, (703) 767-3272. Web, www.dcaai.mil.

Performs all contract audits for the Defense Dept. Provides Defense Dept. personnel responsible for procurement and contract administration with accounting and financial advisory services regarding the negotiation, administration, and settlement of contracts and subcontracts.

Defense Dept., *Acquisition Reform,* 3600 Defense Pentagon, #3E1034 20301-3600; (703) 695-6413. Fax, (703) 695-2760. Stan Z. Soloway, Deputy Under Secretary. Web, www.acq.osd.mil/ar.

Seeks to improve and streamline Defense Dept. policies and practices governing the development and procurement of defense materiel and weapons systems, including associated education and training. Evaluates defense reform initiatives.

Defense Dept., *Acquisition, Technology, and Logistics,* The Pentagon, #3E933 20301-3010; (703) 695-2381. Fax, (703) 693-2576. Jacques S. Gansler, Under Secretary. Web, www.acq.osd.mil.

Formulates and directs policy relating to the department's purchasing system. Oversees all defense procurement and acquisition programs.

Defense Dept., *Armed Services Board of Contract Appeals,* 5109 Leesburg Pike, Falls Church, VA 22041-3208; (703) 681-8500. Fax, (703) 681-8535. Paul Williams, Chair. Web, www.defenselink.mil.

Adjudicates disputes arising under Defense Dept. contracts.

Defense Dept., *Defense Acquisition Regulations Council,* The Pentagon 20301-3062; (703) 602-0131. Fax, (703) 602-0350. Eleanor R. Spector, Director. Web, www.defenselink.mil.

Develops procurement regulations for the Defense Dept.

Defense Dept., *Logistics,* The Pentagon 20301-3500; (703) 697-5530. Fax, (703) 693-0555. Roger W. Kallock, Deputy Under Secretary. Web, www.defenselink.mil.

Formulates and implements department policies and programs regarding spare parts management. Helps determine Defense Dept. spare parts requirements and oversees acquisition of spare parts.

Defense Dept., *Operational Test and Evaluation,* The Pentagon 20301-1700; (703) 697-3654. Fax, (703) 693-5248. Philip E. Coyle III, Director. Web, www.dote.osd.mil.

Ensures that major acquisitions, including weapons systems, are operationally effective and suitable prior to full-scale investment. Provides the secretary of defense and Congress with independent assessment of these programs.

Defense Logistics Agency *(Defense Dept.),* 8725 John Jay Kingman Rd., #2533, Fort Belvoir, VA 22060-6221; (703) 767-5200. Fax, (703) 767-5207. Lt. Gen. Henry T. Glisson (USA), Director; Rear Adm. Raymond Archer,

Deputy Director. Information, (703) 767-6200. Web, www.dla.mil.

Administers defense contracts; acquires, stores, and distributes food, clothing, medical, and other supplies used by the military services and other federal agencies; administers programs related to logistical support for the military services; and assists military services with developing, acquiring, and using technical information and defense materiel and disposing of materiel no longer needed.

Defense Systems Management College *(Defense Dept.),* 9820 Belvoir Rd., #G38, Fort Belvoir, VA 22060-5565; (703) 805-3360. Fax, (703) 805-2639. Brig. Gen. Frank J. Anderson (USAF), Commandant. Registrar, (703) 805-2227. Web, www.dsmc.dsm.mil.

Academic institution that offers courses to military and civilian personnel who specialize in acquisition and procurement. Conducts research to support and improve management of defense systems acquisition programs.

Marine Corps *(Defense Dept.),* *Installations and Logistics, Contracts Division,* 2 Navy Annex 20380-1775; (703) 695-6326. Fax, (703) 695-6382. Philip E. Zanfagna Jr., Assistant Deputy Chief of Staff.

Military office that directs Marine Corps procurement programs.

Navy Dept. *(Defense Dept.),* *Acquisition and Business Management,* 2211 S. Clark Pl., #578, Arlington, VA 22202-3738; (703) 602-2338. Fax, (703) 602-4643. Rear Adm. G. H. Jenkins Jr., Deputy. Web, www.navy.mil.

Directs and reviews Navy acquisition and procurement policy.

Navy Dept. *(Defense Dept.),* *Logistics,* 2000 Navy Pentagon 20350-2000; (703) 695-2154. Fax, (703) 695-1117. Vice Adm. James F. Amerault, Deputy Chief. Web, www.navy.mil.

Military office that directs overall Navy logistics policy.

Navy Dept. *(Defense Dept.),* *Military Sealift Command,* Washington Navy Yard, Bldg. 210 20398-5400; (202) 685-5001. Fax, (202) 685-5020. Rear Adm. Gordon S. Holder, Commander. Web, www.msc.navy.mil.

Transports Defense Dept. and other U.S. government cargo by sea; operates ships that maintain supplies for the armed forces and scientific agencies; transports fuels for the Energy Dept.

U.S. Coast Guard *(Transportation Dept.),* *Acquisition,* 2100 2nd St. S.W., #5120 20593-0001; (202) 267-2007. Fax, (202) 267-4279. Rear Adm. Roy Casto, Chief. Web, www.uscg.mil.

Administers all procurement made through the Acquisition Contract Support division.

U.S. Coast Guard *(Transportation Dept.), Logistics Management,* 2100 2nd St. S.W. 20593-0001; (202) 267-1407. Fax, (202) 267-4516. Capt. Leonard Bosma, Chief. Web, www.uscg.mil.

Sets policy and procedures for the procurement, distribution, maintenance, and replacement of materiel and personnel.

CONGRESS

General Accounting Office, *National Security and International Affairs,* 441 G St. N.W., #4035 20548; (202) 512-2800. Fax, (202) 512-7686. Henry L. Hinton, Assistant Comptroller General.

Independent, nonpartisan agency in the legislative branch. Audits, analyzes, and evaluates Defense Dept. acquisition programs; makes unclassified reports available to the public.

House Armed Services Committee, *Subcommittee on Military Procurement,* 2340 RHOB 20515; (202) 225-4440. Fax, (202) 226-0105. Rep. Duncan Hunter, R-Calif., Chair; Steve Thompson, Professional Staff Member. Web, www.house.gov/hasc.

Jurisdiction over legislation on military procurement (excluding construction) and military contract services.

House Armed Services Committee, *Subcommittee on Military Readiness,* 2117 RHOB 20515; (202) 225-6288. Fax, (202) 225-7102. Rep. Herbert H. Bateman, R-Va., Chair; Peter Steffes, Professional Staff Member. Web, www.house.gov/hasc.

Jurisdiction over legislation on naval petroleum reserves and leasing of capital equipment.

House Government Reform Committee, *Subcommittee on National Security, Veterans Affairs, and International Affairs,* B372 RHOB 20515; (202) 225-2548. Fax, (202) 225-2382. Rep. Christopher Shays, R-Conn., Chair; Lawrence Halloran, Staff Director. Web, www.house.gov/reform.

Oversight of defense procurement.

Senate Armed Services Committee, *SR-228 20510;* (202) 224-3871. Sen. John W. Warner, R-Va., Chair; Les Brownlee, Staff Director. Web, armed_services.senate.gov.

Jurisdiction over legislation on military procurement (excluding construction), naval petroleum reserves, and military contract services.

NONPROFIT

Contract Services Assn., *1200 G St. N.W., #510 20005;* (202) 347-0600. Fax, (202) 347-0608. Gary Engebretson, President. Web, www.csa-dc.org.

Membership: companies that, under contract, provide federal, state, and local governments and other agencies with various technical and support services (particularly in defense, space, transportation, environment, energy, and health care). Analyzes the process by which the government awards contracts to private firms. Monitors legislation and regulations.

Council of Defense and Space Industry Assns., *2111 Wilson Blvd., #400, Arlington, VA 22201-3061; (703) 247-9490. Fax, (703) 243-8539. Timothy Olsen, Administrative Officer.*

Makes recommendations on federal procurement policies. Interests include estimating and accounting systems, contract clauses, defective pricing data, industrial security, management systems control, patents and technical data, property acquisition and control, and contract cost principles.

Electronic Industries Assn., *Government Division,* 2500 Wilson Blvd., #400, Arlington, VA 22201-3834; (703) 907-7500. Fax, (703) 907-7501. Dan C. Heinemeier, Vice President. Web, www.eia.org.

Membership: companies engaged in the research, development, integration, or manufacture of electronic equipment or services for government applications. Monitors federal policy and practices in acquiring electronic products and services; represents the industry's views on acquisition regulations in federal agencies; serves as the focal point through which the government communicates with the electronics industry on procurement policy and other matters affecting the business-government relationship.

National Defense Transportation Assn., *50 S. Pickett St., #220, Alexandria, VA 22304-7296; (703) 751-5011. Fax, (703) 823-8761. Edward Honor, President.*

Membership: transportation users, manufacturers, and mode carriers; information technology firms; and related military, government, and civil interests worldwide. Promotes a strong U.S. transportation capability through coordination of private industry, government, and the military.

17 Science and Technology

GENERAL POLICY

See also Science and Mathematics Education (chap. 6)

AGENCIES

Office of Science *(Energy Dept.)*, 1000 Independence Ave. S.W., #7B058 20585; (202) 586-5430. Fax, (202) 586-4120. James Decker, Director

Advises the secretary on the department's physical science and energy research and development programs; the management of the nonweapons multipurpose laboratories; and education and training activities required for basic and applied research activities. Manages the department's high energy physics, nuclear physics, fusion energy sciences, basic energy sciences, health and environmental research, and computational and technology research. Provides and operates the large-scale facilities required for research in the physical and life sciences.

National Museum of Natural History *(Smithsonian Institution)*, 10th St. and Constitution Ave. N.W. 20560-0106; (202) 357-2664. Fax, (202) 357-4779. Robert W. Fry, Director. Web, www.nmnh.si.edu.

Conducts research and maintains exhibitions and collections relating to the natural sciences. Collections are organized into seven research and curatorial departments: anthropology, botany, entomology, invertebrate zoology, mineral sciences, paleobiology, and vertebrate zoology.

National Science and Technology Council *(Executive Office of the President)*, Dwight D. Eisenhower Executive Office Bldg., #435 20502; (202) 456-6100. Fax, (202) 456-6026. Neal Lane, Chair. General e-mail, information@ostp.eop.gov. Web, www.whitehouse.gov/WH/EOP/OSTP/NSTC/html/charge.html.

Coordinates research and development activities and programs that involve more than one federal agency. Activities concern biotechnology; earth sciences; human subjects; international science; engineering and technology; life sciences; food, agriculture, and forestry; and research, computing, materials, and radiation policy coordination.

National Science Board *(National Science Foundation)*, 4201 Wilson Blvd., #1220, Arlington, VA 22230; (703) 306-2000. Fax, (703) 306-0181. Eamon M. Kelly, Chair; Marta Cehelsky, Executive Officer. Information, (703) 306-1234. Web, www.nsf.gov.

Formulates policy for the National Science Foundation; advises the president on national science policy.

National Science Foundation, 4201 Wilson Blvd., #1205, Arlington, VA 22230; (703) 306-1234. Fax, (703) 306-0109. Rita R. Colwell, Director, (703) 306-1000. TTY, (703) 306-0090. Publications, (301) 947-2722. Government Affairs, (703) 306-1070. General e-mail, info@nsf.gov. Web, www.nsf.gov.

Sponsors scientific and engineering research; develops and helps implement science and engineering education programs; fosters dissemination of scientific information; promotes international cooperation within the scientific community; and assists with national science policy planning.

National Science Foundation, *Science Resources Studies*, 4201 Wilson Blvd., #965, Arlington, VA 22230; (703) 306-1780. Fax, (703) 306-0510. Linda T. Carlson, Director. Web, www.nsf.gov/sbe/srs.

Projects national scientific and technical resources and requirements.

Office of Management and Budget (OMB), *(Executive Office of the President)*, *Energy and Science*, New Executive Office Bldg., #8002 20503; (202) 395-3404. Fax, (202) 395-3049. Kathleen Peroff, Deputy Associate Director. Web, www.whitehouse.gov/omb.

Assists and advises the OMB director in budget preparation; analyzes and evaluates programs in space and science, including the activities of the National Science Foundation and the National Aeronautics and Space Administration; coordinates OMB science, energy, and space policies and programs.

Office of Science and Technology Policy *(Executive Office of the President)*, Dwight D. Eisenhower Executive Office Bldg., #424 20502; (202) 456-7116. Fax, (202) 456-6021. Neal Lane, Director. General e-mail, information@ostp.pop.gov. Web, www.whitehouse.gov/WH/EOP/OSTP/html/OSTP_Home.html.

Serves as the president's principal adviser on science and technology policy. Assists with review of research and development budgets of federal agencies, including the departments of Energy, Commerce, and Health and Human Services; the National Science Foundation; and the National Aeronautics and Space Administration. Works with the Office of Management and Budget, other executive offices, Congress, and federal agencies to develop research programs consistent with the president's science and technology goals. Administers the Federal Coordinating Council for Science, Engineering, and Technology.

Office of Science and Technology Policy *(Executive Office of the President)*, *Science*, Dwight D. Eisenhower Executive Office Bldg., #436 20502; (202) 456-6130. Fax,

(202) 456-6027. Arthur Bienenstock, Associate Director. Web, www.whitehouse.gov/WH/EOP/OSTP/html/ OSTP_Home.html.

Analyzes policies and advises the president on biological, physical, social, and behavioral sciences and on engineering; coordinates executive office and federal agency actions related to these issues. Evaluates the effectiveness of government science programs.

Office of Science and Technology Policy *(Executive Office of the President)*, **Technology,** *Dwight D. Eisenhower Executive Office Bldg., #423 20502; (202) 456-6046. Fax, (202) 456-6023. Duncan Moore, Associate Director. Web, www.whitehouse.gov/WH/EOP/OSTP/html/ OSTP_Home.html.*

Analyzes policies and advises the president on technology and related issues of physical, computational, and space sciences; coordinates executive office and federal agency actions related to these issues.

Technology Administration *(Commerce Dept.)*, *14th St. and Constitution Ave. N.W., #4824 20230; (202) 482-1575. Fax, (202) 501-2492. Dr. Cheryl L. Shavers, Under Secretary. Information, (202) 482-8321. Web, www.ta.doc. gov.*

Seeks to enhance U.S. competitiveness by encouraging the development of new technologies and the conversion of technological knowledge into products and services. Oversees the National Institute of Standards and Technology and the National Technical Information Service.

CONGRESS

General Accounting Office, *Resources, Community, and Economic Development, 441 G St. N.W., #2T23 20548; (202) 512-3200. Fax, (202) 512-8774. Keith Fultz, Assistant Comptroller General. Web, www.gao.gov.*

Independent, nonpartisan agency in the legislative branch. Reviews and analyzes issues involving federal science, technology, and public policy; audits and oversees the National Science Foundation and the Office of Science and Technology Policy; serves as liaison with the National Academy of Sciences and the National Academy of Engineering; audits and evaluates the performance of the Commerce Dept. (including the National Oceanic and Atmospheric Administration and the National Institute of Standards and Technology); makes reports available to the public.

House Administration Committee, *1309 LHOB 20515; (202) 225-8281. Fax, (202) 225-9957. Rep. Bill Thomas, R-Calif., Chair; Cathy Abernathy, Staff Director. Web, www.house.gov/cha.*

Jurisdiction over legislation related to and operations of the Smithsonian Institution (jurisdiction shared with House Government Reform Committee).

House Appropriations Committee, *Subcommittee on Commerce, Justice, State, and Judiciary, H309 CAP 20515; (202) 225-3351. Rep. Harold Rogers, R-Ky., Chair; Jim Kulikowski, Staff Director. Web, www.house.gov/ appropriations.*

Jurisdiction over legislation to appropriate funds for the Commerce Dept., including the National Oceanic and Atmospheric Administration, the National Institute of Standards and Technology, and the National Technical Information Service.

House Appropriations Committee, *Subcommittee on Interior, B308 RHOB 20515; (202) 225-3081. Fax, (202) 225-9069. Rep. Ralph Regula, R-Ohio, Chair; Deborah A. Weatherly, Clerk. Web, www.house.gov/appropriations.*

Jurisdiction over legislation to appropriate funds for the Smithsonian Institution and the U.S. Geological Survey.

House Appropriations Committee, *Subcommittee on VA, HUD, and Independent Agencies, H143 CAP 20515; (202) 225-3241. Rep. James T. Walsh, R-N.Y., Chair; Frank Cushing, Staff Director. Web, www.house.gov/ appropriations.*

Jurisdiction over legislation to appropriate funds for the National Science Foundation and the Office of Science and Technology Policy.

House Science Committee, *2320 RHOB 20515; (202) 225-6371. Fax, (202) 226-0891. Rep. F. James Sensenbrenner Jr., R-Wis., Chair; Todd Schultz, Chief of Staff. Web, www.house.gov/science.*

Jurisdiction over legislation on scientific research and development; science scholarships, programs, policy, resources, employment, and exploration; and technology.

House Science Committee, *Subcommittee on Basic Research, B374 RHOB 20515; (202) 225-7858. Fax, (202) 225-7815. Rep. Nick Smith, R-Mich., Chair; Steve Eule, Staff Director. Web, www.house.gov/science.*

Jurisdiction over legislation on the National Science Foundation and the Office of Science and Technology Policy; science research and development programs; math, science, and engineering education; international scientific cooperation; and nuclear research and development projects.

House Science Committee, *Subcommittee on Technology, 2319 RHOB 20515; (202) 225-8844. Fax, (202)*

225-4438. Rep. Constance A. Morella, R-Md., Chair; Jeffrey Grove, Staff Director. Web, www.house.gov/science.

Jurisdiction over technology policy (including technology transfer), cooperative research and development, patent and intellectual property policy, biotechnology, and recombinant DNA research. Legislative jurisdiction over the National Institute of Standards and Technology and the National Technical Information Service.

Senate Appropriations Committee, *Subcommittee on Commerce, Justice, State, and Judiciary, S-146A CAP 20510; (202) 224-7277. Sen. Judd Gregg, R-N.H., Chair; Jim Morhard, Clerk. Web, appropriations.senate.gov/ commerce.*

Jurisdiction over legislation to appropriate funds for the Commerce Dept., including the National Oceanic and Atmospheric Administration, National Institute of Standards and Technology, and the National Technical Information Service.

Senate Appropriations Committee, *Subcommittee on Interior, SD-131 20510; (202) 224-7233. Sen. Slade Gorton, R-Wash., Chair; Bruce Evans, Clerk. Web, appropriations.senate.gov/interior.*

Jurisdiction over legislation to appropriate funds for the Smithsonian Institution and the U.S. Geological Survey.

Senate Appropriations Committee, *Subcommittee on VA, HUD, and Independent Agencies, SD-130 20510; (202) 224-7211. Sen. Christopher S. Bond, R-Mo., Chair; Jon Kamarck, Staff Director. Web, appropriations.senate. gov/vahud.*

Jurisdiction over legislation to appropriate funds for the National Science Foundation and the Office of Science and Technology Policy.

Senate Commerce, Science, and Transportation Committee, *SD-508 20510; (202) 224-5115. Fax, (202) 224-1259. Sen. John McCain, R-Ariz., Chair; Mark Buse, Staff Director. Web, commerce.senate.gov.*

Jurisdiction over legislation on the Commerce Dept. and its scientific activities and science aspects of the Office of Science and Technology Policy.

Senate Commerce, Science, and Transportation Committee, *Subcommittee on Science, Technology, and Space, SH-428 20510; (202) 224-8172. Fax, (202) 228-0326. Sen. Bill Frist, R-Tenn., Chair; Floyd DesChamps, Professional Staff Member. Web, commerce.senate.gov.*

Oversight of the National Institute of Standards and Technology and other departments and agencies with an emphasis on science. Jurisdiction over scientific research and development; science fellowships, scholarships,

grants, programs, policy, resources, employment, and exploration; and technology. Jurisdiction over international scientific cooperation, technology transfer, and cooperative research and development (including global change and the space station); resolutions of joint cooperation with foreign governments on science and technology.

Senate Health, Education, Labor, and Pensions Committee, *SD-428 20510; (202) 224-5375. Fax, (202) 228-5044. Sen. James M. Jeffords, R-Vt., Chair; Mark Powden, Staff Director. TTY, (202) 224-1975. Web, labor. senate.gov.*

Oversees and has jurisdiction over legislation on the National Science Foundation.

Senate Rules and Administration Committee, *SR-305 20510; (202) 224-6352. Fax, (202) 224-3036. Sen. Mitch McConnell, R-Ky., Chair; Tamara Somerville, Staff Director. Web, rules.senate.gov.*

Jurisdiction over legislation concerning the Smithsonian Institution and the U.S. Botanic Garden.

NONPROFIT

ACIL, *1629 K St. N.W., #400 20006; (202) 887-5872. Fax, (202) 887-0021. Joan Walsh Cassedy, Executive Director. Laboratory Referral Service, (202) 887-5872. Web, www. acil.org.*

Membership: independent commercial laboratories. Promotes professional and ethical business practices in providing analysis, testing, and research in engineering, microbiology, analytical chemistry, life sciences, and environmental geosciences.

American Assn. for Laboratory Accreditation, *5301 Buckeystown Pike, #350, Frederick, MD 21704; (301) 644-3248. Fax, (301) 662-2974. Peter Unger, President. Web, www.a2la.org.*

Accredits and monitors laboratories that test construction materials and perform acoustics and vibration, biological, chemical, electrical, geotechnical, nondestructive, environmental, mechanical, metals and metal fasteners, calibration, asbestos, radon, and thermal testing. Registers laboratory quality systems.

American Assn. for the Advancement of Science, *1200 New York Ave. N.W. 20005; (202) 326-6640. Fax, (202) 371-9526. Richard S. Nicholson, Executive Officer. Information, (202) 326-6400. Web, www.aaas.org.*

Membership: scientists, affiliated scientific organizations, and individuals interested in science. Fosters scientific education; monitors and seeks to influence public policy and public understanding of science and technology; encourages scientific literacy among minorities and women. Sponsors national and international symposia, workshops, and meetings; publishes *Science* magazine.

American Assn. for the Advancement of Science, *Scientific Freedom, Responsibility, and Law Program,* *1200 New York Ave. N.W. 20005; (202) 326-6792. Fax, (202) 289-4950. Mark S. Frankel, Director. Web, www. aaas.org/spp/dspp/SFRL/SFRL.htm.*

Focuses on professional ethics and law in science and engineering and on the social implications of science and technology. Collaborates with other professional groups on these activities; provides technical assistance to organizations developing codes of ethics or educational programs on research integrity.

Assn. for Women in Science, *1200 New York Ave. N.W., #650 20005; (202) 326-8940. Fax, (202) 326-8960. Catherine Didion, Executive Director. General e-mail, awis@awis.org. Web, www.awis.org.*

Promotes equal opportunity for women in scientific professions; provides career and funding information. Interests include international development.

Council of Scientific Society Presidents, *1155 16th St. N.W. 20036; (202) 872-6230. Fax, (202) 872-4079. Martin Apple, President. General e-mail, cssp@acs.org. Web, www.science-presidents.org.*

Membership: presidents, presidents-elect, and immediate past presidents of professional scientific societies and federations. Supports professional science education. Serves as a forum for discussion of emerging scientific issues, formulates national science policy, and develops the nation's scientific leadership.

Federation of American Scientists, *307 Massachusetts Ave. N.E. 20002; (202) 546-3300. Fax, (202) 675-1010. Jeremy J. Stone, President. General e-mail, fas@fas.org. Web, www.fas.org.*

Conducts studies and monitors legislation on issues and problems related to science and technology, especially U.S. nuclear arms policy, energy, arms transfer, and civil aerospace issues.

George C. Marshall Institute, *1730 K St. N.W., #905 20006; (202) 296-9655. Fax, (202) 296-9714. Jeffrey T. Salmon, Executive Director. General e-mail, info@ marshall.org. Web, www.marshall.org.*

Analyzes the technical and scientific aspects of public policy issues; produces publications on environmental science, space, national security, and technology policy.

Government-University-Industry Research Round-table, *2101 Constitution Ave. N.W., #F02014 20418;*

(202) 334-3486. Fax, (202) 334-1505. Thomas H. Moss, Executive Director. Web, www4.national-academy.org.

Forum sponsored by the National Academy of Sciences, National Academy of Engineering, and Institute of Medicine. Provides scientists, engineers, and members of government, academia, and industry with an opportunity to discuss ways of improving the infrastructure for science and technology research.

National Academy of Sciences, *2101 Constitution Ave. N.W. 20418; (202) 334-2000. Fax, (202) 334-2419. Bruce M. Alberts, President; Jack Halpern, Vice President, (202) 334-2151. Library, (202) 334-2125. Press, (202) 334-2138. Publications, (800) 624-6242; in Washington, (202) 334-3313. General e-mail, news@nas.edu. Web, www.nas.edu.*

Congressionally chartered independent organization that advises the federal government on questions of science, technology, and health. Library open to the public by appointment. (Affiliated with the National Academy of Engineering, the Institute of Medicine, and the National Research Council.)

National Geographic Society, *Committee for Research and Exploration,* *1145 17th St. N.W. 20036-4688; (202) 857-7161. Fax, (202) 429-5729. Peter H. Raven, Chair. Web, www.nationalgeographic.com.*

Sponsors basic research grants in the sciences, including anthropology, archeology, astronomy, biology, botany, ecology, physical and human geography, geology, oceanography, paleontology, and zoology. To apply for grants, mail one- to two-page prospectus of project, estimated budget, and curriculum vitae.

National Research Council, *2101 Constitution Ave. N.W. 20418; (202) 334-2000. Fax, (202) 334-2419. Bruce M. Alberts, President; Jack Halpern, Vice President, (202) 334-2151. Library, (202) 334-2125. Press, (202) 334-2138. Publications, (800) 624-6242; in Washington, (202) 334-3313. General e-mail, news@nas.edu. Web, www. nationalacademies.org/nrc.*

Serves as the principal operating agency of the National Academy of Sciences, National Academy of Engineering, and Institute of Medicine. Program units focus on physical, social, and life sciences; applications of science including medicine, transportation, and education; international affairs; and U.S. government policy. Library open to the public by appointment.

SAMA Group of Assns., *225 Reinekers Lane, #625, Alexandria, VA 22314-2875; (703) 836-1360. Fax, (703) 836-6644. Mike Duff, Executive Director.*

Membership: manufacturers and distributors of high technology scientific and industrial instruments and laboratory apparatus. Works to increase worldwide demand for products. (Affiliated with the Analytical and Life Science Systems Assn., the Opto-Precision Instrument Assn., and the Laboratory Products Assn.)

Society of Research Administrators, *1200 19th St. N.W., #300 20036-2412; (202) 857-1141. Fax, (202) 828-6049. Brian Russo, Membership Coordinator. General e-mail, sra@dc.sba.com. Web, sra.rams.com.*

Membership: scientific and medical research administrators in the United States and other countries. Advances public understanding of the profession; offers professional development services; sponsors mentoring and awards programs. Monitors legislation and regulations.

Data, Statistics, and Reference

AGENCIES

National Aeronautics and Space Administration (NASA), *National Space Science Data Center, Goddard Space Flight Center, Code 633, Greenbelt, MD 20771; (301) 286-7355. Fax, (301) 286-1771. Joseph H. King, Head. Web, nssdc.gsfc.nasa.gov.*

Acquires, catalogs, and distributes NASA mission data to the international space science community, including research organizations, universities, and other interested organizations worldwide. Provides software tools and network access to promote collaborative data analysis. (Mail data requests to above address, attention: Code 633.4/Request Coordination Office, or phone [301] 286-6695.)

National Aeronautics and Space Administration, *Space Science Data Operations, Goddard Space Flight Center, Code 630, Greenbelt, MD 20771; (301) 286-7354. Fax, (301) 286-1771. James L. Green, Chief. Information, (301) 286-6695. Web, ssdoo.gsfc.nasa.gov.*

Develops and operates systems for processing, archiving, and disseminating space physics and astrophysics data.

National Institute of Standards and Technology *(Commerce Dept.), Information Services, 100 Bureau Dr., Stop 2500, Gaithersburg, MD 20899-2500; (301) 975-2786. Fax, (301) 869-8071. Mary-Diedre Coraggio, Director (Acting). Reference desk, (301) 975-3052. Web, nvl.nist.gov.*

Conducts publications program for the institute and maintains a research information center, which includes material on engineering, chemistry, physics, mathematics, and the materials and computer sciences.

National Institute of Standards and Technology *(Commerce Dept.), Measurement Services, 820 W. Dia-*

mond Ave., Gaithersburg, MD 20899 (mailing address: Bldg. 820, #306, MS 2000, Gaithersburg, MD 20899); (301) 975-8424. Fax, (301) 971-2183. Richard F. Kayser, Director. Web, www.nist.gov.

Disseminates physical, chemical, and engineering measurement standards and provides services to ensure accurate and compatible measurements, specifications, and codes on a national and international scale.

National Institute of Standards and Technology *(Commerce Dept.), Standard Reference Data, 820 W. Diamond Ave., Bldg. 820, #113, Gaithersburg, MD 20899; (301) 975-2200. Fax, (301) 926-0416. John R. Rumble Jr., Chief. Information and publications, (301) 975-2208. General e-mail, srdata@nist.gov. Web, www.nist.gov/srd.*

Collects and disseminates critically evaluated physical, chemical, and materials properties data in the physical sciences and engineering for use by industry, government, and academic laboratories. Develops databases in a variety of formats, including disk, CD-ROM, online, and magnetic tape.

National Institute of Standards and Technology *(Commerce Dept.), Statistical Engineering, 820 W. Diamond Ave., #353, Gaithersburg, MD 20899; (301) 975-2839. Fax, (301) 990-4127. Keith R. Eberhardt, Chief (Acting). Web, www.nist.gov/itl/div898.*

Promotes within industry and government the use of effective statistical techniques for planning analysis of experiments in the physical sciences; interprets experiments and data collection programs.

National Museum of American History *(Smithsonian Institution), Library, 14th St. and Constitution Ave. N.W., MRC 630 20560; (202) 357-2414. Fax, (202) 357-4256. Rhoda Ratner, Chief Librarian. Web, www.si.edu/nmah/.*

Collection includes materials on the history of science and technology, with concentrations in engineering, transportation, and applied science. Maintains collection of trade catalogs and materials about expositions and world fairs. Open to the public by appointment.

National Oceanic and Atmospheric Administration (NOAA), *(Commerce Dept.), Library and Information Services, 1315 East-West Hwy., SSMC3, 2nd Floor, Silver Spring, MD 20910; (301) 713-2607. Fax, (301) 713-4598. Janice A. Beattie, Director. Reference service, (301) 713-2600. General e-mail, reference@nodc.noaa.gov. Web, www.lib.noaa.gov.*

Collection includes reports, journals, monographs, photographs, and microforms on atmospheric and oceanic science. Maintains bibliographic database of other NOAA libraries, an online service, and reference materials on CD-ROM. Makes interlibrary loans; open to the public.

National Oceanic and Atmospheric Administration *(Commerce Dept.), National Environmental Satellite, Data, and Information Service,* *1335 East-West Hwy., Silver Spring, MD 20910; (301) 713-3578. Fax, (301) 713-1249. Gregory W. Withee, Assistant Administrator. Web, www.nesdis.noaa.gov.*

Acquires and disseminates global environmental (marine, atmospheric, solid earth, and solar-terrestrial) data. Operates the following data facilities: National Climatic Data Center, Asheville, N.C.; National Geophysical Data Center, Boulder, Colo.; and National Oceanographic Data Center, Washington, D.C. Maintains comprehensive data and information referral service.

National Oceanic and Atmospheric Administration *(Commerce Dept.), National Oceanographic Data Center,* *1315 East-West Hwy., SSMC3, 4th Floor, Silver Spring, MD 20910-3282; (301) 713-3270. Fax, (301) 713-3300. Vacant, Director; Kurt Schneble, Deputy Director. Information and requests, (301) 606-4549. General e-mail, services@nodc.noaa.gov. Web, www.noaa.gov.*

Offers a wide range of oceanographic data on the Web, disk, CD-ROM, and hard copy; provides research scientists with data processing services; prepares statistical summaries and graphical data products. (Fee charged for some services.)

National Technical Information Service *(Commerce Dept.), 5285 Port Royal Rd., #200F, Springfield, VA 22161; (703) 605-6400. Fax, (703) 605-6715. Ron R. Lawson, Director. TTY, (703) 605-6043. Sales center, (703) 605-6000; rush orders, (800) 553-6847. Web, www.ntis.gov.*

Distribution center that catalogs and sells U.S. and foreign government-sponsored research, development, and scientific engineering reports and other technical analyses prepared by federal and local government agencies. Offers microfiche and computerized bibliographic search services. Online database available through commercial vendors and in machine-readable form through lease agreement.

Smithsonian Institution, *Central Reference and Loan Services, 10th St. and Constitution Ave. N.W., MRC 154 20560; (202) 357-2139. Fax, (202) 786-2443. Martin A. Smith, Chief Librarian. TTY, (202) 357-2328.*

Maintains collection of general reference, biographical, and interdisciplinary materials; serves as an information resource on institution libraries, a number of which have collections in scientific subjects, including horticulture, botany, science and technology, and anthropology.

Smithsonian Institution, *Dibner Library of the History of Science and Technology, 14th St. and Constitution Ave. N.W., NMAH 5016/MRC 630 20560; (202) 357-1577. Fax, (202) 633-9102. William E. Baxter, Head, Special Collections. Web, www.sil.si.edu.*

Collection includes major holdings in the history of science and technology dating from the fifteenth to the twentieth centuries. Extensive collections in natural history, archeology, almanacs, physical and mathematical sciences, and scientific instrumentation. Open to the public by appointment.

U.S. Geological Survey *(Interior Dept.), Earth Science Information Center, 507 National Center, Reston, VA 20192-1507; (703) 648-5920. Fax, (703) 648-5548. Susan Russell-Robinson, Chief. U.S. maps, (888) 275-8747. Web, www.usgs.gov.*

Collects, organizes, and distributes cartographic, geographic, hydrologic, and other earth science information; offers maps, reports, and other publications, digital cartographic data, aerial photographs, and space imagery and manned spacecraft photographs for sale. Acts as clearinghouse on cartographic and geographic data.

U.S. Geological Survey *(Interior Dept.), Library, 12201 Sunrise Valley Dr., MS 950, Reston, VA 20192; (703) 648-4305. Fax, (703) 648-6373. Nancy Blair, Chief Librarian (Acting). Web, library.usgs.gov.*

Maintains collection of books, periodicals, serials, maps, and technical reports on geology, mineral and water resources, mineralogy, paleontology, petrology, soil and environmental sciences, and physics and chemistry as they relate to earth sciences. Open to the public; makes interlibrary loans.

CONGRESS

General Accounting Office (GAO), *Document Distribution Center, 441 G St. N.W. 20548 (mailing address: P.O. Box 37050 20013); (202) 512-6000. Fax, (202) 512-6061. Angela Childs, Supervisor. Press, (202) 512-4800. Locator, (202) 512-3000. General e-mail, info@www.gao.gov. Web, www.gao.gov.*

Provides information to the public on many federal programs. GAO publications and information about GAO publications are available upon request.

Library of Congress, *Science, Technology, and Business, 10 1st St. S.E. 20540-4750; (202) 707-5664. Fax, (202) 707-1925. William J. Sittig, Chief. Science reading room, (202) 707-6401. Technical reports, (202) 707-5655. Web, 1cweb.loc.gov/rr/scitech.*

Offers reference service by telephone, by correspondence, and in person. Maintains a collection of more than three million technical reports.

NONPROFIT

American Statistical Assn., *1429 Duke St., Alexandria, VA 22314; (703) 684-1221. Fax, (703) 684-2037. Ray Waller, Executive Director. General e-mail, asainfo@ amstat.org. Web, www.amstat.org.*

Membership: individuals interested in statistics and related quantitative fields. Advises government agencies on statistics and methodology in agency research; promotes development of statistical techniques for use in business, industry, finance, government, agriculture, and science.

Commission on Professionals in Science and Technology, *1200 New York Ave. N.W., #390 20005; (202) 326-7080. Fax, (202) 842-1603. Eleanor Babco, Executive Director. Web, www.cpst.org.*

Membership: scientific societies, corporations, academicians, and individuals. Analyzes and publishes data on scientific and engineering human resources in the United States. Interests include employment of minorities and women, salary ranges, and supply and demand of scientists and engineers.

International Programs

See also Information and Exchange Programs (chap. 13)

AGENCIES

International Trade Administration *(Commerce Dept.), Technology and Aerospace Industries, 14th St. and Constitution Ave. N.W., #2800A 20230; (202) 482-1872. Fax, (202) 482-0856. Ellis R. Mottur, Deputy Assistant Secretary. Web, www.ita.doc.gov.*

Conducts analyses and competitive assessments of high-tech industries, including aerospace, telecommunications, computer and business equipment, microelectronics, and medical equipment and instrumentation. Develops trade policies for these industries, negotiates market access for U.S. companies, assists in promoting exports through trade missions, shows, and fairs in major overseas markets.

National Institute of Standards and Technology *(Commerce Dept.), International and Academic Affairs, Route I-270 and Quince Orchard Rd., Administration Bldg., #A505, Gaithersburg, MD 20899; (301) 975-4119. Fax, (301) 975-3530. B. Stephen Carpenter, Director. Web, www.nist.gov/oiaa/oiaa1.htm.*

Represents the institute in international functions; coordinates programs with foreign institutions; assists scientists from foreign countries who visit the institute for consultation. Administers a postdoctoral research associates program.

National Oceanic and Atmospheric Administration *(Commerce Dept.), National Environmental Satellite, Data, and Information Service, 1335 East-West Hwy., Silver Spring, MD 20910; (301) 713-3578. Fax, (301) 713-1249. Gregory W. Withee, Assistant Administrator. Web, www.nesdis.noaa.gov.*

Acquires and disseminates global environmental data: marine, atmospheric, solid earth, and solar-terrestrial. Participates, with National Meteorological Center, in the World Weather Watch Programme developed by the World Meteorological Organization. Manages U.S. civil earth-observing satellite systems and atmospheric, oceanographic, geophysical, and solar data centers. Provides the public, businesses, and government agencies with environmental data and information products and services.

National Science Foundation, *International Programs, 4201 Wilson Blvd., #935, Arlington, VA 22230; (703) 306-1710. Fax, (703) 306-0476. Pierre M. Perrolle, Director. Web, www.nsf.gov/sbe/int.*

Coordinates and manages the foundation's international scientific activities and cooperative research and exchange programs; promotes new partnerships between U.S. scientists and engineers and their foreign colleagues; provides support for U.S. participation in international scientific organizations.

National Weather Service *(National Oceanic and Atmospheric Administration), National Center for Environmental Prediction, 5200 Auth Rd., Camp Springs, MD 20746; (301) 763-8016. Fax, (301) 763-8434. Louis W. Uccellini, Director. Web, www.ncep.noaa.gov.*

The National Center for Environmental Prediction and the National Environmental Satellite, Data, and Information Service are part of the World Weather Watch Programme developed by the United Nations' World Meteorological Organization. Collects data and exchanges it with other nations; provides other national weather service offices, private meteorologists, and government agencies with products, including forecast guidance products.

Office of Science and Technology Policy *(Executive Office of the President), National Security and International Affairs, Dwight D. Eisenhower Executive Office Bldg., #494 20502; (202) 456-2894. Fax, (202) 456-6028. Neal Lane, Director. Web, www.whitehouse.gov/WH/EOP/ OSTP/html/OSTP_Home.html.*

Advises the president on international science and technology matters as they affect national security; coordinates international science and technology initiatives at the interagency level.

Smithsonian Institution, *International Relations,* *1100 Jefferson Dr. S.W., #3123, MRC 705 20560; (202) 357-4282. Fax, (202) 786-2557. Francine C. Berkowitz, Director.*

Fosters the development and coordinates the international aspects of Smithsonian scientific activities; facilitates basic research in the natural sciences and encourages international collaboration among individuals and institutions.

State Dept., *Oceans and International Environmental and Scientific Affairs, 2201 C St. N.W., #7831 20520-7818; (202) 647-1554. Fax, (202) 647-0217. David Sandalow, Assistant Secretary. Press, (202) 647-3486. Web, www.state.gov.*

Formulates and implements policies and proposals for U.S. international scientific, technological, environmental, oceanic and marine, arctic and Antarctic, and space programs; coordinates international science and technology policy with other federal agencies.

State Dept., *Scientific Programs, 2201 C St. N.W., #5336 20520; (202) 647-2752. Fax, (202) 647-8902. Raymond E. Wanner, Deputy Director. Web, www.state.gov.*

Oversees U.S. participation in international scientific and technical organizations, including the International Atomic Energy Agency; the United Nations Environment Programme; the Commission on Sustainable Development; and the United Nations Educational, Scientific, and Cultural Organization. Works to ensure that United Nations agencies follow United Nations Conference on Environment and Development recommendations on sustainable growth.

Technology Administration *(Commerce Dept.), International Technology Policy, 14th St. and Constitution Ave. N.W., #4412 20230; (202) 482-6351. Fax, (202) 501-6849. Cathy Campbell, Director.*

Develops and implements policies to enhance the competitiveness of U.S. technology-based industry. Provides information on foreign research and development; coordinates, on behalf of the Commerce Dept., negotiation of international science and technology agreements. Manages the Japan Technology program, which seeks to ensure access for U.S. researchers and industry to Japanese science and technology.

INTERNATIONAL ORGANIZATIONS

InterAcademy Panel on International Issues, *2101 Constitution Ave. N.W., NAS 243 20418; (202) 334-2800. Fax, (202) 334-3094. John Boright, Executive Director. Web, www.national-academies.org.*

Membership: academies of science in countries worldwide. Promotes communication among leading authorities in the natural and social sciences; advises governments and international organizations; interests include scientific aspects of population, sustainable development, energy and other resources, and environmental protection. (National Academy of Sciences is U.S. member.)

NONPROFIT

American Assn. for the Advancement of Science, *International Programs, 1200 New York Ave. N.W., 7th Floor 20005; (202) 326-6650. Fax, (202) 289-4958. Richard Getzinger, Director. Web, www.aaas.org/ international.*

Administers programs concerned with international science and engineering; works to further understanding of global problems with scientific and technological components; provides policymakers at national and international levels with information from the scientific community.

Japan Information Access Project, *2000 P St. N.W., #620 20036; (202) 822-6040. Fax, (202) 822-6044. Mindy Kotler, Director. General e-mail, access@nmjc.org. Web, www.nmjc.org/jiap.*

Studies Japanese and Northeast Asian Security and public policy. Researches and analyzes issues affecting Japan's relationship with the West.

National Research Council, *International Affairs, 2101 Constitution Ave. N.W., FO 2045 20418; (202) 334-2800. Fax, (202) 334-3094. John Boright, Executive Director. Web, www4.nationalacademies.org/oia/oiahome.nsf.*

Serves the international interests of the National Research Council, National Academy of Sciences, National Academy of Engineering, and Institute of Medicine. Promotes effective application of science and technology to the economic and social problems of industrialized and developing countries; advises U.S. government agencies; participates in international organizations, conferences, and cooperative activities.

Research Applications

AGENCIES

Defense Technical Information Center *(Defense Dept.), 8725 John Jay Kingman Rd., #0944, Fort Belvoir, VA 22060-6221; (703) 767-9100. Fax, (703) 767-9183. Kurt N. Molholm, Administrator. Registration, (703) 767-8273. Web, www.dtic.mil.*

Acts as a central repository for the Defense Dept.'s collection of current and completed research and development efforts in all fields of science and technology. Disseminates research and development information to contractors, grantees, and registered organizations working on government research and development projects, particularly for the Defense Dept. Users must register with the center.

National Aeronautics and Space Administration, *Space Science, 300 E St. S.W. 20546 (mailing address: NASA Headquarters, Mail Code S 20546); (202) 358-1409. Fax, (202) 358-3092. Edward J. Weiler, Associate Administrator. Information, (202) 358-1547. Web, spacescience.nasa.gov.*

Provides information on technology developed during NASA's activities that have practical applications in other fields; maintains a data bank. (Accepts written requests for specific technical information.)

National Institute of Standards and Technology *(Commerce Dept.), Bldg. 101, #A1134, Gaithersburg, MD 20899 (mailing address: 100 Bureau Dr., MS 1000, Gaithersburg, MD 20899); (301) 975-2300. Fax, (301) 869-8972. Raymond G. Kammer, Director. Information, (301) 975-2762. Web, www.nist.gov.*

Nonregulatory agency that serves as national reference and measurement laboratory for the physical and engineering sciences. Works with industry, government agencies, and academia; conducts research in electronics, manufacturing, physics, chemistry, radiation, materials science, applied mathematics, computer science and technology, and engineering sciences.

National Science Foundation, *Human Resource Development, 4201 Wilson Blvd., #815, Arlington, VA 22230; (703) 306-1640. Fax, (703) 306-0423. Dr. Norman L. Fortenberry, Director (Acting). Web, www.ehr.nsf.gov/ EHR/HRD.*

Supports and encourages participation in scientific and engineering research by women, minorities, and people with disabilities. Awards grants and scholarships.

Technology Administration *(Commerce Dept.), Technology Policy, 14th St. and Constitution Ave. N.W., #4814C 20230; (202) 482-5687. Fax, (202) 482-4817. Kelly H. Carnes, Assistant Secretary. Web, www.ta.doc.gov/ OTPolicy/default.html.*

Promotes the removal of barriers to the commercialization of technology; analyzes federal research and development funding; acts as an information clearinghouse.

NONPROFIT

American National Standards Institute, *Conformity Assessment, Washington Office, 1819 L St. N.W., #600 20006; (301) 469-3360. John Donaldson, Vice President. Customer service, (888) 267-4783. General e-mail, info@ ansi.org. Web, www.ansi.org.*

Administers and coordinates the voluntary standardization system for the U.S. private sector; maintains staff contacts for specific industries. Serves as U.S. member of the International Organization for Standardization (ISO) and hosts the U.S. National Committee of the International Electrotechnical Commission (IEC). (ANSI headquarters in New York.)

National Center for Advanced Technologies, *1250 Eye St. N.W., #801 20005-3922; (202) 371-8451. Fax, (202) 371-8573. Stan Siegel, President. General e-mail, ncat@ncat.com. Web, www.ncat.com.*

Encourages U.S. competition in the world market by uniting government, industry, and university efforts to develop advanced technologies. (Affiliated with the Aerospace Industries Assn. of America.)

Public Technology, *1301 Pennsylvania Ave. N.W., #800 20004; (202) 626-2400. Fax, (202) 626-2498. Costis Toregas, President. Information, (800) 852-4934. Library, (202) 626-2456. Press, (202) 626-2412. General e-mail, press@ pti.nw.dc.us. Web, pti.nw.dc.us.*

Cooperative research, development, and technology-transfer organization of cities and counties in North America. Applies available technological innovations and develops other methods to improve public services. Participates in international conferences.

Rand Corporation, *Washington Office, 1333 H St. N.W., #800 20005; (202) 296-5000. Fax, (202) 296-7960. Bruce Hoffman, Director. Web, www.rand.org.*

Research organization. Interests include energy, emerging technologies and critical systems, space and transportation, technology policies, international cooperative research, water resources, ocean and atmospheric sciences, and other technologies in defense and nondefense areas. (Headquarters in Santa Monica, Calif.)

SRI International, *Washington Office, 1611 N. Kent St., #700, Arlington, VA 22209; (703) 524-2053. Fax, (703) 247-8569. William Mohr, Director. Web, www.sri.com.*

Research and consulting organization that conducts basic and applied research for government, industry, and business. Interests include engineering, physical and life sciences, and international research. (Headquarters in Menlo Park, Calif.)

Scientific Research Practices

AGENCIES

Education Dept., *Grants Policy and Oversight Staff: Protection of Human Subjects in Research, 7th and D Sts. S.W., #3652 20202-4248; (202) 260-5353. Fax, (202)*

205-0667. Helene Deramond, Coordinator. Web, ocfo.ed.
gov/humansub.htm.

Advises the grant policy and oversight staff on the
regulations for the protection of human subjects and
provides guidance to the Education Dept. on the requirements for complying with the regulations. Serves as the
primary Education Dept. contact for matters concerning
the protection of human subjects in research.

Energy Dept., *Human Subjects Research Program,*
19901 Germantown Rd., #SC-72, Germantown, MD
20874-1290; (301) 903-4731. Fax, (301) 903-8521. Susan
L. Rose, Program Manager. Web, www.er.doe.gov/
production/ober/humsubj/index.html.

Works to protect the rights and welfare of human
research subjects by establishing guidelines and regulations on scientific research that uses human subjects; acts
as an educational and technical resource to investigators,
administrators, and institutional research boards. Interests include Energy Dept. health-related studies that use
workers as subjects.

Health and Human Services Dept., *Research*
Integrity, 5515 Security Lane, #700, Rockville, MD 20852;
(301) 443-3400. Fax, (301) 443-5351. Chris B. Pascal,
Director (Acting). Web, ori.dhhs.gov/intro.htm.

Seeks to promote the quality of Public Health Service extramural and intramural research programs.
Extramural programs provide funding to research institutions that are not part of the federal government.
Intramural programs provide funding for research conducted within federal government facilities. Develops
policies and regulations that protect individuals who
disclose information about scientific misconduct from
retaliation; administers assurance program; provides
technical assistance to institutions during inquiries and
investigations of scientific misconduct; reviews institutional findings and recommends administrative actions
to the assistant secretary of Health and Human Services;
sponsors educational programs and activities for professionals interested in research integrity.

National Bioethics Advisory Commission *(Health*
and Human Services Dept.), 6100 Executive Blvd.,
#5B01, Rockville, MD 20892-7508; (301) 402-4242. Fax,
(301) 480-6900. Harold Shapiro, Chair. Web, bioethics.gov.

Works to protect the rights and welfare of human
subjects in scientific research; addresses issues concerning the management and use of genetics information;
advises the National Science and Technology Council
and other federal agencies on bioethical issues arising
from research on human biology and behavior; provides
the public with information about its recommendations
on bioethical issues.

Veterans Affairs Dept., *Military and Veterans Health*
Coordinating Board, 810 Vermont Ave., #13H 20420;
(202) 273-9897. Fax, (202) 273-9912. Robert Claypool,
Executive Director.

Works to protect the health of servicemembers, veterans, and families for past, current, and future military
deployments.

NONPROFIT

Do No Harm–The Coalition of Americans for
Research Ethics, *200 Daingerfield Rd., #100, Alexandria,*
VA 22314; (703) 684-8352. Fax, (703) 684-5813. Gene
Tarne, President. Web, www.stemcellresearch.org.

Membership: researchers and health care, bioethic,
and legal professionals opposed to scientific research
conducted on human embryos. Seeks to educate policymakers and the public about the development of medical
treatments and therapies that do not utilize human
embryos.

Humane Society of the United States, *Animal*
Research Issues, 2100 L St. N.W. 20037; (301) 258-3043.
Fax, (301) 258-7760. Martin Stephens, Vice President.
Web, www.hsus.org/programs/research/index.html.

Opposes the use of animals in scientific research and
consumer product testing. Promotes tissue and cell
research as an alternative to research conducted on animals. Sponsors programs that educate the public about
animal research.

 # BIOLOGY AND LIFE SCIENCES

AGENCIES

Animal and Plant Health Inspection Service
(APHIS), *(Agriculture Dept.), National Biological Con-*
trol Institute, 4700 River Rd., Unit 5, Riverdale, MD
20737-1229; (301) 734-4329. Fax, (301) 734-7823. Michael
Oraze, Director (Acting). Web, www.aphis.usda.gov.

Division of APHIS Plant Protection and Quarantine.
Oversees efforts to control animal and plant pests; works
to develop a national and international biological control
network, and to document and improve procedures for
importation, interstate movement, and release of biological control agents.

Armed Forces Radiobiology Research Institute
(Defense Dept.), 8901 Wisconsin Ave., Bethesda, MD
20889-5603; (301) 295-1210. Fax, (301) 295-4967. Col.
Robert Eng (MSUSA), Director. Web, www.afrri.usuhs.mil.

Serves as the principal ionizing radiation radiobiology research laboratory under the jurisdiction of the

Uniformed Services University of the Health Sciences. Participates in international conferences and projects. Library open to the public.

National Aeronautics and Space Administration, *Life Sciences, 300 E St. S.W. 20546; (202) 358-2530. Fax, (202) 358-4168. Joan Vernikos, Director. Web, www.hq. nasa.gov.*

Conducts NASA's life sciences research.

National Institute of General Medical Sciences *(National Institutes of Health), 45 Center Dr., MSC-6200, #2AN12B, Bethesda, MD 20892-6200; (301) 594-2172. Fax, (301) 402-0156. Marvin Cassman, Director. Web, www.nih.gov/nigms.*

Supports basic biomedical research and training that are not targeted to specific diseases; focus includes cell biology, genetics, pharmacology, and systemic response to trauma and anesthesia.

National Museum of Natural History *(Smithsonian Institution), Library, 10th St. and Constitution Ave. N.W., #51 20560; (202) 357-1496. Fax, (202) 357-1896. Ann Juneau, Chief Librarian.*

Maintains reference collections covering systematic biology and taxonomy, invertebrate biology and vertebrate zoology, paleobiology, botany, general geology and mineral sciences, oceanography, entomology, ecology, evolution, limnology, anthropology, and ethnology; permits on-site use of the collections. Open to the public by appointment; makes interlibrary loans.

National Museum of Natural History *(Smithsonian Institution), Naturalist Center, 741 Miller Dr. S.E., #G2, Leesburg, VA 20175; (703) 779-9712. Fax, (703) 779-9715. Richard H. Efthim, Manager. Information, (800) 729-7725. General e-mail, natcenter@aol.com. Web, nmnhgoph.si.edu/museum/learn.html.*

Maintains natural history research and reference library with books and more than 30,000 objects, including minerals, rocks, plants, animals, shells and corals, insects, invertebrates, micro- and macrofossil materials, and microbiological and anthropological materials. Facilities include study equipment such as microscopes, dissecting instruments, and plant presses. Operates a teachers' reference center. Library open to the public. Reservations required for groups of six or more.

National Oceanic and Atmospheric Administration *(Commerce Dept.), National Marine Fisheries Service, 1315 East-West Hwy., Silver Spring, MD 20910; (301) 713-2239. Fax, (301) 713-2258. Penelope Dalton, Assistant Administrator. Press, (301) 713-2370. Web, www.nmfs.gov.*

Conducts research and collects data on marine ecology and biology; collects, analyzes, and provides information through the Marine Resources Monitoring, Assessment, and Prediction Program. Administers the Magnuson Fishery Conservation and Management Act and marine mammals and endangered species protection programs. Works with the Army Corps of Engineers on research into habitat restoration and conservation.

National Science Foundation, *Biological Sciences, 4201 Wilson Blvd., #605, Arlington, VA 22230; (703) 306-1400. Fax, (703) 306-0343. Mary E. Clutter, Assistant Director. Information, (703) 306-1234. Web, www.nsf.gov/bio.*

Directorate that provides grants for research in the cellular and molecular biosciences, environmental biology, integrative biology and neuroscience, and biological infrastructure. Monitors international research.

Naval Medical Research Center *(Defense Dept.), 503 Robert Grant Ave., Silver Spring, MD 20910-7500; (301) 319-7400. Fax, (301) 319-7410. Capt. Richard Hibbs, Commanding Officer. Web, www.nmri.nnmc.navy.mil.*

Performs basic and applied biomedical research in areas of military importance, including infectious diseases, hyperbaric medicine, wound repair enhancement, environmental stress, and immunobiology. Provides support to field laboratories and naval hospitals; monitors research internationally.

U.S. Geological Survey *(Interior Dept.), Biological Resources, 12201 Sunrise Valley Dr., Reston, VA 20192; (703) 648-4050. Fax, (703) 648-7031. Dennis B. Fenn, Chief Biologist. Web, www.nbs.gov.*

Performs research in support of biological resource management. Monitors and reports on the status of the nation's biotic resources. Conducts research on wildlife, fish, insects, and plants, including the effects of disease and environmental contaminants on endangered and other species.

NONPROFIT

American Institute of Biological Sciences, *1444 Eye St. N.W., #200 20005; (202) 628-1500. Fax, (202) 628-1509. Richard O'Grady, Executive Director. Information, (800) 992-2427. Web, www.aibs.org.*

Membership: biologists, biological associations, industrial research laboratories, and others interested in biology. Promotes interdisciplinary cooperation among members engaged in biological research and education; conducts educational programs for members; sponsors Congressional Science Fellowship; administers projects supported by government grants. Monitors legislation and regulations.

American Society for Biochemistry and Molecular Biology, *9650 Rockville Pike, Bethesda, MD 20814; (301) 530-7145. Fax, (301) 571-1824. Charles C. Hancock, Executive Officer. General e-mail, asbmb@asbmb.faseb.org. Web, www.faseb.org/asbmb.*

Professional society of biological chemists; membership by election. Participates in International Union of Biochemistry and Molecular Biology (headquartered in Berlin). Monitors legislation and regulations.

American Society for Cell Biology, *9650 Rockville Pike, Bethesda, MD 20814-3992; (301) 530-7153. Fax, (301) 530-7139. Elizabeth Marincola, Executive Director. General e-mail, ascbinfo@ascb.org. Web, www.ascb.org/ascb.*

Membership: scientists who have education or research experience in cell biology or an allied field. Promotes scientific exchange worldwide; organizes courses, workshops, and symposia. Monitors legislation and regulations.

American Society for Microbiology, *1752 N St. N.W. 20036; (202) 737-3600. Fax, (202) 942-9333. Michael I. Goldberg, Executive Director. Press, (202) 942-9297. General e-mail, oed@asmusa.org. Web, www.asmusa.org.*

Membership: microbiologists. Encourages education, training, scientific investigation, and application of research results in microbiology and related subjects; participates in international research.

American Type Culture Collection, *10801 University Blvd., Manassas, VA 20110-2209; (703) 365-2700. Fax, (703) 365-2750. Raymond H. Cypess, President. Toll-free, (800) 638-6597. General e-mail, help@atcc.org. Web, www.atcc.org.*

Provides biological products, technical services, and educational programs to government agencies, academic institutions, and private industry worldwide. Serves as a repository of living cultures and genetic material.

AOAC International, *481 N. Frederick Ave., #500, Gaithersburg, MD 20877; (301) 924-7077. Fax, (301) 924-7089. E. James Bradford, Executive Director. General e-mail, info@aoac.org. Web, www.aoac.org.*

International association of analytical science professionals, companies, government agencies, nongovernmental organizations, and institutions. Promotes methods validation and quality measurements in the analytical sciences. Supports the development, testing, validation, and publication of reliable chemical and biological methods of analyzing foods, drugs, feed, fertilizers, pesticides, water, forensic materials, and other substances.

Biophysical Society, *9650 Rockville Pike, #L0512, Bethesda, MD 20814-3998; (301) 530-7114. Fax, (301) 530-7133. Rosalba Kampman, Executive Director. Web, www.biophysics.org/biophys.*

Membership: scientists, professors, and researchers engaged in biophysics or related fields. Encourages development and dissemination of knowledge in biophysics.

Carnegie Institution of Washington, *1530 P St. N.W. 20005-1910; (202) 387-6400. Fax, (202) 387-8092. Maxine F. Singer, President. Library, (202) 939-1120. Web, www.ciw.edu.*

Conducts research in the physical and biological sciences at the following centers: the observatories of the Carnegie Institution with headquarters in Pasadena, Calif.; Geophysical Laboratory and Dept. of Terrestrial Magnetism in Washington, D.C.; Dept. of Plant Biology in Stanford, Calif.; and Dept. of Embryology in Baltimore, Md. Refers specific inquiries to appropriate department. Library open to the public by appointment.

Ecological Society of America, *1707 H St. N.W., 4th Floor 20006-3916; (202) 833-8773. Fax, (202) 833-8775. Katherine S. McCarter, Executive Director. General e-mail, esahq@esa.org. Web, esa.sdsc.edu.*

Promotes research in ecology, the scientific study of the relationship between organisms and their past, present, and future environments. Interests include biotechnology; management of natural resources, habitats, and ecosystems to protect biological diversity; and ecologically sound public policies.

Federation of American Societies for Experimental Biology, *9650 Rockville Pike, Bethesda, MD 20814-3998; (301) 530-7090. Fax, (301) 571-0686. Sidney H. Golub, Executive Director. Information, (301) 571-0657. Web, www.faseb.org.*

Federation of seventeen scientific and educational groups: American Physiological Society, American Society for Biochemistry and Molecular Biology, American Society for Pharmacology and Experimental Therapeutics, American Society for Investigative Pathology, American Society for Nutritional Sciences, American Assn. of Immunologists, American Society for Cell Biology, Biophysical Society, The Protein Society, American Assn. of Anatomists, American Society for Bone and Mineral Research, Society for Developmental Biology, American Peptide Society, Assn. of Biomolecular Resource Facilities, American Society for Clinical Investigation, Society for the Study of Reproduction, and Teratology Society. Serves as support group for member societies; participates in international conferences.

Biotechnology

See also Agricultural Research/Education (chap. 2); Genetic Disorders (chap. 11)

AGENCIES

Cooperative State Research, Education, and Extension Service *(Agriculture Dept.), Competitive Research Grants and Awards Management,* 901 D St. S.W., #322 20447; (202) 401-1761. Fax, (202) 401-1782. Sally Rockey, Deputy Administrator.

Administers competitive research grants for biotechnology in the agricultural field. Oversees research in biotechnology.

Environmental Protection Agency, *Prevention, Pesticides, and Toxic Substances,* 401 M St. S.W., MC 7101 20460; (202) 260-2902. Fax, (202) 260-1847. James V. Aidala, Assistant Administrator (Nominee). Pollution prevention and toxic substances control, (202) 260-3810.

Regulates certain agricultural and industrial products of biotechnology.

National Institute of Standards and Technology *(Commerce Dept.), Chemical Science and Technology Laboratory,* Route I-270 and Quince Orchard Rd., Gaithersburg, MD 20899; (301) 975-3145. Fax, (301) 975-3845. Hratch G. Semerjian, Director.

Conducts basic and applied research in biotechnology.

National Institutes of Health (NIH), *(Health and Human Services Dept.), Biotechnology Activities,* 6000 Executive Blvd., #302, MSC 7010, Bethesda, MD 20892-7010; (301) 496-9838. Fax, (301) 496-9839. Amy Patterson, Director. Web, www.nih.gov/od/oba.

Reviews requests submitted to NIH involving genetic testing, recombinant DNA technology, and xenotransplantation, and implements research guidelines.

National Library of Medicine *(National Institutes of Health), National Center for Biotechnology Information,* 8600 Rockville Pike, Bldg. 38A, 8th Floor, Bethesda, MD 20894; (301) 496-2475. Fax, (301) 480-9241. Dr. David J. Lipman, Director. Web, www.ncbi.nlm.nih.gov.

Creates automated systems for storing and analyzing knowledge of molecular biology and genetics. Develops new information technologies to aid in understanding the molecular processes that control human health and disease. Conducts basic research in computational molecular biology.

Office of Science and Technology Policy *(Executive Office of the President), Biotechnology Subcommittee of the Committee on Science,* 4201 Wilson Blvd., #605, Arlington, VA 22250; (703) 306-1400. Fax, (703) 306-0343. Mary E. Clutter, Chair. Web, www.nsf.gov.bio.

Serves as a forum for addressing biotechnology research issues, sharing information, identifying gaps in scientific knowledge, and developing consensus among concerned federal agencies. Facilitates continuing cooperation among federal agencies on topical issues.

NONPROFIT

Biotechnology Industry Organization, 1625 K St. N.W., #1100 20006-1604; (202) 857-0244. Fax, (202) 857-0237. Carl B. Feldbaum, President. General e-mail, bio@bio.org. Web, www.bio.org.

Membership: U.S. and international companies engaged in biotechnology. Monitors government activities at all levels; promotes educational activities; conducts workshops.

Friends of the Earth, 1025 Vermont Ave. N.W., #300 20005-6303; (202) 783-7400. Fax, (202) 783-0444. Brent Blackwelder, President. General e-mail, foe@foe.org. Web, www.foe.org.

Monitors legislation and regulations on issues related to seed industry consolidation and patenting laws and on business developments in agricultural biotechnology and their effect on farming, food production, genetic resources, and the environment.

Kennedy Institute of Ethics *(Georgetown University),* Healy Hall, 4th Floor, 37th and O Sts. N.W. 20057; (202) 687-8099. Fax, (202) 687-8089. Dr. Leroy Walters, Director. Library, (800) 633-3849; in Washington, (202) 687-3885. Web, www.georgetown.edu/research/kie.

Sponsors research on medical ethics, including legal and ethical definitions of death, allocation of scarce health resources, and recombinant DNA and human gene therapy. Supplies National Library of Medicine with online database on bioethics; publishes annual bibliography; conducts international programs and free bibliographic searches. Library open to the public.

Botany

See also Horticulture and Gardening (chap. 2)

AGENCIES

National Arboretum *(Agriculture Dept.),* 3501 New York Ave. N.E. 20002; (202) 245-4539. Fax, (202) 245-4575. Thomas S. Elias, Director. Library, (202) 245-4538.

Maintains public display of plants on 446 acres; provides information and makes referrals concerning cultivated plants (exclusive of field crops and fruits); conducts plant breeding and research; maintains herbarium. Library open to the public by appointment.

National Museum of Natural History *(Smithsonian Institution), Botany, 10th St. and Constitution Ave. N.W., MRC 166 20560-0166; (202) 357-2534. Fax, (202) 786-2563. W. John Kress, Chair. Web, nmnhwww.si.edu/ departments/botany.html.*

Conducts botanical research worldwide; furnishes information on the identification, distribution, and local names of flowering plants; studies threatened and endangered plant species.

Smithsonian Institution, *Botany Branch Library, 10th St. and Constitution Ave. N.W., MRC 166 20560-0166; (202) 357-2715. Fax, (202) 357-1896. Ruth F. Schallert, Librarian. Web, www.sil.si.edu.*

Collections include taxonomic botany, plant morphology, general botany, history of botany, grasses, and algae. Permits on-site use of collections (appointment preferred); makes interlibrary loans. (Housed at the National Museum of Natural History.)

CONGRESS

U.S. Botanic Garden, *245 1st St. S.W. 20024; (202) 225-8333. Fax, (202) 225-1561. Vacant, Executive Director. Web, www.aoc.gov/pages/usbgpage.htm.*

Collects, cultivates, and grows various plants for public display and study; identifies botanic specimens and furnishes information on proper growing methods. Conducts horticultural classes and tours.

NONPROFIT

American Society for Horticultural Science, *113 S. West St., #200, Alexandria, VA 22314; (703) 836-4606. Fax, (703) 836-2024. Michael Neff, Executive Director. General e-mail, ashs@ashs.org. Web, www.ashs.org.*

Membership: educators, government workers, firms, associations, and individuals interested in horticultural science. Promotes scientific research and education in horticulture, including international exchange of information.

American Society of Plant Physiologists, *15501 Monona Dr., Rockville, MD 20855-2768; (301) 251-0560. Fax, (301) 279-2996. John Lisack, Executive Director. Web, www.aspp.org.*

Membership: plant physiologists, plant biochemists, and molecular biologists. Seeks to educate and promote public interest in plant physiology. Publishes journals; provides placement service for members; sponsors annual meeting of plant scientists.

National Assn. of Plant Patent Owners, *1250 Eye St. N.W., #500 20005-3922; (202) 789-2900. Fax, (202) 789-1893. Craig Regelbrugge, Administrator.*

Membership: owners of patents on newly propagated horticultural plants. Informs members of plant patents issued, provisions of patent laws, and changes in practice. Promotes the development, protection, production, and distribution of new varieties of horticultural plants. Works with international organizations of plant breeders on matters of common interest. (Affiliated with the American Nursery and Landscape Assn.)

Zoology

See also Animals and Plants (chap. 9)

AGENCIES

National Museum of Natural History *(Smithsonian Institution), Entomology, 10th St. and Constitution Ave. N.W., MRC 105 20560-0105; (202) 357-2078. Fax, (202) 786-2894. Scott E. Miller, Chair. Library, (202) 357-2354. Web, nmnhwww.si.edu/departments/entom.html.*

Conducts worldwide research in entomology. Maintains the national collection of insects; lends insect specimens to specialists for research and classification. Library open to the public by appointment.

National Museum of Natural History *(Smithsonian Institution), Invertebrate Zoology, 10th St. and Constitution Ave. N.W., MRC 163 20560-0163; (202) 357-3027. Fax, (202) 357-3043. Kristian Fauchald, Chair. Web, nmnhwww.si.edu/departments/invert.html.*

Conducts research on the identity, morphology, histology, life history, distribution, classification, and ecology of marine, terrestrial, and fresh water invertebrate animals (except insects); maintains the national collection of invertebrate animals; aids exhibit and educational programs; conducts pre- and postdoctoral fellowship programs; provides facilities for visiting scientists in the profession.

National Museum of Natural History *(Smithsonian Institution), Vertebrate Zoology, 10th St. and Constitution Ave. N.W., MRC 109 20560-0109; (202) 357-2740. Fax, (202) 786-2979. Dave Johnson, Chief; Lynne R. Parenti, Chair.*

Conducts research worldwide on the systematics, ecology, and behavior of mammals, birds, reptiles, amphibians, and fish; maintains the national collection of specimens.

NONPROFIT

American Zoo and Aquarium Assn., *8403 Colesville Rd., #710, Silver Spring, MD 20910; (301) 562-0777. Fax,*

(301) 562-0888. Sydney J. Butler, Executive Director. Web, www.aza.org.

Membership: interested individuals and professionally run zoos and aquariums in North America. Administers professional accreditation program; participates in worldwide conservation, education, and research activities.

Entomological Society of America, *9301 Annapolis Rd., Lanham, MD 20706; (301) 731-4535. Fax, (301) 731-4538. James Olmes, Executive Director. General e-mail, esa@entsoc.org. Web, www.entsoc.org.*

Scientific association that promotes the science of entomology and the interests of professionals in the field. Advises on crop protection, food chain, and individual and urban health matters dealing with insect pests.

Jane Goodall Institute, *P.O. Box 14890, Silver Spring, MD 20911-4890; (301) 565-0086. Fax, (301) 565-3188. Stewart Hudson, Executive Director. General e-mail, JGIinformation@janegoodall.org. Web, www.janegoodall. org.*

Seeks to increase primate habitat conservation, expand noninvasive primate research, and promote activities that ensure the well-being of primates. (Affiliated with Jane Goodall Institutes in Canada, Europe, Asia, and Africa.)

⌨ ENGINEERING

See also Construction (chap. 12)

AGENCIES

National Institute of Standards and Technology *(Commerce Dept.), Electronics and Electrical Engineering Laboratory, 100 Bureau Dr., Bldg. 220, #B358, MS 8100, Gaithersburg, MD 20899; (301) 975-2220. Fax, (301) 975-4091. William E. Anderson, Director (Acting). General e-mail, eeel@nist.gov. Web, www.eeel.nist.gov.*

Provides focus for research, development, and applications in the fields of electrical, electronic, quantum electric, and electromagnetic materials engineering. Interests include fundamental physical constants, practical data, measurement methods, theory, standards, technology, technical services, and international trade.

National Institute of Standards and Technology *(Commerce Dept.), Manufacturing Engineering Laboratory, Route I-270 and Quince Orchard Rd., Bldg. 220, #B322, Gaithersburg, MD 20899; (301) 975-3400. Fax, (301) 948-5668. Richard H. F. Jackson, Director. Web, www.mel.nist.gov.*

Collects technical data, develops standards in production engineering, and publishes findings; produces the technical base for proposed standards and technology for industrial and mechanical engineering; provides instrument design, fabrication, and repair. Helps establish international standards.

National Science Foundation, *Engineering, 4201 Wilson Blvd., #505, Arlington, VA 22230; (703) 306-1300. Fax, (703) 306-0289. Eugene Wong, Assistant Director. Web, www.eng.nsf.gov.*

Directorate that supports fundamental research and education in engineering through grants and special equipment awards. Programs are designed to enhance international competitiveness and to improve the quality of engineering in the United States. Oversees the following divisions: Electrical and Communications Systems; Chemical and Transport Systems; Engineering Education and Centers; Civil and Mechanical Systems; Design, Manufacture, and Industrial Innovation; and Bioengineering and Environmental Systems.

NONPROFIT

American Assn. of Engineering Societies, *1111 19th St. N.W., #403 20036-3690; (202) 296-2237. Fax, (202) 296-1151. Tom Price, Executive Director. Web, www.aaes. org.*

Federation of engineering societies; members work in industry, construction, government, academia, and private practice. Advances the knowledge, understanding, and practice of engineering. Serves as delegate to the World Federation of Engineering Organizations.

American Consulting Engineers Council, *1015 15th St. N.W., #802 20005; (202) 347-7474. Fax, (202) 898-0068. David Raymond, Executive Vice President. General e-mail, acec@acec.org. Web, www.acec.org.*

Membership: practicing consulting engineering firms and state, local, and regional consulting engineers councils. Serves as an information clearinghouse for member companies in such areas as legislation, legal cases, marketing, management, professional liability, business practices, and insurance. Monitors legislation and regulations.

American Consulting Engineers Council, *Research and Management Foundation, 1015 15th St. N.W., #802 20005; (202) 347-7474. Fax, (202) 898-0068. Florian Kogelnik, Director. General e-mail, acec@acec.org. Web, www.acec.org.*

Conducts research and educational activities to improve engineering practices, professional cooperation, and ties to government. Provides information and training to member organizations on research and analysis, management training, access to international markets, and community involvement.

American Society for Engineering Education, *1818 N St. N.W., #600 20036; (202) 331-3500. Fax, (202) 265-8504. Frank L. Huband, Executive Director. Press, (202) 331-3537. Web, www.asee.org.*

Membership: engineering faculty and administrators, professional engineers, government agencies, and engineering colleges, corporations, and professional societies. Conducts research, conferences, and workshops on engineering education. Monitors legislation and regulations.

American Society of Civil Engineers, *1801 Alexander Bell Dr., Reston, VA 20191-4400; (703) 295-6300. Fax, (703) 295-6333. James E. Davis, Executive Director. Information, (800) 548-2723. Web, www.asce.org.*

Membership: professionals and students in civil engineering. Develops and produces consensus standards for construction documents and building codes. Maintains the Civil Engineering Research Foundation, which focuses national attention and resources on the research needs of the civil engineering profession. Participates in international conferences.

American Society of Mechanical Engineers, *Public Affairs, Washington Office, 1828 L St. N.W., #906 20036; (202) 785-3756. Fax, (202) 429-9417. Philip W. Hamilton, Managing Director. General e-mail, grdept@asme.org. Web, www.asme.org.*

Serves as a clearinghouse for sharing of information among federal, state, and local governments and the engineering profession. Monitors legislation and regulations. (Headquarters in New York.)

ASFE, *8811 Colesville Rd., #G106, Silver Spring, MD 20910; (301) 565-2733. Fax, (301) 589-2017. John P. Bachner, Executive Vice President. General e-mail, info@ asfe.org. Web, www.asfe.org.*

Membership: consulting geotechnical and geoenvironmental engineering firms. Conducts seminars and a peer review program on quality control policies and procedures in geotechnical engineering. Formerly the Assn. of Soil and Foundation Engineers.

Institute of Electrical and Electronics Engineers–United States Activities, *Professional Activities, Washington Office, 1828 L St. N.W., #1202 20036-5104; (202) 785-0017. Fax, (202) 785-0835. W. Thomas Suttle, Managing Director. General e-mail, ieeeusa@ieee.org. Web, www.ieee.org.*

U.S. arm of an international technological and professional organization concerned with all areas of elec-

trotechnology policy, including aerospace, computers, communications, biomedicine, electric power, and consumer electronics.

International Federation of Professional and Technical Engineers, *8630 Fenton St., #400, Silver Spring, MD 20910; (301) 565-9016. Fax, (301) 565-0018. Paul E. Almeida, President. Web, www.ifpte.org.*

Membership: approximately 50,000 technicians, engineers, scientists, professionals, and other workers, including government employees. Helps members negotiate pay, benefits, and better working conditions; conducts training programs and workshops. Monitors legislation and regulations. (Affiliated with the AFL-CIO and the Canadian Labour Congress.)

International Microelectronics and Packaging Society, *1850 Centennial Park Dr., #105, Reston, VA 20191-1517; (703) 758-1060. Fax, (703) 758-1066. Richard Breck, Executive Director. Information, (888) 464-6277. General e-mail, imaps@imaps.org. Web, www.imaps. org.*

Membership: persons involved in the microelectronics industry worldwide. Integrates disciplines of science and engineering; fosters exchange of information among complementary technologies, including ceramics, thin and thick films, surface mounts, semiconductor packaging, discrete semiconductor devices, monolithic circuits, and multichip modules; disseminates technical knowledge.

International Test and Evaluation Assn., *4400 Fair Lakes Court, #104, Fairfax, VA 22033-3899; (703) 631-6220. Fax, (703) 631-6221. R. Alan Plishker, Executive Director. Web, www.itea.org.*

Membership: engineers, scientists, managers, and other industry, government, and academic professionals interested in testing and evaluating products and complex systems. Provides a forum for information exchange; monitors international research.

National Academy of Engineering, *2101 Constitution Ave. N.W., #218 20418; (202) 334-3201. Fax, (202) 334-1680. William A. Wulf, President. Library, (202) 334-2125. Publications, (800) 624-6242; in Washington, (202) 334-3313. Web, www.nae.edu.*

Independent society whose members are elected in recognition of important contributions to the field of engineering and technology. Shares responsibility with the National Academy of Sciences for examining questions of science and technology at the request of the federal government; promotes international cooperation. Library open to the public by appointment. (Affiliated with the National Academy of Sciences.)

National Society of Professional Engineers, *1420 King St., Alexandria, VA 22314-2794; (703) 684-2800. Fax, (703) 836-4875. Patrick J. Natale, Executive Director. Web, www.nspe.org.*

Membership: U.S. licensed professional engineers from all disciplines. Holds engineering seminars; operates an information center; interests include international practice of engineering.

🖳 ENVIRONMENTAL AND EARTH SCIENCES

See also Resources Management (chap. 9)

AGENCIES

Arctic Research Commission, *4350 N. Fairfax Dr., #630, Arlington, VA 22203; (703) 525-0111. Fax, (703) 525-0114. Garrett W. Brass, Executive Director.*

Presidential advisory commission that develops policy for arctic research; assists the interagency Arctic Research Policy Committee in implementing a national plan of arctic research; recommends improvements in logistics, data management, and dissemination of arctic information.

National Aeronautics and Space Administration, *Earth Science, 300 E St. S.W. 20546 (mailing address: NASA Headquarters, Mail Code Y 20546); (202) 358-2165. Fax, (202) 358-3092. Ghassem R. Asrar, Associate Administrator. Web, www.hq.nasa.gov.*

Conducts programs dealing with the earth as observed from space; conducts upper atmospheric and terrestrial studies and meteorological and ocean research.

National Oceanic and Atmospheric Administration *(Commerce Dept.), 14th St. and Constitution Ave. N.W. 20230; (202) 482-3436. Fax, (202) 408-9674. D. James Baker, Under Secretary. Information, (202) 482-2000. Press, (202) 482-6090. Web, www.noaa.gov.*

Conducts research in marine and atmospheric sciences; issues weather forecasts and warnings vital to public safety and the national economy; surveys resources of the sea; analyzes economic aspects of fisheries operations; develops and implements policies on international fisheries; provides states with grants to conserve coastal zone areas; protects marine mammals; maintains a national environmental center with data from satellite observations and other sources including meteorological, oceanic, geodetic, and seismological data centers; provides colleges and universities with grants for

research, education, and marine advisory services; prepares and provides nautical and aeronautical charts and maps.

National Oceanic and Atmospheric Administration *(Commerce Dept.), Library and Information Services, 1315 East-West Hwy., SSMC3, 2nd Floor, Silver Spring, MD 20910; (301) 713-2607. Fax, (301) 713-4598. Janice A. Beattie, Director. Reference service, (301) 713-2600. General e-mail, reference@nodc.noaa.gov. Web, www.lib. noaa.gov.*

Collection includes reports, journals, monographs, photographs, and microforms on atmospheric and oceanic science. Maintains bibliographic database of other NOAA libraries, an online service, and reference materials on CD-ROM. Makes interlibrary loans; open to the public.

National Science Foundation, *Geosciences, 4201 Wilson Blvd., #705N, Arlington, VA 22230; (703) 306-1500. Fax, (703) 306-0372. Margaret S. Leien, Assistant Director. Web, www.geo.nsf.gov.*

Directorate that supports research about the Earth, including its atmosphere, continents, oceans, and interior. Works to improve the education and human resource base for the geosciences; participates in international and multidisciplinary activities, especially to study changes in the global climate.

National Science Foundation, *Polar Programs, 4201 Wilson Blvd., #755S, Arlington, VA 22230; (703) 306-1030. Fax, (703) 306-0645. Karl Erb, Director; Dennis Peacock, Science Head, Antarctica Science, (703) 306-1033. Web, www.nsf.gov/od/opp.*

Funds and manages U.S. activity in Antarctica; provides grants for arctic programs in polar biology and medicine, earth sciences, atmospheric sciences, meteorology, ocean sciences, and glaciology. The Polar Information Program serves as a clearinghouse for polar data and makes referrals on specific questions.

Smithsonian Environmental Research Center *(Smithsonian Institution), 647 Contees Wharf Rd., Edgewater, MD 21037 (mailing address: P.O. Box 28, Edgewater, MD 21037); (410) 798-4424. Fax, (301) 261-7954. Ross B. Simons, Director. Web, www.serc.si.edu.*

Performs laboratory and field research that measures physical, chemical, and biological interactions to determine the mechanisms of environmental responses to humans' use of air, land, and water. Evaluates properties of the environment that affect the functions of living organisms. Maintains research laboratories, public education program, facilities for controlled environments, and estuarine and terrestrial lands.

U.S. Geological Survey *(Interior Dept.), 12201 Sunrise Valley Dr., Reston, VA 20192; (703) 648-7411. Fax, (703) 648-4454. Charles G. Groat, Director. Library, (703) 648-4302. Press, (703) 648-4460. Outreach, (703) 648-4460. Web, www.usgs.gov.*

Provides reports, maps, and databases that describe and analyze water, energy, biological, and mineral resources; the land surface; and the underlying geological structure and dynamic processes of the earth.

U.S. Geological Survey *(Interior Dept.), Library, 12201 Sunrise Valley Dr., MS 950, Reston, VA 20192; (703) 648-4305. Fax, (703) 648-6373. Nancy Blair, Chief Librarian (Acting). Web, library.usgs.gov.*

Maintains collection of books, periodicals, serials, maps, and technical reports on geology, mineral and water resources, mineralogy, paleontology, petrology, soil and environmental sciences, and physics and chemistry as they relate to earth sciences. Open to the public; makes interlibrary loans.

CONGRESS

House Government Reform Committee, *Subcommittee on National Economic Growth, Natural Resources, and Regulatory Affairs, B377 RHOB 20515; (202) 225-4407. Fax, (202) 225-2441. Rep. David M. McIntosh, R-Ind., Chair; Marlo Lewis, Staff Director. Web, www.house.gov/reform.*

Oversees operations of the National Oceanic and Atmospheric Administration.

House Resources Committee, *Subcommittee on Energy and Mineral Resources, 1626 LHOB 20515; (202) 225-9297. Fax, (202) 225-5255. Rep. Barbara Cubin, R-Wyo., Chair; William Condit, Staff Director. General e-mail, resources.committee@mail.house.gov. Web, www.house.gov/resources/energy.*

Jurisdiction over U.S. Geological Survey legislation, except water-related programs.

House Resources Committee, *Subcommittee on Fisheries, Conservation, Wildlife, and Oceans, H2-187 FHOB 20515; (202) 226-0200. Fax, (202) 225-1542. Rep. H. James Saxton, R-N.J., Chair; Harry Burroughs, Staff Director. General e-mail, fishery.subcommittee@mail.house.gov. Web, www.house.gov/resources/fisheries.*

Jurisdiction over legislation on most oceanographic matters, including ocean engineering, ocean charting, and certain programs of the National Oceanic and Atmospheric Administration.

House Resources Committee, *Subcommittee on Water and Power, 1522 LHOB 20515; (202) 225-8331. Fax, (202) 226-6953. Rep. John T. Doolittle, R-Calif.,*

Chair; Robert Faber, Staff Director. General e-mail, water.power@mail.house.gov. Web, www.house.gov/resources/water.

Jurisdiction over water-related programs of the U.S. Geological Survey, saline water research and development, water resources research programs, and matters related to the Water Resources Planning Act.

Senate Commerce, Science, and Transportation Committee, *SD-508 20510; (202) 224-5115. Fax, (202) 224-1259. Sen. John McCain, R-Ariz., Chair; Mark Buse, Staff Director. Web, commerce.senate.gov.*

Jurisdiction over legislation on most oceanographic matters, including ocean charting and the National Oceanic and Atmospheric Administration.

Senate Commerce, Science, and Transportation Committee, *Subcommittee on Oceans and Fisheries, SH-428 20510; (202) 224-8172. Fax, (202) 228-0326. Sen. Olympia J. Snowe, R-Maine, Chair; Sloan Rapoport, Counsel. Web, commerce.senate.gov.*

Studies national ocean policy and programs, including ocean-specific satellite and atmospheric systems of the National Oceanic and Atmospheric Administration. (Subcommittee does not report legislation.)

Senate Energy and Natural Resources Committee, *Subcommittee on Forest and Public Land Management, SD-306 20510; (202) 224-6170. Fax, (202) 228-0539. Sen. Larry E. Craig, R-Idaho, Chair; Mark Rey, Professional Staff Member. General e-mail, forests@energy.senate.gov. Web, energy.senate.gov.*

Jurisdiction over legislation on the U.S. Geological Survey.

NONPROFIT

American Geophysical Union, *2000 Florida Ave. N.W. 20009-1277; (202) 462-6910. Fax, (202) 328-0566. A. F. Spilhaus Jr., Executive Director. Web, www.agu.org.*

Membership: scientists and technologists who study the environments and components of the Earth, Sun, and solar system. Promotes international cooperation; disseminates information.

Atmospheric Sciences

See also Air Pollution (chap. 9)

AGENCIES

National Science Foundation, *Atmospheric Sciences, 4201 Wilson Blvd., #775, Arlington, VA 22230; (703) 306-1520. Fax, (703) 306-0377. Jarvis Moyers, Director. Web, www.geo.nsf.gov/atm.*

Supports research on the earth's atmosphere and the sun's effect on it, including studies of the physics, chemistry, and dynamics of the earth's upper and lower atmospheres and its space environment; climate processes and variations; and the natural global cycles of gases and particles in the earth's atmosphere.

National Weather Service *(National Oceanic and Atmospheric Administration), 1325 East-West Hwy., Silver Spring, MD 20910; (301) 713-0689. Fax, (301) 713-0662. Jack Kelly, Administrator. Web, www.nws.noaa.gov.*

Issues warnings of hurricanes, severe storms, and floods; provides weather forecasts and services for the general public and for aviation and marine interests. National Weather Service forecast office, (703) 260-0107; weather forecast for Washington, D.C., and vicinity, (703) 260-0307; marine forecast, (703) 260-0505; recreational forecast, (703) 260-0705; climate data, (703) 271-4800; river stages, (703) 260-0305; pilot weather, (800) 992-7433.

National Weather Service *(National Oceanic and Atmospheric Administration), National Center for Environmental Prediction, 5200 Auth Rd., Camp Springs, MD 20746; (301) 763-8016. Fax, (301) 763-8434. Louis W. Uccellini, Director. Web, www.ncep.noaa.gov.*

The National Center for Environmental Prediction and the National Environmental Satellite, Data, and Information Service are part of the World Weather Watch Programme developed by the United Nations' World Meteorological Organization. Collects data and exchanges it with other nations; provides other national weather service offices, private meteorologists, and government agencies with products, including forecast guidance products.

U.S. Geological Survey *(Interior Dept.), Earth Surface Dynamics Program, 12201 Sunrise Valley Dr., MS 906, Reston, VA 20192; (703) 648-6517. Fax, (703) 648-6647. Elliot Spiker, Program Coordinator. Web, geochange.er. usgs.gov.*

Conducts research on climate fluctuations and documents the variability of the climate system in the past and future; provides information on global change and its effects on society; examines terrestrial and marine processes and the natural history of global change.

NONPROFIT

Alliance for Responsible Atmospheric Policy, *2111 Wilson Blvd., #850, Arlington, VA 22201; (703) 243-0344. Fax, (703) 243-2874. David Stirpe, Executive Director. Web, www.alcalde-fay.com.*

Coalition of users and producers of chlorofluorocarbons (CFCs). Seeks further study of the ozone depletion theory.

Climate Institute, *333 1/2 Pennsylvania Ave. S.E. 20003-1148; (202) 547-0104. Fax, (202) 547-0111. John C. Topping Jr., President. General e-mail, info@climate.org. Web, www.climate.org.*

Educates the public and policymakers on climate change (greenhouse effect, or global warming) and on the depletion of the ozone layer. Develops strategies on mitigating climate change in developing countries.

Global Climate Coalition, *1275 K St. N.W., #890 20005; (202) 682-9161. Fax, (202) 638-1043. Glenn Kelly, President. General e-mail, gcc@globalclimate.org. Web, www.globalclimate.org.*

Membership: business trade associations and private companies. Promotes scientific research on global climate change; analyzes economic and social impacts of policy options; produces educational materials and conducts programs.

Geology and Earth Sciences

AGENCIES

National Museum of Natural History *(Smithsonian Institution), Mineral Sciences, 10th St. and Constitution Ave. N.W., MRC-119 20560; (202) 357-1412. Fax, (202) 357-2476. James F. Luhr, Chair. Web, www.volcano.si.edu.*

Conducts research on meteorites. Interests include mineralogy, petrology, volcanology, and geochemistry. Maintains the Global Volcanism Network, which reports worldwide volcanic and seismic activity.

National Museum of Natural History *(Smithsonian Institution), Naturalist Center, 741 Miller Dr. S.E., #G2, Leesburg, VA 20175; (703) 779-9712. Fax, (703) 779-9715. Richard H. Efthim, Manager. Information, (800) 729-7725. General e-mail, natcenter@aol.com. Web, nmnhgoph. si.edu/museum/learn.html.*

Maintains natural history research and reference library with books and more than 30,000 objects, including minerals, rocks, plants, animals, shells and corals, insects, invertebrates, micro- and macrofossil materials, and microbiological and anthropological materials. Facilities include study equipment such as microscopes, dissecting instruments, and plant presses. Operates a teachers' reference center. Library open to the public. Reservations required for groups of six or more.

National Museum of Natural History, *Paleobiology, 10th St. and Constitution Ave. N.W., MRC 121 20560; (202) 357-2162. Fax, (202) 786-2832. Richard H. Benson, Chair. Web, nmnhwww.si.edu/departments/paleo.html.*

Conducts research worldwide on invertebrate paleontology, paleobotany, sedimentology, and vertebrate paleontology; provides information on paleontology.

Maintains national collection of fossil organisms and sediment samples.

National Science Foundation, *Earth Sciences,* 4201 *Wilson Blvd., #785, Arlington, VA 22230; (703) 306-1550. Fax, (703) 306-0382. Herman B. Zimmerman, Director. Web, www.geo.nsf.gov/ear.*

Provides grants for research in geology, geophysics, geochemistry, and related fields, including tectonics, hydrologic sciences, and continental dynamics.

U.S. Geological Survey *(Interior Dept.),* **Earthquake** *Hazards, 12201 Sunrise Valley Dr., Reston, VA 20192 (mailing address: 905 National Center, Reston, VA 20192); (703) 648-6714. Fax, (703) 648-6717. John Filson, Program Coordinator.*

Manages geologic, geophysical, and engineering investigations, including assessments of hazards from earthquakes and landslides; conducts research on the mechanisms and occurrences of earthquakes worldwide and their relationship to the behavior of the crust and upper mantle; develops methods for predicting the time, place, and magnitude of earthquakes; conducts engineering and geologic studies on landslides and ground failures.

U.S. Geological Survey *(Interior Dept.),* **Geologic** *Division, 12201 Sunrise Valley Dr., MS 911, Reston, VA 20192; (703) 648-6600. Fax, (703) 648-7031. P. Patrick Leahy, Chief Geologist. Web, geology.usgs.gov.*

Conducts onshore and offshore geologic research and investigation. Produces information on geologic hazards, such as earthquakes and volcanoes; geologic information for use in the management of public lands and national policy determinations; information on the chemistry and physics of the Earth; and geologic, geophysical, and geochemical maps and analyses to address environmental, resource, and geologic hazards concerns. Participates in international research.

U.S. Geological Survey *(Interior Dept.),* **National** *Cooperative Geologic Mapping Program, 12201 Sunrise Valley Dr., MS 908, Reston, VA 20192; (703) 648-6960. Fax, (703) 648-6937. John S. Pallister, Program Coordinator.*

Produces geologic maps; makes maps available to public and private organizations.

U.S. Geological Survey *(Interior Dept.),* **Volcano Hazards,** *12201 Sunrise Valley Dr., Reston, VA 20192 (mailing address: 905 National Center, Reston, VA 20192); (703) 648-6708. Fax, (703) 648-5483. Marianne C. Guffanti, Program Coordinator. Web, volcanoes.usgs.gov.*

Manages geologic, geophysical, and engineering investigations, including assessments of hazards from volcanoes; conducts research worldwide on the mechanisms of volcanoes and on igneous and geothermal systems. Issues warnings of potential volcanic hazards.

NONPROFIT

American Geological Institute, *4220 King St., Alexandria, VA 22302; (703) 379-2480. Fax, (703) 379-7563. Marcus E. Milling, Executive Director. Web, www.agiweb. org.*

Membership: earth science societies and associations. Maintains a computerized database with worldwide information on geology, engineering and environmental geology, oceanography, and other geological fields (available to the public for a fee).

Oceanography

See also Ocean Resources (chap. 9)

AGENCIES

National Museum of Natural History *(Smithsonian Institution),* **Botany,** *10th St. and Constitution Ave. N.W., MRC 166 20560-0166; (202) 357-2534. Fax, (202) 786-2563. Ernani Menez, Marine Biologist. Web, nmnhwww. si.edu/departments/botany.html.*

Investigates the biology, evolution, and classification of tropical and subtropical marine algae and seagrasses. Acts as curator of the national collection in this field. Develops and participates in scholarly programs.

National Museum of Natural History *(Smithsonian Institution),* **Crustaceans,** *10th St. and Constitution Ave. N.W., #51 20560; (202) 357-4673. Fax, (202) 357-3043. Rafael Lemaitre, Curator.*

Conducts worldwide research and answers scientific inquiries on the Smithsonian's marine invertebrate collections; engages in taxonomic identification, community analysis, and specimen and sample data management.

National Museum of Natural History *(Smithsonian Institution),* **Library,** *10th St. and Constitution Ave. N.W., #51 20560; (202) 357-1496. Fax, (202) 357-1896. Ann Juneau, Chief Librarian.*

Maintains collections covering oceanography; permits on-site use of the collections. Open to the public by appointment; makes interlibrary loans.

National Museum of Natural History *(Smithsonian Institution),* **Vertebrate Zoology,** *10th St. and Constitution Ave. N.W., MRC 109 20560-0109; (202) 357-2740. Fax, (202) 786-2979. Dave Johnson, Chief; Lynne R. Parenti, Chair.*

Processes, sorts, and distributes to scientists specimens of marine vertebrates; engages in taxonomic sorting, community analysis, and specimen and sample data management.

National Oceanic and Atmospheric Administration *(Commerce Dept.), Commissioned Corps, 1315 East-West Hwy., 12th Floor, Bldg. #3, Silver Spring, MD 20910-3282; (301) 713-1045. Fax, (301) 713-1541. Rear Adm. Evelyn J. Fields, Director. Recruiting, (301) 713-3470. Web, www.noaa.gov/nchome.*

Uniformed service of the Commerce Dept. that operates and manages NOAA's fleet of hydrographic, oceanographic, and fisheries research ships and aircraft. Supports NOAA's scientific programs.

National Oceanic and Atmospheric Administration *(Commerce Dept.), National Ocean Service, 1305 East-West Hwy., SSMC4, Silver Spring, MD 20910-3074. Fax, (301) 713-4269. Nancy Foster, Assistant Administrator. Web, www.nos.noaa.gov.*

Manages charting and geodetic services, oceanography and marine services, coastal resource coordination, and marine survey operations.

National Oceanic and Atmospheric Administration *(Commerce Dept.), National Oceanographic Data Center, 1315 East-West Hwy., SSMC3, 4th Floor, Silver Spring, MD 20910-3282; (301) 713-3270. Fax, (301) 713-3300. Vacant, Director; Kurt Schneble, Deputy Director. Information and requests, (301) 606-4549. General e-mail, services@nodc.noaa.gov. Web, www.noaa.gov.*

Offers a wide range of oceanographic data on the Web, disk, CD-ROM, and hard copy; provides research scientists with data processing services; prepares statistical summaries and graphical data products. (Fee charged for some services.)

National Science Foundation, *Ocean Sciences Research, 4201 Wilson Blvd., #725, Arlington, VA 22230; (703) 306-1580. Fax, (703) 306-0390. Larry Clark, Head (Acting). Web, www.geo.nsf.gov/oce.*

Awards grants to academic institutions and private corporations for research in all areas of the marine sciences, including biological, chemical, and physical oceanography, marine geology, and marine geophysics.

National Science Foundation, *Oceanographic Centers and Facilities, 4201 Wilson Blvd., #725, Arlington, VA 22230; (703) 306-1576. Fax, (703) 306-0390. Michael R. Reeve, Head.*

Awards grants and contracts for acquiring, upgrading, and operating oceanographic research facilities that lend themselves to shared usage. Facilities supported include ships, submersibles, and shipboard and shore-based data logging and processing equipment. Supports development of new drilling techniques and systems.

U.S. Geological Survey *(Interior Dept.),* **Marine and Coastal Geologic Surveys,** *12201 Sunrise Valley Dr., Reston, VA 20192 (mailing address: 915B National Center, Reston, VA 20192); (703) 648-6511. Fax, (703) 648-5464. S. Jeffress Williams, Program Coordinator.*

Surveys the continental margins and the ocean floor to provide information on the mineral resources potential of submerged lands.

NONPROFIT

Marine Technology Society, *1828 L St. N.W., #906 20036-5104; (202) 775-5966. Fax, (202) 429-9417. Judith Krauthames, Executive Director. General e-mail, mtsadmin@erols.com. Web, www.mtsociety.org.*

Membership: scientists, engineers, technologists, and others interested in marine science and technology. Provides information on marine science, technology, and education.

National Ocean Industries Assn., *1120 G St. N.W., #900 20005; (202) 347-6900. Fax, (202) 347-8650. Robert B. Stewart, President. General e-mail, noia@noia.org. Web, www.noia.org.*

Membership: manufacturers, producers, suppliers, and support and service companies involved in marine, offshore, and ocean work. Interests include offshore oil and gas supply and production, deep-sea mining, ocean thermal energy, and new energy sources.

MATHEMATICAL, COMPUTER, AND PHYSICAL SCIENCES

See also Space Sciences (this chapter)

AGENCIES

National Institute of Standards and Technology *(Commerce Dept.), Bldg. 101, #A1134, Gaithersburg, MD 20899 (mailing address: 100 Bureau Dr., MS 1000, Gaithersburg, MD 20899); (301) 975-2300. Fax, (301) 869-8972. Raymond G. Kammer, Director. Information, (301) 975-2762. Web, www.nist.gov.*

Nonregulatory agency that serves as national reference and measurement laboratory for the physical and engineering sciences. Works with industry, government agencies, and academia; conducts research in electronics, manufacturing, physics, chemistry, radiation, materials science, applied mathematics, computer science and technology, and engineering sciences.

National Institute of Standards and Technology (Commerce Dept.), Information Technology Laboratory, *Bldg. 225, #B264, Gaithersburg, MD 20899; (301) 975-2900. Fax, (301) 840-1357. William O. Mehuron, Director (Acting). Web, www.itl.nist.gov.*

Offers support in mathematical and computer sciences to all institute programs and federal agencies; provides consultations, methods, and research supporting the institute's scientific and engineering projects. Manages and operates NIST central computing facilities.

National Science Foundation, *Mathematical and Physical Sciences, 4201 Wilson Blvd., #1005N, Arlington, VA 22230; (703) 306-1800. Fax, (703) 306-0545. Robert A. Eisenstein, Assistant Director. Web, www.nsf.gov/mps.*

Directorate that supports research in the mathematical and physical sciences; divisions focus on physics, chemistry, materials research, mathematical sciences, and astronomical sciences. Works to improve the education and human resource base for these fields; participates in international and multidisciplinary activities.

NONPROFIT

Carnegie Institution of Washington, *1530 P St. N.W. 20005-1910; (202) 387-6400. Fax, (202) 387-8092. Maxine F. Singer, President. Library, (202) 939-1120. Web, www.ciw.edu.*

Conducts research in the physical and biological sciences at the following centers: the observatories of the Carnegie Institution with headquarters in Pasadena, Calif.; Geophysical Laboratory and Dept. of Terrestrial Magnetism in Washington, D.C.; Dept. of Plant Biology in Stanford, Calif.; and Dept. of Embryology in Baltimore, Md. Refers specific inquiries to appropriate department. Library open to the public by appointment.

Chemistry

AGENCIES

National Institute of Standards and Technology (Commerce Dept.), Chemical Science and Technology Laboratory, *Route I-270 and Quince Orchard Rd., Gaithersburg, MD 20899; (301) 975-3145. Fax, (301) 975-3845. Hratch G. Semerjian, Director.*

Develops uniform chemical measurement methods; provides federal agencies and industry with advisory and research services in the areas of analytical chemistry, biotechnology, chemical engineering, and physical chemistry; conducts interdisciplinary research efforts with other NIST laboratories.

National Institute of Standards and Technology (Commerce Dept.), Materials Science and Engineering

Laboratory, 100 Bureau Dr., MS 8500, Gaithersburg, MD 20899-8500 (mailing address: Bldg. 223, #B309, Gaithersburg, MD 20899); (301) 975-5658. Fax, (301) 975-5012. Leslie E. Smith, Director.

Provides measurements, data, standards, reference materials, concepts, and technical information fundamental to the processing, microstructure, properties, and performance of materials; addresses the scientific basis for new advanced materials; operates a research nuclear reactor for advanced materials characterization measurements; operates four materials data centers.

National Science Foundation, *Chemistry, 4201 Wilson Blvd., #1055, Arlington, VA 22230; (703) 306-1840. Fax, (703) 306-0534. Janet G. Osteryoung, Director. Toll-free fax, (800) 338-3128. Web, www.nsf.gov/chem.*

Awards grants to research programs in organic and macromolecular chemistry, materials chemistry, physical chemistry, analytical and surface chemistry, and inorganic, bioinorganic, and organometallic chemistry; provides funds for instruments needed in chemistry research; coordinates interdisciplinary programs. Monitors international research.

National Science Foundation, *Materials Research, 4201 Wilson Blvd., #1065, Arlington, VA 22230; (703) 306-1813. Fax, (703) 306-0515. Thomas A. Weber, Director. Web, www.nsf.gov.*

Provides grants for research in condensed matter physics; solid state chemistry and polymers; metals, ceramics, and electronic materials; and materials theory. Provides major instrumentation for these activities. Supports multidisciplinary research in these areas through materials research science and engineering centers. Supports national facilities and instrumentation in the areas of synchrotron radiation and high magnetic fields. Monitors international research.

NONPROFIT

American Assn. for Clinical Chemistry, *2101 L St. N.W., #202 20037-1526; (202) 857-0717. Fax, (202) 887-5093. Richard G. Flaherty, Executive Vice President. Web, www.aacc.org.*

International society of chemists, physicians, and other scientists specializing in clinical chemistry. Provides educational and professional development services; presents awards for outstanding achievement. Monitors legislation and regulations.

American Chemical Society, *1155 16th St. N.W. 20036; (202) 872-4600. Fax, (202) 872-4615. John K. Crum, Executive Director. Library, (202) 872-6000. Web, www.acs.org.*

Membership: professional chemists and chemical engineers. Maintains educational programs, including those that evaluate college chemistry departments and high school chemistry curricula. Administers grants and fellowships for basic research; sponsors international exchanges; presents achievement awards. Library open to the public.

American Chemical Society, *Petroleum Research Fund, 1155 16th St. N.W. 20036; (202) 872-4481. Fax, (202) 872-6319. Lawrence A. Funke, Administrator. Web, www.acs.org.*

Makes grants to nonprofit institutions for advanced scientific education and fundamental research related to the petroleum industry (chemistry, geology, engineering).

American Institute of Chemical Engineers, *1300 Eye St. N.W., #1090 East 20005-3314; (202) 962-8690. Fax, (202) 962-8699. Darlene S. Schuster, Director. General e-mail, dc@aiche.org. Web, www.aiche.org.*

Membership: professionals from industry, government, academia, and consulting, including students and retirees. Sponsors research in chemical engineering and promotes public understanding of the profession.

American Institute of Chemists (AIC), *515 King St., #420, Alexandria, VA 22314; (703) 836-2090. Fax, (703) 684-6048. Sharon Dobson, Executive Director. General e-mail, AICoffice@theaic.org. Web, www.theaic.org.*

Professional society of chemists and chemical engineers. Sponsors a national certification program. Publishes an annual professional directory. AIC Foundation sponsors the Student Award Program. Monitors legislation and regulations.

AOAC International, *481 N. Frederick Ave., #500, Gaithersburg, MD 20877; (301) 924-7077. Fax, (301) 924-7089. E. James Bradford, Executive Director. General e-mail, info@aoac.org. Web, www.aoac.org.*

International association of analytical science professionals, companies, government agencies, nongovernmental organizations, and institutions. Promotes methods validation and quality measurements in the analytical sciences. Supports the development, testing, validation, and publication of reliable chemical and biological methods of analyzing foods, drugs, feed, fertilizers, pesticides, water, forensic materials, and other substances.

Chemical Manufacturers Assn., *1300 Wilson Blvd., Arlington, VA 22209; (703) 741-5000. Fax, (703) 741-6097. Frederick L. Webber, President. Web, www.cmahq.com.*

Membership: manufacturers of basic industrial chemicals. Provides members with technical research, communications services, and legal affairs counseling. Interests include environmental safety and health, transportation, energy, and international trade. Monitors legislation and regulations.

Society of the Plastics Industry, *1801 K St. N.W., #600K 20006; (202) 974-5200. Fax, (202) 296-7005. Donald K. Duncan, President. Web, www.plasticsindustry.org.*

Promotes the plastics industry. Monitors legislation and regulations.

Synthetic Organic Chemical Manufacturers Assn., *1850 M St. N.W., #700 20036; (202) 721-4100. Fax, (202) 296-8120. Edmund Fording, President. Web, www.socma.com.*

Membership: companies that manufacture, distribute, and market organic chemicals, and providers of custom chemical services. Interests include international trade, environmental and occupational safety, and health issues; conducts workshops and seminars. Promotes commercial opportunities for members. Monitors legislation and regulations.

Computer Sciences

See also Internet and Related Technologies (chap. 4)

AGENCIES

National Coordination Office for Computing, Information, and Communications, *4201 Wilson Blvd., #690, Arlington, VA 22230; (703) 306-4722. Fax, (703) 306-4727. Kay Howell, Director. Web, www.ccic.gov.*

Coordinates multi-agency research and development projects that involve computing, information, and communications, including the High Performance Computing and Communications (HPCC) Program. Reports to the National Science and Technology Council; provides information to Congress, U.S. and foreign organizations, and the public.

National Institute of Standards and Technology *(Commerce Dept.), Information Technology Laboratory, Bldg. 225, #B264, Gaithersburg, MD 20899; (301) 975-2900. Fax, (301) 840-1357. William O. Mehuron, Director (Acting). Web, www.itl.nist.gov.*

Advises federal agencies on automatic data processing management and use of information technology; helps federal agencies maintain up-to-date computer technology support systems, emphasizing computer security techniques; recommends federal information processing standards; conducts research in computer science and technology.

National Science Foundation (NSF), *Computer and Information Sciences and Engineering, 4201 Wilson Blvd., Arlington, VA 22230; (703) 306-1900. Fax, (703) 306-0577. Ruzena Bajesy, Assistant Director. Web, www.cise.nsf.gov.*

Directorate that promotes basic research and education in computer and information sciences and engineering; helps maintain U.S. preeminence in these fields. Coordinates NSF involvement in the High-Performance Computing and Communications (HPCC) program; develops computer resources for scholarly communication, including links with foreign research and education networks; helps set Internet policy.

National Science Foundation, *Computer Communications Research, 4201 Wilson Blvd., #1145, Arlington, VA 22230; (703) 306-1910. Fax, (703) 306-1947. Michael Evangelist, Director. Web, www.cise.nsf.gov/cise/index.html.*

Awards grants for research in computer science and engineering, including programs in computer and computation theory; numeric, symbolic, and geometric computation; computer systems; and software engineering.

National Science Foundation, *Information and Intelligence Systems, 4201 Wilson Blvd., #1115, Arlington, VA 22230; (703) 306-1930. Fax, (703) 306-0599. Michael E. Lesk, Director. Web, www.cise.nsf.gov/iis.*

Supports research on designing, developing, managing, and using information systems, including database and expert systems, knowledge models and cognitive systems, machine intelligence and robotics, information technology and organizations, and interactive systems.

NONPROFIT

Computer and Communications Industry Assn., *666 11th St. N.W., #600 20001; (202) 783-0070. Fax, (202) 783-0534. Edward J. Black, President. General e-mail, ccia@aol.com. Web, www.ccianet.org.*

Membership: manufacturers and suppliers of computer data processing and communications-related products and services. Interests include telecommunications policy, capital formation and tax policy, federal procurement policy, communications and computer industry standards, intellectual property policies, encryption, international trade, and antitrust reform.

Computer Law Assn., *3028 Javier Rd., #402, Fairfax, VA 22031-4622; (703) 560-7747. Fax, (703) 207-7028. Barbara Fieser, Executive Director. General e-mail, clanet@aol.com. Web, www.cla.org.*

Membership: lawyers, law students, and nonattorneys concerned with the legal aspects of computers and com-

puter communications. Sponsors programs and provides information on such issues as software protection, contracting, telecommunications, international distribution, financing, taxes, copyrights, patents, and electronic data interchange. Focus includes the Internet and e-commerce.

Industry Advisory Council, *3601E Chain Bridge Rd., Fairfax, VA 22030; (703) 218-1965. Fax, (703) 218-1960. Terri K. Beck, Executive Director. Web, www.iaconline.org.*

Membership: producers of computer hardware and software and systems integrators. Serves as liaison between government and industry; offers programs on development and acquisition of information technology. Monitors legislation and regulations. (Affiliated with the Federation of Government Information Processing Councils.)

Information Technology Assn. of America, *1616 N. Fort Myer Dr., #1300, Arlington, VA 22209; (703) 284-5300. Fax, (703) 525-2279. Harris N. Miller, President. Web, www.itaa.org.*

Membership: personal computer software publishing companies. Promotes growth of the software industry worldwide; helps develop electronic commerce. Operates a toll-free hotline to report software piracy; investigates claims of software theft within corporations, financial institutions, academia, state and local governments, and nonprofit organizations. Provides legal counsel and initiates litigation on behalf of members.

Information Technology Industry Council, *1250 Eye St. N.W., #200 20005; (202) 737-8888. Fax, (202) 638-4922. Rhett Dawson, President. Press, (202) 626-5725. General e-mail, webmaster@itic.org. Web, www.itic.org.*

Membership: providers of information technology products and services. Promotes the global competitiveness of its members and advocates free trade. Seeks to protect intellectual property and encourages the use of voluntary standards.

Information Technology Resellers Assn., *11921 Freedom Dr., #550, Reston, VA 20190; (703) 904-4337. Fax, (703) 834-6920. David E. Poisson, President. Web, www.itra.net.*

Membership: companies that buy, sell, and lease new and used computers and other high-technology equipment. Acts as liaison with equipment manufacturers; enforces industry code of ethics; conducts industry surveys. Monitors legislation and regulations.

Institute of Electrical and Electronics Engineers–United States Activities, *Professional Activities, Washington Office, 1828 L St. N.W., #1202 20036-5104; (202) 785-0017. Fax, (202) 785-0835. W. Thomas Suttle,*

Managing Director. General e-mail, ieeeusa@ieee.org. Web, www.ieee.org.

U.S. arm of an international technological and professional organization. Interests include promoting career and technology policy interests of members.

International Council for Computer Communication, *P.O. Box 9745 20016; (703) 836-7787. John D. McKendree, Treasurer. Web, www.icccgovernors.org.*

Membership: industry, government, and academic leaders interested in computer communications issues. Promotes scientific research in and development of computer communication; encourages evaluation of applications of computer communication for educational, scientific, medical, economic, legal, cultural, and other peaceful purposes; sponsors international conferences, seminars, and workshops. (Affiliated with the International Federation for Information Processing in Vienna, Austria.)

Software and Information Industry Assn., *1730 M St. N.W., #700 20036; (202) 452-1600. Fax, (202) 223-8756. Ken Walsh, President. Web, www.siia.net.*

Membership: publishers of microcomputer software. Promotes the industry worldwide; conducts investigations and litigation to protect members' copyrights; collects data, including monthly sales information; offers contracts reference and credit information exchange services; sponsors conferences and seminars. Monitors legislation and regulations.

Mathematics

AGENCIES

National Institute of Standards and Technology (NIST), *(Commerce Dept.), Information Technology Laboratory, Bldg. 225, #B264, Gaithersburg, MD 20899; (301) 975-2900. Fax, (301) 840-1357. William O. Mehuron, Director (Acting). Web, www.itl.nist.gov.*

Develops improved mathematical and statistical models and computational methods; consults on their use. Manages and operates NIST central computing facilities.

National Science Foundation, *Mathematical Sciences, 4201 Wilson Blvd., #1025, Arlington, VA 22230; (703) 306-1870. Fax, (703) 306-0555. Philippe Tondeur, Director. Web, www.nsf.gov/mps/dms.*

Provides grants for research in the mathematical sciences in the following areas: classical and modern analysis, geometric analysis, topology and foundations, algebra and number theory, applied and computational mathematics, and statistics and probability. Maintains special projects program, which supports scientific computing equipment for mathematics research and several research institutes. Sponsors conferences, workshops,

and postdoctoral research fellowships. Monitors international research.

NONPROFIT

American Statistical Assn., *1429 Duke St., Alexandria, VA 22314; (703) 684-1221. Fax, (703) 684-2037. Ray Waller, Executive Director. General e-mail, asainfo@ amstat.org. Web, www.amstat.org.*

Membership: individuals interested in statistics and related quantitative fields. Advises government agencies on statistics and methodology in agency research; promotes development of statistical techniques for use in business, industry, finance, government, agriculture, and science.

Conference Board of the Mathematical Sciences, *1529 18th St. N.W. 20036; (202) 293-1170. Fax, (202) 265-2384. Ronald C. Rosier, Administrative Officer. Web, www.maa.org/cbms/cbms.html.*

Membership: presidents of fifteen mathematical sciences professional societies. Serves as a forum for discussion of issues of concern to the mathematical sciences community.

Mathematical Assn. of America, *1529 18th St. N.W. 20036-1358; (202) 387-5200. Fax, (202) 265-2384. Tina H. Straley, Executive Director. General e-mail, maahq@ maa.org. Web, www.maa.org.*

Membership: mathematics professors and individuals worldwide with a professional interest in mathematics. Seeks to improve the teaching of collegiate mathematics. Conducts professional development programs.

Physics

AGENCIES

National Institute of Standards and Technology *(Commerce Dept.), Materials Science and Engineering Laboratory, 100 Bureau Dr., MS 8500, Gaithersburg, MD 20899-8500 (mailing address: Bldg. 223, #B309, Gaithersburg, MD 20899); (301) 975-5658. Fax, (301) 975-5012. Leslie E. Smith, Director.*

Provides measurements, data, standards, reference materials, concepts, and technical information fundamental to the processing, microstructure, properties, and performance of materials; addresses the scientific basis for new advanced materials; operates a research nuclear reactor for advanced materials characterization measurements; operates four materials data centers.

National Institute of Standards and Technology *(Commerce Dept.), Physics Laboratory, 100 Bureau Dr., Bldg. 221, #B160, Gaithersburg, MD 20899-8400; (301) 975-4200. Fax, (301) 975-3038. Katharine B. Gebbie, Director. Web, physics.nist.gov.*

Conducts research to improve measurement capability and quantitative understanding of basic physical processes that underlie measurement science; investigates structure and dynamics of atoms and molecules; provides national standards for time and frequency and for measurement of radiation; develops radiometric and wavelength standards; analyzes national measurement needs.

National Science Foundation, *Materials Research,* *4201 Wilson Blvd., #1065, Arlington, VA 22230; (703) 306-1813. Fax, (703) 306-0515. Thomas A. Weber, Director. Web, www.nsf.gov.*

Provides grants for research in condensed matter physics; solid state chemistry and polymers; metals, ceramics, and electronic materials; and materials theory. Provides major instrumentation for these activities. Supports multidisciplinary research in these areas through materials research science and engineering centers. Supports national facilities and instrumentation in the areas of synchrotron radiation and high magnetic fields. Monitors international research.

National Science Foundation, *Physics,* *4201 Wilson Blvd., #1015, Arlington, VA 22230; (703) 306-1890. Fax, (703) 306-0566. Joseph L. Dehmer, Director. Web, www.nsf.gov/mps/phy.*

Awards grants for research and special programs in atomic, molecular, and optical physics; elementary particle physics; and nuclear, theoretical, and gravitational physics. Monitors international research.

Science *(Energy Dept.), High Energy and Nuclear Physics,* *19901 Germantown Rd., Germantown, MD 20874-1290; (301) 903-3713. Fax, (301) 903-5079. S. Peter Rosen, Associate Director. Web, www.science.doe.gov.*

Provides grants and facilities for research in high energy and nuclear physics. Constructs, operates, and maintains particle accelerators used in high energy and nuclear physics research.

NONPROFIT

American Institute of Physics, *1 Physics Ellipse, College Park, MD 20740-3843; (301) 209-3000. Fax, (301) 209-0843. Marc H. Brodsky, Executive Director. Web, www.api.org.*

Fosters cooperation among the physics community; improves public understanding of science; disseminates information on scientific research.

American Physical Society, *Public Information, Washington Office,* *529 14th St. N.W., #1050 20045; (202) 662-8700. Fax, (202) 662-8711. Robert L. Park,*

Director. General e-mail, opa@aps.org. Web, www.aps.org.

Scientific and educational society of educators, students, citizens, and scientists, including industrial scientists. Sponsors studies on issues of public concern related to physics, such as reactor safety and energy use. Informs members of national and international developments. (Headquarters in College Park, Md.)

Optical Society of America, *2010 Massachusetts Ave. N.W. 20036; (202) 223-8130. Fax, (202) 223-1096. John Thorner, Executive Director. Web, www.osa.org.*

Membership: researchers, educators, manufacturers, students, and others interested in optics and photonics worldwide. Promotes research and information exchange; conducts conferences. Interests include use of optics in medical imaging and surgery.

Weights and Measures/ Metric System

AGENCIES

National Conference on Weights and Measures, *15245 Shady Grove Rd., #130, Rockville, MD 20850; (240) 632-9454. Fax, (301) 990-9771. Beth W. Palys, Executive Director. General e-mail, ncwm@mgmtsol.com.*

Membership: state and local officials who deal with weights and measures, industry and business representatives, individuals, and associations. Serves as a national forum on issues related to weights and measures administration; develops consensus on uniform laws and regulations, specifications, and tolerances for weighing and measuring devices.

National Institute of Standards and Technology *(Commerce Dept.), Measurement Services,* *820 W. Diamond Ave., Gaithersburg, MD 20899 (mailing address: Bldg. 820, #306, MS 2000, Gaithersburg, MD 20899); (301) 975-8424. Fax, (301) 971-2183. Richard F. Kayser, Director. Web, www.nist.gov.*

Disseminates physical, chemical, and engineering measurement standards and provides services to ensure accurate and compatible measurements, specifications, and codes on a national and international scale.

National Institute of Standards and Technology *(Commerce Dept.), Metric Program,* *100 Bureau Dr., Stop 2000, Gaithersburg, MD 20899-2000; (301) 975-3690. Fax, (301) 948-1416. Gerard Iannelli, Director. General e-mail, metric_prg@nist.gov. Web, www.nist.gov/metric.*

Coordinates federal metric conversion transition to ensure consistency; provides the public with technical and general information about the metric system; assists state and local governments, businesses, and educators with metric conversion activities.

National Institute of Standards and Technology *(Commerce Dept.), Weights and Measures, 820 W. Diamond Ave., #223, Gaithersburg, MD 20878; (301) 975-4004. Fax, (301) 926-0647. Gilbert M. Ugiansky, Chief.*

Promotes uniformity in weights and measures law and enforcement. Provides weights and measures agencies with training and technical assistance; assists state and local agencies in adapting their weights and measures to meet national standards; conducts research; sets uniform standards and regulations.

CONGRESS

House Science Committee, *Subcommittee on Technology, 2319 RHOB 20515; (202) 225-8844. Fax, (202) 225-4438. Rep. Constance A. Morella, R-Md., Chair; Jeffrey Grove, Staff Director. Web, www.house.gov/science.*

Jurisdiction over legislation on weights and measurement systems; monitors the National Institute of Standards and Technology.

Senate Commerce, Science, and Transportation Committee, *Subcommittee on Science, Technology, and Space, SH-428 20510; (202) 224-8172. Fax, (202) 228-0326. Sen. Bill Frist, R-Tenn., Chair; Floyd DesChamps, Professional Staff Member. Web, commerce.senate.gov.*

Jurisdiction over legislation on weights and measurement systems; monitors the National Institute of Standards and Technology.

NONPROFIT

American National Metric Council, *4340 East-West Hwy., #401, Bethesda, MD 20814-4408; (301) 718-6508. Fax, (301) 656-0989. Gian Argenentati, President. General e-mail, anmc@paimgmt.com.*

Membership: companies, libraries, organizations, and individuals. Coordinates voluntary transition to the metric system in the United States and assists with industry transition; serves as information source on U.S. and international metric planning and use.

📠 SOCIAL SCIENCES

See also History and Preservation (chap. 5)

AGENCIES

National Museum of Natural History *(Smithsonian Institution), Anthropology, 10th St. and Constitution Ave. N.W., MRC 112 20560; (202) 357-2363. Fax, (202)*

357-2208. Carolyn Rose, Chair. Information, (202) 357-1592. Web, nmnhwww.si.edu/departments/anthro.html.

Conducts research on paleo-Indian archeology and prehistory, New World origins, and paleoecology. Maintains anthropological and human studies film archives. Museum maintains public exhibitions of human cultures.

National Museum of Natural History *(Smithsonian Institution), Library, 10th St. and Constitution Ave. N.W., #51 20560; (202) 357-1496. Fax, (202) 357-1896. Ann Juneau, Chief Librarian.*

Maintains reference collections covering anthropology and ethnology; permits on-site use of the collections. Open to the public by appointment; makes interlibrary loans.

National Science Foundation, *Social, Behavioral, and Economic Sciences, 4201 Wilson Blvd., #905, Arlington, VA 22230; (703) 306-1700. Fax, (703) 306-0495. Norman M. Bradburn, Assistant Director. Web, www.nsf.gov/sbe.*

Directorate that awards grants for research in behavioral and cognitive sciences, social and economic sciences, science resources studies, and international programs. Provides support for workshops, symposia, and conferences.

NONPROFIT

American Anthropological Assn., *4350 N. Fairfax Dr., #640, Arlington, VA 22203-1620; (703) 528-1902. Fax, (703) 528-3546. William E. Davis III, Executive Director. Web, www.aaanet.org.*

Membership: anthropologists, educators, students, and others interested in anthropological studies. Publishes research studies of member organizations, sponsors workshops, and disseminates to members information concerning developments in anthropology worldwide.

American Institutes for Research, *3333 K St. N.W., #300 20007; (202) 342-5000. Fax, (202) 342-5033. David A. Goslin, President. Web, www.air-dc.org.*

Conducts research and analysis in the behavioral and social sciences, including education and health research and data analysis to assess fairness and equity in the workplace; assists in designing and writing documents; assesses usability of software, systems, and other products; studies human-machine interface.

American Psychological Assn., *750 1st St. N.E. 20002-4242; (202) 336-5500. Fax, (202) 336-6069. Raymond D. Fowler, Executive Vice President. Library, (202) 336-5640. TTY, (202) 336-6123. Web, www.apa.org.*

Membership: professional psychologists, educators, and behavioral research scientists. Supports research, training, and professional services; works toward improving the qualifications, competence, and training programs of psychologists. Monitors international research and U.S. legislation on mental health.

American Sociological Assn., *1307 New York Ave. N.W., #700 20005; (202) 383-9005. Fax, (202) 638-0882. Felice Levine, Executive Officer. TTY, (202) 872-0486. General e-mail, executive.office@asanet.org. Web, www. asanet.org.*

Membership: sociologists, social scientists, and others interested in research, teaching, and application of sociology in the United States and internationally. Sponsors professional development program, teaching resources center, and education programs; offers fellowships for minorities.

Consortium of Social Science Assns., *1522 K St. N.W., #836 20005; (202) 842-3525. Fax, (202) 842-2788. Howard J. Silver, Executive Director. Web, www.cosa.org.*

Consortium of associations in the fields of anthropology, criminology, economics, history, political science, psychology, sociology, statistics, geography, linguistics, law, and social science. Advocates support for research and monitors federal funding in the social and behavioral sciences; conducts seminars.

Human Resources Research Organization, *66 Canal Center Plaza, #400, Alexandria, VA 22314; (703) 549-3611. Fax, (703) 549-9025. Lauress L. Wise II, President. Web, www.humrro.org.*

Research and development organization in the fields of industrial and behavioral psychology. Studies, designs, develops, and evaluates personnel systems, chiefly in the workplace. Interests include personnel selection and promotion, career progression, performance appraisal, training, and program evaluation.

Institute for the Study of Man, *1133 13th St. N.W., #C2 20005-4297; (202) 371-2700. Fax, (202) 371-1523. Roger Pearson, Executive Director. General e-mail, socecon@aol.com. Web, www.mankind.org.*

Publishes academic journals, books, and monographs in areas related to anthropology, psychology, genetics, archeology, linguistics, and cultural history.

Geography and Mapping

AGENCIES

Census Bureau *(Commerce Dept.), Geography, 8903 Presidential Pkwy., Upper Marlboro, MD 20772; (301) 457-2131. Fax, (301) 457-4710. Robert W. Marx, Chief. Web, www.census.geo.gov.*

Manages the TIGER system, a nationwide geographic database; prepares maps for use in conducting censuses and surveys and for showing their results geographically; determines names and current boundaries of legal geographic units; defines names and boundaries of selected statistical areas; develops geographic code schemes; maintains computer files of area measurements, geographic boundaries, and map features with address ranges.

National Archives and Records Administration, Cartographic and Architectural Branch, *8601 Adelphi Rd., #3320, College Park, MD 20740-6001; (301) 713-7030. Fax, (301) 713-7488. Robert Richardson, Director. TTY, (301) 713-7030. General e-mail, carto@arch2.nara. gov.*

Makes information available on federal government cartographic records, architectural drawings, and aerial mapping films; prepares descriptive guides and inventories of records. Library open to the public. Records may be reproduced for a fee.

National Imagery and Mapping Agency *(Defense Dept.), 4600 Sangamore Rd., Bethesda, MD 20816; (301) 227-7300. Fax, (301) 227-3696. Lt. Gen. James C. King, Director. Web, www.nima.mil.*

Combat support agency that provides imagery and geospatial information to national policymakers and military forces in support of national defense objectives; incorporates the missions and functions of the former Defense Mapping Agency, Central Imaging Office, and Defense Dissemination Program Office.

National Oceanic and Atmospheric Administration *(Commerce Dept.), National Geodetic Survey, 1315 East-West Hwy., SSMC3, Silver Spring, MD 20910-3282; (301) 713-3222. Fax, (301) 713-4175. Charles W. Challstrom, Director. Web, www.ngs.noaa.gov.*

Develops and maintains the National Spatial Reference System, a national geodetic reference system which serves as a common reference for latitude, longitude, height, scale, orientation, and gravity measurements. Maps the nation's coastal zone and waterways; conducts research and development programs to improve the collection, distribution, and use of spatial data; coordinates the development and application of new surveying instrumentation and procedures; and assists state, county, and municipal agencies through a variety of cooperative programs.

State Dept., *Office of the Geographer and Global Issues, 2201 C St. N.W., #8742 20520; (202) 647-2021. Fax, (202) 647-0504. William B. Wood, Director. Web, www.state.gov.*

Advises the State Dept. and other federal agencies on geographic and cartographic matters. Furnishes technical and analytical research and advice in the field of geography.

U.S. Board on Geographic Names, *12201 Sunrise Valley Dr., 523 National Center, Reston, VA 20192-0523; (703) 648-4544. Fax, (703) 648-4549. Roger L. Payne, Executive Secretary, Domestic Names Committee; Randall Flynn, Executive Secretary, Foreign Names Committee, (301) 227-3050. Web, mapping.usgs.gov/www/gnis.*

Interagency organization established by Congress to standardize geographic names. Board members are representatives from the Depts. of Agriculture, Commerce, Defense, Interior, and State; the Central Intelligence Agency; the Government Printing Office; the Library of Congress; and the Postal Service. Sets policy governing the use of both domestic and foreign geographic names as well as underseas and Antarctic feature names.

U.S. Geological Survey *(Interior Dept.),* **Data and Information Delivery,** *12201 Sunrise Valley Dr., Reston, VA 20192 (mailing address: 508 National Center, Reston, VA 20192); (703) 648-5780. Fax, (703) 648-5939. Hedy J. Rossmeissl, Senior Program Advisor.*

Plans and coordinates information dissemination activities of the National Mapping Division; manages inventory and assures proper storage and preservation for all products.

U.S. Geological Survey *(Interior Dept.),* **Earth Science Information Center,** *507 National Center, Reston, VA 20192-1507; (703) 648-5920. Fax, (703) 648-5548. Susan Russell-Robinson, Chief. U.S. maps, (888) 275-8747. Web, www.usgs.gov.*

Collects, organizes, and distributes cartographic, geographic, hydrologic, and other earth science information; offers maps, reports, and other publications, digital cartographic data, aerial photographs, and space imagery and manned spacecraft photographs for sale. Acts as clearinghouse on cartographic and geographic data.

U.S. Geological Survey *(Interior Dept.),* **National Mapping,** *12201 Sunrise Valley Dr., MS 516, Reston, VA 20192; (703) 648-5748. Fax, (703) 648-7031. Richard E. Witmer, Chief. Information and data services, (703) 648-5780. Web, www.nmd.usgs.gov.*

Provides government agencies and the public with geographic and cartographic information, maps, and technical assistance; conducts research; collects, compiles, and analyzes information about features of the earth's surface; develops and maintains a digital geographic/cartographic database and assists users in applying spatial data; coordinates federal mapping activities; encourages the development of surveying and mapping techniques.

CONGRESS

Library of Congress, *Geography and Map Division,* *101 Independence Ave. S.E., #B02 20540-4650; (202) 707-8530. Fax, (202) 707-8531. John R. Hébert, Chief. Reference, (202) 707-6277.*

Maintains cartographic collection of maps, atlases, globes, and reference books. Reference service provided; reading room open to the public. Interlibrary loans available through the library's loan division; photocopies, when not limited by copyright or other restriction, available through the library's photoduplication service.

NONPROFIT

American Congress on Surveying and Mapping, *5410 Grosvenor Lane, #100, Bethesda, MD 20814-2122; (301) 493-0200. Fax, (301) 493-8245. Curtis W. Sumner, Executive Director. General e-mail, infoacsm@mindspring.com. Web, www.survmap.org.*

Membership: professionals working worldwide in surveying, cartography, geodesy, and geographic/land information systems (computerized mapping systems used in urban, regional, and environmental planning). Sponsors workshops and seminars for surveyors and mapping scientists; participates in accreditation of college and university surveying and related degree programs; grants fellowships; develops and administers certification programs for hydrographers and technician surveyors. Monitors legislation and regulations.

American Society for Photogrammetry and Remote Sensing, *Imaging and Geospacial Information Society,* *5410 Grosvenor Lane, #210, Bethesda, MD 20814-2160; (301) 493-0290. Fax, (301) 493-0208. James R. Plasker, Executive Director. General e-mail, asprs@asprs.org. Web, www.asprs.org.*

Promotes use of photogrammetry, remote sensing, and geographic information systems (computerized mapping systems used in urban, regional, and environmental planning) for earth resource evaluation and preparation of maps; interests include global applications of mapping. Sponsors continuing education programs.

Assn. of American Geographers, *1710 16th St. N.W. 20009-3198; (202) 234-1450. Fax, (202) 234-2744. Ronald F. Abler, Executive Director. General e-mail, gaia@aag.org. Web, www.aag.org.*

Membership: educators, students, business executives, government employees, and scientists in the field of geography. Seeks to advance professional studies in geography and encourages the application of geographic research in education, government, and business.

National Geographic Maps, *1145 17th St. N.W. 20036-4688; (202) 857-7799. Fax, (202) 429-5704. Allen Carroll, Director. Library, (202) 775-6173. Map orders, (800) 962-1643. Web, www.nationalgeographic.com.*

Educational and scientific organization. Supports and conducts research on cartography, mapping, and geography. Produces and sells to the public political, physical, and thematic maps, atlases, and globes. (Affiliated with National Geographic Society.)

🛰 SPACE SCIENCES

AGENCIES

Air Force Dept. *(Defense Dept.)*, **Space,** *1640 Air Force Pentagon, #4E998 20330-1640; (703) 693-5799. Fax, (703) 693-6567. Richard M. McCormick, Deputy Assistant Secretary. Web, www.af.mil.*

Formulates, reviews, and executes Air Force policies and programs relating to space.

Commerce Dept., *Space Commercialization, 14th St. and Constitution Ave. N.W., #4817 20230; (202) 482-6125. Fax, (202) 482-5173. Gary R. Bachula, Director (Acting). General e-mail, spaceinfo@ta.doc.gov. Web, www.ta.doc.gov/space.*

Promotes private investment in space activities; seeks to remove legal, policy, and institutional impediments to space commerce; represents private sector interests at the federal level; coordinates commercial space policy for the Commerce Dept. Monitors international developments.

Federal Aviation Administration *(Transportation Dept.)*, **Commercial Space Transportation,** *800 Independence Ave. S.W., #331 20591; (202) 267-7793. Fax, (202) 267-5450. Patricia Grace Smith, Associate Administrator. Web, ast.faa.gov.*

Promotes and facilitates the operation of commercial expendable space launch vehicles by the private sector; licenses and regulates these activities.

National Aeronautics and Space Administration (NASA), *300 E St. S.W. 20546 (mailing address: NASA Headquarters, Mail Code A 20546); (202) 358-1010. Fax, (202) 358-2811. Daniel S. Goldin, Administrator. Information, (202) 358-0000. TTY, (800) 877-8339. Locator, (202) 358-0000. Web, www.hq.nasa.gov.*

Conducts research on problems of flight within and outside the earth's atmosphere; develops, constructs, tests, and operates experimental aeronautical and space vehicles; conducts activities for manned and unmanned exploration of space; maintains information center.

National Aeronautics and Space Administration, *Aero-Space Technology, 300 E St. S.W. 20546 (mailing address: NASA Headquarters, Mail Code R 20546); (202) 358-2693. Fax, (202) 358-4066. Sam Venneri, Associate Administrator. Web, www.hq.nasa.gov/office/aero.*

Conducts research in aerodynamics, materials, structures, avionics, propulsion, high performance computing, human factors, aviation safety, and space transportation in support of national space and aeronautical research and technology goals. Manages the following NASA research centers: Ames (Moffett, Calif.); Dryden (Edwards, Calif.); Langley (Hampton, Va.); and Glenn (Cleveland, Ohio).

National Aeronautics and Space Administration, *Goddard Space Flight Center, Code 100, Greenbelt, MD 20771; (301) 286-5121. Fax, (301) 286-1714. Al Diaz, Director. Information, (301) 286-8955. Web, pao.gsfc.nasa.gov.*

Conducts space and earth science research; performs advanced planning for space missions; develops and manages spacecraft and scientific instrumentation; functions as the control center for earth orbital satellites; operates the NASA tracking and data relay satellite system.

National Aeronautics and Space Administration, *International Space Station, 300 E St. S.W. 20546 (mailing address: NASA Headquarters, Mail Code M-4 20546); (202) 358-4424. Fax, (202) 358-2848. W. Michael Hawes, Director. Web, station.nasa.gov.*

Responsible for developing a permanently manned orbiting space station to serve as a research facility for scientific, technological, and commercial activities.

National Aeronautics and Space Administration, *Life and Microgravity Sciences and Applications, 300 E St. S.W. 20546 (mailing address: NASA Headquarters, Mail Code U 20546); (202) 358-0122. Fax, (202) 358-4174. Dr. Arnold E. Nicogossian, Associate Administrator. Web, www.hq.nasa.gov/office/olmsa.*

Conducts all in-orbit exploration of space. Areas of research include life sciences (people, animals, and plants), materials (crystals and minerals), and microgravity effects observed in space. Participates in international projects and conferences.

National Aeronautics and Space Administration, *NASA Advisory Council, 300 E St. S.W. 20546 (mailing*

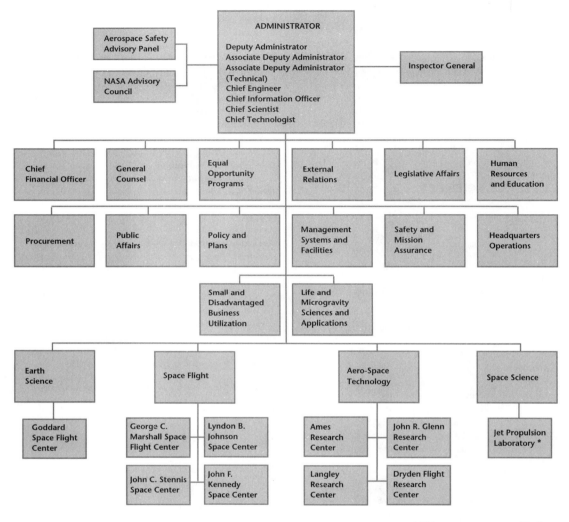

* JPL is a contractor-operated facility

address: NASA Headquarters, Mail Code Z 20546); (202) 358-2096. Fax, (202) 358-4336. Lori B. Garver, Executive Secretary. Web, www.hq.nasa.gov/office/codez/nac/nac.htm.

Advises the administrator on NASA's aeronautics and space plans and programs. The council is comprised of the following advisory committees: Aeronautics, Technology and Commercialization, Life and Microgravity Sciences and Applications, Space Science, International Space Station, Minority Business Resource, and Earth Systems Science and Applications.

National Aeronautics and Space Administration, National Space Science Data Center, Goddard Space Flight Center, Code 633, Greenbelt, MD 20771; (301) 286-7355. Fax, (301) 286-1771. Joseph H. King, Head. Web, nssdc.gsfc.nasa.gov.

Acquires, catalogs, and distributes NASA mission data to the international space science community, including research organizations, universities, and other interested organizations worldwide. Provides software tools and network access to promote collaborative data analysis. (Mail data requests to above address, attention: Code 633.4/Request Coordination Office, or phone [301] 286-6695.)

National Aeronautics and Space Administration, *Safety and Mission Assurance, 300 E St. S.W. 20546 (mailing address: NASA Headquarters, Mail Code Q 20546); (202) 358-2406. Fax, (202) 358-2699. Frederick D. Gregory, Associate Administrator. Web, www.hq.nasa.gov/ office/codeq.*

Evaluates the safety and reliability of NASA systems and programs. Alerts officials to technical execution and physical readiness of NASA projects.

National Aeronautics and Space Administration, *Space Communications, 300 E St. S.W. 20546 (mailing address: NASA Headquarters, Mail Code M-3 20546); (202) 358-2020. Fax, (202) 358-2865. Robert Spearing, Director. Web, www.hq.nasa.gov.*

Plans, develops, and operates worldwide tracking, data acquisition, data processing, and communications systems, facilities, and services essential to the agency's space flight missions, including the Space Tracking Data Network at Goddard Space Flight Center in Greenbelt, Md., and the Deep Space Network operated by the Jet Propulsion Laboratory in Pasadena, Calif. Gives support to planetary spacecraft, earth-orbiting satellites, shuttle missions, sounding rockets, balloons, and aeronautical test vehicles.

National Aeronautics and Space Administration, *Space Flight, 300 E St. S.W. 20546 (mailing address: NASA Headquarters, Mail Code M 20546); (202) 358-2015. Fax, (202) 358-2838. Joseph H. Rothenberg, Associate Administrator. Web, www.hq.nasa.gov/osf.*

Responsible for space transportation systems operations, including U.S. participation in international missions. Manages the Johnson Space Center, Kennedy Space Center, Marshall Space Flight Center, and Stennis Space Center. Administers the development, testing, and production phases of the space shuttle. Manages the shuttle space lab program and the space station.

National Aeronautics and Space Administration, *Space Science, 300 E St. S.W. 20546 (mailing address: NASA Headquarters, Mail Code S 20546); (202) 358-1409. Fax, (202) 358-3092. Edward J. Weiler, Associate Administrator. Information, (202) 358-1547. Web, spacescience.nasa.gov.*

Makes information available on technological developments that have resulted from NASA programs. (Accepts written requests for specific technical information.)

National Aeronautics and Space Administration, *Space Science and Aeronautics, 300 E St. S.W. 20546 (mailing address: NASA Headquarters, Mail Code IS 20546); (202) 358-0900. Fax, (202) 358-3030. P. Diane Rausch, Director. Web, www.hq.nasa.gov.*

Acts as liaison with space agencies of foreign countries; negotiates and implements international agreements for cooperation in space; works with other U.S. government agencies on international issues regarding space and aeronautics.

National Aeronautics and Space Administration, *Space Shuttle, 300 E St. S.W., #7A70, MS M-7 20546; (202) 358-1200. Fax, (202) 358-2848. William F. Readdy, Director. Web, www.hq.nasa.gov.*

Directs policy related to operation of the space shuttle program, including U.S.-Russian cooperative programs and commercial uses of the shuttle.

National Air and Space Museum *(Smithsonian Institution), 6th St. and Independence Ave. S.W. 20560-0310; (202) 357-1745. Fax, (202) 357-2426. Gen. John R. Dailey, Director. Library, (202) 357-3133. Press, (202) 357-1552. TTY, (202) 357-1505. Education office, (202) 786-2106. Daily space and earth phenomena report, (202) 357-2000 (recording). Tours, (202) 357-1400. Web, www.nasm.si.edu.*

Collects, preserves, and exhibits astronautical objects and equipment of historical interest, including manned spacecraft and communications and weather satellites. Library open to the public by appointment.

CONGRESS

General Accounting Office, *National Security and International Affairs, 441 G St. N.W., #4035 20548; (202) 512-2800. Fax, (202) 512-7686. Henry L. Hinton, Assistant Comptroller General.*

Independent, nonpartisan agency in the legislative branch. Audits, analyzes, and evaluates the performance of the National Aeronautics and Space Administration. Makes unclassified reports available to the public.

House Appropriations Committee, *Subcommittee on VA, HUD, and Independent Agencies, H143 CAP 20515; (202) 225-3241. Rep. James T. Walsh, R-N.Y., Chair; Frank Cushing, Staff Director. Web, www.house.gov/ appropriations.*

Jurisdiction over legislation to appropriate funds for the National Aeronautics and Space Administration.

House Government Reform Committee, *Subcommittee on National Security, Veterans Affairs, and International Affairs, B372 RHOB 20515; (202) 225-2548. Fax, (202) 225-2382. Rep. Christopher Shays,*

R-Conn., Chair; Lawrence Halloran, Staff Director. Web, www.house.gov/reform.

Oversees operations of the National Aeronautics and Space Administration (jurisdiction shared with the House Science Committee).

House Science Committee, *Subcommittee on Space and Aeronautics,* B374 RHOB 20515; (202) 225-7858. Fax, (202) 225-6415. Rep. Dana Rohrabacher, R-Calif., Chair; Shana Dale, Staff Director. Web, www.house.gov/science.

Jurisdiction over legislation on space programs, national research and development in space exploration, space commercialization, earth-observing systems, the National Aeronautics and Space Administration (jurisdiction shared with House Government Reform Committee), and space-related activities of the Transportation and Commerce departments.

Senate Appropriations Committee, *Subcommittee on VA, HUD, and Independent Agencies,* SD-130 20510; (202) 224-7211. Sen. Christopher S. Bond, R-Mo., Chair; Jon Kamarck, Staff Director. Web, appropriations.senate.gov/vahud.

Jurisdiction over legislation to appropriate funds for the National Aeronautics and Space Administration.

Senate Commerce, Science, and Transportation Committee, *Subcommittee on Science, Technology, and Space,* SH-428 20510; (202) 224-8172. Fax, (202) 228-0326. Sen. Bill Frist, R-Tenn., Chair; Floyd DesChamps, Professional Staff Member. Web, commerce.senate.gov.

Jurisdiction over legislation on nonmilitary space programs, national research and development in space exploration, space commercialization, and earth-observing systems. Oversight and legislative jurisdiction over the National Aeronautics and Space Administration.

INTERNATIONAL ORGANIZATIONS

European Space Agency, *Washington Office,* 955 L'Enfant Plaza S.W., #7800 20024; (202) 488-4158. Fax, (202) 488-4930. Ian W. Pryke, Head. Web, www.esa.int.

Intergovernmental agency that promotes international collaboration in space research and development and the use of space technology for peaceful purposes. Members include Austria, Belgium, Denmark, Finland, France, Germany, Ireland, Italy, the Netherlands, Norway, Portugal, Spain, Sweden, Switzerland, and the United Kingdom; Canada participates in some programs. (Headquarters in Paris.)

NONPROFIT

Aerospace Education Foundation, 1501 Lee Hwy., Arlington, VA 22209; (703) 247-5839. Fax, (703) 247-

5853. Dan Marrs, Managing Director (Acting). Information, (800) 727-3337. General e-mail, aefstaff@aef.org. Web, www.aef.org.

Promotes knowledge of U.S. military and civilian aerospace development and history. Sponsors educational symposia and scholarships for enlisted personnel and officers on active duty or in the National Guard and Reserves. (Affiliated with the Air Force Assn.)

Aerospace Industries Assn., 1250 Eye St. N.W., #1200 20005-3922; (202) 371-8400. Fax, (202) 371-8470. John W. Douglass, President. Press, (202) 371-8544. Web, www.aia-aerospace.org.

Represents U.S. manufacturers of commercial, military, and business aircraft; helicopters; aircraft engines; missiles; spacecraft; and related components and equipment. Interests include international standards and trade.

American Astronautical Society, 6352 Rolling Mill Pl., #102, Springfield, VA 22152; (703) 866-0020. Fax, (703) 866-3526. Carolyn Brown, Executive Director. General e-mail, aas@astronautical.org. Web, www.astronautical.org.

Scientific and technological society of researchers, scientists, astronauts, and other professionals in the field of astronautics and spaceflight engineering. Organizes national and local meetings and symposia; promotes international cooperation.

American Institute of Aeronautics and Astronautics, 1801 Alexander Bell Dr., #500, Reston, VA 20191; (703) 264-7500. Fax, (703) 264-7551. Cort Durocher, Executive Director. Information, (800) 639-2422. General e-mail, custserv@aiaa.org. Web, www.aiaa.org.

Membership: engineers, scientists, and students in the fields of aeronautics and astronautics. Holds workshops on aerospace technical issues for congressional subcommittees; sponsors international conferences. Offers computerized database through its Technical Information Service in New York.

National Research Council, *Aeronautics and Space Engineering Board,* 2001 Wisconsin Ave. N.W. 20007 (mailing address: 2101 Constitution Ave. N.W., #HA292 20418); (202) 334-2855. Fax, (202) 334-2482. George M. Levin, Director. Library, (202) 334-2125. Press, (202) 334-2138. Publications, (202) 334-2855. Web, www.nas.edu/cets/aseb.

Membership: aeronautics and space experts. Advises government agencies on aeronautics and space engineering research, technology, experiments, international programs, and policy. Library open to the public by appointment.

National Research Council, *Space Studies Board,* 2001 Wisconsin Ave. N.W. 20007 (mailing address: 2101 Constitution Ave. N.W., #HA584 20418); (202) 334-3477. Fax, (202) 334-3701. Joseph K. Alexander, Director. Library, (202) 334-2125. Press, (202) 334-2138. General e-mail, ssb@nas.edu. Web, www.nas.edu/ssb/ssb.html.

Provides assessments for NASA and other federal agencies on space science and applications, including international programs; provides research assessments and long-term research strategies. Interests include astronomy, lunar and planetary exploration, solar and space physics, earth science, space biology and medicine, and microgravity materials research. Library open to the public by appointment.

National Space Society, *600 Pennsylvania Ave. S.E., #201 20003-4316; (202) 543-1900. Fax, (202) 546-4189. Patricia A. Dasch, Executive Director. General e-mail, nsshq@nss.org. Web, www.nss.org.*

Membership: individuals interested in space programs and applications of space technology. Provides information on NASA, commercial space activities, and international cooperation; promotes public education on space exploration and development; conducts conferences and workshops. Monitors legislation and regulations.

Resources for the Future, *1616 P St. N.W. 20036; (202) 328-5000. Fax, (202) 939-3460. Paul Portney, President. Library, (202) 328-5089. General e-mail, info@rff.org. Web, www.rff.org.*

Examines the economic aspects of U.S. space policy, including policy on the space shuttle, unmanned rockets, communications satellites, and the space station. Focuses on the role of private business versus that of government.

Space Policy Institute *(George Washington University),* *2013 G St. N.W., Stuart Hall, #201 20052; (202) 994-7292. Fax, (202) 994-1639. John M. Logsdon, Director. General e-mail, spi@gwu.edu. Web, www.gwu.edu/ ~spi.*

Conducts research on space policy issues; organizes seminars, symposia, and conferences. Focuses on civilian space activities, including competitive and cooperative interactions on space between the United States and other countries.

Young Astronaut Council, *1308 19th St. N.W. 20036; (202) 682-1984. Fax, (202) 775-1773. T. Wendell Butler, President. General e-mail, yac1@aol.com. Web, www.yac. org.*

Promotes improved math and science skills through aerospace activities for children ages three to sixteen. Encourages children to pursue careers in aerospace fields.

Astronomy

AGENCIES

National Aeronautics and Space Administration, Space Science, *300 E St. S.W. 20546 (mailing address: NASA Headquarters, Mail Code S 20546); (202) 358-1409. Fax, (202) 358-3092. Edward J. Weiler, Associate Administrator. Information, (202) 358-1547. Web, spacescience.nasa.gov.*

Administers programs that study the composition, energy, mass, position, size, and properties of celestial bodies within the universe, as observed from Earth; participates in international research efforts. Administers NASA's rocket programs.

National Science Foundation, Astronomical Sciences, *4201 Wilson Blvd., #1045, Arlington, VA 22230; (703) 306-1820. Fax, (703) 306-0525. Hugh M. Van Horn, Director. Web, www.nsf.gov/MPS/ast.*

Provides grants for ground-based astronomy and astronomical research on planetary astronomy, stellar astronomy and astrophysics, galactic astronomy, extragalactic astronomy and cosmology, and advanced technologies and instrumentation. Maintains astronomical facilities; participates in international projects.

U.S. Naval Observatory *(Defense Dept.),* *3450 Massachusetts Ave. N.W. 20392-5420; (202) 762-1467. Fax, (202) 762-1489. Capt. Ben Jaramillo, Superintendent. Information, (202) 762-1438. Web, www.usno.navy.mil.*

Determines the precise positions and motions of celestial bodies. Operates the U.S. master clock. Provides the U.S. Navy and Defense Dept. with astronomical and timing data for navigation, precise positioning, and command, control, and communications.

NONPROFIT

American Astronomical Society, *2000 Florida Ave. N.W., #400 20009-1231; (202) 328-2010. Fax, (202) 234-2560. Robert W. Milkey, Executive Officer. Press, (301) 286-5154. General e-mail, aas@aas.org. Web, www.aas.org.*

Membership: astronomers and other professionals interested in the advancement of astronomy in the United States, Canada, and Mexico. Holds scientific meetings; participates in international organizations; awards research grants.

American Geophysical Union, *2000 Florida Ave. N.W. 20009-1277; (202) 462-6910. Fax, (202) 328-0566. A. F. Spilhaus Jr., Executive Director. Web, www.agu.org.*

Membership: scientists and technologists who study the environments and components of the Earth, Sun, and solar system. Promotes international cooperation; disseminates information.

Assn. of Universities for Research in Astronomy, *1200 New York Ave. N.W., #350 20005; (202) 483-2101. Fax, (202) 483-2106. William S. Smith, President. Web, www.aura-astronomy.org.*

Consortium of universities. Manages three ground-based observatories and the international Gemini Project for the National Science Foundation and manages the Space Telescope Science Institute for the National Aeronautics and Space Administration.

18

Social Services
and Disabilities

⊞ GENERAL POLICY

AGENCIES

Administration for Children and Families *(Health and Human Services Dept.)*, *901 D St. S.W. 20447 (mailing address: 370 L'Enfant Promenade S.W. 20447); (202) 401-9200. Fax, (202) 401-5770. Olivia A. Golden, Assistant Secretary. Information, (202) 401-9215. Web, www. acf.dhhs.gov.*

Administers and funds programs for native Americans, low-income families and individuals, and persons with disabilities. Responsible for Social Services Block Grants to the states; coordinates Health and Human Services Dept. policy and regulations on child protection, day care, foster care, adoption services, child abuse and neglect, and special services for those with disabilities. Administers Head Start program and funds the National Runaway Switchboard, (800) 621-4000, and the Domestic Violence Hotline, (800) 799-7233; TTY, (800) 787-3224.

Administration for Children and Families *(Health and Human Services Dept.)*, *Community Services*, *901 D St. S.W. 20447 (mailing address: 370 L'Enfant Promenade S.W. 20447); (202) 401-9333. Fax, (202) 401-4694. Donald Sykes, Director.*

Administers the Community Services Block Grant and Discretionary Grant programs and the Low Income Home Energy Assistance Block Grant Program for heating, cooling, and weatherizing low-income households.

Administration for Children and Families *(Health and Human Services Dept.)*, *State Systems*, *200 Independence Ave. S.W., 3rd Floor 20447 (mailing address: 370 L'Enfant Promenade S.W. 20447); (202) 401-6959. Fax, (202) 401-6400. Mark Ragan, Director. Web, www.acf. dhhs.gov/programs/oss.*

Oversees the development of state social services information systems; assists states in developing child welfare information systems; coordinates departmental policy regarding state projects with the Office of Child Support Enforcement, the Health Care Financing Administration (Medicaid), and the Food and Nutrition Service (Food Stamp Program).

Administration for Native Americans *(Health and Human Services Dept.)*, *200 Independence Ave. S.W., #348F 20201; (202) 690-7776. Fax, (202) 690-7441. Gary N. Kimble, Commissioner.*

Awards grants for locally determined social and economic development strategies; promotes native American economic and social self-sufficiency; funds tribes

and native American and native Hawaiian organizations. Commissioner chairs the Intradepartmental Council on Indian Affairs, which coordinates native American-related programs.

AmeriCorps *(Corporation for National Service)*, *Volunteers in Service to America (VISTA)*, *1201 New York Ave. N.W., 8th Floor 20525; (202) 606-5000. Fax, (202) 565-2789. Lee Lacy, Deputy Director. TTY, (800) 833-3722. Volunteer recruiting information, (800) 942-2677. Web, www.americorps.org.*

Assigns full-time volunteers to public and private nonprofit organizations to alleviate poverty in local communities. Volunteers receive stipends.

Bureau of Indian Affairs *(Interior Dept.)*, *Social Services*, *1849 C St. N.W., MS 4660 20240-4001; (202) 208-2721. Fax, (202) 208-2648. Larry R. Blair, Chief.*

Gives assistance, in accordance with state payment standards, to native Americans who do not qualify for other forms of direct aid. Provides family and individual counseling and child welfare services. Administers the Indian Child Welfare Act grants to native American tribes and organizations to establish and operate native American child protection services.

Corporation for National Service, *1201 New York Ave. N.W. 20525; (202) 606-5000. Fax, (202) 565-2784. Harris L. Wofford, Chief Executive Officer. TTY, (202) 565-2799. Volunteer recruiting information, (800) 942-2677. Web, www.cns.gov.*

Independent corporation that administers federally sponsored domestic volunteer programs that provide disadvantaged citizens with services, including AmeriCorps, AmeriCorps-VISTA (Volunteers in Service to America), AmeriCorps-NCCC (National Civilian Community Corps), Learn and Serve America, and the National Senior Service Corps.

Food and Nutrition Service *(Agriculture Dept.)*, *3101 Park Center Dr., #803, Alexandria, VA 22302; (703) 305-2062. Fax, (703) 305-2908. Samuel Chambers Jr., Administrator. Information, (703) 305-2286. Web, www.usda. gov/fns.*

Administers all Agriculture Dept. domestic food assistance, including the distribution of funds and food for school breakfast and lunch programs (preschool through secondary) to public and nonprofit private schools; the food stamp program; and a supplemental nutrition program for women, infants, and children (WIC).

Food and Nutrition Service *(Agriculture Dept.)*, *Food Distribution*, *3101 Park Center Dr., #503, Alexandria, VA*

22302; (703) 305-2680. Fax, (703) 305-2420. *Les Johnson, Director.*

Administers the purchasing and distribution of food to state agencies for child care centers, public and private schools, public and nonprofit charitable institutions, and summer camps. Coordinates the distribution of special commodities, including surplus cheese and butter. Administers the National Commodity Processing Program, which facilitates distribution, at reduced prices, of processed foods to state agencies.

Food and Nutrition Service *(Agriculture Dept.), Food Stamp Program, 3101 Park Center Dr., #710, Alexandria, VA 22302; (703) 305-2026. Fax, (703) 305-2454. Susan Carr Gossman, Deputy Administrator.*

Administers, through state welfare agencies, the Food Stamp Program, which provides needy persons with food coupons to increase food purchasing power. Provides matching funds to cover half the cost of coupon issuance.

Health and Human Services Dept., *200 Independence Ave. S.W., #615F 20201; (202) 690-7000. Fax, (202) 690-7203. Donna E. Shalala, Secretary; Kevin Thurm, Deputy Secretary, (202) 690-6133. Press, (202) 690-6343. TTY, (800) 877-8339. Locator, (202) 619-0257. Web, www.os.dhhs.gov.*

Acts as principal adviser to the president on health and welfare plans, policies, and programs of the federal government. Encompasses the Health Care Financing Administration, the Administration for Children and Families, the Public Health Service, and the Centers for Disease Control and Prevention.

Health and Human Services Dept., *Disability, Aging, and Long-Term Care Policy, 200 Independence Ave. S.W., #424E 20201; (202) 690-6443. Fax, (202) 401-7733. Bob Williams, Deputy Assistant Secretary. Web, aspe.dhhs.gov/daltcp/home.htm.*

Coordinates policy and evaluation procedures for social services programs to ensure efficient use of resources. Conducts research and analyses of programs, including long-term care services for the elderly; social services programs for families; and programs for the disabled.

Health and Human Services Dept., *Human Services Policy: Economic Support for Families, 200 Independence Ave. S.W., #404E 20201; (202) 690-7148. Fax, (202) 690-6562. Canta Pian, Director. Web, www.dhhs.gov.*

Collects and disseminates information on human services programs that provide nonelderly populations, including families and their children, with cash, employment, training, and related assistance.

CONGRESS

General Accounting Office, *Health, Education, and Human Services, 441 G St. N.W. 20548; (202) 512-6806. Fax, (202) 512-5806. Victor S. Rezendes, Assistant Comptroller General.*

Independent, nonpartisan agency in the legislative branch. Audits, analyzes, and evaluates Health and Human Services Dept. and Corporation for National Service programs; makes reports available to the public.

House Agriculture Committee, *Subcommittee on Department Operations, Oversight, Nutrition, and Forestry, 1430 LHOB 20515; (202) 225-4913. Fax, (202) 225-4464. Rep. Robert W. Goodlatte, R-Va., Chair; Kevin Kramp, Staff Director. Web, agriculture.house.gov.*

Jurisdiction over food stamp legislation.

House Appropriations Committee, *Subcommittee on Labor, Health and Human Services, and Education, 2358 RHOB 20515; (202) 225-3508. Fax, (202) 225-3509. Rep. John Edward Porter, R-Ill., Chair; Tony McCann, Staff Director. Web, www.house.gov/appropriations.*

Jurisdiction over legislation to appropriate funds for the Health and Human Services Dept. (except the Food and Drug Administration and native American health programs), Corporation for National Service programs, and the National Council on Disability.

House Education and the Workforce Committee, *2181 RHOB 20515; (202) 225-4527. Fax, (202) 225-9571. Rep. Bill Goodling, R-Pa., Chair; Kevin D. Talley, Staff Director. Web, www.house.gov/ed_workforce.*

Jurisdiction over legislation on Community Services Block Grant Program, Head Start, native Americans programs, antipoverty programs, applications of the Older Americans Act (including volunteer older Americans programs under the Corporation for National Service) and related legislation, runaway youth, child and youth development, Child Care Development Block Grant, and child-family services.

House Education and the Workforce Committee, *Subcommittee on Oversight and Investigations, 2181 RHOB 20515; (202) 225-4527. Fax, (202) 225-9571. Rep. Peter Hoekstra, R-Mich., Chair; Kevin D. Talley, Staff Director. Web, www.house.gov/ed_workforce.*

Oversees and investigates matters relating to child abuse and domestic violence, child adoption, education of children with disabilities, vocational rehabilitation for people with disabilities and developmental disabilities, day care, and domestic volunteer programs, including the Corporation for National Service. No legislative jurisdiction.

House Ways and Means Committee, *Subcommittee on Human Resources,* B317 RHOB 20515; (202) 225-1025. Fax, (202) 225-9480. Rep. Nancy L. Johnson, R-Conn., Chair; Ronald Haskins, Staff Director. Web, www.house.gov/ways_means.

Jurisdiction over legislation on welfare programs, child support enforcement, child welfare, child care, foster care, adoption assistance, supplemental security income, unemployment compensation and insurance, low-income energy assistance, eligibility of welfare recipients for food stamps, and social services for the elderly and persons with disabilities.

Senate Agriculture, Nutrition, and Forestry Committee, SR-328A 20510; (202) 224-2035. Fax, (202) 224-1725. Sen. Richard G. Lugar, R-Ind., Chair; Keith Luse, Staff Director. Web, agriculture.senate.gov.

Jurisdiction over legislation on low-income energy assistance programs.

Senate Appropriations Committee, *Subcommittee on Labor, Health and Human Services, and Education,* SD-186 20510; (202) 224-7230. Fax, (202) 224-1360. Sen. Arlen Specter, R-Pa., Chair; Bettilou Taylor, Staff Director. Web, appropriations.senate.gov/labor.

Jurisdiction over legislation to appropriate funds for the Health and Human Services Dept. (except the Food and Drug Administration and native American health programs), Corporation for National Service, and the National Council on Disability.

Senate Finance Committee, *Subcommittee on Social Security and Family Policy,* SD-219 20510; (202) 224-4515. Fax, (202) 224-5920. Sen. Don Nickles, R-Okla., Chair; Alec Bachon, Staff Contact. Web, finance.senate.gov.

Holds hearings on legislation concerning welfare programs, child support enforcement, child welfare, child care, foster care, adoption assistance, supplemental security income, unemployment compensation and insurance, and social services for the elderly and persons with disabilities.

NONPROFIT

American Enterprise Institute for Public Policy Research, *Social and Individual Responsibility Project,* 1150 17th St. N.W. 20036; (202) 862-5904. Fax, (202) 862-5802. Douglas J. Besharov, Director. Web, www.aei.org.

Research and education organization that conducts studies on social welfare policies, including family and welfare policies. Interests include children, child abuse and neglect, divorce, drug abuse, family breakdown, poverty, out-of-wedlock births, and welfare programs.

American Public Human Services Assn., 810 1st St. N.E., #500 20002-4267; (202) 682-0100. Fax, (202) 289-6555. William Waldman, Executive Director. Web, www.aphsa.org.

Membership: state and local human services administrators. Dedicated to developing, promoting, and implementing public human services policies that improve the health and well-being of families, children, and adults. Provides training and technical assistance; operates a job bank.

Assn. of Community Organizations for Reform Now, *Washington Office,* 739 8th St. S.E. 20003; (202) 547-2500. Fax, (202) 547-2483. Melanie Marcus, Head. General e-mail, natacorndc@acorn.org. Web, www.acorn.org.

Works to advance the interests of minority and low-income families through community organizing and action. Interests include jobs, living wages, housing, welfare reform, and community reinvestment. (Headquarters in New Orleans.)

Catholic Charities USA, 1731 King St., #200, Alexandria, VA 22314; (703) 549-1390. Fax, (703) 549-1656. Fred Kammer (SJ), President. Press, (703) 549-1390. Web, catholiccharitiesusa.org.

Member agencies and institutions provide persons of all backgrounds with social services, including adoption, education, counseling, food, and housing services. National office promotes public policies that address human needs and social injustice. Provides members with advocacy and professional support, including technical assistance, training, and resource development; disseminates publications.

Center for Community Change, 1000 Wisconsin Ave. N.W. 20007; (202) 342-0519. Fax, (202) 342-1132. Andy Mott, Executive Director.

Provides community-based organizations serving minorities and the economically disadvantaged with technical assistance. Areas of assistance include community development block grants, housing, economic and resource development, rural development projects, and program planning.

Center for Law and Social Policy, 1616 P St. N.W., #150 20036; (202) 328-5140. Fax, (202) 328-5195. Alan W. Houseman, Director. Web, www.clasp.org.

Public interest organization with expertise in law and policy affecting low-income Americans. Seeks to improve the economic conditions of low-income families with children and to secure access for persons in poverty to the civil justice system.

Center for the Study of Social Policy, *1250 Eye St. N.W., #503 20005-3922; (202) 371-1565. Fax, (202) 371-1472. Frank Faro, Director. Web, www.cssp.org.*

Assists states and communities in organizing, financing, and delivering human services, with a focus on children and families. Helps build capacity for local decision making; helps communities use informal supports in the protection of children; promotes nonadversarial approach to class action litigation on behalf of dependent children.

Center on Budget and Policy Priorities, *820 1st St. N.E., #510 20002; (202) 408-1080. Fax, (202) 408-1056. Robert Greenstein, Executive Director. Web, www.cbpp.org.*

Research group that analyzes federal, state, and local government policies affecting low- and moderate-income Americans.

Christian Relief Services, *8815 Telegraph Rd., Lorton, VA 22079; (703) 550-2472. Fax, (703) 550-2473. Eugene L. Krizek, President. General e-mail, info@christianrelief.org. Web, www.christianrelief.org.*

Promotes economic development and the alleviation of poverty in urban areas of the United States, native American reservations, and developing countries around the world. Donates medical supplies and food; administers housing, hospital, and school construction programs.

Coalition on Human Needs, *1700 K St. N.W., #1150 20006; (202) 736-5885. Fax, (202) 785-0791. Stuart P. Campbell, Executive Director. General e-mail, chn@chn.org. Web, www.chn.org.*

Promotes public policies that address the needs of low-income Americans. Members include civil rights, religious, labor, and professional organizations and individuals concerned with the well-being of children, women, the elderly, and people with disabilities.

Council on Social Work Education, *1725 Duke St., #500, Alexandria, VA 22314-3457; (703) 683-8080. Fax, (703) 683-8099. Donald W. Beless, Executive Director. General e-mail, membership@cswe.org. Web, www.cswe.org.*

Promotes quality education in social work. Accredits social work programs.

Food Research and Action Center, *1875 Connecticut Ave. N.W., #540 20009-5728; (202) 986-2200. Fax, (202) 986-2525. James Weill, President. General e-mail, webmaster@frac.org. Web, www.frac.org.*

Public interest advocacy, research, and legal center that works to end hunger and poverty in the United States; offers legal assistance, organizational aid, training, and information to groups seeking to improve or expand federal food programs, including food stamp, child nutrition, and WIC (women, infants, and children) programs; conducts studies relating to hunger and poverty; coordinates network of antihunger organizations. Monitors legislation and regulations.

Goodwill Industries International, *9200 Rockville Pike, Bethesda, MD 20814-3896; (301) 530-6500. Fax, (301) 530-1516. Fred Grandy, President. Web, www.goodwill.org.*

Membership: 185 autonomous organizations that provide disabled and disadvantaged individuals with Goodwill Industries services, which include vocational rehabilitation evaluation, job training, employment, and placement services.

Grameen Foundation USA, *1709 New York Ave. N.W., #101 20006; (202) 628-3560. Fax, (202) 628-3880. Alex Counts, President. General e-mail, info@grameenfoundation.org. Web, www.grameenfoundation.org.*

Seeks to eliminate poverty through collaboration with public and private institutions; supports and promotes antipoverty programs of the Grameen Bank; educates policymakers about microcredit programs for the poor; offers support services to agencies starting or expanding microcredit programs. Microcredit loans are small amounts of credit given to poor people for self-employment projects.

Hudson Institute, *National Security Studies, Washington Office, 1015 18th St. N.W., #300 20036; (202) 223-7770. Fax, (202) 223-8537. William E. Odom, Director. Web, www.hudson.org.*

Studies welfare policy; helps states create welfare reform programs. (Headquarters in Indianapolis.)

Institute for Women's Policy Research, *1707 L St. N.W., #750 20036; (202) 785-5100. Fax, (202) 833-4362. Heidi I. Hartmann, Director. Web, www.iwpr.org.*

Public policy research organization that focuses on women's issues, including welfare reform, family and work policies, employment and wages, and discrimination based on gender, race, or ethnicity.

National Assn. for the Advancement of Colored People, *Washington Office, 1025 Vermont Ave. N.W., #1120 20005; (202) 638-2269. Fax, (202) 638-5936. Hilary O. Shelton, Director. Web, www.naacp.org.*

Membership: persons interested in civil rights for all minorities. Interests include welfare reform and related social welfare matters. Administers programs that create employment and affordable housing opportunities and that improve health care. Monitors legislation and regulations. (Headquarters in Baltimore.)

National Assn. of Community Action Agencies, *1100 17th St. N.W., #500 20036; (202) 265-7546. Fax, (202) 265-8850. John Buckstead, Executive Director. Web, www.nacaa.org.*

Provides community action agencies with information, training, and technical assistance; advocates, at all levels of government, for low-income people.

National Assn. of Social Workers, *750 1st St. N.E., #700 20002-4241; (202) 408-8600. Fax, (202) 336-8310. Josephine Nieves, Executive Director. General e-mail, nasw@capcon.net. Web, www.socialworkers.org.*

Membership: graduates of accredited social work education programs and students in accredited programs. Promotes the interests of social workers and their clients; promotes professional standards; certifies members of the Academy of Certified Social Workers; conducts research.

National Community Action Foundation, *810 1st St. N.E., #530 20002; (202) 842-2092. Fax, (202) 842-2095. David Bradley, Executive Director. General e-mail, info@ncaf.org. Web, www.ncaf.org.*

Organization for community action agencies concerned with issues that affect the poor. Provides information on Community Services Block Grant, low-income energy assistance, employment and training, weatherization for low-income housing, nutrition, and the Head Start program.

National Urban Coalition, *2120 L St. N.W., #510 20037; (202) 986-1460. Fax, (202) 986-1468. Rhett Louis, President (Acting).*

Membership: urban community action groups. Operates Say Yes to a Youngster's Future, a community-based education program for low-income students in math, science, and technology. M. Carl Holman Leadership Development Institute gives students opportunities to learn from local and national leaders, including scholars, entrepreneurs, and other experts.

National Urban League, *Research and Public Policy, Washington Office, 1111 14th St. N.W., #1001 20005-5603; (202) 898-1604. Fax, (202) 408-1965. William Spriggs, Director. General e-mail, info@nul.org. Web, www.nul.org.*

Social service organization concerned with the social welfare of African Americans and other minorities. Social Welfare Division disseminates welfare rights information to local leagues. (Headquarters in New York.)

Poverty and Race Research Action Council, *3000 Connecticut Ave. N.W., #200 20008; (202) 387-9887. Fax, (202) 387-0764. Chester W. Hartman, Executive Director. General e-mail, info@prrac.org. Web, www.prrac.org.*

Facilitates cooperative links between researchers and activists who work on race and poverty issues. Provides nonprofit organizations with funding for research on race and poverty.

Public Welfare Foundation, *2600 Virginia Ave. N.W., #505 20037-1977; (202) 965-1800. Fax, (202) 625-1348. Larry Kressley, Executive Director. General e-mail, general@publicwelfare.org. Web, www.publicwelfare.org.*

Seeks to assist people to overcome barriers to full participation in society. Awards grants to nonprofits in the following areas: criminal justice, disadvantaged elderly and youths, the environment, health care, population and reproductive health, human rights and global security, and community and economic development.

Salvation Army, *615 Slaters Lane, Alexandria, VA 22314 (mailing address: P.O. Box 269, Alexandria, VA 22313); (703) 684-5500. Fax, (703) 684-3478. John A. Busby, National Commander. Web, www.salvationarmyusa.org.*

International religious social welfare organization that provides social services, including counseling, youth and senior citizens' services, emergency help, foster care, settlement and day care, tutoring for the retarded, programs for people with disabilities, prison work, summer camps, community centers, employment services, rehabilitation programs for alcoholics, missing persons bureaus, and residences for the homeless. (International headquarters in London.)

United Jewish Communities, *Washington Office, 1700 K St. N.W., #1150 20006; (202) 785-5900. Fax, (202) 785-4937. Diana Aviv, Director. Web, www.jewishcommunitiesdc.org.*

Fundraising organization. Sustains and enhances the quality of Jewish life domestically and internationally. Advocates the needs of the Jewish community abroad. Offers marketing, communications, and public relations support; coordinates a speakers bureau and Israeli emissaries. (Headquarters in New York.)

Urban Institute, *2100 M St. N.W. 20037; (202) 833-7200. Fax, (202) 429-0687. Robert D. Reischauer, President. Information, (202) 261-5702. Library, (202) 261-5534. General e-mail, paffairs@ui.urban.org. Web, www.urban.org.*

Nonpartisan, public policy research and education organization. Interests include states' use of federal funds; delivery of social services to specific groups, including children of mothers in welfare reform programs; retirement policy, income, and community-based services for the elderly; job placement and training programs for welfare recipients; health care cost containment and access; food stamps; child nutrition; the homeless; housing; immigration; and tax policy. Library open to the public by appointment.

U.S. Conference of City Human Services Officials, *1620 Eye St. N.W. 20006; (202) 861-6707. Fax, (202) 293-2352. Crystal Swann, Assistant Executive Director.*

Promotes improved social services for specific urban populations through meetings, technical assistance, and training programs for members; fosters information exchange among federal, state, and local governments, human services experts, and other groups concerned with human services issues. (Affiliate of the U.S. Conference of Mayors.)

 CHILDREN AND FAMILIES

See also Caucuses (chap. 20)

AGENCIES

Administration for Children and Families *(Health and Human Services Dept.), 901 D St. S.W. 20447 (mailing address: 370 L'Enfant Promenade S.W. 20447); (202) 401-9200. Fax, (202) 401-5770. Olivia A. Golden, Assistant Secretary. Information, (202) 401-9215. Web, www.acf.dhhs.gov.*

Plans, manages, and coordinates national assistance programs that promote stability, economic security, responsibility, and self-support for families; supervises programs and use of funds to provide the most needy with aid and to increase alternatives to public assistance. Programs include Temporary Assistance to Needy Families, Child Welfare, Head Start, Child Support Enforcement, Low-Income Home Energy Assistance, Community Services Block Grant, and Refugee Resettlement Assistance.

Administration for Children and Families *(Health and Human Services Dept.), Child Support Enforcement, 901 D St. S.W. 20447 (mailing address: 370 L'Enfant Promenade S.W. 20447); (202) 401-9370. Fax, (202) 401-3450. David Gray Ross, Director. Information, (202) 401-9373. Web, www.acf.dhhs.gov.*

Helps states develop, manage, and operate child support programs. Maintains the Federal Parent Locator Service, which provides state and local child support agencies with information for locating absent parents. State enforcement agencies locate absent parents, establish paternity, establish and enforce support orders, and collect child support payments.

Administration for Children and Families *(Health and Human Services Dept.), Temporary Assistance to Needy Families, 901 D St. S.W. 20447 (mailing address: 370 L'Enfant Promenade S.W. 20447); (202) 401-5139. Fax, (202) 205-5887. Alvin C. Collins, Director.*

Provides recipients of Aid to Families with Dependent Children with job search assistance, vocational training, and educational aid (including remedial programs, literacy training, and instruction in English as a second language); focuses on women with young children; provides child care options and other support services to make participation possible. Coordinates programs, under the Family Support Act of 1988, with departments of Education and Labor.

Administration for Children, Youth, and Families *(Health and Human Services Dept.), Children's Bureau, 330 C St. S.W. 20201; (202) 205-8618. Fax, (202) 260-9345. Joseph Semidei, Associate Commissioner. Web, www.acf.dhhs.gov/programs/cb.*

Administers grants to agencies and institutes of higher learning for research projects and for training personnel in the child welfare field. Administers formula grants to strengthen child welfare services provided by state and local public welfare agencies. Provides states with technical assistance in group and foster care, adoption, and family services. Maintains clearinghouse of programs for preventing and treating child abuse.

Administration for Children, Youth, and Families *(Health and Human Services Dept.), Family and Youth Services, 330 C St. S.W. 20447 (mailing address: P.O. Box 1182 20013); (202) 205-8102. Fax, (202) 260-9333. Gilda Lambert, Associate Commissioner.*

Administers federal discretionary grant programs for projects serving runaway and homeless youth and for projects that deter youth involvement in gangs. Provides youth service agencies with training and technical assistance. Monitors federal policies, programs, and legislation. Supports research on youth development issues, including gangs, runaways, and homeless youth. Operates national clearinghouse on families and youth.

Cooperative State Research, Education, and Extension Service *(Agriculture Dept.), Family, 4-H, and Nutrition, 800 9th St. S.W. 20024 (mailing address: P.O. Box 2225 20250-2225); (202) 720-2908. Fax, (202) 690-2469. Alma C. Hobbs, Deputy Administrator. Web, www.reeusda.gov.*

Administers education programs with state land-grant universities and county governments for rural and urban youth ages five to nineteen. Projects provide youth with experience in the fields of science and technological literacy, environment, natural resources, health, leadership, citizenship, service, and personal development.

Food and Nutrition Service *(Agriculture Dept.),* *Analysis, Nutrition, and Evaluation,* 3101 Park Center Dr., #503, Alexandria, VA 22302; (703) 305-2585. Fax, (703) 305-2576. Alberta Frost, Director.

Administers the Nutrition Education and Training Program, which provides states with grants for disseminating nutrition information to children and for inservice training of food service and teaching personnel; administers the Child Nutrition Labeling Program, which certifies that foods served in school lunch and breakfast programs meet nutritional requirements; provides information and technical assistance in nutrition and food service management.

Food and Nutrition Service *(Agriculture Dept.), Child Nutrition,* 3101 Park Center Dr., #1006, Alexandria, VA 22302; (703) 305-2590. Fax, (703) 305-2879. Stanley Garnett, Director. Press, (703) 305-2039.

Administers the transfer of funds to state agencies for the National School Lunch Program; the School Breakfast Program; the Special Milk Program, which helps schools and institutions provide children who do not have access to full meals under other child nutrition programs with fluid milk; the Child and Adult Care Food Program, which provides children in nonresidential child-care centers and family day care homes with year-round meal service; and the Summer Food Service Program, which provides children from low-income families with meals during the summer months.

Food and Nutrition Service *(Agriculture Dept.), Supplemental Food Program,* 3101 Park Center Dr., #540, Alexandria, VA 22302; (703) 305-2746. Fax, (703) 305-2196. Patricia N. Daniels, Director.

Provides health departments and agencies with federal funding for food supplements and administrative expenses to make food, nutrition education, and health services available to infants, young children, and pregnant, nursing, and postpartum women.

Health and Human Services Dept., *Head Start,* 330 C St. S.W., #2212 20447; (202) 205-8572. Fax, (202) 260-9336. Helen Taylor, Associate Commissioner. Web, www.acf.dhhs.gov/programs/hsb/index.htm.

Awards grants to nonprofit organizations and local governments for operating community Head Start programs (comprehensive development programs for children, ages three to five, of low-income families); manages a limited number of parent and child centers for families with children up to age three. Conducts research and manages demonstration programs, including those under the Comprehensive Child Care Development Act of 1988; administers the Child Development Associate

scholarship program, which trains individuals for careers in child development, often as Head Start teachers.

Health and Human Services Dept., *Human Services Policy: Children and Youth Policy,* 200 Independence Ave. S.W., #450G 20201; (202) 690-6461. Fax, (202) 690-5514. Matthew Stagner, Director. Web, www.dhhs.gov.

Develops policies and procedures for programs that benefit children, youth and families. Interests include child protection, domestic violence, family support, gang violence, child care and development, and care for drug-exposed, runaway, and homeless children and their families.

National Institute of Child Health and Human Development *(National Institutes of Health), Center for Research for Mothers and Children,* 6100 Executive Blvd., #4B05, Bethesda, MD 20892-7510; (301) 496-5097. Fax, (301) 480-7773. Dr. Sumner J. Yaffe, Director.

Supports biomedical and behavioral science research and training for maternal and child health care. Areas of study include fetal development, maternal-infant health problems, HIV-related diseases in childbearing women, roles of nutrients and hormones in child growth, developmental disabilities, and behavioral development.

Office of Justice Programs *(Justice Dept.), Juvenile Justice and Delinquency Prevention,* 810 7th St. N.W., 8th Floor 20531; (202) 307-5911. Fax, (202) 307-2093. Shay Bilchik, Administrator. Technical information, (202) 307-0751. Clearinghouse, (800) 638-8736. Web, www.ncjrs.org/ojjhome.htm.

Administers federal programs related to prevention and treatment of juvenile delinquency, missing and exploited children, child victimization, and research and evaluation of juvenile justice system; coordinates with youth programs of the departments of Agriculture, Education, Housing and Urban Development, Interior, and Labor, and of the Substance Abuse and Mental Health Services Administration, including the Center for Studies of Crime and Delinquency. Operates the Juvenile Justice Clearinghouse.

Office of Justice Programs *(Justice Dept.), Violence Against Women,* 800 K St. N.W., #920 20001; (202) 616-8894. Fax, (202) 307-3911. Bonnie Campbell, Director. Web, www.usdoj.gov/vawo.

Seeks more effective policies and services to combat domestic violence, sexual assault, stalking, and other crimes against women. Helps administer grants to states to fund shelters, crisis centers, and hotlines, and to hire law enforcement officers, prosecutors, and counselors specializing in cases of sexual violence and other violent crimes against women.

See also Bureau of Indian Affairs (p. 6)

CONGRESS

House Education and the Workforce Committee, *Subcommittee on Early Childhood, Youth, and Families,* 2181 RHOB 20515; (202) 225-4527. Fax, (202) 225-9571. Rep. Michael N. Castle, R-Del., Chair; Kevin D. Talley, Staff Director. Web, www.house.gov/ed_workforce.

Jurisdiction over legislation on the National School Lunch Program, the School Breakfast Program, the Summer Food Program for Children, the Special Milk Program for Children, and the Special Supplemental Food Program for Women, Infants, and Children (WIC).

Senate Agriculture, Nutrition, and Forestry Committee, *Subcommittee on Research, Nutrition, and General Legislation,* SR-328A 20510; (202) 224-2854. Fax, (202) 224-1725. Sen. Peter G. Fitzgerald, R-Ill., Chair; Terry VanDoren, Legislative Assistant. Web, agriculture. senate.gov.

Jurisdiction over legislation on commodity donations, the Food Stamp Program, the National School Lunch Program, the School Breakfast Program, the Summer Food Program for Children, the Special Milk Program for Children, the Special Supplemental Food Program for Women, Infants, and Children (WIC), and nutritional programs for the elderly.

Senate Health, Education, Labor, and Pensions Committee, *Subcommittee on Children and Families,* SH-615 20510; (202) 224-5800. Fax, (202) 228-0581. Sen. Judd Gregg, R-N.H., Chair; Stephanie Monroe, Staff Director. Web, labor.senate.gov.

Jurisdiction over legislation on day care, child abuse and domestic violence, family and medical leave, low-income energy assistance, adoption reform, Community Services Block Grant Program, Head Start, youth, child and youth development, Child Care Development Block Grant, and child-family services.

NONPROFIT

Adoptees in Search, *P.O. Box 41016, Bethesda, MD 20824; (301) 656-8555. Fax, (301) 652-2106. Joanne W. Small, Executive Director. General e-mail, ais20824@aol. com. Web, www.adopteesinsearch.org.*

Membership: adult adoptees, adoptive parents, and birth relatives. Provides members with professional consultation, guidance, and support services. Promotes awareness of adoption practice and laws that affect adopted people and their families. Advocates legislation that restores full civil rights to adult adoptees.

Adoption Service Information Agency, *7720 Alaska Ave. N.W. 20012; (202) 726-7193. Fax, (202) 722-4928. Theodore Kim, President. Web, www.asia-adopt.org.*

Provides information on international and domestic adoption; sponsors seminars and workshops for adoptive and prospective adoptive parents.

Alliance for Children and Families, *Washington Office,* 1701 K St. N.W., #200 20006-1503; (202) 223-3447. Fax, (202) 331-7476. Carmen Delgado Votaw, Senior Vice President. Web, www.alliance1.org.

Membership: children and family service agencies in the United States and abroad. Provides families with support services and counseling. Promotes affordable and accessible family-centered health and mental health care, affordable housing and safe neighborhoods, education and job training, family and child welfare, and fiscal and workplace policies that strengthen family viability. Monitors legislation. (Headquarters in Milwaukee.)

American Assn. for Marriage and Family Therapy, 1133 15th St. N.W., #300 20005-2710; (202) 452-0109. Fax, (202) 223-2329. Michael Bowers, Executive Director. Web, www.aamft.org.

Membership: professional marriage and family therapists. Promotes professional standards in marriage and family therapy through training programs; provides the public with educational material and referral service for marriage and family therapy.

American Bar Assn., *Center on Children and the Law,* 740 15th St. N.W., 9th Floor 20005-1009; (202) 662-1720. Fax, (202) 662-1755. Howard Davidson, Director. General e-mail, ctrchildlaw@abanet.org. Web, www.abanet.org/child.

Works to increase lawyer representation of children; sponsors speakers and conferences; monitors legislation. Interests include child sexual abuse and exploitation, missing and runaway children, parental kidnapping, child support, foster care, and adoption of children with special needs.

American Humane Assn., *Washington Office,* 236 Massachusetts Ave. N.E., #203 20002; (202) 543-7780. Fax, (202) 546-3266. Adele Douglass, Director. General e-mail, ahaeast@aol.com. Web, www.americanhumane.org.

Membership: humane societies, individuals, and government agencies concerned with child and animal protection laws. Prepares model state legislation on child abuse and its prevention; publishes surveys on child and animal abuse and state abuse laws. (Headquarters in Denver.)

American Youth Work Center, *1200 17th St. N.W. 4th Floor 20036; (202) 785-0764. Fax, (202) 728-0657.*

William Treanor, Executive Director. General e-mail, info@youthtoday.org. Web, www.youthtoday.org.

International citizens' interest group concerned with juvenile justice and community-based youth services, including runaway shelters, hotlines, crisis intervention centers, drug programs, alternative education, and job training and placement. Provides youth programs with technical assistance; works with agencies and individuals dealing with young people; serves as clearinghouse and resource center; sponsors a college internship program.

America's Promise–The Alliance for Youth, *909 N. Washington St., #400, Alexandria, VA 22314-1556; (703) 684-4500. Fax, (703) 535-3900. Gen. Colin Powell, Chair; Peter A. Gallagher, President. General e-mail, commit@ americaspromise.org. Web, www.americaspromise.org.*

Works with national and local organizations to mobilize individuals, groups, and organizations to build and strengthen the character and competence of America's youth; encourages volunteerism and community service among young people; provides information to individuals about state and local mentorship opportunities.

Boy Scouts of America, *Washington Office,* *9190 Rockville Pike, Bethesda, MD 20814; (301) 530-9360. Fax, (301) 564-3648. Ron L. Carroll, Scout Executive. Web, www.bsa.scouting.org.*

Educational services organization for boys ages seven to seventeen. Promotes citizen participation and physical fitness. The Explorers Program, which includes young men and women ages fourteen to twenty, provides vocational opportunities. (Headquarters in Irving, Texas.)

Boys and Girls Clubs of America, *Washington Office,* *600 Jefferson Plaza, #401, Rockville, MD 20852-1150; (301) 251-6676. Fax, (301) 294-3052. Robbie Callaway, Senior Vice President. Web, www.bgca.org.*

Educational service organization for boys and girls, most from disadvantaged circumstances. Works to prevent juvenile delinquency; promotes youth employment, health and fitness, leadership, and citizenship. Interests include child care, child safety and protection, drug and alcohol abuse prevention, runaway and homeless youth, youth employment, child nutrition, tax reform and charitable contributions, and other issues that affect disadvantaged youth. (Headquarters in Atlanta.)

Child Nutrition Forum, *1875 Connecticut Ave. N.W., #540 20009-5728; (202) 986-2200. Fax, (202) 986-2525. Ellen Teller, Coordinator.*

Membership: agriculture, labor, education, and health and nutrition specialists; school food service officials; and consumer and religious groups. Supports federal nutrition programs for children; provides information on school nutrition programs. Monitors legislation and regulations concerning hunger issues.

Child Welfare League of America, *440 1st St. N.W., #310 20001-2085; (202) 638-2952. Fax, (202) 638-4004. Shay Bilchik, Administrator. Web, www.cwla.org.*

Membership: public and private child welfare agencies. Develops standards for the field; provides information on adoption, day care, foster care, group home services, child protection, residential care for children and youth, services to pregnant adolescents and young parents, and other child welfare issues.

Children's Defense Fund, *25 E St. N.W. 20001; (202) 628-8787. Fax, (202) 662-3510. Marian Wright Edelman, President. Web, www.childrensdefense.org.*

Advocacy group concerned with programs and policies for children and youth, particularly poor and minority children. Interests include health care, education, child care, job training and employment, and family support; works to ensure educational and job opportunities for youth.

Children's Defense Fund, *Child Care Division,* *25 E St. N.W. 20001; (202) 628-8787. Fax, (202) 662-3510. Helen Blank, Director. Web, www.childrensdefense.org.*

Advocacy group concerned with federal and state programs for children and youth; provides parents and child-care advocates with information on child-care policy.

Children's Foundation, *725 15th St. N.W., #505 20005-2109; (202) 347-3300. Fax, (202) 347-3382. Kay Hollestelle, Executive Director. General e-mail, cfwashdc@aol.com. Web, www.childrensfoundation.net.*

Advocacy group for children and those who care for them. Works to improve available child care; promotes enforcement of child support; offers information, technical assistance, and professional training to child care providers and parents.

Children's Rights Council, *300 Eye St. N.E., #401 20002-4389; (202) 547-6227. Fax, (202) 546-4272. David L. Levy, President. Web, www.vix.com/crc.*

Membership: parents and professionals. Works to strengthen families through education and advocacy. Supports family formation and preservation. Conducts conferences and serves as an information clearinghouse. Interests include children whose parents are separated, unwed, or divorced.

Christian Children's Fund, *Washington Office,* *1400 16th St. N.W., #715 20036; (202) 462-2161. Fax, (202) 462-0601. Betty Meyer, Director. General e-mail, ccfwash@aol.com. Web, www.christianchildrensfund.org.*

Works internationally to ensure the survival, protection, and development of children. Promotes the improvement in quality of life of children within the context of family, community, and culture. Helps children in unstable situations brought on by war, natural disasters, and other high-risk circumstances. (Headquarters in Richmond, Va.)

Council for Professional Recognition, *Child Development Associate National Credentialing Program,* *2460 16th St. N.W. 20009-3575; (202) 265-9090. Fax, (202) 265-9161. Carol Brunson Day, President. Information, (800) 424-4310. Web, www.cdacouncil.org.*

Promotes and establishes standards for quality child care through an accrediting program. Awards credentials to family day care, preschool, home visitor, and infant-toddler caregivers.

Girl Scouts of the U.S.A., *Government Relations,* *Washington Office, 1025 Connecticut Ave. N.W., #309 20036; (202) 659-3780. Fax, (202) 331-8065. LaVerne Alexander, Director. Web, www.girlscouts.org.*

Educational service organization for girls ages five to seventeen. Promotes personal development through social action, leadership, and other projects. Interests include career education, youth camp safety, prevention of child sexual exploitation, child health care, runaways, and juvenile justice. (Headquarters in New York.)

Mothers at Home, *8310-A Old Courthouse Rd., Vienna, VA 22182; (703) 827-5903. Fax, (703) 790-8587. Betty Walter, Executive Director. Information, (800) 783-4666. Press, (703) 534-7858. General e-mail, mah@mah.org. Web, www.mah.org.*

Provides information and support for mothers who stay home, or who would like to stay home, to raise their children, in the United States and abroad. Monitors legislation and regulations relating to mothers and family issues.

National Assn. for the Education of Young Children, *1509 16th St. N.W. 20036-1426; (202) 232-8777. Fax, (202) 328-1846. Mark R. Ginsberg, Executive Director. Web, www.naeyc.org.*

Membership: early childhood professionals and parents. Works to improve the quality of early childhood care and education. Administers national accreditation system for early childhood programs. Maintains information service.

National Assn. of Child Advocates, *1522 K St. N.W., #600 20005; (202) 289-0777. Fax, (202) 289-0776. Tamara Lucas Copeland, President. General e-mail, naca@childadvocacy.org. Web, www.childadvocacy.org.*

Membership: private, nonprofit, state- and community-based child advocacy organizations. Works for safety, security, health, and education for all children by strengthening and building child advocacy organizations.

National Black Child Development Institute, *1023 15th St. N.W., #600 20005; (202) 387-1281. Fax, (202) 234-1738. Evelyn K. Moore, President. General e-mail, moreinfo@nbcdi.org. Web, www.nbcdi.org.*

Advocacy group for African American children, youth, and families. Interests include child care, foster care, adoption, health, and education. Provides information on government policies that affect African American children, youth, and families.

National Campaign to Prevent Teen Pregnancy, *1776 Massachusetts Ave. N.W., #200 20036; (202) 261-5655. Fax, (202) 331-7735. Sarah S. Brown, Director. General e-mail, campaign@teenpregnancy.org. Web, www.teenpregnancy.org.*

Nonpartisan initiative that seeks to reduce the U.S. teen pregnancy rate by one-third by the year 2005.

National Center for Missing and Exploited Children, *699 Prince St., Alexandria, VA 22314; (703) 274-3900. Fax, (703) 274-2200. Ernest Allen, President. TTY, (800) 826-7653. Toll-free hotline, (800) 843-5678. Web, www.missingkids.org.*

Private organization funded primarily by the Justice Dept. Assists parents and citizens' groups in locating and safely returning missing children; offers technical assistance to law enforcement agencies; coordinates public and private missing children programs; maintains database that coordinates information on missing children.

National Child Support Enforcement Assn., *444 N. Capitol St. N.W., #414 20001-1512; (202) 624-8180. Fax, (202) 624-8828. Joel Bankes, Executive Director. General e-mail, ncsea@sso.org. Web, www.ncsea.org.*

Promotes enforcement of child support obligations and educates professionals on child support issues; fosters exchange of ideas among child support professionals. Monitors legislation and regulations.

National Collaboration for Youth, *1319 F St. N.W. 20004; (202) 347-2080. Fax, (202) 393-4517. Gordon A. Raley, Executive Director.*

Membership: national youth-serving organizations. Works to improve members' youth development programs through information exchange and other support. Raises public awareness of youth issues. Monitors legislation and regulations. (Affiliate of the National Assembly of Health and Human Service Organizations.)

National Congress of Parents and Teachers, Legislation, Washington Office, *1090 Vermont Ave. N.W., #1200 20005; (202) 289-6790. Fax, (202) 289-6791. Maribeth Oakes, Director. Web, www.pta.org.*

Membership: parent-teacher associations at the preschool, elementary, and secondary levels. Supports school lunch and breakfast programs; works as an active member of the Child Nutrition Forum, which supports federally funded nutrition programs for children. (Headquarters in Chicago.)

National Council for Adoption, *1930 17th St. N.W. 20009-6207; (202) 328-1200. Fax, (202) 332-0935. David Malutinok, President. General e-mail, ncfadc@ibm.net. Web, www.ncfa-usa.org.*

Organization of individuals, national and international agencies, and corporations interested in adoption. Supports adoption through legal, ethical agencies; advocates the right to confidentiality in adoption. Conducts research and holds conferences; provides information; supports pregnancy counseling, maternity services, and counseling for infertile couples.

National Family Caregivers Assn., *10400 Connecticut Ave., #500, Kensington, MD 20895-3944; (301) 942-6430. Fax, (301) 942-2302. Suzanne Mintz, President. Information, (800) 896-3650. General e-mail, info@nfcacares.org. Web, www.nfcacares.org.*

Seeks to increase the quality of life of family caregivers by providing support and information; works to raise public awareness of caregiving through educational activities and a speakers bureau.

National 4-H Council, *7100 Connecticut Ave., Chevy Chase, MD 20815-4999; (301) 961-2820. Fax, (301) 961-2894. Richard J. Sauer, President. Press, (301) 961-2915. Web, www.fourhcouncil.edu.*

Educational organization incorporated to expand and strengthen the 4-H program (for young people ages seven to nineteen) of the Cooperative Extension System and state land-grant universities. Programs include citizenship and leadership training.

National Head Start Assn., *1651 Prince St., Alexandria, VA 22314; (703) 739-0875. Fax, (703) 739-0878. Sarah M. Greene, Chief Executive Officer. Web, www.nhsa.org.*

Membership organization that represents Head Start children, families, and staff. Recommends strategies on issues affecting Head Start programs; provides training and professional development opportunities. Monitors legislation and regulations.

National Network for Youth, *1319 F St. N.W., #401 20004; (202) 783-7949. Fax, (202) 783-7955. Della M.*

Hughes, *Executive Director. AIDS hotline for youth-serving agencies, (800) 878-2437. General e-mail, nn4youth@ nn4youth.org. Web, www.nn4youth.org.*

Membership: providers of services related to runaway and homeless youth. Offers technical assistance to new and existing youth projects; operates Safe Choices Project, which provides youth with AIDS prevention education. Monitors legislation and regulations.

National Urban League, *Research and Public Policy, Washington Office,* *1111 14th St. N.W., #1001 20005-5603; (202) 898-1604. Fax, (202) 408-1965. William Spriggs, Director. General e-mail, info@nul.org. Web, www. nul.org.*

Social service organization concerned with the social welfare of African Americans and other minorities. Youth Development division provides local leagues with technical assistance for youth programs and seeks training opportunities for youth within Urban League programs. (Headquarters in New York.)

National Youth Advocate Program, *P.O. Box 39127 20016 (mailing address: 4545 42nd St. N.W., #209 20016); (202) 244-6410. Fax, (202) 244-6396. Mubarak E. Awad, Director. General e-mail, nyap@msn.org. Web, www.nyap. org.*

Supports the development and operation of community-based services for at-risk youth and their families. (Affiliated with Youth Advocate Program International.)

Orphan Foundation of America, *128C Church St. N.W., Vienna, VA 22180-4507; (703) 281-4226. Fax, (703) 281-0116. Eileen McCaffrey, Executive Director. Information, (800) 950-4673. General e-mail, help@orphan.org. Web, www.orphan.org.*

Advocates for orphaned, abandoned, and homeless teenage youths. Provides research, information, scholarships, emergency cash grants, volunteer programs, guidance, and support. Interests include the rights of orphaned children, transition from youth foster care to young adult independence, and breaking the welfare cycle. Learning center provides training and educational materials.

Rape, Abuse, and Incest National Network (RAINN), *635-B Pennsylvania Ave. S.E. 20003-4303; (202) 544-1034. Fax, (202) 544-3556. Debbie Andrews, Executive Director. Toll-free, (800) 656-HOPE. General e-mail, rainnmail@aol.com. Web, www.rainn.org.*

Publicizes the issue of sexual assault and the availability of local counseling services for rape and incest survivors. RAINN's 24-hour sexual assault hotline provides free counseling services through a national network of rape crisis centers.

Stand for Children, *1834 Connecticut Ave. N.W. 20009; (202) 234-0095. Fax, (202) 234-0217. Jonah Martin Edelman, Executive Director. Information, (800) 663-4032. General e-mail, tellstand@stand.org. Web, www.stand.org.*

Works with chapters nationwide to promote the growth, health, education, and safety of children. Provides information to the public about policies that affect children and families. Organizes meetings between parents and community leaders. (Affiliated with the Children's Defense Fund.)

Elderly

See also Health Services for Special Groups (chap. 11); Pensions and Benefits (chap. 7); Senior Citizens (chap. 1); Social Security (this chapter)

AGENCIES

Administration on Aging *(Health and Human Services Dept.), 200 Independence Ave. S.W., #309F 20201; (202) 401-4634. Fax, (202) 401-7741. Jeanette C. Takamura, Assistant Secretary. Press, (202) 401-4541. General e-mail, AoAInfo@aoa.gov. Web, www.aoa.dhhs.gov.*

Acts as advocate for the elderly; serves as the principal agency for implementing programs under the Older Americans Act. Develops programs to promote the economic welfare and personal independence of older people; provides advice and assistance to promote the development of state-administered, community-based social services for older people; supports curriculum development and training in gerontology.

National Senior Service Corps *(Corporation for National Service), Retired and Senior Volunteer Program, Foster Grandparent Program, and Senior Companion Program, 1201 New York Ave. N.W. 20525; (202) 606-5000. Fax, (202) 565-2789. Tom Endres, Director. TTY, (202) 565-2799. Volunteer recruiting information, (800) 942-2677. Web, www.cns.gov.*

Network of programs that help older Americans find service opportunities in their communities, including the Retired and Senior Volunteer Program, which encourages older citizens to use their talents and experience in community service; the Foster Grandparent Program, which gives older citizens opportunities to work with exceptional children and children with special needs; and the Senior Companion Program, which recruits older citizens to help homebound adults, especially seniors, with special needs.

See also Administration for Children and Families (p. 377)

CONGRESS

House Education and the Workforce Committee, *Subcommittee on Postsecondary Education, Training, and Life-Long Learning, 2181 RHOB 20515; (202) 225-4527. Fax, (202) 225-9571. Rep. Howard P. "Buck" McKeon, R-Calif., Chair; Kevin D. Talley, Staff Director. Web, www.house.gov/ed_workforce.*

Jurisdiction over legislation on all matters dealing with programs and services for the elderly, including health and nutrition programs and the Older Americans Act.

Senate Health, Education, Labor, and Pensions Committee, *Subcommittee on Aging, SH-608 20510; (202) 224-2962. Fax, (202) 228-0412. Sen. Mike DeWine, R-Ohio, Chair; Karla Carpenter, Staff Director. Web, labor.senate.gov.*

Jurisdiction over applications of the Older Americans Act and related legislation.

Senate Special Committee on Aging, *SD-G31 20510; (202) 224-5364. Fax, (202) 224-8660. Sen. Charles E. Grassley, R-Iowa, Chair; Ted Totman, Staff Director. Web, aging.senate.gov.*

Oversight of all matters affecting older Americans. Studies and reviews public and private policies and programs that affect the elderly, including retirement income and maintenance, housing, health, welfare, employment, education, recreation, and participation in family and community life; provides other Senate committees with information. Cannot report legislation.

NONPROFIT

AARP, *601 E St. N.W. 20049; (202) 434-2277. Fax, (202) 434-2320. Horace B. Deets, Executive Director. Library, (202) 434-6240. Press, (202) 434-2560. TTY, (202) 434-6561. Web, www.aarp.org.*

Conducts educational and counseling programs in areas concerning the elderly such as widowed persons services, health promotion, housing, and consumer protection. Library open to the public.

Families USA, *1334 G St. N.W., #300 20005; (202) 737-6340. Fax, (202) 347-2417. Ron Pollack, Executive Director. General e-mail, info@familiesusa.org. Web, www.familiesusa.org.*

Organization of American families whose interests include health care and long-term care, Social Security, Medicare, and Medicaid. Monitors legislation and regulations affecting the elderly.

Jewish Council for the Aging, *National Center for Productive Aging, 11820 Parklawn Dr., #200, Rockville,*

MD 20852; (301) 881-8782. Fax, (301) 231-9360. David N. Gamse, Executive Director. TTY, (301) 881-5263. Web, www.jcagw.org.

Nonsectarian organization that provides programs and services to help older people continue living independent lives. Offers employment-related services, computer training, adult day care, in-home care, transportation, information and referrals, volunteer opportunities, and consultation.

National Assn. of Area Agencies on Aging, *927 15th St. N.W., 6th Floor 20005; (202) 296-8130. Fax, (202) 296-8134. Janice Jackson, Executive Director. General e-mail, jjf@n4a.org. Web, www.n4a.org.*

Works to establish an effective national policy on aging; provides local agencies with training and technical assistance; disseminates information to these agencies and the public. Monitors legislation and regulations.

National Assn. of Area Agencies on Aging, *Elder-care Locator, 927 15th St. N.W., 6th Floor 20005; (800) 677-1116. Fax, (202) 296-8134. Angela Heath, Project Officer. Web, www.aoa.dhhs.gov.*

Service that helps older people and caregivers locate local support resources for aging Americans. Refers people to agencies or organizations that deal with meal services, home care transportation, housing alternatives, home repair, recreation, social activities, and legal services.

National Assn. of State Units on Aging, *1225 Eye St. N.W., #725 20005; (202) 898-2578. Fax, (202) 898-2583. Daniel A. Quirk, Executive Director. General e-mail, staff@NASUA.org.*

Membership: state and territorial governmental units that deal with the elderly. Provides members with information, technical assistance, and professional training. Monitors legislation and regulations.

National Caucus and Center on Black Aged, *1424 K St. N.W., #500 20005-2407; (202) 637-8400. Fax, (202) 347-0895. Samuel J. Simmons, President.*

Concerned with issues that affect elderly African Americans. Sponsors employment and housing programs for the elderly and education and training for professionals in gerontology. Monitors legislation and regulations.

National Council of Senior Citizens, *8403 Colesville Rd., #1200, Silver Spring, MD 20910-3314; (301) 578-8800. Fax, (301) 578-8999. Steve Protulis, Executive Director. Web, www.ncscinc.org.*

Seeks to strengthen benefits to the elderly, including improved Social Security payments, increased employment, and education and health programs.

National Council on the Aging, *409 3rd St. S.W., 2nd Floor 20024; (202) 479-1200. Fax, (202) 479-0735. James Firman, President. Information, (202) 479-6653. Library, (202) 479-6669. Press, (202) 479-6975. General e-mail, info@ncoa.org. Web, www.ncoa.org.*

Serves as an information clearinghouse on training, technical assistance, advocacy, and research on every aspect of aging. Provides information on social services for older persons. Monitors legislation and regulations. Library open to the public.

National Hispanic Council on Aging, *2713 Ontario Rd. N.W. 20009; (202) 265-1288. Fax, (202) 745-2522. Marta Sotomayor, President. General e-mail, nhcoa@worldnet.att.net. Web, www.nhcoa.org.*

Membership: senior citizens, health care workers, professionals in the field of aging, and others in the United States and Puerto Rico who are interested in topics related to Hispanics and aging. Provides research training, consulting, and technical assistance; sponsors seminars, workshops, and management internships.

See also Catholic Charities USA (p. 31); National Senior Citizens Law Center (p. 8); Salvation Army (p. 632)

 # DISABILITIES

See also Employment and Training Programs (chap. 7); Special Groups in Education (chap. 6)

AGENCIES

Administration for Children and Families *(Health and Human Services Dept.), Administration on Developmental Disabilities, 200 Independence Ave. S.W., #300F 20201; (202) 690-6590. Fax, (202) 690-6904. Sue Swenson, Commissioner. TTY, (202) 690-6415. Web, www.acf.dhhs.gov/programs/add.*

Establishes state protection and advocacy systems for people with developmental disabilities, including persons with mental retardation, cerebral palsy, epilepsy, and autism; awards discretionary grants to university-affiliated programs and to programs of national significance. Administers formula grants to states for persons who incurred developmental disabilities before the age of twenty-two.

Architectural and Transportation Barriers Compliance Board (Access Board), *1331 F St. N.W., #1000 20004-1111; (202) 272-5434. Fax, (202) 272-5447. Lawrence W. Roffee, Executive Director. TTY, (202) 272-*

5449. Toll-free technical assistance, (800) 872-2253. Web, www.access-board.gov.

Enforces standards requiring that buildings and telecommunications and transportation systems be accessible to persons with disabilities; provides technical assistance and information on designing these facilities; sets accessibility guidelines for the Americans with Disabilities Act (ADA) and the Telecommunications Act of 1996.

Committee for Purchase from People Who Are Blind or Severely Disabled, *1215 Jefferson Davis Hwy., #310, Arlington, VA 22202-4302; (703) 603-7740. Fax, (703) 603-0655. Leon Wilson, Executive Director.*

Presidentially appointed committee. Determines which products and services are suitable for federal procurement from qualified nonprofit agencies that employ people who are blind or have other severe disabilities; seeks to increase employment opportunities for these individuals.

Education Dept., *Special Education and Rehabilitative Services, 330 C St. S.W. 20202-2500; (202) 205-5465. Fax, (202) 205-9252. Judith Heumann, Assistant Secretary. TTY, (202) 205-5465. Main phone is voice and TTY accessible. Web, www.ed.gov.*

Provides information on federal legislation and programs and national organizations concerning individuals with disabilities.

Employment Standards Administration *(Labor Dept.), Coal Mine Workers' Compensation, 200 Constitution Ave. N.W., #C3520 20210; (202) 693-0046. Fax, (202) 693-1395. James L. DeMarce, Director.*

Provides direction for administration of the black lung benefits program. Adjudicates claims filed on or after July 1, 1973; certifies these benefit payments and maintains black lung beneficiary rolls.

(For claims filed before July 1, 1973, contact Social Security Administration, Disability.)

Equal Employment Opportunity Commission, *Americans with Disabilities Act, 1801 L St. N.W., #6027 20507; (202) 663-4503. Fax, (202) 663-4639. Christopher J. Kuczynski, Director. Information, (800) 669-4000. TTY, (800) 669-6820.*

Division of the Office of Legal Counsel. Provides interpretations, opinions, and technical assistance on the ADA provisions relating to employment.

Justice Dept., *Disability Rights, 1425 New York Ave. N.W., #4039 20005 (mailing address: P.O. Box 66738 20035-6738); (202) 307-0663. Fax, (202) 307-1198. John L. Wodatch, Chief. Information, (800) 514-0301. TTY,*

(800) 514-0383. Web, www.usdoj.gov/crt/ada/adahom1.htm.

Litigates cases under Title II and III of the Americans with Disabilities Act, which prohibits discrimination on the basis of disability in places of public accommodation and in all activities of state and local government. Provides technical assistance to business and individuals affected by the law.

National Council on Disability, *1331 F St. N.W., #1050 20004-1107; (202) 272-2004. Fax, (202) 272-2022. Marca Bristo, Chair. Web, www.ncd.gov.*

Reviews and reports to the president on all laws, programs, and policies of the federal government affecting individuals with disabilities. Focus includes health insurance; sponsors conferences for families caring for persons with disabilities.

National Institute of Child Health and Human Development *(National Institutes of Health), National Center for Medical Rehabilitation Research, 6100 Executive Blvd., Bldg. 6100E, #2A-03, Bethesda, MD 20852; (301) 402-2242. Fax, (301) 402-0832. Dr. Michael Weinrich, Director. Web, silk.nih.gov/silk/NCMRR.*

Conducts and supports research to develop improved technologies, techniques, and prosthetic and orthotic devices for people with disabilities; promotes medical rehabilitation training.

National Institute on Disability and Rehabilitation Research *(Education Dept.), 330 C St. S.W., #3060 20202-2572 (mailing address: 400 Maryland Ave. S.W., #3060 20202); (202) 205-8134. Fax, (202) 205-8997. Katherine D. Seelman, Director. TTY, (202) 205-9136. Web, www.ed.gov/offices/osers/nidrr/pubs.html.*

Assists research programs in rehabilitating people with disabilities; provides information on developments in the field; awards grants and contracts for scientific, technical, and methodological research; coordinates federal research programs on rehabilitation; offers fellowships to individuals conducting research in the field.

President's Committee on Employment of People with Disabilities, *1331 F St. N.W., #300 20004-1107; (202) 376-6200. Fax, (202) 376-6219. John Lancaster, Executive Director. TTY, (202) 376-6205. General e-mail, info@pcepd.gov. Web, www.pcepd.gov.*

Seeks to eliminate physical and psychological barriers to the disabled through education and information programs; promotes education, training, rehabilitation, and employment opportunities for people with disabilities.

Rehabilitation Services Administration *(Education Dept.), 330 C St. S.W. 20202-2531; (202) 205-5482. Fax,*

(202) 205-9874. Fredric K. Schroeder, Commissioner. TTY, (202) 205-9295.

Coordinates and directs major federal programs for eligible physically and mentally disabled persons. Administers distribution of grants for training and employment programs and for establishing supported-employment and independent-living programs. Provides vocational training and job placement.

Smithsonian Institution, *Accessibility Program,* 900 Jefferson Dr. S.W., #1239 20560-0426; (202) 786-2942. Fax, (202) 786-2210. Janice Majewski, Coordinator. TTY, (202) 786-2414.

Coordinates Smithsonian efforts to improve accessibility of its programs and facilities to visitors and staff with disabilities. Serves as a resource for museums and individuals nationwide.

Social Security Administration, *Disability,* 6401 Security Blvd., #560, Baltimore, MD 21235; (410) 965-3424. Fax, (410) 965-6503. Kenneth D. Nibali, Associate Commissioner. Information, (410) 965-7700.

Administers and regulates the disability insurance program and disability provisions of the Supplemental Security Income (SSI) program.

CONGRESS

House Appropriations Committee, *Subcommittee on Transportation,* 2358 RHOB 20515; (202) 225-2141. Rep. Frank R. Wolf, R-Va., Chair; John T. Blazey, Staff Director. Web, www.house.gov/appropriations.

Jurisdiction over legislation to appropriate funds for the Architectural and Transportation Barriers Compliance Board.

House Commerce Committee, *Subcommittee on Health and the Environment,* 2125 RHOB 20515; (202) 225-2927. Fax, (202) 225-1919. Rep. Michael Bilirakis, R-Fla., Chair; James E. Derderian, Staff Director. General e-mail, commerce@mail.house.gov. Web, www.house.gov/commerce.

Jurisdiction over developmental disability legislation.

House Education and the Workforce Committee, *Subcommittee on Early Childhood, Youth, and Families,* 2181 RHOB 20515; (202) 225-4527. Fax, (202) 225-9571. Rep. Michael N. Castle, R-Del., Chair; Kevin D. Talley, Staff Director. Web, www.house.gov/ed_workforce.

Jurisdiction over legislation on special education programs including, but not limited to, alcohol and drug abuse and education of the disabled.

Library of Congress, *National Library Service for the Blind and Physically Handicapped,* 1291 Taylor St. N.W.

20542; (202) 707-5104. Fax, (202) 707-0712. Frank Kurt Cylke, Director. TTY, (202) 707-0744. Reference, (202) 707-5100; outside D.C. area, (800) 424-8567. General e-mail, nls@loc.gov. Web, www.loc.gov/nls.

Administers a national program of free library services for persons with physical disabilities in cooperation with regional and subregional libraries. Produces and distributes full-length books and magazines in recorded form (disc and cassette) and in Braille. Reference section answers questions relating to blindness and physical disabilities and on library services available to persons with disabilities.

Senate Appropriations Committee, *Subcommittee on Transportation,* SD-133 20510; (202) 224-2175. Fax, (202) 224-4401. Sen. Richard C. Shelby, R-Ala., Chair; Wally Burnett, Majority Clerk. Web, appropriations.senate.gov/transportation.

Jurisdiction over legislation to appropriate funds for the Architectural and Transportation Barriers Compliance Board.

Senate Health, Education, Labor, and Pensions Committee, SD-428 20510; (202) 224-5375. Fax, (202) 228-5044. Sen. James M. Jeffords, R-Vt., Chair; Mark Powden, Staff Director. TTY, (202) 224-1975. Web, labor.senate.gov.

Jurisdiction over legislation on people with disabilities, including vocational rehabilitation for people with physical and developmental disabilities. Jurisdiction over the Americans with Disabilities Act.

NONPROFIT

American Assn. of University Affiliated Programs for Persons with Developmental Disabilities, 8630 Fenton St., #410, Silver Spring, MD 20910; (301) 588-8252. Fax, (301) 588-2842. George Jesien, Executive Director. Web, www.aauap.org.

Network of facilities that diagnose and treat the developmentally disabled. Trains graduate students and professionals in the field; helps state and local agencies develop services. Interests include interdisciplinary training and services, early screening to prevent developmental disabilities, and development of equipment and programs to serve persons with disabilities.

American Bar Assn., *Commission on Mental and Physical Disability Law,* 740 15th St. N.W. 20005; (202) 662-1570. Fax, (202) 662-1032. John Parry, Director. Web, www.abanet.org/disability/home.html.

Serves as a clearinghouse for information on mental and physical disability law and offers legal research services.

American Counseling Assn., *Rehabilitation, 5999 Stevenson Ave., Alexandria, VA 22304-3300; (703) 823-9800. Fax, (703) 823-0252. Richard Yep, Executive Director. Information, (800) 347-6647. TTY, (703) 370-1943. Web, www.counseling.org.*

Membership: counselors, counselor educators and graduate students in the rehabilitation field, and other interested persons. Establishes counseling and research standards; encourages establishment of rehabilitation facilities; conducts leadership training and continuing education programs; serves as a liaison between counselors and clients. Monitors legislation and regulations. Library open to the public.

American Medical Rehabilitation Providers Assn., *1606 20th St. N.W., 3rd Floor 20009; (202) 265-4404. Fax, (202) 833-9168. Carolyn Zollar, Vice President, Government Relations. Information, (888) 346-4624. Web, www.amrpa.org.*

Promotes improved rehabilitation facilities; sponsors workshops, seminars, and on-the-job training contracts.

American Network of Community Options and Resources, *4200 Evergreen Lane, #315, Annandale, VA 22003-3255; (703) 642-6614. Fax, (703) 642-0497. Renee Pietrangelo, Managing Director. General e-mail, ancor@radix.net. Web, www.ancor.org.*

Membership: privately operated agencies and corporations that provide support and services to people with disabilities. Advises and works with regulatory and consumer agencies that serve people with disabilities; provides information and sponsors seminars and workshops; publishes directory that lists services offered by member agencies. Monitors legislation and regulations.

American Occupational Therapy Assn., *4720 Montgomery Lane, Bethesda, MD 20814 (mailing address: P.O. Box 31220, Bethesda, MD 20824-1220); (301) 652-2682. Fax, (301) 652-7711. Chris Bluhm, Executive Director (Acting). TTY, (800) 377-8555. Web, www.aota.org.*

Membership: registered occupational therapists, certified occupational therapy assistants, and students. Associate members include businesses and organizations supportive of occupational therapy. Accredits colleges and universities and certifies therapists.

American Orthotic and Prosthetic Assn., *1650 King St., #500, Alexandria, VA 22314; (703) 836-7116. Fax, (703) 836-0838. Lance O. Hoxie, Executive Director. Web, www.opoffice.org.*

Membership: companies that manufacture or supply artificial limbs and braces. Provides information on the profession.

American Physical Therapy Assn., *1111 N. Fairfax St., Alexandria, VA 22314-1488; (703) 684-2782. Fax, (703) 684-7343. Francis Mallon, Executive Vice President. Information, (800) 999-2782. TTY, (703) 683-6748. General e-mail, svcctr@apta.org. Web, www.apta.org.*

Membership: physical therapists, assistants, and students. Establishes professional standards and accredits physical therapy programs; seeks to improve physical therapy education, practice, and research.

American Speech-Language-Hearing Assn., *10801 Rockville Pike, Rockville, MD 20852; (301) 897-5700. Fax, (301) 571-0457. Frederick T. Spahr, Executive Director. Press, (301) 897-0156. TTY, (301) 897-0157. Toll-free hotline (except Alaska, Hawaii, and Maryland), (800) 638-8255 (voice and TTY accessible). General e-mail, actioncenter@asha.org. Web, www.asha.org.*

Membership: specialists in speech-language pathology and audiology. Sponsors professional education programs; acts as accrediting agent for graduate college programs and for public clinical education programs in speech-language pathology and audiology. Advocates the rights of the communicatively disabled; provides information on speech, hearing, and language problems. Provides referrals to speech-language pathologists and audiologists. Interests include national and international standards for bioacoustics and noise.

Brain Injury Assn., *105 N. Alfred St., Alexandria, VA 22314; (703) 236-6000. Fax, (703) 236-6001. Allan I. Bergman, President. Family helpline, (800) 444-6443.*

Works to improve the quality of life for persons with traumatic brain injuries and for their families. Promotes the prevention of head injuries through public awareness and education programs. Offers state-level support services for individuals and their families. Monitors legislation and regulations.

Center on Disability and Health, *1522 K St. N.W., #800 20005; (202) 842-4408. Fax, (202) 842-2402. Bob Griss, Director. General e-mail, bgrisscdh@aol.com.*

Promotes changes in the financing and delivery of health care to meet the needs of persons with disabilities and other chronic health conditions. Conducts research; provides technical assistance to disability groups and agencies. Monitors legislation and regulations.

Consortium for Citizens with Disabilities, *1730 K St. N.W., #1212 20006; (202) 785-3388. Fax, (202) 467-4179. Paul Marchand, Chair. General e-mail, info@c-c-d.org. Web, www.c-c-d.org.*

Coalition of national disability organizations. Advocates national public policy that ensures the self-determination, independence, empowerment, and integration in all aspects of society for children and adults with disabilities.

Disability Resource Center, *4400 University Dr., MSN 2E6, Fairfax, VA 22030-4444; (703) 993-2474. Fax, (703) 993-2478. Rhoda Rothschild, Assistant Director. TTY, (703) 993-2474. Web, www.gmu.edu/departments/ advising/dss.html.*

Advocates for the rights of people with physical and mental disabilities; seeks to educate the public about these rights; conducts research. Monitors legislation and regulations.

Disability Rights Education and Defense Fund, *Governmental Affairs, Washington Office, 1629 K St. N.W. 20006; (202) 986-0375. Fax, (202) 775-7465. Pat Wright, Director.*

Law and policy center working to protect and advance the civil rights of people with disabilities through legislation, litigation, advocacy, and technical assistance. Educates and trains attorneys, advocates, persons with disabilities, and parents of children with disabilities. (Headquarters in Berkeley, Calif.)

Disabled American Veterans, *807 Maine Ave. S.W. 20024-2410; (202) 554-3501. Fax, (202) 554-3581. Arthur H. Wilson, National Adjutant. Web, www.dav.org.*

Chartered by Congress to assist veterans with claims for benefits; represents veterans seeking to correct alleged errors in military records. Assists families of veterans with disabilities.

Disabled Sports USA, *451 Hungerford Dr., #100, Rockville, MD 20850; (301) 217-0960. Fax, (301) 217-0968. Kirk M. Bauer, Executive Director. TTY, (301) 217-0963. General e-mail, dsusa@dsusa.org. Web, www.dsusa. org.*

Conducts sports and recreation activities and physical fitness programs for people with disabilities and their families and friends; conducts workshops and competitions; participates in world championships.

Epilepsy Foundation, *4351 Garden City Dr., Landover, MD 20785; (301) 459-3700. Fax, (301) 577-2684. Eric Hargis, Chief Executive Officer. Information, (800) 332-1000. Library, (800) 332-4050. General e-mail, postmaster@ efa.org. Web, www.epilepsyfoundation.org.*

Promotes research and treatment of epilepsy; makes research grants; disseminates information and educational materials. Affiliates provide direct services for people with epilepsy and make referrals when necessary. Library open to the public by appointment.

Girl Scouts of the U.S.A., *Government Relations, Washington Office, 1025 Connecticut Ave. N.W., #309*

20036; (202) 659-3780. Fax, (202) 331-8065. LaVerne Alexander, Director. Web, www.girlscouts.org.

Educational service organization for girls ages five to seventeen. Promotes personal development through social action, leadership, and programs such as Girl Scouting for Handicapped Girls. (Headquarters in New York.)

Goodwill Industries International, *9200 Rockville Pike, Bethesda, MD 20814-3896; (301) 530-6500. Fax, (301) 530-1516. Fred Grandy, President. Web, www. goodwill.org.*

Membership: 185 autonomous organizations that provide disabled and disadvantaged individuals with Goodwill Industries services, which include vocational rehabilitation evaluation, job training, employment, and placement services.

International Code Council, *5203 Leesburg Pike, Falls Church, VA 22041; (703) 931-4533. Fax, (703) 379-1546. Richard P. Kuchnicki, Executive Vice President. Web, www. intlcode.org.*

Provides review board for the American National Standards Institute accessibility standards, which ensure that buildings are accessible to persons with physical disabilities.

National Assn. of Developmental Disabilities Councils, *1234 Massachusetts Ave. N.W., #103 20005; (202) 347-1234. Fax, (202) 347-4023. Susan A. Zierman, Executive Director. General e-mail, NADDC@igc.apc.org. Web, www.naddc.org.*

Membership: state and territorial councils authorized by the Development Disabilities Act, which promotes the interests of people with developmental disabilities and their families. Monitors legislation and regulations.

National Council on Independent Living, *1916 Wilson Blvd., #209, Arlington, VA 22201; (703) 525-3406. Fax, (703) 525-3409. Anne-Marie Hughey, Executive Director. TTY, (703) 525-4153. General e-mail, ncil@ncil.org. Web, www.ncil.org.*

Membership: independent living centers, their staff and volunteers, and individuals with disabilities. Seeks to strengthen independent living centers; facilitates the integration of people with disabilities into society; provides training and technical assistance; sponsors referral service and speakers' bureau.

National Easter Seal Society, *Washington Office, 700 13th St. N.W., #200 20005; (202) 347-3066. Fax, (202) 737-7914. Joseph D. Romer, Executive Vice President. TTY, (202) 347-7385. Web, www.easter-seals.org.*

Federation of state and local groups with programs that help people with disabilities achieve independence.

Washington office monitors legislation and regulations. Affiliates assist individuals with a broad range of disabilities, including muscular dystrophy, cerebral palsy, stroke, speech and hearing loss, blindness, amputation, and learning disabilities. Services include physical, occupational, vocational, and speech therapy; speech, hearing, physical, and vocational evaluation; psychological testing and counseling; personal and family counseling; supported employment; special education programs; social clubs and day and residential camps; and transportation, referral, and follow-up programs. (Headquarters in Chicago.)

National Information Center for Children and Youth with Disabilities, *1825 Connecticut Ave. N.W., 7th Floor 20009 (mailing address: P.O. Box 1492 20013); (202) 884-8200. Fax, (202) 884-8441. Suzanne Ripley, Director. Information, (800) 695-0285. Web, www.nichcy. org.*

Federally funded clearinghouse that provides free information to parents, educators, caregivers, advocates, and others who help children and youth with disabilities become active participants in school, work, and the community. Offers personal responses to specific questions, referrals to other organizations, prepared information packets, and technical assistance to families and professional groups.

National Multiple Sclerosis Society, *Washington Office, 2021 K St. N.W., #715 20006-1003; (202) 296-9891. Fax, (202) 296-3425. Jeanne Oates Angulo, President. Web, www.msandyou.org.*

Seeks to advance medical knowledge of multiple sclerosis, a disease of the central nervous system; disseminates information worldwide. Patient services include individual and family counseling, exercise programs, equipment loans, medical and social service referrals, transportation assistance, back-to-work training programs, and in-service training seminars for nurses, homemakers, and physical and occupational therapists. (Headquarters in New York.)

National Organization on Disability, *910 16th St. N.W., #600 20006-2988; (202) 293-5960. Fax, (202) 293-7999. Allen A. Reich, President. TTY, (202) 293-5968. Web, www.nod.org.*

Administers the Community Partnership Program, a network of communities that works to remove barriers and address educational, employment, social, and transportation needs of people with disabilities. Provides members with information and technical assistance; sponsors annual community awards competition; makes referrals. Monitors legislation and regulations.

National Parent Network on Disabilities, *1130 17th St. N.W., #400 20036; (202) 463-2299. Fax, (202) 463-9405. Patricia McGill Smith, Executive Director. General e-mail, pmcglsmith@aol.com. Web, www.npnd.org.*

Works to improve the lives of people with disabilities by providing parents and family member groups with information, education, and training. Monitors legislation and regulations.

National Rehabilitation Assn., *633 S. Washington St., Alexandria, VA 22314; (703) 836-0850. Fax, (703) 836-0848. Michelle Vaughan, Executive Director. TTY, (703) 836-0849. Web, www.nationalrehab.org.*

Membership: administrators, counselors, therapists, disability examiners, vocational evaluators, instructors, job placement specialists, disability managers in the corporate sector, and others interested in rehabilitation of the physically and mentally disabled. Sponsors conferences and workshops. Monitors legislation and regulations.

National Rehabilitation Information Center, *1010 Wayne Ave., #800, Silver Spring, MD 20910; (301) 562-2400. Fax, (301) 562-2401. Mark Odum, Director. Information, (800) 346-2742. TTY, (301) 495-5626. Web, www. naric.com.*

Provides information on disability and rehabilitation research. Acts as referral agency for disability and rehabilitation facilities and programs.

Paralyzed Veterans of America, *801 18th St. N.W. 20006-3517; (202) 872-1300. Fax, (202) 785-4452. Gordon H. Mansfield, Executive Director. Information, (800) 424-8200. TTY, (202) 416-7622. Web, www.pva.org.*

Congressionally chartered organization that assists veterans with claims for benefits. Distributes information on special education for paralyzed veterans; supports and raises funds for medical research.

RESNA, *1700 N. Moore St., #1540, Arlington, VA 22209-1903; (703) 524-6686. Fax, (703) 524-6630. James R. Geletka, Executive Director. TTY, (703) 524-6639. General e-mail, info@resna.org. Web, www.resna.org.*

Membership: engineers, health professionals, persons with disabilities, and others concerned with rehabilitation engineering technology. Promotes and supports developments in rehabilitation engineering; acts as an information clearinghouse.

Special Olympics International, *1325 G St. N.W., #500 20005; (202) 628-3630. Fax, (202) 824-0200. Robert Sargent Shriver Jr., Chair. General e-mail, soimail@aol.com. Web, www.specialolympics.org.*

Offers individuals with mental retardation opportunities for year-round sports training; sponsors athletic competition worldwide in twenty-two individual and team sports.

Spina Bifida Assn. of America, *4590 MacArthur Blvd. N.W., #250 20007-4226; (202) 944-3285. Fax, (202) 944-3295. Lawrence Pencak, Executive Director. Information, (800) 621-3141. General e-mail, sbaa@sbaa.org. Web, www.sbaa.org.*

Membership: individuals with spina bifida, their supporters, and concerned professionals. Offers educational programs, scholarships, and support services; acts as a clearinghouse; provides referrals. Serves as U.S. member of the International Federation for Hydrocephalus and Spina Bifida, which is headquartered in Geneva. Monitors legislation and regulations.

United Cerebral Palsy Assns., *1660 L St. N.W., #700 20036-5602; (202) 776-0406. Fax, (202) 776-0414. Kirsten Nyrop, Executive Director. Information, (800) 872-5827. Main phone is voice and TTY accessible. Web, www.ucpa.org.*

National network of state and local affiliates that assists individuals with cerebral palsy and other developmental disabilities and their families. Provides parent education, early intervention, employment services, family support and respite programs, therapy, assistive technology, and vocational training. Promotes research on cerebral palsy; supports the use of assistive technology and community-based living arrangements for persons with cerebral palsy and other developmental disabilities.

Very Special Arts, *1300 Connecticut Ave. N.W., #700 20036; (202) 628-2800. Fax, (202) 737-0725. John Kemp, Chief Executive Officer. Information, (800) 933-8721. TTY, (202) 737-0645. Web, www.vsarts.org.*

Initiates and supports research and program development providing arts training and demonstration for persons with disabilities. Provides technical assistance and training to Very Special Arts state organizations; acts as an information clearinghouse for arts and persons with disabilities. (Affiliated with the Kennedy Center education office.)

Blind and Visually Impaired

AGENCIES

Committee for Purchase from People Who Are Blind or Severely Disabled, *1215 Jefferson Davis Hwy., #310, Arlington, VA 22202-4302; (703) 603-7740. Fax, (703) 603-0655. Leon Wilson, Executive Director.*

Presidentially appointed committee. Determines which products and services are suitable for federal procurement from qualified nonprofit agencies that employ people who are blind or have other severe disabilities;

seeks to increase employment opportunities for these individuals.

CONGRESS

Library of Congress, *National Library Service for the Blind and Physically Handicapped, 1291 Taylor St. N.W. 20542; (202) 707-5104. Fax, (202) 707-0712. Frank Kurt Cylke, Director. TTY, (202) 707-0744. Reference, (202) 707-5100; outside D.C. area, (800) 424-8567. General e-mail, nls@loc.gov. Web, www.loc.gov/nls.*

Administers a national program of free library services for persons with physical disabilities in cooperation with regional and subregional libraries. Produces and distributes full-length books and magazines in recorded form (disc and cassette) and in Braille. Reference section answers questions relating to blindness and physical disabilities and on library services available to persons with disabilities.

NONPROFIT

American Blind Lawyers Assn., *1155 15th St. N.W., #1004 20005; (202) 467-5081. Fax, (202) 467-5085. Gary Austin, President.*

Membership: blind lawyers and law students. Provides members with legal information; acts as an information clearinghouse on legal materials available in Braille, in large print, on computer disc, and on tape. (Affiliated with American Council of the Blind.)

American Council of the Blind, *1155 15th St. N.W., #1004 20005-2706; (202) 467-5081. Fax, (202) 467-5085. Charles Crawford, Executive Director. Toll-free, 2:00– 5:00 p.m. E.S.T., (800) 424-8666. Web, www.acb.org.*

Membership organization serving blind and visually impaired individuals. Interests include Social Security, telecommunications, rehabilitation services, transportation, education, and architectural access. Provides blind individuals with information and referral services, including legal referrals; advises state organizations and agencies serving the blind; sponsors scholarships for the blind and visually impaired.

American Foundation for the Blind, *Governmental Relations, Washington Office, 820 1st St. N.E., #400 20002; (202) 408-0200. Fax, (202) 289-7880. Scott Marshall, Vice President. Information, (800) 232-5463. General e-mail, afbgov@afb.net. Web, www.afb.org.*

Advocates equality of access and opportunity for the blind and visually impaired. Provides services; conducts informational and educational programs; develops and implements public policy and legislation. Maintains the Helen Keller Archives and M. C. Migel Memorial Library at its headquarters in N.Y.

Assn. for Education and Rehabilitation of the Blind and Visually Impaired, *P.O. Box 22397, Alexandria, VA 22304; (703) 823-9690. Fax, (703) 823-9695. Denise Rozell, Executive Director. General e-mail, aer@ aerbvi.org. Web, www.aerbvi.org.*

Membership: professionals and paraprofessionals who work with the blind and visually impaired. Provides information on services for people who are blind and visually impaired and on employment opportunities for those who work with them. Works to improve quality of education and rehabilitation services. Monitors legislation and regulations.

Blinded Veterans Assn., *477 H St. N.W. 20001-2699; (202) 371-8880. Fax, (202) 371-8258. John Williams, Director. Information, (800) 669-7079. General e-mail, bva@bva.org. Web, www.bva.org.*

Chartered by Congress to assist veterans with claims for benefits. Seeks out blinded veterans to make them aware of benefits and services available to them.

National Industries for the Blind, *1901 N. Beauregard St., #200, Alexandria, VA 22311-1727; (703) 998-0770. Fax, (703) 671-9053. Pat Beattie, Director, Public Policy. Web, www.nib.org.*

Works to develop and improve opportunities for evaluating, training, employing, and advancing people who are blind and multidisabled blind. Develops business opportunities in the federal, state, and commercial marketplaces for organizations employing people with severe vision disabilities.

Prevention of Blindness Society, *1775 Church St. N.W. 20036; (202) 234-1010. Fax, (202) 234-1020. Michele Hartlove, Executive Director.*

Conducts preschool and elementary school screening program and glaucoma testing; provides information and referral service on eye health care; assists low-income persons in obtaining eye care and provides eyeglasses for a nominal fee to persons experiencing financial stress; conducts macular degeneration support group.

Deaf and Hearing Impaired

AGENCIES

General Services Administration, *Federal Relay Service, 13221 Woodland Park Rd., 3rd Floor, Herndon, VA 20171-3022; (703) 306-6360. Carolyn Thomas, Director. TTY, (800) 877-8339. Customer service, (800) 877-0996. Web, www.gsa.gov/frs.*

Assures that the federal telecommunications system is fully accessible to deaf, hearing-impaired, and speech-

impaired individuals, including federal workers. Operates twenty-four hours a day, seven days a week. Produces a directory of TDD/TTY services within the federal government.

National Institute on Deafness and Other Communication Disorders *(National Institutes of Health), 31 Center Dr., MSC-2320, #3C02, Bethesda, MD 20892-2320; (301) 402-0900. Fax, (301) 402-1590. Dr. James F. Battey Jr., Director. Information, (301) 496-7243. TTY, (301) 496-6596. Web, www.nih.gov/nidcd.*

Conducts and supports research and research training and disseminates information on hearing disorders and other communication processes, including diseases that affect hearing, balance, smell, taste, voice, speech, and language. Monitors international research.

NONPROFIT

Alexander Graham Bell Assn. for the Deaf and Hard of Hearing, *3417 Volta Pl. N.W. 20007-2778; (202) 337-5220. Fax, (202) 337-8314. Donna Sorkin, Executive Director. Main phone is voice and TTY accessible. General e-mail, agbell2@aol.com. Web, www.agbell.org.*

Provides hearing-impaired children in the United States and abroad with information and special education programs; works to improve employment opportunities for deaf persons; acts as a support group for parents of deaf persons.

American Academy of Audiology, *8300 Greensboro Dr., #750, McLean, VA 22102; (703) 790-8466. Fax, (703) 790-8631. Carol Fraser Fisk, Executive Director. Web, www.audiology.org.*

Membership: audiologists. Provides consumer information on testing and treatment for hearing loss; sponsors research, awards, and continuing education for audiologists.

American Speech-Language-Hearing Assn., *10801 Rockville Pike, Rockville, MD 20852; (301) 897-5700. Fax, (301) 571-0457. Frederick T. Spahr, Executive Director. Press, (301) 897-0156. TTY, (301) 897-0157. Toll-free hotline (except Alaska, Hawaii, and Maryland), (800) 638-8255 (voice and TTY accessible). General e-mail, actioncenter@asha.org. Web, www.asha.org.*

Membership: specialists in speech-language pathology and audiology. Sponsors professional education programs; acts as accrediting agent for graduate college programs and for public clinical education programs in speech-language pathology and audiology. Advocates the rights of the communicatively disabled; provides information on speech, hearing, and language problems. Provides referrals to speech-language pathologists and audiologists. Interests include national and international standards for bioacoustics and noise.

Better Hearing Institute, *515 King St., #420, Alexandria, VA 22314-3137; (703) 684-3391. Fax, (703) 684-6048. Mary Beth Zadel, Executive Director. Hearing Helpline, (800) 327-9355. Main phone is voice and TTY accessible. Web, www.betterhearing.org.*

Educational organization that conducts national public information programs on hearing loss, hearing aids, and other treatments.

Gallaudet University, *800 Florida Ave. N.E. 20002-3695; (202) 651-5000. Fax, (202) 651-5508. I. King Jordan, President, (202) 651-5005. Phone numbers are voice and TTY accessible. Web, www.gallaudet.edu.*

Offers undergraduate and graduate degree programs for the deaf and hard of hearing and graduate training for teachers and other professionals who work with the deaf; conducts research; maintains outreach and regional centers and demonstration doctoral, continuing education, secondary, elementary, and preschool programs (Model Secondary School for the Deaf, Kendall Demonstration Elementary School). Sponsors the Center for Global Education, the National Information Center on Deafness, and the National Center for the Law and the Deaf.

Hearing Industries Assn., *515 King St., #420, Alexandria, VA 22314; (703) 684-5744. Fax, (703) 684-6048. Carole M. Rogin, President. Web, www.hearing.org.*

Membership: hearing aid manufacturers and companies that supply hearing aid components. Provides information on hearing loss and hearing aids.

National Assn. of the Deaf, *814 Thayer Ave., Silver Spring, MD 20910-4500; (301) 587-1788. Fax, (301) 587-1791. Nancy J. Bloch, Executive Director. TTY, (301) 587-1789. General e-mail, nadinfo@nad.org. Web, www.nad.org.*

Safeguards the accessibility and civil rights of deaf and hard-of-hearing citizens in education, employment, health care, and telecommunications. Focuses on grassroots advocacy and empowerment, captioned media, deafness-related information and publications, legal assistance, policy development and research, public awareness, and youth leadership development.

National Deaf Education Networking and Clearinghouse, *800 Florida Ave. N.E., #3400 20002-3695; (202) 651-5051. Fax, (202) 651-5054. Randall Gentry, Director. TTY, (202) 651-5052. General e-mail, Clearinghouse.Infotogo@gallaudet.edu. Web, clerccenter.gallaudet.edu.*

Provides information on topics dealing with hearing loss and deafness for children and young adults up to age 21. (Affiliated with Gallaudet University.)

Registry of Interpreters for the Deaf, *8630 Fenton St., #324, Silver Spring, MD 20910; (301) 608-0050. Fax, (301) 608-0508. Ben Hall, President. General e-mail, info@rid.org. Web, www.rid.org.*

Trains and certifies interpreters; maintains registry of certified interpreters; establishes certification standards. Sponsors training workshops and conferences.

Self Help for Hard of Hearing People, *7910 Woodmont Ave., #1200, Bethesda, MD 20814; (301) 657-2248. Fax, (301) 913-9413. John Jaco, Executive Director. TTY, (301) 657-2249. General e-mail, national@shhh.org. Web, www.shhh.org.*

Promotes understanding of the nature, causes, and remedies of hearing loss. Provides hearing-impaired people with support and information. Seeks to educate the public about hearing loss and the problems of the hard of hearing. Provides travelers with information on assistive listening devices in museums, theaters, and places of worship.

Telecommunications for the Deaf, *8630 Fenton St., #604, Silver Spring, MD 20910; (301) 589-3786. Fax, (301) 589-3797. Claude Stout, Executive Director. TTY, (301) 589-3006. Voice via relay, (800) 735-2258. General e-mail, info@tdi-online.org. Web, www.tdi-online.org.*

Membership: individuals, organizations, and businesses using text telephone (TTY) equipment. Provides information on TTY equipment. Interests include closed captioning for television, emergency access (911), TTY relay services, visual alerting systems, and TTY/computer conversion. Publishes a national TTY telephone directory.

Mental Disabilities

AGENCIES

Administration for Children and Families *(Health and Human Services Dept.), Administration on Developmental Disabilities, 200 Independence Ave. S.W., #300F 20201; (202) 690-6590. Fax, (202) 690-6904. Sue Swenson, Commissioner. TTY, (202) 690-6415. Web, www.acf.dhhs.gov/programs/add.*

Establishes state protection and advocacy systems for people with developmental disabilities, including persons with mental retardation, cerebral palsy, epilepsy, and autism; awards discretionary grants to university-affiliated programs and to programs of national significance. Administers formula grants to states for persons who incurred developmental disabilities before the age of twenty-two.

NONPROFIT

American Assn. on Mental Retardation, *444 N. Capitol St. N.W., #846 20001-1512; (202) 387-1968. Fax, (202) 387-2193. Doreen Croser, Executive Director. Information, (800) 424-3688. Web, www.aamr.org.*

Membership: physicians, educators, administrators, social workers, psychologists, psychiatrists, lawyers, students, and others interested in mental retardation and related developmental disabilities. Provides information on legal rights, services, and facilities for people (including children) with mental retardation. Monitors international research.

American Foundation for Autistic Children, *4917 Dorset Ave., Chevy Chase, MD 20815; (301) 656-9213. Mooza V. P. Grant, President.*

Works with children and parents of autistic and self-injurious children. Conducts research and provides information on autism; works with education and health institutions. Interests include developing residential facilities for older children.

The Arc, *Governmental Affairs, Washington Office, 1730 K St. N.W., #1212 20006; (202) 785-3388. Fax, (202) 467-4179. Paul Marchand, Director. General e-mail, thearc@metronet.com. Web, thearc.org.*

Membership: individuals interested in assisting people with mental retardation. Provides information on government programs and legislation concerning mental retardation; oversees and encourages support for local groups that provide direct services for people with mental retardation. (Headquarters in Arlington, Tex.)

Autism Society of America, *7910 Woodmont Ave., #300, Bethesda, MD 20814-3015; (301) 657-0881. Fax, (301) 657-0869. Joan S. Zaro, Executive Director. Information, (800) 328-8476. Web, www.autism-society.org.*

Monitors legislation and regulations affecting support, education, training, research, and other services for individuals with autism. Offers referral service and information to the public.

Best Buddies International, *Washington Office, 1325 G St. N.W., #500 20005; (202) 824-0316. Fax, (202) 824-0351. Lisa Dirx, Director. Information, (800) 892-8339. Web, www.bestbuddies.org.*

Volunteer organization that provides friends and jobs to people with mental retardation worldwide. (Headquarters in Miami.)

International Assn. of Psychosocial Rehabilitation Services, *10025 Gov. Warfield Pkwy., #301, Columbia, MD 21044-3357; (410) 730-7190. Fax, (410) 730-5965. Ruth A. Hughes, Chief Executive Officer. TTY, (410) 730-1723. General e-mail, general@iapsrs.org. Web, www.iapsrs.org.*

Membership: agencies, mental health practitioners, policymakers, family groups, and consumer organizations. Supports the community adjustment of persons with psychiatric disabilities; promotes the role of rehabilitation in mental health systems; opposes discrimination based on mental disability.

Joseph P. Kennedy Jr. Foundation, *1325 G St. N.W., #500 20005-4709; (202) 393-1250. Fax, (202) 824-0351. Margaret McLaughlin, Executive Director. Web, www.familyvillage.wisc.edu/jpkf/.*

Seeks to enhance the quality of life of persons with mental retardation and to prevent retardation by identifying and eliminating its causes. Awards grants for social services and medical research.

National Assn. of Protection and Advocacy Systems, *900 2nd St. N.E., #211 20002; (202) 408-9514. Fax, (202) 408-9520. Curtis Decker, Executive Director. TTY, (202) 408-9521. Web, www.protectionandadvocacy.org.*

Membership: agencies working for the rights of the mentally ill or developmentally disabled and clients of the vocational rehabilitation system. Provides state agencies with training and technical assistance; maintains an electronic mail network. Monitors legislation and regulations.

National Assn. of State Directors of Developmental Disability Services, *113 Oronoco St., Alexandria, VA 22314; (703) 683-4202. Fax, (703) 684-1395. Robert M. Gettings, Executive Director. Web, www.nasddds.org.*

Membership: chief administrators of state mental retardation programs. Coordinates exchange of information on mental retardation programs among the states; provides information on state programs.

National Children's Center, *6200 2nd St. N.W. 20011; (202) 722-2300. Fax, (202) 722-2383. Arthur Ginsberg, Executive Director. Web, www.washingtonpost.com/yp/ncc.*

Provides educational, social, and clinical services to infants, children, and adults with mental retardation and other developmental disabilities. Services provided through a 24-hour intensive treatment program, group homes and independent living programs, educational services, adult treatment programs, and early intervention programs for infants with disabilities or infants at high risk. Operates a child development center for children with and without disabilities.

▦ HOMELESSNESS

AGENCIES

Education Dept., *Adult Education and Literacy,* 330 C St. S.W., #4428 20202-6510 (mailing address: 400 Maryland Ave. S.W. 20202); (202) 205-8270. Fax, (202) 205-8973. Ronald S. Pugsley, Director. Literacy clearinghouse, (202) 205-9996. Web, www.ed.gov.

Provides state and local agencies and community-based organizations with assistance in establishing education programs for homeless adults.

Education Dept., *Education for Homeless Children and Youth,* 400 Maryland Ave. S.W., #3W230 20202; (202) 260-0994. Fax, (202) 260-7764. Patricia McKee, Coordinator, (202) 260-0991. Web, www.ed.gov.

Provides formula grants to education agencies in the states and Puerto Rico to educate homeless children and youth and to establish an office of coordinator of education for homeless children and youth in each jurisdiction.

Federal Emergency Management Agency, *Emergency Food and Shelter National Board Program,* 701 N. Fairfax St., #310, Alexandria, VA 22314-2064; (703) 706-9660. Fax, (703) 706-9677. Carol Coleman, Program Chief, (202) 646-3107; Sharon Bailey, Director. Web, www.efsp.unitedway.org.

Administers the Emergency Food and Shelter Program under the McKinney Act. Gives supplemental assistance to programs that provide the homeless and persons in need with shelter, food, and support services.

Housing and Urban Development Dept., *Community Planning and Development,* 451 7th St. S.W., #7100 20410; (202) 708-2690. Fax, (202) 708-3336. Cardell Cooper, Assistant Secretary. Information, (202) 708-0980. Web, www.hud.gov.

Gives supplemental assistance to facilities that aid the homeless; awards grants for innovative programs that address the needs of homeless families with children.

Housing and Urban Development Dept. (HUD), *Special Needs Assistance Programs,* 451 7th St. S.W., #7262 20410; (202) 708-4300. Fax, (202) 708-3617. John D. Garrity, Director. Web, www.hud.gov.

Advises and represents the secretary on homelessness matters; promotes cooperation among federal agencies on homelessness issues; coordinates assistance programs for the homeless under the McKinney Act. Trains HUD field staff in administering homelessness programs. Distributes funds to eligible nonprofit organizations, cities,

counties, tribes, and territories for shelter, care, transitional housing, and permanent housing for the disabled homeless. Programs provide for acquisition and rehabilitation of buildings, prevention of homelessness, counseling, and medical care. Administers the Federal Surplus Property Program and spearheads the initiative to lease HUD-held homes to the homeless.

NONPROFIT

Housing Assistance Council, 1025 Vermont Ave. N.W., #606 20005-3516; (202) 842-8600. Fax, (202) 347-3441. Moises Loza, Executive Director. Information, (800) 989-4422. General e-mail, hac@ruralhome.org.

Provides low-income housing development groups in rural areas with seed money loans and technical assistance; assesses programs designed to respond to rural housing needs; makes recommendations for federal and state involvement; publishes technical guides and reports on rural housing issues.

National Alliance to End Homelessness, 1518 K St. N.W., #206 20005; (202) 638-1526. Fax, (202) 638-4664. Churchill J. Gibson IV, Executive Director. General e-mail, naeh@naeh.org. Web, www.endhomelessness.org.

Seeks to form a corporate public-private partnership to alleviate problems of the homeless; promotes policies and programs that reduce the homeless population.

National Coalition for Homeless Veterans, 333 1/2 Pennsylvania Ave. S.E. 20003-1148; (202) 546-1969. Fax, (202) 546-2063. Linda Boone, Executive Director. General e-mail, nchv@nchv.org. Web, www.nchv.org.

Provides technical assistance to service providers; advocates on behalf of homeless veterans.

National Coalition for the Homeless, 1012 14th St. N.W., #600 20005-3406; (202) 737-6444. Fax, (202) 737-6445. Mary Ann Gleason, Executive Director. General e-mail, nch@ari.net. Web, nch.ari.net.

Advocacy network of persons who are or have been homeless, state and local coalitions, other activists, service providers, housing developers, and others. Seeks to create the systemic and attitudinal changes necessary to end homelessness. Works to meet the needs of persons who are homeless or at risk of becoming homeless.

National Law Center on Homelessness and Poverty, 1411 K St. N.W., #1400 20005; (202) 638-2535. Fax, (202) 628-2737. Maria Foscarinis, Executive Director. General e-mail, nlchp@nlchp.org. Web, www.nlchp.org.

Legal advocacy group that works to protect and expand the rights of the homeless through impact litigation, and conducts research on homelessness issues. Acts as a clearinghouse for legal information and technical assistance. Monitors legislation and regulations.

Salvation Army, *615 Slaters Lane, Alexandria, VA 22314 (mailing address: P.O. Box 269, Alexandria, VA 22313); (703) 684-5500. Fax, (703) 684-3478. John A. Busby, National Commander. Web, www.salvationarmyusa.org.*

International religious social welfare organization that provides the homeless with residences and social services, including counseling, emergency help, and employment services. (International headquarters in London.)

Share Our Strength, *733 15th St. N.W., #640 20005; (202) 393-2925. Fax, (202) 347-5868. Bill Shore, Executive Director. Information, (800) 969-4767. General e-mail, sos@charitiesusa.com. Web, www.strength.org.*

Works to alleviate and prevent hunger and poverty in the United States and around the world. Meets immediate demands for food by providing food assistance; treats malnutrition and other consequences of hunger; promotes economic independence among people in need, while seeking long-term solutions to hunger and poverty. Helps mobilize industries, organizations, and individuals to contribute their talents to anti-hunger efforts.

U.S. Conference of Mayors, *Task Force on Hunger and Homelessness, 1620 Eye St. N.W. 20006; (202) 861-6707. Fax, (202) 293-2352. Eugene T. Lowe, Assistant Executive Director. Web, www.usmayors.org/uscm.*

Tracks trends in hunger, homelessness, and community programs that address homelessness and hunger in U.S. cities; issues reports. Monitors legislation and regulations.

SOCIAL SECURITY

AGENCIES

Employment Standards Administration *(Labor Dept.), Coal Mine Workers' Compensation, 200 Constitution Ave. N.W., #C3520 20210; (202) 693-0046. Fax, (202) 693-1395. James L. DeMarce, Director.*

Provides direction for administration of the black lung benefits program. Adjudicates claims filed on or after July 1, 1973; certifies these benefit payments and maintains black lung beneficiary rolls.

(For claims filed before July 1, 1973, contact Social Security Administration, Disability.)

Social Security Administration, *6401 Security Blvd., Baltimore, MD 21235; (410) 965-3120. Fax, (410) 966-*

1463. Kenneth Apfel, Commissioner; William Halter, Deputy Commissioner. Information, (800) 772-1213. Press, (410) 965-8904. TTY, (800) 325-0778. Web, www. ssa.gov.

Administers national social security programs and the supplemental security income program.

Social Security Administration, *Central Operations, 1500 Woodlawn Dr., Baltimore, MD 21241 (mailing address: 7000 Security West Tower, Baltimore, MD 21241); (410) 966-7000. Fax, (410) 966-6005. W. Burnell Hurt, Director. Information, (800) 772-1213.*

Reviews and authorizes claims for benefits under the disability insurance program and all claims for beneficiaries living abroad; certifies benefits payments; maintains beneficiary rolls.

Social Security Administration, *Disability, 6401 Security Blvd., #560, Baltimore, MD 21235; (410) 965-3424. Fax, (410) 965-6503. Kenneth D. Nibali, Associate Commissioner. Information, (410) 965-7700.*

Provides direction for administration of the disability insurance program, which is paid out of the Social Security Trust Fund. Administers disability and blindness provisions of the Supplemental Security Income (SSI) program. Responsible for claims filed under black lung benefits program before July 1, 1973.

Social Security Administration, *Hearings and Appeals, 5107 Leesburg Pike, #1600, Falls Church, VA 22041-3255; (703) 605-8200. Fax, (703) 605-8201. Rita S. Geier, Associate Commissioner.*

Administers a nationwide system of administrative law judges who conduct hearings and decide appealed cases concerning benefits provisions. Reviews decisions for appeals council action, if necessary, and renders the secretary's final decision. Reviews benefits cases on health insurance, disability, retirement and survivors' benefits, and supplemental security income.

Social Security Administration, *Operations, 6401 Security Blvd., West High Rise, #1204, Baltimore, MD 21235; (410) 965-3143. Fax, (410) 966-7941. Carolyn W. Colvin, Deputy Commissioner. Information, (800) 772-1213. TTY, (410) 965-4404.*

Issues Social Security numbers, maintains earnings and beneficiary records, authorizes claims, certifies benefits, and makes postadjudicative changes in beneficiary records for retirement, survivors', and disability insurance and black lung claims. Maintains toll-free number for workers who want information on future Social Security benefits.

Social Security Administration, *Program, Benefits, Policy, 6401 Security Blvd., #760, Baltimore, MD 21235;*

SOCIAL SECURITY ADMINISTRATION

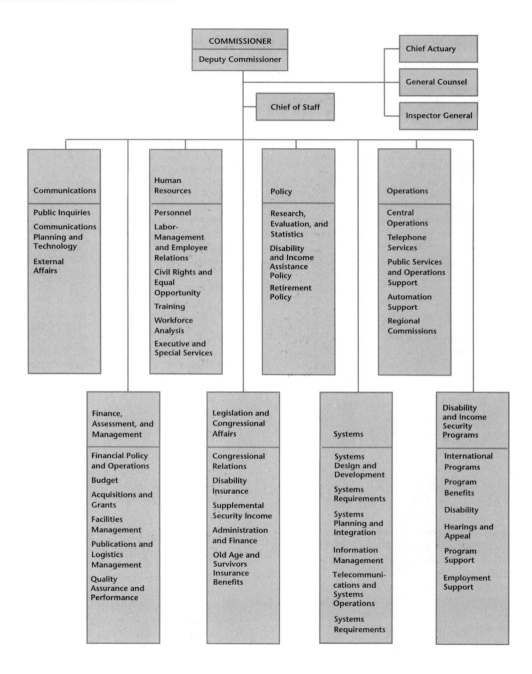

COMMISSIONER

Deputy Commissioner

Chief Actuary

General Counsel

Chief of Staff

Inspector General

Communications

Public Inquiries

Communications
Planning and
Technology

External
Affairs

**Human
Resources**

Personnel

Labor-
Management
and Employee
Relations

Civil Rights and
Equal
Opportunity

Training

Workforce
Analysis

Executive and
Special Services

Policy

Research,
Evaluation, and
Statistics

Disability
and Income
Assistance
Policy

Retirement
Policy

Operations

Central
Operations

Telephone
Services

Public Services
and Operations
Support

Automation
Support

Regional
Commissions

**Finance,
Assessment, and
Management**

Financial Policy
and Operations

Budget

Acquisitions and
Grants

Facilities
Management

Publications and
Logistics
Management

Quality
Assurance and
Performance

**Legislation and
Congressional
Affairs**

Congressional
Relations

Disability
Insurance

Supplemental
Security Income

Administration
and Finance

Old Age and
Survivors
Insurance
Benefits

Systems

Systems
Design and
Development

Systems
Requirements

Systems
Planning and
Integration

Information
Management

Telecommuni-
cations and
Systems
Operations

Systems
Requirements

**Disability
and Income
Security
Programs**

International
Programs

Program
Benefits

Disability

Hearings and
Appeal

Program
Support

Employment
Support

(410) 965-7100. Fax, (410) 965-8582. Frederick Strecke-wald, Associate Commissioner.

Develops policies and procedures for administering the retirement and survivors' insurance programs. Provides direction and technical guidance for administration of the Supplemental Security Income (SSI) program for the elderly, blind, and disabled. Provides guidance on administration of state supplementary benefits programs; monitors state compliance with mandatory minimum federal supplements.

Social Security Administration, *Research, Evaluation, and Statistics, 6401 Security Blvd., Operations Building, #4C-15, Baltimore, MD 21235; (410) 965-2841. Fax, (410) 965-3308. Peter M. Wheeler, Associate Commissioner. Publications, (202) 358-6263.*

Compiles statistics on beneficiaries; conducts research on the economic status of beneficiaries and the relationship between Social Security, the American people, and the economy; analyzes the effects of proposed Social Security legislation, especially on lower- and middle-income individuals and families; disseminates results of research and statistical programs through publications.

CONGRESS

General Accounting Office, *Health, Education, and Human Services, 441 G St. N.W. 20548; (202) 512-6806. Fax, (202) 512-5806. Victor S. Rezendes, Assistant Comptroller General.*

Independent, nonpartisan agency in the legislative branch that audits, analyzes, and evaluates Health and Human Services Dept. programs, including Social Security, Medicare, and Medicaid; makes reports available to the public.

House Appropriations Committee, *Subcommittee on Labor, Health and Human Services, and Education, 2358 RHOB 20515; (202) 225-3508. Fax, (202) 225-3509. Rep. John Edward Porter, R-Ill., Chair; Tony McCann, Staff Director. Web, www.house.gov/appropriations.*

Jurisdiction over legislation to appropriate funds for the Social Security Administration.

House Ways and Means Committee, *Subcommittee on Human Resources, B317 RHOB 20515; (202) 225-1025. Fax, (202) 225-9480. Rep. Nancy L. Johnson, R-Conn., Chair; Ronald Haskins, Staff Director. Web, www.house.gov/ways_means.*

Jurisdiction over legislation on supplemental security income for the elderly, blind, and disabled.

House Ways and Means Committee, *Subcommittee on Social Security, B316 RHOB 20515; (202) 225-9263. Fax, (202) 225-9480. Rep. E. Clay Shaw Jr., R-Fla., Chair; Kim Hildred, Staff Director. Web, www.house.gov/ways_means.*

Jurisdiction over Social Security disability and retirement and survivors' legislation.

Senate Appropriations Committee, *Subcommittee on Labor, Health and Human Services, and Education, SD-186 20510; (202) 224-7230. Fax, (202) 224-1360. Sen. Arlen Specter, R-Pa., Chair; Bettilou Taylor, Staff Director. Web, appropriations.senate.gov/labor.*

Jurisdiction over legislation to appropriate funds for the Social Security Administration.

Senate Finance Committee, *Subcommittee on Social Security and Family Policy, SD-219 20510; (202) 224-4515. Fax, (202) 224-5920. Sen. Don Nickles, R-Okla., Chair; Alec Bachon, Staff Contact. Web, finance.senate.gov.*

Holds hearings on supplemental security income for the elderly, blind, and disabled; Social Security disability; and retirement and survivors' legislation.

Senate Special Committee on Aging, *SD-G31 20510; (202) 224-5364. Fax, (202) 224-8660. Sen. Charles E. Grassley, R-Iowa, Chair; Ted Totman, Staff Director. Web, aging.senate.gov.*

Studies and makes recommendations on Social Security and other retirement benefits for the elderly.

NONPROFIT

National Academy of Social Insurance, *1776 Massachusetts Ave. N.W., #615 20036-1904; (202) 452-8097. Fax, (202) 452-8111. Pamela J. Larson, Executive Vice President. General e-mail, nasi@nasi.org. Web, www.nasi.org.*

Promotes research and education on Social Security, health care financing, and related public and private programs; assesses social insurance programs and their relationship to other programs; supports research and leadership development. Acts as a clearinghouse for social insurance information.

National Committee to Preserve Social Security and Medicare, *10 G St. N.E., #600 20002; (202) 216-0420. Fax, (202) 216-0451. Martha McSteen, President. Web, www.ncpssm.org.*

Educational and advocacy organization that focuses on Social Security and Medicare programs and on related income security and health issues. Interests include retirement income protection, health care reform, and the quality of life of seniors. Monitors legislation and regulations.

2030 Center, *1015 18th St. N.W., #200 20036; (202) 822-6526. Fax, (202) 822-1199. Hans Riemer, Director. General e-mail, 2030@2030.org. Web, www.2030.org.*

Public policy research and advocacy organization. Promotes policies that ensure the long-term viability of the social security system and expanded economic opportunities for younger Americans.

19

Transportation

AGENCIES

Architectural and Transportation Barriers Compliance Board (Access Board), *1331 F St. N.W., #1000 20004-1111; (202) 272-5434. Fax, (202) 272-5447. Lawrence W. Roffee, Executive Director. TTY, (202) 272-5449. Toll-free technical assistance, (800) 872-2253. Web, www.access-board.gov.*

Enforces standards requiring that buildings and telecommunications and transportation systems be accessible to persons with disabilities; provides technical assistance and information on designing these facilities; sets accessibility guidelines for the Americans with Disabilities Act and the Telecommunications Act of 1996.

Bureau of Transportation Statistics *(Transportation Dept.), 400 7th St. S.W. 20590; (202) 366-1270. Fax, (202) 366-3640. Ashish K. Sen, Director. Information, (202) 366-3282. Web, www.bts.gov.*

Works to improve public awareness of the nation's transportation systems. Compiles, analyzes, and makes accessible information on transportation.

Census Bureau *(Commerce Dept.), Services Sector Statistics Division: Vehicle Inventory and Use Survey, Suitland and Silver Hill Rds., Suitland, MD 20746 (mailing address: MS 6500 20233); (301) 457-2668. Fax, (301) 457-8345. Kimberly P. Moore, Survey Statistician. Web, www. census.gov/econ/www/viusmain.html.*

Provides data and explains proper use of data for the bureau's Truck Inventory and Use Survey.

National Transportation Safety Board (NTSB), *490 L'Enfant Plaza East S.W. 20594; (202) 314-6010. Fax, (202) 314-6018. James E. Hall, Chair; Vacant, Vice Chair. Web, www.ntsb.gov.*

Promotes transportation safety through independent investigations of accidents and other safety problems. Makes recommendations for safety improvement.

National Transportation Safety Board, *Research and Engineering, 490 L'Enfant Plaza East S.W. 20594; (202) 314-6500. Fax, (202) 314-6599. Vernon Ellingstad, Director. Web, www.ntsb.gov.*

Evaluates effectiveness of federal, state, and local safety programs. Identifies transportation safety issues not addressed by government or industry. Conducts studies on specific safety problems.

Office of Management and Budget (OMB), *(Executive Office of the President), Transportation, New Executive Office Bldg., #9208 20503; (202) 395-5704. Fax,*

(202) 395-4797. David E. Tornquist, Chief. Web, www. whitehouse.gov/omb.

Assists and advises the OMB director on budget preparation, proposed legislation, and evaluations of Transportation Dept. programs, policies, and activities.

Research and Special Programs Administration *(Transportation Dept.), 400 7th St. S.W., #8410 20590; (202) 366-4433. Fax, (202) 366-3666. Kelley Coyner, Administrator. Web, www.rspa.dot.gov.*

Coordinates research and development programs to improve safety of transportation systems; focus includes hazardous materials shipments, pipeline safety, and preparedness for transportation emergencies. Oversees Volpe National Transportation Systems Center in Cambridge, Mass., and Transportation Safety Institute in Oklahoma City.

Research and Special Programs Administration *(Transportation Dept.), Emergency Transportation, 400 7th St. S.W., #8404 20590-0001; (202) 366-5270. Fax, (202) 366-3769. William M. Medigovich, Director. Web, www.rspa.dot.gov/oet.*

Develops, coordinates, and reviews transportation emergency preparedness programs for use in emergencies affecting national defense and in emergencies caused by natural disasters and crisis situations.

Research and Special Programs Administration *(Transportation Dept.), Innovation, Research, and Education, 400 7th St. S.W., #8417 20590; (202) 366-4434. Fax, (202) 366-3671. Fenton Carey, Associate Administrator. Web, www.rspa.dot.gov/dra.*

Supports transportation innovation research, engineering, education, and safety training. Focus includes intermodal transportation; partnerships among government, universities, and industry; and economic growth and competitiveness through use of new technologies. Monitors international research.

Transportation Dept. (DOT), *400 7th St. S.W. 20590; (202) 366-2222. Fax, (202) 366-7202. Rodney E. Slater, Secretary; Mortimer L. Downey, Deputy Secretary. Press, (202) 366-4570. Locator, (202) 366-4000. Web, www. dot.gov.*

Deals with most areas of transportation. Comprises the Bureau of Transportation Statistics, Coast Guard, Federal Aviation Administration, Federal Highway Administration, Federal Motor Carrier Safety Administration, Federal Railroad Administration, Maritime Administration, National Highway Traffic Safety Administration, Research and Special Programs Administration, Federal Transit Administration, and Saint Lawrence Seaway Development Corp.

NATIONAL TRANSPORTATION SAFETY BOARD

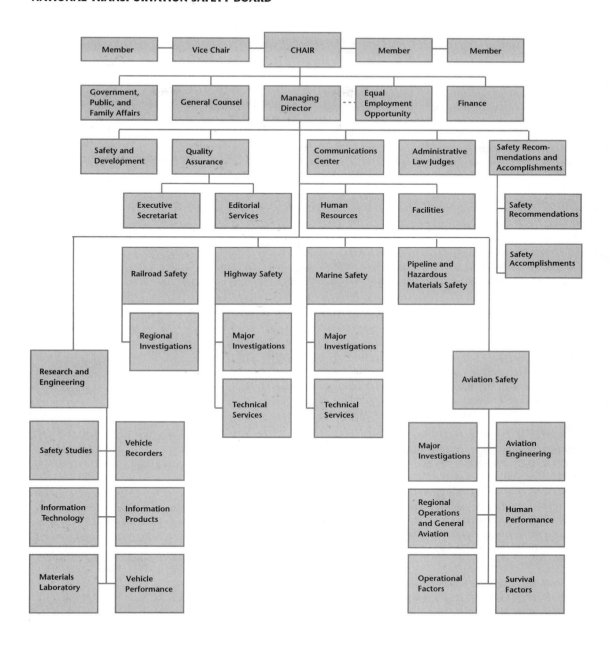

Transportation Dept., *Aviation and International Affairs,* *400 7th St. S.W., #10232 20590; (202) 366-4551. Fax, (202) 493-2005. A. Bradley Mims, Assistant Secretary. Web, www.dot.gov/ost/aviation.*

Formulates domestic aviation policy. Formulates international aviation, maritime, and across-the-border railroad and trucking policy.

Transportation Dept., *Aviation Consumer Protection,*
400 7th St. S.W., #4107 20590 (mailing address: Transportation Dept., C75 20590); (202) 366-2220. Fax, (202) 366-7907. Norman Strickman, Assistant Director (Acting). General e-mail, airconsumer@ost.dot.gov. Web, www.dot.gov/airconsumer.

Refers consumer complaints to appropriate departmental offices; advises the secretary on consumer issues; coordinates citizen participation activities and promotes joint projects with consumer interest groups; serves as ombudsman for consumer protection affairs; publishes educational materials.

Transportation Dept., *Environmental Policies Team,*
400 7th St. S.W., #10309 20590-0001; (202) 366-4861. Fax, (202) 366-7610. Camille Mittelholtz, Team Leader. Web, www.dot.gov.

Develops environmental policy and makes recommendations to the secretary; monitors Transportation Dept. implementation of environmental legislation; serves as liaison with other federal agencies and state and local governments on environmental matters related to transportation.

Transportation Dept., *Intelligence and Security,* 400 7th St. S.W., #10401 20590; (202) 366-6535. Fax, (202) 366-7261. Rear Adm. J. A. Kinghorn (USCG), Director. Web, www.dot.gov.

Advises the secretary on transportation intelligence and security policy. Acts as liaison with the intelligence community, federal agencies, corporations, and interest groups; administers counterterrorism strategic planning processes.

Transportation Dept., *Transportation Policy,* 400 7th St. S.W., #10228 20590; (202) 366-4544. Fax, (202) 366-7127. Eugene A. Conti, Assistant Secretary. Web, www.dot.gov.

Oversees policy development for all domestic transportation except aviation. Assesses the performance of the domestic transportation network; analyzes the effect of government policies on domestic transportation industries.

Transportation Dept., *Transportation Policy Development,* 400 7th St. S.W., P-100, #10305 20590; (202) 366-4416. Fax, (202) 366-7618. Linda L. Lawson, Director. Web, www.dot.gov.

Develops, coordinates, and evaluates public policy with respect to safety, environmental, energy, and accessibility issues affecting all aspects of transportation. Assesses the economic and institutional implications of domestic transportation matters. Oversees legislative and regulatory proposals affecting transportation. Provides advice on research and development requirements. Develops policy proposals to improve the performance, safety, and efficiency of the transportation system.

U.S. Customs Service *(Treasury Dept.), Field Operations,* 1300 Pennsylvania Ave. N.W., #5.5C 20229; (202) 927-0100. Fax, (202) 927-0837. Charles W. Winwood, Assistant Commissioner. Web, www.customs.treas.gov.

Enforces statutes relating to the processing and regulation of people, baggage, cargo, and mail in and out of the United States; assesses and collects customs duties, excise taxes, fees, and penalties due on imported merchandise; administers certain navigation laws.

CONGRESS

General Accounting Office, *Transportation Issues,* 441 G St. N.W., #2T23 20548; (202) 512-3650. Fax, (202) 512-3766. John H. Anderson Jr., Director. Web, www.gao.gov.

Independent, nonpartisan agency in the legislative branch. Audits, analyzes, and evaluates performance of the Transportation Dept. and its component agencies; makes reports available to the public.

House Appropriations Committee, *Subcommittee on Commerce, Justice, State, and Judiciary,* H309 CAP 20515; (202) 225-3351. Rep. Harold Rogers, R-Ky., Chair; Jim Kulikowski, Staff Director. Web, www.house.gov/appropriations.

Jurisdiction over legislation to appropriate funds for the Maritime Administration and Federal Maritime Commission.

House Appropriations Committee, *Subcommittee on Transportation,* 2358 RHOB 20515; (202) 225-2141. Rep. Frank R. Wolf, R-Va., Chair; John T. Blazey, Staff Director. Web, www.house.gov/appropriations.

Jurisdiction over legislation to appropriate funds for the Transportation Dept. (except the Maritime Administration) and related agencies, including the National Transportation Safety Board and the Surface Transportation Board.

House Transportation and Infrastructure Committee, 2165 RHOB 20515; (202) 225-9446. Fax, (202) 225-6782. Rep. Bud Shuster, R-Pa., Chair; Jack Schenendorf, Chief of Staff. General e-mail, transcomm@mail.house.gov. Web, www.house.gov/transportation.

Jurisdiction over legislation on transportation.

Senate Appropriations Committee, *Subcommittee on Commerce, Justice, State, and Judiciary,* S-146A CAP 20510; (202) 224-7277. Sen. Judd Gregg, R-N.H., Chair; Jim Morhard, Clerk. Web, appropriations.senate.gov/commerce.

Jurisdiction over legislation to appropriate funds for the Maritime Administration and the Federal Maritime Commission.

Senate Appropriations Committee, *Subcommittee on Transportation,* *SD-133 20510; (202) 224-2175. Fax, (202) 224-4401. Sen. Richard C. Shelby, R-Ala., Chair; Wally Burnett, Majority Clerk. Web, appropriations.senate. gov/transportation.*

Jurisdiction over legislation to appropriate funds for the Transportation Dept. (except the Maritime Administration) and related agencies, including the National Transportation Safety Board and the Surface Transportation Board.

Senate Commerce, Science, and Transportation Committee, *SD-508 20510; (202) 224-5115. Fax, (202) 224-1259. Sen. John McCain, R-Ariz., Chair; Mark Buse, Staff Director. Web, commerce.senate.gov.*

Jurisdiction over legislation on transportation; oversight of the Transportation Dept. and the National Transportation Safety Board.

Senate Special Committee on Aging, *SD-G31 20510; (202) 224-5364. Fax, (202) 224-8660. Sen. Charles E. Grassley, R-Iowa, Chair; Ted Totman, Staff Director. Web, aging.senate.gov.*

Studies and makes recommendations on the availability of transportation for the elderly.

NONPROFIT

American Public Works Assn., *Washington Office, 1401 K St. N.W., 11th Floor 20005; (202) 408-9541. Fax, (202) 408-9542. Peter B. King, Executive Director. General e-mail, apwa.dc@apwa.net. Web, www.apwa.net.*

Membership: engineers, architects, and others who maintain and manage public works facilities and services. Conducts research and promotes exchange of information on transportation and infrastructure-related issues. (Headquarters in Kansas City.)

Assn. for Transportation Law, Logistics, and Policy, *19564 Club House Rd., Montgomery Village, MD 20886; (301) 670-6733. Fax, (301) 670-6735. E. Dale Jones, Executive Director. General e-mail, atllp@aol.com. Web, www. transportlink.com/atllp.*

Provides members with continuing educational development in transportation law and practice. Interests include railroad, motor, energy, pipeline, antitrust, labor, logistics, safety, and environmental matters.

Assn. of Metropolitan Planning Organizations, Transportation, *1700 K St. N.W., #1300 20036; (202)*

457-0710. Fax, (202) 296-9352. Vacant, Director. Web, www.ampo.org.

Membership: more than 340 metropolitan planning organizations, which are councils of elected officials and transportation professionals that are responsible for planning local transportation systems. Provides a forum for professional and organizational development; sponsors conferences and training programs. (Affiliated with National Assn. of Regional Councils.)

Institute of Navigation, *1800 Diagonal Rd., #480, Alexandria, VA 22314-2840; (703) 683-7101. Fax, (703) 683-7105. Lisa Beaty, Director of Operations. General e-mail, membership@ion.org. Web, www.ion.org.*

Membership: individuals and organizations interested in navigation. Encourages research in navigation and establishment of uniform practices in navigation operations and education; conducts symposia on air, space, marine, and land navigation.

Institute of Transportation Engineers, *525 School St. S.W., #410 20024-2797; (202) 554-8050. Fax, (202) 863-5486. Thomas W. Brahms, Executive Director. Web, www. ite.org.*

Membership: international professional transportation engineers. Conducts research, seminars, and training sessions; provides professional and scientific information on transportation standards and recommended practices.

International Brotherhood of Teamsters, *25 Louisiana Ave. N.W. 20001; (202) 624-6800. Fax, (202) 624-8102. James P. Hoffa, President. Web, www.teamster. org.*

Membership: more than 1.4 million workers in the transportation and construction industries, factories, offices, hospitals, warehouses, and other workplaces. Helps members negotiate pay, benefits, and better working conditions; conducts training programs and workshops. Monitors legislation and regulations. (Affiliated with the AFL-CIO.)

National Defense Transportation Assn., *50 S. Pickett St., #220, Alexandria, VA 22304-7296; (703) 751-5011. Fax, (703) 823-8761. Edward Honor, President.*

Membership: transportation users, manufacturers, and mode carriers; information technology firms; and related military, government, and civil interests worldwide. Promotes a strong U.S. transportation capability through coordination of private industry, government, and the military.

National Research Council, *Transportation Research Board, 2001 Wisconsin Ave. N.W. 20007 (mailing address:*

2101 Constitution Ave. N.W. 20418); (202) 334-2933. Fax, (202) 334-2003. Robert E. Skinner Jr., Executive Director. Information, (202) 334-2933. Library, (202) 334-2990. Publications, (202) 334-3213. Toll-free, (800) 424-9818. Web, www4.nationalacademies.org/trb/homepage.nsf.

Promotes research in transportation systems planning and administration and in the design, construction, maintenance, and operation of transportation facilities. Provides information to state and national highway and transportation departments; operates research information services; conducts special studies, conferences, and workshops; publishes technical reports. Library open to the public by appointment.

Rebuild America Coalition, c/o American Public Works Assn., 1401 K St. N.W., 11th Floor 20005; (202) 408-1325. Fax, (202) 408-9542. Ann McCulloch, Coalition Manager. Web, www.rebuildamerica.org.

Coalition of public and private organizations concerned with maintaining the infrastructure of the United States. Advocates government encouragement of innovative technology, financing, and public-private partnerships to build and rebuild public facilities, including highways, ports, airports, and transit systems.

Sheet Metal Workers' International Assn., 1750 New York Ave. N.W. 20006; (202) 783-5880. Fax, (202) 662-0880. Michael J. Sullivan, General President. Web, smwia.org.

Membership: more than 130,000 U.S. and Canadian workers in the building and construction trades, manufacturing, and the railroad and shipyard industries. Assists members with contract negotiation and grievances; conducts training programs and workshops. Monitors legislation and regulations. (Affiliated with the Sheet Metal and Air Conditioning Contractors' Assn., the AFL-CIO, and the Canadian Labour Congress.)

Surface Transportation Policy Project, 1100 17th St. N.W., 10th Floor 20036; (202) 466-2636. Fax, (202) 466-2247. Roy Kienitz, Executive Director. General e-mail, stpp@transact.org. Web, www.transact.org/stpp.htm.

Advocates transportation policy and investments that conserve energy, protect environmental and aesthetic quality, strengthen the economy, promote social equity, and make communities more livable.

Union of Concerned Scientists, Government Relations, Washington Office, 1616 P St. N.W., #310 20036; (202) 332-0900. Fax, (202) 332-0905. Alden Meyer, Director; Todd Perry, Washington Representative for Arms Control and International Security. General e-mail, ucs@ucsusa.org. Web, www.ucsusa.org.

Develops and promotes market-based strategies to reduce the adverse environmental, economic, and public health effects of the U.S. transportation system. Advocates price incentives to promote transportation reform; development of cleaner, more fuel-efficient vehicles; and advancement of transportation technology and alternative fuels. (Headquarters in Cambridge, Mass.)

United Transportation Union, Washington Office, 304 Pennsylvania Ave. S.E. 20003; (202) 543-7714. Fax, (202) 543-0015. James M. Brunkenhoefer, Legislative Director. Web, www.utu.org.

Membership: approximately 150,000 workers in the transportation industry. Helps members negotiate pay, benefits, and better working conditions; conducts training programs and workshops. Monitors legislation and regulations. (Headquarters in Cleveland, Ohio; affiliated with the AFL-CIO.)

Freight and Intermodalism

See also specific modes of transportation (this chapter)

AGENCIES

Federal Railroad Administration (Transportation Dept.), Policy and Program Development, 1120 Vermont Ave. N.W., #7075 20590; (202) 493-6400. Fax, (202) 493-6401. Charles H. White Jr., Associate Administrator.

Promotes intermodal movement of freight involving rail transportation; studies economics and industry practices.

Maritime Administration (Transportation Dept.), Intermodal Development, 400 7th St. S.W., #7209 20590; (202) 366-8888. Fax, (202) 366-6988. Richard L. Walker, Director. Web, marad.dot.gov/intermodal_development. html.

Promotes development and improved use of marine-related intermodal transportation systems; provides technical information and advice to other agencies and organizations concerned with intermodal development.

Surface Transportation Board (Transportation Dept.), 1925 K St. N.W. 20423-0001; (202) 565-1500. Fax, (202) 565-9004. Wayne Burkes, Vice Chair; Linda J. Morgan, Chair. Web, www.stb.dot.gov.

Regulates rates for intermodal connections to or from water in noncontiguous domestic trade (between the mainland and Alaska, Hawaii, or U.S. territories).

Transportation Dept., Intermodalism, 400 7th St. S.W., #10126 20590; (202) 366-5781. Fax, (202) 366-0263. Stephen D. Van Beek, Director. Web, www.dot.gov.

TRANSPORTATION DEPARTMENT

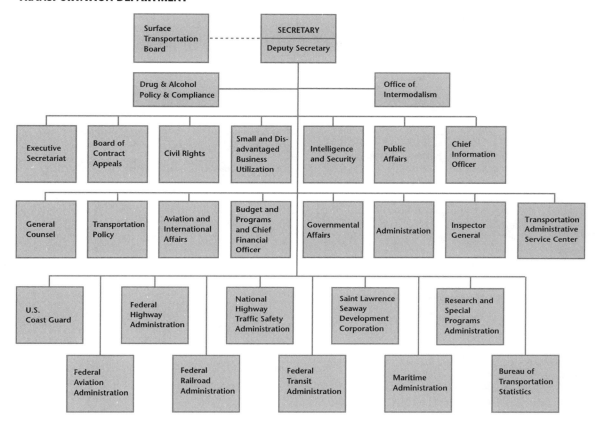

Coordinates departmental efforts to develop an intermodal transportation system to move people and goods; promotes energy efficiency and optimal use of national transportation resources.

NONPROFIT

American Moving and Storage Assn., *1611 Duke St., Alexandria, VA 22314; (703) 683-7410. Fax, (703) 683-7527. Joseph Harrison, President. Web, www.moving.org.*

Represents members' views before the Transportation Dept. and other government agencies. Conducts certification and training programs. Provides financial support for research on the moving and storage industry.

Distribution and LTL Carriers Assn., *200 Mill Rd., #600, Alexandria, VA 22314; (703) 838-1806. Fax, (703) 684-8143. Kevin M. Williams, President.*

Membership: movers of general freight. Provides networking opportunities; conducts workshops and seminars. Monitors legislation and regulations.

Intermodal Assn. of North America, *7501 Greenway Center Dr., #720, Greenbelt, MD 20770; (301) 982-3400. Fax, (301) 982-4815. Joanne Casey, President. General e-mail, IANA@intermodal.org. Web, www.intermodal.org.*

Membership: railroads, stacktrain operators, water carriers, motor carriers, marketing companies, and suppliers to the intermodal industry. Promotes intermodal transportation of freight. Monitors legislation and regulations.

National Assn. of Chemical Distributors (NACD), *1560 Wilson Blvd., #1250, Arlington, VA 22209; (703) 527-6223. Fax, (703) 527-7747. Vacant, Executive Vice President. Web, www.nacd.com.*

Membership: firms involved in purchasing, processing, blending, storing, transporting, and marketing of chemical products. Provides members with information on such topics as training, safe handling and transport of chemicals, liability insurance, and environmental issues.

Manages the NACD Educational Foundation. Monitors legislation and regulations.

National Customs Brokers and Forwarders Assn. of America, *1200 18th St. N.W., #901 20036; (202) 466-0222. Fax, (202) 466-0226. Barbara Reilly, Executive Vice President. General e-mail, staff@ncbfaa.org. Web, www.ncbfaa.org.*

Membership: customs brokers and freight forwarders in the United States. Fosters information exchange within the industry. Monitors legislation and regulations.

National Industrial Transportation League, *1700 N. Moore St., #1900, Arlington, VA 22209-1904; (703) 524-5011. Fax, (703) 524-5017. Edward M. Emmett, President. Web, www.nitl.org.*

Membership: air, water, and surface shippers and receivers, including industries, corporations, chambers of commerce, and trade associations. Monitors legislation and regulations.

✈ AIR TRANSPORTATION

AGENCIES

Civil Air Patrol, *National Capital Wing, Washington Office, Bolling Air Force Base, 222 Luke Ave., #2 20332-5114; (202) 767-4405. Fax, (202) 767-5695. Col. Roland Butler, Wing Commander.*

Official civilian auxiliary of the U.S. Air Force. Primary function is to conduct search-and-rescue missions for the Air Force. Maintains an aerospace education program for adults and a cadet program for junior and senior high school students. (Headquarters at Maxwell Air Force Base, Ala.)

Federal Aviation Administration (FAA), *(Transportation Dept.), 800 Independence Ave. S.W. 20591; (202) 267-3111. Fax, (202) 267-5047. Jane F. Garvey, Administrator. Press, (202) 267-3883. Web, www.faa.gov.*

Regulates air commerce to improve aviation safety; promotes development of a national system of airports; develops and operates a common system of air traffic control and air navigation for both civilian and military aircraft; prepares the annual National Aviation System Plan.

Federal Aviation Administration *(Transportation Dept.), Aviation Policy and Plans, 800 Independence Ave. S.W., #939, APO-1 20591; (202) 267-3274. Fax, (202) 267-3278. John M. Rodgers, Director. Web, www.api.hq.faa.gov.*

Responsible for economic and regulatory policy and analysis, aviation activity forecasts, and strategic planning within the FAA.

Federal Aviation Administration *(Transportation Dept.), Environment and Energy, 800 Independence Ave. S.W., #900W 20591; (202) 267-3576. Fax, (202) 267-5594. James Erickson, Director. Web, www.faa.aee.gov.*

Responsible for environmental affairs and energy conservation for aviation, including implementation and administration of various aviation-related environmental acts.

Federal Aviation Administration *(Transportation Dept.), International Aviation, 800 Independence Ave. S.W., #1028, AIA-1 20591; (202) 267-3213. Fax, (202) 267-5306. Joan W. Bauerlein, Director. Web, www.faa.gov.*

Coordinates all activities of the FAA that involve foreign relations; acts as liaison with the State Dept. and other agencies concerning international aviation; provides other countries with technical assistance on civil aviation problems; formulates international civil aviation policy for the United States.

Federal Aviation Administration *(Transportation Dept.), Research and Acquisitions, 800 Independence Ave. S.W., #1019 20591; (202) 267-7222. Fax, (202) 267-5085. Steven Zaidman, Associate Administrator. Web, www.faa.gov/ara/arahome.htm.*

Advises and assists in developing concepts for applying new technologies to meet long-range national airspace system requirements and for system acquisition, engineering, and management activities.

Federal Aviation Administration *(Transportation Dept.), Statistics and Forecast, 800 Independence Ave. S.W., #935, APO-110 20591; (202) 267-3355. Fax, (202) 267-5370. Robert L. Bowles, Manager. Web, www.faa.gov.*

Maintains statistics relating to civil aircraft, airports, and air personnel, including age and type of pilots, passenger data, activity counts at FAA air traffic control facilities, and related information. Forecasts demand at FAA facilities and demand for commercial and general aviation sectors; holds two annual forecast conferences.

Federal Aviation Administration *(Transportation Dept.), System Architecture and Investment Analysis, 1250 Maryland Ave. S.W. 20202-5175 (mailing address: 800 Independence Ave. S.W., ASD-1 20591); (202) 358-5238. Fax, (202) 358-5207. John Scardina, Director (Acting). Web, www.faa.gov.*

Advises and assists in developing advanced technologies to meet National Airspace System Development requirements. Works with internal FAA customers, other government agencies, and the aviation industry to understand and respond to user requirements.

Justice Dept., *Civil Division: Torts Branch, Aviation/Admiralty Litigation,* 1425 New York Ave. N.W., #10100 20530 (mailing address: P.O. Box 14271 20044-4271); (202) 616-4000. Fax, (202) 616-4002. Gary W. Allen, Director. Web, www.usdoj.gov.

Represents the federal government in civil suits arising from aviation incidents and accidents. Handles tort litigation for the government's varied activities in the operation of the air traffic control system, the regulation of air commerce, weather services, aeronautical charting, and the government's operation of its own civil and military aircraft.

National Aeronautics and Space Administration (NASA), *Aero-Space Technology,* 300 E St. S.W. 20546 (mailing address: NASA Headquarters, Mail Code R 20546); (202) 358-2693. Fax, (202) 358-4066. Sam Venneri, Associate Administrator. Web, www.hq.nasa.gov/office/aero.

Conducts research in aerodynamics, materials, structures, avionics, propulsion, high performance computing, human factors, aviation safety, and space transportation in support of national space and aeronautical research and technology goals. Manages the following NASA research centers: Ames (Moffett, Calif.); Dryden (Edwards, Calif.); Langley (Hampton, Va.); and Glenn (Cleveland, Ohio).

National Air and Space Museum *(Smithsonian Institution),* 6th St. and Independence Ave. S.W. 20560-0310; (202) 357-1745. Fax, (202) 357-2426. Gen. John R. Dailey, Director. Library, (202) 357-3133. Press, (202) 357-1552. TTY, (202) 357-1505. Education office, (202) 786-2106. Daily space and earth phenomena report, (202) 357-2000 (recording). Tours, (202) 357-1400. Web, www.nasm.si.edu.

Maintains exhibits and collections on aeronautics, pioneers of flight, and early aircraft through modern air technology. Library open to the public by appointment.

National Mediation Board, 1301 K St. N.W., #250E 20572; (202) 692-5000. Fax, (202) 692-5080. Stephen E. Crable, Chief of Staff, (202) 692-5030; Ernest DuBester, Chair. Information, (202) 692-5050. TTY, (202) 692-5001.

Mediates labor disputes in the airline industry; determines and certifies labor representatives for the industry.

Transportation Dept., *Airline Information,* 400 7th St. S.W., #4125, MC K-25 20590; (202) 366-9059. Fax, (202) 366-3383. Timothy E. Carmody, Director. Web, www.dot.gov.

Develops, interprets, and enforces accounting and reporting regulations for the aviation industry; issues air carrier reporting instructions, waivers, and due-date extensions.

Transportation Dept., *Aviation Analysis,* 400 7th St. S.W., #6401, X-50 20590; (202) 366-5903. Fax, (202) 366-7638. Randall D. Bennett, Director (Acting). Web, www.dot.gov.

Analyzes essential air service needs of communities; directs subsidy policy and programs; guarantees air service to small communities; conducts research for the department on airline mergers, international route awards, and employee protection programs; administers the air carrier fitness provisions of the Federal Aviation Act; registers domestic and foreign air carriers; enforces charter regulations for tour operators.

Transportation Dept., *Aviation and International Affairs,* 400 7th St. S.W., #10232 20590; (202) 366-4551. Fax, (202) 493-2005. A. Bradley Mims, Assistant Secretary. Web, www.dot.gov/ost/aviation.

Formulates domestic and international aviation policy. Assesses the performance of the U.S. aviation network in meeting public needs. Studies the social and economic conditions of the aviation industry, including airline licensing, antitrust concerns, and the effect of government policies.

Transportation Dept., *Aviation Consumer Protection,* 400 7th St. S.W., #4107 20590 (mailing address: Transportation Dept., C75 20590); (202) 366-2220. Fax, (202) 366-7907. Norman Strickman, Assistant Director (Acting). General e-mail, airconsumer@ost.dot.gov. Web, www.dot.gov/airconsumer.

Addresses complaints about airline service and consumer-protection matters. Conducts investigations, provides assistance, and reviews regulations affecting air carriers.

Transportation Dept., *Information Technology, Financial, and Secretarial Audits,* 400 7th St. S.W., #9228, JA-20 20590-0001; (202) 366-1496. Fax, (202) 366-3530. John Meche, Director. Web, www.dot.gov.

Provides auditing services for airline economic programs.

CONGRESS

House Appropriations Committee, *Subcommittee on Transportation,* 2358 RHOB 20515; (202) 225-2141. Rep. Frank R. Wolf, R-Va., Chair; John T. Blazey, Staff Director. Web, www.house.gov/appropriations.

Jurisdiction over legislation to appropriate funds for the Federal Aviation Administration.

House Science Committee, *Subcommittee on Space and Aeronautics,* B374 RHOB 20515; (202) 225-7858. *Fax, (202) 225-6415. Rep. Dana Rohrabacher, R-Calif., Chair; Shana Dale, Staff Director. Web, www.house.gov/science.*

Legislative jurisdiction over the Transportation Dept. (relating to space activities and aeronautics) and the National Aeronautics and Space Administration.

House Science Committee, *Subcommittee on Technology,* 2319 RHOB 20515; (202) 225-8844. *Fax, (202) 225-4438. Rep. Constance A. Morella, R-Md., Chair; Jeffrey Grove, Staff Director. Web, www.house.gov/science.*

Jurisdiction over legislation on civil aviation research and development, including research programs of the Federal Aviation Administration.

House Transportation and Infrastructure Committee, *Subcommittee on Aviation,* 2251 RHOB 20515; (202) 226-3220. *Fax, (202) 225-4629. Rep. John J. "Jimmy" Duncan Jr., R-Tenn., Chair; David Schaffer, Staff Director. General e-mail, transcomm@mail.house.gov. Web, www.house.gov/transportation.*

Jurisdiction over legislation on civil aviation, including airport funding, airline deregulation, safety issues, the National Transportation Safety Board, and the Federal Aviation Administration (except research and development). Jurisdiction over aviation noise pollution legislation.

Senate Appropriations Committee, *Subcommittee on Transportation,* SD-133 20510; (202) 224-2175. *Fax, (202) 224-4401. Sen. Richard C. Shelby, R-Ala., Chair; Wally Burnett, Majority Clerk. Web, appropriations.senate. gov/transportation.*

Jurisdiction over legislation to appropriate funds for the Federal Aviation Administration.

Senate Commerce, Science, and Transportation Committee, SD-508 20510; (202) 224-5115. *Fax, (202) 224-1259. Sen. John McCain, R-Ariz., Chair; Mark Buse, Staff Director. Web, commerce.senate.gov.*

Jurisdiction over legislation on the National Aeronautics and Space Administration, including nonmilitary aeronautical research and development.

Senate Commerce, Science, and Transportation Committee, *Subcommittee on Aviation,* SH-427 20510; (202) 224-4852. *Fax, (202) 228-0326. Sen. Slade Gorton, R-Wash., Chair; Ann H. Choiniere, Senior Counsel. Web, commerce.senate.gov.*

Jurisdiction over legislation on civil aviation, including airport funding, airline deregulation, safety issues, research and development, the National Transportation

Safety Board, and the Federal Aviation Administration. Jurisdiction over aviation noise pollution legislation.

NONPROFIT

Aeronautical Repair Station Assn., *121 N. Henry St., Alexandria, VA 22314-2903; (703) 739-9543. Fax, (703) 739-9488. Sarah MacLeod, Executive Director. General e-mail, arsa@arsa.org. Web, www.arsa.org.*

Membership: Federal Aviation Administration-certified repair stations; associate members are suppliers and distributors of components and parts. Works to improve relations between repair stations and manufacturers. Interests include reducing costs and problems associated with product liability and establishing uniformity in the application, interpretation, and enforcement of FAA regulations. Monitors legislation and regulations.

Aerospace Education Foundation, *1501 Lee Hwy., Arlington, VA 22209; (703) 247-5839. Fax, (703) 247-5853. Dan Marrs, Managing Director (Acting). Information, (800) 727-3337. General e-mail, aefstaff@aef.org. Web, www.aef.org.*

Promotes knowledge and appreciation of U.S. civilian and military aerospace development and history. (Affiliated with the Air Force Assn.)

Aerospace Industries Assn., *1250 Eye St. N.W., #1200 20005-3922; (202) 371-8400. Fax, (202) 371-8470. John W. Douglass, President. Press, (202) 371-8544. Web, www. aia-aerospace.org.*

Represents U.S. manufacturers of commercial, military, and business aircraft; helicopters; aircraft engines; missiles; spacecraft; and related components and equipment. Interests include international standards and trade.

AIR Conference (Airline Industrial Relations Conference), *1300 19th St. N.W., #750 20036-1609; (202) 861-7550. Fax, (202) 861-7557. Robert J. DeLucia, Vice President. General e-mail, office@aircon.org. Web, www. aircon.org.*

Membership: domestic and international scheduled air carriers. Monitors developments and collects data on trends in airline labor relations.

Air Line Pilots Assn. International, *1625 Massachusetts Ave. N.W. 20036; (703) 689-2270. Fax, (703) 689-4370. Duane Woerth, President. Press, (703) 481-4440. Web, www.alpa.org.*

Membership: airline pilots in the United States and Canada. Promotes air travel safety; assists investigations of aviation accidents. Monitors legislation and regulations. (Affiliated with the AFL-CIO.)

Air Transport Assn. of America, *1301 Pennsylvania Ave. N.W., #1100 20004; (202) 626-4000. Fax, (202) 626-4166. Carol B. Hallett, President. Web, www.air-transport. org.*

Membership: U.S. scheduled air carriers. Promotes aviation safety and the facilitation of air transportation for passengers and cargo. Monitors legislation and regulations.

American Helicopter Society, *217 N. Washington St., Alexandria, VA 22314; (703) 684-6777. Fax, (703) 739-9279. Morris E. Flater, Executive Director. General e-mail, ahs703@aol.com. Web, www.vtol.org.*

Membership: individuals and organizations interested in vertical flight. Acts as an information clearinghouse for technical data on helicopter design improvement, aerodynamics, and safety. Awards the Vertical Flight Foundation Scholarship to students interested in helicopter technology.

American Institute of Aeronautics and Astronautics, *1801 Alexander Bell Dr., #500, Reston, VA 20191; (703) 264-7500. Fax, (703) 264-7551. Cort Durocher, Executive Director. Information, (800) 639-2422. General e-mail, custserv@aiaa.org. Web, www.aiaa.org.*

Membership: engineers, scientists, and students in the fields of aeronautics and astronautics. Holds workshops on aerospace technical issues for congressional subcommittees; sponsors international conferences. Offers computerized database through its Technical Information Service in New York.

AOPA Legislative Affairs, *Washington Office, 500 E St. S.W., #250 20024; (202) 479-4050. Fax, (202) 484-1312. Bill Deere, Executive Director. Web, www.aopa.org.*

Membership: owners and pilots of general aviation aircraft. Washington office monitors legislation and regulations. Headquarters office provides members with maps, trip planning, speakers bureau, and other services; issues airport directory and handbook for pilots; sponsors the Air Safety Foundation. (Headquarters in Frederick, Md.)

Assn. of Flight Attendants, *1275 K St. N.W. 20005-4006; (202) 712-9799. Fax, (202) 712-9798. Patricia A. Friend, President. General e-mail, afatalk@afanet.org. Web, www.afanet.org.*

Membership: approximately 47,000 flight attendants. Helps members negotiate pay, benefits, and better working conditions; conducts training programs and workshops. Monitors legislation and regulations. (Affiliated with the AFL-CIO.)

Aviation Consumer Action Project, *529 14th St. N.W., #1265 20045 (mailing address: P.O. Box 19029*

20036); (202) 638-4000. Fax, (202) 638-0746. Paul S. Hudson, Director. General e-mail, acap71@erols.com. Web, www.acap1971.org.

Consumer advocacy organization that represents interests of airline passengers before the Federal Aviation Administration on safety issues and before the Transportation Dept. on economic and regulatory issues; testifies before Congress.

Cargo Airline, *1220 19th St. N.W., #400 20036; (202) 293-1030. Fax, (202) 293-4377. Stephen A. Alterman, President.*

Membership: cargo airlines and other firms interested in the development and promotion of air freight.

General Aviation Manufacturers Assn., *1400 K St. N.W., #801 20005; (202) 393-1500. Fax, (202) 842-4063. Edward M. Bolen, President. Web, www.generalaviation. org.*

Membership: U.S. manufacturers of business, commuter, and personal aircraft and manufacturers of engines, avionics, and equipment. Monitors legislation and regulations; sponsors safety and public information programs. Interests include international affairs.

Helicopter Assn. International, *1635 Prince St., Alexandria, VA 22314; (703) 683-4646. Fax, (703) 683-4745. Roy Resavage, President. Web, www.rotor.com.*

Membership: owners, manufacturers, and operators of helicopters, and affiliated companies in the civil helicopter industry. Provides information on use and operation of helicopters; offers business management and aviation safety courses; sponsors annual industry exposition. Monitors legislation and regulations.

International Assn. of Machinists and Aerospace Workers, *9000 Machinists Pl., Upper Marlboro, MD 20772-2687; (301) 967-4500. Fax, (301) 967-4588. Thomas Buffenbarger, President. Web, www.iamaw.org.*

Membership: machinists in more than 200 industries. Helps members negotiate pay, benefits, and better working conditions; conducts training programs and workshops. Monitors legislation and regulations. (Affiliated with the AFL-CIO, the Canadian Labour Congress, the Railway Labor Executives Assn., the International Metalworkers Federation, and the International Transport Workers' Federation.)

National Aeronautic Assn., *1815 N. Fort Myer Dr., #700, Arlington, VA 22209; (703) 527-0226. Fax, (703) 527-0229. Donald J. Koranda, President. General e-mail, naa@naa-usa.org. Web, www.naa-usa.org.*

Membership: persons interested in development of general and sporting aviation. Supervises sporting aviation competitions; oversees and approves official U.S. aircraft, aeronautics, and astronautics records. Interests include aeromodeling, aerobatics, helicopters, ultralights, home-built aircraft, parachuting, soaring, hang gliding, and ballooning. Serves as U.S. representative to the International Aeronautical Federation in Lausanne, Switzerland.

National Agricultural Aviation Assn., *1005 E St. S.E. 20003; (202) 546-5722. Fax, (202) 546-5726. James Callan, Executive Director. General e-mail, naaa@aol.com.*

Membership: qualified agricultural pilots; operating companies that seed, fertilize, and spray land by air; and allied industries. Monitors legislation and regulations.

National Air Carrier Assn., *910 17th St. N.W., #800 20006; (202) 833-8200. Fax, (202) 659-9479. Juan Priddy, President.*

Membership: air carriers certified for charter and scheduled operations. Monitors legislation and regulations.

National Air Transportation Assn., *4226 King St., Alexandria, VA 22302-1507; (703) 845-9000. Fax, (703) 845-8176. James K. Coyne, President. Information, (800) 808-6282. Web, www.nata-online.org.*

Membership: companies that provide on-demand air charter, aircraft sales, flight training, maintenance and repair, avionics, and other services. Manages education foundation; compiles statistics; provides business assistance programs. Monitors legislation and regulations.

National Assn. of State Aviation Officials, *8401 Colesville Rd., #505, Silver Spring, MD 20910; (301) 588-0587. Fax, (301) 585-1803. Lori P. Lehnerd, Executive Vice President. Web, www.nasao.org.*

Membership: state aeronautics agencies that deal with aviation issues, including regulation. Seeks uniform aviation laws; manages an aviation research and education foundation.

National Business Aviation Assn., *1200 18th St. N.W., #400 20036; (202) 783-9000. Fax, (202) 331-8364. John W. Olcott, President. Web, www.nbaa.org.*

Membership: companies owning and operating aircraft for business use, suppliers, and maintenance and air fleet service companies. Conducts seminars and workshops in business aviation management. Sponsors annual civilian aviation exposition. Monitors legislation and regulations.

Regional Airline Assn., *1200 19th St. N.W., #300 20036-2422; (202) 857-1170. Fax, (202) 429-5113. Deborah McElroy, President. General e-mail, raa@dc.sba.com. Web, www.raa.org.*

Membership: regional airlines that provide passenger, scheduled cargo, and mail service. Issues annual report on the industry.

RTCA, *1140 Connecticut Ave. N.W., #1020 20036; (202) 833-9339. Fax, (202) 833-9434. David S. Watrous, President. Web, www.rtca.org.*

Membership: federal agencies, aviation organizations, and commercial firms interested in aeronautical systems. Develops and publishes standards for aviation, including minimum operational performance standards for specific equipment; conducts research, makes recommendations, and issues reports on the field of aviation electronics and telecommunications.

Airports

AGENCIES

Animal and Plant Health Inspection Service *(Agriculture Dept.),* **Wildlife Services,** *1400 Independence Ave. S.W., #1624S 20250-3402; (202) 720-2054. Fax, (202) 690-0053. William Clay, Deputy Administrator (Acting). Web, www.aphis.usda.gov/ws.*

Works to minimize damage caused by wildlife to human health and safety. Interests include aviation safety; works with airport managers to reduce the risk of bird strikes. Oversees the National Wildlife Research Center in Ft. Collins, Colo.

Bureau of Land Management *(Interior Dept.),* **Lands and Realty,** *1620 L St. N.W. 20240 (mailing address: 1849 C St. N.W., MC 1000LS 20240); (202) 452-7780. Fax, (202) 452-7708. Ray Brady, Manager. Web, www.blm.gov.*

Operates the Airport Lease Program, which leases public lands for use as public airports.

Federal Aviation Administration *(Transportation Dept.),* **Airports,** *800 Independence Ave. S.W., #600E, ARP-1 20591; (202) 267-9471. Fax, (202) 267-5301. Woodie Woodward, Associate Administrator (Acting). Web, www.faa.gov/arp/arphome.htm.*

Makes grants for development and improvement of publicly operated and owned airports and some privately owned airports; certifies safety design standards for airports; administers the congressional Airport Improvement Program; oversees construction and accessibility standards for people with disabilities. Questions about local airports are usually referred to a local FAA field office.

Maryland Aviation Administration, *P.O. Box 8766, Baltimore, MD 21240; (410) 859-7060. Fax, (410) 850-4729. Vacant, Director, BWI Operations, (410) 859-7022; David Blackshear, Executive Director.*

Responsible for aviation operations, planning, instruction, and safety in Maryland; operates Baltimore/Washington International Airport (BWI).

Metropolitan Washington Airports Authority, *1 Aviation Circle, MA-1 20001-6000; (703) 417-8610. Fax, (703) 417-8949. James A. Wilding, President. Web, www. metwashairports.com.*

Independent interstate agency created by Virginia and the District of Columbia with the consent of Congress; operates Washington Dulles International Airport and Ronald Reagan Washington National Airport.

NONPROFIT

Airports Council International, *1775 K St. N.W., #500 20006; (202) 293-8500. Fax, (202) 331-1362. David Z. Plavin, President. General e-mail, postmaster@aci-na.org. Web, www.aci-na.org.*

Membership: authorities, boards, commissions, and municipal departments operating public airports. Serves as liaison with government agencies and other aviation organizations; works to improve passenger and freight facilitation; acts as clearinghouse on engineering and operational aspects of airport development. Monitors legislation and regulations.

American Assn. of Airport Executives, *601 Madison St., #400, Alexandria, VA 22314; (703) 824-0500. Fax, (703) 820-1395. Charles M. Barclay, President. Web, www. airportnet.org.*

Membership: airport managers, superintendents, consultants, authorities and commissions, government officials, and others interested in the construction, management, and operation of airports. Conducts examination for and awards the professional designation of Accredited Airport Executive.

Aviation Safety and Security

AGENCIES

Federal Aviation Administration *(Transportation Dept.), Accident Investigation, 800 Independence Ave. S.W., AAI-1 20591; (202) 267-9612. Fax, (202) 267-5043. Steven Wallace, Director. Web, www.faa.gov/avr/aai/aii/ home.htm.*

Investigates aviation accidents and incidents to detect unsafe conditions and trends in the national airspace system and to coordinate corrective action.

Federal Aviation Administration *(Transportation Dept.), Air Traffic Services, 800 Independence Ave. S.W., ATS-1 20591; (202) 267-7111. Fax, (202) 267-5621. Steven J. Brown, Associate Administrator (Acting). Web, www.faa.gov/ats/atshome.htm.*

Operates the national air traffic control system; employs air traffic controllers at airport towers, en route air traffic control centers, and flight service stations; maintains the National Flight Data Center.

Federal Aviation Administration *(Transportation Dept.), Aircraft Certification Service, 800 Independence Ave. S.W., AIR-1 20591; (202) 267-8235. Fax, (202) 267-5364. Elizabeth Erickson, Director. Web, www.faa.gov.*

Certifies all aircraft for airworthiness; approves designs and specifications for new aircraft, aircraft engines, propellers, and appliances; supervises aircraft manufacturing and testing.

Federal Aviation Administration *(Transportation Dept.), Airway Facilities, 800 Independence Ave. S.W., #700E, AAF-1 20591; (202) 267-8181. Fax, (202) 267-5015. Alan R. Moore, Director (Acting). Web, www.faa. gov/ats/af.*

Conducts research and development programs aimed at providing procedures, facilities, and devices needed for a safe and efficient system of air navigation and air traffic control.

Federal Aviation Administration *(Transportation Dept.), Aviation Medicine, 800 Independence Ave. S.W., #800W, AAM-1 20591; (202) 267-3535. Fax, (202) 267-5399. Dr. Jon L. Jordan, Federal Air Surgeon. Web, www. faa.gov.*

Responsible for the medical activities and policies of the FAA; designates, through regional offices, aviation medical examiners who conduct periodic medical examinations of all air personnel; maintains a Civil Aeromedical Institute in Oklahoma City.

Federal Aviation Administration *(Transportation Dept.), Civil Aviation Security, 800 Independence Ave. S.W., #300E, ACS-1 20591; (202) 267-9863. Fax, (202) 267-8496. Cathal L. Flynn, Associate Administrator. Web, www.cas.faa.gov.*

Responsible for domestic and foreign air carrier and airport security, including FAA antihijacking, antitheft, and sabotage prevention programs; formulates regulations for airport security, antihijacking controls, air cargo security, and hazardous materials; enforces regulations; inspects airports for compliance.

Federal Aviation Administration *(Transportation Dept.), Flight Standards Service, 800 Independence Ave. S.W., #821, AFS-1 20591; (202) 267-8237. Fax, (202) 267-5230. L. Nicholas Lacey, Director. Web, www.faa.gov/avr/ afshome.htm.*

Sets certification standards for air carriers, commercial operators, air agencies, and air personnel (except air traffic control tower operators); directs and executes certification and inspection of flight procedures, operating methods, air personnel qualification and proficiency, and maintenance aspects of airworthiness programs; manages the registry of civil aircraft and all official air personnel records; supports law enforcement agencies responsible for drug interdiction.

Federal Aviation Administration *(Transportation Dept.), System Safety, 800 Independence Ave. S.W., #1040A, ASY-1 20591; (202) 267-3611. Fax, (202) 267-5496. Christopher A. Hart, Assistant Administrator. Web, www.nasdac.faa.gov.*

Responsible for safety promotion and for the quality and integrity of safety-data studies and analyses.

Federal Bureau of Investigation *(Justice Dept.), Criminal Investigative Division, 935 Pennsylvania Ave. N.W., #7116 20535; (202) 324-4260. Fax, (202) 324-0027. Ruben Garcia Jr., Assistant Director. Web, www.fbi.gov.*

Investigates cases of aircraft hijacking, destruction of aircraft, and air piracy. Works with FAA to ensure security of national air carrier systems in areas of violent crime, organized crime, civil rights, corruption, and financial crimes.

Federal Communications Commission, *Enforcement Information Bureau, 445 12th St. S.W. 20554-0001; (202) 418-1105. David H. Solomon, Chief. Information, (888) 225-5322. TTY, (888) 835-5322. Web, www.fcc.gov/cib.*

Provides technical services to aid the Federal Aviation Administration in locating aircraft in distress; provides interference resolution for air traffic control radio frequencies.

National Oceanic and Atmospheric Administration *(Commerce Dept.), National Ocean Service, 1305 East-West Hwy., SSMC4, Silver Spring, MD 20910; (301) 713-3074. Fax, (301) 713-4269. Nancy Foster, Assistant Administrator. Web, www.nos.noaa.gov.*

Directs programs and conducts research to support fundamental scientific and engineering activities and resource development for safe navigation of national airspace. Maintains the National Spatial Reference System. Prints and distributes aeronautical charts.

National Transportation Safety Board, *Aviation Safety, 490 L'Enfant Plaza East S.W., #5400 20594; (202) 314-6300. Fax, (202) 314-6309. Bernard S. Loeb, Director.*

Responsible for management, policies, and programs in aviation safety and for aviation accident investigations. Manages programs on special investigations, safety issues, and safety objectives. Acts as U.S. representative in international investigations.

Aerospace Medical Assn., *320 S. Henry St., Alexandria, VA 22314-3579; (703) 739-2240. Fax, (703) 739-9652. Dr. Russell B. Rayman, Executive Director. Web, www.asma.org.*

Membership: physicians, flight surgeons, aviation medical examiners, flight nurses, scientists, technicians, and specialists in clinical, operational, and research fields of aerospace medicine. Promotes programs to improve aerospace medicine and maintain safety in aviation by examining and monitoring the health of aviation personnel; participates in aircraft investigation and cockpit design.

Air Traffic Control Assn., *2300 Clarendon Blvd., #711, Arlington, VA 22201; (703) 522-5717. Fax, (703) 527-7251. Gabriel A. Hartl, President. General e-mail, atca@ worldnet.att.net. Web, www.atca.org.*

Membership: air traffic controllers, flight service station specialists, pilots, aviation engineers and manufacturers, and others interested in air traffic control systems. Compiles and publishes information and data concerning air traffic control; provides information to members, Congress, and federal agencies; acts as liaison between members and Congress.

Flight Safety Foundation, *601 Madison St., #300, Alexandria, VA 22314; (703) 739-6700. Fax, (703) 739-6708. Stuart Matthews, President. Web, www.flightsafety. org.*

Membership: aerospace manufacturers, domestic and foreign airlines, energy and insurance companies, educational institutions, and organizations and corporations interested in flight safety. Sponsors seminars and conducts studies and safety audits on air safety for governments and industries. Administers award programs that recognize achievements in air safety. Operates the Q-STAR program, which is a charter-provider verification service.

International Society of Air Safety Investigators, *Technology Trading Park, 5 Export Dr., Sterling, VA 20164-4421; (703) 430-9668. Fax, (703) 450-1745. Ann Schull, Office Manager. General e-mail, isasi@erols.com. Web, www.isasi.org.*

Membership: specialists who investigate and seek to define the causes of aircraft accidents. Encourages improvement of air safety and investigative procedures.

National Air Traffic Controllers Assn., *1150 17th St. N.W., #701 20036; (202) 223-2900. Fax, (202) 659-3991. Michael McNally, President. Web, www.natca.org.*

Seeks to increase air traffic controller staffing levels, improve working conditions, and encourage procurement of more modern, reliable equipment. Concerned with airport safety worldwide.

National Assn. of Air Traffic Specialists, *11303 Amherst Ave., #4, Wheaton, MD 20902; (301) 933-6228. Fax, (301) 933-3902. Walter W. Pike, Chief Executive Officer. General e-mail, naatshq@aol.com. Web, www.naats.org.*

Membership: flight service station controllers from the FAA. Assists members with contract negotiation and grievances; conducts training programs and workshops. Monitors legislation and regulations.

See also National Safety Council (p. 241)

 MARITIME TRANSPORTATION

AGENCIES

Army Corps of Engineers *(Defense Dept.), 20 Massachusetts Ave. N.W., #8228 20314-1000; (202) 761-0001. Fax, (202) 761-4463. Lt. Gen. Joe N. Ballard (USACE), Chief of Engineers. Web, www.usace.army.mil.*

Provides local governments with navigation, flood control, disaster relief, and hydroelectric power services.

Federal Maritime Commission, *800 N. Capitol St. N.W., #1046 20573-0001; (202) 523-5725. Fax, (202) 523-0014. Harold J. Creel Jr., Chair; Bruce A. Dombrowski, Managing Director. Library, (202) 523-5762. TTY, (800) 877-8339. Locator, (202) 523-5773. Web, www.fmc.gov.*

Regulates foreign ocean shipping of the United States; enforces maritime shipping laws and regulations regarding rates and charges, freight forwarding, passengers, and port authorities. Library open to the public.

Federal Maritime Commission, *Tariffs, Certification, and Licensing, 800 N. Capitol St. N.W., 9th Floor 20573; (202) 523-5796. Fax, (202) 523-5830. Austin L. Schmitt, Director. Web, www.fmc.gov.*

Regulates the rates charged for shipping in foreign commerce; licenses and enforces regulations concerning ocean freight forwarders; issues certificates of financial responsibility to ensure that carriers refund fares and meet their liability in case of death, injury, or nonperformance.

Justice Dept., *Civil Division: Torts Branch, Aviation/Admiralty Litigation, 1425 New York Ave. N.W., #10100 20530 (mailing address: P.O. Box 14271 20044-4271); (202) 616-4000. Fax, (202) 616-4002. Gary W. Allen, Director. Web, www.usdoj.gov.*

Represents the federal government in civil suits concerning the maritime industry, including ships, shipping,

and merchant marine personnel. Handles civil cases arising from admiralty incidents and accidents, including oil spills.

Maritime Administration *(Transportation Dept.), 400 7th St. S.W., #7206, MAR-100 20590; (202) 366-5823. Fax, (202) 366-3890. Clyde J. Hart Jr., Administrator. Information, (202) 366-5807. Web, marad.dot.gov.*

Conducts research on shipbuilding and operations; administers subsidy programs; provides financing guarantees and a tax-deferred fund for shipbuilding; operates the U.S. Merchant Marine Academy in Kings Point, N.Y.

Maritime Administration *(Transportation Dept.), Financial and Rate Approvals, 400 7th St. S.W., #8117, MAR-560 20590; (202) 366-2324. Fax, (202) 366-7901. Michael P. Ferris, Director.*

Calculates rates for commercial American steamship lines to enable them to compete with foreign shipping lines that operate at lower cost. Conducts financial analysis of commercial shipping and calculates guideline rates for carriage of preference cargoes.

Maritime Administration *(Transportation Dept.), Insurance and Shipping Analysis, 400 7th St. S.W., #8117, MAR-570 20590; (202) 366-2400. Fax, (202) 366-7901. Edmond J. Fitzgerald, Director.*

Recommends subsidies for ship operation to the Maritime Subsidy Board. Administers war risk insurance.

Maritime Administration *(Transportation Dept.), Maritime Labor, Training, and Safety, 400 7th St. S.W., #7302 20590; (202) 366-5755. Fax, (202) 493-2288. Taylor Jones II, Director. Web, www.marad.dot.gov/labor_training. html.*

Supports the training of merchant marine officers at the U.S. Merchant Marine Academy in Kings Point, N.Y., and at maritime academies in California, Maine, Massachusetts, Michigan, New York, and Texas. Monitors maritime industry labor practices and policies; promotes consonant labor relations and safety practices.

Maritime Administration *(Transportation Dept.), Maritime Subsidy Board, 400 7th St. S.W., #7210, MAR-120 20590; (202) 366-5746. Fax, (202) 366-9206. Joel C. Richard, Secretary.*

Administers subsidy contracts for the construction and operation of U.S.-flag ships engaged in foreign trade.

Maritime Administration *(Transportation Dept.), Policy and International Trade, 400 7th St. S.W., #7218, MAR-400 20590; (202) 366-5772. Fax, (202) 366-7403. Bruce J. Carlton, Associate Administrator. Web, marad.dot. gov/policy.html.*

Conducts economic analyses and makes policy recommendations to the administrator. Negotiates multilateral and bilateral maritime agreements; directs the agency's strategic planning; manages collection and dissemination of official government statistics on ocean-borne foreign commerce; formulates government positions in international maritime policy matters.

Maritime Administration *(Transportation Dept.), Research and Development,* 400 7th St. S.W., #7213, MAR-130 20590; (202) 366-1925. Fax, (202) 366-1922. Alexander C. Landsburg, Coordinator.

Conducts technology assessment activities related to the development and use of water transportation systems for commercial and national security purposes. Makes recommendations concerning future trends in such areas as trade, technologies, fuels, and materials.

Maritime Administration *(Transportation Dept.), Ship Construction,* 400 7th St. S.W., MAR-720 20590; (202) 366-5737. Fax, (202) 366-3954. Marc P. Lasky, Director.

Works with private industry to develop standardized ship designs and improved shipbuilding techniques and materials.

Maritime Administration *(Transportation Dept.), Ship Financing,* 400 7th St. S.W., #8122, MAR-770 20590; (202) 366-5744. Fax, (202) 366-7901. Mitchell D. Lax, Director. Web, marad.dot.gov/title/11/index.html.

Provides ship financing guarantees and administers the Capital Construction Fund Program.

Maritime Administration *(Transportation Dept.), Shipping Analysis and Cargo Preference,* 400 7th St. S.W., #8126, MAR-500 20590; (202) 366-0364. Fax, (202) 366-7901. James J. Zok, Associate Administrator. Web, marad.dot.gov/aa_financial.html.

Administers shipping analysis and cargo preference programs, including Marine Insurance programs.

Navy Dept. *(Defense Dept.), Military Sealift Command,* Washington Navy Yard, Bldg. 210 20398-5400; (202) 685-5001. Fax, (202) 685-5020. Rear Adm. Gordon S. Holder, Commander. Web, www.msc.navy.mil.

Transports Defense Dept. and other U.S. government cargo by sea; operates ships that maintain supplies for the armed forces and scientific agencies; transports fuels for the Energy Dept.

Surface Transportation Board *(Transportation Dept.),* 1925 K St. N.W. 20423-0001; (202) 565-1500. Fax, (202) 565-9004. Wayne Burkes, Vice Chair; Linda J. Morgan, Chair. Web, www.stb.dot.gov.

Regulates rates for water transportation and intermodal connections in noncontiguous domestic trade (between the mainland and Alaska, Hawaii, or U.S. territories).

U.S. Coast Guard *(Transportation Dept.),* 2100 2nd St. S.W. 20593-0001; (202) 267-2390. Fax, (202) 267-4158. Adm. James M. Loy, Commandant. Information, (202) 267-1587. Web, www.uscg.mil.

Carries out search-and-rescue missions in and around navigable waters and on the high seas; enforces federal laws on the high seas and navigable waters of the United States and its possessions; conducts marine environmental protection programs; administers boating safety programs; inspects and regulates construction, safety, and equipment of merchant marine vessels; establishes and maintains a system of navigation aids; carries out domestic icebreaking activities; maintains a state of military readiness to assist the Navy in time of war or when directed by the president.

U.S. Coast Guard *(Transportation Dept.), Investigations and Analysis,* 2100 2nd St. S.W., #2404, G-MOA 20593; (202) 267-1430. Fax, (202) 267-1416. Capt. John L. Grenier, Chief.

Handles disciplinary proceedings for merchant marine personnel. Compiles and analyzes records of marine casualties.

U.S. Coast Guard *(Transportation Dept.), National Maritime Center, Licensing and Evaluation,* 4200 Wilson Blvd., #510, NMC-4C, Arlington, VA 22203-1804; (202) 493-1047. Fax, (202) 493-1064. Stewart Walker, Chief.

Provides guidance to marine licensing and documentation efforts and regional examination centers regarding evaluation of personnel qualifications, licensing, certification, shipment, and discharge of merchant mariners. Monitors operation of the Regional Examination Center; evaluates requests for medical waivers, vessel manning scales, and exemptions from citizenship requirements; advises the State Dept. concerning merchant marine personnel procedures abroad.

U.S. Coast Guard *(Transportation Dept.), Strategic Analysis,* 2100 2nd St. S.W. 20593-0001; (202) 267-2690. Fax, (202) 267-4234. James F. McEntire, Chief.

Makes five-to-fifteen-year projections on trends in politics, economics, sociology, technology, and society and how those trends will affect the Coast Guard.

CONGRESS

House Appropriations Committee, *Subcommittee on Commerce, Justice, State, and Judiciary,* H309 CAP

20515; (202) 225-3351. Rep. Harold Rogers, R-Ky., Chair; Jim Kulikowski, Staff Director. Web, www.house.gov/appropriations.

Jurisdiction over legislation to appropriate funds for the Maritime Administration and Federal Maritime Commission.

House Appropriations Committee, *Subcommittee on Energy and Water Development,* 2362 RHOB 20515; (202) 225-3421. Rep. Ron Packard, R-Calif., Chair; Robert Schmidt, Staff Director. Web, www.house.gov/appropriations.

Jurisdiction over legislation to appropriate funds for the civil programs of the Army Corps of Engineers.

House Appropriations Committee, *Subcommittee on Transportation,* 2358 RHOB 20515; (202) 225-2141. Rep. Frank R. Wolf, R-Va., Chair; John T. Blazey, Staff Director. Web, www.house.gov/appropriations.

Jurisdiction over legislation to appropriate funds for the U.S. Coast Guard, Saint Lawrence Seaway Development Corp., and Panama Canal Commission.

House Government Reform Committee, *Subcommittee on National Economic Growth, Natural Resources, and Regulatory Affairs,* B377 RHOB 20515; (202) 225-4407. Fax, (202) 225-2441. Rep. David M. McIntosh, R-Ind., Chair; Marlo Lewis, Staff Director. Web, www.house.gov/reform.

Oversees operations of the Federal Maritime Commission.

House Science Committee, *Subcommittee on Technology,* 2319 RHOB 20515; (202) 225-8844. Fax, (202) 225-4438. Rep. Constance A. Morella, R-Md., Chair; Jeffrey Grove, Staff Director. Web, www.house.gov/science.

Oversight of research and development activities of the U.S. Coast Guard and the Maritime Administration.

House Transportation and Infrastructure Committee, *Subcommittee on Coast Guard and Maritime Transportation,* 507 FHOB 20515; (202) 226-3552. Fax, (202) 226-2524. Rep. Wayne T. Gilchrest, R-Md., Chair; Rebecca Dye, Counsel. General e-mail, transcomm@mail.house.gov. Web, www.house.gov/transportation.

Jurisdiction over legislation on most merchant marine matters, including government subsidies and assistance; merchant marine personnel programs; port regulation, safety, and security; and ship and freight regulation and rates. Jurisdiction over legislation on maritime safety, marine pollution control and abatement, U.S. Coast Guard, and the Saint Lawrence Seaway (jurisdiction shared with the Subcommittee on Water Resources and Environment).

House Transportation and Infrastructure Committee, *Subcommittee on Water Resources and Environment,* B376 RHOB 20515; (202) 225-4360. Fax, (202) 226-5435. Rep. Sherwood Boehlert, R-N.Y., Chair; Ben Grumbles, Counsel. General e-mail, transcomm@mail.house.gov. Web, www.house.gov/transportation.

Jurisdiction over legislation on deepwater ports and the Saint Lawrence Seaway, including the Saint Lawrence Seaway Development Corp. (jurisdiction shared with the Subcommittee on Coast Guard and Maritime Transportation).

Senate Appropriations Committee, *Subcommittee on Commerce, Justice, State, and Judiciary,* S-146A CAP 20510; (202) 224-7277. Sen. Judd Gregg, R-N.H., Chair; Jim Morhard, Clerk. Web, appropriations.senate.gov/commerce.

Jurisdiction over legislation to appropriate funds for the Maritime Administration and the Federal Maritime Commission.

Senate Appropriations Committee, *Subcommittee on Energy and Water Development,* SD-127 20510; (202) 224-7260. Sen. Pete V. Domenici, R-N.M., Chair; Clay Sell, Clerk. Web, appropriations.senate.gov/energy.

Jurisdiction over legislation to appropriate funds for the Civil Corps of Engineers.

Senate Appropriations Committee, *Subcommittee on Transportation,* SD-133 20510; (202) 224-2175. Fax, (202) 224-4401. Sen. Richard C. Shelby, R-Ala., Chair; Wally Burnett, Majority Clerk. Web, appropriations.senate.gov/transportation.

Jurisdiction over legislation to appropriate funds for the U.S. Coast Guard, Saint Lawrence Seaway Development Corp., and Panama Canal Commission.

Senate Commerce, Science, and Transportation Committee, SD-508 20510; (202) 224-5115. Fax, (202) 224-1259. Sen. John McCain, R-Ariz., Chair; Mark Buse, Staff Director. Web, commerce.senate.gov.

Oversight of and legislative jurisdiction over the U.S. Coast Guard, the Maritime Administration, maritime safety, and ports, including security and regulation; oversight of the Federal Maritime Commission.

Senate Commerce, Science, and Transportation Committee, *Subcommittee on Oceans and Fisheries,* SH-428 20510; (202) 224-8172. Fax, (202) 228-0326. Sen. Olympia J. Snowe, R-Maine, Chair; Sloan Rapoport, Counsel. Web, commerce.senate.gov.

Studies issues involving deepwater ports. (Jurisdiction shared with Senate Energy and Natural Resources and Senate Environment and Public Works committees.)

Studies legislation on the U.S. Coast Guard. (Subcommittee does not report legislation.)

Senate Commerce, Science, and Transportation Committee, *Subcommittee on Surface Transportation and Merchant Marine*, SH-427 20510; (202) 224-4852. Fax, (202) 228-0326. Sen. Kay Bailey Hutchison, R-Texas, Chair; Ann Begeman, Professional Staff Member. Web, commerce.senate.gov.

Jurisdiction over legislation on Saint Lawrence Seaway and merchant marine matters, including ship and freight regulation and rates, merchant marine personnel programs, and government subsidies and assistance to foreign and U.S. vessels.

Senate Energy and Natural Resources Committee, *Subcommittee on Water and Power,* SD-308 20510; (202) 224-4971. Sen. Gordon H. Smith, R-Ore., Chair; Colleen Deegan, Majority Counsel. General e-mail, water&power@energy.senate.gov. Web, energy.senate.gov.

Jurisdiction over legislation on deepwater ports (jurisdiction shared with Senate Commerce, Science, and Transportation and Senate Environment and Public Works committees).

Senate Environment and Public Works Committee, *Subcommittee on Transportation and Infrastructure,* SD-410 20510; (202) 224-6176. Fax, (202) 224-5167. Sen. George V. Voinovich, R-Ohio, Chair; Ellen Stein, Staff Contact. Web, epw.senate.gov.

Jurisdiction over legislation authorizing construction, operation, and maintenance of inland waterways and harbors (jurisdiction on deepwater ports beyond three-mile limit shared with Senate Energy and Natural Resources and Senate Commerce, Science, and Transportation committees).

NONPROFIT

AFL-CIO Maritime Committee, *1150 17th St. N.W., #700 20036; (202) 835-0404. Fax, (202) 872-0912. Talmage E. Simpkins, Executive Director.*

Membership: AFL-CIO maritime unions. Provides information on the maritime industry and unions. Interests include seamen's service contracts and pension plans, maritime safety, U.S. merchant marine, and the rights of Panama Canal residents. Monitors legislation and regulations.

American Maritime Congress, *1300 Eye St. N.W., #250W 20005-3314; (202) 842-4900. Fax, (202) 842-3492. Gloria Cataneo Tosi, President.*

Organization of U.S.-flag carriers engaged in oceanborne transportation. Conducts research and provides information on the U.S.-flag merchant marine.

Boat Owners Assn. of the United States, *Government Affairs, 880 S. Pickett St., Alexandria, VA 22304; (703) 461-2864. Fax, (703) 461-2845. Michael Sciulla, Director.*

Membership: owners of recreational boats. Represents boat-owner interests before the federal government; offers consumer protection and other services to members.

Chamber of Shipping of America, *1730 M St. N.W., #407 20036; (202) 775-4399. Fax, (202) 659-3795. Joseph J. Cox, President.*

Represents U.S.-based companies that own, operate, or charter oceangoing tankers, container ships, and other merchant vessels engaged in domestic and international trade.

Maritime Institute for Research and Industrial Development, *1775 K St. N.W., #200 20006; (202) 463-6505. Fax, (202) 223-9093. C. James Patti, President. General e-mail, miraid2@worldnet.att.net.*

Membership: U.S.-flag ship operators. Promotes the development of the U.S. Merchant Marine. Interests include bilateral shipping agreements, the use of private commercial merchant vessels by the Defense Dept., and enforcement of cargo preference laws for U.S.-flag ships.

National Marine Manufacturers Assn., *Federal Government Relations, Washington Office, 1819 L St. N.W., #700 20036; (202) 861-1180. Fax, (202) 861-1181. Betsy L. Oilman, Director. Web, www.nmma.org.*

Membership: recreational marine equipment manufacturers. Promotes boating safety and the development of boating facilities. Serves as liaison with Congress and regulatory agencies. Monitors legislation and regulations. (Headquarters in Chicago.)

Shipbuilders Council of America, *1600 Wilson Blvd., #1000, Arlington, VA 22209; (703) 351-6734. Fax, (703) 351-6736. Allen Walker, President. Web, www.shipbuilders. org.*

Membership: commercially focused shipyards that repair and build ships, and allied industries and associations. National trade association representing the competitive shipyard industry that makes up the core shipyard industrial base in the United States. Monitors legislation and regulations.

Transportation Institute, *5201 Auth Way, Camp Springs, MD 20746; (301) 423-3335. Fax, (301) 423-0634. James L. Henry, President. Web, www.trans-inst.org.*

Membership: U.S.-flag maritime shipping companies. Conducts research on freight regulation and rates, government subsidies and assistance, domestic and international maritime matters, maritime safety, ports, Saint Lawrence Seaway, shipbuilding, and regulation of shipping.

See also Intermodal Assn. of North America (p. 661)

Maritime Safety

AGENCIES

Federal Communications Commission, *Enforcement Information Bureau,* 445 12th St. S.W. 20554-0001; (202) 418-1105. David H. Solomon, Chief. Information, (888) 225-5322. TTY, (888) 835-5322. Web, www.fcc.gov/cib.

Provides technical services to the U.S. Coast Guard for locating ships in distress. Provides policy and program support for maritime radiotelegraph inspection.

National Oceanic and Atmospheric Administration *(Commerce Dept.), National Ocean Service: Coast Survey,* 1315 East-West Hwy., SSMC3, #6147, Silver Spring, MD 20910-3282; (301) 713-2770. Fax, (301) 713-4019. Capt. David B. MacFarland, Director. Web, www. chartmaker.ncd.noaa.gov.

Directs programs and conducts research to support fundamental scientific and engineering activities and resource development for safe navigation of the nation's waterways and territorial seas. Constructs, prints, and distributes nautical charts.

National Response Center *(Transportation Dept.),* 2100 2nd St. S.W., #2611 20593; (202) 267-2675. Fax, (202) 267-2165. Syed Qadir, Director. Toll-free hotline, (800) 424-8802. Web, www.nrc.uscg.mil.

Maintains 24-hour hotline for reporting oil spills or hazardous materials accidents. Notifies appropriate federal officials to reduce the effects of accidents.

National Transportation Safety Board, *Marine Safety,* 490 L'Enfant Plaza East S.W., #6313 20594; (202) 314-6450. Fax, (202) 314-6454. Marjorie Murtagh, Director. Web, www.ntsb.gov.

Investigates selected marine transportation accidents, including major marine accidents that involve U.S. Coast Guard operations or functions. Determines the facts upon which the board establishes probable cause; makes recommendations on matters pertaining to marine transportation safety and accident prevention.

Occupational Safety and Health Administration *(Labor Dept.), General Industry Compliance,* 200 Constitution Ave. N.W., #N3107, MS-N3603 20210; (202) 693-1850. Fax, (202) 693-1628. Arthur T. Buchanan, Director.

Interprets maritime compliance safety standards for agency field personnel and private employees and employers.

U.S. Coast Guard *(Transportation Dept.), Boating Safety,* 2100 2nd St. S.W., G-OPB 20593-0001; (202) 267-1077. Fax, (202) 267-4285. Capt. M. F. Holmes, Chief. Web, www.uscgboating.org.

Establishes and enforces safety standards for recreational boats and associated equipment; sets boater education standards; coordinates nationwide public awareness and information programs.

U.S. Coast Guard *(Transportation Dept.), Design and Engineering Standards,* 2100 2nd St. S.W., #1218, G-MSE 20593; (202) 267-2967. Fax, (202) 267-4816. Capt. Mark Van Haverbeke, Chief.

Develops standards; responsible for general vessel arrangements, naval architecture, vessel design and construction, and transport of bulk dangerous cargoes. Supports national advisory committees and national professional organizations to achieve industry standards.

U.S. Coast Guard *(Transportation Dept.), Investigations and Analysis,* 2100 2nd St. S.W., #2404, G-MOA 20593; (202) 267-1430. Fax, (202) 267-1416. Capt. John L. Grenier, Chief.

Compiles and analyzes records of accidents involving commercial vessels that result in loss of life, serious injury, or substantial damage.

U.S. Coast Guard *(Transportation Dept.), Marine Safety and Environmental Protection,* 2100 2nd St. S.W., #2408 20593; (202) 267-2200. Fax, (202) 267-4839. Rear Adm. Robert C. North, Assistant Commandant. Web, www. uscg.mil/hq/g-m/gmhome.htm.

Establishes and enforces regulations for port safety; environmental protection; vessel safety, inspection, design, documentation, and investigation; licensing of merchant vessel personnel; and shipment of hazardous materials.

U.S. Coast Guard *(Transportation Dept.), Marine Safety Center,* 400 7th St. S.W., #6302 20590; (202) 366-6480. Fax, (202) 366-3877. Capt. J. G. Lantz, Commanding Officer.

Reviews and approves commercial vessel plans and specifications to ensure technical compliance with federal safety and pollution abatement standards.

U.S. Coast Guard *(Transportation Dept.), Operations Policy Directorate,* 2100 2nd St. S.W. 20593-0001 (mailing address: Commandant G-OP 20593); (202) 267-2267. Fax, (202) 267-4674. Rear Adm. Terry M. Cross, Contact. Web, www.uscg.mil.

Administers Long Range and Short Range Aids to Navigation programs; regulates the construction, maintenance, and operation of bridges across U.S. navigable waters. Conducts search-and-rescue and polar and domestic ice-breaking operations. Regulates waterways under U.S. jurisdiction. Operates the Coast Guard Command Center; participates in defense operations; enforces boating safety; assists with law enforcement/drug interdictions.

NONPROFIT

U.S. Coast Guard Auxiliary, *2100 2nd St. S.W. 20593-0001; (202) 267-1001. Fax, (202) 267-4460. Mark Kern, Chief Director. Web, www.uscg.mil/hq/g-o/cgaux/default. htm.*

Volunteer, nonmilitary organization created by Congress to assist the Coast Guard in promoting water safety. Offers public education programs; administers the Courtesy Marine Examination Program, a safety equipment check free to the public; works with the Coast Guard and state boating officials to maintain marine safety.

Ports and Waterways

AGENCIES

Army Corps of Engineers *(Defense Dept.), Civil Works, 20 Massachusetts Ave. N.W. 20314; (202) 761-0099. Fax, (202) 761-8992. Maj. Gen. Hans A. Van Winkle, Director. Web, www.usace.army.mil.*

Coordinates field offices that oversee harbors, dams, levees, waterways, locks, reservoirs, and other construction projects designed to facilitate transportation and flood control. Major projects include the Mississippi, Missouri, and Ohio Rivers.

Federal Maritime Commission, *Agreements and Information Management, 800 N. Capitol St. N.W. 20573; (202) 523-5793. Fax, (202) 523-4372. Jeremiah D. Hospital, Chief. Web, www.fmc.gov.*

Analyzes agreements between terminal operators and shipping companies for docking facilities and agreements between ocean common carriers.

Maritime Administration *(Transportation Dept.), Inland Waterways and Great Lakes, 400 7th St. S.W., MAR-115 20590; (202) 366-1718. Fax, (202) 366-3890. Bonnie Marie Green, Deputy Administrator.*

Coordinates agency policies affecting U.S. inland waterways and the Great Lakes. Works with industry, unions, state and local governments, and other federal agencies; interests include streamlining of regulatory requirements and improved integration of maritime with other modes of transportation.

Maritime Administration *(Transportation Dept.), Port, Intermodal, and Environmental Activities, 400 7th St. S.W., #7214, MAR-800 20590; (202) 366-4721. Fax, (202) 366-6988. Margaret Blum, Associate Administrator. Web, marad.dot.gov/aa_port_inter_env.html.*

Responsible for direction and administration of port and intermodal transportation development and port readiness for national defense.

Panama Canal Commission, *1850 Eye St. N.W., #1030 20006; (202) 634-6441. Fax, (202) 634-6439. William J. Connolly, Deputy Director. Web, www.pananet.com/pancanal.*

Independent federal agency that manages, operates, and maintains the Panama Canal and its complementary works, installations, and equipment; provides for the orderly transit of vessels through the canal.

Saint Lawrence Seaway Development Corp. *(Transportation Dept.), 400 7th St. S.W., #5424 20590; (202) 366-0118. Fax, (202) 366-7147. Albert S. Jacquez, Administrator. Information, (202) 366-0091. Web, www.dot.gov/slsdc.*

Operates and maintains the Saint Lawrence Seaway within U.S. territorial limits; conducts development programs and coordinates activities with its Canadian counterpart.

Tennessee Valley Authority, *Government Affairs, Washington Office, 1 Massachusetts Ave. N.W., #300 20444; (202) 898-2999. Fax, (202) 898-2998. David Withrow, Vice President. Web, www.tva.gov.*

Coordinates resource conservation, development, and land-use programs in the Tennessee River Valley. Operates the river control system; projects include flood control, navigation development, and multiple-use reservoirs.

U.S. Coast Guard *(Transportation Dept.), 2100 2nd St. S.W. 20593-0001; (202) 267-2390. Fax, (202) 267-4158. Adm. James M. Loy, Commandant. Information, (202) 267-1587. Web, www.uscg.mil.*

Enforces rules and regulations governing the safety and security of ports and anchorages and the movement of vessels in U.S. waters. Supervises cargo transfer operations, storage, and stowage; conducts harbor patrols and waterfront facility inspections; establishes security zones and monitors vessel movement.

NONPROFIT

American Assn. of Port Authorities, *1010 Duke St., Alexandria, VA 22314; (703) 684-5700. Fax, (703) 684-6321. Kurt J. Nagle, President. General e-mail, info@ aapa-ports.org. Web, www.aapa-ports.org.*

Membership: port authorities in the Western Hemisphere. Provides technical and economic information on port finance, construction, operation, and security.

American Waterways Operators, *1600 Wilson Blvd., #1000, Arlington, VA 22209; (703) 841-9300. Fax, (703) 841-0389. Thomas Allegretti, President. Web, www. americanwaterways.com.*

Membership: commercial shipyard owners and operators of barges, tugboats, and towboats on navigable coastal and inland waterways. Monitors legislation and regulations; acts as liaison with Congress, the U.S. Coast Guard, the Army Corps of Engineers, and the Maritime Administration. Monitors legislation and regulations.

International Longshore and Warehouse Union, Washington Office, *1775 K St. N.W., #200 20006; (202) 463-6265. Fax, (202) 467-4875. Lindsay McLaughlin, Legislative Director. Web, www.ilwu.org.*

Membership: approximately 45,000 longshore and warehouse personnel. Helps members negotiate pay, benefits, and better working conditions; conducts training programs and workshops. Monitors legislation and regulations. (Headquarters in San Francisco; affiliated with the AFL-CIO.)

International Longshoremen's Assn., Washington Office, *1101 17th St. N.W., #400 20036; (202) 955-6304. Fax, (202) 955-6048. John Bowers Jr., Legislative Director.*

Membership: approximately 61,000 longshore personnel. Helps members negotiate pay, benefits, and better working conditions; conducts training programs and workshops. Monitors legislation and regulations. (Headquarters in New York; affiliated with the AFL-CIO.)

National Assn. of Waterfront Employers, *2011 Pennsylvania Ave. N.W., #301 20006; (202) 296-2810. Fax, (202) 331-7479. Charles T. Carroll Jr., Executive Director.*

Membership: private stevedore and marine terminal companies, their subsidiaries, and other waterfront-related employers. Legislative interests include trade, antitrust, insurance, and user-fee issues. Monitors legislation and regulations.

National Waterways Conference, *1130 17th St. N.W. 20036-4676; (202) 296-4415. Fax, (202) 835-3861. Harry N. Cook, President. Web, www.waterways.org.*

Membership: petroleum, coal, chemical, electric power, building materials, iron and steel, and grain companies; port authorities; water carriers; and other waterways interests. Conducts research on the economics of water transportation; sponsors educational programs on waterways. Monitors legislation and regulations.

Passenger Vessel Assn., *1600 Wilson Blvd., #1000A, Arlington, VA 22209; (703) 807-0100. Fax, (703) 807-0103. John R. Groundwater, Executive Director. Web, www.passengervessel.com.*

Membership: owners, operators, and suppliers for U.S. and Canadian passenger vessels; and international vessel companies. Interests include dinner and excursion boats, car and passenger ferries, overnight cruise ships, and riverboat casinos. Monitors legislation and regulations.

See also Transportation Institute (p. 672)

MOTOR VEHICLES

See also Air Pollution (chap. 9); Caucuses (chap. 20); Insurance (chap. 3)

AGENCIES

Federal Highway Administration (FHA), *(Transportation Dept.), 400 7th St. S.W., #4218 20590; (202) 366-0650. Fax, (202) 366-3244. Kenneth R. Wykle, Administrator. Information, (202) 366-0660. Web, www.fhwa.dot. gov.*

Administers federal-aid highway programs with money from the Highway Trust Fund; works to improve highway and motor vehicle safety; coordinates research and development programs on highway and traffic safety, construction, costs, and environmental impact of highway transportation; administers regional and territorial highway building programs and the highway beautification program.

Federal Motor Carrier Safety Administration *(Transportation Dept.), Bus and Truck Safety Operations, 400 7th St. S.W., #3107 20590; (202) 366-1790. Fax, (202) 366-8842. John MacGowan, Director (Acting). Web, www.fmcsa.dot.gov.*

Regulates motor vehicle size and weight on federally aided highways; conducts studies on issues relating to motor carrier transportation; promotes uniformity in state and federal motor carrier laws and regulations.

CONGRESS

House Appropriations Committee, *Subcommittee on Transportation, 2358 RHOB 20515; (202) 225-2141. Rep. Frank R. Wolf, R-Va., Chair; John T. Blazey, Staff Director. Web, www.house.gov/appropriations.*

Jurisdiction over legislation to appropriate funds for the Transportation Dept., including the Federal Highway Administration and the National Highway Traffic Safety Administration.

House Commerce Committee, *Subcommittee on Telecommunications, Trade, and Consumer Protection,* 2125 RHOB 20515; (202) 225-2927. Fax, (202) 225-1919. Rep. W. J. "Billy" Tauzin, R-La., Chair; James E. Derderian, Staff Director. General e-mail, commerce@mail.house.gov. Web, www.house.gov/commerce.

Jurisdiction over motor vehicle safety legislation and the National Highway Traffic Safety Administration (jurisdiction shared with House Transportation and Infrastructure Committee).

House Science Committee, *Subcommittee on Technology,* 2319 RHOB 20515; (202) 225-8844. Fax, (202) 225-4438. Rep. Constance A. Morella, R-Md., Chair; Jeffrey Grove, Staff Director. Web, www.house.gov/science.

Special oversight of surface transportation research and development programs of executive branch departments and agencies.

House Transportation and Infrastructure Committee, *Subcommittee on Ground Transportation,* B376 RHOB 20515; (202) 226-0727. Fax, (202) 226-3475. Rep. Tom Petri, R-Wis., Chair; Glenn Scammel, Counsel. General e-mail, transcomm@mail.house.gov. Web, www.house.gov/transportation.

Jurisdiction over legislation on regulation of commercial vehicles and interstate surface transportation, including the Federal Highway Administration, National Highway Traffic Safety Administration (jurisdiction shared with House Commerce Committee), federal aid to highways, and highway trust fund programs and activities.

Senate Appropriations Committee, *Subcommittee on Transportation,* SD-133 20510; (202) 224-2175. Fax, (202) 224-4401. Sen. Richard C. Shelby, R-Ala., Chair; Wally Burnett, Majority Clerk. Web, appropriations.senate.gov/transportation.

Jurisdiction over legislation to appropriate funds for the Transportation Dept., including the Federal Highway Administration and National Highway Traffic Safety Administration.

Senate Commerce, Science, and Transportation Committee, SD-508 20510; (202) 224-5115. Fax, (202) 224-1259. Sen. John McCain, R-Ariz., Chair; Mark Buse, Staff Director. Web, commerce.senate.gov.

Jurisdiction over motor vehicle safety legislation; oversight of the Surface Transportation Board.

Senate Commerce, Science, and Transportation Committee, *Subcommittee on Surface Transportation and Merchant Marine,* SH-427 20510; (202) 224-4852. Fax, (202) 228-0326. Sen. Kay Bailey Hutchison, R-Texas,

Chair; Ann Begeman, Professional Staff Member. Web, commerce.senate.gov.

Jurisdiction over legislation on regulation of commercial motor carriers and interstate buses. Oversight of surface transportation research and development, including Federal Highway Administration activities (but excluding federal highway construction).

Senate Environment and Public Works Committee, *Subcommittee on Transportation and Infrastructure,* SD-410 20510; (202) 224-6176. Fax, (202) 224-5167. Sen. George V. Voinovich, R-Ohio, Chair; Ellen Stein, Staff Contact. Web, epw.senate.gov.

Jurisdiction over legislation on the Federal Highway Administration, National Highway Traffic Safety Administration, highway trust fund programs, and federal aid to highways.

NONPROFIT

American Assn. of Motor Vehicle Administrators, 4301 Wilson Blvd., #400, Arlington, VA 22203; (703) 522-4200. Fax, (703) 522-1553. Kenneth M. Beam, President. Web, www.aamva.net.

Membership: officials responsible for administering and enforcing motor vehicle and traffic laws in the United States and Canada. Promotes uniform laws and regulations for vehicle registration, drivers' licenses, and motor carrier services; provides administrative evaluation services for safety equipment.

American Automobile Assn., *Public Relations, Washington Office,* 1440 New York Ave. N.W., #200 20005-2111; (202) 942-2050. Fax, (202) 783-4798. Steve Hayes, Managing Director. Web, www.aaa.com.

Membership: state and local automobile associations. Provides members with travel services. Interests include all aspects of highway transportation, travel and tourism, safety, drunk driving, economics, federal aid, and legislation that affects motorists. (Headquarters in Heathrow, Fla.)

American Bus Assn., 1100 New York Ave. N.W., #1050 20005-3934; (202) 842-1645. Fax, (202) 842-0850. Peter J. Pantuso, President. General e-mail, abainfo@buses.org. Web, www.buses.org.

Membership: intercity privately owned bus companies, state associations, travel/tourism businesses, bus manufacturers, and those interested in the bus industry. Monitors legislation and regulations.

American Trucking Assns., 2200 Mill Rd., Alexandria, VA 22314-4677; (703) 838-1700. Fax, (703) 684-4326. Walter B. McCormick, President. Information, (800) 282-

5463. Library, (703) 838-1880. Press, (703) 838-1873. General e-mail, membership@trucking.org. Web, www. truckline.org.

Membership: state trucking associations, individual trucking and motor carrier organizations, and related supply companies. Maintains departments on industrial relations, law, management systems, research, safety, traffic, state laws, taxation, communications, legislation, economics, and engineering. Library open to the public by appointment.

Electrical Vehicle Assn. of the Americas, 701 Pennsylvania Ave. 20004; (202) 508-5995. Kateri Callahan, Executive Director. Web, www.evaa.org.

Membership: auto and vehicle companies and manufacturers, electric utilities, EV component suppliers, research institutions, and government agencies. Works to advance electric vehicles and supporting infrastructure through policy, information, and market development initiatives in the U.S.

Highway Loss Data Institute, 1005 N. Glebe Rd., #800, Arlington, VA 22201; (703) 247-1600. Fax, (703) 247-1595. Brian O'Neill, President. Web, www.carsafety.org.

Research organization that gathers, processes, and publishes data on the ways in which insurance losses vary among different kinds of vehicles. (Affiliated with Insurance Institute for Highway Safety.)

International Parking Institute, 701 Kenmore Ave., #200, Fredericksburg, VA 22404-7167 (mailing address: P.O. Box 7167, Fredericksburg, VA 22404-7167); (540) 371-7535. Fax, (540) 371-8022. David Ivey, President. Web, www.parking.org.

Membership: operators, designers, and builders of parking lots and structures. Provides leadership to the parking industry; supports professional development; works with transportation and related fields.

Motor Freight Carriers Assn., 499 S. Capitol St. S.W., #502A 20003; (202) 554-3060. Fax, (202) 554-3160. Timothy P. Lynch, President. Web, www.mfca.org.

Represents trucking employers. Negotiates and administers labor contracts with the Teamsters Union.

Motorcycle Industry Council, *Government Relations, Washington Office,* 1235 Jefferson Davis Hwy., #600, Arlington, VA 22202; (703) 416-0444. Fax, (703) 416-2269. Kathy Van Kleeck, Vice President. Web, www.mic.org.

Membership: manufacturers and distributors of motorcycles, mopeds and related parts, accessories, and equipment. Monitors legislation and regulations. (Headquarters in Irvine, Calif.)

National Assn. of Regulatory Utility Commissioners, 1101 Vermont Ave. N.W., #200 20005; (202) 898-2200. Fax, (202) 898-2213. Charles Gray, Executive Director. Press, (202) 898-2205. Web, www.naruc.org.

Membership: members of federal, state, municipal, and Canadian regulatory commissions that have jurisdiction over motor and common carriers. Interests include motor carriers.

National Institute for Automotive Service Excellence, 13505 Dulles Technology Dr., #2, Herndon, VA 20171-3421; (703) 713-3800. Fax, (703) 713-0727. Ronald H. Weiner, President. Web, www.asecert.org.

Administers program for testing and certifying automotive technicians; researches methods to improve technician training.

National Motor Freight Traffic Assn., 2200 Mill Rd., 4th Floor, Alexandria, VA 22314; (703) 838-1810. Fax, (703) 683-1094. Martin E. Foley, Executive Director. Web, www.erols.com/nmfta.

Membership: motor carriers of general goods in interstate and intrastate commerce. Publishes *National Motor Freight Classification.*

National Parking Assn., 1112 16th St. N.W., #300 20036; (202) 296-4336. Fax, (202) 331-8523. Barbara O'Dell, Executive Director. Web, www.npapark.org.

Membership: parking garage owners, operators, and consultants and university municipalities. Offers information and research services; sponsors seminars and educational programs on garage design and equipment. Monitors legislation and regulations.

National Private Truck Council, 66 Canal Center Plaza, #600, Alexandria, VA 22314; (703) 683-1300. Fax, (703) 683-1217. John A. McQuaid, President. Web, www.nptc.org.

Membership: manufacturers, producers, distributors, and retail establishments that operate fleets of vehicles incidental to their nontransportation businesses. Interests include truck safety, maintenance, and economics. Supports economic deregulation of the trucking industry and uniformity in state taxation of the industry. Private Management Fleet Institute conducts continuing education, truck research, and certification programs.

NATSO, 1199 N. Fairfax St., #801, Alexandria, VA 22314; (703) 549-2100. Fax, (703) 684-4525. W. Dewey Clower, President. General e-mail, natsoinc@aol.com. Web, www. natso.com.

Membership: travel plaza and truck stop operators and suppliers to the truck stop industry. Provides credit information and educational training programs. Monitors legislation and regulations. Operates the NATSO Foundation, which promotes highway safety.

Natural Gas Vehicle Coalition, *1100 Wilson Blvd., #850, Arlington, VA 22209; (703) 527-3022. Fax, (703) 527-3025. Richard R. Kolodziej, President. Web, www.ngvc. org.*

Membership: natural gas distributors; pipeline, automobile, and engine manufacturers; environmental groups; research and development organizations; and state and local government agencies. Advocates installation of compressed natural gas fuel stations and development of industry standards. Helps market new natural gas products and equipment.

Truckload Carriers Assn., *2200 Mill Rd., Alexandria, VA 22314; (703) 838-1950. Fax, (703) 836-6610. Lana R. Batts, President. Web, www.truckload.org.*

Represents intercity common and contract trucking companies before Congress, federal agencies, courts, and the media.

Highways

AGENCIES

Federal Highway Administration *(Transportation Dept.), Infrastructure, 400 7th St. S.W., #3212 20590; (202) 366-0371. Fax, (202) 366-3043. Vincent F. Schimmoller, Program Manager.*

Provides guidance and oversight for planning, design, construction, and maintenance operations relating to federal aid, direct federal construction, and other highway programs; establishes design guidelines and specifications for highways built with federal funds.

Federal Highway Administration *(Transportation Dept.), National Highway Institute, 4600 N. Fairfax Dr., #800, Arlington, VA 22203; (703) 235-0500. Fax, (703) 235-0593. Moges Ayele, Director. Web, www.nhi.fhwa.dot. gov.*

Develops and administers, in cooperation with state highway departments, training programs for agency, state, and local highway department employees.

Federal Highway Administration *(Transportation Dept.), Policy, 400 7th St. S.W., #3317 20590; (202) 366-0585. Fax, (202) 366-9626. King Gee, Director (Acting). Web, www.fhwa.dot.gov.*

Develops policy and administers the Federal Highway Administration's international programs. Conducts policy studies and analyzes legislation; makes recommendations; compiles and reviews highway-related data. Represents the administration at international conferences; administers foreign assistance programs.

Federal Highway Administration *(Transportation Dept.), Real Estate Services, 400 7th St. S.W. 20590; (202) 366-0142. Fax, (202) 366-3713. Susan Lauffer, Director.*

Funds and oversees acquisition of land by states for federally assisted highways; provides financial assistance to relocate people and businesses forced to move by highway construction; cooperates in administering program for the use of air rights in connection with federally aided highways; administers Highway Beautification Act to control billboards and junkyards along interstate and federally aided primary highways.

Federal Highway Administration *(Transportation Dept.), Research, Technology, and Development, 6300 Georgetown Pike, McLean, VA 22101; (202) 493-3165. Fax, (202) 493-3170. Dennis C. Judycki, Director.*

Conducts highway research and development programs; studies safety, location, design, construction, operation, and maintenance of highways; cooperates with state and local highway departments in utilizing results of research.

U.S. Coast Guard *(Transportation Dept.), 2100 2nd St. S.W. 20593-0001; (202) 267-2390. Fax, (202) 267-4158. Adm. James M. Loy, Commandant. Information, (202) 267-1587. Web, www.uscg.mil.*

Regulates the construction, maintenance, and operation of bridges across U.S. navigable waters.

NONPROFIT

American Assn. of State Highway and Transportation Officials, *444 N. Capitol St. N.W., #249 20001; (202) 624-5800. Fax, (202) 624-5806. John Horsley, Executive Director. Web, www.aashto.org.*

Membership: the Federal Highway Administration and transportation departments of the states, District of Columbia, Guam, and Puerto Rico. Maintains committees on transportation planning, finance, maintenance, safety, and construction.

American Road and Transportation Builders Assn., *1010 Massachusetts Ave. N.W., 6th Floor 20001; (202) 289-4434. Fax, (202) 289-4435. T. Peter Ruane, President. General e-mail, artba@artba.com. Web, www.artba-hq. org.*

Membership: highway and transportation contractors; federal, state, and local engineers and officials; construction equipment manufacturers and distributors; and others interested in the transportation construction industry. Serves as liaison with government; provides information on highway engineering and construction developments.

Intelligent Transportation Society of America, *400 Virginia Ave. S.W., #800 20024-2730; (202) 484-4847. Fax, (202) 484-3483. John Collins, President. Publications, (202) 484-4548. Web, www.itsa.org.*

Advocates application of electronic, computer, and communications technology to make surface transportation more efficient and to save lives, time, and money. Coordinates research, development, and implementation of intelligent transportation systems by government, academia, and industry.

International Bridge, Tunnel, and Turnpike Assn., *2120 L St. N.W., #305 20037-1527; (202) 659-4620. Fax, (202) 659-0500. Neil D. Schuster, Executive Director. General e-mail, ibtta@ibtta.org. Web, www.ibtta.org.*

Membership: public and private operators of toll facilities and associated industries. Conducts research; compiles statistics.

International Road Federation, *1010 Massachusetts Ave. N.W., #410 20001; (202) 371-5544. Fax, (202) 371-5565. Gerald P. Shea, Director General. General e-mail, info@irfnet.org. Web, www.irfnet.org.*

Membership: road associations and automobile construction and related industries. Administers fellowship program that allows foreign engineering students to study at U.S. graduate schools. Maintains interest in roads and highways worldwide.

Road Information Program, *1726 M St. N.W., #401 20036; (202) 466-6706. Fax, (202) 785-4722. William M. Wilkins, Executive Director. General e-mail, wilkins@tripnet.org. Web, www.tripnet.org.*

Organization of transportation specialists; conducts research on economic and technical transportation issues; promotes consumer awareness of the condition of the national road and bridge system.

Manufacturing and Sales

AGENCIES

International Trade Administration *(Commerce Dept.), Automotive Affairs, 14th St. and Constitution Ave. N.W., #4036 20230; (202) 482-0554. Fax, (202) 482-0674. Henry P. Misisco, Director. Web, www.ita.doc.gov/auto.*

Promotes the export of U.S. automotive products; compiles and analyzes auto industry data; seeks to secure a favorable position for the U.S. auto industry in global markets through policy and trade agreements.

NONPROFIT

American Automotive Leasing Assn., *700 13th St. N.W., #950 20005; (202) 393-7292. Fax, (202) 393-7293.*

Mary T. Tavenner, Executive Director. General e-mail, amautolsg@aol.com.

Membership: automotive commercial fleet leasing and management companies. Monitors legislation and regulations.

American Car Rental Assn., *11250-8 Roger Bacon Dr., #8, Reston, VA 20190; (703) 234-4148. Fax, (703) 435-4390. William H. Drohan, Director. Web, www.acra.org.*

Membership: companies involved in the short-term renting of automobiles. Acts as liaison with legislative bodies and regulatory agencies. Maintains information clearinghouse and membership directory.

American International Automobile Dealers Assn., *99 Canal Center Plaza, #500, Alexandria, VA 22314; (703) 519-7800. Fax, (703) 519-7810. Walter E. Huizenga, President. Web, www.aiada.org.*

Promotes a free market for international nameplate automobiles in the United States. Monitors legislation and regulations.

Assn. of International Automobile Manufacturers, *1001 N. 19th St., #1200, Arlington, VA 22209; (703) 525-7788. Fax, (703) 525-8817. Philip A. Hutchinson Jr., President. Web, www.aiam.org.*

Membership: importers of cars and automotive equipment. Serves as an information clearinghouse on import regulations at the state and federal levels.

Automotive Aftermarket Industry Assn., *4600 East-West Hwy., #300, Bethesda, MD 20814; (301) 654-6664. Fax, (301) 654-3299. Gene Gardner, President. Web, www.aftermarket.org.*

Membership: domestic and international manufacturers, manufacturers' representatives, retailers, and distributors in the automotive aftermarket industry, which involves service of a vehicle after it leaves the dealership. Offers educational programs, conducts research, and provides members with technical and international trade services; acts as liaison with government; sponsors annual marketing conference and trade shows.

Automotive Parts Rebuilders Assn., *4401 Fair Lakes Court, #210, Fairfax, VA 22033; (703) 968-2772. Fax, (703) 968-2878. William C. Gager, President. General e-mail, mail@apra.org. Web, www.apra.org.*

Membership: rebuilders of automotive parts. Conducts educational programs on transmission, brake, clutch, water pump, air conditioning, electrical parts, heavy-duty brake, and carburetor rebuilding.

Automotive Recyclers Assn., *3975 Fair Ridge Dr., #20 Terrace Level North, Fairfax, VA 22033-2924; (703) 385-*

1001. Fax, (703) 385-1494. William P. Steinkuller, Executive Vice President. Web, www.autorecyc.org.

Membership: retail and wholesale firms selling recycled auto and truck parts. Works to increase the efficiency of businesses in the automotive recycling industry. Cooperates with public and private agencies to encourage further automotive recycling efforts.

Electronic Industries Alliance, *2500 Wilson Blvd., #400, Arlington, VA 22201-3834; (703) 907-7500. Fax, (703) 907-7501. Dave McCurdy, President. Web, www. eia.org.*

Membership: manufacturers, dealers, installers, and distributors of consumer electronics products. Provides consumer information and data on industry trends; advocates an open market. Monitors legislation and regulations.

International Tire and Rubber Assn., Government Affairs, Washington Office, *1707 Pepper Tree Court, Bowie, MD 20721; (301) 577-5040. Fax, (301) 731-0039. Roy Littlefield, Director.*

Membership: manufacturers, distributors, and retailers of retreaded tires. Interests include environmental and small-business issues and quality control in the industry. Promotes government procurement of retreaded tires. Monitors legislation and regulations. (Headquarters in Louisville, Ky.)

Japan Automobile Manufacturers Assn., Washington Office, *1050 17th St. N.W., #410 20036; (202) 296-8537. Fax, (202) 872-1212. William C. Duncan, General Director. Web, www.japanauto.com.*

Membership: Japanese motor vehicle manufacturers. Interests include energy, market, trade, and environmental issues. (Headquarters in Tokyo.)

National Automobile Dealers Assn., *8400 Westpark Dr., McLean, VA 22102-3591; (703) 821-7000. Fax, (703) 821-7075. Frank E. McCarthy, President. General e-mail, nada@nada.org. Web, www.nada.org.*

Membership: domestic and imported franchised new car and truck dealers. Publishes the *National Automobile Dealers Used Car Guide* (Blue Book).

Recreation Vehicle Dealers Assn. of North America, *3930 University Dr., Fairfax, VA 22030-2515; (703) 591-7130. Fax, (703) 591-0734. Michael A. Molino, President. Information, (800) 336-0355. General e-mail, rvda@ aol.com. Web, www.rvda.org.*

Serves as liaison between the recreation vehicle industry and government; interests include government regulation of safety, trade, warranty, and franchising; provides members with educational services; works to improve service standards for consumers.

Recreation Vehicle Industry Assn., *1896 Preston White Dr., Reston, VA 20191 (mailing address: P.O. Box 2999, Reston, VA 20195-0999); (703) 620-6003. Fax, (703) 620-5071. David J. Humphreys, President. General e-mail, rvia@rvia.org. Web, www.rvia.org.*

Membership: manufacturers of recreation vehicles and their suppliers. Compiles shipment statistics and other technical data; provides consumers and the media with information on the industry. Assists members' compliance with American National Standards Institute requirements for recreation vehicles. Monitors legislation and regulations.

Tire Assn. of North America, *11921 Freedom Dr., #550, Reston, VA 20190; (703) 736-8082. Fax, (703) 904-4339. David Poisson, Executive Vice President. Web, www. tana.net.*

Membership: independent tire dealers and retreaders. Conducts seminars and market research. Monitors federal and state legislation and regulations.

Truck Renting and Leasing Assn., *1725 Duke St., #600, Alexandria, VA 22314-3457; (703) 299-9120. Fax, (703) 299-9115. J. Michael Payne, President. Web, www. trala.org.*

Membership: truck renting and leasing companies and system suppliers to the industry. Acts as liaison with legislative bodies and regulatory agencies. Interests include federal motor carrier safety issues, highway funding, operating taxes and registration fees at the state level, and uniformity of state taxes.

Truck Trailer Manufacturers Assn., *1020 Princess St., Alexandria, VA 22314; (703) 549-3010. Fax, (703) 549-3014. Richard P. Bowling, President. Web, www.ttmanet.org.*

Membership: truck trailer manufacturing and supply companies. Serves as liaison between its members and government agencies; works to improve safety standards and industry efficiency.

Union of Needletrades Industrial and Textile Employees, Washington Office, *888 16th St. N.W., #303 20006; (202) 347-7417. Fax, (202) 347-0708. Ann Hoffman, Legislative Director. General e-mail, stopsweatshops@ uniteunion.org. Web, www.uniteunion.org.*

Membership: approximately 285,000 workers in basic apparel and textiles, millinery, shoe, laundry, retail, and related industries; and in auto parts and auto supply. Assists members with contract negotiation and grievances; conducts training programs and workshops. Monitors legislation and regulations. (Headquarters in New York; affiliated with the AFL-CIO.)

United Auto Workers, Washington Office, *1757 N St. N.W. 20036; (202) 828-8500. Fax, (202) 293-3457.*

Stephen P. Yokich, President. Toll-free, (800) 243-8829; in Canada, (800) 387-0538. Web, www.uaw.org.

Membership: approximately 775,000 active and 500,000 retired North American workers in aerospace, automotive, defense, manufacturing, steel, technical, and other industries. Assists members with contract negotiation and grievances; conducts training programs and workshops. Monitors legislation and regulations. (Headquarters in Detroit; affiliated with the AFL-CIO.)

Traffic Safety

See also Beverages (chap. 2)

AGENCIES

Federal Motor Carrier Safety Administration *(Transportation Dept.), 400 7th St. S.W., #3419 20590; (202) 366-2519. Fax, (202) 366-7298. Julie Anna Cirillo, Deputy Administrator (Acting). Web, www.fmcsa.dot.gov.*

Develops roadway safety standards, including standards for traffic control systems and devices. Administers program to make safety improvements to highways. Monitors the federal and state Motor Carrier Safety Assistance programs to improve commercial vehicle safety on U.S. highways.

Federal Motor Carrier Safety Administration *(Transportation Dept.), Bus and Truck Safety Operations, 400 7th St. S.W., #3107 20590; (202) 366-1790. Fax, (202) 366-8842. John MacGowan, Director (Acting). Web, www.fmcsa.dot.gov.*

Interprets and disseminates national safety regulations regarding commercial drivers' qualifications, maximum hours of service, accident reporting, and transportation of hazardous materials. Sets minimum levels of financial liability for trucks and buses. Responsible for Commercial Driver's License Information Program.

Federal Highway Administration *(Transportation Dept.), Operations: Core Business Unit, 400 7th St. S.W., #3401, HOP-1 20590; (202) 366-0408. Fax, (202) 366-3302. Christine M. Johnson, Program Manager.*

Fosters the efficient operation of streets and highways. Facilitates the deployment of transportation management and traveler information ITS technologies. Includes offices of Travel Management, Operations Technology Services, Freight Management and Operations, and Intelligent Transportation Systems ITS.

National Highway Traffic Safety Administration *(Transportation Dept.), 400 7th St. S.W., #5220 20590; (202) 366-1836. Fax, (202) 366-2106. Rosalyn G. Mill-*

man, Administrator (Acting). Information, (202) 366-9550. Toll-free 24-hour hotline, (800) 424-9393; in Washington, (202) 366-0123. Web, www.nhtsa.dot.gov.

Implements motor vehicle safety programs; issues federal motor vehicle safety standards; conducts testing programs to determine compliance with these standards; funds local and state motor vehicle and driver safety programs; conducts research on motor vehicle development, equipment, and auto and traffic safety. The Auto Safety Hotline provides safety information and handles consumer problems and complaints involving safety-related defects.

National Highway Traffic Safety Administration *(Transportation Dept.), Motor Vehicle Safety Research Advisory Committee, 400 7th St. S.W. 20590; (202) 366-1537. Fax, (202) 366-5930. Raymond Owings, Chair (Acting).*

Serves as an independent source of ideas for motor vehicle safety research; provides the National Highway Traffic Safety Administration with information and recommendations.

National Highway Traffic Safety Administration *(Transportation Dept.), National Driver Register, 400 7th St. S.W., #6124 20590; (202) 366-4800. Fax, (202) 366-2746. W. P. Bill Holden, Chief.*

Maintains and operates the National Driver Register, a program in which states exchange information on motor vehicle driving records to ensure that drivers with suspended licenses in one state cannot obtain licenses in any other state.

National Transportation Safety Board, *Highway Safety, 490 L'Enfant Plaza East S.W., HS-1 20594; (202) 314-6440. Fax, (202) 314-6406. Joseph G. Osterman, Director.*

In cooperation with states, investigates selected highway transportation accidents to compile the facts upon which the board determines probable cause; works to prevent similar recurrences; makes recommendations on matters pertaining to highway safety and accident prevention.

NONPROFIT

AAA Foundation for Traffic Safety, *1440 New York Ave. N.W., #201 20005; (202) 638-5944. Fax, (202) 638-5943. David K. Willis, President. Fulfillment, (800) 305-7233. Web, www.aaafts.org/aaa.*

Sponsors "human factor" research on traffic safety issues, including bicycle and pedestrian safety; supplies traffic safety educational materials to elementary and secondary schools, commercial driving schools, law enforcement agencies, motor vehicle administrations, and programs for older drivers.

Advocates for Highway and Auto Safety, *750 1st St. N.E., #901 20002; (202) 408-1711. Fax, (202) 408-1699. Judith Lee Stone, President. General e-mail, advocates@ saferoads.org. Web, www.saferoads.org.*

Coalition of insurers, citizens' groups, and public health and safety organizations. Advocates public policy designed to reduce deaths, injuries, and economic costs associated with motor vehicle crashes and fraud and theft involving motor vehicles. Interests include safety belts and child safety seats, air bags, drunk driving abuse, motorcycle helmets, vehicle crashworthiness, and speed limits. Monitors legislation and regulations.

American Highway Users Alliance, *1776 Massachusetts Ave. N.W., #500 20036; (202) 857-1200. Fax, (202) 857-1220. William D. Fay, President. Web, www.highways. org.*

Membership: companies and associations representing major industry and highway user groups. Develops information, analyzes public policy, and advocates legislation to improve roadway safety and efficiency and to increase the mobility of the American public. (Affiliated with the Roadway Safety Foundation.)

American Trucking Assns., *Safety Policy, 2200 Mill Rd., Alexandria, VA 22314; (703) 838-1847. Fax, (703) 683-1398. David J. Osiecki, Vice President. Web, www. truckline.com.*

Membership: state trucking associations, individual trucking and motor carrier organizations, and related supply companies. Provides information on safety for the trucking industry. Develops safety training programs for motor carriers and drivers.

Center for Auto Safety, *1825 Connecticut Ave., #330 20009; (202) 328-7700. Fax, (202) 387-0140. Clarence M. Ditlow III, Executive Director. Web, www.autosafety.org.*

Public interest organization that receives written consumer complaints against auto manufacturers; monitors federal agencies responsible for regulating and enforcing auto and highway safety rules.

Commercial Vehicle Safety Alliance, *5430 Grosvenor Lane, #130, Bethesda, MD 20814; (301) 564-1623. Fax, (301) 564-0588. Steve Campbell, Executive Director. General e-mail, cvsahq@aol.com. Web, www.cvsa.org.*

Membership: U.S., Canadian, and Mexican officials responsible for administering and enforcing commercial motor carrier safety laws. Works to increase on-highway inspections, prevent duplication of inspections, improve the safety of equipment operated on highways, and improve compliance with hazardous materials transportation regulations.

DANA Foundation, *P.O. Box 1050, Germantown, MD 20875; (301) 540-7295. Joseph Colella, Executive Director.*

Promotes public awareness of child passenger safety issues, including compatibility and proper use of child safety seats.

Institute of Transportation Engineers, *525 School St. S.W., #410 20024-2797; (202) 554-8050. Fax, (202) 863-5486. Thomas W. Brahms, Executive Director. Web, www. ite.org.*

Membership: international professional transportation engineers. Interests include safe and efficient surface transportation; provides professional and scientific information on transportation standards and recommended practices.

Insurance Institute for Highway Safety, *1005 N. Glebe Rd., Arlington, VA 22201; (703) 247-1600. Fax, (703) 247-1678. Brian O'Neill, President. Web, www. highwaysafety.org.*

Membership: property and casualty insurance associations and individual insurance companies. Conducts research and provides data on highway safety; seeks ways to reduce losses from vehicle crashes. (Affiliated with Highway Loss Data Institute.)

Mothers Against Drunk Driving, *Washington Office, 1001 G St. N.W., #400 East 20001; (202) 638-3735. Fax, (202) 638-3516. Tom Howarth, Washington Contact. General e-mail, peyser@ix.netcom.com.*

Works to increase public awareness of the problem of drunk driving; advocates strict enforcement of drunk driving laws; operates sobriety checkpoints; supports victims of drunk driving offenses. Monitors legislation and regulations. (Headquarters in Irving, Texas.)

National Assn. of Governors' Highway Safety Representatives, *750 1st St. N.E., #720 20002-4241; (202) 789-0942. Fax, (202) 789-0946. Barbara L. Harsha, Executive Director. Web, www.naghsr.org.*

Membership: state officials who manage highway safety programs. Maintains information clearinghouse on state highway safety programs; interprets technical data concerning highway safety. Represents the states in policy debates on national highway safety issues.

National Commission Against Drunk Driving, *1900 L St. N.W., #705 20036; (202) 452-6004. Fax, (202) 223-7012. John V. Moulden, President. General e-mail, ncadd@trafficsafety.org. Web, www.ncadd.com.*

Works to increase public awareness of the problem of drunk and impaired drivers, especially repeat offenders. Administers worksite traffic safety programs for corporate managers. Monitors the implementation of recommendations made by the Presidential Commission Against Drunk Driving.

National Crash Analysis Center *(George Washington University),* *20101 Academic Way, Ashburn, VA 20147; (703) 726-8362. Fax, (703) 726-8359. Azim Eskandarian, Director. Web, gwuva.gwu.edu/ncac.*

Conducts advanced research on transportation safety. Serves as a resource for the transportation research community on all Federal Highway Administration and National Highway Traffic Safety Administration crash test films and documentation. Research interests include biomechanics, crash-related injury, vehicle dynamics, and vehicle-to-object analysis.

National Safety Council, *Public Affairs, Washington Office, 1025 Connecticut Ave. N.W., #1200 20036; (202) 293-2270. Fax, (202) 293-0032. Charles A. Hurley, Executive Director. Web, www.nsc.org.*

Chartered by Congress. Conducts research and provides educational and informational services on highway safety, child passenger safety, and motor vehicle crash prevention; promotes policies to reduce accidental deaths and injuries. Monitors legislation and regulations. (Headquarters in Itasca, Ill.)

National School Transportation Assn., *625 Slaters Lane, #205, Alexandria, VA 22314 (mailing address: P.O. Box 2639, Springfield, VA 22152-2639); (703) 684-3200. Fax, (703) 684-3212. Karen E. Finkel, Executive Director. Web, www.schooltrans.com.*

Membership: private owners who operate school buses on contract, bus manufacturers, and allied companies. Primary area of interest and research is school bus safety.

Network of Employers for Traffic Safety, *1900 L St. N.W., #705 20036; (202) 452-6005. Fax, (202) 223-7012. Kathryn A. Lusby-Treber, Executive Director. Information, (888) 221-0045. General e-mail, nets@trafficsafety.org. Web, www.trafficsafety.org.*

Dedicated to reducing the human and economic cost associated with highway crashes. Helps employers develop and implement workplace highway safety programs. Provides technical assistance.

Roadway Safety Foundation, *1776 Massachusetts Ave. N.W., #500 20036; (202) 857-1200. Fax, (202) 857-1220. William D. Fay, President. Web, www.roadwaysafety.org.*

Conducts highway safety programs to reduce automobile-related accidents and deaths. (Affiliated with American Highway Users Alliance.)

Tire Industry Safety Council, *1400 K St. N.W., #900 20005; (202) 783-1022. Fax, (202) 783-3512. Kristen Udowitz, Director. General e-mail, kristen@rma.org. Web, www.tisc.org.*

Membership: American tire manufacturers. Provides consumers with information on tire care and safety.

United Motorcoach Assn., *113 S. West St., 4th Floor, Alexandria, VA 22314; (703) 838-2929. Fax, (703) 838-2950. Victor S. Parra, Chief Executive Officer. Web, www.uma.org.*

Provides information, offers technical assistance, conducts research, and monitors legislation. Interests include insurance, safety programs, and credit.

See also NATSO, Inc. (p. 677)

RAIL TRANSPORTATION

AGENCIES

Federal Railroad Administration *(Transportation Dept.), 1120 Vermont Ave. 20005 (mailing address: 400 7th St. S.W. 20590); (202) 493-6014. Fax, (202) 493-6009. Jolene M. Molitoris, Administrator. Web, www.fra.dot.gov.*

Develops national rail policies; enforces rail safety laws; administers financial assistance programs available to states and the rail industry; conducts research and development on improved rail safety.

Federal Railroad Administration *(Transportation Dept.), Policy and Program Development, 1120 Vermont Ave. N.W., #7075 20590; (202) 493-6400. Fax, (202) 493-6401. Charles H. White Jr., Associate Administrator.*

Plans, coordinates, and administers activities related to railroad economics, finance, traffic and network analysis, labor management, and transportation planning, as well as intermodal, environmental, emergency response, and international programs.

Federal Railroad Administration *(Transportation Dept.), Railroad Development, 1120 Vermont Ave. N.W., 6th Floor 20005 (mailing address: 400 7th St. S.W., MS-20 20590); (202) 493-6381. Fax, (202) 493-6330. Arrigo Montini, Associate Administrator (Acting).*

Administers federal assistance programs for national, regional, and local rail services, including freight service assistance, service continuation, and passenger service.

Conducts research and development on new rail technologies.

Federal Railroad Administration *(Transportation Dept.), Safety, 1120 Vermont Ave. N.W., 6th Floor 20005 (mailing address: 400 7th St. S.W., #25 20590); (202) 493-6300. Fax, (202) 493-6309. George A. Gavalla, Associate Administrator. Web, www.fra.dot.gov/safindex.htm.*

Administers and enforces federal laws and regulations that promote railroad safety, including track maintenance, inspection and equipment standards, operating practices, and transportation of explosives and other hazardous materials. Conducts inspections and reports on railroad equipment facilities and accidents.

National Mediation Board, *1301 K St. N.W., #250E 20572; (202) 692-5000. Fax, (202) 692-5080. Stephen E. Crable, Chief of Staff, (202) 692-5030; Ernest DuBester, Chair. Information, (202) 692-5050. TTY, (202) 692-5001.*

Mediates labor disputes in the railroad industry; determines and certifies labor representatives in the industry.

National Railroad Passenger Corp., *60 Massachusetts Ave. N.E. 20002; (202) 906-3000. Fax, (202) 906-3865. George D. Warrington, President. Press, (202) 906-3860. Consumer relations/complaints, (202) 906-2121; travel and ticket information, (800) 872-7245. Web, www. amtrak.com.*

Quasi-public corporation created by the Rail Passenger Service Act of 1970 to improve and develop intercity passenger rail service.

National Transportation Safety Board, *Railroad Safety, 490 L'Enfant Plaza East S.W. 20594; (202) 314-6430. Fax, (202) 314-6497. Robert C. Lauby, Director.*

Investigates passenger train accidents, including rapid rail transit and rail commuter systems, and freight rail accidents with substantial damage to determine probable cause; investigates all employee and passenger fatalities; makes recommendations on rail transportation safety and accident prevention.

Railroad Retirement Board, *Legislative Affairs, Washington Office, 1310 G St. N.W., #500 20005-3004; (202) 272-7742. Fax, (202) 272-7728. Marian Powers Gibson, Director.*

Assists congressional offices with inquiries on retirement, spouse, survivor, and unemployment benefits for railroad employees and retirees. Assists with legislation. (Headquarters in Chicago.)

Surface Transportation Board *(Transportation Dept.), 1925 K St. N.W. 20423-0001; (202) 565-1500. Fax,*

(202) 565-9004. Linda J. Morgan, Chair; Wayne Burkes, Vice Chair. Web, www.stb.dot.gov.

Regulates rail rate disputes, railroad consolidations, rail line construction proposals, line abandonments, rail car service, and motor carrier undercharge cases.

Surface Transportation Board *(Transportation Dept.), Congressional and Public Services, 1925 K St. N.W. 20423-0001; (202) 565-1592. Fax, (202) 565-9016. Dan King, Director. Web, www.stb.dot.gov.*

Informs members of Congress, the public, and the media of board actions. Prepares testimony for hearings; comments on proposed legislation; assists the public in matters involving transportation regulations.

U.S. Coast Guard *(Transportation Dept.), 2100 2nd St. S.W. 20593-0001; (202) 267-2390. Fax, (202) 267-4158. Adm. James M. Loy, Commandant. Information, (202) 267-1587. Web, www.uscg.mil.*

Regulates the construction, maintenance, and operation of bridges across U.S. navigable waters, including railway bridges.

CONGRESS

House Appropriations Committee, *Subcommittee on Transportation, 2358 RHOB 20515; (202) 225-2141. Rep. Frank R. Wolf, R-Va., Chair; John T. Blazey, Staff Director. Web, www.house.gov/appropriations.*

Jurisdiction over legislation to appropriate funds for the Federal Railroad Administration, National Railroad Passenger Corp. (Amtrak), and Surface Transportation Board.

House Transportation and Infrastructure Committee, *Subcommittee on Ground Transportation, B376 RHOB 20515; (202) 226-0727. Fax, (202) 226-3475. Rep. Tom Petri, R-Wis., Chair; Glenn Scammel, Counsel. General e-mail, transcomm@mail.house.gov. Web, www.house. gov/transportation.*

Jurisdiction over railroad legislation, including railroad labor and retirement. Oversees operations of the Federal Railroad Administration, the Surface Transportation Board, and the National Railroad Passenger Corp. (Amtrak).

Senate Appropriations Committee, *Subcommittee on Transportation, SD-133 20510; (202) 224-2175. Fax, (202) 224-4401. Sen. Richard C. Shelby, R-Ala., Chair; Wally Burnett, Majority Clerk. Web, appropriations.senate. gov/transportation.*

Jurisdiction over legislation to appropriate funds for the Federal Railroad Administration, the National Railroad Passenger Corp. (Amtrak), and the Surface Transportation Board.

Senate Commerce, Science, and Transportation Committee, *Subcommittee on Surface Transportation and Merchant Marine,* SH-427 20510; (202) 224-4852. Fax, (202) 228-0326. Sen. Kay Bailey Hutchison, R-Texas, Chair; Ann Begeman, Professional Staff Member. Web, commerce.senate.gov.

Jurisdiction over railroad legislation (except railroad labor and retirement); oversees the Federal Railroad Administration, Surface Transportation Board, and National Railroad Passenger Corp. (Amtrak).

Senate Health, Education, Labor, and Pensions Committee, SD-428 20510; (202) 224-5375. Fax, (202) 228-5044. Sen. James M. Jeffords, R-Vt., Chair; Mark Powden, Staff Director. TTY, (202) 224-1975. Web, labor. senate.gov.

Jurisdiction over legislation on railroad labor and retirement.

NONPROFIT

American Short Line Regional Railroad Assn., 1120 G St. N.W., #520 20005-3889; (202) 628-4500. Fax, (202) 628-6430. Frank K. Turner, President. Web, www.aslrra. org.

Membership: independently owned short line railroad systems. Assists members with technical and legal questions; compiles information on laws, regulations, and other matters affecting the industry.

Assn. of American Railroads, 50 F St. N.W., 4th Floor 20001; (202) 639-2100. Fax, (202) 639-2558. Edward R. Hamberger, President. Library, (202) 639-2333. Press, (202) 639-2555. Web, www.aar.org.

Provides information on freight railroad operations, safety and maintenance, economics and finance, management, and law and legislation; conducts research; issues statistical reports. Library open to the public by appointment.

Brotherhood of Maintenance of Way Employees, *Washington Office,* 10 G St. N.E., #460 20002; (202) 638-2135. Fax, (202) 737-3085. Mac A. Fleming, President. Web, www.bmwe.org.

Membership: rail industry workers and others. Assists members with contract negotiation and grievances; conducts training programs and workshops. Monitors legislation and regulations. (Headquarters in Southfield, Mich.; affiliated with the AFL-CIO.)

National Assn. of Railroad Passengers, 900 2nd St. N.E., #308 20002-3557; (202) 408-8362. Fax, (202) 408-8287. Ross B. Capon, Executive Director. Web, www. narprail.org.

Consumer organization. Works to expand and improve U.S. intercity and commuter rail passenger service, increase federal funds for mass transit, ensure fair treatment for rail freight transportation, and address environmental concerns pertaining to mass transit. Opposes subsidies for intercity trucking; works with Amtrak on scheduling, new services, fares, and advertising.

National Assn. of Regulatory Utility Commissioners, 1101 Vermont Ave. N.W., #200 20005; (202) 898-2200. Fax, (202) 898-2213. Charles Gray, Executive Director. Press, (202) 898-2205. Web, www.naruc.org.

Membership: members of federal, state, municipal, and Canadian regulatory commissions that have jurisdiction over motor and common carriers. Interests include railroads.

National Railway Labor Conference, 1901 L St. N.W., #500 20036; (202) 862-7200. Fax, (202) 862-7230. Robert F. Allen, Chair.

Assists member railroad lines with labor matters; negotiates with railroad labor representatives.

Railway Progress Institute, 700 N. Fairfax St., #601, Alexandria, VA 22314; (703) 836-2332. Fax, (703) 548-0058. Robert A. Matthews, President. Web, www.rpi.org.

Membership: railroad and rail rapid transit suppliers. Conducts research on safety and new technology; monitors legislation.

Transportation Communications International Union, 3 Research Pl., Rockville, MD 20850; (301) 948-4910. Fax, (301) 948-1369. Robert A. Scardelletti, President. Web, www.tcunion.org.

Membership: approximately 120,000 railway workers. Assists members with contract negotiation and grievances; conducts training programs and workshops. Monitors legislation and regulations. (Affiliated with the AFL-CIO and Canadian Labour Congress.)

See also Intermodal Assn. of North America (p. 661)

TRANSIT SYSTEMS

AGENCIES

Federal Transit Administration *(Transportation Dept.),* 400 7th St. S.W. 20590; (202) 366-4040. Fax, (202) 366-9854. Nuria I. Fernandez, Administrator (Nominee). Information, (202) 366-4319. Web, www.fta.dot.gov.

Responsible for developing improved mass transportation facilities, equipment, techniques, and methods;

assists state and local governments in financing mass transportation systems.

Federal Transit Administration *(Transportation Dept.), Budget and Policy, 400 7th St. S.W., #9310 20590; (202) 366-4050. Fax, (202) 366-7116. Michael A. Winter, Associate Administrator. Web, www.fta.dot.gov/office/ budget.*

Develops budgets, programs, legislative proposals, and policies for the federal transit program; evaluates program proposals and their potential impact on local communities; coordinates private sector initiatives of the agency.

Federal Transit Administration *(Transportation Dept.), Program Management, 400 7th St. S.W., #9315 20590; (202) 366-4020. Fax, (202) 366-7951. Hiram J. Walker, Associate Administrator. Web, www.fta.dot.gov/ office/program.*

Administers capital planning and operating assistance grants and loan activities; monitors transit projects in such areas as environmental impact, special provisions for the elderly and people with disabilities, efficiency, and investment.

Federal Transit Administration *(Transportation Dept.), Research, Demonstration, and Innovation, 400 7th St. S.W., #9401 20590; (202) 366-4052. Fax, (202) 366-3765. Edward L. Thomas, Associate Administrator. Web, www.fta.dot.gov/office/research.*

Provides industry and state and local governments with contracts, cooperative agreements, and grants for testing, developing, and demonstrating methods of improved mass transportation service and technology. Supports security, safety, and drug control efforts in transit systems.

Maryland Mass Transit Administration, *6 St. Paul St., Baltimore, MD 21202; (410) 767-3943. Fax, (410) 333-3279. Ronald L. Freeland, Administrator; Vacant, Director, Operations, (410) 767-8758. Information, (888) 218-2267. TTY, (410) 539-3497. Wheelchair accessibility, (410) MTA-LIFT. Web, www.mtatransit.com.*

Responsible for mass transit programs in Maryland; provides MARC commuter rail service between Baltimore, Washington, and suburbs in Maryland and West Virginia. (Mailing address for MARC: 5 Amtrak Way, P.O. Box 8718, Baltimore, MD 21240-8718.)

National Transportation Safety Board, *Railroad Safety, 490 L'Enfant Plaza East S.W. 20594; (202) 314-6430. Fax, (202) 314-6497. Robert C. Lauby, Director.*

Investigates passenger train accidents, including rapid rail transit and rail commuter systems, and freight rail accidents with substantial damage to determine probable cause; investigates all employee and passenger fatalities; makes recommendations on rail transportation safety and accident prevention.

Surface Transportation Board *(Transportation Dept.), 1925 K St. N.W. 20423-0001; (202) 565-1500. Fax, (202) 565-9004. Wayne Burkes, Vice Chair; Linda J. Morgan, Chair. Web, www.stb.dot.gov.*

Regulates mergers and through-route requirements for the intercity bus industry.

Virginia Railway Express, *1500 King St., #202, Alexandria, VA 22314; (703) 684-1001. Fax, (703) 684-1313. Stephen T. Roberts, Director of Operations. Information, (703) 684-0400. TTY, (703) 684-0551. Toll-free, (800) 743-3873. General e-mail, gotrains@vre.org. Web, www. vre.org.*

Regional transportation partnership that provides commuter rail service from the northern Virginia suburbs to Alexandria, Arlington, and Washington, D.C.

Washington Metropolitan Area Transit Authority, *600 5th St. N.W. 20001; (202) 962-1234. Fax, (202) 962-1133. Richard A. White, General Manager. Information, (202) 637-7000. Web, www.wmata.com.*

Provides bus and rail transit service to Washington, D.C., and the neighboring Maryland and Virginia communities; assesses and plans for transportation needs. Provides fare, schedule, and route information; promotes accessibility for persons with disabilities and the elderly.

CONGRESS

House Appropriations Committee, *Subcommittee on Transportation, 2358 RHOB 20515; (202) 225-2141. Rep. Frank R. Wolf, R-Va., Chair; John T. Blazey, Staff Director. Web, www.house.gov/appropriations.*

Jurisdiction over legislation to appropriate funds for the Federal Transit Administration and intercity mass transit systems, including the Washington Metropolitan Area Transit Authority.

House Transportation and Infrastructure Committee, *Subcommittee on Ground Transportation, B376 RHOB 20515; (202) 226-0727. Fax, (202) 226-3475. Rep. Tom Petri, R-Wis., Chair; Glenn Scammel, Counsel. General e-mail, transcomm@mail.house.gov. Web, www.house. gov/transportation.*

Jurisdiction over legislation on urban mass transportation and intercity mass transit systems.

Senate Appropriations Committee, *Subcommittee on Transportation, SD-133 20510; (202) 224-2175. Fax, (202) 224-4401. Sen. Richard C. Shelby, R-Ala., Chair;*

Wally Burnett, Majority Clerk. Web, appropriations.senate. gov/transportation.

Jurisdiction over legislation to appropriate funds for the Federal Transit Administration, urban mass transportation, and intercity mass transit systems, including the Washington Metropolitan Area Transit Authority.

Senate Banking, Housing, and Urban Affairs Committee, *SD-534 20510; (202) 224-7391. Fax, (202) 224-5137. Sen. Phil Gramm, R-Texas, Chair; Wayne A. Abernathy, Staff Director. Web, banking.senate.gov.*

Jurisdiction over legislation on urban mass transportation and intercity mass transit systems.

NONPROFIT

Amalgamated Transit Union, *5025 Wisconsin Ave. N.W., 3rd Floor 20016-4139; (202) 537-1645. Fax, (202) 244-7824. Jim La Sala, President. Web, www.cais.net/atu.*

Membership: transit workers in the United States and Canada, including bus, van, subway, and light rail operators; clerks, baggage handlers, and maintenance employees in urban transit, over-the-road, and school bus industries; and municipal workers. Assists members with contract negotiations and grievances; conducts training programs and seminars. Monitors legislation and regulations. (Affiliated with the AFL-CIO.)

American Bus Assn., *1100 New York Ave. N.W., #1050 20005-3934; (202) 842-1645. Fax, (202) 842-0850. Peter J. Pantuso, President. General e-mail, abainfo@buses.org. Web, www.buses.org.*

Membership: intercity privately owned bus companies, state associations, travel/tourism businesses, bus manufacturers, and those interested in the bus industry. Monitors legislation and regulations.

American Public Transportation Assn., *1201 New York Ave. N.W., #400 20005; (202) 898-4000. Fax, (202) 898-4070. William W. Millar, President. Information, (202) 898-4089. Web, www.apta.com.*

Membership: rapid rail and motor bus systems and manufacturers, suppliers, and consulting firms. Compiles data on the industry; promotes research. Monitors legislation and regulations.

Assn. for Commuter Transportation, *1518 K St. N.W., #503 20005; (202) 393-3497. Fax, (202) 638-4833.*

Kenneth Sufka, Executive Director. General e-mail, acthq@ aol.com. Web, tmi.cob.fsu.edu/act.

Membership: corporations, public agencies, transit authorities, transport management associations, vanpool management companies, and individuals. Serves as a clearinghouse for ride-sharing information and materials. Monitors legislation and regulations.

Community Transportation Assn. of America, *1341 G St. N.W., #600 20005; (202) 628-1480. Fax, (202) 737-9197. Dale Marsico, Executive Director. Information, (800) 527-8279. Web, www.ctaa.org.*

Works to improve mobility for the elderly, the poor, and persons with disabilities; concerns include rural, small-city, and specialized transportation.

National Assn. of Railroad Passengers, *900 2nd St. N.E., #308 20002-3557; (202) 408-8362. Fax, (202) 408-8287. Ross B. Capon, Executive Director. Web, www. narprail.org.*

Consumer organization. Works to expand and improve U.S. intercity and commuter rail passenger service, increase federal funds for mass transit, ensure fair treatment for rail freight transportation, and address environmental concerns pertaining to mass transit. Opposes subsidies for intercity trucking; works with Amtrak on scheduling, new services, fares, and advertising.

National Research Council, *Transportation Research Board Library, 2001 Wisconsin Ave. N.W. 20007 (mailing address: 2101 Constitution Ave. N.W. 20418); (202) 334-2989. Fax, (202) 334-2527. Donald Martin, Associate Librarian. Web, www.4.nationalacademies.org/trb.*

Provides information on research projects and publications covering such topics as public transportation technology and management, elderly and disabled passenger needs, and rural transport systems. Fee for services.

United Motorcoach Assn., *113 S. West St., 4th Floor, Alexandria, VA 22314; (703) 838-2929. Fax, (703) 838-2950. Victor S. Parra, Chief Executive Officer. Web, www. uma.org.*

Provides information, offers technical assistance, conducts research, and monitors legislation. Interests include insurance, safety programs, and credit.

20 U.S. Congress and Politics

ACCESS TO CONGRESSIONAL INFORMATION

AGENCIES

National Archives and Records Administration, Federal Register, *800 N. Capitol St., #700 20408; (202) 523-5230. Fax, (202) 523-6866. Frances D. McDonald, Editor-in-Chief. TTY, (202) 523-5229. Public Laws Update Service (PLUS), (202) 523-6641. Web, www.nara.gov/ fedreg/.*

Assigns public law numbers to enacted legislation, executive orders, and proclamations; responds to inquiries on public law numbers; assists inquirers in finding presidential signing or veto messages in the *Weekly Compilation of Presidential Documents* and the *Public Papers of the Presidents* series; compiles slip laws and annual *United States Statutes at Large;* compiles indexes for finding statutory provisions. Operates Public Laws Update Service (PLUS), which provides information by telephone on new legislation. Publications available from the U.S. Government Printing Office.

CONGRESS

Government Printing Office, *Documents, 732 N. Capitol St. N.W. 20402 (mailing address: Superintendent of Documents, Government Printing Office 20402); (202) 512-0571. Fax, (202) 512-1434. Francis J. Buckley Jr., Superintendent. Congressional order desk and publications, (202) 512-1808; fax for orders, (202) 512-2168. Web, www. gpo.gov/su_docs.*

Prints, distributes, and sells congressional documents, prints, public laws, reports, and House calendars. Orders, P.O. Box 371954, Pittsburgh, PA 15250-7954.

House Administration Committee, *1309 LHOB 20515; (202) 225-8281. Fax, (202) 225-9957. Rep. Bill Thomas, R-Calif., Chair; Cathy Abernathy, Staff Director. Web, www.house.gov/cha.*

Jurisdiction over the printing, cost of printing, binding, and distribution of congressional publications; jurisdiction (in conjunction with the Senate Rules and Administration Committee and the Joint Committee on Printing) over the Government Printing Office, executive papers, and depository libraries; jurisdiction over federal election law.

Joint Committee on Printing, *1309 LHOB 20515; (202) 225-8281. Rep. Bill Thomas, R-Calif., Chair; Eric C. Peterson, Staff Director. Web, www.house.gov/jcp.*

Controls arrangement and style of the *Congressional Record;* determines which congressional prints, documents, and reports are inserted; oversees public printing, binding, and distribution of government publications; oversees activities of the Government Printing Office (in conjunction with the House Administration and Senate Rules and Administration committees).

Legislative Resource Center, *Records and Registration, B-106 CHOB 20515; (202) 226-5200. Fax, (202) 226-5208. Bob Cuthriell, Director.*

Maintains and distributes House bills, reports, public laws, and documents to members' offices, committee staffs, and the general public. (Telephone requests are accepted.)

Legislative Resource Center, *Resource and Reference, B-106 CHOB 20515; (202) 226-5200. Fax, (202) 226-5204. Lea Uhre, Manager.*

Conducts historical research. Advises members on the disposition of their records and papers; maintains information on manuscript collections of former members; maintains biographical files on former members. Print publications include *Biographical Directory of the United States Congress, 1774–1989; Guide to Research Collections of Former Members of the United States House of Representatives, 1789–1987; Black Americans in Congress, 1870–1989;* and *Women in Congress, 1917–1989.*

Senate Document Room, *SH-B04 20510; (202) 224-7860. Fax, (202) 228-2815. Linda K. Daniels, Superintendent.*

Maintains and distributes Senate bills, reports, public laws, and documents. (To obtain material send a self-addressed mailing label or fax with request. Telephone requests are not accepted.)

Senate Executive Clerk, *S138 CAP 20510; (202) 224-4341. Fax, (202) 228-3935. Michelle Haynes, Executive Clerk.*

Maintains and distributes copies of treaties submitted to the Senate for ratification; provides information on submitted treaties and nominations. (Shares distribution responsibility with Senate Document Room, [202] 224-7860.)

Senate Historical Office, *SH-201 20510; (202) 224-6900. Fax, (202) 224-5329. Richard Baker, Historian. Web, www.senate.gov.*

Serves as an information clearinghouse on Senate history, traditions, and members. Collects, organizes, and distributes to the public previously unpublished Senate documents; collects and preserves photographs and pictures related to Senate history; conducts an oral history program; advises senators and Senate committees on the disposition of their noncurrent papers and records. Produces publications on the history of the Senate.

Senate Office of Conservation and Preservation, *S410 CAP 20510; (202) 224-4550. Carl Fritter, Bookbinder.*

Develops and coordinates programs related to the conservation and preservation of Senate records and materials for the Secretary of the Senate.

Senate Rules and Administration Committee, *SR-305 20510; (202) 224-6352. Fax, (202) 224-3036. Sen. Mitch McConnell, R-Ky., Chair; Tamara Somerville, Staff Director. Web, rules.senate.gov.*

Jurisdiction (in conjunction with the Joint Committee on Printing) over the Government Printing Office and legislation on printing of and corrections to the *Congressional Record.*

NONPROFIT

White House Correspondents Assn., *1067 National Press Bldg. 20045; (202) 737-2934. Fax, (202) 783-0841. Arlene Dillon, President.*

Membership: reporters who cover the White House. Acts as a link between reporters and White House staff.

NEWS SERVICES

Congressional Quarterly, *1414 22nd St. N.W. 20037; (202) 887-8500. Fax, (202) 728-1863. Robert W. Merry, President. Information, (202) 887-6279. Web, www.cq.com.*

Provides news, analysis, and information on government. Products include the *CQ Weekly; online legislative tracking services; print and electronic news updates; abstracts and full text of the Congressional Record; Campaigns and Elections magazine; the Congressional Staff Directory; and books on Congress. (Affiliated with the St. Petersburg Times.)*

See also Media Contacts in Washington (p. 137)

Congressional Record

The *Congressional Record,* published daily when Congress is in session, is a printed account of proceedings on the floor of the House and Senate. A Daily Digest section summarizes the day's action on the floor and in committees, and lists committee meetings scheduled for the following day. An index is published monthly and at the close of sessions of Congress. Since January 1995, House members have not been allowed to edit their remarks before they appear in the *Record,* but senators retain this privilege. Material not spoken on the floor may be inserted through unanimous consent to revise or extend a speech, and is published in a distinctive typeface. Grammatical, typographical, and technical corrections are also permitted.

CONGRESS

Government Printing Office Main Bookstore, *Congressional Order Desk, 710 N. Capitol St. N.W. 20402 (mailing address: Superintendent of Documents, GPO, P.O. Box 371954, Pittsburgh, PA 15250-7954); (202) 512-1808. Fax, (202) 512-2250. Congressional order desk and publications, (202) 512-1800. Web, www.access.gpo.gov/su_docs.*

Sells copies of and subscriptions to the *Congressional Record.* Orders, P.O. Box 371954, Pittsburgh, PA 15250-7954.

Library of Congress, *Law Library, 101 Independence Ave. S.E., #LM240 20540; (202) 707-5065. Fax, (202) 707-1820. Rubens Medina, Law Librarian. Reading room, (202) 707-5080.*

Copies of the *Congressional Record* are available for reading. Terminals in the reading room provide access to a computer system containing bill digests from the 93rd Congress to date.

NONPROFIT

Martin Luther King Memorial Library, *901 G St. N.W., #400 20001; (202) 727-1101. Fax, (202) 727-1129. Mary E. Raphael, Director. Information, (202) 727-0321. Hours of operation, (202) 727-1111 (recording). Web, www.dclibrary.org.*

Maintains collection of *Congressional Record* paperback volumes (1980 to date), bound volumes (1939–1976), microfilm (1827–1964), and microfiche (1977–1985).

Schedules/Status of Legislation

Information can also be obtained from the **Congressional Record** *(Daily Digest) and from individual congressional committees (see 106th Congress, p. 725)*

CONGRESS

Calendars of the U.S. House of Representatives and History of Legislation, *Senate Document Room, SH-B04 20510; (202) 224-7860. Fax, (202) 228-2815. Linda K. Daniels, Superintendent.*

Issued daily when the House is in session. Provides capsule legislative history of all measures reported by House and Senate committees; provides additional reference material. Subject index included in each Monday edition or in the edition published on the first day the House is in session. (Also available from the House Document Room, B-18 Ford Bldg., 2nd and D Sts. S.W. 20515; [202] 225-3456, and from the Superintendent of Documents, Government Printing Office, Washington, DC 20402; [202] 512-1808.)

House Democratic Cloakroom, *H222 CAP 20515; (202) 225-7330. Barry K. Sullivan, Manager. Recorded messages: House floor action, (202) 225-7400; legislative program, (202) 225-1600.*

Provides information about House floor proceedings.

House Republican Cloakroom, *H223 CAP 20515; (202) 225-7350. Timothy J. Harroun, Manager. Recorded messages: House floor action, (202) 225-7430; legislative program, (202) 225-2020.*

Provides information about House floor proceedings.

Legislative Information Service, *B-106 CHOB 20515; (202) 225-1772. Fax, (202) 226-5208. Deborah Turner, Chief.*

Records, stores, and provides legislative status information on all bills and resolutions pending in Congress. Provides information through LEGIS, a computer-based service, on all legislation introduced since the 96th Congress. Measures that became law (public or private) between the 93rd and 96th Congress are also available.

Legislative Resource Center, *Records and Registration, B-106 CHOB 20515; (202) 226-5200. Fax, (202) 226-5208. Bob Cuthriell, Director.*

Provides videotapes of House floor proceedings.

Library of Congress, *Main Reading Room, 101 Independence Ave. 20540; (202) 707-5522. Fax, (202) 707-1957. Barbara Moreland, Head. Web, www.loc.gov.*

Makes available a computer system containing information on all legislation introduced since the 93rd Congress (1973), arranged by member's name, subject, committee, and bill or resolution number.

Senate Democratic Cloakroom, *S225 CAP 20510; (202) 224-4691. Recorded message: Senate floor action, (202) 224-8541.*

Provides information about Senate floor proceedings.

Senate Republican Cloakroom, *S226 CAP 20510; (202) 224-6191. Recorded message: Senate floor action, (202) 224-8601.*

Provides information about Senate floor proceedings.

NEWS SERVICES

Associated Press, *Washington Office, 2021 K St. N.W., #600 20006; (202) 776-9400. Fax, (202) 776-9570. Sandy Johnson, Bureau Chief. Web, www.wire.ap.org.*

Publishes daybook that lists congressional committee meetings and hearings and their location and subject matter. No fee for listing events in daybook. (Headquarters in New York.)

CQ Daily Monitor, *1414 22nd St. N.W. 20037; (202) 887-6515. Fax, (202) 835-1635. Subscriptions, (202) 887-6258.*

Provides daily news and analysis about Congress; lists daily committee meetings and hearings, complete witness list, floor proceedings, and future scheduled committee meetings and hearings. Fee for services. (A publication of Congressional Quarterly Inc.)

CQ.com on Congress, *1414 22nd St. N.W. 20037; (202) 887-8511. Fax, (202) 728-1863. Subscriptions and demonstrations, (202) 887-6279.*

Provides online congressional news and analysis, including legislative summaries, votes, testimony, and archival and reference materials. Provides hearing and markup schedules, including time and location, meeting agendas, and full witness listings. Fee for services. (Affiliated with Congressional Quarterly Inc.)

United Press International, *1510 H St. N.W., #700 20005; (202) 898-8000. Fax, (202) 898-8057. Web, www.upi.com.*

Wire service that lists congressional committee meetings and hearings, location, and subject matter. Fee for services.

Washington Post, *1150 15th St. N.W. 20071; (202) 334-7410. Information, (202) 334-6000. Web, www.washingtonpost.com.*

Lists congressional committee meetings and hearings, locations, and subject matter. Fee for services.

 CAMPAIGNS AND ELECTIONS

See also Standards of Conduct (this chapter)

AGENCIES

Federal Communications Commission, *Complaints and Political Programming, 445 12th St. S.W., 3rd Floor 20554; (202) 418-1440. Fax, (202) 418-2053. Robert Baker, Chief. Information, (202) 418-0200.*

Handles complaints and inquiries concerning the equal time rule, which requires equal broadcast opportunities for all legally qualified candidates for the same office. Enforces related Communications Act provisions, including the requirement for sponsorship identification of all paid broadcast announcements.

Federal Election Commission, *999 E St. N.W. 20463; (202) 694-1000. Fax, (202) 219-3880. Scott E. Thomas, Chair. Information, (202) 694-1100. Library, (202) 694-*

1600. Press, (202) 694-1220. Toll-free information, (800) 424-9530. Web, www.fec.gov.

Formulates, administers, and enforces policy with respect to the Federal Election Campaign Act of 1971 as amended, including campaign disclosure requirements, contribution and expenditure limitations, and public financing of presidential nominating conventions and campaigns. Receives campaign finance reports; makes rules and regulations; conducts audits and investigations. Serves as an election information clearinghouse. Copies of campaign finance reports available for inspection. Library open to the public.

Federal Election Commission, *Election Administration, 999 E St. N.W., #209 20463; (202) 694-1095. Fax, (202) 219-8500. Penelope Bonsall, Director. Information, (800) 424-9530. Web, www.fec.gov.*

Conducts studies on voter registration, voting procedures, and election administration; serves as an information clearinghouse on election administration; provides information on National Voter Registration Act of 1993; provides updates on performance standards for electronic voting systems; produces research publications, which are available through the Government Printing Office.

Federal Election Commission, *Public Records, 999 E St. N.W., #129 20463; (202) 694-1120. Fax, (202) 501-0693. Patricia Young, Assistant Staff Director. Information, (800) 424-9530. Web, www.fec.gov.*

Makes available for public inspection and copying the detailed campaign finance reports on contributions and expenditures filed by candidates for federal office, their supporting political committees, and individuals and committees making expenditures on behalf of a candidate. Maintains copies of all reports and statements filed since 1972.

Justice Dept., *Election Crimes, 1400 New York Ave. N.W. 20530 (mailing address: P.O. Box 27518, McPherson Station 20038); (202) 514-1421. Fax, (202) 514-3003. Craig C. Donsanto, Director. Web, www.usdoj.gov.*

Supervises enforcement of federal criminal laws related to campaigns and elections. Oversees investigation of deprivation of voting rights; intimidation and coercion of voters; denial or promise of federal employment or other benefits; illegal political contributions, expenditures, and solicitations; and all other election violations referred to the division.

CONGRESS

House Administration Committee, *1309 LHOB 20515; (202) 225-8281. Fax, (202) 225-9957. Rep. Bill*

Thomas, R-Calif., Chair; Cathy Abernathy, Staff Director. Web, www.house.gov/cha.

Jurisdiction over legislation and other matters related to all federal elections, including campaign finance; corrupt practices; contested House elections; voter registration; overseas voters; and broadcast of early election projections. Oversees operations of the Federal Election Commission.

House Appropriations Committee, *Subcommittee on Treasury, Postal Service, and General Government, B307 RHOB 20515; (202) 225-5834. Fax, (202) 225-5895. Rep. Jim Kolbe, R-Ariz., Chair; Michelle Mrdeza, Clerk. Web, www.house.gov/appropriations.*

Jurisdiction over legislation to appropriate funds for the Federal Election Commission.

House Commission on Congressional Mailing Standards, *1338 LHOB 20515; (202) 225-9337. Fax, (202) 226-0047. Rep. Bill Thomas, R-Calif., Chair; Jack Dail, Staff Director.*

Receives complaints, conducts investigations, and issues decisions on disputes arising from the alleged abuse of franked mail by House members.

House Government Reform Committee, *Subcommittee on the District of Columbia, B-349A RHOB 20515; (202) 225-6751. Rep. Thomas M. Davis III, R-Va., Chair; Peter Sirh, Staff Director. Web, www.house.gov/reform.*

Oversight of election laws in the District of Columbia.

House Judiciary Committee, *Subcommittee on the Constitution, H2-362 FHOB 20515; (202) 226-7680. Fax, (202) 225-3746. Rep. Charles T. Canady, R-Fla., Chair; Cathy Cleaver, Chief Counsel. General e-mail, Judiciary@ mail.house.gov. Web, www.house.gov/judiciary.*

Jurisdiction over proposed constitutional amendments related to the electoral college, campaign reform, and presidential succession.

House Ways and Means Committee, *1102 LHOB 20515; (202) 225-3625. Fax, (202) 225-2610. Rep. Bill Archer, R-Texas, Chair; A. L. Singleton, Chief of Staff. Web, www.house.gov/ways_means.*

Jurisdiction over legislation on taxes and credits for public financing of federal elections.

Legislative Resource Center, *Records and Registration, B-106 CHOB 20515; (202) 226-5200. Fax, (202) 226-5208. Bob Cuthriell, Director.*

Receives reports of campaign receipts and expenditures of House candidates and committees. Open for public inspection.

FEDERAL ELECTION COMMISSION

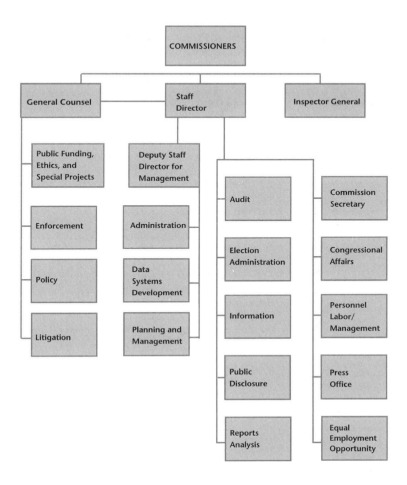

Secretary of the Senate, *Public Records: Campaign Financing,* SH-232 20510; (202) 224-0758. Fax, (202) 224-1851. *Raymond Davis, Chief.*

Receives reports of campaign receipts and expenditures of Senate candidates and committees. Open for public inspection.

Senate Appropriations Committee, *Subcommittee on Treasury and General Government,* SD-188 20510; (202) 224-7337. *Sen. Ben Nighthorse Campbell, R-Colo., Chair; Patricia Raymond, Clerk. Web, appropriations. senate.gov/treasury.*

Jurisdiction over legislation to appropriate funds for the Federal Election Commission.

Senate Finance Committee, *SD-219 20510; (202) 224-4515. Fax, (202) 224-5920. Sen. William V. Roth Jr., R-Del., Chair; Frank Polk, Staff Director. Web, finance.senate.gov.*

Jurisdiction over legislation on taxes and credits for public financing of federal elections.

Senate Governmental Affairs Committee, *Subcommittee on Oversight of Government Management, Restructuring, and the District of Columbia,* SH-601 20510; (202) 224-3682. Fax, (202) 224-3328. *Sen. George V. Voinovich, R-Ohio, Chair; Kristine Simmons, Staff Director. General e-mail, ogm@govt-aff.senate.gov. Web, gov_affairs.senate.gov/ogm.htm.*

Oversight of election laws in the District of Columbia.

Senate Judiciary Committee, *Subcommittee on the Constitution, Federalism, and Property Rights, SD-524 20510; (202) 224-8081. Fax, (202) 228-0544. Sen. John Ashcroft, R-Mo., Chair; Adam Cingoli, Chief Counsel. Web, judiciary.senate.gov/constitu.htm.*

Jurisdiction over proposed constitutional amendments related to the electoral college, campaign reform, and presidential succession.

Senate Rules and Administration Committee, *SR-305 20510; (202) 224-6352. Fax, (202) 224-3036. Sen. Mitch McConnell, R-Ky., Chair; Tamara Somerville, Staff Director. Web, rules.senate.gov.*

Jurisdiction over legislation and other matters related to all federal elections, including presidential succession; campaign finance; corrupt practices; political action committees; election law changes; and broadcast of early election projections. Oversees voter registration by mail and operations of the Federal Election Commission.

NONPROFIT

Alliance for Better Campaigns, *529 14th St. N.W., #320 20045; (202) 879-6755. Fax, (202) 879-6756. Paul Taylor, Executive Director. General e-mail, alliance@ bettercampaigns.org. Web, www.bettercampaigns.org.*

Dedicated to improving the elections process by promoting voluntary, realistic standards of campaign conduct.

American Assn. of Political Consultants, *600 Pennsylvania Ave. S.E., #330 20003; (202) 544-9815. Fax, (202) 544-9816. Raymond Strother, President. General e-mail, aapcmail@aol.com. Web, www.theaapc.org/.*

Membership: political consultants, media specialists, campaign managers, corporate public affairs officers, pollsters, public officials, academicians, fundraisers, lobbyists, and congressional staffers. Focuses on ethics of the profession; provides members with opportunities to meet industry leaders and learn new techniques and emerging technologies.

American Bar Assn., *Standing Committee on Election Law, 740 15th St. N.W. 20005; (202) 662-1692. Fax, (202) 638-3844. Elizabeth M. Yang, Director. Web, www.abanet. org.*

Studies ways to improve the U.S. election and campaign process.

Center for Responsive Politics, *1101 14th St. N.W. 20036; (202) 857-0044. Fax, (202) 857-7809. Larry Makinson, Executive Director. Web, www.opensecrets.org.*

Conducts research on Congress and related issues, with particular interest in campaign finance and congressional operations.

Commission on Presidential Debates, *1200 New Hampshire Ave. N.W., #445 20036; (202) 872-1020. Fax, (202) 783-5923. Frank J. Fahrenkopf Jr., Co-Chair; Paul G. Kirk, Co-Chair.*

Independent, nonpartisan organization established to sponsor general election presidential and vice presidential debates, and to undertake educational and research activities related to the debates.

Common Cause, *1250 Connecticut Ave. N.W., #600 20036; (202) 833-1200. Fax, (202) 659-3716. Scott Harshbarger, President. Press, (202) 736-5770. Web, www. commoncause.org.*

Citizens' legislative interest group. Records and analyzes campaign contributions to congressional candidates and campaign committees, particularly those from political action committees, and soft money contributions to national political parties.

Congressional Accountability Project, *1611 Connecticut Ave. N.W., #3A 20009; (202) 296-2787. Fax, (202) 833-2406. Gary Ruskin, Director. Web, www.essential.org/ orgs/CAP/CAP.html.*

Seeks to reform rules on campaign finance, gifts, pensions, and ethics for members of Congress; advocates free online access to congressional documents; files ethics complaints against individual members of Congress.

Public Campaign, *1320 19th St. N.W., #M1 20036; (202) 293-0222. Fax, (202) 293-0202. Ellen S. Miller, Executive Director. General e-mail, info@publicampaign. org. Web, www.publicampaign.org.*

Grassroots organization interested in campaign finance reform. Supports the Clean Money Campaign, a voluntary program in which candidates receive a set amount of public financing for elections if they reject private money and limit spending.

Election Statistics and Apportionment

AGENCIES

Census Bureau *(Commerce Dept.), Administrative and Customer Services, 4700 Silver Hill Rd., FB3, #1587, Suitland, MD 20746-8500 (mailing address: Customer Service, Bureau of the Census 20233); (301) 457-2155. Fax, (301) 457-2778. Gloria Gutierrez, Chief. Fax after hours (orders only), (301) 457-3842.*

Disseminates census data on counties, municipalities, and other small areas to state legislatures for use in redrawing congressional district boundaries.

Census Bureau *(Commerce Dept.), Population, Suitland and Silver Hill Rds., Suitland, MD 20746; (301) 457-2071. Fax, (301) 457-2644. John F. Long, Chief.*

Computes every ten years the population figures that determine the number of representatives each state may have in the House of Representatives.

CONGRESS

Clerk of the House of Representatives, *H154 CAP 20515; (202) 225-7000. Jeff Trandahl, Clerk. Web, clerkweb.house.gov.*

Publishes biennial compilation of statistics on congressional and presidential elections. Receives population figures compiled by the Census Bureau that form the basis for reapportionment of the House; informs state governors of new apportionment figures.

House Judiciary Committee, *2138 RHOB 20515; (202) 225-3951. Fax, (202) 225-7682. Rep. Henry J. Hyde, R-Ill., Chair; Thomas Mooney, Chief of Staff. General e-mail, Judiciary@mail.house.gov. Web, www.house.gov/judiciary.*

Jurisdiction over reapportionment legislation.

Senate Judiciary Committee, *SD-224 20510; (202) 224-5225. Fax, (202) 224-9102. Sen. Orrin G. Hatch, R-Utah, Chair; Manus Cooney, Chief Counsel. Web, judiciary.senate.gov.*

Jurisdiction over reapportionment legislation.

Senate Rules and Administration Committee, *SR-305 20510; (202) 224-6352. Fax, (202) 224-3036. Sen. Mitch McConnell, R-Ky., Chair; Tamara Somerville, Staff Director. Web, rules.senate.gov.*

Distributes *Senate Election Law Guidebook,* a compilation of Senate campaign information, including federal and state laws governing election to the U.S. Senate. Available from the Senate Document Room.

NONPROFIT

Common Cause, *State Issues Development, 1250 Connecticut Ave. N.W., #600 20036; (202) 833-1200. Fax, (202) 659-3716. Ed Davis, Director. Web, www. commoncause.org.*

Citizens' interest group. Seeks to alter procedures governing redistricting by the establishment of independent redistricting commissions. Serves as an information clearinghouse; provides research and support for regional field offices.

Voting/Political Participation

See also Civil Rights (chap. 1)

NONPROFIT

AARP/VOTE, *601 E St. N.W. 20049; (202) 434-3730. Fax, (202) 434-3745. Molly Daniels, Director. Web, www.aarp. org.*

Nonpartisan voter education program of the American Association of Retired Persons. Maintains nationwide volunteer network that raises issues of concern to older persons in political campaigns.

Arab American Institute, *1600 K St. N.W., #601 20006; (202) 429-9210. Fax, (202) 429-9214. James J. Zogby, President. General e-mail, aai@arab-aai.org. Web, www. aaiusa.org.*

Advocacy group concerned with political issues affecting Arab Americans. Seeks to involve the Arab American community in party politics and the electoral process.

Center for Civic Education, *Government Relations, Washington Office, 1308 19th St. N.W. 20036-1602; (202) 861-8800. Fax, (202) 861-8811. Mark J. Molli, Director. Web, www.civiced.org.*

Fosters the participation in civic life by citizens. Interests include the U.S. Constitution, American political traditions, and the rights and responsibilities of citizens. Develops curriculum and national standards for elementary and secondary school students. (Headquarters in Calabasas, Calif.)

Center for Voting and Democracy, *P.O. Box 60037 20039; (301) 270-4616. Fax, (301) 270-4133. Robert Richie, Executive Director. Information, (202) 828-3062. General e-mail, fairvote@compuserve.com. Web, www. fairvote.org.*

Researches and disseminates information on electoral systems that promote voter participation and fair representation. Supports a broad range of proportional representation systems and reforms in plurality elections. Holds conferences; provides technical assistance to localities.

Coalition of Black Trade Unionists, *1625 L St. N.W. 20036 (mailing address: P.O. Box 66268 20035); (202) 429-1203. Fax, (202) 429-1102. Wil Duncan, Executive Director.*

Monitors legislation affecting African American and other minority trade unionists. Focuses on equal employment opportunity, unemployment, and voter education and registration.

Committee for the Study of the American Electorate, *421 New Jersey Ave. S.E. 20003; (202) 546-3221. Fax, (202) 546-3571. Curtis Gans, Director. Web, www. gspm.org/csae.*

Nonpartisan research group that studies issues involving low and declining American voter participation.

Democracy 21, *1825 Eye St. N.W., #400 20006; (202) 429-2008. Fax, (202) 293-2660. Fred Wertheimer, President. General e-mail, fwertheimer@Democracy21.org.*

Focuses on using the communications revolution to strengthen democracy and on eliminating the influence of big money in American politics.

Democratic National Committee, *Campaign Division, 430 S. Capitol St. S.E. 20003; (202) 863-8000. Fax, (202) 488-5025. Joseph Andrew, National Chair. General e-mail, dnc@democrats.org. Web, www.democrats.org.*

Responsible for electoral activities at the federal, state, and local levels; sponsors workshops to recruit Democratic candidates and to provide instruction in campaign techniques; conducts party constituency outreach programs; coordinates voter registration.

Joint Center for Political and Economic Studies, *1090 Vermont Ave. N.W., #1100 20005-4961; (202) 789-3500. Fax, (202) 789-6390. Eddie N. Williams, President. Web, www.jointctr.org.*

Researches and analyzes issues of concern to African Americans, focusing on economic and social policy issues and African American political participation. Publishes a biannual profile of African American elected officials in federal, state, and local government; holds forums on public policy issues.

Labor Council for Latin American Advancement, *815 16th St. N.W., #310 20006; (202) 347-4223. Fax, (202) 347-5095. Oscar Sanchez, Executive Director. Web, www. lclaa.org.*

Membership: Hispanic trade unionists. Conducts nonpartisan voter registration and education programs; encourages increased participation by Hispanic workers in the political process. (Affiliated with the AFL-CIO.)

League of Women Voters of the United States, *1730 M St. N.W., #1000 20036; (202) 429-1965. Fax, (202) 429-0854. Jane Gruenebaum, Executive Director. Web, www.lwv.org.*

Membership: women and men interested in nonpartisan political action and study. Works to increase participation in government; provides information on voter registration and balloting. Interests include social policy, natural resources, international relations, and representative government.

National Assn. of Latino Elected and Appointed Officials, *Washington Office, 311 Massachusetts Ave. N.E. 20002; (202) 546-2536. Fax, (202) 546-4121. Larry Gonzalez, Director. Web, www.naleo.org.*

Research and advocacy group that provides civic affairs information and assistance on legislation affecting Hispanics. Encourages Hispanic participation in local, state, and national politics. Interests include the health and social, economic, and educational welfare of Hispanics. (Headquarters in Los Angeles.)

National Black Caucus of Local Elected Officials, *c/o National League of Cities, 1301 Pennsylvania Ave. N.W., #550 20004; (202) 626-3169. Fax, (202) 626-3043. Roosevelt Coats, President. Press, (202) 626-3000.*

Membership: elected officials at the local level and other interested individuals. Concerned with issues affecting African Americans, including housing, economics, the family, and human rights.

National Black Caucus of State Legislators, *444 N. Capitol St. N.W., #622 20001; (202) 624-5457. Fax, (202) 508-3826. Ivan Lanier, Executive Director.*

Membership: African American state legislators. Promotes effective leadership among African American state legislators; serves as an information network and clearinghouse for members.

National Coalition on Black Voter Participation, *1629 K St. N.W., #801 20006; (202) 659-4929. Fax, (202) 659-5025. Melanie L. Campbell, Executive Director. General e-mail, ncbvp@hotmail.com. Web, www.bigvote.org.*

Seeks to increase black voter civic participation to eliminate barriers to political participation for African Americans. Sponsors Operation Big Vote, Black Youth Vote, and Black Women's Roundtable that conducts voter education, registration, and get-out-the-vote activities in African American communities. Operates an information resource center. Monitors legislation and regulations.

National Political Congress of Black Women, *8401 Colesville Rd., #400, Silver Spring, MD 20910; (301) 562-8000. Fax, (301) 562-8303. C. DeLores Tucker, Chair. Web, www.npcbw.org.*

Nonpartisan political organization that encourages African American women to participate in the political process. Advocates nonpartisan voter registration and encourages African American women to engage in other political activities. Develops positions and participates in platform development and strategies that address the needs of communities at every level of government.

National Women's Political Caucus, *1630 Connecticut Ave. N.W., #201 20009; (202) 785-1100. Fax, (202) 785-*

3605. Nick Demeter, Political Director; Roselyn O'Connell, President. General e-mail, mailnwpc@aol.com. Web, www. nwpc.org.

Advocacy group that seeks greater involvement of women in politics. Seeks to identify, recruit, and train women for elective and appointive political office, regardless of party affiliation; serves as an information clearinghouse on women in politics, particularly during election campaigns; publishes directory of women holding federal and state offices.

Project Vote, *739 8th St. S.E., #202 20003; (202) 546-3492. Fax, (202) 546-2483. Zachary Polett, Executive Director.*

Civic organization that registers low-income and minority individuals and educates them on the power of the vote.

Republican National Committee, *Political Operations, 310 1st St. S.E. 20003; (202) 863-8600. Fax, (202) 863-8657. David Israelite, Director. Web, www.rnc.org.*

Responsible for electoral activities at the federal, state, and local levels; operates party constituency outreach programs; coordinates voter registration.

 CAPITOL

Capitol switchboard, (202) 224-3121. See also 106th Congress (p. 725) for each member's office.

CONGRESS

Architect of the Capitol, *SB15 CAP 20515; (202) 228-1793. Fax, (202) 228-1893. Alan M. Hantman, Architect. Web, www.aoc.gov.*

Maintains the Capitol and its grounds, the House and Senate office buildings, Capitol power plant, Robert A. Taft Memorial, and buildings and grounds of the Supreme Court and the Library of Congress; operates the Botanic Garden and Senate restaurants. Acquires property and plans and constructs buildings for Congress, the Supreme Court, and the Library of Congress. Assists in deciding which artwork, historical objects, and exhibits are to be accepted for display in the Capitol. Flag office flies American flags over the Capitol at legislators' request.

Architect of the Capitol, *Office of the Curator, HT3 CAP 20515; (202) 228-1222. Fax, (202) 228-4602. Barbara A. Wolanin, Curator. Press, (202) 228-1205. Web, www.aoc.gov.*

Preserves artwork; maintains collection of drawings, photographs, and manuscripts on and about the Capitol and the House and Senate office buildings. Maintains records of the architect of the Capitol. Library open to the public.

Capitol Police, *119 D St. N.E. 20510; (202) 224-9806. Fax, (202) 228-2592. Gary L. Abrecht, Chief.*

Responsible for security for the Capitol, House and Senate office buildings, and Botanic Garden; approves demonstration permits.

House Administration Committee, *1309 LHOB 20515; (202) 225-8281. Fax, (202) 225-9957. Rep. Bill Thomas, R-Calif., Chair; Cathy Abernathy, Staff Director. Web, www.house.gov/cha.*

Responsible for all matters related to security of the House office buildings and the House wing of the Capitol; jurisdiction over operations of the Botanic Garden, Library of Congress, Smithsonian Institution, and Capitol art collection (in conjunction with the Joint Committee on the Library).

House Appropriations Committee, *Subcommittee on Legislative Branch, H147 CAP 20515; (202) 225-5338. Rep. Charles H. Taylor, R-N.C., Chair; Edward E. Lombard, Staff Assistant. Web, www.house.gov/appropriations.*

Jurisdiction over legislation to appropriate funds for the House of Representatives, the Architect of the Capitol (except Senate items), the Botanic Garden, the Library of Congress, and House offices.

House Office Building Commission, *H232 CAP 20515; (202) 225-0600. Fax, (202) 226-0337. Rep. J. Dennis Hastert, R-Ill., Chair; Ted Van Der Meid, Staff Contact.*

Studies and approves all matters related to construction and alterations of House office buildings. Assigns office space to House committees.

House Transportation and Infrastructure Committee, *Subcommittee on Economic Development, Public Buildings, Hazardous Materials, Pipeline Transportation, 586 FHOB 20515; (202) 225-3014. Fax, (202) 226-1898. Rep. Bob Franks, R-N.J., Chair; Richard C. Barnett, Staff Director. General e-mail, transcomm@mail.house. gov. Web, www.house.gov/transportation.*

Jurisdiction over legislation relating to the Capitol and House office buildings, including naming of buildings and facilities. Oversees planning, construction, renovation, maintenance, and care of the grounds and buildings of the Capitol, House, Library of Congress, and Botanic Garden (in conjunction with the Joint Committee on the Library). Participates with other House committees in the oversight of security.

Joint Committee on the Library of Congress, *SR-305 20510; (202) 224-6352. Sen. Ted Stevens, R-Alaska, Chair; Ed Edens, Staff Contact.*

Oversees the placing of all works of art in the Capitol (in conjunction with the House Administration and Senate Rules and Administration committees); oversees development and maintenance of the Botanic Garden and the Library of Congress (in conjunction with the House Transportation and Infrastructure and Senate Rules and Administration committees).

Senate Appropriations Committee, *Subcommittee on Legislative Branch, S125 CAP 20510; (202) 224-8921. Sen. Robert F. Bennett, R-Utah, Chair; Christine Ciccone, Staff Director. Web, appropriations.senate.gov/leg.*

Jurisdiction over legislation to appropriate funds for the Senate, the Architect of the Capitol (except House items), the Botanic Garden, the Library of Congress, and Senate offices.

Senate Commission on Art, *S411 CAP 20510-7102; (202) 224-2955. Fax, (202) 224-8799. Sen. Trent Lott, R-Miss., Chair; Diane K. Skvarla, Curator of the Senate. Web, www.senate.gov/learning/learn_art_about.html.*

Accepts artwork and historical objects for display in Senate office buildings and the Senate wing of the Capitol. Maintains and exhibits Senate collections (paintings, sculpture, furniture, and manuscripts); oversees and maintains old Senate and Supreme Court chambers.

Senate Rules and Administration Committee, *SR-305 20510; (202) 224-6352. Fax, (202) 224-3036. Sen. Mitch McConnell, R-Ky., Chair; Tamara Somerville, Staff Director. Web, rules.senate.gov.*

Responsible for all matters related to the Senate office buildings, including oversight of alterations, and the Senate wing of the Capitol; jurisdiction over authorization of funds for constructing and acquiring additional office space; oversees the maintenance and care of the grounds and buildings of the Botanic Garden and the Library of Congress and the placement of all works of art in the Capitol (in conjunction with the Joint Committee on the Library). Assigns office space to Senate members and committees.

Superintendent of the House Office Buildings, *B341 RHOB 20515; (202) 225-4141. Fax, (202) 225-3003. Robert R. Miley, Superintendent.*

Oversees construction, maintenance, and operation of House office buildings; assigns office space to House members under rules of procedure established by the Speaker's office and the House Office Building Commission.

Superintendent of the Senate Office Buildings, *SD-G45 20510; (202) 224-3141. Fax, (202) 224-0652. Larry R. Stoffel, Superintendent.*

Oversees construction, maintenance, and operation of Senate office buildings.

U.S. Botanic Garden, *245 1st St. S.W. 20024; (202) 225-8333. Fax, (202) 225-1561. Vacant, Executive Director. Web, www.aoc.gov/pages/usbgpage.htm.*

Collects, cultivates, and grows various plants for public display and study.

NONPROFIT

U.S. Capitol Historical Society, *200 Maryland Ave. N.E. 20002; (202) 543-8919. Fax, (202) 544-8244. Ron Sarasin, President. Information, (800) 887-9318. Library, (202) 543-8919, ext. 27. General e-mail, uschs@uschs.org. Web, www.uschs.org.*

Membership: members of Congress, individuals, and organizations interested in the preservation of the history and traditions of the U.S. Capitol. Conducts historical research; offers tours, lectures, and films; maintains information centers in the Capitol; publishes an annual historical calendar.

Tours and Events

CONGRESS

The House and Senate public galleries are open daily from 9:00 a.m.– 4:30 p.m. (Hours are extended when chamber is in session.) Free gallery passes are available from any congressional office.

Capitol Guide Service, *S102 20510; (202) 224-3235. Ted Daniel, Director; David Hauck, Assistant Director, (202) 224-4048. TTY, (202) 224-4049. Visitor information, (202) 225-6827.*

Offers the general public free guided tours of the interior of the U.S. Capitol. For accommodations for visitors with special needs.

Capitol Police, *Protective Services, 119 D St. N.E., #102 20510; (202) 224-9825. Fax, (202) 228-2429. Steven D. Bahrns, Deputy Chief.*

Handles administrative and protective aspects of all special events held on the Capitol grounds. Accepts applications for demonstration permits and for visiting musical performances and submits them to the police board for approval. Coordinates all VIP arrivals.

Sergeant at Arms of the Senate, *S321 CAP 20510-7200; (202) 224-2341. Fax, (202) 224-7690. James W. Ziglar, Sergeant at Arms; Loretta Symms, Deputy Sergeant at Arms.*

Enforces rules and regulations of the Senate public gallery. Approves visiting band performances on the Senate steps; to arrange for performances, contact your senator.

NONPROFIT

U.S. Capitol Historical Society, *200 Maryland Ave. N.E. 20002; (202) 543-8919. Fax, (202) 544-8244. Ron Sarasin, President. Information, (800) 887-9318. Library, (202) 543-8919, ext. 27. General e-mail, uschs@uschs.org. Web, www.uschs.org.*

Offers tours, lectures, and films; maintains information centers in the Capitol.

🏛 CAUCUSES: ORGANIZATIONS OF MEMBERS

HOUSE AND SENATE

Ad Hoc Congressional Committee on Irish Affairs, *403 CHOB 20515; (202) 225-7896. Fax, (202) 226-2279. Rep. Peter T. King, R-N.Y., Co-Chair; Rep. Benjamin A. Gilman, R-N.Y., Co-Chair; Rep. Joseph Crowley, D-N.Y., Co-Chair; Rep. Richard E. Neal, D-Mass., Co-Chair; Robert F. O'Connor, Staff Contact.*

California Democratic Congressional Delegation, *1221 LHOB 20515; (202) 225-2861. Fax, (202) 226-6791. Sherry Greenberg, Staff Contact; Rep. Sam Farr, D-Calif., Chair.*

Commission on Security and Cooperation in Europe *(Helsinki Commission), 234 FHOB 20515; (202) 225-1901. Fax, (202) 226-4199. Rep. Christopher H. Smith, R-N.J., Chair; Sen. Ben Nighthorse Campbell, R-Colo., Co-Chair; Ronald McNamara, Deputy Chief of Staff. Web, www.house.gov/csce.*

Congressional Arts Caucus, *2347 RHOB 20515; (202) 225-3615. Fax, (202) 225-7822. Rep. Louise M. Slaughter, D-N.Y., Chair; Andrew Bernstein, Staff Contact.*

Congressional Asian Pacific American Caucus, *2418 RHOB 20515; (202) 225-1188. Fax, (202) 226-0341. Del. Robert A. Underwood, D-Guam, Chair; Jeannine R. Aguon, Legislative Assistant.*

Congressional Black Caucus, *319 CHOB 20515; (202) 225-3315. Fax, (202) 225-2313. Rep. James E. Clyburn, D-S.C., Chair; Danny Cromer, Legislative Director.*

Congressional Competitiveness Caucus, *c/o CELI, 201 Massachusetts Ave. N.E., #C-8 20002; (202) 546-5007.*

Fax, (202) 546-7037. Sen. Max Baucus, D-Mont., Co-Chair; Sen. Charles E. Grassley, R-Iowa, Co-Chair; Sen. Jeff Bingaman, D-N.M., Co-Chair; Sen. Gordon H. Smith, R-Ore., Co-Chair; Rep. Marcy Kaptur, D-Ohio, Co-Chair; Rep. Jim Kolbe, R-Ariz., Co-Chair; Joleen L. Worsley, Staff Contact. Web, www.celi.org/caucus.htm.

Congressional Fire Services Caucus, *SH-104 20510; (202) 224-2441. Sen. William V. Roth Jr., R-Del., Chair; Rob Book, Staff Contact.*

Congressional Fire Services Institute, *900 2nd St. N.E., #303 20002; (202) 371-1277. Fax, (202) 682-3473. Sen. William V. Roth Jr., R-Del., Chair; William Webb, Executive Director.*

Congressional Grace Caucus, *2402 RHOB 20515; (202) 225-5611. Fax, (202) 225-9177. Rep. Christopher Cox, R-Calif., Chair; Peter M. Uhlmann, Legislative Director.*

Bipartisan coalition; focuses on recommendations made by the Grace commission (President's Private Sector Survey on Cost Control) and other commissions.

Congressional Hispanic Caucus, *2435 RHOB 20515; (202) 225-2410. Fax, (202) 226-0350. Rep. Lucille Roybal-Allard, D-Calif., Chair; Selena Walsh, Executive Director.*

Congressional Task Force on International HIV/AIDS, *1035 LHOB 20515; (202) 225-3106. Fax, (202) 225-6197. Rep. Jim McDermott, D-Wash., Chair; Christopher Dunn, Staff Contact.*

Studies the spread of HIV/AIDS in the developing world; helps plan the U.S. government response.

Fine Arts Board, *SH-522 20510; (202) 224-3004. Fax, (202) 224-2354. Sen. Ted Stevens, R-Alaska, Vice Chair; Liz Connell, Staff Contact.*

Flat Tax Caucus, *301 CHOB 20515; (202) 225-7772. Rep. Dick Armey, R-Texas, Co-Chair; Sen. Richard C. Shelby, R-Ala., Co-Chair; Lisa Vogt, Staff Contact. Web, flattax.gov.*

Global Legislators Organization for a Balanced Environment U.S.A., *2000 P St. N.W., #308 20036; (202) 293-9090. Fax, (202) 293-9098. Rep. John Edward Porter, R-Ill., Chair; William R. Singleton, Director. Web, www.globeusa.org.*

Educates and encourages cooperation among environmentally concerned legislators around the world. Promotes the development of informed, balanced approaches to emerging environmental challenges.

Internet Caucus, *SR-433 20510; (202) 224-4242. Fax, (202) 224-3479. Rep. Robert W. Goodlatte, R-Va., Co-*

Chair; Sen. Patrick J. Leahy, D-Vt., Co-Chair; Sen. Conrad Burns, R-Mont., Co-Chair; Rep. Rick Boucher, D-Va., Co-Chair; Ed Barron, Staff Contact. Web, www.netcaucus.org.

Promotes growth of the Internet, including government participation; educates members and congressional staff about the Internet.

Long Island Congressional Delegation, 2243 RHOB 20515; (202) 225-2601. Fax, (202) 225-1589. Rep. Gary L. Ackerman, D-N.Y., Chair; Jedd Moskowitz, Chief of Staff.

New York Bipartisan Congressional Delegation, 2354 RHOB 20515; (202) 225-4365. Fax, (202) 225-0816. Rep. Charles B. Rangel, D-N.Y., Chair; Maya Rockeymoore, Staff Contact.

Pennsylvania Congressional Delegation, 2423 RHOB 20515; (202) 225-2065. Fax, (202) 225-5709. Rep. John P. Murtha, D-Pa., Chair; Debra Tekavec, Staff Contact.

Porkbusters Coalition, 1415 LHOB 20515; (202) 225-2331. Fax, (202) 226-0836. Rep. David Minge, D-Minn., Co-Chair; Rep. Ed Royce, R-Calif., Co-Chair; Curtis Yoakum, Staff Contact.

U.S. Assn. of Former Members of Congress, 330 A St. N.E. 20002; (202) 543-8676. Fax, (202) 543-7145. Matthew McHugh, President.

Nonpartisan organization of former members of Congress. Acts as a congressional alumni association; sponsors educational projects, including the Congress to Campus program, which provides support for colleges and universities to host visits of former representatives and senators.

U.S. Holocaust Memorial Council, 100 Raoul Wallenberg Pl. S.W. 20024; (202) 488-0490. Fax, (202) 314-7881. Jane Rizer, Staff Contact.

Vietnam Veterans in Congress, 2335 RHOB 20515; (202) 225-5905. Fax, (202) 225-5396. Rep. Lane Evans, D-Ill., Co-Chair; Tom O'Donnell, Staff Contact; Sen. Tom Daschle, D-S.D., Co-Chair; Sen. John Kerry, D-Mass., Co-Chair.

Women's Policy Inc., 409 12th St. S.W., #705 20024; (202) 554-2323. Fax, (202) 554-2346. Mary Anne Leary, Executive Director. General e-mail, webmaster@ womenspolicy.org. Web, www.womenspolicy.org.

Tracks legislative and executive branch actions affecting women and children.

HOUSE

Albanian Issues Caucus, 2303 RHOB 20515; (202) 225-2464. Fax, (202) 225-5513. Rep. Eliot L. Engel, D-N.Y.,

Co-Chair; Rep. Peter T. King, R-N.Y., Co-Chair; Jason Steinbaum, Staff Contact.

Army Caucus, 2441 RHOB 20515; (202) 225-4611. Fax, (202) 226-0621. Rep. John M. McHugh, R-N.Y., Co-Chair; Rep. Chet Edwards, D-Texas, Co-Chair; Anne Lemay, Staff Contact.

The Coalition (Blue Dogs), 1504 LHOB 20515; (202) 225-2031. Fax, (202) 225-5724. Rep. Chris John, D-La., Co-Chair; Rep. Robert E. "Bud" Cramer, D-Ala., Co-Chair; Gordon Taylor, Legislative Director.

Congressional Alcohol Fuels Caucus, 303 CHOB 20515; (202) 225-2911. Fax, (202) 225-9129. Rep. Lane Evans, D-Ill., Co-Chair; Rep. David Minge, D-Minn., Co-Chair; Rep. Jim Nussle, R-Iowa, Co-Chair; Craig Patterson, Staff Contact.

Congressional Automotive Caucus, 2187 RHOB 20515; (202) 225-3611. Fax, (202) 225-6393. Rep. Dale E. Kildee, D-Mich., Co-Chair; Rep. Fred Upton, R-Mich., Co-Chair; Michael Gorges, Staff Contact.

Congressional Bearing Caucus, 2113 RHOB 20515; (202) 225-4476. Fax, (202) 225-4488. Rep. Nancy L. Johnson, R-Conn., Co-Chair; Rep. John M. Spratt Jr., D-S.C., Co-Chair; Todd Funk, Staff Contact.

Congressional Children's Working Group, 2352 RHOB 20515; (202) 225-3915. Fax, (202) 225-6798. Rep. Tim Roemer, D-Ind., Chair; Maggie McDow, Staff Contact.

Congressional Friends of Animals, 2217 RHOB 20515; (202) 225-3531. Rep. Tom Lantos, D-Calif., Co-Chair; Rep. Christopher Shays, R-Conn., Co-Chair; Serena Lin, Staff Contact.

Congressional Hispanic Caucus Institute, 504 C St. N.E. 20002; (202) 543-1771. Fax, (202) 546-2143. Rep. Lucille Roybal-Allard, D-Calif., Chair; Ingrid Duran, Executive Director. Toll-free college scholarship information, (800) 392-3532.

Congressional Human Rights Caucus, 2217 RHOB 20515; (202) 225-3531. Rep. John Edward Porter, R-Ill., Co-Chair; Rep. Tom Lantos, D-Calif., Co-Chair; Hans Hogrefe, Staff Contact.

Congressional Older Americans Caucus, 2309 RHOB 20515; (202) 225-3876. Fax, (202) 225-3059. Rep. Ralph Regula, R-Ohio, Co-Chair; Rep. Constance A. Morella, R-Md., Co-Chair; Pamela Kirby, Staff Contact.

Congressional Pro-Life Caucus, 2370 RHOB 20515; (202) 225-7669. Fax, (202) 225-7768. Rep. Christopher H.

Smith, R-N.J., Co-Chair; Maggie Wynne, Director; Rep. James A. Barcia, D.-Mich., Co-Chair.

Congressional Social Security Caucus, *2407 RHOB 20515; (202) 225-5961. Fax, (202) 225-9764. Rep. C. W. Bill Young, R-Fla., Chair; Brian Mabry, Staff Contact.*

Congressional Space Caucus, *332 CHOB 20515; (202) 225-3671. Fax, (202) 225-3516. Rep. Dave Weldon, R-Fla., Co-Chair; Brendan Curry, Staff Contact.*

Congressional Steel Caucus, *2309 RHOB 20515; (202) 225-3876. Fax, (202) 225-3059. Rep. Ralph Regula, R-Ohio, Chair; Karen Buttaro, Staff Contact.*

Congressional Task Force on Haiti, *2305 RHOB 20515; (202) 225-6231. Fax, (202) 226-0112. Rep. Major R. Owens, D-N.Y., Chair; Jacqueline Ellis, Staff Contact.*

Congressional Task Force on International HIV/AIDS, *1035 LHOB 20515; (202) 225-3106. Fax, (202) 225-6197. Rep. Jim McDermott, D-Wash., Chair; Christopher Dunn, Staff Contact.*

Congressional Task Force on Tobacco and Health, *2434 RHOB 20515; (202) 225-3411. Fax, (202) 226-0771. Rep. Martin T. Meehan, D-Mass., Co-Chair; Rep. James V. Hansen, R-Utah, Co-Chair; Sara Andrews, Staff Contact.*

Congressional Task Force to End the Arab Boycott, *2160 RHOB 20515; (202) 225-3931. Fax, (202) 225-5620. Rep. Ileana Ros-Lehtinen, R-Fla., Chair; Rudy Fernandez, Staff Contact.*

Congressional Urban Caucus, *2416 RHOB 20515; (202) 225-4372. Fax, (202) 226-0333. Rep. Bobby L. Rush, D-Ill., Chair; Tanya Ballard, Staff Contact.*

Congressional Women's Caucus, *1122 LHOB 20515; (202) 225-5441. Fax, (202) 225-3289. Rep. Sue W. Kelly, R-N.Y., Co-Chair; Rep. Carolyn B. Maloney, D-N.Y., Co-Chair; Carolyn Holmes, Staff Contact.*

Congressional Working Group on China, *2457 RHOB 20515; (202) 225-4965. Fax, (202) 225-8259. Rep. Nancy Pelosi, D-Calif., Co-Chair; Rep. Frank R. Wolf, R-Va., Co-Chair; Carolyn Bartholomew, Staff Contact.*

Conservative Action Team, *429 CHOB 20515; (202) 225-2701. Fax, (202) 225-3038. Rep. John Shadegg, R-Ariz., Chair; Neil Bradley, Staff Contact.*

House Republican Task Force on Agriculture, *1527 LHOB 20515; (202) 225-2006. Fax, (202) 225-3392. Rep. George Nethercutt, R-Wash., Chair; Jack Silzel, Staff Contact.*

Long Island Sound Congressional Caucus, *2421 RHOB 20515; (202) 225-6506. Fax, (202) 225-0546. Rep. Nita M. Lowey, D-N.Y., Co-Chair; Esten Perez, Staff Contact; Rep. Christopher Shays, R-Conn., Co-Chair.*

Mainstream Conservative Alliance, *2183 RHOB 20515; (202) 225-4031. Fax, (202) 225-0563. Rep. W. J. "Billy" Tauzin, R-La., Co-Chair; Rep. Zach Wamp, R-Tenn., Co-Chair; James White, Staff Contact.*

Medical Technology Caucus, *103 CHOB 20515; (202) 225-2871. Fax, (202) 225-6351. Rep. Anna G. Eshoo, D-Calif., Co-Chair; Rep. Jim Ramstad, R-Minn., Co-Chair; Megan Ivory, Staff Contact.*

Narcotics Abuse and Control Caucus, *2354 RHOB 20515; (202) 225-4365. Fax, (202) 225-0816. Rep. Charles B. Rangel, D-N.Y., Chair; Emile Milne, Staff Contact.*

Northeast Agricultural Caucus, *2246 RHOB 20515; (202) 225-3665. Fax, (202) 225-1891. Rep. Sherwood Boehlert, R-N.Y., Co-Chair; Rep. Tim Holden, D-Pa., Co-Chair; Sara Gray, Staff Contact.*

Permanent U.S. Congressional Delegation to the European Parliament, *2170 RHOB 20515; (202) 225-5021. Fax, (202) 225-2035. Rep. Benjamin A. Gilman, R-N.Y., Chair; Laura Rush, Staff Contact.*

Rural Health Care Coalition, *303 CHOB 20515; (202) 225-2911. Fax, (202) 225-9129. Rep. Jim Nussle, R-Iowa, Co-Chair; Rep. Mike McIntyre, D-N.C., Co-Chair; Christine Pollack, Staff Contact.*

SENATE

Democratic Technology and Communications Committee, *SH-619 20510; (202) 224-1430. Fax, (202) 224-1431. Sen. John D. Rockefeller IV, D-W.Va., Chair; Robin Schepper, Staff Contact.*

Northeast-Midwest Senate Coalition, *SH-728 20510; (202) 224-0606. Fax, (202) 228-0776. Sen. James M. Jeffords, R-Vt., Co-Chair; Sen. Daniel Patrick Moynihan, D-N.Y., Co-Chair; Cameron Taylor, Staff Contact.*

Senate Auto Caucus, *SR-459 20510; (202) 224-6221. Fax, (202) 224-1388. Sen. Carl Levin, D-Mich., Co-Chair; Sen. Mike DeWine, R-Ohio, Co-Chair; Brennan VanDyke, Staff Contact.*

Senate Cancer Coalition, *SH-517 20510; (202) 224-5274. Fax, (202) 224-8022. Sen. Dianne Feinstein, D-Calif., Co-Chair; Sen. Connie Mack, R-Fla., Co-Chair; Mark Smith, Staff Contact.*

Senate Democratic Task Force on Hispanic Issues, *SH-703 20510; (202) 224-5521. Fax, (202) 224-2852. Sen. Jeff Bingaman, D-N.M., Chair; Angelo Gonzales, Staff Contact.*

Senate Rural Health Caucus, *SH-731 20510; (202) 224-3254. Fax, (202) 224-9369. Sen. Tom Harkin, D-Iowa, Co-Chair; Sen. Craig Thomas, R-Wyo., Co-Chair; Sabrina Corlette, Staff Contact.*

Senate Steel Caucus, *SH-711 20510; (202) 224-4254. Fax, (202) 228-1229. Sen. Arlen Specter, R-Pa., Co-Chair; Sen. John D. Rockefeller IV, D-W.Va., Co-Chair; Peter Grollman, Staff Contact.*

Senate Textile Caucus, *SR-125 20510; (202) 224-6121. Fax, (202) 228-0327. Sen. Ernest F. Hollings, D-S.C., Chair; Greg Elias, Staff Contact.*

U.S. Interparliamentary Group—Canada, *SH-808 20510; (202) 224-3047. Fax, (202) 224-2373. Sen. Frank H. Murkowski, R-Alaska, Chair; Sally Walsh, Director.*

U.S. Interparliamentary Group—Mexico, *SH-808 20510; (202) 224-3047. Fax, (202) 224-2373. Sen. Paul Coverdell, R-Ga., Chair; Sally Walsh, Director.*

U.S. Interparliamentary Group—NATO/U.S. Parliamentary Assembly, *SH-808 20510; (202) 224-3047. Fax, (202) 224-2373. Sen. William V. Roth Jr., R-Del., Chair; Sally Walsh, Director.*

U.S. Senate—Interparliamentary Services, *SH-808 20510; (202) 224-3047. Fax, (202) 224-2373. Vacant, Chair; Sally Walsh, Director.*
Membership: elected parliamentarians throughout the world. All members of Congress are members.

Western States Senate Coalition, *SR-380 20510; (202) 224-5852. Fax, (202) 224-1933. Sen. Ben Nighthorse Campbell, R-Colo., Co-Chair; Sen. Byron L. Dorgan, D-N.D., Co-Chair; Sen. Orrin G. Hatch, R-Utah, Co-Chair; Sen. Ted Stevens, R-Alaska, Co-Chair; Kevin Studer, Staff Contact.*

CONGRESS AT WORK

See 106th Congress (p. 725) for individual members' offices and committee assignments and for rosters of congressional committees and subcommittees.

CONGRESS

House Recording Studio, *Communications Media, B310 RHOB 20515; (202) 225-3941. Fax, (202) 225-0707. Mike Allen, Director. Web, www.onlinecao.house.gov.*

Assists House members in making tape recordings. Provides daily gavel-to-gavel television coverage of House floor proceedings.

House Rules Committee, *H312 CAP 20515; (202) 225-9191. Rep. David Dreier, R-Calif., Chair; Vince Randazzo, Staff Director. Web, www.house.gov/rules.*

Sets rules for floor debate on legislation reported by regular standing committees; grants emergency waivers, under the House rules and the Congressional Budget Act of 1974, of required reporting dates for bills and resolutions authorizing new budget authority; has jurisdiction over resolutions creating committees; has legislative authority to recommend changes in the rules of the House; has jurisdiction over recesses and final adjournments of Congress.

Office of Photography, *B302 RHOB 20515; (202) 225-2840. Fax, (202) 225-5896. Dwight Comedy, Director.*

Provides House members with photographic assistance.

Parliamentarian of the House of Representatives, *H209 CAP 20515; (202) 225-7373. Charles W. Johnson III, Parliamentarian.*

Advises presiding officers on parliamentary procedures and committee jurisdiction over legislation; prepares and maintains a compilation of the precedents of the House.

Parliamentarian of the Senate, *S133 CAP 20510; (202) 224-6128. Fax, (202) 224-5064. Robert B. Dove, Parliamentarian; Alan S. Frumin, Associate Parliamentarian.*

Advises presiding officers on parliamentary procedures and committee jurisdiction over legislation; prepares and maintains a compilation of the precedents of the Senate.

Senate Rules and Administration Committee, *SR-305 20510; (202) 224-6352. Fax, (202) 224-3036. Sen. Mitch McConnell, R-Ky., Chair; Tamara Somerville, Staff Director. Web, rules.senate.gov.*

Jurisdiction over all matters related to the rules governing the conduct of business in the Senate, including floor, committee, and gallery procedures. Also studies and makes recommendations on computer and other technical services in the Senate; oversees operation of the computer information system for the Senate.

Sergeant at Arms of the Senate, *Senate Photographic Studio, SDG-10 20510; (202) 224-3669. Fax, (202) 228-3584. Steve Benza, Supervisor.*

Provides Senate members with photographic assistance.

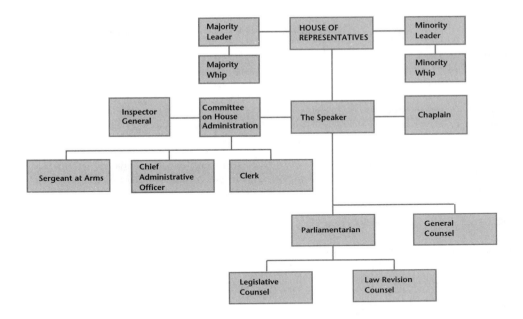

Leadership

HOUSE

House Democratic Caucus, *1420 LHOB 20515; (202) 226-3210. Fax, (202) 225-0282. Rep. Martin Frost, D-Texas, Chair; Matt Angle, Executive Director. Web, dcaucusweb.house.gov.*

Membership: House Democrats. Selects Democratic leadership; formulates party rules and floor strategy; considers caucus members' recommendations on major issues; votes on the Democratic Steering and Policy Committee's recommendations for Democratic committee assignments.

House Democratic Policy Committee, *H302 CAP 20515; (202) 225-6760. Fax, (202) 226-0938. Rep. Richard A. Gephardt, D-Mo., Chair; Craig Hannah, Executive Director. Web, www.house.gov/democrats.*

Sergeant at Arms of the Senate, *Senate Recording Studio, ST71 CAP 20510; (202) 224-4977. Fax, (202) 224-8701. David Bass, Manager.*

Assists Senate members in making radio and video tape recordings and live satellite broadcasts; televises Senate floor proceedings for broadcast by C-SPAN (Cable-Satellite Public Affairs Network).

Studies and makes recommendations to the Democratic leadership on party policy and priorities. Assisted in decision making by the House Democratic Leadership Advisory Group.

House Democratic Steering Committee, *H204 CAP 20515; (202) 225-0100. Fax, (202) 226-0938. Rep. Richard A. Gephardt, D-Mo., Co-Chair; Rep. Steny H. Hoyer, D-Md., Co-Chair; Craig Hannah, Executive Director. Web, www.house.gov/democrats.*

Makes Democratic committee assignments, subject to approval by the House Democratic Caucus.

House Republican Conference, *1010 LHOB 20515; (202) 225-5107. Fax, (202) 225-0809. Rep. J. C. Watts Jr., R-Okla., Chair; Pam Pryor, Executive Director.*

Membership: House Republicans. Selects Republican leadership; formulates party rules and floor strategy, and considers party positions on major legislation; votes on Republican Committee on Committees' recommendations for House committee chairmen and Republican committee assignments; publishes *Legislative Digest* analyzing pending legislation.

House Republican Policy Committee, *2471 RHOB 20515; (202) 225-6168. Fax, (202) 225-0931. Rep. Christo-*

pher Cox, R-Calif., Chair; Benedict Cohen, Executive Director. Web, policy.house.gov.

Studies legislation and makes recommendations on House Republican policies and positions on proposed legislation.

House Republican Steering Committee, H209 CAP 20515; (202) 225-2204. Rep. J. Dennis Hastert, R-Ill., Chair; Karen Haas, Staff Contact.

Makes Republican committee assignments and nominates committee chairmen subject to approval by the House Republican Conference and entire House of Representatives.

Majority Leader of the House of Representatives, H327-A CAP 20515; (202) 225-4000. Fax, (202) 226-8100. Rep. Dick Armey, R-Texas, Majority Leader; Siobhan McGill, Floor Assistant. Web, www.freedom.gov.

Serves as chief strategist and floor spokesman for the majority party in the House.

Majority Whip of the House of Representatives, H107 CAP 20515; (202) 225-0197. Fax, (202) 225-5117. Rep. Tom DeLay, R-Texas, Majority Whip; Susan Hirschmann, Chief of Staff. Web, majoritywhip.house.gov.

Serves as assistant majority leader in the House; helps marshal majority forces in support of party strategy.

Minority Leader of the House of Representatives, H204 CAP 20515-6502; (202) 225-0100. Fax, (202) 225-7414. Rep. Richard A. Gephardt, D-Mo., Minority Leader; Dan Turton, Executive Floor Assistant. Web, www.house.gov/democrats.

Serves as chief strategist and floor spokesman for the minority party in the House.

Minority Whip of the House of Representatives, H307 CAP 20515; (202) 225-3130. Fax, (202) 225-0749. Rep. David E. Bonior, D-Mich., Minority Whip; Sarah Dufendach, Administrative Assistant.

Serves as assistant minority leader in the House; helps marshal minority forces in support of party strategy.

Speaker of the House of Representatives, Speaker's Office, H232 CAP 20515; (202) 225-0600. Fax, (202) 226-1996. Rep. J. Dennis Hastert, R-Ill., Speaker; Scott B. Palmer, Chief of Staff. General e-mail, speaker@mail.house.gov. Web, speaker.house.gov.

Presides over the House while in session; preserves decorum and order; announces vote results; recognizes members for debate and introduction of bills, amendments, and motions; refers bills and resolutions to committees; decides points of order; appoints House members to conference committees; votes at his own discretion.

See House Leadership (p. 754); Partisan Committees (p. 752).

SENATE

Democratic Leader of the Senate, S221 CAP 20510; (202) 224-5556. Fax, (202) 224-7895. Sen. Tom Daschle, D-S.D., Democratic Leader; Peter Rouse, Chief of Staff. Press, (202) 224-2939.

Serves as chief strategist and floor spokesman for the Democratic party in the Senate.

Majority Leader of the Senate, SR 487 20510; (202) 224-6253. Fax, (202) 224-2262. Sen. Trent Lott, R-Miss., Majority Leader; Dave Hoppe, Chief of Staff.

Serves as chief strategist and floor spokesman for the majority party in the Senate.

Majority Whip of the Senate, S208 CAP 20510; (202) 224-2708. Fax, (202) 224-3913. Sen. Don Nickles, R-Okla., Majority Whip; Eric Ueland, Staff Director.

Serves as assistant majority leader in the Senate; helps marshal majority forces in support of party strategy.

Minority Whip of the Senate, S149 CAP 20510 (mailing address: SH-528 20510); (202) 224-2158. Fax, (202) 224-7362. Sen. Harry Reid, D-Nev., Minority Whip; Janice Shelton, Executive Assistant.

Serves as assistant minority leader in the Senate; helps marshal minority forces in support of party strategy.

President Pro Tempore of the Senate, S237 CAP 20510; (202) 224-5972. Fax, (202) 224-1300. Sen. Strom Thurmond, R-S.C., President Pro Tempore; R. J. "Duke" Short, Administrative Assistant.

Presides over the Senate in the absence of the vice president.

Senate Democratic Conference, S309 CAP 20510; (202) 224-3735. Sen. Tom Daschle, D-S.D., Chair; Sen. Barbara A. Mikulski, D-Md., Secretary; Martin P. Paone, Secretary for the Minority.

Membership: Democratic senators. Selects Democratic leadership; formulates party rules and floor strategy and considers party positions on major legislation; votes on Democratic Steering Committee's recommendations for Democratic committee assignments.

Senate Democratic Policy Committee, S118 CAP 20510; (202) 224-3232. Sen. Tom Daschle, D-S.D., Chair; Mark Patterson, Staff Director. General e-mail, postmaster@dpc.senate.gov. Web, www.senate.gov/~dpc.

CONGRESSIONAL LIAISONS AT FEDERAL AGENCIES

DEPARTMENTS

Agriculture, Andrew Fish, (202) 720-7907

Commerce, Debby Kilmer, (202) 482-3663

Defense, John K. Veroneau, (703) 697-6210

  Air Force, Maj. Gen. Tim Mosely, (703) 697-8153

  Army, Maj. Gen. William Lennox, (703) 697-6767

  Navy, Rear Adm. Cutler Dawson, (703) 697-7146

Education, Scott Fleming, (202) 401-0020

Energy, John C. Angell, (202) 586-5450

Health and Human Services, Helen Mathis, (202) 690-6786

Housing and Urban Development, Hal DeCell, (202) 708-0380

Interior, Vacant, (202) 208-7693

Justice, Robert Raben (acting), (202) 514-3752

Labor, Geri D. Palast, (202) 219-4601

State, Barbara Larkin, (202) 647-4204

Transportation, Nadine Hamilton, (202) 366-9714

Treasury, Linda L. Robertson, (202) 622-1900

Veterans Affairs, Phil Riggin, (202) 273-5615

AGENCIES

Agency for International Development, Dorothy Rayburn, (202) 712-4340

Commission on Civil Rights, Vacant, (202) 376-8317

Commodity Futures Trading Commission, Beau Greenwood Jr., (202) 418-5075

Consumer Product Safety Commission, Robert J. Wager, (301) 504-0515

Corporation for National Service, Mark Isaac, (202) 606-5000, ext. 279

Environmental Protection Agency, John Reeder (acting), (202) 260-5200

Equal Employment Opportunity Commission, Sylvia Anderson, (202) 663-4900

Export-Import Bank, Sandy Jackson, (202) 565-3235

Farm Credit Administration, Eileen McMahon, (703) 883-4056

Federal Communications Commission, Cheryl Wilkerson, (202) 418-1900

Federal Deposit Insurance Corporation, Alice C. Goodman, (202) 898-8730

Federal Election Commission, Christina VanBrakle, (202) 694-1006

Federal Emergency Management Agency, Fran McCarthy, (202) 646-4500

Federal Labor Relations Authority, Patty Reilly, (202) 482-6500

Federal Maritime Commission, David Miles, (202) 523-5740

Federal Mediation and Conciliation Service, Kim Beg, (202) 606-8150

Federal Reserve System, Donald J. Winn, (202) 452-3456

Studies and makes recommendations to the Democratic leadership on legislation for consideration by the Senate.

Senate Democratic Steering and Coordination Committee, *SH-712 20510; (202) 224-9048. Sen. John Kerry, D-Mass., Chair; Martin P. Paone, Secretary for the Minority.*

Makes Democratic committee assignments subject to approval by the Senate Democratic Conference.

Senate Republican Committee on Committees, *SH-730 20510; (202) 224-3441. Sen. Slade Gorton, R-Wash., Chair; Tony Williams, Staff Contact.*

Makes Republican committee assignments and selects committee chairmen, subject to approval by the Senate Republican Conference. (The committee con-

venes once every two years at the beginning of each new Congress.)

Senate Republican Conference, *SH-405 20510; (202) 224-2764. Sen. Connie Mack, R-Fla., Chair; Lee Johnson, Staff Director.*

Membership: Republican senators. Serves as caucus and central coordinating body of the party. Organizes and elects Senate Republican leadership; votes on Republican Committee on Committees' recommendations for Senate committee chairs and Republican committee assignments. Staff provides various support and media services for Republican members.

Senate Republican Policy Committee, *SR-347 20510; (202) 224-2946. Sen. Larry E. Craig, R-Idaho, Chair; Jade West, Staff Director. Web, www.senate.gov/~rpc.*

CONGRESSIONAL LIAISONS AT FEDERAL AGENCIES (continued)

Federal Trade Commission, Carol Kando-Pineda (acting), (202) 326-2195

General Services Administration, Bill Ratchford, (202) 501-0563

Legal Services Corporation, Dori Gillman, (202) 336-8800

Merit Systems Protection Board, Susan Williams, (202) 653-7171

National Aeronautics and Space Administration, Mary D. Kerwin, (202) 358-1948

National Credit Union Administration, Robert Loftus, (703) 518-6300

National Endowment for the Arts, Richard Woodruff, (202) 682-5434

National Endowment for the Humanities, Michael Bagley, (202) 606-8328

National Labor Relations Board, John Toner, (202) 273-1944

National Mediation Board, Benetta M. Mansfield, (202) 692-5040

National Science Foundation, David Stonner, (703) 306-1070

National Transportation Safety Board, Betty Scott, (202) 314-6120

Nuclear Regulatory Commission, Dennis K. Rathbun, (301) 415-1776

Occupational Safety and Health Review Commission, Patricia A. Randle, (202) 606-5398

Office of Personnel Management, Cynthia Brock-Smith, (202) 606-1300

Office of Special Counsel, Jane McFarland, (202) 653-7984

Pension Benefit Guaranty Corporation, Judith Schub, (202) 326-4010

Postal Rate Commission, Margaret P. Crenshaw, (202) 789-6840

Securities and Exchange Commission, Susan Wyderko, (202) 942-0010

Selective Service System, Lewis C. Brodsky, (703) 605-4100

Small Business Administration, Jane Merkin, (202) 205-6700

Smithsonian Institution, Vacant, (202) 357-2962

Social Security Administration, Judy Chesser, (410) 965-3737

Surface Transportation Board, Dan King, (202) 565-1594

Tennessee Valley Authority, David Withrow, (202) 898-2999

U.S. International Trade Commission, Nancy Carman, (202) 205-3151

U.S. Postal Service, Deborah Willhite, (202) 268-2506

Studies and makes recommendations to the majority leader on the priorities and scheduling of legislation on the Senate floor; prepares policy papers and develops Republican policy initiatives.

Vice President of the United States, *President of the Senate,* S212 CAP 20510; (202) 224-8391. Albert Gore Jr., Vice President; Ronna Freiberg, Director, Legislative Affairs. Senate office: SD-202 20510; (202) 224-2424. Executive office: White House 20500; (202) 456-2326. General e-mail, vice-president@whitehouse.gov. Web, www. whitehouse.gov.

Presides over the Senate while in session; preserves decorum and order; announces vote results; recognizes members for debate and introduction of bills, amendments, and motions; decides points of order; votes only in the case of a tie. (President pro tempore of the Senate presides in the absence of the vice president.)

See Senate Leadership (p. 824); Partisan Committees (p. 752).

Officers

HOUSE

Chaplain of the House of Representatives, *HB25 CAP 20515; (202) 225-2509. Rev. Daniel Coughlin, Chaplain.*

Opens each day's House session with a prayer and offers other religious services to House members, their families, and staffs. (Prayer sometimes offered by visiting chaplain.)

Chief Administrative Officer of the House of Representatives, *HB30 CAP 20515; (202) 225-6900. Fax,*

(202) 226-6300. James M. "Jay" Eagen III, Chief Administrative Officer.

Responsible for all administrative functions of the House, including services related to employee assistance, placement, finance, payroll, benefits, food service, information resources, telecommunications, furniture, procurement, photography, postal operations, office supplies and equipment, child care center, barber and beauty shop, and press galleries.

Clerk of the House of Representatives, *H154 CAP 20515; (202) 225-7000. Jeff Trandahl, Clerk. Web, clerkweb. house.gov.*

Responsible for direction of duties of House employees; receives lobby registrations and reports of campaign expenditures and receipts of House candidates; disburses funds appropriated for House expenditures; responsible for other activities necessary for the continuing operation of the House.

Floor Assistant to the Speaker of the House of Representatives, *HB13 CAP 20515; (202) 225-4768. Fax, (202) 225-1488. Jay Pierson, Floor Assistant to the Speaker.*

Assists the majority leadership and members on legislative matters.

General Counsel of the House of Representatives, *219 CHOB 20515; (202) 225-9700. Fax, (202) 226-1360. Geraldine R. Gennet, General Counsel.*

Advises House members and committees on legal matters.

Inspector General of the House of Representatives, *385 FHOB 20515-9990; (202) 226-1250. Fax, (202) 225-4240. Steve McNamara, Inspector General (Designate); Robert B. Frey III, Deputy Inspector General. Web, www. house.gov/IG.*

Conducts periodic audits of the financial and administrative functions of the House and joint entities.

Legislative Counsel of the House of Representatives, *136 CHOB 20515; (202) 225-6060. Fax, (202) 225-3437. Pope Barrow, Legislative Counsel.*

Assists House members and committees in drafting legislation.

Sergeant at Arms of the House of Representatives, *H124 CAP 20515; (202) 225-2456. Fax, (202) 225-3233. Wilson L. "Bill" Livingood, Sergeant at Arms.*

Maintains order on the House floor; executes orders from the Speaker of the House. Serves on the Capitol Police Board and Capitol Guide Board; oversees Capitol security (with Senate Sergeant at Arms) and protocol.

SENATE

Chaplain of the Senate, *S332 CAP 20510; (202) 224-2510. Fax, (202) 224-9686. Lloyd Ogilvie, Chaplain.*

Opens each day's Senate session with a prayer and offers other religious services to Senate members, their families, and staffs. (Prayer sometimes offered by visiting chaplain.)

Legal Counsel of the Senate, *SH-642 20510; (202) 224-4435. Fax, (202) 224-3391. Patricia Mack Bryan, Legal Counsel.*

Advises Senate members and committees on legal matters.

Legislative Counsel of the Senate, *SD-668 20510; (202) 224-6461. Fax, (202) 224-0567. James W. Fransen, Legislative Counsel.*

Assists Senate members and committees in drafting legislation.

Majority Secretary of the Senate, *S337 CAP 20510; (202) 224-3835. Elizabeth Letchworth, Secretary; Dave Schiappa, Assistant Secretary.*

Assists the majority leader and majority party in the Senate.

Minority Secretary of the Senate, *S309 CAP 20510; (202) 224-3735. Martin P. Paone, Secretary; Lula Davis, Assistant Secretary.*

Assists the minority leader and the minority party in the Senate.

Secretary of the Senate, *S220 CAP 20510; (202) 224-3622. Gary Sisco, Secretary; Jon Lynn Kerchner, Administrative Assistant. Information, (202) 224-2115. Web, www. senate.gov/learning/learn_leaders_officers_secretary.html.*

Chief administrative officer of the Senate. Responsible for direction of duties of Senate employees and administration of oaths; receives lobby registrations and reports of campaign expenditures and receipts of Senate candidates; responsible for other Senate activities.

Sergeant at Arms of the Senate, *S321 CAP 20510-7200; (202) 224-2341. Fax, (202) 224-7690. James W. Ziglar, Sergeant at Arms; Loretta Symms, Deputy Sergeant at Arms.*

Oversees the Senate wing of the Capitol; doormen; Senate pages; and telecommunication, photographic, supply, and janitorial services. Maintains order on the Senate floor and galleries; oversees Capitol security (with House Sergeant at Arms); sits on the Capitol Police Board and Capitol Guide Board.

Pay and Perquisites

CONGRESS

Attending Physician, *H166 CAP 20515; (202) 225-5421. Dr. John F. Eisold, Attending Physician; Robert J. Burg, Administrative Assistant.*

Provides members with primary care, first-aid, emergency care, and environmental/occupational health services; provides House and Senate employees, visiting dignitaries, and tourists with first-aid and emergency care.

Chief Administrative Office, *Postal Operations of the House of Representatives, B227 LHOB 20515; (202) 225-3856. Fax, (202) 225-6530. Paul Lozito, Director.*

Supervises the postal facilities in the Capitol and the House office buildings.

Clerk of the House of Representatives, *H154 CAP 20515; (202) 225-7000. Jeff Trandahl, Clerk. Web, clerkweb.house.gov.*

Prepares and submits quarterly reports covering the receipts and expenditures of the House for three months, including disbursements by each committee and each member's office and staff. Reports available from the House Document Room, (202) 225-3456.

House Administration Committee, *1309 LHOB 20515; (202) 225-8281. Fax, (202) 225-9957. Rep. Bill Thomas, R-Calif., Chair; Cathy Abernathy, Staff Director. Web, www.house.gov/cha.*

Responsible for all matters related to the House's internal operational budget, including members' allowances and expenses, remuneration of House employees, and such unforeseen expenditures as special investigations. Oversight of the Franking Commission.

House Commission on Congressional Mailing Standards, *1338 LHOB 20515; (202) 225-9337. Fax, (202) 226-0047. Rep. Bill Thomas, R-Calif., Chair; Jack Dail, Staff Director.*

Oversight of the use of franked mail by House members.

House Government Reform Committee, *Subcommittee on Government Management, Information, and Technology, B373 RHOB 20515; (202) 225-5147. Fax, (202) 225-2373. Rep. Steve Horn, R-Calif., Chair; J. Russell George, Staff Director. Web, www.house.gov/reform.*

Jurisdiction over proposed changes in the salary of members of Congress.

Secretary of the Senate, *S220 CAP 20510; (202) 224-3622. Gary Sisco, Secretary; Jon Lynn Kerchner, Adminis-trative Assistant. Information, (202) 224-2115. Web, www.senate.gov/learning/learn_leaders_officers_secretary.html.*

Prepares and submits semiannual reports covering the receipts and expenditures of the Senate for six months, including data on each committee and each member's office and staff. Reports available from the Government Printing Office, (202) 275-3030.

Senate Governmental Affairs Committee, *SD-340 20510; (202) 224-4751. Fax, (202) 224-9603. Sen. Fred Thompson, R-Tenn., Chair; Hannah Sistare, Staff Director. Web, gov_affairs.senate.gov.*

Jurisdiction over proposed changes in the salary of members of Congress.

Senate Rules and Administration Committee, *SR-305 20510; (202) 224-6352. Fax, (202) 224-3036. Sen. Mitch McConnell, R-Ky., Chair; Tamara Somerville, Staff Director. Web, rules.senate.gov.*

Responsible for all matters related to the Senate's internal operational budget, including members' allowances and expenses, remuneration of Senate employees, and such unforeseen expenditures as special investigations. Oversees budgets of the Secretary of the Senate, the Sergeant at Arms, and the Architect of the Capitol. Jurisdiction over Senate use of the franking privilege.

Senate Select Committee on Ethics, *SH-220 20510; (202) 224-2981. Fax, (202) 224-7416. Sen. Pat Roberts, R-Kan., Chair; Victor M. Baird, Staff Director.*

Oversight of the use of franked mail by Senate members; takes action on misuse of the frank.

NONPROFIT

National Taxpayers Union, *Communications, 108 N. Alfred St., 3rd Floor, Alexandria, VA 22314; (703) 683-5700. Fax, (703) 683-5722. Peter Sepp, Vice President. Web, www.ntu.org.*

Citizens' interest group that publishes reports on congressional pay and perquisites, including pensions and the franking privilege.

Standards of Conduct

AGENCIES

Justice Dept., *Public Integrity, 1400 New York Ave. N.W. 20005; (202) 514-1412. Fax, (202) 514-3003. Lee J. Radek, Chief. Web, www.usdoj.gov.*

Conducts investigations of wrongdoing in selected cases that involve alleged corruption of public office or violations of election law by public officials, including members of Congress.

CONGRESS

House Standards of Official Conduct Committee, HT-2 CAP 20515; (202) 225-7103. Fax, (202) 225-7392. Rep. Lamar Smith, R-Texas, Chair; Robert Walker, Chief Counsel. Web, www.house.gov/ethics/.

Enforces the House Code of Official Conduct (rules governing the behavior of House members and employees); has full legislative jurisdiction over all matters under that code; reviews members' financial disclosures.

Legislative Resource Center, Records and Registration, B-106 CHOB 20515; (202) 226-5200. Fax, (202) 226-5208. Bob Cuthriell, Director.

Receives and maintains the financial disclosure records of House members, officers, employees, candidates, and certain legislative organizations. Receives reports from committee chairs on foreign travel by members and staff. Records open for public inspection.

Secretary of the Senate, Public Records: Ethics, SH-232 20510; (202) 224-0322. Fax, (202) 224-1851. Susan Morgan, Senior Information Specialist.

Receives and maintains the financial disclosure records of Senate members, officers, employees, candidates, and legislative organizations. Receives reports from committee chairs on foreign travel by senators and staff. Records open for public inspection.

Senate Select Committee on Ethics, SH-220 20510; (202) 224-2981. Fax, (202) 224-7416. Sen. Pat Roberts, R-Kan., Chair; Victor M. Baird, Staff Director.

Receives complaints and investigates allegations of improper conduct; administers the code of official conduct; recommends disciplinary action; makes recommendations to the Senate on additional laws, rules, and regulations that may be necessary; investigates allegations of unauthorized disclosure of classified information and documents by members, officers, and employees of the Senate.

CONGRESSIONAL SUPPORT GROUPS

CONGRESS

Congressional Budget Office, 402 FHOB 20515; (202) 226-2700. Fax, (202) 225-7509. Dan L. Crippen, Director. Information, (202) 226-2600. Web, www.cbo.gov.

Nonpartisan office that provides the House and Senate with budget-related information and analyses of alternative fiscal policies.

General Accounting Office, 441 G St. N.W. 20548; (202) 512-5500. Fax, (202) 512-5507. David M. Walker, Comptroller General. Information, (202) 512-4800. Library, (202) 512-5180. Documents, (202) 512-6000. Web, www.gao.gov.

Independent, nonpartisan agency in the legislative branch. Serves as the investigating agency for Congress; carries out legal, accounting, auditing, and claims settlement functions; makes recommendations for more effective government operations; publishes monthly lists of reports available to the public. Library open to the public by appointment.

Law Revision Counsel, H2304 FHOB 20515; (202) 226-2411. Fax, (202) 225-0010. John R. Miller, Law Revision Counsel. Web, www.law.house.gov.

Develops and updates an official classification of U.S. laws.

Legislative Counsel of the House of Representatives, 136 CHOB 20515; (202) 225-6060. Fax, (202) 225-3437. Pope Barrow, Legislative Counsel.

Assists House members and committees in drafting legislation.

Legislative Counsel of the Senate, SD-668 20510; (202) 224-6461. Fax, (202) 224-0567. James W. Fransen, Legislative Counsel.

Assists Senate members and committees in drafting legislation.

Library of Congress, Congressional Research Service, 101 Independence Ave. S.E. 20540; (202) 707-5775. Fax, (202) 707-2615. Daniel P. Mulhollan, Director. Information, (202) 707-5700. Services not available to public.

Provides members of Congress and committees with general reference assistance; prepares upon request background reports, analytical studies, reading lists, bibliographies, and pros and cons of policy issues; conducts public issue seminars and workshops for committees, members, and staffs; makes available the services of subject specialists.

Liaison Offices

CONGRESS

Office of Personnel Management, Congressional Liaison, B332 RHOB 20515; (202) 225-4955. Fax, (202) 632-0832. Charlene E. Luskey, Chief.

Provides House and Senate members with information on federal civil service matters, especially those pertaining to federal employment, retirement, and health benefits programs.

HOUSE

Air Force Liaison, *B322 RHOB 20515; (202) 225-6656. Fax, (202) 685-2592. Col. Pete Bunce, Chief.*

Provides House members with services and information on all matters related to the U.S. Air Force.

Army Liaison, *B325 RHOB 20515; (202) 225-3853. Fax, (202) 685-2674. Col. Tony J. Buckles, Chief.*

Provides House members with services and information on all matters related to the U.S. Army.

Navy-Marine Corps Liaison, *B324 RHOB 20515; (202) 225-7124. Fax, (202) 685-6077. Capt. Mike Denkler, Director; Col. Mike Regner, Marine Corps Director.*

Provides House members with services and information on all matters related to the U.S. Navy and the U.S. Marine Corps.

U.S. Coast Guard Liaison, *B320 RHOB 20515; (202) 225-4775. Fax, (202) 426-6081. Cmdr. Al Bernard, Chief.*

Provides House members with services and information on all matters related to the U.S. Coast Guard.

Veterans Affairs Dept. Congressional Liaison Service, *B328 RHOB 20515; (202) 225-2280. Fax, (202) 453-5225. Philip R. Mayo, Director.*

Provides House members with services and information on all matters related to veterans' benefits and services.

White House Legislative Affairs, *White House 20502; (202) 456-2230. Fax, (202) 456-6220. Broderick Johnson, Deputy Assistant (House); Charles Brain, Assistant to the President for Legislative Affairs.*

Serves as a liaison between the president and the House of Representatives.

SENATE

Air Force Liaison, *SR-182 20510; (202) 224-2481. Fax, (202) 685-2575. Lyle Koenig, Chief.*

Provides senators with services and information on all matters related to the U.S. Air Force.

Army Liaison, *SR-183 20510; (202) 224-2881. Fax, (202) 685-2570. Timothy A. Peterson, Chief.*

Provides senators with services and information on all matters related to the U.S. Army.

Navy-Marine Corps Liaison, *SR-182 20510; (202) 224-4681. Fax, (202) 685-6005. Col. Benjamin Cassidy, Marine Corps Director; Capt. Jacob Shuford, Navy Director.*

Provides senators with services and information on all matters related to the U.S. Navy and the U.S. Marine Corps.

U.S. Coast Guard Liaison, *SR-183 20510; (202) 224-2913. Fax, (202) 755-1695. Cmdr. Thomas Richey, Chief.*

Provides senators with services and information on all matters related to the U.S. Coast Guard.

Veterans Affairs Dept. Congressional Liaison Service, *SH-321 20510; (202) 224-5351. Fax, (202) 453-5218. Philip R. Mayo, Director.*

Provides senators with services and information on all matters related to veterans' benefits and services.

White House Legislative Affairs, *White House 20502; (202) 456-2230. Fax, (202) 456-6220. Chuck Brain, Assistant to the President for Legislative Affairs; Karen Robb, Deputy Assistant (Senate).*

Serves as a liaison between the president and the Senate.

Libraries

For Library of Congress divisions, see Libraries and Educational Media (chap. 6)

CONGRESS

House Administration Committee, *1309 LHOB 20515; (202) 225-8281. Fax, (202) 225-9957. Rep. Bill Thomas, R-Calif., Chair; Cathy Abernathy, Staff Director. Web, www.house.gov/cha.*

Jurisdiction over legislation on the House library; manages, in conjunction with the Joint Library and the Senate Rules and Administration committees, policies and programs of the Library of Congress.

Joint Committee on the Library of Congress, *SR-305 20510; (202) 224-6352. Sen. Ted Stevens, R-Alaska, Chair; Ed Edens, Staff Contact.*

Studies and makes recommendations on legislation dealing with the Library of Congress.

Legislative Resource Center, *Library of the House, B-106 CHOB 20515; (202) 226-5200. Fax, (202) 226-5207. Stephen R. Mayer, Senior Library Assistant.*

Serves as the statutory and official depository of House reports, hearings, prints, and documents for the Clerk of the House.

Library of Congress, *Congressional Research Service, 101 Independence Ave. S.E. 20540; (202) 707-5775. Fax, (202) 707-2615. Daniel P. Mulhollan, Director. Information, (202) 707-5700. Services not available to public.*

Provides members of Congress and committees with general reference assistance.

Library of Congress, *Law Library, 101 Independence Ave. S.E., #LM240 20540; (202) 707-5065. Fax, (202) 707-*

1820. Rubens Medina, Law Librarian. Reading room, (202) 707-5080.

Maintains collections of foreign, international, and comparative law organized jurisdictionally by country; covers all legal systems—common, civil, Roman, canon, religious, and ancient and medieval law. Services include a public reading room; a microtext facility, with readers and printers for microfilm and microfiche; and foreign law/rare book reading areas. Staff of legal specialists is competent in approximately forty languages; does not provide advice on legal matters.

Library of the Senate, *SR-B15 20510; (202) 224-7106. Gregory Harness, Librarian.*

Maintains special collection for Senate private use of primary source legislative materials, including reports, hearings, prints, documents, and debate proceedings. (Not open to the public.)

Senate Rules and Administration Committee, *SR-305 20510; (202) 224-6352. Fax, (202) 224-3036. Sen. Mitch McConnell, R-Ky., Chair; Tamara Somerville, Staff Director. Web, rules.senate.gov.*

Manages, in conjunction with the House Administration and the Joint Library committees, policies and programs of the Library of Congress.

Pages

CONGRESS

House of Representatives Page Board, *H154 CAP 20515; (202) 225-7000. Fax, (202) 225-3289. Rep. Sue W. Kelly, R-N.Y., Chair; Grace Crews, Coordinator.*

Oversees and enforces rules and regulations concerning the House page program.

House of Representatives Page School, *LJ-A15, Library of Congress 20540-9996; (202) 225-9000. Fax, (202) 225-9001. Robert F. Knautz, Principal.*

Provides pages of the House with junior year high school education.

Senate Page School, *U.S. Senate 20510-7248; (202) 224-3926. Fax, (202) 224-1838. Kathryn S. Weeden, Principal.*

Provides education for pages of the Senate.

Sergeant at Arms of the Senate, *S321 CAP 20510-7200; (202) 224-2341. Fax, (202) 224-7690. James W. Ziglar, Sergeant at Arms; Loretta Symms, Deputy Sergeant at Arms.*

Oversees and enforces rules and regulations concerning Senate pages after they have been appointed.

Staff

CONGRESS

House Administration Committee, *1309 LHOB 20515; (202) 225-8281. Fax, (202) 225-9957. Rep. Bill Thomas, R-Calif., Chair; Cathy Abernathy, Staff Director. Web, www.house.gov/cha.*

Jurisdiction over employment of persons by the House. Handles issues of compensation, retirement, and other benefits for members, officers, and employees. Oversight of the House contingent fund, office equipment, and police, parking, restaurant, and other related services.

Human Resources/Policy and Administration, *House Resume Referral Service, 263 CHOB 20515-6610; (202) 225-2926. Fax, (202) 226-0098. James M. "Jay" Eagen III, Chief Administrative Officer. Information, (202) 225-2450.*

Provides members, committees, and administrative offices of the House of Representatives with placement and referral services.

Office of Compliance, *Education and Training, 110 2nd St. S.E., #LA-200 20540-1999; (202) 724-9250. Fax, (202) 426-1913. Teresa James, Director. Information, (202) 724-9260. TTY, (202) 426-1912. Web, www.compliance.gov.*

Provides general information to covered employees, applicants, and former employees of the legislative branch about their equal employment rights and protections under the Congressional Accountability Act of 1995.

Senate Placement Office, *SH-142 20510; (202) 224-9167. Yvonne Costello, Manager.*

Provides members, committees, and administrative offices of the Senate with placement and referral services.

Senate Rules and Administration Committee, *SR-305 20510; (202) 224-6352. Fax, (202) 224-3036. Sen. Mitch McConnell, R-Ky., Chair; Tamara Somerville, Staff Director. Web, rules.senate.gov.*

Jurisdiction over Senate contingent fund, which provides salaries for professional committee staff members and general funds for personal Senate staffs.

NONPROFIT

Administrative Assistants Assn. of the U.S. House of Representatives, *123 CHOB 20515; (202) 225-4540. Fax, (202) 225-3402. John W. McCamman, President.*

Professional and social organization of House chiefs of staff. Meets to discuss mutual concerns and exchange information. Sponsors orientation program for new chiefs of staff. Meets with administrative, congressional, and international personnel for off-the-record briefings.

Congressional Legislative Staff Assn., *107 CHOB 20515; (202) 225-5235. Fax, (202) 225-5615. Chris Schloesser, President.*

Nonpartisan professional organization of legislative assistants, legislative directors, legal counsels, and committee staff. Meets to discuss mutual concerns, exchange information, and hear guest speakers; holds seminars on issues pending on the House floor.

Congressional Management Foundation, *513 Capitol Court N.E., #300 20002; (202) 546-0100. Fax, (202) 547-0936. Richard Shapiro, Executive Director. General e-mail, cmf@ricochet.net. Web, www.cmf.web.org.*

Nonpartisan organization that provides members of Congress and their staffs with management information and services through seminars, consultation, research, and publications.

Federal Bar Assn., *2215 M St. N.W. 20037; (202) 785-1614. Fax, (202) 785-1568. Jack D. Lockridge, Executive Director. General e-mail, fba@fedbar.org. Web, www.fedbar.org.*

Organization of bar members who are present or former staff members of the House, Senate, Library of Congress, Supreme Court, General Accounting Office, or Government Printing Office, or attorneys in legislative practice before federal courts or agencies.

Senate Press Secretaries Assn., *SR-416 20510; (202) 224-5401. Fax, (202) 224-8834. Margaret Camp, President.*

Bipartisan organization of present and former senatorial press secretaries and assistant press secretaries. Meets to discuss mutual concerns and to hear guest speakers.

 POLITICAL ADVOCACY

See also Advocacy and Public Service (chap. 1)

AGENCIES

Justice Dept., *Foreign Agents Registration Unit, 1400 New York Ave. N.W., #9500 20530; (202) 514-1216. Fax, (202) 514-2836. Marshall Williams, Chief. Web, www.usdoj.gov/criminal/fara.*

Receives and maintains the registration of agents representing foreign countries, companies, organizations, and individuals. Compiles semi-annual report on foreign agent registrations. Foreign agent registration files are open for public inspection.

CONGRESS

House Judiciary Committee, *Subcommittee on the Constitution, H2-362 FHOB 20515; (202) 226-7680. Fax, (202) 225-3746. Rep. Charles T. Canady, R-Fla., Chair; Cathy Cleaver, Chief Counsel. General e-mail, Judiciary@mail.house.gov. Web, www.house.gov/judiciary.*

Jurisdiction over legislation on regulation of lobbying and disclosure requirements for registered lobbyists.

Legislative Resource Center, *Records and Registration, B-106 CHOB 20515; (202) 226-5200. Fax, (202) 226-5208. Bob Cuthriell, Director.*

Receives and maintains lobby registrations and quarterly financial reports of lobbyists. Administers the statutes of the Federal Regulation of Lobbying Act of 1995 and counsels lobbyists. Receives and maintains agency filings made under the requirements of Section 319 of the Interior Dept. and Related Agencies Appropriations Act for fiscal 1990 (known as the Byrd amendment). Open for public inspection.

Secretary of the Senate, *Public Records: Campaign Financing, SH-232 20510; (202) 224-0758. Fax, (202) 224-1851. Mark W. Ward, Staff Contact.*

Receives and maintains lobby registrations and quarterly financial reports of lobbyists. Open for public inspection.

Senate Governmental Affairs Committee, *SD-340 20510; (202) 224-4751. Fax, (202) 224-9603. Sen. Fred Thompson, R-Tenn., Chair; Hannah Sistare, Staff Director. Web, gov_affairs.senate.gov.*

Jurisdiction over legislation on regulation of lobbying and disclosure requirements for registered lobbyists.

NONPROFIT

American League of Lobbyists, *P.O. Box 30005, Alexandria, VA 22310; (703) 960-3011. Fax, (703) 960-4070. Patti Jo Baber, Executive Director. General e-mail, info@alldc.org. Web, www.alldc.org.*

Membership: lobbyists and government relations and public affairs professionals. Works to improve the skills, ethics, and public image of lobbyists. Monitors lobby legislation; conducts educational programs on public issues, lobbying techniques, and other topics of interest to membership.

Political Action Committees

The following are some key political action committees (PACs) based in Washington. Note that many other organizations listed in this book operate their own PACs.

LABOR

Active Ballot Club *(United Food and Commercial Workers International Union, AFL-CIO), 1775 K St. N.W. 20006; (202) 223-3111. Fax, (202) 728-1802. Joseph T. Hansen, Treasurer.*

Air Line Pilots Assn. PAC, *1625 Massachusetts Ave. N.W., 8th Floor 20036; (202) 797-4033. Fax, (202) 797-4030. Dennis Dolan, Treasurer.*

Amalgamated Transit Union—Cope, *5025 Wisconsin Ave. N.W., 3rd Floor 20016; (202) 537-1645. Fax, (202) 244-7824. Oliver W. Green, Treasurer.*

American Federation of State, County, and Municipal Employees—PEOPLE, Qualified, *1625 L St. N.W. 20036; (202) 429-1000. Fax, (202) 429-1102. William Lucy, Treasurer. Web, www.afscme.org.*

American Federation of Teachers Committee on Political Education, *555 New Jersey Ave. N.W. 20001; (202) 879-4436. Fax, (202) 393-6375. Edward J. McElroy, Treasurer.*

Carpenters' Legislative Improvement Committee *(United Brotherhood of Carpenters and Joiners of America, AFL-CIO), 101 Constitution Ave. N.W. 20001; (202) 546-6206. Fax, (202) 546-3873. William G. Luddy, Treasurer.*

Committee on Letter Carriers Political Education *(National Assn. of Letter Carriers), 100 Indiana Ave. N.W. 20001; (202) 393-4695. Fax, (202) 737-1540. Florence Johnson, Treasurer.*

CWA-COPE Political Contributions Committee *(Communications Workers of America, AFL-CIO), 501 3rd St. N.W., #1070 20001; (202) 434-1410. Fax, (202) 434-1318. Barbara J. Easterling, Treasurer.*

Democratic Republican Independent Voter Education Committee *(International Brotherhood of Teamsters, Chauffeurs, Warehousemen, and Helpers of America), 25 Louisiana Ave. N.W. 20001; (202) 624-8741. Fax, (202) 624-8973. Mike Mathis, Treasurer.*

Engineers Political Education Committee/International Union of Operating Engineers, *1125 17th St. N.W. 20036; (202) 429-9100. Fax, (202) 778-2688. N. Budd Coutts, Treasurer.*

International Brotherhood of Electrical Workers Committee on Political Education, *1125 15th St. N.W., #1202 20005; (202) 728-6020. Fax, (202) 728-6099. Edwin D. Hill, Treasurer.*

Ironworkers Political Action League, *1750 New York Ave. N.W., #400 20006; (202) 383-4800. Fax, (202) 383-6483. Joe Hunt, Treasurer.*

Laborers' Political League of Laborers' International Union of North America, *905 16th St. N.W. 20006; (202) 737-8320. Fax, (202) 737-2754. Carl Booker, Treasurer.*

Machinists Non-Partisan Political League *(International Assn. of Machinists and Aerospace Workers, AFL-CIO), 9000 Machinists Pl., Upper Marlboro, MD 20772; (301) 967-4500. Fax, (301) 967-4588. Donald E. Wharton, Treasurer.*

National Education Assn. PAC, *1201 16th St. N.W. 20036; (202) 822-7300. Fax, (202) 822-7741. Mary Elizabeth Teasley, Director.*

Political Fund Committee of the American Postal Workers Union, AFL-CIO, *1300 L St. N.W. 20005; (202) 842-4210. Fax, (202) 682-2528. Robert Tunstall, Treasurer.*

Seafarers Political Activity Donation *(Seafarers International Union of North America), 5201 Auth Way, Camp Springs, MD 20746; (301) 899-0675. Fax, (301) 899-7355. David Heindel, Treasurer.*

Sheet Metal Workers International Assn. Political Action League, *1750 New York Ave. N.W. 20006; (202) 662-0887. Fax, (202) 662-0895. Alfred T. Zlotopolski, Treasurer.*

United Mine Workers of America, *Coal Miners Political Action Committee, 8315 Lee Hwy., Fairfax, VA 22031; (703) 208-7200. Fax, (703) 208-7264. Carlo Tarley, Secretary-Treasurer.*

NONCONNECTED

American AIDS PAC, *1808 Swann St. N.W. 20009; (202) 462-8061. Fax, (202) 483-1964. Thomas F. Sheridan, Treasurer.*

American Sugarbeet Growers Assn. Political Action Committee, *1156 15th St. N.W., #1101 20005; (202) 833-2398. Fax, (202) 833-2962. Luther Markwart, Treasurer.*

Americans for Free International Trade PAC, *112 S. West St., #310, Alexandria, VA 22314; (703) 684-8880. Fax, (703) 836-5256. Lee Maas, Treasurer.*

Arthur Andersen PAC (FKA) Arthur Andersen/ Andersen Consulting PAC, *1666 K St. N.W. 20006; (202) 481-7000. Sharon Spigelmyer, Treasurer.*

RATINGS OF MEMBERS

The following organizations either publish voting records on selected issues or annually rate members of Congress; organizations marked with an asterisk (*) rate members biennially.

AFL–CIO, 815 16th St. N.W. 20006; (202) 637-5000.

American Conservative Union, 1007 Cameron St., Alexandria, VA 22314; (703) 836-8602.

*American Farm Bureau Federation, 600 Maryland Ave. S.W., #800 20024; (202) 484-3600.

Americans for Democratic Action, 1625 K St. N.W., #210 20006; (202) 785-5980.

*Common Cause, 1250 Connecticut Ave. N.W., #600 20036; (202) 833-1200.

Competitive Enterprise Institute, 1001 Connecticut Ave. N.W., #1250 20036; (202) 331-1010.

Consumer Federation of America, 1424 16th St. N.W., #604 20036; (202) 387-6121.

Human Rights Campaign, 919 18th St. N.W., #800 20006; (202) 628-4160.

Leadership Conference on Civil Rights, 1629 K St. N.W., #1010 20006; (202) 466-3311.

League of Conservation Voters, 1707 L St. N.W., #750 20036; (202) 785-8683.

*Liberty Lobby, 300 Independence Ave. S.E. 20003; (202) 546-5611.

National Abortion and Reproductive Rights Action League-Political Action Committee (NARAL-PAC), 1156 15th St. N.W., 7th Floor 20005; (202) 973-3000.

*National Assn. for the Advancement of Colored People (NAACP), 1025 Vermont Ave. N.W., #1120 20005; (202) 638-2269.

National Assn. of Social Workers-PACE (Political Action for Candidate Election), 750 1st St. N.E., #700 20002; (202) 408-8600.

National Council of Senior Citizens, 8403 Colesville Rd., #1200, Silver Spring, MD 20910; (301) 578-8800.

National Federation of Independent Business, 600 Maryland Ave. S.W., #700 20024; (202) 554-9000.

National Gay and Lesbian Task Force Policy Institute, 1700 Kalorama Rd. N.W. 20009; (202) 332-6483.

National Taxpayers Union, 108 N. Alfred St., Alexandria, VA 22314, (703) 683-5700.

National Women's Political Caucus, 1630 Connecticut Ave. N.W., #201 20009; (202) 785-1100.

Public Citizen, Congress Watch, 215 Pennsylvania Ave. S.E., 3rd Floor 20003; (202) 546-4996.

U.S. Chamber of Commerce Legislative and Public Affairs, 1615 H St. N.W. 20062; (202) 463-5604.

U.S. Student Assn., 1413 K St. N.W., 9th Floor 20005; (202) 347-8772.

*Zero Population Growth, 1400 16th St. N.W., #320 20036; (202) 332-2200.

Black America's PAC, *2029 P St. N.W., #202 20036; (202) 785-9619. Fax, (202) 785-9621. Alvin Williams, Executive Director. General e-mail, bampac@bampac.org. Web, www.bampac.org.*

Council for a Livable World, *110 Maryland Ave. N.E., #409 20002; (202) 543-4100. Fax, (202) 543-6297. John Isaacs, President. General e-mail, clw@clw.org. Web, www. clw.org.*

Supports congressional candidates who advocate arms control and cutting the military budget.

Deloitte and Touche LLP Federal Political Action Committee, *555 12th N.W., #500 20004; (202) 879-5600. Fax, (202) 879-5309. Wade S. Williams, Treasurer.*

EMILY's List, *805 15th St. N.W., #400 20005; (202) 326-1400. Fax, (202) 326-1415. Ann Marie Habershaw, Treasurer. Web, www.emilyslist.org.*

Raises money to support pro-choice Democratic women candidates for political office.

Ernst and Young PAC, *1225 Connecticut Ave. N.W., #200 20036; (202) 327-6410. Fax, (202) 327-8863. Allen W. Urban, Treasurer.*

GOPAC, *122 C St. N.W., #505 20001; (202) 484-2282. Fax, (202) 783-3306. Tony Moonis, Treasurer. Web, www.gopac.org.*

Promotes conservative Republican candidates for local, state, and federal office.

National Committee for an Effective Congress, *122 C St. N.W., #650 20001; (202) 639-8300. Fax, (202) 639-5038. James E. Byron, Treasurer. Web, www.ncec.org.*

Supports liberal or progressive candidates in marginal races.

National PAC, *600 Pennsylvania Ave. S.E., #207 20003; (202) 879-7710. Fax, (202) 879-7728. Marvin Josephson, Treasurer.*

Supports candidates who advocate close U.S.-Israeli relations.

New Republican Majority Fund, *201 N. Union St., #530, Alexandria, VA 22314; (703) 299-6600. Fax, (703) 548-5954. J. Stanley Huckaby, Treasurer; Bret Boyles, Executive Director. General e-mail, nrmf@msn.com.*

Peat Marwick Partners/Principals and Employees Political Action Committee, *P.O. Box 18254 20036; (202) 533-5816. Fax, (202) 533-8516. Stephen E. Allis, Treasurer.*

PricewaterhouseCoopers PAC, *1900 K St. N.W. 20006; (202) 822-4274. Fax, (202) 822-5640. Allen J. Weltmann, Treasurer.*

Voters for Choice, *1010 Wisconsin Ave. N.W., #410 20007-3679; (202) 944-5080. Fax, (202) 944-5081. Mary Jean Collins, Treasurer. General e-mail, vfc@ibm.net.*

WISH List, *3205 N St. N.W. 20007; (202) 342-9111. Fax, (202) 342-9190. Kim Coupounas, Treasurer. General e-mail, WISHpac@aol.com. Web, www.thewishlist.org.*

Raises money for pro-choice Republican women candidates.

TRADE, MEMBERSHIP, AND HEALTH

Action Committee for Rural Electrification, *4301 Wilson Blvd., Arlington, VA 22203; (703) 907-5500. Fax, (703) 907-5516. Patrick E. Gioffre, Treasurer.*

American Bankers Assn. BankPAC, *1120 Connecticut Ave. N.W., 8th Floor 20036; (202) 663-5113. Fax, (202) 663-7544. Gary W. Fields, Treasurer. Web, www.aba.com.*

American Dental PAC, *1111 14th St. N.W., 11th Floor 20005; (202) 898-2424. Fax, (202) 898-2437. Dr. John V. Reitz, Treasurer.*

American Health Care Assn. Political Action Committee, *1201 L St. N.W. 20005; (202) 842-4444. Fax, (202) 842-3860. Mary Ousley, Treasurer. Web, www.ahca.org.*

American Medical Assn. PAC, *1101 Vermont Ave. N.W. 20005; (202) 789-7400. Fax, (202) 789-7469. Kevin Walker, Treasurer.*

Assn. of Trial Lawyers of America PAC, *1050 31st St. N.W. 20007; (202) 965-3500. Fax, (202) 338-8709. Heather Tureen, Director.*

Build PAC of the National Assn. of Home Builders, *1201 15th St. N.W. 20005; (202) 822-0470. Fax, (202) 822-0572. Joe Barney, Treasurer.*

Credit Union Legislative Action Council, *805 15th St. N.W., #300 20005; (202) 682-4200. Fax, (202) 682-9054. Richard Gose, Treasurer.*

Dealers Election Action Committee of the National Automobile Dealers Assn., *8400 Westpark Dr., McLean, VA 22102; (703) 821-7111. Fax, (703) 442-3168. Leonard Fichtner, Treasurer. Web, www.nada.org.*

Human Rights Campaign PAC, *919 18th St. N.W., #800 20006; (202) 628-4160. Fax, (202) 347-5323. Elizabeth Birch, Treasurer. General e-mail, hrc@hrc.org. Web, www.hrc.org.*

Supports candidates for state and federal office who favor gay and lesbian rights.

Independent Insurance Agents of America Political Action Committee, *412 1st St. S.E., #300 20003; (202) 863-7000. Fax, (202) 863-7015. Francis Shelburne, Treasurer. Web, www.independentagent.com.*

National Assn. of Broadcasters Television and Radio Political Action Committee, *1771 N St. N.W. 20036; (202) 429-5300. Fax, (202) 775-2157. Amanda Kornegay, Manager. Web, www.nab.org.*

National Assn. of Insurance and Financial Advisors PAC, *1922 F St. N.W. 20006; (202) 331-6000. Fax, (202) 331-2163. Magenta Ishak, Director. Web, www.naifa.org.*

National Assn. of Retired Federal Employees PAC, *606 N. Washington St., Alexandria, VA 22314; (703) 838-7760. Fax, (703) 838-7784. Charles Fallis, Treasurer. Member relations, (800) 456-8410. General e-mail, narfehq@aol.com. Web, www.narfe.org.*

National Assn. of Social Workers Political Action for Candidate Election, *750 1st St. N.E., #700 20002; (202) 408-8600. Fax, (202) 336-8311. Marisue Hartung, Treasurer.*

National Beer Wholesalers' Assn. PAC, *1100 S. Washington St., Alexandria, VA 22314; (703) 683-4300. Fax, (703) 683-8965. Linda Auglis, Director.*

National Committee to Preserve Social Security and Medicare PAC, *10 G St. N.E., #600 20002; (202) 216-0420. Fax, (202) 216-0451. Shelly C. Shapiro, Treasurer. Web, www.ncpssm.org.*

NRA Political Victory Fund, *11250 Waples Mill Rd., Fairfax, VA 22030; (703) 267-1000. Fax, (703) 267-3918. Wilson Phillips, Treasurer. Web, www.nra.org.*

Physical Therapy Political Action Committee, *1111 N. Fairfax St., Alexandria, VA 22314; (703) 684-2782. Fax, (202) 684-7343. Michael Matlack, Director. Web, www. apta.org.*

Women's Campaign Fund, *734 15th St. N.W., #500 20005; (202) 393-8164. Fax, (202) 393-0649. Lynn Martin, Treasurer. Web, www.wcsonline.org.*

Political Interest Groups

See also Advocacy and Public Service (chap. 1)

NONPROFIT

Alexis de Tocqueville Institution, *1611 N. Kent St., #901, Arlington, VA 22209; (703) 351-4969. Fax, (703) 351-0090. Christian Braunlich, President. Web, www.adti. net.*

Public policy research organization that conducts, sponsors, and publishes research and analysis. Advocates individual political and economic freedom, limited government, and free markets.

American Conservative Union, *1007 Cameron St., Alexandria, VA 22314; (703) 836-8602. Fax, (703) 836-8606. Christian Josi, Executive Director. Information, (800) 228-7345. General e-mail, acu@conservative.org. Web, www.conservative.org.*

Legislative interest organization that focuses on defense, foreign policy, economics, the national budget, taxes, and legal and social issues. Monitors legislation and regulations.

Americans Back in Charge Foundation, *1100 Connecticut Ave. N.W., #330 20036; (202) 861-5900. Fax, (202) 861-6065. Cleta Mitchell, Director. General e-mail, abic@abic.org. Web, www.abic.org.*

Works for congressional passage of a term limits constitutional amendment; provides information on term limits and congressional reform; advocates limited government. Term Limits Legal Institute project handles lawsuits regarding congressional term limits.

Americans for Democratic Action, *1625 K St. N.W., #210 20006; (202) 785-5980. Fax, (202) 785-5969. Jim Jontz, President; Amy F. Isaacs, Director. General e-mail, adaction@ix.netcom.com. Web, www.adaction.org.*

Legislative interest organization that seeks to strengthen civil, constitutional, women's, family, workers', and human rights.

The Brookings Institution, *1775 Massachusetts Ave. N.W. 20036; (202) 797-6000. Fax, (202) 797-6004. Michael H. Armacost, President. General e-mail, brookinfo@ brook.edu. Web, www.brookings.edu.*

Public policy research organization that seeks to improve the performance of American institutions, the effectiveness of government programs, and the quality of public policy through research and analysis. Sponsors lectures, debates, and policy forums.

Campaign for America's Future, *1025 Connecticut Ave. N.W., #205 20036; (202) 955-5665. Fax, (202) 955-5606. Robert L. Borosage, Co-Director; Roger Hickey, Co-Director. General e-mail, info@ourfuture.org. Web, www. ourfuture.org.*

Operates the Campaign for America's Future and the Institute for America's Future. Advocates policies to help working people. Supports improved employee benefits, including health care, child care, and paid family leave; promotes life-long education and training of workers. Seeks full employment, higher wages, and increased productivity. Monitors legislation and regulations.

Cato Institute, *1000 Massachusetts Ave. N.W. 20001-5403; (202) 842-0200. Fax, (202) 842-3490. Edward H. Crane III, President. General e-mail, cato@cato.org. Web, www.cato.org.*

Public policy research organization that advocates limited government and individual liberty. Interests include privatization and deregulation, low and simple taxes, and reduced government spending. Encourages voluntary solutions to social and economic problems.

Center for National Policy, *1 Massachusetts Ave. N.W., #333 20001; (202) 682-1800. Fax, (202) 682-1818. Maureen Steinbruner, President. General e-mail, thecenter@ cnponline.org. Web, www.cnponline.org.*

Public policy research and educational organization that serves as a forum for development of national policy alternatives. Studies issues of national and international concern including problems of governance; sponsors conferences and symposia.

Christian Coalition, *Government Affairs, Washington Office, 227 Massachusetts Ave. N.E., #101 20002; (202) 547-3600. Fax, (202) 543-2978. Jeffrey K. Taylor, Director. Web, www.cc.org.*

Membership: individuals who support traditional, conservative Christian values. Represents members' views to all levels of government and to the media. (Headquarters in Richmond, Va.)

Common Cause, *1250 Connecticut Ave. N.W., #600 20036; (202) 833-1200. Fax, (202) 659-3716. Scott Harsh-*

barger, President. Press, (202) 736-5770. Web, www.commoncause.org.

Citizens' legislative interest group that works for institutional reform in federal and state government. Advocates partial public financing of congressional election campaigns, ethics in government, nuclear arms control, oversight of defense spending, tax reform, and a reduction of political action committee influence in Congress.

Concerned Women for America, *1015 15th St. N.W., #1100 20005; (202) 488-7000. Fax, (202) 488-0806. George Tryfiates, Executive Director. Web, www.cwfa.org.*

Educational organization that seeks to protect the rights of the family and preserve Judeo-Christian values. Monitors legislation affecting family and religious issues.

Concord Coalition, *1819 H St. N.W., #800 20006; (202) 467-6222. Fax, (202) 467-6333. Robert L. Bixby, Executive Director. Web, www.concordcoalition.org.*

Nonpartisan, grassroots organization advocating fiscal responsibility and ensuring Social Security, Medicare, and Medicaid are secure for all generations.

Congressional Economic Leadership Institute, *201 Massachusetts Ave. N.E., #C8 20002; (202) 546-5007. Fax, (202) 546-7037. John Weinfurter, President. Web, www.celi.org.*

Nonpartisan research group that serves as a forum for the discussion of economic issues between Congress and the private sector.

Congressional Institute for the Future, *Hall of the States, 444 N. Capitol St. N.W., #601B 20001; (202) 863-1700. Fax, (202) 479-9447. Tom Hennessy, Executive Director. General e-mail, info@futuretrends.org. Web, www.futuretrends.org.*

Nonpartisan educational organization that offers information about emerging issues and trends to leaders in business and government. Conducts research; sponsors seminars and conferences; compiles and analyzes public opinion data.

Conservative Caucus, *450 Maple Ave. East, #309, Vienna, VA 22180; (703) 938-9626. Fax, (703) 281-4108. Howard Phillips, Chair. Web, www.conservativeusa.org.*

Legislative interest organization that promotes grassroots activity on issues such as national defense and economic and tax policy. The Conservative Caucus Research, Analysis, and Education Foundation studies public issues including Central American affairs, defense policy, and federal funding of political advocacy groups.

Council for Citizens Against Government Waste, *1301 Connecticut Ave. N.W., #400 20036; (202) 467-5300.*

Fax, (202) 467-4253. Thomas A. Schatz, President. Information, (800) 232-6479. Web, www.cagw.org.

Nonpartisan organization that seeks to eliminate waste, mismanagement, and inefficiency in the federal government. Monitors legislation and regulations.

Eagle Forum, *Washington Office, 316 Pennsylvania Ave. S.E., #203 20003; (202) 544-0353. Fax, (202) 547-6996. Sheila Moloney, Executive Director. General e-mail, eagle@eagleforum.org. Web, www.eagleforum.org.*

Legislative interest group that supports conservative, pro-family policies at all levels of government. Concerns include abortion, affirmative action, taxes, and national defense. (Headquarters in St. Louis.)

Empower America, *1701 Pennsylvania Ave. N.W., #900 20006; (202) 452-8200. Fax, (202) 833-0388. James R. Taylor, President. General e-mail, empower1@empower.org. Web, www.empower.org.*

Public policy research organization that seeks to encourage economic growth through lower taxes, less government spending, and regulatory reform. Interests include social policy and the moral impact of popular culture.

Family Research Council, *801 G St. N.W. 20001; (202) 393-2100. Fax, (202) 393-2134. Chuck Donovan, Executive Vice President. Web, www.frc.org.*

Legislative interest organization that analyzes issues affecting the family and seeks to ensure that the interests of the family are considered in the formulation of public policy.

Foundation for Public Affairs, *2033 K St. N.W., #700 20006; (202) 872-1750. Fax, (202) 835-8343. Leslie Swift-Rosenzweig, Executive Director. Web, www.pac.org.*

Public policy research and educational foundation that serves as an information clearinghouse on interest groups and corporate public affairs programs. Monitors the activities of public policy groups and advises on methods of operation, staff, budget size, and other administrative topics. Provides third-party commentary on groups' effectiveness and political orientation. Library open to the public by appointment. (Affiliated with the Public Affairs Council.)

Free Congress Research and Education Foundation, *717 2nd St. N.E. 20002-4368; (202) 546-3000. Fax, (202) 543-5605. Paul M. Weyrich, President. General e-mail, info@freecongress.org. Web, www.freecongress.org.*

Research and education foundation that promotes traditional values, conservative governance, and institutional reform. Studies judicial/political issues, electoral process, and public policy. Trains citizens to participate in a democracy.

Frontiers of Freedom, *1401 Wilson Blvd., #1007, Arlington, VA 22209; (703) 527-8282. Fax, (703) 527-8388. George Landrith, Executive Director. General e-mail, freedom@ff.org. Web, www.ff.org.*

Seeks to increase personal freedom though a reduction in the size of government. Interests include property rights, regulatory and tax reform, global warming, national missile defense, Internet regulation, school vouchers, and second amendment rights. Monitors legislation and regulations.

Fund for the Feminist Majority Foundation, *1600 Wilson Blvd., #801, Arlington, VA 22209; (703) 522-2214. Fax, (703) 522-2219. Eleanor Smeal, President. General e-mail, femmaj@feminist.org. Web, www.feminist.org.*

Legislative interest group that seeks to increase the number of feminists running for public office; promotes a national feminist agenda.

The Heritage Foundation, *214 Massachusetts Ave. N.E. 20002-4999; (202) 546-4400. Fax, (202) 546-0904. Edwin J. Feulner Jr., President. Web, www.heritage.org.*

Public policy research organization that conducts research and analysis and sponsors lectures, debates, and policy forums advocating individual freedom, limited government, the free market system, and a strong national defense.

Interfaith Alliance, *1012 14th St. N.W., #700 20005; (202) 639-6370. Fax, (202) 639-6375. Jane Holmes-Dixon, President. General e-mail, mail@interfaithalliance.org. Web, www.tialliance.org.*

Membership: Protestant, Catholic, Jewish, and Muslim clergy; laity; and others who favor a positive, nonpartisan role for religious faith in public life. Advocates mainstream religious values; promotes tolerance and social opportunity; opposes the use of religion to promote political extremism at national, state, and local levels. Monitors legislation and regulations.

Liberty Lobby, *Board of Policy, 300 Independence Ave. S.E. 20003; (202) 546-5611. Vince Ryan, Chair. General e-mail, libertylobby@earthlink.net. Web, www.spotlight.org.*

Legislative interest organization that opposes, busing, free trade, gun control, hate crimes legislation, the Genocide Convention, foreign aid, and U.S. involvement in the United Nations. Supports states' rights, reduced government spending and lower taxes, protective immigration laws, and repeal of the Sixteenth, Seventeenth, and Twenty-Fifth amendments.

Log Cabin Republicans, *1633 Que St. N.W., #210 20009; (202) 347-5306. Fax, (202) 347-5224. Rich Tafel, Executive Director. General e-mail, info@lcr.org. Web, www.lcr.org.*

Membership: lesbian and gay Republicans. Educates conservative politicians and voters on gay and lesbian issues; disseminates information; conducts seminars for members. Raises campaign funds. Monitors legislation and regulations.

Millennium Institute, *1117 N. 19th St., #900, Arlington, VA 22209-1708; (703) 841-0048. Fax, (703) 841-0050. Gerald O. Barney, President. General e-mail, millennium@igc.apc.org. Web, www.igc.apc.org/millennium.*

Uses the significance of the year 2000 to focus attention on strategies for building a sustainable economic and ecological future. Conducts research; sponsors conferences; supports worldwide information sharing and coalition building.

National Center for Policy Analysis, *Washington Office, 655 15th St. N.W., #375 20005; (202) 628-6671. Fax, (202) 628-6474. Jack Strayer, Vice President. Web, www.ncpa.org.*

Conducts research and policy analysis; disseminates others' outside research in the areas of tax reform, health care, the environment, criminal justice, education, social security, and welfare reform. (Headquarters in Dallas.)

National Jewish Democratic Council, *P.O. Box 75308 20013-5308; (202) 216-9060. Fax, (202) 216-9061. Ira Forman, Executive Director. General e-mail, njdc@njdc.org. Web, www.njdc.org.*

Encourages Jewish involvement in the Democratic party and its political campaigns. Monitors and analyzes domestic and foreign policy issues that concern the American Jewish community.

National Organization for Women, *733 15th St. N.W., 2nd Floor 20005; (202) 628-8669. Fax, (202) 785-8576. Patricia Ireland, President. TTY, (202) 331-9002. General e-mail, now@now.org. Web, www.now.org.*

Advocacy organization that works for women's civil rights. Acts through demonstrations, court cases, and legislative efforts to improve the status of all women. Interests include increasing the number of women in elected and appointed office, improving women's economic status and health coverage, ending violence against women, preserving abortion rights, and abolishing discrimination based on gender, race, age, and sexual orientation.

National Taxpayers Union, *Communications, 108 N. Alfred St., 3rd Floor, Alexandria, VA 22314; (703) 683-5700. Fax, (703) 683-5722. Peter Sepp, Vice President. Web, www.ntu.org.*

Citizens' interest group that promotes tax and spending reduction at all levels of government. Supports constitutional amendments to balance the federal budget and limit taxes.

National Woman's Party, *144 Constitution Ave. N.E. 20002; (202) 546-1210. Fax, (202) 546-3997. Marty Langelan, President. Web, www.natwomanparty.org.*

Membership: women seeking equality under the law. Supports the Equal Rights Amendment and other legislation to eliminate discrimination against women.

People for the American Way, *2000 M St. N.W., #400 20036; (202) 467-4999. Fax, (202) 293-2672. Ralph G. Neas, President. General e-mail, pfaw@pfaw.org. Web, www.pfaw.org.*

Nonpartisan organization that promotes protection of First Amendment rights through a national grassroots network of members and volunteers. Conducts public education programs on constitutional issues. Provides radio, television, and newspaper advertisements; maintains speakers bureau. Library open to the public by appointment.

Progress and Freedom Foundation, *1301 K St. N.W., #550E 20005; (202) 289-8928. Fax, (202) 289-6079. Jeffrey A. Eisenach, President. General e-mail, mail@pff.org. Web, www.pff.org.*

Studies the impact of the digital revolution and its implications for public policy; sponsors seminars, conferences, and broadcasts.

Progressive Policy Institute, *600 Pennsylvania Ave. S.E., #400 20003; (202) 547-0001. Fax, (202) 544-5014. Will Marshall, President. General e-mail, ppiinfo@dlcppi. org. Web, www.dlcppi.org.*

Public policy research and educational organization that supports individual opportunity, equal justice under the law, and popular government.

Public Advocate of the U.S., *5613 Leesburg Pike, #17, Falls Church, VA 22041; (703) 845-1808. Eugene Delgaudio, Executive Director.*

Educational grassroots organization that promotes a limited role for the federal government.

Public Affairs Council, *2033 K St. N.W., #700 20006; (202) 872-1790. Fax, (202) 835-8343. Douglas G. Pinkham, President. Web, www.pac.org.*

Membership: corporate public affairs executives. Informs and counsels members on public affairs programs. Sponsors conferences on election issues, government relations, and political trends. Sponsors the Foundation for Public Affairs.

Public Citizen, *Congress Watch, 215 Pennsylvania Ave. S.E., 3rd Floor 20003; (202) 546-4996. Fax, (202) 547-7392. Frank Clemente, Director. Web, www.citizen.org.*

Citizens' interest group. Interests include consumer protection, financial services, public health and safety, government reform, trade, and the environment.

Rainbow PUSH Coalition, *1002 Wisconsin Ave. N.W. 20007; (202) 333-5270. Fax, (202) 728-1192. Jesse L. Jackson Sr., President. Web, www.rainbowpush.org.*

Independent political organization concerned with U.S. domestic and foreign policy. Interests include D.C. statehood, civil rights, defense policy, agriculture, poverty, the economy, energy, the environment, hate crimes, and social justice.

Republican Jewish Coalition, *415 2nd St. N.E., #100 20002; (202) 547-7701. Fax, (202) 544-2434. Matthew Brooks, Executive Director. Web, www.rjchq.org.*

Legislative interest group that works to build support among Republican party decision makers on issues of concern to the Jewish community; studies domestic and foreign policy issues affecting the Jewish community; supports a strong relationship between the United States and Israel.

Traditional Values Coalition, *Washington Office, 139 C St. S.E. 20003; (202) 547-8570. Fax, (202) 546-6403. Andrea Sheldon Lafferty, Executive Director. Web, www. traditionalvalues.org.*

Legislative interest group that supports traditional, conservative Judeo-Christian values. Interests include anti-abortion issues, decreased federal funding for the arts, and the promotion of school prayer. Opposes gay rights legislation. (Headquarters in Anaheim, Calif.)

20/20 Vision, *1828 Jefferson Pl. N.W. 20036; (202) 833-2020. Fax, (202) 833-5307. Tim Barner, Program Director. General e-mail, vision@2020vision.org. Web, www. 2020vision.org.*

Prodemocracy advocacy group that encourages members to spend twenty minutes each month in communicating their opinions to policymakers. Targets legislative issues in particular districts and provides information on current issues. Interests include reducing military spending and protecting the environment.

Urban Institute, *2100 M St. N.W. 20037; (202) 833-7200. Fax, (202) 429-0687. Robert D. Reischauer, President. Information, (202) 261-5702. Library, (202) 261-5534. General e-mail, paffairs@ui.urban.org. Web, www.urban.org.*

Public policy research and education organization. Investigates U.S. social and economic problems; encourages discussion on solving society's problems, improving and implementing government decisions, and increasing citizens' awareness of public choices. Library open to the public by appointment.

U.S. Chamber of Commerce, *Membership Grassroots Operations, 1615 H St. N.W. 20062-2000; (202) 463-5604. Fax, (202) 463-3190. R. Bruce Josten, Senior Vice President. Press, (202) 463-5682. Web, www.uschamber. org.*

Federation that works to enact probusiness legislation; tracks election law legislation; coordinates the chamber's candidate endorsement program and its grassroots lobbying activities.

U.S. Term Limits, *10 G St. N.W., #410 20002; (202) 379-3000. Fax, (202) 379-3010. Jon Lerner, Executive Director. Web, www.termlimits.org.*

Works with state and local activists to place initiatives before voters; supports term limits at all levels of government; seeks limits of three terms in the House and two in the Senate. Monitors legislation and regulations.

The Woman Activist, *2310 Barbour Rd., Falls Church, VA 22043; (703) 573-8716. Flora Crater, President.*

Advocacy group that conducts research on individuals and groups in elective and appointive office, especially those who make decisions affecting women and minorities. Publishes legislative record and actions of the Virginia Assembly annually.

Women Legislators' Lobby, *Policy and Programs, 110 Maryland Ave. N.E., #205 20002; (202) 543-8505. Fax, (202) 675-6469. Kimberly Robson, Director. General e-mail, will@wand.org. Web, www.wand.org.*

Membership: women state legislators. Sponsors conferences, training workshops, issue briefings, and seminars. Interests include violence against women and children, employment, education, and the environment. Monitors legislation and regulations. (Affiliated with Women's Action for New Directions.)

See also Coalition of Black Trade Unionists (p. 230); Voters for Choice (p. 508)

🏛 POLITICAL PARTY ORGANIZATIONS

Democratic

Democratic Congressional Campaign Committee, *430 S. Capitol St. S.E. 20003; (202) 863-1500. Fax, (202) 485-3512. Rep. Patrick J. Kennedy, D-R.I., Chair; David Plouffe, Executive Director. Web, www.dccc.org.*

Provides Democratic House candidates with financial and other campaign services.

Democratic Governors' Assn., *499 S. Capitol St. S.E., #113 20003; (202) 485-5085. Fax, (202) 479-5156. Gov. Frank L. O'Bannon, D-Ind., Chair; Katherine Whelan, Executive Director.*

Serves as a liaison between governors' offices and Democratic party organizations; assists Democratic gubernatorial candidates.

Democratic Leadership Council, *600 Pennsylvania Ave. S.E., #400 20003; (202) 546-0007. Fax, (202) 544-5002. Sen. Joseph I. Lieberman, D-Conn., Chair; Alvin From, President. Web, www.dlcppi.org.*

Organization of Democratic members of Congress, governors, state and local officials, and concerned citizens. Builds consensus within the Democratic party on public policy issues, including economic growth, national security, national service, and expansion of opportunity for all Americans.

Democratic National Committee (DNC), *6 E St. S.W. 20003; (202) 543-7680. Fax, (202) 543-7686. Joseph Andrew, National Chair. Press, (202) 863-8012. General e-mail, dnc@democrats.org. Web, www.democrats.org.*

Formulates and promotes Democratic party policies and positions; assists Democratic candidates for state and national office; organizes national political activities; works with state and local officials and organizations.

Democratic National Committee, *6 E St. S.W. 20003; (202) 543-7680. Fax, (202) 543-7686. Edward Rendell, General Chair. Press, (202) 863-8012. General e-mail, dnc@democrats.org. Web, www.democrats.org.*

Responsible for legal affairs of the DNC, including campaign finance and election laws, ethics, and related matters.

Democratic National Committee, *Assn. of State Democratic Chairs, 430 S. Capitol St. S.E. 20003; (202) 479-5120. Fax, (202) 479-5123. Ann Fishman, Executive Director. General e-mail, tringhese@dnc.democrats.org.*

Acts as a liaison between state parties and the DNC; works to strengthen state parties for national, state, and local elections; conducts fundraising activities for state parties.

Democratic National Committee, *Communications, 430 S. Capitol St. S.E. 20003; (202) 863-8148. Fax, (202) 863-8012. Jenny Backus, Director.*

Assists federal, state, and local Democratic candidates and officials in delivering a coordinated message on current issues; works to improve and expand relations with the press and to increase the visibility of Democratic officials and the Democratic party.

Democratic National Committee, *Finance,* 430 S. Capitol St. S.E. 20003; (202) 863-7119. Fax, (202) 863-8082. Brian Hardwick, Director.

Responsible for developing the Democratic party's financial base. Coordinates fundraising efforts for and gives financial support to Democratic candidates in national, state, and local campaigns.

Democratic National Committee, *Research,* 430 S. Capitol St. S.E. 20003; (202) 479-5130. Fax, (202) 479-5129. Doug Kelly, Director.

Provides Democratic elected officials, candidates, state party organizations, and the general public with information on Democratic party policy and programs.

Democratic Senatorial Campaign Committee, 430 S. Capitol St. S.E. 20003; (202) 224-2447. Fax, (202) 485-3120. Sen. Robert G. Torricelli, D-N.J., Chair; Jamie Fox, Executive Director. Web, www.dscc.org.

Provides Democratic senatorial candidates with financial, research, and consulting services.

Women's National Democratic Club, *Committee on Public Policy,* 1526 New Hampshire Ave. N.W. 20036; (202) 232-7363. Fax, (202) 986-2791. Anna Stout, President. General e-mail, womansndc@aol.com. Web, www. democraticwoman.org.

Studies issues and presents views to congressional committees, the Democratic Party Platform Committee, Democratic leadership groups, elected officials, and other interested groups.

Republican

College Republican National Committee, 600 Pennsylvania Ave. S.E., #301 20003; (202) 608-1411. Fax, (202) 608-1429. Parker B. Hamilton, Executive Director. Web, www.crnc.org.

Membership: Republican college students. Promotes grassroots support for the Republican party and provides campaign assistance.

National Federation of Republican Women, 124 N. Alfred St., Alexandria, VA 22314; (703) 548-9688. Fax, (703) 548-9836. Marian Miller, President. Web, www.nfrw. org.

Political education and volunteer arm of the Republican party. Organizes volunteers for support of Republican candidates for national, state, and local offices; encourages candidacy of Republican women; sponsors campaign management schools. Recruits Republican women candidates for office.

National Republican Congressional Committee, 320 1st St. S.E. 20003; (202) 479-7000. Fax, (202) 863-0693.

Rep. Thomas M. Davis III, R-Va., Chair; John Guzik, Executive Director (Acting). Web, www.nrcc.org.

Provides Republican House candidates with campaign assistance, including financial, public relations, media, and direct mail services.

National Republican Senatorial Committee, 425 2nd St. N.E. 20002; (202) 675-6000. Fax, (202) 675-6058. Sen. Mitch McConnell, R-Ky., Chair; Steven Law, Executive Director. Web, www.nrsc.org.

Provides Republican senatorial candidates with financial and public relations services.

Republican Governors Assn., 310 1st St. S.E. 20003; (202) 863-8587. Fax, (202) 863-8659. Clinton Key, Executive Director; Gov. Ed T. Schafer, R-N.D., Chair. Web, www.rga.org.

Serves as a liaison between governors' offices and Republican party organizations; assists Republican candidates for governor.

Republican National Committee (RNC), 310 1st St. S.E. 20003; (202) 863-8500. Fax, (202) 863-8820. Jim Nicholson, Chair. Information, (202) 863-8790. Press, (202) 863-8550. Web, www.rnc.org.

Develops and promotes Republican party policies and positions; assists Republican candidates for state and national office; sponsors workshops to recruit Republican candidates and provide instruction in campaign techniques; organizes national political activities; works with state and local officials and organizations.

Republican National Committee, 310 1st St. S.E. 20003; (202) 863-8500. Fax, (202) 863-8820. Michael W. Grebe, General Counsel. Information, (202) 863-8790. Press, (202) 863-8550. Web, www.rnc.org.

Responsible for legal affairs of the RNC, including equal time and fairness cases before the Federal Communications Commission. Advises the RNC and state parties on redistricting and campaign finance law compliance.

Republican National Committee, *Communications,* 310 1st St. S.E. 20003; (202) 863-8614. Fax, (202) 863-8773. Clifford May, Director.

Assists federal, state, and local Republican candidates and officials in delivering a coordinated message on current issues; works to improve and expand relations with the press and to increase the visibility of Republican officials and the Republican message.

Republican National Committee, *Finance,* 310 1st St. S.E. 20003; (202) 863-8720. Fax, (202) 863-8690. Margaret Alexander Parker, Director.

Responsible for developing the Republican party's financial base. Coordinates fundraising efforts for and gives financial support to Republican candidates in national, state, and local campaigns.

Republican National Committee, *Republican National Hispanic Assembly, 600 Pennsylvania Ave. S.E., #300 20003; (202) 544-6700. Fax, (202) 544-6869. Jose Rivera, Chair.*

Seeks to develop a strong, effective, and informed Hispanic Republican constituency. Encourages Hispanic Americans to seek office at all levels of government; provides information and offers advisory services to Republican candidates, officeholders, and party organizations.

Ripon Society, *501 Capitol Court N.E., #300 20002; (202) 546-1292. Fax, (202) 547-6560. Michael Gill, Executive Director. General e-mail, info@riponsoc.org. Web, www.riponsoc.org.*

Membership: moderate Republicans. Works for the adoption of moderate policies within the Republican party.

Other Political Parties

Constitution Party, *450 Maple Ave. East, Vienna, VA 22180; (703) 242-0613. Fax, (703) 242-0796. Alison Potter, Administrative Director. Information, (800) 283-8647. General e-mail, hq@constitutionparty.com. Web, www. constitutionparty.com.*

Nationally organized political party. Favors repeal of the Sixteenth Amendment, which established the federal income tax; elimination of the Education Dept.; termination of federal funding for the arts; appointment of pro-life federal judges; expansion of state powers; and comprehensive regulatory reform.

Libertarian Party, *Libertarian Party of D.C., P.O. Box 12075 20005; (202) 483-6401. Daniel Smith, Chair. Web, www.lp.org.*

Nationally organized political party. Seeks to bring libertarian ideas into the national political debate. Believes in the primacy of the individual over government; supports property rights, free trade, and eventual elimination of taxes.

Natural Law Party, *Washington Office, P.O. Box 22254, Alexandria, VA 22304; (703) 823-6933. Fax, (703) 823-6934. Sarina Grosswald, Treasurer. General e-mail, info@natural-law.org. Web, www.natural-law.org.*

Nationally organized political party that seeks to infuse natural law philosophies with emphasis on prevention and proven solutions into the U.S. political debate. Supports preventive medicine programs, use and development of renewable energy resources, sustainable agricultural practices, and alternative approaches to criminal justice. (Headquarters in Fairfield, Iowa.)

Reform Party, *Washington Office, P.O. Box 76060 20013; (888) 830-5749,ext. 5207. Donna Waks, Chair. General e-mail, chair@dcreformparty.org. Web, www. reformparty.org.*

Nationally organized political party. Promotes a balanced budget; campaign finance reform; congressional term limits; tax reform; Medicare, Medicaid, and Social Security reform; and lobbying restrictions. (Headquarters in Dallas.)

Workers World Party, *Washington Office, P.O. Box 57300 20037; (202) 588-1205. Malcolm Cummins, Contact. General e-mail, dc@workers.org. Web, www.workers. org.*

Nationally organized political party that promotes socialism. Seeks to achieve equal employment, housing, education, and health care for all people. (Headquarters in New York.)

106th Congress

PRONUNCIATION GUIDE FOR CONGRESS

The following is an informal guide for some of the most-often mispronounced names of members of Congress.

SENATE

Evan Bayh, D-Ind. - BY
John B. Breaux, D-La. - BRO
Max Cleland, D-Ga. - CLEE-lend
Michael D. Crapo, R-Idaho - CRAY-poe
Tom Daschle, D-S.D. - DASH-el
Pete V. Domenici, R-N.M. - da-MEN-ih-chee
Michael B. Enzi, R-Wyo. - EN-zee
Russell D. Feingold, D-Wis. - FINE-gold
Dianne Feinstein, D-Calif. - FINE-stine
James M. Inhofe, R-Okla. - IN-hoff
Daniel K. Inouye, D-Hawaii - in-NO-ay
Mary L. Landrieu, D-La. - LAN-drew
Rick Santorum, R-Pa. - san-TORE-um
Robert G. Torricelli, D-N.J. - tor-uh-SELL-ee

HOUSE

Robert B. Aderholt, R-Ala. - ADD-er-holt
Spencer Bachus, R-Ala. - BACK-us
John Baldacci, D-Maine - Ball-DATCH-ee
James A. Barcia, D-Mich. - BAR-sha
Xavier Becerra, D-Calif. - HAH-vee-air beh-SEH-ra
Doug Bereuter, R-Neb. - BEE-right-er
Michael Bilirakis, R-Fla. - bil-lee-RACK-us
Rod R. Blagojevich, D-Ill. - bla-GOY-a-vich
Earl Blumenauer, D-Ore. - BLUM-men-hour
Sherwood Boehlert, R-N.Y. - BO-lert
John A. Boehner, R-Ohio - BAY-ner
Henry Bonilla, R-Texas - bo-NEE-uh
David E. Bonior, D-Mich. - BON-yer
Rick Boucher, D-Va. - BOUGH-cher
Steve Buyer, R-Ind. - BOO-yer
Charles T. Canady, R-Fla. - CAN-uh-dee
Michael E. Capuano, D-Mass. - CAP-oo-ON-oh
Steve Chabot, R-Ohio - SHAB-butt
Saxby Chambliss, R-Ga. - SAX-bee CHAM-bliss
Helen Chenoweth-Hage, R-Idaho - CHEN-o-weth HAY-g
Joseph Crowley, D-N.Y. - KRAU-lee
Barbara Cubin, R-Wyo. - CUE-bin
Peter A. DeFazio, D-Ore. - da-FAH-zee-o
Diana DeGette, D-Colo. - de-GET
Bill Delahunt, D-Mass. - DELL-a-hunt
Rosa DeLauro, D-Conn. - da-LAUR-o
Peter Deutsch, D-Fla. - DOYCH
Lincoln Diaz-Balart, R-Fla. - DEE-az baa-LART
Vernon J. Ehlers, R-Mich. - AY-lurz
Robert L. Ehrlich Jr., R-Md. - ER-lick
Anna G. Eshoo, D-Calif. - EH-shoo
Eni F. H. Faleomavaega, D-Am. Samoa - EN-ee FOL-ee-oh-mav-ah-ENG-uh
Chaka Fattah, D-Pa. - SHOCK-ah fa-TAH
Vito J. Fossella, R-N.Y. - VEE-toe Fuh-SELL-ah
Rodney Frelinghuysen, R-N.J. - FREE-ling-high-zen
Elton Gallegly, R-Calif. - GAL-uh-glee
Greg Ganske, R-Iowa - GAN-skee
Sam Gejdenson, D-Conn. - GAY-den-son
Virgil H. Goode Jr., I-Va. - GOOD (rhymes with "food")
Robert W. Goodlatte, R-Va. - GOOD-lat
Luis V. Gutierrez, D-Ill. - loo-EES goo-tee-AIR-ez
Gil Gutknecht, R-Minn. - GOOT-neck
Van Hilleary, R-Tenn. - HILL-ary

Rubén Hinojosa, D-Texas - ru-BEN ee-na-HO-suh
Joseph M. Hoeffel, D-Pa. - HUFF-ull
Peter Hoekstra, R-Mich. - HOKE-struh
John Hostettler, R-Ind. - HO-stet-lur
Amo Houghton, R-N.Y. - HO-tun
Kenny Hulshof, R-Mo. - HULLZ-hoff
Ernest Istook, R-Okla. - IZ-took
John R. Kasich, R-Ohio - KAY-sick
Gerald D. Kleczka, D-Wis. - KLETCH-kuh
Jim Kolbe, R-Ariz. - COLE-bee
Dennis J. Kucinich, D-Ohio - ku-SIN-itch
Steven T. Kuykendall, R-Calif. - KY-ken-doll
Steven C. LaTourette, R-Ohio - la-TUR-et
Rick A. Lazio, R-N.Y. - LAZZ-ee-o
Frank A. LoBiondo, R-N.J. - lo-bee-ON-dough
Zoe Lofgren, D-Calif. - ZO
Nita M. Lowey, D-N.Y. - LOW-ee
Donald Manzullo, R-Ill. - man-ZOO-low
David Minge, D-Minn. - MING-gee (hard G)
Jerrold Nadler, D-N.Y. - NAD-ler
Bob Ney, R-Ohio - NAY
David R. Obey, D-Wis. - OH-bee
Doug Ose, R-Calif. - OH-see
Frank Pallone Jr., D-N.J. - pa-LOAN
Bill Pascrell Jr., D-N.J. - pas-KRELL
Ed Pastor, D-Ariz. - pas-TORE
Nancy Pelosi, D-Calif. - pa-LOH-see
Tom Petri, R-Wis. - PEE-try
Richard W. Pombo, R-Calif. - POM-bo
George P. Radanovich, R-Calif. - Ruh-DON-o-vitch
Ralph Regula, R-Ohio - REG-you-luh
Silvestre Reyes, D-Texas - sil-VES-treh RAY-ess (rolled 'R')
Dana Rohrabacher, R-Calif. - ROAR-ah-BAH-ker
Carlos A. Romero-Barceló, D-P.R. - ro-MARE-oh bar-sell-O
Ileana Ros-Lehtinen, R-Fla. - il-ee-AH-na ross-LAY-tin-nen
Marge Roukema, R-N.J. - ROCK-ah-muh
Joe Scarborough, R-Fla. - SCAR-burro
Bob Schaffer, R-Colo. - SHAY-fer
Jan Schakowsky, D-Ill. - shuh-COW-ski
José E. Serrano, D-N.Y. - ho-ZAY sa-RAH-no (rolled 'R')
John Shadegg, R-Ariz. - SHAD-egg
John Shimkus, R-Ill. - SHIM-kus
Ronnie Shows, D-Miss. - rhymes with "cows"
Mark Souder, R-Ind. - SOW (rhymes with "now")-dur
Debbie Stabenow, D-Mich. - STAB-uh-now
Bart Stupak, D-Mich. - STEW-pack
Tom Tancredo, R-Colo. - tan-CRAY-doe
Ellen O. Tauscher, D-Calif. - TAU (rhymes with "now")-sher
W. J. "Billy" Tauzin, R-La. - TOE-zan
John Thune, R-S.D. - THOON
Todd Tiahrt, R-Kan. - TEE-hart
Nydia M. Velázquez, D-N.Y. - NID-ee-uh veh-LASS-kez
Peter J. Visclosky, D-Ind. - vis-KLOSS-key
Anthony D. Weiner, D-N.Y. - WEE-ner
Bob Weygand, D-R.I. - WAY-gend (hard G)
Lynn Woolsey, D-Calif. - WOOL-zee

Delegations to the 106th Congress

The list below gives the names of senators and representatives of each state delegation for the 106th Congress, as of April 17, 2000. The senators are listed by seniority and the representatives by district. Italicized names indicate members serving their freshman terms.

ALABAMA

Richard C. Shelby (R)
Jeff Sessions (R)
1. Sonny Callahan (R)
2. Terry Everett (R)
3. Bob Riley (R)
4. Robert B. Aderholt (R)
5. Robert E. "Bud" Cramer (D)
6. Spencer Bachus (R)
7. Earl F. Hilliard (D)

ALASKA

Ted Stevens (R)
Frank H. Murkowski (R)
 AL Don Young (R)

AMERICAN SAMOA

 AL Eni F. H. Faleomavaega (D)

ARIZONA

John McCain (R)
Jon Kyl (R)
1. Matt Salmon (R)
2. Ed Pastor (D)
3. Bob Stump (R)
4. John Shadegg (R)
5. Jim Kolbe (R)
6. J. D. Hayworth (R)

ARKANSAS

Tim Hutchinson (R)
Blanche Lincoln (D)
1. Marion Berry (D)
2. Vic Snyder (D)

3. Asa Hutchinson (R)
4. Jay Dickey (R)

CALIFORNIA

Dianne Feinstein (D)
Barbara Boxer (D)
1. *Mike Thompson (D)*
2. Wally Herger (R)
3. *Doug Ose (R)*
4. John T. Doolittle (R)
5. Robert T. Matsui (D)
6. Lynn Woolsey (D)
7. George Miller (D)
8. Nancy Pelosi (D)
9. Barbara Lee (D)
10. Ellen O. Tauscher (D)
11. Richard W. Pombo (R)
12. Tom Lantos (D)
13. Pete Stark (D)
14. Anna G. Eshoo (D)
15. Tom Campbell (R)
16. Zoe Lofgren (D)
17. Sam Farr (D)
18. Gary A. Condit (D)
19. George P. Radanovich (R)
20. Cal Dooley (D)
21. Bill Thomas (R)
22. Lois Capps (D)
23. Elton Gallegly (R)
24. Brad Sherman (D)
25. Howard P. "Buck" McKeon (R)
26. Howard L. Berman (D)
27. James E. Rogan (R)
28. David Dreier (R)
29. Henry A. Waxman (D)
30. Xavier Becerra (D)

31. Matthew G. Martinez (D)
32. Julian C. Dixon (D)
33. Lucille Roybal-Allard (D)
34. *Grace F. Napolitano (D)*
35. Maxine Waters (D)
36. *Steven T. Kuykendall (R)*
37. Juanita Millender-McDonald (D)
38. Steve Horn (R)
39. Ed Royce (R)
40. Jerry Lewis (R)
41. *Gary Miller (R)*
42. *Joe Baca (D)*
43. Ken Calvert (R)
44. Mary Bono (R)
45. Dana Rohrabacher (R)
46. Loretta Sanchez (D)
47. Christopher Cox (R)
48. Ron Packard (R)
49. Brian P. Bilbray (R)
50. Bob Filner (D)
51. Randy "Duke" Cunningham (R)
52. Duncan Hunter (R)

COLORADO

Ben Nighthorse Campbell (R)
Wayne Allard (R)
1. Diana DeGette (D)
2. *Mark Udall (D)*
3. Scott McInnis (R)
4. Bob Schaffer (R)
5. Joel Hefley (R)
6. *Tom Tancredo (R)*

CONNECTICUT

Christopher J. Dodd (D)
Joseph I. Lieberman (D)

1. John B. Larson (D)
2. Sam Gejdenson (D)
3. Rosa DeLauro (D)
4. Christopher Shays (R)
5. Jim Maloney (D)
6. Nancy L. Johnson (R)

DELAWARE

William V. Roth Jr. (R)
Joseph R. Biden Jr. (D)
AL   Michael N. Castle (R)

DISTRICT OF COLUMBIA

AL   Eleanor Holmes Norton (D)

FLORIDA

Bob Graham (D)
Connie Mack (R)
1. Joe Scarborough (R)
2. Allen Boyd (D)
3. Corrine Brown (D)
4. Tillie Fowler (R)
5. Karen L. Thurman (D)
6. Cliff Stearns (R)
7. John L. Mica (R)
8. Bill McCollum (R)
9. Michael Bilirakis (R)
10. C. W. Bill Young (R)
11. Jim Davis (D)
12. Charles T. Canady (R)
13. Dan Miller (R)
14. Porter J. Goss (R)
15. Dave Weldon (R)
16. Mark Foley (R)
17. Carrie P. Meek (D)
18. Ileana Ros-Lehtinen (R)
19. Robert Wexler (D)
20. Peter Deutsch (D)
21. Lincoln Diaz-Balart (R)
22. E. Clay Shaw Jr. (R)
23. Alcee L. Hastings (D)

GEORGIA

Paul Coverdell (R)
Max Cleland (D)
1. Jack Kingston (R)
2. Sanford D. Bishop Jr. (D)
3. Mac Collins (R)
4. Cynthia A. McKinney (D)
5. John Lewis (D)
6. *Johnny Isakson (R)*

7. Bob Barr (R)
8. Saxby Chambliss (R)
9. Nathan Deal (R)
10. Charlie Norwood (R)
11. John Linder (R)

GUAM

AL   Robert A. Underwood (D)

HAWAII

Daniel K. Inouye (D)
Daniel K. Akaka (D)
1. Neil Abercrombie (D)
2. Patsy T. Mink (D)

IDAHO

Larry E. Craig (R)
Michael D. Crapo (R)
1. Helen Chenoweth-Hage (R)
2. *Mike Simpson (R)*

ILLINOIS

Richard J. Durbin (D)
Peter G. Fitzgerald (R)
1. Bobby L. Rush (D)
2. Jesse L. Jackson Jr. (D)
3. William O. Lipinski (D)
4. Luis V. Gutierrez (D)
5. Rod R. Blagojevich (D)
6. Henry J. Hyde (R)
7. Danny K. Davis (D)
8. Philip M. Crane (R)
9. *Jan Schakowsky (D)*
10. John Edward Porter (R)
11. Jerry Weller (R)
12. Jerry F. Costello (D)
13. *Judy Biggert (R)*
14. J. Dennis Hastert (R)
15. Thomas W. Ewing (R)
16. Donald Manzullo (R)
17. Lane Evans (D)
18. Ray LaHood (R)
19. *David D. Phelps (D)*
20. John Shimkus (R)

INDIANA

Richard G. Lugar (R)
Evan Bayh (D)
1. Peter J. Visclosky (D)
2. David M. McIntosh (R)
3. Tim Roemer (D)

4. Mark Souder (R)
5. Steve Buyer (R)
6. Dan Burton (R)
7. Ed Pease (R)
8. John Hostettler (R)
9. *Baron P. Hill (D)*
10. Julia Carson (D)

IOWA

Charles E. Grassley (R)
Tom Harkin (D)
1. Jim Leach (R)
2. Jim Nussle (R)
3. Leonard L. Boswell (D)
4. Greg Ganske (R)
5. Tom Latham (R)

KANSAS

Sam Brownback (R)
Pat Roberts (R)
1. Jerry Moran (R)
2. Jim Ryun (R)
3. *Dennis Moore (D)*
4. Todd Tiahrt (R)

KENTUCKY

Mitch McConnell (R)
Jim Bunning (R)
1. Edward Whitfield (R)
2. Ron Lewis (R)
3. Anne M. Northup (R)
4. *Ken Lucas (D)*
5. Harold Rogers (R)
6. *Ernie Fletcher (R)*

LOUISIANA

John B. Breaux (D)
Mary L. Landrieu (D)
1. *David Vitter (R)*
2. William J. Jefferson (D)
3. W. J. "Billy" Tauzin (R)
4. Jim McCrery (R)
5. John Cooksey (R)
6. Richard H. Baker (R)
7. Chris John (D)

MAINE

Olympia J. Snowe (R)
Susan Collins (R)
1. Tom Allen (D)
2. John Baldacci (D)

MARYLAND

Paul S. Sarbanes (D)
Barbara A. Mikulski (D)
1. Wayne T. Gilchrest (R)
2. Robert L. Ehrlich Jr. (R)
3. Benjamin L. Cardin (D)
4. Albert R. Wynn (D)
5. Steny H. Hoyer (D)
6. Roscoe G. Bartlett (R)
7. Elijah E. Cummings (D)
8. Constance A. Morella (R)

MASSACHUSETTS

Edward M. Kennedy (D)
John Kerry (D)
1. John W. Olver (D)
2. Richard E. Neal (D)
3. Jim McGovern (D)
4. Barney Frank (D)
5. Martin T. Meehan (D)
6. John F. Tierney (D)
7. Edward J. Markey (D)
8. *Michael E. Capuano (D)*
9. Joe Moakley (D)
10. Bill Delahunt (D)

MICHIGAN

Carl Levin (D)
Spencer Abraham (R)
1. Bart Stupak (D)
2. Peter Hoekstra (R)
3. Vernon J. Ehlers (R)
4. Dave Camp (R)
5. James A. Barcia (D)
6. Fred Upton (R)
7. Nick Smith (R)
8. Debbie Stabenow (D)
9. Dale E. Kildee (D)
10. David E. Bonior (D)
11. Joe Knollenberg (R)
12. Sander M. Levin (D)
13. Lynn Rivers (D)
14. John Conyers Jr. (D)
15. Carolyn Cheeks Kilpatrick (D)
16. John D. Dingell (D)

MINNESOTA

Paul Wellstone (D)
Rod Grams (R)
1. Gil Gutknecht (R)
2. David Minge (D)
3. Jim Ramstad (R)
4. Bruce F. Vento (D)
5. Martin Olav Sabo (D)
6. Bill Luther (D)
7. Collin C. Peterson (D)
8. James L. Oberstar (D)

MISSISSIPPI

Thad Cochran (R)
Trent Lott (R)
1. Roger Wicker (R)
2. Bennie Thompson (D)
3. Charles W. "Chip" Pickering Jr. (R)
4. *Ronnie Shows (D)*
5. Gene Taylor (D)

MISSOURI

Christopher S. Bond (R)
John Ashcroft (R)
1. William L. Clay (D)
2. James M. Talent (R)
3. Richard A. Gephardt (D)
4. Ike Skelton (D)
5. Karen McCarthy (D)
6. Pat Danner (D)
7. Roy Blunt (R)
8. Jo Ann Emerson (R)
9. Kenny Hulshof (R)

MONTANA

Max Baucus (D)
Conrad Burns (R)
AL   Rick Hill (R)

NEBRASKA

Bob Kerrey (D)
Chuck Hagel (R)
1. Doug Bereuter (R)
2. *Lee Terry (R)*
3. Bill Barrett (R)

NEVADA

Harry Reid (D)
Richard H. Bryan (D)
1. *Shelley Berkley (D)*
2. Jim Gibbons (R)

NEW HAMPSHIRE

Robert C. Smith (R)
Judd Gregg (R)
1. John E. Sununu (R)
2. Charles Bass (R)

NEW JERSEY

Frank R. Lautenberg (D)
Robert G. Torricelli (D)
1. Robert E. Andrews (D)
2. Frank A. LoBiondo (R)
3. H. James Saxton (R)
4. Christopher H. Smith (R)
5. Marge Roukema (R)
6. Frank Pallone Jr. (D)
7. Bob Franks (R)
8. Bill Pascrell Jr. (D)
9. Steven R. Rothman (D)
10. Donald M. Payne (D)
11. Rodney Frelinghuysen (R)
12. *Rush D. Holt (D)*
13. Robert Menendez (D)

NEW MEXICO

Pete V. Domenici (R)
Jeff Bingaman (D)
1. Heather A. Wilson (R)
2. Joe Skeen (R)
3. *Tom Udall (D)*

NEW YORK

Daniel Patrick Moynihan (D)
Charles E. Schumer (D)
1. Michael P. Forbes (D)
2. Rick A. Lazio (R)
3. Peter T. King (R)
4. Carolyn McCarthy (D)
5. Gary L. Ackerman (D)
6. Gregory W. Meeks (D)
7. *Joseph Crowley (D)*
8. Jerrold Nadler (D)
9. *Anthony D. Weiner (D)*
10. Edolphus Towns (D)
11. Major R. Owens (D)
12. Nydia M. Velázquez (D)
13. Vito J. Fossella (R)
14. Carolyn B. Maloney (D)
15. Charles B. Rangel (D)
16. José E. Serrano (D)
17. Eliot L. Engel (D)
18. Nita M. Lowey (D)
19. Sue W. Kelly (R)
20. Benjamin A. Gilman (R)
21. Michael R. McNulty (D)
22. *John E. Sweeney (R)*
23. Sherwood Boehlert (R)
24. John M. McHugh (R)
25. James T. Walsh (R)

26. Maurice D. Hinchey (D)
27. *Thomas M. Reynolds (R)*
28. Louise M. Slaughter (D)
29. John J. LaFalce (D)
30. Jack Quinn (R)
31. Amo Houghton (R)

NORTH CAROLINA

Jesse Helms (R)
John Edwards (D)
1. Eva Clayton (D)
2. Bob Etheridge (D)
3. Walter B. Jones Jr. (R)
4. David E. Price (D)
5. Richard M. Burr (R)
6. Howard Coble (R)
7. Mike McIntyre (D)
8. *Robin Hayes (R)*
9. Sue Myrick (R)
10. Cass Ballenger (R)
11. Charles H. Taylor (R)
12. Melvin Watt (D)

NORTH DAKOTA

Kent Conrad (D)
Byron L. Dorgan (D)
AL   Earl Pomeroy (D)

OHIO

Mike DeWine (R)
George V. Voinovich (R)
1. Steve Chabot (R)
2. Rob Portman (R)
3. Tony P. Hall (D)
4. Michael G. Oxley (R)
5. Paul E. Gillmor (R)
6. Ted Strickland (D)
7. David L. Hobson (R)
8. John A. Boehner (R)
9. Marcy Kaptur (D)
10. Dennis J. Kucinich (D)
11. *Stephanie Tubbs Jones (D)*
12. John R. Kasich (R)
13. Sherrod Brown (D)
14. Tom Sawyer (D)
15. Deborah Pryce (R)
16. Ralph Regula (R)
17. James A. Traficant Jr. (D)
18. Bob Ney (R)
19. Steven C. LaTourette (R)

OKLAHOMA

Don Nickles (R)
James M. Inhofe (R)
1. Steve Largent (R)
2. Tom Coburn (R)
3. Wes Watkins (R)
4. J. C. Watts Jr. (R)
5. Ernest Istook (R)
6. Frank D. Lucas (R)

OREGON

Ron Wyden (D)
Gordon H. Smith (R)
1. *David Wu (D)*
2. *Greg Walden (R)*
3. Earl Blumenauer (D)
4. Peter A. DeFazio (D)
5. Darlene Hooley (D)

PENNSYLVANIA

Arlen Specter (R)
Rick Santorum (R)
1. Robert A. Brady (D)
2. Chaka Fattah (D)
3. Robert A. Borski (D)
4. Ron Klink (D)
5. John E. Peterson (R)
6. Tim Holden (D)
7. Curt Weldon (R)
8. James C. Greenwood (R)
9. Bud Shuster (R)
10. *Donald L. Sherwood (R)*
11. Paul E. Kanjorski (D)
12. John P. Murtha (D)
13. *Joseph M. Hoeffel (D)*
14. William J. Coyne (D)
15. *Patrick J. Toomey (R)*
16. Joseph R. Pitts (R)
17. George W. Gekas (R)
18. Mike Doyle (D)
19. Bill Goodling (R)
20. Frank R. Mascara (D)
21. Phil English (R)

PUERTO RICO

AL   Carlos A. Romero-Barceló (D)

RHODE ISLAND

Jack Reed (D)
Lincoln Chafee (R)

1. Patrick J. Kennedy (D)
2. Bob Weygand (D)

SOUTH CAROLINA

Strom Thurmond (R)
Ernest F. Hollings (D)
1. Mark Sanford (R)
2. Floyd D. Spence (R)
3. Lindsey Graham (R)
4. *Jim DeMint (R)*
5. John M. Spratt Jr. (D)
6. James E. Clyburn (D)

SOUTH DAKOTA

Tom Daschle (D)
Tim Johnson (D)
AL   John Thune (R)

TENNESSEE

Fred Thompson (R)
Bill Frist (R)
1. Bill Jenkins (R)
2. John J. "Jimmy" Duncan Jr. (R)
3. Zach Wamp (R)
4. Van Hilleary (R)
5. Bob Clement (D)
6. Bart Gordon (D)
7. Ed Bryant (R)
8. John Tanner (D)
9. Harold E. Ford Jr. (D)

TEXAS

Phil Gramm (R)
Kay Bailey Hutchison (R)
1. Max Sandlin (D)
2. Jim Turner (D)
3. Sam Johnson (R)
4. Ralph M. Hall (D)
5. Pete Sessions (R)
6. Joe L. Barton (R)
7. Bill Archer (R)
8. Kevin Brady (R)
9. Nick Lampson (D)
10. Lloyd Doggett (D)
11. Chet Edwards (D)
12. Kay Granger (R)
13. William "Mac" M. Thornberry (R)
14. Ron Paul (R)

15. Rubén Hinojosa (D)
16. Silvestre Reyes (D)
17. Charles W. Stenholm (D)
18. Sheila Jackson-Lee (D)
19. Larry Combest (R)
20. *Charlie Gonzalez (D)*
21. Lamar Smith (R)
22. Tom DeLay (R)
23. Henry Bonilla (R)
24. Martin Frost (D)
25. Ken Bentsen (D)
26. Dick Armey (R)
27. Solomon P. Ortiz (D)
28. Ciro D. Rodriguez (D)
29. Gene Green (D)
30. Eddie Bernice Johnson (D)

UTAH

Orrin G. Hatch (R)
Robert F. Bennett (R)
1. James V. Hansen (R)
2. Merrill Cook (R)
3. Christopher B. Cannon (R)

VERMONT

Patrick J. Leahy (D)
James M. Jeffords (R)
 AL Bernard Sanders (I)

VIRGIN ISLANDS

 AL Donna M. C. Christensen (D)

VIRGINIA

John W. Warner (R)
Charles S. Robb (D)
1. Herbert H. Bateman (R)
2. Owen B. Pickett (D)
3. Robert C. Scott (D)
4. Norman Sisisky (D)
5. Virgil H. Goode Jr. (I)
6. Robert W. Goodlatte (R)
7. Thomas J. Bliley Jr. (R)
8. James P. Moran (D)
9. Rick Boucher (D)
10. Frank R. Wolf (R)
11. Thomas M. Davis III (R)

WASHINGTON

Slade Gorton (R)
Patty Murray (D)
1. *Jay Inslee (D)*
2. Jack Metcalf (R)
3. *Brian Baird (D)*
4. Richard "Doc" Hastings (R)
5. George Nethercutt (R)
6. Norm Dicks (D)

7. Jim McDermott (D)
8. Jennifer Dunn (R)
9. Adam Smith (D)

WEST VIRGINIA

Robert C. Byrd (D)
John D. Rockefeller IV (D)
1. Alan B. Mollohan (D)
2. Bob Wise (D)
3. Nick J. Rahall II (D)

WISCONSIN

Herb Kohl (D)
Russell D. Feingold (D)
1. *Paul D. Ryan (R)*
2. *Tammy Baldwin (D)*
3. Ron Kind (D)
4. Gerald D. Kleczka (D)
5. Thomas M. Barrett (D)
6. Tom Petri (R)
7. David R. Obey (D)
8. *Mark Green (R)*
9. F. James Sensenbrenner Jr. (R)

WYOMING

Craig Thomas (R)
Michael B. Enzi (R)
 AL Barbara Cubin (R)

House Committees

The standing and select committees of the U.S. House of Representatives are listed below. The listing includes the room number, telephone number, party ratio, and jurisdiction for each full committee. Subcommittees are listed alphabetically under each committee. Membership is listed in order of seniority on the committee or subcommittee.

Members of the majority party, Republicans, are shown in roman type; the minority party, Democrats, are shown in italic type; Independents, in bold italic type. The word vacancy indicates that a committee or subcommittee seat had not been filled as of April 17, 2000. Subcommittee vacancies do not necessarily indicate vacancies on full committees, or vice versa. The partisan committees of the House are listed on p. 752. Members of these committees are listed in alphabetical order, not by seniority. All area codes are (202).

AGRICULTURE

Phone: 225-0029 **Room:** 1301 LHOB
Staff Director: Bill O'Conner; 225-2171; 1301 LHOB
Minority Staff Director: Stephen Haterius; 225-0317; 1305 LHOB

Agriculture generally; forestry in general, and forest reserves other than those created from the public domain; adulteration of seeds, insect pests, and protection of birds and animals in forest reserves; agricultural and industrial chemistry; agricultural colleges and experiment stations; agricultural economics and research; agricultural education extension services; agricultural production and marketing and stabilization of prices of agricultural products, and commodities (not including distribution outside of the United States); animal industry and diseases of animals; commodities exchanges; crop insurance and soil conservation; dairy industry; entomology and plant quarantine; extension of farm credit and farm security; inspection of livestock, poultry, meat products, seafood, and seafood products; human nutrition and home economics; plant industry, soils, and agricultural engineering; rural electrification; rural development; water conservation related to activities of the Agriculture Dept. The chair and ranking minority member are voting members ex officio of all subcommittees of which they are not regular members.
Party Ratio: R 27-D 24

Larry Combest,
  Texas, chair
	*Charles W. Stenholm,
	  Texas, ranking member*

Bill Barrett, Neb.	*Gary A. Condit, Calif.*
John A. Boehner, Ohio	*Collin C. Peterson, Minn.*
Thomas W. Ewing, Ill.	*Cal Dooley, Calif.*
Robert W. Goodlatte, Va.	*Eva Clayton, N.C.*
Richard W. Pombo, Calif.	*David Minge, Minn.*
Charles T. Canady, Fla.	*Earl F. Hilliard, Ala.*
Nick Smith, Mich.	*Earl Pomeroy, N.D.*
Terry Everett, Ala.	*Tim Holden, Pa.*
Frank D. Lucas, Okla.	*Sanford D. Bishop Jr., Ga.*
Helen Chenoweth-Hage, Idaho	*Bennie Thompson, Miss.*
John Hostettler, Ind.	*John Baldacci, Maine*
Saxby Chambliss, Ga.	*Marion Berry, Ark.*
Ray LaHood, Ill.	*Mike McIntyre, N.C.*
Jerry Moran, Kan.	*Debbie Stabenow, Mich.*
Bob Schaffer, Colo.	*Bob Etheridge, N.C.*
John Thune, S.D.	*Chris John, La.*
Bill Jenkins, Tenn.	*Leonard L. Boswell, Iowa*
John Cooksey, La.	*David D. Phelps, Ill.*
Ken Calvert, Calif.	*Ken Lucas, Ky.*
Gil Gutknecht, Minn.	*Mike Thompson, Calif.*
Bob Riley, Ala.	*Baron P. Hill, Ind.*
Greg Walden, Ore.	*Joe Baca, Calif.*
Mike Simpson, Idaho	*Vacancy*
Doug Ose, Calif.	
Robin Hayes, N.C.	
Ernie Fletcher, Ky.	

Subcommittees

Department Operations, Oversight, Nutrition, and Forestry
Phone: 225-0171 **Room:** 1430 LHOB

Goodlatte, chair	*Clayton*
Ewing	*Berry*
Pombo	*Thompson (Miss.)*
Canady	*Phelps*
Hostettler	*Hill (Ind.)*
Chambliss	*Thompson (Calif.)*
LaHood	*Minge*
Moran (Kan.)	*Baca*
Cooksey	*Vacancy*
Walden	

General Farm Commodities, Resource Conservation, and Credit
Phone: 225-0171 **Room:** 1430 LHOB

Barrett (Neb.), chair	*Minge*
Boehner	*Thompson (Miss.)*
Smith (Mich.)	*Phelps*
Lucas (Okla.)	*Hill (Ind.)*
Chambliss	*Clayton*
Moran (Kan.)	*Pomeroy*
Thune	*Holden*
Jenkins	*Bishop*
Ose	*Baldacci*
Hayes	

Livestock and Horticulture

Phone: 225-1564 **Room:** 1400 LHOB

Pombo, chair	*Peterson (Minn.)*
Boehner	*Holden*
Goodlatte	*Condit*
Everett	*Dooley*
Lucas (Okla.)	*Berry*
Chenoweth-Hage	*McIntyre*
Hostettler	*Stabenow*
Schaffer	*Etheridge*
Calvert	*Boswell*
Gutknecht	*Lucas (Ky.)*
Riley	

Risk Management, Research, and Specialty Crops

Phone: 225-4652 **Room:** 1730 LHOB

Ewing, chair	*Condit*
Barrett (Neb.)	*Dooley*
Smith (Mich.)	*Hilliard*
Everett	*Pomeroy*
Lucas (Okla.)	*Bishop*
Chambliss	*Baldacci*
LaHood	*McIntyre*
Moran (Kan.)	*Stabenow*
Thune	*Etheridge*
Jenkins	*John*
Gutknecht	*Boswell*
Riley	*Lucas (Ky.)*
Walden	*Thompson (Calif.)*
Simpson	
Ose	
Hayes	
Fletcher	

APPROPRIATIONS

Phone: 225-2771 **Room:** H-218 CAP
Clerk and Staff Director: James W. Dyer; 225-2771; H-218 CAP
Minority Staff Director: R. Scott Lilly; 225-3481; 1016 LHOB

Appropriation of the revenue for the support of the government; rescissions of appropriations contained in appropriation acts; transfers of unexpended balances; new spending authority under the Congressional Budget Act. The chair and ranking minority member are voting members ex officio of all subcommittees of which they are not regular members.

Party Ratio: R 33-D 27-I 1

C. W. Bill Young, Fla., chair	*David R. Obey, Wis., ranking member*
Ralph Regula, Ohio	*John P. Murtha, Pa.*
Jerry Lewis, Calif.	*Norm Dicks, Wash.*
John Edward Porter, Ill.	*Martin Olav Sabo, Minn.*
Harold Rogers, Ky.	*Julian C. Dixon, Calif.*
Joe Skeen, N.M.	*Steny H. Hoyer, Md.*
Frank R. Wolf, Va.	*Alan B. Mollohan, W.Va.*
Tom DeLay, Texas	*Marcy Kaptur, Ohio*
Jim Kolbe, Ariz.	*Nancy Pelosi, Calif.*
Ron Packard, Calif.	*Peter J. Visclosky, Ind.*
Sonny Callahan, Ala.	*Nita M. Lowey, N.Y.*
James T. Walsh, N.Y.	*José E. Serrano, N.Y.*
Charles H. Taylor, N.C.	*Rosa DeLauro, Conn.*
David L. Hobson, Ohio	*James P. Moran, Va.*
Ernest Istook, Okla.	*John W. Olver, Mass.*
Henry Bonilla, Texas	*Ed Pastor, Ariz.*
Joe Knollenberg, Mich.	*Carrie P. Meek, Fla.*
Dan Miller, Fla.	*David E. Price, N.C.*
Jay Dickey, Ark.	*Michael P. Forbes, N.Y.*
Jack Kingston, Ga.	*Chet Edwards, Texas*
Rodney Frelinghuysen, N.J.	*Robert E. "Bud" Cramer, Ala.*
Roger Wicker, Miss.	*Maurice D. Hinchey, N.Y.*
George Nethercutt, Wash.	*Lucille Roybal-Allard, Calif.*
Randy "Duke" Cunningham, Calif.	*Sam Farr, Calif.*
Todd Tiahrt, Kan.	*Jesse L. Jackson Jr., Ill.*
Zach Wamp, Tenn.	
Tom Latham, Iowa	*Carolyn Cheeks Kilpatrick, Mich.*
Anne M. Northup, Ky.	*Allen Boyd, Fla.*
Robert B. Aderholt, Ala.	
Jo Ann Emerson, Mo.	
John E. Sununu, N.H.	
Kay Granger, Texas	
John E. Peterson, Pa.	
	Virgil H. Goode Jr., Va.

Subcommittees

Agriculture, Rural Development, FDA, and Related Agencies

Phone: 225-2638 **Room:** 2362 RHOB

Skeen, chair	*Kaptur*
Walsh	*DeLauro*
Dickey	*Hinchey*
Kingston	*Farr*
Nethercutt	*Boyd*

APPROPRIATIONS (continued)

Bonilla
Latham
Emerson

Commerce, Justice, State, and Judiciary
Phone: 225-3351 **Room:** H-309 CAP

Rogers, chair	*Serrano*
Kolbe	*Dixon*
Taylor (N.C.)	*Mollohan*
Regula	*Roybal-Allard*
Latham	
Miller (Fla.)	
Wamp	

Defense
Phone: 225-2847 **Room:** H-149 CAP

Lewis (Calif.),	*Murtha*
chair	*Dicks*
Young (Fla.)	*Sabo*
Skeen	*Dixon*
Hobson	*Visclosky*
Bonilla	*Moran (Va.)*
Nethercutt	
Istook	
Cunningham	
Dickey	
Frelinghuysen	

District of Columbia
Phone: 225-5338 **Room:** H-147 CAP

Istook, chair	*Moran (Va.)*
Cunningham	*Dixon*
Tiahrt	*Mollohan*
Aderholt	
Emerson	
Sununu	

Energy and Water Development
Phone: 225-3421 **Room:** 2362 RHOB

Packard, chair	*Visclosky*
Rogers	*Edwards*
Knollenberg	*Pastor*
Frelinghuysen	*Forbes*
Callahan	
Latham	
Wicker	

Foreign Operations, Export Financing, and Related Programs
Phone: 225-2041 **Room:** H-150 CAP

Callahan, chair	*Pelosi*
Porter	*Lowey*
Wolf	*Jackson*
Packard	*Kilpatrick*
Knollenberg	*Sabo*
Kingston	

Lewis (Calif.)
Wicker

Interior
Phone: 225-3081 **Room:** B-308 RHOB

Regula, chair	*Dicks*
Kolbe	*Murtha*
Skeen	*Moran (Va.)*
Taylor (N.C.)	*Cramer*
Nethercutt	*Hinchey*
Wamp	
Kingston	
Peterson (Pa.)	

Labor, Health and Human Services, and Education
Phone: 225-3508 **Room:** 2358 RHOB

Porter, chair	*Obey*
Young (Fla.)	*Hoyer*
Bonilla	*Pelosi*
Istook	*Lowey*
Miller (Fla.)	*DeLauro*
Dickey	*Jackson*
Wicker	
Northup	
Cunningham	

Legislative Branch
Phone: 225-5338 **Room:** H-147 CAP

Taylor (N.C.),	*Pastor*
chair	*Murtha*
Wamp	*Hoyer*
Lewis (Calif.)	
Granger	
Peterson (Pa.)	

Military Construction
Phone: 225-3047 **Room:** B-300 RHOB

Hobson, chair	*Olver*
Porter	*Edwards*
Tiahrt	*Farr*
Walsh	*Boyd*
Miller (Fla.)	*Dicks*
Aderholt	
Granger	
	Goode

Transportation
Phone: 225-2141 **Room:** 2358 RHOB

Wolf, chair	*Sabo*
DeLay	*Olver*
Regula	*Pastor*
Rogers	*Kilpatrick*
Packard	*Serrano*
Callahan	*Forbes*
Tiahrt	
Aderholt	
Granger	

Treasury, Postal Service, and General Government

Phone: 225-5834 **Room:** B-307 RHOB

Kolbe, chair	*Hoyer*
Wolf	*Meek*
Northup	*Price*
Emerson	*Roybal-Allard*
Sununu	
Peterson (Pa.)	
	Goode

Veterans Affairs, Housing and Urban Development, and Independent Agencies

Phone: 225-3241 **Room:** H-143 CAP

Walsh, chair	*Mollohan*
DeLay	*Kaptur*
Hobson	*Meek*
Knollenberg	*Price*
Frelinghuysen	*Cramer*
Northup	
Sununu	
	Goode

ARMED SERVICES

Phone: 225-4151 **Room:** 2120 RHOB

Majority Staff Director: Robert S. Rangel; 225-4151; 2120 RHOB

Minority Staff Director: Jim Schweiter; 225-4158; 2340 RHOB

Ammunition depots; forts; arsenals; Army, Navy, and Air Force reservations and establishments; common defense generally; conservation, development, and use of naval petroleum and oil shale reserves; Defense Dept. generally, including the Army, Navy, and Air Force Depts. generally; interoceanic canals generally, including measures relating to the maintenance, operation, and administration of interoceanic canals; Merchant Marine Academy, and State Maritime Academies; military applications of nuclear energy; tactical intelligence and intelligence related activities of the Defense Dept.; national security aspects of merchant marine, including financial assistance for the construction and operation of vessels, the maintenance of the U.S. shipbuilding and ship repair industrial base, cabotage, cargo preference, and merchant marine officers and seamen as these matters relate to the national security; pay, promotion, retirement, and other benefits and privileges of members of the armed forces; scientific research and development in support of the armed services; selective service; Size and composition of the Army, Navy, Marine Corps, and Air Force; soldiers' and sailors' homes; strategic and critical materials necessary for the common defense. The chair and ranking minority member are non-voting members ex-officio of all subcommittees of which they are not regular members.

Party Ratio: R 32-D 28

Floyd D. Spence, S.C., chair	*Ike Skelton, Mo., ranking member*
Bob Stump, Ariz.	*Norman Sisisky, Va.*
Duncan Hunter, Calif.	*John M. Spratt Jr., S.C.*
John R. Kasich, Ohio	*Solomon P. Ortiz, Texas*
Herbert H. Bateman, Va.	*Owen B. Pickett, Va.*
James V. Hansen, Utah	*Lane Evans, Ill.*
Curt Weldon, Pa.	*Gene Taylor, Miss.*
Joel Hefley, Colo.	*Neil Abercrombie, Hawaii*
H. James Saxton, N.J.	*Martin T. Meehan, Mass.*
Steve Buyer, Ind.	*Robert A. Underwood, Guam*
Tillie Fowler, Fla.	*Patrick J. Kennedy, R.I.*
John M. McHugh, N.Y.	*Rod R. Blagojevich, Ill.*
James M. Talent, Mo.	*Silvestre Reyes, Texas*
Terry Everett, Ala.	*Tom Allen, Maine*
Roscoe G. Bartlett, Md.	*Vic Snyder, Ark.*
Howard P. "Buck" McKeon, Calif.	*Jim Turner, Texas*
J. C. Watts Jr., Okla.	*Adam Smith, Wash.*
William M. "Mac" Thornberry, Texas	*Loretta Sanchez, Calif.*
John Hostettler, Ind.	*Jim Maloney, Conn.*
Saxby Chambliss, Ga.	*Mike McIntyre, N.C.*
Van Hilleary, Tenn.	*Ciro D. Rodriguez, Texas*
Joe Scarborough, Fla.	*Cynthia A. McKinney, Ga.*
Walter B. Jones Jr., N.C.	*Ellen O. Tauscher, Calif.*
Lindsey Graham, S.C.	*Robert A. Brady, Pa.*
Jim Ryun, Kan.	*Robert E. Andrews, N.J.*
Bob Riley, Ala.	*Baron P. Hill, Ind.*
Jim Gibbons, Nev.	*Mike Thompson, Calif.*
Mary Bono, Calif.	*John B. Larson, Conn.*
Joseph R. Pitts, Pa.	
Robin Hayes, N.C.	
Steven T. Kuykendall, Calif.	
Donald L. Sherwood, Pa.	

Subcommittees

Military Installations and Facilities

Phone: 225-7120 **Room:** 2340 RHOB

Hefley, chair	*Taylor (Miss.)*
Fowler	*Ortiz*
McHugh	*Abercrombie*
McKeon	*Underwood*
Hostettler	*Reyes*
Hilleary	*Snyder*
Scarborough	*Brady (Pa.)*
Stump	*Thompson (Calif.)*
Saxton	
Buyer	

Military Personnel

Phone: 225-7560 **Room:** 2340 RHOB

ARMED SERVICES (continued)

Buyer, chair	*Abercrombie*
Bartlett	*Meehan*
Watts	*Kennedy*
Thornberry	*Sanchez*
Graham	*McKinney*
Ryun	*Tauscher*
Bono	*Thompson (Calif.)*
Pitts	*Larson*
Hayes	
Kuykendall	

Military Procurement
Phone: 225-4440 **Room:** 2340 RHOB

Hunter, chair	*Sisisky*
Spence	*Skelton*
Stump	*Spratt*
Hansen	*Evans*
Saxton	*Blagojevich*
Talent	*Allen*
Everett	*Turner*
Watts	*Smith (Wash.)*
Thornberry	*Maloney (Conn.)*
Graham	*McIntyre*
Ryun	*McKinney*
Gibbons	*Tauscher*
Bono	*Brady (Pa.)*
Pitts	
Hayes	

Military Readiness
Phone: 225-6288 **Room:** 2117 RHOB

Bateman, chair	*Ortiz*
Chambliss	*Sisisky*
Jones (N.C.)	*Spratt*
Riley	*Pickett*
Hunter	*Underwood*
Hansen	*Blagojevich*
Weldon (Pa.)	*Smith (Wash.)*
Fowler	*Maloney (Conn.)*
Talent	*McIntyre*
Everett	*Rodriguez*
Gibbons	
Sherwood	

Military Research and Development
Phone: 225-1967 **Room:** 2120 RHOB

Weldon (Pa.), chair	*Pickett*
	Taylor (Miss.)
Bartlett	*Meehan*
Kuykendall	*Kennedy*
Sherwood	*Reyes*
Kasich	*Allen*
Bateman	*Snyder*
Hefley	*Turner*

McHugh	*Sanchez*
McKeon	*Rodriguez*
Hostettler	*Andrews*
Chambliss	*Hill (Ind.)*
Hilleary	*Larson*
Scarborough	
Jones (N.C.)	
Riley	

Oversight Panel on Terrorism
Phone: 225-4151 **Room:** 2340 RHOB

Saxton, chair	*Snyder*
Hunter	*Taylor (Miss.)*
Weldon (Pa.)	*Maloney (Conn.)*
Bateman	*McIntyre*
Bartlett	*Andrews*
Chambliss	*Hill (Ind.)*
Gibbons	
Hayes	

BANKING AND FINANCIAL SERVICES

Phone: 225-7502 **Room:** 2129 RHOB
Staff Director: Anthony F. Cole; 225-7502; 2129 RHOB
Minority Staff Director: Jeanne Roslanowick; 225-4247; B-301C RHOB

Banks and banking, including deposit insurance and federal monetary policy; bank capital markets activities generally; depository institution securities activities generally, including the activities of any affiliates, except for functional regulation under applicable securities laws not involving safety and soundness; economic stabilization, defense production, renegotiation, and control of the price of commodities, rents, and services; financial aid to commerce and industry (other than transportation); international finance; international financial and monetary organizations; money and credit, including currency and the issuance of notes and redemption thereof; gold and silver, including the coinage thereof; valuation and revaluation of the dollar; public and private housing; urban development. The chair and ranking minority member are non-voting members ex officio of all subcommittees of which they are not regular members.

Party Ratio: R 32-D 27-I 1

Jim Leach, Iowa, chair	*John J. LaFalce, N.Y., ranking member*
Bill McCollum, Fla.	*Bruce F. Vento, Minn.*
Marge Roukema, N.J.	*Barney Frank, Mass.*
Doug Bereuter, Neb.	*Paul E. Kanjorski, Pa.*
Richard H. Baker, La.	*Maxine Waters, Calif.*
Rick A. Lazio, N.Y.	*Carolyn B. Maloney, N.Y.*
Spencer Bachus, Ala.	*Luis V. Gutierrez, Ill.*
Michael N. Castle, Del.	*Nydia M. Velázquez, N.Y.*
Peter T. King, N.Y.	*Melvin Watt, N.C.*

Tom Campbell, Calif.
Ed Royce, Calif.
Frank D. Lucas, Okla.
Jack Metcalf, Wash.
Bob Ney, Ohio
Bob Barr, Ga.
Sue W. Kelly, N.Y.
Ron Paul, Texas
Dave Weldon, Fla.
Jim Ryun, Kan.
Merrill Cook, Utah
Bob Riley, Ala.
Rick Hill, Mont.
Steven C. LaTourette,
  Ohio
Donald Manzullo, Ill.
Walter B. Jones Jr., N.C.
Paul D. Ryan, Wis.
Doug Ose, Calif.
John E. Sweeney, N.Y.
Judy Biggert, Ill.
Lee Terry, Neb.
Mark Green, Wis.
Patrick J. Toomey, Pa.

Gary L. Ackerman, N.Y.
Ken Bentsen, Texas
Jim Maloney, Conn.
Darlene Hooley, Ore.
Julia Carson, Ind.
Bob Weygand, R.I.
Brad Sherman, Calif.
Max Sandlin, Texas
Gregory W. Meeks, N.Y.
Barbara Lee, Calif.
Frank R. Mascara, Pa.
Jay Inslee, Wash.
Jan Schakowsky, Ill.
Dennis Moore, Kan.
Charlie Gonzalez, Texas
Stephanie Tubbs Jones,
  Ohio
Michael E. Capuano, Mass.
Michael P. Forbes, N.Y.

Bernard Sanders, Vt.

Subcommittees

Capital Markets, Securities, and Government-Sponsored Enterprises
Phone: 226-0469 **Room:** 2129 RHOB

Baker, chair	*Kanjorski*
Lucas (Okla.)	*Ackerman*
Manzullo	*Velázquez*
Jones (N.C.)	*Bentsen*
Ryan	*Weygand*
Sweeney	*Sandlin*
Biggert	*Waters*
Terry	*Maloney (N.Y.)*
Toomey	*Maloney (Conn.)*
Roukema	*Hooley*
King	*Mascara*
Royce	*Jones (Ohio)*
Paul	*Capuano*
Cook	
Riley	

Domestic and International Monetary Policy
Phone: 226-0473 **Room:** B-304 RHOB

Bachus, chair	*Waters*
Paul	*Frank*
Ose	*Watt*
McCollum	*Carson*
Castle	*Meeks*

Lucas (Okla.)	*Lee*
Metcalf	*Kanjorski*
Ney	*Sherman*
Weldon (Fla.)	*Inslee*
Ryun	*Schakowsky*
Ryan	*Moore*
Biggert	
Green (Wis.)	
Toomey	
	Sanders

Financial Institutions and Consumer Credit
Phone: 225-2258 **Room:** 2129 RHOB

Roukema, chair	*Vento*
McCollum	*Maloney (N.Y.)*
Bereuter	*Watt*
Castle	*Ackerman*
Campbell	*Bentsen*
Royce	*Sherman*
Metcalf	*Sandlin*
Barr	*Meeks*
Kelly	*Gutierrez*
Weldon (Fla.)	*Mascara*
Ryun	*Inslee*
Cook	*Moore*
Riley	*Gonzalez*
Hill (Mont.)	
LaTourette	

General Oversight and Investigations
Phone: 226-3280 **Room:** 212 OHOB

King, chair	*Sanders*
LaTourette	*Gutierrez*
Ney	*Gonzalez*
Barr	*Vacancy*
Paul	
Terry	

Housing and Community Opportunity
Phone: 225-6634 **Room:** B-303 RHOB

Lazio, chair	*Frank*
Ney	*Velázquez*
Green (Wis.)	*Maloney (Conn.)*
Bereuter	*Hooley*
Baker	*Carson*
Campbell	*Weygand*
Barr	*Vento*
Kelly	*Lee*
Hill (Mont.)	*Schakowsky*
Jones (N.C.)	*Jones (Ohio)*
Sweeney	*Capuano*
Terry	*Forbes*
Metcalf	
Roukema	

BUDGET

Phone: 226-7270 **Room:** 309 CHOB
Staff Director: Wayne Struble; 226-7270; 309 CHOB
Minority Staff Director: Thomas S. Kahn; 226-7200; 214 CHOB

Congressional budget process generally; concurrent budget resolutions; measures relating to special controls over the federal budget; Congressional Budget Office.

Party Ratio: R 24-D 19

John R. Kasich, Ohio, chair	*John M. Spratt Jr., S.C., ranking member*
Saxby Chambliss, Ga.	*Jim McDermott, Wash.*
Christopher Shays, Conn.	*Lynn Rivers, Mich.*
Wally Herger, Calif.	*Bennie Thompson, Miss.*
Bob Franks, N.J.	*David Minge, Minn.*
Nick Smith, Mich.	*Ken Bentsen, Texas*
Jim Nussle, Iowa	*Jim Davis, Fla.*
Peter Hoekstra, Mich.	*Bob Weygand, R.I.*
George P. Radanovich, Calif.	*Eva Clayton, N.C.*
	David E. Price, N.C.
Charles Bass, N.H.	*Edward J. Markey, Mass.*
Gil Gutknecht, Minn.	*Gerald D. Kleczka, Wis.*
Van Hilleary, Tenn.	*Bob Clement, Tenn.*
John E. Sununu, N.H.	*James P. Moran, Va.*
Joseph R. Pitts, Pa.	*Darlene Hooley, Ore.*
Joe Knollenberg, Mich.	*Ken Lucas, Ky.*
William M. "Mac" Thornberry, Texas	*Rush D. Holt, N.J.*
Jim Ryun, Kan.	*Joseph M. Hoeffel, Pa.*
Mac Collins, Ga.	*Tammy Baldwin, Wis.*
Zach Wamp, Tenn.	
Mark Green, Wis.	
Ernie Fletcher, Ky.	
Gary Miller, Calif.	
Paul D. Ryan, Wis.	
Patrick J. Toomey, Pa.	

COMMERCE

Phone: 225-2927 **Room:** 2125 RHOB
Staff Director: James E. Derderian; 225-2927; 2125 RHOB
Minority Staff Director and Chief Counsel: Reid Stuntz; 225-3641; 2322 RHOB

Interstate and foreign commerce generally; biomedical research and development; consumer affairs and consumer protection; health and health facilities, except health care supported by payroll deductions; interstate energy compacts; measures relating to the exploration, production, storage, supply, marketing, pricing, and regulation of energy resources, including all fossil fuels, solar energy, and other unconventional or renewable energy resources; measures relating to the conservation of energy resources; measures relating to energy information generally; measures relating to (A) the genera-

tion and marketing of power (except by federally chartered or federal regional power marketing authorities), (B) the reliability and interstate transmission of, and ratemaking for, all power, and (C) the siting of generation facilities, except the installation of interconnections between government water power projects; measures relating to general management of the Energy Dept., and the management and all functions of the Federal Energy Regulatory Commission; national energy policy generally; public health and quarantine; regulation of the domestic nuclear energy industry, including regulation of research and development reactors and nuclear regulatory research; regulation of interstate and foreign communications; securities and exchanges; travel and tourism; nuclear and other energy, and non-military nuclear energy and research and development including the disposal of nuclear waste. The chair and ranking minority member are voting members ex officio of all subcommittees of which they are not regular members.

Party Ratio: R 29-D 24

Thomas J. Bliley Jr., Va., chair	*John D. Dingell, Mich., ranking member*
W. J. "Billy" Tauzin, La.	*Henry A. Waxman, Calif.*
Michael G. Oxley, Ohio	*Edward J. Markey, Mass.*
Michael Bilirakis, Fla.	*Ralph M. Hall, Texas*
Joe L. Barton, Texas	*Rick Boucher, Va.*
Fred Upton, Mich.	*Edolphus Towns, N.Y.*
Cliff Stearns, Fla.	*Frank Pallone Jr., N.J.*
Paul E. Gillmor, Ohio	*Sherrod Brown, Ohio*
James C. Greenwood, Pa.	*Bart Gordon, Tenn.*
Christopher Cox, Calif.	*Peter Deutsch, Fla.*
Nathan Deal, Ga.	*Bobby L. Rush, Ill.*
Steve Largent, Okla.	*Anna G. Eshoo, Calif.*
Richard M. Burr, N.C.	*Ron Klink, Pa.*
Brian P. Bilbray, Calif.	*Bart Stupak, Mich.*
Edward Whitfield, Ky.	*Eliot L. Engel, N.Y.*
Greg Ganske, Iowa	*Tom Sawyer, Ohio*
Charlie Norwood, Ga.	*Albert R. Wynn, Md.*
Tom Coburn, Okla.	*Gene Green, Texas*
Rick A. Lazio, N.Y.	*Karen McCarthy, Mo.*
Barbara Cubin, Wyo.	*Ted Strickland, Ohio*
James E. Rogan, Calif.	*Diana DeGette, Colo.*
John Shimkus, Ill.	*Thomas M. Barrett, Wis.*
Heather A. Wilson, N.M.	*Bill Luther, Minn.*
John Shadegg, Ariz.	*Lois Capps, Calif.*
Charles W. "Chip" Pickering Jr., Miss.	
Vito J. Fossella, N.Y.	
Roy Blunt, Mo.	
Ed Bryant, Tenn.	
Robert L. Ehrlich Jr., Md.	

Subcommittees

Energy and Power

Phone: 225-2927 **Room:** 2125 RHOB

Barton, chair	*Hall (Texas)*
Bilirakis	*McCarthy (Mo.)*
Stearns	*Sawyer*
Largent	*Markey*
Burr	*Boucher*
Whitfield	*Pallone*
Norwood	*Brown (Ohio)*
Coburn	*Gordon*
Rogan	*Rush*
Shimkus	*Wynn*
Wilson	*Strickland*
Shadegg	*Deutsch*
Pickering	*Klink*
Fossella	
Bryant	
Ehrlich	

Finance and Hazardous Materials

Phone: 225-2927 **Room:** 2125 RHOB

Oxley, chair	*Towns*
Tauzin	*Deutsch*
Gillmor	*Stupak*
Greenwood	*Engel*
Cox	*DeGette*
Largent	*Barrett (Wis.)*
Bilbray	*Luther*
Ganske	*Capps*
Lazio	*Markey*
Shimkus	*Hall (Texas)*
Wilson	*Pallone*
Shadegg	*Rush*
Fossella	
Blunt	
Ehrlich	

Health and Environment

Phone: 225-2927 **Room:** 2125 RHOB

Bilirakis, chair	*Brown (Ohio)*
Upton	*Waxman*
Stearns	*Pallone*
Greenwood	*Deutsch*
Deal	*Stupak*
Burr	*Green (Texas)*
Bilbray	*Strickland*
Whitfield	*DeGette*
Ganske	*Barrett (Wis.)*
Norwood	*Capps*
Coburn	*Hall (Texas)*
Lazio	*Towns*

Cubin	*Eshoo*
Shadegg	
Pickering	
Bryant	

Oversight and Investigations

Phone: 225-2927 **Room:** 2125 RHOB

Upton, chair	*Klink*
Barton	*Waxman*
Cox	*Stupak*
Burr	*Green (Texas)*
Bilbray	*McCarthy (Mo.)*
Whitfield	*Strickland*
Ganske	*DeGette*
Blunt	
Bryant	

Telecommunications, Trade, and Consumer Protection

Phone: 225-2927 **Room:** 2125 RHOB

Tauzin, chair	*Markey*
Oxley	*Boucher*
Stearns	*Gordon*
Gillmor	*Rush*
Cox	*Eshoo*
Deal	*Engel*
Largent	*Wynn*
Cubin	*Luther*
Rogan	*Klink*
Shimkus	*Sawyer*
Wilson	*Green (Texas)*
Pickering	*McCarthy (Mo.)*
Fossella	
Blunt	
Ehrlich	

EDUCATION AND THE WORKFORCE

Phone: 225-4527 **Room:** 2181 RHOB
Staff Director: Kevin D. Talley; 225-4527; 2181 RHOB
Minority Staff Director: Gail Weiss; 225-3725; 2101 RHOB

Measures relating to education or labor generally; child labor; Columbia Institution for the Deaf, Dumb, and Blind; Howard University; Freedmen's Hospital; convict labor and the entry of goods made by convicts into interstate commerce; food programs for children in schools; labor standards and statistics; mediation and arbitration of labor disputes; regulation or prevention of importation of foreign laborers under contract; U.S. Employees' Compensation Commission; vocational rehabilitation; wages and hours of labor; welfare of miners; work incentive programs. The chair and ranking minority member are non-voting members ex officio of

EDUCATION AND THE WORKFORCE (continued)
all subcommittees of which they are not regular members.

Party Ratio: R 27-D 22

Bill Goodling, Pa., chair
Tom Petri, Wis.
Marge Roukema, N.J.
Cass Ballenger, N.C.
Bill Barrett, Neb.
John A. Boehner, Ohio
Peter Hoekstra, Mich.
Howard P. "Buck" McKeon, Calif.
Michael N. Castle, Del.
Sam Johnson, Texas
James M. Talent, Mo.
James C. Greenwood, Pa.
Lindsey Graham, S.C.
Mark Souder, Ind.
David M. McIntosh, Ind.
Charlie Norwood, Ga.
Ron Paul, Texas
Bob Schaffer, Colo.
Fred Upton, Mich.
Nathan Deal, Ga.
Van Hilleary, Tenn.
Vernon J. Ehlers, Mich.
Matt Salmon, Ariz.
Tom Tancredo, Colo.
Ernie Fletcher, Ky.
Jim DeMint, S.C.
Johnny Isakson, Ga.

William L. Clay, Mo., ranking member
George Miller, Calif.
Dale E. Kildee, Mich.
Matthew G. Martinez, Calif.
Major R. Owens, N.Y.
Donald M. Payne, N.J.
Patsy T. Mink, Hawaii
Robert E. Andrews, N.J.
Tim Roemer, Ind.
Robert C. Scott, Va.
Lynn Woolsey, Calif.
Carlos A. Romero-Barceló, P.R.
Chaka Fattah, Pa.
Rubén Hinojosa, Texas
Carolyn McCarthy, N.Y.
John F. Tierney, Mass.
Ron Kind, Wis.
Loretta Sanchez, Calif.
Harold E. Ford Jr., Tenn.
Dennis J. Kucinich, Ohio
David Wu, Ore.
Rush D. Holt, N.J.

Subcommittees

Early Childhood, Youth, and Families
Phone: 225-4527 **Room:** 2181 RHOB

Castle, chair	*Kildee*
Johnson (Texas)	*Miller (Calif.)*
Souder	*Payne*
Paul	*Mink*
Goodling	*Scott*
Greenwood	*Kucinich*
McIntosh	*Woolsey*
Upton	*Romero-Barceló*
Hilleary	*Fattah*
Petri	*Hinojosa*
Roukema	*McCarthy (N.Y.)*
Boehner	*Sanchez*
Graham	*Ford*
Schaffer	*Wu*
Salmon	

Tancredo
DeMint

Employer-Employee Relations
Phone: 225-4527 **Room:** 2181 RHOB

Boehner, chair	*Andrews*
Talent	*Kildee*
Petri	*Payne*
Roukema	*Romero-Barceló*
Ballenger	*McCarthy (N.Y.)*
Goodling	*Tierney*
McKeon	*Wu*
Hoekstra	*Holt*
Salmon	
Fletcher	
DeMint	

Oversight and Investigations
Phone: 225-4527 **Room:** 2181 RHOB

Hoekstra, chair	*Roemer*
Norwood	*Scott*
Hilleary	*Kind*
Schaffer	*Ford*
Tancredo	
Fletcher	

Postsecondary Education, Training, and Life-Long Learning
Phone: 225-4527 **Room:** 2181 RHOB

McKeon, chair	*Martinez*
Goodling	*Tierney*
Petri	*Kind*
Barrett (Neb.)	*Holt*
Greenwood	*Owens*
Graham	*Mink*
McIntosh	*Andrews*
Castle	*Roemer*
Souder	*Fattah*
Deal	*Hinojosa*
Ehlers	
Isakson	

Workforce Protections
Phone: 225-4527 **Room:** 2181 RHOB

Ballenger, chair	*Owens*
Barrett (Neb.)	*Miller (Calif.)*
Hoekstra	*Martinez*
Graham	*Woolsey*
Paul	*Sanchez*
Johnson (Texas)	*Kucinich*
Boehner	
Isakson	

GOVERNMENT REFORM

Phone: 225-5074 **Room:** 2157 RHOB
Majority Staff Director: Kevin Binger; 225-5074; 2157 RHOB
Minority Staff Director: Philip Schiliro; 225-5051; B350-A RHOB

Civil service, including intergovernmental personnel; the status of officers and employees of the United States, including their compensation, classification, and retirement; measures relating to the municipal affairs of the District of Columbia in general, other than appropriations; federal paperwork reduction; budget and accounting measures, generally; holidays and celebrations; overall economy, efficiency, and management of government operations and activities, including federal procurement; National Archives; population and demography generally, including the census; Postal Service generally, including the transportation of mail; public information and records; relationship of the federal government to the states and municipalities generally; reorganizations in the executive branch of the government. The chair and ranking minority member are voting members ex officio of all subcommittees of which they are not regular members.

Party Ratio: R 24-D 19-I 1

Dan Burton, Ind., chair
Benjamin A. Gilman, N.Y.
Constance A. Morella, Md.
Christopher Shays, Conn.
Ileana Ros-Lehtinen, Fla.
John M. McHugh, N.Y.
Steve Horn, Calif.
John L. Mica, Fla.
Thomas M. Davis III, Va.
David M. McIntosh, Ind.
Mark Souder, Ind.
Joe Scarborough, Fla.
Steven C. LaTourette, Ohio
Mark Sanford, S.C.
Bob Barr, Ga.
Dan Miller, Fla.
Asa Hutchinson, Ark.
Lee Terry, Neb.
Judy Biggert, Ill.
Greg Walden, Ore.
Doug Ose, Calif.
Paul D. Ryan, Wis.
Helen Chenoweth-Hage, Idaho
David Vitter, La.

Henry A. Waxman, Calif., ranking member
Tom Lantos, Calif.
Bob Wise, W.Va.
Major R. Owens, N.Y.
Edolphus Towns, N.Y.
Paul E. Kanjorski, Pa.
Patsy T. Mink, Hawaii
Carolyn B. Maloney, N.Y.
Eleanor Holmes Norton, D.C.
Chaka Fattah, Pa.
Elijah E. Cummings, Md.
Dennis J. Kucinich, Ohio
Rod R. Blagojevich, Ill.
Danny K. Davis, Ill.
John F. Tierney, Mass.
Jim Turner, Texas
Tom Allen, Maine
Harold E. Ford Jr., Tenn.
Jan Schakowsky, Ill.

Bernard Sanders, Vt.

Subcommittees

Census

Phone: 226-1973 **Room:** 114 OHOB

Miller (Fla.), chair	*Maloney (N.Y.)*
Davis (Va.)	*Davis (Ill.)*
Ryan	*Ford*
Souder	

Civil Service

Phone: 225-6427 **Room:** B-371C RHOB

Scarborough, chair	*Cummings*
Hutchinson	*Norton*
Morella	*Allen*
Mica	
Miller (Fla.)	

Criminal Justice, Drug Policy, and Human Resources

Phone: 225-2577 **Room:** B-373 RHOB

Mica, chair	*Mink*
Barr	*Towns*
Gilman	*Cummings*
Shays	*Kucinich*
Ros-Lehtinen	*Blagojevich*
Souder	*Tierney*
LaTourette	*Turner*
Hutchinson	*Schakowsky*
Ose	
Vitter	

District of Columbia

Phone: 225-6751 **Room:** B-349A RHOB

Davis (Va.), chair	*Norton*
	Maloney (N.Y.)
Morella	*Towns*
Horn	
Scarborough	

Government Management, Information, and Technology

Phone: 225-5147 **Room:** B-373 RHOB

Horn, chair	*Turner*
Biggert	*Kanjorski*
Davis (Va.)	*Owens*
Walden	*Mink*
Ose	*Maloney (N.Y.)*
Ryan	

National Economic Growth, Natural Resources, and Regulatory Affairs

Phone: 225-4407 **Room:** B-377 RHOB

McIntosh, chair	*Kucinich*
Ryan	*Lantos*
Barr	*Kanjorski*
Terry	*Ford*

GOVERNMENT REFORM (continued)

Walden
Chenoweth-Hage
Vitter

Sanders

National Security, Veterans Affairs, and International Relations

Phone: 225-2548 **Room:** B-372 RHOB

Shays, chair	*Blagojevich*
Souder	*Lantos*
Ros-Lehtinen	*Wise*
McHugh	*Condit*
Mica	*Tierney*
McIntosh	*Allen*
Sanford	*Towns*
Terry	*Schakowsky*
Biggert	
Chenoweth-Hage	
	Sanders

Postal Service

Phone: 225-3741 **Room:** B-349C RHOB

McHugh, chair	*Fattah*
Sanford	*Owens*
Gilman	*Davis (Ill.)*
LaTourette	
Miller (Fla.)	

HOUSE ADMINISTRATION

Phone: 225-8281 **Room:** 1309 LHOB
Majority Staff Director: Cathy Abernathy; 225-8281; 1309 LHOB
Minority Staff Director: Bob Bean; 225-2061; 1339 LHOB

Accounts of the house generally; assignment of office space for members and committees; disposition of useless executive papers; matters relating to the election of the president, vice president, or members of congress; corrupt practices; contested elections; credentials and qualifications; federal elections generally; appropriations from accounts for committee salaries and expenses (except for the Committee on Appropriations), House Information Systems, and allowances and expenses of members, House officers and administrative offices of the House; auditing and settling of all such accounts; expenditure of such accounts; employment of persons by the House, including clerks for members and committees, and reporters of debates; Library of Congress and the House Library; statuary and pictures; acceptance or purchase of works of art for the Capitol; the Botanic Garden; management of the Library of Congress; purchase of books and manuscripts; Smithsonian Institution and the incorporation of similar institutions; Franking Commission; printing and correction of the Congressional Record; services to the House,

including the House restaurant, parking facilities and administration of the House office buildings and of the House wing of the Capitol; travel of members of the House; raising, reporting, and use of campaign contributions for candidates for office of representative in the House of Representatives, of delegate, and of resident commissioner to the United States from Puerto Rico; compensation, retirement, and other benefits of the members, officers, and employees of the Congress.

Party Ratio: R 6-D 3

Bill Thomas, Calif., chair	*Steny H. Hoyer, Md., ranking member*
John A. Boehner, Ohio	*Chaka Fattah, Pa.*
Vernon J. Ehlers, Mich.	*Jim Davis, Fla.*
Bob Ney, Ohio	
John L. Mica, Fla.	
Thomas W. Ewing, Ill.	

INTERNATIONAL RELATIONS

Phone: 225-5021 **Room:** 2170 RHOB
Chief of Staff: Richard J. Garon Jr.; 225-5021; 2170 RHOB
Minority Chief of Staff: Kathleen Bertelsen Moazed; 225-6735; B-360 RHOB

Relations of the United States with foreign nations generally; acquisition of land and buildings for embassies and legations in foreign countries; establishment of boundary lines between the United States and foreign nations; export controls, including nonproliferation of nuclear technology and nuclear hardware; foreign loans; international commodity agreements (other than those involving sugar), including all agreements for cooperation in the export of nuclear technology and nuclear hardware; international conferences and congresses; international education; intervention abroad and declarations of war; measures relating to the diplomatic service; measures to foster commercial intercourse with foreign nations and to safeguard American business interests abroad; measures relating to international economic policy; neutrality; protection of American citizens abroad and expatriation; American National Red Cross; trading with the enemy; U.N. organizations. The chair and ranking minority member are non-voting members ex officio of all subcommittees of which they are not regular members.

Party Ratio: R 26-D 23

Benjamin A. Gilman, N.Y., chair	*Sam Gejdenson, Conn., ranking member*
Bill Goodling, Pa.	*Tom Lantos, Calif.*
Jim Leach, Iowa	*Howard L. Berman, Calif.*
Henry J. Hyde, Ill.	*Gary L. Ackerman, N.Y.*
Doug Bereuter, Neb.	*Eni F. H. Faleomavaega, Am. Samoa*
Christopher H. Smith, N.J.	
Dan Burton, Ind.	*Matthew G. Martinez, Calif.*

Elton Gallegly, Calif.
Ileana Ros-Lehtinen, Fla.
Cass Ballenger, N.C.
Dana Rohrabacher, Calif.
Donald Manzullo, Ill.
Ed Royce, Calif.
Peter T. King, N.Y.
Steve Chabot, Ohio
Mark Sanford, S.C.
Matt Salmon, Ariz.
Amo Houghton, N.Y.
Tom Campbell, Calif.
John M. McHugh, N.Y.
Kevin Brady, Texas
Richard M. Burr, N.C.
Paul E. Gillmor, Ohio
George P. Radanovich, Calif.
John Cooksey, La.
Tom Tancredo, Colo.

Donald M. Payne, N.J.
Robert Menendez, N.J.
Sherrod Brown, Ohio
Cynthia A. McKinney, Ga.
Alcee L. Hastings, Fla.
Pat Danner, Mo.
Earl F. Hilliard, Ala.
Brad Sherman, Calif.
Robert Wexler, Fla.
Steven R. Rothman, N.J.
Jim Davis, Fla.
Earl Pomeroy, N.D.
Bill Delahunt, Mass.
Gregory W. Meeks, N.Y.
Barbara Lee, Calif.
Joseph Crowley, N.Y.
Joseph M. Hoeffel, Pa.

Subcommittees

Africa
Phone: 226-7812 **Room:** 255 FHOB

Royce, chair	*Payne*
Houghton	*Hastings (Fla.)*
Campbell	*Meeks*
Chabot	*Lee*
Tancredo	
Radanovich	

Asia and the Pacific
Phone: 226-7825 **Room:** B-359 RHOB

Bereuter, chair	*Lantos*
Leach	*Berman*
Rohrabacher	*Faleomavaega*
King	*Martinez*
Sanford	*Brown (Ohio)*
Salmon	*Wexler*
McHugh	*Davis (Fla.)*
Burr	*Pomeroy*
Gillmor	*Ackerman*
Manzullo	*Hastings (Fla.)*
Royce	
Cooksey	

International Economic Policy and Trade
Phone: 225-3345 **Room:** 257 FHOB

Ros-Lehtinen, chair	*Menendez*
	Danner
Manzullo	*Hilliard*
Chabot	*Sherman*
Brady (Texas)	*Rothman*
Radanovich	*Delahunt*

Cooksey	*Crowley*
Bereuter	*Hoeffel*
Rohrabacher	
Campbell	
Burr	

International Operations and Human Rights
Phone: 225-5748 **Room:** B-358 RHOB

Smith (N.J.), chair	*McKinney*
	Faleomavaega
Goodling	*Hilliard*
Hyde	*Sherman*
Tancredo	*Delahunt*
Burton	*Meeks*
Ballenger	
King	
Salmon	

Western Hemisphere
Phone: 226-7820 **Room:** 2401-A RHOB

Gallegly, chair	*Ackerman*
Burton	*Martinez*
Ballenger	*Menendez*
Smith (N.J.)	*Wexler*
Ros-Lehtinen	*Rothman*
Sanford	*Davis (Fla.)*
Brady (Texas)	*Pomeroy*
Gillmor	

JUDICIARY

Phone: 225-3951 **Room:** 2138 RHOB
Chief Counsel: Thomas Mooney; 225-3951; 2138 RHOB
Minority Chief Counsel: Julian Epstein; 225-6906; B-351C RHOB

The judiciary and judicial proceedings, civil and criminal; administrative practice and procedure; apportionment of representatives; bankruptcy, mutiny, espionage, and counterfeiting; civil liberties; constitutional amendments; federal courts and judges, and local courts in the territories and possessions; immigration and naturalization; interstate compacts, generally; measures relating to claims against the United States; meetings of Congress, attendance of members and their acceptance of incompatible offices; national penitentiaries; patents, the Patent Office, copyrights, and trademarks; presidential succession; protection of trade and commerce against unlawful restraints and monopolies; revision and codification of the Statutes of the United States; state and territorial boundaries; subversive activities affecting the internal security of the United States. The chair and ranking minority member are non-voting members ex officio of all subcommittees of which they are not regular members.

Party Ratio: R 21-D 16

Henry J. Hyde, Ill., chair	*John Conyers Jr., Mich., ranking member*

JUDICIARY (continued)

F. James Sensenbrenner Jr., Wis.	*Barney Frank, Mass.*
Bill McCollum, Fla.	*Howard L. Berman, Calif.*
George W. Gekas, Pa.	*Rick Boucher, Va.*
Howard Coble, N.C.	*Jerrold Nadler, N.Y.*
Lamar Smith, Texas	*Robert C. Scott, Va.*
Elton Gallegly, Calif.	*Melvin Watt, N.C.*
Charles T. Canady, Fla.	*Zoe Lofgren, Calif.*
Robert W. Goodlatte, Va.	*Sheila Jackson-Lee, Texas*
Steve Chabot, Ohio	*Maxine Waters, Calif.*
Bob Barr, Ga.	*Martin T. Meehan, Mass.*
Bill Jenkins, Tenn.	*Bill Delahunt, Mass.*
Asa Hutchinson, Ark.	*Robert Wexler, Fla.*
Ed Pease, Ind.	*Steven R. Rothman, N.J.*
Christopher B. Cannon, Utah	*Tammy Baldwin, Wis.*
James E. Rogan, Calif.	*Anthony D. Weiner, N.Y.*
Lindsey Graham, S.C.	
Mary Bono, Calif.	
Spencer Bachus, Ala.	
Joe Scarborough, Fla.	
David Vitter, La.	

Subcommittees

Commercial and Administrative Law
Phone: 225-2825 **Room:** B-353 RHOB

Gekas, chair	*Nadler*
Graham	*Baldwin*
Chabot	*Watt*
Bachus	*Weiner*
Bono	*Delahunt*
Scarborough	
Vitter	

Constitution
Phone: 226-7680 **Room:** H2-362 FHOB

Canady, chair	*Watt*
Hyde	*Waters*
Hutchinson	*Frank*
Bachus	*Conyers*
Goodlatte	*Nadler*
Barr	
Jenkins	
Graham	

Courts and Intellectual Property
Phone: 225-5741 **Room:** B-351A RHOB

Coble, chair	*Berman*
Sensenbrenner	*Conyers*
Gallegly	*Boucher*
Goodlatte	*Lofgren*
Jenkins	*Delahunt*
Pease	*Wexler*

Cannon
Rogan
Bono

Crime
Phone: 225-3926 **Room:** 207 CHOB

McCollum, chair	*Scott*
Chabot	*Meehan*
Barr	*Rothman*
Gekas	*Weiner*
Coble	*Jackson-Lee*
Smith (Texas)	
Canady	
Hutchinson	

Immigration and Claims
Phone: 225-5727 **Room:** B-370B RHOB

Smith (Texas), chair	*Jackson-Lee*
	Berman
McCollum	*Lofgren*
Gallegly	*Frank*
Pease	*Meehan*
Cannon	
Canady	
Goodlatte	
Scarborough	

RESOURCES

Phone: 225-2761 **Room:** 1324 LHOB
Majority Staff Director: Lloyd Jones; 225-2761; 1324 LHOB
Minority Staff Director: John A. Lawrence; 225-6065; 1329 LHOB

Public lands generally, including entry, easements, and grazing; mining interests generally; fisheries and wildlife, including research, restoration, refuges, and conservation; forest reserves and national parks created from the public domain; forfeiture of land grants and alien ownership, including alien ownership of mineral lands; Geological Survey; international fishing agreements; interstate compacts relating to apportionment of waters for irrigation purposes; irrigation and reclamation, including water supply for reclamation projects, easements of public lands for irrigation projects, and acquisition of private lands when necessary to complete irrigation projects; measures relating to the care and management of Indians, including the care and allotment of Indian lands and general and special measures relating to claims which are paid out of Indian funds; measures relating generally to the insular possessions of the United States, except those affecting the revenue and appropriations; military parks and battlefields, national cemeteries administered by the secretary of the Interior, parks within the District of Columbia, and the erection of monuments to the memory of individuals; mineral land laws and claims and entries thereunder; mineral resources of the public lands; mining schools and experimental stations; marine affairs (including coastal zone management), except for measures relating to oil and other pollution of navigable waters; oceanography; petroleum conservation on the public lands and conservation of the radium supply in the United States; preservation of prehistoric ruins and objects of interest on the public domain; relations of the United States with the Indians and the Indian tribes; Trans-Alaska Oil Pipeline (except ratemaking). The chair and ranking minority member are non-voting members ex officio of all subcommittees of which they are not regular members.

Party Ratio: R 28-D 24

Don Young, Alaska, chair	*George Miller, Calif., ranking member*
W. J. "Billy" Tauzin, La.	*Nick J. Rahall II, W.Va.*
James V. Hansen, Utah	*Bruce F. Vento, Minn.*
H. James Saxton, N.J.	*Dale E. Kildee, Mich.*
Elton Gallegly, Calif.	*Peter A. DeFazio, Ore.*
John J. "Jimmy" Duncan Jr., Tenn.	*Eni F. H. Faleomavaega, Am. Samoa*
Joel Hefley, Colo.	*Neil Abercrombie, Hawaii*
John T. Doolittle, Calif.	*Solomon P. Ortiz, Texas*
Wayne T. Gilchrest, Md.	*Owen B. Pickett, Va.*
Ken Calvert, Calif.	*Frank Pallone Jr., N.J.*
Richard W. Pombo, Calif.	*Cal Dooley, Calif.*
Barbara Cubin, Wyo.	*Carlos A. Romero-Barceló, P.R.*
Helen Chenoweth-Hage, Idaho	*Robert A. Underwood, Guam*
George P. Radanovich, Calif.	*Patrick J. Kennedy, R.I.*
Walter B. Jones Jr., N.C.	*Adam Smith, Wash.*
William M. "Mac" Thornberry, Texas	*Chris John, La.*
Christopher B. Cannon, Utah	*Donna M. C. Christensen, Virgin Is.*
Kevin Brady, Texas	*Ron Kind, Wis.*
John E. Peterson, Pa.	*Jay Inslee, Wash.*
Rick Hill, Mont.	*Grace F. Napolitano, Calif.*
Bob Schaffer, Colo.	*Tom Udall, N.M.*
Jim Gibbons, Nev.	*Mark Udall, Colo.*
Mark Souder, Ind.	*Joseph Crowley, N.Y.*
Greg Walden, Ore.	*Rush D. Holt, N.J.*
Donald L. Sherwood, Pa.	
Robin Hayes, N.C.	
Mike Simpson, Idaho	
Tom Tancredo, Colo.	

Subcommittees

Energy and Mineral Resources
Phone: 225-9297 **Room:** 1626 LHOB

Cubin, chair	*Underwood*
Tauzin	*Rahall*
Thornberry	*Faleomavaega*
Cannon	*Ortiz*
Brady (Texas)	*Dooley*
Schaffer	*Kennedy*
Gibbons	*John*
Walden	*Inslee*
Tancredo	

Fisheries Conservation, Wildlife, and Oceans
Phone: 226-0200 **Room:** 187 FHOB

Saxton, chair	*Faleomavaega*
Tauzin	*Vento*
Hansen	*DeFazio*
Gilchrest	*Abercrombie*
Pombo	*Ortiz*
Jones (N.C.)	*Pallone*
Souder	*Romero-Barceló*
Hayes	*Kennedy*
Simpson	

Forests and Forest Health
Phone: 225-0691 **Room:** 1337 LHOB

Chenoweth-Hage, chair	*Smith (Wash.)*
	Kildee
Duncan	*Pickett*
Doolittle	*Kind*
Gilchrest	*Napolitano*
Peterson (Pa.)	*Udall (N.M.)*
Hill (Mont.)	*Udall (Colo.)*
Schaffer	*Crowley*
Sherwood	
Hayes	

National Parks and Public Lands
Phone: 226-7736 **Room:** 140 CHOB

Hansen, chair	*Romero-Barceló*
Gallegly	*Rahall*
Duncan	*Vento*
Hefley	*Kildee*
Pombo	*Christensen*
Cubin	*Kind*
Radanovich	*Inslee*
Jones (N.C.)	*Udall (N.M.)*
Cannon	*Udall (Colo.)*
Hill (Mont.)	*Crowley*
Gibbons	*Holt*
Souder	
Sherwood	

Water and Power
Phone: 225-8331 **Room:** 1522 LHOB

Doolittle, chair	*Dooley*
Calvert	*Miller (Calif.)*
Pombo	*DeFazio*
Chenoweth-Hage	*Pickett*

RESOURCES (continued)

Radanovich	*Smith (Wash.)*
Thornberry	*Christensen*
Walden	*Napolitano*
Simpson	

RULES

Phone: 225-9191 **Room:** H-312 CAP
Majority Staff Director: Vince Randazzo; 225-9191; H-312 CAP
Minority Staff Director: George C. Crawford; 225-9091; H-152 CAP

Rules and joint rules (other than rules or joint rules relating to the Code of Official Conduct), and order of business of the House; recesses and final adjournments of Congress.

Party Ratio: R 9-D 4

David Dreier, Calif., chair	*Joe Moakley, Mass., ranking member*
Porter J. Goss, Fla.	*Martin Frost, Texas*
John Linder, Ga.	*Tony P. Hall, Ohio*
Deborah Pryce, Ohio	*Louise M. Slaughter, N.Y.*
Lincoln Diaz-Balart, Fla.	
Richard "Doc" Hastings, Wash.	
Sue Myrick, N.C.	
Pete Sessions, Texas	
Thomas M. Reynolds, N.Y.	

Subcommittees

Legislative and Budget Process
Phone: 225-1547 **Room:** 421 CHOB

Goss, chair	*Frost*
Pryce	*Moakley*
Hastings (Wash.)	
Myrick	
Dreier	

Rules and Organization of the House
Phone: 225-8925 **Room:** 421 CHOB

Linder, chair	*Hall (Ohio)*
Diaz-Balart	*Slaughter*
Sessions	
Reynolds	
Dreier	

SCIENCE

Phone: 225-6371 **Room:** 2320 RHOB
Chief of Staff: Todd Schultz; 225-6371; 2320 RHOB
Minority Staff Director: Robert E. Palmer; 225-6375; 822 OHOB

All energy research, development, and demonstration, and projects therefor, and all federally owned or operated nonmilitary energy laboratories; astronautical research and development, including resources, personnel, equipment, and facilities; civil aviation research and development; environmental research and development; marine research; measures relating to the commercial application of energy technology; National Institute of Standards and Technology, standardization of weights and measures and the metric system; National Aeronautics and Space Administration; National Space Council; National Science Foundation; National Weather Service; outer space, including exploration and control thereof; science scholarships; scientific research, development, and demonstration, and projects therefor. The chair and ranking minority member are members ex officio of all subcommittees of which they are not regular members.

Party Ratio: R 25-D 22

F. James Sensenbrenner Jr., Wis., chair	*Ralph M. Hall, Texas, ranking member*
Sherwood Boehlert, N.Y.	*Bart Gordon, Tenn.*
Lamar Smith, Texas	*Jerry F. Costello, Ill.*
Constance A. Morella, Md.	*James A. Barcia, Mich.*
Curt Weldon, Pa.	*Eddie Bernice Johnson, Texas*
Dana Rohrabacher, Calif.	
Joe L. Barton, Texas	*Lynn Woolsey, Calif.*
Ken Calvert, Calif.	*Lynn Rivers, Mich.*
Nick Smith, Mich.	*Zoe Lofgren, Calif.*
Roscoe G. Bartlett, Md.	*Mike Doyle, Pa.*
Vernon J. Ehlers, Mich.	*Sheila Jackson-Lee, Texas*
Dave Weldon, Fla.	*Debbie Stabenow, Mich.*
Gil Gutknecht, Minn.	*Bob Etheridge, N.C.*
Thomas W. Ewing, Ill.	*Nick Lampson, Texas*
Christopher B. Cannon, Utah	*John B. Larson, Conn.*
Kevin Brady, Texas	*Mark Udall, Colo.*
Merrill Cook, Utah	*David Wu, Ore.*
George Nethercutt, Wash.	*Anthony D. Weiner, N.Y.*
Frank D. Lucas, Okla.	*Michael E. Capuano, Mass.*
Mark Green, Wis.	*Brian Baird, Wash.*
Steven T. Kuykendall, Calif.	*Joseph M. Hoeffel, Pa.*
Gary Miller, Calif.	*Dennis Moore, Kan.*
Judy Biggert, Ill.	*Joe Baca, Calif.*
Mark Sanford, S.C.	
Jack Metcalf, Wash.	

Subcommittees

Basic Research
Phone: 225-7858 **Room:** B-374 RHOB

Smith (Mich.) chair	*Johnson (Texas)*
	Etheridge
Boehlert	*Woolsey*
Smith (Texas)	*Larson*
Morella	*Rivers*

Gutknecht *Doyle*
Ewing
Lucas (Okla.)
Biggert

Energy and Environment
Phone: 225-9662 **Room:** 389 FHOB

Calvert, chair *Costello*
Weldon (Pa.) *Doyle*
Barton *Barcia*
Rohrabacher *Johnson (Texas)*
Ehlers *Lofgren*
Weldon (Fla.) *Hoeffel*
Miller (Calif.) *Baca*
Biggert
Metcalf

Space and Aeronautics
Phone: 225-7858 **Room:** B-374 RHOB

Rohrabacher, *Gordon*
  chair *Lofgren*
Smith (Texas) *Jackson-Lee*
Barton *Lampson*
Calvert *Etheridge*
Bartlett *Larson*
Ehlers *Udall (Colo.)*
Weldon (Fla.) *Wu*
Cannon *Weiner*
Brady (Texas) *Moore*
Cook *Capuano*
Nethercutt *Baird*
Lucas (Okla.) *Baca*
Green (Wis.)
Kuykendall
Sanford

Technology
Phone: 225-8844 **Room:** 2319 RHOB

Morella, chair *Barcia*
Weldon (Pa.) *Rivers*
Bartlett *Stabenow*
Gutknecht *Udall (Colo.)*
Ewing *Wu*
Cannon *Weiner*
Brady (Texas) *Capuano*
Cook *Gordon*
Green (Wis.) *Baird*
Kuykendall
Miller (Calif.)

SELECT INTELLIGENCE

Phone: 225-4121 (Majority); 225-7690 (Minority)
Room: H-405 CAP
Staff Director: John I. Millis; 225-4121; H-405 CAP
Minority Counsel: Michael W. Sheehy; 225-7690; H-405
  CAP

Legislative and budget authority over the National Security Agency and the director of central intelligence, the Defense Intelligence Agency, the National Security Agency, intelligence activities of the Federal Bureau of Investigation, and other components of the federal intelligence community. The Speaker of the House and minority leader are non-voting members ex officio of the full committee.

Party Ratio: R 9-D 7

Porter J. Goss, *Julian C. Dixon, Calif.,*
  Fla., chair *ranking member*
Jerry Lewis, Calif. *Nancy Pelosi, Calif.*
Bill McCollum, Fla. *Sanford D. Bishop Jr., Ga.*
Michael N. Castle, Del. *Norman Sisisky, Va.*
Sherwood Boehlert, N.Y. *Gary A. Condit, Calif.*
Charles Bass, N.H. *Tim Roemer, Ind.*
Jim Gibbons, Nev. *Alcee L. Hastings, Fla.*
Ray LaHood, Ill.
Heather A. Wilson, N.M.

Subcommittees

Human Intelligence, Analysis, and Counterintelligence
Phone: 225-4121 **Room:** H-405 CAP

McCollum, chair *Hastings (Fla.)*
Bass *Pelosi*
Lewis (Calif.) *Sisisky*
Gibbons *Condit*
LaHood
Wilson

Technical and Tactical Intelligence
Phone: 225-4121 **Room:** H-405 CAP

Castle, chair *Bishop*
Boehlert *Roemer*
Bass *Condit*
Gibbons *Sisisky*
LaHood
Wilson

SMALL BUSINESS

Phone: 225-5821 **Room:** 2361 RHOB
Chief of Staff: Mark Strand; 225-5821; 2361 RHOB
Minority Staff Director: Michael Day; 225-4038; B-343C
  RHOB

Assistance to and protection of small business, including financial aid, regulatory flexibility, and paperwork reduction; participation of small business enterprises in federal procurement and government contracts.

Party Ratio: R 19-D 17

James M. Talent, *Nydia M. Velázquez, N.Y.,*
  Mo., chair *ranking member*
Larry Combest, Texas *Juanita Millender-*
Joel Hefley, Colo. *McDonald, Calif.*

SMALL BUSINESS (continued)

Donald Manzullo, Ill.	Danny K. Davis, Ill.
Roscoe G. Bartlett, Md.	Carolyn McCarthy, N.Y.
Frank A. LoBiondo, N.J.	Bill Pascrell Jr., N.J.
Sue W. Kelly, N.Y.	Rubén Hinojosa, Texas
Steve Chabot, Ohio	Donna M. C. Christensen,
Phil English, Pa.	Virgin Is.
David M. McIntosh, Ind.	Robert A. Brady, Pa.
Rick Hill, Mont.	Tom Udall, N.M.
Joseph R. Pitts, Pa.	Dennis Moore, Kan.
John E. Sweeney, N.Y.	Stephanie Tubbs Jones,
Patrick J. Toomey, Pa.	Ohio
Jim DeMint, S.C.	Charlie Gonzalez, Texas
Ed Pease, Ind.	David D. Phelps, Ill.
John Thune, S.D.	Grace F. Napolitano,
Mary Bono, Calif.	Calif.
Vacancy	Brian Baird, Wash.
	Shelley Berkley, Nev.
	Mark Udall, Colo.

Subcommittees

Empowerment
Phone: 226-2630 **Room:** B-363 RHOB

Pitts, chair	Millender-McDonald
English	Moore
DeMint	Jones (Ohio)
LoBiondo	Udall (N.M.)
Pease	

Government Programs and Oversight
Phone: 226-2630 **Room:** B-363 RHOB

Bartlett, chair	Davis (Ill.)
Bono	Hinojosa
Toomey	Gonzalez
Hill (Mont.)	Vacancy
Vacancy	

Regulatory Reform and Paperwork Reduction
Phone: 226-2630 **Room:** B-363 RHOB

Kelly, chair	Pascrell
Combest	Brady (Pa.)
McIntosh	Moore
Sweeney	Vacancy
Thune	

Rural Enterprises, Business Opportunities, and Special Small Business Programs
Phone: 226-2630 **Room:** B-363 RHOB

LoBiondo, chair	Christensen
Hill (Mont.)	Phelps
DeMint	Udall (N.M.)
Thune	Baird
Sweeney	

Tax, Finance, and Exports
Phone: 226-2630 **Room:** B-363 RHOB

Manzullo, chair	McCarthy (N.Y.)
Chabot	Hinojosa
English	Gonzalez
Toomey	Napolitano
Vacancy	

STANDARDS OF OFFICIAL CONDUCT

Phone: 225-7103 **Room:** HT-2 CAP
Staff Director and Chief Counsel: Robert Walker; 225-7103; HT-2 CAP

The jurisdiction of the Committee on Standards of Official Conduct is derived from authority granted under House Rules and federal statutes. The scope of the Committee's jurisdiction under the various authorizing rules and statutes. The Committee on Standards of Official Conduct has legislative jurisdiction over all measures relating to the Code of Official Conduct adopted under House Rule XLIII. To assist the House in its analysis, appraisal, and evaluation of existing laws and whether enacting additional legislation is necessary and appropriate, the Committee on Standards of Official Conduct is directed to review and study on a continuing basis the application and effectiveness of those laws whose subject matter is within the jurisdiction of the Committee. With respect to Members, officers, and employees of the U.S. House of Representatives, the Committee on Standards of Official Conduct is authorized to undertake the following actions: A) Recommend administrative actions to establish or enforce standards of official conduct. B) Investigate alleged violations of the Code of Official Conduct or of any applicable rules, laws, or regulations governing the performance of official duties or the discharge of official responsibilities. Such investigations must be made in accordance with Committee rules. C) Report to appropriate federal or State authorities substantial evidence of a violation of any law applicable to the performance of official duties that may have been disclosed in a Committee investigation. Such reports must be approved by the House or by an affirmative vote of two-thirds of the Committee. D) Render advisory opinions regarding the propriety of any current or proposed conduct of a Member, officer, or E) Consider requests for written waivers of the prohibition against receiving gifts when exceptional circumstances make such waivers appropriate.

Party Ratio: R 5-D 5

Lamar Smith, Texas, chair	Howard L. Berman, Calif., ranking member
Joel Hefley, Colo.	Martin Olav Sabo, Minn.
Joe Knollenberg, Mich.	Ed Pastor, Ariz.
Dave Camp, Mich.	Chaka Fattah, Pa.
Rob Portman, Ohio	Zoe Lofgren, Calif.

TRANSPORTATION AND INFRASTRUCTURE

Phone: 225-9446 **Room:** 2165 RHOB
Majority Chief of Staff: Jack Schenendorf; 225-9446; 2165 RHOB
Minority Staff Director: David Heymsfeld; 225-4472; 2163 RHOB

Transportation, including civil aviation, railroads, water transportation, transportation safety (except automobile safety), transportation infrastructure, transportation labor, and railroad retirement and unemployment (except revenue measures); water power; the Coast Guard; federal management of emergencies and natural disasters; flood control and improvement of waterways; inspection of merchant marine vessels; navigation and related laws; rules and international arrangements to prevent collisions at sea; measures, other than appropriations, that relate to construction, maintenance, and safety of roads; buildings and grounds of the Botanic Gardens, the Library of Congress and the Smithsonian Institution, and other governmental buildings within the District of Columbia; post offices, customhouses, federal courthouses, and the merchant marine, except for national security aspects; pollution of navigable waters; and bridges and dams and related transportation regulatory agencies. The chair and ranking minority member are voting members ex officio of all subcommittees of which they are not regular members.

Party Ratio: R 41–D 34

Bud Shuster, Pa., chair
Don Young, Alaska
Tom Petri, Wis.
Sherwood Boehlert, N.Y.
Herbert H. Bateman, Va.
Howard Coble, N.C.
John J. "Jimmy" Duncan Jr., Tenn.
Thomas W. Ewing, Ill.
Wayne T. Gilchrest, Md.
Steve Horn, Calif.
Bob Franks, N.J.
John L. Mica, Fla.
Jack Quinn, N.Y.
Tillie Fowler, Fla.
Vernon J. Ehlers, Mich.
Spencer Bachus, Ala.
Steven C. LaTourette, Ohio
Sue W. Kelly, N.Y.
Ray LaHood, Ill.
Richard H. Baker, La.

James L. Oberstar, Minn., ranking member
Nick J. Rahall II, W.Va.
Robert A. Borski, Pa.
William O. Lipinski, Ill.
Bob Wise, W.Va.
James A. Traficant Jr., Ohio
Peter A. DeFazio, Ore.
Bob Clement, Tenn.
Jerry F. Costello, Ill.
Eleanor Holmes Norton, D.C.
Jerrold Nadler, N.Y.
Pat Danner, Mo.
Robert Menendez, N.J.
Corrine Brown, Fla.
James A. Barcia, Mich.
Bob Filner, Calif.
Eddie Bernice Johnson, Texas
Frank R. Mascara, Pa.
Gene Taylor, Miss.

Charles Bass, N.H.
Bob Ney, Ohio
Jack Metcalf, Wash.
Ed Pease, Ind.
Asa Hutchinson, Ark.
Merrill Cook, Utah
John Cooksey, La.
John Thune, S.D.
Frank A. LoBiondo, N.J.
Jerry Moran, Kan.
John T. Doolittle, Calif.
Lee Terry, Neb.
Donald L. Sherwood, Pa.
Gary Miller, Calif.
John E. Sweeney, N.Y.
Jim DeMint, S.C.
Doug Bereuter, Neb.
Steven T. Kuykendall, Calif.
Mike Simpson, Idaho
Johnny Isakson, Ga.
David Vitter, La.

Juanita Millender-McDonald, Calif.
Elijah E. Cummings, Md.
Earl Blumenauer, Ore.
Max Sandlin, Texas
Ellen O. Tauscher, Calif.
Bill Pascrell Jr., N.J.
Leonard L. Boswell, Iowa
Jim McGovern, Mass.
Tim Holden, Pa.
Nick Lampson, Texas
John Baldacci, Maine
Marion Berry, Ark.
Ronnie Shows, Miss.
Brian Baird, Wash.
Shelley Berkley, Nev.

Subcommittees

Aviation

Phone: 226-3220 **Room:** 2251 RHOB

Duncan, chair
Sweeney
Young (Alaska)
Petri
Ewing
Mica
Quinn
Ehlers
Bachus
LaHood
Bass
Metcalf
Pease
Hutchinson
Cook
Cooksey
Thune
LoBiondo
Moran (Kan.)
Doolittle
Sherwood
Miller (Calif.)
DeMint
Kuykendall
Simpson

Lipinski
Costello
Brown (Fla.)
Johnson (Texas)
Millender-McDonald
Cummings
Boswell
Baldacci
Berry
Norton
Menendez
Tauscher
McGovern
Lampson
Rahall
Traficant
DeFazio
Danner
Filner
Sandlin
Holden

TRANSPORTATION AND INFRASTRUCTURE

(continued)

Isakson
Vitter

Coast Guard and Maritime Transportation

Phone: 226-3552 **Room:** 507 FHOB

Gilchrest, chair	*DeFazio*
LoBiondo	*Taylor (Miss.)*
Young (Alaska)	*Baird*
Coble	
Vitter	

Economic Development, Public Buildings, Hazardous Materials, and Pipeline Transportation

Phone: 225-3014 **Room:** 586 FHOB

Franks, chair	*Wise*
Cooksey	*Norton*
Ewing	*Shows*
LaTourette	
Vitter	

Ground Transportation

Phone: 226-0727 **Room:** B-376 RHOB

Petri, chair	*Rahall*
Franks	*Clement*
Boehlert	*Nadler*
Bateman	*Danner*
Coble	*Barcia*
Duncan	*Filner*
Horn	*Mascara*
Mica	*Sandlin*
Quinn	*Pascrell*
Fowler	*Holden*
Bachus	*Shows*
LaTourette	*Berkley*
Kelly	*Borski*
LaHood	*Lipinski*
Baker	*Wise*
Bass	*Brown (Fla.)*
Ney	*Johnson (Texas)*
Metcalf	*Millender-McDonald*
Pease	*Cummings*
Cook	*Blumenauer*
Thune	*Berry*
Moran (Kan.)	
Terry	
Miller (Calif.)	
Sweeney	
DeMint	
Bereuter	

Oversight, Investigations, and Emergency Management

Phone: 225-5504 **Room:** 589 FHOB

Fowler, chair	*Traficant*
Terry	*Nadler*
Doolittle	*Berkley*
Isakson	

Water Resources and Environment

Phone: 225-4360 **Room:** B-376 RHOB

Boehlert, chair	*Borski*
Sherwood	*Taylor (Miss.)*
Young (Alaska)	*Blumenauer*
Bateman	*Baird*
Gilchrest	*Clement*
Horn	*Costello*
Franks	*Menendez*
Quinn	*Barcia*
Ehlers	*Mascara*
LaTourette	*Tauscher*
Kelly	*Pascrell*
Baker	*Boswell*
Ney	*McGovern*
Hutchinson	*Lampson*
LoBiondo	*Baldacci*
Doolittle	
Bereuter	
Kuykendall	
Simpson	

VETERANS' AFFAIRS

Phone: 225-3527 **Room:** 335 CHOB
Staff Director: Carl Commenator; 225-3527; 335 CHOB
Minority Staff Director: Mike Durishin; 225-9756; 333 CHOB

Veterans' measures generally; cemeteries of the United States in which veterans of any war or conflict are or may be buried, whether in the United States or abroad, except cemeteries administered by the secretary of the Interior; compensation, vocational rehabilitation, and education of veterans; life insurance issued by the government on account of service in the armed forces; pensions of all the wars of the United States; readjustment of servicemen to civil life; soldiers' and sailors' civil relief; veterans' hospitals, medical care, and treatment of veterans.

Party Ratio: R 17–D 14

Bob Stump, Ariz., chair	*Lane Evans, Ill., ranking member*
Christopher H. Smith, N.J.	*Bob Filner, Calif.*
Michael Bilirakis, Fla.	*Luis V. Gutierrez, Ill.*
Floyd D. Spence, S.C.	*Corrine Brown, Fla.*
Terry Everett, Ala.	*Mike Doyle, Pa.*
Steve Buyer, Ind.	*Collin C. Peterson, Minn.*
	Julia Carson, Ind.

Jack Quinn, N.Y.
Cliff Stearns, Fla.
Jerry Moran, Kan.
J. D. Hayworth, Ariz.
Helen Chenoweth-Hage,
    Idaho
Ray LaHood, Ill.
James V. Hansen, Utah
Howard P. "Buck"
    McKeon, Calif.
Jim Gibbons, Nev.
Mike Simpson, Idaho
Richard H. Baker, La.

Silvestre Reyes, Texas
Vic Snyder, Ark.
Ciro D. Rodriguez, Texas
Ronnie Shows, Miss.
Shelley Berkley, Nev.
Baron P. Hill, Ind.
Tom Udall, N.M.

Subcommittees

Benefits

Phone: 225-9164 (majority); 225-9756 (minority)
Room: 337 CHOB

Quinn, chair	*Filner*
Hayworth	*Reyes*
LaHood	*Berkley*
Hansen	*Evans*
Gibbons	

Health

Phone: 225-9154 **Room:** 338 CHOB

Stearns, chair	*Gutierrez*
Smith (N.J.)	*Doyle*
Bilirakis	*Peterson (Minn.)*
Moran (Kan.)	*Carson*
Chenoweth-Hage	*Snyder*
McKeon	*Rodriguez*
Simpson	*Shows*
Baker	
Vacancy	

Oversight and Investigations

Phone: 225-3569 **Room:** 335 CHOB

Everett, chair	*Brown (Fla.)*
Stump	*Hill*
Spence	*Udall (N.M.)*
Buyer	

WAYS AND MEANS

Phone: 225-3625 **Room:** 1102 LHOB
Chief of Staff: A. L. Singleton; 225-3625; 1102 LHOB
Minority Chief Counsel: Janice A. Mays; 225-4021; 1106 LHOB

Revenue measures generally; reciprocal trade agreements; customs, collection districts, and ports of entry and delivery; revenue measures relating to the insular possessions; bonded debt of the United States; deposit of public moneys; transportation of dutiable goods; tax-exempt foundations and charitable trusts; national Social Security, except (A) health care and facilities programs that are supported from general revenues as opposed to payroll deductions and (B) work incentive programs. The chair and ranking minority member are non-voting members ex officio of all subcommittees of which they are not regular members.

Party Ratio: R 23-D 16

Bill Archer, Texas,
    chair
Philip M. Crane, Ill.
Bill Thomas, Calif.
E. Clay Shaw Jr., Fla.
Nancy L. Johnson, Conn.
Amo Houghton, N.Y.
Wally Herger, Calif.
Jim McCrery, La.
Dave Camp, Mich.
Jim Ramstad, Minn.
Jim Nussle, Iowa
Sam Johnson, Texas
Jennifer Dunn, Wash.
Mac Collins, Ga.
Rob Portman, Ohio
Phil English, Pa.
Wes Watkins, Okla.
J. D. Hayworth, Ariz.
Jerry Weller, Ill.
Kenny Hulshof, Mo.
Scott McInnis, Colo.
Ron Lewis, Ky.
Mark Foley, Fla.

Charles B. Rangel, N.Y.,
    ranking member
Pete Stark, Calif.
Robert T. Matsui, Calif.
William J. Coyne, Pa.
Sander M. Levin, Mich.
Benjamin L. Cardin, Md.
Jim McDermott, Wash.
Gerald D. Kleczka, Wis.
John Lewis, Ga.
Richard E. Neal, Mass.
Michael R. McNulty, N.Y.
William J. Jefferson, La.
John Tanner, Tenn.
Xavier Becerra, Calif.
Karen L. Thurman, Fla.
Lloyd Doggett, Texas

Subcommittees

Health

Phone: 225-3943 **Room:** 1136 LHOB

Thomas, chair	*Stark*
Johnson (Conn.)	*Kleczka*
McCrery	*Lewis (Ga.)*
Crane	*McDermott*
Johnson (Texas)	*Thurman*
Camp	
Ramstad	
English	

Human Resources

Phone: 225-1025 **Room:** B-317 RHOB

Johnson (Conn.), chair	*Cardin*
	Stark
English	*Matsui*
Watkins	*Coyne*
Lewis (Ky.)	*Jefferson*
Foley	
McInnis	

WAYS AND MEANS (continued)

McCrery
Camp

Oversight

Phone: 225-7601 **Room:** 1136 LHOB

Houghton, chair	*Coyne*
Portman	*McNulty*
Dunn	*McDermott*
Watkins	*Lewis (Ga.)*
Weller	*Neal*
Hulshof	
Hayworth	
McInnis	

Social Security

Phone: 225-9263 **Room:** B-316 RHOB

Shaw, chair	*Matsui*
Johnson (Texas)	*Levin*
Collins	*Tanner*
Portman	*Doggett*
Hayworth	*Cardin*
Weller	
Hulshof	
McCrery	

Trade

Phone: 225-6649 **Room:** 1104 LHOB

Crane, chair	*Levin*
Thomas	*Rangel*
Shaw	*Neal*
Houghton	*McNulty*
Camp	*Jefferson*
Ramstad	*Becerra*
Dunn	
Herger	
Nussle	

PARTISAN COMMITTEES

DEMOCRATIC CONGRESSIONAL CAMPAIGN COMMITTEE

Phone: 863-1500 **Room:** 430 S. Capitol St. S.E. 20003
Patrick J. Kennedy, R.I., chair

DEMOCRATIC POLICY COMMITTEE

Phone: 225-6760 **Room:** H-302 Capitol
Richard A. Gephardt, Mo., chair

DEMOCRATIC STEERING COMMITTEE

Phone: 225-0100 **Room:** H-204 Capitol
Richard A. Gephardt, Mo., chair
Steny H. Hoyer, Md., co-chair
José E. Serrano, N.Y., vice chair
David E. Bonoir, Mich., vice chair

Benjamin L. Cardin, Md.	*Jim McDermott, Wash.*
James E. Clyburn, S.C.,	*Robert Menendez, N.J.*
Elijah E. Cummings, Md.	*Joe Moakley, Mass.*
Diana DeGette, Colo.	*John P. Murtha, Pa.*
Bill Delahunt, Mass.	*David R. Obey, Wis.*
Rosa DeLauro, Conn.	*Frank Pallone Jr., N.J.*
John D. Dingell, Mich.	*Ed Pastor, Ariz.*
Chet Edwards, Texas	*Nancy Pelosi, Calif.*
Eliot L. Engel, N.Y.	*Collin C. Peterson, Minn.*
Martin Frost, Texas	*Charles B. Rangel, N.Y.*
Bart Gordon, Tenn.	*Lucille Roybal-Allard,*
Gene Green, Texas	*Calif.*
Darlene Hooley, Ore.	*Tom Sawyer, Ohio*
Stephanie Tubbs Jones,	*John M. Spratt Jr., S.C.*
Ohio	*Charles W. Stenholm,*
Patrick J. Kennedy, R.I.	*Texas*
Carolyn Cheeks Kilpatrick,	*John Tanner, Tenn.*
Mich.	*Bennie Thompson, Miss.*
John Lewis, Ga.	*Peter J. Visclosky, Ind.*
William O. Lipinski, Ill.	*Maxine Waters, Calif.*
Edward J. Markey, Mass.	*Melvin Watt, N.C.*
Robert T. Matsui, Calif.	*Henry A. Waxman, Calif.*
Karen McCarthy, Mo.	*Lynn Woolsey, Calif.*

NATIONAL REPUBLICAN CONGRESSIONAL COMMITTEE

Phone: 479-7000 **Room:** 320 First St. S.E. 20003
Thomas M. Davis III, Va., chair
Dave Camp, Mich., executive committee chair
Henry Bonilla, Texas, vice chair
John T. Doolittle, Calif., vice chair
Robert L. Ehrlich Jr., Md., vice chair
Jim McCrery, La., vice chair
Anne M. Northup, Ky., vice chair
John Shadegg, Ariz., vice chair
J. Dennis Hastert, Ill., ex officio
Dick Armey, Texas, ex officio
Tom DeLay, Texas, ex officio
J. C. Watts Jr., Okla., ex officio
Christopher Cox, Calif., ex officio
Thomas M. Davis III, Va., ex officio
Tillie Fowler, Fla., ex officio
Deborah Pryce, Ohio, ex officio

Executive Committee

Roy Blunt, Mo.
Henry Bonilla, Texas
Richard M. Burr, N.C.
Dave Camp, Mich.
John T. Doolittle, Calif.
Robert L. Ehrlich Jr.,
  Md.
Jo Ann Emerson, Mo.
Mark Foley, Fla.
Porter J. Goss, Fla.
Mark Green, Wis.
Richard "Doc" Hastings,
  Wash.
David L. Hobson, Ohio
Sue W. Kelly, N.Y.
Jack Kingston, Ga.
Rick A. Lazio, N.Y.

Jim McCrery, La.
Jerry Moran, Kan.
Bob Ney, Ohio
Anne M. Northup, Ky.
Ed Pease, Ind.
Rob Portman, Ohio
George P. Radanovich,
  Calif.
Thomas M. Reynolds,
  N.Y.
James E. Rogan, Calif.
Ed Royce, Calif.
Pete Sessions, Texas
John Shadegg, Ariz.
John E. Sununu, N.H.
John E. Sweeney, N.Y.
Jerry Weller, Ill.

REPUBLICAN POLICY COMMITTEE

Phone: 225-6168 **Room:** 2471 RHOB
Christopher Cox, Calif., chair
Jerry Weller, Ill., vice chair

Bill Archer, Texas
Dick Armey, Texas
Bob Barr, Ga.
Doug Bereuter, Neb.
Tom Bliley, Va.
Thomas M. Davis III, Va.

Tom DeLay, Texas
David Dreier, Calif.
Phil English, Pa.
Ernie Fletcher, Ky.
Tillie Fowler, Fla.
Benjamin A. Gilman, N.Y.

Robert W. Goodlatte, Va.
Mark Green, Wis.
J. Dennis Hastert, Ill.
Rick Hill, Mont.
John R. Kasich, Ohio
Joe Knollenberg, Mich.
Ron Lewis, Ky.
Jack Metcalf, Wash.
Charles W. "Chip"
  Pickering Jr., Miss.
Richard W. Pombo, Calif.
Rob Portman, Ohio
Deborah Pryce, Ohio

John Shadegg, Ariz.
Nick Smith, Mich.
Floyd D. Spence, S.C.
Cliff Stearns, Fla.
John E. Sununu, N.H.
John Thune, S.D.
Todd Tiahrt, Kan.
Patrick J. Toomey, Pa.
J. C. Watts Jr., Okla.
Curt Weldon, Pa.
Dave Weldon, Fla.
Heather A. Wilson, N.M.
C. W. Bill Young, Fla.

REPUBLICAN STEERING COMMITTEE

Phone: 225-2204 **Room:** H-209 Capitol

J. Dennis Hastert, Ill.
Bill Archer, Texas
Dick Armey, Texas
Cass Ballenger, N.C.
Joe L. Barton, Texas
Thomas J. Bliley Jr., Va.
Roy Blunt, Mo.
Ken Calvert, Calif.
Dave Camp, Mich.
Saxby Chambliss, Ga.
Christopher Cox, Calif.
Thomas M. Davis III, Va.
Tom DeLay, Texas
David Dreier, Calif.

Tillie Fowler, Fla.
John R. Kasich, Ohio
Tom Latham, Iowa
John Linder, Ga.
Bill McCollum, Fla.
John M. McHugh, N.Y.
Jerry Moran, Kan.
Deborah Pryce, Ohio
Bud Shuster, Pa.
Bob Stump, Ariz.
John E. Sweeney, N.Y.
J. C. Watts Jr., Okla.
C. W. Bill Young, Fla.
Don Young, Alaska

House Leadership

DEMOCRATIC LEADERS

Minority Leader *Richard A. Gephardt, Mo.*
Minority Whip *David E. Bonior, Mich.*
Caucus Chair *Martin Frost, Texas*
Caucus Vice Chair *Robert Menendez, N.J.*
Chief Deputy Whips
Chet Edwards, Texas
John Lewis, Ga.
Ed Pastor, Ariz.
Maxine Waters, Calif.
Parliamentarian
Barney Frank, Mass.
Bob Wise, W.Va.
Ex-Officio *Joe Moakley, Mass.*

Deputy Whip

Gene Green, Texas	*Martin Olav Sabo, Minn.*
Eddie Bernice Johnson, Texas	*Charles W. Stenholm, Texas*
Robert T. Matsui, Calif.	*Nydia M. Velázquez, N.Y.*
Charles B. Rangel, N.Y.	*Lynn Woolsey, Calif.*
Bobby L. Rush, Ill.	*Albert R. Wynn, Md.*

At-Large Whip

Neil Abercrombie, Hawaii	*Darleen Hooley, Ore.*
Thomas H. Allen, Maine	*Sheila Jackson-Lee, Texas*
John Baldacci, Maine	*William J. Jefferson, La.*
Thomas M. Barrett, Wis.	*Chris John, La.*
Xavier Becerra, Calif.	*Paul E. Kanjorski, Pa.*
Howard L. Berman, Calif.	*Dale E. Kildee, Mich.*
Marion Berry, Ark.	*Carolyn Cheeks*
Sanford D. Bishop Jr., Ga.	* Kilpatrick, Mich.*
Rod R. Blagojevich, Ill.	*Zoe Lofgren, Calif.*
Rick Boucher, Va.	*Nita M. Lowey, N.Y.*
Sherrod Brown, Ohio	*Frank R. Mascara, Pa.*
Lois Capps, Calif.	*Michael E. McNulty, N.Y.*
Benjamin L. Cardin, Md.	*George Miller, Calif.*
Eva M. Clayton, N.C.	*Alan B. Mollohan, W.Va.*
James E. Clyburn, S.C.	*Richard E. Neal, Mass.*
Joseph Crowley, N.Y.	*James L. Oberstar, Minn.*
Elijah E. Cummings, Md.	*David R. Obey, Wis.*
Jim Davis, Fla.	*John W. Olver, Mass.*
Diana DeGette, Colo.	*Frank Pallone Jr., N.J.*
Norm Dicks, Wash.	*Bill Pascrell Jr., N.J.*
Lloyd Doggett, Texas	*Donald M. Payne, N.J.*
Anna G. Eshoo, Calif.	*Nancy Pelosi, Calif.*
Lane Evans, Ill.	*David E. Price, N.C.*
Bob Filner, Calif.	*Loretta Sanchez, Calif.*
Sam Gejdenson, Conn.	*Max Sandlin, Texas*
Bart Gordon, Tenn.	*Tom C. Sawyer, Ohio*
Luis V. Gutierrez, Ill.	*Jan D. Schakowsky, Ill.*
Maurice D. Hinchey, N.Y.	*José E. Serrano, N.Y.*

Brad Sherman, Calif.	*Robert A. Underwood,*
Louise M. Slaughter, N.Y.	* Guam*
Adam Smith, Wash.	*Bruce F. Vento, Minn.*
Vic Snyder, Ark.	*Peter J. Visclosky, Ind.*
John M. Spratt Jr., S.C.	*Anthony D. Weiner, N.Y.*
John F. Tierney, Mass.	*Bob Weygand, R.I.*
Tom Udall, N.M.	*Bob Wise, W.Va.*

Regional Whip

Brian Baird, Wash.	*Jim McGovern, Mass.*
Robert A. Borski, Pa.	*Juanita Millender-*
Allen Boyd, Fla.	* McDonald, Calif.*
Michael E. Capuano, Mass.	*Patsy T. Mink, Hawaii*
Danny K. Davis, Ill.	*Jerrold Nadler, N.Y.*
Bob Etheridge, N.C.	*Bobby L. Rush, Ill.*
Harold E. Ford Jr., Tenn.	*Bart Stupak, Mich.*
Charlie Gonzalez, Texas	*Bennie Thompson, Miss.*
Maurice D. Hinchey, N.Y.	*Jim Turner, Texas*
Jay Inslee, Wash.	*Mark Udall, Colo.*
Dennis J. Kucinich, Ohio	*Bob Wise, W.Va.*
Barbara Lee, Calif.	*Albert R. Wynn, Md.*
Bill Luther, Minn.	

Steering Committee
Co-Chair *Richard A. Gephardt, Mo.*
Co-Chair *Steny H. Hoyer, Md.*
Democratic Congressional Campaign Committee Chair
Patrick J. Kennedy, R.I.

REPUBLICAN LEADERS

Speaker of the House J. Dennis Hastert, Ill.
Majority Leader Dick Armey, Texas
Majority Whip Tom DeLay, Texas
Conference Chair J. C. Watts Jr., Okla.
Conference Vice Chair Tillie Fowler, Fla.
Conference Secretary Deborah Pryce, Ohio
Chief Deputy Whip Roy Blunt, Mo.

Deputy Whip

Cass Ballenger, N.C.	Mark Foley, Fla.
Barbara Cubin, Wyo.	Porter J. Goss, Fla.
John T. Doolittle, Calif.	Rick A. Lazio, N.Y.
Thomas W. Ewing, Ill.	Bob Ney, Ohio

Assistant Whip

Steve Buyer, Ind.	Thomas M. Davis III, Va.
Sonny Callahan, Ala.	Paul E. Gillmor, Ohio
Dave Camp, Mich.	Robert W. Goodlatte, Va.
Mac Collins, Ga.	Wash.
Randy "Duke"	Van Hilleary, Tenn.
Cunningham, Calif.	David L. Hobson, Ohio

Ernest Istook, Okla.
Sue W. Kelly, N.Y.
Jack Kingston, Ga.
Frank A. LoBiondo, N.J.
Scott McInnis, Colo.
David M. McIntosh, Ind.
Howard P. "Buck"
  McKeon, Calif.

Dan Miller, Fla.
Richard W. Pombo, Calif.
Rob Portman, Ohio
Deborah Pryce, Ohio
Matt Salmon, Ariz.
Jim Saxton, N.J.
John Shadegg, Ariz.
Lamar Smith, Texas

James M. Talent, Mo.
Todd Tiahrt, Kan.
James T. Walsh, N.Y.

Jerry Weller, Ill.
Roger Wicker, Miss.

Policy Committee Chair *Christopher Cox, Calif.*
Steering Committee Chair *J. Dennis Hastert, Ill.*
National Republican Congressional Committee Chair
Thomas M. Davis III, Va.

House Members' Offices

The list below gives the names of House members and their party, state, and district affiliation, followed by addresses and telephone numbers for their Washington offices. The area code for all telephone numbers in Washington, D.C. is (202). The list also gives the name of a top administrative aide for each member.

The address, telephone number, and director for the members' district offices are listed. Each representative's committee assignments are given as the final entry. For partisan committee assignments, see p. 752.

As of April 17, 2000, there were 222 Republicans, 211 Democrats, 2 independents in the House of Representatives. This information was gathered by Congressional Quarterly from House offices in Washington, D.C.

ABERCROMBIE, NEIL, D-HAWAII (1)

Capitol Hill Office: 1502 LHOB 20515; 225-2726; Fax: 225-4580
Web: www.house.gov/abercrombie
E-mail: neil.abercrombie@mail.house.gov
District Office(s): Federal Bldg., Honolulu 96850; (808) 541-2570; Fax: (808) 533-0133; *Chief of Staff:* Alan Yamamoto
Committee Assignment(s): Armed Services; Resources

ACKERMAN, GARY L., D-N.Y. (5)

Capitol Hill Office: 2243 RHOB 20515; 225-2601; Fax: 225-1589; *Administrative Assistant:* Jedd Moskowitz
Web: www.house.gov/ackerman
E-mail: www.house.gov/writerep
District Office(s): 218-14 Northern Blvd., Bayside 11361; (718) 423-2154; *District Administrator:* Anne McShane
229 Main St., Huntington 11743; (516) 423-2154; *Office Manager:* Moya Berry
Committee Assignment(s): Banking and Financial Services; International Relations

ADERHOLT, ROBERT B., R-ALA. (4)

Capitol Hill Office: 1007 LHOB 20515; 225-4876; Fax: 225-5587; *Chief of Staff:* Mark Busching
Web: www.house.gov/aderholt
E-mail: robert.aderholt@mail.house.gov
District Office(s): Federal Bldg., #102-104, Cullman 35055; (256) 734-6043; Fax: (256) 737-0885; *Constituent Services Representative:* Evelyn Stevens
Federal Bldg., #247, Jasper 35501; (205) 221-2310; Fax: (205) 221-9035; *Deputy Chief of Staff:* M. Hood Harris

Federal Bldg., #107, Gadsden 35901; (256) 546-0201; Fax: (256) 546-8778; *Field Representative:* Kevin Rosamond
Committee Assignment(s): Appropriations

ALLEN, TOM, D-MAINE (1)

Capitol Hill Office: 1717 LHOB 20515; 225-6116; Fax: 225-5590; *Chief of Staff:* Jackie Potter
Web: www.house.gov/allen
E-mail: rep.tomallen@mail.house.gov
District Office(s): 234 Oxford St., Portland 04101; (207) 774-5019; Fax: (207) 871-0720; *District Director:* Bill Johnson *Communications Director:* Mark Sullivan
Committee Assignment(s): Armed Services; Government Reform

ANDREWS, ROBERT E., D-N.J. (1)

Capitol Hill Office: 2439 RHOB 20515; 225-6501; Fax: 225-6583; *Chief of Staff:* David Socolow
Web: www.house.gov/andrews
E-mail: rob.andrews@mail.house.gov
District Office(s): 506 A White Horse Pike, Haddon Heights 08035; (856) 546-5100; Fax: (856) 546-9529; *Office Manager:* Christina Morales; *Press Secretary:* Bill Caruso; *Scheduler:* Helene McCarthy
63 N. Broad St., Woodbury 08096; (856) 848-3900; Fax: (856) 848-8341; *District Representative:* Leanne Hasbrouck
Committee Assignment(s): Armed Services; Education and Workforce

ARCHER, BILL, R-TEXAS (7)

Capitol Hill Office: 1236 LHOB 20515; 225-2571; Fax: 225-4381; *Chief of Staff:* Don Carlson

Web: www.house.gov/archer

E-mail: www.house.gov/writerep

District Office(s): 10000 Memorial Dr., Houston 77024; (713) 682-8828; Fax: (713) 680-8070; *District Representative:* Camille Cromwell

Committee Assignment(s): Joint Taxation; Ways and Means

ARMEY, DICK, R-TEXAS (26)

Capitol Hill Office: 301 CHOB 20515; 225-7772; Fax: 226-8101; *Administrative Assistant:* Gayland Barksdale

Web: armey.house.gov

E-mail: www.house.gov/writerep

District Office(s): 9901 Valley Ranch Parkway East, Irving 75063; (972) 556-2500; *District Director:* Jean Campbell

BACA, JOE, D-CALIF. (42)

Capitol Hill Office: 2300 RHOB 20515; 225-6161; Fax: 225-8671; *Chief of Staff:* Linda Macias

Web: www.house.gov/baca

E-mail: www.house.gov/writerep

District Office(s): 201 North E St., San Bernardino 92401; (909) 885-2222; Fax: (909) 888-5959; *District Director:* Michael Townsend

Committee Assignment(s): Agriculture; Science

BACHUS, SPENCER, R-ALA. (6)

Capitol Hill Office: 442 CHOB 20515; 225-4921; Fax: 225-2082; *Chief of Staff:* Jeff Emerson

Web: www.house.gov/bachus

E-mail: www.house.gov/bachus/citizendirect.htm

District Office(s): 1900 International Park Dr., Birmingham 35243; (205) 969-2296; Fax: (205) 969-3958; *District Director:* R. Cameron Ward

3500 McFarland Blvd., Northport 35476; (205) 333-9894; *District Office Manager:* Margaret Pyle

Committee Assignment(s): Banking and Financial Services; Judiciary; Transportation and Infrastructure

BAIRD, BRIAN, D-WASH. (3)

Capitol Hill Office: 1721 LHOB 20515; 225-3536; Fax: 225-3478; *Chief of Staff:* Joe Shoemaker

Web: www.house.gov/baird

E-mail: www.house.gov/writerep

District Office(s): 1220 Main St., #360, Vancouver 98660; (360) 695-6292; Fax: (360) 695-6197; *Scheduler:* Cindy Gipson

Committee Assignment(s): Science; Small Business; Transportation and Infrastructure

BAKER, RICHARD H., R-LA. (6)

Capitol Hill Office: 434 CHOB 20515; 225-3901; Fax: 225-7313; *Administrative Assistant:* Christy Casteel

Web: www.house.gov/baker

E-mail: www.house.gov/writerep

District Office(s): 5555 Hilton Ave., Baton Rouge 70808; (225) 929-7711; Fax: (225) 929-7688; *Press Secretary:* Michael DiResto

Committee Assignment(s): Banking and Financial Services; Transportation and Infrastructure; Veterans' Affairs

BALDACCI, JOHN, D-MAINE (2)

Capitol Hill Office: 1740 LHOB 20515; 225-6306; Fax: 225-2943; *Administrative Assistant:* Larry Benoit

Web: www.house.gov/baldacci

E-mail: baldacci@me02.house.gov

District Office(s): 157 Main St., Lewiston 04240; (207) 782-3704; Fax: (207) 782-5330; *Office Manager:* Judy Cadorette

500 Main St., Madawaska 04756; (207) 728-6160; *Field Representatives:* Barbara Hayslatt, Margaret Chase

Smith Federal Bldg., Bangor 04402; (207) 942-6935; Fax: (207) 942-5907; *Field Representative:* Janet Dennis

445 Main St., Presque Isle 04769; (207) 764-1036; Fax: (207) 764-1060; *Field Representative:* Marcia Gartley

Committee Assignment(s): Agriculture; Transportation and Infrastructure

BALDWIN, TAMMY, D-WIS. (2)

Capitol Hill Office: 1020 LHOB 20515; 225-2906; Fax: 225-6942; *Chief of Staff:* Brad Fitch

Web: www.house.gov/baldwin

E-mail: www.house.gov/writerep

District Office(s): 10 E. Doty St., Madison 53703; (608) 258-9800; Fax: (608) 258-9808; *District Director:* Bill Murat

Committee Assignment(s): Budget; Judiciary

BALLENGER, CASS, R-N.C. (10)

Capitol Hill Office: 2182 RHOB 20515; 225-2576; Fax: 225-0316; *Chief of Staff:* Patrick Murphy

Web: www.house.gov/ballenger

E-mail: cass.ballenger@mail.house.gov

District Office(s): 361 10th Ave. Dr. N.E., #102, Hickory 28603; (704) 327-6100; Fax: (704) 327-8311; *District Director:* Thomas D. Luckadoo

Committee Assignment(s): Education and Workforce; International Relations

BARCIA, JAMES A., D-MICH. (5)

Capitol Hill Office: 2419 RHOB 20515; 225-8171; Fax: 225-2168; *Chief of Staff:* Kristen Valade Day

Web: www.house.gov/barcia

E-mail: jim.barcia-pub@mail.house.gov

District Office(s): 5409 W. Pierson Rd., Flushing 48433; (810) 732-7501; Fax: (810) 732-7504; *Staff Assistant:* Mark Salogar

301 E. Genesee St., Saginaw 48607; (517) 754-6075; Fax: (517) 754-6571; *District Director:* James C. Lewis

503 N. Euclid St., Bay City 48706; (517) 667-0003; Fax: (517) 667-0921; *Staff Assistant:* Marla N. Schutt

Committee Assignment(s): Science; Transportation and Infrastructure

BARR, BOB, R-GA. (7)

Capitol Hill Office: 1207 LHOB 20515; 225-2931; Fax: 225-2944; *Chief of Staff:* Jonathan Blyth

Web: www.house.gov/barr

E-mail: barr.ga@mail.house.gov

District Office(s): 207 Newnan St., Carrollton 30117; (770) 836-1776; Fax: (770) 838-0436; *Constituent Services Representative:* Catherine Brock

200 Ridley Ave., LaGrange 30240; (706) 812-1776; Fax: (706) 885-9019; *Constituent Services Representative:* Jan Haralson

600 E. 1st St., Rome 30161; (706) 290-1776; Fax: (706) 232-7864; *Constituent Services Representative:* Linda Shiver

999 Whitlock Ave., Marietta 30064; (770) 429-1776; Fax: (770) 795-9551; *District Director:* Fred Aiken

Committee Assignment(s): Banking and Financial Services; Government Reform; Judiciary

BARRETT, BILL, R-NEB. (3)

Capitol Hill Office: 2458 RHOB 20515; 225-6435; Fax: 225-0207; *Chief of Staff:* Jeri Finke

Web: www.house.gov/billbarrett

E-mail: www.house.gov/writerep

District Office(s): 312 W. 3rd St., Grand Island 68801; (308) 381-5555; *Deputy Chief of Staff:* Mark Whitacre

1811 Ave. A, Scottsbluff 69361; (308) 632-3333; *District Office Manager:* Esther Benson

Committee Assignment(s): Agriculture; Education and Workforce

BARRETT, THOMAS M., D-WIS. (5)

Capitol Hill Office: 1214 LHOB 20515; 225-3571; Fax: 225-2185; *Chief of Staff:* Sharon Robinson

Web: www.house.gov/barrett

E-mail: telltom@mail.house.gov

District Office(s): 135 W. Wells St., Milwaukee 53203; (414) 297-1331; Fax: (414) 297-1359; *District Director:* Terry Perry

Committee Assignment(s): Commerce

BARTLETT, ROSCOE G., R-MD. (6)

Capitol Hill Office: 2412 RHOB 20515; 225-2721; Fax: 225-2193; *Chief of Staff:* Jim Backlin

Web: www.house.gov/bartlett

E-mail: www.house.gov/writerep

District Office(s): 15 E. Main St., Westminster 21157; (410) 857-1115; Fax: (410) 857-1329; *Projects Administrator:* Phil Straw

5831 Buckeystown Pike, Frederick 21701; (301) 694-3030; Fax: (301) 694-6674; *District Director:* Gregg Cox

50 Broadway, Frostburg 21532; (301) 689-0034; Fax: (301) 689-1871; *Caseworker:* Barbara Callagan

100 W. Franklin St., Hagerstown 21740; (301) 797-6043; Fax: (301) 797-2385; *Caseworker:* Marci Cosens

Committee Assignment(s): Armed Services; Science; Small Business

BARTON, JOE L., R-TEXAS (6)

Capitol Hill Office: 2264 RHOB 20515; 225-2002; Fax: 225-3052; *Chief of Staff:* Heather Stansell

Web: www.house.gov/barton

E-mail: rep.barton@mail.house.gov

District Office(s): 303 W. Knox St., Ennis 75119; (817) 543-1000; *District Representative:* Linda Gillespie

4521 S. Hulen St., Fort Worth 76109; (817) 543-1000; Fax: (817) 926-2618; *Casework Director:* Christi Townsend

805 Washington Dr., Arlington 76011; (817) 543-1000; Fax: (817) 548-7029; *District Director:* Harold Samuels

Committee Assignment(s): Commerce; Science

BASS, CHARLES, R-N.H. (2)

Capitol Hill Office: 218 CHOB 20515; 225-5206; Fax: 225-2946; *Policy Director:* James Martin

Web: www.house.gov/bass

E-mail: cbass@mail.house.gov

District Office(s): 142 N. Main St., Concord 03301; (603) 226-0249; Fax: (603) 226-0476; *Chief of Staff:* Darwin Cusack

2 Cottage St., Littleton 03561; (603) 444-1271; Fax: (603) 444-5343; *Constituent Services Representative:* Bryan Christiansen

One West St., Keene 03431; (603) 358-4094; Fax: (603) 358-5092; *Constituent Services Representative:* Jane Lane

170 Main St., Nashua 03060; (603) 889-8772; Fax: (603) 889-6890; *Constituent Services Representative:* Madeline Saulnier

Committee Assignment(s): Budget; Select Intelligence; Transportation and Infrastructure

BATEMAN, HERBERT H., R-VA. (1)

Capitol Hill Office: 2211 RHOB 20515; 225-4261; Fax: 225-4382; *Administrative Assistant:* Dan Scandling

Web: www.house.gov/bateman

E-mail: www.house.gov/writerep

District Office(s): Massaponax Outlet Center, Fredericksburg 22407; (540) 898-2975; Fax: (540) 898-3280; *District Representative:* John Goolrick

23386 Front St., Accomac 23301; (757) 787-7836; Fax: (757) 787-9540; *District Representative:* Suzanne Beasley

739 Thimble Shoals Blvd., Newport News 23606; (757) 873-1132; Fax: (757) 599-0424; *District Director:* Dee Benton

475 Main St., Warsaw 22572; (804) 333-1412; Fax: (804) 333-5341; *District Representative:* Ruth Jessie

Committee Assignment(s): Armed Services; Transportation and Infrastructure

BECERRA, XAVIER, D-CALIF. (30)

Capitol Hill Office: 1119 LHOB 20515; 225-6235; Fax: 225-2202; *Chief of Staff:* Krista Atteberry

Web: www.house.gov/becerra

E-mail: www.house.gov/writerep

District Office(s): 1910 Sunset Blvd., Los Angeles 90026; (213) 483-1425; Fax: (213) 483-1429; *District Administrative Assistant:* Henry Lozano

Committee Assignment(s): Ways and Means

BENTSEN, KEN, D-TEXAS (25)

Capitol Hill Office: 326 CHOB 20515; 225-7508; Fax: 225-2947; *Chief of Staff:* Stephen H. Brown

Web: www.house.gov/bentsen

E-mail: ken.bentsen@mail.house.gov

District Office(s): 6575 W. Loop South, Bellaire 77401; (713) 667-3554; Fax: (713) 667-4833; *Chief of Staff:* Pat M. Strong

1300 Rollingbrook Dr., Baytown 77521; (281) 837-8225; *Staff Assistant:* Thomas C. Mayo

1001 E. Southmore Ave., Pasadena 77502; (713) 473-4334; Fax: (713) 475-8887; *Staff Assistant:* Diane Patterson

Committee Assignment(s): Banking and Financial Services; Budget

BEREUTER, DOUG, R-NEB. (1)

Capitol Hill Office: 2184 RHOB 20515; 225-4806; *Chief of Staff:* Susan Olson

Web: www.house.gov/bereuter

E-mail: www.house.gov/writerep

District Office(s): 502 N. Broad St., Fremont 68025; (402) 727-0888; Fax: (402) 727-9130; *District Assistant:* Judy Larson

1045 K St., Lincoln 68508; (402) 438-1598; Fax: (402) 438-1604; *District Office Manager:* Roger Massey

Committee Assignment(s): Banking and Financial Services; International Relations; Transportation and Infrastructure

BERKLEY, SHELLEY, D-NEV. (1)

Capitol Hill Office: 1505 LHOB 20515; 225-5965; Fax: 225-3119; *Chief of Staff:* Richard Urey

Web: www.house.gov/berkley

E-mail: shelley.berkley@mail.house.gov

District Office(s): 2340 Paseo Del Prado, Las Vegas 89102; (702) 220-9823; Fax: (702) 220-9841; *District Director:* Tod J. Story

Committee Assignment(s): Small Business; Transportation and Infrastructure; Veterans' Affairs

BERMAN, HOWARD L., D-CALIF. (26)

Capitol Hill Office: 2330 RHOB 20515; 225-4695; *Chief of Staff:* Gene Smith

Web: www.house.gov/berman

E-mail: howard.berman@mail.house.gov

District Office(s): 10200 Sepulveda Blvd., Mission Hills 91345; (818) 891-0543; *Executive Secretary:* Pearl Ricci

Committee Assignment(s): International Relations; Judiciary; Standards of Official Conduct

BERRY, MARION, D-ARK. (1)

Capitol Hill Office: 1113 LHOB 20515; 225-4076; Fax: 225-5602; *Chief of Staff:* H. Thad Huguley

Web: www.house.gov/berry

E-mail: www.house.gov/writerep

District Office(s): 615 S. Main St., Jonesboro 72401; (870) 972-4600; Fax: (870) 972-4605; *District Director:* Jason R. Willett

Committee Assignment(s): Agriculture; Transportation and Infrastructure

BIGGERT, JUDY, R-ILL. (13)

Capitol Hill Office: 508 CHOB 20515; 225-3515; Fax: 225-9420; *Chief of Staff:* Kathy Lydon

Web: www.house.gov/biggert

E-mail: www.house.gov/writerep

District Office(s): 115 W. 55th St., Clarendon Hills 60514; (630) 655-2052; Fax: (630) 655-1061; *District Director:* John Hoffman

Committee Assignment(s): Banking and Financial Services; Government Reform; Science

BILBRAY, BRIAN P., R-CALIF. (49)

Capitol Hill Office: 1530 LHOB 20515; 225-2040; Fax: 225-2948; *Chief of Staff:* John Woodard

Web: www.house.gov/bilbray

E-mail: brian.bilbray@mail.house.gov

District Office(s): 1101 Camino del Rio South, San Diego 92108; (619) 291-1430; Fax: (619) 291-8956; *District Director:* Greg Stein

Committee Assignment(s): Commerce

BILIRAKIS, MICHAEL, R-FLA. (9)

Capitol Hill Office: 2369 RHOB 20515; 225-5755; Fax: 225-4085; *Chief of Staff:* Todd Tuten

Web: www.house.gov/bilirakis

E-mail: www.house.gov/writerep

District Office(s): 1100 Cleveland St., Clearwater 33755; (727) 441-3721; Fax: (727) 442-8180; *District Director:* Sonja B. Stefanadis

4111 Land O'Lakes Blvd., Land O'Lakes 34639; (813) 996-7441; Fax: (813) 996-7762; *Caseworker:* Shirley Miaoulis

Committee Assignment(s): Commerce; Veterans' Affairs

BISHOP, SANFORD D. JR., D-GA. (2)

Capitol Hill Office: 1433 LHOB 20515; 225-3631; Fax: 225-2203; *Chief of Staff:* Beverly Gilyard

Web: www.house.gov/bishop

E-mail: bishop.email@mail.house.gov

District Office(s): 401 N. Patterson St., Valdosta 31601; (912) 247-9705; Fax: (912) 241-1035; *Field Representative:* Michael Bryant

235 Roosevelt Ave., Albany 31701; (912) 439-8067; Fax: (912) 436-2099; *District Director:* Hobby Stripling

City Hall, Dawson 31742; (912) 995-3991; Fax: (912) 995-4894; *Staff Assistant:* Tonya Griggs

Committee Assignment(s): Agriculture; Select Intelligence

BLAGOJEVICH, ROD R., D-ILL. (5)

Capitol Hill Office: 331 CHOB 20515; 225-4061; Fax: 225-5603; *Chief of Staff:* David Stricklin

Web: www.house.gov/blagojevich

E-mail: Rod.Blagojevich@mail.house.gov

District Office(s): 4064 N. Lincoln Ave., Chicago 60618; (773) 868-3240; Fax: (773) 868-0036; *District Director:* Lucy Herman Moog

11 Conti Parkway, Elmwood Park 60717; (708) 583-1948; *Congressional Aide:* Patricia Nino

Committee Assignment(s): Armed Services; Government Reform

BLILEY, THOMAS J. JR., R-VA. (7)

Capitol Hill Office: 2409 RHOB 20515; 225-2815; Fax: 225-0011; *Chief of Staff:* Linda Pedigo

Web: www.house.gov/bliley

E-mail: tom.bliley@mail.house.gov

District Office(s): 763 Madison Rd., Culpeper 22701; (540) 825-8960; *District Office Representative:* Anita Essalih

4914 Fitzhugh Ave., Richmond 23230; (804) 771-2809; *District Director:* Kathy Costigan

Committee Assignment(s): Commerce

BLUMENAUER, EARL, D-ORE. (3)

Capitol Hill Office: 1406 LHOB 20515; 225-4811; Fax: 225-8941; *Staff Director:* Ross Brown

Web: www.house.gov/blumenauer

E-mail: write.earl@mail.house.gov

District Office(s): The Weatherly Bldg., Portland 97214; (503) 231-2300; Fax: (503) 230-5413; *District Director:* Julia Pomeroy

Committee Assignment(s): Transportation and Infrastructure

BLUNT, ROY, R-MO. (7)

Capitol Hill Office: 217 CHOB 20515; 225-6536; Fax: 225-5604; *Chief of Staff:* Gregg Hartley

Web: www.house.gov/blunt

E-mail: www.house.gov/writerep

District Office(s): 2247-B E. Sunshine St., Springfield 65804; (417) 889-1800; *Public Information Officer:* Dan Wadlington

302 Joplin St., Joplin 64801; (417) 781-1041; *Field Representative:* Steve McIntosh

Committee Assignment(s): Commerce

BOEHLERT, SHERWOOD, R-N.Y. (23)

Capitol Hill Office: 2246 RHOB 20515; 225-3665; Fax: 225-1891; *Chief of Staff:* Dean Patrick D'Amore

Web: www.house.gov/boehlert

E-mail: rep.boehlert@mail.house.gov

District Office(s): Alexander Pirnie Federal Bldg., Utica 13501; (315) 793-8146; Fax: (315) 798-4099; *District Director:* Jeanne Donalty

66 S. Broad St., Norwich 13815; (607) 337-2543; *Staff Assistant:* John Baker

41 S. Main St., Oneonta 13820; (607) 432-5524;

Committee Assignment(s): Science; Select Intelligence; Transportation and Infrastructure

BOEHNER, JOHN A., R-OHIO (8)

Capitol Hill Office: 1011 LHOB 20515; 225-6205; Fax: 225-0704; *Chief of Staff:* Barry Jackson

Web: www.house.gov/boehner

E-mail: www.house.gov/writerep

District Office(s): 8200 Beckett Park Dr., Hamilton 45011; (513) 870-0300; Fax: (513) 870-0151; *District Deputy Chief of Staff:* William C. "Mickey" Krieger II

12 S. Plum St., Troy 45373; (937) 339-1524; Fax: (937) 339-1878; *Field Representative:* Kelly Smith

Committee Assignment(s): Agriculture; Education and Workforce; House Administration; Joint Library; Joint Printing

BONILLA, HENRY, R-TEXAS (23)

Capitol Hill Office: 1427 LHOB 20515; 225-4511; Fax: 225-2237; *Chief of Staff:* Steve Ruhlen

Web: www.house.gov/bonilla

E-mail: www.house.gov/writerep

District Office(s): 1300 Matamoros St., Laredo 78040; (956) 726-4682; Fax: (956) 726-4684; *Constituent Liaison:* Viola Martinez

11120 Wurzbach Rd., San Antonio 78230; (210) 697-9055; Fax: (210) 697-9185; *District Director:* Phil Ricks

4400 N. Big Spring St., Midland 79705; (915) 686-8833; Fax: (915) 686-8819; *Constituent Liaison:* Tony Carillo

Federal Courthouse, Del Rio 78840; (830) 774-6547; Fax: (830) 774-5693; *Constituent Liaison:* Ida Gutierrez

Committee Assignment(s): Appropriations

BONIOR, DAVID E., D-MICH. (10)

Capitol Hill Office: 2207 RHOB 20515; 225-2106; Fax: 226-1169; *Administrative Assistant:* Sarah Dufendach

Web: davidbonior.house.gov

E-mail: david.bonior@mail.house.gov

District Office(s): 59 N. Walnut St., Mt. Clemens 48043; (810) 469-3232; *Administrative Assistant:* Christine Koch

Federal Bldg., Port Huron 48060; (810) 987-8889; *Congressional Aide:* Timothy Morse

BONO, MARY, R-CALIF. (44)

Capitol Hill Office: 516 CHOB 20515; 225-5330; Fax: 225-2961; *Chief of Staff:* Frank W. Cullen

Web: www.house.gov/bono

E-mail: www.house.gov/writerep

District Office(s): 155 S. Palm Canyon Dr., Palm Springs 92264; (760) 320-1076; Fax: (760) 320-0596; *District Director:* Kim Waltrip

11401 Heacock St., Moreno Valley 92557; (909) 485-4827; Fax: (909) 485-4897; *Field Representative:* Susan La Belle

1600 E. Florida Ave., Hemet 92544; (909) 658-2312; Fax: (909) 652-2562; *Field Representative:* Alta Armstrong

Committee Assignment(s): Armed Services; Judiciary; Small Business

BORSKI, ROBERT A., D-PA. (3)

Capitol Hill Office: 2267 RHOB 20515; 225-8251; Fax: 225-4628; *Administrative Assistant:* Mark Vieth

Web: www.house.gov/borski

E-mail: borski@mail.house.gov

District Office(s): 2630 Memphis St., Philadelphia 19125; (215) 426-4616; Fax: (215) 426-7741; *Congressional Aide:* Peg Rzepski

7141 Frankford Ave., Philadelphia 19135; (215) 335-3355; Fax: (215) 333-4508; *District Director:* John F. Dempsey; *Press Secretary:* Karen Peck

Committee Assignment(s): Transportation and Infrastructure

BOSWELL, LEONARD L., D-IOWA (3)

Capitol Hill Office: 1029 LHOB 20515; 225-3806; Fax: 225-5608; *Chief of Staff:* Jeani Murray

Web: www.house.gov/boswell

E-mail: www.house.gov/writerep

District Office(s): 709 Furnas Dr., Osceola 50213; (515) 342-4801; Fax: (515) 342-4354; *District Director:* Jay Byers

Committee Assignment(s): Agriculture; Transportation and Infrastructure

BOUCHER, RICK, D-VA. (9)

Capitol Hill Office: 2329 RHOB 20515; 225-3861; Fax: 225-0442

Web: www.house.gov/boucher

E-mail: ninthnet@mail.house.gov

District Office(s): 188 E. Main St., Abingdon 24210; (540) 628-1145; Fax: (540) 628-2203; *Chief of Staff:* Becky Coleman

311 Shawnee Ave. East, Big Stone Gap 24219; (540) 523-5450; Fax: (540) 523-1412; *Casework Specialist:* Eloise Lawson

106 N. Washington Ave., Pulaski 24301; (540) 980-4310; Fax: (540) 980-0529; *Casework Supervisor:* Becki Gunn

Committee Assignment(s): Commerce; Judiciary

BOYD, ALLEN, D-FLA. (2)

Capitol Hill Office: 107 CHOB 20515; 225-5235; Fax: 225-5615; *Administrative Assistant:* Jennifer Cannon

Web: www.house.gov/boyd

E-mail: rep.boyd@mail.house.gov

District Office(s): 301 S. Monroe St., Tallahassee 32301; (850) 561-3979; Fax: (850) 681-2902; *District Director:* Jerry Smithwick

30 W. Government St., Panama City 32401; (850) 785-0812; Fax: (850) 763-3764; *District Representative:* Jim Norton

Committee Assignment(s): Appropriations

BRADY, KEVIN, R-TEXAS (8)

Capitol Hill Office: 1531 LHOB 20515; 225-4901; Fax: 225-5524; *Chief of Staff:* Doug Centilli

Web: www.house.gov/brady

E-mail: rep.brady@mail.house.gov

District Office(s): 616 FM 1960 West Houston 77090; (281) 895-8892; Fax: (281) 895-8912; *Senior Caseworker:* June Kenyon

111 E. University St., College Station 77840; (409) 846-6068; Fax: (409) 260-2916; *Regional District Director:* Scott Pool

200 River Pointe Dr., Conroe 77304; (409) 441-5700; Fax: (409) 441-5757; *District Director:* Heather Montgomery

Committee Assignment(s): International Relations; Resources; Science

BRADY, ROBERT A., D-PA. (1)

Capitol Hill Office: 216 CHOB 20515; 225-4731; Fax: 225-0088; *Chief of Staff:* Stan White

Web: www.house.gov/robertbrady

E-mail: www.house.gov/writerep

District Office(s): 1907 S. Broad St., Philadelphia 19148; (215) 389-4627; Fax: (215) 389-4636; *District Director:* Shirley Gregory

1510 W. Cecil B. Moore Ave., Philadelphia 19121; (215) 236-5430; Fax: (215) 236-5472; *Press Secretary:* Karen Warrington

The Colony Bldg., Chester 19013; (610) 874-7094; Fax: (610) 874-7193; *Office Manager:* Carl Fitzgerald

Committee Assignment(s): Armed Services; Small Business

BROWN, CORRINE, D-FLA. (3)

Capitol Hill Office: 2444 RHOB 20515; 225-0123; Fax: 225-2256; *Administrative Assistant:* Elias Ronnie Simmons

Web: www.house.gov/corrinebrown

E-mail: www.house.gov/writerep

District Office(s): 101 E. Union St., Jacksonville 32202; (904) 354-1652; Fax: (904) 354-2721; *District Director:* Glenel Bowden

Chamber of Commerce Bldg., Orlando 32804; (407) 872-0656; Fax: (407) 872-5763; *Chief Congressional Aide:* Sybrennia Grady

Committee Assignment(s): Transportation and Infrastructure; Veterans' Affairs

BROWN, SHERROD, D-OHIO (13)

Capitol Hill Office: 201 CHOB 20515; 225-3401; Fax: 225-2266; *Chief of Staff:* Donna Pignatelli

Web: www.house.gov/sherrodbrown

E-mail: sherrod@mail.house.gov

District Office(s): 5201 Abbe Rd., Elyria 44035; (440) 934-5100; Fax: (440) 934-5145; *District Director:* Elizabeth Thames

124 W. Washington St., Medina 44256; (330) 722-9262; Fax: (330) 722-2401; *Caseworker:* Colin Cranston

15561 W. High St., Middlefield 44062; (440) 632-5913; Fax: (440) 632-5780; *Caseworker:* Joyce Edelinsky

Committee Assignment(s): Commerce; International Relations

BRYANT, ED, R-TENN. (7)

Capitol Hill Office: 408 CHOB 20515; 225-2811; Fax: 225-2989; *Chief of Staff:* P. K. Rehbein

Web: www.house.gov/bryant

E-mail: www.house.gov/writerep

District Office(s): 330 N. 2nd St., Clarksville 37040; (931) 503-0391; Fax: (931) 503-0393; *Staff Assistant:* Woody Parker

5909 Shelby Oaks Dr., Memphis 38134; (901) 382-5811; Fax: (901) 373-8215; *Staff Assistant:* Susan McCord

810 1/2 S. Garden St., Columbia 38401; (931) 381-8100; Fax: (931) 381-1956; *Field Representative:* Becky Moon

Committee Assignment(s): Commerce

BURR, RICHARD M., R-N.C. (5)

Capitol Hill Office: 1513 LHOB 20515; 225-2071; Fax: 225-2995; *Administrative Assistants:* John Versaggi; Peter Hans

Web: www.house.gov/burr

E-mail: richard.burrnc05@mail.house.gov

District Office(s): Piedmont Plaza Two, Winston Salem 27104; (336) 631-5125; Fax: (336) 725-4493; *District Director:* L. Dean Myers

Alamance County Office Bldg., Graham 27253; (336) 229-0159; *Regional Representative:* Susan Hatfield

Committee Assignment(s): Commerce; International Relations

BURTON, DAN, R-IND. (6)

Capitol Hill Office: 2185 RHOB 20515; 225-2276; Fax: 225-0016; *Chief of Staff:* Mark Walker

Web: www.house.gov/burton

E-mail: www.house.gov/writerep

District Office(s): 435 E. Main St., Greenwood 46142; (317) 882-3640; Fax: (317) 889-3845; *Special Assistant:* Mary Frederick

8900 Keystone at the Crossing, Indianapolis 46240; (317) 848-0201; Fax: (317) 846-7306; *District Director:* Michael A. Delph

Committee Assignment(s): Government Reform; International Relations

BUYER, STEVE, R-IND. (5)

Capitol Hill Office: 227 CHOB 20515; 225-5037; Fax: 225-2267; *Chief of Staff:* Kelly Craven

Web: www.house.gov/buyer

E-mail: www.house.gov/writerep

District Office(s): 215 W. Sycamore St., Kokomo 46901; (765) 454-7551; *District Manager:* Linda Worsham

100 S. Main St., Monticello 47960; (219) 583-9819; *Staff Assistant:* Janet Faker

Committee Assignment(s): Armed Services; Veterans' Affairs

CALLAHAN, SONNY, R-ALA. (1)

Capitol Hill Office: 2466 RHOB 20515; 225-4931; Fax: 225-0562; *Chief of Staff:* Jo Bonner

Web: www.house.gov/callahan

E-mail: sonny.callahan@mail.house.gov

District Office(s): 1141 Montlimar Dr., Mobile 36609; (334) 690-2811; Fax: (334) 342-0404; *District Director:* Eliska Roe

Committee Assignment(s): Appropriations

CALVERT, KEN, R-CALIF. (43)

Capitol Hill Office: 2201 RHOB 20515; 225-1986; Fax: 225-2004; *Chief of Staff:* Dave Ramey

Web: www.house.gov/calvert

E-mail: www.house.gov/writerep

District Office(s): 3400 Central Ave., Riverside 92506; (909) 784-4300; Fax: (909) 784-5255; *District Director:* Linda Fisher

Committee Assignment(s): Agriculture; Resources; Science

CAMP, DAVE, R-MICH. (4)

Capitol Hill Office: 137 CHOB 20515; 225-3561; Fax: 225-9679; *Chief of Staff:* Behrends Foster

Web: www.house.gov/camp

E-mail: davecamp@mail.house.gov

District Office(s): 3508 W. Houghton Lake Dr., Houghton Lake 48629; (517) 366-4922; Fax: (517) 366-4543; *Constituent Representative:* Tarin Eisenga

135 Ashman Dr., Midland 48640; (517) 631-2552; Fax: (517) 631-6271; *District Director:* Brent Neubecker

308 W. Main St., Owosso 48867; (517) 723-6759; Fax: (517) 725-3117; *Constituent Relations Representative:* Lori Particka

Committee Assignment(s): Standards of Official Conduct; Ways and Means

CAMPBELL, TOM, R-CALIF. (15)

Capitol Hill Office: 2442 RHOB 20515; 225-2631; Fax: 225-6788; *Administrative Assistant:* Jackie Corcoran

Web: www.house.gov/campbell

E-mail: campbell@mail.house.gov

District Office(s): 910 Campisi Way, Campbell 95008; (408) 371-7337; Fax: (408) 371-7925; *District Manager:* Casey Beyer

Committee Assignment(s): Banking and Financial Services; International Relations; Joint Economic

CANADY, CHARLES T., R-FLA. (12)

Capitol Hill Office: 2432 RHOB 20515; 225-1252; Fax: 225-2279; *Chief of Staff:* Stacey Windham

Web: www.house.gov/canady

E-mail: rep.charles.canady@mail.house.gov

District Office(s): Federal Bldg., Lakeland 33801; (863) 688-2651; Fax: (863) 683-4453; *District Director:* Sue Loftin

Committee Assignment(s): Agriculture; Judiciary

CANNON, CHRISTOPHER B., R-UTAH (3)

Capitol Hill Office: 118 CHOB 20515; 225-7751; Fax: 225-5629; *Chief of Staff:* Windsor Freemeyer

Web: www.house.gov/cannon

E-mail: cannon.ut03@mail.house.gov

District Office(s): 51 S. University Ave., Provo 84606; (801) 379-2500; Fax: (801) 379-2509; *District Director:* Keith Nash

Committee Assignment(s): Judiciary; Resources; Science

CAPPS, LOIS, D-CALIF. (22)

Capitol Hill Office: 1118 LHOB 20515; 225-3601; Fax: 225-5632; *Chief of Staff:* Jeremy Rabinovitz

Web: www.house.gov/capps

E-mail: lois.capps@mail.house.gov

District Office(s): 1428 Chapala St., Santa Barbara 93101; (805) 730-1710; Fax: (805) 730-9153; *District Director:* Sharon Siegel

1411 March St., San Luis Obispo 93401; (805) 546-8348; Fax: (805) 546-8368; *District Representative:* Anne McMahon

910 E. Stowell Rd., Santa Maria 93454; (805) 349-9313; Fax: (805) 349-1241; *Community Liason:* Yvette Andrade

Committee Assignment(s): Commerce

CAPUANO, MICHAEL E., D-MASS. (8)

Capitol Hill Office: 1232 LHOB 20515; 225-5111; Fax: 225-9322; *Administrative Assistant:* Dan Muroff

Web: www.house.gov/capuano

E-mail: www.house.gov/writerep

District Office(s): 110 1st St., Cambridge 02141; (617) 621-6208; Fax: (617) 621-8628; *District Director:* Mike Gorman

Roxbury Community College, Roxbury 02120; (617) 621-6208; Fax: (617) 541-6909; *District Representative:* Ego Ezedi

Committee Assignment(s): Banking and Financial Services; Science

CARDIN, BENJAMIN L., D-MD. (3)

Capitol Hill Office: 104 CHOB 20515; 225-4016; Fax: 225-9219; *Administrative Assistant:* David Koshgarian

Web: www.house.gov/cardin

E-mail: rep.cardin@mail.house.gov

District Office(s): 540 E. Belvedere Ave., Baltimore 21212; (410) 433-8886; Fax: (410) 433-2110; *Press Secretary:* Susan F. Sullam; *District Office Director:* Bailey E. Fine

Committee Assignment(s): Ways and Means

CARSON, JULIA, D-IND. (10)

Capitol Hill Office: 1541 LHOB 20515; 225-4011; Fax: 225-5633; *Chief of Staff:* Sarge Visher

Web: www.house.gov/carson

E-mail: rep.carson@mail.house.gov

District Office(s): 300 E. Fall Creek Parkway, Indianapolis 46205; (317) 283-6516; Fax: (317) 283-6567; *District Director:* Melody Barber

Committee Assignment(s): Banking and Financial Services; Veterans' Affairs

CASTLE, MICHAEL N., R-DEL. (AL)

Capitol Hill Office: 1227 LHOB 20515; 225-4165; Fax: 225-2291; *Administrative Assistant:* Paul Leonard

Web: www.house.gov/castle

E-mail: delaware@mail.house.gov

District Office(s): 3 Christina Centre, Wilmington 19801; (302) 428-1902; Fax: (302) 428-1950; *District Director:* Jeffrey A. Dayton

Frear Federal Bldg., Dover 19904; (302) 736-1666; Fax: (302) 736-6580; *Field Representative:* Kate Johnson

Committee Assignment(s): Banking and Financial Services; Education and Workforce; Select Intelligence

CHABOT, STEVE, R-OHIO (1)

Capitol Hill Office: 129 CHOB 20515; 225-2216; Fax: 225-3012; *Administrative Assistant:* Gary Lindgren

Web: www.house.gov/chabot

E-mail: www.house.gov/writerep

District Office(s): 105 W. 4th St., Cincinnati 45202; (513) 684-2723; Fax: (513) 421-8722; *District Director:* Mike Cantwell

Committee Assignment(s): International Relations; Judiciary; Small Business

CHAMBLISS, SAXBY, R-GA. (8)

Capitol Hill Office: 1019 LHOB 20515; 225-6531; Fax: 225-3013; *Chief of Staff:* Rob Leebern

Web: www.house.gov/chambliss

E-mail: rep.saxby.chambliss@mail.house.gov

District Office(s): 682 Cherry St., Macon 31210; (912) 752-0800; Fax: (912) 752-0888; *District Director:* Bill Stembridge

208 Tebeau St., Waycross 31501; (912) 287-1180; Fax: (912) 287-1182; *District Representative:* Eric Betts

Committee Assignment(s): Agriculture; Armed Services; Budget

CHENOWETH-HAGE, HELEN, R-IDAHO (1)

Capitol Hill Office: 1727 LHOB 20515; 225-6611; Fax: 225-3029; *Chief of Staff:* Keith Lee Rupp

Web: www.house.gov/chenoweth

E-mail: ask.helen@mail.house.gov

District Office(s): 304 N. 8th St., Boise 83702; (208) 336-9831; Fax: (208) 336-9891; *District Director:* Chad Hyslop

111 Main St., Lewiston 83501; (208) 746-4613; Fax: (208) 746-4655; *Office Assistant:* Valerie Schatz

610 W. Hubbard, Coeur D'Alene 83814; (208) 667-0127; Fax: (208) 667-0310; *District Representative:* Karen Roetter

Committee Assignment(s): Agriculture; Government Reform; Resources; Veterans' Affairs

CHRISTENSEN, DONNA M. C., D-VIRGIN IS. (AL)

Capitol Hill Office: 1711 LHOB 20515; 225-1790; Fax: 225-5517; *Administrative Assistant:* Lorraine Hill

Web: www.house.gov/christian-christensen

E-mail: donna.christensen@mail.house.gov

District Office(s): Vitraco Mall, St. Thomas 00801; (340) 774-4408; Fax: (340) 774-8033; *St. Thomas Office Manager:* Shawn Malone

P.O. Box 5980, Space #3 Mini Mall, St. Croix 00823; (340) 778-5900; Fax: (340) 778-5111; *District Director:* Claire Roker

Committee Assignment(s): Resources; Small Business

CLAY, WILLIAM L., D-MO. (1)

Capitol Hill Office: 2306 RHOB 20515; 225-2406; Fax: 225-1725; *Chief of Staff:* Harriet Pritchett Grigsby

Web: www.house.gov/clay

E-mail: www.house.gov/writerep

District Office(s): 5261 Delmar Blvd., St. Louis 63108; (314) 367-1970; Fax: (314) 367-1341; *District Assistant:* Mark Odom

12755 New Halls Ferry Plaza, Florissant 63033; (314) 839-9148; Fax: (314) 839-9318; *District Coordinator:* Virginia Cook

Committee Assignment(s): Education and Workforce

CLAYTON, EVA, D-N.C. (1)

Capitol Hill Office: 2440 RHOB 20515; 225-3101; Fax: 225-3354; *Administrative Assistant:* Johnny Barnes

Web: www.house.gov/clayton

E-mail: eclayton1@mail.house.gov

District Office(s): Warren Corners Shopping Center, Norlina 27563; (252) 456-4800; Fax: (252) 456-2611; *Administrative Staff Assistant:* Linda Jones

400 Martin Luther King Jr. Dr., Greenville 27834; (252) 758-8800; Fax: (252) 758-1021; *District Manager:* Charles Worth

Committee Assignment(s): Agriculture; Budget

CLEMENT, BOB, D-TENN. (5)

Capitol Hill Office: 2229 RHOB 20515; 225-4311; Fax: 226-1035; *Chief of Staff:* Caroline Nielson

Web: www.house.gov/clement

E-mail: bob.clement@mail.house.gov

District Office(s): 801 Broadway, Nashville 37203; (615) 736-5295; Fax: (615) 736-7479; *Press Secretary:* Christi Ray; *Policy-Communications Director:* William S. Mason

2701 Jefferson St., Nashville 37208; (615) 320-1363; Fax: (615) 321-3873; *Nashville Coordinator:* Gail Stafford

101 5th Ave. West Springfield 37172; (615) 384-6600; Fax: (615) 384-2582; *Field Coordinator:* Caroline Diaz-Barriaga

Committee Assignment(s): Budget; Transportation and Infrastructure

CLYBURN, JAMES E., D-S.C. (6)

Capitol Hill Office: 319 CHOB 20515; 225-3315; Fax: 225-2313; *Chief of Staff:* Yelberton Watkins

Web: www.house.gov/clyburn

E-mail: jclyburn@mail.house.gov

District Office(s): 1703 Gervais St., Columbia 29201; (803) 799-1100; Fax: (803) 799-9060; *District Director:* Robert M. Nance

P.O. Box 6099, Charleston 29405; (843) 965-5578; Fax: (843) 965-5581; *Area Director:* Davis Marshall

Business and Technology Center, Florence 29506; (843) 662-1212; Fax: (843) 662-8474; *Area Director:* Charlene Lowery

COBLE, HOWARD, R-N.C. (6)

Capitol Hill Office: 2468 RHOB 20515; 225-3065; Fax: 225-8611; *Chief of Staff:* Ed McDonald

Web: www.house.gov/coble

E-mail: howard.coble@mail.house.gov

District Office(s): 241 Sunset Ave., Asheboro 27203; (336) 626-3060; Fax: (336) 626-4533; *District Representative:* Rebecca Redding Williams

330 S. Greene St., Greensboro 27401; (336) 333-5005; Fax: (336) 333-5048; *District Representative:* Janine Osborne

155 Northpoint Ave., High Point 27262; (336) 886-5106; Fax: (336) 886-8740; *District Representative:* Carolyn McGahey

Committee Assignment(s): Judiciary; Transportation and Infrastructure

COBURN, TOM, R-OKLA. (2)

Capitol Hill Office: 429 CHOB 20515; 225-2701; Fax: 225-3038

Web: www.house.gov/coburn

E-mail: rep.coburn@mail.house.gov

District Office(s): 215 State St., Muskogee 74401; (918) 687-2533; Fax: (918) 682-8503; *Chief of Staff:* Karl E. Ahlgren

120 S. Missouri Ave., Claremore 74017; (918) 341-9336; Fax: (918) 341-9437; *Field Representative:* Jo Rainbolt

34 A St., Miami 74354; (918) 542-5337; Fax: (918) 542-5367; *Field Representative:* Jo Rainbolt

Committee Assignment(s): Commerce

COLLINS, MAC, R-GA. (3)

Capitol Hill Office: 1131 LHOB 20515; 225-5901; Fax: 225-2515; *Administrative Assistant:* Betty Monro

Web: www.house.gov/maccollins

E-mail: mac.collins@mail.house.gov

District Office(s): 173 N. Main St., Jonesboro 30236; (770) 603-3395; Fax: (770) 603-3402; *Constituent Services Representative:* Audrey M. Bray

2121 Wynnton Rd., Columbus 31906; (706) 327-7228; Fax: (706) 324-7969; *District Director:* Shirley Gillespie

Committee Assignment(s): Budget; Ways and Means

COMBEST, LARRY, R-TEXAS (19)

Capitol Hill Office: 1026 LHOB 20515; 225-4005; *Administrative Assistant:* Rob Lehman

Web: www.house.gov/combest

E-mail: www.house.gov/writerep

District Office(s): 5809 S. Western Ave., Amarillo 79110; (806) 353-3945; *Staff Assistant:* Sherry Sagebiel

George H. Mahon Federal Bldg., Lubbock 79401; (806) 763-1611; *District Representative:* Jimmy Clark

3800 E. 42nd St., Odessa 79762; (915) 550-0743; *Office Manager:* Jenny Welch

Committee Assignment(s): Agriculture; Small Business

CONDIT, GARY A., D-CALIF. (18)

Capitol Hill Office: 2234 RHOB 20515; 225-6131; Fax: 225-0819; *Administrative Assistant:* Mike Dayton

Web: www.house.gov/gcondit

E-mail: gary.condit@mail.house.gov

District Office(s): Federal Bldg., Merced 95340; (209) 383-4455; Fax: (209) 726-1065; *Field Representative:* Brian Griffin

920 16th St., Modesto 95354; (209) 527-1914; Fax: (209) 527-5748; *Chief of Staff:* Mike Lynch

Committee Assignment(s): Agriculture; Select Intelligence

CONYERS, JOHN JR., D-MICH. (14)

Capitol Hill Office: 2426 RHOB 20515; 225-5126; Fax: 225-0072; *Chief of Staff:* Greg Moore

Web: www.house.gov/conyers

E-mail: john.conyers@mail.house.gov

RHOB 48226; 961-5670; Fax: 226-2085

Committee Assignment(s): Judiciary

COOK, MERRILL, R-UTAH (2)

Capital Hill Office: Independence Ave. and S. Capitol St., S.E., Washington 20515; 225-3011; Fax: 225-5638; *Administrative Assistant:* Connie Humphrey

Web: www.house.gov/cook

E-mail: cong.merrill.cook@mail.house.gov

District Office(s): Federal Bldg., Salt Lake City 84138; (801) 524-4394; Fax: (801) 524-5994; *District Director:* Art Martines; *Scheduler:* Lorraine Bennett

Committee Assignment(s): Banking and Financial Services; Science; Transportation and Infrastructure

COOKSEY, JOHN, R-LA. (5)

Capitol Hill Office: 317 CHOB 20515; 225-8490; Fax: 225-5639; *Administrative Assistant:* Lee Fletcher

Web: www.house.gov/cooksey

E-mail: congressman.cooksey@mail.house.gov

District Office(s): 1101 Hudson Lane, Monroe 71201; (318) 330-9998; Fax: (318) 330-9950; *District Director:* Dwight "Del" Vines; *Communications Director:* Robert "Bob" Anderson

2019 MacArthur Dr., Alexandria 71301; (318) 448-1777; Fax: (318) 473-8163; *Co-District Manager:* Susan DeKeyzer

Committee Assignment(s): Agriculture; International Relations; Transportation and Infrastructure

COSTELLO, JERRY F., D-ILL. (12)

Capitol Hill Office: 2454 RHOB 20515; 225-5661; Fax: 225-0285; *Chief of Staff:* Brian Lott
Web: www.house.gov/costello
E-mail: jfc.il12@mail.house.gov
District Office(s): 1363 Neidringhaus Ave., Granite City 62040; (618) 451-7065; Fax: (618) 451-2126; *Staff Assistant:* David Cueto
8787 State St., East St. Louis 62203; (618) 397-8833; *Staff Assistant:* Mel Frierson
327 W. Main St., Belleville 62220; (618) 233-8026; Fax: (618) 233-8765; *District Manager:* Frank Miles
250 W. Cherry St., Carbondale 62901; (618) 529-3791; *Staff Assistant:* Alice Tucker
1330 Swanwick St., Chester 62233; (618) 826-3043; *Staff Assistant:* Patsie Travelstead
Committee Assignment(s): Science; Transportation and Infrastructure

COX, CHRISTOPHER, R-CALIF. (47)

Capitol Hill Office: 2402 RHOB 20515; 225-5611; Fax: 225-9177; *Chief of Staff:* C. Dean McGrath Jr.
Web: www.house.gov/chriscox
E-mail: christopher.cox@mail.house.gov
District Office(s): One Newport Place, Newport Beach 92660; (714) 756-2244; Fax: (714) 251-9309; *District Representative:* Greg Haskin
Committee Assignment(s): Commerce

COYNE, WILLIAM J., D-PA. (14)

Capitol Hill Office: 2455 RHOB 20515; 225-2301; Fax: 225-1844; *Administrative Assistant:* Coleman J. Conroy
Web: www.house.gov/coyne
E-mail: www.house.gov/writerep
District Office(s): William S. Moorhead Federal Bldg., Pittsburgh 15222; (412) 644-2870; Fax: (412) 644-3434; *Executive Assistant:* James Rooney
Committee Assignment(s): Ways and Means

CRAMER, ROBERT E. "BUD," D-ALA. (5)

Capitol Hill Office: 2350 RHOB 20515; 225-4801; *Administrative Assistant:* Jeff Murray
Web: www.house.gov/cramer
E-mail: budmail@mail.house.gov
District Office(s): P.O. Box 668, Decatur 35602; (256) 355-9400; Fax: (256) 355-9404; *Caseworker:* Peggy Allen
1301-C John R St., Muscle Shoals 35661; (256) 381-3450; Fax: (256) 381-3452; *Caseworker:* Mary Ethel McDonald
403 Franklin St., Huntsville 35801; (256) 551-0190; Fax: (256) 551-0194; *District Coordinator:* Joey Ceci
Committee Assignment(s): Appropriations

CRANE, PHILIP M., R-ILL. (8)

Capitol Hill Office: 233 CHOB 20515; 225-3711; Fax: 225-7830; *Chief of Staff:* Ted Schelenski
Web: www.house.gov/crane
E-mail: www.house.gov/writerep
District Office(s): 300 N. Milwaukee Ave., Lake Villa 60046; (847) 265-9000; Fax: (847) 265-9028; *Caseworker:* Carol Toft
1100 W. Northwest Highway, Palatine 60067; (847) 358-9160; Fax: (847) 358-9185; *Caseworker:* Thelma Hummel
Committee Assignment(s): Joint Taxation; Ways and Means

CROWLEY, JOSEPH, D-N.Y. (7)

Capitol Hill Office: 1517 LHOB 20515; 225-3965; Fax: 225-1909; *Administrative Assistant:* Chris McCannell
Web: www.house.gov/crowley
E-mail: write2joecrowley@mail.house.gov
District Office(s): 82-11 37th Ave., Jackson Heights 11372; (718) 779-1400; Fax: (718) 505-0156; *District Director:* Michael McSweeney
2114 Williamsbridge Rd., Bronx 10461; (718) 931-1400; Fax: (718) 931-1340; *District Director:* Fran Mahoney
Committee Assignment(s): International Relations; Resources

CUBIN, BARBARA, R-WYO. (AL)

Capitol Hill Office: 1114 LHOB 20515; 225-2311; Fax: 225-3057; *Administrative Assistant:* Vacant
Web: www.house.gov/cubin
E-mail: barbara.cubin@mail.house.gov
District Office(s): Federal Bldg., Cheyenne 82001; (307) 772-2595; Fax: (307) 772-2597; *Field Representative:* Katie Legerski
Federal Bldg., Casper 82601; (307) 261-6595; Fax: (307) 261-6597; *State Director:* Mantha Phillips
2515 Foothills Blvd., Rock Springs 82901; (307) 362-4095; Fax: (307) 362-4097; *Field Representative:* Bonnie Cannon
Committee Assignment(s): Commerce; Resources

CUMMINGS, ELIJAH E., D-MD. (7)

Capitol Hill Office: 1632 LHOB 20515; 225-4741; Fax: 225-3178; *Chief of Staff:* Deidre Bishop
Web: www.house.gov/cummings
E-mail: rep.cummings@mail.house.gov
District Office(s): 3000 Druid Park Dr., Baltimore 21215; (410) 367-1900; Fax: (410) 367-5331; *District Manager:* Deborah Perry
7900 Liberty Rd., Baltimore 21244; (410) 496-2010; Fax: (410) 496-2015; *District Administrator:* Vernon Simms

754 Frederick Rd., Catonsville 21228; (410) 719-8777; Fax: (410) 455-0110; *Special Assistant:* William Cole; *Press Secretary:* Michael Christianson

Committee Assignment(s): Government Reform; Transportation and Infrastructure

CUNNINGHAM, RANDY "DUKE," R-CALIF. (51)

Capitol Hill Office: 2238 RHOB 20515; 225-5452; Fax: 225-2558; *Chief of Staff:* Trey Hardin

Web: www.house.gov/cunningham

E-mail: www.house.gov/writerep

District Office(s): 613 W. Valley Parkway, Escondido 92025; (760) 737-8438; Fax: (760) 737-9132; *District Director:* Cameron Durckel

Committee Assignment(s): Appropriations

DANNER, PAT, D-MO. (6)

Capitol Hill Office: 2262 RHOB 20515; 225-7041; Fax: 225-8221; *Chief of Staff:* Cathie McCarley

Web: www.house.gov/danner

E-mail: www.house.gov/writerep

District Office(s): 5754 N. Broadway, Kansas City 64118; (816) 455-2256; Fax: (816) 455-2153; *District Congressional Aide:* Irene Delich

U.S. Post Office, St. Joseph 64501; (816) 233-9818; Fax: (816) 233-9848; *District Administrator:* Rose M. Grinstead

Committee Assignment(s): International Relations; Transportation and Infrastructure

DAVIS, DANNY K., D-ILL. (7)

Capitol Hill Office: 1222 LHOB 20515; 225-5006; Fax: 225-5641; *Chief of Staff:* Richard Boykin

Web: www.house.gov/davis

E-mail: www.house.gov/writerep

District Office(s): 3333 W. Arthington St., Chicago 60624; (773) 533-7520; Fax: (773) 533-7530; *District Administrator:* F. Daniel Cantrell; *Communications Director:* Ira Cohen

Committee Assignment(s): Government Reform; Small Business

DAVIS, JIM, D-FLA. (11)

Capitol Hill Office: 418 CHOB 20515; 225-3376; Fax: 225-5652; *Chief of Staff:* Suzanne Farmer

Web: www.house.gov/jimdavis

E-mail: www.house.gov/writerep

District Office(s): 3315 Henderson Blvd., Tampa 33609; (813) 354-9217; Fax: (813) 354-9514; *District Director:* T. Clay Phillips

Committee Assignment(s): Budget; House Administration; International Relations; Joint Library

DAVIS, THOMAS M. III, R-VA. (11)

Capitol Hill Office: 224 CHOB 20515; 225-1492; Fax: 225-3071; *Chief of Staff:* Peter Sirh

Web: www.house.gov/tomdavis

E-mail: tom.davis@mail.house.gov

District Office(s): 7018 Evergreen Court, Annandale 22003; (703) 916-9610; Fax: (703) 916-9617; *District Director:* David Thomas

730 Elden St., 2nd Floor, Herndon 20170; (703) 437-1726; Fax: (703) 437-3004; *Constituent Services Director:* Ann Rust

13554 Minnieville Rd., Woodbridge 22192; (703) 590-4599; Fax: (703) 590-4740; *Constituent Services Representative:* George Massey

Committee Assignment(s): Government Reform

DEAL, NATHAN, R-GA. (9)

Capitol Hill Office: 2437 RHOB 20515; 225-5211; Fax: 225-8272; *Chief of Staff:* Chris Riley

Web: www.house.gov/deal

E-mail: www.house.gov/writerep

District Office(s): 200 Main St., Gainesville 30503; (770) 535-2592; Fax: (770) 535-2765; *District Director:* Jim Adams

415 E. Walnut Ave., Dalton 30721; (706) 226-5320; Fax: (706) 278-0840; *Staff Assistant:* Vivian Campbell

108 W. Lafayette Square, Lafayette 30728; (706) 638-7042; Fax: (706) 638-7049; *Staff Assistant:* Lonna Hightower

Committee Assignment(s): Commerce; Education and Workforce

DEFAZIO, PETER A., D-ORE. (4)

Capitol Hill Office: 2134 RHOB 20515; 225-6416; Fax: 225-0032; *Administrative Assistant:* Penny Dodge

Web: www.house.gov/defazio

E-mail: peter.defazio@mail.house.gov

District Office(s): 151 W. 7th Ave., Eugene 97401; (541) 465-6732; Fax: (541) 465-6458; *District Director:* Betsy Boyd

P.O. Box 1557, Coos Bay 97420; (541) 269-2609; Fax: (541) 269-5760; *Field Representative:* Chris Conroy

P.O. Box 2460, Roseburg 97470; (541) 440-3523; Fax: (541) 440-3525; *Field Representative:* Chris Conroy

Committee Assignment(s): Resources; Transportation and Infrastructure

DEGETTE, DIANA, D-COLO. (1)

Capitol Hill Office: 1339 LHOB 20515; 225-4431; Fax: 225-5657; *Administrative Assistant:* Lisa Cohen

Web: www.house.gov/degette

E-mail: degette@mail.house.gov

District Office(s): 1400 Glenarm Place, Denver 80202; (303) 844-4988; Fax: (303) 844-4996; *District Director:* Greg Diamond

Committee Assignment(s): Commerce

DELAHUNT, BILL, D-MASS. (10)

Capitol Hill Office: 1317 LHOB 20515; 225-3111; Fax: 225-5658; *Administrative Assistant:* Steve Schwadron

Web: www.house.gov/delahunt

E-mail: william.delahunt@mail.house.gov

District Office(s): 1495 Hancock St., Quincy 02169; (617) 770-3700; Fax: (617) 770-2984; *District Director:* Annie Federico

Federal Bldg., Brockton 02401; (508) 584-6666; Fax: (617) 770-2984; *District Representative:* Anestis Kalaitzidis

146 Main St., Hyannis 02601; (508) 771-0666; Fax: (508) 790-1959; *Regional Representative:* Mark Forest

Committee Assignment(s): International Relations; Judiciary

DeLAURO, ROSA, D-CONN. (3)

Capitol Hill Office: 436 CHOB 20515; 225-3661; Fax: 225-4890; *Chief of Staff:* Leah Gurowitz

Web: www.house.gov/delauro

E-mail: www.house.gov/writerep

District Office(s): 59 Elm St., New Haven 06510; (203) 562-3718; Fax: (203) 772-2260; *District Director:* Jennifer Emra

Committee Assignment(s): Appropriations

DeLAY, TOM, R-TEXAS (22)

Capitol Hill Office: 341 CHOB 20515; 225-5951; Fax: 225-5241; *Chief of Staff:* Susan Hirschmann

Web: www.majoritywhip.house.gov

E-mail: thewhip@mail.house.gov

District Office(s): 10701 Corporate Dr., Stafford 77477; (281) 240-3700; Fax: (281) 240-2959; *District Director:* Ann Swisher

Committee Assignment(s): Appropriations

DeMINT, JIM, R-S.C. (4)

Capitol Hill Office: 507 CHOB 20515; 225-6030; Fax: 226-1177; *Chief of Staff:* Marie Wheat

Web: www.demint.house.gov

E-mail: www.house.gov/writerep

District Office(s): 300 E. Washington St., Greenville 29601; (864) 232-1141; Fax: (864) 233-2160; *District Director:* Jason Elliott

201 Magnolia St., Spartanburg 29301; (864) 582-6422; *Field Representative:* Ray Wynn

Committee Assignment(s): Education and Workforce; Small Business; Transportation and Infrastructure

DEUTSCH, PETER, D-FLA. (20)

Capitol Hill Office: 204 CHOB 20515; 225-7931; Fax: 225-8456; *Chief of Staff:* Robin Rorapaugh

Web: www.house.gov/deutsch

E-mail: www.house.gov/writerep

District Office(s): 10100 Pines Blvd., Pembroke Pines 33026; (954) 437-3936; Fax: (954) 437-4776; *Constituent Services Director:* Susan Lewis

1010 Kennedy Dr., Key West 33040; (305) 294-5815; Fax: (305) 294-4193; *Monroe County Representative:* Becky Iannotta

Committee Assignment(s): Commerce

DIAZ-BALART, LINCOLN, R-FLA. (21)

Capitol Hill Office: 404 CHOB 20515; 225-4211; Fax: 225-8576; *Administrative Assistant:* Stephen Vermillion

Web: www.house.gov/diaz-balart

E-mail: www.house.gov/writerep

District Office(s): 8525 N.W. 53rd Terrace, Miami 33166; (305) 470-8555; Fax: (305) 470-8575; *District Director:* Ana M. Carbonell

Committee Assignment(s): Rules

DICKEY, JAY, R-ARK. (4)

Capitol Hill Office: 2453 RHOB 20515; 225-3772; Fax: 225-1314; *Administrative Assistant:* Rob Johnson

Web: www.house.gov/dickey

E-mail: talk2jay@mail.house.gov

District Office(s): 100 Reserve St., Hot Springs National Park 71901; (501) 623-5800; Fax: (501) 623-5363; *District Field Representative:* Glenda Peacock

100 E. 8th Ave., Pine Bluff 76701; (870) 536-3376; Fax: (870) 536-4058; *District Director:* Allen W. Maxwell

Committee Assignment(s): Appropriations

DICKS, NORM, D-WASH. (6)

Capitol Hill Office: 2467 RHOB 20515; 225-5916; Fax: 226-1176

Web: www.house.gov/dicks

E-mail: www.house.gov/writerep

District Office(s): 500 Pacific Ave., Bremerton 98310; (360) 479-4011; Fax: (360) 553-7445; *County Director:* Cheri Williams

1717 Pacific Ave., Tacoma 98402; (253) 593-6536; Fax: (253) 593-6551; *District Director:* Kurt Beckett

Committee Assignment(s): Appropriations

DINGELL, JOHN D., D-MICH. (16)

Capitol Hill Office: 2328 RHOB 20515; 225-4071; *Administrative Assistant:* Marda Robillard

Web: www.house.gov/dingell

E-mail: public.dingell@mail.house.gov

District Office(s): 5465 Schaefer Rd., Dearborn 48126; (313) 846-1276; Fax: (313) 846-5628; *District Administrator:* Terrance Spryzsak

23 E. Front St., Monroe 48161; (313) 243-1849; Fax: (313) 243-5559; *Office Manager:* Donna Hoffer

Committee Assignment(s): Commerce

DIXON, JULIAN C., D-CALIF. (32)

Capitol Hill Office: 2252 RHOB 20515; 225-7084; Fax: 225-4091; *Administrative Assistant:* Andrea Tracy Holmes
Web: www.house.gov/dixon
E-mail: www.house.gov/writerep
District Office(s): 5100 W. Goldleaf Circle, Los Angeles 90056; (323) 678-5424; Fax: (323) 678-6026; *Administrative Assistant:* Patricia Miller
Committee Assignment(s): Appropriations; Select Intelligence

DOGGETT, LLOYD, D-TEXAS (10)

Capitol Hill Office: 328 CHOB 20515; 225-4865; Fax: 225-3073; *Chief of Staff:* Tom Valentine
Web: www.house.gov/doggett
E-mail: lloyd.doggett@mail.house.gov
District Office(s): Federal Bldg., Austin 78701; (512) 916-5921; Fax: (512) 916-5108; *District Director:* Tom Morgan
Committee Assignment(s): Ways and Means

DOOLEY, CAL, D-CALIF. (20)

Capitol Hill Office: 1201 LHOB 20515; 225-3341; Fax: 225-9308; *Chief of Staff:* Lisa Quigley
Web: www.house.gov/dooley
E-mail: www.house.gov/writerep
District Office(s): 530 Kings County Dr., Hanford 93230; (559) 585-8171; Fax: (559) 585-8199; Fax: (559) 585-8241; *District Director:* Nicole Parra
Committee Assignment(s): Agriculture; Resources

DOOLITTLE, JOHN T., R-CALIF. (4)

Capitol Hill Office: 1526 LHOB 20515; 225-2511; Fax: 225-5444; *Chief of Staff:* David Lopez
Web: www.house.gov/doolittle
E-mail: doolittle@mail.house.gov
District Office(s): 2130 Professional Dr., Roseville 95661; (916) 786-5560; Fax: (916) 786-6364; *District Director:* Richard Robinson
Committee Assignment(s): Joint Economic; Resources; Transportation and Infrastructure

DOYLE, MIKE, D-PA. (18)

Capitol Hill Office: 133 CHOB 20515; 225-2135; Fax: 225-3084; *Chief of Staff:* David Lucas
Web: www.house.gov/doyle
E-mail: rep.doyle@mail.house.gov
District Office(s): 541 5th Ave., McKeesport 15132; (412) 664-4049; Fax: (412) 664-6055; *Economic Development Representative:* Kenneth Foltz
11 Duff Rd., Penn Hills 15235; (412) 241-6055; Fax: (412) 241-6820; *District Director:* Paul D'Alesandro
Committee Assignment(s): Science; Veterans' Affairs

DREIER, DAVID, R-CALIF. (28)

Capitol Hill Office: 237 CHOB 20515; 225-2305; Fax: 225-7018; *Chief of Staff:* Brad Smith
Web: www.house.gov/dreier
E-mail: www.house.gov/writerep
District Office(s): 112 N. 2nd Ave., Covina 91723; (909) 592-2857; (626) 339-9078; *District Director:* Mark S. Harmsen
Committee Assignment(s): Rules

DUNCAN, JOHN J. "JIMMY" JR., R-TENN. (2)

Capitol Hill Office: 2400 RHOB 20515; 225-5435; Fax: 225-6440; *Chief of Staff:* Judy Whitbred
Web: www.house.gov/duncan
E-mail: jjduncan@mail.house.gov
District Office(s): Courthouse, Athens 37303; (423) 745-4671; Fax: (423) 745-6025; *Office Manager:* Linda Higdon
800 Market St., Knoxville 37902; (423) 523-3772; Fax: (423) 544-0728; *District Director:* Bob Griffitts
262 E. Broadway, Maryville 37804; (423) 984-5464; Fax: (423) 984-0521; *Office Manager:* Vickie Flynn
Committee Assignment(s): Resources; Transportation and Infrastructure

DUNN, JENNIFER, R-WASH. (8)

Capitol Hill Office: 432 CHOB 20515; 225-7761; Fax: 225-8673; *Chief of Staff:* Kara Kennedy
Web: www.house.gov/dunn
E-mail: dunnwa08@mail.house.gov
District Office(s): 2737 78th Ave. S.E., Mercer Island 98040; (206) 275-3438; Fax: (206) 275-3437; *District Director:* Susan McColley
Committee Assignment(s): Ways and Means

EDWARDS, CHET, D-TEXAS (11)

Capitol Hill Office: 2459 RHOB 20515; 225-6105; Fax: 225-0350; *Administrative Assistant:* Chris Chwastyk
Web: www.house.gov/edwards
E-mail: www.house.gov/writerep
District Office(s): 701 Clay Ave., Waco 76706; (254) 752-9600; Fax: (254) 752-7769; *Deputy District Director:* Myrtle Thompson
116 S. East St., Belton 76513; (254) 933-2904; Fax: (254) 933-2913; *District Director:* Sam Murphey
Committee Assignment(s): Appropriations

EHLERS, VERNON J., R-MICH. (3)

Capitol Hill Office: 1714 LHOB 20515; 225-3831; Fax: 225-5144; *Chief of Staff:* Bill McBride
Web: www.house.gov/ehlers
E-mail: rep.ehlers@mail.house.gov
District Office(s): Federal Bldg., Grand Rapids 49503; (616) 451-8383; Fax: (616) 454-5630; *Constituent Services Director:* Nancy Ostapowicz

Committee Assignment(s): Education and Workforce; House Administration; Joint Library; Science; Transportation and Infrastructure

EHRLICH, ROBERT L. JR., R-MD. (2)

Capitol Hill Office: 315 CHOB 20515; 225-3061; Fax: 225-3094; *Chief of Staff:* Steven Kreseski

Web: www.house.gov/ehrlich

E-mail: ehrlich@mail.house.gov

District Office(s): 1407 York Rd., Lutherville 21093; (410) 337-7222; Fax: (410) 337-0021; *District Director:* Karl Aumann

4231 Postal Court, Pasadena 21122; (410) 255-6983; *District Director:* Karl Aumann

45 N. Main St., Bel Air 21014; (410) 838-2517; Fax: (410) 838-7823; *District Representative:* Shirley Stoyer

1011 Old Eastern Ave., Essex 21221; (410) 780-3911; *District Representative:* Christine Massoni

Committee Assignment(s): Commerce

EMERSON, JO ANN, R-MO. (8)

Capitol Hill Office: 132 CHOB 20515; 225-4404; Fax: 226-0326

Web: www.house.gov/emerson

E-mail: joann.emerson@mail.house.gov

District Office(s): 339 Broadway, Cape Girardeau 63701; (573) 335-0101; Fax: (573) 335-1931; *Chief of Staff:* Lloyd Smith

612 Pine St., Rolla 65401; (573) 364-2455; Fax: (573) 364-1053; *District Office Manager:* Iris Bernhardt

22 E. Columbia St., Farmington 63640; (573) 756-9755; Fax: (573) 756-9762; *District Office Manager:* Melody Cannon

Committee Assignment(s): Appropriations

ENGEL, ELIOT L., D-N.Y. (17)

Capitol Hill Office: 2303 RHOB 20515; 225-2464; Fax: 225-5513; *Administrative Assistant:* John Calvelli

Web: www.house.gov/engel

E-mail: www.house.gov/writerep

District Office(s): 3655 Johnson Ave., Bronx 10463; (718) 796-9700; *Chief of Staff:* Arnold I. Linhardt; *Communications Director:* Joseph O'Brien

87 Nepperhan Ave., Yonkers 10701; (914) 423-0700; *Caseworker:* Cynthia Miller

250 S. 6th Ave., Mount Vernon 10550; (914) 699-4100; *Caseworker:* Cynthia Miller

655 E. 233rd St., Bronx 10466; (718) 652-0400; *Caseworker:* Shirley Saunders

177 Dreiser Loop, Bronx 10475; (718) 320-2314; *Caseworker:* Shirley Saunders

Committee Assignment(s): Commerce

ENGLISH, PHIL, R-PA. (21)

Capitol Hill Office: 1410 LHOB 20515; 225-5406; Fax: 225-3103; *Chief of Staff:* Robert Holste

Web: www.house.gov/english

E-mail: www.house.gov/writerep

District Office(s): 310 French St., Erie 16507; (814) 456-2038; Fax: (814) 454-0163; *Chief of Staff:* Jerry Knight

900 N. Hermitage Rd., Hermitage 16148; (724) 342-6132; Fax: (724) 342-3219; *Office Manager:* Marilyn Magnato

602 Butler Mall, Butler 16001; (724) 285-7005; Fax: (724) 285-5616; *Office Manager:* Marci Mustello

312 Chestnut St., Meadville 16335; (814) 724-8414; Fax: (814) 333-8829; *Office Manager:* Kim Green

Committee Assignment(s): Small Business; Ways and Means

ESHOO, ANNA G., D-CALIF. (14)

Capitol Hill Office: 205 CHOB 20515; 225-8104; Fax: 225-8890; *Chief of Staff:* John Flaherty

Web: www.house.gov/eshoo

E-mail: annagram@mail.house.gov

District Office(s): 698 Emerson St., Palo Alto 94301; (650) 323-2984; Fax: (650) 323-3498; *District Director:* Karen Chapman

Committee Assignment(s): Commerce

ETHERIDGE, BOB, D-N.C. (2)

Capitol Hill Office: 1641 LHOB 20515; 225-4531; Fax: 225-5662; *Chief of Staff:* Julie Dwyer

Web: www.house.gov/etheridge

E-mail: bob.etheridge@mail.house.gov

District Office(s): 225 Hillsborough St., Raleigh 27603; (919) 829-9122; Fax: (919) 829-9883; *District Director:* Russ Swindell

607 N. 1st St., Lillington 27546; (910) 814-0335; Fax: (910) 814-2264; *Office Manager:* Leonore Tuck

Committee Assignment(s): Agriculture; Science

EVANS, LANE, D-ILL. (17)

Capitol Hill Office: 2335 RHOB 20515; 225-5905; Fax: 225-5396; *Administrative Assistant:* Dennis J. King

Web: www.house.gov/evans

E-mail: lane.evans@mail.house.gov

District Office(s): 1535 47th Ave., Moline 61265; (309) 793-5760; Fax: (309) 762-9193; *District Representative:* Philip G. Hare

261 N. Broad St., Galesburg 61401; (309) 342-4411; Fax: (309) 342-9749; *Office Manager:* Joyce Bean

Committee Assignment(s): Armed Services; Veterans' Affairs

EVERETT, TERRY, R-ALA. (2)

Capitol Hill Office: 2312 RHOB 20515; 225-2901; Fax: 225-8913; *Administrative Assistant:* H. Clay Swanzy Jr.

Web: www.house.gov/everett

E-mail: terry.everett@mail.house.gov

District Office(s): 3500 Eastern Blvd., Montgomery 36116; (334) 277-9113; Fax: (334) 277-8534; *District Director:* Steve Pelhem

256 Honeysuckle Rd., Dothan 36305; (334) 794-9680; Fax: (334) 671-1480; *District Aide:* Joe Williams

108 N. Main St., Opp 36467; (334) 493-9253; Fax: (334) 493-6666; *Staff Assistant:* Frances Spurlin

Committee Assignment(s): Agriculture; Armed Services; Veterans' Affairs

EWING, THOMAS W., R-ILL. (15)

Capitol Hill Office: 2417 RHOB 20515; 225-2371; Fax: 225-8071; *Administrative Assistant:* Brad Close

Web: www.house.gov/ewing

E-mail: www.house.gov/writerep

District Office(s): 2401 E. Washington St., Bloomington 61704; (309) 662-9371; Fax: (309) 663-9806; *Caseworker:* Barbara Booth

120 N. Vermilion St., Danville 61832; (217) 431-8230; *Caseworker:* Ginney Mulholland

Busey Plaza, Urbana 61801; (217) 328-0165; Fax: (217) 328-0169; *Chief of Staff:* Terry Greene

210 W. Water St., Pontiac 61764; (815) 844-7660; Fax: (815) 844-3473; *District Assistant:* Joe Alexander

Committee Assignment(s): Agriculture; House Administration; Joint Economic; Science; Transportation and Infrastructure

FALEOMAVAEGA, ENI F. H., D-AM. SAMOA (AL)

Capitol Hill Office: 2422 RHOB 20515; 225-8577; Fax: 225-8757; *Administrative Assistant:* Martin R. Yerick

Web: www.house.gov/faleomavaega

E-mail: faleomavaega@mail.house.gov

District Office(s): P.O. Drawer X, Pago Pago 96799; (684) 633-1372; Fax: (684) 633-2680; *District Manager:* Oreta M. Togafau

Committee Assignment(s): International Relations; Resources

FARR, SAM, D-CALIF. (17)

Capitol Hill Office: 1221 LHOB 20515; 225-2861; Fax: 225-6791; *Administrative Assistant:* Rochelle Dornatt

Web: www.house.gov/farr

E-mail: samfarr@mail.house.gov

District Office(s): 100 W. Alisal St., Salinas 93901; (831) 424-2229; Fax: (831) 424-7099; *District Director:* Donna Blitzer

701 Ocean St., Santa Cruz 95060; (831) 429-1976; *Congressional Aide:* Allison Endert

Committee Assignment(s): Appropriations

FATTAH, CHAKA, D-PA. (2)

Capitol Hill Office: 1205 LHOB 20515; 225-4001; *Chief of Staff:* Claudia Pharis

Web: www.house.gov/fattah

E-mail: www.house.gov/writerep

District Office(s): 6632 Germantown Ave., Philadelphia 19144; (215) 848-9386; *Caseworker:* Phyllis Goode

4104 Walnut St., Philadelphia 19104; (215) 387-6404; *District Director:* Gregory Naylor

Committee Assignment(s): Education and Workforce; Government Reform; House Administration; Joint Printing; Standards of Official Conduct

FILNER, BOB, D-CALIF. (50)

Capitol Hill Office: 2463 RHOB 20515; 225-8045; Fax: 225-9073; *Chief of Staff:* Stan Turesky

Web: www.house.gov/filner

E-mail: TalktoBobFilner@mail.house.gov

District Office(s): 333 F St., Chula Vista 91910; (619) 422-5963; Fax: (619) 422-7290; *District Director:* Francisco Estrada

Committee Assignment(s): Transportation and Infrastructure; Veterans' Affairs

FLETCHER, ERNIE, R-KY. (6)

Capitol Hill Office: 1117 LHOB 20515; 225-4706; Fax: 225-2122; *Chief of Staff:* Daniel Groves

Web: www.house.gov/fletcher

E-mail: www.house.gov/writerep

District Office(s): 860 Corporate Dr., Lexington 40503; (606) 219-1366; Fax: (606) 219-3437; *Field Representative:* Jay Boyd

Committee Assignment(s): Agriculture; Budget; Education and Workforce

FOLEY, MARK, R-FLA. (16)

Capitol Hill Office: 113 CHOB 20515; 225-5792; Fax: 225-3132; *Administrative Assistant:* Kirk Fordham

Web: www.house.gov/foley

E-mail: mark.foley@mail.house.gov

District Office(s): 4440 PGA Blvd., Palm Beach Gardens 33410; (561) 627-6192; Fax: (561) 626-4749; *District Director:* Ed Chase

County Annex Bldg., Port St. Lucie 34986; (561) 878-3181; Fax: (561) 871-0651; *District Manager:* Ann Decker

Committee Assignment(s): Ways and Means

FORBES, MICHAEL P., D-N.Y. (1)

Capitol Hill Office: 125 CHOB 20515; 225-3826; Fax: 225-3143; *Chief of Staff:* David Williams

Web: www.house.gov/forbes

E-mail: mike.forbes@mail.house.gov

District Office(s): 3680 Route 112, Coram 11727; (516) 451-2200; Fax: (516) 451-1977; *District Director:* James Harris

Committee Assignment(s): Appropriations; Banking and Financial Services

FORD, HAROLD E. JR., D-TENN. (9)

Capitol Hill Office: 325 CHOB 20515; 225-3265; Fax: 225-5663; *Chief of Staff:* Marland Buckner

Web: www.house.gov/ford
E-mail: rep.harold.ford.jr@mail.house.gov
District Office(s): Clifford Davis Federal Bldg., Memphis 38103; (901) 544-4131; Fax: (901) 544-4329; *Field Director:* Clay Perry
Committee Assignment(s): Education and Workforce; Government Reform

FOSSELLA, VITO J., R-N.Y. (13)

Capitol Hill Office: 431 CHOB 20515; 225-3371; Fax: 226-1272; *Chief of Staff:* Tom Quaadman
Web: www.house.gov/fossella
E-mail: vito.fossella@mail.house.gov
District Office(s): 4434 Amboy Rd., Staten Island 10312; (718) 356-8400; Fax: (718) 356-1928; *District Director:* Sherry Diamond; *Press Secretary:* Craig Donner
9818 4th Ave., Brooklyn 11209; (718) 630-5277; Fax: (718) 630-5388; *Office Manager:* Eileen Long
Committee Assignment(s): Commerce

FOWLER, TILLIE, R-FLA. (4)

Capitol Hill Office: 106 CHOB 20515; 225-2501; Fax: 225-9318; *Administrative Assistant:* David Gilliland
Web: www.house.gov/fowler
E-mail: www.house.gov/writerep
District Office(s): 140 S. Atlantic Ave., Ormond Beach 32176; (904) 672-0754; Fax: (904) 673-8964; *District Manager:* Chris Calabucci
4452 Hendricks Ave., Jacksonville 32207; (904) 739-6600; Fax: (904) 367-0066; *District Director:* Susan Siegmund
Committee Assignment(s): Armed Services; Transportation and Infrastructure

FRANK, BARNEY, D-MASS. (4)

Capitol Hill Office: 2210 RHOB 20515; 225-5931; Fax: 225-0182; *Chief of Staff:* Peter Kovar
Web: www.house.gov/frank
E-mail: www.house.gov/writerep
District Office(s): 29 Crafts St., Newton 02458; (617) 332-3920; Fax: (617) 332-2822; *District Director:* Dorothy M. Reichard
89 Main St., Bridgewater 02324; (508) 697-9403; Fax: (508) 674-3030; *Office Manager:* Garth Patterson
558 Pleasant St., New Bedford 02740; (508) 999-6462; Fax: (508) 697-0263; *Office Manager:* Elsie Souza
222 Milliken Place, Fall River 02721; (508) 674-3551; *Office Manager:* Amelia Wright
Committee Assignment(s): Banking and Financial Services; Judiciary

FRANKS, BOB, R-N.J. (7)

Capitol Hill Office: 225 CHOB 20515; 225-5361; Fax: 225-9460; *Chief of Staff:* Bill Ulrey
Web: www.house.gov/bobfranks
E-mail: franksnj@mail.house.gov

District Office(s): 2333 Morris Ave., Union 07083; (908) 686-5576; Fax: (908) 688-7390; *Deputy Chief of Staff:* Janet M. Thompson
73 Main St., Woodbridge 07095; (908) 602-0075; *Community Services Director:* Barbara Ballard
Committee Assignment(s): Budget; Transportation and Infrastructure

FRELINGHUYSEN, RODNEY, R-N.J. (11)

Capitol Hill Office: 228 CHOB 20515; 225-5034; Fax: 225-3186; *Administrative Assistant:* Donna F. Mullins
Web: www.house.gov/frelinghuysen
E-mail: rodney.frelinghuysen@mail.house.gov
District Office(s): 30 Schuyler Place, Morristown 07960; (973) 984-0711; *District Director:* Mark Broadhurst
Committee Assignment(s): Appropriations

FROST, MARTIN, D-TEXAS (24)

Capitol Hill Office: 2256 RHOB 20515; 225-3605; Fax: 225-4951; *Chief of Staff:* Matt Angle
Web: www.house.gov/frost
E-mail: martin.frost@mail.house.gov
District Office(s): 100 N. Main St., Corsicana 75110; (903) 874-0760; Fax: (903) 874-0468; *Office Manager:* Penny Jones
400 S. Zang Blvd., Dallas 75208; (214) 948-3401; Fax: (214) 948-3468; *Office Manager:* Marsha Steever-Patykiewicz
3020 S.E. Loop 820, Fort Worth 76140; (817) 293-9231; Fax: (817) 293-0526; *District Director:* Cinda M. Crawford
Committee Assignment(s): Rules

GALLEGLY, ELTON, R-CALIF. (23)

Capitol Hill Office: 2427 RHOB 20515; 225-5811; Fax: 225-1100; *Administrative Assistant:* Joel Kassiday
Web: www.house.gov/gallegly
E-mail: www.house.gov/writerep
District Office(s): 300 Esplanade Dr., Oxnard 93030; (805) 485-2300; Fax: (805) 983-3922; *District Director:* Paula Sheil
Committee Assignment(s): International Relations; Judiciary; Resources

GANSKE, GREG, R-IOWA (4)

Capitol Hill Office: 1108 LHOB 20515; 225-4426; Fax: 225-3193; *Chief of Staff:* Kim D. Schmett
Web: www.house.gov/ganske
E-mail: rep.ganske@mail.house.gov
District Office(s): Federal Bldg., Des Moines 50309; (515) 284-4634; Fax: (515) 280-1412; *District Director:* Sue Steinick
40 Pearl St., Council Bluffs 51503; (712) 323-5976; Fax: (712) 323-7903; *Field Representative:* Ben Post
Committee Assignment(s): Commerce

GEJDENSON, SAM, D-CONN. (2)

Capitol Hill Office: 2304 RHOB 20515; 225-2076; Fax: 225-4977; *Chief of Staff:* Scott Kovarovics
Web: www.house.gov/gejdenson
E-mail: bozrah@mail.house.gov
District Office(s): 2 Courthouse Square, 5th Floor, Norwich 06360; (860) 886-0139; Fax: (860) 886-2974; *District Director:* Michelle Halloran
94 Court St., Middletown 06457; (860) 346-1123; Fax: (860) 344-0530; *Office Director:* Patricia Shea
Committee Assignment(s): International Relations

GEKAS, GEORGE W., R-PA. (17)

Capitol Hill Office: 2410 RHOB 20515; 225-4315; Fax: 225-8440; *Chief of Staff:* Allan Cagnoli
Web: www.house.gov/gekas
E-mail: www.house.gov/writerep
District Office(s): 222 S. Market St., Elizabethtown 17022; (717) 367-6731; Fax: (717) 367-6602; *Office Director:* Shelley Whitcomb
108 B Municipal Bldg., Lebanon 17042; (717) 273-1451; Fax: (717) 273-1673; *Office Director:* Reg Nyman
3605 Vartan Way, Harrisburg 17110; (717) 541-5507; Fax: (717) 541-5518; *District Secretary:* Arlene Eckels
Committee Assignment(s): Judiciary

GEPHARDT, RICHARD A., D-MO. (3)

Capitol Hill Office: 1226 LHOB 20515; 225-2671; Fax: 225-7452; *Chief of Staff:* Steve A. Elmendorf
Web: www.house.gov/gephardt
E-mail: gephardt@mail.house.gov
District Office(s): 11140 S. Towne Square, St. Louis 63123; (314) 894-3400; Fax: (314) 845-7088; *Administrative Assistant:* Mary Renick
998 E. Gannon Dr., Festus 63208; (636) 937-6399; Fax: (636) 937-8098; *County Coordinator:* Chuck Banks

GIBBONS, JIM, R-NEV. (2)

Capitol Hill Office: 100 CHOB 20515; 225-6155; Fax: 225-5629; *Chief of Staff:* Mike Dayton
Web: www.house.gov/gibbons
E-mail: mail.gibbons@mail.house.gov
District Office(s): Bruce Thompson Federal Bldg., Reno 89501; (775) 686-5760; Fax: (775) 686-5711; *District Scheduler:* Deanna Lazovich
850 S. Durango Dr., Las Vegas 89128; (702) 255-1651; Fax: (702) 255-1927; *Regional Field Representative:* Jeanne Rice
Western Folklife Center, Elko 89801; (775) 777-7920; Fax: (775) 777-7922; *Regional Representative:* Gene Marchetti
Committee Assignment(s): Armed Services; Resources; Select Intelligence; Veterans' Affairs

GILCHREST, WAYNE T., R-MD. (1)

Capitol Hill Office: 2245 RHOB 20515; 225-5311; Fax: 225-0254; *Administrative Assistant:* Tony Caligiuri
Web: www.house.gov/gilchrest
E-mail: www.house.gov/writerep
District Office(s): 44 Calvert St., Annapolis 21401; (410) 263-6321; Fax: (410) 263-7619; *District Office Manager:* Susan Dill
One Plaza East, Salisbury 21801; (410) 749-3184; Fax: (410) 749-8458; *District Office Manager:* Jodi Beauchamp
315 High St., Chestertown 21620; (410) 778-9407; Fax: (410) 778-9560; *District Office Manager:* Karen Willis
Committee Assignment(s): Resources; Transportation and Infrastructure

GILLMOR, PAUL E., R-OHIO (5)

Capitol Hill Office: 1203 LHOB 20515; 225-6405; *Administrative Assistant:* Mark S. Wellman
Web: www.house.gov/gillmor
E-mail: www.house.gov/writerep
District Office(s): 120 Jefferson St., Port Clinton 43452; (419) 734-1999; *Office Manager:* Everett Woodel
County Administration Bldg., Norwalk 44857; (419) 668-0206; *District Aide:* Nancy Lehman
148 E. South Boundary St., Perrysburg 43551; (419) 872-2500; *District Representative:* Brian Dicken
613 W. 3rd St., Defiance 43512; (419) 782-1996; Fax: (800) 278-8203; *District Aide:* Barbara Barker
Committee Assignment(s): Commerce; International Relations

GILMAN, BENJAMIN A., R-N.Y. (20)

Capitol Hill Office: 2449 RHOB 20515; 225-3776; Fax: 225-2541; *Administrative Assistant:* Robert Becker
Web: www.house.gov/gilman
E-mail: ben@mail.house.gov
District Office(s): 32 Main St., Hastings-on-Hudson 10706; (914) 478-5550
407 E. Main St., Middletown 10940; (914) 343-6666; Fax: (914) 342-2900; *District Director:* Amalia T. Aumick
377 Route 59, Monsey 10952; (914) 357-9000; Fax: (914) 357-0924; *District Representative:* Joseph S. Salter
Committee Assignment(s): Government Reform; International Relations

GONZALEZ, CHARLIE, D-TEXAS (20)

Capitol Hill Office: 327 CHOB 20515; 225-3236; Fax: 225-1915; *Chief of Staff:* Kevin Kimble
Web: www.house.gov/gonzalez
E-mail: www.house.gov/writerep
District Office(s): 727 E. Durango Blvd., Federal Bldg., San Antonio 78206; (210) 472-6195; Fax: (210) 472-

4009; *Staff Assistant:* Ruben Galdeano; *District Director:* Mary Jessie Rogue

Committee Assignment(s): Banking and Financial Services; Small Business

GOODE, VIRGIL H. JR., I-VA. (5)

Capitol Hill Office: 1520 LHOB 20515; 225-4711; Fax: 225-5681; *Chief of Staff:* Tom Hance

Web: www.house.gov/goode

E-mail: rep.goode@mail.house.gov

District Office(s): 104 S. 1st St., Charlottesville 22902; (804) 295-6372; Fax: (804) 295-6059; *District Office Manager:* Esther Page

70 E. Court St., Rocky Mount 24151; (540) 484-1254; Fax: (540) 484-1459; *Caseworker:* Tonia Dillard

700 Main St., Danville 24541; (804) 792-1280; Fax: (804) 797-5942; *Press Secretary:* Linwood Duncan

103 S. Main St., Farmville 23901; (804) 392-8331; Fax: (804) 392-6448; *Caseworker:* Margaret Watkins

Committee Assignment(s): Appropriations

GOODLATTE, ROBERT W., R-VA. (6)

Capitol Hill Office: 2240 RHOB 20515; 225-5431; Fax: 225-9681; *Chief of Staff:* David E. Lehman

Web: www.house.gov/goodlatte

E-mail: talk2bob@mail.house.gov

District Office(s): Two S. Main St., Harrisonburg 22801; (540) 432-2391; Fax: (540) 432-6593; *District Representative:* Charles Evans-Haywood

10 Franklin Rd. S.E., Roanoke 24011; (540) 857-2672; Fax: (540) 857-2675; *District Director:* Peter S. Larkin

916 Main St., Lynchburg 24504; (804) 845-8306; Fax: (804) 845-8245; *District Representative:* Clarkie Jester

114 N. Central Ave., Staunton 24401; (540) 885-3861; Fax: (540) 885-3930; *District Representative:* Amanda Hagan

Committee Assignment(s): Agriculture; Judiciary

GOODLING, BILL, R-PA. (19)

Capitol Hill Office: 2107 RHOB 20515; 225-5836; Fax: 226-1000; *Chief of Staff:* Kimberly A. Strycharz

Web: www.house.gov/goodling

E-mail: www.house.gov/writerep

District Office(s): 2020 Yale Ave., Camp Hill 17011; (717) 763-1988; *District Director:* Thomas E. Davidson

140 Baltimore St., Gettysburg 17325; (717) 334-3430; *District Secretary:* Georgiana Spangler

Federal Bldg., York 17405; (717) 843-8887; *District Secretary:* Betty Lou Tarasovic

Committee Assignment(s): Education and Workforce; International Relations

GORDON, BART, D-TENN. (6)

Capitol Hill Office: 2368 RHOB 20515; 225-4231; Fax: 225-6887; *Administrative Assistant:* Chuck Atkins

Web: www.house.gov/gordon

E-mail: bart.gordon@mail.house.gov

District Office(s): Courthouse Square, Murfreesboro 37133; (615) 896-1986; Fax: (615) 896-8218; *District Administrative Assistant:* Kent Syler

17 S. Jefferson Ave., Cookville 38503; (615) 528-5907; Fax: (615) 528-1165; *Field Representative:* Billy Smith

Committee Assignment(s): Commerce; Science

GOSS, PORTER J., R-FLA. (14)

Capitol Hill Office: 108 CHOB 20515; 225-2536; Fax: 225-6820; *Administrative Assistant:* Wendy K. D. Selig

Web: www.house.gov/goss

E-mail: www.house.gov/writerep

District Office(s): 2000 Main St., Fort Myers 33901; (941) 332-4677; Fax: (941) 332-1743; *Chief of Staff:* Sheryl V. Wooley; *District Scheduler:* Linda Uhler

3301 Tamiami Trail East Naples 33962; (941) 774-8060; Fax: (941) 774-7262; *Constituent Services Representative:* Hannah Smalley

Charlotte Memorial Auditorium, Punta Gorda 33950; (941) 639-0051; Fax: (941) 639-0714;

Committee Assignment(s): Rules; Select Intelligence

GRAHAM, LINDSEY, R-S.C. (3)

Capitol Hill Office: 1429 LHOB 20515; 225-5301; Fax: 225-3216; *Administrative Assistant:* Richard Perry

Web: www.house.gov/graham

E-mail: www.house.gov/writerep

District Office(s): 315 S. McDuffie St., Anderson 29622; (864) 224-7401; Fax: (864) 225-7049; *District Coordinator:* Jane Goolsby

120 Main St., Greenwood 29646; (864) 223-8251; *Caseworker:* Van Cato

5 Federal Bldg., Aiken 29801; (803) 649-5571; *Caseworker:* Jean Price

Committee Assignment(s): Armed Services; Education and Workforce; Judiciary

GRANGER, KAY, R-TEXAS (12)

Capitol Hill Office: 435 CHOB 20515; 225-5071; Fax: 225-5683; *Chief of Staff:* Bruce Butler

Web: www.house.gov/granger

E-mail: texas.granger@mail.house.gov

District Office(s): 1600 W. 7th St., Ft. Worth 76102; (817) 338-0909; Fax: (817) 335-5852; *District Director:* Barbara Ragland

Committee Assignment(s): Appropriations

GREEN, GENE, D-TEXAS (29)

Capitol Hill Office: 2429 RHOB 20515; 225-1688; Fax: 225-9903; *Administrative Assistant:* Marc Gonzales

Web: www.house.gov/green

E-mail: ask.gene@mail.house.gov

District Office(s): 256 N. Sam Houston Parkway East, Houston 77060; (281) 330-0761; Fax: (713) 330-0807; *Caseworker:* Yuroba Harris *District Director:* Rhonda Jackson

11811 I-10 East, Houston 77029; (713) 477-0761; Fax: (713) 330-0807; *Caseworker:* Marlene Clowers

Committee Assignment(s): Commerce

GREEN, MARK, R-WIS. (8)

Capitol Hill Office: 1218 LHOB 20515; 225-5665; Fax: 225-5729; *Chief of Staff:* Mark Graul

Web: www.house.gov/markgreen

E-mail: mark.green@mail.house.gov

District Office(s): 700 E. Walnut St., Green Bay 54301; (920) 437-1954; Fax: (920) 437-1978; *District Director:* Chad Weininger

Committee Assignment(s): Banking and Financial Services; Budget; Science

GREENWOOD, JAMES C., R-PA. (8)

Capitol Hill Office: 2436 RHOB 20515; 225-4276; Fax: 225-9511; *Chief of Staff:* Jordan "Pete" Krauss

Web: www.house.gov/greenwood

E-mail: www.house.gov/writerep

District Office(s): 69 E. Oakland Ave., Doylestown 18901; (215) 348-7511; Fax: (215) 348-7658; *District Scheduler:* Nancy Lonsdale

One Oxford Valley Rd., Langhorne 19047; (215) 752-7711; Fax: (215) 750-8014; *District Director:* Stephanie Fischer

Committee Assignment(s): Commerce; Education and Workforce

GUTIERREZ, LUIS V., D-ILL. (4)

Capitol Hill Office: 2438 RHOB 20515; 225-8203; Fax: 225-7810; *Chief of Staff:* Doug Scofield

Web: www.house.gov/gutierrez

E-mail: luisg@gutierrez.house.gov

District Office(s): 3181 N. Elston Ave., Chicago 60618; (773) 509-0999; Fax: (773) 509-0152; *Deputy Chief of Staff:* Lori Baas

Committee Assignment(s): Banking and Financial Services; Veterans' Affairs

GUTKNECHT, GIL, R-MINN. (1)

Capitol Hill Office: 425 CHOB 20515; 225-2472; Fax: 225-3246; *Administrative Assistant:* Brent R. Orrell

Web: www.house.gov/gutknecht

E-mail: gil.gutknecht@mail.house.gov

District Office(s): 1530 Greenview Dr., S.W., Rochester 55902; (507) 252-9841; Fax: (507) 252-9915; *Communications Director:* Lee A. Aase

Committee Assignment(s): Agriculture; Budget; Science

HALL, RALPH M., D-TEXAS (4)

Capitol Hill Office: 2221 RHOB 20515; 225-6673; Fax: 225-3332; *Chief of Staff:* Janet Poppleton

Web: www.house.gov/ralphhall

E-mail: www.house.gov/writerep

District Office(s): 104 N. San Jacinto St., Rockwall 75087; (972) 771-9118; Fax: (972) 722-0907; *Administrative Assistant:* Diane Milliken

Federal Bldg., Sherman 75090; (903) 892-1112; Fax: (903) 868-0264; *District Assistant:* Judy Rowton

211 W. Ferguson St., Tyler 75702; (903) 597-3729; Fax: (903) 597-0726; *District Assistant:* Martha Glover

Committee Assignment(s): Commerce; Science

HALL, TONY P., D-OHIO (3)

Capitol Hill Office: 1436 LHOB 20515; 225-6465; Fax: 225-9272; *Chief of Staff:* Rick Carne

Web: www.house.gov/tonyhall

E-mail: www.house.gov/writerep

District Office(s): Federal Bldg., Dayton 45402; (937) 225-2843; Fax: (937) 225-2706; *District Director:* Jim Vangrov

Committee Assignment(s): Rules

HANSEN, JAMES V., R-UTAH (1)

Capitol Hill Office: 242 CHOB 20515; 225-0453; Fax: 225-5857; *Chief of Staff:* Nancee W. Blockinger

Web: www.house.gov/hansen

E-mail: www.house.gov/writerep

District Office(s): Federal Bldg., Ogden 84401; (801) 393-8362; Fax: (801) 621-7846; *District Director:* Steven T. Petersen

435 E. Tabernacle St., St. George 84770; (801) 628-1071; Fax: (801) 634-9289; *Field Office Manager:* Rick Arial

Committee Assignment(s): Armed Services; Resources; Veterans' Affairs

HASTERT, J. DENNIS, R-ILL. (14)

Capitol Hill Office: 2263 RHOB 20515; 225-2976; Fax: 225-0697; *Chief of Staff:* Scott B. Palmer

Web: www.house.gov/hastert

E-mail: dhastert@mail.house.gov

District Office(s): 27 N. River St., Batavia 60510; (630) 406-1114; Fax: (630) 406-1808; *District Director:* Shaye R. Mandle

HASTINGS, ALCEE L., D-FLA. (23)

Capitol Hill Office: 2235 RHOB 20515; 225-1313; Fax: 226-0690

Web: www.house.gov/alceehastings

E-mail: www.house.gov/alceehastings/comments.html

District Office(s): 2701 W. Oakland Park Blvd., Ft. Lauderdale 33311; (954) 733-2800; Fax: (954) 735-9444; *Chief of Staff:* Art W. Kennedy

5725 Corporate Way, West Palm Beach 33407; (561) 684-0565; Fax: (561) 684-3613; *Congressional Aide:* Mikel Jones

Committee Assignment(s): International Relations; Select Intelligence

HASTINGS, RICHARD "DOC," R-WASH. (4)

Capitol Hill Office: 1323 LHOB 20515; 225-5816; Fax: 225-3251; *Chief of Staff:* Ed Cassidy

Web: www.house.gov/hastings

E-mail: www.house.gov/writerep

District Office(s): 2715 St. Andrews Loop, Pasco 99301; (509) 543-9396; Fax: (509) 545-1972; *District Director:* Joyce DeFelice

302 E. Chestnut St., Yakima 98901; (509) 452-3243; Fax: (509) 452-3438; *Staff Assistant:* Ranie Haas

Committee Assignment(s): Rules

HAYES, ROBIN, R-N.C. (8)

Capitol Hill Office: 130 CHOB 20515; 225-3715; Fax: 225-4036; *Chief of Staff:* Chris Cox

Web: www.house.gov/hayes

E-mail: www.house.gov/writerep

District Office(s): 137 Union St. South, Concord 28025; (704) 786-1612; Fax: (704) 782-1004; *District Director:* Richard Hudson

230 E. Franklin St., Rockingham 28379; (910) 997-2070; Fax: (910) 997-7987; *Constituent Liaison:* Paulette Burgess

Committee Assignment(s): Agriculture; Armed Services; Resources

HAYWORTH, J. D., R-ARIZ. (6)

Capitol Hill Office: 1023 LHOB 20515; 225-2190; Fax: 225-3263; *Chief of Staff:* Joseph Eule

Web: www.house.gov/hayworth

E-mail: www.house.gov/writerep

District Office(s): 1017 S. Gilbert St., Mesa 85204; (480) 926-4151; Fax: (480) 926-3998; *District Director:* Doug Nick; *Press Secretary:* Jim Heath

408 N. Sacaton St., Casa Grande 85222; (520) 876-4095; Fax: (520) 876-4096; *District Coordinator:* Miguel Olivas

1300 S. Milton St., Flagstaff 86001; (520) 556-8760; Fax: (520) 556-8764; *Office Manager:* Patty Brookins

Committee Assignment(s): Veterans' Affairs; Ways and Means

HEFLEY, JOEL, R-COLO. (5)

Capitol Hill Office: 2230 RHOB 20515; 225-4422; Fax: 225-1942

E-mail: www.house.gov/writerep

District Office(s): 6059 S. Quebec St., Englewood 80111; (303) 843-0401; Fax: (303) 843-0726; *Office Manager:* Angie D'Aurio

104 S. Cascade Ave., Colorado Springs 80903; (719) 520-0055; Fax: (719) 520-0840; *District Director:* Connie Solomon

Committee Assignment(s): Armed Services; Resources; Small Business; Standards of Official Conduct

HERGER, WALLY, R-CALIF. (2)

Capitol Hill Office: 2433 RHOB 20515; 225-3076; *Administrative Assistant:* John P. Magill

Web: www.house.gov/herger

E-mail: www.house.gov/writerep

District Office(s): 55 Independence Circle, Chico 95926; (530) 893-8363; *District Office Manager:* Fran Peace

410 Hemsted Dr., Redding 96002; (530) 223-5898; *Field Representative:* David Meurer

Committee Assignment(s): Budget; Ways and Means

HILL, BARON P., D-IND. (9)

Capitol Hill Office: 1208 LHOB 20515; 225-5315; Fax: 225-1101; *Chief of Staff:* Matt Pierce

Web: www.house.gov/baronhill

E-mail: www.house.gov/writerep

District Office(s): 1201 E. 10th St., Jeffersonville 47130; (812) 288-3999; Fax: (812) 288-3877; *District Chief of Staff:* Luke H. Clippinger

Committee Assignment(s): Agriculture; Armed Services; Veterans' Affairs

HILL, RICK, R-MONT. (AL)

Capitol Hill Office: 1609 LHOB 20515; 225-3211; Fax: 225-5687; *Chief of Staff:* Larry Akey

Web: www.house.gov/hill

E-mail: rick.hill@mail.house.gov

District Office(s): 33 S. Last Chance Gulch, Helena 59601; (406) 443-7878; Fax: (406) 449-3736; *State Director:* Peggy Olson Trenk

518 2nd St. South, Great Falls 59405; (406) 454-1066; Fax: (406) 454-1130; *Staff Assistant:* Marta Ferguson

200 E. Broadway, Missoula 59601; (406) 543-9550; Fax: (406) 543-9560; *Field Representative:* Julie Altemus

27 N. 27th St., Billings 59101; (406) 256-1019; Fax: (406) 256-3185; *State Director:* Todd A. O'Hair

Committee Assignment(s): Banking and Financial Services; Resources; Small Business

HILLEARY, VAN, R-TENN. (4)

Capitol Hill Office: 114 CHOB 20515; 225-6831; Fax: 225-3272; *Chief of Staff:* Jim Burnett

Web: www.house.gov/hilleary

E-mail: van.hilleary@mail.house.gov

District Office(s): 300 S. Jackson St., Tullahoma 37388; (931) 393-4764; Fax: (931) 393-4767; *District Director:* Janice Bowling

998 N. Main St., Crossville 38555; (931) 484-1114; Fax: (931) 484-5097; *Project Director:* Myra Staggs

400 W. Main St., #304, Morristown 37814; (423) 587-0396; Fax: (423) 587-0065; *District Director:* Paul Chapman

Committee Assignment(s): Armed Services; Budget; Education and Workforce

HILLIARD, EARL F., D-ALA. (7)

Capitol Hill Office: 1314 LHOB 20515; 225-2665; Fax: 226-0772; *Chief of Staff:* Phyllis Hallmon
Web: www.house.gov/hilliard
E-mail: callearl@mail.house.gov
District Office(s): The Penick Bldg., Birmingham 35203; (205) 328-2841; Fax: (205) 251-6816; *District Manager:* Elvira Williams
204 Federal Bldg., Tuscaloosa 35401; (205) 752-3578; Fax: (205) 349-2450; *District Manager:* Kay Presley
3800 Norman Bridge Rd., Montgomery 36105; (334) 281-0531; Fax: (334) 281-1109; *Montgomery District Manager:* Robert A. Lane

Committee Assignment(s): Agriculture; International Relations

HINCHEY, MAURICE D., D-N.Y. (26)

Capitol Hill Office: 2431 RHOB 20515; 225-6335; Fax: 226-0774; *Chief of Staff:* Kiersten Stewart
Web: www.house.gov/hinchey
E-mail: maurice.hinchey@mail.house.gov
District Office(s): 291 Wall St., Kingston 12401; (914) 331-4466; *District Representative:* Kevin O'Connell
123 South Cayuga St., Ithaca 14850; (607) 273-1388; *Federal Liaison:* Marsha McElligott
20 Anawana Lake Rd., Monticello 12701; (914) 791-7116; *Community Liaison:* Julie Allen
15 Henry St., Binghamton 13901; (607) 773-2768; Fax: (607) 772-1789; *District Representative:* Jim Testani

Committee Assignment(s): Appropriations

HINOJOSA, RUBÉN, D-TEXAS (15)

Capitol Hill Office: 1032 LHOB 20515; 225-2531; Fax: 225-5688; *Chief of Staff:* Rita Jaramillo
Web: www.house.gov/hinojosa
E-mail: rep.hinojosa@mail.house.gov
District Office(s): 311 N. 15th St., McAllen 78501; (210) 682-5545; Fax: (210) 687-0141; *District Director:* Rosie Cavazos
101 S. Saint Mary's St., Beeville 78102; (361) 358-8400; Fax: (361) 358-8407;

Committee Assignment(s): Education and Workforce; Small Business

HOBSON, DAVID L., R-OHIO (7)

Capitol Hill Office: 1514 LHOB 20515; 225-4324; *Chief of Staff:* Mary Beth Carozza
Web: www.house.gov/hobson
E-mail: www.house.gov/writerep

District Office(s): 212 S. Broad St., Lancaster 43130; (614) 654-5149; *Senior Constituent Aide:* Bob Clark
5 W. N. St., #200, Springfield 45501; (937) 925-0474; *District Director:* Eileen Austria

Committee Assignment(s): Appropriations

HOEFFEL, JOSEPH M., D-PA. (13)

Capitol Hill Office: 1229 LHOB 20515; 225-6111; Fax: 226-0611; *Chief of Staff:* Joshua D. Shapiro
Web: www.house.gov/hoeffel
E-mail: www.house.gov/writerep
District Office(s): 1768 Markley St., Norristown 19401; (610) 272-8400; Fax: (610) 272-8532; *District Director:* Joan Nagel

Committee Assignment(s): Budget; International Relations; Science

HOEKSTRA, PETER, R-MICH. (2)

Capitol Hill Office: 1124 LHOB 20515; 225-4401; Fax: 226-0779; *Chief of Staff:* Jon Vanden Heuvel
Web: www.house.gov/hoekstra
E-mail: tellhoek@mail.house.gov
District Office(s): 31 E. 8th St., Holland 49423; (616) 395-0030; Fax: (616) 395-0271; *Public Policy Director:* Bill Huizenga
900 3rd St., Muskegon 49440; (231) 722-8386; Fax: (231) 722-0176; *Constituent Services Director:* Jerry Kooiman
210 1/2 N. Mitchell St., Cadillac 49601; (231) 775-0050; Fax: (231) 775-0298; *Cadillac Area Representative:* Jill Brown

Committee Assignment(s): Budget; Education and Workforce

HOLDEN, TIM, D-PA. (6)

Capitol Hill Office: 1421 LHOB 20515; 225-5546; Fax: 226-0996; *Chief of Staff:* Trish Reilly-Hudock
Web: www.house.gov/holden
E-mail: www.house.gov/writerep
District Office(s): 101 N. Centre St., Pottsville 17901; (570) 622-4212; Fax: (570) 628-2561; *Office Manager:* Connie Caldonetti
Berks County Services Center, Reading 19601; (610) 371-9931; Fax: (610) 371-9939; *Staff Assistant:* Tim Smith

Committee Assignment(s): Agriculture; Transportation and Infrastructure

HOLT, RUSH D., D-N.J. (12)

Capitol Hill Office: 1630 LHOB 20515; 225-5801; Fax: 225-6025; *Administrative Assistant:* Steven Mavigilio
Web: www.house.gov/rholt
E-mail: rush.holt@mail.house.gov
District Office(s): 50 Washington Rd., Princeton Junction 08550; (609) 750-9365; Fax: (609) 750-0618; *Chief of Staff:* Mark Matzen

Committee Assignment(s): Budget; Education and Workforce; Resources

HOOLEY, DARLENE, D-ORE. (5)

Capitol Hill Office: 1130 LHOB 20515; 225-5711; Fax: 225-5699; *Chief of Staff:* Joan Mooney
Web: www.house.gov/hooley
E-mail: darlene@mail.house.gov
District Office(s): 315 Mission St., Salem 97302; (503) 588-9100; Fax: (503) 588-5517; *District Director:* Jane Markham
914 Mollalla Ave., Oregon City 97045; (503) 557-1324; Fax: (503) 557-1981; *Staff Assistant:* Jean Eggers
Committee Assignment(s): Banking and Financial Services; Budget

HORN, STEVE, R-CALIF. (38)

Capitol Hill Office: 2331 RHOB 20515; 225-6676; Fax: 226-1012; *Chief of Staff:* David Bartel
Web: www.house.gov/horn
E-mail: steve.horn@mail.house.gov
District Office(s): 4010 Watson Plaza Dr., Lakewood 90712; (562) 425-1336; Fax: (562) 425-4591; *District Director:* Connie Sziebl
Committee Assignment(s): Government Reform; Transportation and Infrastructure

HOSTETTLER, JOHN, R-IND. (8)

Capitol Hill Office: 1507 LHOB 20515; 225-4636; Fax: 225-3284; *Administrative Assistant:* Tom Washburn
Web: www.house.gov/hostettler
E-mail: john.hostettler@mail.house.gov
District Office(s): 120 W. 7th St., Bloomington 47404; (812) 334-1111; Fax: (812) 333-6928; *Deputy District Director:* Chris Crabtree
101 N.W. Martin Luther King Blvd., Evansville 47708; (812) 465-6484; Fax: (812) 422-4761; *District Director:* Robert D. Krieg
Committee Assignment(s): Agriculture; Armed Services

HOUGHTON, AMO, R-N.Y. (31)

Capitol Hill Office: 1110 LHOB 20515; 225-3161; Fax: 225-5574; *Staff Director:* Chet Lunner
Web: www.house.gov/houghton
E-mail: houghton@mail.house.gov
District Office(s): Federal Bldg., #122, Jamestown 14702; (716) 484-0252; Fax: (716) 484-8178; *Economic Development Director:* Mickey Brown
268 Genesee St., Auburn 13021; (315) 255-3045
32 Denison Parkway West Corning 14830; (607) 937-3333; Fax: (607) 937-6047; *District Director:* Robert Iszard
Committee Assignment(s): International Relations; Ways and Means

HOYER, STENY H., D-MD. (5)

Capitol Hill Office: 1705 LHOB 20515; 225-4131; Fax: 225-4300; *Administrative Assistant:* Betsy Bossart

Web: www.house.gov/hoyer
E-mail: www.house.gov/writerep
District Office(s): 6500 Cherrywood Lane, #310, Greenbelt 20770; (301) 474-0119; Fax: (301) 474-4697; *Caseworker:* Betty Richardson
21A Industrial Park Dr., Waldorf 20602; (301) 843-1577; Fax: (301) 843-1331; *District Director:* John Bohanan
Committee Assignment(s): Appropriations; House Administration; Joint Library; Joint Printing

HULSHOF, KENNY, R-MO. (9)

Capitol Hill Office: 412 CHOB 20515; 225-2956; Fax: 225-5712; *Administrative Assistant:* Matt Miller
Web: www.house.gov/hulshof
E-mail: www.house.gov/writerep
District Office(s): 33 E. Broadway St., Columbia 65203; (573) 449-5111; Fax: (573) 449-5312; *District Representative:* Eric W. Feltner
201 N. 3rd St., Hannibal 63401; (573) 221-1200; Fax: (573) 221-5349; *District Representative:* Scott Callicott
317 Lafayette St., Washington 63090; (314) 239-4001; Fax: (314) 239-1987; *District Representative:* David O'Brien
Committee Assignment(s): Ways and Means

HUNTER, DUNCAN, R-CALIF. (52)

Capitol Hill Office: 2265 RHOB 20515; 225-5672; Fax: 225-0235; *Chief of Staff:* Victoria J. Middleton
Web: www.house.gov/hunter
E-mail: www.house.gov/writerep
District Office(s): 366 S. Pierce St., El Cajon 92020; (619) 579-3001; Fax: (619) 579-2251; *District Chief of Staff:* Wendell Cutting
1101 Airport Rd., Imperial 92251; (760) 353-5420; Fax: (760) 353-0653; *Field Representative:* Carole Starr
Committee Assignment(s): Armed Services

HUTCHINSON, ASA, R-ARK. (3)

Capitol Hill Office: 1535 LHOB 20515; 225-4301; Fax: 225-5713; *Chief of Staff:* West Doss
Web: www.house.gov/hutchinson
E-mail: asa.hutchinson@mail.house.gov
District Office(s): 402 N. Walnut St., Harrison 72601; (870) 741-6900; Fax: (870) 741-7741; *District Representative:* Linda Emerson
30 S. 6th St., Fort Smith 72901; (501) 782-7787; Fax: (501) 783-7662; *District Director:* Kathy J. Watson
35 E. Mountain St., Fayetteville 72701; (501) 442-5258; Fax: (501) 442-0937; *District Representative:* Steve Gray
Committee Assignment(s): Government Reform; Judiciary; Transportation and Infrastructure

HYDE, HENRY J., R-ILL. (6)

Capitol Hill Office: 2110 RHOB 20515; 225-4561; Fax: 225-1166; *Chief of Staff:* Judy Wolverton
Web: www.house.gov/hyde
E-mail: www.house.gov/writerep
District Office(s): 50 E. Oak St., Addison 60101; (630) 832-5950; Fax: (630) 832-5969; *Executive Assistant:* Alice Horstman
Committee Assignment(s): International Relations; Judiciary

INSLEE, JAY, D-WASH. (1)

Capitol Hill Office: 308 CHOB 20515; 225-6311; Fax: 226-1606; *Chief of Staff:* Joby Shimomura
Web: www.house.gov/inslee
E-mail: www.house.gov/writerep
District Office(s): 21905 64th Ave. West, Mountlake Terrace 98043; (425) 640-0233; Fax: (425) 776-7168; *District Director:* Michael Mann
Committee Assignment(s): Banking and Financial Services; Resources

ISAKSON, JOHNNY, R-GA. (6)

Capitol Hill Office: 2428 RHOB 20515; 225-4501; Fax: 225-4656; *Administrative Assistant:* David J. Heil
Web: www.house.gov/isakson
E-mail: www.house.gov/writerep
District Office(s): 6000 Lake Forest Dr., Atlanta 30328; (404) 252-5239; Fax: (404) 303-1260; *Chief of Staff:* Heath Garrett
Committee Assignment(s): Education and Workforce; Transportation and Infrastructure

ISTOOK, ERNEST, R-OKLA. (5)

Capitol Hill Office: 2404 RHOB 20515; 225-2132; Fax: 226-1463; *Administrative Assistant:* John C. Albaugh
Web: www.house.gov/istook
E-mail: istook@mail.house.gov
District Office(s): 5400 N. Grand Blvd., Oklahoma City 73112; (405) 942-3636; Fax: (405) 942-3792; *District Director:* Steven Jones
1st Court Place, Bartlesville 74003; (918) 336-5546; Fax: (918) 336-5740; *Northern Region Field Representative:* Ben Harris
5th St. and Grand Ave., Ponca City 74601; (580) 762-6778; Fax: (580) 762-7049; *Northern Region Field Representative:* Ben Harris
Committee Assignment(s): Appropriations

JACKSON, JESSE L. JR., D-ILL. (2)

Capitol Hill Office: 313 CHOB 20515; 225-0773; Fax: 225-0899; *Chief of Staff:* Kenneth A. Edmonds
Web: www.jessejacksonjr.org
E-mail: comments@jessejacksonjr.org
District Office(s): 10331 S. Halsted St., Chicago 60628;

(773) 238-2100; Fax: (773) 238-7984; *Constituent Services Director:* Annette M. deCaussin
17926 S. Halsted St., Homewood 60430; (708) 798-6000; Fax: (708) 798-6160; *District Administrator:* Richard J. Bryant
Committee Assignment(s): Appropriations

JACKSON-LEE, SHEILA, D-TEXAS (18)

Capitol Hill Office: 410 CHOB 20515; 225-3816; Fax: 225-3317; *Chief of Staff:* Earl Smith Jr.
Web: www.house.gov/jacksonlee
E-mail: tx.18@mail.house.gov
District Office(s): 1919 Smith St., Houston 77002; (713) 655-6050; Fax: (713) 655-1612; *Office Manager:* Elaine Oliver
420 W. 19th St., Houston 77008; (713) 861-4070; Fax: (713) 861-4323
6719 W. Montgomery Rd., Houston 77091; (713) 691-4882; Fax: (713) 699-8292; *District Field Representative:* Dorothy Hubbard
Committee Assignment(s): Judiciary; Science

JEFFERSON, WILLIAM J., D-LA. (2)

Capitol Hill Office: 240 CHOB 20515; 225-6636; Fax: 225-1988; *Chief of Staff:* Lionel R. Collins Jr.
Web: www.house.gov/jefferson
E-mail: www.house.gov/writerep
District Office(s): 501 Magazine St., New Orleans 70130; (504) 589-2274; Fax: (504) 589-4513; *Executive Assistant:* Stephanie Butler
Committee Assignment(s): Ways and Means

JENKINS, BILL, R-TENN. (1)

Capitol Hill Office: 1708 LHOB 20515; 225-6356; Fax: 225-5714; *Chief of Staff:* Brenda Otterson
Web: www.house.gov/jenkins
E-mail: rep.jenkins@mail.house.gov
District Office(s): Federal Bldg., #157, Kingsport 37662; (423) 247-8161; Fax: (423) 247-1834; *Field Director:* Bill Snodgrass; *Press Secretary:* Paul Mays
Committee Assignment(s): Agriculture; Judiciary

JOHN, CHRIS, D-LA. (7)

Capitol Hill Office: 1504 LHOB 20515; 225-2031; Fax: 225-5724; *Chief of Staff:* Lynn Hershey
Web: www.house.gov/john
E-mail: chrisjohn@mail.house.gov
District Office(s): 800 Lafayette St., Lafayette 70501; (318) 235-6322; Fax: (318) 235-6072; *Executive Assistant:* Stephen Stefanski
1011 Lakeshore Dr., Lake Charles 70601; (318) 433-1747; Fax: (318) 433-0974; *Executive Assistant:* Lynn Jones
Committee Assignment(s): Agriculture; Resources

JOHNSON, EDDIE BERNICE, D-TEXAS (30)

Capitol Hill Office: 1511 LHOB 20515; 225-8885; Fax: 226-1477; *Chief of Staff:* Karen Huey White
Web: www.house.gov/ebjohnson
E-mail: ejohnson@mail.house.gov
District Office(s): 2501 Cedar Springs Rd., Dallas 75201; (214) 922-8885; Fax: (214) 922-7028; *District Director:* Roscoe Smith
1634-B W. Irving Blvd., Irving 75061; (972) 253-8885; Fax: (972) 253-3034; *Special Assistant:* Bernard Williams
Committee Assignment(s): Science; Transportation and Infrastructure

JOHNSON, NANCY L., R-CONN. (6)

Capitol Hill Office: 2113 RHOB 20515; 225-4476; Fax: 225-4488; *Chief of Staff:* Dave Karvelas
Web: www.house.gov/nancyjohnson
E-mail: njohnson@mail.house.gov
District Office(s): 480 Myrtle St., New Britain 06053; (203) 223-8412; Fax: (203) 827-9009; *District Director:* Ted Fusaro
Committee Assignment(s): Ways and Means

JOHNSON, SAM, R-TEXAS (3)

Capitol Hill Office: 1030 LHOB 20515; 225-4201; Fax: 225-1485; *Chief of Staff:* Michael Hanson
Web: www.house.gov/samjohnson
E-mail: sam.tx03@mail.house.gov
District Office(s): 801 E. Campbell Rd., Richardson 75081; (972) 470-0892; Fax: (972) 470-9937; *District Director:* Mary Lynn Murrell
Committee Assignment(s): Education and Workforce; Ways and Means

JONES, STEPHANIE TUBBS, D-OHIO (11)

Capitol Hill Office: 1516 LHOB 20515; 225-7032; Fax: 225-1339; *Chief of Staff:* Marcia Fudge
Web: www.house.gov/tubbsjones
E-mail: stephanie.tubbs.jones@mail.house.gov
District Office(s): 3645 Warrensville Center Rd., Shaker Heights 44122; (216) 522-4900; Fax: (216) 522-4908; *Legislative Assistant:* Betty K. Pinkney
Committee Assignment(s): Banking and Financial Services; Small Business

JONES, WALTER B. JR., R-N.C. (3)

Capitol Hill Office: 422 CHOB 20515; 225-3415; Fax: 225-3286; *Administrative Assistant:* Glen Downs
Web: www.house.gov/jones
E-mail: congjones@mail.house.gov
District Office(s): 102-C Eastbrook Dr., Greenville 27858; (919) 931-1003; Fax: (919) 931-1002; *District Director:* Millie Lilley
Committee Assignment(s): Armed Services; Banking and Financial Services; Resources

KANJORSKI, PAUL E., D-PA. (11)

Capitol Hill Office: 2353 RHOB 20515; 225-6511; *Chief of Staff:* Karen M. Feather
Web: www.house.gov/kanjorski
E-mail: paul.kanjorski@mail.house.gov
District Office(s): 7 N. Wilkes-Barre Blvd., Wilkes-Barre 18702; (717) 825-2200; *District Director:* Joseph J. Terrana
860 Spruce St., Kulpmont 17834; (717) 373-1541; *District Office Manager:* Henry Sgro
Committee Assignment(s): Banking and Financial Services; Government Reform

KAPTUR, MARCY, D-OHIO (9)

Capitol Hill Office: 2366 RHOB 20515; 225-4146; Fax: 225-7711; *Chief of Staff:* Roger Szemraj
Web: www.house.gov/kaptur
E-mail: rep.kaptur@mail.house.gov
District Office(s): 420 Madison Ave., Toledo 43604; (419) 259-7500; Fax: (419) 255-9623; *District Manager:* Steve Katich
Committee Assignment(s): Appropriations

KASICH, JOHN R., R-OHIO (12)

Capitol Hill Office: 1111 LHOB 20515; 225-5355; *Chief of Staff:* Don Thibaut
Web: www.house.gov/kasich
E-mail: jkasich@mail.house.gov
District Office(s): 2700 E. Dublin-Granville Rd., Columbus 43231; (614) 523-2555; *Office Manager:* Sally Testa
Committee Assignment(s): Armed Services; Budget

KELLY, SUE W., R-N.Y. (19)

Capitol Hill Office: 1122 LHOB 20515; 225-5441; Fax: 225-3289; *Chief of Staff:* Steve V. Hall
Web: www.house.gov/suekelly
E-mail: dearsue@mail.house.gov
District Office(s): 21 Old Main St., #205, Fishkill 12524; (914) 897-5200; Fax: (914) 897-5800; *District Director:* Chris Fish
116 Radio Circle Dr., Mount Kisco 10549; (914) 241-6340; Fax: (914) 241-3502; *Special Assistant:* Jerry Nappi
Committee Assignment(s): Banking and Financial Services; Small Business; Transportation and Infrastructure

KENNEDY, PATRICK J., D-R.I. (1)

Capitol Hill Office: 312 CHOB 20515; 225-4911; Fax: 225-3290; *Chief of Staff:* Anthony C. Marcella
Web: www.house.gov/patrickkennedy
E-mail: patrick.kennedy@mail.house.gov
District Office(s): 249 Roosevelt Ave., Pawtucket 02860; (401) 729-5600; Fax: (401) 729-5608; *District Director:* Larry Ferguson; *Press Secretary:* Larry Berman
Committee Assignment(s): Armed Services; Resources

KILDEE, DALE E., D-MICH. (9)

Capitol Hill Office: 2187 RHOB 20515; 225-3611; Fax: 225-6393; *Administrative Assistant:* Christopher Mansour
Web: www.house.gov/kildee
E-mail: dale.kildee@mail.house.gov
District Office(s): 1829 N. Perry St., Pontiac 48340; (810) 373-9337; Fax: (810) 373-6955; *District Director:* Tiffany Anderson-Flynn
432 N. Saginaw St., Flint 48502; (810) 239-1437; Fax: (810) 239-1439; *Assistant District Director:* Barbara Donnelly
Committee Assignment(s): Education and Workforce; Resources

KILPATRICK, CAROLYN CHEEKS, D-MICH. (15)

Capitol Hill Office: 503 CHOB 20515; 225-2261; Fax: 225-5730; *Chief of Staff:* Jamal Simmons
Web: www.house.gov/kilpatrick
E-mail: www.house.gov/writerep
District Office(s): 1274 Library St., Detroit 48226; (313) 965-9004; Fax: (313) 965-9006; *District Director:* Derrick Miller
Committee Assignment(s): Appropriations

KIND, RON, D-WIS. (3)

Capitol Hill Office: 1713 LHOB 20515; 225-5506; Fax: 225-5739; *Administrative Assistant:* Alan MacLeod
Web: www.house.gov/kind
E-mail: ron.kind@mail.house.gov
District Office(s): 202 5th Ave. South, LaCrosse 54601; (608) 782-2558; Fax: (608) 782-4588; *District Director:* Loren J. Kannenberg
131 S. Barstow St., Eau Claire 54701; (715) 831-9214; Fax: (715) 831-9272; *Caseworker:* Mark Aumann
Committee Assignment(s): Education and Workforce; Resources

KING, PETER T., R-N.Y. (3)

Capitol Hill Office: 403 CHOB 20515; 225-7896; Fax: 226-2279; *Chief of Staff:* Robert F. O'Connor
Web: www.house.gov/king
E-mail: pete.king@mail.house.gov
District Office(s): 1003 Park Blvd., Massapequa Park 11762; (516) 541-4225; Fax: (516) 541-6602; *District Director:* Anne Rosenfeld
Committee Assignment(s): Banking and Financial Services; International Relations

KINGSTON, JACK, R-GA. (1)

Capitol Hill Office: 1034 LHOB 20515; 225-5831; Fax: 226-2269; *Chief of Staff:* Grace Cummings
Web: www.house.gov/kingston
E-mail: jack.kingston@mail.house.gov

District Office(s): 52 N. Main St., #220, Statesboro 30458; (912) 489-8797; Fax: (912) 764-8549; *Staff Assistant:* Keri Copeland
805 Gloucester St., #304, Brunswick 31520; (912) 265-9010; Fax: (912) 265-9013; *Office Manager:* Russ Graham
6605 Abercorn St., #102, Savannah 31405; (912) 352-0101; Fax: (912) 352-0105; *District Director:* Peggy Lee Mowers
Committee Assignment(s): Appropriations

KLECZKA, GERALD D., D-WIS. (4)

Capitol Hill Office: 2301 RHOB 20515; 225-4572; Fax: 225-8135; *Administrative Assistant:* Winfield Boerckel
Web: www.house.gov/kleczka
E-mail: jerry.4wi@mail.house.gov
District Office(s): 414 W. Moreland Blvd., Waukesha 53188; (414) 549-6360; Fax: (414) 549-6723; *Senior Constituent Liaison:* Catherine Vigdahl
5032 W. Forest Home Ave., Milwaukee 53219; (414) 297-1140; Fax: (414) 327-6151; *Chief of Staff:* Kathryn A. Hein; *Communications Director:* David de Felice
Committee Assignment(s): Budget; Ways and Means

KLINK, RON, D-PA. (4)

Capitol Hill Office: 2448 RHOB 20515; 225-2565; Fax: 226-2274; *Administrative Assistant:* Mary Kiernan
Web: www.house.gov/klink
E-mail: www.house.gov/writerep
District Office(s): Beaver Trust Bldg., Beaver 15009; (412) 728-3005; Fax: (412) 728-3095; *District Manager:* Brian J. Hayden
2692 Leechburg Rd., Lower Burrell 15068; (412) 335-4518; *Staff Assistant:* Melanie Polydence
11279 Center Highway, N. Huntingdon 15642; (412) 864-8681; Fax: (412) 864-8691; *District Project Coordinator:* Nancy A. Smith
Cranberry Township Municipal Bldg., Mars 16046; (412) 772-6080; Fax: (412) 772-6099; *District Director:* Joe Brimmeier
The Castleton, New Castle 16101; (412) 654-9036; Fax: (412) 654-9076; *Caseworker:* Rita Foley
Committee Assignment(s): Commerce

KNOLLENBERG, JOE, R-MICH. (11)

Capitol Hill Office: 2349 RHOB 20515; 225-5802; Fax: 226-2356; *Chief of Staff:* Paul Welday
Web: www.house.gov/knollenberg
E-mail: rep.knollenberg@mail.house.gov
District Office(s): 15439 Middlebelt Rd., Livonia 48154; (313) 425-7557; Fax: (313) 425-7691; *District Representative:* Melissa O'Rear

30833 N. Western Highway, Farmington Hills 48334; (248) 851-1366; Fax: (248) 851-0418; *District Field Director:* Shawn Ciavattone *Scheduler:* Glenn Martin

Committee Assignment(s): Appropriations; Budget; Standards of Official Conduct

KOLBE, JIM, R-ARIZ. (5)

Capitol Hill Office: 2266 RHOB 20515; 225-2542; Fax: 225-0378; *Chief of Staff:* Frances C. McNaught
Web: www.house.gov/kolbe
E-mail: www.house.gov/writerep
District Office(s): 77 Calle Portal, Sierra Vista 85635; (520) 459-3115; Fax: (520) 459-5419; *District Aide:* Bernadette Polley
1661 N. Swan Rd., Tucson 85712; (520) 881-3588; Fax: (520) 322-9490; *District Director:* Patricia Klein; *Press Secretary:* Keith D. Rosenblum
Committee Assignment(s): Appropriations

KUCINICH, DENNIS J., D-OHIO (10)

Capitol Hill Office: 1730 LHOB 20515; 225-5871; Fax: 225-5745; *Administrative Assistant:* John R. Edgell
Web: www.house.gov/kucinich
E-mail: www.house.gov/writerep
District Office(s): 14400 Detroit Ave., Lakewood 44107; (216) 228-8850; *District Director:* Patricia Vecchio
Committee Assignment(s): Education and Workforce; Government Reform

KUYKENDALL, STEVEN T., R-CALIF. (36)

Capitol Hill Office: 512 CHOB 20515; 225-8220; Fax: 225-7119; *Chief of Staff:* Katherine Hahn
Web: www.house.gov/kuykendall
E-mail: www.house.gov/writerep
District Office(s): 21311 Hawthorne Blvd., Torrance 90503; (310) 543-1098; Fax: (310) 543-2098; *District Director:* Adam Mendelsohn
Committee Assignment(s): Armed Services; Science; Transportation and Infrastructure

LaFALCE, JOHN J., D-N.Y. (29)

Capitol Hill Office: 2310 RHOB 20515; 225-3231; Fax: 225-8693; *Administrative Assistant:* Roy Dye
Web: www.house.gov/lafalce
E-mail: www.house.gov/writerep
District Office(s): Federal Bldg., Buffalo 14202; (716) 846-4056; Fax: (716) 856-3821; *District Representative:* Mary Brennan-Taylor
Main Post Office Bldg., Niagara Falls 14302; (716) 284-9976; Fax: (716) 284-8870; *Staff Assistant:* Rebecca C. Muscoreil
409 S. Union St., Spencerport 14559; (716) 352-4777; Fax: (716) 352-4747; *District Representative:* Hannelore Heyen
Committee Assignment(s): Banking and Financial Services

LaHOOD, RAY, R-ILL. (18)

Capitol Hill Office: 329 CHOB 20515; 225-6201; Fax: 225-9249; *Chief of Staff:* Diane R. Liesman
Web: www.house.gov/lahood
E-mail: www.house.gov/writerep
District Office(s): 100 N.E. Monroe St., Peoria 61602; (309) 671-7027; Fax: (309) 671-7309; *District Chief of Staff:* Brad McMillan
236 W. State St., Jacksonville 62650; (217) 245-1431; Fax: (217) 243-6852; *Office Manager:* Sally Dahman
3050 Montvale Dr., Springfield 62704; (217) 793-0808; Fax: (217) 793-9724; *Press Secretary:* Tim Butler; *Office Manager:* Donna Rapps Miller
Committee Assignment(s): Agriculture; Select Intelligence; Transportation and Infrastructure; Veterans' Affairs

LAMPSON, NICK, D-TEXAS (9)

Capitol Hill Office: 417 CHOB 20515; 225-6565; Fax: 225-5547; *Chief of Staff:* Tom Combs
Web: www.house.gov/lampson
E-mail: nick.lampson@mail.house.gov
District Office(s): Jack Brooks Federal Bldg., Beaumont 77701; (409) 838-0061; Fax: (409) 832-0738; *District Director:* Joe Arnold
U.S. Post Office Bldg., #216, Galveston 77550; (409) 762-5877; Fax: (409) 763-4133; *Galveston Director:* Dorthea Lewis
Committee Assignment(s): Science; Transportation and Infrastructure

LANTOS, TOM, D-CALIF. (12)

Capitol Hill Office: 2217 RHOB 20515; 225-3531; Fax: 225-7900; *Chief of Staff:* Robert R. King
Web: www.house.gov/lantos
E-mail: talk2tom@mail.house.gov
District Office(s): 400 El Camino Real, San Mateo 94402; (650) 342-0300; Fax: (650) 375-8270; *District Representative:* Evelyn Szelenyi
Committee Assignment(s): Government Reform; International Relations

LARGENT, STEVE, R-OKLA. (1)

Capitol Hill Office: 426 CHOB 20515; 225-2211; Fax: 225-9187; *Chief of Staff:* Terry Allen
Web: www.house.gov/largent
E-mail: ok01.largent@mail.house.gov
District Office(s): 2424 E. 21st St., Tulsa 74114; (918) 749-0014; Fax: (918) 749-0781; *District Director:* Mike Willis
Committee Assignment(s): Commerce

LARSON, JOHN B., D-CONN. (1)

Capitol Hill Office: 1419 LHOB 20515; 225-2265; Fax: 225-1031; *Administrative Assistant:* George Shevlin

Web: www.house.gov/larson

E-mail: www.house.gov/writerep

District Office(s): 221 Main St., 4th Floor, Hartford 06106; (860) 278-8888; Fax: (860) 278-2111; *District Director:* Maureen Moriarty

Committee Assignment(s): Armed Services; Science

LATHAM, TOM, R-IOWA (5)

Capitol Hill Office: 324 CHOB 20515; 225-5476; Fax: 225-3301; *Washington Operations Director:* James D. Carstensen

Web: www.house.gov/latham

E-mail: latham.ia05@mail.house.gov

District Office(s): 1411 1st Ave. South, Fort Dodge 50501; (515) 573-2738; Fax: (515) 576-7141; *Staff Assistant:* Jim Oberhelman

20 W. 6th St., Spencer 51301; (712) 262-6480; Fax: (712) 262-6673; *Staff Assistant:* Lois Clark

526 Pierce St., Sioux City 51101; (712) 277-2114; Fax: (712) 277-0932; *Staff Assistant:* Michele Wing

123 Albany Ave. S.E., Orange City 51041; (712) 737-8708; Fax: (712) 737-3456; *Chief of Staff:* Vicky Vermaat

Committee Assignment(s): Appropriations

LATOURETTE, STEVEN C., R-OHIO (19)

Capitol Hill Office: 1224 LHOB 20515; 225-5731; Fax: 225-3307; *Chief of Staff:* Jennifer Laptook

Web: www.house.gov/latourette

E-mail: www.house.gov/writerep

District Office(s): One Victoria Place, Painesville 44077; (440) 352-3939; Fax: (440) 352-3622; *District Director:* Chris Hess

Parma Heights City Hall, Parma Heights 44130; (440) 887-3900; *District Outreach Representative:* Mary Spada

Committee Assignment(s): Banking and Financial Services; Government Reform; Transportation and Infrastructure

LAZIO, RICK A., R-N.Y. (2)

Capitol Hill Office: 2244 RHOB 20515; 225-3335; Fax: 225-4669; *Chief of Staff:* Andrew Ehrlich

Web: www.house.gov/lazio

E-mail: lazio@mail.house.gov

District Office(s): 126 W. Main St., Babylon 11702; (516) 893-9010; Fax: (516) 893-9017; *District Director:* Barbara Vogl

Committee Assignment(s): Banking and Financial Services; Commerce

LEACH, JIM, R-IOWA (1)

Capitol Hill Office: 2186 RHOB 20515; 225-6576; Fax: 226-1278; *Administrative Assistant:* Bill Tate

Web: www.house.gov/leach

E-mail: talk2jim@mail.house.gov

District Office(s): 1756 1st Ave. N.E., Cedar Rapids 52402; (319) 363-4773; Fax: (319) 363-5008; *Staff Assistant:* Gary Grant; *Press Secretary:* Doug Wagner

209 W. 4th St., Davenport 52801; (319) 326-1841; Fax: (319) 326-5464; *District Office Manager:* Rita Lowry

Plaza Centre One, Iowa City 52240; (319) 351-0789; Fax: (319) 351-5789; *Staff Assistant:* Ginny Burrus

Committee Assignment(s): Banking and Financial Services; International Relations

LEE, BARBARA, D-CALIF. (9)

Capitol Hill Office: 414 CHOB 20515; 225-2661; Fax: 225-9817; *Chief of Staff:* Sandre Swanson

Web: www.house.gov/lee

E-mail: www.house.gov/writerep

District Office(s): 1300 Clay St., Oakland 94612; (510) 763-0370; *District Director:* Sandre Swanson

Committee Assignment(s): Banking and Financial Services; International Relations

LEVIN, SANDER M., D-MICH. (12)

Capitol Hill Office: 2268 RHOB 20515; 225-4961; Fax: 226-1033; *Chief of Staff:* Hilarie Chambers

Web: www.house.gov/levin

E-mail: slevin@mail.house.gov

District Office(s): 2017 E. Fourteen Mile Rd., Sterling Heights 48310; (810) 268-4444; Fax: (810) 268-0918; *District Administrator:* Jennifer Demsko

Committee Assignment(s): Ways and Means

LEWIS, JERRY, R-CALIF. (40)

Capitol Hill Office: 2112 RHOB 20515; 225-5861; Fax: 225-6498; *Administrative Assistant:* Arlene Willis

Web: www.house.gov/jerrylewis

E-mail: www.house.gov/writerep

District Office(s): 1150 Brookside Ave., Redlands 92373; (909) 862-6030; Fax: (909) 335-9155; *District Representative:* Janet Scott

Committee Assignment(s): Appropriations; Select Intelligence

LEWIS, JOHN, D-GA. (5)

Capitol Hill Office: 343 CHOB 20515; 225-3801; Fax: 225-0351; *Chief of Staff:* Linda Earley Chastang

Web: www.house.gov/johnlewis

E-mail: johnlewis@mail.house.gov

District Office(s): Equitable Bldg., Atlanta 30303; (404) 659-0116; Fax: (404) 331-0947; *Constituent Services Director:* Love Williams

Committee Assignment(s): Ways and Means

LEWIS, RON, R-KY. (2)

Capitol Hill Office: 223 CHOB 20515; 225-3501; Fax: 226-2019; *Administrative Assistant:* Greg Van Tatenhove

Web: www.house.gov/ronlewis

E-mail: www.house.gov/writerep

District Office(s): Federal Bldg., Bowling Green 42101; (270) 842-9896; Fax: (270) 842-9081; *District Representative:* Phyllis Causey

312 N. Mulberry St., Elizabethtown 42701; (270) 765-4360; Fax: (270) 766-1580; *District Director:* Keith Rogers

Federal Bldg., Owensboro 42302; (270) 688-8858; *Field Representative:* Scott Miller

Committee Assignment(s): Ways and Means

LINDER, JOHN, R-GA. (11)

Capitol Hill Office: 2447 RHOB 20515; 225-4272; Fax: 225-4696; *Administrative Assistant:* Henry Plaster

Web: www.house.gov/linder

E-mail: john.linder@mail.house.gov

District Office(s): 220 College Ave., Athens 30601; (706) 355-9909; Fax: (706) 355-9968; *District Field Representative:* Jeff Finger

3675 Crestwood Parkway, Duluth 30096; (770) 931-9550; Fax: (770) 931-2775; *District Director:* Allan Hayes

Committee Assignment(s): Rules

LIPINSKI, WILLIAM O., D-ILL. (3)

Capitol Hill Office: 1501 LHOB 20515; 225-5701; Fax: 225-1012; *Administrative Assistant:* Colleen Corr

Web: www.house.gov/lipinski

E-mail: www.house.gov/writerep

District Office(s): 5239 W. 95th St., Oak Lawn 60453; (708) 952-0860; Fax: (708) 952-0862; *Staff Assistant:* Lenore Goodfriend

5832 S. Archer Ave., Chicago 60638; (312) 886-0481; Fax: (773) 767-9395; *District Director:* Jerry Hurkes

19 W. Hillgrove Ave., LaGrange 60525; (708) 352-0524; *Staff Assistant:* Rita Pula

Committee Assignment(s): Transportation and Infrastructure

LoBIONDO, FRANK A., R-N.J. (2)

Capitol Hill Office: 222 CHOB 20515; 225-6572; Fax: 225-3318; *Chief of Staff:* Mary Annie Harper

Web: www.house.gov/lobiondo

E-mail: lobiondo@mail.house.gov

District Office(s): 5914 Main St., Mays Landing 08330; (609) 625-5008; Fax: (609) 625-5071; *District Director:* Joan Dermanoski

Committee Assignment(s): Small Business; Transportation and Infrastructure

LOFGREN, ZOE, D-CALIF. (16)

Capitol Hill Office: 318 CHOB 20515; 225-3072; Fax: 225-3336; *Chief of Staff:* John Flannery

Web: www.house.gov/lofgren

E-mail: zoe@lofgren.house.gov

District Office(s): 635 N. 1st St., San Jose 95112; (408) 271-8700; Fax: (408) 271-8713; *District Chief of Staff:* Sandra Soto

Committee Assignment(s): Judiciary; Science; Standards of Official Conduct

LOWEY, NITA M., D-N.Y. (18)

Capitol Hill Office: 2421 RHOB 20515; 225-6506; Fax: 225-0546; *Chief of Staff:* Matthew Traub

Web: www.house.gov/lowey

E-mail: nita.lowey@mail.house.gov

District Office(s): 222 Mamaroneck Ave., White Plains 10605; (914) 428-1707; Fax: (914) 328-1505; *District Director:* Patricia Keegan

97-45 Queens Blvd., Rego Park 11374; (718) 897-3602; Fax: (718) 897-3804; *District Representative:* Sharon Levy

Committee Assignment(s): Appropriations

LUCAS, FRANK D., R-OKLA. (6)

Capitol Hill Office: 438 CHOB 20515; 225-5565; Fax: 225-8698; *Chief of Staff:* Stacy Glasscock

Web: www.house.gov/lucas

E-mail: www.house.gov/writerep

District Office(s): 500 N. Broadway, Oklahoma City 73102; (405) 235-5311; Fax: (580) 983-2771; *District Director:* Mona Taylor

2728 Williams Ave., Woodward 73802; (580) 256-5752; Fax: (580) 254-3047; *Field Representative:* Tammie Smith

703-A Frisco Ave., Clinton 73601; (580) 323-6232; Fax: (580) 323-3431; *Field Representative:* David Thompson

Federal Bldg., #229, Enid 73701; (580) 233-9224; Fax: (580) 233-8010; *Field Representative:* Tim Milacek

Committee Assignment(s): Agriculture; Banking and Financial Services; Science

LUCAS, KEN, D-KY. (4)

Capitol Hill Office: 1237 LHOB 20515; 225-3465; Fax: 225-8698; *Chief of Staff:* John Lapp

Web: www.house.gov/kenlucas

E-mail: write.kenlucas@mail.house.gov

District Office(s): 277 Buttermilk Pike, Ft. Mitchell 41017; (606) 426-0080; Fax: (606) 426-0061; *District Director:* Angie Dixon

Carl D. Perkins Federal Bldg., #236, Ashland 41101; (606) 324-9898; Fax: (606) 325-9866; *District Representative:* Sue Dowdy

Committee Assignment(s): Agriculture; Budget

LUTHER, BILL, D-MINN. (6)

Capitol Hill Office: 117 CHOB 20515; 225-2271; Fax: 225-3368; *Chief of Staff:* Ted Thompson

Web: www.house.gov/luther

E-mail: bill.luther@mail.house.gov

District Office(s): 1811 Weir Dr., Woodbury 55125; (612) 730-4949; Fax: (612) 730-0507; *Chief of Staff:* Ted Thompson; *District Director:* Corinne Hoeft

Committee Assignment(s): Commerce

MALONEY, CAROLYN B., D-N.Y. (14)

Capitol Hill Office: 2430 RHOB 20515; 225-7944; Fax: 225-4709; *Administrative Assistant:* Ben Chevat

Web: www.house.gov/maloney

E-mail: rep.carolyn.maloney@mail.house.gov

District Office(s): 1651 3rd Ave., New York 10128; (212) 860-0606; Fax: (212) 860-0704; *N.Y. Chief of Staff:* Minna Elias

28-11 Astoria Blvd., Astoria 11102; (718) 932-1804; *District Representative:* Dominick Fucile

Committee Assignment(s): Banking and Financial Services; Government Reform; Joint Economic

MALONEY, JIM, D-CONN. (5)

Capitol Hill Office: 1213 LHOB 20515; 225-3822; Fax: 225-5746; *Chief of Staff:* Jim Hart

Web: www.house.gov/jimmaloney

E-mail: www.house.gov/writerep

District Office(s): 20 E. Main St., Waterbury 06702; (203) 573-1418; Fax: (203) 573-9329; *District Director:* Cheryl Reedy

Committee Assignment(s): Armed Services; Banking and Financial Services

MANZULLO, DONALD, R-ILL. (16)

Capitol Hill Office: 409 CHOB 20515; 225-5676; Fax: 225-5284; *Chief of Staff:* J. Douglas Thomas

Web: www.house.gov/manzullo

E-mail: www.house.gov/writerep

District Office(s): 181 Virginia Ave., Crystal Lake 60014; (815) 356-9800; Fax: (815) 356-9803; *Caseworker:* Nada Johnson

415 S. Mulford Rd., Rockford 61108; (815) 394-1231; *District Director:* Pamela Sexton

Committee Assignment(s): Banking and Financial Services; International Relations; Small Business

MARKEY, EDWARD J., D-MASS. (7)

Capitol Hill Office: 2108 RHOB 20515; 225-2836; *Chief of Staff:* David Moulton

Web: www.house.gov/markey

E-mail: www.house.gov/writerep

District Office(s): 5 High St., Medford 02155; (781) 396-2900; *District Administrative Assistant:* Carol Lederman

188 Concord St., Framingham 01702; (508) 875-2900; *Congressional Aide:* Timothy Sweeney

Committee Assignment(s): Budget; Commerce

MARTINEZ, MATTHEW G., D-CALIF. (31)

Capitol Hill Office: 2269 RHOB 20515; 225-5464; Fax: 225-5467; *Chief of Staff:* Maxine Grant

Web: www.house.gov/martinez

E-mail: www.house.gov/writerep

District Office(s): 2550 W. Main St., Alhambra 91801; (626) 458-4524; Fax: (626) 458-2241; *Office Manager:* Sally Martinez

Committee Assignment(s): Education and Workforce; International Relations

MASCARA, FRANK R., D-PA. (20)

Capitol Hill Office: 314 CHOB 20515; 225-4665; Fax: 225-3377; *Administrative Assistant:* Bill Sember

Web: www.house.gov/mascara

E-mail: www.house.gov/writerep

District Office(s): Professional Plaza, #210, N. Charleroi 15022; (724) 483-9016; Fax: (724) 483-9044; *District Director:* Lou Lignelli; *Press Secretary:* Stephanie Mangini

96 N. Main St., Washington 15301; (724) 228-4326; Fax: (724) 228-5839; *Community Services Representative:* Tina Dallatore

140 N. Beeson Ave., #408, Uniontown 15401; (724) 437-5078; Fax: (724) 437-5189; *Field Representative:* Chris Buckelew

Greene County Office Bldg., Waynesburg 15370; (724) 852-2182; *Field Representative:* Pam Snyder

Greensburg City Hall, Greensburg 15601; (724) 834-6441; Fax: (724) 834-6514; *Field Representative:* David McCormick

Committee Assignment(s): Banking and Financial Services; Transportation and Infrastructure

MATSUI, ROBERT T., D-CALIF. (5)

Capitol Hill Office: 2308 RHOB 20515; 225-7163; Fax: 225-0566; *Administrative Assistant:* Tom Keaney

Web: www.house.gov/matsui

E-mail: www.house.gov/writerep

District Office(s): 12-600 Federal Courthouse, Sacramento 95814; (916) 498-5600; Fax: (916) 444-6117; *District Director:* Anne Valenti

Committee Assignment(s): Ways and Means

McCARTHY, CAROLYN, D-N.Y. (4)

Capitol Hill Office: 1725 LHOB 20515; 225-5516; Fax: 225-5758; *Chief of Staff:* Jim Messina

Web: www.house.gov/carolynmccarthy

E-mail: www.house.gov/writerep

District Office(s): One Fulton Ave., Hempstead 11550; (516) 489-7066; Fax: (516) 489-7283; *District Director:* Mary Ellen Mendelsohn

Committee Assignment(s): Education and Workforce; Small Business

McCARTHY, KAREN, D-MO. (5)

Capitol Hill Office: 1330 LHOB 20515; 225-4535; Fax:
225-4403; *Chief of Staff:* Phil Scaglia
Web: www.house.gov/karenmccarthy
E-mail: www.house.gov/writerep
District Office(s): 400 E. Ninth St., Kansas City 64105;
(816) 842-4545; Fax: (816) 471-5213; *Chief of Staff:*
Phil Scaglia
301 W. Lexington Ave., Independence 64050; (816) 833-
4545; *District Aide:* Tom Wyrsch
Committee Assignment(s): Commerce

McCOLLUM, BILL, R-FLA. (8)

Capitol Hill Office: 2109 RHOB 20515; 225-2176; Fax:
225-0999; *Chief of Staff:* John Ariale
Web: www.house.gov/mccollum
E-mail: www.house.gov/writerep
District Office(s): 605 E. Robinson St., Orlando 32801;
(407) 872-1962; Fax: (407) 872-1944; *District Office
Manager:* Sue Lancaster
Committee Assignment(s): Banking and Financial Ser-
vices; Judiciary; Select Intelligence

McCRERY, JIM, R-LA. (4)

Capitol Hill Office: 2104 RHOB 20515; 225-2777; Fax:
225-8039; *Chief of Staff:* Richard Hunt
Web: www.house.gov/mccrery
E-mail: jim.mccrery@mail.house.gov
District Office(s): 6425 Youree Dr., Shreveport 71105;
(318) 798-2254; Fax: (318) 798-2063; *District Man-
ager:* Linda Sentell Wright
Southgate Plaza Shopping Center, Leesville 71446; (318)
238-0778; Fax: (318) 238-0566; *Caseworker:* Lee
Turner
Committee Assignment(s): Ways and Means

McDERMOTT, JIM, D-WASH. (7)

Capitol Hill Office: 1035 LHOB 20515; 225-3106; *Admin-
istrative Assistant:* Charles M. Williams
Web: www.house.gov/mcdermott
E-mail: www.house.gov/writerep
District Office(s): 1809 7th Ave., Seattle 98101; (206) 553-
7170; Fax: (206) 553-7175; *District Administrator:*
Jane Sanders
Committee Assignment(s): Budget; Ways and Means

McGOVERN, JIM, D-MASS. (3)

Capitol Hill Office: 416 CHOB 20515; 225-6101; Fax: 225-
5759; *Chief of Staff:* Ed Augustus
Web: www.house.gov/mcgovern
E-mail: www.house.gov/mcgovern/send.htm
District Office(s): 34 Mechanic St., Worcester 01608; (508)
831-7356; Fax: (508) 754-0982; *District Director:*
Gladys Rodriguez-Parker

218 S. Main St., Fall River 02721; (508) 677-0140; Fax:
(508) 677-0992; *District Representative:* Patrick Norton
One Park St., Attleboro 02703; (508) 431-8025; Fax:
(508) 431-8017; *District Representative:* Shirley
Coehlo
Committee Assignment(s): Transportation and Infrastructure

McHUGH, JOHN M., R-N.Y. (24)

Capitol Hill Office: 2441 RHOB 20515; 225-4611; Fax:
226-0621; *Chief of Staff:* Robert Taub
Web: www.house.gov/mchugh
E-mail: www.house.gov/writerep
District Office(s): Fulton County Office Bldg., #10, Johns-
town 12095; (518) 762-0379; Fax: (518) 762-0369;
District Office Manager: Diane Henderson
Federal Bldg., #104, Plattsburgh 12901; (518) 563-1406;
Fax: (518) 561-9723; *District Office Manager:* Ruth
Mary Ortloff
#404A, Key Bank Bldg., Watertown 13601; (315) 782-
3150; Fax: (315) 782-1291; *District Office Manager:*
Elaine Grabiec
Committee Assignment(s): Armed Services; Government
Reform; International Relations

McINNIS, SCOTT, R-COLO. (3)

Capitol Hill Office: 320 CHOB 20515; 225-4761; Fax: 226-
0622; *Chief of Staff:* Mike Hesse
Web: www.house.gov/mcinnis
E-mail: www.house.gov/writerep
District Office(s): 134 W. B St., Pueblo 81003; (719) 543-
8200; Fax: (719) 543-8204; *District Director:* Roger
Gomez
Old Main Post Office Professional Bldg., Durango 81301;
(303) 259-2754; Fax: (303) 259-2762; *Office Manager:*
LuAnn Kraemer
Hotel Colorado, Glenwood Springs 81601; (970) 928-
0637; Fax: (970) 928-0630; *Area Representative:* Lynne
Kerst
327 N. 7th St., Grand Junction 81501; (303) 245-7107;
Fax: (303) 245-2194; *Office Manager:* Don Hower
Committee Assignment(s): Ways and Means

McINTOSH, DAVID M., R-IND. (2)

Capitol Hill Office: 1610 LHOB 20515; 225-3021; Fax:
225-3382; *Chief of Staff:* Jeff Taylor
Web: www.house.gov/mcintosh
E-mail: www.house.gov/writerep
District Office(s): 2900 W. Jackson St., #101, Muncie
47304; (765) 747-5566; Fax: (765) 747-5586; *Community Relations Director:* Kim Orlosky
1134 Meridian St., Anderson 46016; (765) 640-2919; Fax:
(765) 640-2922; *Field Representative:* Kathleen Atterholt

50 N. 5th St., Richmond 47374; (317) 962-2883; *Field Representative:* Cliff Wagner

2581 7th St., Columbus 47201; (812) 372-3637; *Field Representative:* Judy Meyer

Committee Assignment(s): Education and Workforce; Government Reform; Small Business

McINTYRE, MIKE, D-N.C. (7)

Capitol Hill Office: 1605 LHOB 20515; 225-2731; Fax: 225-5773; *Chief of Staff:* Dean Mitchell

Web: www.house.gov/mcintyre

E-mail: congmcintyre@mail.house.gov

District Office(s): 218 Federal Bldg., Fayetteville 28301; (910) 323-0260; Fax: (910) 323-0069; *District Director:* Judith Kirchman

Post Office Bldg., Wilmington 28401; (910) 815-4959; Fax: (910) 815-4543; *Constituent Services Assistant:* Pamela Campbell-Dereef

701 N. Elm St., Lumberton 28358; (910) 671-6223; Fax: (910) 739-5085; *District Executive Assistant:* Marie Thompson

Committee Assignment(s): Agriculture; Armed Services

McKEON, HOWARD P. "BUCK," R-CALIF. (25)

Capitol Hill Office: 2242 RHOB 20515; 225-1956; Fax: 226-0683; *Chief of Staff:* Bob Cochran

Web: www.house.gov/mckeon

E-mail: tellbuck@mail.house.gov

District Office(s): 23929 W. Valencia Blvd., Santa Clarita 91355; (805) 254-2111; Fax: (805) 254-2380; *Press Secretary:* David Foy

1008 West Ave. M-14, Palmdale 93551; (805) 274-9688; *Field Representative:* Lew Stults

Committee Assignment(s): Armed Services; Education and Workforce; Veterans' Affairs

McKINNEY, CYNTHIA A., D-GA. (4)

Capitol Hill Office: 124 CHOB 20515; 225-1605; Fax: 226-0691; *Chief of Staff:* Merwyn Scott

Web: www.house.gov/mckinney

E-mail: cymck@mail.house.gov

District Office(s): 246 Sycamore St., Decatur 30030; (404) 377-6900; Fax: (404) 377-6909; *District Director:* Philippa Brown

Committee Assignment(s): Armed Services; International Relations

McNULTY, MICHAEL R., D-N.Y. (21)

Capitol Hill Office: 2161 RHOB 20515; 225-5076; Fax: 225-5077; *Chief of Staff:* Lana Helfrich

Web: www.house.gov/mcnulty

E-mail: mike.mcnulty@mail.house.gov

District Office(s): 2490 Riverfront Center, Amsterdam 12010; (518) 843-3400; *Secretary:* Elaine DeVito

U.S. Post Office, Schenectady 12305; (518) 374-4547; *District Representative:* Bob Carr

Leo W. O'Brien Federal Bldg., Albany 12207; (518) 465-0700; Fax: (518) 427-5107; 33 2nd St., Troy 12180; (518) 271-0822; *District Representative:* Tom Matthews

Committee Assignment(s): Ways and Means

MEEHAN, MARTIN T., D-MASS. (5)

Capitol Hill Office: 2434 RHOB 20515; 225-3411; Fax: 226-0771; *Chief of Staff:* Bill McCann

Web: www.house.gov/meehan

E-mail: martin.meehan@mail.house.gov

District Office(s): Walker Bldg., Marlborough 01752; (508) 460-9292; Fax: (508) 460-6869; *Congressional Aide:* Chris Doherty

11 Kearney Square, 3rd Floor, Lowell 01852; (978) 459-0101; Fax: (978) 459-1907; *District Coordinator:* John Gill

Bay State Bldg., Lawrence 01840; (978) 681-6200; Fax: (978) 682-6070; *Area Coordinator:* June Black

Committee Assignment(s): Armed Services; Judiciary

MEEK, CARRIE P., D-FLA. (17)

Capitol Hill Office: 401 CHOB 20515; 225-4506; Fax: 226-0777; *Chief of Staff:* John Shelbe

Web: www.house.gov/meek

E-mail: www.house.gov/writerep

District Office(s): 3550 Biscayne Blvd., Miami 33137; (305) 576-9303; Fax: (305) 576-9753; *Chief of Staff:* Peggy Demon

Committee Assignment(s): Appropriations

MEEKS, GREGORY W., D-N.Y. (6)

Capitol Hill Office: 1710 LHOB 20515; 225-3461; Fax: 226-4169; *Chief of Staff:* Jameel W. Aalim-Johnson

Web: www.house.gov/meeks

E-mail: www.house.gov/writerep

District Office(s): 19606 Linden Blvd., St. Albans 11412; (718) 949-5600; Fax: (718) 949-5972; *District Chief of Staff:* Josephine Johnson

20-08 Seagirt Blvd., Far Rockaway 11691; (718) 327-9791; Fax: (718) 327-4722; *Community Liaison:* Ed Williams

121-04 Liberty Ave., Richmond Hill 11419; (718) 738-4200; Fax: (718) 738-5588; *Comm. Liaison:* Veronica Beckford

Committee Assignment(s): Banking and Financial Services; International Relations

MENENDEZ, ROBERT, D-N.J. (13)

Capitol Hill Office: 405 CHOB 20515; 225-7919; Fax: 226-0792; *Chief of Staff:* Michael H. Hutton

Web: www.house.gov/menendez

E-mail: www.house.gov/writerep

District Office(s): 654 Ave. C, Bayonne 07002; (201) 823-2900; *Congressional Aide:* Bob Burrows

911 Bergen Ave., Jersey City 07302; (201) 222-2828; Fax: (201) 222-0188; *Executive Assistant:* Kay LiCausi; *District Director:* Jose Alvarez

263 Hobart St., Perth Amboy 08861; (732) 324-6212; Fax: (732) 324-7470; *District Director:* Jose Alvarez

Committee Assignment(s): International Relations; Transportation and Infrastructure

METCALF, JACK, R-WASH. (2)

Capitol Hill Office: 1510 LHOB 20515; 225-2605; Fax: 225-4420; *Chief of Staff:* S. Lewis Moore

Web: www.house.gov/metcalf

E-mail: www.house.gov/writerep

District Office(s): 2930 Wetmore Ave., Everett 98201; (425) 252-3188; Fax: (425) 252-6606; *Chief of Staff:* S. Lewis Moore

322 N. Commerical St., Bellingham 98225; (360) 733-4500; Fax: (360) 733-5144; *Caseworker:* Fairalee Markusen

Committee Assignment(s): Banking and Financial Services; Science; Transportation and Infrastructure

MICA, JOHN L., R-FLA. (7)

Capitol Hill Office: 2445 RHOB 20515; 225-4035; Fax: 226-0821; *Chief of Staff:* Russell Roberts

Web: www.house.gov/mica

E-mail: john.mica@mail.house.gov

District Office(s): 1000 City Center Circle, Port Orange 32119; (904) 756-9798; Fax: (904) 756-9903; *District Aide:* Nora Hall

1211 Semoran Blvd., Casselberry 32707; (407) 657-8080; Fax: (407) 657-5353; *District Representative:* Dick Harkey

840 Deltona Blvd., Deltona 32725; (407) 860-1499; Fax: (407) 860-5730; *Caseworker:* Janet Mines

Committee Assignment(s): Government Reform; House Administration; Transportation and Infrastructure

MILLENDER-McDONALD, JUANITA, D-CALIF. (37)

Capitol Hill Office: 419 CHOB 20515; 225-7924; Fax: 225-7926; *Chief of Staff:* Pearl Marsh

Web: www.house.gov/millender-mcdonald

E-mail: millender.mcdonald@mail.house.gov

District Office(s): 970 W. 190th St., Torrance 90502; (310) 538-1190; Fax: (310) 538-9672; *District Director:* Pat Etienne

Committee Assignment(s): Small Business; Transportation and Infrastructure

MILLER, DAN, R-FLA. (13)

Capitol Hill Office: 102 CHOB 20515; 225-5015; Fax: 226-0828; *Chief of Staff:* Dani Doane

Web: www.house.gov/danmiller

E-mail: miller13@mail.house.gov

District Office(s): 2424 Manatee Ave., Bradenton 34205; (941) 747-9081; Fax: (941) 749-5310; *District Director:* Glenda Wright

1751 Mound St., Sarasota 34236; (941) 951-6643; Fax: (941) 951-2972; *District Representative:* Gee Dee Kerr

Committee Assignment(s): Appropriations; Government Reform

MILLER, GARY, R-CALIF. (41)

Capitol Hill Office: 1037 LHOB 20515; 225-3201; Fax: 226-6926; *Chief of Staff:* John Rothrock

Web: www.house.gov/garymiller

E-mail: www.house.gov/writerep

District Office(s): 22632 Golden Springs Dr., #350, Diamond Bar 91765; (909) 612-4677; Fax: (909) 612-1087; *District Director:* Bill Blankenship

Committee Assignment(s): Budget; Science; Transportation and Infrastructure

MILLER, GEORGE, D-CALIF. (7)

Capitol Hill Office: 2205 RHOB 20515; 225-2095; *Administrative Assistant:* Daniel Weiss

Web: www.house.gov/georgemiller

E-mail: george.miller-pub@mail.house.gov

District Office(s): 1333 Willow Pass Rd., Concord 94520; (925) 602-1880; *District Director:* David Tucker

3220 Blume Dr., Richmond 94806; (510) 262-6500; Fax: (510) 222-1306; *Staff Assistant:* Hank Royal

1410 Georgia St., Vallejo 94590; (707) 645-1888; *Staff Assistant:* Katherine Hoffman

Committee Assignment(s): Education and Workforce; Resources

MINGE, DAVID, D-MINN. (2)

Capitol Hill Office: 1415 LHOB 20515; 225-2331; Fax: 226-0836; *Chief of Staff:* Ross Peterson

Web: www.house.gov/minge

E-mail: www.house.gov/writerep

District Office(s): 205 E. 4th St., Chaska 55318; (612) 448-6567; Fax: (612) 448-6930; *District Director:* Herb Halvorson

938 4th Ave., Windom 56101; (507) 831-0115; Fax: (507) 831-0118; *District Director:* Herb Halvorson

542 1st St. South, Montevideo 56265; (320) 269-9311; Fax: (320) 269-8651; *Constituent Services Representative:* Ruthann Lee

Committee Assignment(s): Agriculture; Budget; Joint Economic

MINK, PATSY T., D-HAWAII (2)

Capitol Hill Office: 2135 RHOB 20515; 225-4906; Fax: 225-4987; *Administrative Assistant:* Helen E. Lewis

Web: www.house.gov/mink

E-mail: www.house.gov/writerep

District Office(s): 5104 Prince Kuhio Federal Bldg., Honolulu 96850; (808) 541-1986; Fax: (808) 538-0233; *Administrative Assistant:* Joan Manke

Committee Assignment(s): Education and Workforce; Government Reform

MOAKLEY, JOE, D-MASS. (9)

Capitol Hill Office: 235 CHOB 20515; 225-8273; Fax: 225-3984; *Chief of Staff:* Kevin Ryan

Web: www.house.gov/moakley

E-mail: jmoakley@mail.house.gov

District Office(s): 3110 U.S. Courthouse, Boston 02210; (617) 428-2000; Fax: (617) 428-2011; *District Director:* Frederick W. Clark

Crocker Bldg., Taunton 02780; (508) 824-6676; Fax: (508) 880-3520; *Congressional Assistant:* Karen Harraghy

Brockton Federal Bldg., Brockton 02401; (508) 586-5555; Fax: (508) 580-4692; *Staff Assistant:* John Montagano

Committee Assignment(s): Rules

MOLLOHAN, ALAN B., D-W.VA. (1)

Capitol Hill Office: 2346 RHOB 20515; 225-4172; Fax: 225-7564; *Chief of Staff:* Sally Moorhead

E-mail: www.house.gov/writerep

District Office(s): Federal Bldg., #315, Wheeling 26003; (304) 232-5390; Fax: (304) 232-5722; *Area Representative:* Cathy Abraham

P.O. Box 1400, Clarksburg 26302; (304) 623-4422; Fax: (304) 623-0571; *Area Representative:* Ann Merandi

Federal Bldg., #232, Morgantown 26505; (304) 292-3019; Fax: (304) 292-3027; *Area Representative:* Lotta Neer

Federal Bldg., #4311, Parkersburg 26102; (304) 428-0493; Fax: (304) 428-5980; *Caseworker:* Betsy Moore

Committee Assignment(s): Appropriations

MOORE, DENNIS, D-KAN. (3)

Capitol Hill Office: 506 CHOB 20515; 225-2865; Fax: 225-2807; *Chief of Staff:* Howard Bauleke

Web: www.house.gov/moore

E-mail: dennis.moore@mail.house.gov

District Office(s): 8417 Santa Fe Dr., #101, Overland Park 66212; (913) 383-2013; Fax: (913) 383-2088; *District Director:* Kaye Cleaver

500 State Ave., Kansas City 66101; (913) 621-0832; Fax: (913) 621-1533; *Constituent Services Aide:* Paul Davidson

647 Massachusetts St., Lawrence 66044; (785) 842-9313; Fax: (785) 843-3289; *Constituent Services Coordinator:* Becky Fast

Committee Assignment(s): Banking and Financial Services; Science; Small Business

MORAN, JAMES P., D-VA. (8)

Capitol Hill Office: 2239 RHOB 20515; 225-4376; Fax: 225-0017; *Administrative Assistant:* Paul Reagan

Web: www.house.gov/moran

E-mail: jim.moran@mail.house.gov

District Office(s): 5115 Franconia Rd., Alexandria 22310; (703) 971-4700; Fax: (703) 922-9436; *District Director:* Susie Warner

Committee Assignment(s): Appropriations; Budget

MORAN, JERRY, R-KAN. (1)

Capitol Hill Office: 1519 LHOB 20515; 225-2715; Fax: 225-5124; *Chief of Staff:* Tom Hemmer

Web: www.house.gov/moranks01

E-mail: jerry.moran@mail.house.gov

District Office(s): #203, Davis Hall, Hays 67601; (913) 628-6401; Fax: (913) 628-3791; *Constituent Services Representative:* Eric Depperschmidt

P.O. Box 1128, Hutchinson 67504; (316) 665-6138; Fax: (316) 665-6360; *District Director:* Kirk Johnson

Committee Assignment(s): Agriculture; Transportation and Infrastructure; Veterans' Affairs

MORELLA, CONSTANCE A., R-MD. (8)

Capitol Hill Office: 2228 RHOB 20515; 225-5341; Fax: 225-1389; *Chief of Staff:* Lisa Boepple

Web: www.house.gov/morella

E-mail: rep.morella@mail.house.gov

District Office(s): 51 Monroe St., Rockville 20850; (301) 424-3501; Fax: (301) 424-5992; *District Director:* Minnie Anderson

Committee Assignment(s): Government Reform; Science

MURTHA, JOHN P., D-PA. (12)

Capitol Hill Office: 2423 RHOB 20515; 225-2065; Fax: 225-5709; *Administrative Assistant:* William Allen

Web: www.house.gov/murtha

E-mail: murtha@mail.house.gov

District Office(s): P.O. Box 780, Johnstown 15907; (814) 535-2642; Fax: (814) 539-6229; *District Administrative Assistant:* John A. Hugya

Committee Assignment(s): Appropriations

MYRICK, SUE, R-N.C. (9)

Capitol Hill Office: 230 CHOB 20515; 225-1976; Fax: 225-3389; *Chief of Staff:* Hal Weatherman; *Administrative Assistant:* David Spooner

Web: www.house.gov/myrick

E-mail: myrick@mail.house.gov

District Office(s): 318 South St., Gastonia 28052; (704) 861-1976; Fax: (704) 864-2445; *District Coordinator:* James White

6525 Morrison Blvd., Charlotte 28211; (704) 362-1060;
Fax: (704) 367-0852; *District Director:* Hal Weatherman
200 S. LaFayette St., Shelby 28150; (704) 484-1976; *District Representative:* Judy Harper
Committee Assignment(s): Rules

NADLER, JERROLD, D-N.Y. (8)

Capitol Hill Office: 2334 RHOB 20515; 225-5635; Fax:
225-6923
Web: www.house.gov/nadler
E-mail: jerrold.nadler@mail.house.gov
District Office(s): 11 Beach St., New York 10013; (212)
334-3207; Fax: (212) 334-5259; *Chief of Staff:* Amy
Rutkin; *District Administrator:* Linda Rosenthal
532 Neptune Ave., Brooklyn 11224; (718) 373-3198; Fax:
(718) 996-0039; *Brooklyn Director:* Robert M. Got-
theim
Committee Assignment(s): Judiciary; Transportation and
Infrastructure

NAPOLITANO, GRACE F., D-CALIF. (34)

Capitol Hill Office: 1407 LHOB 20515; 225-5256; Fax:
225-0027; *Chief of Staff:* Chuck Fuentes
Web: www.house.gov/napolitano
E-mail: grace@mail.house.gov
District Office(s): 1712 W. Beverly Blvd., Montebello
90640; (323) 728-0112; Fax: (323) 728-4113; *District
Director:* Ray Cordova
Committee Assignment(s): Resources; Small Business

NEAL, RICHARD E., D-MASS. (2)

Capitol Hill Office: 2236 RHOB 20515; 225-5601; Fax:
225-8112; *Chief of Staff:* Ann Jablon
Web: www.house.gov/neal
E-mail: www.house.gov/writerep
District Office(s): 1550 Main St., Springfield 01103; (413)
785-0325; Fax: (413) 747-0604; *District Director:*
Kevin Kennedy
4 Congress St., Milford 01757; (508) 634-8198; Fax:
(508) 634-8398; *Office Manager:* Virginia Purcell
Committee Assignment(s): Ways and Means

NETHERCUTT, GEORGE, R-WASH. (5)

Capitol Hill Office: 1527 LHOB 20515; 225-2006; Fax:
225-3392; *Chief of Staff:* Jim Dornan
Web: www.house.gov/nethercutt
E-mail: george.nethercutt-pub@mail.house.gov
District Office(s): W. 920 Riverside, Spokane 99201; (509)
353-2374; Fax: (509) 353-2412; *District Director:*
Nancy Fike
555 S. Main St., Colville 99114; (509) 684-3481; *Legislative Representative:* Shelly Short
29 S. Palouse St., Walla Walla 99362; (509) 529-9358;
Legislative Representative: Jeff Anderson

20 N. Pines, #24, Spokane 99206; (509) 924-7775; *Caseworker:* Stephen Taylor
Committee Assignment(s): Appropriations; Science

NEY, BOB, R-OHIO (18)

Capitol Hill Office: 1024 LHOB 20515; 225-6265; Fax:
225-3394; *Chief of Staff:* Neil Volz
Web: www.house.gov/ney
E-mail: www.house.gov/writerep
District Office(s): 3201 Belmont St., Bellaire 43906; (614)
676-1960; Fax: (614) 676-1983; *Field Representative:*
Dennis Watson
Hilton-Fairfield Bldg., #200, New Philadelphia 44663;
(330) 364-6380; Fax: (330) 364-7675; *Field Represen-
tative:* Lesely Applegarth
Masonic Temple Bldg., Zanesville 43701; (614) 452-7023;
Fax: (614) 452-7191; *District Director:* Joseph Rose
Committee Assignment(s): Banking and Financial Ser-
vices; House Administration; Joint Printing; Trans-
portation and Infrastructure

NORTHUP, ANNE M., R-KY. (3)

Capitol Hill Office: 1004 LHOB 20515; 225-5401; Fax:
225-5776; *Chief of Staff:* Terry Carmack
Web: www.house.gov/northup
E-mail: rep.northup@mail.house.gov
District Office(s): Ron Mazzoli Federal Bldg., Louisville
40202; (502) 582-5129; Fax: (502) 582-5897; *District
Director:* Sherri Craig
Committee Assignment(s): Appropriations

NORTON, ELEANOR HOLMES, D-D.C. (AL)

Capitol Hill Office: 1424 LHOB 20515; 225-8050; Fax:
225-3002; *Chief of Staff:* Donna Brazile
Web: www.house.gov/norton
E-mail: www.house.gov/writerep
District Office(s): 815 15th St. N.W., Washington 20005;
(202) 783-5065; Fax: (202) 783-5211; *District Office
Director:* Sheila Bunn
2041 Martin Luther King Jr. Ave. S.E., Washington 20020;
(202) 678-8900; Fax: (202) 678-8844; *Caseworker:*
Stephanie Knight
Committee Assignment(s): Government Reform; Trans-
portation and Infrastructure

NORWOOD, CHARLIE, R-GA. (10)

Capitol Hill Office: 1707 LHOB 20515; 225-4101; Fax:
225-0279; *Chief of Staff:* John S. Walker
Web: www.house.gov/norwood
E-mail: ga10@hr.house.gov
District Office(s): 1056 Claussen Rd., Augusta 30907;
(706) 733-7066; Fax: (706) 733-7725; *District Director:* Michael Shaffer
Laurens County Courthouse, Dublin 31021; (912) 275-
2814; Fax: (912) 275-2063; *Constituent Services Representative:* Angie Rosengart

1776 N. Jefferson St., Milledgeville 31061; (912) 453-0373; Fax: (912) 453-7302; *Constituent Services Representative:* Angie Rosengart

Committee Assignment(s): Commerce; Education and Workforce

NUSSLE, JIM, R-IOWA (2)

Capitol Hill Office: 303 CHOB 20515; 225-2911; Fax: 225-9129; *Chief of Staff:* Rich Meade

Web: www.house.gov/nussle

E-mail: nussleia@mail.house.gov

District Office(s): 23 3rd St. N.W., Mason City 50401; (515) 423-0303; *District Representative:* Jennifer Pedersen

712 W. Main St., Manchester 52057; (319) 927-5141; Fax: (319) 927-5087; *District Administrator:* Cheryl Madlom

2255 John F. Kennedy Rd., Dubuque 52002; (319) 557-7740; *District Representative:* Kathy Reed

3641 Kimball Ave., Waterloo 50702; (319) 235-1109; *District Representative:* Joseph Huber

Committee Assignment(s): Budget; Ways and Means

OBERSTAR, JAMES L., D-MINN. (8)

Capitol Hill Office: 2365 RHOB 20515; 225-6211; Fax: 225-0699; *Administrative Assistant:* William G. Richard

Web: www.house.gov/oberstar

E-mail: oberstar@mail.house.gov

District Office(s): City Hall, Elk River 55330; (612) 241-0188; Fax: (612) 241-0233; *Staff Assistant:* Ken Hasskamp

Federal Bldg., Duluth 55802; (218) 727-7474; Fax: (218) 727-8270; *District Office Director:* Jackie Morris

City Hall, Brainerd 56401; (218) 828-4400; Fax: (218) 828-1412; *Staff Assistant:* Ken Hasskamp

City Hall, Chisholm 55719; (218) 254-5761; Fax: (218) 254-5132; *Staff Assistant:* Vacant

Committee Assignment(s): Transportation and Infrastructure

OBEY, DAVID R., D-WIS. (7)

Capitol Hill Office: 2314 RHOB 20515; 225-3365; *Staff Director:* William Stone

E-mail: www.house.gov/writerep

District Office(s): Federal Bldg., Wausau 54401; (715) 842-5606; *District Representative:* Doug Hill

Committee Assignment(s): Appropriations

OLVER, JOHN W., D-MASS. (1)

Capitol Hill Office: 1027 LHOB 20515; 225-5335; Fax: 226-1224; *Chief of Staff:* Jennie Kugel

Web: www.house.gov/olver

E-mail: john.olver@mail.house.gov

District Office(s): 57 Suffolk St., Holyoke 01040; (413) 532-7010; Fax: (413) 532-6543; *District Director:* John Niedzielski

Conte Federal Bldg., Pittsfield 01201; (413) 442-0946; Fax: (413) 443-2792; *District Director:* Deborah Guachione

463 Main St., Fitchburg 01420; (508) 342-8722; Fax: (508) 343-8156; *Economic Development Aide:* Patricia Paulsen

Committee Assignment(s): Appropriations

ORTIZ, SOLOMON P., D-TEXAS (27)

Capitol Hill Office: 2136 RHOB 20515; 225-7742; Fax: 226-1134; *Chief of Staff:* Florencio Rendon

Web: www.house.gov/ortiz

E-mail: www.house.gov/writerep

District Office(s): 3649 Leopard St., Corpus Christi 78408; (512) 883-5868; Fax: (512) 884-9201; *Office Manager:* Gerald Sawyer

3505 Boca Chica Blvd., Brownsville 78521; (956) 541-1242; Fax: (956) 544-6915; *District Director:* Denise Blanchard

Committee Assignment(s): Armed Services; Resources

OSE, DOUG, R-CALIF. (3)

Capitol Hill Office: 1508 LHOB 20515; 225-5716; Fax: 226-1298; *Chief of Staff:* Marko Mlikotin

Web: www.house.gov/ose

E-mail: doug.ose@mail.house.gov

District Office(s): 722-B Main St., Woodland 95695; (530) 669-3540; Fax: (530) 669-1395; *Deputy District Director:* Julie Lilleywhite

Committee Assignment(s): Agriculture; Banking and Financial Services; Government Reform

OWENS, MAJOR R., D-N.Y. (11)

Capitol Hill Office: 2305 RHOB 20515; 225-6231; Fax: 226-0112; *Administrative Assistant:* Jacqueline Ellis

Web: www.house.gov/owens

E-mail: www.house.gov/writerep

District Office(s): 289 Utica Ave., Brooklyn 11213; (718) 773-3100; Fax: (718) 735-7143; *District Director:* Clyde Griffith

1414 Corelyou Rd., Brooklyn 11226; (718) 940-3213; Fax: (718) 940-3217

Committee Assignment(s): Education and Workforce; Government Reform

OXLEY, MICHAEL G., R-OHIO (4)

Capitol Hill Office: 2233 RHOB 20515; 225-2676; *Chief of Staff:* Jim Conzelman

Web: www.house.gov/oxley

E-mail: mike.oxley@mail.house.gov

District Office(s): 24 W. 3rd St., Mansfield 44902; (419) 522-5757; *District Representative:* R. Philip Holloway

100 E. Main Cross St., Findlay 45840; (419) 423-3210; *District Representative:* Bonnie Dunbar

3121 W. Elm Plaza, Lima 45805; (419) 999-6455; *District Representative:* Kelly Kirk

Committee Assignment(s): Commerce

PACKARD, RON, R-CALIF. (48)

Capitol Hill Office: 2372 RHOB 20515; 225-3906; Fax: 225-0134; *Chief of Staff:* Eric Mondero

Web: www.house.gov/packard

E-mail: rep.packard@mail.house.gov

District Office(s): 221 E. Vista Way, Vista 92084; (760) 631-1364; Fax: (760) 631-1367; *District Director:* Melissa Dollaghan

629 Camino de los Mares, San Clemente 92673; (949) 496-2343; Fax: (949) 496-2988; *District Representative:* Wyatt Hart

Committee Assignment(s): Appropriations

PALLONE, FRANK JR., D-N.J. (6)

Capitol Hill Office: 420 CHOB 20515; 225-4671; Fax: 225-9665; *Administrative Assistant:* Timothy J. Yehl

Web: www.house.gov/pallone

E-mail: frank.pallone@mail.house.gov

District Office(s): I.E.I. Airport Plaza, Hazlet 07730; (732) 264-9104; Fax: (732) 739-4668; *Staff Assistant:* Wanda Pettiford

504 Broadway, Long Branch 07740; (732) 571-1140; Fax: (732) 870-3890; *District Director:* Michael Beson

Kilmer Square, New Brunswick 08901; (732) 249-8892; Fax: (732) 249-1335; *District Representative:* Jim McCann

Committee Assignment(s): Commerce; Resources

PASCRELL, BILL JR., D-N.J. (8)

Capitol Hill Office: 1722 LHOB 20515; 225-5751; Fax: 225-5782; *Chief of Staff:* Ed Farmer

Web: www.house.gov/pascrell

E-mail: bill.pascrell@mail.house.gov

District Office(s): Robert A. Roe Federal Bldg., Paterson 07505; (973) 523-5152; Fax: (973) 523-0637; *District Director:* Tony Ardis; *Press Secretary:* Joe Waks

Passaic City Hall, 1st Floor, Passaic 07055; (973) 472-4510; *Special Assistant:* Roscoe Baker

Bloomfield Town Hall, #200A, Bloomfield 07003; (973) 680-1361; Fax: (973) 680-1617; *Field Representative:* Brendan Gill

Committee Assignment(s): Small Business; Transportation and Infrastructure

PASTOR, ED, D-ARIZ. (2)

Capitol Hill Office: 2465 RHOB 20515; 225-4065; Fax: 225-1655; *Administrative Assistant:* Laura Campos

Web: www.house.gov/pastor

E-mail: ed.pastor@mail.house.gov

District Office(s): 411 N. Central Ave., Phoenix 85004; (602) 256-0551; Fax: (602) 257-9103; *District Director:* Ron Piceno; *Press Secretary:* Maura Saavedra

2432 E. Broadway Blvd., Tucson 85716; (520) 624-9986; Fax: (520) 624-3872; *South Arizona District Director:* Linda Leatherman

281 W. 24th St., Yuma 85364; (520) 726-2234; Fax: (520) 726-2235; *Caseworker:* Charlene Fernandez

Committee Assignment(s): Appropriations; Standards of Official Conduct

PAUL, RON, R-TEXAS (14)

Capitol Hill Office: 203 CHOB 20515; 225-2831; Fax: 226-4871; *Chief of Staff:* Tom Lizardo

Web: www.house.gov/paul

E-mail: rep.paul@mail.house.gov

District Office(s): 200 W. 2nd St., Freeport 77541; (409) 230-0000; Fax: (409) 230-0030; *Field Representative:* Dianna Gilbert

312 S. Main St., #228, Victoria 77901; (361) 576-1231; Fax: (361) 576-0381; *District Case Manager:* Jackie Gloor

301 N. Guadalupe St., San Marcos 78666; (361) 396-1400; Fax: (361) 396-1434; *Caseworker:* Scott Green

Committee Assignment(s): Banking and Financial Services; Education and Workforce

PAYNE, DONALD M., D-N.J. (10)

Capitol Hill Office: 2209 RHOB 20515; 225-3436; Fax: 225-4160; *Chief of Staff:* Maxine James

Web: www.house.gov/payne

E-mail: donald.payne@mail.house.gov

District Office(s): Martin Luther King Jr. Federal Bldg. and U.S. Courthouse, Newark 07102; (973) 645-3213; Fax: (973) 645-5902; *District Representative:* Robert Cottingham

333 N. Broad St., Elizabeth 07208; (908) 629-0222; Fax: (908) 629-0221; *Special Assistant:* Amiri Settles

Committee Assignment(s): Education and Workforce; International Relations

PEASE, ED, R-IND. (7)

Capitol Hill Office: 119 CHOB 20515; 225-5805; *Chief of Staff:* Brian Kerns

Web: www.house.gov/pease

E-mail: pease@mail.house.gov

District Office(s): Federal Bldg., #107, Terre Haute 47808; (812) 238-1619; Fax: (812) 238-5638; *Press Secretary:* Brian Kerns

355 S. Washington St., Danville 46122; (317) 718-0307; Fax: (317) 718-0310; *Constituent Representative:* Dennis Campbell

107 Charles A. Halleck Federal Bldg., Lafayette 47901; (765) 423-1661; Fax: (765) 423-2808; *District Director:* Brian Kerns

Committee Assignment(s): Judiciary; Small Business; Transportation and Infrastructure

PELOSI, NANCY, D-CALIF. (8)

Capitol Hill Office: 2457 RHOB 20515; 225-4965; Fax: 225-8259; *Administrative Assistant:* Judith Lemons

Web: www.house.gov/pelosi

E-mail: sf.nancy@mail.house.gov

District Office(s): Burton Federal Bldg. #145378, San Francisco 94102; (415) 556-4862; Fax: (415) 861-1670; *District Director:* Carolyn Bartholomew

Committee Assignment(s): Appropriations; Select Intelligence

PETERSON, COLLIN C., D-MINN. (7)

Capitol Hill Office: 2159 RHOB 20515; 225-2165; Fax: 225-1593; *Administrative Assistant:* Mark Brownell

Web: www.house.gov/collinpeterson

E-mail: tocollin.peterson@mail.house.gov

District Office(s): 110 2nd St. South, Waite Park 56387; (320) 259-0559; Fax: (320) 259-0413; *Press Secretary:* Allison Myhre; *Staff Assistant:* Mary Bertram

Minnesota Wheat Growers Bldg., Red Lake Falls 56750; (218) 253-4356; Fax: (218) 253-4373; *Staff Assistant:* Deb Hams

714 Lake Ave., Detroit Lakes 56501; (218) 847-5056; Fax: (218) 847-5109; *District Director:* Tony Kinkel

Committee Assignment(s): Agriculture; Veterans' Affairs

PETERSON, JOHN E., R-PA. (5)

Capitol Hill Office: 307 CHOB 20515; 225-5121; Fax: 225-5796; *Administrative Assistant:* Bob Ferguson

Web: www.house.gov/johnpeterson

E-mail: john.peterson@mail.house.gov

District Office(s): 115 W. Spring St., Titusville 16354; (814) 827-3985; Fax: (814) 827-7307; *District Director:* Peter Winkler

224 Liberty St., Warren 16365; (814) 726-3910; *District Representative:* Leota Mack

1524 W. College Ave., State College 16801; (814) 238-1776; Fax: (814) 238-1918; *Caseworker:* Susan Gurekovich

Committee Assignment(s): Appropriations; Resources

PETRI, TOM, R-WIS. (6)

Capitol Hill Office: 2462 RHOB 20515; 225-2476; Fax: 225-2356; *Administrative Assistant:* Joseph Flader

Web: www.house.gov/petri

E-mail: tompetri@mail.house.gov

District Office(s): 115 Washington Ave., Oshkosh 54901; (920) 231-6333; Fax: (920) 231-0464; *Staff Assistant:* Frank Frassetto

490 W. Rolling Meadows Dr., Fond du Lac 54937; (920) 922-1180; Fax: (920) 922-4498; *District Director:* Sue Kerkman-Jung

Committee Assignment(s): Education and Workforce; Transportation and Infrastructure

PHELPS, DAVID D., D-ILL. (19)

Capitol Hill Office: 1523 LHOB 20515; 225-5201; Fax: 225-1541; *Chief of Staff:* Robert Griner

Web: www.house.gov/phelps

E-mail: gary.meltz@mail.house.gov

District Office(s): 901 State St., #1, Eldorado 62930; (618) 272-8203; Fax: (618) 273-4151; *Constituent Services Director:* Donna Hooper

119 W. Williams St., #201, Decatur 62523; (217) 425-8819; Fax: (217) 425-7053; *District Director:* Joe Handley

219 6th St., Charleston 61920; (217) 345-9166; Fax: (217) 345-9509; *District Representative:* Lela Tapella

606 N. 13th St., Lawrenceville 62439; (618) 943-6036; Fax: (618) 943-6214; *District Representative:* Shirley Stevenson

701 N. Court St., Marion 62959; (618) 997-6004; Fax: (618) 997-8493; *District Representative:* Judy Hampton

201 E. Nolen St., W. Frankfort 62896; (618) 937-6402; Fax: (618) 937-6479; *District Representative:* James Kirkpatrick

Committee Assignment(s): Agriculture; Small Business

PICKERING, CHARLES W. "CHIP" JR., R-MISS. (3)

Capitol Hill Office: 427 CHOB 20515; 225-5031; Fax: 225-5797; *Chief of Staff:* Susan Connell

Web: www.house.gov/pickering

E-mail: c.pickering@mail.house.gov

District Office(s): 110-D Airport Rd., Pearl 39208; (601) 932-2410; Fax: (601) 965-4598; *District Director:* Stanley Shows

Golden Triangle Airport, Columbus 39701; (601) 327-2766; Fax: (601) 328-4570; *District Representative:* Hank Moseley

823 22nd Ave., Meridian 39301; (601) 693-6681; Fax: (601) 693-1801; *Special Assistant:* Lynne Compton

Committee Assignment(s): Commerce

PICKETT, OWEN B., D-VA. (2)

Capitol Hill Office: 2133 RHOB 20515; *Administrative Assistant:* Jeanne Evans

District Office(s): 2710 Virginia Beach Blvd., Virginia Beach 23452; (757) 486-3710; Fax: (757) 498-8253; *Constituent Services Manager:* Norman Langrehr

3841 E. Little Creek Rd., Norfolk 23518; (757) 583-5892; Fax: (757) 583-6189; *Constituent Services Manager:* Julia Jacobs-Hopkins

Committee Assignment(s): Armed Services; Resources

PITTS, JOSEPH R., R-PA. (16)

Capitol Hill Office: 504 CHOB 20515; 225-2411; Fax: 225-2013; *Chief of Staff:* Bill Wichterman
Web: www.house.gov/pitts
E-mail: pitts.pa16@mail.house.gov
District Office(s): 50 N. Duke St., Lancaster 17602; (717) 393-0667; *District Director:* Tom Tillett
P.O. Box 837, Unionville 19375; (610) 429-1540; Fax: (610) 444-5750; *Executive Assistant:* Katie Martin
Committee Assignment(s): Armed Services; Budget; Joint Economic; Small Business

POMBO, RICHARD W., R-CALIF. (11)

Capitol Hill Office: 2411 RHOB 20515; 225-1947; Fax: 226-0861; *Chief of Staff:* Steve Ding
Web: www.house.gov/pombo/pombo.htm
E-mail: rpombo@mail.house.gov
District Office(s): 2495 W. March Lane, Stockton 95207; (209) 951-3091; Fax: (209) 951-1910; *District Director:* Stephen Reid
Committee Assignment(s): Agriculture; Resources

POMEROY, EARL, D-N.D. (AL)

Capitol Hill Office: 1533 LHOB 20515; 225-2611; Fax: 226-0893; *Chief of Staff:* Karen Frederickson
Web: www.house.gov/pomeroy
E-mail: rep.earl.pomeroy@mail.house.gov
District Office(s): Federal Bldg., #266, Fargo 58102; (701) 235-9760; Fax: (701) 235-9767; *Eastern Field Director:* Joan Carlson
220 E. Rosser Ave., Bismarck 58501; (701) 224-0355; Fax: (701) 224-0431; *State Director:* Gail Skaley
Committee Assignment(s): Agriculture; International Relations

PORTER, JOHN EDWARD, R-ILL. (10)

Capitol Hill Office: 2373 RHOB 20515; 225-4835; Fax: 225-0837; *Chief of Staff:* Robert Bradner
Web: www.house.gov/porter
E-mail: www.house.gov/writerep
District Office(s): 115 N. Arlington Heights Rd., Arlington Heights 60004; (847) 392-0303; Fax: (847) 392-5774; *Caseworker:* Mary Beth Hartmann
102 Wilmot Rd., Deerfield 60015; (847) 940-0202; Fax: (847) 940-7143; *Chief of Staff:* Ginny Hotaling
301 W. Washington St., Waukegan 60085; (847) 662-0101; Fax: (847) 662-7519; *Caseworker:* Dee Jay Kweder
Committee Assignment(s): Appropriations

PORTMAN, ROB, R-OHIO (2)

Capitol Hill Office: 238 CHOB 20515; 225-3164; Fax: 225-1992; *Chief of Staff:* Bob Schellhas
Web: www.house.gov/portman
E-mail: portmail@mail.house.gov
District Office(s): 175 E. Main St., Batavia 45103; (513) 732-2948; Fax: (513) 732-3196; *District Representative:* Helen Heistand
8044 Montgomery Rd., Cincinnati 45236; (513) 791-0381; Fax: (513) 791-1696; *District Office Manager:* Gloria Griffiths
Committee Assignment(s): Standards of Official Conduct; Ways and Means

PRICE, DAVID E., D-N.C. (4)

Capitol Hill Office: 2162 RHOB 20515; 225-1784; Fax: 225-2014; *Administrative Assistant:* Billy Moore
Web: www.house.gov/price
E-mail: david.price@mail.house.gov
District Office(s): 16 E. Rowan St., Raleigh 27609; (919) 989-8771; *District Director:* Rose Auman
315 E. Chapel Hill St., Durham 27701; (919) 688-3004; *District Liaison:* Tracy Lovett
1777 Fordham Blvd., Chapel Hill 27514; (919) 967-7924; Fax: (919) 967-8324; *Staff Assistant:* Gay Eddy
Committee Assignment(s): Appropriations; Budget

PRYCE, DEBORAH, R-OHIO (15)

Capitol Hill Office: 221 CHOB 20515; 225-2015; Fax: 225-3529; *Chief of Staff:* Tim Day
Web: www.house.gov/pryce
E-mail: pryce.oh15@mail.house.gov
District Office(s): 500 S. Front St., Columbus 43215; (614) 469-5614; Fax: (614) 469-6937; *District Director:* Marcee C. McCreary
Committee Assignment(s): Rules

QUINN, JACK, R-N.Y. (30)

Capitol Hill Office: 229 CHOB 20515; 225-3306; Fax: 226-0347; *Administrative Assistant:* Mary Lou Palmer
Web: www.house.gov/quinn
E-mail: www.house.gov/writerep
District Office(s): 403 Main St., Buffalo 14203; (716) 845-5257; Fax: (716) 847-0323; *Scheduler:* Erin Herlihy; *Communications Director:* Tracy Cone
Committee Assignment(s): Transportation and Infrastructure; Veterans' Affairs

RADANOVICH, GEORGE P., R-CALIF. (19)

Capitol Hill Office: 123 CHOB 20515; 225-4540; Fax: 225-3402; *Chief of Staff:* John W. McCamman
Web: www.house.gov/radanovich
E-mail: george.radanovich@mail.house.gov
District Office(s): 2377 W. Shaw Ave., Fresno 93711; (559) 248-0800; Fax: (559) 248-0169; *District Director:* Steven N. Samuelian
Committee Assignment(s): Budget; International Relations; Resources

RAHALL, NICK J. II, D-W.VA. (3)

Capitol Hill Office: 2307 RHOB 20515; 225-3452; Fax: 225-9061; *Administrative Assistant:* Kent Keyser

Web: www.house.gov/rahall

E-mail: nrahall@mail.house.gov

District Office(s): Federal Bldg., Bluefield 24701; (304) 325-6222; Fax: (304) 325-0552; *Community Relations:* Deborah Stevens

101 N. Court St., Lewisburg 24901; (304) 647-3228; Fax: (304) 647-3304; *Community Relations:* Teri Booth

R. K. Bldg., Logan 25601; (304) 752-4934; Fax: (304) 752-8797; *Community Relations:* Debrina Workman

106 Main St., Beckley 25801; (304) 252-5000; Fax: (304) 252-9803; *District Representative:* Kelly Dyke

845 5th Ave., Huntington 25701; (304) 522-6425; Fax: (304) 529-5716; *District Representative:* Jo Ann Cook

Committee Assignment(s): Resources; Transportation and Infrastructure

RAMSTAD, JIM, R-MINN. (3)

Capitol Hill Office: 103 CHOB 20515; 225-2871; Fax: 225-6351; *Chief of Staff:* Dean P. Peterson

Web: www.house.gov/ramstad

E-mail: mn03@mail.house.gov

District Office(s): 8120 Penn Ave. South, Bloomington 55431; (612) 881-4600; Fax: (612) 881-1943; *Office Director:* Shari Nichols; *Communications Director:* Lance N. Olson

Committee Assignment(s): Ways and Means

RANGEL, CHARLES B., D-N.Y. (15)

Capitol Hill Office: 2354 RHOB 20515; 225-4365; Fax: 225-0816; *Administrative Assistant:* Maya Rockeymoore

Web: www.house.gov/rangel

E-mail: www.house.gov/writerep

District Office(s): 163 W. 125th St., New York City 10027; (212) 663-3900; Fax: (212) 663-4277; *District Administrator:* Vivian Jones

2110 1st Ave., New York City 10029; (212) 348-9630; Fax: (212) 423-0489; *Community Representative:* Mirian Falcon-Lopez

Committee Assignment(s): Joint Taxation; Ways and Means

REGULA, RALPH, R-OHIO (16)

Capitol Hill Office: 2309 RHOB 20515; 225-3876; Fax: 225-3059; *Chief of Staff:* Connie Ann Veillette

Web: www.house.gov/regula

E-mail: www.house.gov/writerep

District Office(s): 4150 Belden Village St. N.W., Canton 44718; (330) 489-4414; Fax: (330) 489-4448; *District Director:* Daryl L. Revoldt

Committee Assignment(s): Appropriations

REYES, SILVESTRE, D-TEXAS (16)

Capitol Hill Office: 514 CHOB 20515; 225-4831; Fax: 225-2016; *Chief of Staff:* Enrique L. Gallegos

Web: www.house.gov/reyes

E-mail: silvestrereyes@mail.house.gov

District Office(s): 310 N. Mesa St., El Paso 79901; (915) 534-4400; Fax: (915) 534-7426; *District Director:* Salvador Payan

Committee Assignment(s): Armed Services; Veterans' Affairs

REYNOLDS, THOMAS M., R-N.Y. (27)

Capitol Hill Office: 413 CHOB 20515; 225-5265; Fax: 225-5910; *Chief of Staff:* Sally Vastola

Web: www.house.gov/reynolds

E-mail: www.house.gov/writerep

District Office(s): 500 Essjay Rd., Williamsville 14221; (716) 634-2324; Fax: (716) 631-7610; *District Director:* Pamela H. LaGrou

10 E. Main St., Victor 14564; (716) 742-1600; Fax: (716) 742-1976; *District Representative:* Paul Cole

Committee Assignment(s): Rules

RILEY, BOB, R-ALA. (3)

Capitol Hill Office: 322 CHOB 20515; 225-3261; Fax: 225-5827; *Administrative Assistant:* Daniel J. Gans

Web: www.house.gov/riley

E-mail: bob.riley@mail.house.gov

District Office(s): 1129 Noble St., Anniston 36201; (256) 236-5655; Fax: (256) 237-9203; *District Director:* Leland Whaley

701 Ave. A, Opelika 36801; (334) 745-6222; Fax: (334) 742-0109; *Field Representative:* Thomas Casson

114 N. 6th St., Clanton 35045; (205) 755-1522; Fax: (205) 755-1161; *Field Representative:* Betty Bennett

Committee Assignment(s): Agriculture; Armed Services; Banking and Financial Services

RIVERS, LYNN, D-MICH. (13)

Capitol Hill Office: 1724 LHOB 20515; 225-6261; Fax: 225-3404; *Administrative Assistant:* Gayle Boesky

Web: www.house.gov/rivers

E-mail: www.house.gov/writerep

District Office(s): 301 W. Michigan Ave., Ypsilanti 48197; (734) 741-4210; Fax: (734) 741-4214; *District Coordinator:* Marsha Lewis; *Scheduler:* Donna Childers

Committee Assignment(s): Budget; Science

RODRIGUEZ, CIRO D., D-TEXAS (28)

Capitol Hill Office: 323 CHOB 20515; 225-1640; Fax: 225-1641; *Chief of Staff:* Jeff Mendelsohn

Web: www.house.gov/rodriguez

E-mail: www.house.gov/writerep

District Office(s): 1313 S.E. Military Highway, San Antonio 78214; (210) 924-7383; Fax: (210) 927-6222; *District Director:* Norma Reyes

202 E. St. Joseph St., San Diego 78384; (210) 279-3907; Fax: (210) 279-8117; *South Texas Liaison:* J. M. Rodriguez

301 Lincoln St., Roma 78584; (956) 847-1111; Fax: (956) 849-3871; *Constituent Services Liaison:* Norma Pena

Committee Assignment(s): Armed Services; Veterans' Affairs

ROEMER, TIM, D-IND. (3)

Capitol Hill Office: 2352 RHOB 20515; 225-3915; Fax: 225-6798; *Chief of Staff:* Mark H. Brown

Web: www.house.gov/roemer

E-mail: tim.roemer@mail.house.gov

District Office(s): 217 N. Main St., South Bend 46601; (219) 288-3301; Fax: (219) 288-0527; *District Director:* Julie Vuckovich

Committee Assignment(s): Education and Workforce; Select Intelligence

ROGAN, JAMES E., R-CALIF. (27)

Capitol Hill Office: 126 CHOB 20515; 225-4176; Fax: 225-5828; *Chief of Staff:* Dan Revetto

Web: www.house.gov/rogan

E-mail: www.house.gov/writerep

District Office(s): 199 S. Los Robles Ave., Pasadena 91101; (626) 577-3969; Fax: (626) 577-5581; *District Office Manager:* Denise Milinkovich

Committee Assignment(s): Commerce; Judiciary

ROGERS, HAROLD, R-KY. (5)

Capitol Hill Office: 2470 RHOB 20515; 225-4601; Fax: 225-0940; *Administrative Assistant:* Kevin I. Fromer

Web: www.house.gov/rogers

E-mail: www.house.gov/writerep

District Office(s): 806 Hambley Blvd., Pikeville 41501; (606) 432-4388; Fax: (606) 432-4262; *Field Representative:* Sandra B. Runyon

601 Main St., Hazard 41701; (606) 439-0794; Fax: (606) 439-4647; *Field Representative:* Heath Preston

551 Clifty St., Somerset 42501; (606) 679-8346; Fax: (606) 678-4856; *District Administrator:* Robert L. Mitchell

Committee Assignment(s): Appropriations

ROHRABACHER, DANA, R-CALIF. (45)

Capitol Hill Office: 2338 RHOB 20515; 225-2415; Fax: 225-0145; *Chief of Staff:* Rick Dykema

Web: www.house.gov/rohrabacher

E-mail: dana@mail.house.gov

District Office(s): 101 Main St., Huntington Beach 92648; (714) 960-6483; Fax: (714) 960-7806; *District Director:* Kathleen Hollingsworth

Committee Assignment(s): International Relations; Science

ROMERO-BARCELÓ, CARLOS A., D-P.R. (AL)

Capitol Hill Office: 2443 RHOB 20515; 225-2615; Fax: 225-2154; *Chief of Staff:* Astrid Jimenez

Web: www.house.gov/romero-barcelo

E-mail: www.house.gov/writerep

District Office(s): Marvesa Bldg. #404, Ponce 00731; (787) 841-3300; Fax: (787) 841-1008; *Caseworker:* Janet Rodriguez

P.O. Box 9023958, San Juan 00902; (787) 723-6333; Fax: (787) 729-6824; *District Director:* Domingo L. Garcia

Committee Assignment(s): Education and Workforce; Resources

ROS-LEHTINEN, ILEANA, R-FLA. (18)

Capitol Hill Office: 2160 RHOB 20515; 225-3931; Fax: 225-5620; *Administrative Assistant:* Arturo Estopinan

Web: www.house.gov/ros-lehtinen

E-mail: www.house.gov/writerep

District Office(s): 9210 S.W. 72nd St., Miami 33173; (305) 275-1800; Fax: (305) 275-1801; *Administrative Assistant:* Debra Zimmerman

Committee Assignment(s): Government Reform; International Relations

ROTHMAN, STEVEN R., D-N.J. (9)

Capitol Hill Office: 1607 LHOB 20515; 225-5061; Fax: 225-5851; *Administrative Assistant:* Charles L. Young

Web: www.house.gov/rothman

E-mail: steven.rothman@mail.house.gov

District Office(s): 25 Main St., Hackensack 07601; (201) 646-0808; Fax: (201) 646-1944; *District Director:* Adam Zellner

30 Central Ave., Jersey City 07302; (201) 798-1366; Fax: (201) 798-1725; *Staff Assistant:* Al Zampella

Committee Assignment(s): International Relations; Judiciary

ROUKEMA, MARGE, R-N.J. (5)

Capitol Hill Office: 2469 RHOB 20515; 225-4465; Fax: 225-9048; *Chief of Staff:* Steve Wilson

Web: www.house.gov/roukema

E-mail: www.house.gov/writerep

District Office(s): 1200 E. Ridgewood Ave., Ridgewood 07450; (201) 447-3900; Fax: (201) 447-3749; *District Administrator:* David Zuidema

500 Route 517, Hackettstown 07840; (908) 850-4747; Fax: (908) 850-3406; *Staff Assistant:* Carol DeRise

Committee Assignment(s): Banking and Financial Services; Education and Workforce

ROYBAL-ALLARD, LUCILLE, D-CALIF. (33)

Capitol Hill Office: 2435 RHOB 20515; 225-1766; Fax: 226-0350; *Chief of Staff:* Kate G. Emmanuel

Web: www.house.gov/roybal-allard

E-mail: www.house.gov/writerep

District Office(s): Roybal Federal Bldg., Los Angeles 90012; (213) 628-9230; Fax: (213) 628-8578; *District Director:* Ana Figueroa-Davis

Committee Assignment(s): Appropriations

ROYCE, ED, R-CALIF. (39)

Capitol Hill Office: 1133 LHOB 20515; 225-4111; Fax: 226-0335; *Chief of Staff:* Joan Bates Korich

Web: www.house.gov/royce

E-mail: www.house.gov/writerep

District Office(s): 305 N. Harbor Blvd., Fullerton 92632; (562) 992-8081; Fax: (562) 992-1668; *Administrative Assistant:* Marcia Gilchrist

Committee Assignment(s): Banking and Financial Services; International Relations

RUSH, BOBBY L., D-ILL. (1)

Capitol Hill Office: 2416 RHOB 20515; 225-4372; Fax: 226-0333; *Chief of Staff:* Kimberley C. Parker

Web: www.house.gov/rush

E-mail: bobby.rush@mail.house.gov

District Office(s): 655 E. 79th St., Chicago 60619; (773) 224-6500; Fax: (773) 224-9624; *District Director:* Stan Watkins

9730 S. Western Ave., Evergreen Park 60642; (708) 422-4055; Fax: (708) 422-5199; *District Aide:* Loretta Newton

Committee Assignment(s): Commerce

RYAN, PAUL D., R-WIS. (1)

Capitol Hill Office: 1217 LHOB 20515; 225-3031; Fax: 225-3393

Web: www.house.gov/ryan

E-mail: www.house.gov/writerep

District Office(s): 20 S. Main St., Janesville 53545; (608) 752-4050; Fax: (608) 752-4711; *Chief of Staff:* Andy Speth

5712 7th Ave., Kenosha 53140; (414) 654-1901; Fax: (414) 654-2156; *Field Representative:* Dave Duecker

304 6th St., Racine 53403; (414) 637-0510; Fax: (414) 637-5689; *Field Representative:* Teresa Mora

Committee Assignment(s): Banking and Financial Services; Budget; Government Reform; Joint Economic

RYUN, JIM, R-KAN. (2)

Capitol Hill Office: 330 CHOB 20515; 225-6601; Fax: 225-7986; *Administrative Assistant:* Daniel Schneider

Web: www.house.gov/ryun

E-mail: www.house.gov/writerep

District Office(s): 800 S.W. Jackson, Topeka 66612; (785) 232-4500; Fax: (785) 232-4512; *District Director:* Michelle Butler-Latham

The Stillwell Hotel, Pittsburg 66762; (316) 232-6100; Fax: (316) 232-6105; *Regional Representative:* Jim Allen

Committee Assignment(s): Armed Services; Banking and Financial Services; Budget

SABO, MARTIN OLAV, D-MINN. (5)

Capitol Hill Office: 2336 RHOB 20515; 225-4755; Fax: 225-4886; *Chief of Staff:* Michael S. Erlandson

Web: www.house.gov/sabo

E-mail: martin.sabo@mail.house.gov

District Office(s): Commerce at the Crossings, #286, Minneapolis 55401; (612) 664-8000; Fax: (612) 664-8004; *Office Director:* Kathleen C. Anderson

Committee Assignment(s): Appropriations; Standards of Official Conduct

SALMON, MATT, R-ARIZ. (1)

Capitol Hill Office: 115 CHOB 20515; 225-2635; Fax: 225-3405; *Chief of Staff:* Glenn Hamer

Web: www.house.gov/salmon

E-mail: matt.salmon@mail.house.gov

District Office(s): 4110 N. Scottsdale Rd., Scottsdale 85251; (602) 946-3600; Fax: (602) 831-2700; *District Director:* Steve Voeller

Committee Assignment(s): Education and Workforce; International Relations

SANCHEZ, LORETTA, D-CALIF. (46)

Capitol Hill Office: 1529 LHOB 20515; 225-2965; Fax: 225-5859; *Chief of Staff:* Lee Godown

Web: www.house.gov/sanchez

E-mail: loretta@mail.house.gov

District Office(s): 12397 Lewis St., Garden Grove 92840; (714) 621-0102; Fax: (714) 621-0401; *District Director:* Mauro Morales

Committee Assignment(s): Armed Services; Education and Workforce

SANDERS, BERNARD, I-VT. (AL)

Capitol Hill Office: 2202 RHOB 20515; 225-4115; Fax: 225-6790; *Chief of Staff:* Jeff Weaver

Web: www.house.gov/bernie

E-mail: bernie@mail.house.gov

District Office(s): One Church St., Burlington 05401; (802) 862-0697; Fax: (802) 860-6370; *Outreach Director:* Phil Fiermonte

Committee Assignment(s): Banking and Financial Services; Government Reform

SANDLIN, MAX, D-TEXAS (1)

Capitol Hill Office: 214 CHOB 20515; 225-3035; Fax: 225-5866; *Chief of Staff:* Paul F. Rogers

Web: www.house.gov/sandlin

E-mail: www.house.gov/writerep

District Office(s): 1300 E. Pinecrest Dr., Marshall 75670; (903) 938-8386; Fax: (903) 935-5772; *District Assistant:* Cindy McGeorge

P.O. Box 538, Sulphur Springs 75483; (903) 885-8682; Fax: (903) 885-2976; *District Assistant:* Debbie Aikin

P.O. Box 248, New Boston 75570; (903) 628-5594; Fax: (903) 628-3155; *District Assistant:* Marie Martin

Committee Assignment(s): Banking and Financial Services; Transportation and Infrastructure

SANFORD, MARK, R-S.C. (1)

Capitol Hill Office: 1233 LHOB 20515; 225-3176; Fax: 225-3407

Web: www.house.gov/sanford

E-mail: sanford@mail.house.gov

District Office(s): 5900 Core Ave., Charleston 29406; (843) 747-4175; Fax: (843) 577-6522; *Chief of Staff:* April Paris Derr

829-E Front St., Georgetown 29440; (843) 527-6868; Fax: (843) 527-0047; *Caseworker:* Elma Harrelson

206 Laurel St., Conway 29526; (843) 248-2660; Fax: (843) 248-2824; *Caseworker:* Elma Harrelson

Committee Assignment(s): Government Reform; International Relations; Joint Economic; Science

SAWYER, TOM, D-OHIO (14)

Capitol Hill Office: 1414 LHOB 20515; 225-5231; Fax: 225-5278; *Chief of Staff:* Mary Anne Walsh

Web: www.house.gov/sawyer

E-mail: www.house.gov/writerep

District Office(s): 411 Wolf Ledges Parkway, Akron 44311; (330) 375-5710; Fax: (330) 375-5459; *District Director:* Judi Shapiro

Committee Assignment(s): Commerce

SAXTON, H. JAMES, R-N.J. (3)

Capitol Hill Office: 339 CHOB 20515; 225-4765; Fax: 225-0778; *Chief of Staff:* Mark O'Connell

Web: www.house.gov/saxton

E-mail: www.house.gov/writerep

District Office(s): One Maine Ave., Cherry Hill 08002; (609) 428-0520; Fax: (609) 428-2384; *Staff Assistant:* Dee Denton

100 High St., Mt. Holly 08060; (609) 261-5800; Fax: (609) 261-1275; *District Director:* Sandra R. Condit

7 Hadley Ave., Toms River 08753; (732) 914-2020; Fax: (732) 914-8351; *Staff Assistant:* Patricia Brogan

Committee Assignment(s): Armed Services; Joint Economic; Resources

SCARBOROUGH, JOE, R-FLA. (1)

Capitol Hill Office: 127 CHOB 20515; 225-4136; Fax: 225-3414; *Chief of Staff:* Bart B. Roper

Web: www.house.gov/scarborough

E-mail: www.house.gov/writerep

District Office(s): 4300 Bayou Blvd., Pensacola 32503; (850) 479-1183; Fax: (850) 479-9394; *District Director:* Nan Weaver

348 S.W. Miracle Strip Pkwy., Fort Walton Beach 32548; (850) 664-1266; Fax: (850) 664-0851; *District Representative:* Lois Hoyt

Committee Assignment(s): Armed Services; Government Reform; Judiciary

SCHAFFER, BOB, R-COLO. (4)

Capitol Hill Office: 212 CHOB 20515; 225-4676; Fax: 225-5870; *Chief of Staff:* Rob Nanfelt

Web: www.house.gov/schaffer

E-mail: rep.schaffer@mail.house.gov

District Office(s): 123 N. College Ave., Fort Collins 80524; (970) 493-9132; Fax: (970) 493-9144; *District Director:* Marge Klein

Madison and Main Bldg., #220E, Greeley 80631; (970) 353-3507; Fax: (970) 353-3509; *District Aide:* Will Sander

19 W. 4th St., La Junta 81050; (719) 384-7370; Fax: (719) 384-6536; *District Aide:* Jeanette Alberg

705 S. Division Ave., Sterling 80751; (970) 522-1788; Fax: (970) 522-1789; *District Director:* Marge Klein

Committee Assignment(s): Agriculture; Education and Workforce; Resources

SCHAKOWSKY, JAN, D-ILL. (9)

Capitol Hill Office: 515 CHOB 20515; 225-2111; Fax: 226-6890; *Chief of Staff:* Cathy Hurwit

Web: www.house.gov/schakowsky

E-mail: jan.schakowsky@mail.house.gov

District Office(s): 2100 Ridge Ave., Evanston 60201; (847) 328-3399; Fax: (847) 328-3425; *Suburban Director:* Jackie Brown

5533 Broadway St., Chicago 60640; (773) 506-7100; Fax: (773) 506-9202; *District Director:* Leslie Combs

6767 N. Milwaukee Ave., Niles 60714; (847) 647-6955; Fax: (847) 647-6954; *Constituent Advocate:* Roberta McCosh

Committee Assignment(s): Banking and Financial Services; Government Reform

SCOTT, ROBERT C., D-VA. (3)

Capitol Hill Office: 2464 RHOB 20515; 225-8351; Fax: 225-8354; *Chief of Staff:* Joni L. Ivey

Web: www.house.gov/scott

E-mail: www.house.gov/writerep

District Office(s): 501 N. 2nd St., Richmond 23219; (804) 644-4845; Fax: (804) 648-6026; *Legislative Assistant:* Nkechi George

2600 Washington Ave., Newport News 23607; (757) 380-1000; Fax: (757) 928-6694; *District Manager:* Gisele P. Russell

Committee Assignment(s): Education and Workforce; Judiciary

SENSENBRENNER, F. JAMES JR., R-WIS. (9)

Capitol Hill Office: 2332 RHOB 20515; 225-5101; Fax: 225-3190; *Chief of Staff:* Philip G. Kiko
Web: www.house.gov/sensenbrenner
E-mail: sensen09@mail.house.gov
District Office(s): 120 Bishops Way, Brookfield 53005; (262) 784-1111; Fax: (262) 784-9437; *District Director:* Thomas Schreibel
Committee Assignment(s): Judiciary; Science

SERRANO, JOSÉ E., D-N.Y. (16)

Capitol Hill Office: 2342 RHOB 20515; 225-4361; Fax: 225-6001; *Chief of Staff:* Ellyn M. Toscano
Web: www.house.gov/serrano
E-mail: jserrano@mail.house.gov
District Office(s): 890 Grand Concourse, Bronx 10451; (718) 538-5400; Fax: (718) 588-3652; *District Director:* Cheryl Simmons-Oliver
Committee Assignment(s): Appropriations

SESSIONS, PETE, R-TEXAS (5)

Capitol Hill Office: 1318 LHOB 20515; 225-2231; Fax: 225-5878; *Chief of Staff:* Jeffrey W. Koch
Web: www.house.gov/sessions
E-mail: petes@mail.house.gov
District Office(s): 10675 E. Northwest Highway, Dallas 75238; (214) 349-9996; Fax: (214) 349-0738; *District Director:* Chris Homan
104 E. Corsicana St., Athens 75751; (903) 675-8288; Fax: (903) 675-8351; *Regional Director:* Charlie Hawn
Committee Assignment(s): Rules

SHADEGG, JOHN, R-ARIZ. (4)

Capitol Hill Office: 430 CHOB 20515; 225-3361; Fax: 225-3462
Web: www.house.gov/shadegg
E-mail: j.shadegg@mail.house.gov
District Office(s): 301 E. Bethany Home Rd., Phoenix 85012; (602) 263-5300; Fax: (602) 248-7733; *Chief of Staff:* Sean D. Noble
Committee Assignment(s): Commerce

SHAW, E. CLAY JR., R-FLA. (22)

Capitol Hill Office: 2408 RHOB 20515; 225-3026; Fax: 225-8398; *Chief of Staff:* Clint Tarkoe
Web: www.house.gov/shaw
E-mail: www.house.gov/writerep
District Office(s): 1512 E. Broward Blvd., Ft. Lauderdale 33301; (954) 522-1800; Fax: (954) 768-0511; *District Director:* George L. Caldwell
222 Lakeview Ave., West Palm Beach 33401; (561) 832-3007; Fax: (561) 832-0227; *District Representative:* Victoria Duxbury
Committee Assignment(s): Ways and Means

SHAYS, CHRISTOPHER, R-CONN. (4)

Capitol Hill Office: 1126 LHOB 20515; 225-5541; Fax: 225-9629; *Chief of Staff:* Peter Carson
Web: www.house.gov/shays
E-mail: rep.shays@mail.house.gov
District Office(s): 10 Middle St., Bridgeport 06604; (203) 579-5870; Fax: (203) 589-0771; *District Director:* Ralph Loomis
888 Washington Blvd., Stamford 06901; (203) 357-8277; Fax: (203) 357-1050; *Caseworker:* Leslie Mostel
Committee Assignment(s): Budget; Government Reform

SHERMAN, BRAD, D-CALIF. (24)

Capitol Hill Office: 1524 LHOB 20515; 225-5911; Fax: 225-5879; *Chief of Staff:* Peter Loge
Web: www.house.gov/sherman
E-mail: brad.sherman@mail.house.gov
District Office(s): 21031 Ventura Blvd., Woodland Hills 91364; (818) 999-1990; Fax: (818) 999-2287; *District Director:* David Tierney
2100 E. Thousand Oaks Blvd., Thousand Oaks 91362; (805) 449-2372; Fax: (805) 449-2375; *Office Manager:* Larry Horner
Committee Assignment(s): Banking and Financial Services; International Relations

SHERWOOD, DONALD L., R-PA. (10)

Capitol Hill Office: 1223 LHOB 20515; 225-3731; Fax: 225-9594; *Chief of Staff:* John S. Enright
Web: www.house.gov/sherwood
E-mail: www.house.gov/writerep
District Office(s): 330 Pine St., Williamsport 17701; (570) 327-8161; Fax: (570) 327-9359; *District Director:* Ruth Calistri
538 Spruce St., Scranton 18503; (570) 346-3834; Fax: (570) 346-8577; *District Director:* Jerry Morgan
Committee Assignment(s): Armed Services; Resources; Transportation and Infrastructure

SHIMKUS, JOHN, R-ILL. (20)

Capitol Hill Office: 513 CHOB 20515; 225-5271; Fax: 225-5880; *Chief of Staff:* Craig A. Roberts
Web: www.house.gov/shimkus
E-mail: www.house.gov/writerep
District Office(s): 3130 Chatham Rd., Springfield 62704; (217) 492-5090; Fax: (217) 492-5096; *District Director:* Deb Detmers
221 E. Broadway, Centralia 62801; (618) 532-9676; Fax: (618) 344-4215; *District Aide:* Nate Newcomb
508 W. Main St., Collinsville 62234; (618) 344-3065; Fax: (618) 344-4215; *Executive Assistant:* Dora Rohan; *Press Secretary:* Steven G. Tomaszewski
Committee Assignment(s): Commerce

SHOWS, RONNIE, D-MISS. (4)

Capitol Hill Office: 509 CHOB 20515; 225-5865; Fax: 225-5886; *Chief of Staff:* Marshall Lusk
Web: www.house.gov/shows
E-mail: www.house.gov/writerep
District Office(s): 245 E. Capitol St., Jackson 39201; (601) 352-1355; Fax: (601) 352-9044; *District Director:* Glenn Rushing
243 John R. Junkin Dr., Natchez 39120; (601) 446-8825; Fax: (601) 446-7250; *Staff Assistant:* Brenda B. Vines
728 1/2 Sawmill Rd., Laurel 39440; (601) 425-4999; Fax: (601) 425-5428; *Staff Assistant:* Danny Shows
Committee Assignment(s): Transportation and Infrastructure; Veterans' Affairs

SHUSTER, BUD, R-PA. (9)

Capitol Hill Office: 2188 RHOB 20515; 225-2431; *Chief of Staff:* Darrell L. Wilson
Web: www.house.gov/shuster
E-mail: www.house.gov/writerep
District Office(s): RD 2, Altoona 16601; (814) 946-1653; *District Manager:* Judy Giansante
1214 Oldtown Rd., Clearfield 16830; (814) 765-9106; *District Aide:* Robert Young
179 E. Queen St., Chambersburg 17201; (717) 264-8308; *District Aide:* Geoffrey Mosebey
Committee Assignment(s): Transportation and Infrastructure

SIMPSON, MIKE, R-IDAHO (2)

Capitol Hill Office: 1440 LHOB 20515; 225-5531; Fax: 225-8216; *Chief of Staff:* Rhonda Sarantis
Web: www.house.gov/simpson
E-mail: www.house.gov/writerep
District Office(s): 304 N. 8th St., Boise 83702; (208) 334-1953; Fax: (208) 334-9533; *Casework Director:* Marcia Bane
628 Blue Lakes Blvd., Twin Falls 83301; (208) 734-7219; Fax: (208) 734-7244; *Agriculture Director:* Charles Barnes
490 Memorial Dr., Idaho Falls 83301; (208) 523-6701; Fax: (208) 523-2384; *Field Director:* Laurel Hall
801 E. Sherman St., Pocatello 83201; (208) 478-4160; Fax: (208) 478-4162; *Staff Assistant:* Kitty Kunz
Committee Assignment(s): Agriculture; Resources; Transportation and Infrastructure; Veterans' Affairs

SISISKY, NORMAN, D-VA. (4)

Capitol Hill Office: 2371 RHOB 20515; 225-6365; Fax: 226-1170; *Chief of Staff:* Jan B. Faircloth
Web: www.house.gov/sisisky
E-mail: www.house.gov/writerep
District Office(s): Bristol Square I, Portsmouth 23704; (757) 393-2068; Fax: (757) 399-1997; *District Representative:* Jeff Cunningham

43 Rives Rd., Petersburg 23805; (804) 732-2544; Fax: (804) 733-4652; *District Representative:* Rick Franklin
Emporia Executive Center, Emporia 23847; (804) 634-5575; Fax: (804) 634-0511; *District Representative:* Rick Franklin
Committee Assignment(s): Armed Services; Select Intelligence

SKEEN, JOE, R-N.M. (2)

Capitol Hill Office: 2302 RHOB 20515; 225-2365; Fax: 225-9599; *Chief of Staff:* Suzanne Eisold
Web: www.house.gov/skeen
E-mail: www.house.gov/writerep
District Office(s): 1065B S. Main St., Las Cruces 88005; (505) 527-1771; Fax: (505) 527-1774; *District Representative:* Dorothy C. Thomas
1717 W. 2nd St., Roswell 88201; (505) 622-0055; Fax: (505) 625-9608; *District Representative:* Alice Eppers
Committee Assignment(s): Appropriations

SKELTON, IKE, D-MO. (4)

Capitol Hill Office: 2206 RHOB 20515; 225-2876; *Administrative Assistant:* Whitney D. Frost
Web: www.house.gov/skelton
E-mail: www.house.gov/writerep
District Office(s): 514-B Northwest Seven Highway, Blue Springs 64014; (816) 228-4242; *District Representative:* Robert D. Hagedorn
1401 Southwest Blvd., Jefferson City 65109; (573) 635-3499; *Staff Assistant:* Carol Scott
219 N. Adams St., Lebanon 65536; (417) 532-7964; *Staff Assistant:* Melissa Richardson
Federal Bldg., Sedalia 65301; (660) 826-2675; *Staff Assistant:* Arletta Garrett
Committee Assignment(s): Armed Services

SLAUGHTER, LOUISE M., D-N.Y. (28)

Capitol Hill Office: 2347 RHOB 20515; 225-3615; Fax: 225-7822
Web: www.house.gov/slaughter
E-mail: louiseny@mail.house.gov
District Office(s): Federal Bldg., Rochester 14614; (716) 232-4850; Fax: (716) 232-1954; *District Aide:* Mary Eaton
Committee Assignment(s): Rules

SMITH, ADAM, D-WASH. (9)

Capitol Hill Office: 116 CHOB 20515; 225-8901; Fax: 225-5893; *Chief of Staff:* Jeff Bjornstad
Web: www.house.gov/adamsmith
E-mail: adam.smith@mail.house.gov
District Office(s): 3600 Port of Tacoma Rd. East Tacoma 98424; (253) 926-6683; Fax: (253) 926-1321; *District Director:* Linda Danforth
Committee Assignment(s): Armed Services; Resources

SMITH, CHRISTOPHER H., R-N.J. (4)

Capitol Hill Office: 2370 RHOB 20515; 225-3765; Fax: 225-7768; *Chief of Staff:* Mary McDermott Noonan
Web: www.house.gov/chrissmith
E-mail: www.house.gov/writerep
District Office(s): 1540 Kuser Rd., #A9, Hamilton 08619; (609) 585-7878; Fax: (609) 585-9155; *Special Assistant:* Jean (Pidge) Carroll; *Regional Director:* Joyce Golden
100 Lacey Rd., Whiting 08759; (732) 350-2300; Fax: (732) 350-6260; *Regional Director:* Lorretta Charbonneau
Committee Assignment(s): International Relations; Veterans' Affairs

SMITH, LAMAR, R-TEXAS (21)

Capitol Hill Office: 2231 RHOB 20515; 225-4236; Fax: 225-8628; *Chief of Staff:* John Lampmann
Web: www.house.gov/lamarsmith
E-mail: www.house.gov/writerep
District Office(s): 33 E. Twohig St., San Angelo 76903; (915) 653-3971; Fax: (915) 655-4687; *Office Manager:* Jo Anne Powell
1006 Junction Highway, Kerrville 78028; (830) 895-1414; Fax: (830) 895-2091; *Office Manager:* Kathy Mains
4305 N. Garfield, Midland 79705; (915) 687-5232; Fax: (915) 687-5234; *Staff Assistant:* Mina Fitting
1st Federal Bldg., San Antonio 78209; (210) 821-5024; Fax: (210) 821-5947; *District Director:* O'Lene Stone
904 S. Main St., Georgetown 78626; (512) 931-3500; Fax: (512) 868-9766; *Staff Assistant:* Jodell Brooks
Committee Assignment(s): Judiciary; Science; Standards of Official Conduct

SMITH, NICK, R-MICH. (7)

Capitol Hill Office: 306 CHOB 20515; 225-6276; Fax: 225-6281; *Administrative Assistant:* Kurt Schmautz
Web: www.house.gov/nicksmith
E-mail: www.house.gov/writerep
District Office(s): 110 1st St., Jackson 49201; (517) 783-4486; Fax: (517) 783-3012; *Chief of Staff:* Keith Brown
249 W. Michigan St., Battle Creek 49017; (616) 965-9066; Fax: (616) 965-9036; *Field Representative:* Greg Moore
Committee Assignment(s): Agriculture; Budget; Science

SNYDER, VIC, D-ARK. (2)

Capitol Hill Office: 1319 LHOB 20515; 225-2506; Fax: 225-5903; *Chief of Staff:* Edward D. Fry II
Web: www.house.gov/snyder
E-mail: snyder.congress@mail.house.gov
District Office(s): 3118 Federal Bldg., Little Rock 72201; (501) 324-5941; Fax: (501) 324-6029; *District Director:* John R. Yates
Committee Assignment(s): Armed Services; Veterans' Affairs

SOUDER, MARK, R-IND. (4)

Capitol Hill Office: 109 CHOB 20515; 225-4436; Fax: 225-3479; *Chief of Staff:* Christopher A. Donesa
Web: www.house.gov/souder
E-mail: souder@mail.house.gov
District Office(s): Federal Bldg., #3105, Fort Wayne 46802; (219) 424-3041; Fax: (219) 424-4042; *District Director:* Mark A. Wickersham
Committee Assignment(s): Education and Workforce; Government Reform; Resources

SPENCE, FLOYD D., R-S.C. (2)

Capitol Hill Office: 2405 RHOB 20515; 225-2452; Fax: 225-2455; *Chief of Staff:* Craig H. Metz
Web: www.house.gov/spence
E-mail: www.house.gov/writerep
District Office(s): 220 Stoneridge Dr., Columbia 29210; (803) 254-5120; Fax: (803) 779-3406; *District Administrator:* Mary T. Howard
1681 Chestnut St. N.E., Orangeburg 29116; (803) 536-4641; Fax: (803) 536-5754; *District Administrator:* Chessye B. Powell
66 E. Railroad Ave., Estill 29918; (803) 625-3177; Fax: (803) 625-4844; *Field Representative:* Mary Eleanor Bowers
807 Port Republic St., Beaufort 29901; (843) 521-2530; Fax: (843) 521-2535; *Field Representative:* Catherine Ceips
Committee Assignment(s): Armed Services; Veterans' Affairs

SPRATT, JOHN M. JR., D-S.C. (5)

Capitol Hill Office: 1536 LHOB 20515; 225-5501; Fax: 225-0464; *Chief of Staff:* Ellen Wallace Buchanan
Web: www.house.gov/spratt
E-mail: john.spratt@mail.house.gov
District Office(s): 39 E. Calhoun St., Sumter 29150; (803) 773-3362; Fax: (803) 773-7662; *District Aide:* Carolyn McCoy
88 Public Square, Darlington 29532; (803) 393-3998; Fax: (803) 393-0860; *District Aide:* Joanne Langley
Courthouse Square, Rock Hill 29731; (803) 327-1114; Fax: (803) 327-4330; *District Administrator:* Robert H. Hopkins
Committee Assignment(s): Armed Services; Budget

STABENOW, DEBBIE, D-MICH. (8)

Capitol Hill Office: 1039 LHOB 20515; 225-4872; Fax: 225-5820
Web: www.house.gov/stabenow
E-mail: debbie.stabenow@mail.house.com
District Office(s): 3401 E. Saginaw Highway, Lansing 48912; (517) 336-7777; Fax: (517) 336-7236; *Administrative Assistant:* Teresa Plachetka

2503 S. Linden Rd., Flint 48532; (810) 230-8275; Fax: (810) 230-8521; *Congressional Aide:* Connie Feuerstein

2900 E. Grand River Ave., Howell 48843; (517) 545-2195; Fax: (517) 545-2430; *Congressional Aide:* Barbara McCallahan

Committee Assignment(s): Agriculture; Science

STARK, PETE, D-CALIF. (13)

Capitol Hill Office: 239 CHOB 20515; 225-5065; Fax: 225-3805; *Administrative Assistant:* Anne Raffaelli

Web: www.house.gov/stark

E-mail: petemail@stark.house.gov

District Office(s): 39300 Civic Center Dr., Fremont 94538; (510) 494-1388; Fax: (510) 494-5852; *District Director:* Jo Cazenave

Committee Assignment(s): Joint Economic; Joint Taxation; Ways and Means

STEARNS, CLIFF, R-FLA. (6)

Capitol Hill Office: 2227 RHOB 20515; 225-5744; Fax: 225-3973; *Chief of Staff:* Jack Seum

Web: www.house.gov/stearns

E-mail: www.house.gov/writerep

District Office(s): 115 S.E. 25th Ave., Ocala 34471; (352) 351-8777; Fax: (352) 351-8011; *District Director:* Judy Moore

1726 Kingsley Ave., Orange Park 32073; (904) 269-3203; Fax: (904) 269-3343; *North District Aide:* Mary Johnson

Magnolia Place, Leesburg 34748; (352) 326-8285; Fax: (352) 326-9430; *Staff Assistant:* Catherine Potter

Committee Assignment(s): Commerce; Veterans' Affairs

STENHOLM, CHARLES W., D-TEXAS (17)

Capitol Hill Office: 1211 LHOB 20515; 225-6605; Fax: 225-2234; *Chief of Staff:* Stephen Haterius

Web: www.house.gov/stenholm

E-mail: texas17@mail.house.gov

District Office(s): 33 E. Twohig Ave., San Angelo 76903; (915) 655-7994; Fax: (915) 658-2798; *District Aide:* James Beauchamp

1501-A Columbia, Stamford 79553; (915) 773-3623; Fax: (915) 773-2833; *District Manager:* Mark Lundgren

241 Pine St., Abilene 79601; (915) 673-7221; Fax: (915) 676-9547; *Office Manager:* Lori Schoonmaker

Committee Assignment(s): Agriculture

STRICKLAND, TED, D-OHIO (6)

Capitol Hill Office: 336 CHOB 20515; 225-5705; Fax: 225-5907; *Chief of Staff:* John Haseley

Web: www.house.gov/strickland

E-mail: www.house.gov/writerep

District Office(s): 254 Front St., Marietta 45750; (740) 376-0868; Fax: (740) 376-0886; *Field Representative:* Denise Pittenger

1236 Gallia St., Portsmouth 45662; (740) 353-5171; Fax: (740) 353-8014; *District Director:* Greg Hargett

36 E. Locust St., Wilmington 45177; (937) 382-4585; Fax: (937) 383-0038; *Field Representative:* Matt Allen

200 Broadway Ave., Jackson 45640; (740) 286-5199; Fax: (740) 286-7540; *Field Representative:* Judy Newman

Committee Assignment(s): Commerce

STUMP, BOB, R-ARIZ. (3)

Capitol Hill Office: 211 CHOB 20515; 225-4576; Fax: 225-6328; *Chief of Staff:* Lisa Atkins

Web: www.house.gov/va

E-mail: www.house.gov/writerep

District Office(s): Federal Bldg., Phoenix 85025; (602) 379-6923; Fax: (602) 271-0611; *District Assistant:* Bruce C. Bartholomew

Committee Assignment(s): Armed Services; Veterans' Affairs

STUPAK, BART, D-MICH. (1)

Capitol Hill Office: 2348 RHOB 20515; 225-4735; Fax: 225-4744; *Chief of Staff:* Scott Schloegel

Web: www.house.gov/stupak

E-mail: stupak@mail.house.gov

District Office(s): 1120 E. Front St., Traverse City 49686; (231) 929-4711; Fax: (231) 929-7725; *Congressional Aide:* Jo Ann Papenfuss

111 E. Chisholm St., Alpena 49707; (517) 356-0690; Fax: (517) 356-0923; *Congressional Aide:* Sue Norkowski

1229 W. Washington St., Marquette 49855; (906) 228-3700; Fax: (906) 228-2305; *Upper Peninsula District Representative:* Matt Johnson

902 Ludington St., Escanaba 49829; (906) 786-4504; Fax: (906) 786-4534; *Congressional Aide:* Cindy Langdon

Iron County Courthouse, Crystal Falls 49920; (906) 875-3751; Fax: (906) 875-3889; *Congressional Aide:* Dee Ball

Committee Assignment(s): Commerce

SUNUNU, JOHN E., R-N.H. (1)

Capitol Hill Office: 316 CHOB 20515; 225-5456; Fax: 225-5822; *Chief of Staff:* Paul J. Collins

Web: www.house.gov/sununu

E-mail: rep.sununu@mail.house.gov

District Office(s): 1750 Elm St., Manchester 03104; (603) 641-9536; Fax: (603) 641-9561; *Constituent Services Director:* Kathy Schneiderat

104 Washington St., Dover 03820; (603) 743-4813; Fax: (603) 743-5956; *District Director:* Pam Kocher; *Scheduler:* Sheri Keniston

Committee Assignment(s): Appropriations; Budget

SWEENEY, JOHN E., R-N.Y. (22)

Capitol Hill Office: 437 CHOB 20515; 225-5614; Fax: 225-6234; *Chief of Staff:* A. Bradford Card

Web: www.house.gov/sweeney

E-mail: www.house.gov/writerep

District Office(s): 285 Broadway, Saratoga Springs 12866; (518) 587-9800; Fax: (518) 587-1228; *Caseworker:* Barbara Plamer; *Interim Scheduler:* Matt Masterson

21 Bay St., Glens Falls 12801; (518) 792-3031; *Caseworker:* Charlene Aspland

560 Warren St., Hudson 12534; (518) 828-0181; Fax: (518) 828-1657; *Caseworker:* Patricia Hart

Committee Assignment(s): Banking and Financial Services; Small Business; Transportation and Infrastructure

TALENT, JAMES M., R-MO. (2)

Capitol Hill Office: 1022 LHOB 20515; 225-2561; Fax: 225-2563; *Administrative Assistant:* Mark Strand

Web: www.house.gov/talent

E-mail: rep.talent@mail.house.gov

District Office(s): 555 N. New Ballas Rd., St. Louis 63141; (314) 872-9561; Fax: (314) 872-3728; *District Director:* Tony Paraino

820 S. Main St., St. Charles 63301; (636) 949-6826; Fax: (636) 949-3832; *District Director:* Tony Paraino

Committee Assignment(s): Armed Services; Education and Workforce; Small Business

TANCREDO, TOM, R-COLO. (6)

Capitol Hill Office: 1123 LHOB 20515; 225-7882; Fax: 226-4623; *Chief of Staff:* Jacque Ponder

Web: www.house.gov/tancredo

E-mail: tom.tancredo@mail.house.gov

District Office(s): 5601 S. Broadway, Littleton 80121; (720) 283-9772; Fax: (720) 283-9776; *Staff Assistant:* Beth Cooper

Committee Assignment(s): Education and Workforce; International Relations; Resources

TANNER, JOHN, D-TENN. (8)

Capitol Hill Office: 1127 LHOB 20515; 225-4714; Fax: 225-1765; *Chief of Staff:* Vickie Walling

Web: www.house.gov/tanner

E-mail: john.tanner@mail.house.gov

District Office(s): 8120 Highway 51 North, Millington 38053; (901) 873-5690; Fax: (901) 873-5692; *Staff Assistant:* Margaret Black

Federal Bldg., Jackson 38301; (901) 423-4848; Fax: (901) 427-1537; *Constituent Services Director:* Shirlene Mercer

203 W. Church St., Union City 38261; (901) 885-7070; Fax: (901) 885-7094; *District Director:* Joe H. Hill

Committee Assignment(s): Ways and Means

TAUSCHER, ELLEN O., D-CALIF. (10)

Capitol Hill Office: 1239 LHOB 20515; 225-1880; Fax: 225-5914; *Chief of Staff:* Peter Muller

Web: www.house.gov/tauscher

E-mail: ellen.tauscher@mail.house.gov

District Office(s): 100 Civic Plaza, Dublin 94568; (925) 829-0813; Fax: (925) 829-7318; *Deputy District Director:* Jennifer Renk

1801 N. California Blvd., Walnut Creek 94596; (925) 932-8899; Fax: (925) 932-8159; *District Director:* Michelle Westover Henry

420 W. 3rd St., Antioch 94509; (925) 757-7187; Fax: (925) 757-7056; *Assistant Field Representative:* Natalie Miladinovich

Committee Assignment(s): Armed Services; Transportation and Infrastructure

TAUZIN, W. J. "BILLY," R-LA. (3)

Capitol Hill Office: 2183 RHOB 20515; 225-4031; Fax: 225-0563

Web: www.house.gov/tauzin

E-mail: www.house.gov/writerep

District Office(s): Federal Bldg., Houma 70360; (504) 876-3033; Fax: (504) 872-4449; *Office Manager:* Jeri Theriot

Ascension Parish Courthouse East, Gonzales 70737; (504) 621-8490; Fax: (504) 621-8493; *Chief of Staff:* Martin Cancienne

8201 W. Judge Perez Dr., Chalmette 70043; (504) 271-1707; Fax: (504) 271-1756; *District Representative:* Peggy T. Bourgeois

210 E. Main St., New Iberia 70560; (318) 367-8231; Fax: (318) 369-7084; *Staff Assistant:* Jan Viator

Committee Assignment(s): Commerce; Resources

TAYLOR, CHARLES H., R-N.C. (11)

Capitol Hill Office: 231 CHOB 20515; 225-6401; *Chief of Staff:* Roger France

Web: www.house.gov/charlestaylor

E-mail: repcharles.taylor@mail.house.gov

District Office(s): 22 S. Pack Square, Asheville 28801; (828) 251-1988; *District Representative:* Nancy Day

Cherokee County Courthouse, Murphy 28906; (828) 837-3249; *District Representative:* Judy Edwards

Committee Assignment(s): Appropriations

TAYLOR, GENE, D-MISS. (5)

Capitol Hill Office: 2311 RHOB 20515; 225-5772; Fax: 225-7074; *Chief of Staff:* Wayne Weidie

Web: www.house.gov/genetaylor

E-mail: www.house.gov/writerep

District Office(s): Federal Bldg., Hattiesburg 39401; (601) 582-3246; Fax: (601) 582-3247; *District Representative:* Jerry Martin

2424 14th St., Gulfport 39501; (228) 864-7670; Fax: (228) 864-3099; *District Manager:* Beau Gex

1314 Government St., Ocean Springs 39564; (228) 872-7950; Fax: (228) 872-7949; *Office Manager:* Brian Martin

Committee Assignment(s): Armed Services; Transportation and Infrastructure

TERRY, LEE, R-NEB. (2)

Capitol Hill Office: 1728 LHOB 20515; 225-4155; Fax: 226-5452; *Chief of Staff:* Steve Sutton

Web: www.house.gov/terry

E-mail: www.house.gov/writerep

District Office(s): 600 N. 93rd St., Omaha 68114; (402) 397-9944; Fax: (402) 397-8787; *District Director:* Molly Lloyd

Committee Assignment(s): Banking and Financial Services; Government Reform; Transportation and Infrastructure

THOMAS, BILL, R-CALIF. (21)

Capitol Hill Office: 2208 RHOB 20515; 225-2915; Fax: 225-8798; *Administrative Assistant:* Cathy Abernathy

Web: www.house.gov/billthomas

E-mail: www.house.gov/writerep

District Office(s): 319 W. Murray Ave., Visalia 93291; (559) 627-6549; Fax: (559) 627-6924; *Caseworker:* Marjorie Lancaster

4100 Truxtun Ave., Bakersfield 93309; (661) 327-3611; Fax: (661) 631-9535; *Field Representative:* Kevin McCarthy

Committee Assignment(s): House Administration; Joint Library; Joint Printing; Joint Taxation; Ways and Means

THOMPSON, BENNIE, D-MISS. (2)

Capitol Hill Office: 1408 LHOB 20515; 225-5876; Fax: 225-5898; *Administrative Assistant:* Marsha G. McCraven

Web: www.house.gov/thompson

E-mail: thompsonms2nd@mail.house.gov

District Office(s): Quitman County Courthouse, Marks 38646; (662) 326-9003; *Field Representative:* Samuel McCray

107 W. Madison St., Bolton 39041; (601) 866-9003; Fax: (601) 866-9036; *District Director:* Charlie Horhn

910 Courthouse Lane, Greenville 38701; (662) 335-9003; Fax: (662) 334-1304; *Field Director:* Marilyn Hansell

City Hall, Mound Bayou 38762; (662) 741-9003; Fax: (662) 741-9002; *Field Representative:* Geri Havard

509 Highway 82 West, Greenwood 38930; (662) 455-9300; Fax: (662) 453-0118; *Office Manager:* Trina Nichols

Committee Assignment(s): Agriculture; Budget

THOMPSON, MIKE, D-CALIF. (1)

Capitol Hill Office: 415 CHOB 20515; 225-3311; Fax: 225-4335

Web: www.house.gov/mthompson

E-mail: m.thompson@mail.house.gov

District Office(s): 317 3rd St., Eureka 95501; (707) 269-9595; Fax: (707) 269-9598; *District Representative:* Liz Murguia

The Fort Bldg., Ft. Bragg 95437; (707) 962-0933; Fax: (707) 962-0934; *Field Representative:* Kendall Smith

1040 Main St., Napa 94559; (707) 226-9898; Fax: (707) 251-9800; *Chief of Staff:* Ed Matovcik

Committee Assignment(s): Agriculture; Armed Services

THORNBERRY, WILLIAM M. "MAC," R-TEXAS (13)

Capitol Hill Office: 131 CHOB 20515; 225-3706; Fax: 225-3486; *Administrative Assistant:* Clay Sell

Web: www.house.gov/thornberry

E-mail: www.house.gov/writerep

District Office(s): 724 Polk St., Amarillo 79101; (806) 371-8844; Fax: (806) 371-7044; *Chief of Staff:* Sylvia Nugent

4245 Kemp, Wichita Falls 76308; (940) 692-1700; *Office Manager:* Brent Oden

Committee Assignment(s): Armed Services; Budget; Resources

THUNE, JOHN, R-S.D. (AL)

Capitol Hill Office: 1005 LHOB 20515; 225-2801; Fax: 225-5823; *Chief of Staff:* Herb Jones

Web: www.house.gov/thune

E-mail: jthune@mail.house.gov

District Office(s): 2310 W. 41st St., Sioux Falls 57105; (605) 331-1010; Fax: (605) 331-0651; *District Director:* Troy Larson

10 6th Ave., S.W., Aberdeen 57401; (605) 622-7988; Fax: (605) 622-7995; *Northeast Area Director:* Mark Vaux

2525 W. Main St., Rapid City 57702; (605) 342-5135; Fax: (605) 342-5291; *West River Director:* Kory Menken

Committee Assignment(s): Agriculture; Small Business; Transportation and Infrastructure

THURMAN, KAREN L., D-FLA. (5)

Capitol Hill Office: 440 CHOB 20515; 225-1002; Fax: 226-0329; *Chief of Staff:* Nora Matus

Web: www.house.gov/thurman

E-mail: kthurman@mail.house.gov

District Office(s): 5700 S.W. 34th St., Gainesville 32608; (352) 336-6614; Fax: (352) 336-6376; *Caseworker:* Denise Huff

2224 Highway 44 West, Inverness 34456; (352) 344-3044; Fax: (352) 637-1769; *District Administrator:* Anne Morgan

5609 U.S. 19 South, New Port Richey 34652; (727) 849-4496; Fax: (727) 845-0462; *Caseworker:* Peg Heal

Committee Assignment(s): Ways and Means

TIAHRT, TODD, R-KAN. (4)

Capitol Hill Office: 428 CHOB 20515; 225-6216; Fax: 225-3489; *Administrative Assistant:* Matt Schlapp

Web: www.house.gov/tiahrt

E-mail: tiahrt@mail.house.gov

District Office(s): 155 N. Market St., Wichita 67202; (316) 262-8992; Fax: (316) 262-5309; *District Director:* Pam Porvaznik; *Communications Director:* Dave Hanna
Committee Assignment(s): Appropriations

TIERNEY, JOHN F., D-MASS. (6)

Capitol Hill Office: 120 CHOB 20515; 225-8020; Fax: 225-5915; *Administrative Assistant:* Elliot Kaye
Web: www.house.gov/tierney
E-mail: www.house.gov/writerep
District Office(s): 17 Peabody Square, Peabody 01960; (978) 531-1669; Fax: (978) 531-1996; *District Director:* Gary Barrett; *Communications Director:* Carolyn Stewart
Lynn City Hall, Lynn 01902; (781) 595-7375; Fax: (781) 595-7492; *Constituent Representative:* Rose Mary Sargent
160 Main St., Haverhill 01830; (978) 469-1942; Fax: (978) 469-9021; *Constituent Representative:* Colin Mahoney
Committee Assignment(s): Education and Workforce; Government Reform

TOOMEY, PATRICK J., R-PA. (15)

Capitol Hill Office: 511 CHOB 20515; 225-6411; Fax: 226-0778; *Chief of Staff:* Chuck Pike
Web: www.house.gov/toomey
E-mail: www.house.gov/writerep
District Office(s): 2020 Hamilton St., Allentown 18104; (610) 439-8861; Fax: (610) 439-1918; *District Director:* Morrie Pulley
Committee Assignment(s): Banking and Financial Services; Budget; Small Business

TOWNS, EDOLPHUS, D-N.Y. (10)

Capitol Hill Office: 2232 RHOB 20515; 225-5936; Fax: 225-1018; *Chief of Staff:* Brenda Pillors
Web: www.house.gov/towns
E-mail: www.house.gov/writerep
District Office(s): 1110 Pennsylvania Ave., Brooklyn 11207; (718) 272-1175; Fax: (718) 272-1203; *Special Assistant:* Linda Price
26 Court St., Brooklyn 11241; (718) 855-8018; Fax: (718) 858-4542; *New York Chief of Staff:* Karen Johnson
1670 Fulton St., Brooklyn 11213; (718) 774-5682; Fax: (718) 774-5730; *District Director:* Jennifer Joseph
Committee Assignment(s): Commerce; Government Reform

TRAFICANT, JAMES A. JR., D-OHIO (17)

Capitol Hill Office: 2446 RHOB 20515; 225-5261; Fax: 225-3719; *Chief of Staff:* Paul Marcone
Web: www.house.gov/traficant
E-mail: telljim@mail.house.gov

District Office(s): 109 W. 3rd St., East Liverpool 43920; (330) 385-5921; Fax: (330) 385-7582; *Staff Representative:* Carrie Davis
5555 Youngstown-Warren Rd., Niles 44446; (330) 652-5649; Fax: (330) 652-2637; *Staff Representative:* George Buccella
125 Market St., Youngstown 44503; (330) 743-1914; Fax: (330) 743-4920; *Casework Services Director:* Anthony Traficanti
Committee Assignment(s): Transportation and Infrastructure

TURNER, JIM, D-TEXAS (2)

Capitol Hill Office: 208 CHOB 20515; 225-2401; Fax: 225-5955; *Chief of Staff:* Elizabeth Hurley
Web: www.house.gov/turner
E-mail: tx02@mail.house.gov
District Office(s): 701 N. 1st St., Lufkin 75901; (409) 637-1770; Fax: (409) 632-8588; *District Director:* Jerry Huffman
420 W. Green Ave., Orange 77630; (409) 883-4990; Fax: (409) 883-5149; *Field Representative:* Ann Gray
Committee Assignment(s): Armed Services; Government Reform

UDALL, MARK, D-COLO. (2)

Capitol Hill Office: 128 CHOB 20515; 225-2161; Fax: 226-7840
Web: www.house.gov/markudall
E-mail: www.house.gov/writerep
District Office(s): 1333 W. 120th Ave., Westminster 80234; (303) 457-4500; Fax: (303) 457-4504; *Chief of Staff:* Alan Salazar
Committee Assignment(s): Resources; Science; Small Business

UDALL, TOM, D-N.M. (3)

Capitol Hill Office: 502 CHOB 20515; 225-6190; Fax: 226-1331; *Chief of Staff:* Gerald Gonzalez
Web: www.house.gov/tomudall
E-mail: tom.udall@mail.house.gov
District Office(s): Joseph M. Montoya Federal Bldg., Santa Fe 87501; (505) 984-8950; *Director:* Michele Jacquez-Ortiz *Communications Coordinator:* Deborah Martinez
P.O. Box 868, Clovis 88102; (505) 763-7616; *District Representative:* Becky Gear
800 Municipal Dr., Farmington 87401; (505) 324-1005; *District Representative:* Pete Valencia
3900 Southern Blvd. S.E., Rio Rancho 87124; (505) 994-0499; *District Representative:* Bill White
Committee Assignment(s): Resources; Small Business; Veterans' Affairs

UNDERWOOD, ROBERT A., D-GUAM (AL)

Capitol Hill Office: 2418 RHOB 20515; 225-1188; Fax: 226-0341; *Chief of Staff:* Esther Kiaaina
Web: www.house.gov/underwood
E-mail: guamtodc@mail.house.gov
District Office(s): 120 Father Duenas Ave., Hagatna 96910; (671) 477-4272; Fax: (671) 477-2587; *Press Secretary:* Cathy Gault; *District Director:* Vincent A. Leon Guerrero
Committee Assignment(s): Armed Services; Resources

UPTON, FRED, R-MICH. (6)

Capitol Hill Office: 2333 RHOB 20515; 225-3761; Fax: 225-4986; *Chief of Staff:* Joan Hillebrands
Web: www.house.gov/upton
E-mail: talk2.fsu@mail.house.gov
District Office(s): 157 S. Kalamazoo Mall, Kalamazoo 49006; (616) 385-0039; Fax: (616) 385-2888; *District Manager:* Jan Harroun
800 Ship St., St. Joseph 49085; (616) 982-1986; Fax: (616) 982-0237; *District Director:* John Proos
Committee Assignment(s): Commerce; Education and Workforce

VELÁZQUEZ, NYDIA M., D-N.Y. (12)

Capitol Hill Office: 2241 RHOB 20515; 225-2361; Fax: 226-0327; *Chief of Staff:* Michael Day
Web: www.house.gov/velazquez
E-mail: www.house.gov/writerep
District Office(s): 173 Ave. B, New York 10009; (212) 673-3997; Fax: (212) 473-5242; *Community Coordinator:* Miguel Hernandez
815 Broadway, Brooklyn 11206; (718) 599-3658; Fax: (718) 599-4537; *N.Y. Scheduler:* Graciela Howard; *District Director:* Minerva Urrutia
16 Court St., Brooklyn 11201; (718) 222-5819; *Staff Assistant:* Leticia Rodriguez
Committee Assignment(s): Banking and Financial Services; Small Business

VENTO, BRUCE F., D-MINN. (4)

Capitol Hill Office: 2413 RHOB 20515; 225-6631; Fax: 225-1968; *Administrative Assistant:* Larry Romans
Web: www.house.gov/vento
E-mail: vento@mail.house.gov
District Office(s): 111 E. Kellogg Blvd., St. Paul 55101; (651) 224-4503; Fax: (651) 224-0575; *District Director:* John Van Hecke
Committee Assignment(s): Banking and Financial Services; Resources

VISCLOSKY, PETER J., D-IND. (1)

Capitol Hill Office: 2313 RHOB 20515; 225-2461; Fax: 225-2493; *Chief of Staff:* Charles E. Brimmer
Web: www.house.gov/visclosky
E-mail: www.house.gov/writerep

District Office(s): 215 W. 35th Ave., Gary 46408; (219) 884-1177; Fax: (219) 884-0273; *District Director:* Mark Savinski
City Hall, Valparaiso 46383; (219) 464-0315
6070 Central Ave., Portage 46368; (219) 763-2904
Committee Assignment(s): Appropriations

VITTER, DAVID, R-LA. (1)

Capitol Hill Office: 2406 RHOB 20515; 225-3015; Fax: 225-0739; *Chief of Staff:* Marty T. Driesler
Web: www.house.gov/vitter
E-mail: www.house.gov/writerep
District Office(s): 2800 Veterans Blvd., Metairie 70002; (504) 589-2753; Fax: (504) 589-2607; *District Director:* David Doss
300 E. Thomas St., Hammond 70401; (504) 542-9616; Fax: (504) 542-9577; *Staff Assistant:* Carol McGuckin
Committee Assignment(s): Government Reform; Judiciary; Transportation and Infrastructure

WALDEN, GREG, R-ORE. (2)

Capitol Hill Office: 1404 LHOB 20515; 225-6730; Fax: 225-5774; *Chief of Staff:* Brian MacDonald
Web: www.house.gov/walden
E-mail: greg.walden@mail.house.gov
District Office(s): 843 E. Main St., Medford 97504; (541) 776-4646; Fax: (541) 779-0204; *District Director:* John Snider
Committee Assignment(s): Agriculture; Government Reform; Resources

WALSH, JAMES T., R-N.Y. (25)

Capitol Hill Office: 2351 RHOB 20515; 225-3701; Fax: 225-4042; *Administrative Assistant:* Arthur Jutton
Web: www.house.gov/walsh
E-mail: rep.james.walsh@mail.house.gov
District Office(s): 1 Lincoln St., Auburn 13021; (315) 255-0649; Fax: (315) 255-1369; *Staff Assistant:* Susan Dwyer
45 Church St., Cortland 13045; (607) 758-3918; Fax: (607) 758-9007; *Staff Assistant:* Terre Dennis
P.O. Box 7306, Syracuse 13261; (315) 423-5657; Fax: (315) 423-5669; *Press Secretary:* James H. O'Connor; *District Manager:* Ginny Carmody
Committee Assignment(s): Appropriations

WAMP, ZACH, R-TENN. (3)

Capitol Hill Office: 423 CHOB 20515; 225-3271; Fax: 225-3494; *Chief of Staff:* Helen Hardin
Web: www.house.gov/wamp
E-mail: www.house.gov/writerep
District Office(s): Joel W. Solomon Bldg., Chattanooga 37402; (423) 756-2342; Fax: (423) 756-6613; *Deputy Chief of Staff:* Robin Derryberry

Federal Bldg., Oak Ridge 37830; (423) 483-3366; Fax: (423) 576-3221; *District Director:* Melissa Copelan
Committee Assignment(s): Appropriations; Budget

WATERS, MAXINE, D-CALIF. (35)

Capitol Hill Office: 2344 RHOB 20515; 225-2201; Fax: 225-7854; *Chief of Staff:* Rodney Johnson
Web: www.house.gov/waters
E-mail: www.house.gov/writerep
District Office(s): 10124 S. Broadway, Los Angeles 90037; (323) 757-8900; Fax: (323) 757-9506; *District Director:* Mike Murase
Committee Assignment(s): Banking and Financial Services; Judiciary

WATKINS, WES, R-OKLA. (3)

Capitol Hill Office: 1401 LHOB 20515; 225-4565; Fax: 225-5966; *Chief of Staff:* Leslie Belcher
Web: www.house.gov/watkins
E-mail: wes.watkins@mail.house.gov
District Office(s): Carl Albert Federal Bldg., McAlester 74501; (918) 423-5951; Fax: (918) 423-1457; *Caseworker:* Sue Bollinger
115 N. Broadway, Ada 74820; (580) 436-1980; Fax: (580) 332-7421; *Caseworker:* Sonja Jolley
1903 N. Boomer Rd., Stillwater 74075; (405) 743-1400; Fax: (405) 743-0680; *District Director:* Lyndal Whitworth
Committee Assignment(s): Ways and Means

WATT, MELVIN, D-N.C. (12)

Capitol Hill Office: 1230 LHOB 20515; 225-1510; Fax: 225-1512; *Administrative Assistant:* Joyce Brayboy Dalton
Web: www.house.gov/watt
E-mail: nc12.public@mail.house.gov
District Office(s): 324 N. College St., Charlotte 28202; (704) 344-9950; Fax: (704) 344-9971; *District Director:* Don N. Baker
123 S. Main St., Salisbury 28144; (704) 797-9950; *District Liaison:* Morgan C. Jackson
8 W. 3rd St., Winston-Salem 27101; (336) 721-9950; Fax: (336) 721-0026; *District Liaison:* Angelia B. Shackelford
Committee Assignment(s): Banking and Financial Services; Joint Economic; Judiciary

WATTS, J. C. JR., R-OKLA. (4)

Capitol Hill Office: 1210 LHOB 20515; 225-6165; Fax: 225-3512; *Chief of Staff:* Pam Pryor
Web: www.house.gov/watts
E-mail: rep.jcwatts@mail.house.gov
District Office(s): 2420 Springer Dr., Norman 73069; (405) 329-6500; Fax: (405) 321-7369; *District Director:* Janet Henthorn

601 S.W. D Ave., Lawton 73501; (580) 357-2131; Fax: (580) 357-7477; *Field Representative:* Becky Womack
Committee Assignment(s): Armed Services

WAXMAN, HENRY A., D-CALIF. (29)

Capitol Hill Office: 2204 RHOB 20515; 225-3976; Fax: 225-4099; *Chief of Staff:* Philip Schiliro
Web: www.house.gov/waxman
E-mail: www.house.gov/writerep
District Office(s): 8436 W. 3rd St., Los Angeles 90048; (323) 651-1040; Fax: (323) 655-8037; *District Office Director:* Lisa Ellman
Committee Assignment(s): Commerce; Government Reform

WEINER, ANTHONY D., D-N.Y. (9)

Capitol Hill Office: 501 CHOB 20515; 225-6616; Fax: 226-7253; *Chief of Staff:* Kevin Ryan
Web: www.house.gov/weiner
E-mail: www.house.gov/writerep
District Office(s): 1901 Emmons Ave., Brooklyn 11235; (718) 332-9001; Fax: (718) 332-9010; *Chief of Staff:* Christopher Bloitti
118-21 Queens Blvd., Forest Hills 11375; (718) 261-7170
90-16 Rockaway Beach Blvd., Rockaway 11693; (718) 318-9255
Committee Assignment(s): Judiciary; Science

WELDON, CURT, R-PA. (7)

Capitol Hill Office: 2452 RHOB 20515; 225-2011; Fax: 225-8137; *Chief of Staff:* Michael Barbera
Web: www.house.gov/curtweldon
E-mail: curtpa07@mail.house.gov
District Office(s): 1554 Garrett Rd., Upper Darby 19082; (610) 259-0700; Fax: (215) 596-4665; *District Director:* Alex Rahn
30 S. Valley Rd., Paoli 19301; (610) 640-9064; Fax: (610) 640-9071; *District Director:* Alex Rahn
Committee Assignment(s): Armed Services; Science

WELDON, DAVE, R-FLA. (15)

Capitol Hill Office: 332 CHOB 20515; 225-3671; Fax: 225-3516; *Chief of Staff:* Dana G. Gartzke
Web: www.house.gov/weldon
E-mail: fla15@mail.house.gov
District Office(s): Bldg. C, Melbourne 32940; (407) 632-1776; Fax: (407) 639-8595; *District Director:* Brian Chase
Indian River County Courthouse, Vero Beach 32960; (561) 778-3534; Fax: (561) 562-5543; *Caseworker:* Janel Young
Committee Assignment(s): Banking and Financial Services; Science

WELLER, JERRY, R-ILL. (11)

Capitol Hill Office: 424 CHOB 20515; 225-3635; Fax: 225-3521; *Administrative Assistant:* Jim Hayes
Web: www.house.gov/weller
E-mail: www.house.gov/writerep
District Office(s): 2701 Black Rd., Joliet 60435; (815) 740-2028; Fax: (815) 740-2037; *District Director:* Reed Wilson
Committee Assignment(s): Ways and Means

WEXLER, ROBERT, D-FLA. (19)

Capitol Hill Office: 213 CHOB 20515; 225-3001; Fax: 225-5974; *Chief of Staff:* Suzanne M. Stoll
Web: www.house.gov/wexler
E-mail: www.house.gov/writerep
District Office(s): Suite 100, Boca Raton 33431; (561) 988-6302; Fax: (561) 988-6423; *District Administrator:* Wendi Lipsich
Margate City Hall, Margate 33063; (954) 972-6454; Fax: (954) 972-2982; *Broward Coordinator:* Lynne Brenes
Committee Assignment(s): International Relations; Judiciary

WEYGAND, BOB, D-R.I. (2)

Capitol Hill Office: 215 CHOB 20515; 225-2735; Fax: 225-5976
Web: www.house.gov/weygand
E-mail: robert.weygand@mail.house.gov
District Office(s): The Summit East, Warwick 02886; (401) 732-9400; *Chief of Staff:* James M. Russo
Committee Assignment(s): Banking and Financial Services; Budget

WHITFIELD, EDWARD, R-KY. (1)

Capitol Hill Office: 236 CHOB 20515; 225-3115; Fax: 225-3547; *Policy Director:* Larry Van Hoose
Web: www.house.gov/whitfield
E-mail: www.house.gov/writerep
District Office(s): Monroe County Courthouse, Tompkinsville 42167; (502) 487-9509; Fax: (502) 487-0019; *Field Representative:* Sandy Simpson
317 W. Ninth St., Hopkinsville 42240; (502) 885-8079; Fax: (502) 885-8598; *Field Representative:* Michael Pape
222 1st St., Henderson 42420; (502) 826-4180; Fax: (502) 826-6783; *Field Representative:* Joe Bradford
#104, Paducah 42001; (502) 442-6901; Fax: (502) 442-6805; *Field Representative:* Heidi Eyer
Committee Assignment(s): Commerce

WICKER, ROGER, R-MISS. (1)

Capitol Hill Office: 206 CHOB 20515; 225-4306; Fax: 225-3549; *Chief of Staff:* John Keast
Web: www.house.gov/wicker
E-mail: roger.wicker@mail.house.gov

District Office(s): P.O. Box 1482, Tupelo 38802; (601) 844-5437; Fax: (601) 844-9096; *District Director:* Bubba Lollar
P.O. Box 70, Southaven 38671; (601) 342-3942; Fax: (601) 342-3883; *District Director:* Merle Flowers
Committee Assignment(s): Appropriations

WILSON, HEATHER A., R-N.M. (1)

Capitol Hill Office: 226 CHOB 20515; 225-6316; Fax: 225-4975; *Chief of Staff:* Marjorie Strayer
Web: www.house.gov/wilson
E-mail: ask.heather@mail.house.gov
District Office(s): 625 Silver Ave. S.W., Albuquerque 87102; (505) 346-6781; Fax: (505) 346-6723; *District Director:* Julie Dreike
Committee Assignment(s): Commerce; Select Intelligence

WISE, BOB, D-W.VA. (2)

Capitol Hill Office: 2367 RHOB 20515; 225-2711; Fax: 225-7856; *Administrative Assistant:* Lowell Johnson
Web: www.house.gov/wise
E-mail: bobwise@mail.house.gov
District Office(s): 4710 Chimney Dr., Charleston 25302; (304) 965-0865; Fax: (304) 965-0872; *Administrative Assistant:* Lowell E. Johnson
222 W. John St., Martinsburg 25401; (304) 264-8810; Fax: (304) 264-8815; *District Director:* Kara Bennett
Committee Assignment(s): Government Reform; Transportation and Infrastructure

WOLF, FRANK R., R-VA. (10)

Capitol Hill Office: 241 CHOB 20515; 225-5136; Fax: 225-0437; *Administrative Assistant:* Charles E. White
Web: www.house.gov/wolf
E-mail: www.house.gov/writerep
District Office(s): 13873 Park Center Rd., Herndon 20171; (703) 709-5800; Fax: (703) 709-5802; *Constituent Services Director:* Judy McCary
110 N. Cameron St., Winchester 22601; (540) 667-0990; Fax: (540) 678-0402; *Constituent Services Assistant:* Donna Crowley
Committee Assignment(s): Appropriations

WOOLSEY, LYNN, D-CALIF. (6)

Capitol Hill Office: 439 CHOB 20515; 225-5161; Fax: 225-5163; *Chief of Staff:* Janice L. Morris
Web: www.house.gov/woolsey
E-mail: lynn.woolsey@mail.house.gov
District Office(s): Northgate Bldg., San Rafael 94904; (415) 507-9554; Fax: (415) 507-9601; *Field Representative:* Tondrea Stewart
1101 College Ave., Santa Rosa 95404; (707) 542-7182; Fax: (707) 542-2745; *District Director:* Leslie G. Horak
Committee Assignment(s): Education and Workforce; Science

WU, DAVID, D-ORE. (1)

Capitol Hill Office: 510 CHOB 20515; 225-0855; Fax: 225-9497; *Chief of Staff:* Julie Tippens

Web: www.house.gov/wu

E-mail: david.wu@mail.house.gov

District Office(s): 620 S.W. Main St., Portland 97205; (503) 326-2901; Fax: (503) 326-5066; *District Director:* Mary K. Elliott

Committee Assignment(s): Education and Workforce; Science

WYNN, ALBERT R., D-MD. (4)

Capitol Hill Office: 407 CHOB 20515; 225-8699; Fax: 225-8714; *Chief of Staff:* Curt S. Clifton

Web: www.house.gov/wynn

E-mail: albert.wynn@mail.house.gov

District Office(s): 6009 Oxon Hill Rd., Oxon Hill 20745; (301) 839-5570; Fax: (301) 567-3853; *Community Relations Coordinator:* Bill Boston

8601 Georgia Ave., Silver Spring 20910; (301) 588-7328; Fax: (301) 588-1225; *Community Liaison:* Melody Khalatbari

9200 Basil Court, Springdale 20774; (301) 773-4094; Fax: (301) 925-9674; *District Director:* Annie E. Peters

Committee Assignment(s): Commerce

YOUNG, C. W. BILL, R-FLA. (10)

Capitol Hill Office: 2407 RHOB 20515; 225-5961; Fax: 225-9764; *Administrative Assistant:* Harry J. Glenn

Web: www.house.gov/young

E-mail: www.house.gov/writerep

District Office(s): 801 W. Bay Dr., Largo 33770; (727) 581-0980; *District Assistant:* George N. Cretekos

360 Central Ave., St. Petersburg 33701; (727) 893-3191; *District Assistant:* Sharon Ghezzi

Committee Assignment(s): Appropriations

YOUNG, DON, R-ALASKA (AL)

Capitol Hill Office: 2111 RHOB 20515; 225-5765; Fax: 225-0425; *Administrative Assistant:* Colin A. Chapman

Web: www.house.gov/donyoung

E-mail: www.house.gov/writerep

District Office(s): 222 W. 7th Ave., Anchorage 99513; (907) 271-5978; Fax: (907) 271-5950; *District Director:* Bill Sharrow

130 Trading Bay Rd., Kenai 99611; (907) 283-5808; Fax: (907) 283-4363; *Staff Assistant:* Peggy Arness

Federal Bldg., Fairbanks 99701; (907) 456-0210; Fax: (907) 456-0279; *Special Assistant:* Royce Chapman

Federal Bldg., #401, Juneau 99801; (907) 586-7400; Fax: (907) 586-8922; *Staff Assistant:* Lucy Hudson

851 E. Westpoint Dr., Wasilla 99654; (907) 376-7665; *Staff Assistant:* Carol Gustafson

109 Main St., Ketchikan 99901; (907) 225-6880; *Staff Assistant:* Sherrie Slick

Committee Assignment(s): Resources; Transportation and Infrastructure

Joint Committees of Congress

The joint committees of Congress are listed below. The listing includes the room number, telephone number, and jurisdiction for each committee. Membership is drawn from both the Senate and House and from both parties. Membership is given in order of seniority on the committees.

Republicans are shown on the left in roman type; Democrats are on the right in italic type. When a senator serves as chair, the vice chair usually is a representative, and vice versa. The office of chair usually rotates from one chamber to the other at the beginning of each Congress. Area code for all telephone numbers is (202).

JOINT ECONOMIC

Phone: 224-5171; **Room:** SD-G01
Executive Director: Shelly Hymes; 226-3234; 1538 LHOB

Studies and investigates all recommendations in the president's annual Economic Report to Congress. Reports findings and recommendations to the House and Senate.

Senate Members

Connie Mack, Fla., chair	*Jeff Bingaman, N.M., ranking member*
William V. Roth Jr., Del.	*Paul S. Sarbanes, Md.*
Robert F. Bennett, Utah	*Edward M. Kennedy, Mass.*
Rod Grams, Minn.	*Charles S. Robb, Va.*
Sam Brownback, Kan.	
Jeff Sessions, Ala.	

House Members

H. James Saxton, N.J., vice chair	*Pete Stark, Calif., ranking member*
Mark Sanford, S.C.	*Carolyn B. Maloney, N.Y.*
John T. Doolittle, Calif.	*David Minge, Minn.*
Tom Campbell, Calif.	*Melvin Watt, N.C.*
Joseph R. Pitts, Pa.	
Paul D. Ryan, Wis.	

JOINT LIBRARY

Phone: 224-6352 **Room:** SR-305
House Staff Contact: Catherine Fanucchi; 225-8281; 1309 LHOB
Senate Staff Contact: Ed Edens; 224-6352; SR-305

Management and expansion of the Library of Congress; receipt of gifts for the benefit of the library; development and maintenance of the Botanic Garden; placement of statues and other works of art in the Capitol.

Senate Members

Ted Stevens, Alaska, chair	*Christopher J. Dodd, Conn., ranking member*
Mitch McConnell, Ky.	*Daniel Patrick Moynihan, N.Y.*
Thad Cochran, Miss.	

House Members

Bill Thomas, Calif., vice chair	*Steny H. Hoyer, Md., ranking member*
John A. Boehner, Ohio	*Jim Davis, Fla.*
Vernon J. Ehlers, Mich.	

JOINT PRINTING

Phone: 225-8281 **Room:** SH-818
Staff Director: Eric C. Peterson; 225-8281; 1309 LHOB
Minority Staff Director: Michael L. Harrison; 225-8281; 1309 LHOB

Probes inefficiency and waste in the printing, binding, and distribution of federal government publications. Oversees arrangement and style of the *Congressional Record*.

Senate Members

Mitch McConnell, Ky., vice chair	*Diane Feinstein, Calif., ranking member*
Thad Cochran, Miss.	*Daniel K. Inouye, Hawaii*
Don Nickles, Okla.	

House Members

Bill Thomas, Calif., chair	*Steny H. Hoyer, Md.*
John A. Boehner, Ohio	*Chaka Fattah, Pa.*
Bob Ney, Ohio	

JOINT TAXATION

Phone: 225-3621 **Room:** 1015 LHOB
Chief of Staff: Lindy Paull; 225-3621; 1015 LHOB

Operation, effects, and administration of the federal system of internal revenue taxes; measures and methods for simplification of taxes.

Senate Members

William V. Roth Jr., Del., chair

Charles E. Grassley, Iowa

Orrin G. Hatch, Utah

Daniel Patrick Moynihan, N.Y., ranking member

Max Baucus, Mont.

House Members

Bill Archer, Texas, vice chair

Philip M. Crane, Ill.

Bill Thomas, Calif.

Charles B. Rangel, N.Y., ranking member

Pete Stark, Calif.

Senate Committees

The standing and select committees of the U.S. Senate are listed below. The listing includes the room number, telephone number, party ratio, and jurisdiction for each full committee. Subcommittees are listed alphabetically under each committee. Membership is listed in order of seniority on the committee or subcommittee.

Members of the majority party, Republicans, are shown in roman type; the minority party, Democrats, are shown in italic type. The partisan committees of the Senate are listed on p. 822. Members of these committees are listed in alphabetical order, not by seniority. Area code for all telephone numbers is (202).

AGRICULTURE, NUTRITION, AND FORESTRY

Phone: 224-2035 **Room:** SR-328A
Staff Director: Keith Luse; 224-2035; SR-328A
Minority Staff Director: Mark Halverson; 224-2035; SR-328A

Agricultural economics and research; agricultural extension services and experiment stations; agricultural production, marketing, and stabilization of prices; agriculture and agricultural commodities; animal industry and diseases; crop insurance and soil conservation; farm credit and farm security; food from fresh waters; food stamp programs; forestry, and forest reserves and wilderness areas other than those created from the public domain; home economics; human nutrition; inspection of livestock, meat, and agricultural products; pests and pesticides; plant industry, soils, and agricultural engineering; rural development, rural electrification, and watersheds; school nutrition programs. The chair and ranking minority member shall serve as non-voting members ex officio of all subcommittees.

Party Ratio: R 10–D 8

Richard G. Lugar, Ind., chair	*Tom Harkin, Iowa*, ranking member
Jesse Helms, N.C.	*Patrick J. Leahy, Vt.*
Thad Cochran, Miss.	*Kent Conrad, N.D.*
Mitch McConnell, Ky.	*Tom Daschle, S.D.*
Paul Coverdell, Ga.	*Max Baucus, Mont.*
Pat Roberts, Kan.	*Bob Kerrey, Neb.*
Peter G. Fitzgerald, Ill.	*Tim Johnson, S.D.*
Charles E. Grassley, Iowa	*Blanche Lincoln, Ark.*
Larry E. Craig, Idaho	
Rick Santorum, Pa.	

Subcommittees

Forestry, Conservation, and Rural Revitalization
Phone: 224-2035 **Room:** SR-328A

Craig, chair	*Conrad*
Santorum	*Leahy*
Coverdell	*Daschle*
Fitzgerald	*Baucus*
Grassley	

Marketing, Inspection, and Product Promotion
Phone: 224-2035 **Room:** SR-328A

Coverdell, chair	*Baucus*
Helms	*Conrad*
Cochran	*Kerrey*
McConnell	

Production and Price Competitiveness
Phone: 224-2035 **Room:** SR-328A

Roberts, chair	*Kerrey*
Helms	*Daschle*
Cochran	*Johnson*
Grassley	*Lincoln*
Craig	

Research, Nutrition, and General Legislation
Phone: 224-2035 **Room:** SR-328A

Fitzgerald, chair	*Leahy*
McConnell	*Johnson*
Roberts	*Lincoln*
Santorum	

APPROPRIATIONS

Phone: 224-3471 **Room:** S-128 CAP
Staff Director: Steve Cortese; 224-3471; S-128 CAP
Minority Staff Director: James H. English; 224-7200; S-206 CAP

Appropriation of revenue; rescission of appropriations; new spending authority under the Congressional Budget Act. The chair and ranking minority member are non-voting members ex officio of all subcommittees.

Party Ratio: R 15-D 13

Ted Stevens, Alaska, chair	*Robert C. Byrd, W.Va., ranking member*
Thad Cochran, Miss.	*Daniel K. Inouye, Hawaii*
Arlen Specter, Pa.	*Ernest F. Hollings, S.C.*
Pete V. Domenici, N.M.	*Patrick J. Leahy, Vt.*
Christopher S. Bond, Mo.	*Frank R. Lautenberg, N.J.*
Slade Gorton, Wash.	*Tom Harkin, Iowa*
Mitch McConnell, Ky.	*Barbara A. Mikulski, Md.*
Conrad Burns, Mont.	*Harry Reid, Nev.*
Richard C. Shelby, Ala.	*Herb Kohl, Wis.*
Judd Gregg, N.H.	*Patty Murray, Wash.*
Robert F. Bennett, Utah	*Byron L. Dorgan, N.D.*
Ben Nighthorse Campbell, Colo.	*Dianne Feinstein, Calif.*
Larry E. Craig, Idaho	*Richard J. Durbin, Ill.*
Kay Bailey Hutchison, Texas	
Jon Kyl, Ariz.	

Subcommittees

Agriculture, Rural Development, and Related Agencies
Phone: 224-5270 **Room:** SD-136

Cochran, chair	*Kohl*
Specter	*Harkin*
Bond	*Dorgan*
Gorton	*Feinstein*
McConnell	*Durbin*
Burns	

Commerce, Justice, State, and Judiciary
Phone: 224-7277 **Room:** S-146A CAP

Gregg, chair	*Hollings*
Stevens	*Inouye*
Domenici	*Lautenberg*
McConnell	*Mikulski*
Hutchison	*Leahy*
Campbell	

Defense
Phone: 224-7255 **Room:** SD-119

Stevens, chair	*Inouye*
Cochran	*Hollings*
Specter	*Byrd*
Domenici	*Leahy*
Bond	*Lautenberg*
McConnell	*Harkin*
Shelby	*Dorgan*
Gregg	*Durbin*
Hutchison	

District of Columbia
Phone: 224-1526 **Room:** S-128 CAP

Hutchison, chair	*Durbin*
Kyl	

Energy and Water Development
Phone: 224-7260 **Room:** SD-127

Domenici, chair	*Reid*
Cochran	*Byrd*
Gorton	*Hollings*
McConnell	*Murray*
Bennett	*Kohl*
Burns	*Dorgan*
Craig	

Foreign Operations
Phone: 224-2104 **Room:** SD-142

McConnell, chair	*Leahy*
Specter	*Inouye*
Gregg	*Lautenberg*
Shelby	*Harkin*
Bennett	*Mikulski*
Campbell	*Murray*
Bond	

Interior
Phone: 224-7233 **Room:** SD-131

Gorton, chair	*Byrd*
Stevens	*Leahy*
Cochran	*Hollings*
Domenici	*Reid*
Burns	*Dorgan*
Bennett	*Kohl*
Gregg	*Feinstein*
Campbell	

Labor, Health and Human Services, and Education
Phone: 224-7230 **Room:** SD-186

Specter, chair	*Harkin*
Cochran	*Hollings*
Gorton	*Inouye*
Gregg	*Reid*
Craig	*Kohl*
Hutchison	*Murray*
Stevens	*Feinstein*
Kyl	

Legislative Branch
Phone: 224-8921 **Room:** S-125 CAP

Bennett, chair	*Feinstein*
Stevens	*Durbin*
Craig	

Military Construction
Phone: 224-7204 **Room:** SD-140

Burns, chair	*Murray*
Hutchison	*Reid*

APPROPRIATIONS (continued)

Craig   *Inouye*
Kyl

Transportation
Phone: 224-2175 **Room:** SD-133

Shelby, chair	*Lautenberg*
Domenici	*Byrd*
Specter	*Mikulski*
Bond	*Reid*
Gorton	*Kohl*
Bennett	*Murray*
Campbell	

Treasury and General Government
Phone: 224-7337 **Room:** SD-188

Campbell, chair	*Dorgan*
Shelby	*Mikulski*
Kyl	

VA, HUD, and Independent Agencies
Phone: 224-7211 **Room:** SD-130

Bond, chair	*Mikulski*
Burns	*Leahy*
Shelby	*Lautenberg*
Craig	*Harkin*
Hutchison	*Byrd*
Kyl	

ARMED SERVICES

Phone: 224-3871 **Room:** SR-228
Staff Director: Les Brownlee; 224-3871; SR-228
Minority Staff Director: David Lyles; 224-3871; SR-228

Defense and defense policy generally; aeronautical and space activities peculiar to or primarily associated with the development of weapons systems or military operations; maintenance and operation of the Panama Canal, including the Canal Zone; military research and development; national security aspects of nuclear energy; naval petroleum reserves (except Alaska); armed forces generally; Selective Service System; strategic and critical materials. The chair and ranking minority member are non-voting members ex officio of all subcommittees of which they are not regular members.

Party Ratio: R 11-D 9

John W. Warner, Va., chair	*Carl Levin, Mich., ranking member*
Strom Thurmond, S.C.	*Edward M. Kennedy, Mass.*
John McCain, Ariz.	*Jeff Bingaman, N.M.*
Robert C. Smith, N.H.	*Robert C. Byrd, W.Va.*
James M. Inhofe, Okla.	*Charles S. Robb, Va.*
Rick Santorum, Pa.	*Joseph I. Lieberman, Conn.*
Olympia J. Snowe, Maine	
Pat Roberts, Kan.	*Max Cleland, Ga.*
Wayne Allard, Colo.	*Mary L. Landrieu, La.*

Tim Hutchinson, Ark.   *Jack Reed, R.I.*
Jeff Sessions, Ala.

Subcommittees

Airland Forces
Phone: 224-3871 **Room:** SR-228

Santorum, chair	*Lieberman*
Inhofe	*Cleland*
Roberts	*Landrieu*
Allard	*Reed*
Hutchinson	

Emerging Threats and Capabilities
Phone: 224-3871 **Room:** SR-228

Roberts, chair	*Bingaman*
Smith (N.H.)	*Kennedy*
Santorum	*Byrd*
Snowe	*Lieberman*
Sessions	

Personnel
Phone: 224-3871 **Room:** SR-228

Hutchinson, chair	*Cleland*
Thurmond	*Kennedy*
McCain	*Robb*
Snowe	*Reed*
Allard	

Readiness and Management Support
Phone: 224-3871 **Room:** SR-228

Inhofe, chair	*Robb*
Thurmond	*Bingaman*
McCain	*Byrd*
Santorum	*Cleland*
Roberts	*Landrieu*
Hutchinson	

Seapower
Phone: 224-3871 **Room:** SR-228

Snowe, chair	*Kennedy*
McCain	*Robb*
Smith (N.H.)	*Reed*
Sessions	

Strategic Forces
Phone: 224-3871 **Room:** SR-228

Allard, chair	*Landrieu*
Thurmond	*Bingaman*
Smith (N.H.)	*Byrd*
Inhofe	*Lieberman*
Sessions	

BANKING, HOUSING, AND URBAN AFFAIRS

Phone: 224-7391 **Room:** SD-534
Staff Director: Wayne A. Abernathy; 224-7391; SD-534
Minority Staff Director: Steven Harris; 224-7391; SD-542

Banks, banking, and financial institutions; price controls; deposit insurance; economic stabilization and growth; defense production; export and foreign trade promotion; export controls; federal monetary policy, including Federal Reserve System; financial aid to commerce and industry; issuance and redemption of notes; money and credit, including currency and coinage; nursing home construction; public and private housing, including veterans' housing; renegotiation of government contracts; urban development and mass transit; international economic policy. The chair and ranking minority member are non-voting members ex officio of all subcommittees of which they are not regular members.

Party Ratio: R 11-D 9

Phil Gramm, Texas, chair	*Paul S. Sarbanes, Md., ranking member*
Richard C. Shelby, Ala.	*Christopher J. Dodd, Conn.*
Connie Mack, Fla.	
Robert F. Bennett, Utah	*John Kerry, Mass.*
Rod Grams, Minn.	*Richard H. Bryan, Nev.*
Wayne Allard, Colo.	*Tim Johnson, S.D.*
Michael B. Enzi, Wyo.	*Jack Reed, R.I.*
Chuck Hagel, Neb.	*Charles E. Schumer, N.Y.*
Rick Santorum, Pa.	*Evan Bayh, Ind.*
Jim Bunning, Ky.	*John Edwards, N.C.*
Michael D. Crapo, Idaho	

Subcommittees

Economic Policy
Phone: 224-7391 **Room:** SD-534

Mack, chair	*Reed*
Bennett	*Dodd*
Enzi	*Kerry*
Bunning	

Financial Institutions
Phone: 224-7391 **Room:** SD-534

Bennett, chair	*Bryan*
Hagel	*Reed*
Mack	*Schumer*
Enzi	*Edwards*
Santorum	*Johnson*
Bunning	*Bayh*
Crapo	*Sarbanes*
Shelby	
Allard	

Housing and Transportation
Phone: 224-7391 **Room:** SD-534

Allard, chair	*Kerry*
Santorum	*Edwards*
Grams	*Dodd*
Shelby	*Bryan*
Gramm	

International Trade and Finance
Phone: 224-7391 **Room:** SD-534

Enzi, chair	*Johnson*
Crapo	*Kerry*
Grams	*Bayh*
Hagel	*Schumer*
Mack	

Securities
Phone: 224-7391 **Room:** SD-534

Grams, chair	*Dodd*
Bunning	*Schumer*
Shelby	*Bayh*
Allard	*Johnson*
Bennett	*Bryan*
Hagel	*Reed*
Santorum	*Edwards*
Crapo	

BUDGET

Phone: 224-0642 **Room:** SD-621
Staff Director: G. William Hoagland; 224-0642; SD-621
Minority Staff Director: Bruce King; 224-3961; SD-634

Federal budget generally; concurrent budget resolutions; Congressional Budget Office.

Party Ratio: R 12-D 10

Pete V. Domenici, N.M., chair	*Frank R. Lautenberg, N.J., ranking member*
Charles E. Grassley, Iowa	*Ernest F. Hollings, S.C.*
Don Nickles, Okla.	*Kent Conrad, N.D.*
Phil Gramm, Texas	*Paul S. Sarbanes, Md.*
Christopher S. Bond, Mo.	*Barbara Boxer, Calif.*
Slade Gorton, Wash.	*Patty Murray, Wash.*
Judd Gregg, N.H.	*Ron Wyden, Ore.*
Olympia J. Snowe, Maine	*Russell D. Feingold, Wis.*
Spencer Abraham, Mich.	*Tim Johnson, S.D.*
Bill Frist, Tenn.	*Richard J. Durbin, Ill.*
Rod Grams, Minn.	
Gordon H. Smith, Ore.	

COMMERCE, SCIENCE, AND TRANSPORTATION

Phone: 224-5115 **Room:** SD-508
Staff Director: Mark Buse; 224-1251; SR-254
Minority Staff Dir.: Ivan A. Schlager; 224-0427; SD-558

Interstate commerce and transportation generally; Coast Guard; coastal zone management; communications; highway safety; inland waterways, except construction; marine fisheries; Merchant Marine and navigation; non-military aeronautical and space sciences; oceans, weather, and atmospheric activities; interoceanic canals generally; regulation of consumer products and services; science, engineering, and technology research, development and policy; sports; standards and measurement;

COMMERCE, SCIENCE AND TRANSPORTATION

(continued)

transportation and commerce aspects of outer continental shelf lands. The chair and ranking minority member are non-voting members ex officio of all subcommittees of which they are not regular members.

Party Ratio: R 11–D 9

John McCain, Ariz., chair	*Ernest F. Hollings, S.C., ranking member*
Ted Stevens, Alaska	*Daniel K. Inouye, Hawaii*
Conrad Burns, Mont.	*John D. Rockefeller IV, W.Va.*
Slade Gorton, Wash.	
Trent Lott, Miss.	*John Kerry, Mass.*
Kay Bailey Hutchison, Texas	*John B. Breaux, La.*
	Richard H. Bryan, Nev.
Olympia J. Snowe, Maine	*Byron L. Dorgan, N.D.*
John Ashcroft, Mo.	*Ron Wyden, Ore.*
Bill Frist, Tenn.	*Max Cleland, Ga.*
Spencer Abraham, Mich.	
Sam Brownback, Kan.	

Subcommittees

Aviation

Phone: 224-4852 **Room:** SH-427

Gorton, chair	*Rockefeller*
Stevens	*Hollings*
Burns	*Inouye*
Lott	*Bryan*
Hutchison	*Breaux*
Ashcroft	*Dorgan*
Frist	*Wyden*
Snowe	*Cleland*
Brownback	
Abraham	

Communications

Phone: 224-5184 **Room:** SH-227

Burns, chair	*Hollings*
Stevens	*Inouye*
Gorton	*Kerry*
Lott	*Breaux*
Ashcroft	*Rockefeller*
Hutchison	*Dorgan*
Abraham	*Wyden*
Frist	*Cleland*
Brownback	

Consumer Affairs, Foreign Commerce, and Tourism

Phone: 224-5183 **Room:** SH-425

Ashcroft, chair	*Bryan*
Gorton	*Breaux*
Abraham	
Burns	
Brownback	

Manufacturing and Competitiveness

Phone: 224-1745 **Room:** SD-508

Abraham, chair	*Dorgan*
Snowe	*Bryan*
Ashcroft	*Hollings*
Frist	*Rockefeller*
Brownback	

Oceans and Fisheries

Phone: 224-8172 **Room:** SH-428

Snowe, chair	*Kerry*
Stevens	*Inouye*
Gorton	*Breaux*
Hutchison	

Science, Technology, and Space

Phone: 224-8172 **Room:** SH-428

Frist, chair	*Breaux*
Burns	*Rockefeller*
Hutchison	*Kerry*
Stevens	*Dorgan*
Abraham	

Surface Transportation and Merchant Marine

Phone: 224-4852 **Room:** SH-427

Hutchison, chair	*Inouye*
Stevens	*Breaux*
Burns	*Dorgan*
Snowe	*Bryan*
Frist	*Wyden*
Abraham	*Cleland*
Ashcroft	
Brownback	

ENERGY AND NATURAL RESOURCES

Phone: 224-4971 **Room:** SD-304
Staff Director: Andrew Lundquist; 224-4971; SD-304
Minority Staff Director: Robert "Bob" Simon; 224-4103; SD-312

Energy policy, regulation, conservation, research, and development; coal; energy-related aspects of deep-water ports; hydroelectric power, irrigation, and reclamation; mines, mining, and minerals generally; national parks, recreation areas, wilderness areas, wild and scenic rivers, historic sites, military parks, and battlefields; naval petroleum reserves in Alaska; non-military development of nuclear energy; oil and gas production and distribution; public lands and forests; solar energy systems; territorial possessions of the United States. The chair and ranking minority member are non-voting members ex officio of all subcommittees of which they are not regular members.

Party Ratio: R 11–D 9

Frank H. Murkowski, Alaska, chair	*Jeff Bingaman, N.M., ranking member*

Pete V. Domenici, N.M.
Don Nickles, Okla.
Larry E. Craig, Idaho
Ben Nighthorse
    Campbell, Colo.
Craig Thomas, Wyo.
Gordon H. Smith, Ore.
Jim Bunning, Ky.
Peter G. Fitzgerald, Ill.
Slade Gorton, Wash.
Conrad Burns, Mont.

Daniel K. Akaka, Hawaii
Byron L. Dorgan, N.D.
Bob Graham, Fla.
Ron Wyden, Ore.
Tim Johnson, S.D.
Mary L. Landrieu, La.
Evan Bayh, Ind.
Blanche Lincoln, Ark.

Subcommittees

Energy Research, Development, Production, and Regulation
Phone: 224-6567 **Room:** SD-308

Nickles, chair
Domenici
Bunning
Gorton
Craig
Fitzgerald
Smith (Ore.)

Graham
Akaka
Dorgan
Johnson
Landrieu
Bayh

Forests and Public Land Management
Phone: 224-6170 **Room:** SD-306

Craig, chair
Burns
Fitzgerald
Campbell
Domenici
Thomas
Smith (Ore.)

Wyden
Akaka
Johnson
Landrieu
Bayh
Lincoln

National Parks, Historic Preservation, and Recreation
Phone: 224-6969 **Room:** SD-354

Thomas, chair
Campbell
Burns
Nickles
Bunning
Gorton

Akaka
Graham
Landrieu
Bayh
Lincoln

Water and Power
Phone: 224-8115 **Room:** SD-308

Smith (Ore.),
    chair
Gorton
Bunning
Craig
Campbell

Dorgan
Graham
Wyden
Lincoln

ENVIRONMENT AND PUBLIC WORKS

Phone: 224-6176 **Room:** SD-410
Majority Staff Director: Dave Conover; 224-7854; SD-410
Minority Staff Contact: Tom Sliter

Environmental policy, research, and development; air, water, and noise pollution; construction and maintenance of highways; environmental aspects of outer continental shelf lands; environmental effects of toxic substances other than pesticides; fisheries and wildlife; flood control and improvements of rivers and harbors; non-military environmental regulation and control of nuclear energy; ocean dumping; public buildings and grounds; public works, bridges, and dams; regional economic development; solid waste disposal and recycling; water resources. The chair is a non-voting member ex officio of all subcommittees.
Party Ratio: R 10-D 8

Robert C. Smith,
    N.H., chair
John W. Warner, Va.
James M. Inhofe, Okla.
Craig Thomas, Wyo.
Christopher S. Bond, Mo.
George V. Voinovich, Ohio
Michael D. Crapo, Idaho
Robert F. Bennett, Utah
Kay Bailey Hutchison,
    Texas
Lincoln Chafee, R.I.

Max Baucus, Mont.,
    ranking member
Daniel Patrick Moynihan,
    N.Y.
Frank R. Lautenberg, N.J.
Harry Reid, Nev.
Bob Graham, Fla.
Joseph I. Lieberman,
    Conn.
Barbara Boxer, Calif.
Ron Wyden, Ore.

Subcommittees

Clean Air, Wetlands, Private Property, and Nuclear Safety
Phone: 224-6176 **Room:** SD-410

Inhofe, chair
Voinovich
Bennett
Hutchison

Graham
Lieberman
Boxer

Fisheries, Wildlife, and Water
Phone: 224-6176 **Room:** SD-410

Crapo, chair
Thomas
Bond
Warner
Bennett
Hutchison

Reid
Lautenberg
Wyden
Graham
Boxer

Superfund, Waste Control, and Risk Assessment
Phone: 224-6176 **Room:** SD-410

Chafee, chair
Warner
Inhofe
Crapo

Lautenberg
Moynihan
Boxer

ENVIRONMENT AND PUBLIC WORKS (continued)

Transportation and Infrastructure

Phone: 224-6176 **Room:** SD-410

Voinovich, chair	*Baucus*
Warner	*Moynihan*
Bond	*Reid*
Inhofe	*Graham*
Thomas	*Lieberman*
Chafee	

FINANCE

Phone: 224-4515 **Room:** SD-219

Majority Staff Dir. and Chief Counsel: Frank Polk; 224-4515; SD-219

Minority Staff Director: David Podoff; 224-5315; SH-203

Revenue measures generally; taxes; tariffs and import quotas; reciprocal trade agreements; customs; revenue sharing; federal debt limit; Social Security; health programs financed by taxes or trust funds. The chair and ranking minority member are non-voting members ex officio of all subcommittees of which they are not regular members.

Party Ratio: R 11-D 9

William V. Roth Jr., Del., chair	*Daniel Patrick Moynihan, N.Y., ranking member*
Charles E. Grassley, Iowa	*Max Baucus, Mont.*
Orrin G. Hatch, Utah	*John D. Rockefeller IV, W.Va.*
Frank H. Murkowski, Alaska	*John B. Breaux, La.*
Don Nickles, Okla.	*Kent Conrad, N.D.*
Phil Gramm, Texas	*Bob Graham, Fla.*
Trent Lott, Miss.	*Richard H. Bryan, Nev.*
James M. Jeffords, Vt.	*Bob Kerrey, Neb.*
Connie Mack, Fla.	*Charles S. Robb, Va.*
Fred Thompson, Tenn.	
Paul Coverdell, Ga.	

Subcommittees

Health Care

Phone: 224-4515 **Room:** SD-219

Coverdell, chair	*Rockefeller*
Roth	*Baucus*
Jeffords	*Breaux*
Grassley	*Conrad*
Gramm	*Graham*
Nickles	*Bryan*
Hatch	*Kerrey*
Thompson	

International Trade

Phone: 224-4515 **Room:** SD-219

Grassley, chair	*Moynihan*
Thompson	*Baucus*

Murkowski	*Rockefeller*
Roth	*Breaux*
Lott	*Conrad*
Gramm	*Graham*
Hatch	*Kerrey*
Jeffords	*Robb*

Long-Term Growth and Debt Reduction

Phone: 224-4515 **Room:** SD-219

Murkowski, chair	*Graham*
Mack	*Bryan*

Social Security and Family Policy

Phone: 224-4515 **Room:** SD-219

Nickles, chair	*Breaux*
Gramm	*Moynihan*
Lott	*Rockefeller*
Jeffords	*Kerrey*
Thompson	*Robb*

Taxation and IRS Oversight

Phone: 224-4515 **Room:** SD-219

Hatch, chair	*Baucus*
Lott	*Moynihan*
Nickles	*Conrad*
Mack	*Bryan*
Murkowski	*Robb*
Grassley	
Thompson	

FOREIGN RELATIONS

Phone: 224-4651 **Room:** SD-450

Majority Staff Director: Steve Biegun; 224-4651; SD-450

Minority Staff Director: Edwin K. Hall; 224-3953; SD-439

Relations of the United States with foreign nations generally; treaties; foreign economic, military, technical, and humanitarian assistance; foreign loans; diplomatic service; International Red Cross; international aspects of nuclear energy; International Monetary Fund; intervention abroad and declarations of war; foreign trade; national security; oceans and international environmental and scientific affairs; protection of U.S. citizens abroad; United Nations; World Bank and other development assistance organizations. The chair and ranking minority member are non-voting members ex officio of all subcommittees of which they are not regular members.

Party Ratio: R 10-D 8

Jesse Helms, N.C., chair	*Joseph R. Biden Jr., Del. ranking member*
Richard G. Lugar, Ind.	*Paul S. Sarbanes, Md.*
Chuck Hagel, Neb.	*Christopher J. Dodd, Conn.*
Gordon H. Smith, Ore.	
Rod Grams, Minn.	*John Kerry, Mass.*
Sam Brownback, Kan.	*Russell D. Feingold, Wis.*
Craig Thomas, Wyo.	*Paul Wellstone, Minn.*

John Ashcroft, Mo.   *Barbara Boxer, Calif.*
Bill Frist, Tenn.   *Robert G. Torricelli, N.J.*
Lincoln Chafee, R.I.

Subcommittees

African Affairs
Phone: 224-4651 **Room:** SD-450

Frist, chair	*Feingold*
Grams	*Sarbanes*
Brownback	

East Asian and Pacific Affairs
Phone: 224-4651 **Room:** SD-450

Thomas, chair	*Kerry*
Helms	*Feingold*
Hagel	*Wellstone*
Smith (Ore.)	*Torricelli*
Chafee	

European Affairs
Phone: 224-4651 **Room:** SD-450

Smith (Ore.), chair	*Biden*
	Sarbanes
Lugar	*Dodd*
Ashcroft	*Wellstone*
Hagel	
Chafee	

International Economic Policy, Export, and Trade Promotion
Phone: 224-4651 **Room:** SD-450

Hagel, chair	*Sarbanes*
Thomas	*Kerry*
Frist	*Boxer*
Lugar	

International Operations
Phone: 224-4651 **Room:** SD-450

Grams, chair	*Boxer*
Helms	*Kerry*
Brownback	*Feingold*
Frist	

Near Eastern and South Asian Affairs
Phone: 224-4651 **Room:** SD-450

Brownback, chair	*Wellstone*
Ashcroft	*Torricelli*
Smith (Ore.)	*Sarbanes*
Grams	*Dodd*
Thomas	

Western Hemisphere, Peace Corps, Narcotics, and Terrorism
Phone: 224-4651 **Room:** SD-450

Chafee, chair	*Dodd*
	Boxer
Helms	*Torricelli*

Lugar
Ashcroft

GOVERNMENTAL AFFAIRS

Phone: 224-4751 **Room:** SD-340
Staff Director: Hannah Sistare; 224-4751; SD-340
Minority Staff Director: Joyce Rechtschaffen; 224-2627; SD-326

Archives of the United States; budget and accounting measures; census and statistics; federal civil service; congressional organization; intergovernmental relations; government information; District of Columbia; organization and management of nuclear export policy; executive branch organization and reorganization; Postal Service; efficiency, economy and effectiveness of government. The chair and ranking minority member are nonvoting members ex officio of all subcommittees of which they are not regular members.

Party Ratio: R 9-D 7

Fred Thompson, Tenn., chair	*Joseph I. Lieberman, Conn., ranking member*
William V. Roth Jr., Del.	*Carl Levin, Mich.*
Ted Stevens, Alaska	*Daniel K. Akaka, Hawaii*
Susan Collins, Maine	*Richard J. Durbin, Ill.*
George V. Voinovich, Ohio	*Robert G. Torricelli, N.J.*
Pete V. Domenici, N.M.	*Max Cleland, Ga.*
Thad Cochran, Miss.	*John Edwards, N.C.*
Arlen Specter, Pa.	
Judd Gregg, N.H.	

Subcommittees

International Security, Proliferation, and Federal Services
Phone: 224-2254 **Room:** SH-442

Cochran, chair	*Akaka*
Stevens	*Levin*
Collins	*Torricelli*
Domenici	*Cleland*
Specter	*Edwards*
Gregg	

Investigations
Phone: 224-3721 **Room:** SR-100

Collins, chair	*Levin*
Roth	*Akaka*
Stevens	*Durbin*
Voinovich	*Cleland*
Domenici	*Edwards*
Cochran	
Specter	

Oversight of Government Management, Restructuring, and the District of Columbia
Phone: 224-3682 **Room:** SH-601

Voinovich, chair	*Durbin*

GOVERNMENTAL AFFAIRS (continued)

Roth
Gregg
Torricelli

HEALTH, EDUCATION, LABOR, AND PENSIONS

Phone: 224-5375 **Room:** SD-428
Staff Director: Mark Powden; 224-6770; SH-835
Minority Staff Director: Michael Myers; 224-7675; SD-644

Education, labor, health, and public welfare in general; aging; arts and humanities; biomedical research and development; child labor; convict labor; domestic activities of the Red Cross; equal employment opportunity; handicapped people; labor standards and statistics; mediation and arbitration of labor disputes; occupational safety and health; private pensions; public health; railway labor and retirement; regulation of foreign laborers; student loans; wages and hours; agricultural colleges; Gallaudet University; Howard University; St. Elizabeths Hospital in Washington, D.C. The chair and ranking minority member are non-voting members ex officio of all subcommittees of which they are not regular members.

Party Ratio: R 10-D 8

James M. Jeffords, Vt., chair	*Edward M. Kennedy, Mass., ranking member*
Judd Gregg, N.H.	*Christopher J. Dodd, Conn.*
Bill Frist, Tenn.	
Mike DeWine, Ohio	*Tom Harkin, Iowa*
Michael B. Enzi, Wyo.	*Barbara A. Mikulski, Md.*
Tim Hutchinson, Ark.	*Jeff Bingaman, N.M.*
Susan Collins, Maine	*Paul Wellstone, Minn.*
Sam Brownback, Kan.	*Patty Murray, Wash.*
Chuck Hagel, Neb.	*Jack Reed, R.I.*
Jeff Sessions, Ala.	

Subcommittees

Aging

Phone: 224-2962 **Room:** SH-608

DeWine, chair	*Mikulski*
Jeffords	*Murray*
Hutchinson	*Dodd*
Gregg	

Children and Families

Phone: 224-5800 **Room:** SH-615

Gregg, chair	*Dodd*
Frist	*Bingaman*
DeWine	*Wellstone*
Collins	*Murray*
Brownback	*Reed*
Hagel	

Employment, Safety, and Training

Phone: 224-7229 **Room:** SH-607

Enzi, chair	*Wellstone*

Jeffords	*Kennedy*
Hutchinson	*Dodd*
Hagel	*Harkin*
Sessions	

Public Health

Phone: 224-7139 **Room:** SD-424

Frist, chair	*Kennedy*
Gregg	*Harkin*
Enzi	*Mikulski*
Collins	*Bingaman*
Brownback	*Reed*
Sessions	

INDIAN AFFAIRS

Phone: 224-2251 **Room:** SH-838
Staff Director: Paul Moorehead; 224-2251; SH-838
Minority Staff Director: Patricia Zell; 224-2251; SH-838

Problems and opportunities of Indians, including Indian land management and trust responsibilities, education, health, special services, loan programs, and claims against the United States.

Party Ratio: R 8-D 6

Ben Nighthorse Campbell, Colo., chair	*Daniel K. Inouye, Hawaii, ranking member*
Frank H. Murkowski, Alaska	*Kent Conrad, N.D.*
	Harry Reid, Nev.
John McCain, Ariz.	*Daniel K. Akaka, Hawaii*
Slade Gorton, Wash.	*Paul Wellstone, Minn.*
Pete V. Domenici, N.M.	*Byron L. Dorgan, N.D.*
Craig Thomas, Wyo.	
Orrin G. Hatch, Utah	
James M. Inhofe, Okla.	

JUDICIARY

Phone: 224-5225 **Room:** SD-224
Chief Counsel and Staff Director: Manus Cooney; 224-5225; SD-224
Minority Chief Counsel: Bruce Cohen; 224-7703; SD-148

Civil and criminal judicial proceedings in general; penitentiaries; bankruptcy, mutiny, espionage, and counterfeiting; civil liberties; constitutional amendments; apportionment of representatives; government information; immigration and naturalization; interstate compacts in general; claims against the United States; patents, copyrights, and trademarks; monopolies and unlawful restraints of trade; holidays and celebrations. The chair and ranking minority member are non-voting members ex officio of all subcommittees of which they are not regular members.

Party Ratio: R 10-D 8

Orrin G. Hatch, Utah, chair	*Patrick J. Leahy, Vt., ranking member*
Strom Thurmond, S.C.	*Edward M. Kennedy, Mass.*

Charles E. Grassley, Iowa	Joseph R. Biden Jr., Del.
Arlen Specter, Pa.	Herb Kohl, Wis.
Jon Kyl, Ariz.	Dianne Feinstein, Calif.
Mike DeWine, Ohio	Russell D. Feingold, Wis.
John Ashcroft, Mo.	Robert G. Torricelli, N.J.
Spencer Abraham, Mich.	Charles E. Schumer, N.Y.
Jeff Sessions, Ala.	
Robert C. Smith, N.H.	

Subcommittees

Administrative Oversight and the Courts

Phone: 224-6736 **Room:** SH-308

Grassley, chair	Torricelli
Sessions	Feingold
Thurmond	Schumer
Abraham	

Antitrust, Business Rights, and Competition

Phone: 224-9494 **Room:** SD-161

DeWine, chair	Kohl
Hatch	Torricelli
Specter	Leahy
Thurmond	

Constitution, Federalism, and Property Rights

Phone: 224-8081 **Room:** SD-524

Ashcroft, chair	Feingold
Hatch	Kennedy
Smith (N.H.)	Leahy
Specter	
Thurmond	

Criminal Justice Oversight

Phone: 224-4135 **Room:** SD-157

Thurmond, chair	Schumer
DeWine	Biden
Ashcroft	Torricelli
Abraham	Leahy
Sessions	

Immigration

Phone: 224-6098 **Room:** SD-323

Abraham, chair	Kennedy
Specter	Feinstein
Grassley	Schumer
Kyl	

Technology, Terrorism, and Government Information

Phone: 224-6791 **Room:** SH-325

Kyl, chair	Feinstein
Hatch	Biden
Grassley	Kohl
DeWine	

Youth Violence

Phone: 224-7572 **Room:** SD-G13

| Sessions, chair | Biden |

Smith (N.H.)	Feinstein
Kyl	Kohl
Ashcroft	

RULES AND ADMINISTRATION

Phone: 224-6352 **Room:** SR-305
Staff Director: Tamara Somerville; 224-6352; SR-305
Minority Staff Director: Kennie L. Gill; 224-6351; SR-479

Senate administration in general; corrupt practices; qualifications of senators; contested elections; federal elections in general; Government Printing Office; Congressional Record; meetings of Congress and attendance of members; presidential succession; the Capitol, congressional office buildings, the Library of Congress, the Smithsonian Institution, and the Botanic Garden.

Party Ratio: R 9-D 7

Mitch McConnell, Ky., chair	Christopher J. Dodd, Conn., ranking member
Jesse Helms, N.C.	Robert C. Byrd, W.Va.
Ted Stevens, Alaska	Daniel K. Inouye, Hawaii
John W. Warner, Va.	Daniel Patrick Moynihan, N.Y.
Thad Cochran, Miss.	
Rick Santorum, Pa.	Dianne Feinstein, Calif.
Don Nickles, Okla.	Robert G. Torricelli, N.J.
Trent Lott, Miss.	Charles E. Schumer, N.Y.
Kay Bailey Hutchison, Texas	

SELECT ETHICS

Phone: 224-2981 **Room:** SH-220
Staff Director and Chief Counsel: Victor M. Baird; 224-2981; SH-220

Studies and investigates standards and conduct of Senate members and employees and may recommend remedial action.

Party Ratio: R 3-D 3

Pat Roberts, Kan., chair	Harry Reid, Nev., vice chair
Robert C. Smith, N.H.	Kent Conrad, N.D.
George V. Voinovich, Ohio	Richard J. Durbin, Ill.

SELECT INTELLIGENCE

Phone: 224-1700 **Room:** SH-211
Majority Staff Director: Nick Rostow; 224-1700; SH-211
Minority Staff Director: Alfred Cumming; 224-1700; SH-211

Legislative and budgetary authority over the Central Intelligence Agency, the Defense Intelligence Agency, the National Security Agency, and intelligence activities of the Federal Bureau of Investigation and other components of the federal intelligence community. The majority leader and minority leader are members ex officio of the committee.

SELECT INTELLIGENCE (continued)

Party Ratio: R 8-D 7

Richard C. Shelby, Ala., chair
Richard G. Lugar, Ind.
Jon Kyl, Ariz.
James M. Inhofe, Okla.
Orrin G. Hatch, Utah
Pat Roberts, Kan.
Wayne Allard, Colo.
Connie Mack, Fla.

Richard H. Bryan, Nev., vice chair
Bob Graham, Fla.
John Kerry, Mass.
Max Baucus, Mont.
Charles S. Robb, Va.
Frank R. Lautenberg, N.J.
Carl Levin, Mich.

SMALL BUSINESS

Phone: 224-5175 **Room:** SR-428A
Staff Director\and Chief Counsel: Emilia DiSanto; 224-5175; SR-428A
Minority Staff Director: Patricia Forbes; 224-8496

Problems of small business; Small Business Administration.

Party Ratio: R 10-D 8

Christopher S. Bond, Mo., chair
Conrad Burns, Mont.
Paul Coverdell, Ga.
Robert F. Bennett, Utah
Olympia J. Snowe, Maine
Michael B. Enzi, Wyo.
Peter G. Fitzgerald, Ill.
Michael D. Crapo, Idaho
George V. Voinovich, Ohio
Spencer Abraham, Mich.

John Kerry, Mass., ranking member
Carl Levin, Mich.
Tom Harkin, Iowa
Joseph I. Lieberman, Conn.
Paul Wellstone, Minn.
Max Cleland, Ga.
Mary L. Landrieu, La.
John Edwards, N.C.

SPECIAL AGING

Phone: 224-5364 **Room:** SD-G31
Staff Director: Ted Totman; 224-5364; SD-G31
Minority Staff Director: Michelle Prejean; 224-1467; SH-628

Problems and opportunities of older people including health, income, employment, housing and care, and assistance. Reports findings and makes recommendations to the Senate, but cannot report legislation.

Party Ratio: R 11-D 9`

Charles E. Grassley, Iowa, chair
James M. Jeffords, Vt.
Larry E. Craig, Idaho
Conrad Burns, Mont.
Richard C. Shelby, Ala.
Rick Santorum, Pa.
Chuck Hagel, Neb.
Susan Collins, Maine
Michael B. Enzi, Wyo.

John B. Breaux, La., ranking member
Harry Reid, Nev.
Herb Kohl, Wis.
Russell D. Feingold, Wis.
Ron Wyden, Ore.
Jack Reed, R.I.
Richard H. Bryan, Nev.
Evan Bayh, Ind.
Blanche Lincoln, Ark.

Tim Hutchinson, Ark.
Jim Bunning, Ky.

VETERANS' AFFAIRS

Phone: 224-9126 **Room:** SR-412
Staff Director: William Tuerk; 224-9126; SR-412
Minority Staff Director: James R. Gottlieb; 224-2074; SH-202

Veterans' measures in general; compensation; life insurance issued by the government on account of service in the armed forces; national cemeteries; pensions; readjustment benefits; veterans' hospitals, medical care, and treatment; vocational rehabilitation and education.

Party Ratio: R 7-D 5

Arlen Specter, Pa., chair
Strom Thurmond, S.C.
Frank H. Murkowski, Alaska
James M. Jeffords, Vt.
Ben Nighthorse Campbell, Colo.
Larry E. Craig, Idaho
Tim Hutchinson, Ark.

John D. Rockefeller IV, W.Va., ranking member
Bob Graham, Fla.
Daniel K. Akaka, Hawaii
Paul Wellstone, Minn.
Patty Murray, Wash.

PARTISAN COMMITTEES

DEMOCRATIC POLICY COMMITTEE

Phone: 224-3232 **Room:** SH-419
Tom Daschle, S.D., chair
Byron L. Dorgan, N.D., chair
Patty Murray, Wash., regional chair
Jack Reed, R.I., regional chair
Mary L. Landrieu, La., regional chair
Bob Kerrey, Neb., regional chair

Ernest F. Hollings, S.C.
Paul S. Sarbanes, Md.
Daniel Patrick Moynihan, N.Y.
John D. Rockefeller IV, W.Va.
Charles S. Robb, Va.
Daniel K. Akaka, Hawaii
Russell D. Feingold, Wis.
Joseph I. Lieberman, Conn.
Paul Wellstone, Minn.

Dianne Feinstein, Calif.
Ron Wyden, Ore.
Robert G. Torricelli, N.J.
Tim Johnson, S.D.
Charles E. Schumer, N.Y.
Blanche Lincoln, Ark.
Evan Bayh, Ind.
Harry Reid, Nev., ex officio
Barbara A. Mikulski, Md., ex officio

DEMOCRATIC SENATORIAL CAMPAIGN COMMITTEE

Phone: 224-2447 **Room:** 430 S. Capitol St., S.E. 20003
Robert G. Torricelli, N.J., chair
Patty Murray, Wash., vice-chair

Harry Reid, Nev., Majority Trust Co-Chair
Evan Bayh, Ind., Leadership Circle Co-Chair
Richard J. Durbin, Ill., Labor Council Co-Chair
Edward M. Kennedy, Mass., Labor Council Co-Chair
Mary L. Landrieu, La., Roundtable Co-Chair
Jack Reed, R.I., Roundtable Co-Chair
Blanche Lincoln, Ark., Leadership Circle Co-Chair
Charles E. Schumer, N.Y., Majority Trust Co-Chair
Tom Harkin, Iowa, Labor Council Co-Chair
John D. Rockefeller IV, W. Va., Board of Trustees Chair
John Edwards, N.C., Legal Council Co-Chair
Ernest F. Hollings, S.C., Legal Council Co-Chair
Patrick J. Leahy, Vt., High Technology Council Co-Chair
Ron Wyden, Ore., High Technology Council Co-Chair

DEMOCRATIC STEERING AND COORDINATION COMMITTEE

Phone: 224-9048 **Room:** SH-712

John Kerry, Mass., chair	Kent Conrad, N.D.
Daniel K. Inouye, Hawaii	Carl Levin, Mich.
Robert C. Byrd, W.Va.	Richard H. Bryan, Nev.
Edward M. Kennedy, Mass.	Herb Kohl, Wis.
Joseph R. Biden Jr., Del.	Barbara Boxer, Calif.
Patrick J. Leahy, Vt.	John B. Breaux, La.
Christopher J. Dodd, Conn.	Tom Daschle, S.D.
Tom Harkin, Iowa	Frank R. Lautenberg, N.J.

Max Baucus, Mont.	Jeff Bingaman, N.M.
Bob Graham, Fla.	Max Cleland, Ga.

DEMOCRATIC TECHNOLOGY AND COMMUNICATIONS COMMITTEE

Phone: 224-1430 **Room:** SH-619

John D. Rockefeller IV, W.Va., chair	Frank R. Lautenberg, N.J.
	Patty Murray, Wash.
Jeff Bingaman, N.M.	Charles S. Robb, Va.
Kent Conrad, N.D.	Tom Daschle, S.D. , ex officio
Christopher J. Dodd, Conn.	Harry Reid, Nev., ex officio
Ernest F. Hollings, S.C.	Barbara A. Mikulski, Md.,
Tim Johnson, S.D.	ex officio
Ernest F. Hollings, S.C.	John B. Breaux, La., ex officio

NATIONAL REPUBLICAN SENATORIAL COMMITTEE

Phone: 675-6000 **Room:** 425 Second St., N.E. 20002

Mitch McConnell, Ky., chair	Larry E. Craig, Idaho
	James M. Inhofe, Okla.
Wayne Allard, Colo.	Gordon H. Smith, Ore.
Christopher S. Bond, Mo.	Jeff Sessions, Ala.

REPUBLICAN POLICY COMMITTEE

Phone: 224-2946 **Room:** SR-347
Larry E. Craig, Idaho, chair

Senate Leadership

DEMOCRATIC LEADERS

President *Al Gore, Tenn.*
Minority Leader *Tom Daschle, S.D.*
Minority Whip *Harry Reid, Nev.*
Conference Chair *Tom Daschle, S.D.*
Conference Secretary *Barbara A. Mikulski, Md.*
Chief Deputy Whip *John B. Breaux, La.*
Assistant Floor Leader *Richard J. Durbin, Ill.*
Deputy Whip
Jeff Bingaman, N.M.
Max Cleland, Ga.
Jack Reed, R.I.
Barbara Boxer, Calif.
Policy Committee
  Chair *Byron L. Dorgan, N.D.*
Steering and Coordination
  Committee Chair *John Kerry, Mass.*
Technology and Communications
  Committee Chair *John D. Rockefeller IV, W.Va.*
Democratic Senatorial Campaign
  Committee Chair *Robert G. Torricelli, N.J.*

REPUBLICAN LEADERS

President Pro Tempore Strom Thurmond, S.C.
Majority Leader Trent Lott, Miss.
Assistant Majority Leader Don Nickles, Okla.
Conference Chair Connie Mack, Fla.
Conference Secretary Paul Coverdell, Ga.
Chief Deputy Whip Judd Gregg, N.H.
Deputy Whip

Spencer Abraham, Mich.	Jon Kyl, Ariz.
John Ashcroft, Mo.	Mitch McConnell, Ky.
Jim Bunning, Ky.	Gordon H. Smith, Ore.
Susan Collins, Maine	Olympia Snowe, Maine
Bill Frist, Tenn.	Craig Thomas, Wyo.
Chuck Hagel, Neb.	
Kay Bailey Hutchison, Texas	

Policy Committee Chair Larry E. Craig, Idaho
Committee on Committees Chair Slade Gorton, Wash.
National Republican Senatorial Committee Chair Mitch McConnell, Ky.

Senate Members' Offices

The list below gives the names of Senate members and their party and state, followed by addresses and telephone numbers for their Washington offices. The area code for all telephone numbers in Washington, D.C. is (202). The list also gives the name of a top administrative aide for each member.

The address, telephone number, and director for the members' district offices are listed. Each senator's committee assignments are given as the final entry. For partisan committee assignments, see p. 822.

As of April 17, 2000, there were 55 Republicans and 45 Democrats in the Senate. This information was gathered by Congressional Quarterly from Senate offices in Washington, D.C.

ABRAHAM, SPENCER, R-MICH.

Capitol Hill Office: SD-329 20510; 224-4822; Fax: 224-8834; *Chief of Staff:* Jim Pitts
Web: abraham.senate.gov
E-mail: michigan@abraham.senate.gov
District Office(s): 26222 Telegraph Rd., Southfield 48034; (248) 350-0510; Fax: (248) 350-0420; *Regional Director:* Pat Wierzbicki
231 W. Lafayette Blvd., Detroit 48226; (313) 961-2349; Fax: (313) 961-2750; *Regional Director:* Eunice Myles Jeffries
121 E. Front St., Traverse City 49684; (231) 922-0915; Fax: (231) 922-2015; *Regional Director:* Phil Hendges
301 E. Genesee St., Saginaw 48607; (517) 752-4400; Fax: (517) 752-4492; *Regional Director:* John Potbury
3738 28th St. S.E., Grand Rapids 49512; (616) 975-1112; Fax: (616) 975-1119; *Regional Director:* Rene Meyers
115 W. Allegan, Lansing 48933; (517) 484-1984; Fax: (517) 484-3099; *State Director:* Billie Wimmer
200 W. Washington St., Marquette 49855; (906) 226-9466; Fax: (906) 226-9464; *Regional Director:* Greg Andrews
Committee Assignment(s): Budget; Commerce, Science, and Transportation; Judiciary; Small Business

AKAKA, DANIEL K., D-HAWAII

Capitol Hill Office: SH-720 20510; 224-6361; Fax: 224-2126; *Administrative Assistant:* James K. Sakai
Web: akaka.senate.gov
E-mail: senator@akaka.senate.gov
District Office(s): Prince Kuhio Federal Bldg., 300 Ala Moana Blvd., #3-106, P.O. Box 50144, Honolulu 96850; (808) 522-8970; Fax: (808) 545-4683; *State Director:* Mike Kitamura

101 Aupuni St., Hilo 96720; (808) 935-1114; Fax: (808) 935-9064
Committee Assignment(s): Energy and Natural Resources; Governmental Affairs; Indian Affairs; Veterans' Affairs

ALLARD, WAYNE, R-COLO.

Capitol Hill Office: SH-513 20510; 224-5941; Fax: 224-6471; *Administrative Assistant:* Mike Bennett
Web: allard.senate.gov
E-mail: www.senate.gov/~allard/webform.html
District Office(s): 7340 E. Caley, Englewood 80111; (303) 220-7414; Fax: (303) 220-8126; *State Director:* Pete Jacobson
3400 W. 16th St., Greeley 80634; (970) 351-7582; Fax: (970) 351-7585; *Northeast Area Director:* Lewis Frank
228 N. Cascade Ave., Colorado Springs 80903; (719) 634-6071; Fax: (719) 636-2590; *Area Director:* Jim Bensberg
411 Thatcher Bldg., Pueblo 81003; (719) 545-9751; Fax: (719) 545-3832; *Area Director:* Doris Morgan
215 Federal Bldg., Grand Junction 81501; (970) 245-9553; Fax: (970) 245-9523; *Field Representative:* Shane Henry
Committee Assignment(s): Armed Services; Banking, Housing and Urban Affairs; Select Intelligence

ASHCROFT, JOHN, R-MO.

Capitol Hill Office: SH-316 20510; 224-6154; Fax: 228-0998; *Chief of Staff:* Brian Waidmann
Web: ashcroft.senate.gov
E-mail: john_ashcroft@ashcroft.senate.gov
District Office(s): 308 E. High St., Jefferson City 65101; (573) 634-2488; Fax: (573) 635-8659; *Constituent Services Director:* Liz Behrooz

Rivergate Business Center, Kansas City 64105; (816) 471-7141; Fax: (816) 471-7338; *District Office Director:* William Leathem

Federal Bldg., Cape Girardeau 63701; (573) 334-7044; Fax: (573) 334-7352; *District Office Director:* Tom Schulte

7700 Bonhomme, Clayton 63105; (314) 725-4484; Fax: (314) 725-4268; *District Office Director:* Joe Messmer

318 Park Central East, Springfield 65806; (417) 864-8258; Fax: (417) 864-7519; *District Office Director:* Steve Hilton

Committee Assignment(s): Commerce, Science, and Transportation; Foreign Relations; Judiciary

BAUCUS, MAX, D-MONT.

Capitol Hill Office: SH-511 20510; 224-2651; Fax: 228-3687; *Chief of Staff:* Jeff Forbes

Web: baucus.senate.gov

E-mail: max@baucus.senate.gov

District Office(s): 207 N. Broadway, Billings 59101; (406) 657-6790; Fax: (406) 657-6793; *State Director:* Sharon Peterson

Federal Bldg., Bozeman 59715; (406) 586-6104; Fax: (406) 586-9177; *Field Director:* Alicia Bradshaw

220 1st Ave. East, Kalispell 59901; (406) 756-1150; Fax: (406) 756-1152; *Field Director:* Rebecca Manna

211 N. Higgins Ave., Missoula 59802; (406) 329-3123; *Field Director:* Kjersten Forseth

Silver Bow Center, Butte 59701; (406) 782-8700; Fax: (406) 782-6553; *Field Director:* Kim Krueger

18 5th St. South, Great Falls 59401; (406) 761-1574; *Field Director:* Greg Eklund

225 Cruse Ave., Helena 59601; (406) 449-5480; Fax: (406) 449-5484; *Field Representative:* Paula Coleman

Committee Assignment(s): Agriculture, Nutrition, and Forestry; Environment and Public Works; Finance; Joint Taxation; Select Intelligence

BAYH, EVAN, D-IND.

Capitol Hill Office: SH-717 20510; 224-5623; Fax: 228-1377; *Chief of Staff:* Tom Sugar

Web: bayh.senate.gov

E-mail: bayh.senate.gov/WebMail.html

District Office(s): Market Tower, #1650, Indianapolis 46204; (317) 554-0750; Fax: (317) 554-0760; *State Director:* Jane Henegar

Winfield K. Denton Federal Bldg., Evansville 47708; (812) 465-6501; Fax: (812) 465-6503; *Regional Coordinator:* Brian Goffinet

Federal Bldg., Fort Wayne 46802; (219) 426-3151; Fax: (219) 420-0060; *Regional Coordinator:* Joel Miller

Ivy Tech State College, Gary 46409; (219) 884-8528; Fax: (219) 884-8593; *Regional Coordinator:* David Rozmanich

Jeffersonville Federal Center, Jeffersonville 47130; (812) 218-2317; Fax: (812) 218-2370; *Regional Coordinator:* Heidi Kimmick

Committee Assignment(s): Banking, Housing, and Urban Affairs; Energy and Natural Resources; Special Aging

BENNETT, ROBERT F., R-UTAH

Capitol Hill Office: SD-431 20510; 224-5444; Fax: 224-4908; *Chief of Staff:* James C. Barker

Web: bennett.senate.gov

E-mail: senator@bennett.senate.gov

District Office(s): Wallace F. Bennett Federal Bldg., Salt Lake City 84138; (801) 524-5933; Fax: (801) 524-5730; *State Director:* Dixie L. Minson

324 25th St., Ogden 84401; (801) 625-5676; Fax: (801) 625-5692; *Northern Utah Area Director:* Anita Thompson

Federal Bldg., St. George 84770; (435) 628-5514; Fax: (435) 628-4160; *Southern Utah Area Director:* Bruce Richeson

Federal Bldg., Cedar City 84720; (435) 865-1335; Fax: (435) 865-1481; *Southern Utah Area Director:* Bruce Richeson

Old House Bldg., Provo 84601; (801) 379-2525; Fax: (801) 375-3432; *Central Utah Area Director:* Donna Sackett

Committee Assignment(s): Appropriations; Banking, Housing and Urban Affairs; Environment and Public Works; Joint Economic; Small Business

BIDEN, JOSEPH R. JR., D-DEL.

Capitol Hill Office: SR-221 20510; 224-5042; Fax: 224-0139; *Chief of Staff:* Alan L. Hoffman

Web: biden.senate.gov

E-mail: senator@biden.senate.gov

District Office(s): J. Caleb Boggs Federal Bldg., Wilmington 19801; (302) 573-6345; Fax: (302) 573-6351; *State Director:* John Dorsey

Federal Bldg., Dover 19904; (302) 678-9483; Fax: (302) 678-2106; *Kent-Sussex County Coordinator:* Kevin Smith

Georgetown Professional Center, Georgetown 19947; (302) 856-9275; Fax: (302) 856-9685; *Kent-Sussex County Coordinator:* Kevin Smith

Committee Assignment(s): Foreign Relations; Judiciary

BINGAMAN, JEFF, D-N.M.

Capitol Hill Office: SH-703 20510; 224-5521; Fax: 224-2852; *Chief of Staff:* Bernard R. Toon

Web: bingaman.senate.gov

E-mail: senator_bingaman@bingaman.senate.gov

District Office(s): 625 Silver Ave. S.W., Albuquerque 87102; (505) 346-6601; Fax: (505) 346-6780; *State Director:* Susan McGuire

105 W. 3rd, Roswell 88201; (505) 622-7113; Fax: (505) 622-3538; *Issues Director:* Lyn Ditto

118 Bridge St., #3, Las Vegas 87701; (505) 454-8824; Fax: (505) 454-8959; *Constituent Services Representative:* Rebecca Montoya

148 Loretto Towne Center, Las Cruces 88001; (505) 523-6561; Fax: (505) 523-6584; *District Coordinator:* Alice Salcido

119 E. Marcy St., Santa Fe 87501; (505) 988-6647; Fax: (505) 988-6596; *Special Assistant:* Dolores Garcia

Committee Assignment(s): Armed Services; Energy and Natural Resources; Health, Education, Labor, and Pensions; Joint Economic

BOND, CHRISTOPHER S., R-MO.

Capitol Hill Office: SR-274 20510; 224-5721; Fax: 224-8149; *Chief of Staff:* Julie Dammann

Web: bond.senate.gov

E-mail: kit_bond@bond.senate.gov

District Office(s): 7700 Bonhomme, St. Louis 63105; (314) 725-4484; Fax: (314) 725-3548; *District Office Director:* Patrick Werner

Federal Bldg., Cape Girardeau 63701; (573) 334-7044; Fax: (573) 334-7352; *District Office Director:* Tom Schulte

318 Park Central East, Springfield 65806; (417) 864-8258; Fax: (417) 864-7519; *Area Director:* Darren Ethridge

Rivergate Business Center, Kansas City 64105; (816) 471-7141; Fax: (816) 471-7338; *District Office Director:* Nancy Wagoner

308 E. High St., Jefferson City 65101; (573) 634-2488; Fax: (573) 634-6005; *Deputy Chief of Staff:* Jason Van Eaton

Committee Assignment(s): Appropriations; Budget; Environment and Public Works; Small Business

BOXER, BARBARA, D-CALIF.

Capitol Hill Office: SH-112 20510; 224-3553; *Administrative Assistant:* Karen Olick

Web: boxer.senate.gov

E-mail: senator@boxer.senate.gov

District Office(s): 312 N. Spring St., Los Angeles 90012; (213) 894-5000; Fax: (213) 894-5012; *Southern California Director:* Matt Kagan

1700 Montgomery St., San Francisco 94111; (415) 403-0100; Fax: (415) 956-6701; *Chief of Staff:* Sam Chapman

501 I St., Sacramento 95814; (916) 448-2787; Fax: (916) 448-2563; *Field Representative:* Robert Marez

1130 O St., Fresno 93721; (559) 497-5109; Fax: (559) 497-5111; *Northern California Director:* Tom Bohigian

600 B St., San Diego 92101; (619) 239-3884; Fax: (619) 239-5719; *Field Representative:* Amy Denhart

201 N. E St., San Bernardino 92401; (909) 888-8525; Fax: (909) 888-8613; *Field Representative:* Leannah Bradley

Committee Assignment(s): Budget; Environment and Public Works; Foreign Relations

BREAUX, JOHN B., D-LA.

Capitol Hill Office: SH-503 20510; 224-4623; Fax: 228-2577; *Chief of Staff:* Fred Hatfield

Web: breaux.senate.gov

E-mail: senator@breaux.senate.gov

District Office(s): Hale Boggs Federal Bldg., New Orleans 70130; (504) 589-2531; Fax: (504) 589-2533; *Constituent Services Representative:* Shantrice Norman-Dial

1900 N. 18th St., Monroe 71201; (318) 325-3320; Fax: (318) 325-8740; *Constituent Services Representative:* Jean Bates

Federal Bldg., Lafayette 70501; (318) 262-6871; Fax: (318) 262-6874; *Executive Assistant:* Raymond Cordova

One American Place, Baton Rouge 70825; (225) 382-2050; Fax: (225) 382-2059; *State Director:* Robert Mann

Committee Assignment(s): Commerce, Science, and Transportation; Finance; Special Aging

BROWNBACK, SAM, R-KAN.

Capitol Hill Office: SH-303 20510; 224-6521; Fax: 228-1265; *Chief of Staff:* Heather Wingate

Web: brownback.senate.gov

E-mail: sam_brownback@brownback.senate.gov

District Office(s): 612 S. Kansas Ave., Topeka 66603; (785) 233-2503; Fax: (785) 233-2616; *Office Manager:* Niomi Burget

11111 W. 95th St., Overland Park 66214; (913) 492-6378; Fax: (913) 492-7253; *Regional Director:* Macie Houston

225 N. Market St., Wichita 67202; (316) 264-8066; Fax: (316) 264-9078; *Regional Director:* Chuck Alderson

1001-C N. Broadway, Pittsburg 66762; (316) 231-6040; Fax: (316) 231-6347; *State Director:* Anne Emerson

811 N. Main St., Garden City 67846; (316) 275-1124; Fax: (316) 275-1837; *Regional Director:* Dennis Mesa

Committee Assignment(s): Commerce, Science, and Transportation; Foreign Relations; Health, Education, Labor, and Pensions; Joint Economic

BRYAN, RICHARD H., D-NEV.

Capitol Hill Office: SR-269 20510; 224-6244; Fax: 224-1867; *Chief of Staff:* Jean Marie Neal

Web: bryan.senate.gov

E-mail: senator@bryan.senate.gov

District Office(s): 300 Las Vegas Blvd. South, Las Vegas 89101; (702) 388-6605; *Southern Nevada Director:* Sara Besser

400 S. Virginia St., Reno 89501; (775) 686-5770; *Reno Area Director:* Michael Moreno

600 E. William St., Carson City 89701; (775) 885-9111; *Rural Area Director:* Tom Baker

Committee Assignment(s): Banking, Housing, and Urban Affairs; Commerce, Science, and Transportation; Finance; Select Intelligence; Special Aging

BUNNING, JIM, R-KY.

Capitol Hill Office: SH-502 20510; 224-4343; Fax: 228-1373; *Chief of Staff:* David A. York

Web: bunning.senate.gov

E-mail: jim_bunning@bunning.senate.gov

District Office(s): Gorman Education Center, Hazard 41701; (606) 435-2390; Fax: (606) 435-1761; *Field Representative:* Darlynn Barber

Pennyrile Bldg., Hopkinsville 42240; (270) 885-1212; Fax: (270) 881-3975; *Field Representative:* T. C. Freeman

600 Dr. Martin Luther King Jr. Place, Louisville 40202; (502) 582-5341; Fax: (502) 582-5344; *Field Representative:* Colley W. Bell III

423 Frederica St., Owensboro 42301; (270) 689-9085; Fax: (270) 689-9158; *Field Representative:* Jim Askins

Corporate Plaza, Lexington 40503; (606) 219-2239; Fax: (606) 219-3269; *Field Representative:* Bill Lambdin

Lookout Corporate Center, Fort Wright 41011; (606) 341-2602; Fax: (606) 331-7445; *State Director:* Debbie McKinney

Committee Assignment(s): Banking, Housing, and Urban Affairs; Energy and Natural Resources; Special Aging

BURNS, CONRAD, R-MONT.

Capitol Hill Office: SD-187 20510; 224-2644; Fax: 224-8594; *Chief of Staff:* Patty McDonald

Web: burns.senate.gov

E-mail: conrad_burns@burns.senate.gov

District Office(s): 2708 1st Ave. North, Billings 59101; (406) 252-0550; Fax: (406) 252-7768; *State Director:* Dwight McKay

208 N. Montana Ave., Helena 59601; (406) 449-5401; Fax: (406) 449-5462; *Field Representative:* Betsy Allen

211 Haggerty Lane, Bozeman 59715; (406) 586-4450; Fax: (406) 586-7647; *Field Representative:* Mike Harris

575 Sunset Blvd., Kalispell 59901; (406) 257-3360; Fax: (406) 257-3974; *Field Representative:* Lori McDonald

P.O. Box 7729, Missoula 59807; (406) 329-3529; Fax: (406) 728-2193; *Field Representative:* Amy Fisher

125 W. Granite St., Butte 59701; (406) 723-3277; Fax: (406) 782-4717; *Field Representative:* Cindy Perdue Dolan

321 1st Ave. North, Great Falls 59401; (406) 452-9585; Fax: (406) 452-9586; *Deputy State Director:* Mike Brown

324 W. Towne St., Glendive 59330; (406) 365-2391; Fax: (406) 365-8836; *Field Representative:* Pamela Tierney Crisafulli

Committee Assignment(s): Appropriations; Commerce, Science, and Transportation; Energy and Natural Resources; Small Business; Special Aging

BYRD, ROBERT C., D-W.VA.

Capitol Hill Office: SH-311 20510; 224-3954; Fax: 228-0002; *Chief of Staff:* Barbara Videnieks

Web: byrd.senate.gov

E-mail: senator_byrd@byrd.senate.gov

District Office(s): 300 Virginia St. East, Charleston 25301; (304) 342-5855; *State Director:* Anne S. Barth

Committee Assignment(s): Appropriations; Armed Services; Rules and Administration

CAMPBELL, BEN NIGHTHORSE, R-COLO.

Capitol Hill Office: SR-380 20510; 224-5852; Fax: 224-1933; *Chief of Staff:* Ginnie Kontnik

Web: campbell.senate.gov

District Office(s): 6950 E. Belleview Ave., Englewood 80111; (303) 843-4100; Fax: (303) 843-4116; *Assistant to the Chief of Staff:* Carolyn Last

19 Old Town Square, Ft. Collins 80524; (970) 224-1909; Fax: (970) 224-1948; *District Director:* Keith Johnson

212 N. Wahsatch Ave., Colorado Springs 80903; (719) 636-9092; Fax: (719) 636-9165; *District Director:* Catherine Lawton

Federal Bldg., Grand Junction 81501; (970) 241-6631; Fax: (970) 241-8313; *District Director:* Katie Aggeler

503 N. Main St., Pueblo 81003; (719) 542-6987; Fax: (719) 542-2515; *State Director:* Dave Devendorf

Committee Assignment(s): Appropriations; Energy and Natural Resources; Indian Affairs; Veterans' Affairs

CHAFEE, LINCOLN, R-R.I.

Capitol Hill Office: SD-505 20510; 224-2921; *Chief of Staff:* David Griswold

Web: chafee.senate.gov

E-mail: senator_chafee@chafee.senate.gov

District Office(s): 10 Dorrance St., Providence 02903; (401) 453-5294; *State Director:* William E. Smith

Committee Assignment(s): Environment and Public Works; Foreign Relations

CLELAND, MAX, D-GA.

Capitol Hill Office: SD-461 20510; 224-3521; Fax: 224-0072; *Chief of Staff:* Wayne Howell

Web: cleland.senate.gov

E-mail: senator_max_cleland@cleland.senate.gov

District Office(s): 75 Spring St. S.W., Atlanta 30303; (404) 331-4811; Fax: (404) 331-5439; *State Director:* Bill Chapman

120 12th St., Columbus 31902; (706) 649-7705; Fax: (706) 649-7709; *District Representative:* William Eggleston

235 Roosevelt Ave., Albany 31701; (912) 430-7796; Fax: (912) 430-7798; *District Representative:* Joy Jones-Keyes

P.O. Box 1621, Augusta 30903; (706) 722-4040; Fax: (706) 722-4555; *District Representative:* Richard "Dusty" Houser

203 Martin Luther King Jr. Blvd., Dalton 30721; (706) 275-8905; Fax: (706) 275-8909; *District Representative:* Freddie Horton

401 Cherry St., Macon 31201; (912) 755-1779; Fax: (912) 755-1269; *District Representative:* Gene Stuckey

Oglethorpe Office Park, Savannah 31406; (912) 352-8283; Fax: (912) 356-5562; *District Representative:* Thomas Williams

Committee Assignment(s): Armed Services; Commerce, Science, and Transportation; Governmental Affairs; Small Business

COCHRAN, THAD, R-MISS.

Capitol Hill Office: SR-326 20510; 224-5054; *Chief of Staff:* Mark Keenum

Web: cochran.senate.gov

E-mail: senator@cochran.senate.gov

District Office(s): U.S. House, Oxford 38655; (601) 236-1018; Fax: (601) 236-7618; *Office Manager:* Mindy Buchanan

188 E. Capitol St., Jackson 39201; (601) 965-4459; Fax: (601) 965-4919; *Special Counsel:* George Phillips

Committee Assignment(s): Agriculture, Nutrition, and Forestry; Appropriations; Governmental Affairs; Joint Library; Joint Printing; Rules and Administration

COLLINS, SUSAN, R-MAINE

Capitol Hill Office: SR-172 20510; 224-2523; Fax: 224-2693; *Chief of Staff:* Steve Abbott

Web: collins.senate.gov

E-mail: senator@collins.senate.gov

District Office(s): P.O. Box 655, Bangor 04402; (207) 945-0417; Fax: (207) 990-4604; *State Office Representative:* Judy Cuddy

168 Capitol St., Augusta 04330; (207) 622-8414; Fax: (207) 622-5884; *State Office Representative:* Randy Bumps

109 Alfred St., Biddeford 04005; (207) 283-1101; Fax: (207) 283-4054; *State Office Representative:* William Vail

11 Lisbon St., Lewiston 04240; (207) 784-6969; Fax: (207) 782-6475; *State Office Representative:* Dan Demeritt

One City Center, Portland 04101; (207) 780-3575; Fax: (207) 828-0380; *State Office Representative:* Sam Patten

25 Sweden St., Caribou 04736; (207) 493-7873; *State Office Representative:* Phil Bosse

Committee Assignment(s): Governmental Affairs; Health, Education, Labor and Pensions; Special Aging

CONRAD, KENT, D-N.D.

Capitol Hill Office: SH-530 20510; 224-2043; Fax: 224-7776; *Chief of Staff:* Robert "Bob" Van Heuvelen

Web: conrad.senate.gov

E-mail: senator@conrad.senate.gov

District Office(s): Federal Bldg., Fargo 58102; (701) 232-8030; Fax: (701) 232-6449; *State Representative:* Lois E. Schneider

Federal Bldg., Minot 58701; (701) 852-0703; Fax: (701) 838-8196; *State Representative:* Gail Bergstad

Federal Bldg., Bismarck 58501; (701) 258-4648; Fax: (701) 258-1254; *State Director:* Lynn J. Clancy

Federal Bldg., Grand Forks 58201; (701) 775-9601; Fax: (701) 746-1990; *State Representative:* James S. Hand

Committee Assignment(s): Agriculture, Nutrition, and Forestry; Budget; Finance; Indian Affairs; Select Ethics

COVERDELL, PAUL, R-GA.

Capitol Hill Office: SR-200 20510; 224-3643; Fax: 228-3783; *Chief of Staff:* Ziad Ojakli

Web: coverdell.senate.gov

E-mail: senator_coverdell@coverdell.senate.gov

District Office(s): 100 Colony Square, Atlanta 30361; (404) 347-2202; Fax: (404) 347-2243; *State Director for Constituent Services:* Shirley A. Puchalski

10 11th St., Columbus 31901; (706) 322-7920; Fax: (706) 322-7967; *Regional Representative:* John Stacy

582 Walnut St., Macon 31201; (912) 742-0205; Fax: (912) 742-0900; *Regional Representative:* Harry Thompson

2 E. Bryan St., Savannah 31401; (912) 238-3244; Fax: (912) 238-1240; *Regional Representative:* Rich Horne

22 N. Main St., Moultrie 31768; (912) 985-8113; Fax: (912) 985-8018; *Regional Representative:* Jody Redding

Augusta Riverfront Center, Augusta 30901; (706) 722-0032; Fax: (706) 724-1953; *Regional Representative:* Donald Stewart

Committee Assignment(s): Agriculture, Nutrition, and Forestry; Finance; Small Business

CRAIG, LARRY E., R-IDAHO

Capitol Hill Office: SH-520 20510; 224-2752; Fax: 228-1067; *Chief of Staff:* Michael O. Ware

Web: craig.senate.gov

District Office(s): 801 E. Sherman St., Pocatello 83201; (208) 236-6817; Fax: (208) 236-6820; *Regional Assistant:* Francoise Cleveland

846 Main St., Lewiston 83501; (208) 743-0792; Fax: (208) 746-7275; *Regional Assistant:* Scott Turlington

304 N. 8th St., Boise 83702; (208) 342-7985; Fax: (208) 343-2458; *Regional Director:* Ken Burgess

Harbor Plaza, Coeur d'Alene 83814; (208) 667-6130; Fax: (208) 765-1743; *State Director:* Sandra Patano

490 Memorial Dr., Idaho Falls 83402; (208) 523-5541; Fax: (208) 522-0135; *Regional Assistant:* Georgia Dixon

1292 Addison Ave. East, Twin Falls 83301; (208) 734-6780; Fax: (208) 734-3905; *Regional Director:* Michael Mathews

Committee Assignment(s): Agriculture, Nutrition, and Forestry; Appropriations; Energy and Natural Resources; Special Aging; Veterans' Affairs

CRAPO, MICHAEL D., R-IDAHO

Capitol Hill Office: SR-111 20510; 224-6142; Fax: 228-1375

Web: crapo.senate.gov

E-mail: crapo.senate.gov/~crapo/webform.html

District Office(s): 202 Falls Ave., Twin Falls 83301; (208) 734-2515; Fax: (208) 733-0414; *Senior Regional Director:* Linda Norris

490 Memorial Dr., Idaho Falls 83404; (208) 522-9779; Fax: (208) 529-8367; *State Agriculture Director:* Don Dixon

304 N. 8th St., Boise 83702; (208) 334-1776; Fax: (208) 334-9044; *Chief of Staff:* John Hoehne

801 E. Sherman St., Pocatello 83201; (208) 236-6775; Fax: (208) 236-6935; *Regional Director:* John Atkins

704 Blaine St., Caldwell 83605; (208) 455-0360; Fax: (208) 455-0358; *Staff Assistant:* Matt Ellsworth

1000 Northwest Blvd., Coeur D'Alene 83814; (208) 664-5490; Fax: (208) 664-0889; *Regional Director:* Sarah Bigger

111 Main St., Lewiston 83501; (208) 743-1492; Fax: (208) 743-6484; *Regional Director:* Mary Hasenoehrl

220 E. 5th St., Moscow 83843; (208) 883-9783; Fax: (208) 883-8743; *Staff Assistant:* Cindy Agidius

Committee Assignment(s): Banking, Housing, and Urban Affairs; Environment and Public Works; Small Business

DASCHLE, TOM, D-S.D.

Capitol Hill Office: SH-509 20510; 224-2321; Fax: 224-2047; *Chief of Staff:* Peter Rouse

Web: daschle.senate.gov

E-mail: tom_daschle@daschle.senate.gov

District Office(s): P.O. Box 1274, Sioux Falls 57101; (605) 334-9596; Fax: (605) 334-2591; *State Director:* Steve Erpenbach

320 S. 1st St., Aberdeen 57402; (605) 225-8823; Fax: (605) 225-8468; *Area Director:* Beth Smith

P.O. Box 8168, Rapid City 57709; (605) 348-7551; Fax: (605) 348-7208; *Area Director:* Ace Gallagher

Committee Assignment(s): Agriculture, Nutrition, and Forestry

DeWINE, MIKE, R-OHIO

Capitol Hill Office: SR-140 20510; 224-2315; Fax: 224-6519; *Chief of Staff:* Laurel Pressler

Web: dewine.senate.gov

E-mail: senator_dewine@dewine.senate.gov

District Office(s): 37 W. Broad St., Columbus 43215; (614) 469-6774; Fax: (614) 469-7419; *Casework Manager:* Jenny Ogle

600 E. Superior Ave., Cleveland 44114; (216) 522-7272; Fax: (216) 522-2239; *District Representative:* Michelle Gillcrist

200 Putnam St., Marietta 45750; (740) 373-2317; Fax: (740) 373-8689; *District Representative:* Lynne M. Crow

265 S. Allison Ave., Xenia 45385; (937) 376-3080; Fax: (937) 376-3387; *State Director:* Barbara Briggs Schenck

420 Madison Ave., Toledo 43604; (419) 259-7535; Fax: (419) 259-7575; *District Representative:* Kathleen A. Teigland

105 E. 4th St., Cincinnati 45202; (513) 763-8260; Fax: (513) 763-8268; *District Representative:* Jana Morford

37 W. Broad St., Columbus 43215; (614) 469-5186; Fax: (614) 469-2982; *District Representative:* Scott Corbitt

Committee Assignment(s): Health, Education, Labor, and Pensions; Judiciary

DODD, CHRISTOPHER J., D-CONN.

Capitol Hill Office: SR-448 20510; 224-2823; *Chief of Staff:* Sheryl Cohen

Web: dodd.senate.gov

E-mail: senator@dodd.senate.gov

District Office(s): Putnam Park, Wethersfield 06109; (860) 258-6940; Fax: (860) 258-6958; *State Director:* Ed Mann

Committee Assignment(s): Banking, Housing, and Urban Affairs; Foreign Relations; Health, Education, Labor, and Pensions; Joint Library; Rules and Administration

DOMENICI, PETE V., R-N.M.

Capitol Hill Office: SH-328 20510; 224-6621; *Administrative Assistant:* Steve Bell

Web: domenici.senate.gov

E-mail: senator_domenici@domenici.senate.gov

District Office(s): 625 Silver Ave. S.W., Albuquerque 87102; (505) 346-6791; *Communications Director:* Lisa Breeden

1065 S. Main St., Bldg. D-13, Las Cruces 88005; (505) 526-5475; Fax: (505) 523-6589; *Field Coordinator:* Don Manzanares

120 S. Federal Place, Santa Fe 87501; (505) 988-6511; *Office Manager:* Maggie Murray

Federal Bldg., Roswell 88201; (505) 623-6170; Fax: (505) 625-2547; *Regional Director:* Poe R. Corn

Committee Assignment(s): Appropriations; Budget; Energy and Natural Resources; Governmental Affairs; Indian Affairs

DORGAN, BYRON L., D-N.D.

Capitol Hill Office: SH-713 20510; 224-2551; Fax: 224-1193; *Chief of Staff:* Lucy Calautti

Web: dorgan.senate.gov

E-mail: senator@dorgan.senate.gov

District Office(s): Federal Square Bldg., Fargo 58107; (701) 239-5389; Fax: (701) 239-5512; *Area Coordinator:* Kevin Carvell

Federal Bldg., Bismarck 58501; (701) 250-4618; Fax: (701) 250-4484; *State Coordinator:* Bob Valeu

100 1st St. S.W., Minot 58701; (701) 852-0703; Fax: (701) 838-8196; *State Representative:* Gail Bergstad

102 N. 4th St., Grand Forks 58201; (701) 746-8972; Fax: (701) 746-9122; *Area Coordinator:* Kevin Carvell

Committee Assignment(s): Appropriations; Commerce, Science, and Transportation; Energy and Natural Resources; Indian Affairs

DURBIN, RICHARD J., D-ILL.

Capitol Hill Office: SR-364 20510; 224-2152; Fax: 228-0400; *Administrative Assistant:* Ed Greelegs

Web: durbin.senate.gov

E-mail: dick@durbin.senate.gov

District Office(s): 525 S. 8th St., Springfield 62703; (217) 492-4062; Fax: (217) 492-4382; *State Director:* Michael E. Daly

230 S. Dearborn St., Chicago 60604; (312) 353-4952; Fax: (312) 353-0150; *Office Director:* Margaret Houlihan

701 St., Marion 62959; (618) 998-8812; Fax: (618) 997-0176; *Staff Assistant:* Donna Eastman

Committee Assignment(s): Appropriations; Budget; Governmental Affairs; Select Ethics

EDWARDS, JOHN, D-N.C.

Capitol Hill Office: SD-225 20510; 224-3154; Fax: 228-1374; *Chief of Staff:* Karen Robb

Web: edwards.senate.gov

E-mail: senator@edwards.senate.gov

District Office(s): 301 Century Post Office Bldg., Raleigh 27601; (919) 856-4245; Fax: (919) 856-4408; *State Director:* Brad Thompson

Committee Assignment(s): Banking, Housing, and Urban Affairs; Governmental Affairs; Small Business

ENZI, MICHAEL B., R-WYO.

Capitol Hill Office: SR-290 20510; 224-3424; Fax: 228-0359; *Chief of Staff:* Flip McConnaughey

Web: enzi.senate.gov

E-mail: senator@enzi.senate.gov

District Office(s): Federal Bldg., #2007, Cheyenne 82001; (307) 772-2477; Fax: (307) 772-2480; *State Director:* Dee Rodekohr

510 S. Gillette Ave., Gillette 82716; (307) 682-6268; Fax: (307) 682-6501; *State Representative:* Robin Bailey

Federal Center, #3201, Casper 82801; (307) 261-6572; Fax: (307) 261-6574; *State Representative:* Cheri Hilderbrand

1285 Sheridan Ave., #210, Cody 82414; (307) 527-9444; Fax: (307) 527-9478; *State Representative:* Karen McCreery

545 W. Broadway, Jackson 83001; (307) 738-9507; Fax: (307) 739-9520; *State Representative:* Lyn Schanaghy

Committee Assignment(s): Banking, Housing, and Urban Affairs; Health, Education, Labor, and Pensions; Small Business; Special Aging

FEINGOLD, RUSSELL D., D-WIS.

Capitol Hill Office: SH-716 20510; 224-5323; Fax: 224-2725; *Administrative Assistant:* Mary Murphy

Web: feingold.senate.gov

E-mail: senator@feingold.senate.gov

District Office(s): 517 E. Wisconsin Ave., Milwaukee 53202; (414) 276-7282; *Southeastern Regional Coordinator:* Cecilia B. Smith-Robertson

317 1st St., #107, Wausau 54403; (715) 848-5660; *Northern Regional Coordinator:* Karen Graff

8383 Greenway Blvd., Middleton 53562; (608) 828-1200; Fax: (608) 828-1203; *Executive Assistant:* Nancy J. Mitchell

425 State St., La Crosse 54601; (608) 782-5585; *Northern and Western Regional Coordinator:* Matt Nikolay

1640 Main St., Green Bay 54302; (920) 465-7508; *Regional Coordinator:* Vacant

Committee Assignment(s): Budget; Foreign Relations; Judiciary; Special Aging

FEINSTEIN, DIANNE, D-CALIF.

Capitol Hill Office: SH-331 20510; 224-3841; Fax: 228-3954; *Chief of Staff:* Mike McGill

Web: feinstein.senate.gov

E-mail: senator@feinstein.senate.gov

District Office(s): 11111 Santa Monica Blvd., Los Angeles 90025; (310) 914-7300; Fax: (310) 914-7318; *Deputy State Director:* Amy Mall

750 B St., San Diego 92101; (619) 231-9712; Fax: (619) 231-1108; *District Director:* Mike Richmond

Federal Office Bldg., Fresno 93721; (559) 485-7430; Fax: (559) 485-9689; *District Director:* Laura Higareda-Chapa

525 Market St., San Francisco 94105; (415) 536-6868; Fax: (415) 536-6841; *State Director:* Jim Lazarus

Committee Assignment(s): Appropriations; Joint Printing; Judiciary; Rules and Administration

FITZGERALD, PETER G., R-ILL.

Capitol Hill Office: SD-555 20510; 224-2854; Fax: 228-1372; *Chief of Staff:* Richard A. Hertling

Web: fitzgerald.senate.gov

E-mail: senator_fitzgerald@fitzgerald.senate.gov

District Office(s): 230 S. Dearborn, Chicago 60604; (312) 886-3506; Fax: (312) 886-3514; *State Director:* Maggie Hickey

520 S. 8th St., Springfield 62703; (217) 492-5089; Fax: (217) 492-5099; *Field Representative:* David Curtin

Ginger Creek Village #7B, Glen Carbon 62034; (618) 692-0364; Fax: (618) 692-1499; *Southern Illinois Director:* Christine Sullivan

115 W. 1st St. #100, Dixon 61021; (815) 288-3140; Fax: (815) 288-3147; *Northern Illinois Director:* Jason Anderson

Committee Assignment(s): Agriculture, Nutrition, and Forestry; Energy and Natural Resources; Small Business

FRIST, BILL, R-TENN.

Capitol Hill Office: SR-416 20510; 224-3344; Fax: 228-1264; *Administrative Assistant:* Lee Rawls

Web: frist.senate.gov

E-mail: senator_frist@frist.senate.gov

District Office(s): 28 White Bridge Rd., Nashville 37205; (615) 352-9411; Fax: (615) 352-9985; *State Director:* Emily Reynolds

5704 Marlin Rd., Bldg. 6000, Chattanooga 37411; (615) 894-2203; Fax: (615) 894-5278; *Field Representative:* Tyler Owens

S. Royal Depot Bldg., Jackson 38301; (901) 424-9655; Fax: (901) 424-8322; *Field Representative:* Jim Humphreys

10368 Wallace Alley St., Kingsport 37663; (423) 323-1252; Fax: (423) 323-0358; *Field Representative:* Misty Horne

Twelve Oaks Executive Park, Bldg. One, Knoxville 37919; (615) 602-7977; Fax: (615) 602-7979; *Senior Field Representative:* Carolyn Jensen

5100 Poplar Ave., Memphis 38137; (901) 683-1910; Fax: (901) 683-3610; *Field Representative:* John Shannon

Committee Assignment(s): Budget; Commerce, Science, and Transportation; Foreign Relations; Health, Education, Labor, and Pensions

GORTON, SLADE, R-WASH.

Capitol Hill Office: SH-730 20510; 224-3441; Fax: 224-9393; *Chief of Staff:* Tony Williams

Web: gorton.senate.gov

E-mail: senator_gorton@gorton.senate.gov

District Office(s): 10900 N.E. 4th St., Bellevue 98004; (425) 451-0103; Fax: (425) 451-0234; *State Director:* Heidi Kelly

Federal Office Bldg., Vancouver 98660; (360) 696-7838; Fax: (360) 696-7844; *Southwest Washington Director:* Cathy Treadwell

The Tower, Yakima 98901; (509) 248-8084; Fax: (509) 248-6167; *District Representative:* Sandra Linde

West 970 Riverside Ave., Spokane 99201; (509) 353-2507; Fax: (509) 353-2547; *Eastern Washington Director:* Catherine O'Connell

8915 W. Grandridge Blvd., Kennewick 99336; (509) 783-0640; Fax: (509) 735-7559; *District Representative:* Suzanne Heaston

11120 Gravelly Lake Dr. South, Tacoma 98499; (253) 581-1614; Fax: (253) 581-0861; *Staff Assistant:* Doug Kotrba

Committee Assignment(s): Appropriations; Budget; Commerce, Science and Transportation; Energy and Natural Resources; Indian Affairs

GRAHAM, BOB, D-FLA.

Capitol Hill Office: SH-524 20510; 224-3041; Fax: 224-2237; *Chief of Staff:* Ken Klein

Web: graham.senate.gov

E-mail: bob_graham@graham.senate.gov

District Office(s): 2252 Killearn Center Blvd., Tallahassee 32308; (850) 907-1100; Fax: (850) 894-3222; *State Director:* Mary Chiles

150 Americas Center, Miami 33131; (305) 536-7293; Fax: (305) 536-6949; *Regional Director:* Ellen Roth

101 E. Kennedy Blvd., Tampa 33602; (813) 228-2476; Fax: (813) 228-2479; *Regional Director:* Tom Greene

Committee Assignment(s): Energy and Natural Resources; Environment and Public Works; Finance; Select Intelligence; Veterans' Affairs

GRAMM, PHIL, R-TEXAS

Capitol Hill Office: SR-370 20510; 224-2934; Fax: 228-2856; *Chief of Staff:* Ruth Cymber

Web: gramm.senate.gov

E-mail: phil_gramm@gramm.senate.gov

District Office(s): 2323 Bryan St., Dallas 75201; (214)
767-3000; *State Director:* Phil Wilson

404 E. Ramsey Rd., San Antonio 78216; (210) 366-9494;
Regional Director: Shannon Beeding

712 Main St., Houston 77002; (713) 718-4000; *Regional Director:* Court Koenning

100 E. Ferguson St., Tyler 75702; (903) 593-0902;
Regional Director: Matt Schaeffer

222 E. Van Buren St., Harlingen 78550; (956) 423-6118;
Regional Director: Ana Maria Garcia

310 N. Mesa St., El Paso 79901; (915) 534-6896; *Regional Director:* Margie Velez

Federal Bldg., Lubbock 79401; (806) 472-7533; *Regional Director:* Sandra Ziegler

Committee Assignment(s): Banking, Housing, and Urban
Affairs; Budget; Finance

GRAMS, ROD, R-MINN.

Capitol Hill Office: SD-257 20510; 224-3244; Fax: 228-
0956; *Chief of Staff:* Gary Russell

Web: grams.senate.gov

E-mail: mail_grams@grams.senate.gov

District Office(s): 2013 2nd Ave. North, Anoka 55303;
(612) 427-5921; Fax: (612) 427-8872; *Minnesota Director:* Merna Pease

Committee Assignment(s): Banking, Housing, and
Urban Affairs; Budget; Foreign Relations; Joint Economic

GRASSLEY, CHARLES E., R-IOWA

Capitol Hill Office: SH-135 20510; 224-3744; Fax: 224-
6020; *Chief of Staff:* Kenneth C. Cunningham

Web: grassley.senate.gov

E-mail: chuck_grassley@grassley.senate.gov

District Office(s): Federal Bldg., Des Moines 50309; (515)
284-4890; Fax: (515) 284-4069; *Iowa Administrator:*
Henry Wulff

Federal Bldg., Council Bluffs 51501; (712) 322-7103;
Regional Director: Mary Ann Hansua

Federal Bldg., Cedar Rapids 52401; (319) 363-6832; Fax:
(319) 363-7179; *Regional Director:* Mary Day

Federal Bldg., Davenport 52801; (319) 322-4331; Fax:
(319) 322-8552; *Regional Director:* Penny Vacek

Waterloo Bldg., Waterloo 50701; (319) 232-6657; Fax:
(319) 232-9965; *Regional Director:* Fred W. Schuster

Federal Courthouse, Sioux City 51101; (712) 233-1860;
Fax: (712) 233-1634; *Regional Director:* Marliss De
Jong

Committee Assignment(s): Agriculture, Nutrition, and
Forestry; Budget; Finance; Joint Taxation; Judiciary;
Special Aging

GREGG, JUDD, R-N.H.

Capitol Hill Office: SR-393 20510; 224-3324; Fax: 224-
4952; *Administrative Assistant:* Townsend Lange
McNitt

Web: gregg.senate.gov

E-mail: mailbox@gregg.senate.gov

District Office(s): 28 Webster St., Manchester 03104;
(603) 622-7979; Fax: (603) 622-0422; *Caseworker:*
Peg Ouellette

3 Glen Dr., Berlin 03570; (603) 752-2604; Fax: (603) 752-
7351; *Caseworker:* Janet Woodward

99 Pease Blvd., Portsmouth 03801; (603) 431-2171; Fax:
(603) 431-1916; *Projects Assistant:* John Cavanaugh

125 N. Main St., Concord 03301; (603) 225-7115; Fax:
(603) 224-0198; *Chief of Staff:* Joel Maiola

Committee Assignment(s): Appropriations; Budget; Government Affairs; Health, Education, Labor, and
Pensions

HAGEL, CHUCK, R-NEB.

Capitol Hill Office: SR-346 20510; 224-4224; Fax: 224-
5213; *Chief of Staff:* Lou Ann Linehan

Web: hagel.senate.gov

E-mail: chuck_hagel@hagel.senate.gov

District Office(s): 11301 Davenport St., Omaha 68154;
(402) 758-8981; Fax: (402) 758-9165; *Chief of Staff:*
Lou Ann Linehan

Federal Bldg., Lincoln 68508; (402) 476-1400; Fax: (402)
476-0605; *Constituent Services Director:* Dorothy
Anderson

4009 6th Ave., Kearney 68847; (308) 236-7602; Fax: (308)
236-7473; *Constituent Services Representative:* Julie
Brooker

1010 Ave. I, Scottsbluff 69361; (308) 632-6032; Fax: (308)
632-6295; *Constituent Services Representative:* Krisa
Hall

Committee Assignment(s): Banking, Housing, and Urban
Affairs; Foreign Relations; Health, Education, Labor,
and Pensions; Special Aging

HARKIN, TOM, D-IOWA

Capitol Hill Office: SH-731 20510; 224-3254; Fax: 224-
9369; *Chief of Staff:* JoDee Winterhof

Web: harkin.senate.gov

E-mail: tom_harkin@harkin.senate.gov

District Office(s): Federal Bldg., Des Moines 50309; (515)
284-4574; Fax: (515) 284-4937; *State Administrator:*
Dianne Liepa

Federal Bldg., Davenport 52801; (319) 322-1338; Fax:
(319) 322-0417; *Regional Representative:* Rita Vargas

150 1st Ave. N.E., Cedar Rapids 52407; (319) 365-4504;
Fax: (319) 393-6869; *Regional Administrator:* Beth
Freeman

Federal Bldg., Dubuque 52001; (319) 582-2130; Fax: (319) 582-2342; *Regional Representative:* Linda Lucy

Federal Bldg., Sioux City 51101; (712) 252-1550; Fax: (712) 252-1638; *Regional Administrator:* Maureen Wilson

Committee Assignment(s): Agriculture, Nutrition, and Forestry; Appropriations; Health, Education, Labor, and Pensions; Small Business

HATCH, ORRIN G., R-UTAH

Capitol Hill Office: SR-131 20510; 224-5251; Fax: 224-6331; *Chief of Staff:* Patricia Knight

Web: hatch.senate.gov

E-mail: senator_hatch@hatch.senate.gov

District Office(s): Federal Bldg., Salt Lake City 84138; (801) 524-4380; Fax: (801) 524-4379; *State Director:* Melanie Bowen

Federal Bldg., Ogden 84401; (801) 625-5672; Fax: (801) 625-5590; *Area Director:* Norma S. Holmgren

51 S. University Ave., Provo 84606; (801) 375-7881; Fax: (801) 374-5005; *Area Director:* Ronald Dean

P.O. Box 99, Cedar City 84720; (435) 586-8435; Fax: (435) 586-2147; *Area Director:* Jeannine Holt

Washington County Administration Bldg., St. George 84770; (435) 634-1795; Fax: (435) 634-1796; *Director:* Jeannine Holt

Committee Assignment(s): Finance; Indian Affairs; Joint Taxation; Judiciary; Select Intelligence

HELMS, JESSE, R-N.C.

Capitol Hill Office: SD-403 20510; 224-6342; Fax: 228-1339; *Administrative Assistant:* Jimmy Broughton

Web: helms.senate.gov

E-mail: jesse_helms@helms.senate.gov

District Office(s): 310 New Bern Ave., Raleigh 27601; (919) 856-4630; Fax: (919) 856-4053; *State Director:* Marilyn Darnell

Federal Bldg., #210, Hickory 28603; (828) 322-5170; Fax: (828) 322-1255; *Staff Director:* Jo Murray

Committee Assignment(s): Agriculture, Nutrition, and Forestry; Foreign Relations; Rules and Administration

HOLLINGS, ERNEST F., D-S.C.

Capitol Hill Office: SR-125 20510; 224-6121; Fax: 224-4293; *Chief of Staff:* Joey Lesesne

Web: hollings.senate.gov

E-mail: senator@hollings.senate.gov

District Office(s): Federal Bldg., Columbia 29201; (803) 765-5731; Fax: (803) 765-5742; *State Director:* Sam B. "Trip" King

Federal Bldg., Greenville 29603; (864) 233-5366; Fax: (864) 233-2923; *Area Assistant:* John Funderburk

U.S. Custom House, Charleston 29401; (843) 727-4525; Fax: (843) 722-4923; *Area Assistant:* Joe S. Maupin

Committee Assignment(s): Appropriations; Budget; Commerce, Science and Transportation

HUTCHINSON, TIM, R-ARK.

Capitol Hill Office: SD-239 20510; 224-2353; Fax: 228-3973; *Chief of Staff:* Todd Deatherage

Web: hutchinson.senate.gov

E-mail: senator.hutchinson@hutchinson.senate.gov

District Office(s): Federal Bldg., Little Rock 72201; (501) 324-6336; *State Director:* Susan Carter

Federal Bldg., Jonesboro 72401; (870) 935-5022; *Regional Representative:* Andrea Allen

101 N. Washington Ave., El Dorado 71730; (870) 863-6406; *Regional Representative:* Don Travis

1 E. Center St., Fayetteville 72701; (501) 582-1935; *Regional Representative:* Jonathan Knight

Committee Assignment(s): Armed Services; Health, Education, Labor and Pensions; Special Aging; Veterans' Affairs

HUTCHISON, KAY BAILEY, R-TEXAS

Capitol Hill Office: SR-284 20510; 224-5922; Fax: 224-0776; *Chief of Staff:* Lawrence "Larry" DiRita

Web: hutchison.senate.gov

E-mail: senator@hutchison.senate.gov

District Office(s): 10440 N. Central Expressway, Dallas 75231; (214) 361-3500; Fax: (214) 361-3502; *Constituent Services Director:* Mary Fae Kamm

1919 Smith St., Houston 77002; (713) 653-3456; Fax: (713) 209-3459; *Deputy Director:* Jason Fuller

8023 Vantage Dr., San Antonio 78230; (210) 340-2885; Fax: (210) 349-6753; *Regional Director:* Laurie Pugh

Federal Bldg., Austin 78701; (512) 916-5834; Fax: (512) 916-5839; *Regional Director:* Kevin Cooper

500 Chestnut St., Abilene 79602; (915) 676-2839; Fax: (915) 676-2937; *Regional Director:* Shea Woodard

Committee Assignment(s): Appropriations; Commerce, Science, and Transportation; Environment and Public Works; Rules and Administration

INHOFE, JAMES M., R-OKLA.

Capitol Hill Office: SR-453 20510; 224-4721; Fax: 228-0380; *Chief of Staff:* Glenn Powell

Web: inhofe.senate.gov

E-mail: jim_inhofe@inhofe.senate.gov

District Office(s): 1924 S. Utica St., Tulsa 74104; (918) 748-7111; Fax: (918) 581-7770; *Field Director:* Pat Highland

1900 N.W. Expressway, Oklahoma City 73118; (405) 608-4381; Fax: (405) 608-4120; *State Director:* Ragon Gentry

100 S. Main St., McAlester 74502; (918) 426-0933; Fax: (918) 426-0935; *Field Representative:* Tim Gaines

Continental Tower North, Enid 73701; (580) 234-5105; Fax: (580) 234-0929; *Field Representative:* Brent Kisling

Committee Assignment(s): Armed Services; Environment and Public Works; Indian Affairs; Select Intelligence

INOUYE, DANIEL K., D-HAWAII

Capitol Hill Office: SH-722 20510; 224-3934; Fax: 224-6747; *Administrative Assistant:* Patrick DeLeon

Web: inouye.senate.gov

E-mail: inouye.senate.gov/abtform.html

District Office(s): Prince Kuhio Federal Bldg., Honolulu 96850; (808) 541-2542; Fax: (808) 541-2549; *Chief of Staff:* Jennifer Goto Sabas

24 N. Church St., Maui 96793; (808) 242-9702; *Field Representative:* Ryther Barbin

101 Aupuni St., Hilo 96720; (808) 935-0844; *Field Representative:* William Kikuchi

P.O. Box 573, Kaunakakai 96748; (808) 642-0203; *Field Representative:* William Akutagawa

P.O. Box 41, Kealakekua 96750; (808) 935-0844; *Field Representative:* Wayne Tanaka

2853-A Mokoi St., Kauai 96766; (808) 245-4620; *Field Representative:* George Kawakami

Committee Assignment(s): Appropriations; Commerce, Science, and Transportation; Indian Affairs; Joint Printing; Rules and Administration

JEFFORDS, JAMES M., R-VT.

Capitol Hill Office: SH-728 20510; 224-5141; *Chief of Staff:* Susan Boardman Russ

Web: jeffords.senate.gov

E-mail: vermont@jeffords.senate.gov

District Office(s): 30 Main St., Burlington 05401; (802) 658-6001; *Office Coordinator:* Renee Huber

58 State St., Montpelier 05602; (802) 223-5273; *State Director:* Jolinda LaClair

2 S. Main St., Rutland 05701; (802) 773-3875; *Office Coordinator:* Marie Pomainville

Committee Assignment(s): Finance; Health, Education, Labor, and Pensions; Special Aging; Veterans' Affairs

JOHNSON, TIM, D-S.D.

Capitol Hill Office: SH-324 20510; 224-5842; Fax: 228-5765; *Administrative Assistant:* Greg Billings

Web: johnson.senate.gov

E-mail: tim@johnson.senate.gov

District Office(s): P.O. Box 1424, Sioux Falls 57101; (605) 332-8896; Fax: (605) 332-2824; *State Director:* Sharon Boysen

P.O. Box 1554, Aberdeen 57402; (605) 226-3440; Fax: (605) 226-2439; *Area Director:* Sharon Stroschein

P.O. Box 1098, Rapid City 57709; (605) 341-3990; Fax: (605) 341-2207; *Service Representative:* Darrell Shoemaker

Committee Assignment(s): Agriculture, Nutrition, and Forestry; Banking, Housing, and Urban Affairs; Budget; Energy and Natural Resources

KENNEDY, EDWARD M., D-MASS.

Capitol Hill Office: SR-315 20510; 224-4543; Fax: 224-2417; *Chief of Staff:* Gerry Kavanaugh

Web: kennedy.senate.gov

E-mail: senator@kennedy.senate.gov

District Office(s): John F. Kennedy Federal Bldg., Boston 02203; (617) 565-3170; Fax: (617) 565-3183; *Staff Director:* Barbara Souliotis

Committee Assignment(s): Armed Services; Health, Education, Labor and Pensions; Joint Economic; Judiciary

KERREY, BOB, D-NEB.

Capitol Hill Office: SH-141 20510; 224-6551; Fax: 224-7645; *Chief of Staff:* Chris Straub

Web: kerrey.senate.gov

E-mail: kerrey.senate.gov/pages/webform.html

District Office(s): 7602 Pacific St., Omaha 68114; (402) 391-3411; *State Director:* Robert Holmstedt

Federal Bldg., Lincoln 68508; (402) 437-5246; *Agricultural Representative:* Eugene T. Glock

17 E. 21st St., Scottsbluff 69361; (308) 632-3595; *Staff Assistant:* Maria Asmus

Committee Assignment(s): Agriculture, Nutrition, and Forestry; Finance

KERRY, JOHN, D-MASS.

Capitol Hill Office: SR-304 20510; 224-2742; Fax: 224-8525; *Chief of Staff:* David McKean

Web: kerry.senate.gov

E-mail: john_kerry@kerry.senate.gov

District Office(s): One Financial Plaza, Springfield 01103; (413) 785-4610; Fax: (413) 736-1049; *Regional Director:* Michael Vito

1 Bowdoin Square, Boston 02114; (617) 565-8519; Fax: (617) 248-3870; *State Director:* Lisa Mead

90 Madison Place, Worcester 01608; (508) 831-7380; Fax: (508) 831-7381; *Regional Director:* Michael Vito

222 Milliken Place, Fall River 02722; (508) 677-0522; Fax: (508) 677-0275; *Regional Director:* Sheila Capone

Committee Assignment(s): Banking, Housing, and Urban Affairs; Commerce, Science, and Transportation; Foreign Relations; Select Intelligence; Small Business

KOHL, HERB, D-WIS.

Capitol Hill Office: SH-330 20510; 224-5653; Fax: 224-9787; *Chief of Staff:* Paul Bock
Web: kohl.senate.gov
E-mail: senator_kohl@kohl.senate.gov
District Office(s): 310 W. Wisconsin Ave., Milwaukee 53203; (414) 297-4451; Fax: (414) 297-4455; *State Director:* JoAnne Anton
14 W. Mifflin St., Madison 53703; (608) 264-5338; Fax: (608) 264-5473; *Area Director:* Eve Galanter
402 Graham Ave., Eau Claire 54701; (715) 832-8424; Fax: (715) 832-8492; *Regional Representative:* Marjorie Bunce
4321 W. College Ave., Appleton 54914; (920) 738-1640; Fax: (920) 738-1643; *Regional Representative:* Marlene Mielke
425 State St., LaCrosse 54601; (608) 796-0045; *Regional Representative:* Cara Carper
Committee Assignment(s): Appropriations; Judiciary; Special Aging

KYL, JON, R-ARIZ.

Capitol Hill Office: SH-724 20510; 224-4521; Fax: 228-1239; *Chief of Staff:* Laurie Fenton
Web: kyl.senate.gov
E-mail: info@kyl.senate.gov
District Office(s): 2200 E. Camelback Rd., Phoenix 85016; (602) 840-1891; Fax: (602) 957-6838; *State Director:* Kimberly Wold
7315 N. Oracle Rd., Tucson 85704; (520) 575-8633; Fax: (520) 797-3232; *Regional Director:* Hank Kenski
Committee Assignment(s): Appropriations; Judiciary; Select Intelligence

LANDRIEU, MARY L., D-LA.

Capitol Hill Office: SH-702 20510; 224-5824; Fax: 224-9735; *Chief of Staff:* Norma Jane Sabiston
Web: landrieu.senate.gov
E-mail: senator@landrieu.senate.gov
District Office(s): Hale Boggs Federal Bldg., New Orleans 70130; (504) 589-2427; Fax: (504) 589-4023; *Office Manager:* Gina Warner
Old Federal Bldg., Baton Rouge 70801; (225) 389-0395; Fax: (225) 389-0660; *State Director:* Don Hutchinson
U.S. Courthouse, Shreveport 71101; (318) 676-3085; Fax: (318) 676-3100; *Office Manager:* Tari Bradford
921 Moss St., Lake Charles 70601; (318) 436-6650; Fax: (318) 439-3762; *Caseworker:* Mark Hensgens
Committee Assignment(s): Armed Services; Energy and Natural Resources; Small Business

LAUTENBERG, FRANK R., D-N.J.

Capitol Hill Office: SH-506 20510; 224-4744; Fax: 224-9707; *Chief of Staff:* Alexander "Sander" Lurie
Web: lautenberg.senate.gov
E-mail: frank_lautenberg@lautenberg.senate.gov
District Office(s): 1 Newark Center, Newark 07102; (973) 645-3030; Fax: (973) 645-0502; *State Director:* Maggie Moran
Barrington Commons, Barrington 08007; (609) 757-5353; Fax: (609) 546-1526; *Deputy State Director:* Karin Elkis
Committee Assignment(s): Appropriations; Budget; Environment and Public Works; Select Intelligence

LEAHY, PATRICK J., D-VT.

Capitol Hill Office: SR-433 20510; 224-4242; Fax: 224-3479; *Chief of Staff:* Luke Albee
Web: leahy.senate.gov
E-mail: senator_leahy@leahy.senate.gov
District Office(s): Courthouse Plaza, Burlington 05401; (802) 863-2525; *Office Director:* Charles Ross
P.O. Box 933, Montpelier 05602; (802) 229-0569; *Office Director:* Robert Paquin
Committee Assignment(s): Agriculture, Nutrition, and Forestry; Appropriations; Judiciary

LEVIN, CARL, D-MICH.

Capitol Hill Office: SR-459 20510; 224-6221; Fax: 224-1388; *Chief of Staff:* Gordon Kerr
Web: levin.senate.gov
E-mail: senator@levin.senate.gov
District Office(s): 30500 VanDyke, Warren 48093; (810) 573-9145; Fax: (810) 573-8260; *Regional Representative:* Eunice Confer
Federal Bldg., Alpena 49707; (517) 354-5520; Fax: (517) 356-3216; *Community Affairs Specialist:* T. J. Thusat
623 Ludington St., Escanaba 49829; (906) 789-0052; Fax: (906) 789-0015; *Regional Representative:* Diana Charles
207 Grandview Parkway, Traverse City 49684; (231) 947-9569; Fax: (231) 947-9518; *Regional Representative:* Harold Chase
Ford Federal Bldg., Grand Rapids 49503; (616) 456-2531; Fax: (616) 456-5147; *Regional Representative:* Richard Tormala
McNamara Federal Bldg., Detroit 48226; (313) 226-6020; Fax: (313) 226-6948; *State Director:* Charles Wilbur
Commerce Center, Saginaw 48607; (517) 754-2494; Fax: (517) 754-2920; *Community Affairs Specialist:* Mary Washington
1810 Michigan National Tower, Lansing 48933; (517) 377-1508; Fax: (517) 377-1506; *Regional Representative:* James J. Turner
Committee Assignment(s): Armed Services; Governmental Affairs; Select Intelligence; Small Business

LIEBERMAN, JOSEPH I., D-CONN.

Capitol Hill Office: SH-706 20510; 224-4041; Fax: 224-9750; *Administrative Assistant:* William G. Andresen

Web: lieberman.senate.gov

E-mail: senator_lieberman@lieberman.senate.gov

District Office(s): 1 State St., Hartford 06103; (860) 549-8463; Fax: (860) 549-8478; *State Director:* Sherry Brown

Committee Assignment(s): Armed Services; Environment and Public Works; Governmental Affairs; Small Business

LINCOLN, BLANCHE, D-ARK.

Capitol Hill Office: SD-359 20510; 224-4843; Fax: 228-1371; *Chief of Staff:* Steve Patterson

Web: lincoln.senate.gov

E-mail: blanche_lincoln@lincoln.senate.gov

District Office(s): 912 W. 4th St., Little Rock 72201; (501) 375-2993; Fax: (501) 375-7064; *Community Outreach Coordinator:* Charles Miller

Federal Bldg., Jonesboro 72401; (870) 910-6896; *Field Representative:* Kim Konecny

Drew County Courthouse, Monticello 71655; (870) 367-6925; *Field Representative:* Raymond Frazier

101 N. 6th St., Fort Smith 72901; (501) 782-9215; *Field Representative:* Jason Ford

Miller County Courthouse, Texarkana 71854; (870) 774-3106; *Field Representative:* Ed French

Committee Assignment(s): Agriculture, Nutrition, and Forestry; Energy and Natural Resources; Special Aging

LOTT, TRENT, R-MISS.

Capitol Hill Office: SR-487 20510; 224-6253; Fax: 224-2262; *Chief of Staff:* William Gottshall

Web: lott.senate.gov

E-mail: senatorlott@lott.senate.gov

District Office(s): P.O. Box 1474, Oxford 38655; (662) 234-3774; Fax: (662) 234-1744; *Staff Assistant:* Geneise Hitt

200 E. Washington St., Greenwood 38930; (662) 453-5681; Fax: (662) 453-8974; *Staff Assistant:* Carolyn Overstreet

245 E. Capitol St., Jackson 39201; (601) 965-4644; Fax: (601) 965-4007; *State Director:* Guy Hovis

3100 Pascagoula St., Pascagoula 39567; (228) 762-5400; Fax: (228) 762-0137; *Field Representative:* Bill Pope

One Government Plaza, Gulfport 39501; (228) 863-1988; Fax: (228) 863-9960; *Field Representative:* Robbie Maxwell

Committee Assignment(s): Commerce, Science, and Transportation; Finance; Rules and Administration

LUGAR, RICHARD G., R-IND.

Capitol Hill Office: SH-306 20510; *Chief of Staff:* Marty Morris

Web: lugar.senate.gov

E-mail: senator_lugar@lugar.senate.gov

District Office(s): 1180 Market Tower, Indianapolis 46204; (317) 226-5555; *State Director:* Lesley Reser

Federal Bldg., Fort Wayne 46802; *Office Director:* Philip Shaull

Federal Center, Jeffersonville 47130; (812) 288-3377; *Regional Director:* Pat McClain

101 N.W. Martin Luther King Jr. Blvd., Evansville 47708; (812) 465-6313; *Office Director:* Mike Duckworth

8585 Broadway, Merrillville 46410; (219) 736-9084; *Office Director:* Timothy J. Sanders

Committee Assignment(s): Agriculture, Nutrition, and Forestry; Foreign Relations; Select Intelligence

MACK, CONNIE, R-FLA.

Capitol Hill Office: SH-517 20510; 224-5274; Fax: 224-8022; *Chief of Staff:* John Reich

Web: mack.senate.gov

E-mail: connie@mack.senate.gov

District Office(s): 1 San Jose Place, Jacksonville 32257; (904) 268-7915; *Regional Aide:* Shannon Boyette

Sun Bank Bldg., Miami 33131; (305) 530-7100; Fax: (305) 372-3740; *Office Manager:* Gladys Ferrer

1342 Colonial Blvd., Fort Myers 33907; (941) 275-6252; Fax: (941) 275-0120; *Regional Director:* Sharon Thierer

1 N. Palafox St., Pensacola 32501; (850) 438-8875; *Regional Director:* Kris Tande

600 N. Westshore Blvd., Tampa 33609; (813) 225-7683; Fax: (813) 225-7686; *Office Manager:* Barbara DiCairano

150 S. Monroe St., Tallahassee 32301; (850) 425-1995; *Regional Director:* Greg Williams

Committee Assignment(s): Banking, Housing, and Urban Affairs; Finance; Joint Economic; Select Intelligence

McCAIN, JOHN, R-ARIZ.

Capitol Hill Office: SR-241 20510; 224-2235; Fax: 228-2862; *Administrative Assistant:* Mark Salter

Web: mccain.senate.gov

E-mail: john_mccain@mccain.senate.gov

District Office(s): 2400 E. Arizona Biltmore Circle, Phoenix 85016; (602) 952-2410; Fax: (602) 952-8702; *State Director:* Larry Pike

4450 S. Rural Rd., Tempe 85282; (480) 897-6289; Fax: (480) 897-8389; *Office Manager:* Kaye Temple

450 W. Paseo Redondo, Tucson 85701; (520) 670-6334; Fax: (520) 670-6637; *Office Manager:* Rosemary Alexander

Committee Assignment(s): Armed Services; Commerce, Science, and Transportation; Indian Affairs

McCONNELL, MITCH, R-KY.

Capitol Hill Office: SR-361A 20510; 224-2541; Fax: 224-2499; *Chief of Staff:* Kyle Simmons
Web: mcconnell.senate.gov
E-mail: senator@mcconnell.senate.gov
District Office(s): 601 W. Broadway, Louisville 40202; (502) 582-6304; Fax: (502) 582-5326; *State Director:* Larry E. Cox
301 S. Main St., London 40741; (606) 864-2026; Fax: (606) 864-2035; *Field Representative:* Rebecca Webster
1885 Dixie Highway, Fort Wright 41011; (606) 578-0188; Fax: (606) 578-0488; *Field Representative:* Kelly White
Federal Bldg., Bowling Green 42101; (270) 781-1673; Fax: (270) 782-1884; *Field Representative:* Robbin Morrison Taylor
Irvin Cobb Bldg., Paducah 42001; (270) 442-4554; Fax: (270) 443-3102; *Field Representative:* Tim Thomas
771 Corporate Dr., Lexington 40503; (606) 224-8286; Fax: (606) 224-9673; *Field Representative:* Kevin Atkins
Committee Assignment(s): Agriculture, Nutrition, and Forestry; Appropriations; Joint Library; Joint Printing; Rules and Administration

MIKULSKI, BARBARA A., D-MD.

Capitol Hill Office: SH-709 20510; 224-4654; Fax: 224-8858
Web: mikulski.senate.gov
E-mail: senator@mikulski.senate.gov
District Office(s): 6404 Ivy Lane, Greenbelt 20770; (301) 345-5517; Fax: (301) 345-7573; *Assistant to the Senator:* Anthony Lawrence
World Trade Center, Baltimore 21202; (410) 962-4510; Fax: (410) 962-4760; *State Director:* Andrea Vernot
60 W. St., Annapolis 21401; (410) 263-1805; Fax: (410) 263-5949; *Office Director:* Denise Nooe
1201 Pemberton Dr., Salisbury 21801; (410) 546-7711; Fax: (410) 546-9324; *Outreach Representative:* Cindy Betts
94 W. Washington St., Hagerstown 21740; (301) 797-2826; Fax: (301) 797-2241; *Outreach Representative:* Eva Rosvold
Committee Assignment(s): Appropriations; Health, Education, Labor and Pensions

MOYNIHAN, DANIEL PATRICK, D-N.Y.

Capitol Hill Office: SR-464 20510; 224-4451; Fax: 228-0406; *Administrative Assistant:* Tony Bullock
Web: www.senate.gov/~moynihan
E-mail: senator@dpm.senate.gov
District Office(s): 405 Lexington Ave., New York 10174; (212) 661-5150; *Regional Director:* Ross Frommer

189 Main St., Oneonta 13820; (607) 433-2310; *Regional Director:* Joe Caruso Guaranty Bldg., Buffalo 14202; (716) 551-4097; *Regional Director:* James Kane
Committee Assignment(s): Environment and Public Works; Finance; Joint Library; Joint Taxation; Rules and Administration

MURKOWSKI, FRANK H., R-ALASKA

Capitol Hill Office: SH-322 20510; 224-6665; Fax: 224-5301; *Chief of Staff:* David Garman
Web: murkowski.senate.gov
E-mail: murkowski.senate.gov/webmail.html
District Office(s): Federal Bldg., Anchorage 99513; (907) 271-3735; Fax: (907) 276-4081; *State Director:* Patricia B. Heller
130 Trading Bay Rd., Kenai 99611; (907) 283-5808; Fax: (907) 283-4363; *Special Assistant:* Rebecca Hultberg
P.O. Box 21647, Juneau 99802; (907) 586-7400; Fax: (907) 586-8922; *Special Assistant:* Lucy Hudson
851 E. Westpoint Dr., Wasilla 99654; (907) 376-7665; Fax: (907) 376-8526; *Special Assistant:* Carol Gustafson
109 Main St., Ketchikan 99901; (907) 225-6880; Fax: (907) 225-0390; *Special Assistant:* Sherrie Slick
Federal Bldg., Fairbanks 99701; (907) 456-0233; Fax: (907) 456-0240; *Special Assistant:* Althea St. Martin
Committee Assignment(s): Energy and Natural Resources; Finance; Indian Affairs; Veterans' Affairs

MURRAY, PATTY, D-WASH.

Capitol Hill Office: SR-173 20510; 224-2621; Fax: 224-0238; *Chief of Staff:* Rick Desimone
Web: murray.senate.gov
E-mail: senator_murray@murray.senate.gov
District Office(s): 2988 Jackson Federal Bldg., Seattle 98174; (206) 553-5545; Fax: (206) 553-0891; *State Director:* John Engber
402 E. Yakima Ave., Yakima 98901; (509) 453-7462; Fax: (509) 453-7731; *Regional Coordinator:* Corky Mattingly
Federal Bldg., Vancouver 98660; (360) 696-7797; Fax: (360) 696-7798; *Regional Representative:* Kaye Masco
601 W. Main Ave., Spokane 99204; (509) 624-9515; Fax: (509) 624-9561; *Regional Coordinator:* Judy Olson
2930 Wetmore Ave., Everett 98201; (425) 259-6515; Fax: (425) 259-7152; *Regional Coordinator:* Jill McKinnie
Committee Assignment(s): Appropriations; Budget; Health, Education, Labor and Pensions; Veterans' Affairs

NICKLES, DON, R-OKLA.

Capitol Hill Office: SH-133 20510; 224-5754; Fax: 224-6008; *Administrative Assistant:* Bret Bernhardt
Web: nickles.senate.gov
E-mail: senator@nickles.senate.gov

District Office(s): 100 N. Broadway, Oklahoma City 73102; (405) 231-4941; *Field Representative:* Mark Nichols

711 S.W. D Ave., Lawton 73501; (580) 357-9878; *Field Representative:* Billie Jo Penn

409 S. Boston Ave., Tulsa 74103; (918) 581-7651; *Manager:* Sharon K. Keasler

1914 Lake Rd., Ponca City 74601; (580) 767-1270; *State Director:* Cheryl Fletcher

Committee Assignment(s): Budget; Energy and Natural Resources; Finance; Joint Printing; Rules and Administration

REED, JACK, D-R.I.

Capitol Hill Office: SH-320 20510; 224-4642; *Administrative Assistant:* J. B. Poersch

Web: reed.senate.gov

E-mail: jack@reed.senate.gov

District Office(s): 201 Hillside Rd., Cranston 02920; (401) 943-3100; *Chief of Staff:* Raymond Simone

Committee Assignment(s): Armed Services; Banking, Housing and Urban Affairs; Health, Education, Labor, and Pensions; Special Aging

REID, HARRY, D-NEV.

Capitol Hill Office: SH-528 20510; 224-3542; Fax: 224-7327; *Chief of Staff:* Susan McCue

Web: reid.senate.gov

E-mail: senator_reid@reid.senate.gov

District Office(s): 300 Las Vegas Blvd. South, Las Vegas 89101; (702) 474-0041; Fax: (702) 474-0137; *Regional Manager:* Jerry Reynoldson

600 E. William St., Carson City 89701; (775) 882-7343; *Regional Representative:* Karen Denio

400 S. Virginia St., Reno 89501; (775) 686-5750; Fax: (775) 686-5757; *State Director:* Mary Conelly

Committee Assignment(s): Appropriations; Environment and Public Works; Indian Affairs; Select Ethics; Special Aging

ROBB, CHARLES S., D-VA.

Capitol Hill Office: SR-154 20510; 224-4024; Fax: 224-8689; *Chief of Staff:* Thomas Lehner

Web: robb.senate.gov

E-mail: senator@robb.senate.gov

District Office(s): The Ironfronts, Richmond 23219; (804) 771-2221; Fax: (804) 771-8313; *State Director:* Rich Williams

BB&T Bldg., Roanoke 24011; (540) 985-0103; Fax: (540) 985-0266; *Regional Representative:* Debbie Lawson-Goins

First Citizens Bank Bldg., Danville 24541; (804) 791-0330; Fax: (804) 791-0334; *Regional Representative:* Anne Geyer

First Union Bank Bldg., Clintwood 24288; (540) 926-4104; Fax: (540) 926-4823; *Regional Representative:* Jim F. O'Quinn

VA Dominion Towers, Norfolk 23510; (757) 441-3124; Fax: (757) 640-1502; *Regional Representative:* Bobbie Spear

Committee Assignment(s): Armed Services; Finance; Joint Economic; Select Intelligence

ROBERTS, PAT, R-KAN.

Capitol Hill Office: SH-302 20510; 224-4774; Fax: 224-3514; *Chief of Staff:* Leroy Towns

Web: roberts.senate.gov

E-mail: pat_roberts@roberts.senate.gov

District Office(s): 155 N. Market St., Wichita 67202; (316) 263-0416; Fax: (316) 263-0273; *District Director:* Karin Wisdom

100 Military Plaza, #203, Dodge City 67801; (316) 227-2244; Fax: (316) 227-2264; *District Director:* Debbie Pugh

4200 Somerset Dr., Prairie Village 66208; (913) 648-3103; Fax: (913) 648-3106; *State Director:* Mike Harper

Frank Carlson Federal Bldg., Topeka 66683; (785) 295-2745; Fax: (785) 235-3665; *Assistant State Director:* Chuck Banks

Committee Assignment(s): Agriculture, Nutrition, and Forestry; Armed Services; Select Ethics; Select Intelligence

ROCKEFELLER, JOHN D. IV, D-W.VA.

Capitol Hill Office: SH-531 20510; 224-6472; Fax: 224-7665; *Chief of Staff:* Tamera Luzzatto

Web: rockefeller.senate.gov

E-mail: senator@rockefeller.senate.gov

District Office(s): 207 Prince St., Beckley 25801; (304) 253-9704; Fax: (304) 253-2578; *Area Coordinator:* Greg Ball

118 Adams St., Fairmont 26554; (304) 367-0122; Fax: (304) 367-0822; *Area Coordinator:* Larry Lemon

405 Capitol St., Charleston 25301; (304) 347-5372; Fax: (304) 347-5371; *State Director:* Lou Ann Johnson

225 W. King St., Martinsburg 25401; (304) 262-9285; Fax: (304) 262-9288; *Area Coordinator:* Penny Householder

Committee Assignment(s): Commerce, Science, and Transportation; Finance; Veterans' Affairs

ROTH, WILLIAM V. JR., R-DEL.

Capitol Hill Office: SH-104 20510; 224-2441; *Administrative Assistant:* John M. Duncan

Web: roth.senate.gov

E-mail: comments@roth.senate.gov

District Office(s): J. Caleb Boggs Federal Bldg., Wilmington 19801; (302) 573-6291; *County Director:* Verna Hensley

12 The Circle, Georgetown 19947; (302) 856-7690; *State Director:* Marlene Elliott

Federal Bldg., Dover 19904; (302) 674-3308; *Legislative Assistant:* Robert Book

Committee Assignment(s): Finance; Governmental Affairs; Joint Economic; Joint Taxation

SANTORUM, RICK, R-PA.

Capitol Hill Office: SR-120 20510; 224-6324; Fax: 228-0604; *Chief of Staff:* Mark D. Rodgers

Web: santorum.senate.gov

E-mail: senator@santorum.senate.gov

District Office(s): Regency Square, #202, Altoona 16001; (814) 946-7023; Fax: (814) 946-7025; *Field Representative:* Julia Bowser

1705 W. 26th St., Erie 16508; (814) 454-7114; Fax: (814) 459-2096; *Field Representative:* Stephanie Lindenberger

221 Strawberry Square, Harrisburg 17101; (717) 231-7540; Fax: (717) 231-7542; *Economic Development Director:* Emmet Mahon

3804 Federal Bldg., Allentown 18015; (610) 770-0142; Fax: (610) 770-0911; *Community Affairs Director:* Jeff Haberkern

Landmarks Bldg., Pittsburgh 15219; (412) 562-0533; Fax: (412) 562-4313; *Regional Director:* Keith Schmidt

527 Linden St., Scranton 18503; (717) 344-8799; Fax: (717) 344-8906; *Regional Director:* Susan Cox

Widener Bldg., Philadelphia 19107; (215) 864-690 0; Fax: (215) 864-6910; *Regional Director:* Skip Irvine

Committee Assignment(s): Agriculture, Nutrition, and Forestry; Armed Services; Banking, Housing, and Urban Affairs; Rules and Administration; Special Aging

SARBANES, PAUL S., D-MD.

Capitol Hill Office: SH-309 20510; 224-4524; Fax: 224-1651; *Chief of Staff:* Peter Marudas

Web: sarbanes.senate.gov

E-mail: senator@sarbanes.senate.gov

District Office(s): 15499 Potomac River Dr., Cobb Island 20625; (301) 259-2404; *Southern Maryland Representative:* Ursula Culver

141 Baltimore St., Cumberland 21502; (301) 724-0695; Fax: (301) 724-4660; *Western Maryland Representative:* Tim Magrath

110 W. Church St., Salisbury 21801; (410) 860-2131; Fax: (410) 860-2134; *Eastern Shore Representative:* Lee Whaley

Tower I, Baltimore 21201; (410) 962-4436; Fax: (410) 962-4156; *State Office Director:* Sharon Faraone

1110 Bonifant St., Silver Spring 20910; (301) 589-0797; Fax: (301) 589-0598; *Field Representative:* Jeannie Lazerov

Committee Assignment(s): Banking, Housing, and Urban Affairs; Budget; Foreign Relations; Joint Economic

SCHUMER, CHARLES E., D-N.Y.

Capitol Hill Office: SH-313 20510; 224-6542; Fax: 228-3027; *Chief of Staff:* John R. Wyma

Web: schumer.senate.gov

E-mail: senator@schumer.senate.gov

District Office(s): 757 3rd Ave., New York 10017; (212) 486-4430; *State Director:* Michael Lynch

Leo O'Brien Bldg., Albany 12207; (518) 431-4070; Fax: (518) 431-4076; *Regional Representative:* Stephen Mann

P.O. Box 7318, Syracuse 13261; (315) 423-5471; Fax: (315) 423-5185; *Regional Representative:* Jill Harvey

100 State St., Rochester 14614; (716) 263-5866; Fax: (716) 263-3173; *Regional Representative:* Joe Hamm

111 W. Huron St., Buffalo 14202; (716) 846-4111; Fax: (716) 846-4113; *Regional Representative:* Jack O'Donnell

Federal Bldg., Binghamton 13901; (607) 772-8109; Fax: (607) 772-8124; *Regional Representative:* Pat Collins

2 Greenway Plaza, Melville 11747; (631) 753-0978; *Regional Representative:* Jason Goldstein

Committee Assignment(s): Banking, Housing, and Urban Affairs; Judiciary; Rules and Administration

SESSIONS, JEFF, R-ALA.

Capitol Hill Office: SR-493 20510; 224-4124; Fax: 224-3149; *Chief of Staff:* Armand DeKeyser

Web: sessions.senate.gov

E-mail: senator@sessions.senate.gov

District Office(s): The One Square Bldg., Montgomery 36104; (334) 265-9507; Fax: (334) 834-2823; *State Director:* Chuck Spurlock

Vance Federal Bldg., Birmingham 35203; (205) 731-1500; Fax: (205) 731-0221; *Field Representative:* Michael Davis

AmSouth Center, Huntsville 35801; (256) 533-0979; Fax: (256) 533-0745; *Field Representative:* Angela Colvert

Colonial Bank Center, Mobile 36608; (334) 414-3083; Fax: (334) 414-5845; *Field Representative:* Stormie Janzen

Committee Assignment(s): Armed Services; Health, Education, Labor and Pensions; Joint Economic; Judiciary

SHELBY, RICHARD C., R-ALA.

Capitol Hill Office: SH-110 20510; 224-5744; Fax: 224-3416; *Chief of Staff:* Tom Young

Web: shelby.senate.gov

E-mail: senator@shelby.senate.gov

District Office(s): Vance Federal Bldg., Birmingham 35203; (205) 731-1384; Fax: (205) 731-1386; *District Representative:* Blair Agricola

Federal House, Mobile 36602; (334) 694-4164; Fax: (334) 694-4166; *District Representative:* Laura Breland

1118 Greensboro Ave., Tuscaloosa 35401; (205) 759-5047; Fax: (205) 759-5067; *District Representative:* Melissa Davis

15 Lee St., Montgomery 36104; (334) 223-7303; Fax: (334) 223-7317; *District Representative:* Reid Cavnar

Huntsville International Airport, Huntsville 35824; (256) 772-0460; Fax: (256) 772-8387; *District Representative:* LeAnn Hill

Committee Assignment(s): Appropriations; Banking, Housing and Urban Affairs; Select Intelligence; Special Aging

SMITH, GORDON H., R-ORE.

Capitol Hill Office: SR-404 20510; 224-3753; Fax: 228-3997; *Chief of Staff:* Kurt Pfotenhauer

Web: gsmith.senate.gov

E-mail: oregon@gsmith.senate.gov

District Office(s): One World Trade Center, Portland 97204; (503) 326-3386; Fax: (503) 326-2900; *State Director:* Kerry Tymchuk

211 E. 7th Ave., Eugene 97401; (541) 465-6750; Fax: (541) 465-6808; *Regional Representative:* Terri Moffett

Jamison Bldg., Bend 97701; (541) 318-1298; Fax: (541) 318-1396; *Regional Representative:* Susan Fitch

Security Plaza, Medford 97504; (541) 608-9102; Fax: (541) 608-9104; *Regional Representative:* Esther Kennedy

116 S. Main St., Pendleton 97801; (541) 278-1129; Fax: (541) 278-4109; *Regional Representative:* Troy Nichols

Committee Assignment(s): Budget; Energy and Natural Resources; Foreign Relations

SMITH, ROBERT C., R-N.H.

Capitol Hill Office: SD-307 20510; 224-2841; Fax: 224-1353; *Chief of Staff:* Dino Carluccio

Web: smith.senate.gov

E-mail: opinion@smith.senate.gov

District Office(s): 1750 Elm St., Manchester 03104; (603) 634-5000; Fax: (603) 634-5003; *State Director:* Pam Patenaude

1 Harbour Place, Portsmouth 03801; (603) 433-1667; Fax: (603) 433-1885; *Caseworker:* Olga Clough

Committee Assignment(s): Armed Services; Environment and Public Works; Judiciary; Select Ethics

SNOWE, OLYMPIA J., R-MAINE

Capitol Hill Office: SR-250 20510; 224-5344; Fax: 224-1946; *Chief of Staff:* Kevin Raye

Web: snowe.senate.gov

E-mail: olympia@snowe.senate.gov

District Office(s): 231 Main St., Biddeford 04005; (207) 282-4144; Fax: (207) 284-2358; *Regional Representative:* Peter Morin

3 Canal Plaza, Portland 04112; (207) 874-0883; Fax: (207) 874-7631; *State Director:* Charles Summers

68 Sewall St., Augusta 04330; (207) 622-8292; Fax: (207) 622-7295; *Regional Representative:* John Cummings

169 Academy St., Presque Isle 04769; (207) 764-5124; Fax: (207) 764-6420; *Regional Representative:* Ken White

1 Cumberland Place, Bangor 04401; (207) 945-0432; Fax: (207) 941-9525; *Regional Representative:* Gail Kelly

2 Great Falls Plaza, Auburn 04210; (207) 786-2451; Fax: (207) 782-1438; *Regional Representative:* Jane Desaulniers

Committee Assignment(s): Armed Services; Budget; Commerce, Science and Transportation; Small Business

SPECTER, ARLEN, R-PA.

Capitol Hill Office: SH-711 20510; 224-4254; Fax: 228-1229; *Chief of Staff:* David Urban

Web: specter.senate.gov

E-mail: senator_specter@specter.senate.gov

District Office(s): Federal Bldg., Pittsburgh 15222; (412) 644-3400; *Executive Director:* Doug Saltzman

Federal Bldg., Erie 16501; (814) 453-3010; *Executive Director:* Lynda Murphy

Post Office Bldg., Allentown 18101; (610) 434-1444; *Executive Director:* Mary Jo Bierman

Federal Bldg., Harrisburg 17101; (717) 782-3951; *Executive Director:* Gayle Mills

Federal Bldg., Philadelphia 19106; (215) 597-7200; *State Director:* Ken Braithwaite

S. Main Towers, Wilkes-Barre 18701; (717) 826-6265; *Executive Director:* Andrew Wallace

310 Spruce St., Scranton 18503; (717) 346-2006; *Executive Director:* Andrew Wallace

Committee Assignment(s): Appropriations; Governmental Affairs; Judiciary; Veterans' Affairs

STEVENS, TED, R-ALASKA

Capitol Hill Office: SH-522 20510; 224-3004; Fax: 224-2354; *Chief of Staff:* Mitch Rose

Web: stevens.senate.gov

E-mail: senator_stevens@stevens.senate.gov

District Office(s): Federal Bldg., Anchorage 99513; (907) 271-5915; Fax: (907) 258-9305; *State Director:* Marie Nash

130 Trading Bay Rd., Kenai 99611; (907) 283-5808; Fax: (907) 283-4363; *Staff Assistant:* Becky Hultberg

Federal Bldg., Juneau 99802; (907) 586-7400; Fax: (907) 586-8922; *Staff Assistant:* Lucy Hudson

Federal Bldg., Ketchikan 99901; (907) 225-6880; Fax: (907) 225-0390; *Staff Assistant:* Sherrie Slick

Federal Bldg., Fairbanks 99701; (907) 456-0261; Fax: (907) 451-7290; *Staff Assistant:* Ruth Burnett

851 E. Westpoint Dr., Wasilla 99654; (907) 376-7665; Fax: (907) 376-8526; *Staff Assistant:* Carol Gustafson

Committee Assignment(s): Appropriations; Commerce, Science, and Transportation; Governmental Affairs; Joint Library; Rules and Administration

THOMAS, CRAIG, R-WYO.

Capitol Hill Office: SH-109 20510; 224-6441; Fax: 224-1724; *Chief of Staff:* Dan Naatz

Web: thomas.senate.gov

E-mail: craig@thomas.senate.gov

District Office(s): 2120 Capitol Ave., Cheyenne 82001; (307) 772-2451; Fax: (307) 638-3512; *State Scheduler:* Mary Paxson

325 W. Main St., Riverton 82501; (307) 856-6642; Fax: (307) 856-5901; *Field Representative:* Pam Buline

Federal Bldg., Casper 82601; (307) 261-6413; Fax: (307) 265-6706; *State Director:* Bobbi Brown

2632 Foothill Blvd., Rock Springs 82901; (307) 362-5012; Fax: (307) 362-5129; *Field Representative:* Pati Smith

40 S. Main St., Sheridan 82801; (307) 672-6456; Fax: (307) 672-8227; *Field Representative:* Jackie Van Mark

Committee Assignment(s): Energy and Natural Resources; Environment and Public Works; Foreign Relations; Indian Affairs

THOMPSON, FRED, R-TENN.

Capitol Hill Office: SD-523 20510; 224-4944; Fax: 228-3679; *Chief of Staff:* Powell A. Moore

Web: thompson.senate.gov

E-mail: senator_thompson@thompson.senate.gov

District Office(s): Howard H. Baker, Jr. U.S. House, Knoxville 37902; (423) 545-4253; Fax: (423) 545-4252; *Field Representative:* Kirk Cunningham

Federal Bldg., Memphis 38103; (901) 544-4224; Fax: (901) 544-4227; *Field Representative:* Kelley Hankins

3322 W. End Ave., Nashville 37203; (615) 736-5129; Fax: (615) 269-4803; *State Director:* Bob Davis

Joel E. Soloman Federal Bldg., Chattanooga 37402; (423) 752-5337; Fax: (423) 752-5342; *Field Representative:* Chris Devaney

Tri-Cities Regional Airport, Blountville 37617; (423) 325-6217; Fax: (423) 325-6192; *Field Representative:* Tony DeVault

Federal Bldg., Jackson 38301; (901) 423-9344; Fax: (901) 423-8918; *Field Representative:* John Newman

Committee Assignment(s): Finance; Governmental Affairs

THURMOND, STROM, R-S.C.

Capitol Hill Office: SR-217 20510; 224-5972; Fax: 224-1300; *Chief of Staff:* R. J. Duke Short

Web: thurmond.senate.gov

E-mail: senator@thurmond.senate.gov

District Office(s): Thurmond Federal Bldg., Columbia 29201; (803) 765-5494; *State Director:* Warren Abernathy

247 Meeting St., Charleston 29401; (843) 727-4596; Fax: (843) 727-4598; *Office Manager:* Patricia Rones-Sykes

John McMillan Federal Bldg., Florence 29501; (843) 662-8873; *Office Manager:* Raleigh Ward

211 York St. N.E., Aiken 29803; (803) 649-2591; *Office Manager:* Elizabeth McFarland

Committee Assignment(s): Armed Services; Judiciary; Veterans' Affairs

TORRICELLI, ROBERT G., D-N.J.

Capitol Hill Office: SD-113 20510; 224-3224; Fax: 224-8567; *Chief of Staff:* Eric Shuffler

Web: torricelli.senate.gov

E-mail: senator_torricelli@torricelli.senate.com

District Office(s): 1 Riverfront Plaza, Newark 07102; (973) 624-5555; Fax: (973) 639-2878; *State Director:* Sean Jackson

Korman Interstate Business Park, Bellmawr 08031; (856) 933-2245; Fax: (856) 933-2711; *Office Director:* Denise Velazquez

Committee Assignment(s): Foreign Relations; Governmental Affairs; Judiciary; Rules and Administration

VOINOVICH, GEORGE V., R-OHIO

Capitol Hill Office: SH-317 20510; 224-3353; Fax: 228-1382; *Chief of Staff:* Ted Hollingsworth

Web: voinovich.senate.gov

E-mail: senator_voinovich@voinovich.senate.gov

District Office(s): 420 Madison Ave., Toledo 43604; (419) 259-3895; Fax: (419) 259-3899; *District Representative:* Dennis Filgor

36 E. 7th St., Cincinnati 45202; (513) 684-3265; Fax: (513) 684-3269; *District Representative:* Ann Langdon

1240 E. Ninth St, Cleveland 44199; (216) 522-7095; Fax: (216) 522-7097; *State Director:* Beth Hansen

37 W. Broad St., Columbus 43215; (614) 469-6697; Fax: (614) 469-7733; *District Representative:* Jeffrey LaRue

37 W. Broad St., Columbus 43215; (614) 469-6774; Fax: (614) 469-7419; *Constituent Services Director:* Jenny Ogle

Committee Assignment(s): Environment and Public Works; Governmental Affairs; Select Ethics; Small Business

WARNER, JOHN W., R-VA.

Capitol Hill Office: SR-225 20510; 224-2023; Fax: 224-6295; *Chief of Staff:* Susan Magill

Web: warner.senate.gov

E-mail: senator@warner.senate.gov

District Office(s): Main St. Centre II, Richmond 23219; (804) 771-2579; Fax: (804) 782-2131; *Office Manager:* Aljean Peterson

World Trade Center, Norfolk 23510; (757) 441-3079; Fax: (757) 441-6250; *Office Manager:* Loretta Tate

Federal Bldg., Abingdon 24210; (540) 628-8158; Fax: (540) 628-1036; *Office Manager:* Cathie Gollehon

First Union Bank Bldg., Roanoke 24011; (540) 857-2676; Fax: (540) 857-2800; *Caseworker:* Camellia Crowder

Committee Assignment(s): Armed Services; Environment and Public Works; Rules and Administration

WELLSTONE, PAUL, D-MINN.

Capitol Hill Office: SH-136 20510; 224-5641; Fax: 224-8438; *Chief of Staff:* Colin McGinnis

Web: wellstone.senate.gov

E-mail: senator@wellstone.senate.gov

District Office(s): International Bldg., St. Paul 55114; (651) 645-0323; Fax: (651) 645-0704; *State Director:* Connie Lewis

105 2nd Ave. West, Virginia 55792; (218) 741-1074; Fax: (218) 741-8544; *Northern Minnesota Director:* Lisa Radosevich Pattni

417 Litchfield Ave. S.W., Willmar 56201; (320) 231-0001; Fax: (320) 231-0006; *Wilmar Office Director:* Tom Meium

Committee Assignment(s): Foreign Relations; Health, Education, Labor and Pensions; Indian Affairs; Small Business; Veterans' Affairs

WYDEN, RON, D-ORE.

Capitol Hill Office: SH-516 20510; 224-5244; Fax: 228-2717; *Chief of Staff:* Josh R. Kardon

Web: wyden.senate.gov

E-mail: wyden.senate.gov/mail2.htm

District Office(s): 151 W. 7th Ave., Eugene 97401; (541) 431-0229; *Field Representative:* Mary Gautreaux

Federal House, Medford 97501; (541) 858-5122; *Field Representative:* Traci Dow

The Jamison Bldg., Bend 97701; (541) 330-9142; *Field Representative:* David Blair

700 N.E. Multnomah St., Portland 97232; (503) 326-7525; *State Director:* Chris Warner

Sac Annex Bldg., La Grande 97850; (541) 962-7691; *Field Representative:* Wayne Kinney

777 13th St. S.E., Salem 97301; (503) 589-4555; *Field Representative:* Patricia Daniels

Committee Assignment(s): Budget; Commerce, Science, and Transportation; Energy and Natural Resources; Environment and Public Works; Special Aging

Ready Reference Lists

Directory of Government Information on the Internet

Listed below are Web sites for locating executive, legislative, and judicial information on the Internet. Web addresses active as of April 17, 2000.

EXECUTIVE BRANCH

The White House

Main: www.whitehouse.gov
News: www.whitehouse.gov/WH/html/briefroom.html
President's Bio: www.whitehouse.gov/WH/EOP/
  OP/html/OP_Bio.html
Vice President's Bio:
  www.whitehouse.gov/WH/EOP/OVP/
  ovpbio_bottom.html
FY 2001 Budget Proposal: w3.access.gpo.gov/usbudget/
  fy2001/maindown.html

Agriculture Dept.

Main: www.usda.gov
News: www.usda.gov/news/news.htm
Secretary's Bio: www.usda.gov/agencies/gallery/
  glickman.htm
Food Safety (government food safety information): www.
  foodsafety.gov
Employee Directory: www.usda.gov/phonebook
List of Regional Offices: offices.usda.gov/scripts/ndISAPI.
  dll/oip_public/USA_map
FY2000 Budget: www.usda.gov/agency/obpa/
  Budget-Summary/2000/text.html
FY2001 Budget: www.usda.gov/agency/obpa/
  Budget-Summary/2001/text.htm

Commerce Dept.

Main: www.commerce.gov
News: 204.193.246.62/public.nsf/docs/
  opa-media-contacts
Secretary's Bio: 204.193.246.62/public.nsf/docs/
  about-the-secretary
E-Commerce Policy: www.ecommerce.gov/
  usdocume.htm
Employee Directory: 204.193.246.62/public.nsf/docs/
  person-finder
List of Regional Offices:
  Census Bureau: www.census.gov/main/www/lco.html
  Economic Development Administration: www.doc.gov/
  eda/html/regoffic.htm

International Trade Administration:
  infoserv2.ita.doc.gov/NEDHomeP.nsf/
  fc3c9761841e8062852564b2006bc6cc/
  49c1ecbcbeeec42d8525663c006367d8?
  OpenDocument
  Minority Business Development Agency:
  www.mbda.gov/local_MBDAcenters.html
FY2000 Budget: www.doc.gov/bmi/budget/pb2000/
  bibtoc.htm
FY2001 Budget: www.doc.gov/bmi/budget/pb2001/
  bibtoc.htm

Defense Dept.

Main: www.defenselink.mil
News: www.defenselink.mil/news
Secretary's Bio: www.defenselink.mil/bios/
  secdef_bio.html
**EDUGATE (educational programs sponsored by the
  Defense Dept):** 198.3.128.64/edugate
Staff Directory: www.defenselink.mil/faq/pis/
  dod_addresses.html
FY2000/FY2001 Budget: www.defenselink.mil/pubs/
  almanac/almanac/money

Education Dept.

Main: www.ed.gov
News: www.ed.gov/offices/OPA
Secretary's Bio: www.ed.gov/offices/OS/riley.html
The Gateway (online education materials): www.
  thegateway.org
Employee Directory: web99.ed.gov/EDLocator
List of Regional Offices: www.ed.gov/offices/OIIA/
  Regions
FY2000/FY2001 Budget: www.ed.gov/offices/OUS/
  budget.html

Energy Dept.

Main: www.doe.gov
News: www.doe.gov/news.htm
Secretary's Bio: www.doe.gov/glance/secbio.htm
DOE Laboratories: www.doe.gov/people/peopnl.htm
Employee Directory: www.doe.gov/people/doecall.htm

List of Regional Offices: www.doe.gov/people/
peopfo.htm

FY2000 Budget: www.cfo.doe.gov/budget/guidance/
fy2000/index.htm

FY2001 Budget: www.cfo.doe.gov/budget/guidance/
fy2001/index.htm

Health and Human Services Dept.

Main: www.os.dhhs.gov

News: www.hhs.gov/news

Secretary's Bio: www.hhs.gov/about/bios/dhhssec.html

The Healthfinder (consumer health and human services
information): www.healthfinder.gov

Employee Directory: directory.psc.gov/employee.htm

List of Regional Offices: www.hhs.gov/about/
regionmap.html

FY2000/FY2001 Budget: www.hhs.gov/progorg/asmb/
budget/budget.html

Housing and Urban Development Dept.

Main: www.hud.gov

News: www.hud.gov/news.html

Secretary's Bio: www.hud.gov/cuomo.html

Home Buyer's Kit: www.hud.gov/buyhome.html

Employee Directory: www.hud.gov/ahpeop.html

List of Regional Offices: www.hud.gov/local.html

FY2000/FY2001 Budget: www.hud.gov/budget.html

Interior Dept.

Main: www.doi.gov

News: www.doi.gov/testdp/doipress

Secretary's Bio: www.doi.gov/bab_bio.html

Volunteer Opportunities: www.doi.gov/non-profit/
volx.html

Employee Directory: www.doi.gov/keyoff.html

List of Regional Offices:

Bureau of Indian Affairs: www.doi.gov/bia/areas/
00alare.html

Bureau of Land Management: www.blm.gov/nhp/
directory/index.htm

National Park Service: www.nps.gov/legacy/
regions.html

Office of Surface Mining: www.osmre.gov/field.htm

U.S. Fish and Wildlife Service: www.fws.gov/where/
regfield.html

U.S. Geological Survey: interactive.usgs.gov/find_us/
index.asp

FY2000/FY2001 Budget: www.doi.gov/budget

Justice Dept.

Main: www.usdoj.gov

News: www.usdoj.gov/03press/index.html

Secretary's Bio: www.usdoj.gov/ag/jreno.html

FBI Most Wanted Lists: www.fbi.gov/mostwanted.htm

List of Regional Offices:

Drug Enforcement Administration: www.usdoj.gov/dea/
agency/domestic.htm

Federal Bureau of Investigation: www.fbi.gov/contact/
fo/fo.htm

Federal Bureau of Prisons: www.bop.gov/facilnot.html

Immigration and Naturalization Service: www.ins.usdoj.
gov/graphics/fieldoffices

FY2000/FY2001 Budget: www.usdoj.gov/jmd/
2k-summary/2ktoc.html

Labor Dept.

Main: www.dol.gov

News: www.dol.gov/dol/public/media/main.htm

Secretary's Bio: www.dol.gov/dol/opa/public/sec/
secbio.htm

America's Job Bank (public employment service): www.
ajb.dni.us

Employee Directory: www.dol.gov/dol/opa/public/
aboutdol/key_folk.htm

List of Regional Offices:

Bureau of Labor Statistics: www.bls.gov/regnhome.htm

Employment and Training Administration: www.ttrc.
doleta.gov/ETA

Occupational Safety and Health Administration: www.
osha-slc.gov/html/RAmap.html

FY2000/FY2001 Budget: www.dol.gov/dol/_sec/public/
budget/main.htm

State Dept.

Main: www.state.gov

News: secretary.state.gov/www/briefings/statements/
index.html

Secretary's Bio: secretary.state.gov/www/albright/
albright.html

Travel Warnings: travel.state.gov/travel_warnings.html

Employee Directory: www.state.gov/www/about_state/
contacts/phbook/phbook.html

List of Regional Offices:

Passport Services: travel.state.gov/agencies_list.html

FY2000/FY2001 Budget: www.state.gov/www/budget/
numbers.html

Transportation Dept.

Main: www.dot.gov

News: www.dot.gov/news.htm

Secretary's Bio: www.dot.gov/affairs/slatebio.htm

Aviation Consumer Protection Division: www.dot.gov/ost/
ogc/subject/consumer/aviation

Employee Directory: www.dot.gov/contacts.htm

List of Regional Offices:

Federal Aviation Administration: www.faa.gov/
centersinfo.htm

Federal Highway Administration: www.fhwa.dot.gov/
field.html

Federal Railroad Administration: www.fra.dot.gov/o/
safety/20regional.htm
Federal Transit Administration: www.fta.dot.gov/office/
regional
Maritime Administration: www.marad.dot.gov/offices/
index.html
National Highway Traffic Safety Administration: www.
nhtsa.dot.gov/nhtsa/whatis/regions
FY2000/FY2001 Budget: ostpxweb.dot.gov/budget/
4budget.htm

Treasury Dept.

Main: www.ustreas.gov
News: www.ustreas.gov/headlines.html
Secretary's Bio: www.ustreas.gov/opc/opc0080.html
Internal Revenue Service:
Main: www.irs.treas.gov
Glossary of Tax Terms: www.treas.gov/stawrs/
glossary.htm
Tax Information: www.irs.treas.gov/ind_info/
index.html
Employee Directory: www.ustreas.gov/press/officers
List of Regional Offices:
Bureau of Alcohol, Tobacco, and Firearms: www.atf.
treas.gov/field/index.htm
Comptroller of the Currency: www.occ.treas.gov/org.
htm#District Offices
Financial Management Services: www.fms.treas.gov/
numbers.html#region
Internal Revenue Service: www.irs.treas.gov/plain/hot/
atn/index.html
Office of Thrift Supervision: www.ots.treas.gov/
contacts.html#regional
U.S. Customs Service: www.customs.treas.gov/top/
office.htm
FY2000/FY2001 Budget: www.ustreas.gov/budget/
whatnew.htm

Veterans Affairs Dept.

Main: www.va.gov
News: www.va.gov/pressrel
Secretary's Bio: www.va.gov/biographies/west.htm
VA Facilities by State:
www.va.gov/stations97/guide/home.asp?
DIVISION=ALL
Employee Directory: www.va.gov/opa/bios
List of Regional Offices: www.vba.va.gov/benefits/
address.htm#list

LEGISLATIVE BRANCH

Congress

U.S. Constitution: lcweb2.loc.gov/const/const.html
Legislative Process: www.house.gov/house/Legproc.html

How Laws are Made: thomas.loc.gov/home/lawsmade.
toc.html
Biographical Directory of the U.S. Congress: bioguide.
congress.gov
Election Statistics (1920–present): clerkweb.house.gov/
histrecs/history/elections/elections.htm
Glossary of Terms: www.senate.gov/learning/
learn_glossery_more.html

House

Main: www.house.gov
Annual Calendar: www.house.gov/house/
2000_House_Calendar.htm
Daily Business: clerkweb.house.gov/floor/current.htm
Committees: www.house.gov/house/CommitteeWWW.
html
Committee Hearing Schedules: thomas.loc.gov/home/
hcomso.html
Pending Business: www.house.gov/house/floor/
thisweek.htm
List of Roll Call Votes: clerkweb.house.gov/evs/index.htm
Leadership: www.house.gov/house/orgs_pub_hse_ldr_
www.html
Media Galleries: www.house.gov/house/mediagallery.htm

Senate

Main: www.senate.gov
Annual Calendar: www.senate.gov/legislative/index.html
Daily Calendar: www.senate.gov/~nickles/legislative/
today.cfm
Committees: www.senate.gov/committees/index.cfm
Committee Hearing Schedules: www.senate.gov/
legislative/legis_legis_committees.html
Pending Business:
www.senate.gov/legislative/legis_legis_pending.html
List of Roll Call Votes: www.senate.gov/legislative/
legis_act_rollcall.html
Leadership: www.senate.gov/learning/learn_leaders_
leadership.html
Media Galleries: www.senate.gov/galleries
Confirmed Executive Nominations:
Civilian: www.senate.gov/legislative/legis_act_
nominations_confirmed_civilian.html
Non-Civilian: www.senate.gov/legislative/legis_act_
nominations_confirmed_ncivilian.html

General Accounting Office

Main: www.gao.gov
Comptroller General Biography: www.gao.gov/dwbiog.
htm

Government Printing Office

Main: www.access.gpo.gov

Library of Congress

Main: www.loc.gov
Online Catalog: catalog.loc.gov
Thomas (Legislative Information on the Internet):
   thomas.loc.gov
Copyright Office: www.loc.gov/copyright

JUDICIAL BRANCH

The Supreme Court

Main: www.supremecourtus.gov
Biographies of Judges: www.supremecourtus.gov/about/
   biographiescurrent.pdf

Federal Judicial Center

Main: www.fjc.gov
Publications: air.fjc.gov/public/fjcweb.nsf/pages/173

U.S. Federal Courts

Main: www.uscourts.gov
News: www.uscourts.gov/news.html
Publications: www.uscourts.gov/publications.html

GOVERNMENT OF THE UNITED STATES

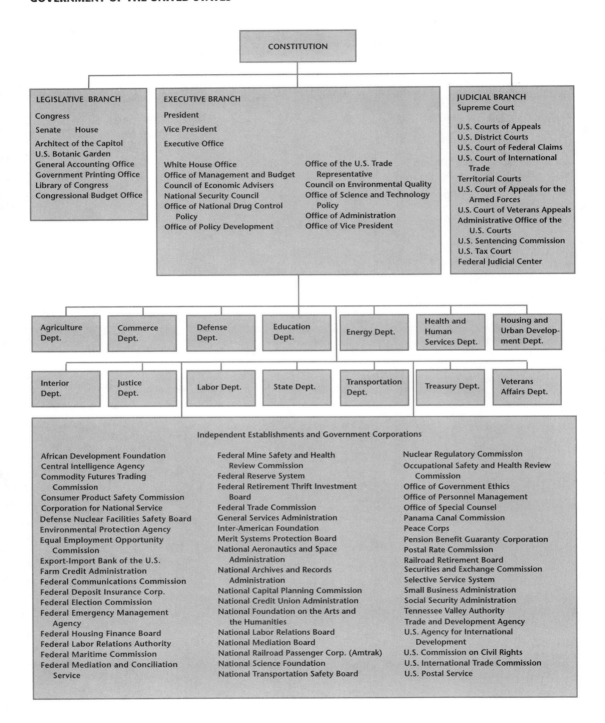

CONSTITUTION

LEGISLATIVE BRANCH

Congress

Senate   House

Architect of the Capitol
U.S. Botanic Garden
General Accounting Office
Government Printing Office
Library of Congress
Congressional Budget Office

EXECUTIVE BRANCH

President

Vice President

Executive Office

White House Office
Office of Management and Budget
Council of Economic Advisers
National Security Council
Office of National Drug Control
　Policy
Office of Policy Development

Office of the U.S. Trade
　Representative
Council on Environmental Quality
Office of Science and Technology
　Policy
Office of Administration
Office of Vice President

JUDICIAL BRANCH
Supreme Court

U.S. Courts of Appeals
U.S. District Courts
U.S. Court of Federal Claims
U.S. Court of International
　Trade
Territorial Courts
U.S. Court of Appeals for the
　Armed Forces
U.S. Court of Veterans Appeals
Administrative Office of the
　U.S. Courts
U.S. Sentencing Commission
U.S. Tax Court
Federal Judicial Center

| Agriculture Dept. | Commerce Dept. | Defense Dept. | Education Dept. | Energy Dept. | Health and Human Services Dept. | Housing and Urban Development Dept. |

| Interior Dept. | Justice Dept. | Labor Dept. | State Dept. | Transportation Dept. | Treasury Dept. | Veterans Affairs Dept. |

Independent Establishments and Government Corporations

African Development Foundation
Central Intelligence Agency
Commodity Futures Trading
　Commission
Consumer Product Safety Commission
Corporation for National Service
Defense Nuclear Facilities Safety Board
Environmental Protection Agency
Equal Employment Opportunity
　Commission
Export-Import Bank of the U.S.
Farm Credit Administration
Federal Communications Commission
Federal Deposit Insurance Corp.
Federal Election Commission
Federal Emergency Management
　Agency
Federal Housing Finance Board
Federal Labor Relations Authority
Federal Maritime Commission
Federal Mediation and Conciliation
　Service

Federal Mine Safety and Health
　Review Commission
Federal Reserve System
Federal Retirement Thrift Investment
　Board
Federal Trade Commission
General Services Administration
Inter-American Foundation
Merit Systems Protection Board
National Aeronautics and Space
　Administration
National Archives and Records
　Administration
National Capital Planning Commission
National Credit Union Administration
National Foundation on the Arts and
　the Humanities
National Labor Relations Board
National Mediation Board
National Railroad Passenger Corp. (Amtrak)
National Science Foundation
National Transportation Safety Board

Nuclear Regulatory Commission
Occupational Safety and Health Review
　Commission
Office of Government Ethics
Office of Personnel Management
Office of Special Counsel
Panama Canal Commission
Peace Corps
Pension Benefit Guaranty Corporation
Postal Rate Commission
Railroad Retirement Board
Securities and Exchange Commission
Selective Service System
Small Business Administration
Social Security Administration
Tennessee Valley Authority
Trade and Development Agency
U.S. Agency for International
　Development
U.S. Commission on Civil Rights
U.S. International Trade Commission
U.S. Postal Service

Governors and Other State Officials

Political affiliations, when available, are indicated as follows: Democrat (D), Independent (I), Republican (R), and Independence Party (Ind). For key officials of the District of Columbia and other Washington area localities, see page 349.

Alabama   Web, www.state.al.us

Gov. Don Siegelman (D), State Capitol, 600 Dexter Ave., #N-104, Montgomery, 36130; Press: Carrie Kurlander, (334) 242-7150

Lt. Gov. Steve Windom (R), Alabama State House, 11 S. Union St., #725, Montgomery, 36130-6050, (334) 242-7900; fax, (334) 242-4661

Secy. of State Jim Bennett (R), State Capitol, 600 Dexter Ave., #S-105, Montgomery, 36103-5616, (334) 242-7200; fax, (334) 242-4993

Atty. Gen. William Holcombe Pryor Jr. (R), Alabama State House, 11 S. Union St., 3rd Floor, Montgomery, 36104-3760, (334) 242-7300; fax, (334) 242-7458

Treasurer Lucy Baxley (D), State Capitol, 600 Dexter Ave., #S-106, Montgomery, 36130-2751, (334) 242-7500; fax, (334) 242-7592

Alaska   Web, www.state.ak.us

Gov. Tony Knowles (D), State Capitol, Juneau, 99811-0001; Press: Robert W. King, (907) 465-3500

Lt. Gov. Fran A. Ulmer (D), State Capitol, Juneau, 99811-0015, (907) 465-3520; fax, (907) 465-5400

(No office of Secretary of State)

Atty. Gen. Bruce M. Botelho, 123 4th St., #450, Juneau, 99801, (907) 465-3600; fax, (907) 465-2075

Treasurer Neil Slotnick, P.O. Box 110400, Juneau, 99811-0400, (907) 465-4660; fax, (907) 465-2576

In Washington, D.C.: John Katz, Special Counsel, Office of State-Federal Relations, State of Alaska, 444 N. Capitol St. N.W., #336 20001-1512, (202) 624-5858; fax, (202) 624-5857

Arizona   Web, www.state.az.us

Gov. Jane Dee Hull (R), State Capitol, 1700 W. Washington St., 9th Floor, Phoenix, 85007; Press: Francie Noyes, (602) 542-1342

(No office of Lieutenant Governor)

Secy. of State Betsey Bayless (R), West Wing, State Capitol, 1700 W. Washington St., 7th Floor, Phoenix, 85007, (602) 542-4285; fax, (602) 542-1575

Atty. Gen. Janet Napolitano (D), 1275 W. Washington St., Phoenix, 85007, (602) 542-5025; fax, (602) 542-1275

Treasurer Carol Springer (R), 1700 W. Washington, 1st Floor, Phoenix, 85007, (602) 542-5815; fax, (602) 542-7176

Arkansas   Web, www.state.ar.us

Gov. Mike Huckabee (R), 250 State Capitol Bldg., Little Rock, 72201; Press: Rex Nelson, (501) 682-2345

Lt. Gov. Winthrop P. Rockefeller (R), State Capitol Bldg., #270, Little Rock, 72201-1061, (501) 682-2144; fax, (501) 682-2894

Secy. of State Sharon Priest (D), State Capitol Bldg., #256, Little Rock, 72201, (501) 682-1010; fax, (501) 682-3510

Atty. Gen. Mark Pryor (D), Tower Bldg., 323 Center St., #200, Little Rock, 72201-2610, (501) 682-2007; fax, (501) 682-8084

Treasurer Jimmie Lou Fisher (D), State Capitol Bldg., #220, Little Rock, 72201, (501) 682-5888; fax, (501) 682-3842

California   Web, www.state.ca.us

Gov. Gray Davis (D), State Capitol, Sacramento, 95814; Press: Michael Bustamante, (916) 445-2841

Lt. Gov. Cruz M. Bustamante (D), State Capitol, #1114, Sacramento, 95814, (916) 445-8994; fax, (916) 323-4998

Secy. of State Bill Jones (R), 1500 11th St., #600, Sacramento, 95814, (916) 653-6814; fax, (916) 653-4620

Atty. Gen. Bill Lockyer (D), 1300 Eye St., #1101, Sacramento, 94244-2550, (916) 445-9555; fax, (916) 324-5205

Treasurer Philip Angelides (D), 915 Capitol Mall, #110, Sacramento, 94209-0001, (916) 653-2995; fax, (916) 653-3125

In Washington, D.C.: Olivia Morgan, Director, Washington Office of the Governor, State of California, 444 N. Capitol St. N.W., #134 20001, (202) 624-5270; fax, (202) 624-5280

Colorado   Web, www.state.co.us

Gov. Bill Owens (R), State Capitol Bldg., #136, Denver, 80203-1792; Press: Dick Wadhams, (303) 866-6324

Lt. Gov. Joe Rogers (R), State Capitol Bldg., #130, Denver, 80203, (303) 866-2087; fax, (303) 866-5469

Secy. of State Donetta Davidson (R), 1560 Broadway, #200, Denver, 80202, (303) 894-2204; fax, (303) 894-2212

Atty. Gen. Ken Salazar (D), 1525 Sherman St., 5th Floor, Denver, 80203, (303) 866-3617; fax, (303) 866-5691

Treasurer Mike Coffman (R), State Capitol Bldg., #140, Denver, 80203, (303) 866-2441; fax, (303) 866-2123

Connecticut   Web, www.state.ct.us

Gov. John G. Rowland (R), State Capitol, 210 Capitol Ave., #202, Hartford, 06106; Press: Dean Pagani, (860) 566-4840

Lt. Gov. M. Jodi Rell (R), State Capitol, 210 Capitol Ave., #304, Hartford, 06106, (860) 524-7384; fax, (860) 524-7304

Secy. of State Susan Bysiewicz (D), State Capitol, 210 Capitol Ave., #104, Hartford, 06106, (860) 509-6200; fax, (860) 509-6209

Atty. Gen. Richard Blumenthal (D), 55 Elm St., Hartford, 06106, (860) 808-5318; fax, (860) 808-5387

Treasurer Denise L. Nappier (D), 55 Elm St., Hartford, 06106-1773, (860) 702-3000; fax, (860) 702-3043

In Washington, D.C.: Alison Kaufman, Director, Washington Office of the Governor, State of Connecticut, 444 N. Capitol St. N.W., #317 20001, (202) 347-4535; fax, (202) 347-7151

Delaware   Web, www.state.de.us

Gov. Thomas R. Carper (D), Carvel State Office Bldg., 820 N. French St., 12th Floor, Wilmington, 19801; Press: Anthony Farina, (302) 577-8711

Lt. Gov. Ruth Ann Minner (D), Tatnall Bldg., 3rd Floor, Dover, 19901, (302) 739-4151; fax, (302) 739-6965

Secy. of State Edward J. Freel, 401 Federal St., #3, Dover, 19901, (302) 739-4111; fax, (302) 739-3811

Atty. Gen. M. Jane Brady (R), Carvel State Office Bldg., 820 N. French St., Wilmington, 19801, (302) 577-8500; fax, (302) 577-2610

Treasurer Jack Markell (D), Thomas Collins Bldg., 540 S. Dupont Hwy., #4, Dover, 19901-4516, (302) 744-1000; fax, (302) 739-5635

In Washington, D.C.: Jonathan Jones, Director, Washington Office of the Governor, State of Delaware, 444 N. Capitol St. N.W., #230 20001, (202) 624-7724; fax, (202) 624-5495

Florida   Web, www.state.fl.us

Gov. Jeb Bush (R), The Capitol, Tallahassee, 32399-0001; Press: Elizabeth Hirst, (850) 488-5394

Lt. Gov. Frank T. Brogan (R), The Capitol, #PL-05, Tallahassee, 32399-0001, (850) 488-4711; fax, (850) 921-6114

Secy. of State Katherine Harris (R), The Capitol, PL-02, Tallahassee, 32399-0250, (850) 488-3680; fax, (850) 487-2214

Atty. Gen. Robert A. Butterworth (D), The Capitol, Tallahassee, 32399-1050, (850) 487-1963; fax, (850) 487-2564

Treasurer Bill Nelson (D), 200 E. Gaines St., Tallahassee, 32301, (850) 922-3100; fax, (850) 488-6581

In Washington, D.C.: Nina Oviedo, Director, Washington Office of the Governor, State of Florida, 444 N. Capitol St. N.W., #349 20001, (202) 624-5885; fax, (202) 624-5886

Georgia   Web, www.state.ga.us

Gov. Roy E. Barnes (D), State Capitol, #203, Atlanta, 30334; Press: Joselyn Butler, (404) 656-1776

Lt. Gov. Mark Taylor (D), State Capitol, #240, Atlanta, 30334, (404) 656-5030; fax, (404) 656-6739

Secy. of State Cathy Cox (D), State Capitol, #214, Atlanta, 30334, (404) 656-2881; fax, (404) 656-0513

Treasurer Dan Ebersole, 200 Piedmont Ave., W. Tower, #1202, Atlanta, 30334, (404) 656-2168; fax, (404) 656-9048

Atty. Gen. Thurbert E. Baker (D), 40 Capitol Square S.W., Atlanta, 30334-1300, (404) 656-3300; fax, (404) 657-8733

Hawaii   Web, www.state.hi.us

Gov. Benjamin J. Cayetano (D), State Capitol, 415 S. Beretania St., Honolulu, 96813; Press: Kathleen Racuya-Markrich, (808) 586-0034

Lt. Gov. Mazie K. Hirono (D), State Capitol, 415 S. Beretania St., Honolulu, 96813, (808) 586-0255; fax, (808) 586-0231

(No office of Secretary of State)

Acting Atty. Gen. Earl I. Anzai, 425 Queen St., Honolulu, 96813, (808) 586-1500; fax, (808) 586-1239

Treasurer Neil Miyahira, 250 S. Hotel St., #305, Honolulu, 96813, (808) 586-1518; fax, (808) 586-1976

Idaho   Web, www.state.id.us

Gov. Dirk Kempthorne (R), State Capitol Bldg., West Wing, 700 W. Jefferson St., 2nd Floor, Boise, 83720-0034; Press: Mark Snider, (208) 334-2100

Lt. Gov. C. L. (Butch) Otter (R), State Capitol Bldg., 700 W. Jefferson St., #225, Boise, 83720-0057, (208) 334-2200; fax, (208) 334-3259

Secy. of State Pete T. Cenarrusa (R), State Capitol Bldg., 700 W. Jefferson St., #203, Boise, 83720-0080, (208) 334-2300; fax, (208) 334-2282

Atty. Gen. Alan G. Lance (R), State Capitol Bldg., 700 W. Jefferson St., Boise, 83720-0010, (208) 334-2400; fax, (208) 334-2530

Treasurer Ron G. Crane (R), State Capitol Bldg., 700 W. Jefferson St., #102, Boise, 83720-0091, (208) 334-3200; fax, (208) 332-2960

Illinois   Web, www.state.il.us

Gov. George H. Ryan (R), State House, #207, Springfield, 62706; Press: David Urbanek, (217) 782-7355

Lt. Gov. Corinne Wood (R), State House, #214, Springfield, 62706, (217) 782-7884; fax, (217) 524-6262

Secy. of State Jesse White (D), State House, #213, Springfield, 62756, (217) 782-2201; fax, (217) 785-0358

Atty. Gen. Jim Ryan (R), 500 S. 2nd St., Springfield, 62706, (217) 782-1090; fax, (217) 782-7046

Treasurer Judy Baar Topinka (R), State House, #219, Springfield, 62706, (217) 782-2211; fax, (217) 785-2777

In Washington, D.C.: Bernie Robinson, Assistant to the Governor, Washington Office of the Governor, State of Illinois, 444 N. Capitol St. N.W., #240 20001, (202) 624-7776; fax, (202) 724-0689

Indiana   Web, www.state.in.us

Gov. Frank L. O'Bannon (D), State House, 200 W. Washington St., #206, Indianapolis, 46204; Press: Phil Bremen, (317) 232-4567

Lt. Gov. Joseph E. Kernan (D), State House, 200 W. Washington St., #333, Indianapolis, 46204-2790, (317) 232-4545; fax, (317) 232-4788

Secy. of State Sue Anne Gilroy (R), State House, 200 W. Washington St., #201, Indianapolis, 46204, (317) 232-6531; fax, (317) 233-3283

Atty. Gen. Jeffrey A. Modisett (D), Indiana Government Center South, 402 W. Washington St., 5th Floor, Indianapolis, 46204-2770, (317) 232-6201; fax, (317) 232-7979

Treasurer Tim Berry (R), State House, 200 W. Washington St., #242, Indianapolis, 46204, (317) 232-6386; fax, (317) 233-1928

In Washington, D.C.: Jeff Viohl, Federal Liaison, Washington Office of the Governor, State of Indiana, 444 N. Capitol St. N.W., #428 20001, (202) 624-1474; fax, (202) 624-1475

Iowa   Web, www.state.ia.us

Gov. Thomas J. Vilsack (D), State Capitol Bldg., Des Moines, 50319; Press: Joe Shannahan, (515) 281-0173

Lt. Gov. Sally Pederson (D), State Capitol Bldg., Des Moines, 50319, (515) 281-5211; fax, (515) 281-6611

Secy. of State Chester J. Culver (D), State Capitol, Hoover Bldg., #105, Des Moines, 50319, (515) 281-5204; fax, (515) 242-5953

Atty. Gen. Thomas J. Miller (D), Hoover Bldg., 2nd Floor, Des Moines, 50319, (515) 281-5164; fax, (515) 281-4209

Treasurer Michael L. Fitzgerald (D), State Capitol Bldg., Des Moines, 50319, (515) 281-5368; fax, (515) 281-7562

In Washington, D.C.: Phil Buchanan, Director, Washington Office of the Governor, State of Iowa, 444 N. Capitol St. N.W., #359 20001, (202) 624-5442; fax, (202) 624-8189

Kansas   Web, www.state.ks.us

Gov. Bill Graves (R), State Capitol, #212-S, Topeka, 66612-1590; Press: Don Brown, (785) 291-3206

Lt. Gov. Gary Sherrer (R), State Capitol, #222-S, Topeka, 66612-1504, (785) 296-2213; fax, (785) 296-5669

Secy. of State Ron Thornburgh (R), Memorial Hall, 120 S.W. 10th St., 1st Floor, Topeka, 66612-1594, (785) 296-4564; fax, (785) 296-4570

Atty. Gen. Carla J. Stovall (R), 127 S.W. 10th St., 2nd Floor, Topeka, 66612-1597, (785) 296-2215; fax, (785) 296-6296

Treasurer Tim Shallenburger (R), Landon State Office Bldg., 900 S.W. Jackson St., #201, Topeka, 66612-1235, (785) 296-3171; fax, (785) 296-7950

Kentucky   Web, www.state. ky.us

Gov. Paul E. Patton (D), State Capitol, 700 Capitol Ave., #100, Frankfort, 40601; Press: Melissa Forsythe, (502) 564-2611

Lt. Gov. Stephen L. Henry (D), State Capitol, 700 Capitol Ave., #100, Frankfort, 40601, (502) 564-2611; fax, (502) 564-2849

Secy. of State John Y. Brown III (D), State Capitol, 700 Capital Ave., #152, Frankfort, 40601, (502) 564-3490; fax, (502) 564-5687

Atty. Gen. Albert B. Chandler III (D), State Capitol, 700 Capitol Ave., #118, Frankfort, 40601, (502) 696-5300; fax, (502) 564-8310

Treasurer Jonathan Miller (D), State Capitol Annex, West Wing, #183, Frankfort, 40601, (502) 564-4722; fax, (502) 564-6545

Louisiana   Web, www.state.la.us

Gov. Murphy J. (Mike) Foster Jr. (R), State Capitol, 900 3rd St., Baton Rouge, 70804-9004; Press: Marsanne Golsby, (225) 342-9037

Lt. Gov. Kathleen Babineaux Blanco (D), 900 N. 3rd St.,

Pentagon Barracks, Bldg. C, 2nd Floor, Baton Rouge, 70802, (225) 342-7009; fax, (225) 342-1949

Secy. of State Walter Fox McKeithen (R), Capitol Bldg., 800 N. 3rd St., 20th Floor, Baton Rouge, 70802, (225) 922-1000; fax, (225) 922-0002

Atty. Gen. Richard P. Ieyoub (D), State Capitol, 300 Capitol Dr., 22nd Floor, Baton Rouge, 70804, (225) 342-7013; fax, (225) 342-7335

Treasurer John Kennedy (D), State Capitol, 900 N. 3rd St., 3rd Floor, Baton Rouge, 70802, (225) 342-0010; fax, (225) 342-0046

Maine   Web, www.state. me.us

Gov. Angus S. King Jr. (I), 1 State House Station, Augusta, 04333-0001; Press: Dennis Bailey, (207) 287-2531

(No office of Lieutenant Governor)

Secy. of State Dan A. Gwadosky (D), Nash Bldg., 148 State House Station, Augusta, 04333-0148, (207) 626-8400; fax, (207) 287-8598

Atty. Gen. Andrew Ketterer (D), 6 State House Station, Augusta, 04333-0006, (207) 626-8800; fax, (207) 287-3145

Treasurer Dale McCormick (D), 39 State House Station, Augusta, 04333-0039, (207) 287-2771; fax, (207) 287-2367

Maryland   Web, www.state.md.us

Gov. Parris N. Glendening (D), State House, 100 State Circle, Annapolis, 21401; Press: Mike Morrill, (410) 974-2316

Lt. Gov. Kathleen Kennedy Townsend (D), State House, 100 State Circle, Annapolis, 21401, (410) 974-2804; fax, (410) 974-5882

Secy. of State John T. Willis (D), Jeffrey Bldg., 16 Francis St., Annapolis, 21401, (410) 974-5521; fax, (410) 974-5190

Atty. Gen. J. Joseph Curran Jr. (D), 200 St. Paul Pl., Baltimore, 21202-2021, (410) 576-6300; fax, (410) 576-6404

Treasurer Richard N. Dixon, Louis L. Goldstein Treasury Bldg., 80 Calvert St., #109, Annapolis, 21401, (410) 260-7533; fax, (410) 974-3530

In Washington, D.C.: Elizabeth Pyke, Federal Relations Director, Washington Office of the Governor, State of Maryland, 444 N. Capitol St. N.W., #311 20001, (202) 624-1430; fax, (202) 783-3061

Massachusetts   Web, www.state.ma.us

Gov. Argeo Paul Cellucci (R), Executive Office, State House, #360, Boston, 02133; Press: John Birtwell, (617) 727-2759

Lt. Gov. Jane M. Swift (R), State House, #360, Boston, 02133, (617) 727-3600; fax, (617) 727-9725

Secy. of the Commonwealth William Francis Galvin (D), State House, #337, Boston, 02133, (617) 727-7030; fax, (617) 742-4722

Atty. Gen. Thomas F. Reilly (D), 1 Ashburton Pl., #2010, Boston, 02108-1698, (617) 727-2200; fax, (617) 727-5768

Treasurer Shannon P. O'Brien (D), State House, #227, Boston, 02133, (617) 367-3900; fax, (617) 227-1622

In Washington, D.C.: Anne Gavin, Director, Washington Office of the Governor, Commonwealth of Massachusetts, 444 N. Capitol St. N.W., #400 20001, (202) 624-7713; fax, (617) 624-7714

Michigan   Web, www.state.mi.us

Gov. John Engler (R), George W. Romney Bldg., 111 S. Capitol, Lansing, 48933; Press: John Truscott, (517) 335-6397

Lt. Gov. Dick Posthumus (R), State Capitol Bldg., George W. Romney Bldg., #S-215, Lansing, 48909, (517) 373-6800; fax, (517) 335-6763

Secy. of State Candice S. Miller (R), Treasury Bldg., 430 W. Allegan St., 1st Floor, Lansing, 48918-9900, (517) 322-1460; fax, (517) 322-1968

Atty. Gen. Jennifer Granholm (D), Williams Bldg., Lansing, 48909, (517) 373-1110; fax, (517) 241-1850

Treasurer Mark A. Murray, Treasury Bldg., 430 W. Allegan St., Lansing, 48922, (517) 373-3200; fax, (517) 373-4968

In Washington, D.C.: LeAnne Wilson, Director, Washington Office of the Governor, State of Michigan, 444 N. Capitol St. N.W., #411 20001, (202) 624-5840; fax, (202) 624-5841

Minnesota   Web, www.state.mn.us

Gov. Jesse Ventura (Ind), State Capitol, 75 Constitution Ave., #130, St. Paul, 55155; Press: John Wodele, (651) 296-0001

Lt. Gov. Mae Schunk (Ind), 130 State Capitol, #130, St. Paul, 55155, (651) 296-3391; fax, (651) 296-0674

Secy. of State Mary Kiffmeyer (R), State Office Bldg., 100 Constitution Ave., #180, St. Paul, 55155-1299, (651) 296-2803; fax, (651) 215-0682

Atty. Gen. Mike Hatch (D), State Capitol, #102, St. Paul, 55155, (651) 296-6196; fax, (651) 297-4193

Treasurer Carol C. Johnson (D), Administration Bldg., 50 Sherburne Ave., #303, St. Paul, 55155, (651) 296-7091; fax, (651) 296-8615

In Washington, D.C.: Amy Gromer, Co-Director, Washington Office of the Governor, State of Minnesota, 444 N. Capitol St. N.W., #365 20001, (202) 624-3642; fax, (202) 624-5425

Mississippi   Web, www.state.ms.us

Gov. Ronnie Musgrove (R), Walter Sillers Bldg., 550 High St., Jackson, 39201; Press: Robbie Wilbur, (601) 359-3100

Lt. Gov. Amy Tuck (D), New Capitol Bldg., 400 High St., 3rd Floor, Jackson, 39201, (601) 359-3200; fax, (601) 359-3935

Secy. of State Eric C. Clark (D), 401 Mississippi St., Jackson, 39205-0136, (601) 359-1350; fax, (601) 359-1499

Atty. Gen. Mike Moore (D), 450 High St., Jackson, 39201, (601) 359-3680; fax, (601) 359-3796

Treasurer Marshall G. Bennett (D), 550 High St., #404, Jackson, 39201, (601) 359-3600; fax, (601) 359-2001

Missouri   Web, www.state.mo.us

Gov. Mel Carnahan (D), State Capitol, #216, Jefferson City, 65102; Press: Jerry Nachtigal, (573) 751-3222

Lt. Gov. Roger B. Wilson (D), State Capitol, #121, Jefferson City, 65101, (573) 751-4727; fax, (573) 751-9422

Secy. of State Rebecca McDowell Cook (D), 600 W. Main St., Jefferson City, 65102, (573) 751-4936; fax, (573) 526-4903

Atty. Gen. Jeremiah W. (Jay) Nixon (D), Supreme Court Bldg., 207 W. High St., Jefferson City, 65101, (573) 751-3321; fax, (573) 751-0774

Treasurer Bob Holden (D), State Capitol, #229, Jefferson City, 65102, (573) 751-2411; fax, (573) 751-9443

In Washington, D.C.: Susan Harris, Director, Washington Office of the Governor, State of Missouri, 400 N. Capital St. N.W., #376 20001, (202) 624-7720; fax, (202) 624-5855

Montana   Web, www.state.mt.us

Gov. Marc Racicot (R), State Capitol, 1625 11th Ave., Helena, 59620; Press: Anastasia Burton, (406) 444-3111

Lt. Gov. Judy Martz (R), Capitol Station, 1625 11th Ave., Helena, 59620, (406) 444-5551; fax, (406) 444-4648

Secy. of State Mike R. Cooney (D), State Capitol, #225, Helena, 59620-2801, (406) 444-2034; fax, (406) 444-3976

Atty. Gen. Joseph P. Mazurek (D), Justice Bldg., 215 N. Sanders St., Helena, 59601, (406) 444-2026; fax, (406) 444-3549

Treasurer Kathy Muri, Sam W. Mitchell Bldg., 125 Roberts St., #176, Helena, 59620-0102, (406) 444-2624; fax, (406) 444-2812

Nebraska   Web, www.state.ne.us

Gov. Mike Johanns (R), State Capitol, 1425 K St., Lincoln, 68509; Press: Chris Peterson, (402) 471-2244

Lt. Gov. David I. Maurstad (R), State Capitol, #2315, Lincoln, 68509-4863, (402) 471-2256; fax, (402) 471-6031

Secy. of State Scott Moore (R), State Capitol, #2300, Lincoln, 68509-4608, (402) 471-2554; fax, (402) 471-3237

Atty. Gen. Donald Stenberg (R), 2115 State Capitol, Lincoln, 68508, (402) 471-2682; fax, (402) 471-3297

Treasurer David E. Heineman (R), State Capitol, #2003, Lincoln, 68509-4788, (402) 471-2455; fax, (402) 471-4390

In Washington, D.C.: Thomas R. Litjen, Director, Washington Office of the Governor, State of Nebraska, 444 N. Capitol St. N.W., #406 20001, (202) 508-3838; fax, (202) 624-7714

Nevada   Web, www.state.nv.us

Gov. Kenny Guinn (R), 101 N. Carson St., Carson City, 89710; Press: Jack Finn, (775) 684-5670

Lt. Gov. Lorraine T. Hunt (R), State Capitol Bldg., 101 N. Carson St., #2, Carson City, 89701, (702) 486-2400; fax, (702) 486-2404

Secy. of State Dean Heller (R), Capitol Complex, 101 N. Carson St., #3, Carson City, 89701-4786, (775) 684-5708; fax, (775) 684-5725

Atty. Gen. Frankie Sue Del Papa (D), Capitol Complex, 100 N. Carson St., Carson City, 89701-4717, (775) 684-1100; fax, (775) 684-1108

Treasurer Brian K. Krolicki (R), Capitol Bldg., 101 N. Carson St., #4, Carson City, 89701-4786, (775) 684-5600; fax, (775) 684-5623

In Washington, D.C.: Michael Pieper, Director, Washington Office of the Governor, State of Nevada, 444 N. Capitol St. N.W., #209 20001, (202) 624-5405; fax, (202) 624-8181

New Hampshire   Web, www.state.nh.us

Gov. Jeanne Shaheen (D), State House, 107 N. Main St., #208-214, Concord, 03301; Press: Pamela Walsh, (603) 271-2121

(No office of Lieutenant Governor)

Secy. of State William M. Gardner (D), State House, 107 N. Main St., #204, Concord, 03301, (603) 271-3242; fax, (603) 271-6316

Atty. Gen. Philip Thomas McLaughlin (D), 33 Capitol St., Concord, 03301-6397, (603) 271-3658; fax, (603) 271-2110

Treasurer Georgie A. Thomas (R), State House Annex, 25 Capitol St., #121, Concord, 03301, (603) 271-2621; fax, (603) 271-3922

New Jersey   Web, www.state.nj.us

Gov. Christine Todd Whitman (R), State House, 125 W. State St., Trenton, 08625-0001; Press: Jayne O'Connor, (609) 777-2600

(No office of Lieutenant Governor)

Secy. of State DeForest B. Soaries Jr. (I), 125 W. State St., Trenton, 08625-0300, (609) 984-1900; fax, (609) 292-7665

Atty. Gen. John J. Farmer Jr., Justice Complex, West Wing, 8th Floor, Trenton, 08625, (609) 292-4925; fax, (609) 292-3508

Treasurer Roland A. Machold Jr., State House, 225 W. State St., Trenton, 08625, (609) 292-5031; fax, (609) 292-6145

In Washington, D.C.: Susan Spencer, Director, Washington Office of the Governor, State of New Jersey, 444 N. Capitol St. N.W., #201 20001, (202) 638-0631; fax, (202) 638-2296

New Mexico   Web, www.state.nm.us

Gov. Gary E. Johnson (R), State Capitol Bldg., #400, Santa Fe, 87503; Press: Diane Kinderwater, (505) 827-3000

Lt. Gov. Walter D. Bradley (R), State Capitol Bldg., #417, Santa Fe, 87503, (505) 827-3050; fax, (505) 827-3057

Secy. of State Rebecca Vigil-Giron (D), 325 Don Gaspar, #300, Santa Fe, 87503, (505) 827-3600; fax, (505) 827-3634

Atty. Gen. Patricia Madrid (D), Bataan Memorial, 407 Galisteo St., #216, Santa Fe, 85701, (505) 827-6000; fax, (505) 827-5826

Treasurer Michael A. Montoya (D), NEA Bldg., 130 S. Capitol, Santa Fe, 85704-0608, (505) 827-6400; fax, (505) 827-6395

New York   Web, www.state.ny.us

Gov. George E. Pataki (R), State Capitol, Albany, 12224; Press: Zenia Mucha, (518) 474-8418

Lt. Gov. Mary O. Donohue (R), Executive Chamber, State Capitol, Albany, 12224, (518) 474-4623; fax, (518) 486-4170

Secy. of State Alexander F. Treadwell (R), 41 State St., Albany, 12231, (518) 474-4750; fax, (518) 474-4765

Atty. Gen. Eliot Spitzer (D), 120 Broadway, New York, 10271-0332, (212) 416-8050; fax, (212) 416-8942

Treasurer George H. Gasser, Alfred E. Smith Office Bldg., 5th Floor, Albany, 12225, (518) 474-4250; fax, (518) 473-9163

In Washington, D.C.: James Mazzarella, Director, Washington Office of the Governor, State of New York, 444 N. Capitol St. N.W., #301 20001, (202) 434-7100; fax, (202) 434-7110

North Carolina   Web, www.state.nc.us

Gov. James B. Hunt Jr. (D), Capitol Square, State Capitol Bldg., Raleigh, 27603-8001; Press: Tad Boggs, (919) 733-5612

Lt. Gov. Dennis A. Wicker (D), State Capitol, Raleigh, 27699-0401, (919) 733-7350; fax, (919) 733-6595

Secy. of State Elaine F. Marshall (D), 300 N. Salisbury St., Raleigh, 27603, (919) 733-4161; fax, (919) 733-1837

Atty. Gen. Michael F. Easley (D), 114 W. Edenton St., Raleigh, 27602, (919) 716-6400; fax, (919) 716-6750

Treasurer Harlan E. Boyles, 325 N. Salisbury St., Raleigh, 27603-1385, (919) 508-5176; fax, (919) 508-5167

In Washington, D.C.: Jim McCleskey, Director, Washington Office of the Governor, State of North Carolina, 444 N. Capitol St. N.W., #332 20001, (202) 624-5830; fax, (202) 624-5836

North Dakota   Web, www.state.nd.us

Gov. Ed T. Schafer (R), 600 E. Boulevard Ave., Dept. 101, Bismarck, 58505-0001; Press: Julie Liffrig, (701) 328-2200

Lt. Gov. Rosemarie Myrdal (R), 600 E. Boulevard Ave., Dept. 101, Bismarck, 58505-0001, (701) 328-2200; fax, (701) 328-2205

Secy. of State Alvin A. Jaeger (R), State Capitol, Dept. 108, 600 E. Boulevard Ave., Bismarck, 58505-0500, (701) 328-2900; fax, (701) 328-2992

Atty. Gen. Heidi Heitkamp (D), State Capitol, Dept. 125, 600 E. Boulevard Ave., 1st Floor, Bismarck, 58505-0040, (701) 328-2210; fax, (701) 328-2226

Treasurer Kathi Gilmore (D), State Capitol, Dept. 120, 600 E. Boulevard Ave., Bismarck, 58505-0600, (701) 328-2643; fax, (701) 328-3002

In Washington, D.C.: Craig Pattee, Director, Washington Office of the Governor, State of North Dakota, 400 N. Capitol St., #585 20001-1512, (202) 347-6607; fax, (202) 434-7110

Ohio   Web, www.state.oh.us

Gov. Bob Taft II (R), Vern Riffe Center, 77 S. High St., 30th Floor, Columbus, 43215; Press: Scott Milburn, (614) 644-0957

Lt. Gov. Maureen O'Connor (R), Vern Riffe Center, 77 S. High St., 30th Floor, Columbus, 43266, (614) 466-3396; fax, (614) 644-0575

Secy. of State J. Kenneth Blackwell (R), 180 E. Broad St., 15th Floor, Columbus, 43215, (614) 466-2655; fax, (614) 644-0649

Atty. Gen. Betty D. Montgomery (R), 30 E. Broad St., 17th Floor, Columbus, 43215-3428, (614) 466-4320; fax, (614) 466-5087

Treasurer Joseph T. Deters (R), 30 E. Broad St., 10th Floor, Columbus, 43266-0421, (614) 466-2160; fax, (614) 644-7313

In Washington, D.C.: June Garvin, Director, Washington Office of the Governor, State of Ohio, 444 N.

Capitol St. N.W., #546 20001, (202) 624-5844; fax, (202) 624-5847

Oklahoma Web, www.state.ok.us

Gov. Frank Keating (R), State Capitol, 2300 N. Lincoln Blvd., #212, Oklahoma City, 73105; Press: Dan Mahoney, (405) 521-2342

Lt. Gov. Mary Fallin (R), State Capitol, 2300 N. Lincoln Blvd., #211, Oklahoma City, 73105, (405) 521-2161; fax, (405) 525-2702

Secy. of State Mike Hunter (R), State Capitol, 2300 N. Lincoln Blvd., #101, Oklahoma City, 73105, (405) 521-3911; fax, (405) 521-3771

Atty. Gen. W. A. (Drew) Edmondson (D), State Capitol, 2300 N. Lincoln Blvd., #112, Oklahoma City, 73105, (405) 521-3921; fax, (405) 521-6246

Treasurer Robert A. Butkin (D), State Capitol, 2300 N. Lincoln Blvd., #217, Oklahoma City, 73105, (405) 521-3191; fax, (405) 521-4994

Oregon Web, www.state.or.us

Gov. John A. Kitzhaber (D), State Capitol, #254, Salem, 97310-4001; Press: Bob Applegate, (503) 378-6496

(No office of Lieutenant Governor)

Secy. of State Bill Bradbury (D), State Capitol, #136, Salem, 97310, (503) 986-1500; fax, (503) 986-1616

Atty. Gen. Hardy Myers (D), Justice Bldg., 1162 Court St. N.E., Salem, 97310, (503) 378-4400; fax, (503) 378-3784

Treasurer Jim Hill (D), 350 Winter St. N.E., #100, Salem, 97301-3896, (503) 378-4000; fax, (503) 373-1500

In Washington, D.C.: Kevin Smith, Director, Washington Office of the Governor, State of Oregon, 444 N. Capitol St. N.W. 20001, (202) 624-3535

Pennsylvania Web, www.state.pa.us

Gov. Thomas J. Ridge (R), Main Capitol Bldg., #225, Harrisburg, 17120; Press: Tim Reeves, (717) 783-1116

Lt. Gov. Mark S. Schweiker (R), Main Capitol Bldg., #200, Harrisburg, 17120, (717) 787-3300; fax, (717) 783-0150

Secy. of the Commonwealth Kim Pizzingrilli, North Office Bldg., #302, Harrisburg, 17120, (717) 787-6458; fax, (717) 787-1734

Atty. Gen. D. Michael Fisher (R), Strawberry Square, 16th Floor, Harrisburg, 17120, (717) 787-3391; fax, (717) 787-8242

Treasurer Barbara Hafer (R), Finance Bldg., #129, Harrisburg, 17120, (717) 787-2991; fax, (717) 772-4234

In Washington, D.C.: Rebecca Halkias, Director, Washington Office of the Governor, Commonwealth of

Pennsylvania, 444 N. Capitol St. N.W., #700 20001, (202) 624-7828; fax, (202) 624-7831

Rhode Island Web, www.state.ri.us

Gov. Lincoln C. Almond (R), State House, Providence, 02903; Press: Lisa Pelosi, (401) 222-2080

Lt. Gov. Charles J. Fogarty (D), State House, #116, Providence, 02903, (401) 222-2371; fax, (401) 222-2012

Secy. of State James R. Langevin (D), State House, #220, Providence, 02903-1105, (401) 222-2357; fax, (401) 222-1356

Atty. Gen. Sheldon Whitehouse (D), 150 S. Main St., Providence, 02903-2856, (401) 274-4400; fax, (401) 222-1331

Treasurer Paul J. Tavares (D), State House, #102, Providence, 02903, (401) 222-2397; fax, (401) 222-6140

In Washington, D.C.: Samuel S. Reid, Director, Washington Office of the Governor, State of Rhode Island, 444 N. Capitol St. N.W., #619 20001, (202) 624-3605; fax, (202) 624-3607

South Carolina Web, www.state.sc.us

Gov. Jim Hodges (D), State House, Columbia, 29211; Press: Nina Brook, (803) 734-9400

Lt. Gov. Robert Lee (Bob) Peeler (R), 1100 Gerbais St., Columbia, 29201, (803) 734-2080; fax, (803) 734-2082

Secy. of State James M. Miles (R), 1205 Pendleton St., #525, Columbia, 29201, (803) 734-2170; fax, (803) 734-1661

Atty. Gen. Charles Molony Condon (R), 1000 Assembly St., #501, Columbia, 29201, (803) 734-3970; fax, (803) 253-6283

Treasurer Grady L. Patterson Jr. (D), Wade Hampton Office Bldg., #118, Columbia, 29211, (803) 734-2101; fax, (803) 734-2039

In Washington, D.C.: Michael Tecklenburg, Director, Washington Office of the Governor, State of South Carolina, 444 N. Capitol St. N.W., #203 20001, (202) 624-7784; fax, (202) 624-7800

South Dakota Web, www.state.sd.us

Gov. William J. Janklow (R), State Capitol, 500 E. Capitol Ave., Pierre, 57501-5070; Press: Bob Mercer, (605) 773-3212

Lt. Gov. Carole Hillard (R), State Capitol, 500 E. Capitol Ave., Pierre, 57501-5070, (605) 773-3661; fax, (605) 773-4711

Secy. of State Joyce Hazeltine (R), State Capitol, 500 E. Capitol Ave., #204, Pierre, 57501-5070, (605) 773-3537; fax, (605) 773-6580

Atty. Gen. Mark Barnett (R), State Capitol, 500 E. Capitol Ave., Pierre, 57501-5070, (605) 773-3215; fax, (605) 773-4106

Treasurer Richard D. Butler (D), State Capitol, 500 E. Capitol Ave., #212, Pierre, 57501-5070, (605) 773-3378; fax, (605) 773-3115

Tennessee   Web, www.state.tn.us

Gov. Don Sundquist (R), State Capitol, 1st Floor, Nashville, 37243-0001; Press: Beth Fortune, (615) 741-1416

Lt. Gov. John S. Wilder (D), 1 Legislative Plaza, Nashville, 37243-0026, (615) 741-2368; fax, (615) 741-9349

Secy. of State Riley C. Darnell (D), State Capitol, 1st Floor, Nashville, 37243-0305, (615) 741-2819; fax, (615) 532-9547

Atty. Gen. Paul G. Summers, 425 5th Ave. North, Cordell Hull Bldg., Nashville, 37243, (615) 741-3491; fax, (615) 741-2009

Treasurer Steve Adams (D), State Capitol, 1st Floor, Nashville, 37243-0225, (615) 741-2956; fax, (615) 253-1591

Texas   Web, www.state.tx.us

Gov. George W. Bush (R), State Capitol, 1100 San Jacinto, Austin, 78701; Press: Linda Edwards, (512) 463-1826

Lt. Gov. Rick Perry (R), State Capitol, Austin, 78711-2068, (512) 463-0001; fax, (512) 463-0039

Secy. of State Elton Bomer, State Capitol, #1E.8, Austin, 78711, (512) 463-5701; fax, (512) 475-2761

Atty. Gen. John Cornyn (R), Price Daniel, Sr. Bldg., 8th Floor, Austin, 78711-2548, (512) 463-2100; fax, (512) 476-2653

Comptroller Carole Keeton Rylander (R), Lyndon B. Johnson State Office Bldg., 111 E. 17th St., Austin, 78774, (512) 463-4000; fax, (512) 475-0352

In Washington, D.C.: Laurie M. Rich, Executive Director, Office of State-Federal Relations, State of Texas, 122 C St. N.W., #200 20001, (202) 638-3927; fax, (202) 463-1984

Utah   Web, www.state.ut.us

Gov. Michael O. Leavitt (R), State Capitol, #210, Salt Lake City, 84114; Press: Vicki Varela, (801) 538-1000

Lt. Gov. Olene S. Walker, State Capitol, #210, Salt Lake City, 84114, (801) 538-1000; fax, (801) 538-1557

(No office of Secretary of State)

Atty. Gen. Jan Graham (D), State Capitol, #236, Salt Lake City, 84114-0810, (801) 366-0260; fax, (801) 538-1121

Treasurer Edward T. Alter (R), State Capitol, #215, Salt Lake City, 84114, (801) 538-1042; fax, (801) 538-1465

In Washington, D.C.: Joanne Snow Neumann, Director, Washington Office of the Governor, State of Utah, 400 N. Capitol St. N.W., #388 20001, (202) 624-7704; fax, (202) 624-7707

Vermont   Web, www.state.vt.us

Gov. Howard B. Dean (D), Pavilion Office Bldg., 109 State St., 5th Floor, Montpelier, 05609; Press: Susan Allen, (802) 828-3333

Lt. Gov. Douglas A. Racine (D), State House, Montpelier, 05633, (802) 828-2226; fax, (802) 828-3198

Secy. of State Deborah L. Markowitz (D), Pavilion Office Bldg., 109 State St., Montpelier, 05609-1101, (802) 828-2363; fax, (802) 828-2496

Atty. Gen. William H. Sorrell (D), Pavilion Office Bldg., 109 State St., Montpelier, 05609-1001, (802) 828-3171; fax, (802) 828-2154

Treasurer James H. Douglas (R), 133 State St., 2nd Floor, Montpelier, 05633-6200, (802) 828-2301; fax, (802) 828-2772

Virginia   Web, www.state.va.us

Gov. James S. Gilmore III (R), State Capitol, Richmond, 23219; Press: Mark Miner, (804) 692-3110

Lt. Gov. John H. Hager (R), 900 E. Main St., #1400, Richmond, 23219-3523, (804) 786-2078; fax, (804) 786-7514

Secy. of the Commonwealth Anne P. Petera, 1 Capitol Square, 830 E. Main St., 14th Floor, Richmond, 23219, (804) 786-2441; fax, (804) 371-0017

Atty. Gen. Mark L. Earley (R), 900 E. Main St., Richmond, 23219, (804) 786-2071; fax, (804) 786-1991

Treasurer Mary G. Morris, 101 N. 14th St., James Monroe Bldg., 3rd Floor, Richmond, 23219, (804) 225-2142; fax, (804) 225-3187

In Washington, D.C.: Michael McSherry, Director, Washington Office of the Governor, Commonwealth of Virginia, 444 N. Capitol St. N.W., #214 20001, (202) 783-1769; fax, (202) 783-7687

Washington   Web, www.state.wa.us

Gov. Gary Locke (D), Legislative Bldg., 2nd Floor, Olympia, 98504-0002; Press: Ed Penhale, (360) 902-4136

Lt. Gov. Bradley Scott Owen (D), Legislative Bldg., #304, Olympia, 98504-0482, (360) 786-7700; fax, (360) 786-7749

Secy. of State Ralph Davies Munro (R), Legislative Bldg., Olympia, 98504-0220, (360) 902-4151; fax, (360) 586-5629

Atty. Gen. Christine O. Gregoire (D), 1125 Washington St. S.E., Olympia, 98504-0100, (360) 753-6200; fax, (360) 586-8474

Treasurer Michael J. Murphy (D), Legislative Bldg., #240, Olympia, 98504-0200, (360) 902-9000; fax, (360) 902-9044

In Washington, D.C.: Jan Shinpoch, Director, Washington Office of the Governor, State of Washington, 444 N. Capitol St. N.W., #617 20001, (202) 624-3680; fax, (202) 624-3682

West Virginia   Web, www.state.wv.us

Gov. Cecil H. Underwood (R), State Capitol Bldg., 1900 Kanawha Blvd. East, Charleston, 25305; Press: Rod Blackstone, (304) 558-6343

(No office of Lieutenant Governor)

Secy. of State Ken Hechler (D), 1900 Kanawha Blvd. East, #157-K, Charleston, 25305-0770, (304) 558-6000; fax, (304) 558-0900

Atty. Gen. Darrell V. McGraw Jr. (D), 1900 Kanawha Blvd. East, #26-E, Charleston, 25305-0220, (304) 558-2021; fax, (304) 558-0140

Treasurer John D. Perdue (D), State Capitol Bldg., #E-145, Charleston, 25305, (304) 558-5000; fax, (304) 558-4097

In Washington, D.C.: Elizabeth Bowen, Director, Washington Office of the Governor, State of West Virginia, 4200 Massachusetts Ave. N.W. 20016, (202) 244-1194; fax, (202) 244-2559

Wisconsin   Web, www.state.wi.us

Gov. Tommy G. Thompson (R), State Capitol, #125-S, Madison, 53707-7863; Press: Darrin Schmitz, (608) 266-1212

Lt. Gov. Scott McCallum (R), 1 S. Pinckney, #330, Madison, 53703, (608) 266-3516; fax, (608) 267-3571

Secy. of State Doug La Follette (D), 30 W. Mifflin St., 10th Floor, Madison, 53707-7848, (608) 266-8888; fax, (608) 266-3159

Atty. Gen. James E. Doyle (D), 123 W. Washington Ave., #117, Madison, 53707-7857, (608) 244-4982; fax, (608) 267-2778

Treasurer Jack Voight (R), 1 S. Pinckney, #550, Madison, 53707, (608) 264-6998; fax, (608) 266-2647

In Washington, D.C.: Schuyler Baab, Director, Washington Office of the Governor, State of Wisconsin, 444 N. Capitol St. N.W., #613 20001, (202) 624-5870; fax, (202) 624-5871

Wyoming   Web, www.state.wy.us/

Gov. Jim Geringer (R), State Capitol, Cheyenne, 82002-0010; Press: Eric Curry, (307) 777-7434

(No office of Lieutenant Governor)

Secy. of State Joseph B. Meyer (R), State Capitol Bldg., Cheyenne, 82002, (307) 777-7378; fax, (307) 777-6217

Atty. Gen. Gay Woodhouse, 123 Capitol Bldg., Cheyenne, 82002, (307) 777-7841; fax, (307) 777-6869

Treasurer Cynthia Lummis (R), 200 W. 24th St., Cheyenne, 82002, (307) 777-7408; fax, (307) 777-5411

Foreign Embassies, U.S. Ambassadors, and Country Desk Officers

The list that follows includes key foreign diplomats in the United States, U.S. Ambassadors or ranking diplomatic officials abroad, and offices or regional desks of the U.S. State Dept. and U.S. Commerce Dept. that follow political, cultural, and economic developments in each country. The Commerce Dept. also provides fax-on-demand services for selected regional desks, including the Business Information Service for the Newly Independent States (BISNIS) at (202) 482-4655, the Central and Eastern Europe Business Information Center (CEEBIC) at (202) 482-2645, the Trade Information Center (TIC) at (800) 872-8723, and the NAFTA Office at (202) 482-4464 or (202) 482-3101.

Afghanistan

Washington embassy suspended operations August 28, 1997.
Consul: Abdul Habib SERAJ.
Chancery (consulate): 360 Lexington Ave., 11th Floor, New York, NY 10017; (212) 972-2276; fax, (212) 972-9046.
Embassy in Kabul temporarily closed.
State Dept.: Jeffrey Lundstead, (202) 647-4324.
Commerce Dept.: Richard Harding, (202) 482-2955.

Albania

Ambassador: Petrit BUSHATI.
Chancery: 2100 S St. N.W. 20008; (202) 223-4942; fax, (202) 628-7342.
U.S. Ambassador in Tirane: Joseph Limprecht.
State Dept.: Andrew Hyde, (202) 647-3747.
Commerce Dept.: CEEBIC, (202) 482-2645.

Algeria

Ambassador: Idriss JAZAIRY.
Chancery: 2118 Kalorama Rd. N.W. 20008; (202) 265-2800; fax, (202) 667-2174.
U.S. Ambassador in Algiers: Cameron R. Hume.
State Dept.: Ronald L. Schlicher, (202) 647-7216.
Commerce Dept.: Cherie Loustaunau, (202) 482-1860.

Andorra

Relations with Andorra are maintained by the U.S. Consulate in Barcelona, Spain.: Edward Romero, ambassador.
Ambassador: Juli MINOVES TRIQUELL.

Chancery (U.N. Mission): 2 United Nations Plaza, 25th Floor, New York, NY 10017; (212) 750-8064; fax, (212) 750-6630.
State Dept.: Richard Weston, (202) 647-1419.

Angola

Ambassador: Antonio Dos Santos FRANCA.
Chancery: 1615 M St. N.W., #900 20036; (202) 785-1156; fax, (202) 785-1258.
U.S. Ambassador in Luanda: Joseph G. Sullivan.
State Dept.: John Sequeria, (202) 647-8434.
Commerce Dept.: Alicia Robinson, (202) 482-4228.

Antigua and Barbuda

Ambassador: Lionel A. HURST.
Chancery: 3216 New Mexico Ave. N.W. 20016; (202) 362-5211; fax, (202) 362-5225.
U.S. Ambassador: Vacant (resident in Bridgetown, Barbados).
State Dept.: Vacant, (202) 647-2620.
Commerce Dept.: Michelle Brooks, (202) 482-1658.

Argentina

Ambassador: Guillermo Enrique GONZALEZ.
Chancery: 1600 New Hampshire Ave. N.W. 20009; (202) 238-6400; fax, (202) 332-3171.
Chargé d'Affaires in Buenos Aires: V. Manuel Rocha.
State Dept.: Milton Charlton, (202) 647-2407.
Commerce Dept.: Valerie Dees, (202) 482-0477.

Armenia

Ambassador: Arman KIRAKOSSIAN.
Chancery: 2225 R St. N.W. 20008; (202) 319-1976; fax, (202) 319-2982.
U.S. Ambassador in Yerevan: Michael Lemmon.

State Dept.: Randy Carlino, (202) 647-6758.
Commerce Dept.: BISNIS, (202) 482-4655.

Australia

Ambassador: Michael Joseph THAWLEY.
Chancery: 1601 Massachusetts Ave. N.W. 20036; (202) 797-3000; fax, (202) 797-3168.
U.S. Ambassador in Canberra: Genta Hawkins Holmes.
State Dept.: Philip Antweiler, (202) 647-7828.
Commerce Dept.: George Paine, (202) 482-2955.

Austria

Ambassador: Peter MOSER.
Chancery: 3524 International Court N.W. 20008; (202) 895-6700; fax, (202) 895-6750.
U.S. Ambassador in Vienna: Kathryn Walt Hall.
State Dept.: Ken Gross, (202) 647-2672.
Commerce Dept.: Lisa Tomlinson, (202) 482-2434.

Azerbaijan

Ambassador: Hafiz Mir Jalal PASHAYEV.
Chancery (temp.): 927 15th St. N.W., #700 20005; (202) 842-0001; fax, (202) 842-0004.
U.S. Ambassador in Baku: Stanley T. Escudero.
State Dept.: Jessica Levine, (202) 647-6048.
Commerce Dept.: BISNIS, (202) 482-4655.

Bahamas

Chargé d'Affaires: Sheila Gweneth CAREY.
Chancery: 2220 Massachusetts Ave. N.W. 20008; (202) 319-2660; fax, (202) 319-2668.
U.S. Ambassador in Nassau: Arthur Schechter.
State Dept.: Kathleen Lange, (202) 647-2621.
Commerce Dept.: Michelle Brooks, (202) 482-1658.

Bahrain

Ambassador: Muhammad ABDUL GHAFFAR.
Chancery: 3502 International Dr. N.W. 20008; (202) 342-0741; fax, (202) 362-2192.
U.S. Ambassador in Manama: Johnny Young.
State Dept.: Greg Sullivan, (202) 647-6571.
Commerce Dept.: David Guglielmi, (202) 482-1860.

Bangladesh

Ambassador: K. M. SHEHABUDDIN.
Chancery: 2201 Wisconsin Ave. N.W. 20007; (202) 342-8372.
U.S. Ambassador in Dhaka: John Holzman.
State Dept.: Jeffrey Lundstead, (202) 647-4324.
Commerce Dept.: George Paine, (202) 482-2955.

Barbados

Ambassador: Courtney N. BLACKMAN.
Chancery: 2144 Wyoming Ave. N.W. 20008; (202) 939-9200.
U.S. Ambassador in Bridgetown: Vacant.
State Dept.: Vacant, (202) 647-2620.
Commerce Dept.: Michelle Brooks, (202) 482-1658.

Belarus

Ambassador: Valery V. TSEPKALO.
Chancery: 1619 New Hampshire Ave. N.W. 20009; (202) 986-1604; fax, (202) 986-1805.
U.S. Ambassador in Minsk: Daniel V. Speckhard.
State Dept.: Daniel Turnbull, (202) 647-6764.
Commerce Dept.: BISNIS, (202) 482-4655.

Belgium

Ambassador: Alex REYN.
Chancery: 3330 Garfield St. N.W. 20008; (202) 333-6900; fax, (202) 333-3079.
U.S. Ambassador in Brussels: Paul Cejas.
State Dept.: Geoffrey Odlum, (202) 647-8027.
Commerce Dept.: Kerry O'Connor, (202) 482-0010.

Belize

Ambassador: James S. MURPHY.
Chancery: 2535 Massachusetts Ave. N.W. 20008; (202) 332-9636; fax, (202) 332-6888.
U.S. Ambassador in Belize City: Carolyn Curiel.
State Dept.: Chris Webster, (202) 647-3543.
Commerce Dept.: Michelle Brooks, (202) 482-1658.

Benin

Ambassador: Lucien Edgar TONOUKOUIN.
Chancery: 2737 Cathedral Ave. N.W. 20008; (202) 232-6656; fax, (202) 265-1996.
U.S. Ambassador in Cotonou: Robert C. Felder.
State Dept.: Donald Boy, (202) 647-1596.
Commerce Dept.: Douglas Wallace, (202) 482-5149.

Bhutan

State Dept.: Diana Wood, (202) 647-1450.
Commerce Dept.: George Paine, (202) 482-2955.

Bolivia

Chargé d'Affaires: Enrique ACKERMANN.
Chancery: 3014 Massachusetts Ave. N.W. 20008; (202) 483-4410; fax, (202) 328-3712.
U.S. Ambassador in La Paz: Donna Jean Hrinak.
State Dept.: Michael Meigs, (202) 647-1715.
Commerce Dept.: Tom Welch, (202) 482-0475.

CORRESPONDING WITH A FOREIGN SERVICE POST

Business correspondence to a foreign service post should be addressed to a section or position rather than to an officer by name in case that officer has transferred to another post. Do not combine any of the following address forms, since this can cause delays in delivery; in some cases the letter may be returned to you.

Posts with APO/FPO addresses:
use use domestic postage
name of section
name of post
PSC or unit number, box number
APO + two-letter code (AA, AE, or AP) + ZIP Code

Posts without APO/FPO addresses (via diplomatic pouch):
use domestic postage
name of section
name of post
Department of State
Washington, DC 20521 + 4-digit postal code

When sending mail via diplomatic pouch (see address form above), add the 4-digit code of the destination post to the 20521 ZIP Code. Following are 4-digit codes for U.S. embassies in foreign capitals and a few key cities.

Abidjan 2010	**Bridgetown** 3120	**Islamabad** 8100	**Monrovia** 8800	**Rome** 9500
Abu Dhabi 6010	**Brussels** 7600	**Jakarta** 8200	**Montevideo** 3360	**St. George's** 3180
Accra 2020	**Bucharest** 5260	**Kampala** 2190	**Moscow** 5430	**San Jose** 3440
Addis Ababa 2030	**Budapest** 5270	**Kathmandu** 6190	**Muscat** 6220	**San Salvador** 3450
Algiers 6030	**Buenos Aires** 3130	**Khartoum** 2200	**Nairobi** 8900	**Sanaa** 6330
Almaty 7030	**Bujumbura** 2100	**Kiev** 5850	**Nassau** 3370	**Santiago** 3460
Amman 6050	**Cairo** 7700	**Kigali** 2210	**N'Djamena** 2410	**Santo Domingo** 3470
Ankara 7000	**Canberra** 7800	**Kingston** 3210	**New Delhi** 9000	**Sarajevo** 7130
Antananarivo 2040	**Caracas** 3140	**Kinshasa** 2220	**Niamey** 2420	**Seoul** 9600
Ashgabat 7070	**Chisinau** 7080	**Kolonia** 4120	**Nicosia** 5450	**Singapore** 4280
Asmara 7170	**Colombo** 6100	**Kuala Lumpur** 4210	**Nouakchott** 2430	**Sofia** 5740
Asunción 3020	**Conakry** 2110	**Kuwait** 6200	**Oslo** 5460	**Stockholm** 5750
Athens 7100	**Copenhagen** 5280	**Lagos** 8300	**Ottawa** 5480	**Suva** 4290
Baku 7050	**Cotonou** 2120	**La Paz** 3220	**Ouagadougou** 2440	**Tallinn** 4530
Bamako 2050	**Dakar** 2130	**Libreville** 2270	**Panama City** 9100	**Tashkent** 7110
Bandar Seri Begawan 4020	**Damascus** 6110	**Lilongwe** 2280	**Paramaribo** 3390	**Tbilisi** 7060
Bangkok 7200	**Dar Es Salaam** 2140	**Lima** 3230	**Paris** 9200	**Tegucigalpa** 3480
Bangui 2060	**Dhaka** 6120	**Lisbon** 5320	**Phnom Penh** 4540	**Tel Aviv** 9700
Banjul 2070	**Djibouti** 2150	**Ljubljana** 7140	**Port-au-Prince** 3400	**Tirane** 9510
Barcelona 5400	**Doha** 6130	**Lome** 2300	**Port Louis** 2450	**Tokyo** 9800
Beijing 7300	**Dublin** 5290	**London** 8400	**Port Moresby** 4240	**Tunis** 6360
Beirut 6070	**Dushanbe** 7090	**Lusaka** 2310	**Port-of-Spain** 3410	**Ulaanbaatar** 4410
Belgrade 5070	**Florence** 5670	**Luxembourg** 5380	**Prague** 5630	**Valletta** 5800
Belize 3050	**Freetown** 2160	**Madrid** 8500	**Praia** 2460	**Vatican City** 5660
Berlin 5090	**Gaborone** 2170	**Majuro** 4380	**Pretoria** 9300	**Vienna** 9900
Bern 5110	**Geneva** 5120	**Malabo** 2320	**Quebec** 5520	**Vientiane** 4350
Bishkek 7040	**Georgetown** 3170	**Managua** 3240	**Quito** 3420	**Vilnius** 4510
Bissau 2080	**Guatemala City** 3190	**Manama** 6210	**Rabat** 9400	**Warsaw** 5010
Bogota 3030	**The Hague** 5770	**Manila** 8600	**Rangoon** 4250	**Wellington** 4360
Bonn 7400	**Hanoi** 4550	**Maputo** 2330	**Reykjavik** 5640	**Windhoek** 2540
Brasilia 7500	**Harare** 2180	**Maseru** 2340	**Riga** 4520	**Yaounde** 2520
Bratislava 5840	**Havana** 3200	**Mbabane** 2350	**Riyadh** 6300	**Yerevan** 7020
Brazzaville 2090	**Helsinki** 5310	**Mexico City** 8700		**Zagreb** 5080
	Hong Kong 8000	**Minsk** 7010		**Zurich** 5130

Bosnia-Herzegovina

Ambassador: Sven ALKALAJ.
Chancery: 2109 E St. N.W. 20037; (202) 337-1500; fax, (202) 337-1502.
U.S. Ambassador in Sarajevo: Thomas J. Miller.
State Dept.: Sherrie Daniels, (202) 647-0608.
Commerce Dept.: CEEBIC, (202) 482-2645.

Botswana

Chargé d'Affaires: Naomi Ellen MAJINDA.
Chancery: 1531-1533 New Hampshire Ave. N.W. 20036; (202) 244-4990; fax, (202) 244-4164.
U.S. Ambassador in Gaborone: John Lange.
State Dept.: Charles Gurney, (202) 647-9856.
Commerce Dept.: Alicia Robinson, (202) 482-4228.

Brazil

Ambassador: Rubens BARBOSA.
Chancery: 3006 Massachusetts Ave. N.W. 20008; (202) 238-2700; fax, (202) 238-2827.
U.S. Ambassador in Brasilia: Anthony S. Harrington.
State Dept.: Milton Charlton, (202) 647-2407.
Commerce Dept.: Carlo Cavagna, (202) 482-0428.

Brunei

Ambassador: Pengiran Anak Dato PUTEH.
Chancery: 3520 International Court N.W., 20008; (202) 342-0159; fax, (202) 342-0158.
U.S. Ambassador in Bandar Seri Begawan: Sylvia Gaye Stanfield.
State Dept.: Joyce Wong, (202) 647-1221.
Commerce Dept.: Susan Abbatecola, (202) 482-1820.

Bulgaria

Ambassador: Philip DIMITROV.
Chancery: 1621 22nd St. N.W. 20008; (202) 387-7969; fax, (202) 234-7973.
U.S. Ambassador in Sofia: Richard Miles.
State Dept.: Lisa Golden, (202) 647-0310.
Commerce Dept.: CEEBIC, (202) 482-2645.

Burkina Faso

Ambassador: Bruno ZIDOUEMBA
Chancery: 2340 Massachusetts Ave. N.W. 20008; (202) 332-5577; fax, (202) 667-1882.
U.S. Ambassador in Ouagadougou: Jimmy J. Kolker.
State Dept.: John Jones, (202) 647-1540.
Commerce Dept.: Philip Michelini, (202) 482-4388.

Burma (See Myanmar)

Burundi

Ambassador: Thomas NDIKUMANA.
Chancery: 2233 Wisconsin Ave. N.W., #212 20007; (202) 342-2574; fax, (202) 342-2578.
U.S. Ambassador in Bujumbura: Mary C. Yates.
State Dept.: Caroline Bargeron, (202) 647-3139.
Commerce Dept.: Philip Michelini, (202) 482-4388.

Cambodia

Ambassador: Roland ENG.
Chancery: 4500 16th St. N.W. 20011; (202) 726-7742; fax, (202) 726-8381.
U.S. Ambassador in Phnom Penh: Kent M. Wiedemann.
State Dept.: Maria Damour, (202) 647-3133.
Commerce Dept.: Hong-Phong Pho, (202) 482-1820.

Cameroon

Ambassador: Jerome MENDOUGA.
Chancery: 2349 Massachusetts Ave. N.W. 20008; (202) 265-8790; fax, (202) 387-3826.
U.S. Ambassador in Yaounde: John M. Yates.
State Dept.: Henry Hand, (202) 647-1707.
Commerce Dept.: Douglas Wallace, (202) 482-5149.

Canada

Ambassador: Raymond A. J. CHRETIEN.
Chancery: 501 Pennsylvania Ave. N.W. 20001; (202) 682-1740; fax, (202) 682-7726.
U.S. Ambassador in Ottawa: Gordon G. Giffin.
State Dept.: Steve Candy, (202) 647-7228.
Commerce Dept.: NAFTA, (202) 482-0305.

Cape Verde

Ambassador: Amilcar Spencer LOPES.
Chancery: 3415 Massachusetts Ave. N.W. 20007; (202) 965-6820; fax, (202) 965-1207.
U.S. Ambassador in Praia: Michael D. Metelits.
State Dept.: John Olson, (202) 647-3469.
Commerce Dept.: Philip Michelini, (202) 482-4388.

Central African Republic

Ambassador: Henry KOBA
Chancery: 1618 22nd St. N.W. 20008; (202) 483-7800; fax, (202) 332-9893.
U.S. Ambassador in Bangui: Robert C. Perry.
State Dept.: Debbie Lopes de Rosa, (202) 647-1707.
Commerce Dept.: Philip Michelini, (202) 482-4388.

Chad

Ambassador: Hassaballah AHMAT SOUBIANE.
Chancery: 2002 R St. N.W. 20009; (202) 462-4009; fax, (202) 265-1937.
U.S. Ambassador in N'Djamena: Christopher E. Goldthwait.
State Dept.: Debbie Lopes de Rosa, (202) 647-1707.
Commerce Dept.: Philip Michelini, (202) 482-4388.

Chile

Ambassador: Mario ARTAZA.
Chancery: 1732 Massachusetts Ave. N.W. 20036; (202) 785-1746; fax, (202) 887-5579.
U.S. Ambassador in Santiago: John O'Leary.
State Dept.: Milton Charlton, (202) 647-2407.
Commerce Dept.: David Schnier, (202) 482-0703.

China

Ambassador: LI Zhao Xing.
Chancery: 2300 Connecticut Ave. N.W. 20008; (202) 328-2500.
U.S. Ambassador in Beijing: Joseph W. Prueher.
State Dept.: Steve Schlaikjer, (202) 647-6803.
Commerce Dept.: Lauren Saadat, (202) 482-4682.

Colombia

Ambassador: Luis Alberto MORENO.
Chancery: 2118 Leroy Pl. N.W. 20008; (202) 387-8338; fax, (202) 232-8643.
U.S. Ambassador in Bogota: Curtis Warren Kamman.
State Dept.: Michael Meigs, (202) 647-1715.
Commerce Dept.: Matt Gaisford, (202) 482-0057.

Comoros

Ambassador: Ahmed DJABIR.
Chancery (U.N. Mission): 420 E. 50th St., New York, NY 10022; (212) 972-8010.
U.S. Ambassador: Mark W. Erwin (resident in Port Louis, Mauritius).
State Dept.: Arlene Ferrill, (202) 647-9742.
Commerce Dept.: Douglas Wallace, (202) 482-5149.

Congo, Democratic Republic of (Zaire)

Ambassador: Faida MITIFU.
Chancery: 1800 New Hampshire Ave. N.W. 20009; (202) 234-7690; fax, (202) 237-0748.
U.S. Ambassador in Kinshasa: William Swing.
State Dept.: Charles Neary, (202) 647-2216.
Commerce Dept.: Philip Michelini, (202) 482-4388.

Congo, Republic of

Chargé d'Affaires: Serge MOMBOULI.
Chancery: 4891 Colorado Ave. N.W. 20011; (202) 726-5500; fax, (202) 726-1860.
U.S. Ambassador in Brazzaville: David H. Kaeuper.
State Dept.: Michael Goldschmidt, (202) 647-1707.
Commerce Dept.: Douglas Wallace, (202) 482-5149.

Costa Rica

Ambassador: Jaime DAREMBLUM.
Chancery: 2114 S St. N.W. 20008; (202) 234-2945; fax, (202) 265-4795.
U.S. Ambassador in San Jose: Thomas J. Dodd.
State Dept.: Chris Webster, (202) 647-3543.
Commerce Dept.: Mark Siegelman, (202) 482-0704.

Côte d'Ivoire

Ambassador: Koffi Moise KOUMOUE.
Chancery (temp.): 3421 Massachusetts Ave. N.W. 20007; (202) 797-0300.
U.S. Ambassador in Abidjan: George Mu.
State Dept.: Donald Boy, (202) 647-1596.
Commerce Dept.: Philip Michelini, (202) 482-4388.

Croatia

Ambassador: Miomir ZUZUL.
Chancery: 2343 Massachusetts Ave. N.W. 20008; (202) 588-5899; fax (202) 588-8936.
U.S. Ambassador in Zagreb: William D. Montgomery.
State Dept.: Colleen Hyland, (202) 647-2452.
Commerce Dept.: CEEBIC, (202) 482-2645.

Cuba

Chancery: Cuba's interests in the United States are represented by Switzerland.
The Cuban Interests Section: is located at 2630 and 2639 16th St. N.W. 20009; (202) 797-8518. Fernando Ramirez, chief of section.
U.S. interests in Cuba are represented through the Swiss Embassy: Vicki Huddleston, U.S. principal officer in Havana.
State Dept.: Michael Witajewski, (202) 647-7488.
Commerce Dept.: Mark Siegelman, (202) 482-0704.

Cyprus

Ambassador: Erato KOZAKOU MARCOULLIS.
Chancery: 2211 R St. N.W. 20008; (202) 462-5772; fax, (202) 483-6710.
U.S. Ambassador in Nicosia: Donald Bandler.
State Dept.: Daniel Lawton, (202) 647-6112.
Commerce Dept.: Ann Corro, (202) 482-3945.

Czech Republic

Ambassador: Alexandr VONDRA.
Chancery: 3900 Spring of Freedom St. N.W. 20008; (202) 274-9100; fax, (202) 966-8540.
U.S. Ambassador in Prague: John Shattuck.
State Dept.: James Donegan, (202) 647-4136.
Commerce Dept.: CEEBIC, (202) 482-2645.

Denmark

Ambassador: K. Erik TYGESEN.
Chancery: 3200 Whitehaven St. N.W. 20008; (202) 234-4300; fax, (202) 328-1470.
U.S. Ambassador in Copenhagen: Richard Swett.
State Dept.: John Hall, (202) 647-6071.
Commerce Dept.: Leaksmy Norin, (202) 482-4414.

Djibouti

Ambassador: Roble OLHAYE.
Chancery: 1156 15th St. N.W., #515 20005; (202) 331-0270; fax, (202) 331-0302.
U.S. Ambassador in Djibouti: Lange Schermerhorn.
State Dept.: Arlene Ferrill, (202) 647-9742.
Commerce Dept.: Douglas Wallace, (202) 482-5149.

Dominica

Ambassador: Nicholas J. O. LIVERPOOL.
Chancery: 3216 New Mexico Ave. N.W. 20016; (202) 364-6781; fax, (202) 364-6791.
U.S. Ambassador: Vacant (resident in Bridgetown, Barbados).
State Dept.: Vacant, (202) 647-2620.
Commerce Dept.: Michelle Brooks, (202) 482-1658.

Dominican Republic

Ambassador: Roberto D. SALADIN SELIN.
Chancery: 1715 22nd St. N.W. 20008; (202) 332-6280; fax, (202) 265-8057.
U.S. Ambassador in Santo Domingo: Charles Manatt.
State Dept.: Vacant, (202) 647-2620.
Commerce Dept.: Mark Siegelman, (202) 482-0704.

Ecuador

Ambassador: Ivonne A-BAKI.
Chancery: 2535 15th St. N.W. 20009; (202) 234-7200; fax, (202) 667-3482.
U.S. Ambassador in Quito: Gwen C. Clare.
State Dept.: Michael Meigs, (202) 647-1715.
Commerce Dept.: Matt Gaisford, (202) 482-0057.

Egypt

Ambassador: M. Nabil FAHMY.
Chancery: 3521 International Court N.W. 20008; (202) 895-5400; fax, (202) 244-4319.
U.S. Ambassador in Cairo: Daniel C. Kurtzer.
State Dept.: Ronald L. Schlicher, (202) 647-7216.
Commerce Dept.: Thomas Sams, (202) 482-1860.

El Salvador

Ambassador: Rene A. LEON.
Chancery: 2308 California St. N.W. 20008; (202) 265-9671.
U.S. Ambassador in San Salvador: Anne Patterson.
State Dept.: Chris Webster, (202) 647-3543.
Commerce Dept.: Elizabeth Jaffee, (202) 482-4302.

Equatorial Guinea

Ambassador: Micha ONDO BILE.
Chancery: 2020 16th St. N.W., #405 20009; (202) 518-5700; fax, (202) 518-5252.
U.S. Ambassador in Malabo: John M. Yates.
State Dept.: Henry Hand, (202) 647-1707.
Commerce Dept.: Douglas Wallace, (202) 482-5149.

Eritrea

Ambassador: Semere RUSSOM.
Chancery: 1708 New Hampshire Ave. N.W. 20009; (202) 319-1991; fax, (202) 319-1304.
U.S. Ambassador in Asmara: William Clarke.
State Dept.: Sylvia Eiriz, (202) 736-4644.
Commerce Dept.: Douglas Wallace, (202) 482-5149.

Estonia

Chargé d'Affaires: Riho KRUUV.
Chancery: 2131 Massachusetts Ave. N.W. 20008; (202) 588-0101; fax, (202) 588-0108.
U.S. Ambassador in Tallinn: Melissa Wells.
State Dept.: Andrew Silski, (202) 647-6071.
Commerce Dept.: CEEBIC, (202) 482-2645.

Ethiopia

Ambassador: Berhane GEBRE-CHRISTOS.
Chancery: 2134 Kalorama Rd. N.W. 20008; (202) 234-2281; fax, (202) 328-7950.
U.S. Ambassador in Addis Ababa: Tibor P. Nagy Jr..
State Dept.: James Knight, (202) 647-8852.
Commerce Dept.: Douglas Wallace, (202) 482-5149.

Fiji

Ambassador: Napolioni MASIREWA.
Chancery: 2233 Wisconsin Ave. N.W., #240 20007; (202) 337-8320; fax, (202) 337-1996.

U.S. Ambassador in Suva: Siddique M. Osman.
State Dept.: Ted Halstead, (202) 736-4741.

Finland

Ambassador: Jaakko LAAJAVA.
Chancery: 3301 Massachusetts Ave. N.W. 20008; (202) 298-5800; fax, (202) 298-6030.
U.S. Ambassador in Helsinki: Eric Edelman.
State Dept.: Stuart Hatcher, (202) 647-6071.
Commerce Dept.: Leaksmy Norin, (202) 482-4414.

France

Ambassador: Francois V. BUJON.
Chancery: 4101 Reservoir Rd. N.W. 20007; (202) 944-6000; fax, (202) 944-6166.
U.S. Ambassador in Paris: Felix George Rohatyn.
State Dept.: Margot Sullivan, (202) 647-4372.
Commerce Dept.: Kerry O'Connor, (202) 482-0010.

Gabon

Ambassador: Paul BUNDUKU-LATHA.
Chancery: 2034 20th St. N.W., #200 20009; (202) 797-1000; fax, (202) 332-0668.
U.S. Ambassador in Libreville: Jim Ledesma.
State Dept.: Michael Goldschmidt, (202) 647-1707.
Commerce Dept.: Douglas Wallace, (202) 482-5149.

Gambia

Ambassador: John Paul BOJANG.
Chancery: 1155 15th St. N.W., #1000 20005; (202) 785-1399; fax, (202) 785-1430.
U.S. Ambassador in Banjul: George W. Haley.
State Dept.: Donald Boy, (202) 647-1596.
Commerce Dept.: Philip Michelini, (202) 482-4388.

Georgia

Ambassador: Tedo JAPARIDZE.
Chancery: 1615 New Hampshire Ave. N.W., #300 20009; (202) 387-2390; fax, (202) 393-4537.
Ambassador in Tbilisi: Ken Yalowitz.
State Dept.: Brook Hefright, (202) 647-6795.
Commerce Dept.: BISNIS, (202) 482-4655.

Germany

Ambassador: Juergen CHROBOG.
Chancery: 4645 Reservoir Rd. N.W. 20007; (202) 298-8141; fax, (202) 298-4249.
U.S. Ambassador in Bonn: John Kornblum.
State Dept.: Shawn Crowley, (202) 647-1484.
Commerce Dept.: Lisa Tomlinson, (202) 482-2434.

Ghana

Ambassador: Kobina Arthur KOOMSON.
Chancery: 3512 International Dr. N.W. 20008; (202) 686-4520; fax, (202) 686-4527.
U.S. Ambassador in Accra: Kathryn D. Robinson.
State Dept.: John Olson, (202) 647-3469.
Commerce Dept.: Douglas Wallace, (202) 482-5149.

Greece

Ambassador: Alexandre PHILON.
Chancery: 2221 Massachusetts Ave. N.W. 20008; (202) 939-5800; fax, (202) 939-5824.
U.S. Ambassador in Athens: R. Nicholas Burns.
State Dept.: Alec Mally, (202) 647-6112.
Commerce Dept.: Ann Corro, (202) 482-3945.

Grenada

Ambassador: Denis G. ANTOINE.
Chancery: 1701 New Hampshire Ave. N.W. 20009; (202) 265-2561.
U.S. Ambassador: Vacant (resident in Bridgetown, Barbados).
State Dept.: Vacant, (202) 647-2620.
Commerce Dept.: Michelle Brooks, (202) 482-1658.

Guatemala

Ambassador: William Howard STIXRUD.
Chancery: 2220 R St. N.W. 20008; (202) 745-4952; fax, (202) 745-1908.
U.S. Ambassador in Guatemala City: Prudence Bushnell.
State Dept.: Chris Webster, (202) 647-3543.
Commerce Dept.: Elizabeth Jaffee, (202) 482-4302.

Guinea

Ambassador: Mohamed Aly THIAM.
Chancery: 2112 Leroy Pl. N.W. 20008; (202) 483-9420; fax, (202) 483-8688.
U.S. Ambassador in Conakry: Joyce E. Leader.
State Dept.: John Jones, (202) 647-1540.
Commerce Dept.: Philip Michelini, (202) 482-4388.

Guinea-Bissau

Ambassador: Mario LOPES DA ROSA.
Chancery: 1511 K St. N.W., #519 20005; (202) 347-3950; fax, (202) 347-3954.
Embassy in Bissau suspended operations June 14, 1998.
State Dept.: John Olson, (202) 647-3469.
Commerce Dept.: Philip Michelini, (202) 482-4388.

Guyana

Ambassador: Mohammed Ali Odeen ISHMAEL.
Chancery: 2490 Tracy Pl. N.W. 20008; (202) 265-6900.
U.S. Ambassador in Georgetown: James F. Mack.
State Dept.: Vacant, (202) 647-2620.
Commerce Dept.: Michelle Brooks, (202) 482-1658.

Haiti

Chargé d'Affaires: Louis Harold JOSEPH.
Chancery: 2311 Massachusetts Ave. N.W. 20008; (202) 332-4090; fax, (202) 745-7215.
U.S. Ambassador in Port-au-Prince: Timothy M. Carney.
State Dept.: Robert Gilchrist, (202) 647-5088.
Commerce Dept.: Scott Smith, (202) 482-1810.

The Holy See

Ambassador: The Most Reverend Gabriele MON-TALVO, apostolic nuncio.
Office: 3339 Massachusetts Ave. N.W. 20008; (202) 333-7121.
U.S. Ambassador in Vatican City: Corrine Claiborne Boggs.
State Dept.: Marta Youth, (202) 647-2632.

Honduras

Ambassador: Hugo NOE PINO.
Chancery: 3007 Tilden St. N.W., #4-M 20008; (202) 966-7702; fax, (202) 966-9751.
U.S. Ambassador in Tegucigalpa: Frank Almaguer.
State Dept.: Chris Webster, (202) 647-3543.
Commerce Dept.: Elizabeth Jaffee, (202) 482-4302.

Hungary

Ambassador: Geza JESZENSZKY.
Chancery: 3910 Shoemaker St. N.W. 20008; (202) 362-6730; fax, (202) 966-8135.
U.S. Ambassador in Budapest: Peter F. Tufo.
State Dept.: Helene Kessler, (202) 647-4136.
Commerce Dept.: CEEBIC, (202) 482-2645.

Iceland

Ambassador: Jon Baldvin HANNIBALSSON.
Chancery: 1156 15th St. N.W., #1200 20005; (202) 265-6653; fax, (202) 265-6656.
U.S. Ambassador in Reykjavik: Barbara J. Griffiths.
State Dept.: Andrew Silski, (202) 647-6071.
Commerce Dept.: Leaksmy Norin, (202) 482-4414.

India

Ambassador: Naresh CHANDRA.
Chancery: 2107 Massachusetts Ave. N.W. 20008; (202) 939-7000; fax, (202) 483-3972.
U.S. Ambassador in New Delhi: Richard F. Celeste.
State Dept.: Gary S. Usrey, (202) 647-4324.
Commerce Dept.: Art Stern, (202) 482-2955.

Indonesia

Ambassador: Dorodjatun KUNTJORO JAKTI.
Chancery: 2020 Massachusetts Ave. N.W. 20036; (202) 775-5200; fax, (202) 775-5365.
U.S. Ambassador in Jakarta: Robert S. Gelbard.
State Dept.: Robert Clark, (202) 647-3276.
Commerce Dept.: Elena Mikalis, (202) 482-1820.

Iran

Chancery: Iran's interests in the United States are represented by Pakistan.
An Iranian Interests Section: is located at 2209 Wisconsin Ave. N.W. 20007; (202) 965-4990. Framarz Fathnezhd, chief of section.
U.S. interests in Iran are represented through the Swiss Embassy in Tehran.
State Dept.: Philo Dibble, (202) 647-7216.
Commerce Dept.: TIC, (202) 482-1860.

Iraq

Chancery: Iraq's interests in the United States are represented by Algeria.
An Iraqi Interests Section: is located at 1801 P St. N.W. 20036; (202) 483-7500; fax, (202) 462-5066. Akram Al-Douri, chief of section.
Embassy in Baghdad temporarily closed.
State Dept.: Philo Dibble, (202) 647-7216.
Commerce Dept.: Thomas Sams, (202) 482-1860.

Ireland

Ambassador: Sean O'HUIGINN.
Chancery: 2234 Massachusetts Ave. N.W. 20008; (202) 462-3939; fax, (202) 232-5993.
U.S. Ambassador in Dublin: Michael J. Sullivan.
State Dept.: Patricia Nelson-Douvelis, (202) 647-6585.
Commerce Dept.: Robert McLaughlin, (202) 482-3748.

Israel

Ambassador: David Elekana IVRY.
Chancery: 3514 International Dr. N.W. 20008; (202) 364-5500; fax, (202) 364-5610.
U.S. Ambassador in Tel Aviv: Martin S. Indyk.
State Dept.: Jacob Walles, (202) 647-3672.
Commerce Dept.: TIC, (202) 482-1860.

Italy

Ambassador: Ferdinando SALLEO.
Chancery: 1601 Fuller St. N.W. 20009; (202) 328-5500; fax, (202) 483-2187.
U.S. Ambassador in Rome: Thomas M. Foglietta.
State Dept.: Clare Pierangelo, (202) 647-4395.
Commerce Dept.: David DeFalco, (202) 482-2178.

Jamaica

Ambassador: Richard Leighton BERNAL.
Chancery: 1520 New Hampshire Ave. N.W. 20036; (202) 452-0660; fax, (202) 452-0081.
U.S. Ambassador in Kingston: Stanley L. McLelland.
State Dept.: Kathleen Lange, (202) 647-2621.
Commerce Dept.: Mark Siegelman, (202) 482-0704.

Japan

Ambassador: Shunji YANAI.
Chancery: 2520 Massachusetts Ave. N.W. 20008; (202) 238-6700; fax, (202) 328-2187.
U.S. Ambassador in Tokyo: Thomas Foley.
State Dept.: Michael Keller, (202) 647-2912.
Commerce Dept.: Bob Francis, (202) 482-2427.

Jordan

Ambassador: Marwan Jamil MUASHER.
Chancery: 3504 International Dr. N.W. 20008; (202) 966-2664; fax, (202) 966-3110.
U.S. Ambassador in Amman: William Burns.
State Dept.: Julia Stanley, (202) 647-1022.
Commerce Dept.: TIC, (202) 482-1860.

Kazakhstan

Ambassador: Bolat K. NURGALIYEV.
Chancery: 1401 16th St. N.W. 20036; (202) 232-5488; fax, (202) 232-5845.
U.S. Ambassador in Almaty: Richard Jones.
State Dept.: Deborah Klepp, (202) 647-6859.
Commerce Dept.: BISNIS, (202) 482-4655.

Kenya

Chargé d'Affaires: Charles M. KANGE.
Chancery: 2249 R St. N.W. 20008; (202) 387-6101; fax, (202) 462-3829.
U.S. Ambassador in Nairobi: Johnnie Carson.
State Dept.: Anne Patchell, (202) 647-6473.
Commerce Dept.: Alicia Robinson, (202) 482-4228.

Kiribati

U.S. Ambassador in Majuro: Joan M. Plaisted.
State Dept.: Tom Steele, (202) 736-4741.

Korea, Democratic People's Republic of (North)

Ambassador: LI Hyong Chol.
U.N. Mission: : 820 E. 2nd Ave., 13th Floor, New York, NY 10017; (212) 972-3105; fax, (212) 972-3154.
State Dept.: Richard Scorza, (202) 647-9330.
Commerce Dept.: William Golike, (202) 482-2523.

Korea, Republic of (South)

Ambassador: Hong Koo LEE.
Chancery: 2450 Massachusetts Ave. N.W. 20008; (202) 939-5600; fax, (202) 387-0205.
U.S. Ambassador in Seoul: Stephen W. Bosworth.
State Dept.: Richard Scorza, (202) 647-9330.
Commerce Dept.: William Golike, (202) 482-2523.

Kuwait

Ambassador: Mohammed Sabah Al-Salim AL-SABAH.
Chancery: 2940 Tilden St. N.W. 20008; (202) 966-0702; fax, (202) 966-0517.
U.S. Ambassador in Kuwait City: James A. Larocco.
State Dept.: Allen Keiswetter, (202) 647-7216.
Commerce Dept.: Cherie Loustaunau, (202) 482-1860.

Kyrgyzstan

Ambassador: Baktybek ABDRISSAEV.
Chancery: 1732 Wisconsin Ave. N.W. 20007; (202) 338-5141; fax, (202) 338-5139.
U.S. Ambassador in Bishkek: Anne Marie Sigmund.
State Dept.: David Morris, (202) 647-6740.
Commerce Dept.: BISNIS, (202) 482-4655.

Laos

Ambassador: Vang RATTANAVONG.
Chancery: 2222 S St. N.W. 20008; (202) 332-6416; fax, (202) 332-4923.
U.S. Ambassador in Vientiane: Vacant.
State Dept.: Sooky Park, (202) 647-3133.
Commerce Dept.: Hong-Phong Pho, (202) 482-1820.

Latvia

Chargé d'Affaires: Peteris VINKELIS.
Chancery: 4325 17th St. N.W. 20011; (202) 726-8213; fax, (202) 726-6785.
U.S. Ambassador in Riga: James H. Holmes.
State Dept.: Andrew Silski, (202) 647-6071.
Commerce Dept.: CEEBIC, (202) 482-2645.

Lebanon

Ambassador: Farid ABBOUD.
Chancery: 2560 28th St. N.W. 20008; (202) 939-6300; fax, (202) 939-6324.

U.S. Ambassador in Beirut: David Satterfield.
State Dept.: Steve Bondy, (202) 647-1030.
Commerce Dept.: Thomas Sams, (202) 482-1860.

Lesotho

Ambassador: Lebohang K. MOLEKO.
Chancery: 2511 Massachusetts Ave. N.W. 20008; (202) 797-5533; fax, (202) 234-6815.
U.S. Ambassador in Maseru: Katherine Peterson.
State Dept.: Kimberly Murphy, (202) 647-8434.
Commerce Dept.: Alicia Robinson, (202) 482-4228.

Liberia

Chargé d'Affaires: Alexander H. N. WALLACE III.
Chancery: 5303 Colorado Ave. N.W. 20011; (202) 723-0437; fax, (202) 723-0436.
Chargé d'Affaires in Monrovia: Bismarck Myrick.
State Dept.: Kathleen List, (202) 647-0252.
Commerce Dept.: Philip Michelini, (202) 482-4388.

Libya

State Dept.: Ronald L. Schlicher, (202) 647-7216.
Commerce Dept.: Cherie Loustaunau, (202) 482-1860.

Liechtenstein

Chancery: Represented by Switzerland, 2900 Cathedral Ave. N.W. 20008; (202) 745-7900; fax, (202) 387-2564.
U.S. Ambassador: J. Richard Fredericks (resident in Bern, Switzerland).
State Dept.: Henry Kelly, (202) 647-2005.

Lithuania

Ambassador: Stasys SAKALAUSKAS.
Chancery: 2622 16th St. N.W. 20009; (202) 234-5860; fax, (202) 328-0466.
U.S. Ambassador in Vilnius: Keith C. Smith.
State Dept.: Andrew Silski, (202) 647-6071.
Commerce Dept.: CEEBIC, (202) 482-2645.

Luxembourg

Ambassador: Arlette CONZEMIUS.
Chancery: 2200 Massachusetts Ave. N.W. 20008; (202) 265-4171; fax, (202) 328-8270.
U.S. Ambassador in Luxembourg: James Hormel.
State Dept.: Cindy Stockbridge, (202) 647-6557.
Commerce Dept.: Kerry O'Connor, (202) 482-0010.

Macedonia

Amassador: Lubica Z. ACEVSKA
Chancery: 3050 K St. N.W., #210 20007; (202) 337-3063; fax, (202) 337-3093.
U.S. Ambassador in Skopje: Michael Einik.

State Dept.: Paul Pfeuffer, (202) 647-0608.
Commerce Dept.: Jonathan Kimball, (202) 482-4915.

Madagascar

Ambassador: Zina ANDRIANARIVELO RAZAFY.
Chancery: 2374 Massachusetts Ave. N.W. 20008; (202) 265-5525.
U.S. Ambassador in Antananarivo: Shirley E. Barnes.
State Dept.: Arlene Ferrill, (202) 647-9742.
Commerce Dept.: Douglas Wallace, (202) 482-5149.

Malawi

Ambassador: Tony KANDIERO.
Chancery: 2408 Massachusetts Ave. N.W. 20008; (202) 797-1007.
U.S. Ambassador in Lilongwe: Ellen Shippy.
State Dept.: Karl Albrecht, (202) 647-8432.
Commerce Dept.: Alicia Robinson, (202) 482-4228.

Malaysia

Ambassador: Dato Sheikh Abdul Khaled GHAZZALI.
Chancery: 2401 Massachusetts Ave. N.W. 20008; (202) 328-2700; fax, (202) 483-7661.
U.S. Ambassador in Kuala Lumpur: Lynn Pascoe.
State Dept.: Joyce Wong, (202) 647-1221.
Commerce Dept.: Susan Abbatecola, (202) 482-1820.

Maldives

Ambassador: Hussain Shihab.
Chancery (U.N. Mission): 800 2nd Ave., #400E, New York, NY 10017; (212) 599-6195; fax (212) 661-6405.
U.S. Ambassador: Shaun E. Donnelly (resident in Colombo, Sri Lanka).
State Dept.: Scott Ticknor, (202) 647-2351.
Commerce Dept.: Art Stern, (202) 482-2955.

Mali

Ambassador: Cheick Oumar DIARRAH.
Chancery: 2130 R St. N.W. 20008; (202) 332-2249; fax, (202) 332-6603.
U.S. Ambassador in Bamako: Michael Ranneberger.
State Dept.: Charles Luoma-Overstreet, (202) 647-2791.
Commerce Dept.: Philip Michelini, (202) 482-4388.

Malta

Ambassador: George SALIBA.
Chancery: 2017 Connecticut Ave. N.W. 20008; (202) 462-3611; fax, (202) 387-5470.
U.S. Ambassador in Valletta: Kathryn L. H. Proffitt.
State Dept.: Richard Weston, (202) 647-1419.
Commerce Dept.: Ann Corro, (202) 482-3945.

Marshall Islands

Ambassador: Banny DE BRUM.
Chancery: 2433 Massachusetts Ave. N.W. 20008; (202) 234-5414; fax, (202) 232-3236.
U.S. Ambassador: Joan M. Plaisted (resident in Majuro, Kiribati).
State Dept.: Tom Steele, (202) 736-4741.

Mauritania

Ambassador: Ahmed Ould Khalifa OULD JIDDOU.
Chancery: 2129 Leroy Pl. N.W. 20008; (202) 232-5700; fax, (202) 319-2623.
U.S. Ambassador in Nouakchott: Timberlake Foster.
State Dept.: Charles Luoma-Overstreet, (202) 647-2791.
Commerce Dept.: Philip Michelini, (202) 482-4388.

Mauritius

Ambassador: Chitmansing JESSERAMSING.
Chancery: 4301 Connecticut Ave. N.W., #441 20008; (202) 244-1491; fax, (202) 966-0983.
U.S. Ambassador in Port Louis: Mark W. Erwin.
State Dept.: Arlene Ferrill, (202) 647-9742.
Commerce Dept.: Alicia Robinson, (202) 482-4228.

Mexico

Ambassador: Jesus REYES HEROLES.
Chancery: 1911 Pennsylvania Ave. N.W. 20006; (202) 728-1600; fax, (202) 728-1698.
U.S. Ambassador in Mexico City: Jeffrey Davidow.
State Dept.: Kevin Whitaker, (202) 647-9894.
Commerce Dept.: NAFTA, (202) 482-0305.

Micronesia

Ambassador: Jesse B. MAREHALAU.
Chancery: 1725 N St. N.W. 20036; (202) 223-4383; fax, (202) 223-4391.
U.S. Ambassador in Kolonia: Diane E. Watson.
State Dept.: Tom Steele, (202) 736-4741.

Moldova

Ambassador: Ceslav CIOBANU.
Chancery: 2101 S St. N.W. 20008; (202) 667-1130; fax, (202) 667-1204.
U.S. Ambassador in Chisinau: Rudolf Perina.
State Dept.: Stephanie Eshelman, (202) 647-6733.
Commerce Dept.: BISNIS, (202) 482-4655.

Monaco

Consul: Maguy MACCARIO-DOYLE.
Chancery (consulate): 565 5th Ave., 23rd Floor, New York, NY 10017; (212) 286-0500; fax, (212) 286-1574.

Relations with Monaco are maintained by the U.S. Embassy in Paris, France.: Felix George Rohatyn, U.S. Ambassador in Paris.
State Dept.: David Van Cleve, (202) 647-4361.

Mongolia

Ambassador: Jalbuu CHOINHOR.
Chancery: 2833 M St. N.W. 20007; (202) 333-7117; fax, (202) 298-9227.
U.S. Ambassador in Ulaanbaatar: Alphonso La Porta.
State Dept.: Jonathan Fritz, (202) 647-6772.
Commerce Dept.: Lauren Saadat, (202) 482-4682.

Morocco

Chargé d'Affaires: Mohammed GHOZLANI.
Chancery: 1601 21st St. N.W. 20009; (202) 462-7979; fax, (202) 265-0161.
U.S. Ambassador in Rabat: Edward M. Gabriel.
State Dept.: Laura Byergo, (202) 647-4675.
Commerce Dept.: David Guglielmi, (202) 482-1860.

Mozambique

Ambassador: Marcos G. NAMASHULUA.
Chancery: 1990 M St. N.W., #570 20036; (202) 293-7146; fax, (202) 835-0245.
U.S. Ambassador in Maputo: Brian Curran.
State Dept.: Cassie L. Ghee, (202) 647-8434.
Commerce Dept.: Alicia Robinson, (202) 482-4228.

Myanmar (Burma)

Ambassador: Tin WINN.
Chancery: 2300 S St. N.W. 20008; (202) 332-9044; fax, (202) 332-9046.
Chargé d'Affaires in Rangoon: Priscilla A. Clapp.
State Dept.: Patrick Murphy, (202) 647-3133.
Commerce Dept.: Susan Abbatecola, (202) 482-1820.

Namibia

Ambassador: Leonard Nangolo IIPUMBU.
Chancery: 1605 New Hampshire Ave. N.W. 20009; (202) 986-0540; fax, (202) 986-0443.
U.S. Ambassador in Windhoek: : Jeffrey A. Bader.
State Dept.: Elizabeth Pratt, (202) 647-8434.
Commerce Dept.: Alicia Robinson, (202) 482-4228.

Nauru

U.S. Ambassador: Siddique M. Osman (resident in Suva, Fiji).
State Dept.: Tom Steele, (202) 736-4741.

Nepal

Ambassador: Damodar GAUTAM.
Chancery: 2131 Leroy Pl. N.W. 20008; (202) 667-4550; fax, (202) 667-5534.
U.S. Ambassador in Kathmandu: Ralph Frank.
State Dept.: Gary S. Usrey, (202) 647-4324.
Commerce Dept.: George Paine, (202) 482-2955.

Netherlands

Ambassador: Joris M. VOS.
Chancery: 4200 Linnean Ave. N.W. 20008; (202) 244-5300; fax, (202) 362-3430.
U.S. Ambassador in The Hague: Cynthia P. Schneider.
State Dept.: Cindy Stockbridge, (202) 647-6557.
Commerce Dept.: Kerry O'Connor, (202) 482-0010.

New Zealand

Ambassador: James B. BOLGER.
Chancery: 37 Observatory Circle N.W. 20008; (202) 328-4800; fax, (202) 667-5227.
U.S. Ambassador in Wellington: Carol Moseley-Braun.
State Dept.: Christopher Rich, (202) 647-4741.
Commerce Dept.: George Paine, (202) 482-2955.

Nicaragua

Ambassador: Francisco Javier AGUIRRE SACASA.
Chancery: 1627 New Hampshire Ave. N.W. 20009; (202) 939-6570; fax, (202) 939-6542.
U.S. Ambassador in Managua: Oliver Garza.
State Dept.: Chris Webster, (202) 647-3543.
Commerce Dept.: Elizabeth Jaffee, (202) 482-4302.

Niger

Ambassador: Joseph DIATTA.
Chancery: 2204 R St. N.W. 20008; (202) 483-4224.
U.S. Ambassador in Niamey: Barbro A. Owens-Kirkpatrick.
State Dept.: Charles Luoma-Overstreet, (202) 647-2791.
Commerce Dept.: Philip Michelini, (202) 482-4388.

Nigeria

Ambassador: Jibril Muhammed AMINU.
Chancery: 1333 16th St. N.W. 20036; (202) 986-8400; (202) 775-1385.
U.S. Ambassador in Lagos: William H. Twaddell.
State Dept.: Alex Martschenko, (202) 647-3407.
Commerce Dept.: Douglas Wallace, (202) 482-5149.

Norway

Ambassador: Tom Eric VRAALSEN.
Chancery: 2720 34th St. N.W. 20008; (202) 333-6000; fax, (202) 337-0870.

U.S. Ambassador in Oslo: David Hermelin.
State Dept.: John Hall, (202) 647-6071.
Commerce Dept.: Leaksmy Norin, (202) 482-4414.

Oman

Ambassador: Abdulla Moh'd Aqeel AL DHAHAB.
Chancery: 2535 Belmont Rd. N.W. 20008; (202) 387-1980; fax, (202) 745-4933.
U.S. Ambassador in Muscat: John Craig.
State Dept.: Allen Keiswetter, (202) 647-7216.
Commerce Dept.: Cherie Loustaunau, (202) 482-1860.

Pakistan

Ambassador: Maleeha LODHI.
Chancery: 2315 Massachusetts Ave. N.W. 20008; (202) 939-6200; fax, (202) 387-0484.
U.S. Ambassador in Islamabad: William Milam.
State Dept.: Jeffrey Lundstead, (202) 647-4324.
Commerce Dept.: Richard Harding, (202) 482-2955.

Palau

Ambassador: Hersey KYOTA.
Chancery: 1150 18th St. N.W., #750 20036; (202) 452-6814; fax, (202) 452-6281.
U.S. Ambassador: Thomas C. Hubbard (resident in Manila, Philippines).
State Dept.: Ted Pierce, (202) 736-4741.

Panama

Ambassador: Guillermo Alfredo FORD BOYD.
Chancery: 2862 McGill Terrace N.W. 20008; (202) 483-1407.
U.S. Ambassador in Panama City: Simon Ferro.
State Dept.: Chris Webster, (202) 647-3543.
Commerce Dept.: Matt Gaisford, (202) 482-0057.

Papua New Guinea

Ambassador: Nagora Y. BOGAN.
Chancery: 1779 Massachusetts Ave. N.W. #805 20036; (202) 745-3680; fax, (202) 745-3679.
U.S. Ambassador in Port Moresby: Arma Jean Karaer.
State Dept.: Ted Pierce, (202) 736-4741.

Paraguay

Ambassador: Juan Esteban AGUIRRE.
Chancery: 2400 Massachusetts Ave. N.W. 20008; (202) 483-6960; fax, (202) 234-4508.
U.S. Ambassador in Asunción: Vacant.
State Dept.: Milton Charlton, (202) 647-2407.
Commerce Dept.: Valerie Dees, (202) 482-0477.

Peru

Ambassador: Alfonso RIVERO.
Chancery: 1700 Massachusetts Ave. N.W. 20036; (202) 833-9860; fax, (202) 659-8124.
U.S. Ambassador in Lima: John R. Hamilton.
State Dept.: Michael Meigs, (202) 647-1715.
Commerce Dept.: Scott Smith, (202) 482-1810.

Philippines

Ambassador: Ernesto M. MACEDA
Chancery: 1600 Massachusetts Ave. N.W. 20036; (202) 467-9300; fax, (202) 328-7614.
U.S. Ambassador in Manila: Thomas C. Hubbard.
State Dept.: William Moore, (202) 647-3276.
Commerce Dept.: Susan Abbatecola, (202) 482-1820.

Poland

Ambassador: Jerzy KOZMINSKI.
Chancery: 2640 16th St. N.W. 20009; (202) 234-3800; fax, (202) 328-6271.
U.S. Ambassador in Warsaw: Daniel Fried.
State Dept.: James Wojtasiewicz, (202) 647-4139.
Commerce Dept.: CEEBIC, (202) 482-2645.

Portugal

Ambassador: Joao ROCHA PARIS.
Chancery: 2125 Kalorama Rd. N.W. 20008; (202) 328-8610; fax, (202) 462-3726.
U.S. Ambassador in Lisbon: Gerald S. McGowan.
State Dept.: Marta Youth, (202) 647-2632.
Commerce Dept.: Ann Corro, (202) 482-3945.

Qatar

Ambassador: Saad Mohamed AL KOBAISI.
Chancery: 4200 Wisconsin Ave. N.W. 20016; (202) 274-1600.
U.S. Ambassador in Doha: Elizabeth McKune.
State Dept.: Harry Kamian, (202) 647-6572.
Commerce Dept.: David Guglielmi, (202) 482-1860.

Romania

Ambassador: Mircea Dan GEOANA.
Chancery: 1607 23rd St. N.W. 20008; (202) 332-4846; fax, (202) 232-4748.
U.S. Ambassador in Bucharest: James C. Rosapepe.
State Dept.: Colin Cleary, (202) 647-4272.
Commerce Dept.: CEEBIC, (202) 482-2645.

Russia

Ambassador: Yuri Viktorovich USHAKOV.
Chancery: 2650 Wisconsin Ave. N.W. 20007; (202) 298-5700; fax, (202) 298-5735.
U.S. Ambassador in Moscow: James F. Collins.
State Dept.: John Mark Pommersheim, (202) 647-6763.
Commerce Dept.: BISNIS, (202) 482-4655.

Rwanda

Ambassador: Richard SEZIBERA.
Chancery: 1714 New Hampshire Ave. N.W. 20009; (202) 232-2882; fax, (202) 232-4544.
U.S. Ambassador in Kigali: George Staples.
State Dept.: Peter Prahar, (202) 647-3139.
Commerce Dept.: Philip Michelini, (202) 482-4388.

Saint Kitts and Nevis

Ambassador: Osbert W. LIBURD.
Chancery: 3216 New Mexico Ave. N.W. 20016; (202) 686-2636; fax, (202) 686-5740.
U.S. Ambassador: William Crotty (resident in Bridgetown, Barbados).
State Dept.: Vacant, (202) 647-2620.
Commerce Dept.: Michelle Brooks, (202) 482-1658.

Saint Lucia

Ambassador: Sonia Merlyn JOHNNY.
Chancery: 3216 New Mexico Ave. N.W. 20016; (202) 364-6792; fax, (202) 364-6728.
U.S. Ambassador: William Crotty (resident in Bridgetown, Barbados).
State Dept.: Vacant, (202) 647-2620.
Commerce Dept.: Michelle Brooks, (202) 482-1658.

Saint Vincent and the Grenadines

Ambassador: Kingsley C. A. LAYNE.
Chancery: 3216 New Mexico Ave. N.W. 20016; (202) 364-6730; fax, (202) 364-6736.
U.S. Ambassador: William Crotty (resident in Bridgetown, Barbados).
State Dept.: Vacant, (202) 647-2620.
Commerce Dept.: Michelle Brooks, (202) 482-1658.

Samoa

Ambassador: Tuiloma Neroni SLADE.
Chancery (U.N. Mission): 800 2nd Ave., #400D, New York, NY 10017; (212) 599-6196; fax, (212) 599-0797.
U.S. Ambassador: Carol Moseley-Braun (resident in Wellington, New Zealand).
State Dept.: Ted Halstead, (202) 736-4741.

San Marino

Consul: Sheila Rabb Weidenfeld, 1899 L St. N.W., #1160 20036; (202) 223-3517.

Relations with San Marino are maintained by the U.S. Consulate in Florence, Italy.: Hilarion Martinez, U.S. consul general.

State Dept.: Debbie Cavin, (202) 647-4395.

São Tomé and Principe

Chargé d'Affaires: Domingos FERREIRA.

Chancery (U.N. Mission): 122 E. 42nd St., #1604, New York, NY 10168; (212) 697-4211; fax, (212) 687-8389.

U.S. Ambassador: Jim Ledesma.

State Dept.: Michael Goldschmidt, (202) 647-1707.

Commerce Dept.: Douglas Wallace, (202) 482-5149.

Saudi Arabia

Ambassador: Prince Bandar BIN SULTAN.

Chancery: 601 New Hampshire Ave. N.W. 20037; (202) 342-3800.

U.S. Ambassador in Riyadh: Wyche Fowler Jr.

State Dept.: Allen Keiswetter, (202) 647-7216.

Commerce Dept.: David Guglielmi, (202) 482-1860.

Senegal

Ambassador: Mamadou Mansour SECK.

Chancery: 2112 Wyoming Ave. N.W. 20008; (202) 234-0540.

U.S. Ambassador in Dakar: Harriet L. Elam-Thomas.

State Dept.: John Jones, (202) 647-1540.

Commerce Dept.: Philip Michelini, (202) 482-4388.

Serbia-Montenegro (See Yugoslavia)

Seychelles

Ambassador: Claude MOREL.

Chancery (U.N. Mission): 800 2nd Ave., #400C, New York, NY 10017; (212) 972-1785; fax, (212) 972-1786.

U.S. Ambassador: Mark W. Erwin (resident in Port Louis, Mauritius).

State Dept.: Arlene Ferrill, (202) 647-9742.

Commerce Dept.: Douglas Wallace, (202) 482-5149.

Sierra Leone

Ambassador: John Ernest LEIGH.

Chancery: 1701 19th St. N.W. 20009; (202) 939-9261; fax, (202) 483-1793.

U.S. Ambassador in Freetown: Joseph H. Melrose.

State Dept.: Michael Thomas, (202) 647-3469.

Commerce Dept.: Philip Michelini, (202) 482-4388.

Singapore

Ambassador: Heng-Chee CHAN.

Chancery: 3501 International Pl. N.W. 20008; (202) 537-3100; fax, (202) 537-0876.

U.S. Ambassador in Singapore: Steven J. Green.

State Dept.: Joyce Wong, (202) 647-1221.

Commerce Dept.: Susan Abbatecola, (202) 482-1820.

Slovakia

Ambassador: Martin BUTORA.

Chancery (temp.): 2201 Wisconsin Ave. N.W., #250 20007; (202) 965-5161; fax, (202) 965-5166.

U.S. Ambassador in Bratislava: Vacant.

State Dept.: Chris Dunnett, (202) 647-4136.

Commerce Dept.: CEEBIC, (202) 482-2645.

Slovenia

Ambassador: Dimitrij RUPEL.

Chancery: 1525 New Hampshire Ave. N.W. 20036; (202) 667-5363; fax, (202) 667-4563.

U.S. Ambassador in Ljubljana: Nancy Ely-Raphel.

State Dept.: Kristina Kvien, (202) 736-7152.

Commerce Dept.: CEEBIC, (202) 482-2645.

Solomon Islands

Ambassador: Rex Stephen HOROI.

Chancery (U.N. Mission): 800 2nd Ave., #400L New York, NY 10017; (212) 599-6192; fax, (212) 661-8925.

U.S. Ambassador: Arma Jean Karaer (resident in Port Moresby, Papua New Guinea).

State Dept.: Ted Pierce, (202) 736-4741.

Somalia

Washington embassy ceased operations May 8, 1991. U.S. embassy in Mogadishu is unstaffed.

State Dept.: Arlene Ferrill, (202) 647-9742.

Commerce Dept.: Douglas Wallace, (202) 482-5149.

South Africa

Ambassador: Makata Sheila SISULU.

Chancery: 3051 Massachusetts Ave. N.W. 20008; (202) 232-4400; fax, (202) 265-1607.

U.S. Ambassador in Pretoria: Delano E. Lewis, Sr.

State Dept.: Donald Gatto, (202) 647-9429.

Commerce Dept.: Finn Holm-Olsen, (202) 482-5148.

Spain

Ambassador: Antonio OYARZABAL.

Chancery: 2375 Pennsylvania Ave. N.W. 20037; (202) 452-0100; fax, (202) 833-5670.

U.S. Ambassador in Madrid: Edward Romero.
State Dept.: Richard Weston, (202) 647-1419.
Commerce Dept.: Ann Corro, (202) 482-3945.

Sri Lanka

Ambassador: Warnasena RASAPUTRAM.
Chancery: 2148 Wyoming Ave. N.W. 20008; (202) 483-4025; fax, (202) 232-7181.
U.S. Ambassador in Colombo: Shaun E. Donnelly.
State Dept.: Gary S. Usrey, (202) 647-4324.
Commerce Dept.: Art Stern, (202) 482-2955.

Sudan

Ambassador: Mahdi Ibrahim MOHAMED.
Chancery: 2210 Massachusetts Ave. N.W. 20008; (202) 338-8565; fax, (202) 667-2406.
Chargé d'Affaires in Khartoum: Vacant.
State Dept.: Sylvia Eiriz, (202) 736-4644.
Commerce Dept.: Philip Michelini, (202) 482-4388.

Suriname

Ambassador: Arnold T. HALFHIDE.
Chancery: 4301 Connecticut Ave. N.W., #460 20008; (202) 244-7488; fax, (202) 244-5878.
U.S. Ambassador in Paramaribo: Dennis K. Hays.
State Dept.: Lisa Kierans, (202) 647-2621.
Commerce Dept.: Michelle Brooks, (202) 482-1658.

Swaziland

Ambassador: Mary M. KANYA.
Chancery: 3400 International Dr. N.W. 20008; (202) 362-6683; fax, (202) 244-8059.
U.S. Ambassador in Mbabane: Alan R. McKee.
State Dept.: Cassie L. Ghee, (202) 647-8434.
Commerce Dept.: Alicia Robinson, (202) 482-4228.

Sweden

Ambassador: Rolf EKEUS.
Chancery: 1501 M St. N.W. 20005-1702; (202) 467-2600; fax, (202) 467-2699.
U.S. Ambassador in Stockholm: Lyndon L. Olson Jr.
State Dept.: Stuart Hatcher, (202) 647-6071.
Commerce Dept.: Leaksmy Norin, (202) 482-4414.

Switzerland

Ambassador: Alfred DEFAGO.
Chancery: 2900 Cathedral Ave. N.W. 20008; (202) 745-7900; fax, (202) 387-2564.
U.S. Ambassador in Bern: J. Richard Fredericks.
State Dept.: Janey Shannon, (202) 647-2448.
Commerce Dept.: Lisa Tomlinson, (202) 482-2434.

Syria

Chargé d'Affaires: Rostom AL ZOUBI.
Chancery: 2215 Wyoming Ave. N.W. 20008; (202) 232-6313; fax, (202) 234-9548.
U.S. Ambassador in Damascus: Ryan Crocker.
State Dept.: Elisabeth Millard, (202) 647-1131.
Commerce Dept.: Thomas Sams, (202) 482-1860.

Taiwan

Representation maintained by the Taipei Economic and Cultural Representatives Office in the United States: 4201 Wisconsin Ave. N.W. 20016; (202) 895-1800.
The United States maintains unofficial relations with Taiwan through the American Institute in Taiwan.
Washington office: 1700 N. Moore St., Arlington, VA 22209-1996; (703) 525-8474; Richard Bush III, managing director.
State Dept.: Keith Jordan, (202) 647-7711.
Commerce Dept.: Laurette Dickerson, (202) 482-1820.

Tajikistan

U.S. Ambassador in Dushanbe: Robert P. J. Finn (resident in Almaty, Kazakhstan).
State Dept.: Jessica Levine (acting), (202) 647-6048.
Commerce Dept.: BISNIS, (202) 482-4655.

Tanzania

Ambassador: Mustafa Salim NYANG'ANYI.
Chancery: 2139 R St. N.W. 20008; (202) 939-6125; fax, (202) 797-7408.
U.S. Ambassador in Dar Es Salaam: Charles R. Stith.
State Dept.: Ricardo Zuniga, (202) 647-6473.
Commerce Dept.: Alicia Robinson, (202) 482-4228.

Thailand

Ambassador: Nitya PIBULSONGGRAM.
Chancery: 1024 Wisconsin Ave. N.W. 20007; (202) 944-3600; fax, (202) 944-3611.
U.S. Ambassador in Bangkok: Richard Hecklinger.
State Dept.: George Kent, (202) 647-0064.
Commerce Dept.: Susan Abbatecola, (202) 482-1820.

Togo

Ambassador: Akoussoulelou BODJONA.
Chancery: 2208 Massachusetts Ave. N.W. 20008; (202) 234-4212; fax, (202) 232-3190.
U.S. Ambassador in Lomé: Brenda B. Schoonover.
State Dept.: Donald Boy, (202) 647-1596.
Commerce Dept.: Douglas Wallace, (202) 482-5149.

Tonga

Ambassador: Akosita FINEANGANOFO (resident in London, England).
Chargé d'Affaires: Siddique M. Osman (resident in Suva, Fiji).
State Dept.: Ted Halstead, (202) 736-4741.

Trinidad and Tobago

Ambassador: Michael ARNEAUD.
Chancery: 1708 Massachusetts Ave. N.W. 20036; (202) 467-6490; fax, (202) 785-3130.
U.S. Ambassador in Port-of-Spain: Edward E. Shumaker III.
State Dept.: Vacant, (202) 647-2620.
Commerce Dept.: Michelle Brooks, (202) 482-1658.

Tunisia

Ambassador: Noureddine MEJDOUB.
Chancery: 1515 Massachusetts Ave. N.W. 20005; (202) 862-1850; fax, (202) 862-1858.
U.S. Ambassador in Tunis: Robin Lynn Raphel.
State Dept.: Jessie Lapenn, (202) 647-4674.
Commerce Dept.: David Guglielmi, (202) 482-1860.

Turkey

Ambassador: Baki ILKIN.
Chancery: 2525 Massachusetts Ave. N.W. 20008; (202) 612-6700; fax, (202) 612-6744.
U.S. Ambassador in Ankara: Mark Robert Parris.
State Dept.: Robert Blake, (202) 647-6114.
Commerce Dept.: David DeFalco, (202) 482-2178.

Turkmenistan

Ambassador: Halil UGUR.
Chancery: 2207 Massachusetts Ave. N.W. 20008; (202) 588-1500; fax, (202) 588-0697.
U.S. Ambassador in Ashgabat: Steven Mann.
State Dept.: David Morris, (202) 647-6740.
Commerce Dept.: BISNIS, (202) 482-4655.

Tuvalu

Chargé d'Affaires: Siddique M. Osman (resident in Suva, Fiji).
State Dept.: Ted Halstead, (202) 736-4741.

Uganda

Ambassador: Edith G. SSEMPALA.
Chancery: 5911 16th St. N.W. 20011; (202) 726-7100; fax, (202) 726-1727.
U.S. Ambassador in Kampala: Martin G. Brennan.
State Dept.: Ricardo Zuniga, (202) 647-6473.
Commerce Dept.: Alicia Robinson, (202) 482-4228.

Ukraine

Ambassador: Kostyantyn GRYSHCHENKO.
Chancery: 3350 M St. N.W. 20007; (202) 333-0606; fax, (202) 333-0817.
U.S. Ambassador in Kiev: Steven K. Piper.
State Dept.: Bruce Lowry, (202) 647-8671.
Commerce Dept.: BISNIS, (202) 482-4655.

United Arab Emirates

Chargé d'Affaires: Hamad Hareb ALHABSI.
Chancery: 1255 22nd St. N.W., #700 20037; (202) 955-7999.
U.S. Ambassador in Abu Dhabi: Theodore E. Kattouf.
State Dept.: Allen Keiswetter, (202) 647-7216.
Commerce Dept.: David Guglielmi, (202) 482-1860.

United Kingdom

Ambassador: Sir Christopher Meyer.
Chancery: 3100 Massachusetts Ave. N.W. 20008; (202) 588-6500; fax, (202) 588-7870.
U.S. Ambassador in London: Philip Lader.
State Dept.: Kenneth Pitterle, (202) 647-6587.
Commerce Dept.: Robert McLaughlin, (202) 482-3748.

Uruguay

Ambassador: Alvaro Mario DIEZ DE MEDINA
Chancery: 2715 M St. N.W. 20007; (202) 331-1313; fax, (202) 331-8142.
U.S. Ambassador in Montevideo: Christopher C. Ashby.
State Dept.: Milton Charlton, (202) 647-2407.
Commerce Dept.: David Schnier, (202) 482-0703.

Uzbekistan

Ambassador: Sodiq SAFAEV.
Chancery: 1746 Massachusetts Ave. N.W. 20036; (202) 887-5300; fax, (202) 293-6804.
U.S. Ambassador in Tashkent: Joseph A. Presel.
State Dept.: Edward Birsner, (202) 647-6765.
Commerce Dept.: BISNIS, (202) 482-4655.

Vanuatu

U.S. Ambassador: Arma Jean Karaer (resident in Port Moresby, Papua New Guinea).
State Dept.: Ted Pierce, (202) 736-4741.

Venezuela

Ambassador: Alfredo TORO HARDY.
Chancery: 1099 30th St. N.W. 20007; (202) 342-2214; fax, (202) 342-6820.
U.S. Ambassador in Caracas: John F. Maisto.

State Dept.: Michael Meigs, (202) 647-1715.
Commerce Dept.: Tom Welch, (202) 482-0475.

Vietnam

Ambassador: Bang LE.
Chancery: 1233 20th St. N.W., #400 20036; (202) 861-0737; fax, (202) 861-0917.
U.S. Ambassador in Hanoi: Pete Peterson.
State Dept.: Josie Papendick, (202) 647-3133.
Commerce Dept.: Hong-Phong Pho, (202) 482-1820.

Western Samoa (See Samoa)

Yemen

Ambassador: Abdulwahab A. AL-HAJJRI.
Chancery: 2600 Virginia Ave. N.W., #705 20037; (202) 965-4760; fax, (202) 337-2017.
U.S. Ambassador in Sanaa: Barbara K. Bodine.
State Dept.: Allen Keiswetter, (202) 647-7216.
Commerce Dept.: David Guglielmi, (202) 482-1860.

Yugoslavia

Washington embassy suspended operations March 25, 1999.

U.S. embassy in Belgrade suspended operations March 20, 1999.
State Dept.: Peggy Walker, (202) 647-0608.
Commerce Dept.: CEEBIC, (202) 482-2645.

Zaire (See Congo)

Zambia

Ambassador: Dunstan Weston KAMANA.
Chancery: 2419 Massachusetts Ave. N.W. 20008; (202) 265-9717; fax, (202) 332-0826.
U.S. Ambassador in Lusaka: David B. Dunn.
State Dept.: Karl Albrecht, (202) 647-8432.
Commerce Dept.: Alicia Robinson, (202) 482-4228.

Zimbabwe

Ambassador: Simbi Veke MUBAKO.
Chancery: 1608 New Hampshire Ave. N.W. 20009; (202) 332-7100; fax, (202) 483-9326.
U.S. Ambassador in Harare: Tom McDonald.
State Dept.: Charles Gurney, (202) 647-9856.
Commerce Dept.: Alicia Robinson, (202) 482-4228.

Freedom of Information Act

Public access to government information remains a key issue in Washington. In 1966 Congress passed legislation to broaden access: the Freedom of Information Act (PL 89–487; codified in 1967 by PL 90–23). Amendments to expand access even further were passed into law over President Ford's veto in 1974 (PL 93–502).

Several organizations in Washington specialize in access to government information. See "Freedom of Information" section in the Communications and the Media chapter for details.

1966 Act

The 1966 act requires executive branch agencies and independent commissions of the federal government to make records, reports, policy statements, and staff manuals available to citizens who request them, unless the materials fall into one of nine exempted categories:

- secret national security or foreign policy information
- internal personnel practices
- information exempted by law (e.g., income tax returns)
- trade secrets, other confidential commercial or financial information
- inter-agency or intra-agency memos
- personal information, personnel, or medical files
- law enforcement investigatory information
- information related to reports on financial institutions
- geological and geophysical information

1974 Amendments

Further clarification of the rights of citizens to gain access to government information came in late 1974, when Congress enacted legislation to remove some of the obstacles that the bureaucracy had erected since 1966. Included in the amendments are provisions that:

- Require federal agencies to publish their indexes of final opinions on settlements of internal cases, policy statements, and administrative staff manuals. If, under special circumstances, the indexes are not published, they are to be furnished to any person requesting them for the cost of duplication. The 1966 law simply required agencies to make such indexes available for public inspection and copying.
- Require agencies to release unlisted documents to someone requesting them with a reasonable description (a change designed to ensure that an agency could not refuse to provide material simply because the applicant could not give its precise title).
- Direct each agency to publish a uniform set of fees for providing documents at the cost of finding and copying them. The amendment allows waiver or reduction of those fees when in the public interest.
- Set time limits for agency responses to requests: 10 working days for an initial request; 20 working days for an appeal from an initial refusal to produce documents; a possible 10–working-day extension which can be granted only once in a single case.
- Set a 30–day time limit for an agency response to a complaint filed in court under the act; provides that such cases should be given priority attention by the courts at the appeal, as well as the trial, level.
- Empower federal district courts to order agencies to produce withheld documents and to examine the contested materials privately *(in camera)* to determine if they are properly exempted.
- Require annual agency reports to Congress, including a list of all agency decisions to withhold information requested under the act; the reasons; the appeals; the results; all relevant rules; the fee schedule; and the names of officials responsible for each denial of information.
- Allow courts to order the government to pay attorneys' fees and court costs for persons winning suits against them under the act.
- Authorize a court to find that an agency employee has acted capriciously or arbitrarily in withholding information; disciplinary action is determined by Civil Service Commission proceedings.
- Amend and clarify the wording of the national defense and national security exemption to make

clear that it applies only to *properly* classified information.

• Amend the wording of the law enforcement exemption to allow withholding of information which, if disclosed, would interfere with enforcement proceedings, deprive someone of a fair trial or hearing, invade personal privacy in an unwarranted way, disclose the identity of a confidential source, disclose investigative techniques, or endanger law enforcement personnel; protect from disclosure all information from a confidential source obtained by a criminal law enforcement agency or a lawful national security investigation.

• Provide that separable non-exempt portions of requested material be released after deletion of the exempt portions.

• Require an annual report from the attorney general to Congress.

1984 Amendments

In 1984 Congress enacted legislation that clarified the requirements of the Central Intelligence Agency to respond to citizen requests for information. Included in the amendments are provisions that:

• Authorize the CIA to close from FOIA review certain operational files that contain information on the identities of sources and methods. The measure removed the requirement that officials search the files for material that might be subject to disclosure.

• Reverse a ruling by the Justice Dept. and the Office of Management and Budget that invoked the Privacy Act to deny individuals FOIA access to information about themselves in CIA records. HR 5164 required the CIA to search files in response to FOIA requests by individuals for information about themselves.

• Require the CIA to respond to FOIA requests for information regarding covert actions or suspected CIA improprieties.

All agencies of the executive branch have issued regulations to implement the Freedom of Information Act. To locate a specific agency's regulations, consult the general index of the *Code of Federal Regulations* under "Information availability."

Electronic Freedom of Information Act of 1996

In 1996 Congress enacted legislation which clarified that electronic documents are subject to the same Freedom of Information Act (FOIA) disclosure rules as printed documents. The 1996 law also requires federal agencies to make records available to the public in various electronic formats, such as e-mail, compact disc, and files accessible via the Internet. An additional measure seeks to improve the government's response time on FOIA requests by requiring agencies to report annually on the number of pending requests and how long it will take to respond.

Privacy Act

To protect citizens from invasions of privacy by the federal government, Congress passed the Privacy Act of 1974 (PL 93–579). The act permitted individuals for the first time to inspect information about themselves contained in federal agency files and to challenge, correct, or amend the material. The major provisions of the act:

• Permit an individual to have access to personal information in federal agency files and to correct or amend that information.

• Prevent an agency maintaining a file on an individual from making it available to another agency without the individual's consent.

• Require federal agencies to keep records that are necessary, lawful, accurate, and current, and to disclose the existence of all data banks and files containing information on individuals.

• Bar the transfer of personal information to other federal agencies for non-routine use without the individual's prior consent or written request.

• Require agencies to keep accurate accountings of transfers of records and make them available to the individual.

• Prohibit agencies from keeping records on an individual's exercise of First Amendment rights unless the records are authorized by statute, approved by the individual, or within the scope of an official law enforcement activity.

• Permit an individual to seek injunctive relief to correct or amend a record maintained by an agency and permit the individual to recover actual damages when an agency acts in a negligent manner that is "willful or intentional."

• Exempt from disclosure: records maintained by the Central Intelligence Agency; records maintained by law enforcement agencies; Secret Service records; statistical information; names of persons providing material used for determining the qualification of an individual for federal government service; federal testing material; and National Archives historical records.

• Provide that an officer or employee of an agency who violates provisions of the act be fined no more than $5,000.

• Prohibit an agency from selling or renting an individual's name or address for mailing list use.

• Require agencies to submit to Congress and to the Office of Management and Budget any plan to establish or alter records.

• Virtually all agencies of the executive branch have issued regulations to implement the Privacy Act. To locate a specific agency's regulations, consult the general index of the *Code of Federal Regulations* under "Privacy Act."

Name Index

In the name index, entries in **boldface** indicate the main entries of senators and representatives.

Alterman, Stephen A., 665
Altman, E. T., 426
Alvarez, Aida, 71, 109
Alvarez, Jose, 788
Alverson, J. M., 545
Alving, Barbara, 392
Ambach, Gordon M., 181
Ambler, Carole A., 82, 105
Ambler, Cynthia L., 220
Amerault, James F., 589
Ames, Fred L., 527, 538
Amey, Earle B., 94
Aminu, Jibril Muhammed, 871
Amorosino, Charles, 183, 205
Amstutz, Daniel G., 51
Andersen, F. Alan, 22
Anderson, Bernard, 218
Anderson, Brooke D., 128
Anderson, Frank J. (USAF), 538, 589
Anderson, George S., 436
Anderson, James A., Jr., 22, 103
Anderson, Jeannette, 53
Anderson, Jeff, 790
Anderson, John A., 257
Anderson, John B., 446
Anderson, John H., Jr., 658
Anderson, Kathleen C., 797
Anderson, Leslie, 180, 445, 563
Anderson, Minnie, 789
Anderson, Philip, 455
Anderson, Robert "Bob," 765
Anderson, Steven C., 62
Anderson, Sylvia, 706
Anderson, Terje, 391
Anderson, William C., 292
Anderson, William E., 258, 606
Anderson-Flynn, Tiffany, 781
Andrade, Yvette, 763
André, Pamela Q. J., 41
Andrew, Joseph, 696, 721
Andrews, A. Michael, 572
Andrews, David R., 456, 498
Andrews, Debbie, 514, 638
Andrews, Robert E., D-N.J., **756**
Andrews, Sara, 701
Andrianarivelo Razafy, Zina, 869
Andringa, Robert, 192
Angell, John C., 706
Angle, Joanne, 376
Angle, Matt, 703, 772
Angle, Robert, 437
Angulo, Jeanne Oates, 400, 645
Ansley, Steve, 573
Anthony, Calvin, 366
Anthony, John Duke, 489
Anthony, Virginia Q., 383, 384, 405, 407
Antoine, Denis G., 866
Antos, Joseph, 359
Anzai, Earl I., 852
Apfel, Kenneth, 651

Apgar, William C., 428, 436
Apple, Martin, 595
Applegarth, Lesely, 790
Applegate, Bob, 857
Araiza, G. Jorge, 529, 585
Aranza, Danny, 491
Arberg, Kathleen, 139
Archer, Bill, R-Texas, 24, 74, 237, 248, 254, 504, 692, **756**
Archer, Raymond, 589
Archey, William T., 132
Ardis, Tony, 792
Argenentati, Gian, 618
Arial, Rick, 775
Ariale, John, 786
Armacost, Michael H., 717
Armey, Dick, R-Texas, 699, 704, **757**
Armstrong, Alta, 761
Armstrong, David A. (USA, ret.), 542
Arneaud, Michael, 875
Arness, Peggy, 809
Arnold, Joe, 782
Arnwine, Barbara, 29
Aron, Nan, 28, 496
Arons, Bernard S., 405
Arredondo, Rudy, 40, 225
Artaza, Mario, 864
Arteaga, Roland, 533
Arthurs, Jean, 555
Asali, Naila, 10
Ashbaugh, Robert, 327
Ashby, Christopher C., 875
Ashcroft, John, R-Mo., 3, 15, 20, 58, 141, 171, 429, 505, 506, 509, 510, 694, **825**
Ashe, Daniel M., 289, 313
Ashley, Ivan R., 107, 109
Ashworth, Russ, 339
Ashworth, Sid, 588
Aspden, William H., Jr., 361, 378
Aspland, Charlene, 803
Asrar, Ghassem R., 608
Atherton, Charles H., 145
Athy, Andrew, 244
Atkins, Chuck, 774
Atkins, Lisa, 802
Atkins, M. Elizabeth, 523
Atteberry, Krista, 759
Atterholt, Kathleen, 786
Attey, Phil, 133
Attias, Chantal, 482
Atwater, Frank, 337
Aubin, Bonnie, 371
Aucella, Frank, 157
Auer, Charlie M., 294
Auer, Ken, 55, 416
Auglis, Linda, 716
Augustus, Ed, 786
Auman, Rose, 794
Aumann, Karl, 770
Aumann, Mark, 781

Aumick, Amalia T., 773
Austin, Gary, 522, 646
Austria, Eileen, 777
Autery, C. Reuben, 99, 262
Auton, Garland, 263
Aviv, Diana, 35, 632
Awad, Mubarak E., 638
Awad, Nihad, 488
Ayele, Moges, 678
Azukas, Charles P., 584

Baab, Schuyler, 859
Baas, Lori, 775
Baas, Marc, 63
Babbitt, Bruce, 275, 302
Babby, Lorna, 7, 310
Babco, Eleanor, 210, 598
Baber, Patti Jo, 713
Baca, Joe, D-Calif., **757**
Baca, Sylvia, 246, 306, 308
Bach, Christopher L., 252, 474
Bachner, John P., 607
Bachon, Alec, 220, 221, 630, 653
Bachula, Gary R., 621
Bachus, Spencer, R-Ala., 80, 94, 475, 726, **757**
Backlin, Jim, 758
Backus, Jenny, 721
Bacon, Elinor R., 432
Bacon, Kenneth H., 128, 138
Baden, Laurence M., 325
Bader, Jeffrey A., 870
Badman, David G., 392, 397
Baer, Ed, 342
Baer, Gregory, 88
Baer, Wendy, 305
Bagin, Richard D., 177
Bagley, Michael, 707
Bahr, Morton, 21, 136
Bahrns, Steven D., 698
Bailey, Dennis, 854
Bailey, Linda, 23
Bailey, Pamela, 364
Bailey, Sharon, 650
Bailey, Sue, 533
Baily, Martin, 69
Bair, Sheila, 93
Baird, Brian, D-Wash., **757**
Baird, Ronald C., 209, 310
Baird, Victor M., 709, 710, 821
Bajesy, Ruzena, 130, 615
Baker, D. James, 277, 608
Baker, Dennis, 352
Baker, Don N., 807
Baker, Edwin W., 434
Baker, James, 51, 66, 277, 608
Baker, John, 760
Baker, Richard, 127, 165, 689
Baker, Richard H., R-La., 361, **757**
Baker, Richard L., 239, 260
Baker, Robert, 114, 691

Knollenberg, Joe, R-Mich., **781**
Knouss, Robert F., 575
Knowles, Donald R., 289
Knudson, Peggy, 446
Knutsen, Arvid, 333
Koba, Henry, 863
Kocak, Richard A., 262
Koch, Christine, 761
Koch, Jeffrey W., 799
Koch, Robert P., 50, 61
Kocher, Pam, 802
Koehnke, Donna R., 126
Koenig, Lyle, 711
Kogelnik, Florian, 606
Koh, Harold Hongju, 460
Kohl, Herb, D-Wis., **836**
Kohl, Kay, 212
Kohn, Donald L. 82
Kohr, Howard, 487
Kolb, Guy, 78
Kolbe, Jim, R-Ariz., 74, 321, 326, 331, 340, 559, 692, 699, 726, **782**
Kolbe, Sherry L., 201
Koleda, Michael, 271
Kolesar, Mary, 418, 433
Kolker, Jimmy J., 863
Kolodziej, Richard R., 263, 678
Kominus, Nicholas, 53
Konnor, Delbert D., 367
Konoshima, Joji, 480
Kooiman, Jerry, 777
Koomson, Kobina Arthur, 866
Koonce, Norman L., 160, 422
Koplovitz, Kay, 71, 109
Koranda, Donald J., 170, 665
Korbel, Kimberly, 99
Koretz, Doreen, 405
Korich, Joan Bates, 797
Kornblum, John, 866
Kornegay, Amanda, 716
Kornkven, Chris, 554
Koshgarian, David, 763
Kostmayer, Peter, 396
Kotch, John, 232
Kotler, Mindy, 479, 599
Koumoue, Koffi Moise, 864
Kovacs, Bill, 40, 249, 302
Kovar, Peter, 772
Kovarovics, Scott, 773
Kozak, Jerome J., 49, 50
Kozakou Marcoullis, Erato, 864
Kozminski, Jerzy, 872
Kraemer, LuAnn, 786
Kramer, Franklin D., 440, 564, 585
Kramerich, Leslie B., 236
Kramp, Kevin, 42, 57, 304, 629
Kraus, Arthur, 102
Krauss, Jordan "Pete," 775
Krauthames, Judith, 311, 612
Krebs, Frederick J., 503
Kreig, Andrew, 122

Krepinevich, Andrew F., 564
Krepon, Michael, 562
Krese, Jenny, 212, 223, 224, 229, 234, 241, 242
Kreseski, Steven, 770
Kresh, Diane N., 185
Kress, W. John, 605
Kressley, Larry, 632
Krieg, Robert D., 778
Krieger, William C. "Mickey" II, 760
Krikorian, Mark, 455
Krissoff, Barry, 41, 50, 52, 53, 82, 244
Krizek, Eugene L., 631
Kroener, William F., III, 498
Kromkowski, John A., 419
Kruse, Dennis K., 573
Kruse, Earl, 428
Kruuv, Riho, 865
Ku, Charlotte, 457
Kuchnicki, Richard P., 424, 644
Kucinich, Dennis J., D-Ohio, 726, **782**
Kuczynski, Christopher J., 641
Kugel, Jennie, 791
Kugler, Mitch, 233, 341
Kuhlman, Richard T., 300
Kuhn, Annelie, 339
Kuhn, Thomas R., 258, 280
Kulik, Bernard, 101, 433, 575
Kulikowski, Jim, 13, 74, 114, 277, 330, 441, 467, 495, 593, 658, 671
Kull, Joseph L., 323
Kullman, Conny, 119
Kumpher, Karol, 403
Kundahl, George G., 527, 539
Kuntjoro Jakti, Dorodjatun, 867
Kuntze, Patricia, 12, 207
Kunz, Kitty, 800
Kupfer, Carl, 376
Kurin, Richard, 166
Kurlander, Carrie, 851
Kursh, Gail, 502
Kurtzer, Daniel C., 865
Kushner, David, 369
Kusumoto, Sandra, 322
Kuykendall, Steven T., R-Calif., 726, **782**
Kvien, Kristina, 873
Kweder, Dee Jay, 794
Kwok, Daphne, 11
Kyl, Jon, R-Ariz., 129, 521, **836**
Kyota, Hersey, 871

La Belle, Susan, 761
La Porta, Alphonso, 870
La Sala, Jim, 687
Laajava, Jaakko, 866
Lacey, L. Nicholas, 667
Lachance, Janice R., 330
Lachatelle, Dorothy, 94
Lackritz, Marc E., 93
Lacy, Lee, 24, 207, 628

Lader, Philip, 875
Ladner, Benjamin, 189
LaFalce, John J., D-N.Y., **782**
Lafferty, Andrea Sheldon, 720
LaFourest, Judith, 148
Lago, Marisa, 456
LaGrou, Pamela H., 795
LaHood, Ray, R-Ill., **782**
Lam, Alvin, 147
Lama, Doris M., 126
Lamb, Shawn, 372
Lambert, Gilda, 513, 633
Lambert, Michael P., 212
Lammon, Robert E., 325
Lamonde, J. R. (USN), 528
Lamp, Gary F., 545
Lampi, Ruth, 366, 515
Lampmann, John, 801
Lampson, Nick, D-Texas, **782**
Lancaster, John, 225, 641
Lancaster, Marjorie, 804
Lancaster, Sue, 786
Lance, Alan G., 853
Landau, Mindy, 12
Landefeld, J. Steven, 81
Landrieu, Mary L., D-La., **836**
Landrith, George, 719
Landsburg, Alexander C., 670
Lane, Jane, 758
Lane, Neal, 41, 246, 277, 440, 573, 592, 598
Lane, Robert A., 777
Langdon, Cindy, 802
Lange, John, 863
Lange, Kathleen, 861, 868
Lange, Robert G., 265
Langelan, Marty, 720
Langley, Joanne, 801
Langrehr, Norman, 793
Lanham, Kerry, 80
Lanier, Ivan, 4, 348, 696
Lannon, George, 171, 458
Lantos, Tom, D-Calif., 700, **782**
Lantz, J. G., 673
Lapenn, Jessie, 875
LaPierre, Wayne, Jr., 516
Lapp, Douglas M., 183, 211
Lapp, John, 784
Lappen, Mark, 107
Laptook, Jennifer, 783
Larcamp, Dan, 257
Largent, Steve, R-Okla., **782**
Larisch, Erich W., 225
Larkin, Barbara, 706
Larkin, J. Stephen, 309
Larkin, Peter S., 774
Larkins, John T., 269
Larmett, Kathleen, 193
Larocco, James A., 868
Larreur, Claude, 171
Larsen, William L., 93, 347

Perlin, Ruth, 148
Perlmutter, Jim, 216
Perlmutter, Sandra, 168
Permuy, Pedro Pablo, 483
Peroff, Kathleen, 246, 592
Perrolle, Pierre M., 598
Perry, Clay, 772
Perry, Daniel, 381
Perry, Deborah, 766
Perry, Glenn, 339
Perry, Richard, 774
Perry, Robert C., 863
Perry, Terry, 758
Perry, Todd, 40, 252, 266, 282, 568, 660
Pertschuk, Michael, 25
Pesachowitz, Alvin, 124
Petera, Anne P., 858
Peters, Annie E., 809
Peters, Debra, 339
Peters, F. Whitten, 557
Peters, Marybeth, 104, 114
Peters, Terry, 372
Petersen, Robert E., Jr., 140
Petersen, Robert R., 51, 52
Petersen, Steven T., 775
Peterson, Charles M., 396
Peterson, Chris, 855
Peterson, Collin C., D-Minn., **793**
Peterson, David A., 216
Peterson, David F., 123, 164
Peterson, Dean P., 795
Peterson, Donald L., 526, 530, 534, 555
Peterson, Eric C., 127, 689, 810
Peterson, John E., R-Pa., **793**
Peterson, Katherine, 869
Peterson, Mark R., 545
Peterson, Patti McGill, 179, 452
Peterson, Pete, 876
Peterson, R. Max, 288, 290
Peterson, Ross, 788
Peterson, Timothy A., 711
Petri, Tom, R-Wis., 676, 684, 686, 726, **793**
Petschek, Evelyn, 24, 83, 235
Pettiford, Wanda, 792
Petty, Brian T., 263
Pfaltzgraff, Robert, Jr., 445, 562
Pfeiffer, W. Dean, 541
Pfeuffer, Paul, 869
Pflaum, William C., 96
Pharis, Claudia, 771
Phelleps, Moya, 261
Phelps, Anne, 241, 260, 368, 388
Phelps, David, 99
Phelps, David D., D-Ill., **793**
Phelps, Thomas C., 185
Phillips, Howard, 562, 718
Phillips, JoAnna, 152, 479
Phillips, John C., 128
Phillips, Mantha, 766
Phillips, T. Clay, 767

Phillips, Wilson, 717
Philon, Alexandre, 866
Pho, Hong-Phong, 863, 868, 876
Pian, Canta, 629
Piatt, William, 325
Piatt, William C., 124
Pibulsonggram, Nitya, 874
Picciano, Lorette, 39, 417
Piceno, Ron, 792
Piché, Diane M., 3
Pichette, David, 226
Pickering, Charles W. "Chip," Jr., R-Miss., 729, **793**
Pickering, Thomas R., 441
Pickett, Owen B., D-Va., **793**
Pieper, Michael, 855
Pierangelo, Clare, 868
Pierce, David, 190
Pierce, Matt, 776
Pierce, Ted, 871, 873, 875
Pierson, Jay, 708
Pierson, Paul, 255
Pietrangelo, Renee, 643
Pigg, B. J., 293, 425
Pignatelli, Donna, 762
Pike, Chuck, 805
Pike, Walter W., 669
Pilipovich, Michele, 228
Pillors, Brenda, 805
Pincus, Andrew J., 498
Pindell, Alvetta, 41
Pinkerton, Sharon, 2, 24, 28, 57, 174, 229, 232, 331, 346, 355, 410, 495, 510, 549
Pinkham, Douglas G., 720
Pinkney, Betty K., 780
Pinn, Vivian W., 404
Pinsky, Robert, 151
Pinson, Tracey L., 109
Pinstrup-Andersen, Per, 65
Piper, Steven K., 875
Pipkin, James, 276
Pirkle, Janice E., 228
Pitkin, Bill, 251, 297, 427
Pitofsky, Robert, 69
Pitra, Mark, 339
Pittenger, Denise, 802
Pitterle, Kenneth, 875
Pitts, Joseph R., R-Pa., 110, 410, **794**
Pitts, Tyrone S., 34
Pizzingrilli, Kim, 857
Place, Michael, 379
Plachetka, Teresa, 801
Plaisted, Joan M., 868, 870
Plamer, Barbara, 803
Planty, Donald J., 485
Plasker, James R., 620
Plaster, Henry, 784
Platzer, Eryl J., 156
Plavin, David Z., 667
Plaza, Eva M., 430

Plesch, Daniel T., 482
Pletka, Danielle, 487
Plewes, Thomas J., 546
Plishker, R. Alan, 182, 607
Plouffe, David, 721
Podesta, John D., 321
Podoff, David, 818
Poe, Mya Thanda, 478, 487
Poisson, David, 680
Poisson, David E., 615
Pokras, Anne, 501
Poleskey, Carl, 218
Polett, Zachary, 697
Polk, Frank, 25, 48, 75, 217, 237, 248, 254, 346, 355, 413, 468, 475, 693, 818
Pollack, Christine, 701
Pollack, Ron, 639
Polley, Bernadette, 782
Polydence, Melanie, 781
Pombo, Richard W., R-Calif., 47, 57, 66, 285, 726, **794**
Pomerantz, Mitch, 332
Pomeroy, Earl, D-N.D., **794**
Pomeroy, Julia, 760
Pommersheim, John Mark, 872
Pompa, Delia, 205
Ponder, Henry, 204
Ponder, Jacque, 803
Poodry, Clifton A., 368, 387
Pool, Scott, 761
Poole, Mark, 452
Pooler, Susanne, 336
Popeo, Daniel J., 499
Poppleton, Janet, 775
Porras, M. Richard, 323
Porter, Daniel E., 124
Porter, Jeffrey, 542
Porter, John Edward, R-Ill., 114, 174, 214, 240, 355, 629, 653, 699, 700, **794**
Portman, Rob, R-Ohio **794**
Portney, Paul, 252, 282, 625
Porvaznik, Pam, 805
Possiel, William, 305
Post, Ben, 772
Post, Diana, 297
Potter, Alison, 723
Potter, Catherine, 802
Potter, Edward E., 215
Potter, Jackie, 756
Potts, Stephen D., 325
Powden, Mark, 2, 15, 25, 28, 58, 146, 174, 186, 190, 196, 200, 203, 355, 359, 361, 379, 512, 594, 642, 685, 820
Powell, Chessye B., 801
Powell, Colin, 636
Powell, Earl A., III, 154
Powell, Edward A., Jr., 322
Powell, Jo Anne, 801
Powell, Russell, 126
Powers, Galen, 363
Powers, Gerard, 446

Subject Index

Entries in **BOLD CAPITALS** are the names of chapters and appendices; those in **bold** indicate major subsections. Page numbers in bold indicate the main entries for congressional committees and subcommittees (**pp. 732–753, 810–823**).

African Development Foundation, 476
Africare, 477
Aged persons. *See Elderly persons*
Agence France-Presse, 137
Agency for Health Care Policy and Research, 352
Agency for International Development (AID)
    Africa Bureau, 476
    Asia and Near East Bureau, 477, 486
    Center for Environment, 252
    Center for Human Capacity Development, 471
    Center for Population, Health, and Nutrition, 448
    congressional liaison, 706
    Europe and Eurasia Bureau, 480, 489
    Financial Officer, 322
    fraud and abuse hotline, 327
    freedom of information contact, 126
    General Counsel, 498
    Global Programs, Field Support and Research Bureau, 472
    Global Technology Network, G/EGAD/BD–GTN Program, 462
    Humanitarian Response Bureau, 448
    Inspector General, 327
    Latin America and the Caribbean Bureau, 483
    library, 187
    Population, 395
    public affairs contact, 128
    small and disadvantaged business contact, 109
    Small and Disadvantaged Business Utilization/Minority Resource Center, 107
    U.S. Foreign Disaster Assistance, 448
Agency for Toxic Substances and Disease Registry, 294
Agribusiness Council, 48
Agricultural Cooperative Development International, 64
Agricultural Marketing Service, 37
    Cotton, 48
    Dairy, 49
    Fruit and Vegetable, 50
    Information, 37
    Livestock and Seed, 50, 65
    Poultry, 66
    Science and Technology, 55
    Seed Regulatory and Testing, 45
    Tobacco, 53
    Transportation and Marketing, 45
Agricultural Research Service, 40, 55
    National Plant Germplasm System, 45
AGRICULTURE AND NUTRITION (chap. 2), 36–67
    commodities, 45–53
    cotton, 48–49
    dairy products, 49–50
    eggs, 49–50
    farm loans, insurance, and subsidies, 53–55
    fertilizer and pesticides, 42–43
    fruits and vegetables, 50
    general policy, 37–40
    grains and oilseeds, 50–52
    horticulture and gardening, 43–44
    livestock and poultry, 65–67
    migrant and seasonal farm workers, 224–225
    nutrition issues. *See Food and Nutrition*
    research and education, 40–42
    soil and watershed conservation, 44–45
    sugar, 52–53
    tobacco and peanuts, 53
    world food assistance, 63–65

Agriculture Department (USDA), 37
    Agricultural Marketing Service. *See that heading*
    Agricultural Research Service. *See that heading*
    Animal and Plant Health Inspection Service. *See that heading*
    Board of Contract Appeals, 37
    Chief Economist, 37
    Commodity Credit Corp., 46, 53
    Communication and Governmental Affairs, 11
    congressional liaison, 706
    consumer contact, 11
    Cooperative State Research, Education, and Extension Service. *See that heading*
    directory of information on the Internet, 846
    Economic Research Service. *See that heading*
    equal employment opportunity contact, 228
    Farm Service Agency. *See that heading*
    Financial Officer, 322
    Food and Nutrition Service. *See that heading*
    Food, Nutrition, and Consumer Services, 37, 55
    Food Safety and Inspection Service. *See that heading*
    Foreign Agricultural Service. *See that heading*
    Forest Service. *See that heading*
    fraud and abuse hotline, 327
    freedom of information contact, 126
    General Counsel, 498
    Graduate School, 189, 211
        International Institute, 451
    Grain Inspection, Packers, and Stockyards Administration, 51, 66
    Information, 37
    Information Officer, 124
    Inspector General, 327
    Internet world wide Web site, 131
    library, 37, 187
    Management Officer, 325
    Marketing and Regulatory Programs, 46
    meat and poultry safety inquiries, 14
    National Agricultural Library, 41, 57, 196
    National Agricultural Statistics Service, 40, 41, 82
    National Arboretum, 43, 153, 604
    Natural Resources and Environment, 275
    Natural Resources Conservation Service, 44, 306
        Pest Management, 42
    organization (chart), 38
    personnel office, 334
    Procurement Officer, 339
    public affairs contact, 128
    publications office, 125
    Research, Education, and Economics, 40, 206
    Risk Management Agency, 54
    Rural Business–Cooperative Service, 41, 46, 271, 415
    Rural Development, 54, 415, 431
    Rural Housing Service, 415, 428, 429
    Rural Utilities Service, 257, 315, 416
    Secretary, 37
    small and disadvantaged business contact, 109
    Special Emphasis Outreach Program, 40
    Women's Executive Leadership Program, 230
    World Agricultural Outlook Board, 63
Agri-Energy Roundtable, 48
AID. *See Agency for International Development*
AIDS Action, 390
AIDS Alliance for Children, Youth, and Families, 391

American Consulting Engineers Council, 606
  Research and Management Foundation, 606
American Corporate Counsel Assn., 503
American Correctional Assn., 519
American Cotton Shippers Assn., 49
American Council for an Energy-Efficient Economy, 251
American Council for Capital Formation, 76
American Council of Life Insurance, 101
American Council of State Savings Supervisors, 89
American Council of Teachers of Russian, 151, 490
American Council of the Blind, 646
American Council of the Blind Government Employees, 332
American Council of Trustees and Alumni, 191
American Council of Young Political Leaders, 452
American Council on Education, 191
American Councils for International Education, 151, 490
American Counseling Assn., 406, 643
American Crop Protection Assn., 43
American Czech and Slovak Assn., 482
American Defense Institute, Pride in America, 535, 561
American Dental Assn., 371
  Political Action Committee, 716
American Dental Trade Assn., 372
American Diabetes Assn., 394
American Dietetic Assn., 58
American Educational Research Assn., 184
American Electronics Assn., 132
American Enterprise Institute for Public Policy Research
  Economic Policy Studies, 76, 215
    Fiscal Policy Studies, 84
    Foreign and Defense Policy Studies, 444, 561
    internship programs, 179
    Social and Individual Responsibility Project, 630
American Ethical Union, Washington Ethical Action, 30
American Farm Bureau Federation, 39, 715
American Farmland Trust, 45
American Federation of Government Employees, 332
American Federation of Musicians, 233
American Federation of Police, 521
American Federation of School Administrators, 181
American Federation of State, County, and Municipal
  Employees—PEOPLE, Qualified, 714
American Federation of Teachers, 181
  Committee on Political Education, 714
American Federation of Television and Radio Artists, 140
American Feed Industry Assn., 51
American Fiber Manufacturers Assn., 98
American Film Institute Theater, 149
American Financial Services Assn., 18
American Fisheries Society, 288
American Folklife Center, 166, 186
American Foreign Service Assn., 233, 448
American Forest and Paper Assn., Regulatory Affairs,
  305, 425
American Forests, 305
American Foundation for AIDS Research, Public Policy, 391
American Foundation for Autistic Children, 649
American Foundation for the Blind, Governmental Relations,
  646
American Friends Service Committee, 30
American Frozen Food Institute, 61
American Gaming Assn., 169
American Gas Assn., 262
  Statistics, 255
American Gastroenterological Assn., 394

American Gear Manufacturers Assn., 99
American Geological Institute, 307, 611
American Geophysical Union, 609, 625
American Gold Star Mothers, 555
American Hardwood Export Council, 305
American Health Care Assn., 365
  Political Action Committee, 716
American Health Lawyers Assn., 369, 523
American Health Quality Assn., 375
American Heart Assn., 398
American Helicopter Society, 665
American Hellenic Institute, 482
American Herbal Products Assn., 58, 285
American Highway Users Alliance, 682
American Hiking Society, 169, 313
American Historical Assn., 162
American history
  genealogy, 165–166
  military history, 542–545
  postal history, 343–344
  Washington area, 167–168
American Homeowners Assn., 433
American Horse Protection Assn., 285
American Horticultural Society, 44
American Hospital Assn., 361
American Hotel and Motel Assn., 172
American Humane Assn., 285, 635
American Immigration Lawyers Assn., 455
American Indian Heritage Foundation, 166
American Indians. *See Native Americans*
American Industrial Health Council, 241, 356
American Industrial Hygiene Assn., 241
American Inns of Court Foundation, 523
American Institute for Cancer Research, 393
American Institute for Conservation of Historic and Artistic
  Works, 162
American Institute for International Steel, 99
American Institute in Taiwan, 479
American Institute of Aeronautics and Astronautics, 624, 665
American Institute of Architects, 160, 422
  American Architectural Foundation, 178
American Institute of Biological Sciences, 602
American Institute of Certified Public Accountants, 89
American Institute of Chemical Engineers, 614
American Institute of Chemists, 614
American Institute of Physics, 617
American Institute of Ultrasound in Medicine, 363
American Institutes for Research, 618
American Insurance Assn., 101, 242
American Intellectual Property Law Assn., 104
American International Automobile Dealers Assn., 679
American Iron and Steel Institute, 309
American Israel Public Affairs Committee, 487
American Jewish Committee, Government and International
  Affairs, 30
American Jewish Congress, 31, 487, 509
American Kidney Fund, 399
American Kurdish Information Network, 487
American Labor Education Center, 222
American Land Title Assn., 433
American League of Financial Institutions, 89, 436
American League of Lobbyists, 713
American Legion National Organization, 549
  Claims Service, 552
  Review and Correction Boards Unit, 552

American Sugarbeet Growers Assn., 52
  Political Action Committee, 714
American Symphony Orchestra League, 158
American Textile Machinery Assn., 98
American Textile Manufacturers Institute, 98
American Tort Reform Assn., 497
American Trauma Society, 388
American Trucking Assns., 676, 682
American Type Culture Collection, 603
American University, 189
American Veterans Committee, 550
American Veterans of World War II, Korea, and Vietnam, 550
American Veterinary Medical Assn., Governmental Relations, 286
American War Mothers, 555
American Water Works Assn., 316
American Waterways Operators, 675
American Wholesale Marketers Assn., 105
American Wind Energy Assn., 272
American Wire Producers Assn., 99
American Women in Radio and Television, 140
American Wood Preservers Institute, 305
American Youth Hostels, 172
American Youth Work Center, 635
American Zinc Assn., 309
American Zoo and Aquarium Assn., 605
Americans Back in Charge Foundation, 717
Americans for Democratic Action, 715, 717
Americans for Free International Trade PAC, 714
Americans for Medical Progress Educational Foundation, 286
Americans for Religious Liberty, 509
Americans for Tax Reform, 84
Americans for the Arts, 147
Americans for the Environment, 279
Americans for the Restitution and Righting of Old Wrongs, 203, 379
Americans United for Separation of Church and State, 31, 198, 509
America's Community Bankers, 89, 436
America's Promise–The Alliance for Youth, 636
Americas Society, 485
AmeriCorps, 23
  National Civilian Community Corps, 23
  VISTA, 24, 207, 628
  volunteer recruiting information, 23
AMIDEAST, 488
Amnesty International USA, 179, 460, 519
Amtrak. *See* National Railroad Passenger Corp.
Anacostia Museum and Center for African American History and Culture, 152, 153
And Justice for All, 5
Animal and Plant Health Inspection Service, 46, 55
  Animal Care, 284
  Investigative and Enforcement Services, 285
  National Biological Control Institute, 601
  Wildlife Services, 288, 666
Animal Health Institute, 66, 286
Animal Welfare Institute, 286, 290
Animals and Plants, 284–291
  fish, 287–288
  livestock and poultry safety, 65–67
  wildlife and marine mammals, 288–291
Annenberg Public Policy Center, 175
Annual Economic Report, 82
ANSER (Analytic Services), 573

Antarctica Project, 284, 457
Anti-Defamation League, 10
Antietam National Battlefield, 161
Antitrust Division (DOJ), 501
  Civil Task Force, 502
  Computers and Finance, 85, 502
  Documents, 502
  Foreign Commerce, 462
  Health Care Task Force, 502
  Telecommunications, 118
  Transportation, Energy, and Agriculture, 502
Antitrust law, 501–503
Anxiety Disorders Assn. of America, 406
AOAC International, 603, 614
AOPA Legislative Affairs, 665
APICS, The Educational Society for Resource Management, 96
Appalachian Regional Commission, 417
Appliances and electronics, 99
Apportionment and election statistics, 694–695
Appraisal Foundation, 434
Appraisal Institute, 434
Apprenticeship programs, 224
Arab American Institute, 695
The Arc, Governmental Affairs, 649
Arca Foundation, 25
Architect of the Capitol, 697
  Office of the Curator, 167, 697
Architectural and Transportation Barriers Compliance Board (Access Board), 423, 640, 656
Architectural Woodwork Institute, 425
Architecture and design, 422–423
Archives. *See Libraries and Educational Media*
Arctic Research Commission, 608
Arlington Arts Center, 153
Arlington County, Va., 349
Arlington House, Robert E. Lee Memorial, 161
Arlington National Cemetery, Internment Services, 544
Armed Forces Benefit Assn., 533
Armed Forces Chaplain Board, 528
Armed Forces Communications and Electronics Assn., 573
Armed Forces Hostess Assn., 532
Armed Forces Institute of Pathology, 385
Armed Forces Radiobiology Research Institute, 297, 385, 601
Armed services. *See Military Personnel and Veterans; specific service departments*
Armenian Assembly of America, 491
Arms Control and Disarmament, 566–570
Arms Control Assn., 567
Army and Air Force Mutual Aid Assn., 533, 555
Army Corps of Engineers, 314, 412, 587, 669
  Civil Emergency Management, 574
  Civil Works, 674
  Research and Development, 572
Army Department, 557
  Acquisition Logistics and Technology, 572
  Arlington National Cemetery, Internment Services, 544
  Army Career and Alumni Program, 536
  Army Clemency and Parole Board, 541
  Army Field Band, 545
  Army Housing, 587
  Army Reserve, 546
  Army Review Boards Agency, 539
  Board for the Correction of Military Records, 541
  Casualty Operations, 530, 555
  Ceremonies and Special Events, 545
    special events coordinator, 545

Federal Mine Safety and Health Review Commission, 239, 260
Federal Motor Carrier Safety Administration, 681
  Bus and Truck Safety Operations, 675, 681
Federal National Mortgage Assn., 436
  Financial Officer, 323
Federal Railroad Administration, 683
  Policy and Program Development, 660, 683
  Railroad Development, 683
  Safety, 684
Federal Register, 123, 319, 689
Federal Reserve System
  Accounting and Budgets, 94
  Banking Supervision and Regulation, 86, 502
  Board of Governors, 69, 79, 87, 91
  congressional liaison, 706
  Consumer and Community Affairs, 11, 17
  equal employment opportunity contact, 228
  Financial Officer, 323
  freedom of information contact, 126
  General Counsel, 499
  International Finance, 474
  Internet world wide Web site, 131
  library, 187
  Management Officer, 325
  Monetary Affairs, 82
  museum education programs, 153
  organization (chart), 87
  personnel office, 334
  Procurement Officer, 339
  public affairs contact, 129
  publications office, 125
  Research and Statistics, 82
Federal Retirement Thrift Investment Board, 235
Federal sector employment, 330–337
  armed services civilian personnel, 529
  congressional pay and perquisites, 709
  dismissals and disputes, 333, 335
  ethics, 325–326
  executive reorganization, 326, 328
  hiring, recruitment, and training, 335
  labor-management relations, 335–336
  pay and employee benefits, 336–337
  personnel offices (box), 334
Federal Service Impasses Panel, 336
Federal Trade Commission (FTC), 69
  Advertising Practices, 23, 107
  Competition, 502
    International Antitrust, 463
  congressional liaison, 707
  Consumer and Business Education, 207
  Consumer Protection, Enforcement, 97
  Economics, 69
  equal employment opportunity contact, 228
  Financial Officer, 323
  Financial Practices, 17, 20
  freedom of information contact, 126
  General Counsel, 499
  Information, 69
  Information Officer, 124
  Internet world wide Web site, 131
  library, 69, 187
  Management Officer, 325
  organization (chart), 71
  personnel office, 334
  Procurement Officer, 339

  public affairs contact, 129
  publications office, 125
Federal Transit Administration, 685
  Budget and Policy, 686
  Information, 685
  Program Management, 686
  Research, Demonstration, and Innovation, 686
Federal Travel Directory, 325
Federal Travel Regulations, 325
The Federalist Society, 497
Federally Employed Women, 231, 333, 344
Federation for American Immigration Reform, 455
Federation of American Health Systems, 362, 363
Federation of American Scientists, 568, 595
Federation of American Societies for Experimental Biology, 603
Federation of International Trade Assns., 470
Federation of Nurses and Health Professionals, 370, 373
Federation of Organizations for Professional Women, 231
Federation of State Humanities Councils, 147
Federation of Tax Administrators, 84
Fellowships and grants, 177–180
Feminists for Life of America, 507
Fertilizer and pesticides, 42–43
Fertilizer Institute, 43
Films and filmmaking, 149–150
Finance and Investments, 85–95
  banking, 85–91
  credit practices, 17–18
  housing mortgages, 435–437
  international affairs, 474–476
  stocks, bonds, and securities, 91–94
  tangible assets, 94–95
Financial aid
  foreign. *See Foreign aid*
  to students, 194–195
Financial Executives Institute, Government Relations, 77
Financial officers, departmental and agency (box), 322–323
Fine Arts Board, 699
Fire prevention and control, 18–19
First Lady, Office of, 321
Fish and fishing
  international agreements, 459–460
  resources, 287–288
Flat Tax Caucus, 699
Fleet Reserve Assn., 527
Flexible Packaging Assn., 20, 96, 299
Flight Safety Foundation, 668
Flood insurance, 15
Fogarty International Center, 385
Folger Shakespeare Library, 152, 153
Folk and native arts, 166–167
Food and Agriculture Organization of the United Nations, Liaison Office for North America, 64, 468–469
Food and Drug Administration (FDA), 23, 352
  Center for Biologics Evaluation and Research, 390
  Center for Devices and Radiological Health, 297, 363
  Center for Drug Evaluation and Research, 365, 390, 514
  Center for Food Safety and Applied Nutrition, 19, 55
  Center for Veterinary Medicine, 285
  Consumer Affairs, 11, 207
  Drug Marketing, Advertising, and Communications, 20, 107
  Generic Drugs, 365
  Information, 352

Gays and lesbians, civil rights advocacy, 5–6
Genealogy, 165–166
General Accounting Office (GAO), 74, 320, 710
    Comptroller General, 74, 320, 710
    directory of information on the Internet, 848
    Document Distribution Center, 127, 597
    Energy, Resources, and Science, 247, 277
    Environmental Protection Issues, 277
    Federal Management and Workforce Issues, 132, 328
    Financial Officer, 323
    Food and Agriculture Issues, 37
    fraud and abuse hotline, 327
    General Government, 494
    Health, Education, and Human Services, 24, 174, 214, 236, 346, 354, 549, 629, 653
    Information, 74, 320, 710
    Information Officer, 124
    Information Resources Management Policies and Issues, 132, 328
    Internet world wide Web site, 131
    internship programs, 179
    libraries, 74, 187, 320, 710
    National Security and International Affairs, 441, 563, 566, 590, 623
    organization (chart), 320
    personnel office, 334
    Procurement Law Division, 338
    public affairs contact, 129
    publications office, 125
    Resources, Community, and Economic Development, 593
    Transportation Issues, 658
General Aviation Manufacturers Assn., 665
General Board of Church and Society of the United Methodist Church, 32
General Conference of Seventh-Day Adventists, 32
General Counsels for Federal Agencies (box), 498–499
General Federation of Women's Clubs, 26, 208
General Services Administration (GSA), 319
    Acquisition Policy, 319, 338
    Board of Contract Appeals, 338
    Business Performance, 324
    congressional liaison, 707
    Consumer Information Center, 11, 12
    Enterprise Development, 108, 338
    Environmental Division, 145, 422
    equal employment opportunity contact, 228
    Federal Acquisition Institute, 324
    Federal Domestic Assistance Catalog Staff, 345, 409
    Federal Information Center, 15, 123, 319
    Federal Protective Service, 324
    Federal Relay Service, 123, 647
    Federal Supply Service, 324
    Federal Telecommunications Service, 121
    Financial Officer, 323
    fraud and abuse hotline, 327
    freedom of information contact, 126
    General Counsel, 499
    Governmentwide Information Systems, 338
    Governmentwide Information Technology Management, 130
    Governmentwide Policy, 319, 338
    Information, 319
    Information Officer, 124
    Inspector General, 327
    Internet world wide Web site, 131
    library, 187, 319
    Living Buildings Program, 145
    National Capital Region, 324
    personnel office, 334
    Procurement Officer, 339
    public affairs contact, 129
    Public Buildings Service, 324, 419, 432
    publications office, 125
    Regulatory Information Service Center, 320
    small and disadvantaged business contact, 109
    Transportation and Property Management, 324
Generic Pharmaceutical Industry Assn., 366
Genetic disorders, 396–397
Genetics Society of America, 397
Geography, 619–621
Geology and earth sciences, 610–611
George and Carol Olmsted Foundation, 539
George C. Marshall Institute, 595
George Mason University, 189
    Center for the Study of Public Choice, 76
George Meany Center for Labor Studies and Memorial Archives, 234
George Washington Parkway, 161
George Washington University, 189
    Cyberspace Policy Institute, 133
    Institute for European, Russian, and Eurasian Studies, 491
    National Crash Analysis Center, 683
    Space Policy Institute, 625
Georgetown University, 189
    Center for Contemporary Arab Studies, 488
    Institute for the Study of Diplomacy, 448
    Institute of Turkish Studies, 488
    Kennedy Institute of Ethics, 397, 604
Geothermal energy, 271
German American Business Council, 482
German Marshall Fund of the United States, 482
Gerontological Society of America, 381
Gifted and talented education, 199–200
Gifts in Kind America, 26
Girl Scouts of the U.S.A., Government Relations, 637, 644
Glass Packaging Institute, 20, 299
Glen Echo Park, 161
Global Climate Coalition, 284, 610
Global Health Council, 356
Global Legislators Organization for a Balanced Environment U.S.A., 699
Goddard Space Flight Center, 621
Gold and precious metals, 94–95
Gold Institute, 94
Goodwill Industries International, 631, 644
GOPAC, 715
Government Accountability Project, 326
Government E-Mail Steering Subcommittee, 130
Government employment. *See Federal sector employment*
Government Ethics Office, 325
    Management Officer, 325
Government Finance Officers Assn., Federal Liaison Center, 347
Government Finance Statistics Yearbook, 469
Government Information, 123–130
    directory of information on the Internet, 846–849
    freedom of information contacts (box), 126
    information officers (box), 124
    public affairs contacts (box), 128–129
    publications offices (box), 125

Government National Mortgage Assn., 436
GOVERNMENT OPERATIONS (chap. 10), 318–350
budget, 80–81
buildings and services, 324–325
census/population data, 328–330
chief management officers (box), 325
civil service. *See Federal sector employment*
claims against the government, 508
coins and currency, 79–80
consumer and emergency hotlines (box), 14–15
directory of government information on the Internet,
846–849
equal employment opportunity contacts (box), 228
ethics, 325–326
executive reorganization, 326, 328
federal contracts and procurement, 338–340
financial officers (box), 322–323
fraud and abuse hotlines (box), 327
freedom of information contacts (box), 126
general policy, 319–324
information access, 123–130
information officers (box), 124
inspectors general (box), 327
Internet world wide Web sites (box), 131
libraries (box), 187
personnel offices (box), 334
post office. *See Postal Service*
Procurement Officers (box), 339
public administration, 344–345
public affairs contacts (box), 128–129
publications offices (box), 125
state and local government. *See that heading*
Government Printing Office, 127
directory of information on the Internet, 848
Documents, 689
Internet world wide Web site, 131
Main Bookstore, Congressional Order Desk, 690
personnel office, 334
public affairs contact, 128
public printer, 127
publications office, 125
Government-University-Industry Research Roundtable, 595
Governors and other state officials (list by state), 851–859
Grain Inspection, Packers, and Stockyards Administration, 51,
66
Grains and oilseeds, 50–52
Grameen Foundation USA, 631
Grantmakers in Health, 26, 357
Grants and fellowships, 177–180
Graphic Communications Assn., 134, 142
Graphic Communications International Union, 142
Gray Panthers Project Fund, 8
Great American Meatout, 63
Great Falls Park, 161
Greater Washington Board of Trade, 77, 417
Greenbelt Park, 161
Greenpeace USA, 284, 290, 296
Greeting Card Assn., 142
Grocery Manufacturers of America, 62
GSA. *See General Services Administration*
Guam's Delegate to Congress, 491
Guaranteed Student Loan/PLUS Program, 194
Guatemala Human Rights Commission/USA, 485
*Guide to Research Collections of Former Members of the United
States House of Representatives,* 689

Gun control, 516
Gun Owners of America, 516
Guttmacher Institute, Public Policy, 383, 395
Gypsum Assn., 425

Habitat for Humanity International, 27, 429
Handgun Control Inc., 516
Handicapped persons. *See Disabled persons*
Hardwood, Plywood, and Veneer Assn., 426
Harmonized Tariff Schedule of the United States, 467
Harper's Ferry National Historic Park, 161
Harry S. Truman Scholarship Foundation, 177
Hazardous materials, 294–297
spills, toll-free numbers, 14
Hazardous Materials Advisory Council, 297
Head Start, 196, 634
HEALTH (chap. 11), 351–407
abortion and reproductive issues, 506–508
AIDS and HIV, 389–391
allergies, 398
arthritis, 391
blood and bone marrow, 392
cancer, 392–394
diabetes and digestive diseases, 394–395
elderly persons, 380–382
family planning and population, 395–396
general policy, 352–359
genetic disorders, 396–397
heart disease and strokes, 398
hospitals, 361–362
infectious diseases, 398
insurance and managed care, 359–361
international organizations, 356
kidney disease, 398–399
lung diseases, 399–400
Medicaid and Medicare, 362–363
medical devices and technology, 363–364
mental health, 405–407
military personnel, 533–534
neurological and muscular disorders, 400–401
nursing homes and hospices, 364–365
pharmaceuticals, 365–367
physicians and other professionals, 367–377
people of color, 401–402
prenatal, maternal, and child health care, 382–385
product safety and testing, 22
radiation protection, 297–298
research and advocacy, 385–405
skin disorders, 402
special groups, 377–385
sports and recreation, 168–171
substance abuse, 402–404
toll-free numbers (box), 14
veterans, 553–555
women, 404–405
workplace safety and health, 238–242
Health and Human Services Department (HHS), 629
Administration for Children and Families. *See that heading*
Administration for Children, Youth, and Families, 513, 633
Administration for Native Americans, 6, 412, 628
Administration on Aging, 7, 639
Agency for Health Care Policy and Research, 352
Agency for Toxic Substances and Disease Registry, 294
AIDS information, 14
cancer information, 14

Minerals Management Service *(cont.)*
    Offshore Minerals Management, 311
    Resources and Environmental Management, 312
    Royalty Management Program, Washington Royalty Office, 308, 310
Minerva Center, 530
Minorities
    civil rights advocacy, 10–11
    education, 201–205
    equal employment opportunities, 229–230
    fair housing, 430–432
    health services, 401–402
Minority Business Development Agency, 109, 338
Minority Business Enterprise Legal Defense and Education Fund, 111
Missing in action, 534–535
Monocacy National Battlefield, 161
Montgomery County, Md., 349
Moorland-Spingarn Research Center, 165
Morris and Gwendolyn Cafritz Foundation, 27
Mortgage Bankers Assn. of America, 90, 436
Mortgage Insurance Companies of America, 102, 436
Mortgages and finance, 435–437
Mothers Against Drunk Driving (MADD), 60, 682
Mothers at Home, 637
Motion Picture Assn. of America, 150
Motor Freight Carriers Assn., 677
Motor Vehicles, 675–683
    auto safety hotline, 14
    highways, 678–679
    manufacturing and sales, 679–681
    traffic safety, 681–683
Motorcycle Industry Council, Government Relations, 677
Mount Vernon, 153
Mount Vernon College, 189
Multicultural education, 205
Multilateral Investment Guarantee Agency, 476
MultiMedia Telecommunications Assn., 121
Multistate Tax Commission, 84, 346
Municipal Securities Rulemaking Board, 93
Municipal Treasurers' Assn. of the United States and Canada, 347
Muscular disorders, 400–401
Museum education programs (box), 153
Museum Services International, 156
Museums, 152–157
Music, 157–158
    military bands, 545
Music Educators National Conference, 158
Mutual/NBC Radio Network, 137

NAACP. *See* National Assn. for the Advancement of Colored People
NAACP Legal Defense and Educational Fund, 3, 204, 229, 506, 520
NAFSA: Assn. of International Educators, 453
NAHB Research Center, 424
    Radon Research and Indoor Air Quality, Laboratory Services, 298
NAIOP, National Assn. of Industrial and Office Properties, 437
Narcotics. *See Drugs and drug abuse*
NASA. *See* National Aeronautics and Space Administration
National Abortion and Reproductive Rights Action League (NARAL), 507
    Political Action Committee, 715

National Abortion Federation, 395, 507
National Academy of Engineering, 607
National Academy of Public Administration, 345
National Academy of Sciences, 595
    Financial Officer, 323
National Academy of Social Insurance, 360, 653
National Academy of Television Arts and Sciences, 140
National Adoption Center, 14
National Aeronautic Assn., 170, 665
National Aeronautics and Space Administration (NASA), 621
    Aero-Space Technology, 621, 663
    congressional liaison, 707
    Earth Science, 608
    equal employment opportunity contact, 228
    Financial Officer, 323
    fraud and abuse hotline, 327
    freedom of information contact, 126
    General Counsel, 499
    Goddard Space Flight Center, 621
    Information, 621
    Information Officer, 124
    Inspector General, 327
    International Space Station, 621
    Internet world wide Web site, 131
    library, 187
    Life and Microgravity Sciences and Applications, 621
    Life Sciences, 602
    NASA Advisory Council, 621
    National Space Science Data Center, 596, 622
    organization (chart), 622
    personnel office, 334
    Procurement Officer, 339
    public affairs contact, 129
    publications office, 125
    Safety and Mission Assurance, 623
    small and disadvantaged business contact, 109
    Space Communications, 623
    Space Flight, 623
    Space Science, 600, 623, 625
    Space Science and Aeronautics, 623
    Space Science Data Operations, 596
    Space Shuttle, 623
National Agricultural Aviation Assn., 43, 666
National Agricultural Library, 41
    D.C. Reference Center, 41
    Food and Nutrition Information Center, 57, 196
National Agricultural Statistics Service, 40, 41, 82
National AIDS Fund, 391
National Air and Space Museum, 153, 623, 663
National Air Carrier Assn., 666
National Air Traffic Controllers Assn., 668
National Air Transportation Assn., 666
National Alcohol Beverage Control Assn., 60
National Alliance for the Mentally Ill, 407
National Alliance of Black School Educators, 204
National Alliance of Business
    Education Reform, 197
    Workforce Adjustment, 208, 222, 226
National Alliance of Hispanic Health, 380, 402
National Alliance of Postal and Federal Employees, 336, 342
National Alliance to End Homelessness, 650
National American Indian Housing Council, 431
National Apartment Assn., 437
National Arboretum, 43, 153, 604
National Architectural Accrediting Board, 422

National Center for Policy Analysis, 719
National Center for Policy Research for Women and Families, 404
National Center for Prosecution of Child Abuse, 514
National Center for State Courts, 498
National Center for Tobacco-Free Kids, 23
National Center for Urban Ethnic Affairs, 419
National Center for Victims of Crime, 513
National Center on Education and the Economy, America's Choice District and School Design, 177, 223
National Center on Institutions and Alternatives, 520
National Certification Commission, 182
National Chamber Litigation Center, 78
National Cheese Institute, 50
National Chicken Council, 67
National Child Support Enforcement Assn., 637
National Children's Center, 649
National Citizens' Coalition for Nursing Home Reform, 365, 381
National Civilian Community Corps, 23
National Clearinghouse for Alcohol and Drug Information, Center for Substance Abuse Prevention, 60
National Clearinghouse for Bilingual Education, 204
National Clearinghouse for Corporate Matching Gifts Information, 177
National Clearinghouse for ESL Literacy Education, 208
National Clearinghouse for Primary Care Information, 354
National Coal Council, 261
National Coalition Against the Misuse of Pesticides, 43
National Coalition for Advanced Manufacturing, 97
National Coalition for Cancer Survivorship, 394
National Coalition for Homeless Veterans, 550, 650
National Coalition for Research in Neurological Disorders, 400
National Coalition for the Homeless, 650
National Coalition on Black Voter Participation, 696
National Coalition on Television Violence, 120
National Coalition to Abolish the Death Penalty, 520
National Collaboration for Youth, 637
National Collegiate Athletic Assn., Federal Relations, 170
National Commission Against Drunk Driving, 682
National Commission for Economic Conversion and Disarmament, 81, 564
National Commission on Libraries and Information Science, 184
National Committee for a Human Life Amendment, 507
National Committee for an Effective Congress, 715
National Committee for Responsive Philanthropy, 27
National Committee on Pay Equity, 229
National Committee to Preserve Social Security and Medicare, 363, 653
    Political Action Committee, 716
National Communications System, 578
National Community Action Foundation, 632
National Community Development Assn., 415
National Community Education Assn., 177
National Community Pharmacists Assn., 366
National Concrete Masonry Assn., 427
National Confectioners Assn., 52
National Conference of Catholic Bishops, 33
    Secretariat for Hispanic Affairs, 5
    Secretariat for Pro-Life Activities, 507
National Conference of Editorial Writers, 137
National Conference of Puerto Rican Women, 5
National Conference of State Historic Preservation Officers, 163

National Conference of State Legislatures, 348
National Conference of States on Building Codes and Standards, 251, 424
National Conference on Ministry to the Armed Forces, 529
    Endorsers Conference for Veterans Affairs Chaplaincy, 554
National Conference on Soviet Jewry, 33, 491
National Conference on Weights and Measures, 617
National Congress for Community Economic Development, 415
National Congress of American Indians, 7
National Congress of Parents and Teachers, Legislation, 198, 199, 638
National Conservatory of Dramatic Arts, 159
National Consortium for Child Mental Health Services, 384, 407
National Constructors Assn., 421
National Consumer Law Center, 29, 523
National Consumers League, 16, 21
National Contact Lens Examiners Board, 376
National Contract Management Assn., 340
National Cooperative Business Assn., 48, 78, 416, 438
National Coordination Office for Computing, Information, and Communications, 614
National Corn Growers Assn., 51
National Cotton Council of America, 49, 98
National Council for Accreditation of Teacher Education, 182
National Council for Adoption, 638
National Council for Community Behavior Healthcare, 407
National Council for International Visitors, 453
National Council for the Social Studies, 182
National Council for the Traditional Arts, 166
National Council of Agricultural Employers, 39
National Council of Architectural Registration Boards, 423
National Council of Catholic Women, 34
National Council of Churches, 34, 199, 509
National Council of Farmer Cooperatives, 42, 48, 416
National Council of Higher Education Loan Programs, 195
National Council of Jewish Women, 34
National Council of La Raza, 5, 205, 230, 431, 455
National Council of Negro Women, 4
National Council of Senior Citizens, 8, 381, 640, 715
National Council of State Education Assns., 182
National Council of State Housing Agencies, 437
National Council of Teachers of Mathematics, 182, 210
National Council of University Research Administrators, 193
National Council on Alcoholism and Drug Dependence, Public Policy, 404
National Council on Disability, 641
National Council on Independent Living, 644
National Council on Patient Information and Education, 367
National Council on Radiation Protection and Measurements, 298
National Council on the Aging, 8, 381, 432, 640
    Senior Community Service Employment Program, 225
National Council on U.S.-Arab Relations, 489
National Court Reporters Assn., 523
National Crash Analysis Center, 683
National Credit Union Administration, 87
    congressional liaison, 707
    equal employment opportunity contact, 228
    Examination and Insurance, 18
    Financial Officer, 323
    freedom of information contact, 126
    General Counsel, 499
    information, 87

National Credit Union Administration *(cont.)*
    library, 187
    Management Officer, 325
    personnel office, 334
    public affairs contact, 129
National Crime Prevention Council, 513
National Criminal Justice Assn., 522
National Customs Brokers and Forwarders Assn. of America, 471, 662
National Deaf Education Networking and Clearinghouse, 648
National Defense Council Foundation, 445
National Defense Industrial Assn., 579
National Defense Transportation Assn., 579, 590, 659
National Defense University, 538
National Democratic Institute for International Affairs, 445
National Dental Assn., 372
National Diabetes Information Clearinghouse, 394
National Digestive Diseases Information Clearinghouse, 394
National District Attorneys Assn., 513
National Drinking Water Advisory Council, 300
National Easter Seal Society, 380, 644
National Economic Council, 70
National Education Assn., 182
    Political Action Committee, 714
National Education Knowledge Industry Assn., 184
National Electrical Contractors Assn., 99, 257, 421
National Electrical Manufacturers Assn., 257
National Employee Benefits Institute, 238
National Endowment for Democracy, 446
National Endowment for the Arts, 145, 177
    Arts Education, Music, Opera, Presenting, and Multidisciplinary, 145, 148, 157
    congressional liaison, 707
    Dance, Design, Media Arts, Museums, and Visual Arts, 119, 145, 149, 154, 159
    Financial Officer, 323
    Folk and Traditional Arts, Literature, Theater, Musical Theater, and Planning and Stabilization, 145, 151, 159, 162, 166, 422
    General Counsel, 499
    Information, 145, 177
    library, 145, 177, 187
    Management Officer, 325
    Partnership, 145
    personnel office, 334
    public affairs contact, 129
National Endowment for the Humanities, 145, 178
    congressional liaison, 707
    equal employment opportunity contact, 228
    Financial Officer, 323
    freedom of information contact, 126
    General Counsel, 499
    library, 145–146, 178, 187
    Management Officer, 325
    personnel office, 334
    Preservation and Access, 162
    public affairs contact, 129
    Public Programs, 149
    Public Programs and Enterprise, 185
    publications office, 125
    Research and Education, 148, 178
National Energy Information Center, 255
National Environmental Development Assn., 281
National Environmental Satellite, Data, and Information Service, 277, 310, 597, 598

National Environmental Trust, 281
National Eye Institute, 376
National Family Caregivers Assn., 638
National Family Planning and Reproductive Health Assn., 396
National Farmers Union, 39
National Federation of Croatian Americans, 483
National Federation of Federal Employees, 336
National Federation of Independent Business, 111, 715
National Federation of Nonprofits, 343
National Federation of Republican Women, 722
National Fire Academy, 18
National Fire Protection Assn., Government Affairs, 19, 424
National Fish and Wildlife Foundation, 291
National Fisheries Institute, 288
National Food Processors Assn., 43, 62, 288
National Football League Players Assn., 170
National Foreign Language Center, 152
National Foreign Trade Council, 471
National Forest Foundation, 305
National Foundation for Brain Research, 400
National Foundation for Infectious Diseases, 398
National Foundation for the Improvement of Education, 183
National Foundation on the Arts and the Humanities
    Federal Council on the Arts and the Humanities, 153
    National Endowment for the Arts. *See that heading*
    National Endowment for the Humanities. *See that heading*
National 4-H Council, 42, 206, 638
National Gallery of Art, 154
    Education Resources, 148
    Information, 154
    museum education programs, 153
National Gay and Lesbian Task Force and Policy Institute, 6, 715
National Genealogical Society, 166
National Geodetic Survey, 619
National Geographic Maps, 621
National Geographic Society, 210
    Committee for Research and Exploration, 595
National Glass Assn., 427
National Governors' Assn., 348
    Center for Policy Research, Training and Employment Program, 223, 224
    Health Policy Studies, 358
    Natural Resources, 249
National Grain and Feed Assn., 51
National Grain Trade Council, 51
National Grange, 39
National Guard Assn. of the United States, 547
National Guard Bureau, 546
    Air National Guard, 546
      Chaplain Service, 528, 546
    Army National Guard, 546
      Chaplain Service, 528, 546
National Gulf War Resource Center, 554
National Head Start Assn., 198, 638
National Health Care Anti-Fraud Assn., 360
National Health Council, 358
National Health Information Center, 354
National Health Law Program, 29, 380
National Health Policy Forum, 358
National Heart, Lung, and Blood Institute, 385
    Blood Disease Program, 396
    Blood Diseases and Resources, 392
    Blood Resources Program, 392
    Heart and Vascular Diseases, 398

National Institutes of Health *(cont.)*
 National Institute of Allergy and Infectious Diseases. *See that heading*
 National Institute of Arthritis and Musculoskeletal and Skin Diseases, 391, 402
  Information Clearinghouse, 391
 National Institute of Child Health and Human Development. *See that heading*
 National Institute of Dental and Craniofacial Research, 371
 National Institute of Diabetes and Digestive and Kidney Diseases. *See that heading*
 National Institute of Environmental Health Sciences, 276
 National Institute of General Medical Sciences, 386, 397, 602
 National Institute of Mental Health, 405
 National Institute of Neurological Disorders and Stroke, 398, 400
 National Institute of Nursing Research, 373
 National Institute on Aging, 381
 National Institute on Alcohol Abuse and Alcoholism, 402
 National Institute on Deafness and Other Communication Disorders, 378, 647
 National Institute on Drug Abuse, 402
 National Library of Medicine, 387, 604
 organization (chart), 386
 personnel office, 334
 Protection from Research Risks, 285, 387
 Research on Minority Health, 387, 402
 Research on Women's Health, 404
 Warren Grant Magnuson Clinical Center, 388, 390, 392
National Insulation Assn., 251, 297, 427
National Insurance Consumer Helpline, 15
National Interreligious Service Board for Conscientious Objectors, Center for Conscience and War, 528, 540, 579
National Investor Relations Institute, 93
National Italian American Foundation, 167
National Jewish Democratic Council, 719
National Journal, 137
National Journalism Center, 180
National Kidney and Urologic Diseases Information Clearinghouse, 399
National Kidney Foundation, Government Relations, 399
National Labor Relations Board (NLRB), 232
 congressional liaison, 707
 equal employment opportunity contact, 228
 Financial Officer, 323
 freedom of information contact, 126
 General Counsel, 499
 library, 187, 232
 personnel office, 334
 Procurement Officer, 339
 public affairs contact, 129
 publications office, 125
National Law Center on Homelessness and Poverty, 650
National Law Enforcement Council, 522
National Lead Information Center, 15
National League of American Pen Women, 148
National League of Cities, 348, 419
National League of Families of American Prisoners and Missing in Southeast Asia, 535
National League of Postmasters, 342
National Leased Housing Assn., 430
National Legal Aid and Defender Assn., 30
National Legal Center for the Public Interest, 30, 498
National Lesbian and Gay Journalists Assn., 6, 137

National Library of Education, 183
National Library of Medicine, 387
 Health Information Programs Development, 387
 library, 187
 National Center for Biotechnology Information, 604
National Library Service for the Blind and Physically Handicapped, 186, 200, 642, 646
National Licensed Beverage Assn., 61
National Literacy Hotline, 15
National Long-Term Care Ombudsman Resource, 382
National Low Income Housing Coalition, 430
National Lumber and Building Material Dealers Assn., 305, 427
National Mall, 161
National Marine Fisheries Service, 287, 459, 602
National Marine Manufacturers Assn., Federal Government Relations, 672
National Maternal and Child Health Clearinghouse, 382
National Meat Canners Assn., 67
National Mediation Board, 232, 663, 684
 congressional liaison, 707
 Financial Officer, 323
 freedom of information contact, 126
 General Counsel, 499
 Information, 232, 663, 684
 personnel office, 334
 Procurement Officer, 339
National Medical Assn., 376
National Mental Health Assn., 407
National Military Family Assn., 532
National Milk Producers Federation, 50
National Mining Assn., 261, 309
 Policy Analysis, 255
National Minority AIDS Council, 391
National Motor Freight Classification, 677
National Motor Freight Traffic Assn., 677
National Multi Housing Council, 438
National MultiCultural Institute, 205
National Multiple Sclerosis Society, 400, 645
National Museum of African Art, 153, 154
National Museum of American Art, 153, 154
National Museum of American History, 154
 Archives Center, 164
 Armed Forces History Collections, 543
 Cultural History, 157, 162
 History Department, 166
 Information, 154
 Library, 154, 596
 museum education programs, 153
 National Numismatic Collection, 79
National Museum of American Jewish Military History, 543
National Museum of Health and Medicine, 154, 543
National Museum of Natural History, 592
 Anthropology, 618
 Botany, 605, 611
 Crustaceans, 611
 Entomology, 605
 Invertebrate Zoology, 605
 Library, 602, 611, 618
 Mineral Sciences, 610
 museum education programs, 153
 Naturalist Center, 209, 602, 610
 Paleobiology, 610
 Vertebrate Zoology, 605, 611
National Museum of the American Indian, 154
National Museum of Women in the Arts, 153, 156

Pax World Service, 474
Pay issues. *See Employee benefits; Wages and salaries*
Peace Action, 568
Peace Corps, 24, 472
    equal employment opportunity contact, 228
    Financial Officer, 323
    freedom of information contact, 126
    General Counsel, 499
    Information, 24, 472
    Internet world wide Web site, 131
    library, 187
    Management Officer, 325
    publications office, 125
Peace Links, 566
Peacekeeping, 564–566
Peanuts, 53
Peat Marwick Partners/Principals and Employees Political
    Action Committee, 716
Pell Grant Program, 194
PEN/Faulkner Foundation, 152
Pennsylvania Congressional Delegation, 700
Pension and Welfare Benefits Administration, 236
Pension Benefit Guaranty Corp., 236
    congressional liaison, 707
    Financial Officer, 323
    freedom of information contact, 126
    General Counsel, 499
    Information, 236
    Internet world wide Web site, 131
    Management Officer, 325
    organization (chart), 236
    public affairs contact, 129
Pension Rights Center, 238
Pensions and Benefits, 235–238
    federal sector, 336–337
    military personnel, 536–537
    Social Security, 651–654
People for the American Way, 720
People for the Ethical Treatment of Animals, 63
People of color. *See Minorities*
PEOPLE, Qualified, 714
Periodical press. *See Communications and the Media*
Perkins Loan Program, 194
Permanent Joint Board on Defense/United States and Canada,
    566
Permanent U.S. Congressional Delegation to the European
    Parliament, 701
Personal Communications Industry Assn., 122
Personnel Offices at Federal Agencies (box), 334
Pesticides, 42–43
    consumer and emergency hotline, 15
Petroleum Marketers Assn. of America, 263
Petroleum resources, 261–264
Pew Center for Civic Journalism, 138
Pharmaceutical Care Management Assn., 367
Pharmaceutical Research and Manufacturers of America, 367
Pharmaceuticals, 365–367
Philanthropy, Public Service, and Voluntarism, 23–28
Phillips Collection, 153, 156
Photography, 149–150
Physical education, 168–171
Physical sciences, 612–618
Physical therapy, 373
Physical Therapy Political Action Committee, 717
Physically disabled. *See Disabled persons*

Physicians and health care professionals, 367–377
Physicians Committee for Responsible Medicine, 59, 287
Physicians for Social Responsibility, 568
Physics, 616–617
Pinchot Institute for Conservation, 284
Planned Parenthood Federation of America, Public Policy, 396
Planning Assistance, 474
PLUS (Public Laws Update Service), 123, 319, 689
PLUS (Student Loan) Program, 194
Points of Light Foundation, 27
Police, law enforcement, 520–522
Police Dept., Metropolitan (D.C.), 138
Police Executive Research Forum, 522
Police Foundation, 522
Political action committees, 713–717
Political activity. *See Congress*
Political Advocacy, 713–721
Political interest groups, 717–721
Political participation, 695–697
Political Party Organizations, 721–723
Pollution and Toxins, 291–302
    air pollution, 292–294
    consumer and emergency hotlines, 15
    hazardous materials, 294–297
    nuclear waste, 268–269
    radiation protection, 297–298
    recycling and solid waste, 298–300
    water pollution, 300–302
Polystyrene Packaging Council, 299
Population Action International, 396
Population Assn. of America, 330
Population data, 328–330
Population-Environment Balance, 282, 396
Population Institute, 396
Population issues, 395–396
Population Reference Bureau, 330, 396
Porkbusters Coalition, 700
Postal Rate Commission, 342
    congressional liaison, 707
    Consumer Advocate, 12
    Financial Officer, 323
    General Counsel, 499
    library, 187
Postal Service, 340–344
    consumer services, 341
    employee and labor relations, 341–342
    to Foreign Service posts (box), 862
    mail rates and classification, 342–343
    stamps/postal history, 343–344
Postsecondary Education, 188–195
    college accreditation, 194
    fellowships and grants, 177–180
    financial aid to students, 194–195
    major Washington colleges (box), 189
    veterans, 552–553
Potomac Heritage American Hiking Assn., 161
Poultry and livestock, 65–67
Poverty and Race Research Action Council, 3, 632
The Preamble Center, 78
Prenatal health care, 382–385
Presbyterian Church (U.S.A.), 34
Preschool, Elementary, Secondary Education, 195–199
Preservation Action, 163
President's Cancer Panel, 393
President's Commission on White House Fellowships, 178, 344

health programs, 355, 359, 379
revenue sharing legislation, 346, 414
social services, 630, 653
subcommittees, **818**
tax-exempt foundations and charitable trusts, 25
tax laws, 504
Senate Foreign Relations Comm., **818–819**
environment and natural resources, 283
international affairs, 443, 447, 449, 457, 460, 468, 475, 477, 478, 481, 484, 487, 490, 511
international broadcasting, 115
international energy policy, 254
national security, 567, 571, 583
subcommittees, **819**
Senate Governmental Affairs Comm., **819**
business and economic policy, 75, 92
congressional salaries, 709
District of Columbia affairs, 350, 693
employment and labor, 229, 232, 237
government operations, 323, 326, 328, 330, 332, 339, 341, 344
international affairs, 457
law and justice, 511
lobbyist regulation, 713
national security, 560, 571
nuclear energy policy, 265
revenue sharing legislation, 346, 414
subcommittees, **819–820**
Senate Health, Education, Labor, and Pensions Comm., **820**
arts and humanities, 146
civil rights, 2
consumer protection, 15, 58
education programs, 174, 186, 190, 196, 200, 203
employment and labor, 214, 219, 220, 221, 229, 233, 237, 240
health programs, 260, 355, 359, 361, 368, 379, 388, 512
Legal Services Corp. oversight, 28
public service organizations oversight, 25
railroad legislation, 685
science programs, 594
social services, 635, 639, 642
subcommittees, **820**
Senate Indian Affairs Comm., 7, 203, 310, 379, **820**
Senate Judiciary Comm., **820–821**
civil liberties and constitutional law, 3, 505, 506, 508, 509, 510
communications and media, 115, 129, 141
consumer privacy, 20
drug abuse issues, 355
elections and apportionment, 694, 695
foreign laborers, 222
holidays and celebrations legislation, 146
housing discrimination, 429
immigration and naturalization, 454
intellectual property protection, 104
international affairs, 449, 583
law and justice, 496, 501, 503, 512, 521
subcommittees, **821**
Senate Permanent Subcomm. on Investigations, 92, 237, 341, 457, 511
Senate Press Gallery, 140
Standing Committee of Correspondents, 139
Senate Press Secretaries Assn., 713
Senate Radio and Television Gallery, 140

Executive Committee of the Radio and Television Correspondents' Galleries, 139
Senate Republican Committee on Committees, 706
Senate Republican Conference, 706
Senate Republican Policy Committee, 706, **823**
Senate Rules and Administration Comm., **821**
elections conduct, 694, 695
government publications jurisdiction, 127
Library of Congress oversight, 186
public buildings oversight, 698
Senate operations, 690, 702, 709, 712
Smithsonian Institution oversight, 147, 594
Senate Rural Health Caucus, 702
Senate Select Comm. on Ethics, 709, 710, **821**
Senate Select Comm. on Intelligence, 512, 583, **821–822**
Senate Small Business Comm., **822**
agricultural policy, 48, 55
antitrust, 503
employment and labor, 241
environment and natural resources, 279
government procurement, 340
housing and development, 410
international affairs, 468
small business programs, 111
Senate Special Comm. on Aging, **822**
civil rights advocacy, 7
employment and labor issues, 222, 237
energy concerns, 248
health care issues, 379
housing issues, 429
social services, 639, 653
transportation concerns, 659
Senate Special Investigations Unit on Gulf War Illnesses, 554
Senate Steel Caucus, 702
Senate Subcomm. on Administrative Oversight and the Courts, 496, 503, **821**
Senate Subcomm. on African Affairs, 477, **819**
Senate Subcomm. on Aging, 221, 639, **820**
Senate Subcomm. on Agriculture, Rural Development, and Related Agencies, 39, 58, 355, **813**
Senate Subcomm. on Airland Forces, 559, **814**
Senate Subcomm. on Antitrust, Business Rights, and Competition, 115, 503, **821**
Senate Subcomm. on Aviation, 664, **816**
Senate Subcomm. on Children and Families, 635, **820**
Senate Subcomm. on Clean Air, Wetlands, Private Property, and Nuclear Safety, 256, 265, 293, 307, 312, 577, **817**
Senate Subcomm. on Commerce, Justice, State, and Judiciary, 13, 75, 114, 279, 330, 442, 468, 496, 594, 658, 671, **813**
Senate Subcomm. on Communications, 115, 132, **816**
Senate Subcomm. on Consumer Affairs, Foreign Commerce, and Tourism, 15, 58, 171, **816**
Senate Subcomm. on Criminal Justice Oversight, **821**
Senate Subcomm. on Defense, 559, **813**
Senate Subcomm. on East Asian and Pacific Affairs, 478, **819**
Senate Subcomm. on Economic Policy, 433, **815**
Senate Subcomm. on Emerging Threats and Capabilities, 571, **814**
Senate Subcomm. on Employment, Safety, and Training, 214, 219, 220, 221, 229, 233, 237, **820**
Senate Subcomm. on Energy and Water Development, 248, 279, 569, 671, **813**
Senate Subcomm. on Energy Research, Development, Production, and Regulation, 248, 256, 265, 307, **817**
Senate Subcomm. on European Affairs, 481, **819**

Telecommunications. *See Communications and the Media*
Telecommunications for the Deaf, 117, 648
Telecommunications Industry Assn., 117
Telephone and telegraph, 121
Telephone Contacts for Data Users, 328
Television, 119–121
    cable services, 117–118
    networks, 137
Tennessee Valley Authority
    congressional liaison, 707
    Government Affairs, 256, 265, 302, 306, 313, 315, 417, 674
Territories and associated states, U.S., 491–492
Textile Museum, 153, 156
Theater, 158–159
Therapeutic Communities of America, 404
Thomas Stone National Historic Site, 161
Time magazine, 137
Tire Assn. of North America, 680
Tire Industry Safety Council, 683
Tobacco
    commodity, 53
    smoking, 22–23
Tobacco Associates, 53
Tourism, 171–172
Town Affiliation Assn. of the U.S., Sister Cities International, 453
Trade policy. *See International Trade and Development*
Trade Promotion Coordinating Committee, 465
Trade Show Exhibitors Assn., 106
Trademarks and patents, 103–105
Traditional Values Coalition, 720
Training. *See Employment and training*
TransAfrica, 477
Transit Systems, 685–687
TRANSPORTATION (chap. 19), 655–687
    air, 662–669
    freight and intermodalism, 660–662
    general policy, 656–660
    maritime, 669–675
    motor vehicles, 675–683
    rail, 683–685
    transit systems, 685–687
Transportation Communications International Union, 685
Transportation Department (DOT), 656
    Airline Information, 663
    airline safety hotline, 14
    auto safety hotline, 41
    Aviation Analysis, 663
    Aviation and International Affairs, 657, 663
    Aviation Consumer Protection, 13, 658, 663
    boating hotline, 14
    Bureau of Transportation Statistics, 656
    congressional liaison, 706
    consumer and emergency hotlines, 14
    consumer contact, 13
    directory of information on the Internet, 847–848
    Environmental Policies Team, 277, 658
    equal employment opportunity contact, 228
    Federal Aviation Administration. *See that heading*
    Federal Highway Administration. *See that heading*
    Federal Motor Carrier Safety Administration, 675, 681
    Federal Railroad Administration, 660, 683, 684
    Federal Transit Administration, 685, 686
    Financial Officer, 322

fraud and abuse hotline, 327
freedom of information contact, 126
General Counsel, 498
hazardous materials, chemical, and oil spills, 14
Information Officer, 124
Information Technology, Financial, and Secretarial Audits, 663
Inspector General, 327
Intelligence and Security, 582, 658
Intermodalism, 660
International Aviation, 456
Internet world wide Web site, 131
library, 187
Management Officer, 325
Maritime Administration. *See that heading*
National Highway Traffic Safety Administration, 681
National Response Center, 295, 673
organization (chart), 661
personnel office, 334
Procurement Officer, 339
public affairs contact, 128
publications office, 125
Research and Special Programs Administration. *See that heading*
Saint Lawrence Seaway Development Corp., 458, 674
Secretary, 656
small and disadvantaged business contact, 109
Surface Transportation Board, 503, 660, 670, 684, 686
Transportation Policy, 658
Transportation Policy Development, 658
U.S. Coast Guard. *See that heading*
Transportation, Elevator, and Grain Merchants' Assn., 52
Transportation Institute, 672
Travel and Tourism, 171–172
    Americans abroad, 457–458
    government, 324–325
Travel Industry Assn. of America, 172
Treasurer of the United States, 79
Treasury Department, 71, 79
    Bureau of Alcohol, Tobacco, and Firearms. *See that heading*
    Bureau of Engraving and Printing, 79
    Bureau of the Public Debt, 80, 91
    Comptroller of the Currency. *See that heading*
    congressional liaison, 706
    consumer and emergency hotlines, 14
    consumer contact, 13
    directory of information on the Internet, 848
    drug smuggling reports, 14
    Economic Policy, 71
    equal employment opportunity contact, 228
    explosive materials discovery, 14
    Federal Finance Policy Analysis, 80
    Federal Financing Bank, 80
    Federal Law Enforcement Training Center, 520
    Financial Crimes Enforcement Network, 521
    Financial Institutions, 88
    Financial Institutions Policy, 92
    Financial Management Service, 72, 79
    Financial Officer, 322
    Fiscal Policy, 74
    Foreign Assets Control, 465, 571
    Foreign Exchange Operations, 475
    fraud and abuse hotline, 327
    freedom of information contact, 126
    General Counsel, 498